2007

This Edition of *Resources for College Libraries* was prepared by:

ACRL & Choice:
Project Editor: Marcus Elmore
Editorial Director, Choice: Francine Graf
Editor & Publisher, Choice: Irving Rockwood

Special Thanks to Our Proofreaders:
Monika Maslowski, Jinna Anderson, Chris Sullivan, Jennifer Donahue, Judith Douville,
Rebecca Bartlett, and Carolyn Wilcox

Record Entry Completed By:
Monika Maslowski, Laurie Trulock, and Sheila Laverty

R. R. Bowker LLC:
John Krafty: Product Manager, RCL
Ashley Ludwig: Managing Editor, RCL
Frank Morris: IT Director
Minh Huynh: Senior Programmer Analyst
Robert Zeisler: Senior Programmer Analyst

Editorial Staff:
Ian Singer: Vice President, Data Services
Roy Crego: Senior Managing Director, Editorial
Eleanor Schubauer: Managing Editor
Michael Olenick: Managing Editor
Beverly Palacio: Associate Editor

Production Department:
Doreen Gravesande: Senior Director, Production
Ralph Coviello, Manager, Manufacturing Services
Myriam Nunez: Project Manager, Product Development & Content Integrity
Kennard McGill: Production Consultant

Research Completed By:
Pat Diaz, Bobbie Ferraro, Kathy Griner, Becky Housel, and Diane Johnson.

Record Entry Completed By:
Jenny Marie DeJesus, Dorothy Perry-Gilchrist, Anthony Giuffra, and Steven Zaffuto

RESOURCES for COLLEGE LIBRARIES

2007

Volume 5:
Science and Technology

Mary Ellen Davis, Executive Director, ACRL

Published by
R. R. Bowker LLC
630 Central Avenue, New Providence
New Jersey 07974

Annie Callanan, President and CEO

URL: http://www.rclweb.net
E-mail address: rclfeedback@bowker.com

Readers may send any corrections and/or updates to the information in this work to:
rclfeedback@bowker.com

International Standard Book Number:

7 Volume Set:	ISBN: 0-8352-4855-0
	ISBN13: 978-0-8352-4855-6
Vol. 1: Humanities:	ISBN: 0-8352-4856-9
	ISBN13: 978-0-8352-4856-3
Vol. 2: Language & Literature:	ISBN: 0-8352-4857-7
	ISBN13: 978-0-8352-4857-0
Vol. 3: History:	ISBN: 0-8352-4858-5
	ISBN13: 978-0-8352-4858-7
Vol. 4: Social Sciences:	ISBN: 0-8352-4859-3
	ISBN13: 978-0-8352-4859-4
Vol. 5: Science and Technology:	ISBN: 0-8352-4860-7
	ISBN13: 978-0-8352-4860-0
Vol. 6: Interdisciplinary & Area Studies:	ISBN: 0-8352-4861-5
	ISBN13: 978-0-8352-4861-7
Vol. 7: Indexes:	ISBN: 0-8352-4862-3
	ISBN13: 978-0-8352-4862-4

Printed and bound in the United States of America

Table of Contents

Resources for College Libraries: General Introduction

Like its predecessors, the three editions of *Books for College Libraries* (BCL) that appeared in 1988, 1975, and 1964, *Resources for College Libraries* (RCL) is a bibliography of carefully selected works spanning the college curriculum and comprising a recommended core collection for all academic libraries. In the tradition of its predecessors, which drew on the such sources as the published catalog of Harvard's Lamont Library (1954), the shelflist of the undergraduate library of the University of Michigan, and, crucially, Charles Shaw's *List of Books for College Libraries* (1931), RCL attempts to balance multiple, often contradictory demands. It seeks to provide a balanced set of recommendations that take note of the weight of the various academic disciplines within the undergraduate curriculum, the degree to which those various disciplines depend on book materials for their essential teaching and research resources, and the extensive pattern of changes that have reshaped the academic curriculum since 1988, the year in which BCL3, the most recent edition of *Books for College Libraries,* appeared.

Of necessity, RCL also embodies a paradox identified by the late Virginia Clark, editor of BCL3: it "can fully succeed only by failing. It would be disastrous should the collection it suggests serve perfectly to ratify the finished work of book selection in any library."[1] Not only will individual institutions create collections significantly larger than the roughly 65,000 titles recommended by RCL, but they will tailor those collections to reflect the size and strength of their own individual departments, majors, and programs. RCL attempts to make general recommendations, within individual subject areas, of those titles most necessary for teaching the subject to undergraduates. In many cases, this means a foundation to which the smallest institutions should aspire but which larger collections will far surpass.

We describe RCL as a successor to, rather than a new edition of, BCL for two reasons. The first is formal, and lies behind the change in nomenclature: RCL includes in its recommendations a variety of electronic resources, including Web sites, subscription databases, e-books, and other electronic materials. The second, procedural reason follows from this: unlike its predecessors, RCL will appear as both a multivolume print edition and a searchable, continuously updated electronic database. In addition, there is a third, tacit distinction which may be made

between RCL and the various editions of BCL: although bibliographers compiling subject lists for RCL often took the titles listed in BCL3 as a starting point, our bibliographic work emphasized building a comprehensive, retrospective list of titles by reference to the current undergraduate curriculum, and thus much of the work on RCL was from scratch. In contrast, the relationship between the various editions of BCL was demonstrably that of revision; from one edition to the next, there was an expectation that a title would be retained unless it was actively removed (if, for instance, it had been superseded by a more recent work). Because so much more time had passed between the appearance of BCL3 and the development of RCL than between any successive editions of BCL, bibliographers faced the simultaneously daunting and liberating prospect of creating a subject list *de novo*. That this same period (1988-2006) has seen momentous sea changes in many of the academic disciplines in the humanities and the sciences, as well as the growth of interdisciplinary study across all the academic disciplines, made this an opportunity to take measure of the way subjects are taught to undergraduates, as well as the sorts of subjects which are taught, when developing our core list.

One result of this reassessment was the decision to recognize and include as separate subject divisions in RCL a number of interdisciplinary fields, e.g., Environmental Studies and Gender Studies. The decision about which fields to include was based primarily on the degree to which those subjects function as areas of formal study at undergraduate institutions in the U.S., whether as major programs, academic minors, or areas of concentration housed within another department (film studies, for instance, is often offered as a program or concentration within the departments of English, Comparative Literature, or Theater). We recognized that the lists of titles recommended for teaching interdisciplinary subjects, e.g., Asian American Studies, might overlap significantly with the corresponding title lists for related traditional fields, e.g., American Literature. At the same time, we were confident that many of the recommended interdisciplinary titles would be unique, and so it has proved. The degree of overlap between the various sections of RCL is, throughout, fortuitous and reflects actual overlap between various undergraduate curricula. Effort was made to regularize the editions selected, but the work of compiling the various subject lists proceeded on an independent basis.

---

1. Virginia Clark, "Introduction," *Books for College Libraries: A Core Collection of 50,000 Titles,* (3rd ed., Chicago: American Library Association, 1988), vii.

The other dramatic difference between RCL and BCL is the decision to move away from Library of Congress classification as the primary framework for the selection and classification of titles. Though this is bound to be regarded by many librarians as a controversial decision, we are confident that it will prove in retrospect to be a sound one. The rationale for doing so is the desire to have titles classified in a fashion which closely follows the contours of the undergraduate curriculum. While LC accomplishes this for some subjects (for instance, British or American Literature, which are taught by chronological periods, and within periods by major authors and by forms such as poetry or drama), other curricula fail to mesh well with LC classification: Business Administration, for example, is responsible for the largest portion of baccalaureate degrees conferred by U.S. colleges and universities,[2] yet the classification of materials in the business curriculum in LC class HB-HJ, while sufficient for cataloging purposes, offers no insight on the relationship between materials so classified and the curriculum in which they are used. It is, furthermore, an arrangement which makes perfect sense to, but only to, librarians. Not all copies of BCL resided in technical services departments, but it seems unlikely that they were much consulted by students or faculty. Our hope is that the new classification scheme will work to the advantage of all the academic library's constituencies: librarians, especially those lacking strong background in a given subject, will be able to see not only the recommended titles but also, in the subject taxonomy, a map of the undergraduate curriculum; faculty will find recommendations of essential works in a form more accessible than LC, and bearing a closer correspondence to the way their courses and departments are organized; students, searching for a place to begin research on a particular topic, will also be able to recognize in the classification scheme something corresponding to their own encounter with the subject matter in the classroom and laboratory. Finally, since each entry in RCL retains its LC classification, those who prefer to search for materials in this fashion will still be able to.

RCL is the result of the collaborative efforts of 332 contributors, almost exclusively teaching faculty or librarians at U.S. colleges and universities. There were three kinds of contributors: subject editors, bibliographers, and referees. Subject editors were selected on the basis of their subject expertise and teaching or collection development experience: eighteen hold doctorates, four are members of the teaching faculty at research universities, two are independent scholars, and the remainder are academic librarians. Many have previously contributed to or authored major bibliographies in their subject areas. They were responsible for developing the subject classification taxonomy for their respective subject areas, for recruiting bibliographers and coordinating their efforts, and for reviewing the results. The subject editors represented a change from the various editions of BCL, where the bibliographers (mainly Choice reviewers) dealt directly with the project editor. By inserting a layer of subject experts we sought to ensure that the titles selected and the taxonomies in which they were classified reflected as much as possible the realities of the contemporary undergraduate curriculum. The second class of RCL contributors, bibliographers, was responsible for the bulk of the actual selection of titles. Like the subject editors, they were faculty and librarians selected for their subject knowledge, often with particular expertise in one specific aspect of a field. Finally, a pool of sixty-four referees, senior faculty or subject-specialist librarians, provided independent assessment of the initial lists developed by the bibliographers; the subject editors used this feedback to further refine their lists prior to publication.

The development of RCL had presumed from the beginning that bibliographers would be manipulating electronic bibliographic records in some sort of online environment, but the decision of the Association of College and Research Libraries (ACRL) Board of Directors to partner with publisher R. R. Bowker to produce RCL allowed us access to Bowker's massive database of bibliographic records, as well as the extensive technical support and expertise Bowker deployed on behalf of the project. Bibliographers selected titles in Bowker's *booksinprint.com* database, in a particular edition, and then imported them to the online RCL Authoring System, where they assigned subject headings and recommended audience levels. In those instances where no bibliographic record existed for a desired title, one was created from a reliable source (preferably with book in hand, though this was not always possible). At the same time, bibliographers submitted corrections to Bowker records when they identified errors or inconsistencies. While this system allowed us to avoid much of the brute effort which was expended on the creation of bibliographic records for the various editions of BCL, it also meant that bibliographers spent thousands of person-hours in the *booksinprint.com* database, identifying the most recent and reliable edition of particular works; in some cases, editors elected to include multiple editions, especially where the differences between them are significant for undergraduate teaching (see, for instance, the decision to include multiple, equally worthwhile translations of Dante's *Divine Comedy* in the Italian literature section).

The use of an online system for the manipulation of electronic bibliographic records was in part a matter of efficiency, but more importantly, it finally addresses one longstanding issue faced by BCL, that of obsolescence.

---

2. http://nces.ed.gov/fastfacts/display.asp?id=37: U.S. Department of Education, National Center for Education Statistics. (2006). *Digest of Education Statistics, 2005* (NCES 2006-030), chapter 3.

When *Choice* magazine was founded in 1964, it was envisioned as, among other things, an ongoing supplement to BCL1. This approach did not prove practical, and the second and third editions of BCL were required. In contrast, RCL will be updated on an ongoing basis beginning almost immediately after its initial publication; bibliographic records will reflect changes in print status, and new titles will be introduced at regular intervals, to supplement or replace extant titles.

In addition to the tireless efforts of the contributors, on whom I cannot lavish sufficient praise, special thanks to the ACRL Board of Directors and Mary Ellen Davis, ACRL Executive Director, without whose approval and generous support this project would not have been possible. Oversight and advice were provided throughout the project by the RCL Editorial Board: Carolyn Sheehy, North Central College, Chair; and other members Joan Ellen Broome, Georgia Southern University; Barbara Burd, College Misericordia; Brian E. Coutts, Western Kentucky University; Bradford Lee Eden, University of California, Santa Barbara; Stacey Marien, American University; and Richard Shaw, Technical College of the Lowcountry.

Thanks are also due the editorial staff of *Choice*, all of whom contributed effort and advice to the production of this work in varying degrees (and all of whom exhibited tremendous kindness in their efforts, especially in the final days): Becky Bartlett, Judith Douville, Fran Graf, Lisa Mitten, and Carolyn Wilcox. Fran Graf and Irv Rockwood, the Publisher of *Choice*, deserve another helping of praise for their advice, encouragement, and oversight of the project, as well as for handling negotiations of our partnership with R. R. Bowker. Judith Douville made superhuman contributions to a number of subject areas in addition to her own responsibilities in Chemistry. Although almost every member of the *Choice* office staff contributed to this work, Sheila Laverty deserves special praise for her work on the Dance section. Finally, the work would not have been completed if it had not been for the tireless effort of a small cadre of freelance staff, namely Jennifer Donahue, Monika Maslowski, Teri Staab, and Laurie Trulock, who proofread and edited subject headings and section notes, entered titles, cataloged records, and helped maintain communication with subject editors, with extraordinary care, intelligence, and persistence.

With our partners at R. R. Bowker, we enjoyed the highest degree of collegiality and cooperation. Special thanks are due to Angela D'Agostino, Vice-President of Marketing; John Krafty, Product Manager of *Books In Print*; Ashley Ludwig, Managing Editor; Todd Rudloff, Project Manager of *Books In Print*; Frank Morris, Senior Programmer; Minh Huynh, Senior Programmer Analyst, all of whom made significant contributions to bringing this work to the light of day.

Finally, my deep thanks to my family, Colleen and Graham, for their patience and support throughout this project.

Marcus Elmore,
Editor

A Note on the RCL Subject Taxonomy

One of the distinctive features of *Resources for College Libraries* is the subject taxonomy used to organize the titles included in RCL. Developed specifically for RCL by the RCL editorial team, and in particular by the subject editors, the RCL taxonomy reflects the contours of today's undergraduate curriculum. The RCL taxonomy's major headings, therefore, generally correspond to academic majors, departments, or courses of study, e.g., anthropology, business administration, or physics. (In some cases an academic discipline has been further subdivided in order to create sections of manageable size, e.g., the subdivision of History by geographical region.) The goal is a classification scheme, which organizes materials as they would be taught by faculty and encountered in the classroom and the laboratory by undergraduate students.

In some subject areas, e.g. British and American literature, the RCL subject taxonomy closely resembles the Library of Congress classification scheme used in *Books for College Libraries*, 3rd edition. In most cases, however, the differences between LC and today's undergraduate curriculum, have been so substantial as to require the development of a new taxonomy from scratch. This has been especially true for the interdisciplinary subjects such as African American Studies, Criminal Justice, and Native American Studies, which draw upon materials from a dizzying range of LC classes. Gender Studies, for example, draws from a large array of academic disciplines, including (but not limited to) psychology, sociology, literature, philosophy, political science, medicine, and history.

The coverage of interdisciplinary subjects in RCL is another of its distinguishing features, and one deemed essential from the very inception of the project. Although there is some overlap between the interdisciplinary title lists and those of related traditional subjects, e.g., American literature and Chicano/a literature (a subsection of Latino Studies), the interdisciplinary sections inevitably include many unique titles. In addition, the inclusion of the interdisciplinary subjects makes it possible to distinguish those titles which have been selected as essential resources for a traditional subject such as American literature (e.g., Carson McCullers' *Collected Novels*), from those selected for an interdisciplinary area (e.g., Pat Mora's *Communion,* selected for Latino Studies > Humanities > Literature > Chicano/a Literature), and also from those selected for both (e.g., Mora's *Borders*).

By making the ways in which titles are actually used in the classroom the focus for our classification of titles in RCL, we hope to both dramatically increase its usefulness to students and faculty members and also to underscore the extent to which titles were selected on the basis of their importance to undergraduate study and teaching.

RCL Contributors

John Abbott, Graduate Student, GSLIS, University of Illinois, Urbana-Champaign.
Subject Editor: European History.

Randy Abbott, Head Reference Librarian, University of Evansville.
Referee.

Anthony Adam, Assistant Director, John B. Coleman Library, Prairie View A&M University.
Bibliographer: GLBT Studies.

Jan Adamczyk, Slavic Reference Service, University of Illinois.
Bibliographer: Russian Languages and Literatures.

Michael Adams, Librarian, CUNY Graduate Center.
Bibliographer: American Literature.

Paulita Aguilar, Curator, Indigenous Nations Library Program, University of New Mexico.
Bibliographer: Native American Studies.

Flavia Alaya, Professor of English, Ramapo College of New Jersey.
Referee.

Jean Alexander, Head of Reference, Hunt Library, Carnegie Mellon University.
Referee.

Duncan Alford, Head of Reference, Law Library, Georgetown University.
Bibliographer: Law.

Karen Antell, Head, Reference Department, University of Oklahoma.
Bibliographer: Technology and Engineering.

Ralph Arcari, Director Emeritus, Health Center Library, University of Connecticut.
Subject Editor: Medicine.

Susan Ariew, University Librarian, University of South Florida.
Bibliographer: Education.

Jan Armstrong, Professor of Education, University of New Mexico.
Referee.

Teresa Arrington, Associate Professor of Modern Languages, Blue Mountain College.
Bibliographer: Spanish Language and Literature.

Susan Awe, Director of Parish Memorial Library, University of New Mexico.
Referee.

David Azzolina, Reference librarian, University of Pennsylvania.
Bibliographer: General Language and Literature.

Pete Banholzer, Technical Information Specialist, NASA.
Bibliographer: Geology.

Ron Banks, Human Subjects Coordinator, Institutional Review Board, University of Illinois.
Bibliographer: Education.

David Bantz, Chief Information Architect, University of Alaska.
Referee.

Adele Barsh, Business and Economics Librarian, Carnegie Mellon University.
Bibliographer: Business Administration.

Jennifer Bartlett, Head of Research & Instructional Services, Murray State University.
Bibliographer: American Literature.

Edwin Battistella, Dean of Arts and Letters and Professor of English, University of Southern Oregon.
Bibliographer: General Language and Literature.

Frederic Baumgartner, Professor of History, Virginia Tech University.
Bibliographer: European History.

Robert Beauregard, Professor, Urban Policy Analysis and Management, New School University.
Referee.

Linda Behrend, Cataloging Librarian, University of Tennessee, Knoxville.
Bibliographer: American Literature.

Penny Beile, Head, Curriculum Materials Center, University of Central Florida.
Bibliographer: Education.

Dean Bell, Dean and Chief Academic Officer, Spertus Institute of Jewish Studies.
Bibliographer: European History.

Dennis Benamati, Director, Ryan-Matura Library, Sacred Heart University.
Referee.

Riva Berleant-Schiller, Professor emerita of Anthropology, University of Connecticut, emerita.
Subject Editor: Anthropology.

Jay Bernstein, Reader Services Librarian, Kingsborough Community College.
Referee.

John Berry, Native American Studies Librarian, University of California, Berkeley.
Subject Editor: Native American Studies.

Sharon Black, Librarian, Annenberg School for Communication, University of Pennsylvania.
Bibliographer: Journalism and Communication.

Steve Blackburn, Library Director, Hartford Seminary.
Referee.

Robert Bland, Associate University Librarian
Automation and Technical Services, University of North
Carolina, Asheville.
Bibliographer: Philosophy.

Richard Bleiler, Humanities Bibliographer, University of
Connecticut.
Bibliographer: General Language and Literature.

Laurel Blewett, Manager of Library Services,
Edward Hospital.
Referee.

Christopher Bloss, Instructional Services Librarian,
University of South Dakota.
Bibliographer: American Literature.

Ellen Bosman, Head of Technical Services, New Mexico
State University.
Subject Editor: GLBT Studies.

Jesús Bottaro, Instructor, CUNY / Medgar Evers
College.
Bibliographer: Spanish Language and Literature.

Steven Botterill, Professor of Italian, University of
California, Berkeley.
Referee.

Sally Bowdoin, Head of Serials, Brooklyn College.
Subject Editor: British Literature.

Linda Bowles-Adarkwa, Subject Specialist, Black
Studies and Women Studies, San Francisco State
University.
Bibliographer: African American Studies.

James Boxall, Director, GIS Centre, Dalhousie University.
Subject Editor: Geography.

James Bracken, Assistant Director for Main Library
Research and Reference Services, Ohio State University.
Subject Editor: Other Literatures in English.

Laura Braunstein, Research and Reference Services,
Dartmouth University.
Bibliographer: General Language and Literature.

Tony Bremholm, Life Sciences Librarian, Texas
A&M University.
Referee.

Karl Bridges, Coordinator of Electronic Instruction
Resources, University of Vermont.
Bibliographer: U.S. and Canadian History.

JoEllen Broome, Reference Specialist, Georgia Southern
University.
Subject Editor: Environmental Studies.

Mitchell Brown, Research Librarian for Chemistry and
Earth System Sciences, University of California,
Irvine.
Referee.

Mary Jane Brustman, Bibliographer for Social Welfare
and Criminal Justice, SUNY Albany.
Subject Editor: Criminal Justice.

Mark Bullock, Graduate Student, History Department,
University of Illinois at Chicago.
Bibliographer: European History.

Merry Burlingham, Chief Bibliographer and Collections
Officer, University of Texas.
**Bibliographer: Asian History, Languages, and
Literatures.**

Angela Cannon, Reference Librarian, Library of
Congress.
**Bibliographer: Russian Languages and
Literatures.**

Karen Cary, Head, Collection Management, Virginia
Commonwealth University.
Bibliographer: Sociology.

Melissa Cast, Reference Librarian and Subject Specialist
for Education, University of Nebraska Omaha.
Bibliographer: Education.

Rafaela Castro, Bibliographer, University of California,
Davis.
Subject Editor: Latino Studies.

Tina Ching, Reference Librarian, Arizona State
University.
Referee.

Diana Chlebek, English and Modern Languages and
Literature Bibliographer, University of Akron.
Bibliographer: French Language and Literature.

Michael Chromey, Humanities Librarian, Atlanta
University Center.
Bibliographer: African American Studies.

Hui Hua Chua, US Documents Librarian, Michigan
State University.
Bibliographer: Journalism and Communication.

Alan Church, Professor of English, University of
Texas at Brownsville.
Referee.

Janet Clarke, Asian American Studies Selector, Stony
Brook University.
Bibliographer: Asian American Studies.

Kim Clarke, Assistant Librarian, Selector for Women's
Studies, University of Minnesota, Twin Cities.
Subject Editor: Gender Studies.

Rudolph Clay, Subject Librarian, African and
African-American Studies, Washington University.
Bibliographer: African American Studies.

Ana Maria Cobos, Library Department Chair, Saddleback
College.
Subject Editor: Latino Studies.

Francesca Colecchia, Professor of Spanish, Duquesne
University.
Referee.

Gerardo Colmenar, Associate Librarian, Asian American Studies, University of California, Santa Barbara.
Subject Editor: Asian American Studies.

Mark Connell, Director, Center for Advancement of Technology in Education, SUNY College at Cortland.
Referee.

Paul Connors, Research Analyst, Michigan Legislative Service Bureau.
Bibliographer: U.S. and Canadian History.

Miriam Conteh-Morgan, Collection Manager for African Studies, Ohio State University.
Bibliographer: African American Studies.

Kate Corby, Education and Psychology Bibliographer, Michigan State University.
Subject Editor: Education.

Ronald Cormier, Professor of French, Longwood College.
Referee.

Alice Crosetto, Acquisitions Librarian, University of Toledo.
Bibliographer: British Literature.

Cynthia Crosser, Social Sciences and Humanities Librarian, University of Maine.
Bibliographer: Education.

Gwyneth Crowley, Coordinator of Collection Development, Social Science Libraries, Yale University.
Subject Editor: Economics.

Alice Daugherty, Reference Librarian, Louisiana State University.
Bibliographer: American Literature.

Stephanie Davis, Librarian, Spring Arbor University.
Bibliographer: Education.

Judith de Luce, Professor of Classics, Miami University of Ohio.
Referee.

Kathy Dean, Humanities Bibliographer, Ohio State University.
Bibliographer: Other Literatures in English.

Louise Deis, Science & Technology Reference Librarian, Princeton University.
Subject Editor: Environmental Sciences; General Science.

JoAnn DeVries, Associate Librarian, Reference/Bibliographer, University of Minnesota.
Bibliographer: Agriculture.

Jan Dixon, Reference Librarian, University of Arkansas.
Bibliographer: Geology.

Deborah Dolan, Social Science Librarian, Hofstra University.
Bibliographer: Psychology.

Travis Dolence, Instruction Librarian, Minnesota State University Moorhead.
Referee.

Michael Doorley, Associate Lecturer in Humanities, American College, Dublin.
Bibliographer: European History.

Judith Douville, Visual Arts, Science and Technology Editor, CHOICE.
Subject Editor: Chemistry.

Bill Drew, Associate Librarian, Systems and Reference, SUNY – Morrisville.
Referee.

Heather Dubnick, Field Bibliographer, Modern Language Assoc.
Subject Editor: Spanish Language and Literature.

Dana Dunn, Professor of Psychology, Moravian College.
Referee.

Lisa Dunn, Head of Reference, Colorado School of Mines.
Bibliographer: Geology.

Karin Durán, Teacher Curriculum Center Librarian, California State University Northridge.
Bibliographer: Latino Studies.

David Eastman, Doctoral Candidate, Department of Religious Studies, Yale University.
Bibliographer: Religion.

Mary Edsall, Professor of Library and Information Science, Catholic University of America.
Subject Editor: Dance.

Marcus Elmore, CHOICE.
Subject Editor: General Language and Literature.

Robert Elsie, Independent scholar.
Bibliographer: European History.

Kimberly Embelton, Literature and Languages Librarian, California State University Northridge.
Bibliographer: British Literature.

Michael Emery, Professor of English, Cottey College.
Bibliographer: GLBT Studies.

Mark Emmons, Head, Instruction Services, University of New Mexico.
Subject Editor: Film.

Carlene Engstrom, Director, D'Arcy McNickle Library, Salish Kootenai College.
Bibliographer: Native American Studies.

Pam Enrici, Associate Librarian, University of Maryland.
Bibliographer: Technology and Engineering.

Robert Entenmann, Professor of History, St. Olaf College.
Referee.

Isabel Espinal, Librarian for Afro American Studies, Anthropology, Native American Indian Studies, University of Massachussetts.
Bibliographer: African American Studies.

James Allan Evans, Professor Emeritus of Classical
Near Eastern and Religious Studies, University of British
Columbia.
Bibliographer: European History.

Angel Falcon, Harvard University, formerly.
Bibliographer: African American Studies.

David Feldman, Professor of Mathematics, University of
New Hampshire.
Referee.

Robert Fernekes, Information Services Librarian,
Business Specialist, Georgia Southern University.
Bibliographer: Business Administration.

Anne Fields, OSU Libraries Coordinator for Research
and Reference, Ohio State University.
Bibliographer: Education.

Jenifer Flaxbart, Head Librarian, Reference and
Information Services, University of Texas, Austin.
Bibliographer: Journalism and Communication.

Adonna Fleming, GIS / Maps Librarian,
University of Nebraska – Lincoln.
Bibliographer: Geology.

Nicole Fluhr, Professor of English, Southern Connecticut
State University.
Referee.

Michael Fosmire, Science Librarian, Purdue University.
Subject Editor: Physics.

Stephen Foster, University Librarian, Wright State
University.
Referee.

Gerri Foudy, Government and Politics, Public Affairs,
and Law Librarian, University of Maryland.
Bibliographer: Political Science.

Kathleen Fountain, Political Science and Social Work
Librarian, California State University, Chico.
Bibliographer: Political Science.

Kristine Fowler, Mathematics Librarian, University of
Minnesota, Twin Cities.
Subject Editor: Mathematics.

Stephen Fowlkes, Bibliographer for Sociology, Social
Work and Reference, Tulane University.
Bibliographer: Sociology.

Ann Fox, Professor of English, Davidson College.
Referee.

Joe Fugate, Professor of German, Kalamazoo College.
Referee.

Steve Fullwood, Manuscripts Librarian, Schomburg
Center for Research in Black Culture, New York Public
Library.
Bibliographer: African American Studies.

Ronald Ganze, Professor of English, Valparaiso
University.
Bibliographer: Medieval Studies.

Bill Gargan, Reference Librarian and Bibliographer,
Brooklyn College.
Bibliographer: British Literature.

Meryle Gaston, Islamic and Middle Eastern Studies
Librarian, University of California, Santa Barbara.
**Subject Editor: Middle Eastern History, Languages,
and Literatures.**

Cameron Gearen, Lecturer in English, Yale University.
**Bibliographer: General Language and
Literature.**

Caroline Geck, Librarian, Kean University.
Referee.

Jennifer Geddes, Research Associate Professor of
Religious Studies, University of Virginia.
Bibliographer: General Language and Literature.

Mary Gilles, Business Reference Librarian,
Washington State University.
Subject Editor: Law.

David Giovacchini, Arabic Librarian, Middle East
Collection, Stanford University.
Referee.

Ed Goedeken, Humanities Bibliographer, Iowa State
University.
Subject Editor: U.S. and Canadian History.

Melissa Goldsmith, Lecturer, Louisiana State University.
Referee.

Millie Gonzalez, Reference Librarian, Framingham
State College.
Bibliographer: Business Administration.

Olympia Gonzalez, Professor of Spanish, Loyola
University of Chicago.
Referee.

David Goodman, Professor of Library and Information
Science, Long Island University.
Subject Editor: Biology.

Candice Goucher, Professor of History, Washington State
University, Vancouver.
Referee.

Malaika Grant, Reference/Instruction Librarian,
University of Minnesota, Twin Cities.
Bibliographer: Gender Studies.

Laura Graves, Professor of History, South Plains
College.
Bibliographer: Native American Studies.

Chip Green, Professor of Geology, University of South
Carolina Upstate.
Referee.

Susan Green, Professor of History, California State
University, Chico.
Referee.

Cheryl Grossman, Electronic Services Supervisor, LearningWork Connection, Ohio State University.
Bibliographer: Education.

Anna Marie Guengerich, Librarian, College of Education, University of Iowa.
Bibliographer: Psychology.

Richard Hacken, European Studies Bibliographer, Brigham Young University.
Referee.

Michael Handis, Associate Librarian for Collection Management, CUNY Graduate Center.
Bibliographer: European History.

Shaun Hardy, Librarian, Carnegie Institution of Washington.
Bibliographer: Geology.

Sara Harrington, Art Librarian, Rutgers University.
Referee.

Jon Harrison, Social Sciences Collections Coordinator, Missouri State University.
Bibliographer: Criminal Justice.

Elizabeth Hartung, Professor of Sociology, California Sate University Channel Islands.
Bibliographer: Sociology.

Laurence Hauptman, Professor of History, SUNY New Paltz.
Bibliographer: Native American Studies.

Peter Hayes, Professor of History, Northwestern University.
Bibliographer: European History.

Charles Hayford, Research Fellow, Department of History, Northwestern University.
Subject Editor: Asian History, Languages, and Literatures.

Jeremy Hein, Professor of Sociology, University of Wisconsin – Eau Claire.
Referee.

Eileen Herring, Agriculture Librarian, University of Hawaii.
Bibliographer: Agriculture.

Martin Hewitt, Head of History Department, Trinity and All Saints College, University of Leeds.
Referee.

Terry Hill, Customer Representative for North America, OTTO HARRASSOWITZ GmbH & Co. KG.
Bibliographer: Political Science.

Baraba Hillson, Public and International Affairs and Psychology Liaison Librarian, George Mason University.
Referee.

Lee Hilyer, Mathematics Subject Librarian, University of Houston.
Bibliographer: Education.

Keith Hitchins, Professor of History, University of Illinois.
Bibliographer: European History.

Adrian Ho, Assistant Librarian, University of Houston.
Bibliographer: Journalism and Communication.

David Hogg, Astronomer, National Radio Astronomy Observatory.
Referee.

Jane Holmquist, Astrophysics Librarian, Princeton University.
Subject Editor: Astronomy.

Emily Horning, Librarian for Philosophy, Religious Studies and Anthropology, Yale University.
Subject Editor: Religion.

John Hunter, Science/Engineering Librarian, Rice University.
Bibliographer: Geology.

Carol Hutchins, Head Librarian, Courant Institute of Mathematical Sciences, New York University.
Subject Editor: Computing.

Robin Imhof, Reference Librarian, University of the Pacific.
Bibliographer: GLBT Studies.

Richard Irving, Associate Librarian, SUNY Albany.
Bibliographer: Criminal Justice.

Kristin Jacobi, Head, Catologing Department, Eastern Connecticut State University.
Bibliographer: Native American Studies.

James Jaffe, Professor of History, University of Wisconsin – Whitewater.
Bibliographer: European History.

Arif Jamal, Social Sciences Bibliographer, University of Pittsburgh.
Bibliographer: African American Studies.

Sylvia James, Sylvia James Consultancy.
Bibliographer: Business Administration.

Fred Jenkins, Head of Collection Management, University of Dayton.
Subject Editor: Ancient History; Classics.

Donald Clay Johnson, Curator, Ames Library of South Asia, University of Minnesota.
Bibliographer: Asian History, Languages, and Literatures.

Melissa Johnson, Reference and Instruction Librarian, Lynn University.
Bibliographer: European History.

Sarah Johnson, Librarian, Eastern Illinois University.
Bibliographer: General Language and Literature.

Lisa Johnston, Head of Public Services, Sweet Briar College.
Bibliographer: British Literature.

Scott Johnston, Librarian, CUNY Graduate Center.
Subject Editor: Urban Studies.

David P. Jordan, Professor of History, University of Illinois at Chicago.
Bibliographer: European History.

Jonathan Judaken, Professor of History, University of Memphis.
Bibliographer: European History.

Jeannie Kamerman, Director, Curriculum Materials Library, University of West Florida.
Bibliographer: Education.

James Kelly, Humanities Bibliographer, University of Massachussetts.
Subject Editor: American Literature.

Marcia Keyser, Instruction and Reference Librarian, Drake University.
Bibliographer: Education.

Shayee Khanaka, Librarian, Middle Eastern Collection, University of California Berkeley.
Bibliographer: Middle Eastern History, Languages, and Literatures.

Sherise Kimura, Reference Librarian, University of San Francisco.
Bibliographer: Asian American Studies.

Douglas King, Librarian, University of South Carolina.
Bibliographer: American Literature.

Laura Kinner, Coordinator, Cataloging Services, University of Toledo.
Bibliographer: British Literature.

Harold Kirkwood, Librarian, Purdue University.
Bibliographer: Business Administration.

Patricia Kirkwood, Science Librarian, University of Arkansas.
Bibliographer: Technology and Engineering.

Sheila Kirven, Education Services Librarian, New Jersey City University.
Bibliographer: Education.

Linda Klein, Reference Librarian, Eastern Kentucky University.
Bibliographer: British Literature.

Michael Knee, Science Bibliographer and Reference Librarian, University of Albany.
Bibliographer: Computing.

Norma Kobzina, Head of Information Services, Marian Koshland Bioscience and Natural Resources Library, University of California, Berkeley.
Subject Editor: Agriculture.

David Koenigstein, Librarian, Brooklyn College.
Bibliographer: British Literature.

Gayla Koerting, Special Collections Librarian, University of South Dakota.
Bibliographer: U.S. and Canadian History.

Laura Koltutsky, Information Services Librarian, University of Houston.
Bibliographer: Education.

Kwasi Konadu, Professor of History, Winston Salem State University.
Bibliographer: African History, Languages, and Literatures.

Svetlana Korolev, Science Librarian, University of Wisconsin, Madison.
Referee.

Wade Kotter, Social Sciences Librarian, Weber State University.
Bibliographer: Criminal Justice.

Joe Kraus, Science Librarian, University of Denver.
Referee.

Eiko Kuwana, Professor of History, University of the Sacred Heart, Tokyo.
Bibliographer: European History.

Sharon Ladenson, Gender Studies and Communications Bibliographer, Michigan State University.
Bibliographer: Journalism and Communication.

Carolyn Laffoon, Earth and Atmospheric Sciences Librarian, Purdue University.
Bibliographer: Geology.

Blake Landor, Bibliographer for Philosophy, Classics, and Religion, University of Florida.
Subject Editor: Philosophy.

Jeffry Larson, Librarian for Romance Languages and Literatures, Linguistics, and Classics, Yale University.
Subject Editor: French Language and Literature; Italian Language and Literature.

Jason E. Lavery, Professor of History, Oklahoma State University.
Bibliographer: European History.

Bernadette Lear, Behavioral Sciences and Education Librarian, Pennsylvania State University.
Bibliographer: Psychology.

Patrick Leary, Research Fellow, Department of History, Northwestern University.
Subject Editor: Victorian Studies.

Richard S. Levy, Professor of History, University of Illinois at Chicago.
Bibliographer: European History.

Kevin Lindstrom, Behavioral Sciences and Education Librarian, University of British Columbia.
Bibliographer: Geology.

Ken Liss, Communication Librarian, Boston College.
Bibliographer: Journalism and Communication.

Carol Loranger, Professor of English, Wright
State University.
Referee.

Jack Lynch, Professor of English, Rutgers University.
Bibliographer: British Literature.

Karen MacDonald, Business Subject Specialist
Librarian, Texas A&M University.
Bibliographer: Business Administration.

Peter Magierski, Librarian for the Middle East Studies,
New York University.
**Bibliographer: Middle Eastern History, Languages,
and Literatures.**

Diane Maher, University Archivist, University of San
Diego.
**Bibliographer: American Literature; British
Literature.**

Janice Mathews, Librarian for Urban Studies and Social
Work, University of Connecticut.
Referee.

Rhonda McGinnis, Business and Economics Librarian,
Wayne State University.
Bibliographer: Business Administration.

Glenn McGuigan, Business Reference Librarian, Penn
State University.
Subject Editor: Business Administration.

Peter McKay, Business Librarian, University of Florida.
Bibliographer: Business Administration.

Paula McMillen, Social Sciences Librarian, Oregon State
University.
Bibliographer: Education.

Lori Mestre, Digital Learning Librarian, University of
Illinois.
Bibliographer: Education.

Sue Metcalf, Social Sciences Librarian, New Mexico
State University.
Referee.

Marion Miller, Professor of History, University of Illinois
at Chicago, emerita.
Bibliographer: European History.

Lisa Mitten, CHOICE.
Subject Editor: Native American Studies.

Sandy Mooney, Design Librarian, Louisiana State
University.
Referee.

Fred Muratori, Bibliographer for Anglo-American and
Comparative Literature and Film, Cornell
University.
Bibliographer: Drama and Theater.

Paula Murphy, Library Consultant.
Referee.

Linda Musser, Head, Fletcher L. Byrom Earth and
Mineral Sciences Library, Pennsylvania State University.
Bibliographer: Geology.

Theodore Natsoulas, Professor of History, University of
Toledo.
Bibliographer: European History.

Sharon Naylor, Education, Psychology and TMC
Division Head, Illinois State University.
Bibliographer: Education.

Antoinette Nelson, Branch Manager, Science and
Engineering Library, University of Texas Arlington.
Subject Editor: Technology and Engineering.

Jan Newberry, Professor of Anthropology, University of
Lethbridge.
Referee.

Shawn Nicholson, Bibliographer for Sociology, Social
Work, Urban Planning, Michigan State University.
Referee.

Jim Niessen, World History Librarian, Rutgers
University.
Bibliographer: European History.

Byron Nordstrom, Professor of History, Gustavus
Adolphus University.
Bibliographer: European History.

Akilah Nosakhere, Manager, Reference and Research
Division, Auburn Avenue Research Library of
African American Culture and History.
Subject Editor: African American Studies.

Nancy O'Brien, Head, Education and Social Science
Library, University of Illinois.
Subject Editor: Education.

Darby Orcutt, Collection Manager for the Humanities
and Data Analysis, North Carolina State
University.
Bibliographer: Journalism and Communication.

Harriet Ottenheimer, Professor of Anthropology,
Kansas State University.
Bibliographer: Anthropology.

Mark Padnos, Coordinator of Public Services, Bronx
Community College.
**Subject Editor: Germanic Languages and
Literatures.**

John Page, Associate Dean, Learning Resources
Division, University of the District of Columbia.
Bibliographer: African American Studies.

Tim Parrish, Professor of English, Southern Connecticut
State University.
Bibliographer: General Language and Literature.

Lucy Patrick, Head of Special Collections, Florida
State University.
Referee.

Christopher Peebles, Associate Vice President for Information Technology and Professor of Anthropology, Indiana University.
Bibliographer: Anthropology.

Ed Peters, Professor of History, University of Pennsylvania.
Bibliographer: European History.

Carmelita Pickett, African American Studies Librarian, Emory University.
Bibliographer: African American Studies.

Lisa Pillow, Collection Development Librarian, University of Wisconsin – River Falls.
Bibliographer: African American Studies.

Chestalene Pintozzi, Science-Engineering Librarian, University of Arizona.
Bibliographer: Geology.

Don Polzella, Professor of Psychology and Associate Dean for Faculty Development and Graduate Programs, University of Dayton.
Subject Editor: Psychology.

Diethelm Prowe, Professor of History, Carleton College.
Bibliographer: European History.

Eleanor Randall, Reference Librarian, Edinboro University of Pennsylvania.
Bibliographer: Biology.

Brenda Reed, Public Services Librarian, Education Library, Queen's University.
Bibliographer: Education.

Ira Revels, Instruction Librarian, Cornell University.
Bibliographer: African American Studies.

Leslie Reynolds, Director of Policy Sciences and Economics Library, Texas A&M University.
Bibliographer: Business Administration.

Amy Robb, Field Librarian for Women's Studies and Communication, University of Michigan.
Bibliographer: Journalism and Communication.

Gloria Roberson, Reference Librarian, Adelphi University.
Bibliographer: African American Studies.

Beth Roberts, Earth and Mineral Sciences Librarian, Pennsylvania State University.
Bibliographer: Geology.

Elizabeth Robertson, Professor of English, University of Colorado.
Bibliographer: British Literature.

Martin Roden, Professor emeritus of Engineering, UCLA.
Bibliographer: Technology and Engineering.

Raquel Rodriguez, Librarian for the African American Collection, University of Pittsburgh.
Bibliographer: African American Studies.

Lisa Romero, Communications Librarian, University of Illinois.
Subject Editor: Journalism and Communication.

Lana Kay Rosenberg, Director, Dance Theatre, Miami University of Ohio.
Referee.

Tony Rosso, Professor of English, Southern Connecticut State University.
Bibliographer: British Literature.

Dana Roth, Chemistry Librarian, Caltech.
Bibliographer: Chemistry.

Linda Salem, Education Librarian, San Diego State University.
Bibliographer: British Literature.

Mark Sanders, Student Outreach Reference Librarian, East Carolina University.
Bibliographer: Environmental Studies.

Rachel Sandoval, Historical Records Project Archivist, University of California, Irvine.
Bibliographer: Latino Studies.

Victoria Santana, Electronic Services Librarian, Oklahoma City University.
Bibliographer: Native American Studies.

Román Santillán, Reference/Instruction Librarian, CUNY / College of Staten Island.
Bibliographer: Spanish Language and Literature.

Vernon Schlotzhauer, Social Science Librarian, Pennsylvania State University.
Bibliographer: Psychology.

Geoff Schmidt, Professor of English, Illinois State University – Edwardsville.
Bibliographer: General Language and Literature.

Alan Schroeder, Business Librarian, California State University Northridge.
Bibliographer: Business Administration.

Kate Schroeder, Doctoral Candidate, History Department, Indiana University.
Subject Editor: African History, Languages, and Literatures.

Friedrich Schuler, Professor of History, Portland State University.
Subject Editor: Latin American History.

Katrin Schultheiss, Professor of History, University of Illinois at Chicago.
Bibliographer: European History.

Jason Schultz, Communications Librarian, Georgia State University.
Bibliographer: African American Studies.

Catherine Shreve, Librarian for Public Policy and Political Science, Duke University.
Subject Editor: Political Science.

Jack Shreve, Professor of English, Allegany College.
Bibliographer: GLBT Studies.

Adam Siegel, Reference Librarian, University of California, Davis.
Bibliographer: Native American Studies.

Dorothy Siles, Librarian, Taylorville Public Library.
Bibliographer: Native American Studies.

Jane Sloan, Media Librarian, Rutgers University.
Subject Editor: Film.

Becky Smith, Head, Business and Economics Library, University of Illinois.
Bibliographer: Business Administration.

Helen Smith, Life Sciences Librarian, Penn State University.
Bibliographer: Agriculture.

Michael Smith, Business Librarian, Texas A&M University.
Bibliographer: Business Administration.

Jacqueline Snider, Librarian, ACT.
Bibliographer: Education.

Doug Southard, DRA International.
Bibliographer: Business Administration.

Roland Spickermann, Professor of History, University of Texas, Permian Basin.
Bibliographer: European History.

Jill Spreitzer, Assistant Librarian, Public Services, University of Detroit Mercy.
Bibliographer: Technology and Engineering.

Jennifer Stevens, Humanities Liaison Librarian, George Mason University.
Bibliographer: Other Literatures in English.

David Stoloff, Professor of Education, Eastern Connecticut State University.
Referee.

Fred Stoss, Biological Science Librarian, SUNY Buffalo.
Subject Editor: Biology.

Stephen Stratton, Head of Collection Development, California State University, Channel Islands.
Subject Editor: Sociology.

Cindy Stretch, Professor of English, Southern Connecticut State University.
Referee.

Leanne Strum, Library Liaison to the School of Business, Regent University.
Bibliographer: Business Administration.

Mila Su, Coordinator of Reference Services, Pennsylvania State University.
Subject Editor: Sport and Recreation.

Helen Sullivan, Head, Slavic Reference Service, University of Illinois.
Subject Editor: Russian Languages and Literatures.

Sarah Sussman, Curator, French and Italian Collections, Stanford University.
Bibliographer: European History.

Marek Suszko, Professor of History, Purdue University North Central.
Bibliographer: European History.

Laura Taddeo, Reference Librarian, SUNY Buffalo.
Bibliographer: British Literature.

Kornelia Tancheva, Director of Instructional Services, Cornell University.
Subject Editor: Drama and Theater.

Wendy Tann, Librarian, Federal Reserve Bank.
Bibliographer: Business Administration.

Cornelia Akins Taylor, Special Collections Librarian, Florida A & M University.
Bibliographer: African American Studies.

Betty Taylor-Thompson, Professor of English, Texas Southern University.
Referee.

Edward Teague, Head, Architecture & Allied Arts Library, University of Oregon.
Subject Editor: Visual Arts.

Samantha Teplitzky, Earth Sciences Librarian and Bibliographer, Stanford University.
Bibliographer: Geology.

Stephen Thompson, Co-Leader, Technical Services Department, Brown University.
Bibliographer: American Literature.

Erik Thomson, Collegiate Assistant Professor, Social Sciences, University of Chicago.
Bibliographer: European History.

Charles Thurston, Reference Librarian and Bibliographer, University of Texas at San Antonio.
Bibliographer: Education.

Judie Triplehorn, Librarian, Geophysical Institute, University of Alaska.
Bibliographer: Geology.

Markel Tumlin, English and American Literature Librarian, San Diego State University.
Bibliographer: American Literature.

Andrea Twiss-Brooks, Bibliographer for Chemical and Geophysical Sciences, University of Chicago.
Subject Editor: Geology.

Kent Underwood, Music Librarian, New York University.
Subject Editor: Music.

Alan Unsworth, Reference Librarian, University of Rochester.
Referee.

David Vaccari, Professor of Engineering, Stevens Institute of Technology.
Bibliographer: Technology and Engineering.

Susan Vega Garcia, Reference & Instruction Librarian, Bibliographer, Iowa State University.
Bibliographer: Latino Studies.

Tom Volkening, Engineering Librarian, Michigan State University.
Bibliographer: Technology and Engineering.

Heather Ward, University of Oregon, formerly.
Subject Editor: Medieval Studies.

Diane Warner, Monographs and Special Formats Cataloger, Texas Tech University.
Bibliographer: American Literature.

Gary Wasdin, Library Director, New School University.
Referee.

Matthew Wayman, Instruction Coordinator, Penn State University.
Bibliographer: U.S. and Canadian History.

Jeneen Willemssen, Librarian, Conserve School.
Bibliographer: Education.

Wendy Williamson, Economics Librarian, University of Minnesota.
Referee.

Suzanne Wise, Collection Development Librarian, Appalachia State University.
Referee.

Ada Woods, Reference Librarian, Towson University.
Bibliographer.

Peng Xu, Reference Librarian, Michigan State University.
Bibliographer: Business Administration.

Lisa Yuro, Reference Librarian/Humanities and Social Sciences Coordinator, University of Alabama.
Bibliographer: Journalism and Communication.

Ann Zawistoski, Reference and Instruction Librarian, Carleton College.
Bibliographer: Geology.

Linda Zellmer, Head, Geology Library, Indiana University.
Subject Editor: Geology.

HOW TO USE
RESOURCES FOR COLLEGE LIBRARIES

Resources for College Libraries (RCL) was designed to be easily searchable by author, title, and the RCL subject taxonomy. The set consists of seven volumes, Volumes 1-6 arranged by RCL Subject, and sorted alphabetically by author. Volume 7 is a comprehensive author, title and subject index. The volumes are arranged by *Resources for College Library* Subject Headings, a full listing of which is present in the Subject Headings Index in volume 7.

Each title in *Resources for College Libraries* has been classified with a specific RCL Subject and/or subjects. Titles can and often do appear within more than one RCL Subject area. Titles have been given a specific readership level through audience code: g=general, l=lower-division undergraduate, u=upper-division undergraduate graduate, and/or f=faculty level resources. Titles previously mentioned in *Books for College Libraries, 3rd Edition*, have been noted with a specific BCL3 icon 𝓑. Non-book entries can be easily identified with the icons for Web 🖳, Ebook 🄴, or CD/DVD-ROM 🗲.

Classification Number, Dewey Decimal Number, Library of Congress Control Number, Audience Code, and whether it has been reviewed in Choice Magazine.

Entries in the Author Index can include the following bibliographic information when available: author, co-author, editor, co-editor, translator, co-translator, along with page number(s) and volume number(s) of the selected works within the 6-volume set. Entries are not cross-referenced by other than primary author and/or first contributor. Entries in the Title Index include the title, page number(s) and volume number(s) of the selected works within the 6-volume set.

Titles in *Resources for College Libraries* have been alphabetized using the following rules:

- Initial articles of titles in English, French, German, Italian, and Spanish are not included for sorting purposes.

- Titles beginning with acronyms appear before those

SAMPLE RCL ENTRY

1 DRAMA AND THEATER ❯ Western Drama ❯ United States

2 Wilmeth, Don B. & Bigsby,   PN2221
     Christopher (Editors)
3 The Cambridge History of American Theater: **4** 1870-1945. **5** Ed. 2
6 Don B. Wilmeth & Christopher Bigsby (Contribution by). **7** Trade Paper.
8 Cambridge University Press. **9** New York, NY. **10** 2006. **11** 608p.
12 Cambridge History of American Theater Ser. **13** ISBN: 0-521-67984-2,
ISBN13: 978-0-521-67984-8. **14** Dewey:792/.0973.
15 LCCN: 00-000000
                 16 Audience: l,u,f. **17** *Choice, 2005* 𝓑

1. RCL Subject Heading
2. Author/First Contributor
3. Title
4. Subtitle
5. Ed. Info
6. Additional Contributors
7. Binding Type
8. Publisher
9. Publisher Location
10. Publication Date
11. Number of Pages
12. Series Title
13. ISBN, ISBN-13
14. Dewey
15. LCCN
16. Audience Code
17. Choice Review and Date

Title entries can include the following bibliographic information, when available: author, co-author, editor, co-editor, translator, co-translator, title, number of volumes, edition, series information, binding type, publisher, publisher location, date of publication, number of pages, ISBN, ISBN-13, Library of Congress

beginning with words. For example, B E A M A Directory would precede Baal, Babylon.

- As a general rule, U.S. and UN are filed in strict alphabetical order.

- Numeric Titles may be found near the end of the Title Index

Authors in *Resources for College Libraries* have been alphabetized using the following rules:

- Proper names beginning with "Mc" and "Mac" are filed in strict alphabetical order. For example, entries for contributors' names such as MacAdam, MacAvory, and MacCarthy are located prior to the pages with entries for names such as McAdam, McCoy, and McDermott.

- When author names are represented with initials, they are alphabetized before author first names. For example, Smith, H. C. appears before Smith, Harold A.

Any errors in bibliographic data should be E-mailed directly to: rclwebfeedback@bowker.com

ABBREVIATIONS AND CODE LIST:

BCL3	*Books for College Libraries, 3rd Edition*
Bk.(s.)	Book(s)
Ed.	Edition
F	Faculty
G	General
Inc.	Incorporated
Jr.	Junior
ISBN	International Standard Book Number
L	Lower-Division Undergraduate
LCCN	Library of Congress Control Number
p.	Pages
RCL	Resources for College Libraries
Ser.	Series
Sr.	Senior
U	Upper-Division Undergraduate

Geographical Abbreviations

AL	Alabama	NJ	New Jersey
AK	Alaska	NM	New Mexico
AB	Alberta	NSW	New South Wales
AE	American Europe	NY	New York
AS	American Samoa	NF	Newfoundland
AZ	Arizona	NC	North Carolina
AR	Arkansas	ND	North Dakota
ACT	Australian Capital Territory	NP	Northern Marianas
BC	British Columbia	N.T.	Northern Territory (Australia)
CA	California	NT	Northwest Territory
CM	Central Marianas	NS	Nova Scotia
CO	Colorado	NU	Nunavut
CT	Connecticut	OH	Ohio
DE	Delaware	OK	Oklahoma
DC	District Of Columbia	ON	Ontario
FM	Federated States Of Micronesia	OR	Oregon
FL	Florida	TT	Pacific Territories
GA	Georgia	PW	Pacific West
GU	Guam	PA	Pennsylvania
HI	Hawaii	PE	Prince Edward Island
ID	Idaho	PR	Puerto Rico
IL	Illinois	PQ	Quebec
IN	Indiana	QLD	Queensland
IA	Iowa	RI	Rhode Island
KS	Kansas	SK	Saskatchewan
KY	Kentucky	SA	South Australia
LA	Louisiana	SC	South Carolina
ME	Maine	SD	South Dakota
MB	Manitoba	TAS	Tasmania
MH	Marshall Islands	TN	Tennessee
MD	Maryland	TX	Texas
MA	Massachusetts	UT	Utah
MI	Michigan	VT	Vermont
MP	Middle Pacific	VIC	Victoria
MN	Minnesota	VI	Virgin Islands
MS	Mississippi	VA	Virginia
MO	Missouri	WA	Washington
MT	Montana	WV	West Virginia
NE	Nebraska	W.A.	Western Australia
NV	Nevada	WI	Wisconsin
NB	New Brunswick	WY	Wyoming
NH	New Hampshire	YT	Yukon Territory

AGRICULTURE

The section on agriculture reflects the fairly rapid growth and expansion of the literature that covers the fields of agriculture and food science that has taken place since the publication of BCL3. The lists are designed to serve the needs of undergraduates and four-year colleges; there are also items that are specifically aimed at community colleges, which often have specialized programs in such fields as horticulture, food service and technology, and fire technology. Materials included also meet the needs of general audiences as well as students, faculty, and researchers in the subject areas.

Many academic programs focus on the broader areas of natural resources, which is now much more interdisciplinary than at the time BCL3 was issued. Publications cover traditional agriculture, conservation, crops and soils, plant biotechnology, entomology, and pest management. Other key subjects are animal science and veterinary medicine, fisheries, forestry, fire management, and rangeland science. The concepts of sustainable agriculture and sustainable forestry were fairly new in the mid- to late-1980s, but have become extremely important since that time.

There is a considerable overlap with the fields of environmental science and it was difficult to make a clear distinction. In the interest of making sure no significant works are excluded, we have put in many titles that relate to soil, water, and wildlife conservation, as well as the economic aspects of the environment.

For this edition, food science and technology has been incorporated under agriculture since much of it is interrelated; the BCL3 categories based on Library of Congress classes TP and TX are now covered in this section.

The classic works in the various sub-disciplines that were in BCL3 are still listed and there are some other retrospective titles, but as a rule, the focus has been on the most important works published after 1988. As much as possible, the latest edition of each title is given. Although some books are out of print, they are included because they are still significant and are heavily cited. When appropriate, electronic equivalents are given as alternate editions. Web sites have been selected based on their currency, reputation of the agencies that created them, and intended audience.

— Norma Kobzina

Agriculture

S493

☐ AgNIC: The Agriculture Network Information Center.
http://agnic.org/
AgNIC.

Audience: **g,l,u,f.**

S493

☐ AGRIS/CARIS: International Information System for the
Agricultural Sciences and Technology.
http://www.fao.org/agris/

Audience: **u,f.**

S539.5

☐ Consultative Group on International Agricultural Research
(CGIAR).
http://www.cgiar.org/
CGIAR.

Audience: **u,f.**

S441

☐ The Core Historical Literature of Agriculture (CHLA).
http://chla.library.cornell.edu/
Albert R. Mann Library, Cornell University.

Audience: **u,f.**

S493

☐ The Food and Agriculture Organization of the United
Nations: WAICENT Information Finder.
http://search.fao.org/opensearch?query=&lang=en
FAO.

Audience: **u,f.**

S494.5.A8

☐ United States Department of Agriculture National
Agricultural Library Catalog (AGRICOLA).
http://agricola.nal.usda.gov/
United States Department of Agriculture.

Audience: **g,u,f.**

HD1769

☐ United States Department of Agriculture National
Agricultural Statistics Service 2002 Census of Agriculture.
http://www.nass.usda.gov/Census_of_Agriculture/index.asp
United States Department of Agriculture.

Audience: **u,f.**

Allen, Robert C.   **HC335.A655 2003**
Farm to Factory: A Reinterpretation of the Soviet Industrial
Revolution. Trade Cloth. Princeton University Press. Princeton,
NJ. 2003. 264p. The Princeton Economic History of the Western
World Ser. ISBN:0-691-00696-2, ISBN13: 978-0-691-00696-3.
Dewey:330.947/0842. LCCN:2002-042718.

Audience: **l,u,f.** *Choice, 2004.*

American Society of   **S671**
  Agricultural Engineers
ASAE Standards: Standards, Engineering Practices and Data
Adopted by the American Society of Agricultural Engineers. Ed.
31. The Society. 1984.

Audience: **u,f.**

Bailey, Liberty Hyde   **SB187.U6 B28**
Cyclopedia of American Agriculture: A Popular Survey of
Agricultural Conditions, Practices and Ideals in the United
States and Canada, Set. Library Binding. Library Reprints, Inc..
Temecula, CA. ISBN:0-7222-3094-X, ISBN13:
978-0-7222-3094-7. Dewey:633/.00973.

Audience: **g,u,f.**

Bakker-Arkema, F. W.   **S675.C54 1999**
  (Editor), et al.
CIGR Handbook of Agricultural Engineering: Agro Processing
Engineering. P. Amirante, J. De Baerdemacker, M. Ruiz-Altisent
& C. J. Studman (Editors). Cloth Text. American Society of
Agricultural Engineers. Saint Joseph, MI. 1999. 540p.
ISBN:1-892769-03-4, ISBN13: 978-1-892769-03-9.
Dewey:631.3. LCCN:98-093767.

Audience: **u,f.**

Ban, A. W. van den, et al.   **S544.B2513 2003**
Communication for Rural Innovation: Rethinking Agricultural
Extension. Ed. 3. H. S. Hawkins, C. Leeuwis & Willem Zijp
(Authors). Trade Paper. Blackwell Publishing, Inc. Malden, MA.
2004. 424p. ISBN:0-632-05249-X, ISBN13: 978-0-632-05249-3.
Dewey:630/.71/5. LCCN:2003-058372.

Audience: **g,l,u.**

Bartali, El Houssine   **S675.C54 1999**
  (Editor), et al.
CIGR Handbook of Agricultural Engineering: Animal
Production and Aquacultural Engineering. Aad Jongebreur, Dand
Moffitt & Frederick Wheaton (Editors). Cloth Text. American
Society of Agricultural Engineers. Saint Joseph, MI. 1999. 395p.
ISBN:0-929355-98-9, ISBN13: 978-0-929355-98-6.
Dewey:631.3. LCCN:98-093767.

Audience: **u,f.**

Berry, Wendell   **S441.B47 2002**
The Art of the Commonplace: The Agrarian Essays of Wendell
Berry. Norman Wirzba (Editor). Trade Cloth. Basic Books. New
York, NY. 2002. 352p. ISBN:1-58243-146-9, ISBN13:
978-1-58243-146-8. Dewey:630/.973. LCCN:2002-000724.

Audience: **g,l,u.** *Choice, 2002.*

Blandford, Percy W.   **S674.5.B55 1976**
Old Farm Tools and Machinery: An Illustrated History. Trade
Cloth. Thomson Gale. Farmington Hills, MI. 1976. 188 p. :p.
ISBN:0-8103-2019-3, ISBN13: 978-0-8103-2019-2.
Dewey:631.3/09. LCCN:75-044376.

Audience: **g,l,u.** *B*

Capinera, John   **SB603.5.C36 2001**
Handbook of Vegetable Pests. Trade Cloth. Elsevier Science &
Technology Books. Saint Louis, MO. 2001. 800p.
ISBN:0-12-158861-0, ISBN13: 978-0-12-158861-8.
Dewey:635/.0497. LCCN:2001-086233.

Audience: **g,l,u.** *Choice, 2001.*

Carstensen, Frederick V.   **S441.O95 1993**
  (Editor), et al.
Outstanding in His Field: Perspectives on American Agricultural
History in Honor of Wayne D. Rasmussen. Morton Rothstein &
Joseph A. Swanson (Editors). Cloth Text. Blackwell Publishing
Professional. Ames, IA. 1993. 176p. Henry A. Wallace Series on
Agricultural History and Rural Studies ISBN:0-8138-0739-5,
ISBN13: 978-0-8138-0739-3. Dewey:338.1/0973.
LCCN:92-045889.

Audience: **g,u,f.**

Audience: g=general, l=lower division undergraduate, u=upper division undergraduate, f=faculty.

3

Collinson, M. P.   S494.5.S95H57 2000
A History of Farming Systems Research. Cloth Text. Oxford
University Press, Inc. New York, NY. 2000. 448p. CABI
Publishing Ser. ISBN:0-85199-405-9, ISBN13:
978-0-85199-405-5. Dewey:630/.72. LCCN:99-042827.
                                                Audience: **u,f.**

Committee on the Role of   S494.5.A65A43 1989
  Alternative Farming Methods Staff
Alternative Agriculture. Paper Text. National Academies Press.
Washington, DC. 1989. 464p. ISBN:0-309-03985-1, ISBN13:
978-0-309-03985-7. Dewey:630/.973. LCCN:88-026997.
                                Audience: **g,l,u.** *Choice, 1990.*

Ebeling, Walter   S441.E23
The Fruited Plain: The Story of American Agriculture. Trade
Cloth. University of California Press. Berkeley, CA. 1979. xiii,
433p. ISBN:0-520-03751-0, ISBN13: 978-0-520-03751-9.
Dewey:338.1/0973. LCCN:78-062837.
                                Audience: **g,l,u,f.** $\mathcal{B}$

Federico, Giovanni   HD1411.F43 2005
Feeding the World: An Economic History of Agriculture,
1800-2000. Trade Cloth. Princeton University Press. Princeton,
NJ. 2005. 520p. The Princeton Economic History of the Western
World Ser. ISBN:0-691-12051-X, ISBN13: 978-0-691-12051-5.
Dewey:338.1/09/034. LCCN:2004-058634.
                                Audience: **g,l,u,f.** *Choice, 2006.*

Fitzgerald, Deborah Kay   HD1761.F564 2003
Every Farm a Factory: The Industrial Ideal in American
Agriculture. Cloth over Boards. Yale University Press.
Cumberland, RI. 2003. 256p. ISBN:0-300-08813-2, ISBN13:
978-0-300-08813-7. Dewey:338.1/0973. LCCN:2002-012135.
                                Audience: **g,l,u,f.** *Choice, 2003.*

Gardner, Bruce L.   HD1761
American Agriculture in the Twentieth Century: How It
Flourished and What It Cost. Trade Paper. Harvard University
Press. Cambridge, MA. 2006. 400p. ISBN:0-674-01989-X,
ISBN13: 978-0-674-01989-8. Dewey:338.1/0973/0904.
                                Audience: **g,l,u.** *Choice, 2003.*

Grigg, David B.   S495.G79 1995
An Introduction to Agricultural Geography. Ed. 2. Trade Paper.
Routledge. New York, NY. 1995. 240p. ISBN:0-415-08443-1,
ISBN13: 978-0-415-08443-7. Dewey:338.1/09.
LCCN:94-012681.
                                          Audience: **u,f.** $\mathcal{B}$

Guohua, Xu & Peel, L. J.   S471.C6A365 1991
  (Editors)
The Agriculture of China. Trade Cloth. Oxford University Press,
Inc. New York, NY. 1991. 320p. Centre for Agricultural Strategy
Ser., No. 2 ISBN:0-19-859208-6, ISBN13: 978-0-19-859208-2.
Dewey:630/.951. LCCN:91-002017.
                                Audience: **l,u,f.** *Choice, 1992.*

Hallam, Arne   HD1470.5.U6.S59 1993
Size, Structure, and the Changing Face of American Agriculture.
Trade Paper. Westview Press. Boulder, CO. 1993. 627p.
ISBN:0-8133-8606-3, ISBN13: 978-0-8133-8606-5.
Dewey:338.160973. LCCN:93-029046.
                                Audience: **g,l,u,f.** *Choice, 1994.*

Harding, T. Swann   S21.C9 H3 1980
Two Blades of Grass: A History of Scientific Development in
the U. S. Department of Agriculture. I. Bernard Cohen (Editor).
Library Binding. Ayer Company Publishers, Inc. Manchester,
NH. 1980. Three Centuries of Science in America Ser.
ISBN:0-405-12547-X, ISBN13: 978-0-405-12547-8.
Dewey:630/.72/073. LCCN:79-007966.
                                          Audience: **u,f.** $\mathcal{B}$

Harlan, Jack Rodney   GN799.A4 H37 1995
The Living Fields: Our Agricultural Heritage. Trade Paper.
Cambridge University Press. New York, NY. 1998. 288p.
ISBN:0-521-64992-7, ISBN13: 978-0-521-64992-6.
Dewey:630.9.
                                Audience: **g,l,u,f.** *Choice, 1996.*

Hays, Samuel P.   S930.H38 1999
Conservation and the Gospel of Efficiency: The Progressive
Conservation Movement, 1890-1920. Trade Paper. University of
Pittsburgh Press. Pittsburgh, PA. 1999. 292p.
ISBN:0-8229-5702-7, ISBN13: 978-0-8229-5702-7.
Dewey:333.7/2/0973. LCCN:98-054700.
                                Audience: **g,l,u,f.** $\mathcal{B}$

Heiser, Charles B. Jr.   S419.H44 1990
Seed to Civilization: The Story of Food. Trade Cloth. Harvard
University Press. Cambridge, MA. 1990. 240p.
ISBN:0-674-79681-0, ISBN13: 978-0-674-79681-2.
Dewey:630.9. LCCN:89-027406.
                                          Audience: **g,l,u.**

Heldman, Dennis R. (Editor)   TP368.2.E57 2003
Encyclopedia of Agricultural, Food, and Biological Engineering.
Paper over Boards. Marcel Dekker Inc. New York, NY. 2003.
1208p. Dekker Encyclopedias Ser. ISBN:0-8247-0938-1,
ISBN13: 978-0-8247-0938-9. Dewey:664/.003.
LCCN:2003-055526.
                                Audience: **g,l,u,f.** *Choice, 2004.*

Hudson, John C.   F351.H858 1994
@ Making the Corn Belt: A Geographical History of
Middle-Western Agriculture. E-Book. Indiana University Press.
Bloomington, IN. 1994. 129p. Midwestern History and Culture
Ser. ISBN:0-253-32832-2, ISBN13: 978-0-253-32832-8.
Dewey:917.8. LCCN:93-035723.
                                          Audience: **f.** *Choice, 1995.*

Hurt, R. Douglas   S441
American Agriculture: A Brief History. Trade Paper. Purdue
University Press. West Lafayette, IN. 2002. 424p.
ISBN:1-55753-281-8, ISBN13: 978-1-55753-281-7.
Dewey:338.1973.
                                          Audience: **g,l,u,f.**

Hurt, R. Douglas   S441.H92
The Dust Bowl: An Agricultural and Social History. Trade
Cloth. Rowman & Littlefield Publishers, Inc. Lanham, MD.
1981. 240p. ISBN:0-88229-541-1, ISBN13: 978-0-88229-541-1.
Dewey:338.1/0978. LCCN:81-004031.
                                Audience: **g,l,u,f.** $\mathcal{B}$

Hurt, R. Douglas   E98.A3
Indian Agriculture in America: Prehistory to the Present. Trade
Paper. University Press of Kansas. Lawrence, KS. 1996. xiv,
290p. ISBN:0-7006-0802-8, ISBN13: 978-0-7006-0802-7.
Dewey:338.1/08997073. LCCN:87-014764.
                                Audience: **g,l,u.** *Choice, 1988.*

Hurt, R. Douglas & Hurt,   **Z5071.H87 1994**
  Mary E.
The History of Agricultural Science and Technology: An
International Annotated Bibliography. Paper over Boards.
Garland Publishing, Inc. New York, NY. 1993. 504p.
Bibliographies on the History of Science and Technology Ser.,
Vol. 20:Reference Library of the Humanities
ISBN:0-8240-7182-4, ISBN13: 978-0-8240-7182-0.
Dewey:016.6309. LCCN:93-028006.
                  Audience: **l,u,f.** *Choice, 1994.*

Kennedy, Roger G.   **E332**
Mr. Jefferson's Lost Cause: Land, Farmers, Slavery, and the
Louisiana Purchase. Trade Paper. Oxford University Press, Inc.
New York, NY. 2004. 368p. ISBN:0-19-517607-3, ISBN13:
978-0-19-517607-0. Dewey:973.4/6/092.
                  Audience: **u,f.** *Choice, 2003.*

King, F. H.   **S471.C6**
Farmers of Forty Centuries or Permanent Agriculture in China,
Korea and Japan. Trade Paper. Kessinger Publishing, LLC.
Whitefish, MT. 2004. ISBN:1-4191-1934-6, ISBN13:
978-1-4191-1934-7. Dewey:630/.951.
                  Audience: **l,u,f.**

Kitani, Osamu (Editor),   **S675.C54 1999**
  et al.
CIGR Handbook of Agricultural Engineering: Energy and
Biomass Engineering. Thomas Jungbluth, Robert M. Peart &
Abdellah Ramdani (Editors). Cloth Text. American Society of
Agricultural Engineers. Saint Joseph, MI. 1999. 330p.
ISBN:0-929355-97-0, ISBN13: 978-0-929355-97-9.
Dewey:631.3. LCCN:98-093767.
                  Audience: **u,f.**

Kulikoff, Allan   **00-029904 [HC]**
From British Peasants to Colonial American Farmers. Trade
Cloth. University of North Carolina Press. Chapel Hill, NC.
2000. 504p. ISBN:0-8078-2569-7, ISBN13: 978-0-8078-2569-3.
Dewey:338.1/0973. LCCN:00-029904.
                  Audience: **u,f.** *Choice, 2001.*

Leigh, G. J.   **S651**
The World's Greatest Fix: A History of Nitrogen and
Agriculture. Trade Cloth. DIANE Publishing Company.
Collingdale, PA. 2006. 242p. ISBN:0-7567-9911-2, ISBN13:
978-0-7567-9911-3. Dewey:631.8/4.
                  Audience: **u,f.** *Choice, 2005.*

Liebman, Matt, et al.   **SB611.5.L54 2001**
Ecological Management of Agricultural Weeds. Charles L.
Mohler & Charles P. Staver (Authors). Trade Cloth. Cambridge
University Press. New York, NY. 2001. 544p.
ISBN:0-521-56068-3, ISBN13: 978-0-521-56068-9.
Dewey:632.5. LCCN:00-068869.
                  Audience: **l,u,f.**

McDowell, George R.   **LB2329.5.M39 2001**
Land-Grant Universities and Extension into the 21st Century:
Renegotiating or Abandoning a Social Contract. Trade Cloth.
Blackwell Publishing Professional. Ames, IA. 2001. 232p.
ISBN:0-8138-1918-0, ISBN13: 978-0-8138-1918-1.
Dewey:378/.054/0973. LCCN:00-063463.
                  Audience: **u,f.**

McWilliams, Carey   **HD1527.C2 M25 2000**
Factories in the Field: The Story of Migratory Farm Labor in
California. Trade Paper. University of California Press. Berkeley,

CA. 2000. 364p. ISBN:0-520-22413-2, ISBN13:
978-0-520-22413-1. Dewey:331.5/44/09794. LCCN:99-045099.
                  Audience: **g,l,u,f.**

Meyer, James H.   **S533.M475 1998**
The Historical Trek of the Land Grant College of Agriculture:
Past, Present and Future. S.I.. 1998.
                  Audience: **u,f.**

Miller, Char (Editor)   **GF503.A84 2003**
The Atlas of U. S. and Canadian Environmental History. Paper
over Boards. Routledge. New York, NY. 2003. 256p.
ISBN:0-415-93781-7, ISBN13: 978-0-415-93781-8.
Dewey:304.2/097/022. LCCN:2003-046799.
               Audience: **g,l,u,f.** *Choice, 2004.*

Mooney, Patrick H. &   **HD6515.A29M66 1995**
  Majka, Theo J.
Farmers' and Farm Workers' Movements. Trade Cloth. Thomson
Gale. Farmington Hills, MI. 1994. 288p. Twayne's Social
Movements Past and Present Ser. ISBN:0-8057-3869-X,
ISBN13: 978-0-8057-3869-8. Dewey:331.88/13/0973.
LCCN:94-018178.
             Audience: **g,l,u.** *Choice, 1995.*

Pillsbury, Richard & Florin,   **G1201.J1 .P5 1996**
  John (Editors)
Atlas of American Agriculture: The American Cornucopia. Trade
Cloth. Macmillan Publishing Company, Inc. Old Tappan, NJ.
1996. 256p. ISBN:0-02-897333-X, ISBN13: 978-0-02-897333-3.
Dewey:338.10973. LCCN:95-046039.
             Audience: **g,l,u.** *Choice, 1997.*

Rao, M. A., et al.   **TP372.5**
Engineering Properties of Foods. Ed. 3. Syed S. H. Rizvi &
Ashim K. Datta (Authors). Paper over Boards. Marcel Dekker
Inc. New York, NY. 2005. 760p. Food Science and Technology
Ser., Vol. 142 ISBN:0-8247-5328-3, ISBN13:
978-0-8247-5328-3. Dewey:664. LCCN:2004-056967.
                  Audience: **u,f.**

Rasmussen, Wayne David
Farmers, Cooperatives, and USDA: A History of Agricultural
Cooperative Service. U.S. Dept. of Agriculture. 1991.
                  Audience: **g,l,u,f.**

Rogal, Samuel J.   **S455**
  (Compiled by)
Agriculture in Britain and America, 1660-1820: An Annotated
Bibliography of the Eighteenth-Century Literature. Cloth Text.
Greenwood Publishing Group, Inc. Portsmouth, NH. 1994. 280p.
Bibliographies and Indexes in World History Ser., No. 33
ISBN:0-313-29352-X, ISBN13: 978-0-313-29352-8.
Dewey:016.630/941. LCCN:94-012323.
                  Audience: **u,f.** *Choice, 1995.*

Rossiter, Margaret W.   **HD1411**
The Emergence of Agricultural Science: Justus Liebig and the
Americans, 1840-1880. Trade Cloth. Yale University Press.
Cumberland, RI. 1975. 288p. Studies in the History of Science
and Medicine, No. 9 ISBN:0-300-01721-9, ISBN13:
978-0-300-01721-2. Dewey:338.1/6. LCCN:74-029737.
                  Audience: **u,f.** *B*

Roth, Lawrence O. & Field,   **S675.R67**
  Harry L.
An Introduction to Agricultural Engineering. Trade Paper. Aspen

Publishers, Inc. New York, NY. 1999. 346p.
ISBN:0-8342-1308-7, ISBN13: 978-0-8342-1308-1.
Dewey:620/.002/4631.

Audience: **u,f.**

Schapsmeier, Frederick H.   **HD1761**
& Schapsmeier, Edward L.
Encyclopedia of American Agricultural History. Cloth Text.
Greenwood Publishing Group, Inc. Portsmouth, NH. 1976. 467p.
ISBN:0-8371-7958-0, ISBN13: 978-0-8371-7958-2.
Dewey:338.1/0973. LCCN:74-034563.

Audience: **g.** *B*

Singh, R. Paul & Heldman,   **TP370.S456 2001**
Dennis R.
Introduction to Food Engineering. Ed. 3. Cloth Text. Elsevier
Science & Technology Books. Saint Louis, MO. 2001. 750p.
Food Science and Technology International Ser.
ISBN:0-12-646384-0, ISBN13: 978-0-12-646384-2. Dewey:664.
LCCN:2001-086670.

Audience: **u,f.**

Slaybaugh, Douglas   **HD1771.5.M97S58 1996**
William I. Myers and the Modernization of American
Agriculture. Cloth Text. Blackwell Publishing Professional.
Ames, IA. 1996. 302p. Henry A. Wallace Series on Agricultural
History and Rural Studies ISBN:0-8138-2038-3, ISBN13:
978-0-8138-2038-5. Dewey:338.1/092 B. LCCN:96-010903.

Audience: **u,f.** *Choice, 1996.*

Stephens, Alan (Editor)   **S411.D573 1998**
Dictionary of Agriculture. Ed. 2. Paper over Boards. Fitzroy
Dearborn Publishers, Inc. Chicago, IL. 1998. 325p.
ISBN:1-57958-076-9, ISBN13: 978-1-57958-076-6.
Dewey:630/.3. LCCN:99-161557.

Audience: **g,l,u.** *Choice, 1999.*

Stock, Catherine McNicol &   **HN57.C69 2001**
Johnston, Robert D. (Editors)
The Countryside in the Age of the Modern State: Political
Histories of Rural America. Book, Other. Cornell University
Press. Ithaca, NY. 2001. 352p. ISBN:0-8014-3850-0, ISBN13:
978-0-8014-3850-9. Dewey:307.72/0973. LCCN:2001-003485.
Audience: **u,f.**

Stout, B. A. & Cheze, B.   **S675.C54 1999**
(Editors)
CIGR Handbook of Agricultural Engineering: Plant Production
Engineering. Cloth Text. American Society of Agricultural
Engineers. Saint Joseph, MI. 1999. 660p. ISBN:1-892769-02-6,
ISBN13: 978-1-892769-02-2. LCCN:98-093767.

Audience: **u,f.**

Tarleton, Raymond J.   **TS2120.T37 2000**
History of the American Association of Cereal Chemists. Trade
Cloth. American Association of Cereal Chemists. Saint Paul,
MN. 2000. 176p. ISBN:1-891127-21-7, ISBN13:
978-1-891127-21-2. Dewey:634.7200257. LCCN:00-108138.
Audience: **u,f.**

Tollner, Ernest W.   **S675.T54 2002**
Natural Resources Engineering. Trade Cloth. Blackwell
Publishing Professional. Ames, IA. 2002. 512p.
ISBN:0-8138-1847-8, ISBN13: 978-0-8138-1847-4. Dewey:627.
LCCN:2001-006117.

Audience: **u,f.**

Troeh, Frederick R. &   **S411.T76 2002**
Donahue, Roy Luther
Dictionary of Agriculture and Environmental Science. Trade
Cloth. Blackwell Publishing Professional. Ames, IA. 2002. 524p.
ISBN:0-8138-0283-0, ISBN13: 978-0-8138-0283-1.
Dewey:630/.3. LCCN:2002-000824.

Audience: **g,l,u,f.**

Van Lier, H. N.   **S675.C54 1999**
(Editor), et al.
CIGR Handbook of Agricultural Engineering: Land and Water
Engineering. L. S. Pereira & F. R. Steiner (Editors). Cloth Text.
American Society of Agricultural Engineers. Saint Joseph, MI.
1999. 570p. ISBN:1-892769-01-8, ISBN13: 978-1-892769-01-5.
Dewey:631.3. LCCN:98-093767.

Audience: **u,f.**

Weber, E.   **SB613.5**
Invasive Plant Species of the World: A Reference Guide to
Environmental Weeds. CAB International Staff (Contribution
by). Cloth Text. Oxford University Press, Inc. New York, NY.
2003. 560p. CABI Publishing Ser. ISBN:0-85199-695-7,
ISBN13: 978-0-85199-695-0. Dewey:632/.5.
LCCN:2003-010034.

Audience: **g,l,u,f.** *Choice, 2004.*

Wegren, Stephen K.   **HD1333.R9W44 1997**
Agriculture and the State in Soviet and Post-Soviet Russia.
Cloth Text. University of Pittsburgh Press. Pittsburgh, PA. 1998.
246p. Pitt Series in Russian and East European Studies
ISBN:0-8229-4062-0, ISBN13: 978-0-8229-4062-3.
Dewey:338.1/847. LCCN:97-045318.

Audience: **u,f.**

Wendel, C. H.   **S674.W46 2004**
Encyclopedia of American Farm Implements and Antiques. Ed.
3. Brian Earnst (Editor). Trade Paper. Krause Publications. Iola,
WI. 2004. 496p. ISBN:0-87349-568-3, ISBN13:
978-0-87349-568-4. Dewey:631.3/03. LCCN:2004-092436.

Audience: **g,u.**

Williams, Robert C.   **S711.W54 1987**
Fordson, Farmall and Poppin' Johnny: A History of the Farm
Tractor and Its Impact on America. Trade Cloth. University of
Illinois Press. Champaign, IL. 1987. 242p.
ISBN:0-252-01328-X, ISBN13: 978-0-252-01328-7.
Dewey:631.3/72/0973. LCCN:86-001359.

Audience: **g,l,u,f.** *Choice, 1987.*

Woods, Thomas A.   **HD1485.P5W66 1991**
Knights of the Plow: Oliver H. Kelley and the Origins of the
Grange in Republican Ideology. Cloth Text. Blackwell
Publishing Professional. Ames, IA. 1990. 276p. Henry A.
Wallace Series on Agricultural History and Rural Studies
ISBN:0-8138-0239-3, ISBN13: 978-0-8138-0239-8.
Dewey:338.1/06073. LCCN:90-004442.

Audience: **g,l,u.** *Choice, 1991.*

Agriculture > Agricultural Biotechnology

Agricultural Biotechnology: Finding Common International
Goals. National Agricultural Biotechnology Council. 2004.

Audience: **u,f.**

SB123.57

☐ Transgenic Crops: An Introduction and Resource Guide.
http://cls.casa.colostate.edu/TransgenicCrops/
Department of Soil and Crop Sciences at Colorado State
University.

Audience: **g,l,u.**

Altman, A & Colwell,   **S494.5.B563.A3715**
Rita R.

ⓔ Agricultural Biotechnology. E-Book. NetLibrary, Inc.
Boulder, CO. 1998. ISBN:0-585-15747-2, ISBN13:
978-0-585-15747-4. Dewey:631.

Audience: **l,u,f.**

Bailey, Britt & Lappe, Marc   **S494.5.G44E54 2002**
(Editors)

Engineering the Farm: The Social and Ethical Aspects of
Agricultural Biotechnology. Trade Cloth. Island Press.
Washington, DC. 2002. 200p. ISBN:1-55963-946-6, ISBN13:
978-1-55963-946-0. Dewey:174/.96315233. LCCN:2002-002893.

Audience: **g,u,f.** *Choice, 2003.*

Bains, William   **TP248.16.B33 2003**

Biotechnology from A to Z. Ed. 3. Trade Paper. Oxford
University Press, Inc. New York, NY. 2004. 422p.
ISBN:0-19-852498-6, ISBN13: 978-0-19-852498-4.
Dewey:660.6/03. LCCN:2004-268929.

Audience: **g,l,u,f.** *Choice, 2004, 1994.*

Bernauer, Thomas   **HD9006.B45 2003**

Genes, Trade, and Regulation: The Seeds of Conflict in Food
Biotechnology. Trade Cloth. Princeton University Press.
Princeton, NJ. 2003. 224p. ISBN:0-691-11348-3, ISBN13:
978-0-691-11348-7. Dewey:338.4/7664. LCCN:2003-051735.

Audience: **l,u,f.**

Chrispeels, Martin J. &   **SB123.57.C48 2002**
Sadava, David E.

Plants, Genes, and Crop Biotechnology. Ed. 2. Trade Cloth.
Jones & Bartlett Publishers, Inc. Sudbury, MA. 2002. 567p.
Botany and Plant Biotechnology Ser. ISBN:0-7637-1586-7,
ISBN13: 978-0-7637-1586-1. Dewey:363.8.
LCCN:2002-067637.

Audience: **g,l,u,f.**

Christou, Paul & Klee,   **TP248.27.P55**
Harry (Editor-In-Chiefs)

Handbook of Plant Biotechnology. Trade Cloth. John Wiley &
Sons, Inc. Hoboken, NJ. 2004. 1488p. ISBN:0-471-85199-X,
ISBN13: 978-0-471-85199-8. Dewey:660.6.
LCCN:2003-027341.

Audience: **g,l,u,f.** *Choice, 2005.*

Cohen, Joel I.   **S494.5.B563M36 1999**

Managing Agricultural Biotechnology: Addressing Research
Program Needs and Policy Implications. Cloth Text. Oxford
University Press, Inc. New York, NY. 2000. 350p.
Biotechnology in Agriculture Ser., Vol. 23 ISBN:0-85199-400-8,
ISBN13: 978-0-85199-400-0. Dewey:631.5/233.
LCCN:99-057155.

Audience: **u,f.**

Cook, R. James & Baker,   **SB732.6 .C66 1983**
Kenneth F.

Nature and Practice of Biological Control of Plant Pathogens.
Trade Cloth. American Phytopathological Society. Saint Paul,

MN. 1983. 539p. ISBN:0-89054-053-5, ISBN13:
978-0-89054-053-4. Dewey:632/.3. LCCN:83-071224.

Audience: **g,l,u,f.**

DeGregori, Thomas   **T14.5.D455 2001**

Agriculture and Modern Technology: A Defense. Cloth Text.
Blackwell Publishing Professional. Ames, IA. 2001. xi, 268p.
ISBN:0-8138-0342-X, ISBN13: 978-0-8138-0342-5.
Dewey:303.48/3. LCCN:00-054147.

Audience: **g,l,u.**

Dennis, E. S. & Llewellyn,   **SB123.57.M65 1991**
D. J. (Editors)

Molecular Approaches to Crop Improvement. Cloth Text.
Springer. New York, NY. 1991. 166p. Plant Gene Research Ser.
ISBN:0-387-82230-5, ISBN13: 978-0-387-82230-3.
Dewey:631.5/23. LCCN:90-024701.

Audience: **g,u,f.** *Choice, 1992.*

Doyle, Jack   **HD9006.D65 1985**

Altered Harvest: Agriculture, Genetics and the Fate of the
World's Food Supply. Trade Cloth. Penguin Group (USA) Inc.
New York, NY. 1985. 512p. ISBN:0-670-11524-X, ISBN13:
978-0-670-11524-2. Dewey:338.1/9/73. LCCN:84-040458.

Audience: **g,l,u,f.** ℬ *Choice, 1986.*

Erbisch, Frederic H.   **K1519.B54I58 2004**
(Editor), et al.

Intellectual Property Rights in Agricultural Biotechnology. Ed.
2. Karim M. Maredia, F. H. Erbisch & K. M. Maredia (Editors).
Cloth Text. Oxford University Press, Inc. New York, NY. 2004.
336p. Biotechnology in Agriculture Ser., Vol. 28:CABI
Publishing Ser. ISBN:0-85199-739-2, ISBN13:
978-0-85199-739-1. Dewey:333.95/316. LCCN:2003-009874.

Audience: **u,f.**

Ervin, David E.   **S494.5.B563**

Transgenic Crops: An Environmental Assessment. Winrock
International. 2001. Variation: Policy Studies Report (Henry A.
Wallace Center for Agricultural & Environmental Policy); no. 15
ISBN:1-893182-22-3, ISBN13: 978-1-893182-22-6.

Audience: **g,l,u,f.**

Food and Agricultural   **HD9000.5**
Organization of the United Nations

☐ Ethical Issues in Food and Agriculture.
http://www.fao.org/documents/show_cdr.asp?url_file=/DOCREP/
003/X9601E/X9601E00.HTM
FAO. ISBN:92-5-104559-3, ISBN13: 978-92-5-104559-6.

Audience: **g,l,u,f.**

Gendel, Steven M. (Editor),   **S0494.5.B56**
et al.

1Agricultural Bioethics: Implications of Agricultural
Biotechnology. A. David Kline, D. Michael Warren & Faye
Yates (Editors). Trade Paper. Books on Demand. Ann Arbor, MI.
1990. 381p. ISBN:0-608-06862-4, ISBN13: 978-0-608-06862-6.
Dewey:174/.963. LCCN:89-015598.

Audience: **g,l,u,f.** *Choice, 1990.*

Halford, Nigel G.   **SB123.57.H35 2003**

Genetically Modified Crops. Trade Cloth. Imperial College
Press. London, 2003. 124p. ISBN:1-86094-353-5, ISBN13:
978-1-86094-353-9. Dewey:631.5/233. LCCN:2005-295947.

Audience: **g,l,u,f.** *Choice, 2004.*

Hokkanen, Heikki M. T. &   SB975.B54 1995
  Lynch, James M. (Editors)
Biological Control: Benefits and Risks. James Lynch
(Contribution by). Trade Paper. Cambridge University Press.
New York, NY. 2003. 326p. Biotechnology Research Ser., Vol. 4
ISBN:0-521-54405-X, ISBN13: 978-0-521-54405-4.
Dewey:632.9/6.

Audience: **g,l,u,f.**

Holden, John H., et al.   SB123.3 .H65 1993
Genes, Crops and the Environment. James Peacock & Trevor A.
Williams (Authors). Cloth Text. Cambridge University Press.
New York, NY. 1993. 176p. ISBN:0-521-43137-9, ISBN13:
978-0-521-43137-8. Dewey:333.95316. LCCN:92-033605.

Audience: **g,l,u,f.** *Choice, 1994.*

Kloppenburg, Jack Ralph   SB117.3.K57 2004
First the Seed: The Political Economy of Plant Biotechnology.
Ed. 2. Trade Paper. University of Wisconsin Press. Chicago, IL.
2005. 468p. Science and Technology in Society Ser.
ISBN:0-299-19244-X, ISBN13: 978-0-299-19244-0.
Dewey:631.5/2. LCCN:2004-053597.

Audience: **u,f.**

Koul, Opender & Dhaliwal,   SB123.57.T723 2004
  G. S. (Editors)
Transgenic Crop Protection: Concepts and Strategies. Book,
Other. Science Publishers. Enfield, NH. 2004. 412p.
ISBN:1-57808-302-8, ISBN13: 978-1-57808-302-2.
Dewey:631.5/233. LCCN:2004-042861.

Audience: **g,l,u.** *Choice, 2005.*

Liang, G. H. & Skinner,   SB123.57.T7255 2004
  D. Z.
Genetically Modified Crops: Their Development, Uses, and
Risks. Cloth Text. Haworth Press, Incorporated, The.
Binghamton, NY. 2004. 380p. ISBN:1-56022-280-8, ISBN13:
978-1-56022-280-4. Dewey:631.5/233. LCCN:2003-022328.

Audience: **g,l,u.** *Choice, 2005.*

Litz, R. E.   SB354.8
Biotechnology of Fruit and Nut Crops. Cloth Text. CAB
International. Wallingford, 2005. 748p. Biotechnology in
Agriculture Ser., Vol. 29:CABI Publishing ISBN:0-85199-662-0,
ISBN13: 978-0-85199-662-2. Dewey:634/.043.
LCCN:2004-007979.

Audience: **l,u,f.**

Lurquin, Paul F.   SB123.57.L88 2004
High Tech Harvest: Understanding Genetically Modified Food
Plants. Trade Paper. Westview Press. Boulder, CO. 2004. 236p.
ISBN:0-8133-4175-2, ISBN13: 978-0-8133-4175-0.
Dewey:631.5/233.

Audience: **l,u,f.** *Choice, 2002.*

Meyers, Robert A. (Editor)   QH506.M66155 1995
Molecular Biology and Biotechnology: A Comprehensive Desk
Reference. Trade Cloth. John Wiley & Sons, Inc. Hoboken, NJ.
1995. xxxviii, 1046p. ISBN:1-56081-569-8, ISBN13:
978-1-56081-569-3. Dewey:574.8/8/03. LCCN:95-009063.

Audience: **g,u,f.** *Choice, 1996.*

Murphy, C. F. & Peterson,   SB123.D47 2000
  D. M. (Editors)
Designing Crops for Added Value. Trade Cloth. American
Society of Agronomy. Madison, WI. 2000. 267p. Agronomy

Ser., No. 40 ISBN:0-89118-144-X, ISBN13: 978-0-89118-144-6.
Dewey:631.5/23. LCCN:00-133615.

Audience: **g,l,u,f.**

Nelson, Gerald C.   QH442.6.G47 2001
Genetically Modified Organisms in Agriculture: Economics and
Politics. Trade Cloth. Elsevier Science & Technology Books.
Saint Louis, MO. 2001. 344p. ISBN:0-12-515422-4, ISBN13:
978-0-12-515422-2. Dewey:338.1/6. LCCN:00-110183.

Audience: **g,l,u.**

Persley, G. J.   SB950.B48 1996
e Biotechnology and Integrated Pest Management. E-Book.
CABI Publishing. Wallingford, ISBN:0-85199-987-5, ISBN13:
978-0-85199-987-6. Dewey:632/.96.

Audience: **g,l,u,f.**

Pinstrup-Andersen, Per &   HD9000.5.P564 2001
  Schiøler, Ebbe
Seeds of Contention: World Hunger and the Global Controversy
over Genetically Modified Crops. Trade Paper. Johns Hopkins
University Press. Baltimore, MD. 2001. 176p.
ISBN:0-8018-6826-2, ISBN13: 978-0-8018-6826-9.
Dewey:338.1/6. LCCN:2001-002303.

Audience: **u,f.**

Poehlman, John M. &   SB185.7.P63 1995
  Sleper, David A.
Breeding Field Crops. Ed. 4. Cloth Text. Blackwell Publishing
Professional. Ames, IA. 1995. 510p. ISBN:0-8138-2427-3,
ISBN13: 978-0-8138-2427-7. Dewey:633/.083.
LCCN:94-036673.

Audience: **u,f.** *Choice, 1987.*

Qaim, Matin, et al.   S494.5.B563A3727
Agricultural Biotechnology in Developing Countries: Towards
Optimizing the Benefits for the Poor. Anatole F. Krattiger &
Joachim Von Braun (Authors). Trade Cloth. Springer. New York,
NY. 2000. 448p. ISBN:0-7923-7230-1, ISBN13:
978-0-7923-7230-1. Dewey:338.1/6/091724. LCCN:00-051429.

Audience: **u,f.**

Rissler, Jane & Mellon,   SB123.57.R564 1996
  Margaret G.
The Ecological Risks of Engineered Crops. Trade Cloth. MIT
Press. Cambridge, MA. 1996. 192p. ISBN:0-262-18171-1,
ISBN13: 978-0-262-18171-6. Dewey:631.5/23.
LCCN:95-038926.

Audience: **l,u.** *Choice, 1996.*

Santaniello, V. & Evenson,   K3925.B56R44 2004
  R. E. (Editors)
The Regulation of Agricultural Biotechnology. International
Consortium on Agricultural Biotechnology Research Staff
(Contribution by). Cloth Text. CAB International. Wallingford,
2004. 320p. CABI Publishing Ser. ISBN:0-85199-742-2,
ISBN13: 978-0-85199-742-1. Dewey:631.5/23.
LCCN:2003-014503.

Audience: **u,f.**

Seiber, James N.   S494.5.B563A3726
Agricultural Biotechnology: Challenges and Prospects. Mahesh
K. Bhalgat, William P. Ridley & Allan S. Felsot (Editors),
American Chemical Society, Division of Agricultural and Food
Chemistry Staff & American Chemical Society, Division of
Agrochemicals Staff (Contribution by). Trade Cloth. Oxford

University Press, Inc. New York, NY. 2004. 232p. ACS
Symposium Ser., Vol. 866 ISBN:0-8412-3815-4, ISBN13:
978-0-8412-3815-2. Dewey:631.5/233. LCCN:2003-057876.

Audience: **u,f.**

Shewry, Peter R. (Editor)   QK495.G74B325 1992
Barley: Genetics, Biochemistry, Molecular Biology and
Biotechnology. Cloth Text. Oxford University Press, Inc. New
York, NY. 1992. 600p. Biotechnology in Agriculture Ser., No. 5
ISBN:0-85198-725-7, ISBN13: 978-0-85198-725-5.
Dewey:584/.93. LCCN:93-183438.

Audience: **u,f.**

Smale, Melinda   SB123.3.V35 2005
Valuing Crop Biodiversity: On-Farm Genetic Resources and
Economic Change. Trade Cloth. CABI Publishing. Wallingford,
2006. 352p. CABI Publishing Ser. ISBN:0-85199-083-5,
ISBN13: 978-0-85199-083-5. Dewey:631.5/23.
LCCN:2005-002725.

Audience: **l,u,f.**

Virchow, Detlef (Editor)   SB123.3.E33 2002
Efficient Conservation of Crop Genetic Diversity: Theoretical
Approaches and Empirical Studies. Trade Cloth. Springer. New
York, NY. 2003. 247p. ISBN:3-540-00006-2, ISBN13:
978-3-540-00006-8. Dewey:333.95/316. LCCN:2002-036474.

Audience: **u,f.**

Agriculture > Agricultural Chemicals

Altieri, Miguel A. &   SB933.3.A38 2003
  Nicholls, Clara I.
Biodiversity and Pest Management in Agroecosystems. Ed. 2.
Cloth Text. Haworth Press, Incorporated, The. Binghamton, NY.
2003. 275p. ISBN:1-56022-922-5, ISBN13: 978-1-56022-922-3.
Dewey:632/.7. LCCN:2002-014860.

Audience: **u,f.** *Choice, 1994.*

Capinera, John L. (Editor)   QL462.3
Encyclopedia of Entomology. Trade Cloth. Springer. New York,
NY. 2006. XLIX, 2580p. ISBN:0-7923-8670-1, ISBN13:
978-0-7923-8670-4. Dewey:595.703. LCCN:2006-275698.

Audience: **g,l,u,f.** *Choice, 2005.*

Clark, J. Marshall &   SB950.93.N48 2004
  Ohkawa, Hideo
New Discoveries in Agrochemicals. American Chemical Society,
Division of Agrochemicals Staff (Contribution by). Trade Cloth.
American Chemical Society. Washington, DC. 2005. 440p. ACS
Symposium Ser., Vol. 892 ISBN:0-8412-3903-7, ISBN13:
978-0-8412-3903-6. Dewey:668.6. LCCN:2004-053129.

Audience: **g,u,f.**

Coats, Joel R. & Yamamoto,   TD196.P38E59 2003
  Hiroki (Editors)
Environmental Fate and Effects of Pesticides. Ed. 3. American
Chemical Society, Division of Agrochemicals Staff (Contribution
by). Trade Cloth. Oxford University Press, Inc. New York, NY.
2003. 314p. ACS Symposium Ser., Vol. 853
ISBN:0-8412-3722-0, ISBN13: 978-0-8412-3722-3.
Dewey:628.5/29. LCCN:2003-048137.

Audience: **l,u,f.** *Choice, 2004.*

Dent, D.   SB931.D45 2000
Insect Pest Management. Ed. 2. Cloth Text. Oxford University
Press, Inc. New York, NY. 2000. 424p. A CAB International

Publication ISBN:0-85199-340-0, ISBN13: 978-0-85199-340-9.
Dewey:632.7. LCCN:99-087126.

Audience: **l,u,f.**

Dunlap, Thomas R.   SB952.D2
DDT: Scientists, Citizens, and Public Policy. Trade Cloth.
Princeton University Press. Princeton, NJ. 1981. 304p.
ISBN:0-691-04680-8, ISBN13: 978-0-691-04680-8.
Dewey:363.7/384. LCCN:80-008546.

Audience: **g,l,u.**

Emden, Helmut F. van &   QH545.P4.V36 1996
  Peakall, David P.
Beyond Silent Spring: Integrated Pest Management and
Chemical Safety. Trade Cloth. Springer. New York, NY. 1996.
344p. ISBN:0-412-72800-1, ISBN13: 978-0-412-72800-6.
Dewey:363.7384. LCCN:95-071377.

Audience: **g,u,f.** *Choice, 1997.*

Flint, Mary Louise   SB950
Pests of the Garden and Small Farm: A Grower's Guide to
Using Less Pesticide. Jack Kelly Clark (Photographer). Trade
Paper. DIANE Publishing Company. Collingdale, PA. 2001.
276p. ISBN:0-7567-5211-6, ISBN13: 978-0-7567-5211-8.
Dewey:632.9.

Audience: **g,l,u,f.**

Flint, Mary Louise &   SB993.3 .F59
  Dreistadt, Steve H.
Natural Enemies Handbook: The Illustrated Guide to Biological
Pest Control. Jack Kelly Clark (Photographer). Paper Text.
DIANE Publishing Company. Collingdale, PA. 2001. 154p.
ISBN:0-7567-5213-2, ISBN13: 978-0-7567-5213-2.
Dewey:632.96.

Audience: **g,l,u,f.**

Hayes, Wayland J.   RA1270.P4
Pesticides Studied in Man. Cloth Text. Lippincott Williams &
Wilkins. Philadelphia, PA. 1982. 672p. ISBN:0-683-03896-6,
ISBN13: 978-0-683-03896-5. Dewey:615.9/02.
LCCN:81-007410.

Audience: **l,u,f.**

Huffaker, Carl B.   SB931
New Technology of Pest Control. Trade Cloth. John Wiley &
Sons, Inc. Hoboken, NJ. 1980. 500p. Environmental Science and
Technology Ser. ISBN:0-471-05336-8, ISBN13:
978-0-471-05336-1. Dewey:632/.7. LCCN:79-004369.

Audience: **u,f.**

Koul, Opender (Editor),   SB950.I4577 2004
  et al.
Integrated Pest Management: Potential, Constraints, and
Challenges. G. S. Dhaliwal & Gerrit W. Cuperus (Editors).
Cloth Text. CAB International. Wallingford, 2004. 352p. CABI
Publishing Ser. ISBN:0-85199-686-8, ISBN13:
978-0-85199-686-8. Dewey:632/.9. LCCN:2003-015419.

Audience: **u,f.**

Krieger, Robert (Editor)   RA1270.P4H36 2001
Principles and Agents, Set. Ed. 2. Trade Cloth. Elsevier Science
& Technology Books. Saint Louis, MO. 2001. 1908p.
ISBN:0-12-426260-0, ISBN13: 978-0-12-426260-7.
Dewey:615.9/51. LCCN:2001-089145.

Audience: **u,f.**

Maredia, Karim M.   SB950.I4575 2003
  (Editor), et al.
Integrated Pest Management in the Global Arena. D. Dakouo, D.
Mota-Sanchez & K. M. Maredia (Editors). Cloth Text. Oxford
University Press, Inc. New York, NY. 2003. 544p. CABI
Publishing Ser. ISBN:0-85199-652-3, ISBN13:
978-0-85199-652-3. Dewey:632/.9. LCCN:2002-154965.
                                    Audience: **u,f.** *Choice, 2004.*

Metcalf, Robert L. &   SB931.I58 1994
  Luckmann, William H. (Editors)
Introduction to Insect Pest Management. Ed. 3. Trade Cloth.
John Wiley & Sons, Inc. Hoboken, NJ. 1994. 672p.
Environmental Science and Technology Ser., Vol. 101:A
Wiley-Interscience Series of Texts and Monographs
ISBN:0-471-58957-8, ISBN13: 978-0-471-58957-0.
Dewey:632/.7. LCCN:93-044141.
                      Audience: **g,l,u,f.** *B Choice, 1994.*

Müller, Franz (Editor)   S585.A57 2000
Agrochemicals: Composition, Production, Toxicology,
Applications. Trade Cloth. John Wiley & Sons, Inc. Hoboken,
NJ. 2000. 1046p. ISBN:3-527-29852-5, ISBN13:
978-3-527-29852-5. Dewey:631.8. LCCN:2001-272087.
                                    Audience: **u,f.**

National Academy Press   SB950.2.A1F88 2000
  Staff
The Future Role of Pesticides in U. S. Agriculture. Trade Cloth.
National Academies Press. Washington, DC. 2000. xx, 301p.
ISBN:0-309-06526-7, ISBN13: 978-0-309-06526-9.
Dewey:632/.95/0973. LCCN:00-011245.
                                    Audience: **g,u,f.**

Neilson, Alasdair   QH545.W3N45 1994
Fate of Organic Chemicals in the Aquatic Environment. Box or
Slipcased. Lewis Publishers. Boca Raton, FL. 1994. 448p.
ISBN:0-87371-597-7, ISBN13: 978-0-87371-597-3.
Dewey:574.5/263. LCCN:94-022460.
                                    Audience: **l,u.** *Choice, 1995.*

Nichols, S. W. & Schuh,   QL462.3
  R. T.
The Torre-Bueno Glossary of Entomology. Trade Cloth.
American Museum of Natural History. New York, NY. 1989.
840p. ISBN:0-913424-13-7, ISBN13: 978-0-913424-13-1.
Dewey:595.7.
                                    Audience: **u,f.**

Norris, Robert F., et al.   SB950.N638 2003
Concepts in Integrated Pest Management. Edward P.
Caswell-Chen & Marcos Kogan (Authors). Cloth Text. Prentice
Hall PTR. Upper Saddle River, NJ. 2002. 586p.
ISBN:0-13-087016-1, ISBN13: 978-0-13-087016-2.
Dewey:632/.9. LCCN:2002-070022.
                                    Audience: **l,u,f.** *Choice, 2003.*

Pimentel, David (Editor)   SB950.7.E53 2002
Encyclopedia of Pest Management. Paper over Boards. Marcel
Dekker Inc. New York, NY. 2002. 954p. ISBN:0-8247-0632-3,
ISBN13: 978-0-8247-0632-6. Dewey:632/.03.
LCCN:2003-265919.
                                    Audience: **g,l,u,f.** *Choice, 2003.*

Racke, Kenneth D.   RA1270.P4.P49 1993
Pesticides in Urban Environments: Fate and Significance. Anne
R. Leslie (Editor). Trade Cloth. John Wiley & Sons, Inc.
Hoboken, NJ. 1993. 385p. ACS Symposium Ser., Vol. 522

ISBN:0-8412-2627-X, ISBN13: 978-0-8412-2627-2.
Dewey:363.17/92/01732. LCCN:92-042060.
                                    Audience: **u,f.** *Choice, 1993.*

Rechcigl, Jack E. &   SB933.3.I53 2000
  Rechcigl, Nancy A.
Insect Pest Management: Techniques for Environmental
Protection. Saddle Stitched. Lewis Publishers. Boca Raton, FL.
1999. 408p. Agriculture and Environment Ser.
ISBN:1-56670-478-2, ISBN13: 978-1-56670-478-6.
Dewey:632/.9517. LCCN:99-040543.
                                    Audience: **u,f.** *Choice, 2000.*

Steinheimer, Thomas R.   TD196.A34A373 2000
  (Editor), et al.
Agrochemical Fate and Movement: Perspectives and Scale of
Study. Lisa Ross & Terry Spittler (Editors). Trade Cloth. Oxford
University Press, Inc. New York, NY. 2000. 384p. ACS
Symposium Ser., No. 751 ISBN:0-8412-3608-9, ISBN13:
978-0-8412-3608-0. Dewey:628.5/29. LCCN:99-053365.
                                    Audience: **u,f.**

Westing, Arthur H. (Editor)   QH545.P4H47 1984
Herbicides in War: The Long Term Ecological and Human
Consequences. Trade Cloth. Taylor & Francis Group.
Philadelphia, PA. 1984. 290p. Peace Studies
ISBN:0-85066-265-6, ISBN13: 978-0-85066-265-8.
Dewey:574.5/2642/09597. LCCN:84-002468.
                                    Audience: **g,l,u.**

Wheeler, Willis B.   SB951.P444 2002
Pesticides in Agriculture and the Environment. Paper over
Boards. Marcel Dekker Inc. New York, NY. 2002. 360p. Books
in Soils, Plants and the Environment, Vol. 90
ISBN:0-8247-0809-1, ISBN13: 978-0-8247-0809-2.
Dewey:632/.95. LCCN:2002-073990.
                                    Audience: **u,f.** *Choice, 2003.*

Whorton, James C.   RA1270.P4
Before Silent Spring: Pesticides in Pre-DDT America. Trade
Cloth. Princeton University Press. Princeton, NJ. 1975. 302p.
ISBN:0-691-08139-5, ISBN13: 978-0-691-08139-7.
Dewey:614.3/1. LCCN:74-002984.
                                    Audience: **g,l.**

Agriculture > Agricultural Ecology

Altieri, Miguel A.   S589.7.A47 1995
Agroecology: The Science of Sustainable Agriculture. Ed. 2.
Trade Paper. Westview Press. Boulder, CO. 1995. 448p.
ISBN:0-8133-1718-5, ISBN13: 978-0-8133-1718-2.
Dewey:338.16/2. LCCN:95-000021.
                                    Audience: **g,l,u,f.**

Altieri, Miguel A. &   SB933.3.A38 2003
  Nicholls, Clara I.
Biodiversity and Pest Management in Agroecosystems. Ed. 2.
Cloth Text. Haworth Press, Incorporated, The. Binghamton, NY.
2003. 275p. ISBN:1-56022-922-5, ISBN13: 978-1-56022-922-3.
Dewey:632/.7. LCCN:2002-014860.
                                    Audience: **u,f.** *Choice, 1994.*

Beeman, Randal S. &   S441.B36 2001
  Pritchard, James A.
A Green and Permanent Land: Ecology and Agriculture in the
Twentieth Century. Trade Cloth. University Press of Kansas.

Lawrence, KS. 2001. 232p. Development of Western Resources Ser. ISBN:0-7006-1066-9, ISBN13: 978-0-7006-1066-2. Dewey:333.76/16/0973. LCCN:00-063334.

Audience: **g,l,u.** *Choice, 2001.*

Boyce, Mark S. & Haney,   **QH75.E295 1997**
Alan W. (Editors)
Ecosystem Management: Applications for Sustainable Forest and Wildlife Resources. Cloth over Boards. Yale University Press. Cumberland, RI. 1997. 384p. ISBN:0-300-06902-2, ISBN13: 978-0-300-06902-0. Dewey:333.95. LCCN:96-003407.

Audience: **u,f.** *Choice, 1997.*

Brookfield, H. C. (Editor),   **S494.5.A43A48 2003**
et al.
Agrodiversity: Learning from Farmers Across the World. Helen Parsons & Muriel Brookfield (Editors). Trade Paper. United Nations Publications. New York, NY. 2005. 368p. ISBN:92-808-1087-1, ISBN13: 978-92-808-1087-5. Dewey:333.76/16. LCCN:2003-010734.

Audience: **g,l,u.** *Choice, 2004.*

Brussaard, L. &   **S589.7.S637 1997**
Ferrara-Cerrato, Ronald
Soil Ecology in Sustainable Agricultural Systems. Library Binding. Lewis Publishers. Boca Raton, FL. 1997. 176p. Advances in Agroecology Ser. ISBN:1-56670-277-1, ISBN13: 978-1-56670-277-5. Dewey:631.4/22. LCCN:96-030093.

Audience: **u,f.** *Choice, 1998.*

Dent, D. R. & Walton, M. P.   **SB933.3.M47 1997**
Methods in Ecological and Agricultural Entomology. Paper Text. Oxford University Press, Inc. New York, NY. 1997. 400p. A CAB International Publication ISBN:0-85199-132-7, ISBN13: 978-0-85199-132-0. Dewey:595.7/072. LCCN:96-048888.

Audience: **u,f.** *Choice, 1998.*

Giampietro, Mario, et al.   **HD1401**
Multi-Scale Integrated Analysis of Agroecosystems: An Integrated Assessment. Charles A. S. Hall & David Pimentel (Authors). Paper over Boards. C R C Press LLC. Boca Raton, FL. 2003. 472p. Advances in Agroecology Ser. ISBN:0-8493-1067-9, ISBN13: 978-0-8493-1067-6. Dewey:338.1. LCCN:2003-059613.

Audience: **u,f.**

Gliessman, Stephen R.   **S589.7.A38 1990**
(Editor)
Agroecology: Ecological Processes in Sustainable Agriculture. Trade Cloth. Springer. New York, NY. 1989. XIV, 380p. Ecological Studies, Vol. 78 ISBN:0-387-97028-2, ISBN13: 978-0-387-97028-8. Dewey:630/.277. LCCN:89-027592.

Audience: **g,l,u,f.** *Choice, 1990.*

Liebman, Matt, et al.   **SB611.5.L54 2001**
Ecological Management of Agricultural Weeds. Charles L. Mohler & Charles P. Staver (Authors). Trade Cloth. Cambridge University Press. New York, NY. 2001. 544p. ISBN:0-521-56068-3, ISBN13: 978-0-521-56068-9. Dewey:632.5. LCCN:00-068869.

Audience: **l,u,f.**

Opie, John   **S616.U6O65 2000**
Ogallala: Water for a Dry Land. Ed. 2. Paper Text. University of Nebraska Press. Lincoln, NE. 2000. 477p. Our Sustainable Future Ser., Vol. 13 ISBN:0-8032-8614-7, ISBN13: 978-0-8032-8614-6. Dewey:333.91/3/0978. LCCN:99-042161.

Audience: **g,l,u.** *Choice, 2000, 1993.*

Pearson, C. J., et al.   **SB176.T76 N67 1995**
The Ecology of Tropical Food Crops. Ed. 2. M. J. T. Norman & P. G. E. Searle (Authors). Cloth Text. Cambridge University Press. New York, NY. 1995. 440p. ISBN:0-521-41062-2, ISBN13: 978-0-521-41062-5. Dewey:630/.2/5745264. LCCN:94-031156.

Audience: **g,l,u.**

Rickerl, Diane & Francis,   **S589.7.A475 2004**
Charles (Editors)
Agroecosystems Analysis. Cloth Text. ASA-CSSA-SSSA. Madison, WI. 2004. xvii, 207p. Agronomy Ser., No. 43 ISBN:0-89118-153-9, ISBN13: 978-0-89118-153-8. Dewey:577.55. LCCN:2003-116111.

Audience: **u,f.** *Choice, 2004.*

Rissler, Jane & Mellon,   **SB123.57.R564 1996**
Margaret G.
The Ecological Risks of Engineered Crops. Trade Cloth. MIT Press. Cambridge, MA. 1996. 192p. ISBN:0-262-18171-1, ISBN13: 978-0-262-18171-6. Dewey:631.5/23. LCCN:95-038926.

Audience: **l,u.** *Choice, 1996.*

Sharpley, Andrew N.   **S587.5.P56P48 2005**
(Editor)
Phosphorus: Agriculture and the Environment. Kivar (or like). ASA-CSSA-SSSA. Madison, WI. 2005. xxiii, 1121p. Agronomy Ser., 46 ISBN:0-89118-157-1, ISBN13: 978-0-89118-157-6. Dewey:631.4/1. LCCN:2005-924646.

Audience: **u,f.**

Smaling, E. M. A. (Editor),   **S589.7.N88 1999**
et al.
Nutrient Disequilibria in Agroecosystems: Concepts and Case Studies. O. Oenema & L. O. Fresco (Editors). Cloth Text. Oxford University Press, Inc. New York, NY. 2000. 336p. CABI Publishing Ser. ISBN:0-85199-268-4, ISBN13: 978-0-85199-268-6. Dewey:577.5/5. LCCN:99-014039.

Audience: **u,f.**

Wood, Stanley   **S589.7 .W66 2000**
Pilot Analysis of Global Ecosystems: Agroecosystems. Trade Cloth. World Resources Institute. Washington, DC. 2000. 100p. ISBN:1-56973-457-7, ISBN13: 978-1-56973-457-5. Dewey:577.5/5. LCCN:00-110966.

Audience: **g,l,u.**

Zimdahl, Robert L.   **SB611.Z55 2004**
Weed-Crop Competition: A Review. Ed. 2. Trade Paper. Blackwell Publishing Professional. Ames, IA. 2004. 232p. ISBN:0-8138-0279-2, ISBN13: 978-0-8138-0279-4. Dewey:632/.5. LCCN:2003-023656.

Audience: **u,f.**

Agriculture > Agricultural Education

National Research Council   **S533.U47 1988**
Staff
Understanding Agriculture: New Directions for Education. Paper Text. National Academies Press. Washington, DC. 1988. 80p. ISBN:0-309-03936-3, ISBN13: 978-0-309-03936-9. Dewey:630/.7/1273. LCCN:88-013126.

Audience: **g,u,f.**

Seevers, Brenda S.   **S544.E48 1997**
Education Through Cooperative Extension. Ed. 1. Paper Text.
Thomson Delmar Learning. Albany, NY. 1997. 304p. Agriculture
Ser. ISBN:0-8273-7172-1, ISBN13: 978-0-8273-7172-9.
Dewey:630/.71/5073. LCCN:96-023113.

Audience: **u,f.**

Agriculture > Agricultural Geography

Grigg, David B.   **S495.G79 1995**
An Introduction to Agricultural Geography. Ed. 2. Paper over
Boards. Routledge. New York, NY. 1995. 240p.
ISBN:0-415-08442-3, ISBN13: 978-0-415-08442-0.
Dewey:338.1/09. LCCN:94-012681.

Audience: **g,l,u.** ℬ

Agriculture > Sustainable Agriculture

S494.5.S86
☐ National Center for Appropriate Technology: Local Solutions
for a Sustainable Future.
http://www.ncat.org/

Audience: **g.**

Allen, Patricia   **HD9005.A69 2004**
Together at the Table: Sustainability and Sustenance in the
American Agrifood System. Trade Cloth. Pennsylvania State
University Press. University Park, PA. 2000. 248p. Rural Studies
Series of the Rural Sociological Society ISBN:0-271-02473-9,
ISBN13: 978-0-271-02473-8. Dewey:338.1/0973.
LCCN:2004-010245.

Audience: **g,u.** *Choice, 2005.*

Allen, Patricia (editor)   **S494.5.S86 I34 1986**
Global Perspectives on Agroecology and Sustainable
Agricultural Systems: Proceedings of the Sixth International
Scientific Conference of the International Federation of Organic
Agriculture Movements. Van Dusen, Debra (editor).
Agroecology Program, University of California. 1988.

Audience: **l,u.**

Atkinson, Giles, et al.   **HC79.E5M4 1997**
Measuring Sustainable Development: Macroeconomics and the
Environment. Richard Dubourg, Kirk Hamilton, Mohan
Munasinghe, David Pearce & Carlos Young (Authors). Trade
Cloth. Edward Elgar Publishing, Inc. Northampton, MA. 1997.
272p. ISBN:1-85898-572-2, ISBN13: 978-1-85898-572-5.
Dewey:338.9. LCCN:96-039592.

Audience: **l,u,f.** *Choice, 1998.*

Borlaug, N. E.   **Z8109.38 .N67 1988 HD9000.5**
Norman E. Borlaug: A Bibliography of Papers and Publications.
CIMMYT. 1988. ISBN:968-6127-27-5, ISBN13:
978-968-6127-27-0.

Audience: **g,u,f.**

Bowler, Ian R. (Editor), et   **HN49.C6S884 2002**
al.
The Sustainability of Rural Systems: Geographical
Interpretations: A Study Initiated by the International
Geographical Union's Commission on the Sustainability of
Rural Systems. Christopher R. Bryant & Chris Cocklin
(Editors). Trade Cloth. Springer. New York, NY. 2002. XIII,

296p. Geojournal Library, Vol. 66 ISBN:1-4020-0513-X,
ISBN13: 978-1-4020-0513-8. Dewey:307.1/412.
LCCN:2002-072968.

Audience: **l,u,f.**

Bruinsma, Jelle (Editor)   **HD9000**
World Agriculture: Towards 2015/2030: An FAO Study. Food
and Agriculture Organization Staff (Contribution by). Trade
Cloth. Earthscan/James & James. London, 2003. 520p.
ISBN:1-84407-008-5, ISBN13: 978-1-84407-008-4.
Dewey:338.1/01/12. LCCN:2004-268402.

Audience: **g,u.**

D'Souza, Gerard E. &   **S494.5.S86S85 1998**
 Gebremedhin, Tesfa G. (Editors)
Sustainability in Agricultural and Rural Development. Ralph
Christy, John Ikerd, Lynndee Kemmet, Luther Tweeten, William
Amponsah, Susan Capalbo & John Antle (Contribution by).
Trade Cloth. Ashgate Publishing, Ltd. Aldershot, 1998. 264p.
ISBN:1-85521-977-8, ISBN13: 978-1-85521-977-9.
Dewey:307.1/412. LCCN:97-051331.

Audience: **u,f.** *Choice, 1999.*

Filson, Glen C. (Editor)   **S451.5.O5I58 2004**
Intensive Agriculture and Sustainability: A Farming Systems
Analysis. Trade Cloth. University of British Columbia Press.
Vancouver, BC. 2004. 256p. Sustainability and the Environment
Ser. ISBN:0-7748-1104-8, ISBN13: 978-0-7748-1104-0.
Dewey:338.1/62/09713. LCCN:2005-440874.

Audience: **u,f.**

Goreham, Gary A., et al.   **Z5074.E3.G69 1992**
The Socioeconomics of Sustainable Agriculture: An Annotated
Bibliography. David L. Watt & Roy M. Jacobsen (Authors).
Paper over Boards. Garland Publishing, Inc. New York, NY.
1992. 360p. ISBN:0-8240-7127-1, ISBN13: 978-0-8240-7127-1.
Dewey:016.3381. LCCN:92-016285.

Audience: **u.** *Choice, 1993.*

Hallberg, M. C. (Editor)   **HD9006.F568 1994**
Food, Agriculture and Rural Policy into the Twenty-First
Century: Issues and Trade-Offs. Trade Paper. Westview Press.
Boulder, CO. 1994. 320p. ISBN:0-8133-8763-9, ISBN13:
978-0-8133-8763-5. Dewey:338.1/973. LCCN:93-050054.

Audience: **u,f.** *Choice, 1994.*

Jackson, Wes (Editor), et al.   **S441**
Meeting the Expectations of the Land: Essays in Sustainable
Agriculture and Stewardship. Wendell Berry & Bruce Colman
(Editors). Trade Cloth. Farrar, Straus & Giroux. New York, NY.
1984. 272p. ISBN:0-86547-171-1, ISBN13: 978-0-86547-171-9.
Dewey:338.1/0973. LCCN:84-060686.

Audience: **g,l,u.**

Ladha, J. K. (Editor), et al.   **SB191.R5I35 2003**
Improving the Sustainability of Rice-Wheat Systems: Issues and
Impacts. J. E. Hill, R. J. Buresh, J. Duxbury & R. K. Gupta
(Editors). Paper Text. ASA-CSSA-SSSA. Madison, WI. 2003.
xix, 231p. Special Publications, 65 ISBN:0-89118-150-4,
ISBN13: 978-0-89118-150-7. Dewey:633.1/8.
LCCN:2003-102422.

Audience: **u,f.**

Liebman, Matt, et al.   **SB611.5.L54 2001**
Ecological Management of Agricultural Weeds. Charles L.
Mohler & Charles P. Staver (Authors). Trade Cloth. Cambridge
University Press. New York, NY. 2001. 544p.

Formats: Web: ☐   Ebook: **ℯ**   CD/DVD-ROM: 🐝   BCL3: ℬ

ISBN:0-521-56068-3, ISBN13: 978-0-521-56068-9.
Dewey:632.5. LCCN:00-068869.

Audience: **l,u,f.**

Lockeretz, William (Editor)   **S441.V57 1997**
Visions of American Agriculture. Trade Cloth. Blackwell
Publishing Professional. Ames, IA. 1999. 564p.
ISBN:0-8138-2044-8, ISBN13: 978-0-8138-2044-6.
Dewey:306.3/49/0973. LCCN:97-005083.

Audience: **g,l,u,f.** *Choice, 1998.*

Moore, Keith M.   **HC1000.Z65C66 2004**
Conflict, Social Capital, and Managing Natural Resources: A
West African Case Study. SANREM Staff (Contribution by).
Cloth Text. CAB International. Wallingford, 2005. 278p. CABI
Publishing Ser. ISBN:0-85199-948-4, ISBN13:
978-0-85199-948-7. Dewey:333.7/0966. LCCN:2004-012409.

Audience: **u,f.**

National Research Council   **S481.N38 1993**
Staff
Sustainable Agriculture and the Environment in the Humid
Tropics. Cloth Text. National Academies Press. Washington, DC.
1993. 720p. ISBN:0-309-04749-8, ISBN13: 978-0-309-04749-4.
Dewey:333.76/15/0913. LCCN:92-036869.

Audience: **l,u,f.** *Choice, 1993.*

Pagiola, Stefano, et al.   **S589.7.P34 1997**
Mainstreaming Biodiversity in Agricultural Development:
Toward Good Practice. John Kellenberg, Lars Vidaeus &
Jitendra Srivastava (Authors). Trade Paper. World Bank
Publications. Washington, DC. 1997. 50p. Environment Papers,
No. 15 ISBN:0-8213-3884-6, ISBN13: 978-0-8213-3884-1.
Dewey:333.95/16. LCCN:97-000994.

Audience: **g,u,f.**

Pearce, David & Barbier,   **HD75.6.P428 2000**
Edward B.
Blueprint for a Sustainable Economy. Trade Cloth.
Earthscan/James & James. London, 2000. 240p. The Blueprint
Ser. ISBN:1-85383-682-6, ISBN13: 978-1-85383-682-4.
Dewey:333.7. LCCN:2003-270749.

Audience: **g,l,u,f.** *Choice, 2000.*

Pretty, Jules N.   **S494.5.S86E27 2005**
The Earthscan Reader in Sustainable Agriculture. Trade Cloth.
Earthscan/James & James. London, 2005. 304p. Earthscan
Readers Ser. ISBN:1-84407-235-5, ISBN13: 978-1-84407-235-4.
Dewey:631.5/8. LCCN:2005-011046.

Audience: **g,l.**

Ruttan, Vernon W. (Editor)   **S589.75**
Agriculture, Environment, and Health: Sustainable Development
in the 21st Century. Book, Other. University of Minnesota Press.
Minneapolis, MN. 1994. 384p. ISBN:0-8166-2291-4, ISBN13:
978-0-8166-2291-7. Dewey:338.1/4. LCCN:93-008527.

Audience: **l,u,f.**

Ruttan, Vernon W. (Editor)   **S494.5.S86.S865 1992**
Sustainable Agriculture and the Environment: Perspectives on
Growth and Constraints. Trade Paper. Westview Press. Boulder,
CO. 1991. 189p. ISBN:0-8133-8507-5, ISBN13:
978-0-8133-8507-5. Dewey:630. LCCN:91-043184.

Audience: **l,u,f.** *Choice, 1992.*

Scanes, Colin G.   **S1**
Perspectives in World Food Agriculture, Vol. 2. Ed. 2. John A.
Miranowski (Editor). Trade Cloth. Blackwell Publishing

Professional. Ames, IA. 2005. 352p. ISBN:0-8138-2031-6,
ISBN13: 978-0-8138-2031-6. Dewey:630.5.
LCCN:2003-009569.

Audience: **g,l,u.**

Thirsk, Joan   **S455.T48 1997**
Alternative Agriculture: A History: From the Black Death to the
Present Day. Trade Cloth. Oxford University Press, Inc. New
York, NY. 1997. 376p. ISBN:0-19-820662-3, ISBN13:
978-0-19-820662-0. Dewey:630.9/41/0903. LCCN:98-115344.

Audience: **g,l,u,f.** *Choice, 1998.*

Agriculture > Urban Agriculture

Council for Agricultural   **S494.5.U72U74 2002**
  Science and Technology Staff (Contribution by)
Urbanization and the New Agriculture. Trade Cloth. Council for
Agricultural Science & Technology (CAST). Ames, IA. 2002.
viii, 124p. ISBN:1-887383-20-4, ISBN13: 978-1-887383-20-2.
Dewey:630/.91732. LCCN:2002-005851.

Audience: **g.**

Agriculture > Women in Agriculture

Kalbagh, Chetana (Editor)   **HD6073.A292**
Women in Agriculture and Rural Development. Discovery Pub.
House. 1992. Women and Development Series; Vol. 2; Variation:
Women and Development Series (New Delhi, India); Vol. 2
ISBN:81-7141-183-5, ISBN13: 978-81-7141-183-2.

Audience: **g,l,u,f.**

Sachs, Carolyn E.   **S441.S25 1983**
Invisible Farmers: Women in Agricultural Production. Trade
Cloth. Rowman & Littlefield Publishers, Inc. Lanham, MD.
1983. 168p. ISBN:0-86598-094-2, ISBN13: 978-0-86598-094-5.
Dewey:305.4/33/0973. LCCN:82-022824.

Audience: **u,f.** *B*

Agriculture > Agricultural Economics

      HD1415
☐ AgEcon Search: Research in Agricultural and Applied
Economics.
http://agecon.lib.umn.edu/
The Regents of the University of Minnesota.

Audience: **g,l,u,f.**

Aglesham, Allan E. (Editor),   **PN2721.S55**
et al.
The Biobased Economy of the Twenty-First Century:
Agriculture Expanding into Health, Energy, Chemicals and
Materials. William F. Brown & Ralph W. F. Hardy (Editors).
Trade Paper. DIANE Publishing Company. Collingdale, PA.
2001. 196p. ISBN:0-7567-1033-2, ISBN13: 978-0-7567-1033-0.
Dewey:792.0947.

Audience: **u,f.**

Browne, William P.   **HD1761.B73 1988**
Private Interests, Public Policy, and American Agriculture. Trade
Paper. University Press of Kansas. Lawrence, KS. 1988. xviii,
294p. Studies in Government and Public Policy
ISBN:0-7006-0335-2, ISBN13: 978-0-7006-0335-0.
Dewey:338.1/873. LCCN:87-023131.

Audience: **g,l,u.** *Choice, 1989.*

Cardwell, Michael (Editor),   K3870.A944 2003
et al.
Agriculture and International Trade: Law, Policy, and the WTO.
Margaret R. Grossman, C. P. Rodgers, M. N. Cardwell, C.
Rogers & M. R. Grossman (Editors). Cloth Text. Oxford
University Press, Inc. New York, NY. 2004. 352p. CABI
Publishing Ser. ISBN:0-85199-663-9, ISBN13:
978-0-85199-663-9. Dewey:341.7/5471. LCCN:2003-004769.
Audience: **l,u,f.**

Carlson, Gerald A. (Editor),   HD1433.A353 1993
et al.
Agricultural and Environmental Resource Economics. David
Zilberman & John A. Miranowski (Editors). Cloth Text. Oxford
University Press, Inc. New York, NY. 1993. 544p. Oxford
Biological Resource Management Ser. ISBN:0-19-507651-6,
ISBN13: 978-0-19-507651-6. Dewey:338.1. LCCN:92-021524.
Audience: **u,f.**

Carlson, Laurie Winn   HD1771.5.S65C37 2005
William J. Spillman and the Birth of Agricultural Economics.
Saddle Stitched, Cloth over Boards, Dust Jacket. University of
Missouri Press. Columbia, MO. 2005. 210p. Missouri Biography
Ser. ISBN:0-8262-1581-5, ISBN13: 978-0-8262-1581-9.
Dewey:338.1/092 B. LCCN:2005-000618.
Audience: **g,u,f.** *Choice, 2005.*

Carter, Sarah   E78.P7.C37
Lost Harvests: Prairie Indian Reserve Farmers and Government
Policy, No. 3. Trade Paper. McGill-Queen's University Press.
Montreal, PQ. 1993. 352p. ISBN:0-7735-0999-2, ISBN13:
978-0-7735-0999-3. Dewey:306.34908997.
Audience: **g,u.**

Clay, Jason & World   S589.75
Wildlife Fund Staff
World Agriculture and the Environment: A
Commodity-by-Commodity Guide to Impacts and Practices.
Trade Cloth. Island Press. Washington, DC. 2004. 282p.
ISBN:1-55963-367-0, ISBN13: 978-1-55963-367-3.
Dewey:363.7. LCCN:2003-016786.
Audience: **g,l,u.** *Choice, 2004.*

Daly, Herman E. & Farley,   HD75.6.E348 2003
Joshua
Ecological Economics: Principles and Applications. Cloth Text.
Island Press. Washington, DC. 2003. 450p.
ISBN:1-55963-312-3, ISBN13: 978-1-55963-312-3.
Dewey:333.7. LCCN:2003-016785.
Audience: **l,u,f.** *Choice, 2004.*

Duraiappah, Anantha   HD75.6.D865 2003
Kumar
Computational Models in the Economics of Environment And.
Trade Cloth. Kluwer Law International. Alphen a/d Rijn, 2003.
248p. Economy and Environment Ser., Vol. 27
ISBN:1-4020-1773-1, ISBN13: 978-1-4020-1773-5.
Dewey:333.7/01/519. LCCN:2003-064067.
Audience: **l,u,f.**

Faucheux, Sylvie   HD75.6.M628 1996
(Editor), et al.
Models of Sustainable Development. David Pearce & John
Proops (Editors). Trade Cloth. Edward Elgar Publishing, Inc.
Northampton, MA. 1996. 384p. New Horizons in Environmental
Economics Ser. ISBN:1-85898-269-3, ISBN13:
978-1-85898-269-4. Dewey:338.9. LCCN:96-004779.
Audience: **u,f.**

Fitzgerald, Deborah Kay   HD1761.F564 2003
Every Farm a Factory: The Industrial Ideal in American
Agriculture. Cloth over Boards. Yale University Press.
Cumberland, RI. 2003. 256p. ISBN:0-300-08813-2, ISBN13:
978-0-300-08813-7. Dewey:338.1/0973. LCCN:2002-012135.
Audience: **g,l,u,f.** *Choice, 2003.*

Hallberg, Milton C.   HD1761.H3529 2001
Economic Trends in U. S. Agriculture and Food Systems since
World War II. Trade Cloth. Blackwell Publishing Professional.
Ames, IA. 2001. 192p. ISBN:0-8138-2845-7, ISBN13:
978-0-8138-2845-9. Dewey:338.1/0973. LCCN:00-047114.
Audience: **l,u,f.**

Ilbery, Brian W. (Editor), et   S494.5.S86A374 1997
al.
Agricultural Restructuring and Sustainability: A Geographical
Perspective. Q. Chiotti & T. Rickard (Editors). Cloth Text.
Oxford University Press, Inc. New York, NY. 1997. 368p. A
CAB International Publication ISBN:0-85199-165-3, ISBN13:
978-0-85199-165-8. Dewey:338.1. LCCN:97-013059.
Audience: **u,f.**

Kauffman, Kyle Dean   HD1401
(Editor)
Advances in Agricultural Economic History, Vol. 2. Audio,
Other. Elsevier Science & Technology Books. Saint Louis, MO.
2003. 174p. Advances in Agricultural Economic History Ser.
ISBN:0-7623-1001-4, ISBN13: 978-0-7623-1001-2.
Dewey:338.1.
Audience: **u,f.**

Lauck, Jon   HD1773.A3L38 2000
American Agriculture and the Problem of Monopoly: The
Political Economy of Grain Belt Farming, 1953-1980. Cloth
Text. University of Nebraska Press. Lincoln, NE. 2000. 259p.
ISBN:0-8032-2932-1, ISBN13: 978-0-8032-2932-7.
Dewey:338.1/0977/09045. LCCN:99-038710.
Audience: **l,u,f.** *Choice, 2000.*

Lerman, Zvi, et al.   HD1333.E852L47 2004
Agriculture in Transition: Land Policies and Evolving Farm
Structures in Post Soviet Countries. Csaba Csaki & Gershon
Feder (Authors). Trade Cloth. Lexington Books. Lanham, MD.
2004. 264p. Rural Economies in Transition Ser.
ISBN:0-7391-0806-9, ISBN13: 978-0-7391-0806-2.
Dewey:333.3/147. LCCN:2003-065846.
Audience: **l,u,f.**

Lyson, Thomas A.   HD1761.L97 2004
Civic Agriculture: Reconnecting Farm, Food, and Community.
Trade Cloth. University Press of New England. Lebanon, NH.
2004. 160p. Civil Society Ser. ISBN:1-58465-413-9, ISBN13:
978-1-58465-413-1. Dewey:338.1/0973. LCCN:2004-005364.
Audience: **g,l,u,f.**

Norton, Roger D.   HD1431
Agricultural Development Policy: Concepts and Experiences.
Trade Cloth. John Wiley & Sons, Inc. Hoboken, NJ. 2004. 540p.
ISBN:0-470-85778-1, ISBN13: 978-0-470-85778-6.
Dewey:338.1/8. LCCN:2003-049480.
Audience: **g,l,u.**

O'Brien, David J., et al.   HD1333.R9R87 2002
Rural Reform in Post-Soviet Russia. Stephen K. Wegren &
Carol Walker (Authors). Trade Cloth. Johns Hopkins University

Press. Baltimore, MD. 2002. 448p. ISBN:0-8018-6960-9, ISBN13: 978-0-8018-6960-0. Dewey:338.1/847. LCCN:2001-006559.

Audience: **u,f.**

Paarlberg, Don &   **S494.5.I5**
Paarlberg, Phillip
The Agricultural Revolution of the 20th Century. Paper Text. Blackwell Publishing Professional. Ames, IA. 2001. 170p. ISBN:0-8138-0409-4, ISBN13: 978-0-8138-0409-5. Dewey:338.1/6.

Audience: **g,u,f.** *Choice, 2001.*

Penson, John B., et al.   **HD1415.P374 2006**
Introduction to Agricultural Economics. Ed. 4. Oral Capps, C. Parr Rosson & Richard Woodward (Authors). Trade Cloth. Prentice Hall PTR. Upper Saddle River, NJ. 2005. 512p. ISBN:0-13-117312-X, ISBN13: 978-0-13-117312-5. Dewey:338.1. LCCN:2005-043042.

Audience: **l,u.**

Peterson, E. Wesley F.   **HD1415.P377 2001**
The Political Economy of Agricultural, Natural Resource, and Environmental Policy Analysis. Trade Cloth. Blackwell Publishing Professional. Ames, IA. 2001. 416p. ISBN:0-8138-0432-9, ISBN13: 978-0-8138-0432-3. Dewey:333.7. LCCN:2001-024285.

Audience: **l,u,f.**

Rothermund, Dietmar   **HB3717**
The Global Impact of the Great Depression, 1929-1939. Trade Paper. Routledge. New York, NY. 1996. 192p. ISBN:0-415-11819-0, ISBN13: 978-0-415-11819-4. Dewey:330.9/043. LCCN:95-025780.

Audience: **g,l,u,f.** *Choice, 1997.*

Santaniello, V.   **SB123.3.A53 2000**
Agriculture and Intellectual Property Rights: Economic, Institutional and Implementation Issues in Biotechnology. Cloth Text. Oxford University Press, Inc. New York, NY. 2000. 272p. CABI Publishing Ser. ISBN:0-85199-457-1, ISBN13: 978-0-85199-457-4. Dewey:631.5/23. LCCN:99-054576.

Audience: **u,f.**

Tangermann, Stefan &   **HD1920.7.C46 2000**
Banse, M. (Editors)
Central and Eastern European Agriculture in an Expanding European Union. Cloth Text. Oxford University Press, Inc. New York, NY. 2000. 224p. A CAB International Publication ISBN:0-85199-425-3, ISBN13: 978-0-85199-425-3. Dewey:338.1/84. LCCN:99-053482.

Audience: **u,f.**

Tweeten, Luther G.   **HD1761.T864 2003**
Terrorism, Radicalism, and Populism in Agriculture. Trade Cloth. Blackwell Publishing Professional. Ames, IA. 2002. 176p. ISBN:0-8138-2158-4, ISBN13: 978-0-8138-2158-0. Dewey:338.1. LCCN:2002-014176.

Audience: **g,l,u.** *Choice, 2003.*

Tweeten, Luther G. &   **HD1761.A62187 2002**
Thompson, Stanley R. (Editors)
Agricultural Policy for the Twenty-First Century. Trade Cloth. Blackwell Publishing Professional. Ames, IA. 2002. xii, 309p. ISBN:0-8138-0899-5, ISBN13: 978-0-8138-0899-4. Dewey:338.1/873. LCCN:2001-008307.

Audience: **g,l,u.**

Agronomy

S22
☐ American Society of Agronomy.
http://www.agronomy.org/
ASA-CSSA-SSSA.

Audience: **u,f.**

Olson, R. A. & Frey, K. J.   **SB189 .N78 1987**
Nutritional Quality of Cereal Grains: Genetic and Agronomic Improvement. Trade Cloth. American Society of Agronomy. Madison, WI. 1987. 512p. Agronomy Monograph Ser., No. 28 ISBN:0-89118-092-3, ISBN13: 978-0-89118-092-0. Dewey:633.1/042. LCCN:87-019600.

Audience: **u,f.**

Poehlman, John M. &   **SB185.7.P63 1995**
Sleper, David A.
Breeding Field Crops. Ed. 4. Cloth Text. Blackwell Publishing Professional. Ames, IA. 1995. 510p. ISBN:0-8138-2427-3, ISBN13: 978-0-8138-2427-7. Dewey:633/.083. LCCN:94-036673.

Audience: **u,f.** *Choice, 1987.*

Simmonds, N. W. & Smartt,   **SB106.I47S56 2000**
Joseph (Editors)
Principles of Crop Improvement. Ed. 2. Trade Cloth. Blackwell Publishing, Inc. Malden, MA. 1999. 424p. ISBN:0-632-04191-9, ISBN13: 978-0-632-04191-6. Dewey:631.5/2. LCCN:99-059354.

Audience: **g,l,u.**

Botany, Agricultural

Balick, Michael J. & Cox,   **GN476.73.B35 1996**
Paul Alan
Plants, People and Culture: The Science of Ethnobotany, a Scientific American Library Book. Trade Cloth. Henry Holt & Company. New York, NY. 1996. 241p. ISBN:0-7167-5061-9, ISBN13: 978-0-7167-5061-1. Dewey:581.6/1. LCCN:96-006493.

Audience: **g,l,u,f.** *Choice, 1996.*

Brown, A. (Editor), et al.   **SB123.3 .U84 1989**
The Use of Plant Genetic Resources. D. H. Frankel, D. R. Marshall & J. T. Williams (Editors). Trade Cloth. Cambridge University Press. New York, NY. 1989. 400p. ISBN:0-521-34584-7, ISBN13: 978-0-521-34584-2. Dewey:631.5/23. LCCN:88-012292.

Audience: **l,u.** *Choice, 1989.*

Cotton, C. M.   **GN476.73.C67 1996**
Ethnobotany: Principles and Applications. Ed. 1. Trade Paper. John Wiley & Sons, Inc. Hoboken, NJ. 1996. 434p. ISBN:0-471-95537-X, ISBN13: 978-0-471-95537-5. Dewey:581.6. LCCN:95-052721.

Audience: **l,u,f.** *Choice, 1997.*

Hartmann, Hudson T., et al.   **SB119.K47 2002**
Hartmann and Kester's Plant Propagation: Principles and Practices. Ed. 7. Dale E. Kester, Fred T. Davies Jr. & Robert L. Geneve (Authors). Mixed Media. Prentice Hall PTR. Upper Saddle River, NJ. 2001. 880p. ISBN:0-13-679235-9, ISBN13: 978-0-13-679235-2. Dewey:631.5/3. LCCN:2001-052334.

Audience: **l,u,f.**

Audience: g=general, l=lower division undergraduate, u=upper division undergraduate, f=faculty.

15

Liang, G. H. & Skinner, D. Z.   SB123.57.T7255 2004

Genetically Modified Crops: Their Development, Uses, and Risks. Cloth Text. Haworth Press, Incorporated, The. Binghamton, NY. 2004. 380p. ISBN:1-56022-280-8, ISBN13: 978-1-56022-280-4. Dewey:631.5/233. LCCN:2003-022328.

Audience: **g,l,u.** *Choice, 2005.*

Martin, Gary J.   GN476.73

Ethnobotany: A Methods Manual. Trade Paper. Earthscan/James & James. London, 2004. 292p. People and Plants Conservation Manual Ser. ISBN:1-84407-084-0, ISBN13: 978-1-84407-084-8. Dewey:581.6/3. LCCN:2004-299832.

Audience: **l,u,f.** *Choice, 1995.*

Botany, Economic

QK96

☐ United States Department of Agriculture Natural Resources Conservation Service PLANTS Database.
http://plants.usda.gov/
United States Department of Agriculture.

Audience: **g,l,u.**

Balick, Michael J. & Cox, Paul Alan   GN476.73.B35 1996

Plants, People and Culture: The Science of Ethnobotany, a Scientific American Library Book. Trade Cloth. Henry Holt & Company. New York, NY. 1996. 241p. ISBN:0-7167-5061-9, ISBN13: 978-0-7167-5061-1. Dewey:581.6/1. LCCN:96-006493.

Audience: **g,l,u,f.** *Choice, 1996.*

Balick, Michael J. (Editor), et al.   RS164.M377 1996

Medicinal Resources of the Tropical Forest: Biodiversity and Its Importance to Human Health. Elaine Elisabetsky & Sarah A. Laird (Editors). Trade Cloth. Edinburgh University Press. Edinburgh, 1996. 440p. Biology and Resource Management in the Tropics Ser. ISBN:0-231-10170-8, ISBN13: 978-0-231-10170-7. Dewey:615/.32/0913. LCCN:95-013809.

Audience: **g,l,u.** *Choice, 1996.*

Cotton, C. M.   GN476.73.C67 1996

Ethnobotany: Principles and Applications. Ed. 1. Trade Paper. John Wiley & Sons, Inc. Hoboken, NJ. 1996. 434p. ISBN:0-471-95537-X, ISBN13: 978-0-471-95537-5. Dewey:581.6. LCCN:95-052721.

Audience: **l,u,f.** *Choice, 1997.*

Cunningham, Anthony   GN476.73.C85 2001

Applied Ethnobotany: People, Wild Plant Use and Conservation. Trade Paper. Earthscan/James & James. London, 2001. 256p. People and Plants Conservation Manual Ser. ISBN:1-85383-697-4, ISBN13: 978-1-85383-697-8. Dewey:581. LCCN:2002-726947.

Audience: **l,u,f.**

Langenheim, Jean H.   SB289.L36 2003

Plant Resins: Chemistry, Evolution, Ecology, and Ethnobotany. Trade Cloth. Timber Press, Inc. Portland, OR. 2003. 612p. ISBN:0-88192-574-8, ISBN13: 978-0-88192-574-6. Dewey:620.1/924. LCCN:2002-028941.

Audience: **u,f.** *Choice, 2003.*

Martin, Gary J.   GN476.73

Ethnobotany: A Methods Manual. Trade Paper. Earthscan/James & James. London, 2004. 292p. People and Plants Conservation

Manual Ser. ISBN:1-84407-084-0, ISBN13: 978-1-84407-084-8. Dewey:581.6/3. LCCN:2004-299832.

Audience: **l,u,f.** *Choice, 1995.*

Piperno, Dolores R. & Pearsall, Deborah M.   E59.A35P56 1998

The Origins of Agriculture in the Lowland Neotropics. Cloth Text. Elsevier Science & Technology Books. Saint Louis, MO. 1998. 400p. ISBN:0-12-557180-1, ISBN13: 978-0-12-557180-7. Dewey:630/.913. LCCN:98-084003.

Audience: **l,u,f.** *Choice, 1998.*

Pollan, Michael   QK46.5.H85 P66

The Botany of Desire: A Plant's-Eye View of the World. Trade Paper. Random House, Inc. New York, NY. 2002. 304p. ISBN:0-375-76039-3, ISBN13: 978-0-375-76039-6. Dewey:306.4/5. LCCN:00-066479.

Audience: **g,l,u,f.** *Choice, 2001.*

Schultes, Richard E., et al.   QK99.A1S39 2001

Plants of the Gods: Their Sacred, Healing and Hallucinogenic Powers. Ed. 2. Albert Hofmann & Christian Ratsch (Authors). Trade Cloth. Inner Traditions International, Ltd. Rochester, VT. 2001. 208p. ISBN:0-89281-979-0, ISBN13: 978-0-89281-979-9. Dewey:394.1/4. LCCN:2001-004425.

Audience: **g,l,u.**

Smale, Melinda   SB123.3.V35 2005

Valuing Crop Biodiversity: On-Farm Genetic Resources and Economic Change. Trade Cloth. CABI Publishing. Wallingford, 2006. 352p. CABI Publishing Ser. ISBN:0-85199-083-5, ISBN13: 978-0-85199-083-5. Dewey:631.5/23. LCCN:2005-002725.

Audience: **l,u,f.**

Sumner, Judith   SB108.U5S85 2004

American Household Botany: A History of Useful Plants, 1620-1900. Trade Cloth. Timber Press, Inc. Portland, OR. 2004. 396p. ISBN:0-88192-652-3, ISBN13: 978-0-88192-652-1. Dewey:581.6/0973. LCCN:2003-026578.

Audience: **g,u.** *Choice, 2005.*

Von Reis, Siri V. & Schultes, Richard E. (Editors)   GN476.73.E84 1995

Ethnobotany: The Evolution of a Discipline. Trade Cloth. Timber Press, Inc. Portland, OR. 2005. 416p. ISBN:0-931146-28-3, ISBN13: 978-0-931146-28-2. Dewey:581.6/1. LCCN:94-015515.

Audience: **u,f.** *Choice, 1996.*

Wickens, G. E.   SB107.W47 2001

Economic Botany: Principles and Practices. Trade Cloth. Springer. New York, NY. 2001. 552p. ISBN:0-7923-6781-2, ISBN13: 978-0-7923-6781-9. Dewey:581.6. LCCN:00-066289.

Audience: **l,u,f.** *Choice, 2002.*

Conservation

QH75.A1

☐ IUCN The World Conservation Union.
http://www.iucn.org/
International Union for Conservation of Nature and Natural Resources.

Audience: **g,l,u,f.**

Bohlen, Janet Trowbridge   QH26.B63 1993
For the Wild Places: Profiles in Conservation. Al Gore
(Foreword by). Trade Cloth. Island Press. Washington, DC.
1993. 228p. ISBN:1-55963-125-2, ISBN13: 978-1-55963-125-9.
Dewey:333.95/16/0922. LCCN:92-038118.
Audience: **g,l,u,f.** *Choice, 1993.*

Dasmann, Raymond F.   TD170
Environmental Conservation. Ed. 5. Trade Cloth. John Wiley &
Sons, Inc. Hoboken, NJ. 1984. 496p. ISBN:0-471-89141-X,
ISBN13: 978-0-471-89141-3. Dewey:333.7/2. LCCN:83-021767.
Audience: **g,l,u,f.** *B*

Gosling, L. Morris &   QH75 .B45 2000
  Sutherland, William J. (Editors)
Behaviour and Conservation. Guy Cowlishaw, John L.
Gittleman, Rosie Woodroffe & Michael J. Samways
(Contribution by). Trade Paper. Cambridge University Press.
New York, NY. 2000. 450p. Conservation Biology Ser., No. 2
ISBN:0-521-66539-6, ISBN13: 978-0-521-66539-1.
Dewey:333.95/16. LCCN:99-026461.
Audience: **l,u,f.** *Choice, 2000.*

Hays, Samuel P.   S930.H38 1999
Conservation and the Gospel of Efficiency: The Progressive
Conservation Movement, 1890-1920. Trade Paper. University of
Pittsburgh Press. Pittsburgh, PA. 1999. 292p.
ISBN:0-8229-5702-7, ISBN13: 978-0-8229-5702-7.
Dewey:333.7/2/0973. LCCN:98-054700.
Audience: **g,l,u,f.** *B*

Leopold, Aldo   QH81.L56 2001
A Sand County Almanac. Michael Sewell (Photographer),
Kenneth Brower (Introduction by). Trade Cloth. Oxford
University Press, Inc. New York, NY. 2001. 192p.
ISBN:0-19-514617-4, ISBN13: 978-0-19-514617-2.
Dewey:508.73. LCCN:2001-034038.
Audience: **g,l,u,f.**

McNeely, Jeffrey A. &   SB481.A2.W67 1982
  Miller, Kenton R. (Editors)
National Parks, Conservation, and Development: The Role of
Protected Areas in Sustaining Society. Trade Paper. Smithsonian
Institution Press. Washington, DC. 1984. 848p.
ISBN:0-87474-663-9, ISBN13: 978-0-87474-663-1.
Dewey:333.78/3. LCCN:84-600007.
Audience: **u,f.** *B*

Michalson, Edgar L.;   S624.N68
  Papendick, Robert I.; Carlson, John E.
Conservation Farming in the United States: The Methods and
Accomplishments of the STEEP Program. CRC Press. 1999.
ISBN:0-8493-1185-3, ISBN13: 978-0-8493-1185-7.
Audience: **g,l,u.**

Nash, Roderick   S930.N36 1976
The American Environment: Readings in the History of
Conservation. Trade Cloth. Addison-Wesley Longman, Inc.
Boston, MA. 1976. xx, 364 p. :p. ISBN:0-201-05239-3,
ISBN13: 978-0-201-05239-8. Dewey:333.7/2/0973.
LCCN:75-010913.
Audience: **g,l,u,f.** *B*

Pinchot, Gifford   S942 .P5
The Fight for Conservation. Trade Paper. Kessinger Publishing,
LLC. Whitefish, MT. 2004. ISBN:1-4192-6217-3, ISBN13:
978-1-4192-6217-3. Dewey:333.7/2/0973.
Audience: **g,u,f.** *B*

Primack, Richard B.   QH75.P7525 2004
A Primer of Conservation Biology. Ed. 3. Trade Cloth. Sinauer
Associates, Inc. Sunderland, MA. 2004. 320p.
ISBN:0-87893-728-5, ISBN13: 978-0-87893-728-8.
Dewey:333.95/16. LCCN:2004-011645.
Audience: **l,u,f.** *Choice, 1996.*

Rutledge, A. J. & Molnar,   SB481.R86 1986
  Donald J.
Anatomy of a Park: The Essentials of Recreation Area Planning
and Design. Ed. 2. Cloth Text. McGraw-Hill Companies, The.
New York, NY. 1986. 224p. ISBN:0-07-054349-6, ISBN13:
978-0-07-054349-2. Dewey:712/.5. LCCN:85-019817.
Audience: **g,u.** *B*

Conservation > Conservation of Natural Resources

Bergstrom, John C., et al.   HD111
Land Use Problems and Conflicts: Causes, Consequences and
Solutions. Stephan J. Goetz & James S. Shortle (Authors). Paper
over Boards. Routledge. New York, NY. 2004. 384p. Routledge
Explorations in Environmental Economics Ser., Vol. 2
ISBN:0-415-70028-0, ISBN13: 978-0-415-70028-3.
Dewey:333.73/13/0973. LCCN:2004-050983.
Audience: **l,u,f.**

Carson, Rachel   QH545
Silent Spring. Ed. 40. Dust Jacket. Houghton Mifflin Company
Trade & Reference Division. Boston, MA. 2002. 400p.
ISBN:0-618-25305-X, ISBN13: 978-0-618-25305-0.
Dewey:363.738/4. LCCN:2002-726803.
Audience: **g,l,u,f.** *B*

Cunningham, Anthony   GN476.73.C85 2001
Applied Ethnobotany: People, Wild Plant Use and Conservation.
Trade Paper. Earthscan/James & James. London, 2001. 256p.
People and Plants Conservation Manual Ser.
ISBN:1-85383-697-4, ISBN13: 978-1-85383-697-8. Dewey:581.
LCCN:2002-726947.
Audience: **l,u,f.**

Geist, Helmut (Editor)   GF90
Our Earth's Changing Land: An Encyclopedia of Land-Use and
Land-Cover Change. Cloth Text. Greenwood Publishing Group,
Inc. Portsmouth, NH. 2005. 792p. ISBN:0-313-32704-1,
ISBN13: 978-0-313-32704-9. Dewey:333.7.
LCCN:2005-019212.
Audience: **g,l,u,f.** *Choice, 2006.*

John H. Heinz III Center   QH104.S73 2002
  for Science, Economics and the Environment
The State of the Nation's Ecosystems: Measuring the Lands,
Waters, and Living Resources of the United States. Trade Paper.
Cambridge University Press. New York, NY. 2002. 288p.
ISBN:0-521-52572-1, ISBN13: 978-0-521-52572-5.
Dewey:333.7/2. LCCN:2002-073890.
Audience: **l,u,f.** *Choice, 2003.*

Moore, Keith M.   HC1000.Z65C66 2004
Conflict, Social Capital, and Managing Natural Resources: A
West African Case Study. SANREM Staff (Contribution by).
Cloth Text. CAB International. Wallingford, 2005. 278p. CABI
Publishing Ser. ISBN:0-85199-948-4, ISBN13:
978-0-85199-948-7. Dewey:333.7/0966. LCCN:2004-012409.
Audience: **u,f.**

National Wildlife Federation   **S920.N3**
  Staff
Conservation Directory: The Guide to Worldwide Environmental
Organizations. Library Binding. Sagebrush Education Resources.
Caledonia, MN. 2003. ISBN:0-613-91697-2, ISBN13:
978-0-613-91697-4. Dewey:333.72.

                                        Audience: **g,l,u,f.**

Neumann, Roderick P.   **SB484.T3N48 1998**
Imposing Wilderness: Struggles over Livelihood and Nature
Preservation in Africa. Trade Cloth. University of California
Press. Berkeley, CA. 1998. 270p. California Studies in Critical
Human Geography, Vol. 4 ISBN:0-520-21178-2, ISBN13:
978-0-520-21178-0. Dewey:333.78/09678. LCCN:98-012746.

                                        Audience: **g,l,u,f.** *Choice, 1999.*

Primack, Richard B.   **QH75.P752 2002**
Essentials of Conservation Biology. Ed. 3. Trade Cloth. Sinauer
Associates, Inc. Sunderland, MA. 2002. 637p.
ISBN:0-87893-719-6, ISBN13: 978-0-87893-719-6.
Dewey:333.95/16. LCCN:2002-008076.

                                        Audience: **l.**

Robinson, Glen O. &   **SD143**
  Robinson, O. F.
The Forest Service: A Study in Public Land Management. Trade
Cloth. Resources for the Future. Washington, DC. 1975. 358p.
ISBN:0-8018-1723-4, ISBN13: 978-0-8018-1723-6.
Dewey:634.9/0973. LCCN:75-011352.

                                        Audience: **u,f.** *B*

Ross, Michael R.   **SH331.R635 1997**
Fisheries Conservation and Management. Cloth Text. Prentice
Hall PTR. Upper Saddle River, NJ. 1996. 374p.
ISBN:0-02-403901-2, ISBN13: 978-0-02-403901-9.
Dewey:333.95/6. LCCN:95-041533.

                                        Audience: **g,l,u.**

Conservation > National Parks and Reserves

Browler, Kenneth &   **SD426.B66 1997**
  National Geographic Society Staff
American Legacy: Our National Forests. Trade Cloth. National
Geographic Society. Washington, DC. 1997.
ISBN:0-7922-3650-5, ISBN13: 978-0-7922-3650-4.
Dewey:333.75/16/0973. LCCN:96-037341.

                                        Audience: **g,u,f.**

Everhart, William C.   **SB482.A4**
The National Park Service. Cloth Text. Westview Press. Boulder,
CO. 1982. 198p. Library of Federal Departments, Agencies, and
Systems Ser. ISBN:0-86531-130-7, ISBN13: 978-0-86531-130-5.
Dewey:719/.32/068. LCCN:82-010884.

                                        Audience: **g,u.** *B*

Foresta, Ronald A.   **SB482.A4**
America's National Parks and Their Keepers. Emery N. Castle
(Foreword by). Trade Cloth. Resources for the Future.
Washington, DC. 1984. 400p. ISBN:0-915707-02-0, ISBN13:
978-0-915707-02-7. Dewey:333.78/3/0973. LCCN:83-043262.

                                        Audience: **g,l,u.**

Forlag, Albert B. & Magoc,   **F722.M23 1999**
  Christopher J.
Yellowstone: The Creation and Selling of an American
Landscape, 1870-1903. Trade Cloth. University of New Mexico
Press. Albuquerque, NM. 1999. 304p. ISBN:0-8263-2119-4,
ISBN13: 978-0-8263-2119-0. Dewey:978.7/52.
LCCN:98-058035.

                                        Audience: **g,l,u,f.** *Choice, 2000.*

Frome, Michael   **SB482.A4F76 1991**
Regreening the National Parks. Trade Paper. University of
Arizona Press. Tucson, AZ. 1992. 289p. ISBN:0-8165-1288-4,
ISBN13: 978-0-8165-1288-1. Dewey:333.78/0973.
LCCN:91-017477.

                                        Audience: **g.** *Choice, 1992.*

Grusin, Richard   **SB484.A4G78 2003**
Culture, Technology, and the Creation of America's National
Parks. Albert Gelpi & Ross Posnock (Contribution by). Trade
Cloth. Cambridge University Press. New York, NY. 2004. 232p.
Cambridge Studies in American Literature and Culture Ser.
ISBN:0-521-82649-7, ISBN13: 978-0-521-82649-5.
Dewey:333.78/3/0973. LCCN:2003-043507.

                                        Audience: **g,l,u,f.** *Choice, 2005.*

MacEachern, Alan   **SB484.C2M23 2001**
Natural Selections: National Parks in Atlantic Canada,
1935-1970. Trade Cloth. McGill-Queen's University Press.
Montreal, PQ. 2001. xiii, 328p. ISBN:0-7735-2157-7, ISBN13:
978-0-7735-2157-5. Dewey:333.78/3/09715.
LCCN:2002-421349.

                                        Audience: **l,u,f.** *Choice, 2001.*

McNeely, Jeffrey A. &   **SB481.A2.W67 1982**
  Miller, Kenton R. (Editors)
National Parks, Conservation, and Development: The Role of
Protected Areas in Sustaining Society. Trade Paper. Smithsonian
Institution Press. Washington, DC. 1984. 848p.
ISBN:0-87474-663-9, ISBN13: 978-0-87474-663-1.
Dewey:333.78/3. LCCN:84-600007.

                                        Audience: **u,f.** *B*

O'Brien, Bob R.   **SB482.A4O37 1999**
Our National Parks and the Search for Sustainability. Gary
O'Brien (Illustrator). Trade Paper. University of Texas Press.
Austin, TX. 1999. 264p. ISBN:0-292-76050-7, ISBN13:
978-0-292-76050-9. Dewey:333.78/315/0973. LCCN:98-009011.

                                        Audience: **g,l.**

Runte, Alfred   **E160**
National Parks: The American Experience. Library Binding.
Sagebrush Education Resources. Caledonia, MN. 1997.
ISBN:0-613-91506-2, ISBN13: 978-0-613-91506-9.
Dewey:719/.32/0973.

                                        Audience: **g,l,u,f.**

Rutledge, A. J. & Molnar,   **SB481.R86 1986**
  Donald J.
Anatomy of a Park: The Essentials of Recreation Area Planning
and Design. Ed. 2. Cloth Text. McGraw-Hill Companies, The.
New York, NY. 1986. 224p. ISBN:0-07-054349-6, ISBN13:
978-0-07-054349-2. Dewey:712/.5. LCCN:85-019817.

                                        Audience: **g,u.** *B*

Sellars, Richard W.   **HC103.7**
Preserving Nature in the National Parks: A History. Trade Paper.
Yale University Press. Cumberland, RI. 1999. 394p.

ISBN:0-300-07578-2, ISBN13: 978-0-300-07578-6.
Dewey:333.7/0973.

Audience: **l,u,f.**

Smith, Darren L. (Editor)   E160.S65 1992
Parks Directory of the United States: A Guide to 4,000 National
and State Parks, Recreational Areas, Historic Sites, Battlefields,
Monuments, Forests, Preserves, Memorials, Seashores, and
Other Designated Recreation Areas in the United States
Administered by National and State Park Agencies. Library
Binding. Omnigraphics, Inc. Detroit, MI. 1992. 360p.
ISBN:1-55888-765-2, ISBN13: 978-1-55888-765-7.
Dewey:917.3/0025. LCCN:91-045072.

Audience: **g,l,u.** *Choice, 1992.*

Conservation > Water Conservation

Gleick, Peter H.   TD345
The World's Water 2004-2005: The Biennial Report on
Freshwater Resources. Trade Paper. Island Press. Washington,
DC. 2004. 362p. ISBN:1-55963-536-3, ISBN13:
978-1-55963-536-3. Dewey:333.9/1.

Audience: **g,l,u,f.**

Grigg, Neil S.   TC423.G75 1985
Water Resources Planning. Cloth Text. McGraw-Hill
Companies, The. New York, NY. 1985. xii, 328 p. :p.
ISBN:0-07-024771-4, ISBN13: 978-0-07-024771-0.
Dewey:333.91. LCCN:84-028868.

Audience: **u,f.** *Choice, 1985.*

Vickers, Amy   TD388.V53 2001
Handbook of Water Use and Conservation: Homes, Landscapes,
Businesses, Industries, Farms. Trade Cloth. WaterPlow Press.
Amherst, MA. 2001. 460p. ISBN:1-931579-07-5, ISBN13:
978-1-931579-07-0. Dewey:333.91/16. LCCN:99-025179.

Audience: **l,u,f.** *Choice, 2001.*

Conservation > Wildlife Conservation

Bolen, Eric G. & Robinson,   SK355.B65 2002
William Laughlin
Wildlife Ecology and Management. Ed. 5. Cloth Text. Prentice
Hall PTR. Upper Saddle River, NJ. 2002. 634p.
ISBN:0-13-066250-X, ISBN13: 978-0-13-066250-7.
Dewey:639.9. LCCN:2002-066251.

Audience: **g,l.**

Neumann, Roderick P.   SB484.T3N48 1998
Imposing Wilderness: Struggles over Livelihood and Nature
Preservation in Africa. Trade Cloth. University of California
Press. Berkeley, CA. 1998. 270p. California Studies in Critical
Human Geography, Vol. 4 ISBN:0-520-21178-2, ISBN13:
978-0-520-21178-0. Dewey:333.78/09678. LCCN:98-012746.

Audience: **g,l,u,f.** *Choice, 1999.*

Crops

                                                           S22
☐ American Society of Agronomy.
http://www.agronomy.org/
ASA-CSSA-SSSA.

Audience: **u,f.**

                                                  SB188.525.I564
☐ CIMMYT International Maize and Wheat Improvement
Center.
http://www.cimmyt.org/

Audience: **g,l,u.**

                                                       SB185.6
☐ ICRISAT: International Crops Research Institute for the
Semi-arid Tropics.
http://www.icrisat.org/
ICRISAT.

Audience: **g,l,u.**

                                                      SB211.P8
☐ International Potato Center: Centro Internacional de la Papa.
http://www.cipotato.org/news_index.asp
International Potato Center (CIP).

Audience: **l,u,f.**

                                                      SB191.R5
☐ IRRI: International Rice Research Institute.
http://irri.org/
International Rice Research Institute.

Audience: **g,l,u,f.**

                                                      SB123.57
☐ Transgenic Crops: An Introduction and Resource Guide.
http://cls.casa.colostate.edu/TransgenicCrops/
Department of Soil and Crop Sciences at Colorado State
University.

Audience: **g,l,u.**

                                                      SB450.97
☐ U.S. Department of Agriculture's Home and Garden Bulletin
Archive.
http://agnic.msu.edu/hgpubs/index.html

Audience: **g,l,u.**

Abbott, A. J. & Atkin, R. K.   SB123 .I465 1987
  (Editors)
Improving Vegetatively-Propagated Crops. Trade Cloth. Elsevier
Science & Technology Books. Saint Louis, MO. 1988. 416p.
Applied Botany and Crop Science Ser. ISBN:0-12-041410-4,
ISBN13: 978-0-12-041410-9. Dewey:631.5/3. LCCN:89-148336.

Audience: **u,f.**

Bajaj, Y. P. S. (Editor)   SB249.C79355 1998
Cotton. Cloth Text. Springer. New York, NY. 1998. 384p.
Biotechnology in Agriculture and Forestry Ser., Vol. 42
ISBN:3-540-62728-6, ISBN13: 978-3-540-62728-9.
Dewey:633.5/123. LCCN:97-045484.

Audience: **g,u,f.**

Bajaj, Y. P. S. (Editor)   SB191.R5R44 1991
Rice, Vol. 14. Cloth Text. Springer. New York, NY. 1991. 648p.
Biotechnology in Agriculture and Forestry Ser.
ISBN:0-387-51810-X, ISBN13: 978-0-387-51810-7.
Dewey:633.1/8. LCCN:90-046033.

Audience: **g,l,u,f.**

Bajaj, Y. P. S. (Editor)   SB191.W5W48 1990
Wheat. Cloth Text. Springer. New York, NY. 1991. 687p.
Biotechnology in Agriculture and Forestry Ser., Vol. 13
ISBN:0-387-51809-6, ISBN13: 978-0-387-51809-1.
Dewey:633.1/1. LCCN:90-009824.

Audience: **u,f.**

Audience: g=general, l=lower division undergraduate, u=upper division undergraduate, f=faculty.

19

Bakker, Henk   **SB231.B26 1999**
Sugar Cane Cultivation and Management. Trade Cloth. Springer.
New York, NY. 1999. 706p. ISBN:0-306-46119-6, ISBN13:
978-0-306-46119-4. Dewey:633.6/1. LCCN:99-031318.

Audience: **u,f.**

Baliger, V. C. & Duncan, R.   **S596.7.C76 1991**
R. (Editors)
Crops As Enhancers of Nutrient Use. Trade Cloth. Elsevier
Science & Technology Books. Saint Louis, MO. 1990. 574p.
ISBN:0-12-077125-X, ISBN13: 978-0-12-077125-7.
Dewey:581.1/335. LCCN:90-000542.

Audience: **g,l,u,f.**

Barnes, R. F. W. & Beard,   **SB45.G57 1992**
J. B. (Editors)
Glossary of Crop Science Terms. Trade Paper. American Society
of Agronomy. Madison, WI. 1992. 88p. ISBN:0-89118-535-6,
ISBN13: 978-0-89118-535-2. Dewey:630/.14. LCCN:92-243632.

Audience: **g,l,u.** *Choice, 1993.*

Barnes, Robert F., et al.   **SB193.F64 2003**
Forages: An Introduction to Grassland Agriculture. Ed. 6.
Michael Collins, Kenneth Moore & Mark Westgate (Authors),
Robert F. Barnes (Editor). Trade Cloth. Blackwell Publishing
Professional. Ames, IA. 2003. 576p. ISBN:0-8138-0421-3,
ISBN13: 978-0-8138-0421-7. Dewey:633.2.
LCCN:2002-014177.

Audience: **l,u.**

Bartholomew, D. (Editor), et   **SB375.P47 2002**
al.
The Pineapple: Botany, Production and Uses. R. E. Paull & K.
Rohrbach (Editors). Cloth Text. Oxford University Press, Inc.
New York, NY. 2003. 328p. CABI Publishing Ser.
ISBN:0-85199-503-9, ISBN13: 978-0-85199-503-8.
Dewey:634/.774. LCCN:2002-005741.

Audience: **u,f.**

Benech-Arnold, Roberto L.   **SB117.H27 2004**
& Sanchez, Rodolfo A.
Handbook of Seed Physiology: Applications to Agriculture.
Paper Text. Haworth Press, Incorporated, The. Binghamton, NY.
2004. 437p. ISBN:1-56022-929-2, ISBN13: 978-1-56022-929-2.
Dewey:631.5/21. LCCN:2003-021276.

Audience: **u,f.** *Choice, 2005.*

Bewley, J. D. & Black, M.   **QK661.B49 1994**
Seeds: Physiology of Development and Germination. Ed. 2.
Trade Cloth. Basic Books. New York, NY. 1994. 462p.
ISBN:0-306-44747-9, ISBN13: 978-0-306-44747-1.
Dewey:582/.0467. LCCN:94-019278.

Audience: **u,f.**

Boerma, H. R. & Specht, J.   **SB205.S7S56 2004**
E. (Editors)
Soybeans: Improvement, Production, and Uses. Ed. 3. Cloth
Text. ASA-CSSA-SSSA. Madison, WI. 2004. xxv, 1144p.
Agronomy Ser., No. 16 ISBN:0-89118-154-7, ISBN13:
978-0-89118-154-5. Dewey:633.3/4. LCCN:2003-114302.

Audience: **g,u.**

Brush, Stephen B.   **SB123.3.B78 2004**
Farmers' Bounty: Locating Crop Diversity in the Contemporary
World. Cloth over Boards. Yale University Press. Cumberland,
RI. 2004. 352p. Yale Agrarian Studies ISBN:0-300-10049-3,

ISBN13: 978-0-300-10049-5. Dewey:631.5/23.
LCCN:2003-020235.

Audience: **l,u,f.** *Choice, 2004.*

Buxton, Dwayne   **SB195.S544 2003**
(Editor), et al.
Silage Science and Technology. Richard Muck & Joseph
Harrison (Editors). Perfect. ASA-CSSA-SSSA. Madison, WI.
2004. xix, 927p. Agronomy Ser., Vol. 42 ISBN:0-89118-151-2,
ISBN13: 978-0-89118-151-4. Dewey:636.08/62.
LCCN:2003-109369.

Audience: **u,f.**

Capinera, John   **SB603.5.C36 2001**
Handbook of Vegetable Pests. Trade Cloth. Elsevier Science &
Technology Books. Saint Louis, MO. 2001. 800p.
ISBN:0-12-158861-0, ISBN13: 978-0-12-158861-8.
Dewey:635/.0497. LCCN:2001-086233.

Audience: **g,l,u.** *Choice, 2001.*

Chopra, V. L. (Editor)   **SB189.E96 2002**
Evolution and Adaptation of Crops: Cereals. Trade Cloth.
Science Publishers. Enfield, NH. 2002. 296p. Evolution and
Adaptation of Crops, Vol. 1:Cereals ISBN:1-57808-190-4,
ISBN13: 978-1-57808-190-5. Dewey:584.9138.
LCCN:2002-728486.

Audience: **u,f.**

Cook, Guy   **SB123.57.C665 2004**
Genetically Modified Language. Paper over Boards. Routledge.
New York, NY. 2004. 176p. ISBN:0-415-31467-4, ISBN13:
978-0-415-31467-1. Dewey:631/.523. LCCN:2004-005597.

Audience: **g,l,u.**

Corley, R. H. V. & Tinker,   **SB299.P3C65 2003**
P. B. H.
The Oil Palm. Ed. 4. Trade Cloth. Blackwell Publishing, Inc.
Malden, MA. 2003. 592p. World Agriculture Ser.
ISBN:0-632-05212-0, ISBN13: 978-0-632-05212-7.
Dewey:633.8/51. LCCN:2003-008646.

Audience: **u,f.**

Cothren, Joe Tom & Smith,   **SB249.C79375 1999**
C. Wayne (Editors)
Cotton: Origin, History, Technology, and Production. Trade
Cloth. John Wiley & Sons, Inc. Hoboken, NJ. 1999. 864p.
Wiley Series in Crop Science, Vol. 4 ISBN:0-471-18045-9,
ISBN13: 978-0-471-18045-6. Dewey:633.5/1. LCCN:99-022020.

Audience: **l,u,f.** *Choice, 2000.*

De Datta, Surajit K.   **SB191.R5**
Principles and Practices of Rice Production. Nyle C. Brady
(Introduction by). Library Binding. Krieger Publishing
Company. Melbourne, FL. 1987. 640p. ISBN:0-89874-994-8,
ISBN13: 978-0-89874-994-6. Dewey:633.1/8. LCCN:86-021370.

Audience: **g,l,u.**

Dennis, E. S. & Llewellyn,   **SB123.57.M65 1991**
D. J. (Editors)
Molecular Approaches to Crop Improvement. Cloth Text.
Springer. New York, NY. 1991. 166p. Plant Gene Research Ser.
ISBN:0-387-82230-5, ISBN13: 978-0-387-82230-3.
Dewey:631.5/23. LCCN:90-024701.

Audience: **g,u,f.** *Choice, 1992.*

Desai, Babasaheb B.   **SB117**
Seeds Handbook: Biology, Production, Processing, and Storage, Vol. 103. Ed. 2. Paper over Boards. Marcel Dekker Inc. New York, NY. 2004. 800p. Books in Soils, Plants, and the Environment Ser., Vol. 100 ISBN:0-8247-4800-X, ISBN13: 978-0-8247-4800-5. Dewey:631.5/21. LCCN:2004-300847.

Audience: **u,f.**

Doggett, Hugh   **SB191.S7D64 1988**
Sorghum. Ed. 2. Trade Cloth. John Wiley & Sons, Inc. Hoboken, NJ. 1989. 512p. Intermediate Tropical Agriculture Ser. ISBN:0-470-20984-4, ISBN13: 978-0-470-20984-4. Dewey:633/.174. LCCN:87-022819.

Audience: **g,l,u.**

Draycott, Philip (Editor)   **SB221.S88 2005**
Sugar Beet. Trade Cloth. Blackwell Publishing, Inc. Malden, MA. 2006. 496p. World Agriculture Ser. ISBN:1-4051-1911-X, ISBN13: 978-1-4051-1911-5. Dewey:633.6/3. LCCN:2005-013771.

Audience: **u,f.**

Ervin, David E.   **S494.5.B563**
Transgenic Crops: An Environmental Assessment. Winrock International. 2001. Variation: Policy Studies Report (Henry A. Wallace Center for Agricultural & Environmental Policy); no. 15 ISBN:1-893182-22-3, ISBN13: 978-1-893182-22-6.

Audience: **g,l,u,f.**

Evans, L. T.   **SB106.O74 E93 1993**
Crop Evolution, Adaptation and Yield. Trade Cloth. Cambridge University Press. New York, NY. 1993. 512p. ISBN:0-521-22571-X, ISBN13: 978-0-521-22571-7. Dewey:630. LCCN:92-028314.

Audience: **l,u,f.** *Choice, 1994.*

Evenson, R. E. & Gollin, D.   **SB185.7.C76 2002**
  (Editors)
Crop Variety Improvement and Its Effect on Productivity: The Impact of International Agricultural Research. Trade Cloth. Oxford University Press, Inc. New York, NY. 2003. 552p. CABI Publishing Ser. ISBN:0-85199-549-7, ISBN13: 978-0-85199-549-6. Dewey:631.5/2. LCCN:2002-011122.

Audience: **u,f.**

Fageria, N. A., et al.   **SB185.5.F34 1997**
Growth and Mineral Nutrition of Field Crops, Vol. 57. Ed. 2. V. C. Baligar & Charles Jones (Authors). Paper over Boards. Marcel Dekker Inc. New York, NY. 1997. 656p. Books in Soils, Plants and the Environment, Vol. 57 ISBN:0-8247-0089-9, ISBN13: 978-0-8247-0089-8. Dewey:631.8. LCCN:97-013975.

Audience: **u,f.**

Fehr, W. R. & Hadley, H. H.   **SB123 .H9**
  (Editors)
Hybridization of Crop Plants. Trade Cloth. American Society of Agronomy. Madison, WI. 1980. 765p. ISBN:0-89118-034-6, ISBN13: 978-0-89118-034-0. Dewey:631.5/23. LCCN:80-012306.

Audience: **g,u,f.**

Ferree, D. C. & Warrington,   **SB363.A67 2003**
  I. (Editors)
Apples: Botany, Production and Uses. Cloth Text. Oxford University Press, Inc. New York, NY. 2003. 704p. CABI Publishing Ser. ISBN:0-85199-592-6, ISBN13: 978-0-85199-592-2. Dewey:634/.11. LCCN:2002-013984.

Audience: **g,u,f.**

Francis, Charles A. (Editor)   **S603.7.M85 1986**
Multiple Cropping Systems. Macmillan. 1986. ISBN:0-02-948610-6, ISBN13: 978-0-02-948610-8.

Audience: **u,f.**

Goodman/RobertM.   **SB45.E486 2004**
Encyclopedia of Plant and Crop Science. Paper over Boards. Marcel Dekker Inc. New York, NY. 2004. 1360p. ISBN:0-8247-0944-6, ISBN13: 978-0-8247-0944-0. Dewey:630/.3. LCCN:2004-043880.

Audience: **g,u.** *Choice, 2004.*

Gupta, U. S.   **SB123**
Crop Improvement: Stress Tolerance. Trade Cloth. Science Publishers. Enfield, NH. 1997. 315p. ISBN:1-57808-005-3, ISBN13: 978-1-57808-005-2. Dewey:631.5/23.

Audience: **u,f.**

Gupta, U. S.   **SB123**
Crop Improvement: Quality Characters. Trade Cloth. Science Publishers. Enfield, NH. 2000. 168p. ISBN:1-57808-126-2, ISBN13: 978-1-57808-126-4. Dewey:631.5/23.

Audience: **u,f.**

Gupta, U. S.   **SB112.5 .G87**
Physiology of Stressed Crops: The Stress of Allelochemicals. Trade Cloth. Science Publishers. Enfield, NH. 2005. 200p. ISBN:1-57808-390-7, ISBN13: 978-1-57808-390-9. Dewey:632/.1.

Audience: **u,f.**

Halford, Nigel G.   **SB123.57.H35 2003**
Genetically Modified Crops. Trade Cloth. Imperial College Press. London, 2003. 124p. ISBN:1-86094-353-5, ISBN13: 978-1-86094-353-9. Dewey:631.5/233. LCCN:2005-295947.

Audience: **g,l,u,f.** *Choice, 2004.*

Hancock, James F. &   **SB106.O74H36 2003**
  Hancock, J. F.
Plant Evolution and the Origin of Crop Species. Ed. 2. Cloth Text. Oxford University Press, Inc. New York, NY. 2004. 336p. CABI Publishing Ser. ISBN:0-85199-685-X, ISBN13: 978-0-85199-685-1. Dewey:633. LCCN:2003-006924.

Audience: **l,u,f.** *Choice, 2004.*

Hanelt, Peter   **SB107.M38 2001**
Mansfeld's World Manual of Agricultural and Horticultural Crops. Institute of Plant Genetics and Crop Plant Research Staff (Editor), R. Kilian & W. Kilian (Drawings by). Trade Cloth. Springer. New York, NY. 2001. 3380p. ISBN:3-540-41017-1, ISBN13: 978-3-540-41017-1. Dewey:630/.3. LCCN:2001-020690.

Audience: **g,l,u.**

Hanson, A. A. (Editor), et al.   **SB205.A4**
Alfalfa and Alfalfa Improvement. D. K. Barnes, R. R. Hill & G. H. Heichel (Editors). Trade Cloth. American Society of Agronomy. Madison, WI. 1988. 1110p. ISBN:0-89118-094-X, ISBN13: 978-0-89118-094-4. Dewey:633.3/1. LCCN:88-003350.

Audience: **u,f.**

Heaton, Donald D.   **SB354.8.H43 1997**
Nature's Harvest: A Produce Reference Guide to Fruits and Vegetables from Around the World. Trade Cloth. Haworth Press, Incorporated, The. Binghamton, NY. 1997. 244p. ISBN:1-56022-865-2, ISBN13: 978-1-56022-865-3. Dewey:641.3/5. LCCN:96-049040.

Audience: **g.** *Choice, 1997.*

Heyne, E. G. (Editor)   SB191.W5 W493 1987
Wheat and Wheat Improvement. Ed. 2. Trade Cloth. American
Society of Agronomy. Madison, WI. 1987. 766p. Agronomy
Monograph Ser., No. 13 ISBN:0-89118-091-5, ISBN13:
978-0-89118-091-3. Dewey:633.1/1. LCCN:87-012564.
Audience: **u,f.**

Holden, John H., et al.   SB123.3 .H65 1993
Genes, Crops and the Environment. James Peacock & Trevor A.
Williams (Authors). Cloth Text. Cambridge University Press.
New York, NY. 1993. 176p. ISBN:0-521-43137-9, ISBN13:
978-0-521-43137-8. Dewey:333.95316. LCCN:92-033605.
Audience: **g,l,u,f.** *Choice, 1994.*

Ishaaya, Isaac   SB931.I43 2004
Insect Pest Management: Field and Protected Crops. A. Rami
Horowitz (Editor). Trade Cloth. Springer. New York, NY. 2004.
XXI, 344p. ISBN:3-540-20755-4, ISBN13: 978-3-540-20755-9.
Dewey:632/.7. LCCN:2003-070422.
Audience: **u,f.**

Koul, Opender & Dhaliwal,   SB123.57.T723 2004
G. S. (Editors)
Transgenic Crop Protection: Concepts and Strategies. Book,
Other. Science Publishers. Enfield, NH. 2004. 412p.
ISBN:1-57808-302-8, ISBN13: 978-1-57808-302-2.
Dewey:631.5/233. LCCN:2004-042861.
Audience: **g,l,u.** *Choice, 2005.*

Kulp, Karel & Ponterotto,   TP434.H36 2000
Joseph G.
Handbook of Cereal Science and Technology, Vol. 99. Ed. 2.
Paper over Boards. Marcel Dekker Inc. New York, NY. 2000.
800p. Food Science and Technology Ser. ISBN:0-8247-8294-1,
ISBN13: 978-0-8247-8294-8. Dewey:664/.7. LCCN:00-022903.
Audience: **u,f.**

Liang, G. H. & Skinner, D.   SB123.57.T7255 2004
Z.
Genetically Modified Crops: Their Development, Uses, and
Risks. Cloth Text. Haworth Press, Incorporated, The.
Binghamton, NY. 2004. 380p. ISBN:1-56022-280-8, ISBN13:
978-1-56022-280-4. Dewey:631.5/233. LCCN:2003-022328.
Audience: **g,l,u.** *Choice, 2005.*

Litz, R. E.   SB354.8
Biotechnology of Fruit and Nut Crops. Cloth Text. CAB
International. Wallingford, 2005. 748p. Biotechnology in
Agriculture Ser., Vol. 29:CABI Publishing ISBN:0-85199-662-0,
ISBN13: 978-0-85199-662-2. Dewey:634/.043.
LCCN:2004-007979.
Audience: **l,u,f.**

Loomis, R. S. & Connor,   S589.7 .L66 1992
D. J.
Crop Ecology: Productivity and Management in Agricultural
Systems. Trade Paper. Cambridge University Press. New York,
NY. 1992. 552p. ISBN:0-521-38776-0, ISBN13:
978-0-521-38776-7. Dewey:631. LCCN:91-029201.
Audience: **l,u,f.** *Choice, 1993.*

Maynard, Donald N. &   SB321.M392 1997
Hochmuth, George J.
Knott's Handbook for Vegetable Growers. Ed. 4. Trade Paper.
John Wiley & Sons, Inc. Hoboken, NJ. 1997. 600p.
ISBN:0-471-13151-2, ISBN13: 978-0-471-13151-9. Dewey:635.
LCCN:96-033492.
Audience: **g.**

McCann, James C.   SB191.M2M14 2005
Maize and Grace: Africa's Encounter with a New World Crop,
1500-2000. Trade Cloth. Harvard University Press. Cambridge,
MA. 2005. 304p. ISBN:0-674-01718-8, ISBN13:
978-0-674-01718-4. Dewey:633.1/5/096. LCCN:2004-054325.
Audience: **g,u,f.** *Choice, 2006.*

Mengel, Konrad, et al.   QK867.P75 2001
Principles of Plant Nutrition. Ed. 5. Ernest A. Kirkby & Thomas
Appel (Authors), Harald Kosegarten (Contribution by). Trade
Cloth. Springer. New York, NY. 2001. 864p.
ISBN:0-7923-7150-X, ISBN13: 978-0-7923-7150-2.
Dewey:575.7/6. LCCN:2001-038360.
Audience: **g,l,u,f.**

Murphy, C. F. & Peterson,   SB123.D47 2000
D. M. (Editors)
Designing Crops for Added Value. Trade Cloth. American
Society of Agronomy. Madison, WI. 2000. 267p. Agronomy
Ser., No. 40 ISBN:0-89118-144-X, ISBN13: 978-0-89118-144-6.
Dewey:631.5/23. LCCN:00-133615.
Audience: **g,l,u,f.**

Nakasone, Henry Y. &   SB359.N275 1998
Paull, Robert E.
Tropical Fruits. Cloth Text. Oxford University Press, Inc. New
York, NY. 1998. 472p. Crop Production Science in Horticulture
Ser., No. 7 ISBN:0-85199-254-4, ISBN13: 978-0-85199-254-9.
Dewey:634/.6. LCCN:97-044048.
Audience: **l,u,f.**

National Research Council   SB123.3.A47 1993
Staff
Agricultural Crop Issues and Policies. Cloth Text. National
Academies Press. Washington, DC. 1994. 480p. Managing
Global Genetic Resources Ser. ISBN:0-309-04430-8, ISBN13:
978-0-309-04430-1. Dewey:333.95/316. LCCN:93-031987.
Audience: **g,l,u,f.** *Choice, 1994.*

Nene, Y. L. (Editor), et al.   SB205.P5
The Pigeonpea. S. D. Hall & V. K. Scheila (Editors). Trade
Cloth. Oxford University Press, Inc. New York, NY. 1991. 490p.
ISBN:0-85198-657-9, ISBN13: 978-0-85198-657-9.
Dewey:635.65.
Audience: **u,f.**

Norman, Geoffrey A.   SB205.S7.S535
(Editor)
Soybean Physiology, Agronomy, and Utilization. Trade Cloth.
Elsevier Science & Technology Books. Saint Louis, MO. 1978.
xii, 249 p. :p. ISBN:0-12-521160-0, ISBN13:
978-0-12-521160-4. Dewey:635/.655. LCCN:78-018399.
Audience: **u,f.** *B*

Nweke, Felix I., et al.   SB211.C3N84 2002
The Cassava Transformation: Africa's Best-Kept Secret. John K.
Lynam & D. S. C. Spencer (Authors). Trade Cloth. Michigan
State University Press. East Lansing, MI. 2002. 250p.
ISBN:0-87013-602-X, ISBN13: 978-0-87013-602-3.
Dewey:633.6/82/096. LCCN:2001-005255.
Audience: **l,u,f.** *Choice, 2002.*

Olsen, Wallace C. (Editor)   SB45.65.L58 1995
The Literature of Crop Science. Book, Other. Cornell University
Press. Ithaca, NY. 1995. 544p. The Literature of the Agricultural
Sciences Ser. ISBN:0-8014-3138-7, ISBN13:
978-0-8014-3138-8. Dewey:630. LCCN:95-020394.
Audience: **u,f.** *Choice, 1996.*

Olson, R. A. & Frey, K. J.   **SB189 .N78 1987**
Nutritional Quality of Cereal Grains: Genetic and Agronomic
Improvement. Trade Cloth. American Society of Agronomy.
Madison, WI. 1987. 512p. Agronomy Monograph Ser., No. 28
ISBN:0-89118-092-3, ISBN13: 978-0-89118-092-0.
Dewey:633.1/042. LCCN:87-019600.

Audience: **u,f.**

Pearson, C. J., et al.   **SB176.T76 N67 1995**
The Ecology of Tropical Food Crops. Ed. 2. M. J. T. Norman &
P. G. E. Searle (Authors). Cloth Text. Cambridge University
Press. New York, NY. 1995. 440p. ISBN:0-521-41062-2,
ISBN13: 978-0-521-41062-5. Dewey:630/.2/5745264.
LCCN:94-031156.

Audience: **g,l,u.**

Poehlman, John M. &   **SB185.7.P63 1995**
Sleper, David A.
Breeding Field Crops. Ed. 4. Cloth Text. Blackwell Publishing
Professional. Ames, IA. 1995. 510p. ISBN:0-8138-2427-3,
ISBN13: 978-0-8138-2427-7. Dewey:633/.083.
LCCN:94-036673.

Audience: **u,f.** *Choice, 1987.*

Pritchard, Seth G. &   **SB112.5.P75 2005**
Amthor, Jeffrey S.
Crops and Environmental Change: An Introduction to Effects of
Global Warming, Increasing Atmospheric CO_2 and O_3
Concentrations, and Soil Salinization on Crop Physiology and
Yield. Trade Cloth. Haworth Press, Incorporated, The.
Binghamton, NY. 2005. 442p. ISBN:1-56022-912-8, ISBN13:
978-1-56022-912-4. Dewey:632/.1. LCCN:2004-016359.

Audience: **g,l,u.** *Choice, 2005.*

Purseglove, J. W.   **SB305**
Spices. Trade Cloth. John Wiley & Sons, Inc. Hoboken, NJ.
1986. 450p. ISBN:0-470-20565-2, ISBN13: 978-0-470-20565-5.
Dewey:633.8/3.

Audience: **g.**

Rasmusson, D. C.   **SB191.B2 B35 1985**
Barley. Trade Cloth. American Society of Agronomy. Madison,
WI. 1985. 522p. Agronomy Monograph Ser., No. 26
ISBN:0-89118-085-0, ISBN13: 978-0-89118-085-2.
Dewey:633.1/6. LCCN:85-072830.

Audience: **u,f.**

Rengel, Zdenko (Editor)   **SB112.5.M56 1999**
Mineral Nutrition of Crops: Fundamental Mechanisms and
Implications. Library Binding. Haworth Press, Incorporated,
The. Binghamton, NY. 1999. 399p. ISBN:1-56022-880-6,
ISBN13: 978-1-56022-880-6. Dewey:631.8/11.
LCCN:98-048697.

Audience: **u,f.** *Choice, 2000.*

Robbelen, G., et al.   **SB298.O32 1989**
Oil Crops of the World. R. K. Downey & A. Ashri (Authors).
Cloth Text. McGraw-Hill Companies, The. New York, NY.
1989. 560p. ISBN:0-07-053081-5, ISBN13: 978-0-07-053081-2.
Dewey:633.8/5. LCCN:89-002546.

Audience: **g,l,u,f.** *Choice, 1989.*

Robinson, J. C.   **SB379.B2R63 1996**
Bananas and Plantains. Cloth Text. Oxford University Press, Inc.
New York, NY. 1996. 256p. Crop Production Science in
Horticulture Ser., No. 5 ISBN:0-85198-985-3, ISBN13:
978-0-85198-985-3. Dewey:634/.772. LCCN:96-214375.

Audience: **g,u,f.**

Sauer, David B. (Editor)   **SB190 .S85 1992**
Storage of Cereal Grains and Their Products. Ed. 4. Cloth Text.
American Association of Cereal Chemists. Saint Paul, MN.
1992. 615p. ISBN:0-913250-74-0, ISBN13: 978-0-913250-74-7.
Dewey:633.1/0468. LCCN:91-078051.

Audience: **u,f.**

Shewry, Peter R. (Editor)   **QK495.G74B325 1992**
Barley: Genetics, Biochemistry, Molecular Biology and
Biotechnology. Cloth Text. Oxford University Press, Inc. New
York, NY. 1992. 600p. Biotechnology in Agriculture Ser., No. 5
ISBN:0-85198-725-7, ISBN13: 978-0-85198-725-5.
Dewey:584/.93. LCCN:93-183438.

Audience: **u,f.**

Simmonds, N. W. & Smartt,   **SB106.I47S56 2000**
Joseph (Editors)
Principles of Crop Improvement. Ed. 2. Trade Cloth. Blackwell
Publishing, Inc. Malden, MA. 1999. 424p. ISBN:0-632-04191-9,
ISBN13: 978-0-632-04191-6. Dewey:631.5/2. LCCN:99-059354.

Audience: **g,l,u.**

Smale, Melinda   **SB123.3.V35 2005**
Valuing Crop Biodiversity: On-Farm Genetic Resources and
Economic Change. Trade Cloth. CABI Publishing. Wallingford,
2006. 352p. CABI Publishing Ser. ISBN:0-85199-083-5,
ISBN13: 978-0-85199-083-5. Dewey:631.5/23.
LCCN:2005-002725.

Audience: **l,u,f.**

Smartt, J.   **SB177.L45 S58 1990**
Grain Legumes: Evolution and Genetic Resources. Trade Cloth.
Cambridge University Press. New York, NY. 1990. 389p.
ISBN:0-521-30797-X, ISBN13: 978-0-521-30797-0.
Dewey:633.3. LCCN:89-007181.

Audience: **u,f.** *Choice, 1990.*

Smartt, Joseph &   **SB106.O74E96 1995**
Simmonds, Norman W. (Editors)
Evolution of Crop Plants. Ed. 2. Trade Cloth. John Wiley &
Sons, Inc. Hoboken, NJ. 1995. 531p. ISBN:0-470-23372-9,
ISBN13: 978-0-470-23372-6. Dewey:631. LCCN:94-025791.

Audience: **g,l,u,f.**

Smith, C. Wayne   **SB187.U6S54 1995**
Crop Production: Evolution, History, and Technology. Trade
Cloth. John Wiley & Sons, Inc. Hoboken, NJ. 1995. 496p.
ISBN:0-471-07972-3, ISBN13: 978-0-471-07972-9.
Dewey:633/.00973. LCCN:95-012070.

Audience: **g,l,u,f.** *Choice, 1996.*

Smith, C. Wayne   **SB191.M2S6127 2004**
(Editor), et al.
Corn: Origin, History, Technology and Production. Javier Betrán
& E. C. A. Runge (Editors). Trade Cloth. John Wiley & Sons,
Inc. Hoboken, NJ. 2004. 968p. Wiley Series in Crop Science
ISBN:0-471-41184-1, ISBN13: 978-0-471-41184-0.
Dewey:633.1/5. LCCN:2003-011399.

Audience: **l,u,f.**

Smith, C. Wayne & Dilday,   **SB191.R5R455 2002**
Robert H. (Editors)
Rice: Origin, History, Technology, and Production. Trade Cloth.
John Wiley & Sons, Inc. Hoboken, NJ. 2002. 656p. Wiley
Series in Crop Science Ser., Vol. 3 ISBN:0-471-34516-4,
ISBN13: 978-0-471-34516-9. Dewey:633.18.
LCCN:2001-057367.

Audience: **l,u,f.**

Smith, C. Wayne &   **SB191.S7S648 2000**
  Frederiksen, Richard A. (Editors)
Sorghum: Origin, History, Technology, and Production. Trade
Cloth. John Wiley & Sons, Inc. Hoboken, NJ. 2000. 840p.
Wiley Series in Crop Science Ser., Vol. 2 ISBN:0-471-24237-3,
ISBN13: 978-0-471-24237-6. Dewey:633.1/74.
LCCN:00-042254.

                                            Audience: **g,u,f.**

Splittstoesser, Walter E   **SB321.S645 1990**
Vegetable Growing Handbook: Organic and Traditional
Methods. Ed. 3. Springer London, Ltd. 1990.
ISBN:0-442-23971-8, ISBN13: 978-0-442-23971-8.

                                            Audience: **g,l,u.**

Sprague, George F. &   **SB191.M2 C78235 1988**
  Dudley, J. W. (Editors)
Corn and Corn Improvement. Ed. 3. Trade Cloth. American
Society of Agronomy. Madison, WI. 1988. 986p. Agronomy
Monograph Ser., No. 18 ISBN:0-89118-099-0, ISBN13:
978-0-89118-099-9. Dewey:633.1/53. LCCN:88-007954.

                                            Audience: **l,u,f.**

Stancey, Gary; Burris,   **QR89.7.B53 1991**
  Robert H; Evans, Harold J
Biological Nitrogen Fixation. Gary Stancey (Editor) ; Robert H.
Burris (Editor) ; Harold J. Evans (Editor). Springer London, Ltd.
1992. ISBN:0-412-02421-7, ISBN13: 978-0-412-02421-4.

                                            Audience: **u,f.**

Taylor, Judith M.   **SB367.T39 2000**
The Olive in California: History of an Immigrant Tree. Kevin
Starr (Foreword by). Trade Paper. Ten Speed Press. Berkeley,
CA. 2004. 256p. Artisanal Foods Ser. ISBN:1-58008-131-2,
ISBN13: 978-1-58008-131-3. Dewey:338.1/7463/09794.
LCCN:99-051302.

                                            Audience: **g,l,u,f.**

Van Wyk, Ben-Erik   **QK98.5.A1V36 2005**
Food Plants of the World. Trade Cloth. Timber Press, Inc.
Portland, OR. 2005. 480p. ISBN:0-88192-743-0, ISBN13:
978-0-88192-743-6. Dewey:581.6/32. LCCN:2005-044048.
                               Audience: **g,l,u,f.** *Choice, 2006.*

Vaughan, J. G., et al.   **SB175.V38 1997**
🄴 The New Oxford Book of Food Plants. Catherine Geissler &
Barbara Nicholson (Authors). E-Book. NetLibrary, Inc. Boulder,
CO. 1997. ISBN:0-585-16358-8, ISBN13: 978-0-585-16358-1.
Dewey:641.303.

                                            Audience: **g,l,u.**

Virchow, Detlef (Editor)   **SB123.3.E33 2002**
Efficient Conservation of Crop Genetic Diversity: Theoretical
Approaches and Empirical Studies. Trade Cloth. Springer. New
York, NY. 2003. 247p. ISBN:3-540-00006-2, ISBN13:
978-3-540-00006-8. Dewey:333.95/316. LCCN:2002-036474.
                                            Audience: **u,f.**

Warman, Arturo   **2002010956 [SB]**
Corn and Capitalism: How a Botanical Bastard Grew to Global
Dominance. Nancy L. Westrate (Translator). Trade Cloth.
University of North Carolina Press. Chapel Hill, NC. 2003.
288p. Latin America in Translation Ser. ISBN:0-8078-2766-5,
ISBN13: 978-0-8078-2766-6. Dewey:633.1/5/09.
LCCN:2002-010956.
                               Audience: **g,l,u.** *Choice, 2003.*

Willson, K. C.   **SB265.W55 1999**
Coffee, Cocoa and Tea. Paper Text. Oxford University Press,
Inc. New York, NY. 1995. 320p. Crop Production Science in
Horticulture Ser. ISBN:0-85198-919-5, ISBN13:
978-0-85198-919-8. Dewey:633.7/3. LCCN:98-034250.
                                            Audience: **g,l,u,f.**

Zimdahl, Robert L.   **SB611.Z55 2004**
Weed-Crop Competition: A Review. Ed. 2. Trade Paper.
Blackwell Publishing Professional. Ames, IA. 2004. 232p.
ISBN:0-8138-0279-2, ISBN13: 978-0-8138-0279-4.
Dewey:632/.5. LCCN:2003-023656.
                                            Audience: **u,f.**

Zohary, Daniel & Hopf,   **GN799.A4Z64 2000**
  Maria
Domestication of Plants in the Old World: The Origin and
Spread of Cultivated Plants in West Asia, Europe, and the Nile
Valley. Ed. 3. Trade Cloth. Oxford University Press, Inc. New
York, NY. 2001. 328p. ISBN:0-19-850357-1, ISBN13:
978-0-19-850357-6. Dewey:631.5/2. LCCN:00-050130.
                                            Audience: **l,u,f.**

Crops > Field Crops

Bajaj, Y. P. S. (Editor)   **SB249.C79355 1998**
Cotton. Cloth Text. Springer. New York, NY. 1998. 384p.
Biotechnology in Agriculture and Forestry Ser., Vol. 42
ISBN:3-540-62728-6, ISBN13: 978-3-540-62728-9.
Dewey:633.5/123. LCCN:97-045484.
                                            Audience: **g,u,f.**

Bajaj, Y. P. S. (Editor)   **SB191.R5R44 1991**
Rice, Vol. 14. Cloth Text. Springer. New York, NY. 1991. 648p.
Biotechnology in Agriculture and Forestry Ser.
ISBN:0-387-51810-X, ISBN13: 978-0-387-51810-7.
Dewey:633.1/8. LCCN:90-046033.
                                            Audience: **g,l,u,f.**

Bajaj, Y. P. S. (Editor)   **SB191.W5W48 1990**
Wheat. Cloth Text. Springer. New York, NY. 1991. 687p.
Biotechnology in Agriculture and Forestry Ser., Vol. 13
ISBN:0-387-51809-6, ISBN13: 978-0-387-51809-1.
Dewey:633.1/1. LCCN:90-009824.
                                            Audience: **u,f.**

Barnes, Robert F., et al.   **SB193.F64 2003**
Forages: An Introduction to Grassland Agriculture. Ed. 6.
Michael Collins, Kenneth Moore & Mark Westgate (Authors),
Robert F. Barnes (Editor). Trade Cloth. Blackwell Publishing
Professional. Ames, IA. 2003. 576p. ISBN:0-8138-0421-3,
ISBN13: 978-0-8138-0421-7. Dewey:633.2.
LCCN:2002-014177.
                                            Audience: **l,u.**

Chopra, V. L. (Editor)   **SB189.E96 2002**
Evolution and Adaptation of Crops: Cereals. Trade Cloth.
Science Publishers. Enfield, NH. 2002. 296p. Evolution and
Adaptation of Crops, Vol. 1:Cereals ISBN:1-57808-190-4,
ISBN13: 978-1-57808-190-5. Dewey:584.9138.
LCCN:2002-728486.
                                            Audience: **u,f.**

Cothren, Joe Tom & Smith,   **SB249.C79375 1999**
  C. Wayne (Editors)
Cotton: Origin, History, Technology, and Production. Trade

Cloth. John Wiley & Sons, Inc. Hoboken, NJ. 1999. 864p. Wiley Series in Crop Science, Vol. 4 ISBN:0-471-18045-9, ISBN13: 978-0-471-18045-6. Dewey:633.5/1. LCCN:99-022020.

Audience: **l,u,f.** *Choice, 2000.*

De Datta, Surajit K.   **SB191.R5**
Principles and Practices of Rice Production. Nyle C. Brady (Introduction by). Library Binding. Krieger Publishing Company. Melbourne, FL. 1987. 640p. ISBN:0-89874-994-8, ISBN13: 978-0-89874-994-6. Dewey:633.1/8. LCCN:86-021370.

Audience: **g,l,u.**

Fageria, N. A., et al.   **SB185.5.F34 1997**
Growth and Mineral Nutrition of Field Crops, Vol. 57. Ed. 2. V. C. Baligar & Charles Jones (Authors). Paper over Boards. Marcel Dekker Inc. New York, NY. 1997. 656p. Books in Soils, Plants and the Environment, Vol. 57 ISBN:0-8247-0089-9, ISBN13: 978-0-8247-0089-8. Dewey:631.8. LCCN:97-013975.

Audience: **u,f.**

Hanson, A. A. (Editor), et al.   **SB205.A4**
Alfalfa and Alfalfa Improvement. D. K. Barnes, R. R. Hill & G. H. Heichel (Editors). Trade Cloth. American Society of Agronomy. Madison, WI. 1988. 1110p. ISBN:0-89118-094-X, ISBN13: 978-0-89118-094-4. Dewey:633.3/1. LCCN:88-003350.

Audience: **u,f.**

Heyne, E. G. (Editor)   **SB191.W5 W493 1987**
Wheat and Wheat Improvement. Ed. 2. Trade Cloth. American Society of Agronomy. Madison, WI. 1987. 766p. Agronomy Monograph Ser., No. 13 ISBN:0-89118-091-5, ISBN13: 978-0-89118-091-3. Dewey:633.1/1. LCCN:87-012564.

Audience: **u,f.**

Norman, Geoffrey A.   **SB205.S7.S535**
  (Editor)
Soybean Physiology, Agronomy, and Utilization. Trade Cloth. Elsevier Science & Technology Books. Saint Louis, MO. 1978. xii, 249 p. :p. ISBN:0-12-521160-0, ISBN13: 978-0-12-521160-4. Dewey:635/.655. LCCN:78-018399.

Audience: **u,f.**

Rasmusson, D. C.   **SB191.B2 B35 1985**
Barley. Trade Cloth. American Society of Agronomy. Madison, WI. 1985. 522p. Agronomy Monograph Ser., No. 26 ISBN:0-89118-085-0, ISBN13: 978-0-89118-085-2. Dewey:633.1/6. LCCN:85-072830.

Audience: **u,f.**

Smith, C. Wayne (Editor), et   **SB191.M2S6127 2004**
  al.
Corn: Origin, History, Technology and Production. Javier Betrán & E. C. A. Runge (Editors). Trade Cloth. John Wiley & Sons, Inc. Hoboken, NJ. 2004. 968p. Wiley Series in Crop Science ISBN:0-471-41184-1, ISBN13: 978-0-471-41184-0. Dewey:633.1/5. LCCN:2003-011399.

Audience: **l,u,f.**

Smith, C. Wayne & Dilday,   **SB191.R5R455 2002**
  Robert H. (Editors)
Rice: Origin, History, Technology, and Production. Trade Cloth. John Wiley & Sons, Inc. Hoboken, NJ. 2002. 656p. Wiley Series in Crop Science Ser., Vol. 3 ISBN:0-471-34516-4, ISBN13: 978-0-471-34516-9. Dewey:633.18. LCCN:2001-057367.

Audience: **l,u,f.**

Crops > Horticultural Crops

Hanelt, Peter   **SB107.M38 2001**
Mansfeld's World Manual of Agricultural and Horticultural Crops. Institute of Plant Genetics and Crop Plant Research Staff (Editor), R. Kilian & W. Kilian (Drawings by). Trade Cloth. Springer. New York, NY. 2001. 3380p. ISBN:3-540-41017-1, ISBN13: 978-3-540-41017-1. Dewey:630/.3. LCCN:2001-020690.

Audience: **g,l,u.**

Crops > Subtropical Crops

                                               SB359
Fruits of Warm Climates.
http://newcrop.hort.purdue.edu/newcrop/morton/index.html
Julia F. Morton. ISBN:0-9610184-1-0, ISBN13: 978-0-9610184-1-2.

Audience: **u,f.**

Bakker, Henk   **SB231.B26 1999**
Sugar Cane Cultivation and Management. Trade Cloth. Springer. New York, NY. 1999. 706p. ISBN:0-306-46119-6, ISBN13: 978-0-306-46119-4. Dewey:633.6/1. LCCN:99-031318.

Audience: **u,f.**

Bartholomew, D. (Editor), et   **SB375.P47 2002**
  al.
The Pineapple: Botany, Production and Uses. R. E. Paull & K. Rohrbach (Editors). Cloth Text. Oxford University Press, Inc. New York, NY. 2003. 328p. CABI Publishing Ser. ISBN:0-85199-503-9, ISBN13: 978-0-85199-503-8. Dewey:634/.774. LCCN:2002-005741.

Audience: **u,f.**

Rehm, S. & Espig, G.   **SB111**
Cultivated Plants of the Tropics and Subtropics: Cultivation, Economic Value, Utilization. Trade Cloth. Backhuys Publishers. Leiden, 1991. 552p. ISBN:3-8236-1169-0, ISBN13: 978-3-8236-1169-1. Dewey:633.

Audience: **u,f.** *Choice, 1992.*

Robinson, J. C.   **SB379.B2R63 1996**
Bananas and Plantains. Cloth Text. Oxford University Press, Inc. New York, NY. 1996. 256p. Crop Production Science in Horticulture Ser., No. 5 ISBN:0-85198-985-3, ISBN13: 978-0-85198-985-3. Dewey:634/.772. LCCN:96-214375.

Audience: **g,u,f.**

Crops > Tropical Crops

                                               SB359
C/T/A/H/R College of Tropical Agriculture and Human Resources University of Hawaii at Manoa: The Noni Website.
http://www.ctahr.hawaii.edu/noni/

Audience: **g,l,u,f.**

                                               SB359
Fruits of Warm Climates.
http://newcrop.hort.purdue.edu/newcrop/morton/index.html
Julia F. Morton. ISBN:0-9610184-1-0, ISBN13: 978-0-9610184-1-2.

Audience: **u,f.**

S494.5.A45

☐ Traditional Tree Initiative.
http://www.traditionaltree.org/
agroforestry.net.

Audience: **g,u.**

Corley, R. H. V. & Tinker, **SB299.P3C65 2003**
P. B. H.
The Oil Palm. Ed. 4. Trade Cloth. Blackwell Publishing, Inc.
Malden, MA. 2003. 592p. World Agriculture Ser.
ISBN:0-632-05212-0, ISBN13: 978-0-632-05212-7.
Dewey:633.8/51. LCCN:2003-008646.

Audience: **u,f.**

Nakasone, Henry Y. & **SB359.N275 1998**
Paull, Robert E.
Tropical Fruits. Cloth Text. Oxford University Press, Inc. New
York, NY. 1998. 472p. Crop Production Science in Horticulture
Ser., No. 7 ISBN:0-85199-254-4, ISBN13: 978-0-85199-254-9.
Dewey:634/.6. LCCN:97-044048.

Audience: **l,u,f.**

Pearson, C. J., et al. **SB176.T76 N67 1995**
The Ecology of Tropical Food Crops. Ed. 2. M. J. T. Norman &
P. G. E. Searle (Authors). Cloth Text. Cambridge University
Press. New York, NY. 1995. 440p. ISBN:0-521-41062-2,
ISBN13: 978-0-521-41062-5. Dewey:630/.2/5745264.
LCCN:94-031156.

Audience: **g,l,u.**

Rehm, S. & Espig, G. **SB111**
Cultivated Plants of the Tropics and Subtropics: Cultivation,
Economic Value, Utilization. Trade Cloth. Backhuys Publishers.
Leiden, 1991. 552p. ISBN:3-8236-1169-0, ISBN13:
978-3-8236-1169-1. Dewey:633.

Audience: **u,f.** *Choice, 1992.*

Crops > Vegetables

Heaton, Donald D. **SB354.8.H43 1997**
Nature's Harvest: A Produce Reference Guide to Fruits and
Vegetables from Around the World. Trade Cloth. Haworth Press,
Incorporated, The. Binghamton, NY. 1997. 244p.
ISBN:1-56022-865-2, ISBN13: 978-1-56022-865-3.
Dewey:641.3/5. LCCN:96-049040.

Audience: **g.** *Choice, 1997.*

Maynard, Donald N. & **SB321.M392 1997**
Hochmuth, George J.
Knott's Handbook for Vegetable Growers. Ed. 4. Trade Paper.
John Wiley & Sons, Inc. Hoboken, NJ. 1997. 600p.
ISBN:0-471-13151-2, ISBN13: 978-0-471-13151-9. Dewey:635.
LCCN:96-033492.

Audience: **g.**

Splittstoesser, Walter E **SB321.S645 1990**
Vegetable Growing Handbook: Organic and Traditional
Methods. Ed. 3. Springer London, Ltd. 1990.
ISBN:0-442-23971-8, ISBN13: 978-0-442-23971-8.

Audience: **g,l,u.**

Crops > Vegetables > Diseases and Pests

Capinera, John **SB603.5.C36 2001**
Handbook of Vegetable Pests. Trade Cloth. Elsevier Science &
Technology Books. Saint Louis, MO. 2001. 800p.

ISBN:0-12-158861-0, ISBN13: 978-0-12-158861-8.
Dewey:635/.0497. LCCN:2001-086233.

Audience: **g,l,u.** *Choice, 2001.*

Entomology

Altieri, Miguel A. & **SB933.3.A38 2003**
Nicholls, Clara I.
Biodiversity and Pest Management in Agroecosystems. Ed. 2.
Cloth Text. Haworth Press, Incorporated, The. Binghamton, NY.
2003. 275p. ISBN:1-56022-922-5, ISBN13: 978-1-56022-922-3.
Dewey:632/.7. LCCN:2002-014860.

Audience: **u,f.** *Choice, 1994.*

Crane, Eva **SF524.C738 1999**
The World History of Beekeeping and Honey Hunting. Library
Binding. Routledge. New York, NY. 1999. 720p.
ISBN:0-415-92467-7, ISBN13: 978-0-415-92467-2.
Dewey:638/.1/09. LCCN:99-025816.

Audience: **g,l,u.** *Choice, 2000.*

Daly, Howell V., et al. **QL463.D34 1998**
Introduction to Insect Biology and Diversity. Ed. 2. John T.
Doyen & Alexander H. Purcell III (Authors). Cloth Text. Oxford
University Press, Inc. New York, NY. 1998. 688p.
ISBN:0-19-510033-6, ISBN13: 978-0-19-510033-4.
Dewey:595.7. LCCN:97-027059.

Audience: **g,l,u.**

Dent, D. **SB931.D45 2000**
Insect Pest Management. Ed. 2. Cloth Text. Oxford University
Press, Inc. New York, NY. 2000. 424p. A CAB International
Publication ISBN:0-85199-340-0, ISBN13: 978-0-85199-340-9.
Dewey:632.7. LCCN:99-087126.

Audience: **l,u,f.**

Ebeling, Walter **QL463**
Urban entomology. Berkeley : Division of Agricultural Sciences,
University of California. 1978. ISBN:0-931876-19-2, ISBN13:
978-0-931876-19-6.

Audience: **g,l,u,f.**

Flint, Mary Louise **SB950**
Pests of the Garden and Small Farm: A Grower's Guide to
Using Less Pesticide. Jack Kelly Clark (Photographer). Trade
Paper. DIANE Publishing Company. Collingdale, PA. 2001.
276p. ISBN:0-7567-5211-6, ISBN13: 978-0-7567-5211-8.
Dewey:632.9.

Audience: **g,l,u,f.**

Flint, Mary Louise & **SB993.3 .F59**
Dreistradt, Steve H.
Natural Enemies Handbook: The Illustrated Guide to Biological
Pest Control. Jack Kelly Clark (Photographer). Paper Text.
DIANE Publishing Company. Collingdale, PA. 2001. 154p.
ISBN:0-7567-5213-2, ISBN13: 978-0-7567-5213-2.
Dewey:632.96.

Audience: **g,l,u,f.**

Gillott, Cedric **QL467.2**
Entomology. Ed. 3. Trade Cloth. Springer. New York, NY. 2005.
XVII, 831p. ISBN:1-4020-3184-X, ISBN13: 978-1-4020-3184-7.
Dewey:595.7.

Audience: **l,u,f.**

Helyer, Neil & Brown,　　　　　　**SB975.H46 2003**
　Kevin
Color Handbook of Biological Control in Plant Protection. Nigel
D. Cattlin (Photographer). Trade Cloth. Timber Press, Inc.
Portland, OR. 2003. 126p. ISBN:0-88192-599-3, ISBN13:
978-0-88192-599-9. Dewey:632.96. LCCN:2003-048404.

　　　　　　　　　　　　　　　Audience: **g,l,u.**　*Choice, 2003.*

Johnson, Norman F. &　　　　　　**QL463.B69 2005**
　Triplehorn, Charles A.
Borror and DeLong's Introduction to the Study of Insects. Ed.
7. Cloth Text. Brooks/Cole. Pacific Grove, CA. 2004. 864p.
ISBN:0-03-096835-6, ISBN13: 978-0-03-096835-8.
Dewey:595.7. LCCN:2004-104139.

　　　　　　　　　　　　　　　　　　Audience: **l,u.**

Metcalf, Robert L. &　　　　　　**SB931.I58 1994**
　Luckmann, William H. (Editors)
Introduction to Insect Pest Management. Ed. 3. Trade Cloth.
John Wiley & Sons, Inc. Hoboken, NJ. 1994. 672p.
Environmental Science and Technology Ser., Vol. 101:A
Wiley-Interscience Series of Texts and Monographs
ISBN:0-471-58957-8, ISBN13: 978-0-471-58957-0.
Dewey:632/.7. LCCN:93-044141.

　　　　　　　　　　Audience: **g,l,u,f.**　*B　Choice, 1994.*

Morse, Roger & Flottum,　　　　　　**SF522.3**
　Kim (Editors)
The ABC and XYZ of Bee Culture: An Encyclopedia of
Beekeeping. Ed. 40. Trade Cloth. A. I. Root Company. Medina,
OH. 1990. 528p. ISBN:0-936028-01-7, ISBN13:
978-0-936028-01-9. Dewey:638.103.

　　　　　　　　　　　　　　　　Audience: **g,l,u,f.**

Norris, Robert F., et al.　　　　　　**SB950.N638 2003**
Concepts in Integrated Pest Management. Edward P.
Caswell-Chen & Marcos Kogan (Authors). Cloth Text. Prentice
Hall PTR. Upper Saddle River, NJ. 2002. 586p.
ISBN:0-13-087016-1, ISBN13: 978-0-13-087016-2.
Dewey:632/.9. LCCN:2002-070022.

　　　　　　　　　　　　　Audience: **l,u,f.**　*Choice, 2003.*

Pimentel, David (Editor)　　　　　　**SB950.7.E53 2002**
Encyclopedia of Pest Management. Paper over Boards. Marcel
Dekker Inc. New York, NY. 2002. 954p. ISBN:0-8247-0632-3,
ISBN13: 978-0-8247-0632-6. Dewey:632/.03.
LCCN:2003-265919.

　　　　　　　　　　　　　Audience: **g,l,u,f.**　*Choice, 2003.*

Resh, Vincent H. & Cardé,　　　　　　**QL462.3.E483 2003**
　Ring T. (Editors)
Encyclopedia of Insects. Trade Cloth. Elsevier Science &
Technology Books. Saint Louis, MO. 2003. 1266p.
ISBN:0-12-586990-8, ISBN13: 978-0-12-586990-4.
Dewey:595.7/03. LCCN:2002-106355.

　　　　　　　　　　　　　Audience: **g,l,u,f.**　*Choice, 2003.*

Sawyer, Richard C.　　　　　　**SB975.5.U6S38 1996**
To Make a Spotless Orange: Biological Control in California.
Cloth Text. Blackwell Publishing Professional. Ames, IA. 1996.
316p. Henry A. Wallace Series on Agricultural History and
Rural Studies ISBN:0-8138-2755-8, ISBN13:
978-0-8138-2755-1. Dewey:634/.304996/09794.
LCCN:96-020194.

　　　　　　　　　　　　　　　　Audience: **g,l,u,f.**

Schoonhoven, Louis M.,　　　　　　**QL496.S38 2005**
　et al.
Insect-Plant Biology. Ed. 2. Joop J. A. van Loon & Marcel
Dicke (Authors). Trade Cloth. Oxford University Press, Inc.
New York, NY. 2006. 440p. ISBN:0-19-852594-X, ISBN13:
978-0-19-852594-3. Dewey:595.717/85. LCCN:2005-019634.

　　　　　　　　　　　　　　　　Audience: **g,l,u.**

Van den Bosch, R., et al.　　　　　　**SB933.3**
An Introduction to Biological Control. P. S. Messenger & A. P.
Gutierrez (Authors). Trade Cloth. Springer. New York, NY.
1982. 262p. ISBN:0-306-40706-X, ISBN13: 978-0-306-40706-2.
Dewey:632/.7. LCCN:81-021125.

　　　　　　　　　　　　　　　　Audience: **g,l,u,f.**

Wheeler, Willis B.　　　　　　**SB951.P444 2002**
Pesticides in Agriculture and the Environment. Paper over
Boards. Marcel Dekker Inc. New York, NY. 2002. 360p. Books
in Soils, Plants and the Environment, Vol. 90
ISBN:0-8247-0809-1, ISBN13: 978-0-8247-0809-2.
Dewey:632/.95. LCCN:2002-073990.

　　　　　　　　　　　　　Audience: **u,f.**　*Choice, 2003.*

Entomology > Insect Pests

Carson, Rachel　　　　　　**QH545**
Silent Spring. Ed. 40. Dust Jacket. Houghton Mifflin Company
Trade & Reference Division. Boston, MA. 2002. 400p.
ISBN:0-618-25305-X, ISBN13: 978-0-618-25305-0.
Dewey:363.738/4. LCCN:2002-726803.

　　　　　　　　　　　　　　Audience: **g,l,u,f.**　*B*

Ishaaya, Isaac　　　　　　**SB931.I43 2004**
Insect Pest Management: Field and Protected Crops. A. Rami
Horowitz (Editor). Trade Cloth. Springer. New York, NY. 2004.
XXI, 344p. ISBN:3-540-20755-4, ISBN13: 978-3-540-20755-9.
Dewey:632/.7. LCCN:2003-070422.

　　　　　　　　　　　　　　　　Audience: **u,f.**

Entomology > Insects

Arnett, Ross H.　　　　　　**QL583**
American Insects: A Handbook of the Insects of America North
of Mexico. Library Binding. Sandhill Crane Press, Inc. Ormond
Beach, FL. 1993. xiv, 850p. ISBN:1-877743-19-4, ISBN13:
978-1-877743-19-1. Dewey:595.7/0973. LCCN:92-041053.

　　　　　　　　　　　　Audience: **g,l,u,f.**　*Choice, 2001, 1985.*

Crane, Eva　　　　　　**SF524.C738 1999**
The World History of Beekeeping and Honey Hunting. Library
Binding. Routledge. New York, NY. 1999. 720p.
ISBN:0-415-92467-7, ISBN13: 978-0-415-92467-2.
Dewey:638/.1/09. LCCN:99-025816.

　　　　　　　　　　　　　Audience: **g,l,u.**　*Choice, 2000.*

Morse, Roger & Flottum,　　　　　　**SF522.3**
　Kim (Editors)
The ABC and XYZ of Bee Culture: An Encyclopedia of
Beekeeping. Ed. 40. Trade Cloth. A. I. Root Company. Medina,
OH. 1990. 528p. ISBN:0-936028-01-7, ISBN13:
978-0-936028-01-9. Dewey:638.103.

　　　　　　　　　　　　　　　　Audience: **g,l,u,f.**

Resh, Vincent H. & Cardé,   QL462.3.E483 2003
  Ring T. (Editors)
Encyclopedia of Insects. Trade Cloth. Elsevier Science &
Technology Books. Saint Louis, MO. 2003. 1266p.
ISBN:0-12-586990-8, ISBN13: 978-0-12-586990-4.
Dewey:595.7/03. LCCN:2002-106355.
            Audience: **g,l,u,f.** *Choice, 2003.*

Environment

Atkinson, Giles, et al.   HC79.E5M4 1997
Measuring Sustainable Development: Macroeconomics and the
Environment. Richard Dubourg, Kirk Hamilton, Mohan
Munasinghe, David Pearce & Carlos Young (Authors). Trade
Cloth. Edward Elgar Publishing, Inc. Northampton, MA. 1997.
272p. ISBN:1-85898-572-2, ISBN13: 978-1-85898-572-5.
Dewey:338.9. LCCN:96-039592.
            Audience: **l,u,f.** *Choice, 1998.*

Calow, Peter (Editor)   GE300.E53 1998
The Encyclopedia of Ecology and Environmental Management.
Trade Cloth. Blackwell Publishing, Inc. Malden, MA. 1998.
832p. ISBN:0-86542-838-7, ISBN13: 978-0-86542-838-6.
Dewey:363.7003. LCCN:97-043092.
            Audience: **g,l,u,f.**

De-Shalit, Avner   GE170.D465 2000
The Environment: Between Theory and Practice. Trade Paper.
Oxford University Press, Inc. New York, NY. 2000. 248p.
ISBN:0-19-924038-8, ISBN13: 978-0-19-924038-8.
Dewey:363.7. LCCN:99-057190.
            Audience: **l,u,f.** *Choice, 2001.*

Halls, Peter, et al.   GE45
GIS for Ecologists and Environmental Scientists. Colin McClean
& Geraldine Newton-Cross (Authors). Trade Paper. John Wiley
& Sons, Inc. Hoboken, NJ. 2006. 320p. ISBN:0-470-84797-2,
ISBN13: 978-0-470-84797-8. Dewey:333.70285.
            Audience: **u,f.**

Jones, Samantha &   HC59.72.E5E24 2004
  Carswell, Grace (Editors)
The Earthscan Reader in Environment, Development and Rural
Livelihoods. Trade Cloth. Earthscan/James & James. London,
2004. 368p. ISBN:1-84407-052-2, ISBN13: 978-1-84407-052-7.
Dewey:333.7. LCCN:2004-011585.
            Audience: **l,u,f.**

McGraw-Hill Staff   GE10
McGraw-Hill Dictionary of Environmental Science. Paper Text.
McGraw-Hill Professional Publishing. New York, NY. 2003.
496p. ISBN:0-07-142177-7, ISBN13: 978-0-07-142177-5.
Dewey:628. LCCN:2003-051208.
            Audience: **g,l,u,f.** *Choice, 2003.*

McNeill, J. R.   GF13.M39 2000
Something New under the Sun: An Environmental History of
the Twentieth-Century World. Trade Cloth. W. W. Norton &
Company, Inc. New York, NY. 2000. 416p.
ISBN:0-393-04917-5, ISBN13: 978-0-393-04917-6.
Dewey:304.2/8/0904. LCCN:99-054900.
            Audience: **g,l.** *Choice, 2000.*

Miller, Char (Editor)   GF503.A84 2003
The Atlas of U. S. and Canadian Environmental History. Paper
over Boards. Routledge. New York, NY. 2003. 256p.

ISBN:0-415-93781-7, ISBN13: 978-0-415-93781-8.
Dewey:304.2/097/022. LCCN:2003-046799.
            Audience: **g,l,u,f.** *Choice, 2004.*

Nash, Roderick   S930.N36 1976
The American Environment: Readings in the History of
Conservation. Trade Cloth. Addison-Wesley Longman, Inc.
Boston, MA. 1976. xx, 364 p. :p. ISBN:0-201-05239-3,
ISBN13: 978-0-201-05239-8. Dewey:333.7/2/0973.
LCCN:75-010913.
            Audience: **g,l,u,f.** *B*

Pearson, C. J., et al.   SB176.T76 N67 1995
The Ecology of Tropical Food Crops. Ed. 2. M. J. T. Norman &
P. G. E. Searle (Authors). Cloth Text. Cambridge University
Press. New York, NY. 1995. 440p. ISBN:0-521-41062-2,
ISBN13: 978-0-521-41062-5. Dewey:630/.2/5745264.
LCCN:94-031156.
            Audience: **g,l,u.**

Pritchard, Seth G. &   SB112.5.P75 2005
  Amthor, Jeffrey S.
Crops and Environmental Change: An Introduction to Effects of
Global Warming, Increasing Atmospheric CO_2 and O_3
Concentrations, and Soil Salinization on Crop Physiology and
Yield. Trade Cloth. Haworth Press, Incorporated, The.
Binghamton, NY. 2005. 442p. ISBN:1-56022-912-8, ISBN13:
978-1-56022-912-4. Dewey:632/.1. LCCN:2004-016359.
            Audience: **g,l,u.** *Choice, 2005.*

Rosenzweig, Cynthia &   S600.7.C54R67 1998
  Hillel, Daniel
Climate Change and the Global Harvest: Potential Impacts of
the Greenhouse Effect on Agriculture. Cloth Text. Oxford
University Press, Inc. New York, NY. 1998. 336p.
ISBN:0-19-508889-1, ISBN13: 978-0-19-508889-2.
Dewey:338.1/4. LCCN:97-027058.
            Audience: **l,u,f.** *Choice, 1998.*

Troeh, Frederick R. &   S411.T76 2002
  Donahue, Roy Luther
Dictionary of Agriculture and Environmental Science. Trade
Cloth. Blackwell Publishing Professional. Ames, IA. 2002. 524p.
ISBN:0-8138-0283-0, ISBN13: 978-0-8138-0283-1.
Dewey:630/.3. LCCN:2002-000824.
            Audience: **g,l,u,f.**

Environment > Environmental Management

Barton, Jonathan   HC79.E5
Environmental Regulation in the New Global Economy: The
Impact on Industry and Competitiveness. Trade Paper. Edward
Elgar Publishing, Inc. Northampton, MA. 2004. 368p.
ISBN:1-84376-845-3, ISBN13: 978-1-84376-845-6.
Dewey:333.7.
            Audience: **l,u,f.**

Boyce, Mark S. & Haney,   QH75
  Alan W. (Editors)
Ecosystem Management: Applications for Sustainable Forest and
Wildlife Resources. Trade Paper. Yale University Press.
Cumberland, RI. 1999. 384p. ISBN:0-300-07858-7, ISBN13:
978-0-300-07858-9. Dewey:333.95.
            Audience: **g,u,f.** *Choice, 1997.*

Dasmann, Raymond F.   **TD170**
Environmental Conservation. Ed. 5. Trade Cloth. John Wiley & Sons, Inc. Hoboken, NJ. 1984. 496p. ISBN:0-471-89141-X, ISBN13: 978-0-471-89141-3. Dewey:333.7/2. LCCN:83-021767.
Audience: **g,l,u,f.** *B*

Mannion, A. M.   **S589.75.M365 1996**
Agriculture and Environmental Change: Temporal and Spatial Dimensions. Trade Paper. John Wiley & Sons, Inc. Hoboken, NJ. 1995. 418p. ISBN:0-471-95478-0, ISBN13: 978-0-471-95478-1. Dewey:306.3/49/09. LCCN:96-106409.
Audience: **u,f.** *Choice, 1996.*

Sampson, Gary & Whalley,   **HF1385**
John (Editors)
The WTO, Trade and the Environment. W. Antweiler, J. Bhagwati, B. Copeland, G. Grossman, A. Krueger, R. E. B. Lucas & T. N. Srinivasan (Contribution by). Trade Cloth. Edward Elgar Publishing, Inc. Northampton, MA. 2005. 736p. Critical Perspectives on the Global Trading System and the Wto Ser., Vol. 5 ISBN:1-84376-839-9, ISBN13: 978-1-84376-839-5. Dewey:382/.92. LCCN:2005-043326.
Audience: **u,f.**

Environment > Environmental Policy

Barry, John & Frankland,   **GE170.I55 2001**
E. Gene (Editors)
International Encyclopedia of Environmental Politics. Paper over Boards. Routledge. New York, NY. 2001. 544p. ISBN:0-415-20285-X, ISBN13: 978-0-415-20285-5. Dewey:363.7/056. LCCN:2001-019754.
Audience: **g,l,f.** *Choice, 2002.*

Carter, Neil   **JA75.8.C38 2001**
The Politics of the Environment: Ideas, Activism, Policy. Cloth Text. Cambridge University Press. New York, NY. 2001. 382p. ISBN:0-521-47037-4, ISBN13: 978-0-521-47037-7. Dewey:320.5. LCCN:2001-035638.
Audience: **g,l,f.** *Choice, 2002.*

Chasek, Pamela S.   **GE149.C42 2001**
Earth Negotiations: Analyzing Thirty Years of Environmental Diplomacy. Trade Paper. United Nations University Press. Tokyo, 2004. 314p. ISBN:92-808-1047-2, ISBN13: 978-92-808-1047-9. Dewey:363.7/0526. LCCN:00-012568.
Audience: **l,u,f.** *Choice, 2002.*

DeSombre, Elizabeth R.   **GE170.D47 2000**
Domestic Sources of International Environmental Policy: Industry, Environmentalists, and U. S. Power. Trade Paper. MIT Press. Cambridge, MA. 2000. 316p. American and Comparative Environmental Policy Ser. ISBN:0-262-54107-6, ISBN13: 978-0-262-54107-7. Dewey:363.7/0526. LCCN:99-041745.
Audience: **u,f.** *Choice, 2001.*

Lindstrom, Matthew J. &   **GE180.L55 2001**
Smith, Zachary A.
The National Environmental Policy Act: Judicial Misconstruciton, Legislative Indifference, and Executive Neglect. Lynton K. Caldwell (Foreword by). Cloth Text. Texas A & M University Press. College Station, TX. 2001. 224p. Environmental History Ser., Vol. 17 ISBN:1-58544-125-2, ISBN13: 978-1-58544-125-9. Dewey:363.7/056/0973. LCCN:2001-002410.
Audience: **l,u,f.** *Choice, 2002.*

Mannion, A. M.   **S589.75.M365 1996**
Agriculture and Environmental Change: Temporal and Spatial Dimensions. Trade Paper. John Wiley & Sons, Inc. Hoboken, NJ. 1995. 418p. ISBN:0-471-95478-0, ISBN13: 978-0-471-95478-1. Dewey:306.3/49/09. LCCN:96-106409.
Audience: **u,f.** *Choice, 1996.*

Farms

Barlett, Peggy F.   **HD1476.U6G43 1993**
American Dreams, Rural Realities: Family Farms in Crisis. Trade Cloth. University of North Carolina Press. Chapel Hill, NC. 1993. 320p. Studies in Rural Culture ISBN:0-8078-4399-7, ISBN13: 978-0-8078-4399-4. Dewey:338.16. LCCN:92-018027.
Audience: **g,l,u,f.** *Choice, 1993.*

Berry, Wendell   **S441 .B4725 1981**
The Gift of Good Land: Further Essays Cultural and Agricultural. Trade Paper. Farrar, Straus & Giroux. New York, NY. 1982. 286p. ISBN:0-86547-052-9, ISBN13: 978-0-86547-052-1. Dewey:630/.973. LCCN:81-081507.
Audience: **g,l,u.**

Borlaug, Norman, et al.   **S471.C6**
Vision of 2050 Agriculture in China: Dare to Dream. Shi Yuanchun, T. C. Tso & David Pimentel (Authors), Shi Yuanchun & T. C. Tso (Editors). Trade Cloth. I D E A L S, Inc. Beltsville, MD. 2004. 750p. ISBN:1-891998-01-3, ISBN13: 978-1-891998-01-0. Dewey:630.951.
Audience: **u,f.**

Clarke, Sally H.   **HD1761 .C53 1994**
Regulation and the Revolution in United States Farm Productivity. Louis Galambos & Robert Gallman (Contribution by). Trade Cloth. Cambridge University Press. New York, NY. 1994. 326p. Studies in Economic History and Policy: The United States in the Twentieth Century ISBN:0-521-44117-X, ISBN13: 978-0-521-44117-9. Dewey:338.1873. LCCN:94-005959.
Audience: **g,u.**

Collinson, M. P.   **S494.5.S95H57 2000**
A History of Farming Systems Research. Cloth Text. Oxford University Press, Inc. New York, NY. 2000. 448p. CABI Publishing Ser. ISBN:0-85199-405-9, ISBN13: 978-0-85199-405-5. Dewey:630/.72. LCCN:99-042827.
Audience: **u,f.**

Faeth, Paul, et al.   **HD1761 .P374 1991**
Paying the Farm Bill: U. S. Agricultural Policy and the Transition to Sustainable Agriculture. Robert C. Repetto, Kim Kroll, Qu Dai & Glenn Helmers (Authors). Trade Paper. World Resources Institute. Washington, DC. 1991. 70p. ISBN:0-915825-64-3, ISBN13: 978-0-915825-64-6. Dewey:338.1/873. LCCN:91-065300.
Audience: **u,f.**

Fitzgerald, Deborah Kay   **HD1761.F564 2003**
Every Farm a Factory: The Industrial Ideal in American Agriculture. Cloth over Boards. Yale University Press. Cumberland, RI. 2003. 256p. ISBN:0-300-08813-2, ISBN13: 978-0-300-08813-7. Dewey:338.1/0973. LCCN:2002-012135.
Audience: **g,l,u,f.** *Choice, 2003.*

Hatfield, J. L. & Baker, J.   **S600.5; S600.7.A37**
M. (Editors)
Micrometeorology in Agricultural Systems. Kivar (or like).

ASA-CSSA-SSSA. Madison, WI. 2005. xix, 584p. Agronomy Ser., No. 47 ISBN:0-89118-158-X, ISBN13: 978-0-89118-158-3. Dewey:630.2/515. LCCN:2005-920031.

Audience: **u,f.**

Huffman, Wallace &   **S541.H84 2006**
  Evenson, Robert
Science for Agriculture: A Long Term Perspective. Ed. 2. Trade Cloth. Blackwell Publishing Professional. Ames, IA. 2006. 328p. ISBN:0-8138-0688-7, ISBN13: 978-0-8138-0688-4. Dewey:630/.72/073. LCCN:2005-011946.

Audience: **l,u,f.**

Hurt, R. Douglas   **S441.H925 2002**
Problems of Plenty: The American Farmer in the Twentieth Century. Trade Cloth. Ivan R. Dee Publisher. Blue Ridge Summit, PA. 2002. 224p. The American Ways Ser. ISBN:1-56663-463-6, ISBN13: 978-1-56663-463-2. Dewey:630/.973/0904. LCCN:2002-067431.

Audience: **g,l,u.** *Choice, 2003.*

Lampkin, N. H. & Padel, S.   **HD1751**
  (Editors)
The Economics of Organic Farming: An International Perspective. Cloth Text. Oxford University Press, Inc. New York, NY. 1994. 480p. CABI Publishing Ser. ISBN:0-85198-911-X, ISBN13: 978-0-85198-911-2. Dewey:338.1/62.

Audience: **l,u,f.**

Lampkin, Nicolas   **S605.5**
Organic Farming. Trade Cloth. Farming Press Ltd. Bridlington, 1990. 720p. ISBN:0-85236-191-2, ISBN13: 978-0-85236-191-7. Dewey:631.5/84.

Audience: **g,l,u.**

Lehman, Tim   **HD256.L44 1995**
Public Values, Private Lands: Farmland Preservation Policy, 1933-1985. Trade Cloth. University of North Carolina Press. Chapel Hill, NC. 1995. 254p. ISBN:0-8078-4491-8, ISBN13: 978-0-8078-4491-5. Dewey:338.76/16/0973. LCCN:94-019636.

Audience: **g,l,u,f.**

McMurry, Sally Ann   **SF274.U6M38 1995**
Transforming Rural Life: Dairying Families and Agricultural Change, 1820-1885. Trade Cloth. Johns Hopkins University Press. Baltimore, MD. 1977. 312p. Revisiting Rural America Ser. ISBN:0-8018-4889-X, ISBN13: 978-0-8018-4889-6. Dewey:306.3/64. LCCN:94-012093.

Audience: **u,f.** *Choice, 1995.*

McWilliams, Carey   **HD1527.C2 M25 2000**
Factories in the Field: The Story of Migratory Farm Labor in California. Trade Paper. University of California Press. Berkeley, CA. 2000. 364p. ISBN:0-520-22413-2, ISBN13: 978-0-520-22413-1. Dewey:331.5/44/09794. LCCN:99-045099.

Audience: **g,l,u,f.**

Michalson, Edgar L.;   **S624.N68**
  Papendick, Robert I.; Carlson, John E.
Conservation Farming in the United States: The Methods and Accomplishments of the STEEP Program. CRC Press. 1999. ISBN:0-8493-1185-3, ISBN13: 978-0-8493-1185-7.

Audience: **g,l,u.**

Wendel, C. H.   **S674.W46 2004**
Encyclopedia of American Farm Implements and Antiques. Ed. 3. Brian Earnst (Editor). Trade Paper. Krause Publications. Iola, WI. 2004. 496p. ISBN:0-87349-568-3, ISBN13: 978-0-87349-568-4. Dewey:631.3/03. LCCN:2004-092436.

Audience: **g,u.**

Williams, Robert C.   **S711.W54 1987**
Fordson, Farmall and Poppin' Johnny: A History of the Farm Tractor and Its Impact on America. Trade Cloth. University of Illinois Press. Champaign, IL. 1987. 242p. ISBN:0-252-01328-X, ISBN13: 978-0-252-01328-7. Dewey:631.3/72/0973. LCCN:86-001359.

Audience: **g,l,u,f.** *Choice, 1987.*

Farms > Family Farms

       S494.5.S86
⬜ LocalHarvest.
http://www.localharvest.org/
LocalHarvest.

Audience: **g.**

Barlett, Peggy F.   **HD1476.U6G43 1993**
American Dreams, Rural Realities: Family Farms in Crisis. Trade Cloth. University of North Carolina Press. Chapel Hill, NC. 1993. 320p. Studies in Rural Culture ISBN:0-8078-4399-7, ISBN13: 978-0-8078-4399-4. Dewey:338.16. LCCN:92-018027.

Audience: **g,l,u,f.** *Choice, 1993.*

McMurry, Sally Ann   **SF274.U6M38 1995**
Transforming Rural Life: Dairying Families and Agricultural Change, 1820-1885. Trade Cloth. Johns Hopkins University Press. Baltimore, MD. 1977. 312p. Revisiting Rural America Ser. ISBN:0-8018-4889-X, ISBN13: 978-0-8018-4889-6. Dewey:306.3/64. LCCN:94-012093.

Audience: **u,f.** *Choice, 1995.*

Mooney, Patrick H. &   **HD6515.A29M66 1995**
  Majka, Theo J.
Farmers' and Farm Workers' Movements. Trade Cloth. Thomson Gale. Farmington Hills, MI. 1994. 288p. Twayne's Social Movements Past and Present Ser. ISBN:0-8057-3869-X, ISBN13: 978-0-8057-3869-8. Dewey:331.88/13/0973. LCCN:94-018178.

Audience: **g,l,u.** *Choice, 1995.*

Farms > Organic Farming

       S494.5.S86
⬜ ATTRA - National Sustainable Agriculture Information Service.
http://attra.ncat.org/
National Center for Appropriate Technology (NCAT).

Audience: **g.**

       S494.5.S86
⬜ LocalHarvest.
http://www.localharvest.org/
LocalHarvest.

Audience: **g.**

Committee on the Role of   **S494.5.A65A43 1989**
  Alternative Farming Methods Staff
Alternative Agriculture. Paper Text. National Academies Press.

Washington, DC. 1989. 464p. ISBN:0-309-03985-1, ISBN13: 978-0-309-03985-7. Dewey:630/.973. LCCN:88-026997.

Audience: **g,l,u.** *Choice, 1990.*

Guthman, Julie   **S605.5 .G88 2004**
Agrarian Dreams: The Paradox of Organic Farming in California. Trade Cloth. University of California Press. Berkeley, CA. 2004. 264p. California Studies in Critical Human Geography Ser. ISBN:0-520-24094-4, ISBN13: 978-0-520-24094-0. Dewey:631.5/84/09794. LCCN:2003-016040.

Audience: **g,l,u,f.** *Choice, 2005.*

Lampkin, N. H. & Padel, S.   **HD1751**
   (Editors)
The Economics of Organic Farming: An International Perspective. Cloth Text. Oxford University Press, Inc. New York, NY. 1994. 480p. CABI Publishing Ser. ISBN:0-85198-911-X, ISBN13: 978-0-85198-911-2. Dewey:338.1/62.

Audience: **l,u,f.**

Lampkin, Nicolas   **S605.5**
Organic Farming. Trade Cloth. Farming Press Ltd. Bridlington, 1990. 720p. ISBN:0-85236-191-2, ISBN13: 978-0-85236-191-7. Dewey:631.5/84.

Audience: **g,l,u.**

Splittstoesser, Walter E   **SB321.S645 1990**
Vegetable Growing Handbook: Organic and Traditional Methods. Ed. 3. Springer London, Ltd. 1990. ISBN:0-442-23971-8, ISBN13: 978-0-442-23971-8.

Audience: **g,l,u.**

Fire

Arno, Stephen F. & Fiedler,   **SD387.F52A76 2005**
   Carl E.
Mimicking Nature's Fire: Restoring Fire-Prone Forests in the West. Trade Cloth. Island Press. Washington, DC. 2005. 256p. ISBN:1-55963-142-2, ISBN13: 978-1-55963-142-6. Dewey:577.2/4/0978. LCCN:2004-025493.

Audience: **u,f.** *Choice, 2005.*

Maclean, Norman F.   **SD421.32.M9M33 1992**
Young Men and Fire. Trade Cloth. University of Chicago Press. Chicago, IL. 1992. 316p. ISBN:0-226-50061-6, ISBN13: 978-0-226-50061-4. Dewey:634.96180978664. LCCN:92-011890.

Audience: **g,l,u.** *Choice, 1993.*

Pyne, Stephen J.   **GN416.P85 2001**
Fire: A Brief History. Trade Cloth. University of Washington Press. Seattle, WA. 2003. 220p. Cycle of Fire Ser. ISBN:0-295-98144-X, ISBN13: 978-0-295-98144-4. Dewey:304.2. LCCN:2001-035593.

Audience: **g,l,u,f.** *Choice, 2002.*

Pyne, Stephen J.   **SD421.3.P96 1997**
Fire in America: A Cultural History of Wildland and Rural Fire. Trade Paper. University of Washington Press. Seattle, WA. 1997. 680p. Weyerhaeuser Environmental Bks. ISBN:0-295-97592-X, ISBN13: 978-0-295-97592-4. Dewey:304.2. LCCN:96-049191.

Audience: **g,l,u,f.** *B*

Pyne, Stephen J.   **SD421.3.P963 2003**
Smokechasing. Trade Cloth. University of Arizona Press. Tucson, AZ. 2003. 270p. ISBN:0-8165-2285-5, ISBN13: 978-0-8165-2285-9. Dewey:634.9/618. LCCN:2002-011504.

Audience: **g,l,u,f.** *Choice, 2003.*

Pyne, Stephen J.   **SD421.3.P96 2004**
Tending Fire: Coping with America's Wildland Fires. Trade Cloth. Island Press. Washington, DC. 2004. 256p. ISBN:1-55963-565-7, ISBN13: 978-1-55963-565-3. Dewey:363.37/9. LCCN:2004-008094.

Audience: **g,l,u,f.** *Choice, 2005.*

Pyne, Stephen J.   **SD421.34.E85P95 1997**
Vestal Fire: An Environmental History, Told Through Fire, of Europe and Europe's Encounter with the World. Trade Cloth. University of Washington Press. Seattle, WA. 1997. 672p. Cycle of Fire Ser. ISBN:0-295-97596-2, ISBN13: 978-0-295-97596-2. Dewey:304.2. LCCN:97-019032.

Audience: **g,l,u,f.** *Choice, 1998.*

Pyne, Stephen J.   **SD421.P95 1997**
World Fire: The Culture of Fire on Earth. Trade Paper. University of Washington Press. Seattle, WA. 1997. 408p. Weyerhaeuser Environmental Bks. ISBN:0-295-97593-8, ISBN13: 978-0-295-97593-1. Dewey:304.2. LCCN:96-052354.

Audience: **g,l,u,f.**

Pyne, Stephen J., et al.   **SD421.P94 1996**
Introduction to Wildland Fire. Ed. 2. Patricia L. Andrews & Richard D. Laven (Authors). Trade Cloth. John Wiley & Sons, Inc. Hoboken, NJ. 1996. 808p. ISBN:0-471-54913-4, ISBN13: 978-0-471-54913-0. Dewey:634.9/618. LCCN:95-044027.

Audience: **g,l,u,f.** *B* *Choice, 1996.*

Fire > Fire Management

                                                     QH545.F5
□ E.V. Komarek Fire Ecology Database.
http://www.ttrs.org/info/fedbintro.htm
Tall Timbers Research Station.

Audience: **u,f.**

Bradstock, Ross A. (Editor),   **QH197.F563 2002**
   et al.
Flammable Australia: The Fire Regimes and Biodiversity of a Continent. Jann E. Williams & Malcolm A. Gill (Editors). Trade Cloth. Cambridge University Press. New York, NY. 2001. 472p. ISBN:0-521-80591-0, ISBN13: 978-0-521-80591-9. Dewey:577.2. LCCN:2001-025479.

Audience: **u,f.** *Choice, 2002.*

Carle, David & Kaufmann,   **SD421**
   Je
Burning Questions: America's Fight with Nature's Fire. Trade Cloth. Greenwood Publishing Group, Inc. Portsmouth, NH. 2002. 312p. ISBN:0-275-97371-9, ISBN13: 978-0-275-97371-1. Dewey:634.9/618/0973. LCCN:2001-059061.

Audience: **u,f.** *Choice, 2003, 2002.*

Fire > Forest Fires

                                                     QH545.F5
□ E.V. Komarek Fire Ecology Database.
http://www.ttrs.org/info/fedbintro.htm
Tall Timbers Research Station.

Audience: **u,f.**

Fuller, Margaret C.   SD421.F84 1991
Forest Fires: An Introduction to Wildland Fire Behavior,
Management, Firefighting, and Prevention. Trade Paper. John
Wiley & Sons, Inc. Hoboken, NJ. 1991. 238p. Nature Editions
Ser. ISBN:0-471-52189-2, ISBN13: 978-0-471-52189-1.
Dewey:634.9/618. LCCN:90-046331.

Audience: **g.**

Fisheries

SH135
☐ AquaNIC: The Aquaculture Network Information Center.
http://www.aquanic.org/

Audience: **g,l,u.**

Bardach, John E. (Editor)   SH135.S87 1997
Sustainable Aquaculture. Trade Cloth. John Wiley & Sons, Inc.
Hoboken, NJ. 1997. 251p. ISBN:0-471-14829-6, ISBN13:
978-0-471-14829-6. Dewey:639/.8. LCCN:96-044727.

Audience: **g,u,f.**

Bennett, George W.   SH159.B38 1983
  (Introduction by)
Management of Lakes and Ponds. Ed. 2. Cloth Text. Krieger
Publishing Company. Melbourne, FL. 1983. 398p.
ISBN:0-89874-626-4, ISBN13: 978-0-89874-626-6.
Dewey:639.3/11. LCCN:83-006091.

Audience: **l,u,f.** 𝐵

Pillay, T. V. R. & Kutty,   SH135.P545 2005
  M. N.
Aquaculture: Principles and Practices. Ed. 2. Trade Cloth.
Fishing News Books, Ltd. Oxford, 2005. 640p.
ISBN:1-4051-0532-1, ISBN13: 978-1-4051-0532-3.
Dewey:639.8. LCCN:2004-065961.

Audience: **g,l,u,f.**

Ross, Michael R.   SH331.R635 1997
Fisheries Conservation and Management. Cloth Text. Prentice
Hall PTR. Upper Saddle River, NJ. 1996. 374p.
ISBN:0-02-403901-2, ISBN13: 978-0-02-403901-9.
Dewey:333.95/6. LCCN:95-041533.

Audience: **g,l,u.**

Southgate, Paul & Lucas,   SH151
  John (Editors)
Aquaculture: Farming Aquatic Animals and Plants. Trade Paper.
Fishing News Books, Ltd. Oxford, 2003. 512p.
ISBN:0-85238-222-7, ISBN13: 978-0-85238-222-6.
Dewey:639.8. LCCN:2004-298527.

Audience: **g,u,f.**

Stickney, Robert R.   SH20.3.E53 2000
Encyclopedia of Aquaculture. Trade Cloth. John Wiley & Sons,
Inc. Hoboken, NJ. 2000. 1088p. ISBN:0-471-29101-3, ISBN13:
978-0-471-29101-5. Dewey:639.8/03. LCCN:99-034744.

Audience: **g,l,u.** *Choice, 2002.*

Woo, P. (Editor)   SH171.F562 2006
Fish Diseases and Disorders: Protozoan and Metazoan
Infections. Ed. 2. Trade Cloth. CABI Publishing. Wallingford,
2006. 800p. CABI Publishing Ser. ISBN:0-85199-015-0,
ISBN13: 978-0-85199-015-6. Dewey:639.3.
LCCN:2005-018533.

Audience: **u,f.**

Food

TP546.L5 1987
Alexis Lichine's New Encyclopedia of Wines and Spirits. Ed. 5.
Trade Cloth. Alfred A. Knopf Inc. New York, NY. 1987. 752p.
ISBN:0-394-56262-3, ISBN13: 978-0-394-56262-9.
Dewey:641.2/22/0321. LCCN:87-002590.

Audience: **g.**

TX643
☐ Epicurious.
http://www.epicurious.com/
CondéNet..

Audience: **g,l,u.**

RA784
☐ Food and Nutrition Information Center at the National
Agricultural Library.
http://nal.usda.gov/fnic/
Food and Nutrition Information Center.

Audience: **g,l,u,f.**

RA601
☐ FoodSafety.gov: Gateway to Government Food Safety
Information.
http://www.foodsafety.gov/
FoodSafety.gov.

Audience: **g,l,u,f.**

SB450.97
☐ U.S. Department of Agriculture's Home and Garden Bulletin
Archive.
http://agnic.msu.edu/hgpubs/index.html

Audience: **g,l,u.**

TX531
☐ USDA National Nutrient Database for Standard Reference,
Release 18. Nutrient Data Laboratory Home Page.
http://www.ars.usda.gov/Services/docs.htm?docid=8964
U.S. Department of Agriculture, Agricultural Research Service.

Audience: **g,l,u,f.**

Adamson, Melitta Weiss   TX641
Food in Medieval Times. Cloth Text. Greenwood Publishing
Group, Inc. Portsmouth, NH. 2004. 288p. Food through History
Ser. ISBN:0-313-32147-7, ISBN13: 978-0-313-32147-4.
Dewey:641.3/0094/0902. LCCN:2004-014054.

Audience: **g,l,u,f.** *Choice, 2005.*

Food and Agricultural   HD9000.5
  Organization of the United Nations
☐ Ethical Issues in Food and Agriculture.
http://www.fao.org/documents/show_cdr.asp?url_file=/DOCREP/
003/X9601E/X9601E00.HTM
FAO. ISBN:92-5-104559-3, ISBN13: 978-92-5-104559-6.

Audience: **g,l,u,f.**

Johnson, Hugh   TP548.J632 1998
Hugh Johnson's Modern Encyclopedia of Wine. Ed. 4. Trade
Cloth. Simon & Schuster. New York, NY. 1998. 592p.
ISBN:0-684-84589-X, ISBN13: 978-0-684-84589-0.
Dewey:641.2/2/0321. LCCN:98-193428.

Audience: **g.** 𝐵

Kulp, Karel & Ponterotto,   TP434.H36 2000
  Joseph G.
Handbook of Cereal Science and Technology, Vol. 99. Ed. 2.

Paper over Boards. Marcel Dekker Inc. New York, NY. 2000. 800p. Food Science and Technology Ser. ISBN:0-8247-8294-1, ISBN13: 978-0-8247-8294-8. Dewey:664/.7. LCCN:00-022903.

Audience: **u,f.**

Purseglove, J. W.   **SB305**
Spices. Trade Cloth. John Wiley & Sons, Inc. Hoboken, NJ. 1986. 450p. ISBN:0-470-20565-2, ISBN13: 978-0-470-20565-5. Dewey:633.8/3.

Audience: **g.**

U. S. Food and Drug   **QR115**
 Administration Dept. of Health and Human Services
☐ The Bad Bug Book.
http://www.cfsan.fda.gov/~mow/intro.html
FDA/Center for Food Safety & Applied Nutrition.

Audience: **g,l,u,f.**

Food > Food Composition

Food Standards Agency   **TX531**
 Staff (Editor)
McCance and Widdowson's the Composition of Foods. Ed. 6. Trade Paper. Royal Society of Chemistry, The. Cambridge, 2002. 538p. ISBN:0-85404-428-0, ISBN13: 978-0-85404-428-3. Dewey:613.2. LCCN:2006-270057.

Audience: **g,l,u,f.**

Winton, Andrew Lincoln &   **TX0541**
 Winton, Kate Grace Barber
The Structure and Composition of Foods, Vol. 4. Trade Paper. Books on Demand. Ann Arbor, MI. 615p. ISBN:0-598-94741-8, ISBN13: 978-0-598-94741-3. Dewey:664.07. LCCN:32-005261.

Audience: **u,f.**

Food > Food Policy

Pinstrup-Andersen, Per &   **HD9000.5.P564 2001**
 Schiøler, Ebbe
Seeds of Contention: World Hunger and the Global Controversy over Genetically Modified Crops. Trade Paper. Johns Hopkins University Press. Baltimore, MD. 2001. 176p. ISBN:0-8018-6826-2, ISBN13: 978-0-8018-6826-9. Dewey:338.1/6. LCCN:2001-002303.

Audience: **u,f.**

Robbins, John   **TX371.R62 1998**
Diet for a New America: How Your Food Choices Affect Your Health, Happiness, and the Future of Life on Earth. Ed. 2. Joanna Macy (Foreword by). Trade Cloth. H. J. Kramer Inc. Tiburon, CA. 1998. 432p. ISBN:0-915811-81-2, ISBN13: 978-0-915811-81-6. Dewey:363.19/29. LCCN:98-010195.

Audience: **g,l,u,f.**

Food > Food Science

                                                                 QP141
☐ Nutrition.gov.
http://www.nutrition.gov/
National Agricultural Library, U.S. Department of Agriculture (USDA).

Audience: **g,l,u,f.**

                                                                 S587
Official Methods of Analysis of the AOAC International. Ed. 16. AOAC International, Arlington, VA. 1995.

Audience: **u,f.**

American Association of   **TX557.A65 2000**
 Cereal Chemists, Approved Methods Committee Staff
 (Contribution by)
Approved Methods of the American Association of Cereal Chemists. Ed. 10. Trade Cloth. American Association of Cereal Chemists. Saint Paul, MN. 2000. 1200p. ISBN:1-891127-12-8, ISBN13: 978-1-891127-12-0. Dewey:664/.7. LCCN:00-100071.

Audience: **g,u,f.**

Bender, David A.   **TX349.B4115 2005**
A Dictionary of Food and Nutrition. Ed. 2. Trade Paper, Perfect. Oxford University Press, Inc. New York, NY. 2005. 592p. Oxford Paperback Reference Ser. ISBN:0-19-860961-2, ISBN13: 978-0-19-860961-2. Dewey:641.3/03. LCCN:2004-021966.

Audience: **g,l,u.**

Bielecki, Stanislaw, et al.   **TP248.65.F66F648**
Food Biotechnology. J Tramper & Jacek Polak (Authors). Trade Cloth. Elsevier Science & Technology Books. Saint Louis, MO. 2000. 448p. Progress in Biotechnology Ser., Vol. 17 ISBN:0-444-50519-9, ISBN13: 978-0-444-50519-4. Dewey:664. LCCN:00-056037.

Audience: **g,l,u,f.**

Bowman, Barbara A. &   **REF 613.2 P933**
 Russell, Robert M. (Editors)
Present Knowledge in Nutrition. Ed. 8. Cloth Text. International Life Sciences Institute/I L S I Press. Washington, DC. 2001. xiv 805p. ISBN:1-57881-107-4, ISBN13: 978-1-57881-107-6. Dewey:613.2.

Audience: **g,l,u,f.**

Charley, Helen G. &   **TX354.C4723 1998**
 Weaver, Connie M.
Foods: A Scientific Approach. Ed. 3. Cloth Text. Prentice Hall PTR. Upper Saddle River, NJ. 1997. 582p. ISBN:0-02-321951-3, ISBN13: 978-0-02-321951-1. Dewey:664. LCCN:97-022861.

Audience: **l,u,f.**

Considine, Douglas M.   **TX349**
 (Editor)
Foods and Food Production Encyclopedia. Considine, Glenn D. (Editor). Van Nostrand Reinhold. 1982. ISBN:0-442-21612-2, ISBN13: 978-0-442-21612-2.

Audience: **g,l,u,f.**

Diehl, J. F.   **RA1258.D54 1995**
Safety of Irradiated Foods, Vol. 68. Ed. 2. Paper over Boards. Marcel Dekker Inc. New York, NY. 1995. 464p. Food Science and Technology Ser., Vol. 68 ISBN:0-8247-9344-7, ISBN13: 978-0-8247-9344-9. Dewey:363.19/2. LCCN:95-009488.

Audience: **g,u,f.**

Doyle, Michael P. (Editor),   **QR115.F654 2001**
 et al.
Food Microbiology: Fundamentals and Frontiers. Ed. 2. Larry R. Beuchat & Thomas J. Montville (Editors). Trade Cloth. ASM Press. Washington, DC. 2001. 888p. ISBN:1-55581-208-2, ISBN13: 978-1-55581-208-9. Dewey:664/.001/579. LCCN:2001-022702.

Audience: **l,u,f.**

Elderidge, Sarah (Editor)   TP248.65.F66F67 2003
Food Biotechnology: Current Issues and Perspectives. Trade
Cloth. Nova Science Publishers, Inc. Hauppauge, NY. 2003.
152p. ISBN:1-59033-848-0, ISBN13: 978-1-59033-848-3.
Dewey:664. LCCN:2003-020169.

Audience: **g,l,u,f.**

Farnworth, Edward R.   QP144.F85H357 2003
(Editor)
Handbook of Fermented Functional Foods. Paper over Boards.
C R C Press LLC. Boca Raton, FL. 2003. 408p. Functional
Foods and Nutraceuticals Ser. ISBN:0-8493-1372-4, ISBN13:
978-0-8493-1372-1. Dewey:613.2/8. LCCN:2002-191169.

Audience: **u,f.**

Firestone, David (Editor)   TP671
Official Methods and Recommended Practices of the AOCS. Ed.
5. Trade Cloth. American Oil Chemists' Society. Champaign, IL.
1998. 1200p. ISBN:0-935315-97-7, ISBN13:
978-0-935315-97-4. Dewey:664.3.

Audience: **g,u,f.**

Fuquay, John W. & Fox,   SF229.E53 2003
Patrick F. (Editors)
Encyclopedia of Dairy Sciences, Set. Hubert Roginski
(Editor-In-Chief). Trade Cloth. Elsevier Science & Technology
Books. Saint Louis, MO. 2002. 2500p. ISBN:0-12-227235-8,
ISBN13: 978-0-12-227235-6. Dewey:636.2/142/03.
LCCN:2002-114095.

Audience: **l,u,f.**

Gurr, M. I.   QP751.G89 1992
Role of Fats in Food and Nutrition. Ed. 2. Trade Cloth. Elsevier
Applied Science Publishers, Ltd. Kidlington, 1992. x, 207p.
ISBN:1-85166-755-5, ISBN13: 978-1-85166-755-0.
Dewey:613.28. LCCN:91-039425.

Audience: **u,f.** 𝐵

Horwitz, Williams (Editor)   S587 .O38
Official Methods of Analysis of AOAC International. Ed. 17.
Ringbound. A O A C International. Gaithersburg, MD. 2000.
2000p. ISBN:0-935584-54-4, ISBN13: 978-0-935584-54-7.
Dewey:630/.2/43.

Audience: **u,f.**

Hui, Yiu H. &   TP370.5
Khachatourians, George G. (Editors)
Food Biotechnology: Microorganisms. Trade Cloth. John Wiley
& Sons, Inc. Hoboken, NJ. 1995. 952p. Food Science and
Technology Ser. ISBN:0-471-18570-1, ISBN13:
978-0-471-18570-3. Dewey:664/.024.

Audience: **u,f.**

International Food   TP368.2
Information Service Staff
Dictionary of Food Science and Technology. Trade Cloth.
Blackwell Publishing, Inc. Malden, MA. 2005. 424p.
ISBN:1-4051-2505-5, ISBN13: 978-1-4051-2505-5.
Dewey:664/.003.

Audience: **g,l,u,f.** *Choice, 2006.*

Katz, Solomon H. &   GT2850.E53 2003
Weaver, William Woys (Editors)
Encyclopedia of Food and Culture. Trade Cloth. Thomson Gale.
Farmington Hills, MI. 2002. 1800p. Scribner Library of Daily
Life ISBN:0-684-80568-5, ISBN13: 978-0-684-80568-9.
Dewey:394.1/2/03. LCCN:2002-014607.

Audience: **g,l,u,f.** *Choice, 2003.*

Kiple, Kenneth F. &   TX353 .C255 2000
Ornelas, Kriemhild Coneè (Editors)
The Cambridge World History of Food, Set. Trade Cloth, Box
or Slipcased. Cambridge University Press. New York, NY. 2000.
1958p. ISBN:0-521-40216-6, ISBN13: 978-0-521-40216-3.
Dewey:641.3/09. LCCN:00-057181.

Audience: **g,l,u,f.** *Choice, 2001.*

Kittler, Pamela Goyan &   TX357.K58 2004
Sucher, Kathryn P.
Food and Culture. Ed. 4. Paper Text. Brooks/Cole. Pacific
Grove, CA. 2003. 560p. ISBN:0-534-56112-8, ISBN13:
978-0-534-56112-3. Dewey:613.2/0973. LCCN:2003-107140.

Audience: **l,u,f.**

Lawrie, Stephen   TX 373 .P74 1993
Lawrie's Meat Science. Ed. 6. Paper over Boards. C R C Press
LLC. Boca Raton, FL. 1998. 336p. ISBN:1-85573-395-1,
ISBN13: 978-1-85573-395-4. Dewey:641.36.

Audience: **g,u.**

Leathers, Howard D. &   HD9018.D44F68 2004
Foster, Phillips
The World Food Problem: Tackling the Causes of
Undernutrition in the Third World. Ed. 3. Library Binding.
Lynne Rienner Publishers, Inc. Boulder, CO. 2004. 420p.
ISBN:1-58826-250-2, ISBN13: 978-1-58826-250-9.
Dewey:363.8/09172/4. LCCN:2004-003785.

Audience: **g,l,u,f.**

Levenstein, Harvey   GT2853.U5 L47 2003
Paradox of Plenty: A Social History of Eating in Modern
America. Trade Paper. University of California Press. Berkeley,
CA. 2003. 376p. California Studies in Food and Culture
ISBN:0-520-23440-5, ISBN13: 978-0-520-23440-6.
Dewey:394.12/0973/0904. LCCN:2002-043916.

Audience: **g,l,u,f.**

Levenstein, Harvey A.   GT2853.U5 L48 2003
Revolution at the Table: The Transformation of the American
Diet. Trade Paper. University of California Press. Berkeley, CA.
2003. 304p. California Studies in Food and Culture, Vol. 7
ISBN:0-520-23439-1, ISBN13: 978-0-520-23439-0.
Dewey:394.1/2/0973. LCCN:2003-040211.

Audience: **g,l,u,f.** *Choice, 1988.*

Marshall, Wayne E.   TS2159.R5 R523 1994
Rice Science and Technology, Vol. 59. James I. Wadsworth
(Editor). Paper over Boards. Marcel Dekker Inc. New York, NY.
1993. 488p. Food Science and Technology Ser., Vol. 59
ISBN:0-8247-8887-7, ISBN13: 978-0-8247-8887-2.
Dewey:664/.725. LCCN:93-028919.

Audience: **u,f.**

Matz, Samuel A.   TP451.S57M37 1993
Snack Food Technology. Ed. 3. Trade Cloth. Chapman & Hall.
New York, NY. 1992. 415p. ISBN:0-442-30893-0, ISBN13:
978-0-442-30893-3. Dewey:664.6. LCCN:92-022849.

Audience: **g,u,f.**

McGee, Harold   TX651.M268 1990
The Curious Cook: More Kitchen Science and Lore. Trade
Cloth. Farrar, Straus & Giroux. New York, NY. 1990. 352p.
ISBN:0-86547-452-4, ISBN13: 978-0-86547-452-9.
Dewey:641.5. LCCN:90-007087.

Audience: **g,l,u,f.**

McGee, Harold   **TX651.M27 2004**
On Food and Cooking: The Science and Lore of the Kitchen.
Trade Cloth. Simon & Schuster. New York, NY. 2004. 896p.
ISBN:0-684-80001-2, ISBN13: 978-0-684-80001-1.
Dewey:641.5. LCCN:2004-058999.

Audience: **g,l,u,f.**

McWilliams, Margaret   **TX531.M38 2005**
Foods: Experimental Perspectives. Ed. 5. Cloth Text. Prentice
Hall PTR. Upper Saddle River, NJ. 2004. 608p.
ISBN:0-13-142536-6, ISBN13: 978-0-13-142536-1. Dewey:664.
LCCN:2004-012300.

Audience: **l,u,f.**

Nestle, Marion   **RA601**
Safe Food: Bacteria, Biotechnology, and Bioterrorism. Trade
Cloth. University of California Press. Berkeley, CA. 2003. 356p.
Studies in Food and Culture, No. 3 ISBN:0-520-23292-5,
ISBN13: 978-0-520-23292-1. Dewey:363.1/926.
LCCN:2002-027172.

Audience: **g,l,u,f.** *Choice, 2003.*

Newman, Jacqueline M.   **GT2853**
Food Culture in China. Cloth Text. Greenwood Publishing
Group, Inc. Portsmouth, NH. 2004. 256p. Food Culture Around
the World Ser. ISBN:0-313-32581-2, ISBN13:
978-0-313-32581-6. Dewey:394.1/2/0951. LCCN:2004-012484.

Audience: **g,u,f.**

Parasecoli, Fabio   **GT2853**
Food Culture in Italy. Cloth Text. Greenwood Publishing Group,
Inc. Portsmouth, NH. 2004. 256p. Food Culture around the
World Ser. ISBN:0-313-32726-2, ISBN13: 978-0-313-32726-1.
Dewey:394.1/2/0945. LCCN:2004-010671.

Audience: **g,l,u,f.**

Pennington, Jean A.   **TX551.P385 2004**
Food Values of Portions Commonly Used. Ed. 18. Trade Paper.
Lippincott Williams & Wilkins. Philadelphia, PA. 2004. 496p.
ISBN:0-7817-4429-6, ISBN13: 978-0-7817-4429-4.
Dewey:641.1. LCCN:2003-066133.

Audience: **g,l,u,f.** *B*

Rao, M. A., et al.   **TP372.5**
Engineering Properties of Foods. Ed. 3. Syed S. H. Rizvi &
Ashim K. Datta (Authors). Paper over Boards. Marcel Dekker
Inc. New York, NY. 2005. 760p. Food Science and Technology
Ser., Vol. 142 ISBN:0-8247-5328-3, ISBN13:
978-0-8247-5328-3. Dewey:664. LCCN:2004-056967.

Audience: **u,f.**

Robbins, John   **TX371.R62 1998**
Diet for a New America: How Your Food Choices Affect Your
Health, Happiness, and the Future of Life on Earth. Ed. 2.
Joanna Macy (Foreword by). Trade Cloth. H. J. Kramer Inc.
Tiburon, CA. 1998. 432p. ISBN:0-915811-81-2, ISBN13:
978-0-915811-81-6. Dewey:363.19/29. LCCN:98-010195.

Audience: **g,l,u,f.**

Sanjur, Diva   **TX357 .S27**
Social and Cultural Perspectives in Nutrition. Cloth Text.
Prentice Hall PTR. Upper Saddle River, NJ. 1981. 352p.
ISBN:0-13-815647-6, ISBN13: 978-0-13-815647-3.
Dewey:641.1. LCCN:81-008693.

Audience: **l,u.** *B*

Schlosser, Eric   **TX945.3**
Fast Food Nation: The Dark Side of the All American Meal.
Library Binding. Sagebrush Education Resources. Caledonia,
MN. 2002. ISBN:0-613-45139-2, ISBN13: 978-0-613-45139-0.
Dewey:394.1/0973.

Audience: **g,l,u,f.**

Singh, R. Paul & Heldman,   **TP370.S456 2001**
Dennis R.
Introduction to Food Engineering. Ed. 3. Cloth Text. Elsevier
Science & Technology Books. Saint Louis, MO. 2001. 750p.
Food Science and Technology International Ser.
ISBN:0-12-646384-0, ISBN13: 978-0-12-646384-2. Dewey:664.
LCCN:2001-086670.

Audience: **u,f.**

Smith, Andrew F. (Editor)   **TX349.E45 2004**
Encyclopedia of Food and Drink in America. Trade Cloth.
Oxford University Press, Inc. New York, NY. 2004. 1584p.
ISBN:0-19-515437-1, ISBN13: 978-0-19-515437-5.
Dewey:641.3/003. LCCN:2003-024873.

Audience: **g,l,u,f.** *Choice, 2005.*

Steinkraus, Keith H.   **TP371.44.H36 1995**
(Editor)
Handbook of Indigenous Fermented Foods, Vol. 73. Ed. 2. Paper
over Boards. Marcel Dekker Inc. New York, NY. 1995. 1053p.
Food Science and Technology Ser., Vol. 73
ISBN:0-8247-9352-8, ISBN13: 978-0-8247-9352-4. Dewey:664.
LCCN:95-041067.

Audience: **g,u,f.**

Thompson, Paul B.   **TP248.65.F66T47 1997**
Food Biotechnology in Ethical Perspective. Trade Cloth.
Springer. New York, NY. 1997. 267p. ISBN:0-412-78380-0,
ISBN13: 978-0-412-78380-7. Dewey:174/.9664.
LCCN:97-072350.

Audience: **l,u,f.**

Trugo, Luiz & Finglas, Paul   **QP141**
(Editors)
Encyclopedia of Food Sciences and Nutrition, Set. Ed. 2.
Benjamin Caballero (Editor-In-Chief). Trade Cloth. Elsevier
Science & Technology Books. Saint Louis, MO. 2003. 6000p.
ISBN:0-12-227055-X, ISBN13: 978-0-12-227055-0.
Dewey:664.003. LCCN:2002-114339.

Audience: **g,l,u.**

Vargas, Luis Alberto &   **GT2853**
Long-Solis, Janet
Food Culture in Mexico. Cloth Text. Greenwood Publishing
Group, Inc. Portsmouth, NH. 2005. 216p. Food Culture Around
the World Ser. ISBN:0-313-32431-X, ISBN13:
978-0-313-32431-4. Dewey:394.1/2/0972. LCCN:2004-025907.

Audience: **u,f.**

Wehr, Michael & Frank,   **SF253**
Joseph H. (Editors)
Standard Methods for the Examination of Dairy Products. Ed.
17. Trade Cloth. American Public Health Association
Publications. Washington, DC. 2004. 570p.
ISBN:0-87553-002-8, ISBN13: 978-0-87553-002-4. Dewey:637.

Audience: **u,f.**

Willson, K. C.   **SB265.W55 1999**
Coffee, Cocoa and Tea. Paper Text. Oxford University Press,
Inc. New York, NY. 1995. 320p. Crop Production Science in

Horticulture Ser. ISBN:0-85198-919-5, ISBN13: 978-0-85198-919-8. Dewey:633.7/3. LCCN:98-034250.

Audience: **g,l,u,f.**

Winkler, A. J., et al.   **SB388 .W5 1974**
General Viticulture. Ed. 2. Lloyd A. Lider, W. M. Kliewer & James A. Cook (Authors). Trade Cloth. University of California Press. Berkeley, CA. 1974. 710p. ISBN:0-520-02591-1, ISBN13: 978-0-520-02591-2. Dewey:634/.8. LCCN:73-087507.

Audience: **g,l,u,f.**

Wood, B. J. B.   **TP370.5**
Microbiology of Fermented Foods, Vols. 1, 2. Ed. 2. Trade Cloth. Springer. New York, NY. 1997. 852p. ISBN:0-7514-0216-8, ISBN13: 978-0-7514-0216-2. Dewey:664/.024. LCCN:97-073963.

Audience: **u,f.**

Wrolstad, Ronald E., et al.   **TX545.H34 2005**
Handbook of Food Analytical Chemistry, Water, Proteins, Enzymes, Lipids, and Carbohydrates, Vol. 1. Eric A. Decker, Steven J. Schwartz & Peter Sporns (Authors). Trade Cloth. John Wiley & Sons, Inc. Hoboken, NJ. 2004. 784p. ISBN:0-471-66378-6, ISBN13: 978-0-471-66378-2. Dewey:664/.07. LCCN:2004-013225.

Audience: **g,u.**

Forestry

QK494
⬜ American Conifer Society.
http://www.conifersociety.org/
American Conifer Society.

Audience: **g,u.**

SD131
⬜ The Forest History Society.
http://www.lib.duke.edu/forest/
Forest History Society.

Audience: **g,u,f.**

SF85.35.W8
⬜ Rangelands West.
http://rangelandswest.org/

Audience: **g,u,f.**

SD131
⬜ Society of American Foresters: Gorwing better all the time.
http://www.safnet.org/index.cfm
Society of American Foresters.

Audience: **g,u.**

Allaby, Michael   **QH541.5.F6A46 2006**
Temperate Forests. Richard Garratt (Illustrator). Trade Cloth. Facts On File, Inc.. New York, NY. 2006. 288p. Biomes of the Earth Ser. ISBN:0-8160-5321-9, ISBN13: 978-0-8160-5321-6. Dewey:577.3. LCCN:2005-007659.

Audience: **l,u,f.**

Arno, Stephen F. & Fiedler,   **SD387.F52A76 2005**
Carl E.
Mimicking Nature's Fire: Restoring Fire-Prone Forests in the West. Trade Cloth. Island Press. Washington, DC. 2005. 256p. ISBN:1-55963-142-2, ISBN13: 978-1-55963-142-6. Dewey:577.2/4/0978. LCCN:2004-025493.

Audience: **u,f.** *Choice, 2005.*

Avery, Thomas Eugene &   **SD555.A93 2002**
Burkhart, Harold E.
Forest Measurements. Ed. 5. Cloth Text. McGraw-Hill Higher Education. Burr Ridge, IL. 2001. 480p. McGraw-Hill Series in Forest Resources ISBN:0-07-366176-7, ISBN13: 978-0-07-366176-6. Dewey:634.9/285. LCCN:00-069940.

Audience: **l,u,f.**

Baker, Mark & Kusel,   **SD565.B35 2003**
Jonathan
Community Forestry in the United States: Learning from the Past, Crafting the Future. Trade Cloth. Island Press. Washington, DC. 2003. 264p. ISBN:1-55963-983-0, ISBN13: 978-1-55963-983-5. Dewey:333.75/152/0973. LCCN:2002-015726.

Audience: **u,f.** *Choice, 2003.*

Balick, Michael J. (Editor),   **RS164.M377 1996**
et al.
Medicinal Resources of the Tropical Forest: Biodiversity and Its Importance to Human Health. Elaine Elisabetsky & Sarah A. Laird (Editors). Trade Cloth. Edinburgh University Press. Edinburgh, 1996. 440p. Biology and Resource Management in the Tropics Ser. ISBN:0-231-10170-8, ISBN13: 978-0-231-10170-7. Dewey:615/.32/0913. LCCN:95-013809.

Audience: **g,l,u.** *Choice, 1996.*

Barraclough, Solon L. &   **SD418.3.D44.B37 1995**
Ghimire, Krishna B.
Forests and Livelihoods: Social Dynamics of Deforestation in Developing Countries. Trade Cloth. Bow Historical Books. New Providence, NJ. 1995. 256p. ISBN:0-333-62889-6, ISBN13: 978-0-333-62889-8. Dewey:333.75/137/091724. LCCN:95-034013.

Audience: **l,u,f.**

Barrett, John W. (Editor)   **SD143.R47 1995**
Regional Silviculture of the United States. Ed. 3. Trade Cloth. John Wiley & Sons, Inc. Hoboken, NJ. 1994. 656p. ISBN:0-471-59817-8, ISBN13: 978-0-471-59817-6. Dewey:634.9/0973. LCCN:94-002514.

Audience: **g,l,u,f.**

Benvie, Sam   **QK110**
The Encyclopedia of North American Trees. Trade Paper. Firefly Books, Ltd. Tonawanda, NY. 2002. 304p. ISBN:1-55297-641-6, ISBN13: 978-1-55297-641-8. Dewey:582.16/097.

Audience: **g,l,u,f.** *Choice, 2000.*

Bettinger, Pete & Wing,   **SD387.R4B48 2004**
Michael G.
Geographic Information Systems: Applications in Forestry and Natural Resources Management. Paper Text. McGraw-Hill Higher Education. Burr Ridge, IL. 2003. 240p. ISBN:0-07-256242-0, ISBN13: 978-0-07-256242-2. Dewey:634.9/028. LCCN:2003-056175.

Audience: **u,f.**

Beuter, John H.   **SD565.C64 1989**
Community Stability in Forest-Based Economies. Dennis C. LeMaster (Editor). Trade Cloth. Timber Press, Inc. Portland, OR. 2003. 198p. ISBN:0-88192-129-7, ISBN13: 978-0-88192-129-8. Dewey:333.75/0973. LCCN:88-024831.

Audience: **l,u,f.**

Bolgiano, Chris   **F106.B673 1998**
The Appalachian Forest: A Search for Roots and Renewal. Trade Cloth. Stackpole Books. Mechanicsburg, PA. 1998. 280p.

ISBN:0-8117-0126-3, ISBN13: 978-0-8117-0126-6.
Dewey:974/.00943. LCCN:98-017747.

Audience: **l,u,f.**

Bunnell, Fred L. & Johnson,   **QH75.P589 1998**
Jacklyn F. (Editors)
Policy and Practices for Biodiversity in Managed Forests: The
Living Dance. Clark S. Binkley (Foreword by). Trade Cloth.
University of British Columbia Press. Vancouver, BC. 1998.
176p. ISBN:0-7748-0690-7, ISBN13: 978-0-7748-0690-9.
Dewey:333.95/16. LCCN:99-192791.

Audience: **u,f.**   *Choice, 1999.*

Clawson, Marion   **SD565**
Forests for Whom and for What? Trade Paper. Resources for the
Future. Washington, DC. 1975. 175p. ISBN:0-8018-1751-X,
ISBN13: 978-0-8018-1751-9. Dewey:333.7/5/0973.
LCCN:74-024399.

Audience: **g,l,u.** ℬ

Clepper, Henry   **SD143 .C56**
Professional Forestry in the United States. Trade Cloth.
Resources for the Future. Washington, DC. 1971. 350p.
ISBN:0-8018-1331-X, ISBN13: 978-0-8018-1331-3.
Dewey:634.9/0973. LCCN:70-171107.

Audience: **u,f.** ℬ

Cox, Thomas R.   **SD0143.T44**
This Well-Wooded Land: Americans and Their Forests from
Colonial Times to the Present. Trade Paper. Books on Demand.
Ann Arbor, MI. 365p. ISBN:0-7837-7048-0, ISBN13:
978-0-7837-7048-2. Dewey:333.750973. LCCN:85-001141.

Audience: **l,u,f.**

Dana, Samuel T. & Fairfax,   **SD565.D3 1980**
Sally K.
Forest and Range Policy. Ed. 2. Trade Cloth. McGraw-Hill
Higher Education. Burr Ridge, IL. 1980. 480p.
ISBN:0-07-015288-8, ISBN13: 978-0-07-015288-5.
Dewey:333.7/4/0973. LCCN:79-013652.

Audience: **l,u.** ℬ

Donahue, Brian   **HD1289.U6D66**
Reclaiming the Commons: Community Farms and Forests in a
New England Town. Trade Paper. Yale University Press.
Cumberland, RI. 2001. 352p. Yale Agrarian Studies
ISBN:0-300-08912-0, ISBN13: 978-0-300-08912-7.
Dewey:333.2.

Audience: **l,u,f.**   *Choice, 1999.*

Earley Lawrenc   **2004000724 [SD]**
Looking for Longleaf. Trade Paper. University of North Carolina
Press. Chapel Hill, NC. 2006. 336p. ISBN:0-8078-5699-1,
ISBN13: 978-0-8078-5699-4. Dewey:634.9/751/0975.

Audience: **u,f.**

Evans, Julian & Turnball,   **SD247.E9 2004**
John W.
Plantation Forestry in the Tropics: The Role, Silviculture, and
Use of Planted Forests for Industrial, Social, Environmental, and
Agroforestry Purposes. Ed. 3. Trade Cloth. Oxford University
Press, Inc. New York, NY. 2004. 481p. ISBN:0-19-852994-5,
ISBN13: 978-0-19-852994-1. Dewey:634.9560913.
LCCN:2004-049287.

Audience: **u,f.**

Fahl, Ronald J.   **Z5991.F33**
North American Forest and Conservation History: A
Bibliography. Trade Cloth. Forest History Society, Inc. Durham,
NC. 1977. 408p. ISBN:0-87436-235-0, ISBN13:
978-0-87436-235-0. Dewey:016.3337/5/0973. LCCN:76-027306.

Audience: **g,l,u,f.** ℬ

Fimbel, Robert A. (Editor),   **QL109.C66 2001**
et al.
The Cutting Edge: Conserving Wildlife in Logged Tropical
Forests. Alejandro Grajal & John G. Robinson (Editors). Trade
Cloth. Columbia University Press. New York, NY. 2001. 700p.
Biology and Resource Management Ser. ISBN:0-231-11454-0,
ISBN13: 978-0-231-11454-7. Dewey:333.95/416/0913.
LCCN:00-031782.

Audience: **l,u,f.**   *Choice, 2002.*

Gelderen, D. M. van   **SB428.G45 1996**
Conifers: The Illustrated Encyclopedia, Vol. 2. J. R. P. Van Hoey
Smith (Photographer). Trade Cloth. Timber Press, Inc. Portland,
OR. 1996. 706p. ISBN:0-88192-354-0, ISBN13:
978-0-88192-354-4. Dewey:635.9/7752. LCCN:95-045149.

Audience: **l,u,f.**

Gordon, Andrew M. &   **S494.5.A45T4625 1997**
Newman, Steven M. (Editors)
Temperate Agroforestry Systems. Paper Text. Oxford University
Press, Inc. New York, NY. 1997. 288p. CABI Publishing Ser.
ISBN:0-85199-147-5, ISBN13: 978-0-85199-147-4.
Dewey:634.9/9. LCCN:97-022710.

Audience: **l,u,f.**   *Choice, 1998.*

Gregersen, Hans (Editor), et   **SD387.P74P46 1989**
al.
People and Trees: The Role of Social Forestry in Sustainable
Development. Sydney Draper & Dieter Elz (Editors). Trade
Paper. World Bank Publications. Washington, DC. 1989. 288p.
EDI Seminar Ser. ISBN:0-8213-1205-7, ISBN13:
978-0-8213-1205-6. Dewey:333.75. LCCN:89-009047.

Audience: **l,u,f.**

Grey, Gene W.   **SB436.G72 1996**
The Urban Forest: Comprehensive Management. Ed. 3. Trade
Cloth. John Wiley & Sons, Inc. Hoboken, NJ. 1995. 156p.
ISBN:0-471-12275-0, ISBN13: 978-0-471-12275-3.
Dewey:635.9/77/091732. LCCN:95-010875.

Audience: **u,f.**   *Choice, 1996.*

Harris, Larry D.   **QH75.H37 1984**
The Fragmented Forest: Island Biogeography Theory and the
Preservation of Biotic Diversity. Kenton R. Miller (Foreword
by). Library Binding. University of Chicago Press. Chicago, IL.
1984. 208p. ISBN:0-226-31763-3, ISBN13: 978-0-226-31763-2.
Dewey:639.9. LCCN:84-000144.

Audience: **l,u,f.**

Hirt, Paul W.   **SD426 .H57**
A Conspiracy of Optimism: Management of the National Forests
since World War Two. Paper Text. University of Nebraska Press.
Lincoln, NE. 1994. 420p. Our Sustainable Future Ser.
ISBN:0-8032-7288-X, ISBN13: 978-0-8032-7288-0.
Dewey:333.75/0973/09045. LCCN:94-003858.

Audience: **g,u,f.**

Hurst, James W.   **KF9949.**
Law and Economic Growth: The Legal History of the Lumber
Industry in Wisconsin, 1836-1915. Trade Paper. Books on
Demand. Ann Arbor, MI. 980p. ISBN:0-608-20442-0, ISBN13:

978-0-608-20442-0. Dewey:343.775/078674/09.
LCCN:83-040287.

Audience: **l,u,f.**

Husch, Bertram, et al.   **SD555.H8 2003**
Forest Mensuration. Ed. 4. Thomas W. Beers & John A.
Kershaw (Authors). Trade Cloth. John Wiley & Sons, Inc.
Hoboken, NJ. 2002. 456p. ISBN:0-471-01850-3, ISBN13:
978-0-471-01850-6. Dewey:634.9/285. LCCN:2002-068995.

Audience: **u,f.** *B*

Hüttermann, Aloys &   **QH541.5.F6E44 1994**
Godbold, Douglas (Editors)
Effects of Acid Rain on Forest Processes. Ed. 1. Trade Cloth.
John Wiley & Sons, Inc. Hoboken, NJ. 1994. 432p. Wiley
Series in Ecological and Applied Microbiology Ser., Vol. 12
ISBN:0-471-51768-2, ISBN13: 978-0-471-51768-9.
Dewey:574.5/2642. LCCN:93-041974.

Audience: **u,f.**

Jackson, Philip L. &   **G1466.G3**
Kimerling, A. Jon (Editors)
Atlas of the Pacific Northwest. Ed. 9. Trade Cloth. Oregon State
University Press. Corvallis, OR. 2003. 160p.
ISBN:0-87071-562-3, ISBN13: 978-0-87071-562-4.
Dewey:333.7/09795/022.

Audience: **g,l,u,f.**

Johnson, Edward A.   **QK110 .J64 1992**
Fire and Vegetation Dynamics: Studies from the North American
Boreal Forest. H. J. B. Birks & J. A. Wiens (Contribution by).
Trade Cloth. Cambridge University Press. New York, NY. 1992.
143p. Cambridge Studies in Ecology ISBN:0-521-34151-5,
ISBN13: 978-0-521-34151-6. Dewey:581.5/2642.
LCCN:91-036693.

Audience: **u,f.** *Choice, 1993.*

Kaufman, Herbert   **SD565.K3 2006**
The Forest Ranger: A Study in Administrative Behavior. Trade
Cloth. Resources for the Future. Washington, DC. 2005. 248p.
ISBN:1-933115-26-2, ISBN13: 978-1-933115-26-9.
Dewey:634.9/2092. LCCN:2005-029327.

Audience: **u,f.**

Kershner, Bruce & Leverett,   **SD387.O43 K47 2004**
Robert T.
The Sierra Club Guide to the Ancient Forests of the Northeast.
Sierra Club Staff (Contribution by). Trade Paper. Sierra Club
Books. San Francisco, CA. 2004. 256p. Adventure Travel
Guides ISBN:1-57805-066-9, ISBN13: 978-1-57805-066-6.
Dewey:333.75/0974. LCCN:2003-053005.

Audience: **g,l,u.** *Choice, 2005.*

Kimmins, J. P.   **QH541.5.F6K55 2004**
Forest Ecology: A Foundation for Sustainable Forest
Management and Environmental Ethics in Forestry. Ed. 3. Cloth
Text. Prentice Hall PTR. Upper Saddle River, NJ. 2003. 720p.
ISBN:0-13-066258-5, ISBN13: 978-0-13-066258-3.
Dewey:577.3. LCCN:2003-054862.

Audience: **l,u,f.**

Kozlowski, T. T.   **SD396.K66**
Tree Growth. Paper Text. Textbook Publishers. Temecula, CA.
2003. 442p. ISBN:0-7581-4666-3, ISBN13: 978-0-7581-4666-3.
Dewey:582/.16/03.

Audience: **l,u,f.**

Kozlowski, Theodore T. &   **QK711.2.K72 1997**
Pallardy, Stephen G.
Physiology of Woody Plants. Ed. 2. Trade Cloth. Elsevier
Science & Technology Books. Saint Louis, MO. 1996. 411p.
ISBN:0-12-424162-X, ISBN13: 978-0-12-424162-6.
Dewey:582.1/5041. LCCN:96-035505.

Audience: **g,l,u,f.** *Choice, 1997.*

Kricher, John C.   **QH104.5.W4**
A Field Guide to the Ecology of Western Forests. Gordon
Morrison (Illustrator), Roger T. Peterson (Foreword by). Trade
Cloth. Houghton Mifflin Company. New York, NY. 1993. 512p.
Peterson Field Guides, No. 45 ISBN:0-395-46725-X, ISBN13:
978-0-395-46725-1. Dewey:574.5/2642/0978. LCCN:92-035792.

Audience: **g,l,u,f.**

Leuschner, William A.   **SD373.L45 1991**
Introduction to Forest Resource Management. Library Binding.
Krieger Publishing Company. Melbourne, FL. 1992. 304p.
ISBN:0-89464-641-9, ISBN13: 978-0-89464-641-6.
Dewey:634.9/28. LCCN:91-021718.

Audience: **l,u.**

Lewis, James G. (James   **SD565**
Graham)
The Forest Service and the greatest good: a centennial history.
Ed. 1. Durham, N.C.: Forest History Society. 2005.
ISBN:0-89030-066-6, ISBN13: 978-0-89030-066-4.

Audience: **g,l,u,f.**

Loomis, John B.   **HD221.L66 2002**
Integrated Public Lands Management: Principles and
Applications to National Forests, Parks, Wildlife Refuges, and
BLM Lands. Ed. 2. Trade Cloth. Edinburgh University Press.
Edinburgh, 2002. 544p. ISBN:0-231-12444-9, ISBN13:
978-0-231-12444-7. Dewey:333.1/0973. LCCN:2001-042390.

Audience: **u,f.** *Choice, 1994.*

MacCleery, Douglas W.   **SD143**
American Forests: A History of Resiliency and Recovery. Paper
Text. DIANE Publishing Company. Collingdale, PA. 1994. 58p.
ISBN:0-7881-0858-1, ISBN13: 978-0-7881-0858-7.
Dewey:333.75/0973.

Audience: **g,l,u,f.**

Manion, Paul D. &   **SB765 .F665 1992**
Lachance, Denis (Editors)
Forest Decline Concepts. Trade Paper. American
Phytopathological Society. Saint Paul, MN. 1992. 249p.
ISBN:0-89054-143-4, ISBN13: 978-0-89054-143-2.
Dewey:634.9/6. LCCN:92-073742.

Audience: **u,f.**

Maser, Chris   **QH541.5.F6M37**
Forest Primeval: The Natural History of an Ancient Forest.
Library Binding. Sagebrush Education Resources. Caledonia,
MN. 2001. ISBN:0-613-92014-7, ISBN13: 978-0-613-92014-8.
Dewey:577.3.

Audience: **g,l,u,f.** *Choice, 1990.*

McDonald, Peter & Lassoie,   **SD387.D6L58 1996**
James P. (Editors)
The Literature of Forestry and Agroforestry. Book, Other.
Cornell University Press. Ithaca, NY. 1996. 456p. The Literature
of the Agricultural Sciences Ser. ISBN:0-8014-3181-6, ISBN13:
978-0-8014-3181-4. Dewey:634.9. LCCN:95-039328.

Audience: **l,u.** *Choice, 1996.*

McEvoy, Thom J.   SD387.S87M389 2004
Positive Impact Forestry: A Sustainable Approach to Managing
Woodlands. James M. Jeffords (Foreword by). Trade Cloth.
Island Press. Washington, DC. 2004. 227p.
ISBN:1-55963-788-9, ISBN13: 978-1-55963-788-6.
Dewey:634.9/2. LCCN:2003-022406.
                                        Audience: **l,u,f.** *Choice, 2004.*

Miller, Char (Editor)   SD143.A596 1997
American Forests: Nature, Culture and Politics. Trade Cloth.
University Press of Kansas. Lawrence, KS. 1997. xiv, 290p.
Development of Western Resources Ser. ISBN:0-7006-0848-6,
ISBN13: 978-0-7006-0848-5. Dewey:333.75/0973/0904.
LCCN:97-014811.
                                        Audience: **l,u,f.** *Choice, 1998.*

Miller, Char   S926.P56M55 2001
Gifford Pinchot and the Making of Modern Environmentalism.
Trade Cloth. Island Press. Washington, DC. 2001. 384p.
ISBN:1-55963-822-2, ISBN13: 978-1-55963-822-7.
Dewey:333.7/2/092 B. LCCN:2001-005665.
                                        Audience: **g,u,f.**

Miller, Char; Staebler,   SD143
  Rebecca
The Greatest Good: 100 Years of Forestry in America. Ed. 2.
Bosworth, Dale N. (Foreword by); Coufal, James E.
(Introduction by). Bethesda, MD: Society of American Foresters.
2004. ISBN:0-939970-89-9, ISBN13: 978-0-939970-89-6.
                                        Audience: **g,l,u,f.**

Nair, P. K. (Editor)   S494.5.A45A39 1989
Agroforestry Systems in the Tropics. Trade Cloth. Springer.
New York, NY. 1989. 672p. Forestry Sciences Ser.
ISBN:90-247-3790-7, ISBN13: 978-90-247-3790-1.
Dewey:634.9/9. LCCN:88-025222.
                                        Audience: **l,u,f.**

Padoch, Christine, et al.   GF696.B67B67 2003
Borneo in Transition: People, Forests, Conservation, and
Development. Ed. 2. Nancy Lee Peluso & Cecilia Danks
(Authors). Trade Cloth. Oxford University Press, Inc. New York,
NY. 2003. ISBN:983-56-0067-8, ISBN13: 978-983-56-0067-8.
Dewey:333.73/15/095983. LCCN:2003-063951.
                                        Audience: **l,u,f.**

Peluso, Nancy L.   SD657.I5P45 1992
Rich Forests, Poor People: Resource Control and Resistance in
Java. Trade Cloth. University of California Press. Berkeley, CA.
1992. 336p. ISBN:0-520-07377-0, ISBN13: 978-0-520-07377-7.
Dewey:333.75/09598/2. LCCN:91-000581.
                                        Audience: **l,u,f.** *Choice, 1993.*

Pinchot, Gifford   S942 .P5
The Fight for Conservation. Trade Paper. Kessinger Publishing,
LLC. Whitefish, MT. 2004. ISBN:1-4192-6217-3, ISBN13:
978-1-4192-6217-3. Dewey:333.7/2/0973.
                                        Audience: **g,u,f.** *B*

Pinchot, Gifford   E664.P62A3 1998
Breaking New Ground. George T. Frampton 2nd, Char Miller &
Alaric Sample (Introduction by). Trade Paper. Island Press.
Washington, DC. 1998. 542p. ISBN:1-55963-670-X, ISBN13:
978-1-55963-670-4. Dewey:333.7/5/0924. LCCN:98-012418.
                                        Audience: **l,u,f.** *B*

Preston, Richard Joseph &   QK110.P74 2002
  Braham, Richard R.
Preston's North American Trees. Ed. 5. Trade Cloth. Blackwell
Publishing Professional. Ames, IA. 2002. 548p.
ISBN:0-8138-1526-6, ISBN13: 978-0-8138-1526-8.
Dewey:582.16/097. LCCN:2002-009404.
                                        Audience: **g,l,u,f.**

Repetto, Robert C.   HD9768.D44R47 1988
Forest for the Trees?: Government Policies and the Misuse of
Forest Resources. Trade Paper. World Resources Institute.
Washington, DC. 1988. 120p. ISBN:0-915825-25-2, ISBN13:
978-0-915825-25-7. Dewey:333.75/09172/4. LCCN:88-050465.
                                        Audience: **g,l,u.** *Choice, 1989.*

Repetto, Robert C. & Gillis,   HD9768.D44 P82 1988
  Malcolm (Editors)
Public Policies and the Misuse of Forest Resources. Trade
Paper. Cambridge University Press. New York, NY. 1988. 448p.
ISBN:0-521-33574-4, ISBN13: 978-0-521-33574-4.
Dewey:333.75/09172/4. LCCN:87-033815.
                                        Audience: **g,l,u,f.** *Choice, 1989.*

Robinson, Glen O.   SD0565.R6
The Forest Service: A Study in Public Land Management. Trade
Paper. Books on Demand. Ann Arbor, MI. 358p.
ISBN:0-598-12042-4, ISBN13: 978-0-598-12042-7.
Dewey:634.9/0973. LCCN:75-011352.
                                        Audience: **u,f.** *B*

Robinson, Glen O. &   SD143
  Robinson, O. F.
The Forest Service: A Study in Public Land Management. Trade
Cloth. Resources for the Future. Washington, DC. 1975. 358p.
ISBN:0-8018-1723-4, ISBN13: 978-0-8018-1723-6.
Dewey:634.9/0973. LCCN:75-011352.
                                        Audience: **u,f.** *B*

Satterfield, Terre   SD387.O43S28 2003
Anatomy of a Conflict: Identity, Knowledge, and Emotion in
Old-Growth Forests. Trade Cloth. University of British
Columbia Press. Vancouver, BC. 2003. x,198p.
ISBN:0-7748-0892-6, ISBN13: 978-0-7748-0892-7.
Dewey:333.75/16/09795. LCCN:2002-004897.
                                        Audience: **l,u,f.** *Choice, 2003.*

Sponsel, Leslie E. (Editor),   SD418.2.T76T75 1996
  et al.
Tropical Deforestation: The Human Dimension. Thomas N.
Headland & Robert C. Bailey (Editors), Jeffrey A. McNeely
(Foreword by). Trade Cloth. Columbia University Press. New
York, NY. 1996. 396p. Methods and Cases in Conservation
Science Ser. ISBN:0-231-10318-2, ISBN13: 978-0-231-10318-3.
Dewey:304.2/8. LCCN:95-047256.
                                        Audience: **u,f.** *Choice, 1997.*

Steen, Harold K.   SD143.F624 1999
Forest and Wildlife Science in America: A History. Trade Cloth.
Forest History Society, Inc. Durham, NC. 1999.
ISBN:0-89030-057-7, ISBN13: 978-0-89030-057-2.
Dewey:634.9/0973. LCCN:98-053507.
                                        Audience: **g,l,u,f.**

Steen, Harold K.   DS822.3.G88 2004
The U. S. Forest Service: A History. Ed. 2. Trade Cloth.
University of Washington Press. Seattle, WA. 2004. 432p.

ISBN:0-295-98402-3, ISBN13: 978-0-295-98402-5.
Dewey:915.204/31/0092. LCCN:2003-066592.

Audience: **l,u,f.**

Stoddard, Charles H.   **SD143**
Essentials of Forestry Practice. Ed. 3. Cloth Text. John Wiley &
Sons, Inc. Hoboken, NJ. 1978. 387p. ISBN:0-471-07262-1,
ISBN13: 978-0-471-07262-1. Dewey:634.9/0973.
LCCN:78-006652.

Audience: **u,f.** 𝓑

Stoddard, Charles H. &   **SD373.S79 1987**
  Stoddard, Glenn M.
Essentials of Forestry Practice. Ed. 4. Trade Cloth. John Wiley
& Sons, Inc. Hoboken, NJ. 1987. 432p. ISBN:0-471-84237-0,
ISBN13: 978-0-471-84237-8. Dewey:634.9/0973.
LCCN:86-022408.

Audience: **l,u.**

Stubbendieck, James, et al.   **SB193.3.N67S88 1997**
North American Range Plants. Ed. 5. Stephan L. Hatch &
Charles H. Butterfield (Authors), Kelly L. Rhodes, Bellamy P.
Jansen & Debra Meier (Illustrators). Trade Cloth. University of
Nebraska Press. Lincoln, NE. 1997. 501p. ISBN:0-8032-4260-3,
ISBN13: 978-0-8032-4260-9. Dewey:581.7/4/097.
LCCN:96-037402.

Audience: **g,l,u.**

Tomback, Diana F. (Editor),   **QK494.5.P66W55 2001**
  et al.
Whitebark Pine Communities: Ecology and Restoration. Stephen
F. Arno & Robert E. Keane (Editors). Trade Cloth. Island Press.
Washington, DC. 2001. 328p. ISBN:1-55963-717-X, ISBN13:
978-1-55963-717-6. Dewey:585/.2. LCCN:00-011161.
Audience: **u,f.** *Choice, 2001.*

Trask, Samuel, et al.   **SD252 .S58**
Forestry Education in America Today and Tomorrow. Dana
Johnson & Evert W. Johnson (Authors), Henry J. Vaux
(Introduction by). Trade Cloth. Society of American Foresters.
Bethesda, MD. 1963. 402p. ISBN:0-939970-12-0, ISBN13:
978-0-939970-12-4. Dewey:634.9072074. LCCN:63-021251.
Audience: **u,f.**

Van Pelt, Robert   **SD397.C7V36 2001**
Forest Giants of the Pacific Coast. Trade Paper. University of
Washington Press. Seattle, WA. 2002. 224p.
ISBN:0-295-98140-7, ISBN13: 978-0-295-98140-6.
Dewey:585/.0979. LCCN:2001-027171.
Audience: **g,l,u,f.** *Choice, 2002.*

Wenger, Karl F. (Editor)   **SD373**
Forestry Handbook. Ed. 2. Trade Cloth. John Wiley & Sons,
Inc. Hoboken, NJ. 1984. 1360p. ISBN:0-471-06227-8, ISBN13:
978-0-471-06227-1. Dewey:634.9. LCCN:83-017110.
Audience: **g,l,u,f.** 𝓑

Williams, Michael   **SD143 .W48 1989**
Americans and Their Forests: A Historical Geography. Alfred W.
Crosby & Donald Worster (Contribution by). Trade Paper.
Cambridge University Press. New York, NY. 1992. 624p.
Cambridge Studies in Environmental History
ISBN:0-521-42837-8, ISBN13: 978-0-521-42837-8.
Dewey:333.75/0973.
Audience: **l,u,f.** *Choice, 1990.*

Wood, Charles H. & Porro,   **SD418.3.A53D44 2002**
  Roberto (Editors)
Deforestation and Land Use in the Amazon. Trade Cloth.
University Press of Florida. Gainesville, FL. 2002. xiii, 385p.
ISBN:0-8130-2464-1, ISBN13: 978-0-8130-2464-6.
Dewey:333.75/137/09811. LCCN:2002-016557.

Audience: **l,u,f.**

Forestry > Agroforestry

                                                    S494.5.A45
⬜ Traditional Tree Initiative.
http://www.traditionaltree.org/
agroforestry.net.

Audience: **g,u.**

Buck, Louise E. & Lassoie,   **S494.5.A45 1999**
  James P.
Agroforestry in Sustainable Agricultural Systems. Saddle
Stitched. Lewis Publishers. Boca Raton, FL. 1998. 432p.
Advances in Agroecology ISBN:1-56670-294-1, ISBN13:
978-1-56670-294-2. Dewey:634.99. LCCN:98-031470.
Audience: **l,u,f.**

Forestry > Deforestation

Cowell, Adrian   **GF532.A4**
The Decade of Destruction: The Crusade to Save the Amazon
Rain Forest. Cloth Text. DIANE Publishing Company.
Collingdale, PA. 1999. 215p. ISBN:0-7881-6688-3, ISBN13:
978-0-7881-6688-4. Dewey:333.75/0981/1.
Audience: **g,l,u,f.**

Lewis, Ronald L.   **HC107.W5L39 1998**
Transforming the Appalachian Countryside: Railroads,
Deforestation, and Social Change in West Virginia, 1880-1920.
Trade Cloth. University of North Carolina Press. Chapel Hill,
NC. 1998. 368p. ISBN:0-8078-2405-4, ISBN13:
978-0-8078-2405-4. Dewey:338.9754. LCCN:97-036616.
Audience: **g.** *Choice, 1998.*

Williams, Michael   **SD131.W53 2002**
Deforesting the Earth: From Prehistory to Global Crisis. Trade
Cloth. University of Chicago Press. Chicago, IL. 2002. 715p.
ISBN:0-226-89926-8, ISBN13: 978-0-226-89926-8.
Dewey:333.75/137. LCCN:2001-007754.

Audience: **l,u,f.**

Forestry > Forest Ecology

Boyce, Mark S. & Haney,   **QH75**
  Alan W. (Editors)
Ecosystem Management: Applications for Sustainable Forest and
Wildlife Resources. Trade Paper. Yale University Press.
Cumberland, RI. 1999. 384p. ISBN:0-300-07858-7, ISBN13:
978-0-300-07858-9. Dewey:333.95.
Audience: **g,u,f.** *Choice, 1997.*

Harris, Larry D.   **QH75.H37 1984**
The Fragmented Forest: Island Biogeography Theory and the
Preservation of Biotic Diversity. Kenton R. Miller (Foreword
by). Library Binding. University of Chicago Press. Chicago, IL.

1984. 208p. ISBN:0-226-31763-3, ISBN13: 978-0-226-31763-2. Dewey:639.9. LCCN:84-000144.

Audience: **l,u,f.**

Laurance, William F. &   QH541.15.F73T76 1997
 Bierregaard, Richard O. Jr. (Editors)
Tropical Forest Remnants: Ecology, Management, and Conservation of Fragmented Communities. Trade Cloth. University of Chicago Press. Chicago, IL. 1997. 632p. ISBN:0-226-46898-4, ISBN13: 978-0-226-46898-3. Dewey:577.34. LCCN:96-038038.

Audience: **l,u,f.** *Choice, 1998.*

Forestry > Forest Policy

Browler, Kenneth &   SD426.B66 1997
 National Geographic Society Staff
American Legacy: Our National Forests. Trade Cloth. National Geographic Society. Washington, DC. 1997. ISBN:0-7922-3650-5, ISBN13: 978-0-7922-3650-4. Dewey:333.75/16/0973. LCCN:96-037341.

Audience: **g,u,f.**

Leuschner, William A.   SD373.L45 1991
Introduction to Forest Resource Management. Library Binding. Krieger Publishing Company. Melbourne, FL. 1992. 304p. ISBN:0-89464-641-9, ISBN13: 978-0-89464-641-6. Dewey:634.9/28. LCCN:91-021718.

Audience: **l,u.**

Forestry > Logging

Fimbel, Robert A. (Editor),   QL109.C66 2001
 et al.
The Cutting Edge: Conserving Wildlife in Logged Tropical Forests. Alejandro Grajal & John G. Robinson (Editors). Trade Cloth. Columbia University Press. New York, NY. 2001. 700p. Biology and Resource Management Ser. ISBN:0-231-11454-0, ISBN13: 978-0-231-11454-7. Dewey:333.95/416/0913. LCCN:00-031782.

Audience: **l,u,f.** *Choice, 2002.*

Satterfield, Terre   SD387.O43S28 2003
Anatomy of a Conflict: Identity, Knowledge, and Emotion in Old-Growth Forests. Trade Cloth. University of British Columbia Press. Vancouver, BC. 2003. x,198p. ISBN:0-7748-0892-6, ISBN13: 978-0-7748-0892-7. Dewey:333.75/16/09795. LCCN:2002-004897.

Audience: **l,u,f.** *Choice, 2003.*

Forestry > Rain Forests

Fisher, William H.   F2520.1.X5F57 2000
Rain Forest Exchanges: Industry and Community on an Amazonian Frontier. Trade Cloth. Smithsonian Institution Press. Washington, DC. 2000. 240p. Series in Ethnographic Inquiry ISBN:1-56098-958-0, ISBN13: 978-1-56098-958-5. Dewey:981.004/984. LCCN:00-028516.

Audience: **l,u,f.** *Choice, 2001.*

Golley, Frank B. & Werger,   QH541.5.J8
 Marinus J. (Editors)
Tropical Rain Forest Ecosystems: Structure and Function. Trade

Cloth. Elsevier. New York, NY. 1983. 382p. Ecosystems of the World Ser., Vol. 14A ISBN:0-444-41986-1, ISBN13: 978-0-444-41986-6. Dewey:574.5/2642/0913. LCCN:81-007861.

Audience: **u,f.**

Forestry > Silviculture

Daniel, Theodore W. &   SD391
 Helms, John
Principles of Silviculture. Ed. 2. Cloth Text. McGraw-Hill Higher Education. Burr Ridge, IL. 1979. 512p. ISBN:0-07-015297-7, ISBN13: 978-0-07-015297-7. Dewey:634.9/5. LCCN:78-012570.

Audience: **l,u,f.**

Duerr, William A.   SD565
Forest Resource Management: Decision-Making Principles and Cases. Cloth Text. Elsevier - Health Sciences Division. Philadelphia, PA. 1979. xv, 612p. ISBN:0-7216-3223-8, ISBN13: 978-0-7216-3223-0. Dewey:333.7/5/0973. LCCN:77-025555.

Audience: **u,f.**

Hardin, Garrett, et al.   QK110.T48 2001
Harlow and Harrar's Textbook of Dendrology. Ed. 9. Donald J. Leopold, Fred M. White & James W. Hardin (Authors). Paper Text. McGraw-Hill Higher Education. Burr Ridge, IL. 2000. 544p. Forestry Ser. ISBN:0-07-366171-6, ISBN13: 978-0-07-366171-1. Dewey:582.16/0973. LCCN:00-024601.

Audience: **l,u,f.**

Harris, Richard W.   SB435
Arboriculture: Care of Trees, Shrubs and Vines in the Landscapes. Cloth Text. Prentice Hall PTR. Upper Saddle River, NJ. 1982. 720p. ISBN:0-13-043935-5, ISBN13: 978-0-13-043935-2. Dewey:634.9. LCCN:82-003867.

Audience: **g,l,u,f.**

Forestry > Trees

                                                 S494.5.A45

☐ Traditional Tree Initiative.
http://www.traditionaltree.org/
agroforestry.net.

Audience: **g,u.**

Forestry > Wood

Core, Harold   SD536 .C67 1979
Wood Structure and Identification. Ed. 2. Trade Paper. Syracuse University Press. Syracuse, NY. 1979. ISBN:0-8156-5043-4, ISBN13: 978-0-8156-5043-0. Dewey:674/.12. LCCN:79-115147.

Audience: **u,f.**

Forestry > Grasslands

                                                 SF85.35.W8

☐ Rangelands West.
http://rangelandswest.org/

Audience: **g,u,f.**

Seidel, K. W., et al.   SD144.A13 A37
The Influence of Cattle Grazing and Grass Seeding on
Coniferous Regeneration after Shelterwood Cutting in Eastern
Oregon. J. Michael Geist & Gerald S. Stricker (Authors). Trade
Paper. Crumb Elbow Publishing. Rhododendron, OR. 1997. 40p.
ISBN:0-89904-642-8, ISBN13: 978-0-89904-642-6.
Dewey:634.909795.

Audience: **u,f.**

Van Dyne, George M.   QH541.5.P7.G74
Grasslands, Systems Analysis and Man. Alicia I. Breymeyer
(Editor). Trade Cloth. Cambridge University Press. New York,
NY. 1980. 976p. International Biological Programme Ser., No.
19 ISBN:0-521-21872-1, ISBN13: 978-0-521-21872-6.
Dewey:574.5/264. LCCN:77-028249.

Audience: **l,u,f.**

Watson, Leslie & Dallwitz,   QK495.G74W38 1992
M. J.
The Grass Genera of the World. Cloth Text. Oxford University
Press, Inc. New York, NY. 1994. 1088p. CABI Publishing Ser.
ISBN:0-85198-802-4, ISBN13: 978-0-85198-802-3.
Dewey:584/.9. LCCN:93-162240.

Audience: **g,u,f.**

Forestry > Rangelands

     SK355 .R36 1996
Rangeland Wildlife. Paper Text. Society for Range Management.
Wheat Ridge, CO. 1995. 1000p. ISBN:1-884930-05-0, ISBN13:
978-1-884930-05-8. Dewey:333.95/4/0978. LCCN:95-072501.

Audience: **l,u,f.**

Board on Agriculture Staff   SF85.3.R36 1993
& National Research Council Staff
Rangeland Health: New Methods to Classify, Inventory, and
Monitor Rangelands. Paper Text. National Academies Press.
Washington, DC. 1993. 200p. ISBN:0-309-04879-6, ISBN13:
978-0-309-04879-8. Dewey:333.74/0973. LCCN:93-039567.

Audience: **l,u,f.**

Heady, Harold F. & Child,   SK355
R. Dennis
Rangeland Ecology and Management. Trade Paper. Westview
Press. Boulder, CO. 1999. 524p. ISBN:0-8133-3799-2, ISBN13:
978-0-8133-3799-9. Dewey:639.9. LCCN:94-002515.

Audience: **g,l,u,f.**

Heath, Maurice E.   SB0193.F65
Forages: The Science of Grassland Agriculture. Ed. 4. Trade
Paper. Books on Demand. Ann Arbor, MI. 1985. 657p.
ISBN:0-608-00127-9, ISBN13: 978-0-608-00127-2.
Dewey:633.2. LCCN:84-015720.

Audience: **u,f.**

Heitschmidt, Rodney K. &   SF85.G73 1991
Stuth, Jerry W. (Editors)
Grazing Management: An Ecological Perspective. Cloth Text.
Timber Press, Inc. Portland, OR. 1991. 264p.
ISBN:0-88192-190-4, ISBN13: 978-0-88192-190-8.
Dewey:636.01. LCCN:90-019900.

Audience: **u,f.** *Choice, 1992.*

Hodgson, J.   SB199
The Ecology and Management of Grazing Systems. Paper Text.
Oxford University Press, Inc. New York, NY. 1998. 480p. CABI

Publishing Ser. ISBN:0-85199-302-8, ISBN13:
978-0-85199-302-7. Dewey:633.2/02.

Audience: **l,u,f.** *Choice, 1997.*

Hodgson, J. & Illius, A. W.   SF85.E26 1996
(Editors)
The Ecology and Management of Grazing Systems. Cloth Text.
Oxford University Press, Inc. New York, NY. 1996. 480p. A
CAB International Publication ISBN:0-85199-107-6, ISBN13:
978-0-85199-107-8. Dewey:633.2/02. LCCN:97-141787.

Audience: **u,f.** *Choice, 1997.*

Hopkins, Alan (Editor)   SB197.G7 2000
Grass: Its Production and Utilization. Ed. 3. Trade Paper.
Blackwell Publishing, Inc. Malden, MA. 2000. 456p.
ISBN:0-632-05017-9, ISBN13: 978-0-632-05017-8.
Dewey:633.2. LCCN:99-059353.

Audience: **l,u,f.**

Kantor, Shawn Everett   HD241.K36 1998
Politics and Property Rights: The Closing of the Open Range in
the Postbellum South. Trade Cloth. University of Chicago Press.
Chicago, IL. 1998. 198p. Studies in Law and Economics
ISBN:0-226-42375-1, ISBN13: 978-0-226-42375-3.
Dewey:333.33/5. LCCN:97-025887.

Audience: **l,u,f.**

Sayre, Nathan F
The New Ranch Handbook: A Guide to Restoring Western
Rangelands. Quivira Coalition. 2001. ISBN:0-9708264-0-0,
ISBN13: 978-0-9708264-0-4.

Audience: **g,l,u,f.**

Seidel, K. W., et al.   SD144.A13 A37
The Influence of Cattle Grazing and Grass Seeding on
Coniferous Regeneration after Shelterwood Cutting in Eastern
Oregon. J. Michael Geist & Gerald S. Stricker (Authors). Trade
Paper. Crumb Elbow Publishing. Rhododendron, OR. 1997. 40p.
ISBN:0-89904-642-8, ISBN13: 978-0-89904-642-6.
Dewey:634.909795.

Audience: **u,f.**

Stoddart, L. A., et al.   SF85 .S75 1975
Range Management. Ed. 3. A. D. Smith & T. W. Boc (Authors).
Cloth Text. McGraw-Hill Companies, The. New York, NY.
1975. 480p. ISBN:0-07-061596-9, ISBN13: 978-0-07-061596-0.
Dewey:636.08/4. LCCN:74-026668.

Audience: **g,l,u,f.**

Stubbendieck, James, et al.   SB193.3.N67S88 1997
North American Range Plants. Ed. 5. Stephan L. Hatch &
Charles H. Butterfield (Authors), Kelly L. Rhodes, Bellamy P.
Jansen & Debra Meier (Illustrators). Trade Cloth. University of
Nebraska Press. Lincoln, NE. 1997. 501p. ISBN:0-8032-4260-3,
ISBN13: 978-0-8032-4260-9. Dewey:581.7/4/097.
LCCN:96-037402.

Audience: **g,l,u.**

Vallentine, John F.   SF85.V35 2001
Grazing Management. Ed. 2. Trade Cloth. Elsevier Science &
Technology Books. Saint Louis, MO. 2000. 659p.
ISBN:0-12-710001-6, ISBN13: 978-0-12-710001-2.
Dewey:633.2/02. LCCN:00-104371.

Audience: **u,f.**

Gardening

SB450.97

☐ U.S. Department of Agriculture's Home and Garden Bulletin Archive.
http://agnic.msu.edu/hgpubs/index.html

Audience: **g,l,u.**

Armitage, Allan M. &   **SB405.A68 2003**
   Laushman, Judy M.
Specialty Cut Flowers: The Production of Annuals, Perennials, Bulbs, and Woody Plants for Fresh and Dried Cut Flowers. Ed. 2. Trade Cloth. Timber Press, Inc. Portland, OR. 2003. 636p. ISBN:0-88192-579-9, ISBN13: 978-0-88192-579-1. Dewey:635.9/66. LCCN:2002-073256.

Audience: **g.**

Beytes, Chris & Hamrick,   **SB405.B254 2003**
   Debbie (Editors)
Crop Production, Vol. 2. Ed. 17. Cloth over Boards. Ball Publishing. Batavia, IL. 2003. 736p. ISBN:1-883052-35-1, ISBN13: 978-1-883052-35-5. Dewey:635.9. LCCN:2003-008491.

Audience: **g.**

Bush-Brown, James &   **SB453.B9 1996**
   Bush-Brown, Louise
America's Garden Book. Ed. 4. Trade Cloth. John Wiley & Sons, Inc. Hoboken, NJ. 1996. 1042p. ISBN:0-02-860995-6, ISBN13: 978-0-02-860995-9. Dewey:635/.0973. LCCN:96-018752.

Audience: **g.** _B_

Chris Beytes (Editor)   **SB405.B254 2003**
Ball Redbook, Vol. 1. Ed. 17. Debbie Hamrick (Editor). Ball Publishing. 2003. ISBN:1-883052-34-3, ISBN13: 978-1-883052-34-8.

Audience: **g.**

Chris Beytes; Debbie   **SB405.B254 2003**
   Hamrick
Ball Redbook. Ed. 17. Chris Beytes (Editor) ; Debbie Hamrick (Editor). Batavia, Ill. : Ball Pub.. 2003. ISBN:1-883052-34-3, ISBN13: 978-1-883052-34-8.

Audience: **g.**

Cloyd, Raymond A., et al.   **SB603.5.C58 2004**
IPM for Gardeners: A Guide to Integrated Pest Management. Philip L. Nixon & Nancy R. Pataky (Authors). Trade Cloth. Timber Press, Inc. Portland, OR. 2004. 252p. ISBN:0-88192-647-7, ISBN13: 978-0-88192-647-7. Dewey:632.9. LCCN:2003-023791.

Audience: **g,l,u.**

Cope, Edward A.   **QK115.C69 2001**
Muenscher's Keys to Woody Plants: An Expanded Guide to Native and Cultivated Species. Book, Other. Cornell University Press. Ithaca, NY. 2001. 336p. A Comstock Book Ser. ISBN:0-8014-3852-7, ISBN13: 978-0-8014-3852-3. Dewey:582.16/0974. LCCN:00-010701.

Audience: **g.** _Choice, 2002._

Halpin, Anne M. (Editor)   **SB419.R74**
Rodale's Encyclopedia of Indoor Gardening. Trade Cloth. Rodale Press, Inc. Emmaus, PA. 1980. 912p.

ISBN:0-87857-319-4, ISBN13: 978-0-87857-319-6. Dewey:635.9/65. LCCN:80-017019.

Audience: **g.** _B_

Harris, Richard Wilson,   **SB435.H317 2004**
   et al.
Arboriculture: Integrated Management of Landscape Trees, Shrubs, and Vines. Ed. 4. James R. Clark & Nelda P. Matheny (Authors). Trade Paper. Prentice Hall PTR. Upper Saddle River, NJ. 2003. 592p. ISBN:0-13-088882-6, ISBN13: 978-0-13-088882-2. Dewey:635.9/77. LCCN:2002-029823.

Audience: **g,l,u.**

Hartmann, Hudson T., et al.   **SB119.K47 2002**
Hartmann and Kester's Plant Propagation: Principles and Practices. Ed. 7. Dale E. Kester, Fred T. Davies Jr. & Robert L. Geneve (Authors). Mixed Media. Prentice Hall PTR. Upper Saddle River, NJ. 2001. 880p. ISBN:0-13-679235-9, ISBN13: 978-0-13-679235-2. Dewey:631.5/3. LCCN:2001-052334.

Audience: **l,u,f.**

Hogan, Sean (Editor)   **SB403.2.F66 2003**
Flora: A Gardener's Encyclopedia, Vol. 2. Trade Cloth, CD-ROM, Box or Slipcased. Timber Press, Inc. Portland, OR. 2003. 2 volumes with slipcase (not sold separately), over 12,000 color photos, 101 color illus., 14 maps, CD-ROM included with first edition 1584p. ISBN:0-88192-538-1, ISBN13: 978-0-88192-538-8. Dewey:635.9/03. LCCN:2003-059663.

Audience: **g.** _Choice, 2004._

Hogan, Sean   **SB403.2**
Flora: A Gardener's Encyclopedia. CD-ROM. Timber Press, Inc. Portland, OR. 2004. ISBN:0-88192-624-8, ISBN13: 978-0-88192-624-8. Dewey:635.9/03.

Audience: **g.** _Choice, 2004._

Huxley, Anthony   **SB450.95.D53 1992**
   (Editor), et al.
The New Royal Horticultural Society Dictionary of Gardening, Set. Mark Griffiths & Margot Levy (Editors). Trade Cloth. Groves Dictionaries, Inc. New York, NY. 1999. 3000p. ISBN:1-56159-001-0, ISBN13: 978-1-56159-001-8. Dewey:635.03. LCCN:92-003261.

Audience: **g.** _Choice, 1993._

LaCroix, Isobyl (Consultant   **SB409.F56 2005**
   Editor)
Flora's Orchids. Trade Cloth. Timber Press, Inc. Portland, OR. 2005. 368p. ISBN:0-88192-721-X, ISBN13: 978-0-88192-721-4. Dewey:635.9/344. LCCN:2005-050591.

Audience: **g.** _Choice, 2006._

Nelson, Paul V.   **SB415.N44 2003**
Greenhouse Operation and Management. Ed. 6. Trade Cloth. Prentice Hall PTR. Upper Saddle River, NJ. 2002. 692p. ISBN:0-13-010577-5, ISBN13: 978-0-13-010577-6. Dewey:635.9/823. LCCN:2002-068446.

Audience: **g,l.**

Northern, Rebecca T.   **SB409.N6 1990**
Home Orchid Growing. Ed. 4. Trade Cloth. Prentice Hall PTR. Upper Saddle River, NJ. 1990. ISBN:0-13-395138-3, ISBN13: 978-0-13-395138-7. Dewey:635.9/3415. LCCN:89-037428.

Audience: **g.**

Olkowski, William, et al.   SB950.O35 1991
Common-Sense Pest Control: Least-Toxic Solutions for Your
Home, Garden, Pets and Community. Sheila Daar & Helga
Olkowski (Authors). Trade Paper. Taunton Press, Inc. Newtown,
CT. 1991. 736p. ISBN:0-942391-63-2, ISBN13:
978-0-942391-63-3. Dewey:635.0496. LCCN:90-026624.
                                    Audience: **g,l,u,f.** *Choice, 1991.*

Poincelot, Raymond P.   SB319.95.P65 2003
Sustainable Horticulture: Today and Tomorrow. Cloth Text.
Prentice Hall PTR. Upper Saddle River, NJ. 2003. 870p.
ISBN:0-13-618554-1, ISBN13: 978-0-13-618554-3.
Dewey:333.76/16. LCCN:2002-034598.
                                    Audience: **g,l,u.** *Choice, 2003.*

Powell, Charles C. &   SB608.O7P69 1997
  Lindquist, Richard K.
Ball Pest and Disease Manual: Disease, Insect, and Mite Control
on Flower and Foliage Crops. Ed. 2. Cloth over Boards. Ball
Publishing. Batavia, IL. 1997. 448p. ISBN:1-883052-13-0,
ISBN13: 978-1-883052-13-3. Dewey:635.9/2. LCCN:96-046954.
                                    Audience: **g,u.** *Choice, 1997.*

Shoemaker, Candace   SB450.95.E49 2001
  (Editor)
Encyclopedia of Gardens: History and Design, Set. Chicago
Botanical Gardens Staff (Produced by). Trade Cloth. Fitzroy
Dearborn Publishers, Inc. Chicago, IL. 1999. 1590p.
ISBN:1-57958-173-0, ISBN13: 978-1-57958-173-2.
Dewey:712/.03. LCCN:2003-267339.
                                    Audience: **g,l,u,f.** *Choice, 2002.*

Staples, George & Herbst,   QK473.H4S75 2005
  Derral R.
A Tropical Garden Flora: Plants Cultivated in the Hawaiian
Islands and Other Tropical Places. Trade Cloth. Bishop Museum
Press. Honolulu, HI. 2005. 918p. ISBN:1-58178-039-7, ISBN13:
978-1-58178-039-0. Dewey:635.9/523. LCCN:2004-028423.
                                    Audience: **g.**

Taylor, Patrick & Dorling   SB450.95.A45 2003
  Kindersley Publishing Staff
American Horticultural Society Encyclopedia of Gardening.
Trade Cloth. Dorling Kindersley Publishing, Inc. New York, NY.
2003. 648p. ISBN:0-7894-9653-4, ISBN13: 978-0-7894-9653-9.
Dewey:635. LCCN:2003-279089.
                                    Audience: **g.** *Choice, 2004.*

Valder, Peter   SB407.V347 1999
The Garden Plants of China. Trade Cloth. Timber Press, Inc.
Portland, OR. 1999. 400p. ISBN:0-88192-470-9, ISBN13:
978-0-88192-470-1. Dewey:635.9/0951. LCCN:99-021156.
                                    Audience: **g,f.** *Choice, 1999.*

Wickens, Gerald E.   SB107
Economic Botany. Trade Paper. Springer. New York, NY. 2004.
556p. ISBN:1-4020-2228-X, ISBN13: 978-1-4020-2228-9.
Dewey:581.6.
                                    Audience: **l,u,f.**

Gardening > Horticulture

Everett, T. H. (Editor)   SB450.95
New York Botanical Garden Illustrated Encyclopaedia of
Horticulture, Vol. 4. Cloth Text. Garland Publishing, Inc. New
York, NY. 1981. 1059p. ISBN:0-8240-7234-0, ISBN13:
978-0-8240-7234-6. Dewey:635/.03/21. LCCN:80-065941.
                                    Audience: **g.**

Everett, T. H. (Editor)   SB450.95
New York Botanical Garden Illustrated Encyclopaedia of
Horticulture, Vol. 3. Cloth Text. Garland Publishing, Inc. New
York, NY. 1980. 500p. ISBN:0-8240-7233-2, ISBN13:
978-0-8240-7233-9. Dewey:635/.03/21. LCCN:80-065941.
                                    Audience: **g,u.**

Everett, T. H. (Editor)   SB450.95
New York Botanical Garden Illustrated Encyclopaedia of
Horticulture, Vol. 2. Cloth Text. Garland Publishing, Inc. New
York, NY. 1980. 500p. ISBN:0-8240-7232-4, ISBN13:
978-0-8240-7232-2. Dewey:635/.03/21. LCCN:80-065941.
                                    Audience: **g,u.**

Everett, T.H. (Editor)   SB317.58
New York Botanical Garden Illustrated Encyclopaedia of
Horticulture, Vol. 1. Paper over Boards. Garland Publishing, Inc.
New York, NY. 1980. 3601p. ISBN:0-8240-7231-6, ISBN13:
978-0-8240-7231-5. Dewey:635.03. LCCN:80-065941.
                                    Audience: **g.** *B*

Hortorium, L. H. Bailey &   SB45 .B22
  Hortorium, Bailey
Hortus Third: A Concise Dictionary of Plants Cultivated in the
United States and Canada. Marion R. Sheehan & Mitsu
Nakayama (Illustrators), David M. Bates (Introduction by).
Trade Cloth. John Wiley & Sons, Inc. Hoboken, NJ. 1976.
1290p. ISBN:0-02-505470-8, ISBN13: 978-0-02-505470-7.
Dewey:582/.06/1. LCCN:77-352066.
                                    Audience: **g,u.**

Janick, Jules   SB318.J35 1986
Horticultural Science. Ed. 4. Cloth over Boards. Worth
Publishers, Inc. New York, NY. 1986. 746p.
ISBN:0-7167-1742-5, ISBN13: 978-0-7167-1742-3. Dewey:635.
LCCN:85-020521.
                                    Audience: **u,f.** *B*

Rogers, Elizabeth Barlow   SB470.5.R64 2001
Landscape Design: A Cultural and Architectural History. Trade
Cloth. Harry N. Abrams, Inc. New York, NY. 2001. 544p.
ISBN:0-8109-4253-4, ISBN13: 978-0-8109-4253-0.
Dewey:712/.09. LCCN:00-048480.
                                    Audience: **g,l,u,f.** *Choice, 2002.*

Van Wyk, Ben-Erik   QK98.5.A1V36 2005
Food Plants of the World. Trade Cloth. Timber Press, Inc.
Portland, OR. 2005. 480p. ISBN:0-88192-743-0, ISBN13:
978-0-88192-743-6. Dewey:581.6/32. LCCN:2005-044048.
                                    Audience: **g,l,u,f.** *Choice, 2006.*

Gardening > Organic Gardening

S494.5.S86

☐ ATTRA - National Sustainable Agriculture Information
Service.
http://attra.ncat.org/
National Center for Appropriate Technology (NCAT).

Audience: **g.**

Plants

SB359

☐ C/T/A/H/R College of Tropical Agriculture and Human
Resources University of Hawaii at Manoa: The Noni Website.
http://www.ctahr.hawaii.edu/noni/

Audience: **g,l,u,f.**

QK96

☐ United States Department of Agriculture Natural Resources
Conservation Service PLANTS Database.
http://plants.usda.gov/
United States Department of Agriculture.

Audience: **g,l,u.**

Epstein, Emanuel & Bloom,   **QK867**
Arnold J.
Mineral Nutrition of Plants. Ed. 2. Trade Cloth. Sinauer
Associates, Inc. Sunderland, MA. 2004. 380p.
ISBN:0-87893-172-4, ISBN13: 978-0-87893-172-9.
Dewey:572/.514. LCCN:2005-278769.

Audience: **l,u,f.**

Hancock, James F. &   **SB106.O74H36 2003**
Hancock, J. F.
Plant Evolution and the Origin of Crop Species. Ed. 2. Cloth
Text. Oxford University Press, Inc. New York, NY. 2004. 336p.
CABI Publishing Ser. ISBN:0-85199-685-X, ISBN13:
978-0-85199-685-1. Dewey:633. LCCN:2003-006924.

Audience: **l,u,f.** *Choice, 2004.*

Kirk, P. M. (Editor), et al.   **QK600.35.A35 2001**
Ainsworth and Bisby's Dictionary of the Fungi. Ed. 9. J. C.
David & J. A. Staplers (Editors). Cloth Text. Oxford University
Press, Inc. New York, NY. 2002. 672p. CABI Publishing Ser.
ISBN:0-85199-377-X, ISBN13: 978-0-85199-377-5.
Dewey:579.5/03. LCCN:2001-043748.

Audience: **g,l,u,f.**

Mengel, Konrad, et al.   **QK867.P75 2001**
Principles of Plant Nutrition. Ed. 5. Ernest A. Kirkby & Thomas
Appel (Authors), Harald Kosegarten (Contribution by). Trade
Cloth. Springer. New York, NY. 2001. 864p.
ISBN:0-7923-7150-X, ISBN13: 978-0-7923-7150-2.
Dewey:575.7/6. LCCN:2001-038360.

Audience: **g,l,u,f.**

Pollan, Michael   **QK46.5.H85 P66**
The Botany of Desire: A Plant's-Eye View of the World. Trade
Paper. Random House, Inc. New York, NY. 2002. 304p.
ISBN:0-375-76039-3, ISBN13: 978-0-375-76039-6.
Dewey:306.4/5. LCCN:00-066479.

Audience: **g,l,u,f.** *Choice, 2001.*

Stout, B. A. & Cheze, B.   **S675.C54 1999**
(Editors)
CIGR Handbook of Agricultural Engineering: Plant Production
Engineering. Cloth Text. American Society of Agricultural
Engineers. Saint Joseph, MI. 1999. 660p. ISBN:1-892769-02-6,
ISBN13: 978-1-892769-02-2. LCCN:98-093767.

Audience: **u,f.**

Toogood, Alan   **SB119.A46 1999**
American Horticultural Society Plant Propagation: The Fully
Illustrated Plant-by-Plant Manual of Practical Techniques. Paul
Anderson (Photographer). Trade Cloth. Dorling Kindersley
Publishing, Inc. New York, NY. 1999. 320p.
ISBN:0-7894-4116-0, ISBN13: 978-0-7894-4116-4.
Dewey:635/.043. LCCN:98-038933.

Audience: **l,u,f.**

Zohary, Daniel & Hopf,   **GN799.A4Z64 2000**
Maria
Domestication of Plants in the Old World: The Origin and
Spread of Cultivated Plants in West Asia, Europe, and the Nile
Valley. Ed. 3. Trade Cloth. Oxford University Press, Inc. New
York, NY. 2001. 328p. ISBN:0-19-850357-1, ISBN13:
978-0-19-850357-6. Dewey:631.5/2. LCCN:00-050130.

Audience: **l,u,f.**

Plants > Plant Biotechnology

Holden, John H., et al.   **SB123.3 .H65 1993**
Genes, Crops and the Environment. James Peacock & Trevor A.
Williams (Authors). Cloth Text. Cambridge University Press.
New York, NY. 1993. 176p. ISBN:0-521-43137-9, ISBN13:
978-0-521-43137-8. Dewey:333.95316. LCCN:92-033605.

Audience: **g,l,u,f.** *Choice, 1994.*

Smartt, J.   **SB177.L45 S58 1990**
Grain Legumes: Evolution and Genetic Resources. Trade Cloth.
Cambridge University Press. New York, NY. 1990. 389p.
ISBN:0-521-30797-X, ISBN13: 978-0-521-30797-0.
Dewey:633.3. LCCN:89-007181.

Audience: **u,f.** *Choice, 1990.*

Stout, B. A. & Cheze, B.   **S675.C54 1999**
(Editors)
CIGR Handbook of Agricultural Engineering: Plant Production
Engineering. Cloth Text. American Society of Agricultural
Engineers. Saint Joseph, MI. 1999. 660p. ISBN:1-892769-02-6,
ISBN13: 978-1-892769-02-2. LCCN:98-093767.

Audience: **u,f.**

Plants > Plant Diseases

Agrios, George N.   **SB731.A35 2004**
Plant Pathology. Ed. 5. Cloth Text. Elsevier Science &
Technology Books. Saint Louis, MO. 2004. 952p.
ISBN:0-12-044565-4, ISBN13: 978-0-12-044565-3.
Dewey:571.9/2. LCCN:2004-011924.

Audience: **l,u,f.**

Campbell, C. Lee (Editor),   **SB950.73.U6C36 1999**
et al.
The Formative Years of Plant Pathology in the United States.
Paul D. Peterson & Clay S. Griffith (Editors). Trade Cloth.
American Phytopathological Society. Saint Paul, MN. 1999.
448p. ISBN:0-89054-233-3, ISBN13: 978-0-89054-233-0.
Dewey:632/.3/072073. LCCN:99-061684.

Audience: **u,f.**

Campbell, Christy   **SB608.G7**
Phylloxera: How Wine Was Saved for the World. Trade Cloth.
HarperCollins Publishers. New York, NY. 2004. 256p.
ISBN:0-00-711535-0, ISBN13: 978-0-00-711535-8.
Dewey:634.8/2/0944/09034. LCCN:2004-401740.

Audience: g,l,u,f.

Clark, C. A. & Moyer, J. W.   **SB608.S98C53 1988**
Compendium of Sweet Potato Diseases. Trade Paper. American
Phytopathological Society. Saint Paul, MN. 1988. 75p.
Compendium of Plant Disease Ser. ISBN:0-89054-089-6,
ISBN13: 978-0-89054-089-3. Dewey:635/.229.
LCCN:88-070995.

Audience: g,u,f.

Dhingra, Onkar D. &   **SB732.5.D45 1995**
  Sinclair, James B.
Basic Plant Pathology Methods. Ed. 2. Paper over Boards.
Lewis Publishers. Boca Raton, FL. 1995. 448p.
ISBN:0-87371-638-8, ISBN13: 978-0-87371-638-3.
Dewey:632/.3/072. LCCN:94-031201.

Audience: l,u,f.

Dickinson, Matthew J.   **SB732.65**
Molecular Plant Pathology. UK-B Format Paperback. Taylor &
Francis Group. Philadelphia, PA. 2003. 244p. Advanced Texts
ISBN:1-85996-044-8, ISBN13: 978-1-85996-044-8.
Dewey:572.82. LCCN:2004-351315.

Audience: u,f.

Erwin, D. C. & Stuteville,   **SB608.A5C65 1990**
  Donald L. (Editors)
Compendium of Alfalfa Diseases. Ed. 2. Trade Paper. American
Phytopathological Society. Saint Paul, MN. 1990. 112p.
Compendium of Plant Disease Ser. ISBN:0-89054-108-6,
ISBN13: 978-0-89054-108-1. Dewey:633.319.
LCCN:90-082462.

Audience: g,u,f.

Erwin, Donald C. &   **SB741.P58E79 1996**
  Ribeiro, Olaf K.
Phytophthora Diseases Worldwide. Trade Cloth. American
Phytopathological Society. Saint Paul, MN. 1996. 592p.
ISBN:0-89054-212-0, ISBN13: 978-0-89054-212-5.
Dewey:632/.4. LCCN:95-083805.

Audience: g,l,u,f.

Frederiksen, R. A. &   **SB608.S6C66 2000**
  Odvody, G. N. (Editors)
Compendium of Sorghum Diseases. Ed. 2. Trade Paper.
American Phytopathological Society. Saint Paul, MN. 2000.
128p. Compendium of Plant Disease Ser. ISBN:0-89054-240-6,
ISBN13: 978-0-89054-240-8. Dewey:633.1/7493.
LCCN:00-104853.

Audience: g,u,f.

Hartman, G. L. (Editor), et   **SB608.S7C58 1999**
  al.
Compendium of Soybean Diseases. Ed. 4. James B. Sinclair &
J. C. Rupe (Editors). Trade Paper. American Phytopathological
Society. Saint Paul, MN. 1999. 128p. Compendium of Plant
Disease Ser. ISBN:0-89054-238-4, ISBN13: 978-0-89054-238-5.
Dewey:633.3/493. LCCN:99-065061.

Audience: g,u,f.

Holliday, Paul   **SB728 .H65 1998**
A Dictionary of Plant Pathology. Ed. 2. Trade Paper. Cambridge
University Press. New York, NY. 2001. 560p.

ISBN:0-521-59458-8, ISBN13: 978-0-521-59458-5.
Dewey:632/.3/03.

Audience: g. Choice, 1999, 1990.

Kraft, John M. & Pfleger,   **SB608.P25C66 2001**
  Frank L. (Editors)
Compendium of Pea Diseases. Ed. 2. Trade Paper. American
Phytopathological Society. Saint Paul, MN. 2001. 90p.
Compendium of Plant Disease Ser. ISBN:0-89054-269-4,
ISBN13: 978-0-89054-269-9. Dewey:635/.6569.
LCCN:2001-090988.

Audience: g,u,f.

Large, E. C. (Ernest   **SB733**
  Charles)
The Advance of the Fungi. American Phytopathological Society.
2003. ISBN:0-89054-308-9, ISBN13: 978-0-89054-308-5.

Audience: u,f.

Maloy, Otis C. & Murray,   **SB728.E53 2001**
  Timothy D.
Encyclopedia of Plant Pathology. Trade Cloth. John Wiley &
Sons, Inc. Hoboken, NJ. 2000. 1368p. ISBN:0-471-29817-4,
ISBN13: 978-0-471-29817-5. Dewey:631/.3/03.
LCCN:00-043323.

Audience: g,u,f. Choice, 2001.

Mathre, D. E. (Editor)   **SB608.B2C65 1997**
Compendium of Barley Diseases. Ed. 2. Trade Paper. American
Phytopathological Society. Saint Paul, MN. 1997. 120p.
Compendium of Plant Disease Ser. ISBN:0-89054-180-9,
ISBN13: 978-0-89054-180-7. Dewey:633.1/693.
LCCN:97-075001.

Audience: g,u,f.

National Research Council   **SB608.G7C35 2004**
  (U.S.), Committee on California Agricultural Research
  Priorities: Pierce's Disease Staff (Contribution by)
🄮 California Agricultural Research Priorities: Pierce's Disease.
E-Book. National Academies Press. Washington, DC. 2004. xv,
161p. ISBN:0-309-54493-9, ISBN13: 978-0-309-54493-1.
Dewey:632/.32. LCCN:2004-114396.

Audience: u,f.

Ou, S. H.   **SB608.R5**
Rice Diseases. Ed. 2. Cloth Text. Oxford University Press, Inc.
New York, NY. 1985. 380p. CABI Publishing Ser.
ISBN:0-85198-545-9, ISBN13: 978-0-85198-545-9.
Dewey:633/.1/89. LCCN:95-947154.

Audience: u,f.

Punja, Zamir K.   **SB733.F86 2004**
Fungal Disease Resistance in Plants: Biochemistry, Molecular
Biology, and Genetic Engineering. Paper Text. Haworth Press,
Incorporated, The. Binghamton, NY. 2004. 275p.
ISBN:1-56022-961-6, ISBN13: 978-1-56022-961-2.
Dewey:632/.4. LCCN:2003-024391.

Audience: u,f. Choice, 2005.

Punja, Zamir K.   **SB733.F86 2004**
Fungal Disease Resistance in Plants: Biochemistry, Molecular
Biology, and Genetic Engineering. Mixed Media. Haworth
Press, Incorporated, The. Binghamton, NY. 2004. 275p.
ISBN:1-56022-960-8, ISBN13: 978-1-56022-960-5.
Dewey:632/.4. LCCN:2003-024391.

Audience: l,u,f. Choice, 2005.

Schwartz, Howard F.   **SB608.B3C66 2005**
  (Editor), et al.
Compendium of Bean Diseases. Ed. 2. James R. Steadman,
Robert L. Forster & Robert Hall (Editors). Paper Text. American
Phytopathological Society. Saint Paul, MN. 2005. 120p.
Compendium of Plant Disease Ser. ISBN:0-89054-327-5,
ISBN13: 978-0-89054-327-6. Dewey:635/.65.
LCCN:2005-930061.

                                        Audience: **g,u,f.**

Sigee, David C.   **SB734 .S54 1993**
Bacterial Plant Pathology: Cell and Molecular Aspects. Trade
Paper. Cambridge University Press. New York, NY. 2005. 337p.
ISBN:0-521-61967-X, ISBN13: 978-0-521-61967-7.
Dewey:632.32. LCCN:2005-283487.
                            Audience: **u,f.** *Choice, 1994.*

Sinclair, Wayne A. & Lyon,   **SB762.S56 2005**
  Howard H.
Diseases of Trees and Shrubs. Ed. 2. Dust Jacket. Cornell
University Press. Ithaca, NY. 2005. 660p. ISBN:0-8014-4371-7,
ISBN13: 978-0-8014-4371-8. Dewey:634.9/6.
LCCN:2005-012282.
                        Audience: **u,f.** *Choice, 2006, 1987.*

Stakman, E. C.   **SB731 .S77**
Principles of Plant Pathology. Paper Text. Textbook Publishers.
Temecula, CA. 2003. xi, 581p. ISBN:0-7581-4646-9, ISBN13:
978-0-7581-4646-5. Dewey:632.

                                        Audience: **l,u,f.**

Strange, Richard N.   **SB599**
Introduction to Plant Pathology. Trade Cloth. John Wiley &
Sons, Inc. Hoboken, NJ. 2003. 480p. ISBN:0-470-84972-X,
ISBN13: 978-0-470-84972-9. Dewey:632/.3.
LCCN:2003-016087.

                                        Audience: **l,f.**

Thurston, H. David   **SB731.T48 1991**
Sustainable Practices for Plant Disease Management in
Traditional Farming Systems. Trade Paper. Westview Press.
Boulder, CO. 1991. 280p. ISBN:0-8133-8363-3, ISBN13:
978-0-8133-8363-7. Dewey:632/.9. LCCN:91-015953.
                            Audience: **u,f.** *Choice, 1992.*

Vidhyasekaran, P.   **SB728.V525 2003**
Concise Encyclopedia of Plant Pathology. Trade Cloth. Haworth
Press, Incorporated, The. Binghamton, NY. 2004. 563p.
ISBN:1-56022-942-X, ISBN13: 978-1-56022-942-1.
Dewey:632/.3/03. LCCN:2003-002492.
                            Audience: **g,l.** *Choice, 2004.*

Webster, Robert K. &   **SB608.R5 C63 1992**
  Gunnell, Pamela S. (Editors)
Compendium of Rice Diseases. Trade Paper. American
Phytopathological Society. Saint Paul, MN. 1992. 86p.
Compendium of Plant Disease Ser. ISBN:0-89054-126-4,
ISBN13: 978-0-89054-126-5. Dewey:633.1/893.
LCCN:92-071949.

                                        Audience: **u,f.**

Westcott, Cynthia & Horst,   **SB731.W47 2001**
  R. Kenneth
Westcott's Plant Disease Handbook. Ed. 6. Trade Cloth.
Springer. New York, NY. 2001. 1032p. ISBN:0-7923-8663-9,
ISBN13: 978-0-7923-8663-6. Dewey:632/.3.
LCCN:2001-016021.

                                        Audience: **g,l,u,f.**

White, Donald G. (Editor)   **SB608.M2C65 1999**
Compendium of Corn Diseases. Ed. 3. Trade Paper. American
Phytopathological Society. Saint Paul, MN. 1999. 128p.
Compendium of Plant Disease Ser. ISBN:0-89054-234-1,
ISBN13: 978-0-89054-234-7. Dewey:633.1/593.
LCCN:99-061963.

                                        Audience: **g,u,f.**

Seeds

Baker, C. J., et al.   **S604.B36 1996**
No-Tillage Seeding: Science and Practice. K. E. Saxton & W. R.
Ritchie (Authors). Cloth Text. Oxford University Press, Inc.
New York, NY. 1996. 272p. A CAB International Publication
ISBN:0-85199-103-3, ISBN13: 978-0-85199-103-0.
Dewey:631.5/31. LCCN:97-142324.
                            Audience: **l,u,f.** *Choice, 1997.*

Benech-Arnold, Roberto L.   **SB117.H27 2004**
  & Sanchez, Rodolfo A.
Handbook of Seed Physiology: Applications to Agriculture.
Paper Text. Haworth Press, Incorporated, The. Binghamton, NY.
2004. 437p. ISBN:1-56022-929-2, ISBN13: 978-1-56022-929-2.
Dewey:631.5/21. LCCN:2003-021276.
                            Audience: **u,f.** *Choice, 2005.*

Bewley, J. D. & Black, M.   **QK661.B49 1994**
Seeds: Physiology of Development and Germination. Ed. 2.
Trade Cloth. Basic Books. New York, NY. 1994. 462p.
ISBN:0-306-44747-9, ISBN13: 978-0-306-44747-1.
Dewey:582/.0467. LCCN:94-019278.

                                        Audience: **u,f.**

Desai, Babasaheb B.   **SB117**
Seeds Handbook: Biology, Production, Processing, and Storage,
Vol. 103. Ed. 2. Paper over Boards. Marcel Dekker Inc. New
York, NY. 2004. 800p. Books in Soils, Plants, and the
Environment Ser., Vol. 100 ISBN:0-8247-4800-X, ISBN13:
978-0-8247-4800-5. Dewey:631.5/21. LCCN:2004-300847.

                                        Audience: **u,f.**

Kelly, A.F.   **SB117.K45 1988**
Seed Production of Agricultural Crops. Trade Cloth. Bow
Historical Books. New Providence, NJ. 1988. 243p.
ISBN:0-582-40410-X, ISBN13: 978-0-582-40410-6.
Dewey:631.5/21. LCCN:87-002923.

                                        Audience: **u,f.**

Kloppenburg, Jack Ralph   **SB117.3.K57 2004**
First the Seed: The Political Economy of Plant Biotechnology.
Ed. 2. Trade Paper. University of Wisconsin Press. Chicago, IL.
2005. 468p. Science and Technology in Society Ser.
ISBN:0-299-19244-X, ISBN13: 978-0-299-19244-0.
Dewey:631.5/2. LCCN:2004-053597.

                                        Audience: **u,f.**

Mayer, A. M. &   **QK740**
  Poljakoff-Mayber, A.
The Germination of Seeds. Ed. 3. Cloth Text. Elsevier Science
& Technology Books. Saint Louis, MO. 1982. 212p.
ISBN:0-08-028854-5, ISBN13: 978-0-08-028854-3.
Dewey:581.3/33.

                                        Audience: **u,f.**

McDonald, Miller B. & Copeland, Lawrence O.   SB117.M36 1997
Seed Production: Principles and Practices. Trade Cloth. Springer. New York, NY. 1997. 768p. ISBN:0-412-07551-2, ISBN13: 978-0-412-07551-3. Dewey:338.1/7. LCCN:95-009326.

Audience: **u,f.**

Soils

S22
▢ American Society of Agronomy.
http://www.agronomy.org/
ASA-CSSA-SSSA.

Audience: **u,f.**

G3201.J3 S5000
FAO/Unesco: Soil Map of the World: Revised Legend. Trade Cloth. Food and Agriculture Organization of the United Nations. Rome, 1989. 123p. ISBN:92-5-103022-7, ISBN13: 978-92-5-103022-6. Dewey:912.

Audience: **g,f.**

S593
Methods of Soil Analysis: Physical Methods. Trade Cloth. ASA-CSSA-SSSA. Madison, WI. 2002. 1,692p. SSSA Book Ser., Vol. 5 ISBN:0-89118-841-X, ISBN: 978-0-89118-841-4. Dewey:631.4.

Audience: **u,f.**

S590
▢ Soil Science Society of America.
http://www.soils.org/
ASA-CSSA-SSSA.

Audience: **g,l,u,f.**

S592
▢ U.S. Dept. of Agriculture NRCS National Resources Conservation Service: Keys to Soil Taxonomy. http://soils.usda.gov/technical/classification/tax_keys/ Ed. 9. U.S. Dept. of Agriculture, National Resources Conservation Service.

Audience: **g,l,u.**

S592
▢ United States Department of Agriculture NCRS Natural Resources Conservation Service Web Soil Survey. http://websoilsurvey.nrcs.usda.gov/app/

Audience: **g,l,u,f.**

S590
▢ United States Department of Agriculture NRCS National Resources Conservation Service Soils. http://soils.usda.gov/

Audience: **g,l,u,f.**

Akin, Wallace E.   QC981.45.A38 1990
Global Patterns: Climate, Vegetation and Soils. Trade Cloth. University of Oklahoma Press. Norman, OK. 1991. 384p. ISBN:0-8061-2309-5, ISBN13: 978-0-8061-2309-7. Dewey:581.5/22. LCCN:90-050227.

Audience: **u,f.** *Choice, 1991.*

Anderson, J. M. & Ingram, J. S. (Editors)   S599.9.T76T76 1993
Tropical Soil Biology and Fertility: A Handbook of Methods.

Ed. 2. Paper Text. CAB International. Wallingford, 1993. 240p. CABI Publishing Ser. ISBN:0-85198-821-0, ISBN13: 978-0-85198-821-4. Dewey:574.526404.

Audience: **u,f.**

Benbi, D. K. & Nieder, R. (Editors)   S596.7.H36 2003
Handbook of Processes and Modeling in the Soil-Plant System. Trade Cloth. Haworth Press, Incorporated, The. Binghamton, NY. 2003. 1008p. ISBN:1-56022-914-4, ISBN13: 978-1-56022-914-8. Dewey:631.4/01/5118. LCCN:2002-072066.

Audience: **u,f.** *Choice, 2004.*

Birkeland, Peter W.   S592.2.B57 1999
Soils and Geomorphology. Ed. 3. Trade Paper. Oxford University Press, Inc. New York, NY. 1999. 432p. ISBN:0-19-507886-1, ISBN13: 978-0-19-507886-2. Dewey:631.4. LCCN:98-003589.

Audience: **u,f.** *B*

Boersma, L. L. (Editor)   S590.2 .F88 1987
Future Developments in Soil Science Research. Trade Cloth. ASA-CSSA-SSSA. Madison, WI. 1987. 538p. ISBN:0-89118-786-3, ISBN13: 978-0-89118-786-8. Dewey:631.4. LCCN:87-201329.

Audience: **u,f.**

Bohn, Hinrich L., et al.   S592.5.B63 2001
Soil Chemistry. Ed. 3. Brian L. McNeal & George A. O'Connor (Authors). Trade Cloth. John Wiley & Sons, Inc. Hoboken, NJ. 2001. 320p. ISBN:0-471-36339-1, ISBN13: 978-0-471-36339-2. Dewey:631.4/1. LCCN:2001-017914.

Audience: **l,u,f.** *B*

Brady, Nyle C. & Weil, Ray R.   S591.B792 2004
Elements of the Nature and Properties of Soils. Ed. 2. Cloth Text. Prentice Hall PTR. Upper Saddle River, NJ. 2003. 624p. ISBN:0-13-048038-X, ISBN13: 978-0-13-048038-5. Dewey:631.4. LCCN:2003-043399.

Audience: **l,u,f.**

Brady, Nyle C. & Weil, Ray R.   S591.B79 2002
The Nature and Properties of Soils. Ed. 13. Trade Cloth. Prentice Hall PTR. Upper Saddle River, NJ. 2001. 960p. ISBN:0-13-016763-0, ISBN13: 978-0-13-016763-7. Dewey:631.4. LCCN:2001-034595.

Audience: **l,u,f.** *B*

Bridges, E. M.   S591 .B85 1997
World Soils. Ed. 3. Trade Paper. Cambridge University Press. New York, NY. 1997. 176p. ISBN:0-521-49777-9, ISBN13: 978-0-521-49777-0. Dewey:631.4.

Audience: **u,f.**

Buol, S. W.   S591.B887 2002
Soil Genesis and Classification. Ed. 5. Trade Cloth. Blackwell Publishing Professional. Ames, IA. 2002. 544p. ISBN:0-8138-2873-2, ISBN13: 978-0-8138-2873-2. Dewey:631.4. LCCN:2002-009252.

Audience: **l,u,f.** *B*

CA Plant Health Association Staff   S633.W45 2002
Western Fertilizer Handbook. Ed. 9. Trade Paper. Prentice Hall

PTR. Upper Saddle River, NJ. 2002. 351p.
ISBN:0-8134-3210-3, ISBN13: 978-0-8134-3210-6.
Dewey:631.8/0978. LCCN:2001-090561.

Audience: **g.**

Campbell, Gaylon S. &   QH505.C34 1998
 Norman, John M.
An Introduction to Environmental Biophysics. Ed. 2. Trade
Paper. Springer. New York, NY. 2000. XXI, 286p.
ISBN:0-387-94937-2, ISBN13: 978-0-387-94937-6.
Dewey:571.4. LCCN:97-015706.

Audience: **u,f.**

Canarache, A., et al.   S592
Elsevier's Dictionary of Soil Science: Definitions in English
with French, German, and Spanish Word Translations. I. I.
Vintila & I. Munteanu (Authors). Trade Cloth. Elsevier Science
& Technology Books. Saint Louis, MO. 2006. 1355p.
ISBN:0-444-82478-2, ISBN13: 978-0-444-82478-3.
Dewey:631.403.

Audience: **l,u,f.**

Cheng, H. H. (Editor)   TD879.P37P47 1990
Pesticides in the Soil Environment: Processes, Impacts, and
Modeling. Trade Cloth. ASA-CSSA-SSSA. Madison, WI. 1990.
554p. Book Ser., No. 2 ISBN:0-89118-791-X, ISBN13:
978-0-89118-791-2. Dewey:628.5/5. LCCN:90-010070.

Audience: **u,f.**

Clive A. Edwards (Editor)   QL391.A6E25 2004
Earthworm Ecology. Ed. 2. CRC Press. 2004.
ISBN:0-8493-1819-X, ISBN13: 978-0-8493-1819-1.

Audience: **g,l,u,f.**

Conklin, Alfred R.   S592.5.C655 2005
Introduction to Soil Chemistry: Analysis and Instrumentation.
Trade Cloth. John Wiley & Sons, Inc. Hoboken, NJ. 2005. 240p.
Chemical Analysis Ser., Vol. 167:A Series of Monographs on
Analytical Chemistry and Its Applications Ser.
ISBN:0-471-46056-7, ISBN13: 978-0-471-46056-5.
Dewey:631.4/1. LCCN:2004-025912.

Audience: **l,u,f.** *Choice, 2006.*

Dick, Warren A. & Hatfield,   S596.7.S87 2001
 Jerry L. (Editors)
Sustaining Soil Fertility in West Africa. Trade Paper.
ASA-CSSA-SSSA. Madison, WI. 2001. 321p. Special
Publications, No. 58 ISBN:0-89118-838-X, ISBN13:
978-0-89118-838-4. Dewey:631.4/22/0966. LCCN:2001-132918.

Audience: **l,u,f.** *Choice, 2002.*

Dixon, J. B. & Weed, S. B.   S592.55.M56 1989
 (Editors)
Minerals in Soil Environments. Ed. 2. Trade Cloth.
ASA-CSSA-SSSA. Madison, WI. 1989. 1264p. Book Ser., No. 1
ISBN:0-89118-787-1, ISBN13: 978-0-89118-787-5.
Dewey:631.4/1. LCCN:88-034929.

Audience: **l,u,f.**

Dixon, Joe B. & Schulze,   S592.55.S655 2002
 Darrell G. (Editors)
Soil Mineralogy with Environmental Applications. Trade Cloth.
American Society of Agronomy. Madison, WI. 2002. 866p. Soil
Science Society of America Bks., No. 7 ISBN:0-89118-839-8,
ISBN13: 978-0-89118-839-1. Dewey:631.4/1.
LCCN:2002-100258.

Audience: **l,u,f.** *Choice, 2003.*

Foth, H. D. & Ellis, Boyd G.   S596.7.F68 1997
Soil Fertility. Ed. 2. Saddle Stitched. Lewis Publishers. Boca
Raton, FL. 1996. 304p. ISBN:1-56670-243-7, ISBN13:
978-1-56670-243-0. Dewey:631.4/2. LCCN:96-027155.

Audience: **l,u,f.**

Foth, Henry D.   S591.F68 1990
Fundamentals of Soil Science. Ed. 8. Trade Paper. John Wiley &
Sons, Inc. Hoboken, NJ. 1990. 384p. ISBN:0-471-52279-1,
ISBN13: 978-0-471-52279-9. Dewey:631.4. LCCN:90-033890.

Audience: **l,u,f.**

Gobat, Jean-Michel (Editor),   S591.G61713 2003
 et al.
The Living Soil: Fundamentals of Soil Science and Soil
Biology. Michel Aragno & Willy Matthey (Editors). Trade
Cloth. Science Publishers. Enfield, NH. 2004. 546p.
ISBN:1-57808-212-9, ISBN13: 978-1-57808-212-4.
Dewey:631.4/6. LCCN:2003-055629.

Audience: **l,u.** *Choice, 2005.*

Griffith, John F. (Editor)   S600.5.H36 1994
Handbook of Agricultural Meteorology. Cloth Text. Oxford
University Press, Inc. New York, NY. 1994. 336p.
ISBN:0-19-506240-X, ISBN13: 978-0-19-506240-3.
Dewey:630.2515. LCCN:92-020614.

Audience: **g,l,u,f.**

Hillel, Daniel   S592.3
Introduction to Environmental Soil Physics. Cloth Text. Elsevier
Science & Technology Books. Saint Louis, MO. 2003. 494p.
ISBN:0-12-348655-6, ISBN13: 978-0-12-348655-4.
Dewey:631.4/3. LCCN:2004-044074.

Audience: **l,u,f.**

Hillel, Daniel J.   S596
 (Editor-In-Chief)
Encyclopedia of Soils in the Environment, Set. Trade Cloth.
Elsevier Science & Technology Books. Saint Louis, MO. 2004.
2200p. ISBN:0-12-348530-4, ISBN13: 978-0-12-348530-4.
Dewey:631.403. LCCN:2004-104447.

Audience: **g,l,u,f.** *Choice, 2005.*

Hillel, Daniel & Elrick,   S593.S28 1990
 David E.
Scaling in Soil Physics: Principles and Applications. Trade
Cloth. ASA-CSSA-SSSA. Madison, WI. 1990. 122p. SSSA
Special Publications, No. 25 ISBN:0-89118-792-8, ISBN13:
978-0-89118-792-9. Dewey:631.4/3. LCCN:90-045642.

Audience: **u,f.**

Jenny, Hans   S592.2.J455 1994
Factors of Soil Formation: A System of Quantitative Pedology.
Trade Paper. Dover Publications, Inc. Mineola, NY. 1994. 288p.
ISBN:0-486-68128-9, ISBN13: 978-0-486-68128-3.
Dewey:551.3/05. LCCN:94-017606.

Audience: **u,f.**

Jones, J. Benton Jr.   SB91.J66 2002
Agronomic Handbook: Management of Crops, Soils and Their
Fertility. Paper over Boards. C R C Press LLC. Boca Raton, FL.
2002. 480p. ISBN:0-8493-0897-6, ISBN13: 978-0-8493-0897-0.
Dewey:630. LCCN:2002-073651.

Audience: **g,l,u,f.**

Jury, William A. & Horton,   S592.3.J86 2004
 Robert
Soil Physics. Ed. 6. Trade Cloth. John Wiley & Sons, Inc.

Hoboken, NJ. 2004. 384p. ISBN:0-471-05965-X, ISBN13: 978-0-471-05965-3. Dewey:631.4/3. LCCN:2003-057625.

Audience: **l,u,f.**

Klute, Ed A. (Editor)   **S593**
Methods of Soil Analysis: Physical and Mineralogical Methods. Ed. 2. Trade Cloth. American Society of Agronomy. Madison, WI. 1986. 1188p. SSSA Book Ser., No. 5 ISBN:0-89118-811-8, ISBN13: 978-0-89118-811-7. Dewey:631.41.

Audience: **g,l,u,f.**

Lal, R   **S494.5.S86L34 1995**
e Sustainable Management of Soil Resources in the Humid Tropics. E-Book. NetLibrary, Inc. Boulder, CO. 1995. ISBN:0-585-17808-9, ISBN13: 978-0-585-17808-0. Dewey:333.76.

Audience: **u,f.**

Landon, J. R.   **SB301.V64 1993**
Booker Tropical Soil Manual: A Handbook for Soil Survey and Agriculture and Evaluation in the Tropics and Subtropics. Trade Paper. Addison-Wesley Longman, Ltd. Harlow, 1991. xiv, 185p. ISBN:0-582-00557-4, ISBN13: 978-0-582-00557-0. Dewey:633.8. LCCN:93-028153.

Audience: **l,u,f.**

Lecomte, Paul   **TD878**
Polluted Sites: Remediation of Soils and Groundwater. Paper over Boards. Taylor & Francis Group. Abingdon, 1999. 220p. ISBN:90-5410-784-7, ISBN13: 978-90-5410-784-2. Dewey:628.5.

Audience: **u,f.** *Choice, 2000.*

Leigh, G. J. (Editor)   **QR89.7.L45 2002**
Nitrogen Fixation at the Millennium. Trade Cloth. Elsevier Science & Technology Books. Saint Louis, MO. 2002. 470p. ISBN:0-444-50965-8, ISBN13: 978-0-444-50965-9. Dewey:572/.545. LCCN:2002-033873.

Audience: **u,f.**

Malcolm E. Sumner (editor)   **S591.H23 2000**
Handbook of Soil Science. CRC Press. 2000. ISBN:0-8493-3136-6, ISBN13: 978-0-8493-3136-7.

Audience: **g,l,u,f.**

Margesin, Rosa & Schinner,   **S593.M4412 2005**
Franz (Contribution by)
Manual of Soil Analysis: Monitoring and Assessing Soil Bioremediation. Trade Cloth. Springer. New York, NY. 2005. XVI, 366p. Soil Biology Ser., Vol. 5 ISBN:3-540-25346-7, ISBN13: 978-3-540-25346-4. Dewey:631.4/1. LCCN:2005-926091.

Audience: **l,u,f.**

McDonald, Peter (Editor)   **S590.45.L58 1994**
The Literature of Soil Science. Book, Other. Cornell University Press. Ithaca, NY. 1994. 456p. The Literature of the Agricultural Sciences Ser. ISBN:0-8014-2921-8, ISBN13: 978-0-8014-2921-7. Dewey:631.4. LCCN:93-027394.

Audience: **u,f.** *Choice, 1994.*

Miller, Ray & Donahue,   **S591.M733 1990**
Roy L.
Soils: An Introduction to Soils and Plant Growth. Ed. 6. Cloth Text. Prentice Hall PTR. Upper Saddle River, NJ. 1990. 752p. ISBN:0-13-820226-5, ISBN13: 978-0-13-820226-2. Dewey:631.4. LCCN:89-026455.

Audience: **l,u,f.**

Mortvedt, J. J. (Editor),   **S587.5.T7M5 1991**
et al.
Micronutrients in Agriculture. Ed. 2. F. R. Cox, L. M. Shuman & R. M. Welch (Editors). Trade Cloth. American Society of Agronomy. Madison, WI. 1991. 760p. SSSA Book Ser., No. 4 ISBN:0-89118-797-9, ISBN13: 978-0-89118-797-4. Dewey:631.8/1. LCCN:91-017987.

Audience: **l,u,f.**

Moser, L. E., et al.   **SB197 .C67**
Cool Season Forage Grasses. D. R. Buxton & M. D. Caster (Authors). Trade Cloth. American Society of Agronomy. Madison, WI. 1996. 841p. Agronomy Monograph Ser., Vol. 34 ISBN:0-89118-130-X, ISBN13: 978-0-89118-130-9. Dewey:633.2.

Audience: **u,f.**

Paul, Eldor A. & Clark,   **QR111.S672 1996**
Francis E.
Soil Microbiology and Biochemistry. Ed. 2. Cloth Text. Elsevier Science & Technology Books. Saint Louis, MO. 1996. 340p. ISBN:0-12-546806-7, ISBN13: 978-0-12-546806-0. Dewey:576/.190948. LCCN:96-013958.

Audience: **l,u,f.**

Postgate, John Raymond   **QR89.7 .P675 1998**
Nitrogen Fixation. Ed. 3. Trade Paper. Cambridge University Press. New York, NY. 1998. 120p. ISBN:0-521-64853-X, ISBN13: 978-0-521-64853-0. Dewey:572/.545. LCCN:98-015362.

Audience: **l,u,f.**

Power, J. F. (Editor,   **SB317.L43R65 1987**
Introduction by)
The Role of Legumes in Conservation Tillage Systems. Paper Text. Soil & Water Conservation Society. Ankeny, IA. 1987. 153p. ISBN:0-935734-15-5, ISBN13: 978-0-935734-15-7. Dewey:633.3. LCCN:87-402220.

Audience: **u,f.**

Power, James F. (Editor)   **S633 .L238 2000**
Land Application of Agricultural, Industrial and Municipal By-Products. Trade Cloth. American Society of Agronomy. Madison, WI. 2000. 653p. Soil Science Society of America Bks., No. 6 ISBN:0-89118-834-7, ISBN13: 978-0-89118-834-6. Dewey:631.8. LCCN:00-131536.

Audience: **u,f.**

Rauschkolb, Roy S. &   **S619.N57R38 1994**
Hornsby, Arthur G.
Nitrogen Management in Irrigated Agriculture. Cloth Text. Oxford University Press, Inc. New York, NY. 1994. 252p. ISBN:0-19-507835-7, ISBN13: 978-0-19-507835-0. Dewey:631.8/4. LCCN:93-037138.

Audience: **u,f.** *Choice, 1994.*

Ritchie, J. T. & Hanks, R. J.   **S596.7.M62 1991**
Modeling Plant and Soil Systems. Trade Cloth. American Society of Agronomy. Madison, WI. 1991. 565p. Agronomy Monograph Ser., Vol. 31 ISBN:0-89118-106-7, ISBN13: 978-0-89118-106-4. Dewey:631.5/01/13. LCCN:91-019991.

Audience: **g,l,u,f.**

Rowell, David L.   **S591.R68 1994**
Soil Science: Methods and Applications. Trade Paper. Prentice Hall PTR. Upper Saddle River, NJ. 1996. 368p.

ISBN:0-582-08784-8, ISBN13: 978-0-582-08784-2.
Dewey:631.4. LCCN:93-012830.

Audience: **l,u,f.**

Sparks, D. L., et al.   **S593.M4453 1996**
Methods of Soil Analysis: Chemical Methods. A. L. Page, P. A.
Helmke, R. H. Loeppert, R. N. Soltanpour, M. A. Tabatabai, C.
T. Johnson & M. E. Sumner (Authors). Trade Cloth.
ASA-CSSA-SSSA. Madison, WI. 1986. 1358p. SSSA Book
Ser., No. 5 ISBN:0-89118-825-8, ISBN13: 978-0-89118-825-4.
Dewey:631.4. LCCN:96-070096.

Audience: **l,u,f.**

Sparks, Donald L.   **S592.5**
Environmental Soil Chemistry. Ed. 2. Cloth Text. Elsevier
Science & Technology Books. Saint Louis, MO. 2002. 352p.
ISBN:0-12-656446-9, ISBN13: 978-0-12-656446-4.
Dewey:631.4/1. LCCN:2002-104258.

Audience: **l,u,f.** *Choice, 2003.*

Sposito, Garrison   **S592.5.S66 1994**
Chemical Equilibria and Kinetics in Soils. Trade Cloth. Oxford
University Press, Inc. New York, NY. 1994. 278p.
ISBN:0-19-507564-1, ISBN13: 978-0-19-507564-9.
Dewey:631.4/1. LCCN:93-046714.

Audience: **u,f.** *Choice, 1995.*

Sposito, Garrison   **S592.5.S656 1989**
The Chemistry of Soils. Trade Cloth. Oxford University Press,
Inc. New York, NY. 1989. 290p. ISBN:0-19-504615-3, ISBN13:
978-0-19-504615-1. Dewey:631.4/1. LCCN:88-011768.

Audience: **l,u,f.** *Choice, 1990.*

Sprague, Milton A. &   **S604.N62 1986**
  Triplett, Golver B. (Editors)
No-Tillage and Surface Tillage Agriculture: The Tillage
Revolution. Trade Cloth. John Wiley & Sons, Inc. Hoboken, NJ.
1986. 467p. ISBN:0-471-88410-3, ISBN13: 978-0-471-88410-1.
Dewey:631.5/8. LCCN:85-026587.

Audience: **l,u,f.** *Choice, 1986.*

Stancey, Gary; Burris,   **QR89.7.B53 1991**
  Robert H; Evans, Harold J
Biological Nitrogen Fixation. Gary Stancey (Editor) ; Robert H.
Burris (Editor) ; Harold J. Evans (Editor). Springer London, Ltd.
1992. ISBN:0-412-02421-7, ISBN13: 978-0-412-02421-4.

Audience: **u,f.**

Stevenson, F. J.   **S592.8.S76 1994**
Humus Chemistry: Genesis, Composition, Reactions. Ed. 2.
Trade Cloth. John Wiley & Sons, Inc. Hoboken, NJ. 1994. 512p.
ISBN:0-471-59474-1, ISBN13: 978-0-471-59474-1.
Dewey:631.4/17. LCCN:93-046704.

Audience: **u,f.**

Stevenson, F. J. & Cole,   **S592.7.S73 1999**
  M. A.
Cycles of Soils: Carbon, Nitrogen, Phosphorus, Sulfur,
Micronutrients. Ed. 2. Trade Cloth. John Wiley & Sons, Inc.
Hoboken, NJ. 1999. 448p. ISBN:0-471-32071-4, ISBN13:
978-0-471-32071-5. Dewey:631.4/1. LCCN:99-012460.

Audience: **u,f.** ℬ *Choice, 1986.*

Stewart, B. A. & Lal, Rattan   **S590**
  (Editors)
Soil Degradation. Cloth Text. Springer. New York, NY. 1989.

345p. Advances in Soil Science Ser., Vol. 11
ISBN:0-387-97126-2, ISBN13: 978-0-387-97126-1.
Dewey:631.4.

Audience: **u,f.**

Storer, Donald
The Chemistry of Soil Analysis. Spiral. Terrific Science Press.
Middletown, OH. 2005. 58p. ISBN:1-883822-38-6, ISBN13:
978-1-883822-38-5.

Audience: **u,f.**

Tabatabai, M. Ali & Sparks,   **S592.5.C46 2005**
  Donald L. (Editors)
Chemical Processes in Soils. Kivar (or like). ASA-CSSA-SSSA.
Madison, WI. 2005. xix, 723p. SSSA Book Ser., 8
ISBN:0-89118-843-6, ISBN13: 978-0-89118-843-8.
Dewey:631.4/1. LCCN:2005-924447.

Audience: **u,f.**

Tan, Kim H.   **S592.5.T36 1998**
Principles of Soil Chemistry, Vol. 65. Ed. 3. Paper over Boards.
Marcel Dekker Inc. New York, NY. 1998. 560p. Books in Soils,
Plants and the Environment ISBN:0-8247-0147-X, ISBN13:
978-0-8247-0147-5. Dewey:631.4/1. LCCN:97-044103.

Audience: **u,f.**

Tan, Kim H.   **S593.T35 2005**
Soil Sampling, Preparation, and Analysis. Ed. 2. Perfect, Paper
over Boards. Marcel Dekker Inc. New York, NY. 2005. 664p.
Books in Soils, Plants, and the Environment Ser.
ISBN:0-8493-3499-3, ISBN13: 978-0-8493-3499-3.
Dewey:631.4/1/0287. LCCN:2005-041311.

Audience: **u,f.**

Tate, Robert L.   **QR111.T28 2000**
Soil Microbiology. Ed. 2. Trade Cloth. John Wiley & Sons, Inc.
Hoboken, NJ. 2000. 536p. ISBN:0-471-31791-8, ISBN13:
978-0-471-31791-3. Dewey:579/.1757. LCCN:99-021922.

Audience: **l,u,f.**

Tisdale, Samuel L., et al.   **S633.S715 2005**
Soil Fertility and Fertilizers: An Introduction to Nutrient
Management. Ed. 7. Werner Lind Nelson, James D. Beaton &
John L. Havlin (Authors). Cloth Text. Prentice Hall PTR. Upper
Saddle River, NJ. 2004. 528p. ISBN:0-13-027824-6, ISBN13:
978-0-13-027824-1. Dewey:631.8. LCCN:2004-044751.

Audience: **l,u,f.**

Troeh, Frederick R;   **S591.T72 2004**
  Thompson, Louis M.
Soils and Soil Fertility. Ed. 6. Blackwell Pub.. 2005.
ISBN:0-8138-0955-X, ISBN13: 978-0-8138-0955-7.

Audience: **l,u,f.**

U.S. Department of   **S592.16**
  Agriculture
Keys to Soil Taxonomy. Trade Paper. University Press of the
Pacific. Miami, FL. 2005. 336p. ISBN:1-4102-2474-0, ISBN13:
978-1-4102-2474-3. Dewey:631.4.

Audience: **g,l,u,f.**

Weaver, R. W. (Editor)   **QR111.M34 1994**
Methods of Soil Analysis: Microbiological and Biochemical
Properties. Trade Cloth. ASA-CSSA-SSSA. Madison, WI. 1994.
1121p. Bk., Vol. 5 ISBN:0-89118-810-X, ISBN13:
978-0-89118-810-0. Dewey:631.4/17/0287. LCCN:94-020752.

Audience: **l,u,f.**

Webster, R. & Oliver, M. A.   **S592.14.W4 1990**
Statistical Methods in Soil and Land Resource Survey. Cloth
Text. Oxford University Press, Inc. New York, NY. 1990. 328p.
Spatial Information Systems Ser. ISBN:0-19-823317-5, ISBN13:
978-0-19-823317-6. Dewey:631.4/7/072. LCCN:90-035409.

Audience: **l,u,f**. *Choice, 1991.*

Westerman, R. L. (Editor)   **S593.S743 1990**
Soil Testing and Plant Analysis. Ed. 3. Trade Cloth. American
Society of Agronomy. Madison, WI. 1990. 812p. SSSA Book
Ser., No. 3 ISBN:0-89118-793-6, ISBN13: 978-0-89118-793-6.
Dewey:631.4/1. LCCN:90-049801.

Audience: **u,f.**

Yi, Xiong; Qingkui, Li   **S599.6.C5C4913 1990**
The Soils of China. Science Press. 1990. ISBN:7-03-000520-1,
ISBN13: 978-7-03-000520-5.

Audience: **u,f.**

Soils > Soil Chemistry

Barber, Stanley A.   **S596.7.B37 1995**
Soil Nutrient Bioavailability: A Mechanistic Approach. Ed. 2.
Trade Cloth. John Wiley & Sons, Inc. Hoboken, NJ. 1995. 384p.
ISBN:0-471-58747-8, ISBN13: 978-0-471-58747-7.
Dewey:631.4/22. LCCN:94-022899.

Audience: **u,f.**

Wolt, Jeffrey D.   **S594.W7 1994**
Soil Solution Chemistry: Applications to Environmental Science
and Agriculture. Ed. 1. Trade Cloth. John Wiley & Sons, Inc.
Hoboken, NJ. 1994. 360p. ISBN:0-471-58554-8, ISBN13:
978-0-471-58554-1. Dewey:631.4/1. LCCN:94-010959.

Audience: **l,u,f.** *Choice, 1995.*

Soils > Soil Classification

Jenny, Hans   **S592.2.J455 1994**
Factors of Soil Formation: A System of Quantitative Pedology.
Trade Paper. Dover Publications, Inc. Mineola, NY. 1994. 288p.
ISBN:0-486-68128-9, ISBN13: 978-0-486-68128-3.
Dewey:551.3/05. LCCN:94-017606.

Audience: **u,f.**

Viticulture

Amerine, M. A., et al.   **TP548.A47 1980**
Technology of Wine Making. Ed. 4. H. W. Berg & William V.
Cruess (Authors). Cloth Text. A V I Publishing Company, Inc.
New York, NY. 1980. xi, 794 p. :p. ISBN:0-87055-333-X,
ISBN13: 978-0-87055-333-2. Dewey:663/.2. LCCN:79-015483.

Audience: **g,l,u,f.**

Amerine, Maynard A. &   **TP548**
Roessler, Edward B.
Wines: Their Sensory Evaluation. Ed. 2. Cloth Text. W. H.
Freeman & Company. New York, NY. 1983. 432p.
ISBN:0-7167-1479-5, ISBN13: 978-0-7167-1479-8.
Dewey:641.2/2. LCCN:83-001539.

Audience: **g,u,f.**

Amerine, Maynard A. &   **TP548**
Singleton, Vernon L.
Wine: An Introduction. Ed. 2. Trade Cloth. University of

California Press. Berkeley, CA. 1977. 384p.
ISBN:0-520-03202-0, ISBN13: 978-0-520-03202-6.
Dewey:641.2/2. LCCN:75-046031.

Audience: **g,l,u.**

Campbell, Christy   **SB608.G7C3199 2005**
The Botanist and the Vintner: How Wine Was Saved for the
World. Trade Cloth. Algonquin Books of Chapel Hill. Chapel
Hill, NC. 2005. 360p. ISBN:1-56512-460-X, ISBN13:
978-1-56512-460-8. Dewey:634.8/27/094409034.
LCCN:2004-059781.

Audience: **g,l,u,f.** *Choice, 2005.*

Ensrud, Barbara   **TP557**
American Vineyards. Trade Cloth. Random House Value
Publishing. New York, NY. 1990. ISBN:0-517-05278-4,
ISBN13: 978-0-517-05278-5. Dewey:641.2/22/0973.

Audience: **g,l,u,f.**

Harkness, E. M.   **TP548.V4844 2002**
Winemaking: From Grape Growing to Marketplace. Ed. 2.
Richard P. Vine & Sally J. Linton (Editors). Trade Cloth.
Springer. New York, NY. 2002. 476p. ISBN:0-306-47272-4,
ISBN13: 978-0-306-47272-5. Dewey:663/.2.
LCCN:2002-024122.

Audience: **g,l,u,f.** *Choice, 2003.*

Jackson, Ron S.   **TP548.J15 2000**
Wine Science: Principles, Practice, Perception. Ed. 2. Trade
Cloth. Elsevier Science & Technology Books. Saint Louis, MO.
2000. 645p. Food Science and Technology International Ser.
ISBN:0-12-379062-X, ISBN13: 978-0-12-379062-0.
Dewey:663/.2. LCCN:00-100487.

Audience: **l,u,f.**

Joslyn, M. A. & Amerine,   **TP557**
M. A.
Dessert, Appetizer and Related Flavored Wines. Trade Cloth. A
N R Publications. Oakland, CA. 1964. 483p.
ISBN:0-931876-09-5, ISBN13: 978-0-931876-09-7.
Dewey:663.2.

Audience: **g,l,u,f.**

McGovern, Patrick E.   **TP559.M53M34 2003**
Ancient Wine: The Search for the Origins of Viniculture. Trade
Cloth. Princeton University Press. Princeton, NJ. 2003. 360p.
ISBN:0-691-07080-6, ISBN13: 978-0-691-07080-3.
Dewey:641.2/0956. LCCN:2002-042714.

Audience: **l,u,f.**

Muscatine, Doris   **TP557**
(Editor), et al.
University of California Sotheby Book of California Wine.
Maynard A. Amerine & Bob Thompson (Editors). Trade Cloth.
University of California Press. Berkeley, CA. 1984. 640p.
ISBN:0-520-05085-1, ISBN13: 978-0-520-05085-3.
Dewey:641.2/2/09794. LCCN:83-047666.

Audience: **g,l,u,f.**

Ough, Cornelius S.   **TP548.O74 1991**
Winemaking Basics. Library Binding. Haworth Press,
Incorporated, The. Binghamton, NY. 1992. 340p.
ISBN:1-56022-005-8, ISBN13: 978-1-56022-005-3.
Dewey:663/.2. LCCN:91-002253.

Audience: **g,u,f.**

Ribéreau-Gayon, Pascal   **TR548**
  (Editor), et al.
Handbook of Enology, the Chemistry of Wine: Stabilization and
Treatments. Ed. 2. Denis Dubourdieu, Y. Glories & A. Maujean
(Editors). Trade Cloth. John Wiley & Sons, Inc. Hoboken, NJ.
2006. 450p. ISBN:0-470-01037-1, ISBN13: 978-0-470-01037-2.
Dewey:663.2. LCCN:2005-013973.

                                          Audience: **l,u,f.**

Rombough, Lon   **SB389**
The Grape Grower: A Guide to Organic Viticulture. Trade Cloth.
Chelsea Green Publishing. White River Junction, VT. 2004.
304p. The House That Jack Built Ser. ISBN:1-931498-30-X,
ISBN13: 978-1-931498-30-2. Dewey:634.8/0973.

                           Audience: **g,l,u,f.** *Choice, 2003.*

Stevenson, Tom   **TP546**
The Sotheby's Wine Encyclopedia. Ed. 4. Trade Cloth. Dorling
Kindersley Publishing, Inc. New York, NY. 2005. 664p.
ISBN:0-7566-1324-8, ISBN13: 978-0-7566-1324-2.
Dewey:641.2/203. LCCN:2005-283793.

                                        Audience: **g,l,u,f.**

Sullivan, Charles L.   **TP557 .S768 1998**
A Companion to California Wine: An Encyclopedia of Wine and
Winemaking from the Mission Period to the Present. Trade
Cloth. University of California Press. Berkeley, CA. 1998. 456p.
ISBN:0-520-21351-3, ISBN13: 978-0-520-21351-7.
Dewey:641.2/2/0979403. LCCN:97-032186.

                                        Audience: **g,l,u,f.**

Thompson, Bob   **TP557 .T491 1993**
The Wine Atlas of California. Trade Cloth. Octopus Publishing
Group. London, 1997. 240p. ISBN:1-85732-162-6, ISBN13:
978-1-85732-162-3. Dewey:641.220973.

                                        Audience: **g,l,u,f.**

Varela, Lucia G; Smith,   **SB608.G7**
  Rhonda J.;Phillips, Phil A.; Purcell, Alexander
Pierce's Disease. University of California, Agriculture and
Natural Resources Communication Services. 2001. Publication /
University of California, Agriculture and Natural Resources;
21600; Variation: Leaflet (University of California (System).
Division of Agriculture and Natural Resources); 21600.

                                         Audience: **g,u,f.**

Wetlands

Cox, Donald D.   **QK115.C72 2002**
A Naturalist's Guide to Wetland Plants: An Ecology for Eastern
North America. Shirley A. Peron (Illustrator). Trade Paper.
Syracuse University Press. Syracuse, NY. 2002. 168p.
ISBN:0-8156-0740-7, ISBN13: 978-0-8156-0740-3.
Dewey:581.7/68/0974. LCCN:2002-004522.

                           Audience: **g,l,u,f.** *Choice, 2003.*

Cronk, Julie K. & Fennessy,   **QK938.M3C76 2001**
  M. Siobhan
Wetland Plants: Biology and Ecology. Paper over Boards. Lewis
Publishers. Boca Raton, FL. 2001. 488p. ISBN:1-56670-372-7,
ISBN13: 978-1-56670-372-7. Dewey:581.7/68.
LCCN:2001-020390.

                             Audience: **u,f.** *Choice, 2002.*

Dugan, Patrick (Editor)   **QH541.5.M3 2005**
Guide to Wetlands: A Comprehensive and Fascinating Guide to
the Wetlands of the World. Trade Paper. Firefly Books, Ltd.
Tonawanda, NY. 2005. 304p. Firefly Pocket Reference Ser.
ISBN:1-55407-111-9, ISBN13: 978-1-55407-111-1.
Dewey:578.768. LCCN:2006-276145.

                             Audience: **g,l.** *Choice, 2006.*

Giblett, Rod   **GB622.G53 1996**
Postmodern Wetlands: Culture, History, Ecology. Trade Paper.
Edinburgh University Press. Edinburgh, 1997. 256p. Postmodern
Theory Ser. ISBN:0-7486-0844-3, ISBN13: 978-0-7486-0844-7.
Dewey:333.91/8. LCCN:97-113104.

                                          Audience: **u,f.**

Good, Ralph E.   **QH541.5.M3.F74**
  (Editor), et al.
Freshwater Wetlands: Ecological Processes and Management
Potential. Dennis F. Whigham & Robert L. Simpson (Editors).
Trade Cloth. Elsevier Science & Technology Books. Saint
Louis, MO. 1978. xvii, 378p. ISBN:0-12-290150-9, ISBN13:
978-0-12-290150-8. Dewey:574.5/2632. LCCN:78-002836.

                                          Audience: **u,f.**

Moser, Michael E. &   **QH87.3.W46 1991**
  Finlayson, Max (Editors)
Wetlands. Trade Cloth. Facts On File, Inc.. New York, NY.
1991. 224p. ISBN:0-8160-2556-8, ISBN13: 978-0-8160-2556-5.
Dewey:574.5/26325. LCCN:91-023683.
                             Audience: **g,l.** *Choice, 1992.*

Odum, Howard T.   **TD196.M4H434 2000**
Heavy Metals in the Environment: Using Wetlands for Their
Removal. Paper over Boards. Lewis Publishers. Boca Raton, FL.
2000. 344p. ISBN:1-56670-401-4, ISBN13: 978-1-56670-401-4.
Dewey:628.5/2. LCCN:99-089022.

                                          Audience: **u,f.**

Animal Science

                                            SF95.N32 NO. 15
[e] Nutrient Requirements of Goats: Angora, Dairy, and Meat
Goats in Temperate and Tropical Countries. E-Book. NetLibrary,
Inc. Boulder, CO. 1981. ISBN:0-585-03745-0, ISBN13:
978-0-585-03745-5. Dewey:636.08/52.

                                          Audience: **u,f.**

Department of Animal
  Science Oklahoma State University
[⬜] Breeds of Poultry.
http://www.ansi.okstate.edu/poultry/
Oklahoma State University Board of Regents.

                                          Audience: **u,f.**

American Kennel Club Staff   **SF426.C66 2006**
  (Contribution by)
The Complete Dog Book. Ed. 20. Trade Cloth. Ballantine
Books. New York, NY. 2006. ISBN:0-345-48092-9, ISBN13:
978-0-345-48092-7. Dewey:636.7/1. LCCN:2005-048263.
                                       Audience: **g,l,u.** *B*

American Sheep Industry   **SF375**
  Association
SID sheep production handbook. Ed. 7. American Sheep
Industry Association. 2003. ISBN:0-9742857-0-6, ISBN13:
978-0-9742857-0-2.
                                          Audience: **l,u,f.**

Anderson, Virginia DeJohn   **SF51.A655 2004**
Creatures of Empire: How Domestic Animals Transformed Early America. Trade Cloth. Oxford University Press, Inc. New York, NY. 2004. 336p. ISBN:0-19-515860-1, ISBN13: 978-0-19-515860-1. Dewey:636/.0973. LCCN:2004-043401.
                         Audience: **g,l,u.**

Bekoff, Marc (Editor)   **QL750**
Encyclopedia of Animal Behavior. Jane Goodall (Foreword by). Cloth Text. Greenwood Publishing Group, Inc. Portsmouth, NH. 2004. 1424p. ISBN:0-313-32745-9, ISBN13: 978-0-313-32745-2. Dewey:591.5/03. LCCN:2004-056073.
            Audience: **g,l,u,f.** *Choice, 2005.*

Bickert, William G., et al.   **SF206.D35 2000**
Dairy Freestall Housing and Equipment, MWPS-7. Ed. 7. Brian Holmes, Kevin Janni, David W. Kammel & Richard R. Stowell (Authors). Trade Paper. MidWest Plan Service. Ames, IA. 2000. 152p. ISBN:0-89373-095-5, ISBN13: 978-0-89373-095-6. Dewey:636.2/142. LCCN:00-061665.
                         Audience: **l,u,f.**

Boden, Edward   **SF609**
Black's Veterinary Dictionary. Ed. 20. Trade Cloth. Rowman & Littlefield Publishers, Inc. Lanham, MD. 2002. 608p. ISBN:0-389-21024-2, ISBN13: 978-0-389-21024-5. Dewey:636/.089/03.
            Audience: **g,u,f.** *Choice, 2002.*

Case, Linda P.   **SF426.C375 2005**
The Dog: Its Behavior, Nutrition and Health. Ed. 2. Trade Cloth. Blackwell Publishing Professional. Ames, IA. 2005. 496p. ISBN:0-8138-1254-2, ISBN13: 978-0-8138-1254-0. Dewey:636.7. LCCN:2004-022582.
                         Audience: **g,l,u.**

Cheeke, Peter R.   **SF95.C463 2005**
Applied Animal Nutrition: Feeds and Feeding. Ed. 3. Cloth Text. Prentice Hall PTR. Upper Saddle River, NJ. 2004. 624p. ISBN:0-13-113331-4, ISBN13: 978-0-13-113331-0. Dewey:636.08/5. LCCN:2004-044341.
                         Audience: **g,u,f.**

Committee on Animal   **SF203.N883 2001**
   Nutrition & National Research Council Staff
Nutrient Requirements of Dairy Cattle, 2001. Ed. 7. Trade Paper. National Academies Press. Washington, DC. 2000. xxi, 381p. ISBN:0-309-06997-1, ISBN13: 978-0-309-06997-7. Dewey:636.2/13. LCCN:00-012828.
                         Audience: **u,f.**

Crane, Eva   **SF524.C738 1999**
The World History of Beekeeping and Honey Hunting. Library Binding. Routledge. New York, NY. 1999. 720p. ISBN:0-415-92467-7, ISBN13: 978-0-415-92467-2. Dewey:638/.1/09. LCCN:99-025816.
            Audience: **g,l,u.** *Choice, 2000.*

Department of Animal   **SF105.B74**
   Science Oklahoma State University
▢ Breeds of Livestock.
http://www.ansi.okstate.edu/breeds/
Oklahoma State University Board of Regents.
                         Audience: **u,f.**

Dukes, H. H. & Reece,   **SF768.D77 2004**
   William O.
Dukes' Physiology of Domestic Animals. Ed. 12. Book, Other.

Cornell University Press. Ithaca, NY. 2004. 1024p. ISBN:0-8014-4238-9, ISBN13: 978-0-8014-4238-4. Dewey:636.089/2/008. LCCN:2003-063492.
                         Audience: **l,u,f.**

Dunlop, Robert H. &   **SF615.D86 1996**
   Williams, David J.
Veterinary Medicine: An Illustrated History. Trade Cloth. Elsevier - Health Sciences Division. Philadelphia, PA. 1995. 704p. ISBN:0-8016-3209-9, ISBN13: 978-0-8016-3209-9. Dewey:636.089/09. LCCN:95-005238.
                         Audience: **u,f.**

Elton, Charles S.   **QH541.E398 2001**
Animal Ecology. Mathew A. Leibold & J. Timothy Wootton (Introduction by). Trade Paper. University of Chicago Press. Chicago, IL. 2001. 296p. ISBN:0-226-20639-4, ISBN13: 978-0-226-20639-4. Dewey:591.7. LCCN:00-069087.
            Audience: **l,u,f.** *B Choice, 2001.*

Ettinger, Stephen J. &   **SF991.T48 2000**
   Feldman, Edward C. (Editors)
Textbook of Veterinary Internal Medicine: Diseases of the Dog and Cat. Ed. 5. Trade Cloth. Elsevier - Health Sciences Division. Philadelphia, PA. 2000. xlvi, 1996p. ISBN:0-7216-7257-4, ISBN13: 978-0-7216-7257-1. Dewey:636.7/0896. LCCN:98-034212.
                         Audience: **u,f.**

Evans, Warren J., et al.   **SF285.H748 1990**
The Horse. Ed. 2. Anthony Borton, Harold F. Hintz & L. Dale Van Vleck (Authors). Cloth over Boards. Worth Publishers, Inc. New York, NY. 1990. 784p. ISBN:0-7167-1811-1, ISBN13: 978-0-7167-1811-6. Dewey:636.1. LCCN:89-017027.
                         Audience: **g,l,u,f.**

Field, Thomas G. & Taylor,   **HD9433.U4T39 2002**
   Robert W.
Beef Production and Management Decisions. Ed. 4. Cloth Text. Prentice Hall PTR. Upper Saddle River, NJ. 2002. 747p. ISBN:0-13-088879-6, ISBN13: 978-0-13-088879-2. Dewey:636.2/13/068. LCCN:2001-055151.
                         Audience: **u,f.**

Fuquay, John W. & Fox,   **SF229.E53 2003**
   Patrick F. (Editors)
Encyclopedia of Dairy Sciences, Set. Hubert Roginski (Editor-In-Chief). Trade Cloth. Elsevier Science & Technology Books. Saint Louis, MO. 2002. 2500p. ISBN:0-12-227235-8, ISBN13: 978-0-12-227235-6. Dewey:636.2/142/03. LCCN:2002-114095.
                         Audience: **l,u,f.**

Gall, C. (Editor)   **SF383**
Goat Production: Breeding and Management. Trade Cloth. Elsevier Science & Technology Books. Saint Louis, MO. 1981. xix, 619p. ISBN:0-12-273980-9, ISBN13: 978-0-12-273980-4. Dewey:636.3/9. LCCN:81-066393.
                         Audience: **u,f.**

Getty, Robert   **SF761**
Sisson and Grossman's The Anatomy of the Domestic Animal, Vol. 2. Ed. 5. Cloth Text. Elsevier - Health Sciences Division. Philadelphia, PA. 1975. 2110p. ISBN:0-7216-4107-5, ISBN13: 978-0-7216-4107-2. Dewey:636.089/1. LCCN:78-081821.
                         Audience: **l,u,f.**

Harmon, Jay, et al.   **SF396.3.S89 2000**
Swine Breeding and Gestation Facilities Handbook. Ed. 2.
Steven J. Hoff, Joseph Zulovich & Donald Levis (Authors).
Trade Paper. MidWest Plan Service. Ames, IA. 2000. 104p.
ISBN:0-89373-078-5, ISBN13: 978-0-89373-078-9.
Dewey:636.4/082/0284. LCCN:00-064717.
                                                    Audience: **u,f.**

Hirning, Harvey J.   **SF375.8 .S43 1994**
Sheep Housing and Equipment Handbook. Ed. 4. C. J. Huffman
(Editor). Trade Paper. MidWest Plan Service. Ames, IA. 1994.
90p. ISBN:0-89373-090-4, ISBN13: 978-0-89373-090-1.
Dewey:636.3/08/31. LCCN:93-026802.
                                                    Audience: **g,u,f.**

Holden, Palmer J., et al.   **SF395.H74 2005**
Swine Science. Ed. 7. M. Eugene Ensminger & Iowa State
Animal Science Staff (Authors). Cloth Text. Prentice Hall PTR.
Upper Saddle River, NJ. 2005. 576p. ISBN:0-13-113461-2,
ISBN13: 978-0-13-113461-4. Dewey:636.4.
LCCN:2004-018854.
                                                    Audience: **g,u,f.**

Houpt, Katherine A.   **SF756.7**
Domestic Animal Behavior for Veterinarians and Animal
Scientists. Ed. 4. Trade Cloth. Blackwell Publishing
Professional. Ames, IA. 2004. 528p. ISBN:0-8138-0334-9,
ISBN13: 978-0-8138-0334-0. Dewey:636/.001/9.
LCCN:2004-017616.
                                                    Audience: **u,f.**

Kahn, Cynthia M. (Editor)   **SF754**
The Merck Veterinary Manual. Ed. 9. Scott Line (Associate
Editor). Trade Cloth. John Wiley & Sons, Inc. Hoboken, NJ.
2005. 2700p. ISBN:0-911910-50-6, ISBN13:
978-0-911910-50-6. Dewey:636.089. LCCN:2004-111348.
                                                    Audience: **g,u,f.**

Mason, I. L.   **SF41**
Evolution of Domesticated Animals. Trade Cloth. John Wiley &
Sons, Inc. Hoboken, NJ. 1986. 320p. ISBN:0-470-20397-8,
ISBN13: 978-0-470-20397-2. Dewey:636/.009.
                                                    Audience: **u,f.**

Midwest Plan Service   **SF206.B44 1986**
   Engineers Staff
Beef Housing and Equipment Handbook. Ed. 4. MWPS Staff
(Editor). Trade Paper. MidWest Plan Service. Ames, IA. 1987.
ISBN:0-89373-068-8, ISBN13: 978-0-89373-068-0.
Dewey:636.2/0831. LCCN:85-028358.
                                                    Audience: **g,u,f.**

Midwest Plan Service   **TD930 .L58**
   Personnel
Livestock Waste Facilities Handbook. Trade Paper. MidWest
Plan Service. Ames, IA. 1998. 94p. ISBN:0-89373-012-2,
ISBN13: 978-0-89373-012-3. Dewey:628/.7466.
                                                    Audience: **u,f.**

Morse, Roger & Flottum,   **SF522.3**
   Kim (Editors)
The ABC and XYZ of Bee Culture: An Encyclopedia of
Beekeeping. Ed. 40. Trade Cloth. A. I. Root Company. Medina,
OH. 1990. 528p. ISBN:0-936028-01-7, ISBN13:
978-0-936028-01-9. Dewey:638.103.
                                                    Audience: **g,l,u,f.**

National Research Council   **SF203.N88 2000**
   Staff
Nutrient Requirements of Beef Cattle: Update 2000. Ed. 7.
Trade Paper. National Academies Press. Washington, DC. 1996.
248p. ISBN:0-309-06934-3, ISBN13: 978-0-309-06934-2.
Dewey:636.2/13.
                                                    Audience: **u,f.**

National Research Council   **SF427.4N38 2006**
   Staff
Nutrient Requirements of Dogs and Cats. Trade Cloth. National
Academies Press. Washington, DC. 2006. 424p.
ISBN:0-309-08628-0, ISBN13: 978-0-309-08628-8.
Dewey:636.7/0852. LCCN:2005-037411.
                                                    Audience: **g,l,u,f.**

National Research Council   **SF427.4.N38 1985**
   Staff
Nutrient Requirements of Dogs, 1985. Ed. 2. Paper Text.
National Academies Press. Washington, DC. 1985. 88p. Nutrient
Requirements of Domestic Animals Ser. ISBN:0-309-03496-5,
ISBN13: 978-0-309-03496-8. Dewey:636.7/085.
LCCN:85-002955.
                                                    Audience: **g,l,u,f.**

National Research Council   **SF285.5.N37 1989**
   Staff
Nutrient Requirements of Horses, Set. Ed. 5. Paper Text.
National Academies Press. Washington, DC. 1989. 112p.
Nutrient Requirements of Domestic Animals Ser.
ISBN:0-309-03989-4, ISBN13: 978-0-309-03989-5.
Dewey:636.1/08/52. LCCN:89-003061.
                                                    Audience: **g,u,f.**

National Research Council   **SF376 .N85 1985**
   Staff
Nutrient Requirements of Sheep. Ed. 6. Paper Text. National
Academies Press. Washington, DC. 1985. 112p. Nutrient
Requirements of Domestic Animals Ser. ISBN:0-309-03596-1,
ISBN13: 978-0-309-03596-5. Dewey:636.3/0852.
LCCN:85-021562.
                                                    Audience: **g,u,f.**

National Research Council   **SF396.5.N87 1998**
   Staff
Nutrient Requirements of Swine. Ed. 10. Paper Text. National
Academies Press. Washington, DC. 1998. 210p. Agriculture Ser.
ISBN:0-309-05993-3, ISBN13: 978-0-309-05993-0.
Dewey:636.4/0852. LCCN:98-009007.
                                                    Audience: **g,u,f.**

National Research Council   **SF396.5.N87 1988**
   Staff
Nutrient Requirements of Swine, 1988. Ed. 9. Paper Text.
National Academies Press. Washington, DC. 1988. 104p.
ISBN:0-309-03779-4, ISBN13: 978-0-309-03779-2.
Dewey:636.4/0852. LCCN:87-034967.
                                                    Audience: **g,u,f.**

National Research Council   **SF0097.U56**
   Staff
United States-Canadian Tables of Feed Composition: Nutritional
Data for United States and Canadian Feeds. Trade Paper. Books
on Demand. Ann Arbor, MI. 156p. ISBN:0-598-09684-1,
ISBN13: 978-0-598-09684-5. Dewey:636.08/55.
LCCN:82-003625.
                                                    Audience: **g,u.**

Pond, Wilson & Bell, Alan SF61.E496 2005
Encyclopedia of Animal Science. Trade Cloth. Marcel Dekker
Inc. New York, NY. 2004. 800p. ISBN:0-8247-4796-8, ISBN13:
978-0-8247-4796-1. Dewey:636.003. LCCN:2005-297469.
Audience: **g,l,u,f.**

Radostits, O. M., et al. SF745 .R331 2000
Veterinary Medicine: A Textbook of the Diseases of Cattle,
Sheep, Pigs, Goats and Horses. Ed. 9. Douglas C. Blood, Clive
C. Gay & Kenneth W. Hinchcliff (Authors). Cloth Text. Elsevier
- Health Sciences Division. Philadelphia, PA. 2000. 1880p.
ISBN:0-7020-2604-2, ISBN13: 978-0-7020-2604-1.
Dewey:636.089.
Audience: **u,f.**

Sambereus SF75.2 .S313 1992
Color Atlas of Livestock Breeds. Trade Cloth. Harcourt Health
Sciences Group. Saint Louis, MO. 1992. 272p.
ISBN:0-7234-1891-8, ISBN13: 978-0-7234-1891-7.
Dewey:636.08.
Audience: **g,l,u,f.**

Scanes, C. G. SF768.S26 2003
Biology of Growth of Domestic Animals. Trade Cloth.
Blackwell Publishing Professional. Ames, IA. 2003. 408p.
ISBN:0-8138-2906-2, ISBN13: 978-0-8138-2906-7.
Dewey:636.089/266. LCCN:2002-155124.
Audience: **u,f.**

Siegal, Mordecai SF442 .C385 2004
The Cat Fanciers' Association Complete Cat Book. Trade Cloth.
HarperCollins Publishers. New York, NY. 2004. 528p.
ISBN:0-06-270233-5, ISBN13: 978-0-06-270233-3.
Dewey:636.8. LCCN:2004-559176.
Audience: **g,l,u.**

Sterba, Gunther & Mills, SF456.5.L4913 1983
Dick (Editors)
The Aquarium Encyclopedia. Trade Cloth. MIT Press.
Cambridge, MA. 1983. 607p. ISBN:0-262-19207-1, ISBN13:
978-0-262-19207-1. Dewey:639.3/4/0321. LCCN:82-000247.
Audience: **g,l,u.** *B*

Subcommittee on Poultry SF494.N37 1994
Nutrition Staff, Committee
Nutrient Requirements of Poultry. Ed. 9. Paper Text. National
Academies Press. Washington, DC. 1994. 176p. Nutrient
Requirements of Domestic Animals Ser. ISBN:0-309-04892-3,
ISBN13: 978-0-309-04892-7. Dewey:636.5/0852.
LCCN:94-003084.
Audience: **g,u,f.**

Swayne, David & Fadly, SF995.D69 2003
Aly M.
Diseases of Poultry. Ed. 11. Y. M. Saif, H. John Barnes, John R.
Glisson & Larry R. McDougald (Editors). Trade Cloth.
Blackwell Publishing Professional. Ames, IA. 2003. 1260p.
ISBN:0-8138-0423-X, ISBN13: 978-0-8138-0423-1.
Dewey:636.5/0896. LCCN:2002-014178.
Audience: **u,f.**

The Animal Welfare HV4708
Information Center, U.S. Department of Agriculture,
Agricultural Research Service, National Agricultural
Library
☐ AWIC: Animal Welfare Information Center.

http://www.nal.usda.gov/awic/index.html
U.S. Department of Agriculture, Agricultural Research Service,
National Agricultural Library.
Audience: **g,l,u,f.**

Tyler, Howard, et al. SF208.T95 2006
Dairy Cattle Science. Ed. 4. M. E. Ensminger & Iowa State
Animal Science Staff (Authors). Cloth Text. Prentice Hall PTR.
Upper Saddle River, NJ. 2005. 432p. ISBN:0-13-113412-4,
ISBN13: 978-0-13-113412-6. Dewey:636.2/142.
LCCN:2005-043003.
Audience: **u,f.**

Universities Federation for SF406
Animal Welfare Staff
Terrestrial Vertebrates. Ed. 7. Trevor B. Poole (Editor). Trade
Cloth. Blackwell Publishing Ltd. Oxford, 1999. 864p.
ISBN:0-632-05131-0, ISBN13: 978-0-632-05131-1.
Dewey:636.088/5. LCCN:98-051409.
Audience: **l,u,f.**

Weaver, William D. Jr. & SF487.N77 2001
North, Mack O.
Commercial Chicken Meat and Egg Production. Ed. 5. Donald
D. Bell (Editor). Trade Cloth. Springer. New York, NY. 2001.
1416p. ISBN:0-7923-7200-X, ISBN13: 978-0-7923-7200-4.
Dewey:636.5. LCCN:00-045232.
Audience: **u,f.**

Wheeler, Eileen TH4930.H67 2005
Horse Facilities Handbook. Trade Cloth. MidWest Plan Service.
Ames, IA. 2005. vii, 232p. ISBN:0-89373-098-X, ISBN13:
978-0-89373-098-7. Dewey:636.1/0831. LCCN:2004-061036.
Audience: **g,u.**

White, Maurice E. SF 771
☐ Consultant: A Diagnostic Support System for Veterinary
Medicine.
http://www.vet.cornell.edu/consultant/consult.asp
Cornell University College of Veterinary Medicine.
Audience: **u,f.**

Veterinary Medicine

Boden, Edward SF609
Black's Veterinary Dictionary. Ed. 20. Trade Cloth. Rowman &
Littlefield Publishers, Inc. Lanham, MD. 2002. 608p.
ISBN:0-389-21024-2, ISBN13: 978-0-389-21024-5.
Dewey:636/.089/03.
Audience: **g,u,f.** *Choice, 2002.*

Case, Linda P. SF426.C375 2005
The Dog: Its Behavior, Nutrition and Health. Ed. 2. Trade Cloth.
Blackwell Publishing Professional. Ames, IA. 2005. 496p.
ISBN:0-8138-1254-2, ISBN13: 978-0-8138-1254-0.
Dewey:636.7. LCCN:2004-022582.
Audience: **g,l,u.**

Dunlop, Robert H. & SF615.D86 1996
Williams, David J.
Veterinary Medicine: An Illustrated History. Trade Cloth.
Elsevier - Health Sciences Division. Philadelphia, PA. 1995.
704p. ISBN:0-8016-3209-9, ISBN13: 978-0-8016-3209-9.
Dewey:636.089/09. LCCN:95-005238.
Audience: **u,f.**

Ettinger, Stephen J. &   SF991.T48 2000
  Feldman, Edward C. (Editors)
Textbook of Veterinary Internal Medicine: Diseases of the Dog and Cat. Ed. 5. Trade Cloth. Elsevier - Health Sciences Division. Philadelphia, PA. 2000. xlvi, 1996p. ISBN:0-7216-7257-4, ISBN13: 978-0-7216-7257-1. Dewey:636.7/0896. LCCN:98-034212.

                         Audience: **u,f.**

Houpt, Katherine A.   SF756.7
Domestic Animal Behavior for Veterinarians and Animal Scientists. Ed. 4. Trade Cloth. Blackwell Publishing Professional. Ames, IA. 2004. 528p. ISBN:0-8138-0334-9, ISBN13: 978-0-8138-0334-0. Dewey:636/.001/9. LCCN:2004-017616.

                         Audience: **u,f.**

Kahn, Cynthia M. (Editor)   SF754
The Merck Veterinary Manual. Ed. 9. Scott Line (Associate Editor). Trade Cloth. John Wiley & Sons, Inc. Hoboken, NJ. 2005. 2700p. ISBN:0-911910-50-6, ISBN13: 978-0-911910-50-6. Dewey:636.089. LCCN:2004-111348.

                         Audience: **g,u,f.**

Radostits, O. M., et al.   SF745 .R331 2000
Veterinary Medicine: A Textbook of the Diseases of Cattle, Sheep, Pigs, Goats and Horses. Ed. 9. Douglas C. Blood, Clive C. Gay & Kenneth W. Hinchcliff (Authors). Cloth Text. Elsevier - Health Sciences Division. Philadelphia, PA. 2000. 1880p. ISBN:0-7020-2604-2, ISBN13: 978-0-7020-2604-1. Dewey:636.089.

                         Audience: **u,f.**

Swayne, David & Fadly,   SF995.D69 2003
  Aly M.
Diseases of Poultry. Ed. 11. Y. M. Saif, H. John Barnes, John R. Glisson & Larry R. McDougald (Editors). Trade Cloth. Blackwell Publishing Professional. Ames, IA. 2003. 1260p. ISBN:0-8138-0423-X, ISBN13: 978-0-8138-0423-1. Dewey:636.5/0896. LCCN:2002-014178.

                         Audience: **u,f.**

The Animal Welfare   HV4708
  Information Center, U.S. Department of Agriculture, Agricultural Research Service, National Agricultural Library
☐ AWIC: Animal Welfare Information Center. http://www.nal.usda.gov/awic/index.html
U.S. Department of Agriculture, Agricultural Research Service, National Agricultural Library.

                         Audience: **g,l,u,f.**

White, Maurice E.   SF 771
☐ Consultant: A Diagnostic Support System for Veterinary Medicine.
http://www.vet.cornell.edu/consultant/consult.asp
Cornell University College of Veterinary Medicine.

                         Audience: **u,f.**

ASTRONOMY

The astronomy and astrophysics resources appearing in this section encompass not only standard college-level textbooks and teaching resources to support the undergraduate liberal arts curriculum, but also resources at the popular level, to whet the interest of the general reader in the excitement of discoveries made daily by telescopes observing our universe and by space missions to distant planets. A significant portion of the list is devoted to the history of astronomy and biographies of individuals who laid the foundations for our current understanding. Textbooks selected are those currently used for course reserve in many American colleges; many of the books chosen are those most frequently borrowed and cited by undergraduates. Topics range from descriptive astronomy to theoretical astrophysics, with the tools of each included. Many of the classic handbooks, atlases and catalogs traditionally in print form are now available online and websites most often used by professional astronomers and amateur enthusiasts are included. It has been said that most of the information needed by astronomers and astrophysicists nowadays is available online, but it is my hope that students will continue to browse the book collections in their college libraries and discover the treasures to be found.

—Jane Holmquis

General Astronomy

☐ Google Directory : Astronomy.
http://directory.google.com/Top/Science/Astronomy/
Audience: **g,l,u,f.**

TK5105.875.I57
☐ Librarians' Internet Index : Astronomy.
http://lii.org/pub/topic/astronomy
Audience: **g,l,u,f.**

☐ National Aeronautics and Space Administration (NASA).
http://www.nasa.gov
Audience: **g,l,u,f.**

QB495
☐ Sky & Telescope Astronomy Web Sites.
http://skyandtelescope.com/resources/internet/article_330_1.asp
Audience: **g,l.**

General Astronomy > Histories

Bartusiak, Marcia   **QB15.A75 2004**
Archives of the Universe: A Treasury of Astronomy's Historic Works of Discovery. Trade Cloth. Knopf Publishing Group. New York, NY. 2004. 720p. ISBN:0-375-42170-X, ISBN13: 978-0-375-42170-9. Dewey:520/.9. LCCN:2004-040057.
Audience: **g,l,u,f.** *Choice, 2005.*

Brashear, Ronald & Lewis,   **QB15.B67 2001**
Daniel
Star Struck: One Thousand Years of the Art and Science of Astronomy. Trade Cloth. University of Washington Press. Seattle, WA. 2001. 144p. ISBN:0-295-98096-6, ISBN13: 978-0-295-98096-6. Dewey:520/.9. LCCN:00-053975.
Audience: **g,l,u,f.** *Choice, 2001.*

Chandrasekhar, S.   **QA808.2**
Newton's Principia for the Common Reader. Trade Paper. Oxford University Press, Inc. New York, NY. 2003. 618p. ISBN:0-19-852675-X, ISBN13: 978-0-19-852675-9. Dewey:531.
Audience: **g,l,u,f.**

Evans, James   **QB16.E93 1998**
The History and Practice of Ancient Astronomy. Cloth Text. Oxford University Press, Inc. New York, NY. 1998. 496p. ISBN:0-19-509539-1, ISBN13: 978-0-19-509539-5. Dewey:520/.09. LCCN:97-016539.
Audience: **g,u,f.** *Choice, 1999.*

Ferguson, Kitty   **QB981.F346 1999**
Measuring the Universe: Our Historic Quest to Chart the horizons of Space and Time. Cloth over Boards. Walker & Company. New York, NY. 1999. 352p. ISBN:0-8027-1351-3, ISBN13: 978-0-8027-1351-3. Dewey:523.1. LCCN:99-019476.
Audience: **g,l,u,f.** *Choice, 2000.*

Ferris, Timothy   **Q125**
Coming of Age in the Milky Way. Trade Paper. HarperCollins Publishers. New York, NY. 2003. 512p. ISBN:0-06-053595-4, ISBN13: 978-0-06-053595-7. Dewey:509. LCCN:2004-273573.
Audience: **g,l,u,f.** *Choice, 1988.*

Galilei, Galileo   **QB41.G129413 2001**
Dialogue Concerning the Two Chief World Systems. Stillman Drake (Translator), Albert Einstein (Foreword by), John Heilbron (Introduction by). UK-Trade Paper. Random House Adult Trade Publishing Group. New York, NY. 2001. 640p. ISBN:0-375-75766-X, ISBN13: 978-0-375-75766-2. Dewey:520. LCCN:2001-030842.
Audience: **g,u,f.**

Gingerich, Owen   **QB15.G563 1993**
The Eye of Heaven: Ptolemy, Copernicus, Kepler. Cloth Text. Springer. New York, NY. 1997. 300p. Masters of Modern Physics Ser., Vol. 7 ISBN:0-88318-863-5, ISBN13: 978-0-88318-863-7. Dewey:520/.9. LCCN:91-026227.
Audience: **g,l,u,f.** *Choice, 1993.*

Gingerich, Owen   **QB461**
Astrophysics and Twentieth-Century Astronomy to 1950. Cambridge University Press. 1984. The General history of astronomy; vol. 4A ISBN:0-521-24256-8, ISBN13: 978-0-521-24256-1.
Audience: **g,u,f.**

Grant, Edward   **QB981.G664 1994**
Planets, Stars, and Orbs: The Medieval Cosmos, 1200-1687. Trade Cloth. Cambridge University Press. New York, NY. 1994. 842p. ISBN:0-521-43344-4, ISBN13: 978-0-521-43344-0. Dewey:523.1/0902. LCCN:93-025899.
Audience: **g,l,u,f.** *Choice, 1995.*

Hoskin, Michael   **QB15.C36 1997**
The Cambridge Illustrated History of Astronomy. Jane Holmquist (Astronomy). Cambridge University Press. 1997. ISBN:0-521-41158-0, ISBN13: 978-0-521-41158-5.
Audience: **g,l,u,f.**

Kepler, Johannes   **QB41.K4213 2003**
Kepler's Somnium: The Dream: or Posthumous Work on Lunar Astronomy. Edward Rosen (Translator). Trade Paper. Dover Publications, Inc. Mineola, NY. 2003. 288p. ISBN:0-486-43282-3, ISBN13: 978-0-486-43282-3. Dewey:523.3. LCCN:2003-050230.
Audience: **g,u,f.**

Kuhn, Thomas S.   **QB41.C815**
The Copernican Revolution: Planetary Astronomy in the Development of Western Thought. Trade Paper. Harvard University Press. Cambridge, MA. 1992. 320p. ISBN:0-674-17103-9, ISBN13: 978-0-674-17103-9. Dewey:523.2. LCCN:57-076121.
Audience: **g,u,f.** *B*

Lang, Kenneth R. &   **QB51**
Gingerich, Owen (Editors)
Source Book in Astronomy and Astrophysics, 1900-1975. Trade Cloth. Harvard University Press. Cambridge, MA. 1979. 942p. Source Books in the History of the Sciences ISBN:0-674-82200-5, ISBN13: 978-0-674-82200-9. Dewey:520. LCCN:78-009463.
Audience: **u,f.** *B*

Lankford, John &   **QB15.H624 1997**
Rothenberg, Marc (Editors)
History of Astronomy: An Encyclopedia. Trade Cloth. Garland Publishing, Inc. New York, NY. 1997. 650p. Encyclopedias in the History of Science Ser., Vol. 1 ISBN:0-8153-0322-X, ISBN13: 978-0-8153-0322-0. Dewey:520/.3. LCCN:96-028558.
Audience: **g,l,u,f.** *Choice, 1997.*

Linton, C. M.   **QB47.L56 2004**
From Eudoxus to Einstein: A History of Mathematical
Astronomy. Trade Cloth. Cambridge University Press. New
York, NY. 2004. 528p. ISBN:0-521-82750-7, ISBN13:
978-0-521-82750-8. Dewey:520.151. LCCN:2003-067569.
Audience: **g,u,f.** *Choice, 2005.*

Longair, Malcolm S.   **QB460.72.H69**
The Cosmic Century: A History of Astrophysics and Cosmology.
Cloth Text. Cambridge University Press. New York, NY. 2006.
565p. ISBN:0-521-47436-1, ISBN13: 978-0-521-47436-8.
Dewey:523.010904.

Audience: **g,l,u,f.**

North, John   **QB981**
Norton History of Astronomy and Cosmology. Trade Paper. W.
W. Norton & Company, Inc. New York, NY. 1995.
ISBN:0-393-31193-7, ISBN13: 978-0-393-31193-8.
Dewey:523.1.

Audience: **g,l,u,f.**

Smith, Robert W.   **QB500.268**
The Space Telescope: A Study of NASA, Science, Technology
and Politics. Trade Paper. Cambridge University Press. New
York, NY. 1993. 528p. ISBN:0-521-45768-8, ISBN13:
978-0-521-45768-2. Dewey:522/.29.
Audience: **g,l,u,f.** *Choice, 1990.*

Whitfield, Peter   **BF1671.W55 2001**
Astrology: A History. Trade Cloth. Harry N. Abrams, Inc. New
York, NY. 2001. 208p. ISBN:0-8109-4235-6, ISBN13:
978-0-8109-4235-6. Dewey:133.5/09. LCCN:2001-022135.
Audience: **g,l.** *Choice, 2002.*

General Astronomy > Biographies

Biagioli, Mario   **Q180.55.M67B53 2006**
Galileo's Instruments of Credit: Telescopes, Images, Secrecy.
Trade Cloth. University of Chicago Press. Chicago, IL. 2006.
316p. ISBN:0-226-04561-7, ISBN13: 978-0-226-04561-0.
Dewey:520/.92 B. LCCN:2005-014562.
Audience: **u,f.**

DeVorkin, David H.   **QB36.R78D49 2000**
Henry Norris Russell: Dean of American Aastronomers.
Princeton University Press. 2000. ISBN:0-691-04918-1,
ISBN13: 978-0-691-04918-2.
Audience: **g,u,f.**

Ferguson, Kitty   **QB36.B8F47 2002**
Tycho and Kepler: The Unlikely Partnership That Forever
Changed Our Understanding of the Heavens. Cloth over Boards.
Walker & Company. New York, NY. 2002. 416p.
ISBN:0-8027-1390-4, ISBN13: 978-0-8027-1390-2.
Dewey:520/.92/2 B. LCCN:2002-027445.
Audience: **g,l,u.** *Choice, 2003.*

Galilei, Galileo & Drake,   **QB41.G123 1990**
  Stillman
Discoveries and Opinions of Galileo. Trade Paper. Doubleday
Publishing. New York, NY. 1957. 320p. ISBN:0-385-09239-3,
ISBN13: 978-0-385-09239-5. Dewey:520. LCCN:57-006305.
Audience: **g,u,f.**

Glass, Ian   **QB36**
Revolutionaries of the Cosmos: The Astro-Physicists. Trade
Cloth. Oxford University Press, Inc. New York, NY. 2006. 336p.

ISBN:0-19-857099-6, ISBN13: 978-0-19-857099-8.
Dewey:523.010922. LCCN:2006-295615.
Audience: **g,l,u,f.** *Choice, 2006.*

Johnson, George   **QB807.J64 2005**
Miss Leavitt's Stars: The Untold Story of the Forgotten Woman
Who Discovered How to Measure the Universe. Trade Cloth. W.
W. Norton & Company, Inc. New York, NY. 2005. 256p. Great
Discoveries Ser. ISBN:0-393-05128-5, ISBN13:
978-0-393-05128-5. Dewey:522/.09/04. LCCN:2005-002823.
Audience: **g,l,u.**

Kolb, Rocky   **QB981.K689 1996**
Blind Watchers of the Sky: The People and Ideas That Shaped
Our View of the Universe. Cloth Text. Perseus Books Group.
New York, NY. 1996. 338p. ISBN:0-201-48992-9, ISBN13:
978-0-201-48992-7. Dewey:523.1. LCCN:95-041438.
Audience: **g,l.** *Choice, 1996.*

Miller, Arthur I.   **QB35.M55 2005**
Empire of the Stars: Obsession, Friendship, and Betrayal in the
Quest for Black Holes. Trade Cloth. Houghton Mifflin Company
Trade & Reference Division. Boston, MA. 2005. 320p.
ISBN:0-618-34151-X, ISBN13: 978-0-618-34151-1.
Dewey:520/.92/2 B. LCCN:2004-060909.
Audience: **g,l,u,f.** *Choice, 2005.*

Mitton, Simon   **QB36.H75M58 2005**
Conflict in the Cosmos: Fred Hoyle's Life in Science. Trade
Cloth. National Academies Press. Washington, DC. 2005. 320p.
ISBN:0-309-09313-9, ISBN13: 978-0-309-09313-2.
Dewey:520/.92 B. LCCN:2004-030638.
Audience: **g,l,u,f.** *Choice, 2005.*

Porter, Roy & Ogilvie,   **Q141.B528 2000**
  Marilyn B. (Editors)
The Biographical Dictionary of Scientists, Set. Ed. 3. Cloth
Text. Oxford University Press, Inc. New York, NY. 2000. 1214p.
ISBN:0-19-521663-6, ISBN13: 978-0-19-521663-9.
Dewey:509.2/2 B. LCCN:00-036752.
Audience: **g,l,u,f.** *Choice, 2001, 1995.*

Trimble, Virginia &   **QB35**
  Williams, Thomas
The Biographical Encyclopedia of Astronomers. Katherine
Bracher & Marvin Bolt (Editors), Thomas Hockey
(Editor-In-Chief), Richard Jarrell, Jordan Marché, Joanne
Palmeri & Jamil Rajep (Editorial Board Members). Trade Cloth.
Springer. New York, NY. 2006. 2000p. ISBN:0-387-31022-3,
ISBN13: 978-0-387-31022-0. Dewey:520.922.
Audience: **g,l,u,f.**

General Astronomy > Dictionaries and Encyclopedias

Darling, David   **QB14.D37 2003**
The Universal Book of Astronomy: From the Andromeda
Galaxy to the Zone of Avoidance. Trade Cloth. John Wiley &
Sons, Inc. Hoboken, NJ. 2003. 576p. ISBN:0-471-26569-1,
ISBN13: 978-0-471-26569-6. Dewey:520/.3.
LCCN:2003-013941.
Audience: **g,l,u.** *Choice, 2004.*

Illingworth, Valerie   **QB14.F3 2006**
The Facts on File Dictionary of Astronomy. Ed. 5. Trade Cloth.
Facts On File, Inc.. New York, NY. 2006. 560p.

ISBN:0-8160-5998-5, ISBN13: 978-0-8160-5998-0.
Dewey:520.3. LCCN:2006-040860.
Audience: **g,l,u,f.** ℞ *Choice, 2001, 1995, 1986.*

Kelley, David H. & Milone,   QB16.K45 2002
E. F.
Exploring Ancient Skies: An Encyclopedic of
Archaeoastronomy. A. F. Aveni (Foreword by). Trade Cloth.
Springer. New York, NY. 2004. 384 schw.-w. u. 8 farb. Abb., 95
schw.-w. Tab., 253 schw.-w. u. 8 farb. Fotos, 131 schw.-w.
Zeichn., Four-page color insert XXVI, 614p.
ISBN:0-387-95310-8, ISBN13: 978-0-387-95310-6.
Dewey:520/.93. LCCN:2001-032842.
Audience: **u,f.** *Choice, 2005.*

Matzner, Richard A., ed.   QB14.D53 2001
Dictionary of Geophysics, Astrophysics, and Astronomy. CRC
Press. 2001. ISBN:0-8493-2891-8, ISBN13: 978-0-8493-2891-6.
Audience: **l,u,f.**

Murdin, Paul (Editor)   QB14.E525 2001
Encyclopedia of Astronomy and Astrophysics, Set. Trade Cloth.
Nature Publishing Group. New York, NY. 2000. 3760p.
ISBN:1-56159-268-4, ISBN13: 978-1-56159-268-5.
Dewey:520.3. LCCN:2002-319017.
Audience: **g,l,u,f.** *Choice, 2001.*

Murdin, Paul & Penston,   QB14.F48 2004
Margaret (Editors)
The Firefly Encyclopedia of Astronomy. Trade Cloth. Firefly
Books, Ltd. Tonawanda, NY. 2004. 472p. ISBN:1-55297-797-8,
ISBN13: 978-1-55297-797-2. Dewey:520/.3.
LCCN:2005-357162.
Audience: **g,l,u,f.** *Choice, 2005.*

Weisstein, Eric   Q121
▢ Eric Weisstein's World of Astronomy.
http://scienceworld.wolfram.com/astronomy/
Audience: **g,l,u,f.**

General Astronomy > Handbooks, Tables and Formulas

                                        QB65
Astronomical Almanac for the Year 2006 and Its Companion,
the Astronomical Almanac Online: Data for Astronomy, Space
Sciences, Geodesy, Surveying, Navigation and Other
Applications. Trade Cloth. United States Government Printing
Office. Washington, DC. 2004. 578p. ISBN:0-11-887333-4,
ISBN13: 978-0-11-887333-8. Dewey:522.
Audience: **g,l,u,f.**

Cox, A.   QB461
Allen's Astrophysical Quantities. Ed. 4. Mixed Media. Springer.
New York, NY. 2001. XVIII, 719p. ISBN:0-387-95189-X,
ISBN13: 978-0-387-95189-8. Dewey:523.01/021.
Audience: **g,l,u,f.**

Gradshteyn, I. S.   QA55.G6613 2000
Table of Integrals, Series, and Products. Ed. 6. Alan Jeffrey &
Daniel Zwillinger (Editors). Cloth Text. Elsevier Science &
Technology Books. Saint Louis, MO. 2000. 1163p.
ISBN:0-12-294757-6, ISBN13: 978-0-12-294757-5.
Dewey:515/.0212. LCCN:00-104373.
Audience: **u,f.**

Jerrard, H G; McNeill, D B
A Dictionary of Scientific Units Including Dimensionless
Numbers and Scales. Ed. 6. Chapman & Hall. 1992.
ISBN:0-412-46720-8, ISBN13: 978-0-412-46720-2.
Audience: **g,l,u,f.**

Lang, Kenneth R.   QB461
Astrophysical Formulae: Volume I: Radiation, Gas Processes
and High Energy AstrophysicsVolume II: Space, Time, Matter
and Cosmology. Ed. 3. Trade Paper. Springer. New York, NY.
2006. XL, 1054p. ISBN:3-540-29692-1, ISBN13:
978-3-540-29692-8. Dewey:523.010212.
Audience: **u,f.**

Mobberley, Martin   QB63.M595 2004
The New Amateur Astronomer. Trade Paper. Springer. New
York, NY. 2004. X, 229p. Patrick Moore's Practical Astronomy
Ser. ISBN:1-85233-663-3, ISBN13: 978-1-85233-663-9.
Dewey:520. LCCN:2004-041728.
Audience: **g,l,u.** *Choice, 2005.*

Pennington, H. C.   QB64.P46 1997
The Year-Round Messier Marathon Field Guide: With Complete
Maps, Charts and Tips to Guide You to Enjoying the Most
Famous List of Deep-Sky Objects. Trade Cloth. Willmann-Bell,
Inc. Richmond, VA. 1998. x, 196 p. :p. ISBN:0-943396-54-9,
ISBN13: 978-0-943396-54-5. Dewey:523.8. LCCN:97-018168.
Audience: **g,l,u,f.** *Choice, 1998.*

U.S. Naval Observatory   QB82
▢ Astronomical Applications Department. U.S. Naval
Observatory.
http://aa.usno.navy.mil/
Audience: **g,l,u,f.**

General Astronomy > Atlases and Catalogs

                                        QB61
▢ NASA/IPAC Extragalactic Database (NED).
http://nedwww.ipac.caltech.edu/
Audience: **g,l,u,f.**

                                        QB601
▢ The Planetary Data System (PDS).
http://pds.jpl.nasa.gov/
Audience: **g,l,u,f.**

                                        QB51.3.E43
▢ The SIMBAD Astronomical Database.
http://cdsweb.u-strasbg.fr/Simbad.html
Audience: **l,u,f.**

                                        QB47
▢ Sloan Digital Sky Survey.
http://www.sdss.org
Audience: **g,l,u,f.**

Greeley, Ronald & Batson,   G1000 .G68 2002
Raymond
The Compact NASA Atlas of the Solar System. Trade Cloth.
Cambridge University Press. New York, NY. 2001. 406p.
ISBN:0-521-80633-X, ISBN13: 978-0-521-80633-6.
Dewey:523.2.
Audience: **g,l,u,f.**

Hoffleit, Dorrit & Jaschek, Carlos   QB843.B75
The Bright Star Catalogue. Ed. 4. Trade Paper. Yale University, Observatory. New Haven, CT. 1982. xv, 472p. ISBN:0-914753-00-2, ISBN13: 978-0-914753-00-1. Dewey:523.89.

Audience: **g,l,u,f.**

Hoffleit, Dorrit, et al.   QB843.B75 B74 SUPPL.
A Supplement to the Bright Star Catalogue. Michael Saladyga & Peter Wlasuk (Authors). Trade Paper. Yale University, Observatory. New Haven, CT. 1984. vi, 135p. ISBN:0-914753-01-0, ISBN13: 978-0-914753-01-8. Dewey:523.8/908. LCCN:83-019834.

Audience: **g,l,u,f.**

Ridpath, Ian (Editor)   QB64.R43 2004
Norton's Star Atlas and Reference Handbook. Ed. 20. Trade Cloth. Penguin Group (USA) Inc. New York, NY. 2003. 208p. ISBN:0-13-145164-2, ISBN13: 978-0-13-145164-3. Dewey:523. LCCN:2003-060520.

Audience: **g,l,u,f.**

Rukl, Antonin   G1000.3.R813 2004
Atlas of the Moon. Gary Seronik (Editor). Saddle Stitched, Cloth over Boards, Dust Jacket. Sky Publishing. Cambridge, MA. 2004. 224p. ISBN:1-931559-07-4, ISBN13: 978-1-931559-07-2. Dewey:523.30223. LCCN:2004-045003.

Audience: **g,l,u.**

Sandage, Allan & Bedke, John   QB857.S256 1994
The Carnegie Atlas of Galaxies. Trade Cloth, Box or Slipcased. Carnegie Institution of Washington. Washington, DC. 1996. 768p. ISBN:0-87279-667-1, ISBN13: 978-0-87279-667-6. Dewey:523.1/12/0216. LCCN:93-071702.

Audience: **g,l,u,f.** *Choice, 1995.*

Tully, R. Brent & Fisher, J. Richard   QB857 .T85 1987
Atlas of Nearby Galaxies. Trade Cloth. Cambridge University Press. New York, NY. 1987. 29p. ISBN:0-521-30136-X, ISBN13: 978-0-521-30136-7. Dewey:519.2/87. LCCN:87-011689.

Audience: **g,l,u,f.** *Choice, 1988.*

General Astronomy > Abstracts and Indexes

                                                 Q113
☐ Astrophysics E-Print Archive.
http://www.arxiv.org/archive/astro-ph

Audience: **u,f.**

                                                 QB43.2
☐ The NASA Astrophysics Data System (ADS).
http://adswww.harvard.edu/

Audience: **g,l,u,f.**

General Astronomy > Yearbooks

                                                 QB1 .A2884
Annual Review of Astronomy and Astrophysics. Trade Cloth. Annual Reviews, Inc. Palo Alto, CA. 2006. ISBN:0-8243-0944-8, ISBN13: 978-0-8243-0944-2. Dewey:520.

Audience: **g,l,u,f.**

Astronomy Texts and Textbooks > Mathematical Methods (QA)

Babu, Gutti Jogesh, 1949- .   QB149 .B328 1996
Astrostatistics. Chapman & Hall. 1996. ISBN:0-412-98391-5, ISBN13: 978-0-412-98391-7.

Audience: **u,f.**

Bevington, Philip R. & Robinson, D. Keith   QA278.B48 2002
Data Reduction and Error Analysis for the Physical Sciences. Ed. 3. Paper Text. McGraw-Hill Higher Education. Burr Ridge, IL. 2002. 336p. ISBN:0-07-247227-8, ISBN13: 978-0-07-247227-1. Dewey:511/.43. LCCN:2002-070896.

Audience: **g,l,u,f.**

Bracewell, Ronald Newbold   QA403.5.B7 2000
The Fourier Transform and Its Applications. Ed. 3. Cloth Text. McGraw-Hill Higher Education. Burr Ridge, IL. 1999. 624p. McGraw-Hill Series in Electrical and Computer Engineering ISBN:0-07-303938-1, ISBN13: 978-0-07-303938-1. Dewey:515/.723. LCCN:99-021139.

Audience: **u,f.**

Goldstein, Herbert, et al.   QA805 .G6 2002
Classical Mechanics. Ed. 3. Charles P. Poole & John L. Safko (Authors). Cloth Text. Addison-Wesley Longman, Inc. Boston, MA. 2001. 680p. ISBN:0-201-65702-3, ISBN13: 978-0-201-65702-9. Dewey:531.

Audience: **u,f.** *B*

Kendall, Maurice   QA279.5
Kendall's Advanced Theory of Statistics, Set. Trade Cloth. Hodder Education. London, 2005. A Hodder Arnold Publication ISBN:0-340-81493-4, ISBN13: 978-0-340-81493-2. Dewey:519.5/42.

Audience: **u,f.**

Lupton, Robert   QA276.L83 1993
Statistics in Theory and Practice. Trade Cloth. Princeton University Press. Princeton, NJ. 1993. 198p. ISBN:0-691-07429-1, ISBN13: 978-0-691-07429-0. Dewey:519.5. LCCN:92-036396.

Audience: **u,f.**

Meeus, Jean H.   QB51.3.E43M42 1998
Astronomical Algorithms. Trade Cloth. Willmann-Bell, Inc. Richmond, VA. 1998. ISBN:0-943396-61-1, ISBN13: 978-0-943396-61-3. Dewey:520. LCCN:98-055091.

Audience: **g,l,u,f.** *Choice, 1992.*

Taylor, John R.   QC39.T4 1997
An Introduction to Error Analysis: The Study of Uncertainties in Physical Measurements. Ed. 2. Trade Cloth. University Science Books. Sausalito, CA. 1997. 448p. ISBN:0-935702-42-3, ISBN13: 978-0-935702-42-2. Dewey:500. LCCN:96-000953.

Audience: **l,u.** *Choice, 1997.*

Astronomy Texts and Textbooks > General and Introductory

Bennett, Jeffrey O., et al.   QB43.3.C68 2007
The Cosmic Perspective. Ed. 4. Megan Donahue, Nicholas Schneider & Mark Voit (Authors). Book, Other.

Benjamin-Cummings Publishing Company. San Francisco, CA. 2005. 736p. ISBN:0-8053-9269-6, ISBN13: 978-0-8053-9269-2. Dewey:520. LCCN:2005-054811.

Audience: **g,l,u.**

Dinwiddie, Robert, et al. QB983.U554 2005
Universe. Robert Eales, David Hughes, Ian Nicholson, Ian Ridpath, Giles Sparrow, Pam Spence, Carole Stott & Kevin Tildsley (Authors), Martin Rees (Editor). Trade Cloth. Dorling Kindersley Publishing, Inc. New York, NY. 2005. 512p. ISBN:0-7566-1364-7, ISBN13: 978-0-7566-1364-8. Dewey:523.1. LCCN:2005-004794.

Audience: **g,l,u.**

Freedman, Roger A. QB43.3.F74 2004
Universe. Ed. 7. Paper Text. W. H. Freeman & Company. New York, NY. 2004. 800p. ISBN:0-7167-9884-0, ISBN13: 978-0-7167-9884-2. Dewey:523.11. LCCN:2004-103077.

Audience: **g,l,u.**

Karttunen, Hannu (Editor), QB43.2.T2613 2003
et al.
Fundamental Astronomy. Ed. 4. Karl Johan Donner, Heikki Oja, Markku Poutanen & Pekka Kröger (Editors). Trade Cloth. Springer. New York, NY. 2003. XI, 468p. ISBN:3-540-00179-4, ISBN13: 978-3-540-00179-9. Dewey:520. LCCN:2002-042569.

Audience: **g,l.**

Petersen, Carolyn Collins & QB68.P46 2003
Brandt, John C.
Visions of the Cosmos. Trade Cloth. Cambridge University Press. New York, NY. 2003. 226p. ISBN:0-521-81898-2, ISBN13: 978-0-521-81898-8. Dewey:520/.22/2. LCCN:2003-043043.

Audience: **g,l.**

Unsöld, Albrecht & QB43.3.U5713 2001
Baschek, Bodo
The New Cosmos: An Introduction to Astronomy and Astrophysics. Ed. 5. W. D. Brewer (Translator). Trade Cloth. Springer. New York, NY. 2001. XIV, 557p. ISBN:3-540-67877-8, ISBN13: 978-3-540-67877-9. Dewey:520. LCCN:2001-034462.

Audience: **g,l.**

Astronomy Texts and Textbooks > Astronomical Instrumentation

Berry, Richard & Burnell, QB51.3.I45B46 2000
James
The Handbook of Astronomical Image Processing. Trade Cloth. Willmann-Bell, Inc. Richmond, VA. 2000. 624p. ISBN:0-943396-67-0, ISBN13: 978-0-943396-67-5. Dewey:522/.63/028. LCCN:00-057193.

Audience: **g,l,u,f.**

Bradt, Hale QB45.2.B73 2003
Astronomy Methods: A Physical Approach to Astronomical Observations. Cloth Text. Cambridge University Press. New York, NY. 2003. 458p. ISBN:0-521-36440-X, ISBN13: 978-0-521-36440-9. Dewey:520. LCCN:2002-041703.
Audience: **u,f.** *Choice, 2004.*

Brunier, Serge & Lagrange, Q11
Anne-Marie
Great Observatories of the World. Catherine J. Cesarsky

(Foreword by). Trade Cloth. Firefly Books, Ltd. Tonawanda, NY. 2005. 200 full color photographs and illustrations, map, list of observatories, appendices, bibliography, index 240p. ISBN:1-55407-055-4, ISBN13: 978-1-55407-055-8. Dewey:522/.1.

Audience: **g,l,u,f.**

Emerson, D. QB465
Interpreting Astronomical Spectra. Trade Paper. John Wiley & Sons, Inc. Hoboken, NJ. 1999. 472p. ISBN:0-471-97679-2, ISBN13: 978-0-471-97679-0. Dewey:522.6/7.

Audience: **u,f.**

Hearnshaw, J. B. QB815 .H43 1996
The Measurement of Starlight: Two Centuries of Astronomical Photometry. Trade Cloth. Cambridge University Press. New York, NY. 1996. 525p. ISBN:0-521-40393-6, ISBN13: 978-0-521-40393-1. Dewey:522.6/2. LCCN:95-034046.
Audience: **g,l,u,f.** *Choice, 1997.*

Kitchin, C. R. QB461.K57 2003
Astrophysical Techniques. Ed. 2. Perfect. Institute of Physics Publishing. Philadelphia, PA. 2003. 510p. ISBN:0-7503-0946-6, ISBN13: 978-0-7503-0946-2. Dewey:522. LCCN:2004-266402.
Audience: **g,l,u,f.** *Choice, 1992.*

Lena, Pierre & Lebrun, QB461.L4613 1998
Francoise
Observational Astrophysics. Ed. 2. Trade Cloth. Springer. New York, NY. 1998. XV, 512p. Astronomy and Astrophysics Library ISBN:3-540-63482-7, ISBN13: 978-3-540-63482-9. Dewey:522. LCCN:97-047092.

Audience: **u,f.**

McCray, W. Patrick QB90.M33 2003
Giant Telescopes: Astronomical Ambition and the Promise of Technology. Trade Cloth. Harvard University Press. Cambridge, MA. 2004. 376p. ISBN:0-674-01147-3, ISBN13: 978-0-674-01147-2. Dewey:522/.29. LCCN:2003-059141.
Audience: **g,l,u,f.** *Choice, 2004.*

Mobberly, Martin QB86.M62 1999
Astronomical Equipment for Amateurs. Patrick Moore (Editor). Trade Paper. Springer. New York, NY. 1998. 266p. Practical Astronomy Ser. ISBN:1-85233-019-8, ISBN13: 978-1-85233-019-4. Dewey:522/.2. LCCN:98-007025.

Audience: **g,l.**

Reeves, Robert QB121.R446 2005
Introduction to Digital Astrophotography: Imaging the Universe with a Digital Camera. Trade Cloth. Willmann-Bell, Inc. Richmond, VA. 2005. xviii, 412p. ISBN:0-943396-83-2, ISBN13: 978-0-943396-83-5. Dewey:522/.63. LCCN:2004-063706.

Audience: **g,l,u,f.**

Reeves, Robert QB121
Wide-Field Astrophotography: Exposing the Universe, Starting with a Common Camera. Cloth Text. Willmann-Bell, Inc. Richmond, VA. 2000. ISBN:0-943396-64-6, ISBN13: 978-0-943396-64-4. Dewey:522/.63.

Audience: **g,l,u,f.**

Rieke, George QC373.O59R54 2002
Detection of Light: From the Ultraviolet to the Submillimeter. Ed. 2. Cloth Text. Cambridge University Press. New York, NY.

2002. 376p. ISBN:0-521-81636-X, ISBN13: 978-0-521-81636-6. Dewey:621.36/2. LCCN:2002-023375.

Audience: **u,f.** *Choice, 2004.*

Scagell, Robin   **QB63.S365 2005**
Stargazing with a Telescope. Trade Paper. Firefly Books, Ltd. Tonawanda, NY. 2005. 192p. ISBN:1-55407-027-9, ISBN13: 978-1-55407-027-5. Dewey:522/.2. LCCN:2005-280331.

Audience: **g,l,u.**

Schroeder, Daniel J.   **QB86.S35 2000**
Astronomical Optics. Ed. 2. Trade Cloth. Elsevier Science & Technology Books. Saint Louis, MO. 1999. 478p. ISBN:0-12-629810-6, ISBN13: 978-0-12-629810-9. Dewey:522.2. LCCN:99-065098.

Audience: **u,f.** *Choice, 1988.*

Stephenson, Bruce, et al.   **QB86 .S74 2000**
The Universe Unveiled: Instruments and Images Through History. Marvin Bolt & Anna Felicity Friedman (Authors). Trade Cloth. Cambridge University Press. New York, NY. 2000. 152p. ISBN:0-521-79143-X, ISBN13: 978-0-521-79143-4. Dewey:522/.2. LCCN:00-059883.

Audience: **g,l,u,f.**

Watson, Fred   **QB88**
Stargazer: The Life and Times of the Telescope. Trade Cloth. Da Capo Press, Inc. Cambridge, MA. 2005. 360p. ISBN:0-306-81432-3, ISBN13: 978-0-306-81432-7. Dewey:522.2/09. LCCN:2006-296717.

Audience: **g,l,u,f.** *Choice, 2005.*

Astronomy Texts and Textbooks > Practical and Spherical Astronomy

Seidelmann, P. Kenneth   **QB8**
  (Editor)
Explanatory Supplement to the Astronomical Almanac. Paper Text. University Science Books. Sausalito, CA. 2005. 752p. ISBN:1-891389-45-9, ISBN13: 978-1-891389-45-0. Dewey:528. LCCN:2005-930073.

Audience: **u,f.** *Choice, 1993.*

Astronomy Texts and Textbooks > Theoretical Astronomy and Celestial Mechanics

Danby, J. M. A.   **QB351.D3 1988**
Fundamentals of Celestial Mechanics. Ed. 2. Trade Cloth. Willmann-Bell, Inc. Richmond, VA. 1988. 467p. ISBN:0-943396-20-4, ISBN13: 978-0-943396-20-0. Dewey:521/.1. LCCN:88-020566.

Audience: **g,l,u,f.**

Diacu, Florin & Holmes,   **QB362.M3D53 1996**
  Philip
Celestial Encounters: The Origins of Chaos and Stability. Trade Cloth. Princeton University Press. Princeton, NJ. 1996. 280p. Princeton Science Library ISBN:0-691-02743-9, ISBN13: 978-0-691-02743-2. Dewey:521. LCCN:96-000108.

Audience: **u.** *Choice, 1997.*

Grossman, Nathaniel   **QB351.G69 1996**
The Sheer Joy of Celestial Mechanics. Trade Cloth. Springer. New York, NY. 1996. 160p. ISBN:0-8176-3832-6, ISBN13: 978-0-8176-3832-0. Dewey:521. LCCN:95-034467.

Audience: **u.** *Choice, 1996.*

Poincare, Henri   **QB351.P7513 1993**
New Methods of Celestial Mechanics, Set. Daniel Goroff (Introduction by). Cloth Text. Springer. New York, NY. 1992. 1200p. History of Modern Physics and Astronomy Ser., Vol. 13 ISBN:1-56396-117-2, ISBN13: 978-1-56396-117-5. Dewey:521. LCCN:89-014884.

Audience: **u,f.** *Choice, 1993.*

Szebehely, Victor G. &   **QB355.S974 1998**
  Mark, Hans
Adventures in Celestial Mechanics. Ed. 2. Trade Cloth. John Wiley & Sons, Inc. Hoboken, NJ. 1998. 320p. ISBN:0-471-13317-5, ISBN13: 978-0-471-13317-9. Dewey:521/.3. LCCN:97-012770.

Audience: **g,l,u.** *Choice, 1998.*

Astronomy Texts and Textbooks > Astrophysics

Carroll, Bradley W. &   **QB461.C35 1996**
  Ostlie, Dale A.
An Introduction to Modern Astrophysics. Julie Berisford (Editor). Cloth Text. Addison-Wesley Longman, Inc. Boston, MA. 1995. 1326p. ISBN:0-201-54730-9, ISBN13: 978-0-201-54730-6. Dewey:523.01. LCCN:95-045144.

Audience: **u,f.**

Frank, Juhan, et al.   **QB466.A25 F73 2001**
Accretion Power in Astrophysics. Ed. 3. Andrew King & Derek J. Raine (Authors). Trade Cloth. Cambridge University Press. New York, NY. 2002. 398p. ISBN:0-521-62053-8, ISBN13: 978-0-521-62053-6. Dewey:523.841. LCCN:2001-037846.

Audience: **u,f.**

Hartquist, T. W., et al.   **QB529.H37 2003**
Blowing Bubbles in the Cosmos: Astronomical Winds, Jets, and Explosions. J. E. Dyson, D. P. Ruffle, John E. Dyson & Deborah P. Ruffle (Authors). Trade Cloth. Oxford University Press, Inc. New York, NY. 2004. 180p. ISBN:0-19-513054-5, ISBN13: 978-0-19-513054-6. Dewey:523.01. LCCN:2003-051706.

Audience: **g,l,u,f.** *Choice, 2004.*

Harwit, Martin D.   **QB461.H37 1998**
Astrophysical Concepts. Ed. 3. Trade Cloth. Springer. New York, NY. 2000. XIV, 651p. Astronomy and Astrophysics Library ISBN:0-387-94943-7, ISBN13: 978-0-387-94943-7. Dewey:523.01. LCCN:97-031962.

Audience: **u,f.**

Longair, Malcolm S.   **QB464.L66 1994**
High Energy Astrophysics: Stars, the Galaxy and the Interstellar Medium. Ed. 2. Trade Paper. Cambridge University Press. New York, NY. 1994. 411p. ISBN:0-521-43584-6, ISBN13: 978-0-521-43584-0. Dewey:523.01976.

Audience: **u,f.**

Longair, Malcolm S.   **QB464 .L66 1992**
High Energy Astrophysics: Particles, Photons and Their Detection, Vol. 1. Ed. 2. Trade Cloth. Cambridge University

Press. New York, NY. 1992. 436p. ISBN:0-521-38374-9, ISBN13: 978-0-521-38374-5. Dewey:523.01976. LCCN:92-191337.

Audience: **u,f.**

Osterbrock, Donald E. &   QB855.55.O88 2005
  Ferland, Gary J.
Astrophysics of Gaseous Nebulae and Active Galactic Nuclei. Ed. 2. Trade Cloth. University Science Books. Sausalito, CA. 2005. 480p. ISBN:1-891389-34-3, ISBN13: 978-1-891389-34-4. Dewey:523.1/125. LCCN:2005-042206.

Audience: **u,f.** *Choice, 1989.*

Rybicki, George B. &   QB991.C64
  Lightman, Alan P.
Radiative Processes in Astrophysics. Ed. 1. Trade Paper. John Wiley & Sons, Inc. Hoboken, NJ. 1985. 400p. ISBN:0-471-82759-2, ISBN13: 978-0-471-82759-7. Dewey:523.01/9/2.

Audience: **g,l,u,f.**

Schneider, P., et al.   QB857.5.G7S36 1999
Gravitational Lenses. J. Ehlers & E. E. Falco (Authors). Trade Paper. Springer. New York, NY. 1999. XIV, 560p. Astronomy and Astrophysics Library ISBN:3-540-66506-4, ISBN13: 978-3-540-66506-9. Dewey:522/.6. LCCN:99-049728.

Audience: **u,f.**

Shu, Frank H.   QB461 .S448 1991
The Physics of Astrophysics: Gas Dynamics. Trade Cloth. University Science Books. Sausalito, CA. 1992. 280p. ISBN:0-935702-65-2, ISBN13: 978-0-935702-65-1. Dewey:523.01. LCCN:91-065168.

Audience: **u.**

Shu, Frank H.   QB461.S448 1991
The Physics of Astrophysics: Radiation Processes. Trade Cloth. University Science Books. Sausalito, CA. 1991. 310p. ISBN:0-935702-64-4, ISBN13: 978-0-935702-64-4. Dewey:523.01. LCCN:91-065168.

Audience: **u.** *Choice, 1992.*

Wheeler, J. Craig   QB843.S95
Cosmic Catastrophes: Supernovae, Gamma-ray Bursts, and Adventures in Hyperspace. Ed. 2. Cloth Text. Cambridge University Press. New York, NY. 2007. 360p. ISBN:0-521-85714-7, ISBN13: 978-0-521-85714-7. Dewey:523.8/4465.

Audience: **g,l.**

Astronomy Texts and Textbooks > Non-optical Methods of Astronomy

Burke, Bernard F. &   QB476.5 .B87 2002
  Graham-Smith, Francis
An Introduction to Radio Astronomy. Ed. 2. Trade Cloth. Cambridge University Press. New York, NY. 2002. 406p. ISBN:0-521-80889-8, ISBN13: 978-0-521-80889-7. Dewey:522.6/82. LCCN:96-013176.

Audience: **u,f.** *Choice, 1997.*

Fabian, Andrew   QB472.F76 2003
  (Editor), et al.
Frontiers of X-Ray Astronomy. Kenneth Pounds & Roger

Blandford (Editors). Trade Cloth. Cambridge University Press. New York, NY. 2004. 256p. ISBN:0-521-82759-0, ISBN13: 978-0-521-82759-1. Dewey:522/.6863. LCCN:2003-053213.

Audience: **u,f.**

Glass, I. S.   QB47 .G53 1999
Handbook of Infrared Astronomy. Richard Ellis, John Huchra, Steven Kahn, George Rieke & Peter B. Stetson (Contribution by). Trade Cloth. Cambridge University Press. New York, NY. 1999. 196p. Cambridge Observing Handbooks for Research Astronomers, No. 1 ISBN:0-521-63311-7, ISBN13: 978-0-521-63311-6. Dewey:522/.683. LCCN:98-047980.

Audience: **u,f.**

Rohlfs, K. & Wilson, T. L.   QB476.5
Tools of Radio Astronomy. Ed. 4. Trade Cloth. Springer. New York, NY. 2006. XVI, 461p. Astronomy and Astrophysics Library ISBN:3-540-40387-6, ISBN13: 978-3-540-40387-6. Dewey:522/.682. LCCN:2004-270196.

Audience: **u,f.** ℬ *Choice, 1997, 1987.*

Schilling, Govert   N/A
Flash!: The Hunt for the Biggest Explosions in the Universe. Naomi Greenberg-Slovin (Translator). Trade Cloth. Cambridge University Press. New York, NY. 2002. 304p. ISBN:0-521-80053-6, ISBN13: 978-0-521-80053-2. Dewey:522/.6862. LCCN:2002-283188.

Audience: **g,l,u,f.** *Choice, 2003, 2002.*

Schlegel, Eric M.   QB472.S35 2002
The Restless Universe: Understanding X-Ray Astronomy in the Age of Chandra and Newton. Trade Cloth. Oxford University Press, Inc. New York, NY. 2002. 228p. ISBN:0-19-514847-9, ISBN13: 978-0-19-514847-3. Dewey:522/.6863. LCCN:2002-072755.

Audience: **g,l.** *Choice, 2003.*

Schönfelder, Volker   QB471.U55 2001
The Universe in Gamma Rays. Trade Cloth. Springer. New York, NY. 2001. XIV, 407p. Astronomy and Astrophysics Library ISBN:3-540-67874-3, ISBN13: 978-3-540-67874-8. Dewey:522/.6862. LCCN:2001-020676.

Audience: **u,f.**

Thompson, A. Richard,   QB479.3.T47 2001
  et al.
Interferometry and Synthesis in Radio Astronomy. Ed. 2. James M. Moran & George W. Swenson Jr. (Authors). Trade Cloth. John Wiley & Sons, Inc. Hoboken, NJ. 2001. 715p. ISBN:0-471-25492-4, ISBN13: 978-0-471-25492-8. Dewey:522/.682. LCCN:00-038130.

Audience: **u,f.**

Tucker, Wallace & Tucker,   QB472.T82 2001
  Karen
Revealing the Universe: The Making of the Chandra X-Ray Observatory. Trade Cloth. Harvard University Press. Cambridge, MA. 2001. 312p. ISBN:0-674-00497-3, ISBN13: 978-0-674-00497-9. Dewey:522/.6863. LCCN:00-053862.

Audience: **g,l.** *Choice, 2001.*

Astronomy Texts and Textbooks > Descriptive Astronomy

Cheng, K. S. & Romero, G.   **QB471.A1**
E. (Editors)
Cosmic Gamma-Ray Sources. Trade Cloth. Springer. New York, NY. 2004. CDXIII, 7p. Astrophysics and Space Science Library, Vol. 304 ISBN:1-4020-2255-7, ISBN13: 978-1-4020-2255-5. Dewey:522.6862.

Audience: **u,f.**

De Young, David   **QB479.5.D4 2000**
The Physics of Extragalactic Radio Sources. Trade Cloth. University of Chicago Press. Chicago, IL. 2001. 569p. ISBN:0-226-14415-1, ISBN13: 978-0-226-14415-3. Dewey:523.1/12. LCCN:2001-037796.

Audience: **u,f.**

Katz, Jonathan I.   **QB471.7.B85K38 2002**
The Biggest Bangs: The Mystery of Gamma-Ray Bursts, the Most Violent Explosions in the Universe. Trade Cloth. Oxford University Press, Inc. New York, NY. 2002. 232p. ISBN:0-19-514570-4, ISBN13: 978-0-19-514570-0. Dewey:522/.6862. LCCN:2001-036545.

Audience: **g,l.**

Astronomy Texts and Textbooks > Descriptive Astronomy > Universe

Croswell, Ken   **QB981.C884 2001**
The Universe at Midnight: Observations Illuminating the Cosmos. Trade Cloth. Simon & Schuster. New York, NY. 2001. 352p. ISBN:0-684-85931-9, ISBN13: 978-0-684-85931-6. Dewey:523.1. LCCN:2001-040232.

Audience: **g,l.**

Lang, Kenneth R.   **QB46**
Parting the Cosmic Veil. Trade Cloth. Springer. New York, NY. 2006. xii, 236p. ISBN:0-387-30735-4, ISBN13: 978-0-387-30735-0. Dewey:520.

Audience: **g,l,u,f.**

Astronomy Texts and Textbooks > Descriptive Astronomy > Solar System

Beatty, J. Kelly (Editor),   **QB501**
et al.
The New Solar System. Ed. 4. Carolyn Collins Petersen & Andrew L. Chaikin (Editors). Trade Paper. Cambridge University Press. New York, NY. 1999. 430p. ISBN:0-521-64587-5, ISBN13: 978-0-521-64587-4. Dewey:523.2. LCCN:98-034472.

Audience: **g,l,u.**

Golub, Leon & Pasachoff,   **QB521.G65 2001**
Jay M.
Nearest Star: The Surprising Science of Our Sun. Trade Cloth. Harvard University Press. Cambridge, MA. 2001. 288p. ISBN:0-674-00467-1, ISBN13: 978-0-674-00467-2. Dewey:523.7. LCCN:00-063213.

Audience: **g,l.**   *Choice, 2001.*

Greeley, Ronald & Batson,   **G1000 .G68 2002**
Raymond
The Compact NASA Atlas of the Solar System. Trade Cloth. Cambridge University Press. New York, NY. 2001. 406p. ISBN:0-521-80633-X, ISBN13: 978-0-521-80633-6. Dewey:523.2.

Audience: **g,l,u,f.**

Hartmann, William K. &   **QB501.2.M54 2005**
Miller, Ron
The Grand Tour: A Traveler's Guide to the Solar System. Ed. 3. Trade Cloth. Workman Publishing Company, Inc. New York, NY. 2005. 304p. ISBN:0-7611-3909-5, ISBN13: 978-0-7611-3909-6. Dewey:523.2. LCCN:2005-043655.

Audience: **g,l,u.**

Lang, Kenneth R.   **QB521.L25 2000**
The Sun from Space. Trade Cloth. Springer. New York, NY. 2000. XVI, 357p. Astronomy and Astrophysics Library ISBN:3-540-66944-2, ISBN13: 978-3-540-66944-9. Dewey:523.7. LCCN:00-041038.

Audience: **g,l,u,f.**   *Choice, 2001.*

Lewis, John S.   **QB501**
Physics and Chemistry of the Solar System. Ed. 2. Paper Text. Elsevier Science & Technology Books. Saint Louis, MO. 2004. 655p. International Geophysics Ser., Vol. 87 ISBN:0-12-446744-X, ISBN13: 978-0-12-446744-6. Dewey:523.2. LCCN:2003-064281.

Audience: **u,f.**   *Choice, 1999, 1995.*

Murray, Carl D. & Dermott,   **QB500.5 .M87 1999**
Stanley F.
Solar System Dynamics. Cloth Text. Cambridge University Press. New York, NY. 2000. 606p. ISBN:0-521-57295-9, ISBN13: 978-0-521-57295-8. Dewey:523.2. LCCN:99-019679.

Audience: **u.**   *Choice, 2000.*

Sheehan, William   **QB601.S543 1992**
Worlds in the Sky: Planetary Discovery from Earliest Times Through Voyager and Magellan. Trade Paper. University of Arizona Press. Tucson, AZ. 1992. 243p. ISBN:0-8165-1308-2, ISBN13: 978-0-8165-1308-6. Dewey:523.2. LCCN:91-039398.

Audience: **g,l,u.**   *Choice, 1993.*

Taylor, Stuart Ross   **QB501 .T25 2001**
Solar System Evolution: A New Perspective. Ed. 2. Cloth Text. Cambridge University Press. New York, NY. 2001. 484p. ISBN:0-521-64130-6, ISBN13: 978-0-521-64130-2. Dewey:523.2. LCCN:00-068903.

Audience: **l,u.**

Astronomy Texts and Textbooks > Descriptive Astronomy > Planets

QB601

The Planetary Data System (PDS).
http://pds.jpl.nasa.gov/

Audience: **g,l,u,f.**

Bagenal, Fran (Editor),   **QB661**
et al.
Jupiter: The Planet, Satellites and Magnetosphere. Timothy Dowling, Bill McKinnon & William B McKinnon (Editors),

Fran Bagenal, Jim Bell, David Jewitt, Ralph Lorenz, Carl Murray & Francis Nimmo (Contribution by). Trade Cloth. Cambridge University Press. New York, NY. 2004. 748p. Cambridge Planetary Science Ser., Vol. 1 ISBN:0-521-81808-7, ISBN13: 978-0-521-81808-7. Dewey:523.45. LCCN:2004-040789.

Audience: **u,f.** *Choice, 2005.*

Cole, G. H. A. & Woolfson,   QB601 .C656 2002
M. M.
Planetary Science: The Science of Planets Around Stars. Institute of Physics Staff (Contribution by). Perfect. Institute of Physics Publishing. Philadelphia, PA. 2002. 528p. ISBN:0-7503-0815-X, ISBN13: 978-0-7503-0815-1. Dewey:523.4/015. LCCN:96-043614.

Audience: **l,u.** *Choice, 2002.*

Croswell, Ken (Contribution   QB601.C76 1997
by)
Planet Quest: The Epic Discovery of Alien Solar Systems. Trade Cloth. Oxford University Press, Inc. New York, NY. 1997. 336p. ISBN:0-19-850198-6, ISBN13: 978-0-19-850198-5. Dewey:523. LCCN:97-027751.

Audience: **g,l.** *Choice, 1998.*

De Pater, Imke & Lissauer,   QB601 .D38 2001
Jack Jonathan
Planetary Sciences. Cloth Text. Cambridge University Press. New York, NY. 2001. 544p. ISBN:0-521-48219-4, ISBN13: 978-0-521-48219-6. Dewey:559.9/2. LCCN:00-052938.

Audience: **u,f.**

Greeley, Ronald & Batson,   G1000 .G68 2002
Raymond
The Compact NASA Atlas of the Solar System. Trade Cloth. Cambridge University Press. New York, NY. 2001. 406p. ISBN:0-521-80633-X, ISBN13: 978-0-521-80633-6. Dewey:523.2.

Audience: **g,l,u,f.**

Harland, David M.   QB671.H195 2002
Mission to Saturn: Cassini and the Huygens Probe. Trade Paper. Springer. New York, NY. 2002. XVII, 290p. Springer-Praxis Books in Astronomy and Space Sciences ISBN:1-85233-656-0, ISBN13: 978-1-85233-656-1. Dewey:629.43/546. LCCN:2002-070844.

Audience: **g,l,u,f.** *Choice, 2003.*

Hartmann, William K.   QB601.H34 2005
Moons and Planets. Ed. 5. Cloth Text. Brooks/Cole. Pacific Grove, CA. 2004. 456p. ISBN:0-534-49393-9, ISBN13: 978-0-534-49393-6. Dewey:523.2. LCCN:2004-091448.

Audience: **g,l,u,f.**

Kargel, J. S.   QB641
Mars: A Warmer, Wetter Mars. Trade Paper. Springer. New York, NY. 2004. XLVIII, 557p. Springer-Praxis Books in Astronomy and Space Sciences ISBN:1-85233-568-8, ISBN13: 978-1-85233-568-7. Dewey:523.43. LCCN:2003-065305.

Audience: **g,l,u,f.** *Choice, 2005.*

Lodders, Katharina &   QB601.L84 1998
Fegley, Bruce Jr.
The Planetary Scientist's Companion. Trade Paper. Oxford University Press, Inc. New York, NY. 1998. 400p. ISBN:0-19-511694-1, ISBN13: 978-0-19-511694-6. Dewey:523.2. LCCN:97-048465.

Audience: **g,l,u,f.** *Choice, 1999.*

Morrison, David & Owen,   QB601.M76 2003
Tobias C.
The Planetary System. Ed. 3. Trade Paper. Addison-Wesley Longman, Inc. Boston, MA. 2002. 570p. ISBN:0-8053-8734-X, ISBN13: 978-0-8053-8734-6. Dewey:523.2. LCCN:2002-034522.

Audience: **g,l.**

Read, Peter L. & Lewis,   QB641.R355 2003
Stephen R.
The Martian Climate Revisited: Atmosphere and Environment of a Desert Planet. Trade Cloth. Springer. New York, NY. 2004. XXVI, 326p. Springer-Praxis Books in Geophysical Sciences ISBN:3-540-40743-X, ISBN13: 978-3-540-40743-0. Dewey:551.6999/23. LCCN:2003-058610.

Audience: **u,f.** *Choice, 2004.*

Strom, Robert G. &   QB611
Sprague, Anne L.
Exploring Mercury: The Iron Planet. Mixed Media. Springer. New York, NY. 2003. XXX, 216p. Springer-Praxis Books in Astronomy and Space Sciences ISBN:1-85233-731-1, ISBN13: 978-1-85233-731-5. Dewey:523.41. LCCN:2003-042781.

Audience: **g,l,u.** *Choice, 2004.*

Astronomy Texts and Textbooks > Descriptive Astronomy > Meteors

Bevan, Alex & de Laeter,   QB755.B48 2002
J. R.
Meteorites: A Journey Through Space and Time. Trade Cloth. Smithsonian Institution Press. Washington, DC. 2002. 256p. ISBN:1-58834-021-X, ISBN13: 978-1-58834-021-4. Dewey:523.5/1. LCCN:2001-049551.

Audience: **g,l,u.** *Choice, 2003.*

Festou, Michel (Editor)   QB721.C42 2005
Comets II. Trade Cloth. University of Arizona Press. Tucson, AZ. 2004. 780p. Space Science Ser. ISBN:0-8165-2450-5, ISBN13: 978-0-8165-2450-1. Dewey:523.6. LCCN:2004-024020.

Audience: **u,f.**

Norton, O. Richard   QB755 .N65 2002
The Cambridge Encyclopedia of Meteorites. Cloth Text. Cambridge University Press. New York, NY. 2002. 374p. ISBN:0-521-62143-7, ISBN13: 978-0-521-62143-4. Dewey:523.5/1/03. LCCN:2001-035621.

Audience: **g,l,u,f.** *Choice, 2002.*

Astronomy Texts and Textbooks > Descriptive Astronomy > Interstellar Matter

Kwok, Sun   QB855.5 .K96 2000
The Origin and Evolution of Planetary Nebulae. Andrew King, Douglas Lin, Stephen Maran, Jim Pringle & Martin Ward (Contribution by). Trade Cloth. Cambridge University Press. New York, NY. 2000. 260p. Cambridge Astrophysics Ser., No. 33 ISBN:0-521-62313-8, ISBN13: 978-0-521-62313-1. Dewey:523.1/135. LCCN:99-021392.

Audience: **u,f.**

Spitzer, Lyman   **QB790**
Physical Processes in the Interstellar Medium. Ed. 1. Trade
Paper. John Wiley & Sons, Inc. Hoboken, NJ. 1998. 335p.
Wiley Classics Library, Vol. 69 ISBN:0-471-29335-0, ISBN13:
978-0-471-29335-4. Dewey:523.1/125. LCCN:77-014273.
                                                    Audience: **u,f.**

Astronomy Texts and Textbooks > Descriptive Astronomy > Stars

Allen, Richard Hinck   **QB802 .A4**
Star Names and Their Meanings. Trade Paper. Kessinger
Publishing, LLC. Whitefish, MT. 2003. ISBN:0-7661-4028-8,
ISBN13: 978-0-7661-4028-8. Dewey:523.8.
                                                Audience: **g,l,u,f.**

Arnett, David   **QB981.A66 1996**
Supernovae and Nucleosynthesis: An Investigation of the
History of Matter, from the Big Bang to the Present. Trade
Paper. Princeton University Press. Princeton, NJ. 1996. 618p.
Princeton Series in Astrophysics ISBN:0-691-01147-8, ISBN13:
978-0-691-01147-9. Dewey:523.1. LCCN:95-041534.
                                        Audience: **u,f.** *Choice, 1996.*

Ashman, Keith M. & Zepf,   **QB853.5 .A84 1998**
Stephen E.
Globular Cluster Systems. Trade Cloth. Cambridge University
Press. New York, NY. 1998. 181p. Cambridge Astrophysics Ser.,
No. 30 ISBN:0-521-55057-2, ISBN13: 978-0-521-55057-4.
Dewey:523.8/55. LCCN:97-017391.
                                                    Audience: **u,f.**

Böhm-Vitense, Erika   **QB801.B64 1989**
Introduction to Stellar Astrophysics, Vol. 2. Cloth Text.
Cambridge University Press. New York, NY. 1989. 264p.
ISBN:0-521-34403-4, ISBN13: 978-0-521-34403-6.
Dewey:523.8.
                                        Audience: **u,f.** *Choice, 1991.*

Böhm-Vitense, Erika   **QB801.B64 1992**
Introduction to Stellar Astrophysics, Vol. 3. Trade Paper.
Cambridge University Press. New York, NY. 1992. 301p.
ISBN:0-521-34871-4, ISBN13: 978-0-521-34871-3.
Dewey:523.8.
                                        Audience: **u,f.** *Choice, 1991.*

Böhm-Vitense, Erika   **QB801 .B64 1989**
Introduction to Stellar Astrophysics: Basic Stellar Observations
and Data, Vol. 1. Trade Paper. Cambridge University Press. New
York, NY. 1989. 256p. ISBN:0-521-34869-2, ISBN13:
978-0-521-34869-0. Dewey:523.8. LCCN:88-020310.
                                        Audience: **u,f.** *Choice, 1990.*

Good, Gerry A.   **QB835.G58 2003**
Observing Variable Stars. Trade Paper. Springer. New York, NY.
2003. VIII, 274p. Patrick Moore's Practical Astronomy Ser.
ISBN:1-85233-498-3, ISBN13: 978-1-85233-498-7.
Dewey:523.8/44. LCCN:2002-190895.
                                        Audience: **g,l,u.** *Choice, 2003.*

Habing, H. J. & Olofsson,   **QB843.A89A78 2003**
Hans (Editors)
Asymptotic Giant Branch Stars. Trade Cloth. Springer. New

York, NY. 2003. IX, 559p. Astronomy and Astrophysics Library
ISBN:0-387-00880-2, ISBN13: 978-0-387-00880-6.
Dewey:523.8/8. LCCN:2003-045456.
                                                    Audience: **u,f.**

Kaler, James B.   **QB801 .K23 2001**
Extreme Stars: At the Edge of Creation. Cloth Text. Cambridge
University Press. New York, NY. 2001. 248p.
ISBN:0-521-40262-X, ISBN13: 978-0-521-40262-0.
Dewey:523.8. LCCN:00-058522.
                                    Audience: **g,l,u,f.** *Choice, 2002.*

Kippenhahn, Rudolph &   **QB808.K57 1990**
Weigert, A.
Stellar Structure and Evolution. Ed. 2. Paper Text. Springer.
New York, NY. 1996. 468p. Astronomy and Astrophysics
Library ISBN:0-387-58013-1, ISBN13: 978-0-387-58013-5.
Dewey:523.8. LCCN:94-019141.
                                        Audience: **u,f.** *Choice, 1990.*

Manchester, Richard N. &   **QB843.P8.M36**
Taylor, Joseph H.
Pulsars. Cloth Text. W. H. Freeman & Company. New York,
NY. 1977. 281p. Astronomy and Astrophysics Ser.
ISBN:0-7167-0358-0, ISBN13: 978-0-7167-0358-7. Dewey:523.
LCCN:77-004206.
                                                    Audience: **u,f.**

O'Dell, C. Robert   **QB855.9.O75O34 2003**
The Orion Nebula: Where Stars Are Born. Trade Cloth. Harvard
University Press. Cambridge, MA. 2003. 192p. Belknap Ser.
ISBN:0-674-01183-X, ISBN13: 978-0-674-01183-0.
Dewey:523.1/13. LCCN:2003-050332.
                                        Audience: **g,l.** *Choice, 2004.*

Rey, H. A.   **QB63**
The Stars: A New Way to See Them. Ed. 3. Dust Jacket.
Houghton Mifflin Company Trade & Reference Division.
Boston, MA. 1973. 160p. ISBN:0-395-08121-1, ISBN13:
978-0-395-08121-1. Dewey:523.8.
                                                    Audience: **g,l.**

Schaaf, Fred   **QB64.S435 2003**
A Year of the Stars: A Month-by-Month Journey of
Skywatching. Trade Cloth. Prometheus Books, Publishers.
Amherst, NY. 2003. 325p. ISBN:1-59102-092-1, ISBN13:
978-1-59102-092-9. Dewey:522. LCCN:2003-008108.
                                    Audience: **g,l,u.** *Choice, 2004.*

Schulz, Norbert   **QB806.S38 2005**
From Dust to Stars: Studies of the Formation and Early
Evolution of Stars. Trade Cloth. Springer. New York, NY. 2005.
XVI, 390p. Springer Praxis Books / Astrophysics and
Astronomy Ser. ISBN:3-540-23711-9, ISBN13:
978-3-540-23711-2. Dewey:523.8/8. LCCN:2004-115080.
                                        Audience: **u,f.** *Choice, 2005.*

Schwarzschild, Martin   **QB801 .S35**
Structure and Evolution of the Stars. Paper Text. Textbook
Publishers. Temecula, CA. 2003. xvii, 296p.
ISBN:0-7581-5644-8, ISBN13: 978-0-7581-5644-0.
Dewey:523.8.
                                                Audience: **g,l,u,f.**

Astronomy Texts and Textbooks > Descriptive Astronomy > Galaxies

Berendzen, Richard, et al.   QB32.B47 1984
Man Discovers the Galaxies. Richard Hart & Daniel Seeley
(Authors). Trade Paper. Columbia University Press. New York,
NY. 1984. 228p. ISBN:0-231-05827-6, ISBN13:
978-0-231-05827-8. Dewey:520/.9/04. LCCN:84-001770.
                                          Audience: **g,l,u,f.**

Binney, James J. &   QB857.B524 1987
  Tremaine, Scot
Galactic Dynamics. Trade Paper. Princeton University Press.
Princeton, NJ. 1988. 755p. Princeton Series in Astrophysics
ISBN:0-691-08445-9, ISBN13: 978-0-691-08445-9.
Dewey:523.1/12. LCCN:86-043129.
                                 Audience: **u,f.** *Choice, 1988.*

Binney, James & Merrifield,   QB857.B522 1998
  Michael
Galactic Astronomy. Trade Cloth. Princeton University Press.
Princeton, NJ. 1998. 810p. Princeton Series in Astrophysics
ISBN:0-691-00402-1, ISBN13: 978-0-691-00402-0.
Dewey:523.1. LCCN:98-024385.
                                 Audience: **u,f.** *Choice, 1999.*

Croswell, Ken   QB857.7.C76 1995
The Alchemy of the Heavens: Searching for Meaning in the
Milky Way. Philippe Van (Illustrator). Trade Cloth. Doubleday
Publishing. New York, NY. 1995. 52p. ISBN:0-385-47213-7,
ISBN13: 978-0-385-47213-5. Dewey:523.1/13.
LCCN:94-030452.
                                          Audience: **g,l.**

Kanipe, Jeff   QB500.262.K36 2006
Chasing Hubble's Shadows: The Search for Galaxies at the
Edge of Time. Cloth over Boards. Farrar, Straus & Giroux. New
York, NY. 2006. 224p. ISBN:0-8090-3406-9, ISBN13:
978-0-8090-3406-2. Dewey:523.1/12. LCCN:2005-009652.
                                 Audience: **g,l.** *Choice, 2006.*

Krolik, Julian H.   QB858.3.K76 1999
Active Galactic Nuclei: From the Central Black Hole to the
Galactic Environment. Trade Cloth. Princeton University Press.
Princeton, NJ. 1998. 620p. Princeton Series in Astrophysics
ISBN:0-691-01152-4, ISBN13: 978-0-691-01152-3.
Dewey:523.1/12. LCCN:98-021857.
                                          Audience: **u,f.**

Melia, Fulvio   QB843.B55M45 2003
The Black Hole at the Center of Our Galaxy. Trade Cloth.
Princeton University Press. Princeton, NJ. 2003. 204p.
ISBN:0-691-09505-1, ISBN13: 978-0-691-09505-9.
Dewey:523.8/875. LCCN:2002-034625.
                                 Audience: **g,l,u.** *Choice, 2003.*

Sparke, Linda S. &   QB857 .S63 2000
  Gallagher, John S.
Galaxies in the Universe: An Introduction. Cloth Text.
Cambridge University Press. New York, NY. 2000. 416p.
ISBN:0-521-59241-0, ISBN13: 978-0-521-59241-3.
Dewey:523.1/12. LCCN:99-044950.
                                 Audience: **u,f.** *Choice, 2001.*

Spinrad, Hyron   QB857.5.E96S65 2005
Galaxy Formation and Evolution. Trade Cloth. Springer. New
York, NY. 2005. xiii, 196p. Springer Praxis Books /
Astrophysics and Astronomy Ser. ISBN:3-540-25498-6, ISBN13:
978-3-540-25498-0. Dewey:523.1/12. LCCN:2005-924538.
                                 Audience: **g,l.** *Choice, 2006.*

Astronomy Texts and Textbooks > Descriptive Astronomy > Quasars

Kembhavi, Ajit K. &   QB860 .K46 1999
  Narlikar, Jayant V.
Quasars and Active Galactic Nuclei: An Introduction. Trade
Cloth. Cambridge University Press. New York, NY. 1999. 476p.
ISBN:0-521-47477-9, ISBN13: 978-0-521-47477-1.
Dewey:523.1/15. LCCN:97-028655.
                                          Audience: **u,f.**

Cosmology

Clark, Stuart   QB981.C593 1999
Towards the Edge of the Universe: A Review of Modern
Cosmology. Ed. 2. Trade Paper. Springer. New York, NY. 1999.
255p. Wiley-Praxis Series in Astronomy and Astrophysics
ISBN:1-85233-098-8, ISBN13: 978-1-85233-098-9.
Dewey:523.1. LCCN:99-035673.
                                          Audience: **u,f.**

Dodelson, Scott   QB981.D63 2003
Modern Cosmology. Cloth Text. Elsevier Science & Technology
Books. Saint Louis, MO. 2003. 440p. ISBN:0-12-219141-2,
ISBN13: 978-0-12-219141-1. Dewey:523.1.
LCCN:2002-117793.
                                 Audience: **u,f.** *Choice, 2003.*

Ferris, Timothy   QB981 .F36 1983
The Red Limit: The Search for the Edge of the Universe. Ed. 2.
Trade Paper. HarperCollins Publishers. New York, NY. 1983.
368p. ISBN:0-688-01836-X, ISBN13: 978-0-688-01836-8.
Dewey:523.1/09. LCCN:83-003068.
                                          Audience: **g.**

Goldsmith, Donald   QB981.G594 1995
Einstein's Greatest Blunder?: The Cosmological Constant and
Other Fudge Factors in the Physics of the Universe. Trade
Cloth. Harvard University Press. Cambridge, MA. 1995. 248p.
Questions of Science Ser. ISBN:0-674-24241-6, ISBN13:
978-0-674-24241-8. Dewey:523.1. LCCN:95-014762.
                                 Audience: **g,l,u.** *Choice, 1996.*

Guth, Alan H.   QB991.B54
The Inflationary Universe: The Quest for a New Theory of
Cosmic Origins. Trade Paper. Perseus Books Group. New York,
NY. 1998. 384p. ISBN:0-201-32840-2, ISBN13:
978-0-201-32840-0. Dewey:523.1/8. LCCN:96-046117.
                                 Audience: **g,l,u,f.** *Choice, 1997.*

Harland, David M. (Editor)   QB991.B54
The Big Bang: A View from the 21st Century. Trade Paper.
Springer. New York, NY. 2003. XXIV, 262p. Springer-Praxis
Books in Astronomy and Space Sciences ISBN:1-85233-713-3,
ISBN13: 978-1-85233-713-1. Dewey:523.18.
LCCN:2003-278459.
                                 Audience: **g,l,u.** *Choice, 2004.*

Harrison, Edward R.   **QB981 .H32 2000**
Cosmology: The Science of the Universe. Ed. 2. Cloth Text.
Cambridge University Press. New York, NY. 2000. 578p.
ISBN:0-521-66148-X, ISBN13: 978-0-521-66148-5.
Dewey:523.1. LCCN:99-010172.
                                      Audience: **g,l,u,f.** *Choice, 2000.*

Hawking, Stephen W.   **QB981.H377 1998**
A Brief History of Time: From the Big Bang to Black Holes.
Ed. 10. Trade Cloth. Bantam Books. New York, NY. 1998.
224p. ISBN:0-553-10953-7, ISBN13: 978-0-553-10953-5.
Dewey:523.1. LCCN:98-021874.
                                      Audience: **g,l,u.** *Choice, 1988.*

Kolb, Edward W. & Turner,   **QB981.K687 1989**
  Michael S.
The Early Universe. Cloth Text. Addison-Wesley Longman, Inc.
Boston, MA. 1990. 576p. Frontiers in Physics Ser.
ISBN:0-201-11603-0, ISBN13: 978-0-201-11603-8.
Dewey:523.1. LCCN:89-000139.
                                      Audience: **u,f.**

Liddle, Andrew   **QB981**
An Introduction to Modern Cosmology. Ed. 2. Trade Cloth. John
Wiley & Sons, Inc. Hoboken, NJ. 2003. 188p.
ISBN:0-470-84834-0, ISBN13: 978-0-470-84834-0.
Dewey:523.1. LCCN:2003-269979.
                                      Audience: **u,f.** *Choice, 2004, 1999.*

Padmanabhan, T.   **QB981 .P245 1993**
Structure Formation in the Universe. Trade Paper. Cambridge
University Press. New York, NY. 1993. 499p.
ISBN:0-521-42486-0, ISBN13: 978-0-521-42486-8.
Dewey:523.1. LCCN:92-014397.
                                      Audience: **u,f.**

Padmanabhan, Thanu   **QB981 .P243 1998**
After the First Three Minutes: The Story of Our Universe. Trade
Cloth. Cambridge University Press. New York, NY. 1998. 227p.
ISBN:0-521-62039-2, ISBN13: 978-0-521-62039-0.
Dewey:523.1. LCCN:97-011060.
                                      Audience: **g,l,u.** *Choice, 1998.*

Peacock, John A.   **QB981 .P37 1999**
Cosmological Physics. Trade Paper. Cambridge University Press.
New York, NY. 1998. 702p. ISBN:0-521-42270-1, ISBN13:
978-0-521-42270-3. Dewey:523.1. LCCN:98-029460.
                                      Audience: **g,l,u,f.**

Peebles, P. J.   **QB857 .P43**
Large-Scale Structure of the Universe. Trade Paper. Princeton
University Press. Princeton, NJ. 1980. 440p. Princeton Series in
Physics ISBN:0-691-08240-5, ISBN13: 978-0-691-08240-0.
Dewey:523.1/12. LCCN:79-084008.
                                      Audience: **u,f.**

Peebles, Phillip James   **QB981 .P424 1993**
  Edwin
Principles of Physical Cosmology. Trade Paper. Princeton
University Press. Princeton, NJ. 1993. 736p. Princeton Series in
Physics ISBN:0-691-01933-9, ISBN13: 978-0-691-01933-8.
Dewey:523.1. LCCN:92-033370.
                                      Audience: **g,u,f.** *Choice, 1993.*

Shu, Frank H.   **QB43.2.S54 1982**
The Physical Universe. Trade Cloth. University Science Books.
Sausalito, CA. 1982. 584p. Series of Books in Astronomy

ISBN:0-935702-05-9, ISBN13: 978-0-935702-05-7. Dewey:523.
LCCN:81-051271.
                                      Audience: **g,l,u,f.** *B*

Silk, Joseph   **QB981**
The Big Bang. Ed. 3. Trade Paper. Henry Holt & Company.
New York, NY. 2000. 512p. ISBN:0-8050-7256-X, ISBN13:
978-0-8050-7256-3. Dewey:523.1/8.
                                      Audience: **g,l,u,f.**

Webb, Stephen   **QB991.C66W43 1999**
Measuring the Universe: The Cosmological Distance Ladder.
Trade Paper. Springer. New York, NY. 1999. XVI, 342p. Series
in Astronomy and Astrophysics ISBN:1-85233-106-2, ISBN13:
978-1-85233-106-1. Dewey:523.1. LCCN:98-043764.
                                      Audience: **l,u.**

Physics -- General Relativity

Begelman, Mitchell & Rees,   **QB843.B55**
  Martin
Gravity's Fatal Attraction: Black Holes in the Universe. Trade
Paper. W. H. Freeman & Company. New York, NY. 1998. 256p.
Scientific American Library Ser., Vol. 58 ISBN:0-7167-6029-0,
ISBN13: 978-0-7167-6029-0. Dewey:523.8/875.
LCCN:95-042959.
                                      Audience: **g,l,u.**

Cheng, Ta-Pei   **QC173.6.C4724 2005**
Relativity, Gravitation and Cosmology: A Basic Introduction.
Trade Paper. Oxford University Press, Inc. New York, NY. 2005.
354p. Oxford Master Series in Physics Ser.
ISBN:0-19-852957-0, ISBN13: 978-0-19-852957-6.
Dewey:530.11. LCCN:2004-019733.
                                      Audience: **u.** *Choice, 2005.*

Ferguson, Kitty   **QB843.B55 F54 1996**
Prisons of Light - Black Holes. Trade Paper. Cambridge
University Press. New York, NY. 1998. 224p.
ISBN:0-521-62571-8, ISBN13: 978-0-521-62571-5.
Dewey:523.8/875.
                                      Audience: **g,l,u.** *Choice, 1997.*

Gott, J. Richard   **QC173.6**
Time Travel in Einstein's Universe: The Physical Possibilities of
Travel Through Time. Trade Paper. Houghton Mifflin Company
Trade & Reference Division. Boston, MA. 2002. 304p.
ISBN:0-618-25735-7, ISBN13: 978-0-618-25735-5.
Dewey:530.1/1.
                                      Audience: **g,l.**

Misner, Charles W., et al.   **QC178 .M57**
Gravitation. Kip S. Thorne & John A. Wheeler (Authors). Trade
Paper. Worth Publishers, Inc. New York, NY. 1973. 1215p.
Physics Ser. ISBN:0-7167-0344-0, ISBN13: 978-0-7167-0344-0.
Dewey:531/.14. LCCN:78-156043.
                                      Audience: **u,f.** *B*

Schutz, Bernard F.   **QC173.6 .S38 1985**
A First Course in General Relativity. Trade Paper. Cambridge
University Press. New York, NY. 1985. 392p.
ISBN:0-521-27703-5, ISBN13: 978-0-521-27703-7.
Dewey:530.1/1. LCCN:83-023205.
                                      Audience: **u,f.** *B* *Choice, 1985.*

Taylor, Edwin F. & Wheeler,   QC173.65T37 1991
  John Archibald
Spacetime Physics. Ed. 2. Trade Paper. Worth Publishers, Inc.
New York, NY. 1992. 32p. ISBN:0-7167-2327-1, ISBN13:
978-0-7167-2327-1. Dewey:530.11. LCCN:92-000722.
                                Audience: **u,f.** *B*

Thorne, Kip S.   QC6.T526 1993
Black Holes and Time Warps: Einstein's Outrageous Legacy.
Frederick Seitz (Introduction by), Stephen W. Hawking
(Foreword by). Trade Paper. W. W. Norton & Company, Inc.
New York, NY. 1995. 640p. ISBN:0-393-31276-3, ISBN13:
978-0-393-31276-8. Dewey:530.1/1. LCCN:93-002014.
                          Audience: **l,u.** *Choice, 1994.*

Weinberg, Steven   QB461
Gravitation and Cosmology: Principles and Applications of the
General Theory of Relativity. Trade Cloth. John Wiley & Sons,
Inc. Hoboken, NJ. 1972. 688p. ISBN:0-471-92567-5, ISBN13:
978-0-471-92567-5. Dewey:523.01. LCCN:78-037175.
                                  Audience: **u,f.** *B*

Wheeler, John A.   QC178
A Journey into Gravity and Spacetime. Trade Paper. Henry Holt
& Company. New York, NY. 1999. 258p. ISBN:0-7167-6034-7,
ISBN13: 978-0-7167-6034-4. Dewey:531.1/4.
                        Audience: **l,u,f.** *Choice, 1990.*

Light and Optics

Bass, Michael   QC369.H35 2001
e Handbook of Optics. Ed. 2. E-Book. McGraw-Hill
Professional Publishing. New York, NY. ISBN:0-07-141479-7,
ISBN13: 978-0-07-141479-1. Dewey:535.
                                Audience: **u,f.**

Bohren, Craig F. &   QC882 .B63 1998
  Huffman, Donald R.
Absorption and Scattering of Light by Small Particles. Trade
Paper. John Wiley & Sons, Inc. Hoboken, NJ. 1998. 544p.
ISBN:0-471-29340-7, ISBN13: 978-0-471-29340-8. Dewey:535.
                                Audience: **u,f.**

Born, Max & Wolf, Emil   QC355.2.B67 1999
Principles of Optics: Electromagnetic Theory of Propagation,
Interference and Diffraction of Light. Ed. 7. A. B. Bhatia, P. C.
Clemmow, D. Gabor, A. R. Stokes, A. M. Taylor, P. A. Wayman
& W. L. Wilcock (Contribution by). Trade Cloth. Cambridge
University Press. New York, NY. 1999. 986p.
ISBN:0-521-64222-1, ISBN13: 978-0-521-64222-4. Dewey:535.
LCCN:98-049429.
                          Audience: **u,f.** *B*

Hecht, Eugene   QC355.3.H43 2002
Optics. Ed. 4. Cloth Text. Addison-Wesley Longman, Inc.
Boston, MA. 2001. 680p. ISBN:0-8053-8566-5, ISBN13:
978-0-8053-8566-3. Dewey:535. LCCN:2001-032540.
                                Audience: **u,f.**

Jenkins, Francis A. &   QC355.2 .J46 2001
  White, Harvey E.
Fundamentals of Optics. Ed. 4. Paper Text. McGraw-Hill Higher
Education. Burr Ridge, IL. 2001. 768p. ISBN:0-07-256191-2,
ISBN13: 978-0-07-256191-3. Dewey:535.
                          Audience: **u,f.** *B*

King, Terry A. & Smith, F.   QC446.2.G73 2000
  Graham
Optics and Photonics: An Introduction. Trade Paper. John Wiley
& Sons, Inc. Hoboken, NJ. 2000. 456p. ISBN:0-471-48925-5,
ISBN13: 978-0-471-48925-2. Dewey:535. LCCN:99-087078.
                                Audience: **u,f.**

Lynch, David K. &   QC335.2 .L96 2001
  Livingston, William
Color and Light in Nature. Ed. 2. Trade Paper. Cambridge
University Press. New York, NY. 2001. 292p.
ISBN:0-521-77504-3, ISBN13: 978-0-521-77504-5. Dewey:535.
LCCN:00-064230.
                      Audience: **g,l,u,f.** *Choice, 1996.*

Radiation Physics -- Cosmic Rays

Friedlander, Michael W.   QC485.F75 2000
A Thin Cosmic Rain: Particles from Outer Space. Trade Paper.
Harvard University Press. Cambridge, MA. 2002. 256p.
ISBN:0-674-00989-4, ISBN13: 978-0-674-00989-9.
Dewey:539.7/223.
                        Audience: **g,l,u.** *Choice, 2001.*

Geophysics -- Cosmic Physics (QC)

Carlowicz, Michael J. &   QB505
  Lopez, Ramon E.
Storms from the Sun: The Emerging Science of Space Weather.
Trade Paper. National Academies Press. Washington, DC. 2003.
256p. ISBN:0-309-08940-9, ISBN13: 978-0-309-08940-1.
Dewey:629.4/16.
                    Audience: **g,l,u.** *Choice, 2003, 2002.*

Davis, T. Neil   QC971.D38 1992
The Aurora Watcher's Handbook. Trade Cloth. University of
Alaska Press. Fairbanks, AK. 1992. 240p. ISBN:0-912006-59-5,
ISBN13: 978-0-912006-59-8. Dewey:538/.768.
LCCN:91-043080.
                        Audience: **g,l.** *Choice, 1992.*

Gombosi, Tamas I.   QC861.2 .G64 1998
Physics of the Space Environment. Alexander J. Dessler, John T.
Houghton & Michael J. Rycroft (Contribution by). Trade Paper.
Cambridge University Press. New York, NY. 2004. 357p.
Cambridge Atmospheric and Space Science Ser.
ISBN:0-521-60768-X, ISBN13: 978-0-521-60768-1.
Dewey:551.51/4.
                        Audience: **u,f.** *Choice, 1999.*

Savage, Candace   QC971 .S27 2001
Aurora: The Mysterious Northern Lights. Trade Paper. Firefly
Books, Ltd. Tonawanda, NY. 2001. 144p. ISBN:1-55209-583-5,
ISBN13: 978-1-55209-583-6. Dewey:538.
                              Audience: **g,l,u.**

Astrobiology

Bennett, Jeffrey O., et al.   QH327 .B45
Life in the Universe. Ed. 2. Seth Shostak & Bruce Jakosky
(Authors). Trade Paper. Addison-Wesley Longman, Inc. Boston,
MA. 2006. 450p. ISBN:0-8053-4753-4, ISBN13:
978-0-8053-4753-1. Dewey:576.8/39. LCCN:2006-025657.
                              Audience: **g,l,u.**

Croswell, Ken (Contribution by)   QB601.C76 1997

Planet Quest: The Epic Discovery of Alien Solar Systems. Trade Cloth. Oxford University Press, Inc. New York, NY. 1997. 336p. ISBN:0-19-850198-6, ISBN13: 978-0-19-850198-5. Dewey:523. LCCN:97-027751.

Audience: **g,l.** *Choice, 1998.*

Gilmour, Iain & Sephton, Mark A. (Editors)   QB54

An Introduction to Astrobiology. Trade Paper. Cambridge University Press. New York, NY. 2004. 364p. ISBN:0-521-54621-4, ISBN13: 978-0-521-54621-8. Dewey:576.8/39. LCCN:2004-557906.

Audience: **g,l,u,f.** *Choice, 2005.*

Goldsmith, Donald (Author, Author)   QB54.G58 2001

The Search for Life in the Universe. Ed. 3. Tobias Owen (Author). Trade Cloth. University Science Books. Sausalito, CA. 2001. 400p. ISBN:1-891389-16-5, ISBN13: 978-1-891389-16-0. Dewey:576.8/39. LCCN:00-048009.

Audience: **g,l.**

Lemonick, Michael D.   QB54.L43 1998

Other Worlds: The Search for Life in the Universe. Trade Cloth. Simon & Schuster. New York, NY. 1998. 272p. ISBN:0-684-83294-1, ISBN13: 978-0-684-83294-4. Dewey:999. LCCN:97-049006.

Audience: **g.**

Lunine, Jonathan I.   QH325.L86 2004

Astrobiology: Multi Disciplinary Approach. Trade Paper. Addison-Wesley Longman, Inc. Boston, MA. 2004. 450p. ISBN:0-8053-8042-6, ISBN13: 978-0-8053-8042-2. Dewey:576.8/3. LCCN:2004-053408.

Audience: **g,l,u,f.**

Ward, Peter D. & Brownlee, Donald   QB54.W336 2000

Rare Earth: Why Complex Life Is Uncommon in the Universe. Cloth Text. Springer. New York, NY. 2000. 368p. ISBN:0-387-98701-0, ISBN13: 978-0-387-98701-9. Dewey:576.8/39. LCCN:99-020532.

Audience: **l,u,f.** *Choice, 2000.*

BIOLOGY

Tremendous achievements in biological research are measured by the production of the information and data created. More than 50,000 English-language, nonfiction, non-juvenile, book titles held in 100 or more libraries were published in fields related to the biological sciences between 1988 and 2006. This is roughly 20,000 more biology titles published in the five decades prior to 1988. It is a formidable task to cull from such an inventory the most significant titles appropriate for college library collections.

Selection for the section on biology took into account several monumental "explosions" in the biological world over the past twenty years. First and foremost was the emergence of entirely new subdisciplines spawning off of the fields of molecular and structural biology and genetics. This is the core of a "New Biology" of genomics, bioinformatics, proteomics, chemical biology, systems biology, all of which share a common thread of organizing the genetic data of genomes from viruses to humans and deciphering the nucleic acid sequences and subsequent protein configurations for which they code. The New Biology is the application of knowledge for discerning the precise mechanisms by which the genomes direct the structure and function of the genetic codes and the biochemical, physiological, anatomical, and cellular processes they direct.

This New Biology is changing not only the production of information in the traditional STM Literature (Science, Technology, Medical Literature), but is changing the ways by which biology curricula and programs are being presented and taught. The ramifications of the New Biology are influencing all other aspects of biological and life science research and teaching, cutting across the disciplines to produce modern hybrid studies of molecular ecology, fishery genomics, microbial genomics, and proteomics of oncology.

The Committee on Undergraduate Biology Education to Prepare Research Scientists for the 21st Century of the Board on Life Sciences in the Division on Earth and Life Studies of the National Research Council of the U.S. National Academies published a 2003 report, BIO2010: Transforming Undergraduate Education for Future Research Biologists. This report clearly outlines the changes needed in undergraduate education to guide students, faculty, and college administrators to prepare the next generation of researchers and educators in biological and life sciences. BIO2010 sets forth the paradigm by which the pedagogy of biological education will be directed in the foreseeable future, and is reflected in the selections for this (and other) section of resources for biology.

— Fred Stoss

History of Biology

☐ Bioexplorer.Net: History of Biology.
http://www.bioexplorer.net/History_of_Biology/
LabBBPM.

Audience: **g,l.**

☐ Google Directory: History of Biology.
http://www.google.com/Top/Science/Biology/History/
Google.

Audience: **g,l.**

☐ University of California Berkeley: Museum of Paleontology
History of Biology.
http://www.ucmp.berkeley.edu/help/topic/history.html
UCMP.

Audience: **g,l.**

Ankerberg, John & Weldon,   **QH360.5.A55 1998**
John
Darwin's Leap of Faith: Exposing the False Religion of
Evolution. Trade Paper. Harvest House Publishers. Eugene, OR.
1998. 396p. ISBN:1-56507-657-5, ISBN13: 978-1-56507-657-0.
Dewey:576.8/01. LCCN:97-040444.

Audience: **u,f.**

Bailey, Ronald   **TP248.23.B35 2005**
Liberation Biology: The Scientific and Moral Case for the
Biotech Revolution. Trade Cloth. Prometheus Books, Publishers.
Amherst, NY. 2005. 310p. ISBN:1-59102-227-4, ISBN13:
978-1-59102-227-5. Dewey:303.48/3. LCCN:2005-005875.

Audience: **u,f.** *Choice, 2006.*

Banks, Cameron   **QH349.B27 2002**
History's Mysteries: Bizarre Beings. Trade Paper. Scholastic,
Inc. New York, NY. 2002. 80p. The History Channel
Presents...Ser. ISBN:0-439-40149-6, ISBN13:
978-0-439-40149-4. LCCN:2003-269315.

Audience: **l,u.**

Barrow, Mark V.   **QL672.73.U6B37 1998**
A Passion for Birds: American Ornithology after Audubon.
Cloth Text. Princeton University Press. Princeton, NJ. 1998.
336p. ISBN:0-691-04402-3, ISBN13: 978-0-691-04402-6.
Dewey:598/.0973. LCCN:97-018600.

Audience: **g,l,u.** *Choice, 1998.*

Bayertz, Kurt (Editor)   **QH333**
From Physico-Theology to Bio-Technology: Essays in the Social
and Cultural History of Biosciences: A Festschrift for Mikul'as
Teich. Porter, Roy (Editor). Amsterdam ; Atlanta, GA : Rodopi.
1998. The Wellcome Institute series in the history of medicine;
Clio medica,; 48; Variation: Clio medica (Amsterdam,
Netherlands) ;; 48 ISBN:90-420-0491-6, ISBN13:
978-90-420-0491-7.

Audience: **u,f.**

Beebe, William (Editor)   **QH81.B715 1988**
The Book of Naturalists: An Anthology of the Best Natural
History. Trade Paper. Princeton University Press. Princeton, NJ.
1988. 520p. ISBN:0-691-02408-1, ISBN13: 978-0-691-02408-0.
Dewey:508. LCCN:87-032727.

Audience: **l,u,f.**

Bogue, Margaret Beattie   **SH219.6.B64 2000**
Fishing the Great Lakes: An Environmental History, 1783-1933.
Trade Paper. University of Wisconsin Press. Chicago, IL. 2000.
464p. ISBN:0-299-16764-X, ISBN13: 978-0-299-16764-6.
Dewey:333.95/613/0977. LCCN:00-008601.

Audience: **l,u,f.** *Choice, 2001.*

Booher, Harold R.   **QH361.B66 1998**
Origins, Icons and Illusions. Trade Paper. Warren H. Green Inc.
Saint Louis, MO. 1997. 17p. ISBN:0-87527-515-X, ISBN13:
978-0-87527-515-4. Dewey:576.8/09. LCCN:98-159250.

Audience: **u,f.** *Choice, 1999.*

Borland, Hal, et al.   **QH81.B414 1989**
Beginnings. Rachel Louise Carson, Douglas Chadwick, Annie
Dillard, Mercie Hans, Sue Hubbell, Aldo Leopold, Faith
McNulty, Sylvia Plath & Carl Sandburg (Authors). Trade Cloth.
National Wildlife Federation. Reston, VA. 1989. 48p. Gifts of
Nature Ser. ISBN:0-945051-10-7, ISBN13: 978-0-945051-10-7.
Dewey:508. LCCN:89-008276.

Audience: **l,u,f.**

Bowden, Valmai   **QH314.B69 2000**
Managing to Make a Difference: Making an Impact on the
Careers of Men and Women Scientists. Trade Cloth. Ashgate
Publishing, Ltd. Aldershot, 2000. 398p. ISBN:1-84014-859-4,
ISBN13: 978-1-84014-859-6. Dewey:570/.23/41.
LCCN:00-132801.

Audience: **l,u.**

Bowler, Peter J.   **QH361 .B69 2003**
Evolution: The History of an Idea. Ed. 3. Trade Paper.
University of California Press. Berkeley, CA. 2003. 488p.
ISBN:0-520-23693-9, ISBN13: 978-0-520-23693-6.
Dewey:576.8. LCCN:2002-007569.

Audience: **u,f.**

Bowler, Peter J.   **QH361.B685 1996**
Life's Splendid Drama: Evolutionary Biology and the
Reconstruction of Life's Ancestry, 1860-1940. Trade Cloth.
University of Chicago Press. Chicago, IL. 1996. 540p. Science
and Its Conceptual Foundations Ser. ISBN:0-226-06921-4,
ISBN13: 978-0-226-06921-0. Dewey:575/.009.
LCCN:95-025394.

Audience: **u,f.** *Choice, 1997.*

Bowler, Peter J.   **QH333.B69 1993**
Biology and Social Thought 1850-1914. John L. Heilbron
(Editor). Paper Text. University of California, Office for History
of Science & Technology. Berkeley, CA. 1993. 95p. Berkeley
Papers in History of Science, No. 15 ISBN:0-918102-19-7,
ISBN13: 978-0-918102-19-5. Dewey:575/.009.
LCCN:92-064057.

Audience: **u,f.**

Bramwell, Martyn   **QH81**
Warwick Illustrated Encyclopedia of Nature. Trade Paper.
Scholastic Library Publishing. Danbury, CT. 1989.
ISBN:0-531-19051-X, ISBN13: 978-0-531-19051-7. Dewey:574.
LCCN:88-051103.

Audience: **l,u.**

Branch, Michael P. (Editor)   **QH104.R43 2004**
Reading the Roots: American Nature Writing Before Walden.
Trade Cloth. University of Georgia Press. Athens, GA. 2005.
424p. ISBN:0-8203-2547-3, ISBN13: 978-0-8203-2547-7.
Dewey:508.73. LCCN:2003-016613.

Audience: **l,u,f.**

Brown, Andrew   **QH375**
The Darwin Wars: The Scientific Battle for the Soul of Man.
Trade Paper. Simon & Schuster, Ltd. London, 2002. 256p.
ISBN:0-7432-0343-7, ISBN13: 978-0-7432-0343-2.
Dewey:576.8/2.
                                                   Audience: **u,f.**

Brown, Andrew   **QH360.5**
The Darwin Wars: How Stupid Genes Became Selfish Gods.
Simon & Schuster, London. 1999. ISBN:0-684-85144-X,
ISBN13: 978-0-684-85144-0.
                                                   Audience: **u,f.**

Brubaker, David C. &   **QH315.L47 2000**
  Ostroff, Joel H. (Editors)
Life, Learning, and Community: Concepts and Models for
Service-Learning in Biology. Perfect. American Association for
Higher Education. Washington, DC. 2000. 176p. AAHE's Series
on Service-Learning in the Disciplines, Vol. 2
ISBN:1-56377-018-0, ISBN13: 978-1-56377-018-0.
Dewey:570/.71/1. LCCN:2001-272836.
                                                   Audience: **l,u,f.**

Buchanan, Bob B. (Editor),   **QK728**
  et al.
Biochemistry and Molecular Biology of Plants. Wilhelm
Gruissem & Russell L. Jones (Editors). Trade Paper. John Wiley
& Sons, Inc. Hoboken, NJ. 2002. 1408p. ISBN:0-943088-39-9,
ISBN13: 978-0-943088-39-6. Dewey:572.8/2. LCCN:00-040591.
                                       Audience: **u,f.** *Choice, 2001.*

Bud, Robert F.   **TP248.18**
The Uses of Life: A History of Biotechnology. Mark F. Cantley
(Foreword by). Trade Paper. Cambridge University Press. New
York, NY. 1994. 319p. ISBN:0-521-47699-2, ISBN13:
978-0-521-47699-7. Dewey:660.6/09.
                                                   Audience: **l,u.**

Caras, Roger A. (Editor)   **QH81**
Roger Caras' Treasury of Classic Nature Tales. Trade Cloth.
BBS Publishing Corporation. Edison, NJ. 1997. 528p.
ISBN:1-57866-009-2, ISBN13: 978-1-57866-009-4. Dewey:508.
                                                   Audience: **l,u,f.**

Carson, Rachel Louise   **QH308.2**
Lost Woods: The Discovered Writing of Rachel Carson. Linda
Lear (Introduction by). Trade Paper. Beacon Press. Boston, MA.
1999. 288p. ISBN:0-8070-8547-2, ISBN13: 978-0-8070-8547-9.
Dewey:570. LCCN:98-020058.
                                     Audience: **l,u,f.** *Choice, 1999.*

Caudill, Edward   **QH360.5.C38 1997**
Darwinian Myths: The Legends and Misuses of a Theory. Cloth
Text. University of Tennessee Press. Knoxville, TN. 1997. 208p.
ISBN:0-87049-984-X, ISBN13: 978-0-87049-984-5.
Dewey:576.8/2. LCCN:97-004691.
                                       Audience: **u,f.** *Choice, 1998.*

Coates, Peter   **GF13**
Nature: Western Attitudes since Ancient Times. Trade Paper.
University of California Press. Berkeley, CA. 2004. 254p.
ISBN:0-520-24478-8, ISBN13: 978-0-520-24478-8.
Dewey:304.2/09.
                                       Audience: **u,f.** *Choice, 1999.*

Cohen, Michael   **QH76.C64 1988**
The History of the Sierra Club, 1892-1970. Trade Cloth. Sierra
Club Books. San Francisco, CA. 1988. 576p.
ISBN:0-87156-732-6, ISBN13: 978-0-87156-732-1.
Dewey:333.95/16/0973. LCCN:88-042550.
                                                   Audience: **u,f.**

Comstock, Gary (Editor)   **QH332.L54 2002**
Life Science Ethics. Trade Cloth. Blackwell Publishing
Professional. Ames, IA. 2002. 448p. ISBN:0-8138-2835-X,
ISBN13: 978-0-8138-2835-0. Dewey:174/.957.
LCCN:2002-003327.
                                       Audience: **u,f.** *Choice, 2003.*

Cooper, Susan Fenimore   **QH81.C793 1998**
Rural Hours. Rochelle Johnson & Daniel Patterson (Editors).
Trade Paper. University of Georgia Press. Athens, GA. 1998.
376p. ISBN:0-8203-2000-5, ISBN13: 978-0-8203-2000-7.
Dewey:508. LCCN:98-002689.
                                                   Audience: **g,l.**

Cooper, William S.   **QH331 .C847 2001**
The Evolution of Reason: Logic as a Branch of Biology.
Michael Ruse (Contribution by). Trade Cloth. Cambridge
University Press. New York, NY. 2001. 236p. Studies in
Philosophy and Biology ISBN:0-521-79196-0, ISBN13:
978-0-521-79196-0. Dewey:570.1. LCCN:00-034260.
                                                   Audience: **u,f.**

de Duve, Christian   **QH325.D418 2005**
Singularities: Landmarks on the Pathways of Life. Cloth Text.
Cambridge University Press. New York, NY. 2005. 274p.
ISBN:0-521-84195-X, ISBN13: 978-0-521-84195-5.
Dewey:576.8/3. LCCN:2004-054761.
                                       Audience: **u,f.** *Choice, 2006.*

Deming, Alison H.   **QH81**
The Edges of the Civilized World: A Journey in Nature and
Culture. Trade Paper. Picador. New York, NY. 1999. 256p.
ISBN:0-312-20406-X, ISBN13: 978-0-312-20406-8. Dewey:508.
                                                   Audience: **u,f.**

Elphick, Jonathan   **QL674.4.E46 2005**
Birds: The Art of Ornithology. Trade Cloth. Rizzoli International
Publications, Inc. New York, NY. 2005. 336p.
ISBN:0-8478-2706-2, ISBN13: 978-0-8478-2706-0.
Dewey:598/.022/2. LCCN:2004-096830.
                                     Audience: **g,l,u.** *Choice, 2005.*

Forsdyke, Donald   **QH361.F58 2001**
The Origin of Species, Revisited: The Search for a Victorian
Who Anticipated Modern Developments in Darwin's Theory.
Trade Cloth. McGill-Queen's University Press. Montreal, PQ.
2001. x, 275p. ISBN:0-7735-2259-X, ISBN13:
978-0-7735-2259-6. Dewey:576.8/2/094109034.
LCCN:2003-275763.
                                       Audience: **u,f.** *Choice, 2002.*

Friedberg, Errol   **QH506.F746 2004**
The Writing Life of James D. Watson: Professor, Promoter,
Provocateur. Trade Cloth. Cold Spring Harbor Laboratory Press.
Woodbury, NY. 2004. 160p. ISBN:0-87969-700-8, ISBN13:
978-0-87969-700-6. Dewey:572.8. LCCN:2004-015640.
                                     Audience: **l,u,f.** *Choice, 2005.*

Glick, Thomas F. (Editor) QH361.C66 1988
The Comparative Reception of Darwinism. Trade Paper.
University of Chicago Press. Chicago, IL. 2003. 534p.
ISBN:0-226-29977-5, ISBN13: 978-0-226-29977-8.
Dewey:575.01/62. LCCN:87-035814.

Audience: **u,f.**

Glick, Thomas F. (Editor), Q174.B67 VOL.221
et al.
The Reception of Darwinism in the Iberian World: Spain,
Spanish America and Brazil. Miguel Angel Puig-Samper &
Rosaura Ruiz (Editors). Trade Cloth. Springer Dordrecht.
Dordrecht, 2001. 282p. Boston Studies in the Philosophy of
Science, Vol. 221 ISBN:1-4020-0082-0, ISBN13:
978-1-4020-0082-9. Dewey:001/.01 s576.8/0946.
LCCN:2001-045953.

Audience: **u,f.**

Gould, Stephen Jay QH366.2.G6593 1996
Full House: The Spread of Excellence from Plato to Darwin.
Trade Cloth. Crown Publishing Group. New York, NY. 1996.
256p. ISBN:0-517-70394-7, ISBN13: 978-0-517-70394-6.
Dewey:576.8. LCCN:96-196285.

Audience: **l,u,f.**

Grafton, Anthony (Editor) QH81
Natural Particulars: Nature and the Disciplines in Renaissance
Europe. Siraisi, Nancy G. (Editor). MIT Press, Cambridge,
Mass.. 1999. Dibner Institute Studies in the History of Science
and Technology ISBN:0-262-07193-2, ISBN13:
978-0-262-07193-2.

Audience: **u,f.**

Greene, John C. QH361.G7 1996
The Death of Adam: Evolution and Its Impact on Western
Thought. Trade Paper. Blackwell Publishing Professional. Ames,
IA. 1981. 388p. ISBN:0-8138-0390-X, ISBN13:
978-0-8138-0390-6. Dewey:575/.009. LCCN:95-044513.

Audience: **u,f.**

Grene, Marjorie & Depew, QH331.G736 2004
David
The Philosophy of Biology: An Episodic History. Paul Guyer &
Gary Hatfield (Contribution by). Trade Cloth. Cambridge
University Press. New York, NY. 2004. 438p. The Evolution of
Modern Philosophy Ser. ISBN:0-521-64371-6, ISBN13:
978-0-521-64371-9. LCCN:2003-055891.

Audience: **u,f.** *Choice, 2005.*

Grove, A. T. & Rackham, QH150
Oliver
The Nature of Mediterranean Europe: An Ecological History.
Trade Paper. Yale University Press. Cumberland, RI. 2003.
384p. ISBN:0-300-10055-8, ISBN13: 978-0-300-10055-6.
Dewey:577.4/6/094. LCCN:2003-101909.

Audience: **l,u,f.** *Choice, 2001.*

Harris, Henry QH325.H35 2002
Things Come to Life: Spontaneous Generation Revisited. Trade
Cloth. Oxford University Press, Inc. New York, NY. 2002. 186p.
ISBN:0-19-851538-3, ISBN13: 978-0-19-851538-8.
Dewey:576.8/3. LCCN:2001-054856.

Audience: **u,f.** *Choice, 2003, 2002.*

Hodge, Michael J. QH361.H63 1991
Origins and Species: A Study on the Historical Sources of
Darwinism and the Contexts of Some Other Accounts of
Organic Diversity from Plato and Aristotle On. Owen Gingerich

(Editor). Trade Cloth. Garland Publishing, Inc. New York, NY.
1991. 824p. Harvard Dissertations in the History of Science Ser.
ISBN:0-8240-7252-9, ISBN13: 978-0-8240-7252-0.
Dewey:575/.009. LCCN:91-010335.

Audience: **u,f.**

Hunter, Graeme K. QP514.2.H86 2002
Vital Forces: The Discovery of the Molecular Basis of Life.
Trade Cloth. Elsevier Science & Technology Books. Saint
Louis, MO. 2000. 364p. ISBN:0-12-361810-X, ISBN13:
978-0-12-361810-8. Dewey:572/.09. LCCN:99-067772.

Audience: **l,u.**

Huth, Hans QH76.H88 1991
Nature and the American: Three Centuries of Changing
Attitudes. Douglas H. Strong (Introduction by). Trade Cloth.
University of Nebraska Press. Lincoln, NE. 1990. 314p.
ISBN:0-8032-7247-2, ISBN13: 978-0-8032-7247-7.
Dewey:333.95/16/0973. LCCN:90-035727.

Audience: **g,l,u,f.**

Israel, G. & Gasca, A. M. QH323.5.I86 2002
The Biology of Numbers: The Correspondence of Vito Volterra
on Mathematical Biology. Trade Cloth. Birkhauser Boston.
Cambridge, MA. 2002. ix, 405p. Science Networks Historical
Studies, Vol. 26 ISBN:3-7643-6514-5, ISBN13:
978-3-7643-6514-1. Dewey:570/.1/51. LCCN:2002-023671.

Audience: **u,f.**

Kline, David BX8695.S6
Great Possessions: An Amish Farmer's Journal. Wendell Berry
(Foreword by). Trade Paper. Farrar, Straus & Giroux. New York,
NY. 1991. 272p. ISBN:0-86547-471-0, ISBN13:
978-0-86547-471-0. Dewey:289.3092.

Audience: **g,l,u,f.**

Knowles, Karen (Editor) QH81.C38 1992
Celebrating the Land: Women's Nature Writings, 1850-1991.
Trade Paper. Northland Publishing. Flagstaff, AZ. 1992. 144p.
ISBN:0-87358-545-3, ISBN13: 978-0-87358-545-3.
Dewey:508/.082. LCCN:92-018071.

Audience: **g,l,u,f.**

Krutch, Joseph Wood QH81.K828 1995
The Best Nature Writing of Joseph Wood Krutch. Edward
Lenders (Foreword by). Trade Paper. University of Utah Press.
Salt Lake City, UT. 1995. 392p. ISBN:0-87480-480-9, ISBN13:
978-0-87480-480-5. Dewey:508. LCCN:95-004976.

Audience: **l,u,f.**

Lambert, Robert A. CS477.F49
Contested Mountains: Nature, Development and Environment in
the Cairngorms Region of Scotland, 1880-1980. Trade Cloth.
White Horse Press. Cambridge, 2001. 320p.
ISBN:1-874267-44-8, ISBN13: 978-1-874267-44-7.
Dewey:941.24.

Audience: **u,f.**

Lane, John QH81.W765 1999
The Woods Stretched for Miles: An Anthology of Contemporary
Nature Writing from the South. Trade Cloth. University of
Georgia Press. Athens, GA. 1999. 256p. ISBN:0-8203-2087-0,
ISBN13: 978-0-8203-2087-8. Dewey:508.75. LCCN:98-020339.

Audience: **l,u,f.**

Larson, Edward J. QH361.L27 2004
Evolution: The Remarkable History of a Scientific Theory. Trade
Cloth. Random House, Inc. New York, NY. 2004. 368p.

ISBN:0-679-64288-9, ISBN13: 978-0-679-64288-6.
Dewey:576.8. LCCN:2003-064888.

Audience: **l,u,f.** *Choice, 2004.*

Lennox, James G.   **QH331 .L528 2001**
Aristotle's Philosophy of Biology: Studies in the Origins of Life
Science. Michael Ruse (Contribution by). Trade Cloth.
Cambridge University Press. New York, NY. 2000. 346p.
Cambridge Studies in Philosophy and Biology
ISBN:0-521-65027-5, ISBN13: 978-0-521-65027-4.
Dewey:570/.1. LCCN:00-026070.

Audience: **u,f.** *Choice, 2001.*

Lewis, Ricki   **QH506.L4365 2001**
Discovery: Windows of the Life Sciences. Trade Paper.
Blackwell Publishing, Inc. Malden, MA. 2001. 248p.
ISBN:0-632-04452-7, ISBN13: 978-0-632-04452-8.
Dewey:572.8. LCCN:00-034229.

Audience: **l,u,f.**

Lewontin, Richard C.   **QH506**
The Triple Helix: Gene, Organism, and Environment. Trade
Paper. Harvard University Press. Cambridge, MA. 2002. 144p.
ISBN:0-674-00677-1, ISBN13: 978-0-674-00677-5.
Dewey:572.8/01.

Audience: **l,u,f.** *Choice, 2000.*

Magner, Lois N.   **QH305.M22 2002**
A History of the Life Sciences. Ed. 3. Paper over Boards.
Marcel Dekker Inc. New York, NY. 2002. 512p.
ISBN:0-8247-0824-5, ISBN13: 978-0-8247-0824-5.
Dewey:570/.9. LCCN:2002-031313.

Audience: **l,u,f.**

Mahowald, Mary Briody   **RB155.M3135 2000**
Genes, Women, Equality. Trade Cloth. Oxford University Press,
Inc. New York, NY. 1999. 334p. ISBN:0-19-512110-4, ISBN13:
978-0-19-512110-0. Dewey:616/.042/082. LCCN:99-014296.

Audience: **l,u,f.**

Mayr, Ernst   **QH331.M375 2004**
What Makes Biology Unique?: Considerations on the Autonomy
of a Scientific Discipline. Cloth Text. Cambridge University
Press. New York, NY. 2004. 246p. ISBN:0-521-84114-3,
ISBN13: 978-0-521-84114-6. Dewey:570/.1.
LCCN:2004-045888.

Audience: **l,u,f.** *Choice, 2005.*

McKibben, Bill (Editor)   **QH81 .B917 1992**
Birch Browsings: A John Burroughs Reader. Trade Paper.
Penguin Group (USA) Inc. New York, NY. 1992. 240p. Nature
Library ISBN:0-14-017016-2, ISBN13: 978-0-14-017016-0.
Dewey:508. LCCN:92-009466.

Audience: **l,u,f.**

Morange, Michel   **QH506**
A History of Molecular Biology. Trade Paper. Harvard
University Press. Cambridge, MA. 2000. 348p.
ISBN:0-674-00169-9, ISBN13: 978-0-674-00169-5.
Dewey:572.8/09.

Audience: **u,f.** *Choice, 1999.*

Mortenson, Philip B.   **QH83.M69 2003**
This Is Not a Weasel: A Close Look at Nature's Most Confusing
Terms. Trade Paper. John Wiley & Sons, Inc. Hoboken, NJ.
2003. 272p. ISBN:0-471-27396-1, ISBN13: 978-0-471-27396-7.
Dewey:570/.1/4. LCCN:2003-005318.

Audience: **g,l,u,f.** *Choice, 2004.*

New York Times Staff   **Q141.S2945 2000**
Scientists at Work. Laura Chang (Editor), Stephen Jay Gould
(Foreword by), Cornelia Dean (Introduction by). Trade Paper.
McGraw-Hill Trade. New York, NY. 2000. 372p.
ISBN:0-07-135882-X, ISBN13: 978-0-07-135882-8.
Dewey:509.2/2 B. LCCN:00-712544.

Audience: **g,l,u.**

Nurse, Paul   **QH305**
The Great Ideas of Biology: The Romanes Lecture for 2003.
Trade Paper. Oxford University Press, Inc. New York, NY. 2004.
28p. Romanes Lectures, Vol. 2003 ISBN:0-19-951897-1,
ISBN13: 978-0-19-951897-5. Dewey:570/.9.
LCCN:2004-302080.

Audience: **g,l,u,f.**

Olson, Sigurd F.   **QH102.O386 2001**
The Meaning of Wilderness: Essential Articles and Speeches.
David Backes (Editor, Introduction by). Trade Cloth. University
of Minnesota Press. Minneapolis, MN. 2001. 232p.
ISBN:0-8166-3708-3, ISBN13: 978-0-8166-3708-9.
Dewey:508.7. LCCN:00-011869.

Audience: **g,l,u,f.**

Pasternak, Charles A.   **QH431**
Quest: The Essence of Humanity. Baruch S. Blumberg
(Foreword by). Trade Cloth. John Wiley & Sons, Inc. Hoboken,
NJ. 2003. 432p. ISBN:0-470-85144-9, ISBN13:
978-0-470-85144-9. Dewey:599.93/8. LCCN:2003-273366.

Audience: **l,u,f.**

Persell, Stuart M.   **QH361.P47 1999**
Neo-Lamarckism and the Evolution Controversy in France,
1870-1920. Trade Cloth. Edwin Mellen Press, The. Lewiston,
NY. 1999. 304p. Studies in French Civilization, Vol. 14
ISBN:0-7734-8275-X, ISBN13: 978-0-7734-8275-3.
Dewey:576.8/0944/09034. LCCN:98-048633.

Audience: **u,f.** *Choice, 1999.*

Plum, Sydney L. (Editor,   **QH81.S8725 1996**
Introduction by)
Coming Through the Swamp: The Nature Writings of Gene
Stratton Porter. Cloth Text. University of Utah Press. Salt Lake
City, UT. 1996. 300p. ISBN:0-87480-497-3, ISBN13:
978-0-87480-497-3. Dewey:813/.52. LCCN:95-048024.

Audience: **g,l,u,f.** *Choice, 1996.*

Pomata, Gianna & Siraisi,   **QH135.H57 2005**
Nancy G. (Editors)
Historia: Empiricism and Erudition in Early Modern Europe.
Trade Cloth. MIT Press. Cambridge, MA. 2005. 472p.
Transformations Ser., :Studies in the History of Science and
Technology ISBN:0-262-16229-6, ISBN13: 978-0-262-16229-6.
Dewey:508/.094. LCCN:2005-041560.

Audience: **u,f.**

Rainger, Ronald (Editor),   **QH305.2.U6A54 1991**
et al.
The American Development of Biology. Keith R. Benson &
Jane Maienschein (Editors). Paper Text. Rutgers University
Press. Piscataway, NJ. 1991. 380p. ISBN:0-8135-1702-8,
ISBN13: 978-0-8135-1702-5. Dewey:574/.0973.
LCCN:91-011533.

Audience: **u,f.** *Choice, 1988.*

Reilly, Philip R.   **QH431.R38 2000**
Abraham Lincoln's DNA and Other Adventures in Genetics.
Trade Cloth. Cold Spring Harbor Laboratory Press. Woodbury,

NY. 2000. xx, 339p. ISBN:0-87969-580-3, ISBN13: 978-0-87969-580-4. Dewey:599.93/5. LCCN:00-029467.
Audience: **l,u,f.** *Choice, 2001.*

Ruse, Michael (Editor)   **QH360.5.B87 1996**
But Is It Science?: The Philosophical Question in the Creation/Evolution Controversy. Trade Paper. Prometheus Books, Publishers. Amherst, NY. 1996. 406p. ISBN:1-57392-087-8, ISBN13: 978-1-57392-087-2. Dewey:575/.001. LCCN:96-004218.
Audience: **g,l,u,f.**

Ruse, Michael   **QH360.5.R87 1996**
Monad to Man: The Concept of Progress in Evolutionary Biology. Trade Cloth. Harvard University Press. Cambridge, MA. 1997. 640p. ISBN:0-674-58220-9, ISBN13: 978-0-674-58220-0. Dewey:575. LCCN:96-018951.
Audience: **u,f.**

Sapp, Jan   **QH305.S27 2003**
Genesis: The Evolution of Biology. Trade Paper. Oxford University Press, Inc. New York, NY. 2003. 384p. ISBN:0-19-515619-6, ISBN13: 978-0-19-515619-5. Dewey:570. LCCN:2002-152271.
Audience: **g,l,u,f.**

Schopf, J. William (Editor)   **QH325 .L694 2002**
Life's Origin: The Beginnings of Biological Evolution. Trade Cloth. University of California Press. Berkeley, CA. 2002. 256p. ISBN:0-520-23390-5, ISBN13: 978-0-520-23390-4. Dewey:576.8/3. LCCN:2002-002071.
Audience: **g,l,u,f.** *Choice, 2003.*

Schopf, J. William (Editor)   **QH359.M35 1992**
Major Events in the History of Life. Trade Paper. Jones & Bartlett Publishers, Inc. Sudbury, MA. 1991. 208p. ISBN:0-86720-268-8, ISBN13: 978-0-86720-268-7. Dewey:575. LCCN:91-036263.
Audience: **u,f.** *Choice, 1992.*

Senker, Cath   **QH506.S484 2002**
Rosalind Franklin. Cloth Text. Raintree. Crystal Lake, IL. 2002. 48p. Scientists Who Made History Ser. ISBN:0-7398-5226-4, ISBN13: 978-0-7398-5226-2. Dewey:572.8/092 B. LCCN:2001-048961.
Audience: **l,u,f.**

Serafini, Anthony   **QH305.S48 1993**
The Epic History of Biology. Trade Paper. Perseus Books Group. New York, NY. 2001. 408p. ISBN:0-7382-0577-X, ISBN13: 978-0-7382-0577-9. Dewey:574.09.
Audience: **u,f.** *Choice, 1994.*

Shore, William H.   **QH81.N315 1994**
The Nature of Nature: New Essays from America's Finest Writers on Science. Trade Cloth. Harcourt Trade Publishers. New York, NY. 1994. 356p. ISBN:0-15-100080-8, ISBN13: 978-0-15-100080-7. Dewey:508. LCCN:94-003123.
Audience: **g,l,u.**

Shreeve, James   **QH431.S5577 2004**
The Genome War: How Craig Venter Tried to Capture the Code of Life and Save the World. Trade Cloth. Alfred A. Knopf Inc. New York, NY. 2004. 416p. ISBN:0-375-40629-8, ISBN13: 978-0-375-40629-4. Dewey:611/.01816. LCCN:2003-047580.
Audience: **u,f.** *Choice, 2004.*

Smocovitis, Vassiliki B.   **QH361.S64 1996**
Unifying Biology: The Evolutionary Synthesis and Evolutionary Biology. Trade Cloth. Princeton University Press. Princeton, NJ. 1996. 254p. ISBN:0-691-03343-9, ISBN13: 978-0-691-03343-3. Dewey:575/.009. LCCN:96-005605.
Audience: **g,l,u,f.** *Choice, 1997.*

Sorenson, W. Conner   **QL474.S67 1995**
Brethren of the Net: American Entomology, 1840-1880. Trade Cloth. University of Alabama Press. Tuscaloosa, AL. 1995. 376p. History of American Science and Technology Ser. ISBN:0-8173-0755-9, ISBN13: 978-0-8173-0755-4. Dewey:595.7/00973. LCCN:94-005258.
Audience: **l,u.** *Choice, 1996.*

Spary, E. C.   **QH147.S62 2000**
Utopia's Garden: French Natural History from Old Regime to Revolution. Trade Cloth. University of Chicago Press. Chicago, IL. 2000. 304p. ISBN:0-226-76862-7, ISBN13: 978-0-226-76862-5. Dewey:508.44/09/033. LCCN:00-029897.
Audience: **g,l,u,f.**

Stahl, Franklin W. &   **QH506.W425 2000**
  Hershey, A. D.
We Can Sleep Later: Alfred D. Hershey and the Origins of Molecular Biology. Trade Cloth. Cold Spring Harbor Laboratory Press. Woodbury, NY. 2000. xii, 359p. ISBN:0-87969-567-6, ISBN13: 978-0-87969-567-5. Dewey:572.8. LCCN:99-086195.
Audience: **u,f.**

Strick, James Edgar   **QH325.S85 2000**
Sparks of Life: Darwinism and the Victorian Debates over Spontaneous Generation. Trade Cloth. Harvard University Press. Cambridge, MA. 2000. 304p. ISBN:0-674-00292-X, ISBN13: 978-0-674-00292-0. Dewey:576.8/8. LCCN:00-031915.
Audience: **u,f.** *Choice, 2001.*

Titterington, D. M. & Cox,   **QH301.T55 2001**
  D. R. (Editors)
Biometrika: One Hundred Years. Ed. 2. Trade Cloth. Oxford University Press, Inc. New York, NY. 2001. 392p. ISBN:0-19-850993-6, ISBN13: 978-0-19-850993-6. Dewey:570/.1/5195. LCCN:2001-036127.
Audience: **u,f.**

Tracy, Kathleen   **QP620.T73 2005**
Friedrich Miescher and the Story of Nucleic Acid. Library Binding. Mitchell Lane Publishers, Inc. Hockessin, DE. 2005. 48p. Uncharted, Unexplored, and Unexplained Ser., :Scientific Advancements of the 19th Century ISBN:1-58415-369-5, ISBN13: 978-1-58415-369-6. Dewey:572.8. LCCN:2005-004252.
Audience: **u,f.**

Turner, Tom   **QH76.T87 1991**
Sierra Club: One Hundred Years of Protecting Nature. Frederick Turner (Foreword by), Richard Leonard & Susan Merrow (Introduction by). Trade Cloth. Harry N. Abrams, Inc. New York, NY. 1991. 288p. ISBN:0-8109-3820-0, ISBN13: 978-0-8109-3820-5. Dewey:333.9516/06073. LCCN:91-009866.
Audience: **g.**

Walters, Michael   **QL672.7.W36 2003**
A Concise History of Ornithology. Cloth over Boards. Yale University Press. Cumberland, RI. 2003. 256p. ISBN:0-300-09073-0, ISBN13: 978-0-300-09073-4. Dewey:598/.09. LCCN:2003-104752.
Audience: **l,u.** *Choice, 2004.*

Watson, James D.   **QH506**
Genes, Girls and Gamow: After the Double Helix. Trade Paper. Knopf Publishing Group. New York, NY. 2003. 336p. ISBN:0-375-72715-9, ISBN13: 978-0-375-72715-3. Dewey:572.8/092 B.

Audience: **l,u,f.** *Choice, 2002.*

Wickelgren, Ingrid   **QH431.W483 2002**
The Gene Masters: How a New Breed of Scientific Entrepeneurs Raced for the Biggest Prize in Biology. Trade Cloth. Henry Holt & Company. New York, NY. 2002. 288p. ISBN:0-8050-7174-1, ISBN13: 978-0-8050-7174-0. Dewey:611/.01816. LCCN:2002-067321.

Audience: **u,f.**

Wiggins, Arthur W. &   **Q163**
  Wynn, Charles M.
The Five Biggest Unsolved Problems in Science. Sidney Harris (Commentaries by). Trade Paper. John Wiley & Sons, Inc. Hoboken, NJ. 2003. 234p. ISBN:0-471-26808-9, ISBN13: 978-0-471-26808-6. Dewey:500. LCCN:2003-284262.

Audience: **g,l.**

Witkowski, Jan   **QH506.I45 2000**
Illuminating Life: Selected Papers from Cold Spring Harbor, 1903-1969. Trade Cloth. Cold Spring Harbor Laboratory Press. Woodbury, NY. 1999. xvi, 383p. ISBN:0-87969-566-8, ISBN13: 978-0-87969-566-8. Dewey:572.8. LCCN:99-045419.

Audience: **u,f.**

Young, David G.   **QH361.Y695 1992**
The Discovery of Evolution. Cloth Text. Cambridge University Press. New York, NY. 1992. 256p. ISBN:0-521-43441-6, ISBN13: 978-0-521-43441-6. Dewey:575/.009. LCCN:93-116579.

Audience: **g,l,u.** *Choice, 1993.*

Biological Techniques

📖 Google Directory: Biological Laboratories. http://www.google.com/Top/Science/Biology/Institutions/ Google.

Audience: **g,l.**

Brubaker, David C. &   **QH315.L47 2000**
  Ostroff, Joel H. (Editors)
Life, Learning, and Community: Concepts and Models for Service-Learning in Biology. Perfect. American Association for Higher Education. Washington, DC. 2000. 176p. AAHE's Series on Service-Learning in the Disciplines, Vol. 2 ISBN:1-56377-018-0, ISBN13: 978-1-56377-018-0. Dewey:570/.71/1. LCCN:2001-272836.

Audience: **l,u,f.**

Chang, Raymond   **QH345.C425 2004**
Physical Chemistry for the Biosciences. Perfect, Paper over Boards. University Science Books. Sausalito, CA. 2005. 677p. ISBN:1-891389-33-5, ISBN13: 978-1-891389-33-7. Dewey:572. LCCN:2004-049612.

Audience: **u,f.** *Choice, 2005.*

Grove, Noel   **QH76.K73 1992**
Preserving Eden: The Nature Conservancy. Stephen J. Krasemann (Photographer). Trade Cloth. Harry N. Abrams, Inc.

New York, NY. 1992. 192p. ISBN:0-8109-3663-1, ISBN13: 978-0-8109-3663-8. Dewey:333.95/16/06073. LCCN:91-024551.

Audience: **g,l,u,f.**

Biological Techniques > Zoos and Botanical Gardens

📖 Google Directory: Zoos and Aquariums. http://www.google.com/Top/Science/Institutions/ Zoos_and_Aquariums/ Google.

Audience: **g,l.**

     QH431

📖 The Jackson Laboratory. http://www.jax.org/

Audience: **l,u,f.**

     QL9.2

📖 ZooWeb. http://www.zooweb.com/

Audience: **l,u,f.**

Anderson, Frank J.   **QK98.3.A53 1990**
A Treasury of Flowers: Rare Illustrations from the Collection of the New York Botanical Garden. Trade Cloth. Bulfinch Press. Boston, MA. 1990. ISBN:0-8212-1758-5, ISBN13: 978-0-8212-1758-0. Dewey:582.13/022/2. LCCN:89-064181.

Audience: **g,l,u,f.**

Banerjee, Subhankar   **QH105.A4B36 2003**
Arctic National Wildlife Refuge: Seasons of Life and Land. Jimmy Carter, Peter Mattiessen, David Sibley, George Schaller, Bill Meadows, Debbie Miller & Fran Mauer (Contribution by). Cloth Text. Mountaineers Books, The. Seattle, WA. 2005. 160p. ISBN:0-89886-909-9, ISBN13: 978-0-89886-909-5. Dewey:508.798/7. LCCN:2002-154578.

Audience: **g,l.**

Baratay, Eric &   **QL76.B3713 2002**
  Hardouin-Fugier, Elisabeth
Zoo: A History of Zoological Gardens in the West. Oliver Welsh (Translator). Trade Cloth. Reaktion Books, Ltd. London, 2004. 356p. ISBN:1-86189-111-3, ISBN13: 978-1-86189-111-2. Dewey:590.73. LCCN:2004-426245.

Audience: **g,l,u,f.** *Choice, 2003.*

Barton, Miles   **QL76.B29 1988**
Zoos and Game Reserves. Franklin Watts, Inc. Staff (Editor). Trade Paper. Scholastic Library Publishing. Danbury, CT. 1988. 32p. Survival Ser. ISBN:0-531-17090-X, ISBN13: 978-0-531-17090-8. Dewey:590/.74/4. LCCN:87-082889.

Audience: **g,l.**

Bell, Catharine (Editor)   **QL76.E53 2001**
Encyclopedia of the World's Zoos, Set. Lester Fisher (Contribution by). Trade Cloth. Fitzroy Dearborn Publishers, Inc. Chicago, IL. 2001. 1600p. ISBN:1-57958-174-9, ISBN13: 978-1-57958-174-9. Dewey:590/.7/303. LCCN:2002-265421.

Audience: **g,l,u,f.** *Choice, 2001.*

Benyus, Janine M.   QL751 .B368 1992
What Makes the Lion Yawn?: A Zoogoer's Guide to Animal
Behavior. Trade Cloth. Addison-Wesley Longman, Inc. Boston,
MA. 1992. 400p. ISBN:0-201-57008-4, ISBN13:
978-0-201-57008-3. Dewey:591.51.

Audience: **g,l.**

Bonner, Jeffrey P.   QL76.B66 2006
Sailing with Noah: Stories from the World of Zoos. Trade Cloth.
University of Missouri Press. Columbia, MO. 2006. 312p.
ISBN:0-8262-1636-6, ISBN13: 978-0-8262-1636-6.
Dewey:590.73. LCCN:2005-031401.

Audience: **g,l.**

Bostock, Stephen S.   HV4708
Zoos and Animal Rights: The Ethics of Keeping Animals. Paper
over Boards. Routledge. New York, NY. 1993. 240p.
ISBN:0-415-05057-X, ISBN13: 978-0-415-05057-9.
Dewey:179.3. LCCN:92-035167.

Audience: **l,u,f.**

Bry, Charlene   QK73.U62M573 1989
World of Plants: The Missouri Botanical Garden. Trade Cloth.
Harry N. Abrams, Inc. New York, NY. 1990. 192p.
ISBN:0-8109-1772-6, ISBN13: 978-0-8109-1772-9.
Dewey:580/.74/477866. LCCN:89-000204.

Audience: **g,l,u,f.** *Choice, 1990.*

Butcher, Russell D.   QL84.2 .B88 2003
America's National Wildlife Refuges: A Complete Guide. Karen
Hollingsworth & John Hollingsworth (Photographers). Trade
Paper. Roberts Rinehart Publishers. Boulder, CO. 2003. 512p.
ISBN:1-57098-379-8, ISBN13: 978-1-57098-379-5.
Dewey:333.95/4160973. LCCN:2002-114660.

Audience: **g,l,u,f.** *Choice, 2003.*

Cogwell, Mathew T.   KFA1653.8.A73A73
Arctic National Wildlife Refuge. Trade Cloth. Nova Science
Publishers, Inc. Hauppauge, NY. 2002. 150p.
ISBN:1-59033-327-6, ISBN13: 978-1-59033-327-3.
Dewey:343.798/076995. LCCN:2002-070313.

Audience: **g,l.** *Choice, 2003.*

Cunningham, Anne S.   NA8360.C86 2000
Crystal Palaces: American Garden Conservatories. Paul Bennett
(Introduction by). Trade Cloth. Princeton Architectural Press.
New York, NY. 2000. xiii, 178p. ISBN:1-56898-242-9, ISBN13:
978-1-56898-242-7. Dewey:728/.924/0973. LCCN:00-008825.

Audience: **g,l,u,f.** *Choice, 2001.*

Dolin, Eric Jay   QL84.2.D65 2003
Smithsonian Book of National Wildlife Refuges. John
Hollingsworth & Karen Hollingsworth (Photographers). Trade
Cloth. Smithsonian Institution Press. Washington, DC. 2003.
256p. ISBN:1-58834-117-8, ISBN13: 978-1-58834-117-4.
Dewey:333.95/16/0973. LCCN:2002-030254.

Audience: **g,l,u,f.**

Earle, Sylvia A. & Wolcott,   QH91.75.U6E18 1999
  Henry
Wild Ocean: America's Parks under the Sea. Trade Cloth.
National Geographic Society. Washington, DC. 1999. 224p.
ISBN:0-7922-7471-7, ISBN13: 978-0-7922-7471-1.
Dewey:333.78/3/097309162. LCCN:99-026847.

Audience: **g,l,u,f.**

Emory, Jerry   QH105.C2 E56 1999
The Monterey Bay Shoreline Guide. Trade Cloth. University of
California Press. Berkeley, CA. 1999. 320p. University of
California Press/Monterey Bay Aquarium Ser., Vol. 1
ISBN:0-520-21153-7, ISBN13: 978-0-520-21153-7.
Dewey:508.794/76. LCCN:98-036120.

Audience: **l,u.**

Fisher, Lester E.   QL31.F527
Dr. Fisher's Life on the Ark: Green Alligators, Bushman, and
Other. Evanston, IL : Racom. 2005. ISBN:0-9704515-6-3,
ISBN13: 978-0-9704515-6-9.

Audience: **g.**

Folzenlogen, Darcy &   QL76.5.U6F64 1993
  Folzenlogen, Robert
A Guide to American Zoos and Aquariums. Trade Paper. Willow
Press. Columbia, MO. 1993. 324p. ISBN:0-9620685-4-3,
ISBN13: 978-0-9620685-4-6. Dewey:590/.74/473025.
LCCN:93-093806.

Audience: **g,l,f.**

Hancocks, David   QL76 .H35 2001
A Different Nature: The Paradoxical World of Zoos and Their
Uncertain Future. Trade Cloth. University of California Press.
Berkeley, CA. 2001. 301p. ISBN:0-520-21879-5, ISBN13:
978-0-520-21879-6. Dewey:590/.7/3. LCCN:00-053209.

Audience: **g,l.** *Choice, 2001.*

Hanson, Elizabeth   QL76.5.U6H36 2002
Animal Attractions: Nature on Display in American Zoos. Trade
Cloth. Princeton University Press. Princeton, NJ. 2002. 256p.
ISBN:0-691-05992-6, ISBN13: 978-0-691-05992-1.
Dewey:590.7/373. LCCN:2001-055198.

Audience: **g,l,u.** *Choice, 2003.*

Hillard, James M.   QL79.N7H55 1995
Aquariums of North America: A Guidebook to Appreciating
North America's Aquatic Treasures. Trade Cloth. Scarecrow
Press, Inc. Lanham, MD. 1995. 199p. ISBN:0-8108-2923-1,
ISBN13: 978-0-8108-2923-7. Dewey:597/.0074/73.
LCCN:94-018440.

Audience: **g,l,u.**

Hoage, Robert J. & Deiss,   QL76.N48 1996
  William A.
New Worlds, New Animals: From Menagerie to Zoological Park
in the Nineteenth Century. Michael H. Robinson (Foreword by).
Trade Paper. Johns Hopkins University Press. Baltimore, MD.
1996. 224p. ISBN:0-8018-5373-7, ISBN13: 978-0-8018-5373-9.
Dewey:590.7/44/09034. LCCN:95-033006.

Audience: **g,l,u.**

Houk, Walter   QK73.U62H866 1996
The Botanical Gardens at the Huntington. Peggy P. Bernal
(Editor), Don Normark (Photographer), James Folsom
(Contribution by). Trade Cloth. Huntington Library Press. San
Marino, CA. 1996. 192p. ISBN:0-87328-155-1, ISBN13:
978-0-87328-155-3. Dewey:580/.74/479493. LCCN:95-045328.

Audience: **g,l,f.**

Hutchins, Michael (Editor),   SF408.3.E84 1995
  et al.
Ethics on the Ark: Zoos, Animal Welfare, and Wildlife
Conservation. Bryan G. Norton, Terry L. Maple & Elizabeth F.
Stevens (Editors). Trade Cloth. Smithsonian Institution Press.

Washington, DC. 1995. 432p. Zoo and Aquarium Biology and Conservation Ser. ISBN:1-56098-515-1, ISBN13: 978-1-56098-515-0. Dewey:639.9/3/01. LCCN:94-037139.

Audience: **g,l,u.** *Choice, 1996.*

Keenan, Philip E.   **QL681.K44 2002**
  (Photographer, Text by)
Birding Across North America: A Naturalist's Observations. Trade Cloth. Timber Press, Inc. Portland, OR. 2002. 260p. ISBN:0-88192-528-4, ISBN13: 978-0-88192-528-9. Dewey:598/.07/2347. LCCN:2001-037623.

Audience: **g,l,u,f.** *Choice, 2002.*

Kisling, Vernon N.   **QL76**
Zoo and Aquarium History: Ancient Animal Collections to Zoological Gardens. Boca Raton, Fla. : CRC Press. 2001. ISBN:0-8493-2100-X, ISBN13: 978-0-8493-2100-9.

Audience: **g,l.**

Koebner, Linda   **QL76.K63 1994**
Zoo Book. Trade Cloth. Tom Doherty Associates, LLC. New York, NY. 1994. 224p. ISBN:0-312-85322-X, ISBN13: 978-0-312-85322-8. Dewey:590/.74/4. LCCN:94-000121.

Audience: **g,l,f.**

Langstroth, Lovell &   **QH105.C2L36 2000**
  Langstroth, Libby
A Living Bay: The Underwater World of Monterey Bay. Trade Cloth. University of California Press. Berkeley, CA. 2000. 304p. University of California Press/Monterey Bay Aquarium Ser., Vol. 2 ISBN:0-520-21686-5, ISBN13: 978-0-520-21686-0. Dewey:577.7/432. LCCN:00-022014.

Audience: **g,l,u,f.** *Choice, 2001.*

Malamud, Randy   **HV4708.M35 1998**
Reading Zoos: Representations of Animals and Captivity. Trade Cloth. New York University Press. New York, NY. 1998. 238p. ISBN:0-8147-5602-6, ISBN13: 978-0-8147-5602-7. Dewey:809.9/33/62. LCCN:97-038182.

Audience: **g,l,u,f.**

Marshall, Anthony D.   **QL76.5.U6M37 1994**
Zoos. Trade Paper. Random House, Inc. New York, NY. 1994. ISBN:0-679-74687-0, ISBN13: 978-0-679-74687-4. Dewey:590/.74/473. LCCN:93-033984.

Audience: **g,l.**

Mazur, Nicole   **QL76**
After the Ark?: Environmental Policy-Making and the Zoo. Trade Paper. Melbourne University Publishing. Carlton, VIC. 2001. 276p. ISBN:0-522-84947-4, ISBN13: 978-0-522-84947-9. Dewey:590/.7/3.

Audience: **g,l,u.** *Choice, 2002.*

Murphy, James B., et al.   **QL666.L29K66 2002**
Komodo Dragons: Biology and Conservation. Claudio Ciofi, Columba De la Panouse & Trooper Walsh (Authors). Trade Cloth. Smithsonian Institution Press. Washington, DC. 2002. 248p. Zoo and Aquarium Biology and Conservation Ser. ISBN:1-58834-073-2, ISBN13: 978-1-58834-073-3. Dewey:597.95. LCCN:2002-021681.

Audience: **l,u.**

Nichols, Mike   **QL76.5.U6N535 1996**
  (Photographer)
Keepers of the Kingdom: The New American Zoo. Trade Cloth.

Lickle Publishing, Inc. Palm Beach, FL. 1996. 132p. ISBN:0-9650308-2-2, ISBN13: 978-0-9650308-2-3. LCCN:95-023922.

Audience: **g,l.**

Novacek, Michael J. (Editor)   **QH541.15.B56B573**
The Biodiversity Crisis: Losing What Counts. Trade Paper. New Press, The. New York, NY. 2001. 224p. American Museum of Natural History Ser. ISBN:1-56584-570-6, ISBN13: 978-1-56584-570-1. Dewey:333.95/16. LCCN:99-054732.

Audience: **l,u.**

Nyhuis, Allen W.   **QL76.5.U6N94 1994**
The Zoo Book: A Guide to America's Best. Trade Paper. Carousel Press. Berkeley, CA. 1994. 288p. ISBN:0-917120-13-2, ISBN13: 978-0-917120-13-8. Dewey:590/.74/473. LCCN:93-046925.

Audience: **g,l,u,f.**

O'Brien, Tim   **QL76.5.N7 O27 1992**
Where the Animals Are: A Guide to the Best Zoos, Aquariums and Wildlife Attractions in North America. Trade Paper. Globe Pequot Press, The. Guilford, CT. 1992. 320p. ISBN:1-56440-077-8, ISBN13: 978-1-56440-077-2. Dewey:590/.74/473. LCCN:92-020081.

Audience: **g,l,u,f.**

O'Neill, Michael J.   **QL77.5.O54 1991**
Zoobabies. Carolyn Fireside (Photographer). Trade Cloth. Random House Adult Trade Publishing Group. New York, NY. 1991. 64p. ISBN:0-679-40698-0, ISBN13: 978-0-679-40698-3. Dewey:636.088/9. LCCN:91-050271.

Audience: **g,l.**

Page, Jake   **QL82.P34 1989**
Smithsonian's New Zoo. Trade Cloth. Smithsonian Institution Press. Washington, DC. 1990. 208p. ISBN:0-87474-734-1, ISBN13: 978-0-87474-734-8. Dewey:639.9. LCCN:89-029626.

Audience: **g,l.**

Page, Jake   **QL76.P29 1990**
Zoo: The Modern Ark. Franz Maier (Photographer). Trade Cloth. Facts On File, Inc.. New York, NY. 1990. 192p. ISBN:0-8160-2345-X, ISBN13: 978-0-8160-2345-5. Dewey:590/.74/4. LCCN:89-029634.

Audience: **g,l.**

Phillips, Roger & Rix,   **SB450.97.P536 2002**
  Martyn
The Botanical Garden: Trees and Shrubs. Trade Cloth. Firefly Books, Ltd. Tonawanda, NY. 2002. 492p. ISBN:1-55297-591-6, ISBN13: 978-1-55297-591-6. Dewey:635.9. LCCN:2003-275969.

Audience: **l,u,f.** *Choice, 2002.*

Phillips, Roger & Rix,   **SB450.97.P536 2002**
  Martyn
The Botanical Garden: Perennials and Annuals. Trade Cloth. Firefly Books, Ltd. Tonawanda, NY. 2002. 540p. ISBN:1-55297-592-4, ISBN13: 978-1-55297-592-3. Dewey:635.9. LCCN:2003-275969.

Audience: **l,u.** *Choice, 2002.*

Riley, Laura & Riley,   **QH76 .R54 1993**
  William
Guide to the National Wildlife Refuges. Ed. 2. Trade Cloth. John Wiley & Sons, Inc. Hoboken, NJ. 1996. 704p.

ISBN:0-02-063660-1, ISBN13: 978-0-02-063660-1.
Dewey:333.95/0973. LCCN:92-015459.

Audience: **g,l,u,f.**

Robinson, Phillip T.   **QL76.R64 2004**
Life at the Zoo: Behind the Scenes with the Animal Doctors.
Trade Cloth. Edinburgh University Press. Edinburgh, 2004.
320p. ISBN:0-231-13248-4, ISBN13: 978-0-231-13248-0.
Dewey:590.73. LCCN:2004-043893.

Audience: **g,l,u,f.**

Rosenthal, Mark, et al.   **QL76.5.U62C487 2003**
The Ark in the Park: The Story of Lincoln Park Zoo. Carol
Tauber & Edward Uhlir (Authors). Trade Cloth. University of
Illinois Press. Champaign, IL. 2003. 216p. ISBN:0-252-02861-9,
ISBN13: 978-0-252-02861-8. Dewey:590/.7/377311.
LCCN:2003-001101.

Audience: **g,l.** *Choice, 2004.*

Rothfels, Nigel   **QL76.5.G3R68 2002**
Savages and Beasts: The Birth of the Modern Zoo. Trade Cloth.
Johns Hopkins University Press. Baltimore, MD. 2002. 288p.
Animals, History, Culture Ser. ISBN:0-8018-6910-2, ISBN13:
978-0-8018-6910-5. Dewey:590/.7/343. LCCN:2001-005689.

Audience: **g,l,u.** *Choice, 2003.*

Salem, Deborah J. &   **HV4708**
  Rowan, Andrew N. (Editors)
The State of the Animals, 2001. Trade Paper. Humane Society
of the United States, The. League City, TX. 2001. 212p.
ISBN:0-9658942-3-1, ISBN13: 978-0-9658942-3-4.
Dewey:179.3.

Audience: **g,l,u.** *Choice, 2001.*

Schaffer, Moselle   **SF416.S32 1990**
Camel Lot: The True Story of a Zoo-Illogical Farm. Trade
Cloth. Penguin Group (USA) Inc. New York, NY. 1990. 288p.
ISBN:0-670-82884-X, ISBN13: 978-0-670-82884-5. Dewey:636.
LCCN:89-040305.

Audience: **g,l.**

Sedgwick, John   **QL77.5.S38 1988**
The Peaceable Kingdom: A Year in the Life of America's Oldest
Zoo. Trade Cloth. HarperCollins Publishers. New York, NY.
1988. 352p. ISBN:0-688-06367-5, ISBN13: 978-0-688-06367-2.
Dewey:590/.74/774811. LCCN:87-024491.

Audience: **g,l.**

Shepherdson, David J.   **SF408.S435 1998**
  (Editor), et al.
Second Nature: Environmental Enrichment for Captive Animals.
Jill D. Mellen & Michael Hutchins (Editors). Trade Cloth.
Smithsonian Institution Press. Washington, DC. 1998. 336p. Zoo
and Aquarium Biology and Conservation Ser.
ISBN:1-56098-745-6, ISBN13: 978-1-56098-745-1.
Dewey:636.088/9. LCCN:97-037840.

Audience: **g,l.**

Stiff, Ruth L.   **QK1.C9 SUPPL.**
Flowers from the Royal Gardens of Kew: Two Centuries of
Curtis's Botanical Magazine. Trade Paper. University Press of
New England. Lebanon, NH. 1988. 80p. ISBN:0-87451-464-9,
ISBN13: 978-0-87451-464-3. Dewey:635.9/05.
LCCN:88-040130.

Audience: **l,u,f.**

Tanner, Ogden &   **QK73.U62N497 1991**
  Auchincloss, Adele
The New York Botanical Garden: An Illustrated Chronicle of
Plants and People. Trade Cloth. Walker & Company. New York,
NY. 1991. 192p. ISBN:0-8027-1141-3, ISBN13:
978-0-8027-1141-0. Dewey:580/.74/47471. LCCN:90-043704.

Audience: **g,l,u,f.**

Taylor, Leighton R.   **QL78.T39 1993**
Aquariums: Windows to Nature. Trade Cloth. John Wiley &
Sons, Inc. Hoboken, NJ. 1993. 192p. ISBN:0-671-85019-9,
ISBN13: 978-0-671-85019-7. Dewey:574.92/074.
LCCN:92-025083.

Audience: **g,l.**

Wexo, John Bonnett   **QL737.C214W49 1989**
Giant Pandas. Library Binding. Creative Company, The.
Mankato, MN. 1995. 24p. Zoobooks Ser. ISBN:0-88682-228-9,
ISBN13: 978-0-88682-228-6. Dewey:599.74/443.
LCCN:88-029966.

Audience: **g,l.**

Winsor, Mary P.   **QL71.U62C358 1991**
Reading the Shape of Nature: Comparative Zoology at the
Agassiz Museum. Trade Cloth. University of Chicago Press.
Chicago, IL. 1991. 342p. Science and Its Conceptual
Foundations Ser. ISBN:0-226-90214-5, ISBN13:
978-0-226-90214-2. Dewey:574/.012. LCCN:91-008742.

Audience: **g,l,u.** *Choice, 1992.*

Biological Techniques > Herbaria, Museums, and Culture Collections

☐ Google Directory: Biology Museums.
http://www.google.com/Top/Reference/Museums/Science/
Biology/
Google.

Audience: **g,l.**

Fish, L.   **QK61**
Preparing Herbarium Specimens. Trade Paper. National
Botanical Institute. Pretoria, 57p. ISBN:1-919795-38-3, ISBN13:
978-1-919795-38-6. Dewey:580.75.

Audience: **u,f.**

Hay, Ashley & Stacey,   **QK77.N368S73 2004**
  Robyn
Herbarium. Trade Cloth. Cambridge University Press. New
York, NY. 2004. 164p. ISBN:0-521-84277-8, ISBN13:
978-0-521-84277-8. Dewey:580/.74/0994. LCCN:2004-015795.

Audience: **g,l,u,f.** *Choice, 2005.*

Metsger, Deborah A. &   **QK75.M36 1999**
  Byers, Sheila C.
Managing the Modern Herbarium: An Interdisciplinary
Approach. Society for the Preservation of Natural History
Collections Staff & Royal Ontario Museum Staff (Contribution
by). Trade Cloth. Society for the Preservation of Natural History
Collections. Washington, DC. 1999. ISBN:0-9635476-2-3,
ISBN13: 978-0-9635476-2-0. Dewey:580/.74/068.
LCCN:99-064548.

Audience: **u,f.**

Biological Techniques > Microscopy

TK5105.5

☐ WWW Virtual Library: Microscopy.
http://www.ou.edu/research/electron/www-vl/
Samuel Roberts Electron Microscopy Laboratory; University of Oklahoma.

Audience: **g,l.**

Conn, P. Michael (Volume Editor)   QP601

Imaging in Biological Research, Vol. 385, Pt. A. Trade Cloth. Elsevier Science & Technology Books. Saint Louis, MO. 2004. 440p. Methods in Enzymology Ser. ISBN:0-12-182790-9, ISBN13: 978-0-12-182790-8. Dewey:616.0754.

Audience: **u,f.**

Conn, P. Michael (Volume Editor)   QP601

Imaging in Biological Research, Part B, Vol. 386. Trade Cloth. Elsevier Science & Technology Books. Saint Louis, MO. 2004. 540p. Methods in Enzymology Ser. ISBN:0-12-182791-7, ISBN13: 978-0-12-182791-5.

Audience: **u,f.**

Furukawa, T. (Editor)   R857.O6B556 2002

Biological Imaging and Sensing. Trade Cloth. Springer. New York, NY. 2004. XVI, 298p. Biological and Medical Physics Ser. ISBN:3-540-43898-X, ISBN13: 978-3-540-43898-4. Dewey:616.07/54. LCCN:2002-030563.

Audience: **u,f.**

Heath, Julian   QH203

Dictionary of Microscopy. Trade Paper. John Wiley & Sons, Inc. Hoboken, NJ. 2005. 358p. ISBN:0-470-01199-8, ISBN13: 978-0-470-01199-7. Dewey:502/.8/203. LCCN:2005-016322.

Audience: **l,u,f.** *Choice, 2006.*

Hibbs, Alan R.   QH224.H53 2004

Confocal Microscopy for Biologists. Trade Cloth. Springer. New York, NY. 2004. 474p. ISBN:0-306-48468-4, ISBN13: 978-0-306-48468-1. Dewey:570/.28/2. LCCN:2004-044172.

Audience: **l,u,f.**

Kiernan, J. A. & Mason, I. (Editors)   QH207.M57 2002

Microscopy and Histology for Molecular Biologists: A User's Guide. Trade Cloth. Portland Press, Ltd. London, 2002. 408p. ISBN:1-85578-141-7, ISBN13: 978-1-85578-141-2. Dewey:570/.28/2. LCCN:2002-483827.

Audience: **u,f.**

Matsumoto, Brian   QH585.M47 VOL.70

Cell Biological Applications of Confocal Microscopy, Vol. 70. Ed. 2. Trade Cloth. Elsevier Science & Technology Books. Saint Louis, MO. 2002. 507p. Methods in Cell Biology Ser., Vol. 70 ISBN:0-12-480277-X, ISBN13: 978-0-12-480277-3. Dewey:571.6 s 571.6. LCCN:2003-272552.

Audience: **u,f.**

Mayer, Frank & Hoppert, Michael   QH207.H566 2003

Microscopic Techniques in Biotechnology. Trade Cloth. John Wiley & Sons, Inc. Hoboken, NJ. 2003. 342p. ISBN:3-527-30198-4, ISBN13: 978-3-527-30198-0. Dewey:660.6. LCCN:2003-274435.

Audience: **u,f.**

Murphy, Douglas B.   QH211.M87 2001

Fundamentals of Light Microscopy and Electronic Imaging. Trade Cloth. John Wiley & Sons, Inc. Hoboken, NJ. 2001. 384p. ISBN:0-471-25391-X, ISBN13: 978-0-471-25391-4. Dewey:502/.8/2. LCCN:2001-024021.

Audience: **l,u,f.**

Oldfield, Ronald Jowett & Rost, Fred W. D.   QH251 .R67 2000

Photography with a Microscope. Trade Cloth. Cambridge University Press. New York, NY. 2000. 288p. ISBN:0-521-77096-3, ISBN13: 978-0-521-77096-5. Dewey:570/.28/2. LCCN:00-702638.

Audience: **l,u.**

Sideman, S. & Landesberg, Amir (Editors)   Q11.N5 VOL.972

Visualization and Imaging in Transport Phenomena. Trade Cloth. New York Academy of Sciences. New York, NY. 2002. xiv, 346p. Annals of the New York Academy of Sciences Ser., Vol. 972 ISBN:1-57331-370-X, ISBN13: 978-1-57331-370-4. Dewey:500 s 616.07/54. LCCN:2002-011259.

Audience: **u,f.**

Spector, David L. & Goldman, Robert D.   QH207.B27 2005

Basic Methods in Microscopy: Protocols and Concepts from Cells. Saddle Stitched, Cloth over Boards. Cold Spring Harbor Laboratory Press. Woodbury, NY. 2005. 382p. ISBN:0-87969-747-4, ISBN13: 978-0-87969-747-1. Dewey:570/.28/2. LCCN:2004-030135.

Audience: **l,u.**

Swenberg, Charles E. & Conklin, James J. (Editors)   R857.O6I46 1988

Imaging Techniques in Biology and Medicine. Trade Cloth. Elsevier Science & Technology Books. Saint Louis, MO. 1988. 369p. Physical Techniques in Biology and Medicine Ser. ISBN:0-12-679070-1, ISBN13: 978-0-12-679070-2. Dewey:616.07/57. LCCN:87-019469.

Audience: **u,f.**

Taatjes, Douglas J. & Mossman, Brooke T. (Editors)   QH585.C463 2005

Cell Imaging Techniques: Methods and Protocols. Book, Other. Humana Press. Totowa, NJ. 1999. 560p. Methods in Molecular Biology Ser. ISBN:1-58829-157-X, ISBN13: 978-1-58829-157-8. Dewey:611/.0181. LCCN:2005-046145.

Audience: **u,f.**

Taylor, D. Lansing & Wang, Yu-Li (Volume Editors)   QH212.F55

Flourescence Microscopy of Living Cells in Culture: Quantitaive Flourescence Microscopy-Imaging and Spectroscopy. Paul T. Matsudaira & Leslie Wilson (Contribution by). Trade Paper. Elsevier Science & Technology Books. Saint Louis, MO. 1990. 503p. Methods in Cell Biology Ser. ISBN:0-12-684755-X, ISBN13: 978-0-12-684755-0. Dewey:578/.4.

Audience: **u,f.**

Wilson, Leslie (Editor), et al.   QH212.F55

Methods in Cell Biology: Fluorescence Microscopy of Living Cells in Culture: Fluorescent Analogs, Labeling Cells and Basic Microscopy. Lansing Taylor & Yu-Li Wang (Editors). Trade

Cloth. Elsevier Science & Technology Books. Saint Louis, MO. 1988. 441p. ISBN:0-12-564129-X, ISBN13: 978-0-12-564129-6. Dewey:578/.4.

Audience: **u,f.**

Biological Techniques > General Field Methods

Dindal, Daniel L. (Editor)   **QH84.8.S632 1990**
Soil Biology Guide. Trade Cloth. John Wiley & Sons, Inc. Hoboken, NJ. 1990. 1376p. ISBN:0-471-04551-9, ISBN13: 978-0-471-04551-9. Dewey:574.909/48. LCCN:88-028016.

Audience: **u,f.**

Hatfield, J. L. & Stewart, B.   **QH84.8.S6315 1994**
A. (Editors)
Soil Biology: Effects on Soil Quality. Paper over Boards. Lewis Publishers. Boca Raton, FL. 1993. 176p. ISBN:0-87371-927-1, ISBN13: 978-0-87371-927-8. Dewey:574.909/48.

Audience: **u,f.**

Keenan, Philip E.   **QL681.K44 2002**
(Photographer, Text by)
Birding Across North America: A Naturalist's Observations. Trade Cloth. Timber Press, Inc. Portland, OR. 2002. 260p. ISBN:0-88192-528-4, ISBN13: 978-0-88192-528-9. Dewey:598/.07/2347. LCCN:2001-037623.

Audience: **g,l,u,f.** *Choice, 2002.*

Millington, Andrew C.   **QH84.G47 2001**
(Editor), et al.
GIS and Remote Sensing Applications in Biogeography and Ecology. Stephen J. Walsh & Patrick E. Osborne (Editors). Trade Cloth. Springer. New York, NY. 2001. 344p. The Kluwer International Series in Engineering and Computer Science, Vol. 626 ISBN:0-7923-7454-1, ISBN13: 978-0-7923-7454-1. Dewey:578/.09. LCCN:2001-038306.

Audience: **u,f.**

Biological Techniques > General Laboratory Methods

QH431
☐ The Jackson Laboratory.
http://www.jax.org/

Audience: **l,u,f.**

Adams, R. L.   **QH585.A28**
Cell Culture for Biochemists. Ed. 2. Trade Cloth. Elsevier. New York, NY. 1990. 364p. Laboratory Techniques in Biochemistry and Molecular Biology Ser., Vol. 8 ISBN:0-444-81306-3, ISBN13: 978-0-444-81306-0. Dewey:574.87/028.

Audience: **l,u.**

Allen, Connie   **QL813.P54**
Fetal Pig Dissection: A Laboratory Guide. Ed. 2. Trade Paper. John Wiley & Sons, Inc. Hoboken, NJ. 2005. 32p. ISBN:0-471-70138-6, ISBN13: 978-0-471-70138-5. Dewey:571.3/19633. LCCN:2005-280852.

Audience: **l,u.**

Ausubel, Frederick M.   **QH506.S54 2002**
(Editor), et al.
Short Protocols in Molecular Biology. Ed. 5. Roger Brent,

Robert E. Kingston, David D. Moore, J. G. Seidman, John A. Smith & Kevin Struhl (Editors). Trade Paper. John Wiley & Sons, Inc. Hoboken, NJ. 2002. 1512p. ISBN:0-471-25092-9, ISBN13: 978-0-471-25092-0. Dewey:572.8/028. LCCN:2002-027224.

Audience: **u,f.**

Baxevanis, Andreas D.   **QH441.2.C876 2002**
(Editor)
Current Protocols in Bioinformatics. Ringbound. John Wiley & Sons, Inc. Hoboken, NJ. 2003. ISBN:0-471-25093-7, ISBN13: 978-0-471-25093-7. Dewey:570/.285. LCCN:2002-191048.

Audience: **u,f.**

Bienvenut, Willy Vincent   **QP551**
(Editor)
Acceleration and Improvement of Protein Identification by Mass Spectrometry. Trade Cloth. Springer. New York, NY. 2005. XXII, 298p. ISBN:1-4020-3318-4, ISBN13: 978-1-4020-3318-6. Dewey:572/.636. LCCN:2005-299257.

Audience: **u,f.**

Bonifacino, Juan S. (Editor),   **QH585.2.S65 2003**
et al.
Short Protocols in Cell Biology. Mary Dasso, Joe B. Harford, Jennifer Lippincott-Schwartz & Kenneth M. Yamada (Editors). Trade Paper. John Wiley & Sons, Inc. Hoboken, NJ. 2004. 826p. ISBN:0-471-48339-7, ISBN13: 978-0-471-48339-7. Dewey:571.6/38. LCCN:2003-017781.

Audience: **u,f.**

Burlingame, A. L. (Volume   **QP601**
Editor)
Biological Mass Spectrometry. Trade Cloth. Elsevier Science & Technology Books. Saint Louis, MO. 2005. 512p. ISBN:0-12-182807-7, ISBN13: 978-0-12-182807-3. Dewey:574.028.

Audience: **u,f.**

Cassella, J. P., et al.   **QL737.R666C37 1997**
The Rat Nervous System: An Introduction to Preparatory Techniques. J. B. Hay & S. J. Lawson (Authors). Trade Paper. John Wiley & Sons, Inc. Hoboken, NJ. 1997. 116p. ISBN:0-471-96967-2, ISBN13: 978-0-471-96967-9. Dewey:599.32/33. LCCN:96-030347.

Audience: **l,u.**

Chiasson, Robert B.   **QL737.R6**
Laboratory Anatomy of the White Rat. Ed. 5. Spiral. McGraw-Hill Higher Education. Burr Ridge, IL. 1987. 144p. Laboratory Anatomy Ser. ISBN:0-697-05132-3, ISBN13: 978-0-697-05132-5. Dewey:599.3233.

Audience: **l,u.**

Claugher, D. (Editor)   **QH83.S32 1990**
Scanning Electron Microscopy in Taxonomy and Functional Morphology. Cloth Text. Oxford University Press, Inc. New York, NY. 1990. 328p. Systematics Association Publications, Vol. 41 ISBN:0-19-857714-1, ISBN13: 978-0-19-857714-0. Dewey:574/.012. LCCN:89-023042.

Audience: **u,f.**

Coligan, John E.   **QR183.S54 2005**
Short Protocols in Immunology. Trade Paper. John Wiley & Sons, Inc. Hoboken, NJ. 2005. 872p. ISBN:0-471-71578-6, ISBN13: 978-0-471-71578-8. Dewey:616.07/9/078. LCCN:2004-024584.

Audience: **u,f.**

Crawley, Jacqueline N.   QP357.C87 1999
  (Editor), et al.
Current Protocols in Neuroscience. Charles Gerfen, Ron McKay,
Michael Rogawski, David Sibley & Phil Skolnick (Editors).
Ringbound. John Wiley & Sons, Inc. Hoboken, NJ. 1997. 700p.
ISBN:0-471-16359-7, ISBN13: 978-0-471-16359-6.
Dewey:612.8. LCCN:97-014252.

                                           Audience: **u,f.**

Desharnais, Robert, et al   QH362
[BiologyLabs On-Line; EvolutionLab; Evolution Lab] Lab
Manual for BiologyLabs On-Line: EvolutionLab. Bell, Jeffrey
Ray & Palladino, Michael A. (Authors). San Francisco :
Addison Wesley Longman ; [S.l.] : California State University,
Center for Distributed Learning 2000. BiologyLabs on-line
ISBN:0-321-05849-6, ISBN13: 978-0-321-05849-2.

                                           Audience: **u,f.**

Diaspro, Alberto (Editor)   QH224
Confocal and Two-Photon Microscopy: Foundations,
Applications and Advances. Trade Cloth. John Wiley & Sons,
Inc. Hoboken, NJ. 2001. 576p. ISBN:0-471-40920-0, ISBN13:
978-0-471-40920-5. Dewey:502/.8/2. LCCN:2001-039010.

                                           Audience: **u,f.**

Dracopoli, Nicolas C.   QH440.5.S54 2004
  (Editor), et al.
Short Protocols in Human Genetics. Jonathan L. Haines, Bruce
R. Korf, Cynthia C. Morton, Anthony Rosenzweig, Christine E.
Seidman, J. G. Seidman & Douglas R. Smith (Editors). Trade
Paper. John Wiley & Sons, Inc. Hoboken, NJ. 2004. 898p.
ISBN:0-471-69418-5, ISBN13: 978-0-471-69418-2.
Dewey:599.93/5. LCCN:2004-009131.

                                           Audience: **u,f.**

Dunn, Ben M., et al.   QP551.S536 2003
Short Protocols in Protein Science. David W. Speicher & Paul T.
Wingfield (Authors), John E. Coligan (Editor). Trade Paper.
John Wiley & Sons, Inc. Hoboken, NJ. 2003. 810p.
ISBN:0-471-48338-9, ISBN13: 978-0-471-48338-0.
Dewey:572/.6. LCCN:2003-012325.

                                           Audience: **u,f.**

Eddison, John (John C.)   QH323.5
Quantitative Investigations in the Biosciences Using Minitab.
Chapman & Hall. 2000. ISBN:1-58488-033-3, ISBN13:
978-1-58488-033-2.

                                           Audience: **u,f.**

Egerton, Ray   QH212.E4E354 2005
Physical Principles of Electron Microscopy: An Introduction to
TEM, SEM, and AEM. Trade Cloth. Springer. New York, NY.
2005. XII, 202p. ISBN:0-387-25800-0, ISBN13:
978-0-387-25800-3. LCCN:2005-924717.

                              Audience: **l,u.** *Choice, 2006.*

Evans, Howard E. &   QL813.D64M54 1996
  DeLahunta, Alexander
Miller's Guide to the Dissection of the Dog. Ed. 4. Cloth Text.
Elsevier - Health Sciences Division. Philadelphia, PA. 1995.
420p. ISBN:0-7216-5748-6, ISBN13: 978-0-7216-5748-6.
Dewey:599.7/4442. LCCN:95-070473.

                                           Audience: **l,u.**

Giberson, Richard T. &   QH207.M59 2001
  Demaree, Richard S. Jr. (Editors)
Microwave Techniques and Protocols. Book, Other. Humana
Press. Totowa, NJ. 2001. 230p. ISBN:0-89603-903-X, ISBN13:
978-0-89603-903-2. Dewey:570/.28/25. LCCN:2001-016992.

                                           Audience: **u,f.**

Gould, Jay E.   QH315
Concise Handbook of Experimental Methods for the Behavioral
and Biological Sciences. CRC Press, Boca Raton. 2002.
ISBN:0-8493-1104-7, ISBN13: 978-0-8493-1104-8.

                                           Audience: **u,f.**

Hamdan, Mahmoud H. &   QP551.M315 2005
  Righetti, Pier G.
Proteomics Today: Protein Assessment and Biomarkers Using
Mass Spectrometry, 2D Electrophoresis, and Microarray
Technology. Trade Cloth. John Wiley & Sons, Inc. Hoboken,
NJ. 2005. 448p. Wiley - Interscience Series on Mass
Spectrometry Ser. ISBN:0-471-64817-5, ISBN13:
978-0-471-64817-8. Dewey:572/.6. LCCN:2004-050921.

                                           Audience: **u,f.**

Horobin, R. W. & Kiernan,
  J. A. (Editors)
Conn's Biological Stains. Ed. 10. Paper over Boards. Taylor &
Francis Group. Philadelphia, PA. 2002. 576p.
ISBN:1-85996-099-5, ISBN13: 978-1-85996-099-8.
Dewey:502.82.

                                           Audience: **l,u.**

Housby, J. Nicholas (Editor)   QP625.N89M375 2001
Mass Spectrometry and Genomic Analysis. Trade Cloth.
Springer. New York, NY. 2001. 162p. Focus on Structural
Biology Ser., Vol. 2 ISBN:0-7923-7173-9, ISBN13:
978-0-7923-7173-1. Dewey:572.8/633. LCCN:2001-038884.

                                           Audience: **l,u.**

James, Thomas L. (Volume   QC762
  Editor)
Nuclear Magnetic Resonance of Biological Macromolecules,
Part C: Methods in Enzymology. Trade Cloth. Elsevier Science
& Technology Books. Saint Louis, MO. 2005. 672p.
ISBN:0-12-182799-2, ISBN13: 978-0-12-182799-1.
Dewey:538.362.

                                           Audience: **l,u.**

Lee, Mike S.   RS189.5.S65I55 2005
Integrated Strategies for Drug Discovery Using Mass
Spectrometry. Trade Cloth. John Wiley & Sons, Inc. Hoboken,
NJ. 2005. 568p. ISBN:0-471-46127-X, ISBN13:
978-0-471-46127-2. Dewey:615/.19. LCCN:2005-003235.

                                           Audience: **u,f.**

Lörinczy, Dénes   QH324.9.C3
The Nature of Biological Systems As Revealed by Thermal
Methods. Trade Cloth. Springer. New York, NY. 2004. IX, 353p.
Hot Topics in Thermal Analysis and Calorimetry Ser., Vol. 5
ISBN:1-4020-2218-2, ISBN13: 978-1-4020-2218-0.
Dewey:570/.28. LCCN:2004-048471.

                                           Audience: **u,f.**

Millington, Andrew C.   QH84.G47 2001
  (Editor), et al.
GIS and Remote Sensing Applications in Biogeography and
Ecology. Stephen J. Walsh & Patrick E. Osborne (Editors).

         Formats: Web: ☐   Ebook: 🄴   CD/DVD-ROM: 🎽   BCL3: 𝓑

Trade Cloth. Springer. New York, NY. 2001. 344p. The Kluwer International Series in Engineering and Computer Science, Vol. 626 ISBN:0-7923-7454-1, ISBN13: 978-0-7923-7454-1. Dewey:578/.09. LCCN:2001-038306.

Audience: **u,f.**

Morel, Gérard; Raccurt,   **QH207**
  Mireille
PCR/RT-PCR in Situ Light and Electron Microscopy. CRC Press: Boca Raton, Fla.. 2003. Methods in Visualization ISBN:0-8493-0041-X, ISBN13: 978-0-8493-0041-7.

Audience: **u,f.**

Murray, Graeme I. &   **QH506.L25 2005**
  Curran, Stephanie
Laser Capture Microdissection: Methods and Protocols. Trade Cloth. Humana Press. Totowa, NJ. 2005. 310p. Methods in Molecular Biology Ser. ISBN:1-58829-260-6, ISBN13: 978-1-58829-260-5. Dewey:572.8/028. LCCN:2004-021929.

Audience: **u,f.**

Pankhurst, C. (Editor), et al.   **QH84.8.B54 1997**
Biological Indicators of Soil Health. B. Doube & V. V. Gupta (Editors). Cloth Text. Oxford University Press, Inc. New York, NY. 1997. 464p. CABI Publishing Ser. ISBN:0-85199-158-0, ISBN13: 978-0-85199-158-0. Dewey:578.75/7. LCCN:97-013061.

Audience: **l,u.**

Pingoud, Alfred, et al.   **QH345.B5118 2002**
Biochemical Methods: A Concise Guide for Students and Researchers. Claus Urbanke, Jim Hoggett & Albert Jeltsch (Authors). Trade Cloth. John Wiley & Sons, Inc. Hoboken, NJ. 2002. 374p. ISBN:3-527-30299-9, ISBN13: 978-3-527-30299-4. Dewey:572. LCCN:2003-269482.

Audience: **l,u.**

Rabilloud, T. (Editor)   **QP551.P7564 2000**
Proteome Research: Two-Dimensional Gel Electrophoresis and Identification Methods. Trade Cloth. Springer. New York, NY. 1999. XVI, 248p. Principles and Practice Ser. ISBN:3-540-65689-8, ISBN13: 978-3-540-65689-0. Dewey:572/.633. LCCN:99-015544.

Audience: **u,f.**

Ream, Walt & Field,   **QH506**
  Katharine G.
Molecular Biology Techniques: An Intensive Laboratory Course. Paper Text. Elsevier Science & Technology Books. Saint Louis, MO. 1998. 234p. ISBN:0-12-583990-1, ISBN13: 978-0-12-583990-7. Dewey:572.8.

Audience: **u,f.**

Righetti, P. G., et al.   **QP551.R525 2001**
The Proteome Revisited: Theory and Practice of All Relevant Electrophoretic Steps. Alexandre Stoyanov & Michael Y. Zhukov (Authors). Trade Cloth. Elsevier Science & Technology Books. Saint Louis, MO. 2001. 410p. Journal of Chromatography Ser., Vol. 63 ISBN:0-444-50526-1, ISBN13: 978-0-444-50526-2. Dewey:572/.6. LCCN:2001-040228.

Audience: **u,f.**

Salinas (Editor)   **QK495.C9A735 2005**
Arabidopsis Protocols. Ed. 2. Trade Cloth. Humana Press. Totowa, NJ. 2005. 525p. Methods in Molecular Biology Ser. ISBN:1-58829-395-5, ISBN13: 978-1-58829-395-4. Dewey:583/.64. LCCN:2005-016343.

Audience: **u,f.**

Schinner, Franz F. (Editor),   **QH84.8.B5713 1995**
  et al.
Methods in Soil Biology. R. Ohlinger, E. Kandeler & R. Margesin (Editors). Paper Text. Springer. New York, NY. 1996. 256p. Springer Lab Manuals Ser. ISBN:3-540-59055-2, ISBN13: 978-3-540-59055-2. Dewey:574.5/26404. LCCN:95-035558.

Audience: **u,f.**

Shields, Martin   **QH315**
Biology Inquiries: Standards-Based Labs, Assessments, and Discussion Lessons; Grades 7-12. Trade Paper, Perfect. John Wiley & Sons, Inc. Hoboken, NJ. 2005. 296p. ISBN:0-7879-7652-0, ISBN13: 978-0-7879-7652-1. Dewey:574.07.

Audience: **l.**

Simpson, Richard J.   **QP551.P84 2004**
Purifying Proteins for Proteomics: A Laboratory Manual. Trade Cloth. Cold Spring Harbor Laboratory Press. Woodbury, NY. 2003. 750p. ISBN:0-87969-695-8, ISBN13: 978-0-87969-695-5. Dewey:572/.6. LCCN:2003-019058.

Audience: **u,f.**

Smith, David & Schenk,   **QL813.P54**
  Michael
Dissection Guide and Atlas of the Fetal Pig. Ed. 2. Perfect. Morton Publishing Company. Englewood, CO. 2003. ISBN:0-89582-626-7, ISBN13: 978-0-89582-626-8. Dewey:599.633.

Audience: **l,u.**

Sprackland, Robert G.   **QH68.S67**
Animals and Fishes in Aquaterrariums. Trade Cloth. T F H Publications, Inc. Neptune, NJ. 1995. 160p. ISBN:0-7938-0125-7, ISBN13: 978-0-7938-0125-1. Dewey:639.

Audience: **l,u,f.**

Strege, Mark A. & Lagu,   **QP519.9.C36C355 2004**
  Avinash L.
Capillary Electrophoresis of Proteins and Peptides. Book, Other. Humana Press. Totowa, NJ. 2004. 344p. Methods in Molecular Biology Ser. ISBN:1-58829-017-4, ISBN13: 978-1-58829-017-5. Dewey:572/.636. LCCN:2003-028088.

Audience: **u,f.**

Tank, Patrick W.   **QM34.T36 2005**
Grant's Dissector: Essentials of Pulmonary and Critical Care Medicine. Ed. 13. Spiral. Lippincott Williams & Wilkins. Philadelphia, PA. 2005. 219p. ISBN:0-7817-5484-4, ISBN13: 978-0-7817-5484-2. LCCN:2004-063357.

Audience: **l,u.**

Walker, Warren F. Jr. &   **QL812**
  Homberger, Dominique G.
Vertebrate Dissection. Ed. 8. Paper Text. Saunders College Publishing. Orlando, FL. 1992. 416p. ISBN:0-03-047434-5, ISBN13: 978-0-03-047434-7. Dewey:596/.04/028. LCCN:91-050763.

Audience: **l,u.**

Walker, Warren F. &   **QL813.P54**
  Homberger, Dominique G.
Anatomy and Dissection of the Fetal Pig. Ed. 5. Trade Paper. Worth Publishers, Inc. New York, NY. 1997. 120p. ISBN:0-7167-2637-8, ISBN13: 978-0-7167-2637-1. Dewey:571.3/1/9633/078.

Audience: **l,u,f.**

Weiler, C. Susan & Penhale,   **QH84.2.U515 1994**
  Polly A. (Editors)
Ultraviolet Radiation in Antarctica: Measurements and
Biological Effects. Trade Cloth. American Geophysical Union.
Washington, DC. 1994. 257p. Antarctic Research Ser., Vol. 62
ISBN:0-87590-841-1, ISBN13: 978-0-87590-841-0.
Dewey:574.98/9. LCCN:94-001422.

Audience: **u,f.**

Westermeier, Reiner   **QP519.9.E434 W47713**
Electrophoresis in Practice: A Guide to Methods and
Applications of DNA and Protein Separations. Ed. 4. Trade
Cloth. John Wiley & Sons, Inc. Hoboken, NJ. 2005. 426p.
ISBN:3-527-31181-5, ISBN13: 978-3-527-31181-1.
Dewey:543/.4. LCCN:2006-280306.

Audience: **u,f.**

White, Bruce A. (Editor)   **QP606.D46P363 1993**
PCR Protocols: Current Methods and Applications. Humana
Press: New Jersey. 1993. Methods in Molecular Biology, 15
ISBN:0-89603-244-2, ISBN13: 978-0-89603-244-6.

Audience: **u,f.**

Wingerd, Bruce D.   **QL813.R37W57 1988**
Rat Dissection Manual. Geoffrey Stein (Illustrator). Trade Paper.
Johns Hopkins University Press. Baltimore, MD. 1988. 62p.
ISBN:0-8018-3690-5, ISBN13: 978-0-8018-3690-9.
Dewey:599.32/33. LCCN:89-120489.

Audience: **l,u.**

Wischnitzer, Saul   **QL812**
Atlas and Dissection Guide for Comparative Anatomy. Ed. 5.
Trade Paper. Worth Publishers, Inc. New York, NY. 1993. 32p.
ISBN:0-7167-2374-3, ISBN13: 978-0-7167-2374-5.
Dewey:596/.04/028. LCCN:92-030800.

Audience: **l,u.**

Wood, M.   **QH541.5.S6**
Soil Biology. Mass Market. Chapman & Hall. New York, NY.
1989. 200p. ISBN:0-412-00951-X, ISBN13: 978-0-412-00951-8.
Dewey:574.526404.

Audience: **l,u.** *Choice, 1990.*

Wood, Martin   **QH541.5.S6**
Environmental Soil Biology. Ed. 2. Trade Paper. Springer. New
York, NY. 1995. 160p. ISBN:0-7514-0343-1, ISBN13:
978-0-7514-0343-5. Dewey:574.5/264/04. LCCN:95-077024.

Audience: **l,u.**

Biological Techniques > Statistical Analysis and Mathematics

Bmsa   **QH323.5.M376 2005**
Mathematics and 21st Century Biology. Trade Paper. National
Academies Press. Washington, DC. 2005. xi, 149p.
ISBN:0-309-09584-0, ISBN13: 978-0-309-09584-6.
Dewey:570/.151. LCCN:2005-924164.

Audience: **u,f.**

Farkas, Miklós   **QH323.5.F37 2001**
Dynamical Models in Biology. Trade Cloth. Elsevier Science &
Technology Books. Saint Louis, MO. 2001. 187p.
ISBN:0-12-249103-3, ISBN13: 978-0-12-249103-0.
Dewey:570/.1/5118. LCCN:00-111107.

Audience: **u,f.**

Hawkins, Dawn   **QH315**
Biomeasurement: Understanding, Analysing and Communicating
Data in the Biosciences. Paper Text. Oxford University Press,
Inc. New York, NY. 2005. 310p. ISBN:0-19-926515-1, ISBN13:
978-0-19-926515-2. Dewey:570.72. LCCN:2005-299556.

Audience: **u,f.**

Konopka, Andrzej &   **QH324.2**
  Crabbe, M. James C.
Compact Handbook of Computational Biology. Paper over
Boards. Marcel Dekker Inc. New York, NY. 2004. 568p.
ISBN:0-8247-0982-9, ISBN13: 978-0-8247-0982-2.
Dewey:570/.285. LCCN:2004-559904.

Audience: **u,f.**

Shipley, Bill   **QH323.5 .S477 2000**
Cause and Correlation in Biology: A User's Guide to Path
Analysis, Structural Equations and Causal Inference. Trade
Paper. Cambridge University Press. New York, NY. 2002. 330p.
ISBN:0-521-52921-2, ISBN13: 978-0-521-52921-1.
Dewey:570.15195.

Audience: **l,u,f.**

Stephenson, Frank H.   **QH323.5**
Calculations for Molecular Biology and Biotechnology: A Guide
to Mathematics in the Laboratory. Trade Paper. Elsevier Science
& Technology Books. Saint Louis, MO. 2003. 302p.
ISBN:0-12-665751-3, ISBN13: 978-0-12-665751-7.
Dewey:572.8/01/51. LCCN:2003-106049.

Audience: **u,f.**

Stewart, Ian   **QH323.5.S747 2001**
What Shape Is a Snowflake?: Magical Numbers in Nature. Cloth
over Boards. Henry Holt & Company. New York, NY. 2001.
200p. ISBN:0-7167-4794-4, ISBN13: 978-0-7167-4794-9.
Dewey:510. LCCN:2002-280019.

Audience: **g.**

Titterington, D. M. & Cox,   **QH301.T55 2001**
  D. R. (Editors)
Biometrika: One Hundred Years. Ed. 2. Trade Cloth. Oxford
University Press, Inc. New York, NY. 2001. 392p.
ISBN:0-19-850993-6, ISBN13: 978-0-19-850993-6.
Dewey:570/.1/5195. LCCN:2001-036127.

Audience: **u,f.**

Van Belle, Gerald, et al.   **QH323.5**
Biostatistics: A Methodology for the Health Sciences. Ed. 2.
Lloyd D. Fisher, Patrick J. Heagerty & Thomas S. Lumley
(Authors). Trade Cloth. John Wiley & Sons, Inc. Hoboken, NJ.
2004. 896p. Wiley Series in Probability and Statistics Ser.
ISBN:0-471-03185-2, ISBN13: 978-0-471-03185-7.
Dewey:610/.1/5195. LCCN:2004-040491.

Audience: **u,f.** *Choice, 1993.*

Biological Techniques > Statistical Analysis and Mathematics > Applied Mathematics (Biology)

Bookstein, Fred L.   **QH351 .B67 1992**
Morphometric Tools for Landmark Data: Geometry and Biology.
Trade Cloth. Cambridge University Press. New York, NY. 1992.
455p. ISBN:0-521-38385-4, ISBN13: 978-0-521-38385-1.
Dewey:571.3/015/195. LCCN:91-039063.

Audience: **u,f.**

Formats: Web: ☐   Ebook: **ⓔ**   CD/DVD-ROM: 🖪   BCL3: *B*

Brauer, Fred &   **QH352.B73 2001**
    Castillo-Chavez, Carlos
Mathematical Models in Population Biology and Epidemiology.
Trade Cloth. Springer. New York, NY. 2001. XXIII, 448p. Texts
in Applied Mathematics, Vol. 40 ISBN:0-387-98902-1, ISBN13:
978-0-387-98902-0. Dewey:577.8/8/015118. LCCN:00-045033.
                               Audience: **u,f.**

Britton, N. F.   **QH323.5**
Essential Mathematical Biology. Trade Paper. Springer. New
York, NY. 2004. XV, 335p. Springer Undergraduate
Mathematics Ser. ISBN:1-85233-536-X, ISBN13:
978-1-85233-536-6. Dewey:570/.1/51. LCCN:2002-036455.
                               Audience: **l,u.**

Day, William H. E. &   **QH323.5.D39 2003**
    McMorris, F. R.
Axiomatic Concensus Theory in Group Choice and
Biomathematics. Trade Cloth. Society for Industrial & Applied
Mathematics. Philadelphia, PA. 2003. xvi + 155p. Frontiers in
Applied Mathematics Ser., Vol. 29 ISBN:0-89871-551-2,
ISBN13: 978-0-89871-551-4. Dewey:570/.15/1.
LCCN:2003-061618.
                               Audience: **u,f.**

Edelstein-Keshet, Leah   **QH323.5.E34 2005**
Mathematical Models in Biology. Trade Paper, Perfect. Society
for Industrial & Applied Mathematics. Philadelphia, PA. 2005.
586p. Classics in Applied Mathematics Ser., Vol. 46
ISBN:0-89871-554-7, ISBN13: 978-0-89871-554-5.
Dewey:570.1/5118. LCCN:2004-117719.
                               Audience: **u,f.**

Feldman, Marcus W.   **QH0371.M295**
    (Editor)
Mathematical Evolutionary Theory. Trade Paper. Books on
Demand. Ann Arbor, MI. 351p. ISBN:0-608-06320-7, ISBN13:
978-0-608-06320-1. Dewey:575.01/51. LCCN:88-015591.
                               Audience: **u,f.**

Gilpin, Michael E. &   **QL752**
    Hanski, Ilkka A. (Editors)
Metapopulation Dynamics: Empirical and Theoretical
Investigations. Trade Paper. Elsevier Science & Technology
Books. Saint Louis, MO. 1991. 336p. ISBN:0-12-284120-4,
ISBN13: 978-0-12-284120-0. Dewey:591.5248.
                               Audience: **u,f.**

Haefner, James W.   **QH323.5.H34 2005**
Modeling Biological Systems: Principles and Applications. Ed.
2. Mixed Media. Springer. New York, NY. 2005. XVI, 480p.
ISBN:0-387-25011-5, ISBN13: 978-0-387-25011-3.
Dewey:570.1/1. LCCN:2005-042543.
                               Audience: **u.**

Hastings, A.   **QH352.S96 1987**
Some Mathematical Questions in Biology - Models in
Population Biology. Trade Paper. American Mathematical
Society. Providence, RI. 1989. 123p. Lectures in Mathematics in
the Life Sciences, Vol. 20 ISBN:0-8218-1170-3, ISBN13:
978-0-8218-1170-2. Dewey:574.5/248/011. LCCN:89-015119.
                               Audience: **u,f.**

Israel, G. & Gasca, A. M.   **QH323.5.I86 2002**
The Biology of Numbers: The Correspondence of Vito Volterra
on Mathematical Biology. Trade Cloth. Birkhauser Boston.

Cambridge, MA. 2002. ix, 405p. Science Networks Historical
Studies, Vol. 26 ISBN:3-7643-6514-5, ISBN13:
978-3-7643-6514-1. Dewey:570/.1/51. LCCN:2002-023671.
                               Audience: **u,f.**

Jones, D. S. (Douglas   **QH323.5**
    Samuel); Sleeman, B. D.
Differential Equations and Mathematical Biology. Chapman &
Hall/CRC. Boca Raton, FL. 2003. Chapman & Hall/CRC
Mathematical Biology and Medicine Series
ISBN:1-58488-296-4, ISBN13: 978-1-58488-296-1.
                               Audience: **u,f.**

Keck, Robert & Patterson,
    Richard R.
Biomath: Problem Solving for Biology Students. Paper Text.
Benjamin-Cummings Publishing Company. San Francisco, CA.
1999. 318p. ISBN:0-8053-6524-9, ISBN13: 978-0-8053-6524-5.
Dewey:510.2/457.
                               Audience: **u,f.**

Kot, Mark   **QH352 .K66 2001**
Elements of Mathematical Ecology. Cloth Text. Cambridge
University Press. New York, NY. 2001. 464p.
ISBN:0-521-80213-X, ISBN13: 978-0-521-80213-0.
Dewey:577/.01/51. LCCN:00-065165.
                  Audience: **u,f.** *Choice, 2002.*

Lestrel, Pete E. (Editor)   **QH351 .F685 1997**
Fourier Descriptors and Their Applications in Biology. Trade
Cloth. Cambridge University Press. New York, NY. 1997. 480p.
ISBN:0-521-45201-5, ISBN13: 978-0-521-45201-4.
Dewey:570.1/5152433. LCCN:96-028577.
                               Audience: **u,f.**

Murray, James D.   **QH323.5.M88 2001**
Mathematical Biology: An Introduction. Ed. 3. Trade Cloth.
Springer. New York, NY. 2004. XXIII, 551p. Interdisciplinary
Applied Mathematics Ser. ISBN:0-387-95223-3, ISBN13:
978-0-387-95223-9. Dewey:570/.1/5118. LCCN:2001-020448.
                               Audience: **u,f.**

Murray, James D.   **QH323.5.M88 2001**
Mathematical Biology: Spatial Models and Biomedical
Applications. Ed. 3. Trade Cloth. Springer. New York, NY.
2004. XXV, 811p. Interdisciplinary Applied Mathematics Ser.
ISBN:0-387-95228-4, ISBN13: 978-0-387-95228-4.
Dewey:570/.1/5118. LCCN:2001-020448.
                               Audience: **u,f.**

Neuhauser, Claudia   **QH323.5.N46 2003**
Calculus for Biology and Medicine. Ed. 2. Cloth Text. Prentice
Hall PTR. Upper Saddle River, NJ. 2003. 822p.
ISBN:0-13-045516-4, ISBN13: 978-0-13-045516-1. Dewey:515.
LCCN:2003-048212.
                               Audience: **l,u.**

Rhodes, John A. & Allman,   **QH323.5.A44 2003**
    Elizabeth S.
Mathematical Models in Biology: An Introduction. Cloth Text.
Cambridge University Press. New York, NY. 2003. 384p.
ISBN:0-521-81980-6, ISBN13: 978-0-521-81980-0.
Dewey:570.1/5118. LCCN:2003-043929.
                     Audience: **l.** *Choice, 2004.*

Ruan, Shigui (Editor), et al.   **QH323.5.D95 2003**
Dynamical Systems and Their Applications in Biology. Gail S.
K. Wolkowicz & Jianhong Wu (Editors), Fields Institute for

Research in Mathematical Sciences Staff (Contribution by).
Trade Cloth. American Mathematical Society. Providence, RI.
2003. 268p. Fields Institute Communications Ser., Vol. 36
ISBN:0-8218-3163-1, ISBN13: 978-0-8218-3163-2.
Dewey:570/.1/5118. LCCN:2002-038530.

Audience: **u,f.**

Swishchuk, Anatoly V. &   **QH323.5**
  Jianhong Wu,
Evolution of Biological Systems in Random Media: Limit
Theorems. Trade Cloth. Kluwer Law International. Alphen a/d
Rijn, 2003. 216p. Mathematical Modelling Ser.
ISBN:1-4020-1554-2, ISBN13: 978-1-4020-1554-0.
Dewey:570/.1/1. LCCN:2003-061857.

Audience: **u,f.**

Taubes, Clifford Henry   **QH323.5.T38 2001**
Modeling Differential Equations in Biology. Cloth Text. Prentice
Hall PTR. Upper Saddle River, NJ. 2000. 479p.
ISBN:0-13-017325-8, ISBN13: 978-0-13-017325-6.
Dewey:570/.1/5195. LCCN:00-064254.

Audience: **l,u.**

Thieme, Horst R.   **QH352.T45 2003**
Mathematics in Population Biology. Trade Cloth. Princeton
University Press. Princeton, NJ. 2003. 568p. Mathematical
Biology Ser. ISBN:0-691-09290-7, ISBN13: 978-0-691-09290-4.
Dewey:577.8/8/015118. LCCN:2002-192472.

Audience: **u,f.**

Vicsek, Tamas & Vicsek,   **QH323.5.F59 2001**
  Thomas (Editors)
Fluctuations and Scaling in Biology. Paper Text. Oxford
University Press, Inc. New York, NY. 2001. 256p.
ISBN:0-19-850790-9, ISBN13: 978-0-19-850790-1.
Dewey:570/.1/5195. LCCN:2001-016281.

Audience: **u,f.**

Voit, Eberhard O.   **QH323.5 .V65 2000**
Computational Analysis of Biochemical Systems: A Practical
Guide for Biochemists and Molecular Biologists. Cloth Text.
Cambridge University Press. New York, NY. 2000. 544p.
ISBN:0-521-78087-X, ISBN13: 978-0-521-78087-2.
Dewey:570/.1/5118. LCCN:00-021913.

Audience: **u,f.**

Wainwright, Stephen A.   **QH351.W25 1988**
Axis and Circumference: The Cylindrical Shape of Plants and
Animals. Trade Cloth. Harvard University Press. Cambridge,
MA. 1988. 176p. ISBN:0-674-05700-7, ISBN13:
978-0-674-05700-5. Dewey:574.4. LCCN:87-021099.

Audience: **u,f.** *Choice, 1989.*

Young, Simon S.   **QH324.2 .Y68 2001**
Computerized Data Acquisition and Analysis for the Life
Sciences: A Hands-on Guide. Trade Cloth. Cambridge
University Press. New York, NY. 2001. 248p.
ISBN:0-521-56281-3, ISBN13: 978-0-521-56281-2.
Dewey:570/.285. LCCN:00-045436.

Audience: **u,f.**

Biological Techniques > Statistical Analysis and Mathematics > Statistics and Biostatistics

Buckland, S. T., et al.   **QL752.D57 1993**
Distance Sampling: Estimating Abundance of Biological
Populations. K. P. Burnham, D. R. Anderson & J. L. Laake
(Authors). Trade Cloth. Chapman & Hall. New York, NY. 1993.
400p. ISBN:0-412-42660-9, ISBN13: 978-0-412-42660-5.
Dewey:591.5248. LCCN:92-039560.

Audience: **u,f.**

Buckland, S.T. (Editor),   **QH352**
  et al.
Advanced Distance Sampling: Estimating Abundance of
Biological Populations. D.R. Anderson & K.P. Burnham
(Editors). Trade Cloth. Oxford University Press, Inc. New York,
NY. 2004. 434p. ISBN:0-19-850783-6, ISBN13:
978-0-19-850783-3. Dewey:591.7/88/0727. LCCN:2004-303414.

Audience: **u,f.**

Burnham, Kenneth P. &   **QH323.5.B87 2002**
  Anderson, D. R.
Model Selection and Multi-Model Inference: A Practical
Information-Theoretic Approach. Ed. 2. Trade Cloth. Springer.
New York, NY. 2003. XXVI, 488p. ISBN:0-387-95364-7,
ISBN13: 978-0-387-95364-9. Dewey:570/.1/51.
LCCN:2001-057677.

Audience: **u,f.**

Denny, Mark W. & Gaines,   **QH323.5.D46 2002**
  Steven
Chance in Biology: Using Probability to Explore Nature. Trade
Paper. Princeton University Press. Princeton, NJ. 2002. 416p.
ISBN:0-691-09494-2, ISBN13: 978-0-691-09494-6.
Dewey:570/.1/5192.

Audience: **u,f.**

Dytham, Calvin   **QH323.5.D98 2003**
Choosing and Using Statistics: A Biologist's Guide. Ed. 2. Trade
Paper. Blackwell Publishing, Inc. Malden, MA. 2003. 264p.
ISBN:1-4051-0243-8, ISBN13: 978-1-4051-0243-8.
Dewey:570/.1/5195. LCCN:2002-074760.

Audience: **u,f.**

Gould, Grant F. & Gould,   **QH323.5.G67 2001**
  James L.
BioStats Basics: A Student Handbook. Spiral. Worth Publishers,
Inc. New York, NY. 2001. 422p. ISBN:0-7167-3416-8, ISBN13:
978-0-7167-3416-1. Dewey:570/.1/5195. LCCN:2001-004467.

Audience: **u,f.**

Govindarajulu, Z.   **QH323.5.G68 2001**
Statistical Techniques in Bioassay. Ed. 2. Trade Cloth. S. Karger
AG. Farmington, CT. 2001. xviii + 234p. ISBN:3-8055-7119-4,
ISBN13: 978-3-8055-7119-7. Dewey:572/.36/0727.
LCCN:00-063292.

Audience: **u,f.**

Pachter, L. & Sturmfels, B.   **QH323.5.A43 2005**
  (Editors)
Algebraic Statistics for Computational Biology. Trade Cloth.
Cambridge University Press. New York, NY. 2005. 432p.
ISBN:0-521-85700-7, ISBN13: 978-0-521-85700-0.
Dewey:572.8/6. LCCN:2005-050070.

Audience: **l,u.**

Pagano, Robert R., et al.   QH323.5.P34 2000
Principles of Biostatistics. Ed. 2. Marcello Pagano & Kimberlee
Gauvreau (Authors). Cloth Text. Brooks/Cole. Pacific Grove,
CA. 2000. 592p. Statistics Ser. ISBN:0-534-22902-6, ISBN13:
978-0-534-22902-3. Dewey:570/.1/5195. LCCN:00-027943.

Audience: **l,u.**

Rosner, Bernard   QH323.5.R674 2006
Fundamentals of Biostatistics. Ed. 6. Cloth Text. Brooks/Cole.
Pacific Grove, CA. 2005. 896p. ISBN:0-534-41820-1, ISBN13:
978-0-534-41820-5. Dewey:570.1/5195. LCCN:2004-117046.

Audience: **l,u.**

Samuels, Myra L. &   QH323.5.S23 2002
Witmer, Jeffrey A.
Statistics for the Life Sciences. Ed. 3. Mixed Media. Prentice
Hall PTR. Upper Saddle River, NJ. 2002. 736p.
ISBN:0-13-041316-X, ISBN13: 978-0-13-041316-1.
Dewey:570/.1/5195. LCCN:2002-074908.

Audience: **l,u.**

Schork, M. Anthony &   QH323.5.S357 2000
Remington, Richard D.
Statistics with Applications to the Biological and Health
Sciences. Ed. 3. Trade Paper. Prentice Hall PTR. Upper Saddle
River, NJ. 2000. 496p. ISBN:0-13-022327-1, ISBN13:
978-0-13-022327-2. Dewey:570/.1/195. LCCN:99-059004.

Audience: **l,u.**

Thomas, Duncan C.   RB155.T468 2004
Statistical Methods in Genetic Epidemiology. Trade Cloth.
Oxford University Press, Inc. New York, NY. 2004. 458p.
ISBN:0-19-515939-X, ISBN13: 978-0-19-515939-4.
Dewey:616/.042. LCCN:2003-053096.

Audience: **u,f.**

Van Belle, Gerald, et al.   QH323.5
Biostatistics: A Methodology for the Health Sciences. Ed. 2.
Lloyd D. Fisher, Patrick J. Heagerty & Thomas S. Lumley
(Authors). Trade Cloth. John Wiley & Sons, Inc. Hoboken, NJ.
2004. 896p. Wiley Series in Probability and Statistics Ser.
ISBN:0-471-03185-2, ISBN13: 978-0-471-03185-7.
Dewey:610/.1/5195. LCCN:2004-040491.

Audience: **u,f.** *Choice, 1993.*

Wardlaw, Alastair C.   QH323.5.W37 2000
Practical Statistics for Experimental Biologists. Ed. 2. Trade
Cloth. John Wiley & Sons, Inc. Hoboken, NJ. 2000. 260p.
ISBN:0-471-98821-9, ISBN13: 978-0-471-98821-2.
Dewey:570/.7/27. LCCN:99-035926.

Audience: **u,f.**

Young, Simon S.   QH324.2 .Y68 2001
Computerized Data Acquisition and Analysis for the Life
Sciences: A Hands-on Guide. Trade Cloth. Cambridge
University Press. New York, NY. 2001. 248p.
ISBN:0-521-56281-3, ISBN13: 978-0-521-56281-2.
Dewey:570/.285. LCCN:00-045436.

Audience: **u,f.**

Zhang, Wei & Shmulevich,   QH438.4.M3C65 2002
Ilya (Editors)
Computational and Statistical Approaches to Genomics. Trade
Cloth. Springer. New York, NY. 2002. 344p.
ISBN:1-4020-7023-3, ISBN13: 978-1-4020-7023-5.
Dewey:572.8/6/015118. LCCN:2002-023676.

Audience: **u,f.**

Biological Techniques > Statistical Analysis and Mathematics > Computer Modeling and Simulation

QH447

☐ Trans-NIH Mouse Initiatives.
http://www.nih.gov/science/models/mouse/

Audience: **u.**

Bernstein, Ruth   QH352.B458 2003
Population Ecology: An Introduction to Computer Simulations.
Trade Paper. John Wiley & Sons, Inc. Hoboken, NJ. 2003. 170p.
ISBN:0-470-85148-1, ISBN13: 978-0-470-85148-7.
Dewey:577.8/8. LCCN:2002-155483.

Audience: **u,f.**

Bookstein, Fred L.   QH351 .B67 1992
Morphometric Tools for Landmark Data: Geometry and Biology.
Trade Cloth. Cambridge University Press. New York, NY. 1992.
455p. ISBN:0-521-38385-4, ISBN13: 978-0-521-38385-1.
Dewey:571.3/015/195. LCCN:91-039063.

Audience: **u,f.**

Brauer, Fred &   QH352.B73 2001
Castillo-Chavez, Carlos
Mathematical Models in Population Biology and Epidemiology.
Trade Cloth. Springer. New York, NY. 2001. XXIII, 448p. Texts
in Applied Mathematics, Vol. 40 ISBN:0-387-98902-1, ISBN13:
978-0-387-98902-0. Dewey:577.8/8/015118. LCCN:00-045033.

Audience: **u,f.**

Burnham, Kenneth P. &   QH323.5.B87 2002
Anderson, D. R.
Model Selection and Multi-Model Inference: A Practical
Information-Theoretic Approach. Ed. 2. Trade Cloth. Springer.
New York, NY. 2003. XXVI, 488p. ISBN:0-387-95364-7,
ISBN13: 978-0-387-95364-9. Dewey:570/.1/51.
LCCN:2001-057677.

Audience: **u,f.**

Dopazo, Joaquin & Azuaje,   QH447
Francisco (Editors)
Data Analysis and Visualization in Genomics and Proteomics.
Trade Cloth. John Wiley & Sons, Inc. Hoboken, NJ. 2005. 284p.
ISBN:0-470-09439-7, ISBN13: 978-0-470-09439-6.
Dewey:572.8/6. LCCN:2005-006838.

Audience: **u,f.**

Gheorghe, Marian   QH506.M66434 2005
Molecular Computation Models: Unconventional Approaches.
Trade Cloth. Idea Group Publishing. Hershey, PA. 2005. 304p.
ISBN:1-59140-333-2, ISBN13: 978-1-59140-333-3.
Dewey:570/.1/1. LCCN:2004-023592.

Audience: **u,f.**

Haefner, James W.   QH323.5.H34 2005
Modeling Biological Systems: Principles and Applications. Ed.
2. Mixed Media. Springer. New York, NY. 2005. XVI, 480p.
ISBN:0-387-25011-5, ISBN13: 978-0-387-25011-3.
Dewey:570.1/1. LCCN:2005-042543.

Audience: **u.**

Hastings, A.   QH352.S96 1987
Some Mathematical Questions in Biology - Models in
Population Biology. Trade Paper. American Mathematical

Society. Providence, RI. 1989. 123p. Lectures in Mathematics in the Life Sciences, Vol. 20 ISBN:0-8218-1170-3, ISBN13: 978-0-8218-1170-2. Dewey:574.5/248/011. LCCN:89-015119.

Audience: **u,f.**

Hastings, Alan   **QH352 .H38**
Population Biology: Concepts and Models. Ed. 2. Trade Cloth. Springer. New York, NY. 2005. 320p. ISBN:0-387-98852-1, ISBN13: 978-0-387-98852-8. Dewey:574.5/248/0151.

Audience: **u.**

Hoppensteadt, Frank C. &   **QH323.5.H67 2002**
Peskin, Charles S.
Modeling and Simulation in Medicine and the Life Sciences. Ed. 2. J. E. Marsden, L. Sirovich, M. Golubitsky & W. Jager (Editors). Trade Cloth. Springer. New York, NY. 2004. XIV, 354p. Texts in Applied Mathematics, Vol. 10 ISBN:0-387-95072-9, ISBN13: 978-0-387-95072-3. Dewey:570./1/51. LCCN:2001-032010.

Audience: **u,f.**

Lestrel, Pete E. (Editor)   **QH351 .F685 1997**
Fourier Descriptors and Their Applications in Biology. Trade Cloth. Cambridge University Press. New York, NY. 1997. 480p. ISBN:0-521-45201-5, ISBN13: 978-0-521-45201-4. Dewey:570.1/5152433. LCCN:96-028577.

Audience: **u,f.**

Millington, Andrew C.   **QH84.G47 2001**
(Editor), et al.
GIS and Remote Sensing Applications in Biogeography and Ecology. Stephen J. Walsh & Patrick E. Osborne (Editors). Trade Cloth. Springer. New York, NY. 2001. 344p. The Kluwer International Series in Engineering and Computer Science, Vol. 626 ISBN:0-7923-7454-1, ISBN13: 978-0-7923-7454-1. Dewey:578/.09. LCCN:2001-038306.

Audience: **u,f.**

Murray, James D.   **QH323.5.M88 2001**
Mathematical Biology: Spatial Models and Biomedical Applications. Ed. 3. Trade Cloth. Springer. New York, NY. 2004. XXV, 811p. Interdisciplinary Applied Mathematics Ser. ISBN:0-387-95228-4, ISBN13: 978-0-387-95228-4. Dewey:570/.1/5118. LCCN:2001-020448.

Audience: **u,f.**

Rhodes, John A. & Allman,   **QH323.5.A44 2003**
Elizabeth S.
Mathematical Models in Biology: An Introduction. Cloth Text. Cambridge University Press. New York, NY. 2003. 384p. ISBN:0-521-81980-6, ISBN13: 978-0-521-81980-0. Dewey:570/.1/5118. LCCN:2003-043929.

Audience: **l.** *Choice, 2004.*

Taubes, Clifford Henry   **QH323.5.T38 2001**
Modeling Differential Equations in Biology. Cloth Text. Prentice Hall PTR. Upper Saddle River, NJ. 2000. 479p. ISBN:0-13-017325-8, ISBN13: 978-0-13-017325-6. Dewey:570/.1/5195. LCCN:00-064254.

Audience: **l,u.**

Voit, Eberhard O.   **QH323.5 .V65 2000**
Computational Analysis of Biochemical Systems: A Practical Guide for Biochemists and Molecular Biologists. Cloth Text. Cambridge University Press. New York, NY. 2000. 544p. ISBN:0-521-78087-X, ISBN13: 978-0-521-78087-2. Dewey:570/.1/5118. LCCN:00-021913.

Audience: **u,f.**

Young, Simon S.   **QH324.2 .Y68 2001**
Computerized Data Acquisition and Analysis for the Life Sciences: A Hands-on Guide. Trade Cloth. Cambridge University Press. New York, NY. 2001. 248p. ISBN:0-521-56281-3, ISBN13: 978-0-521-56281-2. Dewey:570/.285. LCCN:00-045436.

Audience: **u,f.**

Biological Techniques > Associations and Organizations

☐ Google Directory: Biology Associations.
http://www.google.com/Top/Science/Biology/Associations/
Google.

Audience: **u,f.**

☐ Google Directory: Biology Directories.
http://www.google.com/Top/Science/Biology/Directories/
Google.

Audience: **l,u,f.**

☐ Google Directory: Biology Meetings.
http://www.google.com/Top/Science/Biology/Meetings/
Google.

Audience: **u,f.**

☐ Google Directory: Biology Products and Services.
http://www.google.com/Top/Science/Biology/
Products_and_Services/
Google.

Audience: **l,u,f.**

Biological Techniques > Library and Reference Works

☐ Columbia University Libraries Biological Sciences Library Biology Internet Resources.
http://www.columbia.edu/cu/lweb/indiv/biology/
internet_resources.html
Columbia University Libraries.

Audience: **g,l,u,f.**

☐ Google Directory: Biology.
http://www.google.com/Top/Science/Biology/
Google.

Audience: **g,l,u,f.**

☐ Google Directory: Biology Associations.
http://www.google.com/Top/Science/Biology/Associations/
Google.

Audience: **u,f.**

☐ Google Directory: Biology Directories.
http://www.google.com/Top/Science/Biology/Directories/
Google.

Audience: **l,u,f.**

☐ Google Directory: Biology Meetings.
http://www.google.com/Top/Science/Biology/Meetings/
Google.

Audience: **u,f.**

☐ Google Directory: Biology Products and Services.
http://www.google.com/Top/Science/Biology/
Products_and_Services/
Google.

Audience: **l,u,f.**

**Adler, Kraig & Halliday,   QL640.7.F57 2002
Tim (Editors)**
Firefly Encyclopedia of Reptiles and Amphibians. Trade Cloth.
Firefly Books, Ltd. Tonawanda, NY. 2002. 240p.
ISBN:1-55297-613-0, ISBN13: 978-1-55297-613-5.
Dewey:597.9. LCCN:2003-542845.

Audience: **g,l,u.** *Choice, 2003.*

Anderson, D. T.   QL363.A53 1996
Atlas of Invertebrate Anatomy. Paper Text. University of New
South Wales Press. Sydney, NSW. 1996. 127p.
ISBN:0-86840-207-9, ISBN13: 978-0-86840-207-9.
Dewey:571.1/2/0223. LCCN:97-112121.

Audience: **l,u.**

Banks, John C., et al.   QM25.A796 2005
Atlas of Clinical Gross Anatomy. Pedro B. Nava, Darrell
Petersen & Kenneth P. Moses (Authors), Martein Moningka
(Contribution by). Paper Text. Elsevier - Health Sciences
Division. Philadelphia, PA. 2005. 524p. ISBN:0-323-03744-5,
ISBN13: 978-0-323-03744-0. Dewey:611/.0022/2.
LCCN:2005-045078.

Audience: **g,l,u,f.**

Bell, Catharine (Editor)   QL76.E53 2001
Encyclopedia of the World's Zoos, Set. Lester Fisher
(Contribution by). Trade Cloth. Fitzroy Dearborn Publishers,
Inc. Chicago, IL. 2001. 1600p. ISBN:1-57958-174-9, ISBN13:
978-1-57958-174-9. Dewey:590/.7/303. LCCN:2002-265421.

Audience: **g,l,u,f.** *Choice, 2001.*

Bobick, James, et al.   QH349.H36 2004
The Handy Biology Answer Book. Naomi Malaban, Sandra
Bobick & Laurel Bridges Roberts (Authors). Library Binding.
Omnigraphics, Inc. Detroit, MI. 2004. xxxiv, 565p. Handy
Answer Book Ser. ISBN:0-7808-0778-2, ISBN13:
978-0-7808-0778-5. Dewey:570. LCCN:2004-017808.

Audience: **g,l,u.**

**Brooke, Michael &   QL673
Birkhead, Tim R.**
The Cambridge Encyclopedia of Ornithology. Trade Cloth.
Cambridge University Press. New York, NY. 1991. 372p.
ISBN:0-521-36205-9, ISBN13: 978-0-521-36205-4. Dewey:598.
LCCN:91-214229.

Audience: **g,l,u.** *Choice, 1992.*

Clemente, Carmine D.   QM531.C57 2007
Anatomy: A Regional Atlas of the Human Body. Ed. 5. Trade
Paper. Lippincott Williams & Wilkins. Philadelphia, PA. 2006.
640p. ISBN:0-7817-5103-9, ISBN13: 978-0-7817-5103-2.
Dewey:611. LCCN:2006-005516.

Audience: **g,l,u,f.**

**Cogger, Harold C. &   QL640.7.E53 1998
Zweifel, Richard G. (Editors)**
Encyclopedia of Reptiles and Amphibians. Ed. 2. David
Kirshner (Illustrator). Trade Cloth. Elsevier Science &
Technology Books. Saint Louis, MO. 1998. 240p.
ISBN:0-12-178560-2, ISBN13: 978-0-12-178560-4.
Dewey:597.9/03. LCCN:98-088226.

Audience: **l,u.** *Choice, 1999.*

Diagram Group   QH308.2
The Facts on File Biology Handbook. Ed. 2. Trade Cloth. Facts
On File, Inc.. New York, NY. 2006. 272p. Science Handbook
Ser. ISBN:0-8160-5877-6, ISBN13: 978-0-8160-5877-8.
Dewey:570.

Audience: **g,l,u.**

Dye, Frank J.   QH491.D94 2002
Dictionary of Developmental Biology and Embryology. Trade
Cloth. John Wiley & Sons, Inc. Hoboken, NJ. 2002. 165p.
ISBN:0-471-44357-3, ISBN13: 978-0-471-44357-5.
Dewey:571.8/03. LCCN:2002-265882.

Audience: **u,f.**

**Frank, Norman & Ramus,   QL645.F73 1995
Erica**
A Complete Guide to Scientific and Common Names of Reptiles
and Amphibians of the World. Trade Paper. Reptile &
Amphibian Magazine. Pottsville, PA. 1996. 300p.
ISBN:0-9641032-3-0, ISBN13: 978-0-9641032-3-8.
Dewey:597.9/01/4. LCCN:95-068825.

Audience: **l,u,f.** *Choice, 1996.*

Gad, Shayne Cox (Editor)   RM301.25.D784 2005
Drug Discovery Handbook. Trade Cloth. John Wiley & Sons,
Inc. Hoboken, NJ. 2005. 1496p. ISBN:0-471-21384-5, ISBN13:
978-0-471-21384-0. Dewey:615/.19. LCCN:2004-027077.

Audience: **u,f.**

**Gale Research Staff &   QP11.W67 2002
McGrath, Kimberley A.**
World of Anatomy and Physiology, Set. Trade Cloth. Thomson
Gale. Farmington Hills, MI. 2002. 600p. ISBN:0-7876-5684-4,
ISBN13: 978-0-7876-5684-3. Dewey:612/.003.
LCCN:2002-005517.

Audience: **g,l,u.** *Choice, 2003.*

Ganti, Tibor   QH341.G26 2003
The Principles of Life. Eors Szathmary & James Griesemer
(Editors). Trade Cloth. Oxford University Press, Inc. New York,
NY. 2003. 220p. ISBN:0-19-850726-7, ISBN13:
978-0-19-850726-0. Dewey:576.8/3. LCCN:2002-038125.

Audience: **l.**

Giovannetti, J.   QH441.2.R365 2002
Genomes and Databases on the Internet: A Practical Guide to
Functions and Applications. Trade Cloth. Horizon Scientific
Press. Norwich, 2001. 224p. ISBN:1-898486-31-X, ISBN13:
978-1-898486-31-2. Dewey:025/.06/5765. LCCN:2002-392506.

Audience: **u,f.** *Choice, 2002.*

Headrick, David   **QL462.3.G67 2001**
A Dictionary of Entomology. George Gordh (Compiled by).
Cloth Text. Oxford University Press, Inc. New York, NY. 2001.
1042p. CABI Publishing Ser. ISBN:0-85199-291-9, ISBN13:
978-0-85199-291-4. Dewey:595.7/03. LCCN:00-044427.
Audience: **g,l,u,f.**

Immelmann, Klaus & Beer,   **QL750.3.I4513 1989**
  Colin
A Dictionary of Ethology. Trade Cloth. Harvard University
Press. Cambridge, MA. 1989. 352p. ISBN:0-674-20506-5,
ISBN13: 978-0-674-20506-2. Dewey:591.5/1/0321.
LCCN:88-021360.
Audience: **g,l,u,f.** *Choice, 1989.*

J., Stangroom   **QH309.W44 2005**
What Scientists Think. Paper over Boards. Routledge. New
York, NY. 2005. XIV, 194p. ISBN:0-415-33426-8, ISBN13:
978-0-415-33426-6. Dewey:570. LCCN:2004-025418.
Audience: **g,l,u.**

Jackson, Betty P. et al.   **RS190.P55**
Atlas of Microscopy of Medicinal Plants, Culinary Herbs, and
Spices. Snowdon, Derek W.; Jackson, Betty P.. Boca Raton,
CRC Press. 1990. ISBN:0-8493-7705-6, ISBN13:
978-0-8493-7705-1.
Audience: **l,u.**

Jeffrey, Charles; Systematics   **QH83**
  Association
Biological Nomenclature. Ed. 3. Edward Arnold. 1989.
ISBN:0-7131-2983-2, ISBN13: 978-0-7131-2983-0.
Audience: **l,u.**

Meyers, Robert A.   **QH506**
Encyclopedia of Molecular Cell Biology and Molecular
Medicine, Set. Ed. 2. Trade Cloth. John Wiley & Sons, Inc.
Hoboken, NJ. 2006. 9600p. ISBN:3-527-30542-4, ISBN13:
978-3-527-30542-1. Dewey:572.8/03. LCCN:2004-275355.
Audience: **u,f.**

Netter, Frank H.   **QM25.N46 2003**
Atlas of Human Anatomy. Ed. 3. John T. Hansen (Editor). Paper
Text. Elsevier - Health Sciences Division. Philadelphia, PA.
2002. 612p. ISBN:1-929007-11-6, ISBN13: 978-1-929007-11-0.
Dewey:611/.0022/2. LCCN:2002-110663.
Audience: **g,l,u,f.** *Choice, 1990.*

Rédei, George P.   **QH427.R43 2003**
Encyclopedic Dictionary of Genetics, Genomics, and
Proteomics. Ed. 2. Trade Cloth. John Wiley & Sons, Inc.
Hoboken, NJ. 2003. 1392p. ISBN:0-471-26821-6, ISBN13:
978-0-471-26821-5. Dewey:576.5/03. LCCN:2002-011131.
Audience: **g,l,u,f.** *Choice, 2004.*

Saccone, Cecilia & Pesole,   **QH447.S23 2003**
  Graziano
Handbook of Comparative Genomics: Principles and
Methodology. Trade Cloth. John Wiley & Sons, Inc. Hoboken,
NJ. 2003. 442p. ISBN:0-471-39128-X, ISBN13:
978-0-471-39128-9. Dewey:572.8. LCCN:2002-011158.
Audience: **u,f.**

Samet, James M., et al.   **QH506.I46 2003**
An Illustrated Chinese-English Guide for Biomedical Scientists.
Weidong Wu, Yuh-Chin T. Huang & XinChao Wang (Authors).

Trade Cloth. Cold Spring Harbor Laboratory Press. Woodbury,
NY. 2004. 115p. ISBN:0-87969-701-6, ISBN13:
978-0-87969-701-3. Dewey:572.8/072. LCCN:2003-070118.
Audience: **u,f.**

Shepherd, Elizabeth   **QL362.S537 1988**
No Bones: A Key to Bugs and Slugs, Worms, and Ticks, Spiders
and Centipedes, and Other Creepy Crawlies. Ippy Patterson
(Illustrator). Trade Cloth. Simon & Schuster Children's
Publishing. New York, NY. 1988. 96p. ISBN:0-02-782880-8,
ISBN13: 978-0-02-782880-1. Dewey:592. LCCN:87-001549.
Audience: **g,l.**

Stachowitsch, Michael   **QL362.S82 1991**
The Invertebrates: An Illustrated Glossary. Ed. 1. Sylvie Proidl
(Illustrator). Trade Cloth. John Wiley & Sons, Inc. Hoboken, NJ.
1992. 690p. ISBN:0-471-83294-4, ISBN13: 978-0-471-83294-2.
Dewey:592. LCCN:91-021129.
Audience: **g,l,u.**

Steinberg, Mark L. &   **TP248.16.S84 2006**
  Cosloy, Sharon D.
The Facts on File Dictionary of Biotechnology and Genetic
Engineering. Trade Cloth. Facts On File, Inc.. New York, NY.
2006. 288p. ISBN:0-8160-6351-6, ISBN13: 978-0-8160-6351-2.
Dewey:660.603. LCCN:2005-056751.
Audience: **g,l,u.** *Choice, 2001, 1994.*

Whitaker, Allan   **TP248.16.W35 1995**
The Language of Biotechnology: A Dictionary of Terms. Ed. 2.
Michael Cox & John M. Walker (Editors), Stephen Hall
(Contribution by). Paper Text. Oxford University Press, Inc.
New York, NY. 1995. 300p. Professional Reference Book
ISBN:0-8412-2982-1, ISBN13: 978-0-8412-2982-2.
Dewey:660/.6/03. LCCN:94-023812.
Audience: **g,l,u,f.** *Choice, 1996.*

Zimmer, Marc   **QP552.G73Z56 2005**
Glowing Genes: A Revolution in Biotechnology. Trade Cloth.
Prometheus Books, Publishers. Amherst, NY. 2005. 250p.
ISBN:1-59102-253-3, ISBN13: 978-1-59102-253-4.
Dewey:572/.4358. LCCN:2004-022817.
Audience: **g,l,u,f.** *Choice, 2005.*

Bioinformatics

Google Directory: Biology Bioinformatics.
http://www.google.com/Top/Science/Biology/Bioinformatics/
Google.
Audience: **g,l.**

University of Washington HealthLinks BioResearcher
Toolkit.
http://healthlinks.washington.edu/bioresearcher
University of Washington Health Sciences Libraries.
Audience: **g,l.**

Bajic, Vladimir B. & Wee,   **QH324.2**
  Tan Tin (Editors)
Information Processing and Living Systems. Saddle Stitched,
Cloth over Boards. Imperial College Press. London, 2005. 777p.
Series on Advances in Bioinformatics and Computational
Biology ISBN:1-86094-563-5, ISBN13: 978-1-86094-563-2.
Dewey:570/.285.
Audience: **u,f.**

Barbieri, Marcello   **QH331.B247 2002**
The Organic Codes: An Introduction to Semantic Biology. Trade
Cloth. Cambridge University Press. New York, NY. 2002. 316p.
ISBN:0-521-82414-1, ISBN13: 978-0-521-82414-9.
Dewey:570/.1. LCCN:2002-073767.
Audience: **u,f.**

Batiza, Ann   **QH324.2B38 2005**
Bioinformatics, Genomics, and Proteomics: Getting the Big
Picture. Trade Cloth, Laminated. Facts On File, Inc.. New York,
NY. 2005. 112p. Biotechnology in the 21st Century Ser.
ISBN:0-7910-8517-1, ISBN13: 978-0-7910-8517-2.
Dewey:572.8/0285. LCCN:2005-017232.
Audience: **u,f.**

Brown, Stuart M.   **QH506.B767 2000**
Bioinformatics: A Biologist's Guide to Biocomputing and the
Internet. Trade Cloth. Eaton Publishing Company/Bio
Techniques Books Division. Westborough, MA. 2000. xi, 188p.
ISBN:1-881299-18-X, ISBN13: 978-1-881299-18-9.
Dewey:570/.285. LCCN:00-046247.
Audience: **l,u,f.**

Buehler, Lukas K. (Editor)   **QH324.2**
Bioinformatics Basics: Applications in Biological Science and
Medicine. Ed. 2. Rashidi, Hooman H. (Editor). Boca Raton :;
Taylor & Francis. 2005. ISBN:0-8493-1283-3, ISBN13:
978-0-8493-1283-0.
Audience: **l,u.**

Cabibbo, A. & Citterich, M.   **QH324.2.I567 2002**
Helmer
The Internet for Cell and Molecular Biologists. Trade Cloth.
Horizon Scientific Press. Norwich, 2002. 328p.
ISBN:1-898486-32-8, ISBN13: 978-1-898486-32-9.
Dewey:025.06/5716. LCCN:2002-437246.
Audience: **l,u,f.**

Campbell, A. Malcolm &   **QH447.C35 2002**
Heyer, Laurie J.
Discovering Genomics, Proteomics, and Bioinformatics. Mixed
Media, Book, Other, Paper Text, CD-ROM.
Benjamin-Cummings Publishing Company. San Francisco, CA.
2002. 352p. ISBN:0-8053-4722-4, ISBN13: 978-0-8053-4722-7.
Dewey:572.8/6. LCCN:2002-067456.
Audience: **u,f.**

Claverie, Jean-Michel &   **QH324.2**
Notredame, Cedric
Bioinformatics for Dummies. Trade Paper. John Wiley & Sons,
Inc. Hoboken, NJ. 2003. 480p. ISBN:0-7645-1696-5, ISBN13:
978-0-7645-1696-2. Dewey:570/.285. LCCN:2002-114813.
Audience: **l,u,f.**

Eils, Roland & Kriete,   **QH324.2.C638 2005**
Andres (Editors)
Computational Systems Biology. Trade Cloth. Elsevier Science
& Technology Books. Saint Louis, MO. 2005. 424p.
ISBN:0-12-088786-X, ISBN13: 978-0-12-088786-6.
Dewey:570/.1/13. LCCN:2005-020831.
Audience: **u,f.**

Gascuel, Olivier & Sagot,   **QH324.2.I557 2000**
Marie-Frances
Computational Biology: First International Conference on
Biology, Informatics, and Mathematics, JOBIM 2000: Selected
Papers. Trade Paper. Springer. New York, NY. 2001. X, 165p.

Lecture Notes in Computer Science, Vol. 2066
ISBN:3-540-42242-0, ISBN13: 978-3-540-42242-6.
Dewey:570/.285. LCCN:2001-041098.
Audience: **u,f.**

Hancock, John M. &   **QH324.2.W54 2004**
Zvelebil, Marketa J. (Editors)
Dictionary of Bioinformatics and Computational Biology. Trade
Cloth. John Wiley & Sons, Inc. Hoboken, NJ. 2004. 664p.
ISBN:0-471-43622-4, ISBN13: 978-0-471-43622-5.
Dewey:570/.285. LCCN:2003-018952.
Audience: **u,f.** *Choice, 2004.*

Higgins, Des & Taylor,   **QH323.5 .B456 2000**
Willie (Editors)
Bioinformatics: A Practical Approach. Trade Paper. Oxford
University Press, Inc. New York, NY. 2000. 270p. The Practical
Approach Ser., 236 ISBN:0-19-963790-3, ISBN13:
978-0-19-963790-4. Dewey:570/.285. LCCN:2001-267557.
Audience: **l,u,f.**

Husmeier, Dirk (Editor), et   **Q11**
al.
Probabilistic Modeling in Bioinformatics and Medical
Informatics. Richard Dybowski & Stephen Roberts (Editors).
Trade Cloth. Springer. New York, NY. 2004. XX, 508p.
Advanced Information and Knowledge Processing Ser.
ISBN:1-85233-778-8, ISBN13: 978-1-85233-778-0.
Dewey:572.8/0285. LCCN:2004-051826.
Audience: **u,f.**

Ignacimuthu, S.
Basic Bioinformatics. Alpha Science International. 2005.
ISBN:1-84265-231-1, ISBN13: 978-1-84265-231-2.
Audience: **u,f.**

Krane, Dan E. & Raymer,   **QH324.2.K72 2002**
Michael L.
Fundamental Concepts of Bioinformatics. Trade Paper.
Benjamin-Cummings Publishing Company. San Francisco, CA.
2002. 320p. ISBN:0-8053-4633-3, ISBN13: 978-0-8053-4633-6.
Dewey:570.285. LCCN:2002-012574.
Audience: **u,f.**

Krawetz, Stephen A. &   **QH507.I575 2002**
Womble, David D. (Editors)
Introduction to Bioinformatics: A Theoretical and Practical
Approach. Book, Other. Humana Press. Totowa, NJ. 2003. 728p.
ISBN:1-58829-064-6, ISBN13: 978-1-58829-064-9.
Dewey:570/.285. LCCN:2002-190207.
Audience: **u,f.**

Lacroix, Zoé & Critchlow,   **QH324.2**
Terence (Editors)
Bioinformatics: Managing Scientific Data. Trade Cloth. Elsevier
Science & Technology Books. Saint Louis, MO. 2003. 441p.
Morgan Kaufmann Series in Multimedia Information and
Systems ISBN:1-55860-829-X, ISBN13: 978-1-55860-829-0.
Dewey:570/.285. LCCN:2003-044603.
Audience: **u,f.**

Lengauer, Thomas (Editor)   **QH506**
Bioinformatics-From Genomes to Drugs, Set. Hugo Kubinyi,
Raimund Mannhold & Hendrik Timmerman (Contribution by).
Trade Cloth. John Wiley & Sons, Inc. Hoboken, NJ. 2002. 668p.

Methods and Principles in Medicinal Chemistry Ser., Vol. 14
ISBN:3-527-29988-2, ISBN13: 978-3-527-29988-1.
Dewey:572.80285. LCCN:2002-524729.

Audience: **u,f.**

Lesk, Arthur M.   **QH324.2**
Introduction to Bioinformatics. Library Binding. Sagebrush
Education Resources. Caledonia, MN. 2002.
ISBN:0-613-91949-1, ISBN13: 978-0-613-91949-4.
Dewey:570/.285.

Audience: **u,f.**

Lesk, Arthur M.   **QH441.2**
Introduction to Bioinformatics. Ed. 2. Paper Text. Oxford
University Press, Inc. New York, NY. 2005. 390p.
ISBN:0-19-927787-7, ISBN13: 978-0-19-927787-2.
Dewey:570/.285. LCCN:2005-279076.

Audience: **u,f.**

Moody, Glyn   **HG4527**
Digital Code of Life: How Bioinformatics Is Revolutionizing
Science, Medicine, and Business. Trade Cloth. John Wiley &
Sons, Inc. Hoboken, NJ. 2004. 400p. ISBN:0-471-32788-3,
ISBN13: 978-0-471-32788-2. Dewey:332.6722.
LCCN:2003-022631.

Audience: **u,f.** *Choice, 2004.*

Orengo, C.A. (Editor), et al.   **QH447**
Bioinformatics. J.M. Thornton & D.T. Jones (Editors). UK-B
Format Paperback. Taylor & Francis Group. Philadelphia, PA.
2003. 320p. ISBN:1-85996-054-5, ISBN13: 978-1-85996-054-7.
Dewey:572.86.

Audience: **l,u.**

Pevsner, Jonathan   **QH441.2.P48 2003**
Bioinformatics and Functional Genomics. Trade Paper. John
Wiley & Sons, Inc. Hoboken, NJ. 2003. 792p.
ISBN:0-471-21004-8, ISBN13: 978-0-471-21004-7.
Dewey:572/.0285. LCCN:2002-156139.

Audience: **u,f.** *Choice, 2004.*

Ramsden, Jeremy   **QH324.2.R35 2004**
Bioinformatics: An Introduction. Trade Cloth. Springer. New
York, NY. 2004. XIV, 244p. Computational Biology Ser., Vol. 3
ISBN:1-4020-2141-0, ISBN13: 978-1-4020-2141-1.
Dewey:572.8/0285. LCCN:2004-053858.

Audience: **u,f.**

Rashidi, Hooman H.;   **QH324.2.R37 2003**
  Buehler, Lukas K.
Bioinformatics Basics: Applications in Biological Science and
Medicine. CRC Press. 2006. ISBN:0-8493-1283-3, ISBN13:
978-0-8493-1283-0.

Audience: **u,f.**

Seckbach, Joseph & Rubin,   **QH324.2 .N49 2004**
  Eitan (Editors)
The New Avenues in Bioinformat. Trade Cloth. Springer. New
York, NY. 2005. XXVI, 281p. Cellular Origin, Life in Extreme
Habitats and Astrobiology Ser. ISBN:1-4020-2639-0, ISBN13:
978-1-4020-2639-3. Dewey:572.86330285.

Audience: **u,f.**

Sensen, Christoph W.   **QH447.E87 2002**
  (Editor)
Essentials of Genomics and Bioinformatics. Trade Paper. John

Wiley & Sons, Inc. Hoboken, NJ. 2002. 442p.
ISBN:3-527-30541-6, ISBN13: 978-3-527-30541-4.
Dewey:572.86. LCCN:2002-523891.

Audience: **u,f.**

Takeuchi, Y.   **QH352.T35 1996**
Global Dynamical Properties of Lotka-Volterra Systems. Cloth
Text. World Scientific Publishing Company, Inc. Hackensack,
NJ. 1996. 280p. ISBN:981-02-2471-0, ISBN13:
978-981-02-2471-4. Dewey:577.8/8/0151. LCCN:96-200751.

Audience: **u,f.**

Tozeren, Aydin & Byers,   **QH506.T68 2003**
  Stephen W.
New Biology for Engineers and Computer Scientists. Cloth
Text. Prentice Hall PTR. Upper Saddle River, NJ. 2003. 286p.
ISBN:0-13-066463-4, ISBN13: 978-0-13-066463-1.
Dewey:572.8. LCCN:2003-040485.

Audience: **u,f.**

Umar, Asad (Editor), et al.   **Q11.N5 VOL.1020**
Applications of Bioinformatics in Cancer Detection. Izet M.
Kapetanovic & Javed Khan (Editors). Trade Cloth. New York
Academy of Sciences. New York, NY. 2004. 300p. Annals of
the New York Academy of Sciences Ser., Vol. 1020
ISBN:1-57331-510-9, ISBN13: 978-1-57331-510-4. Dewey:500
s 616.99/4075. LCCN:2004-006687.

Audience: **u,f.**

Valafar, Faramarz (Editor)   **Q11.N5 NO.980**
Techniques in Bioinformatics and Medical Informatics. Trade
Cloth. New York Academy of Sciences. New York, NY. 2002.
316p. Annals of the New York Academy of Sciences Ser., Vol.
980 ISBN:1-57331-432-3, ISBN13: 978-1-57331-432-9.
Dewey:500 s 570/.285. LCCN:2002-153014.

Audience: **u,f.**

Wang, Jason T. L. (Editor),   **QA76.9.D343**
  et al.
Data Mining in Bioinformatics. Dennis E. Shasha, Hannu T. T.
Toivonen & Mohammed J. Zaki (Editors). Trade Cloth.
Springer. New York, NY. 2004. XI, 340p. Advanced Information
and Knowledge Processing Ser. ISBN:1-85233-671-4, ISBN13:
978-1-85233-671-4. Dewey:572.8/0285/6312.
LCCN:2004-048546.

Audience: **u,f.**

Wang, Jason T. L. (Editor),   **QH324.2.C635 2003**
  et al.
Computational Biology and Genome Informatics. Cathy H. Wu
& Paul P. Wang (Editors). Trade Cloth. World Scientific
Publishing Company, Inc. Hackensack, NJ. 2003. 270p.
ISBN:981-238-257-7, ISBN13: 978-981-238-257-3.
Dewey:572.86. LCCN:2003-544795.

Audience: **u,f.**

Westehead, D. R. & Parish,   **QH441.2**
  J. H.
Instant Notes in Bioinformatics. UK-B Format Paperback.
Taylor & Francis Group. Philadelphia, PA. 2002. 272p. Instant
Notes Ser. ISBN:1-85996-272-6, ISBN13: 978-1-85996-272-5.
Dewey:572.8/0825.

Audience: **u,f.**

Willis, Delta   QH351.W55 1995
The Sand Dollar and the Slide Rule: Drawing Blueprints from Nature. Trade Cloth. Addison-Wesley Longman, Inc. Boston, MA. 1995. 234p. ISBN:0-201-63275-6, ISBN13: 978-0-201-63275-0. Dewey:574.4. LCCN:94-037157.
Audience: **g,l.**

Wong, Limsoon   QH324.2P73 2004
ⓔ The Practical Bioinformatician. E-Book. World Scientific Publishing Company, Inc. Hackensack, NJ. ISBN:981-256-234-6, ISBN13: 978-981-256-234-0. Dewey:570.285.
Audience: **u,f.**

Wu, Catherine H. &   QH441.2.W8 2000
  McLarty, Jerry W.
Neural Networks and Genome Informatics. Trade Cloth. Elsevier Science & Technology Books. Saint Louis, MO. 2000. 220p. Methods in Computational and Theoretical Molecular Biology Ser., 1 ISBN:0-08-042800-2, ISBN13: 978-0-08-042800-0. Dewey:576.5/0285/632. LCCN:00-056153.
Audience: **u,f.**

Xiong, Jin   QH324.2.X56 2006
Essential Bioinformatics. Cloth Text. Cambridge University Press. New York, NY. 2006. 352p. ISBN:0-521-84098-8, ISBN13: 978-0-521-84098-9. Dewey:572.80285. LCCN:2005-029453.
Audience: **u,f.**

Yan, Peter V. (Editor)   QH324.2.B555 2004
Bioinformatics: New Research. Trade Cloth. Nova Science Publishers, Inc. Hauppauge, NY. 2005. 173p. ISBN:1-59454-242-2, ISBN13: 978-1-59454-242-8. Dewey:572.8/0285. LCCN:2004-028388.
Audience: **u,f.**

Yan, Peter V. (Editor)   QH324.2.T74 2005
Trends in Bioinformatics Research. Nova Science Pub Inc. 2006. ISBN:1-59454-739-4, ISBN13: 978-1-59454-739-3.
Audience: **u,f.**

Young, Paul   QH447
Exploring Genomes: Web-Based Bioinformatic Excercises. Trade Paper. Worth Publishers, Inc. New York, NY. 2002. 51p. ISBN:0-7167-5738-9, ISBN13: 978-0-7167-5738-2. Dewey:572.8/6.
Audience: **u,f.**

Young, Simon S.   QH324.2 .Y68 2001
Computerized Data Acquisition and Analysis for the Life Sciences: A Hands-on Guide. Trade Cloth. Cambridge University Press. New York, NY. 2001. 248p. ISBN:0-521-56281-3, ISBN13: 978-0-521-56281-2. Dewey:570/.285. LCCN:00-045436.
Audience: **u,f.**

Bioinformatics > Analytic Methods

Baxevanis, Andreas D.   QH441.2.C876 2002
  (Editor)
Current Protocols in Bioinformatics. Ringbound. John Wiley & Sons, Inc. Hoboken, NJ. 2003. ISBN:0-471-25093-7, ISBN13: 978-0-471-25093-7. Dewey:570/.285. LCCN:2002-191048.
Audience: **u,f.**

Baxevanis, Andreas D. &   QP551
  Ouellette, B. F. Francis (Editors)
Bioinformatics: A Practical Guide to the Analysis of Genes and Proteins. Ed. 3. Trade Cloth. John Wiley & Sons, Inc. Hoboken, NJ. 2004. 560p. ISBN:0-471-47878-4, ISBN13: 978-0-471-47878-2. Dewey:572.8/633/0285. LCCN:2004-011822.
Audience: **u,f.**

Buckland, S.T. (Editor),   QH352
  et al.
Advanced Distance Sampling: Estimating Abundance of Biological Populations. D.R. Anderson & K.P. Burnham (Editors). Trade Cloth. Oxford University Press, Inc. New York, NY. 2004. 434p. ISBN:0-19-850783-6, ISBN13: 978-0-19-850783-3. Dewey:591.7/88/0727. LCCN:2004-303414.
Audience: **u,f.**

Gentleman, Robert (Editor),   QH324.2
  et al.
Bioinformatics and Computational Biology Solutions Using R and Bioconductor. Wolfgang Huber, Sandrine Dudoit, Vincent J. Carey & Rafael A. Irizarry (Editors). Trade Cloth. Springer. New York, NY. 2005. XIX, 473p. Statistics for Biology and Health Ser. ISBN:0-387-25146-4, ISBN13: 978-0-387-25146-2. Dewey:570.285. LCCN:2005-923843.
Audience: **u,f.**

Glover, Thomas & Mitchell,   QH323.5
  Kevin
An Introduction to Biostatistics. Paper Text. Waveland Press, Inc. Prospect Heights, IL. 2006. 416p. ISBN:1-57766-458-2, ISBN13: 978-1-57766-458-1. Dewey:570/.1/5195.
Audience: **u,f.**

Griffiths, Anthony J. F.,   QH430.I62 2004
  et al.
An Introduction to Genetic Analysis. Ed. 8. William M. Gelbart, Richard C. Lewontin, Susan R. Wessler, David Suzuki & Jeffrey H. Miller (Authors). Cloth over Boards. W. H. Freeman & Company. New York, NY. 2004. 800p. ISBN:0-7167-4939-4, ISBN13: 978-0-7167-4939-4. Dewey:576.5. LCCN:2004-102340.
Audience: **u,f.**

Hartl, Daniel L. & Jones,   QH430.H3733 2001
  Elizabeth
Genetics: Analysis of Genes and Genomes. Ed. 5. Cloth Text. Jones & Bartlett Publishers, Inc. Sudbury, MA. 2000. 858p. Genetics Ser. ISBN:0-7637-0913-1, ISBN13: 978-0-7637-0913-6. Dewey:576.5. LCCN:00-038440.
Audience: **u,f.**

Hartl, Daniel L. & Jones,   QH430.H3733 2005
  Elizabeth W.
Genetics: Analysis of Genes and Genomes. Ed. 6. Trade Cloth. Jones & Bartlett Publishers, Inc. Sudbury, MA. 2004. 854p. ISBN:0-7637-1511-5, ISBN13: 978-0-7637-1511-3. Dewey:576.5. LCCN:2004-042183.
Audience: **u,f.**

Istas, Jacques   QH323.5.I866 2005
Mathematical Modeling for the Life Sciences. Trade Paper. Springer. New York, NY. 2005. VII, 164p. Universitext Ser. ISBN:3-540-25305-X, ISBN13: 978-3-540-25305-1. Dewey:570.1/5118. LCCN:2005-926252.
Audience: **u,f.** *Choice, 2006.*

Knudsen, Steen   QP624.5.D726K68 2002
A Biologist's Guide to Analysis of DNA Microarray Data. Trade
Cloth. John Wiley & Sons, Inc. Hoboken, NJ. 2002. 144p.
ISBN:0-471-22490-1, ISBN13: 978-0-471-22490-7.
Dewey:572.8/636. LCCN:2002-072380.

Audience: **u,f.**

Knudsen, Steen   QP624.5.D726K68 2004
Guide to Analysis of DNA Microarray Data. Ed. 2. Trade Paper.
John Wiley & Sons, Inc. Hoboken, NJ. 2004. 184p.
ISBN:0-471-65604-6, ISBN13: 978-0-471-65604-3.
Dewey:572.8/636. LCCN:2003-026036.

Audience: **u,f.**

Kohane, Isaac S., et al.   QP624.5.D726K686
Microarrays for an Integrative Genomics. Alvin Kho & Atul J.
Butte (Authors). Trade Cloth. MIT Press. Cambridge, MA.
2002. 326p. Computational Molecular Biology Ser.
ISBN:0-262-11271-X, ISBN13: 978-0-262-11271-0.
Dewey:572.8/6. LCCN:2002-022663.

Audience: **u,f.**

Kordal, Richard Joseph,   QP624.5.D726M53 2002
et al.
Microfabricated Sensors: Application of Optical Technology for
DNA Analysis. Arthur M. Usmani & Wai Tak Law (Authors),
American Chemical Society, Division of Industrial and
Engineering Chemistry Staff & American Chemical Society Staff
(Contribution by). Cloth Text. Oxford University Press, Inc.
New York, NY. 2002. 170p. ACS Symposium Ser., Vol. 815
ISBN:0-8412-3763-8, ISBN13: 978-0-8412-3763-6.
Dewey:610/.28. LCCN:2001-056737.

Audience: **u,f.**

Le, Chap T.   QH323.5
Introductory Biostatistics. Trade Cloth. John Wiley & Sons, Inc.
Hoboken, NJ. 2003. 552p. ISBN:0-471-41816-1, ISBN13:
978-0-471-41816-0. Dewey:610.15195. LCCN:2003-273311.

Audience: **u,f.**

Lefkovitch, L. P.   QH83.L429 1993
Optimal Set Covering for Biological Classification: Theory of
Conditional Clustering and Its Use in Biological Classification
and Identification. Trade Paper. Canadian Government
Publishing. Aylmer, PQ. 1993. 454p. ISBN:0-660-14821-8,
ISBN13: 978-0-660-14821-2. Dewey:574/.014.
LCCN:93-245195.

Audience: **u,f.**

Lele, Subhash; Richtsmeier,   QH351
Joan T.
An Invariant Approach to Statistical Analysis of Shapes.
Chapman & Hall/CRC: Boca Raton, Fla.. 2001. Interdisciplinary
statistics ISBN:0-8493-0319-2, ISBN13: 978-0-8493-0319-7.

Audience: **u,f.**

Lin, Simon M. & Johnson,   QP624.5.D726M48 2002
Kimberly F. (Editors)
Methods of Microarray Data Analysis. Trade Cloth. Springer.
New York, NY. 2001. 208p. ISBN:0-7923-7564-5, ISBN13:
978-0-7923-7564-7. Dewey:572.8/636. LCCN:2001-050241.

Audience: **u,f.**

Looney, Stephen W.   QH323.5
Biostatistical Methods. Humana Press: Totowa, N.J.. 2002.
Methods in Molecular Biology ;; Vol. 184; Variation: Methods
in Molecular Biology (Clifton, N.J.); Vol. 184
ISBN:0-89603-951-X, ISBN13: 978-0-89603-951-3.

Audience: **u,f.**

Magnello, Eileen & Hardy,   QH323.5.R565 2002
Anne (Editors)
The Road to Medical Statistis. Trade Cloth. Rodopi. Kenilworth,
NY. 2002. 175p. Clio Medica/The Wellcome Institute Series in
the History of Medicine, 67 ISBN:90-420-1208-0, ISBN13:
978-90-420-1208-0. Dewey:610/.72/7.

Audience: **u,f.**

Manly, Bryan F.   QH352.M35 1990
Stage-Structured Populations: Sampling, Analysis and
Simulation. Trade Cloth. Chapman & Hall. New York, NY.
1990. 160p. Population and Community Biology Ser.
ISBN:0-412-35060-2, ISBN13: 978-0-412-35060-3.
Dewey:574.5/248/072. LCCN:89-023878.
Audience: **u,f.** *Choice, 1990.*

Marcus, Leslie F. (Editor),   QH351.A38 1996
et al.
Advances in Morphometrics: Proceedings of the NATO ASI
Held in IL Ciocco, Tuscany, Italy, July 18-30,1993. M. Corti &
A. Loy (Editors). Trade Cloth. Basic Books. New York, NY.
1996. 588p. NATO ASI Series A, Life Sciences, No. 284
ISBN:0-306-45301-0, ISBN13: 978-0-306-45301-4.
Dewey:574/.012. LCCN:96-018484.

Audience: **u,f.**

Matis, James H. & Kiffe,   QH352.M383 2000
Thomas R.
Stochastic Population Models: A Compartmental Perspective.
Trade Paper. Springer. New York, NY. 2000. X, 202p. Lecture
Notes in Statistics, Vol. 145 ISBN:0-387-98657-X, ISBN13:
978-0-387-98657-9. Dewey:577.8/8/015118. LCCN:00-030462.
Audience: **u,f.**

Maurer, Brian A.   QH352.M39 1994
Geologic Population Analysis: Tools for the Analysis of
Biodiversity. Ed. 2. Trade Paper. Blackwell Publishing, Inc.
Malden, MA. 1994. 144p. Methods in Ecology Ser.
ISBN:0-632-03741-5, ISBN13: 978-0-632-03741-4.
Dewey:574.5/248. LCCN:94-184019.

Audience: **u,f.**

McCallum, Hamish   QH352
Population Parameters: Estimation for Ecological Models. Trade
Paper. Blackwell Publishing, Inc. Malden, MA. 2000. 360p.
Methods in Ecology Ser. ISBN:0-86542-740-2, ISBN13:
978-0-86542-740-2. Dewey:577.8/8/0151.

Audience: **u,f.**

Misener, Stephen &   QH506.B535 2000
Krawetz, Stephen A. (Editors)
Bioinformatics Methods and Protocols. Book, Other. Humana
Press. Totowa, NJ. 1999. 512p. Methods in Molecular Biology
Ser., Vol. 132 ISBN:0-89603-732-0, ISBN13:
978-0-89603-732-8. Dewey:572.8/0285. LCCN:99-017054.

Audience: **u,f.**

Misra, J. C. (Editor)   QH323.5.U53 2002
Uncertainty and Optimality: Probability, Statistics and
Operations Research. Cloth Text. World Scientific Publishing

Company, Inc. Hackensack, NJ. 2002. 572p.
ISBN:981-238-082-5, ISBN13: 978-981-238-082-1.
Dewey:519.5.

Audience: **u,f.**

Motulsky, Harvey &   QH323.5.M68 2003
  Christopoulos, Arthur
Fitting Models to Biological Data Using Linear and Nonlinear
Regression: A Practical Guide to Curve Fitting. Trade Cloth.
Oxford University Press, Inc. New York, NY. 2004. 352p.
ISBN:0-19-517179-9, ISBN13: 978-0-19-517179-2.
Dewey:570/.1/5118. LCCN:2003-057957.

Audience: **u,f.**

Roff, Derek   QH324.2
Introduction to Computer-Intensive Methods of Data Analysis in
Biology. Trade Cloth. Cambridge University Press. New York,
NY. 2006. 376p. ISBN:0-521-84628-5, ISBN13:
978-0-521-84628-8. Dewey:570.285. LCCN:2006-001857.

Audience: **u,f.**

Shoemaker, J. S. & Lin, S.   QP624.5.D726M483
  M. (Editors)
Methods of Microarray Data Analysis, Vol. 4. Trade Cloth.
Springer. New York, NY. 2004. XVI, 256p.
ISBN:0-387-23074-2, ISBN13: 978-0-387-23074-0.
Dewey:572.8636. LCCN:2005-297773.

Audience: **u,f.**

Simon, Richard M.   QP624.5.D726D475
Design and Analysis of DNA Microarray Investigations. Trade
Cloth. Springer. New York, NY. 2004. X, 199p. Statistics for
Biology and Health Ser. ISBN:0-387-00135-2, ISBN13:
978-0-387-00135-7. Dewey:572.8/65. LCCN:2003-054790.

Audience: **u,f.**

Speed, Terry (ed.)   QP624.5.D726 S73 2003
Statistical Analysis of Gene Expression Microarray Data. CRC
Press. 2003. Interdisciplinary Statistics Ser.
ISBN:1-58488-327-8, ISBN13: 978-1-58488-327-2.

Audience: **u,f.**

Stekel, Dov   QP624.5.D726S74 2003
Microarray Bioinformatics. Trade Cloth. Cambridge University
Press. New York, NY. 2003. 280p. ISBN:0-521-81982-2,
ISBN13: 978-0-521-81982-4. Dewey:572.8/636.
LCCN:2003-043959.

Audience: **u,f.**

White, Bruce A. (Editor)   QP606.D46P363 1993
PCR Protocols: Current Methods and Applications. Humana
Press: New Jersey. 1993. Methods in Molecular Biology, 15
ISBN:0-89603-244-2, ISBN13: 978-0-89603-244-6.

Audience: **u,f.**

Wit, Ernst & McClure,   QP624.5.D726
  John
Statistics for Microarrays: Design, Analysis and Inference. Trade
Cloth. John Wiley & Sons, Inc. Hoboken, NJ. 2004. 278p.
ISBN:0-470-84993-2, ISBN13: 978-0-470-84993-4.
Dewey:629.04. LCCN:2004-045909.

Audience: **u,f.**

Zhang, Wei, et al.   QP624.5.D726Z438
Microarray Quality Control. Ilya Shmulevich & Jaakko Astola
(Authors). Trade Cloth. John Wiley & Sons, Inc. Hoboken, NJ.
2004. 136p. ISBN:0-471-45344-7, ISBN13: 978-0-471-45344-4.
Dewey:572.8/636. LCCN:2003-026922.

Audience: **u,f.**

Bioinformatics > Gene Sequencing

Augen, Jeff   QH441.2
Bioinformatics in the Post-Genomic Era: Genome,
Transcriptome, Proteome, and Information-Based Medicine.
Trade Paper. Addison Wesley Professional. Boston, MA. 2004.
400p. ISBN:0-321-17386-4, ISBN13: 978-0-321-17386-7.
Dewey:572.8/0285. LCCN:2004-106573.

Audience: **u,f.**

Baxevanis, Andreas D.   QH441.2.C876 2002
  (Editor)
Current Protocols in Bioinformatics. Ringbound. John Wiley &
Sons, Inc. Hoboken, NJ. 2003. ISBN:0-471-25093-7, ISBN13:
978-0-471-25093-7. Dewey:570/.285. LCCN:2002-191048.

Audience: **u,f.**

Baxevanis, Andreas D. &   QP551
  Ouellette, B. F. Francis (Editors)
Bioinformatics: A Practical Guide to the Analysis of Genes and
Proteins. Ed. 3. Trade Cloth. John Wiley & Sons, Inc. Hoboken,
NJ. 2004. 560p. ISBN:0-471-47878-4, ISBN13:
978-0-471-47878-2. Dewey:572.8/633/0285.
LCCN:2004-011822.

Audience: **u,f.**

Bernot, Alain   QH447.B4813 2004
⒠ Genome Transcriptome and Proteome Analysis. E-Book.
John Wiley & Sons, Inc. Hoboken, NJ. 2006. 248p.
ISBN:0-470-02079-2, ISBN13: 978-0-470-02079-1.
Dewey:572.8.

Audience: **u,f.** *Choice, 2005.*

Chapman, K. E. & Higgins,   QH450
  S. J. (Editors)
Essays in Biochemistry: Regulation of Gene Expression, Vol.
37. Trade Paper. Portland Press, Ltd. London, 2001. 131p.
ISBN:1-85578-138-7, ISBN13: 978-1-85578-138-2.
Dewey:572.865.

Audience: **u,f.**

Collado-Vides, Julio &   QH438.4.M3G46 2002
  Hofestädt, Ralf (Editors)
Gene Regulation and Metabolism: Post-Genomic Computational
Approaches. Cloth Text. MIT Press. Cambridge, MA. 2002.
320p. Computational Molecular Biology Ser.
ISBN:0-262-03297-X, ISBN13: 978-0-262-03297-1.
Dewey:572.8/01/5118. LCCN:2001-056247.

Audience: **u,f.**

Higgins, D. & Taylor, Willie   QP517.M3
  (Editors)
Bioinformatics: Sequence, Structure and Databanks: A Practical
Approach. Cloth Text. Oxford University Press, Inc. New York,
NY. 2000. 272p. The Practical Approach Ser., No. 236
ISBN:0-19-963791-1, ISBN13: 978-0-19-963791-1.
Dewey:572/.0285.

Audience: **u,f.**

Jordan, Bertrand   QP624.5.D726D634
DNA Microarrays: Gene Expression Applications. Trade Cloth.
Springer. New York, NY. 2001. IX, 140p. Principles and
Practice Ser. ISBN:3-540-41507-6, ISBN13: 978-3-540-41507-7.
Dewey:572.8/65. LCCN:2001-032237.
Audience: **u,f.**

Kolchanov, Nikolay &   QH447
  Hofestaedt, Ralf (Editors)
Bioinformatics of Genome Regulation and Structure. Trade
Cloth. Springer. New York, NY. 2004. 396p.
ISBN:1-4020-7735-1, ISBN13: 978-1-4020-7735-7.
Dewey:572.8/6. LCCN:2003-070159.
Audience: **u,f.**

Koonin, Eugene V. &   QH447.K665 2002
  Galperin, Michael Y.
Sequence - Evolution - Function: Computational Approaches in
Comparative Genomics. Trade Cloth. Springer. New York, NY.
2002. 488p. ISBN:1-4020-7274-0, ISBN13: 978-1-4020-7274-1.
Dewey:572.8/6. LCCN:2002-034045.
Audience: **u,f.**

Lee, Mei-Ling Ting   QP624.5.D726
Analysis of Microarray Gene Expression Data. Trade Cloth.
Springer. New York, NY. 2004. 400p. ISBN:0-7923-7087-2,
ISBN13: 978-0-7923-7087-1. Dewey:572.8/636.
LCCN:2004-041531.
Audience: **u,f.**

Markel, Scott & León,   QP625.N89
  Darryl
Sequence Analysis in a Nutshell: A Guide to Tools and
Databases. Trade Paper, Perfect. O'Reilly Media, Inc.
Sebastopol, CA. 2003. 302p. ISBN:0-596-00494-X, ISBN13:
978-0-596-00494-1. Dewey:572.8633. LCCN:2003-271321.
Audience: **u,f.**

McLachlan, Geoffrey J.,   QP624.5.D726
  et al.
Analyzing Microarray Gene Expression Data. Kim-Anh Do &
Christophe Ambroise (Authors). Trade Cloth. John Wiley &
Sons, Inc. Hoboken, NJ. 2004. 352p. Wiley Series in Probability
and Statistics Ser. ISBN:0-471-22616-5, ISBN13:
978-0-471-22616-1. Dewey:572.8/636. LCCN:2004-042239.
Audience: **u,f.**

Mount, David   QH441.2.M68 2004
Bioinformatics: Sequence and Genome Analysis. Ed. 2. Trade
Cloth. Cold Spring Harbor Laboratory Press. Woodbury, NY.
2004. 600p. ISBN:0-87969-687-7, ISBN13: 978-0-87969-687-0.
Dewey:572.8/633. LCCN:2004-009760.
Audience: **u,f.**

Parmigiani, Giovanni   QP624.5.D726A53 2003
  (Editor), et al.
The Analysis of Gene Expression Data: Methods and Software.
Elizabeth S. Garrett, Rafael A. Irizarry & Scott Zeger (Editors).
Trade Cloth. Springer. New York, NY. 2003. XIX, 455p.
Statistics for Biology and Health Ser. ISBN:0-387-95577-1,
ISBN13: 978-0-387-95577-3. Dewey:572. LCCN:2002-030572.
Audience: **u,f.**

Speed, Terry (ed.)   QP624.5.D726 S73 2003
Statistical Analysis of Gene Expression Microarray Data. CRC
Press. 2003. Interdisciplinary Statistics Ser.
ISBN:1-58488-327-8, ISBN13: 978-1-58488-327-2.
Audience: **u,f.**

Zhang, Wei, et al.   QP624.5.D726Z438
Microarray Quality Control. Ilya Shmulevich & Jaakko Astola
(Authors). Trade Cloth. John Wiley & Sons, Inc. Hoboken, NJ.
2004. 136p. ISBN:0-471-45344-7, ISBN13: 978-0-471-45344-4.
Dewey:572.8/636. LCCN:2003-026922.
Audience: **u,f.**

Bioinformatics > methods of gene sequencing

Baxevanis, Andreas D.   QH441.2.C876 2002
  (Editor)
Current Protocols in Bioinformatics. Ringbound. John Wiley &
Sons, Inc. Hoboken, NJ. 2003. ISBN:0-471-25093-7, ISBN13:
978-0-471-25093-7. Dewey:570/.285. LCCN:2002-191048.
Audience: **u,f.**

Kolchanov, Nikolay &   QH447
  Hofestaedt, Ralf (Editors)
Bioinformatics of Genome Regulation and Structure. Trade
Cloth. Springer. New York, NY. 2004. 396p.
ISBN:1-4020-7735-1, ISBN13: 978-1-4020-7735-7.
Dewey:572.8/6. LCCN:2003-070159.
Audience: **u,f.**

White, Bruce A. (Editor)   QP606.D46P363 1993
PCR Protocols: Current Methods and Applications. Humana
Press: New Jersey. 1993. Methods in Molecular Biology, 15
ISBN:0-89603-244-2, ISBN13: 978-0-89603-244-6.
Audience: **u,f.**

Bioinformatics > Protein Sequences

                                              QH447
☐ Entrez Genome.
http://www.ncbi.nlm.nih.gov:80/entrez/query.fcgi?db=Genome
Audience: **u,f.**

                                              QH447
☐ Trans-NIH Mouse Initiatives.
http://www.nih.gov/science/models/mouse/
Audience: **u.**

Albala, Joanna S. &   QH506.P796 2003
  Humphery-Smith, Ian
Protein Arrays, Biochips, and Proteomics: The Next Phase of
Genomics Discovery. Paper over Boards. Marcel Dekker Inc.
New York, NY. 2003. 304p. ISBN:0-8247-4312-1, ISBN13:
978-0-8247-4312-3. Dewey:572/.6. LCCN:2004-296024.
Audience: **u,f.**

Augen, Jeff   QH441.2
Bioinformatics in the Post-Genomic Era: Genome,
Transcriptome, Proteome, and Information-Based Medicine.
Trade Paper. Addison Wesley Professional. Boston, MA. 2004.
400p. ISBN:0-321-17386-4, ISBN13: 978-0-321-17386-7.
Dewey:572.8/0285. LCCN:2004-106573.
Audience: **u,f.**

Baxevanis, Andreas D. &   QP551
  Ouellette, B. F. Francis (Editors)
Bioinformatics: A Practical Guide to the Analysis of Genes and
Proteins. Ed. 3. Trade Cloth. John Wiley & Sons, Inc. Hoboken,

NJ. 2004. 560p. ISBN:0-471-47878-4, ISBN13: 978-0-471-47878-2. Dewey:572.8/633/0285. LCCN:2004-011822.

Audience: **u,f.**

Bernot, Alain   **QH447.B4813 2004**
🔲 Genome Transcriptome and Proteome Analysis. E-Book. John Wiley & Sons, Inc. Hoboken, NJ. 2006. 248p. ISBN:0-470-02079-2, ISBN13: 978-0-470-02079-1. Dewey:572.8.

Audience: **u,f.** *Choice, 2005.*

Blalock, Eric M. (Editor)   **QP624.5.D726B456**
A Beginner's Guide to Microarrays. Trade Cloth. Springer. New York, NY. 2003. 368p. ISBN:1-4020-7472-7, ISBN13: 978-1-4020-7472-1. Dewey:572.8/636. LCCN:2003-051408.

Audience: **u,f.**

Bourne, Philip E. & Weissig,   **QP517.M3S776 2003**
Helge (Editors)
Structural Bioinformatics. Trade Cloth. John Wiley & Sons, Inc. Hoboken, NJ. 2003. 649p. Methods of Biochemical Analysis Ser., Vol. 44 ISBN:0-471-20200-2, ISBN13: 978-0-471-20200-4. Dewey:572.8/733. LCCN:2002-011156.

Audience: **u,f.**

Campbell, A. Malcolm &   **QH447.C35 2002**
Heyer, Laurie J.
Discovering Genomics, Proteomics, and Bioinformatics. Mixed Media, Book, Other, Paper Text, CD-ROM. Benjamin-Cummings Publishing Company. San Francisco, CA. 2002. 352p. ISBN:0-8053-4722-4, ISBN13: 978-0-8053-4722-7. Dewey:572.8/6. LCCN:2002-067456.

Audience: **u,f.**

Smith, Bryan John (Editor)   **QP625.N89P76 2002**
Protein Sequencing Protocols. Ed. 2. Book, Other. Humana Press. Totowa, NJ. 2003. 430p. Methods in Molecular Biology Ser., Vol. 211 ISBN:0-89603-975-7, ISBN13: 978-0-89603-975-9. Dewey:572.8/633. LCCN:2002-022740.

Audience: **u,f.**

Srivastava, Sudhir (Editor)   **QP551.I46 2005**
Informatics in Proteomics. Perfect, Paper over Boards. Marcel Dekker Inc. New York, NY. 2005. 500p. ISBN:1-57444-480-8, ISBN13: 978-1-57444-480-3. Dewey:572/.6. LCCN:2004-063438.

Audience: **u,f.**

Bioinformatics > DNA and RNA Sequences

                        QH303.5
🔲 BLAST.
http://www.ncbi.nlm.nih.gov/Education/BLASTinfo/information3.html

Audience: **u,f.**

                        QH447
🔲 Entrez Genome.
http://www.ncbi.nlm.nih.gov:80/entrez/query.fcgi?db=Genome

Audience: **u,f.**

                        QH447
🔲 Mouse Genome Resources.
http://www.ncbi.nlm.nih.gov/genome/guide/mouse/

Audience: **u,f.**

                        QH447
🔲 Trans-NIH Mouse Initiatives.
http://www.nih.gov/science/models/mouse/

Audience: **u.**

Baxevanis, Andreas D. &   **QP551**
Ouellette, B. F. Francis (Editors)
Bioinformatics: A Practical Guide to the Analysis of Genes and Proteins. Ed. 3. Trade Cloth. John Wiley & Sons, Inc. Hoboken, NJ. 2004. 560p. ISBN:0-471-47878-4, ISBN13: 978-0-471-47878-2. Dewey:572.8/633/0285. LCCN:2004-011822.

Audience: **u,f.**

Berrar, Daniel P. (Editor), et   **QP624.5.D726P73 2002**
al.
A Practical Approach to Microarray Data Analysis. Werner Dubitzky & Martin Granzow (Editors). Trade Cloth. Springer. New York, NY. 2002. 384p. ISBN:1-4020-7260-0, ISBN13: 978-1-4020-7260-4. Dewey:572.8/633. LCCN:2002-034174.

Audience: **u,f.**

Blalock, Eric M. (Editor)   **QP624.5.D726B456**
A Beginner's Guide to Microarrays. Trade Cloth. Springer. New York, NY. 2003. 368p. ISBN:1-4020-7472-7, ISBN13: 978-1-4020-7472-1. Dewey:572.8/636. LCCN:2003-051408.

Audience: **u,f.**

Knudsen, Steen   **QP624.5.D726K68 2002**
A Biologist's Guide to Analysis of DNA Microarray Data. Trade Cloth. John Wiley & Sons, Inc. Hoboken, NJ. 2002. 144p. ISBN:0-471-22490-1, ISBN13: 978-0-471-22490-7. Dewey:572.8/636. LCCN:2002-072380.

Audience: **u,f.**

Korf, Ian F., et al.   **QH324.2**
BLAST. Mark Yandell & Joseph Bedell (Authors). Trade Paper, Perfect. O'Reilly Media, Inc. Sebastopol, CA. 2003. 339p. ISBN:0-596-00299-8, ISBN13: 978-0-596-00299-2. Dewey:572.8/0285/536. LCCN:2004-272804.

Audience: **u,f.**

Rampal, Jang B. (Editor)   **QP624.5.D726D62 2001**
DNA Arrays: Methods and Protocols. Book, Other. Humana Press. Totowa, NJ. 2001. 280p. Methods in Molecular Biology Ser., Vol. 170 ISBN:0-89603-822-X, ISBN13: 978-0-89603-822-6. Dewey:572.8/6. LCCN:00-040791.

Audience: **u,f.**

Westermeier, Reiner   **QP519.9.E434 W47713**
Electrophoresis in Practice: A Guide to Methods and Applications of DNA and Protein Separations. Ed. 4. Trade Cloth. John Wiley & Sons, Inc. Hoboken, NJ. 2005. 426p. ISBN:3-527-31181-5, ISBN13: 978-3-527-31181-1. Dewey:543/.4. LCCN:2006-280306.

Audience: **u,f.**

Bioinformatics > Proteomics

QH447

□ Entrez Genome.
http://www.ncbi.nlm.nih.gov:80/entrez/query.fcgi?db=Genome
Audience: **u,f.**

QD431.E9

□ ExPASy Proteomics Server.
http://www.expasy.ch/
Audience: **u,f.**

QH447

□ Zebrafish Genome Resources.
http://www.ncbi.nlm.nih.gov/genome/guide/zebrafish/
Audience: **u,f.**

Albala, Joanna S. &   **QH506.P796 2003**
  Humphery-Smith, Ian
Protein Arrays, Biochips, and Proteomics: The Next Phase of
Genomics Discovery. Paper over Boards. Marcel Dekker Inc.
New York, NY. 2003. 304p. ISBN:0-8247-4312-1, ISBN13:
978-0-8247-4312-3. Dewey:572/.6. LCCN:2004-296024.
Audience: **u,f.**

Augen, Jeff   **QH441.2**
Bioinformatics in the Post-Genomic Era: Genome,
Transcriptome, Proteome, and Information-Based Medicine.
Trade Paper. Addison Wesley Professional. Boston, MA. 2004.
400p. ISBN:0-321-17386-4, ISBN13: 978-0-321-17386-7.
Dewey:572.8/0285. LCCN:2004-106573.
Audience: **u,f.**

Batiza, Ann   **QH324.2B38 2005**
Bioinformatics, Genomics, and Proteomics: Getting the Big
Picture. Trade Cloth, Laminated. Facts On File, Inc.. New York,
NY. 2005. 112p. Biotechnology in the 21st Century Ser.
ISBN:0-7910-8517-1, ISBN13: 978-0-7910-8517-2.
Dewey:572.8/0285. LCCN:2005-017232.
Audience: **u,f.**

Baxevanis, Andreas D. &   **QP551**
  Ouellette, B. F. Francis (Editors)
Bioinformatics: A Practical Guide to the Analysis of Genes and
Proteins. Ed. 3. Trade Cloth. John Wiley & Sons, Inc. Hoboken,
NJ. 2004. 560p. ISBN:0-471-47878-4, ISBN13:
978-0-471-47878-2. Dewey:572.8/633/0285.
LCCN:2004-011822.
Audience: **u,f.**

Bourne, Philip E. & Weissig,   **QP517.M3S776 2003**
  Helge (Editors)
Structural Bioinformatics. Trade Cloth. John Wiley & Sons, Inc.
Hoboken, NJ. 2003. 649p. Methods of Biochemical Analysis
Ser., Vol. 44 ISBN:0-471-20200-2, ISBN13: 978-0-471-20200-4.
Dewey:572.8/733. LCCN:2002-011156.
Audience: **u,f.**

Burczynski, Michael E.   **QH438.4.B55**
  (Editor)
Surrogate Tissue Analysis: Genomic, Proteomic and
Metabolomic Approaches. Rockett, John C. (Editor). CRC Press:
Boca Raton. 2006. ISBN:0-8493-2840-3, ISBN13:
978-0-8493-2840-4.
Audience: **u,f.**

Campbell, A. Malcolm &   **QH447.C35 2002**
  Heyer, Laurie J.
Discovering Genomics, Proteomics, and Bioinformatics. Mixed
Media, Book, Other, Paper Text, CD-ROM.
Benjamin-Cummings Publishing Company. San Francisco, CA.
2002. 352p. ISBN:0-8053-4722-4, ISBN13: 978-0-8053-4722-7.
Dewey:572.8/6. LCCN:2002-067456.
Audience: **u,f.**

Cheng, R Holland &   **QP801.P64**
  Hammar, Lena (Editors)
Conformational Proteomics of Macromolecular Architecture:
Approaching the Structure of Large Molecular Assemblies and
Their Mechanisms of Action. CD-ROM, Trade Cloth. World
Scientific Publishing Company, Inc. Hackensack, NJ. 2004.
432p. ISBN:981-238-614-9, ISBN13: 978-981-238-614-4.
Dewey:547.7.
Audience: **u,f.**

Dopazo, Joaquin & Azuaje,   **QH447**
  Francisco (Editors)
Data Analysis and Visualization in Genomics and Proteomics.
Trade Cloth. John Wiley & Sons, Inc. Hoboken, NJ. 2005. 284p.
ISBN:0-470-09439-7, ISBN13: 978-0-470-09439-6.
Dewey:572.8/6. LCCN:2005-006838.
Audience: **u,f.**

Dunn, Michael J. (Editor)   **QP551.F94 2000**
From Genome to Proteome: Advances in the Practice and
Application of Proteomics. Trade Cloth. John Wiley & Sons,
Inc. Hoboken, NJ. 2000. 552p. ISBN:3-527-30154-2, ISBN13:
978-3-527-30154-6. Dewey:572/.6. LCCN:00-697886.
Audience: **u,f.**

Gad, Shayne Cox (Editor)   **RM301.25.D784 2005**
Drug Discovery Handbook. Trade Cloth. John Wiley & Sons,
Inc. Hoboken, NJ. 2005. 1496p. ISBN:0-471-21384-5, ISBN13:
978-0-471-21384-0. Dewey:615/.19. LCCN:2004-027077.
Audience: **u,f.**

Moussa, Naima Moustaid &   **QP171**
  Berdanier, Carolyn
Genomics and Proteomics in Nutrition. Paper over Boards.
Marcel Dekker Inc. New York, NY. 2004. 528p. Nutrition in
Health and Disease Ser., Vol. 1 ISBN:0-8247-5430-1, ISBN13:
978-0-8247-5430-3. Dewey:612.3. LCCN:2004-275369.
Audience: **u,f.**

Raghavachari, Ramesh &   **TP248.6.G523 2001**
  Tan, Weihong
Genomics and Proteomics Technologies. Trade Paper. S P I
E-International Society for Optical Engineering. Bellingham,
WA. 2001. v, 82p. Proceeding Ser., No. 2 ISBN:0-8194-3942-8,
ISBN13: 978-0-8194-3942-0. Dewey:660.6/5.
LCCN:2001-279171.
Audience: **u,f.**

Rédei, George P.   **QH427.R43 2003**
Encyclopedic Dictionary of Genetics, Genomics, and
Proteomics. Ed. 2. Trade Cloth. John Wiley & Sons, Inc.
Hoboken, NJ. 2003. 1392p. ISBN:0-471-26821-6, ISBN13:
978-0-471-26821-5. Dewey:576.5/03. LCCN:2002-011131.
Audience: **g,l,u,f.** *Choice, 2004.*

Sanchez, Jean-Charles   **QP551**
  (Editor), et al.
Biomedical Applications of Proteomics. Garry L. Corthals &
Denis F. Hochstrasser (Editors). Trade Cloth. John Wiley &

Sons, Inc. Hoboken, NJ. 2004. 452p. ISBN:3-527-30807-5, ISBN13: 978-3-527-30807-1. Dewey:616.07. LCCN:2004-425115.

Audience: **u,f.**

Sensen, Christoph W.   **QH447**
(Editor)
Handbook of Genome Research: Genomics, Proteomics, Metabolomics, Bioinformatics, Ethical and Legal Issues. Trade Cloth. John Wiley & Sons, Inc. Hoboken, NJ. 2005. 646p. ISBN:3-527-31348-6, ISBN13: 978-3-527-31348-8. Dewey:572.86.

Audience: **u,f.** *Choice, 2006.*

Speicher, David W. (Editor)   **QP551**
Proteome Analysis: Interpreting the Genome. Trade Cloth. Elsevier Science & Technology Books. Saint Louis, MO. 2004. 394p. ISBN:0-444-51024-9, ISBN13: 978-0-444-51024-2. Dewey:572.8/6. LCCN:2006-273067.

Audience: **u,f.**

Wilkins, M. R.   **QP551.P756 1997**
Proteome Research: New Frontiers in Functional Genomics. Ron D. Appel, Denis F. Hochstrasser & Keith L. Williams (Volume Editors). Trade Paper. Springer. New York, NY. 1997. XVIII, 243p. Principles and Practice Ser. ISBN:3-540-62753-7, ISBN13: 978-3-540-62753-1. Dewey:572/.6. LCCN:97-030956.

Audience: **u,f.**

Woodford, Neil & Johnson,   **QR74.G46 2004**
Alan (Editors)
Genomics, Proteomics, and Clinical Bacteriology: Methods and Reviews. Book, Other. Humana Press. Totowa, NJ. 2004. 408p. Methods in Molecular Biologytm Ser. ISBN:1-58829-218-5, ISBN13: 978-1-58829-218-6. Dewey:616.9/201. LCCN:2004-000332.

Audience: **u,f.**

Bioinformatics > Computational Molecular Biology

                                            QD431.E9
ExPASy Proteomics Server.
http://www.expasy.ch/

Audience: **u,f.**

Amos, Martyn (Editor)   **QH324.2.C35 2004**
Cellular Computing. Trade Cloth. Oxford University Press, Inc. New York, NY. 2004. 238p. Genomics and Bioinformatics Ser. ISBN:0-19-515539-4, ISBN13: 978-0-19-515539-6. Dewey:571.6. LCCN:2003-058013.

Audience: **u,f.**

Andrade, M. A. (Editor)   **QH447**
Bioinformatics and Genomes. Trade Cloth. Horizon Scientific Press. Norwich, 2003. 227p. ISBN:1-898486-47-6, ISBN13: 978-1-898486-47-3. Dewey:572.8/6/0285.

Audience: **u,f.**

Baclawski, Kenneth & Niu,   **QH324.2.B33 2005**
Tianhua
Ontologies for Bioinformatics. Trade Cloth. MIT Press. Cambridge, MA. 2005. 440p. Computational Molecular Biology Ser. ISBN:0-262-02591-4, ISBN13: 978-0-262-02591-1. Dewey:572.8/0285. LCCN:2005-042803.

Audience: **u,f.**

Barnes, Michael R. & Gray,   **QH438.4**
Ian C. (Editors)
Bioinformatics for Geneticists. Trade Cloth. John Wiley & Sons, Inc. Hoboken, NJ. 2003. 422p. Hierarchical Exotoxicology Mini Ser. ISBN:0-470-84393-4, ISBN13: 978-0-470-84393-2. Dewey:576.50285. LCCN:2003-535288.

Audience: **u,f.**

Bourne, Philip E. & Weissig,   **QP517.M3S776 2003**
Helge (Editors)
Structural Bioinformatics. Trade Cloth. John Wiley & Sons, Inc. Hoboken, NJ. 2003. 649p. Methods of Biochemical Analysis Ser., Vol. 44 ISBN:0-471-20200-2, ISBN13: 978-0-471-20200-4. Dewey:572.8/733. LCCN:2002-011156.

Audience: **u,f.**

Brown, Stuart M.   **QH506.B767 2000**
Bioinformatics: A Biologist's Guide to Biocomputing and the Internet. Trade Cloth. Eaton Publishing Company/Bio Techniques Books Division. Westborough, MA. 2000. xi, 188p. ISBN:1-881299-18-X, ISBN13: 978-1-881299-18-9. Dewey:570/.285. LCCN:00-046247.

Audience: **l,u,f.**

Clote, Peter & Backofen,   **QH438.4.M3C565 2000**
Rolf
Computational Molecular Biology: An Introduction. Trade Cloth. John Wiley & Sons, Inc. Hoboken, NJ. 2000. 300p. Wiley Series in Mathematical and Computational Biology Ser., Vol. 1 ISBN:0-471-87251-2, ISBN13: 978-0-471-87251-1. Dewey:572.8/01/5118. LCCN:00-038169.

Audience: **u,f.**

Dopazo, Joaquin & Azuaje,   **QH447**
Francisco (Editors)
Data Analysis and Visualization in Genomics and Proteomics. Trade Cloth. John Wiley & Sons, Inc. Hoboken, NJ. 2005. 284p. ISBN:0-470-09439-7, ISBN13: 978-0-470-09439-6. Dewey:572.8/6. LCCN:2005-006838.

Audience: **u,f.**

Eils, Roland & Kriete,   **QH324.2.C638 2005**
Andres (Editors)
Computational Systems Biology. Trade Cloth. Elsevier Science & Technology Books. Saint Louis, MO. 2005. 424p. ISBN:0-12-088786-X, ISBN13: 978-0-12-088786-6. Dewey:570/.1/13. LCCN:2005-020831.

Audience: **u,f.**

Fortuner, Renaud   **QH324.2**
Advances in Computer Methods for Systematic Biology: Artificial Intelligence, Databases, Computer Vision. Trade Cloth. Johns Hopkins University Press. Baltimore, MD. 1993. 574p. ISBN:0-8018-4492-4, ISBN13: 978-0-8018-4492-8. Dewey:574.0113. LCCN:92-024949.

Audience: **u,f.**

Gheorghe, Marian   **QH506.M66434 2005**
Molecular Computation Models: Unconventional Approaches. Trade Cloth. Idea Group Publishing. Hershey, PA. 2005. 304p. ISBN:1-59140-333-2, ISBN13: 978-1-59140-333-3. Dewey:570/.1/1. LCCN:2004-023592.

Audience: **u,f.**

Giovannetti, J.   **QH441.2.R365 2002**
Genomes and Databases on the Internet: A Practical Guide to Functions and Applications. Trade Cloth. Horizon Scientific

Press. Norwich, 2001. 224p. ISBN:1-898486-31-X, ISBN13: 978-1-898486-31-2. Dewey:025/.06/5765. LCCN:2002-392506.

Audience: **u,f.** *Choice, 2002.*

Grant, Richard P. (Editor)   **QH477**
Computational Genomics: Theory and Application. Paper over Boards. Taylor & Francis Group. Philadelphia, PA. 2004. 350p. ISBN:1-904933-01-7, ISBN13: 978-1-904933-01-4. Dewey:572.8/6.

Audience: **u,f.**

Hsu, Hui-Hwang   **QH324.2.A38 2006**
Advanced Data Mining Technologies in Bioinformatics. Trade Cloth. Idea Group Publishing. Hershey, PA. 2006. x, 329p. ISBN:1-59140-863-6, ISBN13: 978-1-59140-863-5. Dewey:572.8/0285. LCCN:2006-003556.

Audience: **u,f.**

Istrail, Sorin, et al.   **QH506**
Computational Molecular Biology. Pavel Pevzner & Ron Shamir (Authors). Trade Cloth. Elsevier Science & Technology Books. Saint Louis, MO. 2003. 184p. Topics in Discrete Mathematics Ser., Vol. 12 ISBN:0-444-51384-1, ISBN13: 978-0-444-51384-7. Dewey:572.8. LCCN:2003-051360.

Audience: **u,f.**

Jagota, Arun K.   **QH506**
Data Analysis and Classification for Bioinformatics. Paper Text. Bioinformatics By the Bay. Sunnyvale, CA. 2001. 80p. ISBN:0-9700297-0-5, ISBN13: 978-0-9700297-0-6. Dewey:576.50285.

Audience: **u,f.**

Kitano, Hiroaki (Editor)   **QH313.F66 2002**
Foundations of Systems Biology. Trade Cloth. MIT Press. Cambridge, MA. 2001. 320p. ISBN:0-262-11266-3, ISBN13: 978-0-262-11266-6. Dewey:573. LCCN:2001-042807.

Audience: **l,u.**

Laplante, Phillip A.   **QH324.2.B535 2003**
Biocomputing. Trade Paper. Nova Science Publishers, Inc. Hauppauge, NY. 2003. 116p. ISBN:1-59033-889-8, ISBN13: 978-1-59033-889-6. Dewey:570/.1/13. LCCN:2004-299233.

Audience: **u,f.**

Mewes, H. W. (Editor), et al.   **QH441.2.B545 2002**
Bioinformatics and Genome Analysis. B. Weiss & H. Seidel (Editors). Trade Cloth. Springer. New York, NY. 2003. XV, 296p. Ernst Schering Research Foundation Workshop Ser., Vol. 38 ISBN:3-540-42893-3, ISBN13: 978-3-540-42893-0. Dewey:570/.285. LCCN:2002-066917.

Audience: **u,f.**

Rapoport, Basil   **QH506.X53 2000**
Data Analysis in Molecular Biology and Evolution. Trade Cloth. Springer. New York, NY. 2000. 296p. ISBN:0-7923-7767-2, ISBN13: 978-0-7923-7767-2. Dewey:572.8/0285. LCCN:00-022032.

Audience: **u,f.**

Raychaudhuri, Soumya   **QH452.7**
Computational Text Analysis: For Functional Genomics and Bioinformatics. Trade Cloth. Oxford University Press, Inc. New York, NY. 2006. 312p. ISBN:0-19-856740-5, ISBN13: 978-0-19-856740-0. Dewey:572.86. LCCN:2006-296260.

Audience: **u,f.**

Rigoutsos, Isidore &   **QH324.2.S97 2006**
Stephanopoulos, G.
Systems Biology. Trade Cloth. Oxford University Press, Inc. New York, NY. 2006. 366p. Series in Systems Biology ISBN:0-19-530080-7, ISBN13: 978-0-19-530080-2. Dewey:570. LCCN:2005-031826.

Audience: **u,f.**

Rédei, George P.   **QH427.R43 2003**
Encyclopedic Dictionary of Genetics, Genomics, and Proteomics. Ed. 2. Trade Cloth. John Wiley & Sons, Inc. Hoboken, NJ. 2003. 1392p. ISBN:0-471-26821-6, ISBN13: 978-0-471-26821-5. Dewey:576.5/03. LCCN:2002-011131.

Audience: **g,l,u,f.** *Choice, 2004.*

Seiffert, Udo (Editor), et al.   **QH324.2.B557 2005**
Bioinformatics Using Computational Intelligence Paradigms. L. C. Jain & Patric Schweizer (Editors). Trade Cloth. Springer. New York, NY. 2005. VIII, 216p. Studies in Fuzziness and Soft Computing Ser., Vol. 176 ISBN:3-540-22901-9, ISBN13: 978-3-540-22901-8. Dewey:572.80285. LCCN:2004-117076.

Audience: **u,f.**

Sensen, Christoph W.   **QH447**
(Editor)
Handbook of Genome Research: Genomics, Proteomics, Metabolomics, Bioinformatics, Ethical and Legal Issues. Trade Cloth. John Wiley & Sons, Inc. Hoboken, NJ. 2005. 646p. ISBN:3-527-31348-6, ISBN13: 978-3-527-31348-8. Dewey:572.86.

Audience: **u,f.** *Choice, 2006.*

Suhai, Sándor   **QH445.2.G473 2000**
Genomics and Proteomics: Functional and Computational Aspects. Trade Cloth. Springer. New York, NY. 2000. 258p. ISBN:0-306-46312-1, ISBN13: 978-0-306-46312-9. Dewey:572.8/633/0285. LCCN:00-022525.

Audience: **u,f.**

Tavani, Herman T.   **QH441.2.T38 2006**
Ethics, Computing, and Genomics. Trade Paper. Jones & Bartlett Publishers, Inc. Sudbury, MA. 2005. 356p. ISBN:0-7637-3620-1, ISBN13: 978-0-7637-3620-0. Dewey:174/.957. LCCN:2005-007396.

Audience: **u,f.**

Wünschiers, Röbbe   **QH324.2W86 2004**
Computational Biology. Trade Paper. Springer. New York, NY. 2004. XVII, 284p. ISBN:3-540-21142-X, ISBN13: 978-3-540-21142-6. Dewey:570.285. LCCN:2004-102411.

Audience: **u,f.** *Choice, 2004.*

Zomaya, Albert Y. (Editor)   **QH324.2**
Parallel Computing for Bioinformatics and Computational Biology: Models, Enabling Technologies and Case Studies. Trade Cloth. John Wiley & Sons, Inc. Hoboken, NJ. 2006. 816p. Wiley Series on Parallel and Distributed Computing Ser. ISBN:0-471-71848-3, ISBN13: 978-0-471-71848-2. Dewey:572.8/0285. LCCN:2005-010253.

Audience: **u,f.**

Bioinformatics > Computational Molecular Biology > Statistics and Mathematics

Corne, David W. & Fogel,   QH324.2.E95 2003
Gary B. (Editors)
Evolutionary Computation in Bioinformatics. Trade Cloth.
Elsevier Science & Technology Books. Saint Louis, MO. 2002.
393p. The Morgan Kaufmann Series in Artificial Intelligence
Ser. ISBN:1-55860-797-8, ISBN13: 978-1-55860-797-2.
Dewey:570.2/85631. LCCN:2002-104302.

Audience: **u,f.**

Ewens, W. J. & Grant,   R858.E986 2001
Gregory
Statistical Methods in Bioinformatics: An Introduction. Cloth
Text. Springer. New York, NY. 2001. 495p. Statistics for
Biology and Health Ser. ISBN:0-387-95229-2, ISBN13:
978-0-387-95229-1. Dewey:570/.1/5195. LCCN:00-067923.

Audience: **u,f.**

Ewens, Warren J. & Grant,   QH324.2.E97 2004
Gregory
Statistical Methods in Bioinformatics: An Introduction. Ed. 2.
Trade Cloth. Springer. New York, NY. 2005. XX, 588p.
Statistics for Biology and Health Ser. ISBN:0-387-40082-6,
ISBN13: 978-0-387-40082-2. Dewey:572.8/0285.
LCCN:2004-056491.

Audience: **u,f.**

Isaev, Alexander   QH324.2.I78 2004
Introduction to Mathematical Methods in Bioinformatics. Trade
Paper. Springer. New York, NY. 2006. XIV, 298p. Universitext
Ser. ISBN:3-540-21973-0, ISBN13: 978-3-540-21973-6.
Dewey:572.8/0285. LCCN:2004-104981.

Audience: **u,f.** *Choice, 2005.*

Jones, Neil C. & Pevzner,   QH324.2.J66 2004
Pavel
An Introduction to Bioinformatics Algorithms. Cloth Text. MIT
Press. Cambridge, MA. 2004. 448p. Computational Molecular
Biology Ser. ISBN:0-262-10106-8, ISBN13: 978-0-262-10106-6.
Dewey:570/.285. LCCN:2004-048289.

Audience: **u,f.**

Konopka, Andrzej &   QH324.2
Crabbe, M. James C.
Compact Handbook of Computational Biology. Paper over
Boards. Marcel Dekker Inc. New York, NY. 2004. 568p.
ISBN:0-8247-0982-9, ISBN13: 978-0-8247-0982-2.
Dewey:570/.285. LCCN:2004-559904.

Audience: **u,f.**

Pachter, L. & Sturmfels, B.   QH323.5.A43 2005
(Editors)
Algebraic Statistics for Computational Biology. Trade Cloth.
Cambridge University Press. New York, NY. 2005. 432p.
ISBN:0-521-85700-7, ISBN13: 978-0-521-85700-0.
Dewey:572.8/6. LCCN:2005-050070.

Audience: **l,u.**

Pevzner, Pavel A.   QH506.P47 2000
Computational Molecular Biology: An Algorithmic Approach.
Trade Cloth. MIT Press. Cambridge, MA. 2000. 332p.
Computational Molecular Biology Ser. ISBN:0-262-16197-4,
ISBN13: 978-0-262-16197-8. Dewey:572.8. LCCN:00-032461.

Audience: **u,f.**

Robin, Stephane, et al.   QP624
DNA, Words and Models: Statistics of Exceptional Words.
Francois Rodolphe & Sophie Schbath (Authors). Trade Cloth.
Cambridge University Press. New York, NY. 2005. 158p.
ISBN:0-521-84729-X, ISBN13: 978-0-521-84729-2.
Dewey:572.8/633. LCCN:2005-047088.

Audience: **u,f.**

Schölkopf, Bernhard   QH324.2.K47 2004
(Editor), et al.
Kernel Methods in Computational Biology. Koji Tsuda &
Jean-Philippe Vert (Editors). Trade Cloth. MIT Press.
Cambridge, MA. 2004. 416p. Computational Molecular Biology
Ser. ISBN:0-262-19509-7, ISBN13: 978-0-262-19509-6.
Dewey:570/.285. LCCN:2003-068640.

Audience: **l,u,f.**

Stephenson, Frank H.   QH323.5
Calculations for Molecular Biology and Biotechnology: A Guide
to Mathematics in the Laboratory. Trade Paper. Elsevier Science
& Technology Books. Saint Louis, MO. 2003. 302p.
ISBN:0-12-665751-3, ISBN13: 978-0-12-665751-7.
Dewey:572.8/01/51. LCCN:2003-106049.

Audience: **u,f.**

Bioinformatics > Computer Applications

    QH303.5
☐ Taxonomy Browser.
http://www.ncbi.nlm.nih.gov/Taxonomy/taxonomyhome.html/

Audience: **l,u,f.**

Andrade, M. A. (Editor)   QH447
Bioinformatics and Genomes. Trade Cloth. Horizon Scientific
Press. Norwich, 2003. 227p. ISBN:1-898486-47-6, ISBN13:
978-1-898486-47-3. Dewey:572.8/6/0285.

Audience: **u,f.**

Baldi, Pierre & Brunak,   QH506.B35 2001
Søren
Bioinformatics: The Machine Learning Approach. Ed. 2. Trade
Cloth. MIT Press. Cambridge, MA. 2001. 400p. Adaptive
Computation and Machine Learning Ser. ISBN:0-262-02506-X,
ISBN13: 978-0-262-02506-5. Dewey:572.8/01/13.
LCCN:2001-030210.

Audience: **u,f.**

Bergeron, Bryan   QH506.B47 2002
Bioinformatics Computing. Trade Paper. Prentice Hall PTR.
Upper Saddle River, NJ. 2002. 464p. ISBN:0-13-100825-0,
ISBN13: 978-0-13-100825-0. Dewey:572.8.
LCCN:2002-038177.

Audience: **u,f.**

Chen, Yi-Ping Phoebe   QH324.2
(Editor)
Bioinformatics Technologies. Trade Cloth. Springer. New York,
NY. 2005. XV, 396p. ISBN:3-540-20873-9, ISBN13:
978-3-540-20873-0. Dewey:570.285.

Audience: **u,f.**

Corne, David W. & Fogel, Gary B. (Editors)   QH324.2.E95 2003
Evolutionary Computation in Bioinformatics. Trade Cloth. Elsevier Science & Technology Books. Saint Louis, MO. 2002. 393p. The Morgan Kaufmann Series in Artificial Intelligence Ser. ISBN:1-55860-797-8, ISBN13: 978-1-55860-797-2. Dewey:570.2/85631. LCCN:2002-104302.

Audience: **u,f.**

CSTB Staff   QH324.2.C28 2005
Catalyzing Inquiry at the Interface of Computing and Biology. Trade Cloth. National Academies Press. Washington, DC. 2005. 466p. ISBN:0-309-09612-X, ISBN13: 978-0-309-09612-6. Dewey:570.285. LCCN:2005-936580.

Audience: **u,f.**

Dopazo, Joaquin & Azuaje, Francisco (Editors)   QH447
Data Analysis and Visualization in Genomics and Proteomics. Trade Cloth. John Wiley & Sons, Inc. Hoboken, NJ. 2005. 284p. ISBN:0-470-09439-7, ISBN13: 978-0-470-09439-6. Dewey:572.8/6. LCCN:2005-006838.

Audience: **u,f.**

Eils, Roland & Kriete, Andres (Editors)   QH324.2.C638 2005
Computational Systems Biology. Trade Cloth. Elsevier Science & Technology Books. Saint Louis, MO. 2005. 424p. ISBN:0-12-088786-X, ISBN13: 978-0-12-088786-6. Dewey:570/.1/13. LCCN:2005-020831.

Audience: **u,f.**

Gibas, Cynthia & Jambeck, Per   QH324.2.G53 2001
Developing Bioinformatics Computer Skills. Lorrie LeJeune (Editor). Trade Paper, Perfect. O'Reilly Media, Inc. Sebastopol, CA. 2001. 446p. ISBN:1-56592-664-1, ISBN13: 978-1-56592-664-6. Dewey:570/.285. LCCN:2001-273989.

Audience: **u,f.**

Giovannetti, J.   QH441.2.R365 2002
Genomes and Databases on the Internet: A Practical Guide to Functions and Applications. Trade Cloth. Horizon Scientific Press. Norwich, 2001. 224p. ISBN:1-898486-31-X, ISBN13: 978-1-898486-31-2. Dewey:025/.06/5765. LCCN:2002-392506.

Audience: **u,f.** *Choice, 2002.*

Grant, Richard P. (Editor)   QH477
Computational Genomics: Theory and Application. Paper over Boards. Taylor & Francis Group. Philadelphia, PA. 2004. 350p. ISBN:1-904933-01-7, ISBN13: 978-1-904933-01-4. Dewey:572.8/6.

Audience: **u,f.**

Jagota, Arun K.   QH506
Data Analysis and Classification for Bioinformatics. Paper Text. Bioinformatics By the Bay. Sunnyvale, CA. 2001. 80p. ISBN:0-9700297-0-5, ISBN13: 978-0-9700297-0-6. Dewey:576.50285.

Audience: **u,f.**

Laplante, Phillip A.   QH324.2.B535 2003
Biocomputing. Trade Paper. Nova Science Publishers, Inc. Hauppauge, NY. 2003. 116p. ISBN:1-59033-889-8, ISBN13: 978-1-59033-889-6. Dewey:570/.1/13. LCCN:2004-299233.

Audience: **u,f.**

Sensen, Christoph W. (Editor)   QH447
Handbook of Genome Research: Genomics, Proteomics, Metabolomics, Bioinformatics, Ethical and Legal Issues. Trade Cloth. John Wiley & Sons, Inc. Hoboken, NJ. 2005. 646p. ISBN:3-527-31348-6, ISBN13: 978-3-527-31348-8. Dewey:572.86.

Audience: **u,f.** *Choice, 2006.*

Stephenson, Frank H.   QH323.5
Calculations for Molecular Biology and Biotechnology: A Guide to Mathematics in the Laboratory. Trade Paper. Elsevier Science & Technology Books. Saint Louis, MO. 2003. 302p. ISBN:0-12-665751-3, ISBN13: 978-0-12-665751-7. Dewey:572.8/01/51. LCCN:2003-106049.

Audience: **u,f.**

Vaidyanathan, Seetharaman (Editor), et al.   QP171.M382 2005
Metabolome Analyses: Strategies for Systems Biology. George G. Harrigan & Royston Goodacre (Editors). Trade Cloth. Springer. New York, NY. 2005. XXII, 394p. ISBN:0-387-25239-8, ISBN13: 978-0-387-25239-1. Dewey:572/.4. LCCN:2005-047906.

Audience: **u,f.**

Bioinformatics > Computer Applications > Computer Hardware

     QH447
☐ Mouse Genome Resources.
http://www.ncbi.nlm.nih.gov/genome/guide/mouse/

Audience: **u,f.**

Fortuner, Renaud   QH324.2
Advances in Computer Methods for Systematic Biology: Artificial Intelligence, Databases, Computer Vision. Trade Cloth. Johns Hopkins University Press. Baltimore, MD. 1993. 574p. ISBN:0-8018-4492-4, ISBN13: 978-0-8018-4492-8. Dewey:574.0113. LCCN:92-024949.

Audience: **u,f.**

Zomaya, Albert Y. (Editor)   QH324.2
Parallel Computing for Bioinformatics and Computational Biology: Models, Enabling Technologies and Case Studies. Trade Cloth. John Wiley & Sons, Inc. Hoboken, NJ. 2006. 816p. Wiley Series on Parallel and Distributed Computing Ser. ISBN:0-471-71848-3, ISBN13: 978-0-471-71848-2. Dewey:572.8/0285. LCCN:2005-010253.

Audience: **u,f.**

Bioinformatics > Computer Applications > Computer Software

     QH303.5
☐ BLAST.
http://www.ncbi.nlm.nih.gov/Education/BLASTinfo/information3.html

Audience: **u,f.**

     QH447
☐ Entrez Genome.
http://www.ncbi.nlm.nih.gov:80/entrez/query.fcgi?db=Genome

Audience: **u,f.**

QH470.D7

☐ FlyBase.
http://flybase.bio.indiana.edu/

Audience: **u,f.**

QH447

☐ Trans-NIH Mouse Initiatives.
http://www.nih.gov/science/models/mouse/

Audience: **u.**

QH447

☐ Zebrafish Genome Resources.
http://www.ncbi.nlm.nih.gov/genome/guide/zebrafish/

Audience: **u,f.**

Fortuner, Renaud **QH324.2**
Advances in Computer Methods for Systematic Biology:
Artificial Intelligence, Databases, Computer Vision. Trade Cloth.
Johns Hopkins University Press. Baltimore, MD. 1993. 574p.
ISBN:0-8018-4492-4, ISBN13: 978-0-8018-4492-8.
Dewey:574.0113. LCCN:92-024949.

Audience: **u,f.**

Hsu, Hui-Hwang **QH324.2.A38 2006**
Advanced Data Mining Technologies in Bioinformatics. Trade
Cloth. Idea Group Publishing. Hershey, PA. 2006. x, 329p.
ISBN:1-59140-863-6, ISBN13: 978-1-59140-863-5.
Dewey:572.8/0285. LCCN:2006-003556.

Audience: **u,f.**

Jamison, D. Curtis **QH324.2.J36 2003**
Perl Programming for Biologists. Trade Paper. John Wiley &
Sons, Inc. Hoboken, NJ. 2003. 208p. ISBN:0-471-43059-5,
ISBN13: 978-0-471-43059-9. Dewey:570/.28/55133.
LCCN:2002-152547.

Audience: **u,f.**

Moorhouse, Michael & **QH324.2**
Barry, Paul
Bioinformatics Biocomputing and Perl: An Introduction to
Bioinformatics Computing Skills and Practice. Trade Paper. John
Wiley & Sons, Inc. Hoboken, NJ. 2004. 506p.
ISBN:0-470-85331-X, ISBN13: 978-0-470-85331-3.
Dewey:570.285571262. LCCN:2004-301645.

Audience: **u,f.**

Schölkopf, Bernhard **QH324.2.K47 2004**
(Editor), et al.
Kernel Methods in Computational Biology. Koji Tsuda &
Jean-Philippe Vert (Editors). Trade Cloth. MIT Press.
Cambridge, MA. 2004. 416p. Computational Molecular Biology
Ser. ISBN:0-262-19509-7, ISBN13: 978-0-262-19509-6.
Dewey:570/.285. LCCN:2003-068640.

Audience: **l,u,f.**

Seiffert, Udo (Editor), et al. **QH324.2.B557 2005**
Bioinformatics Using Computational Intelligence Paradigms. L.
C. Jain & Patric Schweizer (Editors). Trade Cloth. Springer.
New York, NY. 2005. VIII, 216p. Studies in Fuzziness and Soft
Computing Ser., Vol. 176 ISBN:3-540-22901-9, ISBN13:
978-3-540-22901-8. Dewey:572.80285. LCCN:2004-117076.

Audience: **u,f.**

Shamir, R. & Frasconi, P. **QH506.A775 2003**
(Editors)
Artificial Intelligence and Heuristic Methods in Bioinformatics,
Vol. 183. Trade Cloth. I O S Press, Inc. Burke, VA. 2003. 256p.
NATO Science Ser., Vol. 183 ISBN:1-58603-294-1, ISBN13:
978-1-58603-294-4. Dewey:572.8/0285. LCCN:2003-106826.

Audience: **u,f.**

Weston, Paul **QH441.2**
Bioinformatics Software Engineering: Delivering Effective
Applications. Trade Paper. John Wiley & Sons, Inc. Hoboken,
NJ. 2004. 140p. ISBN:0-470-85772-2, ISBN13:
978-0-470-85772-4. Dewey:572.8/0285. LCCN:2004-016911.

Audience: **u,f.**

Zomaya, Albert Y. (Editor) **QH324.2**
Parallel Computing for Bioinformatics and Computational
Biology: Models, Enabling Technologies and Case Studies.
Trade Cloth. John Wiley & Sons, Inc. Hoboken, NJ. 2006. 816p.
Wiley Series on Parallel and Distributed Computing Ser.
ISBN:0-471-71848-3, ISBN13: 978-0-471-71848-2.
Dewey:572.8/0285. LCCN:2005-010253.

Audience: **u,f.**

Bioinformatics > Microarray Data Analysis and Sequence Analysis

QH447

☐ Entrez Genome.
http://www.ncbi.nlm.nih.gov:80/entrez/query.fcgi?db=Genome

Audience: **u,f.**

QH447

☐ Zebrafish Genome Resources.
http://www.ncbi.nlm.nih.gov/genome/guide/zebrafish/

Audience: **u,f.**

Albala, Joanna S. & **QH506.P796 2003**
Humphery-Smith, Ian
Protein Arrays, Biochips, and Proteomics: The Next Phase of
Genomics Discovery. Paper over Boards. Marcel Dekker Inc.
New York, NY. 2003. 304p. ISBN:0-8247-4312-1, ISBN13:
978-0-8247-4312-3. Dewey:572/.6. LCCN:2004-296024.

Audience: **u,f.**

Allison, David B., et al. **QP624.5.D726.D636**
DNA Microarrays and Related Genomic Techniques: Statistical
Design, Analysis, and Interpretation of Experiments. Grier P.
Page, T. Mark Beasley & Jode W. Edwards (Authors). Paper
over Boards. Marcel Dekker Inc. New York, NY. 2005. 392p.
Biostatistics Ser., Vol. 16 ISBN:0-8247-5461-1, ISBN13:
978-0-8247-5461-7. Dewey:572.8/636. LCCN:2005-050488.

Audience: **u,f.**

Baldi, Pierre & Hatfield, G. **QP624.5.D726.B353**
Wesley
DNA Microarrays and Gene Expression: From Experiments to
Data Analysis and Modeling. Trade Cloth. Cambridge University
Press. New York, NY. 2002. 230p. ISBN:0-521-80022-6,
ISBN13: 978-0-521-80022-8. Dewey:572.8/65.
LCCN:2001-052862.

Audience: **u,f.**

Baxevanis, Andreas D.   QH441.2.C876 2002
  (Editor)
Current Protocols in Bioinformatics. Ringbound. John Wiley &
Sons, Inc. Hoboken, NJ. 2003. ISBN:0-471-25093-7, ISBN13:
978-0-471-25093-7. Dewey:570/.285. LCCN:2002-191048.
                                Audience: **u,f.**

Berrar, Daniel P. (Editor),   QP624.5.D726P73 2002
  et al.
A Practical Approach to Microarray Data Analysis. Werner
Dubitzky & Martin Granzow (Editors). Trade Cloth. Springer.
New York, NY. 2002. 384p. ISBN:1-4020-7260-0, ISBN13:
978-1-4020-7260-4. Dewey:572.8/633. LCCN:2002-034174.
                                Audience: **u,f.**

Blalock, Eric M. (Editor)   QP624.5.D726B456
A Beginner's Guide to Microarrays. Trade Cloth. Springer. New
York, NY. 2003. 368p. ISBN:1-4020-7472-7, ISBN13:
978-1-4020-7472-1. Dewey:572.8/636. LCCN:2003-051408.
                                Audience: **u,f.**

Bowtell, David & Sambrook,   QP624.5.D726B69 2002
  Joseph (Editors)
DNA Microarrays: A Molecular Cloning Manual. Cloth Text.
Cold Spring Harbor Laboratory Press. Woodbury, NY. 2002.
712p. ISBN:0-87969-624-9, ISBN13: 978-0-87969-624-5.
Dewey:572.8/6. LCCN:2002-071255.
                                Audience: **u,f.**

Causton, Helen, et al.   QP624.5.D726C38 2003
Microarray Gene Expression Data Analysis: A Beginner's
Guide. Alvis Brazma & John Quackenbush (Authors). Trade
Paper. Blackwell Publishing, Inc. Malden, MA. 2003. 176p.
ISBN:1-4051-0682-4, ISBN13: 978-1-4051-0682-5.
Dewey:572.8/633. LCCN:2002-034224.
                                Audience: **u,f.**

Day, I. N. M. & Ye, S.   QP624.5.D726.M5 2003
  (Editors)
Microarrays and Microplates: Applications in Biomedical
Sciences. UK-B Format Paperback. Taylor & Francis Group.
Philadelphia, PA. 2003. 192p. ISBN:1-85996-074-X, ISBN13:
978-1-85996-074-5. Dewey:572.8636.
                                Audience: **u,f.**

Hamdan, Mahmoud H. &   QP551.M315 2005
  Righetti, Pier G.
Proteomics Today: Protein Assessment and Biomarkers Using
Mass Spectrometry, 2D Electrophoresis, and Microarray
Technology. Trade Cloth. John Wiley & Sons, Inc. Hoboken,
NJ. 2005. 448p. Wiley - Interscience Series on Mass
Spectrometry Ser. ISBN:0-471-64817-5, ISBN13:
978-0-471-64817-8. Dewey:572/.6. LCCN:2004-050921.
                                Audience: **u,f.**

Jagota, Arun K.   QH506
Data Analysis and Classification for Bioinformatics. Paper Text.
Bioinformatics By the Bay. Sunnyvale, CA. 2001. 80p.
ISBN:0-9700297-0-5, ISBN13: 978-0-9700297-0-6.
Dewey:576.50285.
                                Audience: **u,f.**

Knudsen, Steen   QP624.5.D726K68 2002
A Biologist's Guide to Analysis of DNA Microarray Data. Trade
Cloth. John Wiley & Sons, Inc. Hoboken, NJ. 2002. 144p.
ISBN:0-471-22490-1, ISBN13: 978-0-471-22490-7.
Dewey:572.8/636. LCCN:2002-072380.
                                Audience: **u,f.**

Knudsen, Steen   QP624.5.D726K68 2004
Guide to Analysis of DNA Microarray Data. Ed. 2. Trade Paper.
John Wiley & Sons, Inc. Hoboken, NJ. 2004. 184p.
ISBN:0-471-65604-6, ISBN13: 978-0-471-65604-3.
Dewey:572.8/636. LCCN:2003-026036.
                                Audience: **u,f.**

Kohane, Isaac S., et al.   QP624.5.D726K686
Microarrays for an Integrative Genomics. Alvin Kho & Atul J.
Butte (Authors). Trade Cloth. MIT Press. Cambridge, MA.
2002. 326p. Computational Molecular Biology Ser.
ISBN:0-262-11271-X, ISBN13: 978-0-262-11271-0.
Dewey:572.8/6. LCCN:2002-022663.
                                Audience: **u,f.**

Lin, Simon M. & Johnson,   QP624.5.D726M48 2002
  Kimberly F. (Editors)
Methods of Microarray Data Analysis. Trade Cloth. Springer.
New York, NY. 2001. 208p. ISBN:0-7923-7564-5, ISBN13:
978-0-7923-7564-7. Dewey:572.8/636. LCCN:2001-050241.
                                Audience: **u,f.**

Müller, H. J. & Roeder,   QP624.5.D726M85 2006
  Thomas
Microarrays. Paper Text. Elsevier Science & Technology Books.
Saint Louis, MO. 2005. 232p. The Experimenter Ser.
ISBN:0-12-088543-3, ISBN13: 978-0-12-088543-5.
Dewey:572.8/636. LCCN:2005-024163.
                                Audience: **u,f.**

Nicolau, Dan (Editor)   QP624.5.D726M514
Microarray Technology and Its Applications. Trade Cloth.
Springer. New York, NY. 2004. XXII, 400p. Biological and
Medical Physics, Biomedical Engineering Ser.
ISBN:3-540-22931-0, ISBN13: 978-3-540-22931-5.
Dewey:572.8636. LCCN:2004-117075.
                                Audience: **u,f.**

Schena, Mark (Editor)   QP624.5.D726D63 2000
DNA Microarrays: A Practical Approach. Cloth Text. Oxford
University Press, Inc. New York, NY. 1999. 232p. The Practical
Approach Ser., No. 205 ISBN:0-19-963777-6, ISBN13:
978-0-19-963777-5. Dewey:572.8/65. LCCN:99-013842.
                                Audience: **u,f.**

Schena, Mark   QP624.5.D726S34 2002
Microarray Analysis: Mining the Human Genome. Trade Cloth.
John Wiley & Sons, Inc. Hoboken, NJ. 2002. 648p.
ISBN:0-471-41443-3, ISBN13: 978-0-471-41443-8.
Dewey:572.8/636. LCCN:2002-011157.
                                Audience: **u,f.**

Biochemistry and Biophysics

☐ Google Directory: Biology, Biochemistry and Molecular
Biology.
http://www.google.com/Top/Science/Biology/
Biochemistry_and_Molecular_Biology/
Google.
                                Audience: **g,l.**

☐ Google Directory: Biology, Biogeochemistry.
http://www.google.com/Top/Science/Earth_Sciences/
Geochemistry/
Google.

Audience: **g,l.**

☐ Google Directory: Biology, Biophysics.
http://www.google.com/Top/Science/Biology/Biophysics/
Google.

Audience: **g,l.**

QH431

☐ The Jackson Laboratory.
http://www.jax.org/

Audience: **l,u,f.**

☐ PROWL - a resource for protein chemistry and mass
spectrometry - Amino Acid Information.
http://prowl.rockefeller.edu/aainfo/contents.htm
ProteoMetrics.

Audience: **g,l.**

Alberty, Robert A.   **QP517.T48A42 2003**
Thermodynamics of Biochemical Reactions. Trade Cloth. John
Wiley & Sons, Inc. Hoboken, NJ. 2003. 408p.
ISBN:0-471-22851-6, ISBN13: 978-0-471-22851-6.
Dewey:547/.2. LCCN:2002-155481.

Audience: **u,f.** *Choice, 2003.*

Alexander, R. McNeill   **QP176.A44 1999**
Energy for Animal Life. Trade Cloth. Oxford University Press,
Inc. New York, NY. 1999. 174p. Oxford Animal Biology Ser.
ISBN:0-19-850053-X, ISBN13: 978-0-19-850053-7.
Dewey:572/.431. LCCN:00-500326.

Audience: **u,f.**

Bower, James M. & Bolouri,   **QP517.M3C638 2004**
  Hamid (Editors)
Computational Modeling of Genetic and Biochemical Networks.
Trade Paper. MIT Press. Cambridge, MA. 2004. 390p.
Computational Molecular Biology Ser. ISBN:0-262-52423-6,
ISBN13: 978-0-262-52423-0. Dewey:572/.01/5118.

Audience: **u,f.**

Lehninger, Albert L., et al.   **QD415.L44 2004**
Principles of Biochemisrty. Ed. 4. Michael M. Cox & David L.
Nelson (Authors). Cloth over Boards. W. H. Freeman &
Company. New York, NY. 2004. 1100p. ISBN:0-7167-4339-6,
ISBN13: 978-0-7167-4339-2. Dewey:572. LCCN:2004-101716.

Audience: **l,u,f.**

Murray, Robert K., et al.   **QP514.2**
Harper's Illustrated Biochemistry. Ed. 26. Darryl K. Granner,
Peter A. Mayes & Victor W. Rodwell (Authors). Paper Text.
McGraw-Hill Professional Publishing. New York, NY. 2003.
693p. ISBN:0-07-138901-6, ISBN13: 978-0-07-138901-3.
Dewey:572.

Audience: **l,u,f.**

Vance, Dennis E. & Vance,   **QP751**
  Jean E. (Editors)
Biochemistry of Lipids, Lipoproteins and Membranes. Ed. 4.
Trade Cloth. Elsevier Science & Technology Books. Saint

Louis, MO. 2002. 648p. New Comprehensive Biochemistry Ser.,
Vol. 36 ISBN:0-444-51138-5, ISBN13: 978-0-444-51138-6.
Dewey:572 s 572/.57. LCCN:2002-192786.

Audience: **u,f.**

Biochemistry and Biophysics > General Biochemistry

QP514.2
☐ The Medical Biochemistry Page.
http://www.indstate.edu/thcme/mwking/home.html

Audience: **u,f.**

QD415.A2
☐ Metabolic Pathways of Biochemistry.
http://www.gwu.edu/~mpb/

Audience: **u,f.**

QD480
☐ Molecular Models for Biochemistry.
http://www.bio.cmu.edu/Courses/BiochemMols/
BCMolecules.html

Audience: **u,f.**

Alberts, Bruce   **QH581.2.M64 2002**
Molecular Biology of the Cell. Ed. 4. Paper over Boards.
Garland Publishing, Inc. New York, NY. 2002. 1616p.
ISBN:0-8153-3218-1, ISBN13: 978-0-8153-3218-3.
Dewey:571.6. LCCN:2001-054471.

Audience: **u,f.**

Behe, Michael J.   **QH325**
Darwin's Black Box: The Biochemical Challenge to Evolution.
Trade Paper. Simon & Schuster. New York, NY. 2006. 336p.
ISBN:0-7432-9031-3, ISBN13: 978-0-7432-9031-9. Dewey:575.

Audience: **u,f.**

Bergethon, P. R.   **QH505.B398 1998**
The Physical Basis of Biochemistry: The Foundations of
Molecular Biophysics. Trade Cloth. Springer. New York, NY.
2000. XXII, 567p. ISBN:0-387-98262-0, ISBN13:
978-0-387-98262-5. Dewey:572. LCCN:97-026975.

Audience: **u,f.**

Bienvenut, Willy Vincent   **QP551**
  (Editor)
Acceleration and Improvement of Protein Identification by Mass
Spectrometry. Trade Cloth. Springer. New York, NY. 2005.
XXII, 298p. ISBN:1-4020-3318-4, ISBN13: 978-1-4020-3318-6.
Dewey:572/.636. LCCN:2005-299257.

Audience: **u,f.**

Brimblecombe, Peter &   **QH344.E86 1989**
  Lein, Alla Yu (Editors)
Evolution of the Global Biogeochemical Sulphur Cycle. Trade
Cloth. John Wiley & Sons, Inc. Hoboken, NJ. 1989. 276p.
ISBN:0-471-92251-X, ISBN13: 978-0-471-92251-3.
Dewey:574.5/222. LCCN:89-005806.

Audience: **u,f.**

Buchanan, Bob B. (Editor),   **QK728**
  et al.
Biochemistry and Molecular Biology of Plants. Wilhelm
Gruissem & Russell L. Jones (Editors). Trade Paper. John Wiley

& Sons, Inc. Hoboken, NJ. 2002. 1408p. ISBN:0-943088-39-9, ISBN13: 978-0-943088-39-6. Dewey:572.8/2. LCCN:00-040591.

Audience: **u,f.** *Choice, 2001.*

Cai, Yong & Braids, Olin C.   QH344.B5723 2002
Biogeochemistry of Environmentally Important Trace Elements. Yong Cai (Editor), American Chemical Society Staff (Contribution by). Cloth Text. Oxford University Press, Inc. New York, NY. 2002. 448p. ACS Symposium Ser., Vol. 835:An American Chemical Society Publication Ser. ISBN:0-8412-3805-7, ISBN13: 978-0-8412-3805-3. Dewey:628.5/2. LCCN:2002-026272.

Audience: **u,f.**

Chameides, William L. &   QH344.C45 1997
Perdue, E. M.
Biogeochemical Cycles: A Computer-Interactive Study of Earth System Science and Global Change. Trade Cloth. Oxford University Press, Inc. New York, NY. 1997. 234p. Computer-Based Earth System Science Ser. ISBN:0-19-509279-1, ISBN13: 978-0-19-509279-0. Dewey:577.1/4/0285/5369. LCCN:96-038035.

Audience: **u,f.**

Champe, Pamela C. &   QP514.2.C48 2004
Harvey, Richard A.
Biochemistry. Ed. 3. Trade Paper. Lippincott Williams & Wilkins. Philadelphia, PA. 2004. 608p. Lippincotts' Illustrated Reviews Ser. ISBN:0-7817-2265-9, ISBN13: 978-0-7817-2265-0. LCCN:2004-557613.

Audience: **u,f.**

Chang, Raymond   QH345.C425 2004
Physical Chemistry for the Biosciences. Perfect, Paper over Boards. University Science Books. Sausalito, CA. 2005. 677p. ISBN:1-891389-33-5, ISBN13: 978-1-891389-33-7. Dewey:572. LCCN:2004-049612.

Audience: **u,f.** *Choice, 2005.*

Chapman, K. E. & Higgins,   QH450
S. J. (Editors)
Essays in Biochemistry: Regulation of Gene Expression, Vol. 37. Trade Paper. Portland Press, Ltd. London, 2001. 131p. ISBN:1-85578-138-7, ISBN13: 978-1-85578-138-2. Dewey:572.865.

Audience: **u,f.**

Cooper, C. & Darley-Usmar,   QP527.B56 2003
V. (Editors)
Free Radicals: Enzymology, Signalling and Disease. Trade Cloth. Portland Press, Ltd. London, 2004. 230p. Biochemical Symposia Ser., Vol. 71 ISBN:1-85578-161-1, ISBN13: 978-1-85578-161-0. Dewey:572 s 612/.0151. LCCN:2004-401709.

Audience: **u,f.**

Cornish-Bowden, Athel   QH325
The Pursuit of Perfection: Aspects of Biochemical Evolution. Trade Cloth. Oxford University Press, Inc. New York, NY. 2004. 170p. ISBN:0-19-852095-6, ISBN13: 978-0-19-852095-5. Dewey:572.8/38. LCCN:2004-304884.

Audience: **u,f.**

Cowan, J. A.   QP531.C68 1997
Inorganic Biochemistry: An Introduction. Ed. 2. Trade Cloth. John Wiley & Sons, Inc. Hoboken, NJ. 1997. 456p.

ISBN:0-471-18895-6, ISBN13: 978-0-471-18895-7. Dewey:572.5/1. LCCN:96-014100.

Audience: **u,f.** *Choice, 1998.*

Daintith, John (Editor)   QP512.F33 2002
The Facts on File Dictionary of Biochemistry. Trade Cloth. Facts On File, Inc.. New York, NY. 2002. 256p. Science Dictionary Ser. ISBN:0-8160-4914-9, ISBN13: 978-0-8160-4914-1. Dewey:572/.03. LCCN:2002-035203.

Audience: **u,f.** *Choice, 2003.*

Danson, M. J. (Editor),
et al.
The Archaebacteria: Biochemistry and Biotechnology. D. W. Hough & George G. Lunt (Editors). Trade Cloth. Portland Press, Ltd. London, 1992. 222p. Biochemical Society Symposium Ser., Vol. 58 ISBN:1-85578-010-0, ISBN13: 978-1-85578-010-1. Dewey:589.9.

Audience: **u,f.**

Davies, Paul
The Fifth Miracle: The Search for the Origin and Meaning of Life. Trade Paper. Simon & Schuster. New York, NY. 2000. 304p. ISBN:0-684-86309-X, ISBN13: 978-0-684-86309-2. Dewey:576.8/3. LCCN:98-033421.

Audience: **u,f.** *Choice, 1999.*

Delmas, Robert J. (Editor)   QH344.I34 1995
Ice Core Studies of Global Biogeochemical Cycles. Cloth Text. Springer. New York, NY. 1995. 496p. NATO ASI Ser., Vol. 30:Global Environmental Change ISBN:3-540-59274-1, ISBN13: 978-3-540-59274-7. Dewey:574.5/222. LCCN:95-015268.

Audience: **u,f.**

Drickamer, Karen D. &   QH345.B522 NO.69
Dell, A. (Editors)
Glycogenomics: The Impact of Genomics and Informatics in Glycobiology. Trade Cloth. Portland Press, Ltd. London, 2002. 170p. Biochemical Society Symposia Ser., Vol. 69 ISBN:1-85578-154-9, ISBN13: 978-1-85578-154-2. Dewey:572 s 572/.567. LCCN:2003-386012.

Audience: **u,f.**

Eiseman, Elisa, et al.   RD127.C375 2004
Case Studies of Existing Human Tissue Repositories: Best Practices for a Biospecimen Resource for the Genomic and Proteomic Era. Gabrielle Bloom & Jennifer Brower (Authors). Trade Cloth. RAND Corporation, The. Santa Monica, CA. 2003. 246p. ISBN:0-8330-3527-4, ISBN13: 978-0-8330-3527-1. Dewey:362.17/83. LCCN:2003-024742.

Audience: **u,f.**

Ernst, Erika J. & Rogers, P.   RM410.A55 2005
David
Antifungal Agents: Methods and Protocols. Trade Cloth. Humana Press. Totowa, NJ. 2005. 198p. Methods in Molecular Medicine Ser., Vol. 118 ISBN:1-58829-277-0, ISBN13: 978-1-58829-277-3. Dewey:616.9/69061. LCCN:2004-027210.

Audience: **u,f.**

Fasham, M. J. R. (Editor)   QH344.O25 2003
Ocean Biogeochemistry: A Synthesis of the Joint Global Ocean Flux Study (JGOFS). Joint Global Ocean Flux Study Staff (Contribution by). Trade Cloth. Springer. New York, NY. 2003.

XVIII, 297p. Global Change, :The IGBP Ser.
ISBN:3-540-42398-2, ISBN13: 978-3-540-42398-0.
Dewey:551.46/01. LCCN:2002-044503.

Audience: **u,f.**

Flanagan, Lawrence B.   **QH344**
  (Editor), et al.
Stable Isotopes and Biosphere - Atmosphere Interactions:
Processes and Biological Controls. James R. Ehleringer & Diane
E. Pataki (Editors), Harold A. Mooney (Contribution by). Trade
Cloth. Elsevier Science & Technology Books. Saint Louis, MO.
2004. 400p. Physiological Ecology Ser. ISBN:0-12-088447-X,
ISBN13: 978-0-12-088447-6. Dewey:577.14.

Audience: **u,f.**

Food and Agriculture   **QH344**
  Organization of the United Nations. ; Global Terrestrial
  Observing System (Organization) ; Integrated Global
  Observing Strategy Partnership. ; Food and Agriculture
  Organization of the United Nations.; Sustainable
  Development Dept.
Terrestrial Carbon Observation: The Rio de Janeiro
Recommendations for Terrestrial and Atmospheric
Measurements. Cihlar, Josef (Editor); Denning, A. Scott
(Editor). Food and Agriculture Organization of the United
Nations: Rome. 2002. ISBN:92-5-104802-9, ISBN13:
978-92-5-104802-3.

Audience: **u,f.**

Gad, Shayne Cox (Editor)   **RM301.25.D784 2005**
Drug Discovery Handbook. Trade Cloth. John Wiley & Sons,
Inc. Hoboken, NJ. 2005. 1496p. ISBN:0-471-21384-5, ISBN13:
978-0-471-21384-0. Dewey:615/.19. LCCN:2004-027077.

Audience: **u,f.**

Graur, Dan & Li,   **QH325.G69 2000**
  Wen-Hsiung
Fundamentals of Molecular Evolution. Ed. 2. Trade Cloth.
Sinauer Associates, Inc. Sunderland, MA. 1999. 443p.
ISBN:0-87893-266-6, ISBN13: 978-0-87893-266-5.
Dewey:572.8/38. LCCN:99-016706.

Audience: **u,f.**

Harris, Henry   **QH325.H35 2002**
Things Come to Life: Spontaneous Generation Revisited. Trade
Cloth. Oxford University Press, Inc. New York, NY. 2002. 186p.
ISBN:0-19-851538-3, ISBN13: 978-0-19-851538-8.
Dewey:576.8/3. LCCN:2001-054856.

Audience: **u,f.** *Choice, 2003, 2002.*

Hassid, Aviv   **QP535.N1N557 2004**
Nitric Oxide Protocols. Ed. 2. Book, Other. Humana Press.
Totowa, NJ. 2004. 260p. Methods in Molecular Biology Ser.
ISBN:1-58829-237-1, ISBN13: 978-1-58829-237-7.
Dewey:612/.01585. LCCN:2003-027923.

Audience: **u,f.**

Higgins, S. J. & Banting, G.   **QP514.2**
  (Editors)
Essays in Biochemistry: Molecular Motors, Vol. 35. Trade
Paper. Portland Press, Ltd. London, 2000. 177p.
ISBN:1-85578-103-4, ISBN13: 978-1-85578-103-0.
Dewey:574.192.

Audience: **u,f.**

Kooijman, S. A. L. M.   **QH323.5 .K66 2000**
Dynamic Energy and Mass Budgets in Biological Systems. Ed.
2. Trade Paper. Cambridge University Press. New York, NY.
2000. 442p. ISBN:0-521-78608-8, ISBN13: 978-0-521-78608-9.
Dewey:570/.1/5118. LCCN:2001-276473.

Audience: **u,f.**

Lörinczy, Dénes   **QH324.9.C3**
The Nature of Biological Systems As Revealed by Thermal
Methods. Trade Cloth. Springer. New York, NY. 2004. IX, 353p.
Hot Topics in Thermal Analysis and Calorimetry Ser., Vol. 5
ISBN:1-4020-2218-2, ISBN13: 978-1-4020-2218-0.
Dewey:570/.28. LCCN:2004-048471.

Audience: **u,f.**

Metzler, David   **QH345.M39 2001**
Biochemistry: The Chemical Reactions of Living Cells. Ed. 2.
Cloth Text. Elsevier Science & Technology Books. Saint Louis,
MO. 2003. 1900p. ISBN:0-12-492543-X, ISBN13:
978-0-12-492543-4. Dewey:572. LCCN:00-106082.

Audience: **l,u,f.** *Choice, 2003.*

Michal, Gerhard (Editor)   **QP171.B685 1999**
Biochemical Pathways: An Atlas of Biochemistry and Molecular
Biology. Trade Cloth. John Wiley & Sons, Inc. Hoboken, NJ.
1998. 288p. ISBN:0-471-33130-9, ISBN13: 978-0-471-33130-8.
Dewey:572.8/4. LCCN:98-033226.

Audience: **u,f.** *Choice, 1999.*

Müller, Werner E. G.   **QH506.P76 NO.33**
Silicon Biomineralization: Biology, Biochemistry, Molecular
Biology, Biotechnology. Trade Cloth. Springer. New York, NY.
2003. 88 schw.-w. u. 17 farb. Abb., 16 schw.-w. Tab., 59
schw.-w. u. 9 farb. Fotos, 46 schw.-w. u. 8 farb. Zeichn. XIII,
340p. Progress in Molecular and Subcellular Biology Ser., Vol.
33 ISBN:3-540-00537-4, ISBN13: 978-3-540-00537-7.
Dewey:572.8 s 572/.55. LCCN:2003-045414.

Audience: **u,f.**

Novartis Foundation   **QP33.D38**
  Symposium Staff
'In Silico' Simulation of Biological Processes, No. 247. Gregory
Bock & Jamie A. Goode (Editors). Trade Cloth. John Wiley &
Sons, Inc. Hoboken, NJ. 2003. 270p. Novartis Foundation
Symposium Ser., Vol. 247 ISBN:0-470-84480-9, ISBN13:
978-0-470-84480-9. Dewey:617.4/72. LCCN:2002-035730.

Audience: **u,f.**

Olson, Marc O. J. (Editor)   **QH596.N83 2004**
The Nucleolus. Trade Cloth. Springer. New York, NY. 2004.
364p. Molecular Biology Intelligence Unit Ser.
ISBN:0-306-47873-0, ISBN13: 978-0-306-47873-4.
LCCN:40-017530.

Audience: **l,u.**

Paul, Eldor A. & Clark,   **QR111.S672 1996**
  Francis E.
Soil Microbiology and Biochemistry. Ed. 2. Cloth Text. Elsevier
Science & Technology Books. Saint Louis, MO. 1996. 340p.
ISBN:0-12-546806-7, ISBN13: 978-0-12-546806-0.
Dewey:576/.190948. LCCN:96-013958.

Audience: **l,u,f.**

Peacocke, Arthur R.   QH345.P37 1989
An Introduction to the Physical Chemistry of Biological Organization. Trade Paper. Oxford University Press, Inc. New York, NY. 1989. 328p. ISBN:0-19-855557-1, ISBN13: 978-0-19-855557-5. Dewey:574.19/283. LCCN:89-016158.
Audience: **l,u.**

Pechkova, Eugenia &   QP551.P37 2003
  Nicolini, Claudio A.
Proteomics and Nanocrystallography. Trade Cloth. Springer. New York, NY. 2003. 200p. ISBN:0-306-47902-8, ISBN13: 978-0-306-47902-1. Dewey:572/.6. LCCN:2003-058935.
Audience: **l,u.**

Pingoud, Alfred, et al.   QH345.B5118 2002
Biochemical Methods: A Concise Guide for Students and Researchers. Claus Urbanke, Jim Hoggett & Albert Jeltsch (Authors). Trade Cloth. John Wiley & Sons, Inc. Hoboken, NJ. 2002. 374p. ISBN:3-527-30299-9, ISBN13: 978-3-527-30299-4. Dewey:572. LCCN:2003-269482.
Audience: **l,u.**

Reydon, Thomas A. C. &   QH303
  Hemerik, Lia (Editors)
Current Themes in Theoretical Biology: A Dutch Perspective. Trade Paper. Springer. New York, NY. 2005. VII, 310p. ISBN:1-4020-2901-2, ISBN13: 978-1-4020-2901-1. Dewey:570.15118.
Audience: **u,f.**

Rigoutsos, Isidore &   QH324.2.S97 2006
  Stephanopoulos, G.
Systems Biology. Trade Cloth. Oxford University Press, Inc. New York, NY. 2006. 366p. Series in Systems Biology ISBN:0-19-530080-7, ISBN13: 978-0-19-530080-2. Dewey:570. LCCN:2005-031826.
Audience: **u,f.**

Rigoutsos, Isidore &   QH324.2.S97 2006
  Stephanopoulos, Gregory (Editors)
Systems Biology: Volume 1: Genomics. Trade Cloth. Oxford University Press, Inc. New York, NY. 2006. 416p. Series in Systems Biology ISBN:0-19-530081-5, ISBN13: 978-0-19-530081-9. Dewey:570. LCCN:2005-031826.
Audience: **u,f.**

Saftig, Paul (Volume Editor)   QH603.L9S24 2005
Lysosomes. Trade Cloth. Springer. New York, NY. 2005. 209p. Medical Intelligence Unit Ser. ISBN:0-387-25562-1, ISBN13: 978-0-387-25562-0. Dewey:571.6/55. LCCN:2005-013404.
Audience: **u,f.**

Saklatvala, J. (Editor), et al.   QH345.B522 NO.70
Biochemical Society Symposia: Proteases and the Regulation of Biological Processes, Vol. 70. G. Salvesen & H. Nagase (Editors). Trade Cloth. Portland Press, Ltd. London, 2003. 300p. Biochemical Symposia Ser., Vol. 70 ISBN:1-85578-155-7, ISBN13: 978-1-85578-155-9. Dewey:572 s 572/.76. LCCN:2003-495529.
Audience: **u,f.**

Schliwa, Manfred (Editor)   QH506
Molecular Motors. Trade Cloth. John Wiley & Sons, Inc. Hoboken, NJ. 2003. 604p. ISBN:3-527-30594-7, ISBN13: 978-3-527-30594-0. Dewey:572.8. LCCN:2003-268622.
Audience: **u,f.**

Scott, Thomas A. & Mercer,   QD415.A25B713 1997
  E. Ian (Translators)
Concise Encyclopedia Biochemistry and Molecular Biology. Ed. 3. Thomas A. Scott & E. Ian Mercer (Revised by). Cloth Text. Walter De Gruyter Inc. Ossining, NY. 1996. 737p. ISBN:3-11-014535-9, ISBN13: 978-3-11-014535-9. Dewey:572/.03. LCCN:96-047538.
Audience: **u,f.** *Choice, 1997.*

Smith, A. D. (Editor)   QP512.O94 2003
Oxford Dictionary of Biochemistry and Molecular Biology. Ed. 2. Trade Cloth. Oxford University Press, Inc. New York, NY. 2000. 672p. ISBN:0-19-850673-2, ISBN13: 978-0-19-850673-7. Dewey:572/.03. LCCN:2004-556931.
Audience: **u,f.** *Choice, 1998.*

Stenesh, Jochanan   QP512.S73 1989
Dictionary of Biochemistry and Molecular Biology. Ed. 2. Trade Cloth. John Wiley & Sons, Inc. Hoboken, NJ. 1989. 536p. ISBN:0-471-84089-0, ISBN13: 978-0-471-84089-3. Dewey:574.19/2/0321. LCCN:88-036561.
Audience: **u,f.**

Sterner, Robert Warner &   QH345.S74 2002
  Elser, James J.
Ecological Stoichiometry: The Biology of Elements from Molecules to the Biosphere. Peter M. Vitousek (Foreword by). Trade Cloth. Princeton University Press. Princeton, NJ. 2002. 440p. ISBN:0-691-07490-9, ISBN13: 978-0-691-07490-0. Dewey:572. LCCN:2002-072262.
Audience: **l,u,f.**

Stryer, Lubert, et al.   QP514.2
Student Companion to Accompany Biochemistry. Ed. 5. Jeremy M. Berg, Nancy Counts Gerber & Frank H. Deis (Authors). Trade Paper. Worth Publishers, Inc. New York, NY. 2002. 600p. ISBN:0-7167-4383-3, ISBN13: 978-0-7167-4383-5. Dewey:574.192.
Audience: **u,f.**

Svensson, Birte   QH344.T73 1992
Trace Gas Exchange in a Global Perspective. Dennis S. Ojima & Bo H. Svensson (Editors). Trade Cloth. Blackwell Publishing, Inc. Malden, MA. 1992. 206p. Ecological Bulletins Ser., No. 42 ISBN:87-16-15009-0, ISBN13: 978-87-16-15009-7. Dewey:574.5222. LCCN:2003-445115.
Audience: **u,f.**

Tinoco, Ignacio, et al.   QH345.T56 2002
Physical Chemistry: Principles and Applications in Biological Sciences. Ed. 4. Joseph D. Puglisi, Kenneth Sauer & James C. Wang (Authors). Cloth Text. Prentice Hall PTR. Upper Saddle River, NJ. 2001. 740p. ISBN:0-13-095943-X, ISBN13: 978-0-13-095943-0. Dewey:541/.02457. LCCN:2001-280599.
Audience: **u,f.**

Voit, Eberhard O.   QH323.5 .V65 2000
Computational Analysis of Biochemical Systems: A Practical Guide for Biochemists and Molecular Biologists. Cloth Text. Cambridge University Press. New York, NY. 2000. 544p. ISBN:0-521-78087-X, ISBN13: 978-0-521-78087-2. Dewey:570/.1/5118. LCCN:00-021913.
Audience: **u,f.**

Williams, Roger J.   **QH345.W49 1998**
Biochemical Individuality. Ed. 2. Trade Paper. McGraw-Hill
Companies, The. New York, NY. 1998. 272p.
ISBN:0-87983-893-0, ISBN13: 978-0-87983-893-5.
Dewey:612/.015. LCCN:98-005055.

Audience: **l,u.**

Zimmer, Elizabeth A. &   **QH390**
  Roalson, Eric (Volume Editors)
Molecular Evolution, Producing the Biochemical Data, Part B.
Trade Cloth. Elsevier Science & Technology Books. Saint
Louis, MO. 2005. 896p. ISBN:0-12-182800-X, ISBN13:
978-0-12-182800-4. Dewey:572.838.

Audience: **u,f.**

Biochemistry and Biophysics > Specific Substances > Proteins

Abelson, John N. & Simon,   **QP551**
  Melvin I. (Editor-In-Chiefs)
Guide to Protein Purification, Vol. 182. Murray P. Deutscher
(Volume Editor). Trade Cloth. Elsevier Science & Technology
Books. Saint Louis, MO. 1990. 894p. Methods in Enzymology
Ser., Vol. 182 ISBN:0-12-182083-1, ISBN13:
978-0-12-182083-1. Dewey:547.7/5.

Audience: **u,f.**

Arnstein, H. R. & Cox,   **QP551.A693 1991**
  R. H.
Protein Biosynthesis: In Focus. Paper Text. Oxford University
Press, Inc. New York, NY. 1992. 128p. In Focus Ser.
ISBN:0-19-963040-2, ISBN13: 978-0-19-963040-0.
Dewey:574.19/296. LCCN:91-003653.

Audience: **u,f.** *Choice, 1993.*

Ballard, F. J.   **QH345.B522 NO.55**
Gene Expression Regulation at the RNA and Protein Levels. J.
Kay & R. John Mayer (Editors). Cloth Text. Portland Press, Ltd.
London, 1989. 203p. Biochemical Society Symposium Ser.,
Symposia 55 ISBN:0-904498-24-7, ISBN13:
978-0-904498-24-0. Dewey:574.19/2 s. LCCN:90-148591.

Audience: **u,f.**

Baxevanis, Andreas D. &   **QP551**
  Ouellette, B. F. Francis (Editors)
Bioinformatics: A Practical Guide to the Analysis of Genes and
Proteins. Ed. 3. Trade Cloth. John Wiley & Sons, Inc. Hoboken,
NJ. 2004. 560p. ISBN:0-471-47878-4, ISBN13:
978-0-471-47878-2. Dewey:572.8/633/0285.
LCCN:2004-011822.

Audience: **u,f.**

Berry, A. & Radford, S.   **QP551**
  (Editors)
From Protein Folding to New Enzymes, Vol. 68. Trade Cloth.
Portland Press, Ltd. London, 2001. 156p. Biochemical Society
Symposium Ser., Vol. 68 ISBN:1-85578-143-3, ISBN13:
978-1-85578-143-6. Dewey:572.633.

Audience: **u,f.**

Branden, Carl-Ivar &   **QP551.B7635 1999**
  Tooze, John
Introduction to Structural Biology. Ed. 2. Paper over Boards.

Garland Publishing, Inc. New York, NY. 1998. 410p.
ISBN:0-8153-2304-2, ISBN13: 978-0-8153-2304-4.
Dewey:572/.633. LCCN:98-034487.

Audience: **u,f.**

Cesareni, Giovanni (Editor),   **QP551.5**
  et al.
Modular Protein Domains. Mario Gimona, Marius Sudol &
Michael Yaffe (Editors). Trade Cloth. John Wiley & Sons, Inc.
Hoboken, NJ. 2005. 524p. ISBN:3-527-30813-X, ISBN13:
978-3-527-30813-2. Dewey:572.6. LCCN:2006-280499.

Audience: **u,f.**

Cheng, R Holland &   **QP801.P64**
  Hammar, Lena (Editors)
Conformational Proteomics of Macromolecular Architecture:
Approaching the Structure of Large Molecular Assemblies and
Their Mechanisms of Action. CD-ROM, Trade Cloth. World
Scientific Publishing Company, Inc. Hackensack, NJ. 2004.
432p. ISBN:981-238-614-9, ISBN13: 978-981-238-614-4.
Dewey:547.7.

Audience: **u,f.**

Conn, P. Michael   **QP551**
Handbook of Proteomic Methods. Humana Press: Totowa, NJ.
2003. ISBN:1-58829-340-8, ISBN13: 978-1-58829-340-4.

Audience: **u,f.**

Creighton, Thomas E.   **QP551.P69583 1997**
  (Editor)
Protein Structure and Protein Function: A Practical Approach,
Set. Ed. 2. Cloth Text. Oxford University Press, Inc. New York,
NY. 1997. xxiii, 383p. The Practical Approach Ser., No. 174,
175 ISBN:0-19-963617-6, ISBN13: 978-0-19-963617-4.
Dewey:547/.75. LCCN:97-006741.

Audience: **u,f.**

DelVecchio, V.G. &   **QH434.A66 2003**
  Krcmery, V. (Editors)
Applications of Genomics and Proteomics for Analysis of
Bacterial Biological Warfare Agents. Trade Cloth. I O S Press,
Inc. Burke, VA. 2003. 196p. NATO Science Ser., Vol. 352
ISBN:1-58603-343-3, ISBN13: 978-1-58603-343-9.
Dewey:623.4/594. LCCN:2003-104680.

Audience: **u,f.**

Dopazo, Joaquin & Azuaje,   **QH447**
  Francisco (Editors)
Data Analysis and Visualization in Genomics and Proteomics.
Trade Cloth. John Wiley & Sons, Inc. Hoboken, NJ. 2005. 284p.
ISBN:0-470-09439-7, ISBN13: 978-0-470-09439-6.
Dewey:572.8/6. LCCN:2005-006838.

Audience: **u,f.**

Dunn, Michael J. (Editor)   **QP551.F94 2000**
From Genome to Proteome: Advances in the Practice and
Application of Proteomics. Trade Cloth. John Wiley & Sons,
Inc. Hoboken, NJ. 2000. 552p. ISBN:3-527-30154-2, ISBN13:
978-3-527-30154-6. Dewey:572/.6. LCCN:00-697886.

Audience: **u,f.**

Dunn, Michael J. (Editor),   **QH431.E62 2005**
  et al.
Encyclopedia of Genetics, Genomics, Proteomics and
Bioinformatics. Lynn B. Jorde, Peter F. R. Little & Shankar

Subramaniam (Editors). Trade Cloth. John Wiley & Sons, Inc. Hoboken, NJ. 2005. 4096p. ISBN:0-470-84974-6, ISBN13: 978-0-470-84974-3. Dewey:599.93/5. LCCN:2005-017410.

Audience: **u,f.**

Eyk, Jennifer E.Van &   **RC666**
  Dunn, Michael J. (Editors)
Proteomic and Genomic Analysis of Cardiovascular Disease. Trade Cloth. John Wiley & Sons, Inc. Hoboken, NJ. 2003. 423p. ISBN:3-527-30596-3, ISBN13: 978-3-527-30596-4. Dewey:616.1/042. LCCN:2003-279641.

Audience: **u,f.**

Fruton, Joseph S.   **QP511.F783 1999**
Proteins, Enzymes and Genes: The Interplay of Chemistry and Biology. Cloth over Boards. Yale University Press. Cumberland, RI. 1999. 800p. ISBN:0-300-07608-8, ISBN13: 978-0-300-07608-0. Dewey:572/.09. LCCN:98-038892.

Audience: **u,f.** *Choice, 1999.*

Fuchs, Jurgen & Podda,   **RB155.E54 2005**
  Maurizio (Editors)
Encyclopedia of Diagnostic Proteomics and Genomics. Trade Cloth. Marcel Dekker Inc. New York, NY. 2005. 1600p. ISBN:0-8247-5564-2, ISBN13: 978-0-8247-5564-5. Dewey:616/.042/03. LCCN:2005-297370.

Audience: **u,f.**

Grandi, Guido (Editor)   **QH447**
Genomics, Proteomics and Vaccines. Trade Cloth. John Wiley & Sons, Inc. Hoboken, NJ. 2004. 336p. ISBN:0-470-85616-5, ISBN13: 978-0-470-85616-1. Dewey:572.8/6. LCCN:2004-273717.

Audience: **u,f.**

Gupta, G. S.   **QP255.G83 2005**
Proteomics of Spermatogenesis. Trade Cloth. Springer. New York, NY. 2005. XXVI, 855p. ISBN:0-387-25398-X, ISBN13: 978-0-387-25398-5. Dewey:612.6/1. LCCN:2005-279130.

Audience: **u,f.**

Hamdan, Mahmoud H. &   **QP551.M315 2005**
  Righetti, Pier G.
Proteomics Today: Protein Assessment and Biomarkers Using Mass Spectrometry, 2D Electrophoresis, and Microarray Technology. Trade Cloth. John Wiley & Sons, Inc. Hoboken, NJ. 2005. 448p. Wiley - Interscience Series on Mass Spectrometry Ser. ISBN:0-471-64817-5, ISBN13: 978-0-471-64817-8. Dewey:572/.6. LCCN:2004-050921.

Audience: **u,f.**

Hondermarck, Hubert   **QP551.P75667 2004**
  (Editor)
Proteomics: Biomedical and Pharmaceutical Applications. Trade Cloth. Springer. New York, NY. 2004. XII, 396p. ISBN:1-4020-2322-7, ISBN13: 978-1-4020-2322-4. Dewey:572/.6. LCCN:2004-050446.

Audience: **u,f.**

Howard, Gary C. (Editor)   **QP551**
Modern Protein Chemistry: Practical Aspects. Brown, William E. (Editor). CRC Press: Boca Raton. 2002. ISBN:0-8493-9453-8, ISBN13: 978-0-8493-9453-9.

Audience: **u,f.**

International Symposium on   **RC270.3.T84**
  Circulating Nucleic Acids in Plasma/Serum 2003 : Santa Monica, Calif.)

Circulating Nucleic Acids in Plasma/Serum III and Serum Proteomics. Hoon, Dave S. B. (Editor); Taback, Bret (Editor). New York : New York Academy of Sciences. 2004. Annals of the New York Academy of Sciences, v. 1022 ISBN:1-57331-551-6, ISBN13: 978-1-57331-551-7.

Audience: **u,f.**

James, P. (Editor)   **QP551.P7558 2001**
Proteome Research: Mass Spectrometry. Trade Cloth. Springer. New York, NY. 2000. XXI, 274p. Principles and Practice Ser. ISBN:3-540-67255-9, ISBN13: 978-3-540-67255-5. Dewey:572/.636. LCCN:00-032205.

Audience: **u,f.**

Jolles, P. & Jornvall, H.   **QP551.P7567 2000**
  (Editors)
Proteomics in functional Genomics: Protein Structure Analysis. Trade Cloth. Springer. New York, NY. 2000. 256p. Experientia Supplementum Ser., 88 ISBN:3-7643-5885-8, ISBN13: 978-3-7643-5885-3. Dewey:572/.633. LCCN:99-059890.

Audience: **u,f.**

Jurisica, Igor & Wigle, Dennis   **QP551**
Knowledge Discovery in Proteomics. Chapman & Hall/CRC: Boca Raton, FL.. 2005. Chapman & Hall/CRC Mathematical Biology & Medicine series; Vol. 8; Variation: Chapman & Hall/CRC Mathematical Biology and Medicine Series ISBN:1-58488-439-8, ISBN13: 978-1-58488-439-2.

Audience: **u,f.**

Kahl, Günter   **QH442**
The Dictionary of Gene Technology: Genomics, Transcriptomics, Proteomics. Ed. 3. Trade Cloth. John Wiley & Sons, Inc. Hoboken, NJ. 2004. 1314p. ISBN:3-527-30765-6, ISBN13: 978-3-527-30765-4. Dewey:572.803. LCCN:2006-280310.

Audience: **u,f.** *Choice, 2005.*

Kamp, R. M. &   **QP551.M399 2004**
  Choli-Papadopoulou, Theodora
Methods in Proteome and Protein Analysis. Juan J. Calvete (Editor). Trade Cloth. Springer. New York, NY. 2004. 125 schw.-w. u. 19 farb. Abb., 18 schw.-w. Tab., 13 schw.-w. u. 5 farb. Fotos, 112 schw.-w. u. 14 farb. Zeichn. XXXII, 404p. Principles and Practice Ser. ISBN:3-540-20222-6, ISBN13: 978-3-540-20222-6. Dewey:572/.6. LCCN:2003-066408.

Audience: **u,f.**

Kannicht, Christoph   **QH450.6.P685 2002**
  (Editor)
Post-Translational Modification of Proteins: Tools for Functional Proteomics. Book, Other. Humana Press. Totowa, NJ. 2002. 336p. Methods in Molecular Biology Ser., Vol. 194 ISBN:0-89603-678-2, ISBN13: 978-0-89603-678-9. Dewey:572/.6. LCCN:2001-051864.

Audience: **u,f.**

Kyte, Jack   **QP551.K98 1995**
Structure in Protein Chemistry, Vol. 1. Paper over Boards. Garland Publishing, Inc. New York, NY. 1995. 616p. Structure in Protein Chemistry Ser., Vol. 1 ISBN:0-8153-1701-8, ISBN13: 978-0-8153-1701-2. Dewey:572.633. LCCN:94-023417.

Audience: **u,f.** *Choice, 1995.*

Formats: Web: ☐   Ebook: **ℯ**   CD/DVD-ROM: ✇   BCL3: **ℬ**

Liebler, Daniel C. (Editor)   QP551.L467 2002
Introduction to Proteomics: Tools for the New Biology. Book,
Other. Humana Press. Totowa, NJ. 2002. 150p.
ISBN:0-89603-991-9, ISBN13: 978-0-89603-991-9.
Dewey:572/.6/072. LCCN:2001-051465.
                                                    Audience: **u,f.**

Liebler, Daniel C. (Editor),   RC267.P775 2005
  et al.
Proteomics in Cancer Research. Lance A. Liotta & Emanuel F.
Petricoin (Editors). Trade Cloth. John Wiley & Sons, Inc.
Hoboken, NJ. 2005. 201p. ISBN:0-471-44476-6, ISBN13:
978-0-471-44476-3. Dewey:616.99/4. LCCN:2004-028131.
                                                    Audience: **u,f.**

Link, Andrew J.   QP551.A14 1999
2-D Proteome Analysis Protocols. Book, Other. Humana Press.
Totowa, NJ. 1999. 450p. Methods in Molecular Biology Ser.,
Vol. 112 ISBN:0-89603-524-7, ISBN13: 978-0-89603-524-9.
Dewey:572/.6. LCCN:98-038677.
                                                    Audience: **u,f.**

Lundblad, Roger L.   QP551
The Evolution from Protein Chemistry to Proteomics: Basic
Science to Clinical Application. CRC/Taylor & Francis: Boca
Raton. 2006. ISBN:0-8493-9678-6, ISBN13: 978-0-8493-9678-6.
                                                    Audience: **u,f.**

Milligan, George   QH345 .B522
  (Editor), et al.
G Proteins and Signal Transduction. J. Kay & M. J. Wakelam
(Editors). Trade Cloth. Portland Press, Ltd. London, 1990. 172p.
Biochemical Society Symposium Ser., Vol. 56
ISBN:1-85578-001-1, ISBN13: 978-1-85578-001-9.
Dewey:574.19/2 s 574.87/5.
                                                    Audience: **u,f.**

Moussa, Naima Moustaid &   QP171
  Berdanier, Carolyn
Genomics and Proteomics in Nutrition. Paper over Boards.
Marcel Dekker Inc. New York, NY. 2004. 528p. Nutrition in
Health and Disease Ser., Vol. 1 ISBN:0-8247-5430-1, ISBN13:
978-0-8247-5430-3. Dewey:612.3. LCCN:2004-275369.
                                                    Audience: **u,f.**

Mullner, S.   TP248.3
Proteomics of Microorganisms: Fundamental Aspects and
Application. M. Hecker (Contribution by), Michael Hecker
(Volume Editor), D. J. Cahill, P. Cash & S. J. Cordwell
(Contribution by). Mixed Media. Springer. New York, NY. 2003.
XI, 228p. Advances in Biochemical Engineering / Biotechnology
Ser. ISBN:3-540-00546-3, ISBN13: 978-3-540-00546-9.
Dewey:660.6/3.
                                                    Audience: **u,f.**

Nedelkov, Dobrin & Nelson,   QP551.N49 2006
  Randall W.
New and Emerging Proteomic Techniques. Trade Cloth. Humana
Press. Totowa, NJ. 2006. xi, 232p. ISBN:1-58829-519-2,
ISBN13: 978-1-58829-519-4. Dewey:572/.6/078.
LCCN:2005-016815.
                                                    Audience: **u,f.**

Neuhold, Lisa A. (Volume   RC341
  Editor)
Human Brain Proteome, Vol. 61. Trade Cloth. Elsevier Science
& Technology Books. Saint Louis, MO. 2004. 352p.

International Review of Neurobiology Ser., Vol. 61
ISBN:0-12-366863-8, ISBN13: 978-0-12-366863-9.
Dewey:612.822. LCCN:2005-273628.
                                                    Audience: **u,f.**

Noel, Joseph P. &   TP248.65.E59
  Robertson, Dan
Protein Engineering, Vol. 388. Trade Cloth. Elsevier Science &
Technology Books. Saint Louis, MO. 2004. 456p.
ISBN:0-12-182793-3, ISBN13: 978-0-12-182793-9.
Dewey:660.634.
                                                    Audience: **u,f.**

Nölting, Bengt   QP551
Protein Folding Kinetics: Biophysical Methods. Ed. 2. Trade
Cloth. Springer. New York, NY. 2005. XVI, 222p.
ISBN:3-540-27277-1, ISBN13: 978-3-540-27277-9.
Dewey:572/.633. LCCN:2005-929411.
                                                    Audience: **u,f.**

Palzkill, Timothy   QP551.P295 2002
Proteomics. Trade Cloth. Springer. New York, NY. 2001. 136p.
ISBN:0-7923-7565-3, ISBN13: 978-0-7923-7565-4.
Dewey:572/.6. LCCN:2001-050242.
                                                    Audience: **l,u.**

Pechkova, Eugenia &   QP551.P37 2003
  Nicolini, Claudio A.
Proteomics and Nanocrystallography. Trade Cloth. Springer.
New York, NY. 2003. 200p. ISBN:0-306-47902-8, ISBN13:
978-0-306-47902-1. Dewey:572/.6. LCCN:2003-058935.
                                                    Audience: **l,u.**

Pennington, S. & Dunn, M.   QH447.P76 2001
  J. (Editors)
Proteomics: From Protein Sequence to Function. Paper Text.
Springer. New York, NY. 2000. 335p. ISBN:0-387-91589-3,
ISBN13: 978-0-387-91589-0. Dewey:572/.6.
LCCN:2002-510768.
                                                    Audience: **u,f.**

Petsko, Gregory A. & Ringe,   QP551.P3974 2004
  Dagmar
Protein Structure and Function. Trade Paper. Sinauer Associates,
Inc. Sunderland, MA. 2004. 195p. Primers in Biology Ser.
ISBN:0-87893-663-7, ISBN13: 978-0-87893-663-2.
Dewey:572/.633. LCCN:2004-351320.
                                          Audience: **u,f.** *Choice, 2004.*

Rabilloud, T. (Editor)   QP551.P7564 2000
Proteome Research: Two-Dimensional Gel Electrophoresis and
Identification Methods. Trade Cloth. Springer. New York, NY.
1999. XVI, 248p. Principles and Practice Ser.
ISBN:3-540-65689-8, ISBN13: 978-3-540-65689-0.
Dewey:572/.633. LCCN:99-015544.
                                                    Audience: **u,f.**

Raghavachari, Ramesh &   TP248.6.G523 2001
  Tan, Weihong
Genomics and Proteomics Technologies. Trade Paper. S P I
E-International Society for Optical Engineering. Bellingham,
WA. 2001. v, 82p. Proceeding Ser., No. 2 ISBN:0-8194-3942-8,
ISBN13: 978-0-8194-3942-0. Dewey:660.6/5.
LCCN:2001-279171.
                                                    Audience: **u,f.**

Rehm, Hubert QP551
Protein Biochemistry and Proteomics. Paper Text. Elsevier Science & Technology Books. Saint Louis, MO. 2006. 256p. ISBN:0-12-088545-X, ISBN13: 978-0-12-088545-9. Dewey:572.60724.

Audience: **u,f.**

Reyes Mateo, C. (Editor), QP752.M45P76 2006
et al.
Protein-Lipid Interactions: New Approaches and Emerging Concepts. J. Gómez Perez, José Villalaín & José M. Gonzaléz Ros (Editors). Trade Cloth. Springer. New York, NY. 2005. xiv, 236p. Springer Series in Biophysics Ser. ISBN:3-540-28400-1, ISBN13: 978-3-540-28400-0. Dewey:572/.577. LCCN:2005-930633.

Audience: **u,f.**

Righetti, P. G., et al. QP551.R525 2001
The Proteome Revisited: Theory and Practice of All Relevant Electrophoretic Steps. Alexandre Stoyanov & Michael Y. Zhukov (Authors). Trade Cloth. Elsevier Science & Technology Books. Saint Louis, MO. 2001. 410p. Journal of Chromatography Ser., Vol. 63 ISBN:0-444-50526-1, ISBN13: 978-0-444-50526-2. Dewey:572/.6. LCCN:2001-040228.

Audience: **u,f.**

Rule, Gordon & Hitchens, QP801.P64
T. Kevin
Fundamentals of Protein NMR Spectroscopy. Trade Cloth. Springer. New York, NY. 2005. xxvi, 530p. Focus on Structural Biology Ser. ISBN:1-4020-3499-7, ISBN13: 978-1-4020-3499-2. Dewey:620.19204223.

Audience: **u,f.**

Sanchez, Jean-Charles QP551
(Editor), et al.
Biomedical Applications of Proteomics. Garry L. Corthals & Denis F. Hochstrasser (Editors). Trade Cloth. John Wiley & Sons, Inc. Hoboken, NJ. 2004. 452p. ISBN:3-527-30807-5, ISBN13: 978-3-527-30807-1. Dewey:616.07. LCCN:2004-425115.

Audience: **u,f.**

Sensen, Christoph W. QH447
(Editor)
Handbook of Genome Research: Genomics, Proteomics, Metabolomics, Bioinformatics, Ethical and Legal Issues. Trade Cloth. John Wiley & Sons, Inc. Hoboken, NJ. 2005. 646p. ISBN:3-527-31348-6, ISBN13: 978-3-527-31348-8. Dewey:572.86.

Audience: **u,f.** *Choice, 2006.*

Simpson, Richard J. QP551.P84 2004
Purifying Proteins for Proteomics: A Laboratory Manual. Trade Cloth. Cold Spring Harbor Laboratory Press. Woodbury, NY. 2003. 750p. ISBN:0-87969-695-8, ISBN13: 978-0-87969-695-5. Dewey:572/.6. LCCN:2003-019058.

Audience: **u,f.**

Smejkal, Gary B. (Editor) QP551
Separation Methods in Proteomics. Lazarev, Alexander (Editor). CRC Taylor & Francis: Boca Raton, FL.. 2006. ISBN:0-8247-2699-5, ISBN13: 978-0-8247-2699-7.

Audience: **u,f.**

Speicher, David W. (Editor) QP551
Proteome Analysis: Interpreting the Genome. Trade Cloth. Elsevier Science & Technology Books. Saint Louis, MO. 2004. 394p. ISBN:0-444-51024-9, ISBN13: 978-0-444-51024-2. Dewey:572.8/6. LCCN:2006-273067.

Audience: **u,f.**

Suhai, Sándor QH445.2.G473 2000
Genomics and Proteomics: Functional and Computational Aspects. Trade Cloth. Springer. New York, NY. 2000. 258p. ISBN:0-306-46312-1, ISBN13: 978-0-306-46312-9. Dewey:572.8/633/0285. LCCN:00-022525.

Audience: **u,f.**

Sundstrom, Michael, et al. QP551.S815 2005
Structural Proteomics. Martin Norin & Aled Edwards (Authors). Paper over Boards. Marcel Dekker Inc. New York, NY. 2005. 304p. ISBN:0-8247-5335-6, ISBN13: 978-0-8247-5335-1. Dewey:572/.633. LCCN:2005-044002.

Audience: **u,f.**

Twyman, Richard M. QD431
Principles of Proteomics. UK-B Format Paperback. Taylor & Francis Group. Abingdon, 2004. 266p. Advanced Texts Ser. ISBN:1-85996-273-4, ISBN13: 978-1-85996-273-2. Dewey:572/.6. LCCN:2004-011210.

Audience: **u,f.**

Veenstra, Timothy D. & QP551
Smith, Richard D. (Editors)
Proteome Characterization and Proteomics, Vol. 65. Trade Cloth. Elsevier Science & Technology Books. Saint Louis, MO. 2003. 413p. ISBN:0-12-034265-0, ISBN13: 978-0-12-034265-5. Dewey:547.7/5.

Audience: **u,f.**

Vo-Dinh QP551.P697225 2005
Protein Nanotechnology: Protocols, Instrumentation, and Applications. Saddle Stitched, Cloth over Boards. Humana Press. Totowa, NJ. 2005. 463p. Methods in Molecular Biology Ser. ISBN:1-58829-310-6, ISBN13: 978-1-58829-310-7. Dewey:572/.6. LCCN:2004-010385.

Audience: **u,f.**

Waksman, Gabriel (Editor) QP551.5.P765 2005
Proteomics and Protein-Protein Interactions: Biology, Chemistry, Bionformatics, and Drug Design. Trade Cloth. Springer. New York, NY. 2005. 27 schw.-w. u. 43 farb. Abb., 8 schw.-w. Tab., 1 schw.-w. u. 30 farb. Fotos, 26 schw.-w. u. 13 farb. Zeichn. VIII, 324p. Protein Reviews Ser. ISBN:0-387-24531-6, ISBN13: 978-0-387-24531-7. Dewey:612/.01575. LCCN:2005-040224.

Audience: **u,f.**

Walker, John M. QP551.P75675 2005
ⓔ Proteomics Protocols Handbook. Trade Cloth, CD-ROM, E-Book. Humana Press. Totowa, NJ. 2005. 1016p. ISBN:1-58829-343-2, ISBN13: 978-1-58829-343-5. Dewey:572/.6. LCCN:2004-016126.

Audience: **u,f.**

Walz, Wolfgang QP43.I585 2005
Integrative Physiology in the Proteomics and Post-Genomics Age. Trade Cloth. Humana Press. Totowa, NJ. 2005. 280p. ISBN:1-58829-315-7, ISBN13: 978-1-58829-315-2. Dewey:571/.072. LCCN:2004-020035.

Audience: **l,u,f.**

Formats: Web: ☐ Ebook: ⓔ CD/DVD-ROM: 🦋 BCL3: 𝐵

Westermeier, Reiner &   QP551.W46 2002
  Naven, Tom
Proteomics in Practice: A Laboratory Manual of Proteome
Analysis. Trade Cloth. John Wiley & Sons, Inc. Hoboken, NJ.
2002. 342p. ISBN:3-527-30354-5, ISBN13: 978-3-527-30354-0.
Dewey:572.64. LCCN:2002-514963.
             Audience: **u,f.**

Woodford, Neil & Johnson,   QR74.G46 2004
  Alan (Editors)
Genomics, Proteomics, and Clinical Bacteriology: Methods and
Reviews. Book, Other. Humana Press. Totowa, NJ. 2004. 408p.
Methods in Molecular Biologytm Ser. ISBN:1-58829-218-5,
ISBN13: 978-1-58829-218-6. Dewey:616.9/201.
LCCN:2004-000332.
             Audience: **u,f.**

Biochemistry and Biophysics > Specific Substances > Enzymes

Chaplin, Martin F. &   TP248.65.E59C48 1990
  Bucke, Christopher
Enzyme Technology. Trade Cloth. Cambridge University Press.
New York, NY. 1990. 280p. ISBN:0-521-34429-8, ISBN13:
978-0-521-34429-6. Dewey:660/.634. LCCN:89-007372.
        Audience: **u,f.** *Choice, 1991.*

Copeland, Robert A.   QP601.C753 2000
Enzymes: A Practical Introduction to Structure, Mechanism, and
Data Analysis. Ed. 2. Trade Cloth. John Wiley & Sons, Inc.
Hoboken, NJ. 2000. 416p. ISBN:0-471-35929-7, ISBN13:
978-0-471-35929-6. Dewey:572.7. LCCN:99-050087.
        Audience: **u,f.** *Choice, 2001.*

Cornish-Bowden, A.   QP601.3
Fundamentals of Enzyme Kinetics. Ed. 2. Paper Text. Portland
Press, Ltd. London, 1995. 343p. ISBN:1-85578-072-0, ISBN13:
978-1-85578-072-9. Dewey:547.7/58/04594.
        Audience: **u,f.** *Choice, 1996.*

Dressler, David   QP601.D69 1990
Enzymes. Trade Cloth. Henry Holt & Company. New York, NY.
1990. 208p. Scientific American Library, No. 34
ISBN:0-7167-5013-9, ISBN13: 978-0-7167-5013-0.
Dewey:574.19/25. LCCN:90-004448.
             Audience: **u,f.**

Dugas, H.   QP601.D78 1989
Bioorganic Chemistry. Ed. 2. Trade Cloth. Springer. New York,
NY. 1988. 651p. Advanced Texts in Chemistry Ser.
ISBN:0-387-96795-8, ISBN13: 978-0-387-96795-0.
Dewey:574.19/25. LCCN:89-117705.
             Audience: **u,f.**

Dugas, Hermann   QP601
Bioorganic Chemistry: A Chemical Approach to Enzyme Action.
Ed. 3. Trade Paper. Springer. New York, NY. 1999. XVII, 700p.
Advanced Texts in Chemistry Ser. ISBN:0-387-98910-2,
ISBN13: 978-0-387-98910-5. Dewey:574.19/25.
             Audience: **u,f.**

Fersht, Alan   QD431.25.S85F47 1998
Structure and Mechanism in Protein Science: A Guide to
Enzyme Catalysis and Protein Folding. Ed. 3. Cloth over

Boards. Worth Publishers, Inc. New York, NY. 1998. 650p.
ISBN:0-7167-3268-8, ISBN13: 978-0-7167-3268-6.
Dewey:547/.75. LCCN:98-036703.
             Audience: **u,f.**

Fruton, Joseph S.   QP511.F783 1999
Proteins, Enzymes and Genes: The Interplay of Chemistry and
Biology. Cloth over Boards. Yale University Press. Cumberland,
RI. 1999. 800p. ISBN:0-300-07608-8, ISBN13:
978-0-300-07608-0. Dewey:572/.09. LCCN:98-038892.
        Audience: **u,f.** *Choice, 1999.*

Kornberg, Arthur   Q183.4.G73
For the Love of Enzymes: The Odyssey of a Biochemist. Trade
Paper. Harvard University Press. Cambridge, MA. 1991. 352p.
ISBN:0-674-30776-3, ISBN13: 978-0-674-30776-6.
Dewey:574.19/2/0924 B.
      Audience: **l,u,f.** *Choice, 1989.*

Marangoni, Alejandro G.   QP601.3.M37 2003
Enzyme Kinetics: A Modern Approach. Trade Cloth. John Wiley
& Sons, Inc. Hoboken, NJ. 2002. 248p. ISBN:0-471-15985-9,
ISBN13: 978-0-471-15985-8. Dewey:572/.7.
LCCN:2002-014042.
        Audience: **u,f.** *Choice, 2003.*

NC-IUBMB & Webb, Edwin   QP601.I56 1992
  C. (Editors)
Enzyme Nomenclature 1992. Ed. 2. Trade Cloth. Elsevier
Science & Technology Books. Saint Louis, MO. 1992. 862p.
ISBN:0-12-227164-5, ISBN13: 978-0-12-227164-9.
Dewey:574.1925014. LCCN:92-025248.
             Audience: **u,f.**

Roberts, S. M., et al.   TP248.27.M53 I57 19
Introduction to Biocatalysis Using Enzymes and
Microorganisms. Nicholas J. Turner, Andrew J. Willetts &
Michael K. Turner (Authors). Trade Cloth. Cambridge
University Press. New York, NY. 1995. 207p.
ISBN:0-521-43070-4, ISBN13: 978-0-521-43070-8.
Dewey:660/.63. LCCN:93-048247.
        Audience: **u,f.** *Choice, 1995.*

Wong, C. -H & Whitesides,   QD262.W65 1994
  G. M.
Enzymes in Synthetic Organic Chemistry. Trade Cloth. Elsevier
Science & Technology Books. Saint Louis, MO. 1994. 388p.
Tetrahedron Organic Chemistry Ser., Vol. 12
ISBN:0-08-035942-6, ISBN13: 978-0-08-035942-7.
Dewey:547.7/0459. LCCN:94-002329.
             Audience: **u,f.**

Biochemistry and Biophysics > Specific Substances > Nucleic Acids

Anker, Philippe & Stroun,   Q11.N5 VOL.906
  Maurice (Editors)
Circulating Nucleic Acids in Plasma or Serum, Vol. 906. Trade
Cloth. New York Academy of Sciences. New York, NY. 2000. x,
188p. Annals of the New York Academy of Sciences Ser., Vol.
906 ISBN:1-57331-269-X, ISBN13: 978-1-57331-269-1.
Dewey:500 s 616.07. LCCN:00-027098.
             Audience: **u,f.**

Beaucage, Serge L. QP620.C87 2000
Current Protocols in Nucleic Acid Chemistry. Ringbound. John Wiley & Sons, Inc. Hoboken, NJ. 2000. ISBN:0-471-24662-X, ISBN13: 978-0-471-24662-6. Dewey:572.8. LCCN:99-015481.
Audience: **u,f.**

Bloomfield, Victor A., et al. QP620.B64 1999
Nucleic Acids: Structures, Properties, and Functions. Donald M. Crothers & Ignacio Tinoco Jr. (Authors). Trade Cloth. University Science Books. Sausalito, CA. 2000. 672p. ISBN:0-935702-49-0, ISBN13: 978-0-935702-49-1. Dewey:572.8. LCCN:98-045268.
Audience: **l,u,f.**

Bowien, Botho & Durre, Peter (Editors) QP620.N7983 2003
Nucleic Acids Isolation Methods. Trade Cloth. American Scientific Publishers. Stevenson Ranch, CA. 2002. 184p. ISBN:1-58883-018-7, ISBN13: 978-1-58883-018-0. Dewey:572.8. LCCN:2002-114111.
Audience: **u,f.**

Doonan, S. QP620
Nucleic Acids. Royal Society of Chemistry. 2004. ISBN:0-85404-481-7, ISBN13: 978-0-85404-481-8.
Audience: **u,f.**

International Symposium on Circulating Nucleic Acids in Plasma/Serum 2003 : Santa Monica, Calif.) RC270.3.T84
Circulating Nucleic Acids in Plasma/Serum III and Serum Proteomics. Hoon, Dave S. B. (Editor); Taback, Bret (Editor). New York : New York Academy of Sciences. 2004. Annals of the New York Academy of Sciences, v. 1022 ISBN:1-57331-551-6, ISBN13: 978-1-57331-551-7.
Audience: **u,f.**

Markoff, Arseni (Editor) QH441.2.A53 2005
Analytical Tools for DNA, Genes and Genomes: Nuts and Bolts. Trade Paper, Perfect. DNA Press. Eagleville, PA. 2005. 220p. Nuts and Bolts Ser. ISBN:0-9748765-1-8, ISBN13: 978-0-9748765-1-1. Dewey:572.8/6. LCCN:2005-003674.
Audience: **u,f.**

Mitchelson, Keith R. (Editor) QP620.C36 2001
Capillary Electrophoresis of Nucleic Acids, Vol. II: Practical Applications of Capillary Electrophoresis. Cheng, Jing (Editor). Humana Press. 2001. Methods in Molecular Biology Ser. ISBN:0-89603-765-7, ISBN13: 978-0-89603-765-6.
Audience: **u,f.**

Mitchelson, Keith R. & Cheng, Jing (Editors) QP620.C36 2001
Capillary Electrophoresis of Nucleic Acids: The Capillary Electrophoresis System as an Analytical Tool. Book, Other. Humana Press. Totowa, NJ. 2000. 504p. Methods in Molecular Biology Ser., Vol. 162 ISBN:0-89603-779-7, ISBN13: 978-0-89603-779-3. Dewey:572.8. LCCN:00-038911.
Audience: **u,f.**

Ronot, Xavier; Usson, Yves QP620.I43 2001
Imaging of Nucleic Acids and Quantitation in Photonic Microscopy. CRC Press. 2000. ISBN:0-8493-0817-8, ISBN13: 978-0-8493-0817-8.
Audience: **u,f.**

Tracy, Kathleen QP620.T73 2005
Friedrich Miescher and the Story of Nucleic Acid. Library Binding. Mitchell Lane Publishers, Inc. Hockessin, DE. 2005. 48p. Uncharted, Unexplored, and Unexplained Ser., :Scientific Advancements of the 19th Century ISBN:1-58415-369-5, ISBN13: 978-1-58415-369-6. Dewey:572.8. LCCN:2005-004252.
Audience: **u,f.**

Walker, Jim QP620.N7987 2000
The Nucleic Acid Protocols Handbook. Ralph Rapley (Editor). Trade Paper. Humana Press. Totowa, NJ. 2000. 1072p. ISBN:0-89603-841-6, ISBN13: 978-0-89603-841-7. Dewey:572.8. LCCN:98-043385.
Audience: **u,f.**

Biochemistry and Biophysics > Specific Substances > DNA

QH465.A1
Biological Responses to DNA Damage. Trade Cloth. Cold Spring Harbor Laboratory Press. Woodbury, NY. 2001. 613p. Symposia on Quantitative Biology Ser., Vol. LXV ISBN:0-87969-605-2, ISBN13: 978-0-87969-605-4. Dewey:572.86.
Audience: **u,f.**

Abelson, John N. & Stone, Melvin I. (Editor-In-Chiefs) QH366.2
Molecular Evolution: Computer Analysis of Protein and Nucleic Acid Sequences. Russell F. Doolittle (Volume Editor), Melvin I. Simon (Editor-In-Chief). Trade Cloth. Elsevier Science & Technology Books. Saint Louis, MO. 1990. 736p. Methods in Enzymology Ser., Vol. 183 ISBN:0-12-182084-X, ISBN13: 978-0-12-182084-8. Dewey:575. LCCN:54-009110.
Audience: **u,f.**

Allison, David B., et al. QP624.5.D726.D636
DNA Microarrays and Related Genomic Techniques: Statistical Design, Analysis, and Interpretation of Experiments. Grier P. Page, T. Mark Beasley & Jode W. Edwards (Authors). Paper over Boards. Marcel Dekker Inc. New York, NY. 2005. 392p. Biostatistics Ser., Vol. 16 ISBN:0-8247-5461-1, ISBN13: 978-0-8247-5461-7. Dewey:572.8/636. LCCN:2005-050488.
Audience: **u,f.**

Amaratunga, Dhammika & Cabrera, Javier QP624.5.D726
Exploration and Analysis of DNA Microarray and Protein Array Data. Trade Cloth. John Wiley & Sons, Inc. Hoboken, NJ. 2003. 272p. Wiley Series in Probability and Statistics Ser. ISBN:0-471-27398-8, ISBN13: 978-0-471-27398-1. Dewey:572.8/636. LCCN:2003-050097.
Audience: **u,f.**

Baldi, Pierre & Hatfield, G. Wesley QP624.5.D726.B353
DNA Microarrays and Gene Expression: From Experiments to Data Analysis and Modeling. Trade Cloth. Cambridge University Press. New York, NY. 2002. 230p. ISBN:0-521-80022-6, ISBN13: 978-0-521-80022-8. Dewey:572.8/65. LCCN:2001-052862.
Audience: **u,f.**

Calladine, Chris R., et al. QP624
Understanding DNA: The Molecule and How it Works. Ed. 3. Andrew Travers, Horace R. Drew & Ben Luisi (Authors). Trade

Cloth. Elsevier Science & Technology Books. Saint Louis, MO. 2004. 352p. ISBN:0-12-155089-3, ISBN13: 978-0-12-155089-9. Dewey:572.86.

Audience: **u,f.**

Chatenay, Didier (Volume   QP620 .E36 2004
   Editor), et al.
Multiple Aspects of DNA and RNA from Biophysics to Bioinformatics: Lecture Notes of the les Houches Summer School 2004. Simona Cocco, Remi Monasson, Denis Thieffry & Jean Dalibard (Volume Editors). Trade Cloth. Elsevier Science & Technology Books. Saint Louis, MO. 2005. 378p. Les Houches Ser. ISBN:0-444-52081-3, ISBN13: 978-0-444-52081-4. Dewey:572.86.

Audience: **u,f.**

Clayton, Julie & Dennis,   QP624.A15 2003
   Carina (Editors)
50 Years of DNA. Cloth over Boards. Palgrave Macmillan. New York, NY. 2003. 120p. ISBN:1-4039-1479-6, ISBN13: 978-1-4039-1479-8. Dewey:572.8/6. LCCN:2003-049848.

Audience: **u,f.**

Corrigan, Oonagh & Tutton,   QH441.2.D66 2004
   Richard
Donating and Exploiting DNA: Social and Ethical Aspects of Public Participation in Genetic Databases. Trade Cloth. Routledge. New York, NY. 2004. 208p. ISBN:0-415-31679-0, ISBN13: 978-0-415-31679-8. Dewey:303.48/3. LCCN:2003-066779.

Audience: **l,u,f.**

Davidson, J. N.   QP624
The Biochemistry of the Nucleic Acids. Paper Text. Textbook Publishers. Temecula, CA. 2003. 288p. ISBN:0-7581-8165-5, ISBN13: 978-0-7581-8165-7. Dewey:574.8/732.

Audience: **u,f.**

Davies, Kevin   QH445.2.D37 2001
Cracking the Genome: Inside the Race to Unlock Human DNA. Trade Cloth. Simon & Schuster. New York, NY. 2001. 320p. ISBN:0-7432-0479-4, ISBN13: 978-0-7432-0479-8. Dewey:599.93. LCCN:00-048430.

Audience: **u,f.**

Day, I. N. M. & Ye, S.   QP624.5.D726.M5 2003
   (Editors)
Microarrays and Microplates: Applications in Biomedical Sciences. UK-B Format Paperback. Taylor & Francis Group. Philadelphia, PA. 2003. 192p. ISBN:1-85996-074-X, ISBN13: 978-1-85996-074-5. Dewey:572.8636.

Audience: **u,f.**

Demeunynck, Martine   QP620
   (Editor), et al.
DNA and RNA Binders, from Small Molecules to Drugs, Vol. 1. Christian Bailly & W. David Wilson (Editors). Trade Cloth. John Wiley & Sons, Inc. Hoboken, NJ. 2003. 754p. ISBN:3-527-30595-5, ISBN13: 978-3-527-30595-7. Dewey:572.8. LCCN:2003-279167.

Audience: **u,f.**

Draghici, Soren   QP624.5.D726
Data Analysis Tools for DNA Microarrays. CRC Press. 2003. ISBN:1-58488-315-4, ISBN13: 978-1-58488-315-9.

Audience: **u,f.**

Drlica, Karl   QH430
Understanding DNA and Gene Cloning: A Guide for the Curious. Ed. 4. Library Binding. Sagebrush Education Resources. Caledonia, MN. 2003. 369p. ISBN:0-613-91363-9, ISBN13: 978-0-613-91363-8. Dewey:576.5. LCCN:2003-043077.

Audience: **u,f.** *Choice, 1997, 1992.*

Duncan, David Ewing   QH429.D86 2005
The Geneticist Who Played Hoops with My DNA: And Other Masterminds from the Frontiers of Research. Trade Cloth. HarperCollins Publishers. New York, NY. 2005. 288p. ISBN:0-06-053738-8, ISBN13: 978-0-06-053738-8. Dewey:660.6/5/0922. LCCN:2005-041507.

Audience: **u,f.**

Durbin, R., et al.   QP620 .B576 1998
Biological Sequence Analysis: Probabilistic Models of Proteins and Nucleic Acids. S. Eddy, A. Krogh & G. Mitchison (Authors). Cloth Text. Cambridge University Press. New York, NY. 1998. 368p. ISBN:0-521-62041-4, ISBN13: 978-0-521-62041-3. Dewey:572.8/633. LCCN:97-046769.

Audience: **u,f.**

Erlich, H.   QP606.D46P37 1989
PCR Technology: Principles and Applications for DNA Amplification. Paper Text. Groves Dictionaries, Inc. New York, NY. 1989. 176p. Breakthroughs in Molecular Biology Ser. ISBN:0-935859-56-X, ISBN13: 978-0-935859-56-0. Dewey:574.87/3282. LCCN:89-004342.

Audience: **u,f.**

Freidberg, Errol, et al.   QH467.F753 1995
DNA Repair and Mutagenesis. G. C. Walker & Wolfram Siede (Authors). Trade Cloth. ASM Press. Washington, DC. 1995. 780p. ISBN:1-55581-088-8, ISBN13: 978-1-55581-088-7. Dewey:574.87/328. LCCN:94-043983.

Audience: **u,f.**

Gesteland, Raymond F.   QP623.R6 2006
   (Editor), et al.
The RNA World. Ed. 3. Thomas R. Cech & John F. Atkins (Editors). Book, Other. Cold Spring Harbor Laboratory Press. Woodbury, NY. 2005. 750p. Cold Spring Harbor Monograph Ser., Vol. 43 ISBN:0-87969-739-3, ISBN13: 978-0-87969-739-6. Dewey:572.8/8. LCCN:2005-019647.

Audience: **u,f.** *Choice, 2006.*

Grigorenko, E.V.   QP624.5.D726 D624 2002
DNA Arrays: Technologies and Experimental Strategies. CRC Press. 2001. Methods and New Frontiers in Neuroscience ISBN:0-8493-2285-5, ISBN13: 978-0-8493-2285-3.

Audience: **u,f.**

Hecht, Sidney M. (Editor)   QP620.B58 1996
Bioorganic Chemistry: Nucleic Acids. Cloth Text. Oxford University Press, Inc. New York, NY. 1996. 512p. International Series of Monographs on Chemistry ISBN:0-19-508467-5, ISBN13: 978-0-19-508467-2. Dewey:547.7/9. LCCN:95-021401.

Audience: **u,f.**

Hermann, Bernd &   QP620.A53 1994
   Hummel, Susanne (Editors)
Ancient DNA. Trade Cloth. Springer. New York, NY. 1993. 263p. ISBN:0-387-97929-8, ISBN13: 978-0-387-97929-8. Dewey:574.873282. LCCN:92-049549.

Audience: **u,f.** *Choice, 1994.*

Holmes, Frederic Lawrence   QP624.H654 2001
Meselson, Stahl, and the Replication of DNA: A History of
"The Most Beautiful Experiment in Biology". Cloth over
Boards. Yale University Press. Cumberland, RI. 2001. 528p.
ISBN:0-300-08540-0, ISBN13: 978-0-300-08540-2.
Dewey:572.8/6. LCCN:2001-017701.

Audience: **u,f.**

Jones, Martin   CC79.5.H85J66 2002
The Molecule Hunt: Archaeology and the Search for Ancient
DNA. Trade Cloth. Arcade Publishing, Inc. New York, NY.
2002. 279p. ISBN:1-55970-611-2, ISBN13: 978-1-55970-611-7.
Dewey:569.9. LCCN:2002-016323.

Audience: **u,f.**

Jordan, Bertrand   QP624.5.D726D634
DNA Microarrays: Gene Expression Applications. Trade Cloth.
Springer. New York, NY. 2001. IX, 140p. Principles and
Practice Ser. ISBN:3-540-41507-6, ISBN13: 978-3-540-41507-7.
Dewey:572.8/65. LCCN:2001-032237.

Audience: **u,f.**

Kay, Lily E.   QH450.2.K39
Who Wrote the Book of Life?: A History of the Genetic Code.
Trade Paper. Stanford University Press. Palo Alto, CA. 2000.
464p. Writing Science Ser. ISBN:0-8047-3417-8, ISBN13:
978-0-8047-3417-2. Dewey:572.8/633. LCCN:99-039446.

Audience: **u,f.** *Choice, 2000.*

Kirby, Lorne T.   RA1057.55.K57 1990
DNA Fingerprinting: An Introduction. Paper Text. Groves
Dictionaries, Inc. New York, NY. 1990. 256p. Breakthroughs in
Molecular Biology Ser. ISBN:0-935859-94-2, ISBN13:
978-0-935859-94-2. Dewey:614/.1. LCCN:90-009527.

Audience: **u,f.** *Choice, 1991.*

Knudsen, Steen   QP624.5.D726K68 2004
Guide to Analysis of DNA Microarray Data. Ed. 2. Trade Paper.
John Wiley & Sons, Inc. Hoboken, NJ. 2004. 184p.
ISBN:0-471-65604-6, ISBN13: 978-0-471-65604-3.
Dewey:572.8/636. LCCN:2003-026036.

Audience: **u,f.**

Kordal, Richard Joseph,   QP624.5.D726M53 2002
 et al.
Microfabricated Sensors: Application of Optical Technology for
DNA Analysis. Arthur M. Usmani & Wai Tak Law (Authors),
American Chemical Society, Division of Industrial and
Engineering Chemistry Staff & American Chemical Society Staff
(Contribution by). Cloth Text. Oxford University Press, Inc.
New York, NY. 2002. 170p. ACS Symposium Ser., Vol. 815
ISBN:0-8412-3763-8, ISBN13: 978-0-8412-3763-6.
Dewey:610/.28. LCCN:2001-056737.

Audience: **u,f.**

Kornberg, Arthur & Baker,   QP624.K668 2005
 Tania
DNA Replication. Ed. 2. Trade Paper. University Science Books.
Sausalito, CA. 2005. 932p. ISBN:1-891389-44-0, ISBN13:
978-1-891389-44-3. Dewey:572.8645.

Audience: **u,f.**

Lagerkvist, Ulf   QP624.L34 1998
DNA Pioneers and Their Legacy. Cloth over Boards. Yale
University Press. Cumberland, RI. 1998. 168p.
ISBN:0-300-07184-1, ISBN13: 978-0-300-07184-9.
Dewey:572.8/6/0072. LCCN:97-037281.

Audience: **u,f.** *Choice, 1998.*

Landweber, Laura F. &   QH75.G454 1999
 Dobson, Andrew P. (Editors)
Genetics and the Extinction of Species: DNA and the
Conservation of Biodiversity. Trade Paper. Princeton University
Press. Princeton, NJ. 1999. 208p. ISBN:0-691-00971-6, ISBN13:
978-0-691-00971-1. Dewey:576.5/8. LCCN:99-024114.

Audience: **u,f.**

Lewin, Benjamin   QH430.L4 2004
Genes VIII. Trade Cloth. Prentice Hall PTR. Upper Saddle
River, NJ. 2004. xxi, 1027p. ISBN:0-13-145140-5, ISBN13:
978-0-13-145140-7. Dewey:576.5. LCCN:2003-015721.

Audience: **u,f.**

Lewontin, Richard C.   QH331 .L535 1993
Biology as Ideology: The Doctrine of DNA. Trade Paper.
HarperCollins Publishers. New York, NY. 1993. 144p.
ISBN:0-06-097519-9, ISBN13: 978-0-06-097519-7.
Dewey:574/.01. LCCN:92-054487.

Audience: **u,f.**

Maddox, Brenda   QH506.F72M33 2002
Rosalind Franklin: The Dark Lady of DNA. Trade Cloth.
HarperCollins Publishers. New York, NY. 2002. 400p.
ISBN:0-06-018407-8, ISBN13: 978-0-06-018407-0.
Dewey:572.8/092 B. LCCN:2002-068898.

Audience: **l,u,f.**

Markoff, Arseni (Editor)   QH441.2.A53 2005
Analytical Tools for DNA, Genes and Genomes: Nuts and Bolts.
Trade Paper, Perfect. DNA Press. Eagleville, PA. 2005. 220p.
Nuts and Bolts Ser. ISBN:0-9748765-1-8, ISBN13:
978-0-9748765-1-1. Dewey:572.8/6. LCCN:2005-003674.

Audience: **u,f.**

McElheny, Victor K.   QP624
Watson and DNA: Making a Scientific Revolution. Trade Cloth.
Basic Books. New York, NY. 2002. 400p. ISBN:0-7382-0341-6,
ISBN13: 978-0-7382-0341-6. Dewey:572.8/092 B.
LCCN:2002-114461.

Audience: **l,u,f.** *Choice, 2003.*

McGee, Glenn   QH447.M356 2003
Beyond Genetics: Putting the Power of DNA to Work in Your
Life. Trade Cloth. HarperCollins Publishers. New York, NY.
2003. 240p. ISBN:0-06-000800-8, ISBN13: 978-0-06-000800-0.
Dewey:306.4/6. LCCN:2002-044864.

Audience: **l,u,f.** *Choice, 2004.*

Messina, Lynn   TP248.215
Biotechnology. H.W. Wilson: New York. 2000. The Reference
Shelf; Vol. 72, No. 4. ISBN:0-8242-0985-0, ISBN13:
978-0-8242-0985-8.

Audience: **u,f.**

Micklos, David & Freyer,   QH506.M54 2002
 Greg
DNA Science: A First Course. Ed. 2. Trade Cloth. Cold Spring
Harbor Laboratory Press. Woodbury, NY. 2003. 575p.
ISBN:0-87969-636-2, ISBN13: 978-0-87969-636-8.
Dewey:572.8/6. LCCN:2002-034893.

Audience: **u,f.**

Miyamoto, Michael M. &   QH371.P47 1992
 Cracraft, Joel (Editors)
Phylogenetic Analysis of DNA Sequences. Trade Cloth. Oxford

University Press, Inc. New York, NY. 1991. 368p.
ISBN:0-19-506698-7, ISBN13: 978-0-19-506698-2.
Dewey:574.87/3282. LCCN:90-028771.

Audience: **u,f.**

Omoto, Charlotte K. &   **QH430.O47 2004**
  Lurquin, Paul F.
Genes and DNA: A Beginner's Guide to Genetics and Its
Applications. Trade Paper. Kegan Paul International, Ltd.
London, 2004. 224p. ISBN:0-231-13013-9, ISBN13:
978-0-231-13013-4. Dewey:576.5. LCCN:2003-062584.

Audience: **u,f.** *Choice, 2004.*

Pasternak, Jack J.   **TP248.2.G58 2003**
Molecular Biotechnology: Principles and Applications of
Recombinant DNA. Ed. 3. Bernard R. Glick (Editor). Trade
Paper. ASM Press. Washington, DC. 2003. 860p.
ISBN:1-55581-269-4, ISBN13: 978-1-55581-269-0.
Dewey:660/.65. LCCN:2002-013148.

Audience: **u,f.** *Choice, 1995.*

Pevzner, Pavel A.   **QH506.P47 2000**
Computational Molecular Biology: An Algorithmic Approach.
Trade Cloth. MIT Press. Cambridge, MA. 2000. 332p.
Computational Molecular Biology Ser. ISBN:0-262-16197-4,
ISBN13: 978-0-262-16197-8. Dewey:572.8. LCCN:00-032461.

Audience: **u,f.**

Pollack, Robert   **QH437.P65 1994**
Signs of Life: The Language and Meanings of DNA. Trade
Cloth. Houghton Mifflin Company. New York, NY. 1994. 224p.
ISBN:0-395-64498-4, ISBN13: 978-0-395-64498-0.
Dewey:574.8/73282. LCCN:93-032474.

Audience: **u,f.**

Reilly, Philip R.   **QH431.R38 2000**
Abraham Lincoln's DNA and Other Adventures in Genetics.
Trade Cloth. Cold Spring Harbor Laboratory Press. Woodbury,
NY. 2000. xx, 339p. ISBN:0-87969-580-3, ISBN13:
978-0-87969-580-4. Dewey:599.93/5. LCCN:00-029467.

Audience: **l,u,f.** *Choice, 2001.*

Rickwood, David & Hames,   **QP620.G45 1990**
  B. D. (Editors)
Gel Electrophoresis of Nucleic Acids: A Practical Approach. Ed.
2. Trade Cloth. Oxford University Press, Inc. New York, NY.
1990. 336p. The Practical Approach Ser. ISBN:0-19-963082-8,
ISBN13: 978-0-19-963082-0. Dewey:574.87/328/028.
LCCN:90-004348.

Audience: **u,f.**

Ridley, Matt   **QH431.R475 1999**
Genome: The Autobiography of a Species in 23 Chapters. Trade
Cloth. HarperCollins Publishers. New York, NY. 2000. 352p.
ISBN:0-06-019497-9, ISBN13: 978-0-06-019497-0.
Dewey:599.935. LCCN:99-040933.

Audience: **u,f.**

Robin, Stephane, et al.   **QP624**
DNA, Words and Models: Statistics of Exceptional Words.
Francois Rodolphe & Sophie Schbath (Authors). Trade Cloth.
Cambridge University Press. New York, NY. 2005. 158p.
ISBN:0-521-84729-X, ISBN13: 978-0-521-84729-2.
Dewey:572.8/633. LCCN:2005-047088.

Audience: **u,f.**

Simon, Richard M.   **QP624.5.D726D475**
Design and Analysis of DNA Microarray Investigations. Trade
Cloth. Springer. New York, NY. 2004. X, 199p. Statistics for
Biology and Health Ser. ISBN:0-387-00135-2, ISBN13:
978-0-387-00135-7. Dewey:572.8/65. LCCN:2003-054790.

Audience: **u,f.**

Sinden, Richard R.   **QP624.S56 1994**
DNA Structure and Function. Trade Cloth. Elsevier Science &
Technology Books. Saint Louis, MO. 1994. 398p.
ISBN:0-12-645750-6, ISBN13: 978-0-12-645750-6.
Dewey:574.87/3282. LCCN:94-010464.

Audience: **u,f.** *Choice, 1995.*

Watson, James D. & Berry,   **QH437.W387 2003**
  Andrew
DNA: The Secret of Life. Trade Cloth. Alfred A. Knopf Inc.
New York, NY. 2003. 464p. ISBN:0-375-41546-7, ISBN13:
978-0-375-41546-3. Dewey:576.5. LCCN:2002-190725.

Audience: **u,f.** *Choice, 2003.*

Watson, James D., et al.   **QH442**
Recombinant DNA: Genes and Genomes:A Short Course. Ed. 3.
Amy Caudy, Meyers Richard & Jan Witkowski (Authors). Trade
Paper. W. H. Freeman & Company. New York, NY. 2006. 474p.
ISBN:0-7167-2866-4, ISBN13: 978-0-7167-2866-5.

Audience: **u,f.**

Watson, James D.   **QH445.2**
The Double Helix: A Personal Account of the Discovery of the
Structure of DNA. Sylvia Nasar (Introduction by). Trade Paper.
Simon & Schuster. New York, NY. 2001. 256p.
ISBN:0-7432-1630-X, ISBN13: 978-0-7432-1630-2.
Dewey:572.8/633.

Audience: **u,f.**

Witherly, Jeffre L., et al.   **QH427.W58 2001**
An A to Z of DNA Science: What Scientists Mean When They
Talk about Genes and Genomes. Galen P. Perry & Darryl L.
Leja (Authors). Trade Paper. Cold Spring Harbor Laboratory
Press. Woodbury, NY. 2001. 136p. ISBN:0-87969-600-1,
ISBN13: 978-0-87969-600-9. Dewey:576.5/03.
LCCN:2001-042138.

Audience: **l,u,f.** *Choice, 2002.*

Biochemistry and Biophysics > Specific Substances > RNA

Ballard, F. J.   **QH345.B522 NO.55**
Gene Expression Regulation at the RNA and Protein Levels. J.
Kay & R. John Mayer (Editors). Cloth Text. Portland Press, Ltd.
London, 1989. 203p. Biochemical Society Symposium Ser.,
Symposia 55 ISBN:0-904498-24-7, ISBN13:
978-0-904498-24-0. Dewey:574.19/2 s. LCCN:90-148591.

Audience: **u,f.**

Chatenay, Didier (Volume   **QP620 .E36 2004**
  Editor), et al.
Multiple Aspects of DNA and RNA from Biophysics to
Bioinformatics: Lecture Notes of the les Houches Summer
School 2004. Simona Cocco, Remi Monasson, Denis Thieffry &
Jean Dalibard (Volume Editors). Trade Cloth. Elsevier Science
& Technology Books. Saint Louis, MO. 2005. 378p. Les
Houches Ser. ISBN:0-444-52081-3, ISBN13:
978-0-444-52081-4. Dewey:572.86.

Audience: **u,f.**

Demeunynck, Martine   **QP620**
  (Editor), et al.
DNA and RNA Binders, from Small Molecules to Drugs, Vol. 1.
Christian Bailly & W. David Wilson (Editors). Trade Cloth.
John Wiley & Sons, Inc. Hoboken, NJ. 2003. 754p.
ISBN:3-527-30595-5, ISBN13: 978-3-527-30595-7.
Dewey:572.8. LCCN:2003-279167.

         Audience: **u,f.**

Jeanteur, Ph   **QP623.R595 2003**
RNA Trafficking and Nuclear Structure Dynamics. Trade Cloth.
Springer. New York, NY. 2004. 28 schw.-w. u. 8 farb. Abb., 2
schw.-w. Tab., 8 schw.-w. u. 7 farb. Fotos, 20 schw.-w. u. 1 farb.
Zeichn. X, 153p. Progress in Molecular and Subcellular Biology
Ser. ISBN:3-540-40451-1, ISBN13: 978-3-540-40451-4.
Dewey:572.8/8. LCCN:2003-059041.

         Audience: **u,f.**

Biochemistry and Biophysics > Plant Biochemistry

         QD480
☐ Molecular Models for Biochemistry.
http://www.bio.cmu.edu/Courses/BiochemMols/
BCMolecules.html

         Audience: **u,f.**

Anderson, John W. &   **QK725**
  Beardall, John
Molecular Activities of Plant Cells. Box or Slipcased. Blackwell
Publishing, Inc. Malden, MA. 384p. ISBN:0-632-02457-7,
ISBN13: 978-0-632-02457-5. Dewey:581.876.

         Audience: **u,f.**

Bowles, D. J. (Editor), et al.   **QK728.B56 1993**
Molecular Botany: Signals and the Environment. J. P. Knox &
P. M. Gilmartin (Editors). Cloth Text. Portland Press, Ltd.
London, 1994. 290p. Biochemical Society Symposium Ser., Vol.
60 ISBN:1-85578-050-X, ISBN13: 978-1-85578-050-7.
Dewey:581.8/8. LCCN:95-182887.

         Audience: **u,f.**

Buchanan, Bob B. (Editor),   **QK861.B45 2000**
  et al.
Biochemistry and Molecular Biology of Plants. Wilhelm
Gruissem & Russell L. Jones (Editors). Trade Cloth. John Wiley
& Sons, Inc. Hoboken, NJ. 2002. 1408p. ISBN:0-943088-37-2,
ISBN13: 978-0-943088-37-2. Dewey:572.8/2. LCCN:00-040591.
         Audience: **u,f.** *Choice, 2001.*

Cullis, Christopher A.   **QK981.C85 2004**
Plant Genomics and Proteomics. Trade Cloth. John Wiley &
Sons, Inc. Hoboken, NJ. 2004. 232p. ISBN:0-471-37314-1,
ISBN13: 978-0-471-37314-8. Dewey:572.8/62.
LCCN:2003-013088.
         Audience: **u,f.** *Choice, 2004.*

Davies, Peter J. (Editor)   **QK731.P594 1995**
Plant Hormones: Physiology, Biochemistry and Molecular
Biology. Ed. 2. Trade Cloth. Springer. New York, NY. 1995.
836p. ISBN:0-7923-2984-8, ISBN13: 978-0-7923-2984-8.
Dewey:581.19/27. LCCN:94-045154.

         Audience: **u,f.**

Dennis, David   **QK881**
Plant Metabolism. Ed. 2. Trade Paper. Prentice Hall PTR. Upper
Saddle River, NJ. 1997. 648p. ISBN:0-582-25906-1, ISBN13:
978-0-582-25906-5. Dewey:572.4/2.

         Audience: **u,f.**

Dennis, David T.   **QK45.2**
Plant Metabolism. Cloth Text. Addison-Wesley Longman, Inc.
Boston, MA. 1996. 530p. ISBN:0-582-46052-2, ISBN13:
978-0-582-46052-2. Dewey:581.

         Audience: **u,f.**

Devi, Prathibha   **QK728**
Principles and Methods in Plant Molecular Biology,
Biochemistry and Genetics. Agrobios, Jodhpur. 2000.
ISBN:81-7754-051-3, ISBN13: 978-81-7754-051-2.

         Audience: **l,u,f.**

Dey, P. M. & Harborne,   **QK861**
  J. B.
Plant Biochemistry. Trade Paper. Elsevier Science & Technology
Books. Saint Louis, MO. 1999. 554p. ISBN:0-12-799214-6,
ISBN13: 978-0-12-799214-3. Dewey:572.2.

         Audience: **u,f.**

Gausman, Harold W.   **SB128.P48 1991**
Plant Biochemical Regulators, Vol. 21. Paper over Boards.
Marcel Dekker Inc. New York, NY. 1991. 368p. Books in Soils,
Plants and the Environment, Vol. 21 ISBN:0-8247-8536-3,
ISBN13: 978-0-8247-8536-9. Dewey:631.8. LCCN:91-020253.
         Audience: **u,f.**

Jones, Hamlyn G. (Editor),   **SB112.5 .P54 1989**
  et al.
Plants under Stress. T. J. Flowers & M. B. Jones (Editors).
Trade Cloth. Cambridge University Press. New York, NY. 1989.
272p. Society for Experimental Biology Seminar Ser., No. 39
ISBN:0-521-34423-9, ISBN13: 978-0-521-34423-4. Dewey:632.
LCCN:88-036689.
         Audience: **u,f.**

Lang, G. A. (Editor)   **QK761.P58 1996**
Plant Dormancy: Physiology, Biochemistry and Molecular
Biology. Cloth Text. Oxford University Press, Inc. New York,
NY. 1997. 408p. A CAB International Publication
ISBN:0-85198-978-0, ISBN13: 978-0-85198-978-5.
Dewey:571.7/82. LCCN:97-142321.
         Audience: **u,f.** *Choice, 1997.*

Lea, Peter J. & Leegood, R.   **QK861.P52 1993**
  C. (Editors)
Plant Biochemistry and Molecular Biology. Trade Paper. John
Wiley & Sons, Inc. Hoboken, NJ. 1993. 324p.
ISBN:0-471-93313-9, ISBN13: 978-0-471-93313-7.
Dewey:572/.2. LCCN:92-022064.

         Audience: **u,f.**

Linder, M. C. (Editor)   **QP141.N86**
Nutritional Biochemistry and Metabolism, with Clinical
Applications. Ed. 2. Paper Text. Appleton & Lange. Stamford,
CT. 1991. 310p. ISBN:0-8385-7084-4, ISBN13:
978-0-8385-7084-5. Dewey:612/.3.

         Audience: **u,f.**

Prade, Rolf   QK602.G465 2003
Genomics of Plants and Fungi, Vol. 18. Paper over Boards.
Marcel Dekker Inc. New York, NY. 2003. 440p. Mycology Ser.,
18 ISBN:0-8247-4125-0, ISBN13: 978-0-8247-4125-9.
Dewey:581.3/5. LCCN:2004-296915.

Audience: **u,f.**

Sharma, A. K. & Sharma,   QK981
  A. (Editors)
Plant Genome:Cryptogams: Lower Groups. Book, Other.
Science Publishers. Enfield, NH. 2004. 274p.
ISBN:1-57808-298-6, ISBN13: 978-1-57808-298-8.
Dewey:581.3. LCCN:2003-042378.

Audience: **u,f.**

Sharma, Arun Kumar &   QK981.P53 2003
  Sharma, Archana (Editors)
Plant Genome:Phanerogams: Biodiversity and Evolution. Trade
Cloth. Science Publishers. Enfield, NH. 2003. c.370p.
ISBN:1-57808-238-2, ISBN13: 978-1-57808-238-4.
Dewey:581.3. LCCN:2003-042378.

Audience: **u,f.**

Wink, Michael (Editor)   QK881
Biochemistry of Plant Secondary Metabolism. Sheffield, England
: Sheffield Academic Press ; CRC Press: Boca Raton, FL. 1999.
ISBN:0-8493-4085-3, ISBN13: 978-0-8493-4085-7.

Audience: **u.**

Biochemistry and Biophysics > Biophysics

Nölting, Bengt   QH505.N65 2003
Methods in Modern Biophysics. Ed. 2. Trade Paper. Springer.
New York, NY. 2005. XVI, 257p. ISBN:3-540-27703-X,
ISBN13: 978-3-540-27703-3. Dewey:571.4.
LCCN:2003-278615.

Audience: **l,u.**

Sneppen, Kim & Zocchi,   QH506
  Giovanni
Physics in Molecular Biology. Cloth Text. Cambridge University
Press. New York, NY. 2005. 320p. ISBN:0-521-84419-3,
ISBN13: 978-0-521-84419-2. Dewey:572.8015118.
LCCN:2006-272422.

Audience: **u,f.** *Choice, 2006.*

Tuszynski, Jack A.   QH506.T877 2003
Introduction to Molecular Biophysics. CRC Press. 2003.
ISBN:0-8493-0039-8, ISBN13: 978-0-8493-0039-4.

Audience: **u,f.**

Yeargers, Edward K.   QH505
Basic Biophysics for Biology. CRC Press: Boca Raton. 1992.
ISBN:0-8493-4424-7, ISBN13: 978-0-8493-4424-4.

Audience: **u,f.**

Cellular and Molecular Biology, Genetics

                                            QH431
☐ The Jackson Laboratory.
http://www.jax.org/

Audience: **l,u,f.**

Cellular and Molecular Biology, Genetics > Molecular Biology, General

                                            QH506
☐ Harvard University Department of Molecular and Cellular
Biology - Biology Links.
http://www.mcb.harvard.edu/BioLinks.html

Audience: **l,u,f.**

                                            QH506
☐ Molecular Biology Gateway: The Gateway to Web Resources
for Molecular Biology, Genomics, PCR, Protocols,
Microbiology, and Biochemistry.
http://www.horizonpress.com/gateway/
Horizon Scientific Press.

Audience: **g,l.**

Alon, Uri   QH324.2.A46 2006
Introduction to Systems Biology and the Design Principles of
Biological Circuits. CRC Press. 2006. ISBN:1-58488-642-0,
ISBN13: 978-1-58488-642-6.

Audience: **u,f.**

Anderson, John W. &   QK725
  Beardall, John
Molecular Activities of Plant Cells. Box or Slipcased. Blackwell
Publishing, Inc. Malden, MA. 384p. ISBN:0-632-02457-7,
ISBN13: 978-0-632-02457-5. Dewey:581.876.

Audience: **u,f.**

Ausubel, Frederick M.   QH506.S54 2002
  (Editor), et al.
Short Protocols in Molecular Biology. Ed. 5. Roger Brent,
Robert E. Kingston, David D. Moore, J. G. Seidman, John A.
Smith & Kevin Struhl (Editors). Trade Paper. John Wiley &
Sons, Inc. Hoboken, NJ. 2002. 1512p. ISBN:0-471-25092-9,
ISBN13: 978-0-471-25092-0. Dewey:572.8/028.
LCCN:2002-027224.

Audience: **u,f.**

Blackwell Science Inc.,   QH506.R35 2001
  Publishing Staff, et al.
Introduction to Molecular Biology. Deanna Raineri & X. Raineri
(Authors). Trade Paper. Blackwell Publishing, Inc. Malden, MA.
2000. 200p. Eleventh Hour Ser. ISBN:0-632-04379-2, ISBN13:
978-0-632-04379-8. Dewey:572.8. LCCN:00-037954.

Audience: **u,f.**

Borlak, Jürgen (Editor)   RB155
Handbook of Toxicogenomics: Strategies and Applications.
Trade Cloth. John Wiley & Sons, Inc. Hoboken, NJ. 2005. 705p.
ISBN:3-527-30342-1, ISBN13: 978-3-527-30342-7.
Dewey:616.042.

Audience: **u,f.**

Bradley, John R., et al.   QH506
Lecture Notes on Molecular Medicine. Ed. 2. David R. Johnson
& David Rubenstein (Authors). Trade Paper. Blackwell
Publishing, Inc. Malden, MA. 2001. 152p. Lecture Notes
ISBN:0-632-05839-0, ISBN13: 978-0-632-05839-6.
Dewey:616/.042. LCCN:2001-025377.

Audience: **u,f.**

Burczynski, Michael E.   RA1224.3
(Editor)
An Introduction to Toxicogenomics. CRC Press: Boca Raton,
FL. 2003. ISBN:0-8493-1334-1, ISBN13: 978-0-8493-1334-9.
Audience: **u,f.**

Cabibbo, A. & Citterich, M.   QH324.2.I567 2002
Helmer
The Internet for Cell and Molecular Biologists. Trade Cloth.
Horizon Scientific Press. Norwich, 2002. 328p.
ISBN:1-898486-32-8, ISBN13: 978-1-898486-32-9.
Dewey:025.06/5716. LCCN:2002-437246.
Audience: **l,u,f.**

Cech, Thomas R. & Pines,   QH447
Maya
The Genes We Share with Yeast, Flies, Worms, and Mice: New
Clues to Human Health and Disease. Trade Paper. DIANE
Publishing Company. Collingdale, PA. 2001. 100p.
ISBN:0-7567-2019-2, ISBN13: 978-0-7567-2019-3.
Dewey:572.86.
Audience: **l,u,f.**

Chadarevian, Soraya de   N/A
Designs for Life: Molecular Biology after World War II. Trade
Cloth. Cambridge University Press. New York, NY. 2002. 444p.
ISBN:0-521-57078-6, ISBN13: 978-0-521-57078-7.
Dewey:572.8/0941/0904. LCCN:2001-025916.
Audience: **u,f.** *Choice, 2003.*

Chitty, Mary (Compiled and
Edited by)
☐ Cambridge Healthtech Institute BioPharmaceutical Glossary,
Taxonomies and Guide to 21st Century Therapeutics,
Technologies and Trends.
http://genomicglossaries.com/
Cambridge Healthtech Institute.
Audience: **g,l.**

Ciobanu, Gabriel (Editor)   QH506
Modelling in Molecular Biology. Trade Cloth. Springer. New
York, NY. 2004. X, 304p. Natural Computing Ser.
ISBN:3-540-40799-5, ISBN13: 978-3-540-40799-7.
Dewey:572.8/01/13. LCCN:2004-106401.
Audience: **u,f.**

Clark, David P.   QH506.C533 2005
Molecular Biology: Understanding the Genetic Revolution.
Cloth Text. Elsevier Science & Technology Books. Saint Louis,
MO. 2005. 816p. ISBN:0-12-175551-7, ISBN13:
978-0-12-175551-5. Dewey:572.8. LCCN:2004-017736.
Audience: **l,u,f.**

Crotty, Shane   QH506 .C76 2001
Ahead of the Curve: David Baltimore's Life in Science. Trade
Cloth. University of California Press. Berkeley, CA. 2001. 270p.
ISBN:0-520-22557-0, ISBN13: 978-0-520-22557-2.
Dewey:572.8/092 B. LCCN:00-051170.
Audience: **l,u,f.** *Choice, 2001.*

Cseke, Leland J.; Kaufman,   QH506.H36 2003
Peter B.
Handbook of Molecular and Cellular Methods in Biology and
Medicine. CRC Press. 2004. ISBN:0-8493-0815-1, ISBN13:
978-0-8493-0815-4.
Audience: **u,f.**

Daniell, Henry & Chase,   QK725.M745 2004
Christine D. (Editors)
Molecular Biology and Biotechnology of Plant Organelles:
Chloroplasts and Mitochondria. Trade Cloth. Springer. New
York, NY. 2005. XXVI, 659p. ISBN:1-4020-2713-3, ISBN13:
978-1-4020-2713-0. Dewey:581.0724.
Audience: **u,f.** *Choice, 2005.*

de Duve, Christian   QH325.D418 2005
Singularities: Landmarks on the Pathways of Life. Cloth Text.
Cambridge University Press. New York, NY. 2005. 274p.
ISBN:0-521-84195-X, ISBN13: 978-0-521-84195-5.
Dewey:576.8/3. LCCN:2004-054761.
Audience: **u,f.** *Choice, 2006.*

DeSalle, Rob (Editor), et al.   QH83.M67 2001
Molecular Systematics and Evolution: Theory and Practice.
Gonzalo Giribet & Ward Wheeler (Editors). Trade Cloth.
Birkhauser Boston. Cambridge, MA. 2002. IX, 309p. EXS Ser.,
Vol. 92: ISBN:3-7643-6544-7, ISBN13: 978-3-7643-6544-8.
Dewey:572.8/38. LCCN:2001-037878.
Audience: **u,f.**

Dickerson, Richard Earl   QH506.D53 2005
Present at the Flood: How Structural Molecular Biology Came
About. Trade Paper. Sinauer Associates, Inc. Sunderland, MA.
2005. 250p. ISBN:0-87893-168-6, ISBN13: 978-0-87893-168-2.
Dewey:572.8/09/04. LCCN:2005-008575.
Audience: **l,u,f.**

Dopazo, Joaquin & Azuaje,   QH447
Francisco (Editors)
Data Analysis and Visualization in Genomics and Proteomics.
Trade Cloth. John Wiley & Sons, Inc. Hoboken, NJ. 2005. 284p.
ISBN:0-470-09439-7, ISBN13: 978-0-470-09439-6.
Dewey:572.8/6. LCCN:2005-006838.
Audience: **u,f.**

Echols, Harrison &   QH506.E246 2001
Grossman, Carol
Operators and Promoters: The Story of Molecular Biology and
Its Creators. Trade Cloth. University of California Press.
Berkeley, CA. 2001. 488p. ISBN:0-520-21331-9, ISBN13:
978-0-520-21331-9. Dewey:572.8/09. LCCN:00-061523.
Audience: **l,u,f.** *Choice, 2001.*

Endo, I. (Editor), et al.   QH506.M636 2002
Molecular Anatomy of Cellular Systems. Ed. 10. T. Kudo, H.
Kudo, T. Shibata, I. Yamaguchi & H. Osada (Editors). Trade
Cloth. Elsevier Science & Technology Books. Saint Louis, MO.
2002. 240p. Progress in Biotechnology Ser., Vol. 22
ISBN:0-444-50739-6, ISBN13: 978-0-444-50739-6.
Dewey:572.8. LCCN:2002-066823.
Audience: **u,f.**

Epstein, Richard J.   QH506.E66 2001
Human Molecular Biology: An Introduction to the Molecular
Basis of Health and Disease. Cloth Text. Cambridge University
Press. New York, NY. 2002. 656p. ISBN:0-521-64285-X,
ISBN13: 978-0-521-64285-9. Dewey:612. LCCN:2001-035238.
Audience: **u,f.**

Fleissner, Erwin   QH506.F545 2004
Vital Harmonies: Molecular Biology and Our Shared Humanity.
Trade Cloth. Edinburgh University Press. Edinburgh, 2004.
176p. ISBN:0-231-13112-7, ISBN13: 978-0-231-13112-4.
Dewey:572.8. LCCN:2004-041313.
Audience: **l,u,f.** *Choice, 2005.*

Friedberg, Errol   **QH506.F746 2004**
The Writing Life of James D. Watson: Professor, Promoter, Provocateur. Trade Cloth. Cold Spring Harbor Laboratory Press. Woodbury, NY. 2004. 160p. ISBN:0-87969-700-8, ISBN13: 978-0-87969-700-6. Dewey:572.8. LCCN:2004-015640.
Audience: **l,u,f.** *Choice, 2005.*

Gerstein, Alan S.   **QH506.M6629 2001**
Molecular Biology Problem Solver: A Laboratory Guide. Trade Paper. John Wiley & Sons, Inc. Hoboken, NJ. 2001. 596p. ISBN:0-471-37972-7, ISBN13: 978-0-471-37972-0. Dewey:572.8/078. LCCN:2001-023491.
Audience: **u,f.**

Gheorghe, Marian   **QH506.M66434 2005**
Molecular Computation Models: Unconventional Approaches. Trade Cloth. Idea Group Publishing. Hershey, PA. 2005. 304p. ISBN:1-59140-333-2, ISBN13: 978-1-59140-333-3. Dewey:570/.1/1. LCCN:2004-023592.
Audience: **u,f.**

Giovannetti, J.   **QH441.2.R365 2002**
Genomes and Databases on the Internet: A Practical Guide to Functions and Applications. Trade Cloth. Horizon Scientific Press. Norwich, 2001. 224p. ISBN:1-898486-31-X, ISBN13: 978-1-898486-31-2. Dewey:025/.06/5765. LCCN:2002-392506.
Audience: **u,f.** *Choice, 2002.*

Hardiman, Gary   **QP624.5.D726M515**
Microarrays Methods and Applications. Trade Paper, Perfect. DNA Press. Eagleville, PA. 2003. 384p. The Nuts and Bolts Ser. ISBN:0-9664027-6-6, ISBN13: 978-0-9664027-6-6. Dewey:572.8/636. LCCN:2002-156708.
Audience: **u,f.**

Harrigan, George G. &   **QP171.M3775 2003**
  Goodacre, Royston (Editors)
Metabolic Profiling: Its Role in Biomarker Discovery and Gene Function Analysis. Trade Cloth. Springer. New York, NY. 2003. 352p. ISBN:1-4020-7370-4, ISBN13: 978-1-4020-7370-0. Dewey:612.3/9. LCCN:2002-192457.
Audience: **u,f.**

Hausmann, Rudolf   **QH506.H37513 2003**
To Grasp the Essence of Life: A History of Molecular Biology. Trade Cloth. Springer. New York, NY. 2003. 322p. ISBN:1-4020-1092-3, ISBN13: 978-1-4020-1092-7. Dewey:572.8. LCCN:2002-038499.
Audience: **l,u,f.** *Choice, 2003.*

Hillis, David M.   **QH83.M665 1996**
  (Editor), et al.
Molecular Systematics. Ed. 2. Craig Moritz & Barbara K. Mable (Editors). Trade Cloth. Sinauer Associates, Inc. Sunderland, MA. 1996. 655p. ISBN:0-87893-282-8, ISBN13: 978-0-87893-282-5. Dewey:574.8/8. LCCN:95-041159.
Audience: **u,f.**

Holmes, David, et al.   **QH506.P73 2003**
Practical Skills in Biomolecular Sciences. Ed. 2. Allan Jones, Rob Reed & Jonathan Weyers (Authors). Trade Paper. Prentice Hall PTR. Upper Saddle River, NJ. 2003. 552p. ISBN:0-13-045142-8, ISBN13: 978-0-13-045142-2. Dewey:572.8. LCCN:2002-035564.
Audience: **l,u,f.**

Hunter, Graeme K.   **QP514.2.H86 2002**
Vital Forces: The Discovery of the Molecular Basis of Life. Trade Cloth. Elsevier Science & Technology Books. Saint Louis, MO. 2000. 364p. ISBN:0-12-361810-X, ISBN13: 978-0-12-361810-8. Dewey:572/.09. LCCN:99-067772.
Audience: **l,u.**

Istrail, Sorin, et al.   **QH506**
Computational Molecular Biology. Pavel Pevzner & Ron Shamir (Authors). Trade Cloth. Elsevier Science & Technology Books. Saint Louis, MO. 2003. 184p. Topics in Discrete Mathematics Ser., Vol. 12 ISBN:0-444-51384-1, ISBN13: 978-0-444-51384-7. Dewey:572.8. LCCN:2003-051360.
Audience: **u,f.**

Jackson, S. P. (Editor), et al.   **QH607**
Extracellular Regulators of Differentiation. K. E. Chapman & D. Wilkinson (Editors). Cloth Text. Portland Press, Ltd. London, 1996. 192p. Biochemical Society Symposium Ser., Vol. 62 ISBN:1-85578-070-4, ISBN13: 978-1-85578-070-5. Dewey:574.8761.
Audience: **u,f.**

Jiang, Tao (Editor), et al.   **QH506.C88 2002**
Current Topics in Computational Molecular Biology. Ying Xu & Michael Zhang (Editors). Trade Cloth. MIT Press. Cambridge, MA. 2002. 556p. Computational Molecular Biology Ser. ISBN:0-262-10092-4, ISBN13: 978-0-262-10092-2. Dewey:572.8/01/51. LCCN:2001-044430.
Audience: **u,f.**

Kauffman, Stuart A.   **QH325**
Investigations. Trade Paper. Oxford University Press, Inc. New York, NY. 2002. 300p. ISBN:0-19-512105-8, ISBN13: 978-0-19-512105-6. Dewey:576.8/8/01.
Audience: **u,f.**

Kitano, Hiroaki (Editor)   **QH313.F66 2002**
Foundations of Systems Biology. Trade Cloth. MIT Press. Cambridge, MA. 2001. 320p. ISBN:0-262-11266-3, ISBN13: 978-0-262-11266-6. Dewey:573. LCCN:2001-042807.
Audience: **l,u.**

Kohane, Isaac S., et al.   **QP624.5.D726K686**
Microarrays for an Integrative Genomics. Alvin Kho & Atul J. Butte (Authors). Trade Cloth. MIT Press. Cambridge, MA. 2002. 326p. Computational Molecular Biology Ser. ISBN:0-262-11271-X, ISBN13: 978-0-262-11271-0. Dewey:572.8/6. LCCN:2002-022663.
Audience: **u,f.**

Kolchanov, Nikolay &   **QH447**
  Hofestaedt, Ralf (Editors)
Bioinformatics of Genome Regulation and Structure. Trade Cloth. Springer. New York, NY. 2004. 396p. ISBN:1-4020-7735-1, ISBN13: 978-1-4020-7735-7. Dewey:572.8/6. LCCN:2003-070159.
Audience: **u,f.**

Koonin, Eugene V. (Volume   **QH447.P69 2006**
  Editor), et al.
Power Laws, Scale-Free Networks and Genome Biology. Georgy Karev & Yuri Wolf (Volume Editors). Trade Cloth. Springer. New York, NY. 2006. XIX, 257p. Molecular Biology Intelligence Unit Ser. ISBN:0-387-25883-3, ISBN13: 978-0-387-25883-6. Dewey:572.8/6. LCCN:2006-001285.
Audience: **u,f.**

Kumar, A. & Srivastava,   QH506.K83 2001
  A. K.
Advanced Topics in Molecular Biology. Cloth Text. Taylor &
Francis Group. Philadelphia, PA. 2001. 160p.
ISBN:1-898486-28-X, ISBN13: 978-1-898486-28-2.
Dewey:572.8.

                                    Audience: **u,f.**

Lea, Peter J. & Leegood, R.   QK861.P52 1993
  C. (Editors)
Plant Biochemistry and Molecular Biology. Trade Paper. John
Wiley & Sons, Inc. Hoboken, NJ. 1993. 324p.
ISBN:0-471-93313-9, ISBN13: 978-0-471-93313-7.
Dewey:572/.2. LCCN:92-022064.

                                    Audience: **u,f.**

Lesk, Arthur M. (Editor)   QH506
Database Annotation in Molecular Biology: Principles and
Practice. Trade Cloth. John Wiley & Sons, Inc. Hoboken, NJ.
2005. 266p. ISBN:0-470-85681-5, ISBN13: 978-0-470-85681-9.
Dewey:572.8. LCCN:2004-024635.

                                    Audience: **u,f.**

Leuba, S. H. & Zlatanova,   QH506.B5524 2001
  J. (Editors)
Biology at the Single Molecule Level. Trade Cloth. Elsevier
Science & Technology Books. Saint Louis, MO. 2001. 262p.
ISBN:0-08-044031-2, ISBN13: 978-0-08-044031-6.
Dewey:572.8. LCCN:2001-058092.

                                    Audience: **u,f.**

Lewontin, Richard C.   QH506
The Triple Helix: Gene, Organism, and Environment. Trade
Paper. Harvard University Press. Cambridge, MA. 2002. 144p.
ISBN:0-674-00677-1, ISBN13: 978-0-674-00677-5.
Dewey:572.8/01.

                        Audience: **l,u,f.** *Choice, 2000.*

Malacinski, George M.   QH506.M368 2002
Essentials of Molecular Biology. Ed. 4. Trade Cloth. Jones &
Bartlett Publishers, Inc. Sudbury, MA. 2003. 545p. Molecular
Biology Ser. ISBN:0-7637-2133-6, ISBN13: 978-0-7637-2133-6.
Dewey:572.8. LCCN:2002-072756.

                                    Audience: **u,f.**

McLennan, A.G., et al.   QH506
Instant Notes in Molecular Biology. Ed. 3. M.R.H. White & P.
Turner (Authors). UK-B Format Paperback. Taylor & Francis
Group. Philadelphia, PA. 2005. 360p. Instant Notes Ser.
ISBN:0-415-35167-7, ISBN13: 978-0-415-35167-6.
Dewey:572.8. LCCN:2005-027956.

                                    Audience: **u,f.**

Morange, Michel   QH506
A History of Molecular Biology. Trade Paper. Harvard
University Press. Cambridge, MA. 2000. 348p.
ISBN:0-674-00169-9, ISBN13: 978-0-674-00169-5.
Dewey:572.8/09.

                        Audience: **u,f.** *Choice, 1999.*

Opresko, Lee   QH313.A386 2004
Advances in Systems Biology. Julie M. Gephart & Michaela B.
Mann (Editors). Trade Cloth. Springer. New York, NY. 2004.
116p. Advances in Experimental Medicine and Biology Ser.,
Vol. 547 ISBN:0-306-48314-9, ISBN13: 978-0-306-48314-1.
Dewey:571. LCCN:2003-068653.

                                    Audience: **u,f.**

Palsson, Bernhard O.   QH324.2.P35 2006
Systems Biology: Properties of Reconstructed Networks. Cloth
Text. Cambridge University Press. New York, NY. 2006. 334p.
ISBN:0-521-85903-4, ISBN13: 978-0-521-85903-5.
Dewey:572.80285. LCCN:2005-035008.

                                    Audience: **u,f.**

Pevzner, Pavel A.   QH506.P47 2000
Computational Molecular Biology: An Algorithmic Approach.
Trade Cloth. MIT Press. Cambridge, MA. 2000. 332p.
Computational Molecular Biology Ser. ISBN:0-262-16197-4,
ISBN13: 978-0-262-16197-8. Dewey:572.8. LCCN:00-032461.

                                    Audience: **u,f.**

Priami, Corrado   QH506.T73 2005
  (Contribution by)
Transactions on Computational Systems Biology I. Mixed
Media. Springer. New York, NY. 2005. IX, 111p. Lecture Notes
in Computer Science / Lecture Notes in Bioinformatics Ser.
ISBN:3-540-25422-6, ISBN13: 978-3-540-25422-5.
Dewey:572.80285. LCCN:2005-922555.

                                    Audience: **u,f.**

Rapley, Ralph & Harbron,   QH506
  Stuart (Editors)
Molecular Analysis and Genome Discovery. Trade Cloth. John
Wiley & Sons, Inc. Hoboken, NJ. 2004. 388p.
ISBN:0-471-49847-5, ISBN13: 978-0-471-49847-6.
Dewey:615/.7. LCCN:2004-001166.

                                    Audience: **u.**

Razin, Shmuel &   QR201.M97M635 2002
  Herrmann, Richard (Editors)
Molecular Biology and Pathogenicity of Mycoplasmas. Trade
Cloth. Springer. New York, NY. 2002. 588p.
ISBN:0-306-47287-2, ISBN13: 978-0-306-47287-9.
Dewey:616/.01428. LCCN:2002-072761.

                                    Audience: **u,f.**

Ream, Walt & Field,   QH506
  Katharine G.
Molecular Biology Techniques: An Intensive Laboratory Course.
Paper Text. Elsevier Science & Technology Books. Saint Louis,
MO. 1998. 234p. ISBN:0-12-583990-1, ISBN13:
978-0-12-583990-7. Dewey:572.8.

                                    Audience: **u,f.**

Rigoutsos, Isidore &   QH324.2.S97 2006
  Stephanopoulos, Gregory (Editors)
Systems Biology: Volume 1: Genomics. Trade Cloth. Oxford
University Press, Inc. New York, NY. 2006. 416p. Series in
Systems Biology ISBN:0-19-530081-5, ISBN13:
978-0-19-530081-9. Dewey:570. LCCN:2005-031826.

                                    Audience: **u,f.**

Ross, Michael H.   QM551.R67 2005
Ross, Histology a Text and Atlas: With Correlated Cell and
Molecular Biology. Ed. 5. Trade Paper. Lippincott Williams &
Wilkins. Philadelphia, PA. 2005. 906p. ISBN:0-7817-5056-3,
ISBN13: 978-0-7817-5056-1. Dewey:611/.018.
LCCN:2005-050445.

                                    Audience: **u,f.**

Salinas (Editor)　　　　QK495.C9A735 2005
Arabidopsis Protocols. Ed. 2. Trade Cloth. Humana Press.
Totowa, NJ. 2005. 525p. Methods in Molecular Biology Ser.
ISBN:1-58829-395-5, ISBN13: 978-1-58829-395-4.
Dewey:583/.64. LCCN:2005-016343.
　　　　　　　　　　　　　　Audience: **u,f.**

Sarkar, Sahotra　　　　QH506.S28 2004
Molecular Models of Life: Philosophical Papers on Molecular
Biology. Trade Cloth. MIT Press. Cambridge, MA. 2005. 352p.
Life and Mind Ser. ISBN:0-262-19512-7, ISBN13:
978-0-262-19512-6. Dewey:572.8/01. LCCN:2004-042614.
　　　　　　　　　　　　　　Audience: **u,f.**

Shreeve, James　　　　QH431.S5577 2004
The Genome War: How Craig Venter Tried to Capture the Code
of Life and Save the World. Trade Cloth. Alfred A. Knopf Inc.
New York, NY. 2004. 416p. ISBN:0-375-40629-8, ISBN13:
978-0-375-40629-4. Dewey:611/.01816. LCCN:2003-047580.
　　　　　　　　　　　　Audience: **u,f.** *Choice, 2004.*

Sneppen, Kim & Zocchi,　　　　QH506
　Giovanni
Physics in Molecular Biology. Cloth Text. Cambridge University
Press. New York, NY. 2005. 320p. ISBN:0-521-84419-3,
ISBN13: 978-0-521-84419-2. Dewey:572.8015118.
LCCN:2006-272422.
　　　　　　　　　　　　Audience: **u,f.** *Choice, 2006.*

Stahl, Franklin W. &　　　　QH506.W425 2000
　Hershey, A. D.
We Can Sleep Later: Alfred D. Hershey and the Origins of
Molecular Biology. Trade Cloth. Cold Spring Harbor Laboratory
Press. Woodbury, NY. 2000. xii, 359p. ISBN:0-87969-567-6,
ISBN13: 978-0-87969-567-5. Dewey:572.8. LCCN:99-086195.
　　　　　　　　　　　　　　Audience: **u,f.**

Stansfield, William D., et al.　　　　QH506
Schaum's Easy Outline Molecular and Cell Biology. Jaime S.
Colome & Raul J. Cano (Authors). Paper Text. McGraw-Hill
Companies, The. New York, NY. 2003. 144p. Schaum's Outline
Ser. ISBN:0-07-139881-3, ISBN13: 978-0-07-139881-7.
Dewey:572.8. LCCN:2003-272771.
　　　　　　　　　　　　　　Audience: **l,u,f.**

Stephenson, Frank H.　　　　QH323.5
Calculations for Molecular Biology and Biotechnology: A Guide
to Mathematics in the Laboratory. Trade Paper. Elsevier Science
& Technology Books. Saint Louis, MO. 2003. 302p.
ISBN:0-12-665751-3, ISBN13: 978-0-12-665751-7.
Dewey:572.8/01/51. LCCN:2003-106049.
　　　　　　　　　　　　　　Audience: **u,f.**

Stillman, Bruce (Editor)　　　　QH603.R5
The Ribosome. Trade Cloth. Cold Spring Harbor Laboratory
Press. Woodbury, NY. 2002. 620p. Symposia on Quantitative
Biology Ser., LXVI ISBN:0-87969-619-2, ISBN13:
978-0-87969-619-1. Dewey:571.658.
　　　　　　　　　　　　　　Audience: **u,f.**

Surzycki, Stefan　　　　QH506.S89 2000
Basic Techniques in Molecular Biology. Trade Paper. Springer.
New York, NY. 2000. VIII, 434p. Lab Manuals Ser.
ISBN:3-540-66678-8, ISBN13: 978-3-540-66678-3.
Dewey:572.8. LCCN:99-055150.
　　　　　　　　　　　　　　Audience: **u,f.**

Surzycki, Stefan　　　　QH506.S893 2002
Human Molecular Biology. Trade Paper. Blackwell Publishing,
Inc. Malden, MA. 2003. 248p. ISBN:0-632-04676-7, ISBN13:
978-0-632-04676-8. Dewey:611/.01816. LCCN:2002-071215.
　　　　　　　　　　　　　　Audience: **u,f.**

Tavani, Herman T.　　　　QH441.2.T38 2006
Ethics, Computing, and Genomics. Trade Paper. Jones & Bartlett
Publishers, Inc. Sudbury, MA. 2005. 356p.
ISBN:0-7637-3620-1, ISBN13: 978-0-7637-3620-0.
Dewey:174/.957. LCCN:2005-007396.
　　　　　　　　　　　　　　Audience: **u,f.**

Thacker, Eugene　　　　QH506.T47 2004
Biomedia. Trade Cloth. University of Minnesota Press.
Minneapolis, MN. 2004. 392p. Electronic Mediations Ser., Vol.
11 ISBN:0-8166-4352-0, ISBN13: 978-0-8166-4352-3.
Dewey:303.48/3. LCCN:2003-017201.
　　　　　　　　　　　　　　Audience: **u,f.**

Thiel, Teresa, et al.　　　　QH506.T48 2002
Biotechnology: DNA to Protein--A Laboratory Project in
Molecular Biology. Shirley T. Bissen & Eilene M. Lyons
(Authors). Spiral. McGraw-Hill Higher Education. Burr Ridge,
IL. 2001. 192p. ISBN:0-07-241664-5, ISBN13:
978-0-07-241664-0. Dewey:572.8. LCCN:2001-030676.
　　　　　　　　　　　　　　Audience: **u,f.**

Trent, R. J.　　　　RB155.T728 2005
Molecular Medicine. Ed. 3. Cloth Text. Elsevier Science &
Technology Books. Saint Louis, MO. 2005. 320p.
ISBN:0-12-699057-3, ISBN13: 978-0-12-699057-7.
Dewey:616/.042. LCCN:2004-028087.
　　　　　　　　　　　　　　Audience: **u,f.**

Warshawsky, David (Editor)　　　　RC268.6
Molecular Carcinogenesis and the Molecular Biology of Human
Cancer. Landolph, Joseph R. (Editor). CRC. Taylor and Francis:
Boca Raton. 2005. ISBN:0-8493-1167-5, ISBN13:
978-0-8493-1167-3.
　　　　　　　　　　　　　　Audience: **u,f.**

Weaver, Robert Franklin　　　　QH506.W43 2004
Molecular Biology. Ed. 3. Cloth Text. McGraw-Hill Higher
Education. Burr Ridge, IL. 2004. 912p. ISBN:0-07-284611-9,
ISBN13: 978-0-07-284611-9. Dewey:572.8.
LCCN:2003-026882.
　　　　　　　　　　　　　　Audience: **u,f.**

Wood, E. J., et al.　　　　QD415
Life Chemistry and Molecular Biology: An Introduction Text. C.
A. Smith & W. R. Pickering (Authors). Paper Text. Portland
Press, Ltd. London, 1996. 224p. ISBN:1-85578-064-X, ISBN13:
978-1-85578-064-4. Dewey:572.
　　　　　　　　　　　　　　Audience: **l,u.**

Wood, Edward J. et al　　　　QH345
Life Chemistry and Molecular Biology. Smith, Christopher &
Pickering, W. R. (W. Roy) (Authors). Portland Press: London.
1997. ISBN:1-85578-064-X, ISBN13: 978-1-85578-064-4.
　　　　　　　　　　　　　　Audience: **l,u.**

Wu, Tai Te (Editor)　　　　QH506.W8 2001
Analytical Molecular Biology. Trade Cloth. Springer. New York,
NY. 2001. 276p. ISBN:0-7923-7447-9, ISBN13:
978-0-7923-7447-3. Dewey:572.8/01/51. LCCN:2001-038129.
　　　　　　　　　　　　　　Audience: **u,f.**

Xing, Wan-Li & Cheng, Jing (Editors)   R857.B5B55 2003

Biochips: Technology and Applications. Trade Cloth. Springer. New York, NY. 2003. VII, 134p. Biological and Medical Physics Ser. ISBN:3-540-00423-8, ISBN13: 978-3-540-00423-3. Dewey:610/.28. LCCN:2003-054291.

Audience: **u,f.**

Zhang, Wei & Shmulevich, Ilya (Editors)   QH438.4.M3C65 2002

Computational and Statistical Approaches to Genomics. Trade Cloth. Springer. New York, NY. 2002. 344p. ISBN:1-4020-7023-3, ISBN13: 978-1-4020-7023-5. Dewey:572.8/6/015118. LCCN:2002-023676.

Audience: **u,f.**

Zweiger, Gary   QH431

Transducing the Genome: Information, Anarchy, and Revolution in the Biomedical Sciences. Trade Paper. McGraw-Hill Companies, The. New York, NY. 2002. 288p. ISBN:0-07-138761-7, ISBN13: 978-0-07-138761-3. Dewey:599.93/5.

Audience: **u,f.** *Choice, 2001.*

Cellular and Molecular Biology, Genetics > Genetics (General)

QH465.A1

Biological Responses to DNA Damage. Trade Cloth. Cold Spring Harbor Laboratory Press. Woodbury, NY. 2001. 613p. Symposia on Quantitative Biology Ser., Vol. LXV ISBN:0-87969-605-2, ISBN13: 978-0-87969-605-4. Dewey:572.86.

Audience: **u,f.**

Google Directory: Biology, Genetics. http://google.com/Top/Science/Biology/Genetics/ Google.

Audience: **g,l.**

TP248.2

NCBI: National Center for Biotechnology Information. http://www.ncbi.nih.gov/ National Center for Biotechnology Information, U.S. National Library of Medicine.

Audience: **g,l.**

NCBI: National Center for Biotechnology Information, A Science Primer. http://www.ncbi.nih.gov/About/primer/index.html National Center for Biotechnology Information, U.S. National Library of Medicine.

Audience: **l.**

QH431

OMIN--Online Mendelian Inheritance in Man. http://www.ncbi.nlm.nih.gov/entrez/query.fcgi?db=omim

Audience: **l,u,f.**

Ackerman, Jennifer G.   QH431.A25 2001

Chance in the House of Fate: A Natural History of Heredity. Trade Cloth. Houghton Mifflin Company Trade & Reference

Division. Boston, MA. 2001. 272p. ISBN:0-618-08287-5, ISBN13: 978-0-618-08287-2. Dewey:599.93/5. LCCN:00-054122.

Audience: **u,f.**

Adhya, Sankar & Garges, Susan (Editors)   QP606.R53

RNA Polymerase and Associated Factors, Vol. 370, Pt. C. Trade Cloth. Elsevier Science & Technology Books. Saint Louis, MO. 2003. 789p. ISBN:0-12-182273-7, ISBN13: 978-0-12-182273-6. Dewey:574.873283.

Audience: **u,f.**

Albright, Matthew   RB155

Profits Pending: How Life Patents Represent the Biggest Swindle of the Twenty-First Century. Trade Paper. Common Courage Press. Monroe, ME. 2003. 224p. ISBN:1-56751-230-5, ISBN13: 978-1-56751-230-4. Dewey:616.042.

Audience: **u,f.**

Alcamo, I. Edward   QH442.A42 2000

DNA Technology: The Awesome Skill. Ed. 2. Cloth Text. Elsevier Science & Technology Books. Saint Louis, MO. 2000. 348p. ISBN:0-12-048920-1, ISBN13: 978-0-12-048920-6. Dewey:611/.01816. LCCN:99-068792.

Audience: **u,f.**

Alper, Joseph S. & Geller, Lisa N.   QH438.7.D68 2002

The Double-Edged Helix: Social Implications of Genetics in a Diverse Society. Catherine Ard, Adrienne Asch & Jon Beckwith (Editors). Trade Cloth. Johns Hopkins University Press. Baltimore, MD. 2002. 312p. ISBN:0-8018-6964-1, ISBN13: 978-0-8018-6964-8. Dewey:599.93/5. LCCN:2001-006618.

Audience: **u,f.** *Choice, 2003.*

American Museum of Natural History Staff, et al.   QH437

Welcome to the Genome: A User's Guide to the Genetic Past, Present, and Future. Rob DeSalle & Michael Yudell (Authors). Trade Cloth. John Wiley & Sons, Inc. Hoboken, NJ. 2004. 240p. ISBN:0-471-45331-5, ISBN13: 978-0-471-45331-4. Dewey:611/.01816. LCCN:2004-558824.

Audience: **u,f.** *Choice, 2005.*

Bailey, Jill   QH430.B34 1995

Genetics and Evolution: The Molecules of Inheritance. Trade Cloth. Oxford University Press, Inc. New York, NY. 1995. 160p. The New Encyclopedia of Science Ser. ISBN:0-19-521137-5, ISBN13: 978-0-19-521137-5. Dewey:575.1. LCCN:95-017141.

Audience: **u,f.**

Baldi, Pierre & Hatfield, G. Wesley   QP624.5.D726.B353

DNA Microarrays and Gene Expression: From Experiments to Data Analysis and Modeling. Trade Cloth. Cambridge University Press. New York, NY. 2002. 230p. ISBN:0-521-80022-6, ISBN13: 978-0-521-80022-8. Dewey:572.8/65. LCCN:2001-052862.

Audience: **u,f.**

Ballard, F. J.   QH345.B522 NO.55

Gene Expression Regulation at the RNA and Protein Levels. J. Kay & R. John Mayer (Editors). Cloth Text. Portland Press, Ltd. London, 1989. 203p. Biochemical Society Symposium Ser., Symposia 55 ISBN:0-904498-24-7, ISBN13: 978-0-904498-24-0. Dewey:574.19/2 s. LCCN:90-148591.

Audience: **u,f.**

Formats: Web: ☐ Ebook: 🅴 CD/DVD-ROM: 🥏 BCL3: 𝓑

Barnes, Michael R. & Gray,   QH438.4
  Ian C. (Editors)
Bioinformatics for Geneticists. Trade Cloth. John Wiley & Sons, Inc. Hoboken, NJ. 2003. 422p. Hierarchical Exotoxicology Mini Ser. ISBN:0-470-84393-4, ISBN13: 978-0-470-84393-2. Dewey:576.50285. LCCN:2003-535288.

                   Audience: **u,f.**

Bishop, Jerry E.   RB155.5.B57 1990
Genome. Trade Cloth. Simon & Schuster. New York, NY. 1990. 352p. ISBN:0-671-67094-8, ISBN13: 978-0-671-67094-8. Dewey:616/.042. LCCN:90-009940.

                   Audience: **l,u.**

Blackburn, G. Meredith &   QD433.N83 1990
  Gait, Michael J.
Nucleic Acids in Chemistry and Biology. Cloth Text. Oxford University Press, Inc. New York, NY. 1991. 464p. ISBN:0-19-963120-4, ISBN13: 978-0-19-963120-9. Dewey:547.7/9. LCCN:90-014187.

                   Audience: **u,f.**

Bodmer, Walter   QH445.2.B63 1995
Book of Man. Trade Cloth. Simon & Schuster. New York, NY. 1995. ix, 259p. ISBN:0-684-80102-7, ISBN13: 978-0-684-80102-5. Dewey:573.2/1. LCCN:94-038081.

                   Audience: **l,u.**

Brown, T. A.   QP624
DNA Sequencing. IRL Press at Oxford University Press: Oxford ; New York. 1995. The Basics; Variation: Basics (Oxford, England) ISBN:0-19-963421-1, ISBN13: 978-0-19-963421-7.

                   Audience: **u,f.**

Brown, Terence A. & BIOS   QH447.B76 2002
  Scientific Publishers Staff (Editors)
Genomes. Ed. 2. Trade Cloth. John Wiley & Sons, Inc. Hoboken, NJ. 2002. 520p. ISBN:0-471-25046-5, ISBN13: 978-0-471-25046-3. Dewey:572.8/6. LCCN:2002-003471.

                   Audience: **u,f.**

Buchanan, Allen, et al.   QH431.F8765 2000
From Chance to Choice: Genetics and Justice. Dan Brock, Norman Daniels & Daniel Wikler (Authors). Trade Cloth. Cambridge University Press. New York, NY. 2000. 412p. ISBN:0-521-66001-7, ISBN13: 978-0-521-66001-3. Dewey:174/.25. LCCN:99-024025.

             Audience: **l,u,f.** *Choice, 2000.*

Cain, Joe   QH361.U7 2004
Upgrading Evolution: Documents of the Committee on Common Problems of Genetics, Paleontology, and Systematics. Committee on Common Problems of Genetics, Paleontology, and Systematics Staff (Contribution by). Trade Paper. American Philosophical Society. Canton, MA. 2004. xlii, 160p. Transactions of the American Philosophical Society Ser., Pt. 94 ISBN:0-87169-942-7, ISBN13: 978-0-87169-942-8. Dewey:576.8. LCCN:2004-054784.

                   Audience: **u,f.**

Campbell, Judith L. &   QH467
  Modrich, Paul (Volume Editors)
DNA Repair, Pt. A. Trade Cloth. Elsevier Science & Technology Books. Saint Louis, MO. 2006. 624p. ISBN:0-12-182813-1, ISBN13: 978-0-12-182813-4. Dewey:572.86459.

                   Audience: **u,f.**

Carey, Gregory   QH431.C243 2002
Human Genetics for the Social Sciences, Vol. 4. Cloth Text. SAGE Publications, Inc. Thousand Oaks, CA. 2002. 536p. Advanced Texts in Psychology Ser., Vol. 4 ISBN:0-7619-2345-4, ISBN13: 978-0-7619-2345-9. Dewey:599.93/5. LCCN:2002-005571.

                   Audience: **u,f.**

Carlson, Elof Axel   QH428.C248 2004
Mendel's Legacy: The Origin of Classical Genetics. Trade Cloth. Cold Spring Harbor Laboratory Press. Woodbury, NY. 2004. 400p. ISBN:0-87969-675-3, ISBN13: 978-0-87969-675-7. Dewey:576.5/072/073. LCCN:2003-023295.

             Audience: **u,f.** *Choice, 2004.*

Carmichael, Gordon   QP623.5.S63R634 2005
  (Editor)
RNA Silencing. Trade Cloth. Humana Press. Totowa, NJ. 2005. 450p. Methods in Molecular Biology Ser. ISBN:1-58829-436-6, ISBN13: 978-1-58829-436-4. Dewey:572.8/65. LCCN:2004-023107.

                   Audience: **u,f.**

Carroll, Sean B.   QH453.C37 2005
Endless Forms Most Beautiful: The New Science of Evo Devo and the Making of the Animal Kingdom. Trade Cloth. W. W. Norton & Company, Inc. New York, NY. 2005. 288p. ISBN:0-393-06016-0, ISBN13: 978-0-393-06016-4. Dewey:571.8/5. LCCN:2004-029388.

                   Audience: **u,f.**

Carroll, Sean B., et al.   QH390.C37 2005
From DNA to Diversity: Molecular Genetics and the Evolution of Animal Design. Ed. 2. Jennifer K. Grenier & Scott D. Weatherbee (Authors). Trade Paper. Blackwell Publishing, Inc. Malden, MA. 2004. 272p. ISBN:1-4051-1950-0, ISBN13: 978-1-4051-1950-4. Dewey:572.8/38. LCCN:2003-027991.

             Audience: **u,f.** *Choice, 2002.*

Chambers, Donald A.   Q11.N5 VOL. 758
  (Editor)
DNA: The Double Helix: Perspective and Prospective at Forty Years. Trade Cloth. New York Academy of Sciences. New York, NY. 1995. 300p. Annals Ser., Vol. 758 ISBN:0-89766-905-3, ISBN13: 978-0-89766-905-4. Dewey:500 s. LCCN:95-008848.

                   Audience: **u,f.**

Comfort, Nathaniel C.   QH429.2.M38C66 2001
The Tangled Field: Barbara McClintock's Search for the Patterns of Genetic Control. Trade Cloth. Harvard University Press. Cambridge, MA. 2001. 368p. ISBN:0-674-00456-6, ISBN13: 978-0-674-00456-6. Dewey:576.5/092 B. LCCN:00-069712.

             Audience: **u,f.** *Choice, 2001.*

Conner, Jeffrey K. & Hartl,   QH456
  Daniel L.
A Primer of Ecological Genetics. Trade Cloth. Sinauer Associates, Inc. Sunderland, MA. 2004. 270p. ISBN:0-87893-202-X, ISBN13: 978-0-87893-202-3. Dewey:576.5/8. LCCN:2003-022664.

                   Audience: **u,f.**

Consumer Dummies Staff &   QH430
  Robinson , Tara Rodden
Genetics for Dummies. Trade Paper. John Wiley & Sons, Inc.

Hoboken, NJ. 2005. 384p. ISBN:0-7645-9554-7, ISBN13: 978-0-7645-9554-7. Dewey:576.5. LCCN:2005-924624.

Audience: **l,u,f.**

Cook-Deegan, Robert M.   **QH445.2**
The Gene Wars: Science, Politics and the Human Genome. Trade Paper. W. W. Norton & Company, Inc. New York, NY. 1996. 416p. ISBN:0-393-31399-9, ISBN13: 978-0-393-31399-4. Dewey:573.212.

Audience: **g,l,u.** *Choice, 1994.*

Cooper, Necia (Editor)   **QH431.H837 1994**
The Human Genome Project. Paul Berg (Foreword by). Cloth Text. University Science Books. Sausalito, CA. 1994. 327p. ISBN:0-935702-29-6, ISBN13: 978-0-935702-29-3. Dewey:611/.01816. LCCN:93-085290.

Audience: **g,l,u,f.** *Choice, 1994.*

Cummings, Michael R.   **QH431.C897 2000**
Human Heredity: Principles and Issues. Ed. 5. Trade Cloth. Thomson Wadsworth. Belmont, CA. 1999. xxvi, 488p. Environmental Science Ser. ISBN:0-534-52372-2, ISBN13: 978-0-534-52372-5. Dewey:599.93/5. LCCN:99-037549.

Audience: **l,u,f.**

Czepulkowski, B. H.   **QH431.A535 2001**
 (Editor)
Analyzing Chromosomes. Trade Paper. Taylor & Francis Group. Philadelphia, PA. 2000. 224p. ISBN:1-85996-188-6, ISBN13: 978-1-85996-188-9. Dewey:611.01816. LCCN:2002-510821.

Audience: **u,f.**

Dale, Jeremy W. & Park,   **QH434.D35 2004**
 Simon F.
Molecular Genetics of Bacteria. Ed. 4. Trade Cloth. John Wiley & Sons, Inc. Hoboken, NJ. 2004. 358p. ISBN:0-470-85084-1, ISBN13: 978-0-470-85084-8. Dewey:572.8/293. LCCN:2003-023103.

Audience: **u,f.** *Choice, 1989.*

Dale, Jeremy & Schantz,   **QH442**
 Malcolm von
From Genes to Genomes: Concepts and Applications of DNA Technology. Trade Cloth. John Wiley & Sons, Inc. Hoboken, NJ. 2002. 372p. ISBN:0-471-49782-7, ISBN13: 978-0-471-49782-0. Dewey:572.86. LCCN:2002-726713.

Audience: **u,f.** *Choice, 2003.*

Davidson, Eric H.   **QH453.D384 2001**
Genomic Regulatory Systems: In Development and Evolution. Cloth Text. Elsevier Science & Technology Books. Saint Louis, MO. 2001. 261p. ISBN:0-12-205351-6, ISBN13: 978-0-12-205351-1. Dewey:571.8/5. LCCN:00-110671.

Audience: **u,f.**

Davies, Kevin   **QH445.2.D37 2003**
Cracking the Genome: Inside the Race to Unlock Human DNA. Trade Paper. Johns Hopkins University Press. Baltimore, MD. 2002. 352p. ISBN:0-8018-7140-9, ISBN13: 978-0-8018-7140-5. Dewey:599.93. LCCN:2002-028250.

Audience: **g,l,u,f.**

Davis, Joel L.   **QH445.2.D38 1990**
Mapping the Code: The Human Genome Project and the Choices of Modern Science. Trade Cloth. John Wiley & Sons, Inc. Hoboken, NJ. 1991. 294p. Wiley Science Editions Ser., Vol.

40 ISBN:0-471-50383-5, ISBN13: 978-0-471-50383-5. Dewey:573.2/12. LCCN:90-012572.

Audience: **g,l,u,f.**

Davis, Rowland H.   **QH506.D395 2003**
The Microbial Models of Molecular Biology: From Genes to Genomes. Trade Cloth. Oxford University Press, Inc. New York, NY. 2003. 352p. ISBN:0-19-515436-3, ISBN13: 978-0-19-515436-8. Dewey:572.8. LCCN:2002-152360.

Audience: **u,f.** *Choice, 2004.*

Desalle, Rob   **QH437.G46 2002**
The Genomic Revolution: Unveiling the Unity of Life. Michael Yudell (Editor). Trade Cloth. National Academies Press. Washington, DC. 2002. 250p. ISBN:0-309-07436-3, ISBN13: 978-0-309-07436-0. Dewey:611/.01816. LCCN:2002-004016.

Audience: **g,l,u.** *Choice, 2003.*

Dorrell, Nick (Volume   **QH434**
 Editor), et al.
Functional Microbial Genomics, Vol. 33. Brendan Wren & Fred Rainey (Volume Editors). Trade Cloth. Elsevier Science & Technology Books. Saint Louis, MO. 2002. 428p. Methods in Microbiology Ser. ISBN:0-12-521533-9, ISBN13: 978-0-12-521533-6. Dewey:576.

Audience: **u,f.**

Dyson, Freeman J.   **QC20.D98 1999**
The Sun, the Genome and the Internet: Tools of Scientific Revolutions. Trade Cloth. Oxford University Press, Inc. New York, NY. 1999. 144p. New York Public Library Lectures in Humanities Ser. ISBN:0-19-512942-3, ISBN13: 978-0-19-512942-7. Dewey:303.48/3. LCCN:98-053830.

Audience: **g,l,f.**

Edelson, Edward   **QH430.E335 1990**
Genetics and Heredity. Library Binding. Chelsea House Publishers. Langhorne, PA. 1991. 116p. The Encyclopedia of Health Ser., :The Healthy Body ISBN:0-7910-0018-4, ISBN13: 978-0-7910-0018-2. Dewey:575.1. LCCN:89-013994.

Audience: **l,u,f.**

Enriquez, Juan   **HM846.E57 2001**
As the Future Catches You: How Genomics and Other Forces Are Changing Your Life, Work, Health and Wealth. Trade Cloth. Crown Publishing Group. New York, NY. 2001. 272p. ISBN:0-609-60903-3, ISBN13: 978-0-609-60903-3. Dewey:303.48/3. LCCN:2001-028239.

Audience: **g,l,u.**

Esteller, Manel (Editor)   **QP624.5.M46**
DNA Methylation: Approaches, Methods, and Applications. CRC Press: Boca Raton. 2005. ISBN:0-8493-2050-X, ISBN13: 978-0-8493-2050-7.

Audience: **u,f.**

Fedoroff, Nina & Botstein,   **QH429.2.M38**
 David (Editors)
The Dynamic Genome: Barbara McClintock's Ideas in the Century of Genetics. Trade Paper. Cold Spring Harbor Laboratory Press. Woodbury, NY. 1992. 422p. ISBN:0-87969-396-7, ISBN13: 978-0-87969-396-1. Dewey:575.1/092. LCCN:92-010074.

Audience: **l,u.** *Choice, 1993.*

Frankham, Richard, et al.   **QH456.F73 2003**
A Primer of Conservation Genetics. Jonathan D. Ballou & David A. Briscoe (Authors), Karina H. McInnes (Illustrator).

Cloth Text. Cambridge University Press. New York, NY. 2004. 234p. ISBN:0-521-83110-5, ISBN13: 978-0-521-83110-9. Dewey:576.5/8. LCCN:2003-055125.

Audience: **u,f.**

Friedberg, Errol C.   **QH467.F748 1996**
Correcting the Blueprint of Life: An Historical Account of the Discovery of DNA Repair Mechanisms. Trade Cloth. Cold Spring Harbor Laboratory Press. Woodbury, NY. 1997. 230p. ISBN:0-87969-507-2, ISBN13: 978-0-87969-507-1. Dewey:574.87/3282. LCCN:96-045981.

Audience: **u,f.** *Choice, 1997.*

Friedberg, Errol C.   **QH467.F753 2005**
DNA Repair and Mutagenesis. Ed. 2. Trade Cloth. ASM Press. Washington, DC. 2005. 1452p. ISBN:1-55581-319-4, ISBN13: 978-1-55581-319-2. Dewey:572.8/6459. LCCN:2005-045353.

Audience: **u,f.**

Galun, Esra   **QP623.5.S63G34 2005**
RNA Silencing. Cloth Text. World Scientific Publishing Company, Inc. Hackensack, NJ. 2005. 468p. ISBN:981-256-206-0, ISBN13: 978-981-256-206-7. Dewey:572.8/65. LCCN:2005-283945.

Audience: **u,f.**

Gee, Henry   **QH437G44 2004**
Jacob's Ladder: The History of the Human Genome. Trade Cloth. W. W. Norton & Company, Inc. New York, NY. 2004. 352p. ISBN:0-393-05083-1, ISBN13: 978-0-393-05083-7. Dewey:599.93/5. LCCN:2004-049504.

Audience: **g,l,u,f.**

Gelfand, David H. (Editor), et al.   **QP606.D46P346 1999**
PCR Methods Manual. Michael A. Innis & John J. Sninsky (Editors). Trade Cloth. Elsevier Science & Technology Books. Saint Louis, MO. 1999. 566p. ISBN:0-12-372185-7, ISBN13: 978-0-12-372185-3. Dewey:572.8/6. LCCN:99-211203.

Audience: **u,f.**

Gerdes, Louise I.   **QH438.7.G413 2005**
Genetic Engineering. Trade Cloth. Thomson Gale. Farmington Hills, MI. 2004. 221p. ISBN:0-7377-2236-3, ISBN13: 978-0-7377-2236-9. Dewey:306.4/6. LCCN:2004-043660.

Audience: **u,f.**

Gibson, Greg & Muse, Spencer V.   **QH447.G534 2002**
A Primer of Genome Science. Paper Text. Sinauer Associates, Inc. Sunderland, MA. 2001. 347p. ISBN:0-87893-234-8, ISBN13: 978-0-87893-234-4. Dewey:572.8/6. LCCN:2001-054236.

Audience: **u,f.** *Choice, 2002.*

Glick, Bernard R. (Editor)   **QK728**
Methods in Plant Molecular Biology and Biotechnology. Thompson, John E. (Editor). CRC Press: Boca Raton. 1993. ISBN:0-8493-5164-2, ISBN13: 978-0-8493-5164-8.

Audience: **u,f.**

Glick, Bernard & Pasternak, Jack (Editors)   **TP248.2.G58 2003**
Molecular Biotechnology: Principles and Applications of Recombinant DNA. Ed. 3. Book, Other. ASM Press. Washington, DC. 2003. 860p. ISBN:1-55581-224-4, ISBN13: 978-1-55581-224-9. Dewey:660/.65. LCCN:2002-013148.

Audience: **u,f.**

Graham, Gordon   **QH447.G73 2002**
Genes: A Philosophical Inquiry. Paper over Boards. Routledge. New York, NY. 2002. 208p. ISBN:0-415-25257-1, ISBN13: 978-0-415-25257-7. Dewey:174/.25. LCCN:2002-028461.

Audience: **l,u,f.**

Greenspan, Ralph   **QH470.D7G74 2004**
Fly Pushing: The Theory and Practice of Drosophila Genetics. Ed. 2. Spiral. Cold Spring Harbor Laboratory Press. Woodbury, NY. 2004. 200p. ISBN:0-87969-711-3, ISBN13: 978-0-87969-711-2. Dewey:595.77/4. LCCN:2004-002342.

Audience: **u,f.**

Griffiths, Anthony J. F., et al.   **QH430.I62 2004**
An Introduction to Genetic Analysis. Ed. 8. William M. Gelbart, Richard C. Lewontin, Susan R. Wessler, David Suzuki & Jeffrey H. Miller (Authors). Cloth over Boards. W. H. Freeman & Company. New York, NY. 2004. 800p. ISBN:0-7167-4939-4, ISBN13: 978-0-7167-4939-4. Dewey:576.5. LCCN:2004-102340.

Audience: **u,f.**

Griffiths, A., et al.   **QH430**
Genetics: A Beginner's Guide. B. J. Guttmann, D. Suzuki & T. Cullis (Authors). Trade Paper. Oneworld Publications. Oxford, 2003. 256p. ISBN:1-85168-304-6, ISBN13: 978-1-85168-304-8. Dewey:576.5.

Audience: **l,u,f.** *Choice, 2003.*

Grotewold, Erich (Editor)   **QK981.4.P56 2003**
Plant functional Genomics. Humana Press: Totowa, N.J.. 2003. Methods in molecular biology ;; v. 236; Variation: Methods in molecular biology (Clifton, N.J.); v. 236 ISBN:1-58829-145-6, ISBN13: 978-1-58829-145-5.

Audience: **u,f.**

Hall, Jeffrey C. (Editor), et al.   **RB155.G3834 2001**
Genetic Dissection of Complex Traits, Vol. 42. Jay C. Dunlap, Theodore Friedmann & Francesco Gianelli (Editors), D. C. Rao (Volume Editor). Trade Cloth. Elsevier Science & Technology Books. Saint Louis, MO. 2000. 583p. Advances in Genetics Ser., Vol. 42 ISBN:0-12-017642-4, ISBN13: 978-0-12-017642-7. Dewey:616.042.

Audience: **u,f.**

Hanski, Ilkka A. & Gaggiotti, Oscar E. (Editors)   **QH352**
Ecology, Genetics and Evolution of Metapopulations. Paper Text. Elsevier Science & Technology Books. Saint Louis, MO. 2004. 696p. ISBN:0-12-323448-4, ISBN13: 978-0-12-323448-3. Dewey:577.8/8. LCCN:2004-044073.

Audience: **u,f.**

Hartl, Daniel L. & Jones, Elizabeth   **QH430.H3733 2001**
Genetics: Analysis of Genes and Genomes. Ed. 5. Cloth Text. Jones & Bartlett Publishers, Inc. Sudbury, MA. 2000. 858p. Genetics Ser. ISBN:0-7637-0913-1, ISBN13: 978-0-7637-0913-6. Dewey:576.5. LCCN:00-038440.

Audience: **u,f.**

Hartl, Daniel L. & Jones, Elizabeth W.   **QH430.H3732 2006**
Essential Genetics: A Genomic Perspective. Ed. 4. Trade Paper.

Jones & Bartlett Publishers, Inc. Sudbury, MA. 2005. 600p.
ISBN:0-7637-3527-2, ISBN13: 978-0-7637-3527-2.
Dewey:572.8/6. LCCN:2005-013813.

Audience: **u,f.**

Hartl, Daniel L. & Jones,   **QH430.H3733 2005**
   Elizabeth W.
Genetics: Analysis of Genes and Genomes. Ed. 6. Trade Cloth.
Jones & Bartlett Publishers, Inc. Sudbury, MA. 2004. 854p.
ISBN:0-7637-1511-5, ISBN13: 978-0-7637-1511-3.
Dewey:576.5. LCCN:2004-042183.

Audience: **u,f.**

Hartwell, Leland, et al.   **QH430.G458 2004**
Genetics: From Genes to Genomes. Ed. 2. Michael L. Goldberg,
Leroy Hood, Ann Reynolds, Lee M. Silver & Ruth C. Veres
(Authors). Trade Cloth. McGraw-Hill Higher Education. Burr
Ridge, IL. 2003. 896p. ISBN:0-07-246248-5, ISBN13:
978-0-07-246248-7. Dewey:576.5. LCCN:2002-012767.

Audience: **l,u,f.**

Hawley, Scott & Mori,   **QH431.H353 1999**
   Catherine A.
The Human Genome: A User's Guide. Trade Paper. Elsevier
Science & Technology Books. Saint Louis, MO. 1998. 413p.
ISBN:0-12-333460-8, ISBN13: 978-0-12-333460-2.
Dewey:611/.01816. LCCN:98-085438.

Audience: **l,u,f.**   *Choice, 1999.*

Hedrick, Philip W.   **QH455.H43 2005**
Genetics of Populations. Ed. 3. Trade Cloth. Jones & Bartlett
Publishers, Inc. Sudbury, MA. 2004. 737p.
ISBN:0-7637-4772-6, ISBN13: 978-0-7637-4772-5.
Dewey:576.5/8. LCCN:2004-056666.

Audience: **u,f.**

Hey, Jody   **QH83.H53 2001**
Genes, Categories, and Species: The Evolutionary and Cognitive
Causes of the Species Problem. Trade Cloth. Oxford University
Press, Inc. New York, NY. 2001. 236p. ISBN:0-19-514477-5,
ISBN13: 978-0-19-514477-2. Dewey:576.8/6. LCCN:00-045655.
Audience: **u,f.**   *Choice, 2002.*

Hunter, William   **RA1057.5.H86 2006**
DNA Analysis. Library Binding, Paper over Boards. Mason
Crest Publishers. Broomall, PA. 2005. 112p. Forensics, the
Science of Crime-Solving Ser. ISBN:1-4222-0026-4, ISBN13:
978-1-4222-0026-1. Dewey:614.1. LCCN:2005-010082.

Audience: **u,f.**

Inglis, John (Editor), et al.   **QH506.W4I55 2003**
Inspiring Science: Jim Watson and the Age of DNA. Jan
Witkowski & Joseph Sambrook (Editors). Trade Cloth. Cold
Spring Harbor Laboratory Press. Woodbury, NY. 2003. 503p.
ISBN:0-87969-698-2, ISBN13: 978-0-87969-698-6.
Dewey:572.8/092 B. LCCN:2003-013791.

Audience: **l,u,f.**   *Choice, 2004.*

James, Thomas L. (Volume   **QC762**
   Editor)
Nuclear Magnetic Resonance and Nucleic Acids, Vol. 261. John
N. Abelson & Melvin I. Simon (Editor-In-Chiefs). Trade Cloth.
Elsevier Science & Technology Books. Saint Louis, MO. 1995.
644p. Methods in Enzymology Ser., Vol. 261
ISBN:0-12-182162-5, ISBN13: 978-0-12-182162-3.
Dewey:538.362.

Audience: **u,f.**

Jenkins, Morton   **QH430**
Teach Yourself 101 Key Ideas: Genetics. Trade Paper.
McGraw-Hill Companies, The. New York, NY. 2001. 112p.
Teach Yourself Ser. ISBN:0-658-01208-8, ISBN13:
978-0-658-01208-2. Dewey:576.5.

Audience: **l,u,f.**

Jobling, Mark, et al.   **QH431.J53 2004**
Human Evolutionary Genetics. Matthew Hurles & Chris
Tyler-Smith (Authors). UK-B Format Paperback. Garland
Publishing, Inc. New York, NY. 2003. 458p.
ISBN:0-8153-4185-7, ISBN13: 978-0-8153-4185-7.
Dewey:599.93/5. LCCN:2003-018294.

Audience: **u,f.**   *Choice, 2004.*

Johnson, Rebecca L.   **QH447.J645 2003**
You and Your Genes. Trade Paper. National Geographic Society.
Washington, DC. 2003. 32p. Life Science Ser.
ISBN:0-7922-8866-1, ISBN13: 978-0-7922-8866-4.
Dewey:576.5. LCCN:2003-271539.

Audience: **g,l,u,f.**

Jones, Steve   **QH431.J575 1994**
The Language of Genes: Unraveling the Mysteries of Human
Genetics. Trade Cloth. Doubleday Publishing. New York, NY.
1994. 272p. ISBN:0-385-47372-9, ISBN13: 978-0-385-47372-9.
Dewey:573.2/1. LCCN:93-044626.

Audience: **u,f.**

Keller, Evelyn Fox &   **QH430**
   Winship, L. L.
The Century of the Gene. Trade Paper. Harvard University
Press. Cambridge, MA. 2002. 192p. ISBN:0-674-00825-1,
ISBN13: 978-0-674-00825-0. Dewey:576.5.

Audience: **u,f.**   *Choice, 2001.*

King, Robert C., et al.   **QH427.K55 2006**
A Dictionary of Genetics. Ed. 7. William D. Stansfield &
Pamela K. Mulligan (Authors). Trade Paper. Oxford University
Press, Inc. New York, NY. 2006. 608p. ISBN:0-19-530761-5,
ISBN13: 978-0-19-530761-0. Dewey:576.503.
LCCN:2005-045610.

Audience: **u,f.**   *Choice, 2003, 1991.*

Klug, William S. &   **QH430.K574 2003**
   Cummings, Michael R.
Concepts of Genetics. Ed. 7. Cloth Text. Prentice Hall PTR.
Upper Saddle River, NJ. 2002. 800p. ISBN:0-13-092998-0,
ISBN13: 978-0-13-092998-3. Dewey:575.1.
LCCN:2002-074822.

Audience: **l,u,f.**

Klug, William S. &   **QH430.K576 2005**
   Cummings, Michael R.
Essentials of Genetics. Ed. 5. Trade Paper. Prentice Hall PTR.
Upper Saddle River, NJ. 2004. 640p. ISBN:0-13-143510-8,
ISBN13: 978-0-13-143510-0. Dewey:576.5.
LCCN:2003-066437.

Audience: **l,u,f.**

Klug, William S. &   **QH430.K576 2002**
   Cummings, Michael R.
Essentials of Genetics. Ed. 4. Paper Text. Prentice Hall PTR.
Upper Saddle River, NJ. 2001. 508p. ISBN:0-13-091264-6,
ISBN13: 978-0-13-091264-0. Dewey:576.5.
LCCN:2001-034589.

Audience: **l,u,f.**

Kohane, Isaac S., et al. QP624.5.D726K686
Microarrays for an Integrative Genomics. Alvin Kho & Atul J. Butte (Authors). Trade Cloth. MIT Press. Cambridge, MA. 2002. 326p. Computational Molecular Biology Ser. ISBN:0-262-11271-X, ISBN13: 978-0-262-11271-0. Dewey:572.8/6. LCCN:2002-022663.
Audience: **u,f.**

Korf, Bruce R. RB155.K666 2000
Human Genetics: A Problem Based Approach. Ed. 2. Trade Paper. Blackwell Publishing, Inc. Malden, MA. 2000. 400p. ISBN:0-632-04425-X, ISBN13: 978-0-632-04425-2. Dewey:616/.042. LCCN:99-030762.
Audience: **u,f.**

Lamb, B. C. QH430.L35 2000
Applied Genetics. Trade Cloth. World Scientific Publishing Company, Inc. Hackensack, NJ. 1999. 300p. ISBN:1-86094-179-6, ISBN13: 978-1-86094-179-5. Dewey:660.6/5. LCCN:2004-351154.
Audience: **u,f.**

Lee, Thomas F. QH447.L44 1991
The Human Genome Project: Cracking the Genetic Code of Life. Trade Cloth. Da Capo Press, Inc. Cambridge, MA. 1991. 332p. ISBN:0-306-43965-4, ISBN13: 978-0-306-43965-0. Dewey:573.2/12. LCCN:91-021358.
Audience: **u,f.** *Choice, 1992.*

Levine, Carol R724
Taking Sides: Clashing Views on Controversial Bioethical Issues. Ed. 11. Paper Text. McGraw-Hill Higher Education. Burr Ridge, IL. 2005. 408p. ISBN:0-07-312955-0, ISBN13: 978-0-07-312955-6. Dewey:174.9574.
Audience: **u,f.**

Lewin, Benjamin QH430.L4 2004
Genes VIII. Cloth Text. Prentice Hall PTR. Upper Saddle River, NJ. 2003. 1056p. ISBN:0-13-143981-2, ISBN13: 978-0-13-143981-8. Dewey:576.5. LCCN:2003-015721.
Audience: **u,f.**

Lewis, Ricki QH431.L41855 2001
Human Genetics. Ed. 4. Trade Cloth. McGraw-Hill Higher Education. Burr Ridge, IL. 2000. 480p. ISBN:0-07-231898-8, ISBN13: 978-0-07-231898-2. Dewey:599.935. LCCN:00-031884.
Audience: **l,u,f.**

Lewontin, Richard C. QH506
The Triple Helix: Gene, Organism, and Environment. Trade Paper. Harvard University Press. Cambridge, MA. 2002. 144p. ISBN:0-674-00677-1, ISBN13: 978-0-674-00677-5. Dewey:572.8/01.
Audience: **l,u,f.** *Choice, 2000.*

Little, Peter (Editor) QH431.L475 2002
Genetic Destinies. Trade Cloth. Oxford University Press, Inc. New York, NY. 2002. 275p. ISBN:0-19-850454-3, ISBN13: 978-0-19-850454-2. Dewey:576.5. LCCN:2002-283784.
Audience: **u,f.** *Choice, 2002.*

Mahowald, Mary Briody RB155.M3135 2000
Genes, Women, Equality. Trade Cloth. Oxford University Press, Inc. New York, NY. 1999. 334p. ISBN:0-19-512110-4, ISBN13: 978-0-19-512110-0. Dewey:616/.042/082. LCCN:99-014296.
Audience: **l,u,f.**

Markoff, Arseni (Editor) QH441.2.A53 2005
Analytical Tools for DNA, Genes and Genomes: Nuts and Bolts. Trade Paper, Perfect. DNA Press. Eagleville, PA. 2005. 220p. Nuts and Bolts Ser. ISBN:0-9748765-1-8, ISBN13: 978-0-9748765-1-1. Dewey:572.8/6. LCCN:2005-003674.
Audience: **u,f.**

Maroni, Gustavo (Editor) QH431.M3226 2001
Molecular and Genetic Analysis of Human Traits. Trade Paper. Blackwell Publishing, Inc. Malden, MA. 2000. 288p. ISBN:0-632-04369-5, ISBN13: 978-0-632-04369-9. Dewey:599.93/5. LCCN:00-023792.
Audience: **u,f.**

Marshall, Elizabeth L. QH445.2.M37 1996
The Human Genome Project: Cracking the Code Within Us. Trade Cloth. Scholastic Library Publishing. Danbury, CT. 1996. 128p. ISBN:0-531-11299-3, ISBN13: 978-0-531-11299-1. Dewey:574.87/3282. LCCN:95-045975.
Audience: **l,u.**

McConkey, Edwin H. QH447.M353 2004
How the Human Genome Works. Trade Paper. Jones & Bartlett Publishers, Inc. Sudbury, MA. 2004. 118p. ISBN:0-7637-2384-3, ISBN13: 978-0-7637-2384-2. Dewey:611/.01816. LCCN:2003-017746.
Audience: **u,f.**

McGee, Glenn QH447.M356 2003
Beyond Genetics: Putting the Power of DNA to Work in Your Life. Trade Cloth. HarperCollins Publishers. New York, NY. 2003. 240p. ISBN:0-06-000800-8, ISBN13: 978-0-06-000800-0. Dewey:306.4/6. LCCN:2002-044864.
Audience: **l,u,f.** *Choice, 2004.*

**Mehlman, Maxwell J. & ** QH431.M366 1998
Botkin, Jeffrey R.
Access to the Genome: The Challenge to Equality. Trade Cloth. Georgetown University Press. Washington, DC. 1998. 160p. ISBN:0-87840-677-8, ISBN13: 978-0-87840-677-7. Dewey:599.93/5. LCCN:97-037974.
Audience: **l,u,f.** *Choice, 1998.*

Miglani, Gurbachen S. QH430
Advanced Genetics. CRC Press. 2002. ISBN:0-8493-2425-4, ISBN13: 978-0-8493-2425-3.
Audience: **u,f.**

Moore, John A. QH367 .M813 2002
From Genesis to Genetics: The Case of Evolution and Creationism. Trade Cloth. University of California Press. Berkeley, CA. 2002. 239p. ISBN:0-520-22441-8, ISBN13: 978-0-520-22441-4. Dewey:231.7/652. LCCN:2001-044419.
Audience: **u,f.** *Choice, 2002.*

Morange, Michel QH447.M6713 2001
The Misunderstood Gene. Trade Cloth. Harvard University Press. Cambridge, MA. 2001. 238p. ISBN:0-674-00336-5, ISBN13: 978-0-674-00336-1. Dewey:572.8/6. LCCN:00-053916.
Audience: **u,f.** *Choice, 2001.*

Moss, Lenny QH430.M674 2002
What Genes Can't Do. Trade Cloth. MIT Press. Cambridge, MA. 2002. 256p. Basic Bioethics Ser. ISBN:0-262-13411-X, ISBN13: 978-0-262-13411-8. Dewey:660.6/5. LCCN:2001-056298.
Audience: **l,u,f.** *Choice, 2003.*

Mulhall, Douglas   **T174.7.M85 2002**
Our Molecular Future: How Nanotechnology, Robotics, Genetics, and Artificial Intelligence Will Transform Our World. Trade Cloth. Prometheus Books, Publishers. Amherst, NY. 2002. 392p. ISBN:1-57392-992-1, ISBN13: 978-1-57392-992-9. Dewey:303.48/3. LCCN:2002-021992.
Audience: **u,f.** *Choice, 2003.*

Nabhan, Gary Paul   **QH431.N28 2004**
Why Some Like It Hot: Food, Genes, and Cultural Diversity. Trade Cloth. Island Press. Washington, DC. 2004. 240p. ISBN:1-55963-466-9, ISBN13: 978-1-55963-466-3. LCCN:2004-005033.
Audience: **u,f.** *Choice, 2005.*

National Research Council   **QK981.45.N28 2002**
Staff
The National Plant Genome Initiative: Objectives for 2003-2008. Perfect. National Academies Press. Washington, DC. 2002. 92p. ISBN:0-309-08521-7, ISBN13: 978-0-309-08521-2. Dewey:572.8/633. LCCN:2003-271259.
Audience: **u,f.**

Ness, Bryan D. (Editor)   **QH427.E53 2004**
Encyclopedia of Genetics, Revised Edition, Vol. 2. Ed. 2. Dawn P. Dawson (Editor-In-Chief), Christina J. Moose & Tracy Irons-Georges (Editorial Coordinators). Library Binding. Salem Press, Inc. Hackensack, NJ. 2004. 936p. ISBN:1-58765-149-1, ISBN13: 978-1-58765-149-6. Dewey:576.5/03. LCCN:2003-026056.
Audience: **u,f.** *Choice, 2004.*

Nicholl, Desmond S.   **QH442.N53 1994**
An Introduction to Genetic Engineering. Cloth Text. Cambridge University Press. New York, NY. 1994. 182p. Studies in Biology ISBN:0-521-43054-2, ISBN13: 978-0-521-43054-8. Dewey:575.10724. LCCN:93-008176.
Audience: **u,f.** *Choice, 1995.*

Nunnally, Brian K.   **QP625.N89A53 2005**
Analytical Techniques in DNA Sequencing. Perfect, Paper over Boards. Marcel Dekker Inc. New York, NY. 2005. 296p. ISBN:0-8247-5342-9, ISBN13: 978-0-8247-5342-9. Dewey:611/.01816. LCCN:2004-066429.
Audience: **u,f.**

Omoto, Charlotte K. &   **QH430.O47 2004**
Lurquin, Paul F.
Genes and DNA: A Beginner's Guide to Genetics and Its Applications. Trade Cloth. Kegan Paul International, Ltd. London, 2004. 224p. ISBN:0-231-13012-0, ISBN13: 978-0-231-13012-7. Dewey:576.5. LCCN:2003-062584.
Audience: **l,u,f.** *Choice, 2004.*

Palladino, Michael A.   **QH447.P35 2002**
Understanding the Human Genome Project. Paper Text. Benjamin-Cummings Publishing Company. San Francisco, CA. 2001. 32p. ISBN:0-8053-6774-8, ISBN13: 978-0-8053-6774-4. Dewey:611/.01816. LCCN:2003-266927.
Audience: **u,f.**

Pennington, Sandra (Editor)   **QH430.P46 2000**
Introduction to Genetics. Trade Paper. Blackwell Publishing, Inc. Malden, MA. 2000. 224p. Eleventh Hour Ser. ISBN:0-632-04438-1, ISBN13: 978-0-632-04438-2. Dewey:576.5. LCCN:99-025401.
Audience: **l,u,f.**

Percus, Jerome K.   **QH438.4.M3 P47 2002**
Mathematics of Genome Analysis. C. Cannings, F. C. Hoppensteadt & L. A. Segel (Contribution by). Cloth Text. Cambridge University Press. New York, NY. 2001. 150p. Studies in Mathematical Biology, Vol. 17 ISBN:0-521-58517-1, ISBN13: 978-0-521-58517-0. Dewey:572.860151. LCCN:2001-035087.
Audience: **u,f.** *Choice, 2002.*

Prade, Rolf   **QK602.G465 2003**
Genomics of Plants and Fungi, Vol. 18. Paper over Boards. Marcel Dekker Inc. New York, NY. 2003. 440p. Mycology Ser., 18 ISBN:0-8247-4125-0, ISBN13: 978-0-8247-4125-9. Dewey:581.3/5. LCCN:2004-296915.
Audience: **u,f.**

Quatrano, Ralph (Editor)   **QK981.P54 2001**
Plant Genomics: Emerging Tools. Trade Cloth. American Society of Plant Physiologists. Rockville, MD. 2001. ISBN:0-943088-42-9, ISBN13: 978-0-943088-42-6. Dewey:572.8/2. LCCN:2001-022412.
Audience: **u,f.**

Reardon, Jenny   **QH431.R248 2004**
Race to the Finish: Identity and Governance in an Age of Genomics. Trade Cloth. Princeton University Press. Princeton, NJ. 2004. 312p. In-formation Ser. ISBN:0-691-11856-6, ISBN13: 978-0-691-11856-7. Dewey:306.4/5. LCCN:2004-050569.
Audience: **u,f.**

Reece, Richard J.   **QH442.R445 2003**
Analysis of Genes and Genomes. Trade Cloth. John Wiley & Sons, Inc. Hoboken, NJ. 2004. 490p. ISBN:0-470-84379-9, ISBN13: 978-0-470-84379-6. Dewey:572.86. LCCN:2003-012937.
Audience: **u,f.**

Resnik, David B.   **QH332**
Owning the Genome: A Moral Analysis of DNA Patenting. Cloth Text. State University of New York Press. Albany, NY. 2004. 272p. ISBN:0-7914-5931-4, ISBN13: 978-0-7914-5931-7. Dewey:346.7304/86. LCCN:2004-041648.
Audience: **u,f.**

Ridley, Matt   **QH429.2.C75R53 2006**
Francis Crick: Discoverer of the Genetic Code. Trade Cloth. HarperCollins Publishers. New York, NY. 2006. 224p. Eminent Lives Ser. ISBN:0-06-082333-X, ISBN13: 978-0-06-082333-7. Dewey:576.5/092 B. LCCN:2005-055878.
Audience: **l,u,f.**

Ringo, John   **QH430.R55 2003**
Fundamental Genetics. Cloth Text. Cambridge University Press. New York, NY. 2004. 476p. ISBN:0-521-80934-7, ISBN13: 978-0-521-80934-4. Dewey:576.5. LCCN:2003-048463.
Audience: **l,u,f.**

Russell, Peter J.   **QH430.R876 2002**
I-Genetics. Mixed Media. Benjamin-Cummings Publishing Company. San Francisco, CA. 2001. 850p. ISBN:0-8053-4553-1, ISBN13: 978-0-8053-4553-7. Dewey:576.5. LCCN:2001-037116.
Audience: **u,f.**

Formats: Web: Ebook: **e**   CD/DVD-ROM: BCL3: **B**

Salemi, Marco &   QP624.P485 2003
  Vandamme, Anne-Mieke (Editors)
The Phylogenetic Handbook: A Practical Approach to DNA and
Protein Phylogeny. Cloth Text. Cambridge University Press.
New York, NY. 2003. 430p. ISBN:0-521-80390-X, ISBN13:
978-0-521-80390-8. Dewey:572.8/633. LCCN:2002-073927.
Audience: **u,f.**

Schepers, Ute   QH450.25
RNA Interference in Practice: Principles, Basics, and Methods
for Gene Silencing in C. elegans, Drosophila, and Mammals.
Trade Cloth. John Wiley & Sons, Inc. Hoboken, NJ. 2005. 336p.
ISBN:3-527-31020-7, ISBN13: 978-3-527-31020-3.
Dewey:572.8845. LCCN:2006-280303.
Audience: **u,f.**

Shawker, Thomas H.   RB155.S44 2004
Unlocking Your Genetic History: A Step-by-Step Guide to
Discovering Your Family's Medical and Genetic Heritage. Trade
Paper. Rutledge Hill Press. Nashville, TN. 2004. 320p. National
Genealogical Society Guides Ser. ISBN:1-4016-0144-8, ISBN13:
978-1-4016-0144-7. Dewey:616/.042. LCCN:2004-006461.
Audience: **l,u,f.**

Shoemaker, J. S. & Lin, S.   QP624.5.D726M483
  M. (Editors)
Methods of Microarray Data Analysis, Vol. 4. Trade Cloth.
Springer. New York, NY. 2004. XVI, 256p.
ISBN:0-387-23074-2, ISBN13: 978-0-387-23074-0.
Dewey:572.8636. LCCN:2005-297773.
Audience: **u,f.**

Shreeve, James   QH431.S5577 2004
The Genome War: How Craig Venter Tried to Capture the Code
of Life and Save the World. Trade Cloth. Alfred A. Knopf Inc.
New York, NY. 2004. 416p. ISBN:0-375-40629-8, ISBN13:
978-0-375-40629-4. Dewey:611/.01816. LCCN:2003-047580.
Audience: **u,f.** *Choice, 2004.*

Snustad, D. Peter &   QH430.S6 2005
  Simmons, Michael J.
Principles of Genetics. Ed. 4. Trade Cloth. John Wiley & Sons,
Inc. Hoboken, NJ. 2005. 888p. ISBN:0-471-69939-X, ISBN13:
978-0-471-69939-2. Dewey:576.5. LCCN:2006-271886.
Audience: **l,u,f.**

Snustad, D. Peter &   QH430
  Simmons, Michael J.
Principles of Genetics. Ed. 3. H. James Price (Editor), James F.
Crow (Epilogue by). Trade Cloth. John Wiley & Sons, Inc.
Hoboken, NJ. 2002. 864p. ISBN:0-471-44180-5, ISBN13:
978-0-471-44180-9. Dewey:576.5. LCCN:2002-190820.
Audience: **l,u,f.**

Sohail, Muhammad (Editor)   QH450
Gene Silencing by RNA Interference: Technology and
Application. CRC Press: Boca Raton, FL. 2005.
ISBN:0-8493-2141-7, ISBN13: 978-0-8493-2141-2.
Audience: **u,f.**

Stansfield, William   QH431.S694 2002
Easy Outline of Genetics. Paper Text. McGraw-Hill Companies,
The. New York, NY. 2002. 144p. Easy Outlines Ser.
ISBN:0-07-138317-4, ISBN13: 978-0-07-138317-2.
Dewey:576.5. LCCN:2002-728306.
Audience: **l,u,f.**

Thistlethwaite, Susan   QH438.7.A33 2003
  Brooks
Adam, Eve, and The Genome: The Human Genome Project and
Theology. Trade Paper. Augsburg Fortress, Publishers.
Minneapolis, MN. 2003. 200p. Theology and the Sciences Ser.
ISBN:0-8006-3614-7, ISBN13: 978-0-8006-3614-2.
Dewey:201/.666065. LCCN:2004-298526.
Audience: **g,l,u.** *Choice, 2004.*

Thomas, Alison   QH430
Introducing Genetics: From Mendel to Molecules. Trade Paper.
Taylor & Francis Group. Philadelphia, PA. 2004. 224p.
ISBN:0-7487-6440-2, ISBN13: 978-0-7487-6440-2.
Dewey:576.5. LCCN:2003-447937.
Audience: **l,u,f.**

Trainor, Lynn E. H.   QH431
The Triplet Genetic Code: Key to Living Organisms. Cloth Text.
World Scientific Publishing Company, Inc. Hackensack, NJ.
2001. 140p. ISBN:981-02-4467-3, ISBN13: 978-981-02-4467-5.
Dewey:576.
Audience: **u,f.**

Trun, Nancy Jo & Trempy,   QH434.T78 2004
  J. E.
Fundamental Bacterial Genetics. Trade Paper. Blackwell
Publishing, Inc. Malden, MA. 2003. 304p. ISBN:0-632-04448-9,
ISBN13: 978-0-632-04448-1. Dewey:579.3/135.
LCCN:2003-000141.
Audience: **l,u.**

Vandermeer, John   QH333.V36 1995
Reconstructing Biology: Genetics and Ecology in the New
World Order. Trade Paper. John Wiley & Sons, Inc. Hoboken,
NJ. 1996. 496p. ISBN:0-471-10917-7, ISBN13:
978-0-471-10917-4. Dewey:304.2. LCCN:95-012076.
Audience: **u,f.** *Choice, 1996.*

Wade, Nicholas   RB155.W326 2001
Life Script: How the Human Genome Discoveries Will
Transform Medicine and Enhance Your Health. Trade Cloth.
Simon & Schuster. New York, NY. 2001. 208p.
ISBN:0-7432-1605-9, ISBN13: 978-0-7432-1605-0.
Dewey:616/.042. LCCN:2001-042627.
Audience: **l,u,f.**

Watson, James D.   QH506
Genes, Girls and Gamow: After the Double Helix. Trade Paper.
Knopf Publishing Group. New York, NY. 2003. 336p.
ISBN:0-375-72715-9, ISBN13: 978-0-375-72715-3.
Dewey:572.8/092 B.
Audience: **l,u,f.** *Choice, 2002.*

Weiss, Kenneth M. &   QH390.W45 2004
  Buchanan, Anne V.
Genetics and the Logic of Evolution. Trade Cloth. John Wiley &
Sons, Inc. Hoboken, NJ. 2004. 560p. ISBN:0-471-23805-8,
ISBN13: 978-0-471-23805-8. Dewey:572.8/38.
LCCN:2003-014905.
Audience: **u,f.** *Choice, 2004.*

Willett, Edward   PR9199.3.W49115
Genetics Demystified. Trade Paper, Perfect. McGraw-Hill
Professional Publishing. New York, NY. 2005. 210p.
ISBN:0-07-145930-8, ISBN13: 978-0-07-145930-3.
Dewey:576.5. LCCN:2005-054730.
Audience: **l,u,f.**

Wilson, Robert   QH331.W558 2004
Genes and the Agents of Life: The Individual in the Fragile
Sciences Biology. Trade Cloth. Cambridge University Press.
New York, NY. 2004. 312p. ISBN:0-521-83646-8, ISBN13:
978-0-521-83646-3. Dewey:570/.1. LCCN:2004-047297.
                                        Audience: **u,f.**

Wingerson, Lois   RB155.6.W56 1990
Mapping Our Genes: The Genome Project and the Future of
Medicine. Trade Cloth. Penguin Group (USA) Inc. New York,
NY. 1990. ISBN:0-525-24877-3, ISBN13: 978-0-525-24877-4.
Dewey:616/.042/0112. LCCN:89-048560.
                                        Audience: **l,u.**

Woolfson, Adrian   QH430
Life Without Genes. HarperCollins. 2000. ISBN:0-00-255618-9,
ISBN13: 978-0-00-255618-7.
                                        Audience: **l,u,f.**

Wyandt, Herman Edwin &   QH431.A76 2003
  Tonk, Vijay S. (Editors)
Atlas of Human Chromosome Heteromorphisms. Trade Cloth.
Springer. New York, NY. 2003. 300p. ISBN:1-4020-1303-5,
ISBN13: 978-1-4020-1303-4. Dewey:611/.01816.
LCCN:2003-051681.
                                        Audience: **u,f.**

Yount, Lisa   TP248.23.Y684 2004
Biotechnology and Genetic Engineering. Ed. 2. Trade Cloth.
Facts On File, Inc.. New York, NY. 2004. 320p. Library in a
Book ISBN:0-8160-5059-7, ISBN13: 978-0-8160-5059-8.
Dewey:303.48/3. LCCN:2003-064223.
                              Audience: **u,f.** *Choice, 2001.*

Cellular and Molecular Biology, Genetics > Genetics (General) > Molecular Genetics

                                              QH470.D7
FlyBase.
http://flybase.bio.indiana.edu/
                                        Audience: **u,f.**

Albala, Joanna S. &   QH506.P796 2003
  Humphery-Smith, Ian
Protein Arrays, Biochips, and Proteomics: The Next Phase of
Genomics Discovery. Paper over Boards. Marcel Dekker Inc.
New York, NY. 2003. 304p. ISBN:0-8247-4312-1, ISBN13:
978-0-8247-4312-3. Dewey:572/.6. LCCN:2004-296024.
                                        Audience: **u,f.**

Alon, Uri   QH324.2.A46 2006
Introduction to Systems Biology and the Design Principles of
Biological Circuits. CRC Press. 2006. ISBN:1-58488-642-0,
ISBN13: 978-1-58488-642-6.
                                        Audience: **u,f.**

Baker, Tania A., et al.   QH506.M6627 2003
Molecular Biology of the Gene. Ed. 5. Stephen P. Bell, Gann
Alexander, Michael Levine, Richard Losick, James D. Watson &
Alexander Gann (Authors). Trade Cloth. Benjamin-Cummings
Publishing Company. San Francisco, CA. 2003. 768p.
ISBN:0-8053-4635-X, ISBN13: 978-0-8053-4635-0.
Dewey:572.8. LCCN:2003-042863.
                                        Audience: **u,f.**

Barash, David P.   QH431.B226 2001
Revolutionary Biology: The New, Gene-Centered View of Life.
Trade Cloth. Transaction Publishers. Somerset, NJ. 2001. 213p.
ISBN:0-7658-0067-5, ISBN13: 978-0-7658-0067-1.
Dewey:599.93/5. LCCN:2001-017123.
                              Audience: **u,f.** *Choice, 2001.*

Baxevanis, Andreas D. &   QP551
  Ouellette, B. F. Francis (Editors)
Bioinformatics: A Practical Guide to the Analysis of Genes and
Proteins. Ed. 3. Trade Cloth. John Wiley & Sons, Inc. Hoboken,
NJ. 2004. 560p. ISBN:0-471-47878-4, ISBN13:
978-0-471-47878-2. Dewey:572.8/633/0285.
LCCN:2004-011822.
                                        Audience: **u,f.**

Benfey, Philip   QH447
Essentials of Genomics. Paper Text. Prentice Hall PTR. Upper
Saddle River, NJ. 2004. 180p. ISBN:0-13-047018-X, ISBN13:
978-0-13-047018-8. Dewey:572.860711. LCCN:2004-018859.
                                        Audience: **u,f.**

Bernot, Alain   QH447.B4813 2004
Genome Transcriptome and Proteome Analysis. E-Book.
John Wiley & Sons, Inc. Hoboken, NJ. 2006. 248p.
ISBN:0-470-02079-2, ISBN13: 978-0-470-02079-1.
Dewey:572.8.
                              Audience: **u,f.** *Choice, 2005.*

Blake, R. D.   QH447.B57 2004
Informational Biopolymers of Genes and Gene Expression.
Trade Cloth. University Science Books. Sausalito, CA. 2004.
700p. ISBN:1-891389-28-9, ISBN13: 978-1-891389-28-3.
Dewey:572.8/6. LCCN:2004-043051.
                                        Audience: **u,f.**

Borlak, Jürgen (Editor)   RB155
Handbook of Toxicogenomics: Strategies and Applications.
Trade Cloth. John Wiley & Sons, Inc. Hoboken, NJ. 2005. 705p.
ISBN:3-527-30342-1, ISBN13: 978-3-527-30342-7.
Dewey:616.042.
                                        Audience: **u,f.**

Brownstein, Michael J. &   QP624.5.D726F86 2003
  Khodursky, Arkady (Editors)
Functional Genomics: Methods and Protocols. Book, Other.
Humana Press. Totowa, NJ. 2003. 250p. Methods in Molecular
Biology Ser., Vol. 224 ISBN:1-58829-291-6, ISBN13:
978-1-58829-291-9. Dewey:572.8/636. LCCN:2003-040707.
                                        Audience: **u,f.**

Cellura, A. Raymond   QH447.C45 2005
The Genomic Environment and Niche-Experience. Trade Cloth.
Cedar Springs Publishers. Abbeville, SC. 2006. xxiii, 176p.
ISBN:0-9760561-3-5, ISBN13: 978-0-9760561-3-3.
Dewey:611/.0181663. LCCN:2005-016919.
                                        Audience: **u,f.**

Cherfas, Jeremy   QH431.C454 2002
The Human Genome: A Beginner's Guide to the Chemical Code
of Life. John Gribbin (Editor). Trade Paper. Dorling Kindersley
Publishing, Inc. New York, NY. 2002. 72p. Essential Science
Ser. ISBN:0-7894-8415-3, ISBN13: 978-0-7894-8415-4.
Dewey:611/.01816. LCCN:2001-047932.
                                        Audience: **l,u,f.**

**Chitty, Mary (Compiled and
Edited by)**
☐ Cambridge Healthtech Institute BioPharmaceutical Glossary,
Taxonomies and Guide to 21st Century Therapeutics,
Technologies and Trends.
http://genomicglossaries.com/
Cambridge Healthtech Institute.

Audience: **g,l.**

Clark, Melody (Editor)   QH447.C65 2000
Comparative Genomics. Trade Cloth. Springer. New York, NY.
2000. 256p. ISBN:0-412-83080-9, ISBN13: 978-0-412-83080-8.
Dewey:572.8/6. LCCN:00-058730.

Audience: **u,f.**

Collado-Vides, Julio &   QH438.4.M3G46 2002
Hofestädt, Ralf (Editors)
Gene Regulation and Metabolism: Post-Genomic Computational
Approaches. Cloth Text. MIT Press. Cambridge, MA. 2002.
320p. Computational Molecular Biology Ser.
ISBN:0-262-03297-X, ISBN13: 978-0-262-03297-1.
Dewey:572.8/01/5118. LCCN:2001-056247.

Audience: **u,f.**

Cooper, David (Editor)   QH447.N38 2003
Nature Encyclopedia of the Human Genome. Trade Cloth.
Nature Publishing Group. New York, NY. 2003. 5159p.
ISBN:0-333-80386-8, ISBN13: 978-0-333-80386-8.
Dewey:611.0181603. LCCN:2004-351190.
Audience: **u,f.** *Choice, 2004.*

Cullis, Christopher A.   QK981.C85 2004
Plant Genomics and Proteomics. Trade Cloth. John Wiley &
Sons, Inc. Hoboken, NJ. 2004. 232p. ISBN:0-471-37314-1,
ISBN13: 978-0-471-37314-8. Dewey:572.8/62.
LCCN:2003-013088.
Audience: **u,f.** *Choice, 2004.*

Danchin, Antoine   QH447.D3613 2002
The Delphic Boat: What Genomes Tell Us. Alison Quayle
(Translator). Trade Cloth. Harvard University Press. Cambridge,
MA. 2003. 380p. ISBN:0-674-00930-4, ISBN13:
978-0-674-00930-1. Dewey:572.8/6. LCCN:2002-027273.
Audience: **u,f.**

Darvas, Ferenc, et al.   RM301.42
Chemical Genomics. Andras Guttman & Gyorgy Dorman
(Authors). Paper over Boards. Marcel Dekker Inc. New York,
NY. 2004. 280p. ISBN:0-8247-5490-5, ISBN13:
978-0-8247-5490-7. Dewey:572.8/6. LCCN:2004-056843.
Audience: **u,f.**

DelVecchio, V.G. &   QH434.A66 2003
Krcmery, V. (Editors)
Applications of Genomics and Proteomics for Analysis of
Bacterial Biological Warfare Agents. Trade Cloth. I O S Press,
Inc. Burke, VA. 2003. 196p. NATO Science Ser., Vol. 352
ISBN:1-58603-343-3, ISBN13: 978-1-58603-343-9.
Dewey:623.4/594. LCCN:2003-104680.
Audience: **u,f.**

Dennis, Carina & Gallagher,   QH447.H835 2001
Richard B. (Editors)
The Human Genome. James D. Watson (Foreword by). Cloth
over Boards. Palgrave Macmillan. New York, NY. 2002. 184p.
ISBN:0-333-97143-4, ISBN13: 978-0-333-97143-7.
Dewey:599.93/5. LCCN:2001-133051.
Audience: **u,f.**

Drickamer, Karen D. &   QH345.B522 NO.69
Dell, A. (Editors)
Glycogenomics: The Impact of Genomics and Informatics in
Glycobiology. Trade Cloth. Portland Press, Ltd. London, 2002.
170p. Biochemical Society Symposia Ser., Vol. 69
ISBN:1-85578-154-9, ISBN13: 978-1-85578-154-2. Dewey:572
s 572/.567. LCCN:2003-386012.

Audience: **u,f.**

Dunn, Michael J. (Editor),   QH431.E62 2005
et al.
Encyclopedia of Genetics, Genomics, Proteomics and
Bioinformatics. Lynn B. Jorde, Peter F. R. Little & Shankar
Subramaniam (Editors). Trade Cloth. John Wiley & Sons, Inc.
Hoboken, NJ. 2005. 4096p. ISBN:0-470-84974-6, ISBN13:
978-0-470-84974-3. Dewey:599.93/5. LCCN:2005-017410.

Audience: **u,f.**

Exbrayat, Jean-Marie   QP620.E93 2001
Genome Visualization by Classic Methods in Light Microscopy.
CRC Press. 2001. ISBN:0-8493-0043-6, ISBN13:
978-0-8493-0043-1.

Audience: **u,f.**

Fink, Gerald   QH447
Seeking Security: Pathogens, Open Access, and Genome
Databases. Board on Life Sciences. National Academies Press.
2004. ISBN:0-309-09305-8, ISBN13: 978-0-309-09305-7.
Audience: **u,f.**

Fraser, Claire M. (Editor),   QH434.M527 2004
et al.
Microbial Genomes. Timothy Ready & Karen E. Nelson
(Editors). Book, Other. Humana Press. Totowa, NJ. 2004. 552p.
Infectious Disease Ser. ISBN:1-58829-189-8, ISBN13:
978-1-58829-189-9. Dewey:572.8/6293. LCCN:2003-025478.
Audience: **u,f.**

Fuchs, Jurgen & Podda,   RB155.E54 2005
Maurizio (Editors)
Encyclopedia of Diagnostic Proteomics and Genomics. Trade
Cloth. Marcel Dekker Inc. New York, NY. 2005. 1600p.
ISBN:0-8247-5564-2, ISBN13: 978-0-8247-5564-5.
Dewey:616/.042/03. LCCN:2005-297370.

Audience: **u,f.**

Galas, David &   QH447.G4653 2002
McCormack, Stephen (Editors)
Genomic Technologies: Present and Future. Trade Cloth. Caister
Academic Press. Norwich, 2002. 418p. Functional Genomics
Ser., Vol. 1 ISBN:0-9542464-2-X, ISBN13: 978-0-9542464-2-6.
Dewey:572.8/6. LCCN:2003-467031.

Audience: **u,f.**

Galperin, Michael Y. &   QH447.F766 2003
Koonin, Eugene V. (Editors)
Frontiers in Computational Genomics: Functional Genomics.
Trade Cloth. Caister Academic Press. Norwich, 2003. 358p.
Functional Genomics Ser., Vol. 3 ISBN:0-9542464-4-6, ISBN13:
978-0-9542464-4-0. Dewey:572.8/6. LCCN:2003-464293.
Audience: **u,f.**

Gibson, Greg & Muse,   QH447.G534 2002
Spencer V.
A Primer of Genome Science. Paper Text. Sinauer Associates,
Inc. Sunderland, MA. 2001. 347p. ISBN:0-87893-234-8,

ISBN13: 978-0-87893-234-4. Dewey:572.8/6.
LCCN:2001-054236.

Audience: **u,f.** *Choice, 2002.*

Gibson, Greg & Muse,   **QH447.G534 2004**
Spencer V.
A Primer of Genome Science. Ed. 2. Trade Cloth. Sinauer
Associates, Inc. Sunderland, MA. 2004. 350p.
ISBN:0-87893-232-1, ISBN13: 978-0-87893-232-0.
Dewey:572.8/6. LCCN:2004-024285.

Audience: **u,f.** *Choice, 2002.*

Grandi, Guido (Editor)   **QH447**
Genomics, Proteomics and Vaccines. Trade Cloth. John Wiley &
Sons, Inc. Hoboken, NJ. 2004. 336p. ISBN:0-470-85616-5,
ISBN13: 978-0-470-85616-1. Dewey:572.8/6.
LCCN:2004-273717.

Audience: **u,f.**

Grant, Richard P. (Editor)   **QH477**
Computational Genomics: Theory and Application. Paper over
Boards. Taylor & Francis Group. Philadelphia, PA. 2004. 350p.
ISBN:1-904933-01-7, ISBN13: 978-1-904933-01-4.
Dewey:572.8/6.

Audience: **u,f.**

Gregory, T. Ryan (Editor)   **QH447.E9626 2005**
The Evolution of the Genome. Cloth Text. Elsevier Science &
Technology Books. Saint Louis, MO. 2004. 768p.
ISBN:0-12-301463-8, ISBN13: 978-0-12-301463-4.
Dewey:572.8/633. LCCN:2005-272318.

Audience: **u,f.** *Choice, 2005.*

Hawley, R. Scott, et al.   **QH431**
The Human Genome: A User's Guide. Ed. 2. Catherine A. Mori
& Julia E. Richards (Authors). Paper Text. Elsevier Science &
Technology Books. Saint Louis, MO. 2004. 480p. Elsevier
Science in Society Ser. ISBN:0-12-333462-4, ISBN13:
978-0-12-333462-6. Dewey:611/.01816. LCCN:2004-559151.

Audience: **u,f.**

Hein, Jotun, et al.   **QH455**
Gene Genealogies, Variation and Evolution: A Primer in
Coalescent Theory. Mikkel Schierup & Carsten Wiuf (Authors).
Trade Cloth. Oxford University Press, Inc. New York, NY. 2005.
296p. ISBN:0-19-852995-3, ISBN13: 978-0-19-852995-8.
Dewey:576.5/8/015118. LCCN:2005-295782.

Audience: **u,f.**

HumanGenome Project (ed.)   **QH447**
☐ The Human Genome Project: Exploring our Molecular
Selves.
http://www.genome.gov/Pages/EducationKit/online.htm
National Human Genome Research Institute (NHGRI).

Audience: **u,f.**

Jackson, M., et al.   **QH431**
Human Genome Evolution: Human Molecular Genetics. T.
Strachan & G. Dover (Authors). Cloth Text. Taylor & Francis
Group. Abingdon, 1996. 256p. Human Molecular Genetics Ser.
ISBN:1-85996-095-2, ISBN13: 978-1-85996-095-0.
Dewey:599.9/35.

Audience: **u,f.** *Choice, 1997.*

Kahl, Günter   **QH442**
The Dictionary of Gene Technology: Genomics,
Transcriptomics, Proteomics. Ed. 3. Trade Cloth. John Wiley &

Sons, Inc. Hoboken, NJ. 2004. 1314p. ISBN:3-527-30765-6,
ISBN13: 978-3-527-30765-4. Dewey:572.803.
LCCN:2006-280310.

Audience: **u,f.** *Choice, 2005.*

Kaplan, Jonathan Michael   **RB155.K36 2000**
Limits and Lies of Human Genetic Research: Dangers for Social
Policy. Paper over Boards. Routledge. New York, NY. 2000.
240p. Reflective Bioethics Ser. ISBN:0-415-92637-8, ISBN13:
978-0-415-92637-9. Dewey:174/.28. LCCN:99-044899.

Audience: **l,u,f.** *Choice, 2001.*

Kerr, Anne   **T14.5**
Genetic Politics. Trade Cloth. New Clarion Press, Ltd.
Cheltenham, 2002. 211p. Issues in Social Policy Series Ser.
ISBN:1-873797-26-5, ISBN13: 978-1-873797-26-6.
Dewey:303.4/83.

Audience: **l,u,f.**

Kerr, Anne   **RB155.K477 2004**
Genetics and Society. Paper over Boards. Routledge. New York,
NY. 2004. 208p. ISBN:0-415-30081-9, ISBN13:
978-0-415-30081-0. Dewey:362.196/042. LCCN:2004-001266.

Audience: **l,u,f.**

Kieff, F. Scott (Editor)   **QH447**
Perspectives on Properties of the Human Genome Project, Vol.
50. Trade Cloth. Elsevier Science & Technology Books. Saint
Louis, MO. 2003. 538p. Advances in Genetics Ser., Vol. 50
ISBN:0-12-017650-5, ISBN13: 978-0-12-017650-2.
Dewey:599.935. LCCN:2004-298559.

Audience: **u,f.**

Kolchanov, Nikolay &   **QH447**
Hofestaedt, Ralf (Editors)
Bioinformatics of Genome Regulation and Structure. Trade
Cloth. Springer. New York, NY. 2004. 396p.
ISBN:1-4020-7735-1, ISBN13: 978-1-4020-7735-7.
Dewey:572.8/6. LCCN:2003-070159.

Audience: **u,f.**

Koonin, Eugene V. &   **QH447.K665 2002**
Galperin, Michael Y.
Sequence - Evolution - Function: Computational Approaches in
Comparative Genomics. Trade Cloth. Springer. New York, NY.
2002. 488p. ISBN:1-4020-7274-0, ISBN13: 978-1-4020-7274-1.
Dewey:572.8/6. LCCN:2002-034045.

Audience: **u,f.**

Lagergren, Jens (Editor)   **QH447.C654 2005**
Comparative Genomics: Recomb 2004 International Workshop,
Rcg 2004, Bertinoro, Italy, October 16-19, 2004, Revised
Selected Papers. Mixed Media. Springer. New York, NY. 2005.
VII, 133p. Lecture Notes in Computer Science / Lecture Notes
in Bioinformatics Ser., Vol. 3388 ISBN:3-540-24455-7, ISBN13:
978-3-540-24455-4. Dewey:572.8/6. LCCN:2004-118127.

Audience: **u,f.**

Lister, T.   **QH447**
Chemistry and the Human Genome. Trade Cloth. Springer. New
York, NY. 2002. 46p. ISBN:0-85404-396-9, ISBN13:
978-0-85404-396-5. Dewey:599.935.

Audience: **u,f.**

McConkey, Edwin H.   **QH447.M353 2004**
How the Human Genome Works. Trade Paper. Jones & Bartlett
Publishers, Inc. Sudbury, MA. 2004. 118p. ISBN:0-7637-2384-3,
ISBN13: 978-0-7637-2384-2. Dewey:611/.01816.
LCCN:2003-017746.

Audience: **u,f.**

McLachlan, Geoffrey J.,   **QP624.5.D726**
  et al.
Analyzing Microarray Gene Expression Data. Kim-Anh Do &
Christophe Ambroise (Authors). Trade Cloth. John Wiley &
Sons, Inc. Hoboken, NJ. 2004. 352p. Wiley Series in Probability
and Statistics Ser. ISBN:0-471-22616-5, ISBN13:
978-0-471-22616-1. Dewey:572.8/636. LCCN:2004-042239.

Audience: **u,f.**

Melville, Sara E.   **QL757.P25 2004**
Parasite Genomics Protocols. Book, Other. Humana Press.
Totowa, NJ. 2004. 472p. Methods in Molecular Biology Ser.
ISBN:1-58829-062-X, ISBN13: 978-1-58829-062-5.
Dewey:616.9/6. LCCN:2003-025343.

Audience: **u,f.**

Mewes, H. W. (Editor), et al.   **QH441.2.B545 2002**
Bioinformatics and Genome Analysis. B. Weiss & H. Seidel
(Editors). Trade Cloth. Springer. New York, NY. 2003. XV,
296p. Ernst Schering Research Foundation Workshop Ser., Vol.
38 ISBN:3-540-42893-3, ISBN13: 978-3-540-42893-0.
Dewey:570/.285. LCCN:2002-066917.

Audience: **u,f.**

Meyers, Robert A.   **QH506.E534 2004**
Encyclopedia of Molecular Cell Biology and Molecular
Medicine, Vol. 5. Ed. 2. Trade Cloth. John Wiley & Sons, Inc.
Hoboken, NJ. 2004. 698p. Encyclopedia of Molecular Biology
and Molecular Medicine Ser. ISBN:3-527-30547-5, ISBN13:
978-3-527-30547-6. Dewey:572.8/03. LCCN:2004-275355.

Audience: **u,f.**

Meyers, Robert A.   **QH506.E534 2004**
Encyclopedia of Molecular Cell Biology and Molecular
Medicine, Vol. 3. Ed. 2. Trade Cloth. John Wiley & Sons, Inc.
Hoboken, NJ. 2004. 720p. Encyclopedia of Molecular Biology
and Molecular Medicine Ser. ISBN:3-527-30545-9, ISBN13:
978-3-527-30545-2. Dewey:572.8/03. LCCN:2004-275355.

Audience: **u,f.**

Meyers, Robert A.   **QH506**
Encyclopedia of Molecular Cell Biology and Molecular
Medicine, Vol. 6. Ed. 2. Trade Cloth. John Wiley & Sons, Inc.
Hoboken, NJ. 2005. 670p. Encyclopedia of Molecular Biology
and Molecular Medicine 16Vset Ser. ISBN:3-527-30548-3,
ISBN13: 978-3-527-30548-3. Dewey:572.8/03.

Audience: **u,f.**

Meyers, Robert A.   **QH506**
Encyclopedia of Molecular Cell Biology and Molecular
Medicine, Vol. 10. Ed. 2. Trade Cloth. John Wiley & Sons, Inc.
Hoboken, NJ. 2005. 714p. Encyclopedia of Molecular Biology
and Molecular Medicine 16Vset Ser. ISBN:3-527-30552-1,
ISBN13: 978-3-527-30552-0. Dewey:572.8/03.

Audience: **u,f.**

Meyers, Robert A.   **QH506**
Encyclopedia of Molecular Cell Biology and Molecular
Medicine, Vol. 7. Ed. 2. Trade Cloth. John Wiley & Sons, Inc.

Hoboken, NJ. 2005. 662p. Encyclopedia of Molecular Biology
and Molecular Medicine 16Vset Ser. ISBN:3-527-30549-1,
ISBN13: 978-3-527-30549-0. Dewey:572.8/03.

Audience: **u,f.**

Meyers, Robert A.   **QH506.E534 2004**
Encyclopedia of Molecular Cell Biology and Molecular
Medicine, Vol. 2. Ed. 2. Trade Cloth. John Wiley & Sons, Inc.
Hoboken, NJ. 2004. 696p. Encyclopedia of Molecular Biology
and Molecular Medicine Ser. ISBN:3-527-30544-0, ISBN13:
978-3-527-30544-5. Dewey:572.8/03. LCCN:2004-275355.

Audience: **u,f.**

Meyers, Robert A.   **QH506.E534 2004**
Encyclopedia of Molecular Cell Biology and Molecular
Medicine, Vol. 1. Ed. 2. Trade Cloth. John Wiley & Sons, Inc.
Hoboken, NJ. 2004. 716p. Encyclopedia of Molecular Biology
and Molecular Medicine Ser. ISBN:3-527-30543-2, ISBN13:
978-3-527-30543-8. Dewey:572.8/03. LCCN:2004-275355.

Audience: **u,f.**

Meyers, Robert A.   **QH506.E534 2004**
Encyclopedia of Molecular Cell Biology and Molecular
Medicine, Vol. 4. Ed. 2. Trade Cloth. John Wiley & Sons, Inc.
Hoboken, NJ. 2004. 726p. Encyclopedia of Molecular Biology
and Molecular Medicine Ser. ISBN:3-527-30546-7, ISBN13:
978-3-527-30546-9. Dewey:572.8/03. LCCN:2004-275355.

Audience: **u,f.**

Meyers, Robert A.   **QH506**
Encyclopedia of Molecular Cell Biology and Molecular
Medicine, Vol. 8. Ed. 2. Trade Cloth. John Wiley & Sons, Inc.
Hoboken, NJ. 2005. 692p. Encyclopedia of Molecular Biology
and Molecular Medicine 16Vset Ser. ISBN:3-527-30550-5,
ISBN13: 978-3-527-30550-6. Dewey:572.8/03.

Audience: **u,f.**

Meyers, Robert A.   **QH506**
Encyclopedia of Molecular Cell Biology and Molecular
Medicine, Vol. 9. Ed. 2. Trade Cloth. John Wiley & Sons, Inc.
Hoboken, NJ. 2005. 634p. Encyclopedia of Molecular Biology
and Molecular Medicine 16Vset Ser. ISBN:3-527-30551-3,
ISBN13: 978-3-527-30551-3. Dewey:572.8/03.

Audience: **u,f.**

Meyers, Robert A.   **QH506**
Encyclopedia of Molecular Cell Biology and Molecular
Medicine, Index, Vol. 16. Ed. 2. Trade Cloth. John Wiley &
Sons, Inc. Hoboken, NJ. 2006. 334p. Encyclopedia of Molecular
Biology and Molecular Medicine 16Vset Ser.
ISBN:3-527-30653-6, ISBN13: 978-3-527-30653-4.
Dewey:572.803.

Audience: **u,f.**

Meyers, Robert A.   **QH506**
Encyclopedia of Molecular Cell Biology and Molecular
Medicine, Proteasomes to Receptor, Transporter and Ion
Channel Diseases, Vol. 11. Ed. 2. Trade Cloth. John Wiley &
Sons, Inc. Hoboken, NJ. 2005. 776p. Encyclopedia of Molecular
Biology and Molecular Medicine 16Vset Ser.
ISBN:3-527-30648-X, ISBN13: 978-3-527-30648-0.
Dewey:572.8/03.

Audience: **u,f.**

Meyers, Robert A.   **QH506**
Encyclopedia of Molecular Cell Biology and Molecular
Medicine, Recombination and Genome Rearrangements to Serial
Analysis of Gene Expression, Vol. 12. Ed. 2. Trade Cloth. John

Wiley & Sons, Inc. Hoboken, NJ. 2005. 796p. Encyclopedia of Molecular Biology and Molecular Medicine 16Vset Ser. ISBN:3-527-30649-8, ISBN13: 978-3-527-30649-7. Dewey:572.8/03.

Audience: **u,f.**

Meyers, Robert A.   **QH506**
Encyclopedia of Molecular Cell Biology and Molecular Medicine, Sex Hormones (Male): Analogs and Antagonists to Synchrotron Infrared Microspectroscopy, Vol. 13. Ed. 2. Trade Cloth. John Wiley & Sons, Inc. Hoboken, NJ. 2005. 760p. Encyclopedia of Molecular Biology and Molecular Medicine 16Vset Ser. ISBN:3-527-30650-1, ISBN13: 978-3-527-30650-3. Dewey:572.8/03.

Audience: **u,f.**

Meyers, Robert A.   **QH506**
Encyclopedia of Molecular Cell Biology and Molecular Medicine, Syngamy and Cell Cycle Control to Triacylglyerol Storage and Mobilization, Regulation Of, Vol. 14. Ed. 2. Trade Cloth. John Wiley & Sons, Inc. Hoboken, NJ. 2005. 766p. Encyclopedia of Molecular Biology and Molecular Medicine 16Vset Ser. ISBN:3-527-30651-X, ISBN13: 978-3-527-30651-0. Dewey:572.8/03.

Audience: **u,f.**

Meyers, Robert A.   **QH506**
Encyclopedia of Molecular Cell Biology and Molecular Medicine, Triplet Repeat Diseases to Zebrafish (Danio rerio) Genome and Genetics, Vol. 15. Ed. 2. Trade Cloth. John Wiley & Sons, Inc. Hoboken, NJ. 2005. 676p. Encyclopedia of Molecular Biology and Molecular Medicine 16Vset Ser. ISBN:3-527-30652-8, ISBN13: 978-3-527-30652-7. Dewey:572.8/03.

Audience: **u,f.**

Miller, O. J. & Therman,   **QH431.T436 2001**
  Eeva
Human Chromosomes. Ed. 4. Trade Cloth. Springer. New York, NY. 2000. XVI, 501p. ISBN:0-387-95031-1, ISBN13: 978-0-387-95031-0. Dewey:611/.01816. LCCN:00-044007.
Audience: **u,f.**

Mount, David   **QH441.2.M68 2004**
Bioinformatics: Sequence and Genome Analysis. Ed. 2. Trade Cloth. Cold Spring Harbor Laboratory Press. Woodbury, NY. 2004. 600p. ISBN:0-87969-687-7, ISBN13: 978-0-87969-687-0. Dewey:572.8/633. LCCN:2004-009760.

Audience: **u,f.**

Opresko, Lee   **QH313.A386 2004**
Advances in Systems Biology. Julie M. Gephart & Michaela B. Mann (Editors). Trade Cloth. Springer. New York, NY. 2004. 116p. Advances in Experimental Medicine and Biology Ser., Vol. 547 ISBN:0-306-48314-9, ISBN13: 978-0-306-48314-1. Dewey:571. LCCN:2003-068653.

Audience: **u,f.**

Palsson, Bernhard O.   **QH324.2.P35 2006**
Systems Biology: Properties of Reconstructed Networks. Cloth Text. Cambridge University Press. New York, NY. 2006. 334p. ISBN:0-521-85903-4, ISBN13: 978-0-521-85903-5. Dewey:572.80285. LCCN:2005-035008.

Audience: **u,f.**

Percus, Jerome K.   **QH438.4.M3 P47 2002**
Mathematics of Genome Analysis. C. Cannings, F. C. Hoppensteadt & L. A. Segel (Contribution by). Cloth Text.

Cambridge University Press. New York, NY. 2001. 150p. Studies in Mathematical Biology, Vol. 17 ISBN:0-521-58517-1, ISBN13: 978-0-521-58517-0. Dewey:572.860151. LCCN:2001-035087.

Audience: **u,f.** *Choice, 2002.*

Pevsner, Jonathan   **QH441.2.P48 2003**
Bioinformatics and Functional Genomics. Trade Paper. John Wiley & Sons, Inc. Hoboken, NJ. 2003. 792p. ISBN:0-471-21004-8, ISBN13: 978-0-471-21004-7. Dewey:572/.0285. LCCN:2002-156139.

Audience: **u,f.** *Choice, 2004.*

Priami, Corrado   **QH506.T73 2005**
  (Contribution by)
Transactions on Computational Systems Biology I. Mixed Media. Springer. New York, NY. 2005. IX, 111p. Lecture Notes in Computer Science / Lecture Notes in Bioinformatics Ser. ISBN:3-540-25422-6, ISBN13: 978-3-540-25422-5. Dewey:572.80285. LCCN:2005-922555.

Audience: **u,f.**

Primrose, Sandy, et al.   **QH442.O42 2006**
Principles of Gene Manipulation and Genomics. Ed. 7. Richard Twyman, Bob Old & Giuseppe Bertola (Authors). Trade Paper. Blackwell Publishing, Inc. Malden, MA. 2006. 668p. ISBN:1-4051-3544-1, ISBN13: 978-1-4051-3544-3. Dewey:660.6/5. LCCN:2005-018202.

Audience: **u,f.**

Raychaudhuri, Soumya   **QH452.7**
Computational Text Analysis: For Functional Genomics and Bioinformatics. Trade Cloth. Oxford University Press, Inc. New York, NY. 2006. 312p. ISBN:0-19-856740-5, ISBN13: 978-0-19-856740-0. Dewey:572.86. LCCN:2006-296260.

Audience: **u,f.**

Rigoutsos, Isidore &   **QH324.2.S97 2006**
  Stephanopoulos, G.
Systems Biology. Trade Cloth. Oxford University Press, Inc. New York, NY. 2006. 366p. Series in Systems Biology ISBN:0-19-530080-7, ISBN13: 978-0-19-530080-2. Dewey:570. LCCN:2005-031826.

Audience: **u,f.**

Rigoutsos, Isidore &   **QH324.2.S97 2006**
  Stephanopoulos, Gregory (Editors)
Systems Biology: Volume 1: Genomics. Trade Cloth. Oxford University Press, Inc. New York, NY. 2006. 416p. Series in Systems Biology ISBN:0-19-530081-5, ISBN13: 978-0-19-530081-9. Dewey:570. LCCN:2005-031826.

Audience: **u,f.**

Rosenthal, A. &   **QH447.H845 2002**
  Vakalopoulou, L. (Editors)
The Human Genome: Biology and Medicine. Cloth Text. Springer. New York, NY. 2002. 156p. Ernst Schering Research Foundation Workshop Ser., Vol. 36 ISBN:3-540-42316-8, ISBN13: 978-3-540-42316-4. Dewey:611/.01816. LCCN:2002-283754.

Audience: **u,f.**

Sensen, Christoph W.   **QH447.E87 2002**
  (Editor)
Essentials of Genomics and Bioinformatics. Trade Paper. John

Wiley & Sons, Inc. Hoboken, NJ. 2002. 442p.
ISBN:3-527-30541-6, ISBN13: 978-3-527-30541-4.
Dewey:572.86. LCCN:2002-523891.

Audience: **u,f.**

Sensen, Christoph W.   **QH447**
  (Editor)
Handbook of Genome Research: Genomics, Proteomics,
Metabolomics, Bioinformatics, Ethical and Legal Issues. Trade
Cloth. John Wiley & Sons, Inc. Hoboken, NJ. 2005. 646p.
ISBN:3-527-31348-6, ISBN13: 978-3-527-31348-8.
Dewey:572.86.

Audience: **u,f.** *Choice, 2006.*

Stillman, Bruce & Stewart,   **QH301**
  David (Editors)
Epigenetics, Vol. 69. Trade Cloth. Cold Spring Harbor
Laboratory Press. Woodbury, NY. 2005. 520p. Cold Spring
Harbor Symposia on Quantitative Biology Ser., No. LXIX
ISBN:0-87969-729-6, ISBN13: 978-0-87969-729-7.
Dewey:570.6.

Audience: **u,f.**

Strachan, Tom & Read,   **QH431.S787 2003**
  Andrew P. (Translators)
Human Molecular Genetics. Ed. 3. Paper over Boards. Garland
Publishing, Inc. New York, NY. 2003. 696p.
ISBN:0-8153-4182-2, ISBN13: 978-0-8153-4182-6.
Dewey:611/.01816. LCCN:2003-017961.

Audience: **u,f.**

Vaidyanathan, Seetharaman   **QP171.M382 2005**
  (Editor), et al.
Metabolome Analyses: Strategies for Systems Biology. George
G. Harrigan & Royston Goodacre (Editors). Trade Cloth.
Springer. New York, NY. 2005. XXII, 394p.
ISBN:0-387-25239-8, ISBN13: 978-0-387-25239-1.
Dewey:572/.4. LCCN:2005-047906.

Audience: **u,f.**

Wade, Nicholas   **RB155.W326 2001**
Life Script: How the Human Genome Discoveries Will
Transform Medicine and Enhance Your Health. Trade Cloth.
Simon & Schuster. New York, NY. 2001. 208p.
ISBN:0-7432-1605-9, ISBN13: 978-0-7432-1605-0.
Dewey:616/.042. LCCN:2001-042627.

Audience: **l,u,f.**

Wang, Jason T. L. (Editor),   **QH324.2.C635 2003**
  et al.
Computational Biology and Genome Informatics. Cathy H. Wu
& Paul P. Wang (Editors). Trade Cloth. World Scientific
Publishing Company, Inc. Hackensack, NJ. 2003. 270p.
ISBN:981-238-257-7, ISBN13: 978-981-238-257-3.
Dewey:572.86. LCCN:2003-544795.

Audience: **u,f.**

Warshawsky, David (Editor)   **RC268.6**
Molecular Carcinogenesis and the Molecular Biology of Human
Cancer. Landolph, Joseph R. (Editor). CRC. Taylor and Francis:
Boca Raton. 2005. ISBN:0-8493-1167-5, ISBN13:
978-0-8493-1167-3.

Audience: **u,f.**

Williams, Clyde R. (Editor)   **QH447.F638 2004**
Focus on Genome Research. Trade Cloth. Nova Science
Publishers, Inc. Hauppauge, NY. 2004. 424p.
ISBN:1-59033-960-6, ISBN13: 978-1-59033-960-2.
Dewey:572.8/6. LCCN:2004-003036.

Audience: **u,f.**

Woodford, Neil & Johnson,   **QR74.G46 2004**
  Alan (Editors)
Genomics, Proteomics, and Clinical Bacteriology: Methods and
Reviews. Book, Other. Humana Press. Totowa, NJ. 2004. 408p.
Methods in Molecular Biologytm Ser. ISBN:1-58829-218-5,
ISBN13: 978-1-58829-218-6. Dewey:616.9/201.
LCCN:2004-000332.

Audience: **u,f.**

Wu, Carl & Allis, C. David
Chromatin and Chromatin Remodeling Enzymes, Pt. C. Trade
Cloth. Elsevier Science & Technology Books. Saint Louis, MO.
2004. 546p. Methods in Enzymology Ser. ISBN:0-12-182781-X,
ISBN13: 978-0-12-182781-6. Dewey:572.87.

Audience: **u,f.**

Wu, Catherine H. &   **QH441.2.W8 2000**
  McLarty, Jerry W.
Neural Networks and Genome Informatics. Trade Cloth. Elsevier
Science & Technology Books. Saint Louis, MO. 2000. 220p.
Methods in Computational and Theoretical Molecular Biology
Ser., 1 ISBN:0-08-042800-2, ISBN13: 978-0-08-042800-0.
Dewey:576.5/0285/632. LCCN:00-056153.

Audience: **u,f.**

Young, Paul   **QH447**
Exploring Genomes: Web-Based Bioinformatic Excercises.
Trade Paper. Worth Publishers, Inc. New York, NY. 2002. 51p.
ISBN:0-7167-5738-9, ISBN13: 978-0-7167-5738-2.
Dewey:572.8/6.

Audience: **u,f.**

Cellular and Molecular Biology, Genetics > Genetics (General) > Population Genetics

Cappuccino, Naomi & Price,   **QH352.P626 1995**
  Peter W. (Editors)
Population Dynamics: New Approaches and Synthesis. Trade
Cloth. Elsevier Science & Technology Books. Saint Louis, MO.
1995. 429p. ISBN:0-12-159270-7, ISBN13: 978-0-12-159270-7.
Dewey:574.5/248. LCCN:95-014616.

Audience: **u,f.**

Dawkins, Richard &   **QH375.D38 1999**
  Dennett, Daniel Clement
The Extended Phenotype: The Long Reach of the Gene. Ed. 2.
Trade Paper. Oxford University Press, Inc. New York, NY. 1999.
324p. Popular Science Ser. ISBN:0-19-288051-9, ISBN13:
978-0-19-288051-2. Dewey:576.8/2. LCCN:98-044794.

Audience: **u,f.**

Edwards, Anthony W. F.   **QH438.4.M3 E37 2000**
Foundations of Mathematical Genetics. Ed. 2. Trade Paper.
Cambridge University Press. New York, NY. 2000. 133p.
ISBN:0-521-77544-2, ISBN13: 978-0-521-77544-1.
Dewey:576.5/8/015118. LCCN:00-702895.

Audience: **u,f.**

Hughes, Austin L.   **QH390.H84 1999**
Adaptive Evolution of Genes and Genomes. Trade Cloth.
Oxford University Press, Inc. New York, NY. 2000. 282p.
ISBN:0-19-511626-7, ISBN13: 978-0-19-511626-7.
Dewey:572.8/38. LCCN:98-046584.
                                               Audience: **u,f.**

Thomas, Duncan C.   **RB155.T468 2004**
Statistical Methods in Genetic Epidemiology. Trade Cloth.
Oxford University Press, Inc. New York, NY. 2004. 458p.
ISBN:0-19-515939-X, ISBN13: 978-0-19-515939-4.
Dewey:616/.042. LCCN:2003-053096.
                                               Audience: **u,f.**

Cellular and Molecular Biology, Genetics > Genetics (General) > Genomics

☐ ASL Arts & Sciences Libraries Genomics Research and Bioinformatics.
http://ublib.buffalo.edu/libraries/asl/guides/bio/genome/
human_genome.html
University at Buffalo, The State University of New York.
                                               Audience: **g,l.**

☐ ASL Arts & Sciences Libraries: Biodiversity.
http://ublib.buffalo.edu/libraries/asl/guides/environment/
biodiversity
Univertstiy at Buffalo, The State University of New York.
                                               Audience: **g,l.**

                                               QH447
☐ Entrez Genome.
http://www.ncbi.nlm.nih.gov:80/entrez/query.fcgi?db=Genome
                                               Audience: **u,f.**

                                               QH470.D7
☐ FlyBase.
http://flybase.bio.indiana.edu/
                                               Audience: **u,f.**

☐ Google Directory: Biology, Genetics, Genomics.
http://google.com/Top/Science/Biology/Genetics/Genomics/
Google.
                                               Audience: **g,l.**

                                               Z692.C65
☐ HHMI Howard Hughes Medical Institute: Blazing a Genetic Trail.
http://hhmi.org/genetictrail/
Howard Hughes Medical Institute.
                                               Audience: **g,l.**

                                               QH438.4.S73
☐ The Human Genome Project Information DOE HGP Genomics Primers.
http://www.ornl.gov/sci/techresources/Human_Genome/publicat/
primer/index.shtml
U.S. Department of Energy Office of Science, Office of
Biological and Environmental Research.
                                               Audience: **g,l.**

☐ The Human Genome Project Publications.
http://www.ornl.gov/sci/techresources/Human_Genome/
publications.shtml
U.S. Department of Energy Office of Science, Office of
Biological and Environmental Research.
                                               Audience: **g,l.**

☐ The Human Genome Project Resources.
http://www.ornl.gov/sci/techresources/Human_Genome/publicat/
tko/09_resources.html
U.S. Department of Energy Office of Science, Office of
Biological and Environmental Research.
                                               Audience: **g,l.**

☐ The Human Genome Project: Exlploring the Genomic Landscape.
http://ornl.gov/sci/techresources/Human_Genome/publicat/tko/
04_exploring.html
U.S. Department of Energy Office of Science, Office of
Biological and Environmental Research.
                                               Audience: **g,l.**

                                               QH447
☐ Mouse Genome Resources.
http://www.ncbi.nlm.nih.gov/genome/guide/mouse/
                                               Audience: **u,f.**

☐ National Library of Medicine PubMed Tutorial.
http://www.nlm.nih.gov/bsd/pubmed_tutorial/m1001.html
National Library of Medicine; National Institutes of Health;
Department of Health and Human Services.
                                               Audience: **g,l.**

                                               QH447
☐ Trans-NIH Mouse Initiatives.
http://www.nih.gov/science/models/mouse/
                                               Audience: **u.**

                                               Z5322.G4
☐ Virtual Library of Genetics.
http://www.ornl.gov/sci/techresources/Human_Genome/
genetics.shtml
U.S. Department of Energy Office of Science, Office of
Biological and Environmental Research.
                                               Audience: **g,l.**

Alon, Uri   **QH324.2.A46 2006**
Introduction to Systems Biology and the Design Principles of
Biological Circuits. CRC Press. 2006. ISBN:1-58488-642-0,
ISBN13: 978-1-58488-642-6.
                                               Audience: **u,f.**

Augen, Jeff   **QH441.2**
Bioinformatics in the Post-Genomic Era: Genome,
Transcriptome, Proteome, and Information-Based Medicine.
Trade Paper. Addison Wesley Professional. Boston, MA. 2004.
400p. ISBN:0-321-17386-4, ISBN13: 978-0-321-17386-7.
Dewey:572.8/0285. LCCN:2004-106573.
                                               Audience: **u,f.**

Batiza, Ann   **QH324.2B38 2005**
Bioinformatics, Genomics, and Proteomics: Getting the Big
Picture. Trade Cloth, Laminated. Facts On File, Inc.. New York,

NY. 2005. 112p. Biotechnology in the 21st Century Ser. ISBN:0-7910-8517-1, ISBN13: 978-0-7910-8517-2. Dewey:572.8/0285. LCCN:2005-017232.

Audience: **u,f.**

Baxevanis, Andreas D. &   **QP551**
Ouellette, B. F. Francis (Editors)
Bioinformatics: A Practical Guide to the Analysis of Genes and Proteins. Ed. 3. Trade Cloth. John Wiley & Sons, Inc. Hoboken, NJ. 2004. 560p. ISBN:0-471-47878-4, ISBN13: 978-0-471-47878-2. Dewey:572.8/633/0285. LCCN:2004-011822.

Audience: **u,f.**

Blot, Michel (Editor)   **QH434.P764 2002**
Prokaryotic Genomics. Trade Cloth. Birkhauser Boston. Cambridge, MA. 2003. XII, 208p. Methods and Tools in Biosciences and Medicine Ser. ISBN:3-7643-6597-8, ISBN13: 978-3-7643-6597-4. Dewey:579.3/135. LCCN:2002-027928.

Audience: **u,f.**

Borlak, Jürgen (Editor)   **RB155**
Handbook of Toxicogenomics: Strategies and Applications. Trade Cloth. John Wiley & Sons, Inc. Hoboken, NJ. 2005. 705p. ISBN:3-527-30342-1, ISBN13: 978-3-527-30342-7. Dewey:616.042.

Audience: **u,f.**

Bower, James M. & Bolouri,   **QP517.M3C638 2004**
Hamid (Editors)
Computational Modeling of Genetic and Biochemical Networks. Trade Paper. MIT Press. Cambridge, MA. 2004. 390p. Computational Molecular Biology Ser. ISBN:0-262-52423-6, ISBN13: 978-0-262-52423-0. Dewey:572/.01/5118.

Audience: **u,f.**

Burczynski, Michael E.   **QH438.4.B55**
(Editor)
Surrogate Tissue Analysis: Genomic, Proteomic and Metabolomic Approaches. Rockett, John C. (Editor). CRC Press: Boca Raton. 2006. ISBN:0-8493-2840-3, ISBN13: 978-0-8493-2840-4.

Audience: **u,f.**

Campbell, A. Malcolm &   **QH447.C35 2002**
Heyer, Laurie J.
Discovering Genomics, Proteomics, and Bioinformatics. Mixed Media, Book, Other, Paper Text, CD-ROM. Benjamin-Cummings Publishing Company. San Francisco, CA. 2002. 352p. ISBN:0-8053-4722-4, ISBN13: 978-0-8053-4722-7. Dewey:572.8/6. LCCN:2002-067456.

Audience: **u,f.**

Cantor, Charles R. & Smith,   **QP624.C36 1999**
Cassandra L.
Genomics: The Science and Technology Behind the Human Genome Project. Trade Cloth. John Wiley & Sons, Inc. Hoboken, NJ. 1999. 624p. Baker Lecture Ser., Vol. 6 ISBN:0-471-59908-5, ISBN13: 978-0-471-59908-1. Dewey:572.8/6. LCCN:98-040448.

Audience: **l,u,f.** *Choice, 1999.*

Caporale, Lynn Helena   **QH366.2.C367 2002**
Darwin in the Genome: Molecular Strategies in Biological Evolution. Trade Cloth. McGraw-Hill Companies, The. New York, NY. 2002. 256p. ISBN:0-07-137822-7, ISBN13: 978-0-07-137822-2. Dewey:576. LCCN:2002-009570.

Audience: **u,f.**

Caporale, Lynn Helena   **QH390.I47 2006**
(Editor)
The Implicit Genome. Trade Cloth. Oxford University Press, Inc. New York, NY. 2006. 398p. ISBN:0-19-517270-1, ISBN13: 978-0-19-517270-6. Dewey:572.8/38. LCCN:2005-011590.

Audience: **u,f.**

Dawkins, Richard &   **QH375.D38 1999**
Dennett, Daniel Clement
The Extended Phenotype: The Long Reach of the Gene. Ed. 2. Trade Paper. Oxford University Press, Inc. New York, NY. 1999. 324p. Popular Science Ser. ISBN:0-19-288051-9, ISBN13: 978-0-19-288051-2. Dewey:576.8/2. LCCN:98-044794.

Audience: **u,f.**

Dunn, Michael J. (Editor)   **QP551.F94 2000**
From Genome to Proteome: Advances in the Practice and Application of Proteomics. Trade Cloth. John Wiley & Sons, Inc. Hoboken, NJ. 2000. 552p. ISBN:3-527-30154-2, ISBN13: 978-3-527-30154-6. Dewey:572/.6. LCCN:00-697886.

Audience: **u,f.**

Finnish Metla Forest
Research Institute
WWW Virtual Library: Forestry, Forest Genetics & Tree Breeding. http://www.metla.fi/info/vlib/forestgen/ Finnish Metla Forest Research Institute.

Audience: **g,l.**

Gad, Shayne Cox (Editor)   **RM301.25.D784 2005**
Drug Discovery Handbook. Trade Cloth. John Wiley & Sons, Inc. Hoboken, NJ. 2005. 1496p. ISBN:0-471-21384-5, ISBN13: 978-0-471-21384-0. Dewey:615/.19. LCCN:2004-027077.

Audience: **u,f.**

Hughes, Austin L.   **QH390.H84 1999**
Adaptive Evolution of Genes and Genomes. Trade Cloth. Oxford University Press, Inc. New York, NY. 2000. 282p. ISBN:0-19-511626-7, ISBN13: 978-0-19-511626-7. Dewey:572.8/38. LCCN:98-046584.

Audience: **u,f.**

HumanGenome Project (ed.)   **QH447**
The Human Genome Project: Exploring our Molecular Selves. http://www.genome.gov/Pages/EducationKit/online.htm National Human Genome Research Institute (NHGRI).

Audience: **u,f.**

Jackson, M., et al.   **QH431**
Human Genome Evolution: Human Molecular Genetics. T. Strachan & G. Dover (Authors). Cloth Text. Taylor & Francis Group. Abingdon, 1996. 256p. Human Molecular Genetics Ser. ISBN:1-85996-095-2, ISBN13: 978-1-85996-095-0. Dewey:599.9/35.

Audience: **u,f.** *Choice, 1997.*

Kanehisa, Minoru   **QH447.K365 2000**
Post-Genome Informatics. Trade Paper. Oxford University Press, Inc. New York, NY. 2000. 158p. ISBN:0-19-850326-1, ISBN13: 978-0-19-850326-2. Dewey:572.8/6/0285. LCCN:99-049584.

Audience: **u,f.**

Kitano, Hiroaki (Editor)   QH313.F66 2002
Foundations of Systems Biology. Trade Cloth. MIT Press. Cambridge, MA. 2001. 320p. ISBN:0-262-11266-3, ISBN13: 978-0-262-11266-6. Dewey:573. LCCN:2001-042807.

Audience: **l,u.**

Lengauer, Thomas (Editor)   QH506
Bioinformatics-From Genomes to Drugs, Set. Hugo Kubinyi, Raimund Mannhold & Hendrik Timmerman (Contribution by). Trade Cloth. John Wiley & Sons, Inc. Hoboken, NJ. 2002. 668p. Methods and Principles in Medicinal Chemistry Ser., Vol. 14 ISBN:3-527-29988-2, ISBN13: 978-3-527-29988-1. Dewey:572.80285. LCCN:2002-524729.

Audience: **u,f.**

Mewes, H. W. (Editor), et al.   QH441.2.B545 2002
Bioinformatics and Genome Analysis. B. Weiss & H. Seidel (Editors). Trade Cloth. Springer. New York, NY. 2003. XV, 296p. Ernst Schering Research Foundation Workshop Ser., Vol. 38 ISBN:3-540-42893-3, ISBN13: 978-3-540-42893-0. Dewey:570/.285. LCCN:2002-066917.

Audience: **u,f.**

Moussa, Naima Moustaid &   QP171
  Berdanier, Carolyn
Genomics and Proteomics in Nutrition. Paper over Boards. Marcel Dekker Inc. New York, NY. 2004. 528p. Nutrition in Health and Disease Ser., Vol. 1 ISBN:0-8247-5430-1, ISBN13: 978-0-8247-5430-3. Dewey:612.3. LCCN:2004-275369.

Audience: **u,f.**

Pevsner, Jonathan   QH441.2.P48 2003
Bioinformatics and Functional Genomics. Trade Paper. John Wiley & Sons, Inc. Hoboken, NJ. 2003. 792p. ISBN:0-471-21004-8, ISBN13: 978-0-471-21004-7. Dewey:572/.0285. LCCN:2002-156139.

Audience: **u,f.** *Choice, 2004.*

Primrose, S. B. & Twyman,   QH445.2.P75 2002
  Richard M.
Principles of Genome Analysis and Genomics. Ed. 3. Trade Paper. Blackwell Publishing, Inc. Malden, MA. 2002. 288p. ISBN:1-4051-0120-2, ISBN13: 978-1-4051-0120-2. Dewey:572.8/633. LCCN:2002-070937.

Audience: **u,f.**

Raghavachari, Ramesh &   TP248.6.G523 2001
  Tan, Weihong
Genomics and Proteomics Technologies. Trade Paper. S P I E-International Society for Optical Engineering. Bellingham, WA. 2001. v, 82p. Proceeding Ser., No. 2 ISBN:0-8194-3942-8, ISBN13: 978-0-8194-3942-0. Dewey:660.6/5. LCCN:2001-279171.

Audience: **u,f.**

Raychaudhuri, Soumya   QH452.7
Computational Text Analysis: For Functional Genomics and Bioinformatics. Trade Cloth. Oxford University Press, Inc. New York, NY. 2006. 312p. ISBN:0-19-856740-5, ISBN13: 978-0-19-856740-0. Dewey:572.86. LCCN:2006-296260.

Audience: **u,f.**

Reardon, Jenny   QH431.R248 2004
Race to the Finish: Identity and Governance in an Age of Genomics. Trade Cloth. Princeton University Press. Princeton,

NJ. 2004. 312p. In-formation Ser. ISBN:0-691-11856-6, ISBN13: 978-0-691-11856-7. Dewey:306.4/5. LCCN:2004-050569.

Audience: **u,f.**

Rigoutsos, Isidore &   QH324.2.S97 2006
  Stephanopoulos, Gregory (Editors)
Systems Biology: Volume 1: Genomics. Trade Cloth. Oxford University Press, Inc. New York, NY. 2006. 416p. Series in Systems Biology ISBN:0-19-530081-5, ISBN13: 978-0-19-530081-9. Dewey:570. LCCN:2005-031826.

Audience: **u,f.**

Robin, Stephane, et al.   QP624
DNA, Words and Models: Statistics of Exceptional Words. Francois Rodolphe & Sophie Schbath (Authors). Trade Cloth. Cambridge University Press. New York, NY. 2005. 158p. ISBN:0-521-84729-X, ISBN13: 978-0-521-84729-2. Dewey:572.8/633. LCCN:2005-047088.

Audience: **u,f.**

Rosenthal, A. &   QH447.H845 2002
  Vakalopoulou, L. (Editors)
The Human Genome: Biology and Medicine. Cloth Text. Springer. New York, NY. 2002. 156p. Ernst Schering Research Foundation Workshop Ser., Vol. 36 ISBN:3-540-42316-8, ISBN13: 978-3-540-42316-4. Dewey:611/.01816. LCCN:2002-283754.

Audience: **u,f.**

Rédei, George P.   QH427.R43 2003
Encyclopedic Dictionary of Genetics, Genomics, and Proteomics. Ed. 2. Trade Cloth. John Wiley & Sons, Inc. Hoboken, NJ. 2003. 1392p. ISBN:0-471-26821-6, ISBN13: 978-0-471-26821-5. Dewey:576.5/03. LCCN:2002-011131.
Audience: **g,l,u,f.** *Choice, 2004.*

Saccone, Cecilia & Pesole,   QH447.S23 2003
  Graziano
Handbook of Comparative Genomics: Principles and Methodology. Trade Cloth. John Wiley & Sons, Inc. Hoboken, NJ. 2003. 442p. ISBN:0-471-39128-X, ISBN13: 978-0-471-39128-9. Dewey:572.8. LCCN:2002-011158.
Audience: **u,f.**

Salinas (Editor)   QK495.C9A735 2005
Arabidopsis Protocols. Ed. 2. Trade Cloth. Humana Press. Totowa, NJ. 2005. 525p. Methods in Molecular Biology Ser. ISBN:1-58829-395-5, ISBN13: 978-1-58829-395-4. Dewey:583/.64. LCCN:2005-016343.

Audience: **u,f.**

Schena, Mark   QP624.5.D726S34 2002
Microarray Analysis: Mining the Human Genome. Trade Cloth. John Wiley & Sons, Inc. Hoboken, NJ. 2002. 648p. ISBN:0-471-41443-3, ISBN13: 978-0-471-41443-8. Dewey:572.8/636. LCCN:2002-011157.

Audience: **u,f.**

Scientific American Staff   QH447.O45 2002
Understanding the Genome. Trade Paper. Warner Books, Inc. New York, NY. 2002. 160p. Science Made Accessible Ser. ISBN:0-446-67872-4, ISBN13: 978-0-446-67872-8. Dewey:611/.01816. LCCN:2001-093742.

Audience: **u,f.**

Sensen, Christoph W.   QH447.E87 2002
  (Editor)
Essentials of Genomics and Bioinformatics. Trade Paper. John
Wiley & Sons, Inc. Hoboken, NJ. 2002. 442p.
ISBN:3-527-30541-6, ISBN13: 978-3-527-30541-4.
Dewey:572.86. LCCN:2002-523891.
                                            Audience: **u,f.**

Sensen, Christoph W.   QH447
  (Editor)
Handbook of Genome Research: Genomics, Proteomics,
Metabolomics, Bioinformatics, Ethical and Legal Issues. Trade
Cloth. John Wiley & Sons, Inc. Hoboken, NJ. 2005. 646p.
ISBN:3-527-31348-6, ISBN13: 978-3-527-31348-8.
Dewey:572.86.
                          Audience: **u,f.** *Choice, 2006.*

Stillman, Bruce & Stewart,   DS597.367.K4 2003
  David (Editors)
The Genome of Homo Sapiens. Trade Cloth. Cold Spring
Harbor Laboratory Press. Woodbury, NY. 2004. 650p. Symposia
on Quantitative Biology Ser., LXVIII ISBN:0-87969-709-1,
ISBN13: 978-0-87969-709-9. Dewey:599.935.
                                            Audience: **u,f.**

Suhai, Sándor   QH445.2.G473 2000
Genomics and Proteomics: Functional and Computational
Aspects. Trade Cloth. Springer. New York, NY. 2000. 258p.
ISBN:0-306-46312-1, ISBN13: 978-0-306-46312-9.
Dewey:572.8/633/0285. LCCN:00-022525.
                                            Audience: **u,f.**

Sussman, Hillary E. & Smit,   QH447.G46515 2006
  Maria A. (Editors)
Genomes. Trade Cloth. Cold Spring Harbor Laboratory Press.
Woodbury, NY. 2006. 488p. Cold Spring Harbor Monograph
Ser., Vol. 46 ISBN:0-87969-806-3, ISBN13: 978-0-87969-806-5.
Dewey:572.8/6. LCCN:2006-001768.
                                            Audience: **u,f.**

Tavani, Herman T.   QH441.2.T38 2006
Ethics, Computing, and Genomics. Trade Paper. Jones & Bartlett
Publishers, Inc. Sudbury, MA. 2005. 356p.
ISBN:0-7637-3620-1, ISBN13: 978-0-7637-3620-0.
Dewey:174/.957. LCCN:2005-007396.
                                            Audience: **u,f.**

Townsend, Chris   QK981.4.F864 2002
Functional Genomics. Trade Cloth. Springer. New York, NY.
2002. 208p. ISBN:1-4020-0456-7, ISBN13: 978-1-4020-0456-8.
Dewey:572.8/2. LCCN:2002-283373.
                                            Audience: **u,f.**

Vaidyanathan, Seetharaman   QP171.M382 2005
  (Editor), et al.
Metabolome Analyses: Strategies for Systems Biology. George
G. Harrigan & Royston Goodacre (Editors). Trade Cloth.
Springer. New York, NY. 2005. XXII, 394p.
ISBN:0-387-25239-8, ISBN13: 978-0-387-25239-1.
Dewey:572/.4. LCCN:2005-047906.
                                            Audience: **u,f.**

Wang, Jason T. L. (Editor),   QH324.2.C635 2003
  et al.
Computational Biology and Genome Informatics. Cathy H. Wu
& Paul P. Wang (Editors). Trade Cloth. World Scientific

Publishing Company, Inc. Hackensack, NJ. 2003. 270p.
ISBN:981-238-257-7, ISBN13: 978-981-238-257-3.
Dewey:572.86. LCCN:2003-544795.
                                            Audience: **u,f.**

Wilkins, M. R.   QP551.P756 1997
Proteome Research: New Frontiers in Functional Genomics. Ron
D. Appel, Denis F. Hochstrasser & Keith L. Williams (Volume
Editors). Trade Paper. Springer. New York, NY. 1997. XVIII,
243p. Principles and Practice Ser. ISBN:3-540-62753-7,
ISBN13: 978-3-540-62753-1. Dewey:572/.6. LCCN:97-030956.
                                            Audience: **u,f.**

Williams, Clyde R. (Editor)   QH447.F638 2004
Focus on Genome Research. Trade Cloth. Nova Science
Publishers, Inc. Hauppauge, NY. 2004. 424p.
ISBN:1-59033-960-6, ISBN13: 978-1-59033-960-2.
Dewey:572.8/6. LCCN:2004-003036.
                                            Audience: **u,f.**

Woodford, Neil & Johnson,   QR74.G46 2004
  Alan (Editors)
Genomics, Proteomics, and Clinical Bacteriology: Methods and
Reviews. Book, Other. Humana Press. Totowa, NJ. 2004. 408p.
Methods in Molecular Biologytm Ser. ISBN:1-58829-218-5,
ISBN13: 978-1-58829-218-6. Dewey:616.9/201.
LCCN:2004-000332.
                                            Audience: **u,f.**

Wu, Catherine H. &   QH441.2.W8 2000
  McLarty, Jerry W.
Neural Networks and Genome Informatics. Trade Cloth. Elsevier
Science & Technology Books. Saint Louis, MO. 2000. 220p.
Methods in Computational and Theoretical Molecular Biology
Ser., 1 ISBN:0-08-042800-2, ISBN13: 978-0-08-042800-0.
Dewey:576.5/0285/632. LCCN:00-056153.
                                            Audience: **u,f.**

Young, Paul   QH447
Exploring Genomes: Web-Based Bioinformatic Excercises.
Trade Paper. Worth Publishers, Inc. New York, NY. 2002. 51p.
ISBN:0-7167-5738-9, ISBN13: 978-0-7167-5738-2.
Dewey:572.8/6.
                                            Audience: **u,f.**

Zanders (Editor)   QH431.C45197 2005
Chemical Genomics. Trade Cloth. Humana Press. Totowa, NJ.
2005. 300p. Methods in Molecular Biology Ser., Vol. 310
ISBN:1-58829-399-8, ISBN13: 978-1-58829-399-2.
Dewey:572.8/6. LCCN:2005-013118.
                                            Audience: **u,f.**

Zhang, Wei & Shmulevich,   QH438.4.M3C65 2002
  Ilya (Editors)
Computational and Statistical Approaches to Genomics. Trade
Cloth. Springer. New York, NY. 2002. 344p.
ISBN:1-4020-7023-3, ISBN13: 978-1-4020-7023-5.
Dewey:572.8/6/015118. LCCN:2002-023676.
                                            Audience: **u,f.**

Cellular and Molecular Biology, Genetics > Medical Genetics

QH447.W67 2002

ⓔ Genomics and World Health: Report of the Advisory Committee on Health Research. E-Book. NetLibrary, Inc. Boulder, CO. 2002. ISBN:0-585-46938-5, ISBN13: 978-0-585-46938-6. Dewey:572.8633.

Audience: **u,f.**

QH431

▢ OMIN--Online Mendelian Inheritance in Man. http://www.ncbi.nlm.nih.gov/entrez/query.fcgi?db=omim

Audience: **l,u,f.**

Alon, Uri　　　　**QH324.2.A46 2006**
Introduction to Systems Biology and the Design Principles of Biological Circuits. CRC Press. 2006. ISBN:1-58488-642-0, ISBN13: 978-1-58488-642-6.

Audience: **u,f.**

Batiza, Ann　　　　**QH324.2B38 2005**
Bioinformatics, Genomics, and Proteomics: Getting the Big Picture. Trade Cloth, Laminated. Facts On File, Inc.. New York, NY. 2005. 112p. Biotechnology in the 21st Century Ser. ISBN:0-7910-8517-1, ISBN13: 978-0-7910-8517-2. Dewey:572.8/0285. LCCN:2005-017232.

Audience: **u,f.**

Brenner, Charles & Duggan,　　**RC268.4.O49 2004**
David J. (Editors)
Oncogenomics: Molecular Approaches to Cancer. Trade Cloth. John Wiley & Sons, Inc. Hoboken, NJ. 2004. 382p. ISBN:0-471-22592-4, ISBN13: 978-0-471-22592-8. Dewey:616.99/4042. LCCN:2003-009480.

Audience: **u,f.**

Brown, Stuart M.　　　　**RB155.B674 2003**
Essentials of Medical Genomics. Trade Cloth. John Wiley & Sons, Inc. Hoboken, NJ. 2002. 288p. ISBN:0-471-21003-X, ISBN13: 978-0-471-21003-0. Dewey:616/.042. LCCN:2002-011163.

Audience: **u,f.**

Brown, Terence A. & BIOS　　**QH447.B76 2002**
Scientific Publishers Staff (Editors)
Genomes. Ed. 2. Trade Cloth. John Wiley & Sons, Inc. Hoboken, NJ. 2002. 520p. ISBN:0-471-25046-5, ISBN13: 978-0-471-25046-3. Dewey:572.8/6. LCCN:2002-003471.

Audience: **u,f.**

Bunton, Robin & Peterson,　　**RB155.P48 2001**
Alan
New Genetics and New Public Health. Paper over Boards. Routledge. New York, NY. 2001. 264p. ISBN:0-415-22141-2, ISBN13: 978-0-415-22141-2. Dewey:616/.042. LCCN:2001-048171.

Audience: **u,f.**

Burdette, Walter J.　　　　**RB155.B87 2001**
The Basis for Gene Therapy. Trade Cloth. Charles C Thomas Publisher, Ltd. Springfield, IL. 2001. xxv, 204p. ISBN:0-398-07158-6, ISBN13: 978-0-398-07158-5. Dewey:616/.042. LCCN:00-050784.

Audience: **u,f.**

Carlson, Rick J. &　　　　**RB155.C375 2002**
Stimeling, Gary
Terrible Gift: The Brave New World of Genetic Medicine. Trade Cloth. PublicAffairs. New York, NY. 2002. 320p. ISBN:1-891620-65-7, ISBN13: 978-1-891620-65-2. Dewey:616/.042. LCCN:2001-060392.

Audience: **l,u,f.** *Choice, 2003, 2002.*

Collado-Vides, Julio &　　**QH438.4.M3G46 2002**
Hofestädt, Ralf (Editors)
Gene Regulation and Metabolism: Post-Genomic Computational Approaches. Cloth Text. MIT Press. Cambridge, MA. 2002. 320p. Computational Molecular Biology Ser. ISBN:0-262-03297-X, ISBN13: 978-0-262-03297-1. Dewey:572.8/01/5118. LCCN:2001-056247.

Audience: **u,f.**

Day, I. N. M. & Ye, S.　　**QP624.5.D726.M5 2003**
(Editors)
Microarrays and Microplates: Applications in Biomedical Sciences. UK-B Format Paperback. Taylor & Francis Group. Philadelphia, PA. 2003. 192p. ISBN:1-85996-074-X, ISBN13: 978-1-85996-074-5. Dewey:572.8636.

Audience: **u,f.**

DeBusk, Ruth M.　　　　**QH431.D344 2002**
Genetics: The Nutrition Connection. Trade Cloth. American Dietetic Association. Chicago, IL. 2002. ix, 206p. ISBN:0-88091-195-6, ISBN13: 978-0-88091-195-5. Dewey:616/.042. LCCN:2002-013150.

Audience: **l,u,f.**

Eiseman, Elisa, et al.　　　　**RD127.C375 2004**
Case Studies of Existing Human Tissue Repositories: Best Practices for a Biospecimen Resource for the Genomic and Proteomic Era. Gabrielle Bloom & Jennifer Brower (Authors). Trade Cloth. RAND Corporation, The. Santa Monica, CA. 2003. 246p. ISBN:0-8330-3527-4, ISBN13: 978-0-8330-3527-1. Dewey:362.17/83. LCCN:2003-024742.

Audience: **u,f.**

Eyk, Jennifer E.Van &　　　　**RC666**
Dunn, Michael J. (Editors)
Proteomic and Genomic Analysis of Cardiovascular Disease. Trade Cloth. John Wiley & Sons, Inc. Hoboken, NJ. 2003. 423p. ISBN:3-527-30596-3, ISBN13: 978-3-527-30596-4. Dewey:616.1/042. LCCN:2003-279641.

Audience: **u,f.**

Feinendegen, Ludwig E.　　　　**RC78.7.R4M65 2003**
Molecular Nuclear Medicine: The Challenge of Genomics and Proteomics to Clinical Practice. Y. W. Bahk, W. C. Eckelman, W. W. Shreeve & H. N. Wagner Jr. (Editors). Trade Cloth. Springer. New York, NY. 2003. XX, 795p. ISBN:3-540-00132-8, ISBN13: 978-3-540-00132-4. Dewey:616.07/575. LCCN:2003-042530.

Audience: **u,f.**

Friedman, Herman (Editor),　　**RC88.9.T47M53 2006**
et al.
Microorganisms and Bioterrorism. Burt Anderson & Mauro Bendinelli (Editors). Trade Cloth. Springer. New York, NY. 2006. XX, 240p. Infectious Agents and Pathogenesis Ser. ISBN:0-387-28156-8, ISBN13: 978-0-387-28156-8. Dewey:363.325/3. LCCN:2005-930722.

Audience: **u,f.** *Choice, 2006.*

Grandi, Guido (Editor) QH447
Genomics, Proteomics and Vaccines. Trade Cloth. John Wiley & Sons, Inc. Hoboken, NJ. 2004. 336p. ISBN:0-470-85616-5, ISBN13: 978-0-470-85616-1. Dewey:572.8/6. LCCN:2004-273717.

Audience: **u,f.**

Hamadeh, Hisham K. & RA1224.3.T6975 2004
Afshari, Cynthia A. (Editors)
Toxicogenomics: Principles and Applications. Trade Cloth. John Wiley & Sons, Inc. Hoboken, NJ. 2004. 361p. ISBN:0-471-43417-5, ISBN13: 978-0-471-43417-7. Dewey:616/.042. LCCN:2003-024163.

Audience: **u,f.**

Horwitz, Marshall QH430
Basic Concepts in Medical Genetics. Kris Carroll (Illustrator), Mary Beth Dinulos (Contribution by). Paper Text. McGraw-Hill Professional Publishing. New York, NY. 2000. 192p. Basic Concept Ser. ISBN:0-07-134500-0, ISBN13: 978-0-07-134500-2. Dewey:616/.042. LCCN:99-053279.

Audience: **l,u,f.**

HumanGenome Project (ed.) QH447
☐ The Human Genome Project: Exploring our Molecular Selves.
http://www.genome.gov/Pages/EducationKit/online.htm
National Human Genome Research Institute (NHGRI).

Audience: **u,f.**

Jackson, M., et al. QH431
Human Genome Evolution: Human Molecular Genetics. T. Strachan & G. Dover (Authors). Cloth Text. Taylor & Francis Group. Abingdon, 1996. 256p. Human Molecular Genetics Ser. ISBN:1-85996-095-2, ISBN13: 978-1-85996-095-0. Dewey:599.9/35.

Audience: **u,f.** *Choice, 1997.*

Jorde, Lynn B. RB155.J67 2002
Medical Genetics. Ed. 3. Cloth Text. Elsevier - Health Sciences Division. Philadelphia, PA. 2003. 350p. ISBN:0-323-02025-9, ISBN13: 978-0-323-02025-1. Dewey:616/.042. LCCN:2003-278342.

Audience: **u,f.**

Jorde, Lynn B., et al. RB155
Medical Genetics. Ed. 2. John C. Carey, Raymond L. White & Michael J. Bamshad (Authors). Paper Text. Elsevier - Health Sciences Division. Philadelphia, PA. 2000. 388p. ISBN:0-323-01253-1, ISBN13: 978-0-323-01253-9. Dewey:616/.042.

Audience: **u,f.**

King, Richard A. (Editor), RB155.G3593 2002
et al.
The Genetic Basis of Common Diseases. Ed. 2. Jerome I. Rotter & Arno G. Motulsky (Editors). Trade Cloth. Oxford University Press, Inc. New York, NY. 2002. 1,090p. Oxford Monographs on Medical Genetics, Vol. 44 ISBN:0-19-512582-7, ISBN13: 978-0-19-512582-5. Dewey:616/.042. LCCN:2002-018390.

Audience: **l,u,f.**

Kingston, Helen M. RB155
ABC of Clinical Genetics. Ed. 3. Trade Paper. BMJ Publishing Group. London, 2002. 120p. ABC Ser. ISBN:0-7279-1627-0, ISBN13: 978-0-7279-1627-3. Dewey:616.042.

Audience: **u,f.**

Kitano, Hiroaki (Editor) QH313.F66 2002
Foundations of Systems Biology. Trade Cloth. MIT Press. Cambridge, MA. 2001. 320p. ISBN:0-262-11266-3, ISBN13: 978-0-262-11266-6. Dewey:573. LCCN:2001-042807.

Audience: **l,u.**

Knoppers, Bartha Maria QH447
Genomics, Health and Society: Emerging Issues for Public Policy. Scriver, Charles. Policy Research Initiative. 2004. ISBN:0-662-35154-1, ISBN13: 978-0-662-35154-2.

Audience: **u,f.**

Kresina, Thomas F. (Editor) RB155.I58 2001
An Introduction to Molecular Medicine and Gene Therapy. Trade Cloth. John Wiley & Sons, Inc. Hoboken, NJ. 2000. 416p. ISBN:0-471-39188-3, ISBN13: 978-0-471-39188-3. Dewey:616/.042. LCCN:00-042890.

Audience: **u,f.**

Lashley, Felissa R. RB155.L37 2005
Clinical Genetics in Nursing Practice, Third Edition. Ed. 3. Trade Cloth. Springer Publishing Company, Inc. New York, NY. 2005. xii, 571p. ISBN:0-8261-2366-X, ISBN13: 978-0-8261-2366-4. Dewey:616/.042/024613. LCCN:2004-028505.

Audience: **u,f.**

Lengauer, Thomas (Editor) QH506
Bioinformatics-From Genomes to Drugs, Set. Hugo Kubinyi, Raimund Mannhold & Hendrik Timmerman (Contribution by). Trade Cloth. John Wiley & Sons, Inc. Hoboken, NJ. 2002. 668p. Methods and Principles in Medicinal Chemistry Ser., Vol. 14 ISBN:3-527-29988-2, ISBN13: 978-3-527-29988-1. Dewey:572.80285. LCCN:2002-524729.

Audience: **u,f.**

Lindee, M. Susan RB155.L555 2005
Moments of Truth in Genetic Medicine. Trade Cloth. Johns Hopkins University Press. Baltimore, MD. 2005. 288p. ISBN:0-8018-8175-7, ISBN13: 978-0-8018-8175-6. Dewey:616/.042. LCCN:2004-028267.

Audience: **u,f.** *Choice, 2006.*

Mahowald, Mary B., et al. RB155
Genetics in the Clinic: Clinical, Ethical, and Social Implications for Primary Care. Timothy Aspinwall, Victor A. McKusick & Angela Scheuerle (Authors). Trade Paper. Elsevier - Health Sciences Division. Philadelphia, PA. 2001. 315p. ISBN:0-323-01203-5, ISBN13: 978-0-323-01203-4. Dewey:616.042. LCCN:00-135004.

Audience: **u,f.**

Meyers, Robert A. QH506.E534 2004
Encyclopedia of Molecular Cell Biology and Molecular Medicine, Vol. 5. Ed. 2. Trade Cloth. John Wiley & Sons, Inc. Hoboken, NJ. 2004. 698p. Encyclopedia of Molecular Biology and Molecular Medicine Ser. ISBN:3-527-30547-5, ISBN13: 978-3-527-30547-6. Dewey:572.8/03. LCCN:2004-275355.

Audience: **u,f.**

Meyers, Robert A. QH506.E534 2004
Encyclopedia of Molecular Cell Biology and Molecular Medicine, Vol. 3. Ed. 2. Trade Cloth. John Wiley & Sons, Inc. Hoboken, NJ. 2004. 720p. Encyclopedia of Molecular Biology and Molecular Medicine Ser. ISBN:3-527-30545-9, ISBN13: 978-3-527-30545-2. Dewey:572.8/03. LCCN:2004-275355.

Audience: **u,f.**

Meyers, Robert A.   **QH506**
Encyclopedia of Molecular Cell Biology and Molecular
Medicine, Vol. 6. Ed. 2. Trade Cloth. John Wiley & Sons, Inc.
Hoboken, NJ. 2005. 670p. Encyclopedia of Molecular Biology
and Molecular Medicine 16Vset Ser. ISBN:3-527-30548-3,
ISBN13: 978-3-527-30548-3. Dewey:572.8/03.
                                    Audience: **u,f.**

Meyers, Robert A.   **QH506**
Encyclopedia of Molecular Cell Biology and Molecular
Medicine, Vol. 10. Ed. 2. Trade Cloth. John Wiley & Sons, Inc.
Hoboken, NJ. 2005. 714p. Encyclopedia of Molecular Biology
and Molecular Medicine 16Vset Ser. ISBN:3-527-30552-1,
ISBN13: 978-3-527-30552-0. Dewey:572.8/03.
                                    Audience: **u,f.**

Meyers, Robert A.   **QH506**
Encyclopedia of Molecular Cell Biology and Molecular
Medicine, Vol. 7. Ed. 2. Trade Cloth. John Wiley & Sons, Inc.
Hoboken, NJ. 2005. 662p. Encyclopedia of Molecular Biology
and Molecular Medicine 16Vset Ser. ISBN:3-527-30549-1,
ISBN13: 978-3-527-30549-0. Dewey:572.8/03.
                                    Audience: **u,f.**

Meyers, Robert A.   **QH506.E534 2004**
Encyclopedia of Molecular Cell Biology and Molecular
Medicine, Vol. 2. Ed. 2. Trade Cloth. John Wiley & Sons, Inc.
Hoboken, NJ. 2004. 696p. Encyclopedia of Molecular Biology
and Molecular Medicine Ser. ISBN:3-527-30544-0, ISBN13:
978-3-527-30544-5. Dewey:572.8/03. LCCN:2004-275355.
                                    Audience: **u,f.**

Meyers, Robert A.   **QH506.E534 2004**
Encyclopedia of Molecular Cell Biology and Molecular
Medicine, Vol. 1. Ed. 2. Trade Cloth. John Wiley & Sons, Inc.
Hoboken, NJ. 2004. 716p. Encyclopedia of Molecular Biology
and Molecular Medicine Ser. ISBN:3-527-30543-2, ISBN13:
978-3-527-30543-8. Dewey:572.8/03. LCCN:2004-275355.
                                    Audience: **u,f.**

Meyers, Robert A.   **QH506.E534 2004**
Encyclopedia of Molecular Cell Biology and Molecular
Medicine, Vol. 4. Ed. 2. Trade Cloth. John Wiley & Sons, Inc.
Hoboken, NJ. 2004. 726p. Encyclopedia of Molecular Biology
and Molecular Medicine Ser. ISBN:3-527-30546-7, ISBN13:
978-3-527-30546-9. Dewey:572.8/03. LCCN:2004-275355.
                                    Audience: **u,f.**

Meyers, Robert A.   **QH506**
Encyclopedia of Molecular Cell Biology and Molecular
Medicine, Vol. 8. Ed. 2. Trade Cloth. John Wiley & Sons, Inc.
Hoboken, NJ. 2005. 692p. Encyclopedia of Molecular Biology
and Molecular Medicine 16Vset Ser. ISBN:3-527-30550-5,
ISBN13: 978-3-527-30550-6. Dewey:572.8/03.
                                    Audience: **u,f.**

Meyers, Robert A.   **QH506**
Encyclopedia of Molecular Cell Biology and Molecular
Medicine, Vol. 9. Ed. 2. Trade Cloth. John Wiley & Sons, Inc.
Hoboken, NJ. 2005. 634p. Encyclopedia of Molecular Biology
and Molecular Medicine 16Vset Ser. ISBN:3-527-30551-3,
ISBN13: 978-3-527-30551-3. Dewey:572.8/03.
                                    Audience: **u,f.**

Meyers, Robert A.   **QH506**
Encyclopedia of Molecular Cell Biology and Molecular
Medicine, Index, Vol. 16. Ed. 2. Trade Cloth. John Wiley &
Sons, Inc. Hoboken, NJ. 2006. 334p. Encyclopedia of Molecular

Biology and Molecular Medicine 16Vset Ser.
ISBN:3-527-30653-6, ISBN13: 978-3-527-30653-4.
Dewey:572.803.
                                    Audience: **u,f.**

Meyers, Robert A.   **QH506**
Encyclopedia of Molecular Cell Biology and Molecular
Medicine, Proteasomes to Receptor, Transporter and Ion
Channel Diseases, Vol. 11. Ed. 2. Trade Cloth. John Wiley &
Sons, Inc. Hoboken, NJ. 2005. 776p. Encyclopedia of Molecular
Biology and Molecular Medicine 16Vset Ser.
ISBN:3-527-30648-X, ISBN13: 978-3-527-30648-0.
Dewey:572.8/03.
                                    Audience: **u,f.**

Meyers, Robert A.   **QH506**
Encyclopedia of Molecular Cell Biology and Molecular
Medicine, Recombination and Genome Rearrangements to Serial
Analysis of Gene Expression, Vol. 12. Ed. 2. Trade Cloth. John
Wiley & Sons, Inc. Hoboken, NJ. 2005. 796p. Encyclopedia of
Molecular Biology and Molecular Medicine 16Vset Ser.
ISBN:3-527-30649-8, ISBN13: 978-3-527-30649-7.
Dewey:572.8/03.
                                    Audience: **u,f.**

Meyers, Robert A.   **QH506**
Encyclopedia of Molecular Cell Biology and Molecular
Medicine, Sex Hormones (Male): Analogs and Antagonists to
Synchrotron Infrared Microspectroscopy, Vol. 13. Ed. 2. Trade
Cloth. John Wiley & Sons, Inc. Hoboken, NJ. 2005. 760p.
Encyclopedia of Molecular Biology and Molecular Medicine
16Vset Ser. ISBN:3-527-30650-1, ISBN13: 978-3-527-30650-3.
Dewey:572.8/03.
                                    Audience: **u,f.**

Meyers, Robert A.   **QH506**
Encyclopedia of Molecular Cell Biology and Molecular
Medicine, Syngamy and Cell Cycle Control to Triacylglyerol
Storage and Mobilization, Regulation Of, Vol. 14. Ed. 2. Trade
Cloth. John Wiley & Sons, Inc. Hoboken, NJ. 2005. 766p.
Encyclopedia of Molecular Biology and Molecular Medicine
16Vset Ser. ISBN:3-527-30651-X, ISBN13: 978-3-527-30651-0.
Dewey:572.8/03.
                                    Audience: **u,f.**

Meyers, Robert A.   **QH506**
Encyclopedia of Molecular Cell Biology and Molecular
Medicine, Triplet Repeat Diseases to Zebrafish (Danio rerio)
Genome and Genetics, Vol. 15. Ed. 2. Trade Cloth. John Wiley
& Sons, Inc. Hoboken, NJ. 2005. 676p. Encyclopedia of
Molecular Biology and Molecular Medicine 16Vset Ser.
ISBN:3-527-30652-8, ISBN13: 978-3-527-30652-7.
Dewey:572.8/03.
                                    Audience: **u,f.**

Meyers, Robert A.   **QH506**
Encylopedia of Molecular Cell Biology and Molecular
Medicine, Set. Ed. 2. Trade Cloth. John Wiley & Sons, Inc.
Hoboken, NJ. 2006. 9600p. ISBN:3-527-30542-4, ISBN13:
978-3-527-30542-1. Dewey:572.8/03. LCCN:2004-275355.
                                    Audience: **u,f.**

Nussbaum, Robert L., et al.   **RB155.T52 2004**
Thompson and Thompson Genetics in Medicine. Ed. 6.
Roderick R. McInnes, Huntington F. Willard & Margaret W.
Thompson (Authors). Paper Text. Elsevier - Health Sciences

Division. Philadelphia, PA. 2004. 540p. ISBN:0-7216-0244-4, ISBN13: 978-0-7216-0244-8. Dewey:616/.042. LCCN:2004-042739.

Audience: **u,f.**

Opresko, Lee   **QH313.A386 2004**
Advances in Systems Biology. Julie M. Gephart & Michaela B. Mann (Editors). Trade Cloth. Springer. New York, NY. 2004. 116p. Advances in Experimental Medicine and Biology Ser., Vol. 547 ISBN:0-306-48314-9, ISBN13: 978-0-306-48314-1. Dewey:571. LCCN:2003-068653.

Audience: **u,f.**

Palsson, Bernhard O.   **QH324.2.P35 2006**
Systems Biology: Properties of Reconstructed Networks. Cloth Text. Cambridge University Press. New York, NY. 2006. 334p. ISBN:0-521-85903-4, ISBN13: 978-0-521-85903-5. Dewey:572.80285. LCCN:2005-035008.

Audience: **u,f.**

Pasternak, Jack J.   **QH431**
An Introduction to Human Molecular Genetics: Mechanisms of Inherited Diseases. Ed. 2. Trade Cloth. John Wiley & Sons, Inc. Hoboken, NJ. 2005. 656p. ISBN:0-471-47426-6, ISBN13: 978-0-471-47426-5. Dewey:616/.042. LCCN:2005-278472.

Audience: **u,f.**

Priami, Corrado   **QH506.T73 2005**
  (Contribution by)
Transactions on Computational Systems Biology I. Mixed Media. Springer. New York, NY. 2005. IX, 111p. Lecture Notes in Computer Science / Lecture Notes in Bioinformatics Ser. ISBN:3-540-25422-6, ISBN13: 978-3-540-25422-5. Dewey:572.80285. LCCN:2005-922555.

Audience: **u,f.**

Pritchard, D. J. & Korf,   **RB155.P6965 2002**
  Bruce R.
Medical Genetics at a Glance. Trade Paper. Blackwell Publishing Ltd. Oxford, 2003. 112p. At a Glance Ser. ISBN:0-632-06372-6, ISBN13: 978-0-632-06372-7. Dewey:616/.042. LCCN:2002-009523.

Audience: **u,f.**

Quesenberry, Peter J.   **RB155.8.S84 1998**
Stem Cell Biology and Gene Therapy. Stein, Gary S.; Forget, Bernard; Weissman, Sherman. John Wiley & Sons Inc. 1998.

Audience: **u,f.**

Reilly, Philip R.   **QH431.R38 2000**
Abraham Lincoln's DNA and Other Adventures in Genetics. Trade Cloth. Cold Spring Harbor Laboratory Press. Woodbury, NY. 2000. xx, 339p. ISBN:0-87969-580-3, ISBN13: 978-0-87969-580-4. Dewey:599.93/5. LCCN:00-029467.

Audience: **l,u,f.** *Choice, 2001.*

Reilly, Philip R.   **RB155.R42 2004**
Is It in Your Genes?: How Genes Influence Common Disorders and Diseases That Affect You and Your Family. Trade Cloth. Cold Spring Harbor Laboratory Press. Woodbury, NY. 2004. 288p. ISBN:0-87969-719-9, ISBN13: 978-0-87969-719-8. Dewey:599.93/5. LCCN:2004-002458.

Audience: **l,u,f.** *Choice, 2004.*

Rigoutsos, Isidore &   **QH324.2.S97 2006**
  Stephanopoulos, G.
Systems Biology. Trade Cloth. Oxford University Press, Inc.

New York, NY. 2006. 366p. Series in Systems Biology ISBN:0-19-530080-7, ISBN13: 978-0-19-530080-2. Dewey:570. LCCN:2005-031826.

Audience: **u,f.**

Rimoin, David L., et al.   **RB155**
Principles and Practice of Medical Genetics, Set. Ed. 4. J. M. Connor, Reed E. Pyeritz, Alan E. H. Emery & Bruce R. Korf (Authors). Trade Cloth. Elsevier - Health Sciences Division. Philadelphia, PA. 2002. 4936p. ISBN:0-443-06434-2, ISBN13: 978-0-443-06434-0. Dewey:616/.042.

Audience: **u,f.**

Rosenthal, A. &   **QH447.H845 2002**
  Vakalopoulou, L. (Editors)
The Human Genome: Biology and Medicine. Cloth Text. Springer. New York, NY. 2002. 156p. Ernst Schering Research Foundation Workshop Ser., Vol. 36 ISBN:3-540-42316-8, ISBN13: 978-3-540-42316-4. Dewey:611/.01816. LCCN:2002-283754.

Audience: **u,f.**

Ross, D. W.   **RB155.R78 2002**
Introduction to Molecular Medicine. Ed. 3. Trade Paper. Springer. New York, NY. 2002. XV, 153p. ISBN:0-387-95372-8, ISBN13: 978-0-387-95372-4. Dewey:616/.042. LCCN:2001-054921.

Audience: **u,f.**

Scheuerle, Angela   **RB155**
Understanding Genetics: A Primer for Couples and Families. Trade Cloth. Greenwood Publishing Group, Inc. Portsmouth, NH. 2005. 224p. ISBN:0-275-98189-4, ISBN13: 978-0-275-98189-1. Dewey:616/.042. LCCN:2004-028072.

Audience: **l,u,f.** *Choice, 2005.*

Shannon, Thomas A. &   **RB155.S43 2003**
  Walter, James J.
The New Genetic Medicine: Theological and Ethical Reflections. Book, Other. Rowman & Littlefield Publishers, Inc. Lanham, MD. 2003. 176p. ISBN:0-7425-3170-8, ISBN13: 978-0-7425-3170-3. Dewey:174/.296042. LCCN:2003-008463.

Audience: **u,f.** *Choice, 2004.*

Simpson, Joe L. & Elias,   **RB155.S492 2003**
  Sherman
Genetics in Obstetrics and Gynecology. Ed. 3. Trade Cloth. Elsevier - Health Sciences Division. Philadelphia, PA. 2002. 512p. ISBN:0-7216-4164-4, ISBN13: 978-0-7216-4164-5. Dewey:616/.042. LCCN:2002-036648.

Audience: **u,f.**

Skirton, H. & Patch, C.   **RB155**
Genetics for Healthcare Professionals: A Lifestage Approach. UK-B Format Paperback. Taylor & Francis Group. Philadelphia, PA. 2002. 224p. ISBN:1-85996-043-X, ISBN13: 978-1-85996-043-1. Dewey:616/.042.

Audience: **u,f.**

Stillman, Bruce & Stewart,   **DS597.367.K4 2003**
  David (Editors)
The Genome of Homo Sapiens. Trade Cloth. Cold Spring Harbor Laboratory Press. Woodbury, NY. 2004. 650p. Symposia on Quantitative Biology Ser., LXVIII ISBN:0-87969-709-1, ISBN13: 978-0-87969-709-9. Dewey:599.935.

Audience: **u,f.**

Thomas, Duncan C.　　　　　**RB155.T468 2004**
Statistical Methods in Genetic Epidemiology. Trade Cloth.
Oxford University Press, Inc. New York, NY. 2004. 458p.
ISBN:0-19-515939-X, ISBN13: 978-0-19-515939-4.
Dewey:616/.042. LCCN:2003-053096.
　　　　　　　　　　　　　　　　　Audience: **u,f.**

Turnpenny, Peter D. &　　　　　　　　**RB155**
　Ellard, Sian
Emery's Elements of Medical Genetics: With Student Consult
Access. Ed. 12. Paper Text. Elsevier - Health Sciences Division.
Philadelphia, PA. 2004. 416p. ISBN:0-443-10045-4, ISBN13:
978-0-443-10045-1. Dewey:616/.042. LCCN:2005-273703.
　　　　　　　　　　　　　　　　　Audience: **u,f.**

Vaidyanathan, Seetharaman　　　　**QP171.M382 2005**
　(Editor), et al.
Metabolome Analyses: Strategies for Systems Biology. George
G. Harrigan & Royston Goodacre (Editors). Trade Cloth.
Springer. New York, NY. 2005. XXII, 394p.
ISBN:0-387-25239-8, ISBN13: 978-0-387-25239-1.
Dewey:572/.4. LCCN:2005-047906.
　　　　　　　　　　　　　　　　　Audience: **u,f.**

Wade, Nicholas　　　　　　　**RB155.W326 2001**
Life Script: How the Human Genome Discoveries Will
Transform Medicine and Enhance Your Health. Trade Cloth.
Simon & Schuster. New York, NY. 2001. 208p.
ISBN:0-7432-1605-9, ISBN13: 978-0-7432-1605-0.
Dewey:616/.042. LCCN:2001-042627.
　　　　　　　　　　　　　　　　　Audience: **l,u,f.**

Wilson, Golder N.　　　　　　**RB155.W552 2000**
Clinical Genetics: A Short Course. Trade Paper. John Wiley &
Sons, Inc. Hoboken, NJ. 2000. 496p. ISBN:0-471-29806-9,
ISBN13: 978-0-471-29806-9. Dewey:616/.042.
LCCN:99-040663.
　　　　　　　　　　　　　　　　　Audience: **u,f.**

Cellular and Molecular Biology, Genetics
> Genetic Engineering

Duster, Troy　　　　　　　　**RB155.D87 2003**
Backdoor to Eugenics. Ed. 2. Paper over Boards. Routledge.
New York, NY. 2003. 256p. ISBN:0-415-94805-3, ISBN13:
978-0-415-94805-0. Dewey:363.9/2. LCCN:2003-010961.
　　　　　　　　　　　　　　　　　Audience: **l,u,f.**

Jeanteur, Ph　　　　　　　**QH506.P76 NO.31**
Regulation of Alternative Splicing. Trade Cloth. Springer. New
York, NY. 2002. 245p. Progress in Molecular and Subcellular
Biology Ser., Vol. 31 ISBN:3-540-43833-5, ISBN13:
978-3-540-43833-5. Dewey:572.8 s 572/.645.
LCCN:2002-070835.
　　　　　　　　　　　　　　　　　Audience: **u,f.**

Kresina, Thomas F. (Editor)　　　　**RB155.I58 2001**
An Introduction to Molecular Medicine and Gene Therapy.
Trade Cloth. John Wiley & Sons, Inc. Hoboken, NJ. 2000. 416p.
ISBN:0-471-39188-3, ISBN13: 978-0-471-39188-3.
Dewey:616/.042. LCCN:00-042890.
　　　　　　　　　　　　　　　　　Audience: **u,f.**

Lengauer, Thomas (Editor)　　　　　　**QH506**
Bioinformatics-From Genomes to Drugs, Set. Hugo Kubinyi,
Raimund Mannhold & Hendrik Timmerman (Contribution by).

Trade Cloth. John Wiley & Sons, Inc. Hoboken, NJ. 2002. 668p.
Methods and Principles in Medicinal Chemistry Ser., Vol. 14
ISBN:3-527-29988-2, ISBN13: 978-3-527-29988-1.
Dewey:572.80285. LCCN:2002-524729.
　　　　　　　　　　　　　　　　　Audience: **u,f.**

Macieira-Coelho, Alvaro　　　　**QH506.P76 NO.24**
　(Editor)
Cell Immortalization. Trade Cloth. Springer. New York, NY.
1999. VII, 207p. Progress in Molecular and Subcellular Biology
Ser., Vol. 24 ISBN:3-540-65618-9, ISBN13: 978-3-540-65618-0.
Dewey:572.8 s 571.8/4. LCCN:99-015705.
　　　　　　　　　　　　　　　　　Audience: **u,f.**

Naam, Ramez　　　　　　　**RB155.N27 2005**
More Than Human: Embracing the Promise of Biological
Enhancement. Trade Cloth. Doubleday Canada, Ltd. Toronto,
ON. 2005. 288p. ISBN:0-7679-1843-6, ISBN13:
978-0-7679-1843-5. Dewey:616/.042. LCCN:2004-054507.
　　　　　　　　　　　　　　　　　Audience: **l,u,f.**

Nigg, Erich A. (Editor)　　　　　　　**QH597**
Centrosomes in Development and Disease. Trade Cloth. John
Wiley & Sons, Inc. Hoboken, NJ. 2004. 474p.
ISBN:3-527-30980-2, ISBN13: 978-3-527-30980-1.
Dewey:571.65. LCCN:2004-303455.
　　　　　　　　　　　　　　　　　Audience: **u,f.**

Quesenberry, Peter J.　　　　　**RB155.8.S84 1998**
Stem Cell Biology and Gene Therapy. Stein, Gary S.; Forget,
Bernard; Weissman, Sherman. John Wiley & Sons Inc. 1998.
　　　　　　　　　　　　　　　　　Audience: **u,f.**

Quesenberry, Peter J.　　　　　**RB155.8.S84 1998**
　(Editor), et al.
Stem Cell Biology and Gene Therapy. Gary S. Stein, Bernard G.
Forget & Sherman M. Weissman (Editors). Trade Cloth. John
Wiley & Sons, Inc. Hoboken, NJ. 1998. 584p.
ISBN:0-471-14656-0, ISBN13: 978-0-471-14656-8.
Dewey:616/.042. LCCN:97-048252.
　　　　　　　　　　　　　　　　　Audience: **u,f.**

Stock, Gregory B. &　　　　　**RB155.E56 2000**
　Campbell, John
Engineering the Human Germline: An Exploration of the
Science and Ethics of Altering the Genes We Pass to Our
Children. Trade Cloth. Oxford University Press, Inc. New York,
NY. 2000. 192p. ISBN:0-19-513302-1, ISBN13:
978-0-19-513302-8. Dewey:174/.25. LCCN:99-015224.
　　　　　　　　　　　Audience: **l,u,f.** *Choice, 2001.*

Cellular and Molecular Biology, Genetics
> Cell Biology, Eucaryotes

☐ Google Directory: Biology, Cell Biology.
http://www.google.com/Top/Science/Biology/Cell_Biology/
Google.
　　　　　　　　　　　　　　　　　Audience: **g,l.**

　　　　　　　　　　　　　　　　　QH506
☐ Harvard University Department of Molecular and Cellular
Biology - Biology Links.
http://www.mcb.harvard.edu/BioLinks.html
　　　　　　　　　　　　　　　　　Audience: **l,u,f.**

Cogoli, Augusto (Editor)   **QH577**
Cell Biology and Biotechnology in Space. Trade Cloth. Elsevier Science & Technology Books. Saint Louis, MO. 2002. 262p. Advances in Space Biology and Medicine Ser. ISBN:0-444-50735-3, ISBN13: 978-0-444-50735-8. Dewey:571.6/0919.

Audience: **u,f.**

Cole, Stewart T.   **QR201.T6**
Tuberculosis and the Tubercle Bacillus. Trade Cloth. ASM Press. Washington, DC. 2004. 603p. ISBN:1-55581-295-3, ISBN13: 978-1-55581-295-9. Dewey:616.9/95. LCCN:2004-017059.

Audience: **u,f.**

Dorrell, Nick (Volume   **QH434**
  Editor), et al.
Functional Microbial Genomics, Vol. 33. Brendan Wren & Fred Rainey (Volume Editors). Trade Cloth. Elsevier Science & Technology Books. Saint Louis, MO. 2002. 428p. Methods in Microbiology Ser. ISBN:0-12-521533-9, ISBN13: 978-0-12-521533-6. Dewey:576.

Audience: **u,f.**

Downes, C. P.   **QH345.B522 NO. 64**
Cellular Responses to Stress, Vol. 64. Trade Cloth. Princeton University Press. Princeton, NJ. 1999. 168p. ISBN:0-691-00951-1, ISBN13: 978-0-691-00951-3. Dewey:572 s. LCCN:98-089203.

Audience: **u,f.**

Dyer, Betsey D. & Obar,   **QH371.D93 1993**
  Robert A.
Tracing the History of Eukaryotic Cells: The Enigmatic Smile. Trade Cloth. Columbia University Press. New York, NY. 1984. 335p. Critical Moments in Paleobiology and Earth History Ser. ISBN:0-231-07592-8, ISBN13: 978-0-231-07592-3. Dewey:574.87. LCCN:93-026798.

Audience: **u,f.** *Choice, 1995.*

Gupta, G. S.   **QP255.G83 2005**
Proteomics of Spermatogenesis. Trade Cloth. Springer. New York, NY. 2005. XXVI, 855p. ISBN:0-387-25398-X, ISBN13: 978-0-387-25398-5. Dewey:612.6/1. LCCN:2005-279130.

Audience: **u,f.**

Guthrie, Christine & Fink,   **QK623.S23**
  Gerald R. (Volume Editors)
Guide to Yeast Genetics and Molecular and Cell Biology, Vol. 351, Pt. C. Trade Cloth. Elsevier Science & Technology Books. Saint Louis, MO. 2002. 735p. ISBN:0-12-182254-0, ISBN13: 978-0-12-182254-5. Dewey:571.2/9562.

Audience: **u,f.**

Guthrie, Christine & Fink,   **QK617.5**
  Gerald R. (Volume Editors)
Guide to Yeast Genetics and Molecular Cell Biology, Vol. 350, Pt. B. Trade Cloth. Elsevier Science & Technology Books. Saint Louis, MO. 2002. 623p. ISBN:0-12-182253-2, ISBN13: 978-0-12-182253-8. Dewey:579.562.

Audience: **u,f.**

Hodgson, David A. &   **QH450.S635 2002**
  Thomas, Christopher M. (Editors)
Signals, Switches, Regulons, and Cascades: Control of Bacterial Gene Expression. Melanie Scourfield (Contribution by). Trade

Cloth. Cambridge University Press. New York, NY. 2002. 304p. Society for General Microbiology Symposia Ser., Vol. 61 ISBN:0-521-81388-3, ISBN13: 978-0-521-81388-4. Dewey:572.865. LCCN:2002-510923.

Audience: **u,f.**

Kierszenbaum, Abraham L.   **RB25.K54 2002**
Histology and Cell Biology: An Introduction to Pathology. Paper Text. Elsevier - Health Sciences Division. Philadelphia, PA. 2002. 640p. ISBN:0-323-01639-1, ISBN13: 978-0-323-01639-1. Dewey:616.07. LCCN:2001-051399.

Audience: **l,u.**

Lackie, J. M.   **QH345.B522 NO.65**
Cell Behaviour: Control and Mechanism of Motility, Vol. 65. Cloth Text. Princeton University Press. Princeton, NJ. 1999. 346p. Biochemical Society Symposium Ser., Vol. 65 ISBN:0-691-00950-3, ISBN13: 978-0-691-00950-6. Dewey:572 s. LCCN:98-089202.

Audience: **u,f.**

Meyers, Robert A.   **QH506**
Encyclopedia of Molecular Cell Biology and Molecular Medicine, Set. Ed. 2. Trade Cloth. John Wiley & Sons, Inc. Hoboken, NJ. 2006. 9600p. ISBN:3-527-30542-4, ISBN13: 978-3-527-30542-1. Dewey:572.8/03. LCCN:2004-275355.

Audience: **u,f.**

Rochelle, A. (Editor)   **QR100**
Environmental Molecular Microbiology: Protocols and Applications. Cloth Text. Taylor & Francis Group. Philadelphia, PA. 2001. 263p. ISBN:1-898486-29-8, ISBN13: 978-1-898486-29-9. Dewey:579.1/7.

Audience: **u,f.**

Ross, Michael H.   **QM551.R67 2005**
Ross, Histology a Text and Atlas: With Correlated Cell and Molecular Biology. Ed. 5. Trade Paper. Lippincott Williams & Wilkins. Philadelphia, PA. 2005. 906p. ISBN:0-7817-5056-3, ISBN13: 978-0-7817-5056-1. Dewey:611/.018. LCCN:2005-050445.

Audience: **u,f.**

Zhou, Jizhong, et al.   **QH447.M53 2004**
Microbial Functional Genomics. Dorothea K. Thompson, James M. Tiedje & Ying Xu (Authors). Trade Cloth. John Wiley & Sons, Inc. Hoboken, NJ. 2004. 624p. ISBN:0-471-07190-0, ISBN13: 978-0-471-07190-7. Dewey:579/.135. LCCN:2003-017519.

Audience: **u,f.**

Cellular and Molecular Biology, Genetics > Developmental Biology

QH431
☐ OMIN--Online Mendelian Inheritance in Man.
http://www.ncbi.nlm.nih.gov/entrez/query.fcgi?db=omim
Audience: **l,u,f.**

Alberts, Bruce   **QH581.2.M64 2002**
Molecular Biology of the Cell. Ed. 4. Paper over Boards. Garland Publishing, Inc. New York, NY. 2002. 1616p. ISBN:0-8153-3218-1, ISBN13: 978-0-8153-3218-3. Dewey:571.6. LCCN:2001-054471.

Audience: **u,f.**

Alberts, Bruce, et al.   QH581.2.E78 2003
Essential Cell Biology. Ed. 2. Alexander Johnson, Julian Lewis, Martin Raff, Keith Roberts, Peter Walter & Dennis Bray (Authors), Karen Hopkin (Editor). Paper over Boards. Taylor & Francis Group. Philadelphia, PA. 2003. 860p. ISBN:0-8153-3480-X, ISBN13: 978-0-8153-3480-4. Dewey:571.6. LCCN:2003-011505.

Audience: **u,f.**

Celis, Julio E. (Editor), et al.   QH583.2.C45 2006
Cell Biology, Set. Ed. 3. Nigel Carter, Kai Simons, J. Victor Small, Tony Hunter & David Shotton (Editors). Trade Cloth. Elsevier Science & Technology Books. Saint Louis, MO. 2005. 2328p. ISBN:0-12-164730-7, ISBN13: 978-0-12-164730-8. Dewey:571.6072. LCCN:2006-271194.

Audience: **u,f.**

Cooper, Geoffrey M.   QH581.2
The Cell: A Molecular Approach. Ed. 3. Trade Cloth, CD-ROM. Sinauer Associates, Inc. Sunderland, MA. 739p. ISBN:0-87893-215-1, ISBN13: 978-0-87893-215-3. Dewey:571.6.

Audience: **u,f.** *Choice, 1997.*

Darnell, J. E. & Lodish,   QH581.2.D37 1995
Harvey
Molecular Cell Biology. Ed. 3. Cloth Text. W. H. Freeman & Company. New York, NY. 1995. 1152p. ISBN:0-7167-2380-8, ISBN13: 978-0-7167-2380-6. Dewey:574.87/6042. LCCN:94-022376.

Audience: **u,f.**

Fan, Gordon L.   QP363.F35 1999
Molecular and Cellular Physiology of Neurons. Trade Cloth. Harvard University Press. Cambridge, MA. 1999. 692p. ISBN:0-674-58155-5, ISBN13: 978-0-674-58155-5. Dewey:573.8/536. LCCN:98-044886.

Audience: **u,f.** *Choice, 2000.*

Gilbert, Scott F.   QL955.G48 2003
Developmental Biology. Ed. 7. Trade Cloth, CD-ROM. Sinauer Associates, Inc. Sunderland, MA. 2003. 784p. ISBN:0-87893-258-5, ISBN13: 978-0-87893-258-0. Dewey:571.8. LCCN:2003-001670.

Audience: **u,f.**

Harold, Frank M.   QH582.4.H37 2001
The Way of the Cell: Molecules, Organisms, and the Order of Life. Trade Cloth. Oxford University Press, Inc. New York, NY. 2001. 320p. ISBN:0-19-513512-1, ISBN13: 978-0-19-513512-1. Dewey:571.6. LCCN:00-056670.

Audience: **u,f.**

Hawes, Chris &   QK673.P58 2001
Satiat-Jeunemaitre, Beatrice (Editors)
Plant Cell Biology: A Practical Approach. Ed. 2. Trade Paper. Oxford University Press, Inc. New York, NY. 2001. 358p. The Practical Approach Ser., Vol. 250 ISBN:0-19-963865-9, ISBN13: 978-0-19-963865-9. Dewey:571.6/2. LCCN:00-054847.

Audience: **u,f.** *Choice, 2002.*

Hine, Robert (Editor)   QH575.F33 2002
The Facts on File Dictionary of Cell and Molecular Biology. Facts on File, Inc. Staff (Contribution by). Trade Cloth. Facts On File, Inc.. New York, NY. 2002. 256p. The Facts on File Science Library ISBN:0-8160-4912-2, ISBN13: 978-0-8160-4912-7. Dewey:571.6/03. LCCN:2002-032540.

Audience: **u,f.** *Choice, 2003.*

Hunter, Graeme K.   QP514.2.H86 2002
Vital Forces: The Discovery of the Molecular Basis of Life. Trade Cloth. Elsevier Science & Technology Books. Saint Louis, MO. 2000. 364p. ISBN:0-12-361810-X, ISBN13: 978-0-12-361810-8. Dewey:572/.09. LCCN:99-067772.

Audience: **l,u.**

Kimmel, Marek   QH323.5.K53 2001
Branching Processes in Biology. Trade Cloth. Springer. New York, NY. 2002. XVIII, 230p. Interdisciplinary Applied Mathematics Ser., Vol. 19 ISBN:0-387-95340-X, ISBN13: 978-0-387-95340-3. Dewey:570/.1/5118. LCCN:2001-042966.

Audience: **u,f.**

Levine, Joseph & Suzuki,   QH431
David
The Secret of Life: Redesigning the Living World. Trade Paper. W. H. Freeman & Company. New York, NY. 1998. 280p. ISBN:0-7167-3311-0, ISBN13: 978-0-7167-3311-9. Dewey:599.935. LCCN:93-004817.

Audience: **u,f.** *Choice, 1994.*

Loewenstein, Werner R.   QH581.2
The Touchstone of Life: Molecular Information, Cell Communication, and the Foundations of Life. Trade Paper. Oxford University Press, Inc. New York, NY. 2000. 384p. ISBN:0-19-514057-5, ISBN13: 978-0-19-514057-6. Dewey:571.6.

Audience: **u,f.**

Michal, Gerhard (Editor)   QP171.B685 1999
Biochemical Pathways: An Atlas of Biochemistry and Molecular Biology. Trade Cloth. John Wiley & Sons, Inc. Hoboken, NJ. 1998. 288p. ISBN:0-471-33130-9, ISBN13: 978-0-471-33130-8. Dewey:572.8/4. LCCN:98-033226.

Audience: **u,f.** *Choice, 1999.*

Moore   RG626 .M57
The Developing Human. Ed. 7. Cloth Text. Elsevier - Health Sciences Division. Philadelphia, PA. 2003. ISBN:0-8089-2265-3, ISBN13: 978-0-8089-2265-0. Dewey:618.3/2.

Audience: **l,u,f.**

Mullis, Kary B. & Gibbs,   QP606.D46P653 1994
Richard (Editors)
The Polymerase Chain Reaction: A Textbook. Trade Cloth. Springer. New York, NY. 1994. 550p. ISBN:0-8176-3607-2, ISBN13: 978-0-8176-3607-4. Dewey:574.87/3282. LCCN:94-162449.

Audience: **u,f.**

Panno, Joseph   QH582.4.P36 2004
The Cell: Evolution of the First Organism. Trade Cloth. Facts On File, Inc.. New York, NY. 2004. 208p. The Facts on File Science Library ISBN:0-8160-4946-7, ISBN13: 978-0-8160-4946-2. Dewey:571.6. LCCN:2003-025841.

Audience: **u,f.**

Twyman, Richard M.   QH506.T98 1998
Advanced Molecular Biology: A Concise Reference. UK-B Format Paperback. Taylor & Francis Group. Abingdon, 1998. 512p. ISBN:1-85996-141-X, ISBN13: 978-1-85996-141-4. Dewey:572.8. LCCN:00-302572.

Audience: **u,f.** *Choice, 1998.*

Organismic Biology (Anatomy, Physiology) > Anatomy and Morphology

☐ Google Directory: Biology, Biomechanics.
http://google.com/Top/Science/Biology/Biomechanics/
Google.

Audience: **g,l.**

Camazine, Scott   **QH313.S477 2001**
Self-Organization in Biological Systems. Cloth Text. Princeton
University Press. Princeton, NJ. 2001. 535p. Princeton Studies
in Complexity ISBN:0-691-01211-3, ISBN13:
978-0-691-01211-7. Dewey:570/.1/1. LCCN:00-045329.

Audience: **u,f.** *Choice, 2002.*

Kunin, W. & Gaston, Kevin   **QH352.B556 1997**
  J. (Editors)
Biology of Rarity: Causes and Consequences of Rare-Common
Differences. Trade Cloth. Springer. New York, NY. 1996. 300p.
Population and Community Biology Ser. ISBN:0-412-63380-9,
ISBN13: 978-0-412-63380-5. Dewey:577.8/8. LCCN:96-071014.

Audience: **u,f.**

Laporte, Joseph   **QH331.L29 2003**
Natural Kinds and Conceptual Change. Trade Cloth. Cambridge
University Press. New York, NY. 2003. 232p. Cambridge
Studies in Philosophy and Biology Ser. ISBN:0-521-82599-7,
ISBN13: 978-0-521-82599-3. LCCN:2003-055148.

Audience: **u,f.** *Choice, 2004.*

Lestrel, Pete E.   **QH351**
Morphometrics for the Life Sciences. Trade Cloth. World
Scientific Publishing Company, Inc. Hackensack, NJ. 1999.
261p. Recent Advances in Human Biology Ser.
ISBN:981-02-3610-7, ISBN13: 978-981-02-3610-6.
Dewey:574.4.

Audience: **u,f.**

MacLeod, Norman (Editor)   **QH351**
Morphology, Shape and Phylogeny. Forey, Peter L. (Editor).
Taylor & Francis, London; New York. 2002. Systematics
Association special volume series ;; 64; Variation: Systematics
Association special volume ;; no. 64 ISBN:0-415-24074-3,
ISBN13: 978-0-415-24074-1.

Audience: **u,f.**

McGhee, George R. Jr.   **QH351.M335 1998**
Theoretical Morphology: The Concept and Its Applications.
Trade Cloth. Columbia University Press. New York, NY. 1999.
378p. Perspectives in Paleobiology and Earth History Ser.
ISBN:0-231-10616-5, ISBN13: 978-0-231-10616-0.
Dewey:571.3/01/51. LCCN:98-008660.

Audience: **u,f.**

Wiens, John J. (Editor)   **QH351.P58 2000**
Phylogenetic Analysis of Morphological Data. Trade Cloth.
Smithsonian Institution Press. Washington, DC. 2000. x, 220p.
Smithsonian Series in Comparative Evolutionary Biology
ISBN:1-56098-841-X, ISBN13: 978-1-56098-841-0.
Dewey:571.3. LCCN:00-023910.

Audience: **u,f.** *Choice, 2001.*

Zelditch, Miriam, et al.   **QH351**
Geometric Morphometrics for Biologists. Donald Swiderski,
David H. Sheets & William Fink (Authors). Cloth Text. Elsevier

Science & Technology Books. Saint Louis, MO. 2004. 416p.
ISBN:0-12-778460-8, ISBN13: 978-0-12-778460-1.
Dewey:571.3/015195. LCCN:2004-107927.

Audience: **u,f.**

Organismic Biology (Anatomy, Physiology) > Anatomy and Morphology > Plant Anatomy

American Institute of   **QE980**
  Biological Sciences; Meeting ; (1993 : Ames, Iowa)
Flowering Plant Origin, Evolution & Phylogeny. Taylor, David
W. (Editor); Hickey, Leo J. (Editor). Chapman & Hall, New
York :. 1996. ISBN:0-412-05341-1, ISBN13:
978-0-412-05341-2.

Audience: **l,u.**

D'Arcy, William G. &   **QK658 .A57 1996**
  Keating, Richard C. (Editors)
The Anther: Form, Function and Phylogeny. Trade Cloth.
Cambridge University Press. New York, NY. 1996. 363p.
ISBN:0-521-48063-9, ISBN13: 978-0-521-48063-5.
Dewey:582.13/04463. LCCN:95-020222.

Audience: **l,u.** *Choice, 1997.*

Fahn, A.   **QK641.F313 1990**
Plant Anatomy. Ed. 4. Trade Cloth. Elsevier Science &
Technology Books. Saint Louis, MO. 1990. 600p.
ISBN:0-08-037490-5, ISBN13: 978-0-08-037490-1.
Dewey:581.4. LCCN:89-022889.

Audience: **l,u.**

Gartner, Barbara L.   **QK646.P58 1995**
  (Editor)
Plant Stems: Physiology and Functional Morphology. Trade
Cloth. Elsevier Science & Technology Books. Saint Louis, MO.
1995. 440p. Physiological Ecology Ser. ISBN:0-12-276460-9,
ISBN13: 978-0-12-276460-8. Dewey:581.4/95.
LCCN:95-002197.

Audience: **l,u.**

Gibson, Arthur C.   **QK922.G53 1996**
Structure-Function Relations of Warm Desert Plants. Cloth Text.
Springer. New York, NY. 1996. 313p. Adaptations of Desert
Organisms Ser. ISBN:3-540-59267-9, ISBN13:
978-3-540-59267-9. Dewey:581.5/2652. LCCN:96-018699.

Audience: **l,u.**

Hanna, Thomas P.   **QK641.H315 1999**
Microscopic and Chemical Parts of Plants. Trade Cloth. Nova
Science Publishers, Inc. Hauppauge, NY. 1999. 211p.
ISBN:1-56072-547-8, ISBN13: 978-1-56072-547-3.
Dewey:571.3/2.

Audience: **l,u.**

Jackson, Betty P. et al.   **RS190.P55**
Atlas of Microscopy of Medicinal Plants, Culinary Herbs, and
Spices. Snowdon, Derek W.; Jackson, Betty P.. Boca Raton,
CRC Press. 1990. ISBN:0-8493-7705-6, ISBN13:
978-0-8493-7705-1.

Audience: **l,u.**

Mabberley, David   **NC730**
Arthur Harry Church: The Anatomy of Flowers. Trade Cloth.
Merrell Publishers Ltd. London, 2005. 128p.

ISBN:1-85894-116-4, ISBN13: 978-1-85894-116-5.
Dewey:743.9/34.

Audience: **g,l,u.**

Romberger, John A., et al.   QK641.R64 2004
Plant Structure: Function and Development. Zygmunt Hejnowicz
& Jane F. Hill (Authors). Perfect. Blackburn Press, The.
Caldwell, NJ. 2004. 524p. ISBN:1-930665-95-4, ISBN13:
978-1-930665-95-8. Dewey:571.3/2. LCCN:2004-100206.

Audience: **l,u.**

Rudall, Paula   QK641
Anatomy of Flowering Plants: An Introduction to Structure and
Development. Ed. 3. Paper Text. Cambridge University Press.
New York, NY. 2006. 200p. ISBN:0-521-69245-8, ISBN13:
978-0-521-69245-8. Dewey:582.13/044.

Audience: **l,u.**

Russell, Sharman Apt   QK653 .R88
Anatomy of a Rose: Exploring the Secret Life of Flowers. Trade
Paper. Perseus Books Group. New York, NY. 2002. 232p.
ISBN:0-7382-0669-5, ISBN13: 978-0-7382-0669-1.
Dewey:582.13.

Audience: **g,l,u.**

Shigo, Alex L.   QK474.87.S56 1994
Tree Anatomy. Trade Cloth. Shigo & Trees, Associates. Durham,
NH. 1994. 104p. Dr. Shigo's Tree Ser. ISBN:0-943563-14-3,
ISBN13: 978-0-943563-14-5. Dewey:582.16/04.
LCCN:94-184815.

Audience: **u.**

Trigiano, R. N. (Robert Nicholas) &   QK725
  Gray, Dennis J. (Editors)
Plant Development and Biotechnology. CRC Press, Boca Raton,
Fl.. 2005. ISBN:0-8493-1614-6, ISBN13: 978-0-8493-1614-2.

Audience: **l,u.**

Wainwright, Stephen A.   QH351.W25 1988
Axis and Circumference: The Cylindrical Shape of Plants and
Animals. Trade Cloth. Harvard University Press. Cambridge,
MA. 1988. 176p. ISBN:0-674-05700-7, ISBN13:
978-0-674-05700-5. Dewey:574.4. LCCN:87-021099.

Audience: **u,f.**   *Choice, 1989.*

Organismic Biology (Anatomy, Physiology) > Anatomy and Morphology > Plant Anatomy > Higher Plants

Evert, Ray F. & Eichhorn,   QK641
  Susan E.
Esau's Plant Anatomy: Meristems, Cells, and Tissues of the
Plant Body: Their Structure, Function, and Development. Ed. 3.
Trade Cloth. John Wiley & Sons, Inc. Hoboken, NJ. 2006. 602p.
ISBN:0-471-73843-3, ISBN13: 978-0-471-73843-5.
Dewey:571.3/2. LCCN:2006-022118.

Audience: **u,f.**

Organismic Biology (Anatomy, Physiology) > Anatomy and Morphology > Animal Anatomy > General

Bone, Jesse F.   SF761.B64 1988
Animal Anatomy and Physiology. Ed. 3. Trade Cloth. Prentice
Hall PTR. Upper Saddle River, NJ. 1996. ISBN:0-8359-0099-1,
ISBN13: 978-0-8359-0099-7. Dewey:636.089/2.
LCCN:87-007335.

Audience: **l,u.**

Gale Research Staff &   QP11.W67 2002
  McGrath, Kimberley A.
World of Anatomy and Physiology, Set. Trade Cloth. Thomson
Gale. Farmington Hills, MI. 2002. 600p. ISBN:0-7876-5684-4,
ISBN13: 978-0-7876-5684-3. Dewey:612/.003.
LCCN:2002-005517.

Audience: **g,l,u.**   *Choice, 2003.*

Organismic Biology (Anatomy, Physiology) > Anatomy and Morphology > Animal Anatomy > Invertebrate

Anderson, D. T.   QL363.A53 1996
Atlas of Invertebrate Anatomy. Paper Text. University of New
South Wales Press. Sydney, NSW. 1996. 127p.
ISBN:0-86840-207-9, ISBN13: 978-0-86840-207-9.
Dewey:571.1/2/0223. LCCN:97-112121.

Audience: **l,u.**

Conniff, Richard   QL362.C66 1996
Spineless Wonders: Strange Tales from the Invertabrate World.
Trade Cloth. Henry Holt & Company. New York, NY. 1996.
240p. ISBN:0-8050-4218-0, ISBN13: 978-0-8050-4218-4.
Dewey:592. LCCN:96-011748.

Audience: **g,l.**   *Choice, 1997.*

Hubbell, Sue   QL362.H835 1999
Waiting for Aphrodite: Journeys into the Time Before Bones.
Trade Cloth. Houghton Mifflin Company Trade & Reference
Division. Boston, MA. 1999. 256p. ISBN:0-395-83703-0,
ISBN13: 978-0-395-83703-0. Dewey:592. LCCN:98-049811.

Audience: **g,l.**   *Choice, 1999.*

Loewer, Peter H.   QL362.L64 1990
The Inside-Out Stomach: An Introduction to Animals without
Backbones. Jean Jenkins (Illustrator). Trade Cloth. Simon &
Schuster Children's Publishing. New York, NY. 1990. 64p.
ISBN:0-689-31432-9, ISBN13: 978-0-689-31432-2. Dewey:592.
LCCN:89-006499.

Audience: **l,u.**

Losito, Linda, et al.   QL362.S85 1989
Simple Animals. Christopher O'Toole, Robin Kerrod & John
Stidworthy (Authors). Trade Cloth. Facts On File, Inc.. New
York, NY. 1989. 96p. Encyclopedia of the Animal World Ser.
ISBN:0-8160-1968-1, ISBN13: 978-0-8160-1968-7. Dewey:592.
LCCN:89-035005.

Audience: **l.**

Ruppert, Edward E., et al.   QL362.R76 2003
Invertebrate Zoology: A Functional Evolutionary Approach. Ed.
7. Richard S. Fox & Robert D. Barnes (Authors). Cloth Text.

Brooks/Cole. Pacific Grove, CA. 2003. 1008p.
ISBN:0-03-025982-7, ISBN13: 978-0-03-025982-1. Dewey:592.
LCCN:2003-107287.

Audience: **l,u.**

Shepherd, Elizabeth   **QL362.S537 1988**
No Bones: A Key to Bugs and Slugs, Worms, and Ticks, Spiders
and Centipedes, and Other Creepy Crawlies. Ippy Patterson
(Illustrator). Trade Cloth. Simon & Schuster Children's
Publishing. New York, NY. 1988. 96p. ISBN:0-02-782880-8,
ISBN13: 978-0-02-782880-1. Dewey:592. LCCN:87-001549.

Audience: **g,l.**

Stachowitsch, Michael   **QL362.S82 1991**
The Invertebrates: An Illustrated Glossary. Ed. 1. Sylvie Proidl
(Illustrator). Trade Cloth. John Wiley & Sons, Inc. Hoboken, NJ.
1992. 690p. ISBN:0-471-83294-4, ISBN13: 978-0-471-83294-2.
Dewey:592. LCCN:91-021129.

Audience: **g,l,u.**

Organismic Biology (Anatomy, Physiology) > Anatomy and Morphology > Animal Anatomy > Vertebrate

Bemis, William, et al.   **QL805.W35**
Functional Anatomy of Vertebrates: An Evolutionary
Perspective. Ed. 4. Karel F. Liem, Warren F. Walker Jr, Lance
Grande & Lauder (Authors). Cloth Text. Brooks/Cole. Pacific
Grove, CA. 2006. ISBN:0-534-41919-4, ISBN13:
978-0-534-41919-6. Dewey:571.3/16.

Audience: **u.**

Bird, David M.   **QL673.B55 2004**
The Bird Almanac: A Guide to Essential Facts and Figures of
the World's Birds. Ed. 2. Trade Paper. Firefly Books, Ltd.
Tonawanda, NY. 2004. 460p. ISBN:1-55297-925-3, ISBN13:
978-1-55297-925-9. Dewey:598. LCCN:2004-273747.

Audience: **l,u.**

Dutta, Hiran M. & Datta   **QL805.V47 2001**
  Munshi, J. S.
Vertebrate Functional Morphology: Horizon of Research in the
21st Century. Book, Other. Science Publishers. Enfield, NH.
2000. 492p. ISBN:1-57808-098-3, ISBN13: 978-1-57808-098-4.
Dewey:571.3/16. LCCN:00-063495.

Audience: **l,u.** *Choice, 2001.*

Hildebrand, Milton &   **QL805.H64 2001**
  Goslow, George Jr.
Analysis of Vertebrate Structure. Ed. 5. Viola Hildebrand
(Illustrator). Trade Cloth. John Wiley & Sons, Inc. Hoboken, NJ.
2001. 660p. ISBN:0-471-29505-1, ISBN13: 978-0-471-29505-1.
Dewey:571.3/16. LCCN:00-068604.

Audience: **l,u.**

Kardong, Kenneth V.   **QL805.K35 2002**
Vertebrates: Comparative Anatomy, Function, Evolution. Ed. 3.
Cloth Text. McGraw-Hill Higher Education. Burr Ridge, IL.
2001. 784p. ISBN:0-07-290956-0, ISBN13: 978-0-07-290956-2.
Dewey:571.3/16. LCCN:2001-030631.

Audience: **l,u.**

Kent, George C. & Carr,   **QL805.K43 2001**
  Robert K.
Comparative Anatomy of the Vertebrates. Ed. 9. Cloth Text.

McGraw-Hill Higher Education. Burr Ridge, IL. 2000. 544p.
ISBN:0-07-303869-5, ISBN13: 978-0-07-303869-8.
Dewey:596.04. LCCN:00-038680.

Audience: **l,u.**

McGowan, Christopher   **QL805 .M36 1999**
A Practical Guide to Vertebrate Mechanics. Cloth Text.
Cambridge University Press. New York, NY. 1999. 316p.
ISBN:0-521-57194-4, ISBN13: 978-0-521-57194-4.
Dewey:571.3/196. LCCN:98-029462.

Audience: **l,u.** *Choice, 1999.*

Parry-Jones, Jemima   **SF473.O85P37 1998**
Understanding Owls. Trade Cloth. Sterling Publishing Co., Inc..
New York, NY. 1998. 120p. ISBN:0-7153-0643-X, ISBN13:
978-0-7153-0643-7. Dewey:636.6. LCCN:99-182014.

Audience: **g,l.**

Popesko, Peter, et al.   **SF761**
Color Atlas of Anatomy of Small Laboratory Animals, Vol. 1.
Jindrich Horak & Viera Rajtova (Authors). Trade Cloth. Elsevier
- Health Sciences Division. Philadelphia, PA. 2003. 256p.
ISBN:0-7020-2699-9, ISBN13: 978-0-7020-2699-7.
Dewey:599.32/0449/0222.

Audience: **g,l,u.**

Popesko, Peter, et al.   **SF761**
Color Atlas of Anatomy of Small Laboratory Animals, Vol. 2.
Viera Rajtova & Jindrich Horak (Authors). Trade Cloth. Elsevier
- Health Sciences Division. Philadelphia, PA. 2003. 256p.
ISBN:0-7020-2703-0, ISBN13: 978-0-7020-2703-1.
Dewey:599.32/0449/0222.

Audience: **g,l,u.**

Wake, Marvalee H. (Editor)   **QL805**
Hyman's Comparative Vertebrate Anatomy. Ed. 3. Library
Binding. University of Chicago Press. Chicago, IL. 1993. xi,
788p. ISBN:0-226-87011-1, ISBN13: 978-0-226-87011-3.
Dewey:596/.04. LCCN:79-000731.

Audience: **u,f.**

Walker, Warren F. Jr. &   **QL812**
  Homberger, Dominique G.
Vertebrate Dissection. Ed. 8. Paper Text. Saunders College
Publishing. Orlando, FL. 1992. 416p. ISBN:0-03-047434-5,
ISBN13: 978-0-03-047434-7. Dewey:596/.04/028.
LCCN:91-050763.

Audience: **l,u.**

Wolff, Ronald G.   **QL805.W75 1991**
Functional Chordate Anatomy. Cloth Text. Houghton Mifflin
Company Trade & Reference Division. Boston, MA. 2000.
710p. ISBN:0-669-21895-2, ISBN13: 978-0-669-21895-4.
Dewey:596/.04. LCCN:90-082265.

Audience: **u.**

Organismic Biology (Anatomy, Physiology) > Anatomy and Morphology > Animal Anatomy > Human Anatomy

     QM26
A.D.A.M. Interactive Anatomy 4. A.D.A.M. Software, Inc..
2004. ISBN:1-57245-301-X, ISBN13: 978-1-57245-301-2.

Audience: **l,u.**

☐ United States National Library of Medicine National Institutes of Health: The Visible Human Project®. http://www.nlm.nih.gov/research/visible/visible_human.html U.S. National Library of Medicine.

Audience: **g,l,u,f.**

Abrahams, Peter H., et al.   **QM25.M23 2003**
McMinn's Color Atlas of Human Anatomy. Ed. 5. R. M. H. McMinn, S. C. Marks & R. T. Hutchings (Authors). Trade Cloth. Mosby, Inc. Saint Louis, MO. 2002. 392p. ISBN:0-7234-3213-9, ISBN13: 978-0-7234-3213-5. Dewey:611. LCCN:2002-029923.

Audience: **g,l,u,f.**

Agur, Anne M. (Author,   **QM25**
   Author)
Grant's Atlas of Anatomy. Ed. 11. Trade Cloth. Lippincott Williams & Wilkins. Philadelphia, PA. 2004. 848p. ISBN:0-7817-4256-0, ISBN13: 978-0-7817-4256-6. Dewey:611/.0022/2. LCCN:2004-273130.

Audience: **g,l,u,f.**

Banks, John C., et al.   **QM25.A796 2005**
Atlas of Clinical Gross Anatomy. Pedro B. Nava, Darrell Petersen & Kenneth P. Moses (Authors), Martein Moningka (Contribution by). Paper Text. Elsevier - Health Sciences Division. Philadelphia, PA. 2005. 524p. ISBN:0-323-03744-5, ISBN13: 978-0-323-03744-0. Dewey:611/.0022/2. LCCN:2005-045078.

Audience: **g,l,u,f.**

Clemente, Carmine D.   **QM531.C57 2007**
Anatomy: A Regional Atlas of the Human Body. Ed. 5. Trade Paper. Lippincott Williams & Wilkins. Philadelphia, PA. 2006. 640p. ISBN:0-7817-5103-9, ISBN13: 978-0-7817-5103-2. Dewey:611. LCCN:2006-005516.

Audience: **g,l,u,f.**

Drake, Richard L., et al.   **QM23.2.D73 2005**
Gray's Anatomy for Students. Wayne Vogl & Adam W. M. Mitchell (Authors), Richard Tibbitts & Paul Richardson (Illustrators). Cloth Text. Elsevier - Health Sciences Division. Philadelphia, PA. 2004. 1150p. ISBN:0-443-06612-4, ISBN13: 978-0-443-06612-2. Dewey:611. LCCN:2004-050179.

Audience: **l,u,f.**

Kass, Leon   **QH332.B44 2004**
Being Human. Trade Paper. W. W. Norton & Company, Inc. New York, NY. 2004. 628p. ISBN:0-393-92639-7, ISBN13: 978-0-393-92639-2. Dewey:128. LCCN:2004-015017.

Audience: **g,l,u.**

Moore, Keith L. & Dalley,   **QM23.2.M67 2006**
   Arthur F. II
Clinically Oriented Anatomy. Ed. 5. Trade Paper, Perfect. Lippincott Williams & Wilkins. Philadelphia, PA. 2005. 1248p. ISBN:0-7817-3639-0, ISBN13: 978-0-7817-3639-8. Dewey:611. LCCN:2004-028886.

Audience: **u,f.**

Netter, Frank H.   **QM25.N46 2003**
Atlas of Human Anatomy. Ed. 3. John T. Hansen (Editor). Paper Text. Elsevier - Health Sciences Division. Philadelphia, PA. 2002. 612p. ISBN:1-929007-11-6, ISBN13: 978-1-929007-11-0. Dewey:611/.0022/2. LCCN:2002-110663.

Audience: **g,l,u,f.** *Choice, 1990.*

Rohen, Johannes W., et al.   **QM25.R55 2001**
Color Atlas of Anatomy: A Photographic Study of the Human Body. Ed. 5. Chihiro Yokochi & Elke Lutjen-Drecoll (Authors). Trade Cloth. Lippincott Williams & Wilkins. Philadelphia, PA. 2002. 528p. ISBN:0-7817-3194-1, ISBN13: 978-0-7817-3194-2. Dewey:611/.0022/2. LCCN:2001-050416.

Audience: **l,u,f.**

Romanes, George J.   **QM23.2**
Cunningham's Manual of Practical Anatomy: Thorax and Abdomen. Ed. 15. Trade Paper. Oxford University Press, Inc. New York, NY. 1986. 304p. ISBN:0-19-263139-X, ISBN13: 978-0-19-263139-8. Dewey:611.

Audience: **u,f.**

Romanes, George J.   **QM23.2**
Cunningham's Manual of Practical Anatomy: Head, Neck and Brain. Ed. 15. Trade Paper. Oxford University Press, Inc. New York, NY. 1986. 352p. ISBN:0-19-263140-3, ISBN13: 978-0-19-263140-4. Dewey:611.

Audience: **u,f.**

Romanes, George J.   **QM23.2 .C915 1986**
Cunningham's Manual of Practical Anatomy: Upper and Lower Limbs. Ed. 15. G. Jgeorge Romanes (Photographer). Trade Paper. Oxford University Press, Inc. New York, NY. 1986. 272p. ISBN:0-19-263138-1, ISBN13: 978-0-19-263138-1. Dewey:611. LCCN:86-016313.

Audience: **u,f.**

Snell, Richard S.   **QM23.2.S55 2003**
Clinical Anatomy. Ed. 7. Trade Paper. Lippincott Williams & Wilkins. Philadelphia, PA. 2003. 1012p. ISBN:0-7817-4315-X, ISBN13: 978-0-7817-4315-0. Dewey:611. LCCN:2003-044695.

Audience: **u,f.**

Standring, Susan   **QM23.2**
Gray's Anatomy Edition: The Anatomical Basis of Clinical Practice. Ed. 39. Mixed Media, Trade Cloth, Digital, Other. Elsevier - Health Sciences Division. Philadelphia, PA. 2004. 1600p. ISBN:0-443-06676-0, ISBN13: 978-0-443-06676-4. Dewey:611.

Audience: **g,l,u,f.** *Choice, 2005.*

Organismic Biology (Anatomy, Physiology) > Histology

☐ Google Directory: Biology, Histology. http://google.com/Top/Science/Biology/Histology/ Google.

Audience: **g,l.**

Ali (Editor)   **QP517.C45T736 2006**
Transmembrane Signaling Protocols. Ed. 2. Trade Cloth. Humana Press. Totowa, NJ. 2006. 376p. Methods in Molecular Biology Ser., Vol. 332 ISBN:1-58829-546-X, ISBN13: 978-1-58829-546-0. Dewey:571.7/4. LCCN:2005-022678.

Audience: **u,f.**

Cole, Stewart T.   **QR201.T6**
Tuberculosis and the Tubercle Bacillus. Trade Cloth. ASM Press. Washington, DC. 2004. 603p. ISBN:1-55581-295-3, ISBN13: 978-1-55581-295-9. Dewey:616.9/95. LCCN:2004-017059.

Audience: **u,f.**

Gartner, Leslie P. & Hiatt,   **QM557.G38 2006**
  James L.
Color Atlas of Histology. Ed. 4. Dumpbin Filled. Lippincott
Williams & Wilkins. Philadelphia, PA. 2005. 462p.
ISBN:0-7817-9828-0, ISBN13: 978-0-7817-9828-0.
Dewey:611/.018/0222. LCCN:2005-002800.
                                              Audience: **u,f.**

Kiernan, J. A. & Mason, I.   **QH207.M57 2002**
  (Editors)
Microscopy and Histology for Molecular Biologists: A User's
Guide. Trade Cloth. Portland Press, Ltd. London, 2002. 408p.
ISBN:1-85578-141-7, ISBN13: 978-1-85578-141-2.
Dewey:570/.28/2. LCCN:2002-483827.
                                              Audience: **u,f.**

Kierszenbaum, Abraham L.   **RB25.K54 2002**
Histology and Cell Biology: An Introduction to Pathology. Paper
Text. Elsevier - Health Sciences Division. Philadelphia, PA.
2002. 640p. ISBN:0-323-01639-1, ISBN13: 978-0-323-01639-1.
Dewey:616.07. LCCN:2001-051399.
                                              Audience: **l,u.**

Lockshin, Richard A. &   **QH671.W482 2004**
  Zakeri, Zahra (Editors)
When Cells Die II: A Comprehensive Evaluation of Apoptosis
and Programmed Cell Death. Ed. 2. Trade Cloth. John Wiley &
Sons, Inc. Hoboken, NJ. 2003. 568p. ISBN:0-471-21947-9,
ISBN13: 978-0-471-21947-7. Dewey:571.9/36.
LCCN:2003-009326.
                                              Audience: **u,f.**

Odorico, J. S. (Editor), et al.   **QH442**
Human Embryonic Stem Cells. Roger A. Pedersen & S-C Zhang
(Editors). Paper over Boards. Taylor & Francis Group.
Philadelphia, PA. 2005. 391p. Advanced Methods Ser.
ISBN:1-85996-278-5, ISBN13: 978-1-85996-278-7.
Dewey:616/.02774.
                                              Audience: **u,f.**

Pavelka, Margit & Roth,   **QP88**
  Jurgen
Functional Ultrastructure: An Atlas of Tissue Biology and
Pathology. Trade Cloth. Springer. New York, NY. 2005. XVI,
326p. ISBN:3-211-83564-4, ISBN13: 978-3-211-83564-7.
Dewey:571.6/33. LCCN:2004-106811.
                                              Audience: **l,u.**

Ross, Jeffrey S. &   **RC280.B8M585 2005**
  Hortobagyi, Gabriel N. (Editors)
Molecular Oncology of Breast Cancer. Trade Cloth. Jones &
Bartlett Publishers, Inc. Sudbury, MA. 2004. 500p.
ISBN:0-7637-4810-2, ISBN13: 978-0-7637-4810-4.
Dewey:616.99/449. LCCN:2004-022163.
                                              Audience: **u,f.**

Ross, Michael H.   **QM551.R67 2005**
Ross, Histology a Text and Atlas: With Correlated Cell and
Molecular Biology. Ed. 5. Trade Paper. Lippincott Williams &
Wilkins. Philadelphia, PA. 2005. 906p. ISBN:0-7817-5056-3,
ISBN13: 978-0-7817-5056-1. Dewey:611/.018.
LCCN:2005-050445.
                                              Audience: **u,f.**

Rothman, S. S.   **QH331.R857 2001**
Lessons from the Living Cell: The Culture of Science and the
Limits of Reductionism. Trade Cloth. McGraw-Hill Companies,

The. New York, NY. 2001. 272p. ISBN:0-07-137820-0, ISBN13:
978-0-07-137820-8. Dewey:571.6/01. LCCN:2001-034235.
                                              Audience: **g,l,u.**

Young, Barbara, et al.   **QM551**
Wheater's Functional Histology: A Text and Colour Atlas. Ed. 5.
Alan Stevens, James S. Lowe & John W. Heath (Authors).
Paper Text. Elsevier - Health Sciences Division. Philadelphia,
PA. 2006. 448p. ISBN:0-443-06850-X, ISBN13:
978-0-443-06850-8. Dewey:611/.018. LCCN:2006-280114.
                                              Audience: **l,u.**

Organismic Biology (Anatomy, Physiology) > Embryology

Google Directory: Biology, Developmental Biology.
http://google.com/Top/Science/Biology/Developmental_Biology/
Google.
                                              Audience: **g,l.**

Amundson, Ronald   **QH360.5.A48 2005**
The Changing Role of the Embryo in Evolutionary Thought:
Roots of Evo-Devo. Michael Ruse (Contribution by). Trade
Cloth. Cambridge University Press. New York, NY. 2005. 294p.
Cambridge Studies in Philosophy and Biology Ser.
ISBN:0-521-80699-2, ISBN13: 978-0-521-80699-2.
Dewey:576.8/01. LCCN:2004-054409.
                                              Audience: **u,f.**   *Choice, 2005.*

Arthur, Wallace   **QH491.A768 2003**
Biased Embryos and Evolution. Cloth Text. Cambridge
University Press. New York, NY. 2004. 248p.
ISBN:0-521-83382-5, ISBN13: 978-0-521-83382-0.
Dewey:571.8. LCCN:2003-062621.
                                              Audience: **u,f.**

Bard, Jonathan B. L.   **QH491**
  (Editor)
Embryos: Color Atlas of Development. Cloth Text. Wolfe
Publishing. London, 1993. 224p. ISBN:0-7234-1740-7, ISBN13:
978-0-7234-1740-8. Dewey:574.33.
                                              Audience: **u,f.**

Bard, Jonathan B. L.   **QH491 .B37 1990**
Morphogenesis: The Cellular and Molecular Processes of
Developmental Anatomy. Trade Cloth. Cambridge University
Press. New York, NY. 1990. 315p. Developmental and Cell
Biology Monographs, No. 23 ISBN:0-521-36196-6, ISBN13:
978-0-521-36196-5. Dewey:571.3. LCCN:89-017415.
                                              Audience: **u,f.**

Bonner, John Tyler   **QH491.B595 2001**
First Signals: The Evolution of Multicellular Development.
Cloth Text. Princeton University Press. Princeton, NJ. 2001.
156p. ISBN:0-691-07037-7, ISBN13: 978-0-691-07037-7.
Dewey:571.8/35. LCCN:00-039976.
                                              Audience: **u,f.**   *Choice, 2001.*

Carroll, Sean B.   **QH453.C37 2005**
Endless Forms Most Beautiful: The New Science of Evo Devo
and the Making of the Animal Kingdom. Trade Cloth. W. W.
Norton & Company, Inc. New York, NY. 2005. 288p.
ISBN:0-393-06016-0, ISBN13: 978-0-393-06016-4.
Dewey:571.8/5. LCCN:2004-029388.
                                              Audience: **u,f.**

Dye, Frank J.   QH491.D94 2002
Dictionary of Developmental Biology and Embryology. Trade
Cloth. John Wiley & Sons, Inc. Hoboken, NJ. 2002. 165p.
ISBN:0-471-44357-3, ISBN13: 978-0-471-44357-5.
Dewey:571.8/03. LCCN:2002-265882.
                                                Audience: **u,f.**

Edelman, Gerald M.   QH491
Topobiology: An Introduction to Molecular Embryology. Trade
Paper. Basic Books. New York, NY. 1993. 256p.
ISBN:0-465-08653-5, ISBN13: 978-0-465-08653-5.
Dewey:574.3/3. LCCN:88-047678.
                                                Audience: **u,f.**

Gerhart, John & Kirschner,   QH366.2.G463 1997
  Marc
Cells, Embryos and Evolution: Toward a Cellular and
Developmental Understanding of Phenotypic Variation and
Evolutionary Adaptability. Trade Paper. Blackwell Publishing,
Inc. Malden, MA. 1997. 656p. ISBN:0-86542-574-4, ISBN13:
978-0-86542-574-3. Dewey:576.8. LCCN:96-051650.
                                                Audience: **u,f.**

Gilbert, Scott F.   QL955.G48 2003
Developmental Biology. Ed. 7. Trade Cloth, CD-ROM. Sinauer
Associates, Inc. Sunderland, MA. 2003. 784p.
ISBN:0-87893-258-5, ISBN13: 978-0-87893-258-0.
Dewey:571.8. LCCN:2003-001670.
                                                Audience: **u,f.**

Glover, David M. & Hames,   QL955.G36 1989
  B. David (Editors)
Genes and Embryos: Frontiers in Molecular Biology. Cloth Text.
Oxford University Press, Inc. New York, NY. 1989. 244p.
Frontiers in Molecular Biology Ser. ISBN:0-19-963028-3,
ISBN13: 978-0-19-963028-8. Dewey:591.3/3. LCCN:89-002202.
                                                Audience: **u,f.**

Hall, Brian K.   QH366.2
Evolutionary Developmental Biology. Ed. 2. Trade Cloth.
Springer. New York, NY. 1998. 512p. ISBN:0-412-78580-3,
ISBN13: 978-0-412-78580-1. Dewey:576.8. LCCN:98-070275.
                                                Audience: **u,f.**

Hall, Brian Keith & Olson,   QH491.K49 2003
  Wendy (Editors)
Keywords and Concepts in Evolutionary Developmental
Biology. Trade Cloth. Harvard University Press. Cambridge,
MA. 2003. 496p. Harvard University Press Reference Library
ISBN:0-674-00904-5, ISBN13: 978-0-674-00904-2.
Dewey:571.8. LCCN:2002-192201.
                                      Audience: **u,f.** *Choice, 2003.*

Hamburger, Viktor   QL961.H34 1988
The Heritage of Experimental Embryology: Hans Spemann and
the Organizer. Cloth Text. Oxford University Press, Inc. New
York, NY. 1988. C08p. Monographs in History and Philosophy
of Biology ISBN:0-19-505110-6, ISBN13: 978-0-19-505110-0.
Dewey:574.3/3/09. LCCN:87-020416.
                                      Audience: **u,f.** *Choice, 1988.*

Malacinski, George M.   QH453.D48 1988
  (Editor)
Developmental Genetics of Higher Organisms: A Primer in
Developmental Biology. Trade Cloth. Simon & Schuster. New
York, NY. 1987. 400p. ISBN:0-02-948730-7, ISBN13:
978-0-02-948730-3. Dewey:574.3. LCCN:87-015366.
                                                Audience: **u,f.**

Maynard Smith, John   QH546.M285 1999
Shaping Life: Genes, Embryos and Evolution. Cloth over
Boards. Yale University Press. Cumberland, RI. 1999. 64p.
Darwinism Today Ser. ISBN:0-300-08022-0, ISBN13:
978-0-300-08022-3. Dewey:572.8/38. LCCN:99-015177.
                                                Audience: **l,u,f.**

Moore   RG626 .M57
The Developing Human. Ed. 7. Cloth Text. Elsevier - Health
Sciences Division. Philadelphia, PA. 2003. ISBN:0-8089-2265-3,
ISBN13: 978-0-8089-2265-0. Dewey:618.3/2.
                                                Audience: **l,u,f.**

Müller, Gerd & Newman,   QH491.O576 2003
  Stuart (Editors)
Origination of Organismal Form: Beyond the Gene in
Developmental and Evolutionary Biology. Trade Cloth. MIT
Press. Cambridge, MA. 2003. 368p. The Vienna Series in
Theoretical Biology ISBN:0-262-13419-5, ISBN13:
978-0-262-13419-4. Dewey:571.3. LCCN:2002-070314.
                                      Audience: **u,f.** *Choice, 2003.*

Oyama, Susan   QH507.O93 2000
The Ontogeny of Information: Developmental Systems and
Evolution. Ed. 2. Cloth Text. Duke University Press. Durham,
NC. 2000. 280p. Science and Cultural Theory Ser.
ISBN:0-8223-2431-8, ISBN13: 978-0-8223-2431-7.
Dewey:576.8. LCCN:99-034735.
                                                Audience: **u,f.**

Robert, Jason Scott   QH491.R63 2004
Embryology, Epigenesis and Evolution: Taking Development
Seriously. Michael Ruse (Contribution by). Trade Cloth.
Cambridge University Press. New York, NY. 2004. 174p.
Cambridge Studies in Philosophy and Biology Ser.
ISBN:0-521-82467-2, ISBN13: 978-0-521-82467-5.
Dewey:571.8. LCCN:2003-048461.
                                      Audience: **u,f.** *Choice, 2004.*

Sadler, Thomas   QM601.L35 2003
Langman's Medical Embryology. Ed. 9. Book, Other. Lippincott
Williams & Wilkins. Philadelphia, PA. 2003. 544p.
ISBN:0-7817-4310-9, ISBN13: 978-0-7817-4310-5.
Dewey:612.6/4. LCCN:2002-043361.
                                                Audience: **u,f.**

Singer, Peter Albert David   RG135 .E43 1990
  (Editor), et al.
Embryo Experimentation: Ethical, Legal and Social Issues.
Helga Kuhse, Stephen Buckle, Karen Dawson & Pascal
Kasimba (Editors). Cloth Text. Cambridge University Press.
New York, NY. 1990. 279p. ISBN:0-521-38359-5, ISBN13:
978-0-521-38359-2. Dewey:174.2/8. LCCN:89-025220.
                                                Audience: **u,f.**

Slack, J. M.   QL955 .S54 1990
From Egg to Embryo: Regional Specification in Early
Development. Ed. 2. Jonathan B. L. Bard, Peter W. Barlow &
David L. Kirk (Contribution by). Trade Paper. Cambridge
University Press. New York, NY. 1991. 348p. Developmental
and Cell Biology Monographs, No. 26 ISBN:0-521-40943-8,
ISBN13: 978-0-521-40943-8. Dewey:591.3/3. LCCN:90-002670.
                                                Audience: **u,f.**

Society for Developmental   **TK5105.875.I57**
Biology (SDB)
☐ The WWW Virtual Library - Developmental Biology.
http://www.sdbonline.org/archive/Other/VL_DB.html
Society for Developmental Biology (SDB).

Audience: **g,l.**

Stern, Claudio (Editor)   **QL955.G34 2004**
Gastrulation: From Cells to Embryo. Trade Cloth. Cold Spring
Harbor Laboratory Press. Woodbury, NY. 2004. 800p.
ISBN:0-87969-707-5, ISBN13: 978-0-87969-707-5.
Dewey:571.8/65. LCCN:2004-009562.

Audience: **u,f.**   *Choice, 2005.*

Sweeney, Lauren J.   **QM601.S94 1998**
Basic Concepts in Embryology: A Student's Survival Guide.
Cloth Text. McGraw-Hill Professional Publishing. New York,
NY. 1997. 480p. Basic Concepts Ser. ISBN:0-07-063308-8,
ISBN13: 978-0-07-063308-7. Dewey:612.6/4. LCCN:97-026599.

Audience: **l,u,f.**

Tuan, Rocky S. & Lo,   **RC280.G5**
Cecilia W. (Editors)
Developmental Biology Protocols, 3 Vol. Set. Book, Other.
Humana Press. Totowa, NJ. 1995. 1700p. Methods in Molecular
Biology Ser. ISBN:0-89603-855-6, ISBN13: 978-0-89603-855-4.
Dewey:616.99/465.

Audience: **u,f.**

Organismic Biology (Anatomy, Physiology) > Embryology > Plant Embryology

Lyndon, R. F.   **QK645 .L96 1998**
The Shoot Apical Meristem: Its Growth and Development.
Jonathan B. L. Bard, Peter W. Barlow & David L. Kirk
(Contribution by). Trade Cloth. Cambridge University Press.
New York, NY. 1998. 295p. Developmental and Cell Biology
Ser., No. 34 ISBN:0-521-40457-6, ISBN13: 978-0-521-40457-0.
Dewey:575.4/85. LCCN:98-010719.

Audience: **u,f.**

Moore, David   **QK601 .M648 1998**
Fungal Morphogenesis. Jonathan B. L. Bard, Peter W. Barlow &
David L. Kirk (Contribution by). Trade Paper. Cambridge
University Press. New York, NY. 2003. 485p. Developmental
and Cell Biology Ser. ISBN:0-521-52857-7, ISBN13:
978-0-521-52857-3. Dewey:571.8/295.

Audience: **u,f.**   *Choice, 1999.*

Raghavan, V.   **QK731.R26 2000**
Developmental Biology of Flowering Plants. Cloth Text.
Springer. New York, NY. 1999. 400p. ISBN:0-387-98781-9,
ISBN13: 978-0-387-98781-1. Dewey:571.8/2. LCCN:99-010027.

Audience: **l,u,f.**   *Choice, 2000.*

Raghavan, Valayamghat   **QK665 .R34 1997**
Molecular Embryology of Flowering Plants. Trade Cloth.
Cambridge University Press. New York, NY. 1997. 712p.
ISBN:0-521-55246-X, ISBN13: 978-0-521-55246-2.
Dewey:571.8/6/2. LCCN:96-044410.

Audience: **u,f.**   *Choice, 1998.*

Raghavan, V.   **QK521 .R34 1989**
Developmental Biology of Fern Gametophytes. Jonathan B. L.
Bard, Peter W. Barlow & David L. Kirk (Contribution by).

Trade Cloth. Cambridge University Press. New York, NY. 1989.
384p. Developmental and Cell Biology Ser.
ISBN:0-521-33022-X, ISBN13: 978-0-521-33022-0.
Dewey:587/.3. LCCN:2006-271692.

Audience: **l,u,f.**   *Choice, 1990.*

Organismic Biology (Anatomy, Physiology) > Embryology > Animal Embryology

Arthur, Wallace   **QH491 .A77 1997**
The Origin of Animal Body Plans: A Study in Evolutionary
Developmental Biology. Trade Cloth. Cambridge University
Press. New York, NY. 1997. 357p. ISBN:0-521-55014-9,
ISBN13: 978-0-521-55014-7. Dewey:571.8/1. LCCN:97-003021.

Audience: **u,f.**

Atkinson, D. &   **QH491**
Thorndyke, M.
Environment and Animal Development: Genes, Life Histories
and Plasticity. Paper over Boards. Taylor & Francis Group.
Philadelphia, PA. 2001. 376p. SEB Seminar Ser.
ISBN:1-85996-184-3, ISBN13: 978-1-85996-184-1.
Dewey:571.81.

Audience: **u.**

De Pomerai, David   **QH453.D4 1990**
From Gene to Animal: An Introduction to the Molecular
Biology of Animal Development. Ed. 2. Trade Cloth. Cambridge
University Press. New York, NY. 1990. 431p.
ISBN:0-521-38192-4, ISBN13: 978-0-521-38192-5.
Dewey:591.3. LCCN:90-001468.

Audience: **u.**

Deeming, D. Charles &   **QL959 .E33 1991**
Ferguson, Mark W. J. (Editors)
Egg Incubation: Its Effects on Embryonic Development in Birds
and Reptiles. Trade Cloth. Cambridge University Press. New
York, NY. 1991. 462p. ISBN:0-521-39071-0, ISBN13:
978-0-521-39071-2. Dewey:571.8/616. LCCN:2005-278208.

Audience: **u,f.**   *Choice, 1992.*

Gilbert, Scott F. & Raunio,   **QL955.E43 1997**
Anne M. (Editors)
Embryology: Constructing the Organism. Cloth Text. Sinauer
Associates, Inc. Sunderland, MA. 1997. 513p.
ISBN:0-87893-237-2, ISBN13: 978-0-87893-237-5.
Dewey:571.8/61. LCCN:97-013045.

Audience: **u,f.**   *Choice, 1998.*

Gilbert, Scott F. & Singer,   **QL955.G48 2006**
Susan R.
Developmental Biology. Ed. 8. Cloth Text. Sinauer Associates,
Inc. Sunderland, MA. 2006. 750p. ISBN:0-87893-250-X,
ISBN13: 978-0-87893-250-4. Dewey:571.8.
LCCN:2006-004780.

Audience: **l,u,f.**

Hennig, W. (Editor)   **QL981**
Early Embryonic Development of Animals. Cloth Text. Springer.
New York, NY. 1992. 236p. Results and Problems in Cell
Differentiation Ser., Vol. 18 ISBN:0-387-55508-0, ISBN13:
978-0-387-55508-9. Dewey:591.334. LCCN:92-020781.

Audience: **u,f.**

Satoh, Noriyuki   **QL613**
Developmental Biology of Ascidians. Trade Cloth. Cambridge
University Press. New York, NY. 1994. 251p. Developmental
and Cell Biology Ser., No. 29 ISBN:0-521-35221-5, ISBN13:
978-0-521-35221-5. Dewey:596.2. LCCN:93-007159.
Audience: **u,f.**

Wall, Robert   **QL971 .W35 1990**
This Side Up: Spatial Determination in the Early Development
of Animals. Jonathan B. L. Bard, Peter W. Barlow & David L.
Kirk (Contribution by). Trade Paper. Cambridge University
Press. New York, NY. 2005. 448p. Developmental and Cell
Biology Ser., Vol. 24 ISBN:0-521-01726-2, ISBN13:
978-0-521-01726-8. Dewey:591.3/3.
Audience: **u,f.**

Wolpert, Lewis   **QM603.W65 1991**
The Triumph of the Embryo. Trade Cloth. Oxford University
Press, Inc. New York, NY. 1991. 224p. ISBN:0-19-854243-7,
ISBN13: 978-0-19-854243-8. Dewey:612.6/4. LCCN:91-007583.
Audience: **u,f.** *Choice, 1992.*

Organismic Biology (Anatomy, Physiology) > Embryology > Animal Embryology > Human Embryology

Amundson, Ronald   **QH360.5.A48 2005**
The Changing Role of the Embryo in Evolutionary Thought:
Roots of Evo-Devo. Michael Ruse (Contribution by). Trade
Cloth. Cambridge University Press. New York, NY. 2005. 294p.
Cambridge Studies in Philosophy and Biology Ser.
ISBN:0-521-80699-2, ISBN13: 978-0-521-80699-2.
Dewey:576.8/01. LCCN:2004-054409.
Audience: **u,f.** *Choice, 2005.*

Brookes, Murray; Zietman,   **QM601**
Anthony
Clinical embryology: a color atlas and text. Boca Raton : CRC
Press. 1998. ISBN:0-8493-1255-8, ISBN13: 978-0-8493-1255-7.
Audience: **u,f.**

Carlson, Bruce M.   **QM601.C29 2004**
Human Embryology and Developmental Biology. Ed. 3. Paper
Text. Elsevier - Health Sciences Division. Philadelphia, PA.
2004. 512p. ISBN:0-323-01487-9, ISBN13: 978-0-323-01487-8.
Dewey:612.6/4. LCCN:2004-040246.
Audience: **u,f.**

Carlson, Bruce M.   **QM601.C29 2004**
Human Embryology and Developmental Biology: With Student
Consult Access. Ed. 3. Cloth Text. Elsevier - Health Sciences
Division. Philadelphia, PA. 2004. xv, 527p.
ISBN:0-323-03649-X, ISBN13: 978-0-323-03649-8.
Dewey:612.64.
Audience: **l,u,f.**

Espejo, Roman (Editor)   **QP277.H85 2002**
Human Embryo Experimentation. Trade Cloth. Thomson Gale.
Farmington Hills, MI. 2002. 79p. Opposing Viewpoints Ser.
ISBN:0-7377-1285-6, ISBN13: 978-0-7377-1285-8.
Dewey:174/.28. LCCN:2002-023637.
Audience: **u,f.**

Gilbert, Stephen G.   **QM602.G55 1989**
Pictorial Human Embryology. Trade Cloth. University of
Washington Press. Seattle, WA. 1988. 176p.

ISBN:0-295-96632-7, ISBN13: 978-0-295-96632-8.
Dewey:612.64. LCCN:87-034642.
Audience: **u,f.** *Choice, 1990.*

Jirásek, Jan E. (Jan   **RG613**
Evangelista)
An Atlas of the Human Embryo and Fetus: A Photographic
Review of Human Prenatal Development. Keith, Louis G.
(Foreword by). Parthenon Pub. Group, New York. 2001.
ISBN:1-85070-659-X, ISBN13: 978-1-85070-659-5.
Audience: **l,u,f.**

Kiessling, Ann & Anderson,   **QP277.K54 2003**
Scott C.
Human Embryonic Stem Cells: An Introduction to the Science
and Therapeutic Potential. Trade Paper. Jones & Bartlett
Publishers, Inc. Sudbury, MA. 2003. 240p. Molecular Biology
Ser. ISBN:0-7637-2341-X, ISBN13: 978-0-7637-2341-5.
Dewey:612.6/46. LCCN:2003-044634.
Audience: **u,f.**

Larsen, William J.   **QM601.L37 2001**
Human Embryology. Ed. 3. Paper Text. Elsevier - Health
Sciences Division. Philadelphia, PA. 2001. 575p.
ISBN:0-443-06583-7, ISBN13: 978-0-443-06583-5.
Dewey:612.6/4. LCCN:2001-017467.
Audience: **u,f.**

Lauritzen, Paul (Editor)   **QH442.2.C566 2001**
Cloning and the Future of Human Embryo Research. Trade
Cloth. Oxford University Press, Inc. New York, NY. 2001. 304p.
ISBN:0-19-512858-3, ISBN13: 978-0-19-512858-1. Dewey:176.
LCCN:00-024562.
Audience: **u,f.**

Moore, Keith L. & Persaud,   **QM601.M757 2003**
T. V. N.
Before We Are Born: Essentials of Embryology and Birth
Defects. Ed. 6. Paper Text. Elsevier - Health Sciences Division.
Philadelphia, PA. 2002. 460p. ISBN:0-7216-9408-X, ISBN13:
978-0-7216-9408-5. Dewey:612.6/4. LCCN:2002-021796.
Audience: **u,f.**

Moore, Keith L. & Persaud,   **QM601.M76 2003**
T. V. N.
The Developing Human: Clinically Oriented Embryology. Ed. 7.
Paper Text. Elsevier - Health Sciences Division. Philadelphia,
PA. 2002. 544p. ISBN:0-7216-9412-8, ISBN13:
978-0-7216-9412-2. Dewey:612.6/4. LCCN:2002-021797.
Audience: **u,f.**

Moore, Keith L., et al.   **QM601**
Color Atlas of Clinical Embryology. Ed. 2. T. V. N. Persaud &
Kohei Shiota (Authors). Trade Cloth. Elsevier - Health Sciences
Division. Philadelphia, PA. 2000. 294p. ISBN:0-7216-8263-4,
ISBN13: 978-0-7216-8263-1. Dewey:611/.013/0222.
LCCN:00-020037.
Audience: **u,f.**

Organismic Biology (Anatomy, Physiology) > Physiology

☐ Google Directory: Biology, Biomechanics.
http://google.com/Top/Science/Biology/Biomechanics/
Google.

Audience: **g,l.**

☐ Google Directory: Biology, Physiology.
http://google.com/Top/Science/Biology/Physiology/
Google.

Audience: **g,l.**

DeAngelis, D. L. (Donald Lee)   **QH344**
Dynamics of nutrient cycling and food webs. London ; New York : Chapman & Hall. 1992. Population and community biology series ;; 9 ISBN:0-412-29830-9, ISBN13: 978-0-412-29830-1.

Audience: **u,f.**

Gordon, Jon   **QH341**
Become an Energy Addict: Simple, Powerful Ways to Energize Your Life. Trade Cloth. Longstreet Press, Inc. Athens, GA. 2003. 192p. ISBN:1-56352-718-9, ISBN13: 978-1-56352-718-0. Dewey:615.89.

Audience: **l,u.**

Gordon, Jon   **QH341.G67 2004**
Energy Addict®: 101 Physical, Mental, and Spiritual Ways to Energize Your Life. Trade Paper. Penguin Group (USA) Inc. New York, NY. 2004. 272p. ISBN:0-399-53089-4, ISBN13: 978-0-399-53089-0.

Audience: **l,u.**

Hazon, N. & Flik, G. (Editors)   **QH508**
Osmoregulation and Drinking in Vertebrates. Paper over Boards. Taylor & Francis Group. Philadelphia, PA. 2002. 208p. SEB Symposium Ser. ISBN:1-85996-094-4, ISBN13: 978-1-85996-094-3. Dewey:571.751.

Audience: **u,f.**

Isfort, Robert J. & Lederberg, Joshua (Editors)   **Q11.N5 VOL.919**
Toxicology for the Next Millennium. Trade Cloth. New York Academy of Sciences. New York, NY. 2000. 500p. Annals of the New York Academy of Sciences Ser., Vol. 919 ISBN:1-57331-265-7, ISBN13: 978-1-57331-265-3. Dewey:500 s 615.9. LCCN:00-058423.

Audience: **u,f.**

Rice-Evans, Catherine A. & Halliwell, B.   **QH345.B522 NO.61**
Free Radicals and Oxidative Stress: Environment, Drugs and Food Additives. Trade Cloth. Portland Press, Ltd. London, 1995. 288p. Biochemical Society Symposium Ser., Vol. 61 ISBN:1-85578-069-0, ISBN13: 978-1-85578-069-9. Dewey:616.07. LCCN:96-101772.

Audience: **u,f.**

Rockson, Stanley G. (Editor)   **Q11.N5 VOL.979**
The Lymphatic Continuum: Lymphatic Biology and Disease. Trade Cloth. New York Academy of Sciences. New York, NY. 2002. x, 235p. Annals of the New York Academy of Sciences Ser., Vol. 979 ISBN:1-57331-414-5, ISBN13: 978-1-57331-414-5. Dewey:500 s 612.4/2. LCCN:2002-153061.

Audience: **u,f.**

Ross, Jeffrey S. & Hortobagyi, Gabriel N. (Editors)   **RC280.B8M585 2005**
Molecular Oncology of Breast Cancer. Trade Cloth. Jones & Bartlett Publishers, Inc. Sudbury, MA. 2004. 500p. ISBN:0-7637-4810-2, ISBN13: 978-0-7637-4810-4. Dewey:616.99/449. LCCN:2004-022163.

Audience: **u,f.**

Rothman, S. S.   **QH331.R857 2001**
Lessons from the Living Cell: The Culture of Science and the Limits of Reductionism. Trade Cloth. McGraw-Hill Companies, The. New York, NY. 2001. 272p. ISBN:0-07-137820-0, ISBN13: 978-0-07-137820-8. Dewey:571.6/01. LCCN:2001-034235.

Audience: **g,l,u.**

The Department of Physiology and Biophysics, Weill Medical College of Cornell University   **Z6662**
☐ The World-Wide Web Virtual Library: Physiology & Biophysics (Biosciences).
http://neocortex.med.cornell.edu/VL-Physio/
Cornell University.

Audience: **g,l.**

Walz, Wolfgang   **QP43.I585 2005**
Integrative Physiology in the Proteomics and Post-Genomics Age. Trade Cloth. Humana Press. Totowa, NJ. 2005. 280p. ISBN:1-58829-315-7, ISBN13: 978-1-58829-315-2. Dewey:571/.072. LCCN:2004-020035.

Audience: **l,u,f.**

Organismic Biology (Anatomy, Physiology) > Physiology > Plant Physiology

Daniell, Henry & Chase, Christine D. (Editors)   **QK725.M745 2004**
Molecular Biology and Biotechnology of Plant Organelles: Chloroplasts and Mitochondria. Trade Cloth. Springer. New York, NY. 2005. XXVI, 659p. ISBN:1-4020-2713-3, ISBN13: 978-1-4020-2713-0. Dewey:581.0724.

Audience: **u,f.** *Choice, 2005.*

Organismic Biology (Anatomy, Physiology) > Physiology > Animal Physiology

QH301
The Cardiovascular System. Trade Cloth. Cold Spring Harbor Laboratory Press. Woodbury, NY. 2003. 600p. Symposia on Quantitative Biology Ser., LXVII ISBN:0-87969-678-8, ISBN13: 978-0-87969-678-8. Dewey:570.6.

Audience: **u,f.**

Feder, Martin E. & Burggren, Warren W. (Editors)   **QL669.2.E58 1992**
Environmental Physiology of the Amphibians. Trade Cloth. University of Chicago Press. Chicago, IL. 1992. 472p. ISBN:0-226-23943-8, ISBN13: 978-0-226-23943-9. Dewey:597.6/041. LCCN:91-030944.

Audience: **l,u.** *Choice, 1993.*

Macieira-Coelho, Alvaro   QH506.P76 NO.30
  (Editor)
Biology of Aging. Trade Cloth. Springer. New York, NY. 2002.
VIII, 192p. Progress in Molecular and Subcellular Biology Ser.,
Vol. 28 ISBN:3-540-43827-0, ISBN13: 978-3-540-43827-4.
Dewey:572.8 s 612.6/7. LCCN:2002-070834.

                                    Audience: **u,f.**

Martinez Arias, Alfonso &   QH506.M376 2002
  Stewart, Alison
Molecular Principles of Animal Development. Paper Text.
Oxford University Press, Inc. New York, NY. 2002. 424p.
ISBN:0-19-879284-0, ISBN13: 978-0-19-879284-0.
Dewey:571.8/1. LCCN:2002-283918.

                                    Audience: **u,f.**

Pollock, Raphael E. &   RC262.5.M36 2003
  O'Sullivan, Brian
UICC Manual of Clinical Oncology. Ed. 8. James H. Doroshow,
David Khayat & Akimasa Nakao (Editors). Trade Paper. John
Wiley & Sons, Inc. Hoboken, NJ. 2004. 936p.
ISBN:0-471-22289-5, ISBN13: 978-0-471-22289-7.
Dewey:616.99/4. LCCN:2003-043069.

                                    Audience: **u,f.**

Organismic Biology (Anatomy, Physiology) > Physiology > Animal Physiology > Human Physiology

☐ United States National Library of Medicine National
Institutes of Health: The Visible Human Project®.
http://www.nlm.nih.gov/research/visible/visible_human.html
U.S. National Library of Medicine.

                                Audience: **g,l,u,f.**

Boron, Walter F. &   QP34.5.B65 2005
  Boulpaep, Emile L.
Medical Physiology: With Student Consult Access. Cloth Text.
Elsevier - Health Sciences Division. Philadelphia, PA. 2004.
1344p. ISBN:1-4160-2328-3, ISBN13: 978-1-4160-2328-9.
Dewey:612. LCCN:2004-051158.

                                    Audience: **u,f.**

Cohen, Barbara Janson   QP36.M54 2005
Memmler's Structure and Function of the Human Body. Ed. 8.
Trade Cloth. Lippincott Williams & Wilkins. Philadelphia, PA.
2005. 544p. ISBN:0-7817-5184-5, ISBN13: 978-0-7817-5184-1.
Dewey:612. LCCN:2004-030916.

                                    Audience: **u,f.**

Ganong, William F.   QP31.2.G36 2005
Review of Medical Physiology. Ed. 22. Paper Text.
McGraw-Hill Companies, The. New York, NY. 2005. 928p.
ISBN:0-07-144040-2, ISBN13: 978-0-07-144040-0. Dewey:612.

                                    Audience: **l,u,f.**

Guyton, Arthur C. & Hall,   QP34.5.G9 2005
  John E.
Textbook of Medical Physiology: With Student Consult Access.
Ed. 11. Cloth Text. Elsevier - Health Sciences Division.
Philadelphia, PA. 2005. 1104p. ISBN:0-7216-0240-1, ISBN13:
978-0-7216-0240-0. Dewey:612. LCCN:2004-051421.

                                    Audience: **u,f.**

Johnson, Leonard R.   QP34.5
  (Editor)
Essential Medical Physiology. Ed. 3. Cloth Text. Elsevier
Science & Technology Books. Saint Louis, MO. 2003. 1008p.
ISBN:0-12-387584-6, ISBN13: 978-0-12-387584-6. Dewey:612.
LCCN:2003-109363.

                                    Audience: **u,f.**

Marieb, Elaine N.   QP34.5.M264 2006
Essentials of Human Anatomy and Physiology. Ed. 8. Trade
Cloth. Benjamin-Cummings Publishing Company. San
Francisco, CA. 2005. xviii, 606p. ISBN:0-8053-7328-4,
ISBN13: 978-0-8053-7328-8. Dewey:612. LCCN:2004-060029.

                                    Audience: **l,u.**

Mielke, James H., et al.   QH431.M525 2006
Human Biological Variation. Lyle W. Konigsberg & John
Relethford (Authors). Trade Paper. Oxford University Press, Inc.
New York, NY. 2005. 432p. ISBN:0-19-518871-3, ISBN13:
978-0-19-518871-4. Dewey:599.9/4. LCCN:2005-040639.

                                    Audience: **l,u,f.**

Scanlon, Valerie C. &   QP34.5.S288 2002
  Sanders, Tina
Essentials of Anatomy and Physiology. Ed. 4. Trade Paper. F. A.
Davis Company. Philadelphia, PA. 2003. 575p.
ISBN:0-8036-1007-6, ISBN13: 978-0-8036-1007-1. Dewey:612.
LCCN:2002-073776.

                                    Audience: **l,u.**

Thibodeau, Gary A. &   QP34.5
  Patton, Kevin T.
Anatomy and Physiology. Ed. 6. Cloth Text. Elsevier - Health
Sciences Division. Philadelphia, PA. 2006. 1272p.
ISBN:0-323-03718-6, ISBN13: 978-0-323-03718-1. Dewey:612.

                                    Audience: **l,u,f.**

Thibodeau, Gary A. &   QP34.5.T5 2000
  Patton, Kevin T.
Structure and Function of the Body. Ed. 11. Trade Cloth.
Elsevier - Health Sciences Division. Philadelphia, PA. 2000.
528p. ISBN:0-323-01082-2, ISBN13: 978-0-323-01082-5.
Dewey:612. LCCN:99-059495.

                                    Audience: **l,u.**

Organismic Biology (Anatomy, Physiology) > Neurobiology

☐ Google Directory: Biology, Neurobiology.
http://google.com/Top/Science/Biology/Neurobiology/
Google.

                                Audience: **g,l.**

The Department of   Z6663.N5
  Neurology and Neuroscience at
  Cornell University Medical College
☐ The World-Wide Web Virtual Library: Neuroscience
(Biosciences).
http://neuro.med.cornell.edu/
The WWW Virtual Library (WWWVL).

                                Audience: **g,l.**

Waxman, Stephen   **RC349.8**
From Neuroscience to Neurology: Neuroscience, Molecular
Medicine and the Therapeutic Transformation of Neurology.
Trade Cloth. Elsevier Science & Technology Books. Saint
Louis, MO. 2004. 552p. ISBN:0-12-738903-2, ISBN13:
978-0-12-738903-5. Dewey:616.8/046. LCCN:2004-018953.
Audience: **u,f.**

Organismic Biology (Anatomy, Physiology) > Neurobiology > Cellular neurobiology

Miyan, J. A. (Editor), et al.   **QP376.8**
Brain Stem Cells. M. Thorndyke, P. W. Beesley & C. M.
Bannister (Editors). Paper over Boards. Taylor & Francis Group.
Philadelphia, PA. 2001. 152p. SEB Seminar Ser.
ISBN:1-85996-222-X, ISBN13: 978-1-85996-222-0.
Dewey:612.826.
Audience: **u,f.**

Organismic Biology (Anatomy, Physiology) > Neurobiology > CNS

O'Neill, C. & Anderton, B.   **QP361**
Neuronal Signal Transduction and Alzheimer's Disease, Vol. 67.
Trade Cloth. Portland Press, Ltd. London, 2001. 213p.
Biochemical Society Symposium Ser., Vol. 67
ISBN:1-85578-133-6, ISBN13: 978-1-85578-133-7.
Dewey:616.831007. LCCN:2003-386010.
Audience: **u,f.**

Organismic Biology (Anatomy, Physiology) > Immunology

□ Google Directory: Biology, Immunology.
http://google.com/Top/Science/Biology/Immunology/
Google.
Audience: **g,l.**

Coligan, John E.   **QR183.S54 2005**
Short Protocols in Immunology. Trade Paper. John Wiley &
Sons, Inc. Hoboken, NJ. 2005. 872p. ISBN:0-471-71578-6,
ISBN13: 978-0-471-71578-8. Dewey:616.07/9/078.
LCCN:2004-024584.
Audience: **u,f.**

Hornick (Editor)   **QR188.8T732 2006**
Transplantation Immunology. Trade Cloth. Humana Press.
Totowa, NJ. 2005. 400p. Methods in Molecular Biology Ser.
ISBN:1-58829-544-3, ISBN13: 978-1-58829-544-6.
Dewey:617.9/5. LCCN:2005-028830.
Audience: **u,f.**

Ludewig, Burkhard &   **RC271.I45A335 2005**
Hoffmann, Matthias W.
Adoptive Immunotherapy: Methods and Protocols. Trade Cloth.
Humana Press. Totowa, NJ. 2005. 520p. Methods in Molecular
Medicine Ser., Vol. 109 ISBN:1-58829-406-4, ISBN13:
978-1-58829-406-7. Dewey:616.99/4061. LCCN:2004-010540.
Audience: **u,f.**

Steinman, Ralph M.   **Q11.N5 VOL.1062**
Human Immunology: Patient-Based Research. New York
Academy of Sciences Staff (Contribution by). Trade Cloth. New
York Academy of Sciences. New York, NY. 2005. xi, 254p.
Annals of the New York Academy of Sciences Ser., Vol. 1062
ISBN:1-57331-606-7, ISBN13: 978-1-57331-606-4. Dewey:500
s 616.07/9. LCCN:2005-033672.
Audience: **u,f.**

Organismic Biology (Anatomy, Physiology) > Immunology > Cancer Immunology

El-Deiry, Safik S. (Editor)   **Q11.N5 VOL.1059**
Tumor Progression and Therapeutic Resistance. Trade Cloth.
New York Academy of Sciences. New York, NY. 2005. 350p.
Annals of the New York Academy of Sciences Ser., Vol. 1059
ISBN:1-57331-543-5, ISBN13: 978-1-57331-543-2. Dewey:500
s 616.99/407. LCCN:2005-029003.
Audience: **u,f.**

Rudland, S. (Editor), et al.   **QH345.B522 NO.63**
Mammary Development and Cancer. D. Fernig & S. Leinster
(Editors). Cloth Text. Portland Press, Ltd. London, 1997. 35p.
Biochemical Society Symposium Ser., Vol. 63
ISBN:1-85578-087-9, ISBN13: 978-1-85578-087-3. Dewey:572
s. LCCN:98-110810.
Audience: **u,f.**

Shimkets, Richard A.   **RC268.4.O54 2005**
(Editor), et al.
The Oncogenomics Handbook: Understanding and Treating
Cancer in the 21st Century. William J. LaRochelle & Beverly A.
Teicher (Editors). Trade Cloth. Humana Press. Totowa, NJ.
2005. 752p. Cancer Drug Discovery and Developmenttm Ser.
ISBN:1-58829-425-0, ISBN13: 978-1-58829-425-8.
Dewey:616.99/4042. LCCN:2004-027753.
Audience: **u,f.**

Von Hoff, Daniel D. &   **RC280.P25P342 2005**
Hruban, Ralph H.
Pancreatic Cancer Cb. Trade Cloth. Jones & Bartlett Publishers,
Inc. Sudbury, MA. 2005. 832p. ISBN:0-7637-2178-6, ISBN13:
978-0-7637-2178-7. Dewey:616.99/437. LCCN:2004-013095.
Audience: **u,f.**

Behavioral Biology

Balda, Russell P., et al.   **QL785.A7228 1997**
Animal Cognition in Nature: The Convergence of Psychology
and Biology in Laboratory and Field. Irene M. Pepperberg & A.
C. Kamil (Authors). Trade Cloth. Elsevier Science &
Technology Books. Saint Louis, MO. 1998. 465p.
ISBN:0-12-077030-X, ISBN13: 978-0-12-077030-4.
Dewey:591.5. LCCN:99-211220.
Audience: **u.**

Caro, Tim (Editor)   **QL751.B3425 1998**
Behavioral Ecology and Conservation Biology. Trade Cloth.
Oxford University Press, Inc. New York, NY. 1998. 598p.
ISBN:0-19-510489-7, ISBN13: 978-0-19-510489-9.
Dewey:591.5. LCCN:97-018005.
Audience: **l,u.**

Dimijian, Greg & Dimijian,　QL50.D54 1996
Mary B. (Photographers)
Animalwatch: Behavior, Biology and Beauty. Greg Dimijian &
Mary B. Dimijian (Text by), Jane Goodall (Foreword by). Trade
Cloth. Harry N. Abrams, Inc. New York, NY. 1996. 144p.
ISBN:0-8109-1975-3, ISBN13: 978-0-8109-1975-4.
Dewey:591.5/1. LCCN:96-001668.

Audience: **g,l.**

Grier, James W. &　QL751
Burk, Ted
Biology of Animal Behavior. Ed. 2. Trade Cloth. McGraw-Hill
Higher Education. Burr Ridge, IL. 1993. 800p.
ISBN:0-697-23492-4, ISBN13: 978-0-697-23492-6.
Dewey:591.51.

Audience: **l,u.**

Houck, Lynne D. &　QL751.6.F66 1996
Drickamer, Lee C. (Editors)
Foundations of Animal Behavior: Classic Papers with
Commentaries. Trade Cloth. University of Chicago Press.
Chicago, IL. 1996. 858p. ISBN:0-226-35456-3, ISBN13:
978-0-226-35456-9. Dewey:591.51. LCCN:96-033734.

Audience: **l,u.**

Immelmann, Klaus & Beer,　QL750.3.I4513 1989
Colin
A Dictionary of Ethology. Trade Cloth. Harvard University
Press. Cambridge, MA. 1989. 352p. ISBN:0-674-20506-5,
ISBN13: 978-0-674-20506-2. Dewey:591.5/1/0321.
LCCN:88-021360.

Audience: **g,l,u,f.**　*Choice, 1989.*

McFarland, David J.　QL751
Animal Behaviour: Psychobiology, Ethology, and Evolution. Ed.
2. Paper Text. Prentice Hall PTR. Upper Saddle River, NJ.
1993. 585p. ISBN:0-582-06721-9, ISBN13: 978-0-582-06721-9.
Dewey:591.51. LCCN:92-016276.

Audience: **l,u.**

Moberg, G. & Mench, J. A.　QP82.2.S8B55 2000
(Editors)
The Biology of Animal Stress: Basic Principles and Implications
for Animal Welfare. Cloth Text. Oxford University Press, Inc.
New York, NY. 2000. 392p. A CAB International Publication
ISBN:0-85199-359-1, ISBN13: 978-0-85199-359-1.
Dewey:571.9/51. LCCN:99-058357.

Audience: **g,l.**

Oller, D. Kimbrough &　P90.E86 2004
Griebel, Ulrike (Editors)
The Evolution of Communication Systems: A Comparative
Approach. Trade Cloth. MIT Press. Cambridge, MA. 2004.
352p. The Vienna Series in Theoretical Biology
ISBN:0-262-15111-1, ISBN13: 978-0-262-15111-5.
Dewey:302.2/09. LCCN:2004-042788.

Audience: **l,u.**

Serpell, James (Editor)　SF433 .D66 1995
The Domestic Dog: Its Evolution, Behaviour and Interactions
with People. Priscilla Barrett (Illustrator). Trade Cloth.
Cambridge University Press. New York, NY. 1995. 280p.
ISBN:0-521-41529-2, ISBN13: 978-0-521-41529-3.
Dewey:636.7. LCCN:95-013800.

Audience: **g,l.**　*Choice, 1996.*

Slater, Peter J. B.　QL751 .S616 1999
Essentials of Animal Behaviour. Cloth Text. Cambridge
University Press. New York, NY. 1999. 244p. Studies in Biology
ISBN:0-521-62004-X, ISBN13: 978-0-521-62004-8.
Dewey:591.5. LCCN:98-034540.

Audience: **l,u.**　*Choice, 2000.*

Behavioral Biology > Behavior of Microorganisms

Clark, Virginia L. & Bavoil,　QP632.B3
Patrik M. (Volume Editors)
Bacterial Pathogenesis: Identification, Regulation and Function
of Virulence Factors. Trade Cloth. Elsevier Science &
Technology Books. Saint Louis, MO. 2002. 527p.
ISBN:0-12-182261-3, ISBN13: 978-0-12-182261-3.
Dewey:579.3165.

Audience: **u,f.**

Friedman, Herman (Editor),　RC88.9.T47M53 2006
et al.
Microorganisms and Bioterrorism. Burt Anderson & Mauro
Bendinelli (Editors). Trade Cloth. Springer. New York, NY.
2006. XX, 240p. Infectious Agents and Pathogenesis Ser.
ISBN:0-387-28156-8, ISBN13: 978-0-387-28156-8.
Dewey:363.325/3. LCCN:2005-930722.

Audience: **u,f.**　*Choice, 2006.*

Behavioral Biology > Plant Behavior

Devine, Robert S.　QH353.D48 1998
Alien Invasion: America's Battle with Non-Native Animals and
Plants. Trade Cloth. National Geographic Society. Washington,
DC. 1998. 277p. ISBN:0-7922-7372-9, ISBN13:
978-0-7922-7372-1. Dewey:577.18. LCCN:98-009730.

Audience: **l,u,f.**

Behavioral Biology > Animal behavior

Benyus, Janine M.　QL751 .B368 1992
What Makes the Lion Yawn?: A Zoogoer's Guide to Animal
Behavior. Trade Cloth. Addison-Wesley Longman, Inc. Boston,
MA. 1992. 400p. ISBN:0-201-57008-4, ISBN13:
978-0-201-57008-3. Dewey:591.51.

Audience: **g,l.**

Goldsmith, Timothy H.　GN365.9
The Biological Roots of Human Nature: Forging Links Between
Evolution and Behavior. Trade Paper. Oxford University Press,
Inc. New York, NY. 1994. 176p. ISBN:0-19-509393-3, ISBN13:
978-0-19-509393-3. Dewey:304.5.

Audience: **u,f.**　*Choice, 1992.*

Houck, Lynne D. &　QL751.6.F66 1996
Drickamer, Lee C. (Editors)
Foundations of Animal Behavior: Classic Papers with
Commentaries. Trade Cloth. University of Chicago Press.
Chicago, IL. 1996. 858p. ISBN:0-226-35456-3, ISBN13:
978-0-226-35456-9. Dewey:591.51. LCCN:96-033734.

Audience: **l,u.**

Formats: Web: ☐　Ebook: 🄴　CD/DVD-ROM: 💥　BCL3: 𝓑

Behavioral Biology > Social Behavior

Anitpa, Sebastian   **QH352.A54 2000**
Analysis and Control of Age-Dependent Population Dynamics.
Trade Cloth. Springer. New York, NY. 2000. 212p.
Mathematical Modelling Ser., Vol. 11:Theory and Applications
ISBN:0-7923-6639-5, ISBN13: 978-0-7923-6639-3.
Dewey:577.8/8/015118. LCCN:00-064699.

                                    Audience: **u,f.**

Eldredge, Niles & Grene,   **QH333 .E43**
  Marjorie
Interactions: The Biological Context of Social Systems. Trade
Cloth. Columbia University Press. New York, NY. 1992. 242p.
ISBN:0-231-07946-X, ISBN13: 978-0-231-07946-4.
Dewey:575/.01. LCCN:92-009432.

                                    Audience: **l,u,f.**

Filk, G. (Editor), et al.   **QP517.M67**
Host-Parasite Interactions. G. F. Wiegertjes & S. E. Wendelaar
Bonga (Editors). Paper over Boards. Taylor & Francis Group.
Abingdon, 2004. 256p. Experimental Biology Reviews Ser.
ISBN:1-85996-298-X, ISBN13: 978-1-85996-298-5.
Dewey:577.8/57. LCCN:2004-005857.

                                    Audience: **l,u,f.**

Goldsmith, Timothy H.   **GN365.9**
The Biological Roots of Human Nature: Forging Links Between
Evolution and Behavior. Trade Paper. Oxford University Press,
Inc. New York, NY. 1994. 176p. ISBN:0-19-509393-3, ISBN13:
978-0-19-509393-3. Dewey:304.5.

                        Audience: **u,f.** *Choice, 1992.*

Leach, Melissa (Editor),   **QH333.S365 2005**
  et al.
Science and Citizens: Globalization and the Challenge of
Engagement. Ian Scoones & Brian Wynne (Editors). Cloth over
Boards. Zed Books, Ltd. London, 2005. 256p. Claiming
Citizenship Ser. ISBN:1-84277-550-2, ISBN13:
978-1-84277-550-9. Dewey:306.4/5. LCCN:2004-057236.

                                    Audience: **u,f.**

Integrative Biology > Biogeography

Allofs, Theo   **QH117**
Pantanal: South America's Wetland Jewel. Russell A.
Mittermeier, Christina G. Mittermeier, Monica Barcellos Harris,
Reinaldo Lourival, Gustavo A. B. da Fonseca & Jose Maria
Cardos da Silva (Text by). Trade Cloth. Firefly Books, Ltd.
Tonawanda, NY. 2005. 176p. ISBN:1-55407-090-2, ISBN13:
978-1-55407-090-9. Dewey:508.81/71. LCCN:2006-445101.

                                  Audience: **l,u,f.**

Beerling, D. J. &   **QH344 .B43 2001**
  Woodward, F. I.
Vegetation and the Terrestrial Carbon Cycle: The First 400
Million Years. Trade Cloth. Cambridge University Press. New
York, NY. 2001. 416p. ISBN:0-521-80196-6, ISBN13:
978-0-521-80196-6. Dewey:577/.144/015118.
LCCN:2001-025553.

                        Audience: **u,f.** *Choice, 2002.*

Bradshaw, G. A.   **QH101.H69 2002**
  (Editor), et al.
How Landscapes Change: Human Disturbance and Ecosystem
Fragmentation in the Americas. P. A. Marquet & Kathryn L.
Ronnenberg (Editors). Trade Cloth. Springer. New York, NY.
2003. XXII, 361p. ISBN:3-540-43697-9, ISBN13:
978-3-540-43697-3. Dewey:304.2/8/097. LCCN:2002-030229.

                                  Audience: **u,f.**

Bradstock, Ross A. (Editor),   **QH197.F563 2002**
  et al.
Flammable Australia: The Fire Regimes and Biodiversity of a
Continent. Jann E. Williams & Malcolm A. Gill (Editors). Trade
Cloth. Cambridge University Press. New York, NY. 2001. 472p.
ISBN:0-521-80591-0, ISBN13: 978-0-521-80591-9.
Dewey:577.2. LCCN:2001-025479.

                      Audience: **u,f.** *Choice, 2002.*

Briggs, John C.   **QH84.B745 1995**
Global Biogeography. Trade Cloth. Elsevier Science &
Technology Books. Saint Louis, MO. 1995. 472p. Developments
in Palaeontology and Stratigraphy Ser. ISBN:0-444-88297-9,
ISBN13: 978-0-444-88297-4. Dewey:578/.09. LCCN:95-030597.

                                  Audience: **l,u,f.**

Bunce, R. G. & Howard, D.   **QH137.S63 1990**
  C. (Editors)
Species Dispersal in Agricultural Habitats. Cloth Text. St.
Martin's Press. Gordonville, VA. 1992. 296p.
ISBN:1-85293-076-4, ISBN13: 978-1-85293-076-9.
Dewey:574.5/264. LCCN:90-037137.

                                    Audience: **u,f.**

Butcher, Samuel S. (Editor),   **QH344.G593 1992**
  et al.
Global Biogeochemical Cycles. Gordon H. Orians, Robert J.
Charlson & Gordon V. Wolfe (Editors). Trade Cloth. Elsevier
Science & Technology Books. Saint Louis, MO. 1992. 379p.
International Geophysics Ser., Vol. 50 ISBN:0-12-147685-5,
ISBN13: 978-0-12-147685-4. Dewey:574.5/222.
LCCN:93-159050.

                      Audience: **u,f.** *Choice, 1993.*

Carey, James R.   **QH352.C36 1993**
Applied Demography for Biologists: With Special Emphasis on
Insects. Trade Paper. Oxford University Press, Inc. New York,
NY. 1993. 222p. ISBN:0-19-506687-1, ISBN13:
978-0-19-506687-6. Dewey:574.5/248/072. LCCN:91-045843.

                      Audience: **u,f.** *Choice, 1993.*

Case, Ted J., et al.   **QH107.I85 2002**
A New Island Biogeography of the Sea of Cortes. Ed. 2. Martin
L. Cody & Exequiel Ezcurra (Authors), Ted J. Case, Martin L.
Cody & Exequiel Ezcurra (Editors). Trade Cloth. Oxford
University Press, Inc. New York, NY. 2002. 688p.
ISBN:0-19-513346-3, ISBN13: 978-0-19-513346-2.
Dewey:577.5/2/091641. LCCN:2001-050007.

                                  Audience: **u,f.**

Chapin, F. Stuart III &   **QH84.1.A7 1995**
  Orner, Christian K. (Editors)
Arctic and Alpine Biodiversity: Patterns, Causes, and Ecosystem
Consequences. Trade Cloth. Springer. New York, NY. 1995.
322p. Ecological Studies, Vol. 113 ISBN:3-540-57948-6,
ISBN13: 978-3-540-57948-9. Dewey:574.5/2621.
LCCN:94-040221.

                                  Audience: **u,f.**

Cox, C. Barry & Moore, Peter D.   QH84.C65 2005
Biogeography: An Ecological and Evolutionary Approach. Ed. 7.
Trade Paper. Blackwell Publishing, Inc. Malden, MA. 2005.
440p. ISBN:1-4051-1898-9, ISBN13: 978-1-4051-1898-9.
Dewey:578/.09. LCCN:2004-009770.
Audience: **u,f.**

Craw, Robin C., et al.   QH84.C678 1999
Panbiogeography: Tracking the History of Life. John R. Grehan
& Michael J. Heads (Authors). Trade Cloth. Oxford University
Press, Inc. New York, NY. 1999. 238p. Oxford Biogeography
Ser., No. 11 ISBN:0-19-507441-6, ISBN13: 978-0-19-507441-3.
Dewey:576.8/5. LCCN:97-041638.
Audience: **l,u,f.** *Choice, 2000.*

Crisci, Jorge Victor, et al.   QH84.C6798 2003
Historical Biogeography: An Introduction. Liliana Katinas &
Paula Posadas (Authors). Trade Cloth. Harvard University Press.
Cambridge, MA. 2003. 264p. ISBN:0-674-01059-0, ISBN13:
978-0-674-01059-8. Dewey:578/.09. LCCN:2002-192236.
Audience: **l,u,f.** *Choice, 2004.*

Flannery, Tim   QH102
The Eternal Frontier: An Ecological History of North America
and Its Peoples. Trade Paper. Grove/Atlantic, Inc. New York,
NY. 2002. 432p. ISBN:0-8021-3888-8, ISBN13:
978-0-8021-3888-0. Dewey:508.7.
Audience: **g,l,f.** *Choice, 2001.*

Foreman, Dave   QH76.F67 1992
The Big Outside: A Descriptive Inventory of the Big Wilderness
Areas of the United States. Trade Paper. Crown Publishing
Group. New York, NY. 1992. ISBN:0-517-58737-8, ISBN13:
978-0-517-58737-9. Dewey:333.78/2/0973.
Audience: **l,u,f.**

Gaston, Kevin J.   QH84
The Structure and Dynamics of Geographic Ranges. Trade
Cloth. Oxford University Press, Inc. New York, NY. 2003. 280p.
Oxford Series in Ecology and Evolution ISBN:0-19-852640-7,
ISBN13: 978-0-19-852640-7. Dewey:577. LCCN:2003-273626.
Audience: **l,u,f.**

Greenaway, Theresa & Dorling Kindersley Publishing Staff   QH86.G73 2004
Jungle. Geoff Dann (Photographer). Library Binding. Dorling
Kindersley Publishing, Inc. New York, NY. 2004. 72p.
Eyewitness Books ISBN:0-7566-0693-4, ISBN13:
978-0-7566-0693-0. Dewey:578.734. LCCN:2004-558978.
Audience: **l,u,f.**

Grove, A. T. & Rackham, Oliver   QH150
The Nature of Mediterranean Europe: An Ecological History.
Trade Paper. Yale University Press. Cumberland, RI. 2003.
384p. ISBN:0-300-10055-8, ISBN13: 978-0-300-10055-6.
Dewey:577.4/6/094. LCCN:2003-101909.
Audience: **l,u,f.** *Choice, 2001.*

Groves, R. H. & Di Castri, F. (Editors)   QH353 .B54 1991
Biogeography of Mediterranean Invasions. Trade Cloth.
Cambridge University Press. New York, NY. 1991. 501p.
ISBN:0-521-36040-4, ISBN13: 978-0-521-36040-1.
Dewey:574.909/822. LCCN:90-045682.
Audience: **u,f.** *Choice, 1992.*

Hammond, D. (Editor)   QH125
Tropical Rainforests of the Guianan Shield. Trade Cloth. CAB
International. Wallingford, 2005. 544p. CABI Publishing Ser.
ISBN:0-85199-536-5, ISBN13: 978-0-85199-536-6.
Dewey:578.734/098. LCCN:2004-021133.
Audience: **u,f.**

Hengeveld, R.   QH84
Dynamic Biogeography. H. John B. Birks & J. A. Wiens
(Contribution by). Trade Paper. Cambridge University Press.
New York, NY. 1992. 263p. Cambridge Studies in Ecology
ISBN:0-521-43756-3, ISBN13: 978-0-521-43756-1.
Dewey:574.9.
Audience: **u,f.**

Huggett, Richard J.   QH84.H84 2004
Fundamentals of Biogeography. Ed. 2. Paper over Boards.
Routledge. New York, NY. 2005. 456p. Routledge Fundamentals
of Physical Geography Ser. ISBN:0-415-32346-0, ISBN13:
978-0-415-32346-8. Dewey:578/.09. LCCN:2003-027028.
Audience: **l,u.**

Jacobson, Michael, et al.   QH344 .E37 2000
Earth System Science: From Biogeochemical Cycles to Global
Changes. Ed. 2. Robert J. Charlson, Gordon H. Orians &
Henning Rodhe (Authors). Paper Text. Elsevier Science &
Technology Books. Saint Louis, MO. 2000. 527p. International
Geophysics Ser., Vol. 73 ISBN:0-12-379370-X, ISBN13:
978-0-12-379370-6. Dewey:550.
Audience: **u.**

Lomolino, Mark V. & Heaney, Lawrence R.   QH84.F76 2004
Frontiers of Biogeography: New Directions in the Geography of
Nature. Trade Cloth. Sinauer Associates, Inc. Sunderland, MA.
2004. 410p. ISBN:0-87893-479-0, ISBN13: 978-0-87893-479-9.
Dewey:578/.09. LCCN:2004-021324.
Audience: **u,f.** *Choice, 2005.*

Lomolino, Mark V. (Editor), et al.   QH84.F68 2004
Foundations of Biogeography: Classic Papers with
Commentaries. Dov F. Sax & James H. Brown (Editors). Trade
Cloth. University of Chicago Press. Chicago, IL. 2004. 1328p.
ISBN:0-226-49236-2, ISBN13: 978-0-226-49236-0.
Dewey:578/.09. LCCN:2003-018272.
Audience: **u,f.**

MacArthur, Robert H. & Wilson, Edward O.   QH85.M3 2001
The Theory of Island Biogeography. Ed. 2. Trade Paper.
Princeton University Press. Princeton, NJ. 2001. 220p. Princeton
Landmarks in Biology Ser. ISBN:0-691-08836-5, ISBN13:
978-0-691-08836-5. Dewey:578.75/2. LCCN:00-051495.
Audience: **u,f.**

MacDonald, Glen M.   QH84
Biogeography: Introduction to Space, Time, and Life. Trade
Cloth. John Wiley & Sons, Inc. Hoboken, NJ. 2002. 512p.
ISBN:0-471-24193-8, ISBN13: 978-0-471-24193-5.
Dewey:578/.09.
Audience: **l,u,f.**

Mielke, Howard   QH84.M54 1989
Patterns of Life: Biogeography of a Changing World. Trade
Cloth. Routledge. New York, NY. 1989. 370p.

ISBN:0-04-574032-1, ISBN13: 978-0-04-574032-1.
Dewey:574.9. LCCN:87-034694.

Audience: **l,u,f.**

Millington, Andrew C.   **QH84.G47 2001**
   (Editor), et al.
GIS and Remote Sensing Applications in Biogeography and
Ecology. Stephen J. Walsh & Patrick E. Osborne (Editors).
Trade Cloth. Springer. New York, NY. 2001. 344p. The Kluwer
International Series in Engineering and Computer Science, Vol.
626 ISBN:0-7923-7454-1, ISBN13: 978-0-7923-7454-1.
Dewey:578/.09. LCCN:2001-038306.

Audience: **u,f.**

Myers, Alan A. & Giller,   **QH84.A53 1988**
   Paul S.
Analytical Biogeography: An Integrated Approach to the Study
of Animal and Plant Distributions. Cloth Text. Chapman & Hall.
New York, NY. 1988. 584p. ISBN:0-412-28260-7, ISBN13:
978-0-412-28260-7. Dewey:574.9. LCCN:88-000307.

Audience: **u,f.** *Choice, 1989.*

Nagy, L. (Editor), et al.   **QH135.A47 2003**
Alpine Biodiversity in Europe. Georg Grabherr, Christian
Körner & D. B. A. Thompson (Editors). Trade Cloth. Springer.
New York, NY. 2003. XXXI, 477p. Ecological Studies, Vol. 167
ISBN:3-540-00108-5, ISBN13: 978-3-540-00108-9.
Dewey:577.5/3/094. LCCN:2003-042503.

Audience: **u,f.**

Petrovskii, Sergei V. & Li,   **QH353**
   Bai-Lian
Exactly Solvable Models of Biological Invasion. Chapman &
Hall/CRC, Boca Raton. 2006. ISBN:1-58488-521-1, ISBN13:
978-1-58488-521-4.

Audience: **l,u.**

Primack, Richard & Corlett,   **QH86.P75 2005**
   Richard
Tropical Rain Forests: An Ecological and Biogeographical
Comparison. Trade Cloth. Blackwell Publishing, Inc. Malden,
MA. 2002. 336p. ISBN:0-632-04513-2, ISBN13:
978-0-632-04513-6. Dewey:577.34. LCCN:2004-009785.

Audience: **l,u,f.** *Choice, 2005.*

Ricketts, Taylor H., et al.   **QH77.N56T47 1999**
Terrestrial Ecoregions of North America: A Conservation
Assessment. Eric Dinerstein, David M. Olson, Colby J. Loucks,
William Eichbaum, Dominick Dellassala, Kevin Kavanaugh,
Prashant Hedao, Patrick Hurley, Robin Abell, Karen L. Carney
& Steven Walters (Authors). Trade Paper. Island Press.
Washington, DC. 1999. 508p. ISBN:1-55963-722-6, ISBN13:
978-1-55963-722-0. Dewey:333.95/16/097. LCCN:99-018912.

Audience: **g,l,u,f.** *Choice, 2000.*

Riddle, Brett R., et al.   **QH84.B76 2005**
Biogeography. Ed. 3. James H. Brown & Mark V. Lomolino
(Authors). Trade Cloth. Sinauer Associates, Inc. Sunderland,
MA. 2005. 560p. ISBN:0-87893-062-0, ISBN13:
978-0-87893-062-3. Dewey:578/.09. LCCN:2005-014443.

Audience: **l,u,f.**

Sax, Dov F. (Editor), et al.   **QH353.S29 2005**
Species Invasions: Insights into Ecology, Evolution, and
Biogeography. John J. Stachowicz & Steven D. Gaines

(Editors). Trade Paper. Sinauer Associates, Inc. Sunderland, MA.
2005. 380p. ISBN:0-87893-811-7, ISBN13: 978-0-87893-811-7.
Dewey:577/.18. LCCN:2005-013019.

Audience: **u,f.**

Spellerberg, Ian F. &   **QH84 .S7 1999**
   Sawyer, John W. D.
An Introduction to Applied Biogeography. Tony Whitten
(Foreword by). Cloth Text. Cambridge University Press. New
York, NY. 1999. 257p. ISBN:0-521-45102-7, ISBN13:
978-0-521-45102-4. Dewey:578.09. LCCN:98-021967.

Audience: **l,u,f.** *Choice, 1999.*

Woods, Charles A. and   **QH109.A1**
   Sergile, Florence E.
Biogeography of the West Indies: Patterns and Perspectives.
CRC Press. 2001. ISBN:0-8493-2001-1, ISBN13:
978-0-8493-2001-9.

Audience: **u,f.**

Integrative Biology > General Ecology

☐ Google Directory: Biology, Ecology.
http://google.com/Top/Science/Biology/Ecology/
Google.

Audience: **g,l.**

☐ Google Directory: Biology, Flora and Fauna.
http://google.com/Top/Science/Biology/Flora_and_Fauna/
Google.

Audience: **g,l.**

Bass, Rick   **QH81**
Wild to the Heart. Trade Paper. W. W. Norton & Company, Inc.
New York, NY. 1997. 176p. ISBN:0-393-31487-1, ISBN13:
978-0-393-31487-8. Dewey:508.

Audience: **l,u,f.**

Brach, Anthony R.
☐ Ecology WWW page.
http://www.people.fas.harvard.edu/~brach/Ecology-WWW.html
Audience: **g,l.**

Cook, Laurence Martin   **QH75**
Genetic and Ecological Diversity: The Sport of Nature.
Chapman & Hall, London ; New York. 1991.
ISBN:0-412-35620-1, ISBN13: 978-0-412-35620-9.

Audience: **l,u,f.**

Curtin, Philip D., et al.   **GF504.C54D47 2001**
Discovering the Chesapeake: The History of an Ecosystem.
Grace Somers Brush & George Wescott Fisher (Authors). Trade
Paper. Johns Hopkins University Press. Baltimore, MD. 2001.
416p. ISBN:0-8018-6468-2, ISBN13: 978-0-8018-6468-1.
LCCN:00-042405.

Audience: **l,u.**

Gotelli, Nicholas J.   **QH352.G67 1998**
A Primer of Ecology. Ed. 2. Trade Paper. Sinauer Associates,
Inc. Sunderland, MA. 1998. ISBN:0-87893-274-7, ISBN13:
978-0-87893-274-0. Dewey:577.8/8/0151. LCCN:98-003508.

Audience: **l,u,f.** *Choice, 1995.*

Huffaker, Carl B. &   QL496.4.E36 1999
  Gutierrez, Andrew Paul (Editors)
Ecological Entomology. Ed. 2. Trade Cloth. John Wiley & Sons,
Inc. Hoboken, NJ. 1998. 776p. ISBN:0-471-24483-X, ISBN13:
978-0-471-24483-7. Dewey:595.7/17. LCCN:98-018923.

                                                      Audience: **u.**

Humphries, Christopher J.   QH83.H86 1999
  & Parenti, Lynne R.
Cladistic Biogeography: Interpreting Patterns of Plant and
Animal Distributions. Ed. 2. Trade Cloth. Oxford University
Press, Inc. New York, NY. 1999. 199p. Oxford Biogeography
Ser., No. 12 ISBN:0-19-854818-4, ISBN13: 978-0-19-854818-8.
Dewey:578/.01/2. LCCN:98-047313.

                                                    Audience: **u,f.**

John H. Heinz III Center   QH104.S73 2002
  for Science, Economics and the Environment
The State of the Nation's Ecosystems: Measuring the Lands,
Waters, and Living Resources of the United States. Trade Paper.
Cambridge University Press. New York, NY. 2002. 288p.
ISBN:0-521-52572-1, ISBN13: 978-0-521-52572-5.
Dewey:333.7/2. LCCN:2002-073890.

                         Audience: **l,u,f.** *Choice, 2003.*

Knapp, Alan K. (Editor), et   QH105.K3G73 1998
al.
Grassland Dynamics: Long-Term Ecological Research in
Tallgrass Prairie. John M. Briggs, David C. Hartnett & Scott L.
Collins (Editors). Trade Cloth. Oxford University Press, Inc.
New York, NY. 1998. 380p. The Long-Term Ecological
Research Network Ser. ISBN:0-19-511486-8, ISBN13:
978-0-19-511486-7. Dewey:577.4/4/09/7813. LCCN:97-008334.

                                Audience: **u,f.** *Choice, 1999.*

Kot, Mark   QH352 .K66 2001
Elements of Mathematical Ecology. Cloth Text. Cambridge
University Press. New York, NY. 2001. 464p.
ISBN:0-521-80213-X, ISBN13: 978-0-521-80213-0.
Dewey:577/.01/51. LCCN:00-065165.

                                Audience: **u,f.** *Choice, 2002.*

Krebs, Charles J.   QH541.15.S72K74 1998
Ecological Methodology. Ed. 2. Cloth Text.
Benjamin-Cummings Publishing Company. San Francisco, CA.
1998. 624p. ISBN:0-321-02173-8, ISBN13: 978-0-321-02173-1.
Dewey:577/.07/27. LCCN:98-008681.

                                              Audience: **u,f.**

Lawton, John H. & May,   QH78.E95 1995
  Robert M. (Editors)
Extinction Rates. Trade Paper. Oxford University Press, Inc.
New York, NY. 1995. 246p. ISBN:0-19-854829-X, ISBN13:
978-0-19-854829-4. Dewey:575/.7. LCCN:95-169009.

                                Audience: **u,f.** *Choice, 1995.*

McFarland, David J.   QL751
Animal Behaviour: Psychobiology, Ethology, and Evolution. Ed.
2. Paper Text. Prentice Hall PTR. Upper Saddle River, NJ.
1993. 585p. ISBN:0-582-06721-9, ISBN13: 978-0-582-06721-9.
Dewey:591.51. LCCN:92-016276.

                                              Audience: **l,u.**

McLaughlin, Peter   QH331 .M377 2001
What Functions Explain: Functional Explanation and
Self-Reproducing Systems. Michael Ruse (Contribution by).
Trade Cloth. Cambridge University Press. New York, NY. 2000.

272p. Cambridge Studies in Philosophy and Biology
ISBN:0-521-78233-3, ISBN13: 978-0-521-78233-3.
Dewey:570.1. LCCN:00-031179.

                                        Audience: **u,f.**

Mitchell, Sandra D.   QH331.M49 2003
Biological Complexity and Integrative Pluralism. Trade Cloth.
Cambridge University Press. New York, NY. 2003. 260p.
Cambridge Studies in Philosophy and Biology
ISBN:0-521-81753-6, ISBN13: 978-0-521-81753-0. Dewey:570.
LCCN:2002-038843.

                                        Audience: **u,f.**

Mueller, Laurence D.   QH352.M94 2000
Stability in Model Populations. Cloth Text. Princeton University
Press. Princeton, NJ. 2000. 336p. Monographs in Population
Biology, Vol. 31 ISBN:0-691-00732-2, ISBN13:
978-0-691-00732-8. Dewey:577.8/8. LCCN:00-038493.

                                        Audience: **u,f.**

Neal, Dick   QH352.N43 2003
Introduction to Population Biology. Cloth Text. Cambridge
University Press. New York, NY. 2003. 408p.
ISBN:0-521-82537-7, ISBN13: 978-0-521-82537-5.
Dewey:577.8/8. LCCN:2003-046029.

                                        Audience: **l,u.**

Oyama, Susan   QH507.O93 2000
The Ontogeny of Information: Developmental Systems and
Evolution. Ed. 2. Cloth Text. Duke University Press. Durham,
NC. 2000. 280p. Science and Cultural Theory Ser.
ISBN:0-8223-2431-8, ISBN13: 978-0-8223-2431-7.
Dewey:576.8. LCCN:99-034735.

                                        Audience: **u,f.**

Pankhurst, Richard J.   QH83
Practical Taxonomic Computing. Trade Cloth. Cambridge
University Press. New York, NY. 1991. 214p.
ISBN:0-521-41760-0, ISBN13: 978-0-521-41760-0.
Dewey:574.012.

                                        Audience: **l,u.**

Prasad, M. N. V. (Editor)   QH545.T7
Trace Elements in the Environment: Biogeochemistry,
Biotechnology, and Bioremediation. (Majeti Narasimha Vara)
(Editor); Sajwan, Kenneth S. (Editor); Naidu, R. (Editor).
CRC/Taylor and Francis, Boca Raton. 2006.
ISBN:1-56670-685-8, ISBN13: 978-1-56670-685-8.

                                        Audience: **l,u.**

Quicke, Donald L. J.   QH83
Principles and Techniques of Contemporary Taxonomy. Blackie
Academic & Professional, London ; New York. 1993. Tertiary
level biology ISBN:0-7514-0019-X, ISBN13:
978-0-7514-0019-9.

                                        Audience: **l,u.**

Renshaw, Eric   QH352.R46 1993
Modelling Biological Populations in Space and Time. C.
Cannings, F. C. Hoppensteadt & L. A. Segel (Contribution by).
Trade Paper. Cambridge University Press. New York, NY. 1993.
421p. Cambridge Studies in Mathematical Biology, No. 11
ISBN:0-521-44855-7, ISBN13: 978-0-521-44855-0.
Dewey:577.8/8/0151.

                                        Audience: **u,f.**

Ryan, Michael J.   QL668.E2A58 2001
Anuran Communication. Trade Cloth. Smithsonian Institution
Press. Washington, DC. 2001. ix, 252p. ISBN:1-56098-973-4,
ISBN13: 978-1-56098-973-8. Dewey:597.8/159.
LCCN:00-047006.

Audience: **u.** *Choice, 2001.*

Scheiner, Samuel M. &   QH541.15.S72D47 2001
  Gurevitch, Jessica
Design and Analysis of Ecological Experiments. Ed. 2. Trade
Paper. Oxford University Press, Inc. New York, NY. 2001. 432p.
ISBN:0-19-513188-6, ISBN13: 978-0-19-513188-8.
Dewey:577/.07/27. LCCN:00-035647.

Audience: **u,f.**

Schuh, Randall T.   QH83.S345 2000
Biological Systematics: Principles and Applications. Trade
Cloth. Cornell University Press. Ithaca, NY. 2000. 256p.
ISBN:0-8014-3675-3, ISBN13: 978-0-8014-3675-8.
Dewey:570/.1/2. LCCN:99-042377.

Audience: **l,u,f.**

Scott-Ram, N. R.   QH83 .S36 1990
Transformed Cladistics, Taxonomy and Evolution. Trade Cloth.
Cambridge University Press. New York, NY. 1990. 250p.
ISBN:0-521-34086-1, ISBN13: 978-0-521-34086-1.
Dewey:574/.012. LCCN:89-009754.

Audience: **u,f.**

Seitz, A. & Loeschcke, V.   QH76.S64 1991
  (Editors)
Species Conservation: A Population-Biological Approach. Trade
Cloth. Birkhauser Boston. Cambridge, MA. 1991. vii, 281p.
Advances in Life Sciences Ser. ISBN:0-8176-2493-7, ISBN13:
978-0-8176-2493-4. Dewey:574.5/24. LCCN:91-019264.

Audience: **u,f.**

Smith, Robert H., et al.   QH352.C52 2000
Chaos in Real Data: Analysis of Non-Linear Dynamics in Short
Ecological Space. Ian P. Woiwod & David R. Morse (Authors),
Joe N. Perry (Editor). Trade Cloth. Springer Dordrecht.
Dordrecht, 2000. 236p. Population and Community Biology
Ser., Vol. 27 ISBN:0-412-79690-2, ISBN13: 978-0-412-79690-6.
Dewey:577.8/8/05118. LCCN:00-037060.

Audience: **u,f.**

Stevens, Peter F.   QH83.S76 1994
The Development of Biological Systematics: Antoine-Laurent de
Jussieu, Nature, and the Natural System. Trade Cloth. Columbia
University Press. New York, NY. 1994. 616p.
ISBN:0-231-06440-3, ISBN13: 978-0-231-06440-8.
Dewey:574/.012. LCCN:94-027231.

Audience: **u,f.** *Choice, 1995.*

Sutherland, William J.   QH541.15.S95 E26 19
  (Editor)
Ecological Census Techniques: A Handbook. Trade Paper.
Cambridge University Press. New York, NY. 1996. 352p.
ISBN:0-521-47815-4, ISBN13: 978-0-521-47815-1.
Dewey:574.5/028. LCCN:95-031985.

Audience: **u,f.**

Swishchuk, Anatoly V. &   QH323.5
  Jianhong Wu,
Evolution of Biological Systems in Random Media: Limit
Theorems. Trade Cloth. Kluwer Law International. Alphen a/d

Rijn, 2003. 216p. Mathematical Modelling Ser.
ISBN:1-4020-1554-2, ISBN13: 978-1-4020-1554-0.
Dewey:570/.1/1. LCCN:2003-061857.

Audience: **u,f.**

Vandermeer, John H. &   QH352.V36 2003
  Goldberg, Deborah Esther
Population Ecology: First Principles. Trade Cloth. Princeton
University Press. Princeton, NJ. 2003. 296p.
ISBN:0-691-11440-4, ISBN13: 978-0-691-11440-8.
Dewey:577.8/8. LCCN:2002-035478.

Audience: **u,f.** *Choice, 2004.*

Williams, David M. &   QH83
  Forey, Peter (Editors)
Milestones in Systematics. Paper over Boards. Taylor & Francis
Group. Philadelphia, PA. 2004. 312p. The Systematics
Association Special Volume Ser., No. 67 ISBN:0-415-28032-X,
ISBN13: 978-0-415-28032-7. Dewey:578/.01/2.
LCCN:2003-065587.

Audience: **u,f.** *Choice, 2005.*

Zhao, Xiao-Qiang   QH352.Z53 2003
Dynamical Systems in Population Biology. Trade Cloth.
Springer. New York, NY. 2003. XIII, 276p. CMS Books in
Mathematics, Vol. 16 ISBN:0-387-00308-8, ISBN13:
978-0-387-00308-5. Dewey:577.8/8. LCCN:2002-044507.

Audience: **u,f.**

Integrative Biology > General Ecology > Marine Habitats

Castro, Peter & Huber,   QH91.C37 2007
  Michael E.
Marine Biology. Ed. 6. Trade Cloth. McGraw-Hill Companies,
The. New York, NY. 2005. xix, 460p. ISBN:0-07-283064-6,
ISBN13: 978-0-07-283064-4. Dewey:578.77.
LCCN:2005-027560.

Audience: **l,u,f.**

Gray, John S. (Editor), et al.   QH344.N37 1997
Biochemical Cycling and Sediment Ecology. William G.
Ambrose & Anna Szaniawska (Editors). Trade Cloth. Springer
London, Ltd. Guildford, 1999. 252p. NATO Advanced Science
Institutes Ser. ISBN:0-7923-5770-1, ISBN13:
978-0-7923-5770-4. Dewey:577.7. LCCN:99-029598.

Audience: **u,f.**

Morton, Brian (Editor)   QH181.I58 1998
Marine Flora and Fauna of Hong Kong and Southern China,
Vol. 5. Trade Paper. Hong Kong University Press. Hong Kong,
2001. 696p. ISBN:962-209-525-9, ISBN13: 978-962-209-525-0.
Dewey:578.77/095125.

Audience: **u,f.**

Nybakken, James W.   QH91.N9 2001
Marine Biology: An Ecological Approach. Ed. 5. Trade Cloth.
Benjamin-Cummings Publishing Company. San Francisco, CA.
2000. 516p. ISBN:0-321-03076-1, ISBN13: 978-0-321-03076-4.
Dewey:577.7. LCCN:00-058603.

Audience: **l,u.**

Riseng, Karen & Jensen, Montambault — QH130 B55 2003

A Biological Assessment of the Aquatic Ecosystems of the Caura River Basin, Bolivar State, Venezuela: RAP Bulletin of Biological Assessment 28. Barry Chernoff (Editor), Antonio Machado-Allison (Editor, Translator), Ana Liz Flores (Translator), Mark Denil (Illustrator), Montambault Jensen (Photographer), Kim Meek (Designed by). Trade Paper. Conservation International. Washington, DC. 2003. 284p. Conservation International Rapid Assessment Program Ser. ISBN:1-881173-69-0, ISBN13: 978-1-881173-69-4. Dewey:577. LCCN:2002-116698.

Audience: **u,f.**

Somervill, Barbara A. — QH91.S67 2004

Oceans, Seas, and Reefs. Trade Cloth. Tradition Publishing Company. Maple Plain, MN. 2004. ISBN:1-59187-045-3, ISBN13: 978-1-59187-045-6. Dewey:577.7. LCCN:2004-009385.

Audience: **g.**

Sumich, James L. — QH91.S95 2004

Introduction to the Biology of Marine Life. Ed. 8. Trade Paper. Jones & Bartlett Publishers, Inc. Sudbury, MA. 2004. 449p. ISBN:0-7637-3313-X, ISBN13: 978-0-7637-3313-1. Dewey:578.77. LCCN:2004-043812.

Audience: **l,u.**

Tuljapurkar, Shripad & Caswell, Hal — QH352.S86 1996

Structured-Population Models in Marine, Terrestrial, and Freshwater Systems. Trade Cloth. Chapman & Hall. New York, NY. 1996. 496p. ISBN:0-412-07261-0, ISBN13: 978-0-412-07261-1. Dewey:574.5/248/0151. LCCN:96-002940.

Audience: **u,f.**

Wetzel, Robert G. — QH96.W47 2001

Limnology: Lake and River Ecosystems. Ed. 3. Cloth Text. Elsevier Science & Technology Books. Saint Louis, MO. 2001. 1006p. ISBN:0-12-744760-1, ISBN13: 978-0-12-744760-5. Dewey:577.6. LCCN:00-110178.

Audience: **u,f.**

Willink, Philip W. (Editor), et al. — QH117.B485 2000

A Biological Assessment of the Aquatic Ecosystems of the Pantanal, Mato Grosso do Sul, Brasil. Barry Chernoff, Leeanne E. Alonso, Jensen R. Montambault & Reinaldo Lourival (Editors). Trade Paper. Conservation International. Washington, DC. 2000. 306p. Conservation International Rapid Assessment Program Ser. ISBN:1-881173-35-6, ISBN13: 978-1-881173-35-9. Dewey:577.63098171. LCCN:00-108756.

Audience: **u,f.**

Wohl, Ellen E. — QH104.W637 2004

Disconnected Rivers: Linking Rivers to Landscapes. Cloth over Boards. Yale University Press. Cumberland, RI. 2004. 320p. ISBN:0-300-10332-8, ISBN13: 978-0-300-10332-8. Dewey:577.6/4/0973. LCCN:2004-011610.

Audience: **g,l,u,f.** *Choice, 2005.*

Integrative Biology > General Ecology > Marine Habitats > Ocean Habitats

Allen, Gerald R. — QH95.8

Marine Life of the Pacific and Indian Oceans. Trade Paper. Tuttle Publishing. Boston, MA. 1997. 96p. Periplus Nature Ser.

ISBN:962-593-016-7, ISBN13: 978-962-593-016-9. Dewey:574.526367.

Audience: **l,u,f.**

American Society of Ichthyologists and Herpetologists; Food and Agriculture Organization; European Commission — QH92

The Living Marine Resources of the Western Central Atlantic: Vol. 2, Pt. 1, Bony fishes., Acipenseridae to Grammatidae. Carpenter, Kent E. (Editor). Food and Agriculture Organization of the United Nations, Rome. 2002. FAO species identification guide for fishery purposes; Special publication / American Society of Ichthyologists and Herpetologists; no. 5; Variation: Special publication (American Society of Ichthyologists and Herpetologists); no. 5 ISBN:92-5-104826-6, ISBN13: 978-92-5-104826-9.

Audience: **u,f.**

Bowen, James & Bowen, Margarita — QH197.B69 2002

The Great Barrier Reef: History, Science, Heritage. Cloth Text. Cambridge University Press. New York, NY. 2002. 474p. ISBN:0-521-82430-3, ISBN13: 978-0-521-82430-9. Dewey:578.7789476. LCCN:2002-073922.

Audience: **l,u,f.** *Choice, 2003.*

Byatt, Andrew et. al — QH91

The Blue Planet: A Natural History of the Oceans. Fothergill, Alastair; Holmes, Martha. BBC Worldwide, London. 2001. ISBN:0-563-38498-0, ISBN13: 978-0-563-38498-4.

Audience: **l,u,f.**

Case, Ted J., et al. — QH107.I85 2002

A New Island Biogeography of the Sea of Cortes. Ed. 2. Martin L. Cody & Exequiel Ezcurra (Authors), Ted J. Case, Martin L. Cody & Exequiel Ezcurra (Editors). Trade Cloth. Oxford University Press, Inc. New York, NY. 2002. 688p. ISBN:0-19-513346-3, ISBN13: 978-0-19-513346-2. Dewey:577.5/2/091641. LCCN:2001-050007.

Audience: **u,f.**

Fasham, M. J. R. (Editor) — QH344.O25 2003

Ocean Biogeochemistry: A Synthesis of the Joint Global Ocean Flux Study (JGOFS). Joint Global Ocean Flux Study Staff (Contribution by). Trade Cloth. Springer. New York, NY. 2003. XVIII, 297p. Global Change, :The IGBP Ser. ISBN:3-540-42398-2, ISBN13: 978-3-540-42398-0. Dewey:551.46/01. LCCN:2002-044503.

Audience: **u,f.**

Food and Agriculture Organization Staff, et al. — GC481

The Living Marine Resources of the Western Central Atlantic: Introduction, Molluscs, Crustaceans, Hagfishes, Sharks, Batoid Fishes and Chimaeras, Vol. 1. American Society of Ichthyologists and Herpetologists Staff & European Communities Commission (Authors), Kent E. Carpenter (Editor). Trade Paper. Food and Agriculture Organization of the United Nations. Rome, 2002. 614p. Fao Species Identification Guide for Fishery Purposes Ser. ISBN:92-5-104825-8, ISBN13: 978-92-5-104825-2. Dewey:578.773.

Audience: **l,u,f.**

Gibson, Ray, et al. — QH137.G53 2001

Photographic Guide to Sea and Shore Life of Britain and North-West Europe. Ben Hextall & Alex Rogers (Authors). Cloth Text. Oxford University Press, Inc. New York, NY. 2001.

Formats: Web: ⬜ Ebook: 🄴 CD/DVD-ROM: 🐟 BCL3: *B*

456p. ISBN:0-19-850041-6, ISBN13: 978-0-19-850041-4. Dewey:578.769/9/0941. LCCN:2001-021772.

Audience: **l,u,f.**

Lawrence, David, et al.   **QH77.A8L385 2002**
The Great Barrier Reef: Finding the Right Balance. Richard Kenchington & Simon Woodley (Authors). Trade Paper. Melbourne University Publishing. Carlton, VIC. 2002. 296p. ISBN:0-522-84992-X, ISBN13: 978-0-522-84992-9. Dewey:333.95/6/09943. LCCN:2003-446349.

Audience: **u,f.** *Choice, 2003.*

Love, Rosaleen   **QH197.L68 2001**
Reefscape: Reflections on the Great Barrier Reef. Trade Cloth. National Academies Press. Washington, DC. 2001. v, 255p. ISBN:0-309-07260-3, ISBN13: 978-0-309-07260-1. Dewey:508.943. LCCN:2001-024281.

Audience: **g,l,u,f.** *Choice, 2001.*

Morgan, Sally & Lalor,   **QH91**
  Pauline
Ocean Life. Trade Paper. Sterling Publishing Co., Inc.. New York, NY. 2001. 512p. ISBN:1-85648-591-9, ISBN13: 978-1-85648-591-3. Dewey:551.46.

Audience: **l,u,f.**

Wolanski, Eric (Editor)   **QH197**
Oceanographic Processes of Coral Reefs: Physical and Biological Links in the Great Barrier Reef. CRC Press, Boca Raton. 2001. ISBN:0-8493-0833-X, ISBN13: 978-0-8493-0833-8.

Audience: **u,f.**

Integrative Biology > General Ecology > Marine Habitats > Deep Sea Habitats

Andersen, Tom   **QH344.A53 1997**
Pelagic Nutrient Cycles: Herbivores As Sources and Sinks. Trade Cloth. Springer. New York, NY. 1997. XII, 300p. Ecological Studies, Vol. 129 ISBN:3-540-61881-3, ISBN13: 978-3-540-61881-2. Dewey:577.7/16. LCCN:96-049478.

Audience: **u,f.**

Herring, Peter   **QH91.H44 2002**
The Biology of the Deep Ocean. Trade Paper. Oxford University Press, Inc. New York, NY. 2002. 324p. Biology of Habitats Ser. ISBN:0-19-854955-5, ISBN13: 978-0-19-854955-0. Dewey:578.77/7. LCCN:2002-277653.

Audience: **l,u.**

Integrative Biology > General Ecology > Marine Habitats > Costal Habitats

Andrew, Neil (Editor)   **QH197**
Under Southern Seas: The Ecology of Australia's Rocky Reefs. Trade Cloth. Krieger Publishing Company. Melbourne, FL. 2000. 256p. ISBN:1-57524-141-2, ISBN13: 978-1-57524-141-8. Dewey:577.7/8957.

Audience: **l,u,f.** *Choice, 2000.*

Blackburn, T. Henry &   **QH344.N54 1988**
  Sorensen, Jan (Editors)
Nitrogen Cycling in Coastal Marine Environments: Scope 33.

Trade Cloth. John Wiley & Sons, Inc. Hoboken, NJ. 1988. 478p. Scientific Committee on Problems of the Environment Ser. ISBN:0-471-91404-5, ISBN13: 978-0-471-91404-4. Dewey:574.5/2638. LCCN:86-026803.

Audience: **u,f.**

Byford, Jim   **QH81.B9985 1999**
Close to the Land: Reflections on Re-Connecting. Trade Paper. University of Tennessee Press. Knoxville, TN. 1999. 192p. Outdoor Tennessee Ser. ISBN:1-57233-029-5, ISBN13: 978-1-57233-029-0. Dewey:508. LCCN:98-025371.

Audience: **l,u,f.**

Faranda, F. M., et al.   **QH93.M42 2001**
Structure and Processes in the Mediterranean Ecosystem. L. Guglielmo & G. Spezie (Authors). Trade Cloth. Springer. New York, NY. 2001. XVIII, 503p. ISBN:88-470-0114-5, ISBN13: 978-88-470-0114-5. Dewey:577.7/38. LCCN:00-066115.

Audience: **u,f.**

Livingston, Robert J.   **QH104**
Trophic Organization in Coastal Systems. CRC Press, Boca Raton, Fla.. 2003. Marine science series ISBN:0-8493-1110-1, ISBN13: 978-0-8493-1110-9.

Audience: **u,f.**

Integrative Biology > General Ecology > Marine Habitats > Marsh and River habitats

Benke, Arthur C. &   **QH102.R58 2005**
  Cushing, Colbert E. (Editors)
Rivers of North America. Trade Cloth. Elsevier Science & Technology Books. Saint Louis, MO. 2005. 1168p. ISBN:0-12-088253-1, ISBN13: 978-0-12-088253-3. Dewey:551.48/3. LCCN:2005-008909.

Audience: **l,u,f.** *Choice, 2006.*

Howarth, R. W., et al.   **QH344.S85 1992**
Sulphur Cycling on the Continents: Wetlands, Terrestrial Ecosystems and Associated Water Bodies. J. W. Stewart & M. V. Ivanov (Authors). Trade Cloth. John Wiley & Sons, Inc. Hoboken, NJ. 1992. 372p. Scientific Committee on Problems of the Environment Ser. ISBN:0-471-93153-5, ISBN13: 978-0-471-93153-9. Dewey:574.5/222. LCCN:91-026109.

Audience: **u,f.**

Kalff, Jacob   **QH96.K24 2002**
Limnology. Paper Text. Prentice Hall PTR. Upper Saddle River, NJ. 2001. 592p. ISBN:0-13-033775-7, ISBN13: 978-0-13-033775-7. Dewey:577.6. LCCN:2001-032745.

Audience: **l,u,f.**

Kentula, Mary E., et al.   **QH76.W47 1992**
Wetlands: An Approach to Improving Decision Making in Wetland Restoration and Creation. Robert P. Brooks, Stephanie E. Gwin, Cindy Holland, Arthur D. Sherman & Jean C. Sifneos (Authors), Ann J. Hairston (Editor). Trade Cloth. Island Press. Washington, DC. 1992. 176p. ISBN:1-55963-221-6, ISBN13: 978-1-55963-221-8. Dewey:333.91/8/0973. LCCN:92-005675.

Audience: **u,f.**

National Research Council   **QH104.R55 2002**
  Staff, et al.
Riparian Areas: Functions and Strategies for Management.

Division on Earth and Life Studies Staff & Committee on Riparian Zone Functioning and Strategies for Management (Authors). Perfect. National Academies Press. Washington, DC. 2002. 444p. ISBN:0-309-08295-1, ISBN13: 978-0-309-08295-2. Dewey:577.68. LCCN:2002-105957.

Audience: **u,f.**

Palmer, Tim   **QH76.P36 1993**
The Wild and Scenic Rivers of America. Trade Cloth. Island Press. Washington, DC. 1993. 338p. ISBN:1-55963-145-7, ISBN13: 978-1-55963-145-7. Dewey:333.91/62/0973. LCCN:92-032660.

Audience: **g,l,u,f.** *Choice, 1993.*

Integrative Biology > General Ecology > Marine Habitats > Lake and Freshwater Habitats

Abell, Robin A., et al.   **QH77.N56F69 2000**
Freshwater Ecoregions of North America: A Conservation Assessment. David M. Olson, Eric Dinerstein, Patrick T. Hurley, James T. Diggs, William Eichbaum, Steven Walters, Wesley Wettengel, Tom Allnutt, Colby J. Loucks & Prashant Hedao (Authors). Trade Paper. Island Press. Washington, DC. 1999. 368p. ISBN:1-55963-734-X, ISBN13: 978-1-55963-734-3. Dewey:577.6. LCCN:99-016796.

Audience: **g,l,u,f.** *Choice, 2000.*

Bronmark, Christer &   **QH96.B724 2005**
Hansson, Lars-Anders
Biology of Lakes and Ponds. Ed. 2. Trade Cloth. Oxford University Press, Inc. New York, NY. 2005. 300p. Biology of Habitats Ser. ISBN:0-19-851612-6, ISBN13: 978-0-19-851612-5. Dewey:577.63. LCCN:2004-025884.

Audience: **u,f.**

Claudi, Renata & Leach,   **QH102.C56 2000**
Joseph H. (Editors)
Nonindigenous Freshwater Organisms: Vectors, Biology and Impacts. Saddle Stitched. Lewis Publishers. Boca Raton, FL. 1999. 480p. ISBN:1-56670-449-9, ISBN13: 978-1-56670-449-6. Dewey:577.6/097. LCCN:99-028607.

Audience: **u,f.** *Choice, 2000.*

Doppelt, Bob, et al.   **QH76**
Entering the Watershed: A New Approach to Save America's River Ecosystems. Mary Scurlock, Chris Frissell, Robert Doppelt & James R. Karr (Authors), James Karr (Editor). Trade Paper. Island Press. Washington, DC. 1993. 504p. ISBN:1-55963-275-5, ISBN13: 978-1-55963-275-1. Dewey:333.91/6216/0973. LCCN:93-008895.

Audience: **l,u,f.** *Choice, 1994.*

Harding, James H.   **QL653.G74H37 1997**
Amphibians and Reptiles of the Great Lakes Region. Cloth over Boards. University of Michigan Press. Chicago, IL. 1997. 400p. Great Lakes Environment Ser. ISBN:0-472-09628-1, ISBN13: 978-0-472-09628-2. Dewey:597.6/0978. LCCN:96-025343.

Audience: **l,u.** *Choice, 1998.*

Kalff, Jacob   **QH96.K24 2002**
Limnology. Paper Text. Prentice Hall PTR. Upper Saddle River, NJ. 2001. 592p. ISBN:0-13-033775-7, ISBN13: 978-0-13-033775-7. Dewey:577.6. LCCN:2001-032745.

Audience: **l,u,f.**

Kelso, J. R. & Hartig, J. H.   **SH157.8**
(Editors)
Methods of Modifying Habitat to Benefit the Great Lakes Ecosystem. Trade Paper. NRC Research Press National Research Council of Canada. Ottawa, ON. 1995. 294p. CISTI Occasional Paper Ser., No. 1 ISBN:0-660-16047-1, ISBN13: 978-0-660-16047-4. Dewey:333.95/2153/09713.

Audience: **u,f.**

Minoura, K. (Editor)   **QH541.5.L3**
Lake Baikal: A Mirror in Time and Space for Understanding Global Change Processes. Trade Cloth. Elsevier Science & Technology Books. Saint Louis, MO. 2000. 348p. ISBN:0-444-50434-6, ISBN13: 978-0-444-50434-0. Dewey:577.6309575.

Audience: **u,f.**

Pienitz , Reinhar (Editor), et   **GB1603.2**
al.
Long-Term Environmental Change in Arctic and Antarctic Lakes. Marianne S. V. Douglas & John P. Smol (Editors). Trade Cloth. Springer. New York, NY. 2005. XXX, 562p. Developments in Paleoenvironmental Research Ser. ISBN:1-4020-2125-9, ISBN13: 978-1-4020-2125-1. Dewey:333.9163091632.

Audience: **u,f.**

Reynolds, C. S. &   **QH96.L29 2004**
O'Sullivan, P. (Editors)
Lakes Handbook, Vol. 1,Set. Trade Cloth. Blackwell Publishing, Inc. Malden, MA. 2005. 528p. ISBN:0-632-04794-1, ISBN13: 978-0-632-04794-9. Dewey:551.4/82.

Audience: **u,f.**

Rossiter, Andrew &   **QH98**
Kawanabe, Hiroya (Volume Editors)
Ancient Lakes: Biodiversity, Ecology and Evolution. Trade Cloth. Elsevier Science & Technology Books. Saint Louis, MO. 2000. 680p. Advances in Ecological Research Ser., Vol. 31 ISBN:0-12-013931-6, ISBN13: 978-0-12-013931-6. Dewey:578.76.

Audience: **u,f.**

Integrative Biology > General Ecology > Land Habitats

Allaby, Michael   **QH541.5.D4A438 2006**
Deserts. Richard Garratt (Illustrator). Trade Cloth. Facts On File, Inc.. New York, NY. 2006. 272p. Biomes of the Earth Ser. ISBN:0-8160-5320-0, ISBN13: 978-0-8160-5320-9. Dewey:577.54. LCCN:2005-005611.

Audience: **l,u,f.**

Bates, H. E.   **QH138.S8**
Through the Woods: The English Woodland - April to April. Agnes Miller Parker (Illustrator). Trade Cloth. Lincoln Frances Ltd. London, 1995. 144p. ISBN:0-7112-0992-8, ISBN13: 978-0-7112-0992-3. Dewey:574.5/2642/0942.

Audience: **l,u,f.**

Bermingham, Eldredge   **QH86.T764 2005**
(Editor), et al.
Tropical Rainforests: Past, Present, and Future. Craig Moritz & Christopher W. Dick (Editors). Trade Cloth. University of

Chicago Press. Chicago, IL. 2005. 672p. ISBN:0-226-04466-1, ISBN13: 978-0-226-04466-8. Dewey:577.34. LCCN:2004-019348.

Audience: **l,u,f.**

Berry, R. J.   **QH141.B47**
Natural History of Orkney. Trade Cloth. A & C Black. London, 2000. 320p. Poyser Natural History Ser. ISBN:0-85661-104-2, ISBN13: 978-0-85661-104-9. Dewey:578/.0941132.

Audience: **l,u,f.** *Choice, 2001.*

Bierregaard, Richard O.   **QH112.L48 2001**
  (Editor), et al.
Lessons from Amazonia: The Ecology and Conservation of a Fragmented Forest. Claude Gascon, Thomas Lovejoy & Rita Mesquita (Editors), Edward O. Wilson (Foreword by). Cloth over Boards. Yale University Press. Cumberland, RI. 2001. 496p. ISBN:0-300-08483-8, ISBN13: 978-0-300-08483-2. Dewey:577.34/0981/1. LCCN:2001-026535.

Audience: **l,u,f.** *Choice, 2002.*

Bonnicksen, Thomas M.   **QH104.B635 2000**
America's Ancient Forests: From the Ice Age to the Age of Discovery. Trade Cloth. John Wiley & Sons, Inc. Hoboken, NJ. 2000. 608p. ISBN:0-471-13622-0, ISBN13: 978-0-471-13622-4. Dewey:577.3/0973. LCCN:98-024396.

Audience: **l,u,f.**

Buckley, Martin   **QH88**
Grains of Sand. London : Hutchinson. 2000. ISBN:0-09-180136-2, ISBN13: 978-0-09-180136-6.

Audience: **l,u,f.**

Campbell, David G.   **QH84.2**
The Crystal Desert: Summers in Antarctica. Trade Paper. Houghton Mifflin Company Trade & Reference Division. Boston, MA. 2002. 308p. ISBN:0-618-21921-8, ISBN13: 978-0-618-21921-6. Dewey:508.989.

Audience: **l,u,f.** *Choice, 1993.*

Campbell, SueEllen   **QH81.C3525 1996**
Bringing the Mountain Home. Trade Cloth. University of Arizona Press. Tucson, AZ. 1996. 118p. ISBN:0-8165-1616-2, ISBN13: 978-0-8165-1616-2. Dewey:508. LCCN:96-004466.

Audience: **l,u,f.**

Chapin, F. Stuart III &   **QH84.1.A7 1995**
  Orner, Christian K. (Editors)
Arctic and Alpine Biodiversity: Patterns, Causes, and Ecosystem Consequences. Trade Cloth. Springer. New York, NY. 1995. 322p. Ecological Studies, Vol. 113 ISBN:3-540-57948-6, ISBN13: 978-3-540-57948-9. Dewey:574.5/2621. LCCN:94-040221.

Audience: **u,f.**

Chernoff, Barry   **QH127**
  (Editor), et al.
A Biological Assessment of the Aquatic Ecosystems of the Rio Paraguay Basin, Alto Paraguay, Paraguay. Jensen R. Montambault & Philip W. Willink (Editors). Trade Paper. University of Chicago Press. Chicago, IL. 2001. 156p. Conservation International Rapid Assessment Program Ser. ISBN:1-881173-40-2, ISBN13: 978-1-881173-40-3. Dewey:577.609892.

Audience: **u,f.**

Crawford, R. M.   **QH84.1.D57 1997**
Disturbance and Recovery in Arctic Lands: An Ecological Perspective: Proceedings of the NATO Advanced Research Workshop on Disturbance and Recovery of Arctic Terrestrial Ecosystems, Rovaniemi, Finland, 24-30 Sept. 1995. Trade Cloth. Springer London, Ltd. Guildford, 1997. 632p. NATO Advanced Science Institutes Ser., Vol. 2:Environment ISBN:0-7923-4418-9, ISBN13: 978-0-7923-4418-6. Dewey:577.27/0911/3. LCCN:96-051038.

Audience: **u,f.**

De Villiers, Marq & Hirtle,   **DT333**
  Sheila
Sahara: A Natural History. Trade Paper. McClelland & Stewart. Toronto, ON. 2004. 336p. ISBN:0-7710-2638-2, ISBN13: 978-0-7710-2638-6. Dewey:916.604/329.

Audience: **g,l,u,f.** *Choice, 2003.*

Dubasak, Marilyn   **QH76.D83 1990**
Wilderness Preservation: A Cross-Cultural Comparison of Canada and the United States. Trade Cloth. Garland Publishing, Inc. New York, NY. 1991. 248p. The Environment: Problems and Solutions Ser. ISBN:0-8240-2517-2, ISBN13: 978-0-8240-2517-5. Dewey:333.78/216/0973. LCCN:90-023934.

Audience: **u,f.**

Fitzharris, Tim   **QH86**
Forests: A Journey into North America's Vanishing Wilderness. Li-leger, Don (Drawings by). Stoddart, Toronto. 1991. ISBN:0-7737-2498-2, ISBN13: 978-0-7737-2498-3.

Audience: **l,u,f.**

Flegg, Jim   **GB612**
Deserts: Miracle of Life. Library Binding. Replica Books. Bridgewater, NJ. 1999. 162p. ISBN:0-7351-0201-5, ISBN13: 978-0-7351-0201-9. Dewey:910/.02154.

Audience: **l,u,f.** *Choice, 1994.*

Fothergill, Alastair   **QH84.2.F68 1995**
A Natural History of the Antarctic: Life in the Freezer. Ben Osborne (Illustrator), David Attenborough (Foreword by). Trade Cloth. Sterling Publishing Co., Inc.. New York, NY. 1995. 224p. ISBN:0-8069-1346-0, ISBN13: 978-0-8069-1346-9. Dewey:508.98/9. LCCN:94-023841.

Audience: **l,u,f.**

Gallagher, Nora (Editor)   **QH81.P3428 1999**
Patagonia: Notes from the Field. Yvon Chouinard (Introduction by). Trade Cloth. Chronicle Books LLC. San Francisco, CA. 1999. 144p. ISBN:0-8118-2604-X, ISBN13: 978-0-8118-2604-4. Dewey:508. LCCN:99-018491.

Audience: **l,u,f.**

Goldsmith, F. B. (Editor)   **QH86.T73 1998**
Tropical Rain Forest: A Wider Perspective. Cloth Text. Chapman & Hall. New York, NY. 1998. 424p. ISBN:0-412-81510-9, ISBN13: 978-0-412-81510-2. Dewey:333.7/5. LCCN:97-069618.

Audience: **l,u,f.**

Greenaway, Theresa &   **QH86.G73 2004**
  Dorling Kindersley Publishing Staff
Jungle. Geoff Dann (Photographer). Library Binding. Dorling Kindersley Publishing, Inc. New York, NY. 2004. 72p. Eyewitness Books ISBN:0-7566-0693-4, ISBN13: 978-0-7566-0693-0. Dewey:578.734. LCCN:2004-558978.

Audience: **l,u,f.**

Grove, A. T. & Rackham,   **QH150**
Oliver
The Nature of Mediterranean Europe: An Ecological History.
Trade Paper. Yale University Press. Cumberland, RI. 2003.
384p. ISBN:0-300-10055-8, ISBN13: 978-0-300-10055-6.
Dewey:577.4/6/094. LCCN:2003-101909.

Audience: **l,u,f.** *Choice, 2001.*

Hammond, D. (Editor)   **QH125**
Tropical Rainforests of the Guianan Shield. Trade Cloth. CAB
International. Wallingford, 2005. 544p. CABI Publishing Ser.
ISBN:0-85199-536-5, ISBN13: 978-0-85199-536-6.
Dewey:578.734/098. LCCN:2004-021133.

Audience: **u,f.**

Hatfield, J. L. & Stewart, B.   **QH84.8.S6315 1994**
A. (Editors)
Soil Biology: Effects on Soil Quality. Paper over Boards. Lewis
Publishers. Boca Raton, FL. 1993. 176p. ISBN:0-87371-927-1,
ISBN13: 978-0-87371-927-8. Dewey:574.909/48.

Audience: **u,f.**

Henry, J. David   **QH106.H46 2002**
Canada's Boreal Forest. Trade Cloth. Smithsonian Institution
Press. Washington, DC. 2002. 208p. Smithsonian Natural
History Ser. ISBN:1-58834-057-0, ISBN13: 978-1-58834-057-3.
Dewey:508.415. LCCN:2002-070687.

Audience: **g,l,u.**

Holst, B., et al.   **QH128 B57 2001**
A Rapid Biological Assessment of the Northern Cordillera
Vilcabamba, Peru. L. Emmons, M. Romo, L. Luna, A.
Chicchon, G. Servat, H. Beltizan & B. Boyle (Authors), Thomas
S. Schulenberg (Editor). Trade Paper. Conservation International.
Washington, DC. 1999. 200p. RAP Working Papers, No. 12
ISBN:1-881173-51-8, ISBN13: 978-1-881173-51-9. Dewey:577.

Audience: **u,f.**

Hosking, Eric & Hosking,   **G590**
David (Photographers)
Poles Apart: The Natural Worlds of the Arctic and Antarctic.
Jim Flegg (Text by). Trade Cloth. Penguin Group (USA) Inc.
New York, NY. 1990. 192p. ISBN:0-7207-1838-4, ISBN13:
978-0-7207-1838-6. Dewey:998. LCCN:89-063771.

Audience: **l,u,f.**

Johnson, D. W. & Van   **QH344.A52 1989**
Hook, R. I. (Editors)
Analysis of Biogeochemical Cycling Process in Walker Branch
Watershed. Cloth Text. Springer. New York, NY. 1988. 401p.
ISBN:0-387-96745-1, ISBN13: 978-0-387-96745-5.
Dewey:551.9. LCCN:88-039675.

Audience: **u,f.** *Choice, 1989.*

Jones, Stephen R. &   **QH102.J54 2004**
Cushman, Ruth Carol
The North American Prairie. Trade Cloth. Houghton Mifflin
Company Trade & Reference Division. Boston, MA. 2004.
528p. Peterson Field Guides ISBN:0-618-17929-1, ISBN13:
978-0-618-17929-9. Dewey:578.74/4/097. LCCN:2002-191338.

Audience: **g,l,u.**

Jukofsky, Diane   **QH86**
Encyclopedia of Rainforests: Diane Jukofsky for the Rainforest
Alliance. Cloth Text. Greenwood Publishing Group, Inc.
Portsmouth, NH. 2001. 384p. ISBN:1-57356-259-9, ISBN13:
978-1-57356-259-1. Dewey:578.734/03. LCCN:2001-032154.

Audience: **g,l,u.** *Choice, 2002.*

Körner, Christian &   **QH541.5.F6**
Schulze, Ernst-Detlef (Editors)
Forest Diversity and Function: Temperate and Boreal Systems.
Michael Scherer-Lorenzen (Volume Editor). Trade Cloth.
Springer. New York, NY. 2004. XIX, 400p. Ecological Studies,
Vol. 176 ISBN:3-540-22191-3, ISBN13: 978-3-540-22191-3.
Dewey:577.3. LCCN:2004-110616.

Audience: **u,f.**

Laws, Richard   **QH84.2**
Antarctica the Last Frontier. Trade Cloth. Pan Macmillan.
London, 1990. 192p. ISBN:1-85283-247-9, ISBN13:
978-1-85283-247-6. Dewey:508.98/9.

Audience: **l,u,f.**

Marshall Cavendish   **QH86.R39 2002**
Corporation Staff (Contribution by)
Rain Forests of the World, Set. Trade Cloth. Marshall Cavendish
Corporation. Tarrytown, NY. 2002. 704p. ISBN:0-7614-7254-1,
ISBN13: 978-0-7614-7254-4. Dewey:578.734.
LCCN:2001-028460.

Audience: **l,u,f.**

Martin, Michael   **GB611**
Deserts of the Earth. Trade Cloth. Thames & Hudson. New
York, NY. 2004. 372p. ISBN:0-500-51194-2, ISBN13:
978-0-500-51194-7. Dewey:551.41/5. LCCN:2004-104540.

Audience: **l,u,f.**

Martin, Vance & Tyler,   **QH77.A68W67 1993**
Nicholas (Editors)
Arctic Wilderness: The 5th World Wilderness Congress. Vance
Martin (Preface by), Nicholas Tyler (Introduction by). Trade
Paper. Fulcrum Publishing. Golden, CO. 1995. 368p.
ISBN:1-55591-931-6, ISBN13: 978-1-55591-931-3.
Dewey:333.7/16/0911. LCCN:95-004201.

Audience: **u,f.**

Matzner, Egbert (Volume   **QH343.7**
Editor)
Biogeochemistry of Forested Catchments in a Changing
Environment. Trade Cloth. Springer. New York, NY. 2004.
XXII, 501p. Ecological Studies, Vol. 172 ISBN:3-540-20973-5,
ISBN13: 978-3-540-20973-7. Dewey:577.3.
LCCN:2004-104100.

Audience: **u,f.**

McMenamin, Mark A. &   **QH360.5.M36 1994**
McMenamin, Dianna L.
Hypersea: Life on the Land. Cloth Text. Columbia University
Press. New York, NY. 1994. 262p. ISBN:0-231-07530-8,
ISBN13: 978-0-231-07530-5. Dewey:575. LCCN:94-015324.

Audience: **l,u,f.** *Choice, 1995.*

Nakashizuka, T. &   **QH188.D58 2001**
Matsumoto, Y. (Editors)
Diversity and Interactions in a Temperate Forest Community:
Ogawa Forest Reserve of Japan. Trade Cloth. Springer. New
York, NY. 2001. 360p. Ecological Studies, Vol. 158
ISBN:4-431-70322-5, ISBN13: 978-4-431-70322-8.
Dewey:577.3/0952. LCCN:2001-057643.

Audience: **u,f.**

National Wetlands Policy   **QH76.I76 1990**
Forum Staff
Issues in Wetlands Protection: Background Papers Prepared for
the National Wetlands Policy Forum. Gail Bingham, Edwin H.

Clark II, Leah V. Haygood & Michele Leslie (Editors). Trade Paper. World Wildlife Fund. Washington, DC. 1990. 256p. ISBN:0-89164-119-X, ISBN13: 978-0-89164-119-3. Dewey:333.91/8/0973. LCCN:90-001631.

Audience: **g,l,u.**

Okuda, T. (Editor), et al.   **QH185.P37 2003**
Pasoh. N. Manokaran, Y. Matsumoto & K. Niiyama (Editors). Trade Cloth. Springer. New York, NY. 2003. XVIII, 628p. ISBN:4-431-00660-5, ISBN13: 978-4-431-00660-2. Dewey:578.095951. LCCN:2004-296280.

Audience: **g,l,u,f.**

Osborne, Graham   **QH86.O82 1998**
   (Photographer)
Rain Forest: Ancient Realm of the Pacific Northwest. Wade Davis (Text by). Trade Cloth. Chelsea Green Publishing. White River Junction, VT. 1999. 128p. ISBN:1-890132-24-1, ISBN13: 978-1-890132-24-8. Dewey:333.75/09795/022. LCCN:00-501376.

Audience: **l,u,f.**

Porter, Douglas R. &   **QH76.C65 1995**
   Salveson, David A. (Editors)
Collaborative Planning for Wetlands and Wildlife: Issues and Examples. John De Grove (Foreword by). Trade Paper. Island Press. Washington, DC. 1995. 303p. ISBN:1-55963-287-9, ISBN13: 978-1-55963-287-4. Dewey:333.91/816/0973. LCCN:94-030143.

Audience: **u,f.** *Choice, 1995.*

Prance, Ghillean   **QH86.W64 1997**
Rainforests of the World: Water, Fire, Earth and Air. Art Wolfe (Photographer). Trade Cloth. Crown Publishing Group. New York, NY. 1998. 304p. ISBN:0-609-60364-7, ISBN13: 978-0-609-60364-2. Dewey:578.734. LCCN:97-004087.

Audience: **g,l,u,f.**

Primack, Richard & Corlett,   **QH86.P75 2005**
   Richard
Tropical Rain Forests: An Ecological and Biogeographical Comparison. Trade Cloth. Blackwell Publishing, Inc. Malden, MA. 2002. 336p. ISBN:0-632-04513-2, ISBN13: 978-0-632-04513-6. Dewey:577.34. LCCN:2004-009785.

Audience: **l,u,f.** *Choice, 2005.*

Reddy, K. Ramesh   **QH344.P5 1999**
Phosphorus Biogeochemistry in Sub-Tropical Ecosystemst. Saddle Stitched. Lewis Publishers. Boca Raton, FL. 1999. 728p. ISBN:1-56670-331-X, ISBN13: 978-1-56670-331-4. Dewey:577/.14. LCCN:98-050246.

Audience: **u,f.**

Roberts, Jerry   **Z7408.L29R63 1999**
Rain Forest Bibliography: An Annotated Guide to over 1600 Nonfiction Books about Central and South American Jungles. Cloth Text. McFarland & Company, Incorporated Publishers. Jefferson, NC. 1999. 320p. ISBN:0-7864-0717-4, ISBN13: 978-0-7864-0717-0. Dewey:016.33375/098. LCCN:99-26061.

Audience: **g,l,u,f.** *Choice, 2000.*

Robichaux, Robert H. &   **QH107.T76 2000**
   Yetman, David A.
The Tropical Deciduous Forest of Alamos: Biodiversity of a Threatened Ecosystem in Mexico. Trade Cloth. University of

Arizona Press. Tucson, AZ. 2000. 259p. ISBN:0-8165-1922-6, ISBN13: 978-0-8165-1922-4. Dewey:333.95/11/097217. LCCN:99-050867.

Audience: **u,f.**

Salvesen, David   **QH76.S25 1994**
Wetlands: Mitigating and Regulating Development Impacts. Ed. 2. Paper Text. Urban Land Institute. Washington, DC. 1994. 150p. ISBN:0-87420-752-5, ISBN13: 978-0-87420-752-1. Dewey:333.91/8/0973. LCCN:93-061896.

Audience: **u,f.**

Scodari, Paul F.   **QH76.S395 1997**
Measuring the Benefits of Federal Wetland Programs. Trade Cloth. Environmental Law Institute. Washington, DC. 1997. 104p. ISBN:0-911937-71-4, ISBN13: 978-0-911937-71-8. Dewey:333.91/8/0973. LCCN:97-133033.

Audience: **l,u,f.**

Slater, Candace   **QH86.I5 2003**
In Search of the Rain Forest. Arturo Escobar & Dianne Rocheleau (Editors), Scott L. Fedick, Alexis Greene, Paul R. Greenough, Nancy L. Peluso & Suzana Sawyer (Contribution by). Trade Cloth. Duke University Press. Durham, NC. 2003. 320p. New Ecologies for the Twenty-First Century Ser. ISBN:0-8223-3205-1, ISBN13: 978-0-8223-3205-3. Dewey:333.95. LCCN:2003-016614.

Audience: **g,l,u,f.**

Sowell, John   **QH102.S69 2001**
Desert Ecology: An Introduction to Life in the Arid Southwest. Trade Paper. University of Utah Press. Salt Lake City, UT. 2001. xii, 193p. ISBN:0-87480-678-X, ISBN13: 978-0-87480-678-6. Dewey:577.54/097. LCCN:00-011599.

Audience: **g,l,u,f.** *Choice, 2001.*

St. Martin's Press Staff &   **QH86.Y68 2001**
   Young, Allen M.
Tropical Rainforests: A Golden Guide from St. Martin's Press. Judith Huf (Illustrator). Trade Paper. St. Martin's Press. Gordonville, VA. 2001. 160p. Golden Guides Ser. ISBN:1-58238-080-5, ISBN13: 978-1-58238-080-3. Dewey:578.734.

Audience: **g,l.**

Sweden.; Statens   **QH84.1**
   naturvårdsverk
Boreal Ecosystems and Landscapes: Structures, Processes and Conservation of Biodiversity. Hansson, Lennart (Editor). Malden, MA : Published and distributed by MUNKSGAARD International Publishers, Copenhagen, Denmark. 1997. Ecological bulletins,; no. 46 ISBN:87-16-15236-0, ISBN13: 978-87-16-15236-7.

Audience: **u,f.**

Trigo Boix, Nuri   **QH107.E374 2003**
Ecology and Man in Mexico's Central Volcanoes Area. G. W. Heil & Roland Bobbink (Editors). Mixed Media. Springer. New York, NY. 2003. IX, 222p. Geobotany Ser., Vol. 29 ISBN:1-4020-1708-1, ISBN13: 978-1-4020-1708-7. Dewey:333.76/0972. LCCN:2003-062042.

Audience: **u,f.**

Tweit, Susan J.   **QH88**
Seasons in the Desert: A Naturalist's Notebook. Kirk Caldwell
(Illustrator). Trade Cloth. DIANE Publishing Company.
Collingdale, PA. 1998. 224p. ISBN:0-7567-5788-6, ISBN13:
978-0-7567-5788-5. Dewey:578.754.

Audience: **g.**

Valentini, Riccardo (Editor)   **QH344.F58 2002**
Fluxes of Carbon, Water and Energy of European Forests. Trade
Cloth. Springer. New York, NY. 2003. XX, 274p. Ecological
Studies, Vol. 163 ISBN:3-540-43791-6, ISBN13:
978-3-540-43791-8. Dewey:577.3/144/094. LCCN:2002-030469.

Audience: **u,f.**

Ward, J. V. & Uehlinger, U.   **QH175.E36 2003**
Ecology of a Glacial Flood Plain. Trade Cloth. Springer
London, Ltd. Guildford, 2003. 320p. Aquatic Ecology Ser., Vol.
1 ISBN:1-4020-1792-8, ISBN13: 978-1-4020-1792-6.
Dewey:577.6/6. LCCN:2003-064056.

Audience: **u,f.**

Wong, Ming H.   **QH179**
Wetlands Ecosystems in Asia: Function and Management. Trade
Cloth. Elsevier Science & Technology Books. Saint Louis, MO.
2004. 480p. Developments in Ecosystems Ser., Vol. 1
ISBN:0-444-51691-3, ISBN13: 978-0-444-51691-6.
Dewey:577.68095. LCCN:2006-273069.

Audience: **u,f.**

Woodin, S. & British   **QH84.1.E26 1997**
  Ecological Society
Ecology of Arctic Environments. M. Marquiss (Editor). Book,
Other. Blackwell Publishing, Inc. Malden, MA. 1997. 292p.
British Ecological Society Special Publications, Vol. 36
ISBN:0-632-04218-4, ISBN13: 978-0-632-04218-0.
Dewey:574.5/2621. LCCN:96-043822.

Audience: **u,f.**

World Wildlife Fund Staff   **QH76.S665**
Statewide Wetlands Strategies: A Guide to Protecting and
Managing the Resource. Trade Cloth. Island Press. Washington,
DC. 1992. 285p. ISBN:1-55963-205-4, ISBN13:
978-1-55963-205-8. Dewey:353.9/382326. LCCN:92-003563.
Audience: **g,l,u,f.**

Zubov, B. V. (Editor)   **QH86.R345 2002**
Rainforests: Overview, Current Abstracts with Indexes. Trade
Cloth. Nova Science Publishers, Inc. Hauppauge, NY. 2002.
226p. ISBN:1-59033-481-7, ISBN13: 978-1-59033-481-2.
Dewey:577.34. LCCN:2002-037872.

Audience: **l,u.**

Integrative Biology > General Ecology > Conservation

Bean, Michael J., et al.   **QH0076.B43**
Reconciling Conflicts under the Endangered Species Act: The
Habitat Conservation Planning Experience. Sarah G. Fitzgerald
& Michael A. O'Connell (Authors). Trade Paper. Books on
Demand. Ann Arbor, MI. 127p. ISBN:0-608-09123-5, ISBN13:
978-0-608-09123-5. Dewey:333.95/16/0973. LCCN:91-021750.
Audience: **u,f.**

Bohlen, Janet Trowbridge   **QH26.B63 1993**
For the Wild Places: Profiles in Conservation. Al Gore
(Foreword by). Trade Cloth. Island Press. Washington, DC.

1993. 228p. ISBN:1-55963-125-2, ISBN13: 978-1-55963-125-9.
Dewey:333.95/16/0922. LCCN:92-038118.
Audience: **g,l,u,f.** *Choice, 1993.*

Bradshaw, G. A. (Editor), et   **QH101.H69 2002**
  al.
How Landscapes Change: Human Disturbance and Ecosystem
Fragmentation in the Americas. P. A. Marquet & Kathryn L.
Ronnenberg (Editors). Trade Cloth. Springer. New York, NY.
2003. XXII, 361p. ISBN:3-540-43697-9, ISBN13:
978-3-540-43697-3. Dewey:304.2/8/097. LCCN:2002-030229.
Audience: **u,f.**

Bright, Chris   **QH353.B75 1998**
Life Out of Bounds: Bioinvasion in a Borderless World. Trade
Paper. W. W. Norton & Company, Inc. New York, NY. 1998.
224p. Worldwatch Environmental Alert Ser.
ISBN:0-393-31814-1, ISBN13: 978-0-393-31814-2.
Dewey:333.9/5/16. LCCN:99-163011.
Audience: **l,u,f.** *Choice, 1999.*

Caro, Tim (Editor)   **QL751.B3425 1998**
Behavioral Ecology and Conservation Biology. Trade Cloth.
Oxford University Press, Inc. New York, NY. 1998. 598p.
ISBN:0-19-510489-7, ISBN13: 978-0-19-510489-9.
Dewey:591.5. LCCN:97-018005.

Audience: **l,u.**

Cartron, Jean-Luc E., et al.   **QH107.B525 2004**
Biodiversity, Ecosystems, and Conservation in Northern Mexico.
Gerardo Ceballos & Richard Stephen Felger (Authors). Trade
Cloth. Oxford University Press, Inc. New York, NY. 2005. 513p.
ISBN:0-19-515672-2, ISBN13: 978-0-19-515672-0.
Dewey:333.95/16/0972. LCCN:2004-012002.

Audience: **l,u,f.**

Clemmons, Janine R. &   **QH76 .B44 1997**
  Buchholz, Richard (Editors)
Behavioural Approaches to Conservation in the Wild. Trade
Cloth. Cambridge University Press. New York, NY. 1997. 398p.
ISBN:0-521-58054-4, ISBN13: 978-0-521-58054-0.
Dewey:639.9. LCCN:96-031559.

Audience: **l,u,f.**

Committee on Scientific   **QH76.S38 1995**
  Issues in the Endangered-A
Science and the Endangered Species Act. Cloth Text. National
Academies Press. Washington, DC. 1995. 288p.
ISBN:0-309-05291-2, ISBN13: 978-0-309-05291-7.
Dewey:333.9516/0973. LCCN:95-033322.

Audience: **l,u,f.**

Crawford, Mark   **QH76.C73 1999**
Habitats and Ecosystems: An Encyclopedia of Endangered
America. Library Binding. ABC-CLIO, Inc. Santa Barbara, CA.
1999. xvii, 398p. ISBN:0-87436-997-5, ISBN13:
978-0-87436-997-7. Dewey:333.78/0973. LCCN:00-698072.
Audience: **u,f.** *Choice, 2000.*

Crisman, Thomas L.   **QH194.C66 2003**
Conservation, Ecology, and Management of African Fresh
Waters. Trade Cloth. University Press of Florida. Gainesville,
FL. 2003. 544p. ISBN:0-8130-2597-4, ISBN13:
978-0-8130-2597-1. Dewey:333.95/28/096. LCCN:2002-043032.
Audience: **u,f.**

Formats: Web: ☐ Ebook: ℮ CD/DVD-ROM: ✇ BCL3: ℬ

Crump, Donald J. (Editor)   QH76.A45 1988
America's Hidden Wilderness: Lands of Seclusion. Trade Cloth.
National Geographic Society. Washington, DC. 1988. 200p.
Special Publications Series 23, No. 1 ISBN:0-87044-666-5,
ISBN13: 978-0-87044-666-5. Dewey:917. LCCN:88-009977.
Audience: **l,u,f.**

DiSilvestro, Roger L.   QH76.D58 1993
Reclaiming the Last Wild Places: A New Agenda for
Biodiversity. Trade Cloth. John Wiley & Sons, Inc. Hoboken,
NJ. 1993. 288p. Wiley Nature Editions Ser., Vol. 10
ISBN:0-471-57244-6, ISBN13: 978-0-471-57244-2.
Dewey:333.95160973. LCCN:92-046457.
Audience: **l,u,f.** *Choice, 1993.*

Dubasak, Marilyn   QH76.D83 1990
Wilderness Preservation: A Cross-Cultural Comparison of
Canada and the United States. Trade Cloth. Garland Publishing,
Inc. New York, NY. 1991. 248p. The Environment: Problems
and Solutions Ser. ISBN:0-8240-2517-2, ISBN13:
978-0-8240-2517-5. Dewey:333.78/216/0973. LCCN:90-023934.
Audience: **u,f.**

Edwards, Victoria H.   QH76 .E34 1995
Dealing in Diversity: America's Market for Nature
Conservation. Trade Cloth. Cambridge University Press. New
York, NY. 1995. 200p. ISBN:0-521-46567-2, ISBN13:
978-0-521-46567-0. Dewey:333.78/216/0973. LCCN:94-036811.
Audience: **l,u,f.** *Choice, 1996.*

Fiedler, Peggy Lee (Editor)   QH75
Conservation Biology: For the Coming Decade. Ed. 2. Kareiva,
Peter M. (Editor). Chapman & Hall, New York. 1998.
ISBN:0-412-09651-X, ISBN13: 978-0-412-09651-8.
Audience: **u,f.**

Fitzsimmons, Allan K.   QH76.F58 1999
Defending Illusions: Federal Protection of Ecosystems. Book,
Other. Rowman & Littlefield Publishers, Inc. Lanham, MD.
1999. 348p. Political Economy Forum Ser. ISBN:0-8476-9421-6,
ISBN13: 978-0-8476-9421-1. Dewey:577/.0973.
LCCN:99-017318.
Audience: **u,f.** *Choice, 2000.*

Galan, Mark   QH76.G33 1997
There's Still Time: The Success of the Endangered Species Act.
Trade Cloth. National Geographic Society. Washington, DC.
1997. 40p. ISBN:0-7922-7092-4, ISBN13: 978-0-7922-7092-8.
Dewey:333.95/22/0973. LCCN:97-011564.
Audience: **l,u,f.**

Gil, Patricio Robles, et al.   QH107
The Great Tamaulipan Natural Province. Exequiel Ezcurra,
Eduardo Peters, Eugenia Pallares & Ana Ezcurra (Authors).
Trade Cloth. Conservation International. Washington, DC. 2005.
360p. ISBN:968-6397-73-6, ISBN13: 978-968-6397-73-4.
Dewey:508.7212.
Audience: **u,f.**

Grove, Noel   QH76.K73 1992
Preserving Eden: The Nature Conservancy. Stephen J.
Krasemann (Photographer). Trade Cloth. Harry N. Abrams, Inc.
New York, NY. 1992. 192p. ISBN:0-8109-3663-1, ISBN13:
978-0-8109-3663-8. Dewey:333.95/16/06073. LCCN:91-024551.
Audience: **g,l,u,f.**

Haisston, Ann J.   QH76
An Approach to Improving Decision Making in Wetland
Restoration and Creation. Trade Cloth, Box or Slipcased. Lewis
Publishers. Boca Raton, FL. 1992. 192p. ISBN:0-87371-937-9,
ISBN13: 978-0-87371-937-7. Dewey:639.9.
Audience: **u,f.** *Choice, 1993.*

Hansson, Lennart   QH75
The Ecological principles of nature conservation: applications in
temperate and boreal environments. London ; New York :
Elsevier Applied Science ; New York, NY : Elsevier Science
Pub. [distributor]. 1992. Conservation ecology series
ISBN:1-85166-718-0, ISBN13: 978-1-85166-718-5.
Audience: **l,u,f.**

Harding, Lee E. &   QH77.C2
  McCullum, Emily (Editors)
Biodiversity in British Columbia: Our Changing Environment.
Trade Paper. University of Washington Press. Seattle, WA. 1994.
426p. ISBN:0-662-20671-1, ISBN13: 978-0-662-20671-2.
Dewey:574.5/09711.
Audience: **l,u,f.**

Harris, Larry D., et al.   QH76.P73 1989
In Defense of Wildlife: Preserving Communities and Corridors.
Aubrey S. Johnson, Ginger M. Meese, John Fitzgerald, Albert
M. Manville & Gay Mackintosh (Authors), M. Rupert Cutler
(Introduction by). Paper Text. Defenders of Wildlife.
Washington, DC. 1989. 96p. ISBN:0-926549-00-6, ISBN13:
978-0-926549-00-5. Dewey:639.9. LCCN:89-138839.
Audience: **l,u,f.**

Hawksworth, D. L.   QH75
Biodiversity: Measurement and Estimation. Chapman & Hall,
London : Royal Society ; London ; New York. 1995.
ISBN:92-64-17059-6, ISBN13: 978-92-64-17059-9.
Audience: **u,f.**

Hummel, Monte   QH77.C2
Protecting Canada's Endangered Spaces: An Owner's Manual.
Key Porter Books, Toronto. 1995. Henderson book series; no.
27 ISBN:1-55013-710-7, ISBN13: 978-1-55013-710-1.
Audience: **u,f.**

Hunt, Constance E., et al.   QH76.C655 1997
Conservation on Private Lands: An Owner's Manual. World
Wildlife Fund Staff, Wildlife Habitat Council Staff & Land Trust
Alliance Staff (Authors). Trade Paper. World Wildlife Fund.
Washington, DC. 1997. ISBN:0-89164-153-X, ISBN13:
978-0-89164-153-7. Dewey:333.95/16/0973. LCCN:97-014714.
Audience: **u,f.**

Hutchins, Michael (Editor),   SF408.3.E84 1995
  et al.
Ethics on the Ark: Zoos, Animal Welfare, and Wildlife
Conservation. Bryan G. Norton, Terry L. Maple & Elizabeth F.
Stevens (Editors). Trade Cloth. Smithsonian Institution Press.
Washington, DC. 1995. 432p. Zoo and Aquarium Biology and
Conservation Ser. ISBN:1-56098-515-1, ISBN13:
978-1-56098-515-0. Dewey:639.9/3/01. LCCN:94-037139.
Audience: **g,l,u.** *Choice, 1996.*

Kentula, Mary E., et al.   QH76.W47 1992
Wetlands: An Approach to Improving Decision Making in
Wetland Restoration and Creation. Robert P. Brooks, Stephanie
E. Gwin, Cindy Holland, Arthur D. Sherman & Jean C. Sifneos

(Authors), Ann J. Hairston (Editor). Trade Cloth. Island Press. Washington, DC. 1992. 176p. ISBN:1-55963-221-6, ISBN13: 978-1-55963-221-8. Dewey:333.91/8/0973. LCCN:92-005675.

Audience: **u,f.**

Kerry, K. R. & Hempel, G.   **QH84.2.A583 1990**
    (Editors)
Antarctic Ecosystems: Change and Conservation. Trade Cloth. Springer. New York, NY. 1990. 432p. ISBN:0-387-52101-1, ISBN13: 978-0-387-52101-5. Dewey:574.5/2621. LCCN:90-009930.

Audience: **g,l,u.**

Körner, Christian &   **QH541.5.F6**
    Schulze, Ernst-Detlef (Editors)
Forest Diversity and Function: Temperate and Boreal Systems. Michael Scherer-Lorenzen (Volume Editor). Trade Cloth. Springer. New York, NY. 2004. XIX, 400p. Ecological Studies, Vol. 176 ISBN:3-540-22191-3, ISBN13: 978-3-540-22191-3. Dewey:577.3. LCCN:2004-110616.

Audience: **u,f.**

Lande, Russell, et al.   **QL752**
Stochastic Population Dynamics in Ecology and Conservation. Steinar Engen & Bernt-Erik Saether (Authors). Trade Cloth. Oxford University Press, Inc. New York, NY. 2003. 224p. Oxford Series in Ecology and Evolution ISBN:0-19-852524-9, ISBN13: 978-0-19-852524-0. Dewey:577.8801518. LCCN:2002-042559.

Audience: **u,f.**

Mann, Charles C. &   **QH76.M36 1995**
    Plummer, Mark L.
Noah's Choice: The Future of Endangered Species. Trade Cloth. Alfred A. Knopf Inc. New York, NY. 1995. 302p. ISBN:0-679-42002-9, ISBN13: 978-0-679-42002-6. Dewey:574.5/29/0973. LCCN:94-025807.

Audience: **l,u,f.** *Choice, 1995.*

Middleton, Susan   **QH76.M525 1991**
Here Today Vanishing Species. Trade Cloth. Chronicle Books LLC. San Francisco, CA. 1991. 144p. ISBN:0-8118-0041-5, ISBN13: 978-0-8118-0041-9. Dewey:574.5/29/0973022. LCCN:91-013547.

Audience: **l,u,f.**

Mooney, Harold A. &   **QH353.I59 2000**
    Hobbs, Richard J. (Editors)
Invasive Species in a Changing World. Trade Cloth. Island Press. Washington, DC. 2000. 384p. ISBN:1-55963-781-1, ISBN13: 978-1-55963-781-7. Dewey:577/.18. LCCN:00-008791.
Audience: **l,u,f.** *Choice, 2001.*

Mooney, Harold A. (Editor),   **SB990**
    et al.
Invasive Alien Species: A New Synthesis. Richard N. Mack, Jeffrey A. McNeely, Laurie E. Neville, Peter Johan Schei & Jeffrey K. Waage (Editors), SCOPE Staff (Other Primary Creator). Trade Paper, Perfect. Island Press. Washington, DC. 2005. 368p. Scope Ser. ISBN:1-55963-363-8, ISBN13: 978-1-55963-363-5. Dewey:578.6/2. LCCN:2004-029420.
Audience: **l,u,f.** *Choice, 2006.*

Morine, David E.   **QH76.M67 1990**
Good Dirt: Confessions of a Conservationist. Trade Paper. Globe Pequot Press, The. Guilford, CT. 1990. ISBN:0-87106-444-8, ISBN13: 978-0-87106-444-8. Dewey:333.7/2. LCCN:90-043074.
Audience: **l,u,f.**

Moss, Dorian & Roy, David   **QH83**
Towards a European Habitat Classification: Background Review 1989-1995. Office for Official Publications of the European Communities ; Lanham, Md. : Bernan Associates [distributor], Luxembourg 1998. Topic report / European Environment Agency ;; 28, 1996; Variation: Topic report (European Environment Agency) ;; no. 28/1996 ISBN:92-9167-115-0, ISBN13: 978-92-9167-115-1.
Audience: **u,f.**

National Science Teachers   **QH353**
    Association; United States; Environmental Protection
    Agency; Office of Research and Development
Introduced Species. National Science Teachers Association, Arlington, Va.. 1998. Global environmental change ISBN:0-87355-192-3, ISBN13: 978-0-87355-192-2.
Audience: **g,l,u.**

Noss, Reed F. &   **QH76.N67 1994**
    Cooperrider, Allen Y.
Saving Nature's Legacy: Protecting and Restoring Biodiversity. Defenders of Wildlife Staff (Other Primary Creator), Rodger Schlickeisen (Foreword by). Trade Cloth. Island Press. Washington, DC. 1994. 443p. ISBN:1-55963-247-X, ISBN13: 978-1-55963-247-8. Dewey:333.95/16/0973. LCCN:93-048895.
Audience: **g,l,u,f.** *Choice, 1994.*

Noss, Reed F., et al.   **QH76.N676 1997**
The Science of Conservation Planning: Habitat Conservation under the Endangered Species Act. Michael A. O'Connell & Dennis D. Murphy (Authors). Trade Cloth. Island Press. Washington, DC. 1997. 263p. ISBN:1-55963-566-5, ISBN13: 978-1-55963-566-0. Dewey:333.7/2/0973. LCCN:97-034520.
Audience: **g,l,u,f.** *Choice, 1998.*

Palmer, Tim   **QH76.P355 2004**
Lifelines: The Case for River Conservation. Ed. 2. Book, Other. Rowman & Littlefield Publishers, Inc. Lanham, MD. 2004. 256p. ISBN:0-7425-3138-4, ISBN13: 978-0-7425-3138-3. Dewey:333.91/62. LCCN:2003-020107.
Audience: **l,u.** *Choice, 1995.*

Pederson, Judith (Editor)   **QH353.I568 2001**
Marine Bioinvasions: Patterns, Processes, and Perspectives. Trade Cloth. Springer. New York, NY. 2003. 152p. ISBN:1-4020-1449-X, ISBN13: 978-1-4020-1449-9. Dewey:577.7/18. LCCN:2003-054973.
Audience: **l,u.**

Perrings, Charles (Editor),   **QH353.E36 2000**
    et al.
The Economics of Biological Invasions. Mark Williamson & Silvana Dalmazzone (Editors). Trade Cloth. Edward Elgar Publishing, Inc. Northampton, MA. 2000. 264p. ISBN:1-84064-378-1, ISBN13: 978-1-84064-378-7. Dewey:577/.18. LCCN:00-026460.
Audience: **u,f.**

Pickett, Steward T. (Editor)   **QH75**
The Ecological Basis of Conservation: Heterogeneity, Ecosystems, and Biodiversity. Cary Conference ; (6th :; 1995 :; Institute of Ecosystem Studies). Chapman & Hall, New York :. 1997. ISBN:0-412-09851-2, ISBN13: 978-0-412-09851-2.
Audience: **u,f.**

Porter, Douglas R. &   **QH76.C65 1995**
  Salveson, David A. (Editors)
Collaborative Planning for Wetlands and Wildlife: Issues and
Examples. John De Grove (Foreword by). Trade Paper. Island
Press. Washington, DC. 1995. 303p. ISBN:1-55963-287-9,
ISBN13: 978-1-55963-287-4. Dewey:333.91/816/0973.
LCCN:94-030143.
                       Audience: **u,f.** *Choice, 1995.*

Primack, Richard & Corlett,   **QH86.P75 2005**
  Richard
Tropical Rain Forests: An Ecological and Biogeographical
Comparison. Trade Cloth. Blackwell Publishing, Inc. Malden,
MA. 2002. 336p. ISBN:0-632-04513-2, ISBN13:
978-0-632-04513-6. Dewey:577.34. LCCN:2004-009785.
                      Audience: **l,u,f.** *Choice, 2005.*

Raup, David M.   **QE721.2.E97**
Extinction: Bad Genes or Bad Luck? Trade Paper. W. W. Norton
& Company, Inc. New York, NY. 1992. 228p.
ISBN:0-393-30927-4, ISBN13: 978-0-393-30927-0.
Dewey:575/.7.
                       Audience: **g,l,u.** *Choice, 1992.*

Roberts, Jerry   **Z7408.L29R63 1999**
Rain Forest Bibliography: An Annotated Guide to over 1600
Nonfiction Books about Central and South American Jungles.
Cloth Text. McFarland & Company, Incorporated Publishers.
Jefferson, NC. 1999. 320p. ISBN:0-7864-0717-4, ISBN13:
978-0-7864-0717-0. Dewey:016.33375/098. LCCN:99-26061.
                      Audience: **g,l,u,f.** *Choice, 2000.*

Rosenberg, Kenneth A.   **QH76.R66 1994**
Wilderness Preservation: A Reference Handbook. Library
Binding. ABC-CLIO, Inc. Santa Barbara, CA. 1994. 292p.
Contemporary World Issues Ser. ISBN:0-87436-731-X, ISBN13:
978-0-87436-731-7. Dewey:333.78/216/0973. LCCN:94-019336.
                      Audience: **g,l,u,f.** *Choice, 1995.*

Ruiz, Gregory M. &   **QH353.I62 2003**
  Carlton, James T. (Editors)
Invasive Species: Vectors and Management Strategies. Trade
Cloth. Island Press. Washington, DC. 2003. 484p.
ISBN:1-55963-902-4, ISBN13: 978-1-55963-902-6.
Dewey:577/.18. LCCN:2003-007223.
                              Audience: **u,f.**

Sandlund, O. T. (Odd Terje)   **QH75**
  (Editor)
Conservation of Biodiversity for Sustainable Development.
Hindar, K. (Kjetil) (Editor); Brown, A. H. D. (Editor).
Scandinavian University Press, Oslo, Norway. 1992.
ISBN:82-00-21508-3, ISBN13: 978-82-00-21508-0.
                              Audience: **u,f.**

Sax, Dov F. (Editor), et al.   **QH353.S29 2005**
Species Invasions: Insights into Ecology, Evolution, and
Biogeography. John J. Stachowicz & Steven D. Gaines
(Editors). Trade Paper. Sinauer Associates, Inc. Sunderland, MA.
2005. 380p. ISBN:0-87893-811-7, ISBN13: 978-0-87893-811-7.
Dewey:577/.18. LCCN:2005-013019.
                              Audience: **u,f.**

Scodari, Paul F.   **QH76.S395 1997**
Measuring the Benefits of Federal Wetland Programs. Trade
Cloth. Environmental Law Institute. Washington, DC. 1997.

104p. ISBN:0-911937-71-4, ISBN13: 978-0-911937-71-8.
Dewey:333.91/8/0973. LCCN:97-133033.
                              Audience: **l,u,f.**

Seitz, A. & Loeschcke, V.   **QH76.S64 1991**
  (Editors)
Species Conservation: A Population-Biological Approach. Trade
Cloth. Birkhauser Boston. Cambridge, MA. 1991. vii, 281p.
Advances in Life Sciences Ser. ISBN:0-8176-2493-7, ISBN13:
978-0-8176-2493-4. Dewey:574.5/24. LCCN:91-019264.
                              Audience: **u,f.**

Shigesada, Nanako &   **QH353.S54 1997**
  Kawasaki, Kohkichi
Biological Invasions: Theory and Practice. Trade Paper. Oxford
University Press, Inc. New York, NY. 1997. 218p. Oxford Series
in Ecology and Evolution ISBN:0-19-854851-6, ISBN13:
978-0-19-854851-5. Dewey:574.5/247. LCCN:96-034591.
                      Audience: **u,f.** *Choice, 1998.*

Stearns, Beverly P. &   **QH78.S734 1999**
  Stearns, Stephen C.
Watching, from the Edge of Extinction. Cloth over Boards. Yale
University Press. Cumberland, RI. 1999. 288p.
ISBN:0-300-07606-1, ISBN13: 978-0-300-07606-6.
Dewey:578.68. LCCN:98-034087.
                              Audience: **g,l,u.**

Sweden.; Statens   **QH84.1**
  naturvårdsverk
Boreal Ecosystems and Landscapes: Structures, Processes and
Conservation of Biodiversity. Hansson, Lennart (Editor).
Malden, MA : Published and distributed by MUNKSGAARD
International Publishers, Copenhagen, Denmark. 1997.
Ecological bulletins,; no. 46 ISBN:87-16-15236-0, ISBN13:
978-87-16-15236-7.
                              Audience: **u,f.**

Tellman, Barbara (Editor)   **QH353.I584 2002**
Invasive Exotic Species in the Sonoran Region. Trade Cloth.
University of Arizona Press. Tucson, AZ. 2002. 460p.
Arizona-Sonora Desert Museum Studies in Natural History
ISBN:0-8165-2178-6, ISBN13: 978-0-8165-2178-4.
Dewey:577/.18. LCCN:2001-005992.
                              Audience: **l,u,f.**

Tobin, Richard   **QH76.T63 1990**
The Expendable Future: U. S. Politics and the Protection of
Biological Diversity. Cloth Text. Duke University Press.
Durham, NC. 1990. 304p. ISBN:0-8223-1053-8, ISBN13:
978-0-8223-1053-2. Dewey:333.95. LCCN:90-002867.
                      Audience: **g,u,f.** *Choice, 1991.*

Ulfstrand, Staffan   **QH194.U43 2002**
Savannah Lives: Animal Life and the Human Evolution of
Africa. Ed. 1. Trade Cloth. Oxford University Press, Inc. New
York, NY. 2003. 330p. ISBN:0-19-850925-1, ISBN13:
978-0-19-850925-7. Dewey:577.4/8/096. LCCN:2003-268550.
                              Audience: **g,l.**

United States. Congress.   **QH76**
  House. Committee on Natural Resources
Ecosystem Management: Sustaining the Nation's Natural
Resources Trust : Majority Staff Report of the Committee on
Natural Resources of the U.S. House of Representatives, One
Hundred Third Congress, Second Session. U.S. G.P.O. : For sale

---

by the U.S. G.P.O., Supt. of Docs., Congressional Sales Office, Washington. 1994. ISBN:0-16-044381-4, ISBN13: 978-0-16-044381-7.

Audience: **g,l,u,f.**

United States;   **QH352**
Environmental Protection Agency; Office of Policy, Planning, and Evaluation
Biological Populations as Indicators of Environmental Change, Vol. 1. Office of Policy, Planning, and Evaluation, U.S. Environmental Protection Agency : For sale by the U.S. G.P.O., Supt. of Docs.,Washington, DC 1992. ISBN:0-16-042615-4, ISBN13: 978-0-16-042615-5.

Audience: **g,l,u,f.**

Van Driesche, Jason & Van   **QH353.V36 2000**
Driesche, Roy G.
Nature Out of Place: Biological Invasions in the Global Age. Trade Cloth. Island Press. Washington, DC. 2000. 352p. ISBN:1-55963-757-9, ISBN13: 978-1-55963-757-2. Dewey:577.1/8. LCCN:00-010477.

Audience: **g,l,u.** *Choice, 2001.*

Weidensaul, Scott   **QH102.W45 2005**
Return to Wild America: A Yearlong Search for the Continent's Natural Soul. Cloth over Boards. Farrar, Straus & Giroux. New York, NY. 2005. 416p. ISBN:0-86547-688-8, ISBN13: 978-0-86547-688-2. Dewey:578/.097. LCCN:2005-047720.

Audience: **g,l.**

Whitmore, T. C. (Timothy   **QH78**
Charles) (Editor)
Tropical Deforestation and Species Extinction. Sayer, Jeffrey (Editor); International Union for Conservation of Nature and Natural Resources; General Assembly; (18th :; 1990 :; Perth, W.A.); International Union for Conservation of Nature and Natural Resources; Commission on Ecology; IUCN Forest Conservation Programme. Chapman & Hall, London ; New York. 1992. ISBN:0-412-45520-X, ISBN13: 978-0-412-45520-9.

Audience: **l,u,f.**

Williamson, Mark   **QH353.W54 1996**
Biological Invasions. Trade Cloth. Springer. New York, NY. 1996. 256p. ISBN:0-412-31170-4, ISBN13: 978-0-412-31170-3. Dewey:577/.18. LCCN:96-084897.

Audience: **u,f.**

World Wildlife Fund Staff   **QH76.S665**
Statewide Wetlands Strategies: A Guide to Protecting and Managing the Resource. Trade Cloth. Island Press. Washington, DC. 1992. 285p. ISBN:1-55963-205-4, ISBN13: 978-1-55963-205-8. Dewey:353.9/382326. LCCN:92-003563.

Audience: **g,l,u,f.**

Integrative Biology > General Ecology > Conservation > Plants

Devine, Robert S.   **QH353.D48 1998**
Alien Invasion: America's Battle with Non-Native Animals and Plants. Trade Cloth. National Geographic Society. Washington, DC. 1998. 277p. ISBN:0-7922-7372-9, ISBN13: 978-0-7922-7372-1. Dewey:577.18. LCCN:98-009730.

Audience: **l,u,f.**

Little, Colin   **QH371 .L58 1990**
The Terrestrial Invasion: An Ecophysiological Approach to the Origins of Land Animals. Trade Cloth. Cambridge University Press. New York, NY. 1990. 314p. Cambridge Studies in Ecology ISBN:0-521-33447-0, ISBN13: 978-0-521-33447-1. Dewey:560/.45. LCCN:89-017471.

Audience: **u,f.** *Choice, 1991.*

May, Elizabeth   **QH77.C2**
Paradise Won. Trade Cloth. McClelland & Stewart/Tundra Books. Plattsburgh, NY. 1990. ISBN:0-7710-5772-5, ISBN13: 978-0-7710-5772-4. LCCN:90-176798.

Audience: **l,u,f.**

Integrative Biology > General Ecology > Environmental Ecology

Agren, Gvran I. & Bosatta,   **QH344 .A35 1998**
Ernesto
Theoretical Ecosystem Ecology: Understanding Nutrient Cycles. Trade Cloth. Cambridge University Press. New York, NY. 1996. 250p. ISBN:0-521-58022-6, ISBN13: 978-0-521-58022-9. Dewey:574.5/222. LCCN:96-018908.

Audience: **u,f.**

Akcakaya, H. Resit, et al.   **QH352**
Applied Population Ecology Using RAMAS Ecolab: Principles and Computer Exercises Using RAMAS EcoLab 2. 0. Ed. 2. Mark A. Burgman & Lev R. Ginzburg (Authors). Paper Text, CD-ROM. Sinauer Associates, Inc. Sunderland, MA. 1999. 285p. ISBN:0-87893-028-0, ISBN13: 978-0-87893-028-9. Dewey:577.8/8/015118.

Audience: **u,f.**

Alexander, Brian   **QH86.A58 1995**
Green Cathedrals: A Wayward Traveler in the Rainforest. Cloth over Boards. Globe Pequot Press, The. Guilford, CT. 1995. 220p. ISBN:1-55821-399-6, ISBN13: 978-1-55821-399-9. Dewey:304.2. LCCN:95-023739.

Audience: **l,u,f.**

Almekinder, Connie & De   **SB123.3**
Boef, Walter
Encouraging Diversity: The Conversation and Development of Plant Genetic Resources. Trade Paper. Intermediate Technology Publications (ITDG). Rugby, 2000. 368p. ISBN:1-85339-510-2, ISBN13: 978-1-85339-510-9. Dewey:333.9/534/16.

Audience: **l,u,f.**

Andersen, Alan N. (Editor),   **QH197.F5624 2003**
et al.
Fire in Tropical Savannas: The Kapalga Experiment. Garry D. Cook & Richard J. Williams (Editors). Trade Cloth. Springer. New York, NY. 2003. XIII, 195p. Ecological Studies, Vol. 169 ISBN:0-387-00291-X, ISBN13: 978-0-387-00291-0. Dewey:577.2. LCCN:2002-044505.

Audience: **u,f.**

Baskin, Yvonne   **QH353.B28 2003**
A Plague of Rats and Rubbervines: The Growing Threat of Species Invasions. Trade Paper. Island Press. Washington, DC. 2003. 330p. ISBN:1-55963-051-5, ISBN13: 978-1-55963-051-1. Dewey:577/.18. LCCN:2002-004029.

Audience: **l,u,f.** *Choice, 2003.*

Begon, Michael, et al. **QH352.B43 1996**
Population Ecology: A Unified Study of Animals and Plants. Ed.
3. Martin Mortimer & D. J. Thompson (Authors). Trade Paper.
Blackwell Publishing, Inc. Malden, MA. 1996. 256p.
ISBN:0-632-03478-5, ISBN13: 978-0-632-03478-9.
Dewey:574.5/248. LCCN:95-023676.

Audience: **l,u,f.**

Benman, B. E. & Persson, **QH352.S59 1988**
L. (Editors)
Size-Structured Populations: Ecology and Evolution. Cloth Text.
Springer. New York, NY. 1989. 284p. ISBN:0-387-50188-6,
ISBN13: 978-0-387-50188-8. Dewey:574.5/248.
LCCN:88-026561.

Audience: **u,f.**

Beran, Max A. **QH344.C39 1995**
Carbon Sequestration in the Biosphere: Processes and Prospects.
Cloth Text. Springer. New York, NY. 1995. 320p. NATO ASI
Ser., Vol. 33:Global Environmental Change
ISBN:3-540-60190-2, ISBN13: 978-3-540-60190-6.
Dewey:574.5/222. LCCN:95-031118.

Audience: **u,f.**

Bernstein, Ruth **QH352.B458 2003**
Population Ecology: An Introduction to Computer Simulations.
Trade Paper. John Wiley & Sons, Inc. Hoboken, NJ. 2003. 170p.
ISBN:0-470-85148-1, ISBN13: 978-0-470-85148-7.
Dewey:577.8/8. LCCN:2002-155483.

Audience: **u,f.**

Berryman, Alan A. **QH352**
Principles of Population Dynamics and Their Application. UK-B
Format Paperback. Nelson Thornes Ltd. Cheltenham, 2000.
256p. ISBN:0-7487-4015-5, ISBN13: 978-0-7487-4015-4.
Dewey:577.88.

Audience: **u,f.**

Borlak, Jürgen (Editor) **RB155**
Handbook of Toxicogenomics: Strategies and Applications.
Trade Cloth. John Wiley & Sons, Inc. Hoboken, NJ. 2005. 705p.
ISBN:3-527-30342-1, ISBN13: 978-3-527-30342-7.
Dewey:616.042.

Audience: **u,f.**

Butcher, Samuel S. (Editor), **QH344.G593 1992**
et al.
Global Biogeochemical Cycles. Gordon H. Orians, Robert J.
Charlson & Gordon V. Wolfe (Editors). Trade Cloth. Elsevier
Science & Technology Books. Saint Louis, MO. 1992. 379p.
International Geophysics Ser., Vol. 50 ISBN:0-12-147685-5,
ISBN13: 978-0-12-147685-4. Dewey:574.5/222.
LCCN:93-159050.

Audience: **u,f.** *Choice, 1993.*

Cappuccino, Naomi & Price, **QH352.P626 1995**
Peter W. (Editors)
Population Dynamics: New Approaches and Synthesis. Trade
Cloth. Elsevier Science & Technology Books. Saint Louis, MO.
1995. 429p. ISBN:0-12-159270-7, ISBN13: 978-0-12-159270-7.
Dewey:574.5/248. LCCN:95-014616.

Audience: **u,f.**

Cartron, Jean-Luc E., et al. **QH107.B525 2004**
Biodiversity, Ecosystems, and Conservation in Northern Mexico.
Gerardo Ceballos & Richard Stephen Felger (Authors). Trade
Cloth. Oxford University Press, Inc. New York, NY. 2005. 513p.

ISBN:0-19-515672-2, ISBN13: 978-0-19-515672-0.
Dewey:333.95/16/0972. LCCN:2004-012002.

Audience: **l,u,f.**

Chela Flores, Julian **QH327.C54 2001**
The New Science of Astrobiology: From Genesis of the Living
Cell to Evolution of Intelligent Behavior in the Universe. Trade
Cloth. Springer. New York, NY. 2001. 288p. Cellular Origin and
Life in Extreme Habitats and Astrobiology Ser., Vol. 5
ISBN:0-7923-7125-9, ISBN13: 978-0-7923-7125-0.
Dewey:576.8/39. LCCN:2001-038285.

Audience: **u,f.** *Choice, 2002.*

Clancy, Paul, et al. **QH325**
Looking for Life, Searching the Solar System. André Brack &
Gerda Horneck (Authors). Cloth Text. Cambridge University
Press. New York, NY. 2005. 364p. ISBN:0-521-82450-8,
ISBN13: 978-0-521-82450-7. Dewey:576.839.
LCCN:2006-271630.

Audience: **u,f.**

Conway Morris, Simon **QH360.5.C66 2004**
Life's Solution: Inevitable Humans in a Lonely Universe. Trade
Paper. Cambridge University Press. New York, NY. 2004. 486p.
ISBN:0-521-60325-0, ISBN13: 978-0-521-60325-6.
Dewey:576.8/01.

Audience: **u,f.** *Choice, 2004.*

Crawford, R. M. **QH84.1.D57 1997**
Disturbance and Recovery in Arctic Lands: An Ecological
Perspective: Proceedings of the NATO Advanced Research
Workshop on Disturbance and Recovery of Arctic Terrestrial
Ecosystems, Rovaniemi, Finland, 24-30 Sept. 1995. Trade Cloth.
Springer London, Ltd. Guildford, 1997. 632p. NATO Advanced
Science Institutes Ser., Vol. 2:Environment ISBN:0-7923-4418-9,
ISBN13: 978-0-7923-4418-6. Dewey:577.27/0911/3.
LCCN:96-051038.

Audience: **u,f.**

Cushing, J. M. **QH352.C87 1998**
An Introduction to Structured Population Dynamics. Trade
Cloth. Society for Industrial & Applied Mathematics.
Philadelphia, PA. 1998. xiv + 193p. CBMS-NSF Regional
Conference Series in Applied Mathematics, No. CB71
ISBN:0-89871-417-6, ISBN13: 978-0-89871-417-3.
Dewey:577.8/8/015118. LCCN:98-019033.

Audience: **u,f.**

Darling, David **QH327.D37 2001**
Life Everywhere: The New Science of Astrobiology. Trade
Cloth. Basic Books. New York, NY. 2001. 224p.
ISBN:0-465-01563-8, ISBN13: 978-0-465-01563-4.
Dewey:576.8/39. LCCN:2001-025147.

Audience: **u,f.** *Choice, 2001.*

DeAngelis, D. L. (Donald **QH352**
Lee) (Editor)
Individual-based models and approaches in ecology:
populations, communities, and ecosystems. Gross, Louis J.
(Editor). New York : Chapman & Hall. 1992.
ISBN:0-412-03161-2, ISBN13: 978-0-412-03161-8.

Audience: **u,f.**

Dick, Steven J. & Strick, **QH325.D53 2004**
James E.
The Living Universe: NASA and the Development of
Astrobiology. Trade Paper. Rutgers University Press. Piscataway,

NJ. 2005. 328p. ISBN:0-8135-3733-9, ISBN13: 978-0-8135-3733-7. Dewey:576.8/39. LCCN:2004-004037.

Audience: **u,f.** *Choice, 2005.*

Feder, Martin E. &   **QL669.2.E58 1992**
Burggren, Warren W. (Editors)
Environmental Physiology of the Amphibians. Trade Cloth. University of Chicago Press. Chicago, IL. 1992. 472p. ISBN:0-226-23943-8, ISBN13: 978-0-226-23943-9. Dewey:597.6/041. LCCN:91-030944.

Audience: **l,u.** *Choice, 1993.*

Floyd, R. B., et al.   **QH352.F76 1996**
Frontiers of Population Ecology. A. W. Sheppard & P. J. De Barro (Authors). Trade Cloth. CSIRO Publishing. Collingwood, VIC. 1996. 450p. ISBN:0-643-05781-1, ISBN13: 978-0-643-05781-4. Dewey:577.8/8. LCCN:97-121379.

Audience: **u,f.**

Getz, Wayne M. & Haight,   **QH352.G47 1989**
Robert G.
Population Harvesting: Demographic Models of Fish, Forest, and Animal Resources. Trade Paper. Princeton University Press. Princeton, NJ. 1989. 408p. Monographs in Population Biology Ser. ISBN:0-691-08516-1, ISBN13: 978-0-691-08516-6. Dewey:574.5/248. LCCN:88-019950.

Audience: **u,f.**

Gilpin, Michael E. &   **QL752**
Hanski, Ilkka A. (Editors)
Metapopulation Dynamics: Empirical and Theoretical Investigations. Trade Paper. Elsevier Science & Technology Books. Saint Louis, MO. 1991. 336p. ISBN:0-12-284120-4, ISBN13: 978-0-12-284120-0. Dewey:591.5248.

Audience: **u,f.**

Ginzburg, Lev R. &   **QH352.G55 2003**
Colyvan, Mark
Ecological Orbits: How Planets Move and Populations Grow. Trade Cloth. Oxford University Press, Inc. New York, NY. 2004. 184p. ISBN:0-19-516816-X, ISBN13: 978-0-19-516816-7. Dewey:577.8/8. LCCN:2003-048690.

Audience: **u,f.** *Choice, 2005.*

Gutierrez, Andrew Paul   **QH352.G87 1996**
Applied Population Ecology: A Supply-Demand Approach. C. K. Ellis (Contribution by). Trade Cloth. John Wiley & Sons, Inc. Hoboken, NJ. 1996. 320p. ISBN:0-471-13586-0, ISBN13: 978-0-471-13586-9. Dewey:591.5/2/48. LCCN:95-043654.

Audience: **u,f.** *Choice, 1996.*

Haccou, Patsy, et al.   **QA274.76.H33 2005**
Branching Processes: Variation, Growth, and Extinction of Populations. Peter Jagers & Vladimir A. Vatutin (Authors), Ulf Dieckmann, Richard Law & Hans Metz (Contribution by). Trade Cloth. Cambridge University Press. New York, NY. 2005. 330p. Cambridge Studies in Adaptive Dynamics Ser., Vol. 5 ISBN:0-521-83220-9, ISBN13: 978-0-521-83220-5. Dewey:577.8801519234. LCCN:2006-531079.

Audience: **u,f.**

Hanski, Ilkka A.   **QH352.H358 1999**
Metapopulation Ecology. Trade Paper. Oxford University Press, Inc. New York, NY. 1999. 324p. Oxford Series in Ecology and Evolution ISBN:0-19-854065-5, ISBN13: 978-0-19-854065-6. Dewey:577.8/8. LCCN:98-031723.

Audience: **u,f.**

Hanski, Ilkka A. &   **QH352**
Gaggiotti, Oscar E. (Editors)
Ecology, Genetics and Evolution of Metapopulations. Paper Text. Elsevier Science & Technology Books. Saint Louis, MO. 2004. 696p. ISBN:0-12-323448-4, ISBN13: 978-0-12-323448-3. Dewey:577.8/8. LCCN:2004-044073.

Audience: **u,f.**

Hanski, Ilkka A. & Gilpin,   **QH352**
Michael E. (Editors)
Metapopulation Biology: Ecology, Genetics, and Evolution. Trade Paper. Elsevier Science & Technology Books. Saint Louis, MO. 1997. 512p. ISBN:0-12-323446-8, ISBN13: 978-0-12-323446-9. Dewey:577.8/8. LCCN:96-028242.

Audience: **u,f.** *Choice, 1997.*

Harrison, A. F. (Editor)   **QH344**
Nutrient Cycling in Terrestrial Ecosystems: Field Methods, Application, and Interpretation. Ineson, P. (Philip) (Editor); Heal, O. W. (Editor). Elsevier Applied Science, London ; New York. 1990. ISBN:1-85166-388-6, ISBN13: 978-1-85166-388-0.

Audience: **u,f.**

Hengeveld, R.   **QH353.H46 1989**
The Dynamics of Biological Invasions. Cloth Text. Chapman & Hall. New York, NY. 1990. 176p. ISBN:0-412-31470-3, ISBN13: 978-0-412-31470-4. Dewey:574.5. LCCN:90-176043.

Audience: **u,f.** *Choice, 1989.*

Huber, Bernhard A.   **QH194.I497 2004**
(Editor), et al.
African Biodiversity: Molecules, Organisms, Ecosystems. Bradley J. Sinclair & Karl-Heinz Lampe (Editors). Trade Cloth. Springer. New York, NY. 2001. XX, 443p. ISBN:0-387-24315-1, ISBN13: 978-0-387-24315-3. Dewey:577.096. LCCN:2005-299985.

Audience: **u,f.**

Johnson, David W., et al.   **HC79.E5**
Ecological Stewardship: A Common Reference for Ecosystem Management. Sexton, Robert C. Szaro & Malk (Authors). CD-ROM, Trade Cloth. Elsevier Science & Technology Books. Saint Louis, MO. 1999. 1788p. ISBN:0-08-043206-9, ISBN13: 978-0-08-043206-9. Dewey:333.7.

Audience: **g,l,u,f.**

Kingsland, Sharon E.   **QH352.K56 1985**
Modeling Nature: Episodes in the History of Population Ecology. Trade Cloth. University of Chicago Press. Chicago, IL. 1995. x, 268p. Science and Its Conceptual Foundations Ser. ISBN:0-226-43726-4, ISBN13: 978-0-226-43726-2. Dewey:574.5/248. LCCN:85-001414.

Audience: **l,u.** *Choice, 1986.*

Lomnicki, Adam   **QH352.L66 1988**
Population Ecology of Individuals. Robert M. May (Editor). Trade Paper. Princeton University Press. Princeton, NJ. 1988. 240p. Monographs in Population Biology, No. 25 ISBN:0-691-08462-9, ISBN13: 978-0-691-08462-6. Dewey:591.52/48. LCCN:87-003439.

Audience: **u,f.**

Looijen, Rick C.   **QH331.L64 1999**
Holism and Reductionism in Biology and Ecology: The Mutual Dependence of Higher and Lower Level Research Programmes.

Trade Cloth. Springer. New York, NY. 1999. 372p. Episteme Ser. ISBN:0-7923-6076-1, ISBN13: 978-0-7923-6076-6. Dewey:570/.1. LCCN:99-052308.

Audience: **u,f.**

Low, Tim   **QH353.L68 2002**
Feral Future: The Untold Story of Australia's Exotic Invaders. Ed. 2. Trade Cloth. University of Chicago Press. Chicago, IL. 2002. 425p. ISBN:0-226-49419-5, ISBN13: 978-0-226-49419-7. Dewey:577/.18. LCCN:2002-067534.

Audience: **l,u,f.** *Choice, 2003.*

Margulis, Lynn &   **QH366.2.E59 1992**
  Olendzenski, Lorraine (Editors)
Environmental Evolution: Effects of the Origin and Evolution of Life on Planet Earth. Trade Cloth. MIT Press. Cambridge, MA. 1992. 400p. ISBN:0-262-13273-7, ISBN13: 978-0-262-13273-2. Dewey:576.8. LCCN:91-017981.

Audience: **u,f.** *Choice, 1992.*

McShea, William J. &   **QH102.O24 2003**
  Healy, William M.
Oak Forest Ecosystems: Ecology and Management for Wildlife. Trade Paper. Johns Hopkins University Press. Baltimore, MD. 2003. 432p. ISBN:0-8018-7747-4, ISBN13: 978-0-8018-7747-6. Dewey:577.3/0973.

Audience: **l,u,f.** *Choice, 2002.*

Millington, Andrew C.   **QH84.G47 2001**
  (Editor), et al.
GIS and Remote Sensing Applications in Biogeography and Ecology. Stephen J. Walsh & Patrick E. Osborne (Editors). Trade Cloth. Springer. New York, NY. 2001. 344p. The Kluwer International Series in Engineering and Computer Science, Vol. 626 ISBN:0-7923-7454-1, ISBN13: 978-0-7923-7454-1. Dewey:578/.09. LCCN:2001-038306.

Audience: **u,f.**

Okuda, T. (Editor), et al.   **QH185.P37 2003**
Pasoh. N. Manokaran, Y. Matsumoto & K. Niiyama (Editors). Trade Cloth. Springer. New York, NY. 2003. XVIII, 628p. ISBN:4-431-00660-5, ISBN13: 978-4-431-00660-2. Dewey:578.095951. LCCN:2004-296280.

Audience: **g,l,u,f.**

Petrovskii, Sergei V. & Li,   **QH353**
  Bai-Lian
Exactly Solvable Models of Biological Invasion. Chapman & Hall/CRC, Boca Raton. 2006. ISBN:1-58488-521-1, ISBN13: 978-1-58488-521-4.

Audience: **l,u.**

Pickett, Steward T. (Editor)   **QH75**
The Ecological Basis of Conservation: Heterogeneity, Ecosystems, and Biodiversity. Cary Conference ; (6th :; 1995 :; Institute of Ecosystem Studies). Chapman & Hall, New York :. 1997. ISBN:0-412-09851-2, ISBN13: 978-0-412-09851-2.

Audience: **u,f.**

Priscu, John C. (Editor)   **QH84.2.E276 1998**
Ecosystem Dynamics in a Polar Desert: The McMurdo Dry Valleys, Antarctica. Trade Cloth. American Geophysical Union. Washington, DC. 1998. Antarctic Research Ser., Vol. 72 ISBN:0-87590-899-3, ISBN13: 978-0-87590-899-1. Dewey:577.54/098/9. LCCN:97-046526.

Audience: **u,f.**

Ricketts, Taylor H., et al.   **QH77.N56T47 1999**
Terrestrial Ecoregions of North America: A Conservation Assessment. Eric Dinerstein, David M. Olson, Colby J. Loucks, William Eichbaum, Dominick Dellassala, Kevin Kavanaugh, Prashant Hedao, Patrick Hurley, Robin Abell, Karen L. Carney & Steven Walters (Authors). Trade Paper. Island Press. Washington, DC. 1999. 508p. ISBN:1-55963-722-6, ISBN13: 978-1-55963-722-0. Dewey:333.95/16/097. LCCN:99-018912.

Audience: **g,l,u,f.** *Choice, 2000.*

Riseng, Karen & Jensen,   **QH130 B55 2003**
  Montambault
A Biological Assessment of the Aquatic Ecosystems of the Caura River Basin, Bolivar State, Venezuela: RAP Bulletin of Biological Assessment 28. Barry Chernoff (Editor), Antonio Machado-Allison (Editor, Translator), Ana Liz Flores (Translator), Mark Denil (Illustrator), Montambault Jensen (Photographer), Kim Meek (Designed by). Trade Paper. Conservation International. Washington, DC. 2003. 284p. Conservation International Rapid Assessment Program Ser. ISBN:1-881173-69-0, ISBN13: 978-1-881173-69-4. Dewey:577. LCCN:2002-116698.

Audience: **u,f.**

Robichaux, Robert H. &   **QH107.T76 2000**
  Yetman, David A.
The Tropical Deciduous Forest of Alamos: Biodiversity of a Threatened Ecosystem in Mexico. Trade Cloth. University of Arizona Press. Tucson, AZ. 2000. 259p. ISBN:0-8165-1922-6, ISBN13: 978-0-8165-1922-4. Dewey:333.95/11/097217. LCCN:99-050867.

Audience: **u,f.**

Roubik, David W. (Editor),   **QH185.E29 2005**
  et al.
Pollination Ecology and the Rain Forest: Sarawak Studies. Shoko Sakai & Abdul Hamid Abg (Editors). Trade Cloth. Springer. New York, NY. 2005. XVIII, 318p. Ecological Studies, Vol. 174 ISBN:0-387-21309-0, ISBN13: 978-0-387-21309-5. Dewey:577.34/09595/4. LCCN:2004-052210.

Audience: **u,f.**

Schultz, Jnrgen   **QH84**
The Ecozones of the World: The Ecological Divisions of the Geosphere. Ed. 2. Trade Cloth. Springer. New York, NY. 2005. XII, 252p. ISBN:3-540-20014-2, ISBN13: 978-3-540-20014-7. Dewey:577.8/2. LCCN:2005-924522.

Audience: **u,f.**

Schulze, Ernst-Detlef   **QH344.C35 2000**
  (Editor)
Carbon and Nitrogen Cycling in European Forest Ecosystems. Mixed Media. Springer. New York, NY. 2000. xx, 500p. Ecological Studies, Vol. 142 ISBN:3-540-67025-4, ISBN13: 978-3-540-67025-4. Dewey:577.3/144/094. LCCN:00-030754.

Audience: **u,f.**

Sener, Bilge (Editor)   **QH345.B528 2003**
Biodiversity: Biomolecular Aspects of Biodiversity and Innovative Utilization. Trade Cloth. Springer. New York, NY. 2003. 426p. ISBN:0-306-47477-8, ISBN13: 978-0-306-47477-4. Dewey:577. LCCN:2002-037011.

Audience: **u,f.**

Sterner, Robert Warner &   **QH345.S74 2002**
  Elser, James J.
Ecological Stoichiometry: The Biology of Elements from Molecules to the Biosphere. Peter M. Vitousek (Foreword by).

Trade Cloth. Princeton University Press. Princeton, NJ. 2002. 440p. ISBN:0-691-07490-9, ISBN13: 978-0-691-07490-0. Dewey:572. LCCN:2002-072262.

Audience: **l,u,f.**

Stonehouse, B.   **QH84.1.S78 1989**
Polar Ecology. Cloth Text. Chapman & Hall. New York, NY. 1988. viii, 222p. Tertiary Level Biology Ser. ISBN:0-412-01701-6, ISBN13: 978-0-412-01701-8. Dewey:574.5/2621. LCCN:89-015809.

Audience: **g,l.**

Turchin, Peter   **QH352.T83 2003**
Complex Population Dynamics: A Theoretical/Empirical Synthesis. Trade Cloth. Princeton University Press. Princeton, NJ. 2003. 456p. Monographs in Population Biology, Vol. 35 ISBN:0-691-09020-3, ISBN13: 978-0-691-09020-7. Dewey:577.8/8. LCCN:2002-022721.

Audience: **u,f.**

United States. Congress.   **QH76**
  House. Committee on Natural Resources
Ecosystem Management: Sustaining the Nation's Natural Resources Trust : Majority Staff Report of the Committee on Natural Resources of the U.S. House of Representatives, One Hundred Third Congress, Second Session. U.S. G.P.O. : For sale by the U.S. G.P.O., Supt. of Docs., Congressional Sales Office, Washington. 1994. ISBN:0-16-044381-4, ISBN13: 978-0-16-044381-7.

Audience: **g,l,u,f.**

Weber, William (Editor),   **QH194.A38 2001**
  et al.
African Rain Forest Ecology and Conservation: An Interdisciplinary Perspective. Lisa Naughton-Treves, Amy Vedder & Lee White (Editors). Cloth over Boards. Yale University Press. Cumberland, RI. 2001. 608p. ISBN:0-300-08433-1, ISBN13: 978-0-300-08433-7. Dewey:577.34/096. LCCN:00-043678.

Audience: **u,f.** *Choice, 2001.*

Willink, Philip W. (Editor),   **QH117.B485 2000**
  et al.
A Biological Assessment of the Aquatic Ecosystems of the Pantanal, Mato Grosso do Sul, Brasil. Barry Chernoff, Leeanne E. Alonso, Jensen R. Montambault & Reinaldo Lourival (Editors). Trade Paper. Conservation International. Washington, DC. 2000. 306p. Conservation International Rapid Assessment Program Ser. ISBN:1-881173-35-6, ISBN13: 978-1-881173-35-9. Dewey:577.63098171. LCCN:00-108756.

Audience: **u,f.**

Yaffee, Steven L., et al.   **QH76.E336 1996**
Ecosystem Management in the United States: An Assessment of Current Experience. Ali F. Phillips, Irene C. Frentz & Paul W. Hardy (Authors). Trade Paper. Island Press. Washington, DC. 1996. 368p. ISBN:1-55963-502-9, ISBN13: 978-1-55963-502-8. Dewey:333.7/0973. LCCN:96-021825.

Audience: **g,l,u,f.** *Choice, 1997.*

Integrative Biology > General Ecology > Ecological Change

Baskin, Yvonne   **QH353.B28 2003**
A Plague of Rats and Rubbervines: The Growing Threat of Species Invasions. Trade Paper. Island Press. Washington, DC. 2003. 330p. ISBN:1-55963-051-5, ISBN13: 978-1-55963-051-1. Dewey:577/.18. LCCN:2002-004029.

Audience: **l,u,f.** *Choice, 2003.*

Beran, Max A.   **QH344.C39 1995**
Carbon Sequestration in the Biosphere: Processes and Prospects. Cloth Text. Springer. New York, NY. 1995. 320p. NATO ASI Ser., Vol. 33:Global Environmental Change ISBN:3-540-60190-2, ISBN13: 978-3-540-60190-6. Dewey:574.5/222. LCCN:95-031118.

Audience: **u,f.**

Bradshaw, G. A. (Editor),   **QH101.H69 2002**
  et al.
How Landscapes Change: Human Disturbance and Ecosystem Fragmentation in the Americas. P. A. Marquet & Kathryn L. Ronnenberg (Editors). Trade Cloth. Springer. New York, NY. 2003. XXII, 361p. ISBN:3-540-43697-9, ISBN13: 978-3-540-43697-3. Dewey:304.2/8/097. LCCN:2002-030229.

Audience: **u,f.**

Burdick, Alan   **QH353.B87 2005**
Out of Eden: An Odyssey of Ecological Invasion. Cloth over Boards. Farrar, Straus & Giroux. New York, NY. 2005. 336p. ISBN:0-374-21973-7, ISBN13: 978-0-374-21973-4. Dewey:577. LCCN:2005-922517.

Audience: **l,u,f.**

Campbell, SueEllen   **QH105.C6C26 2003**
Even Mountains Vanish: Searching for Solace in an Age of Extinction. Trade Paper. University of Utah Press. Salt Lake City, UT. 2003. 150p. ISBN:0-87480-771-9, ISBN13: 978-0-87480-771-4. Dewey:508.7. LCCN:2003-010945.

Audience: **l,u,f.**

Cox, George W.   **QH353.C69 2004**
Alien Species and Evolution: The Evolutionary Ecology of Exotic Plants, Animals, Microbes, and Interacting Native Species. Trade Cloth. Island Press. Washington, DC. 2004. 400p. ISBN:1-55963-008-6, ISBN13: 978-1-55963-008-5. Dewey:578.6/2. LCCN:2003-027299.

Audience: **u,f.** *Choice, 2005.*

Drake, J. A. & Mooney,   **QH353.B56 1989**
  Harold A.
Biological Invasions: A Global Perspective. Trade Cloth. John Wiley & Sons, Inc. Hoboken, NJ. 1989. 550p. Scientific Committee on Problems of the Environment Ser. ISBN:0-471-92085-1, ISBN13: 978-0-471-92085-4. Dewey:574.5. LCCN:88-020765.

Audience: **u,f.**

Krasny, Marianne E.   **QH353.I5835 2002**
Invasion Ecology. Trade Paper. National Science Teachers Association. Arlington, VA. 2002. xi, 176p. Cornell Scientific Inquiry Ser. ISBN:0-87355-211-3, ISBN13: 978-0-87355-211-0. Dewey:577/.18. LCCN:2002-011620.

Audience: **l,u,f.**

Lal, Rattan   **QH101.G58 2000**
Global Climate Change and Tropical Ecosystems: Cold. Saddle
Stitched. Lewis Publishers. Boca Raton, FL. 1999. 456p.
Advances in Soil Science Ser. ISBN:1-56670-485-5, ISBN13:
978-1-56670-485-4. Dewey:577.5/7/0913. LCCN:99-047136.
                                                    Audience: **u,f.**

Leland, John   **QH353.L49 2005**
Aliens in the Backyard: Plant and Animal Imports into America.
Perfect, Paper over Boards, Dust Jacket. University of South
Carolina Press. Columbia, SC. 2005. 235p.
ISBN:1-57003-582-2, ISBN13: 978-1-57003-582-1.
Dewey:578.6/2. LCCN:2005-000544.
                               Audience: **l,u,f.** *Choice, 2006.*

Margulis, Lynn &   **QH366.2.E59 1992**
  Olendzenski, Lorraine (Editors)
Environmental Evolution: Effects of the Origin and Evolution of
Life on Planet Earth. Trade Cloth. MIT Press. Cambridge, MA.
1992. 400p. ISBN:0-262-13273-7, ISBN13: 978-0-262-13273-2.
Dewey:576.8. LCCN:91-017981.
                               Audience: **u,f.** *Choice, 1992.*

Minoura, K. (Editor)   **QH541.5.L3**
Lake Baikal: A Mirror in Time and Space for Understanding
Global Change Processes. Trade Cloth. Elsevier Science &
Technology Books. Saint Louis, MO. 2000. 348p.
ISBN:0-444-50434-6, ISBN13: 978-0-444-50434-0.
Dewey:577.6309575.
                                                    Audience: **u,f.**

Petrovskii, Sergei V. & Li,   **QH353**
  Bai-Lian
Exactly Solvable Models of Biological Invasion. Chapman &
Hall/CRC, Boca Raton. 2006. ISBN:1-58488-521-1, ISBN13:
978-1-58488-521-4.
                                                    Audience: **l,u.**

Pienitz , Reinhar (Editor),   **GB1603.2**
  et al.
Long-Term Environmental Change in Arctic and Antarctic
Lakes. Marianne S. V. Douglas & John P. Smol (Editors). Trade
Cloth. Springer. New York, NY. 2005. XXX, 562p.
Developments in Paleoenvironmental Research Ser.
ISBN:1-4020-2125-9, ISBN13: 978-1-4020-2125-1.
Dewey:333.9163091632.
                                                    Audience: **u,f.**

Priscu, John C. (Editor)   **QH84.2.E276 1998**
Ecosystem Dynamics in a Polar Desert: The McMurdo Dry
Valleys, Antarctica. Trade Cloth. American Geophysical Union.
Washington, DC. 1998. Antarctic Research Ser., Vol. 72
ISBN:0-87590-899-3, ISBN13: 978-0-87590-899-1.
Dewey:577.54/098/9. LCCN:97-046526.
                                                    Audience: **u,f.**

Tamm, C. O.   **QH344.T36 1990**
Nitrogen in Terrestrial Ecosystems: Questions of Productivity,
Vegetational Changes and Ecosystem Stability. Hermann
Remmert, William D. Billings, O. L. Lange, J. S. Olson &
Frank B. Golley (Editors). Cloth Text. Springer. New York, NY.
1991. 116p. Ecological Studies, Vol. 81 ISBN:0-387-51807-X,
ISBN13: 978-0-387-51807-7. Dewey:574.5/2642.
LCCN:90-010292.
                                                    Audience: **u,f.**

United States;   **QH352**
  Environmental Protection Agency; Office of Policy,
  Planning, and Evaluation
Biological Populations as Indicators of Environmental Change,
Vol. 1. Office of Policy, Planning, and Evaluation, U.S.
Environmental Protection Agency : For sale by the U.S. G.P.O.,
Supt. of Docs.,Washington, DC 1992. ISBN:0-16-042615-4,
ISBN13: 978-0-16-042615-5.
                                              Audience: **g,l,u,f.**

Integrative Biology > General Ecology > Population Ecology

Akcakaya, H. Resit, et al.   **QH352**
Applied Population Ecology Using RAMAS Ecolab: Principles
and Computer Exercises Using RAMAS EcoLab 2. 0. Ed. 2.
Mark A. Burgman & Lev R. Ginzburg (Authors). Paper Text,
CD-ROM. Sinauer Associates, Inc. Sunderland, MA. 1999.
285p. ISBN:0-87893-028-0, ISBN13: 978-0-87893-028-9.
Dewey:577.8/8/015118.
                                                    Audience: **u,f.**

Baskin, Yvonne   **QH353.B28 2003**
A Plague of Rats and Rubbervines: The Growing Threat of
Species Invasions. Trade Paper. Island Press. Washington, DC.
2003. 330p. ISBN:1-55963-051-5, ISBN13: 978-1-55963-051-1.
Dewey:577/.18. LCCN:2002-004029.
                               Audience: **l,u,f.** *Choice, 2003.*

Bazykin, Alexander   **QH352.B39 1998**
Nonlinear Dynamics of Interacting Populations. Cloth Text.
World Scientific Publishing Company, Inc. Hackensack, NJ.
1997. 193p. Neural Systems Ser. ISBN:981-02-1685-8, ISBN13:
978-981-02-1685-6. Dewey:577.8/8/0151. LCCN:98-011768.
                                                    Audience: **u,f.**

Begon, Michael, et al.   **QH352.B43 1996**
Population Ecology: A Unified Study of Animals and Plants. Ed.
3. Martin Mortimer & D. J. Thompson (Authors). Trade Paper.
Blackwell Publishing, Inc. Malden, MA. 1996. 256p.
ISBN:0-632-03478-5, ISBN13: 978-0-632-03478-9.
Dewey:574.5/248. LCCN:95-023676.
                                                    Audience: **l,u,f.**

Benman, B. E. & Persson,   **QH352.S59 1988**
  L. (Editors)
Size-Structured Populations: Ecology and Evolution. Cloth Text.
Springer. New York, NY. 1989. 284p. ISBN:0-387-50188-6,
ISBN13: 978-0-387-50188-8. Dewey:574.5/248.
LCCN:88-026561.
                                                    Audience: **u,f.**

Bernstein, Ruth   **QH352.B458 2003**
Population Ecology: An Introduction to Computer Simulations.
Trade Paper. John Wiley & Sons, Inc. Hoboken, NJ. 2003. 170p.
ISBN:0-470-85148-1, ISBN13: 978-0-470-85148-7.
Dewey:577.8/8. LCCN:2002-155483.
                                                    Audience: **u,f.**

Berryman, Alan A.   **QH352**
Principles of Population Dynamics and Their Application. UK-B
Format Paperback. Nelson Thornes Ltd. Cheltenham, 2000.
256p. ISBN:0-7487-4015-5, ISBN13: 978-0-7487-4015-4.
Dewey:577.88.
                                                    Audience: **u,f.**

Brauer, Fred & QH352.B73 2001
  Castillo-Chavez, Carlos
Mathematical Models in Population Biology and Epidemiology.
Trade Cloth. Springer. New York, NY. 2001. XXIII, 448p. Texts
in Applied Mathematics, Vol. 40 ISBN:0-387-98902-1, ISBN13:
978-0-387-98902-0. Dewey:577.8/8/015118. LCCN:00-045033.
Audience: **u,f.**

Buckland, S. T., et al. QL752.D57 1993
Distance Sampling: Estimating Abundance of Biological
Populations. K. P. Burnham, D. R. Anderson & J. L. Laake
(Authors). Trade Cloth. Chapman & Hall. New York, NY. 1993.
400p. ISBN:0-412-42660-9, ISBN13: 978-0-412-42660-5.
Dewey:591.5248. LCCN:92-039560.
Audience: **u,f.**

Buckland, S.T. (Editor), QH352
  et al.
Advanced Distance Sampling: Estimating Abundance of
Biological Populations. D.R. Anderson & K.P. Burnham
(Editors). Trade Cloth. Oxford University Press, Inc. New York,
NY. 2004. 434p. ISBN:0-19-850783-6, ISBN13:
978-0-19-850783-3. Dewey:591.7/88/0727. LCCN:2004-303414.
Audience: **u,f.**

Cappuccino, Naomi & Price, QH352.P626 1995
  Peter W. (Editors)
Population Dynamics: New Approaches and Synthesis. Trade
Cloth. Elsevier Science & Technology Books. Saint Louis, MO.
1995. 429p. ISBN:0-12-159270-7, ISBN13: 978-0-12-159270-7.
Dewey:574.5/248. LCCN:95-014616.
Audience: **u,f.**

Chesser, Ronald K. & QH352.P628 1996
  Smith, Michael H.
Population Dynamics in Ecological Space and Time. Olin E.
Rhodes Jr. (Editor). Trade Cloth. University of Chicago Press.
Chicago, IL. 1996. 396p. ISBN:0-226-71057-2, ISBN13:
978-0-226-71057-0. Dewey:574.5/248. LCCN:96-003246.
Audience: **u,f.** *Choice, 1996.*

Cushing, J. M. QH352.C87 1998
An Introduction to Structured Population Dynamics. Trade
Cloth. Society for Industrial & Applied Mathematics.
Philadelphia, PA. 1998. xiv + 193p. CBMS-NSF Regional
Conference Series in Applied Mathematics, No. CB71
ISBN:0-89871-417-6, ISBN13: 978-0-89871-417-3.
Dewey:577.8/8/015118. LCCN:98-019033.
Audience: **u,f.**

Ebert, Thomas A. QH352.E24 1999
Plant and Animal Populations: Methods in Demography. Trade
Cloth. Elsevier Science & Technology Books. Saint Louis, MO.
1998. 312p. ISBN:0-12-228740-1, ISBN13: 978-0-12-228740-4.
Dewey:577.8/8. LCCN:98-086238.
Audience: **u,f.**

Floyd, R. B., et al. QH352.F76 1996
Frontiers of Population Ecology. A. W. Sheppard & P. J. De
Barro (Authors). Trade Cloth. CSIRO Publishing. Collingwood,
VIC. 1996. 450p. ISBN:0-643-05781-1, ISBN13:
978-0-643-05781-4. Dewey:577.8/8. LCCN:97-121379.
Audience: **u,f.**

Getz, Wayne M. & Haight, QH352.G47 1989
  Robert G.
Population Harvesting: Demographic Models of Fish, Forest,
and Animal Resources. Trade Paper. Princeton University Press.

Princeton, NJ. 1989. 408p. Monographs in Population Biology
Ser. ISBN:0-691-08516-1, ISBN13: 978-0-691-08516-6.
Dewey:574.5/248. LCCN:88-019950.
Audience: **u,f.**

Gilpin, Michael E. & QL752
  Hanski, Ilkka A. (Editors)
Metapopulation Dynamics: Empirical and Theoretical
Investigations. Trade Paper. Elsevier Science & Technology
Books. Saint Louis, MO. 1991. 336p. ISBN:0-12-284120-4,
ISBN13: 978-0-12-284120-0. Dewey:591.5248.
Audience: **u,f.**

Ginzburg, Lev R. & QH352.G55 2003
  Colyvan, Mark
Ecological Orbits: How Planets Move and Populations Grow.
Trade Cloth. Oxford University Press, Inc. New York, NY. 2004.
184p. ISBN:0-19-516816-X, ISBN13: 978-0-19-516816-7.
Dewey:577.8/8. LCCN:2003-048690.
Audience: **u,f.** *Choice, 2005.*

Gutierrez, Andrew Paul QH352.G87 1996
Applied Population Ecology: A Supply-Demand Approach. C.
K. Ellis (Contribution by). Trade Cloth. John Wiley & Sons,
Inc. Hoboken, NJ. 1996. 320p. ISBN:0-471-13586-0, ISBN13:
978-0-471-13586-9. Dewey:591.5/2/48. LCCN:95-043654.
Audience: **u,f.** *Choice, 1996.*

Haccou, Patsy, et al. QA274.76.H33 2005
Branching Processes: Variation, Growth, and Extinction of
Populations. Peter Jagers & Vladimir A. Vatutin (Authors), Ulf
Dieckmann, Richard Law & Hans Metz (Contribution by). Trade
Cloth. Cambridge University Press. New York, NY. 2005. 330p.
Cambridge Studies in Adaptive Dynamics Ser., Vol. 5
ISBN:0-521-83220-9, ISBN13: 978-0-521-83220-5.
Dewey:577.8801519234. LCCN:2006-531079.
Audience: **u,f.**

Hanski, Ilkka A. QH352.H358 1999
Metapopulation Ecology. Trade Paper. Oxford University Press,
Inc. New York, NY. 1999. 324p. Oxford Series in Ecology and
Evolution ISBN:0-19-854065-5, ISBN13: 978-0-19-854065-6.
Dewey:577.8/8. LCCN:98-031723.
Audience: **u,f.**

Hanski, Ilkka A. & QH352
  Gaggiotti, Oscar E. (Editors)
Ecology, Genetics and Evolution of Metapopulations. Paper
Text. Elsevier Science & Technology Books. Saint Louis, MO.
2004. 696p. ISBN:0-12-323448-4, ISBN13: 978-0-12-323448-3.
Dewey:577.8/8. LCCN:2004-044073.
Audience: **u,f.**

Hanski, Ilkka A. & Gilpin, QH352
  Michael E. (Editors)
Metapopulation Biology: Ecology, Genetics, and Evolution.
Trade Paper. Elsevier Science & Technology Books. Saint
Louis, MO. 1997. 512p. ISBN:0-12-323446-8, ISBN13:
978-0-12-323446-9. Dewey:577.8/8. LCCN:96-028242.
Audience: **u,f.** *Choice, 1997.*

Hastings, A. QH352.S96 1987
Some Mathematical Questions in Biology - Models in
Population Biology. Trade Paper. American Mathematical
Society. Providence, RI. 1989. 123p. Lectures in Mathematics in
the Life Sciences, Vol. 20 ISBN:0-8218-1170-3, ISBN13:
978-0-8218-1170-2. Dewey:574.5/248/011. LCCN:89-015119.
Audience: **u,f.**

Formats: Web: ☐ Ebook: 🄴 CD/DVD-ROM: 🐟 BCL3: 𝓑

Hastings, Alan   QH352 .H38
Population Biology: Concepts and Models. Ed. 2. Trade Cloth.
Springer. New York, NY. 2005. 320p. ISBN:0-387-98852-1,
ISBN13: 978-0-387-98852-8. Dewey:574.5/248/0151.
                                        Audience: **u.**

Hayek, Lee-Ann C. &   QH352.H39 1997
  Buzas, Martin A.
Surveying Natural Populations. Trade Cloth. Columbia
University Press. New York, NY. 1997. 448p.
ISBN:0-231-10240-2, ISBN13: 978-0-231-10240-7.
Dewey:574.5/248/072. LCCN:96-022434.
                          Audience: **l,u,f.** *Choice, 1998.*

Hickman, Cleveland P.,   QL47.2.H527 2003
  et al.
Animal Diversity. Ed. 3. Larry S. Roberts & Allan Larson
(Authors). Paper Text. McGraw-Hill Companies, The. New
York, NY. 2002. xvi, 447p. ISBN:0-07-119549-1, ISBN13:
978-0-07-119549-2. Dewey:590. LCCN:2002-022113.
                                        Audience: **l,u.**

Jain, Subodh K. & Botsford,   QH352
  L. W. (Editors)
Applied Population Biology. Trade Cloth. Springer London, Ltd.
Guildford, 1992. 304p. Monographiae Biologicae
ISBN:0-7923-1425-5, ISBN13: 978-0-7923-1425-7. Dewey:574
s. LCCN:91-029384.
                                        Audience: **u,f.**

Jain, Subodh K. &   QH352.P574 1990
  Wohrmann, K. (Editors)
Population Biology. Cloth Text. Springer. New York, NY. 1990.
456p. ISBN:0-387-50802-3, ISBN13: 978-0-387-50802-3.
Dewey:574.5/248. LCCN:89-021933.
                                        Audience: **u,f.**

Lande, Russell, et al.   QL752
Stochastic Population Dynamics in Ecology and Conservation.
Steinar Engen & Bernt-Erik Saether (Authors). Trade Cloth.
Oxford University Press, Inc. New York, NY. 2003. 224p.
Oxford Series in Ecology and Evolution ISBN:0-19-852524-9,
ISBN13: 978-0-19-852524-0. Dewey:577.8801518.
LCCN:2002-042559.
                                        Audience: **u,f.**

Lomnicki, Adam   QH352.L66 1988
Population Ecology of Individuals. Robert M. May (Editor).
Trade Paper. Princeton University Press. Princeton, NJ. 1988.
240p. Monographs in Population Biology, No. 25
ISBN:0-691-08462-9, ISBN13: 978-0-691-08462-6.
Dewey:591.52/48. LCCN:87-003439.
                                        Audience: **u,f.**

Mitton, Jeffry B.   QH371.M68 1997
Selection in Natural Populations. Cloth Text. Oxford University
Press, Inc. New York, NY. 1997. 256p. ISBN:0-19-506352-X,
ISBN13: 978-0-19-506352-3. Dewey:572.8/38.
LCCN:96-049688.
                          Audience: **u,f.** *Choice, 1998.*

Thieme, Horst R.   QH352.T45 2003
Mathematics in Population Biology. Trade Cloth. Princeton
University Press. Princeton, NJ. 2003. 568p. Mathematical
Biology Ser. ISBN:0-691-09290-7, ISBN13: 978-0-691-09290-4.
Dewey:577.8/8/015118. LCCN:2002-192472.
                                        Audience: **u,f.**

Integrative Biology > General Ecology > Theoretical Ecology

Agren, Gvran I. & Bosatta,   QH344 .A35 1998
  Ernesto
Theoretical Ecosystem Ecology: Understanding Nutrient Cycles.
Trade Cloth. Cambridge University Press. New York, NY. 1996.
250p. ISBN:0-521-58022-6, ISBN13: 978-0-521-58022-9.
Dewey:574.5/222. LCCN:96-018908.
                                        Audience: **u,f.**

Akcakaya, H. Resit, et al.   QH352
Applied Population Ecology Using RAMAS Ecolab: Principles
and Computer Exercises Using RAMAS EcoLab 2. 0. Ed. 2.
Mark A. Burgman & Lev R. Ginzburg (Authors). Paper Text,
CD-ROM. Sinauer Associates, Inc. Sunderland, MA. 1999.
285p. ISBN:0-87893-028-0, ISBN13: 978-0-87893-028-9.
Dewey:577.8/8/015118.
                                        Audience: **u,f.**

Bazykin, Alexander   QH352.B39 1998
Nonlinear Dynamics of Interacting Populations. Cloth Text.
World Scientific Publishing Company, Inc. Hackensack, NJ.
1997. 193p. Neural Systems Ser. ISBN:981-02-1685-8, ISBN13:
978-981-02-1685-6. Dewey:577.8/8/0151. LCCN:98-011768.
                                        Audience: **u,f.**

Brauer, Fred &   QH352.B73 2001
  Castillo-Chavez, Carlos
Mathematical Models in Population Biology and Epidemiology.
Trade Cloth. Springer. New York, NY. 2001. XXIII, 448p. Texts
in Applied Mathematics, Vol. 40 ISBN:0-387-98902-1, ISBN13:
978-0-387-98902-0. Dewey:577.8/8/015118. LCCN:00-045033.
                                        Audience: **u,f.**

Buckland, S.T. (Editor),   QH352
  et al.
Advanced Distance Sampling: Estimating Abundance of
Biological Populations. D.R. Anderson & K.P. Burnham
(Editors). Trade Cloth. Oxford University Press, Inc. New York,
NY. 2004. 434p. ISBN:0-19-850783-6, ISBN13:
978-0-19-850783-3. Dewey:591.7/88/0727. LCCN:2004-303414.
                                        Audience: **u,f.**

Integrative Biology > Evolution

                                             QH83.A785 2005
The Applications and Limitations of Taxonomy (in Classification
of Organisms): An Anthology of Current Thought. Library
Binding, Paper over Boards. Rosen Publishing Group,
Incorporated, The. New York, NY. 2005. 158p. Contemporary
Discourse in the Field of Biology Ser. ISBN:1-4042-0400-8,
ISBN13: 978-1-4042-0400-3. Dewey:570.12.
LCCN:2004-021800.
                                        Audience: **l,u,f.**

▢ Google Directory: Biology, Evolution.
http://google.com/Top/Science/Biology/Evolution/
Google.
                                        Audience: **g,l.**

Adams, Fred   QH325.A278 2002
Origins of Existence: How Life Emerged in the Universe. Trade
Cloth. Simon & Schuster. New York, NY. 2002. 272p.
ISBN:0-7432-1262-2, ISBN13: 978-0-7432-1262-5.
Dewey:576.8/3. LCCN:2002-073877.

Audience: **u,f.**

Alexander, R. McNeil   QH371.A45 1996
Optima for Animals. Cloth Text. Princeton University Press.
Princeton, NJ. 1996. 176p. ISBN:0-691-02799-4, ISBN13:
978-0-691-02799-9. Dewey:591/.01/51. LCCN:96-012454.

Audience: **u,f.** *Choice, 1997.*

American Institute of   QE980
  Biological Sciences; Meeting ; (1993 : Ames, Iowa)
Flowering Plant Origin, Evolution & Phylogeny. Taylor, David
W. (Editor); Hickey, Leo J. (Editor). Chapman & Hall, New
York :. 1996. ISBN:0-412-05341-1, ISBN13:
978-0-412-05341-2.

Audience: **l,u.**

Amundson, Ronald   QH360.5.A48 2005
The Changing Role of the Embryo in Evolutionary Thought:
Roots of Evo-Devo. Michael Ruse (Contribution by). Trade
Cloth. Cambridge University Press. New York, NY. 2005. 294p.
Cambridge Studies in Philosophy and Biology Ser.
ISBN:0-521-80699-2, ISBN13: 978-0-521-80699-2.
Dewey:576.8/01. LCCN:2004-054409.

Audience: **u,f.** *Choice, 2005.*

Arthur, Wallace   QH371.A765 1988
A Theory of the Evolution of Development. Ed. 1. Trade Cloth.
John Wiley & Sons, Inc. Hoboken, NJ. 1988. 104p.
ISBN:0-471-91974-8, ISBN13: 978-0-471-91974-2.
Dewey:574.4. LCCN:88-005628.

Audience: **u,f.** *Choice, 1989.*

Avers, Charlotte J.   QH366.2.A933 1989
Process and Pattern in Evolution. Trade Cloth. Oxford
University Press, Inc. New York, NY. 1989. 606p.
ISBN:0-19-505275-7, ISBN13: 978-0-19-505275-6. Dewey:575.
LCCN:88-005368.

Audience: **u,f.** *Choice, 1989.*

Avery, John   QH366.2.A94 2003
Information Theory and Evolution. Trade Cloth. World Scientific
Publishing Company, Inc. Hackensack, NJ. 2003. 232p.
ISBN:981-238-399-9, ISBN13: 978-981-238-399-0.
Dewey:576.8. LCCN:2003-050156.

Audience: **u,f.** *Choice, 2004.*

Beals, Kevin, et al.   QH362.B43 2002
Life Through Time: Evolutionary Activities for Grades 5-8.
Nicole Parizeau, Rick MacPherson & Lincoln Bergman
(Authors), Lisa Baker (Illustrator), Lisa Klofkorn (Illustrator,
Photographer). Trade Paper. University of California, Berkeley,
Lawrence Hall of Science. Berkeley, CA. 2003. 358p. Great
Explorations in Math and Science Ser. ISBN:0-924886-67-6,
ISBN13: 978-0-924886-67-6. Dewey:372.3/5.
LCCN:2002-151772.

Audience: **l.**

Beerling, D. J. &   QH344 .B43 2001
  Woodward, F. I.
Vegetation and the Terrestrial Carbon Cycle: The First 400
Million Years. Trade Cloth. Cambridge University Press. New

York, NY. 2001. 416p. ISBN:0-521-80196-6, ISBN13:
978-0-521-80196-6. Dewey:577/.144/015118.
LCCN:2001-025553.

Audience: **u,f.** *Choice, 2002.*

Bell, Graham   QH375.B43 1997
Basics of Selection. Trade Paper. Springer. New York, NY. 1996.
404p. ISBN:0-412-05531-7, ISBN13: 978-0-412-05531-7.
Dewey:576.82. LCCN:95-017458.

Audience: **u,f.**

Bell, Graham   QH375.B44 1997
Selection: The Mechanism of Evolution. Trade Cloth. Springer.
New York, NY. 1996. 688p. ISBN:0-412-05521-X, ISBN13:
978-0-412-05521-8. Dewey:575.01/62. LCCN:95-017458.

Audience: **u,f.** *Choice, 1997.*

Bemis, William, et al.   QL805.W35
Functional Anatomy of Vertebrates: An Evolutionary
Perspective. Ed. 4. Karel F. Liem, Warren F. Walker Jr, Lance
Grande & Lauder (Authors). Cloth Text. Brooks/Cole. Pacific
Grove, CA. 2006. ISBN:0-534-41919-4, ISBN13:
978-0-534-41919-6. Dewey:571.3/16.

Audience: **u.**

Bennett, Jeffrey O., et al.   QH327 .B45
Life in the Universe. Ed. 2. Seth Shostak & Bruce Jakosky
(Authors). Trade Paper. Addison-Wesley Longman, Inc. Boston,
MA. 2006. 450p. ISBN:0-8053-4753-4, ISBN13:
978-0-8053-4753-1. Dewey:576.8/39. LCCN:2006-025657.

Audience: **g,l,u.**

Berra, Tim M.   QH371.B47 1990
Evolution and the Myth of Creationism: A Basic Guide to the
Facts in the Evolution Debate. Trade Cloth. Stanford University
Press. Palo Alto, CA. 1990. 220p. ISBN:0-8047-1548-3,
ISBN13: 978-0-8047-1548-5. Dewey:213. LCCN:89-051484.

Audience: **g,l,u,f.** *Choice, 1991.*

Bird, Richard J.   QH331.B525 2003
Chaos and Life: Complexity and Order in Evolution and
Thought. Trade Cloth. Eastern European Monographs.
Bradenton, FL. 2003. 352p. ISBN:0-231-12662-X, ISBN13:
978-0-231-12662-5. Dewey:570/.1. LCCN:2003-051637.

Audience: **u,f.** *Choice, 2004.*

Bonner, John T.   QH371.B65 1988
The Evolution of Complexity by Means of Natural Selection.
Trade Cloth. Princeton University Press. Princeton, NJ. 1988.
344p. ISBN:0-691-08493-9, ISBN13: 978-0-691-08493-0.
Dewey:575. LCCN:87-038490.

Audience: **u,f.**

Bowler, Peter J.   QH361 .B69 2003
Evolution: The History of an Idea. Ed. 3. Trade Paper.
University of California Press. Berkeley, CA. 2003. 488p.
ISBN:0-520-23693-9, ISBN13: 978-0-520-23693-6.
Dewey:576.8. LCCN:2002-007569.

Audience: **u,f.**

Bowler, Peter J.   QH361.B685 1996
Life's Splendid Drama: Evolutionary Biology and the
Reconstruction of Life's Ancestry, 1860-1940. Trade Cloth.
University of Chicago Press. Chicago, IL. 1996. 540p. Science
and Its Conceptual Foundations Ser. ISBN:0-226-06921-4,
ISBN13: 978-0-226-06921-0. Dewey:575/.009.
LCCN:95-025394.

Audience: **u,f.** *Choice, 1997.*

Brandon, Robert N.   QH360.5 .B73 1996
Concepts and Methods in Evolutionary Biology. Michael Ruse
(Contribution by). Trade Cloth. Cambridge University Press.
New York, NY. 1996. 237p. Cambridge Studies in Philosophy
and Biology ISBN:0-521-49545-8, ISBN13: 978-0-521-49545-5.
Dewey:575/.001. LCCN:95-005990.
Audience: **l,u,f.** *Choice, 1996.*

Brooks, Daniel R. & Wiley,   QH371.B69 1988
  Edward O.
Evolution As Entropy: Toward a Unified Theory of Biology. Ed.
2. Library Binding. University of Chicago Press. Chicago, IL.
1996. 432p. Science and Its Conceptual Foundations Ser.
ISBN:0-226-07573-7, ISBN13: 978-0-226-07573-0.
Dewey:575.01/6. LCCN:88-010688.
Audience: **u,f.**

Bybee, Rodger W. (Editor)   QH362.E853 2003
Evolution in Perspective: The Science Teacher's Compendium.
Perfect. National Science Teachers Association. Arlington, VA.
2003. xxii, 99p. ISBN:0-87355-234-2, ISBN13:
978-0-87355-234-9. Dewey:576.8. LCCN:2003-021609.
Audience: **l,u,f.**

Cain, Joe   QH361.U7 2004
Upgrading Evolution: Documents of the Committee on Common
Problems of Genetics, Paleontology, and Systematics.
Committee on Common Problems of Genetics, Paleontology,
and Systematics Staff (Contribution by). Trade Paper. American
Philosophical Society. Canton, MA. 2004. xlii, 160p.
Transactions of the American Philosophical Society Ser., Pt. 94
ISBN:0-87169-942-7, ISBN13: 978-0-87169-942-8.
Dewey:576.8. LCCN:2004-054784.
Audience: **u,f.**

Corning, Peter   QH366.2.C73 2003
Nature's Magic: Synergy in Evolution and the Fate of
Humankind. Trade Cloth. Cambridge University Press. New
York, NY. 2003. 464p. ISBN:0-521-82547-4, ISBN13:
978-0-521-82547-4. Dewey:576.8. LCCN:2002-031552.
Audience: **u,f.** *Choice, 2004.*

Cox, George W.   QH353.C69 2004
Alien Species and Evolution: The Evolutionary Ecology of
Exotic Plants, Animals, Microbes, and Interacting Native
Species. Trade Cloth. Island Press. Washington, DC. 2004. 400p.
ISBN:1-55963-008-6, ISBN13: 978-1-55963-008-5.
Dewey:578.6/2. LCCN:2003-027299.
Audience: **u,f.** *Choice, 2005.*

Cracraft, Joel & Donoghue,   QH83.A86 2004
  Michael J. (Editors)
Assembling the Tree of Life. Trade Cloth. Oxford University
Press, Inc. New York, NY. 2004. 591p. ISBN:0-19-517234-5,
ISBN13: 978-0-19-517234-8. Dewey:578/.01/2.
LCCN:2003-058012.
Audience: **u,f.** *Choice, 2005.*

Crawford, Michael   QH371.C88 1989
Driving Force. Trade Cloth. HarperCollins Publishers. New
York, NY. 1989. ISBN:0-06-039069-7, ISBN13:
978-0-06-039069-3. Dewey:575/.016. LCCN:88-045891.
Audience: **u,f.**

Davies, Paul S.   QH375.D36 2001
Norms of Nature: Naturalism and the Nature of Functions.
Trade Cloth. MIT Press. Cambridge, MA. 2001. 250p. Life and
Mind Ser., :Philosophical Issues in Biology and Psychology

ISBN:0-262-04187-1, ISBN13: 978-0-262-04187-4.
Dewey:570/.1. LCCN:00-055403.
Audience: **u,f.** *Choice, 2001.*

Dawkins, Richard   QH366.2.D37 1996
The Blind Watchmaker: Why the Evidence of Evolution Reveals
a Universe Without Design. Trade Paper. W. W. Norton &
Company, Inc. New York, NY. 1996. 400p.
ISBN:0-393-31570-3, ISBN13: 978-0-393-31570-7.
Dewey:576.8/2. LCCN:96-229669.
Audience: **l,u,f.**

Dawkins, Richard   QH308.2
Climbing Mount Improbable. Trade Paper. W. W. Norton &
Company, Inc. New York, NY. 1997. 352p.
ISBN:0-393-31682-3, ISBN13: 978-0-393-31682-7. Dewey:574.
Audience: **l,u,f.** *Choice, 1997.*

Dawkins, Richard   QH366.2.D373 2003
A Devil's Chaplain: Reflections on Hope, Lies, Science, and
Love. Reinforced. Houghton Mifflin Company Trade &
Reference Division. Boston, MA. 2003. 272p.
ISBN:0-618-33540-4, ISBN13: 978-0-618-33540-4. Dewey:500.
LCCN:2003-050859.
Audience: **l,u,f.**

Dawkins, Richard   QH361.D39 2004
The Ancestor's Tale: A Pilgrimage to the Dawn of Evolution.
Yan Wong (Read by). Trade Cloth. Houghton Mifflin Company
Trade & Reference Division. Boston, MA. 2004. 688p.
ISBN:0-618-00583-8, ISBN13: 978-0-618-00583-3.
Dewey:576.8. LCCN:2004-059864.
Audience: **l,u,f.** *Choice, 2005.*

Dembski, William A.   QH360.5.D46 2001
No Free Lunch: Why Specified Complexity Cannot Be
Purchased Without Intelligence. Book, Other. Rowman &
Littlefield Publishers, Inc. Lanham, MD. 2001. 432p.
ISBN:0-7425-1297-5, ISBN13: 978-0-7425-1297-9.
Dewey:576.8/01. LCCN:2001-031791.
Audience: **u,f.**

Dyer, Betsey D. & Obar,   QH371.D93 1993
  Robert A.
Tracing the History of Eukaryotic Cells: The Enigmatic Smile.
Trade Cloth. Columbia University Press. New York, NY. 1984.
335p. Critical Moments in Paleobiology and Earth History Ser.
ISBN:0-231-07592-8, ISBN13: 978-0-231-07592-3.
Dewey:574.87. LCCN:93-026798.
Audience: **u,f.** *Choice, 1995.*

Edey, Maitland A.   QH361.E34 1989
Blueprints: Solving the Mystery of Evolution. Donald C.
Johanson (Editor). Trade Cloth. Little Brown & Company. New
York, NY. 1989. 456p. ISBN:0-316-21076-5, ISBN13:
978-0-316-21076-8. Dewey:575. LCCN:88-031737.
Audience: **u,f.** *Choice, 1989.*

Eldredge, Niles   QH366.2.E535 1998
The Pattern of Evolution. Trade Cloth. W. H. Freeman &
Company. New York, NY. 1998. 250p. ISBN:0-7167-3046-4,
ISBN13: 978-0-7167-3046-0. Dewey:576.8. LCCN:98-034754.
Audience: **u,f.** *Choice, 1999.*

Erickson, Jonathon S.   QH372.E75 1989
The Living Earth: The Coevolution of the Planet and Life. Trade
Cloth. McGraw-Hill School Education Group. Columbus, OH.

1989. 212p. Discovering Earth Science Ser.
ISBN:0-8306-8942-7, ISBN13: 978-0-8306-8942-2. Dewey:577.
LCCN:88-026557.

Audience: **l,u,f.**

Feldman, Marcus W.   **QH0371.M295**
  (Editor)
Mathematical Evolutionary Theory. Trade Paper. Books on
Demand. Ann Arbor, MI. 351p. ISBN:0-608-06320-7, ISBN13:
978-0-608-06320-1. Dewey:575.01/51. LCCN:88-015591.

Audience: **u,f.**

Fenchel, T. M. & Fenchel,   **QH366.2**
  Tom
The Origin and Early Evolution of Life. Trade Cloth. Oxford
University Press, Inc. New York, NY. 2003. 180p.
ISBN:0-19-852635-0, ISBN13: 978-0-19-852635-3.
Dewey:576.8/3. LCCN:2002-070193.

Audience: **l,u,f.**

Fortey, Richard   **QH366.2.F69 1998**
Life: A Natural History of the First Four Billion Years of Life
on Earth. Trade Cloth. Alfred A. Knopf Inc. New York, NY.
1998. 368p. ISBN:0-375-40119-9, ISBN13: 978-0-375-40119-0.
Dewey:576.8. LCCN:97-049466.

Audience: **l,u,f.**

Fox, Ronald F.   **QH371.F62 1988**
Energy and the Evolution of Life. Cloth Text. W. H. Freeman &
Company. New York, NY. 1988. 704p. ISBN:0-7167-1849-9,
ISBN13: 978-0-7167-1849-9. Dewey:575. LCCN:87-021458.

Audience: **l,u,f.**

Frank, Steven A.   **QH375.F735 1998**
Foundations of Social Evolution. Cloth Text. Princeton
University Press. Princeton, NJ. 1998. 280p. Monographs in
Behavior and Ecology ISBN:0-691-05933-0, ISBN13:
978-0-691-05933-4. Dewey:576.8/2/011. LCCN:97-052086.

Audience: **l,u,f.**

Fry, Iris   **QH325.F78 2000**
The Emergence of Life on Earth: A Historical and Scientific
Overview. Cloth Text. Rutgers University Press. Piscataway, NJ.
2000. ix, 327p. ISBN:0-8135-2739-2, ISBN13:
978-0-8135-2739-0. Dewey:576.8/3. LCCN:99-023153.

Audience: **l,u,f.** *Choice, 2000.*

Futuyma, Douglas J.   **QH366.2.F87 1997**
Evolutionary Biology. Ed. 3. Trade Cloth. Sinauer Associates,
Inc. Sunderland, MA. 1997. 751p. ISBN:0-87893-189-9,
ISBN13: 978-0-87893-189-7. Dewey:576.8. LCCN:97-037947.

Audience: **u,f.**

Futuyma, Douglas J.   **QH366.2.F88 1995**
Science on Trial: The Case for Evolution. Trade Paper. Sinauer
Associates, Inc. Sunderland, MA. 1995. 223p.
ISBN:0-87893-184-8, ISBN13: 978-0-87893-184-2. Dewey:575.
LCCN:95-005980.

Audience: **l,u,f.**

Gardner, James N.   **QH366.2.G38 2003**
Biocosm: The New Scientific Theory of Evolution: Intelligent
Life Is the Architect of the Universe. Trade Paper, Pictures or
Photographs. Inner Ocean Publishing/Innisfree Press. Makawao,
HI. 2003. 344p. ISBN:1-930722-22-2, ISBN13:
978-1-930722-22-4. Dewey:576.8/3. LCCN:2004-300254.

Audience: **u,f.** *Choice, 2004.*

Gerhart, John & Kirschner,   **QH366.2.G463 1997**
  Marc
Cells, Embryos and Evolution: Toward a Cellular and
Developmental Understanding of Phenotypic Variation and
Evolutionary Adaptability. Trade Paper. Blackwell Publishing,
Inc. Malden, MA. 1997. 656p. ISBN:0-86542-574-4, ISBN13:
978-0-86542-574-3. Dewey:576.8. LCCN:96-051650.

Audience: **u,f.**

Ghiselin, Michael T.   **QH360.5.G48 1997**
Metaphysics and the Origin of Species. Cloth Text. State
University of New York Press. Albany, NY. 1997. 377p. SUNY
Series in Philosophy and Biology ISBN:0-7914-3467-2,
ISBN13: 978-0-7914-3467-3. Dewey:576.8/01.
LCCN:96-038957.

Audience: **u,f.** *Choice, 1998.*

Goldsmith, Timothy H.   **GN365.9**
The Biological Roots of Human Nature: Forging Links Between
Evolution and Behavior. Trade Paper. Oxford University Press,
Inc. New York, NY. 1994. 176p. ISBN:0-19-509393-3, ISBN13:
978-0-19-509393-3. Dewey:304.5.

Audience: **u,f.** *Choice, 1992.*

Goodwin, Brian   **QH366.2.G655 1994**
How the Leopard Changed Its Spots: The Evolution of
Complexity. Trade Cloth. Simon & Schuster. New York, NY.
1994. 320p. ISBN:0-02-544710-6, ISBN13: 978-0-02-544710-3.
Dewey:576.8. LCCN:94-016891.

Audience: **u,f.** *Choice, 1995.*

Gould, Stephen Jay   **QH366.2.G659 1995**
Dinosaur in a Haystack: Reflections in Natural History. Trade
Cloth. Crown Publishing Group. New York, NY. 1995. 496p.
ISBN:0-517-70393-9, ISBN13: 978-0-517-70393-9. Dewey:508.
LCCN:95-051333.

Audience: **l,u,f.**

Gould, Stephen Jay   **QH366.2.G663 2002**
The Structure of Evolutionary Theory. Trade Cloth. Harvard
University Press. Cambridge, MA. 2002. 1464p.
ISBN:0-674-00613-5, ISBN13: 978-0-674-00613-3.
Dewey:576.8. LCCN:2001-043556.

Audience: **l,u,f.** *Choice, 2002.*

Greene, John C.   **QH361.G7 1996**
The Death of Adam: Evolution and Its Impact on Western
Thought. Trade Paper. Blackwell Publishing Professional. Ames,
IA. 1981. 388p. ISBN:0-8138-0390-X, ISBN13:
978-0-8138-0390-6. Dewey:575/.009. LCCN:95-044513.

Audience: **u,f.**

Hall, Brian K. &   **QH401.V37 2005**
  Hallgrímsson, Benedikt (Editors)
Variation: A Central Concept in Biology. Trade Cloth. Elsevier
Science & Technology Books. Saint Louis, MO. 2005. 592p.
ISBN:0-12-088777-0, ISBN13: 978-0-12-088777-4.
Dewey:576.5/4. LCCN:2005-047332.

Audience: **l,u,f.** *Choice, 2005.*

Harvey, Paul H. & Pagel,   **QH366.2.H385 1991**
  Mark D.
The Comparative Method in Evolutionary Biology. Trade Cloth.
Oxford University Press, Inc. New York, NY. 1991. 248p.
Oxford Series in Ecology and Evolution ISBN:0-19-854641-6,
ISBN13: 978-0-19-854641-2. Dewey:575/.0072.
LCCN:90-021148.

Audience: **l,u,f.** *Choice, 1992.*

   Formats: Web: ☐   Ebook: 🄴   CD/DVD-ROM: 🐟   BCL3: *B*

Hemelrijk, Charlotte   **QH313**
  (Editor)
Self-Organisation and Evolution of Biological and Social
Systems. Trade Cloth. Cambridge University Press. New York,
NY. 2005. 204p. ISBN:0-521-84655-2, ISBN13:
978-0-521-84655-4. Dewey:577.88. LCCN:2006-276106.
                           Audience: **u,f.**

Hooper, Judith   **QH375.H66 2002**
Of Moths and Men: An Evolutionary Tale: The Untold Story of
Science and the Peppered Moth. Trade Cloth. W. W. Norton &
Company, Inc. New York, NY. 2002. 320p.
ISBN:0-393-05121-8, ISBN13: 978-0-393-05121-6.
Dewey:576.8/2. LCCN:2002-026315.
                           Audience: **l,u,f.**

Hough, Derek   **QH360.5**
Evolution: A Case of Stating the Obvious. Berkeley Pub.,
Berkeley, Gloucestershire. 1997. ISBN:0-9529358-0-5, ISBN13:
978-0-9529358-0-3.
                           Audience: **g,l,u.**

Hull, David L. (Editor)   **QH371.H85 1989**
The Metaphysics of Evolution. Cloth Text. State University of
New York Press. Albany, NY. 1989. 331p. SUNY Series in
Philosophy and Biology ISBN:0-7914-0211-8, ISBN13:
978-0-7914-0211-5. Dewey:575/.001. LCCN:89-031776.
                           Audience: **u,f.**

Hull, David L.   **QH360.5 .H86 2001**
Science and Selection: Essays on Biological Evolution and the
Philosophy of Science. Michael Ruse (Contribution by). Cloth
Text. Cambridge University Press. New York, NY. 2000. 288p.
Cambridge Studies in Philosophy and Biology
ISBN:0-521-64339-2, ISBN13: 978-0-521-64339-9.
Dewey:576.8/01. LCCN:00-027938.
                 Audience: **u,f.** *Choice, 2001.*

Itzkoff, Seymour W.   **QH360.5.I89 2000**
The Inevitable Domination by Man: An Evolutionary Detective
Story. Trade Cloth. Paideia Publishers. Ashfield, MA. 2000. xvi,
386p. ISBN:0-913993-16-6, ISBN13: 978-0-913993-16-3.
Dewey:576.8/01. LCCN:00-021970.
                 Audience: **u,f.** *Choice, 2000.*

Jablonka, Eva & Lamb,   **QH366.2.J322 2005**
  Marion J.
Evolution in Four Dimensions: Genetic, Epigenetic, Behavioral,
and Symbolic Variation in the History of Life. Anna Zeligowski
(Illustrator). Trade Cloth. MIT Press. Cambridge, MA. 2005.
472p. Life and Mind Ser. ISBN:0-262-10107-6, ISBN13:
978-0-262-10107-3. Dewey:576.8. LCCN:2004-058193.
                 Audience: **u,f.** *Choice, 2005.*

Kardong, Kenneth V.   **QL805.K35 2002**
Vertebrates: Comparative Anatomy, Function, Evolution. Ed. 3.
Cloth Text. McGraw-Hill Higher Education. Burr Ridge, IL.
2001. 784p. ISBN:0-07-290956-0, ISBN13: 978-0-07-290956-2.
Dewey:571.3/16. LCCN:2001-030631.
                           Audience: **l,u.**

Keller, Laurent (Editor)   **QH375.L48 1999**
Levels of Selection in Evolution. Cloth Text. Princeton
University Press. Princeton, NJ. 1999. 272p. Monographs in
Behavior and Ecology ISBN:0-691-00703-9, ISBN13:
978-0-691-00703-8. Dewey:576.8/2. LCCN:99-022314.
                 Audience: **u,f.** *Choice, 2000.*

Khakhina, Liya N.   **QH378.K4313 1992**
Concepts of Symbiogenesis: A Historical and Critical Study of
the Research of Russian Botanists. Lynn Margulis, Mark
McMenamin & Robert Coalson (Editors), Stephanie Merkel
(Translator). Cloth over Boards. Yale University Press.
Cumberland, RI. 1992. 160p. Bio-Origins Ser.
ISBN:0-300-04816-5, ISBN13: 978-0-300-04816-2.
Dewey:575.0160922. LCCN:92-014466.
                           Audience: **u,f.**

Knoll, Andrew H.   **QH325.K54 2004**
Life on a Young Planet: The First Three Billion Years of
Evolution on Earth. Trade Paper. Princeton University Press.
Princeton, NJ. 2004. 304p. Princeton Science Library
ISBN:0-691-12029-3, ISBN13: 978-0-691-12029-4.
Dewey:576.8/3.
                 Audience: **l,u,f.** *Choice, 2003.*

Larson, Edward J.   **QH361.L27 2004**
Evolution: The Remarkable History of a Scientific Theory. Trade
Cloth. Random House, Inc. New York, NY. 2004. 368p.
ISBN:0-679-64288-9, ISBN13: 978-0-679-64288-6.
Dewey:576.8. LCCN:2003-064888.
                 Audience: **l,u,f.** *Choice, 2004.*

Larson, Edward J.   **QH366.2.L375 2001**
Evolution's Workshop: God and Science on the Galapagos
Islands. Trade Cloth. Basic Books. New York, NY. 2001. 336p.
ISBN:0-465-03810-7, ISBN13: 978-0-465-03810-7.
Dewey:576.8. LCCN:00-065159.
                 Audience: **l,u,f.** *Choice, 2001.*

Lees, D. R. & Edwards, D.   **QH359.E935 1993**
  (Editors)
Evolutionary Patterns and Processes. Trade Cloth. Elsevier
Science & Technology Books. Saint Louis, MO. 1993. 325p.
Linnean Society Symposium Ser., No. 14 ISBN:0-12-440895-8,
ISBN13: 978-0-12-440895-1. Dewey:575.01/6.
LCCN:94-105236.
                           Audience: **u,f.**

Levinton, Jeffrey S.   **QH366.2.L47 1988**
Genetics, Paleontology and Macroevolution. Cloth Text.
Cambridge University Press. New York, NY. 1988. 656p.
ISBN:0-521-24933-3, ISBN13: 978-0-521-24933-1. Dewey:575.
LCCN:87-011730.
                 Audience: **u,f.** *Choice, 1988.*

Levy, Charles K.   **QH375.L54 1999**
Evolutionary Wars. Trudy Nicholson (Illustrator). Trade Cloth.
W. H. Freeman & Company. New York, NY. 1999. 278p.
ISBN:0-7167-3483-4, ISBN13: 978-0-7167-3483-3.
Dewey:576.8/2. LCCN:99-039982.
                           Audience: **u,f.**

Little, Colin   **QH371 .L58 1990**
The Terrestrial Invasion: An Ecophysiological Approach to the
Origins of Land Animals. Trade Cloth. Cambridge University
Press. New York, NY. 1990. 314p. Cambridge Studies in
Ecology ISBN:0-521-33447-0, ISBN13: 978-0-521-33447-1.
Dewey:560/.45. LCCN:89-017471.
                 Audience: **u,f.** *Choice, 1991.*

Loomis, William F.   **QH371.L65 1988**
Four Billion Years: An Essay on the Evolution of Genes and
Organisms. Cloth Text. Sinauer Associates, Inc. Sunderland,

MA. 1988. 286p. ISBN:0-87893-475-8, ISBN13:
978-0-87893-475-1. Dewey:575. LCCN:88-001848.
Audience: **u,f.** *Choice, 1988.*

Lurquin, Paul F.   QH325.L87 2003
The Origins of Life and the Universe. Trade Cloth. Columbia
University Press. New York, NY. 2003. 248p.
ISBN:0-231-12654-9, ISBN13: 978-0-231-12654-0.
Dewey:576.8/3. LCCN:2002-035166.
Audience: **l,u,f.** *Choice, 2003.*

Margulis, Lynn & Dolan,   QH325.M29 2002
Michael
Early Life: Evolution on the PreCambrian Earth. Ed. 2. Trade
Paper. Jones & Bartlett Publishers, Inc. Sudbury, MA. 2002.
224p. Evolution Ser. ISBN:0-7637-1463-1, ISBN13:
978-0-7637-1463-5. Dewey:576.8/3. LCCN:2001-046290.
Audience: **l,u,f.**

Margulis, Lynn &   QH366.2.E59 1992
Olendzenski, Lorraine (Editors)
Environmental Evolution: Effects of the Origin and Evolution of
Life on Planet Earth. Trade Cloth. MIT Press. Cambridge, MA.
1992. 400p. ISBN:0-262-13273-7, ISBN13: 978-0-262-13273-2.
Dewey:576.8. LCCN:91-017981.
Audience: **u,f.** *Choice, 1992.*

Markos, Anton   QH331.M315 2002
Readers of the Book of Life: Contextualizing Developmental
Evolutionary Biology. Trade Cloth. Oxford University Press,
Inc. New York, NY. 2002. 256p. ISBN:0-19-514948-3, ISBN13:
978-0-19-514948-7. Dewey:570/.1. LCCN:2001-051352.
Audience: **u,f.** *Choice, 2003.*

Maynard Smith, John   QH371.M327 1989
Evolutionary Genetics. Paper Text. Oxford University Press, Inc.
New York, NY. 1989. 344p. ISBN:0-19-854215-1, ISBN13:
978-0-19-854215-5. Dewey:575.1/5. LCCN:88-017041.
Audience: **u,f.**

Maynard Smith, John &   QH366.2
Szathmary, Eors
The Major Transitions in Evolution. Trade Paper. Oxford
University Press, Inc. New York, NY. 1998. 360p.
ISBN:0-19-850294-X, ISBN13: 978-0-19-850294-4.
Dewey:576.8.
Audience: **u,f.**

Maynard Smith, John &   QH366.2.M39194 1999
Szathmary, Eors
The Origins of Life: From the Birth of Life to the Origin of
Language. Trade Cloth. Oxford University Press, Inc. New York,
NY. 1999. 192p. ISBN:0-19-850493-4, ISBN13:
978-0-19-850493-1. Dewey:576.8. LCCN:99-230990.
Audience: **l,u,f.** *Choice, 1999.*

Mayr, Ernst   QH366.2.M3933 2001
What Evolution Is. Jared M. Diamond (Introduction by). Trade
Cloth. Basic Books. New York, NY. 2001. 336p.
ISBN:0-465-04425-5, ISBN13: 978-0-465-04425-2.
Dewey:576.8. LCCN:2001-036562.
Audience: **u,f.** *Choice, 2002.*

McFadden, Johnjoe   QH366.2.M396 2001
Quantum Evolution: The New Science of Life. Trade Cloth. W.
W. Norton & Company, Inc. New York, NY. 2001. 352p.

ISBN:0-393-05041-6, ISBN13: 978-0-393-05041-7.
Dewey:576.8. LCCN:00-053320.
Audience: **u,f.** *Choice, 2001.*

McKinney, M. L.   QH395.H47 1988
Heterochrony in Evolution: A Multidisciplinary Approach. Trade
Cloth. Springer. New York, NY. 1988. 366p. Topics in
Geobiology Ser., Vol. 7 ISBN:0-306-42947-0, ISBN13:
978-0-306-42947-7. Dewey:575. LCCN:88-022573.
Audience: **u,f.**

McKinney, M. L. &   QH395.M34 1991
McNamara, K. J.
Heterochrony: The Evolution of Ontogeny. Trade Cloth.
Springer. New York, NY. 1991. 456p. ISBN:0-306-43638-8,
ISBN13: 978-0-306-43638-3. Dewey:575. LCCN:91-006371.
Audience: **u,f.**

McLaughlin, Peter   QH331 .M377 2001
What Functions Explain: Functional Explanation and
Self-Reproducing Systems. Michael Ruse (Contribution by).
Trade Cloth. Cambridge University Press. New York, NY. 2000.
272p. Cambridge Studies in Philosophy and Biology
ISBN:0-521-78233-3, ISBN13: 978-0-521-78233-3.
Dewey:570.1. LCCN:00-031179.
Audience: **u,f.**

McNamara, Kenneth J.   QH395.M36 1997
Shapes of Time: The Evolution of Growth and Development.
Trade Cloth. Johns Hopkins University Press. Baltimore, MD.
1997. 360p. ISBN:0-8018-5571-3, ISBN13: 978-0-8018-5571-9.
Dewey:576.8. LCCN:96-029775.
Audience: **u,f.** *Choice, 1998.*

Mills, Cynthia   QH366.2.M55 2004
The Theory of Evolution: What It Is, Where It Came from, and
Why It Works. Trade Paper. John Wiley & Sons, Inc. Hoboken,
NJ. 2004. 224p. ISBN:0-471-21484-1, ISBN13:
978-0-471-21484-7. Dewey:576.8. LCCN:2004-003618.
Audience: **l,u,f.**

Mindell, David P.   QH371.M54 2006
The Evolving World: Evolution in Everyday Life. Trade Cloth.
Harvard University Press. Cambridge, MA. 2006. 352p.
ISBN:0-674-02191-6, ISBN13: 978-0-674-02191-4.
Dewey:576.8. LCCN:2005-058131.
Audience: **l,u,f.** *Choice, 2006.*

Mitton, Jeffry B.   QH371.M68 1997
Selection in Natural Populations. Cloth Text. Oxford University
Press, Inc. New York, NY. 1997. 256p. ISBN:0-19-506352-X,
ISBN13: 978-0-19-506352-3. Dewey:572.8/38.
LCCN:96-049688.
Audience: **u,f.** *Choice, 1998.*

Miyamoto, Michael M. &   QH371.P47 1992
Cracraft, Joel (Editors)
Phylogenetic Analysis of DNA Sequences. Trade Cloth. Oxford
University Press, Inc. New York, NY. 1991. 368p.
ISBN:0-19-506698-7, ISBN13: 978-0-19-506698-2.
Dewey:574.87/3282. LCCN:90-028771.
Audience: **u,f.**

Formats: Web: ▢ Ebook: 🄴 CD/DVD-ROM: 🧷 BCL3: 𝐵

Mousseau, Timothy A., et al.   QH401.A395 2000
Adaptive Genetic Variation in the Wild. Barry Sinervo & John
A. Endler (Authors). Trade Cloth. Oxford University Press, Inc.
New York, NY. 2000. 276p. ISBN:0-19-512183-X, ISBN13:
978-0-19-512183-4. Dewey:576.5/4. LCCN:99-013844.
Audience: **u,f.**

National Academy of   QH362.T435 1998
  Sciences Staff & Vedral, Joyce L.
Teaching about Evolution and the Nature of Science. Trade
Paper. National Academies Press. Washington, DC. 1998. 150p.
ISBN:0-309-06364-7, ISBN13: 978-0-309-06364-7.
Dewey:576.8/071. LCCN:98-016100.
Audience: **u,f.**

National Academy Press   QH366.2.S425 1999
  (Created by)
Science and Creationism: A View from the National Academy of
Sciences. Ed. 2. Trade Paper. National Academies Press.
Washington, DC. 1998. 35p. ISBN:0-309-06406-6, ISBN13:
978-0-309-06406-4. LCCN:99-006259.
Audience: **l,u,f.**

Nitecki, Matthew H.   QH371.E929 1988
  (Editor)
Evolutionary Progress. Trade Cloth. University of Chicago
Press. Chicago, IL. 2000. 362p. ISBN:0-226-58692-8, ISBN13:
978-0-226-58692-2. Dewey:575. LCCN:88-020835.
Audience: **u,f.**

Oller, D. Kimbrough &   P90.E86 2004
  Griebel, Ulrike (Editors)
The Evolution of Communication Systems: A Comparative
Approach. Trade Cloth. MIT Press. Cambridge, MA. 2004.
352p. The Vienna Series in Theoretical Biology
ISBN:0-262-15111-1, ISBN13: 978-0-262-15111-5.
Dewey:302.2/09. LCCN:2004-042788.
Audience: **l,u.**

Olson, Steve   QH362.T435 2004
Evolution in Hawaii: A Supplement to Teaching about Evolution
and the Nature of Science. National Academy of Sciences (U.S.)
Staff (Contribution by). Trade Cloth. National Academies Press.
Washington, DC. 2004. viii, 48p. ISBN:0-309-08991-3, ISBN13:
978-0-309-08991-3. LCCN:2004-298464.
Audience: **g,l,u.**

Oyama, Susan   QH507.O93 2000
The Ontogeny of Information: Developmental Systems and
Evolution. Ed. 2. Cloth Text. Duke University Press. Durham,
NC. 2000. 280p. Science and Cultural Theory Ser.
ISBN:0-8223-2431-8, ISBN13: 978-0-8223-2431-7.
Dewey:576.8. LCCN:99-034735.
Audience: **u,f.**

Pagel, Mark D. (Editor)   QH360.2.O83 2002
Encyclopedia of Evolution, Set. Trade Cloth. Oxford University
Press, Inc. New York, NY. 2002. 1,234p. ISBN:0-19-512200-3,
ISBN13: 978-0-19-512200-8. Dewey:576.8/03.
LCCN:2001-021588.
Audience: **g,l,u,f.** *Choice, 2002.*

Palumbi, Stephen R.   QH371.P25 2001
The Evolution Explosion: How Humans Cause Rapid
Evolutionary Change. Trade Cloth. W. W. Norton & Company,
Inc. New York, NY. 2001. 288p. ISBN:0-393-02011-8, ISBN13:
978-0-393-02011-3. Dewey:576.8. LCCN:00-067004.
Audience: **l,u,f.** *Choice, 2001.*

Patterson, Colin   QH366.2.P37 1999
Evolution. Ed. 2. Trade Cloth. Cornell University Press. Ithaca,
NY. 1999. 176p. Comstock Book Ser. ISBN:0-8014-3642-7,
ISBN13: 978-0-8014-3642-0. Dewey:576.8. LCCN:98-041312.
Audience: **l,u,f.** *Choice, 1999.*

Pennock, Robert T.   QH366.2.P428 1999
Tower of Babel: The Evidence Against the New Creationism.
Trade Cloth. MIT Press. Cambridge, MA. 1999. 440p. Bradford
Bks. ISBN:0-262-16180-X, ISBN13: 978-0-262-16180-0.
Dewey:576.8. LCCN:98-027286.
Audience: **u,f.** *Choice, 1999.*

Persell, Stuart M.   QH361.P47 1999
Neo-Lamarckism and the Evolution Controversy in France,
1870-1920. Trade Cloth. Edwin Mellen Press, The. Lewiston,
NY. 1999. 304p. Studies in French Civilization, Vol. 14
ISBN:0-7734-8275-X, ISBN13: 978-0-7734-8275-3.
Dewey:576.8/0944/09034. LCCN:98-048633.
Audience: **u,f.** *Choice, 1999.*

Pigliucci, Massimo   QH366.2.P54 2002
Denying Evolution: Creationism, Scientism, and the Nature of
Science. Trade Cloth. Sinauer Associates, Inc. Sunderland, MA.
2002. 275p. ISBN:0-87893-659-9, ISBN13: 978-0-87893-659-5.
Dewey:576.8. LCCN:2002-005190.
Audience: **l,u,f.** *Choice, 2003.*

Plotkin, Henry C. (Editor)   QH371.R63 1988
The Role of Behavior in Evolution. Trade Cloth. MIT Press.
Cambridge, MA. 1988. 208p. Bradford Bks.
ISBN:0-262-16107-9, ISBN13: 978-0-262-16107-7.
Dewey:575.01. LCCN:87-029693.
Audience: **u,f.** *Choice, 1989.*

Quicke, Donald L. J.   QH83
Principles and Techniques of Contemporary Taxonomy. Blackie
Academic & Professional, London ; New York. 1993. Tertiary
level biology ISBN:0-7514-0019-X, ISBN13:
978-0-7514-0019-9.
Audience: **l,u.**

Rana, Fazale & Ross, Hugh   QH325.R36 2004
Origins of Life: Biblical and Evolutionary Models Face Off.
Trade Cloth. NavPress Publishing Group. Colorado Springs, CO.
2004. 297p. ISBN:1-57683-344-5, ISBN13: 978-1-57683-344-5.
Dewey:576.8/3. LCCN:2003-017389.
Audience: **l,u,f.**

Ridley, Mark (Editor)   QH366.2.E846 1997
Evolution: An Oxford Reader. Trade Paper. Oxford University
Press, Inc. New York, NY. 1998. 438p. Oxford Readers Ser.
ISBN:0-19-289287-8, ISBN13: 978-0-19-289287-4.
Dewey:576.8. LCCN:97-028965.
Audience: **l,u,f.**

Ridley, Matt   QH366.2.R527 1997
The Origins of Virtue: Human Instincts and the Evolution of
Cooperation. Trade Cloth. Penguin Group (USA) Inc. New
York, NY. 1997. 304p. ISBN:0-670-87449-3, ISBN13:
978-0-670-87449-1. Dewey:303.5. LCCN:96-044907.
Audience: **g,l,u,f.**

Roff, Derek A.   QH401.R64 2001
Life History Evolution. Trade Cloth. Sinauer Associates, Inc.
Sunderland, MA. 2001. 465p. ISBN:0-87893-756-0, ISBN13:
978-0-87893-756-1. Dewey:576.5/4. LCCN:2001-049533.
Audience: **l,u,f.**

Rose, Michael   **QH361.R874 2001**
The Evolution Wars: A Guide to the Debates. Paper Text.
Rutgers University Press. Piscataway, NJ. 2001. 328p.
ISBN:0-8135-3036-9, ISBN13: 978-0-8135-3036-9.
Dewey:576.8/09. LCCN:2001-041686.

Audience: **g,l,u,f.**

Ross, Robert M. & Allmon,   **QH366.2.C39 1990**
  Warren D. (Editors)
Causes of Evolution: A Paleontological Perspective. Stephen Jay
Gould (Foreword by). Trade Cloth. University of Chicago Press.
Chicago, IL. 1990. 494p. ISBN:0-226-72823-4, ISBN13:
978-0-226-72823-0. Dewey:575. LCCN:90-011049.

Audience: **l,u,f.**   *Choice, 1991.*

Rossiter, Andrew &   **QH98**
  Kawanabe, Hiroya (Volume Editors)
Ancient Lakes: Biodiversity, Ecology and Evolution. Trade
Cloth. Elsevier Science & Technology Books. Saint Louis, MO.
2000. 680p. Advances in Ecological Research Ser., Vol. 31
ISBN:0-12-013931-6, ISBN13: 978-0-12-013931-6.
Dewey:578.76.

Audience: **u,f.**

Rothschild, Lynn & Lister,   **QH366.2**
  Adrian (Editors)
Evolution on Planet Earth: Impact of the Physical Environment.
Cloth Text. Elsevier Science & Technology Books. Saint Louis,
MO. 2003. 456p. ISBN:0-12-598655-6, ISBN13:
978-0-12-598655-7. Dewey:576.8. LCCN:2002-115394.

Audience: **l,u,f.**   *Choice, 2004.*

Ruppert, Edward E., et al.   **QL362.R76 2003**
Invertebrate Zoology: A Functional Evolutionary Approach. Ed.
7. Richard S. Fox & Robert D. Barnes (Authors). Cloth Text.
Brooks/Cole. Pacific Grove, CA. 2003. 1008p.
ISBN:0-03-025982-7, ISBN13: 978-0-03-025982-1. Dewey:592.
LCCN:2003-107287.

Audience: **l,u.**

Ruse, Michael (Editor)   **QH371.B78 1988**
But Is It Science?: The Philosophical Question in the
Evolution-Creation Controversy. Trade Cloth. Prometheus
Books, Publishers. Amherst, NY. 1988. 375p. Frontiers of
Philosophy Ser. ISBN:0-87975-439-7, ISBN13:
978-0-87975-439-6. Dewey:575/.001. LCCN:87-035818.

Audience: **l,u,f.**

Ruse, Michael (Editor)   **QH360.5.B87 1996**
But Is It Science?: The Philosophical Question in the
Creation/Evolution Controversy. Trade Paper. Prometheus
Books, Publishers. Amherst, NY. 1996. 406p.
ISBN:1-57392-087-8, ISBN13: 978-1-57392-087-2.
Dewey:575/.001. LCCN:96-004218.

Audience: **g,l,u,f.**

Ruse, Michael   **QH360.5.R87 1996**
Monad to Man: The Concept of Progress in Evolutionary
Biology. Trade Cloth. Harvard University Press. Cambridge,
MA. 1997. 640p. ISBN:0-674-58220-9, ISBN13:
978-0-674-58220-0. Dewey:575. LCCN:96-018951.

Audience: **u,f.**

Ruse, Michael   **QH360.5.R874 1999**
Mystery of Mysteries: Is Evolution a Social Construction? Trade
Cloth. Harvard University Press. Cambridge, MA. 1999. 320p.

ISBN:0-674-46706-X, ISBN13: 978-0-674-46706-4.
Dewey:576.8/01. LCCN:98-041969.

Audience: **g,l,u,f.**   *Choice, 1999.*

Schmidt-Kittler, N. & Vogel,   **QH351.C65 1991**
  K. (Editors)
Constructional Morphology and Evolution. Cloth Text. Springer.
New York, NY. 1991. 424p. ISBN:0-387-53279-X, ISBN13:
978-0-387-53279-0. Dewey:574.4. LCCN:91-012697.

Audience: **u,f.**

Schopf, J. William (Editor)   **QH359.E926 1999**
Evolution!: Facts and Fallacies. Paper Text. Elsevier Science &
Technology Books. Saint Louis, MO. 1998. 159p.
ISBN:0-12-628860-7, ISBN13: 978-0-12-628860-5.
Dewey:576.8. LCCN:98-084494.

Audience: **g,l,u,f.**   *Choice, 1999.*

Schopf, J. William (Editor)   **QH325 .L694 2002**
Life's Origin: The Beginnings of Biological Evolution. Trade
Cloth. University of California Press. Berkeley, CA. 2002. 256p.
ISBN:0-520-23390-5, ISBN13: 978-0-520-23390-4.
Dewey:576.8/3. LCCN:2002-002071.

Audience: **g,l,u,f.**   *Choice, 2003.*

Seckbach, Joseph (Editor)   **QH325**
Origins: Genesis, Evolution and Diversity of Life. Trade Cloth.
Springer. New York, NY. 2004. XXXI, 709p. Cellular Origin,
Life in Extreme Habitats and Astrobiology Ser., Vol. 6
ISBN:1-4020-1813-4, ISBN13: 978-1-4020-1813-8.
Dewey:576.8/3. LCCN:2004-303161.

Audience: **u,f.**

Smith, J. Maynard   **QH359.O74**
Organization Constraints on the Dynamics of Evolution. Trade
Cloth. John Wiley & Sons, Inc. Hoboken, NJ. 1992. 454p.
Proceedings in Nonlinear Science Ser. ISBN:0-471-93500-X,
ISBN13: 978-0-471-93500-1. Dewey:575.

Audience: **u,f.**

Smocovitis, Vassiliki B.   **QH361.S64 1996**
Unifying Biology: The Evolutionary Synthesis and Evolutionary
Biology. Trade Cloth. Princeton University Press. Princeton, NJ.
1996. 254p. ISBN:0-691-03343-9, ISBN13: 978-0-691-03343-3.
Dewey:575/.009. LCCN:96-005605.

Audience: **g,l,u,f.**   *Choice, 1997.*

Sober, Elliott   **QH371.S62 1993**
Philosophy of Biology. Trade Paper. Westview Press. Boulder,
CO. 1993. 231p. Dimensions of Philosophy Ser.
ISBN:0-8133-0785-6, ISBN13: 978-0-8133-0785-5.
Dewey:574.01. LCCN:92-037484.

Audience: **u,f.**   *Choice, 1994.*

Sober, Elliott   **QH371.S63 1988**
Reconstructing the Past: Parsimony, Evolution, and Inference.
Trade Cloth. MIT Press. Cambridge, MA. 1989. 288p.
ISBN:0-262-19273-X, ISBN13: 978-0-262-19273-6.
Dewey:574/.01. LCCN:88-009324.

Audience: **u,f.**

Stearns, Stephen C.   **QH366.2**
The Evolution of Life Histories. Trade Paper. Oxford University
Press, Inc. New York, NY. 1992. 262p. ISBN:0-19-857741-9,
ISBN13: 978-0-19-857741-6. Dewey:575. LCCN:91-034726.

Audience: **u,f.**

Steen, Wim J. van der   **QH360**
Evolution As Natural History: A Philosophical Analysis. Trade Cloth. Greenwood Publishing Group, Inc. Portsmouth, NH. 2000. 200p. Human Evolution, Behavior, and Intelligence Ser. ISBN:0-275-96870-7, ISBN13: 978-0-275-96870-0. LCCN:99-052983.
Audience: **l,u,f.**

Sterelny, Kim   **QH366.2**
Dawkins vs. Gould: Survival of the Fittest. Trade Paper. Totem Books. Cambridge, 2001. 106p. Revolutions in Science Ser. ISBN:1-84046-249-3, ISBN13: 978-1-84046-249-4. Dewey:576.8.
Audience: **g,l.**

Sterelny, Kim   **QH360.5 .S76 2001**
The Evolution of Agency and Other Essays. Michael Ruse (Contribution by). Trade Cloth. Cambridge University Press. New York, NY. 2000. 328p. Studies in Philosophy and Biology ISBN:0-521-64231-0, ISBN13: 978-0-521-64231-6. Dewey:576.8/01. LCCN:00-025317.
Audience: **u,f.** *Choice, 2001.*

Stevens, Peter F.   **QH83.S76 1994**
The Development of Biological Systematics: Antoine-Laurent de Jussieu, Nature, and the Natural System. Trade Cloth. Columbia University Press. New York, NY. 1994. 616p. ISBN:0-231-06440-3, ISBN13: 978-0-231-06440-8. Dewey:574/.012. LCCN:94-027231.
Audience: **u,f.** *Choice, 1995.*

Takeuchi, Y.   **QH352.T35 1996**
Global Dynamical Properties of Lotka-Volterra Systems. Cloth Text. World Scientific Publishing Company, Inc. Hackensack, NJ. 1996. 280p. ISBN:981-02-2471-0, ISBN13: 978-981-02-2471-4. Dewey:577.8/8/0151. LCCN:96-200751.
Audience: **u,f.**

Thompson, John N.   **QH372.T48 1994**
The Coevolutionary Process. Trade Cloth. University of Chicago Press. Chicago, IL. 1994. 383p. ISBN:0-226-79759-7, ISBN13: 978-0-226-79759-5. Dewey:575. LCCN:94-014140.
Audience: **u,f.** *Choice, 1995.*

Thompson, John N.   **QH372.T482 2005**
The Geographic Mosaic of Coevolution. Trade Cloth. University of Chicago Press. Chicago, IL. 2005. 400p. Interspecific Interactions Ser. ISBN:0-226-79761-9, ISBN13: 978-0-226-79761-8. Dewey:576.8/7. LCCN:2004-023861.
Audience: **u,f.** *Choice, 2005.*

Thompson, Paul   **QH371.T494 1989**
The Structure of Biological Theories. Cloth Text. State University of New York Press. Albany, NY. 1989. 148p. SUNY Series in Philosophy and Biology ISBN:0-88706-933-9, ISBN13: 978-0-88706-933-8. Dewey:575.01. LCCN:88-015376.
Audience: **u,f.** *Choice, 1989.*

Van De Vijver, Gertrudis, et al.   **QH360.5.E96 1998**
Evolutionary Systems: Biological and Epistemological Perspectives on Selection and Self-Organization. Stanley N. Salthe & Manuela Delpos (Authors). Trade Cloth. Springer. New York, NY. 1998. 450p. ISBN:0-7923-5260-2, ISBN13: 978-0-7923-5260-0. Dewey:576.8/01. LCCN:98-036791.
Audience: **u,f.**

Wainwright, Peter C. & Reilly, Stephen M. (Editors)   **QH351.E37 1994**
Ecological Morphology: Integrative Organismal Biology. Trade Cloth. University of Chicago Press. Chicago, IL. 1994. 376p. ISBN:0-226-86994-6, ISBN13: 978-0-226-86994-0. Dewey:591.5. LCCN:93-040993.
Audience: **u,f.**

Wallace, Alfred R.   **QH366.2.W342 2002**
Infinite Tropics: An Alfred Russel Wallace Anthology. Andrew Berry (Editor), Stephen Jay Gould (Foreword by). Trade Cloth. Verso Books. London, 2003. 320p. ISBN:1-85984-652-1, ISBN13: 978-1-85984-652-0. Dewey:570. LCCN:2002-280978.
Audience: **l,u,f.** *Choice, 2002.*

Wallace, Alfred R.   **QH375.W332 2002**
The Alfred Russel Wallace Reader: A Selection of Writings from the Field. Jane R. Camerini (Author, Editor), David Quammen (Foreword by). Trade Paper. Johns Hopkins University Press. Baltimore, MD. 2001. 248p. Center Books in Natural History ISBN:0-8018-6789-4, ISBN13: 978-0-8018-6789-7. Dewey:576.8/2. LCCN:2001-000539.
Audience: **l,u,f.** *Choice, 2002.*

Wallace, David Rains   **QH366.2.W35 1997**
The Monkey's Bridge: Mysteries of Evolution in Central America. Trade Cloth. Sierra Club Books. San Francisco, CA. 1997. 304p. ISBN:0-87156-586-2, ISBN13: 978-0-87156-586-0. Dewey:578/.09728. LCCN:97-008046.
Audience: **u,f.** *Choice, 1998.*

Ward-Jackson, Peter   **QH366.2.W37 2001**
Future Evolution: An Illuminated History of Life to Come. Alexis Rockman (Illustrator). Cloth over Boards. W. H. Freeman & Company. New York, NY. 2002. 208p. ISBN:0-7167-3496-6, ISBN13: 978-0-7167-3496-3. Dewey:576.8. LCCN:2001-003607.
Audience: **l,u,f.**

Weber, Bruce H. (Editor), et al.   **QH359.E57 1988**
Entropy, Information, and Evolution: New Perspectives on Physical and Biological Evolution. David J. Depew & James D. Smith (Editors). Trade Cloth. MIT Press. Cambridge, MA. 1988. 370p. Bradford Bks. ISBN:0-262-23132-8, ISBN13: 978-0-262-23132-9. Dewey:575. LCCN:87-003822.
Audience: **u,f.** *Choice, 1988.*

Wells, Jonathan   **QH366.2.W45 2000**
Icons of Evolution: Science or Myth? Trade Cloth. Regnery Publishing, Incorporated, An Eagle Publishing Company. Washington, DC. 2000. 240p. ISBN:0-89526-276-2, ISBN13: 978-0-89526-276-9. Dewey:576.8. LCCN:00-062544.
Audience: **u,f.**

Wesson, Robert   **QH366.2.W47 1991**
Beyond Natural Selection. Trade Cloth. MIT Press. Cambridge, MA. 1991. 370p. ISBN:0-262-23161-1, ISBN13: 978-0-262-23161-9. Dewey:575.01. LCCN:90-021977.
Audience: **u,f.** *Choice, 1992.*

Whitfield, Philip   **QH366.2.W53 1993**
From So Simple a Beginning: The Book of Evolution. Rodger Lewin (Foreword by). Trade Cloth. Macmillan Publishing Company, Inc. Old Tappan, NJ. 1993. 224p. ISBN:0-02-627115-X, ISBN13: 978-0-02-627115-8. Dewey:575. LCCN:93-006883.
Audience: **l,u,f.** *Choice, 1994.*

Williams, George C.   QH375.W52 1992
Natural Selection: Domains, Levels, and Challenges. Paper Text.
Oxford University Press, Inc. New York, NY. 1992. 224p.
Oxford Series in Ecology and Evolution ISBN:0-19-506933-1,
ISBN13: 978-0-19-506933-4. Dewey:577.01/62.
LCCN:91-038938.

Audience: **u,f.** *Choice, 1993.*

Willis, Christopher   QH371.W55 1989
The Wisdom of the Genes: New Pathways in Evolution. Trade
Cloth. Basic Books. New York, NY. 1989. 368p.
ISBN:0-465-09195-4, ISBN13: 978-0-465-09195-9. Dewey:575.
LCCN:89-042526.

Audience: **u,f.**

Yockey, Hubert P.   QH506.Y634 2004
Information Theory, Evolution and the Origin of Life. Ed. 2.
Trade Cloth. Cambridge University Press. New York, NY. 2005.
272p. ISBN:0-521-80293-8, ISBN13: 978-0-521-80293-2.
Dewey:572.8. LCCN:2004-054518.

Audience: **u,f.**

Young, David G.   QH361.Y695 1992
The Discovery of Evolution. Cloth Text. Cambridge University
Press. New York, NY. 1992. 256p. ISBN:0-521-43441-6,
ISBN13: 978-0-521-43441-6. Dewey:575/.009.
LCCN:93-116579.

Audience: **g,l,u.** *Choice, 1993.*

Zelditch, Miriam Leah   QH395.B49 2001
(Editor)
Beyond Heterochrony: The Evolution of Development. Trade
Cloth. John Wiley & Sons, Inc. Hoboken, NJ. 2001. 392p.
ISBN:0-471-37973-5, ISBN13: 978-0-471-37973-7.
Dewey:576.8. LCCN:2001-023742.

Audience: **u,f.**

Zimmer, Carl   QH361.Z48 2006
Evolution: The Triumph of an Idea. Trade Paper. HarperCollins
Publishers. New York, NY. 2006. 528p. ISBN:0-06-113840-1,
ISBN13: 978-0-06-113840-9. Dewey:576.809.
LCCN:2006-043640.

Audience: **g.**

Integrative Biology > Evolution > Speciation

Ayala, Francisco J. (Editor)   QH380.S97 2005
Systematics and the Origin of Species: On Ernst Mayr's 100th
Anniversary. Saddle Stitched, Cloth over Boards. National
Academies Press. Washington, DC. 2005. 367p.
ISBN:0-309-09536-0, ISBN13: 978-0-309-09536-5.
Dewey:576.8/6. LCCN:2005-017917.

Audience: **u,f.**

Bateson, William   QH401
Materials for the Study of Variation: Treated with Especial
Regard to Discontinuity in the Origin of Species. Peter Bowler
& Gerry Webster (Introduction by). Trade Cloth. Johns Hopkins
University Press. Baltimore, MD. 1992. 652p. Foundations of
Natural History Ser. ISBN:0-8018-4419-3, ISBN13:
978-0-8018-4419-5. Dewey:575.2. LCCN:91-045926.

Audience: **u,f.**

Benman, B. E. & Persson,   QH352.S59 1988
L. (Editors)
Size-Structured Populations: Ecology and Evolution. Cloth Text.
Springer. New York, NY. 1989. 284p. ISBN:0-387-50188-6,
ISBN13: 978-0-387-50188-8. Dewey:574.5/248.
LCCN:88-026561.

Audience: **u,f.**

Bunce, R. G. & Howard, D.   QH137.S63 1990
C. (Editors)
Species Dispersal in Agricultural Habitats. Cloth Text. St.
Martin's Press. Gordonville, VA. 1992. 296p.
ISBN:1-85293-076-4, ISBN13: 978-1-85293-076-9.
Dewey:574.5/264. LCCN:90-037137.

Audience: **u,f.**

Claridge, M. F. (Editor),   QH380.S655 1997
et al.
Species: The Units of Biodiversity. H. A. Dawah & M. R.
Wilson (Editors). Trade Cloth. Springer. New York, NY. 1997.
460p. Systematics Association Ser. ISBN:0-412-63120-2,
ISBN13: 978-0-412-63120-7. Dewey:578.01/2.
LCCN:96-070872.

Audience: **u,f.**

Coyne, Jerry A. & Orr, H.   QH380.C68 2004
Allen
Speciation. Trade Cloth. Sinauer Associates, Inc. Sunderland,
MA. 2004. 545p. ISBN:0-87893-091-4, ISBN13:
978-0-87893-091-3. Dewey:576.8/6. LCCN:2004-009505.
Audience: **u,f.** *Choice, 2005.*

Cracraft, Joel & Donoghue,   QH83.A86 2004
Michael J. (Editors)
Assembling the Tree of Life. Trade Cloth. Oxford University
Press, Inc. New York, NY. 2004. 591p. ISBN:0-19-517234-5,
ISBN13: 978-0-19-517234-8. Dewey:578/.01/2.
LCCN:2003-058012.
Audience: **u,f.** *Choice, 2005.*

Eldridge, Niles   QH366.2.E52 1989
Macroevolutionary Dynamics: Species, Niches and Adaptive
Peaks. Trade Cloth. McGraw-Hill Companies, The. New York,
NY. 1989. 226p. ISBN:0-07-019474-2, ISBN13:
978-0-07-019474-8. Dewey:575. LCCN:88-032585.
Audience: **u,f.** *Choice, 1989.*

Ereshefsky, Marc (Editor)   QH380.U54 1992
The Units of Evolution: Essays on the Nature of the Species.
Trade Paper. MIT Press. Cambridge, MA. 1991. 424p. Bradford
Bks. ISBN:0-262-55020-2, ISBN13: 978-0-262-55020-8.
Dewey:574/.012. LCCN:91-004097.

Audience: **l,u,f.**

Gordon, Malcolm S., et al.   QH366.2.G657 1995
Invasions of the Land: The Transitions of Organisms from
Aquatic to Terrestrial Life. Everett C. Olson & David J.
Chapman (Authors). Trade Cloth. Columbia University Press.
New York, NY. 1994. 312p. ISBN:0-231-06876-X, ISBN13:
978-0-231-06876-5. Dewey:575. LCCN:94-020344.
Audience: **u,f.** *Choice, 1995.*

Hey, Jody   QH83.H53 2001
Genes, Categories, and Species: The Evolutionary and Cognitive
Causes of the Species Problem. Trade Cloth. Oxford University
Press, Inc. New York, NY. 2001. 236p. ISBN:0-19-514477-5,
ISBN13: 978-0-19-514477-2. Dewey:576.8/6. LCCN:00-045655.
Audience: **u,f.** *Choice, 2002.*

Howard, Daniel J. &   **QH380.E54 1998**
Berlocher, Stewart H. (Editors)
Endless Forms: Species and Speciation. Trade Paper. Oxford
University Press, Inc. New York, NY. 1998. 482p.
ISBN:0-19-510901-5, ISBN13: 978-0-19-510901-6.
Dewey:576.8/6. LCCN:97-031461.

Audience: **u,f.**

King, Max   **QH380.K56 1993**
The Evolution of Species. Trade Cloth. Cambridge University
Press. New York, NY. 1993. 358p. ISBN:0-521-35308-4,
ISBN13: 978-0-521-35308-3. Dewey:575.1. LCCN:92-033870.

Audience: **l,u,f.** *Choice, 1994.*

Kitching, Ian, et al.   **QH83.C486 1998**
Cladistics: The Theory and Practice of Parsimony Analysis. Ed.
2. Peter Forey, Christopher Humphries & David Williams
(Authors). Cloth Text. Oxford University Press, Inc. New York,
NY. 1998. 248p. Systematics Association Publications, No. 11
ISBN:0-19-850139-0, ISBN13: 978-0-19-850139-8.
Dewey:570/.1/2. LCCN:98-010352.

Audience: **u,f.**

Lambert, David M. &   **QH380.S64 1995**
Spencer, Hamish G.
Speciation and the Recognition Concept: Theory and
Application. Trade Cloth. Johns Hopkins University Press.
Baltimore, MD. 1994. 504p. ISBN:0-8018-4740-0, ISBN13:
978-0-8018-4740-0. Dewey:575.1/3. LCCN:94-027980.

Audience: **u,f.**

MacLeod, Norman (Editor)   **QH351**
Morphology, Shape and Phylogeny. Forey, Peter L. (Editor).
Taylor & Francis, London; New York. 2002. Systematics
Association special volume series ;; 64; Variation: Systematics
Association special volume ;; no. 64 ISBN:0-415-24074-3,
ISBN13: 978-0-415-24074-1.

Audience: **u,f.**

Margulis, Lynn & Sagan,   **QH380**
Dorion
Acquiring Genomes: A Theory of the Origins of Species. Trade
Cloth. Basic Books. New York, NY. 2002. 256p.
ISBN:0-465-04391-7, ISBN13: 978-0-465-04391-0.
Dewey:576.8/6. LCCN:2002-001521.

Audience: **u,f.**

Minelli, A.   **QH83.M655 1993**
Biological Systematics: The State of the Art. Trade Cloth.
Chapman & Hall. New York, NY. 1993. 408p.
ISBN:0-412-36440-9, ISBN13: 978-0-412-36440-2.
Dewey:578/.012. LCCN:93-003578.

Audience: **u,f.** *Choice, 1995.*

Otte, Daniel & Endler, John   **QH83.S685 1989**
A. (Editors)
Speciation and Its Consequences. Cloth Text. Sinauer
Associates, Inc. Sunderland, MA. 1989. 679p.
ISBN:0-87893-657-2, ISBN13: 978-0-87893-657-1. Dewey:575.
LCCN:89-005867.

Audience: **u,f.** *Choice, 1990.*

Paterson, Hugh E. &   **QH380.P38 1993**
McEvey, Shane F.
Evolution and the Recognition Concept of Species: Collected
Writings. Trade Cloth. Johns Hopkins University Press.

Baltimore, MD. 1976. 256p. ISBN:0-8018-4409-6, ISBN13:
978-0-8018-4409-6. Dewey:575. LCCN:92-004779.

Audience: **u,f.** *Choice, 1993.*

Schilthuizen, Menno   **QH380.S35 2001**
Frogs, Flies, and Dandelions: Speciation--The Evolution of New
Species. Trade Cloth. Oxford University Press, Inc. New York,
NY. 2001. 256p. ISBN:0-19-850393-8, ISBN13:
978-0-19-850393-4. Dewey:576.8/6. LCCN:2001-270180.

Audience: **u,f.**

Schwartz, Jeffrey H.   **QH366.2.S386 1999**
Sudden Origins: Fossils, Genes, and the Emergence of Species.
Trade Cloth. John Wiley & Sons, Inc. Hoboken, NJ. 1999. 432p.
ISBN:0-471-32985-1, ISBN13: 978-0-471-32985-5.
Dewey:576.8. LCCN:98-045724.

Audience: **u,f.** *Choice, 1999.*

Wheeler, Quentin & Meier,   **QH83.S695 2000**
Rudolf
Species Concepts and Phylogenetic Theory: A Debate. Trade
Cloth. Columbia University Press. New York, NY. 2000. 256p.
ISBN:0-231-10142-2, ISBN13: 978-0-231-10142-4.
Dewey:576.8/6. LCCN:99-044163.

Audience: **u,f.**

Wiens, John J. (Editor)   **QH351.P58 2000**
Phylogenetic Analysis of Morphological Data. Trade Cloth.
Smithsonian Institution Press. Washington, DC. 2000. x, 220p.
Smithsonian Series in Comparative Evolutionary Biology
ISBN:1-56098-841-X, ISBN13: 978-1-56098-841-0.
Dewey:571.3. LCCN:00-023910.

Audience: **u,f.** *Choice, 2001.*

Winston, Judith E.   **QH83.W57 1999**
Describing Species: Practical Taxonomic Procedure for
Biologists. Trade Cloth. Columbia University Press. New York,
NY. 1999. 512p. ISBN:0-231-06824-7, ISBN13:
978-0-231-06824-6. LCCN:99-014019.

Audience: **u,f.** *Choice, 2000.*

Integrative Biology > Evolution > Molecular Evolution

Barbieri, Marcello   **QH331.B247 2002**
The Organic Codes: An Introduction to Semantic Biology. Trade
Cloth. Cambridge University Press. New York, NY. 2002. 316p.
ISBN:0-521-82414-1, ISBN13: 978-0-521-82414-9.
Dewey:570/.1. LCCN:2002-073767.

Audience: **u,f.**

Behe, Michael J.   **QH325**
Darwin's Black Box: The Biochemical Challenge to Evolution.
Trade Paper. Simon & Schuster. New York, NY. 2006. 336p.
ISBN:0-7432-9031-3, ISBN13: 978-0-7432-9031-9. Dewey:575.

Audience: **u,f.**

Caporale, Lynn H. (Editor)   **Q11.N5 VOL. 870**
Molecular Strategies in Biological Evolution. Cloth Text. New
York Academy of Sciences. New York, NY. 1999. 350p.
ISBN:1-57331-192-8, ISBN13: 978-1-57331-192-2. Dewey:500
s. LCCN:99-028213.

Audience: **u,f.**

Caporale, Lynn Helena   QH390.I47 2006
  (Editor)
The Implicit Genome. Trade Cloth. Oxford University Press, Inc. New York, NY. 2006. 398p. ISBN:0-19-517270-1, ISBN13: 978-0-19-517270-6. Dewey:572.8/38. LCCN:2005-011590.
Audience: u,f.

Carroll, Sean B., et al.   QH390.C37 2005
From DNA to Diversity: Molecular Genetics and the Evolution of Animal Design. Ed. 2. Jennifer K. Grenier & Scott D. Weatherbee (Authors). Trade Paper. Blackwell Publishing, Inc. Malden, MA. 2004. 272p. ISBN:1-4051-1950-0, ISBN13: 978-1-4051-1950-4. Dewey:572.8/38. LCCN:2003-027991.
Audience: u,f. Choice, 2002.

De Duve, Christian   QH325.D415 2002
Life Evolving: Molecules, Mind, and Meaning. Trade Cloth. Oxford University Press, Inc. New York, NY. 2002. 358p. ISBN:0-19-515605-6, ISBN13: 978-0-19-515605-8. Dewey:576.8/8. LCCN:2002-075407.
Audience: u,f. Choice, 2003.

De Pouplana, Lluis Ribbas   QH390.G445 2004
  (Editor)
The Genetic Code and the Origin of Life. Trade Cloth. Springer. New York, NY. 2004. 272p. ISBN:0-306-47843-9, ISBN13: 978-0-306-47843-7. Dewey:572.8/633. LCCN:2004-015694.
Audience: u,f.

DeSalle, Rob (Editor), et al.   QH83.M67 2001
Molecular Systematics and Evolution: Theory and Practice. Gonzalo Giribet & Ward Wheeler (Editors). Trade Cloth. Birkhauser Boston. Cambridge, MA. 2002. IX, 309p. EXS Ser., Vol. 92: ISBN:3-7643-6544-7, ISBN13: 978-3-7643-6544-8. Dewey:572.8/38. LCCN:2001-037878.
Audience: u,f.

Givnish, Thomas J. &   QH83 .M664 1997
  Sytsma, Kenneth J. (Editors)
Molecular Evolution and Adaptive Radiation. Trade Cloth. Cambridge University Press. New York, NY. 1997. 638p. ISBN:0-521-57329-7, ISBN13: 978-0-521-57329-0. Dewey:572.8/38. LCCN:97-005995.
Audience: u,f.

Gouyon, Pierre-Henri, et al.   QH390.G6813 2002
Gene Avatars: Neo-Darwinian Theory of Evolution. Jean-Pierre Henry & Jacques Arnould (Authors). Trade Cloth. Springer. New York, NY. 2002. 278p. ISBN:0-306-46616-3, ISBN13: 978-0-306-46616-8. Dewey:572.8/38. LCCN:2001-038767.
Audience: u,f.

Hughes, Austin L.   QH390.H84 1999
Adaptive Evolution of Genes and Genomes. Trade Cloth. Oxford University Press, Inc. New York, NY. 2000. 282p. ISBN:0-19-511626-7, ISBN13: 978-0-19-511626-7. Dewey:572.8/38. LCCN:98-046584.
Audience: u,f.

Lewontin, Richard C.   QH506
The Triple Helix: Gene, Organism, and Environment. Trade Paper. Harvard University Press. Cambridge, MA. 2002. 144p. ISBN:0-674-00677-1, ISBN13: 978-0-674-00677-5. Dewey:572.8/01.
Audience: l,u,f. Choice, 2000.

Maynard Smith, John   QH371.M327 1989
Evolutionary Genetics. Paper Text. Oxford University Press, Inc. New York, NY. 1989. 344p. ISBN:0-19-854215-1, ISBN13: 978-0-19-854215-5. Dewey:575.1/5. LCCN:88-017041.
Audience: u,f.

Nei, Masatoshi & Kumar,   QH390.N45 2000
  Sudhir
Molecular Evolution and Phylogenetics. Trade Paper. Oxford University Press, Inc. New York, NY. 2000. 348p. ISBN:0-19-513585-7, ISBN13: 978-0-19-513585-5. Dewey:572.8/38. LCCN:99-039160.
Audience: u,f.

Osawa, Syozo   QH390.O83 1995
Evolution of the Genetic Code. Cloth Text. Oxford University Press, Inc. New York, NY. 1995. 232p. ISBN:0-19-854781-1, ISBN13: 978-0-19-854781-5. Dewey:575. LCCN:94-045539.
Audience: u,f.

Page, Roderic D. & Holmes,   QH390.P34 1998
  Edward C.
Molecular Evolution: A Phylogenetic Approach. Trade Paper. Blackwell Publishing, Inc. Malden, MA. 1998. 352p. Evolutionary Biology Ser. ISBN:0-86542-889-1, ISBN13: 978-0-86542-889-8. Dewey:572.8/38. LCCN:98-004696.
Audience: u,f.

Raff, Rudolf A.   QH390.R325 1996
The Shape of Life: Genes, Development, and the Evolution of Animal Form. Trade Paper. University of Chicago Press. Chicago, IL. 1996. 544p. ISBN:0-226-70266-9, ISBN13: 978-0-226-70266-7. Dewey:575.1. LCCN:95-049224.
Audience: u,f. Choice, 1996.

Rapoport, Basil   QH506.X53 2000
Data Analysis in Molecular Biology and Evolution. Trade Cloth. Springer. New York, NY. 2000. 296p. ISBN:0-7923-7767-2, ISBN13: 978-0-7923-7767-2. Dewey:572.8/0285. LCCN:00-022032.
Audience: u,f.

Sener, Bilge (Editor)   QH345.B528 2003
Biodiversity: Biomolecular Aspects of Biodiversity and Innovative Utilization. Trade Cloth. Springer. New York, NY. 2003. 426p. ISBN:0-306-47477-8, ISBN13: 978-0-306-47477-4. Dewey:577. LCCN:2002-037011.
Audience: u,f.

Singh, Rama S. & Krimbas,   QH390.E96 2000
  Costas B. (Editors)
Evolutionary Genetics: From Molecules to Morphology. Trade Cloth. Cambridge University Press. New York, NY. 2000. 720p. ISBN:0-521-57123-5, ISBN13: 978-0-521-57123-4. Dewey:576.8. LCCN:99-014415.
Audience: u,f.

Sterner, Robert Warner &   QH345.S74 2002
  Elser, James J.
Ecological Stoichiometry: The Biology of Elements from Molecules to the Biosphere. Peter M. Vitousek (Foreword by). Trade Cloth. Princeton University Press. Princeton, NJ. 2002. 440p. ISBN:0-691-07490-9, ISBN13: 978-0-691-07490-0. Dewey:572. LCCN:2002-072262.
Audience: l,u,f.

Takahata, Naoyuki & Clark,   **QH352**
  Andrew G. (Editors)
Mechanisms of Molecular Evolution. Cloth Text. Sinauer
Associates, Inc. Sunderland, MA. 1993. 250p.
ISBN:0-87893-825-7, ISBN13: 978-0-87893-825-4.
Dewey:574.87328.

Audience: **u,f.**

Wagner, Andreas   **QH390.W356 2005**
Robustness and Evolvability in Living Systems. Trade Cloth.
Princeton University Press. Princeton, NJ. 2005. 408p. Princeton
Studies in Complexity Ser. ISBN:0-691-12240-7, ISBN13:
978-0-691-12240-3. Dewey:572.8/38. LCCN:2004-054936.

Audience: **u,f.** *Choice, 2006.*

Wiens, John J. (Editor)   **QH351.P58 2000**
Phylogenetic Analysis of Morphological Data. Trade Cloth.
Smithsonian Institution Press. Washington, DC. 2000. x, 220p.
Smithsonian Series in Comparative Evolutionary Biology
ISBN:1-56098-841-X, ISBN13: 978-1-56098-841-0.
Dewey:571.3. LCCN:00-023910.

Audience: **u,f.** *Choice, 2001.*

Zimmer, Elizabeth A. &   **QH390**
  Roalson, Eric (Volume Editors)
Molecular Evolution, Producing the Biochemical Data, Part B.
Trade Cloth. Elsevier Science & Technology Books. Saint
Louis, MO. 2005. 896p. ISBN:0-12-182800-X, ISBN13:
978-0-12-182800-4. Dewey:572.838.

Audience: **u,f.**

Integrative Biology > Evolution > Human Evolution

Bonnette, Dennis   **GN281 .B63**
Origin of the Human Species. Trade Paper. Rodopi. Kenilworth,
NY. 2001. XV,202p. Value Inquiry Book Ser., Vol. 106
ISBN:90-420-1374-5, ISBN13: 978-90-420-1374-2.
Dewey:599.93/8.

Audience: **u,f.** *Choice, 2001.*

Corning, Peter   **QH366.2.C73 2003**
Nature's Magic: Synergy in Evolution and the Fate of
Humankind. Trade Cloth. Cambridge University Press. New
York, NY. 2003. 464p. ISBN:0-521-82547-4, ISBN13:
978-0-521-82547-4. Dewey:576.8. LCCN:2002-031552.

Audience: **u,f.** *Choice, 2004.*

Jackson, M., et al.   **QH431**
Human Genome Evolution: Human Molecular Genetics. T.
Strachan & G. Dover (Authors). Cloth Text. Taylor & Francis
Group. Abingdon, 1996. 256p. Human Molecular Genetics Ser.
ISBN:1-85996-095-2, ISBN13: 978-1-85996-095-0.
Dewey:599.9/35.

Audience: **u,f.** *Choice, 1997.*

Morris, Desmond   **GN280.7.M675 2005**
Naked Ape: A Zoologist's Study of the Human Animal. UK-B
Format Paperback. Knopf Publishing Group. New York, NY.
2005. 192p. ISBN:0-09-948201-0, ISBN13: 978-0-09-948201-7.
Dewey:156.

Audience: **l,u,f.**

Relethford, John H.   **QH390.R45 2001**
Genetics and the Search for Modern Human Origins. Trade
Cloth. John Wiley & Sons, Inc. Hoboken, NJ. 2001. 264p.
ISBN:0-471-38413-5, ISBN13: 978-0-471-38413-7.
Dewey:572.8/38. LCCN:00-068633.

Audience: **u,f.**

Stillman, Bruce & Stewart,   **DS597.367.K4 2003**
  David (Editors)
The Genome of Homo Sapiens. Trade Cloth. Cold Spring
Harbor Laboratory Press. Woodbury, NY. 2004. 650p. Symposia
on Quantitative Biology Ser., LXVIII ISBN:0-87969-709-1,
ISBN13: 978-0-87969-709-9. Dewey:599.935.

Audience: **u,f.**

Integrative Biology > Evolution > Cladistics

Cracraft, Joel & Donoghue,   **QH83.A86 2004**
  Michael J. (Editors)
Assembling the Tree of Life. Trade Cloth. Oxford University
Press, Inc. New York, NY. 2004. 591p. ISBN:0-19-517234-5,
ISBN13: 978-0-19-517234-8. Dewey:578/.01/2.
LCCN:2003-058012.

Audience: **u,f.** *Choice, 2005.*

Gee, Henry   **QH82**
Deep Time: Cladistics, the Revolution in Evolution. Fourth
Estate, London. 2001. ISBN:1-85702-987-9, ISBN13:
978-1-85702-987-1.

Audience: **u,f.**

Humphries, Christopher J.   **QH83.H86 1999**
  & Parenti, Lynne R.
Cladistic Biogeography: Interpreting Patterns of Plant and
Animal Distributions. Ed. 2. Trade Cloth. Oxford University
Press, Inc. New York, NY. 1999. 199p. Oxford Biogeography
Ser., No. 12 ISBN:0-19-854818-4, ISBN13: 978-0-19-854818-8.
Dewey:578/.01/2. LCCN:98-047313.

Audience: **u,f.**

Kitching, Ian, et al.   **QH83.C486 1998**
Cladistics: The Theory and Practice of Parsimony Analysis. Ed.
2. Peter Forey, Christopher Humphries & David Williams
(Authors). Cloth Text. Oxford University Press, Inc. New York,
NY. 1998. 248p. Systematics Association Publications, No. 11
ISBN:0-19-850139-0, ISBN13: 978-0-19-850139-8.
Dewey:570/.1/2. LCCN:98-010352.

Audience: **u,f.**

Panchen, Alec L.   **QH83 .P35 1992**
Classification, Evolution, and the Nature of Biology. Trade
Paper. Cambridge University Press. New York, NY. 1992. 415p.
ISBN:0-521-31578-6, ISBN13: 978-0-521-31578-4.
Dewey:574.012. LCCN:91-026274.

Audience: **l,u.**

Scott-Ram, N. R.   **QH83 .S36 1990**
Transformed Cladistics, Taxonomy and Evolution. Trade Cloth.
Cambridge University Press. New York, NY. 1990. 250p.
ISBN:0-521-34086-1, ISBN13: 978-0-521-34086-1.
Dewey:574/.012. LCCN:89-009754.

Audience: **u,f.**

Skelton, Peter, et al.   **QH83**
Cladistics: A Practical Primer. Andrew Smith & Neale Monks
(Authors). CD-ROM, Cloth Text, Mixed Media. Cambridge
University Press. New York, NY. 2002. 92p.
ISBN:0-521-52341-9, ISBN13: 978-0-521-52341-7.
Dewey:578.012.

Audience: **l,u.** *Choice, 2003.*

Integrative Biology > Evolution > Darwin and Darwinism

Alters, Brian J.   **QH362.A628 2005**
Teaching Evolution in Higher Education: Methodological,
Religious, and Nonreligious Issues. Trade Paper. Jones &
Bartlett Publishers, Inc. Sudbury, MA. 2004. 136p.
ISBN:0-7637-2889-6, ISBN13: 978-0-7637-2889-2.
Dewey:576.8/071/1. LCCN:2004-054945.

Audience: **l,u,f.**

Alters, Brian J. & Alters,   **QH362.A62 2001**
  Sandra M.
Defending Evolution in the Classroom: A Guide to the
Creation/Evolution Controversy. Trade Cloth. Jones & Bartlett
Publishers, Inc. Sudbury, MA. 2001. 272p. Evolution Ser.
ISBN:0-7637-1923-4, ISBN13: 978-0-7637-1923-4.
Dewey:576.8/071. LCCN:2001-029193.

Audience: **l,u,f.**

Ankerberg, John & Weldon,   **QH360.5.A55 1998**
  John
Darwin's Leap of Faith: Exposing the False Religion of
Evolution. Trade Paper. Harvest House Publishers. Eugene, OR.
1998. 396p. ISBN:1-56507-657-5, ISBN13: 978-1-56507-657-0.
Dewey:576.8/01. LCCN:97-040444.

Audience: **u,f.**

Behe, Michael J.   **QH325**
Darwin's Black Box: The Biochemical Challenge to Evolution.
Trade Paper. Simon & Schuster. New York, NY. 2006. 336p.
ISBN:0-7432-9031-3, ISBN13: 978-0-7432-9031-9. Dewey:575.

Audience: **u,f.**

Bird, Wendell R.   **QH371.B58**
The Origin of Species Revisited, Set. Trade Cloth. Philosophical
Library, Inc. New York, NY. 1989. 700p. ISBN:0-8022-2545-4,
ISBN13: 978-0-8022-2545-0. Dewey:575. LCCN:87-014066.

Audience: **l,u,f.**

Bowler, Peter J.   **QH366.2.B675 1993**
Darwinism. Trade Cloth. Thomson Gale. Farmington Hills, MI.
1993. 155p. Twayne's Studies in Intellectual and Cultural
History, Vol. 6 ISBN:0-8057-8613-9, ISBN13:
978-0-8057-8613-2. Dewey:575.01/62/09. LCCN:93-000431.

Audience: **l,u,f.** *Choice, 1994.*

Bowler, Peter J.   **QH361**
The Non-Darwinian Revolution: Reinterpreting a Historical
Myth. Trade Paper. Johns Hopkins University Press. Baltimore,
MD. 1982. 256p. ISBN:0-8018-4367-7, ISBN13:
978-0-8018-4367-9. Dewey:575/.009. LCCN:88-009738.

Audience: **u,f.** *Choice, 1989.*

Brown, Andrew   **QH375**
The Darwin Wars: The Scientific Battle for the Soul of Man.
Trade Paper. Simon & Schuster, Ltd. London, 2002. 256p.
ISBN:0-7432-0343-7, ISBN13: 978-0-7432-0343-2.
Dewey:576.8/2.

Audience: **u,f.**

Brown, Andrew   **QH360.5**
The Darwin Wars: How Stupid Genes Became Selfish Gods.
Simon & Schuster, London. 1999. ISBN:0-684-85144-X,
ISBN13: 978-0-684-85144-0.

Audience: **u,f.**

Caporale, Lynn Helena   **QH366.2.C367 2002**
Darwin in the Genome: Molecular Strategies in Biological
Evolution. Trade Cloth. McGraw-Hill Companies, The. New
York, NY. 2002. 256p. ISBN:0-07-137822-7, ISBN13:
978-0-07-137822-2. Dewey:576. LCCN:2002-009570.

Audience: **u,f.**

Caudill, Edward   **QH360.5.C38 1997**
Darwinian Myths: The Legends and Misuses of a Theory. Cloth
Text. University of Tennessee Press. Knoxville, TN. 1997. 208p.
ISBN:0-87049-984-X, ISBN13: 978-0-87049-984-5.
Dewey:576.8/2. LCCN:97-004691.

Audience: **u,f.** *Choice, 1998.*

Cziko, Gary   **QH360.5**
Without Miracles: Universal Selection Theory and the Second
Darwinian Revolution. Trade Paper. MIT Press. Cambridge,
MA. 1997. 400p. Bradford Bks. ISBN:0-262-53147-X, ISBN13:
978-0-262-53147-4. Dewey:576.8/2. LCCN:95-000943.

Audience: **u,f.** *Choice, 1996.*

Dembski, William A. &   **QH360.5.D42 2004**
  Ruse, Michael (Editors)
Debating Design: From Darwin to DNA. Cloth Text. Cambridge
University Press. New York, NY. 2004. 422p.
ISBN:0-521-82949-6, ISBN13: 978-0-521-82949-6.
Dewey:576.8. LCCN:2004-047363.

Audience: **u,f.**

Dennett, Daniel C.   **QH365**
Darwin's Dangerous Idea: Evolution and the Meanings of Life.
Trade Paper. Simon & Schuster. New York, NY. 1996. 592p.
ISBN:0-684-82471-X, ISBN13: 978-0-684-82471-0.
Dewey:575/.0162.

Audience: **l,u,f.**

Depew, David J. & Weber,   **QH365**
  Bruce H.
Darwinism Evolving: Systems Dynamics and the Genealogy of
Natural Selection. Trade Paper. MIT Press. Cambridge, MA.
1996. 608p. Bradford Bks. ISBN:0-262-54083-5, ISBN13:
978-0-262-54083-4. Dewey:575.01/62.

Audience: **u,f.** *Choice, 1995.*

Dover, Gabriel   **QH366.2 .D67 2000**
Dear Mr. Darwin: Letters on the Evolution of Life and Human
Nature. Trade Cloth. University of California Press. Berkeley,
CA. 2000. 262p. ISBN:0-520-22790-5, ISBN13:
978-0-520-22790-3. Dewey:576.8. LCCN:00-042615.

Audience: **l,u,f.** *Choice, 2001.*

Eldredge, Niles   **QH360.5.E44 1995**
Reinventing Darwin: The Great Debate at the High Table of
Evolutionary Theory. Trade Cloth. John Wiley & Sons, Inc.
Hoboken, NJ. 1995. 244p. ISBN:0-471-30301-1, ISBN13:
978-0-471-30301-5. Dewey:575/.001. LCCN:94-032861.
Audience: u,f.

Forsdyke, Donald   **QH361.F58 2001**
The Origin of Species, Revisited: The Search for a Victorian
Who Anticipated Modern Developments in Darwin's Theory.
Trade Cloth. McGill-Queen's University Press. Montreal, PQ.
2001. x, 275p. ISBN:0-7735-2259-X, ISBN13:
978-0-7735-2259-6. Dewey:576.8/2/094109034.
LCCN:2003-275763.
Audience: u,f. Choice, 2002.

Gayon, Jean   **QH375 .G3813 1998**
Darwinism's Struggle for Survival: Heredity and the Hypothesis
of Natural Selection. Matthew Cobb (Translator). Trade Cloth.
Cambridge University Press. New York, NY. 1998. 532p.
Cambridge Studies in Philosophy and Biology
ISBN:0-521-56250-3, ISBN13: 978-0-521-56250-8.
Dewey:576.8/2. LCCN:97-020559.
Audience: u,f.

Glick, Thomas F. (Editor)   **QH361.C66 1988**
The Comparative Reception of Darwinism. Trade Paper.
University of Chicago Press. Chicago, IL. 2003. 534p.
ISBN:0-226-29977-5, ISBN13: 978-0-226-29977-8.
Dewey:575.01/62. LCCN:87-035814.
Audience: u,f.

Glick, Thomas F. (Editor),   **Q174.B67 VOL.221**
  et al.
The Reception of Darwinism in the Iberian World: Spain,
Spanish America and Brazil. Miguel Angel Puig-Samper &
Rosaura Ruiz (Editors). Trade Cloth. Springer Dordrecht.
Dordrecht, 2001. 282p. Boston Studies in the Philosophy of
Science, Vol. 221 ISBN:1-4020-0082-0, ISBN13:
978-1-4020-0082-9. Dewey:001/.01 s576.8/0946.
LCCN:2001-045953.
Audience: u,f.

Hodge, Michael J.   **QH361.H63 1991**
Origins and Species: A Study on the Historical Sources of
Darwinism and the Contexts of Some Other Accounts of
Organic Diversity from Plato and Aristotle On. Owen Gingerich
(Editor). Trade Cloth. Garland Publishing, Inc. New York, NY.
1991. 824p. Harvard Dissertations in the History of Science Ser.
ISBN:0-8240-7252-9, ISBN13: 978-0-8240-7252-0.
Dewey:575/.009. LCCN:91-010335.
Audience: u,f.

Johnson, Phillip E.   **QH375**
Darwin on Trial. Ed. 2. Trade Paper. InterVarsity Press.
Downers Grove, IL. 1993. 220p. ISBN:0-8308-1324-1, ISBN13:
978-0-8308-1324-7. Dewey:576.8/2. LCCN:90-026218.
Audience: u,f. Choice, 1992.

Johnson, Phillip E.   **QH366.2.J655 1997**
Defeating Darwinism by Opening Minds. Trade Cloth.
InterVarsity Press. Downers Grove, IL. 1997. 131p.
ISBN:0-8308-1362-4, ISBN13: 978-0-8308-1362-9.
Dewey:576.8/2. LCCN:97-012916.
Audience: u,f.

Jones, Steve   **QH375**
Darwin's Ghost: The Origin of the Species Updated. Trade
Paper. Ballantine Books. New York, NY. 2001. 416p.
ISBN:0-345-42277-5, ISBN13: 978-0-345-42277-4.
Dewey:576.8/2.
Audience: g,l,u,f. Choice, 2000.

Joseph, Rhawn   **Q175**
Astrobiology, the Origin of Life, and the Death of Darwinism:
Evolutionary Metamorphosis. Ed. 2. Trade Paper.
UniversityPress.Info. San Jose, CA. 2001. 370p.
ISBN:0-9700733-8-0, ISBN13: 978-0-9700733-8-9. Dewey:501.
Audience: l,u.

Kirschner, Marc W. &   **QH366.2.K57 2005**
  Gerhart, John C.
The Plausibility of Life: Resolving Darwin's Dilemma. John
Norton (Illustrator). Cloth over Boards. Yale University Press.
Cumberland, RI. 2005. 336p. ISBN:0-300-10865-6, ISBN13:
978-0-300-10865-1. Dewey:576.8. LCCN:2005-040113.
Audience: u,f. Choice, 2006.

Mayr, Ernst W.   **QH371.M336 1991**
One Long Argument: Charles Darwin and the Genesis of
Modern Evolutionary Thought. Trade Cloth. Harvard University
Press. Cambridge, MA. 1991. 214p. ISBN:0-674-63905-7,
ISBN13: 978-0-674-63905-8. Dewey:575. LCCN:91-011051.
Audience: u,f. Choice, 1992.

Michod, Richard E.   **QH375.M535 1999**
Darwinian Dynamics: Evolutionary Transitions in Fitness and
Individuality. Trade Cloth. Princeton University Press. Princeton,
NJ. 1998. 280p. ISBN:0-691-02699-8, ISBN13:
978-0-691-02699-2. Dewey:576.8/2. LCCN:98-004166.
Audience: u,f. Choice, 1999.

Milton, Richard   **QH375**
Shattering the Myths of Darwinism. Trade Cloth. Inner
Traditions International, Ltd. Rochester, VT. 2000. 320p.
ISBN:0-89281-884-0, ISBN13: 978-0-89281-884-6.
Dewey:576.8/2.
Audience: l,u,f.

Rose, Michael R.   **QH371.R683 1998**
Darwin's Spectre: Evolutionary Biology in the Modern World.
Cloth Text. Princeton University Press. Princeton, NJ. 1998.
227p. ISBN:0-691-01217-2, ISBN13: 978-0-691-01217-9.
Dewey:576.8/2. LCCN:98-011494.
Audience: u,f. Choice, 1999.

Ruse, Michael   **QH360.5R867 2003**
Darwin and Design: Does Evolution Have a Purpose? Trade
Cloth. Harvard University Press. Cambridge, MA. 2003. 384p.
ISBN:0-674-01023-X, ISBN13: 978-0-674-01023-9.
Dewey:576.8/01. LCCN:2002-038819.
Audience: u,f. Choice, 2003.

Ruse, Michael   **QH371.R75 1989**
The Darwinian Paradigm: Essays on Its History, Philosophy and
Religious Implications. Paper over Boards. Routledge. New
York, NY. 1989. 310p. ISBN:0-415-00300-8, ISBN13:
978-0-415-00300-1. Dewey:575. LCCN:88-023985.
Audience: u,f.

Ruse, Michael   **QH361.R87 1999**
The Darwinian Revolution: Science Red in Tooth and Claw. Ed.
2. Trade Cloth. University of Chicago Press. Chicago, IL. 1999.

368p. ISBN:0-226-73168-5, ISBN13: 978-0-226-73168-1. Dewey:576.8/2. LCCN:99-023377.

Audience: **u,f.** *Choice, 2000.*

Ruse, Michael   **QH360.5.R878 1998**
Taking Darwin Seriously: A Naturalistic Approach to Philosophy. Trade Paper. Prometheus Books, Publishers. Amherst, NY. 1998. 340p. ISBN:1-57392-242-0, ISBN13: 978-1-57392-242-5. Dewey:128. LCCN:98-038272.

Audience: **u,f.**

Ryan, Frank   **QH366.2.R93 2002**
Darwin's Blind Spot: Evolution Beyond Natural Selection. Trade Cloth. Houghton Mifflin Company Trade & Reference Division. Boston, MA. 2002. 320p. ISBN:0-618-11812-8, ISBN13: 978-0-618-11812-0. Dewey:576.8. LCCN:2002-032284.

Audience: **u,f.** *Choice, 2003.*

Shanahan, Timothy   **QH361.S43 2004**
The Evolution of Darwinism: Selection, Adaptation and Progress in Evolutionary Biology. Cloth Text. Cambridge University Press. New York, NY. 2004. 352p. ISBN:0-521-83413-9, ISBN13: 978-0-521-83413-1. Dewey:576.8/2. LCCN:2003-058439.

Audience: **g,l,u,f.**

Smith, John M.   **QH371.M298 1989**
Did Darwin Get It Right? Mass Market. Chapman & Hall. New York, NY. 1988. 264p. ISBN:0-412-01911-6, ISBN13: 978-0-412-01911-1. Dewey:575. LCCN:88-021809.

Audience: **u,f.**

Wills, Christopher & Bada, Jeffrey   **QH325**
Spark of Life: Darwin and the Primeval Soup. Trade Paper. Basic Books. New York, NY. 2001. 320p. ISBN:0-7382-0493-5, ISBN13: 978-0-7382-0493-2. Dewey:570.1.

Audience: **g,l,u,f.**

Descriptive Biology: General

☐ Google Directory: Biology, Taxonomy.
http://google.com/Top/Science/Biology/Taxonomy/
Google.

Audience: **g,l.**

     QH303.5
☐ Taxonomy Browser.
http://www.ncbi.nlm.nih.gov/Taxonomy/taxonomyhome.html/
Audience: **l,u,f.**

☐ The WWW Virtual Library: Model Organisms.
http://ceolas.org/VL/mo/
The WWW Virtual Library (WWWVL).

Audience: **g,l.**

Avise, John C.   **QH84.A95 2000**
Phylogeography: The History and Formation of Species. Trade Cloth. Harvard University Press. Cambridge, MA. 2000. 458p. ISBN:0-674-66638-0, ISBN13: 978-0-674-66638-2. Dewey:578/.09. LCCN:99-019648.

Audience: **l,u,f.** *Choice, 2000.*

Barnes, Richard S. K. (Editor)   **QH83.D58 1997**
The Diversity of Living Organisms. Trade Paper. Blackwell Publishing, Inc. Malden, MA. 1998. 360p. ISBN:0-632-04917-0, ISBN13: 978-0-632-04917-2. Dewey:570/.1/2. LCCN:97-015026.

Audience: **l,u,f.**

Battaglia, Bruno (Editor), et al.   **QH84.2 .A57 1997**
Antarctic Communities: Species, Structure and Survival. Jose Valencia & David Walton (Editors). Trade Cloth. Cambridge University Press. New York, NY. 1997. 480p. ISBN:0-521-48033-7, ISBN13: 978-0-521-48033-8. Dewey:333.9/5/16/09989. LCCN:96-037973.

Audience: **l,u,f.**

Blair, Cornelia B. (Editor)   **QH76**
Endangered Species: Must They Disappear? Trade Paper. Thomson Gale. Farmington Hills, MI. 1996. 144p. ISBN:1-57302-024-9, ISBN13: 978-1-57302-024-4. Dewey:578.680973.

Audience: **l,u,f.**

Center for Biological Informatics of the U.S. Geological Survey   **TD169**
☐ The National Biological Information Infrastructure (NBII): Systematics.
http://nbii.gov/disciplines/systematics.html
Center for Biological Informatics of the U.S. Geological Survey.
Audience: **g,l.**

Claudi, Renata & Leach, Joseph H. (Editors)   **QH102.C56 2000**
Nonindigenous Freshwater Organisms: Vectors, Biology and Impacts. Saddle Stitched. Lewis Publishers. Boca Raton, FL. 1999. 480p. ISBN:1-56670-449-9, ISBN13: 978-1-56670-449-6. Dewey:577.6/097. LCCN:99-028607.

Audience: **u,f.** *Choice, 2000.*

Claugher, D. (Editor)   **QH83.S32 1990**
Scanning Electron Microscopy in Taxonomy and Functional Morphology. Cloth Text. Oxford University Press, Inc. New York, NY. 1990. 328p. Systematics Association Publications, Vol. 41 ISBN:0-19-857714-1, ISBN13: 978-0-19-857714-0. Dewey:574/.012. LCCN:89-023042.

Audience: **u,f.**

Elewa, Ashraf M. T. (Editor)   **QH351.M6195 2004**
Morphometrics. Trade Cloth. Springer. New York, NY. 2004. XIV, 263p. ISBN:3-540-21429-1, ISBN13: 978-3-540-21429-8. Dewey:571.3/072/7. LCCN:2004-103476.

Audience: **u,f.**

Ereshefsky, Marc   **QH83 .E73 2001**
The Poverty of the Linnaean Hierarchy: A Philosophical Study of Biological Taxonomy. Michael Ruse, John Bell & James Crawford (Contribution by). Trade Cloth. Cambridge University Press. New York, NY. 2000. 328p. Studies in Philosophy and Biology ISBN:0-521-78170-1, ISBN13: 978-0-521-78170-1. Dewey:578.012. LCCN:00-028945.

Audience: **u,f.**

Felsenstein, Joseph   **QH83.F45 2003**
Inferring Phylogenies. Trade Cloth. Sinauer Associates, Inc. Sunderland, MA. 2003. 664p. ISBN:0-87893-177-5, ISBN13: 978-0-87893-177-4. Dewey:578/.01/2. LCCN:2003-008942.

Audience: **u,f.**

Forey, Peter L., et al.   **QH83**
Cladistics: A Practical Course in Systematics. Christopher J. Humphries, Ian J. Kitching, R. W. Scotland & D. J. Siebert (Authors). Paper Text. Oxford University Press, Inc. New York, NY. 1993. 208p. Systematics Association Publications, Vol. 10 ISBN:0-19-857766-4, ISBN13: 978-0-19-857766-9. Dewey:578/.012.

Audience: **u,f.**

Funk, V. A., et al.   **QH83.C613 1991**
The Compleat Cladist: A Primer of Phylogenetic Procedures. D. R. Brooks, Edward O. Wiley & Douglas Siegel-Causey (Authors). Trade Paper. University of Kansas, Natural History Museum. Lawrence, KS. 1991. 168p. Special Publications, No. 19 ISBN:0-89338-035-0, ISBN13: 978-0-89338-035-9. Dewey:575.

Audience: **u,f.**

Gaston, Kevin J.   **QH352**
Rarity. Chapman & Hall, London ; New York. 1994. Population and community biology series; 13 ISBN:0-412-47510-3, ISBN13: 978-0-412-47510-8.

Audience: **l,u,f.**

Gee, Henry   **QH82**
Deep Time: Cladistics, the Revolution in Evolution. Fourth Estate, London. 2001. ISBN:1-85702-987-9, ISBN13: 978-1-85702-987-1.

Audience: **u,f.**

Hawksworth, David L.   **QH83.P767 1988**
  (Editor)
Prospects in Systematics. Trade Cloth. Oxford University Press, Inc. New York, NY. 1988. 480p. Systematics Association Publications, Vol. 36 ISBN:0-19-857707-9, ISBN13: 978-0-19-857707-2. Dewey:574/.012. LCCN:88-001820.

Audience: **u,f.**

Margulis, Lynn, et al.   **QH83.M357 1999**
Diversity of Life: The Illustrated Guide to the Five Kingdoms. Ed. 2. Karlene V. Schwartz & Michael Dolan (Authors). Trade Paper. Jones & Bartlett Publishers, Inc. Sudbury, MA. 1999. 248p. ISBN:0-7637-0862-3, ISBN13: 978-0-7637-0862-7. LCCN:99-011879.

Audience: **l,u,f.**

National Center for   **QH83**
  Biotechnology Information, U.S. National Library of
  Medicine
☐ NCBI: The NCBI Taxonomy Homepage.
http://www.ncbi.nlm.nih.gov/Taxonomy/taxonomyhome.html/index.cgi
NCBI, U.S. National Library of Medicine.

Audience: **g,l.**

Schmidt-Kittler, N. & Vogel,   **QH351.C65 1991**
  K. (Editors)
Constructional Morphology and Evolution. Cloth Text. Springer. New York, NY. 1991. 424p. ISBN:0-387-53279-X, ISBN13: 978-0-387-53279-0. Dewey:574.4. LCCN:91-012697.

Audience: **u,f.**

Schwartz, Karlene V. &   **QH83.M36 1998**
  Margulis, Alexander R.
Five Kingdoms: An Illustrated Guide to the Phyla of Life on Earth. Ed. 3. Trade Cloth. W. H. Freeman & Company. New

York, NY. 1997. 520p. ISBN:0-7167-3026-X, ISBN13: 978-0-7167-3026-2. Dewey:570/.1/2. LCCN:97-021338.

Audience: **l,u,f.**

Semple, Charles & Steel,   **QH83.S45 2003**
  Mike
Phylogenetics. Trade Cloth. Oxford University Press, Inc. New York, NY. 2003. 256p. Oxford Lecture Series in Mathematics and Its Applications, Vol. 24 ISBN:0-19-850942-1, ISBN13: 978-0-19-850942-4. Dewey:572.8/38/0151. LCCN:2002-027406.

Audience: **u,f.**

Wilson, Robert A. (Editor)   **QH83.S725 1999**
Species: New Interdisciplinary Essays. Trade Paper. MIT Press. Cambridge, MA. 1999. 338p. A Bradford Book Ser. ISBN:0-262-73123-1, ISBN13: 978-0-262-73123-2. Dewey:576.8/6. LCCN:98-034713.

Audience: **u,f.** *Choice, 2000.*

Winston, Judith E.   **QH83.W57 1999**
Describing Species: Practical Taxonomic Procedure for Biologists. Trade Cloth. Columbia University Press. New York, NY. 1999. 512p. ISBN:0-231-06824-7, ISBN13: 978-0-231-06824-6. LCCN:99-014019.

Audience: **u,f.** *Choice, 2000.*

Descriptive Biology: Microorganisms

☐ Google Directory: Biology, Microbiology.
http://google.com/Top/Science/Biology/Microbiology/
Google.

Audience: **g,l.**

                  TK5105.875.I57
☐ The Microbiology Network.
http://microbiol.org/

Audience: **g,l.**

                  QH303.5
☐ Taxonomy Browser.
http://www.ncbi.nlm.nih.gov/Taxonomy/taxonomyhome.html/
Audience: **l,u,f.**

Danson, M. J. (Editor),
  et al.
The Archaebacteria: Biochemistry and Biotechnology. D. W. Hough & George G. Lunt (Editors). Trade Cloth. Portland Press, Ltd. London, 1992. 222p. Biochemical Society Symposium Ser., Vol. 58 ISBN:1-85578-010-0, ISBN13: 978-1-85578-010-1. Dewey:589.9.

Audience: **u,f.**

Mullner, S.   **TP248.3**
Proteomics of Microorganisms: Fundamental Aspects and Application. M. Hecker (Contribution by), Michael Hecker (Volume Editor), D. J. Cahill, P. Cash & S. J. Cordwell (Contribution by). Mixed Media. Springer. New York, NY. 2003. XI, 228p. Advances in Biochemical Engineering / Biotechnology Ser. ISBN:3-540-00546-3, ISBN13: 978-3-540-00546-9. Dewey:660.6/3.

Audience: **u,f.**

Sherman, Irwin W.   QR201.M3M647 2005
Molecular Approaches to Malaria. Trade Cloth. ASM Press.
Washington, DC. 2005. 575p. ISBN:1-55581-330-5, ISBN13:
978-1-55581-330-7. Dewey:616.9/362. LCCN:2005-010990.
Audience: **u,f.**

Descriptive Biology: Microorganisms > Virology

Flint, S. J., et al.   QR360.P697 2004
Principles of Virology: Molecular Biology, Pathogenesis, and
Control of Animal Viruses. Ed. 2. L. W. Enquist, V. R.
Racaniello & A. M. Skalka (Authors). Trade Cloth. ASM Press.
Washington, DC. 2003. 820p. ISBN:1-55581-259-7, ISBN13:
978-1-55581-259-1. Dewey:579.2. LCCN:2003-009529.
Audience: **u,f.**

Hechemy, Karim E.   Q11.N5 VOL.1063
Rickettsioses: From Genome to Proteome, Pathobiology, and
Rickettsiae As an International Threat. New York Academy of
Sciences Staff (Contribution by). Trade Cloth. New York
Academy of Sciences. New York, NY. 2005. xx, 474p. Annals
of the New York Academy of Sciences Ser., Vol. 1063
ISBN:1-57331-600-8, ISBN13: 978-1-57331-600-2.
Dewey:616.9/22. LCCN:2005-035059.
Audience: **u,f.**

Descriptive Biology: Microorganisms > Bacteriology

Garrity, George (Editor)   QR81.B46 2004
Bergey's Manual of Systematic Bacteriology: The
Proteobacteria. Ed. 2. Trade Cloth. Springer. New York, NY.
2000. LXXXII, 2816p. ISBN:0-387-95040-0, ISBN13:
978-0-387-95040-2. Dewey:579.3012.
Audience: **l,u,f.**

Garrity, George M. (Editor)   QR81.B46 2001
Bergey's Manual of Systematic Bacteriology: The Archaea, and
the Deeply Branching and Phototropic Bateria. Ed. 2. Trade
Cloth. Springer. New York, NY. 2001. XXI, 721p.
Biotechnology Intelligence Unit Ser., Vol. 1
ISBN:0-387-98771-1, ISBN13: 978-0-387-98771-2.
Dewey:579.3/01/2. LCCN:2001-020400.
Audience: **l,u,f.**

Hodgson, David A. &   QH450.S635 2002
  Thomas, Christopher M. (Editors)
Signals, Switches, Regulons, and Cascades: Control of Bacterial
Gene Expression. Melanie Scourfield (Contribution by). Trade
Cloth. Cambridge University Press. New York, NY. 2002. 304p.
Society for General Microbiology Symposia Ser., Vol. 61
ISBN:0-521-81388-3, ISBN13: 978-0-521-81388-4.
Dewey:572.865. LCCN:2002-510923.
Audience: **u,f.**

Descriptive Biology: Plants

☐ Google Directory: Biology, Mycology.
http://google.com/Top/Science/Biology/Mycology/
Google.
Audience: **g,l.**

                    QH303.5
☐ Taxonomy Browser.
http://www.ncbi.nlm.nih.gov/Taxonomy/taxonomyhome.html/
Audience: **l,u,f.**

☐ The Virtual Library of Botany / Plant Biology (Biosciences).
http://www.ou.edu/cas/botany-micro/www-vl/
The WWW Virtual Library (WWWVL).
Audience: **g,l.**

                    SD248.8
☐ WWW Virtual Library: Forestry.
http://www.metla.fi/info/vlib/Forestry/
The WWW Virtual Library (WWWVL).
Audience: **g,l.**

Salinas (Editor)   QK495.C9A735 2005
Arabidopsis Protocols. Ed. 2. Trade Cloth. Humana Press.
Totowa, NJ. 2005. 525p. Methods in Molecular Biology Ser.
ISBN:1-58829-395-5, ISBN13: 978-1-58829-395-4.
Dewey:583/.64. LCCN:2005-016343.
Audience: **u,f.**

Descriptive Biology: Plants > General

☐ Google Directory: Biology, Botany.
http://google.com/Top/Science/Biology/Botany/
Google.
Audience: **g,l.**

                    QK10
☐ GRIN Taxonomy for Plants.
http://www.ars-grin.gov/cgi-bin/npgs/html/index.pl
Audience: **u,f.**

Adair, W. Steven (Editor)   QH603.E93O74 1990
Organization and Assembly of Plant and Animal Extracellular
Matrix. Academic Press. 1990. Biology of Extracellular Matrix
Ser. ISBN:0-12-044060-1, ISBN13: 978-0-12-044060-3.
Audience: **u.**

Lloyd, David G. (Editor)   QK653
Floral Biology: Studies on Floral Evolution in Animal-Pollinated
Plants. Barrett, Spencer Charles Hilton (Editor). Chapman &
Hall, New York. 1996. ISBN:0-412-04341-6, ISBN13:
978-0-412-04341-3.
Audience: **u.**

Pritchard, Hayden N. &   QK505 .P84 1984
  Bradt, Patricia T.
Biology of Nonvascular Plants. Cloth Text. Mosby, Inc. Saint
Louis, MO. 1983. 576p. ISBN:0-8016-4043-1, ISBN13:
978-0-8016-4043-8. Dewey:586. LCCN:83-001018.
Audience: **l,u,f.**

Scagel, R. F., et al.   QK505.N66 1982
Nonvascular Plants: An Evolutionary Survey. Ed. 1. Robert J.
Bandoni, Glenn E. Rouse, W. D. Schofield, Janet R. Stein &
Jack Maze (Authors). Cloth Text. Thomson Wadsworth.
Belmont, CA. 1982. 570p. ISBN:0-534-01029-6, ISBN13:
978-0-534-01029-4. Dewey:586. LCCN:81-024066.
Audience: **u,f.** 𝓑

Descriptive Biology: Plants > Nomenclature

QK10

GRIN Taxonomy for Plants.
http://www.ars-grin.gov/cgi-bin/npgs/html/index.pl

Audience: **u,f.**

QK96.R4 VOL. 111

International Code of Botanical Nomenclature. Trade Cloth.
Bow Historical Books. New Providence, NJ. 1983. xv, 472 p.
;p. ISBN:90-313-0572-3, ISBN13: 978-90-313-0572-8.
Dewey:581/.012. LCCN:83-012277.

Audience: **u,f.**

Brako, Lois (Editor), et al.   **QK96.B68 1995**
Scientific and Common Names of 7,000 Vascular Plants in the
United States. David F. Farr & Amy Y. Rossman (Editors), U. S.
National Fungus Collections Staff (Contribution by). Trade
Paper. American Phytopathological Society. Saint Paul, MN.
1995. 301p. U. S. National Fungus Collections
ISBN:0-89054-171-X, ISBN13: 978-0-89054-171-5.
Dewey:581.973/014. LCCN:94-079381.

Audience: **u,f.**

Cronquist, Arthur   **QK495.A1**
An Integrated System of Classification of Flowering Plants.
Armen Takhtajan (Foreword by). Trade Cloth. Columbia
University Press. New York, NY. 1992. 1262p.
ISBN:0-231-03880-1, ISBN13: 978-0-231-03880-5.
Dewey:582.13/012. LCCN:80-039556.

Audience: **u,f.**

Gledhill, David   **QK13**
The Names of Plants. Ed. 4. Cloth Text. Cambridge University
Press. New York, NY. 2006. 475p. ISBN:0-521-86645-6,
ISBN13: 978-0-521-86645-3. Dewey:580/.14.

Audience: **g,l,u,f.** *Choice, 2003, 1986.*

Greuter, W. (Editor), et al.   **QK96**
International Code of Botanical Nomenclature (St. Louis Code):
Adopted by the 16th International Botanical Congress, St. Louis
August 1999. J. McNeill & F. R. Barrie (Editors). Cloth Text. A.
R. Gartner Verlag KG. Liechtenstein, 2000. xviii, 474p. Regnum
Vegetabile Ser., Vol. 138 ISBN:3-904144-22-7, ISBN13:
978-3-904144-22-3. Dewey:581.014.

Audience: **u,f.**

Harris, James G. & Harris,   **QK9.H37 2001**
  Melinda Woolf
Plant Identification Terminology: An Illustrated Glossary. Ed. 2.
Perfect. Spring Lake Publishing. Payson, UT. 2001. 216p.
ISBN:0-9640221-6-8, ISBN13: 978-0-9640221-6-4.
Dewey:580/.1/4. LCCN:00-191714.

Audience: **g,l.** *Choice, 1994.*

Linné, Carl von & Freer,   **QK91**
  Stephen
Linnaeus' Philosophia Botanica. Trade Paper. Oxford University
Press, Inc. New York, NY. 2005. 432p. ISBN:0-19-856934-3,
ISBN13: 978-0-19-856934-3. Dewey:580.12.
LCCN:2002-030761.

Audience: **u,f.**

Naqshi, A. R.   **QK11**
An Introduction to Botanical Nomenclature. Trade Paper.
Scientific Publishers. Jodhpur, RJ, 1993. 96p.
ISBN:81-7233-051-0, ISBN13: 978-81-7233-051-4.
Dewey:580.3.

Audience: **l,u.**

Pankhurst, Richard J.   **QK96.P35 1995**
Plants and Their Names: A Concise Dictionary. Trade Cloth.
Oxford University Press, Inc. New York, NY. 1995. 558p.
ISBN:0-19-866189-4, ISBN13: 978-0-19-866189-4.
Dewey:581/.014. LCCN:94-005024.

Audience: **g,l,u.** *Choice, 1995.*

Radcliffe-Smith, A.   **QK13.R16 1998**
Three-Language List of Botanical Name Components. Trade
Paper. Royal Botanic Gardens, Kew. Brough, 1998. 143p.
ISBN:1-900347-50-4, ISBN13: 978-1-900347-50-1.
Dewey:580/.1/4. LCCN:2001-411897.

Audience: **u,f.**

Stearn, William T.   **QK13**
Botanical Latin. Ed. 4. Trade Paper. Timber Press, Inc. Portland,
OR. 2004. 560p. ISBN:0-88192-627-2, ISBN13:
978-0-88192-627-9. Dewey:580.1/4.

Audience: **l,u,f.**

Descriptive Biology: Plants > Lower Plants (Cryptograms)

QK10

GRIN Taxonomy for Plants.
http://www.ars-grin.gov/cgi-bin/npgs/html/index.pl

Audience: **u,f.**

Pritchard, Hayden N. &   **QK505 .P84 1984**
  Bradt, Patricia T.
Biology of Nonvascular Plants. Cloth Text. Mosby, Inc. Saint
Louis, MO. 1983. 576p. ISBN:0-8016-4043-1, ISBN13:
978-0-8016-4043-8. Dewey:586. LCCN:83-001018.

Audience: **l,u,f.**

Scagel, R. F., et al.   **QK505.N66 1982**
Nonvascular Plants: An Evolutionary Survey. Ed. 1. Robert J.
Bandoni, Glenn E. Rouse, W. D. Schofield, Janet R. Stein &
Jack Maze (Authors). Cloth Text. Thomson Wadsworth.
Belmont, CA. 1982. 570p. ISBN:0-534-01029-6, ISBN13:
978-0-534-01029-4. Dewey:586. LCCN:81-024066.

Audience: **u,f.**

Descriptive Biology: Plants > Lower Plants (Cryptograms) > Algae

Andersen, Robert A.   **QK565.2.A44 2005**
  (Editor)
Algal Culturing Techniques. Trade Cloth. Elsevier Science &
Technology Books. Saint Louis, MO. 2005. 596p.
ISBN:0-12-088426-7, ISBN13: 978-0-12-088426-1.
Dewey:579.8. LCCN:2004-061905.

Audience: **l,u,f.** *Choice, 2005.*

Bold, Harold C., et al.   **QK641.B596 1987**
Morphology of Plants and Fungi. Ed. 5. Constantine
Alexopoulos & Theodore Delevoryas (Authors). Trade Cloth.

Addison-Wesley Educational Publishers, Inc. Boston, MA. 1997. 928p. ISBN:0-06-040839-1, ISBN13: 978-0-06-040839-8. Dewey:581.4. LCCN:86-014294.

Audience: **l,u,f.** *B*

Bold, Harold C. & Wynne,   QK566.B64 1985
Michael J.
Introduction to the Algae. Ed. 2. Trade Paper. Prentice Hall PTR. Upper Saddle River, NJ. 1997. 848p. ISBN:0-13-477746-8, ISBN13: 978-0-13-477746-7. Dewey:589.3. LCCN:84-004696.

Audience: **l,u,f.** *B*

Cole, Kathleen M. &   QK569.R4 B56 1990
Sheath, Robert G. (Editors)
Biology of the Red Algae. Trade Cloth. Cambridge University Press. New York, NY. 1990. 525p. ISBN:0-521-34301-1, ISBN13: 978-0-521-34301-5. Dewey:589.4/1. LCCN:89-071274.
Audience: **u,f.** *Choice, 1991.*

Cox, E. J.   QK569.D54C69 1996
Identification of Freshwater Diatoms from Live Material. Trade Cloth. Springer. New York, NY. 1996. 128p. ISBN:0-412-49380-2, ISBN13: 978-0-412-49380-5. Dewey:589.4/81. LCCN:96-084346.

Audience: **u,f.**

Druehl, Louis   QK570.5
Pacific Seaweeds: A Guide to Common Seaweeds of the Pacific Northwest. Trade Paper. Harbour Publishing Company, Ltd. Madeira Park, BC. 192p. ISBN:1-55017-240-9, ISBN13: 978-1-55017-240-9. Dewey:579.8/817743.

Audience: **u,f.**

Graham, Linda E. &   QK566.G735 2000
Wilcox, Lee W.
Algae. Cloth Text. Prentice Hall PTR. Upper Saddle River, NJ. 1999. 700p. ISBN:0-13-660333-5, ISBN13: 978-0-13-660333-7. Dewey:579.8. LCCN:99-024517.
Audience: **u,f.** *Choice, 2000.*

Larkum, Anthony W. D.,   QK565.P495 2003
et al.
Photosynthesis in Algae. Susan E. Douglas & John A. Raven (Authors). Trade Cloth. Kluwer Law International. Alphen a/d Rijn, 2003. 500p. Advances in Photosynthesis and Respiration Ser., Vol. 14 ISBN:0-7923-6333-7, ISBN13: 978-0-7923-6333-0. Dewey:572/.46298. LCCN:2003-066347.

Audience: **u,f.**

Lee, Robert E.   QK566 .L44 1999
Phycology. Ed. 3. Trade Paper. Cambridge University Press. New York, NY. 1999. 624p. ISBN:0-521-63883-6, ISBN13: 978-0-521-63883-8. Dewey:579.8. LCCN:98-053255.
Audience: **u,f.** *B Choice, 2000.*

Lobban, Christopher S. &   QK570.2 .L64 1994
Harrison, Paul J.
Seaweed Ecology and Physiology. P. K. Dayton, M. Harlin, D. S. Littler & M. M. Littler (Contribution by). Trade Paper. Cambridge University Press. New York, NY. 1996. 376p. ISBN:0-521-40897-0, ISBN13: 978-0-521-40897-4. Dewey:589.4/5/041. LCCN:93-021306.
Audience: **u,f.** *Choice, 1995.*

Meinesz, Alexandre   QK569
Killer Algae: The True Story of a Biological Invasion. Daniel Simberloff (Translator), David Quammen (Foreword by). Trade

Paper. University of Chicago Press. Chicago, IL. 2001. 360p. ISBN:0-226-51923-6, ISBN13: 978-0-226-51923-4. Dewey:579.8/35. LCCN:2002-511824.

Audience: **l,u,f.**

Patrick, Ruth & Reimer,   QK569.D54P28
Charles W.
The Diatoms of the United States (Exclusive of Alaska and Hawaii), Vol. 2, Pt. 1. Su-ing Yong (Illustrator). Library Binding. Academy of Natural Sciences Philadelphia. Philadelphia, PA. 1975. 213p. Monograph, No. 13-2 ISBN:0-910006-21-0, ISBN13: 978-0-910006-21-7. Dewey:589/.62/0973.

Audience: **u,f.**

Prescott, G. W. (Gerald   QK571.P67
Webber)
Algae of the Western Great Lakes Area, with an Illustrated Key to the Genera of Desmids and Freshwater Diatoms. Paper Text. Textbook Publishers. Temecula, CA. 2003. xiii, 977p. ISBN:0-7581-0788-9, ISBN13: 978-0-7581-0788-6. Dewey:589.30977.

Audience: **u,f.**

Prud'homme van Reine, W.   QK575.A785 C79 2001
F. & Trono, G. C. Jr. (Editors)
Cryptogams: Algae. Trade Cloth. Backhuys Publishers. Leiden, 2001. 318p. Plant Resources of South-East Asia Ser., No. 15.1 ISBN:90-5782-096-X, ISBN13: 978-90-5782-096-0. Dewey:579.8/0959. LCCN:2003-376665.

Audience: **u,f.**

Subba Rao, D. V.   QK565.2.A438 2005
Algal Cultures, Analogues of Blooms and Applications. Trade Cloth. Science Publishers. Enfield, NH. 2006. 954p. ISBN:1-57808-393-1, ISBN13: 978-1-57808-393-0. Dewey:579.8. LCCN:2005-051701.

Audience: **u.**

Tomas, Carmelo R. (Editor)   QK934.I44 1997
Identifying Marine Phytoplankton. Trade Paper. Elsevier Science & Technology Books. Saint Louis, MO. 1997. 858p. ISBN:0-12-693018-X, ISBN13: 978-0-12-693018-4. Dewey:579.8/1776. LCCN:97-013861.
Audience: **u,f.** *Choice, 1998.*

Wehr, John D. & Sheath,   QK570.5.F74 2003
Robert G.
Freshwater Algae of North America: Ecology and Classification. James H. Thorp (Contribution by). Trade Cloth. Elsevier Science & Technology Books. Saint Louis, MO. 2002. 917p. Aquatic Ecology Ser. ISBN:0-12-741550-5, ISBN13: 978-0-12-741550-5. Dewey:579.8/176/097. LCCN:2002-107708.
Audience: **l,u,f.** *Choice, 2003.*

Whitton, Brian A. (Editor),   QK573 .F74 2002
et al.
The Freshwater Algal Flora of the British Isles: An Identification Guide to Freshwater and Terrestrial Algae. Alan J. Brook & David M. John (Editors). Trade Cloth, CD-ROM, Mixed Media. Cambridge University Press. New York, NY. 2002. 714p. ISBN:0-521-77051-3, ISBN13: 978-0-521-77051-4. Dewey:579.8/176/0941. LCCN:2001-025917.
Audience: **l,u,f.** *Choice, 2003.*

   Formats: Web: ☐ Ebook: **e** CD/DVD-ROM: ✎ BCL3: *B*

Descriptive Biology: Plants > Lower Plants (Cryptograms) > Fungi

Alexopoulos, Constantine J.,   **QK603.A55 1996**
et al.
Introductory Mycology. Ed. 4. Charles W. Mims & M. Blackwell (Authors). Trade Cloth. John Wiley & Sons, Inc. Hoboken, NJ. 1996. 880p. ISBN:0-471-52229-5, ISBN13: 978-0-471-52229-4. Dewey:589.2. LCCN:95-020699.
     Audience: **l,u,f.**

Burnett, John   **QK602.B86 2003**
Fungal Populations and Species. Trade Paper. Oxford University Press, Inc. New York, NY. 2003. 362p. ISBN:0-19-851553-7, ISBN13: 978-0-19-851553-1. Dewey:579.5/13. LCCN:2002-030818.
     Audience: **l,u,f.** *Choice, 2003.*

Cooke, R. C. & Whipps, J.   **QK604.2.E28.C66 1993**
M.
Eco-Physiology of Fungi. Trade Cloth. Blackwell Publishing, Inc. Malden, MA. 1993. 352p. ISBN:0-632-02168-3, ISBN13: 978-0-632-02168-0. Dewey:589.2045222. LCCN:92-031283.
     Audience: **u,f.** *Choice, 1994.*

Dix, Neville J; Webster,
John
Fungal Ecology. Chapman & Hall. 1995. ISBN:0-412-64130-5, ISBN13: 978-0-412-64130-5.
     Audience: **u,f.**

Esser, K. (Editor), et al.   **QK603.M87 2004**
The Mycota: A Comprehensive Treatise on Fungi As Experimental Systems for Basic and Applied Research. Ed. 2. Paul A. Lemke & Ulrich Kuck (Editors). Trade Cloth. Springer. New York, NY. 2004. xv, 375p. ISBN:3-540-58003-4, ISBN13: 978-3-540-58003-4. Dewey:579.5. LCCN:2004-274073.
     Audience: **u,f.**

Maheshwari, Ramesh   **QK603.M34 2005**
Fungi: Experimental Methods in Biology. Perfect, Paper over Boards. Marcel Dekker Inc. New York, NY. 2005. 240p. Mycology Ser., Vol. 24 ISBN:1-57444-468-9, ISBN13: 978-1-57444-468-1. Dewey:579.5. LCCN:2005-041276.
     Audience: **u,f.**

Descriptive Biology: Plants > Lower Plants (Cryptograms) > Fungi > Mushrooms

Bessette, Alan E.   **QK617.B483 1997**
Mushrooms of Northeastern North America. Trade Paper. Syracuse University Press. Syracuse, NY. 1997. xiv, 582p. ISBN:0-8156-0388-6, ISBN13: 978-0-8156-0388-7. Dewey:589.2/22/097485. LCCN:96-005729.
     Audience: **l,u,f.** *Choice, 1998.*

Hudler, George W.   **QK603 .H79 1998**
Magical Mushrooms, Mischievous Molds. Trade Paper. Princeton University Press. Princeton, NJ. 2000. 264p. ISBN:0-691-07016-4, ISBN13: 978-0-691-07016-2. Dewey:579.5.
     Audience: **l,u,f.** *Choice, 1999.*

Kuo, Michael   **QK623.M65K86 2005**
Morels. Trade Paper, Perfect. University of Michigan Press. Chicago, IL. 2005. 216p. ISBN:0-472-03036-1, ISBN13: 978-0-472-03036-1. Dewey:579.5/78. LCCN:2005-002490.
     Audience: **l,u,f.** *Choice, 2006.*

Schaechter, Elio   **QK617 S32 1998**
In the Company of Mushrooms: A Biologist's Tale. Trade Paper. Harvard University Press. Cambridge, MA. 1998. 296p. ISBN:0-674-44555-4, ISBN13: 978-0-674-44555-0. Dewey:579.6.
     Audience: **l,u,f.** *Choice, 1997.*

Turner, Nancy J. &   **QK100.A1T87 1991**
Szczawinski, Adam F.
Common Poisonous Plants and Mushrooms of North America. Ed. 2. Trade Cloth. Timber Press, Inc. Portland, OR. 2003. 324p. ISBN:0-88192-179-3, ISBN13: 978-0-88192-179-3. Dewey:581.6/9/097. LCCN:90-037574.
     Audience: **g,l,u,f.** *Choice, 1991.*

Descriptive Biology: Plants > Lower Plants (Cryptograms) > Mosses

Crum, Howard A. &   **QK540.5**
Anderson, Lewis E.
Mosses of Eastern North America. Trade Cloth. Columbia University Press. New York, NY. 1981. 1330p. ISBN:0-231-04516-6, ISBN13: 978-0-231-04516-2. Dewey:588/.2/097. LCCN:79-024789.
     Audience: **l,u,f.** *B*

Grout, A. J.   **QK541 .G82**
Mosses with Hand Lens and Microscope. Trade Cloth. John Johnson Natural History History Books. North Bennington, VT. 1972. ISBN:0-910914-03-6, ISBN13: 978-0-910914-03-1. Dewey:588.2.
     Audience: **l,u,f.**

Malcolm, Bill & Malcolm,   **QK537.M35 2000**
Nancy
Mosses and Other Bryophytes: An Illustrated Glossary. Trade Cloth. Micro Optics Press. Nelson, 2000. 226p. ISBN:0-473-06730-7, ISBN13: 978-0-473-06730-4. Dewey:588/.03. LCCN:2001-411832.
     Audience: **l,u,f.** *Choice, 2001.*

Schofield, W. B.   **QK556.5.P16S36 2000**
Field Guide to Liverwort General of Pacific North America. Trade Paper. University of Washington Press. Seattle, WA. 2002. 320p. ISBN:0-295-98194-6, ISBN13: 978-0-295-98194-9. Dewey:588/.3/09795. LCCN:2001-055654.
     Audience: **l,u.** *Choice, 2003.*

Schofield, W. B.   **QK533.S36 2001**
Introduction to Bryology. Perfect. Blackburn Press, The. Caldwell, NJ. 2001. 431p. ISBN:1-930665-26-1, ISBN13: 978-1-930665-26-2. Dewey:588. LCCN:2001-088824.
     Audience: **l,u,f.**

Shaw, A. Jonathan &   **QK533 .B48 2000**
Goffinet, Bernard (Editors)
Bryophyte Biology. Cloth Text. Cambridge University Press. New York, NY. 2000. 486p. ISBN:0-521-66097-1, ISBN13: 978-0-521-66097-6. Dewey:588. LCCN:99-462301.
     Audience: **l,u,f.**

Descriptive Biology: Plants > Lower Plants (Cryptograms) > Lichens

Ahmadjian, Vernon   **QK581.A35 1993**
The Lichen Symbiosis. Trade Cloth. John Wiley & Sons, Inc. Hoboken, NJ. 1993. 266p. ISBN:0-471-57885-1, ISBN13: 978-0-471-57885-7. Dewey:589.1. LCCN:92-042873.
Audience: **l,u,f.** *Choice, 1993.*

Bates, Jeffrey W. & Farmer,   **QK533.B72 1992**
Andrew M. (Editors)
Bryophytes and Lichens in a Changing Environment. Cloth Text. Oxford University Press, Inc. New York, NY. 1992. 416p. ISBN:0-19-854291-7, ISBN13: 978-0-19-854291-9. Dewey:588/.045. LCCN:91-043550.
Audience: **l,u,f.** *Choice, 1993.*

Brodo, Irwin M., et al.   **QK586.5.B76 2001**
Lichens of North America. Sylvia Duran Sharnoff & Stephen Sharnoff (Authors), Susan Laurie-Bourque (Contribution by), Peter Raven (Foreword by). Cloth over Boards. Yale University Press. Cumberland, RI. 2001. 828p. ISBN:0-300-08249-5, ISBN13: 978-0-300-08249-4. Dewey:579.7/097. LCCN:00-049541.
Audience: **g,l.** *Choice, 2002.*

Galun, Margalith (Editor)   **QK583 .C73 1988**
Handbook of Lichenology. Children's Board Books. Marcel Dekker Inc. New York, NY. 2005. 688p. ISBN:0-8493-3580-9, ISBN13: 978-0-8493-3580-8. Dewey:589.1. LCCN:87-023848.
Audience: **u,f.**

Hale, Mason E.   **QK1**
The Biology of Lichens. Ed. 3. Trade Paper. Cambridge University Press. New York, NY. 1991. 198p. ISBN:0-521-42771-1, ISBN13: 978-0-521-42771-5. Dewey:589.1.
Audience: **l,u,f.** *B*

Hale, Mason E., et al.   **QK587**
How to Know the Lichens. Ed. 2. John Bamrick, Edward T. Cawley & William G. Jaques (Authors). Paper Text. McGraw-Hill Higher Education. Burr Ridge, IL. 1979. 256p. Pictured Key Nature Ser. ISBN:0-697-04763-6, ISBN13: 978-0-697-04763-2. Dewey:589/.1/097.
Audience: **g,l.**

Descriptive Biology: Plants > Lower Plants (Cryptograms) > Other Crypograms (Ferns, etc.)

de Winter, W. P. & Aroroso,   **SB108.A785**
V. B. (Editors)
Cryptogams: Ferns and Fern Allies. Trade Cloth. Backhuys Publishers. Leiden, 2003. 268p. PROSEA Ser., No. 15.2 ISBN:90-5782-128-1, ISBN13: 978-90-5782-128-8. Dewey:581.6.
Audience: **u,f.**

Jermy, A. Clive   **QK527**
Illustrated Field Guide to Ferns and Allied Plants of the British Isles. Trade Paper. Stationery Office, The. London, 1993. xiv, 194p. ISBN:0-11-310009-4, ISBN13: 978-0-11-310009-5. Dewey:587/.0941.
Audience: **g,l,u,f.**

Lellinger, David B.   **QK523.L45 2002**
A Modern Multilingual Glossary for Taxonomic Pteridology. Trade Cloth. American Fern Society. Brevard, NC. 2002. 263p. Pteridologia Ser., Vol. 3 ISBN:0-933500-02-5, ISBN13: 978-0-933500-02-0. Dewey:587/.03. LCCN:2002-007337.
Audience: **u,f.**

Lellinger, David B.   **QK524.5.L45 1985**
A Field Manual of the Ferns and Fern-Allies of the United States and Canada. A. Murray Evans (Photographer). Trade Paper. Smithsonian Institution Press. Washington, DC. 1985. 446p. ISBN:0-87474-603-5, ISBN13: 978-0-87474-603-7. Dewey:587. LCCN:84-022216.
Audience: **l,u.** *B Choice, 1986.*

Moran, Robbin Craig   **QK522.M67 2004**
A Natural History of Ferns. Trade Cloth. Timber Press, Inc. Portland, OR. 2004. 302p. ISBN:0-88192-667-1, ISBN13: 978-0-88192-667-5. Dewey:587/.3. LCCN:2004-001299.
Audience: **g,l,u,f.** *Choice, 2005.*

Nayar, B. K.   **QK522.P84 2003**
Pteridology in the New Millennium: NBRI Golden Jubilee Volume (in Honor of Prof. B.K. Nayar). Subhash Chandra & Mrittunjai Srivastava (Editors), National Botanical Research Institute (India) Staff (Contribution by). Trade Cloth. Springer. New York, NY. 2003. 544p. ISBN:1-4020-1128-8, ISBN13: 978-1-4020-1128-3. Dewey:587. LCCN:2003-040010.
Audience: **u,f.**

Page, C. N.   **QK527 .P26 1997**
Ferns of Britain and Ireland. Ed. 2. Trade Paper. Cambridge University Press. New York, NY. 1997. 558p. ISBN:0-521-58658-5, ISBN13: 978-0-521-58658-0. Dewey:587/.3/0941. LCCN:96-038838.
Audience: **g,l,u,f.** *Choice, 1998.*

Palmer, Daniel D.   **QK511.H3P36 2002**
Hawaii's Ferns and Fern Allies. Trade Cloth. University of Hawaii Press. Honolulu, HI. 2002. 336p. ISBN:0-8248-2522-5, ISBN13: 978-0-8248-2522-5. Dewey:587.3/09969. LCCN:2002-003574.
Audience: **g,l,u,f.** *Choice, 2003.*

Raghavan, Valayamghat   **QK521 .R34 1989**
Developmental Biology of Fern Gametophytes. Jonathan B. L. Bard, Peter W. Barlow & David L. Kirk (Contribution by). Trade Paper. Cambridge University Press. New York, NY. 2005. 375p. Developmental and Cell Biology Ser., Vol. 20 ISBN:0-521-01725-4, ISBN13: 978-0-521-01725-1. Dewey:587/.3. LCCN:2006-271692.
Audience: **u,f.**

Verdoorn, Frans (Editor)   **QK523 .V47**
Manual of Pteridology. Trade Cloth. Lubrecht & Cramer, Ltd. Port Jervis, NY. 1967. ISBN:90-6123-093-4, ISBN13: 978-90-6123-093-9. Dewey:587.
Audience: **l,u,f.**

Descriptive Biology: Plants > Higher Plants

QK10

☐ GRIN Taxonomy for Plants.
http://www.ars-grin.gov/cgi-bin/npgs/html/index.pl
Audience: **u,f.**

Barrett, Marilyn   **RM666.H33**
The Handbook of Clinically Tested Herbal Remedies. Trade
Cloth. Haworth Press, Incorporated, The. Binghamton, NY.
2004. 1435p. Haworth Series in Evidence-Based Phytotherapy
ISBN:0-7890-1068-2, ISBN13: 978-0-7890-1068-1.
Dewey:615/.321. LCCN:2003-025270.
Audience: **u,f.** *Choice, 2005.*

Christophe, Christophe   **RM666.H33**
  Wiart (Author, Editor)
Medicinal Plants of Asia and the Pacific. Trade Cloth. Humana
Press. Totowa, NJ. 2006. 500p. ISBN:1-58829-748-9, ISBN13:
978-1-58829-748-8. Dewey:615/.321. LCCN:2006-015502.
Audience: **u,f.**

Daniel, M.   **QK99.A1D36 2005**
Medicinal Plants: Chemistry and Properties. Trade Cloth.
Science Publishers. Enfield, NH. 2005. 260p.
ISBN:1-57808-395-8, ISBN13: 978-1-57808-395-4.
Dewey:615/.321. LCCN:2005-054084.
Audience: **u,f.**

Hanson, Bryan   **RS164.H276 2005**
Understanding Medicinal Plants: Their Chemistry and
Therapeutic Action. Saddle Stitched, Cloth over Boards.
Haworth Press, Incorporated, The. Binghamton, NY. 2005. 307p.
ISBN:0-7890-1551-X, ISBN13: 978-0-7890-1551-8.
Dewey:615/.321. LCCN:2004-024495.
Audience: **u,f.** *Choice, 2006.*

Henry, J. David   **QH106.H46 2002**
Canada's Boreal Forest. Trade Cloth. Smithsonian Institution
Press. Washington, DC. 2002. 208p. Smithsonian Natural
History Ser. ISBN:1-58834-057-0, ISBN13: 978-1-58834-057-3.
Dewey:508.415. LCCN:2002-070687.
Audience: **g,l,u.**

Jukofsky, Diane   **QH86**
Encyclopedia of Rainforests: Diane Jukofsky for the Rainforest
Alliance. Cloth Text. Greenwood Publishing Group, Inc.
Portsmouth, NH. 2001. 384p. ISBN:1-57356-259-9, ISBN13:
978-1-57356-259-1. Dewey:578.734/03. LCCN:2001-032154.
Audience: **g,l,u.** *Choice, 2002.*

Ross, Ivan A.   **RS164.R676 2003**
Medicinal Plants of the World: Chemical Constituents,
Traditional and Modern Medicinal Uses, Vol. 1. Ed. 2. Saddle
Stitched, Cloth over Boards. Humana Press. Totowa, NJ. 2003.
489p. ISBN:1-58829-281-9, ISBN13: 978-1-58829-281-0.
Dewey:615/.32. LCCN:02-032933.
Audience: **u,f.** *Choice, 1999.*

Ross, Ivan A.   **RS164.R676 1999**
Medicinal Plants of the World: Chemical Constituents,
Traditional and Modern Medicinal Uses, Vol. 1. Book, Other.
Humana Press. Totowa, NJ. 1994. a; Organic and
Pharmaceutical Chemistry a; Pharmacology and Toxicology a;

Plant Biology a; Pharmacognosy 432p. ISBN:0-89603-542-5,
ISBN13: 978-0-89603-542-3. Dewey:615/.32. LCCN:98-034758.
Audience: **u,f.** *Choice, 1999.*

Ross, Ivan A.   **RS164**
Medicinal Plants of the World: Chemical Constituents,
Traditional and Modern Medicinal Uses. Trade Cloth. Humana
Press. Totowa, NJ. 2005. 648p. ISBN:1-58829-129-4, ISBN13:
978-1-58829-129-5. Dewey:615/.32.
Audience: **u,f.**

Ross, Ivan A. (Editor)   **RS164.R676 1999**
Medicinal Plants of the World: Chemical Constituents,
Traditional and Modern Medicinal Uses. Book, Other. Humana
Press. Totowa, NJ. 2001. a; Organic and Pharmaceutical
Chemistry a; Pharmacology and Toxicology a; Plant Biology a;
Pharmacognosy 504p. ISBN:0-89603-877-7, ISBN13:
978-0-89603-877-6. Dewey:615/.32. LCCN:98-034758.
Audience: **u,f.** *Choice, 2001.*

Wiart   **RS179**
Medicinal Plants of the Asia-Pacific: Drugs for the Future?
Trade Cloth. World Scientific Publishing Company, Inc.
Hackensack, NJ. 2005. 800p. ISBN:981-256-341-5, ISBN13:
978-981-256-341-5. Dewey:615.321.
Audience: **u,f.**

Descriptive Biology: Animals

☐ Google Directory: Biology, Zoology.
http://google.com/Top/Science/Biology/Zoology/
Google.
Audience: **g,l.**

☐ Google Directory: Biology, Zoology, Chordates, Ornithology
[Birds].
http://google.com/Top/Science/Biology/Zoology/Chordates/
Ornithology/
Google.
Audience: **g,l.**

QH303.5

☐ Taxonomy Browser.
http://www.ncbi.nlm.nih.gov/Taxonomy/taxonomyhome.html/
Audience: **l,u,f.**

Allaby, Michael (Editor)   **QL9**
The Concise Oxford Dictionary of Zoology. Trade Paper. Oxford
University Press, Inc. New York, NY. 1992. 512p. Oxford
Paperback Reference Ser. ISBN:0-19-286093-3, ISBN13:
978-0-19-286093-4. Dewey:591/.03. LCCN:91-045531.
Audience: **g,l,u,f.** *Choice, 1992.*

Allaby, Michael (Editor)   **QL9**
A Dictionary of Zoology. Ed. 2. Trade Paper. Oxford University
Press, Inc. New York, NY. 2003. 606p. Oxford Paperback
Reference Ser. ISBN:0-19-860758-X, ISBN13:
978-0-19-860758-8. Dewey:590/.3. LCCN:2003-278285.
Audience: **g,l,u,f.** *Choice, 2004.*

Biewener, Andrew A. QP301
Animal Locomotion. Trade Cloth. Oxford University Press, Inc.
New York, NY. 2003. 296p. Oxford Animal Biology Ser.
ISBN:0-19-850023-8, ISBN13: 978-0-19-850023-0.
Dewey:573.791. LCCN:2003-545378.

Audience: **l,u.**

Carey, James R. & Judge, QP85
Debra S. (Debra Suzan)
Longevity Records: Life Spans of Mammals, Birds, Amphibians,
Reptiles, and Fish. Odense University Press, Odense. 2000.
Monographs on population aging,; 8 ISBN:87-7838-539-3,
ISBN13: 978-87-7838-539-0.

Audience: **g,l,u.**

Getz, Wayne Marcus & QH352
Haight, Robert G.
Population Harvesting: Demographic Models of Fish, Forest,
and Animal Resources. Princeton University Press, Princeton,
N.J.. 1989. Monographs in population biology ;; 27
ISBN:0-691-08515-3, ISBN13: 978-0-691-08515-9.

Audience: **u.**

Hansell, Michael H. QL756
Animal Architecture. Trade Cloth. Oxford University Press, Inc.
New York, NY. 2005. 336p. Oxford Animal Biology Ser.
ISBN:0-19-850751-8, ISBN13: 978-0-19-850751-2.
Dewey:591.5'64. LCCN:2005-297193.

Audience: **l,u.** *Choice, 2005.*

Jurd, Richard D. QL47.2
Instant Notes in Animal Biology. Ed. 2. UK-B Format
Paperback. Taylor & Francis Group. Abingdon, 2004. 312p.
ISBN:1-85996-325-0, ISBN13: 978-1-85996-325-8. Dewey:590.
LCCN:2003-058333.

Audience: **l,u.**

Mayr, Ernst & Ashlock, QL351
Peter D.
Principles of Systematic Zoology. Ed. 2. McGraw-Hill, New
York. 1991. ISBN:0-07-041144-1, ISBN13: 978-0-07-041144-9.

Audience: **l,u.**

Nollman, Jim (Editor) QL713.2
☐ The WWW Virtual Library Whale Watching Web.
http://www.helsinki.fi/~lauhakan/whale/
Lauhakangas, Rauno (Editor). The WWW Virtual Library
(WWWVL).

Audience: **g,l.**

Reader's Digest Editors QL7.E53
Encyclopedia of Animals: Mammals, Birds, Reptiles,
Amphibians. Trade Cloth. Reader's Digest Association,
Incorporated, The. Pleasantville, NY. 1994. 688p.
ISBN:1-875137-49-1, ISBN13: 978-1-875137-49-7.
Dewey:591.03.

Audience: **g,l,u.**

Descriptive Biology: Animals > Invertebrates

QH447
☐ Mouse Genome Resources.
http://www.ncbi.nlm.nih.gov/genome/guide/mouse/

Audience: **u,f.**

Anderson, D. T. (Editor) QL362.I58 2001
Invertebrate Zoology. Ed. 2. Paper Text. Oxford University
Press, Inc. New York, NY. 2002. 476p. ISBN:0-19-551368-1,
ISBN13: 978-0-19-551368-4. Dewey:592. LCCN:2002-276846.

Audience: **l,u.**

Capinera, John L. (Editor) QL462.3
Encyclopedia of Entomology. Trade Cloth. Springer. New York,
NY. 2006. XLIX, 2580p. ISBN:0-7923-8670-1, ISBN13:
978-0-7923-8670-4. Dewey:595.703. LCCN:2006-275698.

Audience: **g,l,u,f.** *Choice, 2005.*

Carey, James R. QH352.C36 1993
Applied Demography for Biologists: With Special Emphasis on
Insects. Trade Paper. Oxford University Press, Inc. New York,
NY. 1993. 222p. ISBN:0-19-506687-1, ISBN13:
978-0-19-506687-6. Dewey:574.5/248/072. LCCN:91-045843.

Audience: **u,f.** *Choice, 1993.*

Coleman, David C. & QL364.4.I58 2000
Hendrix, Paul F.
Invertebrates as Webmasters in Ecosystems. Cloth Text. Oxford
University Press, Inc. New York, NY. 2000. 350p. CABI
Publishing Ser. ISBN:0-85199-394-X, ISBN13:
978-0-85199-394-2. Dewey:592.17. LCCN:99-041246.

Audience: **u,f.**

Davies, R. G. QL463.D38 1988
Outlines of Entomology. Ed. 7. Paper Text. Chapman & Hall.
New York, NY. 1988. 350p. ISBN:0-412-26680-6, ISBN13:
978-0-412-26680-5. Dewey:595.7. LCCN:88-010865.

Audience: **l,u.**

Doris, Ellen QL467.2
Entomology. Rubenstein, Len (Photographer); produced in
association with The Children's School of Science, Woods Hole,
Massachusetts. New York : Thames and Hudson. 1993. Real
kids real science books; Variation: Doris, Ellen.; Real kids real
science books ISBN:0-500-19004-6, ISBN13:
978-0-500-19004-3.

Audience: **u.**

Elzinga, Richard J. QL463.E48 2003
Fundamentals of Entomology. Ed. 6. Cloth Text. Prentice Hall
PTR. Upper Saddle River, NJ. 2003. 512p.
ISBN:0-13-048030-4, ISBN13: 978-0-13-048030-9.
Dewey:595.7. LCCN:2002-034583.

Audience: **u.**

Flint, S. J., et al. QR360.P697 2004
Principles of Virology: Molecular Biology, Pathogenesis, and
Control of Animal Viruses. Ed. 2. L. W. Enquist, V. R.
Racaniello & A. M. Skalka (Authors). Trade Cloth. ASM Press.
Washington, DC. 2003. 820p. ISBN:1-55581-259-7, ISBN13:
978-1-55581-259-1. Dewey:579.2. LCCN:2003-009529.

Audience: **u,f.**

Food and Agriculture GC481
Organization Staff, et al.
The Living Marine Resources of the Western Central Atlantic:
Introduction, Molluscs, Crustaceans, Hagfishes, Sharks, Batoid
Fishes and Chimaeras, Vol. 1. American Society of
Ichthyologists and Herpetologists Staff & European
Communities Commission (Authors), Kent E. Carpenter
(Editor). Trade Paper. Food and Agriculture Organization of the
United Nations. Rome, 2002. 614p. Fao Species Identification

Guide for Fishery Purposes Ser. ISBN:92-5-104825-8, ISBN13: 978-92-5-104825-2. Dewey:578.773.

Audience: **l,u,f.**

Gilbert, Pamela &   **Z5856.G52 1990**
Hamilton, Chris J.
Entomology: A Guide to Information Sources. Ed. 2. Trade Cloth. Continuum International Publishing Group, Ltd. London, 1990. 272p. ISBN:0-7201-2052-7, ISBN13: 978-0-7201-2052-3. Dewey:595.7/007. LCCN:89-013268.

Audience: **l,u.**

Gullan, P. J. & Cranston, P.   **QL463.G85 2004**
S.
The Insects: An Outline of Entomology. Ed. 3. Trade Cloth. Blackwell Publishing, Inc. Malden, MA. 2004. 528p. ISBN:1-4051-1113-5, ISBN13: 978-1-4051-1113-3. Dewey:595.7. LCCN:2004-000124.

Audience: **g,l,u.**

Gullan, P. J.; Cranston, P. S.   **QL463**
The insects: an outline of entomology. McInnes, K. Hansen (Illustrator). London ; New York : Chapman & Hall. 1994. ISBN:0-412-49360-8, ISBN13: 978-0-412-49360-7.

Audience: **l,u.**

Headrick, David   **QL462.3.G67 2001**
A Dictionary of Entomology. George Gordh (Compiled by). Cloth Text. Oxford University Press, Inc. New York, NY. 2001. 1042p. CABI Publishing Ser. ISBN:0-85199-291-9, ISBN13: 978-0-85199-291-4. Dewey:595.7/03. LCCN:00-044427.

Audience: **g,l,u,f.**

Huffaker, Carl B. &   **QL496.4.E36 1999**
Gutierrez, Andrew Paul (Editors)
Ecological Entomology. Ed. 2. Trade Cloth. John Wiley & Sons, Inc. Hoboken, NJ. 1998. 776p. ISBN:0-471-24483-X, ISBN13: 978-0-471-24483-7. Dewey:595.7/17. LCCN:98-018923.

Audience: **u.**

McGavin, George C.   **QL467.2**
Essential Entomology: An Order-by-Order Introduction. Richard Lewington (Illustrator). Paper Text. Oxford University Press, Inc. New York, NY. 2001. 324p. ISBN:0-19-850002-5, ISBN13: 978-0-19-850002-5. Dewey:595.7.

Audience: **u.**

Meglitsch, Paul A. &   **QL362.M4 1991**
Schram, Frederick R.
Invertebrate Zoology. Ed. 3. Cloth Text. Oxford University Press, Inc. New York, NY. 1991. 640p. ISBN:0-19-504900-4, ISBN13: 978-0-19-504900-8. Dewey:592. LCCN:89-026592.

Audience: **l,u.**

Nation, James L.   **QL495**
Insect Physiology and Biochemistry. CRC Press, Boca Raton. 2002. ISBN:0-8493-1181-0, ISBN13: 978-0-8493-1181-9.

Audience: **u.**

Noble, Elmer R.   **QL757.P34 1989**
Parasitology: The Biology of Animal Parasites. Ed. 6. Trade Cloth. Lippincott Williams & Wilkins. Philadelphia, PA. 1989. 574p. ISBN:0-8121-1155-9, ISBN13: 978-0-8121-1155-2. Dewey:591.52/49. LCCN:88-009235.

Audience: **l,u.**

Robinson, W. H.   **QL472.7.R63 1996**
Urban Entomology: Insect and Mite Pests. UK-B Format Paperback. Chapman & Hall. New York, NY. 1996. 448p. ISBN:0-412-60750-6, ISBN13: 978-0-412-60750-9. Dewey:595.7/09173/2. LCCN:96-083463.

Audience: **g,l,u.**

Ruppert, Edward E., et al.   **QL362.R76 2003**
Invertebrate Zoology: A Functional Evolutionary Approach. Ed. 7. Richard S. Fox & Robert D. Barnes (Authors). Cloth Text. Brooks/Cole. Pacific Grove, CA. 2003. 1008p. ISBN:0-03-025982-7, ISBN13: 978-0-03-025982-1. Dewey:592. LCCN:2003-107287.

Audience: **l,u.**

Sorenson, W. Conner   **QL474.S67 1995**
Brethren of the Net: American Entomology, 1840-1880. Trade Cloth. University of Alabama Press. Tuscaloosa, AL. 1995. 376p. History of American Science and Technology Ser. ISBN:0-8173-0755-9, ISBN13: 978-0-8173-0755-4. Dewey:595.7/00973. LCCN:94-005258.

Audience: **l,u.** *Choice, 1996.*

Wallace, Robert L. &   **QL362 .W33**
Taylor, Walter K.
Invertebrate Zoology. Ed. 6. Trade Paper. Prentice Hall PTR. Upper Saddle River, NJ. 2002. 356p. ISBN:0-13-042937-6, ISBN13: 978-0-13-042937-7. Dewey:592.

Audience: **l,u.**

Williamson, D. I. (Donald   **QL362.75**
Irving)
Larvae and Evolution: Toward A New Zoology. Margulis, Lynn (Foreword by); Tauber, Alfred I. (Foreword by). Chapman and Hall, New York. 1992. ISBN:0-412-03081-0, ISBN13: 978-0-412-03081-9.

Audience: **u.**

Wolanski, Eric (Editor)   **QH197**
Oceanographic Processes of Coral Reefs: Physical and Biological Links in the Great Barrier Reef. CRC Press, Boca Raton. 2001. ISBN:0-8493-0833-X, ISBN13: 978-0-8493-0833-8.

Audience: **u,f.**

Descriptive Biology: Animals > Vertebrates

GC481
The Living Marine Resource of the Western Central Atlantic: Bony Fishes (Opistognathidae to Molidae), Sea Turtles and Marine Mammals, Vol. 3, Pt. 2. Trade Cloth. Food and Agriculture Organization of the United Nations. Rome, 2002. 758p. Fao Species Identification Guide for Fishery Purposes Ser. ISBN:92-5-104827-4, ISBN13: 978-92-5-104827-6. Dewey:578.773.

Audience: **u,f.**

QH447
Zebrafish Genome Resources.
http://www.ncbi.nlm.nih.gov/genome/guide/zebrafish/

Audience: **u,f.**

Adams, S. M.   SH177.S75B56 1990
Biological Indicators of Stress in Fish. Trade Paper. American
Fisheries Society. Bethesda, MD. 1990. 191p. Symposium Ser.,
No. 8 ISBN:0-913235-62-8, ISBN13: 978-0-913235-62-1.
Dewey:639.3. LCCN:90-083452.

Audience: **u,f.**

Adler, Kraig & Halliday,   QL640.7.F57 2002
  Tim (Editors)
Firefly Encyclopedia of Reptiles and Amphibians. Trade Cloth.
Firefly Books, Ltd. Tonawanda, NY. 2002. 240p.
ISBN:1-55297-613-0, ISBN13: 978-1-55297-613-5.
Dewey:597.9. LCCN:2003-542845.

Audience: **g,l,u.** *Choice, 2003.*

Banks, John C., et al.   QM25.A796 2005
Atlas of Clinical Gross Anatomy. Pedro B. Nava, Darrell
Petersen & Kenneth P. Moses (Authors), Martein Moningka
(Contribution by). Paper Text. Elsevier - Health Sciences
Division. Philadelphia, PA. 2005. 524p. ISBN:0-323-03744-5,
ISBN13: 978-0-323-03744-0. Dewey:611/.0022/2.
LCCN:2005-045078.

Audience: **g,l,u,f.**

Barrow, Mark V.   QL672.73.U6B37 1998
A Passion for Birds: American Ornithology after Audubon.
Cloth Text. Princeton University Press. Princeton, NJ. 1998.
336p. ISBN:0-691-04402-3, ISBN13: 978-0-691-04402-6.
Dewey:598/.0973. LCCN:97-018600.

Audience: **g,l,u.** *Choice, 1998.*

Berthold, Peter, et al.   QL698.9.B4813 2001
Bird Migration: A General Survey. Ed. 2. Hans-Gunther Bauer
& Valarie Westhead (Authors). Cloth Text. Oxford University
Press, Inc. New York, NY. 2001. 266p. Oxford Ornithology Ser.,
Vol. 12 ISBN:0-19-850786-0, ISBN13: 978-0-19-850786-4.
Dewey:598.156/8. LCCN:2001-021810.

Audience: **g,l,u.**

Bird, David M.   QL673.B55 2004
The Bird Almanac: A Guide to Essential Facts and Figures of
the World's Birds. Ed. 2. Trade Paper. Firefly Books, Ltd.
Tonawanda, NY. 2004. 460p. ISBN:1-55297-925-3, ISBN13:
978-1-55297-925-9. Dewey:598. LCCN:2004-273747.

Audience: **l,u.**

Bone, Q.; Marshall, N. B.;   QL615.B66
  Blaxter, J. S. H.
Biology of Fishes. Ed. 2. Routledge. 1995.
ISBN:0-7514-0243-5, ISBN13: 978-0-7514-0243-8.

Audience: **l,u.**

Brooke, Michael &   QL673
  Birkhead, Tim R.
The Cambridge Encyclopedia of Ornithology. Trade Cloth.
Cambridge University Press. New York, NY. 1991. 372p.
ISBN:0-521-36205-9, ISBN13: 978-0-521-36205-4. Dewey:598.
LCCN:91-214229.

Audience: **g,l,u.** *Choice, 1992.*

Carrier, Jeffrey C. (Editor)   QL638.93
Biology of Sharks and Their Relatives. Musick, John A.
(Editor); Heithaus, Michael R. (Editor). CRC PRess. 2004.
ISBN:0-8493-1514-X, ISBN13: 978-0-8493-1514-5.

Audience: **l,u.**

Chapman and Hall Staff   QL668.E2
Ecology and Conservation of Amphibians. Trade Cloth.
Chapman & Hall. New York, NY. 224p. ISBN:0-412-62410-9,
ISBN13: 978-0-412-62410-0. Dewey:597.817.
LCCN:95-071856.

Audience: **l,u.** *Choice, 1997.*

Cloudsley-Thompson, John   QL641.C57 1999
  L.
The Diversity of Amphibians and Reptiles: An Introduction.
Cloth Text. Springer. New York, NY. 1999. 254p.
ISBN:3-540-65056-3, ISBN13: 978-3-540-65056-0.
Dewey:597.9. LCCN:98-045640.

Audience: **l,u.**

Cogger, Harold C. &   QL640.7.E53 1998
  Zweifel, Richard G. (Editors)
Encyclopedia of Reptiles and Amphibians. Ed. 2. David
Kirshner (Illustrator). Trade Cloth. Elsevier Science &
Technology Books. Saint Louis, MO. 1998. 240p.
ISBN:0-12-178560-2, ISBN13: 978-0-12-178560-4.
Dewey:597.9/03. LCCN:98-088226.

Audience: **l,u.** *Choice, 1999.*

Conant, Roger & Collins,   QL651.C65 1998
  Joseph T.
A Field Guide to Reptiles and Amphibians: Eastern and Central
North America. Ed. 3. Isabelle Hunt Conant & Tom R. Johnson
(Illustrators). Trade Paper. Houghton Mifflin Company Trade &
Reference Division. Boston, MA. 1998. 634p. Peterson Field
Guides ISBN:0-395-90452-8, ISBN13: 978-0-395-90452-7.
Dewey:597.6/097. LCCN:98-013622.

Audience: **g,l,u.**

Duellman, William E. &   QL667.D84 1994
  Trueb, Linda
Biology of Amphibians. Trade Paper. Johns Hopkins University
Press. Baltimore, MD. 1981. 696p. ISBN:0-8018-4780-X,
ISBN13: 978-0-8018-4780-6. Dewey:597.6. LCCN:93-024401.

Audience: **l,u.**

Elphick, Jonathan   QL674.4.E46 2005
Birds: The Art of Ornithology. Trade Cloth. Rizzoli International
Publications, Inc. New York, NY. 2005. 336p.
ISBN:0-8478-2706-2, ISBN13: 978-0-8478-2706-0.
Dewey:598/.022/2. LCCN:2004-096830.

Audience: **g,l,u.** *Choice, 2005.*

Evans, David H. (Editor)   QL639.1.P49 2005
The Physiology of Fishes. Ed. 3. Claiborne, James B. (Editor).
CRC Press. 2005. ISBN:0-8493-2022-4, ISBN13:
978-0-8493-2022-4.

Audience: **l,u.**

Feder, Martin E. &   QL669.2.E58 1992
  Burggren, Warren W. (Editors)
Environmental Physiology of the Amphibians. Trade Cloth.
University of Chicago Press. Chicago, IL. 1992. 472p.
ISBN:0-226-23943-8, ISBN13: 978-0-226-23943-9.
Dewey:597.6/041. LCCN:91-030944.

Audience: **l,u.** *Choice, 1993.*

Filisky, Michael   QL625.F55 1989
Peterson First Guide to Fishes. Sarah Landry (Illustrator). Trade
Paper. Houghton Mifflin Company. New York, NY. 1989. 128p.
ISBN:0-395-50219-5, ISBN13: 978-0-395-50219-8.
Dewey:597.097. LCCN:88-032887.

Audience: **g,l,u.**

Food and Agriculture   **GC481**
  Organization Staff, et al.
The Living Marine Resources of the Western Central Atlantic:
Introduction, Molluscs, Crustaceans, Hagfishes, Sharks, Batoid
Fishes and Chimaeras, Vol. 1. American Society of
Ichthyologists and Herpetologists Staff & European
Communities Commission (Authors), Kent E. Carpenter
(Editor). Trade Paper. Food and Agriculture Organization of the
United Nations. Rome, 2002. 614p. Fao Species Identification
Guide for Fishery Purposes Ser. ISBN:92-5-104825-8, ISBN13:
978-92-5-104825-2. Dewey:578.773.
                                        Audience: **l,u,f.**

Frank, Norman & Ramus,   **QL645.F73 1995**
  Erica
A Complete Guide to Scientific and Common Names of Reptiles
and Amphibians of the World. Trade Paper. Reptile &
Amphibian Magazine. Pottsville, PA. 1996. 300p.
ISBN:0-9641032-3-0, ISBN13: 978-0-9641032-3-8.
Dewey:597.9/01/4. LCCN:95-068825.
                            Audience: **l,u,f.** *Choice, 1996.*

Gerking, Shelby D.   **QL639.1.G47 1994**
Feeding Ecology of Fish. Trade Cloth. Elsevier Science &
Technology Books. Saint Louis, MO. 1994. 416p.
ISBN:0-12-280780-4, ISBN13: 978-0-12-280780-0.
Dewey:597/.053. LCCN:93-042569.
                                        Audience: **l,u.**

Gerthold, Peter   **QL698.9.B4813 1993**
Bird Migration: A General Survey. Hans-Gunther Baueer &
Tricia Tomlinson (Translators). Trade Cloth. Oxford University
Press, Inc. New York, NY. 1994. 250p. Ornithology Ser., No. 3
ISBN:0-19-854692-0, ISBN13: 978-0-19-854692-4.
Dewey:598.252/5. LCCN:93-033020.
                            Audience: **g,l,u.** *Choice, 1994.*

Getz, Wayne M. & Haight,   **QH352.G47 1989**
  Robert G.
Population Harvesting: Demographic Models of Fish, Forest,
and Animal Resources. Trade Paper. Princeton University Press.
Princeton, NJ. 1989. 408p. Monographs in Population Biology
Ser. ISBN:0-691-08516-1, ISBN13: 978-0-691-08516-6.
Dewey:574.5/248. LCCN:88-019950.
                                        Audience: **u,f.**

Graham, Jeffrey B. (Editor)   **QL615.G73 1997**
Air-Breathing Fishes: Evolution, Diversity, and Adaptation.
Trade Cloth. Elsevier Science & Technology Books. Saint
Louis, MO. 1997. 299p. ISBN:0-12-294860-2, ISBN13:
978-0-12-294860-2. Dewey:573.2/17. LCCN:96-047586.
                            Audience: **l,u.** *Choice, 1997.*

Harding, James H.   **QL653.G74H37 1997**
Amphibians and Reptiles of the Great Lakes Region. Cloth over
Boards. University of Michigan Press. Chicago, IL. 1997. 400p.
Great Lakes Environment Ser. ISBN:0-472-09628-1, ISBN13:
978-0-472-09628-2. Dewey:597.6/0978. LCCN:96-025343.
                            Audience: **l,u.** *Choice, 1998.*

Hart, Paul & Reynolds,   **QL615.H36 2004**
  John (Editors)
The Handbook of Fish Biology and Fisheries, Vol. 2. Trade
Cloth. Blackwell Publishing, Inc. Malden, MA. 2002. 424p.
ISBN:0-632-06482-X, ISBN13: 978-0-632-06482-3. Dewey:597.
LCCN:2004-351189.
                            Audience: **g,l,u.** *Choice, 2003.*

Hickman, Cleveland P., et   **QL47.2.H527 2003**
  al.
Animal Diversity. Ed. 3. Larry S. Roberts & Allan Larson
(Authors). Paper Text. McGraw-Hill Companies, The. New
York, NY. 2002. xvi, 447p. ISBN:0-07-119549-1, ISBN13:
978-0-07-119549-2. Dewey:590. LCCN:2002-022113.
                                        Audience: **l,u.**

Hofrichter, Robert (Editor)   **QL641.A4713 2000**
Amphibians: The World of Frogs, Toads, Salamanders and
Newts. Trade Cloth. Firefly Books, Ltd. Tonawanda, NY. 2000.
264p. ISBN:1-55209-541-X, ISBN13: 978-1-55209-541-6.
Dewey:597.8. LCCN:2001-368012.
                            Audience: **l,u.** *Choice, 2001.*

Hubbs, Carl L. & Lagler,   **QL625.5.H814 2004**
  Karl F.
Fishes of the Great Lakes Region. Gerald R. Smith (Editor).
Trade Paper. University of Michigan Press. Chicago, IL. 2004.
332p. ISBN:0-472-11371-2, ISBN13: 978-0-472-11371-2.
Dewey:597.176/0977. LCCN:2004-047986.
                            Audience: **l,u,f.** *Choice, 2005.*

Jedicke, Peter & Scientific   **QH349.C43 2001**
  American Editors
Extreme Science: Chasing the Ghost Bat: Extreme Science and
Other Mysteries of Nature. Trade Paper. St. Martin's Press.
Gordonville, VA. 2001. 257p. Extreme Science Ser.
ISBN:0-312-26818-1, ISBN13: 978-0-312-26818-3. Dewey:570.
LCCN:2001-042406.
                                        Audience: **g,l,u.**

Jobling, Malcom   **QL639.8**
Environmental Biology of Fishes. Springer. 1995. Fish &
Fisheries Series ISBN:0-412-58080-2, ISBN13:
978-0-412-58080-2.
                                        Audience: **u,f.**

Keenan, Philip E.   **QL681.K44 2002**
  (Photographer, Text by)
Birding Across North America: A Naturalist's Observations.
Trade Cloth. Timber Press, Inc. Portland, OR. 2002. 260p.
ISBN:0-88192-528-4, ISBN13: 978-0-88192-528-9.
Dewey:598/.07/2347. LCCN:2001-037623.
                            Audience: **g,l,u,f.** *Choice, 2002.*

Lannoo, Michael J. (Editor)   **QL644.7 .A48 2005**
Amphibian Declines: The Conservation Status of United States
Species. Trade Cloth. University of California Press. Berkeley,
CA. 2005. 1024p. ISBN:0-520-23592-4, ISBN13:
978-0-520-23592-2. Dewey:333.95/78. LCCN:2004-015272.
                                        Audience: **l,u.**

Long, John A.   **QL618.2.L66 1995**
The Rise of Fishes: 500 Million Years of Evolution. Trade
Cloth. Johns Hopkins University Press. Baltimore, MD. 1961.
224p. ISBN:0-8018-4992-6, ISBN13: 978-0-8018-4992-3.
Dewey:597/.038. LCCN:94-024692.
                                        Audience: **l,u.**

Maisy, John   **QE851.M35 1996**
Discovering Fossil Fishes: Your Guide to the Wonders of
Prehistoric Ocean Life. Trade Cloth. Henry Holt & Company.
New York, NY. 1996. 224p. ISBN:0-8050-4366-7, ISBN13:
978-0-8050-4366-2. Dewey:567. LCCN:96-006907.
                            Audience: **g,l,u.** *Choice, 1996.*

Matthews, William J.   QL624.M38 1998
Patterns in Freshwater Fish Ecology. Trade Cloth. Springer. New York, NY. 1998. 784p. ISBN:0-412-02831-X, ISBN13: 978-0-412-02831-1. Dewey:597.176. LCCN:97-021339.

Audience: **l,u.**

Moyle, Peter B. & Cech,   QL615.M64 2004
  Joseph J.
Fishes: An Introduction to Ichthyology. Ed. 5. Cloth Text. Prentice Hall PTR. Upper Saddle River, NJ. 2003. 744p. ISBN:0-13-100847-1, ISBN13: 978-0-13-100847-2. Dewey:597. LCCN:2003-054863.

Audience: **l,u.**

National Audubon Society   QL625.G56 2002
  Staff, et al.
National Audubon Society Field Guide to Fishes: North America. Ed. 2. James D. Williams & Carter R. Gilbert (Authors). Trade Cloth. Alfred A. Knopf Inc. New York, NY. 2002. 896p. National Audubon Society Ser. ISBN:0-375-41224-7, ISBN13: 978-0-375-41224-0. Dewey:597/.097. LCCN:2002-020773.

Audience: **g,l,u.**

Palika, Liz   SF459.R4P33 1998
The Complete Idiot's Guide to Reptiles and Amphibians. Trade Paper. Penguin Group (USA) Inc. New York, NY. 2003. 320p. The Complete Idiot's Guide Ser. ISBN:0-87605-145-X, ISBN13: 978-0-87605-145-0. Dewey:639.3/9. LCCN:98-015972.

Audience: **g,l,u.**

Paxton, John R. &   QL614.7.E535 1998
  Eschmeyer, William N. (Editors)
Encyclopedia of Fishes. Ed. 2. David Kirshner (Illustrator). Trade Cloth. Elsevier Science & Technology Books. Saint Louis, MO. 1998. 240p. Natural World Ser. ISBN:0-12-547665-5, ISBN13: 978-0-12-547665-2. Dewey:597/.03. LCCN:98-088228.

Audience: **g,l,u,f.** *Choice, 1999.*

Perrine, C. M. (Editor),   QL677.4.B57 1991
  et al.
Bird Populations Studies: Relevance to Conservation and Management. J. D. Lebreton & G. J. Hirons (Editors). Trade Cloth. Oxford University Press, Inc. New York, NY. 1991. 704p. Oxford Ornithology Ser., No. 1 ISBN:0-19-857730-3, ISBN13: 978-0-19-857730-0. Dewey:639.9/78. LCCN:90-041974.

Audience: **u.** *Choice, 1992.*

Pitkin, Linda M.   QL620.45.P58 2001
Coral Fish. Trade Paper. Smithsonian Institution Press. Washington, DC. 2001. 112p. ISBN:1-56098-818-5, ISBN13: 978-1-56098-818-2. Dewey:597.177/89. LCCN:00-046320.

Audience: **g,l,u.**

Playfair, Susan R.   HD8039.F66U536 2003
Vanishing Species?: Saving the Fish, Sacrificing the Fisherman. Trade Cloth. University Press of New England. Lebanon, NH. 2003. 292p. ISBN:1-58465-318-3, ISBN13: 978-1-58465-318-9. Dewey:338.3/727/0974. LCCN:2002-153373.

Audience: **l,u,f.**

Robins, C. Richard   QL627.C66 1991
Common and Scientific Names of Fishes from the United States and Canada. Ed. 5. Trade Cloth. American Fisheries Society. Bethesda, MD. 1991. 183p. Special Publication Ser., No. 20

ISBN:0-913235-70-9, ISBN13: 978-0-913235-70-6. Dewey:597.097/014. LCCN:90-086052.

Audience: **l,u,f.**

Rohde, Fred C., et al.   93-32535 [QL]
Freshwater Fishes of the Carolinas, Virginia, Maryland, and Delaware. Rudolf G. Arndt, David G. Lindquist & James F. Parnell (Authors). Trade Cloth. University of North Carolina Press. Chapel Hill, NC. 1994. 228p. ISBN:0-8078-2130-6, ISBN13: 978-0-8078-2130-5. Dewey:597.092/975. LCCN:93-032535.

Audience: **l,u,f.** *Choice, 1995.*

Satchell, Geoffrey H.   QL639.1 .S28 1991
Physiology and Form of Fish Circulation. Trade Cloth. Cambridge University Press. New York, NY. 1991. 253p. ISBN:0-521-39519-4, ISBN13: 978-0-521-39519-9. Dewey:597/.011. LCCN:90-038675.

Audience: **l,u.** *Choice, 1991.*

Schreck, C. B. & Moyle,   QL618.5.M47 1990
  Peter B. (Editors)
Methods for Fish Biology. Cloth Text. American Fisheries Society. Bethesda, MD. 1990. 684p. ISBN:0-913235-58-X, ISBN13: 978-0-913235-58-4. Dewey:597/.0072. LCCN:90-083196.

Audience: **l,u.**

Tomelleri, Joseph R. &   QL628.M53T66 1990
  Eberle, Mark E.
Fishes of the Central United States. Trade Cloth. University Press of Kansas. Lawrence, KS. 2004. xviii, 230p. ISBN:0-7006-0457-X, ISBN13: 978-0-7006-0457-9. Dewey:597.092/978. LCCN:89-038658.

Audience: **l,u,f.**

Wade, Nicholas (Editor)   QL614.5.S35 1997
The Science Times Book of Fish. Cloth over Boards. Globe Pequot Press, The. Guilford, CT. 1997. 240p. Science Times Ser. ISBN:1-55821-604-9, ISBN13: 978-1-55821-604-4. Dewey:597. LCCN:97-019471.

Audience: **g,l,u.**

Walters, Michael   QL672.7.W36 2003
A Concise History of Ornithology. Cloth over Boards. Yale University Press. Cumberland, RI. 2003. 256p. ISBN:0-300-09073-0, ISBN13: 978-0-300-09073-4. Dewey:598/.09. LCCN:2003-104752.

Audience: **l,u.** *Choice, 2004.*

Wilson, Josleen & National   QL625.W55 1991
  Audubon Society Staff
North American Fish. Trade Cloth. Random House Value Publishing. New York, NY. 1992. 80p. National Audubon Society Nature Ser. ISBN:0-517-03765-3, ISBN13: 978-0-517-03765-2. Dewey:597.097. LCCN:91-011789.

Audience: **g,l,u.**

Wootton, R. J.   QL639.8.W66 1992
Fish Ecology. Mass Market. Chapman & Hall. New York, NY. 1992. 200p. Tertiary Level Biology Ser. ISBN:0-412-02921-9, ISBN13: 978-0-412-02921-9. Dewey:597/.05. LCCN:91-028996.

Audience: **l,u.**

Formats: Web: ☐   Ebook: 🄴   CD/DVD-ROM: 💥   BCL3: 𝓑

Wootton, Robert J.   QL615.W63 1998
Ecology of Teleost Fishes. Ed. 2. Trade Cloth. Springer. New York, NY. 1998. 392p. ISBN:0-412-84590-3, ISBN13: 978-0-412-84590-1. Dewey:597.5045. LCCN:98-070538.
                                        Audience: **l,u.**

Zug, George R., et al.   QL641.Z84 2001
Herpetology: An Introductory Biology of Amphibians and Reptiles. Ed. 2. Janalee Caldwell & Laurie J. Vitt (Authors). Cloth Text. Elsevier Science & Technology Books. Saint Louis, MO. 2001. 630p. ISBN:0-12-782622-X, ISBN13: 978-0-12-782622-6. Dewey:597.9. LCCN:00-111103.
                                        Audience: **l,u.**

Biotechnology

☐ Google Directory: Biology, Biotechnology.
http://google.com/Top/Science/Biology/Biotechnology/
Google.
                                        Audience: **g,l.**

                                        TP248.2
☐ National Center for Biotechnology Information (NCBI).
http://www.ncbi.nih.gov/
                                        Audience: **l,u,f.**

Abate, Tom   HD9999.B442A2 2003
The Biotech Investor: How to Profit from the Coming Boom in Biotechnology. Cloth over Boards. Henry Holt & Company. New York, NY. 2003. 304p. ISBN:0-8050-7069-9, ISBN13: 978-0-8050-7069-9. Dewey:332.63/22. LCCN:2002-028765.
                                        Audience: **u,f.**

Albright, Matthew   RB155
Profits Pending: How Life Patents Represent the Biggest Swindle of the Twenty-First Century. Trade Paper. Common Courage Press. Monroe, ME. 2003. 224p. ISBN:1-56751-230-5, ISBN13: 978-1-56751-230-4. Dewey:616.042.
                                        Audience: **u,f.**

Bergeron, Bryan & Chan,   HD9999.B442B47 2004
 Paul
Biotech Industry: A Global, Economic, and Financing Overview. Trade Cloth. John Wiley & Sons, Inc. Hoboken, NJ. 2004. 362p. ISBN:0-471-46561-5, ISBN13: 978-0-471-46561-4. Dewey:338.4/76606. LCCN:2003-017976.
                                        Audience: **u,f.**

Bourgaize, David B., et al.   QH506.B67 2000
Biotechnology: Demystifying the Concepts. Rodolfo G. Buiser & Thomas R. Jewell (Authors). Trade Paper. Benjamin-Cummings Publishing Company. San Francisco, CA. 1999. 416p. ISBN:0-8053-4602-3, ISBN13: 978-0-8053-4602-2. Dewey:572.8. LCCN:99-036737.
                                        Audience: **l,u,f.**

Bowring, Finn   TP248.6.B695 2003
Science, Seeds, and Cyborgs: Biotechnology and the Appropriation of Life. Trade Cloth. Verso Books. London, 2003. 320p. ISBN:1-85984-687-4, ISBN13: 978-1-85984-687-2. Dewey:306.4/6. LCCN:2002-032950.
                                        Audience: **g,l,u.** *Choice, 2003.*

Bud, Robert F.   TP248.18
The Uses of Life: A History of Biotechnology. Mark F. Cantley (Foreword by). Trade Paper. Cambridge University Press. New York, NY. 1994. 319p. ISBN:0-521-47699-2, ISBN13: 978-0-521-47699-7. Dewey:660.6/09.
                                        Audience: **l,u.**

Cato Research
☐ The World Wide Web Virtual Library: Biotechnology Information Directory Section.
http://cato.com/biotech/
Cato Research.
                                        Audience: **g,l.**

Cogoli, Augusto (Editor)   QH577
Cell Biology and Biotechnology in Space. Trade Cloth. Elsevier Science & Technology Books. Saint Louis, MO. 2002. 262p. Advances in Space Biology and Medicine Ser. ISBN:0-444-50735-3, ISBN13: 978-0-444-50735-8. Dewey:571.6/0919.
                                        Audience: **u,f.**

DelVecchio, V.G. &   QH434.A66 2003
 Krcmery, V. (Editors)
Applications of Genomics and Proteomics for Analysis of Bacterial Biological Warfare Agents. Trade Cloth. I O S Press, Inc. Burke, VA. 2003. 196p. NATO Science Ser., Vol. 352 ISBN:1-58603-343-3, ISBN13: 978-1-58603-343-9. Dewey:623.4/594. LCCN:2003-104680.
                                        Audience: **u,f.**

Figeys, Daniel (Editor)   TP248.65.P76
Industrial Proteomics: Applications for Biotechnology and Pharmaceuticals. Digital, Other. John Wiley & Sons, Inc. Hoboken, NJ. 2005. 320p. Methods of Biochemical Analysis Ser. ISBN:0-471-70375-3, ISBN13: 978-0-471-70375-4. Dewey:660.6/3.
                                        Audience: **u,f.**

Finegold, David L., et al.   HD9999.B442B542 2005
Bioindustry Ethics. Cecile Bensimon, Abdallah S. Daar, Margaret Eaton, Beatrice Godard, Bartha Maria Knoppers, Peter A. Singer & Jocelyn MacKie (Authors). Trade Paper, Perfect. Elsevier Science & Technology Books. Saint Louis, MO. 2005. 384p. ISBN:0-12-369370-5, ISBN13: 978-0-12-369370-9. Dewey:174/.96606. LCCN:2005-040638.
                                        Audience: **u,f.**

Fukuyama, Francis   TP248.23.F85 2002
Our Posthuman Future: Consequences of the Biotechnology Revolution. Cloth over Boards. Farrar, Straus & Giroux. New York, NY. 2002. 272p. ISBN:0-374-23643-7, ISBN13: 978-0-374-23643-4. Dewey:303.48/3. LCCN:2002-100914.
                                        Audience: **l,u,f.** *Choice, 2002.*

Fumento, Michael   TP248.215.F86 2003
BioEvolution: How Biotech Is Changing Our World. Trade Cloth. Encounter Books. New York, NY. 2005. 510p. Ser. ISBN:1-893554-75-9, ISBN13: 978-1-893554-75-7. Dewey:303.48/3. LCCN:2003-049372.
                                        Audience: **g,l,u.** *Choice, 2004.*

Gad, Shayne Cox (Editor)   RM301.25.D784 2005
Drug Discovery Handbook. Trade Cloth. John Wiley & Sons, Inc. Hoboken, NJ. 2005. 1496p. ISBN:0-471-21384-5, ISBN13: 978-0-471-21384-0. Dewey:615/.19. LCCN:2004-027077.
                                        Audience: **u,f.**

Gaisford, James D., et al. HD9999.B442E25 2001
The Economics of Biotechnology. Jill E. Hobbs, William A. Kerr, Nicholas Perdikis & Marni D. Plunkett (Authors). Trade Cloth. Edward Elgar Publishing, Inc. Northampton, MA. 2001. 264p. ISBN:1-84064-595-4, ISBN13: 978-1-84064-595-8. Dewey:338.4/76606. LCCN:2001-031534.

Audience: **u,f.**

Gough, Leo HD9999.B442G68 2001
Investing in Biotechnology Stocks. Trade Cloth. John Wiley & Sons, Inc. Hoboken, NJ. 2001. 228p. ISBN:0-471-47914-4, ISBN13: 978-0-471-47914-7. Dewey:332.6/322. LCCN:2001-273955.

Audience: **u,f.**

Grand, Steve QH324.2.G73 2001
Creation: Life and How to Make It. Trade Cloth. Harvard University Press. Cambridge, MA. 2001. 240p. ISBN:0-674-00654-2, ISBN13: 978-0-674-00654-6. Dewey:570/.1/13. LCCN:2001-024165.

Audience: **l,u,f.** *Choice, 2002.*

Halford, Nigel G. (Editor) SB106.B56P582 2006
Plant Biotechnology: Current and Future Applications of Genetically Modified Crops. Trade Cloth. John Wiley & Sons, Inc. Hoboken, NJ. 2006. 316p. ISBN:0-470-02181-0, ISBN13: 978-0-470-02181-1. Dewey:631.5/233. LCCN:2005-024912.

Audience: **l,u.**

Ho, Rodney J. Y. & Gibaldi, Milo RS380.H6 2003
Biotechnology and Biopharmaceuticals: Transforming Proteins and Genes into Drugs. Trade Paper. John Wiley & Sons, Inc. Hoboken, NJ. 2003. 576p. ISBN:0-471-20690-3, ISBN13: 978-0-471-20690-3. Dewey:615/.19. LCCN:2002-153462.

Audience: **u,f.**

Institute for Research HF5381.A1
(Chicago, Ill.)
Career as A Biochemist: Cutting Edge Scientific Research, Practical Applications in Industry, New Specialties: Biotechnology and Bioengineering, Many Yop Professional Positions in Medicine, Pharmaceuticals, Nutrition. Institute for Research, Chicago. 1999. Institute research; no. 156; Variation: Careers research monographs ;; no. 156 ISBN:1-58511-156-2, ISBN13: 978-1-58511-156-5.

Audience: **g,l,u,f.**

Institute for Research HF5381.A1
(Chicago, Ill.)
Careers in Biotechnology, Bolecular Biology: Genetic Engineering-- Gene Therapy. Institute for Research, Chicago. 2000. Research; no. 3; Variation: Careers; no. 3 ISBN:1-58511-003-5, ISBN13: 978-1-58511-003-2.

Audience: **g,l,u,f.**

Juma, Calestous S494.5.B563J86 1989
The Gene Hunters: Biotechnology and the Scramble for Seeds. Trade Cloth. Princeton University Press. Princeton, NJ. 1989. 304p. ISBN:0-691-04258-6, ISBN13: 978-0-691-04258-9. Dewey:338.1/6. LCCN:89-003643.

Audience: **l,u.** *Choice, 1989.*

Kleinman, Daniel Lee QH315.K54 2003
Impure Cultures: University Biology and the World of Commerce. Trade Paper. University of Wisconsin Press. Chicago, IL. 2003. xv, 205p. Science and Technology in Society

Ser. ISBN:0-299-19233-4, ISBN13: 978-0-299-19233-4. Dewey:570/.72. LCCN:2003-007233.

Audience: **g,u,f.**

Leach, Melissa (Editor), et al. QH333.S365 2005
Science and Citizens: Globalization and the Challenge of Engagement. Ian Scoones & Brian Wynne (Editors). Cloth over Boards. Zed Books, Ltd. London, 2005. 256p. Claiming Citizenship Ser. ISBN:1-84277-550-2, ISBN13: 978-1-84277-550-9. Dewey:306.4/5. LCCN:2004-057236.

Audience: **u,f.**

Lee, Mike S. RS189.5.S65I55 2005
Integrated Strategies for Drug Discovery Using Mass Spectrometry. Trade Cloth. John Wiley & Sons, Inc. Hoboken, NJ. 2005. 568p. ISBN:0-471-46127-X, ISBN13: 978-0-471-46127-2. Dewey:615/.19. LCCN:2005-003235.

Audience: **u,f.**

Mayer, Frank & Hoppert, Michael QH207.H566 2003
Microscopic Techniques in Biotechnology. Trade Cloth. John Wiley & Sons, Inc. Hoboken, NJ. 2003. 342p. ISBN:3-527-30198-4, ISBN13: 978-3-527-30198-0. Dewey:660.6. LCCN:2003-274435.

Audience: **u,f.**

McCamant, James D. HD9999.B442
Biotech Investing: Every Investor's Guide. Trade Cloth. Perseus Books Group. New York, NY. 2002. 208p. ISBN:0-7382-0509-5, ISBN13: 978-0-7382-0509-0. Dewey:332.6/722.

Audience: **u,f.**

Messina, Lynn TP248.215
Biotechnology. H.W. Wilson: New York. 2000. The Reference Shelf; Vol. 72, No. 4. ISBN:0-8242-0985-0, ISBN13: 978-0-8242-0985-8.

Audience: **u,f.**

Mortensen, Vigo (Editor) QH332.L52 1995
Life and Death: Moral Implications of Biotechnology. Trade Paper. World Council of Churches/Conseil Oecumenique des Eglises. Geneva, 1996. 110p. ISBN:2-8254-1170-1, ISBN13: 978-2-8254-1170-4. Dewey:174/.2. LCCN:96-206033.

Audience: **u,f.**

Nicholl, Desmond S. QH442.N53 1994
An Introduction to Genetic Engineering. Cloth Text. Cambridge University Press. New York, NY. 1994. 182p. Studies in Biology ISBN:0-521-43054-2, ISBN13: 978-0-521-43054-8. Dewey:575.10724. LCCN:93-008176.

Audience: **u,f.** *Choice, 1995.*

Novartis Staff RM301.3.G45F76 2000
From Genome to Therapy: Integrating New Technologies with Drug Development. Trade Cloth. John Wiley & Sons, Inc. Hoboken, NJ. 2000. 174p. CIBA Foundation Symposia Ser., Vol. 229 ISBN:0-471-62744-5, ISBN13: 978-0-471-62744-9. LCCN:00-043348.

Audience: **u,f.**

Oliver, Richard L. HD9999.B442O438 2003
The Biotech Age: The Business of Biotech and How to Profit from It. Ed. 2. Trade Paper. McGraw-Hill Companies, The. New York, NY. 2003. 256p. ISBN:0-07-141489-4, ISBN13: 978-0-07-141489-0. Dewey:338.4/76606. LCCN:2003-002228.

Audience: **u,f.**

Oliver, Richard W.   HD9999.B442O44 2000
The Coming Biotech Age: The Business of Bio-Materials. Trade
Cloth. McGraw-Hill Trade. New York, NY. 1999. 266p.
ISBN:0-07-135020-9, ISBN13: 978-0-07-135020-4.
Dewey:338.4/76606. LCCN:99-053282.
                                        Audience: **u,f.**

Prasad, M. N. V. (Editor)   QH545.T7
Trace Elements in the Environment: Biogeochemistry,
Biotechnology, and Bioremediation. (Majeti Narasimha Vara)
(Editor); Sajwan, Kenneth S. (Editor); Naidu, R. (Editor).
CRC/Taylor and Francis, Boca Raton. 2006.
ISBN:1-56670-685-8, ISBN13: 978-1-56670-685-8.
                                        Audience: **l,u.**

Prasad, Paras N.   QH515.P73 2003
Introduction to Biophotonics. Trade Cloth. John Wiley & Sons,
Inc. Hoboken, NJ. 2003. 616p. ISBN:0-471-28770-9, ISBN13:
978-0-471-28770-4. Dewey:571.4/55. LCCN:2003-000578.
                                        Audience: **l,u.**

Prentis, Steve   TP248.2.P74 1984
Biotechnology. Trade Cloth. George Braziller Inc. New York,
NY. 1984. 192p. ISBN:0-8076-1094-1, ISBN13:
978-0-8076-1094-7. Dewey:660/.62. LCCN:83-026571.
                                        Audience: **u,f.**

Rabinow, Paul   QP606.D46 R33
Making PCR: Story of Biotechnology. Library Binding.
Sagebrush Education Resources. Caledonia, MN. 1997.
ISBN:0-613-91117-2, ISBN13: 978-0-613-91117-7.
Dewey:574.87/3282.
                                        Audience: **g,l.**

Rauter, Amélia Pilar   QH345.N346 2003
  (Editor), et al.
Natural Products in the New Millennium: Prospects and
Industrial Application. Fernando Brito Palma, Jorge Justino,
Maria Eduarda Araújo & Susana Pina dos Santos (Editors).
Trade Cloth. Springer. New York, NY. 2002. 540p. Proceedings
of the Phytochemical Society Ser., Vol. 49 ISBN:1-4020-1047-8,
ISBN13: 978-1-4020-1047-7. Dewey:660.6.
LCCN:2002-043265.
                                        Audience: **u,f.**

Robbins-Roth, Cynthia   T14.5
From Alchemy to IPO: The Business of Biotechnology. Trade
Cloth. Perseus Books Group. New York, NY. 2000. 272p.
ISBN:0-7382-0253-3, ISBN13: 978-0-7382-0253-2.
Dewey:303.48/3.
                                        Audience: **u,f.**

Robin, Stephane, et al.   QP624
DNA, Words and Models: Statistics of Exceptional Words.
Francois Rodolphe & Sophie Schbath (Authors). Trade Cloth.
Cambridge University Press. New York, NY. 2005. 158p.
ISBN:0-521-84729-X, ISBN13: 978-0-521-84729-2.
Dewey:572.8/633. LCCN:2005-047088.
                                        Audience: **u,f.**

Roerdink, F. H. & Kroon, A.   QH345.H66 VOL. 9
  M. (Editors)
Drug Carrier Systems. Trade Cloth. John Wiley & Sons, Inc.
Hoboken, NJ. 1989. 342p. Horizons in Biochemistry and
Biophysics Ser. ISBN:0-471-92317-6, ISBN13:
978-0-471-92317-6. Dewey:574.19 s. LCCN:88-036668.
                                        Audience: **u,f.**

Rudolph, Frederick B. &   TP248.2.B574 1996
  McIntire, Larry V. (Editors)
Biotechnology: Science, Engineering, and Ethical Challenges for
the 21st Century. Trade Cloth. National Academies Press.
Washington, DC. 1996. 296p. ISBN:0-309-05282-3, ISBN13:
978-0-309-05282-5. Dewey:660.6. LCCN:95-044203.
                                Audience: **g,l,u.** *Choice, 1997.*

Ruse, Michael & Castle,   TP248.65.F66G458
  David (Editors)
Genetically Modified Foods: Debating Biotechnology. Trade
Paper. Prometheus Books, Publishers. Amherst, NY. 2004. 350p.
Contemporary Issues Ser. ISBN:1-57392-996-4, ISBN13:
978-1-57392-996-7. Dewey:363.19/29. LCCN:2002-070510.
                                        Audience: **g,l,u,f.**

Sapienza, Alice M. & Stork,   HD9999.B442S27 2001
  Diana
Leading Biotechnology Alliances: Right from the Start. Trade
Cloth. John Wiley & Sons, Inc. Hoboken, NJ. 2001. 216p.
ISBN:0-471-18248-6, ISBN13: 978-0-471-18248-1.
Dewey:660.6/068/1. LCCN:2001-017900.
                                        Audience: **u,f.**

Schacter, Bernice   TP248
Issues and Dilemmas of Biotechnology: A Reference Guide.
Cloth Text. Greenwood Publishing Group, Inc. Portsmouth, NH.
1999. 224p. ISBN:0-313-30642-7, ISBN13: 978-0-313-30642-6.
Dewey:660.6. LCCN:99-015457.
                                Audience: **l,u.** *Choice, 2000.*

Seethala, Ramakrishna &   RM301.25.H36 2001
  Fernandes, P. B. (Editors)
Handbook of Drug Screening, Vol. 114. Paper over Boards.
Marcel Dekker Inc. New York, NY. 2001. 648p. Drugs and the
Pharmaceutical Sciences Ser., Vol. 114 ISBN:0-8247-0562-9,
ISBN13: 978-0-8247-0562-6. Dewey:615/.19.
LCCN:2001-032412.
                                        Audience: **u,f.**

Simon, Francoise & Kotler,   HD9999.B442S56 2003
  Philip
Building Global Biobrands: Taking Biotechnology to Market.
Kevin Sharer (Foreword by). Trade Cloth. Simon & Schuster.
New York, NY. 2003. 352p. ISBN:0-7432-2244-X, ISBN13:
978-0-7432-2244-0. Dewey:660.6/068/8. LCCN:2003-040810.
                                        Audience: **u,f.**

Singh, Shailendra   QH442
Gene Biotechnology. Trade Cloth. Laurier Books, Ltd. Ottawa,
ON. 2005. 225p. ISBN:81-8030-078-1, ISBN13:
978-81-8030-078-3. Dewey:572.8.
                                        Audience: **l,u.**

Sklar, Larry A. (Editor)   TP248.25.F57F57 2004
Flow Cytometry in Biotechnology. Trade Paper. Oxford
University Press, Inc. New York, NY. 2005. 400p.
ISBN:0-19-515234-4, ISBN13: 978-0-19-515234-0.
Dewey:660.6. LCCN:2004-000655.
                                        Audience: **u,f.**

Slater, Adrian, et al.   TP248.27.P55
Plant Biotechnology: The Genetic Manipulation of Plants. Nigel
W. Scott & Mark R. Fowler (Authors). Paper Text. Oxford
University Press, Inc. New York, NY. 2003. 368p.
ISBN:0-19-925468-0, ISBN13: 978-0-19-925468-2.
Dewey:631.5/23. LCCN:2003-273349.
                                Audience: **u,f.** *Choice, 2003.*

Smith, George Patrick   **TP248.2**
The New Biology: Law, Ethics, and Biotechnology. Plenum Press, New York. 1989. ISBN:0-89885-448-2, ISBN13: 978-0-89885-448-0.

Audience: **g,l,u,f.**

Smith, John E.   **TP248.2.S66 2004**
Biotechnology. Ed. 4. Cloth Text. Cambridge University Press. New York, NY. 2004. 284p. Studies in Biology Ser. ISBN:0-521-83332-9, ISBN13: 978-0-521-83332-5. Dewey:660.6. LCCN:2003-065269.

Audience: **u,f.**

Steinberg, Mark L. &   **TP248.16.S84 2006**
  Cosloy, Sharon D.
The Facts on File Dictionary of Biotechnology and Genetic Engineering. Trade Cloth. Facts On File, Inc.. New York, NY. 2006. 288p. ISBN:0-8160-6351-6, ISBN13: 978-0-8160-6351-2. Dewey:660.603. LCCN:2005-056751.

Audience: **g,l,u.** *Choice, 2001, 1994.*

Thacker, Eugene   **QH506.T47 2004**
Biomedia. Trade Cloth. University of Minnesota Press. Minneapolis, MN. 2004. 392p. Electronic Mediations Ser., Vol. 11 ISBN:0-8166-4352-0, ISBN13: 978-0-8166-4352-3. Dewey:303.48/3. LCCN:2003-017201.

Audience: **u,f.**

Thacker, Eugene   **HD9999.B442T453 2005**
The Global Genome: Biotechnology, Politics, and Culture. Trade Cloth. MIT Press. Cambridge, MA. 2005. 464p. Leonardo Bks. ISBN:0-262-20155-0, ISBN13: 978-0-262-20155-1. Dewey:338.4/76606. LCCN:2004-061148.

Audience: **u,f.** *Choice, 2005.*

Thackray, Arnold W.   **TP248.18.P75 1998**
  (Editor)
Private Science: Biotechnology and the Rise of the Molecular Sciences. Book, Other. University of Pennsylvania Press. Philadelphia, PA. 1998. 304p. Chemical Sciences in Society Ser. ISBN:0-8122-3428-6, ISBN13: 978-0-8122-3428-2. Dewey:306.4/6. LCCN:97-031823.

Audience: **l,u.** *Choice, 1998.*

Thiel, Teresa, et al.   **QH506.T48 2002**
Biotechnology: DNA to Protein--A Laboratory Project in Molecular Biology. Shirley T. Bissen & Eilene M. Lyons (Authors). Spiral. McGraw-Hill Higher Education. Burr Ridge, IL. 2001. 192p. ISBN:0-07-241664-5, ISBN13: 978-0-07-241664-0. Dewey:572.8. LCCN:2001-030676.

Audience: **u,f.**

Vo-Dinh   **QP551.P697225 2005**
Protein Nanotechnology: Protocols, Instrumentation, and Applications. Saddle Stitched, Cloth over Boards. Humana Press. Totowa, NJ. 2005. 463p. Methods in Molecular Biology Ser. ISBN:1-58829-310-6, ISBN13: 978-1-58829-310-7. Dewey:572/.6. LCCN:2004-010385.

Audience: **u,f.**

Waksman, Gabriel (Editor)   **QP551.5.P765 2005**
Proteomics and Protein-Protein Interactions: Biology, Chemistry, Bionformatics, and Drug Design. Trade Cloth. Springer. New York, NY. 2005. 27 schw.-w. u. 43 farb. Abb., 8 schw.-w. Tab., 1 schw.-w. u. 30 farb. Fotos, 26 schw.-w. u. 13 farb. Zeichn. VIII, 324p. Protein Reviews Ser. ISBN:0-387-24531-6, ISBN13: 978-0-387-24531-7. Dewey:612/.01575. LCCN:2005-040224.

Audience: **u,f.**

Whitaker, Allan   **TP248.16.W35 1995**
The Language of Biotechnology: A Dictionary of Terms. Ed. 2. Michael Cox & John M. Walker (Editors), Stephen Hall (Contribution by). Paper Text. Oxford University Press, Inc. New York, NY. 1995. 300p. Professional Reference Book ISBN:0-8412-2982-1, ISBN13: 978-0-8412-2982-2. Dewey:660/.6/03. LCCN:94-023812.

Audience: **g,l,u,f.** *Choice, 1996.*

Wickelgren, Ingrid   **QH431.W483 2002**
The Gene Masters: How a New Breed of Scientific Entrepeneurs Raced for the Biggest Prize in Biology. Trade Cloth. Henry Holt & Company. New York, NY. 2002. 288p. ISBN:0-8050-7174-1, ISBN13: 978-0-8050-7174-0. Dewey:611/.01816. LCCN:2002-067321.

Audience: **u,f.**

Wolff, George   **HD9999.B442W65 2001**
The Biotech Investor's Bible. Trade Cloth. John Wiley & Sons, Inc. Hoboken, NJ. 2001. 336p. ISBN:0-471-41279-1, ISBN13: 978-0-471-41279-3. Dewey:338.4/36606. LCCN:2001-024898.

Audience: **u,f.**

Yount, Lisa   **TP248.23.Y684 2004**
Biotechnology and Genetic Engineering. Ed. 2. Trade Cloth. Facts On File, Inc.. New York, NY. 2004. 320p. Library in a Book ISBN:0-8160-5059-7, ISBN13: 978-0-8160-5059-8. Dewey:303.48/3. LCCN:2003-064223.

Audience: **u,f.** *Choice, 2001.*

Zimmer, Marc   **QP552.G73Z56 2005**
Glowing Genes: A Revolution in Biotechnology. Trade Cloth. Prometheus Books, Publishers. Amherst, NY. 2005. 250p. ISBN:1-59102-253-3, ISBN13: 978-1-59102-253-4. Dewey:572/.4358. LCCN:2004-022817.

Audience: **g,l,u,f.** *Choice, 2005.*

Natural History

                    QH61
Guidelines for Institutional Policies and Planning in Natural History Collections. Trade Cloth. Natural Science Collections Alliance. Washington, DC. 1994. ISBN:0-942924-17-7, ISBN13: 978-0-942924-17-6. Dewey:508.074.

Audience: **u,f.**

Bass, Rick   **QH81**
Wild to the Heart. Trade Paper. W. W. Norton & Company, Inc. New York, NY. 1997. 176p. ISBN:0-393-31487-1, ISBN13: 978-0-393-31487-8. Dewey:508.

Audience: **l,u,f.**

Beazley, John D.   **QH81**
The Way Nature Works. Trade Cloth. Macmillan Publishing Company, Inc. Old Tappan, NJ. 1992. 360p. ISBN:0-02-508110-1, ISBN13: 978-0-02-508110-9. Dewey:508.

Audience: **g,l.**

Buffon, Georges-Louis   **QH81**
  Leclerc
Natural History, General and Particular. Ed. 3. William Smellie (Translator). Trade Cloth. Continuum International Publishing Group, Ltd. London, 2001. 3100p. ISBN:1-85506-842-7, ISBN13: 978-1-85506-842-1. Dewey:508.

Audience: **g,l,u,f.**

Carter, David A. & Walker, Annette K. QH61
Care and Conservation of Natural History Collections. Trade
Cloth. Elsevier Science & Technology Books. Saint Louis, MO.
1998. 288p. ISBN:0-7506-0961-3, ISBN13: 978-0-7506-0961-6.
Dewey:508/.075.

Audience: **u,f.**

Coates, Peter GF13
Nature: Western Attitudes since Ancient Times. Trade Paper.
University of California Press. Berkeley, CA. 2004. 254p.
ISBN:0-520-24478-8, ISBN13: 978-0-520-24478-8.
Dewey:304.2/09.

Audience: **u,f.** *Choice, 1999.*

Cooper, Susan Fenimore QH81.C793 1998
Rural Hours. Rochelle Johnson & Daniel Patterson (Editors).
Trade Paper. University of Georgia Press. Athens, GA. 1998.
376p. ISBN:0-8203-2000-5, ISBN13: 978-0-8203-2000-7.
Dewey:508. LCCN:98-002689.

Audience: **g,l.**

Costain, Meredith SB419
Our Plant Home. Library Binding. Sagebrush Education
Resources. Caledonia, MN. 2000. ISBN:0-613-30655-4,
ISBN13: 978-0-613-30655-3. Dewey:635.965.

Audience: **g,l,u,f.**

Curtis, Will QH81.C876 1992
The Second Nature of Things. Nora S. Unwin (Illustrator).
Trade Cloth. HarperCollins Publishers. New York, NY. 1992.
xii, 290p. ISBN:0-88001-285-4, ISBN13: 978-0-88001-285-0.
Dewey:508. LCCN:92-016806.

Audience: **g,l,u,f.**

Dalton, Stephen (Author, Photographer) TR647
Secret Worlds. Trade Paper. Firefly Books, Ltd. Tonawanda, NY.
2003. 160p. ISBN:1-55297-806-0, ISBN13: 978-1-55297-806-1.
Dewey:779.3092. LCCN:2003-277594.

Audience: **g,l,u,f.**

Dunlap, Thomas QH15 .D85 1999
Nature and the English Diaspora: Environment and History in
the United States, Canada, Australia, and New Zealand. Alfred
W. Crosby & Donald Worster (Contribution by). Cloth Text.
Cambridge University Press. New York, NY. 1999. 365p.
Studies in Environment and History, No. 17
ISBN:0-521-65173-5, ISBN13: 978-0-521-65173-8.
Dewey:508/.09. LCCN:98-043736.

Audience: **u,f.** *Choice, 2000.*

Eiseley, Loren C. QH81.E6 1997
The Night Country. Leonard Everett Fisher (Illustrator), Gale E.
Christianson (Introduction by). Trade Paper. University of
Nebraska Press. Lincoln, NE. 1997. 241p. ISBN:0-8032-6735-5,
ISBN13: 978-0-8032-6735-0. Dewey:500.9. LCCN:97-001507.

Audience: **g,l,u,f.**

Elliott, Doug QH81.E65
Wildwoods Wisdom: Encounters with the Natural World. Cloth
Text. Granite Publishing, LLC. Columbus, NC. 1992. 204p.
ISBN:1-893183-36-X, ISBN13: 978-1-893183-36-0. Dewey:508.
LCCN:91-035712.

Audience: **g,l,u,f.**

Emanoil, Mary (Editor) in association with IUCN-The World Conservation Union QH75
Encyclopedia of Endangered Species. Gale Research, Detroit.
1994. Gale environmental library ISBN:0-8103-8857-X,
ISBN13: 978-0-8103-8857-4.

Audience: **l,u,f.**

French, Roger QH15.F74 1994
Ancient Natural History: Histories of Nature. Paper over Boards.
Routledge. New York, NY. 1994. 384p. Sciences of Antiquity
Ser. ISBN:0-415-08880-1, ISBN13: 978-0-415-08880-0.
Dewey:508/.09/01. LCCN:94-005131.

Audience: **u,f.**

Gessner, David QH81
Sick of Nature. Trade Paper, Perfect. University Press of New
England. Lebanon, NH. 2005. 234p. ISBN:1-58465-464-3,
ISBN13: 978-1-58465-464-3. Dewey:508.

Audience: **l,u,f.**

Goodenough, Ursula QH331
The Sacred Depths of Nature. Trade Paper. Oxford University
Press, Inc. New York, NY. 2000. 220p. ISBN:0-19-513629-2,
ISBN13: 978-0-19-513629-6. Dewey:574/.01. LCCN:98-006579.

Audience: **l,u,f.** *Choice, 1999.*

Gould, Stephen Jay QH366.2.G659 1995
Dinosaur in a Haystack: Reflections in Natural History. Trade
Cloth. Crown Publishing Group. New York, NY. 1995. 496p.
ISBN:0-517-70393-9, ISBN13: 978-0-517-70393-9. Dewey:508.
LCCN:95-051333.

Audience: **l,u,f.**

Gould, Stephen Jay QH375
Ever since Darwin: Reflections in Natural History. Trade Paper.
W. W. Norton & Company, Inc. New York, NY. 1992. 288p.
ISBN:0-393-30818-9, ISBN13: 978-0-393-30818-1.
Dewey:576.8/2. LCCN:77-022504.

Audience: **l,u,f.**

Gould, Stephen Jay QH366.2
The Panda's Thumb: More Reflections in Natural History. Trade
Paper. W. W. Norton & Company, Inc. New York, NY. 1992.
344p. ISBN:0-393-30819-7, ISBN13: 978-0-393-30819-8.
Dewey:575.01.

Audience: **l,u,f.**

Grinstein, Louise S. (Editor), et al. QH26
Women in the Biological Sciences: A Biobibliographic
Sourcebook. Carol A. Biermann & Rose K. Rose (Editors).
Cloth Text. Greenwood Publishing Group, Inc. Portsmouth, NH.
1997. 640p. ISBN:0-313-29180-2, ISBN13: 978-0-313-29180-7.
Dewey:574/.082 B. LCCN:96-043783.

Audience: **l,u,f.** *Choice, 1998.*

Grove, Noel QH76.K73 1992
Preserving Eden: The Nature Conservancy. Stephen J.
Krasemann (Photographer). Trade Cloth. Harry N. Abrams, Inc.
New York, NY. 1992. 192p. ISBN:0-8109-3663-1, ISBN13:
978-0-8109-3663-8. Dewey:333.95/16/06073. LCCN:91-024551.

Audience: **g,l,u,f.**

Hay, John QH81.H368 1998
In the Company of Light. Trade Cloth. Beacon Press. Boston,
MA. 1998. 144p. Concord Library ISBN:0-8070-8538-3,

Audience: g=general, l=lower division undergraduate, u=upper division undergraduate, f=faculty.

221

ISBN13: 978-0-8070-8538-7. Dewey:508.741.
LCCN:97-014415.

Audience: **l,u,f.**

Heinemann, Bruce W. **QH46**
Art of Nature: Reflections on the Grand Design. Trade Cloth.
Prior Publishing Company. Anacortes, WA. 1993. 154p.
ISBN:0-930861-05-1, ISBN13: 978-0-930861-05-6.
Dewey:778.93.

Audience: **l,u,f.**

Hopes, David B. **QH81.H73 1990**
A Sense of the Morning. Trade Paper. Simon & Schuster. New
York, NY. 1990. ISBN:0-671-68241-5, ISBN13:
978-0-671-68241-5. Dewey:508. LCCN:89-037629.

Audience: **g,l,u,f.**

Jardine, N. (Editor), et al. **QH15 .C85 1996**
Cultures of Natural History. J. A. Secord & E. C. Spary
(Editors). Trade Paper. Cambridge University Press. New York,
NY. 1996. 523p. ISBN:0-521-55894-8, ISBN13:
978-0-521-55894-5. Dewey:508/.09. LCCN:94-039445.

Audience: **u,f.**

Jedicke, Peter & Scientific **QH349.C43 2001**
American Editors
Extreme Science: Chasing the Ghost Bat: Extreme Science and
Other Mysteries of Nature. Trade Paper. St. Martin's Press.
Gordonville, VA. 2001. 257p. Extreme Science Ser.
ISBN:0-312-26818-1, ISBN13: 978-0-312-26818-3. Dewey:570.
LCCN:2001-042406.

Audience: **g,l,u.**

Kahn, Jetty **QH26.K34 1999**
Women in Life Science Careers. Library Binding. Capstone
Press, Inc. Mankato, MN. 1998. 48p. Short Biographies Ser.
ISBN:0-7368-0014-X, ISBN13: 978-0-7368-0014-3. Dewey:[B].
LCCN:98-004251.

Audience: **l,u,f.**

Katz, Cathie **QH82.K38 2000**
Nature a Day at a Time: An Uncommon Look at Common
Wildlife. Trade Cloth. Sierra Club Books. San Francisco, CA.
2000. 392p. ISBN:1-57805-050-2, ISBN13: 978-1-57805-050-5.
Dewey:508. LCCN:99-086436.

Audience: **g,l,u,f.**

Keynes, Randal **QH31.D2**
Annie's box: Charles Darwin, his daughter, and human
evolution. London :; Fourth Estate. 2001. ISBN:1-84115-060-6,
ISBN13: 978-1-84115-060-4.

Audience: **u,f.**

Kinch, John A. **QH104.K54 2000**
A Journey for All Seasons: A Nature Conservancy Book. Cloth
over Boards. Globe Pequot Press, The. Guilford, CT. 2000.
180p. Nature Conservancy Bks. ISBN:1-55821-943-9, ISBN13:
978-1-55821-943-4. Dewey:508.73. LCCN:99-040930.

Audience: **g,l,u,f.**

Klein, William J. **QH53 .K57 1988**
Learning under the Sun. Trade Paper. Blackwell Publishing
Professional. Ames, IA. 1988. 392p. ISBN:0-8138-1038-8,
ISBN13: 978-0-8138-1038-6. Dewey:574/.076.

Audience: **l,u,f.**

Knopp, Lisa **BF241.K62 1996**
Field of Vision. Trade Paper. University of Iowa Press. Iowa
City, IA. 1996. 156p. ISBN:0-87745-551-1, ISBN13:
978-0-87745-551-6. Dewey:814/.54. LCCN:95-052045.

Audience: **g,l,u,f.** *Choice, 1996.*

Krogh, David **QH308.2**
Biology: A Guide to the Natural World. Trade Paper. Prentice
Hall PTR. Upper Saddle River, NJ. 2002. 370p.
ISBN:0-13-092242-0, ISBN13: 978-0-13-092242-7. Dewey:570.

Audience: **l,u,f.**

Lauder, Everlyn H. **QH46.L38 1994**
Seasons Observed. Trade Cloth. Harry N. Abrams, Inc. New
York, NY. 1994. 96p. ISBN:0-8109-4455-3, ISBN13:
978-0-8109-4455-8. Dewey:508/.022/2. LCCN:94-008418.

Audience: **l,u,f.**

Lembke, Janet **QH81.L54 1990**
Looking for Eagles: Reflections of a Classical Naturalist. Trade
Cloth. Globe Pequot Press, The. Guilford, CT. 1990. 192p.
ISBN:1-55821-077-6, ISBN13: 978-1-55821-077-6. Dewey:508.
LCCN:90-041041.

Audience: **l,u,f.**

Lembke, Janet **QH81.L545 1994**
Skinny Dipping: And Other Immersions in Water, Myth and
Being Human. Cloth over Boards. Globe Pequot Press, The.
Guilford, CT. 1994. 196p. ISBN:1-55821-274-4, ISBN13:
978-1-55821-274-9. Dewey:508. LCCN:94-015378.

Audience: **l,u,f.**

Levin, Ted **QH81.L65 1992**
Blood Brook. Trade Cloth. Chelsea Green Publishing. White
River Junction, VT. 1992. 208p. ISBN:0-930031-56-3, ISBN13:
978-0-930031-56-5. Dewey:508.743/6.

Audience: **l,u,f.**

Lewens, Tim **QH331.L533 2004**
Organisms and Artifacts: Design in Nature and Elsewhere. Trade
Cloth. MIT Press. Cambridge, MA. 2004. 240p. Life and Mind
Ser. ISBN:0-262-12261-8, ISBN13: 978-0-262-12261-0.
Dewey:570/.1. LCCN:2003-061768.

Audience: **u,f.**

Longoria, Arturo **QH107.L675 2000**
Keepers of the Wilderness. Trade Cloth. Texas A & M
University Press. College Station, TX. 2004. 128p.
Environmental History Ser., Vol. 15 ISBN:0-89096-929-9,
ISBN13: 978-0-89096-929-8. Dewey:508.72/12.
LCCN:99-053326.

Audience: **l,u,f.**

Macmillan Publishing **QH13 .W38**
Company Staff
The Way Nature Works. Trade Cloth. John Wiley & Sons, Inc.
Hoboken, NJ. 1997. 359p. ISBN:0-02-862281-2, ISBN13:
978-0-02-862281-1. Dewey:508. LCCN:92-012283.

Audience: **l,u,f.**

Marchand, Peter J. **QH81.M2653 2000**
Autumn: A Season of Change. Trade Paper. University Press of
New England. Lebanon, NH. 2000. 214p. ISBN:0-87451-870-9,
ISBN13: 978-0-87451-870-2. Dewey:508.2. LCCN:99-054701.

Audience: **l,u,f.**

Mitchell, Andrew W.   **QH48**
The Young Naturalist. Trade Paper. EDC Publishing. Tulsa, OK. 1989. 32p. Hobby Guides Ser. ISBN:0-86020-653-X, ISBN13: 978-0-86020-653-8. Dewey:508.
Audience: **l,u,f.**

Montgomery, Sy   **QH104.M66 2000**
The Curious Naturalist: Nature's Everyday Mysteries. Trade Paper. Down East Books. Camden, ME. 2000. 221p. ISBN:0-89272-510-9, ISBN13: 978-0-89272-510-6. Dewey:508.73. LCCN:00-043113.
Audience: **g,l,u,f.** *Choice, 2001.*

Organisation for Economic   **QH75**
  Co-operation and Development
Handbook of Market Creation for Biodiversity: Issues in Implementation. OECD, Paris. 2004. ISBN:92-64-01861-1, ISBN13: 978-92-64-01861-7.
Audience: **u,f.**

Organisation for Economic   **QH75**
  Co-operation and Development.; Working Group on Economic Aspects of Biodiversity
Handbook of Incentive Measures for Niodiversity: Design and Implementation. Organisation for Economic Co-operation and Development,, Paris, France. 1999. ISBN:92-64-17059-6, ISBN13: 978-92-64-17059-9.
Audience: **u,f.**

Pitt, David C.   **QH75**
The Future of the Environment: The Social Dimensions of Conservation and Ecological Alternatives. Routledge, London ; New York. 1988. ISBN:0-415-00455-1, ISBN13: 978-0-415-00455-8.
Audience: **u,f.**

Pliny the Elder   **QH41.P721713 2004**
Natural History: A Selection. John F. Healey (Translator, Introduction by, Notes by). Trade Paper. Penguin Group (USA) Inc. New York, NY. 1991. 448p. Classics Ser. ISBN:0-14-044413-0, ISBN13: 978-0-14-044413-1. Dewey:508. LCCN:91-220670.
Audience: **u,f.**

Quammen, David   **QH81.Q17 2000**
The Boilerplate Rhino: Nature in the Eye of the Beholder. Trade Cloth. Simon & Schuster. New York, NY. 2000. 288p. ISBN:0-684-83728-5, ISBN13: 978-0-684-83728-4. Dewey:508. LCCN:99-056894.
Audience: **g,l.**

Quammen, David   **QH81**
Wild Thoughts from Wild Places. Trade Paper. Simon & Schuster. New York, NY. 1999. 304p. ISBN:0-684-85208-X, ISBN13: 978-0-684-85208-9. Dewey:508. LCCN:97-029090.
Audience: **g,l.**

Rice, Anthony   **QH15.R44 1999**
Voyages of Discovery: Three Centuries of Natural History Exploration. Trade Cloth. Crown Publishing Group. New York, NY. 1999. 336p. ISBN:0-609-60536-4, ISBN13: 978-0-609-60536-3. Dewey:508/.09. LCCN:99-032989.
Audience: **l,u,f.**

Roth, Dennis M.   **QH76**
The Wilderness Movement and the National Forests. Ed. 2. Trade Paper. Intaglio Press. College Station, TX. 1995. 105p.

ISBN:0-944091-05-9, ISBN13: 978-0-944091-05-0. Dewey:333.78/2/0973.
Audience: **g,l,u,f.**

Roucoux, Katherine   **TR692**
Heaven and Earth: Unseen by the Naked Eye. David Malin (Introduction by). Trade Cloth. Phaidon Press. London, 2002. 384p. ISBN:0-7148-4280-X, ISBN13: 978-0-7148-4280-6. Dewey:502.2/2. LCCN:2003-283290.
Audience: **u,f.**

Shorrocks, Brian &   **QH352.L58 1990**
  Swingland, Ian R. (Editors)
Living in a Patchy Environment. Trade Cloth. Oxford University Press, Inc. New York, NY. 1990. 256p. ISBN:0-19-854591-6, ISBN13: 978-0-19-854591-0. Dewey:574.5/247. LCCN:89-026608.
Audience: **u,f.**

Starfield, A. M. ; Bleloch, A.   **QH75**
  L. (Andrew L.)
Building Models for Conservation and Wildlife Management. Ed. 2. Burgess International Group, Edina, MN. 1991. ISBN:0-8087-7790-4, ISBN13: 978-0-8087-7790-8.
Audience: **u,f.**

TERC Staff   **QH54.G66**
Global Lab - An Integrated Science Program: Investigating Our Earth: Water, Unit III. Perfect. Kendall/Hunt Publishing Company. Dubuque, IA. 2000. 280p. ISBN:0-7872-6339-7, ISBN13: 978-0-7872-6339-3. Dewey:500.
Audience: **u,f.**

TERC Staff   **QH54.G66**
Global Lab - An Integrated Science Program: Becoming a Global Community, Unit I. Paper Text. Kendall/Hunt Publishing Company. Dubuque, IA. 2000. 92p. ISBN:0-7872-6342-7, ISBN13: 978-0-7872-6342-3. Dewey:500.
Audience: **u,f.**

Trigo Boix, Nuri   **QH107.E374 2003**
Ecology and Man in Mexico's Central Volcanoes Area. G. W. Heil & Roland Bobbink (Editors). Mixed Media. Springer. New York, NY. 2003. IX, 222p. Geobotany Ser., Vol. 29 ISBN:1-4020-1708-1, ISBN13: 978-1-4020-1708-7. Dewey:333.76/0972. LCCN:2003-062042.
Audience: **u,f.**

Tudge, Colin   **QH83.T84 2000**
The Variety of Life: A Survey and a Celebration of All the Creatures that Have Ever Lived. Trade Cloth. Oxford University Press, Inc. New York, NY. 2000. 684p. ISBN:0-19-850311-3, ISBN13: 978-0-19-850311-8. Dewey:578/.01/2. LCCN:99-050043.
Audience: **g,l.** *Choice, 2000.*

Turner, Jack   **QH81.T87 1996**
The Abstract Wild. Trade Cloth. University of Arizona Press. Tucson, AZ. 1996. 136p. ISBN:0-8165-1394-5, ISBN13: 978-0-8165-1394-9. Dewey:508. LCCN:96-010099.
Audience: **g,l,u,f.**

Ward, Alan   **QH308.2**
Experimenting with Nature Study. Zena Flax (Illustrator). Library Binding. Chelsea House Publishers. Langhorne, PA. 1991. 48p. Experimenting With Ser. ISBN:0-7910-1515-7, ISBN13: 978-0-7910-1515-5. Dewey:574.
Audience: **l,u,f.**

Waterman, Laura & **QH76.W38 1993**
Waterman, Guy
Wilderness Ethics: Preserving the Spirit of Wildness. Ed. 2.
Roderick Nash (Foreword by). Trade Paper. Countryman Press.
Woodstock, VT. 1993. 240p. ISBN:0-88150-256-1, ISBN13:
978-0-88150-256-5. Dewey:333.78/2. LCCN:93-018436.
Audience: **g,l,u,f.**

Wiley, John P. Jr. **QH81.W556 1993**
Natural High. Trade Paper. University Press of New England.
Lebanon, NH. 1993. 128p. ISBN:0-87451-624-2, ISBN13:
978-0-87451-624-1. Dewey:508. LCCN:92-056912.
Audience: **g,l.**

Wolgemuth, Ken **QH81.W63 1991**
The Old Marlborough Road: "A Journey into Wonder". Trade
Paper. Steerforth Press. Hanover, NH. 1991. 160p.
ISBN:0-944072-16-X, ISBN13: 978-0-944072-16-5.
Dewey:508.748/45. LCCN:91-065384.
Audience: **g,l.**

Natural History > Reference

QH84
☐ Wildfinder - Mapping the World's Species.
http://www.worldwildlife.org/wildfinder
Audience: **g,l,u,f.**

Bridson, Gavin **Z7405.H6B75 1994**
The History of Natural History: An Annotated Bibliography.
Cloth Text. Garland Publishing, Inc. New York, NY. 1994. 776p.
Bibliographies on the History of Science and Technology Ser.,
Vol. 24 ISBN:0-8240-2319-6, ISBN13: 978-0-8240-2319-5.
Dewey:508/.09. LCCN:94-002658.
Audience: **g.**

Bright, Michael **QH46.B745 2005**
1001 Natural Wonders: Places You Must See Before You Die.
Trade Cloth. Barron's Educational Series, Inc. Hauppauge, NY.
2005. 960p. ISBN:0-7641-5817-1, ISBN13: 978-0-7641-5817-9.
Dewey:508. LCCN:2004-106565.
Audience: **g.**

Dillard, Annie **QH81**
Pilgrim at Tinker Creek. Library Binding. Sagebrush Education
Resources. Caledonia, MN. 1998. ISBN:0-613-37649-8,
ISBN13: 978-0-613-37649-5. Dewey:508.755/792.
Audience: **l,u,f.**

Leopold, Aldo **QH104**
A Sand County Almanac: And Sketches Here and There. Charles
W. Schwartz (Illustrator), Robert Finch (Introduction by). Trade
Paper. Oxford University Press, Inc. New York, NY. 1989. 256p.
ISBN:0-19-505928-X, ISBN13: 978-0-19-505928-1.
Dewey:508.73.
Audience: **l,u,f.**

Müsch, Irmgard, et al. **QH81**
Albertus Seba: Cabinet of Natural Curiosities. Rainer Willmann
& Jes Rust (Authors), Den Haag Konlinklijke Bibliotheek Staff
(Illustrator). Trade Cloth. Taschen America, LLC. Los Angeles,
CA. 2001. 636p. ISBN:3-8228-1600-0, ISBN13:
978-3-8228-1600-4. Dewey:508.
Audience: **u,f.**

Olson, Sigurd F. **QH102.O386 2001**
The Meaning of Wilderness: Essential Articles and Speeches.
David Backes (Editor, Introduction by). Trade Cloth. University
of Minnesota Press. Minneapolis, MN. 2001. 232p.
ISBN:0-8166-3708-3, ISBN13: 978-0-8166-3708-9.
Dewey:508.7. LCCN:00-011869.
Audience: **g,l,u,f.**

Roberts, Jerry **Z7408.L29R63 1999**
Rain Forest Bibliography: An Annotated Guide to over 1600
Nonfiction Books about Central and South American Jungles.
Cloth Text. McFarland & Company, Incorporated Publishers.
Jefferson, NC. 1999. 320p. ISBN:0-7864-0717-4, ISBN13:
978-0-7864-0717-0. Dewey:016.33375/098. LCCN:99-26061.
Audience: **g,l,u,f.** *Choice, 2000.*

Roederer, Juan G. **QH507.R62 2005**
Information and Its Role in Nature. Trade Cloth. Springer. New
York, NY. 2005. XII, 235p. The Frontiers Collection
ISBN:3-540-23075-0, ISBN13: 978-3-540-23075-5.
Dewey:570.285. LCCN:2005-924951.
Audience: **l,u,f.**

Shearer, Benjamin F. & **QH26**
Shearer, Barbara S. (Editors)
Notable Women in the Life Sciences: A Biographical Dictionary.
Cloth Text. Greenwood Publishing Group, Inc. Portsmouth, NH.
1996. 456p. ISBN:0-313-29302-3, ISBN13: 978-0-313-29302-3.
Dewey:574/.092/2. LCCN:95-025603.
Audience: **l,u,f.** *Choice, 1996.*

World Conservation **QH75**
Monitoring Centre
Checklist of CITES Species: A Reference to the Appendices to
the Convention on International Trade in Endangered Species of
Wild Fauna and Flora. CITES Secretariat, Genève ; Great
Britain. 2001. ISBN:1-899628-17-7, ISBN13:
978-1-899628-17-9.
Audience: **u,f.**

Natural History > Reference > Encyclopedias, Dictionaries, Handbooks

QH12
The Mitchell Beazley Family Encyclopedia of Nature. Mitchell
Beazley. 1992. ISBN:1-85732-925-2, ISBN13:
978-1-85732-925-4.
Audience: **g,l,u,f.**

Abercrombie, Michael, et al. **QH302.5**
The New Penguin Dictionary of Biology. Ed. 8. Michael
Hickman, M. L. Johnson & Michael Thain (Authors). Trade
Paper. Penguin Group (USA) Inc. New York, NY. 1991. 624p.
Dictionary Ser. ISBN:0-14-051177-6, ISBN13:
978-0-14-051177-2. Dewey:574.03.
Audience: **g.**

Beacham, Walton (Editor) **QH75**
World Wildlife Fund Guide to Extinct Species of Modern Times.
Beacham Pub., Osprey, FL. 1997. ISBN:0-933833-40-7,
ISBN13: 978-0-933833-40-1.
Audience: **l,u,f.**

Bell, Catharine (Editor) **QL76.E53 2001**
Encyclopedia of the World's Zoos, Set. Lester Fisher
(Contribution by). Trade Cloth. Fitzroy Dearborn Publishers,

Inc. Chicago, IL. 2001. 1600p. ISBN:1-57958-174-9, ISBN13: 978-1-57958-174-9. Dewey:590/.7/303. LCCN:2002-265421.
Audience: **g,l,u,f.** *Choice, 2001.*

Borror, Donald J.   **QH13.B68**
Dictionary of Word Roots and Combining Forms. Paper Text. McGraw-Hill Higher Education. Burr Ridge, IL. 1960. 134p. ISBN:0-87484-053-8, ISBN13: 978-0-87484-053-7. Dewey:574.03. LCCN:60-015564.
Audience: **g.**

Bramwell, Martyn   **QH81**
Warwick Illustrated Encyclopedia of Nature. Trade Paper. Scholastic Library Publishing. Danbury, CT. 1989. ISBN:0-531-19051-X, ISBN13: 978-0-531-19051-7. Dewey:574. LCCN:88-051103.
Audience: **l,u.**

Brooks, Felicity   **AG5**
First Encyclopedia of Our World. Library Binding. EDC Publishing. Tulsa, OK. 2000. 64p. Usborne First Encyclopedia Library ISBN:1-58086-265-9, ISBN13: 978-1-58086-265-3. Dewey:032.
Audience: **g.**

Colvin, Leslie   **QH302.5**
Living World Encyclopedia. Library Binding. Sagebrush Education Resources. Caledonia, MN. 1999. ISBN:0-613-74482-9, ISBN13: 978-0-613-74482-9. Dewey:570.3.
Audience: **l,u,f.**

Emanoil, Mary (Editor) in   **QH75**
  association with IUCN-The World Conservation Union
Encyclopedia of Endangered Species. Gale Research, Detroit. 1994. Gale environmental library ISBN:0-8103-8857-X, ISBN13: 978-0-8103-8857-4.
Audience: **l,u,f.**

Gaither, Carl C. &   **QH81**
  Cavazos-Gaither, Alma E.
Naturally Speaking: A Dictionary of Quotations on Biology, Botany, Nature and Zoology. Perfect. Institute of Physics Publishing. Philadelphia, PA. 2001. 596p. ISBN:0-7503-0681-5, ISBN13: 978-0-7503-0681-2. Dewey:508.
Audience: **l,u,f.**

Jukofsky, Diane   **QH86**
Encyclopedia of Rainforests: Diane Jukofsky for the Rainforest Alliance. Cloth Text. Greenwood Publishing Group, Inc. Portsmouth, NH. 2001. 384p. ISBN:1-57356-259-9, ISBN13: 978-1-57356-259-1. Dewey:578.734/03. LCCN:2001-032154.
Audience: **g,l,u.** *Choice, 2002.*

Lawrence, Eleanor   **QH302.5.H65 1995**
Henderson's Dictionary of Biological Terms. Ed. 11. Trade Cloth. John Wiley & Sons, Inc. Hoboken, NJ. 1995. 693p. ISBN:0-470-23507-1, ISBN13: 978-0-470-23507-2. Dewey:570.3. LCCN:95-030517.
Audience: **l,u,f.** *Choice, 1990.*

Lincoln, R. J. & Boxshall,   **QH48**
  G. A.
The Cambridge Illustrated Dictionary of Natural History. Roberta Smith (Illustrator). Trade Paper. Cambridge University Press. New York, NY. 1990. 417p. ISBN:0-521-39941-6, ISBN13: 978-0-521-39941-8. Dewey:508/.03.
Audience: **l,u,f.** *Choice, 1988.*

Murphy, Trevor   **QH41**
Pliny the Elder's Natural History: The Empire in the Encyclopedia. Trade Cloth. Oxford University Press, Inc. New York, NY. 2004. 320p. ISBN:0-19-926288-8, ISBN13: 978-0-19-926288-5. Dewey:937.06. LCCN:2004-300657.
Audience: **u,f.** *Choice, 2005.*

Oxford University Press   **QH13.N27 2001**
  Staff (Compiled by)
The Nature Encyclopedia: An A-Z Guide to Life on Earth. Trade Cloth. Oxford University Press, Inc. New York, NY. 2001. 480p. ISBN:0-19-521834-5, ISBN13: 978-0-19-521834-3. Dewey:508/.03. LCCN:2002-265654.
Audience: **g,l,u,f.** *Choice, 2002.*

Pouchet, F.-A.   **QH13**
  (Félix-Archimède)
The Universe: Encyclopaedia of Natural History. Bhavana Books & Prints, New Delhi. 2001. ISBN:81-86505-22-9, ISBN13: 978-81-86505-22-9.
Audience: **u,f.**

Thain, Michael & Hickman,   **QH302.5**
  Michael
The Penguin Dictionary of Biology. Ed. 11. Michael Abercrombie, C. J. J. Hickman & N. I. Johnson (Compiled by). Trade Paper. Penguin Group (USA) Inc. New York, NY. 2004. 720p. Dictionary, Penguin Ser. ISBN:0-14-101396-6, ISBN13: 978-0-14-101396-1. Dewey:570/.3. LCCN:2004-276653.
Audience: **l,u,f.**

Tootill, Elizabeth (Editor)   **QH13.F35 1988**
The Facts on File Dictionary of Biology. Ed. 2. Trade Cloth. Facts On File, Inc.. New York, NY. 1988. 336p. Science Dictionaries Ser. ISBN:0-8160-1865-0, ISBN13: 978-0-8160-1865-9. Dewey:574/.03/21. LCCN:88-045476.
Audience: **l,u,f.**

Zykov, C.   **QH13**
Elsevier's Dictionary of Nature and Hunting: In English, French, Russian, German and Latin. Trade Cloth. Elsevier Science & Technology Books. Saint Louis, MO. 2002. 518p. ISBN:0-444-50420-6, ISBN13: 978-0-444-50420-3. Dewey:508/.03. LCCN:2002-034665.
Audience: **u,f.**

Natural History > Reference > Anthologies

Allison, Linda (Author,   **QH48 .A44**
  Illustrator)
The Sierra Club Summer Book. Trade Paper. Little Brown & Company. New York, NY. 1989. 160p. ISBN:0-316-03433-9, ISBN13: 978-0-316-03433-3. Dewey:796.5.
Audience: **g,l,f.**

Beebe, William (Editor)   **QH81.B715 1988**
The Book of Naturalists: An Anthology of the Best Natural History. Trade Paper. Princeton University Press. Princeton, NJ. 1988. 520p. ISBN:0-691-02408-1, ISBN13: 978-0-691-02408-0. Dewey:508. LCCN:87-032727.
Audience: **l,u,f.**

Camazine, Scott   **QH46.C32 1991**
Velvet Mites and Silken Webs: The Wonderful Details of Nature in Photographs and Essays. Trade Cloth. John Wiley & Sons, Inc. Hoboken, NJ. 1991. 192p. Wiley Science Editions, Vol. 93 ISBN:0-471-61485-8, ISBN13: 978-0-471-61485-2. Dewey:508. LCCN:91-002395.

Audience: **g,l,u,f.**

Caras, Roger A. (Editor)   **QH81**
Roger Caras' Treasury of Classic Nature Tales. Trade Cloth. BBS Publishing Corporation. Edison, NJ. 1997. 528p. ISBN:1-57866-009-2, ISBN13: 978-1-57866-009-4. Dewey:508.

Audience: **l,u,f.**

Daniel, John   **QH81**
The Trail Home: Essays. Trade Paper. Knopf Publishing Group. New York, NY. 1994. 272p. ISBN:0-679-75438-5, ISBN13: 978-0-679-75438-1. Dewey:508.

Audience: **l,u,f.**

Dunne, Pete   **QH81.D837 1995**
Before the Echo: Essays on Nature. Diana Marlinski (Illustrator). Trade Cloth. University of Texas Press. Austin, TX. 1995. 156p. Corrie Herring Hooks Ser., Vol. 28 ISBN:0-292-71578-1, ISBN13: 978-0-292-71578-3. Dewey:508. LCCN:94-022910.

Audience: **l,u,f.**

Ereshefsky, Marc (Editor)   **QH380.U54 1992**
The Units of Evolution: Essays on the Nature of the Species. Trade Paper. MIT Press. Cambridge, MA. 1991. 424p. Bradford Bks. ISBN:0-262-55020-2, ISBN13: 978-0-262-55020-8. Dewey:574/.012. LCCN:91-004097.

Audience: **l,u,f.**

Finch, Robert   **QH81.N67 1990**
The Norton Book of Nature Writing. John C. Elder (Editor). Trade Cloth. W. W. Norton & Company, Inc. New York, NY. 1990. 921p. ISBN:0-393-02799-6, ISBN13: 978-0-393-02799-0. Dewey:508. LCCN:89-035531.

Audience: **l,u,f.**

Finch, Robert & Elder, John   **QH81.N67 2002**
E. (Editors)
Nature Writing: The Tradition in English. Ed. 2. Trade Cloth. W. W. Norton & Company, Inc. New York, NY. 2002. 1024p. ISBN:0-393-04966-3, ISBN13: 978-0-393-04966-4. Dewey:508. LCCN:2001-055825.

Audience: **l,u,f.**

Gould, Stephen Jay   **QH81.G67323 1998**
Leonardo's Mountain of Clams and the Diet of Worms: Essays on Natural History. Trade Cloth. Crown Publishing Group. New York, NY. 1998. 432p. ISBN:0-609-60141-5, ISBN13: 978-0-609-60141-9. Dewey:500. LCCN:98-011500.

Audience: **l,u,f.**

Hull, David L.   **QH360.5 .H86 2001**
Science and Selection: Essays on Biological Evolution and the Philosophy of Science. Michael Ruse (Contribution by). Cloth Text. Cambridge University Press. New York, NY. 2000. 288p. Cambridge Studies in Philosophy and Biology ISBN:0-521-64339-2, ISBN13: 978-0-521-64339-9. Dewey:576.8/01. LCCN:00-027938.

Audience: **u,f.** *Choice, 2001.*

Leopold, Aldo   **QH81.L557 1991**
The River of the Mother of God: And Other Essays by Aldo Leopold. Susan L. Flader & J. Baird Callicott (Editors). Trade Cloth. University of Wisconsin Press. Chicago, IL. 1991. 400p. ISBN:0-299-12760-5, ISBN13: 978-0-299-12760-2. Dewey:333.9516. LCCN:90-045491.

Audience: **l,u,f.** *Choice, 1991.*

Lomolino, Mark V. (Editor),   **QH84.F68 2004**
et al.
Foundations of Biogeography: Classic Papers with Commentaries. Dov F. Sax & James H. Brown (Editors). Trade Cloth. University of Chicago Press. Chicago, IL. 2004. 1328p. ISBN:0-226-49236-2, ISBN13: 978-0-226-49236-0. Dewey:578/.09. LCCN:2003-018272.

Audience: **u,f.**

McKibben, Bill (Editor)   **QH81 .B917 1992**
Birch Browsings: A John Burroughs Reader. Trade Paper. Penguin Group (USA) Inc. New York, NY. 1992. 240p. Nature Library ISBN:0-14-017016-2, ISBN13: 978-0-14-017016-0. Dewey:508. LCCN:92-009466.

Audience: **l,u,f.**

Moore, Kathleen Dean   **QH81.M853 1999**
Holdfast: At Home in the Natural World. Cloth over Boards. Globe Pequot Press, The. Guilford, CT. 1999. 184p. ISBN:1-55821-780-0, ISBN13: 978-1-55821-780-5. LCCN:98-030763.

Audience: **g,l,u,f.**

Ridley, Mark (Editor)   **QH366.2.E846 1997**
Evolution: An Oxford Reader. Trade Paper. Oxford University Press, Inc. New York, NY. 1998. 438p. Oxford Readers Ser. ISBN:0-19-289287-8, ISBN13: 978-0-19-289287-4. Dewey:576.8. LCCN:97-028965.

Audience: **l,u,f.**

Ruse, Michael   **QH371.R75 1989**
The Darwinian Paradigm: Essays on Its History, Philosophy and Religious Implications. Paper over Boards. Routledge. New York, NY. 1989. 310p. ISBN:0-415-00300-8, ISBN13: 978-0-415-00300-1. Dewey:575. LCCN:88-023985.

Audience: **u,f.**

Shepard, Paul   **QH81.S572 1999**
Encounters with Nature: Essays by Paul Shepard. Florence R. Shepard (Editor), David Petersen (Introduction by). Trade Cloth. Island Press. Washington, DC. 1999. 252p. ISBN:1-55963-529-0, ISBN13: 978-1-55963-529-5. Dewey:508. LCCN:99-033862.

Audience: **g,l,u,f.** *Choice, 2000.*

Shore, William H.   **QH81.N315 1994**
The Nature of Nature: New Essays from America's Finest Writers on Science. Trade Cloth. Harcourt Trade Publishers. New York, NY. 1994. 356p. ISBN:0-15-100080-8, ISBN13: 978-0-15-100080-7. Dewey:508. LCCN:94-003123.

Audience: **g,l,u.**

Thomson, Keith S.   **QH81.T61115 1993**
The Common but Less Frequent Loon and Other Essays. Linda P. Thomson (Illustrator). Cloth over Boards. Yale University Press. Cumberland, RI. 1993. 192p. ISBN:0-300-05630-3, ISBN13: 978-0-300-05630-3. Dewey:508. LCCN:93-017240.

Audience: **g,l.**

Thoreau, Henry David   QH81.T6122 1989
The Natural History Essays. Robert Sattelmeyer (Introduction by). Trade Paper. Gibbs Smith, Publisher. Layton, UT. 1980. 304p. Peregrine Smith Literary Naturalists Ser. ISBN:0-87905-298-8, ISBN13: 978-0-87905-298-0. Dewey:917.44/02. LCCN:88-034468.

        Audience: **g,l,u,f.**

Watkins, T. H. & Byrnes,   QH76.W67 1995
   Patricia (Editors)
World of Wilderness: Essays on the Power and Purpose of Wild Country. Trade Paper. Roberts Rinehart Publishers. Boulder, CO. 1995. 288p. ISBN:1-57098-016-0, ISBN13: 978-1-57098-016-9. Dewey:333.78/2/0973. LCCN:94-074947.

        Audience: **g,l.**

Wood, Paul (Editor)   QH45.R39 1996
Thomas Reid on the Animate Creation: Papers Relating to the Life Sciences. Trade Cloth. Pennsylvania State University Press. University Park, PA. 1996. 288p. ISBN:0-271-01571-3, ISBN13: 978-0-271-01571-2. Dewey:508. LCCN:95-039165.

        Audience: **u,f.** *Choice, 1996.*

Zimmer, Marc   QP552.G73Z56 2005
Glowing Genes: A Revolution in Biotechnology. Trade Cloth. Prometheus Books, Publishers. Amherst, NY. 2005. 250p. ISBN:1-59102-253-3, ISBN13: 978-1-59102-253-4. Dewey:572/.4358. LCCN:2004-022817.

        Audience: **g,l,u,f.** *Choice, 2005.*

Natural History > Education

        QH54.G66
Global Lab - An Integrated Science Program: Extended Investigations, Unit V. Trade Cloth. Kendall/Hunt Publishing Company. Dubuque, IA. ISBN:0-7872-6346-X, ISBN13: 978-0-7872-6346-1. Dewey:500.

        Audience: **u,f.**

        QL9.2
☐ ZooWeb.
http://www.zooweb.com/

        Audience: **l,u,f.**

Anderson, Dennis   QH81.A565 1993
An Hour Before Dawn: Stories of the Outdoors. Trade Paper. Voyageur Press, Inc. Saint Paul, MN. 1993. 240p. ISBN:0-89658-180-2, ISBN13: 978-0-89658-180-7. Dewey:508.

        Audience: **g,l.**

Anderson, Tom   QH81.A574 1989
Learning Nature by a Country Road. Charles K. Johnston (Illustrator). Trade Cloth. Voyageur Press, Inc. Saint Paul, MN. 1990. 256p. ISBN:0-89658-085-7, ISBN13: 978-0-89658-085-5. Dewey:508. LCCN:89-005543.

        Audience: **g,l.**

Bates, Marston   QH308.2
The Nature of Natural History. Paper Text. Textbook Publishers. Temecula, CA. 2003. 309p. ISBN:0-7581-4043-6, ISBN13: 978-0-7581-4043-2. Dewey:574.

        Audience: **g,l.**

Cornell, Joseph   QH53
Sharing Nature with Children. Ed. 20. Trade Paper. Dawn Publications. Nevada City, CA. 1998. 176p. ISBN:1-883220-73-4, ISBN13: 978-1-883220-73-0. Dewey:508.

        Audience: **g,l,u,f.**

Cvancara, Alan M.   QH81.C88 1992
Exploring Nature in Winter. Daniel Richards (Illustrator). Trade Paper. Walker & Company. New York, NY. 1992. 194p. The Naturalist's Bookshelf Ser. ISBN:0-8027-7385-0, ISBN13: 978-0-8027-7385-2. Dewey:508. LCCN:92-012560.

        Audience: **g,l,u,f.**

Diagram Group   QH55.N38 1992
Nature Projects on File. Book, Other. Facts On File, Inc.. New York, NY. 1992. 290p. ISBN:0-8160-2705-6, ISBN13: 978-0-8160-2705-7. Dewey:508. LCCN:91-040846.

        Audience: **l,u,f.**

Dillard, Annie   QH81
Teaching a Stone to Talk: Expeditions and Encounters. Trade Paper. HarperCollins Publishers. New York, NY. 1988. 176p. ISBN:0-06-091541-2, ISBN13: 978-0-06-091541-4. Dewey:508. LCCN:82-045720.

        Audience: **l,u,f.**

Durrell, Gerald   QL31.G58
My Family and Other Animals. Trade Paper. Penguin Group (USA) Inc. New York, NY. 2004. 288p. ISBN:0-14-200441-3, ISBN13: 978-0-14-200441-8. Dewey:590.9/2.

        Audience: **g,l,u,f.**

Herholdt, Elizabeth M.   QH60
Natural History Collections: their management and value. Pretoria : Transvaal Museum. 1990. Special publication ;; no. 1 = Spesiale publikasie ; Nr. 1; Variation: Special publication (Transvaal Museum) ;; no. 1. ISBN:0-907990-11-8, ISBN13: 978-0-907990-11-6.

        Audience: **u,f.**

Johnson, Cathy   QH53.J643 1991
The Naturalist's Path: A Handbook for Beginning the Study of Nature. Trade Paper. Walker & Company. New York, NY. 1991. 208p. ISBN:0-8027-7360-5, ISBN13: 978-0-8027-7360-9. Dewey:508. LCCN:91-018612.

        Audience: **l,u,f.**

Johnson, Cathy   QH81.J6 1989
The Nocturnal Naturalist: Exploring the Outdoors at Night. David R. Wallace (Foreword by). Trade Cloth. Globe Pequot Press, The. Guilford, CT. 1989. 244p. ISBN:0-87106-524-X, ISBN13: 978-0-87106-524-7. Dewey:508. LCCN:89-007549.

        Audience: **g,l,u.**

Montgomery, Sy   QH81.M83 1993
Nature's Everyday Mysteries: A Field Guide to the World in Your Backyard. Rodica Prato (Illustrator), Roger T. Peterson (Foreword by). Trade Paper. Houghton Mifflin Company Trade & Reference Division. Boston, MA. 1993. 152p. Curious Naturalist Ser. ISBN:0-9631591-9-4, ISBN13: 978-0-9631591-9-9. Dewey:508. LCCN:92-036189.

        Audience: **g,l,u,f.**

Nudds, J. R. & Pettitt, C.   Q105.A1
   W. (Editors)
Value and Valuation of Natural Science Collections. Trade

Cloth. Geological Society Publishing House. Bath, 1996. 230p. ISBN:1-897799-76-4, ISBN13: 978-1-897799-76-5. Dewey:507.4.

Audience: **u,f.**

Roberts, Mervin F.   **QH68**
Terrariums for Your New Pet. Trade Paper. T F H Publications, Inc. Neptune, NJ. 1990. 64p. ISBN:0-86622-525-0, ISBN13: 978-0-86622-525-0. LCCN:90-196101.

Audience: **g,l,u.**

Rose, Carolyn L. (Editor),   **QH61.S84 1995**
   et al.
Storage of Natural History Collections: A Preventive Conservation Approach, Vol. 1. Catharine A. Hawks, Hugh H. Genoways, Karen Ackoff, Anna J. Norville & Jennifer Tung (Editors). Trade Cloth. Society for the Preservation of Natural History Collections. Washington, DC. 1995. ISBN:0-9635476-1-5, ISBN13: 978-0-9635476-1-3. Dewey:508/.075/3. LCCN:95-000223.

Audience: **u,f.**

Swain, Roger B.   **QH81.S883 1991**
Saving Graces: Sojourns of a Backyard Biologist. Trade Cloth. Little Brown & Company. New York, NY. 1991. 138p. ISBN:0-316-82471-2, ISBN13: 978-0-316-82471-2. Dewey:508. LCCN:91-007767.

Audience: **g.**

TERC Staff   **QH54.G66**
Global Lab: An Integrated Science Program. Paper Text. Kendall/Hunt Publishing Company. Dubuque, IA. 2000. 88p. ISBN:0-7872-6347-8, ISBN13: 978-0-7872-6347-8. Dewey:500.

Audience: **u,f.**

TERC Staff   **QH54.G66**
Global Lab - An Integrated Science Program: Extended Investigations, Unit V. Perfect. Kendall/Hunt Publishing Company. Dubuque, IA. 2000. 176p. ISBN:0-7872-6341-9, ISBN13: 978-0-7872-6341-6. Dewey:500.

Audience: **u,f.**

TERC Staff   **QH54.G66**
Global Lab - An Integrated Science Program: Investigating Our Earth, Unit IV. Perfect. Kendall/Hunt Publishing Company. Dubuque, IA. 2000. 324p. ISBN:0-7872-6340-0, ISBN13: 978-0-7872-6340-9. Dewey:500.

Audience: **u,f.**

TERC Staff   **QH54.G66**
Global Lab - An Integrated Science Program: Investigating Our Earth: Land, Unit II. Paper Text. Kendall/Hunt Publishing Company. Dubuque, IA. 2000. 92p. ISBN:0-7872-6343-5, ISBN13: 978-0-7872-6343-0. Dewey:500.

Audience: **u,f.**

Tucker, Priscilla M.   **QH55.T83 1995**
Basic Nature Projects: 101 Fun Explorations. Trade Paper. Stackpole Books. Mechanicsburg, PA. 1995. 256p. ISBN:0-8117-2511-1, ISBN13: 978-0-8117-2511-8. Dewey:508. LCCN:95-003821.

Audience: **l,u,f.**

Natural History > Education > Curricula and Class Development

☐ Internet4Classrooms Gateway - Biology. http://internet4classrooms.com/gateway_biology.htm Internet4Classrooms.

Audience: **g,l,u,f.**

Bates, H. E.   **QH138.S8**
Through the Woods: The English Woodland - April to April. Agnes Miller Parker (Illustrator). Trade Cloth. Lincoln Frances Ltd. London, 1995. 144p. ISBN:0-7112-0992-8, ISBN13: 978-0-7112-0992-3. Dewey:574.5/2642/0942.

Audience: **l,u,f.**

Carnibucci, Patricia   **QH48**
Our Living World: Over 15 Complete Printable Unit Studies with Interactive Links. CD-ROM. Champion Press, Ltd. Belgium, WI. 2002. 160p. ISBN:1-891400-71-1, ISBN13: 978-1-891400-71-1. Dewey:508.

Audience: **l,u,f.**

Chichester, Page   **QH55.C48 1997**
National Wildlife Federation Book of Family Nature Activities: 50 Simple Projects and Activities. Trade Paper. Henry Holt & Company. New York, NY. 1997. ISBN:0-8050-4686-0, ISBN13: 978-0-8050-4686-1. Dewey:508. LCCN:97-000812.

Audience: **l,u,f.**

Dashefsky, H. Steven   **QL468.5.D36 1994**
Entomology: High-School Science Fair Experiments. Cloth Text. McGraw-Hill School Education Group. Columbus, OH. 1993. ISBN:0-07-015661-1, ISBN13: 978-0-07-015661-6. Dewey:595.7/0078. LCCN:93-039693.

Audience: **g,l,u,f.**

Dashefsky, H. Steven
Zoology: Forty-Nine Science Fair Projects. Library Binding. Sagebrush Education Resources. Caledonia, MN. 1994. ISBN:0-613-71545-4, ISBN13: 978-0-613-71545-4. Dewey:591/.078.

Audience: **g,l,u,f.**

Dashefsky, H. Steven   **QL52.6.D375 1995**
Zoology: High-School Science Fair Experiments. Trade Cloth. McGraw-Hill School Education Group. Columbus, OH. 1994. 160p. ISBN:0-07-015686-7, ISBN13: 978-0-07-015686-9. Dewey:591/.076. LCCN:94-029631.

Audience: **g,l,u,f.**

Duensing, Edward   **QH81.D835 1997**
Talking to Fireflies, Shrinking the Moon: Nature Activities for All Ages. Trade Paper. Fulcrum Publishing. Golden, CO. 1997. 144p. ISBN:1-55591-310-5, ISBN13: 978-1-55591-310-6. Dewey:508. LCCN:96-048840.

Audience: **g,l.**

Duensing, Edward   **QH81.D835 1990**
Talking to Fireflies, Shrinking the Moon: A Parent's Guide to Nature Activities. Trade Paper. Penguin Group (USA) Inc. New York, NY. 1990. 192p. ISBN:0-452-26511-8, ISBN13: 978-0-452-26511-0. Dewey:508. LCCN:90-034703.

Audience: **g,l.**

Fitzsimons, Cecilia   **QH48**
Step-by-Step: Nature Craft Projects for Kids. Trade Cloth.
Smithmark Publishers, Inc. New York, NY. 1995. 96p.
ISBN:0-8317-7793-1, ISBN13: 978-0-8317-7793-7.
Dewey:745.5.

Audience: **g,l,u.**

Hoover, Evalyn & Mercier,   **QH47**
  Sheryl
Exploring Environments, Grades K-6. Betty Cordel (Editor).
Trade Paper. AIMS Education Foundation. Fresno, CA. 1999.
168p. ISBN:1-881431-77-0, ISBN13: 978-1-881431-77-0.
Dewey:375.0083.

Audience: **g,l,u.**

Hosoume, Kimi & Barber,   **QH68.H835 1994**
  Jacqueline
Terrarium Habitats. Kay Fairwell, Lincoln Bergman & Carl
Babcock (Editors), Rose Craig (Illustrator), Richard Hoyt
(Photographer). Trade Paper. University of California, Berkeley,
Lawrence Hall of Science. Berkeley, CA. 1994. 92p. Great
Explorations in Math and Science Ser. ISBN:0-912511-85-0,
ISBN13: 978-0-912511-85-6. LCCN:95-194169.

Audience: **g,l,u.**

Hosoume, Kimi & Barber,   **QH68**
  Jacqueline
Terrarium Habitats, Grades K-6. Kay Fairwell, Lincoln Bergman
& Carl Babcock (Editors), Rose Craig (Illustrator), Richard
Hoyt (Photographer). Trade Paper. University of California,
Berkeley, Lawrence Hall of Science. Berkeley, CA. 2000. 92p.
Great Explorations in Math and Science Ser.
ISBN:0-924886-51-X, ISBN13: 978-0-924886-51-5.
Dewey:372.357.

Audience: **g,l,u.**

Walmsley, Sean A. (Editor)   **LB1570.C487 1994**
Children Exploring Their World: Theme Teaching in Elementary
School. Trade Paper. Heinemann. Portsmouth, NH. 1994. 304p.
ISBN:0-435-08804-1, ISBN13: 978-0-435-08804-0.
Dewey:372.13. LCCN:93-31221.

Audience: **g,l,u.**

Natural History > Education > Laboratory and Field

▢ Internet4Classrooms Gateway - Biology.
http://internet4classrooms.com/gateway_biology.htm
Internet4Classrooms.

Audience: **g,l,u,f.**

Bartlett, Richard   **QH68**
Digest for the Successful Terrarium. Trade Cloth. Tetra Press.
Blacksburg, VA. 80p. ISBN:3-89356-035-1, ISBN13:
978-3-89356-035-6. Dewey:578.073.

Audience: **g,l,f.**

Birchard, William Jr. &   **TE304.B572 2000**
  Proudman, Robert D.
Appalachian Trail Design, Construction, and Maintenance. Ed.
2. Trade Paper. Appalachian Trail Conference. Harpers Ferry,
WV. 2000. 248p. ISBN:0-917953-72-X, ISBN13:
978-0-917953-72-9. Dewey:624.

Audience: **g,u,f.**

Daley, Allen & Daley, Stella   **QH68**
Making and Using Terrariums and Planters. Trade Paper.
Blandford Press. London, 1989. 144p. ISBN:0-7137-2091-3,
ISBN13: 978-0-7137-2091-4. Dewey:635.9/824.

Audience: **g,l,u,f.**

Dashefsky, H. Steven   **QL468.5.D36 1994**
Entomology: High-School Science Fair Experiments. Cloth Text.
McGraw-Hill School Education Group. Columbus, OH. 1993.
ISBN:0-07-015661-1, ISBN13: 978-0-07-015661-6.
Dewey:595.7/0078. LCCN:93-039693.

Audience: **g,l,u,f.**

Dashefsky, H. Steven
Zoology: Forty-Nine Science Fair Projects. Library Binding.
Sagebrush Education Resources. Caledonia, MN. 1994.
ISBN:0-613-71545-4, ISBN13: 978-0-613-71545-4.
Dewey:591/.078.

Audience: **g,l,u,f.**

Dashefsky, H. Steven   **QL52.6.D375 1995**
Zoology: High-School Science Fair Experiments. Trade Cloth.
McGraw-Hill School Education Group. Columbus, OH. 1994.
160p. ISBN:0-07-015686-7, ISBN13: 978-0-07-015686-9.
Dewey:591/.076. LCCN:94-029631.

Audience: **g,l,u,f.**

Keenan, Philip E.   **QL681.K44 2002**
  (Photographer, Text by)
Birding Across North America: A Naturalist's Observations.
Trade Cloth. Timber Press, Inc. Portland, OR. 2002. 260p.
ISBN:0-88192-528-4, ISBN13: 978-0-88192-528-9.
Dewey:598/.07/2347. LCCN:2001-037623.

Audience: **g,l,u,f.** *Choice, 2002.*

Stewart, Ian   **QH323.5.S747 2001**
What Shape Is a Snowflake?: Magical Numbers in Nature. Cloth
over Boards. Henry Holt & Company. New York, NY. 2001.
200p. ISBN:0-7167-4794-4, ISBN13: 978-0-7167-4794-9.
Dewey:510. LCCN:2002-280019.

Audience: **g.**

Westland, Pamela   **SB415**
Terrariums: An easy guide to growing a host of miniature
gardens, using traditional terrariums, glass bottles and decorative
dishes. Trade Cloth. Book Sales, Inc. Edison, NJ. 1993.
ISBN:1-55521-845-8, ISBN13: 978-1-55521-845-4.
Dewey:635.9824.

Audience: **g,l,u,f.**

Natural History > Biographies

Allardyce, Gilbert   **QH31**
On the Track of the New Brunswick Panther: The Story of
Bruce Wright and the Eastern Panther. G. Allardyce,
Fredericton, N.B.. 2001. ISBN:0-9688897-0-0, ISBN13:
978-0-9688897-0-1.

Audience: **g,l,f.**

Bonta, Marcia M.   **QH26.B66 1991**
Women in the Field: America's Pioneering Women Naturalists.
Trade Paper. Texas A & M University Press. College Station,
TX. 1992. 320p. ISBN:0-89096-489-0, ISBN13:
978-0-89096-489-7. Dewey:508/.092/2 B. LCCN:90-020729.

Audience: **g,l,u,f.** *Choice, 1991.*

Breidbach, Olaf QH46.H213 1998
  (Contribution by), et al.
Art Forms in Nature: The Prints of Ernst Haeckel. Irenaus
Eibl-Eibesfeld & Richard Hartman (Contribution by). Trade
Paper. Prestel Publishing. New York, NY. 1998. 140p.
ISBN:3-7913-1990-6, ISBN13: 978-3-7913-1990-2.
Dewey:570/.22/2. LCCN:98-231776.

Audience: **g,l,u,f.** *Choice, 1999.*

Carty, Winthrop P. QH26.C28 1992
The Rhino Man and Other Uncommon Environmentalists:
Portraits of Global 500. Trade Paper. Clarendon House.
Arlington, VA. 1992. xi, 177p. ISBN:0-9631509-0-1, ISBN13:
978-0-9631509-0-5. LCCN:92-009166.

Audience: **l,u,f.**

Corsi, Pietro QH15.C6713 1988
The Age of Lamark. Jonathan Mandelbaum (Translator). Trade
Cloth. University of California Press. Berkeley, CA. 1988. 384p.
ISBN:0-520-05830-5, ISBN13: 978-0-520-05830-9.
Dewey:575/.009/034. LCCN:88-004839.

Audience: **l,u,f.**

Evans, Howard E. QH26.E77 1993
Pioneer Naturalists: The Discovery and Naming of North
American Plants and Animals. Michael G. Kippenhan
(Illustrator). Trade Cloth. Henry Holt & Company. New York,
NY. 1993. 224p. ISBN:0-8050-2337-2, ISBN13:
978-0-8050-2337-4. Dewey:508.7/014. LCCN:93-012501.

Audience: **l,u,f.**

Gratzer, Walter Bruno Q125.B375 1997
A Bedside Nature: Genius and Eccentricity in Science,
1869-1953. Trade Cloth. W. H. Freeman & Company. New
York, NY. 1997. 266p. ISBN:0-7167-3139-8, ISBN13:
978-0-7167-3139-9. Dewey:509/.034. LCCN:97-015964.

Audience: **u,f.**

Haeckel, Ernst QH46
Haeckel's Art Forms from Nature. CD-ROM, Trade Paper.
Dover Publications, Inc. Mineola, NY. 2004. 48p. Pictorial
Archive Ser., :Dover Full-Color Electronic Design Ser.
ISBN:0-486-99602-6, ISBN13: 978-0-486-99602-8.
Dewey:570.2/22.

Audience: **u,f.**

Henig, Robin Marantz QH31
Monk and Two Peas: The Story of Gregor Mendel and the
Discovery of Genetics. Phoenix, London. 2001.
ISBN:0-7538-1122-7, ISBN13: 978-0-7538-1122-1.

Audience: **l,u,f.**

Henricksson, John (Editor) QH14.N68 1997
North Writers: Our Place in the Woods. Trade Paper. University
of Minnesota Press. Minneapolis, MN. 1997. 176p.
ISBN:0-8166-2903-X, ISBN13: 978-0-8166-2903-9. Dewey:508.
LCCN:97-011452.

Audience: **l,u,f.**

Henricksson, John (Editor) QH14.N67 1991
North Writers: A Strong Woods Collection. Book, Other.
University of Minnesota Press. Minneapolis, MN. 1991. xviii,
292p. ISBN:0-8166-1950-6, ISBN13: 978-0-8166-1950-4.
Dewey:508. LCCN:91-012035.

Audience: **l,u,f.**

Krensky, Stephen QH26
Four Against the Odds: The Struggle to Save Our Environment.
Prebound. Turtleback Books. Madison, WI. 1992.
ISBN:0-606-21605-7, ISBN13: 978-0-606-21605-0.
Dewey:J363.7092.

Audience: **l,u,f.**

Krutch, Joseph Wood QH81.K828 1995
The Best Nature Writing of Joseph Wood Krutch. Edward
Lenders (Foreword by). Trade Paper. University of Utah Press.
Salt Lake City, UT. 1995. 392p. ISBN:0-87480-480-9, ISBN13:
978-0-87480-480-5. Dewey:508. LCCN:95-004976.

Audience: **l,u,f.**

Meyers, Steven J. QH81.M583 1989
Lime Creek Odyssey. Trade Cloth. Fulcrum Publishing. Golden,
CO. 1989. 132p. ISBN:1-55591-037-8, ISBN13:
978-1-55591-037-2. Dewey:508. LCCN:88-032705.

Audience: **l,u,f.**

Mitchell, John G. QH75
The Man Who Would Dam the Amazon and Other Accounts
from Afield. Trade Paper. University of Nebraska Press. Lincoln,
NE. 1990. xiv, 368p. ISBN:0-8032-8187-0, ISBN13:
978-0-8032-8187-5. Dewey:333.7/2. LCCN:89-078517.

Audience: **l,u,f.**

Morine, David E. QH76.M67 1990
Good Dirt: Confessions of a Conservationist. Trade Paper. Globe
Pequot Press, The. Guilford, CT. 1990. ISBN:0-87106-444-8,
ISBN13: 978-0-87106-444-8. Dewey:333.7/2. LCCN:90-043074.

Audience: **l,u,f.**

New York Times Staff Q141.S2945 2000
Scientists at Work. Laura Chang (Editor), Stephen Jay Gould
(Foreword by), Cornelia Dean (Introduction by). Trade Paper.
McGraw-Hill Trade. New York, NY. 2000. 372p.
ISBN:0-07-135882-X, ISBN13: 978-0-07-135882-8.
Dewey:509.2/2 B. LCCN:00-712544.

Audience: **g,l,u.**

Norwood, Vera 92-22562 [QH]
Made from This Earth: American Women and Nature. Trade
Paper. University of North Carolina Press. Chapel Hill, NC.
1993. 392p. Gender and American Culture Ser.
ISBN:0-8078-4396-2, ISBN13: 978-0-8078-4396-3.
Dewey:508.73/082. LCCN:92-022562.

Audience: **l,u,f.** *Choice, 1993.*

Rice, Anthony QH15.R44 1999
Voyages of Discovery: Three Centuries of Natural History
Exploration. Trade Cloth. Crown Publishing Group. New York,
NY. 1999. 336p. ISBN:0-609-60536-4, ISBN13:
978-0-609-60536-3. Dewey:508/.09. LCCN:99-032989.

Audience: **l,u,f.**

Richardson, Bob QH31
A Face Beside the Fire: Memories of Dawn Grey
Owl-Richardson. Trafford, Victoria, B.C.. 2001.
ISBN:1-55212-719-2, ISBN13: 978-1-55212-719-3.

Audience: **u,f.**

Stangroom, J. (Jeremy) QH309.W44 2005
What Scientists Think. Paper over Boards. Routledge. New
York, NY. 2005. XIV, 194p. ISBN:0-415-33426-8, ISBN13:
978-0-415-33426-6. Dewey:570. LCCN:2004-025418.

Audience: **g,l,u.**

Formats: Web: ▢ Ebook: 🄴 CD/DVD-ROM: 🌠 BCL3: 𝐵

Sterling, Keir B. (Editor),   **QH26**
et al.
Biographical Dictionary of American and Canadian Naturalists
and Environmentalists. Richard P. Harmond, George A. Cevasco
& Lorne F. Hammond (Editors). Cloth Text. Greenwood
Publishing Group, Inc. Portsmouth, NH. 1997. 960p.
ISBN:0-313-23047-1, ISBN13: 978-0-313-23047-9.
Dewey:508/.092/273 B. LCCN:96-000156.
         Audience: **u,f.** *Choice, 1998.*

Thomson, Keith S.   **QH81.T61115 1993**
The Common but Less Frequent Loon and Other Essays. Linda
P. Thomson (Illustrator). Cloth over Boards. Yale University
Press. Cumberland, RI. 1993. 192p. ISBN:0-300-05630-3,
ISBN13: 978-0-300-05630-3. Dewey:508. LCCN:93-017240.
         Audience: **g,l.**

Vickery, James D.   **QH26.V53 1988**
Wilderness Visionaries. Trade Paper. Globe Pequot Press, The.
Guilford, CT. 1988. 250p. ISBN:0-934802-28-9, ISBN13:
978-0-934802-28-4. Dewey:508.73/092/2 B. LCCN:85-030589.
         Audience: **l,u,f.**

Warner, William W.   **QH81.W29**
Into the Porcupine Cave and Other Odysseys: Adventures of an
Occasional Naturalist. Trade Cloth. National Geographic
Society. Washington, DC. 1999. ISBN:0-7922-7611-6, ISBN13:
978-0-7922-7611-1. Dewey:508.
         Audience: **g,l.**

Zwinger, Ann   **QH81.Z94 1998**
The Nearsighted Naturalist. Trade Cloth. University of Arizona
Press. Tucson, AZ. 1998. 294p. ISBN:0-8165-1880-7, ISBN13:
978-0-8165-1880-7. Dewey:508. LCCN:98-008881.
         Audience: **g,l.**

Zwinger, Ann Haymond   **QH14.Z95 2000**
Shaped by Wind and Water: Reflections of a Naturalist. Cloth
over Boards. Milkweed Editions. Minneapolis, MN. 2000. 200p.
Credo Ser. ISBN:1-57131-241-2, ISBN13: 978-1-57131-241-9.
Dewey:508. LCCN:99-055767.
         Audience: **l,u,f.**

Natural History > Biographies > Darwin

Darwin, Charles   **QH365**
The Voyage of the Beagle: Charles Darwin's Journal of
Researches. Janet Browne & Michael Neve (Editors), Janet
Browne & Michael Neve (Introduction by). Trade Paper.
Penguin Group (USA) Inc. New York, NY. 1989. 448p. Penguin
Classics Ser. ISBN:0-14-043268-X, ISBN13:
978-0-14-043268-8. Dewey:508/.092. LCCN:89-212506.
         Audience: **l,u,f.**

Keynes, R. D. & Darwin,   **QH365.Z9 K4 2000**
Charles
Charles Darwin's Zoology Notes and Specimen Lists from H.
M. S. Beagle. Richard Keynes (Editor). Trade Cloth. Cambridge
University Press. New York, NY. 2000. 464p.
ISBN:0-521-46569-9, ISBN13: 978-0-521-46569-4.
Dewey:508.8. LCCN:2001-269276.
         Audience: **g,l,u.** *Choice, 2001.*

Stott, Rebecca   **QH375.S76 2003**
Darwin and the Barnacle: The Story of the One Tiny Creature
and History's Most Spectacular Scientific Breakthrough. Trade

Cloth. W. W. Norton & Company, Inc. New York, NY. 2003.
256p. ISBN:0-393-05745-3, ISBN13: 978-0-393-05745-4.
Dewey:576.8092. LCCN:2003-002215.
         Audience: **u,f.**

Natural History > Biographies > Linnaes

Blunt, Wilfrid   **QH44**
Linnaeus: The Compleat Naturalist. Trade Cloth. Princeton
University Press. Princeton, NJ. 2002. 288p.
ISBN:0-691-09636-8, ISBN13: 978-0-691-09636-0.
Dewey:580.9/2.
         Audience: **l,u,f.**

Blunt, Wilfrid; Stearn,   **QH44**
William T. (William Thomas)
The compleat naturalist: a life of Linnaeus. London : Frances
Lincoln. 2001. ISBN:0-7112-1841-2, ISBN13:
978-0-7112-1841-3.
         Audience: **l,u,f.**

Fara, Patricia   **QK26.F37 2004**
Sex, Botany and Empire: The Story of Carl Linnaeus and
Joseph Banks. Trade Cloth. Columbia University Press. New
York, NY. 2004. 176p. ISBN:0-231-13426-6, ISBN13:
978-0-231-13426-2. Dewey:580.9/22. LCCN:2004-049391.
         Audience: **l,u,f.**

Frangsmyr, Tore   **QH44.L56 1994**
(Introduction by)
Linnaeus: The Man and His Work. Sten Lindroth, Gunnar
Eriksson & Gunnar Broberg (Contribution by). Library Binding.
Watson Publishing International. Sagamore Beach, MA. 1994.
232p. Upsala Studies in History of Science, Vol. 18
ISBN:0-88135-155-5, ISBN13: 978-0-88135-155-2.
Dewey:580/.92 B. LCCN:94-010558.
         Audience: **u,f.**

Koerner, Lisbet   **QH44**
Linnaeus: Nature and Nation. Trade Paper. Harvard University
Press. Cambridge, MA. 2001. 320p. ISBN:0-674-00565-1,
ISBN13: 978-0-674-00565-5. Dewey:580/.92 B.
         Audience: **u,f.**

Koerner, Lisbet   **QH44.K58 1999**
Linnaeus: Nature and Nation. Trade Cloth. Harvard University
Press. Cambridge, MA. 1999. 320p. ISBN:0-674-09745-9,
ISBN13: 978-0-674-09745-2. Dewey:580/.92 B.
LCCN:99-034570.
         Audience: **u,f.**

Natural History > Biographies > Wallace

Wilson, John G. (John   **QH31.W2**
Grenell)
The Forgotten Naturalist: In Search of Alfred Russel Wallace.
Arcadia, Tennyson, S.A.. 2000. ISBN:1-875606-72-6, ISBN13:
978-1-875606-72-6.
         Audience: **l,u,f.**

Natural History > Nature Writing

Gardner, Jason (Editor)   QH81.S194 1998
The Sacred Earth: Writers on Nature and Spirit. David Brower (Foreword by). Trade Paper. New World Library. Novato, CA. 1998. 208p. ISBN:1-57731-068-3, ISBN13: 978-1-57731-068-6. Dewey:508. LCCN:98-023015.

Audience: **l,u,f.**

Great Books Foundation   QH311.N33 2001
Staff (Contribution by)
The Nature of Life: Readings in Biology. Trade Paper. Great Books Foundation. Chicago, IL. 2001. xvi, 291p. ISBN:1-880323-86-9, ISBN13: 978-1-880323-86-1. Dewey:570. LCCN:2001-033681.

Audience: **l,u,f.**

Halpern, Daniel   QH81.N317 1996
The Nature Reader. Dan Frank (Editor). Trade Cloth. HarperCollins Publishers. New York, NY. 1997. 208p. ISBN:0-88001-491-1, ISBN13: 978-0-88001-491-5. Dewey:820.8/036. LCCN:96-042420.

Audience: **g,l,u,f.**

Heintzman, James   QH14.H45 1988
Making the Right Connections: A Guide for Nature Writers. Michael Gross & Ronald Zimmerman (Editors), Sylvia Myrhe (Illustrator). Paper Text. University of Wisconsin-Stevens Point Foundation Press. Stevens Point, WI. 1988. 54p. Interpreter's Handbook Ser. ISBN:0-932310-07-9, ISBN13: 978-0-932310-07-1. Dewey:808/.066508.

Audience: **u,f.**

Hinchman, Hannah   QH14.H46 1997
A Trail Through Leaves: The Journal As a Path to Place. Trade Cloth. W. W. Norton & Company, Inc. New York, NY. 1997. 224p. ISBN:0-393-04101-8, ISBN13: 978-0-393-04101-9. Dewey:808/.066508. LCCN:96-037100.

Audience: **l,u,f.**

Hodgson, Barbara   QH46
Naturalists: A Journal. Greystone Books, Vancouver. 2003. ISBN:1-55054-927-8, ISBN13: 978-1-55054-927-0.

Audience: **l,u,f.**

Leslie, Clare Walker &   QH81.L595 1998
Roth, Charles E.
Nature Journaling: Learning to Observe and Connect with the World Around You. Trade Cloth. Storey Publishing, LLC. Pownal, VT. 1998. 192p. ISBN:1-58017-088-9, ISBN13: 978-1-58017-088-8. Dewey:508. LCCN:98-014497.

Audience: **l,u,f.**

Lueders, Edward, et al.   QH14.W75 1989
Writing Natural History: Dialogues with Authors. Barry Lopez & Gary Paul Nabhan (Authors). Trade Paper. University of Utah Press. Salt Lake City, UT. 1989. 124p. ISBN:0-87480-323-3, ISBN13: 978-0-87480-323-5. Dewey:808/.066. LCCN:89-004764.

Audience: **u,f.**

Lyon, Thomas J.   QH81.T355 1989
(Introduction by)
This Incomparable Land: A Book of American Nature Writing. Trade Cloth. Houghton Mifflin Company. New York, NY. 1989.

495p. ISBN:0-395-48312-3, ISBN13: 978-0-395-48312-1. Dewey:508.73. LCCN:88-013451.

Audience: **g,l,u,f.**

Mabberley, David   NC730
Arthur Harry Church: The Anatomy of Flowers. Trade Cloth. Merrell Publishers Ltd. London, 2005. 128p. ISBN:1-85894-116-4, ISBN13: 978-1-85894-116-5. Dewey:743.9/34.

Audience: **g,l,u.**

Mabey, Richard (Editor)   QH81.O97 1995
The Oxford Book of Nature Writing. Trade Cloth. Oxford University Press, Inc. New York, NY. 1995. 272p. ISBN:0-19-214172-4, ISBN13: 978-0-19-214172-9. Dewey:809.9/336. LCCN:94-020026.

Audience: **g,l,u,f.**

Manguel, Alberto   QH81.M254 1998
By the Light of the Glow-Worm Lamp: Three Centuries of Reflections on Nature. Trade Paper. Perseus Books Group. New York, NY. 1998. 384p. ISBN:0-306-45992-2, ISBN13: 978-0-306-45992-4. Dewey:508. LCCN:98-026198.

Audience: **l,u,f.**

Murray, John A.   QH14.M87 1995
The Sierra Club Nature Writing Handbook: A Creative Guide. Trade Paper. Sierra Club Books. San Francisco, CA. 1995. 208p. ISBN:0-87156-436-X, ISBN13: 978-0-87156-436-8. Dewey:808/.066508. LCCN:95-005601.

Audience: **l,u,f.**

Murray, John A.   QH14.M87 2003
Writing about Nature. Trade Paper. University of New Mexico Press. Albuquerque, NM. 2003. 202p. ISBN:0-8263-3085-1, ISBN13: 978-0-8263-3085-7. Dewey:808/.066508. LCCN:2003-007238.

Audience: **l,u,f.**

Petersen, David   QH14.P48 2001
Writing Naturally: A Down-to-Earth Guide to Nature Writing. Trade Paper. Johnson Books. Boulder, CO. 2004. 224p. ISBN:1-55566-273-0, ISBN13: 978-1-55566-273-8. Dewey:808/.066508. LCCN:00-054962.

Audience: **l,u,f.**

Plum, Sydney L. (Editor,   QH81.S8725 1996
Introduction by)
Coming Through the Swamp: The Nature Writings of Gene Stratton Porter. Cloth Text. University of Utah Press. Salt Lake City, UT. 1996. 300p. ISBN:0-87480-497-3, ISBN13: 978-0-87480-497-3. Dewey:813/.52. LCCN:95-048024.

Audience: **g,l,u,f.** *Choice, 1996.*

Sterling, Keir B. (Editor),   QH26
et al.
Biographical Dictionary of American and Canadian Naturalists and Environmentalists. Richard P. Harmond, George A. Cevasco & Lorne F. Hammond (Editors). Cloth Text. Greenwood Publishing Group, Inc. Portsmouth, NH. 1997. 960p. ISBN:0-313-23047-1, ISBN13: 978-0-313-23047-9. Dewey:508/.092/273 B. LCCN:96-000156.

Audience: **u,f.** *Choice, 1998.*

Tweit, Susan J.   **QH88**
Seasons in the Desert: A Naturalist's Notebook. Kirk Caldwell
(Illustrator). Trade Cloth. DIANE Publishing Company.
Collingdale, PA. 1998. 224p. ISBN:0-7567-5788-6, ISBN13:
978-0-7567-5788-5. Dewey:578.754.

Audience: **g.**

Natural History > Bioregions and Bioregionalism

QH84

☐ Wildfinder - Mapping the World's Species.
http://www.worldwildlife.org/wildfinder

Audience: **g,l,u,f.**

Deutsches Nationalkomitee   **QH75**
  MAB; Unesco
Full of Life: UNESCO Biosphere Reserves, Model Regions for
Sustainable Development. Springer-Verlag, SpringerBerlin. 2005.
ISBN:3-540-20077-0, ISBN13: 978-3-540-20077-2.

Audience: **u,f.**

Friederici, Peter   **QH81.F8424 1999**
The Suburban Wild. Trade Cloth. University of Georgia Press.
Athens, GA. 1999. 125p. ISBN:0-8203-2134-6, ISBN13:
978-0-8203-2134-9. Dewey:508. LCCN:99-025399.

Audience: **l,u,f.**

Frome, Michael   **QH76.F76 1997**
Battle for the Wilderness. Trade Paper. University of Utah Press.
Salt Lake City, UT. 1997. 278p. ISBN:0-87480-552-X, ISBN13:
978-0-87480-552-9. Dewey:333.78/2/0973. LCCN:97-030314.

Audience: **u,f.**   *Choice, 1998.*

Kanze, Edward   **QH197.K34 2000**
Kangaroo Dreaming: An Australian Wildlife Odyssey. Trade
Cloth. Sierra Club Books. San Francisco, CA. 2000. 416p.
ISBN:0-609-60796-0, ISBN13: 978-0-609-60796-1.
Dewey:508.94. LCCN:00-030102.

Audience: **l,u,f.**   *Choice, 2001.*

Keynes, R. D.   **QH11.K49 2003**
Fossils, Finches, and Fuegians: Darwin's Adventures and
Discoveries on the Beagle. Trade Cloth. Oxford University
Press, Inc. New York, NY. 2003. 460p. ISBN:0-19-516649-3,
ISBN13: 978-0-19-516649-1. Dewey:576.8/2/092.
LCCN:2002-154176.

Audience: **l,u,f.**   *Choice, 2004.*

Klinkenborg, Verlyn   **QH104**
The Rural Life. Trade Paper. Little Brown & Company. New
York, NY. 2004. 224p. ISBN:0-316-73551-5, ISBN13:
978-0-316-73551-3. Dewey:508.73.

Audience: **g,l,u,f.**

Larkin, David   **QH81.L324 1998**
Country Wild. Trade Cloth. Houghton Mifflin Company Trade &
Reference Division. Boston, MA. 1998. 160p.
ISBN:0-395-77190-0, ISBN13: 978-0-395-77190-7. Dewey:508.
LCCN:99-176039.

Audience: **l,u,f.**

Natural History > Bioregions and Bioregionalism > North America (United States, Canada, Mexico, Central America)

Abell, Robin A., et al.   **QH77.N56F69 2000**
Freshwater Ecoregions of North America: A Conservation
Assessment. David M. Olson, Eric Dinerstein, Patrick T. Hurley,
James T. Diggs, William Eichbaum, Steven Walters, Wesley
Wettengel, Tom Allnutt, Colby J. Loucks & Prashant Hedao
(Authors). Trade Paper. Island Press. Washington, DC. 1999.
368p. ISBN:1-55963-734-X, ISBN13: 978-1-55963-734-3.
Dewey:577.6. LCCN:99-016796.

Audience: **g,l,u,f.**   *Choice, 2000.*

Adelman, Charlotte &   **QH104.A53 2001**
  Schwartz, Bernard L.
Prairie Directory of North America: The United States and
Canada. Trade Paper. Lawndale Enterprises. Wilmette, IL. 2001.
352p. ISBN:0-9715096-0-3, ISBN13: 978-0-9715096-0-3.
Dewey:577.4/4/097. LCCN:2001-098353.

Audience: **l,u,f.**

Benke, Arthur C. &   **QH102.R58 2005**
  Cushing, Colbert E. (Editors)
Rivers of North America. Trade Cloth. Elsevier Science &
Technology Books. Saint Louis, MO. 2005. 1168p.
ISBN:0-12-088253-1, ISBN13: 978-0-12-088253-3.
Dewey:551.48/3. LCCN:2005-008909.

Audience: **l,u,f.**   *Choice, 2006.*

Cartron, Jean-Luc E., et al.   **QH107.B525 2004**
Biodiversity, Ecosystems, and Conservation in Northern Mexico.
Gerardo Ceballos & Richard Stephen Felger (Authors). Trade
Cloth. Oxford University Press, Inc. New York, NY. 2005. 513p.
ISBN:0-19-515672-2, ISBN13: 978-0-19-515672-0.
Dewey:333.95/16/0972. LCCN:2004-012002.

Audience: **l,u,f.**

City of Ann Arbor Natural   **QH58.A46 1999**
  Area Preservation Division Satff
Along the Huron: The Natural Communities of the Huron River
Corridor in Ann Arbor, Michigan. Trade Paper. University of
Michigan Press. Chicago, IL. 1999. 136p. ISBN:0-472-08651-0,
ISBN13: 978-0-472-08651-1. LCCN:00-699024.

Audience: **l,u.**

Covel, Paul F.   **QH26.C64 1988**
Beacons along a Naturalist's Trail: California Naturalists and
Innovators. Rex Burress (Illustrator, Preface by), James F. Covel
(Foreword by). Trade Paper. Western Interpretive Press.
Oakland, CA. 1988. xii, 153p. ISBN:0-931430-01-1, ISBN13:
978-0-931430-01-5. Dewey:508/.092/2 B. LCCN:87-034691.

Audience: **g,l,u,f.**

Crump, Donald J. (Editor)   **QH76.A45 1988**
America's Hidden Wilderness: Lands of Seclusion. Trade Cloth.
National Geographic Society. Washington, DC. 1988. 200p.
Special Publications Series 23, No. 1 ISBN:0-87044-666-5,
ISBN13: 978-0-87044-666-5. Dewey:917. LCCN:88-009977.

Audience: **l,u,f.**

Curtin, Philip D., et al.   **GF504.C54D47 2001**
Discovering the Chesapeake: The History of an Ecosystem.
Grace Somers Brush & George Wescott Fisher (Authors). Trade

Paper. Johns Hopkins University Press. Baltimore, MD. 2001.
416p. ISBN:0-8018-6468-2, ISBN13: 978-0-8018-6468-1.
LCCN:00-042405.

Audience: **l,u.**

Doppelt, Bob, et al.   **QH76**
Entering the Watershed: A New Approach to Save America's
River Ecosystems. Mary Scurlock, Chris Frissell, Robert
Doppelt & James R. Karr (Authors), James Karr (Editor). Trade
Paper. Island Press. Washington, DC. 1993. 504p.
ISBN:1-55963-275-5, ISBN13: 978-1-55963-275-1.
Dewey:333.91/6216/0973. LCCN:93-008895.

Audience: **l,u,f.** *Choice, 1994.*

Fitzharris, Tim   **QH86**
Forests: A Journey into North America's Vanishing Wilderness.
Li-leger, Don (Drawings by). Stoddart, Toronto. 1991.
ISBN:0-7737-2498-2, ISBN13: 978-0-7737-2498-3.

Audience: **l,u,f.**

Foreman, Dave   **QH76.F67 1992**
The Big Outside: A Descriptive Inventory of the Big Wilderness
Areas of the United States. Trade Paper. Crown Publishing
Group. New York, NY. 1992. ISBN:0-517-58737-8, ISBN13:
978-0-517-58737-9. Dewey:333.78/2/0973.

Audience: **l,u,f.**

Frome, Michael   **QH76.F765 1994**
Promised Land: Adventures and Encounters in Wild America.
Ed. 2. Trade Paper. University of Tennessee Press. Knoxville,
TN. 1994. 360p. ISBN:0-87049-851-7, ISBN13:
978-0-87049-851-0. Dewey:508.73. LCCN:94-004691.

Audience: **l,u,f.**

Gil, Patricio Robles, et al.   **QH107**
The Great Tamaulipan Natural Province. Exequiel Ezcurra,
Eduardo Peters, Eugenia Pallares & Ana Ezcurra (Authors).
Trade Cloth. Conservation International. Washington, DC. 2005.
360p. ISBN:968-6397-73-6, ISBN13: 978-968-6397-73-4.
Dewey:508.7212.

Audience: **u,f.**

Harding, James H.   **QL653.G74H37 1997**
Amphibians and Reptiles of the Great Lakes Region. Cloth over
Boards. University of Michigan Press. Chicago, IL. 1997. 400p.
Great Lakes Environment Ser. ISBN:0-472-09628-1, ISBN13:
978-0-472-09628-2. Dewey:597.6/0978. LCCN:96-025343.
Audience: **l,u.** *Choice, 1998.*

Harding, Lee E. &   **QH77.C2**
  McCullum, Emily (Editors)
Biodiversity in British Columbia: Our Changing Environment.
Trade Paper. University of Washington Press. Seattle, WA. 1994.
426p. ISBN:0-662-20671-1, ISBN13: 978-0-662-20671-2.
Dewey:574.5/09711.

Audience: **l,u,f.**

Heacox, Kim   **QH26.H38 1996**
Visions of Wild America. National Geographic Society Staff
(Contribution by). Trade Cloth. National Geographic Society.
Washington, DC. 1996. 200p. ISBN:0-7922-2944-4, ISBN13:
978-0-7922-2944-5. Dewey:333.7/2/0973. LCCN:96-018715.
Audience: **l,u,f.**

Henry, J. David   **QH106.H46 2002**
Canada's Boreal Forest. Trade Cloth. Smithsonian Institution
Press. Washington, DC. 2002. 208p. Smithsonian Natural

History Ser. ISBN:1-58834-057-0, ISBN13: 978-1-58834-057-3.
Dewey:508.415. LCCN:2002-070687.

Audience: **g,l,u.**

Hernandez, Francisco   **QH107.H53 2000**
The Mexican Treasury: The Writings of Dr. Francisco
Hernández. Simon Varey (Editor). Trade Cloth. Stanford
University Press. Palo Alto, CA. 2001. xix, 281p.
ISBN:0-8047-3963-3, ISBN13: 978-0-8047-3963-4.
Dewey:508.72. LCCN:00-026519.

Audience: **g,l,u,f.**

Hummel, Monte   **QH77.C2**
Protecting Canada's Endangered Spaces: An Owner's Manual.
Key Porter Books, Toronto. 1995. Henderson book series; no.
27 ISBN:1-55013-710-7, ISBN13: 978-1-55013-710-1.

Audience: **u,f.**

Huth, Hans   **QH76.H88 1991**
Nature and the American: Three Centuries of Changing
Attitudes. Douglas H. Strong (Introduction by). Trade Cloth.
University of Nebraska Press. Lincoln, NE. 1990. 314p.
ISBN:0-8032-7247-2, ISBN13: 978-0-8032-7247-7.
Dewey:333.95/16/0973. LCCN:90-035727.

Audience: **g,l,u,f.**

Kelso, J. R. & Hartig, J. H.   **SH157.8**
  (Editors)
Methods of Modifying Habitat to Benefit the Great Lakes
Ecosystem. Trade Paper. NRC Research Press National Research
Council of Canada. Ottawa, ON. 1995. 294p. CISTI Occasional
Paper Ser., No. 1 ISBN:0-660-16047-1, ISBN13:
978-0-660-16047-4. Dewey:333.95/2153/09713.

Audience: **u,f.**

Kingsolver, Barbara   **QH104.K55 2002**
Last Stand: America's Virgin Lands. Annie Griffiths Belt
(Photographer). Trade Cloth. National Geographic Society.
Washington, DC. 2002. 192p. ISBN:0-7922-6909-8, ISBN13:
978-0-7922-6909-0. Dewey:333.95/16/0973.
LCCN:2002-075105.

Audience: **g,l,u.**

Lane, John   **QH81.W765 1999**
The Woods Stretched for Miles: An Anthology of Contemporary
Nature Writing from the South. Trade Cloth. University of
Georgia Press. Athens, GA. 1999. 256p. ISBN:0-8203-2087-0,
ISBN13: 978-0-8203-2087-8. Dewey:508.75. LCCN:98-020339.
Audience: **l,u,f.**

Larson, Peggy   **QH88.L37 2000**
The Deserts of the Southwest: A Sierra Club Naturalist's Guide.
Ed. 2. Book, Other. Sierra Club Books. San Francisco, CA.
2000. 304p. Naturalist's Guides ISBN:1-57805-052-9, ISBN13:
978-1-57805-052-9. Dewey:578.754/0979. LCCN:99-056996.
Audience: **l,u,f.**

Lazaroff, David W. &   **QH88.L39 1998**
  Arizona-Sonora Desert Museum Staff
Arizona-Sonora Desert Museum Book of Answers. Trade Paper.
Arizona Sonora Desert Museum Press. Tucson, AZ. 1998. 198p.
ISBN:1-886679-09-6, ISBN13: 978-1-886679-09-2.
Dewey:578.754. LCCN:97-031829.

Audience: **l,u,f.**

MacPherson, Allen   GV199.44.C22O58 2000
Ontario Provincial Park Trail Guide. Trade Paper. Boston Mills
Press. Erin, ON. 2000. 168p. ISBN:1-55046-290-3, ISBN13:
978-1-55046-290-6. Dewey:508.713. LCCN:2001-272984.
                                    Audience: **l,u,f.**

Olson, Steve   QH362.T435 2004
Evolution in Hawaii: A Supplement to Teaching about Evolution
and the Nature of Science. National Academy of Sciences (U.S.)
Staff (Contribution by). Trade Cloth. National Academies Press.
Washington, DC. 2004. viii, 48p. ISBN:0-309-08991-3, ISBN13:
978-0-309-08991-3. LCCN:2004-298464.
                                    Audience: **g,l,u.**

Osborne, Graham   QH86.O82 1998
  (Photographer)
Rain Forest: Ancient Realm of the Pacific Northwest. Wade
Davis (Text by). Trade Cloth. Chelsea Green Publishing. White
River Junction, VT. 1999. 128p. ISBN:1-890132-24-1, ISBN13:
978-1-890132-24-8. Dewey:333.75/09795/022.
LCCN:00-501376.
                                    Audience: **l,u,f.**

Price, Jennifer   QH104
Flight Maps: Adventures with Nature in Modern America. Trade
Paper. Basic Books. New York, NY. 2000. 352p.
ISBN:0-465-02486-6, ISBN13: 978-0-465-02486-5.
Dewey:508.73.
                         Audience: **g,l,u,f.** *Choice, 1999.*

Ricketts, Taylor H., et al.   QH77.N56T47 1999
Terrestrial Ecoregions of North America: A Conservation
Assessment. Eric Dinerstein, David M. Olson, Colby J. Loucks,
William Eichbaum, Dominick Dellassala, Kevin Kavanaugh,
Prashant Hedao, Patrick Hurley, Robin Abell, Karen L. Carney
& Steven Walters (Authors). Trade Paper. Island Press.
Washington, DC. 1999. 508p. ISBN:1-55963-722-6, ISBN13:
978-1-55963-722-0. Dewey:333.95/16/097. LCCN:99-018912.
                         Audience: **g,l,u,f.** *Choice, 2000.*

Riley, Laura & Riley,   QH76 .R54 1993
  William
Guide to the National Wildlife Refuges. Ed. 2. Trade Cloth.
John Wiley & Sons, Inc. Hoboken, NJ. 1996. 704p.
ISBN:0-02-063660-1, ISBN13: 978-0-02-063660-1.
Dewey:333.95/0973. LCCN:92-015459.
                                    Audience: **g,l,u,f.**

Roth, Dennis M.   QH76
The Wilderness Movement and the National Forests. Ed. 2.
Trade Paper. Intaglio Press. College Station, TX. 1995. 105p.
ISBN:0-944091-05-9, ISBN13: 978-0-944091-05-0.
Dewey:333.78/2/0973.
                                    Audience: **g,l,u,f.**

Smith, Scott T.   QH46.S558 1996
  (Photographer)
Nevada: Magnificent Wilderness. Trade Cloth. Westcliffe
Publishers. Englewood, CO. 1996. 128p. ISBN:1-56579-153-3,
ISBN13: 978-1-56579-153-4. Dewey:779/.36793.
LCCN:96-060392.
                                    Audience: **l,u,f.**

Trimble, Stephen (Editor)   QH81.W779 1995
Words from the Land. Trade Paper. University of Nevada Press.
Reno, NV. 1995. 416p. ISBN:0-87417-264-0, ISBN13:
978-0-87417-264-5. Dewey:508. LCCN:95-009831.
                                    Audience: **g,l,u,f.**

Ward, Kennan   QH105.W367 2000
Denali: Reflection of a Naturalist. Trade Cloth. T&N Children's
Publishing. Minnetonka, MN. 1999. 160p. ISBN:1-55971-716-5,
ISBN13: 978-1-55971-716-8. Dewey:508.798/3.
LCCN:99-026465.
                                    Audience: **g.**

Wessels, Tom   QH104.W47 2001
The Granite Landscape: A Natural History of America's
Mountain Domes, from Acadia to Yosemite. Brian D. Cohen
(Illustrator). Trade Cloth. Countryman Press. Woodstock, VT.
2001. 216p. ISBN:0-88150-429-7, ISBN13: 978-0-88150-429-3.
Dewey:508.73. LCCN:2002-067718.
                                    Audience: **g.**

Wright, Mabel Osgood &   QH81.W794 1999
  Philippon, Daniel J.
The Friendship of Nature: A New England Chronicle of Birds
and Flowers. Mabel Osgood Wright (Photographer, Contribution
by), Daniel J. Philippon (Contribution by). Trade Cloth. Johns
Hopkins University Press. Baltimore, MD. 1999. 192p.
American Land Classics Ser. ISBN:0-8018-6234-5, ISBN13:
978-0-8018-6234-2. Dewey:508.74. LCCN:99-020198.
                                    Audience: **g,l,u,f.**

Yaffee, Steven L., et al.   QH76.E336 1996
Ecosystem Management in the United States: An Assessment of
Current Experience. Ali F. Phillips, Irene C. Frentz & Paul W.
Hardy (Authors). Trade Paper. Island Press. Washington, DC.
1996. 368p. ISBN:1-55963-502-9, ISBN13: 978-1-55963-502-8.
Dewey:333.7/0973. LCCN:96-021825.
                         Audience: **g,l,u,f.** *Choice, 1997.*

Zwinger, Ann   QH81.Z9 1988
Beyond the Aspen Grove. Trade Paper. University of Arizona
Press. Tucson, AZ. 1988. 345p. ISBN:0-8165-1054-7, ISBN13:
978-0-8165-1054-2. Dewey:508.788/3. LCCN:87-034274.
                                    Audience: **g,l.**

Natural History > Bioregions and Bioregionalism > South America

Allofs, Theo   QH117
Pantanal: South America's Wetland Jewel. Russell A.
Mittermeier, Christina G. Mittermeier, Monica Barcellos Harris,
Reinaldo Lourival, Gustavo A. B. da Fonseca & Jose Maria
Cardos da Silva (Text by). Trade Cloth. Firefly Books, Ltd.
Tonawanda, NY. 2005. 176p. ISBN:1-55407-090-2, ISBN13:
978-1-55407-090-9. Dewey:508.81/71. LCCN:2006-445101.
                                    Audience: **l,u,f.**

Bierregaard, Richard O.   QH112.L48 2001
  (Editor), et al.
Lessons from Amazonia: The Ecology and Conservation of a
Fragmented Forest. Claude Gascon, Thomas Lovejoy & Rita
Mesquita (Editors), Edward O. Wilson (Foreword by). Cloth
over Boards. Yale University Press. Cumberland, RI. 2001.
496p. ISBN:0-300-08483-8, ISBN13: 978-0-300-08483-2.
Dewey:577.34/0981/1. LCCN:2001-026535.
                         Audience: **l,u,f.** *Choice, 2002.*

Chernoff, Barry (Editor),   QH127
  et al.
A Biological Assessment of the Aquatic Ecosystems of the Rio
Paraguay Basin, Alto Paraguay, Paraguay. Jensen R.

Montambault & Philip W. Willink (Editors). Trade Paper. University of Chicago Press. Chicago, IL. 2001. 156p. Conservation International Rapid Assessment Program Ser. ISBN:1-881173-40-2, ISBN13: 978-1-881173-40-3. Dewey:577.609892.

Audience: **u,f.**

Darwin, Charles   **QH11.D2 2001**
The Voyage of the Beagle: Journal of Researches into the Natural History and Geology of the Countries Visited During the Voyage of H. M. S. Beagle Round the World. Trade Paper. Random House Adult Trade Publishing Group. New York, NY. 2001. 496p. ISBN:0-375-75680-9, ISBN13: 978-0-375-75680-1. Dewey:508.8. LCCN:00-046294.

Audience: **l,u,f.**

Gallagher, Nora (Editor)   **QH81.P3428 1999**
Patagonia: Notes from the Field. Yvon Chouinard (Introduction by). Trade Cloth. Chronicle Books LLC. San Francisco, CA. 1999. 144p. ISBN:0-8118-2604-X, ISBN13: 978-0-8118-2604-4. Dewey:508. LCCN:99-018491.

Audience: **l,u,f.**

Hammond, D. (Editor)   **QH125**
Tropical Rainforests of the Guianan Shield. Trade Cloth. CAB International. Wallingford, 2005. 544p. CABI Publishing Ser. ISBN:0-85199-536-5, ISBN13: 978-0-85199-536-6. Dewey:578.734/098. LCCN:2004-021133.

Audience: **u,f.**

Holst, B., et al.   **QH128 B57 2001**
A Rapid Biological Assessment of the Northern Cordillera Vilcabamba, Peru. L. Emmons, M. Romo, L. Luna, A. Chicchon, G. Servat, H. Beltizan & B. Boyle (Authors), Thomas S. Schulenberg (Editor). Trade Paper. Conservation International. Washington, DC. 1999. 200p. RAP Working Papers, No. 12 ISBN:1-881173-51-8, ISBN13: 978-1-881173-51-9. Dewey:577.

Audience: **u,f.**

Larson, Edward J.   **QH366.2.L375 2001**
Evolution's Workshop: God and Science on the Galapagos Islands. Trade Cloth. Basic Books. New York, NY. 2001. 336p. ISBN:0-465-03810-7, ISBN13: 978-0-465-03810-7. Dewey:576.8. LCCN:00-065159.

Audience: **l,u,f.** *Choice, 2001.*

Maslow, Jonathan Evan   **QH26.M27 1996**
Footsteps in the Jungle: Adventures in the Scientific Exploration of the American Tropics. Trade Cloth. Ivan R. Dee Publisher. Blue Ridge Summit, PA. 1996. 75p. ISBN:1-56663-137-8, ISBN13: 978-1-56663-137-2. Dewey:508.8/092/2 B. LCCN:96-019161.

Audience: **l,u,f.** *Choice, 1997.*

Oliveira, Paulo S. &   **QH117.C52 2002**
Marquis, Robert J.
The Cerrados of Brazil: Ecology and Natural History of a Neotropical Savanna. Trade Cloth. Columbia University Press. New York, NY. 2002. 424p. ISBN:0-231-12042-7, ISBN13: 978-0-231-12042-5. Dewey:577.4/8/0981. LCCN:2002-022739.

Audience: **l,u,f.** *Choice, 2003.*

Riseng, Karen & Jensen,   **QH130 B55 2003**
Montambault
A Biological Assessment of the Aquatic Ecosystems of the Caura River Basin, Bolivar State, Venezuela: RAP Bulletin of Biological Assessment 28. Barry Chernoff (Editor), Antonio

Machado-Allison (Editor, Translator), Ana Liz Flores (Translator), Mark Denil (Illustrator), Montambault Jensen (Photographer), Kim Meek (Designed by). Trade Paper. Conservation International. Washington, DC. 2003. 284p. Conservation International Rapid Assessment Program Ser. ISBN:1-881173-69-0, ISBN13: 978-1-881173-69-4. Dewey:577. LCCN:2002-116698.

Audience: **u,f.**

Natural History > Bioregions and Bioregionalism > Africa

Crisman, Thomas L.   **QH194.C66 2003**
Conservation, Ecology, and Management of African Fresh Waters. Trade Cloth. University Press of Florida. Gainesville, FL. 2003. 544p. ISBN:0-8130-2597-4, ISBN13: 978-0-8130-2597-1. Dewey:333.95/28/096. LCCN:2002-043032.

Audience: **u,f.**

Huber, Bernhard A.   **QH194.I497 2004**
(Editor), et al.
African Biodiversity: Molecules, Organisms, Ecosystems. Bradley J. Sinclair & Karl-Heinz Lampe (Editors). Trade Cloth. Springer. New York, NY. 2001. XX, 443p. ISBN:0-387-24315-1, ISBN13: 978-0-387-24315-3. Dewey:577.096. LCCN:2005-299985.

Audience: **u,f.**

Jashemski, Wilhelmina   **QH152.N36 2001**
Feemster & Meyer, Frederick G. (Editors)
The Natural History of Pompeii. Trade Cloth. Cambridge University Press. New York, NY. 2002. 528p. ISBN:0-521-80054-4, ISBN13: 978-0-521-80054-9. Dewey:508.337/7. LCCN:2001-025503.

Audience: **g,l,u,f.**

Morris, Patrick, et al.   **QH194.W55 2002**
Wild Africa. Amanda Barrett, Andrew Murray, Marguerite Smits van Oyen & Dorling Kindersley Publishing Staff (Authors). Trade Cloth. Dorling Kindersley Publishing, Inc. New York, NY. 2001. 240p. ISBN:0-7894-8158-8, ISBN13: 978-0-7894-8158-0. Dewey:508.6. LCCN:2001-281190.

Audience: **g,l,u.**

Natural History > Bioregions and Bioregionalism > Europe

Allen, David Elliston   **QH137.N28 2001**
(Editor)
Naturalists and Society: The Culture of Natural History in Britain, 1700-1900. Trade Cloth. Ashgate Publishing, Ltd. Aldershot, 2001. 314p. Variorum Collected Studies, No. 724 ISBN:0-86078-863-6, ISBN13: 978-0-86078-863-8. Dewey:508.41/09. LCCN:2001-022813.

Audience: **l,u,f.**

Berry, R. J.   **QH141.B47**
Natural History of Orkney. Trade Cloth. A & C Black. London, 2000. 320p. Poyser Natural History Ser. ISBN:0-85661-104-2, ISBN13: 978-0-85661-104-9. Dewey:578/.0941132.

Audience: **l,u,f.** *Choice, 2001.*

Botting, Douglas   QH137.B67 1999
Wild Britain: A Traveller's Guide. Trade Cloth. Interlink
Publishing Group, Inc. Northampton, MA. 2004. 224p. Wild
Guides ISBN:1-56656-321-6, ISBN13: 978-1-56656-321-5.
Dewey:508.41. LCCN:99-027825.
                                              Audience: **l,u,f.**

Botting, Douglas   QH147.B68 1999
Wild France: A Traveller's Guide. Trade Cloth. Interlink
Publishing Group, Inc. Northampton, MA. 2004. 224p. Wild
Guides ISBN:1-56656-333-X, ISBN13: 978-1-56656-333-8.
Dewey:508.44. LCCN:99-039121.
                                              Audience: **l,u,f.**

Faranda, F. M., et al.   QH93.M42 2001
Structure and Processes in the Mediterranean Ecosystem. L.
Guglielmo & G. Spezie (Authors). Trade Cloth. Springer. New
York, NY. 2001. XVIII, 503p. ISBN:88-470-0114-5, ISBN13:
978-88-470-0114-5. Dewey:577.7/38. LCCN:00-066115.
                                              Audience: **u,f.**

Foster, John W. & Chesney,   QH81.N319 1997
Helena C.
Nature in Ireland: A Scientific and Cultural History. Trade Cloth.
Dufour Editions, Inc. Chester Springs, PA. 1997. 700p.
ISBN:1-874675-29-5, ISBN13: 978-1-874675-29-7.
Dewey:508.415. LCCN:97-164170.
                                 Audience: **l,u,f.** *Choice, 1998.*

Gibbons, Bob & Walters,   DA650
Martin
Britain: Travellers' Nature Guide. Trade Paper. Oxford
University Press, Inc. New York, NY. 2003. 384p. Nature
Guides ISBN:0-19-850433-0, ISBN13: 978-0-19-850433-7.
Dewey:914.104/86. LCCN:2003-282054.
                                              Audience: **l,u,f.**

Gibbons, Bob   DC16
France: Travellers' Nature Guide. Martin Walters (Editor). Trade
Paper. Oxford University Press, Inc. New York, NY. 2003. 344p.
Nature Guides ISBN:0-19-850431-4, ISBN13:
978-0-19-850431-3. Dewey:914.40484. LCCN:2003-279700.
                                              Audience: **l,u,f.**

Gibson, Ray, et al.   QH137.G53 2001
Photographic Guide to Sea and Shore Life of Britain and
North-West Europe. Ben Hextall & Alex Rogers (Authors).
Cloth Text. Oxford University Press, Inc. New York, NY. 2001.
456p. ISBN:0-19-850041-6, ISBN13: 978-0-19-850041-4.
Dewey:578.769/9/0941. LCCN:2001-021772.
                                              Audience: **l,u,f.**

Grafton, Anthony (Editor)   QH81
Natural Particulars: Nature and the Disciplines in Renaissance
Europe. Siraisi, Nancy G. (Editor). MIT Press, Cambridge,
Mass.. 1999. Dibner Institute Studies in the History of Science
and Technology ISBN:0-262-07193-2, ISBN13:
978-0-262-07193-2.
                                              Audience: **u,f.**

Grove, A. T. & Rackham,   QH150
Oliver
The Nature of Mediterranean Europe: An Ecological History.
Trade Paper. Yale University Press. Cumberland, RI. 2003.
384p. ISBN:0-300-10055-8, ISBN13: 978-0-300-10055-6.
Dewey:577.4/6/094. LCCN:2003-101909.
                                 Audience: **l,u,f.** *Choice, 2001.*

Groves, R. H. & Di Castri,   QH353 .B54 1991
F. (Editors)
Biogeography of Mediterranean Invasions. Trade Cloth.
Cambridge University Press. New York, NY. 1991. 501p.
ISBN:0-521-36040-4, ISBN13: 978-0-521-36040-1.
Dewey:574.909/822. LCCN:90-045682.
                                 Audience: **u,f.** *Choice, 1992.*

Grunfeld, Frederic V.   QH171.G785 1999
Wild Spain: A Traveller's Guide. Trade Cloth. Interlink
Publishing Group, Inc. Northampton, MA. 2004. 224p. Wild
Guides ISBN:1-56656-322-4, ISBN13: 978-1-56656-322-2.
Dewey:508.46. LCCN:99-017868.
                                              Audience: **l,u,f.**

Hawksworth, D. L. (Editor)   QH137
The Changing Wildlife of Great Britain and Ireland. Taylor &
Francis, London ; New York. 2001. ISBN:0-7484-0957-2,
ISBN13: 978-0-7484-0957-0.
                                              Audience: **u,f.**

Lambert, Robert A.   CS477.F49
Contested Mountains: Nature, Development and Environment in
the Cairngorms Region of Scotland, 1880-1980. Trade Cloth.
White Horse Press. Cambridge, 2001. 320p.
ISBN:1-874267-44-8, ISBN13: 978-1-874267-44-7.
Dewey:941.24.
                                              Audience: **u,f.**

Lehane, Brendan   QH143.L43 2000
Wild Ireland: A Traveller's Guide. Trade Cloth. Interlink
Publishing Group, Inc. Northampton, MA. 2004. 224p. Wild
Guides ISBN:1-56656-363-1, ISBN13: 978-1-56656-363-5.
Dewey:914.1504824. LCCN:99-087775.
                                              Audience: **l,u,f.**

Trabaud, Louis (Editor)   QH150.L54 2000
Life and Environment in the Mediterranean. Trade Cloth. WIT
Press. Ashurst, 2000. 400p. Advances in Ecological Sciences
Ser., Vol. 3 ISBN:1-85312-680-2, ISBN13: 978-1-85312-680-2.
Dewey:577/.09182/2. LCCN:99-065489.
                                              Audience: **u,f.**

Viney, Michael   QH143
Ireland. Trade Cloth. Smithsonian Institution Press. Washington,
DC. 2003. 328p. Smithsonian Natural History Ser.
ISBN:1-58834-110-0, ISBN13: 978-1-58834-110-5.
Dewey:508.4/15.
                                              Audience: **g.**

Natural History > Bioregions and Bioregionalism > Asia

Imanishi, Kinji   QH331.I537 2002
A Japanese View of Nature: The World of Living Things by
Kinji Imanishi. Pamela J. Asquith (Editor, Introduction by).
Paper over Boards. Taylor & Francis Group. Abingdon, 2002.
160p. Japan Anthropology Workshop ISBN:0-7007-1631-9,
ISBN13: 978-0-7007-1631-9. Dewey:570/.1.
LCCN:2002-028456.
                                              Audience: **u,f.**

Minoura, K. (Editor)   QH541.5.L3
Lake Baikal: A Mirror in Time and Space for Understanding
Global Change Processes. Trade Cloth. Elsevier Science &

Technology Books. Saint Louis, MO. 2000. 348p. ISBN:0-444-50434-6, ISBN13: 978-0-444-50434-0. Dewey:577.6309575.

Audience: **u,f.**

Natural History > Bioregions and Bioregionalism > Arctic/Antarctic

Campbell, David G.   **QH84.2**
The Crystal Desert: Summers in Antarctica. Trade Paper. Houghton Mifflin Company Trade & Reference Division. Boston, MA. 2002. 308p. ISBN:0-618-21921-8, ISBN13: 978-0-618-21921-6. Dewey:508.989.

Audience: **l,u,f.** *Choice, 1993.*

Chapin, F. Stuart III &   **QH84.1.A7 1995**
  Orner, Christian K. (Editors)
Arctic and Alpine Biodiversity: Patterns, Causes, and Ecosystem Consequences. Trade Cloth. Springer. New York, NY. 1995. 322p. Ecological Studies, Vol. 113 ISBN:3-540-57948-6, ISBN13: 978-3-540-57948-9. Dewey:574.5/2621. LCCN:94-040221.

Audience: **u,f.**

Crawford, R. M.   **QH84.1.D57 1997**
Disturbance and Recovery in Arctic Lands: An Ecological Perspective: Proceedings of the NATO Advanced Research Workshop on Disturbance and Recovery of Arctic Terrestrial Ecosystems, Rovaniemi, Finland, 24-30 Sept. 1995. Trade Cloth. Springer London, Ltd. Guildford, 1997. 632p. NATO Advanced Science Institutes Ser., Vol. 2:Environment ISBN:0-7923-4418-9, ISBN13: 978-0-7923-4418-6. Dewey:577.27/0911/3. LCCN:96-051038.

Audience: **u,f.**

Fothergill, Alastair   **QH84.2.F68 1995**
A Natural History of the Antarctic: Life in the Freezer. Ben Osborne (Illustrator), David Attenborough (Foreword by). Trade Cloth. Sterling Publishing Co., Inc.. New York, NY. 1995. 224p. ISBN:0-8069-1346-0, ISBN13: 978-0-8069-1346-9. Dewey:508.98/9. LCCN:94-023841.

Audience: **l,u,f.**

Hosking, Eric & Hosking,   **G590**
  David (Photographers)
Poles Apart: The Natural Worlds of the Arctic and Antarctic. Jim Flegg (Text by). Trade Cloth. Penguin Group (USA) Inc. New York, NY. 1990. 192p. ISBN:0-7207-1838-4, ISBN13: 978-0-7207-1838-6. Dewey:998. LCCN:89-063771.

Audience: **l,u,f.**

Kerry, K. R. & Hempel, G.   **QH84.2.A583 1990**
  (Editors)
Antarctic Ecosystems: Change and Conservation. Trade Cloth. Springer. New York, NY. 1990. 432p. ISBN:0-387-52101-1, ISBN13: 978-0-387-52101-5. Dewey:574.5/2621. LCCN:90-009930.

Audience: **g,l,u.**

Krasemann, Stephen J.   **QH84.1.K73 1991**
Diary of an Arctic Year. Trade Cloth. Chronicle Books LLC. San Francisco, CA. 1991. 192p. ISBN:0-8118-0027-X, ISBN13: 978-0-8118-0027-3. Dewey:574.9091632. LCCN:91-009358.

Audience: **l,u,f.**

Laws, Richard   **QH84.2**
Antarctica the Last Frontier. Trade Cloth. Pan Macmillan. London, 1990. 192p. ISBN:1-85283-247-9, ISBN13: 978-1-85283-247-6. Dewey:508.98/9.

Audience: **l,u,f.**

Lopez, Barry   **QH84.1.L67 1989**
Arctic Dreams: Imagination and Desire in a Northern Landscape. Trade Paper. Bantam Books. New York, NY. 1988. 496p. ISBN:0-553-34664-4, ISBN13: 978-0-553-34664-0. Dewey:508.719/9. LCCN:88-047877.

Audience: **l,u,f.** *Choice, 1986.*

Martin, Vance & Tyler,   **QH77.A68W67 1993**
  Nicholas (Editors)
Arctic Wilderness: The 5th World Wilderness Congress. Vance Martin (Preface by), Nicholas Tyler (Introduction by). Trade Paper. Fulcrum Publishing. Golden, CO. 1995. 368p. ISBN:1-55591-931-6, ISBN13: 978-1-55591-931-3. Dewey:333.7/16/0911. LCCN:95-004201.

Audience: **u,f.**

Moss, Sanford   **QH84.2**
Natural History of the Antarctic Peninsula. Lucia DeLeiris (Illustrator). Trade Paper. Columbia University Press. New York, NY. 1990. 208p. ISBN:0-231-06269-9, ISBN13: 978-0-231-06269-5. Dewey:508.98/9.

Audience: **l,u,f.** *Choice, 1988.*

Pielou, E. C.   **QH84.1.P54 1994**
A Naturalist's Guide to the Arctic. Trade Cloth. University of Chicago Press. Chicago, IL. 1995. 344p. ISBN:0-226-66813-4, ISBN13: 978-0-226-66813-0. Dewey:508.98. LCCN:94-002555.

Audience: **g,l,u,f.** *Choice, 1995.*

Wallace, Joseph E.   **QH84.1**
The Arctic. New York, N.Y. : Gallery Books. 1988. ISBN:0-8317-0391-1, ISBN13: 978-0-8317-0391-2.

Audience: **g,l.**

Young, Steven B.   **QH84.1**
To the Arctic: An Introduction to the Far Northern World. Trade Paper. John Wiley & Sons, Inc. Hoboken, NJ. 1994. 354p. Science Editions Ser. ISBN:0-471-07889-1, ISBN13: 978-0-471-07889-0. Dewey:508.311/3. LCCN:88-017423.

Audience: **g,l,u,f.** *Choice, 1989.*

Natural History > Bioregions and Bioregionalism > Rainforests

Alexander, Brian   **QH86.A58 1995**
Green Cathedrals: A Wayward Traveler in the Rainforest. Cloth over Boards. Globe Pequot Press, The. Guilford, CT. 1995. 220p. ISBN:1-55821-399-6, ISBN13: 978-1-55821-399-9. Dewey:304.2. LCCN:95-023739.

Audience: **l,u,f.**

Bermingham, Eldredge   **QH86.T764 2005**
  (Editor), et al.
Tropical Rainforests: Past, Present, and Future. Craig Moritz & Christopher W. Dick (Editors). Trade Cloth. University of Chicago Press. Chicago, IL. 2005. 672p. ISBN:0-226-04466-1, ISBN13: 978-0-226-04466-8. Dewey:577.34. LCCN:2004-019348.

Audience: **l,u,f.**

Bierregaard, Richard O.   QH112.L48 2001
   (Editor), et al.
Lessons from Amazonia: The Ecology and Conservation of a
Fragmented Forest. Claude Gascon, Thomas Lovejoy & Rita
Mesquita (Editors), Edward O. Wilson (Foreword by). Cloth
over Boards. Yale University Press. Cumberland, RI. 2001.
496p. ISBN:0-300-08483-8, ISBN13: 978-0-300-08483-2.
Dewey:577.34/0981/1. LCCN:2001-026535.
                              Audience: **l,u,f.** *Choice, 2002.*

Goldsmith, F. B. (Editor)   QH86.T73 1998
Tropical Rain Forest: A Wider Perspective. Cloth Text. Chapman
& Hall. New York, NY. 1998. 424p. ISBN:0-412-81510-9,
ISBN13: 978-0-412-81510-2. Dewey:333.7/5. LCCN:97-069618.
                              Audience: **l,u,f.**

Hammond, D. (Editor)   QH125
Tropical Rainforests of the Guianan Shield. Trade Cloth. CAB
International. Wallingford, 2005. 544p. CABI Publishing Ser.
ISBN:0-85199-536-5, ISBN13: 978-0-85199-536-6.
Dewey:578.734/098. LCCN:2004-021133.
                              Audience: **u,f.**

Jukofsky, Diane   QH86
Encyclopedia of Rainforests: Diane Jukofsky for the Rainforest
Alliance. Cloth Text. Greenwood Publishing Group, Inc.
Portsmouth, NH. 2001. 384p. ISBN:1-57356-259-9, ISBN13:
978-1-57356-259-1. Dewey:578.734/03. LCCN:2001-032154.
                              Audience: **g,l,u.** *Choice, 2002.*

Laurance, William F.   QH197.L38 2000
Stinging Trees and Wait-a-Whiles: Confessions of a Rainforest
Biologist. Trade Cloth. University of Chicago Press. Chicago,
IL. 2000. 196p. ISBN:0-226-46896-8, ISBN13:
978-0-226-46896-9. Dewey:577.34/09943/6. LCCN:00-020543.
                              Audience: **l,u,f.**

Marshall Cavendish   QH86.R39 2002
   Corporation Staff (Contribution by)
Rain Forests of the World, Set. Trade Cloth. Marshall Cavendish
Corporation. Tarrytown, NY. 2002. 704p. ISBN:0-7614-7254-1,
ISBN13: 978-0-7614-7254-4. Dewey:578.734.
LCCN:2001-028460.
                              Audience: **l,u,f.**

Maslow, Jonathan Evan   QH26.M27 1996
Footsteps in the Jungle: Adventures in the Scientific Exploration
of the American Tropics. Trade Cloth. Ivan R. Dee Publisher.
Blue Ridge Summit, PA. 1996. 75p. ISBN:1-56663-137-8,
ISBN13: 978-1-56663-137-2. Dewey:508.8/092/2 B.
LCCN:96-019161.
                              Audience: **l,u,f.** *Choice, 1997.*

Oldfield, Sara   QH86.O43 2003
Rainforest. Bruce Coleman (Photographer), Mark Rose
(Foreword by). Trade Cloth. MIT Press. Cambridge, MA. 2003.
160p. ISBN:0-262-15106-5, ISBN13: 978-0-262-15106-1.
Dewey:578.734. LCCN:2002-029559.
                              Audience: **g,l,u.** *Choice, 2003.*

Osborne, Graham   QH86.O82 1998
   (Photographer)
Rain Forest: Ancient Realm of the Pacific Northwest. Wade
Davis (Text by). Trade Cloth. Chelsea Green Publishing. White
River Junction, VT. 1999. 128p. ISBN:1-890132-24-1, ISBN13:
978-1-890132-24-8. Dewey:333.75/09795/022.
LCCN:00-501376.
                              Audience: **l,u,f.**

Prance, Ghillean   QH86.W64 1997
Rainforests of the World: Water, Fire, Earth and Air. Art Wolfe
(Photographer). Trade Cloth. Crown Publishing Group. New
York, NY. 1998. 304p. ISBN:0-609-60364-7, ISBN13:
978-0-609-60364-2. Dewey:578.734. LCCN:97-004087.
                              Audience: **g,l,u,f.**

Reader's Digest Editors   QH86.M97 1998
Mysteries of the Rain Forest. Trade Cloth. Reader's Digest
Association, Incorporated, The. Pleasantville, NY. 2002. 160p.
The Earth, Its Wonders, Its Secrets Ser. ISBN:0-7621-0110-5,
ISBN13: 978-0-7621-0110-8. Dewey:578.734.
LCCN:98-021012.
                              Audience: **g,l.**

Roberts, Jerry   Z7408.L29R63 1999
Rain Forest Bibliography: An Annotated Guide to over 1600
Nonfiction Books about Central and South American Jungles.
Cloth Text. McFarland & Company, Incorporated Publishers.
Jefferson, NC. 1999. 320p. ISBN:0-7864-0717-4, ISBN13:
978-0-7864-0717-0. Dewey:016.33375/098. LCCN:99-26061.
                              Audience: **g,l,u,f.** *Choice, 2000.*

Roubik, David W. (Editor),   QH185.E29 2005
   et al.
Pollination Ecology and the Rain Forest: Sarawak Studies.
Shoko Sakai & Abdul Hamid Abg (Editors). Trade Cloth.
Springer. New York, NY. 2005. XVIII, 318p. Ecological Studies,
Vol. 174 ISBN:0-387-21309-0, ISBN13: 978-0-387-21309-5.
Dewey:577.34/09595/4. LCCN:2004-052210.
                              Audience: **u,f.**

St. Martin's Press Staff &   QH86.Y68 2001
   Young, Allen M.
Tropical Rainforests: A Golden Guide from St. Martin's Press.
Judith Huf (Illustrator). Trade Paper. St. Martin's Press.
Gordonville, VA. 2001. 160p. Golden Guides Ser.
ISBN:1-58238-080-5, ISBN13: 978-1-58238-080-3.
Dewey:578.734.
                              Audience: **g,l.**

Natural History > Bioregions and Bioregionalism > Forests

Bonnicksen, Thomas M.   QH104.B635 2000
America's Ancient Forests: From the Ice Age to the Age of
Discovery. Trade Cloth. John Wiley & Sons, Inc. Hoboken, NJ.
2000. 608p. ISBN:0-471-13622-0, ISBN13: 978-0-471-13622-4.
Dewey:577.3/0973. LCCN:98-024396.
                              Audience: **l,u,f.**

Fitzharris, Tim   QH86
Forests: A Journey into North America's Vanishing Wilderness.
Li-leger, Don (Drawings by). Stoddart, Toronto. 1991.
ISBN:0-7737-2498-2, ISBN13: 978-0-7737-2498-3.
                              Audience: **l,u,f.**

Henry, J. David   QH106.H46 2002
Canada's Boreal Forest. Trade Cloth. Smithsonian Institution
Press. Washington, DC. 2002. 208p. Smithsonian Natural
History Ser. ISBN:1-58834-057-0, ISBN13: 978-1-58834-057-3.
Dewey:508.415. LCCN:2002-070687.
                              Audience: **g,l,u.**

McShea, William J. &   **QH102.O24 2003**
  Healy, William M.
Oak Forest Ecosystems: Ecology and Management for Wildlife.
Trade Paper. Johns Hopkins University Press. Baltimore, MD.
2003. 432p. ISBN:0-8018-7747-4, ISBN13: 978-0-8018-7747-6.
Dewey:577.3/0973.

Audience: **l,u,f.** *Choice, 2002.*

Raffan, James (Editor)   **QH106**
Rendezvous with the Wild: The Boreal Forest. Trade Cloth.
Boston Mills Press. Erin, ON. 2004. 188p. ISBN:1-55046-422-1,
ISBN13: 978-1-55046-422-1. Dewey:508.71.

Audience: **g,l.**

Natural History > Bioregions and Bioregionalism > Deserts

Allaby, Michael   **QH541.5.D4A438 2006**
Deserts. Richard Garratt (Illustrator). Trade Cloth. Facts On File,
Inc.. New York, NY. 2006. 272p. Biomes of the Earth Ser.
ISBN:0-8160-5320-0, ISBN13: 978-0-8160-5320-9.
Dewey:577.54. LCCN:2005-005611.

Audience: **l,u,f.**

Campbell, David G.   **QH84.2**
The Crystal Desert: Summers in Antarctica. Trade Paper.
Houghton Mifflin Company Trade & Reference Division.
Boston, MA. 2002. 308p. ISBN:0-618-21921-8, ISBN13:
978-0-618-21921-6. Dewey:508.989.

Audience: **l,u,f.** *Choice, 1993.*

De Villiers, Marq & Hirtle,   **DT333**
  Sheila
Sahara: A Natural History. Trade Paper. McClelland & Stewart.
Toronto, ON. 2004. 336p. ISBN:0-7710-2638-2, ISBN13:
978-0-7710-2638-6. Dewey:916.604/329.

Audience: **g,l,u,f.** *Choice, 2003.*

Flegg, Jim   **GB612**
Deserts: Miracle of Life. Library Binding. Replica Books.
Bridgewater, NJ. 1999. 162p. ISBN:0-7351-0201-5, ISBN13:
978-0-7351-0201-9. Dewey:910/.02154.

Audience: **l,u,f.** *Choice, 1994.*

Gibson, Arthur C.   **QK922.G53 1996**
Structure-Function Relations of Warm Desert Plants. Cloth Text.
Springer. New York, NY. 1996. 313p. Adaptations of Desert
Organisms Ser. ISBN:3-540-59267-9, ISBN13:
978-3-540-59267-9. Dewey:581.5/2652. LCCN:96-018699.

Audience: **l,u.**

Larson, Peggy   **QH88.L37 2000**
The Deserts of the Southwest: A Sierra Club Naturalist's Guide.
Ed. 2. Book, Other. Sierra Club Books. San Francisco, CA.
2000. 304p. Naturalist's Guides ISBN:1-57805-052-9, ISBN13:
978-1-57805-052-9. Dewey:578.754/0979. LCCN:99-056996.

Audience: **l,u,f.**

Lazaroff, David W. &   **QH88.L39 1998**
  Arizona-Sonora Desert Museum Staff
Arizona-Sonora Desert Museum Book of Answers. Trade Paper.
Arizona Sonora Desert Museum Press. Tucson, AZ. 1998. 198p.
ISBN:1-886679-09-6, ISBN13: 978-1-886679-09-2.
Dewey:578.754. LCCN:97-031829.

Audience: **l,u,f.**

Martin, Michael   **GB611**
Deserts of the Earth. Trade Cloth. Thames & Hudson. New
York, NY. 2004. 372p. ISBN:0-500-51194-2, ISBN13:
978-0-500-51194-7. Dewey:551.41/5. LCCN:2004-104540.

Audience: **l,u,f.**

Oldfield, Sara   **QH88.O43 2004**
Deserts: The Living Drylands. Trade Cloth. MIT Press.
Cambridge, MA. 2004. 180p. ISBN:0-262-15112-X, ISBN13:
978-0-262-15112-2. Dewey:577.54/. LCCN:2004-044860.

Audience: **g,l,u.**

Sowell, John   **QH102.S69 2001**
Desert Ecology: An Introduction to Life in the Arid Southwest.
Trade Paper. University of Utah Press. Salt Lake City, UT.
2001. xii, 193p. ISBN:0-87480-678-X, ISBN13:
978-0-87480-678-6. Dewey:577.54/097. LCCN:00-011599.

Audience: **g,l,u,f.** *Choice, 2001.*

Natural History > Bioregions and Bioregionalism > Prairie Grasslands

Adelman, Charlotte &   **QH104.A53 2001**
  Schwartz, Bernard L.
Prairie Directory of North America: The United States and
Canada. Trade Paper. Lawndale Enterprises. Wilmette, IL. 2001.
352p. ISBN:0-9715096-0-3, ISBN13: 978-0-9715096-0-3.
Dewey:577.4/4/097. LCCN:2001-098353.

Audience: **l,u,f.**

Andersen, Alan N. (Editor),   **QH197.F5624 2003**
  et al.
Fire in Tropical Savannas: The Kapalga Experiment. Garry D.
Cook & Richard J. Williams (Editors). Trade Cloth. Springer.
New York, NY. 2003. XIII, 195p. Ecological Studies, Vol. 169
ISBN:0-387-00291-X, ISBN13: 978-0-387-00291-0.
Dewey:577.2. LCCN:2002-044505.

Audience: **u,f.**

Jones, Stephen R. &   **QH102.J54 2004**
  Cushman, Ruth Carol
The North American Prairie. Trade Cloth. Houghton Mifflin
Company Trade & Reference Division. Boston, MA. 2004.
528p. Peterson Field Guides ISBN:0-618-17929-1, ISBN13:
978-0-618-17929-9. Dewey:578.74/4/097. LCCN:2002-191338.

Audience: **g,l,u.**

Knapp, Alan K. (Editor),   **QH105.K3G73 1998**
  et al.
Grassland Dynamics: Long-Term Ecological Research in
Tallgrass Prairie. John M. Briggs, David C. Hartnett & Scott L.
Collins (Editors). Trade Cloth. Oxford University Press, Inc.
New York, NY. 1998. 380p. The Long-Term Ecological
Research Network Ser. ISBN:0-19-511486-8, ISBN13:
978-0-19-511486-7. Dewey:577.4/4/09/7813. LCCN:97-008334.

Audience: **u,f.** *Choice, 1999.*

Larrabee, Aimée & Altman,   **QH104**
  John
Last Stand of the Tallgrass Prairie. Friedman/Fairfax, New York
: Distributed by Sterling Pub. Co.. 2001. ISBN:1-58663-134-9,
ISBN13: 978-1-58663-134-5.

Audience: **l,u,f.**

Lynch, Wayne   **QH102.L96 2004**
Windswept: A Passionate View of the Prairie Grasslands. Trade
Paper. X Y Z Publishing. Montreal, PQ. 2004. 144p.
ISBN:1-894856-25-2, ISBN13: 978-1-894856-25-6.
Dewey:577.4/4/097. LCCN:2004-381280.
Audience: **l,u,f.**

Madson, John   **QH104.M3 2004**
Where the Sky Began: Land of the Tallgrass Prairie. Dycie
Madson (Illustrator). Trade Paper. University of Iowa Press.
Iowa City, IA. 2004. 340p. A Bur Oak Book Ser.
ISBN:0-87745-861-8, ISBN13: 978-0-87745-861-6.
Dewey:577.4/4/0973. LCCN:2003-066307.
Audience: **l,u,f.**

Savage, Candace   **QH102.S38 2004**
Prairie: A Natural History. Cloth over Boards. Douglas &
McIntyre, Ltd. Vancouver, BC. 2004. 320p.
ISBN:1-55054-985-5, ISBN13: 978-1-55054-985-0.
Dewey:508.3153/097. LCCN:2004-040623.
Audience: **g,l.**

Natural History > Bioregions and Bioregionalism > Oceans

American Society of   **QH92**
Ichthyologists and Herpetologists; Food and Agriculture
Organization; European Commission
The Living Marine Resources of the Western Central Atlantic:
Vol. 2, Pt. 1, Bony fishes., Acipenseridae to Grammatidae.
Carpenter, Kent E. (Editor). Food and Agriculture Organization
of the United Nations, Rome. 2002. FAO species identification
guide for fishery purposes; Special publication / American
Society of Ichthyologists and Herpetologists; no. 5; Variation:
Special publication (American Society of Ichthyologists and
Herpetologists); no. 5 ISBN:92-5-104826-6, ISBN13:
978-92-5-104826-9.
Audience: **u,f.**

Byatt, Andrew et. al   **QH91**
The Blue Planet: A Natural History of the Oceans. Fothergill,
Alastair; Holmes, Martha. BBC Worldwide, London. 2001.
ISBN:0-563-38498-0, ISBN13: 978-0-563-38498-4.
Audience: **l,u,f.**

Goodman, Jordan   **QH11**
The Rattlesnake: A voyage of discovery to the Coral Sea. Faber
and Faber, London. 2005. ISBN:0-571-21073-2, ISBN13:
978-0-571-21073-2.
Audience: **l,u,f.**

Hinrichsen, Don   **QH75**
Our Common Seas. Earthscan, London. 1990.
ISBN:1-85383-030-5, ISBN13: 978-1-85383-030-3.
Audience: **l,u,f.**

Love, Rosaleen   **QH197.L68 2001**
Reefscape: Reflections on the Great Barrier Reef. Trade Cloth.
National Academies Press. Washington, DC. 2001. v, 255p.
ISBN:0-309-07260-3, ISBN13: 978-0-309-07260-1.
Dewey:508.943. LCCN:2001-024281.
Audience: **g,l,u,f.** *Choice, 2001.*

Morris, Rod & Balance,   **QH1**
Alison
South Sea Islands: A Natural History. Trade Cloth. Firefly

Books, Ltd. Tonawanda, NY. 2003. 160p. ISBN:1-55297-609-2,
ISBN13: 978-1-55297-609-8. Dewey:508.95.
Audience: **g,l,u,f.**

Vanstrum, Glenn S.   **QH91.V36 2003**
The Saltwater Wilderness. Trade Cloth. Oxford University Press,
Inc. New York, NY. 2003. 360p. ISBN:0-19-515937-3, ISBN13:
978-0-19-515937-0. Dewey:508.3162. LCCN:2002-066348.
Audience: **g,l.**

Wolanski, Eric (Editor)   **QH197**
Oceanographic Processes of Coral Reefs: Physical and
Biological Links in the Great Barrier Reef. CRC Press, Boca
Raton. 2001. ISBN:0-8493-0833-X, ISBN13:
978-0-8493-0833-8.
Audience: **u,f.**

Zedler, Joy B.   **QH75**
Handbook for Restoring Tidal Wetlands. CRC Press, Boca
Raton, Fla.. 2001.
Audience: **u,f.**

Natural History > Bioregions and Bioregionalism > Aquatic Freshwaters (Rivers, Lakes Streams, Ponds, Swamps)

Abell, Robin A., et al.   **QH77.N56F69 2000**
Freshwater Ecoregions of North America: A Conservation
Assessment. David M. Olson, Eric Dinerstein, Patrick T. Hurley,
James T. Diggs, William Eichbaum, Steven Walters, Wesley
Wettengel, Tom Allnutt, Colby J. Loucks & Prashant Hedao
(Authors). Trade Paper. Island Press. Washington, DC. 1999.
368p. ISBN:1-55963-734-X, ISBN13: 978-1-55963-734-3.
Dewey:577.6. LCCN:99-016796.
Audience: **g,l,u,f.** *Choice, 2000.*

Allofs, Theo   **QH117**
Pantanal: South America's Wetland Jewel. Russell A.
Mittermeier, Christina G. Mittermeier, Monica Barcellos Harris,
Reinaldo Lourival, Gustavo A. B. da Fonseca & Jose Maria
Cardos da Silva (Text by). Trade Cloth. Firefly Books, Ltd.
Tonawanda, NY. 2005. 176p. ISBN:1-55407-090-2, ISBN13:
978-1-55407-090-9. Dewey:508.81/71. LCCN:2006-445101.
Audience: **l,u,f.**

Benke, Arthur C. &   **QH102.R58 2005**
Cushing, Colbert E. (Editors)
Rivers of North America. Trade Cloth. Elsevier Science &
Technology Books. Saint Louis, MO. 2005. 1168p.
ISBN:0-12-088253-1, ISBN13: 978-0-12-088253-3.
Dewey:551.48/3. LCCN:2005-008909.
Audience: **l,u,f.** *Choice, 2006.*

Crisman, Thomas L.   **QH194.C66 2003**
Conservation, Ecology, and Management of African Fresh
Waters. Trade Cloth. University Press of Florida. Gainesville,
FL. 2003. 544p. ISBN:0-8130-2597-4, ISBN13:
978-0-8130-2597-1. Dewey:333.95/28/096. LCCN:2002-043032.
Audience: **u,f.**

Doppelt, Bob, et al.   **QH76**
Entering the Watershed: A New Approach to Save America's
River Ecosystems. Mary Scurlock, Chris Frissell, Robert
Doppelt & James R. Karr (Authors), James Karr (Editor). Trade

Paper. Island Press. Washington, DC. 1993. 504p.
ISBN:1-55963-275-5, ISBN13: 978-1-55963-275-1.
Dewey:333.91/6216/0973. LCCN:93-008895.
Audience: **l,u,f.** *Choice, 1994.*

Gray, Elaine   **QH75**
Wetlands: An Overview of the Issues. Council of Planning
Librarians, Chicago, Ill.. 1990. CPL bibliography ;; no. 265
ISBN:0-86602-265-1, ISBN13: 978-0-86602-265-1.
Audience: **u,f.**

Kentula, Mary E., et al.   **QH76.W47 1992**
Wetlands: An Approach to Improving Decision Making in
Wetland Restoration and Creation. Robert P. Brooks, Stephanie
E. Gwin, Cindy Holland, Arthur D. Sherman & Jean C. Sifneos
(Authors), Ann J. Hairston (Editor). Trade Cloth. Island Press.
Washington, DC. 1992. 176p. ISBN:1-55963-221-6, ISBN13:
978-1-55963-221-8. Dewey:333.91/8/0973. LCCN:92-005675.
Audience: **u,f.**

Minoura, K. (Editor)   **QH541.5.L3**
Lake Baikal: A Mirror in Time and Space for Understanding
Global Change Processes. Trade Cloth. Elsevier Science &
Technology Books. Saint Louis, MO. 2000. 348p.
ISBN:0-444-50434-6, ISBN13: 978-0-444-50434-0.
Dewey:577.6309575.
Audience: **u,f.**

Moore, Kathleen D.   **QH81.M854 1996**
Riverwalking: Reflections on Moving Water. Trade Paper.
Harcourt Trade Publishers. New York, NY. 1996. 224p. Harvest
Book Ser. ISBN:0-15-600461-5, ISBN13: 978-0-15-600461-9.
Dewey:508. LCCN:96-011364.
Audience: **g,l,u,f.**

Wilson, Sam   **QH76.S58 1996**
The Sierra Club Wetlands Reader: A Literary Companion. Tom
Moritz (Editor). Trade Paper. Sierra Club Books. San Francisco,
CA. 1996. 288p. ISBN:0-87156-425-4, ISBN13:
978-0-87156-425-2. Dewey:333.91/8/0973. LCCN:95-005602.
Audience: **g,l.**

Wohl, Ellen E.   **QH104.W637 2004**
Disconnected Rivers: Linking Rivers to Landscapes. Cloth over
Boards. Yale University Press. Cumberland, RI. 2004. 320p.
ISBN:0-300-10332-8, ISBN13: 978-0-300-10332-8.
Dewey:577.6/4/0973. LCCN:2004-011610.
Audience: **g,l,u,f.** *Choice, 2005.*

Zedler, Joy B.   **QH75**
Handbook for Restoring Tidal Wetlands. CRC Press, Boca
Raton, Fla.. 2001.
Audience: **u,f.**

Natural History > Bioregions and Bioregionalism > Urban Environments

Siebert, Charles   **QH81.S59 1998**
Wickerby: An Urban Pastoral. Trade Cloth. Crown Publishing
Group. New York, NY. 1998. 216p. ISBN:0-609-60237-3,
ISBN13: 978-0-609-60237-9. Dewey:508. LCCN:97-024546.
Audience: **g,l.**

Astrobiology and Exobiology

Adams, Fred   **QH325.A278 2002**
Origins of Existence: How Life Emerged in the Universe. Trade
Cloth. Simon & Schuster. New York, NY. 2002. 272p.
ISBN:0-7432-1262-2, ISBN13: 978-0-7432-1262-5.
Dewey:576.8/3. LCCN:2002-073877.
Audience: **u,f.**

Bennett, Jeffrey O., et al.   **QH327 .B45**
Life in the Universe. Ed. 2. Seth Shostak & Bruce Jakosky
(Authors). Trade Paper. Addison-Wesley Longman, Inc. Boston,
MA. 2006. 450p. ISBN:0-8053-4753-4, ISBN13:
978-0-8053-4753-1. Dewey:576.8/39. LCCN:2006-025657.
Audience: **g,l,u.**

Chela Flores, Julian   **QH327.C54 2001**
The New Science of Astrobiology: From Genesis of the Living
Cell to Evolution of Intelligent Behavior in the Universe. Trade
Cloth. Springer. New York, NY. 2001. 288p. Cellular Origin and
Life in Extreme Habitats and Astrobiology Ser., Vol. 5
ISBN:0-7923-7125-9, ISBN13: 978-0-7923-7125-0.
Dewey:576.8/39. LCCN:2001-038285.
Audience: **u,f.** *Choice, 2002.*

Clancy, Paul, et al.   **QH325**
Looking for Life, Searching the Solar System. André Brack &
Gerda Horneck (Authors). Cloth Text. Cambridge University
Press. New York, NY. 2005. 364p. ISBN:0-521-82450-8,
ISBN13: 978-0-521-82450-7. Dewey:576.839.
LCCN:2006-271630.
Audience: **u,f.**

Conway Morris, Simon   **QH360.5.C66 2004**
Life's Solution: Inevitable Humans in a Lonely Universe. Trade
Paper. Cambridge University Press. New York, NY. 2004. 486p.
ISBN:0-521-60325-0, ISBN13: 978-0-521-60325-6.
Dewey:576.8/01.
Audience: **u,f.** *Choice, 2004.*

Darling, David   **QH327.D37 2001**
Life Everywhere: The New Science of Astrobiology. Trade
Cloth. Basic Books. New York, NY. 2001. 224p.
ISBN:0-465-01563-8, ISBN13: 978-0-465-01563-4.
Dewey:576.8/39. LCCN:2001-025147.
Audience: **u,f.** *Choice, 2001.*

Davies, Paul
The Fifth Miracle: The Search for the Origin and Meaning of
Life. Trade Paper. Simon & Schuster. New York, NY. 2000.
304p. ISBN:0-684-86309-X, ISBN13: 978-0-684-86309-2.
Dewey:576.8/3. LCCN:98-033421.
Audience: **u,f.** *Choice, 1999.*

Dick, Steven J. & Strick,   **QH325.D53 2004**
James E.
The Living Universe: NASA and the Development of
Astrobiology. Trade Paper. Rutgers University Press. Piscataway,
NJ. 2005. 328p. ISBN:0-8135-3733-9, ISBN13:
978-0-8135-3733-7. Dewey:576.8/39. LCCN:2004-004037.
Audience: **u,f.** *Choice, 2005.*

Ehrenfreund, Pascale   **QH325.A77 2004**
(Editor), et al.
Astrobiology: Future Perspectives. Luann Becker, Jen Blank &
J. R. Brucato (Editors). Trade Cloth. Springer. New York, NY.

2004. XVI, 518p. Astrophysics and Space Science Library, Vol. 305 ISBN:1-4020-2304-9, ISBN13: 978-1-4020-2304-0. Dewey:576.8/39. LCCN:2004-301893.

Audience: **u,f.**

Gardner, James N.   QH366.2.G38 2003
Biocosm: The New Scientific Theory of Evolution: Intelligent Life Is the Architect of the Universe. Trade Paper, Pictures or Photographs. Inner Ocean Publishing/Innisfree Press. Makawao, HI. 2003. 344p. ISBN:1-930722-22-2, ISBN13: 978-1-930722-22-4. Dewey:576.8/3. LCCN:2004-300254.

Audience: **u,f.** *Choice, 2004.*

Grossinger, Richard   QH341.G76 2003
Embryos, Galaxies, and Sentient Beings: How the Universe Makes Life. Harold B. Dowse (Preface by), John E. Upledger (Foreword by). Trade Paper, Pictures or Photographs. North Atlantic Books. Berkeley, CA. 2003. 400p. ISBN:1-55643-419-7, ISBN13: 978-1-55643-419-8. Dewey:576.8/3. LCCN:2003-008751.

Audience: **u,f.**

Horneck, G. & Baumstark-Khan, C.   QH325.A78 2001
Astrobiology: The Quest for the Conditions of Life. Trade Cloth. Springer. New York, NY. 2003. XV, 411p. Physics and Astronomy Online Library ISBN:3-540-42101-7, ISBN13: 978-3-540-42101-6. Dewey:576.8/3. LCCN:2001-049849.

Audience: **l,u.**

Joseph, Rhawn   Q175
Astrobiology, the Origin of Life, and the Death of Darwinism: Evolutionary Metamorphosis. Ed. 2. Trade Paper. UniversityPress.Info. San Jose, CA. 2001. 370p. ISBN:0-9700733-8-0, ISBN13: 978-0-9700733-8-9. Dewey:501.

Audience: **l,u.**

Lunine, Jonathan I.   QH325.L86 2004
Astrobiology: Multi Disciplinary Approach. Trade Paper. Addison-Wesley Longman, Inc. Boston, MA. 2004. 450p. ISBN:0-8053-8042-6, ISBN13: 978-0-8053-8042-2. Dewey:576.8/3. LCCN:2004-053408.

Audience: **g,l,u,f.**

Lurquin, Paul F.   QH325.L87 2003
The Origins of Life and the Universe. Trade Cloth. Columbia University Press. New York, NY. 2003. 248p. ISBN:0-231-12654-9, ISBN13: 978-0-231-12654-0. Dewey:576.8/3. LCCN:2002-035166.

Audience: **l,u,f.** *Choice, 2003.*

Owen, Tobias (Editor), et al.   QH325.C76 2003
Life in the Universe: From the Miller Experiment to the Search for Life on Other Worlds. Francois Raulin, Joseph Seckbach & Julian Chela-Flores (Editors). Saddle Stitched, Cloth over Boards. Springer. New York, NY. 2004. 387p. Cellular Origins, Life in Extreme Habitats and Astrobiology Ser., Vol. 7 ISBN:1-4020-2371-5, ISBN13: 978-1-4020-2371-2. Dewey:576.8/3. LCCN:2004-051581.

Audience: **l,u.**

Planel, Hubert   QH327.P5213 2004
Space and Life. Paper over Boards. Taylor & Francis Group. Philadelphia, PA. 2004. 192p. ISBN:0-415-31759-2, ISBN13: 978-0-415-31759-7. Dewey:571/.0919. LCCN:2003-065508.

Audience: **l,u.**

Popa, Radu   QH325.P67 2004
Between Necessity and Probability: Searching for the Definition and Origin of Life. Trade Cloth. Springer. New York, NY. 2004. XIV, 258p. Advances in Astrobiology and Biogeophysics Ser. ISBN:3-540-20490-3, ISBN13: 978-3-540-20490-9. Dewey:576.8/3. LCCN:2003-067260.

Audience: **u,f.**

Schulze-Makuch, Dirk & Irwin, Louis N.   QH341.S339 2004
Life in the Universe: Expectations and Constraints. Trade Cloth. Springer. New York, NY. 2004. XIV, 172p. Advances in Astrobiology and Biogeophysics Ser. ISBN:3-540-20627-2, ISBN13: 978-3-540-20627-9. Dewey:576.8/39. LCCN:2004-041072.

Audience: **l,u,f.** *Choice, 2005.*

Seckbach, Joseph & Rubin, Eitan (Editors)   QH324.2 .N49 2004
The New Avenues in Bioinformat. Trade Cloth. Springer. New York, NY. 2005. XXVI, 281p. Cellular Origin, Life in Extreme Habitats and Astrobiology Ser. ISBN:1-4020-2639-0, ISBN13: 978-1-4020-2639-3. Dewey:572.86330285.

Audience: **u,f.**

Simon, Anne   QH308.2
The Real Science Behind the X-Files: Microbes, Meteorites, and Mutants. Trade Paper. Simon & Schuster. New York, NY. 2001. 320p. ISBN:0-684-85618-2, ISBN13: 978-0-684-85618-6. Dewey:570.

Audience: **g,l.**

Ssb   QH327.A865 2005
The Astrophysical Context of Life. Trade Paper. National Academies Press. Washington, DC. 2005. xiv, 79p. ISBN:0-309-09627-8, ISBN13: 978-0-309-09627-0. Dewey:576.8/39072073. LCCN:2005-284601.

Audience: **u,f.**

Trotman, Clive   QH325
The Feathered Onion: Creation of Life in the Universe. Trade Paper. John Wiley & Sons, Inc. Hoboken, NJ. 2004. 272p. ISBN:0-470-87187-3, ISBN13: 978-0-470-87187-4. Dewey:576.8/3. LCCN:2004-302788.

Audience: **g,l.**

Ulmschneider, Peter   QH325.U46 2002
Intelligent Life in the Universe: Principles and Requirements Behind Its Emergence. Trade Cloth. Springer. New York, NY. 2004. X, 251p. Advances in Astrobiology and Biogeophysics Ser. ISBN:3-540-43988-9, ISBN13: 978-3-540-43988-2. Dewey:576.8/3. LCCN:2002-035967.

Audience: **u,f.** *Choice, 2003.*

Wickramasinghe, Chandra   QH325.W53 2001
Cosmic Dragons: Life and Death on Our Planet. Cloth over Boards. Souvenir Press Ltd. London, 2003. 192p. ISBN:0-285-63606-5, ISBN13: 978-0-285-63606-4. Dewey:576.8/8. LCCN:2002-318404.

Audience: **g,l.** *Choice, 2003.*

Zubay, Geoffrey L.   QH325.Z83 2000
Origins of Life: On Earth and in the Cosmos. Ed. 2. Paper Text. Elsevier Science & Technology Books. Saint Louis, MO. 2000. 564p. Origins of Life Ser., Vol. 2 ISBN:0-12-781910-X, ISBN13: 978-0-12-781910-5. Dewey:576.8/3. LCCN:99-064634.

Audience: **l,u,f.**

Biology Education

☐ Google Directory: Biology Education.
http://www.google.com/Top/Science/Biology/Education/
Google.

Audience: **g,l.**

☐ Google Directory: Biology Humor.
http://www.google.com/Top/Recreation/Humor/Science/Biology/
Google.

Audience: **g,l.**

☐ Google Directory: Biotechnology and Pharmaceuticals
Employment.
http://www.google.com/Top/Business/
Biotechnology_and_Pharmaceuticals/Employment/
Google.

Audience: **g,l.**

☐ Internet4Classrooms Gateway - Biology.
http://internet4classrooms.com/gateway_biology.htm
Internet4Classrooms.

Audience: **g,l,u,f.**

TK5105.5

☐ The WWW Virtual Library: Science Fairs.
http://physics.usc.edu/ScienceFairs/
USC.

Audience: **g,l.**

Alters, Brian J.   **QH362.A628 2005**
Teaching Evolution in Higher Education: Methodological,
Religious, and Nonreligious Issues. Trade Paper. Jones &
Bartlett Publishers, Inc. Sudbury, MA. 2004. 136p.
ISBN:0-7637-2889-6, ISBN13: 978-0-7637-2889-2.
Dewey:576.8/071/1. LCCN:2004-054945.

Audience: **l,u,f.**

Alters, Brian J. & Alters,   **QH362.A62 2001**
  Sandra M.
Defending Evolution in the Classroom: A Guide to the
Creation/Evolution Controversy. Trade Cloth. Jones & Bartlett
Publishers, Inc. Sudbury, MA. 2001. 272p. Evolution Ser.
ISBN:0-7637-1923-4, ISBN13: 978-0-7637-1923-4.
Dewey:576.8/071. LCCN:2001-029193.

Audience: **l,u,f.**

Appel, Toby A.   **QH319.A1A66 2000**
Shaping Biology: The National Science Foundation and
American Biological Research, 1945-1975. Trade Cloth. Johns
Hopkins University Press. Baltimore, MD. 2000. 408p.
ISBN:0-8018-6321-X, ISBN13: 978-0-8018-6321-9.
LCCN:99-089620.

Audience: **u,f.**

Arco Staff   **QH316**
Master AP Biology. Ed. 17. Trade Paper. Peterson's.
Lawrenceville, NJ. 2003. 320p. Master the AP Ser.
ISBN:0-7689-0988-0, ISBN13: 978-0-7689-0988-3.
Dewey:570.76.

Audience: **l.**

Astor, Bart   **HF5381**
What Can You Do with a Major in Biology: Real People. Real
Jobs. Real Rewards. Trade Paper. John Wiley & Sons, Inc.
Hoboken, NJ. 2005. 144p. What Can You Do with a Major In...
Ser. ISBN:0-7645-7606-2, ISBN13: 978-0-7645-7606-5.
Dewey:570/.23. LCCN:2005-277450.

Audience: **l,u.**

Beals, Kevin, et al.   **QH362.B43 2002**
Life Through Time: Evolutionary Activities for Grades 5-8.
Nicole Parizeau, Rick MacPherson & Lincoln Bergman
(Authors), Lisa Baker (Illustrator), Lisa Klofkorn (Illustrator,
Photographer). Trade Paper. University of California, Berkeley,
Lawrence Hall of Science. Berkeley, CA. 2003. 358p. Great
Explorations in Math and Science Ser. ISBN:0-924886-67-6,
ISBN13: 978-0-924886-67-6. Dewey:372.3/5.
LCCN:2002-151772.

Audience: **l.**

Beynon, R. J.   **QH323.5**
Postgraduate Studies in the Biological Sciences: A Researcher's
Companion. Trade Paper. Portland Press, Ltd. London, 1993.
150p. ISBN:1-85578-009-7, ISBN13: 978-1-85578-009-5.
Dewey:574.072.

Audience: **u,f.**

Bowden, Valmai   **QH314.B69 2000**
Managing to Make a Difference: Making an Impact on the
Careers of Men and Women Scientists. Trade Cloth. Ashgate
Publishing, Ltd. Aldershot, 2000. 398p. ISBN:1-84014-859-4,
ISBN13: 978-1-84014-859-6. Dewey:570/.23/41.
LCCN:00-132801.

Audience: **l,u.**

Bybee, Rodger W. (Editor)   **QH362.E853 2003**
Evolution in Perspective: The Science Teacher's Compendium.
Perfect. National Science Teachers Association. Arlington, VA.
2003. xxii, 99p. ISBN:0-87355-234-2, ISBN13:
978-0-87355-234-9. Dewey:576.8. LCCN:2003-021609.

Audience: **l,u,f.**

Callihan, Laurie Ann   **QH316**
  (Author, Editor)
The Best Test Preparation for the CLEP Biology. Trade Paper.
Research & Education Association. Piscataway, NJ. 2004. 280p.
Test Prep Ser. ISBN:0-87891-269-X, ISBN13:
978-0-87891-269-8. Dewey:570/.76.

Audience: **l,u.**

Dashefsky, H. Steven   **QL468.5.D36 1994**
Entomology: High-School Science Fair Experiments. Cloth Text.
McGraw-Hill School Education Group. Columbus, OH. 1993.
ISBN:0-07-015661-1, ISBN13: 978-0-07-015661-6.
Dewey:595.7/0078. LCCN:93-039693.

Audience: **g,l,u,f.**

Dashefsky, H. Steven
Zoology: Forty-Nine Science Fair Projects. Library Binding.
Sagebrush Education Resources. Caledonia, MN. 1994.
ISBN:0-613-71545-4, ISBN13: 978-0-613-71545-4.
Dewey:591/.078.

Audience: **g,l,u,f.**

Dashefsky, H. Steven   **QL52.6.D375 1995**
Zoology: High-School Science Fair Experiments. Trade Cloth.
McGraw-Hill School Education Group. Columbus, OH. 1994.

160p. ISBN:0-07-015686-7, ISBN13: 978-0-07-015686-9. Dewey:591/.076. LCCN:94-029631.

Audience: **g,l,u,f.**

Duensing, Edward   **QH81.D835 1997**
Talking to Fireflies, Shrinking the Moon: Nature Activities for All Ages. Trade Paper. Fulcrum Publishing. Golden, CO. 1997. 144p. ISBN:1-55591-310-5, ISBN13: 978-1-55591-310-6. Dewey:508. LCCN:96-048840.

Audience: **g,l.**

Duensing, Edward   **QH81.D835 1990**
Talking to Fireflies, Shrinking the Moon: A Parent's Guide to Nature Activities. Trade Paper. Penguin Group (USA) Inc. New York, NY. 1990. 192p. ISBN:0-452-26511-8, ISBN13: 978-0-452-26511-0. Dewey:508. LCCN:90-034703.

Audience: **g,l.**

Dyer, Gloria, et al.   **QH308.2**
SAT II Success Biology E/M. Ed. 3. Gordon Chenery & Tracy Halward (Authors). Trade Paper. Peterson's. Lawrenceville, NJ. 2002. 329p. SAT II Success Ser. ISBN:0-7689-0907-4, ISBN13: 978-0-7689-0907-4. Dewey:570.

Audience: **l.**

Fisher, Kathleen M., et al.   **QH315**
Mapping Biology Knowledge. James H. Wandersee & David E. Moody (Authors). Trade Cloth. Springer. New York, NY. 2000. 224p. Science and Technology Education Library ISBN:0-7923-6575-5, ISBN13: 978-0-7923-6575-4. Dewey:570.71. LCCN:2001-057425.

Audience: **u,f.**

Fleming, Michael F.   **QH315.F59 2002**
Biology Teacher's Survival Guide: Tips, Techniques and Materials for Success in the Classroom. Trade Paper. John Wiley & Sons, Inc. Hoboken, NJ. 2002. 304p. ISBN:0-13-045051-0, ISBN13: 978-0-13-045051-7. Dewey:570/.71/2. LCCN:2002-282821.

Audience: **u,f.**

Garber, Steven D.   **QH316.G37 2002**
Biology: A Self-Teaching Guide. Ed. 2. Trade Paper. John Wiley & Sons, Inc. Hoboken, NJ. 2002. 368p. Self-Teaching Guides, Vol. 161 ISBN:0-471-22330-1, ISBN13: 978-0-471-22330-6. Dewey:570. LCCN:2002-513136.

Audience: **l,u.**

Gier, Paul, et al.   **QH316**
Biology 2007. Mark Metz & Linda Brooke Stabler (Authors), Kaplan Staff (Editor). Trade Paper. Simon & Schuster, Inc. New York, NY. 2006. 408p. ISBN:1-4195-5053-5, ISBN13: 978-1-4195-5053-9. Dewey:570/.76.

Audience: **l.**

Goldberg, Deborah T.   **QH316.G57 2006**
Barron's How to Prepare for the AP Biology Exam. Trade Cloth. Barron's Educational Series, Inc. Hauppauge, NY. 2006. 487p. ISBN:0-7641-8308-7, ISBN13: 978-0-7641-8308-9. Dewey:570/.76. LCCN:2005-051211.

Audience: **l,u.**

Hatano, Giyoo & Inagaki,   **QH315.I55 2002**
  Kayoko
Young Children's Thinking about Biological World. Paper over Boards. Taylor & Francis Group. Abingdon, 2002. 224p. Essays

in Developmental Psychology Ser. ISBN:1-84169-041-4, ISBN13: 978-1-84169-041-4. Dewey:372.3/57. LCCN:2002-017789.

Audience: **g,l.**

HumanGenome Project (ed.)   **QH447**
☐ The Human Genome Project: Exploring our Molecular Selves. http://www.genome.gov/Pages/EducationKit/online.htm National Human Genome Research Institute (NHGRI).

Audience: **u,f.**

Janovy, John Jr.   **QH314.J36 2004**
On Becoming a Biologist. Ed. 2. Trade Cloth. University of Nebraska Press. Lincoln, NE. 2005. 176p. ISBN:0-8032-7620-6, ISBN13: 978-0-8032-7620-8. Dewey:570/.23. LCCN:2004-010902.

Audience: **g,l,u.** *Choice, 1986.*

Kaplan   **QH316**
Kaplan AP Biology 2006. Trade Paper. Kaplan Books. New York, NY. 2006. 408p. ISBN:0-7432-6560-2, ISBN13: 978-0-7432-6560-7. Dewey:570.76.

Audience: **g,l.**

King, Rita M.   **QH309.K54 2003**
Biology Made Simple. Trade Paper. Broadway Books. New York, NY. 2003. 208p. ISBN:0-7679-1542-9, ISBN13: 978-0-7679-1542-7. Dewey:570. LCCN:2003-041908.

Audience: **g,l.**

Knisely, Karen   **QH304.K59 2004**
A Student Handbook for Writing in Biology. Ed. 2. Trade Paper. W. H. Freeman & Company. New York, NY. 2004. 224p. ISBN:0-7167-6709-0, ISBN13: 978-0-7167-6709-1. Dewey:808/.06657. LCCN:2004-025038.

Audience: **l,u.**

Layman, Dale P.   **QH309.L38 2003**
Biology Demystified. Paper Text. McGraw-Hill Professional Publishing. New York, NY. 2003. 401p. ISBN:0-07-141040-6, ISBN13: 978-0-07-141040-3. Dewey:570. LCCN:2003-052659.

Audience: **l,u,f.**

McGraw-Hill Staff   **QH315**
Biology: The Dynamics of Life Student Edition) 2004. Trade Cloth. Glencoe/McGraw-Hill. Columbus, OH. 2004. ISBN:0-07-829900-4, ISBN13: 978-0-07-829900-1. Dewey:574.

Audience: **u.**

McMillan, Victoria E.   **QH304**
Writing Papers in the Biological Sciences. Ed. 4. Spiral. Bedford/Saint Martin's. New York, NY. 2006. 288p. ISBN:0-312-44083-9, ISBN13: 978-0-312-44083-1. Dewey:808/.066/57.

Audience: **l,u.**

Minkoff, Eli C. & Baker,   **QH315.M63 2004**
  Pamela J.
Biology Today: An Issues Approach. Ed. 3. UK-B Format Paperback. Taylor & Francis Group. Philadelphia, PA. 2003. 768p. ISBN:0-8153-4157-1, ISBN13: 978-0-8153-4157-4. Dewey:570. LCCN:2003-011485.

Audience: **l,u.**

Mortenson, Philip B. QH83.M69 2003
This Is Not a Weasel: A Close Look at Nature's Most Confusing Terms. Trade Paper. John Wiley & Sons, Inc. Hoboken, NJ. 2003. 272p. ISBN:0-471-27396-1, ISBN13: 978-0-471-27396-7. Dewey:570/.1/4. LCCN:2003-005318.

Audience: **g,l,u,f.** *Choice, 2004.*

National Academy of QH362.T435 1998
Sciences Staff & Vedral, Joyce L.
Teaching about Evolution and the Nature of Science. Trade Paper. National Academies Press. Washington, DC. 1998. 150p. ISBN:0-309-06364-7, ISBN13: 978-0-309-06364-7. Dewey:576.8/071. LCCN:98-016100.

Audience: **u,f.**

National Research Council QH319.A1
Staff
Fulfilling the Promise: Biology Education in the Nation's Schools. Paper Text. National Academies Press. Washington, DC. 1990. 168p. ISBN:0-309-05147-9, ISBN13: 978-0-309-05147-7. Dewey:574/.071/0973.

Audience: **g,l,u,f.** *Choice, 1991.*

National Research Council, QH319.A1B56 2002
Committee on Undergraduate Biology Education to Prepare Research Scientists for the 21st Century (Contribution by)
Bio2010: Transforming Undergraduate Education for Future Research Biologists. Trade Paper. National Academies Press. Washington, DC. 2002. xv, 191p. ISBN:0-309-08535-7, ISBN13: 978-0-309-08535-9. Dewey:570/.71/173. LCCN:2002-152267.

Audience: **u,f.**

Pack, Phillip E. QH316.P34 2001
Biology. Ed. 2. Trade Paper. John Wiley & Sons, Inc. Hoboken, NJ. 2001. 416p. CliffsAP Ser. ISBN:0-7645-8682-3, ISBN13: 978-0-7645-8682-8. Dewey:570.76. LCCN:00-112069.

Audience: **l,u.**

Pechenik, Jan A. QH304.P43 2007
A Short Guide to Writing about Biology. Ed. 6. Trade Paper. Longman Publishing. Boston, MA. 2006. 256p. ISBN:0-321-38592-6, ISBN13: 978-0-321-38592-5. Dewey:808/.06657. LCCN:2006-044759.

Audience: **g,l,u,f.**

Peterson's Guides Staff QH316
AP Success - Biology. Ed. 5. Trade Paper. Peterson's. Lawrenceville, NJ. 2003. ISBN:0-7689-1260-1, ISBN13: 978-0-7689-1260-9. Dewey:570/.76.

Audience: **l,u.**

Princeton Review Staff QH316
Cracking the AP Biology Exam, 2006-2007 Edition. Trade Paper. Random House Information Group. New York, NY. 2006. 352p. ISBN:0-375-76525-5, ISBN13: 978-0-375-76525-4. Dewey:570.76.

Audience: **l.**

Princeton Review Staff QH316
Cracking the GRE Biology Test. Ed. 5. Trade Paper. Random House Information Group. New York, NY. 2005. 352p. ISBN:0-375-76488-7, ISBN13: 978-0-375-76488-2. Dewey:570/.76.

Audience: **u.**

Princeton Review Staff & QH316
Wright, Judene
Cracking the SAT II Biology E/M Subject Test: 2005-2006. Trade Paper. Random House Information Group. New York, NY. 2005. 384p. ISBN:0-375-76447-X, ISBN13: 978-0-375-76447-9. Dewey:570.76.

Audience: **l.**

Shields, Martin QH315
Biology Inquiries: Standards-Based Labs, Assessments, and Discussion Lessons; Grades 7-12. Trade Paper, Perfect. John Wiley & Sons, Inc. Hoboken, NJ. 2005. 296p. ISBN:0-7879-7652-0, ISBN13: 978-0-7879-7652-1. Dewey:574.07.

Audience: **l.**

Steen, Lynn Arthur (Editor) QH323.5.M36367 2005
Math and Bio 2010: Linking Undergraduate Disciplines. Trade Paper. Mathematical Association of America. Washington, DC. 2005. Reports ISBN:0-88385-818-5, ISBN13: 978-0-88385-818-9. LCCN:2004-115954.

Audience: **f.**

Tsur, Samuel A. QH83.T77 1999
Elsevier's Dictionary of the Genera of Life: In English (with Definitions). Trade Cloth. Elsevier Science & Technology Books. Saint Louis, MO. 1999. 564p. ISBN:0-444-82905-9, ISBN13: 978-0-444-82905-4. Dewey:570/.3. LCCN:99-017292.

Audience: **l,u,f.** *Choice, 2000.*

Walmsley, Sean A. (Editor) LB1570.C487 1994
Children Exploring Their World: Theme Teaching in Elementary School. Trade Paper. Heinemann. Portsmouth, NH. 1994. 304p. ISBN:0-435-08804-1, ISBN13: 978-0-435-08804-0. Dewey:372.13. LCCN:93-31221.

Audience: **g,l,u.**

Bioethics

Becker, Gerhold K. (Editor) QH322.M67
The Moral Status of Persons: Perspectives on Bioethics. Trade Paper. Rodopi. Kenilworth, NY. 2000. VII, 246p. Value Inquiry Book Ser., Vol. 96 ISBN:90-420-1201-3, ISBN13: 978-90-420-1201-1. Dewey:353.008232.

Audience: **u,f.**

Bryant, John A. (Editor), QH332.B51725 2002
et al.
Bioethics for Scientists. John Searle & Linda Baggott la Velle (Editors). Trade Cloth. John Wiley & Sons, Inc. Hoboken, NJ. 2002. 372p. ISBN:0-471-49532-8, ISBN13: 978-0-471-49532-1. Dewey:174/.957. LCCN:2002-280924.

Audience: **u,f.**

Bryant, John, et al. QH332
Introduction to Bioethics. John Searle & Linda Baggott la Velle (Authors). Trade Cloth. John Wiley & Sons, Inc. Hoboken, NJ. 2005. 250p. ISBN:0-470-02197-7, ISBN13: 978-0-470-02197-2. Dewey:174/.957. LCCN:2005-019920.

Audience: **l,u,f.**

Bulger, Ruth Ellen (Editor), QH332 .E73 2002
et al.
The Ethical Dimensions of the Biological and Health Sciences. Ed. 2. Elizabeth Heitman & Stanley Joel Reiser (Editors). Cloth

Text. Cambridge University Press. New York, NY. 2002. 386p.
ISBN:0-521-81053-1, ISBN13: 978-0-521-81053-1.
Dewey:174/.957. LCCN:2001-043382.

Audience: **u,f.**

Bulger, Ruth E. (Editor),   QH332.E73 1993
  et al.
The Ethical Dimensions of the Biological Sciences. Elizabeth
Heitman & Stanley J. Reiser (Editors). Cloth Text. Cambridge
University Press. New York, NY. 1993. 308p.
ISBN:0-521-43463-7, ISBN13: 978-0-521-43463-8.
Dewey:174.9574. LCCN:92-026258.

Audience: **u,f.**

Cahill, Lisa Sowle   QH332.C344 2004
Bioethics and the Common Good. Trade Cloth. Marquette
University Press. Milwaukee, WI. 2004. 88p. The Pere
Marquette Lecture in Theology Ser., Vol. 2004
ISBN:0-87462-584-X, ISBN13: 978-0-87462-584-4.
Dewey:241/.64957. LCCN:2004-001874.

Audience: **u,f.**

Cameron, Nigel M. de S.   QH332.B515 2000
  (Editor), et al.
BioEngagement: Making a Christian Difference Through
Bioethics Today. Scott E. Daniels & Barbara J. White (Editors).
Trade Paper. William B. Eerdmans Publishing Company. Grand
Rapids, MI. 2000. 278p. Horizons in Bioethics Ser.
ISBN:0-8028-4793-5, ISBN13: 978-0-8028-4793-5.
Dewey:179/.1. LCCN:00-056181.

Audience: **u,f.**

Comstock, Gary (Editor)   QH332.L54 2002
Life Science Ethics. Trade Cloth. Blackwell Publishing
Professional. Ames, IA. 2002. 448p. ISBN:0-8138-2835-X,
ISBN13: 978-0-8138-2835-0. Dewey:174/.957.
LCCN:2002-003327.

Audience: **u,f.** *Choice, 2003.*

Crawford, S. Cromwell   QH332
Hindu Bioethics for the Twenty-First Century. Paper Text. State
University of New York Press. Albany, NY. 2003. 256p. SUNY
Series in Religious Studies ISBN:0-7914-5780-X, ISBN13:
978-0-7914-5780-1. Dewey:174/.957.

Audience: **u,f.** *Choice, 2004.*

Creath, Richard &   QH331 .B475 2000
  Maienschein, Jane (Editors)
Biology and Epistemology. Michael Ruse (Contribution by).
Cloth Text. Cambridge University Press. New York, NY. 1999.
313p. Cambridge Studies in Philosophy and Biology
ISBN:0-521-59290-9, ISBN13: 978-0-521-59290-1.
Dewey:570/.1. LCCN:99-022990.

Audience: **u,f.** *Choice, 2000.*

De Risio, Sergio & Orsucci,   QH332.B5155 2004
  Franco F. (Editors)
Bioethics in Complexity: Foundations and Evolutions. Trade
Cloth. Imperial College Press. London, 2004. 90p.
ISBN:1-86094-399-3, ISBN13: 978-1-86094-399-7.
Dewey:174/.957. LCCN:2006-386500.

Audience: **u,f.**

Demers, Patricia A.   QH332.S3825 2001
Science and Ethics (La Science et I'Ethique), Vol. 11. Trade
Paper. University of Toronto Press. Toronto, ON. 2001. 270p.
ISBN:0-8020-8476-1, ISBN13: 978-0-8020-8476-7.
Dewey:174/.2. LCCN:2002-284182.

Audience: **u,f.**

Donchin, Anne & Purdy,   QH332.E43 1999
  Laura M. (Editors)
Embodying Bioethics: Recent Feminist Advances. Trade Cloth.
Rowman & Littlefield Publishers, Inc. Lanham, MD. 1999.
296p. New Feminist Perspectives Ser. ISBN:0-8476-8924-7,
ISBN13: 978-0-8476-8924-8. Dewey:174/.2. LCCN:98-028146.

Audience: **u,f.** *Choice, 1999.*

Eiseman, Elisa   QH332.E36 2003
The National Bioethics Advisory Commission: Contributing to
Public Policy. Trade Paper. RAND Corporation, The. Santa
Monica, CA. 2004. 200p. ISBN:0-8330-3364-6, ISBN13:
978-0-8330-3364-2. Dewey:174/.957/0973. LCCN:2003-008549.

Audience: **u,f.**

Engelhardt, H. Tristram   QH332.E54 1991
Bioethics and Secular Humanism: The Search for a Common
Morality. Trade Cloth. Bow Historical Books. New Providence,
NJ. 1991. xvii, 206p. ISBN:0-334-02495-1, ISBN13:
978-0-334-02495-8. Dewey:179/.1. LCCN:90-023377.

Audience: **u,f.** *Choice, 1992.*

Espejo, Roman (Editor)   QP277.H85 2002
Human Embryo Experimentation. Trade Cloth. Thomson Gale.
Farmington Hills, MI. 2002. 79p. Opposing Viewpoints Ser.
ISBN:0-7377-1285-6, ISBN13: 978-0-7377-1285-8.
Dewey:174/.28. LCCN:2002-023637.

Audience: **u,f.**

Finegold, David L., et al.   HD9999.B442B542 2005
Bioindustry Ethics. Cecile Bensimon, Abdallah S. Daar,
Margaret Eaton, Beatrice Godard, Bartha Maria Knoppers, Peter
A. Singer & Jocelyn MacKie (Authors). Trade Paper, Perfect.
Elsevier Science & Technology Books. Saint Louis, MO. 2005.
384p. ISBN:0-12-369370-5, ISBN13: 978-0-12-369370-9.
Dewey:174/.96606. LCCN:2005-040638.

Audience: **u,f.**

Fox, Michael W.   QH332.F68 2001
Bringing Life to Ethics: Global Bioethics for a Humane Society.
Bernard E. Rollin (Foreword by). Cloth Text. State University of
New York Press. Albany, NY. 2001. xiii, 251p.
ISBN:0-7914-4801-0, ISBN13: 978-0-7914-4801-4.
Dewey:174/.957. LCCN:00-026522.

Audience: **u,f.** *Choice, 2001.*

Fukuyama, Francis   TP248.23.F85 2002
Our Posthuman Future: Consequences of the Biotechnology
Revolution. Cloth over Boards. Farrar, Straus & Giroux. New
York, NY. 2002. 272p. ISBN:0-374-23643-7, ISBN13:
978-0-374-23643-4. Dewey:303.48/3. LCCN:2002-100914.

Audience: **l,u,f.** *Choice, 2002.*

Galston, Arthur W. &   QH332.E96 2005
  Peppard, Christiana Z. (Editors)
Expanding Horizons in Bioethics. Trade Cloth. Springer. New
York, NY. 2005. XXIV, 256p. ISBN:1-4020-3061-4, ISBN13:
978-1-4020-3061-1. Dewey:174/.957. LCCN:2005-279048.

Audience: **u,f.**

Ganti, Tibor   QH325.G355 2003
Chemoton Theory: Theory of Living Systems. Trade Cloth.
Springer. New York, NY. 2003. 455p. Mathematical and
Computational Chemistry Ser. ISBN:0-306-47785-8, ISBN13:
978-0-306-47785-0. Dewey:576.8/3. LCCN:2003-050647.

Audience: **u,f.**

Hooft, Stan Van   QH332
Life, Death, and Subjectivity: Moral Sources in Bioethics. Trade
Paper. Rodopi. Kenilworth, NY. 2004. 247p. Value Inquiry Book
Ser., 160 ISBN:90-420-1912-3, ISBN13: 978-90-420-1912-6.
Dewey:174.957.

Audience: **l,u.**

Hutchins, Michael (Editor),   SF408.3.E84 1995
  et al.
Ethics on the Ark: Zoos, Animal Welfare, and Wildlife
Conservation. Bryan G. Norton, Terry L. Maple & Elizabeth F.
Stevens (Editors). Trade Cloth. Smithsonian Institution Press.
Washington, DC. 1995. 432p. Zoo and Aquarium Biology and
Conservation Ser. ISBN:1-56098-515-1, ISBN13:
978-1-56098-515-0. Dewey:639.9/3/01. LCCN:94-037139.

Audience: **g,l,u.**   *Choice, 1996.*

Kaczor, Christopher   QH332.K325 2005
The Edge of Life: Human Dignity and Contemporary Bioethics.
Trade Cloth. Springer. New York, NY. 2005. vii, 155p.
Philosophy and Medicine / Catholic Studies in Bioethics Ser.
ISBN:1-4020-3155-6, ISBN13: 978-1-4020-3155-7.
Dewey:179.7. LCCN:2005-296446.

Audience: **l,u,f.**

Kass, Leon R.   QH332.K37 2002
Life, Liberty, and Defense of Dignity: The Challenge for
Bioethics. Trade Cloth. Encounter Books. New York, NY. 2005.
312p. Ser. ISBN:1-893554-55-4, ISBN13: 978-1-893554-55-9.
Dewey:174/.957. LCCN:2002-074225.

Audience: **g,l,u.**   *Choice, 2003.*

Korthals, Michiel & Bogers,   QH331.E712 2004
  Robert J. (Editors)
Ethics for Life Scientists. Trade Cloth. Springer. New York, NY.
2005. IX, 236p. Wageningen Ur Frontis Ser., Vol. 5
ISBN:1-4020-3178-5, ISBN13: 978-1-4020-3178-6.
Dewey:174/.957. LCCN:2005-275578.

Audience: **g,l,u,f.**

Kump, Lee R., et al.   QH331.K798 2004
The Earth System. Ed. 2. James F. Kasting & Robert G. Crane
(Authors). Trade Paper. Prentice Hall PTR. Upper Saddle River,
NJ. 2003. 432p. ISBN:0-13-142059-3, ISBN13:
978-0-13-142059-5. Dewey:577/.1. LCCN:2003-012099.

Audience: **l,u,f.**

Leach, Melissa (Editor),   QH333.S365 2005
  et al.
Science and Citizens: Globalization and the Challenge of
Engagement. Ian Scoones & Brian Wynne (Editors). Cloth over
Boards. Zed Books, Ltd. London, 2005. 256p. Claiming
Citizenship Ser. ISBN:1-84277-550-2, ISBN13:
978-1-84277-550-9. Dewey:306.4/5. LCCN:2004-057236.

Audience: **u,f.**

Levine, Carol   R724
Taking Sides: Clashing Views on Controversial Bioethical
Issues. Ed. 11. Paper Text. McGraw-Hill Higher Education. Burr
Ridge, IL. 2005. 408p. ISBN:0-07-312955-0, ISBN13:
978-0-07-312955-6. Dewey:174.9574.

Audience: **u,f.**

Levinson, Ralph & Reiss,   QH332
  Michael (Editors)
Key Issues in Bioethics: A Guide for Teachers. Paper over
Boards. Routledge. New York, NY. 2003. 200p.
ISBN:0-415-30914-X, ISBN13: 978-0-415-30914-1.
Dewey:174.9/57/071.

Audience: **u,f.**

Lovelock, James   QH313.L68 2000
Gaia: A New Look at Life on Earth. Trade Paper. Oxford
University Press, Inc. New York, NY. 2000. 176p.
ISBN:0-19-286218-9, ISBN13: 978-0-19-286218-1. Dewey:577.
LCCN:2001-266301.

Audience: **l,u,f.**

Mepham, Ben   QH332
Bioethics for the Biosciences: An Introduction. Paper Text.
Oxford University Press, Inc. New York, NY. 2005. 402p.
ISBN:0-19-926715-4, ISBN13: 978-0-19-926715-6.
Dewey:174.957. LCCN:2005-440974.

Audience: **l,u,f.**

Mortensen, Vigo (Editor)   QH332.L52 1995
Life and Death: Moral Implications of Biotechnology. Trade
Paper. World Council of Churches/Conseil Oecumenique des
Eglises. Geneva, 1996. 110p. ISBN:2-8254-1170-1, ISBN13:
978-2-8254-1170-4. Dewey:174/.2. LCCN:96-206033.

Audience: **u,f.**

O'Hear, Anthony (Editor)   QH331.P4677 2005
Philosophy, Biology and Life. Trade Paper. Cambridge
University Press. New York, NY. 2005. 336p. Royal Institute of
Philosophy Supplement Ser., Vol. 56 ISBN:0-521-67845-5,
ISBN13: 978-0-521-67845-2. Dewey:570/.1.
LCCN:2005-053182.

Audience: **g,l,u,f.**

Potter, Van R.   QH332.P68 1988
Global Bioethics: Building on the Leopold Legacy. Trade Paper.
Michigan State University Press. East Lansing, MI. 1988. 203p.
ISBN:0-87013-264-4, ISBN13: 978-0-87013-264-3.
Dewey:179/.1. LCCN:88-042901.

Audience: **u,f.**

Qiu, Renzong   QH332.B5172 2004
Bioethics: Asian Perspectives - A Quest for Moral Diversity.
Trade Cloth. Springer. New York, NY. 2003. 246p. Philosophy
and Medicine Ser., Vol. 80 ISBN:1-4020-1795-2, ISBN13:
978-1-4020-1795-7. Dewey:174/.957/095. LCCN:2003-064113.

Audience: **l,u,f.**

Robertson, George (Editor)   QH81.F88 1996
FutureNatural: Nature, Science, Culture. Paper over Boards.
Routledge. New York, NY. 1996. 328p. Futures, New
Perspectives for Cultural Analysis Ser. ISBN:0-415-07013-9,
ISBN13: 978-0-415-07013-3. Dewey:508. LCCN:95-025912.

Audience: **l,u,f.**   *Choice, 1997.*

Rogers, Arthur & Durand   QH332.R63 1995
  de Bousingen, Denis
Bioethics in Europe. Trade Cloth. Council of Europe.

Strasbourg, 1995. 366p. European Issues Ser.
ISBN:92-871-2566-X, ISBN13: 978-92-871-2566-8.
LCCN:95-209684.

Audience: **l,u,f.**

Rudolph, Frederick B. &   **TP248.2.B574 1996**
  McIntire, Larry V. (Editors)
Biotechnology: Science, Engineering, and Ethical Challenges for
the 21st Century. Trade Cloth. National Academies Press.
Washington, DC. 1996. 296p. ISBN:0-309-05282-3, ISBN13:
978-0-309-05282-5. Dewey:660.6. LCCN:95-044203.

Audience: **g,l,u.** *Choice, 1997.*

Schacter, Bernice   **TP248**
Issues and Dilemmas of Biotechnology: A Reference Guide.
Cloth Text. Greenwood Publishing Group, Inc. Portsmouth, NH.
1999. 224p. ISBN:0-313-30642-7, ISBN13: 978-0-313-30642-6.
Dewey:660.6. LCCN:99-015457.

Audience: **l,u.** *Choice, 2000.*

Scheper-Hughes, Nancy &   **QH332.C653 2002**
  Wacquant, Loic (Editors)
Commodifying Bodies. Trade Paper. SAGE Publications, Inc.
Thousand Oaks, CA. 2003. 200p. Theory, Culture and Society
Ser. ISBN:0-7619-4034-0, ISBN13: 978-0-7619-4034-0.
Dewey:306.4. LCCN:2002-105445.

Audience: **l,u,f.**

Schneider, Stephen Henry   **QH331.S324 2004**
  (Editor), et al.
Scientists Debate Gaia: The Next Century. Penelope J. Boston,
Eileen Crist & James R. Miller (Editors). Trade Cloth. MIT
Press. Cambridge, MA. 2004. 400p. ISBN:0-262-19498-8,
ISBN13: 978-0-262-19498-3. Dewey:577. LCCN:2003-061532.

Audience: **u,f.** *Choice, 2005.*

Sensen, Christoph W.   **QH447**
  (Editor)
Handbook of Genome Research: Genomics, Proteomics,
Metabolomics, Bioinformatics, Ethical and Legal Issues. Trade
Cloth. John Wiley & Sons, Inc. Hoboken, NJ. 2005. 646p.
ISBN:3-527-31348-6, ISBN13: 978-3-527-31348-8.
Dewey:572.86.

Audience: **u,f.** *Choice, 2006.*

Singer, Peter Albert David   **RG135 .E43 1990**
  (Editor), et al.
Embryo Experimentation: Ethical, Legal and Social Issues.
Helga Kuhse, Stephen Buckle, Karen Dawson & Pascal
Kasimba (Editors). Cloth Text. Cambridge University Press.
New York, NY. 1990. 279p. ISBN:0-521-38359-5, ISBN13:
978-0-521-38359-2. Dewey:174.2/8. LCCN:89-025220.

Audience: **u,f.**

Singer, S. Jonathan   **QH331 .S47 2001**
The Splendid Feast of Reason. Trade Cloth. University of
California Press. Berkeley, CA. 2001. 270p.
ISBN:0-520-22425-6, ISBN13: 978-0-520-22425-4.
Dewey:570/.1. LCCN:00-069957.

Audience: **g,l,u,f.** *Choice, 2001.*

Smith, George Patrick   **TP248.2**
The New Biology: Law, Ethics, and Biotechnology. Plenum
Press, New York. 1989. ISBN:0-89885-448-2, ISBN13:
978-0-89885-448-0.

Audience: **g,l,u,f.**

Sober, Elliott   **QH360.5.S63 1999**
Philosophy of Biology. Ed. 2. Trade Paper. Westview Press.
Boulder, CO. 1999. 256p. Dimensions of Philosophy Ser.
ISBN:0-8133-9126-1, ISBN13: 978-0-8133-9126-7.
Dewey:574.01. LCCN:99-049091.

Audience: **u,f.** *Choice, 1994.*

Southwood, Richard &   **QH367**
  Southwood, R.
The Story of Life. Trade Paper. Oxford University Press, Inc.
New York, NY. 2004. 272p. ISBN:0-19-860786-5, ISBN13:
978-0-19-860786-1. Dewey:576.8.

Audience: **g,l.**

Sprinkle, Robert H.   **QH333.S68 1994**
Profession of Conscience: The Making and Meaning of
Life-Sciences Liberalism. Cloth Text. Princeton University
Press. Princeton, NJ. 1994. 272p. ISBN:0-691-03365-X,
ISBN13: 978-0-691-03365-5. Dewey:174/.957.
LCCN:94-009662.

Audience: **l,u,f.** *Choice, 1995.*

Stamos, David N.   **QH83.S75 2003**
The Species Problem: Biological Species, Ontology, and the
Metaphysics of Biology. Trade Cloth. Lexington Books.
Lanham, MD. 2003. 390p. ISBN:0-7391-0503-5, ISBN13:
978-0-7391-0503-0. Dewey:576.8/6. LCCN:2002-155405.

Audience: **l,u,f.**

Stansfield, William D.   **QH309.S78 2000**
Death of a Rat: Understandings and Appreciations of Science.
Trade Cloth. Prometheus Books, Publishers. Amherst, NY. 2000.
360p. ISBN:1-57392-814-3, ISBN13: 978-1-57392-814-4.
Dewey:174/.957. LCCN:00-020932.

Audience: **g,l,u.** *Choice, 2001.*

Steen, Wim J. van der   **QH360**
Evolution As Natural History: A Philosophical Analysis. Trade
Cloth. Greenwood Publishing Group, Inc. Portsmouth, NH.
2000. 200p. Human Evolution, Behavior, and Intelligence Ser.
ISBN:0-275-96870-7, ISBN13: 978-0-275-96870-0.
LCCN:99-052983.

Audience: **l,u,f.**

Takahashi, Takao (Editor)   **QH332**
Taking Life and Death Seriously - Bioethics from Japan. Trade
Cloth. Elsevier Science & Technology Books. Saint Louis, MO.
2005. 333p. Advances in Bioethics Ser. ISBN:0-7623-1206-8,
ISBN13: 978-0-7623-1206-1. Dewey:174.957.

Audience: **u,f.**

Tavani, Herman T.   **QH441.2.T38 2006**
Ethics, Computing, and Genomics. Trade Paper. Jones & Bartlett
Publishers, Inc. Sudbury, MA. 2005. 356p.
ISBN:0-7637-3620-1, ISBN13: 978-0-7637-3620-0.
Dewey:174/.957. LCCN:2005-007396.

Audience: **u,f.**

Taylor, Peter J., et al.   **QH333.C48 1997**
Changing Life: Genomes, Ecologies, Bodies and Commodities.
Saul E. Halforn & Paul N. Edwards (Authors). Book, Other.
University of Minnesota Press. Minneapolis, MN. 1997. 240p.
Cultural Politics Ser. ISBN:0-8166-3012-7, ISBN13:
978-0-8166-3012-7. Dewey:570/.1. LCCN:97-014055.

Audience: **u,f.**

The European Commission   QH332
Modern Biology and Visions of Humanity. Trade Paper. Multi
Science Publishing Company Ltd. Brentwood, 2004. 212p.
ISBN:0-906522-30-7, ISBN13: 978-0-906522-30-1.
Dewey:174.957.

Audience: **l,u,f.**

Thiele, Felix & R.E.   QH332
  Ashcroft, Imperial College of Science (Editors)
Bioethics in a Small World. Trade Cloth. Springer. New York,
NY. 2004. XV, 138p. Wissenschaftsethik und
Technikfolgenbeurteilung Ser. ISBN:3-540-23595-7, ISBN13:
978-3-540-23595-8. Dewey:174.957.

Audience: **l,u,f.**

Tong, Rosemarie, et al.   R724.G596 2001
Globalizing Feminist Bioethics: Crosscultural Perspectives.
Gwen Anderson & Aida Santos-Maranan (Authors). Trade Paper.
Westview Press. Boulder, CO. 2000. 384p. ISBN:0-8133-6615-1,
ISBN13: 978-0-8133-6615-9. Dewey:174.9/57.
LCCN:2001-267722.

Audience: **l,u,f.**

Turney, Jon   QH331.T792 2004
Lovelock and Gaia: Signs of Life. Trade Cloth. Columbia
University Press. New York, NY. 2004. 168p. Revolutions in
Science Ser. ISBN:0-231-13430-4, ISBN13: 978-0-231-13430-9.
Dewey:550. LCCN:2004-049392.

Audience: **g,l.**

UNESCO Staff   QH332
The Ethics of Life. Trade Paper. UNESCO Publishing. Paris,
1998. 238p. Ethics Ser., Vol. 02014565 ISBN:92-3-103422-7,
ISBN13: 978-92-3-103422-0. Dewey:100.

Audience: **g,l,u,f.**

Volk, Tyler   QH331.V714 2003
Gaia's Body: Toward a Physiology of Earth. Trade Paper. MIT
Press. Cambridge, MA. 2003. 291p. ISBN:0-262-72042-6,
ISBN13: 978-0-262-72042-7. Dewey:577/.01.
LCCN:2003-041343.

Audience: **l,u,f.** *Choice, 1998.*

Walter, Jennifer & Klein,   QH332.S77 2003
  Eran (Editors)
The Story of Bioethics: From Seminal Works to Contemporary
Explorations. Book, Other. Georgetown University Press.
Washington, DC. 2003. 264p. ISBN:0-87840-138-5, ISBN13:
978-0-87840-138-3. Dewey:174/.957. LCCN:2003-004678.

Audience: **g,l,u,f.**

Wasserman, Gerhard   QH360.5.W38 1996
  (Editor)
Keys to Life: Philosophy and New Mechanism of Evolution and
Development. Trade Cloth. Ashgate Publishing, Ltd. Aldershot,
1996. 256p. Avebury Series in Philosophy ISBN:1-85972-142-7,
ISBN13: 978-1-85972-142-1. Dewey:576.8/01.
LCCN:95-083600.

Audience: **l,u,f.**

Waterman, Laura &   QH76.W38 1993
  Waterman, Guy
Wilderness Ethics: Preserving the Spirit of Wildness. Ed. 2.
Roderick Nash (Foreword by). Trade Paper. Countryman Press.
Woodstock, VT. 1993. 240p. ISBN:0-88150-256-1, ISBN13:
978-0-88150-256-5. Dewey:333.78/2. LCCN:93-018436.

Audience: **g,l,u,f.**

Biology Careers

Brazaitis, Peter   QL77.5.B72 2003
You Belong in a Zoo!: Tales from a Lifetime Spent with Cobras,
Crocs, and Other Creatures. Trade Cloth. Random House Adult
Trade Publishing Group. New York, NY. 2003. 368p.
ISBN:1-4000-6012-5, ISBN13: 978-1-4000-6012-2.
Dewey:636.088/9/092 B. LCCN:2003-047997.

Audience: **g,l,f.**

Brown, Sheldon S.   TP248.215.B766 2001
Biotechnology Careers. Trade Cloth.
McGraw-Hill/Contemporary. Lincolnwood, IL. 2000. 160p.
Opportunities in... Ser. ISBN:0-658-00479-4, ISBN13:
978-0-658-00479-7. Dewey:660.6/023. LCCN:00-043261.

Audience: **g,l,f.**

Camenson, Blythe   QH314.C35 2003
Great Jobs for Biology Majors. Ed. 2. Trade Paper.
McGraw-Hill Companies, The. New York, NY. 2003. 240p.
ISBN:0-07-140898-3, ISBN13: 978-0-07-140898-1.
Dewey:570/.23. LCCN:2003-050180.

Audience: **g,l,u,f.**

Camenson, Blythe   SB469.384.C35 1998
Opportunities in Landscape Architecture, Botanical Gardens, and
Arboreta Careers. Trade Cloth. McGraw-Hill Companies, The.
New York, NY. 1998. 160p. Opportunities in... Ser.
ISBN:0-8442-6483-0, ISBN13: 978-0-8442-6483-7.
Dewey:712/.023/73. LCCN:98-018216.

Audience: **g,l,f.**

Camenson, Blythe   QL76.C35 1998
Opportunities in Zoo Careers. Trade Paper. McGraw-Hill Trade.
New York, NY. 2003. 202p. Opportunities in... Ser.
ISBN:0-8442-2313-1, ISBN13: 978-0-8442-2313-1.
Dewey:590/.7/3023. LCCN:97-021798.

Audience: **g,l,f.**

Fanning, Odom   GE60.F36 2002
Opportunities in Environmental Careers. Ed. 2. Trade Cloth.
McGraw-Hill Trade. New York, NY. 2003. 160p. Opportunities
in... Ser. ISBN:0-07-138723-4, ISBN13: 978-0-07-138723-1.
Dewey:363.7/0023/73. LCCN:2001-052607.

Audience: **g,l,f.**

Fasulo, Michael, et al.   GE60.F365 2001
Careers for Environmental Types and Others Who Respect the
Earth. Ed. 2. Jane Kinney & Mike Fasulo (Authors). Trade
Paper. McGraw-Hill Companies, The. New York, NY. 2001.
192p. VGM Careers for You Ser. ISBN:0-658-01649-0, ISBN13:
978-0-658-01649-3. Dewey:363.7/0023. LCCN:2001-026433.

Audience: **g,l,f.**

Gimble, Jeffrey   HD9999.B443U6385
Academia to Biotechnology: Career Changes at any Stage.
Paper Text. Elsevier Science & Technology Books. Saint Louis,
MO. 2004. 186p. ISBN:0-12-284151-4, ISBN13:
978-0-12-284151-4. Dewey:338.4/76606. LCCN:2005-271919.

Audience: **g,l,u,f.**

Institute for Career   HF5381.A1
  Research
A Career as An Environmental Engineer: Using Technology to
Help Save the Planet. Institute for Career Research, Chicago,

Ill.. 2003. Institute research ;; no. 313; Variation: Careers ;; no. 313 ISBN:1-58511-313-1, ISBN13: 978-1-58511-313-2.

Audience: **g,l,f.**

Institute for Career HF5381.A1
  Research
Careers in Bioinformatics: Fusing High-Powered Computing and Biology to Revolutionize Healthcare. Institute for Career Research, Chicago, Ill.. 2005. Institute research ;; no. 417; Variation: Careers ;; no. 415 ISBN:1-58511-417-0, ISBN13: 978-1-58511-417-7.

Audience: **g,l,f.**

Institute for Career HF5381.A1
  Research
Careers in Genetics Research: Cell Biology. Institute for Career Research, Chicago, Ill.. 2002. Institute research ;; no. 300; Variation: Careers ;; no. 300 ISBN:1-58511-300-X, ISBN13: 978-1-58511-300-2.

Audience: **g,l,f.**

Institute for Career RC963
  Research
Careers in Industrial Hygiene: Occupational and Environmental Health and Safety. Institute for Career Research, Chicago, Ill.. 2005. Institute research ;; no. 250; Variation: Careers ;; no. 250 ISBN:1-58511-250-X, ISBN13: 978-1-58511-250-0.

Audience: **g,l,f.**

Institute for Research HF5381.A1
  (Chicago, Ill.)
Career as A Biochemist: Cutting Edge Scientific Research, Practical Applications in Industry, New Specialties: Biotechnology and Bioengineering, Many Yop Professional Positions in Medicine, Pharmaceuticals, Nutrition. Institute for Research, Chicago. 1999. Institute research; no. 156; Variation: Careers research monographs ;; no. 156 ISBN:1-58511-156-2, ISBN13: 978-1-58511-156-5.

Audience: **g,l,u,f.**

Institute for Research HF5381.A1
  (Chicago, Ill.)
Career as a biochemist: cutting edge scientific research, practical applications in industry, new specialties: biotechnology and bioengineering, many top professional positions in medicine, pharmaceuticals, nutrition. Institute for Research (Chicago, Ill.). 1999. Institute research ;; no. 156; Variation: Careers research monographs ;; no. 156 ISBN:1-58511-156-2, ISBN13: 978-1-58511-156-5.

Audience: **g,l,f.**

Institute for Research HF5381.A1
  (Chicago, Ill.)
Careers in Biotechnology, Bolecular Biology: Genetic Engineering-- Gene Therapy. Institute for Research, Chicago. 2000. Research; no. 3; Variation: Careers; no. 3 ISBN:1-58511-003-5, ISBN13: 978-1-58511-003-2.

Audience: **g,l,u,f.**

Institute for Research HF5381.A1
  (Chicago, Ill.)
Careers in biotechnology, molecular biology: genetic engineering-- gene therapy. Chicago : Institute for Research. 2000. Research ;; no. 3; Variation: Careers ;; no. 3 ISBN:1-58511-003-5, ISBN13: 978-1-58511-003-2.

Audience: **g,l,f.**

Louise, Chandra B. QH314 .L68 1998
Jump Start Your Career in Bio Science. Trade Paper. Peer Productions. Durham, NC. 1998. 220p. ISBN:0-9661790-0-5, ISBN13: 978-0-9661790-0-2. Dewey:570/.23. LCCN:97-075974.

Audience: **g,l,f.**

Moussalli, Carole TP248.22.M68 2004
Vault Career Guide to Biotech. Trade Paper. Vault.com. New York, NY. 2004. 128p. ISBN:1-58131-268-7, ISBN13: 978-1-58131-268-3. Dewey:660.6/023. LCCN:2004-009491.

Audience: **g,l,f.**

Pavia, Audrey SF80.P29 2001
Careers with Animals. Trade Paper. Barron's Educational Series, Inc. Hauppauge, NY. 2001. 176p. Success Without College Ser. ISBN:0-7641-1621-5, ISBN13: 978-0-7641-1621-6. Dewey:636/.023. LCCN:00-051884.

Audience: **g.**

Robinson, Phillip T. QL76.R64 2004
Life at the Zoo: Behind the Scenes with the Animal Doctors. Trade Cloth. Edinburgh University Press. Edinburgh, 2004. 320p. ISBN:0-231-13248-4, ISBN13: 978-0-231-13248-0. Dewey:590.73. LCCN:2004-043893.

Audience: **g,l,u,f.**

Rutter, Michael SH456.R868 1995
Fly Fishing for the Compleat Idiot: A No-Nonsense Guide to Fly Casting. Kathleen Ort (Editor), Greg Siple & Ed Jenne (Illustrators). Trade Paper. Mountain Press Publishing Company, Inc. Missoula, MT. 1995. 200p. ISBN:0-87842-313-3, ISBN13: 978-0-87842-313-2. Dewey:799.1/2. LCCN:95-006709.

Audience: **g,f.**

Shenk, Ellen HF5381.S542 2000
Outdoor Careers: Exploring Occupations in Outdoor Fields. Ed. 2. Trade Paper. Stackpole Books. Mechanicsburg, PA. 2004. 224p. ISBN:0-8117-2873-0, ISBN13: 978-0-8117-2873-7. Dewey:331.7/02. LCCN:99-047776.

Audience: **g,l,f.**

VGM Career Books Staff HF5383.R437 1994
Resumes for Environmental Careers. Trade Paper. McGraw-Hill Trade. New York, NY. 2003. 462p. VGM Professional Resumes Ser. ISBN:0-8442-4159-8, ISBN13: 978-0-8442-4159-3. Dewey:808/.06665. LCCN:93-045864.

Audience: **l,u.**

WetFeet HD9666.5
Careers in Biotech Pharmaceuticals: WetFeet Insider Guide. Trade Paper. WetFeet, Inc. San Francisco, CA. 2004. 140p. ISBN:1-58207-441-0, ISBN13: 978-1-58207-441-2. Dewey:338.476151.

Audience: **g,l,f.**

Winter, Charles A. QH314.W525 2004
Opportunities in Biological Science Careers. Trade Paper. McGraw-Hill Companies, The. New York, NY. 2004. 160p. VGM Opportunities Ser. ISBN:0-07-143187-X, ISBN13: 978-0-07-143187-3. Dewey:570/.23. LCCN:2003-025821.

Audience: **g,l,u,f.**

CHEMISTRY

Chemistry is one of the very basic sciences, just above mathematics and physics, next to astronomy and earth sciences, and below the more elaborate biological sciences and applied areas of engineering, materials sciences, health sciences, and emerging areas such as nanotechnology.

Chemistry is taught at all four college and university undergraduate levels, each level the prerequisite for the next, as complexity in the subject area develops. This listing reflects the most important works that undergraduate students will encounter as they visit their academic libraries for further help in their studies. Those libraries, if properly stocked with useful works, will have all or nearly all the items on this list. All have been vetted for undergraduate level, usefulness, and value to student and scholar alike. There are serial entities such as Chemical Abstracts; review works; monographs; Web sites; and handbooks, encyclopedias, dictionaries, directories, and a host of works not imaginable even fifteen years ago. Added since BCL3 are Web sites and new areas of chemistry such as biotechnology (on the cusp between chemistry and biology), nanotechnology (on the cusps among materials science, physics, and chemistry), and the still-emerging area of environmental chemistry.

There are classic works, some textbooks that are timeless, popular-level works, biographies, special topic monographs, desktop reference works, foreign-language dictionaries, glossaries—everything that the well-rounded chemical student or practitioner will need.

— Judith Douville

Basic Chemistry > Guides to the Literature

QD8.5

☐ ACS Publications.
http://pubs.acs.org/
American Chemical Society.

Audience: **l,u,f.**

QD9.3

☐ CHEMINFO, Chemical Information Sources from Indiana University.
http://www.indiana.edu/~cheminfo/
The Trustees of Indiana University.

Audience: **l,u,f.**

QD8.5

☐ Chemistry Index.
http://www.chemie.fu-berlin.de/chemistry/index_en.html
Freie Universitat Berlin.

Audience: **u,f.**

QD8

☐ Comprehensive Chemistry Sites.
http://library.stanford.edu/depts/swain/help/webdirs/
subject.html#comprehensive
Stanford University.

Audience: **l,u,f.**

QD9.3

☐ Links for Chemists, the Chemistry Section of the WWW Virtual Library.
http://www.liv.ac.uk/chemistry/links/links.html
The University of Liverpool.

Audience: **l,u,f.**

QD8.3

☐ Martindale's the.
http://www.martindalecenter.com/GradChemistry.html

Audience: **u,f.**

QD803

☐ MolData--General Chemistry.
http://pages.pomona.edu/~wsteinmetz/GenChem.htm

Audience: **l,u,f.**

QD8.5

☐ NIST Virtual Library--Chemistry.
http://nvl.nist.gov/nvl2.cfm?dynamic=3Dres_subj&subjectid=3D7
NIST.

Audience: **l,u,f.**

QD9.3

☐ SIRCh (Selected Internet Resources for Chemistry).
http://www.indiana.edu/~cheminfo/cis_ca.html
Indiana University.

Audience: **l,u,f.**

QD9.3

☐ U.S. Food and Drug Administration. Library of Chemistry Information.
http://www.cfsan.fda.gov/~dms/chemist.html
U.S. F.D.A..

Audience: **l,u,f.**

QD8.3

☐ Yahoo! Search Directory.
http://dir.yahoo.com/Science/Chemistry/
Yahoo! Inc..

Audience: **l,u,f.**

Allan, Barbara & Livesey, Brian   **QD9.A43 1994**
How to Use Biological Abstracts, Chemical Abstracts and Index Chemicus. Ed. 2. Trade Cloth. Ashgate Publishing, Ltd. Aldershot, 1994. 114p. ISBN:0-566-07556-3, ISBN13: 978-0-566-07556-8. Dewey:025.06/54. LCCN:94-012968.

Audience: **l,u,f.** *Choice, 1995.*

Antony, Arthur   **QD8.3**
Guide to Basic Information Sources in Chemistry. Trade Cloth. John Wiley & Sons, Inc. Hoboken, NJ. 1979. 219p. Information Resources Ser. ISBN:0-470-26587-6, ISBN13: 978-0-470-26587-1. Dewey:540/.7. LCCN:79-000330.

Audience: **l,u,f.**

Douville, Judith A.   **Z675.C47D68 2004**
The Literature of Chemistry: Recommended Titles for Undergraduate Chemistry Library Collections. Trade Paper. Association of College & Research Libraries. Chicago, IL. 2004. xii, 191p. ISBN:0-8389-8308-1, ISBN13: 978-0-8389-8308-9. Dewey:016.54. LCCN:2004-018053.

Audience: **l,u,f.** *Choice, 2005.*

Huber, Charles F.
☐ Chemistry Resources on the Internet.
http://www.library.ucsb.edu/istl/98-winter/interne1.html

Audience: **l,u,f.**

Lees, Nigel   **QD8.5**
How to Find Information - Chemistry: A Guide to Searching in Published Sources. Trade Paper. British Library Science Reference & Information Service (S R I S). London, 1995. 68p. How to Find Ser. ISBN:0-7123-0806-7, ISBN13: 978-0-7123-0806-9. Dewey:016.54.

Audience: **u,f.**

Maizell, Robert E.   **QD8.5.M34 1998**
How to Find Chemical Information: A Guide for Practicing Chemists, Educators, and Students. Ed. 3. Trade Cloth. John Wiley & Sons, Inc. Hoboken, NJ. 1998. 544p. ISBN:0-471-12579-2, ISBN13: 978-0-471-12579-2. Dewey:540/.7. LCCN:97-029120.

Audience: **u,f.** *Choice, 1998.*

Mellon, M. G.   **QD8.5.M44 1982**
Chemical Publications. Ed. 5. Cloth Text. McGraw-Hill Companies, The. New York, NY. 1982. 352p. ISBN:0-07-041514-5, ISBN13: 978-0-07-041514-0. Dewey:540/.72. LCCN:81-020947.

Audience: **u,f.** *B*

Ridley, Damon D.   **QA76.9.D3R543 2002**
Information Retrieval: SciFinder and SciFinder Scholar. Trade Cloth. John Wiley & Sons, Inc. Hoboken, NJ. 2002. 252p. ISBN:0-470-84350-0, ISBN13: 978-0-470-84350-5. Dewey:025/.06/5. LCCN:2002-280282.

Audience: **u,f.** *Choice, 2003, 2002.*

Ridley, Damon D.   **Z699.5.S3R53 1996**
Online Searching: A Scientist's Perspective. Trade Cloth. John
Wiley & Sons, Inc. Hoboken, NJ. 1997. 364p.
ISBN:0-471-96520-0, ISBN13: 978-0-471-96520-6.
Dewey:025.5/24. LCCN:95-054160.

Audience: **u,f.**

Rowland, Fytton & Rhodes,   **QD8.5.I47 1993**
  Peter (Editors)
Information Sources in Chemistry. Ed. 4. Library Binding. K. G.
Saur Verlag GmbH & Company. Munchen 70, 1993. 350p.
Guides to Information Sources Ser. ISBN:1-85739-016-4,
ISBN13: 978-1-85739-016-2. Dewey:540/.72. LCCN:92-017946.

Audience: **l,u,f.** *Choice, 1993.*

Singer, T. E. (Editor)   **QD1.A355**
Searching the Chemical Literature. Trade Cloth. American
Chemical Society. Washington, DC. 1961. Advances in
Chemistry Ser., No. 30 ISBN:0-8412-0031-9, ISBN13:
978-0-8412-0031-9. Dewey:540.5. LCCN:61-011330.

Audience: **u,f.**

Wiggins, Gary D.   **QD8.5**
Chemical Information Sources. Cloth Text. McGraw-Hill
Companies, The. New York, NY. 1991. 256p. Advanced
Chemistry Ser. ISBN:0-07-909939-4, ISBN13:
978-0-07-909939-6. Dewey:540/.072.

Audience: **u,f.** *Choice, 1992.*

Wolman, Yecheskel   **QD8.5.W64 1988**
Chemical Information: A Practical Guide to Utilization. Ed. 2.
Trade Cloth. John Wiley & Sons, Inc. Hoboken, NJ. 1988. 306p.
ISBN:0-471-91704-4, ISBN13: 978-0-471-91704-5.
Dewey:540/.72. LCCN:87-023119.

Audience: **u,f.** *ẞ Choice, 1989.*

Basic Chemistry > Abstracting and Indexing Services

QD9
Abstracting and Indexing Resources for Historical Chemistry
Journals.
http://library.caltech.edu/collections/rpb/chemistry/
Hist.Chem.Index.pdf
Royal Society Catalogue of Scientific Papers.

Audience: **u,f.**

QD8.5
ACS Journals.
http://pubs.acs.org/journals/query/subscriberSearch.jsp
American Chemical Society.

Audience: **l,u,f.**

QD9
CAS DDS Title Search.
http://www.cas.org/Support/DDS/ddssearch.html
Chemical Abstracts.

Audience: **l,u,f.**

QD9
CAS, a Division of the American Chemical Society.
http://www.cas.org/
American Chemical Society.

Audience: **l,u,f.**

QD
Chemical Abstracts. American Chemical Society, 1907-.

Audience: **u,f.**

QD1
Chemisches Zentralblatt. Berlin: Verlag Chemie, 1830-1969.

Audience: **u,f.**

QD9
Core Journals Covered in CAplus.
http://www.cas.org/sent.html
Chemical Abstracts.

Audience: **l,u,f.**

QD9
DiscoveryGate.
http://www.discoverygate.com/iss/servlet/App?Action+ShowApp

Audience: **l,u,f.**

Z7401
Journal Citation Reports.
http://scientific.thomson.com/products/jcr/
Thomson.com.

Audience: **u,f.**

QD8.5
RSC Publishing--Journals.
http://www.rsc.org/Publishing/Journals/fjournalsearch.asp
Royal Society of Chemistry.

Audience: **l,u,f.**

QD1
SciFinder Scholar.
http://www.cas.org/SCIFINDER/SCHOLAR/
Chemical Abstracts Service.

Audience: **l,u,f.**

AI3
Web of Science.
http://scientific.thomson.com/products/wos/
Thomson.com.

Audience: **u,f.**

American Chemical Society;   **QD9**
  Chemical Abstracts Service
Chemical Abstracts Service Source Index (CASSI). ACS.

Audience: **u,f.**

Basic Chemistry > Encyclopedias

QD40
Chemistry Hypermedia Project--General Chemistry
Cross-Index.
http://www.chem.vt.edu/chem-ed/genchem.html
Virginia Technical Institute.

Audience: **l,u,f.**

QD4
Eric Weisstein's World of Chemistry.
http://scienceworld.wolfram.com/chemistry/
Wolfram.

Audience: **l,u,f.**

TP9

Kirk-Othmer Concise Encyclopedia of Chemical Technology, 2 vols. Ed. 4. John Wiley & Sons. 2003. ISBN:0-471-64686-5, ISBN13: 978-0-471-64686-0.

Audience: **l,u,f.**

TP9

⬚ Kirk-Othmer encyclopedia of chemical technology [electronic resource].
http://www3.interscience.wiley.com/cgi-bin/homepage/?isbn=0471238961
Ed. 5. NY: Wiley, 2004-.

Audience: **u,f.**

Considine, Douglas M.   **QD4**
  (Editor)
Van Nostrand Rheinhold Encyclopedia of Chemistry. Ed. 4. Cloth Text. John Wiley & Sons, Inc. Hoboken, NJ. 1984. 1168p. ISBN:0-442-22572-5, ISBN13: 978-0-442-22572-8. Dewey:540/.3/21. LCCN:83-023336.

Audience: **l,u,f.** *B*

Hampel, Clifford A.   **QD46**
The Encyclopedia of the Chemical Elements. Reinhold Book Corp.. 1968.

Audience: **l,u,f.**

Herman Mark, John J.   **TP9**
  McKetta, Jr., Donald F. Othmer, ed. board
[Kirk-Othmer] Encyclopedia of chemical technology. Ed. 2. NY: Interscience, 1963-70. 22 v..

Audience: **u,f.**

Kirk-Othmer   **TP9**
Kirk-Othmer Encyclopedia of Chemical Technology. Ed. 5. Trade Cloth. John Wiley & Sons, Inc. Hoboken, NJ. 2006. 869p. ISBN:0-471-48502-0, ISBN13: 978-0-471-48502-5. Dewey:660/.03/21.

Audience: **u,f.**

Kroschwitz, Jacqueline I.   **TP9**
  (Executive Editor)
Kirk-Othmer Encyclopedia of Chemical Technology. Ed. 4. Wiley. 1991. ISBN:0-471-52669-X, ISBN13: 978-0-471-52669-8.

Audience: **u,f.**

Kroschwitz, Jacqueline I.   **TP9**
Kirk-Othmer Encyclopedia of Chemical Technology. Ed. 5. Seidel, Arza (Editors). Wiley-Interscience. 2004. ISBN:0-471-48494-6, ISBN13: 978-0-471-48494-3.

Audience: **u,f.**

Lagowski, Joseph J. (Editor)   **QD4.M33 1997**
Macmillan Encyclopedia of Chemistry, Set. Trade Cloth. Thomson Gale. Farmington Hills, MI. 1997. 1696p. ISBN:0-02-897225-2, ISBN13: 978-0-02-897225-1. Dewey:540/.3. LCCN:97-001824.

Audience: **l,u,f.** *Choice, 1998.*

Martin Grayson and David   **TP9**
  Eckroth, executive eds.
[Kirk-Othmer] Encyclopedia of chemical technology. Ed. 3. NY: Wiley, 1978-84. 31 v.. 1978. ISBN:0-471-02037-0, ISBN13: 978-0-471-02037-0.

Audience: **u,f.**

Basic Chemistry > Dictionaries

QD7

⬚ Abbreviations of Chemical Compounds.
http://www.chemie.fu-berlin.de/cgi-bin/abbscomp
Freie Universitat Berlin.

Audience: **u,f.**

⬚ Abkurtzungen Chemischer Verbindungen/Abbreviations of Chemical Compounds.
http://www.chemie.fu-berlin.de/cgi-bin/abbscomp
Freie Universitat Berlin.

Audience: **u,f.**

QD7

⬚ CAS Standard Abbreviations and Acronyms.
http://www.cas.org/ONLINE/standards.html
Chemical Abstracts.

Audience: **l,u,f.**

QD7

⬚ Indiana University Chemistry Library Acronyms Database.
http://www.oscar.chem.indiana.edu/cfdocs/libchem/acronyms/titleu.cfm
Indiana University.

Audience: **l,u,f.**

QD5

McGraw-Hill Dictionary of Chemistry. Ed. 2. McGraw-Hill. 2003. ISBN:0-07-141046-5, ISBN13: 978-0-07-141046-5.

Audience: **l,u,f.**

QD9.3

⬚ The Sheffield Chemdex: The Directory of Chemistry on the WWW since 1993.
http://www.chemdex.org/

Audience: **l,u,f.**

QD7

⬚ Stereochemical Glossary.
http://www.rsc.org/pdf/tct/stereochemgloss.pdf
Royal Society of Chemistry.

Audience: **u,f.**

QD5

⬚ Wiley Interscience Reference Tables.
http://www3.interscience.wiley.com/stats/refTables.html
Wiley-Interscience.

Audience: **l,u,f.**

Bennett, H.   **QD5.B4**
Concise Chemical and Technical Dictionary. Ed. 4. Trade Cloth. Chemical Publishing Company, Inc. New York, NY. 1986. ISBN:0-8206-0310-4, ISBN13: 978-0-8206-0310-0. Dewey:540/.3/21.

Audience: **l,u,f.**

Daintith, John (Editor)   **QD5.D4985**
A Dictionary of Chemistry. Ed. 4. Trade Paper. Oxford University Press, Inc. New York, NY. 2000. 592p. Oxford Paperback Reference Ser. ISBN:0-19-280101-5, ISBN13: 978-0-19-280101-2. Dewey:540/.3. LCCN:2001-268453.

Audience: **l,u,f.**

FIZ Chemie, Berlin (Editor)   **QD291**
Dictionary of Common Names = Trivialnamen-Handbuch. VCH.
1993. ISBN:1-56081-720-8, ISBN13: 978-1-56081-720-8.
                                        Audience: **u,f.**

Hackh, Ingo Waldemar   **QD5.H3 1987**
  Dagobert
Grant and Hackh's Chemical Dictionary. Ed. 5. R. A. Grant
(Editor). Cloth Text. McGraw-Hill Companies, The. New York,
NY. 1987. 656p. ISBN:0-07-024067-1, ISBN13:
978-0-07-024067-4. Dewey:540/.3. LCCN:86-007496.
                                        Audience: **l,u,f.** *B*

Hampel, Clifford A. &   **QD4**
  Hawley, Gessner G.
Glossary of Chemical Terms. Ed. 2. Trade Cloth. John Wiley &
Sons, Inc. Hoboken, NJ. 1982. 464p. ISBN:0-442-23871-1,
ISBN13: 978-0-442-23871-1. Dewey:540/.3/21.
LCCN:81-011482.
                                        Audience: **l,u,f.** *B*

Howard, Philip H. & Neal,   **TP9.H65 1992**
  Michael W.
Dictionary of Chemical Names and Synonyms. Paper over
Boards. Lewis Publishers. Boca Raton, FL. 1992. 2544p.
ISBN:0-87371-396-6, ISBN13: 978-0-87371-396-2.
Dewey:660.03. LCCN:92-009160.
                            Audience: **l,u,f.** *Choice, 1993.*

Lewis, Richard J.   **QD5.C5**
Hawley's Condensed Chemical Dictionary, Set. Ed. 14. Trade
Cloth, Compact Disc, Mixed Media. John Wiley & Sons, Inc.
Hoboken, NJ. 2002. xiii, 1223p. ISBN:0-471-05533-6, ISBN13:
978-0-471-05533-4. Dewey:540/.3.
                                        Audience: **u,f.**

Sharp, David W. A.   **QD5.P4 2003**
The Dictionary of Chemistry. Ed. 3. Trade Paper. Penguin
Group (USA) Inc. New York, NY. 2003. 448p. Dictionary,
Penguin Ser. ISBN:0-14-051445-7, ISBN13: 978-0-14-051445-2.
Dewey:540/.3. LCCN:2003-278225.
                            Audience: **l,u,f.** *Choice, 2004.*

Wohlauer, Gabriele E.   **QD7.W6**
German Chemical Abbreviations. H. D. Gholston (Editor). Trade
Cloth. Special Libraries Association. Alexandria, VA. 1966.
ISBN:0-87111-165-9, ISBN13: 978-0-87111-165-4.
Dewey:540.148. LCCN:66-013627.
                                        Audience: **u,f.**

Basic Chemistry > Foreign Language Dictionaries

Callaham, Ludmilla   **QD5.C33 1996**
  Ignatiev, et al.
Callaham's Russian-English Dictionary of Science and
Technology. Ed. 4. Patricia E. Newman & John R. Callaham
(Authors). Trade Cloth. John Wiley & Sons, Inc. Hoboken, NJ.
1996. 848p. ISBN:0-471-61139-5, ISBN13: 978-0-471-61139-4.
Dewey:603. LCCN:94-037599.
                            Audience: **u,f.** *Choice, 1996.*

Cox, James C., et al.   **QD5.P3 1991**
Patterson's German-English Dictionary for Chemists. Ed. 4.
George E. Condoyannis & Austin M. Patterson (Authors). Trade

Cloth. John Wiley & Sons, Inc. Hoboken, NJ. 1992. 944p.
ISBN:0-471-66991-1, ISBN13: 978-0-471-66991-3.
Dewey:540/.3. LCCN:90-045365.
                            Audience: **l,u,f.** *Choice, 1992.*

Kaplan, Steven M.   **QD5.K294 1998**
Wiley's English-Spanish Spanish-English Chemistry Dictionary,
1. Ed. 1. Trade Cloth. John Wiley & Sons, Inc. Hoboken, NJ.
1998. 530p. ISBN:0-471-19288-0, ISBN13: 978-0-471-19288-6.
Dewey:540.3. LCCN:97-034936.
                                        Audience: **l,u,f.**

Kryt, Dobromila (Editor)   **QD5**
Dictionary of Chemical Terminology. Trade Cloth. Elsevier.
New York, NY. 1980. 612p. ISBN:0-444-99788-1, ISBN13:
978-0-444-99788-3. Dewey:540/.3. LCCN:79-020852.
                                        Audience: **u,f.**

Patterson, Austin McDowell   **QD5.P25 1954**
French-English Dictionary for Chemists. Ed. 2. Wiley. 1954.
                                        Audience: **u,f.**

Technical University of   **QD5.L26 1997**
  Dresden Staff (Editor)
Langenscheidt Routledge German Dictionary of Chemistry and
Chemical Technology: Germanenglish, Vol. 1. Ed. 6. Library
Binding. Routledge. New York, NY. 1997. 769p. Bilingual
Specialist Dictionaries Ser. ISBN:0-415-17128-8, ISBN13:
978-0-415-17128-1. Dewey:540/.3. LCCN:97-033480.
                            Audience: **u,f.** *Choice, 1999.*

Technische Universitat   **QD5.L26 1997**
  Dresden Staff (Editor)
Langenscheidt Routledge German Dictionary of Chemistry and
Chemical Technology, Vol. 2. Ed. 5. Library Binding. Routledge.
New York, NY. 1997. 807p. Bilingual Specialist Dictionaries
Ser. ISBN:0-415-17336-1, ISBN13: 978-0-415-17336-0.
Dewey:540/.3. LCCN:97-033480.
                            Audience: **u,f.** *Choice, 1999.*

Wenske, Gerhard   **QD5.W565**
Wörterbuch Chemie Deutsch/Englisch: Dictionary of Chemistry
German/English. Hans-Dieter Junge (Editor). Trade Cloth. John
Wiley & Sons, Inc. Hoboken, NJ. 1993. 2055p. Parat Ser., Vol.
23 ISBN:3-527-26429-9, ISBN13: 978-3-527-26429-2.
Dewey:540/.3.
                                        Audience: **u,f.**

Basic Chemistry > Handbooks and Tables of Data

                                                    TP202
☐ Aldrich Catalog.
http://www.sigmaaldrich.com/Brands/Aldrich.html
Sigma-Aldrich.
                                        Audience: **u,f.**

                                                    QD9.3
☐ ChemFinder.com Database & Internet Searching.
http://chemfinder.cambridgesoft.com/reference/
CambridgeSoft Corporation.
                                        Audience: **l,u,f.**

QD467

☐ ChemiCool Periodic Table.
http://www.chemicool.com/

Audience: **l,u,f.**

QD461

☐ ChemIDplus.
http://www.sis.nlm.nih.gov/chemical.html
National Library of Medicine.

Audience: **u,f.**

QD5

☐ Combined Chemical Dictionary.
http://www.chemnetbase.com/scripts/ccdweb.exe
CRC Press.

Audience: **u,f.**

QD6

✈ Composite Index for CRC Handbooks, Version 1.1. Ed. 3.
CRC Press. 1992. ISBN:0-8493-0290-0, ISBN13:
978-0-8493-0290-9.

Audience: **u,f.**

☐ Handbook of Chemistry and Physics.
http://www.hbcpnetbase.com/
Ed. 86.

Audience: **l,u,f.**

RS51

☐ The Merck Index, Internet Edition.
http://chemfinder.cambridgesoft.com/reference/
TheMerckIndex.asp
Via Cambridge ChemFinder.com.

Audience: **l,u,f.**

TP202

☐ Sigma-Aldrich.
http://www.sigmaaldrich.com/Area_of_Interest/The_Americas/
United_States.html
Sigma-Aldrich Co..

Audience: **u,f.**

Aldrich Chemical Company   **TP202**
Catalog Handbook of Fine Chemicals. Aldrich Chemical Co..
Audience: **u,f.**

Coyne, Gary S.   **QD53.C69 1997**
The Laboratory Companion: A Practical Guide to Materials,
Equipment, and Technique. Ed. 2. Trade Cloth. John Wiley &
Sons, Inc. Hoboken, NJ. 1997. 552p. ISBN:0-471-18422-5,
ISBN13: 978-0-471-18422-5. Dewey:542. LCCN:97-016689.
Audience: **l,u,f.** *Choice, 1998.*

Dean, John A. (Editor)   **QD65 .L36 1999**
Lange's Handbook of Chemistry. Ed. 15. Trade Cloth.
McGraw-Hill Professional Publishing. New York, NY. 1998.
1424p. Handbook Ser. ISBN:0-07-016384-7, ISBN13:
978-0-07-016384-3. Dewey:540. LCCN:84-643191.
Audience: **l,u,f.** ℬ *Choice, 1992.*

Faust, Rüdiger, et al.   **QD37.F3813 1999**
World Records in Chemistry. Günter Knaus & Ulrich Siemeling
(Authors), Hans-Jürgen Quadbeck-Seeger (Editor). Trade Paper.
John Wiley & Sons, Inc. Hoboken, NJ. 1999. 377p.

ISBN:3-527-29574-7, ISBN13: 978-3-527-29574-6. Dewey:540.
LCCN:99-230079.
Audience: **u,f.** *Choice, 1999.*

Gordon, Arnold J. & Ford,   **QD31.2**
  Richard A.
The Chemist's Companion: A Handbook of Practical Data,
Techniques, and References. Trade Cloth. John Wiley & Sons,
Inc. Hoboken, NJ. 1973. 560p. ISBN:0-471-31590-7, ISBN13:
978-0-471-31590-2. Dewey:540. LCCN:72-006660.
Audience: **l,u,f.** ℬ

Lide, David R.   **QD65**
  (Editor-in-Chief)
CRC Handbook of Chemistry and Physics: A Ready-Reference
Book of Chemical and Physical Data. Ed. 84. CRC Press. 2003.
ISBN:0-8493-0484-9, ISBN13: 978-0-8493-0484-2.
Audience: **l,u,f.**

Milne, George W. (Editor)   **TP9.G286 1999**
Gardner's Chemical Synonyms and Trade Names. Ed. 11. Trade
Cloth. John Wiley & Sons, Inc. Hoboken, NJ. 1999. 1434p.
ISBN:0-566-08190-3, ISBN13: 978-0-566-08190-3.
Dewey:660/.03. LCCN:98-051143.
Audience: **u,f.** *Choice, 2000.*

Ockerman, Herbert W.   **QD51**
Illustrated Chemistry Laboratory Terminology. CRC. 1991.
ISBN:0-8493-0152-1, ISBN13: 978-0-8493-0152-0.
Audience: **l,u,f.**

O'Neil, Maryadele J.   **RS51.M4 2001**
  (Editor), et al.
The Merck Index: An Encyclopedia of Chemicals, Drugs, and
Biologicals. Ed. 13. Susan Budavari & Patricia Heckelman
(Editors), Ann Smith (Associate Editor). Trade Cloth. John
Wiley & Sons, Inc. Hoboken, NJ. 2001. 1741p.
ISBN:0-911910-13-1, ISBN13: 978-0-911910-13-1.
Dewey:615/.1/03. LCCN:2003-267062.
Audience: **l,u,f.**

Shugar, Gershon J.; Dean,   **QD65**
  John A.
The Chemist's Ready Reference Handbook. Shugar, Ronald A.
et al. (Consulting Editors). McGraw-Hill. 1990.
ISBN:0-07-057178-3, ISBN13: 978-0-07-057178-5.
Audience: **l,u,f.**

Shugar, Gershon J. &   **QD61.S58 1996**
  Ballinger, Jack T.
Chemical Technicians' Ready Reference Handbook. Ed. 4. Trade
Cloth. McGraw-Hill Professional Publishing. New York, NY.
1996. 972p. Harvard Business Review Book Ser.
ISBN:0-07-057186-4, ISBN13: 978-0-07-057186-0. Dewey:542.
LCCN:95-052614.
Audience: **l,u,f.** ℬ

Basic Chemistry > Directories

QD8

☐ Chemistry.org.
http://www.acs.org/portal/a/c/s/1/home.html
American Chemical Society.

Audience: **l,u,f.**

QD8

☐ Chemsoc: The RSC's Chemical Science Network.
http://www.chemsoc.org/
Royal Society of Chemistry.

Audience: **l,u,f.**

QD8

☐ General Guide for Chemists and Chemical Engineers.
http://library.stanford.edu/depts/swain/help/subjectguides/general/index.html
Stanford University.

Audience: **l,u,f.**

Q180.56

☐ LabGuide Online.
http://mediabrains.com/client/LabGuide/bg1/search.asp

Audience: **u,f.**

QD1

☐ Royal Society of Chemistry.
http://www.rsc.org/

Audience: **l,u,f.**

QD8

☐ Yahoo! Search Directory Science: Chemistry.
http://dir.yahoo.com/science/chemistry/
Yahoo! Inc..

Audience: **l,u,f.**

American Chemical Society,   **Z5524.U5**
  Committee on Professional Training
☐ DGR Web 2005 (Directory of Graduate Research).
http://dgr.rints.com/
The Society.

Audience: **u,f.**

American Chemical Society,   **Z5525.U5**
  Committee on Professional Training
Directory of Graduate Research. The Society.

Audience: **u,f.**

Warr, Wendy A. (Editor),   **QD39.3.C6 D57**
  et al.
Directory of Chemistry Software, 1992. Peter Willett & Geoff Downs (Editors). Trade Paper. American Chemical Society. Washington, DC. 1992. 204p. ISBN:0-9518236-0-4, ISBN13: 978-0-9518236-0-6. Dewey:5.30296.

Audience: **u,f.** *Choice, 1992.*

Basic Chemistry > Style Guide

QD8.5

☐ Reference Style Guidelines.
http://pubs.acs.org/books/references.shtml
American Chemical Society.

Audience: **u,f.**

Dodd, Janet S. (Editor)   **QD8.5.A25 1997**
The ACS Style Guide: A Manual for Authors and Editors. Ed. 2. Trade Paper. Oxford University Press, Inc. New York, NY. 1997. 472p. An American Chemical Society Publication ISBN:0-8412-3462-0, ISBN13: 978-0-8412-3462-8. Dewey:808/.06654. LCCN:96-049413.

Audience: **u,f.** 𝓑

Basic Chemistry > Biographies

QD21

☐ 100 Distinguished European Chemists (18th, 19th, and 20th Centuries).
http://www.euchems.org/Distinguished/index.asp

Audience: **l,u,f.**

QD21

☐ Biographical Snapshots of Famous Women and Minority Chemists.
http://jchemed.chem.wisc.edu/JCEWWW/Features/eChemists/Bios/index.html
Journal of Chemical Education.

Audience: **l,u,f.**

QD21

☐ Biographies of Famous Chemists.
http://www.liv.ac.uk/Chemistry/Links/refbiog.html

Audience: **l,u,f.**

QD39

🐝 Chemistry, 1901-1995 [electronic resource]. [Singapore]: World Scientific. 1999. ISBN:981-02-3571-2, ISBN13: 978-981-02-3571-0.

Audience: **u,f.**

Barkan, Diana Kormos   **QD22.N39 B37 1999**
Walther Nernst and the Transition to Modern Physical Science. Trade Cloth. Cambridge University Press. New York, NY. 1999. 300p. ISBN:0-521-44456-X, ISBN13: 978-0-521-44456-9. Dewey:540/.092. LCCN:98-022028.

Audience: **l,u,f.** *Choice, 1999.*

Basolo, Fred   **QD22.B258A3 2002**
From Coello to Inorganic Chemistry: A Lifetime of Reactions. Trade Cloth. Springer. New York, NY. 2002. 266p. Profiles in Inorganic Chemistry Ser. ISBN:0-306-46774-7, ISBN13: 978-0-306-46774-5. Dewey:540/.92 B. LCCN:2002-022220.

Audience: **l,u,f.**

Bowden, Mary E.   **QD21.B67**
Chemical Achievers: The Human Face of the Chemical Sciences. Trade Paper. Chemical Heritage Foundation. Philadelphia, PA. 1997. 187p. ISBN:0-941901-12-2, ISBN13: 978-0-941901-12-3. Dewey:540/.92/2 B.

Audience: **l,u,f.** *Choice, 1998.*

Djerassi, Carl   **QD22.D63 A3**
The Pill, Pygmy Chimps, and Degas' Horse: The Remarkable Autobiography of the Award Winning Scientist Who Synthesized the Pill. Trade Paper. Basic Books. New York, NY. 1993. 352p. ISBN:0-465-05758-6, ISBN13: 978-0-465-05758-0. Dewey:540/.92 B. LCCN:91-058599.

Audience: **u,f.**

Farber, Eduard   **QD21**
Great Chemists. Interscience Publishers. 1961.

Audience: **l,u,f.**

Goertzel, Ted & Goertzel,   **Q143.P25G6**
  Ben
Linus Pauling: A Life in Science and Politics. Trade Paper. Basic Books. New York, NY. 1996. 320p. ISBN:0-465-00673-6, ISBN13: 978-0-465-00673-1. Dewey:509.2.

Audience: **u,f.** *Choice, 1996.*

Formats: Web: ☐   Ebook: 🄴   CD/DVD-ROM: 🐝   BCL3: 𝓑

Grenthe, Ingmar (Editor)   QD39.C4862
Nobel Lectures in Chemistry: 1996-2000. Trade Paper. World
Scientific Publishing Company, Inc. Hackensack, NJ. 2003.
476p. ISBN:981-02-4959-4, ISBN13: 978-981-02-4959-5.
Dewey:540.

Audience: **u,f.**

Grinstein, Louise S.   QD21
  (Editor), et al.
Women in Chemistry and Physics: A Biobibliographic
Sourcebook. Miriam H. Rafailovich & Rose K. Rose (Editors).
Cloth Text. Greenwood Publishing Group, Inc. Portsmouth, NH.
1993. 736p. ISBN:0-313-27382-0, ISBN13: 978-0-313-27382-7.
Dewey:509.22. LCCN:92-040224.

Audience: **l,u,f.** *Choice, 1994.*

Hahn, Otto   QD22.H2
Otto Hahn: A Scientific Autobiography. Scribner's Sons. 1966.

Audience: **l,u,f.**

Hargittai, Istvan   QD21.H294 2000
Candid Science: Conversations with Famous Chemists.
Magdolna Hargittai (Editor). Trade Cloth. Imperial College
Press. London, 2000. 300p. ISBN:1-86094-151-6, ISBN13:
978-1-86094-151-1. Dewey:540.

Audience: **l,u,f.**

Jaffe, Bernard   QD21.J3
Crucibles: The Story of Chemistry from Ancient Alchemy to
Nuclear Fission. Ed. 4. Trade Cloth. Peter Smith Publisher, Inc.
Magnolia, MA. 1990. ISBN:0-8446-5486-8, ISBN13:
978-0-8446-5486-7. Dewey:540/.9.

Audience: **l,u,f.** *B*

Jaffe, Bernard   QD21.J3
Crucibles: The Lives and Achievements of the Great Chemists.
Simon and Schuster. 1930.

Audience: **l,u,f.**

James, Laylin K. (Editor)   QD21.N63 1993
Nobel Laureates in Chemistry: 1901-1992. Saddle Stitched,
Cloth over Boards. John Wiley & Sons, Inc. Hoboken, NJ.
1993. 798p. History of Modern Chemical Sciences Ser.
ISBN:0-8412-2459-5, ISBN13: 978-0-8412-2459-9. Dewey:B.
LCCN:93-017902.

Audience: **l,u,f.** *Choice, 1994.*

Knight, David (Author,   QD22.D3
  Contribution by)
Humphry Davy: Science and Power. Sally Gregory Kohlstedt
(Contribution by). Trade Paper. Cambridge University Press.
New York, NY. 1998. 232p. Science Biographies Ser.
ISBN:0-521-56539-1, ISBN13: 978-0-521-56539-4.
Dewey:509.2.

Audience: **u,f.** *Choice, 1993.*

Lewis, Edward S.   QD22.L57L48 1998
A Biography of Distinguished Scientist Gilbert Newton Lewis.
Trade Cloth. Edwin Mellen Press, The. Lewiston, NY. 1998.
152p. ISBN:0-7734-8284-9, ISBN13: 978-0-7734-8284-5.
Dewey:540/.92 B. LCCN:98-025084.

Audience: **l,u,f.** *Choice, 1999.*

McGrayne, Sharon Bertsch   TP18.M34 2001
Prometheans in the Lab: Chemistry and the Making of the
Modern World. Trade Cloth. McGraw-Hill Trade. New York,

NY. 2001. 224p. ISBN:0-07-135007-1, ISBN13:
978-0-07-135007-5. Dewey:660/.0922. LCCN:2001-030671.

Audience: **l,u,f.** *Choice, 2002.*

Miles, Wyndham D   QD21.A43
American Chemists and Chemical Engineers. Wyndham D.
Miles (Editor). American Chemical Society. 1976.
ISBN:0-8412-0278-8, ISBN13: 978-0-8412-0278-8.

Audience: **u,f.**

Morris, Peter J. T. &   QD22.W67R63 2001
  Benfrey, Otto Theodor (Editors)
Robert Burns Woodward: Architect and Artist in the World of
Molecules. Trade Cloth. Chemical Heritage Foundation.
Philadelphia, PA. 2001. 497p. History of Modern Chemical
Sciences Ser. ISBN:0-941901-25-4, ISBN13:
978-0-941901-25-3. Dewey:547/.0092. LCCN:00-050876.

Audience: **l,u,f.** *Choice, 2001.*

Olah, George A.   QD22.O43A3 2001
A Life of Magic Chemistry: Autobiographical Reflections of a
Nobel Prize Winner. Trade Cloth. John Wiley & Sons, Inc.
Hoboken, NJ. 2000. 296p. ISBN:0-471-15743-0, ISBN13:
978-0-471-15743-4. Dewey:540.92. LCCN:00-043638.

Audience: **l,u,f.**

Poirier, Jean-Pierre   QD22.L4P6513 1996
Lavoisier: Chemist, Biologist, Economist. Rebecca Balinski
(Translator). Trade Cloth. University of Pennsylvania Press.
Philadelphia, PA. 1996. 544p. Chemical Sciences in Society Ser.
ISBN:0-8122-3365-4, ISBN13: 978-0-8122-3365-0.
Dewey:540/.92 B. LCCN:96-035738.

Audience: **l,u,f.** *Choice, 1997.*

Rayner-Canham, Marelene   QC15.R39 1997
  F. & Rayner-Canham, Geoffrey W.
A Devotion to Their Science: Pioneer Women of Radioactivity.
Trade Cloth. Chemical Heritage Foundation. Philadelphia, PA.
1997. 280p. ISBN:0-941901-16-5, ISBN13: 978-0-941901-16-1.
Dewey:539.7/52/0922. LCCN:98-131383.

Audience: **l,u,f.** *Choice, 1997.*

Rayner-Canham, Marelene   QD20.R39 1998
  F. & Rayner-Canham, Geoffrey W.
Women in Chemistry: Their Changing Roles from Alchemical
Times to the Mid-20th Century. Trade Cloth. American
Chemical Society. Washington, DC. 1998. 284p. History of
Modern Chemical Sciences Ser. ISBN:0-8412-3522-8, ISBN13:
978-0-8412-3522-9. Dewey:540/.82. LCCN:98-003890.

Audience: **l,u.** *Choice, 1999.*

Russell, Colin A.   QD22.F65 R86 1996
Edward Frankland: Chemistry, Controversy and Conspiracy in
Victorian England. Trade Cloth. Cambridge University Press.
New York, NY. 1996. 555p. ISBN:0-521-49636-5, ISBN13:
978-0-521-49636-0. Dewey:540.9/2. LCCN:95-040319.

Audience: **l,u,f.** *Choice, 1997.*

Schutt, Hans-Werner   QD22.M58S3813 1996
Eilhard Mitscherlich: Prince of Prussian Chemistry. William E.
Russwy (Translator). Trade Cloth. American Chemical Society.
Washington, DC. 1996. 239p. History of Modern Chemical
Sciences Ser. ISBN:0-8412-3345-4, ISBN13:
978-0-8412-3345-4. Dewey:[B]. LCCN:96-033322.

Audience: **l,u,f.** *Choice, 1997.*

Seaborg, Glenn T. &   QD22.S436A3 2001
  Seaborg, Eric
Adventures in the Atomic Age: From Watts to Washington.
Cloth over Boards. Farrar, Straus & Giroux. New York, NY.
2001. 356p. ISBN:0-374-29991-9, ISBN13: 978-0-374-29991-0.
Dewey:327.1/74/092 B. LCCN:00-049522.
                                  Audience: **l,u,f.** *Choice, 2002.*

Thackray, Arnold W. &   Q185.T52 2000
  Myers, Minor Jr.
Arnold O. Beckman: One Hundred Years of Excellence. Trade
Cloth. Chemical Heritage Foundation. Philadelphia, PA. 2000.
397p. Chemical Heritage Foundation Series in Innovation and
Entrepreneurship Ser., Vol. 3 ISBN:0-941901-23-8, ISBN13:
978-0-941901-23-9. Dewey:338.7/681/092 B. LCCN:00-027014.
                                  Audience: **l,u,f.** *Choice, 2001.*

Zewail, Ahmed   QD22.Z46A3 2002
Voyage Through Time: Walks of Life to the Nobel Prize. Trade
Cloth. American University in Cairo Press. New York, NY.
2002. 256p. ISBN:977-424-677-2, ISBN13: 978-977-424-677-7.
Dewey:540/.92 B. LCCN:2002-332902.
                                  Audience: **l,u,f.** *Choice, 2002.*

Basic Chemistry > History of Chemistry

                                              QD11
☐ Chem Soc Timeline.
http://www.chemsoc.org/timeline/
Royal Society of Chemistry.
                                  Audience: **l,u,f.**

                                              QD11
☐ Historical Chemistry--Full Text and Miscellaneous Sites.
http://www.rsc.org/library/researchers/selectsites/
selectsites10c.asp
Royal Society of Chemistry.
                                  Audience: **l,u,f.**

                                              QD11
☐ History of Chemistry.
http://www.chemistrycoach.com/history_of_chemistry.htm
                                  Audience: **l,u,f.**

                                              QD11
☐ Royal Society of Chemistry--Historical Chemistry
Information Service.
http://www.rsc.org/library/lichelp/historicalchemistry/index.asp
Royal Society of Chemistry.
                                  Audience: **u,f.**

                                              QD11
☐ Selected Classic Papers from the History of Chemistry.
http://web.lemoyne.edu/~giunta/papers.html
Le Moyne College.
                                  Audience: **l,u,f.**

                                              QD11
☐ Virtual library: Science: Chemistry: History of Chemistry.
http://www.liv.ac.uk/Chemistry/Links/refhistory.html
                                  Audience: **u,f.**

Benfey, Otto Theodor   QD455 .C49 1981
  (Editor)
Classics in the Theory of Chemical Combination. Ed. 3. Trade

Cloth. Krieger Publishing Company. Melbourne, FL. 1981. xii,
192p. ISBN:0-89874-368-0, ISBN13: 978-0-89874-368-5.
Dewey:541. LCCN:81-008300.
                                  Audience: **u,f.**

Berson, Jerome A.   QD11.B48 1999
Chemical Creativity: Ideas from the Work of Woodward,
Hückel, Meerwein, and Others. Trade Paper. John Wiley &
Sons, Inc. Hoboken, NJ. 1999. 207p. ISBN:3-527-29754-5,
ISBN13: 978-3-527-29754-2. Dewey:540/.9. LCCN:99-206238.
                                  Audience: **u,f.** *Choice, 2000.*

Brock, William H.   QD11.B76
The Norton History of Chemistry. Trade Paper. W. W. Norton &
Company, Inc. New York, NY. 1993. 768p. Norton History of
Science Ser. ISBN:0-393-31043-4, ISBN13: 978-0-393-31043-6.
Dewey:540/.9. LCCN:93-019054.
                                  Audience: **u,f.** *Choice, 1994.*

Cobb, Cathy & Goldwhite,   QD11 .C59 1995
  Harold
Creations of Fire: Chemistry's Lively History from Alchemy to
the Atomic Age. Trade Paper. Perseus Books Group. New York,
NY. 2001. 496p. ISBN:0-7382-0594-X, ISBN13:
978-0-7382-0594-6. Dewey:540.9.
                                  Audience: **g,l,u,f.** *Choice, 1996.*

Donovan, Arthur   QD22.L4 D58 1996
Antoine Lavoisier: Science, Administration and Revolution.
Sally Gregory Kohlstedt (Contribution by), David Knight
(Contribution by, Preface by). Trade Paper. Cambridge
University Press. New York, NY. 1996. 367p. Science
Biographies Ser. ISBN:0-521-56672-X, ISBN13:
978-0-521-56672-8. Dewey:540.9/2. LCCN:96-178046.
                                  Audience: **u,f.**

Duncan, Alistair M.   QD18.E85
Laws and Order in Eighteenth-Century Chemistry. Oxford
University Press. 1996. ISBN:0-19-855806-6, ISBN13:
978-0-19-855806-4.
                                  Audience: **u,f.**

Ferry, Georgina   QD903.6.H63F47 2000
Dorothy Hodgkin: A Life. Book, Other. Cold Spring Harbor
Laboratory Press. Woodbury, NY. 2000. vi, 423p.
ISBN:0-87969-590-0, ISBN13: 978-0-87969-590-3.
Dewey:548/.092 B. LCCN:00-022666.
                                  Audience: **u,f.** *Choice, 2001.*

Garfield, Simon   TP140.P46G37 2001
Mauve: How One Man Invented a Color That Changed the
World. Trade Cloth. W. W. Norton & Company, Inc. New York,
NY. 2001. 222p. ISBN:0-393-02005-3, ISBN13:
978-0-393-02005-2. Dewey:666/.257. LCCN:00-069533.
                                  Audience: **u,f.** *Choice, 2001.*

Greenberg, Arthur   QD11.G74 2000
A Chemical History Tour: Picturing Chemistry from Alchemy to
Modern Molecular Science. Trade Cloth. John Wiley & Sons,
Inc. Hoboken, NJ. 2000. 336p. ISBN:0-471-35408-2, ISBN13:
978-0-471-35408-6. Dewey:540/.9. LCCN:99-038865.
                                  Audience: **l,u,f.**

Henry M. Leicester,   **QD11**
  ed.-in-chief.
Chymia. American Chemical Society, Division of the History of
Chemistry; Edgar F. Smith Memorial Collection, Univ. of
Pennsylvania. v. 1-12, 1948-1967
                                         Audience: **u,f.**

Holmes, Frederic L. &   **QD53.I57 2000**
  Levere, Trevor Harvey (Editors)
Instruments and Experimentation in the History of Chemistry.
Trade Cloth. MIT Press. Cambridge, MA. 2000. 437p. Dibner
Institute Studies in the History of Science and Technology
ISBN:0-262-08282-9, ISBN13: 978-0-262-08282-2. Dewey:542.
LCCN:99-021064.
                                    Audience: **u,f.** *Choice, 2001.*

Hudson, John   **QD11.H84 1992**
The History of Chemistry. Chapman & Hall. 1992.
ISBN:0-412-03651-7, ISBN13: 978-0-412-03651-4.
                                         Audience: **u,f.**

Ihde, Aaron J.   **QD11.I44 1984**
The Development of Modern Chemistry. Trade Paper. Dover
Publications, Inc. Mineola, NY. 1984. 851p.
ISBN:0-486-64235-6, ISBN13: 978-0-486-64235-2.
Dewey:540/.9. LCCN:82-018245.
                                    Audience: **u,f.** *B*

Knight, David (Editor)   **QD18.E85D48 1998**
Development of Chemistry. Library Binding. Routledge. New
York, NY. 1998. 4144p. ISBN:0-415-17912-2, ISBN13:
978-0-415-17912-6. Dewey:540/.94. LCCN:98-004837.
                                         Audience: **u,f.**

Knight, David   **QD11.K53 1992**
Ideas in Chemistry: A History of the Science. Cloth Text.
Rutgers University Press. Piscataway, NJ. 1992. 325p.
ISBN:0-8135-1835-0, ISBN13: 978-0-8135-1835-0.
Dewey:540.9. LCCN:91-047598.
                                    Audience: **u,f.** *Choice, 1993.*

Krebs, Robert E.   **QD466**
The History and Use of Our Earth's Chemical Elements: A
Reference Guide. Book, Other. Greenwood Publishing Group,
Inc. Portsmouth, NH. 1998. 360p. ISBN:0-313-30123-9,
ISBN13: 978-0-313-30123-0. Dewey:546. LCCN:96-049735.
                                    Audience: **l,u,f.** *Choice, 1998.*

Lambert, Joseph B.   **CC79.C5 L36 1997**
Traces of the Past: Unraveling the Secrets of Archaeology
Through Chemistry. Trade Paper. Perseus Books Group. New
York, NY. 1998. 336p. ISBN:0-7382-0027-1, ISBN13:
978-0-7382-0027-9. Dewey:930.1/028. LCCN:98-087038.
                                    Audience: **u,f.** *Choice, 1998.*

Levere, Trevor Harvey   **QD11.L45 2001**
Transforming Matter: A History of Chemistry from Alchemy to
the Buckyball. Trade Paper. Johns Hopkins University Press.
Baltimore, MD. 2001. 232p. Introductory Studies in the History
of Science ISBN:0-8018-6610-3, ISBN13: 978-0-8018-6610-4.
Dewey:540/.9. LCCN:00-011487.
                                    Audience: **u,f.** *Choice, 2002.*

Mason, Stephen Finney   **QH325**
Chemical Evolution: Origins of the Elements, Molecules, and
Living Systems. Oxford University Press. 1991.
ISBN:0-19-855272-6, ISBN13: 978-0-19-855272-7.
                                         Audience: **u,f.**

Mauskopf, Seymour H.   **QD11.C48 1993**
  (Editor)
Chemical Sciences in the Modern World. Trade Cloth.
University of Pennsylvania Press. Philadelphia, PA. 1994. 448p.
Chemical Sciences in Society Ser. ISBN:0-8122-3156-2,
ISBN13: 978-0-8122-3156-4. Dewey:540. LCCN:93-030055.
                                    Audience: **u,f.** *Choice, 1994.*

Melhado, Evan M. &   **QD22.B5 E55 1992**
  Frängsmyr, Tore (Editors)
Enlightenment Science in the Romantic Era: The Chemistry of
Berzelius and Its Cultural Setting. Trade Cloth. Cambridge
University Press. New York, NY. 1992. 260p.
ISBN:0-521-41775-9, ISBN13: 978-0-521-41775-4.
Dewey:540.92. LCCN:91-045939.
                                    Audience: **u,f.** *Choice, 1993.*

Nye, Mary J.   **QD452.N94 1993**
From Chemical Philosophy to Theoretical Chemistry: Dynamics
of Matter and Dynamics of Disciplines, 1800-1950. Trade Cloth.
University of California Press. Berkeley, CA. 1994. 346p.
ISBN:0-520-08210-9, ISBN13: 978-0-520-08210-6. Dewey:540.
LCCN:92-043114.
                                    Audience: **u.** *Choice, 1994.*

Orna, Mary V. (Editor)   **CC79.C5A73 1996**
Archaeological Chemistry: Organic, Inorganic, and Biochemical
Analysis. Cloth Text. Oxford University Press, Inc. New York,
NY. 1996. 472p. ACS Symposium Ser., No. 625
ISBN:0-8412-3395-0, ISBN13: 978-0-8412-3395-9.
Dewey:930.1/028. LCCN:96-004812.
                                    Audience: **u,f.** *Choice, 1996.*

Partington, James R.   **QD11.P28**
History of Chemistry. Trade Cloth. Martino Publishing.
Mansfield Centre, CT. 1996. 3154p. ISBN:1-888262-12-5,
ISBN13: 978-1-888262-12-4. Dewey:540/.9.
                                         Audience: **u,f.**

Partington, James R.   **QD11.P3 1989**
A Short History of Chemistry. Ed. 3. Trade Paper. Dover
Publications, Inc. Mineola, NY. 1989. 428p.
ISBN:0-486-65977-1, ISBN13: 978-0-486-65977-0.
Dewey:540/.9. LCCN:89-001216.
                                         Audience: **u,f.**

Salzberg, Hugh W.   **QD11.S23 1990**
From Caveman to Chemist: Circumstances and Achievements.
Trade Paper. American Chemical Society. Washington, DC.
1991. 294p. An American Chemical Society Publication
ISBN:0-8412-1787-4, ISBN13: 978-0-8412-1787-4.
Dewey:540/.9. LCCN:90-044612.
                                    Audience: **u,f.** *Choice, 1992.*

Skolnik, Herman   **QD1**
A Century of Chemistry: The Role of Chemists and the
American Chemical Society. Reese, Kenneth M. (Editors).
American Chemical Society. 1976. ISBN:0-8412-0307-5,
ISBN13: 978-0-8412-0307-5.
                                         Audience: **l,u,f.**

Stillman, John Maxson   **QD11.S84**
Story of Alchemy and Early Chemistry. Trade Paper. Kessinger
Publishing, LLC. Whitefish, MT. 2003. ISBN:0-7661-3230-7,
ISBN13: 978-0-7661-3230-6. Dewey:540.1.
                                         Audience: **l,u,f.**

Weeks, Mary Elvira   QD466.W4
Discovery of the Elements. Trade Paper. Kessinger Publishing, LLC. Whitefish, MT. 2003. ISBN:0-7661-3872-0, ISBN13: 978-0-7661-3872-8. Dewey:546/.11.

Audience: **l,u,f.** *B*

Williams, R. J. P.; da Silva,   QD33
  J. J. R. Frausto
Bringing Chemistry to Life: From Matter to Man. Oxford University Press. 1999. ISBN:0-19-850546-9, ISBN13: 978-0-19-850546-4.

Audience: **u,f.**

Basic Chemistry > Chemistry Today

Atkins, P. W.   QD466.A845
The Periodic Kingdom: A Journey into the Land of the Chemical Elements. Paper Text. DIANE Publishing Company. Collingdale, PA. 1998. 163p. ISBN:0-7881-5518-0, ISBN13: 978-0-7881-5518-5. Dewey:546.8.

Audience: **l.** *Choice, 1996.*

Ball, Philip   QD461.B228 2001
Stories of the Invisible: A Guided Tour of Molecules. Trade Cloth. Oxford University Press, Inc. New York, NY. 2001. 224p. ISBN:0-19-280214-3, ISBN13: 978-0-19-280214-9. Dewey:541.2/2. LCCN:2001-036601.

Audience: **l.** *Choice, 2002.*

Bhushan, Nalini &   QD6.O34 2000
  Rosenfeld, Stuart (Editors)
Of Minds and Molecules: New Philosophical Perspectives on Chemistry. Trade Cloth. Oxford University Press, Inc. New York, NY. 2000. 316p. ISBN:0-19-512834-6, ISBN13: 978-0-19-512834-5. Dewey:540/.1. LCCN:99-040329.

Audience: **u,f.**

Breslow, Ronald   QD31.2.B75 1997
Chemistry Today and Tomorrow: The Central, Useful, and Creative Science. Trade Paper. American Chemical Society. Washington, DC. 1996. 144p. ISBN:0-8412-3460-4, ISBN13: 978-0-8412-3460-4. Dewey:540. LCCN:96-045078.

Audience: **l,u,f.** *Choice, 1997.*

Emsley, John   QD466.E48 1998
The Elements. Ed. 3. Trade Cloth. Oxford University Press, Inc. New York, NY. 1998. 304p. ISBN:0-19-855819-8, ISBN13: 978-0-19-855819-4. Dewey:546. LCCN:98-213249.

Audience: **l,u.** *Choice, 1999, 1992.*

Emsley, John   QP514.2.E47 1998
Molecules at an Exhibition: Portraits of Intriguing Materials in Everyday Life. Trade Cloth. Oxford University Press, Inc. New York, NY. 1998. 264p. ISBN:0-19-850266-4, ISBN13: 978-0-19-850266-1. Dewey:540. LCCN:97-036754.

Audience: **u.** *Choice, 1998.*

Emsley, John   QD466
Nature's Building Blocks: An A-Z Guide to the Elements. Trade Paper. Oxford University Press, Inc. New York, NY. 2003. 552p. ISBN:0-19-850340-7, ISBN13: 978-0-19-850340-8. Dewey:546.

Audience: **l,u.**

Hoenig, Steven L.   QD31.2.H58 2001
Basic Training in Chemistry. Trade Cloth. Springer. New York, NY. 2001. 198p. ISBN:0-306-46546-9, ISBN13: 978-0-306-46546-8. Dewey:540. LCCN:00-067108.

Audience: **l,u,f.**

Hoffmann, Roald   QD37.H612 1995
The Same and Not the Same. Trade Cloth. Columbia University Press. New York, NY. 1995. 294p. ISBN:0-231-10138-4, ISBN13: 978-0-231-10138-7. Dewey:540. LCCN:94-039457.

Audience: **u,f.** *Choice, 1996.*

Karukstis, Kerry K. & Van   QD31.2
  Hecke, Gerald R.
Chemistry Connections: The Chemical Basis of Everyday Phenomena. Ed. 2. Paper Text. Elsevier Science & Technology Books. Saint Louis, MO. 2003. 250p. Complementary Science Ser. ISBN:0-12-400151-3, ISBN13: 978-0-12-400151-0. Dewey:540. LCCN:2003-102993.

Audience: **l,u,f.** *Choice, 2004.*

Lewis, Grace Ross   TP200.L49 1999
1001 Chemicals in Everyday Products. Ed. 2. Trade Paper. John Wiley & Sons, Inc. Hoboken, NJ. 1998. 400p. ISBN:0-471-29212-5, ISBN13: 978-0-471-29212-8. Dewey:363.179. LCCN:98-006419.

Audience: **l.** *Choice, 1999.*

McEvoy, James E. (Editor)   QD40.P293 1991
Partnerships in Chemical Research and Education. Trade Cloth. Oxford University Press, Inc. New York, NY. 1992. 250p. ACS Symposium Ser., No. 478 ISBN:0-8412-2173-1, ISBN13: 978-0-8412-2173-4. Dewey:540/.72. LCCN:91-032420.

Audience: **u,f.** *Choice, 1992.*

Newton, David E.   QD31.2.N49 1999
Chemistry. Cloth Text. Greenwood Publishing Group, Inc. Portsmouth, NH. 1998. 304p. Oryx Frontiers of Science Ser., No. 1 ISBN:1-57356-160-6, ISBN13: 978-1-57356-160-0. Dewey:540. LCCN:98-040880.

Audience: **u,f.** *Choice, 1999.*

Prepared by the Committee   QD
  on Patents and Related Matters
☐ What Every Chemist Should Know about Patents. http://www.chemistry.org/portal/resources/ACS/ACSContent/ government/publications/Chem_patent2001.pdf American Chemical Society.

Audience: **u,f.**

Taber, K.   QD40.T33
Chemical Misconceptions: Prevention, Diagnosis and Cure. Trade Paper. Royal Society of Chemistry, The. Cambridge, 2002. x + 180p. ISBN:0-85404-386-1, ISBN13: 978-0-85404-386-6. Dewey:540.7/1241.

Audience: **l,u.**

Taber, K.   QD40.T33
Chemical Misconceptions: Prevention, Diagnosis and Cure. Trade Paper. Royal Society of Chemistry, The. Cambridge, 2002. viii + 238p. ISBN:0-85404-381-0, ISBN13: 978-0-85404-381-1. Dewey:540.7/1241.

Audience: **l,u.**

Vögtle, Fritz (Editor), et al.   QD39.S83 2000
Stimulating Concepts in Chemistry. J. Fraser Stoddart &
Masakatsu Shibasaki (Editors). Trade Cloth. John Wiley & Sons,
Inc. Hoboken, NJ. 2001. 413p. ISBN:3-527-29978-5, ISBN13:
978-3-527-29978-2. Dewey:540. LCCN:2001-274155.
Audience: **u,f.**

Basic Chemistry > The Future of Chemistry

Atkinson, William Illsey   T174
Nanocosm: Nanotechnology and the Big Changes Coming from
the Inconceivably Small. AMACOM. 2003.
ISBN:0-8144-7181-1, ISBN13: 978-0-8144-7181-4.
Audience: **l,u,f.**

Drexler, K. Eric   T174
Nanosystems: Molecular Machinery, Manufacturing, and
Computation. Wiley-Interscience. 1992. ISBN:0-471-57547-X,
ISBN13: 978-0-471-57547-4.
Audience: **u,f.**

Drexler, K. Eric   T45
Unbounding the Future: The Nanotechnology Revolution. W.
Morrow. 1991. ISBN:0-688-09124-5, ISBN13:
978-0-688-09124-8.
Audience: **u,f.**

Fabbrizzi, Luigi & Poggi,   QD1.C742 2000
  Antonio (Editors)
Chemistry at the Beginning of the Third Millennium: Molecular
Design, Supramolecules, Nanotechnology and Beyond. Trade
Cloth. Springer. New York, NY. 2000. VIII, 356p.
ISBN:3-540-67460-8, ISBN13: 978-3-540-67460-3.
Dewey:540/.1/12. LCCN:00-041048.
Audience: **u,f.**

Hall, Nina (Editor)   QD39 .N47 2000
The New Chemistry. Cloth Text. Cambridge University Press.
New York, NY. 2000. 506p. ISBN:0-521-45224-4, ISBN13:
978-0-521-45224-3. Dewey:540. LCCN:99-016729.
Audience: **u,f.** *Choice, 2001.*

Lister, Ted (Editor)   QD31.2.C77 2000
Cutting Edge Chemistry. Trade Paper. Royal Society of
Chemistry, The. Cambridge, 2000. 196p. ISBN:0-85404-914-2,
ISBN13: 978-0-85404-914-1. Dewey:540.
Audience: **u,f.**

Mulhall, Douglas   T174
Our Molecular Future: How Nanotechnology, Robotics,
Genetics, and Artificial Intelligence Will Transform Our World.
Prometheus Books. 2002. ISBN:1-57392-992-1, ISBN13:
978-1-57392-992-9.
Audience: **l,u,f.**

Wilson, Michael, et al.   T174
Nanotechnology: Basic Science and Emerging Technologies.
Chapman & Hall/CRC. 2002. ISBN:1-58488-339-1, ISBN13:
978-1-58488-339-5.
Audience: **l,u,f.**

Basic Chemistry > Safety Literature

                                                          QD63.5
☐ ACS Division of Chemical Health and Safety.
http://membership.acs.org/c/chas/
American Chemical Society.
Audience: **u,f.**

                                                          QD63.5
☐ Chemical and Engineering News Safety Letters (1993+).
http://pubs.acs.org/cen/safety/index.html
American Chemical Society.
Audience: **u,f.**

                                                          QD63.5
☐ Chemical Laboratory Safety (Stanford University).
http://library.stanford.edu/depts/swain/help/subjectguides/
chemsafety.html
Stanford University.
Audience: **u,f.**

                                                          QD63.5
☐ Chemical Safety--Web Guide (Stanford University).
http://library.stanford.edu/depts/swain/help/webdirs/
subject.html#safety
Stanford University.
Audience: **u,f.**

                                                          QD63.5
☐ LAB SAFETY--Online Safety Course.
http://www.practicingsafescience.org/
Audience: **u,f.**

                                                          QD63.5
☐ Materials Safety Data Sheets.
http://www.sigmaaldrich.com/
Sigma-Aldrich.
Audience: **u,f.**

                                                          QD63.5
☐ MSDS Hyper Glossary.
http://www.ilpi.com/msds/ref/index.html
Audience: **u,f.**

                                                          QD63.5
Safety in Academic Chemistry Laboratories. Ed. 6. American
Chemical Society. 1995. ISBN:0-8412-3259-8, ISBN13:
978-0-8412-3259-4.
Audience: **u,f.**

ACS Task Force on   QD51
  Laboratory Waste Management
Less Is Better: Laboratory Chemical Management for Waste
Reduction. Ed. 2. American Chemical Society, Dept. of Govt.
Relations and Science Policy. 1993.
Audience: **u,f.**

American Chemical Society,   TD899.L32L33 1994
  Task Force on Laboratory Waste Management Staff
Laboratory Waste Management: A Guidebook. Trade Cloth.
Oxford University Press, Inc. New York, NY. 1994. 250p. An
American Chemical Society Publication ISBN:0-8412-2735-7,
ISBN13: 978-0-8412-2735-4. Dewey:660. LCCN:93-045546.
Audience: **u,f.** *Choice, 1994.*

Armour, M. A.   **QD64.A76 2003**
Hazardous Laboratory Chemicals Disposal Guide. Ed. 3. Trade
Paper. Lewis Publishers. Boca Raton, FL. 2003. 592p.
ISBN:1-56670-567-3, ISBN13: 978-1-56670-567-7.
Dewey:542/.89. LCCN:2002-043358.
                              Audience: **u,f**. *Choice, 2003.*

Furr, A. Keith(Editory)   **QD51**
CRC Handbook of Laboratory Safety. Ed. 5. CRC Press. 2000.
ISBN:0-8493-2523-4, ISBN13: 978-0-8493-2523-6.
                              Audience: **u,f**.

Hajian, Harry G.   **QD63.5.H34**
Working Safely in the Chemistry Laboratory. Robert L. Pecsok
(Author, Editor). Trade Paper. John Wiley & Sons, Inc.
Hoboken, NJ. 1994. 250p. ISBN:0-8412-2707-1, ISBN13:
978-0-8412-2707-1. Dewey:542/.1/0289. LCCN:93-045353.
                              Audience: **l,u,f**. *Choice, 1994.*

Hall, Steven K.   **TP187.H35 1994**
Chemical Safety in the Laboratory. Paper over Boards. Lewis
Publishers. Boca Raton, FL. 1993. 288p. ISBN:0-87371-896-8,
ISBN13: 978-0-87371-896-7. Dewey:660/.2804.
LCCN:93-028653.
                              Audience: **u,f**. *Choice, 1994.*

Kaufman, James A. (Editor)   **QD64.W37 1990**
Waste Disposal in Academic Institutions. Paper over Boards.
Lewis Publishers. Boca Raton, FL. 1990. 208p.
ISBN:0-87371-256-0, ISBN13: 978-0-87371-256-9.
Dewey:363.72/87/02437. LCCN:90-005400.
                              Audience: **u,f**. *Choice, 1990.*

Lefevre, Marc J.   **RC963.3.L4313 1989**
First Aid Manual for Chemical Accidents. Ed. 2. Shirley A.
Conibear (Revised by). Trade Paper. John Wiley & Sons, Inc.
Hoboken, NJ. 1989. 272p. ISBN:0-442-20490-6, ISBN13:
978-0-442-20490-7. Dewey:615.9/08. LCCN:88-027996.
                              Audience: **u,f**.

Luxon, S. G. (Editor)   **QD63.5**
Hazards in the Chemical Laboratory. Ed. 5. Royal Society of
Chemistry. 1992. ISBN:0-85186-229-2, ISBN13:
978-0-85186-229-3.
                              Audience: **u,f**.

National Research Council   **T55.3.H3P78 1995**
Staff
Prudent Practices in the Laboratory: Handling and Disposal of
Chemicals. Ringbound. National Academies Press. Washington,
DC. 1995. 427p. ISBN:0-309-05229-7, ISBN13:
978-0-309-05229-0. Dewey:660/.2804. LCCN:95-032461.
                              Audience: **u,f**. *Choice, 1996.*

Saunders, G. Thomas   **QD54.F85S38 1993**
Laboratory Fume Hoods: A User's Manual. Ed. 1. Trade Cloth.
John Wiley & Sons, Inc. Hoboken, NJ. 1993. 144p.
ISBN:0-471-56935-6, ISBN13: 978-0-471-56935-0.
Dewey:542.1. LCCN:92-039024.
                              Audience: **u,f**.

Stricoff, R. Scott & Walters,   **QD51.S92 1995**
Douglas B.
Handbook of Laboratory Health and Safety. Ed. 2. Trade Cloth.
John Wiley & Sons, Inc. Hoboken, NJ. 1995. 480p.
ISBN:0-471-02628-X, ISBN13: 978-0-471-02628-0.
Dewey:001.4/028/9. LCCN:94-019358.
                              Audience: **u,f**. *Choice, 1995.*

The Forum for Scientific   **T55.3**
Excellence, Inc. (Editor)
Concise Manual of Chemical and Environmental Safety in
Schools and Colleges. Lippincott.
                              Audience: **u,f**.

Young, Jay A. (Editor)   **QD51.I48 1991**
Improving Safety in the Chemical Laboratory: A Practical
Guide. Ed. 2. Trade Cloth. John Wiley & Sons, Inc. Hoboken,
NJ. 1991. 432p. ISBN:0-471-53036-0, ISBN13:
978-0-471-53036-7. Dewey:542/.0289. LCCN:90-024189.
                              Audience: **u,f**. *Choice, 1992.*

Young, Jay A.; Kinglsey,   **QD51**
Warren K.; Wahl, George H., Jr.
Developing a Chemical Hygiene Plan. American Chemical
Society. 1990. ISBN:0-8412-1876-5, ISBN13:
978-0-8412-1876-5.
                              Audience: **u,f**.

Basic Chemistry > Problem Manuals, Educational Materials, and Computer Materials

                                                        QD45
☐ CCIIM (Clearinghouse for Chemical Information
Instructional Materials).
http://www.indiana.edu/~cheminfo/cciimnro.html
Indiana University.
                              Audience: **u,f**.

                                                        QD45
☐ Chem Tutor.
http://www.chemtutor.com/
                              Audience: **l,u,f**.

                                                        QD45
☐ Chemical Education--Web Guide (Stanford University).
http://library.stanford.edu/depts/swain/help/webdirs/
subject.html#chemed
Stanford University.
                              Audience: **l,u,f**.

                                                        QD99.3
☐ Computational Chemistry List (CCL Links).
http://www.ccl.net/chemistry/links/index.shtml
                              Audience: **u,f**.

                                                        QD31.3
☐ General Chemistry Virtual Textbook (Stephen Lower).
http://www.chem1.com/acad/webtext/virtualtextbook.html
Stephen Lower.
                              Audience: **l,u,f**.

                                                        QD1
☐ JCE (Journal of Chemical Education) Digital Library.
http://www.jce.divched.org/JCEDLib
Journal of Chemical Education.
                              Audience: **l,u,f**.

                                                        QD1
☐ JCE Online: Journal of Chemical Education.
http://jchemed.chem.wisc.edu/
American Chemical Society.
                              Audience: **l,u,f**.

QD45

☐ Journal of Chemical Education Chemical Education Resource Shelf.
http://www.umsl.edu/~chemist/books/texts.html
Division of Chemical Education, Inc., American Chemical Society.

Audience: **l,u,f.**

Alley, Michael   **Q223.A38 2003**
The Craft of Scientific Presentations: Critical Steps to Succeed and Critical Errors to Avoid. Trade Paper. Springer. New York, NY. 2005. XV, 241p. ISBN:0-387-95555-0, ISBN13: 978-0-387-95555-1. Dewey:808/.0665. LCCN:2002-030237.

Audience: **u,f.**

Billo, E. Joseph   **QD39.3.S67B55 2001**
Excel for Chemists: A Comprehensive Guide. Ed. 2. Trade Paper. John Wiley & Sons, Inc. Hoboken, NJ. 2001. 512p. ISBN:0-471-39462-9, ISBN13: 978-0-471-39462-4. Dewey:542/.85/5369. LCCN:2001-024022.

Audience: **u,f.**   *Choice, 1998.*

Diamond, Dermot &   **QD39.3.S7D53 1997**
 Hanratty, Venita C. A.
Spreadsheet Applications in Chemistry Using Microsoft Excel. Trade Paper. John Wiley & Sons, Inc. Hoboken, NJ. 1997. 256p. ISBN:0-471-14087-2, ISBN13: 978-0-471-14087-0. Dewey:540/.285/5369. LCCN:96-026223.

Audience: **u,f.**   *Choice, 1997.*

Jurs, Peter C.   **QD39.3.E46J873 1996**
Computer Software Applications in Chemistry. Ed. 2. Trade Cloth. John Wiley & Sons, Inc. Hoboken, NJ. 1996. 304p. ISBN:0-471-10587-2, ISBN13: 978-0-471-10587-9. Dewey:542/.8. LCCN:95-041349.

Audience: **u,f.**   *Choice, 1996, 1987.*

Kenkel, John V., et al.   **QD33.K415 2000**
Chemistry: An Industry-Based Introduction with CD-ROM. Paul B. Kelter & David S. Hage (Authors). Paper over Boards. Lewis Publishers. Boca Raton, FL. 2000. 544p. ISBN:1-56670-303-4, ISBN13: 978-1-56670-303-1. Dewey:540. LCCN:00-030343.

Audience: **u,f.**   *Choice, 2001.*

Steiner, Erich   **QA37.2.S7985 1996**
The Chemistry Maths Book. Paper Text. Oxford University Press, Inc. New York, NY. 1996. 560p. ISBN:0-19-855913-5, ISBN13: 978-0-19-855913-9. Dewey:510/.2454. LCCN:95-051779.

Audience: **u,f.**   *Choice, 1997.*

Tebbutt, Peter   **QA37.2.T43**
Basic Mathematics for Chemists. Ed. 2. Trade Paper. John Wiley & Sons, Inc. Hoboken, NJ. 1998. 292p. ISBN:0-471-97284-3, ISBN13: 978-0-471-97284-6. Dewey:510.2/4/541.

Audience: **l,u,f.**

Zielinski, T. J. & Swift, M.   **QD39.3.E46U84 1997**
 (Editors)
Using Computers in Chemistry and Chemical Education. Cloth Text. Oxford University Press, Inc. New York, NY. 1997. 416p. ACS Professional Reference Bks. ISBN:0-8412-3465-5, ISBN13: 978-0-8412-3465-9. Dewey:542/.85. LCCN:97-014325.

Audience: **u,f.**   *Choice, 1998.*

Analytical Chemistry > Encyclopedias

LB2806.45

☐ Chemistry Hypermedia Project--Analytical Chemistry Cross-Index.
http://www.chem.vt.edu/chem-ed/ac-basic.html

Audience: **u,f.**

Meyers, Robert A.   **QD71.5.E52 2000**
 (Editor-In-Chief)
Encyclopedia of Analytical Chemistry: Applications, Theory, and Instrumentation, Vol. 1-15. Trade Cloth. John Wiley & Sons, Inc. Hoboken, NJ. 2001. 14344p. ISBN:0-471-97670-9, ISBN13: 978-0-471-97670-7. Dewey:543/.003. LCCN:00-042282.

Audience: **l,u,f.**   *Choice, 2001.*

Townshend, Alan (Editor)   **QD71.5**
Encyclopedia of Analytical Science, 10 vols. Academic Press. 1995. ISBN:0-12-226700-1, ISBN13: 978-0-12-226700-0.

Audience: **l,u,f.**

Analytical Chemistry > General Handbooks and Data Compilations

American Chemical Society   **QD77.A54 2005**
 Staff (Contribution by)
Reagent Chemicals: American Chemical Society Specifications, Official from January 1, 2006. Ed. 10. Trade Cloth. American Chemical Society. Washington, DC. 2005. 832p. An American Chemical Society Publication ISBN:0-8412-3945-2, ISBN13: 978-0-8412-3945-6. Dewey:543/.028/4. LCCN:2005-045502.

Audience: **u,f.**

Association of Official   **QD71**
 Analytical Chemists
Handbook for AOAC members. Ed. 6. Arlington, VA: Association of Official Analytical Chemists. 1989. ISBN:0-935584-41-2, ISBN13: 978-0-935584-41-7.

Audience: **u,f.**

Bruno, Thomas J.;   **QD78**
 Svoronos, Paris D. N.
CRC Handbook of Basic Tables for Chemical Analysis. CRC Press, Boca Raton, FL. 1989. ISBN:0-8493-3935-9, ISBN13: 978-0-8493-3935-6.

Audience: **l,u,f.**

Dean, John Aurie   **QD78**
Analytical Chemistry Handbook. McGraw-Hill. 1995. ISBN:0-07-016197-6, ISBN13: 978-0-07-016197-9.

Audience: **l,u,f.**

Ewing, Galen Wood (Editor)   **QD79.I5A49 1997**
🄮 Analytical Instrumentation Handbook. Ed. 2. E-Book. NetLibrary, Inc. Boulder, CO. 1997. ISBN:0-585-08205-7, ISBN13: 978-0-585-08205-9. Dewey:543/.07.

Audience: **u,f.**

Günzler, Helmut &   **QD75.22.H36 2001**
 Williams, Alex (Editors)
Handbook of Analytical Techniques, Set. Trade Cloth. John Wiley & Sons, Inc. Hoboken, NJ. 2001. 1198p. ISBN:3-527-30165-8, ISBN13: 978-3-527-30165-2. Dewey:543. LCCN:2001-269238.

Audience: **u,f.**

Settle, Frank A. (Editor)   QD79.I5
Handbook of Instrumental Techniques for Analytical Chemistry.
Prentice-Hall PTR, Upper Saddle River, NJ. 1997.
ISBN:0-13-177338-0, ISBN13: 978-0-13-177338-7.
                                        Audience: **u,f.**

Analytical Chemistry > Analytical Methods > Standard Methods

                                              QD75.2
☐ NIOSH Manual of Analytical Methods (NMAM).
http://www.cdc.gov/niosh/nmam/
                                        Audience: **u,f.**

                                                S587
Official Methods of Analysis of the AOAC International. Ed. 16.
AOAC International, Arlington, VA. 1995.
                                        Audience: **u,f.**

Furman, N. Howell (Editor)   QD131.S68
Standard Methods of Chemical Analysis, Set. Trade Cloth.
Krieger Publishing Company. Melbourne, FL. 1975. 6202p.
ISBN:0-88275-940-X, ISBN13: 978-0-88275-940-1. Dewey:543.
LCCN:74-023465.
                                        Audience: **u,f.**

Keith, Lawrence H. (Editor)   TD193
Compilation of EPA's Sampling and Analysis Methods. Ed. 2.
CRC/Lewis Publishers. 1996. ISBN:1-56670-170-8, ISBN13:
978-1-56670-170-9.
                                        Audience: **u,f.**

Scholz, Eugen   QD111 .S41513 1984
Karl Fischer Titration. D. Lee (Translator). Cloth Text. Springer.
New York, NY. 1984. 138p. ISBN:0-387-13734-3, ISBN13:
978-0-387-13734-6. Dewey:544. LCCN:84-014165.
                                        Audience: **u,f.**

Thurman, E. M. & Mills,   QD63.E88T58 1998
M. S.
Solid-Phase Extraction: Principles and Practice. Trade Cloth.
John Wiley & Sons, Inc. Hoboken, NJ. 1998. 372p. Chemical
Analysis, Vol. 150:A Series of Monographs on Analytical
Chemistry and Its Applications ISBN:0-471-61422-X, ISBN13:
978-0-471-61422-7. Dewey:543/.0892. LCCN:97-027535.
                              Audience: **u,f.** *Choice, 1998.*

Watson, C. A.   QD75.2 .W377 1994
Official and Standardized Methods of Analysis. Ed. 3. Trade
Cloth. Springer. New York, NY. 1994. 802p.
ISBN:0-85186-441-4, ISBN13: 978-0-85186-441-9. Dewey:545.
                                        Audience: **u,f.**

Analytical Chemistry > Analytical Methods > General Methods

                                              LB2806.45
☐ Chemistry Hypermedia Project--Encyclopedia of Analytical
Instrumentation.
http://www.chem.vt.edu/chem-ed/ac-meths.html
                                        Audience: **u,f.**

Budevsky, O.   QD71
Foundations of Chemical Analysis. Chalmers, R. A.; Masson, M.
R. (Editors). Halsted Press. 1979. Ellis Horwood Series in
Analytical Chemistry ISBN:0-470-26692-9, ISBN13:
978-0-470-26692-2.
                                        Audience: **u,f.**

Fritz, James S.   QD63.E88F68 1999
Analytical Solid-Phase Extraction. Trade Cloth. John Wiley &
Sons, Inc. Hoboken, NJ. 1999. 224p. ISBN:0-471-24667-0,
ISBN13: 978-0-471-24667-1. Dewey:543/.0892.
LCCN:98-043758.
                              Audience: **u,f.** *Choice, 2000.*

Kolthoff, I. M.; Stenger, V.   QD111
A.
Volumetric Analysis, 1942-1957, 3 vols. Ed. 2. Furman, N. H.
(Translator). Interscience Publishers.
                                        Audience: **u,f.**

Kuwana, Theodore (Editor)   QD75.2
Physical Methods in Modern Chemical Analysis, 1978-1983, 3
vols. Academic Press. ISBN:0-12-430801-5, ISBN13:
978-0-12-430801-5.
                                        Audience: **u,f.**

Levinson, R.   QD75.22.L48 2001
More Modern Chemical Techniques. Trade Paper. Royal Society
of Chemistry, The. Cambridge, 2002. x + 183p.
ISBN:0-85404-929-0, ISBN13: 978-0-85404-929-5. Dewey:543.
                                        Audience: **u,f.**

Mueller-Harvey, I. & Baker,   QD75.22.M84 2002
R. M.
Chemical Analysis in the Laboratory: A Basic Guide. Trade
Paper. Royal Society of Chemistry, The. Cambridge, 2002. xvi +
92p. ISBN:0-85404-646-1, ISBN13: 978-0-85404-646-1.
Dewey:543.
                                        Audience: **u,f.**

Reilly, C. N. (Editor)   QD71
Advances in Analytical Chemistry and Instrumentation,
1960-1973, Vols. 1-11. Wiley-Interscience.
                                        Audience: **u,f.**

Rouessac, Annick &   QD79.I5R6813 2000
Rouessac, Francis
Chemical Analysis: Modern Instrumental Methods and
Techniques. Trade Paper. John Wiley & Sons, Inc. Hoboken, NJ.
2000. 470p. ISBN:0-471-97261-4, ISBN13: 978-0-471-97261-7.
Dewey:543. LCCN:99-058872.
                                        Audience: **l,u,f.**

Smart, L. E. (Editor)   QD81
Separation, Purification and Identification. Mixed Media. Royal
Society of Chemistry, The. Cambridge, 2002. 120p. The
Molecular World Ser. ISBN:0-85404-685-2, ISBN13:
978-0-85404-685-0. Dewey:544.
                            Audience: **l,u,f.** *Choice, 2003.*

Smyth, Malcolm R. (Editor)   QD75.2
Chemical Analysis in Complex Matrices. PTR Prentice Hall.
1992. Ellis Horwood PTR Prentice Hall Analytical Chemistry
Series ISBN:0-13-127671-9, ISBN13: 978-0-13-127671-0.
                                        Audience: **u,f.**

Taylor, Larry R., et al.   **QD79.I5T39 1994**
Instrumental Methods for Determining Elements: Selection and
Applications. Richard B. Papp & Bruce D. Pollard (Authors).
Trade Cloth. John Wiley & Sons, Inc. Hoboken, NJ. 1994. ix,
322p. ISBN:1-56081-038-6, ISBN13: 978-1-56081-038-4.
Dewey:543. LCCN:93-038305.
                                    Audience: **u,f.** *Choice, 1995.*

Thomas, Leslie C.;   **QD113**
  Chamberlin, Gordon J.
Colorimetric Chemical Analytical Methods. Ed. 9. Shute, G.
(Reviser). Tintometer; NY: distr. by Wiley. 1980.
ISBN:0-471-27605-7, ISBN13: 978-0-471-27605-0.
                                         Audience: **u,f.**

Walton, Harold F.; Rocklin,   **QD79.C453**
  Roy D.
Ion Exchange in Analytical Chemistry. CRC Press, Boca Raton,
FL. 1990. ISBN:0-8493-6199-0, ISBN13: 978-0-8493-6199-9.
                                         Audience: **u,f.**

Analytical Chemistry > Special Topics > Chromatography

Bartle, Keith D. & Myers,   **QP519.9.C36**
  Peter (Editors)
Capillary Electrochromatography. Trade Cloth. Royal Society of
Chemistry, The. Cambridge, 2001. xvi + 150p.
ISBN:0-85404-530-9, ISBN13: 978-0-85404-530-3.
Dewey:544.9/2. LCCN:2001-131677.
                                    Audience: **u,f.** *Choice, 2002.*

Cazes, Jack (Editor)   **QD79.C4E63 2001**
Encyclopedia of Chromatography. Paper over Boards. Marcel
Dekker Inc. New York, NY. 2001. 927p. New Encyclopedias
Ser. ISBN:0-8247-0511-4, ISBN13: 978-0-8247-0511-4.
Dewey:543/.8. LCCN:2001-028927.
                                         Audience: **u,f.**

Grob, Robert L. & Barry,   **QD79.C45M63 2004**
  Eugene F. (Editors)
Modern Practice of Gas Chromatography. Ed. 4. Trade Cloth.
John Wiley & Sons, Inc. Hoboken, NJ. 2004. 1064p.
ISBN:0-471-22983-0, ISBN13: 978-0-471-22983-4.
Dewey:543/.85. LCCN:2003-062033.
                                    Audience: **u,f.** *Choice, 2005, 1996.*

Heftmann, E. (Editor)   **QD79.C4**
Chromatography: Fundamentals and Applications of
Chromatography and Related Differential Migration Methods.
Ed. 6. Cloth Text. Elsevier Science & Technology Books. Saint
Louis, MO. 2004. 490p. Journal of Chromatography Library
ISBN:0-444-51106-7, ISBN13: 978-0-444-51106-5.
Dewey:543.8.
                                         Audience: **u,f.**

Heftmann, E. (Editor)   **QD79**
Chromatography: A Laboratory Handbook of Chromatographic
and Electrophoretic Methods. Van Nostrand Reinhold. 1975.
ISBN:0-442-23280-2, ISBN13: 978-0-442-23280-1.
                                         Audience: **u,f.**

Jennings, Walter, et al.   **QD79.C45J458 1997**
Analytical Gas Chromatography. Ed. 2. Eric Mittlefehldt &
Phillip Stremple (Authors). Trade Cloth. Elsevier Science &

Technology Books. Saint Louis, MO. 1997. 389p.
ISBN:0-12-384357-X, ISBN13: 978-0-12-384357-9.
Dewey:543/.0896. LCCN:97-215353.
                                    Audience: **u,f.** *Choice, 1998.*

McMaster, Marvin C.   **QD79.C454M36 1994**
HPLC, a Practical User's Guide. Trade Cloth. John Wiley &
Sons, Inc. Hoboken, NJ. 1994. xii, 211 p. :p.
ISBN:1-56081-636-8, ISBN13: 978-1-56081-636-2.
Dewey:543/.0894. LCCN:93-042139.
                                    Audience: **u,f.** *Choice, 1995.*

McNair, Harold M. &   **QD79.C45M425 1998**
  Miller, James M.
Basic Gas Chromatography. Trade Paper. John Wiley & Sons,
Inc. Hoboken, NJ. 1997. 224p. Techniques in Analytical
Chemistry Ser., Vol. 12 ISBN:0-471-17261-8, ISBN13:
978-0-471-17261-1. Dewey:543/.0896. LCCN:97-018151.
                                    Audience: **u,f.** *Choice, 1998.*

Sadek, Paul C.   **QD79**
The HPLC Solvent Guide. Ed. 2. Trade Cloth. John Wiley &
Sons, Inc. Hoboken, NJ. 2002. 664p. ISBN:0-471-41138-8,
ISBN13: 978-0-471-41138-3. Dewey:543/.0894.
LCCN:2002-275754.
                                         Audience: **u,f.**

Snyder, Lloyd R., et al.   **QP519.9.H53S69 1997**
Practical HPLC Method Development. Ed. 2. Joseph J. Kirkland
& Joseph L. Glajch (Authors). Trade Cloth. John Wiley & Sons,
Inc. Hoboken, NJ. 1997. 800p. ISBN:0-471-00703-X, ISBN13:
978-0-471-00703-6. Dewey:543/.0894. LCCN:96-034296.
                                    Audience: **u,f.** *Choice, 1997.*

Tebbett, Ian (Editor)   **RA1057**
Gas Chromatography in Forensic Science. E. Horwood. 1992.
Ellis Horwood Series in Forensic Science ISBN:0-13-327198-6,
ISBN13: 978-0-13-327198-0.
                                         Audience: **u,f.**

Weston, Andrea   **QD79.C454**
HPLC and CE: Principles and Practice. Brown, Phyllis R.
(Editors). Academic Press. 1997. ISBN:0-12-136640-5, ISBN13:
978-0-12-136640-7.
                                         Audience: **u,f.**

Zweig, Gunter and Joseph   **QD117.C5**
  Sherma (eds.)
CRC Handbook of Chromatography. CRC Press. 1972.
ISBN:0-87819-560-2, ISBN13: 978-0-87819-560-2.
                                         Audience: **u,f.**

Analytical Chemistry > Special Topics > Spectroscopy > Reference Works

☐ Biophysical Chemistry Online Resources (UW,
Madison)--Techniques.
http://chemistry.library.wisc.edu/biophysics/techniques.htm
                                         Audience: **u,f.**

☐ Colby College. Chemistry Department.
http://www.colby edu/chemistry/NMR/NMR.html
                                         Audience: **u,f.**

☐ SIRCh: Analytical Chemistry--Spectral Sources.
http://www.indiana.edu/~cheminfo/ca-accc.html#spectral
Audience: **u,f.**

☐ Spectral Information Resources (Stanford University).
http://library.stanford.edu/depts/swain/help/subjectguides/
spectral.html
Audience: **u,f.**

☐ Wiki Spectroscopy.
http://scienceofspectroscopy.info/
Audience: **u,f.**

Denney, Ronald C.   **QC450.3**
A Dictionary of Spectroscopy. Ed. 2. Wiley. 1982.
Wiley-Interscience Publication ISBN:0-471-87478-7, ISBN13:
978-0-471-87478-2.
Audience: **u,f.**

Herzberg, Gerhard   **QC454.M6H4713 1989**
Molecular Spectra and Molecular Structure: Spectra of Diatomic
Molecules, Vol. 1. Ed. 2. Library Binding. Krieger Publishing
Company. Melbourne, FL. 1989. 678p. Molecular Spectra and
Molecular Structure Ser. ISBN:0-89464-268-5, ISBN13:
978-0-89464-268-5. Dewey:535.8/4. LCCN:88-002933.
Audience: **u,f.**

Herzberg, Gerhard   **QC454.M6 H4713**
Molecular Spectra and Molecular Structure: Electronic Spectra
and Electronic Structure of Polyatomic Molecules, Vol. 3. Trade
Cloth. Krieger Publishing Company. Melbourne, FL. 1991.
784p. Molecular Spectra and Molecular Structure Ser.
ISBN:0-89464-270-7, ISBN13: 978-0-89464-270-8.
Dewey:535.8/4. LCCN:88-002933.
Audience: **u,f.** 𝔅

Herzberg, Gerhard   **QC454.M6 H4713**
Molecular Spectra and Molecular Structure: Infrared and Raman
of Polyatomic Molecules, Vol. 2. Library Binding. Krieger
Publishing Company. Melbourne, FL. 1990. 650p. Molecular
Spectra and Molecular Structure Ser. ISBN:0-89464-269-3,
ISBN13: 978-0-89464-269-2. Dewey:535.8/4. LCCN:88-002933.
Audience: **u,f.**

Perkampus, Heinz-Helmut   **QD450.3**
Encyclopedia of Spectroscopy. Grinter, Heide-Charlotte; Grinter,
Roger (Translators). VCH. 1995. ISBN:3-527-29281-0, ISBN13:
978-3-527-29281-3.
Audience: **u,f.**

Robinson, J. W. (Editor)   **QD95**
Handbook of Spectroscopy. CRC Press. 1974.
ISBN:0-87819-333-2, ISBN13: 978-0-87819-333-2.
Audience: **u,f.**

Tranter, George E. &   **QC450.3.E53**
  Holmes, John L. (Editors)
Encyclopedia of Spectroscopy and Spectrometry, Set. John C.
Lindon (Editor-In-Chief). Trade Cloth. Elsevier Science &
Technology Books. Saint Louis, MO. 2000. 2581p.
ISBN:0-12-226680-3, ISBN13: 978-0-12-226680-5.
Dewey:543/.0858/03. LCCN:98-087952.
Audience: **u,f.** *Choice, 2000.*

Analytical Chemistry > Special Topics > Spectroscopy > Infrared Spectroscopy

QC457
The Atlas of Near Infrared Spectra. Trade Cloth. Sadtler
Research Laboratories. Philadelphia, PA. 1981. 1000p.
ISBN:0-8456-0063-X, ISBN13: 978-0-8456-0063-4.
Dewey:535.8/42. LCCN:80-052913.
Audience: **u,f.**

Bellamy, L J   **QD476**
Infrared Spectra of Complex Molecules, Vol. 2. Ed. 3. Chapman
& Hall. 1980. ISBN:0-412-22350-3, ISBN13:
978-0-412-22350-1.
Audience: **u,f.**

Hershenson, Herbert M.   **QD96**
Infrared Absorption Spectra, 1959-1964, 2 vols. Academic Press.
Audience: **u,f.**

Nyquist, Richard A.   **QD96.I5N96 2001**
Interpreting Infrared, Raman, and Nuclear Magnetic Resonance
Spectra. Trade Cloth. Elsevier Science & Technology Books.
Saint Louis, MO. 2001. xv, 447p. ISBN:0-12-523470-8,
ISBN13: 978-0-12-523470-2. Dewey:543/.0858.
LCCN:00-108478.
Audience: **u,f.** *Choice, 2001.*

Nyquist, Richard A.   **QC457.N94 1984**
The Interpretation of Vapor-Phase Infrared Spectra. Sadtler.
1984.
Audience: **u,f.**

Nyquist, Richard A.   **QD305**
IR and NMR spectral data-structure correlations for the carbonyl
group. Philadelphia, PA: Sadtler Research Laboratories. 1986.
ISBN:0-8456-0135-0, ISBN13: 978-0-8456-0135-8.
Audience: **u,f.**

Pouchert, Charles J.   **QC457.P87 1997**
The Aldrich Library of FT-IR Spectra. Trade Cloth.
Sigma-Aldrich Corporation. Saint Louis, MO. 1989.
ISBN:0-941633-39-X, ISBN13: 978-0-941633-39-0.
Dewey:543/.08583. LCCN:97-073684.
Audience: **u,f.**

Pouchert, Charles J.   **QD96.I5**
The Aldrich Library of Infrared Spectra. Ed. 3. Aldrich
Chemical Co.. 1981.
Audience: **u,f.**

Sadtler Research Labs, Inc.,   **QC453 .S73 1978**
  Staff
The Sadtler Handbook of Infrared Spectra. Trade Paper. Sadtler
Research Laboratories. Philadelphia, PA. 1978. The Sadtler
Handbooks Ser. ISBN:0-8456-0034-6, ISBN13:
978-0-8456-0034-4. Dewey:547/.3/085. LCCN:77-095458.
Audience: **u,f.**

Smith, Brian C.   **QD96.I5**
Infrared Spectral Interpretation: A Systematic Approach. CRC
Press, Boca Raton, FL. 1999. ISBN:0-8493-2463-7, ISBN13:
978-0-8493-2463-5.
Audience: **u,f.**

Stuart, Barbara **QD96.I5**
Modern Infrared Spectroscopy. Ando, David J. (Editor). Wiley.
1996. Analytical Chemistry by Open Learning
ISBN:0-471-95916-2, ISBN13: 978-0-471-95916-8.
Audience: **u,f.**

Analytical Chemistry > Special Topics > Spectroscopy > Mass Spectroscopy

QC454.A8

i-mass.com (Mass spectrometry Web address).
http://www.i-mass.com/
Audience: **u,f.**

Barker, James **QD96.M3D38 1999**
Mass Spectrometry: Analytical Chemistry by Open Learning.
Ed. 2. David J. Ando (Editor). Trade Paper. John Wiley & Sons,
Inc. Hoboken, NJ. 1999. 532p. Analytical Chemistry by Open
Learning Ser., Pt. B ISBN:0-471-96762-9, ISBN13:
978-0-471-96762-0. Dewey:543/.0873. LCCN:98-003127.
Audience: **u,f.**

Caprioli, Richard M. & **QD96.M3**
Gross, Michael L. (Editors)
The Encyclopedia of Mass Spectrometry: Biological
Applications. M. L. Gross (Contribution by). Trade Cloth.
Elsevier Science & Technology Books. Saint Louis, MO. 2004.
400p. ISBN:0-08-043800-8, ISBN13: 978-0-08-043800-9.
Dewey:543/.0873. LCCN:2003-107670.
Audience: **u,f.**

de Hoffmann, Edmond & **QD96.M3H6413 2001**
Stroobant, Vincent
Mass Spectrometry: Principles and Applications. Ed. 2. Trade
Paper. John Wiley & Sons, Inc. Hoboken, NJ. 2001. 420p.
ISBN:0-471-48566-7, ISBN13: 978-0-471-48566-7.
Dewey:543/.0873. LCCN:2001-033254.
Audience: **u,f.** *Choice, 1997.*

Grayson, Michael A. **QD96.M3M43 2002**
(Editor)
Measuring Mass: From Positive Rays to Proteins. Trade Cloth.
Chemical Heritage Foundation. Philadelphia, PA. 2005. 149p.
ISBN:0-941901-31-9, ISBN13: 978-0-941901-31-4.
Dewey:543/.0873/09. LCCN:2001-007646.
Audience: **u,f.** *Choice, 2003.*

Gross, M. L. & Caprioli, R. **QD96.M3**
The Encyclopedia of Mass Spectrometry: Methods of Mass
Analysis and Associated Instrumentation. Trade Cloth. Elsevier
Science & Technology Books. Saint Louis, MO. 2006. 600p.
ISBN:0-08-043805-9, ISBN13: 978-0-08-043805-4.
Dewey:543/.0873.
Audience: **u,f.**

Gross, M. L. & Caprioli, R. **QD96.M3**
The Encyclopedia of Mass Spectrometry: Theory and Ion
Chemistry. Patricia Armentrout (Editor). Trade Cloth. Elsevier
Science & Technology Books. Saint Louis, MO. 2003. 940p.
ISBN:0-08-043802-4, ISBN13: 978-0-08-043802-3.
Dewey:543/.0873. LCCN:2003-107670.
Audience: **u,f.**

Gross, M. L. & Caprioli, R. **QD96.M3**
The Encyclopedia of Mass Spectrometry: Fundamentals of and
Applications to Organic (and Organometallic) Compounds. Nico
M. Nibbering (Editor). Trade Cloth. Elsevier Science &
Technology Books. Saint Louis, MO. 2004. 950p.
ISBN:0-08-043846-6, ISBN13: 978-0-08-043846-7.
Dewey:543/.0873. LCCN:2003-107670.
Audience: **u,f.**

Gross, M. L. & Caprioli, R. **QD96.M3**
The Encyclopedia of Mass Spectrometry: Hyphenated Methods.
Wilfried M. A. Niessen (Volume Editor). Trade Cloth. Elsevier
Science & Technology Books. Saint Louis, MO. 2006. 1000p.
ISBN:0-08-043847-4, ISBN13: 978-0-08-043847-4.
Dewey:543/.0873.
Audience: **u,f.**

Gross, Michael L. & **QD96.M3**
Caprioli, Richard M. (Editors)
The Encyclopedia of Mass Spectrometry: Biological
Applications: Carbohydrates, Nucleic Acids and Other
Biological Compounds. Trade Cloth. Elsevier Science &
Technology Books. Saint Louis, MO. 2005. 600p.
ISBN:0-08-043803-2, ISBN13: 978-0-08-043803-0.
Dewey:543.65. LCCN:2003-107670.
Audience: **u,f.**

McLafferty, Fred W. **QC454.M3 M395**
Wiley Registry of Mass Spectral Data: With NIST 2005 Spectral
Data. Ed. 7. Digital, Other. John Wiley & Sons, Inc. Hoboken,
NJ. 2005. ISBN:0-471-47325-1, ISBN13: 978-0-471-47325-1.
Dewey:545/.33.
Audience: **u,f.**

McLafferty, Fred W. & **QC454.M3M395 1989**
Stauffer, Douglas B.
Wiley/NBS Registry of Mass Spectral Data. Ed. 1. Trade Cloth.
John Wiley & Sons, Inc. Hoboken, NJ. 1989. 7872p.
ISBN:0-471-62886-7, ISBN13: 978-0-471-62886-6.
Dewey:539/.6/028. LCCN:87-031645.
Audience: **u,f.**

McLafferty, Fred W. & **QC454.M3.M39 1993**
Turecek, Frantisek
Interpretation of Mass Spectra. Ed. 4. John Choi (Illustrator).
Trade Cloth. University Science Books. Sausalito, CA. 1993.
370p. ISBN:0-935702-25-3, ISBN13: 978-0-935702-25-5.
Dewey:543/.0873. LCCN:92-082536.
Audience: **u,f.** *Choice, 1994.*

McMaster, Marvin & **QD79.C45M423 1998**
McMaster, Christopher
Gc/Ms: A Practical User's Guide. Trade Cloth. John Wiley &
Sons, Inc. Hoboken, NJ. 1998. 184p. ISBN:0-471-24826-6,
ISBN13: 978-0-471-24826-2. Dewey:543/.0873.
LCCN:97-048529.
Audience: **u,f.** *Choice, 1999.*

Smith, R. Martin & Busch, **QD96.M3S65 1999**
Kenneth L.
Understanding Mass Spectra: A Basic Approach. Trade Cloth.
John Wiley & Sons, Inc. Hoboken, NJ. 1998. 320p.
ISBN:0-471-29704-6, ISBN13: 978-0-471-29704-8.
Dewey:543/.0873. LCCN:98-018136.
Audience: **u,f.** *Choice, 2005, 1999.*

Sparkman, O. David   QD96.M3S73 2000
Mass Spec Desk Reference. Paper Text. Global View
Publishing. Pittsburgh, PA. 2000. xvi, 106p.
ISBN:0-9660813-2-3, ISBN13: 978-0-9660813-2-9.
Dewey:543/.0873/014. LCCN:00-100995.
                                        Audience: **u,f.** *Choice, 2001.*

Analytical Chemistry > Special Topics > Spectroscopy > Nuclear Magnetic Resonance Spectroscopy

                                                    QC462.85
Aldrich/ACD Library of FT NMR Spectra. Aldrich,
Milwaukee, WI; Advanced Chemistry Development. 1998.
                                        Audience: **u,f.**

Enhanced NMR Periodic Table.
http://www.chem.tamu.edu/services/NMR/periodic/index.shtml
                                        Audience: **u,f.**

                                            QC762 .S28 1983
Sadtler Guide to Carbon-13 NMR Spectra. Trade Cloth. Sadtler
Research Laboratories. Philadelphia, PA. 1983.
ISBN:0-8456-0087-7, ISBN13: 978-0-8456-0087-0.
Dewey:547.3/0877. LCCN:82-050006.
                                        Audience: **u,f.**

Bigler, Peter   QD96.N8B54 2000
NMR Spectroscopy: Processing Strategies. Ed. 2. Trade Cloth,
CD-ROM. John Wiley & Sons, Inc. Hoboken, NJ. 2000. 271p.
Spectroscopic Techniques Ser. ISBN:3-527-29990-4, ISBN13:
978-3-527-29990-4. Dewey:543/.0877. LCCN:00-266560.
                                        Audience: **u,f.** *Choice, 1998.*

Breitmaier, Eberhard and   QD96.N8
  Gerhard Bauer
Carbon-13 NMR spectroscopy: high-resolution methods and
applications in organic chemistry and biochemistry. NY: VCH
Publishers. 1987. ISBN:0-89573-493-1, ISBN13:
978-0-89573-493-8.
                                        Audience: **u,f.**

Cowan, Brian   QC762 .C69 1997
Nuclear Magnetic Resonance and Relaxation. Trade Cloth.
Cambridge University Press. New York, NY. 1997. 458p.
ISBN:0-521-30393-1, ISBN13: 978-0-521-30393-4.
Dewey:538/.362. LCCN:96-046614.
                                        Audience: **u,f.** *Choice, 1998.*

Freeman, Ray   RC78.7.N83 F74
Spin Choreography: Basic Steps in High Resolution NMR.
Trade Cloth. Oxford University Press, Inc. New York, NY. 1998.
404p. ISBN:0-19-850481-0, ISBN13: 978-0-19-850481-8.
Dewey:543/.0877.
                                        Audience: **u,f.** *Choice, 1997.*

Friebolin, Horst   QP519.9.N83F7513
Basic One- and Two-Dimensional NMR Spectroscopy. Ed. 3.
Trade Paper. John Wiley & Sons, Inc. Hoboken, NJ. 1998. 410p.
ISBN:3-527-29513-5, ISBN13: 978-3-527-29513-5.
Dewey:543/.0877. LCCN:99-184404.
                                        Audience: **u,f.** *Choice, 2005.*

Macomber, Roger S.   QD96.N8M3 1998
A Complete Introduction to Modern NMR Spectroscopy. Ed. 1.
Trade Paper. John Wiley & Sons, Inc. Hoboken, NJ. 1997. 400p.
ISBN:0-471-15736-8, ISBN13: 978-0-471-15736-6.
Dewey:543/.0877. LCCN:97-017106.
                                        Audience: **u,f.** *Choice, 1998.*

Pouchert, Charles J.   QD96.N8
The Aldrich Library of NMR Spectra. Ed. 2. Aldrich Chemical
Co.. 1983.
                                        Audience: **u,f.**

Pouchert, Charles J.   QC462.85
The Aldrich Library of 13C and 1H FT-NMR Spectra, 3 vols.
Behnke, Jacqlynn (Editors). Aldrich Chemical Co.. 1993.
ISBN:0-941633-34-9, ISBN13: 978-0-941633-34-5.
                                        Audience: **u,f.**

Roberts, John D.   QC437 .R58
An Introduction to the Analysis of Spin-Spin Splitting in
High-Resolution Nuclear Magnetic Resonance Spectra. W. A.
Benjamin. 1961.
                                        Audience: **u,f.**

Sadtler Research Labs, Inc.,   QC762 .S3 1978
  Staff
The Sadtler Handbook of Proton NMR Spectra. Trade Cloth.
Sadtler Research Laboratories. Philadelphia, PA. 1978. The
Sadtler Handbooks Ser. ISBN:0-8456-0035-4, ISBN13:
978-0-8456-0035-1. Dewey:543/.08. LCCN:78-054281.
                                        Audience: **u,f.**

Simons, W. W. &   QC490
  Zanger, M.
Sadtler Guide to NMR Spectra. Trade Paper. Sadtler Research
Laboratories. Philadelphia, PA. 1972. ISBN:0-8456-0001-X,
ISBN13: 978-0-8456-0001-6. Dewey:547/.308/5.
LCCN:72-075379.
                                        Audience: **u,f.**

Analytical Chemistry > Special Topics > Spectroscopy > Ultraviolet Spectroscopy

Frost, T
Ultra Violet Spectrometry: Practical Techniques, Instrumentation
and Data Handling. Springer London, Ltd. 1993.
ISBN:0-412-40530-X, ISBN13: 978-0-412-40530-3.
                                        Audience: **u,f.**

Hershenson, Herbert M.   Z7144.S7 U4
Ultraviolet and Visible Absorption Spectra: Index for 1930-1954.
Trade Cloth. Elsevier Science & Technology Books. Saint
Louis, MO. 1956. ISBN:0-12-343265-0, ISBN13:
978-0-12-343265-0. Dewey:16.5353.
                                        Audience: **u,f.**

Sadtler Research Labs, Inc.,   QC459 .S25 1979
  Staff
The Sadtler Handbook of Ultraviolet Spectra. William Simons
(Editor). Trade Cloth. Sadtler Research Laboratories.
Philadelphia, PA. 1978. The Sadtler Handbooks Ser.
ISBN:0-8456-0033-8, ISBN13: 978-0-8456-0033-7.
Dewey:547.3/08585. LCCN:79-065539.
                                        Audience: **u,f.**

Analytical Chemistry > Special Topics > Spectroscopy > Other Spectroscopic Techniques

Alkemade, C. Theodorus J.; Herrmann, R. QD96.F5
Fundamentals of Analytical Flame Spectroscopy. Auerbach, R.; Gilbert, Paul T., Jr. (Translators). Wiley. 1979. A Halsted Press Book ISBN:0-470-26710-0, ISBN13: 978-0-470-26710-3.
Audience: **u,f.**

Barr, Tery Lynn QD96.E44
Modern ESCA: The Principles and Practice of X-ray Photoelectron Spectroscopy. CRC Press, Boca Raton, FL. 1994. ISBN:0-8493-8653-5, ISBN13: 978-0-8493-8653-4.
Audience: **u,f.**

Hollas, J. Michael QD96.A8H65 2002
Basic Atomic and Molecular Spectroscopy. Trade Paper. John Wiley & Sons, Inc. Hoboken, NJ. 2002. 186p. Basic Concepts in Chemistry Ser. ISBN:0-471-28162-X, ISBN13: 978-0-471-28162-7. Dewey:541.2/2. LCCN:2002-727722.
Audience: **u,f.**

Hollas, J. Michael QC454.H618H64 1998
High Resolution Spectroscopy. Ed. 2. Trade Cloth. John Wiley & Sons, Inc. Hoboken, NJ. 1998. 762p. ISBN:0-471-97421-8, ISBN13: 978-0-471-97421-5. Dewey:535.8/4. LCCN:97-044183.
Audience: **u,f.**

Jenkins, Ron QD96.X2J47 1999
X-Ray Fluorescence Spectrometry. Ed. 2. Trade Cloth. John Wiley & Sons, Inc. Hoboken, NJ. 1999. 232p. Chemical Analysis, Vol. 212:A Series of Monographs on Analytical Chemistry and Its Applications ISBN:0-471-29942-1, ISBN13: 978-0-471-29942-4. Dewey:543/.08586. LCCN:98-039008.
Audience: **u,f.**

Johansson, Sven A. E. (Editor), et al. QD96.X2P37 1995
Particle-Induced X-Ray Emission Spectrometry (PIXE). John L. Campbell & Klas G. Malmqvist (Editors). Trade Cloth. John Wiley & Sons, Inc. Hoboken, NJ. 1995. 451p. Chemical Analysis, Vol. 184:A Series of Monographs on Analytical Chemistry and Its Applications ISBN:0-471-58944-6, ISBN13: 978-0-471-58944-0. Dewey:545/.836. LCCN:94-044471.
Audience: **u,f.** *Choice, 1996.*

Mirabella, Francis M. (Editor) QD96.M65M63 1998
Modern Techniques in Applied Molecular Spectroscopy. Trade Cloth. John Wiley & Sons, Inc. Hoboken, NJ. 1998. 409p. Techniques in Analytical Chemistry Ser., Vol. 14 ISBN:0-471-12359-5, ISBN13: 978-0-471-12359-0. Dewey:543/.0858. LCCN:97-013437.
Audience: **u,f.**

Van Loon, Jon C. QD96
Analytical Atomic Absorption Spectroscopy: Selected Methods. Academic Press. 1980. ISBN:0-12-714050-6, ISBN13: 978-0-12-714050-6.
Audience: **u,f.**

Analytical Chemistry > Special Topics > Polarography

Thomas, Francis G. & Henze, Gunter QD116.V4 T4813 2001
Introduction to Voltammetic Analysis. Trade Paper. CSIRO Publishing. Collingwood, VIC. 2000. 264p. ISBN:0-643-06593-8, ISBN13: 978-0-643-06593-2. Dewey:543.0871.
Audience: **u,f.** *Choice, 2002.*

Analytical Chemistry > Treatises

Cases, Miguel Valcarcel QD75.2.V35 2000
Principles of Analytical Chemistry: A Textbook. Trade Cloth. Springer. New York, NY. 2000. XV, 371p. ISBN:3-540-64007-X, ISBN13: 978-3-540-64007-3. Dewey:543. LCCN:00-033829.
Audience: **u,f.** *Choice, 2001.*

Kellner, R. (Editor) QD101.2
Analytical Chemistry: The Approved Text to the FECS Curriculum Analytical Chemistry. WIley-VCH. 1998. ISBN:3-527-28881-3, ISBN13: 978-3-527-28881-6.
Audience: **l,u,f.**

Kolthoff, Izaak M. QD75
Treatise on Analytical Chemistry. Elving, Philip J. (Editors). Wiley-Interscience. 1959.
Audience: **l,u,f.**

Kolthoff, Izaak M. QD75.2
Treatise on Analytical Chemistry: Theory and Practice, Vol. 8, Pt. 1. Ed. 2. Philip J. Elving & Edward J. Meehan (Editors). Trade Cloth. John Wiley & Sons, Inc. Hoboken, NJ. 1986. 767p. Treatise on Analytical Chemistry Ser. ISBN:0-471-07995-2, ISBN13: 978-0-471-07995-8. Dewey:543. LCCN:78-001707.
Audience: **u,f.**

Wang, Joseph QD115.W33 2000
Analytical Electrochemistry. Ed. 2. Trade Cloth. John Wiley & Sons, Inc. Hoboken, NJ. 2000. 232p. ISBN:0-471-28272-3, ISBN13: 978-0-471-28272-3. Dewey:543/.4. LCCN:99-089637.
Audience: **u,f.** *Choice, 2006, 2001, 1995.*

Wilson, Cecil L. QD75
Comprehensive Analytical Chemistry. Wilson, David W. (Editors). Elsevier.
Audience: **l,u,f.**

Analytical Chemistry > Sampling and Statistical Methodology

Beebe, Kenneth R., et al. QD75.4.S8B44 1998
Chemometrics: A Practical Guide. Randy J. Pell & Mary Beth Seasholtz (Authors). Trade Cloth. John Wiley & Sons, Inc. Hoboken, NJ. 1998. 360p. Wiley-Interscience Series on Laboratory Automation Ser., Vol. 4 ISBN:0-471-12451-6, ISBN13: 978-0-471-12451-1. Dewey:543/.001/5195. LCCN:97-017970.
Audience: **u,f.**

Crawford, Karen & Heaton, Alan   QD75.9 .C739 1998
Problem Solving in Analytical Chemistry. Denise Rafferty & Sara Sleigh (Editors). Trade Paper. Springer. New York, NY. 2000. 159p. ISBN:1-870343-46-8, ISBN13: 978-1-870343-46-6. Dewey:543.

Audience: **l,u,f.**

Meloan, Clifton E.   QD63.S4M44 1999
Chemical Separations: Principles, Techniques and Experiments. Trade Cloth. John Wiley & Sons, Inc. Hoboken, NJ. 1999. 768p. ISBN:0-471-35197-0, ISBN13: 978-0-471-35197-9. Dewey:543/.078. LCCN:99-036208.

Audience: **u,f.**

Otto, Matthias   QD75.4.S8O88 1999
Chemometrics: Statistics and Computer Applications in Analytical Chemistry. Trade Paper. John Wiley & Sons, Inc. Hoboken, NJ. 1999. 330p. ISBN:3-527-29628-X, ISBN13: 978-3-527-29628-6. Dewey:543/.007/27. LCCN:99-186538.

Audience: **u,f.** *Choice, 1999.*

Analytical Chemistry > History and Bibliography

Issaq, Haleem J.   QD79.C4C36 2002
A Century of Separation Science. Paper over Boards. Marcel Dekker Inc. New York, NY. 2001. 776p. ISBN:0-8247-0576-9, ISBN13: 978-0-8247-0576-3. Dewey:660/.2842. LCCN:2001-059229.

Audience: **u,f.**

Laitinen, Herbert A.   QD72
A History of Analytical Chemistry. Ewing, Galen W. (Editors). American Chemical Society. 1977.

Audience: **l,u,f.**

Analytical Chemistry > Problem Manuals and Software

Kenkel, John V.   QD75.22.K445 2002
Analytical Chemistry for Technicians. Ed. 3. Paper over Boards. Lewis Publishers. Boca Raton, FL. 2002. 584p. ISBN:1-56670-519-3, ISBN13: 978-1-56670-519-6. Dewey:543. LCCN:2002-029654.

Audience: **l,u,f.** *Choice, 2003.*

Analytical Chemistry > Guides to the Literature

☐ Analytical Chemistry Network.
http://www.chemsoc.org/networks/acn/about.htm

Audience: **u,f.**

QD71
☐ Analytical Chemistry Springboard.
http://www.anachem.umu.se/jumpstation.htm

Audience: **u,f.**

☐ Analytical Chemistry--Subject Guide (Stanford University).
http://library.stanford.edu/depts/swain/help/subjectguides/analytical.html

Audience: **u,f.**

☐ Analytical Chemistry--Web Links (Stanford University).
http://library.stanford.edu/depts/swain/help/webdirs/subject.html#analytical

Audience: **u,f.**

☐ Analytical Sciences Digital Library.
http://www.asdlib.org/

Audience: **u,f.**

☐ MolData--Analytical Chemistry.
http://pages.pomona.edu/~wsteinmetz/AnalChem.htm

Audience: **u,f.**

☐ SIRCh: Analytical Chemistry.
http://www.indiana.edu/~cheminfo/ca_accc.html

Audience: **u,f.**

Analytical Chemistry > Nomenclature

QD75.3
☐ Compendium of Analytical Nomenclature.
http://www.iupac.org/publications/analytical_compendium/

Audience: **u,f.**

Physical Chemistry > Literature Retrieval

Q199
Journal of Physical and Chemical Reference Data. American Chemical Society.

Audience: **u,f.**

☐ MolData--Physical Chemistry.
http://pages.pomona.edu/~wsteinmetz/PChem.htm

Audience: **u,f.**

Arny, Linda Ray   QC5.3
The Search for Data in the Physical and Chemical Sciences. Special Libraries Association. 1984. ISBN:0-87111-308-2, ISBN13: 978-0-87111-308-5.

Audience: **u,f.**

Parker, Sybil P.   QD451.P49 1988
Physical Chemistry Source Book. Trade Cloth. McGraw-Hill Companies, The. New York, NY. 1988. 416p. Science Reference Ser. ISBN:0-07-045504-X, ISBN13: 978-0-07-045504-7. Dewey:541.3. LCCN:87-036629.

Audience: **u,f.** *Choice, 1988.*

Physical Chemistry > Encyclopedias

Guggenheim, E. A.   QD453
The International Encyclopedia of Physical Chemistry and
Chemical Physics (22 v.). Meyer, Joseph Edward; Tompkins,
Frederick Clifford (Editors). Macmillan. 1965.
                                 Audience: **u,f.**

Nalwa, Hari Singh, (Editor)   T174
Encyclopedia of Nanoscience and Nanotechnology. American
Scientific Publishers. 2004. ISBN:1-58883-001-2, ISBN13:
978-1-58883-001-2.
                                 Audience: **u,f.**

Schleyer, Paul von Ragué   QD39.3.E46 E53 1998
Encyclopedia of Computational Chemistry, Set. Trade Cloth.
John Wiley & Sons, Inc. Hoboken, NJ. 1998. 3580p.
ISBN:0-471-96588-X, ISBN13: 978-0-471-96588-6.
Dewey:542.8/5. LCCN:98-037164.
                   Audience: **u,f.** *Choice, 1999.*

Schwarz, James A.   T174
Dekker Encyclopedia of Nanoscience and Nanotechnology.
Contescu, Cristian I.; Putyera, Karaol (Editors). Marcel Dekker.
2004. ISBN:0-8247-5047-0, ISBN13: 978-0-8247-5047-3.
                              Audience: **l,u,f.**

Physical Chemistry > Dictionary

Ulicky, Ladislav &   QD5.C4555 1992
  Kemp, T. J.
Comprehensive Dictionary of Physical Chemistry. Cloth Text.
Prentice Hall PTR. Upper Saddle River, NJ. 1992. 550p.
ISBN:0-13-151747-3, ISBN13: 978-0-13-151747-9.
Dewey:540/.3. LCCN:91-024322.
                                 Audience: **u,f.**

Physical Chemistry > General Handbooks

Condon, E. W. & Odishaw,   QC21.C7
  Hugh (Editors)
Handbook of Physics. Ed. 2. Cloth Text. McGraw-Hill
Companies, The. New York, NY. 1967. ISBN:0-07-012403-5,
ISBN13: 978-0-07-012403-5. Dewey:530.
                                 Audience: **u,f.**

Lide, David R. and Henry V.   QC173.397.L53 1994
  Kehiaian
CRC Handbook of Thermophysical and Thermochemical Data.
CRC Press. 1994. ISBN:0-8493-0197-1, ISBN13:
978-0-8493-0197-1.
                                 Audience: **u,f.**

Lide, David R.; Kehiaian,   QC173.397.L53 1994
  Henry V.
CRC Handbook of Thermophysical and Thermochemical
Data. CRC Press. 1994. ISBN:0-8493-0197-1, ISBN13:
978-0-8493-0197-1.
                                 Audience: **u,f.**

Physical Chemistry > Databases and Literature Reviews

Electronic Materials Information Service (EMIS) database.
Stevanage, Herts, UK: INSPEC, 1980-.
                                 Audience: **u,f.**

DIPPR (AIChE Design
  Institute for Physical Property Data)
Data Compilation of Pure Compound Properties Database.
http://dippr.byu.edu/
American Institute of Chemical Engineers; Office of Standard
Reference Data, National Bureau of Standards
                                 Audience: **u,f.**

Physical Chemistry > Treatises, Monographs, and Advanced Textbooks

                                 QD1
Annual Review of Physical Chemistry. Annual Reviews.
                                 Audience: **u,f.**

Alberty, Robert A. & Silbey,   QD453.2.A45 2001
  Robert J.
Physical Chemistry. Ed. 3. Trade Cloth. John Wiley & Sons,
Inc. Hoboken, NJ. 2000. 980p. ISBN:0-471-38311-2, ISBN13:
978-0-471-38311-6. Dewey:541.3. LCCN:00-020734.
                               Audience: **u,f.**

Baetzold, Roger C. &   QP61
  Rossiter, Bryant W. (Editors)
Physical Methods of Chemistry, Supplement and Cumulative
Index, Vol. 10. Ed. 2. Trade Cloth. John Wiley & Sons, Inc.
Hoboken, NJ. 1993. 408p. Physical Methods of Chemistry Ser.,
Vol. 10 ISBN:0-471-57086-9, ISBN13: 978-0-471-57086-8.
Dewey:542. LCCN:92-024512.
                                 Audience: **u,f.**

Bernasek, S.   QD461.B45 1995
Heterogeneous Reaction Dynamics. Trade Paper. John Wiley &
Sons, Inc. Hoboken, NJ. 1995. 158p. ISBN:0-89573-742-6,
ISBN13: 978-0-89573-742-7. Dewey:541.3/93.
LCCN:95-014954.
                   Audience: **u,f.** *Choice, 1996.*

Berry, R. Stephen, et al.   QD453.2.B48 2000
Physical Chemistry. Ed. 2. Stuart A. Rice & John Ross
(Authors). Cloth Text. Oxford University Press, Inc. New York,
NY. 2000. 1080p. Topics in Physical Chemistry Ser.
ISBN:0-19-510589-3, ISBN13: 978-0-19-510589-6.
Dewey:541.3. LCCN:00-024923.
                                 Audience: **u,f.**

Bromberg, J. Philip   QD453.2 .B76 1984
Physical Chemistry. Ed. 2. Cloth Text. Prentice Hall PTR. Upper
Saddle River, NJ. 1983. ISBN:0-205-08019-7, ISBN13:
978-0-205-08019-9. Dewey:541.3. LCCN:83-021531.
                                 Audience: **u,f.**

Dack, M. R.   **QD540**
Techniques of Chemistry: Solutions and Solubilities, Vol. 8. Trade Cloth. John Wiley & Sons, Inc. Hoboken, NJ. 1975. 475p. ISBN:0-471-93266-3, ISBN13: 978-0-471-93266-6. Dewey:541.3/4. LCCN:75-002331.
Audience: **u,f.**

Drago, Russell S.   **QD95**
Physical Methods in Chemistry. Ed. 2. Cloth Text. Elsevier - Health Sciences Division. Philadelphia, PA. 1977. xvi, 660p. ISBN:0-7216-3184-3, ISBN13: 978-0-7216-3184-4. Dewey:543/.0858. LCCN:76-008572.
Audience: **u,f.**

Eyring, Henry   **QD453**
Physical Chemistry, an Advanced Treatise. Henderson, Douglas; Jost, Wilhelm (Editors). Academic Press.
Audience: **u,f.**

Gil, Victor   **QD461 .G52 2000**
Orbitals in Chemistry: A Modern Guide for Students. Cloth Text. Cambridge University Press. New York, NY. 2000. 326p. ISBN:0-521-66167-6, ISBN13: 978-0-521-66167-6. Dewey:541.2/8. LCCN:99-461968.
Audience: **u,f.** *Choice, 2001.*

Glasstone, Samuel S.   **QD453**
Textbook of Physical Chemistry. Ed. 2. Van Nostrand. 1965.
Audience: **u,f.**

Hargittai, I. & Hargittai, M.   **QD461.H268 1995**
Symmetry Through the Eyes of a Chemist. Ed. 2. Trade Cloth. Basic Books. New York, NY. 1995. 484p. ISBN:0-306-44851-3, ISBN13: 978-0-306-44851-5. Dewey:541.2/2. LCCN:95-030533.
Audience: **u,f.** *Choice, 1996.*

Kettle, Sidney F.   **QD471.K47516 1985**
Symmetry and Structure. Trade Cloth. John Wiley & Sons, Inc. Hoboken, NJ. 1985. 340p. ISBN:0-471-90501-1, ISBN13: 978-0-471-90501-1. Dewey:541.2/2. LCCN:84-017365.
Audience: **u,f.** *B Choice, 1985.*

Moelwyn Hughes, E. A.   **QD453**
Physical Chemistry. Ed. 2. Pergamon. 1965.
Audience: **u,f.**

Moelwyn-Hughes, E. A.   **QD453..3**
Physical Chemistry. Paper Text. Textbook Publishers. Temecula, CA. 2003. 1333p. ISBN:0-7581-6500-5, ISBN13: 978-0-7581-6500-8. Dewey:541.
Audience: **u,f.**

Moore, W. J.   **QD453.2**
Physical Chemistry. Ed. 5. Trade Paper. Addison-Wesley Longman, Ltd. Harlow, 1972. 992p. ISBN:0-582-44234-6, ISBN13: 978-0-582-44234-4. Dewey:541/.3.
Audience: **u,f.**

Nonhebel, D. C., et al.   **QD471**
Radicals. J. M. Tedder & J. C. Walton (Authors). Trade Cloth. Cambridge University Press. New York, NY. 1979. 216p. Cambridge Texts in Chemistry and Biochemistry Ser. ISBN:0-521-22004-1, ISBN13: 978-0-521-22004-0. Dewey:541.2/24. LCCN:78-054721.
Audience: **u,f.**

Pilling, Michael J. & Seakins, Paul W.   **QD502.P54 1995**
Reaction Kinetics. Ed. 2. Cloth Text. Oxford University Press, Inc. New York, NY. 1996. 320p. ISBN:0-19-855528-8, ISBN13: 978-0-19-855528-5. Dewey:541.3/94. LCCN:94-046221.
Audience: **u,f.** *Choice, 1997.*

Prigogine, Ilya (Editor)   **QD453**
Advances in Chemical Physics. Wiley.
Audience: **u,f.**

Rappe, Anthony K. & Casewit, Carla J.   **QD461.R26 1996**
Molecular Mechanics Across Chemistry. John Choi (Illustrator). Trade Cloth. University Science Books. Sausalito, CA. 1997. 420p. ISBN:0-935702-77-6, ISBN13: 978-0-935702-77-4. Dewey:541.2/2. LCCN:96-013315.
Audience: **u,f.** *Choice, 1997.*

Rossiter, Bryant W.   **QD61.P47 1986**
Physical Methods of Chemistry: Determination of Electronic and Optical Properties, Vol. 8. Ed. 2. Roger C. Baetzold (Editor). Trade Cloth. John Wiley & Sons, Inc. Hoboken, NJ. 1993. 544p. Physical Methods of Chemistry, Vol. 9 ISBN:0-471-54407-8, ISBN13: 978-0-471-54407-4. Dewey:541.3. LCCN:92-024323.
Audience: **u,f.**

Rossiter, Bryant W. & Baetzold, Roger C. (Editors)   **QD61.P47 1986**
Physical Methods of Chemistry: Investigations of Surfaces and Interfaces. Ed. 2. Trade Cloth. John Wiley & Sons, Inc. Hoboken, NJ. 1992. 528p. Physical Methods of Chemistry, Vol. 8 ISBN:0-471-54406-X, ISBN13: 978-0-471-54406-7. Dewey:541.3. LCCN:91-039605.
Audience: **u,f.**

Rossiter, Bryant W. & Baetzold, Roger C. (Editors)   **QD61.P47 1986**
Physical Methods of Chemistry: Investigations of Surfaces and Interfaces. Ed. 2. Trade Cloth. John Wiley & Sons, Inc. Hoboken, NJ. 1993. 768p. Physical Methods of Chemistry, Vol. 7 ISBN:0-471-54405-1, ISBN13: 978-0-471-54405-0. Dewey:541.3. LCCN:92-024513.
Audience: **u,f.**

Rossiter, Bryant W. (Editor), et al.   **QD61.P47 1986 VOL. 7**
Physical Methods of Chemistry: Determination of Elastic and Mechanical Properties. Ed. 2. Roger C. Baetzold & John F. Hamilton (Editors). Trade Cloth. John Wiley & Sons, Inc. Hoboken, NJ. 1991. 313p. Physical Methods of Chemistry, Vol. 6 ISBN:0-471-53438-2, ISBN13: 978-0-471-53438-9. Dewey:542 s. LCCN:90-013009.
Audience: **u,f.**

Rossiter, Bryant W. & Hamilton, John F. (Editors)   **QD453.2**
Components of Scientific Instruments and Applications of Computers to Chemical Research, Vol. 1. Ed. 2. Trade Cloth. John Wiley & Sons, Inc. Hoboken, NJ. 1986. 834p. Physical Methods of Chemistry Ser., Vol. 2 ISBN:0-471-08034-9, ISBN13: 978-0-471-08034-3. Dewey:541.3. LCCN:85-006386.
Audience: **u,f.**

Rossiter, Bryant W. & Hamilton, John F. (Editors)   **QD81**
Determination of Chemical Composition and Molecular Structure. Ed. 2. Trade Cloth. John Wiley & Sons, Inc.

Hoboken, NJ. 1987. 624p. Physical Methods of Chemistry Ser., Vol. 3 ISBN:0-471-85041-1, ISBN13: 978-0-471-85041-0. Dewey:542. LCCN:87-410717.

Audience: **u,f.**

Rossiter, Bryant W. &   **QD61.P47 1986**
Hamilton, John F. (Editors)
Determination of Chemical Composition and Molecular Structure. Ed. 2. Trade Cloth. John Wiley & Sons, Inc. Hoboken, NJ. 1989. 992p. Physical Methods of Chemistry, Vol. 3 ISBN:0-471-85051-9, ISBN13: 978-0-471-85051-9. Dewey:542. LCCN:85-006386.

Audience: **u,f.**

Rossiter, Bryant W.   **QD61.P47 1986**
Physical Methods of Chemistry: Microscopy, Vol. 4. Ed. 2. John F. Hamilton (Editor). Trade Cloth. John Wiley & Sons, Inc. Hoboken, NJ. 1991. 560p. Physical Methods of Chemistry Ser., Vol. 4 ISBN:0-471-08026-8, ISBN13: 978-0-471-08026-8. Dewey:542. LCCN:90-024799.

Audience: **u,f.**

Rossiter, Bryant W.   **QD61.P47 1986**
Physical Methods of Chemistry: Determination of Structural Features of Crystalline and Amorphous Solids, Vol. 5. Ed. 2. John F. Hamilton (Editor). Trade Cloth. John Wiley & Sons, Inc. Hoboken, NJ. 1990. 618p. Physical Methods of Chemistry Ser., Vol. 5 ISBN:0-471-52509-X, ISBN13: 978-0-471-52509-7. Dewey:542. LCCN:85-006386.

Audience: **u,f.**

Rossiter, Bryant W. &   **QD61.P47 1986**
Hamilton, John F. (Editors)
Physical Methods of Chemistry, Electrochemical Methods, Vol. 2. Ed. 2. Trade Cloth. John Wiley & Sons, Inc. Hoboken, NJ. 1986. 928p. Physical Methods of Chemistry Ser., Vol. 1 ISBN:0-471-08027-6, ISBN13: 978-0-471-08027-5. Dewey:542. LCCN:85-006386.

Audience: **u,f.**

Rossiter, Bryant W. (Editor),   **QD 61 P47 1986 V.2**
et al.
Physical Methods of Chemistry, Determination of Thermodynamic Properties, Vol. 6. Ed. 2. John F. Hamilton & Roger C. Baetzold (Editors). Trade Cloth. John Wiley & Sons, Inc. Hoboken, NJ. 1992. 760p. Physical Methods of Chemistry Ser., Vol. 11 ISBN:0-471-57087-7, ISBN13: 978-0-471-57087-5. Dewey:541.369. LCCN:85-006386.

Audience: **u,f.**

Seddon, John M. & Gale,   **QD504.S43 2002**
Julian D.
Thermodynamics and Statistical Mechanics. Trade Paper. John Wiley & Sons, Inc. Hoboken, NJ. 2002. 161p. Basic Concepts in Chemistry Ser. ISBN:0-471-28165-4, ISBN13: 978-0-471-28165-8. Dewey:541.3/69. LCCN:2002-491824.
Audience: **u,f.**

Tabor, David   **QC173 .T25 1991**
Gases, Liquids and Solids: And Other States of Matter. Ed. 3. Cloth Text. Cambridge University Press. New York, NY. 1991. 440p. ISBN:0-521-40488-6, ISBN13: 978-0-521-40488-4. Dewey:530.4. LCCN:91-009214.
Audience: **u,f.** *Choice, 1992.*

Verkade, John G.   **QD461.V45 1996**
A Pictorial Approach to Molecular Bonding and Vibrations. Ed. 2. Cloth Text. Springer. New York, NY. 1996. 367p.

ISBN:0-387-94811-2, ISBN13: 978-0-387-94811-9. Dewey:541.2/24. LCCN:96-019135.
Audience: **u,f.** *Choice, 1997.*

Warren, Warren S.   **QD475.W27 2000**
The Physical Basis of Chemistry. Ed. 2. Paper Text. Elsevier Science & Technology Books. Saint Louis, MO. 2000. 211p. Complementary Science Ser. ISBN:0-12-735855-2, ISBN13: 978-0-12-735855-0. Dewey:541/.01/53. LCCN:99-068993.
Audience: **u,f.** *Choice, 2000, 1994.*

Weissberger, Arnold   **QD61**
Physical Methods of Chemistry. Wiley-Interscience.
Audience: **u,f.**

Weissberger, Arnold (Editor)   **QD61**
Techniques of Chemistry. Wiley.
Audience: **u,f.**

Physical Chemistry > Treatises, Monographs, and Advanced Textbooks > Thermodynamics

Anderson, Greg   **QC311**
Thermodynamics of Natural Systems. Ed. 2. Cloth Text. Cambridge University Press. New York, NY. 2005. 662p. ISBN:0-521-84772-9, ISBN13: 978-0-521-84772-8. Dewey:541/.369. LCCN:2005-284189.
Audience: **u,f.**

Dugdale, J.S   **QC318**
Entropy and its Physical Meaning. Taylor & Francis. 1996. ISBN:0-7484-0568-2, ISBN13: 978-0-7484-0568-8.
Audience: **u,f.**

Hinchliffe, Alan   **QD455.3.C64H46 1999**
Chemical Modeling: From Atoms to Liquids. Trade Cloth. John Wiley & Sons, Inc. Hoboken, NJ. 1999. 314p. ISBN:0-471-99903-2, ISBN13: 978-0-471-99903-4. Dewey:541/.01/13. LCCN:99-032077.
Audience: **u,f.** *Choice, 2000.*

Honig, J. M. (Editor)   **QD504.H66 1999**
Thermodynamics: Principles Characterizing Physical and Chemical Processes. Ed. 2. Trade Cloth. Elsevier Science & Technology Books. Saint Louis, MO. 1999. 608p. ISBN:0-12-355045-9, ISBN13: 978-0-12-355045-3. Dewey:536.7. LCCN:98-086761.
Audience: **u,f.**

Jeffrey, G. A.   **QD461.J44 1997**
An Introduction to Hydrogen Bonding. Cloth Text. Oxford University Press, Inc. New York, NY. 1997. 320p. Topics in Physical Chemistry Ser. ISBN:0-19-509548-0, ISBN13: 978-0-19-509548-7. Dewey:541.2/26. LCCN:96-026792.
Audience: **u,f.** *Choice, 1998.*

Kondepudi, Dilip K. &   **QC311.K66 1998**
Prigogine, Ilya
Modern Thermodynamics: From Heat Engines to Dissipative Structures. Trade Cloth. John Wiley & Sons, Inc. Hoboken, NJ. 1998. 508p. ISBN:0-471-97393-9, ISBN13: 978-0-471-97393-5. Dewey:536/.7. LCCN:97-048745.
Audience: **u,f.** *Choice, 1999.*

Kudryavtsev, A. B., et al.   QD503.K83 2001
The Law of Mass Action: And Its Statistical Mechanical Basis.
Reginald F. Jameson & Wolfgang Linert (Authors). Trade Cloth.
Springer. New York, NY. 2001. XIV, 348p.
ISBN:3-540-41078-3, ISBN13: 978-3-540-41078-2.
Dewey:541.3/92. LCCN:2001-017048.

Audience: **u,f.**

McQuarrie, Donald A. &   QD453.2.M394 1997
Simon, John D.
Physical Chemistry: A Molecular Approach. John Choi
(Illustrator). Trade Cloth. University Science Books. Sausalito,
CA. 1997. 1270p. ISBN:0-935702-99-7, ISBN13:
978-0-935702-99-6. Dewey:541. LCCN:97-000142.

Audience: **u,f.** *Choice, 1998.*

McQuarrie, Donald &   QD504.M335 1999
Simon, John
Molecular Thermodynamics. Trade Cloth. University Science
Books. Sausalito, CA. 1999. 656p. ISBN:1-891389-05-X,
ISBN13: 978-1-891389-05-4. Dewey:541.3/69.
LCCN:98-048543.

Audience: **u,f.** *Choice, 1999.*

Mortimer, Robert G.   QD453.2.M67 2000
Physical Chemistry. Ed. 2. Cloth Text. Elsevier Science &
Technology Books. Saint Louis, MO. 2000. 1116p.
ISBN:0-12-508345-9, ISBN13: 978-0-12-508345-4.
Dewey:541.3. LCCN:99-068611.

Audience: **u,f.**

Rock, Peter A.   QD504
Chemical Thermodynamics. Trade Cloth. University Science
Books. Sausalito, CA. 1983. 548p. Physical Chemistry Ser.
ISBN:0-935702-12-1, ISBN13: 978-0-935702-12-5.
Dewey:541.3/69. LCCN:82-051233.

Audience: **u,f.**

Whalen, James W.   QD504.W47 1991
Molecular Thermodynamics: A Statistical Approach. Trade
Cloth. John Wiley & Sons, Inc. Hoboken, NJ. 1991. 381p.
ISBN:0-471-51478-0, ISBN13: 978-0-471-51478-7.
Dewey:541.3/69. LCCN:90-039767.

Audience: **u,f.** *Choice, 1992.*

Physical Chemistry > Treatises, Monographs, and Advanced Textbooks > Catalysis

Gates, Bruce C.   QD505.G38 1991
Catalytic Chemistry: An Introductory Text. Trade Cloth. John
Wiley & Sons, Inc. Hoboken, NJ. 1991. 480p.
ISBN:0-471-51761-5, ISBN13: 978-0-471-51761-0.
Dewey:541.3/95. LCCN:91-004192.

Audience: **u,f.** *Choice, 1992.*

Horvath, Istvan T.   QD505.E53 2003
(Editor-In-Chief)
Encyclopedia of Catalysis, Set. Trade Cloth. John Wiley &
Sons, Inc. Hoboken, NJ. 2002. 4772p. ISBN:0-471-24183-0,
ISBN13: 978-0-471-24183-6. Dewey:660/.2995/03.
LCCN:2002-027422.

Audience: **u,f.** *Choice, 2003.*

Weitkamp, Jens & Puppe,   TP245.S5C39 1999
Lothar (Editors)
Catalysis and Zeolites: Fundamentals and Applications. Trade
Cloth. Springer. New York, NY. 1999. XVIII, 564p.
ISBN:3-540-63650-1, ISBN13: 978-3-540-63650-2.
Dewey:660/.2995. LCCN:98-048578.

Audience: **u,f.**

Physical Chemistry > Treatises, Monographs, and Advanced Textbooks > Photochemistry

Calvert, Jack G.; Pitts,   QD601
James N.
Photochemistry. Wiley. 1966.

Audience: **u,f.**

Kopecký, Jan   QD275.K6613 1991
Organic Photochemistry: A Visual Approach. Trade Paper. John
Wiley & Sons, Inc. Hoboken, NJ. 1992. 285p.
ISBN:0-89573-296-3, ISBN13: 978-0-89573-296-5.
Dewey:547.135. LCCN:91-036270.

Audience: **u,f.** *Choice, 1992.*

Ramamurthy,   QD714.O74 1998
Vaidhyanathan & Schanze, Kirk S. (Editors)
Organic and Inorganic Photochemsitry, Vol. 2. Paper over
Boards. Marcel Dekker Inc. New York, NY. 1998. 368p.
Molecular and Supramolecular Photochemistry Ser.
ISBN:0-8247-0174-7, ISBN13: 978-0-8247-0174-1.
Dewey:541.3/5. LCCN:98-035550.

Audience: **u,f.**

Van Hecke, Gerald R. &   QD63.L3 V36 1998
Karukstis, Kerry K.
A Guide to Lasers in Chemistry. Cloth Text. Jones & Bartlett
Publishers, Inc. Sudbury, MA. 1997. 288p. Chemistry Ser.
ISBN:0-7637-0412-1, ISBN13: 978-0-7637-0412-4.
Dewey:542/.8. LCCN:97-013440.

Audience: **u,f.** *Choice, 1998.*

Physical Chemistry > Treatises, Monographs, and Advanced Textbooks > Quantum Chemistry

☐ JCE LivTexts: Physical Chemistry [Quantum States of Atoms
and Molecules].
http://www.jce.divched.org/jcedlib/livtexts/pchem

Audience: **u,f.**

Atkins, P. W. & Friedman,   QD462.A84 1996
R. S.
Molecular Quantum Mechanics. Ed. 3. Cloth Text. Oxford
University Press, Inc. New York, NY. 1996. 564p.
ISBN:0-19-855948-8, ISBN13: 978-0-19-855948-1.
Dewey:541/.28. LCCN:96-023892.

Audience: **u,f.** *B̶ Choice, 1998.*

Baggott, Jim   QC174.12.B34 1992
The Meaning of Quantum Chemistry: A Guide for Students of
Chemistry and Physics. Trade Cloth. Oxford University Press,
Inc. New York, NY. 1992. 248p. ISBN:0-19-855576-8, ISBN13:
978-0-19-855576-6. Dewey:530.12. LCCN:91-034937.

Audience: **u,f.** *Choice, 1993.*

Bates, D. R. (Editor)   QC174.1 .B3
Quantum Theory. Trade Cloth. Elsevier Science & Technology
Books. Saint Louis, MO. 9999. ISBN:0-318-50352-2, ISBN13:
978-0-318-50352-3. Dewey:530.12.

Audience: **u,f.**

Bates, David R.   QC174
Quantum Theory: Aggregates of Particles. Academic Press.
1961.

Audience: **u,f.**

Bates, David R.   QC174
Quantum Theory: Elements. Academic Press. 1961.

Audience: **u,f.**

Bates, David R.   QC174
Quantum Theory: Radiation and High Energy Physics.
Academic Press. 1962.

Audience: **u,f.**

Clark, Tim & Koch, Rainer   QD461 .C415 1999
Chemist's Electronic Book of Orbitals. Mixed Media. Springer.
New York, NY. 1999. VIII, 96p. ISBN:3-540-63726-5, ISBN13:
978-3-540-63726-4. Dewey:541.2/2. LCCN:98-046052.

Audience: **u,f.**

Dykstra, Clifford E.   QD462.D95 1991
Quantum Chemistry and Molecular Spectroscopy. Paper Text.
Prentice Hall PTR. Upper Saddle River, NJ. 1991. 480p.
ISBN:0-13-747312-5, ISBN13: 978-0-13-747312-0.
Dewey:541.2/8. LCCN:91-025868.

Audience: **u,f.** *Choice, 1992.*

Fitts, Donald D.   QD462 .F55 1999
Principles of Quantum Mechanics: As Applied to Chemistry and
Chemical Physics. Cloth Text. Cambridge University Press. New
York, NY. 1999. 362p. ISBN:0-521-65124-7, ISBN13:
978-0-521-65124-0. Dewey:541.28. LCCN:98-039486.

Audience: **u,f.** *Choice, 2000.*

Grunwald, Ernest   QD504.G78 1997
Thermodynamics of Molecular Species. Ed. 1. Trade Cloth. John
Wiley & Sons, Inc. Hoboken, NJ. 1996. 323p.
ISBN:0-471-01254-8, ISBN13: 978-0-471-01254-2.
Dewey:541.3/69. LCCN:96-014103.

Audience: **u,f.** *Choice, 1997.*

Ratner, Mark A. & Schatz,   QD462.R28 2000
George C.
Introduction to Quantum Mechanics in Chemistry. Trade Cloth.
Prentice Hall PTR. Upper Saddle River, NJ. 2000. 305p.
ISBN:0-13-895491-7, ISBN13: 978-0-13-895491-8.
Dewey:541.2/8. LCCN:00-029130.

Audience: **u,f.**

Physical Chemistry > Treatises, Monographs, and Advanced Textbooks > Other Special Topics

☐ Wavelet Tutorial.
http://engineering.rowan.edu/~polikan/WAVELETS/
WTtutorial.html

Audience: **u,f.**

Borghi, R. P. & Destriau, M.   QD516.B6713 1998
Combustion and Flames: Chemical and Physical Principles.
Trade Cloth. Editions Technip. Paris Cedex 15, 1998. 371p.
ISBN:2-7108-0740-8, ISBN13: 978-2-7108-0740-7.
Dewey:541.3/61. LCCN:99-208655.

Audience: **u,f.** *Choice, 1999.*

Franklin, J. L.   QD501 .F7454 1979
Ion-Molecule Reactions. Trade Cloth. John Wiley & Sons, Inc.
Hoboken, NJ. 1983. Benchmark Papers in Physical Chemistry
and Chemical Physics, 3 ISBN:0-87933-331-6, ISBN13:
978-0-87933-331-7. Dewey:541/.39. LCCN:78-016358.

Audience: **u,f.**

Glassman, Irvin   QD516.G55 1996
Combustion. Ed. 3. Cloth Text. Elsevier Science & Technology
Books. Saint Louis, MO. 1996. 631p. ISBN:0-12-285852-2,
ISBN13: 978-0-12-285852-9. Dewey:541.3/61.
LCCN:96-003069.

Audience: **u,f.** *B Choice, 1997.*

Jordan, Peter C.   QD501.J7573
Chemical Kinetics and Transport. Trade Cloth. Basic Books.
New York, NY. 1979. 384p. ISBN:0-306-40122-3, ISBN13:
978-0-306-40122-0. Dewey:541/.39. LCCN:78-020999.

Audience: **u,f.** *B*

Levine, Ira N.   QD462.L48 2000
Quantum Chemistry. Ed. 5. Trade Cloth. Prentice Hall PTR.
Upper Saddle River, NJ. 1999. 739p. ISBN:0-13-685512-1,
ISBN13: 978-0-13-685512-5. Dewey:541.2/8. LCCN:99-028558.

Audience: **u,f.** *B*

Masel, Richard I.   QD502.M35 2001
Chemical Kinetics and Catalysis. Trade Cloth. John Wiley &
Sons, Inc. Hoboken, NJ. 2001. 968p. ISBN:0-471-24197-0,
ISBN13: 978-0-471-24197-3. Dewey:541.3/94.
LCCN:00-043303.

Audience: **u,f.**

Mortimer, M. & Taylor, P.   QD502.C44 2002
G. (Editors)
Chemical Kinetics and Mechanism. Mixed Media. Royal Society
of Chemistry, The. Cambridge, 2002. 256p. The Molecular
World Ser. ISBN:0-85404-670-4, ISBN13: 978-0-85404-670-6.
Dewey:541.3/94.

Audience: **u,f.** *Choice, 2003.*

Simons, Jack & Nichols, Jeff   QD462.S53 1997
Quantum Mechanics in Chemistry. Cloth Text. Oxford
University Press, Inc. New York, NY. 1997. 640p. Topics in
Physical Chemistry Ser. ISBN:0-19-508200-1, ISBN13:
978-0-19-508200-5. Dewey:541.2/8. LCCN:96-034013.

Audience: **u,f.** *Choice, 1998.*

Tsukerblat, Boris S.   QD455.3.G75
Group Theory in Chemistry and Spectroscopy. Trade Cloth.
Elsevier Science & Technology Books. Saint Louis, MO. 1994.
430p. Theoretical Chemistry Ser. ISBN:0-12-702285-6, ISBN13:
978-0-12-702285-7. Dewey:540.15122.
Audience: **u,f.** *Choice, 1994.*

Physical Chemistry > Physicochemical Calculations

▭ Computational Chemistry Comparison and Benchmark
Database.
http://srdata.nist.gov/cccbdb/
Audience: **u,f.**

▭ Conversion Factors.
http://www.google.com/help/features.html#calculator
Audience: **u,f.**

TP155
▭ Data & Property Calculation Websites.
http://tigger.uic.edu/~mansoori/
Thermodynamic.Data.and.Property_html
Audience: **u,f.**

▭ Molecular Structure Calculations.
http://www.colby.edu/chemistry/webmo/mointro.html
Audience: **u,f.**

Daubert, T. E. & Danner, R.   TP200 .D38 1985
P. (Editors)
Data Compilation Tables of Properties of Pure Compounds.
Ringbound. American Institute of Chemical Engineers. New
York, NY. 1985. 400p. ISBN:0-8169-0341-7, ISBN13:
978-0-8169-0341-2. Dewey:660.2/0212. LCCN:85-071969.
Audience: **u,f.**

Malinowski, Edmund R.   QD39.3.F33M35 2001
Factor Analysis in Chemistry. Ed. 3. Trade Cloth. John Wiley &
Sons, Inc. Hoboken, NJ. 2002. 432p. ISBN:0-471-13479-1,
ISBN13: 978-0-471-13479-4. Dewey:542. LCCN:2001-046660.
Audience: **u,f.** *Choice, 2002.*

Mills, Ian (Compiled by)   QD451.5.Q36 1993
Quantities, Units, and Symbols in Physical Chemistry. Ed. 2.
Trade Cloth. Blackwell Publishing, Inc. Malden, MA. 1993.
176p. ISBN:0-632-03572-2, ISBN13: 978-0-632-03572-4.
Dewey:541.3014. LCCN:92-040104.
Audience: **u,f.**

Wilson, S   QD39.3.E46
Methods in Computational Chemistry: Electron Correlation in
Atoms and Molecules. Trade Cloth. Springer. New York, NY.
1987. 382p. ISBN:0-306-42645-5, ISBN13: 978-0-306-42645-2.
Dewey:542/.8. LCCN:87-007249.
Audience: **u,f.**

Physical Chemistry > Physicochemical Properties and Data Compilations > Physical Property Data

QC161.5
▭ [Critical] Properties of Various Gases.
http://www.flexwareinc.com/gasprop.htm
Audience: **u,f.**

▭ Atomic and Molecular Orbitals.
http://www.shef.ac.uk/chemistry/orbitron
Audience: **u,f.**

▭ Atomic Radii Tables.
http://www.monroecc.edu/wusers/flanzafame/PerRadii.pdf
Audience: **u,f.**

▭ Enhanced NMR Periodic Table.
http://www.chem.tamu.edu/services/NMR/periodic/index.shtml
Audience: **u,f.**

TN690.2
▭ FACT (Facility for the Analysis of Chemical
Thermodynamics).
http://www.crct.polymtl.ca/fact/index.php
Audience: **u,f.**

▭ Finding Physical and Chemical Properties.
http://www.library.vanderbilt.edu/science/property.htm
Audience: **u,f.**

QD65
▭ Index to Physical, Chemical and Other Property Data.
http://www.asu.edu/lib/noble/chem/property.htm
Audience: **u,f.**

QD511
▭ NIST Chemistry WebBook.
http://webbook.nist.gov/chemistry/
National Institute of Standards and Technology (NIST).
Audience: **u,f.**

QD467
▭ WebElements Periodic Table.
http://www.webelements.com/
Mark Winter [The University of Sheffield and WebElements Ltd,
UK].
Audience: **u,f.**

American Institute of   QC271
Physics
Temperature, Its Measurement and Control in Science and
Industry; Papers Presented at a Symposium Held in New York
City, November 1939. Reinhold.
Audience: **u,f.**

Baum, Edward J.   TD193.B38 1998
Chemical Property Estimation: Theory and Application. Paper
over Boards. Lewis Publishers. Boca Raton, FL. 1997. 400p.

ISBN:0-87371-938-7, ISBN13: 978-0-87371-938-4.
Dewey:628.5. LCCN:97-033124.

Audience: **u,f.** *Choice, 1998.*

Daubert, T. E. & Foster, Diane (Editors) TP200.D39 1989

Physical and Thermodynamic Properties of Pure Chemicals: Data Compilation. Paper over Boards. Hemisphere Publishing Corporation. Philadelphia, PA. 1989. 1100p. ISBN:0-89116-948-2, ISBN13: 978-0-89116-948-2. Dewey:661/.00212. LCCN:89-031740.

Audience: **u,f.** *Choice, 1990.*

Dreisbach, Robert Rickert QD1

Physical Properties of Chemical Compounds; Advances in Chemistry Series, Nos. 15, 22, 29. American Chemical Society.

Audience: **u,f.**

Firestone, Richard B. & Chu, S. Y. Frank QD601.2.F57

Table of Isotopes: 1999. Ed. 8. Coral M. Baglin (Editor). CD-ROM, Trade Paper, Mixed Media. John Wiley & Sons, Inc. Hoboken, NJ. 1999. 224p. ISBN:0-471-35633-6, ISBN13: 978-0-471-35633-2. Dewey:541.38840212. LCCN:99-025447.

Audience: **u,f.**

Forsythe, William E. QC61 .S6 1964

Smithsonian Physical Tables. Ed. 9. Trade Cloth. Smithsonian Institution Press. Washington, DC. 1964. ISBN:0-87474-015-0, ISBN13: 978-0-87474-015-8. Dewey:530. LCCN:54-060067.

Audience: **u,f.**

Jordan, Thomas Earl QD476.J6

Vapor Pressure of Organic Compounds. Interscience Publishers. 1954.

Audience: **u,f.**

Kaye, G. W. C. & Laby, T. H. QC61.K3 1995

Tables of Physical and Chemical Constants. Ed. 16. Trade Cloth. Addison-Wesley Longman, Inc. Boston, MA. 1995. 624p. ISBN:0-582-22629-5, ISBN13: 978-0-582-22629-6. Dewey:530/.0212. LCCN:95-015665.

Audience: **u,f.**

National Research Council, Office of Critical Tables QD65

Consolidated Index of Selected Property Values: Physical Chemistry and Thermodynamics. National Academy of Sciences National Research Council. 1962.

Audience: **u,f.**

Simrock, K. H., et al. QD65

Critical Data of Pure Substances, Set, Vol. 2, Pts. 1 & 2. R. Janowsky & A. Ohnsorge (Authors). Library Binding. Dechema. 60061 Frankfurt, 1986. 1500p. Dechema Chemistry Data Ser. ISBN:3-921567-77-7, ISBN13: 978-3-921567-77-7. Dewey:540/.212.

Audience: **u,f.**

Physical Chemistry > Physicochemical Properties and Data Compilations > Azeotropes and Solutions

QD543

▢ IUPAC-NIST Solubility Data Series Database. http://srdata.nist.gov/solubility

Audience: **u,f.**

QD543

Solubility Data Series. Pergamon.

Audience: **u,f.**

TP247.5

▢ SOLV-DB (Solvents Database). http://solvdb.ncms.org/index.html

Audience: **u,f.**

Burgess, John ML420.M388

Ions in Solution. Ed. 2. Trade Paper. Horwood Publishing Ltd. Chichester, 1999. 240p. ISBN:1-898563-50-0, ISBN13: 978-1-898563-50-1. Dewey:781.63.

Audience: **u,f.**

Butler, James N. & Cogley, David R. QD561.B985 1998

Ionic Equilibrium: Solubility and pH Calculations. Ed. 2. Trade Cloth. John Wiley & Sons, Inc. Hoboken, NJ. 1998. 576p. ISBN:0-471-58526-2, ISBN13: 978-0-471-58526-8. Dewey:541.3/723. LCCN:97-013435.

Audience: **u,f.** *Choice, 1998.*

Dow Chemical Company Staff QD1.A355 NO. 6, ETC.

Azeotropic Data. Trade Cloth. American Chemical Society. Washington, DC. 1952. ISBN:0-8412-0166-8, ISBN13: 978-0-8412-0166-8. Dewey:541.36. LCCN:52-003085.

Audience: **u,f.**

Fogg, P. G. & Gerrard, W. QD543.F633 1990

Solubility of Gases in Liquids: A Critical Evaluation of Gas-Liquid Systems in Theory and Practice. Trade Cloth. John Wiley & Sons, Inc. Hoboken, NJ. 1991. 344p. ISBN:0-471-92925-5, ISBN13: 978-0-471-92925-3. Dewey:541.3/422. LCCN:90-045670.

Audience: **u,f.** *Choice, 1991.*

Gmehling, J. QD526.A94 1994

Azeotropic Data. Trade Cloth. John Wiley & Sons, Inc. Hoboken, NJ. 1994. 1766p. ISBN:3-527-28671-3, ISBN13: 978-3-527-28671-3. Dewey:660.28425. LCCN:95-115329.

Audience: **u,f.**

Gmehling, J. & Onken, U. QD503.G59

Vapor-Liquid Equilibrium Data Collection Tables and Diagrams of Data for Binary and Multicomponent Mixtures up to Moderate Pressures: Constants of Correlation Equations for Computer Use: Part 2a: Organic Hydroxy Compounds: Alcohols, Vol. 1. J. M. Prausnitz (Introduction by). Cloth Text. Dechema. 60061 Frankfurt, 1978. Dechema Chemistry Data Ser. ISBN:3-921567-09-2, ISBN13: 978-3-921567-09-8. Dewey:541.3/63. LCCN:79-670289.

Audience: **u,f.**

Hansen, Charles M.   QD543.H258
Hansen Solubility Parameters: A User's Handbook. CRC Press. 2000. ISBN:0-8493-1525-5, ISBN13: 978-0-8493-1525-1.
Audience: **u,f.**

Hartley, F. R., et al.   QD503
Solution Equilibria. C. Burgess & R. M. Alcock (Authors). Trade Cloth. John Wiley & Sons, Inc. Hoboken, NJ. 1980. 361p. ISBN:0-470-26880-8, ISBN13: 978-0-470-26880-3. Dewey:541/.341. LCCN:79-042956.
Audience: **u,f.** *B*

Hildebrand, Joel, et al.   QD541
Regular and Related Solutions: The Solubility of Gases, Liquids and Solids. John M. Prausnitz & Robert L. Scott (Authors). Trade Cloth. John Wiley & Sons, Inc. Hoboken, NJ. 1979. 238p. ISBN:0-442-15665-0, ISBN13: 978-0-442-15665-7. Dewey:541/.34. LCCN:79-122670.
Audience: **u,f.**

Hillert, Mats   QD503 .H554 1998
Phase Equilibria, Phase Diagrams and Phase Transformations: Their Thermodynamic Basis. Cloth Text. Cambridge University Press. New York, NY. 1998. 554p. ISBN:0-521-56270-8, ISBN13: 978-0-521-56270-6. Dewey:541.3/63. LCCN:97-012280.
Audience: **u,f.** *Choice, 1998.*

Horsley, L. H.; Tamplin,   QD1.A355
Wlliam S.
Azeotropic Data, Vol. 2. American Chemical Society. 1952.
Audience: **u,f.**

Horvath, Ari L.   QD565
Handbook of Aqueous Electrolyte Solutions: Physical Properties, Estimation and Correlation Methods. Trade Cloth. Prentice Hall PTR. Upper Saddle River, NJ. 1985. 631p. Physical Chemistry Ser. ISBN:0-470-20214-9, ISBN13: 978-0-470-20214-2. Dewey:541.3/72. LCCN:85-014039.
Audience: **u,f.**

Lias, Sharon G.   S494.5.B563
Gas-Phase Ion and Neutral Thermochemistry. Cloth Text. Springer. New York, NY. 1988. 872p. ISBN:0-88318-562-8, ISBN13: 978-0-88318-562-9. Dewey:338.16.
Audience: **u,f.**

Linke, William F.   QD66
Solubilities, Inorganic and Metal Organic Compounds; A Compilation of Solubility Data from the Periodical Literature, 2 volumes. Ed. 4. American Chemical Society. 1958.
Audience: **u,f.**

Marcus, Yizhak   QD544.M37 1999
The Properties of Solvents. Trade Cloth. John Wiley & Sons, Inc. Hoboken, NJ. 1998. 254p. Wiley Series in Solutions Chemistry Ser., Vol. 4 ISBN:0-471-98369-1, ISBN13: 978-0-471-98369-9. Dewey:541.3/482. LCCN:98-018212.
Audience: **u,f.**

Murrell, J. N. & Boucher, E.   QD
A.
Properties of Liquids and Solutions. Trade Cloth. John Wiley & Sons, Inc. Hoboken, NJ. 1982. 298p. ISBN:0-471-10201-6, ISBN13: 978-0-471-10201-4. Dewey:540/.0422. LCCN:81-021921.
Audience: **u,f.** *B*

Poling, Bruce E., et al.   TP242.P62 2001
The Properties of Gases and Liquids. Ed. 5. John O'Connell & John M. Prausnitz (Authors). Cloth Text. McGraw-Hill Professional Publishing. New York, NY. 2000. 768p. ISBN:0-07-011682-2, ISBN13: 978-0-07-011682-5. Dewey:660/.042. LCCN:00-061622.
Audience: **u,f.** *Choice, 2001.*

Seidell, Atherton   QD66
Solubilities of Inorganic and Metal Organic Compounds; A Compilation of Quantitative Solubility Data from the Periodical Literature, 2 vols. Van Nostrand. 1940.
Audience: **u,f.**

Sillén, Lars Gunnar   QD503
Stability Constants of Metal Ion Complexes. Ed. 2. The Chemical Society. 1964.
Audience: **u,f.**

Stephen, H., et al.   QD543
Solubilities of Inorganic and Organic Compounds, Set. T. Stephen & H. Silcock (Authors). Trade Cloth. Pergamon Press. Kidlington, 1979. 7300p. ISBN:0-08-023599-9, ISBN13: 978-0-08-023599-8. Dewey:541.3/42/0212. LCCN:79-040319.
Audience: **u,f.**

Timmermans, Jean   QD453
The Physico-Chemical Constants of Binary Systems in Concentrated Solutions. Interscience.
Audience: **u,f.**

Young, David A.   QD503.Y68 1991
Phase Diagrams of the Elements. Trade Cloth. University of California Press. Berkeley, CA. 1991. 280p. ISBN:0-520-07483-1, ISBN13: 978-0-520-07483-5. Dewey:541.3/63. LCCN:90-025978.
Audience: **u,f.** *Choice, 1992.*

Physical Chemistry > Physicochemical Properties and Data Compilations > The Chemical Bond

Pauling, Linus   QD469.P38
The Nature of the Chemical Bond and the Structure of Molecules and Crystals: An Introduction to Modern Structural Chemistry. Ed. 3. Trade Cloth. Cornell University Press. Ithaca, NY. 1960. 664p. George Fisher Baker Non-Resident Lecture Ser. ISBN:0-8014-0333-2, ISBN13: 978-0-8014-0333-0. Dewey:541.22.
Audience: **u,f.** *B*

Stranges, Anthony N.   QD469 .S73 1982
Electrons and Valence: Development of the Theory, 1900-1925. Trade Cloth. Texas A & M University Press. College Station, TX. 1982. 304p. ISBN:0-89096-124-7, ISBN13: 978-0-89096-124-7. Dewey:541.2/24. LCCN:81-048378.
Audience: **u,f.** *B*

Zewail, Ahmed H. (Editor)   QD461.C422 1992
The Chemical Bond: Structure and Dynamics. Trade Cloth. Elsevier Science & Technology Books. Saint Louis, MO. 1992. 313p. ISBN:0-12-779620-7, ISBN13: 978-0-12-779620-8. Dewey:541.2/24. LCCN:91-029643.
Audience: **u,f.** *Choice, 1993.*

Physical Chemistry > Physicochemical Properties and Data Compilations > Colloids, Surfaces, and Interfaces

Adamson, Arthur W. &   **QD506.A3 1997**
Gast, Alice P.
Physical Chemistry of Surfaces. Ed. 6. Trade Cloth. John Wiley & Sons, Inc. Hoboken, NJ. 1997. 808p. ISBN:0-471-14873-3, ISBN13: 978-0-471-14873-9. Dewey:541.3/3. LCCN:97-005929.
Audience: **u,f.** *B Choice, 1998.*

Birdi, K. S. (Editor)   **QD508**
Surface and Colloid Chemistry Handbook. CRCnetBASE. 1999. 1523-3138
Audience: **u,f.**

Birdi, K.S.   **QD508.H36**
Handbook of Surface and Colloid Chemistry. CRC Press. 2003. ISBN:0-8493-1079-2, ISBN13: 978-0-8493-1079-9.
Audience: **u,f.**

Evans, D. Fennell &   **QD549.E93 1999**
Wennerström, Håkan
The Colloidal Domain: Where Physics, Chemistry, Biology, and Technology Meet. Ed. 2. Trade Cloth. John Wiley & Sons, Inc. Hoboken, NJ. 1999. 672p. Advances in Interfacial Engineering, Vol. 1 ISBN:0-471-24247-0, ISBN13: 978-0-471-24247-5. Dewey:541.3/45. LCCN:98-023227.
Audience: **u,f.** *Choice, 1999, 1995.*

Hiemenez, Paul C. &   **QD549.H53 1997**
Rajagopalan, Raj
Principles of Colloid and Surface Chemistry. Ed. 3. Paper over Boards. Marcel Dekker Inc. New York, NY. 1997. 672p. Undergraduate Chemistry Ser. ISBN:0-8247-9397-8, ISBN13: 978-0-8247-9397-5. Dewey:541.3/45. LCCN:97-004015.
Audience: **u,f.**

Hubbard, Arthur T.   **QD506.E63 2002**
Encyclopedia of Surface and Colloid Science. Paper over Boards. Marcel Dekker Inc. New York, NY. 2002. xlix, 5667p. ISBN:0-8247-0633-1, ISBN13: 978-0-8247-0633-3. Dewey:541/.33/03. LCCN:2003-279548.
Audience: **u,f.**

McCash, Elaine M.   **QD506.M35 2001**
Surface Chemistry. Paper Text. Oxford University Press, Inc. New York, NY. 2001. 188p. ISBN:0-19-850328-8, ISBN13: 978-0-19-850328-6. Dewey:541.3/3. LCCN:2001-270027.
Audience: **u,f.** *Choice, 2002.*

Myers, Drew   **QD506.M93 1999**
Surfaces, Interfaces, and Colloids: Principles and Applications. Ed. 2. Trade Cloth. John Wiley & Sons, Inc. Hoboken, NJ. 1999. 528p. ISBN:0-471-33060-4, ISBN13: 978-0-471-33060-8. Dewey:541.3/3. LCCN:98-038906.
Audience: **u,f.** *Choice, 1999, 1992.*

Stein, H. N. (Editor)   **QD549.S7896 1996**
The Preparation of Dispersions in Liquids, Vol. 58. Paper over Boards. Marcel Dekker Inc. New York, NY. 1995. 240p. Surfactant Science Ser., Vol. 58 ISBN:0-8247-9674-8, ISBN13: 978-0-8247-9674-7. Dewey:541.3/45. LCCN:95-040714.
Audience: **u,f.** *Choice, 1996.*

Toth, Jozsef   **QD547.A395 2002**
Adsorption: Theory, Modeling, and Analysis, Vol. 107. Paper over Boards. Marcel Dekker Inc. New York, NY. 2002. 904p. Surfactant Science Ser., Vol. 107 ISBN:0-8247-0747-8, ISBN13: 978-0-8247-0747-7. Dewey:541.3/3. LCCN:2002-067806.
Audience: **u.**

Physical Chemistry > Physicochemical Properties and Data Compilations > Crystallography

                                                        QD921
American Mineralogist Crystal Structure Database.
http://rruff.geo.arizona.edu/AMS/amcsd.php
Audience: **u,f.**

Cambridge Structural Database--Tutorial.
http://stanley.chem.lsu.edu/webpub/7770-Lecture-5-Cambridge-Crystal-Database.pdf
Audience: **u,f.**

Crystallography Links.
http://www.iumsc.indiana.edu/usefulLinks/crystalLinks.html
Audience: **u,f.**

                                                        QD901
Crystallography Online.
http://journals.iucr.org/cww-top/crystal.index.html
Audience: **u,f.**

                                                        QD901
Crystallography Online.
http://www.iucr.ac.uk/cww-top/crystal.index.html
International Union of Crystallography.
Audience: **u,f.**

Crystallography Open Database.
http://www.crystallography.net/
Audience: **u,f.**

Crystallography Subject Guide (Stanford University).
http://library.stanford.edu/depts/swain/help/subjectguides/crystallography.html
Audience: **u,f.**

                                                        QD111
Interactive Tutorial about Diffraction.
http://www.uni-wuerzburg.de/mineralogie/crystal/teaching/teaching.html
Audience: **u,f.**

Notes on Individual Crystallographyers--History of Crystallography--People.
http://www.iucr.ac.uk/
Audience: **u,f.**

☐ Reciprocal Net: Common Molecules.
http://www.reciprocalnet.org/edumodules/commonmolecules/
index.html

Audience: **u,f.**

☐ X-Ray Crystallography Research Guide (U.
Wisconsin-Madison).
http://chemistry.library.wisc.edu/instruction/
xraycrystallography.htm

Audience: **u,f.**

Borchardt-Ott, W.   QD905.2.B713 1993
Crystallography: An Introduction. R. Gould (Translator). Trade
Paper. Springer. New York, NY. 1993. xiii, 290p.
ISBN:3-540-56679-1, ISBN13: 978-3-540-56679-3. Dewey:548.
LCCN:93-044956.

Audience: **u,f.** *Choice, 1994.*

Giacovazzo, Carmelo   QD921.G46 1998
Direct Phasing in Crystallography: Fundamentals and
Applications. Trade Cloth. Oxford University Press, Inc. New
York, NY. 1999. 528p. International Union of Crystallography
Texts on Crystallography, No. 8 ISBN:0-19-850072-6, ISBN13:
978-0-19-850072-8. Dewey:548/.8. LCCN:99-193578.

Audience: **u,f.** *Choice, 1999.*

Glusker, Jenny P., et al.   QD945.G583 1994
Crystal Structure Analysis for Chemists and Biologists. Mitchell
Lewis & Miriam Rossi (Authors). Trade Cloth. John Wiley &
Sons, Inc. Hoboken, NJ. 1994. xviii, 854p. Methods in
Stereochemical Analysis Ser. ISBN:0-89573-273-4, ISBN13:
978-0-89573-273-6. Dewey:548.83. LCCN:92-007886.

Audience: **u,f.** *Choice, 1995.*

Hammond, Christopher   QD905.2.H355 2001
The Basics of Crystallography and Diffraction. Ed. 2. Trade
Cloth. Oxford University Press, Inc. New York, NY. 2001. 320p.
International Union of Crystallography Texts on Crystallography,
Vol. 5 ISBN:0-19-850553-1, ISBN13: 978-0-19-850553-2.
Dewey:548. LCCN:00-053086.

Audience: **u,f.** *Choice, 2001.*

Ladd, Mark   QD921.L26 1999
Crystal Structures, Lattices and Solids in Stereoview. Trade
Paper. Horwood Publishing Ltd. Chichester, 2002. 180p.
Horwood Series in Science ISBN:1-898563-63-2, ISBN13:
978-1-898563-63-1. Dewey:548/.81. LCCN:00-690733.

Audience: **u,f.** *Choice, 2000.*

Mak, Thomas C. W. &   QD945.M244 1992
Zhou, Gong-Du
Crystallography in Modern Chemistry: A Resource Book of
Crystal Structures. Trade Cloth. John Wiley & Sons, Inc.
Hoboken, NJ. 1992. 1323p. ISBN:0-471-54702-6, ISBN13:
978-0-471-54702-0. Dewey:548.8. LCCN:91-023395.

Audience: **u,f.** *Choice, 1993.*

Massa, Werner   QD945.M37713 2000
Crystal Structure Determination. R. O. Gould (Translator). Trade
Paper. Springer. New York, NY. 2000. XI, 206p.
ISBN:3-540-65970-6, ISBN13: 978-3-540-65970-9.
Dewey:548/.83. LCCN:99-036317.

Audience: **u,f.** *Choice, 2004, 2000.*

Mersmann, A. (Editor)   TP156.C7C795 2001
Crystallization Technology Handbook. Ed. 2. Paper over Boards.
Marcel Dekker Inc. New York, NY. 2001. 840p.
ISBN:0-8247-0528-9, ISBN13: 978-0-8247-0528-2.
Dewey:660/.284298. LCCN:2001-028553.

Audience: **u,f.**

O'Keeffe, Michael &   QD461
Navrotsky, Alexandra (Editors)
Structure and Bonding in Crystals, Vol. 2. Trade Cloth. Elsevier
Science & Technology Books. Saint Louis, MO. 1981. xviii,
357p. ISBN:0-12-525102-5, ISBN13: 978-0-12-525102-0.
Dewey:548/.81. LCCN:81-007924.

Audience: **u,f.**

O'Keeffe, Michael &   QD478
Navrotsky, Alexandra (Editors)
Structure and Bonding in Crystals, Vol. 1. Trade Cloth. Elsevier
Science & Technology Books. Saint Louis, MO. 1981. xviii,
327p. ISBN:0-12-525101-7, ISBN13: 978-0-12-525101-3.
Dewey:548/.81. LCCN:81-007924.

Audience: **u,f.**

Woolfson, Michael & Hai-fu,   QD945 .W59 1995
Fan
Physical and Non-Physical Methods of Solving Crystal
Structures. Trade Cloth. Cambridge University Press. New York,
NY. 1995. 288p. ISBN:0-521-41299-4, ISBN13:
978-0-521-41299-5. Dewey:548/.83. LCCN:94-008254.

Audience: **u,f.** *Choice, 1996.*

Physical Chemistry > Physicochemical Properties and Data Compilations > Electrochemistry

QD553

☐ Electrochemical Science and Technology Information
Resource (ESTIR).
http://electrochem.cwru.edu/estir/

Audience: **u,f.**

Bard   QD551 .B37
Encyclopedia of Electrochemistry, Vol. 1. Trade Cloth. Marcel
Dekker Inc. New York, NY. 1986. ISBN:0-8247-6093-X,
ISBN13: 978-0-8247-6093-9. Dewey:541/.37. LCCN:73-088796.

Audience: **u,f.**

Bard, Allen J. & Faulkner,   QD553.B37 2001
Larry R.
Electrochemical Methods: Fundamentals and Applications. Ed.
2. Trade Cloth. John Wiley & Sons, Inc. Hoboken, NJ. 2000.
856p. ISBN:0-471-04372-9, ISBN13: 978-0-471-04372-0.
Dewey:541.3/7. LCCN:00-038210.

Audience: **u,f.** *B*

Bockris, John O'M.; K. N.   QD553
Amulya, Reddy
Modern Electrochemistry, 3 vols. Plenum Press. 1998.
ISBN:0-306-46597-3, ISBN13: 978-0-306-46597-0.

Audience: **u,f.**

Bockris, John O'M. &   QD553.B63 1998
  Reddy, A. K.
Modern Electrochemistry 1: Ionics. Ed. 2. Trade Cloth. Basic
Books. New York, NY. 1998. 666p. ISBN:0-306-45554-4,
ISBN13: 978-0-306-45554-4. Dewey:541.3/7. LCCN:97-024151.
Audience: **u,f.**

Bockris, John O'M. &   QD553.B63 1998
  Reddy, Amulya K. N.
Modern Electrochemistry: Electrodics in Chemistry,
Engineering, Biology and Environmental Science. Ed. 2. Trade
Cloth. Springer. New York, NY. 2001. 542p.
ISBN:0-306-46324-5, ISBN13: 978-0-306-46324-2.
Dewey:541.3/7. LCCN:97-024151.
Audience: **u,f.**

Bockris, John O'M.   QD553.B63 1998
Modern Electrochemistry: Electrodics in Chemistry,
Engineering, Biology and Environmental Science. Ed. 2.
Amulya K. N. Reddy (Editor). Trade Paper. Springer. New York,
NY. 2001. 564p. ISBN:0-306-46325-3, ISBN13:
978-0-306-46325-9. Dewey:541.3/7. LCCN:97-024151.
Audience: **u,f.**

Bockris, John O'M., et al.   QD553.B63
Modern Electrochemistry: Fundamentals of Electrodics. Ed. 2.
Amulya K. N. Reddy & Maria E. Gamboa-Aldeco (Authors).
Trade Cloth. Springer. New York, NY. 2001. 788p.
ISBN:0-306-46166-8, ISBN13: 978-0-306-46166-8.
Dewey:541.3/7.
Audience: **u,f.**

Bockris, John O'M., et al.   QD553.B63
Modern Electrochemistry: Fundamentals of Electrodics. Ed. 2.
Amulya K. N. Reddy & Maria E. Gamboa-Aldeco (Authors).
Trade Paper. Springer. New York, NY. 2001. 820p.
ISBN:0-306-46167-6, ISBN13: 978-0-306-46167-5.
Dewey:541.3/7.
Audience: **u,f.**

Conway, Brian E.   QD560 .C65 1969
Electrochemical Data. Trade Cloth. Greenwood Publishing
Group, Inc. Portsmouth, NH. 1971. 374p. ISBN:0-8371-1630-9,
ISBN13: 978-0-8371-1630-3. Dewey:541/.37/0212.
LCCN:69-010078.
Audience: **u,f.**

Crow, D. R. (Editor)   QD553.C92 1998
Principles and Applications of Electrochemistry. Ed. 4. Trade
Paper. Nelson Thornes Ltd. Cheltenham, 1994. 296p.
ISBN:0-7487-4378-2, ISBN13: 978-0-7487-4378-0.
Dewey:621.31/242. LCCN:00-304342.
Audience: **u,f.** *B*

Dell, R. M. & Rand, D. A. J.   TK2901.D45
Understanding Batteries. Trade Paper. Royal Society of
Chemistry, The. Cambridge, 2001. xxx + 224p. RSC Paperbacks
Ser. ISBN:0-85404-605-4, ISBN13: 978-0-85404-605-8.
Dewey:621.3/1242.
Audience: **u,f.**

Hamnett, Andrew, et al.   QD553.H29 1998
Electrochemistry. Carl H. Hamann & Wolf Vielstich (Authors).
Trade Paper. John Wiley & Sons, Inc. Hoboken, NJ. 1999. 437p.
ISBN:3-527-29096-6, ISBN13: 978-3-527-29096-3.
Dewey:541.3/7. LCCN:98-155076.
Audience: **u,f.** *Choice, 1999.*

Hampel, Clifford A. (Editor)   QD553.H3
Encyclopedia of Electrochemistry. Trade Cloth. Krieger
Publishing Company. Melbourne, FL. 1972. 1224p.
ISBN:0-88275-023-2, ISBN13: 978-0-88275-023-1.
Dewey:541.3703. LCCN:64-022288.
Audience: **u,f.**

Latimer, Wendell Mitchell   QD561
The Oxidation States of the Elements and Their Potentials in
Aqueous Solutions [Known As Oxidation Potentials].
Prentice-Hall. 1964. Prentice-Hall Chemistry Series
Audience: **u,f.**

Orbakh, Doron   QD555.5.N66 1999
Nonaqueous Electrochemistry. Paper over Boards. Marcel
Dekker Inc. New York, NY. 1999. 608p. ISBN:0-8247-7334-9,
ISBN13: 978-0-8247-7334-2. Dewey:541.3/7. LCCN:99-035915.
Audience: **u,f.** *Choice, 2000.*

Sawyer, Donald T., et al.   QD553.S32 1995
Electrochemistry for Chemists. Ed. 2. Andrzej Sobkowiak &
Julian L. Roberts Jr. (Authors). Trade Cloth. John Wiley &
Sons, Inc. Hoboken, NJ. 1995. 528p. ISBN:0-471-59468-7,
ISBN13: 978-0-471-59468-0. Dewey:541.3/7. LCCN:95-002738.
Audience: **u,f.** *Choice, 1996.*

Physical Chemistry > Physicochemical Properties and Data Compilations > Thermochemical and Thermophysical Data

     QD504.C62
☐ CODATA Key Values for Thermodynamics.
http://www.codata.org/resources/databases/key1.html
Audience: **u,f.**

     TJ265
☐ Thermodex: An Index of Selected Thermodynamic and
Physical Property Resources.
http://www.lib.utexas.edu/thermodex/
Audience: **u,f.**

Barin, Ihsan, et al.   QD511.8.B369 1993
Thermochemical Data of Pure Substances. Ed. 2. Fried Sauert,
Ernst Schultze-Rhonhof & Wang Shu Sheng (Authors). Trade
Cloth. John Wiley & Sons, Inc. Hoboken, NJ. 1992. 1874p.
ISBN:1-56081-717-8, ISBN13: 978-1-56081-717-8.
Dewey:541.369. LCCN:92-046891.
Audience: **u,f.** *Choice, 1993.*

Baulch, D. L.   QD502.E9
Evaluated Kinetic Data for High Temperature Reactions. Cloth
Text. Springer. New York, NY. 1982. 721p.
ISBN:0-88318-281-5, ISBN13: 978-0-88318-281-9.
Dewey:541.394.
Audience: **u,f.**

Baulch, D. L., et al.   QD502
Evaluated Kinetic Data for High Temperature Reactions.
Durbury, J. (Author). Butterworths. ISBN:0-408-70346-6,
ISBN13: 978-0-408-70346-8.
Audience: **u,f.**

Chase, M. W. & National   QD511.N57 1998
  Institute of Standards and Technology Staff
NIST-JANAF Thermochemical Tables. Ed. 4. Trade Cloth.
American Institute of Physics. Melville, NY. 1998. xi, 1951p.
Journal of Physical and Chemical Reference Data Ser.
ISBN:1-56396-820-7, ISBN13: 978-1-56396-820-4.
Dewey:541.3/6/0212. LCCN:98-086732.

Audience: **u,f.**

Chase, Malcolm W.   QD511
NIST-JANAF Thermochemical Tables, 2 v. Ed. 4. American
Institute of Physics for the National Institute of Standards and
Technology. 1998. ISBN:1-56396-831-2, ISBN13:
978-1-56396-831-0.

Audience: **u,f.**

Chase, Malcolm W.   QD511
NIST-JANAF Thermochemical Tables, Pt. 1. American Institute
of Physics for the National Institute of Standards and
Technology. 1998. ISBN:1-56396-819-3, ISBN13:
978-1-56396-819-8.

Audience: **u,f.**

Domalski, Eugene S.,   QC145.4.T5 D66
  William H. Evans, and Elizabeth D. Hearing
Heat Capacities and Entropies of Organic Compounds in the
Condensed Phase. American Chemical Society; NY, American
Institute of Physics for National Bureau of Standards. 1984.
ISBN:0-88318-447-8, ISBN13: 978-0-88318-447-9.

Audience: **u,f.**

Dreisbach, Robert Rickert,   QD518
  compiler
Pressure Volume Temperature Relationship of Organic
Compounds; a Reference Volume for Reading Directly the
Variation of Vapor Pressure with Temperature of a Compound
Belonging to one of the Twenty Three Cox Chart Families ...
Ed. 3. Handbook Publishers. 1952.

Audience: **u,f.**

Gammon, Bruce E.   QD541.G36
Transport Properties and Related Thermodynamic Data of
Binary Mixtures, Vol. 2. Trade Cloth. American Institute of
Chemical Engineers. New York, NY. 1994. 584p. Design
Institute for Physical Property Data Ser. ISBN:0-8169-0622-X,
ISBN13: 978-0-8169-0622-2. Dewey:661.8/00212.
LCCN:93-033434.

Audience: **u,f.**

Gammon, Bruce E.   QD541.G36 1993
Transport Properties and Related Thermodynamic Data of
Binary Mixtures, Vol. 1. Kenneth N. Marsh, Q. Dong & A. K.
R. Dewan (Editors). Trade Cloth. American Institute of
Chemical Engineers. New York, NY. 1993. 994p. Design
Institute for Physical Property Data Ser. ISBN:0-8169-0580-0,
ISBN13: 978-0-8169-0580-5. Dewey:661.8/00212.
LCCN:93-033434.

Audience: **u,f.**

Gurvich, L. V.; Veyts, I. V.;   QD504
  Alcock, C. B.
Thermodynamic Properties of Individual Substances, Various
Volumes. Begell House. 1996. ISBN:1-56700-075-4, ISBN13:
978-1-56700-075-7.

Audience: **u,f.**

Ho, C. Y.   QD466 .H7
Thermal Conductivity of the Elements: A Comprehensive
Review. Paper Text. Springer. New York, NY. 1974. 796p.
ISBN:0-88318-216-5, ISBN13: 978-0-88318-216-1.
Dewey:541/.36. LCCN:75-004440.

Audience: **u,f.**

Hultgren, Ralph R. et al.   QD171
Selected Values of Thermodynamic Properties of Binary Alloys.
American Society for Metals. 1973.

Audience: **u,f.**

Hultgren, Ralph; Desai,   QD171
  Pramod D.
Selected Values of the Thermodynamic Properties of the
Elements. American Society of Metals. 1973.

Audience: **u,f.**

Inorganic Chemistry Staff,   QD511.8.B56 1999
  et al.
Thermochemical Data of Elements and Compounds. Michael
Binnewies & E. Milke (Authors). Trade Cloth. John Wiley &
Sons, Inc. Hoboken, NJ. 1999. 934p. ISBN:3-527-29775-8,
ISBN13: 978-3-527-29775-7. Dewey:541.3/6/021.
LCCN:99-190836.

Audience: **u,f.**

IUPAC, Physical Chemistry   QD511
  Division
Experimental Chemical Thermodynamics, v. 1: Combustion
Calorimetry. Pergamon Press. 1978. ISBN:0-08-020923-8,
ISBN13: 978-0-08-020923-4.

Audience: **u,f.**

IUPAC. Commission on   QD511
  Thermodynamics and Thermochemistry.
Experimental Thermochemistry: Measurement of Heats of
Reaction, 2v. Interscience. 1956.

Audience: **u,f.**

Mackay, Donald   TD196
Physicochemical Properties and Environmental Fate
Handbook. Shiu, Wan-Ying; Ma, Kuo-Ching (Editors). Chapman
& Hall/CRCnetBase. 1999.

Audience: **u,f.**

Rossini, Frederick D. [and   QC100
  others]
Selected Values of Chemical Thermodynamic Properties. U.S.
Government Printing Office. 1952.

Audience: **u,f.**

Rossini, Frederick D., et al   QD305.H5
Selected Values of Physical and Thermodynamic Properties of
Hydrocarbons and Related Compounds. American Petroleum
Institute by Carnegie Press. 1953.

Audience: **u,f.**

Stull, D. R.; Prophet,   QD511
  Harold
JANAF Thermodynamical Tables. U.S. Government Printing
Office. 1971.

Audience: **u,f.**

U.S. National Bureau of Standards   QC100
Tables of Chemical Kinetics, Homogeneous Reactions. U.S. Government Printing Office. 1951.

Audience: **u,f.**

Wagman, Donald D.; Rossini, Frederick D.   QC100
Selected Values of Chemical Thermodynamic Properties. U.S. Government Printing Office. 1965.

Audience: **u,f.**

Wilhoit, R. C. and B. J. Zwolinski   QD305.A4 W39 1973
Physical and Thermodynamic Properties of Aliphatic Alcohols. American Chemical Society. 1973. ISBN:0-88318-202-5, ISBN13: 978-0-88318-202-4.

Audience: **u,f.**

Yaws, Carl L.   TP200.Y39 2005
Yaws' Handbook of Physical Properties for Hydrocarbons and Chemicals: Physical Properties for More Than 41,000 Organic and Inorganic Chemical Compounds: Coverage for C1 to C100 Organics and Ac to Zr Inorganics. Trade Cloth. Gulf Publishing Company. Houston, TX. 2005. 812p. ISBN:0-9765113-7-1, ISBN13: 978-0-9765113-7-3. Dewey:660.02/1. LCCN:2005-052830.

Audience: **u,f.**

Yaws, Carl L.   QD504
Thermodynamic and Physical Property Data. Gulf Publ. Co.. 1992. ISBN:0-88415-031-3, ISBN13: 978-0-88415-031-2.

Audience: **u,f.**

Yungman, V. S. (Editor), et al.   TA418.52.T4313 1999
Thermal Constants of Substances, Set. V. P. Glushko, V. A. Medvedev & L. V. Gurvich (Editors). Trade Cloth. John Wiley & Sons, Inc. Hoboken, NJ. 1999. 6592p. ISBN:0-471-31855-8, ISBN13: 978-0-471-31855-2. Dewey:620.1/1296. LCCN:98-029638.

Audience: **u,f.**

Physical Chemistry > Physicochemical Properties and Data Compilations > Atomic and Molecular Data

Brauman, J. I. & Streitwieser, Andrew Jr.   QD461 .S9
Supplemental Tables of Molecular Orbital Calculations. Trade Cloth. Pergamon Press. Kidlington, 1965. ISBN:0-08-010219-0, ISBN13: 978-0-08-010219-1. Dewey:547.122.

Audience: **u,f.**

Haile, J. M.   QC168.7.H35
Molecular Dynamics Simulation: Elementary Methods. Trade Cloth. John Wiley & Sons, Inc. Hoboken, NJ. 1992. 489p. Monographs in Physical Chemistry ISBN:0-471-81966-2, ISBN13: 978-0-471-81966-0. Dewey:541.3/94. LCCN:91-031963.

Audience: **u,f.**

Howell, M. G., et al.   QD291 .H6
Formula Index to NMR Literature Data, Vol. 2. A. S. Kende & J. S. Webb (Authors). Trade Cloth. Springer. New York, NY. 1966. 206p. ISBN:0-306-67002-X, ISBN13: 978-0-306-67002-2. Dewey:547. LCCN:64-007756.

Audience: **u,f.**

Howell, M. G.   QD291
Formula Index to NMR Literature Data, Vol. 1. Kende, A. S.; Webb, J. S. (Editors). Plenum. 1965.

Audience: **u,f.**

McClellan, A. L.   QC571.M27
Tables of Experimental Dipole Moments. Cloth Text. W. H. Freeman & Company. New York, NY. 1995. 713p. ISBN:0-7167-0122-7, ISBN13: 978-0-7167-0122-4. Dewey:541.377. LCCN:63-014844.

Audience: **u,f.**

Streitwieser, Andrew, Jr.; Brauman, John I.   QD461
Supplemental Tables of Molecular Orbital Calculations. With a Dictionary of Pi Electron Calculations, 2 v. Pergamon Press. 1965.

Audience: **u,f.**

Physical Chemistry > Physicochemical Properties and Data Compilations > Spectroscopy

The Science of Spectroscopy.
http://scienceofspectroscopy.info/wiki/index.php?title=Main_Page
Audience: **u,f.**

Physical Chemistry > Laboratory Texts and Manuals

Daniels, Farrington   QD457
Experimental Physical Chemistry. Ed. 7. Cloth Text. McGraw-Hill Companies, The. New York, NY. 1970. xv, 669p. ISBN:0-07-015339-6, ISBN13: 978-0-07-015339-4. Dewey:541/.3/0724. LCCN:75-077952.

Audience: **u,f.** *B*

Salzberg, Hugh, Jack I. Morrow, and Stephen R. Cohen   QD457
Laboratory Course in Physical Chemistry. Academic Press. 1966.

Audience: **u,f.**

Shoemaker, David P., et al.   QD457.G37 2002
Experiments in Physical Chemistry. Ed. 7. Carl W. Garland & Joseph W. Nibler (Authors). Cloth Text. McGraw-Hill Higher Education. Burr Ridge, IL. 2002. 800p. ISBN:0-07-231821-X, ISBN13: 978-0-07-231821-0. Dewey:541.3/078. LCCN:2001-058652.

Audience: **u,f.**

White, John M   QD457
Physical Chemistry Laboratory Experiments. Prentice Hall. 1975. ISBN:0-13-665927-6, ISBN13: 978-0-13-665927-3.

Audience: **u,f.**

Physical Chemistry > Problem Manuals and Physical Chemistry Software

Cropper, William H.   QD455.3.E4C76 1998
Mathematica Programs for Physical Chemistry. Mixed Media.
Springer. New York, NY. 1998. XI, 246p. ISBN:0-387-98337-6,
ISBN13: 978-0-387-98337-0. Dewey:541.3/0285/53.
LCCN:97-034136.
                                        Audience: **u,f.** *Choice, 1999.*

Field, Martin J.   QD480 .F5 1999
A Practical Introduction to the Simulation of Molecular
Systems. Trade Paper. Cambridge University Press. New York,
NY. 2005. 335p. ISBN:0-521-01799-8, ISBN13:
978-0-521-01799-2. Dewey:541.220113.
                                        Audience: **u,f.** *Choice, 2000.*

Francl, Michelle   QD458
Survival Guide for Physical Chemistry. Perfect. Physics
Curriculum & Instruction, Inc. Lakeville, MN. 2001. 136p.
ISBN:0-9713134-0-7, ISBN13: 978-0-9713134-0-8.
Dewey:541.06. LCCN:2001-093987.
                                        Audience: **u.**

Metz, Clyde R.   QD456.M4 1989
Schaum's Outline of Physical Chemistry. Ed. 2. Paper Text.
McGraw-Hill Companies, The. New York, NY. 1988. 512p.
Schaum's Outline Ser. ISBN:0-07-041715-6, ISBN13:
978-0-07-041715-1. Dewey:541.3/076. LCCN:87-029839.
                                        Audience: **u.**

Watson, P.   QD453.2
Physical Chemistry: Interactive Software. CD-ROM. John Wiley
& Sons, Inc. Hoboken, NJ. 1997. ISBN:0-471-16226-4,
ISBN13: 978-0-471-16226-1. Dewey:541.3.
                                        Audience: **u,f.**

Whitakker, G., et al.   QD453.2
Instant Notes in Physical Chemistry. A. Mount & M. Heal
(Authors). Paper Text. Springer. New York, NY. 2000. 320p.
Instant Notes Ser. ISBN:0-387-91619-9, ISBN13:
978-0-387-91619-4. Dewey:541.3.
                                        Audience: **u.** *Choice, 2001.*

Organic Chemistry > Guides to the Literature

☐ MolData--Organic Chemistry.
http://pages.pomona.edu/~wsteinmetz/OrgChem.htm
                                        Audience: **l,u,f.**

☐ Organic Chemistry Info (Hans Reich--UW-Madison).
http://www.chem.wisc.edu/areas/organic/index-chem.htm
                                        Audience: **l,u,f.**

Heller, Stephen R. (Editor)   QD257.7.B394 1998
The Beilstein System: Strategies for Effective Searching. Cloth
Text. Oxford University Press, Inc. New York, NY. 1997. 224p.
Computer Applications in Chemistry Collection
ISBN:0-8412-3523-6, ISBN13: 978-0-8412-3523-6.
Dewey:025.06/547. LCCN:97-035536.
                                        Audience: **u,f.** *Choice, 1998.*

Organic Chemistry > Bibliographies, Indexes, and Reviews

⚙ ChemPrep [Electronic Resource]. Institute for Scientific
Information. 1091-8558
                                        Audience: **u,f.**

                                                    QD262
⚙ Current Chemical Reactions. Institute for Scientific
Information. 0163-6278
                                        Audience: **u,f.**

                                                  QD251.B43
⚙ Current Facts [Computer File]; (Beilstein Current Facts in
Chemistry). Springer Verlag. 0939-7698
                                        Audience: **u,f.**

Infochem Gmbh Staff   QD291
ChemReact41/InfoChem: Reaction Database/Reaction Display
File. CD-ROM, Trade Cloth. Springer. New York, NY. 1996.
100p. ISBN:3-540-14563-X, ISBN13: 978-3-540-14563-9.
Dewey:541.3902856.
                                        Audience: **u,f.**

Patterson, Austin McDowell   QD291
The Ring Index. Ed. 2. Capell, Leonard, T.; Walker, D. F.
(Editors). American Chemical Society. 1960.
                                        Audience: **u,f.**

Organic Chemistry > Nomenclature

☐ Common Reactive Intermediates in Organic Chemistry.
http://www.chem.wisc.edu/areas/reich/handouts/Reactive-
Intermediates.GIF
                                        Audience: **l,u,f.**

                                                    QD291
☐ Common Reactive Intermediates in Organic Chemistry.
http://www.chem.wisc.edu/areas/reich/handouts/Reactive-
Intermediates.GIF
University of Wisconsin.
                                        Audience: **u,f.**

                                                    QD291
☐ Glossary of Class Names of Organic Compounds and
Reactive Intermediates Based on Structures.
http://www.chem.qmw.ac.uk/iupac/class/
Pure and Applied Chemistry.
                                        Audience: **u,f.**

☐ Glossary of Class Names of Organic Compounds and
Reactive Intermediates Based on Structuresbased on structure.
http://www.chem.qmw.ac.uk/iupac/class/
                                        Audience: **u,f.**

                                                     QD5
☐ Glossary of Terms Used in Physical Organic Chemistry.
http://www.chem.qmw.ac.uk/iupac/gtpoc/cont.html
IUPAC.
                                        Audience: **u,f.**

□ Glossary of Terms Used in Physical Organic Chemistry.
http://www.chem.qmw.ac.uk/iupac/class/

Audience: **u,f.**

□ IUPAC Nomenclature of Organic Chemistry
(Recommendations 1979/1993).
http://www.acdlabs.com/iupac/nomenclature/

Audience: **u,f.**

QD291

□ IUPAC Nomenclature of Organic Chemistry
(Recommendations 1979/1993).
http://www.acdlabs.com/iupac/nomenclature/
IUPAC.

Audience: **u,f.**

Fox, Robert B. & Powell,   **QD291.F6 2001**
Warren H.
Nomenclature of Organic Compounds: Principles and Practice.
Ed. 2. Trade Cloth. Oxford University Press, Inc. New York,
NY. 2001. 458p. An American Chemical Society Publication
ISBN:0-8412-3648-8, ISBN13: 978-0-8412-3648-6.
Dewey:547/.0014. LCCN:99-043801.

Audience: **l,u,f.**

Fresenius, Philipp   **QD291.F7413 1989**
Organic Chemical Nomenclature. Trade Cloth. Prentice Hall
PTR. Upper Saddle River, NJ. 1989. 294p. Organic Chemistry
Ser. ISBN:0-470-21098-2, ISBN13: 978-0-470-21098-7.
Dewey:547/.0014. LCCN:88-021599.

Audience: **l,u,f.**

Giese, F.   **QD291.G53 1986**
Beilstein's Index. Cloth Text. Springer. New York, NY. 1986.
253p. ISBN:0-387-16142-2, ISBN13: 978-0-387-16142-6.
Dewey:547/.0014. LCCN:85-027914.

Audience: **l,u,f.**

Godly, Edward W.   **QD291.G63 1995**
Naming Organic Compounds: A Systematic Instruction Manual.
Ed. 2. Trade Cloth. Prentice Hall PTR. Upper Saddle River, NJ.
1995. 280p. Ellis Horwood Series in Organic Chemistry Ser.
ISBN:0-13-103623-8, ISBN13: 978-0-13-103623-9.
Dewey:547/.0014. LCCN:94-027486.

Audience: **l,u,f.**

Hellwinkel, D.   **QD291.H3913 2001**
Systematic Nomenclature in Organic Chemistry: A Directory to
Comprehension and Application of It's Basic Principles. Trade
Paper. Springer. New York, NY. 2001. X, 228p.
ISBN:3-540-41138-0, ISBN13: 978-3-540-41138-3.
Dewey:547/.001/4. LCCN:2001-020540.

Audience: **l,u,f.**

International Union of Pure   **QD291**
and Applied Chemistry
Nomenclature of Organic Chemistry: Sections A, B and C. Ed.
4. Trade Cloth. Elsevier Science & Technology Books. Saint
Louis, MO. 1979. 352p. ISBN:0-08-022369-9, ISBN13:
978-0-08-022369-8. Dewey:547/.0014. LCCN:79-040358.

Audience: **u,f.**

Kaplan, Fred, et al.   **QD291**
The Vocabulary of Organic Chemistry. Roger S. Macomber,
Milton M. Orchin, R. Marshall Wilson & Hans W. Zimmer

(Authors). Trade Cloth. John Wiley & Sons, Inc. Hoboken, NJ.
1980. 609p. ISBN:0-471-04491-1, ISBN13: 978-0-471-04491-8.
Dewey:547/.0014. LCCN:79-025930.

Audience: **l,u,f.**

Lide, David R., Milne,   **QD291**
G.W.A.
Names, Synonyms, and Structures of Organic Compounds: a
CRC Reference Handbook, 3 v. CRC Press. 1995.
ISBN:0-8493-0405-9, ISBN13: 978-0-8493-0405-7.

Audience: **l,u,f.**

Organic Chemistry > Encyclopedias

Paquette, L. A.   **QD77.E53**
Encyclopedia of Reagents for Organic Synthesis. Ed. 11. Digital,
Other. John Wiley & Sons, Inc. Hoboken, NJ. 2003. 6234p.
ISBN:0-470-84289-X, ISBN13: 978-0-470-84289-8.
Dewey:547.2.

Audience: **u,f.**

Paquette, Leo A.   **QD77.E53 1995**
Encyclopedia of Reagents for Organic Synthesis, Set. Trade
Cloth. John Wiley & Sons, Inc. Hoboken, NJ. 1995. 6234p.
ISBN:0-471-93623-5, ISBN13: 978-0-471-93623-7.
Dewey:547.2. LCCN:95-032803.

Audience: **u,f.**

Organic Chemistry > Dictionaries

QD251

□ Beilstein Dictionary.
http://www-sul.stanford/edu/depts/swain/beilstein/bedict1.html
Stanford University.

Audience: **u,f.**

QD246

□ Named Rules and Effects in Organic Chemistry.
http://www.chem.wisc.edu/areas/reigh/handouts/Nameeffect/
named-effects.htm
University of Wisconsin.

Audience: **l,u,f.**

□ Named Rules and Effects in Organic Chemistry.
http://www.chem.wisc.edu/areas/reich/handouts/Nameeffect/
named-effects.htm

Audience: **l,u,f.**

Patai, Saul   **QD251**
Glossary of Organic Chemistry, Including Physical Organic
Chemistry. Interscience Publishers. 1962.

Audience: **l,u,f.**

Organic Chemistry > Handbooks and Tables of Data

□ CrossFire Beilstein.
http://www.mdl.com/products/knowledge/crossfire_beilstein/
Elsevier MDL.

Audience: **u,f.**

QD246
⚙ Dictionary of Organic Compounds on CD-ROM. Chapman & Hall Chemical Database. 1993.
Audience: **u,f.**

QD246.D5
Dictionary of Organic Compounds, Set. Ed. 6. Chapman & Hall. 1996. ISBN:0-412-54090-8, ISBN13: 978-0-412-54090-5.
Audience: **u,f.**

QV 55
▢ DrugBank.
http://redpoll.pharmacy.ualberta.ca/drugbank
Audience: **u,f.**

QD77
▢ Named Reagents.
http://www.chem.wisc.edu/areas/reigh/handouts/NameReagents/namedreag.htm
University of Wisconsin.
Audience: **u,f.**

▢ Named Reagents.
http://www.chem.wisc.edu/areas/reich/handouts/NameReagents/namedreag.htm
Audience: **u,f.**

▢ PKa Values (Acids, Bases, Alcohols, etc.).
http://research.chem.psu.edu/brpgroup/pKa_compilation.pdf
Audience: **u,f.**

Beilstein, Friedrich Konrad **QD251**
Handbuch der Organischen Chemie, Various Vols. & Eds.,1918 - Present. Springer. 1918.
Audience: **u,f.**

Beyer, Hans & Walter, QD251.2.B4813 1996 Wolfgang
Handbook of Organic Chemistry. Douglas R. Lloyd (Translator). Cloth Text. Prentice Hall Books. Old Tappan, NJ. 1996. 1015p. ISBN:0-13-010356-X, ISBN13: 978-0-13-010356-7. Dewey:547. LCCN:93-011632.
Audience: **u,f.** *Choice, 1996.*

Bovey, Frank A. **QC762.B6**
NMR Data Tables for Organic Compounds, 1. Ed. 99. Trade Cloth. John Wiley & Sons, Inc. Hoboken, NJ. 1967. 610p. ISBN:0-470-09210-6, ISBN13: 978-0-470-09210-1. Dewey:547/.1/280212. LCCN:67-020258.
Audience: **u,f.**

Chatani, N. **QD262.S35 2000**
Science of Synthesis: Houben-Weyl Methods of Molecular Transformations. Ed. 5. M. Lautens (Editor). Trade Cloth. George Thieme Verlag. Stuttgart, 2001. 1112p. ISBN:3-13-112131-9, ISBN13: 978-3-13-112131-8. Dewey:547/.2. LCCN:00-061560.
Audience: **u,f.**

Coates, Robert M. & QD77.H37 1999 Denmark, Scott E. (Editors)
Reagents, Auxiliaries and Catalysts for C-C Bond Formation. Trade Cloth. John Wiley & Sons, Inc. Hoboken, NJ. 1999. 764p. Hdbk of Reagents for Organic Synthesis Ser.

ISBN:0-471-97924-4, ISBN13: 978-0-471-97924-1.
Dewey:547/.2. LCCN:98-053088.
Audience: **u,f.** *Choice, 2000.*

Dean, John A. & Gokel, QD251.3.G65 2004 George W.
Dean's Handbook of Organic Chemistry. Ed. 2. Trade Cloth. McGraw-Hill Professional Publishing. New York, NY. 2003. 800p. ISBN:0-07-137593-7, ISBN13: 978-0-07-137593-1. Dewey:547. LCCN:2003-277466.
Audience: **l,u,f.** *Choice, 2004.*

Egloff, Gustav **QD291**
Physical Constants of Hydrocarbons, 5 vols., 1939-. Reinhold. 1939.
Audience: **l,u,f.**

Fieser, Mary (Editor) **QD262**
Reagents for Organic Synthesis (Fieser and Fieser's Reagents for Organic Synthesis). Wiley.
Audience: **u,f.**

Gmehling, J. (Editor) **TP156.E65**
Vapor-Liquid Equilibrium Data Collection: Aqueous-Organic Systems. Ed. 2. Cloth Text. Dechema. 60061 Frankfurt, 1991. 750p. Dechema Chemistry Data Ser., Vol. 1, Pt. 1 ISBN:3-926959-30-4, ISBN13: 978-3-926959-30-0. Dewey:547.1363.
Audience: **u,f.**

Lautens, M. **QD262.S35 2000**
Science of Synthesis - Houben-Weyl Methods of Molecular Transformations: Category One - Organometallics. Ed. 5. Trade Cloth. Thieme Medical Publishers, Inc. New York, NY. 2001. 1112p. ISBN:0-86577-940-6, ISBN13: 978-0-86577-940-2. Dewey:547/.2. LCCN:00-061560.
Audience: **u,f.**

Lide, David R. **TP247**
Handbook of Organic Solvents. CRC Press. 1995. ISBN:0-8493-8930-5, ISBN13: 978-0-8493-8930-6.
Audience: **l,u,f.**

Lide, David R., Milne, QD257 G.W.A.
Handbook of Data on Common Organic Compounds, 3 v. CRC Press. 1995. ISBN:0-8493-0404-0, ISBN13: 978-0-8493-0404-0.
Audience: **u,f.**

Lide, David, Milne, G.W. A. QD257 (eds.)
Handbook of Data on Organic Compounds, 7 v. CRC Press. 1994. ISBN:0-8493-0445-8, ISBN13: 978-0-8493-0445-3.
Audience: **u,f.**

Mettes, L. & Zuman, Petr **QD272.E4**
Handbook Series in Organic Electrochemistry, Set. Trade Cloth. Franklin Book Company, Inc. Newtown Sq, PA. ISBN:0-8493-7220-8, ISBN13: 978-0-8493-7220-9. Dewey:QD272.E4C7. LCCN:77-024273.
Audience: **u,f.**

Pearson, Anthony J. & QD77.H37 1999 Roush, William R. (Editors)
Activating Agents and Protecting Groups. Trade Cloth. John Wiley & Sons, Inc. Hoboken, NJ. 1999. 528p. Handbook of

Reagents for Organic Synthesis Ser., Vol. 4
ISBN:0-471-97927-9, ISBN13: 978-0-471-97927-2.
Dewey:547/.2. LCCN:98-053088.

Audience: **u,f.** *Choice, 2000.*

Pretsch, Ernho, et al.   **QC462.85.T313 2000**
Structure Determination of Organic Compounds: Tables of
Spectral Data. Ed. 3. C. Affolter & P Bühlm (Authors). Mixed
Media. Springer. New York, NY. 2004. XV, 421p.
ISBN:3-540-67815-8, ISBN13: 978-3-540-67815-1.
Dewey:547/.122. LCCN:00-063719.

Audience: **u,f.**

Rappoport, Zvi, (Comjpiler)   **QD291**
CRC Handbook of Tables for Organic Compound Identification.
Ed. 3. CRC Press. 1967. ISBN:0-8493-0303-6, ISBN13:
978-0-8493-0303-6.

Audience: **l,u,f.**

Reich, Hans J. & Rigby,   **QD77.H37 1999**
James H. (Editors)
Handbook of Reagents for Organic Synthesis, Acidic and Basic
Reagents, Vol. 2. Trade Cloth. John Wiley & Sons, Inc.
Hoboken, NJ. 1999. 508p. Hdbk of Reagents for Organic
Synthesis Ser. ISBN:0-471-97925-2, ISBN13:
978-0-471-97925-8. Dewey:547/.2. LCCN:98-053088.

Audience: **u,f.** *Choice, 2000.*

Riddick, John A., Bunger,   **QD61**
William B., Sakano,Theodore K.
Organic Solvents, Vol. 1: Physical Properties and Methods of
Purification. Ed. 4. Wiley. 1986. ISBN:0-471-08467-0, ISBN13:
978-0-471-08467-9.

Audience: **u,f.**

Rigby, James H.   **QD77.H37 1999**
Oxidizing and Reducing Agents. Steven D. Burke & Rick L.
Danheiser (Editors). Trade Cloth. John Wiley & Sons, Inc.
Hoboken, NJ. 1999. 564p. Handbook of Reagents for Organic
Synthesis Ser., Vol. 3 ISBN:0-471-97926-0, ISBN13:
978-0-471-97926-5. Dewey:547/.2. LCCN:98-053088.

Audience: **u,f.** *Choice, 2000.*

Sakano, Theodore K., et al.   **QD61.T4 VOL. 2, 1986**
Organic Solvents: Physical Properties and Methods of
Purification. Ed. 4. William B. Bunger, John A. Riddick &
Weissberger (Authors). Trade Cloth. John Wiley & Sons, Inc.
Hoboken, NJ. 1986. 1344p. Techniques of Chemistry Ser., Vol.
40 ISBN:0-471-08467-0, ISBN13: 978-0-471-08467-9.
Dewey:542 s. LCCN:86-015698.

Audience: **u,f.**

Ueno, Keihei, Toshiaki   **QD77**
Imamura, and K.L. Cheng
Handbook of Organic Analytical Reagents. Ed. 2. CRC Press.
1992. ISBN:0-8493-4287-2, ISBN13: 978-0-8493-4287-5.

Audience: **u,f.**

Utermark, Walther; Schicke,   **QD518**
Walter
Schmelzpunkt Tabellen Organischer Verbindungen/Melting Point
Tables of Organic Compounds. Ed. 2. Interscience Publishers.
1963.

Audience: **u,f.**

Weast, Robert C.   **QD257**
Handbook of Data on Organic Compounds (HODOC), Vol. 1.
Grasselli, Jeanette G. (Editors). CRC Press. 1989.
ISBN:0-8493-0441-5, ISBN13: 978-0-8493-0441-5.

Audience: **u,f.**

Organic Chemistry > History

☐ An Archive of Famous Organic Chemists.
http://orgchem.chem.uconn.edu/colleges/oldchemists.html

Audience: **l,u,f.**

     QD21
☐ An Archive of Famous Organic Chemists.
http://orgchem.chem.uconn.edu/colleges/oldchemists.html
University of Connecticut.

Audience: **l,u,f.**

Ball, Philip   **QD31.2.B35 1994**
Designing the Molecular World: Chemistry at the Frontier. Trade
Cloth. Princeton University Press. Princeton, NJ. 1994. 384p.
Princeton Science Library ISBN:0-691-00058-1, ISBN13:
978-0-691-00058-9. Dewey:540. LCCN:93-038151.

Audience: **l,u,f.** *Choice, 1995.*

Benfey, Otto Theodor   **QD476.B4**
From Vital Force to Structural Formulas. Trade Paper. Chemical
Heritage Foundation. Philadelphia, PA. 1964. 115p. BCHOC
Publication, No. 10 ISBN:0-941901-09-2, ISBN13:
978-0-941901-09-3. Dewey:547.12.

Audience: **l,u,f.**

Hopf, Henning   **QD305.H5 H67**
Classics in Hydrocarbon Chemistry: Syntheses, Concepts,
Perspectives. Trade Cloth. John Wiley & Sons, Inc. Hoboken,
NJ. 2001. 562p. ISBN:3-527-30216-6, ISBN13:
978-3-527-30216-1. Dewey:547/.010459.

Audience: **u,f.** *Choice, 2001.*

Tarbell, Dean S. & Tarbell,   **QD248.5.U6 T37 1986**
Ann T.
Essays on the History of Organic Chemistry in the United
States, 1875-1955. Cloth Text. Folio Publishers Tarbell.
Nashville, TN. 1986. x, 434p. ISBN:0-939454-03-3, ISBN13:
978-0-939454-03-7. Dewey:547/.009. LCCN:86-012062.

Audience: **l,u,f.**

Traynham, James G.   **QD248.E87 1986**
(Editor)
Essays on the History of Organic Chemistry. Cloth Text.
Louisiana State University Press. Baton Rouge, LA. 1986. 208p.
ISBN:0-8071-1293-3, ISBN13: 978-0-8071-1293-9.
Dewey:547/.009. LCCN:86-014377.

Audience: **l,u,f.** *Choice, 1988.*

Organic Chemistry > Compilations and Treatises

Ando, Wataru (Editor)   **QD305.E7.O7 1992**
Organic Peroxides. Trade Cloth. John Wiley & Sons, Inc.
Hoboken, NJ. 1992. 862p. ISBN:0-471-93438-0, ISBN13:
978-0-471-93438-7. Dewey:547.23. LCCN:92-001320.

Audience: **u,f.** *Choice, 1993.*

Carey, Francis A. &   QD251.2.C36 1990
  Sundberg, Richard J.
Advanced Organic Chemistry: Structure and Mechanisms, Pt. A.
Ed. 3. Trade Paper. Springer. New York, NY. 1990. 832p.
ISBN:0-306-43447-4, ISBN13: 978-0-306-43447-1. Dewey:547.
LCCN:90-006851.

                                         Audience: **u,f.**

Carey, Francis A. &   QD251.2.C36 1990
  Sundberg, Richard J.
Advanced Organic Chemistry: Reactions and Synthesis. Ed. 3.
Trade Cloth. Springer. New York, NY. 1990. 830p.
ISBN:0-306-43456-3, ISBN13: 978-0-306-43456-3. Dewey:547.
LCCN:90-006851.

                                         Audience: **u,f.**

Coffey, S. (Editor)   QD251.2
Rodd's Chemistry of Carbon Compounds: Heterocyclic
Compounds, Fused-Ring Heterocycles with Three or More N
Atoms, Vol. 4. Ed. 2. Trade Cloth. Elsevier. New York, NY.
1980. 506p. ISBN:0-444-40664-6, ISBN13: 978-0-444-40664-4.
Dewey:547. LCCN:64-004605.

                                 Audience: **u,f.** *B*

Coffey, S. (Editor)   QD251.R6 1964
Rodd's Chemistry of Carbon Compounds; A Modern
Comprehensive Treatise. Ed. 2. Elsevier Pub. Co..
ISBN:0-444-40664-6, ISBN13: 978-0-444-40664-4.

                                         Audience: **u,f.**

Coffey, Samuel (Editor)   QD251
Rodd's Chemistry of Carbon Compounds; A Modern
Comprehensive Treatise. Ed. 2. Elsevier. ISBN:0-444-40664-6,
ISBN13: 978-0-444-40664-4.

                                         Audience: **u,f.**

Cohen, S. G.   QD476
Progress in Physical Organic Chemistry. Streitweiser, A.; Taft,
R. W. (Editors). NY: Wiley, 1963- ..

                                         Audience: **u,f.**

Dyson, George Malcolm   QD251
Manual of Organic Chemistry for Advanced Students.
Longmans, Green. 1950.

                                         Audience: **u,f.**

Fieser, Louis F.; Fieser,   QD251
  Mary
Advanced Organic Chemistry. Reinhold Pub. Corp.. 1961.
                                         Audience: **u,f.**

Fieser, Louis Frederick   QD251.F44
Advanced Organic Chemistry. Paper Text. Textbook Publishers.
Temecula, CA. 2003. 1158p. ISBN:0-7581-4927-1, ISBN13:
978-0-7581-4927-5. Dewey:547.

                                         Audience: **u,f.**

Harvey, Ronald G.   QD341.H9H34 1997
Polycyclic Aromatic Hydrocarbons. Trade Cloth. John Wiley &
Sons, Inc. Hoboken, NJ. 1996. 300p. ISBN:1-56081-686-4,
ISBN13: 978-1-56081-686-7. Dewey:547/.61. LCCN:96-019742.
                              Audience: **u,f.** *Choice, 1998.*

Harwood, L. M.   QD281.R35H37 1991
Polar Rearrangements. Cloth Text. Oxford University Press, Inc.
New York, NY. 1992. 100p. Chemistry Primers Ser., No. 5

ISBN:0-19-855671-3, ISBN13: 978-0-19-855671-8.
Dewey:547.1/22. LCCN:91-026884.
                              Audience: **u,f.** *Choice, 1993.*

Hine, Jack   QD476.H5
Physical Organic Chemistry. Ed. 2. Cloth Text. McGraw-Hill
Companies, The. New York, NY. 1962. Advanced Chemistry
Ser. ISBN:0-07-028929-8, ISBN13: 978-0-07-028929-1.
Dewey:547.1.

                                         Audience: **u,f.**

Hine, Jack Sylvester   QD476.H5
Physical Organic Chemistry. Paper Text. Textbook Publishers.
Temecula, CA. 2003. 552p. ISBN:0-7581-8456-5, ISBN13:
978-0-7581-8456-6. Dewey:547.1.

                                  Audience: **u,f.** *B*

Jones, William, ed.   TA418
Organic Molecular Solids: Properties and Applications. CRC
Press. 1997. ISBN:0-8493-9428-7, ISBN13: 978-0-8493-9428-7.
                                         Audience: **u,f.**

Leonard, J
Advanced Practical Organic Chemistry. Ed. 2. Blackie Academic
& Professional. 1994. ISBN:0-7514-0200-1, ISBN13:
978-0-7514-0200-1.
                                         Audience: **u,f.**

Olah, George A. & Molnár,   QD305.H5
Árpád
Hydrocarbon Chemistry. Ed. 2. Trade Cloth. John Wiley &
Sons, Inc. Hoboken, NJ. 2003. 871p. ISBN:0-471-41782-3,
ISBN13: 978-0-471-41782-8. Dewey:547/.01.
LCCN:2002-154116.
                          Audience: **l,u,f.** *Choice, 2003, 1995.*

Roberts, John D.; Stewart,   QD253.R73 1971b
Ross; Caserio, Marjorie
Organic Chemistry: Methane to Macromolecules. W. A.
Benjamin. 1971.
                                         Audience: **u,f.**

Rodd, E. H. (Editor)   QD251
Chemistry of Carbon Compounds: a Modern Comprehensive
Treatise, Various Vols., 1951-1989. Elsevier. 1951.
                                         Audience: **u,f.**

Sainsbury, M.   QD331.S25 1992
Aromatic Chemistry. Cloth Text. Oxford University Press, Inc.
New York, NY. 1992. 96p. Chemistry Primers Ser., No. 4
ISBN:0-19-855675-6, ISBN13: 978-0-19-855675-6.
Dewey:547/.6. LCCN:91-047606.
                           Audience: **u.** *Choice, 1993.*

Sykes, Peter   QD476 .S89 1986
A Guidebook to Mechanism in Organic Chemistry. Ed. 60.
Trade Paper. John Wiley & Sons, Inc. Hoboken, NJ. 1986. 416p.
ISBN:0-470-20663-2, ISBN13: 978-0-470-20663-8.
Dewey:547.1/39. LCCN:85-024067.
                                         Audience: **u,f.**

Vogel, A. I., et al.   QD261.V63 1989
Vogel's Textbook of Practical Organic Chemistry. Ed. 5. Antony
J. Hannaford, Brian S. Furniss & Peter W. Smith (Authors).
Trade Cloth. John Wiley & Sons, Inc. Hoboken, NJ. 1989.
1514p. ISBN:0-470-21414-7, ISBN13: 978-0-470-21414-5.
Dewey:547. LCCN:88-036786.
                                         Audience: **l,u,f.**

Wiberg, Kenneth B.   **QD476**
Physical Organic Chemistry. Wiley. 1964.

Audience: **u,f.**

Organic Chemistry > Structure and Properties: Electronic/Physical

Dewar, Michael James   **QD461**
  Steuart
The Molecular Orbital Theory of Organic Chemistry.
McGraw-Hill. 1969. McGraw-Hill Series in Advanced
Chemistry

Audience: **u,f.**

Jorgensen, William L. &   **QD461**
  Salem, Lionel
The Organic Chemist's Book of Orbitals. Trade Cloth. Elsevier
Science & Technology Books. Saint Louis, MO. 1973. xii, 305p.
ISBN:0-12-390250-9, ISBN13: 978-0-12-390250-4.
Dewey:547/.1/28. LCCN:72-009990.

Audience: **u,f.** 𝕭

Lund, Henning &   **QD273.O73 2001**
  Hammerich, Ole
Organic Electrochemistry: An Introduction and a Guide. Ed. 4.
Paper over Boards. Marcel Dekker Inc. New York, NY. 2000.
1392p. ISBN:0-8247-0430-4, ISBN13: 978-0-8247-0430-8.
Dewey:547/.137. LCCN:00-047593.

Audience: **u,f.**

MacKay, Don   **QD271.H3186 2000**
Handbook of Property Estimation Methods for Chemicals:
Enviornmental and Health Sciences. Paper over Boards. Lewis
Publishers. Boca Raton, FL. 2000. 504p. ISBN:1-56670-456-1,
ISBN13: 978-1-56670-456-4. Dewey:547/.3. LCCN:99-058377.

Audience: **u,f.**

Mackay, Donald   **TD196.O73**
Handbook of Physical-Chemical Properties and Environmental
Fate for Organic Chemicals. Ed. 2. Taylor & Francis. 2005.
ISBN:1-56670-687-4, ISBN13: 978-1-56670-687-2.

Audience: **u,f.**

Moore, Elaine   **QD480.M654 2002**
Molecular Modelling and Bonding. Mixed Media. Royal Society
of Chemistry, The. Cambridge, 2002. 154p. The Molecular
World Ser. ISBN:0-85404-675-5, ISBN13: 978-0-85404-675-1.
Dewey:541.2/2.

Audience: **u,f.** *Choice, 2003.*

Quinkert, Gerhard, et al.   **QD255.5.S78 Q5513**
Aspects of Organic Chemistry: Structure. Ernst Egert &
Christian Griesinger (Authors). Trade Cloth. John Wiley &
Sons, Inc. Hoboken, NJ. 1996. 506p. ISBN:3-906390-15-2,
ISBN13: 978-3-906390-15-4. Dewey:547.

Audience: **u,f.** *Choice, 1997.*

Rauk, Arvi   **QD461.R33 1994**
Orbital Interaction Theory of Organic Chemistry. Ed. 1. Trade
Cloth. John Wiley & Sons, Inc. Hoboken, NJ. 1994. 336p.
ISBN:0-471-59389-3, ISBN13: 978-0-471-59389-8.
Dewey:547/.128. LCCN:93-027021.

Audience: **u,f.** *Choice, 2001, 1994.*

Roberts, John D.   **QD476**
Notes on Molecular Orbital Calculations. W. A. Benjamin. 1961.

Audience: **u,f.**

Smart, L. E. & Gagan, J.   **QD921 .T457 2002**
  M. F. (Editors)
The Third Dimension. Mixed Media. Royal Society of
Chemistry, The. Cambridge, 2002. 254p. The Molecular World
Ser. ISBN:0-85404-660-7, ISBN13: 978-0-85404-660-7.
Dewey:541.2/2.

Audience: **u,f.** *Choice, 2003.*

Smith, William B.   **QD476.S567 1996**
Introduction to Theoretical Organic Chemistry and Molecular
Modelling. Trade Cloth. John Wiley & Sons, Inc. Hoboken, NJ.
1996. 200p. ISBN:1-56081-937-5, ISBN13: 978-1-56081-937-0.
Dewey:547.1/2. LCCN:95-042883.

Audience: **u,f.** *Choice, 1997.*

Organic Chemistry > Synthetic Methods: > Annuals and Other Serial Publications

Gilman, Henry(Editor-in-   **QD262**
  Chief)
Organic Syntheses. WIley.

Audience: **l,u,f.**

Liotta, Dennis C. & Volmer,   **QD262**
  Mark
Organic Syntheses: Reaction Guide. Trade Cloth. John Wiley &
Sons, Inc. Hoboken, NJ. 1991. 872p. Organic Syntheses
Collective Volumes, Vol. 10 ISBN:0-471-54261-X, ISBN13:
978-0-471-54261-2. Dewey:547.2.

Audience: **u,f.**

Sugasawa, Shigehiko; Nakai,   **QD262**
  Seijiro
Reaction Index of Organic Syntheses. Wiley. 1967.

Audience: **l,u,f.**

Organic Chemistry > Synthetic Methods: > Compendia of Synthetic Methods

Anand, Nitya, et al.   **QD262.A528 1988**
Art in Organic Synthesis. Ed. 2. S. Randanathan & Jasjit S.
Bindra (Authors). Trade Cloth. John Wiley & Sons, Inc.
Hoboken, NJ. 1988. 448p. ISBN:0-471-88738-2, ISBN13:
978-0-471-88738-6. Dewey:547/.2. LCCN:87-014762.

Audience: **u,f.**

Buehler   **QD262**
Survey of Organic Syntheses. Trade Cloth. John Wiley & Sons,
Inc. Hoboken, NJ. 1970. 1166p. ISBN:0-471-11670-X, ISBN13:
978-0-471-11670-7. Dewey:547/.2. LCCN:73-112590.

Audience: **l,u,f.** 𝕭

Carruthers, W.   **QD262 .C33 1986**
Some Modern Methods of Organic Synthesis. Ed. 3. Cloth Text.
Cambridge University Press. New York, NY. 1987. 544p.
Cambridge Texts in Chemistry and Biochemistry Ser.
ISBN:0-521-32234-0, ISBN13: 978-0-521-32234-8.
Dewey:547.2. LCCN:85-021270.

Audience: **u,f.**

Corey, Elias James &   QD262.C577 1989
  Cheng, Xue-Min
The Logic of Chemistry Synthesis. Trade Cloth. John Wiley &
Sons, Inc. Hoboken, NJ. 1989. 436p. ISBN:0-471-50979-5,
ISBN13: 978-0-471-50979-0. Dewey:547.2. LCCN:89-005335.
                                       Audience: **u,f.**

Harrison, Ian T. &   QD262
  Harrison, Shuyen
Compendium of Organic Synthetic Methods, Vol. 1. Ed. 1.
Trade Cloth. John Wiley & Sons, Inc. Hoboken, NJ. 1971. 560p.
Compendium of Organic Synthetic Methods Ser., Vol. 1
ISBN:0-471-35550-X, ISBN13: 978-0-471-35550-2.
Dewey:547/.2. LCCN:71-162800.
                                    Audience: **u,f.** *B*

House, Herbert O.   QD262.H67
Modern Synthetic Reactions. Ed. 2. Cloth Text.
Benjamin-Cummings Publishing Company. San Francisco, CA.
1972. ISBN:0-8053-4501-9, ISBN13: 978-0-8053-4501-8.
Dewey:547/.2. LCCN:78-173958.
                                    Audience: **u,f.** *B*

Ireland, Robert E.   QD262
Organic Synthesis. Prentice-Hill. 1969. ISBN:0-13-640839-7,
ISBN13: 978-0-13-640839-0.
                                    Audience: **u,f.**

Katritzky, Alan R. (Editor),   QD262.C534 1995
  et al.
Comprehensive Organic Functional Group Transformations, Set.
Otto Meth-Cohn & Charles W. Rees (Editors). Trade Cloth.
Elsevier Science & Technology Books. Saint Louis, MO. 1995.
8878p. ISBN:0-08-040604-1, ISBN13: 978-0-08-040604-6.
Dewey:547/.2. LCCN:95-031088.
                         Audience: **u,f.** *Choice, 1996.*

Larock, Richard C.   QD262.L355
Comprehensive Organic Transformations: A Guide to Functional
Group Preparations. CD-ROM, Mixed Media, Digital, Other.
John Wiley & Sons, Inc. Hoboken, NJ. 1996. 27p.
ISBN:0-471-18649-X, ISBN13: 978-0-471-18649-6.
Dewey:547/.2.
                                    Audience: **u,f.**

Larock, Richard C.   QD262.L355 1999
Comprehensive Organic Transformations: A Guide to Functional
Group Preparations. Ed. 2. Trade Cloth. John Wiley & Sons,
Inc. Hoboken, NJ. 1999. 2640p. ISBN:0-471-19031-4, ISBN13:
978-0-471-19031-8. Dewey:547/.2. LCCN:98-037314.
                                    Audience: **u,f.**

Mulzer, Johann, et al.   QD262.O72445 1990
Organic Synthesis Highlights. Hans-Josef Altenbach, Manfred
Braun, Karsten Krohn & Hans-Ulrich Reissig (Authors). Trade
Cloth. John Wiley & Sons, Inc. Hoboken, NJ. 1990. 410p.
ISBN:3-527-27955-5, ISBN13: 978-3-527-27955-5.
Dewey:547.2. LCCN:90-013003.
                                    Audience: **u,f.**

Smit, W. A., et al.   QD262.B6313 1998
Organic Synthesis: The Science Behind the Art. A. F. Bochkov
& R. Caple (Authors). Trade Cloth. Springer. New York, NY.
1998. xx + 475p. ISBN:0-85404-544-9, ISBN13:
978-0-85404-544-0. Dewey:547.2.
                                    Audience: **u,f.**

Trost, B. M. & Fleming, I.   QD262.C535 1991
  (Editors)
Comprehensive Organic Synthesis, Set. Ed. 3. Trade Cloth.
Elsevier Science & Technology Books. Saint Louis, MO. 1991.
10400p. ISBN:0-08-035929-9, ISBN13: 978-0-08-035929-8.
LCCN:90-026621.
                         Audience: **u,f.** *Choice, 1992.*

Waldmann, Herbert (Editor)   QD262.O72445 1990
Organic Synthesis Highlights II. Trade Paper. John Wiley &
Sons, Inc. Hoboken, NJ. 1997. 424p. ISBN:3-527-29378-7,
ISBN13: 978-3-527-29378-0. Dewey:547.2. LCCN:90-013003.
                                    Audience: **u,f.**

Williams, Johnathan M.   QD305.H7P74 1996
  (Editor)
Preparation of Alkenes: A Practical Approach. Cloth Text.
Oxford University Press, Inc. New York, NY. 1996. 272p. The
Practical Approach in Chemistry Ser. ISBN:0-19-855795-7,
ISBN13: 978-0-19-855795-1. Dewey:547.4/12/0459.
LCCN:96-013456.
                         Audience: **u,f.** *Choice, 1997.*

Organic Chemistry > Synthetic Methods: > Special Techniques in Synthesis

Aitken, R. Alan (Editor)   QD262.A79 1992
Asymmetric Synthesis. Trade Cloth. Chapman & Hall. New
York, NY. 1991. 256p. ISBN:0-412-02451-9, ISBN13:
978-0-412-02451-1. Dewey:547.2. LCCN:91-046601.
                         Audience: **u,f.** *Choice, 1993.*

Giese, Bernd   QD471
Radicals in Organic Synthesis. Cloth Text. Franklin Book
Company, Inc. Newtown Sq, PA. 1986. 350p. Organic
Chemistry Ser., Vol. 5 ISBN:0-08-032493-2, ISBN13:
978-0-08-032493-7. Dewey:547.1/224. LCCN:86-017052.
                         Audience: **u,f.** *Choice, 1987.*

Greene, Theodora   QD262.G665 1999
Protective Groups in Organic Synthesis. Ed. 3. Peter G. Wuts
(Editor). Trade Cloth. John Wiley & Sons, Inc. Hoboken, NJ.
1999. 816p. ISBN:0-471-16019-9, ISBN13: 978-0-471-16019-9.
Dewey:547.2. LCCN:98-038182.
                                    Audience: **u,f.**

Hassner, Alfred &   QD262.H324 2002
  Stumer, C.
Organic Syntheses Based on Name Reactions. Ed. 2. J. E.
Baldwin & Robert M. Williams (Contribution by). Trade Cloth.
Elsevier Science & Technology Books. Saint Louis, MO. 2002.
454p. Tetrahedron Organic Chemistry Ser., Vol. 22
ISBN:0-08-043260-3, ISBN13: 978-0-08-043260-1.
Dewey:547/.2. LCCN:2002-024278.
                                    Audience: **u,f.**

Kyriacou, Demetrios K.   QD262
Basics of Electroorganic Synthesis. Trade Cloth. John Wiley &
Sons, Inc. Hoboken, NJ. 1981. 153p. ISBN:0-471-07975-8,
ISBN13: 978-0-471-07975-0. Dewey:547/.2. LCCN:80-025326.
                                    Audience: **u,f.**

Morrison, James D. (Editor) QD481 .A78 1983
Asymmetric Synthesis, Vol. 1: Analytical Methods. Trade Cloth.
Elsevier Science & Technology Books. Saint Louis, MO. 1983.
ISBN:0-12-507701-7, ISBN13: 978-0-12-507701-9.
Dewey:541.3/93. LCCN:83-004620.

Audience: **u,f.**

Nogradi, M. QD481.N64 1995
Stereoselective Synthesis: A Practical Approach. Ed. 2. Trade
Cloth. John Wiley & Sons, Inc. Hoboken, NJ. 1994. 369p.
ISBN:3-527-29242-X, ISBN13: 978-3-527-29242-4.
Dewey:541.2/23. LCCN:97-165615.

Audience: **u,f.**

Noyori, Ryoji QD262.N69 1994
Asymmetric Catalysis in Organic Synthesis. Ed. 1. Trade Cloth.
John Wiley & Sons, Inc. Hoboken, NJ. 1994. 400p. Baker
Lecture Ser., Vol. 4 ISBN:0-471-57267-5, ISBN13:
978-0-471-57267-1. Dewey:547.2. LCCN:93-003884.

Audience: **u,f.** *Choice, 1995.*

Ono, Noboru QD262.O62 2001
The Nitro Group in Organic Synthesis. Trade Cloth. John Wiley
& Sons, Inc. Hoboken, NJ. 2001. 392p. Organic Nitro
Chemistry Ser., Vol. 7 ISBN:0-471-31611-3, ISBN13:
978-0-471-31611-4. Dewey:547/.2. LCCN:00-047762.

Audience: **u,f.** *Choice, 2002.*

Procter, Garry QD262.P76 1996
Asymmetric Synthesis. Trade Cloth. Oxford University Press,
Inc. New York, NY. 1997. 248p. ISBN:0-19-855726-4, ISBN13:
978-0-19-855726-5. Dewey:547/.2. LCCN:95-035780.

Audience: **u,f.** *Choice, 1998.*

Sandler, Stanley R. QD262 .S23 1983
Organic Functional Group Preparations, Vol. I. Ed. 2. Trade
Cloth. Elsevier Science & Technology Books. Saint Louis, MO.
1983. 657p. Organic Chemistry Ser. ISBN:0-12-618601-4,
ISBN13: 978-0-12-618601-7. Dewey:547/.2. LCCN:83-002555.

Audience: **u,f.**

Santelli, Maurice and QD262
  Jean-Marc Pons
Lewis Acids and Selectivity in Organic Synthesis. CRC Press.
1996. New Directions in Organic and Biological Chemistry
ISBN:0-8493-7866-4, ISBN13: 978-0-8493-7866-9.

Audience: **u,f.**

Seneci, Pierfausto QD262.S465 2000
Solid-Phase Synthesis and Combinatorial Technologies. Trade
Cloth. John Wiley & Sons, Inc. Hoboken, NJ. 2000. 656p.
ISBN:0-471-33195-3, ISBN13: 978-0-471-33195-7.
Dewey:547.2. LCCN:99-086954.

Audience: **u,f.**

Stowell, John C. QD305.C3 S76
Carbanions in Organic Synthesis. Trade Cloth. John Wiley &
Sons, Inc. Hoboken, NJ. 1979. 247p. ISBN:0-471-02953-X,
ISBN13: 978-0-471-02953-3. Dewey:547/.1/372.
LCCN:79-000373.

Audience: **u,f.**

Tsuji, Jiro QD505.T785 2000
Transition Metal Reagents and Catalysts: Innovations in Organic
Synthesis. Trade Cloth. John Wiley & Sons, Inc. Hoboken, NJ.
2000. 494p. ISBN:0-471-63498-0, ISBN13: 978-0-471-63498-0.
Dewey:547/.2. LCCN:2001-271784.

Audience: **u,f.**

Wong, C. -H & Whitesides, QD262.W65 1994
G. M.
Enzymes in Synthetic Organic Chemistry. Trade Cloth. Elsevier
Science & Technology Books. Saint Louis, MO. 1994. 388p.
Tetrahedron Organic Chemistry Ser., Vol. 12
ISBN:0-08-035942-6, ISBN13: 978-0-08-035942-7.
Dewey:547.7/0459. LCCN:94-002329.

Audience: **u,f.**

Organic Chemistry > Reactions

Al's Notebook.
http://www.alsnotebook.com/

Audience: **u,f.**

Classic Organic Reactions.
http://www.chempensoftware.com/organicreactions.htm

Audience: **l,u,f.**

QD291
Named Reactions in Organic Chemistry.
http://orgchem.chem.uconn.edu/namereact/named.html
University of Connecticut.

Audience: **u,f.**

Named Reactions in Organic Chemistry.
http://orgchem.chem.uconn.edu/namereact/named.html

Audience: **u,f.**

Reactivity and Structure: Concepts in Organic Chemistry.
Springer-Verlag.

Audience: **u,f.**

Adams, Roger (Editor) QD251
Organic Reactions. John Wiley & Sons.

Audience: **u,f.**

Grossman, Robert B. QD502.5.G76 2002
The Art of Writing Reasonable Organic Reaction Mechanisms.
Ed. 2. Trade Cloth. Springer. New York, NY. 2006. XVI, 355p.
ISBN:0-387-95468-6, ISBN13: 978-0-387-95468-4.
Dewey:547/.139. LCCN:2002-024189.

Audience: **u,f.** *Choice, 2003.*

Haines, Alan H. QD281.O9H24 1985
Methods for the Oxidation of Organic Compounds: Alkanes,
Alkenes, Alkynes, and Arenes, Vol. 1. Trade Cloth. Elsevier
Science & Technology Books. Saint Louis, MO. 1985. xix,
388p. Best Synthetic Methods Ser. ISBN:0-12-315501-0,
ISBN13: 978-0-12-315501-6. Dewey:547/.23. LCCN:84-012465.

Audience: **u,f.**

Kharasch, Morris Selig and QD77
  Otto Reinmuth
Grignard Reactions of Nonmetallic Substances. Prentice-Hall.
1954. Prentice-Hall Chemistry Series

Audience: **u,f.**

Laue, Thomas M. & QD291.L35 1998
  Plagens, Andreas
Named Organic Reactions. Claus Vogel (Translator). Trade

Cloth. John Wiley & Sons, Inc. Hoboken, NJ. 1998. 298p.
ISBN:0-471-97142-1, ISBN13: 978-0-471-97142-9.
Dewey:547.1/39.

Audience: **u,f.** *Choice, 1999.*

Li, Chao-Jun & Chan,   **QD255.4.L5 1997**
Tak-Hang
Organic Reactions in Aqueous Media. Ed. 1. Trade Cloth. John
Wiley & Sons, Inc. Hoboken, NJ. 1997. 216p.
ISBN:0-471-16395-3, ISBN13: 978-0-471-16395-4.
Dewey:547/.13422. LCCN:96-029886.

Audience: **u,f.** *Choice, 1998.*

Li, J. J.   **QD291**
Name Reactions: A Collection of Detailed Reaction
Mechanisms. Ed. 2. Trade Cloth. Springer. New York, NY.
2003. XVIII, 465p. ISBN:3-540-40203-9, ISBN13:
978-3-540-40203-9. Dewey:547/.2. LCCN:2003-284063.

Audience: **u,f** *Choice, 2004, 2002.*

Miller, Audrey & Solomon,   **QD502.5.M53 2000**
Philippa H.
Writing Reaction Mechanisms in Organic Chemistry. Ed. 2.
Paper Text. Elsevier Science & Technology Books. Saint Louis,
MO. 1999. 471p. Advanced Organic Chemistry Ser.
ISBN:0-12-496712-4, ISBN13: 978-0-12-496712-0.
Dewey:547.1/39. LCCN:99-061410.

Audience: **u,f** *Choice, 1992.*

Moody, Christopher J. &   **QD476.M66 1992**
Whitham, Gordon H.
Reactive Intermediates. Cloth Text. Oxford University Press,
Inc. New York, NY. 1992. 96p. Chemistry Primers Ser., No. 8
ISBN:0-19-855673-X, ISBN13: 978-0-19-855673-2.
Dewey:547.2. LCCN:92-012267.

Audience: **u,f** *Choice, 1993.*

Mundy, Bradford P. &   **QD291.M86 1988**
Ellerd, Michael G.
Name Reactions and Reagents in Organic Synthesis. Ed. 1.
Trade Cloth. John Wiley & Sons, Inc. Hoboken, NJ. 1988. 560p.
ISBN:0-471-83626-5, ISBN13: 978-0-471-83626-1.
Dewey:541/.39. LCCN:88-014915.

Audience: **u,f** *Choice, 2005.*

Olah, George A.   **QD501**
Friedel Crafts and Related Reactions. Interscience Publishers,
1963-65. 4 v. in 6. 1963.

Audience: **u,f.**

Patai, Saul E.   **QD251.2.P34 1989**
Patai's Guide to the Chemistry of Functional Groups. Trade
Cloth. John Wiley & Sons, Inc. Hoboken, NJ. 1989. 466p.
ISBN:0-471-91526-2, ISBN13: 978-0-471-91526-3. Dewey:547.
LCCN:88-020707.

Audience: **u,f.**

Pross, Addy   **QD476.P755 1995**
Theoretical and Physical Principles of Organic Reactivity. Ed. 1.
Trade Cloth. John Wiley & Sons, Inc. Hoboken, NJ. 1995. 312p.
ISBN:0-471-55599-1, ISBN13: 978-0-471-55599-5.
Dewey:547.1. LCCN:95-021389.

Audience: **u,f.** *Choice, 1996.*

Organic Chemistry > Organic Chemistry of Special Elements

Brook, Michael A.   **QD412.S6B76 2000**
Silicon in Organic, Organometallic, and Polymer Chemistry.
Trade Cloth. John Wiley & Sons, Inc. Hoboken, NJ. 1999. 704p.
ISBN:0-471-19658-4, ISBN13: 978-0-471-19658-7.
Dewey:547/.08. LCCN:98-049722.

Audience: **u,f.** *Choice, 2001.*

Brown, Herbert C.   **QD281.H78 B7**
Hydroboration. W.A. Benjamin. 1962.

Audience: **u,f.**

Colvim, E. W.   **QD412.S6 C65 1988**
Silicon Reagents. Trade Cloth. Elsevier Science & Technology
Books. Saint Louis, MO. 1988. 147p. ISBN:0-12-182560-4,
ISBN13: 978-0-12-182560-7. Dewey:547/.2. LCCN:89-164624.

Audience: **u,f.**

Goldwhite, Harold   **QD181.P1**
Introduction to Phosphorus Chemistry. Trade Cloth. Cambridge
University Press. New York, NY. 1981. 128p. Cambridge Texts
in Chemistry and Biochemistry Ser. ISBN:0-521-22978-2,
ISBN13: 978-0-521-22978-4. Dewey:546/.7122.
LCCN:79-027141.

Audience: **u,f.** *B*

Hudlicky, Milos   **QD305.H15 H82 1992**
Chemistry of Organic Flourine Compounds. Ed. 2. Cloth Text.
Prentice Hall PTR. Upper Saddle River, NJ. 1992. 918p.
ISBN:0-13-131673-7, ISBN13: 978-0-13-131673-7.
Dewey:547/.02. LCCN:92-241426.

Audience: **u,f.**

Hudlicky, Milos   **QD305.H15C48 1995**
Chemistry of Organic Fluorine Compounds II: A Critical
Review. Attila E. Pavlath (Editor). Cloth Text. Oxford
University Press, Inc. New York, NY. 1995. 1200p. ACS
Monographs, No. 187 ISBN:0-8412-2515-X, ISBN13:
978-0-8412-2515-2. Dewey:547/.02. LCCN:95-020195.

Audience: **u,f.** *Choice, 1996.*

Quin, Louis D.   **QD305.P46Q56 2000**
A Guide to Organophosphorus Chemistry. Trade Cloth. John
Wiley & Sons, Inc. Hoboken, NJ. 2000. 408p.
ISBN:0-471-31824-8, ISBN13: 978-0-471-31824-8.
Dewey:547/.07. LCCN:99-043429.

Audience: **u,f.**

Thomas, Susan E.   **QD412.B1T56 1991**
Organic Synthesis: The Roles of Boron and Silicon. Cloth Text.
Oxford University Press, Inc. New York, NY. 1992. 96p.
Chemistry Primers Ser., No. 1 ISBN:0-19-855663-2, ISBN13:
978-0-19-855663-3. Dewey:547/.05671. LCCN:91-013680.

Audience: **u,f.** *Choice, 1992.*

Organic Chemistry > Special Topics in Organic Chemistry > Spectroscopy

                                                QD466.5.C1

C-13 and Proton Chemical Shifts.

http://www.chem.wisc.edu/areas/reich/Handouts/nmr-c13/
cdata.htm
University of Wisconsin.

Audience: **u,f.**

☐ C-13 and Proton Chemical Shifts.
http://www.chem.wisc.edu/areas/reich/Handouts/nmr-c13/
cdata.htm

Audience: **u,f.**

QC463.S72 I54 1983
Infrared Spectra Handbook of Common Organic Solvents. Trade
Cloth. Sadtler Research Laboratories. Philadelphia, PA. 1983.
ISBN:0-8456-0093-1, ISBN13: 978-0-8456-0093-1.
Dewey:547.1/3482. LCCN:83-050550.

Audience: **u,f.**

QC462.85 .I54 1987
Infrared Spectra Handbook of Intermediates. Trade Cloth.
Sadtler Research Laboratories. Philadelphia, PA. 1987.
ISBN:0-8456-0133-4, ISBN13: 978-0-8456-0133-4.
Dewey:547.3/08583/0222. LCCN:86-061363.

Audience: **u,f.**

QC437
Organic Electronic Spectral Data. WIley & Sons.

Audience: **u,f.**

QC462.85
☐ Spectral Database for Organic Compounds, SDBS.
http://www.aist.go.jp/RIODB/SDBS/cgi-bin/cre_index.cgi

Audience: **u,f.**

QC462.85
☐ Spectral Database for Organic Compunds, SDBS.
http://www.aist.go.jp/RIODB/SDBS/cgi-bin/cre_index.cgi
National Institute of Advanced Industrial Science and
Technology (AIST), Japan.

Audience: **u,f.**

Cooper, James W.   **QD272.S6**
Spectroscopic Techniques for Organic Chemists. Trade Cloth.
John Wiley & Sons, Inc. Hoboken, NJ. 1980. 376p.
ISBN:0-471-05166-7, ISBN13: 978-0-471-05166-4.
Dewey:547.3/0858. LCCN:79-023952.

Audience: **u,f.** ℬ

Dollish, Francis R.   **QC454.R36**
Characteristic Raman Frequencies of Organic Compounds. Ed.
99. Trade Cloth. Krieger Publishing Company. Melbourne, FL.
1974. 443p. ISBN:0-471-21769-7, ISBN13: 978-0-471-21769-5.
Dewey:547/.34/64. LCCN:73-012157.

Audience: **u,f.**

Field, L. D., et al.   **QD272.S6S74 1995**
Organic Structures from Spectra. Ed. 2. S. Sternhall & J. R.
Kalman (Authors). Trade Cloth. John Wiley & Sons, Inc.
Hoboken, NJ. 1995. 220p. ISBN:0-471-95630-9, ISBN13:
978-0-471-95630-3. Dewey:547.3/0858. LCCN:95-031574.

Audience: **u,f.**

Friedel, Robert A. and   **QC459.F7**
  Milton Orchin
Ultraviolet Spectra of Aromatic Compounds. Wiley. 1951.

Audience: **u,f.**

Grasselli, Jeanette G.,   **QD257**
  Ritchey, William M. (eds.)
Atlas of Spectral Data and Physical Constants for Organic
Compounds. Ed. 2. Cleveland, OH: CRC Press. 6 v.. 1975.
ISBN:0-87819-317-0, ISBN13: 978-0-87819-317-2.

Audience: **u,f.**

Klessinger, Martin & Michl,   **QD476.K53 1995**
  Josef
Excited States and Photochemistry of Organic Molecules. Trade
Paper. John Wiley & Sons, Inc. Hoboken, NJ. 1995. 537p.
ISBN:1-56081-588-4, ISBN13: 978-1-56081-588-4.
Dewey:547.1/35. LCCN:92-046464.

Audience: **u,f.** *Choice, 1996.*

Lambert, Joseph B., et al.   **QD272.S6O74 1998**
Organic Structural Spectroscopy. Ed. 1. Herbert F. Shurvell,
David A. Lightner & Robert Graham Cooks (Authors). Cloth
Text. Prentice Hall PTR. Upper Saddle River, NJ. 1997. 568p.
ISBN:0-13-258690-8, ISBN13: 978-0-13-258690-0.
Dewey:547/.122. LCCN:97-040522.

Audience: **u,f.** *Choice, 1998.*

Perkampus, Heinz-Helmut   **QD96**
UV-VIS-Spektroskopie und Ihre Anwendungen. Springer Verlag.
1986. ISBN:0-387-15467-1, ISBN13: 978-0-387-15467-1.

Audience: **u,f.**

Roberts, John D.   **QD591 .R6**
Nuclear Magnetic Resonance: Applications to Organic
Chemistry. McGraw-Hill. 1959. McGraw-Hill Series in
Advanced Chemistry

Audience: **u,f.**

Silverstein, Robert M. &   **QD272.S6S55 1998**
  Webster, Francis X.
Spectrometric Identification of Organic Compounds. Ed. 6.
Trade Cloth. John Wiley & Sons, Inc. Hoboken, NJ. 1997. 496p.
ISBN:0-471-13457-0, ISBN13: 978-0-471-13457-2.
Dewey:543.5. LCCN:97-021336.

Audience: **u,f.** ℬ

Organic Chemistry > Special Topics in
Organic Chemistry > Stereochemistry

Buckingham, J.; Hill, R. A.   **QD481**
Atlas of Stereochemistry: Absolute Configurations of Organic
Molecules. Ed. 2. Chapman and Hall. 1986.
ISBN:0-412-26000-X, ISBN13: 978-0-412-26000-1.

Audience: **u,f.**

Eliel, Ernest L. (Editor)   **QD481 .C68 1981**
Conformational Analysis. Trade Cloth. American Chemical
Society. Washington, DC. 1965. ISBN:0-8412-0653-8, ISBN13:
978-0-8412-0653-3. Dewey:547.1/223. LCCN:81-010783.

Audience: **u,f.**

Eliel, Ernest Ludwig, et al.   **QD481.E515 2001**
Basic Organic Stereochemistry. Michael P. Doyle & Samuel H.
Wilen (Authors). Trade Paper. John Wiley & Sons, Inc.
Hoboken, NJ. 2001. 704p. ISBN:0-471-37499-7, ISBN13:
978-0-471-37499-2. Dewey:547/.1223. LCCN:2001-017847.

Audience: **l,u,f.**

Eliel, Ernest L. & Wilen,   **QD481.E525 1994**
Samuel H.
Stereochemistry of Organic Compounds. Ed. 1. Trade Cloth.
John Wiley & Sons, Inc. Hoboken, NJ. 1994. 1267p.
ISBN:0-471-01670-5, ISBN13: 978-0-471-01670-0.
Dewey:547.1/223. LCCN:93-012476.

                  Audience: **u,f.** *Choice, 1995.*

Flapan, Erica   **QD455.3.T65 F53 2000**
When Topology Meets Chemistry: A Topological Look at
Molecular Chirality. John Barrow, Fan Chung, Ingrid
Daubechies, Persi W. Diaconis, Ronald Graham & Don Zagier
(Contribution by). Cloth Text. Cambridge University Press. New
York, NY. 2000. 256p. Outlooks Ser. ISBN:0-521-66254-0,
ISBN13: 978-0-521-66254-3. Dewey:541/.01/514.
LCCN:00-027517.

                  Audience: **u,f.** *Choice, 2001.*

Kagan, Henri   **QD481.K2513**
Organic Stereochemistry. M. C. Whiting & U. H. Whiting
(Translators). Trade Paper. John Wiley & Sons, Inc. Hoboken,
NJ. 1979. 166p. ISBN:0-470-26725-9, ISBN13:
978-0-470-26725-7. Dewey:547/.1/223. LCCN:79-011500.
                  Audience: **u,f.**

Klyne, W. & Buckingham,   **QD481 .K64 1978**
John B.
Atlas of Stereochemistry: Absolute Configurations of Organic
Molecules, I. Ed. 2. Trade Cloth. Oxford University Press, Inc.
New York, NY. 1978. ISBN:0-19-520058-6, ISBN13:
978-0-19-520058-4. Dewey:547.1/223. LCCN:78-002366.
                  Audience: **u,f.**

Mezey, Paul G.   **QD461.M583 1993**
Shape in Chemistry: An Introduction to Molecular Shape and
Topology. Trade Paper. John Wiley & Sons, Inc. Hoboken, NJ.
1993. 224p. ISBN:0-89573-727-2, ISBN13: 978-0-89573-727-4.
Dewey:541.2/2. LCCN:93-015622.

                  Audience: **u,f.** *Choice, 1994.*

Mislow, Kurt   **QD481.M53 2002**
Introduction to Stereochemistry and Conformational Analysis.
Trade Paper. Dover Publications, Inc. Mineola, NY. 2003. 208p.
ISBN:0-486-42530-4, ISBN13: 978-0-486-42530-6.
Dewey:547/.1223. LCCN:2002-074187.

                  Audience: **u,f.**

Morris, David G. & Abel,   **QD481.M67 2002**
Eddie
Stereochemistry. Trade Paper. John Wiley & Sons, Inc.
Hoboken, NJ. 2002. 200p. Basic Concepts in Chemistry Ser.
ISBN:0-471-22477-4, ISBN13: 978-0-471-22477-8.
Dewey:547/.1223. LCCN:2002-511021.

                  Audience: **u,f.**

Norman L. Allinger,   **QD481**
Norman L.
Topics in Stereochemistry. Eliel, Ernest L. (Editors). John Wiley
& Sons.

                  Audience: **u,f.**

Ramsay, O. Bertrand   **QD481.R24 1981**
Stereochemistry. Trade Cloth. Heyden & Son, Inc. Philadelphia,
PA. 1981. xv, 256 p. :p. ISBN:0-85501-682-5, ISBN13:
978-0-85501-682-1. Dewey:547.1/223. LCCN:82-106278.
                  Audience: **u,f.** *B*

Organic Chemistry > Special Topics in Organic Chemistry > Heterocyclics

                           QD400
Journal of Heterocyclic Chemistry (search).
http://www.jhetchem.com/
Journal of Heterocyclic Chemistry.

                  Audience: **u,f.**

Journal of Heterocyclic Chemistry (search).
http://www.jhetchem.com/
                  Audience: **u,f.**

Davies, David T.   **QD400 .D38 1991**
Aromatic Heterocyclic Chemistry. Paper Text. Oxford University
Press, Inc. New York, NY. 1992. 96p. Chemistry Primers Ser.,
No. 2 ISBN:0-19-855660-8, ISBN13: 978-0-19-855660-2.
Dewey:547.59. LCCN:91-034831.
                  Audience: **u,f.** *Choice, 1993.*

Katritzky, Alan R.   **QD400.K29 1985**
Handbook of Heterocyclic Chemistry. Cloth Text. Elsevier
Science & Technology Books. Saint Louis, MO. 1985. 542p.
ISBN:0-08-026217-1, ISBN13: 978-0-08-026217-8.
Dewey:547/.59. LCCN:84-025492.
                  Audience: **u,f.**

Katritzky, Alan R. & Rees,   **QD400**
C. W. (Editors)
Comprehensive Heterocyclic Chemistry: The Structure,
Reactions, Synthesis and Uses of Heterocyclic Compounds.
Trade Cloth. Elsevier Science & Technology Books. Saint
Louis, MO. 1984. 8000p. ISBN:0-08-026200-7, ISBN13:
978-0-08-026200-0. Dewey:547/.59. LCCN:83-004264.
                  Audience: **u,f.** *B*

Sainsbury, Malcolm   **QD400.S25 2002**
Heterocyclic Chemistry. Trade Paper. John Wiley & Sons, Inc.
Hoboken, NJ. 2002. 142p. Basic Concepts in Chemistry Ser.
ISBN:0-471-28164-6, ISBN13: 978-0-471-28164-1.
Dewey:547/.59. LCCN:2002-725621.
                  Audience: **u,f.**

Scriven, Katritzky R., et al.   **QD400.C65 1996**
Comprehensive Heterocyclic Chemistry II: An Extended and
Updated Review of the Literature (1982-1995), Set. Ed. 2. Alan
R. Katritzky & Rees (Authors). Trade Cloth. Elsevier Science &
Technology Books. Saint Louis, MO. 1996. 11628p.
ISBN:0-08-042072-9, ISBN13: 978-0-08-042072-1.
Dewey:547/.59. LCCN:96-017870.
                  Audience: **u,f.** *Choice, 1998.*

Organic Chemistry > Special Topics in Organic Chemistry > Chemistry of Natural Products, Including Alkaloids

                        QD415.A25 D53
Dictionary of Natural Products on CD-ROM. Chapman and
Hall. 1996. ISBN:0-412-49150-8, ISBN13: 978-0-412-49150-4.
                  Audience: **u,f.**

☐ Heterocycles (Natural Products) Databases (1975+).
http://www2.heterocycles.jp/
Audience: **u,f.**

QD400

☐ Heterocycles (Natural Products) Databases (1975+).
http://www2.heterocycles.jp/
Audience: **u,f.**

Apsimon, John W. (Editor)   **QD262**
The Total Synthesis of Natural Products, Vol. 1. Ed. 1. Trade
Cloth. John Wiley & Sons, Inc. Hoboken, NJ. 1973. 624p. Total
Synthesis of Natural Products Ser., Vol. 1 ISBN:0-471-03251-4,
ISBN13: 978-0-471-03251-9. Dewey:547.7/0459/05.
LCCN:72-004075.
Audience: **u,f.**

Hesse, Manfred   **QK898.A4H4713 2002**
Alkaloids: Nature's Curse or Blessing. Trade Cloth. John Wiley
& Sons, Inc. Hoboken, NJ. 2002. 414p. ISBN:3-906390-24-1,
ISBN13: 978-3-906390-24-6. Dewey:572/.5492.
LCCN:2003-275828.
Audience: **u,f.**

Hostettmann, K., et al.   **QD272.C4H67 1998**
Preparative Chromatography Techniques: Applications in Natural
Product Isolation. Ed. 2. A. Marston & M. Hostettmann
(Authors). Trade Cloth. Springer. New York, NY. 1997. XI,
244p. ISBN:3-540-62459-7, ISBN13: 978-3-540-62459-2.
Dewey:543/.089. LCCN:98-116711.
Audience: **u,f.** *Choice, 1998.*

Nakanishi, Koji &   **QD415.C63 1999**
  Meth-Cohn, Otto (Editors)
Comprehensive Natural Products Chemistry, Set. Derek H.
Barton & David Barton (Editor-In-Chiefs). Trade Cloth. Elsevier
Science & Technology Books. Saint Louis, MO. 1999. 8500p.
ISBN:0-08-042709-X, ISBN13: 978-0-08-042709-6.
Dewey:547.7. LCCN:98-015249.
Audience: **u,f.** *Choice, 1999.*

Nakanishi, Koji   **QD22.N24A3 1991**
Koji Nakanishi: A Wandering Natural Products Chemist. Jeffrey
I. Seeman (Editor). Cloth Text. Oxford University Press, Inc.
New York, NY. 1991. 230p. Profiles, Pathways and Dreams Ser.
ISBN:0-8412-1775-0, ISBN13: 978-0-8412-1775-1.
Dewey:540/.92 B. LCCN:90-045062.
Audience: **u,f.**

Southon, Ian   **RS431**
Dictionary of Alkaloids. Buckingham, John (Editors). Chapman
and Hall. 1989. ISBN:0-412-24910-3, ISBN13:
978-0-412-24910-5.
Audience: **u,f.**

Organic Chemistry > Special Topics in Organic Chemistry > Organometallics and Coordination Compounds

QD501

☐ Organometallic HyperTextBook (OH).
http://www.ilpi.com/organomet/
Audience: **u,f.**

Aylett, B. J.   **QD411**
Organometallic Compounds: Groups IV and V. Ed. 4. Trade
Cloth. Chapman & Hall. New York, NY. 1979. xiii, 521p.
ISBN:0-412-13020-3, ISBN13: 978-0-412-13020-5.
Dewey:547/.05. LCCN:79-042877.
Audience: **u,f.**

Constable, Edwin C.   **QD474.C655**
Metals and Ligand Reactivity: An Introduction to the Organic
Chemistry of Metal Complexes. Trade Cloth. John Wiley &
Sons, Inc. Hoboken, NJ. 1996. 308p. ISBN:3-527-29278-0,
ISBN13: 978-3-527-29278-3. Dewey:547/.05.
Audience: **u,f.** *Choice, 1996.*

Cundari, Thomas R.   **QD411.C69 2001**
  (Editor)
Computational Organometallic Chemistry. Paper over Boards.
Marcel Dekker Inc. New York, NY. 2001. 448p.
ISBN:0-8247-0478-9, ISBN13: 978-0-8247-0478-0.
Dewey:547/.05. LCCN:2001-028072.
Audience: **u,f.**

Davies, Alwyn G.   **QD412.S7**
Organotin Chemistry. Ed. 2. Trade Cloth. John Wiley & Sons,
Inc. Hoboken, NJ. 2004. 438p. ISBN:3-527-31023-1, ISBN13:
978-3-527-31023-4. Dewey:547/.05686. LCCN:2004-300189.
Audience: **u,f.**

Dodziuk, Helena   **QD878.D63 2001**
Introduction to Supramolecular Chemistry. Trade Cloth.
Springer. New York, NY. 2001. 368p. ISBN:1-4020-0214-9,
ISBN13: 978-1-4020-0214-4. Dewey:547/.1226.
LCCN:2001-050614.
Audience: **u,f.** *Choice, 2002.*

Hegedus, Louis   **QD262.H35 1999**
Transition Metals in the Synthesis of Complex Organic
Molecules. Ed. 2. Trade Cloth. University Science Books.
Sausalito, CA. 1999. 337p. ISBN:1-891389-04-1, ISBN13:
978-1-891389-04-7. Dewey:547/.2. LCCN:99-010276.
Audience: **u,f.** *Choice, 1999.*

Houghton, R. P.   **QD262**
Metal Complexes in Organic Chemistry. Trade Cloth.
Cambridge University Press. New York, NY. 1979. 318p.
Cambridge Texts in Chemistry and Biochemistry Ser.
ISBN:0-521-21992-2, ISBN13: 978-0-521-21992-1.
Dewey:547/.2. LCCN:78-051685.
Audience: **u,f.**

McCleverty, J. A. & Meyer,   **QD474**
  Thomas J. (Editors)
Comprehensive Coordination Chemistry II: From Biology to
Nanotechnology, Set. Ed. 2. Trade Cloth. Elsevier Science &
Technology Books. Saint Louis, MO. 2003. 8400p.
ISBN:0-08-043748-6, ISBN13: 978-0-08-043748-4.
Dewey:541.2/242. LCCN:2003-113706.
Audience: **u,f.** *Choice, 2004.*

Negishi, Ei-ichi & Meijere,   **QD262.H267 2002**
  Armin De (Editors)
Handbook of Organopalladium Chemistry for Organic Synthesis.
Trade Cloth. John Wiley & Sons, Inc. Hoboken, NJ. 2002.
3424p. ISBN:0-471-31506-0, ISBN13: 978-0-471-31506-3.
Dewey:547/.2. LCCN:2002-726894.
Audience: **u,f.** *Choice, 2003.*

Audience: g=general, l=lower division undergraduate, u=upper division undergraduate, f=faculty.

299

Robinson, Gregory H.   QD474.C67 1993
  (Editor)
Coordination Chemistry of Aluminum. Trade Cloth. John Wiley
& Sons, Inc. Hoboken, NJ. 1993. xiii, 234p.
ISBN:1-56081-059-9, ISBN13: 978-1-56081-059-9.
Dewey:546.673. LCCN:93-012703.
                                        Audience: **u,f.** *Choice, 1994.*

Vogtle, Fritz (Editor), et al.   QD411.C66 1996
Comprehensive Supramolecular Chemistry, Set. J. Eric Davies,
J. M. Lehn, Jerry L. Atwood & David D. MacNicol (Editors).
Trade Cloth. Elsevier Science & Technology Books. Saint
Louis, MO. 1996. 7660p. ISBN:0-08-040610-6, ISBN13:
978-0-08-040610-7. Dewey:547.7. LCCN:96-021927.
                                        Audience: **u,f.** *Choice, 1997.*

Wilkinson, Geoffrey (Editor)   QD474.C65 1987
Comprehensive Coordination Chemistry: The Synthesis,
Reactions, Properties and Applications of Coordination
Compounds, Set. Trade Cloth. Franklin Book Company, Inc.
Newtown Sq, PA. 1987. 7500p. ISBN:0-08-026232-5, ISBN13:
978-0-08-026232-1. Dewey:541.2/242. LCCN:86-012319.
                                        Audience: **u,f.** *Choice, 1988.*

Organic Chemistry > Organic Analytical Procedures

📖 Library Resources for Identifying Unknowns (Stanford
University).
http://library.stanford.edu/depts/swain/services/courses/chem130/
index.html
                                        Audience: **u,f.**

                                                        QD561
📖 PKa Values (Acids, Bases, Alcohols, etc.).
http://research.chem.psu.edu/brpgroup/pKa_compilation.pdf
Pennsylvania State University.
                                        Audience: **u,f.**

Blackburn, Stanley   QD79
Amino Acids and Amines, v. 2. CRC Press. 1983.
ISBN:0-8493-3066-1, ISBN13: 978-0-8493-3066-7.
                                        Audience: **u,f.**

Blackburn, Stanley (Editor)   QD79.C4
Handbook of Chromatography: Amino Acids and Amines.
Library Binding. Franklin Book Company, Inc. Newtown Sq,
PA. 1983. 312p. Series in Chromatography
ISBN:0-8493-3064-5, ISBN13: 978-0-8493-3064-3.
Dewey:543/.089. LCCN:82-009561.
                                        Audience: **u,f.**

Clarke, H. T.   QD271.C58
A Handbook of Organic Analysis. Ed. 5. B. Haynes (Editor).
Trade Paper. Taylor & Francis Group. Philadelphia, PA. 1975.
320p. ISBN:0-8448-0662-5, ISBN13: 978-0-8448-0662-4.
Dewey:547.3. LCCN:74-083479.
                                        Audience: **l,u,f.**

Crews, Phillip, et al.   QD272.S6C74 1998
Organic Structure Analysis. Marcel Jaspars & Jamie Rodriquez
(Authors). Cloth Text. Oxford University Press, Inc. New York,
NY. 1998. 576p. Topics in Organic Chemistry Ser.

ISBN:0-19-510102-2, ISBN13: 978-0-19-510102-7.
Dewey:547/.122. LCCN:97-031686.
                                        Audience: **u,f.** *Choice, 1999.*

Feigl, Fritz; Anger, Vinzenz   QD271
Spot Tests in Organic Analysis. Ed. 7. Oesper, Ralph E.
(Translator). Elsevier Pub. Co.. 1966.
                                        Audience: **l,u,f.**

Feinstein, Karen   QD272
Guide to Spectroscopic Identification of Organic Compounds.
CRC Press. 1995. ISBN:0-8493-9448-1, ISBN13:
978-0-8493-9448-5.
                                        Audience: **u,f.**

Kortum, G.; Vogel, Gustav   QD273
  W.; Andrussow, K.
Dissociation Constants of Organic Acids in Aqueous Solution.
Butterworth. 1961.
                                        Audience: **u,f.**

Majer, Vladimir; Vaclav   QC304
  Svoboda; H. V. Kehiaian
Enthalpies of Vaporization of Organic Compounds: A Critical
Review and Data Compilation. Blackwell Scientific. 1985.
Chemical Data Series; No. 32 ISBN:0-632-01529-2, ISBN13:
978-0-632-01529-0.
                                        Audience: **u,f.**

Pedley, J. B., et al.   QD511.8.P43 1985
Thermochemical Data of Organic Compounds. Ed. 2. R. D.
Naylor & S. B. Kirby (Authors). Cloth Text. Chapman & Hall.
New York, NY. 1986. 750p. ISBN:0-412-27100-1, ISBN13:
978-0-412-27100-7. Dewey:547.1/36. LCCN:85-013206.
                                        Audience: **u,f.**

Perrin, D. D.   QD273.P35
Dissociation Constants of Organic Bases in Aqueous Solution.
Trade Cloth. Elsevier Science & Technology Books. Saint
Louis, MO. 1976. ISBN:0-08-020826-6, ISBN13:
978-0-08-020826-8. Dewey:547.134.
                                        Audience: **u,f.**

Serjeant, E. P. & Dempsey,   QD561
  B. (Editors)
Ionization Constants of Organic Acids in Aqueous Solution.
Trade Cloth. Pergamon Press. Kidlington, 1979. ix, 989p.
Chemical Data Ser., Vol. 23 ISBN:0-08-022339-7, ISBN13:
978-0-08-022339-1. Dewey:547.1/3723. LCCN:78-040988.
                                        Audience: **u,f.**

Shriner, Ralph L., et al.   QD261.S965 1998
The Systematic Identification of Organic Compounds. Ed. 7.
Reynold C. Fuson, David Y. Curtin, Christine K. F. Hermann &
Terence C. Morrill (Authors). Trade Cloth. John Wiley & Sons,
Inc. Hoboken, NJ. 1997. 700p. ISBN:0-471-59748-1, ISBN13:
978-0-471-59748-3. Dewey:547/.34/078. LCCN:97-005545.
                                        Audience: **l,u,f.**

Timmermans, Jean   QD291
Physico Chemical Constants of Pure Organic Compounds,v. 1.
Elsevier. 1950.
                                        Audience: **u,f.**

Organic Chemistry > Laboratory Procedure Manuals

Armarego, W. L. & Perrin, D. D.   TP156.P83P47 1996
Purification of Laboratory Chemicals. Ed. 4. Trade Cloth. Elsevier Science & Technology Books. Saint Louis, MO. 1996. 448p. ISBN:0-7506-2839-1, ISBN13: 978-0-7506-2839-6. Dewey:542. LCCN:97-109714.
                                                        Audience: **u,f.**

Landgrebe, John A.   QD261 .L34 1993
Theory and Practice in the Organic Laboratory: With Microscale and Standard Scale Experiments. Ed. 4. Mass Market. Brooks/Cole. Pacific Grove, CA. 1993. 573p. ISBN:0-534-16854-X, ISBN13: 978-0-534-16854-4. Dewey:547/.0078. LCCN:92-032949.
                                                        Audience: **l,u,f.**

Menger, F. M. & Mandell, L.   QD502.M46
Electronic Interpretation of Organic Chemistry: A Problems-Oriented Text. Trade Cloth. Basic Books. New York, NY. 1980. 224p. ISBN:0-306-40379-X, ISBN13: 978-0-306-40379-8. Dewey:547/.1/39. LCCN:79-021718.
                                                        Audience: **l,u,f.** *B*

Williamson   QD261.F5 1998
Organic Experiments. Ed. 8. Trade Cloth. Houghton Mifflin Company. New York, NY. 1997. 672p. ISBN:0-395-86519-0, ISBN13: 978-0-395-86519-4. Dewey:547/.0078. LCCN:97-072467.
                                                        Audience: **l,u,f.**

Zubrick, James W.   QD261.Z83 1997
The Organic Chem Lab Survival Manual: A Student's Guide to Techniques. Ed. 4. Trade Paper. John Wiley & Sons, Inc. Hoboken, NJ. 1997. 400p. ISBN:0-471-12948-8, ISBN13: 978-0-471-12948-6. Dewey:547/.0078. LCCN:96-035813.
                                                        Audience: **l,u,f.**

Organic Chemistry > Problem Manuals

Ghiron, Chiara & Thomas, Russell   QD262.G47 1997
Exercises in Synthetic Organic Chemistry. Cloth Text. Oxford University Press, Inc. New York, NY. 1997. 144p. ISBN:0-19-855944-5, ISBN13: 978-0-19-855944-3. Dewey:547.2/076. LCCN:96-047593.
                                Audience: **l,u,f.** *Choice, 1998.*

Meislich, Herbert, et al.   QD257.M44 1999
Schaum's Outline of Organic Chemistry. Ed. 3. George J. Hademenos, Howard Nechamkin & Jacob Sharefkin (Authors). Paper Text. McGraw-Hill Companies, The. New York, NY. 1999. 464p. Schaum's Outline Ser. ISBN:0-07-134165-X, ISBN13: 978-0-07-134165-3. Dewey:547. LCCN:99-028581.
                                                        Audience: **u,f.**

Patrick, Graham L.   QD256.5.P37 2003
Organic Chemistry. Ed. 2. UK-B Format Paperback. Taylor & Francis Group. Abingdon, 2003. 328p. Instant Notes Ser. ISBN:1-85996-264-5, ISBN13: 978-1-85996-264-0. Dewey:547. LCCN:2003-062938.
                                                        Audience: **l,u,f.**

Inorganic Chemistry > General Surveys

Mackay, K. M., et al.   QD151.2 .M33 1996
Introduction to Modern Inorganic Chemistry. Ed. 5. R. Ann Mackay & W. Henderson (Authors). Trade Paper. Nelson Thornes Ltd. Cheltenham, 1996. xvi, 468p. ISBN:0-7487-3983-1, ISBN13: 978-0-7487-3983-7. Dewey:546. LCCN:2003-446783.
                                                        Audience: **u,f.**

Mark, James E., et al.   QD196.M37 2004
Inorganic Polymers. Ed. 2. H. R. Allcock & Robert West (Authors). Trade Cloth. Oxford University Press, Inc. New York, NY. 2005. 352p. ISBN:0-19-513119-3, ISBN13: 978-0-19-513119-2. Dewey:546. LCCN:2004-043395.
                                Audience: **u,f.** *Choice, 1992.*

Mingos, D. M.   QD467.M64 1998
Essential Trends in Inorganic Chemistry. Cloth Text. Oxford University Press, Inc. New York, NY. 1998. 400p. ISBN:0-19-850109-9, ISBN13: 978-0-19-850109-1. Dewey:546. LCCN:97-035359.
                                                        Audience: **u,f.**

Moeller, Therald B.   QD151.2.M63
Inorganic Chemistry: A Modern Introduction. Library Binding. Krieger Publishing Company. Melbourne, FL. 1991. 856p. ISBN:0-89464-453-X, ISBN13: 978-0-89464-453-5. Dewey:546. LCCN:81-016455.
                                                        Audience: **u,f.**

Sidgwick, Nevil Vincent   QD466
Chemical Elements and Their Compounds. Clarendon Press. 1950.
                                                        Audience: **u,f.**

Inorganic Chemistry > Nomenclature

                                                        QP512
☐ Glossary of Terms Used in Bioinorganic Chemistry. http://www.chem.qmw.ac.uk/iupac/bioinorg/ Pure & Applied Chem.
                                                        Audience: **u,f.**

☐ Glossary of Terms Used in Bioinorganic Chemistry. http://www.chem.qmw.ac.uk/iupac/bioinorg/
                                                        Audience: **u,f.**

Brock, B. Peter (Editor), et al.   QD149.B59 1990
Inorganic Chemical Nomenclature: Principles and Practice. Warren H. Powell & W. Conard Fernelius (Editors). Cloth Text. Oxford University Press, Inc. New York, NY. 1990. 148p. ISBN:0-8412-1697-5, ISBN13: 978-0-8412-1697-6. Dewey:546/.014. LCCN:90-000760.
                                Audience: **u,f.** *Choice, 1991.*

Connelly, N. G. (Editor), et al.   QD149
Nomenclature of Inorganic Chemistry: Recommendations 2005. R. M. Hartshorn, T. Damhus & A. T. Hutton (Editors). Trade Cloth. Royal Society of Chemistry, The. Cambridge, 2005. 340p. ISBN:0-85404-438-8, ISBN13: 978-0-85404-438-2. Dewey:546.014.
                                                        Audience: **u,f.**

Royal Society of Chemistry   QD149.I57
  Staff
Nomenclature of Inorganic Chemistry II: Recommendations
2000. J. A. McCleverty & N. G. Connelly (Editors). Trade
Cloth. Royal Society of Chemistry, The. Cambridge, 2001. x +
130p. ISBN:0-85404-487-6, ISBN13: 978-0-85404-487-0.
Dewey:546/.014.

                    Audience: **u,f**

Inorganic Chemistry > Encyclopedia

King, R. Bruce (Editor)   QD148.E53 2005
Encyclopedia of Inorganic Chemistry, Set. Ed. 2. Trade Cloth.
John Wiley & Sons, Inc. Hoboken, NJ. 2005. 6696p.
ISBN:0-470-86078-2, ISBN13: 978-0-470-86078-6.
Dewey:546/.03. LCCN:2005-013416.
            Audience: **u,f.** *Choice, 2006.*

King, R. Bruce (Editor),   QD148.E53 1994
  et al.
Encyclopedia of Inorganic Chemistry, Set. Jeremy K. Burdett,
Robert H. Crabtree, C. M. Lukehart, R. A. Scott & R. L. Wells
(Editors). Trade Cloth. John Wiley & Sons, Inc. Hoboken, NJ.
1994. 5000p. ISBN:0-471-93620-0, ISBN13:
978-0-471-93620-6. Dewey:546/.03. LCCN:94-019739.
            Audience: **u,f.** *Choice, 2006.*

Inorganic Chemistry > Handbooks and Tables of Data

☐ CrossFire Gmelin.
http://www.mdl.com/products/knowledge/crossfire_gmelin/
index.jsp
Elsevier MDL.
                    Audience: **u,f**

Knacke, O., Kubaschewski,   QD511
  O., Hesselmann, K.
Thermochemical Properties of Inorganic Substances, v. 1. Ed. 2.
Springer Verlag. 1991. ISBN:3-540-54014-8, ISBN13:
978-3-540-54014-4.
                    Audience: **u,f**

Knacke, O., et al.   QD511.8 .T47 1991
Thermochemical Properties of Inorganic Substances, Set. Ed. 2.
Ortrud Kubaschewski & K. Hesselmann (Authors). Trade Cloth.
Woodhead Publishing, Ltd. Cambridge, 1995. 2500p.
ISBN:3-514-00363-7, ISBN13: 978-3-514-00363-7.
Dewey:541.3/6. LCCN:91-025087.
                    Audience: **u,f**

Knacke, O. (Editor), et al.   QD511.8.T47 1991
Thermochemical Properties of Inorganic Substances. Ed. 2.
Ortrud Kubaschewski & K. Hesselmann (Editors). Cloth Text.
Springer. New York, NY. 1991. 2500p. ISBN:0-387-54014-8,
ISBN13: 978-0-387-54014-6. Dewey:541.3/6. LCCN:91-025087.
                    Audience: **u,f**

Macintyre, J. E. (Executive   QD148
  Editor)
Dictionary of Inorganic Compounds. Chapman and Hall. 1992.
ISBN:0-412-30120-2, ISBN13: 978-0-412-30120-9.
                    Audience: **u,f**

Macintyre, Jane E. &   E195.O82
  Hodgson, A.J.
Dictionary of Inorganic and Organometallic Compounds:
Version 6.1. Compact Disc. Chapman & Hall. New York, NY.
2000. ISBN:0-412-63330-2, ISBN13: 978-0-412-63330-0.
Dewey:973.2.
                    Audience: **u,f**

Martell, Arthur Earl; Smith,   QD503
  Robert M.
Critical Stability Constants. Plenum Press.
                    Audience: **u,f**

Meyer, von R. J.   QD151
Gmelins Handbuch der Anorganischen Chemie, 590 vols.
Springer Verlag. 1924.
                    Audience: **u,f**

Patnaik, Pradyot   QD155.5P37 2002
Handbook of Inorganic Chemicals. Trade Cloth. McGraw-Hill
Professional Publishing. New York, NY. 2002. 1086p.
ISBN:0-07-049439-8, ISBN13: 978-0-07-049439-8. Dewey:546.
LCCN:2002-029526.
            Audience: **u,f.** *Choice, 2003.*

Perrin, D. D. (Editor)   QD561
Ionization Constants of Inorganic Acids and Bases in Aqueous
Solution, No.29. Ed. 2. Trade Cloth. Pergamon Press.
Kidlington, 1982. 194p. Chemical Data Ser.
ISBN:0-08-029214-3, ISBN13: 978-0-08-029214-4.
Dewey:541.3/723. LCCN:82-016524.
                    Audience: **u,f**

Perry, Dale L.   QD155
Handbook of Inorganic Compounds. Phillips, Sidney L.
(Editors). CRC Press. 1995. ISBN:0-8493-8671-3, ISBN13:
978-0-8493-8671-8.
                    Audience: **u,f**

Wagman, Donald D. et   QD511
  al.(Editors)
The NBS Tables of Chemical Thermodynamic Properties:
Selected Values for Inorganic and Cl and C2 Organic Substances
in SI Units. American Chemical Society and the American
Institute of Physics for the National Bureau of Standards. 1982.
ISBN:0-88318-417-6, ISBN13: 978-0-88318-417-2.
                    Audience: **u,f**

Inorganic Chemistry > Compilations and Treatises

Bailar, J. C. (Editor)   QD151.2
Comprehensive Inorganic Chemistry, Set. Trade Cloth.
Pergamon Press. Kidlington, 1973. ISBN:0-08-017275-X,
ISBN13: 978-0-08-017275-0. Dewey:546. LCCN:77-189736.
              Audience: **u,f.** *B*

Cotton, F. Albert, et al.   QD151.2.C68 1999
Advanced Inorganic Chemistry. Ed. 6. Geoffrey Wilkinson,
Manfred Bochmann & Carlos A. Murillo (Authors). Trade
Cloth. John Wiley & Sons, Inc. Hoboken, NJ. 1999. 1376p.
ISBN:0-471-19957-5, ISBN13: 978-0-471-19957-1. Dewey:546.
LCCN:98-008020.
            Audience: **u,f.** *Choice, 1999.*

Cox, P. A.   QD31.2.C682 1995
The Elements on Earth: Inorganic Chemistry in the
Environment. Trade Cloth. Oxford University Press, Inc. New
York, NY. 1995. 304p. ISBN:0-19-856241-1, ISBN13:
978-0-19-856241-2. Dewey:546. LCCN:94-042633.
Audience: **l,u,f.** *Choice, 1996.*

Cox, P. A.   QD153.5.C69 2000
Instant Notes in Inorganic Chemistry. Paper Text. Springer. New
York, NY. 2000. 320p. Instant Notes Ser. ISBN:0-387-91604-0,
ISBN13: 978-0-387-91604-0. Dewey:546/.02/02.
LCCN:00-039829.
Audience: **l,u,f.**

Greenwood, Norman &   QD466.G74 1997
  Earnshaw, A.
Chemistry of the Elements. Ed. 2. Trade Paper. Elsevier Science
& Technology Books. Saint Louis, MO. 1997. 1600p.
ISBN:0-7506-3365-4, ISBN13: 978-0-7506-3365-9. Dewey:546.
LCCN:97-036336.
Audience: **l,u,f.** *B*

Harding, C. J. (Editor),   QD466.E446 2002
  et al.
Elements of the p Block. D. A. Johnson & R. Janes (Editors).
Mixed Media. Royal Society of Chemistry, The. Cambridge,
2002. 312p. The Molecular World Ser. ISBN:0-85404-690-9,
ISBN13: 978-0-85404-690-4. Dewey:546.
Audience: **u,f.** *Choice, 2003.*

Henderson, William & Abel,   QD151.3.H46 2002
  Eddie
Main Group Chemistry. Trade Paper. John Wiley & Sons, Inc.
Hoboken, NJ. 2002. 196p. Basic Concepts in Chemistry Ser.
ISBN:0-471-22478-2, ISBN13: 978-0-471-22478-5. Dewey:546.
LCCN:2002-006102.
Audience: **u,f.**

Jones, Chris J. & Abel,   QD172.T6J66 2002
  Eddie
d- and f- Block Chemistry. Trade Paper. John Wiley & Sons,
Inc. Hoboken, NJ. 2002. 200p. Basic Concepts in Chemistry
Ser. ISBN:0-471-22476-6, ISBN13: 978-0-471-22476-1.
LCCN:2002-009098.
Audience: **u,f.**

Kettle, S. F.   QD475.K46 1996
Physical Inorganic Chemistry: A Coordination Chemistry
Approach. Cloth Text. Oxford University Press, Inc. New York,
NY. 1998. 512p. ISBN:0-19-850405-5, ISBN13:
978-0-19-850405-4. Dewey:541.2/242. LCCN:95-044747.
Audience: **u,f.**

Mellor, Joseph William   QD31
A Comprehensive Treatise on Inorganic and Theoretical
Chemistry, 16 v. Longmans. 1922.
Audience: **u,f.**

Remy, H.   QD151.R443
Treatise on Inorganic Chemistry. J. Kleinberg (Editor). Other.
Elsevier. New York, NY. 1956. ISBN:0-318-51827-9, ISBN13:
978-0-318-51827-5. Dewey:546.
Audience: **u,f.**

Sneed, M. Cannon   QD151.2.S64
Comprehensive Inorganic Chemistry. Paper Text. Textbook
Publishers. Temecula, CA. 2003. ISBN:0-7581-1034-0, ISBN13:
978-0-7581-1034-3. Dewey:546.
Audience: **u,f.**

Swaddle, Thomas W.   QD151.5.S93 1997
Inorganic Chemistry: An Industrial and Environmental
Perspective. Trade Cloth. Elsevier Science & Technology Books.
Saint Louis, MO. 1997. 482p. ISBN:0-12-678550-3, ISBN13:
978-0-12-678550-0. Dewey:546. LCCN:97-001552.
Audience: **l,u,f.** *Choice, 1997.*

Van der Put, P. J.   QD151.2.P89 1998
The Inorganic Chemistry of Materials: How to Make Things
Out of Elements. Trade Cloth. Basic Books. New York, NY.
1998. 394p. ISBN:0-306-45731-8, ISBN13: 978-0-306-45731-9.
Dewey:546. LCCN:98-033993.
Audience: **l,u,f.** *Choice, 1999.*

Inorganic Chemistry > Structure and Properties

Ballhausen, Carl Johan;
  Gray, Harry B.
Molecular Oribital Theory: An Introductory Lecture Note and
Reprint Volume. Ed. 2. Benjamin/Cummings Publishing Co..
1965.
Audience: **u,f.**

Barrett, Jack & Abel, Eddie   QD461.B265 2002
Structure and Bonding. Trade Paper. John Wiley & Sons, Inc.
Hoboken, NJ. 2002. 181p. Basic Concepts in Chemistry Ser.,
Vol. 1 ISBN:0-471-22479-0, ISBN13: 978-0-471-22479-2.
Dewey:541.2/24. LCCN:2002-284913.
Audience: **u,f.**

Bartecki, Adam & Burgess,   QD113.B3713 2002
  John
The Colour of Metal Compounds. Cloth Text. Gordon & Breach
Publishing Group. New York, NY. 2000. 209p.
ISBN:90-5699-250-3, ISBN13: 978-90-5699-250-7.
Dewey:546.3. LCCN:2002-391685.
Audience: **u,f.** *Choice, 2001.*

Comba, Peter & Hambley,   QD480.C66 1995
  Trevor W.
Molecular Modeling of Inorganic Compounds. Trade Cloth.
John Wiley & Sons, Inc. Hoboken, NJ. 1995. 207p.
ISBN:3-527-29076-1, ISBN13: 978-3-527-29076-5.
Dewey:541.2/2/015118. LCCN:95-024487.
Audience: **u,f.** *Choice, 1996.*

Ebsworth, E.A.V., et al.   QD95 .E29 1991
Structural Methods in Inorganic Chemistry. Ed. 2. D.W.H.
Rankin & S. Cradock (Authors). Trade Cloth. Blackwell
Publishing, Inc. Malden, MA. 528p. ISBN:0-632-02965-X,
ISBN13: 978-0-632-02965-5. Dewey:546.
Audience: **u,f.**

Figgis, Brian N. &   QD475.F54 2000
  Hitchman, Michael A.
Ligand Field Theory and Its Applications. Trade Cloth. John
Wiley & Sons, Inc. Hoboken, NJ. 1999. 376p. Special Topics in

Inorganic Chemistry Ser., Vol. 2 ISBN:0-471-31776-4, ISBN13: 978-0-471-31776-0. Dewey:541.2/242. LCCN:99-028986.

Audience: **u,f.** *Choice, 2001.*

Hyde, Bruce & Andersson,   **QD921.H93 1989**
Sten
Inorganic Crystal Structures. Ed. 1. Trade Cloth. John Wiley & Sons, Inc. Hoboken, NJ. 1989. 430p. ISBN:0-471-62897-2, ISBN13: 978-0-471-62897-2. Dewey:548. LCCN:88-005492.

Audience: **u,f.** *Choice, 1989.*

Jean, Yves & Volatron,   **QD461.J4313 1993**
Francois
An Introduction to Molecular Orbitals. Jeremy K. Burdett (Editor, Translator). Cloth Text. Oxford University Press, Inc. New York, NY. 1993. 352p. ISBN:0-19-506918-8, ISBN13: 978-0-19-506918-1. Dewey:514.2/24. LCCN:92-045676.

Audience: **u,f.** *Choice, 1993.*

Kosuge, K.   **QD921.K676613 1994**
Chemistry of Non-Stoichiometric Compounds. Trade Cloth. Oxford University Press, Inc. New York, NY. 1994. 272p. ISBN:0-19-855555-5, ISBN13: 978-0-19-855555-1. Dewey:548/.8. LCCN:93-021864.

Audience: **u,f.** *Choice, 1994.*

Sanderson, R. T.   **QD467.S3**
Chemical Periodicity. Paper Text. Textbook Publishers. Temecula, CA. 2003. x, 330p. ISBN:0-7581-4901-8, ISBN13: 978-0-7581-4901-5. Dewey:541.901.

Audience: **l,u,f.**

Sanderson, Robert Thomas   **QD467**
Chemical Periodicity. Reinhold Publ. Corp.. 1960.

Audience: **l,u,f.**

Solomon, Edward I., Lever,   **QD95**
A.B.P. (eds.)
Inorganic Electronic Structure and Spectroscopy, 2 v. Wiley. 1999. ISBN:0-471-32683-6, ISBN13: 978-0-471-32683-0.

Audience: **u,f.**

Solomon, Edward I. &   **QD95.I486 1999**
Lever, A. B. P. (Editors)
Inorganic Electronic Structure and Spectroscopy, Applications and Case Studies, Vol. 2. Trade Cloth. John Wiley & Sons, Inc. Hoboken, NJ. 1999. 672p. ISBN:0-471-32682-8, ISBN13: 978-0-471-32682-3. Dewey:543/.0858. LCCN:98-038180.

Audience: **u,f.**

Solomon, Edward I. &   **QD95.I486**
Lever, A. B. P.
Inorganic Electronic Structure and Spectroscopy, Applications and Case Studies. Trade Paper. John Wiley & Sons, Inc. Hoboken, NJ. 2006. 658p. ISBN:0-471-97114-6, ISBN13: 978-0-471-97114-6. Dewey:543/.0858. LCCN:2006-276064.

Audience: **u,f.**

Solomon, Edward I. &   **QD95.I486 1999**
Lever, A. B. P. (Editors)
Inorganic Electronic Structure and Spectroscopy, Methodology, Vol. 1. Trade Cloth. John Wiley & Sons, Inc. Hoboken, NJ. 1999. 752p. Inorganic Reactions and Methods Ser., Vol. 1 ISBN:0-471-15406-7, ISBN13: 978-0-471-15406-8. Dewey:543/.0858. LCCN:98-038180.

Audience: **u,f.**

Solomon, Edward I. &   **QD95.I486**
Lever, A. Barry P. (Editors)
Inorganic Electronic Structure and Spectroscopy, Methodology. Trade Paper. John Wiley & Sons, Inc. Hoboken, NJ. 2006. 732p. ISBN:0-471-97124-3, ISBN13: 978-0-471-97124-5. Dewey:543/.0858. LCCN:2006-276064.

Audience: **u,f.**

Von Zelewsky, Alexander   **QD474.Z45 1996**
Stereochemistry of Coordination Compounds. Ed. 1. Trade Cloth. John Wiley & Sons, Inc. Hoboken, NJ. 1996. 266p. Inorganic Chemistry Ser., Vol. 2:A Textbook Ser. ISBN:0-471-95057-2, ISBN13: 978-0-471-95057-8. Dewey:541.2/23. LCCN:95-019754.

Audience: **u,f.** *Choice, 1996.*

Inorganic Chemistry > Synthetic Methods

Booth, Harold Simmons   **QD156**
Inorganic Syntheses. McGraw-Hill Book Co..

Audience: **u,f.**

Langford, Cooper Harold;   **QD471 .L23**
Gray, Harry B.
Ligand Substitution Processes. W. A. Benjamin. 1965.

Audience: **u,f.**

Walton, Harold Frederic   **QD155**
Inorganic Preparations: A Laboratory Manual. Prentice=Hall. 1948. Prentice-Hall Chemistry Series

Audience: **u,f.**

Inorganic Chemistry > Reactions

Basolo, Fred and Ralph G.   **QD171**
Pearson
Mechanisms of Inorganic Reactions: A Study of Metal Complexes in Solution. Ed. 2. Wiley. 1967.

Audience: **u,f.**

Gould, Edwin S.   **QD31**
Inorganic Reactions and Structure. Holt, Rinehart and Winston. 1962.

Audience: **u,f.**

Jacobson, Carl Alfred (ed.)   **QD155**
Encyclopedia of Chemical Reactions, 8 v. Reinhold Pub. Corp.. 1946.

Audience: **u,f.**

Jordan, Robert B.   **QD502.J67 1998**
Reaction Mechanisms of Inorganic and Organometallic Systems. Ed. 2. Cloth Text. Oxford University Press, Inc. New York, NY. 1998. 380p. Topics in Inorganic Chemistry Ser. ISBN:0-19-511555-4, ISBN13: 978-0-19-511555-0. Dewey:541.3/9. LCCN:97-031222.

Audience: **u,f.** *Choice, 1998, 1992.*

Lappin, A. G.   **QD63.O9L37 1994**
Redox Mechanisms in Inorganic Chemistry. Cloth Text. Prentice Hall PTR. Upper Saddle River, NJ. 1994. 250p. ISBN:0-13-770751-7, ISBN13: 978-0-13-770751-5. Dewey:541.3/93. LCCN:93-050189.

Audience: **u,f.** *Choice, 1995.*

Zuckerman, J J
Inorganic Reactions and Methods: Formation of Bonds to
Transition and Inner-Transition Metals, Set. J. J. Zuckerman
(Editor). John Wiley & Sons, Inc. ISBN:0-89573-250-5,
ISBN13: 978-0-89573-250-7.

Audience: **u,f.**

Inorganic Chemistry > Special Topics > Spectroscopy

QC457 .I5265 1984
Infrared Spectra Handbook of Inorganic Compounds. Trade
Paper. Sadtler Research Laboratories. Philadelphia, PA. 1984.
ISBN:0-8456-0112-1, ISBN13: 978-0-8456-0112-9.
Dewey:544/.63. LCCN:84-052117.

Audience: **u,f.**

Duckworth, Douglas C. &   **QD95.I488 2000**
Smith, D. H.
Inorganic Mass Spectrometry: Fundamentals and Applications,
Vol. 23. Christopher M. Barshick (Editor). Paper over Boards.
Marcel Dekker Inc. New York, NY. 2000. 528p. Practical
Spectroscopy Ser. ISBN:0-8247-0243-3, ISBN13:
978-0-8247-0243-4. Dewey:543/.0873. LCCN:99-087830.

Audience: **u,f.**

Nakamoto, Kazuo   **QD96.I5N33 1997**
Applications in Coordination, Organometallic and Bioinorganic
Chemistry, Pt. B. Ed. 5. Trade Cloth. John Wiley & Sons, Inc.
Hoboken, NJ. 1997. 400p. Infrared and Raman Spectra of
Inorganic and Coordination Chemistry Ser., Vol. 2
ISBN:0-471-16392-9, ISBN13: 978-0-471-16392-3.
Dewey:543/.08583. LCCN:96-033456.

Audience: **u,f.** *Choice, 1998.*

Nakamoto, Kazuo   **QD96.I5.N33 1997**
Infrared and Raman Spectra of Inorganic and Coordination
Compounds, Pts. A&B, Set. Ed. 5. Trade Cloth. John Wiley &
Sons, Inc. Hoboken, NJ. 1997. 771p. ISBN:0-471-19406-9,
ISBN13: 978-0-471-19406-4. Dewey:543/.08583.
LCCN:96-033456.

Audience: **u,f.** **℟** *Choice, 1998.*

Nakamoto, Kazuo   **QD96.I5N33 1997**
Theory and Applications in Inorganic Chemistry. Ed. 5. Trade
Cloth. John Wiley & Sons, Inc. Hoboken, NJ. 1997. 408p.
Infrared and Raman Spectra of Inorganic and Coordination
Chemistry Ser., Vol. 1 ISBN:0-471-16394-5, ISBN13:
978-0-471-16394-7. Dewey:543/.08583. LCCN:96-033456.

Audience: **u,f.** *Choice, 1998.*

Nyquist, Richard A., et al.   **QC457.N927 1997**
Handbook of Infrared and Raman Spectra of Inorganic
Compounds and Organic Salts, Set. Ronald O. Kagel, Curtis L.
Putzig & M. Anne Leugers (Authors). Trade Cloth. Elsevier
Science & Technology Books. Saint Louis, MO. 1996. 1184p.
ISBN:0-12-523444-9, ISBN13: 978-0-12-523444-3.
Dewey:543/.08583. LCCN:96-022175.

Audience: **u,f.** *Choice, 1997.*

Parish, R. V.   **QD95.P25 1990**
NMR, NQR, EPR, and Mossbauer Spectroscopy in Inorganic
Chemistry. Trade Cloth. Ellis Horwood Ltd. Hempstead, 1990.
223 p. :p. ISBN:0-13-625518-3, ISBN13: 978-0-13-625518-5.
Dewey:543/.087. LCCN:90-004873.

Audience: **u,f.**

Inorganic Chemistry > Special Topics > Solid State Chemistry

TA455.C43
Ceramics WebBook.
http://www.ceramics.nist.gov/webbook/evaluate.htm

Audience: **u,f.**

The Graphite Page.
http://www.phy.mtu.edu/~jaszczak/graphite.html

Audience: **u,f.**

Kim Allen's Fullerene Page.
http://www.mindspring.com/~kimall/Fuller/

Audience: **u,f.**

Abel, Eddie & Dann,   **QD478.D36 2002**
Sandra E.
Reactions and Characterization of Solids. Trade Paper. John
Wiley & Sons, Inc. Hoboken, NJ. 2002. 201p. Basic Concepts
in Chemistry Ser. ISBN:0-471-22481-2, ISBN13:
978-0-471-22481-5. Dewey:541/.0421. LCCN:2002-511022.

Audience: **u,f.**

Aldersey-Williams, Hugh   **QD181.C1A43 1995**
The Most Beautiful Molecule: The Discovery of the Buckyball.
Trade Cloth. John Wiley & Sons, Inc. Hoboken, NJ. 1995. 340p.
ISBN:0-471-10938-X, ISBN13: 978-0-471-10938-9.
Dewey:546.6/81. LCCN:95-012422.

Audience: **u,f.** *Choice, 1996.*

Baggott, Jim   **QD181.C1B28 1994**
Perfect Symmetry: The Accidental Discovery of
Buckminsterfullerene. Cloth Text. Oxford University Press, Inc.
New York, NY. 1995. 328p. ISBN:0-19-855790-6, ISBN13:
978-0-19-855790-6. Dewey:546.6/812. LCCN:94-014068.

Audience: **u,f.** *Choice, 1995.*

Cheetham, A. K. & Day,   **QD478.S6334 1991**
Peter (Editors)
Solid State Chemistry: Compounds, Vol. 2. Cloth Text. Oxford
University Press, Inc. New York, NY. 1992. 318p.
ISBN:0-19-855166-5, ISBN13: 978-0-19-855166-9.
Dewey:541/.0421. LCCN:91-012173.

Audience: **u,f.** *Choice, 1993.*

Cheetham, A. K. & Day,   **QD478.S634 1987**
Peter
Solid-State Chemistry: Techniques. Trade Cloth. Oxford
University Press, Inc. New York, NY. 1987. 412p.
ISBN:0-19-855165-7, ISBN13: 978-0-19-855165-2.
Dewey:541/.0421. LCCN:85-003121.

Audience: **u,f.** *Choice, 1988.*

Elliott, Stephen   **QC183.A3**
The Physics and Chemistry of Solids. Trade Cloth. John Wiley
& Sons, Inc. Hoboken, NJ. 1998. 794p. ISBN:0-471-98194-X,
ISBN13: 978-0-471-98194-7. Dewey:530.4/1.

Audience: **u,f.**

Hannay, Norman B.   **QD478**
Treatise on Solid State Chemistry, 6 vols..in 7. Plenum Press.
1973. ISBN:0-306-35050-5, ISBN13: 978-0-306-35050-4.

Audience: **u,f.**

Hirsch, A. QD181.C1 H57
The Chemistry of the Fullerenes. Trade Paper. Thieme Medical
Publishers, Inc. New York, NY. 1994. 203p. Organic Chemistry
Monograph Ser. ISBN:0-86577-560-5, ISBN13:
978-0-86577-560-2. Dewey:546/.681.
Audience: **u,f.**

Kadish, Karl M. & Ruoff, QD181.C1F843 2000
Rodney S. (Editors)
Fullerenes: Chemistry, Physics, and Technology. Trade Cloth.
John Wiley & Sons, Inc. Hoboken, NJ. 2000. 978p.
ISBN:0-471-29089-0, ISBN13: 978-0-471-29089-6.
Dewey:546/.681. LCCN:00-033402.
Audience: **u,f.**

Ladd, M. F. QD461
Structure and Bonding in Solid State Chemistry. Trade Cloth.
John Wiley & Sons, Inc. Hoboken, NJ. 1979. 326p. Ellis
Horwood Series in Chemical Science Ser. ISBN:0-470-26597-3,
ISBN13: 978-0-470-26597-0. Dewey:541/.224.
LCCN:78-041289.
Audience: **u,f.**

Inorganic Chemistry > Special Topics > Organometallic Chemistry

Brauer QD411.S96
Copper, Silver, Gold, Zinc, Cadmium, and Mercury, Vol. 5. W.
A. Herrmann (Editor). Trade Cloth. Thieme Medical Publishers,
Inc. New York, NY. 1998. 258p. ISBN:0-86577-662-8, ISBN13:
978-0-86577-662-3. Dewey:541.3/9.
Audience: **u,f.**

Hermann, W. A. QD411.S96 1996
Synthetic Methods of Organometallic and Inorganic Chemistry:
(Herman/Brauer). Trade Cloth. George Thieme Verlag. Stuttgart,
1998. 244p. ISBN:3-13-103051-8, ISBN13: 978-3-13-103051-1.
Dewey:541.3/9. LCCN:95-049908.
Audience: **u,f.**

Herrmann, W. A. (Editor) QD411.S96
Synthetic Methods of Organometallic and Inorganic Chemistry:
Lanthanides and Actinides. Trade Cloth. Thieme Medical
Publishers, Inc. New York, NY. 1997. 236p.
ISBN:0-86577-663-6, ISBN13: 978-0-86577-663-0.
Dewey:541.3/9.
Audience: **u,f.**

Herrmann, W. A. (Editor) QD411.S96 1996
Synthetic Methods of Organometallic and Inorganic Chemistry:
Phosphorus, Arsenic, Antimony, and Bismuth. Trade Cloth.
Thieme Medical Publishers, Inc. New York, NY. 1996. 240p.
ISBN:0-86577-654-7, ISBN13: 978-0-86577-654-8.
Dewey:541.3/9. LCCN:95-049908.
Audience: **u,f.**

Herrmann, W. A. (Editor) QD411.S96 1996
Synthetic Methods of Organometallic and Inorganic Chemistry:
Groups 1, 2, 13, and 14. Trade Cloth. Thieme Medical
Publishers, Inc. New York, NY. 1996. 320p.
ISBN:0-86577-653-9, ISBN13: 978-0-86577-653-1.
Dewey:541.3/9. LCCN:95-049908.
Audience: **u,f.**

Herrmann, W. A. (Editor) QD411.S96
Synthetic Methods of Organometallic and Inorganic Chemistry:
Sulfur, Selenium, and Tellurium, Vol. 4. Trade Cloth. Thieme
Medical Publishers, Inc. New York, NY. 1998. 244p.
ISBN:0-86577-661-X, ISBN13: 978-0-86577-661-6.
Dewey:541.39.
Audience: **u,f.**

Herrmann, W. A. & Brauer QD411.S96
Synthetic Methods of Organometallic and Inorganic Chemistry:
Transition Metals, Pt. 1. Trade Cloth. Thieme Medical
Publishers, Inc. New York, NY. 1997. 306p.
ISBN:0-86577-664-4, ISBN13: 978-0-86577-664-7.
Dewey:541.3/9.
Audience: **u,f.**

Herrmann, W. A. & Brauer QD411.S96
Synthetic Methods of Organometallic and Inorganic Chemistry:
Transition Metals, Vol. 2. Trade Cloth. Thieme Medical
Publishers, Inc. New York, NY. 1997. 266p.
ISBN:0-86577-665-2, ISBN13: 978-0-86577-665-4.
Dewey:541.3/9.
Audience: **u,f.**

Herrmann, W. A. & QD411.S96
Brauer, G.
Transition Metals, Vol. 3. Trade Cloth. Thieme Medical
Publishers, Inc. New York, NY. 1999. 233p. Synthetic Methods
of Organometallic and Inorganic Chemistry Ser., Vol. 9
ISBN:0-86577-971-6, ISBN13: 978-0-86577-971-6.
Dewey:541.3/9.
Audience: **u,f.**

Herrmann, Wolfgang A. QD411.S96
(Editor)
Synthetic Methods of Organometallic and Inorganic Chemistry,
Vol. 2. Trade Cloth. George Thieme Verlag. Stuttgart, 1996.
320p. ISBN:3-13-103031-3, ISBN13: 978-3-13-103031-3.
Dewey:541.3/9.
Audience: **u,f.**

Herrmann, Wolfgang A. QD411.S96
(Editor)
Synthetic Methods of Organometallic and Inorganic Chemistry,
Vol. 2. Trade Cloth. George Thieme Verlag. Stuttgart, 1997.
266p. ISBN:3-13-103091-7, ISBN13: 978-3-13-103091-7.
Dewey:541.3/9.
Audience: **u,f.**

Herrmann, Wolfgang A. QD411.S96
(Editor)
Synthetic Methods of Organometallic and Inorganic Chemistry,
Vol. 3. Trade Cloth. George Thieme Verlag. Stuttgart, 1996.
240p. ISBN:3-13-103041-0, ISBN13: 978-3-13-103041-2.
Dewey:541.3/9.
Audience: **u,f.**

Herrmann, Wolfgang A. QD411.S96
(Editor)
Synthetic Methods of Organometallic and Inorganic Chemistry,
Vol. 6. Trade Cloth. George Thieme Verlag. Stuttgart, 1997.
236p. ISBN:3-13-103071-2, ISBN13: 978-3-13-103071-9.
Dewey:541.3/9.
Audience: **u,f.**

Formats: Web: ☐ Ebook: 🅔 CD/DVD-ROM: 🏵 BCL3: 𝓑

Herrmann, Wolfgang A.   **QD411.S96**
  (Editor)
Synthetic Methods of Organometallic and Inorganic Chemistry,
Vol. 3. Trade Cloth. George Thieme Verlag. Stuttgart, 1999.
233p. ISBN:3-13-115141-2, ISBN13: 978-3-13-115141-4.
Dewey:541.3/9.
                                              Audience: **u,f.**

Herrmann, Wolfgang A.   **QD411.S96**
  (Editor)
Synthetic Methods of Organometallic and Inorganic Chemistry,
Vol. 5. Trade Cloth. George Thieme Verlag. Stuttgart, 1998.
258p. ISBN:3-13-103061-5, ISBN13: 978-3-13-103061-0.
Dewey:541.3/9.
                                              Audience: **u,f.**

Herrmann, Wolfgang A.   **QD411.S96**
  (Editor)
Synthetic Methods of Organometallic and Inorganic Chemistry,
Vol. 7. Trade Cloth. George Thieme Verlag. Stuttgart, 1997.
306p. ISBN:3-13-103081-X, ISBN13: 978-3-13-103081-8.
Dewey:541.3/9.
                                              Audience: **u,f.**

Herrmann, Wolfgang A.   **QD411.S96 1996**
  (Editor)
Synthetic Methods of Organometallic and Inorganic Chemistry.
Trade Cloth. George Thieme Verlag. Stuttgart, 1996. 192p.
ISBN:3-13-103021-6, ISBN13: 978-3-13-103021-4.
Dewey:541.3/9. LCCN:95-049908.
                                              Audience: **u,f.**

Herrmann, Wolfgang A.   **QD411.S96 1996**
  (Editor)
Synthetic Methods of Organometallic and Inorganic Chemistry:
Literature, Laboratory Techniques, and COmmon Starting
Materials. Trade Cloth. Thieme Medical Publishers, Inc. New
York, NY. 1996. 192p. ISBN:0-86577-627-X, ISBN13:
978-0-86577-627-2. Dewey:541.3/9. LCCN:95-049908.
                                              Audience: **u,f.**

Hill, Anthony F.   **QD411.8.T73H55 2002**
Organotransition Metal Chemistry. Trade Paper. John Wiley &
Sons, Inc. Hoboken, NJ. 2002. 185p. Basic Concepts in
Chemistry Ser. ISBN:0-471-28163-8, ISBN13:
978-0-471-28163-4. Dewey:547/.056. LCCN:2002-727723.
                                              Audience: **u,f.**

Liebau, F.   **QD181.S6.L614 1985**
Structural Chemistry of Silicates: Structure, Bonding and
Classification. Cloth Text. Springer. New York, NY. 1985. 347p.
ISBN:0-387-13747-5, ISBN13: 978-0-387-13747-6.
Dewey:546/.68324. LCCN:84-023532.
                          Audience: **u,f.** *B* *Choice, 1985.*

Wilkinson, Geoffrey   **QD411**
Comprehensive Organometallic Chemistry: The Synthesis,
Reactions and Structures of Organometallic Compounds. F.
Gordon Stone & Edward W. Abel (Editors). Trade Cloth.
Elsevier Science & Technology Books. Saint Louis, MO. 1982.
9460p. ISBN:0-08-025269-9, ISBN13: 978-0-08-025269-8.
Dewey:547/.05. LCCN:82-007595.
                                      Audience: **u,f.** *B*

Wilkinson, Geoffrey   **QD411.C652 1995**
Comprehensive Organometallic Chemistry II: A Review of the
Literature 1982-1994. Ed. 2. F. Gordon Stone & Edward W.
Abel (Editors). Trade Cloth. Elsevier Science & Technology

Books. Saint Louis, MO. 1995. 9666p. ISBN:0-08-040608-4,
ISBN13: 978-0-08-040608-4. Dewey:547/.05. LCCN:95-007030.
                          Audience: **u,f.** *Choice, 1996.*

Yamamoto, Akio   **QD411.Y3613 1986**
Organotransition Metal Chemistry: Fundamental Concepts and
Applications. Ed. 1. Trade Cloth. John Wiley & Sons, Inc.
Hoboken, NJ. 1986. 480p. ISBN:0-471-89171-1, ISBN13:
978-0-471-89171-0. Dewey:547/.05. LCCN:85-026349.
                                              Audience: **u,f.**

Inorganic Chemistry > Special Topics > Lanthanides, Actinides, and Nuclear Chemistry

                                               QD601.2
▢ Table of Isotopes.
http://ie.lbl.gov/toi.htm
Lawrence National Radiation Laboratory, Berkeley.
                                              Audience: **u,f.**

Adloff, J. P.; Guillaumont,   **QD601**
  Robert
Fundamentals of Radiochemistry. CRC Press. 1993.
ISBN:0-8493-4244-9, ISBN13: 978-0-8493-4244-8.
                                              Audience: **u,f.**

Choppin, Gregory R., et al.   **QD601.3.C48 2001**
Radiochemistry and Nuclear Chemistry. Ed. 3. Jan-Olov
Liljenzin & Jan Rydberg (Authors). Cloth Text. Elsevier Science
& Technology Books. Saint Louis, MO. 2001. 720p.
ISBN:0-7506-7463-6, ISBN13: 978-0-7506-7463-8.
Dewey:541.3/8. LCCN:2001-043430.
                                              Audience: **u,f.**

Cotton, Simon   **QD172.R2C67 1991**
Lanthanides and Actinides. Trade Cloth. Oxford University
Press, Inc. New York, NY. 1991. 202p. ISBN:0-19-507366-5,
ISBN13: 978-0-19-507366-9. Dewey:546/.41. LCCN:91-017815.
                          Audience: **u,f.** *Choice, 1992.*

Freeman, A. J. & Keller, C.   **QD172.A3H36 1984**
  (Editors)
Handbook on the Physics and Chemistry of the Actinides, Vol.
3. Trade Cloth. Elsevier Science & Technology Books. Saint
Louis, MO. 1986. 516p. ISBN:0-444-86926-3, ISBN13:
978-0-444-86926-5. Dewey:546/.4. LCCN:84-020698.
                                              Audience: **u,f.**

Freeman, A. J. & Keller, C.   **QD172.A3H36 1984**
  (Editors)
Handbook on the Physics and Chemistry of the Actinides, Vol.
6. Trade Cloth. Elsevier Science & Technology Books. Saint
Louis, MO. 1991. x, 742p. ISBN:0-444-87447-X, ISBN13:
978-0-444-87447-4. Dewey:546/.4. LCCN:84-020698.
                                              Audience: **u,f.**

Freeman, A. J. & Keller, C.   **QD172.A3H36 1984**
  (Editors)
Handbook on the Physics and Chemistry of the Actinides, Vol.
4. Trade Cloth. Elsevier. New York, NY. 1986. 574p.
ISBN:0-444-86983-2, ISBN13: 978-0-444-86983-8.
Dewey:546/.4. LCCN:84-020698.
                                              Audience: **u,f.**

Freeman, A. J. & Lander,   QD172.A3H36 1984
  G. H. (Editors)
Handbook on the Physics and Chemistry of the Actinides, Vol.
1. Trade Cloth. Elsevier Science & Technology Books. Saint
Louis, MO. 1985. 530p. ISBN:0-444-86903-4, ISBN13:
978-0-444-86903-6. Dewey:546/.4. LCCN:84-020698.
                          Audience: **u,f.**

Freeman, A. J. & Lander,   QD172.A3H36 1984
  G. H.
Handbook on the Physics and Chemistry of the Actinides. Trade
Cloth. Elsevier. New York, NY. 1988. ISBN:0-444-87056-3,
ISBN13: 978-0-444-87056-8. Dewey:546/.4. LCCN:84-020698.
                          Audience: **u,f.**

Freeman, A. J. & Lander,   QD172.A3H36 1984
  G. H.
Handbook on the Physics and Chemistry of the Actinides, Pt. 1:
Physics, Vol. 2. Trade Cloth. Elsevier Science & Technology
Books. Saint Louis, MO. 1985. 504p. ISBN:0-444-86907-7,
ISBN13: 978-0-444-86907-4. Dewey:546/.4. LCCN:84-020698.
                          Audience: **u,f.**

Friedlander, G., et al.   QD601.2
Nuclear and Radiochemistry. Ed. 3. J. M. Miller, E. S. Macias
& J. W. Kennedy (Authors). Trade Cloth. John Wiley & Sons,
Inc. Hoboken, NJ. 1981. 684p. ISBN:0-471-28021-6, ISBN13:
978-0-471-28021-7. Dewey:541.3/8. LCCN:81-001000.
                          Audience: **u,f.**

Gschneidner, K. A. Jr. &   QD172.R2H26
  Eyring, LeRoy
Handbook on the Physics and Chemistry of Rare Earths. Trade
Cloth. Elsevier. New York, NY. 1978. xxv, 894p.
ISBN:0-444-85022-8, ISBN13: 978-0-444-85022-5.
Dewey:546/.4. LCCN:78-012371.
                          Audience: **u,f.**

Gschneidner, K. A. Jr. &   QD172.R2
  Eyring, Leroy (Editors)
Handbook on the Physics and Chemistry of Rare Earths, Vol.
15. Trade Cloth. Elsevier Science & Technology Books. Saint
Louis, MO. 1991. 530p. ISBN:0-444-88966-3, ISBN13:
978-0-444-88966-9. Dewey:546/.4.
                          Audience: **u,f.**

Hoffman, Darleane C., et al.   QD602.4 .H64 2000
The Transuranium People: The Inside Story. Albert Ghiorso &
Glenn T. Seaborg (Authors). Trade Cloth. Imperial College
Press. London, 2000. 564p. ISBN:1-86094-087-0, ISBN13:
978-1-86094-087-3. Dewey:546/.44/092273.
LCCN:2004-267047.
                          Audience: **l,u,f.**

Katz, J J; Seaborg, Glenn   QD172.A3C46 1986
  Theodore; Morss, L R
The Chemistry of the Actinide Elements, Vol. 2. Ed. 2. J. J.
Katz (Editor) ; Glenn Theodore Seaborg (Editor) ; L. R. Morss
(Editor). Chapman & Hall. 1986. ISBN:0-412-27370-5, ISBN13:
978-0-412-27370-4.
                          Audience: **u,f.**

Katz, J. J. (Editor), et al.   QD172.A3C46 1986
The Chemistry of the Actinide Elements, Vol. I. Ed. 2. Glenn
Theodore Seaborg & L. R. Morss (Editors). Cloth Text.

Chapman & Hall. New York, NY. 1986. 998p.
ISBN:0-412-10550-0, ISBN13: 978-0-412-10550-0.
Dewey:546/.7. LCCN:86-008284.
                          Audience: **u,f.**

Lieser, Karl Heinrich   QD601.3.L54 2001
Nuclear and Radiochemistry: Fundamentals and Applications.
Ed. 2. Trade Cloth. John Wiley & Sons, Inc. Hoboken, NJ.
2001. 474p. ISBN:3-527-30317-0, ISBN13: 978-3-527-30317-5.
Dewey:541.3/8. LCCN:2001-272382.
                          Audience: **u,f.**

Loveland, Walter D.;   QD601.3
  Morrissey, David J.; Seaborg, Glenn T.
Modern Nuclear Chemistry. Wiley-Interscience. 2006.
ISBN:0-471-11532-0, ISBN13: 978-0-471-11532-8.
                          Audience: **u,f.**

Morss, Lester R.   QD172.T7.T69 1992
Transuranium Elements: A Half Century. Jean Fuger (Editor).
Trade Cloth. Oxford University Press, Inc. New York, NY. 1992.
562p. An American Chemical Society Publication
ISBN:0-8412-2219-3, ISBN13: 978-0-8412-2219-9.
Dewey:546/.44. LCCN:92-007475.
                  Audience: **u,f.** *Choice, 1993.*

Trenn, Thaddeus J.   QC794.5.T73
Transmutation: Natural and Artificial. Trade Cloth. John Wiley
& Sons, Inc. Hoboken, NJ. 1982. 144p. Nobel Prize Topics in
Chemistry Ser. ISBN:0-471-26105-X, ISBN13:
978-0-471-26105-6. Dewey:539.7/5.
                          Audience: **u,f.**

Vertes, Attila; Nagy, Sandor;   QD601.3
  Klencsar, Zoltan
Handbook of Nuclear Chemistry, 5 vols. Kluwer Academic
Publishers. 2003. ISBN:1-4020-1305-1, ISBN13:
978-1-4020-1305-8.
                          Audience: **u,f.**

Inorganic Chemistry > Special Topics > Chemistry of Specific Elements

Akiba, Kin-ya (Editor)   QD255.4.C48 1999
Chemistry of Hypervalent Compounds. Ed. 1. Trade Cloth. John
Wiley & Sons, Inc. Hoboken, NJ. 1998. 432p.
ISBN:0-471-24019-2, ISBN13: 978-0-471-24019-8.
Dewey:541.2/24. LCCN:98-006578.
                  Audience: **u,f.** *Choice, 1999.*

Banks, R. E. (Editor)   QD181.F1.F54 2000
Fluorine Chemistry at the Millennium: Fascinated by Fluorine.
Trade Cloth. Elsevier Science & Technology Books. Saint
Louis, MO. 2000. 660p. ISBN:0-08-043405-3, ISBN13:
978-0-08-043405-6. Dewey:546/.731. LCCN:00-026273.
                          Audience: **u,f.**

Emsley, John   QD181.P1E447 2000
The 13th Element: The Sordid Tale of Murder, Fire and
Phosphorus. Trade Cloth. John Wiley & Sons, Inc. Hoboken,
NJ. 2000. 352p. ISBN:0-471-39455-6, ISBN13:
978-0-471-39455-6. Dewey:546/.712. LCCN:00-703013.
                        Audience: **l,u,f.**

Gutmann, Viktor   **QD165**
Halogen Chemistry, 3 v. Academic Press. 1967.
                                    Audience: **u,f.**

Rao, C. N. & Raveau,   **QD172.T6R36 1995**
  Bernard
Transition Metal Oxides. Trade Paper. John Wiley & Sons, Inc.
Hoboken, NJ. 1995. 338p. ISBN:1-56081-647-3, ISBN13:
978-1-56081-647-8. Dewey:546/.6. LCCN:95-010717.
                                    Audience: **u,f.** *Choice, 1995.*

Rigden, John S.   **QD181.H1R54 2002**
Hydrogen: The Essential Element. Trade Cloth. Harvard
University Press. Cambridge, MA. 2002. 288p.
ISBN:0-674-00738-7, ISBN13: 978-0-674-00738-3.
Dewey:546/.2. LCCN:2001-051708.
                            Audience: **l,u,f.** *Choice, 2003, 2002.*

Sawyer, Donald T.   **QD181.O1S18 1991**
Oxygen Chemistry. Trade Cloth. Oxford University Press, Inc.
New York, NY. 1991. 236p. International Series of Monographs
on Chemistry ISBN:0-19-505798-8, ISBN13:
978-0-19-505798-0. Dewey:546/.721. LCCN:91-006766.
                                    Audience: **u,f.** *Choice, 1992.*

Schmidbauer, Hubert   **QD181.A9G65 1999**
Gold: Chemistry, Biochemistry, and Technology. Trade Cloth.
John Wiley & Sons, Inc. Hoboken, NJ. 1999. 908p.
ISBN:0-471-97369-6, ISBN13: 978-0-471-97369-0.
Dewey:546/.656. LCCN:98-007028.
                                    Audience: **u,f.** *Choice, 1999.*

Silver, J   **QD181.F4C48 1993**
Chemistry of Iron. J. Silver (Editor). Blackie Academic &
Professional. 1993. ISBN:0-7514-0062-9, ISBN13:
978-0-7514-0062-5.
                                    Audience: **u,f.**

Inorganic Chemistry > Special Topics > Analytical Methods and Procedures, Including Chromatography

Albert, Adrien & Serjeant,   **QD561**
  E. P.
The Determination of Ionization Constants: A Laboratory
Manual. Ed. 3. Trade Cloth. Chapman & Hall. New York, NY.
1984. 150p. ISBN:0-412-24290-7, ISBN13: 978-0-412-24290-8.
Dewey:546/.24. LCCN:84-007497.
                                    Audience: **u,f.** *B*

Feigl, F. & Anger, V.   **QD81**
Spot Tests in Inorganic Analysis. Ed. 6. Trade Cloth. Elsevier
Science & Technology Books. Saint Louis, MO. 1982. 700p.
ISBN:0-444-40929-7, ISBN13: 978-0-444-40929-4.
Dewey:544/.834. LCCN:76-135494.
                                    Audience: **l,u,f.** *B*

Lederer, Michael   **QD79.C4L44 1994**
Chromatography for Organic Chemistry. Trade Cloth. John
Wiley & Sons, Inc. Hoboken, NJ. 1994. 230p.
ISBN:0-471-94285-5, ISBN13: 978-0-471-94285-6.
Dewey:543/.089. LCCN:93-031657.
                                    Audience: **u,f.**

Qureshi, Mohsin (Editor)   **QD117**
Inorganics. CRC Press. 1987. ISBN:0-8493-3049-1, ISBN13:
978-0-8493-3049-0.
                                    Audience: **u,f.**

Vogel, Arthur Israel   **QD101**
Vogel's Textbook of Quantitative Inorganic Analysis. Ed. 6.
Prentice Hall. 2000. ISBN:0-582-22628-7, ISBN13:
978-0-582-22628-9.
                                    Audience: **l,u,f.**

Inorganic Chemistry > Guides to the Literature

☐ MolChem--Inorganic Chemistry.
http://pages.pomona.edu/~wsteinmetz/InorChem.htm
                                    Audience: **l,u,f.**

Environmental Chemistry > Guides to the Literature

☐ Green Chemistry.
http://reenchem.uoregon.edu/gems.html
                                    Audience: **l,u,f.**

☐ MolData--Environmental Chemistry.
http://pages.pomona.edu/~wsteinmetz/EnvChem.htm
                                    Audience: **l,u,f.**

Hutchinson, Barbara S. &   **S494.5.A39U75 2002**
  Greider, Antoinette Paris (Editors)
Using the Agricultural, Environmental, and Food Literature, Vol.
61. Paper over Boards. Marcel Dekker Inc. New York, NY.
2002. 536p. Books in Library and Information Science, Vol. 61
ISBN:0-8247-0800-8, ISBN13: 978-0-8247-0800-9.
Dewey:630/.7/2. LCCN:2002-073403.
                                    Audience: **u,f.** *Choice, 2003.*

Webster, James K. (Editor)   **Z7914**
Toxic and Hazardous Materials: A Sourcebook and Guide to
Information Sources. Greenwood Press. 1987.
ISBN:0-313-24575-4, ISBN13: 978-0-313-24575-6.
                                    Audience: **u,f.**

Environmental Chemistry > Abstracting and Indexing Services

                                    TD172
☐ Pollution Abstracts.
http://www.csa.com/factsheets/pollution-set-c.php
CSA.
                                    Audience: **u,f.**

                                    TD172
Pollution Abstracts. Cambridge Scientific Abstracts.
                                    Audience: **u,f.**

RA1215

☐ TOXLINE.
http://toxnet.nlm.nih.gov/cgi-bin/sis/htmlgen?TOXLINE
Audience: **u,f.**

RA1215

☐ TOXNET. National Library of Medicine.
http://sis.nlm.nih.gov/sis1/
Audience: **u,f.**

Environmental Chemistry > General Environmental Chemistry

Anastas, Paul T.   **TP155**
Green Chemistry: Frontiers in Benign Chemical Syntheses and Processes. Williamson, Tracy C. (Editors). Oxford University Press. 1998. ISBN:0-19-850170-6, ISBN13: 978-0-19-850170-1.
Audience: **u,f.**

Anastas, Paul T. & Warner,   **TP155.A657 1998**
John
Green Chemistry: Theory and Practice. Trade Cloth. Oxford University Press, Inc. New York, NY. 1998. 152p. ISBN:0-19-850234-6, ISBN13: 978-0-19-850234-0. Dewey:660/.2/0286. LCCN:98-036292.
Audience: **u,f.**

Connell, Des. W. et al.   **TD193**
(Editors)
Basic Concepts of Environmental Chemistry. Lewis Pubishers. 1997. ISBN:0-87371-998-0, ISBN13: 978-0-87371-998-8.
Audience: **l,u,f.**

DeVito, Stephen C.   **TP155.D43 1996**
Designing Safer Chemicals: Green Chemistry for Pollution Prevention. Garrett, Roger L. (Editors). American Chemical Society. 1996. (ACS Symposium Series 640) ISBN:0-8412-3443-4, ISBN13: 978-0-8412-3443-7.
Audience: **u,f.**

Fergusson, J. E.   **TD196.H43F47 1990**
The Heavy Elements: Chemistry, Environmental Impact and Health Effects. Trade Cloth. Elsevier Science & Technology Books. Saint Louis, MO. 1990. 614p. ISBN:0-08-034860-2, ISBN13: 978-0-08-034860-5. Dewey:363.17/91. LCCN:90-006783.
Audience: **u,f.**

Harrison, R. M. (Editor)   **TD174**
Pollution: Causes, Effects and Control. Ed. 4. Trade Paper. Royal Society of Chemistry, The. Cambridge, 2001. xxiv + 580p. ISBN:0-85404-621-6, ISBN13: 978-0-85404-621-8. Dewey:363.7/3.
Audience: **l,u,f.**

Harrison, R. M. (Editor),   **QD31.2.I572 1991**
et al.
Introductory Chemistry for the Environmental Sciences. W. R. Johnston, Spyridon Rapsomanikis & S. J. De Mora (Editors). Cloth Text. Cambridge University Press. New York, NY. 1991. 364p. Cambridge Environmental Chemistry Ser., No. 4 ISBN:0-521-25673-9, ISBN13: 978-0-521-25673-5. Dewey:540. LCCN:90-002370.
Audience: **l,u,f.** *Choice, 1992.*

Lancaster, M.   **TP155.2.E58**
Green Chemistry: An Introductory Text. Royal Society of Chemistry Staff (Contribution by). Trade Paper. Royal Society of Chemistry, The. Cambridge, 2002. 334p. RSC Paperbacks Ser. ISBN:0-85404-620-8, ISBN13: 978-0-85404-620-1. Dewey:660.2/0286. LCCN:2002-025908.
Audience: **u,f.** *Choice, 2003.*

Macalady, Donald L.   **TD193.P45 1998**
(Editor)
Perspectives in Environmental Chemistry. Cloth Text. Oxford University Press, Inc. New York, NY. 1997. 526p. Topics in Environmental Chemistry Ser. ISBN:0-19-510208-8, ISBN13: 978-0-19-510208-6. Dewey:628.5. LCCN:97-004123.
Audience: **u,f.** *Choice, 1998.*

Manahan, Stanley E.   **QD31.2.M35 1994**
Environmental Chemistry. Ed. 6. Trade Cloth, Box or Slipcased. Lewis Publishers. Boca Raton, FL. 1994. 832p. ISBN:1-56670-088-4, ISBN13: 978-1-56670-088-7. Dewey:628.5/01/54. LCCN:94-018437.
Audience: **u,f.**

Matlack, Albert S.   **TP155.2.E58**
Introduction to Green Chemistry. M. Dekker. 2001. ISBN:0-8247-0411-8, ISBN13: 978-0-8247-0411-7.
Audience: **u,f.**

Sawyer, Clair N., et al.   **TD193.S28 1994**
Chemistry for Environmental Engineering. Ed. 4. Perry L. McCarty & Gene F. Parkin (Authors). Cloth Text. McGraw-Hill Higher Education. Burr Ridge, IL. 1994. 608p. Water Resources, Environmental Engineering and Chemical Engineering Ser. ISBN:0-07-054978-8, ISBN13: 978-0-07-054978-4. Dewey:628/.01/54. LCCN:94-000261.
Audience: **l,u,f.**

Schwarzenbach, René   **TD196.O73S39 2003**
P., et al.
ⓔ Environmental Organic Chemistry. Ed. 2. Philip M. Gschwend & Dieter M. Imboden (Authors). E-Book. John Wiley & Sons, Inc. Hoboken, NJ. 2005. ISBN:0-471-74399-2, ISBN13: 978-0-471-74399-6. Dewey:628.1/68.
Audience: **u,f.**

Winter, Carl K.   **TX531.C518 1990**
Chemicals in the Human Food Chain. Cloth Text. John Wiley & Sons, Inc. Hoboken, NJ. 1990. ISBN:0-442-00421-4, ISBN13: 978-0-442-00421-7. Dewey:363.1/92. LCCN:89-070670.
Audience: **l,u,f.**

Environmental Chemistry > Dictionaries and Encyclopedia

☐ Chemistry and Environmental Dictionary.
http://environmentalchemistry.com/yogi/chemistry/dictionary/
Audience: **l,u,f.**

Ayres,   **TD196.C45A97 1998**
Dictionary of Environmentally Important Chemicals. Blackie Academic & Professional. 1997. ISBN:0-7514-0256-7, ISBN13: 978-0-7514-0256-8.
Audience: **u,f.**

Coleman, Ronny J.   **T55**
Hazardous Materials Dictionary. Ed. 2. Technomic Publ. Co..
1994. ISBN:1-56676-160-3, ISBN13: 978-1-56676-160-4.
Audience: **l,u,f.**

Gangolli, S. (Editor)   **RA1193.D53 1999**
The Dictionary of Substances and Their Effects. Ed. 2. Trade
Cloth. Springer. New York, NY. 1999. 6526p.
ISBN:0-85404-803-0, ISBN13: 978-0-85404-803-8.
Dewey:615.9003. LCCN:2003-389391.
Audience: **u,f.**

Gregorich, E. G. et al.   **S592**
   (Editors)
Soil and Environmental Science Dictionary. CRC Press. 2001.
ISBN:0-8493-3115-3, ISBN13: 978-0-8493-3115-2.
Audience: **u,f.**

Hodgson, Ernest, et al.   **RA1193.D535 2000**
Dictionary of Toxicology. Ed. 2. Richard B. Mailman & Janice
E. Chambers (Authors). Trade Cloth. Nature Publishing Group.
New York, NY. 1998. 608p. ISBN:1-56159-216-1, ISBN13:
978-1-56159-216-6. Dewey:615.9003. LCCN:2002-319014.
Audience: **u,f.** *Choice, 1989.*

Lewis, Robert A. (Editor)   **RA1193.L48 1996**
Dictionary of Toxicology. Paper over Boards. Lewis Publishers.
Boca Raton, FL. 1998. 1136p. ISBN:1-56670-223-2, ISBN13:
978-1-56670-223-2. Dewey:615.9/003. LCCN:96-035759.
Audience: **u,f.** *Choice, 1998.*

Meyers, Robert A.   **TD173.E53 1999**
The Encyclopedia of Environmental Pollution and Cleanup, Set.
Diane Kender Dittrick (Editor). Trade Cloth. John Wiley &
Sons, Inc. Hoboken, NJ. 1999. 1936p. ISBN:0-471-31612-1,
ISBN13: 978-0-471-31612-1. Dewey:628.5. LCCN:99-017884.
Audience: **u,f.** *Choice, 1999.*

Environmental Chemistry > Handbooks and Desk References

☐ EPA Estimation Program Interface (EPI) Suite.
http://www.epa.gov/oppt/exposure/docs/episuite.htm
Audience: **u,f.**

                                                     RA1190
☐ Hazardous Substances Data Bank (HSDB).
http://www.nlm.nih.gov/pubs/factsheets/hsdbfs.html
Audience: **u,f.**

☐ HazMap: Occupational Exposure to Hazardous Materials.
http://hazmap.nlm.nih.gov/
Audience: **u,f.**

☐ Household Products Database.
http://www.nlm.nih.gov/news/press_releases/
householdprod03.html
Audience: **l,u,f.**

                                                     TD173
☐ National Park Service Environmental Contaminants
Encyclopedia.
http://www.nature.nps.gov/hazardssafety/toxic/index.cfm
Audience: **u,f.**

                                                     T55.3.H3
☐ Sax's Dangerous Properties of Industrial Materials.
http://www.knovel.com/knovel2/Toc.jsp?BookID=707
Ed. 10. Knovel Library.
Audience: **l,u,f.**

Clark, James   **TP155.2.E58**
Handbook of Green Chemistry and Technology. Macquarrie,
Duncan (Editors). Blackwell Science. 2002.
ISBN:0-632-05715-7, ISBN13: 978-0-632-05715-3.
Audience: **l,u,f.**

De Renzo, D. J. (Editor)   **TP247.5.S63 1986**
Solvents Safety Handbook. Trade Cloth. Noyes Data
Corporation/Noyes Publications. Park Ridge, NJ. 1986. 696p.
ISBN:0-8155-1074-8, ISBN13: 978-0-8155-1074-1.
Dewey:660.2/9482/0289. LCCN:86-005208.
Audience: **u,f.**

Hoffman, David J.   **RA1226.H36 2002**
Handbook of Ecotoxicology. Ed. 2. Paper over Boards. Lewis
Publishers. Boca Raton, FL. 2002. 1312p. ISBN:1-56670-546-0,
ISBN13: 978-1-56670-546-2. Dewey:615.9/02.
LCCN:2002-075228.
Audience: **u,f.** *Choice, 1995.*

Howard, Philip H.   **TD176.4.H69 1989**
Handbook of Environmental Fate and Exposure Data for
Organic Chemicals, Vol. 1. Paper over Boards. Lewis
Publishers. Boca Raton, FL. 1989. 600p. Handbook of
Environmental Fate and Exposure Data for Organic Chemicals
Ser., Vol. 1 ISBN:0-87371-151-3, ISBN13: 978-0-87371-151-7.
Dewey:363.7/38. LCCN:89-002436.
Audience: **u,f.**

Howard, Philip H.   **TD176.4.H69**
Handbook of Environmental Fate and Exposure Data for
Organic Chemicals: Solvents, Vol. 2. Paper over Boards. Lewis
Publishers. Boca Raton, FL. 1990. 576p. Handbook of
Environmental Fate and Exposure Data for Organic Chemicals
Ser., Vol. 2 ISBN:0-87371-204-8, ISBN13: 978-0-87371-204-0.
Dewey:363.7/38. LCCN:89-002436.
Audience: **u,f.**

Lewis, Richard J.   **T55.3.H3L49 2002**
Hazardous Chemicals Desk Reference. Ed. 5. Trade Cloth. John
Wiley & Sons, Inc. Hoboken, NJ. 2002. 1728p.
ISBN:0-471-44165-1, ISBN13: 978-0-471-44165-6.
Dewey:604.7. LCCN:2001-046947.
Audience: **u,f.** *Choice, 1993.*

Lewis, Richard J.   **T55.3.H3L494 2004**
Sax's Dangerous Properties of Industrial Materials. Ed. 11.
Trade Cloth. John Wiley & Sons, Inc. Hoboken, NJ. 2005.
4860p. ISBN:0-471-70133-5, ISBN13: 978-0-471-70133-0.
Dewey:604.7. LCCN:2005-273086.
Audience: **u,f.** *Choice, 2005, 2000, 1999, 1997.*

Lewis, Richard J., Sr.   **T55**
Sax's dangerous properties of industrial materials. Ed. 11.
Wiley-Interscience, 3 v.. 2004. ISBN:0-471-47662-5, ISBN13:
978-0-471-47662-7.

Audience: **u,f.**

O. S. H. A. Staff   **RA1229.3.C48 1995**
Chemical Information Manual. Ed. 3. Trade Paper. Government
Institutes. Blue Ridge Summit, PA. 1995. 341p.
ISBN:0-86587-469-7, ISBN13: 978-0-86587-469-5.
Dewey:615.9/02. LCCN:95-077857.

Audience: **u,f.**

Patnaik, Pradyot   **RA1211.P38 1999**
A Comprehensive Guide to the Hazardous Properties of
Chemical Substances. Ed. 2. Trade Cloth. John Wiley & Sons,
Inc. Hoboken, NJ. 1999. 1008p. ISBN:0-471-29175-7, ISBN13:
978-0-471-29175-6. Dewey:615.9. LCCN:98-039972.

Audience: **u,f.** *Choice, 2000, 1993.*

Urben, Peter (Revised by)   **T55.3.H3B73 1995**
Bretherick's Handbook of Reactive Chemical Hazards, Set. Ed.
5. Trade Cloth. Elsevier Science & Technology Books. Saint
Louis, MO. 1991. 2100p. ISBN:0-7506-1557-5, ISBN13:
978-0-7506-1557-0. Dewey:660/.2804. LCCN:95-199154.

Audience: **u,f.**

Urben, Peter   **TP149**
Bretherick's Handbook of Reactive Chemical Hazards. Ed. 6.
Trade Paper. Elsevier Science & Technology Books. Saint
Louis, MO. 2000. 2100p. ISBN:0-7506-4725-6, ISBN13:
978-0-7506-4725-0. Dewey:660/.2804.

Audience: **u,f.**

Verschueren, Karel   **TD196.O73V47 2001**
Handbook of Environmental Data on Organic Chemicals, Set.
Ed. 4. Trade Cloth. John Wiley & Sons, Inc. Hoboken, NJ.
2001. 2416p. ISBN:0-471-37490-3, ISBN13:
978-0-471-37490-9. Dewey:363.738. LCCN:00-069254.

Audience: **u,f.** *B Choice, 2002, 1999, 1997.*

Environmental Chemistry > Chemical Analysis of Environmental Samples

QD142 .A5
Standard Methods for the Examination of Water and Wastewater.
CD-ROM, Compact Disc. American Public Health Association
Publications. Washington, DC. 2004. ISBN:0-87553-239-X,
ISBN13: 978-0-87553-239-4. Dewey:543.3.

Audience: **l,u,f.**

QD142
Standard methods for the examination of water and
wastewater [computer file]. American Public Health Association;
American Water Works Association; Water Environment
Federation, 1999.

Audience: **u,f.**

Carter, M. R. (Editor)   **S593.S7425 1993**
Soil Sampling and Methods of Analysis. Paper over Boards.
Lewis Publishers. Boca Raton, FL. 1993. 864p.
ISBN:0-87371-861-5, ISBN13: 978-0-87371-861-5.
Dewey:631.40287. LCCN:92-038583.

Audience: **u,f.** *Choice, 1994.*

Stafford, Charles J., et al.   **SB951**
The U. S. EPA Manual of Chemical Methods for Pesticides and
Devices. Ed. 2. Everett S. Greer & Adrian W. Burns (Authors).
Ringbound. A O A C International. Gaithersburg, MD. 1992.
790p. ISBN:0-935584-47-1, ISBN13: 978-0-935584-47-9.
Dewey:668.65.

Audience: **u,f.**

Environmental Chemistry > Special Topics in Environmental Chemistry > Pesticides and Agrochemicals

Briggs, Shirley A.; Rachel   **RA1270**
  Carson Council Staff
Basic Guide to Pesticides: Their Characteristics and Hazards.
Hemisphere Pub. Corp.. 1992. ISBN:1-56032-253-5, ISBN13:
978-1-56032-253-5.

Audience: **l,u,f.**

Krieger, Robert (Editor)   **RA1270.P4H36 2001**
Principles and Agents, Set. Ed. 2. Trade Cloth. Elsevier Science
& Technology Books. Saint Louis, MO. 2001. 1908p.
ISBN:0-12-426260-0, ISBN13: 978-0-12-426260-7.
Dewey:615.9/51. LCCN:2001-089145.

Audience: **u,f.**

Milne, G. W. A. (Editor)   **SB951.A786 2000**
Ashgate Handbook of Pesticides and Agricultural Chemicals.
Trade Cloth. John Wiley & Sons, Inc. Hoboken, NJ. 2000. 226p.
ISBN:0-566-08388-4, ISBN13: 978-0-566-08388-4.
Dewey:631.8. LCCN:00-102728.

Audience: **u,f.** *Choice, 2001.*

Milne, G. W. A. (Editor)   **SB961**
CRC Handbook of Pesticides. CRC Press. 1995.
ISBN:0-8493-2447-5, ISBN13: 978-0-8493-2447-5.

Audience: **u,f.**

Montgomery, John H.   **TD196**
Agrochemicals Desk Reference. Ed. 2. CRC Press. 1997.
ISBN:1-56670-167-8, ISBN13: 978-1-56670-167-9.

Audience: **u,f.**

Environmental Chemistry > Special Topics in Environmental Chemistry > Air Pollution and Atmospheric Chemistry

Berner, Elizabeth K. &   **QC880.4.A8B47 1996**
  Berner, Robert A.
Global Environment: Water, Air, and Geochemical Cycles. Trade
Paper. Prentice Hall PTR. Upper Saddle River, NJ. 1995. 376p.
ISBN:0-13-301169-0, ISBN13: 978-0-13-301169-2.
Dewey:551.5. LCCN:95-025174.

Audience: **l,u,f.** *Choice, 1996.*

Blewett, Stephen E.   **TD883.B59 1998**
What's in the Air: Natural and Man-Made Air Pollution. Trade
Cloth. Ozone Research Group, Inc. Altadena, CA. 1998. 140p.
ISBN:0-9640565-2-6, ISBN13: 978-0-9640565-2-7.
Dewey:363.739/2. LCCN:98-070936.

Audience: **l,u,f.** *Choice, 1999.*

Butler, J. D. **TD890**
Air Pollution Chemistry. Trade Cloth. Elsevier Science & Technology Books. Saint Louis, MO. 1979. viii, 408p. ISBN:0-12-147950-1, ISBN13: 978-0-12-147950-3. Dewey:628.5/3/2. LCCN:78-018677.

Audience: **u,f.**

Miller, E. Willard & Miller, **TD883.M52 1998**
Ruby M.
Indoor Pollution: A Reference Handbook. Library Binding. ABC-CLIO, Inc. Santa Barbara, CA. 1998. 330p. Contemporary World Issues Ser. ISBN:0-87436-895-2, ISBN13: 978-0-87436-895-6. Dewey:363.739/2. LCCN:98-025606.

Audience: **l,u,f.** *Choice, 1999.*

Seinfeld, John H. & Pandis, **QC879.6.S45 1998**
Spyros N.
Atmospheric Chemistry and Physics: From Air Pollution to Climate Change. Trade Cloth. John Wiley & Sons, Inc. Hoboken, NJ. 1997. 1360p. ISBN:0-471-17815-2, ISBN13: 978-0-471-17815-6. Dewey:551.5/11. LCCN:97-007638.

Audience: **u,f.** *Choice, 1998.*

Environmental Chemistry > Special Topics in Environmental Chemistry > Soil and Water Chemistry

Ball, Philip **GB661.2.B35 2000**
Life's Matrix: A Biography of Water. Trade Cloth. Farrar, Straus & Giroux. New York, NY. 2000. xii, 417p. ISBN:0-374-18628-6, ISBN13: 978-0-374-18628-9. Dewey:553.7. LCCN:99-059110.

Audience: **l,u,f.** *Choice, 2000.*

Evangelou, V. P. **TD878.E93 1998**
Environmental Soil and Water Chemistry: Principles and Applications. Trade Cloth. John Wiley & Sons, Inc. Hoboken, NJ. 1998. 592p. ISBN:0-471-16515-8, ISBN13: 978-0-471-16515-6. Dewey:628.5. LCCN:98-013433.

Audience: **u,f.** *Choice, 1999.*

Franks, F. **QD169.W3 F72 2000**
Water: A Matrix of Life. Ed. 2. Trade Paper. Springer. New York, NY. 2000. xii + 226p. ISBN:0-85404-583-X, ISBN13: 978-0-85404-583-9. Dewey:553.7. LCCN:2003-389066.

Audience: **l,u,f.** *Choice, 2001.*

Montgomery, John H. **TD426.M66 2000**
Groundwater Chemicals Desk Reference. Ed. 3. Paper over Boards. Lewis Publishers. Boca Raton, FL. 2000. 1384p. ISBN:1-56670-498-7, ISBN13: 978-1-56670-498-4. Dewey:628.1/61. LCCN:00-037077.

Audience: **u,f.** *Choice, 2000, 1992.*

Pankow, James F. **GB855**
Aquatic Chemistry Concepts. Lewis Publishers. 1991. ISBN:0-87371-150-5, ISBN13: 978-0-87371-150-0.

Audience: **u,f.**

Stumm, Werner **GB855.S79 1992**
Chemistry of the Solid-Water Interface: Processes at the Mineral-Water and Particle-Water Interface in Natural Systems. Ed. 1. Trade Paper. John Wiley & Sons, Inc. Hoboken, NJ. 1992. 448p. ISBN:0-471-57672-7, ISBN13: 978-0-471-57672-3. Dewey:551.46. LCCN:92-009701.

Audience: **u,f.** *Choice, 1993.*

Stumm, Werner & Morgan, **GB855.S78 1995**
James J.
Aquatic Chemistry: Chemical Equilibria and Rates in Natural Waters. Ed. 3. Trade Cloth. John Wiley & Sons, Inc. Hoboken, NJ. 1995. 1040p. ISBN:0-471-51184-6, ISBN13: 978-0-471-51184-7. Dewey:359.9. LCCN:94-048319.

Audience: **u,f.** *Choice, 1996.*

Van der Leeden, Frits **TD351.V36 1990**
(Editor), et al.
The Water Encyclopedia. Ed. 2. Fred L. Troise & David K. Todd (Editors). Paper over Boards. Lewis Publishers. Boca Raton, FL. 1990. 824p. Geraghty and Miller Environmental Science and Engineering Ser. ISBN:0-87371-120-3, ISBN13: 978-0-87371-120-3. Dewey:553.7/021. LCCN:89-014011.

Audience: **l,u,f.** *Choice, 1990.*

Environmental Chemistry > Special Topics in Environmental Chemistry > Metals

Katz, Sidney A. & Salem, **RA1231.C5K38 1994**
Harry
The Biological and Environmental Chemistry of Chromium. Trade Paper. John Wiley & Sons, Inc. Hoboken, NJ. 1994. 214p. ISBN:1-56081-629-5, ISBN13: 978-1-56081-629-4. Dewey:574.19/214. LCCN:94-005417.

Audience: **u,f.** *Choice, 1995.*

Environmental Chemistry > Special Topics in Environmental Chemistry > Hazardous Materials Handling

Blackman, William C. Jr. **TD1040.B53 2001**
Basic Hazardous Waste Management. Ed. 3. Paper over Boards. Lewis Publishers. Boca Raton, FL. 2001. 488p. ISBN:1-56670-533-9, ISBN13: 978-1-56670-533-2. Dewey:363.72/87. LCCN:2001-020391.

Audience: **u,f.**

Burgess, William A. **RC967.B83 1995**
Recognition of Health Hazards in Industry: A Review of Materials Processes. Ed. 2. Trade Cloth. John Wiley & Sons, Inc. Hoboken, NJ. 1995. 560p. ISBN:0-471-57716-2, ISBN13: 978-0-471-57716-4. Dewey:363.11. LCCN:94-018498.

Audience: **u,f.** *Choice, 1995.*

Burke, Robert **T55**
Hazardous Materials Chemistry for Emergency Responders. CRC Press. 1997. ISBN:1-56670-174-0, ISBN13: 978-1-56670-174-7.

Audience: **l,u,f.**

Lewis, Richard J. **T55.3.H3R37 2000**
Rapid Guide to Hazardous Chemicals in the Workplace. Ed. 4. Trade Paper. John Wiley & Sons, Inc. Hoboken, NJ. 2000. 261p. ISBN:0-471-35542-9, ISBN13: 978-0-471-35542-7. Dewey:604.7/03. LCCN:99-086808.

Audience: **l,u,f.**

Lunn, George & Sansone, **TD1050.S24L86 1994**
Eric B.
Destruction of Hazardous Chemicals in the Laboratory. Ed. 2.

Trade Cloth. John Wiley & Sons, Inc. Hoboken, NJ. 1994. 520p. ISBN:0-471-57399-X, ISBN13: 978-0-471-57399-9. Dewey:604.7. LCCN:93-035634.

Audience: **u,f.** *Choice, 1990.*

Manahan, Stanley E.   **TD1030.M37 1990**
Hazardous Waste Chemistry: Toxicology and Treatment. Paper over Boards. Lewis Publishers. Boca Raton, FL. 1990. 392p. ISBN:0-87371-209-9, ISBN13: 978-0-87371-209-5. Dewey:628.4/2. LCCN:90-033889.

Audience: **u,f.** *Choice, 1991.*

Wentz, Charles A.   **TD1030.W46 1995**
Hazardous Waste Management. Ed. 2. Trade Cloth. McGraw-Hill Higher Education. Burr Ridge, IL. 1995. 560p. Engineering Ser. ISBN:0-07-069308-0, ISBN13: 978-0-07-069308-1. Dewey:363.7/28. LCCN:94-003996.

Audience: **u,f.** *Choice, 1989.*

World Health Organization   **QD63.5.C47 1992**
  Staff & International Union of Pure and Applied
  Chemistry Staff
Chemical Safety Matters: Safe Use and Disposal of Chemicals in Laboratories. Trade Cloth. Cambridge University Press. New York, NY. 1992. 304p. ISBN:0-521-41375-3, ISBN13: 978-0-521-41375-6. Dewey:542/.028/9. LCCN:91-028312.

Audience: **u,f.**

Environmental Chemistry > Special Topics in Environmental Chemistry > Toxicology

                    RA1229
Patty's Toxicology (vol. 1-8).
http://www.knovel.com/knovel2/Toc.jsp?BookID=706
Ed. 5. Knovel Library.

Audience: **u,f.**

                    RA1190
TOXNET.
http://tox.nlm.nih.gov/

Audience: **u,f.**

Clayton, George D. &   **RC967.P37 1991**
  Clayton, Florence E. (Editors)
Patty's Industrial Hygiene and Toxicology: General Principles, Vol. 1, Pt. A. Ed. 4. Trade Cloth. John Wiley & Sons, Inc. Hoboken, NJ. 1991. 1104p. Patty's Industrial Hygiene and Toxicology Ser., Vol. A ISBN:0-471-50197-2, ISBN13: 978-0-471-50197-8. Dewey:613.6/2. LCCN:90-013080.

Audience: **u,f.**

Clayton, George D. &   **RC967.P37 1991**
  Clayton, Florence E. (Editors)
Patty's Industrial Hygiene and Toxicology: General Principles, Vol. 1, Pt. B, General Principles. Ed. 4. Trade Cloth. John Wiley & Sons, Inc. Hoboken, NJ. 1991. 1120p. Patty's Industrial Hygiene and Toxicology Ser., Vol. B ISBN:0-471-50196-4, ISBN13: 978-0-471-50196-1. Dewey:613.6/2. LCCN:90-013080.

Audience: **u,f.**

Crosby, Donald G.   **RA1226.C76 1998**
Environmental Toxicology and Chemistry. Cloth Text. Oxford University Press, Inc. New York, NY. 1998. 352p. Topics in

Environmental Chemistry Ser. ISBN:0-19-511713-1, ISBN13: 978-0-19-511713-4. Dewey:615.9/02. LCCN:97-022438.

Audience: **u,f.** *Choice, 1998.*

Fenton, John Joseph   **RA1219**
Toxicology: A Case-Oriented Approach. CRC Press. 2002. ISBN:0-8493-0371-0, ISBN13: 978-0-8493-0371-5.

Audience: **u,f.**

Harris, Robert L. (Editor)   **RC967.P37**
Patty's Industrial Hygiene, Vol. 4. Ed. 5. Trade Cloth. John Wiley & Sons, Inc. Hoboken, NJ. 2000. 3552p. ISBN:0-471-29784-4, ISBN13: 978-0-471-29784-0. Dewey:613.6/2. LCCN:99-032462.

Audience: **u,f.** *Choice, 2002.*

Harris, Robert L. (Editor)   **RC967.P37 2000**
Patty's Industrial Hygiene, I: Introduction to Industrial Hygiene, II: Recognition and Evaluation of Chemical Agents. Ed. 5. Trade Cloth. John Wiley & Sons, Inc. Hoboken, NJ. 2000. 756p. ISBN:0-471-29756-9, ISBN13: 978-0-471-29756-7. Dewey:613.6/2. LCCN:99-032462.

Audience: **u,f.**

Harris, Robert L. (Editor)   **RC967.P37**
Patty's Industrial Hygiene, III: Physical Agents IV: Biohazards V: Engineering Control and Personal Protection. Ed. 5. Trade Cloth. John Wiley & Sons, Inc. Hoboken, NJ. 2000. 864p. Patty's Industrial Hygiene and Toxicology Ser., Vol. 2 ISBN:0-471-29754-2, ISBN13: 978-0-471-29754-3. Dewey:613.6/2. LCCN:99-032462.

Audience: **u,f.**

Harris, Robert L. (Editor)   **RC967.P37**
Patty's Industrial Hygiene, VI: Law, Regulation, and Management. Ed. 5. Trade Cloth. John Wiley & Sons, Inc. Hoboken, NJ. 2000. 792p. Patty's Industrial Hygiene and Toxicology Ser., Vol. 3 ISBN:0-471-29753-4, ISBN13: 978-0-471-29753-6. Dewey:613.6/2. LCCN:99-032462.

Audience: **u,f.**

Himonas, Alex   **RC967.P37**
Patty's Industrial Hygiene VII: Specialty Areas and Allied Professions. Ed. 5. Robert L. Harris (Editor). Trade Cloth. John Wiley & Sons, Inc. Hoboken, NJ. 2000. 1067p. Patty's Industrial Hygiene and Toxicology Ser., Vol. 4 ISBN:0-471-29749-6, ISBN13: 978-0-471-29749-9. Dewey:613.6/2. LCCN:99-032462.

Audience: **u,f.**

Manahan, Stanley E.   **RA1219.3.M36 2002**
Toxicological Chemistry and Biochemistry. Ed. 3. Paper over Boards. Lewis Publishers. Boca Raton, FL. 2002. 448p. ISBN:1-56670-618-1, ISBN13: 978-1-56670-618-6. Dewey:815.9/001/54. LCCN:2002-072486.

Audience: **u,f.**

Ottoboni, M. Alice   **RA 1213 .O88 1997**
The Dose Makes the Poison: A Plain-Language Guide to Toxicology. Ed. 2. Trade Paper. John Wiley & Sons, Inc. Hoboken, NJ. 1997. 256p. ISBN:0-471-28837-3, ISBN13: 978-0-471-28837-4. Dewey:615.9.

Audience: **g,l,u,f.**

Sipes, I. G. (Editor), et al.   **RA1199.C648 1997**
Comprehensive Toxicology. C. A. McQueen & A. J. Gandolfi (Editors). Trade Cloth. Elsevier Science & Technology Books.

Formats: Web: ☐ Ebook: **e** CD/DVD-ROM: ✿ BCL3: *B*

Saint Louis, MO. 1997. 7482p. ISBN:0-08-042301-9, ISBN13: 978-0-08-042301-2. Dewey:615.9. LCCN:96-033052.

Audience: **u,f.** *Choice, 1997.*

Sittig, Marshall   **RA1215.S58 2002**
Handbook of Toxic and Hazardous Chemicals and Carcinogens. Ed. 4. Richard P. Pohanish (Editor). Trade Cloth. Noyes Data Corporation/Noyes Publications. Park Ridge, NJ. 2002. 2300p. ISBN:0-8155-1459-X, ISBN13: 978-0-8155-1459-6. Dewey:615.9/02. LCCN:2001-056289.

Audience: **u,f.** *Choice, 2003, 2002.*

Sterner, Olov   **RA1226 .S74 1999**
Chemistry, Health and Environment. Trade Paper. John Wiley & Sons, Inc. Hoboken, NJ. 1999. 360p. ISBN:3-527-30087-2, ISBN13: 978-3-527-30087-7. Dewey:615.902.

Audience: **u,f.** *Choice, 2000.*

Thornton, Joe   **RA1242.C436T48 2000**
Pandora's Poison: Chlorine, Health, and a New Environmental Strategy. Trade Cloth. MIT Press. Cambridge, MA. 2000. 611p. ISBN:0-262-20124-0, ISBN13: 978-0-262-20124-7. Dewey:615.9/51. LCCN:99-057011.

Audience: **u,f.** *Choice, 2000.*

Environmental Chemistry > Special Topics in Environmental Chemistry > Regulatory and Legislative Concerns

     RA1229 .N55
NIOSH Pocket Guide to Chemical Hazards. Perfect. United States Government Printing Office. Washington, DC. 2003. 463p. ISBN:0-16-051257-3, ISBN13: 978-0-16-051257-5. Dewey:615.9/02.

Audience: **l,u,f.**

     KF3945
☐ NIOSH Pocket Guide to Chemical Hazards.
http://www.cdc.gov/niosh/npg/
National Institute for Occupational Safety and Health (NIOSH).

Audience: **u,f.**

Sweet, Doris V. (Editor)   **RA1215 .N37A**
Registry of Toxic Effects of Chemical Substances, 1985-1986 Edition: Addendum and User's Guide. Trade Paper. United States Government Printing Office. Washington, DC. 1987. ISBN:0-16-009168-3, ISBN13: 978-0-16-009168-1. Dewey:615.9/02/0212.

Audience: **u,f.**

Sweet, Doris V. (Editor)   **RA1196**
Registry of Toxic Effects of Chemical Substances, RTECS: A Comprehensive Guide. Paper Text. DIANE Publishing Company. Collingdale, PA. 1994. 70p. ISBN:0-7881-0565-5, ISBN13: 978-0-7881-0565-4. Dewey:615.9.

Audience: **u,f.**

Utterback, Paul J. &   **QD63.5.E38 1998**
  Nelson, David A. (Editors)
Educating for OSHA Savvy Chemists. Cloth Text. Oxford University Press, Inc. New York, NY. 1998. 206p. ACS Symposium Ser., No. 700 ISBN:0-8412-3569-4, ISBN13: 978-0-8412-3569-4. Dewey:542/.1/0289. LCCN:98-016896.

Audience: **u,f.** *Choice, 1999.*

Environmental Chemistry > Special Topics in Environmental Chemistry > Environmental Chemistry Databases

     TD193
☐ Chemical Information System.
http://www.nisc.com/cis/
National Information Services Corporation (NISC).

Audience: **u,f.**

     TD171
☐ Envirofacts Data Warehouse.
http://www.epa.gov/enviro/html/ef_overview.html

Audience: **u,f.**

     Z7890x
✱ TOXLINE on SilverPlatter. Boston: SilverPlatter Information, Inc., 1989- . quarterly; cumulative discs..

Audience: **u,f.**

Environmental Chemistry > Educational Materials

☐ Greener Education Materials.
http://greenchem.uoregon.edu/gems.html

Audience: **l,u,f.**

Industrial Chemistry > Handbooks and Encyclopedias

     TP151
☐ Perry's Chemical Engineers' Handbook.
http://www.knovel.com/knovel2/Toc.jsp?BookID=48
Ed. 7. Knovel Library.

Audience: **u,f.**

Ali, M. & El, Ali Bassam   **TP151.A57 2005**
Handbook of Industrial Chemistry. Trade Cloth. McGraw-Hill Professional Publishing. New York, NY. 2004. 628p. McGraw-Hill Handbooks ISBN:0-07-141037-6, ISBN13: 978-0-07-141037-3. Dewey:661/.8. LCCN:2004-063172.

Audience: **u,f.** *Choice, 2005.*

Austin, G. T.   **TP155**
Shreve's Chemical Process Industries. Ed. 5. Cloth Text. McGraw-Hill Companies, The. New York, NY. 1984. xiii, 859p. ISBN:0-07-057147-3, ISBN13: 978-0-07-057147-1. Dewey:660. LCCN:83-013629.

Audience: **u,f.**

Bohnet, Matthias, et. al.   **TP9**
  (Editors)
Ullmann's Encyclopedia of Industrial Chemistry. Ed. 6. Wiley-VCH. 2003. ISBN:3-527-30385-5, ISBN13: 978-3-527-30385-4.

Audience: **u,f.**

Lide, David R.   **QD64**
Basic Laboratory and Industrial Chemicals: A CRC Quick
Reference Handbook. CRC Press. 1993. ISBN:0-8493-4498-0,
ISBN13: 978-0-8493-4498-5.

Audience: **u,f.**

Perry, Robert H. & Green,   **TP151.P45 1997**
  Donald W.
Perry's Chemical Engineers' Handbook. Ed. 7. Trade Cloth.
McGraw-Hill Professional Publishing. New York, NY. 1997.
2640p. Handbook Ser. ISBN:0-07-049841-5, ISBN13:
978-0-07-049841-9. Dewey:660. LCCN:96-051648.

Audience: **u,f.** *B* *Choice, 1998.*

Riegel, Emil Raymond   **TP145**
Riegel's handbook of industrial chemistry. Ed. 10. James A.
Kent, ed.. NY: Kluwer Academic/Plenum Publishers. 2003.
ISBN:0-306-47411-5, ISBN13: 978-0-306-47411-8.

Audience: **u,f.**

Riegel, Emil Raymond   **TP145**
☐ Riegel's Handbook of Industrial Chemistry.
http://ebooks.springerlink.com/Details.aspx
Ed. 10. Kent, James A. (Editor). SpringerLink ebook.
ISBN:0-306-48541-9, ISBN13: 978-0-306-48541-1.

Audience: **u,f.**

Riegel, Emil Raymond   **TP145.R53 2003**
Riegel's Handbook of Industrial Chemistry. Ed. 10. James
Albert Kent (Editor). Trade Cloth. Springer. New York, NY.
2003. 1374p. ISBN:0-306-47411-5, ISBN13:
978-0-306-47411-8. Dewey:660. LCCN:2002-040615.

Audience: **u,f.** *Choice, 2004.*

Shackelford, James M.   **TA403**
CRC Materials Science and Engineering Handbook. Ed. 3.
Alexander, William (Editors). CRC Press. 2001.
ISBN:0-8493-2696-6, ISBN13: 978-0-8493-2696-7.

Audience: **u,f.**

Ullmann, Fritz   **TP9**
☐ Ullmann's Encyclopedia of Industrial Chemistry.
http://www3.interscience.wiley.com/cgi-bin/mrwhome/
104554801/HOME?CRETRY=1&SRETRY=0
Ed. 6. Wiley-VCH.

Audience: **u,f.**

Ullmann, Fritz   **TP9.U57 1985**
Ullmann's Encyclopedia of Industrial Chemistry: A1-A28,
B1-B8. Ed. 5. Wolfgang Gerhartz, Y. Stephen Yamamoto, F.
Thomas Campbell, Rudolf Pfefferkorn & James F. Rounsaville
(Editors). Trade Paper. John Wiley & Sons, Inc. Hoboken, NJ.
1996. v. A1-A7, A9-p. ISBN:0-89573-151-7, ISBN13:
978-0-89573-151-7. Dewey:660/.03/21. LCCN:84-025829.

Audience: **u,f.**

Yaws, Carl   **TP761.C65B7 2001**
Matheson Gas Data Book. Ed. 7. Trade Cloth. McGraw-Hill
Professional Publishing. New York, NY. 2001. 982p. Chemical
Engineering Ser. ISBN:0-07-135854-4, ISBN13:
978-0-07-135854-5. Dewey:665.7/0212. LCCN:2001-030867.

Audience: **u,f.**

Industrial Chemistry > Dictionaries and Thesauri

Ash, Irene (Editor)   **Z695.1.C5.I52 1992**
Industrial Chemical Thesaurus: Chemical to Tradename
Reference and Tradename to Chemical Cross Reference and
Manufacturers Directory. Ed. 2. Michael Ash (Compiled by).
Trade Cloth. John Wiley & Sons, Inc. Hoboken, NJ. 1992.
1312p. ISBN:1-56081-615-5, ISBN13: 978-1-56081-615-7.
Dewey:025.4/954. LCCN:92-022095.

Audience: **u,f.** *Choice, 1993.*

Ashford, Robert D.   **TP200.A79 2001**
Ashford's Dictionary of Industrial Chemicals. Trade Cloth. Bow
Historical Books. New Providence, NJ. 2001. viii, 1269p.
ISBN:0-9522674-2-X, ISBN13: 978-0-9522674-2-3.
Dewey:660/.03. LCCN:2003-428034.

Audience: **u,f.**

Noether, D. & Noeter,   **TP9.N64 1993**
  Herman
Encyclopedic Dictionary of Chemical Technology. Trade Paper.
John Wiley & Sons, Inc. Hoboken, NJ. 1993. 297p.
ISBN:0-89573-329-3, ISBN13: 978-0-89573-329-0.
Dewey:660/.03. LCCN:93-105705.

Audience: **u,f.** *Choice, 1994.*

Technische Universitat   **QD5**
  Dresden, Zentrum für Angewandte Sprachwissenschaft
Fachwörterbuch, Chemie und Chemische Technik:
Deutsch-Englisch, mit etwa 62 000 Wortstellen=Technical
Dictionary of Chemistry and Chemical Technology; German
English: with About : 62,000 Entries. Ed. 4. A. Hatier. 1992.
ISBN:3-86117-035-3, ISBN13: 978-3-86117-035-8.

Audience: **u,f.**

Industrial Chemistry > History and Development of Chemical Industry

Brandt, E. N.   **HD9651.9.D6B73 1997**
Growth Company: Dow Chemical's First Century. Trade Paper.
Michigan State University Press. East Lansing, MI. 1997. 649p.
ISBN:0-87013-426-4, ISBN13: 978-0-87013-426-5.
Dewey:338.7/66/00973. LCCN:97-000749.

Audience: **u,f.** *Choice, 1998.*

Cain, Gordon   **HD9651.95.C34**
Everybody Wins!: A Life in Free Enterprise. Ed. 2. Chemical
Heritage Press. 2001. ISBN:0-941901-28-9, ISBN13:
978-0-941901-28-4.

Audience: **u,f.**

Campbell, W. A.   **HD9652.5 .M55 1991**
Milestones in 150 Years of the Chemical Industry, No. 96. H. L.
Roberts (Editor). Trade Cloth. Royal Society of Chemistry, The.
Cambridge, 1991. 318p. Special Publications
ISBN:0-85186-456-2, ISBN13: 978-0-85186-456-3.
Dewey:338.4766009. LCCN:92-115112.

Audience: **u,f.**

Hermes, Matthew E.   **QD22.C35H47 1996**
  (Editor)
Enough for One Lifetime: Wallace Carothers, Inventor of Nylon.
Trade Cloth. American Chemical Society. Washington, DC.

1996. 345p. History of Modern Chemical Sciences Ser. ISBN:0-8412-3331-4, ISBN13: 978-0-8412-3331-7. Dewey:677.4/73/092. LCCN:96-005560.

Audience: **u,f.** *Choice, 1996.*

Multhauf, Robert P.   **Z7914.C4**
The History of Chemical Technology: An Annotated Bibliography. Library Binding. Garland Publishing, Inc. New York, NY. 1983. 299p. Bibliographies of the History of Science and Technology Ser., Vol. 5 ISBN:0-8240-9255-4, ISBN13: 978-0-8240-9255-9. Dewey:016.66/009. LCCN:82-048272.

Audience: **u,f.** *B*

Smiley, Robert A.; Jackson,   **TP145**
  Harold L.
Chemistry and the Chemical Industry: A Practical Guide for Non-Chemists. CRC Press. 2002. ISBN:1-58716-054-4, ISBN13: 978-1-58716-054-7.

Audience: **l,u,f.**

Industrial Chemistry > Product Sources

☐ BuyersGuideChem.
http://www.buyersguidechem.de/

Audience: **u,f.**

☐ CE (Chemical Engineering) Buyer's Guide.
http://www.che.com/buyersguide/index.php

Audience: **u,f.**

☐ ChemACX Pro.
http://chemacx.cambridgesoft.com/chemacx/index.asp

Audience: **u,f.**

☐ ChemCats (STN or SciFinder/SciFinder Scholar).
http://www.cas.org/CASFILES/chemcats.html

Audience: **u,f.**

TP155
☐ Chemcyclopedia.
http://www.mediabrains.com/client/chemcyclop/BG1/search.asp

Audience: **u,f.**

☐ ChemExper.com.
http://www.chemexper.com/

Audience: **u,f.**

☐ Chemical Week buyer's guide.
http://www.chemweekbuyersguide/com/public/

Audience: **u,f.**

QD33.L8725
☐ ChemIndustry.com.
http://www.chemindustry.com
ChemIndustry.com, Inc..

Audience: **l,u,f.**

Ash, Michael & Ash, Irene   **TP12.A69 2000**
  (Compiled by)
Chemical Manufacturers Directory of Trade Name Products. Ed.

2. Trade Cloth. Synapse Information Resources, Inc. Endicott, NY. 2000. 1130p. ISBN:1-890595-23-3, ISBN13: 978-1-890595-23-4. Dewey:660/.029. LCCN:99-096850.

Audience: **u,f.**

Ash, Michael & Ash, Irene   **TP200.A78 2001**
  (Compiled by)
Specialty Chemicals Source Book, Vol. 2. Ed. 2. Kivar (or like). Synapse Information Resources, Inc. Endicott, NY. 2000. 2156p. Synapse Chemical Library ISBN:1-890595-32-2, ISBN13: 978-1-890595-32-6. Dewey:660. LCCN:00-192312.

Audience: **u,f.** *Choice, 1998.*

Industrial Chemistry > Economic and Financial Information > Monographic Sources

Dun and Bradstreet   **HF5035.D78**
  Information Services Staff
Dun and Bradstreet/Gale Industry Reference Handbooks. Linda D. Hall (Contribution by). Trade Cloth. Thomson Gale. Farmington Hills, MI. 1998. 600p. Dun and Bradstreet/Gale Industry Reference Handbooks Ser. ISBN:0-7876-3004-7, ISBN13: 978-0-7876-3004-1. Dewey:338.761.

Audience: **u,f.** *Choice, 1999.*

Dun and Bradstreet   **HG4907.D86 1998**
  Information Services Staff
Industry Reference Handbooks, Set. Linda D. Hall (Contribution by). Trade Cloth. Thomson Gale. Farmington Hills, MI. 1998. 3600p. ISBN:0-7876-3040-3, ISBN13: 978-0-7876-3040-9. Dewey:338.7/4/0973. LCCN:00-500443.

Audience: **u,f.**

Dun and Bradstreet Staff &   **HG4907**
  Thomson Gale Staff
D and B/Gale Industry Reference Handbook: Health and Medical Services. Trade Cloth. Thomson Gale. Farmington Hills, MI. 1998. 600p. ISBN:0-7876-3003-9, ISBN13: 978-0-7876-3003-4. Dewey:338.7/4/0973.

Audience: **u,f.** *Choice, 1999.*

Dun and Bradstreet Staff &   **HE7775**
  Thomson Gale Staff
D and B/Gale Industry Reference Handbook: Telecommunications. Trade Cloth. Thomson Gale. Farmington Hills, MI. 1998. 600p. ISBN:0-7876-3005-5, ISBN13: 978-0-7876-3005-8. Dewey:384.02573.

Audience: **u,f.** *Choice, 1999.*

Dun and Bradstreet Staff &   **HD9696.23.U6**
  Thomson Gale Staff
D and B/Gale Industry Reference Handbook: Electronics and Software. Trade Cloth. Thomson Gale. Farmington Hills, MI. 1998. 600p. ISBN:0-7876-3002-0, ISBN13: 978-0-7876-3002-7. Dewey:338.47004.

Audience: **u,f.**

Dun and Bradstreet Staff &   **HD9651.5**
  Thomson Gale Staff
Industry Reference Handbooks. Ed. 1. Trade Cloth. Thomson Gale. Farmington Hills, MI. 1999. 600p. ISBN:0-7876-3839-0, ISBN13: 978-0-7876-3839-9. Dewey:338.4766.

Audience: **u,f.** *Choice, 1999.*

Eveleth, William T. (Editor)   **HD9651**
Kline Guide to the U.S. Chemical Industry. Kline. 1990.

Audience: **u,f.**

Industrial Chemistry > Standards and Specifications

American Society for   **TA401**
  Testing and Materials
Annual Book of ASTM Standards, Annual Compilation; 71 vols. in 16 sections. ASTM.

Audience: **u,f.**

Industrial Chemistry > Treatises and Comprehensive Works

Backhurst, J. R. & Harker,   **TP155.C69 1996**
  J. H.
Chemical Engineering: Solutions to the Problems in Chemical Engineering. Ed. 2. Trade Paper. Elsevier Science & Technology Books. Saint Louis, MO. 1997. 264p. ISBN:0-7506-2612-7, ISBN13: 978-0-7506-2612-5. Dewey:660.2. LCCN:95-023187.

Audience: **u,f.**

Cahn, Robert W. (Editor), et   **TA403.M347 1991**
  al.
Materials Science and Technology: A Comprehensive Treatment, Set. Peter Haasen & E. J. Kramer (Editors). Trade Cloth. John Wiley & Sons, Inc. Hoboken, NJ. 1996. 999p. Materials Science and Technology Ser., :A Comprehensive Treatment Ser. ISBN:3-527-26813-8, ISBN13: 978-3-527-26813-9. Dewey:620.1/1. LCCN:90-021936.

Audience: **u,f.**

Cahn, Robert W.   **TA403 .M347 1991**
Processing of Polymers. Han E. H. Meijer (Editor). Trade Cloth. John Wiley & Sons, Inc. Hoboken, NJ. 1997. 906p. Materials Science and Technology Ser., Vol. 18:A Comprehensive Treatment Ser. ISBN:3-527-26831-6, ISBN13: 978-3-527-26831-3. Dewey:620.11. LCCN:90-021936.

Audience: **u,f.**

Cahn, Robert W.   **TA403**
Materials Science and Technology, Synthesis of Polymers. A. Dieter Schluter (Editor). Trade Cloth. John Wiley & Sons, Inc. Hoboken, NJ. 1999. 686p. Materials Science and Technology Ser., :A Comprehensive Treatment Ser. ISBN:3-527-29449-X, ISBN13: 978-3-527-29449-7. Dewey:547.7/045/9. LCCN:99-186707.

Audience: **u,f.** *Choice, 1999.*

Chen, Gang   **TJ265**
Nanoscale energy transport and conversion: a parallel treatment of electrons, molecules, phonons, and photons. Oxford. 2005. ISBN:0-19-515942-X, ISBN13: 978-0-19-515942-4.

Audience: **u,f.**

Coulson, J. M., et al.   **TP155.C69 1996**
Chemical Engineering: Fluid Flow, Heat Transfer and Mass Transfer. Ed. 5. J. F. Richardson, J. R. Backhurst & J. H. Harker (Authors). Trade Paper. Elsevier Science & Technology Books. Saint Louis, MO. 1996. 732p. Chemical Engineering Ser., Vol. 1 ISBN:0-7506-2557-0, ISBN13: 978-0-7506-2557-9. Dewey:660. LCCN:95-023187.

Audience: **u,f.**

Coulson, J. & Richardson, J   **TP155.C69 1996**
Chemical Engineering: Design. Ed. 2. Trade Paper. Elsevier Science & Technology Books. Saint Louis, MO. 1996. 976p. Chemical Engineering Ser., Vol. 6 ISBN:0-7506-2558-9, ISBN13: 978-0-7506-2558-6. Dewey:660.2/812. LCCN:95-023187.

Audience: **u,f.**

Theodore, Louis; Kunz,   **T174**
  Robert G.
Nanotechnology: Environmental Implications and Solutions. Wiley-Interscience. 2005. ISBN:0-471-69976-4, ISBN13: 978-0-471-69976-7.

Audience: **u,f.**

Wittcoff, Harold A. &   **TP247.W59 1996**
  Reuben, Bryan G.
Industrial Organic Chemicals. Ed. 1. Trade Cloth. John Wiley & Sons, Inc. Hoboken, NJ. 1996. 560p. ISBN:0-471-54036-6, ISBN13: 978-0-471-54036-6. Dewey:661.8. LCCN:95-035580.

Audience: **u,f.** *Choice, 1996.*

Industrial Chemistry > Special Topics in Industrial Chemistry > Chemical Technology > Handbooks and Data Compilations

Archer, Wesley L.   **TP247.5**
☐ Industrial Solvents Handbook.
http://www.netlibrary.com
NetLibrary.

Audience: **u,f.**

Ash, Michael & Ash, Irene   **TP994.A85 1997**
Handbook of Industrial Surfactants: An International Guide to More Than 21,000 Products by Trade Name, Composition, Function and Manufacturer. Ed. 2. Trade Cloth. Ashgate Publishing, Ltd. Aldershot, 1997. 2440p. ISBN:0-566-07892-9, ISBN13: 978-0-566-07892-7. Dewey:668/.1/0294. LCCN:96-029925.

Audience: **u,f.**

Flick, E. W.   **TP247.5**
☐ Industrial Solvents Handbook.
http://www.knovel.com/knovel2/Toc.jsp?BookID=363
Ed. 5. Knovel Library.

Audience: **u,f.**

Howard, Philip H.   **QD257**
Handbook of Physical Properties of Organic Chemicals. Meylan, William M. (Editors). Lewis Publishers. 1997. ISBN:1-56670-227-5, ISBN13: 978-1-56670-227-0.

Audience: **u,f.**

Industrial Chemistry > Special Topics in Industrial Chemistry > Chemical Technology > Treatises

Interrante, Leonard V. &   **TA403.C43 1998**
  Hampden-Smith, Mark J. (Editors)
Chemistry of Advanced Materials: An Overview. Trade Cloth.

John Wiley & Sons, Inc. Hoboken, NJ. 1997. 592p.
ISBN:0-471-18590-6, ISBN13: 978-0-471-18590-1.
Dewey:620.1/1. LCCN:97-011898.

Audience: **u,f.** *Choice, 1998.*

McDonough, William &   **TD794.5.M395 2002**
** Braungart, Michael**
Cradle to Cradle: Remaking the Way We Make Things. Trade
Paper. Farrar, Straus & Giroux. New York, NY. 2002. 208p.
ISBN:0-86547-587-3, ISBN13: 978-0-86547-587-8.
Dewey:745.2. LCCN:2001-044245.

Audience: **u,f.** *Choice, 2002.*

Murray, G. T.   **TA403.M84 1993**
Introduction to Engineering Materials: Behavior, Properties, and
Selection, Vol. 2. Paper over Boards. Marcel Dekker Inc. New
York, NY. 1993. 688p. Engineering Materials Ser., Vol. 2
ISBN:0-8247-8965-2, ISBN13: 978-0-8247-8965-7.
Dewey:620.1/1. LCCN:93-012660.

Audience: **u,f.** *Choice, 1994.*

Rao, C. N. R.; Muller, A.;   **QC176**
** Cheetham, A. K.**
The Chemistry of Nanomaterials: Synthesis, Properties and
Applications. Wiley-VCH. 2004. ISBN:3-527-30686-2, ISBN13:
978-3-527-30686-2.

Audience: **u,f.**

Industrial Chemistry > Special Topics in Industrial Chemistry > Minerals and Metals

Kurlansky, Mark   **TN900.K865 2002**
Salt: A World History. Cloth over Boards. Walker & Company.
New York, NY. 2002. 496p. ISBN:0-8027-1373-4, ISBN13:
978-0-8027-1373-5. Dewey:553.6/3/09. LCCN:2004-533381.

Audience: **l,u,f.** *Choice, 2002.*

Laszlo, Pierre   **TN900.L3713 2001**
Salt: Grain of Life. Mary Beth Mader (Translator). Trade Cloth.
Columbia University Press. New York, NY. 2001. 256p. Arts
and Traditions of the Table Ser., :Perspectives on Culinary
History Ser. ISBN:0-231-12198-9, ISBN13: 978-0-231-12198-9.
Dewey:553.6/3. LCCN:2001-028227.

Audience: **l,u,f.** *Choice, 2002.*

Smithells, Colin J., et al.   **TN671.S55 1998**
Smithells Metals Reference Book. Ed. 7. Eric A. Brandes & G.
B. Brook (Authors). Trade Paper. Elsevier Science &
Technology Books. Saint Louis, MO. 1998. 1800p.
ISBN:0-7506-3624-6, ISBN13: 978-0-7506-3624-7.
Dewey:669/.02/12. LCCN:97-027401.

Audience: **u,f.**

Industrial Chemistry > Special Topics in Industrial Chemistry > Perfumes

Pybus, D. & Sell, C.   **TP983.P93**
The Chemistry of Fragrances. Trade Cloth. Springer. New York,
NY. 1999. xvi + 278p. RSC Paperback Ser.
ISBN:0-85404-528-7, ISBN13: 978-0-85404-528-0.
Dewey:668.5/4.

Audience: **u,f.**

Industrial Chemistry > Special Topics in Industrial Chemistry > Plastics > Handbook and Encyclopedia

□ Glossary of Acronyms.   **TP1110**
http://www.plastics.com/acronyms/

Audience: **u,f.**

□ Glossary of Acronyms.
http://www.plastics.com/acronyms/

Audience: **u,f.**

Harper, Charles A. (Editor)   **TP1130.H36 1996**
Handbook of Plastics, Elastomers and Composites. Ed. 3. Trade
Cloth. McGraw-Hill Professional Publishing. New York, NY.
1996. 848p. ISBN:0-07-026693-X, ISBN13: 978-0-07-026693-3.
Dewey:668.4. LCCN:96-020787.

Audience: **u,f.**

Industrial Chemistry > Special Topics in Industrial Chemistry > Plastics > History and Development

Fenichell, Stephen   **TP1116.F46 1996**
Plastic: The Making of a Synthetic Century. Trade Cloth.
HarperCollins Publishers. New York, NY. 1996. 320p.
ISBN:0-88730-732-9, ISBN13: 978-0-88730-732-4.
Dewey:303.4/83. LCCN:96-000364.

Audience: **l,u,f.** *Choice, 1997.*

Meikle, Jeffrey L.   **TP1117.M45 1995**
American Plastic: A Cultural History. Cloth Text. Rutgers
University Press. Piscataway, NJ. 1995. 500p.
ISBN:0-8135-2234-X, ISBN13: 978-0-8135-2234-0.
Dewey:303.48/3. LCCN:95-015187.

Audience: **l,u,f.** *Choice, 1996.*

Sparke, Penny (Editor)   **TP1122.P554 1993**
The Plastics Age: From Bakelite to Beanbags and Beyond.
Trade Cloth. Overlook Press, The. New York, NY. 1993. 160p.
ISBN:0-87951-471-X, ISBN13: 978-0-87951-471-6.
Dewey:668.4. LCCN:92-035039.

Audience: **l,u,f.** *Choice, 1993.*

Industrial Chemistry > Special Topics in Industrial Chemistry > Plastics > Properties

Brydson, J. A.   **TP1120.B7 1999**
Plastics Materials. Ed. 7. Cloth Text. Elsevier Science &
Technology Books. Saint Louis, MO. 1999. 920p.
ISBN:0-7506-4132-0, ISBN13: 978-0-7506-4132-6.
Dewey:668.4. LCCN:99-030623.

Audience: **l,u,f.**

Gruenwald, Geza
Structural Plastics: Composition - Properties - Processing. Oxford University Press, Inc. 1992. Hanser Publishers Ser.: Progress in Polymer Processing ISBN:0-19-520958-3, ISBN13: 978-0-19-520958-7.

Audience: **u,f.**

Grunwald, Geza   **TA455.P5.G74 1993**
Plastics: How Structure Determines Properties. Trade Cloth. Hanser-Gardner Publications. Cincinnati, OH. 1993. 371p. ISBN:3-446-16520-7, ISBN13: 978-3-446-16520-5. Dewey:620.1/923. LCCN:92-053928.

Audience: **u,f.**

Industrial Chemistry > Special Topics in Industrial Chemistry > Plastics > Environmental Considerations

Environmental Action   **TD798.W64 1990**
  Coalition Staff, et al.
Plastics: America's Packaging Dilemma. Nancy Wolf & Ellen Feldman (Authors). Trade Cloth. Island Press. Washington, DC. 1990. 133p. ISBN:1-55963-063-9, ISBN13: 978-1-55963-063-4. Dewey:363.72/88. LCCN:90-043801.

Audience: **l,u,f.** *Choice, 1991.*

Stevens, E. S.   **TP1180.B55S74 2002**
Green Plastics: An Introduction to the New Science of Biodegradable Plastics. Trade Cloth. Princeton University Press. Princeton, NJ. 2001. 248p. ISBN:0-691-04967-X, ISBN13: 978-0-691-04967-0. Dewey:668.4. LCCN:2001-036257.

Audience: **l,u,f.** *Choice, 2002.*

Wallace, Deborah   **TH9446**
In the Mouth of the Dragon. Avery Pub. Group. 1990. ISBN:0-89529-440-0, ISBN13: 978-0-89529-440-1.

Audience: **l,u,f.**

Industrial Chemistry > Special Topics in Industrial Chemistry > Petrochemicals

Berkowitz, Norbert   **TP343.B38 1997**
Fossil Hydrocarbons: Chemistry and Technology. Trade Cloth. Elsevier Science & Technology Books. Saint Louis, MO. 1997. 351p. ISBN:0-12-091090-X, ISBN13: 978-0-12-091090-8. Dewey:553.2. LCCN:97-023439.

Audience: **u,f.** *Choice, 1998.*

Industrial Chemistry > Special Topics in Industrial Chemistry > Rubber and Composite Materials

White, James L.   **TS1890.W54 1995**
Rubber Processing: Technology, Materials, Principles. Trade Cloth. Hanser-Gardner Publications. Cincinnati, OH. 1994. 620p. ISBN:1-56990-165-1, ISBN13: 978-1-56990-165-6. Dewey:678/.2. LCCN:93-048549.

Audience: **u,f.** *Choice, 1996.*

Industrial Chemistry > Special Topics in Industrial Chemistry > Dyes and Colorants

Balfour-Paul, Jenny   **TP923.B34 1998**
Indigo. Trade Cloth. British Museum Press. London, 1998. vii, 264p. ISBN:0-7141-1776-5, ISBN13: 978-0-7141-1776-8. Dewey:667.26. LCCN:99-223017.

Audience: **l,u,f.** *Choice, 2001.*

Christie, R. M.   **TP910TP910.C374 2001**
Colour Chemistry. Trade Paper. Royal Society of Chemistry, The. Cambridge, 2001. xii + 206p. ISBN:0-85404-573-2, ISBN13: 978-0-85404-573-0. Dewey:667.2.

Audience: **l,u,f.**

Industrial Chemistry > Special Topics in Industrial Chemistry > Paper Chemistry

Roberts, J. C.   **TS1120.P37 1991**
Paper Chemistry. Trade Cloth. Bow Historical Books. New Providence, NJ. 1991. xiii, 234p. ISBN:0-216-92909-1, ISBN13: 978-0-216-92909-8. Dewey:676/.2. LCCN:90-027806.

Audience: **u,f.** *Choice, 1996.*

Industrial Chemistry > Special Topics in Industrial Chemistry > Pyrotechnics and Explosives

                                                    TP149
☐ Database of Gas Explosion Hazards.
http://www.aist.go.jp/RIODB/gasexpl/index_e.html
AIST, Japan.

Audience: **u,f.**

☐ Database of Gas Explosion Hazards.
http://www.aist.go.jp/RIODB/gasexpl/index_e.html

Audience: **u,f.**

Russell, Michael S.   **TP300.R87**
The Chemistry of Fireworks. Trade Paper. Royal Society of Chemistry, The. Cambridge, 2000. xviii + 118p. ISBN:0-85404-598-8, ISBN13: 978-0-85404-598-3. Dewey:662.1.

Audience: **l,u,f.**

Industrial Chemistry > Guides to the Internet

☐ Chemie.de Information Service.
http://www.chemie.de/

Audience: **u,f.**

☐ ChemIndustry.com.
http://www.chemindustry.com/

Audience: **u,f.**

☐ ChemSpy.com.
http://www.chemspy.com/

Audience: **u,f.**

☐ NanoTechWeb news.
http://nanotechweb.org/

Audience: **u,f.**

Polymer Chemistry > Guides to the Literature

☐ Polymer Chemistry--Subject Guide (Stanford University).
http://library.stanford.edu/depts/swain/help/subjectguides/
polymer.html

Audience: **u,f.**

☐ Polymer Search on the Internet (RAPRA).
http://www.polymer-search.com/home/default.asp

Audience: **u,f.**

Adkins, R. T. (Editor) Z5524
Information Sources in Polymers and Plastics. Bowker-Saur.
1989. ISBN:0-408-02027-X, ISBN13: 978-0-408-02027-5.

Audience: **u,f.**

Polymer Chemistry > General Resources

QD281.P6
☐ The Macrogalleria; A Cyberland of Polymer Fun.
http://www.psic.ws/macrog/index.htm

Audience: **u,f.**

Carraher, Jr., Charles QD381
Seymour/Carraher's Polymer Chemistry, Vol. 16. Ed. 6. Paper
over Boards. Marcel Dekker Inc. New York, NY. 2003. 960p.
Undergraduate Chemistry: a Series of Textbooks Ser., 16
ISBN:0-8247-0806-7, ISBN13: 978-0-8247-0806-1.
Dewey:547/.7. LCCN:2004-269342.

Audience: **u,f.**

Tonelli, Alan E. QD381.T65 2001
Polymers from the Inside Out: An Introduction to
Macromolecules. Trade Cloth. John Wiley & Sons, Inc.
Hoboken, NJ. 2001. 280p. ISBN:0-471-38138-1, ISBN13:
978-0-471-38138-9. Dewey:547/.7. LCCN:00-047990.

Audience: **u,f.** *Choice, 2001.*

Polymer Chemistry > Nomenclature

☐ Glossary of Basic Terms in Polymer Science.
http://www.iupac.org/reports/1996/6812jenkins/

Audience: **u,f.**

☐ Guide to Polymer Abbreviations/Tradenames.
http://www.theotherpages.org/abbrev.html

Audience: **u,f.**

Loening, K. L. (Editor) QD380.3
List of Standard Abbreviations, (Symbols) for Synthetic
Polymers and Polymeric Materials: Basic Definitions of Terms
Relating to Polymers. Trade Paper. Pergamon Press. Kidlington,
1978. ISBN:0-08-022371-0, ISBN13: 978-0-08-022371-1.
Dewey:547.280321.

Audience: **u,f.**

Polymer Chemistry > Encyclopedias

Cheremisinoff, Nicholas P. TP1087.C477 2001
Condensed Encyclopedia of Polymer Engineering Terms. Ed.
169. Trade Cloth. Elsevier Science & Technology Books. Saint
Louis, MO. 2001. 800p. ISBN:0-7506-7210-2, ISBN13:
978-0-7506-7210-8. Dewey:668.9/03. LCCN:00-068904.

Audience: **u,f.** *Choice, 2001.*

Kroschwitz, Jacqueline I. & TP1087.C66 1990
 Menges, George
Concise Encyclopedia of Polymer Science and Engineering.
Herman F. Mark, Norbert Bikales & Charles G. Overberger
(Editors). Trade Cloth. John Wiley & Sons, Inc. Hoboken, NJ.
1990. 1376p. ISBN:0-471-51253-2, ISBN13:
978-0-471-51253-0. Dewey:668.9/03. LCCN:89-070674.

Audience: **u,f.** *Choice, 1991.*

Mark, Herman F. TP1087.E46 2003
Encyclopedia of Polymer Science and Technology, Vol. 14, Pt.
1. Ed. 3. Trade Cloth. John Wiley & Sons, Inc. Hoboken, NJ.
2003. 3005p. ISBN:0-471-28824-1, ISBN13:
978-0-471-28824-4. Dewey:668.9. LCCN:2003-041107.

Audience: **u,f.** *Choice, 2003.*

Mark, Herman F. (Editorial QD281.P6
 Board Member), et al.
Acid-Base Interactions to Vinyl Chloride Polymers. Ed. 2.
Norbert Bikales, Charles G. Overberger & Georg Menges
(Editorial Board Members), Jacqueline I. Kroschwitz
(Editor-In-Chief). Trade Cloth. John Wiley & Sons, Inc.
Hoboken, NJ. 1989. 889p. Encyclopedia of Polymer Science and
Engineering Ser. ISBN:0-471-80948-9, ISBN13:
978-0-471-80948-7. Dewey:547.7. LCCN:84-019713.

Audience: **u,f.**

Mark, Herman F. (Editorial TP1087
 Board Member), et al.
Encyclopedia of Polymer Science and Engineering, A to
Amorphous Polymers, Vol. 1. Ed. 2. Norbert Bikales, Charles G.
Overberger & Georg Menges (Editorial Board Members),
Jacqueline I. Kroschwitz (Editor-In-Chief). Trade Cloth. John
Wiley & Sons, Inc. Hoboken, NJ. 1985. 912p.
ISBN:0-471-89540-7, ISBN13: 978-0-471-89540-4.
Dewey:547.7/03/21. LCCN:84-019713.

Audience: **u,f.** *B*

Salamone, Joseph C. TP1110
 (Editor)
Concise Polymeric Materials Encyclopedia. CRC Press. 1999.
ISBN:0-8493-2226-X, ISBN13: 978-0-8493-2226-6.

Audience: **u,f.**

Salamone, Joseph C. TP1110
 (Editor)
Polymeric Materials Encyclopedia. CRC Press. 1996.
ISBN:0-8493-2651-6, ISBN13: 978-0-8493-2651-6.

Audience: **u,f.**

Audience: g=general, l=lower division undergraduate, u=upper division undergraduate, f=faculty.

321

Salamone, Joseph C.   **TP1110**
  (Editor)
Polymeric Materials Encyclopedia (Set). CRC Press. 1996.
ISBN:0-8493-2470-X, ISBN13: 978-0-8493-2470-3.
                              Audience: **u,f.**

Polymer Chemistry > Handbooks

Brandrup, J.   **QD388.P65 1999**
Polymer Handbook. Ed. 4. Edmund H. Immergut, E. A. Grulk,
A. Abe & D. Bloch (Editors). Trade Cloth. John Wiley & Sons,
Inc. Hoboken, NJ. 1999. 2336p. Polymer Handbook Ser.
ISBN:0-471-16628-6, ISBN13: 978-0-471-16628-3.
Dewey:547/.7. LCCN:98-037261.
                      Audience: **u,f.** *Choice, 1999, 1990.*

Shackelford, James F., ed.   **TA403.4.C74**
CRC Materials Science and Engineering Handbook. Ed. 2. CRC
Press. 1994. ISBN:0-8493-4250-3, ISBN13: 978-0-8493-4250-9.
                              Audience: **u,f.**

Polymer Chemistry > Dictionary

Alger, Mark   **QD380.3.A52 1989**
Polymer Science Dictionary. Mass Market. Elsevier. New York,
NY. 1989. 544p. ISBN:1-85166-220-0, ISBN13:
978-1-85166-220-3. Dewey:668.9/03. LCCN:88-011034.
                      Audience: **u,f.** *Choice, 1990.*

Polymer Chemistry > History

Furukawa, Yasu   **QD381.F87 1998**
Inventing Polymer Science: Staudinger, Carothers, and the
Emergence of Macromolecular Chemistry. Trade Cloth.
University of Pennsylvania Press. Philadelphia, PA. 1998. 310p.
Chemical Sciences in Society Ser. ISBN:0-8122-3336-0,
ISBN13: 978-0-8122-3336-0. Dewey:547/.7. LCCN:97-036390.
                      Audience: **u,f.** *Choice, 1998.*

Polymer Chemistry > Treatises and Comprehensive Works

Allen, Geoffrey &   **QD381.C66 1989**
  Bevington, J. C.
Comprehensive Polymer Science Series: The Synthesis,
Characterization, Reactions and Applications of Polymers, Set.
Trade Cloth. Elsevier Science & Technology Books. Saint
Louis, MO. 1988. 5367p. ISBN:0-08-032515-7, ISBN13:
978-0-08-032515-6. Dewey:547.7. LCCN:88-025548.
                              Audience: **u,f.**

Billmeyer, Fred W. Jr.   **QD381**
Textbook of Polymer Science. Ed. 3. Trade Cloth. John Wiley &
Sons, Inc. Hoboken, NJ. 1984. 608p. ISBN:0-471-03196-8,
ISBN13: 978-0-471-03196-3. Dewey:547.7. LCCN:83-019870.
                              Audience: **u,f.** *B*

Boyd, Richard H. &   **QD281.P6 B677 1993**
  Phillips, Paul J.
The Science of Polymer Molecules. D. R. Clarke, S. Suresh & I.

M. Ward (Contribution by). Trade Cloth. Cambridge University
Press. New York, NY. 1993. 428p. Solid State Science Ser.
ISBN:0-521-32076-3, ISBN13: 978-0-521-32076-4.
Dewey:547.7. LCCN:94-153475.
                      Audience: **u,f.** *Choice, 1994.*

Hall, Christopher D.   **TA455.P58H35 1989**
Polymer Materials: An Introduction for Technologists and
Scientists. Ed. 2. Cloth Text. John Wiley & Sons, Inc. Hoboken,
NJ. 1988. 243p. ISBN:0-470-21092-3, ISBN13:
978-0-470-21092-5. Dewey:620.1/92. LCCN:88-005520.
                              Audience: **u,f.**

Misra, Gauri S.   **QD381.I59 1991**
Introductory Polymer Chemistry. Trade Cloth. John Wiley &
Sons, Inc. Hoboken, NJ. 1993. 253p. ISBN:0-470-21720-0,
ISBN13: 978-0-470-21720-7. Dewey:547.7. LCCN:90-021092.
                      Audience: **u,f.** *Choice, 1994.*

Munk, Petr & Aminabhavi,   **QD381.M85 2001**
  Tejraj M.
Introduction to Macromolecular Science. Ed. 2. Trade Cloth.
John Wiley & Sons, Inc. Hoboken, NJ. 2002. 609p.
ISBN:0-471-41716-5, ISBN13: 978-0-471-41716-3.
Dewey:547/.7. LCCN:2001-045583.
                      Audience: **u,f.** *Choice, 2002, 1990.*

Painter, Paul C.; Coleman,   **QD381**
  Michael M.
Fundamentals of Polymer Science: An Introductory Text. Ed. 2.
Technomic Pub. Co.. 1997. ISBN:1-56676-559-5, ISBN13:
978-1-56676-559-6.
                              Audience: **u,f.**

Ravve, A.   **QD381.R38 1995**
Principles of Polymer Chemistry. Trade Cloth. Springer. New
York, NY. 1995. 510p. ISBN:0-306-44873-4, ISBN13:
978-0-306-44873-7. Dewey:547/.7. LCCN:95-007219.
                      Audience: **u,f.** *Choice, 1995.*

Stevens, Malcolm P.   **QD381.S73 1999**
Polymer Chemistry: An Introduction. Ed. 3. Cloth Text. Oxford
University Press, Inc. New York, NY. 1998. 574p.
ISBN:0-19-512444-8, ISBN13: 978-0-19-512444-6.
Dewey:547/.84. LCCN:98-023083.
                      Audience: **u,f.** *Choice, 1999.*

Polymer Chemistry > Techniques in Polymer Chemistry

Akelah, A; Moet,   **TP1087.A4 1990**
  Abdelsamie
Functionalized Polymers: Synthesis, Properties and Applications.
Chapman & Hall. 1990. ISBN:0-412-30290-X, ISBN13:
978-0-412-30290-9.
                              Audience: **u,f.**

Collins, Edward A., et al.   **QD385**
Experiments in Polymer Science. Fred W. Billmeyer & Jan
Bares (Authors). Trade Paper. John Wiley & Sons, Inc.
Hoboken, NJ. 1973. 530p. ISBN:0-471-16585-9, ISBN13:
978-0-471-16585-9. Dewey:547/.84/028. LCCN:73-000650.
                              Audience: **u,f.**

Sandler, Stanley R. & Karo, Wolf   QD281.P6S27 1992
Polymer Syntheses, Vol. 1. Ed. 2. Trade Cloth. Elsevier Science & Technology Books. Saint Louis, MO. 1991. 512p. Polymer Syntheses Ser., Vol. 29-I ISBN:0-12-618511-5, ISBN13: 978-0-12-618511-9. Dewey:547.2/8. LCCN:91-029659.

Audience: **u,f.** B

Sandler, Stanley R. & Karo, Wolf   QD262.S24 1992
Sourcebook of Advanced Organic Laboratory Preparations. Paper Text. Elsevier Science & Technology Books. Saint Louis, MO. 1992. 352p. ISBN:0-12-618506-9, ISBN13: 978-0-12-618506-5. Dewey:547.2/078. LCCN:92-013631.

Audience: **u,f.** *Choice, 1993.*

Seymour, Raymond B.   TP156.P6S44 1990
Engineering Polymer Sourcebook. Cloth Text. McGraw-Hill Companies, The. New York, NY. 1990. xvii, 300p. ISBN:0-07-056360-8, ISBN13: 978-0-07-056360-5. Dewey:668.9. LCCN:89-035066.

Audience: **u,f.** *Choice, 1990.*

Sorenson, Wayne R.; Campbell, Tod W.   QD281
Preparative Methods of Polymer Chemistry. Ed. 2. Interscience Publishers. 1968. ISBN:0-471-81379-6, ISBN13: 978-0-471-81379-8.

Audience: **u,f.**

Polymer Chemistry > Characterization of Polymers > General Methods

Hunt, B J; James, M I   QD139.P6P64 1993
Polymer Characterization. B. J. Hunt (Editor) ; M. I. James (Editor). Blackie Academic & Professional. 1993. ISBN:0-7514-0082-3, ISBN13: 978-0-7514-0082-3.

Audience: **u,f.**

Tong, Ho-Ming, et al.   TA455.P58C472 1994
Characterization of Polymers: Surfaces, Interfaces, Thin Films. Ned J. Chou, Ravi F. Saraf & Steven P. Kowalczyk (Authors). Trade Cloth. Elsevier Science & Technology Books. Saint Louis, MO. 1993. 250p. Materials Characterization Ser. ISBN:0-7506-9287-1, ISBN13: 978-0-7506-9287-8. Dewey:620.192. LCCN:93-001909.

Audience: **u,f.** *Choice, 1994.*

White, J. R. & Campbell, D.   QD139.P6C36 1989
Polymer Characterization: Physical Techniques. Trade Cloth. Chapman & Hall. New York, NY. 1989. 380p. ISBN:0-412-27160-5, ISBN13: 978-0-412-27160-1. Dewey:547.8/4046. LCCN:89-007292.

Audience: **u,f.** *Choice, 1990.*

Polymer Chemistry > Characterization of Polymers > Spectroscopy

QC463.P5 I53
The Infrared Spectra Atlas of Monomers and Polymers. Trade Paper. Sadtler Research Laboratories. Philadelphia, PA. 1980. ISBN:0-8456-0064-8, ISBN13: 978-0-8456-0064-1. Dewey:547.3/08583. LCCN:80-053761.

Audience: **u,f.**

QC462.85 .N97 1989
The Infrared Spectra Building Blocks of Polymers. Trade Cloth. Sadtler Research Laboratories. Philadelphia, PA. 1989. ISBN:0-8456-0151-2, ISBN13: 978-0-8456-0151-8. Dewey:547.3/08583. LCCN:88-060355.

Audience: **u,f.**

QC762 .S29 1988
Sadtler Guide to Carbon-13 NMR Spectra of Polymers and Resins. Trade Cloth. Sadtler Research Laboratories. Philadelphia, PA. 1988. ISBN:0-8456-0150-4, ISBN13: 978-0-8456-0150-1. Dewey:547.7046. LCCN:88-060354.

Audience: **u,f.**

Bovey, Frank A. & Mirau, Peter A.   QP519.9.N83B68 1996
NMR of Polymers. Trade Cloth. Elsevier Science & Technology Books. Saint Louis, MO. 1996. 459p. ISBN:0-12-119765-4, ISBN13: 978-0-12-119765-0. Dewey:574.19/285. LCCN:96-028240.

Audience: **u,f.** *Choice, 1997.*

Bower, D. I. & Maddams, W. F.   QD381.8 .B69 1988
The Vibrational Spectroscopy of Polymers. Cloth Text. Cambridge University Press. New York, NY. 1989. 352p. Cambridge Solid State Science Ser. ISBN:0-521-24633-4, ISBN13: 978-0-521-24633-0. Dewey:547.8/43. LCCN:88-002956.

Audience: **u,f.** *Choice, 1990.*

Koenig, Jack L.   QD139.P6K64 1999
Spectroscopy of Polymers. Ed. 2. Trade Cloth. Elsevier Science & Technology Books. Saint Louis, MO. 1999. 376p. ISBN:0-444-10031-8, ISBN13: 978-0-444-10031-3. Dewey:547.7/046. LCCN:99-037577.

Audience: **u,f.** *Choice, 2000.*

Montaudo, Giorgio   QD139
Mass Spectrometry of Polymers. Lattimer, Robert P. (Editors). CRC Press. 2002. ISBN:0-8493-3127-7, ISBN13: 978-0-8493-3127-5.

Audience: **u,f.**

Simons, W. W. & Zanger, M.   QD139.P6 S52
Sadtler Guide to the NMR Spectra of Polymers. Trade Paper. Sadtler Research Laboratories. Philadelphia, PA. 1973. ISBN:0-8456-0002-8, ISBN13: 978-0-8456-0002-3. Dewey:547/.308/5. LCCN:73-090432.

Audience: **u,f.**

Polymer Chemistry > Characterization of Polymers > Miscellaneous Methods

Hatakeyama, T & Quinn, F. X.   QD79.T38H38 1999
Thermal Analysis: Fundamentals and Applications to Polymer Science. Ed. 2. Trade Cloth. John Wiley & Sons, Inc. Hoboken, NJ. 1999. 190p. ISBN:0-471-98362-4, ISBN13: 978-0-471-98362-0. Dewey:543/.086. LCCN:98-049129.

Audience: **u,f.**

Woodward, Arthur E.   TP1087.W66 1995
Understanding Polymer Morphology. Trade Paper. Hanser-Gardner Publications. Cincinnati, OH. 1994. 128p.

Audience: g=general, l=lower division undergraduate, u=upper division undergraduate, f=faculty.

323

ISBN:1-56990-141-4, ISBN13: 978-1-56990-141-0.
Dewey:668.9. LCCN:94-037332.

Audience: **u,f.** *Choice, 1996.*

Polymer Chemistry > Mechanical and Chemical Behavior of Polymers

Courtney, Thomas H.   **TA405**
Mechanical Behavior of Materials. Ed. 2. McGraw-Hill. 2000.
ISBN:0-07-028594-2, ISBN13: 978-0-07-028594-1.

Audience: **u,f.**

Hamid, S. Halim; Amin,   **QC381,9**
  Mohamed B. & Maadhah, Ali G.
Handbook of Polymer Degradation. M. Dekker. 1992.
Environmental Science and Pollution Control Series, No. 2
ISBN:0-8247-8671-8, ISBN13: 978-0-8247-8671-7.

Audience: **u,f.**

Polymer Chemistry > Physical and Chemical Properties of Polymers

☐ Table of the Properties of 200 Linear Macromolecules and Small Molecules.
http://web.utk.edu/~athas/databank/intro.html

Audience: **u,f.**

Mark, James E. (Editor)   **TA455.P58P475 1996**
Physical Properties of Polymers Handbook. Cloth Text. Springer.
New York, NY. 1996. ISBN:1-56396-599-2, ISBN13:
978-1-56396-599-9. Dewey:620.1/92. LCCN:95-050256.

Audience: **u,f.** *Choice, 1996.*

Mark, James E. (Editor)   **TA455.P58P475 1996**
Physical Properties of Polymers Handbook. Cloth Text. Springer.
New York, NY. 1996. 744p. Polymers and Complex Materials
Ser. ISBN:1-56396-295-0, ISBN13: 978-1-56396-295-0.
Dewey:620.1/92. LCCN:95-050256.

Audience: **u,f.** *Choice, 1996.*

Mark, James E. (Editor)   **TA455**
🔷 Physical Properties of Polymers Handbook. AIP Press. 1996.
ISBN:1-56396-598-4, ISBN13: 978-1-56396-598-2.

Audience: **u,f.**

Ragone, David V.   **TA418.52.R34 1995**
Thermodynamics of Materials, Vol. 1. Trade Cloth. John Wiley
& Sons, Inc. Hoboken, NJ. 1994. 336p. MIT Series in Materials
Science and Engineering, Vol. 1 ISBN:0-471-30885-4, ISBN13:
978-0-471-30885-0. Dewey:536/.7. LCCN:94-025647.

Audience: **u,f.** *Choice, 1995.*

Ragone, David V.   **TA418.52.R34**
Thermodynamics of Materials, Vol. 2. Trade Cloth. John Wiley
& Sons, Inc. Hoboken, NJ. 1994. 256p. MIT Series in Materials
Science and Engineering, Vol. 2 ISBN:0-471-30886-2, ISBN13:
978-0-471-30886-7. Dewey:536/.7. LCCN:94-025647.

Audience: **u,f.** *Choice, 1995.*

Strobl, Gert R.   **QC173.4.P65S77 1997**
The Physics of Polymers: Concepts for Understanding Their
Structures and Behavior. Ed. 2. Trade Paper. Springer. New
York, NY. 1997. xii, 439p. ISBN:3-540-63203-4, ISBN13:
978-3-540-63203-0. Dewey:530.413. LCCN:97-028362.

Audience: **u,f.** *Choice, 1997.*

Zoller, Paul; Walsh,   **QD381**
  David J.
Standard Pressure-Volume-Temperature Data for Polymers.
Technomic Pub. Co.. 1995. ISBN:1-56676-328-2, ISBN13:
978-1-56676-328-8.

Audience: **u,f.**

Polymer Chemistry > Multicomponent Systems

Sperling, L. H.   **QD381.S6348 1997**
Polymeric Multicomponent Materials: An Introduction. Ed. 2.
Trade Cloth. John Wiley & Sons, Inc. Hoboken, NJ. 1997. 416p.
ISBN:0-471-04138-6, ISBN13: 978-0-471-04138-2.
Dewey:620.1/92. LCCN:97-006509.

Audience: **u,f.** *Choice, 1998.*

Biological Chemistry > Guides to the Literature

☐ Biology and Biochemistry--Web Guide (Stanford University).
http://library.stanford.edu/depts/swain/help/webdirs/
subject.html#biology

Audience: **u,f.**

☐ Biophysical Chemistry Online Resources (UW,
Madison)--Databases.
http://chemistry.library.wisc.edu/biophysics/databases.htm

Audience: **u,f.**

☐ Biotechnology--Subject Guide (Stanford University).
http://library.stanford.edu/depts/swain/help/subjectguides/
biotechnology/index.html

Audience: **u,f.**

☐ Biotechnology--Web Guide (Stanford University).
http://library.stanford.edu/depts/swain/help/webdirs/
subject.html#biotech

Audience: **u,f.**

☐ MolData--Biochemistry.
http://pages.pomona.edu/~wsteinmetz/BioChem.htm

Audience: **u,f.**

Schmidt, Diane, et al.   **QH303.6.D38 2002**
Using the Biological Literature: A Practical Guide, Vol. 60. Ed.
3. Elisabeth B. Davis & Pamela F. Jacobs (Authors). Paper over
Boards. Marcel Dekker Inc. New York, NY. 2001. 479p. Books
in Library and Information Science, Vol. 60
ISBN:0-8247-0667-6, ISBN13: 978-0-8247-0667-8.
Dewey:570/.7/2. LCCN:2001-058392.

Audience: **u,f.** *Choice, 2002.*

Wyatt, H. V. (Editor)   QH303.6
Information Sources in the Life Sciences. Ed. 4. Trade Cloth. R.
R. Bowker LLC. East Grinstead, 1994. 250p. Guides to
Information Sources Ser. ISBN:1-85739-032-6, ISBN13:
978-1-85739-032-2. Dewey:016.57.
                                        Audience: **u,f.** *Choice, 1988.*

Biological Chemistry > Abstracting and Indexing Services

                                                          QH301
☐ BasicBIOSIS.
http://scientific.thomson.com/products/basic/
Biological Abstracts--Thomson Scientific.
                                        Audience: **u,f.**

                                                          QH301
Biological Abstracts. BioSciences Information Service of
Biological Abstracts.
                                        Audience: **u,f.**

☐ Biological Abstracts.
http://scientific.thomson.com/products/ba/
Biological Abstracts--Thomson Scientific.
                                        Audience: **u,f.**

☐ Biological Abstracts/RRM.
http://scientific.thomson.com/products/barrm/
Biological Abstracts/RRM--Thomson Scientific.
                                        Audience: **u,f.**

                                                          QH301
☐ BIOSIS Previews.
http://scientific.thomson.com/products/bp/
BIOSIS Previews--Thomson Scientific.
                                        Audience: **u,f.**

                                                          QH301
☐ PubMed.
http://ncbi.nlm.nih.gov/entrez/.
                                        Audience: **u,f.**

Biological Chemistry > Encyclopedias

Flickinger, Michael C. &   TP248.3.E52 1999
Drew, Stephen W.
Encyclopedia of Bioprocess Technology, Set. Trade Cloth. John
Wiley & Sons, Inc. Hoboken, NJ. 1999. 2798p.
ISBN:0-471-13822-3, ISBN13: 978-0-471-13822-8.
Dewey:660.6/03. LCCN:99-011576.
                                        Audience: **u,f.** *Choice, 1999.*

Kendrew, John & Lawrence,   QH506.E53
Elleanor (Editors)
The Encyclopedia of Molecular Biology. Trade Paper. Blackwell
Publishing, Inc. Malden, MA. 1995. 1192p.
ISBN:0-86542-621-X, ISBN13: 978-0-86542-621-4.
Dewey:574.8803.
                                        Audience: **u,f.**

Scott, Thomas A. & Mercer,   QD415.A25B713 1997
E. Ian (Translators)
Concise Encyclopedia Biochemistry and Molecular Biology. Ed.
3. Thomas A. Scott & E. Ian Mercer (Revised by). Cloth Text.
Walter De Gruyter Inc. Ossining, NY. 1996. 737p.
ISBN:3-11-014535-9, ISBN13: 978-3-11-014535-9.
Dewey:572/.03. LCCN:96-047538.
                                        Audience: **u,f.** *Choice, 1997.*

Biological Chemistry > Nomenclature

                                                          QP601.I54
Enzyme Nomenclature 1984 Z Cth. Trade Cloth. Elsevier
Science & Technology Books. Saint Louis, MO. 1984.
ISBN:0-12-227162-9, ISBN13: 978-0-12-227162-5.
Dewey:574.19/25/014.
                                        Audience: **u,f.**

NC-IUBMB & Webb, Edwin   QP601.I56 1992
C. (Editors)
Enzyme Nomenclature 1992. Ed. 2. Trade Cloth. Elsevier
Science & Technology Books. Saint Louis, MO. 1992. 862p.
ISBN:0-12-227164-5, ISBN13: 978-0-12-227164-9.
Dewey:574.1925014. LCCN:92-025248.
                                        Audience: **u,f.**

Biological Chemistry > Dictionaries

Dorland, Newman W.   R121 .D73 1994
Dorland's Illustrated Medical Dictionary. Ed. 28. Cloth Text.
Elsevier - Health Sciences Division. Philadelphia, PA. 1994.
1992p. ISBN:0-7216-2859-1, ISBN13: 978-0-7216-2859-2.
Dewey:610.3. LCCN:78-050050.
                                        Audience: **l,u,f.** *B*

Smith, A. D. (Editor), et al.   QP512.O94 1997
Oxford Dictionary of Biochemistry and Molecular Biology. S. P.
Datta, G. H. Smith, P. N. Campbell, R Bentley & H. A.
McKenzie (Editors). Trade Cloth. Oxford University Press, Inc.
New York, NY. 1997. 752p. ISBN:0-19-854768-4, ISBN13:
978-0-19-854768-6. Dewey:572/.03. LCCN:97-225841.
                                        Audience: **u,f.** *Choice, 1998.*

Stedman, Thomas L.   R121.S8 1995
Stedman's Medical Dictionary, 1995. Ed. 26. Trade Cloth.
Lippincott Williams & Wilkins. Philadelphia, PA. 1995. 2192p.
ISBN:0-683-07922-0, ISBN13: 978-0-683-07922-7.
Dewey:610.3. LCCN:94-038190.
                                        Audience: **l,u,f.**

Biological Chemistry > Glossaries

Bains, William   TP248.16
Biotechnology from A to Z. Ed. 2. Trade Paper. Oxford
University Press, Inc. New York, NY. 1998. 422p.
ISBN:0-19-963693-1, ISBN13: 978-0-19-963693-8.
Dewey:660.6/03. LCCN:93-215815.
                                        Audience: **u,f.** *Choice, 2004, 1994.*

Glick, David   QP512.G55
Glossary of Biochemistry and Molecular Biology. Ed. 2. Paper
Text. Portland Press, Ltd. London, 1996. 250p.

ISBN:1-85578-088-7, ISBN13: 978-1-85578-088-0.
Dewey:574.1/92/014.

Audience: **u,f.** *Choice, 1997.*

Biological Chemistry > Review Literature

QP601

Methods in Enzymology. Academic Press.

Audience: **u,f.**

QD271

Methods of Biochemical Analysis. Wiley.

Audience: **u,f.**

Biological Chemistry > History

Bowden, Mary Ellen, et al.   **RM301.25.B69 2002**
Pharmaceutical Achievers: The Human Face of Pharmaceutical
Research. Amy Beth Crow & Tracy Sullivan (Authors). Trade
Paper, Perfect. Chemical Heritage Foundation. Philadelphia, PA.
2005. 214p. ISBN:0-941901-30-0, ISBN13: 978-0-941901-30-7.
Dewey:615/.1/0922. LCCN:2001-055313.

Audience: **u,f.**

Fruton, Joseph S.   **QP511**
A Bio-Bibliography for the History of the Biochemical Sciences
since 1800. Trade Cloth. American Philosophical Society.
Canton, MA. 1982. Special Publications, Vol. 39
ISBN:0-87169-983-4, ISBN13: 978-0-87169-983-1.
Dewey:016.57419/2. LCCN:82-072158.

Audience: **u,f.**

Fruton, Joseph S.   **QD415.F78 1992**
A Skeptical Biochemist. Trade Cloth. Harvard University Press.
Cambridge, MA. 1992. 342p. ISBN:0-674-81077-5, ISBN13:
978-0-674-81077-8. Dewey:574.19/2/09. LCCN:91-029378.

Audience: **u,f.** *Choice, 1993.*

Hargittai, Istvan   **QP511.7.H37 2002**
Candid Science II: Conversations with Famous Biomedical
Scientists. Magdolna Hargittai (Editor). Trade Cloth. Imperial
College Press. London, 2002. 616p. ISBN:1-86094-280-6,
ISBN13: 978-1-86094-280-8. Dewey:572/.092/2.
LCCN:2002-510095.

Audience: **u,f.** *Choice, 2003, 2002.*

Kohler, Robert E.   **QP511.5.U5**
From Medical Chemistry to Biochemistry: The Making of a
Biomedical Discipline. Trade Cloth. Cambridge University
Press. New York, NY. 1982. 380p. Cambridge Monographs on
the History of Medicine ISBN:0-521-24312-2, ISBN13:
978-0-521-24312-4. Dewey:572/.09. LCCN:81-010189.

Audience: **u,f.**

Sacks, Oliver   **RC339.52.S23A3 2001**
Uncle Tungsten: Memories of a Chemical Boyhood. Trade
Cloth. Alfred A. Knopf Inc. New York, NY. 2001. 352p.
ISBN:0-375-40448-1, ISBN13: 978-0-375-40448-1.
Dewey:509.2. LCCN:2001-033738.

Audience: **l,u,f.** *Choice, 2002.*

Biological Chemistry > Laboratory Methods

Cunico, Robert L., et al.   **QP519.9.H53C86 1998**
Basic HPLC and CE of Biomolecules. Karen M. Gooding &
Tim Wehr (Authors). Trade Paper. Bay Bioanalytical Laboratory,
Inc. Hercules, CA. 1998. 400p. ISBN:0-9663229-0-8, ISBN13:
978-0-9663229-0-3. Dewey:547/.30894. LCCN:98-070600.

Audience: **u,f.** *Choice, 1999.*

Fini, Carlo   **QP551**
Laboratory Methodology in Biochemistry: Amino Acid Analysis
and Protein Sequencing. Floridi, Ardesio; Finelli, Vincent N.
(Editors). CRC Press. 1990. ISBN:0-8493-4400-X, ISBN13:
978-0-8493-4400-8.

Audience: **u,f.**

Inman, Keith; Rudin, Norah   **RA1057**
An Introduction to Forensic DNA Analysis. CRC Press. 1997.
ISBN:0-8493-8117-7, ISBN13: 978-0-8493-8117-1.

Audience: **u,f.**

Martin, R.   **QP620 .M37 1996**
Gel Electrophoresis: Nucleic Acids. UK-B Format Paperback.
Springer. New York, NY. 1996. 192p. Introduction to
Biotechniques Ser. ISBN:1-872748-28-7, ISBN13:
978-1-872748-28-3. Dewey:574.87328.

Audience: **u,f.** *Choice, 1997.*

Neuberger, A. & Van   **QD415.N48**
  Deenen, L. L. (Editors)
Modern Physical Methods in Biochemistry, Pt. A. Trade Cloth.
Elsevier. New York, NY. 1985. 428p. New Comprehensive
Biochemistry Ser., Vol. 11 ISBN:0-444-80649-0, ISBN13:
978-0-444-80649-9. Dewey:574.19/2 s. LCCN:85-004402.

Audience: **u,f.**

Biological Chemistry > Tables of Data

Lentner, Cornelus (Editor)   **QP33**
Geigy Scientific Tables, 4 vols.. Ed. 8. CIBA-Geigy. 1981.
ISBN:0-914168-50-9, ISBN13: 978-0-914168-50-8.

Audience: **u,f.**

Biological Chemistry > Treatises

QD415

New Comprehensive Biochemistry. Elsevier/North Holland
Biomedical Press.

Audience: **u,f.**

Barry, John Michael; Barry,   **QP514**
  E. M.
An Introduction to the Structure of Biological Molecules.
Prentice-Hall. 1969. Prentice-Hall Biological Science Series

Audience: **u,f.**

Baszkin, Adam & Norde,   **QP517.S87P48 2000**
  Willem (Contribution by)
Physical Chemistry of Biological Interfaces. Paper over Boards.
Marcel Dekker Inc. New York, NY. 1999. 856p.
ISBN:0-8247-7581-3, ISBN13: 978-0-8247-7581-0.
Dewey:570/.1/5413. LCCN:99-051471.

Audience: **u,f.**

Chang, Raymond   QH345.C425 2004
Physical Chemistry for the Biosciences. Perfect, Paper over
Boards. University Science Books. Sausalito, CA. 2005. 677p.
ISBN:1-891389-33-5, ISBN13: 978-1-891389-33-7. Dewey:572.
LCCN:2004-049612.
                                              Audience: **u,f.** *Choice, 2005.*

Cowan, J. A.   QP531.C68 1997
Inorganic Biochemistry: An Introduction. Ed. 2. Trade Cloth.
John Wiley & Sons, Inc. Hoboken, NJ. 1997. 456p.
ISBN:0-471-18895-6, ISBN13: 978-0-471-18895-7.
Dewey:572.5/1. LCCN:96-014100.
                                              Audience: **u,f.** *Choice, 1998.*

Cowan, James A.   QP531.C68 1997
Inorganic Biochemistry: An Introduction. Ed. 2. Trade Cloth.
John Wiley & Sons, Inc. Hoboken, NJ. 1996. 400p.
ISBN:1-56081-923-5, ISBN13: 978-1-56081-923-3.
Dewey:574.19/214. LCCN:96-014100.
                                              Audience: **u,f.**

Dugas, H.   QP601.D78 1989
Bioorganic Chemistry. Ed. 2. Trade Cloth. Springer. New York,
NY. 1988. 651p. Advanced Texts in Chemistry Ser.
ISBN:0-387-96795-8, ISBN13: 978-0-387-96795-0.
Dewey:574.19/25. LCCN:89-117705.
                                              Audience: **u,f.**

Dugas, Hermann   QP601
Bioorganic Chemistry: A Chemical Approach to Enzyme Action.
Ed. 3. Trade Paper. Springer. New York, NY. 1999. XVII, 700p.
Advanced Texts in Chemistry Ser. ISBN:0-387-98910-2,
ISBN13: 978-0-387-98910-5. Dewey:574.19/25.
                                              Audience: **u,f.**

Fessner, Wolf-Dieter   TP248.65.E59B563
    (Editor)
Biocatalysis - From Discovery to Application. Trade Paper.
Springer. New York, NY. 2000. IX, 254p. Desktop Editions in
Chemistry Ser. ISBN:3-540-66970-1, ISBN13:
978-3-540-66970-8. Dewey:660.6/34. LCCN:00-020456.
                                              Audience: **u,f.**

Florkin, Marcel   QH345
Comparative Biochemistry: A Comprehensive Treatise, 7 Vols.
Mason, Howard S. (Editors). Academic Press. 1960.
                                              Audience: **u,f.**

Florkin, Marcel   QD415
Comprehensive Biochemistry (Set). Stotz, Elmer H. (Editors).
Elsevier. 0000. ISBN:0-444-80151-0, ISBN13:
978-0-444-80151-7.
                                              Audience: **u,f.**

Frausto da Silva, J. J. R. &   QP531.S54 1991
    Williams, R. J.
The Biological Chemistry of the Elements: The Inorganic
Chemistry of Life. Trade Cloth. Oxford University Press, Inc.
New York, NY. 1991. 582p. ISBN:0-19-855598-9, ISBN13:
978-0-19-855598-8. Dewey:572/.51. LCCN:91-011585.
                                              Audience: **u,f.** *Choice, 1992.*

Hammes, Gordon G.   QP517.P49H35 2000
Thermodynamics and Kinetics for the Biological Sciences.
Trade Paper. John Wiley & Sons, Inc. Hoboken, NJ. 2000. 176p.
ISBN:0-471-37491-1, ISBN13: 978-0-471-37491-6. Dewey:572.
LCCN:99-086233.
                                              Audience: **u,f.**

Jevons, Frederick Raphael   QP514.J47 1968
The Biochemical Approach to Life. Ed. 2. Sanger, F. (fr.). Basic
Books. 1968.
                                              Audience: **l,u,f.**

Karlson, P.   QP514.2
Introduction to Modern Biochemistry. Ed. 4. Charles Doering
(Translator). Trade Cloth. Elsevier Science & Technology
Books. Saint Louis, MO. 1975. xiii, 545p.
ISBN:0-12-399764-X, ISBN13: 978-0-12-399764-7.
Dewey:574.19/2. LCCN:73-009429.
                                              Audience: **u,f.**

Klotz, Irwing M.   QP517.L54K57 1997
Ligand-Receptor Energetics: A Guide for the Perplexed. Trade
Paper. John Wiley & Sons, Inc. Hoboken, NJ. 1997. 192p.
ISBN:0-471-17626-5, ISBN13: 978-0-471-17626-8.
Dewey:574.19/283. LCCN:96-034518.
                                              Audience: **u,f.** *Choice, 1998.*

Lehninger, Albert L.   QH511.L4
Bioenergetics. Ed. 2. Paper Text. Benjamin-Cummings
Publishing Company. San Francisco, CA. 1971. Biology
Teaching Monographs ISBN:0-8053-6103-0, ISBN13:
978-0-8053-6103-2. Dewey:574.1/9121.
                                              Audience: **u,f.** *B*

Lehninger, Albert L.   QD415.L44 2000
Principles of Biochemistry. Ed. 3. Cloth Text. Worth Publishers,
Inc. New York, NY. 2000. ISBN:1-57259-153-6, ISBN13:
978-1-57259-153-0. Dewey:572. LCCN:99-049137.
                                              Audience: **l,u,f.**

Lehninger, Albert L., et al.   QD415 .L44 2000
Lehninger Principles of Biochemistry. David L. Nelson &
Michael M. Cox (Authors). Trade Cloth. Worth Publishers, Inc.
New York, NY. 2000. ISBN:0-7167-3867-8, ISBN13:
978-0-7167-3867-1. Dewey:572. LCCN:99-049137.
                                              Audience: **l,u,f.**

Mahler, Henry R. & Cordes,   QP514.2
    Eugene H.
Biological Chemistry. Ed. 2. Cloth Text. HarperCollins
Publishers. New York, NY. 1971. xiv, 1009p.
ISBN:0-06-044172-0, ISBN13: 978-0-06-044172-2.
Dewey:574.19/2. LCCN:76-141169.
                                              Audience: **u,f.**

Mathews   QD415.M34
Biochemistry. Ed. 3. Cloth Text. Benjamin-Cummings
Publishing Company. San Francisco, CA. 1999.
ISBN:0-8053-3067-4, ISBN13: 978-0-8053-3067-0. Dewey:572.
                                              Audience: **l,u,f.**

Mathews, Christopher K., et   QD415.M34 1999
    al.
Biochemistry. Ed. 3. Kevin G. Ahern & Kensal E. Van Holde
(Authors). Cloth Text. Benjamin-Cummings Publishing
Company. San Francisco, CA. 1999. 1200p.
ISBN:0-8053-3066-6, ISBN13: 978-0-8053-3066-3. Dewey:572.
LCCN:99-043683.
                                              Audience: **l,u,f.**

Stryer, Lubert   QP514.2.S66 1995
Biochemistry. Ed. 4. Cloth Text. W. H. Freeman & Company.
New York, NY. 1995. 1064p. ISBN:0-7167-2009-4, ISBN13:
978-0-7167-2009-6. Dewey:574.1/92. LCCN:94-022832.
                                              Audience: **l,u,f.** *B*

Suckling, Colin J. &   QP514.2
  Suckling, Keith E.
Biological Chemistry. Cloth Text. Cambridge University Press.
New York, NY. 1980. 393p. Cambridge Texts in Chemistry and
Biochemistry Ser. ISBN:0-521-22852-2, ISBN13:
978-0-521-22852-7. Dewey:574.19/2. LCCN:79-051830.

                                Audience: **l,u,f.**

Taylor, P. G. (Editor)   QH506 .M42 2002
Mechanism and Synthesis. Mixed Media. Royal Society of
Chemistry, The. Cambridge, 2002. 368p. The Molecular World
Ser. ISBN:0-85404-695-X, ISBN13: 978-0-85404-695-9.
Dewey:547.2.

                  Audience: **u,f.** *Choice, 2003.*

Terrett, Nicholas K.   RS419.T47 1998
Combinatorial Chemistry. Cloth Text. Oxford University Press,
Inc. New York, NY. 1998. 200p. Chemistry Masters Ser.
ISBN:0-19-850220-6, ISBN13: 978-0-19-850220-3.
Dewey:615.1/9. LCCN:97-032698.

                  Audience: **u,f.** *Choice, 1999.*

Tinoco, Ignacio, et al.   QH345.T56 2002
Physical Chemistry: Principles and Applications in Biological
Sciences. Ed. 4. Joseph D. Puglisi, Kenneth Sauer & James C.
Wang (Authors). Cloth Text. Prentice Hall PTR. Upper Saddle
River, NJ. 2001. 740p. ISBN:0-13-095943-X, ISBN13:
978-0-13-095943-0. Dewey:541/.02457. LCCN:2001-280599.

                                  Audience: **u,f.**

Voet, Donald & Voet, Judith   QP514.2.V64 1995
G.
Biochemistry. Ed. 2. Trade Cloth. John Wiley & Sons, Inc.
Hoboken, NJ. 1995. 1392p. ISBN:0-471-58651-X, ISBN13:
978-0-471-58651-7. Dewey:572. LCCN:94-049605.

                              Audience: **l,u,f.**

Biological Chemistry > Special Topics

☐ Entrez, the Life Science Search Engine.
http://www.ncbi.nlm.nih.gov/gquery/gquery.fcgi

                              Audience: **u,f.**

                                   QD381
☐ Image Library of Biological Macromolecules.
http://www.imb-jena.de/IMAGE.html

                              Audience: **u,f.**

Biological Chemistry > Special Topics > Proteins and Nucleic Acids

☐ Antibody Explorer.
http://www.sigmaaldrich.com/Area_of_Interest/Life_Science/
Antibody_Explorer.html

                              Audience: **u,f.**

☐ Human Protein Atlas.
http://www.proteinatlas.org/

                              Audience: **u,f.**

☐ Protein Data Bank.
http://mmcif.pdb.org/index.html

                              Audience: **u,f.**

☐ RNA World Website.
http://www.imb-jena.de/RNA.html

                              Audience: **u,f.**

Adams, R L; Knowler, J T;
  Leader, D P
The Biochemistry of the Nucleic Acids. Ed. 11. Chapman &
Hall. 1992. ISBN:0-412-46030-0, ISBN13: 978-0-412-46030-2.

                          Audience: **u,f.** *ℬ*

Barrett, G. C. & Elmore,   QD431 .B28 1998
D. T.
Amino Acids and Peptides. Cloth Text. Cambridge University
Press. New York, NY. 1998. 240p. ISBN:0-521-46292-4,
ISBN13: 978-0-521-46292-1. Dewey:572.65. LCCN:97-031093.

                  Audience: **u,f.** *Choice, 1999.*

Blackburn, G. Meredith &   QD433.N83 1990
Gait, Michael J.
Nucleic Acids in Chemistry and Biology. Cloth Text. Oxford
University Press, Inc. New York, NY. 1991. 464p.
ISBN:0-19-963120-4, ISBN13: 978-0-19-963120-9.
Dewey:547.7/9. LCCN:90-014187.

                          Audience: **u,f.**

Fricker, Lloyd D. (Editor)   QP552
Peptide Biosynthesis and Processing. CRC Press. 1991.
ISBN:0-8493-8852-X, ISBN13: 978-0-8493-8852-1.

                          Audience: **u,f.**

Janson, Jan-Christer &   QP551.P69754 1997
Rydén, Lars (Editors)
Protein Purification: Principles, High-Resolution Methods, and
Applications. Ed. 2. Trade Cloth. John Wiley & Sons, Inc.
Hoboken, NJ. 1997. 712p. ISBN:0-471-18626-0, ISBN13:
978-0-471-18626-7. Dewey:572/.6. LCCN:97-013875.

                  Audience: **u,f.** *Choice, 1998.*

Jones, John   QD431
Amino Acid and Peptide Synthesis. Ed. 2. Paper Text. Oxford
University Press, Inc. New York, NY. 2002. 96p. Oxford
Chemistry Primers Ser., Vol. 7 ISBN:0-19-925738-8, ISBN13:
978-0-19-925738-6. Dewey:547/.750459. LCCN:2002-511930.

                          Audience: **u,f.**

Lister, T.   QH447
Chemistry and the Human Genome. Trade Cloth. Springer. New
York, NY. 2002. 46p. ISBN:0-85404-396-9, ISBN13:
978-0-85404-396-5. Dewey:599.935.

                          Audience: **u,f.**

Rhodes, Gale   QP519.9.X72R48 2000
Crystallography Made Crystal Clear: A Guide for Users of
Macromolecular Models. Ed. 2. Trade Paper. Elsevier Science &
Technology Books. Saint Louis, MO. 1999. 286p.
ISBN:0-12-587072-8, ISBN13: 978-0-12-587072-6.
Dewey:547/.7. LCCN:99-063088.

                Audience: **u,f.** *Choice, 2000, 1993.*

Wilkinson, A. J. & Moody,   TP248.65.P76M66 1990
P. C.
Protein Engineering: In Focus. Paper Text. Oxford University
Press, Inc. New York, NY. 1991. 96p. In Focus Ser.
ISBN:0-19-963194-8, ISBN13: 978-0-19-963194-0.
Dewey:660/.63. LCCN:90-007728.
Audience: **u,f.** *Choice, 1992.*

Biological Chemistry > Special Topics > Lipid Biochemistry

Gunstone, Frank D.,   QP751
Harwood, John L.
The Lipid Handbook. Padley, Fred B. (Editors). Chapman and
Hall. 1986. ISBN:0-412-24480-2, ISBN13: 978-0-412-24480-3.
Audience: **u,f.**

Biological Chemistry > Special Topics > Foods and Nutrition

Barham, Peter   TX651.B147 2001
The Science of Cooking. Trade Cloth. Springer. New York, NY.
2001. VII, 244p. ISBN:3-540-67466-7, ISBN13:
978-3-540-67466-5. Dewey:641.5. LCCN:00-059559.
Audience: **l,u,f.**

Beckett, Sheilah   TP640.B43 2000
The Science of Chocolate. Trade Paper. Royal Society of
Chemistry, The. Cambridge, 2000. xiv + 176p.
ISBN:0-85404-600-3, ISBN13: 978-0-85404-600-3.
Dewey:664.5.
Audience: **l,u,f.** *Choice, 2001.*

Bender, David A.   QP771 .B44 1992
Nutritional Biochemistry of the Vitamins. Trade Cloth.
Cambridge University Press. New York, NY. 1992. 451p.
ISBN:0-521-38144-4, ISBN13: 978-0-521-38144-4.
Dewey:613.2/86. LCCN:91-034082.
Audience: **u,f.** *Choice, 1993.*

Berdanier, Carolyn D.   QP141
CRC Desk Reference for Nutrition. CRC Press. 1998.
ISBN:0-8493-9682-4, ISBN13: 978-0-8493-9682-3.
Audience: **l,u,f.**

Brody, Tom   QP141.B853 1999
Nutritional Biochemistry. Ed. 2. Cloth Text. Elsevier Science &
Technology Books. Saint Louis, MO. 1998. 1006p.
ISBN:0-12-134836-9, ISBN13: 978-0-12-134836-6.
Dewey:612.3/9. LCCN:98-040384.
Audience: **u,f.** *Choice, 1999.*

Coultate, T. P.   TX531.C757 2002
Food: The Chemistry of Its Components. Ed. 4. Trade Paper.
Royal Society of Chemistry, The. Cambridge, 2002. xii + 432p.
RSC Paperbacks Ser. ISBN:0-85404-615-1, ISBN13:
978-0-85404-615-7. Dewey:641.1.
Audience: **l,u,f.**

Davies & Austin   QP722.A8D38 1991
Vitamin C: Its Chemistry and Biochemistry. Trade Cloth.
Springer. New York, NY. 1991. x + 154p. ISBN:0-85186-333-7,
ISBN13: 978-0-85186-333-7. Dewey:612.399.
Audience: **u,f.** *Choice, 1992.*

Ensminger, Audrey H. et al.   TX349
(Editors)
The Concise Encyclopedia of Foods and Nutrition. CRC Press.
1995. ISBN:0-8493-4455-7, ISBN13: 978-0-8493-4455-8.
Audience: **l,u,f.**

Navarra, Tova & Lipowitz,   QP771.E53 1996
Myron A.
Encyclopedia of Vitamins, Minerals, and Supplements. John G.
Navarra Jr. (Foreword by). Trade Cloth. Facts On File, Inc..
New York, NY. 1995. 304p. ISBN:0-8160-3183-5, ISBN13:
978-0-8160-3183-2. Dewey:615.3/28/03. LCCN:95-012645.
Audience: **l,u,f.** *Choice, 1996.*

Pike, Ruth L.   TX353
Nutrition: An Integrated Approach. Ed. 3. Cloth Text. John
Wiley & Sons, Inc. Hoboken, NJ. 1984. 1068p.
ISBN:0-471-09004-2, ISBN13: 978-0-471-09004-5.
Dewey:612/.3. LCCN:83-016766.
Audience: **u,f.** ℬ

Sikorski, Zdzislaw E.   TX545
(Editor)
Chemical and Functional Properties of Food Components.
Technomic Pub. Co.. 1997. ISBN:1-56676-464-5, ISBN13:
978-1-56676-464-3.
Audience: **u,f.**

Somer, Elizabeth & Health   QP771.S66
Media of America Staff
The Essential Guide to Vitamins and Minerals. Ed. 2. Trade
Paper. HarperCollins Publishers. New York, NY. 1996. 464p.
ISBN:0-06-273345-1, ISBN13: 978-0-06-273345-0.
Dewey:612.3.
Audience: **l,u,f.**

Spallholz, Julian E.   QP141
Nutrition: Chemistry and Biology. Ed. 2. Boylan, L. Mallory;
Driskell, Judy A. (Editors). CRC Press. 1998.
ISBN:0-8493-8504-0, ISBN13: 978-0-8493-8504-9.
Audience: **u,f.**

Biological Chemistry > Special Topics > Medical Biochemistry and Pharmacology

Bhagavan, Nadhipuram V.   QP514.2.B45 1991
Medical Biochemistry. Trade Cloth. Jones & Bartlett Publishers,
Inc. Sudbury, MA. 1992. 992p. ISBN:0-86720-030-8, ISBN13:
978-0-86720-030-0. Dewey:612/.015. LCCN:91-007015.
Audience: **u,f.** *Choice, 1993.*

Cannon, Joseph   RM300.C36 1998
Pharmacology for Chemists. Trade Cloth. Oxford University
Press, Inc. New York, NY. 1999. 288p. ACS Professional
Reference Bks. ISBN:0-8412-3524-4, ISBN13:
978-0-8412-3524-3. Dewey:615/.1/024541. LCCN:98-025069.
Audience: **u,f.** *Choice, 1999.*

Gringauz, Alex   RS403.G76
Introduction to Medicinal Chemistry: How Drugs Act and Why.
Ed. 2. Trade Cloth. John Wiley & Sons, Inc. Hoboken, NJ.
1996. 736p. ISBN:0-471-18545-0, ISBN13: 978-0-471-18545-1.
Dewey:615.1/9. LCCN:95-049331.
Audience: **u,f.** *Choice, 1998.*

Hansch, Corwin (Editor)   RS402.C65 1990
Comprehensive Medicinal Chemistry. Trade Cloth. Elsevier
Science & Technology Books. Saint Louis, MO. 1990. 6000p.
The Rational Design, Mechanistic Study and Therapeutic
Application of Chemical Compounds Ser. ISBN:0-08-032530-0,
ISBN13: 978-0-08-032530-9. Dewey:615.19. LCCN:89-016329.
       Audience: **u,f.** *Choice, 1990.*

Hardie, D. Grahame   QP517.C45H37 1991
Biochemical Messengers: Hormones, Neurotransmitters and
Growth Factors. Trade Cloth. Chapman & Hall. New York, NY.
1990. 250p. ISBN:0-412-30340-X, ISBN13: 978-0-412-30340-1.
Dewey:574.87/6. LCCN:91-008226.
       Audience: **u,f.** *Choice, 1992.*

Repic, Oljan   RS403.R46 1998
Principles of Process Research and Chemical Development in
the Pharmaceutical Industry. Ed. 1. Trade Cloth. John Wiley &
Sons, Inc. Hoboken, NJ. 1998. 240p. ISBN:0-471-16516-6,
ISBN13: 978-0-471-16516-3. Dewey:615/.19. LCCN:97-013904.
       Audience: **u,f.** *Choice, 1998.*

Sherma, Joseph & Zweig,
G.   RS189 .D79
Handbook of Chromatography, Set. Trade Cloth. Franklin Book
Company, Inc. Newtown Sq, PA. 1981. Handbook of
Chromatography Ser. ISBN:0-8493-3030-0, ISBN13:
978-0-8493-3030-8. Dewey:615/.19015. LCCN:81-010157.
       Audience: **u,f.**

Biological Chemistry > Special Topics > Toxicology and Environmental Concerns

Landis, Wayne G. & Yu,
Ming-Ho   QH545.A1L35 1999
Introduction to Environmental Toxicology. Ed. 2. Box or
Slipcased. Lewis Publishers. Boca Raton, FL. 1998. 416p.
ISBN:1-56670-265-8, ISBN13: 978-1-56670-265-2.
Dewey:571.9/5. LCCN:97-050324.
       Audience: **u,f.**

Biological Chemistry > Special Topics > Plant and Animal Biochemistry

Specarb: Raman Spectra of Carbohydrates.
http://www.models.kvl.dk/users/engelsen/specarb/specarb.html
       Audience: **u,f.**

Specarb: Raman Spectra of Carbohydrates.
http://www.models.kvl.dk/users/engelsen/specarb/specarb.html
       Audience: **u,f.**

Britton, G.   QP670
The Biochemistry of Natural Pigments. Trade Cloth. Cambridge
University Press. New York, NY. 1983. 376p. Cambridge Texts
in Chemistry and Biochemistry Ser. ISBN:0-521-24892-2,
ISBN13: 978-0-521-24892-1. Dewey:574.19/218.
LCCN:82-009512.
       Audience: **u,f.**

David, Serge   QP701.D3813 1997
The Molecular and Supramolecular Chemistry of Carbohydrates:
A Chemical Introduction to the Glycosciences. Rosemary G.
Beau (Translator). Cloth Text. Oxford University Press, Inc.
New York, NY. 1998. 336p. ISBN:0-19-850047-5, ISBN13:
978-0-19-850047-6. Dewey:572/.56. LCCN:97-018604.
       Audience: **u,f.** *Choice, 1998.*

Milgrom, Lionel R.   QD441.M55 1997
The Colours of Life: An Introduction to the Chemistry of
Porphyrins and Related Compounds. Cloth Text. Oxford
University Press, Inc. New York, NY. 1997. 255p.
ISBN:0-19-855380-3, ISBN13: 978-0-19-855380-9.
Dewey:547.5/93. LCCN:96-027452.
       Audience: **u,f.** *Choice, 1998.*

Pigman, Ward & Horton,
Derek   QD321
The Carbohydrates: Chemistry and Biochemistry, Vol. 2A. Trade
Cloth. Elsevier Science & Technology Books. Saint Louis, MO.
1970. xix, 469p. ISBN:0-12-556302-7, ISBN13:
978-0-12-556302-4. Dewey:547/.78.
       Audience: **u,f.** *B*

Robyt, John F.   QD321.R667 1998
Essentials of Carbohydrate Chemistry. Trade Cloth. Springer.
New York, NY. 1997. XV, 399p. Advanced Texts in Chemistry
Ser. ISBN:0-387-94951-8, ISBN13: 978-0-387-94951-2.
Dewey:572/.56. LCCN:97-019019.
       Audience: **u,f.** *Choice, 1998.*

Stick, Robert V.   QD321 .S84 2001
Carbohydrates: The Sweet Molecules of Life. Cloth Text.
Elsevier Science & Technology Books. Saint Louis, MO. 2001.
256p. ISBN:0-12-670960-2, ISBN13: 978-0-12-670960-5.
Dewey:547.78.
       Audience: **l,u,f.** *Choice, 2001.*

Biological Chemistry > Special Topics > Steroids

Richards, John H.;
Hendrickson, James B.   QD415.R5
The Biosynthesis of Steroids, Terpenes, and Acetogenins. W.A.
Benjamin. 1964.
       Audience: **u,f.**

Biological Chemistry > Laboratory Safety

Prokopetz, Andrew T.   QD63.5.P5313 1995
Safety in the Chemistry and Biochemistry Laboratory. Andre
Picot, Philippe Grenouillet & Douglas B. Walters (Editors),
Robert H. Dodd (Translator). Trade Cloth. John Wiley & Sons,
Inc. Hoboken, NJ. 1994. 332p. ISBN:1-56081-040-8, ISBN13:
978-1-56081-040-7. Dewey:542/.1/0289. LCCN:94-038824.
       Audience: **l,u,f.** *Choice, 1995.*

Biological Chemistry > Problem Manuals and Educational Materials

☐ The Biochemical Periodic Table.
http://umbbd.ahc.umn.edu/periodic/spiral.html
Audience: **u,f.**

☐ NCBI Education.
http://www.ncbi.nlm.nih.gov/Education/
Audience: **l,u,f.**

Hames, B. D. & Hooper, N. M.   QP518.3
Biochemistry. Ed. 2. UK-B Format Paperback. Taylor & Francis Group. Philadelphia, PA. 2000. 432p. Instant Notes Ser. ISBN:1-85996-142-8, ISBN13: 978-1-85996-142-1. Dewey:572.
Audience: **l,u,f.**

Kuchel, Philip W.   QP518.3.S3 1998
Schaum's Outline of Biochemistry. Ed. 2. Paper Text. McGraw-Hill Companies, The. New York, NY. 1997. 576p. Schaum's Outline Ser. ISBN:0-07-036149-5, ISBN13: 978-0-07-036149-2. Dewey:572. LCCN:97-023525.
Audience: **l,u,f.**

COMPUTING

The RCL Computing section has been informed by the notions of topics of study as outlined in "Computing Curricula 2005" prepared under auspices of ACM and IEEE. In that document the growth and development of the study of computing is clear. In fact, several types of programs are observed: Computer Engineering, Computer Science, Information Systems, Information Technology, and Software Engineering.

The taxonomy is a simplified version of the ACM Computing Classification System 1998. While this scheme admits classification of almost any topical area, most applications of computing will be found in other RCL sections. Specially important areas of interplay, aside from scientific disciplines and engineering, are business administration and quantitatively-grounded social sciences. However, indication of titles in bioinformatics and computational biology under this section intends to underscore the very significant and overarching interaction between computer scientists and biologists today. Even undergraduate level curricula are being influenced by such developments.

Relatively few titles from the last edition of BCL made it into the present update. This reflects the churn and dynamism in a field developed only over the last 50 years. In addition, students will use a vast array of freely available materials supporting particular programming tools. As librarians' budget resources allow, many book needs may be satisfied with one or more aggregations of computing monographs. Review and recommendation of these aggregations was deemed beyond our scope.

—Carol Hutchins

Data Structures

Mehta, Dinesh P. & Sahni,   **QA76.9.S88H363 2004**
Sartaj (Editors)
Handbook of Data Structures and Applications. Chapman &
Hall/CRC. 2005. Computer and Information Science Series
ISBN:1-58488-435-5, ISBN13: 978-1-58488-435-4.
Audience: **u,f.**

Samet, Hanan   **QA76.9.D3**
Foundations of Multidimensional and Metric Data Structures.
Trade Cloth. Elsevier Science & Technology Books. Saint
Louis, MO. 2006. 1024p. The Morgan Kaufmann Series in
Computer Graphics and Geometric Modeling Ser.
ISBN:0-12-369446-9, ISBN13: 978-0-12-369446-1.
Dewey:005.7/3. LCCN:2005-054165.
Audience: **u,f.**

Shekhar, Shashi & Chawla,   **G70.212.S54 2003**
Sanjay
Spatial Databases: A Tour. Cloth Text. Prentice Hall PTR. Upper
Saddle River, NJ. 2002. 262p. ISBN:0-13-017480-7, ISBN13:
978-0-13-017480-2. Dewey:910/.285. LCCN:2002-003694.
Audience: **u.**

Data Encryption

Garfinkel, Simson, et al.   **QA76.76.O63**
Practical UNIX and Internet Security. Ed. 3. Gene Spafford &
Alan Schwartz (Authors). Trade Paper, Perfect. O'Reilly Media,
Inc. Sebastopol, CA. 2003. 984p. ISBN:0-596-00323-4, ISBN13:
978-0-596-00323-4. Dewey:005.8. LCCN:2004-557663.
Audience: **l,u,f.**

Goldreich, Oded   **QA268 .G5745 2001**
Foundations of Cryptography: Basic Tools, Vol. 1. Trade Cloth.
Cambridge University Press. New York, NY. 2001. 392p.
ISBN:0-521-79172-3, ISBN13: 978-0-521-79172-4.
Dewey:652/.8. LCCN:00-049362.
Audience: **u,f.**

Goldreich, Oded   **QA76.9**
Foundations of Cryptography: Basic Applications. Trade Cloth.
Cambridge University Press. New York, NY. 2004. 448p.
ISBN:0-521-83084-2, ISBN13: 978-0-521-83084-3.
Dewey:005.8/2.
Audience: **u,f.**

Salomon, David   **QA76.9.D33S25 2004**
Data Compression: The Complete Reference. Ed. 3. Trade
Cloth. Springer. New York, NY. 2004. XX, 900p.
ISBN:0-387-40697-2, ISBN13: 978-0-387-40697-8.
Dewey:005.74/6. LCCN:2003-065725.
Audience: **u,f.**

Schneier, Bruce   **QA76.9.A25S35 1996**
Applied Cryptography: Protocols, Algorithms, and Source Code
in C. Ed. 2. Trade Paper. John Wiley & Sons, Inc. Hoboken, NJ.
1995. 784p. ISBN:0-471-11709-9, ISBN13: 978-0-471-11709-4.
Dewey:005.8/2. LCCN:95-012398.
Audience: **u,f.**

Schneier, Bruce   **QA76.9.A25S352 2004**
Secrets and Lies: Digital Security in a Networked World. Trade
Paper. John Wiley & Sons, Inc. Hoboken, NJ. 2004. 448p.

ISBN:0-471-45380-3, ISBN13: 978-0-471-45380-2.
Dewey:005.8. LCCN:00-042252.
Audience: **g,l,u,f.** *Choice, 2001.*

Stallings, William   **TK5105.59**
Cryptography and Network Security. Ed. 4. Cloth Text. Prentice
Hall PTR. Upper Saddle River, NJ. 2005. 592p.
ISBN:0-13-187316-4, ISBN13: 978-0-13-187316-2. Dewey:5.8.
LCCN:2006-276085.
Audience: **u.**

Coding and Information Theory

Roman, Steven A.   **QA268 .R66**
An Introduction to Coding and Information Theory. Trade Cloth.
Springer. New York, NY. 1996. Undergraduate Texts in
Mathematics ISBN:0-614-14030-7, ISBN13: 978-0-614-14030-9.
Dewey:005.7/2. LCCN:96-011738.
Audience: **l,u.**

Salomon, David   **QA76.9.D33S25 2004**
Data Compression: The Complete Reference. Ed. 3. Trade
Cloth. Springer. New York, NY. 2004. XX, 900p.
ISBN:0-387-40697-2, ISBN13: 978-0-387-40697-8.
Dewey:005.74/6. LCCN:2003-065725.
Audience: **u,f.**

Theory of Computation > General

Cormen, Thomas H., et al.   **QA76.6**
Introduction to Algorithms. Ed. 2. Charles E. Leiserson, Ronald
L. Rivest & Clifford Stein (Authors). Cloth Text. McGraw-Hill
Higher Education. Burr Ridge, IL. 2001. 1056p.
ISBN:0-07-013151-1, ISBN13: 978-0-07-013151-4.
Dewey:005.1. LCCN:2001-031277.
Audience: **u,f.**

Davis, Martin   **QA76.17.D38 2000**
The Universal Computer: The Road from Leibniz to Turing.
Trade Cloth. W. W. Norton & Company, Inc. New York, NY.
2000. 256p. ISBN:0-393-04785-7, ISBN13: 978-0-393-04785-1.
Dewey:004/.09. LCCN:00-040200.
Audience: **g,l,u,f.** *Choice, 2001.*

Goldreich, Oded   **QA268 .G5745 2001**
Foundations of Cryptography: Basic Tools, Vol. 1. Trade Cloth.
Cambridge University Press. New York, NY. 2001. 392p.
ISBN:0-521-79172-3, ISBN13: 978-0-521-79172-4.
Dewey:652/.8. LCCN:00-049362.
Audience: **u,f.**

Goldreich, Oded   **QA76.9**
Foundations of Cryptography: Basic Applications. Trade Cloth.
Cambridge University Press. New York, NY. 2004. 448p.
ISBN:0-521-83084-2, ISBN13: 978-0-521-83084-3.
Dewey:005.8/2.
Audience: **u,f.**

Harel, David & Feldman,   **QA76.9.A43H37 2004**
Yishai A.
Algorithmics: The Spirit of Computing. Ed. 3. Trade Paper.
Addison-Wesley Longman, Inc. Boston, MA. 2004. 536p.
ISBN:0-321-11784-0, ISBN13: 978-0-321-11784-7.
Dewey:005.1. LCCN:2004-041063.
Audience: **g,l.**

Jones, Neil C. & Pevzner, **QH324.2.J66 2004**
  Pavel
An Introduction to Bioinformatics Algorithms. Cloth Text. MIT
Press. Cambridge, MA. 2004. 448p. Computational Molecular
Biology Ser. ISBN:0-262-10106-8, ISBN13: 978-0-262-10106-6.
Dewey:570/.285. LCCN:2004-048289.

Audience: **u,f.**

Sedgewick, Robert **QA76.73.J38S4 1998**
Algorithms in Java, Pt. 1-4. Ed. 3. Trade Paper. Addison Wesley
Professional. Boston, MA. 2002. 768p. ISBN:0-201-36120-5,
ISBN13: 978-0-201-36120-9. Dewey:005.13/3.
LCCN:98-025050.

Audience: **u.**

Sedgewick, Robert **QA76.9.A43**
Algorithms in Java: Graph Algorithms. Ed. 3. Trade Paper.
Addison Wesley Professional. Boston, MA. 2003. 528p.
ISBN:0-201-36121-3, ISBN13: 978-0-201-36121-6.
Dewey:005.13/3. LCCN:92-000901.

Audience: **u.**

Watts, Duncan J. **QA166.W38 1999**
Small Worlds: The Dynamics of Networks Between Order and
Randomness. Cloth Text. Princeton University Press. Princeton,
NJ. 1999. 266p. Princeton Studies in Complexity
ISBN:0-691-00541-9, ISBN13: 978-0-691-00541-6.
Dewey:511/.5. LCCN:98-056088.

Audience: **g,u.** *Choice, 2000.*

Theory of Computation > Analysis of Algorithms and Complexity

Baase, Sara & Van Gelder, **QA76.9.A43B33 2000**
  Allen
Computer Algorithms: Introduction to Design and Analysis. Ed.
3. Cloth Text. Addison-Wesley Longman, Inc. Boston, MA.
1999. 688p. ISBN:0-201-61244-5, ISBN13: 978-0-201-61244-8.
Dewey:519.7. LCCN:99-014185.

Audience: **l,u.** *B*

Cormen, Thomas H., et al. **QA76.6**
Introduction to Algorithms. Ed. 2. Charles E. Leiserson, Ronald
L. Rivest & Clifford Stein (Authors). Cloth Text. McGraw-Hill
Higher Education. Burr Ridge, IL. 2001. 1056p.
ISBN:0-07-013151-1, ISBN13: 978-0-07-013151-4.
Dewey:005.1. LCCN:2001-031277.

Audience: **u,f.**

Davis, Martin D., et al. **QA267.D38 1994**
Computability, Complexity, and Languages: Fundamentals of
Theoretical Computer Science. Ed. 2. Elaine J. Weyuker & Ron
Sigal (Authors). Cloth Text. Elsevier Science & Technology
Books. Saint Louis, MO. 1994. 609p. Computer Science and
Scientific Computing Ser. ISBN:0-12-206382-1, ISBN13:
978-0-12-206382-4. Dewey:511.3. LCCN:93-026807.

Audience: **u.** *Choice, 1994.*

Garey, Michael R. & **QA76.6.G35**
  Johnson, David S.
Computers and Intractability: A Guide to the Theory of
NP-Completeness. Cloth Text. W. H. Freeman & Company. New
York, NY. 1979. 338p. Mathematical Sciences Ser.
ISBN:0-7167-1044-7, ISBN13: 978-0-7167-1044-8.
Dewey:519.4/0285. LCCN:78-012361.

Audience: **l,u.**

Knuth, Donald E. **QA76.6.K64 1997**
The Art of Computer Programming: Sorting and Searching. Ed.
2. Trade Cloth. Addison Wesley Professional. Boston, MA.
1998. 800p. Art of Computer Programming Ser., Vol. 3
ISBN:0-201-89685-0, ISBN13: 978-0-201-89685-5.
Dewey:005.1. LCCN:97-002147.

Audience: **u,f.**

Knuth, Donald E. **QA76.6.K64 1997**
Art of Computer Programming: Fundamental Algorithms. Ed. 3.
Trade Cloth. Addison Wesley Professional. Boston, MA. 1997.
672p. ISBN:0-201-89683-4, ISBN13: 978-0-201-89683-1.
Dewey:005.1. LCCN:97-002147.

Audience: **u,f.** *B*

Knuth, Donald E. **QA76.6.K64 1997**
The Art of Computer Programming: Seminumerical Algorithms.
Ed. 3. Trade Cloth. Addison Wesley Professional. Boston, MA.
1997. 784p. Art of Computer Programming Ser., Vol. 2
ISBN:0-201-89684-2, ISBN13: 978-0-201-89684-8.
Dewey:005.1. LCCN:97-002147.

Audience: **u,f.**

Papadimitriou, Christos H. **QA267.7 .P36 1994**
Computational Complexity. Cloth Text. Addison-Wesley
Longman, Inc. Boston, MA. 1993. 500p. ISBN:0-201-53082-1,
ISBN13: 978-0-201-53082-7. Dewey:511.3. LCCN:93-005662.

Audience: **u.**

Proakis, John G. & **TK5102.9.P757 1996**
  Manolakis, Dimitris G.
Digital Signal Processing: Principles, Algorithms and
Applications. Ed. 3. Trade Cloth. Prentice Hall PTR. Upper
Saddle River, NJ. 1995. 1016p. ISBN:0-13-373762-4, ISBN13:
978-0-13-373762-2. Dewey:621.382/2. LCCN:95-009117.

Audience: **u.**

Sankoff, David & Kruskal, **QA292.T55 1999**
  Joseph P.
Time Warps, String Edits, and Macromolecules: The Theory and
Practice of Sequence Comparision. David Sankoff & Joseph P.
Kruskal (Editors). Trade Paper. C S L I Publications/Center for
the Study of Language & Information. Stanford, CA. 2001.
408p. The David Hume Ser., :The Philosophy and Cognitive
Science Reissues ISBN:1-57586-217-4, ISBN13:
978-1-57586-217-0. Dewey:515/.24. LCCN:99-042488.

Audience: **l,u.**

Theory of Computation > Logic and Semantics of Programs

Winskel, Glynn **QA76.7.**
The Formal Semantics of Programming Languages: An
Introduction. Trade Paper. MIT Press. Cambridge, MA. 1993.
384p. Foundations of Computing Ser. ISBN:0-262-73103-7,
ISBN13: 978-0-262-73103-4. Dewey:005.131.

Audience: **u,f.** *Choice, 1993.*

Theory of Computation > Mathematical Logic and Formal Languages

Davis, Martin **QA76.17.D38 2000**
The Universal Computer: The Road from Leibniz to Turing.
Trade Cloth. W. W. Norton & Company, Inc. New York, NY.

2000. 256p. ISBN:0-393-04785-7, ISBN13: 978-0-393-04785-1. Dewey:004/.09. LCCN:00-040200.

Audience: **g,l,u,f.** *Choice, 2001.*

Sipser, Michael   **QA267.S56 1997**
Introduction to the Theory of Computation. Ed. 1. Cloth Text. Thomson Course Technology. Boston, MA. 1996. 416p. Computer Science Ser. ISBN:0-534-94728-X, ISBN13: 978-0-534-94728-6. Dewey:511.3/5. LCCN:96-035322.

Audience: **u.**

Math of Computing > Numerical Analysis and Scientific Computing

Brodlie, K. W. (Editor),   **Q175.S4242 1992**
   et al.
Scientific Visualization: Techniques and Applications. L. Carpenter, Rae A. Earnshaw, J. R. Gallop, R. J. Hubbold, A. M. Mumford, C. D. Osland & P. Quarendon (Editors). Cloth Text. Springer. New York, NY. 1992. 284p. ISBN:0-387-54565-4, ISBN13: 978-0-387-54565-3. Dewey:502.8. LCCN:91-035638.

Audience: **u,f.**

Heath, Michael T.   **Q183.9.H4 2002**
Scientific Computing: An Introductory Survey. Ed. 2. Paper Text. McGraw-Hill Companies, The. New York, NY. 2001. xii, 563p. ISBN:0-07-112229-X, ISBN13: 978-0-07-112229-0. Dewey:519.4/0285. LCCN:2001-031265.

Audience: **u.**

Press, William H., et al.   **QA76.73.C153 N85 20**
Numerical Recipes in C++: The Art of Scientific Computing. Ed. 2. Saul A. Teukolsky, William T. Vetterling & Brian P. Flannery (Authors). Cloth Text. Cambridge University Press. New York, NY. 2002. 1032p. ISBN:0-521-75033-4, ISBN13: 978-0-521-75033-2. Dewey:519.4/0285/5133. LCCN:2001-052699.

Audience: **g,u,f.**

Math of Computing > Discrete Mathematics

Biggs, Norman L.   **QA76.9.M35B54 2002**
Discrete Mathematics. Ed. 2. Cloth Text. Oxford University Press, Inc. New York, NY. 2003. 440p. ISBN:0-19-850718-6, ISBN13: 978-0-19-850718-5. Dewey:510. LCCN:2002-029063.

Audience: **l,u.**

Goodman, Jacob E. &   **QA167.H36 2004**
   O'Rourke, Joseph
Handbook of Discrete and Computational Geometry. Ed. 2. Paper over Boards. Chapman & Hall. New York, NY. 2004. 1560p. The CRC Press Series on Discrete Mathematics and Its Applications ISBN:1-58488-301-4, ISBN13: 978-1-58488-301-2. Dewey:516/.13. LCCN:2004-040662.

Audience: **u,f.** *Choice, 1998.*

Graham, Ronald L., et al.   **QA39.2.G733 1994**
Concrete Mathematics: A Foundation for Computer Science. Ed. 2. Donald E. Knuth & Oren Patashnik (Authors). Trade Cloth. Addison Wesley Professional. Boston, MA. 1994. 672p. ISBN:0-201-55802-5, ISBN13: 978-0-201-55802-9. Dewey:510. LCCN:93-040325.

Audience: **u.**

O'Rourke, Joseph   **QA448.D38 O76 1998**
Computational Geometry in C. Ed. 2. Cloth Text. Cambridge University Press. New York, NY. 1998. 392p. ISBN:0-521-64010-5, ISBN13: 978-0-521-64010-7. Dewey:516/.0285/5133. LCCN:98-015363.

Audience: **u.** *Choice, 1999.*

Information Systems > Database Management

Berry, Michael W. (Editor)   **QA76.9.D343S69 2003**
Survey of Text Mining: Clustering, Classification, and Retrieval. Trade Cloth. Springer. New York, NY. 2003. XVII, 244p. ISBN:0-387-95563-1, ISBN13: 978-0-387-95563-6. Dewey:006.3. LCCN:2003-042434.

Audience: **u.**

Date, C. J.   **QA76.9.D3D3659 2003**
An Introduction to Database Systems. Ed. 8. Cloth Text. Addison-Wesley Longman, Inc. Boston, MA. 2003. 1024p. ISBN:0-321-19784-4, ISBN13: 978-0-321-19784-9. Dewey:005.74. LCCN:2003-052442.

Audience: **u.**

Gray, Jim & Reuter,   **QA76.545 .G73 1993**
   Andreas
Transaction Processing: Concepts and Techniques. Elsevier Science and Technology. 1993. Morgan Kaufman Series in Data Management Systems ISBN:1-55860-190-2, ISBN13: 978-1-55860-190-1.

Audience: **u,f.**

Han, Jiawei & Kamber,   **QA76.9 D343 H36 2006**
   Micheline
Data Mining: Concepts and Techniques. Ed. 2. Trade Cloth. Elsevier Science & Technology Books. Saint Louis, MO. 2006. 800p. The Morgan Kaufmann Series in Data Management Systems Ser. ISBN:1-55860-901-6, ISBN13: 978-1-55860-901-3. Dewey:005.741. LCCN:2006-296324.

Audience: **u,f.**

Muller, Robert J.   **QA76.9.D26M85 1999**
Database Design for Smarties: Using UML for Data Modeling. Trade Paper. Elsevier Science & Technology Books. Saint Louis, MO. 1999. 464p. The Morgan Kaufmann Series in Data Management Systems Ser. ISBN:1-55860-515-0, ISBN13: 978-1-55860-515-2. Dewey:005.74. LCCN:98-054436.

Audience: **l,u.**

Shekhar, Shashi & Chawla,   **G70.212.S54 2003**
   Sanjay
Spatial Databases: A Tour. Cloth Text. Prentice Hall PTR. Upper Saddle River, NJ. 2002. 262p. ISBN:0-13-017480-7, ISBN13: 978-0-13-017480-2. Dewey:910/.285. LCCN:2002-003694.

Audience: **u.**

Teorey, Toby; Lightstone,   **QA76.9.D26T45 2005**
   Sam & Nadeau, Tom
Database Modeling and Design. Ed. 4. Elsevier. 2006. Morgan Kaufmann Series in Data Management Systems ISBN:0-12-685352-5, ISBN13: 978-0-12-685352-0.

Audience: **l,u.**

Ullman, Jeffrey D. &   **QA76.9.D3U42 2002**
   Widom, Jennifer
A First Course in Database Systems. Ed. 2. Cloth Text. Prentice

---

Hall PTR. Upper Saddle River, NJ. 2001. 528p.
ISBN:0-13-035300-0, ISBN13: 978-0-13-035300-9.
Dewey:005.7/4. LCCN:2001-045937.

Audience: **l,u.**

Information Systems > Information Storage and Retrieval

Baeza-Yates, Ricardo &   **Z667.B34 1999**
  Ribeiro-Neto, Berthier
Modern Information Retrieval. Trade Paper. Addison-Wesley
Longman, Inc. Boston, MA. 1999. 544p. ACM Press Ser.
ISBN:0-201-39829-X, ISBN13: 978-0-201-39829-8.
Dewey:025.04. LCCN:99-010033.

Audience: **u.**

Berry, Michael W. (Editor)   **QA76.9.D343S69 2003**
Survey of Text Mining: Clustering, Classification, and Retrieval.
Trade Cloth. Springer. New York, NY. 2003. XVII, 244p.
ISBN:0-387-95563-1, ISBN13: 978-0-387-95563-6.
Dewey:006.3. LCCN:2003-042434.

Audience: **u.**

Berry, Michael W. &   **TK5105.884.B47 2005**
  Browne, Murray
Understanding Search Engines: Mathematical Modeling and
Text Retrieval. Ed. 2. Trade Paper, Perfect. Society for Industrial
& Applied Mathematics. Philadelphia, PA. 2005. 117p.
ISBN:0-89871-581-4, ISBN13: 978-0-89871-581-1.
Dewey:025.04. LCCN:2005-042539.

Audience: **u.** *Choice, 2006, 2000.*

Information Systems > World Wide Web

Andersson, Eve Astrid, et al.   **QA76.625.A55 2006**
Software Engineering for Internet Applications. Philip
Greenspun & Andrew Grumet (Authors). Trade Paper. MIT
Press. Cambridge, MA. 2006. 376p. ISBN:0-262-51191-6,
ISBN13: 978-0-262-51191-9. Dewey:005.2/76.
LCCN:2005-049144.

Audience: **l,u.**

Berners-Lee, Tim &   **TK5105.875.I57**
  Fischetti, Mark
Weaving the Web: The Original Design and Ultimate Destiny of
the World Wide Web by Its Inventor. Tim Berners-Lee (Read
by). Audio Cassette. HarperCollins Publishers. New York, NY.
1999. ISBN:0-694-52125-6, ISBN13: 978-0-694-52125-8.
Dewey:025.04.

Audience: **g,l,u.**

Berry, Michael W. &   **TK5105.884.B47 2005**
  Browne, Murray
Understanding Search Engines: Mathematical Modeling and
Text Retrieval. Ed. 2. Trade Paper, Perfect. Society for Industrial
& Applied Mathematics. Philadelphia, PA. 2005. 117p.
ISBN:0-89871-581-4, ISBN13: 978-0-89871-581-1.
Dewey:025.04. LCCN:2005-042539.

Audience: **u.** *Choice, 2006, 2000.*

Johnson, Jeff   **TK5105**
Web Bloopers: 60 Common Web Design Mistakes, and How to
Avoid. Elsevier Science & Technology. 2003. Morgan Kaufmann

Series in Interactive Technologies ISBN:1-55860-840-0,
ISBN13: 978-1-55860-840-5.

Audience: **g,l,u.**

Krug, Steve   **TK5105.888**
Don't Make Me Think: A Common Sense Approach to the Web
Usability. Ed. 2. Trade Paper. New Riders Publishing. Berkeley,
CA. 2005. 224p. ISBN:0-321-34475-8, ISBN13:
978-0-321-34475-5. Dewey:006.7. LCCN:2006-277850.

Audience: **g,u.**

Maruyama, Hiroshi, et al.   **QA76.76.H94X418 2002**
XML and Java: Developing Web Applications. Ed. 2. Andy
Clark, Satoshi Hada, Kazuya Kosaka, Makoto Murata, Yuichi
Nakamura, Ryo Neyama, Kent Tamura & Naohiko Uramoto
(Authors). Trade Paper. Addison Wesley Professional. Boston,
MA. 2002. 688p. ISBN:0-201-77004-0, ISBN13:
978-0-201-77004-9. Dewey:005.7/2. LCCN:2002-018354.

Audience: **u.**

Musciano, Chuck &   **QA76.76.H94**
  Kennedy, Bill
HTML and XHTML: The Definitive Guide. Ed. 5. Trade Paper,
Perfect. O'Reilly Media, Inc. Sebastopol, CA. 2002. 670p.
ISBN:0-596-00382-X, ISBN13: 978-0-596-00382-1.
Dewey:006.7/4. LCCN:2003-269735.

Audience: **g,l,u,f.**

Nielsen, Jakob   **TK5105.888.N55 2000**
Designing Web Usability: The Practice of Simplicity. Trade
Paper. New Riders Publishing. Berkeley, CA. 1999. 432p.
Landmark Ser. ISBN:1-56205-810-X, ISBN13:
978-1-56205-810-4. Dewey:005.7/2. LCCN:99-063014.

Audience: **g,l,u.**

Pastor-Satorras, Romualdo   **TK5105.875.I57P385**
  & Vespignani, Alessandro
Evolution and Structure of the Internet: A Statistical Physics
Approach. Trade Cloth. Cambridge University Press. New York,
NY. 2004. 284p. ISBN:0-521-82698-5, ISBN13:
978-0-521-82698-3. Dewey:004.67/8. LCCN:2003-047257.

Audience: **u,f.**

Information Systems > Information Systems Applications

Andersson, Eve Astrid, et al.   **QA76.625.A55 2006**
Software Engineering for Internet Applications. Philip
Greenspun & Andrew Grumet (Authors). Trade Paper. MIT
Press. Cambridge, MA. 2006. 376p. ISBN:0-262-51191-6,
ISBN13: 978-0-262-51191-9. Dewey:005.2/76.
LCCN:2005-049144.

Audience: **l,u.**

Gray, Jim & Reuter,   **QA76.545 .G73 1993**
  Andreas
Transaction Processing: Concepts and Techniques. Elsevier
Science and Technology. 1993. Morgan Kaufman Series in Data
Management Systems ISBN:1-55860-190-2, ISBN13:
978-1-55860-190-1.

Audience: **u,f.**

Krug, Steve TK5105.888
Don't Make Me Think: A Common Sense Approach to the Web Usability. Ed. 2. Trade Paper. New Riders Publishing. Berkeley, CA. 2005. 224p. ISBN:0-321-34475-8, ISBN13: 978-0-321-34475-5. Dewey:006.7. LCCN:2006-277850.
Audience: **g,u.**

Nielsen, Jakob TK5105.888.N55 2000
Designing Web Usability: The Practice of Simplicity. Trade Paper. New Riders Publishing. Berkeley, CA. 1999. 432p. Landmark Ser. ISBN:1-56205-810-X, ISBN13: 978-1-56205-810-4. Dewey:005.7/2. LCCN:99-063014.
Audience: **g,l,u.**

Shneiderman, Ben & QA76.9.H85S54 2004
  Plaisant, Catherine
Designing the User Interface: Strategies for Effective Human-Computer Interaction. Ed. 4. Cloth Text. Addison-Wesley Longman, Inc. Boston, MA. 2004. 672p. ISBN:0-321-19786-0, ISBN13: 978-0-321-19786-3. Dewey:005.1. LCCN:2003-068940.
Audience: **g,u,f.**

Spolsky, Joel QA76.6
User Interface Design for Programmers. Trade Paper. Apress L. P.. Berkeley, CA. 2001. 144p. ISBN:1-893115-94-1, ISBN13: 978-1-893115-94-1. Dewey:005.1.
Audience: **u.**

Artificial Intelligence

Anthony, M. H. & Biggs, Q325.5.A58 1992
  Norman L.
Computational Learning Theory. Trade Cloth. Cambridge University Press. New York, NY. 1992. 171p. Cambridge Tracts in Theoretical Computer Science Ser., No. 30 ISBN:0-521-41603-5, ISBN13: 978-0-521-41603-0. Dewey:006.3/1. LCCN:92-191126.
Audience: **u,f.**

Dreyfus, Hubert L. Q335.D74 1992
What Computers Still Can't Do: A Critique of Artificial Reason. Trade Paper. MIT Press. Cambridge, MA. 1992. 429p. ISBN:0-262-54067-3, ISBN13: 978-0-262-54067-4. Dewey:006.3. LCCN:92-027715.
Audience: **g,l,u,f.**

Funge, John David QA76.76.C672F86 1999
AI for Games and Animation: A Cognitive Modeling Approach. Cloth Text. A K Peters, Ltd. Wellesley, MA. 1999. 212p. ISBN:1-56881-103-9, ISBN13: 978-1-56881-103-1. Dewey:794.8/163. LCCN:99-032421.
Audience: **u.**

Iwanska, Lucja M. & QA76.9.N38N3843 2000
  Shapiro, Stuart C. (Editors)
Natural Language Processing and Knowledge Representation: Language for Knowledge and Knowledge for Language. Trade Paper. MIT Press. Cambridge, MA. 2000. 350p. AAAI Press Ser. ISBN:0-262-59021-2, ISBN13: 978-0-262-59021-1. Dewey:006.3/5. LCCN:99-087360.
Audience: **u,f.**

Jones, Joseph L., et al. TJ211.415.J65 1998
Mobile Robots: Inspiration to Implementation. Ed. 2. Anita M. Flynn & Bruce A. Seiger (Authors). Paper Text. A K Peters,

Ltd. Wellesley, MA. 1998. 457p. ISBN:1-56881-097-0, ISBN13: 978-1-56881-097-3. Dewey:629.8/92. LCCN:98-042605.
Audience: **l,u.** *Choice, 1994.*

Mitchell, Thomas M. Q325.5.M58 1997
Machine Learning. Cloth Text. McGraw-Hill Higher Education. Burr Ridge, IL. 1997. 432p. ISBN:0-07-042807-7, ISBN13: 978-0-07-042807-2. Dewey:006.3/1. LCCN:97-007692.
Audience: **u.**

Moravec, Hans TJ211.M655 1999
Robot: Mere Machine to Transcendent Mind. Trade Cloth. Oxford University Press, Inc. New York, NY. 1998. 240p. ISBN:0-19-511630-5, ISBN13: 978-0-19-511630-4. Dewey:303.48/34/0112. LCCN:97-047328.
Audience: **g,l.** *Choice, 1999.*

Pearl, Judea BD541 .P43 2000
Causality: Models, Reasoning, and Inference. Trade Cloth. Cambridge University Press. New York, NY. 2000. 400p. ISBN:0-521-77362-8, ISBN13: 978-0-521-77362-1. Dewey:122. LCCN:99-042108.
Audience: **u.** *Choice, 2000.*

Russell, Stuart J. & Norvig, Q335.R86 2003
  Peter
Artificial Intelligence: A Modern Approach. Ed. 2. John F. Canny (Contribution by). Cloth Text. Prentice Hall PTR. Upper Saddle River, NJ. 2002. 1132p. Prentice Hall Series in Artificial Intelligence ISBN:0-13-790395-2, ISBN13: 978-0-13-790395-5. Dewey:006.3. LCCN:2003-269366.
Audience: **u.** *Choice, 1995.*

Schölkopf, Bernhard QH324.2.K47 2004
  (Editor), et al.
Kernel Methods in Computational Biology. Koji Tsuda & Jean-Philippe Vert (Editors). Trade Cloth. MIT Press. Cambridge, MA. 2004. 416p. Computational Molecular Biology Ser. ISBN:0-262-19509-7, ISBN13: 978-0-262-19509-6. Dewey:570/.285. LCCN:2003-068640.
Audience: **l,u,f.**

Siegwart, Roland & TJ211.415.S54 2004
  Nourbakhsh, Illah Reza
Introduction to Autonomous Mobile Robots. Trade Cloth. MIT Press. Cambridge, MA. 2004. 331p. Intelligent Robots and Autonomous Agents Ser. ISBN:0-262-19502-X, ISBN13: 978-0-262-19502-7. Dewey:629.8/92. LCCN:2003-059349.
Audience: **u.**

Weiss, Sholom M. & Q325.5.W45 1990
  Kulikowski, Casimir A. (Editors)
Computer Systems That Learn: Classification and Prediction Methods from Statistics, Neural Nets, Machine Learning and Expert Systems. Trade Cloth. Elsevier Science & Technology Books. Saint Louis, MO. 1990. 223p. Machine Learning Ser. ISBN:1-55860-065-5, ISBN13: 978-1-55860-065-2. Dewey:006.3. LCCN:90-048187.
Audience: **g,l,u.**

Computer Graphics

Brodlie, K. W. (Editor), Q175.S4242 1992
  et al.
Scientific Visualization: Techniques and Applications. L. Carpenter, Rae A. Earnshaw, J. R. Gallop, R. J. Hubbold, A. M.

Mumford, C. D. Osland & P. Quarendon (Editors). Cloth Text. Springer. New York, NY. 1992. 284p. ISBN:0-387-54565-4, ISBN13: 978-0-387-54565-3. Dewey:502.8. LCCN:91-035638.

Audience: **u,f.**

Foley, James D.　　　　　　　**T385 .C5735**
Computer Graphics: Principles and Practices. Ed. 3. Cloth Text. Addison-Wesley Longman, Inc. Boston, MA. 2000. 1296p. ISBN:0-201-35717-8, ISBN13: 978-0-201-35717-2. Dewey:006.6/6.

Audience: **u.**

Funge, John David　　　　　**QA76.76.C672F86 1999**
AI for Games and Animation: A Cognitive Modeling Approach. Cloth Text. A K Peters, Ltd. Wellesley, MA. 1999. 212p. ISBN:1-56881-103-9, ISBN13: 978-1-56881-103-1. Dewey:794.8/163. LCCN:99-032421.

Audience: **u.**

Glassner, Andrew S.　　　　**QA76.76.I59G55 2004**
Interactive Storytelling: Techniques for 21st Century Fiction. Paper Text. A K Peters, Ltd. Wellesley, MA. 2004. 510p. ISBN:1-56881-221-3, ISBN13: 978-1-56881-221-2. Dewey:006.7. LCCN:2003-068957.

Audience: **g,u.**

Glassner, Andrew S.　　　　　**T385.G578 1999**
Andrew Glassner's Notebook: Recreational Computer Graphics. Brian A. Barsky (Editor). Trade Paper. Elsevier Science & Technology Books. Saint Louis, MO. 1999. 420p. Computer Graphics and Geometric Modeling Ser. ISBN:1-55860-598-3, ISBN13: 978-1-55860-598-5. Dewey:006.6. LCCN:99-028111.

Audience: **g,l,u,f.** *Choice, 2000.*

Goodman, Jacob E. &　　　　　**QA167.H36 2004**
　O'Rourke, Joseph
Handbook of Discrete and Computational Geometry. Ed. 2. Paper over Boards. Chapman & Hall. New York, NY. 2004. 1560p. The CRC Press Series on Discrete Mathematics and Its Applications ISBN:1-58488-301-4, ISBN13: 978-1-58488-301-2. Dewey:516/.13. LCCN:2004-040662.

Audience: **u,f.** *Choice, 1998.*

Murray, James D. &　　　　　**T385.M87 1996**
　VanRyper, William
Encyclopedia of Graphics File Formats: The Complete Reference on CD-ROM with Links to Internet Resources. Ed. 2. Deborah Russell (Editor). Trade Paper. O'Reilly Media, Inc. Sebastopol, CA. 1996. 1116p. ISBN:1-56592-161-5, ISBN13: 978-1-56592-161-0. Dewey:006.603. LCCN:97-140158.

Audience: **l,u.**

O'Rourke, Joseph　　　　　**QA448.D38 O76 1998**
Computational Geometry in C. Ed. 2. Cloth Text. Cambridge University Press. New York, NY. 1998. 392p. ISBN:0-521-64010-5, ISBN13: 978-0-521-64010-7. Dewey:516/.0285/5133. LCCN:98-015363.

Audience: **u.** *Choice, 1999.*

Samet, Hanan　　　　　　**QA76.9.D3**
Foundations of Multidimensional and Metric Data Structures. Trade Cloth. Elsevier Science & Technology Books. Saint Louis, MO. 2006. 1024p. The Morgan Kaufmann Series in Computer Graphics and Geometric Modeling Ser. ISBN:0-12-369446-9, ISBN13: 978-0-12-369446-1. Dewey:005.7/3. LCCN:2005-054165.

Audience: **u,f.**

Shirley, Peter & Morley, R.　　　**T385.S438 2003**
　Keith
Realistic Ray Tracing. Ed. 2. Cloth Text. A K Peters, Ltd. Wellesley, MA. 2003. 225p. ISBN:1-56881-198-5, ISBN13: 978-1-56881-198-7. Dewey:006.6/2. LCCN:2003-051411.

Audience: **u.**

Image Processing and Computer Vision

Davies, E. R.　　　　　　**TA1634.D39 2005**
Machine Vision: Theory, Algorithms, Practicalities. Ed. 3. Cloth Text. Elsevier Science & Technology Books. Saint Louis, MO. 2004. 934p. ISBN:0-12-206093-8, ISBN13: 978-0-12-206093-9. Dewey:006.3/7. LCCN:2005-270146.

Audience: **u,f.**

Pattern Recognition

Anthony, M. H. & Biggs,　　　**Q325.5.A58 1992**
　Norman L.
Computational Learning Theory. Trade Cloth. Cambridge University Press. New York, NY. 1992. 171p. Cambridge Tracts in Theoretical Computer Science Ser., No. 30 ISBN:0-521-41603-5, ISBN13: 978-0-521-41603-0. Dewey:006.3/1. LCCN:92-191126.

Audience: **u,f.**

Cristianini, Nello &　　　　　**TK7882.P3**
　Shawe-Taylor, John
Kernel Methods for Pattern Analysis. Trade Cloth. Cambridge University Press. New York, NY. 2004. 476p. ISBN:0-521-81397-2, ISBN13: 978-0-521-81397-6. Dewey:006.31. LCCN:30-695900.

Audience: **u,f.**

Davies, E. R.　　　　　　**TA1634.D39 2005**
Machine Vision: Theory, Algorithms, Practicalities. Ed. 3. Cloth Text. Elsevier Science & Technology Books. Saint Louis, MO. 2004. 934p. ISBN:0-12-206093-8, ISBN13: 978-0-12-206093-9. Dewey:006.3/7. LCCN:2005-270146.

Audience: **u,f.**

Duda, Richard O., et al.　　　**Q327.D83 2000**
Pattern Classification, Part 1. Ed. 2. Peter E. Hart & David G. Stork (Authors). Trade Cloth. John Wiley & Sons, Inc. Hoboken, NJ. 2000. 680p. ISBN:0-471-05669-3, ISBN13: 978-0-471-05669-0. Dewey:006.4. LCCN:99-029981.

Audience: **u,f.**

Simulation

Brodlie, K. W. (Editor),　　　**Q175.S4242 1992**
　et al.
Scientific Visualization: Techniques and Applications. L. Carpenter, Rae A. Earnshaw, J. R. Gallop, R. J. Hubbold, A. M. Mumford, C. D. Osland & P. Quarendon (Editors). Cloth Text. Springer. New York, NY. 1992. 284p. ISBN:0-387-54565-4, ISBN13: 978-0-387-54565-3. Dewey:502.8. LCCN:91-035638.

Audience: **u,f.**

Kohonen, Teuvo　　　　　**QA76.87.K65 1995**
Self-Organizing Maps. Ed. 2. Trade Cloth. Springer. New York, NY. 1995. 362p. Information Sciences Ser., Vol. 30 ISBN:3-540-58600-8, ISBN13: 978-3-540-58600-5. Dewey:006.4/2. LCCN:95-004098.

Audience: **u,f.**

Robinson, Stewart   **T57.62**
Simulation: The Practice of Model Development and Use. Trade
Paper. John Wiley & Sons, Inc. Hoboken, NJ. 2004. 336p.
ISBN:0-470-84772-7, ISBN13: 978-0-470-84772-5.
Dewey:003.3. LCCN:2003-063093.

Audience: **l,u.**

Document and Text Processing

Berry, Michael W. (Editor)   **QA76.9.D343S69 2003**
Survey of Text Mining: Clustering, Classification, and Retrieval.
Trade Cloth. Springer. New York, NY. 2003. XVII, 244p.
ISBN:0-387-95563-1, ISBN13: 978-0-387-95563-6.
Dewey:006.3. LCCN:2003-042434.

Audience: **u.**

Iwanska, Lucja M. &   **QA76.9.N38N3843 2000**
Shapiro, Stuart C. (Editors)
Natural Language Processing and Knowledge Representation:
Language for Knowledge and Knowledge for Language. Trade
Paper. MIT Press. Cambridge, MA. 2000. 350p. AAAI Press
Ser. ISBN:0-262-59021-2, ISBN13: 978-0-262-59021-1.
Dewey:006.3/5. LCCN:99-087360.

Audience: **u,f.**

Witten, Ian H., et al.   **TA1637.W58 1999**
Managing Gigabytes: Compressing and Indexing Documents and
Images. Ed. 2. Alistair Moffat & Timothy C. Bell (Authors), Ed
Fox (Editor). Cloth Text. Elsevier Science & Technology Books.
Saint Louis, MO. 1999. 550p. Morgan Kaufmann Series in
Multimedia Information and Systems ISBN:1-55860-570-3,
ISBN13: 978-1-55860-570-1. Dewey:651.5/0285574.
LCCN:99-026345.

Audience: **u,f.**

Applications

☐ ACM Computing Reviews.
http://www.reviews.com
Reviews.com.

Audience: **g,l,u,f.**

Casey, Eoghan   **HV8079.C65**
Handbook of Computer Crime Investigation: Forensic Tools and
Technology. Library Binding. Sagebrush Education Resources.
Caledonia, MN. 2001. ISBN:0-613-91981-5, ISBN13:
978-0-613-91981-4. Dewey:363.25/968.

Audience: **l,u,f.**

Clote, Peter & Backofen,   **QH438.4.M3C565 2000**
Rolf
Computational Molecular Biology: An Introduction. Trade Cloth.
John Wiley & Sons, Inc. Hoboken, NJ. 2000. 300p. Wiley
Series in Mathematical and Computational Biology Ser., Vol. 1
ISBN:0-471-87251-2, ISBN13: 978-0-471-87251-1.
Dewey:572.8/01/5118. LCCN:00-038169.

Audience: **u,f.**

Gentleman, Robert (Editor),   **QH324.2**
et al.
Bioinformatics and Computational Biology Solutions Using R
and Bioconductor. Wolfgang Huber, Sandrine Dudoit, Vincent J.

Carey & Rafael A. Irizarry (Editors). Trade Cloth. Springer.
New York, NY. 2005. XIX, 473p. Statistics for Biology and
Health Ser. ISBN:0-387-25146-4, ISBN13: 978-0-387-25146-2.
Dewey:570.285. LCCN:2005-923843.

Audience: **u,f.**

Glassner, Andrew S.   **QA76.76.I59G55 2004**
Interactive Storytelling: Techniques for 21st Century Fiction.
Paper Text. A K Peters, Ltd. Wellesley, MA. 2004. 510p.
ISBN:1-56881-221-3, ISBN13: 978-1-56881-221-2.
Dewey:006.7. LCCN:2003-068957.

Audience: **g,u.**

Jones, Joseph L., et al.   **TJ211.415.J65 1998**
Mobile Robots: Inspiration to Implementation. Ed. 2. Anita M.
Flynn & Bruce A. Seiger (Authors). Paper Text. A K Peters,
Ltd. Wellesley, MA. 1998. 457p. ISBN:1-56881-097-0, ISBN13:
978-1-56881-097-3. Dewey:629.8/92. LCCN:98-042605.

Audience: **l,u.** *Choice, 1994.*

Jones, Neil C. & Pevzner,   **QH324.2.J66 2004**
Pavel
An Introduction to Bioinformatics Algorithms. Cloth Text. MIT
Press. Cambridge, MA. 2004. 448p. Computational Molecular
Biology Ser. ISBN:0-262-10106-8, ISBN13: 978-0-262-10106-6.
Dewey:570/.285. LCCN:2004-048289.

Audience: **u,f.**

Murray, Janet Horowitz   **QA76.76.I59M87 1998**
Hamlet on the Holodeck: The Future of Narrative in
Cyberspace. Trade Paper. MIT Press. Cambridge, MA. 1998.
336p. ISBN:0-262-63187-3, ISBN13: 978-0-262-63187-7.
Dewey:809/.00285/67. LCCN:98-017955.

Audience: **u,f.** *Choice, 1997.*

Proakis, John G. &   **TK5102.9.P757 1996**
Manolakis, Dimitris G.
Digital Signal Processing: Principles, Algorithms and
Applications. Ed. 3. Trade Cloth. Prentice Hall PTR. Upper
Saddle River, NJ. 1995. 1016p. ISBN:0-13-373762-4, ISBN13:
978-0-13-373762-2. Dewey:621.382/2. LCCN:95-009117.

Audience: **u.**

Raychaudhuri, Soumya   **QH452.7**
Computational Text Analysis: For Functional Genomics and
Bioinformatics. Trade Cloth. Oxford University Press, Inc. New
York, NY. 2006. 312p. ISBN:0-19-856740-5, ISBN13:
978-0-19-856740-0. Dewey:572.86. LCCN:2006-296260.

Audience: **u,f.**

Sankoff, David & Kruskal,   **QA292.T55 1999**
Joseph P.
Time Warps, String Edits, and Macromolecules: The Theory and
Practice of Sequence Comparision. David Sankoff & Joseph P.
Kruskal (Editors). Trade Paper. C S L I Publications/Center for
the Study of Language & Information. Stanford, CA. 2001.
408p. The David Hume Ser., :The Philosophy and Cognitive
Science Reissues ISBN:1-57586-217-4, ISBN13:
978-1-57586-217-0. Dewey:515/.24. LCCN:99-042488.

Audience: **l,u.**

Schölkopf, Bernhard   **QH324.2.K47 2004**
(Editor), et al.
Kernel Methods in Computational Biology. Koji Tsuda &
Jean-Philippe Vert (Editors). Trade Cloth. MIT Press.
Cambridge, MA. 2004. 416p. Computational Molecular Biology

Ser. ISBN:0-262-19509-7, ISBN13: 978-0-262-19509-6. Dewey:570/.285. LCCN:2003-068640.

Audience: **l,u,f.**

Siegwart, Roland &   TJ211.415.S54 2004
  Nourbakhsh, Illah Reza
Introduction to Autonomous Mobile Robots. Trade Cloth. MIT Press. Cambridge, MA. 2004. 331p. Intelligent Robots and Autonomous Agents Ser. ISBN:0-262-19502-X, ISBN13: 978-0-262-19502-7. Dewey:629.8/92. LCCN:2003-059349.

Audience: **u.**

Waterman, Michael   QH438.4.M33 W38 1995
Introduction to Computational Biology: Maps, Sequences and Genomes. Chapman and Hall/CRC. 1995. ISBN:0-412-99391-0, ISBN13: 978-0-412-99391-6.

Audience: **u.**

Witten, Ian H., et al.   TA1637.W58 1999
Managing Gigabytes: Compressing and Indexing Documents and Images. Ed. 2. Alistair Moffat & Timothy C. Bell (Authors), Ed Fox (Editor). Cloth Text. Elsevier Science & Technology Books. Saint Louis, MO. 1999. 550p. Morgan Kaufmann Series in Multimedia Information and Systems ISBN:1-55860-570-3, ISBN13: 978-1-55860-570-1. Dewey:651.5/0285574. LCCN:99-026345.

Audience: **u,f.**

Millieux > Computer Industry

                                              ZA4150
☐ Slashdot: News for Nerds, Stuff That Matters. http://slashdot.org

Audience: **g,l,u,f.**

Raymond, Eric S.   QA76.76.O63R397 2001
The Cathedral and the Bazaar: Musings on Linux and Open Source by an Accidental Revolutionary. Ed. 2. Bob Young (Foreword by). Cloth Text. O'Reilly Media, Inc. Sebastopol, CA. 2001. 255p. ISBN:0-596-00131-2, ISBN13: 978-0-596-00131-5. Dewey:005.4/32. LCCN:2001-021087.

Audience: **g,l,u,f.** *Choice, 2002.*

Millieux > History of Computing

Berners-Lee, Tim &   TK5105.875.I57
  Fischetti, Mark
Weaving the Web: The Original Design and Ultimate Destiny of the World Wide Web by Its Inventor. Tim Berners-Lee (Read by). Audio Cassette. HarperCollins Publishers. New York, NY. 1999. ISBN:0-694-52125-6, ISBN13: 978-0-694-52125-8. Dewey:025.04.

Audience: **g,l,u.**

Campbell-Kelly, Martin &   QA76.17.C36 2004
  Aspray, William
Computer: A History of the Information Machine. Ed. 2. Trade Paper. Westview Press. Boulder, CO. 2004. 360p. The Sloan Technology Ser. ISBN:0-8133-4264-3, ISBN13: 978-0-8133-4264-1. Dewey:004/.09. LCCN:2004-006325.

Audience: **g,l,u,f.** *Choice, 2005.*

Ceruzzi, Paul E.   004/.09/045
History of Modern Computing. Library Binding. Sagebrush Education Resources. Caledonia, MN. 2003.

ISBN:0-613-91131-8, ISBN13: 978-0-613-91131-3. Dewey:QA76.17.

Audience: **g,l,u,f.**

Davis, Martin   QA76.17.D38 2000
The Universal Computer: The Road from Leibniz to Turing. Trade Cloth. W. W. Norton & Company, Inc. New York, NY. 2000. 256p. ISBN:0-393-04785-7, ISBN13: 978-0-393-04785-1. Dewey:004/.09. LCCN:00-040200.

Audience: **g,l,u,f.** *Choice, 2001.*

Shasha, Dennis E. & Lazere,   QA76.2.A2S53 1995
  Cathy
Out of Their Minds: The Lives and Discoveries of 15 Great Computer Scientists. Trade Cloth. Springer. New York, NY. 1995. 304p. ISBN:0-387-97992-1, ISBN13: 978-0-387-97992-2. Dewey:004/.092/2 B. LCCN:95-008360.

Audience: **g,l,u.** *Choice, 1996.*

Millieux > Computers and Society

                                              ZA4150
☐ Slashdot: News for Nerds, Stuff That Matters. http://slashdot.org

Audience: **g,l,u,f.**

Baase, Sara   QA76.9
A Gift of Fire: Social, Legal, and Ethical Issues for Computers and the Internet. Ed. 2. Trade Paper. Prentice Hall PTR. Upper Saddle River, NJ. 2002. 464p. ISBN:0-13-008215-5, ISBN13: 978-0-13-008215-2. Dewey:5.75.

Audience: **l,u.**

Berners-Lee, Tim &   TK5105.875.I57
  Fischetti, Mark
Weaving the Web: The Original Design and Ultimate Destiny of the World Wide Web by Its Inventor. Tim Berners-Lee (Read by). Audio Cassette. HarperCollins Publishers. New York, NY. 1999. ISBN:0-694-52125-6, ISBN13: 978-0-694-52125-8. Dewey:025.04.

Audience: **g,l,u.**

Cohoon, J. McGrath   QA76.9.W65W66 2006
Women and Information Technology: Research on Under-Representation. William Aspray (Editor). Trade Cloth. MIT Press. Cambridge, MA. 2006. 512p. ISBN:0-262-03345-3, ISBN13: 978-0-262-03345-9. Dewey:004/.082. LCCN:2005-052253.

Audience: **l,u,f.**

Cooper, Jonathan   K564.C6 L53
Liberating Cyberspace: Civil Liberties, Human Rights and the Internet. Library Binding. Sagebrush Education Resources. Caledonia, MN. 1999. ISBN:0-613-92346-4, ISBN13: 978-0-613-92346-0. Dewey:342/.0858.

Audience: **g,l,u.**

Murray, Janet Horowitz   QA76.76.I59M87 1998
Hamlet on the Holodeck: The Future of Narrative in Cyberspace. Trade Paper. MIT Press. Cambridge, MA. 1998. 336p. ISBN:0-262-63187-3, ISBN13: 978-0-262-63187-7. Dewey:809/.00285/67. LCCN:98-017955.

Audience: **u,f.** *Choice, 1997.*

Schneier, Bruce   QA76.9.A25S352 2004
Secrets and Lies: Digital Security in a Networked World. Trade Paper. John Wiley & Sons, Inc. Hoboken, NJ. 2004. 448p.

ISBN:0-471-45380-3, ISBN13: 978-0-471-45380-2.
Dewey:005.8. LCCN:00-042252.

Audience: **g,l,u,f.** *Choice, 2001.*

Shneiderman, Ben   QA76.S5145 2003
Leonardo's Laptop: Human Needs and the New Computing
Technologies. Trade Paper. MIT Press. Cambridge, MA. 2003.
281p. ISBN:0-262-69299-6, ISBN13: 978-0-262-69299-1.
Dewey:004. LCCN:2001-056277.

Audience: **g,l,u.**

Millieux > Legal Aspects

Baase, Sara   QA76.9
A Gift of Fire: Social, Legal, and Ethical Issues for Computers
and the Internet. Ed. 2. Trade Paper. Prentice Hall PTR. Upper
Saddle River, NJ. 2002. 464p. ISBN:0-13-008215-5, ISBN13:
978-0-13-008215-2. Dewey:5.75.

Audience: **l,u.**

Casey, Eoghan   HV8079.C65
Handbook of Computer Crime Investigation: Forensic Tools and
Technology. Library Binding. Sagebrush Education Resources.
Caledonia, MN. 2001. ISBN:0-613-91981-5, ISBN13:
978-0-613-91981-4. Dewey:363.25/968.

Audience: **l,u,f.**

Cooper, Jonathan   K564.C6 L53
Liberating Cyberspace: Civil Liberties, Human Rights and the
Internet. Library Binding. Sagebrush Education Resources.
Caledonia, MN. 1999. ISBN:0-613-92346-4, ISBN13:
978-0-613-92346-0. Dewey:342/.0858.

Audience: **g,l,u.**

Raymond, Eric S.   QA76.76.O63R397 2001
The Cathedral and the Bazaar: Musings on Linux and Open
Source by an Accidental Revolutionary. Ed. 2. Bob Young
(Foreword by). Cloth Text. O'Reilly Media, Inc. Sebastopol,
CA. 2001. 255p. ISBN:0-596-00131-2, ISBN13:
978-0-596-00131-5. Dewey:005.4/32. LCCN:2001-021087.

Audience: **g,l,u,f.** *Choice, 2002.*

General

☐ ACM Computing Reviews.
http://www.reviews.com
Reviews.com.

Audience: **g,l,u,f.**

ZA4150

☐ Slashdot: News for Nerds, Stuff That Matters.
http://slashdot.org

Audience: **g,l,u,f.**

Campbell-Kelly, Martin &   QA76.17.C36 2004
  Aspray, William
Computer: A History of the Information Machine. Ed. 2. Trade
Paper. Westview Press. Boulder, CO. 2004. 360p. The Sloan
Technology Ser. ISBN:0-8133-4264-3, ISBN13:
978-0-8133-4264-1. Dewey:004/.09. LCCN:2004-006325.

Audience: **g,l,u,f.** *Choice, 2005.*

Dean, Thomas L.   QA76.D3333328 2004
Talking with Computers: Explorations in the Science and
Technology of Computing. Cloth Text. Cambridge University
Press. New York, NY. 2004. 314p. ISBN:0-521-83425-2,
ISBN13: 978-0-521-83425-4. Dewey:004. LCCN:2003-065531.

Audience: **g,l.** *Choice, 2004.*

Dreyfus, Hubert L.   Q335.D74 1992
What Computers Still Can't Do: A Critique of Artificial Reason.
Trade Paper. MIT Press. Cambridge, MA. 1992. 429p.
ISBN:0-262-54067-3, ISBN13: 978-0-262-54067-4.
Dewey:006.3. LCCN:92-027715.

Audience: **g,l,u,f.**

Harel, David   QA76.5.H3575 2000
Computers Ltd: What They Really Can't Do. Trade Cloth.
Oxford University Press, Inc. New York, NY. 2006. 240p.
ISBN:0-19-850555-8, ISBN13: 978-0-19-850555-6. Dewey:004.
LCCN:00-023751.

Audience: **g,l.**

Harel, David & Feldman,   QA76.9.A43H37 2004
  Yishai A.
Algorithmics: The Spirit of Computing. Ed. 3. Trade Paper.
Addison-Wesley Longman, Inc. Boston, MA. 2004. 536p.
ISBN:0-321-11784-0, ISBN13: 978-0-321-11784-7.
Dewey:005.1. LCCN:2004-041063.

Audience: **g,l.**

Moravec, Hans   TJ211.M655 1999
Robot: Mere Machine to Transcendent Mind. Trade Cloth.
Oxford University Press, Inc. New York, NY. 1998. 240p.
ISBN:0-19-511630-5, ISBN13: 978-0-19-511630-4.
Dewey:303.48/34/0112. LCCN:97-047328.

Audience: **g,l.** *Choice, 1999.*

Myers, Brad
☐ Computer Almanac: Interesting and Useful Numbers About
Computers.
http://www-cgi.cs.cmu.edu/afs/cs.cmu.edu/user/bam/www/
numbers.html

Audience: **g,l,u.**

Ralston, Anthony (Editor),   QA76.15.E48 2003
  et al.
Encyclopedia of Computer Science. Ed. 4. Edwin Reilly &
David Hemmendinger (Editors). Trade Cloth. John Wiley &
Sons, Inc. Hoboken, NJ. 2003. 2064p. ISBN:0-470-86412-5,
ISBN13: 978-0-470-86412-8. Dewey:004/.03.
LCCN:2003-283283.

Audience: **l,u.** *Choice, 2001.*

Resource Discovery Network   TA7
☐ EEVL: Computing.
http://www.eevl.ac.uk/computing/
Herriot Watt University.

Audience: **g,l.**

Schneier, Bruce   QA76.9.A25S352 2004
Secrets and Lies: Digital Security in a Networked World. Trade
Paper. John Wiley & Sons, Inc. Hoboken, NJ. 2004. 448p.
ISBN:0-471-45380-3, ISBN13: 978-0-471-45380-2.
Dewey:005.8. LCCN:00-042252.

Audience: **g,l,u,f.** *Choice, 2001.*

Shasha, Dennis E. & Lazere, Cathy   QA76.2.A2S53 1995
Out of Their Minds: The Lives and Discoveries of 15 Great Computer Scientists. Trade Cloth. Springer. New York, NY. 1995. 304p. ISBN:0-387-97992-1, ISBN13: 978-0-387-97992-2. Dewey:004/.092/2 B. LCCN:95-008360.
Audience: **g,l,u.** *Choice, 1996.*

Shneiderman, Ben   QA76.S5145 2003
Leonardo's Laptop: Human Needs and the New Computing Technologies. Trade Paper. MIT Press. Cambridge, MA. 2003. 281p. ISBN:0-262-69299-6, ISBN13: 978-0-262-69299-1. Dewey:004. LCCN:2001-056277.
Audience: **g,l,u.**

Reference

☐ ACM Computing Reviews.
http://www.reviews.com
Reviews.com.
Audience: **g,l,u,f.**

   QA76
☐ Association for Computing Machinery.
http://www.acm.org
Audience: **g,l,u,f.**

   TK7885.A1
☐ IEEE Computer Society.
http://www.computer.org
Audience: **g,l,u,f.**

Dr. Dobbs Magazine
☐ Electronic Review of Computer Books.
http://www.ercb.com
Audience: **g,l,u,f.**

Howe, Dennis   QA76.15
☐ FOLDOC: Free Online Dictionary of Computing.
http://foldoc.org
Imperial College Dept of Computing.
Audience: **g,l,u,f.**

Knee, Michael   K5640
Computer Science and Computing: A Guide to the Literature. Trade Cloth. Libraries Unlimited, Inc. Westport, CT. 2005. 184p. Reference Sources in Science and Technology Ser. ISBN:1-59158-160-5, ISBN13: 978-1-59158-160-4. Dewey:016.004. LCCN:2005-028597.
Audience: **g,l,u,f.** *Choice, 2006.*

Mehta, Dinesh P. & Sahni, Sartaj (Editors)   QA76.9.S88H363 2004
Handbook of Data Structures and Applications. Chapman & Hall/CRC. 2005. Computer and Information Science Series ISBN:1-58488-435-5, ISBN13: 978-1-58488-435-4.
Audience: **u,f.**

Myers, Brad
☐ Computer Almanac: Interesting and Useful Numbers About Computers.
http://www-cgi.cs.cmu.edu/afs/cs.cmu.edu/user/bam/www/numbers.html
Audience: **g,l,u.**

Ralston, Anthony (Editor), et al.   QA76.15.E48 2003
Encyclopedia of Computer Science. Ed. 4. Edwin Reilly & David Hemmendinger (Editors). Trade Cloth. John Wiley & Sons, Inc. Hoboken, NJ. 2003. 2064p. ISBN:0-470-86412-5, ISBN13: 978-0-470-86412-8. Dewey:004/.03. LCCN:2003-283283.
Audience: **l,u.** *Choice, 2001.*

Resource Discovery Network   TA7
☐ EEVL: Computing.
http://www.eevl.ac.uk/computing/
Herriot Watt University.
Audience: **g,l.**

Hardware

Hennessy, John L. & Patterson, David A.   QA76.9.A73P377 2003
Computer Architecture: A Quantitative Approach. Ed. 3. Cloth Text. Elsevier Science & Technology Books. Saint Louis, MO. 2002. 1136p. The Morgan Kaufmann Series in Computer Architecture and Design Ser. ISBN:1-55860-596-7, ISBN13: 978-1-55860-596-1. Dewey:004.2/2. LCCN:2001-099789.
Audience: **l,u.**

Parhami, Behrooz   QA76.9.A73P375 2005
Computer Architecture: From Microprocessors to Supercomputers. Cloth Text. Oxford University Press, Inc. New York, NY. 2005. 575p. The Oxford Series in Electrical and Computer Engineering ISBN:0-19-515455-X, ISBN13: 978-0-19-515455-9. Dewey:004.2/2. LCCN:2004-052063.
Audience: **u.**

Rafiquzzaman, M.   TK7888.4.R34 2005
Fundamentals of Digital Logic and Microcomputer Design. Ed. 5. Trade Cloth, CD-ROM. John Wiley & Sons, Inc. Hoboken, NJ. 2005. 840p. ISBN:0-471-72784-9, ISBN13: 978-0-471-72784-2. Dewey:621.39/5. LCCN:2004-065974.
Audience: **u,f.**

Thompson, Robert Bruce & Thompson, Barbara Fritchman   QA76.5
PC Hardware in a Nutshell. Ed. 3. Trade Paper, Perfect. O'Reilly Media, Inc. Sebastopol, CA. 2003. 850p. ISBN:0-596-00513-X, ISBN13: 978-0-596-00513-9. Dewey:621.39/16. LCCN:2004-268182.
Audience: **g,l,u,f.**

Tocci, Ronald J. & Ambrosio, Frank J.   QA76.5.T556 2002
Microprocessors and Microcomputers: Hardware and Software. Ed. 6. Trade Cloth. Prentice Hall PTR. Upper Saddle River, NJ. 2002. 612p. ISBN:0-13-060904-8, ISBN13: 978-0-13-060904-5. Dewey:004.16. LCCN:2001-051151.
Audience: **u,f.**

Uffenbeck, John E.   QA76.5.U35 2000
Microcomputers and Microprocessors: The 8080, 8085, and Z-80 Programming, Interfacing, and Troubleshooting. Ed. 3. Cloth Text. Prentice Hall PTR. Upper Saddle River, NJ. 1999. 729p. ISBN:0-13-209198-4, ISBN13: 978-0-13-209198-5. Dewey:004.165. LCCN:98-050972.
Audience: **l.**

System Organization > Processor Architecture

Berger, Arnold S.   **QA76.9.C643B47 2005**
Hardware and Computer Organization. Cloth Text. Elsevier
Science & Technology Books. Saint Louis, MO. 2005. 512p.
Embedded Technology Ser. ISBN:0-7506-7886-0, ISBN13:
978-0-7506-7886-5. Dewey:004.2/2. LCCN:2005-040553.
                                        Audience: **g,u,f.**

Hennessy, John L. &   **QA76.9.A73P377 2003**
  Patterson, David A.
Computer Architecture: A Quantitative Approach. Ed. 3. Cloth
Text. Elsevier Science & Technology Books. Saint Louis, MO.
2002. 1136p. The Morgan Kaufmann Series in Computer
Architecture and Design Ser. ISBN:1-55860-596-7, ISBN13:
978-1-55860-596-1. Dewey:004.2/2. LCCN:2001-099789.
                                        Audience: **l,u.**

Parhami, Behrooz   **QA76.9.A73P375 2005**
Computer Architecture: From Microprocessors to
Supercomputers. Cloth Text. Oxford University Press, Inc. New
York, NY. 2005. 575p. The Oxford Series in Electrical and
Computer Engineering ISBN:0-19-515455-X, ISBN13:
978-0-19-515455-9. Dewey:004.2/2. LCCN:2004-052063.
                                        Audience: **u.**

System Organization > Computer and Communication Networks

Comer, Douglas E. &   **TK5105.5**
  Droms, Ralph E.
Computer Networks and Internets with Internet Applications.
Ed. 4. Cloth Text. Prentice Hall PTR. Upper Saddle River, NJ.
2003. 768p. ISBN:0-13-143351-2, ISBN13: 978-0-13-143351-9.
Dewey:004.6. LCCN:2004-270063.
                                        Audience: **u.**

Garfinkel, Simson, et al.   **QA76.76.O63**
Practical UNIX and Internet Security. Ed. 3. Gene Spafford &
Alan Schwartz (Authors). Trade Paper, Perfect. O'Reilly Media,
Inc. Sebastopol, CA. 2003. 984p. ISBN:0-596-00323-4, ISBN13:
978-0-596-00323-4. Dewey:005.8. LCCN:2004-557663.
                                        Audience: **l,u,f.**

Lynch, Nancy A.   **QA76.9.A43L96 1997**
Distributed Algorithms. Cloth Text. Elsevier Science &
Technology Books. Saint Louis, MO. 1996. 904p. Morgan
Kaufmann Series in Data Management System
ISBN:1-55860-348-4, ISBN13: 978-1-55860-348-6.
Dewey:005.2/76. LCCN:97-041375.
                                        Audience: **u,f.**

Mullender, Sape   **QA76.9.D5D5937 1993**
Distributed Systems. Ed. 2. Trade Cloth. Addison-Wesley
Longman, Inc. Boston, MA. 1993. 580p. ACM Press Frontier
Ser. ISBN:0-201-62427-3, ISBN13: 978-0-201-62427-4.
Dewey:004/.36. LCCN:93-234489.
                                        Audience: **u,f.**

Pastor-Satorras, Romualdo   **TK5105.875.I57P385**
  & Vespignani, Alessandro
Evolution and Structure of the Internet: A Statistical Physics
Approach. Trade Cloth. Cambridge University Press. New York,
NY. 2004. 284p. ISBN:0-521-82698-5, ISBN13:
978-0-521-82698-3. Dewey:004.67/8. LCCN:2003-047257.
                                        Audience: **u,f.**

Peterson, Larry L. & Davie,   **TK5015.5.P479 2003**
  Bruce S.
Computer Networks: A Systems Approach. Ed. 3. Cloth Text.
Elsevier Science & Technology Books. Saint Louis, MO. 2003.
813p. The Morgan Kaufmann Series in Networking
ISBN:1-55860-832-X, ISBN13: 978-1-55860-832-0.
Dewey:004.6/5. LCCN:2003-047589.
                                        Audience: **u,f.**

Stallings, William   **TK5105.59**
Cryptography and Network Security. Ed. 4. Cloth Text. Prentice
Hall PTR. Upper Saddle River, NJ. 2005. 592p.
ISBN:0-13-187316-4, ISBN13: 978-0-13-187316-2. Dewey:5.8.
LCCN:2006-276085.
                                        Audience: **u.**

Watts, Duncan J.   **QA166.W38 1999**
Small Worlds: The Dynamics of Networks Between Order and
Randomness. Cloth Text. Princeton University Press. Princeton,
NJ. 1999. 266p. Princeton Studies in Complexity
ISBN:0-691-00541-9, ISBN13: 978-0-691-00541-6.
Dewey:511/.5. LCCN:98-056088.
                                        Audience: **g,u.** *Choice, 2000.*

System Organization > Performance

Lynch, Nancy A.   **QA76.9.A43L96 1997**
Distributed Algorithms. Cloth Text. Elsevier Science &
Technology Books. Saint Louis, MO. 1996. 904p. Morgan
Kaufmann Series in Data Management System
ISBN:1-55860-348-4, ISBN13: 978-1-55860-348-6.
Dewey:005.2/76. LCCN:97-041375.
                                        Audience: **u,f.**

Mullender, Sape   **QA76.9.D5D5937 1993**
Distributed Systems. Ed. 2. Trade Cloth. Addison-Wesley
Longman, Inc. Boston, MA. 1993. 580p. ACM Press Frontier
Ser. ISBN:0-201-62427-3, ISBN13: 978-0-201-62427-4.
Dewey:004/.36. LCCN:93-234489.
                                        Audience: **u,f.**

Software > Software Engineering

Booch, Grady, et al.   **QA76.76.D47B655 2005**
The Unified Modeling Language User Guide. Ed. 2. James
Rumbaugh & Ivar Jacobson (Authors). Trade Cloth. Addison
Wesley Professional. Boston, MA. 2005. 512p.
ISBN:0-321-26797-4, ISBN13: 978-0-321-26797-9.
Dewey:005.1. LCCN:2005-005678.
                                        Audience: **l,u,f.**

Brooks, Frederick P. Jr.   **QA76.758.B75 1995**
The Mythical Man-Month: Essays on Software Engineering. Ed.
2. Trade Paper. Addison Wesley Professional. Boston, MA.
1995. 336p. ISBN:0-201-83595-9, ISBN13: 978-0-201-83595-3.
Dewey:005.1/068. LCCN:94-036653.
                                        Audience: **g,l,u,f.** *Choice, 1996.*

Chan, Patrick & Bentley, Jon   QA76.6.B454 2000
Programming Pearls. Ed. 2. Trade Paper. Addison Wesley
Professional. Boston, MA. 1999. 256p. ISBN:0-201-65788-0,
ISBN13: 978-0-201-65788-3. Dewey:005.1. LCCN:99-046520.
                                        Audience: **g,u.**

Gamma, Erich, et al.   QA76.64.D47 1995
Design Patterns: Elements of Reusable Object-Oriented
Software. Richard Helm, Ralph Johnson & John M. Vlissides
(Authors), Grady Booch (Foreword by). Other. Addison Wesley
Professional. Boston, MA. 1994. 416p. Professional Computing
Ser. ISBN:0-201-63361-2, ISBN13: 978-0-201-63361-0.
Dewey:005.1/2. LCCN:94-034264.
                                        Audience: **g,l,u,f.**

Hetzel, Bill   QA76.76.T48
The Complete Guide to Software Testing. Ed. 2. Trade Cloth.
John Wiley & Sons, Inc. Hoboken, NJ. 1993. 296p.
ISBN:0-471-56567-9, ISBN13: 978-0-471-56567-3.
Dewey:005.1/4.
                                        Audience: **u.**

McConnell, Steve   QA76.76.D47M39 2004
Code Complete. Ed. 2. Trade Paper. Microsoft Press. Redmond,
WA. 2004. 900p. ISBN:0-7356-1967-0, ISBN13:
978-0-7356-1967-8. Dewey:005.1. LCCN:2004-049981.
                                        Audience: **u,f.**

Plauger, P. J.   QA76.76.D47P55 1993
Programming on Purpose: Essays on Programming Design. Ed.
1. Trade Paper. Prentice Hall PTR. Upper Saddle River, NJ.
1993. 256p. ISBN:0-13-721374-3, ISBN13: 978-0-13-721374-0.
Dewey:005.12. LCCN:92-045905.
                                        Audience: **g,u.**

Sommerville, Ian   QA76.758S657 2004
Software Engineering. Ed. 7. Cloth Text. Addison-Wesley
Longman, Inc. Boston, MA. 2004. 784p. International Computer
Science Ser. ISBN:0-321-21026-3, ISBN13: 978-0-321-21026-5.
Dewey:005.1. LCCN:2004-007038.
                                        Audience: **u.**

Spolsky, Joel   QA76.6
User Interface Design for Programmers. Trade Paper. Apress L.
P.. Berkeley, CA. 2001. 144p. ISBN:1-893115-94-1, ISBN13:
978-1-893115-94-1. Dewey:005.1.
                                        Audience: **u.**

Software > Programming Languages

Abelson, Harold, et al.   QA76.6.A255 1996
Structure and Interpretation of Computer Programs. Ed. 2.
Gerald J. Sussman & Julie Sussman (Authors). Cloth Text.
McGraw-Hill Higher Education. Burr Ridge, IL. 1996. 556p.
ISBN:0-07-000484-6, ISBN13: 978-0-07-000484-9.
Dewey:005.1. LCCN:96-017756.
                                Audience: **l,u.** *B Choice, 1997.*

Aho, Alfred V., et al.   QA76.76.C65A37 1986
Compilers: Principles, Techniques, and Tools. Ravi Sethi &
Jeffrey D. Ullman (Authors). Cloth Text. Addison-Wesley
Longman, Inc. Boston, MA. 1986. 500p. ISBN:0-201-10088-6,
ISBN13: 978-0-201-10088-4. Dewey:005.4/53.
LCCN:85-015647.
                                        Audience: **l,u.** *B*

Barron, David W.   QA76.6.B3715 2000
The World of Scripting Languages. Trade Paper. John Wiley &
Sons, Inc. Hoboken, NJ. 2000. 506p. Worldwide Series in
Computer Science Ser., Vol. 2 ISBN:0-471-99886-9, ISBN13:
978-0-471-99886-0. Dewey:005.2/762. LCCN:99-089450.
                                        Audience: **l,u.**

Clocksin, W. F. & Mellish, C. S.   QA76.73.P76C57 2003
Programming in Prolog: Using the ISO Standard. Ed. 5. Trade
Paper. Springer. New York, NY. 2003. XV, 293p.
ISBN:3-540-00678-8, ISBN13: 978-3-540-00678-7.
Dewey:005.13/3. LCCN:2003-044177.
                                        Audience: **l,u.**

Dybvig, R. Kent   QA76.73.S34D93 2003
The Scheme Programming Language. Ed. 3. Trade Paper. MIT
Press. Cambridge, MA. 2003. 329p. ISBN:0-262-54148-3,
ISBN13: 978-0-262-54148-0. Dewey:005.13/3.
LCCN:2003-046449.
                                        Audience: **l,u.**

Feuer, Alan R.   QA76.73.C15F48 1999
The C Puzzle Book. Ed. 3. Trade Paper. Addison Wesley
Professional. Boston, MA. 1998. 192p. ISBN:0-201-60461-2,
ISBN13: 978-0-201-60461-0. Dewey:005.13/3.
LCCN:98-045561.
                                        Audience: **g,l,u.**

Flanagan, David   QA76.73.J38
Java in a Nutshell. Ed. 5. Trade Paper, Perfect. O'Reilly Media,
Inc. Sebastopol, CA. 2005. 1252p. ISBN:0-596-00773-6,
ISBN13: 978-0-596-00773-7. Dewey:005.13/3.
LCCN:2005-277917.
                                        Audience: **g,u,f.**

Gosling, James, et al.   QA76.73.J38
The Java(tm) Language Specification. Ed. 3. Gilad Bracha, Bill
Joy & Guy L. Steele Jr. (Authors). Trade Paper, Perfect.
Addison Wesley Professional. Boston, MA. 2005. 624p. Java
Ser. ISBN:0-321-24678-0, ISBN13: 978-0-321-24678-3.
Dewey:005.13/3.
                                        Audience: **u,f.**

Gosling, James, et al.   QA76.73.J38A76 2005
The Java Programming Language. Ed. 4. David Holmes & Ken
Arnold (Authors). Trade Paper. Addison Wesley Professional.
Boston, MA. 2005. 928p. ISBN:0-321-34980-6, ISBN13:
978-0-321-34980-4. Dewey:005.13/3. LCCN:2005-017029.
                                        Audience: **u,f.**

Harold, Elliotte Rusty   QA76.76.H94H34 2004
XML 1. 1 Bible. Ed. 3. Trade Paper. John Wiley & Sons, Inc.
Hoboken, NJ. 2004. 1054p. Bible Ser. ISBN:0-7645-4986-3,
ISBN13: 978-0-7645-4986-1. Dewey:005.72.
LCCN:2004-101453.
                                        Audience: **l,u.**

Hejlsberg, Anders; Wiltamuth, Scott; Golde, Peter   QA76.76.C154H45 2003
The C# Programming Language. Addison-Wesley. 2003.
Microsoft .NET development Series ISBN:0-321-15491-6,
ISBN13: 978-0-321-15491-0.
                                        Audience: **l,u,f.**

Horstmann, Cay & Cornell, Gary   QA76.73.J38
Core Java(TM) 2: Fundamentals. Ed. 7. Trade Paper. Prentice

Formats: Web: ⬜ Ebook: 🅔 CD/DVD-ROM: 🪱 BCL3: *B*

Hall PTR. Upper Saddle River, NJ. 2004. 784p. Sun Microsystems Press Java Ser. ISBN:0-13-148202-5, ISBN13: 978-0-13-148202-9. Dewey:005.133. LCCN:2004-109876.

Audience: **l,u.**

Horstmann, Cay & Cornell,   **QA76.73.J38**
Gary
Core Java(TM) 2 Advanced Features, Vol. II. Ed. 7. Trade Paper. Prentice Hall PTR. Upper Saddle River, NJ. 2004. 256p. ISBN:0-13-111826-9, ISBN13: 978-0-13-111826-3. Dewey:005.2762.

Audience: **l,u.**

Kernighan, Brian W. &   **QA76.73.C15K47 1988**
Ritchie, Dennis M.
The C Programming Language: ANSI C Version. Ed. 2. Cloth Text. Prentice Hall PTR. Upper Saddle River, NJ. 1988. 288p. ISBN:0-13-110370-9, ISBN13: 978-0-13-110370-2. Dewey:005.13/3. LCCN:88-005934.

Audience: **u,f.**

Lippman, Stanley B. &   **QA76.73.C15L57 1998**
Lajoie, Jose
C++ Primer. Ed. 3. Trade Paper. Addison Wesley Professional. Boston, MA. 1998. 1264p. ISBN:0-201-82470-1, ISBN13: 978-0-201-82470-4. Dewey:005.13/3. LCCN:98-009464.

Audience: **u.**

Lomax, Paul, et al.   **QA76.73.B3**
Visual Basic 2005 in a Nutshell. Ed. 3. Ron Petrusha, Steven Roman & Tim Patrick (Authors). Trade Paper, Perfect. O'Reilly Media, Inc. Sebastopol, CA. 2006. 766p. ISBN:0-596-10152-X, ISBN13: 978-0-596-10152-7. Dewey:005.2768.

Audience: **u,f.**

Metcalf, Michael, et al.   **QA76.73.F**
Fortran 95/2003 Explained. Ed. 3. John Reid Jr. & Malcolm Cohen (Authors). Trade Paper. Oxford University Press, Inc. New York, NY. 2004. 434p. Numerical Mathematics and Scientific Computation Ser. ISBN:0-19-852693-8, ISBN13: 978-0-19-852693-3. Dewey:005.13/3. LCCN:2004-273807.

Audience: **u,f.** *Choice, 2005.*

Musciano, Chuck &   **QA76.76.H94**
Kennedy, Bill
HTML and XHTML: The Definitive Guide. Ed. 5. Trade Paper, Perfect. O'Reilly Media, Inc. Sebastopol, CA. 2002. 670p. ISBN:0-596-00382-X, ISBN13: 978-0-596-00382-1. Dewey:006.7/4. LCCN:2003-269735.

Audience: **g,l,u,f.**

Paulson, L. C.   **QA76.73.M6 P38 1996**
ML for the Working Programmer. Ed. 2. Cloth Text. Cambridge University Press. New York, NY. 1996. 496p. ISBN:0-521-57050-6, ISBN13: 978-0-521-57050-3. Dewey:005.1/33. LCCN:96-013574.

Audience: **u.**

Plauger, P. J., et al.   **QA76.73.C153C17 2001**
The C++ Standard Template Library: A Definitive Approach to C++ Programming Using Stl. Meng Lee, Alexander A. Stepanov & David R. Musser (Authors). Trade Paper. Prentice Hall PTR. Upper Saddle River, NJ. 2000. 512p. ISBN:0-13-437633-1, ISBN13: 978-0-13-437633-2. Dewey:005.13/3. LCCN:00-065273.

Audience: **u.**

Press, William H., et al.   **QA76.73.C153 N85 20**
Numerical Recipes in C++: The Art of Scientific Computing. Ed. 2. Saul A. Teukolsky, William T. Vetterling & Brian P. Flannery (Authors). Cloth Text. Cambridge University Press. New York, NY. 2002. 1032p. ISBN:0-521-75033-4, ISBN13: 978-0-521-75033-2. Dewey:519.4/0285/5133. LCCN:2001-052699.

Audience: **g,u,f.**

Rumbaugh, James, et al.   **QA76.76.D47R86 2004**
The Unified Modeling Language Reference Manual. Ed. 2. Ivar Jacobson & Grady Booch (Authors). Trade Paper. Addison Wesley Professional. Boston, MA. 2004. 752p. The Addison-Wesley Object Technology Ser. ISBN:0-321-24562-8, ISBN13: 978-0-321-24562-5. Dewey:005.3. LCCN:2004-012580.

Audience: **g,u,f.**

Scott, Michael L.   **QA76.7**
Programming Language Pragmatics. Ed. 2. Paper Text. Elsevier Science & Technology Books. Saint Louis, MO. 2005. 912p. ISBN:0-12-633951-1, ISBN13: 978-0-12-633951-2. Dewey:005.13.

Audience: **u,f.**

Sedgewick, Robert   **QA76.73.J38S4 1998**
Algorithms in Java, Pt. 1-4. Ed. 3. Trade Paper. Addison Wesley Professional. Boston, MA. 2002. 768p. ISBN:0-201-36120-5, ISBN13: 978-0-201-36120-9. Dewey:005.13/3. LCCN:98-025050.

Audience: **u.**

Sedgewick, Robert   **QA76.9.A43**
Algorithms in Java: Graph Algorithms. Ed. 3. Trade Paper. Addison Wesley Professional. Boston, MA. 2003. 528p. ISBN:0-201-36121-3, ISBN13: 978-0-201-36121-6. Dewey:005.13/3. LCCN:92-000901.

Audience: **u.**

Sethi, Ravi   **QA76.7.S48 1996**
Programming Languages: Concepts and Constructs. Ed. 2. Tom Stone (Editor). Other. Addison-Wesley Longman, Inc. Boston, MA. 1995. 624p. ISBN:0-201-59065-4, ISBN13: 978-0-201-59065-4. Dewey:005.13. LCCN:95-040528.

Audience: **u.**

Steele, Guy Jr.   **QA76.73.L23S73 1990**
Common LISP: The Language. Ed. 2. Trade Paper. Elsevier Science & Technology Books. Saint Louis, MO. 1984. 1029p. LISP Ser. ISBN:1-55558-041-6, ISBN13: 978-1-55558-041-4. Dewey:005.13/3. LCCN:89-026016.

Audience: **l,u.**

Sutter, Herb   **QA76.73.C153S88 2000**
Exceptional C++: 47 Engineering Puzzles, Programming Problems, and Solutions. Trade Paper. Addison Wesley Professional. Boston, MA. 1999. 240p. The C++ In-Depth Ser. ISBN:0-201-61562-2, ISBN13: 978-0-201-61562-3. Dewey:005.13/3. LCCN:99-046115.

Audience: **l,u.**

Winskel, Glynn   **QA76.7.**
The Formal Semantics of Programming Languages: An Introduction. Trade Paper. MIT Press. Cambridge, MA. 1993. 384p. Foundations of Computing Ser. ISBN:0-262-73103-7, ISBN13: 978-0-262-73103-4. Dewey:005.131.

Audience: **u,f.** *Choice, 1993.*

Software > Operating Systems

Brinch Hansen, Per QA76.76.O63B7425
Classic Operating Systems: from Batch Processing to Distributed Systems. Springer. 2000. ISBN:0-387-95113-X, ISBN13: 978-0-387-95113-3.

Audience: **u,f.**

Garfinkel, Simson, et al. QA76.76.O63
Practical UNIX and Internet Security. Ed. 3. Gene Spafford & Alan Schwartz (Authors). Trade Paper, Perfect. O'Reilly Media, Inc. Sebastopol, CA. 2003. 984p. ISBN:0-596-00323-4, ISBN13: 978-0-596-00323-4. Dewey:005.8. LCCN:2004-557663.

Audience: **l,u,f.**

Powers, Shelley, et al. QA76.76.O63
UNIX Power Tools. Ed. 3. Jerry Peek, Tim O'Reilly & Michael Kosta Loukides (Authors). Trade Paper, Perfect. O'Reilly Media, Inc. Sebastopol, CA. 2002. 1156p. ISBN:0-596-00330-7, ISBN13: 978-0-596-00330-2. Dewey:005.4/32. LCCN:2003-269689.

Audience: **u,f.**

Rago, Stephen A. & Stevens, QA76.76.O63S754 2005
W. Richard
Advanced Programming in the UNIX Environment. Ed. 2. Trade Cloth. Addison Wesley Professional. Boston, MA. 2005. 904p. ISBN:0-201-43307-9, ISBN13: 978-0-201-43307-4. Dewey:005.4/32. LCCN:2005-007943.

Audience: **u,f.**

Sobell, Mark G. QA76.76.O63.S59483
A Practical Guide to Linux Commands, Editors, and Shell Programming. Trade Paper. Prentice Hall PTR. Upper Saddle River, NJ. 2005. 976p. ISBN:0-13-147823-0, ISBN13: 978-0-13-147823-7. Dewey:005.4/46. LCCN:2005-050051.

Audience: **g,l,u.**

Tanenbaum, Andrew S. QA76.76.O63T359 2001
Modern Operating Systems. Ed. 2. Cloth Text. Prentice Hall PTR. Upper Saddle River, NJ. 2001. 976p. ISBN:0-13-031358-0, ISBN13: 978-0-13-031358-4. Dewey:005.4/3. LCCN:00-051666.

Audience: **u.**

Software > Miscellany

ZA4150
☐ Slashdot: News for Nerds, Stuff That Matters.
http://slashdot.org

Audience: **g,l,u,f.**

Myers, Brad
☐ Computer Almanac: Interesting and Useful Numbers About Computers.
http://www-cgi.cs.cmu.edu/afs/cs.cmu.edu/user/bam/www/numbers.html

Audience: **g,l,u.**

Software > General

Aho, Alfred V., et al. QA76.76.C65A37 1986
Compilers: Principles, Techniques, and Tools. Ravi Sethi & Jeffrey D. Ullman (Authors). Cloth Text. Addison-Wesley

Longman, Inc. Boston, MA. 1986. 500p. ISBN:0-201-10088-6, ISBN13: 978-0-201-10088-4. Dewey:005.4/53. LCCN:85-015647.

Audience: **l,u.** ℬ

Appel, Andrew W. QA76.73.J38A65 2002
Modern Compiler Implementation in Java. Ed. 2. Jens Palsberg (As told to). Cloth Text. Cambridge University Press. New York, NY. 2002. 512p. ISBN:0-521-82060-X, ISBN13: 978-0-521-82060-8. Dewey:005.4/53. LCCN:2002-073453.

Audience: **l,u.**

Gamma, Erich, et al. QA76.64.D47 1995
Design Patterns: Elements of Reusable Object-Oriented Software. Richard Helm, Ralph Johnson & John M. Vlissides (Authors), Grady Booch (Foreword by). Other. Addison Wesley Professional. Boston, MA. 1994. 416p. Professional Computing Ser. ISBN:0-201-63361-2, ISBN13: 978-0-201-63361-0. Dewey:005.1/2. LCCN:94-034264.

Audience: **g,l,u,f.**

McConnell, Steve QA76.76.D47M39 2004
Code Complete. Ed. 2. Trade Paper. Microsoft Press. Redmond, WA. 2004. 900p. ISBN:0-7356-1967-0, ISBN13: 978-0-7356-1967-8. Dewey:005.1. LCCN:2004-049981.

Audience: **u,f.**

Plauger, P. J. QA76.76.D47P55 1993
Programming on Purpose: Essays on Programming Design. Ed. 1. Trade Paper. Prentice Hall PTR. Upper Saddle River, NJ. 1993. 256p. ISBN:0-13-721374-3, ISBN13: 978-0-13-721374-0. Dewey:005.12. LCCN:92-045905.

Audience: **g,u.**

Raymond, Eric S. QA76.76.O63R397 2001
The Cathedral and the Bazaar: Musings on Linux and Open Source by an Accidental Revolutionary. Ed. 2. Bob Young (Foreword by). Cloth Text. O'Reilly Media, Inc. Sebastopol, CA. 2001. 255p. ISBN:0-596-00131-2, ISBN13: 978-0-596-00131-5. Dewey:005.4/32. LCCN:2001-021087.

Audience: **g,l,u,f.** *Choice, 2002.*

Rumbaugh, James, et al. QA76.76.D47R86 2004
The Unified Modeling Language Reference Manual. Ed. 2. Ivar Jacobson & Grady Booch (Authors). Trade Paper. Addison Wesley Professional. Boston, MA. 2004. 752p. The Addison-Wesley Object Technology Ser. ISBN:0-321-24562-8, ISBN13: 978-0-321-24562-5. Dewey:005.3. LCCN:2004-012580.

Audience: **g,u,f.**

Salomon, David QA76.9.D33S25 2004
Data Compression: The Complete Reference. Ed. 3. Trade Cloth. Springer. New York, NY. 2004. XX, 900p. ISBN:0-387-40697-2, ISBN13: 978-0-387-40697-8. Dewey:005.74/6. LCCN:2003-065725.

Audience: **u,f.**

Sommerville, Ian QA76.758S657 2004
Software Engineering. Ed. 7. Cloth Text. Addison-Wesley Longman, Inc. Boston, MA. 2004. 784p. International Computer Science Ser. ISBN:0-321-21026-3, ISBN13: 978-0-321-21026-5. Dewey:005.1. LCCN:2004-007038.

Audience: **u.**

Formats: Web: ☐ Ebook: ℯ CD/DVD-ROM: 🦡 BCL3: ℬ

Winskel, Glynn   QA76.7.
The Formal Semantics of Programming Languages: An
Introduction. Trade Paper. MIT Press. Cambridge, MA. 1993.
384p. Foundations of Computing Ser. ISBN:0-262-73103-7,
ISBN13: 978-0-262-73103-4. Dewey:005.131.

Audience: **u,f.** *Choice, 1993.*

Software > Programming Techniques

Abelson, Harold, et al.   QA76.6.A255 1996
Structure and Interpretation of Computer Programs. Ed. 2.
Gerald J. Sussman & Julie Sussman (Authors). Cloth Text.
McGraw-Hill Higher Education. Burr Ridge, IL. 1996. 556p.
ISBN:0-07-000484-6, ISBN13: 978-0-07-000484-9.
Dewey:005.1. LCCN:96-017756.

Audience: **l,u.** *B Choice, 1997.*

Andersson, Eve Astrid, et al.   QA76.625.A55 2006
Software Engineering for Internet Applications. Philip
Greenspun & Andrew Grumet (Authors). Trade Paper. MIT
Press. Cambridge, MA. 2006. 376p. ISBN:0-262-51191-6,
ISBN13: 978-0-262-51191-9. Dewey:005.2/76.
LCCN:2005-049144.

Audience: **l,u.**

Booch, Grady et al.   QA76.64
Object-Oriented Design with Applications. Ed. 3.
Addison-Wesley Longman. 2006. Object Technology Series
ISBN:0-201-89551-X, ISBN13: 978-0-201-89551-3.

Audience: **u,f.**

Booch, Grady, et al.   QA76.76.D47B655 2005
The Unified Modeling Language User Guide. Ed. 2. James
Rumbaugh & Ivar Jacobson (Authors). Trade Cloth. Addison
Wesley Professional. Boston, MA. 2005. 512p.
ISBN:0-321-26797-4, ISBN13: 978-0-321-26797-9.
Dewey:005.1. LCCN:2005-005678.

Audience: **l,u,f.**

Chan, Patrick & Bentley,   QA76.6.B454 2000
  Jon
Programming Pearls. Ed. 2. Trade Paper. Addison Wesley
Professional. Boston, MA. 1999. 256p. ISBN:0-201-65788-0,
ISBN13: 978-0-201-65788-3. Dewey:005.1. LCCN:99-046520.

Audience: **g,u.**

Dongarra, Jack (Editor),   QA76.58
  et al.
The Sourcebook of Parallel Computing. Ian Foster, Geoffrey C.
Fox, William Gropp, Ken Kennedy, Linda Torczon & Andy
White (Editors). Trade Cloth. Elsevier Science & Technology
Books. Saint Louis, MO. 2002. 842p. The Morgan Kaufmann
Series in Computer Architecture and Design Ser.
ISBN:1-55860-871-0, ISBN13: 978-1-55860-871-9.
Dewey:004/.35. LCCN:2002-107244.

Audience: **u,f.** *Choice, 2003.*

Gamma, Erich, et al.   QA76.64.D47 1995
Design Patterns: Elements of Reusable Object-Oriented
Software. Richard Helm, Ralph Johnson & John M. Vlissides
(Authors), Grady Booch (Foreword by). Other. Addison Wesley
Professional. Boston, MA. 1994. 416p. Professional Computing
Ser. ISBN:0-201-63361-2, ISBN13: 978-0-201-63361-0.
Dewey:005.1/2. LCCN:94-034264.

Audience: **g,l,u,f.**

Maruyama, Hiroshi, et al.   QA76.76.H94X418 2002
XML and Java: Developing Web Applications. Ed. 2. Andy
Clark, Satoshi Hada, Kazuya Kosaka, Makoto Murata, Yuichi
Nakamura, Ryo Neyama, Kent Tamura & Naohiko Uramoto
(Authors). Trade Paper. Addison Wesley Professional. Boston,
MA. 2002. 688p. ISBN:0-201-77004-0, ISBN13:
978-0-201-77004-9. Dewey:005.7/2. LCCN:2002-018354.

Audience: **u.**

Metcalf, Michael, et al.   QA76.73.F
Fortran 95/2003 Explained. Ed. 3. John Reid Jr. & Malcolm
Cohen (Authors). Trade Paper. Oxford University Press, Inc.
New York, NY. 2004. 434p. Numerical Mathematics and
Scientific Computation Ser. ISBN:0-19-852693-8, ISBN13:
978-0-19-852693-3. Dewey:005.13/3. LCCN:2004-273807.

Audience: **u,f.** *Choice, 2005.*

Plauger, P. J., et al.   QA76.73.C153C17 2001
The C++ Standard Template Library: A Definitive Approach to
C++ Programming Using Stl. Meng Lee, Alexander A. Stepanov
& David R. Musser (Authors). Trade Paper. Prentice Hall PTR.
Upper Saddle River, NJ. 2000. 512p. ISBN:0-13-437633-1,
ISBN13: 978-0-13-437633-2. Dewey:005.13/3.
LCCN:00-065273.

Audience: **u.**

Powers, Shelley, et al.   QA76.76.O63
UNIX Power Tools. Ed. 3. Jerry Peek, Tim O'Reilly & Michael
Kosta Loukides (Authors). Trade Paper, Perfect. O'Reilly
Media, Inc. Sebastopol, CA. 2002. 1156p. ISBN:0-596-00330-7,
ISBN13: 978-0-596-00330-2. Dewey:005.4/32.
LCCN:2003-269689.

Audience: **u,f.**

Rago, Stephen A. & Stevens,   QA76.76.O63S754 2005
  W. Richard
Advanced Programming in the UNIX Environment. Ed. 2. Trade
Cloth. Addison Wesley Professional. Boston, MA. 2005. 904p.
ISBN:0-201-43307-9, ISBN13: 978-0-201-43307-4.
Dewey:005.4/32. LCCN:2005-007943.

Audience: **u,f.**

Sobell, Mark G.   QA76.76.O63.S59483
A Practical Guide to Linux Commands, Editors, and Shell
Programming. Trade Paper. Prentice Hall PTR. Upper Saddle
River, NJ. 2005. 976p. ISBN:0-13-147823-0, ISBN13:
978-0-13-147823-7. Dewey:005.4/46. LCCN:2005-050051.

Audience: **g,l,u.**

Spolsky, Joel   QA76.6
User Interface Design for Programmers. Trade Paper. Apress L.
P.. Berkeley, CA. 2001. 144p. ISBN:1-893115-94-1, ISBN13:
978-1-893115-94-1. Dewey:005.1.

Audience: **u.**

Sutter, Herb   QA76.73.C153S88 2000
Exceptional C++: 47 Engineering Puzzles, Programming
Problems, and Solutions. Trade Paper. Addison Wesley
Professional. Boston, MA. 1999. 240p. The C++ In-Depth Ser.
ISBN:0-201-61562-2, ISBN13: 978-0-201-61562-3.
Dewey:005.13/3. LCCN:99-046115.

Audience: **l,u.**

ENVIRONMENTAL SCIENCES

Environmental sciences are a multifaceted interdisciplinary subject — the study of the impact of living organisms, especially humans, and natural processes and materials on, in, and surrounding planet Earth. Environmental sciences involve biology, chemistry, physics, geology, mathematics, modeling and analysis, engineering, technology, and management. It has especially developed from the realization of pollution of air, water, and soils. It impinges on medicine with toxicology, contamination, epidemiology, and public health. Agriculture and forestry are inextricably involved with water, pesticides, desertification, deforestation, biodiversity, and biotechnology issues. This holistic nature of environmental sciences has given rise to new coinage such as biogeochemistry and bioremediation, brownfields, and green chemistry.

In the Environmental Sciences section I have tried to complement the Environmental Studies section. I have concentrated on the scientific and technical aspects of the environment, so most of the material is at a more specialized level. Engineering is well represented in this collection. I have included resources in energy, climatology, pollution, waste, conservation, toxicology, and epidemiology. The taxonomy was created using environmental sciences thesauri, topical concerns in the media, and class offerings, besides book reviews and special listings. I took the liberty of adding a few classics and resources on environmental disasters.

— Louise Deis

Azeiteiro, Ulisses　　　　　　　**GE70.W68 2004**
World Trends in Environmental Education. Trade Cloth. Peter
Lang Publishing, Inc. New York, NY. 2004. 268p.
Environmental Education, Communication and Sustainability
Ser. ISBN:0-8204-6526-7, ISBN13: 978-0-8204-6526-5.
Dewey:363.7/0071. LCCN:2004-044111.

Audience: **f.**

Crump, Andy　　　　　　　**GE10**
Dictionary of Environment and Development: People, Places,
Ideas, and Organizations. Trade Cloth. MIT Press. Cambridge,
MA. 1993. 272p. ISBN:0-262-03207-4, ISBN13:
978-0-262-03207-0. Dewey:363.7/003. LCCN:92-036484.

Audience: **g,l,u,f.**

Cunningham, William P.　　　　　　　**GE10.E58 1998**
(Editor)
Environmental Encyclopedia, 1998. Ed. 2. Trade Cloth.
Thomson Gale. Farmington Hills, MI. 1997. 1196p.
ISBN:0-8103-9314-X, ISBN13: 978-0-8103-9314-1.
Dewey:363.7/003. LCCN:98-153941.

Audience: **g.**

Miller, Char (Editor)　　　　　　　**GF503.A84 2003**
The Atlas of U. S. and Canadian Environmental History. Paper
over Boards. Routledge. New York, NY. 2003. 256p.
ISBN:0-415-93781-7, ISBN13: 978-0-415-93781-8.
Dewey:304.2/097/022. LCCN:2003-046799.

Audience: **g,l,u,f.**　*Choice, 2004.*

Pfafflin, James R. & Ziegler,　　　　　　　**TD9.E5 1998**
Edward N. (Editors)
Encyclopedia of Environmental Science and Engineering. Ed. 4.
Cloth Text. G + B Science Publishers. 1998. 1408p.
ISBN:90-5699-636-3, ISBN13: 978-90-5699-636-9. Dewey:628.
LCCN:99-459973.

Audience: **l,u,f.**

United Nations Environment
Programme
▢ Global Environment Outlook 3: Past, Present, and Future
Perspectives.
http://www.unep.org/GEO/geo3/
Earthscan Publications Ltd..

Audience: **g,l,u,f.**

Agricultural Pollution

Feigin, A., et al.　　　　　　　**TD760.F45 1990**
Irrigation with Treated Sewage Effluent: Management for
Environmental Protection. I. Ravina & J. Shalhevet (Authors),
E. Bresler, G. W. Thomas, L. Dale Van Vleck & B. Yaron
(Editors). Cloth Text. Springer. New York, NY. 1991. 224p.
Advanced Series in Agricultural Sciences, Vol. 17
ISBN:0-387-50804-X, ISBN13: 978-0-387-50804-7.
Dewey:628.3/623. LCCN:90-010199.

Audience: **u,f.**　*Choice, 1991.*

National Research Council　　　　　　　**TD427.N87N38 2000**
Staff, et al.
Clean Coastal Waters: Understanding and Reducing the Effects
of Nutrient Pollution. Ocean Studies Board Staff & Water
Science and Technology Board Staff (Authors). Trade Cloth.
National Academies Press. Washington, DC. 2000. xvi, 405p.

ISBN:0-309-06948-3, ISBN13: 978-0-309-06948-9.
Dewey:363.739/4. LCCN:00-009621.

Audience: **g,u,f.**　*Choice, 2001.*

Wilson, Duff　　　　　　　**TD195.F46W55 2001**
Fateful Harvest: The True Story of a Small Town, a Global
Industry, and a Toxic Secret. Trade Cloth. HarperCollins
Publishers. New York, NY. 2001. 336p. ISBN:0-06-019369-7,
ISBN13: 978-0-06-019369-0. Dewey:363.19/2.
LCCN:2001-024208.

Audience: **g,l.**

Agricultural Pollution > Deforestation

Balick, Michael J. (Editor),　　　　　　　**RS164.M377 1996**
et al.
Medicinal Resources of the Tropical Forest: Biodiversity and Its
Importance to Human Health. Elaine Elisabetsky & Sarah A.
Laird (Editors). Trade Cloth. Edinburgh University Press.
Edinburgh, 1996. 440p. Biology and Resource Management in
the Tropics Ser. ISBN:0-231-10170-8, ISBN13:
978-0-231-10170-7. Dewey:615/.32/0913. LCCN:95-013809.

Audience: **g,l,u.**　*Choice, 1996.*

Cowell, Adrian　　　　　　　**GF532.A4**
The Decade of Destruction: The Crusade to Save the Amazon
Rain Forest. Cloth Text. DIANE Publishing Company.
Collingdale, PA. 1999. 215p. ISBN:0-7881-6688-3, ISBN13:
978-0-7881-6688-4. Dewey:333.75/0981/1.

Audience: **g,l,u,f.**

Cowell, Adrian (Produced　　　　　　　**GF532.A4**
by, Directed By)
🎞 The Decade of Destruction Series. Video, VHS Format.
Bullfrog Films, Inc. Oley, PA. 1990. ISBN:1-56029-027-7,
ISBN13: 978-1-56029-027-8. Dewey:333.75/0981/1.

Audience: **g,l,u,f.**

Fimbel, Robert A. (Editor),　　　　　　　**QL109.C66 2001**
et al.
The Cutting Edge: Conserving Wildlife in Logged Tropical
Forests. Alejandro Grajal & John G. Robinson (Editors). Trade
Cloth. Columbia University Press. New York, NY. 2001. 700p.
Biology and Resource Management Ser. ISBN:0-231-11454-0,
ISBN13: 978-0-231-11454-7. Dewey:333.95/416/0913.
LCCN:00-031782.

Audience: **l,u,f.**　*Choice, 2002.*

Golley, Frank B. & Werger,　　　　　　　**QH541.5.J8**
Marinus J. (Editors)
Tropical Rain Forest Ecosystems: Structure and Function. Trade
Cloth. Elsevier. New York, NY. 1983. 382p. Ecosystems of the
World Ser., Vol. 14A ISBN:0-444-41986-1, ISBN13:
978-0-444-41986-6. Dewey:574.5/2642/0913. LCCN:81-007861.

Audience: **u,f.**

Laurance, William F. &　　　　　　　**QH541.15.F73T76 1997**
Bierregaard, Richard O. Jr. (Editors)
Tropical Forest Remnants: Ecology, Management, and
Conservation of Fragmented Communities. Trade Cloth.
University of Chicago Press. Chicago, IL. 1997. 632p.
ISBN:0-226-46898-4, ISBN13: 978-0-226-46898-3.
Dewey:577.34. LCCN:96-038038.

Audience: **l,u,f.**　*Choice, 1998.*

Leuschner, William A.   **SD373.L45 1991**
Introduction to Forest Resource Management. Library Binding.
Krieger Publishing Company. Melbourne, FL. 1992. 304p.
ISBN:0-89464-641-9, ISBN13: 978-0-89464-641-6.
Dewey:634.9/28. LCCN:91-021718.

Audience: **l,u.**

Lewis, Ronald L.   **HC107.W5L39 1998**
Transforming the Appalachian Countryside: Railroads,
Deforestation, and Social Change in West Virginia, 1880-1920.
Trade Cloth. University of North Carolina Press. Chapel Hill,
NC. 1998. 368p. ISBN:0-8078-2405-4, ISBN13:
978-0-8078-2405-4. Dewey:338.9754. LCCN:97-036616.
Audience: **g.** *Choice, 1998.*

Marsh, George Perkins   **GF31.M35 2003**
Man and Nature, or, Physical Geography As Modified by
Human Action. David Lowenthal (Editor, Annotations by,
Foreword by), William Cronon (Foreword by). Trade Cloth.
University of Washington Press. Seattle, WA. 2003. 512p.
Weyerhaeuser Environmental Classics Ser. ISBN:0-295-98316-7,
ISBN13: 978-0-295-98316-5. Dewey:304.2.
LCCN:2003-040286.

Audience: **g.** *Choice, 2003.*

Stoddard, Charles H. &   **SD373.S79 1987**
    Stoddard, Glenn M.
Essentials of Forestry Practice. Ed. 4. Trade Cloth. John Wiley
& Sons, Inc. Hoboken, NJ. 1987. 432p. ISBN:0-471-84237-0,
ISBN13: 978-0-471-84237-8. Dewey:634.9/0973.
LCCN:86-022408.

Audience: **l,u.**

Agricultural Pollution > Groundwater Pollution

Bradl, Heike   **TD196.M4**
Heavy Metals in the Environment: Origin, Interaction and
Remediation. Elsevier. 2005. ISBN:0-12-088381-3, ISBN13:
978-0-12-088381-3.

Audience: **g,l,u,f.**

Agricultural Pollution > Pesticides

Carson, Rachel   **QH545**
Silent Spring. Ed. 40. Dust Jacket. Houghton Mifflin Company
Trade & Reference Division. Boston, MA. 2002. 400p.
ISBN:0-618-25305-X, ISBN13: 978-0-618-25305-0.
Dewey:363.738/4. LCCN:2002-726803.
Audience: **g,l,u,f.** *B*

Dunlap, Thomas R.   **SB952.D2**
DDT: Scientists, Citizens, and Public Policy. Trade Cloth.
Princeton University Press. Princeton, NJ. 1981. 304p.
ISBN:0-691-04680-8, ISBN13: 978-0-691-04680-8.
Dewey:363.7/384. LCCN:80-008546.

Audience: **g,l,u.**

Hayes, Wayland J.   **RA1270.P4**
Pesticides Studied in Man. Cloth Text. Lippincott Williams &
Wilkins. Philadelphia, PA. 1982. 672p. ISBN:0-683-03896-6,
ISBN13: 978-0-683-03896-5. Dewey:615.9/02.
LCCN:81-007410.

Audience: **l,u,f.**

Krieger, Robert (Editor)   **RA1270.P4H36 2001**
Principles and Agents, Set. Ed. 2. Trade Cloth. Elsevier Science
& Technology Books. Saint Louis, MO. 2001. 1908p.
ISBN:0-12-426260-0, ISBN13: 978-0-12-426260-7.
Dewey:615.9/51. LCCN:2001-089145.

Audience: **u,f.**

Westing, Arthur H. (Editor)   **QH545.P4H47 1984**
Herbicides in War: The Long Term Ecological and Human
Consequences. Trade Cloth. Taylor & Francis Group.
Philadelphia, PA. 1984. 290p. Peace Studies
ISBN:0-85066-265-6, ISBN13: 978-0-85066-265-8.
Dewey:574.5/2642/09597. LCCN:84-002468.

Audience: **g,l,u.**

Whorton, James C.   **RA1270.P4**
Before Silent Spring: Pesticides in Pre-DDT America. Trade
Cloth. Princeton University Press. Princeton, NJ. 1975. 302p.
ISBN:0-691-08139-5, ISBN13: 978-0-691-08139-7.
Dewey:614.3/1. LCCN:74-002984.

Audience: **g,l.**

Air Pollution

Bardana, Emil J.   **RA577.5.I55 1997**
Indoor Air Pollution and Health, Vol. 9. Anthony Montanaro
(Editor). Paper over Boards. Marcel Dekker Inc. New York, NY.
1996. 520p. Clinical Allergy and Immunology Ser., Vol. 9
ISBN:0-8247-9479-6, ISBN13: 978-0-8247-9479-8.
Dewey:613/.5. LCCN:96-036591.

Audience: **u,f.**

Bubenick, David V.   **TD196.A25.A29 1984**
Acid Rain Information Book. Ed. 2. Trade Cloth. Noyes Data
Corporation/Noyes Publications. Park Ridge, NJ. 1984. 397p.
ISBN:0-8155-0967-7, ISBN13: 978-0-8155-0967-7.
Dewey:363.7/394. LCCN:83-021986.

Audience: **u,f.**

Gruden, Dusan (Volume   **QD31**
    Editor)
Traffic and Environment. D. Gruden, W. Berg & K. Borgmann
(Contribution by). Mixed Media. Springer. New York, NY. 2004.
XIV, 294p. ISBN:3-540-00050-X, ISBN13: 978-3-540-00050-1.
Dewey:540.

Audience: **u,f.**

Heinsohn, Robert Jennings   **TD883.1**
    & Cimbala, John M.
Indoor Air Quality Engineering: Environmental Health and
Control of Indoor Pollutants. Paper over Boards. Marcel Dekker
Inc. New York, NY. 2003. 920p. ISBN:0-8247-4061-0, ISBN13:
978-0-8247-4061-0. Dewey:628.53.

Audience: **u,f.**

Iqbal, Mohammed & Yunus,   **QK751.P57 1996**
    Mohammed (Editors)
Plant Response to Air Pollution. Trade Cloth. John Wiley &
Sons, Inc. Hoboken, NJ. 1996. 558p. ISBN:0-471-96061-6,
ISBN13: 978-0-471-96061-4. Dewey:581.5/222.
LCCN:95-042780.

Audience: **g.** *Choice, 1997.*

Lumsden, Peter (Editor)   **QK757 .P53 1997**
Plants and UV-B: Responses to Environmental Change. Trade
Cloth. Cambridge University Press. New York, NY. 1997. 375p.

Society for Experimental Biology Seminar Ser., Vol. 64
ISBN:0-521-57222-3, ISBN13: 978-0-521-57222-4.
Dewey:571.4/56/2. LCCN:96-030065.

Audience: **l,u,f.**

McDermott, Henry J.   **TD890.M38 2004**
Air Monitoring for Toxic Exposures. Ed. 2. Trade Cloth. John
Wiley & Sons, Inc. Hoboken, NJ. 2004. 688p.
ISBN:0-471-45435-4, ISBN13: 978-0-471-45435-9.
Dewey:628.5/3/0287. LCCN:2003-026039.

Audience: **g,u,f.** *Choice, 2005.*

Pfafflin, James R. &   **TD9.E5 2006**
  Edward N. Ziegler
Encyclopedia of Environmental Science and Engineering. Ed. 5.
CRC Press. 2006. ISBN:0-8493-9843-6, ISBN13:
978-0-8493-9843-8.

Audience: **g,l,u,f.**

Pluschke, Peter (Editor)   **TD883.17**
Indoor Air Pollution. Mixed Media. Springer. New York, NY.
2004. xi, 270p. The Handbook of Environmental Chemistry Ser.,
Vol. 4:Air Pollution, Part F ISBN:3-540-21098-9, ISBN13:
978-3-540-21098-6. Dewey:363.7/392. LCCN:2004-104243.

Audience: **l,u,f.** *Choice, 2005.*

Singh, Hanwant B. (Editor)   **QC861.2**
Composition Chemistry, and Climate of the Atmosphere. Trade
Cloth. John Wiley & Sons, Inc. Hoboken, NJ. 1995. 544p.
Industrial Engineering Ser. ISBN:0-471-28514-5, ISBN13:
978-0-471-28514-4. Dewey:551.5.

Audience: **g,l,u,f.**

Trapp, Stefan & McFarlane,   **QK753.X45P58 1994**
  Craig (Editors)
Plant Contamination: Modeling and Simulation of Organic
Chemical Processes. Paper over Boards. Lewis Publishers. Boca
Raton, FL. 1994. 272p. ISBN:1-56670-078-7, ISBN13:
978-1-56670-078-8. Dewey:581.2. LCCN:94-009734.

Audience: **u,f.** *Choice, 1996.*

United States; Clean Air Act   **QH76**
  Advisory Committee; United States; Environmental
  Protection Agency
Clean Air Act of 1990: A Primer on Consensus-Building. U.S.
Environmental Protection Agency: Washington, DC: For sale by
the Supt. of Docs., U.S. G.P.O.. 1990. ISBN:0-16-036250-4,
ISBN13: 978-0-16-036250-7.

Audience: **u,f.**

Westing, Arthur H. (Editor)   **QH545.P4H47 1984**
Herbicides in War: The Long Term Ecological and Human
Consequences. Trade Cloth. Taylor & Francis Group.
Philadelphia, PA. 1984. 290p. Peace Studies
ISBN:0-85066-265-6, ISBN13: 978-0-85066-265-8.
Dewey:574.5/2642/09597. LCCN:84-002468.

Audience: **g,l,u.**

Biodegradation

Maier, Raina M., et al.   **QR100.M345 2000**
Environmental Microbiology. Ian L. Pepper & Charles P. Gerba
(Authors). Cloth Text. Elsevier Science & Technology Books.
Saint Louis, MO. 2000. 585p. ISBN:0-12-497570-4, ISBN13:
978-0-12-497570-5. Dewey:579/.17. LCCN:00-267828.

Audience: **u,f.**

Marsh, George Perkins   **GF31.M35 2003**
Man and Nature, or, Physical Geography As Modified by
Human Action. David Lowenthal (Editor, Annotations by,
Foreword by), William Cronon (Foreword by). Trade Cloth.
University of Washington Press. Seattle, WA. 2003. 512p.
Weyerhaeuser Environmental Classics Ser. ISBN:0-295-98316-7,
ISBN13: 978-0-295-98316-5. Dewey:304.2.
LCCN:2003-040286.

Audience: **g.** *Choice, 2003.*

Bioremediation

Bradl, Heike   **TD196.M4**
Heavy Metals in the Environment: Origin, Interaction and
Remediation. Elsevier. 2005. ISBN:0-12-088381-3, ISBN13:
978-0-12-088381-3.

Audience: **g,l,u,f.**

Maier, Raina M., et al.   **QR100.M345 2000**
Environmental Microbiology. Ian L. Pepper & Charles P. Gerba
(Authors). Cloth Text. Elsevier Science & Technology Books.
Saint Louis, MO. 2000. 585p. ISBN:0-12-497570-4, ISBN13:
978-0-12-497570-5. Dewey:579/.17. LCCN:00-267828.

Audience: **u,f.**

Brownfields

Krimsky, Sheldon   **RC649**
Hormonal Chaos: The Scientific and Social Origins of the
Environmental Endocrine Hypothesis. Lynn R. Goldman
(Foreword by). Trade Cloth. DIANE Publishing Company.
Collingdale, PA. 2004. 284p. ISBN:0-7567-7113-7, ISBN13:
978-0-7567-7113-3. Dewey:616.4/071.

Audience: **g,l.**

Wilson, Duff   **TD195.F46W55 2001**
Fateful Harvest: The True Story of a Small Town, a Global
Industry, and a Toxic Secret. Trade Cloth. HarperCollins
Publishers. New York, NY. 2001. 336p. ISBN:0-06-019369-7,
ISBN13: 978-0-06-019369-0. Dewey:363.19/2.
LCCN:2001-024208.

Audience: **g,l.**

Carbon

Kellogg, William W. &   **QC879.8 .K44**
  Schware, Robert
Climate Change and Society: Consequences of Increasing
Atmospheric Carbon Dioxide. Walter O. Roberts (Foreword by).
Paper Text. Westview Press. Boulder, CO. 1981. 170p. Special
Studies ISBN:0-86531-180-3, ISBN13: 978-0-86531-180-0.
Dewey:363.7/392. LCCN:80-054157.

Audience: **l,u.**

Ruddiman, William F.   **QC981.R763 2005**
Plows, Plagues, and Petroleum: How Humans Took Control of
Climate. Trade Cloth. Princeton University Press. Princeton, NJ.
2005. 272p. ISBN:0-691-12164-8, ISBN13: 978-0-691-12164-2.
Dewey:363.738/74. LCCN:2004-062444.

Audience: **g,l,u,f.** *Choice, 2006.*

Sweet, William   TJ808.S87 2006
Kicking the Carbon Habit: Global Warming and the Case for
Renewable Energy. Trade Cloth. Columbia University Press.
New York, NY. 2006. 272p. ISBN:0-231-13710-9, ISBN13:
978-0-231-13710-2. Dewey:333.79/4. LCCN:2005-035034.
                                        Audience: **g,l.**

Dams

Postel, Sandra & Richter,   QH75.P67 2003
  Brian D.
Rivers for Life: Managing Water for People and Nature. Trade
Cloth. Island Press. Washington, DC. 2003. 220p.
ISBN:1-55963-443-X, ISBN13: 978-1-55963-443-4.
Dewey:333.91/6216. LCCN:2003-006051.
                            Audience: **g,l,u,f.** *Choice, 2004.*

Ecosystem Decline

Bailey, Robert G.   QH540.7.B35 1996
Ecosystem Geography. Lev Ropes (Illustrator). Trade Cloth.
Springer. New York, NY. 1995. XII, 204p. ISBN:0-387-94354-4,
ISBN13: 978-0-387-94354-1. Dewey:574.5/012.
LCCN:95-034178.
                            Audience: **u,f.** *Choice, 1996.*

Barber, Stanley A.   S596.7.B37 1995
Soil Nutrient Bioavailability: A Mechanistic Approach. Ed. 2.
Trade Cloth. John Wiley & Sons, Inc. Hoboken, NJ. 1995. 384p.
ISBN:0-471-58747-8, ISBN13: 978-0-471-58747-7.
Dewey:631.4/22. LCCN:94-022899.
                                        Audience: **u,f.**

Bolen, Eric G. & Robinson,   SK355.B65 2002
  William Laughlin
Wildlife Ecology and Management. Ed. 5. Cloth Text. Prentice
Hall PTR. Upper Saddle River, NJ. 2002. 634p.
ISBN:0-13-066250-X, ISBN13: 978-0-13-066250-7.
Dewey:639.9. LCCN:2002-066251.
                                        Audience: **g,l.**

Boyce, Mark S. & Haney,   QH75
  Alan W. (Editors)
Ecosystem Management: Applications for Sustainable Forest and
Wildlife Resources. Trade Paper. Yale University Press.
Cumberland, RI. 1999. 384p. ISBN:0-300-07858-7, ISBN13:
978-0-300-07858-9. Dewey:333.95.
                            Audience: **g,u,f.** *Choice, 1997.*

Cowell, Adrian   GF532.A4
The Decade of Destruction: The Crusade to Save the Amazon
Rain Forest. Cloth Text. DIANE Publishing Company.
Collingdale, PA. 1999. 215p. ISBN:0-7881-6688-3, ISBN13:
978-0-7881-6688-4. Dewey:333.75/0981/1.
                            Audience: **g,l,u,f.**

Crawford, Mark   QH76.C73 1999
Habitats and Ecosystems: An Encyclopedia of Endangered
America. Library Binding. ABC-CLIO, Inc. Santa Barbara, CA.
1999. xvii, 398p. ISBN:0-87436-997-5, ISBN13:
978-0-87436-997-7. Dewey:333.78/0973. LCCN:00-698072.
                            Audience: **u,f.** *Choice, 2000.*

Denny, Mark W.   QH541.5.S35D46 1988
Biology and the Mechanics of the Wave-Swept Environment.
Trade Cloth. Princeton University Press. Princeton, NJ. 1988.
400p. ISBN:0-691-08486-6, ISBN13: 978-0-691-08486-2.
Dewey:574.5/2638/01532593. LCCN:87-032806.
                            Audience: **u,f.** *Choice, 1989.*

Harrison, Gordon   RA644.M2.H37 1978
Mosquitoes, Malaria, and Man: A History of the Hostilities since
1880. Trade Cloth. Penguin Group (USA) Inc. New York, NY.
1978. viii, 314p. ISBN:0-525-16025-6, ISBN13:
978-0-525-16025-0. Dewey:614.5/3/2009. LCCN:77-021725.
                                        Audience: **g,l.**

John H. Heinz III Center   QH104.S73 2002
  for Science, Economics and the Environment
The State of the Nation's Ecosystems: Measuring the Lands,
Waters, and Living Resources of the United States. Trade Paper.
Cambridge University Press. New York, NY. 2002. 288p.
ISBN:0-521-52572-1, ISBN13: 978-0-521-52572-5.
Dewey:333.7/2. LCCN:2002-073890.
                            Audience: **l,u,f.** *Choice, 2003.*

Lewis, Ronald L.   HC107.W5L39 1998
Transforming the Appalachian Countryside: Railroads,
Deforestation, and Social Change in West Virginia, 1880-1920.
Trade Cloth. University of North Carolina Press. Chapel Hill,
NC. 1998. 368p. ISBN:0-8078-2405-4, ISBN13:
978-0-8078-2405-4. Dewey:338.9754. LCCN:97-036616.
                            Audience: **g.** *Choice, 1998.*

Lumsden, Peter (Editor)   QK757 .P53 1997
Plants and UV-B: Responses to Environmental Change. Trade
Cloth. Cambridge University Press. New York, NY. 1997. 375p.
Society for Experimental Biology Seminar Ser., Vol. 64
ISBN:0-521-57222-3, ISBN13: 978-0-521-57222-4.
Dewey:571.4/56/2. LCCN:96-030065.
                                        Audience: **l,u,f.**

Maier, Raina M., et al.   QR100.M345 2000
Environmental Microbiology. Ian L. Pepper & Charles P. Gerba
(Authors). Cloth Text. Elsevier Science & Technology Books.
Saint Louis, MO. 2000. 585p. ISBN:0-12-497570-4, ISBN13:
978-0-12-497570-5. Dewey:579/.17. LCCN:00-267828.
                                        Audience: **u,f.**

McNeill, J. R.   GF13.M39 2000
Something New under the Sun: An Environmental History of
the Twentieth-Century World. Trade Cloth. W. W. Norton &
Company, Inc. New York, NY. 2000. 416p.
ISBN:0-393-04917-5, ISBN13: 978-0-393-04917-6.
Dewey:304.2/8/0904. LCCN:99-054900.
                            Audience: **g,l.** *Choice, 2000.*

Mittermeier, Russell A.,   QH75.H675 2004
  et al.
Hotspots Revisited: Earth's Biologically Richest and Most
Endangered Terrestrial Ecoregions. Patricio Robles Gil, John
Pilgrim, Cristina Goettsch Mittermeier, Thomas Brooks, Michael
Hoffman, Gustavo A. B. da Fonseca & John Lamoreux
(Authors), Peter A. Seligmann (Preface by), Harrison Ford
(Foreword by). Trade Cloth. Conservation International.
Washington, DC. 2005. 392p. ISBN:968-6397-77-9, ISBN13:
978-968-6397-77-2. Dewey:577.
                            Audience: **g,l,u,f.** *Choice, 2006.*

Moser, Michael E. &   **QH87.3.W46 1991**
  Finlayson, Max (Editors)
Wetlands. Trade Cloth. Facts On File, Inc.. New York, NY.
1991. 224p. ISBN:0-8160-2556-8, ISBN13: 978-0-8160-2556-5.
Dewey:574.5/26325. LCCN:91-023683.
                                    Audience: **g,l.** *Choice, 1992.*

Mulamoottil, George   **GB621**
Wetlands: Environmental Gradients, Boundaries, and Buffers.
Lewis. 1996. ISBN:1-56670-147-3, ISBN13:
978-1-56670-147-1.
                                    Audience: **u,f.**

National Research Council   **TD427.N87N38 2000**
  Staff, et al.
Clean Coastal Waters: Understanding and Reducing the Effects
of Nutrient Pollution. Ocean Studies Board Staff & Water
Science and Technology Board Staff (Authors). Trade Cloth.
National Academies Press. Washington, DC. 2000. xvi, 405p.
ISBN:0-309-06948-3, ISBN13: 978-0-309-06948-9.
Dewey:363.739/4. LCCN:00-009621.
                                    Audience: **g,u,f.** *Choice, 2001.*

Nierenberg, William A.   **QH540.4.E52 1995**
  (Editor-In-Chief)
Encyclopedia of Environmental Biology, Set. Trade Cloth.
Elsevier Science & Technology Books. Saint Louis, MO. 1995.
2168p. ISBN:0-12-226730-3, ISBN13: 978-0-12-226730-7.
Dewey:577/.03. LCCN:94-024917.
                                    Audience: **g,l,u,f.** *Choice, 1996.*

Norton, Bryan G.   **QH75.N66 2002**
Searching for Sustainability: Interdisciplinary Essays in the
Philosophy of Conservation Biology. Trade Cloth. Cambridge
University Press. New York, NY. 2002. 564p. Cambridge
Studies in Philosophy and Biology ISBN:0-521-80990-8,
ISBN13: 978-0-521-80990-0. Dewey:333.95/16.
LCCN:2002-017404.
                                    Audience: **u,f.** *Choice, 2003.*

Pimm, Stuart L.   **GE140.P56 2001**
The World According to Pimm: A Scientist Audits the Earth.
Trade Cloth. McGraw-Hill Companies, The. New York, NY.
2001. 304p. ISBN:0-07-137490-6, ISBN13: 978-0-07-137490-3.
Dewey:333.7/2. LCCN:2001-030229.
                                    Audience: **g,l,u,f.** *Choice, 2002.*

Postel, Sandra   **TD345.P67 1992**
The Last Oasis: Facing Water Scarcity. Trade Cloth. W. W.
Norton & Company, Inc. New York, NY. 1992. 128p.
Worldwatch Environmental Alert Ser. ISBN:0-393-03428-3,
ISBN13: 978-0-393-03428-8. Dewey:333.91. LCCN:92-030356.
                                    Audience: **g,l.** *Choice, 1993.*

Primack, Richard B.   **QH75.P7525 2004**
A Primer of Conservation Biology. Ed. 3. Trade Cloth. Sinauer
Associates, Inc. Sunderland, MA. 2004. 320p.
ISBN:0-87893-728-5, ISBN13: 978-0-87893-728-8.
Dewey:333.95/16. LCCN:2004-011645.
                                    Audience: **l,u,f.** *Choice, 1996.*

Willmer, Pat, et al.   **QP82.W48 2004**
Environmental Physiology of Animals. Ed. 2. Graham Stone &
Ian A. Johnston (Authors). Trade Cloth. Blackwell Publishing,
Inc. Malden, MA. 2004. 768p. ISBN:1-4051-0724-3, ISBN13:
978-1-4051-0724-2. Dewey:571.1. LCCN:2003-023170.
                                    Audience: **l,u,f.**

World Resources Institute   **HC79.E5**
  Staff
World Resources, 1992-93: A Guide to the Global Environment.
Paper Text. Oxford University Press, Inc. New York, NY. 1992.
400p. ISBN:0-19-506231-0, ISBN13: 978-0-19-506231-1.
Dewey:333.7.
                                    Audience: **g,l,u,f.**

Worldwatch Institute   **QE29**
Vital Signs 2006: the Trends That Are Shaping Our Future.
Trade Paper. W. W. Norton & Company, Inc. New York, NY.
2006. 144p. ISBN:0-393-32872-4, ISBN13: 978-0-393-32872-1.
Dewey:550.
                                    Audience: **g,l,u,f.**

Ecosystem Decline > Anthropogenic Impact

Bourliere, F.   **QH541.5.P7**
Tropical Savannas. Trade Cloth. Elsevier. New York, NY. 1983.
730p. Ecosystems of the World Ser., Vol. 13
ISBN:0-444-42035-5, ISBN13: 978-0-444-42035-0.
Dewey:574.5/2643/0913. LCCN:81-019415.
                                    Audience: **l,u,f.**

Callicott, J. Baird   **QH81.L563C66 1987**
Companion to a Sand County Almanac: Interpretive and Critical
Essays. Trade Paper. University of Wisconsin Press. Chicago,
IL. 1987. 320p. ISBN:0-299-11234-9, ISBN13:
978-0-299-11234-9. Dewey:508.73. LCCN:87-010396.
                                    Audience: **l,u.** *Choice, 1988.*

Cowell, Adrian (Produced   **GF532.A4**
  by, Directed By)
The Decade of Destruction Series. Video, VHS Format.
Bullfrog Films, Inc. Oley, PA. 1990. ISBN:1-56029-027-7,
ISBN13: 978-1-56029-027-8. Dewey:333.75/0981/1.
                                    Audience: **g,l,u,f.**

Foster, David R. & Aber,   **QH104.5.N4.F67 2004**
  John D. (Editors)
Forests in Time: The Environmental Consequences of 1,000
Years of Change in New England. Cloth over Boards. Yale
University Press. Cumberland, RI. 2004. 496p.
ISBN:0-300-09235-0, ISBN13: 978-0-300-09235-6.
Dewey:577.3/0974. LCCN:2003-012715.
                                    Audience: **g,l,u,f.** *Choice, 2004.*

Golley, Frank B. & Werger,   **QH541.5.J8**
  Marinus J. (Editors)
Tropical Rain Forest Ecosystems: Structure and Function. Trade
Cloth. Elsevier. New York, NY. 1983. 382p. Ecosystems of the
World Ser., Vol. 14A ISBN:0-444-41986-1, ISBN13:
978-0-444-41986-6. Dewey:574.5/2642/0913. LCCN:81-007861.
                                    Audience: **u,f.**

Hall, Colin Michael & Boyd,   **G156.5.E26N28 2005**
  Stephen W.
Nature-Based Tourism in Peripheral Areas: Development or
Disaster? Trade Cloth. Channel View Publications. Clevedon,
2005. 296p. Aspects of Tourism Collection, No. 21
ISBN:1-84541-001-7, ISBN13: 978-1-84541-001-8.
Dewey:338.4/791. LCCN:2004-016905.
                                    Audience: **g,l,u.**

Hertsgaard, Mark   GE149.H47 1998
Earth Odyssey: Around the World in Search of Our
Environmental Future. Trade Cloth. Broadway Books. New
York, NY. 1998. 384p. ISBN:0-7679-0058-8, ISBN13:
978-0-7679-0058-4. Dewey:363.7. LCCN:98-028202.
                                        Audience: **g.**

Hoyle   TJ163.2
Energy or Extinction. Trade Paper. Heinemann. Portsmouth, NH.
1985. ix, 81p. ISBN:0-435-54430-6, ISBN13:
978-0-435-54430-0. Dewey:333.79. LCCN:77-376795.
                                        Audience: **g.**

Huggett, Richard J.   GF23.M35.H85 1993
Modelling the Human Impact on Nature: Systems Analysis of
Environmental Problems. Trade Cloth. Oxford University Press,
Inc. New York, NY. 1993. 224p. ISBN:0-19-874170-7, ISBN13:
978-0-19-874170-1. Dewey:304.2/01/5118. LCCN:93-012093.
                                Audience: **u,f.** *Choice, 1994.*

Koren, Herman & Bisesi,   RA565.K67 2002
  Michael S.
Handbook of Environmental Health, Vol. 1. Ed. 4. Paper over
Boards. Lewis Publishers. Boca Raton, FL. 2002. 824p.
ISBN:1-56670-536-3, ISBN13: 978-1-56670-536-3.
Dewey:363.7. LCCN:2002-016110.
                                Audience: **l,u,f.** *Choice, 2003.*

McNeill, J. R.   GF13.M39 2000
Something New under the Sun: An Environmental History of
the Twentieth-Century World. Trade Cloth. W. W. Norton &
Company, Inc. New York, NY. 2000. 416p.
ISBN:0-393-04917-5, ISBN13: 978-0-393-04917-6.
Dewey:304.2/8/0904. LCCN:99-054900.
                                Audience: **g,l.** *Choice, 2000.*

Miller, Julia R., et al.   GF4
The Encyclopedia of Human Ecology. Richard M. Lerner,
Lawrence B. Schiamberg & Trustees of Tufts University Staff
(Authors). Library Binding. ABC-CLIO, Inc. Santa Barbara, CA.
2003. 760p. ISBN:1-57607-852-3, ISBN13: 978-1-57607-852-5.
Dewey:304.2/03. LCCN:2003-004178.
                                Audience: **g.** *Choice, 2004.*

Quammen, David   QH541.5.I8Q35 1996
The Song of the Dodo: Island Biogeography in an Age of
Extinctions. Trade Cloth. Simon & Schuster. New York, NY.
1996. 704p. ISBN:0-684-80083-7, ISBN13: 978-0-684-80083-7.
Dewey:574.5/267. LCCN:95-044972.
                                Audience: **g,l,u,f.** *Choice, 1996.*

Ruddiman, William F.   QC981.R763 2005
Plows, Plagues, and Petroleum: How Humans Took Control of
Climate. Trade Cloth. Princeton University Press. Princeton, NJ.
2005. 272p. ISBN:0-691-12164-8, ISBN13: 978-0-691-12164-2.
Dewey:363.738/74. LCCN:2004-062444.
                                Audience: **g,l,u,f.** *Choice, 2006.*

Sinclair, A. R. & Arcese,   QL337.T3S42 1995
  Peter (Editors)
Serengeti II: Dynamics, Management, and Conservation of an
Ecosystem. Trade Cloth. University of Chicago Press. Chicago,
IL. 1995. 673p. ISBN:0-226-76031-6, ISBN13:
978-0-226-76031-5. Dewey:574.5/264. LCCN:94-045542.
                                Audience: **u,f.** *Choice, 1996.*

Speth, James Gustave   GE149.S64 2004
Red Sky at Morning: America and the Crisis of the Global
Environment. Cloth over Boards. Yale University Press.
Cumberland, RI. 2004. 320p. ISBN:0-300-10232-1, ISBN13:
978-0-300-10232-1. Dewey:363.7/00973. LCCN:2003-020223.
                                Audience: **g.** *Choice, 2004.*

Tarr, Joel A.   TD180.T37 1996
The Search for the Ultimate Sink: Urban Pollution in Historical
Perspective. Trade Paper. University of Akron Press, The.
Akron, OH. 1996. 419p. Series on Technology and the
Environment ISBN:1-884836-06-2, ISBN13: 978-1-884836-06-0.
Dewey:363.73/09173/2. LCCN:96-038383.
                                Audience: **l,u,f.** *Choice, 1997.*

Van Dyne, George M.   QH541.5.P7.G74
Grasslands, Systems Analysis and Man. Alicia I. Breymeyer
(Editor). Trade Cloth. Cambridge University Press. New York,
NY. 1980. 976p. International Biological Programme Ser., No.
19 ISBN:0-521-21872-1, ISBN13: 978-0-521-21872-6.
Dewey:574.5/264. LCCN:77-028249.
                                Audience: **l,u,f.**

Ecosystem Decline > Biodiversity

Fuller, Margaret C.   SD421.F84 1991
Forest Fires: An Introduction to Wildland Fire Behavior,
Management, Firefighting, and Prevention. Trade Paper. John
Wiley & Sons, Inc. Hoboken, NJ. 1991. 238p. Nature Editions
Ser. ISBN:0-471-52189-2, ISBN13: 978-0-471-52189-1.
Dewey:634.9/618. LCCN:90-046331.
                                        Audience: **g.**

Gorke, Martin   QH540.5.G6713 2003
The Death of Our Planet's Species: A Challenge to Ecology and
Ethics. Trade Cloth. Island Press. Washington, DC. 2003. 408p.
ISBN:1-55963-957-1, ISBN13: 978-1-55963-957-6.
Dewey:333.95. LCCN:2003-006059.
                                Audience: **g,l,u,f.** *Choice, 2004.*

Harris, Larry D.   QH75.H37 1984
The Fragmented Forest: Island Biogeography Theory and the
Preservation of Biotic Diversity. Kenton R. Miller (Foreword
by). Library Binding. University of Chicago Press. Chicago, IL.
1984. 208p. ISBN:0-226-31763-3, ISBN13: 978-0-226-31763-2.
Dewey:639.9. LCCN:84-000144.
                                        Audience: **l,u,f.**

Middleton, Susan &   QH76.5
  Liittschwager, David
Archipelago: Portraits of Life in the World's Most Remote
Island Sanctuary. Trade Cloth. National Geographic Society.
Washington, DC. 2005. 264p. ISBN:0-7922-4188-6, ISBN13:
978-0-7922-4188-1. Dewey:578.68/09969/0222.
LCCN:2006-278389.
                                        Audience: **g.**

Primack, Richard B.   QH75.P752 2002
Essentials of Conservation Biology. Ed. 3. Trade Cloth. Sinauer
Associates, Inc. Sunderland, MA. 2002. 637p.
ISBN:0-87893-719-6, ISBN13: 978-0-87893-719-6.
Dewey:333.95/16. LCCN:2002-008076.
                                        Audience: **l.**

Quammen, David   **QH541.5.I8Q35 1996**
The Song of the Dodo: Island Biogeography in an Age of
Extinctions. Trade Cloth. Simon & Schuster. New York, NY.
1996. 704p. ISBN:0-684-80083-7, ISBN13: 978-0-684-80083-7.
Dewey:574.5/267. LCCN:95-044972.
Audience: **g,l,u,f.** *Choice, 1996.*

Spellerberg, Ian F.   **QH75.S6355 1992**
Evaluation and Assessment for Conservation. Trade Cloth.
Chapman & Hall. New York, NY. 1992. 300p.
ISBN:0-412-44270-1, ISBN13: 978-0-412-44270-4.
Dewey:333.9516. LCCN:92-239653.
Audience: **u,f.** *Choice, 1993.*

Wilson, Don E. (Editor),   **QL708.5.M435 1996**
  et al.
Measuring and Monitoring Biological Diversity: Standard
Methods for Mammals. Mercedes S. Foster, F. Russell Cole,
James D. Nichols & Rasanayagam Rudran (Editors). Trade
Cloth. Smithsonian Institution Press. Washington, DC. 1996.
480p. Biodiversity Handbook Ser. ISBN:1-56098-636-0,
ISBN13: 978-1-56098-636-2. Dewey:599.052/48/0723.
LCCN:96-001554.
Audience: **u.**

Wilson, Edward O.   **QH75**
The Diversity of Life. Trade Cloth, Box or Slipcased. Harvard
University Press. Cambridge, MA. 1993. 432p. Questions of
Science Ser. ISBN:0-674-21299-1, ISBN13: 978-0-674-21299-2.
Dewey:333.95.
Audience: **g,l.** *Choice, 1993.*

Ecosystem Decline > Coral Reefs

Bryant, Dirk, et al.   **QE565**
Reefs at Risk: A Map-Based Indicator of Threats to the World's
Coral Reefs. Lauretta Burke, John McManus & Mark Spalding
(Authors). Trade Cloth. World Resources Institute. Washington,
DC. 1998. 56p. ISBN:1-56973-257-4, ISBN13:
978-1-56973-257-1. Dewey:551.4/24. LCCN:98-086375.
Audience: **g,l,u,f.**

Middleton, Susan &   **QH76.5**
  Liittschwager, David
Archipelago: Portraits of Life in the World's Most Remote
Island Sanctuary. Trade Cloth. National Geographic Society.
Washington, DC. 2005. 264p. ISBN:0-7922-4188-6, ISBN13:
978-0-7922-4188-1. Dewey:578.68/09969/0222.
LCCN:2006-278389.
Audience: **g.**

Ecosystem Decline > Desertification

Shiklomanov, I. A. &   **GB661.2**
  Rodda, John C. (Editors)
World Water Resources at the Beginning of the Twenty-First
Century. Trade Paper. Cambridge University Press. New York,
NY. 2004. 449p. International Hydrology Ser.
ISBN:0-521-61722-7, ISBN13: 978-0-521-61722-2.
Dewey:553.7/09/05. LCCN:2002-031201.
Audience: **u,f.** *Choice, 2004.*

Ecosystem Decline > Erosion

Lal, Rattan   **S590.2.S6289 1999**
Soil Quality and Soil Erosion. Saddle Stitched. Saint Lucie
Press. Boca Raton, FL. 1998. 352p. ISBN:1-57444-100-0,
ISBN13: 978-1-57444-100-0. Dewey:631.4. LCCN:99-166567.
Audience: **u,f.** *Choice, 1999.*

Energy Use

     T174.3.D64
Department of Energy New Technology: Sharing New Frontiers.
Paper Text. DIANE Publishing Company. Collingdale, PA. 1993.
167p. ISBN:1-56806-205-2, ISBN13: 978-1-56806-205-1.
Dewey:607.
Audience: **g.**

Alters, Sandra M.   **TJ163.24**
Energy: Supplies, Sustainability, and Costs. Ed. 2005. Trade
Paper, Perfect. Thomson Gale. Farmington Hills, MI. 2005.
162p. Information Plus Ser. ISBN:0-7876-9072-4, ISBN13:
978-0-7876-9072-4. Dewey:333.79.
Audience: **g.**

Angelo, Joseph A.   **TK9145**
Nuclear Technology. Cloth Text. Greenwood Publishing Group,
Inc. Portsmouth, NH. 2004. 656p. Sourcebooks in Modern
Technology ISBN:1-57356-336-6, ISBN13: 978-1-57356-336-9.
Dewey:621.48. LCCN:2004-011238.
Audience: **u,f.** *Choice, 2005.*

Angrist, Stanley W.   **TK2896.A6 1982**
Direct Energy Conversion. Ed. 4. Cloth Text. Prentice Hall PTR.
Upper Saddle River, NJ. 1982. 520p. ISBN:0-205-07758-7,
ISBN13: 978-0-205-07758-8. Dewey:621.31/24.
LCCN:81-020591.
Audience: **l,u,f.**

Bisio, Attilio & Boots,   **TJ163.235.E53 1995**
  Sharon (Editors)
Encyclopedia of Energy Technology and the Environment, Set.
Trade Cloth. John Wiley & Sons, Inc. Hoboken, NJ. 1995.
3024p. Encyclopedia Series in Environmental Science
ISBN:0-471-54458-2, ISBN13: 978-0-471-54458-6.
Dewey:333.79/03. LCCN:94-044119.
Audience: **g,l,u,f.** *Choice, 1995.*

Bisio, Attilio & Boots,   **TJ163.235.W55 1997**
  Sharon (Editors)
The Wiley Encyclopedia of Energy and the Environment, Set.
Trade Cloth. John Wiley & Sons, Inc. Hoboken, NJ. 1996.
1562p. Encyclopedia of Energy and the Environment Ser., Vol. 2
ISBN:0-471-14827-X, ISBN13: 978-0-471-14827-2.
Dewey:333.79/03. LCCN:96-002734.
Audience: **g.** *Choice, 1997.*

Cleveland, Cutler J.   **TJ163.28.E53 2004**
  (Editor-In-Chief)
Encyclopedia of Energy, Set. Robert Ayres, Robert Costanza,
Jose Goldemberg, Marija D. Ilic, Eberhard Jochem, Robert
Kaufmann, Amory Lovins, Mohan Munasinghe, Claudia
Sheinbaum Pardo, Per Peterson, Lee Schipper, Margaret Slade,
Vaclav Smil, Ernst Worrell & R. K. Pachauri (Contribution by).
Trade Cloth. Elsevier Science & Technology Books. Saint

Louis, MO. 2004. 5376p. ISBN:0-12-176480-X, ISBN13: 978-0-12-176480-7. Dewey:333.79/03. LCCN:2003-116610.
Audience: **g,l,u,f.** *Choice, 2004.*

Cuff, David J. & Young,   **TJ163.25.U6C83 1986**
  William J.
Energy Atlas, United States. Ed. 2. Trade Cloth. Macmillan Publishing Company, Inc. Old Tappan, NJ. 1985. 420p. ISBN:0-02-691240-6, ISBN13: 978-0-02-691240-2. Dewey:333.99/0973. LCCN:85-004867.
Audience: **g,l.** *Choice, 1986.*

Decher, Reiner   **TK2896.D43 1997**
Direct Energy Conversion: Fundamentals of Electric Power Production. Cloth Text. Oxford University Press, Inc. New York, NY. 1996. 272p. ISBN:0-19-509572-3, ISBN13: 978-0-19-509572-2. Dewey:621.3/124. LCCN:96-004842.
Audience: **u,f.** *Choice, 1998.*

Denny, Fred I.   **TK1001**
Power System Operations and Electricity Markets. CRC Press. 2002. ISBN:0-8493-0813-5, ISBN13: 978-0-8493-0813-0.
Audience: **g,u.**

Duffy, Robert J.   **HD9698.U5D76 1997**
Nuclear Politics in America: A History and Theory of Government Regulation. Trade Cloth. University Press of Kansas. Lawrence, KS. 1997. viii, 304p. Studies in Government and Public Policy ISBN:0-7006-0852-4, ISBN13: 978-0-7006-0852-2. Dewey:333.792/4/0973. LCCN:97-019146.
Audience: **g.** *Choice, 1998.*

Edwards, Lyman (Editor),   **TJ280.7**
  et al.
Handbook of Geothermal Energy. Herman H. Rieke III, George V. Chilingar & Walter H. Fertl (Editors). Other. Elsevier Science & Technology Books. Saint Louis, MO. 1983. 614p. ISBN:0-87201-322-7, ISBN13: 978-0-87201-322-3. Dewey:621.44. LCCN:81-020246.
Audience: **l,u.**

Glasstone, Samuel   **TK9202**
Nuclear Reactor Engineering. Ed. 4. Chapman & Hall. 1994. ISBN:0-412-98521-7, ISBN13: 978-0-412-98521-8.
Audience: **u,f.**

Glasstone, Samuel &   **GE105**
  Jordan, Walter H.
Nuclear Power and Its Environmental Effects. Trade Paper. American Nuclear Society. La Grange Park, IL. 1980. 400p. ISBN:0-89448-024-3, ISBN13: 978-0-89448-024-9. Dewey:363.7. LCCN:80-067303.
Audience: **g,l,u,f.**

Hoyle   **TJ163.2**
Energy or Extinction. Trade Paper. Heinemann. Portsmouth, NH. 1985. ix, 81p. ISBN:0-435-54430-6, ISBN13: 978-0-435-54430-0. Dewey:333.79. LCCN:77-376795.
Audience: **g.**

Hunn, Bruce D. (Editor)   **TJ163.5.B84F86 1996**
Fundamentals of Building Energy Dynamics. Trade Cloth. MIT Press. Cambridge, MA. 1996. 550p. Solar Heat Technologies Ser., Vol. 4 ISBN:0-262-08238-1, ISBN13: 978-0-262-08238-9. Dewey:696. LCCN:95-046158.
Audience: **g,u,f.** *Choice, 1997.*

Inhaber, Herbert   **TD195.E49**
Energy Risk Assessment. Bernard L. Cohen (Introduction by). Cloth Text. Gordon & Breach Publishing Group. New York, NY. 1982. 396p. ISBN:0-677-05980-9, ISBN13: 978-0-677-05980-8. Dewey:333.79. LCCN:82-003060.
Audience: **l,u,f.**

Ruddiman, William F.   **QC981.R763 2005**
Plows, Plagues, and Petroleum: How Humans Took Control of Climate. Trade Cloth. Princeton University Press. Princeton, NJ. 2005. 272p. ISBN:0-691-12164-8, ISBN13: 978-0-691-12164-2. Dewey:363.738/74. LCCN:2004-062444.
Audience: **g,l,u,f.** *Choice, 2006.*

Saccomanno, Fabio   **TK1007**
Electric Power Systems: Analysis and Control. Trade Cloth. John Wiley & Sons, Inc. Hoboken, NJ. 2003. 744p. IEEE Press Series on Power Engineering, Series Editor Ser., :Paul M. Anderson Ser. ISBN:0-471-23439-7, ISBN13: 978-0-471-23439-5. Dewey:621.3/1.
Audience: **u,f.** *Choice, 2003.*

Short, Tom   **TK3001.S47 2003**
Electric power distribution handbook. CRC Press. 2004. ISBN:0-8493-1791-6, ISBN13: 978-0-8493-1791-0.
Audience: **u,f.**

Suppes, Galen J. &   **QC173**
  Storvick, Truman
Sustainable Nuclear Power. Trade Cloth. Elsevier Science & Technology Books. Saint Louis, MO. 2006. 416p. ISBN:0-12-370602-5, ISBN13: 978-0-12-370602-7. Dewey:539.
Audience: **u,f.**

Teller, Edward   **TJ163.2.T4**
Energy from Heaven and Earth. Cloth Text. W. H. Freeman & Company. New York, NY. 1979. 322p. ISBN:0-7167-1063-3, ISBN13: 978-0-7167-1063-9. Dewey:333.7. LCCN:79-004049.
Audience: **g.**

Walker, Peter (Editor)   **TK9009.C48 1992**
Chambers Nuclear Energy and Radiation Dictionary. Trade Cloth. Chambers Harrap Publishers Limited.. Edinburgh, 1992. 352p. ISBN:0-550-13246-5, ISBN13: 978-0-550-13246-8. Dewey:621.48/03. LCCN:93-111539.
Audience: **u,f.** *Choice, 1993.*

Wolfson, Richard   **TK9148**
Nuclear Choices: A Citizen's Guide to Nuclear Technology. Trade Cloth. MIT Press. Cambridge, MA. 1991. 428p. ISBN:0-262-23158-1, ISBN13: 978-0-262-23158-9. Dewey:333.7924. LCCN:90-013545.
Audience: **g,l.** *Choice, 1992, 1991.*

Worldwatch Institute   **QE29**
Vital Signs 2006: the Trends That Are Shaping Our Future. Trade Paper. W. W. Norton & Company, Inc. New York, NY. 2006. 144p. ISBN:0-393-32872-4, ISBN13: 978-0-393-32872-1. Dewey:550.
Audience: **g,l,u,f.**

Zumerchik, John   **TJ163.28.M33 2001**
Macmillan Encyclopedia of Energy. Ed. 3. Trade Cloth. Macmillan Publishing Company, Inc. Old Tappan, NJ. 2000. ISBN:0-02-865020-4, ISBN13: 978-0-02-865020-3. Dewey:621.042/03. LCCN:00-062498.
Audience: **g,l,u,f.**

Energy Use > Energy Conservation

Beggs, Clive   **TJ163.5.B84**
Energy: Management, Supply and Conservation. Paper Text.
Elsevier Science & Technology Books. Saint Louis, MO. 2002.
284p. ISBN:0-7506-5096-6, ISBN13: 978-0-7506-5096-0.
Dewey:696.
Audience: **g,l,u.**

Hordeski, Michael F.   **TJ163.28.H67 2004**
Encyclopedia of Energy Conservation Technology. Paper over
Boards. Marcel Dekker Inc. New York, NY. 2004. 350p.
ISBN:0-8247-4810-7, ISBN13: 978-0-8247-4810-4.
Dewey:621.042/03. LCCN:2004-047095.
Audience: **u,f.**

Hunn, Bruce D. (Editor)   **TJ163.5.B84F86 1996**
Fundamentals of Building Energy Dynamics. Trade Cloth. MIT
Press. Cambridge, MA. 1996. 550p. Solar Heat Technologies
Ser., Vol. 4 ISBN:0-262-08238-1, ISBN13: 978-0-262-08238-9.
Dewey:696. LCCN:95-046158.
Audience: **g,u,f.**   *Choice, 1997.*

Miller, Bruce G.   **TP325.M55 2005**
Coal Energy Systems. Cloth Text. Elsevier Science &
Technology Books. Saint Louis, MO. 2004. 544p. Sustainable
World Ser. ISBN:0-12-497451-1, ISBN13: 978-0-12-497451-7.
Dewey:662.6/2. LCCN:2005-270338.
Audience: **g,l.**

Ramage, Janet   **TJ163.2.R345 1997**
Energy: A Guidebook. Ed. 2. Trade Paper. Oxford University
Press, Inc. New York, NY. 1997. 416p. ISBN:0-19-288022-5,
ISBN13: 978-0-19-288022-2. Dewey:333.79. LCCN:96-052364.
Audience: **g,l.**   *Choice, 1998.*

Yeang, Kenneth   **NA6230.Y43 1999**
The Green Skyscraper: The Basis for Designing Sustainable
Intensive Buildings. Trade Paper. Prestel Publishing. New York,
NY. 1999. 304p. ISBN:3-7913-1993-0, ISBN13:
978-3-7913-1993-3. Dewey:720/.47. LCCN:98-034625.
Audience: **g.**

Energy Use > Renewable Energy Sources

Charlier, Roger H.   **TC147**
Tidal Energy. Trade Cloth. John Wiley & Sons, Inc. Hoboken,
NJ. 1982. xi, 351p. ISBN:0-442-24425-8, ISBN13:
978-0-442-24425-5. Dewey:621.31/2134. LCCN:81-013111.
Audience: **l,u,f.**

Cuff, David J. & Young,   **TJ163.25.U6C83 1986**
  William J.
Energy Atlas, United States. Ed. 2. Trade Cloth. Macmillan
Publishing Company, Inc. Old Tappan, NJ. 1985. 420p.
ISBN:0-02-691240-6, ISBN13: 978-0-02-691240-2.
Dewey:333.99/0973. LCCN:85-004867.
Audience: **g,l.**   *Choice, 1986.*

da Rosa, Aldo V.   **TJ163.2**
Fundamentals of Renewable Energy Processes. Cloth Text.
Elsevier Science & Technology Books. Saint Louis, MO. 2005.
712p. ISBN:0-12-088510-7, ISBN13: 978-0-12-088510-7.
Dewey:621.042. LCCN:2005-282302.
Audience: **l,u.**   *Choice, 2006.*

Golob, Richard & Brus,   **TJ808.3.G65 1993**
  Eric
The Almanac of Renewable Energy: The Complete Guide to
Emerging Energy Technologies. Trade Cloth. Henry Holt &
Company. New York, NY. 1993. 352p. ISBN:0-8050-1948-0,
ISBN13: 978-0-8050-1948-3. Dewey:333.79/4.
LCCN:92-013963.
Audience: **g,l.**   *Choice, 1993.*

Masters, Gilbert M.   **TK1005.M33 2004**
Renewable and Efficient Electric Power Systems. Trade Cloth.
John Wiley & Sons, Inc. Hoboken, NJ. 2004. 680p.
ISBN:0-471-28060-7, ISBN13: 978-0-471-28060-6.
Dewey:621.31. LCCN:2003-062035.
Audience: **g,u,f.**   *Choice, 2005.*

Plunkett, Jack W. (Editor)   **HD9502.U52 P625**
Plunkett's Renewable, Alternative and Hydrogen Energy
Industry Almanac 2006: The Only Complete Guide to the
Business of Renewable, Alternative and Hydrogen Energy. Trade
Paper, CD-ROM. Plunkett Research, Ltd. Houston, TX. 2005.
354p. ISBN:1-59392-037-7, ISBN13: 978-1-59392-037-1.
Dewey:333.
Audience: **g,f.**

Quaschning, Volker   **TD195.E49**
Understanding Renewable Energy Systems. Trade Cloth.
Earthscan Canada. Toronto, ON. 2005. 192p.
ISBN:1-84407-136-7, ISBN13: 978-1-84407-136-4.
Dewey:333.79/4. LCCN:2004-022852.
Audience: **g,l,u.**   *Choice, 2005.*

Sorensen, Bent   **TJ808**
Renewable Energy. Ed. 3. Cloth Text. Elsevier Science &
Technology Books. Saint Louis, MO. 2004. 952p.
ISBN:0-12-656153-2, ISBN13: 978-0-12-656153-1.
Dewey:333.79/4. LCCN:2004-557471.
Audience: **u,f.**   *Choice, 2001.*

Sweet, William   **TJ808.S87 2006**
Kicking the Carbon Habit: Global Warming and the Case for
Renewable Energy. Trade Cloth. Columbia University Press.
New York, NY. 2006. 272p. ISBN:0-231-13710-9, ISBN13:
978-0-231-13710-2. Dewey:333.79/4. LCCN:2005-035034.
Audience: **g,l.**

Twidell, John, et al.   **TJ808**
Renewable Energy Resources. Ed. 2. Anthony D. Weir & Tony
Weir (Authors). Paper over Boards. Taylor & Francis Group.
Philadelphia, PA. 2005. 624p. ISBN:0-419-25320-3, ISBN13:
978-0-419-25320-4. Dewey:621.042. LCCN:2005-015300.
Audience: **l,u.**

Energy Use > Renewable Energy Sources > Biomass

Clarke, Anthony J.   **QR160**
Biodegradation of cellulose: enzymology and biotechnology.
Technomic. 1997. ISBN:1-56676-414-9, ISBN13:
978-1-56676-414-8.
Audience: **u,f.**

Clarke, Anthony J.   QR160.C519 1997
Biodegradation of cellulose: enzymology and biotechnology.
Technomic. 1997. ISBN:1-56676-414-9, ISBN13:
978-1-56676-414-8.

Audience: **u,f.**

Klass, Donald L.   TP339.K54 1998
Biomass for Renewable Energy, Fuels, and Chemicals. Trade
Cloth. Elsevier Science & Technology Books. Saint Louis, MO.
1998. 651p. ISBN:0-12-410950-0, ISBN13: 978-0-12-410950-6.
Dewey:662.8/8. LCCN:98-084422.

Audience: **u,f.** *Choice, 1999.*

Energy Use > Renewable Energy Sources > Geothermal

Armstead, H. C.   TJ280.7 .A74 1978
Geothermal Energy: It's Past, Present and Future Contributions
to the Energy Needs of Man. Ed. 99. Trade Cloth. John Wiley
& Sons, Inc. Hoboken, NJ. 1978. 357p. ISBN:0-470-26337-7,
ISBN13: 978-0-470-26337-2. Dewey:553.7. LCCN:78-002545.

Audience: **g,f.**

Dickson, Mary H. & Fanelli,   TJ280.7.G443 2005
Mario (Editors)
Geothermal Energy: Utilization and Technology. Perfect, Paper
over Boards. Earthscan/James & James. London, 2005. 205p.
ISBN:1-84407-184-7, ISBN13: 978-1-84407-184-5.
Dewey:621.44. LCCN:2005-006659.

Audience: **g,l,u,f.** *Choice, 2005.*

Edwards, Lyman (Editor),   TJ280.7
et al.
Handbook of Geothermal Energy. Herman H. Rieke III, George
V. Chilingar & Walter H. Fertl (Editors). Other. Elsevier Science
& Technology Books. Saint Louis, MO. 1983. 614p.
ISBN:0-87201-322-7, ISBN13: 978-0-87201-322-3.
Dewey:621.44. LCCN:81-020246.

Audience: **l,u.**

Energy Use > Renewable Energy Sources > Hydroelectric

Baker, A. C.   TC147 .B28 1991
Tidal Power. Trade Cloth. Institution of Engineering and
Technology (IET). Edison, NJ. 1991. 260p. Energy Ser., No. 5
ISBN:0-86341-189-4, ISBN13: 978-0-86341-189-2.
Dewey:621.31/2134. LCCN:92-131476.

Audience: **l,u,f.**

Energy Use > Renewable Energy Sources > Hydrogen

Fowler, T. Kenneth   QC791.73.F69 1997
The Fusion Quest. Trade Cloth. Johns Hopkins University Press.
Baltimore, MD. 1997. 272p. ISBN:0-8018-5456-3, ISBN13:
978-0-8018-5456-9. Dewey:621.48/4. LCCN:96-034254.

Audience: **g,l,u,f.** *Choice, 1997.*

Hoogers, Gregor   TK2931.F785 2003
Fuel Cell Technology Handbook. Trade Cloth. Society of
Automotive Engineers, Inc. Warrendale, PA. 2002. 800p.

ISBN:0-7680-0706-2, ISBN13: 978-0-7680-0706-0.
Dewey:621.31/2429.

Audience: **g,l,u,f.** *Choice, 2003.*

Vaitheeswaran, Vijay V.   TJ163.2.V335 2003
Power to the People: How the Coming Energy Revolution Will
Transform an Industry, Change Our Lives, and Maybe Even
Save the Planet. Cloth over Boards. Farrar, Straus & Giroux.
New York, NY. 2003. 368p. ISBN:0-374-23675-5, ISBN13:
978-0-374-23675-5. Dewey:333.79. LCCN:2003-006985.

Audience: **g,l,u,f.** *Choice, 2004.*

Energy Use > Renewable Energy Sources > Solar Power

Archer, Mary D. & Hill,   TK1087 .C573 2001
Robert (Editors)
Clean Electricity from Photovoltaics. Trade Cloth. Imperial
College Press. London, 2001. 868p. Series on Photoconversion
of Solar Energy, Vol. 1 ISBN:1-86094-161-3, ISBN13:
978-1-86094-161-0. Dewey:621.381542. LCCN:2004-267046.

Audience: **l,u,f.**

Hamakawa, Yoshihiro   TK2960.T45 2003
(Volume Editor)
Thin-Film Solar Cells: Next Generation Photovoltaics and Its
Applications. Trade Cloth. Springer. New York, NY. 2004. XV,
244p. Springer Series in Photonics, Vol. 13
ISBN:3-540-43945-5, ISBN13: 978-3-540-43945-5.
Dewey:621.31/244. LCCN:2003-057384.

Audience: **u,f.**

Hunn, Bruce D. (Editor)   TJ163.5.B84F86 1996
Fundamentals of Building Energy Dynamics. Trade Cloth. MIT
Press. Cambridge, MA. 1996. 550p. Solar Heat Technologies
Ser., Vol. 4 ISBN:0-262-08238-1, ISBN13: 978-0-262-08238-9.
Dewey:696. LCCN:95-046158.

Audience: **g,u,f.** *Choice, 1997.*

Markvart, Tomas (Editor)   TK1087.S66 2000
Solar Electricity. Ed. 2. Trade Cloth. John Wiley & Sons, Inc.
Hoboken, NJ. 2000. 298p. UNESCO Energy Engineering Ser.,
Vol. 6 ISBN:0-471-98852-9, ISBN13: 978-0-471-98852-6.
Dewey:621.31/244. LCCN:00-033028.

Audience: **g,l,u,f.**

Perlin, John   TK1085.P47 2002
From Space to Earth: The Story of Solar Electricity. Trade
Paper. Harvard University Press. Cambridge, MA. 2002. 240p.
ISBN:0-674-01013-2, ISBN13: 978-0-674-01013-0.
Dewey:621.31/244. LCCN:2002-027606.

Audience: **g,u.**

Zweibel, Ken   TK2960.Z945 1990
Harnessing Solar Power: The Photovoltaics Challenge. Cloth
Text. Perseus Books Group. New York, NY. 1990. 330p.
ISBN:0-306-43564-0, ISBN13: 978-0-306-43564-5.
Dewey:621.31/244. LCCN:90-039905.

Audience: **g,l,u.** *Choice, 1991.*

Energy Use > Renewable Energy Sources > Wind Power

Baker, A. C.   **TC147 .B28 1991**
Tidal Power. Trade Cloth. Institution of Engineering and
Technology (IET). Edison, NJ. 1991. 260p. Energy Ser., No. 5
ISBN:0-86341-189-4, ISBN13: 978-0-86341-189-2.
Dewey:621.31/2134. LCCN:92-131476.
                    Audience: **l,u,f.**

Gipe, Paul   **TJ820.G56 1995**
Wind Energy Comes of Age. Ed. 1. Trade Cloth. John Wiley &
Sons, Inc. Hoboken, NJ. 1995. 560p. Wiley Series in
Sustainable Design Ser., Vol. 4 ISBN:0-471-10924-X, ISBN13:
978-0-471-10924-2. Dewey:333.792. LCCN:94-036564.
                    Audience: **l,u,f.** *Choice, 1995.*

Gipe, Paul   **TJ820**
Wind Power: Renewable Energy for Home, Farm, and Business.
Trade Cloth. Chelsea Green Publishing. White River Junction,
VT. 2004. 512p. ISBN:1-931498-60-1, ISBN13:
978-1-931498-60-9. Dewey:621.4/5.
                    Audience: **g,l.** *Choice, 2004.*

Spera, David A. (Editor)   **TJ828.W563 1994**
Wind Turbine Technology: Fundamental Concepts of Wind
Turbine Engineering. Trade Cloth. A S M E Press. New York,
NY. 1994. 656p. ISBN:0-7918-1205-7, ISBN13:
978-0-7918-1205-1. Dewey:621.4/5. LCCN:94-011137.
                    Audience: **g,l,u,f.**

Environmental Chemistry

Dorfman, Mark, et al.   **TD899.C5.D66 1992**
Environmental Dividends: Cutting More Chemical Wastes.
Catherine Miller & Warren Muir (Authors). Trade Paper.
INFORM, Inc. New York, NY. 1992. 288p.
ISBN:0-918780-50-0, ISBN13: 978-0-918780-50-8. Dewey:660.
LCCN:92-012251.
                    Audience: **g,l,u.** *Choice, 1993.*

Durham, Jack L. & Teasley,   **QC925 .C44 1984**
John I. (Editors)
Chemistry of Particles, Fogs and Rains. Trade Cloth. Elsevier
Science & Technology Books. Saint Louis, MO. 1984. 288p.
Acid Precipitation Ser., Vol. 2 ISBN:0-250-40567-9, ISBN13:
978-0-250-40567-1. Dewey:628.1/683. LCCN:83-015272.
                    Audience: **l,u.**

Holland, H. D. & Turekian,   **QE515**
K. K.
Treatise on Geochemistry, Set. Trade Cloth. Elsevier Science &
Technology Books. Saint Louis, MO. 2003. 7800p.
ISBN:0-08-043751-6, ISBN13: 978-0-08-043751-4.
Dewey:551.9. LCCN:2003-113648.
                    Audience: **l,u,f.** *Choice, 2004.*

Saxena, Jitendra (Editor)   **QH545.A1 H38**
Hazard Assessment of Chemicals, Vol. 6. Library Binding.
Hemisphere Publishing Corporation. Philadelphia, PA. 1988.
400p. Hazard Assessment of Chemicals Ser.
ISBN:0-89116-835-4, ISBN13: 978-0-89116-835-5.
Dewey:363.7/384.
                    Audience: **l,u.**

Saxena, Jitendra & Fischer,   **QH545.A1 H38**
Farley (Editors)
Hazard Assessment of Chemicals: Vol. 1, Current Developments.
Trade Cloth. Elsevier Science & Technology Books. Saint
Louis, MO. 1981. Serial Publication Ser. ISBN:0-12-312401-8,
ISBN13: 978-0-12-312401-2. Dewey:363.7/384.
                    Audience: **l,u.**

Seinfeld, John H. & Pandis,   **QC879.6.S45 2006**
Spyros N.
Atmospheric Chemistry and Physics: From Air Pollution to
Climate Change. Ed. 2. Trade Cloth. John Wiley & Sons, Inc.
Hoboken, NJ. 2006. 1203p. ISBN:0-471-72017-8, ISBN13:
978-0-471-72017-1. Dewey:551.5/11.
                    Audience: **l,u,f.** *Choice, 1998.*

Tinsley, Ian J.   **TD174**
Chemical Concepts in Pollutant Behavior. Ed. 2. Trade Cloth.
John Wiley & Sons, Inc. Hoboken, NJ. 2004. 402p.
ISBN:0-471-09525-7, ISBN13: 978-0-471-09525-5.
Dewey:577.27. LCCN:2003-025152.
                    Audience: **l,u.**

Verschueren, Karel   **TD196.O73V47 2001**
Handbook of Environmental Data on Organic Chemicals, Set.
Ed. 4. Trade Cloth. John Wiley & Sons, Inc. Hoboken, NJ.
2001. 2416p. ISBN:0-471-37490-3, ISBN13:
978-0-471-37490-9. Dewey:363.738. LCCN:00-069254.
                    Audience: **u,f.** *B* *Choice, 2002, 1999, 1997.*

Walker, C. H. &   **QH541.5.S3**
Livingstone, D. R.
Persistent Pollutants in Marine Ecosystems. Trade Cloth.
Elsevier Science & Technology Books. Saint Louis, MO. 1992.
192p. Society of Environment Toxicology and Chemistry Ser.
ISBN:0-08-041874-0, ISBN13: 978-0-08-041874-2.
Dewey:574.52636. LCCN:92-006423.
                    Audience: **l,u,f.**

Warren, Christian   **RA1231.L4W37 2000**
Brush with Death: A Social History of Lead Poisoning. Trade
Cloth. Johns Hopkins University Press. Baltimore, MD. 2000.
384p. ISBN:0-8018-6289-2, ISBN13: 978-0-8018-6289-2.
Dewey:615.9/25688/0973. LCCN:99-046329.
                    Audience: **l,u.** *Choice, 2000.*

Environmental Disasters

Burger, Joanna (Editor)   **QH545.O5B44 1994**
Before and after an Oil Spill: The Arthur Kill. Cloth Text.
Rutgers University Press. Piscataway, NJ. 1994. 320p.
ISBN:0-8135-2095-9, ISBN13: 978-0-8135-2095-7.
Dewey:363.73/82/0916346. LCCN:93-043803.
                    Audience: **u,f.** *Choice, 1995.*

Burger, Joanna   **TD196.P4B87 1997**
Oil Spills. Cloth Text. Rutgers University Press. Piscataway, NJ.
1997. 228p. ISBN:0-8135-2338-9, ISBN13: 978-0-8135-2338-5.
Dewey:363.73/82. LCCN:96-008340.
                    Audience: **u,f.** *Choice, 1997.*

Cowell, Adrian   **GF532.A4**
The Decade of Destruction: The Crusade to Save the Amazon
Rain Forest. Cloth Text. DIANE Publishing Company.
Collingdale, PA. 1999. 215p. ISBN:0-7881-6688-3, ISBN13:
978-0-7881-6688-4. Dewey:333.75/0981/1.
                    Audience: **g,l,u,f.**

Gerber, Michele S.   TD898.12.W2G47 2002
On the Home Front: The Cold War Legacy of the Hanford
Nuclear Site. Ed. 2. Trade Cloth. University of Nebraska Press.
Lincoln, NE. 2005. 363p. ISBN:0-8032-7101-8, ISBN13:
978-0-8032-7101-2. Dewey:363.72/89/0979751.
LCCN:2001-027956.
                              Audience: **g,l.** *Choice, 2003, 2002, 1993.*

Jasanoff, Sheila (Editor)   T174.5.L415 1994
Learning from Disaster: Risk Management after Bhopal. Trade
Cloth. University of Pennsylvania Press. Philadelphia, PA. 1994.
336p. Law in Social Context Ser. ISBN:0-8122-3250-X,
ISBN13: 978-0-8122-3250-9. Dewey:363.17/91/0954.
LCCN:93-048100.
                              Audience: **l,u.** *Choice, 1994.*

Mycio, Mary   QH543.5.M93 2005
Wormwood Forest: A Natural History of Chernobyl. Trade
Cloth. National Academies Press. Washington, DC. 2005. 304p.
ISBN:0-309-09430-5, ISBN13: 978-0-309-09430-6.
Dewey:577.27/7/094777. LCCN:2005-012715.
                              Audience: **g,l,u,f.** *Choice, 2006.*

Osif, Bonnie A.; Baratta,   TK1345.H37
  Anthony J. & Conkling, Thomas W.
TMI 25 Years Later: The Three Mile Island Nuclear Power
Plant Accident and Its Impact. Pennsylvania State University
Press. 2004. ISBN:0-271-02383-X, ISBN13: 978-0-271-02383-0.
                                          Audience: **l,u.**

Smith, Jim & Beresford,   TD196.R3
  Nicholas A.
Chernobyl: Catastrophe, Consequences and Solutions. Trade
Cloth. Springer. New York, NY. 2005. XXVI, 310p. Springer
Praxis Books / Environmental Sciences Ser.
ISBN:3-540-23866-2, ISBN13: 978-3-540-23866-9.
Dewey:363.1799094776. LCCN:2005-928344.
                              Audience: **g,l,u,f.** *Choice, 2006.*

Walker, J. Samuel   TK1345.H37 W35 2004
Three Mile Island: A Nuclear Crisis in Historical Perspective.
Trade Cloth. University of California Press. Berkeley, CA. 2004.
315p. ISBN:0-520-23940-7, ISBN13: 978-0-520-23940-1.
Dewey:363.17/99/0974818. LCCN:2003-010137.
                              Audience: **g,l,u,f.** *Choice, 2004.*

Environmental Diseases and Health

Adriano, D. C.   QH545.T7A37 2001
Trace Elements in Terrestrial Environments: Biogeochemistry,
Bioavailability and Risks of Metals. Ed. 2. Trade Cloth.
Springer. New York, NY. 2001. XII, 867p. ISBN:0-387-98678-2,
ISBN13: 978-0-387-98678-4. Dewey:577./.14. LCCN:00-061263.
                              Audience: **l,u,f.**

Aldrich, Tim E. & Griffith,   RA566
  Jack
Environmental Epidemiology and Risk Assessment. Christopher
Cooke (Editor). Trade Cloth. John Wiley & Sons, Inc. Hoboken,
NJ. 2002. 288p. Industrial Health and Safety Ser.
ISBN:0-471-29066-1, ISBN13: 978-0-471-29066-7.
Dewey:616.9/8.
                                          Audience: **g.**

Bingham, Eula, et al.   RA1229 .P38
Patty's Industrial Hygiene and Toxicology, Set. Ed. 5. Barbara
Cohrssen & Charles H. Powell (Authors). CD-ROM. John Wiley

& Sons, Inc. Hoboken, NJ. 2005. ISBN:0-471-70057-6,
ISBN13: 978-0-471-70057-9. Dewey:613.6/2.
                                          Audience: **g,l,u,f.**

Calabrese, Edward J.   RA566
Nutrition and Environmental Health, Vol. 1. Trade Cloth. John
Wiley & Sons, Inc. Hoboken, NJ. 1980. 585p.
ISBN:0-471-04833-X, ISBN13: 978-0-471-04833-6.
Dewey:615.9. LCCN:79-021089.
                                          Audience: **l,u,f.**

Committee on   RA565.N323 1991
  Environmental Epidemiolgy, National R
Environmental Epidemiology: Use of the Gray Literature and
Other Data in Environmental Epidemiology. Trade Cloth.
National Academies Press. Washington, DC. 1997. 200p.
ISBN:0-309-05737-X, ISBN13: 978-0-309-05737-0.
Dewey:363.72/87. LCCN:91-028051.
                              Audience: **f.** *Choice, 1998.*

Gofman, John W.   RA1231.R2.G56
Radiation and Human Health: A Comprehensive Investigation of
the Evidence Relating Low-Level Radiation to Cancer and Other
Diseases. Trade Cloth. Sierra Club Books. San Francisco, CA.
1981. 928p. Guides ISBN:0-87156-275-8, ISBN13:
978-0-87156-275-3. Dewey:616.9/897. LCCN:80-026484.
                                          Audience: **g,l.**

Harrison, Gordon   RA644.M2.H37 1978
Mosquitoes, Malaria, and Man: A History of the Hostilities since
1880. Trade Cloth. Penguin Group (USA) Inc. New York, NY.
1978. viii, 314p. ISBN:0-525-16025-6, ISBN13:
978-0-525-16025-0. Dewey:614.5/3/2009. LCCN:77-021725.
                                          Audience: **g,l.**

Higginson, John, et al.   RC261.48 .H54 1991
Human Cancer: Epidemiology and Environmental Causes.
Calum S. Muir & Nubia Muñoz (Authors). Trade Paper.
Cambridge University Press. New York, NY. 2005. 603p.
Cambridge Monographs on Cancer Research Ser.
ISBN:0-521-02196-0, ISBN13: 978-0-521-02196-8.
Dewey:614.5/999. LCCN:91-023259.
                                          Audience: **u,f.**

Kirsch-Volders, Micheline   RA1229.M87 1984
  (Editor)
Mutagenicity, Carcinogenicity, and Teratogenicity of Industrial
Pollutants. Trade Cloth. Basic Books. New York, NY. 1984.
350p. ISBN:0-306-41148-2, ISBN13: 978-0-306-41148-9.
Dewey:615.9/02. LCCN:83-011126.
                                          Audience: **u,f.**

Koren, Herman & Bisesi,   RA565.K67 2002
  Michael S.
Handbook of Environmental Health, Vol. 1. Ed. 4. Paper over
Boards. Lewis Publishers. Boca Raton, FL. 2002. 824p.
ISBN:1-56670-536-3, ISBN13: 978-1-56670-536-3.
Dewey:363.7. LCCN:2002-016110.
                              Audience: **l,u,f.** *Choice, 2003.*

Kryter, Karl D.   RA772.N7.K78 1985
The Effects of Noise on Man. Ed. 2. Trade Cloth. Elsevier
Science & Technology Books. Saint Louis, MO. 1985. xi, 688
p. :p. ISBN:0-12-427460-9, ISBN13: 978-0-12-427460-0.
Dewey:616.9/896. LCCN:83-003892.
                                          Audience: **g,l,u,f.**

Lippmann, Morton   **RA565.E58 2000**
Environmental Toxicants: Human Exposures and Their Health Effects. Ed. 2. Trade Cloth. John Wiley & Sons, Inc. Hoboken, NJ. 1999. 1008p. ISBN:0-471-29298-2, ISBN13: 978-0-471-29298-2. Dewey:363.7. LCCN:99-021927.
Audience: **g.** *Choice, 1993.*

Mager Stellman, Jeanne &   **RC963A3**
International Labor Office Staff (Editors)
Encyclopaedia of Occupational Health and Safety. Ed. 4. CD-ROM. International Labour Office. Washington, DC. 2003. ISBN:92-2-109818-4, ISBN13: 978-92-2-109818-8. Dewey:613.6/2/0321.
Audience: **g,l,u,f.** *Choice, 2000, 1998.*

National Research Council   **RA565.N323 1991**
Staff
Environmental Epidemiology: Public Health and Hazardous Wastes. Cloth Text. National Academies Press. Washington, DC. 1992. 296p. Environmental Epidemiology Ser. ISBN:0-309-04496-0, ISBN13: 978-0-309-04496-7. Dewey:363.72/87. LCCN:91-028051.
Audience: **u,f.** *Choice, 1992.*

Neely, W. Brock   **RA566.27.N44 1994**
Introduction to Chemical Exposure and Risk Assessment. Paper over Boards. Lewis Publishers. Boca Raton, FL. 1994. 208p. ISBN:1-56670-094-9, ISBN13: 978-1-56670-094-8. Dewey:615.9/02. LCCN:94-022452.
Audience: **u,f.** *Choice, 1995.*

Nieuwenhuijsen, Mark   **RA427.3**
(Editor)
Exposure Assessment in Occupational and Environmental Epidemiology. Trade Paper. Oxford University Press, Inc. New York, NY. 2003. 298p. Oxford Medical Publications ISBN:0-19-852861-2, ISBN13: 978-0-19-852861-6. Dewey:614.4. LCCN:2004-296186.
Audience: **g,l,u,f.**

Peakall, David   **QH545x**
Animal biomarkers as pollution indicators. Chapman & Hall. 1992. ISBN:0-412-40200-9, ISBN13: 978-0-412-40200-5.
Audience: **g,l,u,f.**

Randolph, Theron G. &   **RC584**
Moss, Ralph W.
An Alternative Approach to Allergies: The New Field of Clinical Ecology Unravels the Environmental Causes of Mental and Physical Ills. Trade Paper. HarperCollins Publishers. New York, NY. 1990. 352p. ISBN:0-06-091693-1, ISBN13: 978-0-06-091693-0. Dewey:616.97. LCCN:88-045902.
Audience: **g.**

Ring, Johannes and Heidrun   **RC584.N484 2002**
Behrendt
New Trends in Allergy V. Springer. 2002. ISBN:3-540-43082-2, ISBN13: 978-3-540-43082-7.
Audience: **u,f.**

Ring, Johannes, et al.   **RC584.N483 1997**
New Trends in Allergy IV, Together with Environmental Allergy and Allergotoxicology III: Joint International Symposium, Hamburg, April 29-May 1, 1995. H. Behrendt & D. Vieluf (Authors). Cloth Text. Springer. New York, NY. 1996. 376p. ISBN:3-540-61120-7, ISBN13: 978-3-540-61120-2. Dewey:616.97. LCCN:96-042937.
Audience: **l,u,f.**

Rothera, Ellen   **RC584 .R68 1991**
Encyclopedia of Allergy and Environmental Illness. Trade Paper. David & Charles Publishers. Newton Abbot, 1991. 256p. ISBN:0-7153-9954-3, ISBN13: 978-0-7153-9954-5. Dewey:616.97/003. LCCN:92-129380.
Audience: **g,l.**

Sipes, I. G. (Editor), et al.   **RA1199.C648 1997**
Comprehensive Toxicology. C. A. McQueen & A. J. Gandolfi (Editors). Trade Cloth. Elsevier Science & Technology Books. Saint Louis, MO. 1997. 7482p. ISBN:0-08-042301-9, ISBN13: 978-0-08-042301-2. Dewey:615.9. LCCN:96-033052.
Audience: **u,f.** *Choice, 1997.*

Steenland, Kyle & Savitz,   **RA566.T67 1997**
David A. (Editors)
Topics in Environmental Epidemiology. Trade Cloth. Oxford University Press, Inc. New York, NY. 1997. 376p. ISBN:0-19-509564-2, ISBN13: 978-0-19-509564-7. Dewey:614.4/2. LCCN:96-029398.
Audience: **u,f.**

Environmental Diseases and Health > Infectious Diseases

Aldrich, Tim E. & Griffith,   **RA566**
Jack
Environmental Epidemiology and Risk Assessment. Christopher Cooke (Editor). Trade Cloth. John Wiley & Sons, Inc. Hoboken, NJ. 2002. 288p. Industrial Health and Safety Ser. ISBN:0-471-29066-1, ISBN13: 978-0-471-29066-7. Dewey:616.9/8.
Audience: **g.**

Stolley, Paul D. & Lasky,   **RA651.S75 1995**
Tamar
Investigating Disease Patterns: The Science of Epidemiology. Trade Cloth. Henry Holt & Company. New York, NY. 1995. 224p. ISBN:0-7167-5058-9, ISBN13: 978-0-7167-5058-1. Dewey:614.4. LCCN:95-014250.
Audience: **l,u,f.** *Choice, 1996.*

Webber, Roger   **RA643.W37 1996**
Communicable Disease Epidemiology and Control. CAB International. 1996. ISBN:0-85199-138-6, ISBN13: 978-0-85199-138-2.
Audience: **u,f.**

Environmental Diseases and Health > Infectious Diseases > Plagues

Davis, Mike   **RA644.I6D387 2005**
The Monster at Our Door: The Global Threat of Bird Flu. Trade Cloth. New Press, The. New York, NY. 2005. 192p. ISBN:1-59558-011-5, ISBN13: 978-1-59558-011-5. Dewey:636.5/0896203. LCCN:2005-043853.
Audience: **g,l.**

Wills, Christopher   **RA649.W55 1996**
Yellow Fever, Black Goddess: The Coevolution of People and Plagues. Heather Mimnaugh (Editor). Trade Cloth. Addison-Wesley Longman, Inc. Boston, MA. 1996. 324p. ISBN:0-201-44235-3, ISBN13: 978-0-201-44235-9. Dewey:614.4/9. LCCN:96-023934.
Audience: **g,l.** *Choice, 1997.*

Zinsser, Hans   **RC199.1.Z54 1996**
Rats, Lice and History: A Chronicle of Disease, Plagues, and Pestilence. Trade Cloth. Black Dog & Leventhal Publishers, Inc. New York, NY. 1996. 320p. ISBN:1-884822-47-9, ISBN13: 978-1-884822-47-6. Dewey:616.9/222/009. LCCN:96-004123.
Audience: **g,l.**

Environmental Diseases and Health > Toxicology

Hayes, Wayland J.   **RA1270.P4**
Pesticides Studied in Man. Cloth Text. Lippincott Williams & Wilkins. Philadelphia, PA. 1982. 672p. ISBN:0-683-03896-6, ISBN13: 978-0-683-03896-5. Dewey:615.9/02. LCCN:81-007410.
Audience: **l,u,f.**

Jarvinen, Alfred W. &   **QH90.57.B5J37 1999**
Ankley, Gerald T.
Linkage of Effects to Tissue Residues: Development of a Comprehensive Database for Aquatic Organisms Exposed to Inorganic and Organic Chemicals. Trade Cloth. Society of Environmental Toxicology and Chemistry. Pensacola, FL. 1998. 15p. ISBN:1-880611-13-9, ISBN13: 978-1-880611-13-5. Dewey:577.6/27. LCCN:98-022670.
Audience: **u,f.**

Krimsky, Sheldon   **RC649**
Hormonal Chaos: The Scientific and Social Origins of the Environmental Endocrine Hypothesis. Lynn R. Goldman (Foreword by). Trade Cloth. DIANE Publishing Company. Collingdale, PA. 2004. 284p. ISBN:0-7567-7113-7, ISBN13: 978-0-7567-7113-3. Dewey:616.4/071.
Audience: **g,l.**

Lippmann, Morton   **RA565.E58 2000**
Environmental Toxicants: Human Exposures and Their Health Effects. Ed. 2. Trade Cloth. John Wiley & Sons, Inc. Hoboken, NJ. 1999. 1008p. ISBN:0-471-29298-2, ISBN13: 978-0-471-29298-2. Dewey:363.7. LCCN:99-021927.
Audience: **g.** *Choice, 1993.*

Nieboer, Evert & Nriagu,   **TD180.A38 VOL. 25**
Jerome O. (Editors)
Nickel and Human Health: Current Perspectives. Ed. 1. Trade Cloth. John Wiley & Sons, Inc. Hoboken, NJ. 1992. 704p. Advances in Environmental Science and Technology Ser., Vol. 23 ISBN:0-471-50076-3, ISBN13: 978-0-471-50076-6. Dewey:628 s. LCCN:91-031093.
Audience: **u,f.** *Choice, 1993.*

Norris, David O. & Carr,   **RA1224.2.N675 2005**
James A.
Endocrine Disruption: Biological Basis for Health Effects in Wildlife and Humans. Trade Cloth. Oxford University Press, Inc. New York, NY. 2005. 491p. ISBN:0-19-513749-3, ISBN13: 978-0-19-513749-1. Dewey:571.9/51. LCCN:2004-053111.
Audience: **l,u,f.**

Nriagu, Jerome O. (Editor)   **QD181.A7**
Arsenic in the Environment: Human Health and Ecosystem Effects, Vol. 2. Trade Cloth. John Wiley & Sons, Inc. Hoboken, NJ. 1994. 320p. Advances in Environmental Science and Technology Ser., Vol. 29 ISBN:0-471-30436-0, ISBN13: 978-0-471-30436-4. Dewey:546.715. LCCN:93-023141.
Audience: **l,u,f.** *Choice, 1994.*

Turiel, Isaac   **RA575.5.T87 1985**
Indoor Air Quality and Human Health. Trade Cloth. Stanford University Press. Palo Alto, CA. 1985. xiv, 174p. ISBN:0-8047-1255-7, ISBN13: 978-0-8047-1255-2. Dewey:613/.5. LCCN:84-050638.
Audience: **l,u,f.** *Choice, 1985.*

Wedeen, Richard P.   **RC918.N37**
Poison in the Pot: The Legacy of Lead. Cloth Text. DIANE Publishing Company. Collingdale, PA. 2000. 274p. ISBN:0-7881-9172-1, ISBN13: 978-0-7881-9172-5. Dewey:616.6/12.
Audience: **g,l.**

Weeks, J. M.
Encyclopedia of Ecological and Environmental Toxicology. Trade Cloth. John Wiley & Sons, Inc. Hoboken, NJ. 2004. 2000p. ISBN:0-471-49559-X, ISBN13: 978-0-471-49559-8.
Audience: **g,l,u,f.**

Wise, Marian & Kenworthy,   **TD1050.C57.K47 1993**
Lauren
Preventing Industrial Toxic Hazards: A Guide for Communities. Ed. 2. Trade Paper. INFORM, Inc. New York, NY. 1993. 208p. ISBN:0-918780-60-8, ISBN13: 978-0-918780-60-7. Dewey:363.72/87525. LCCN:92-041873.
Audience: **g,l.** *Choice, 1994.*

Environmental Geology (A T-B)

Carter, R. W. & Woodroffe,   **QE501.4.P3C63 1994**
C. D. (Editors)
Coastal Evolution: Late Quaternary Shoreline Morphodynamics. Trade Cloth. Cambridge University Press. New York, NY. 1995. 539p. ISBN:0-521-41976-X, ISBN13: 978-0-521-41976-5. Dewey:551.4/57. LCCN:94-007763.
Audience: **u,f.** *Choice, 1995.*

Ehlers, Manfred   **GE45.R44R46 2003**
Remote Sensing for Environmental Monitoring, GIS Applications, and Geology II. Trade Paper. S P I E-International Society for Optical Engineering. Bellingham, WA. 2003. 682p. Proceeding Ser. ISBN:0-8194-4668-8, ISBN13: 978-0-8194-4668-8. Dewey:621.36/78. LCCN:2003-545337.
Audience: **u,f.**

Ehlers, Manfred & Michel,   **GE45.R44S65 2003**
Ulrich
Remote Sensing for Environmental Monitoring, GIS Applications, and Geology III. Trade Paper. S P I E-International Society for Optical Engineering. Bellingham, WA. 2004. 562p. Proceedings of SPIE Ser. ISBN:0-8194-5122-3, ISBN13: 978-0-8194-5122-4. Dewey:621.36/78. LCCN:2004-302624.
Audience: **u,f.**

Foth, Henry D. & Schafer,   **S591**
John
Soil Geography and Land Use. Cloth Text. John Wiley & Sons, Inc. Hoboken, NJ. 1980. 484p. ISBN:0-471-01710-8, ISBN13: 978-0-471-01710-3. Dewey:631.4. LCCN:79-027731.
Audience: **u,f.**

Haslett, Simon K.   **QE741.Q28 2002**
Quaternary Environmental Micropalaeontology. Cloth Text. Oxford University Press, Inc. New York, NY. 2002. 288p.

ISBN:0-340-76197-0, ISBN13: 978-0-340-76197-7.
Dewey:560.779. LCCN:2003-268637.

Audience: **u.** *Choice, 2003.*

Holland, H. D. & Turekian, QE515
K. K.
Treatise on Geochemistry, Set. Trade Cloth. Elsevier Science &
Technology Books. Saint Louis, MO. 2003. 7800p.
ISBN:0-08-043751-6, ISBN13: 978-0-08-043751-4.
Dewey:551.9. LCCN:2003-113648.

Audience: **l,u,f.** *Choice, 2004.*

Hoskins, P. W. O. (Editor) TD898.2
Geology and Mineralogy of Radioactive Waste Repositories.
Trade Cloth. Springer. New York, NY. 2005. 450p.
Environmental Science Ser. ISBN:3-540-43919-6, ISBN13:
978-3-540-43919-6. Dewey:621.4/838.

Audience: **u,f.**

Lal, Rattan S590.2.S6289 1999
Soil Quality and Soil Erosion. Saddle Stitched. Saint Lucie
Press. Boca Raton, FL. 1998. 352p. ISBN:1-57444-100-0,
ISBN13: 978-1-57444-100-0. Dewey:631.4. LCCN:99-166567.

Audience: **u,f.** *Choice, 1999.*

Posa, Francesco & Ehlers, GE45.R44R46 2004
Manfred
Remote Sensing for Environmental Monitoring, Gis
Applications, and Geology, IV. Trade Paper. S P I
E-International Society for Optical Engineering. Bellingham,
WA. 2004. 494p. ISBN:0-8194-5521-0, ISBN13:
978-0-8194-5521-5. Dewey:621.36/78. LCCN:2005-278217.

Audience: **u,f.**

Rowe, R. K. TA705.G427 2001
Geotechnical and Geoenvironmental Engineering Handbook.
Trade Cloth. Springer. New York, NY. 2001. 1160p.
ISBN:0-7923-8613-2, ISBN13: 978-0-7923-8613-1.
Dewey:624.1/51. LCCN:99-037319.

Audience: **u,f.**

Environmental Impact Analysis

Black, Peter E. TD194.6.B53
Environmental Impact Analysis. Trade Cloth. Greenwood
Publishing Group, Inc. Portsmouth, NH. 1981. xii, 146 p. :p.
ISBN:0-03-059618-1, ISBN13: 978-0-03-059618-6.
Dewey:333.7/1/0973. LCCN:81-007339.

Audience: **g.**

Kidder, Stanley Q. & QC879.5.K53 1995
Vonder Haar, Thomas H.
Satellite Meteorology: An Introduction. Cloth Text. Elsevier
Science & Technology Books. Saint Louis, MO. 1995. 466p.
ISBN:0-12-406430-2, ISBN13: 978-0-12-406430-0.
Dewey:551.6/354. LCCN:94-042859.

Audience: **u,f.** *Choice, 1996.*

United Nations Environment TD194.6
Programme Staff
Environmental Impact Assessment: Issues, Trends and Practice.
Trade Paper. United Nations Publications. New York, NY. 1996.
96p. ISBN:0-614-26930-X, ISBN13: 978-0-614-26930-7.
Dewey:333.714.

Audience: **g.**

World Resources Institute HC79.E5
Staff
World Resources, 1992-93: A Guide to the Global Environment.
Paper Text. Oxford University Press, Inc. New York, NY. 1992.
400p. ISBN:0-19-506231-0, ISBN13: 978-0-19-506231-1.
Dewey:333.7.

Audience: **g,l,u,f.**

Worldwatch Institute QE29
Vital Signs 2006: the Trends That Are Shaping Our Future.
Trade Paper. W. W. Norton & Company, Inc. New York, NY.
2006. 144p. ISBN:0-393-32872-4, ISBN13: 978-0-393-32872-1.
Dewey:550.

Audience: **g,l,u,f.**

Yeang, Ken NA2542.35
Ecodesign: A Manual for Ecological Eesign. Wiley US. 2006.
ISBN:0-470-85291-7, ISBN13: 978-0-470-85291-0.

Audience: **g.**

Environmental Impact Analysis >
Environmental Engineering.
Environmental Audits

Bingham, Eula, et al. RA1229 .P38
Patty's Industrial Hygiene and Toxicology, Set. Ed. 5. Barbara
Cohrssen & Charles H. Powell (Authors). CD-ROM. John Wiley
& Sons, Inc. Hoboken, NJ. 2005. ISBN:0-471-70057-6,
ISBN13: 978-0-471-70057-9. Dewey:613.6/2.

Audience: **g,l,u,f.**

Canter, Larry W. TD194.6.C36 1996
Environmental Impact Assessment. Ed. 2. Cloth Text.
McGraw-Hill Higher Education. Burr Ridge, IL. 1995. 480p.
Water Resources and Environmental Engineering Ser.
ISBN:0-07-009767-4, ISBN13: 978-0-07-009767-4.
Dewey:333.7/14. LCCN:95-000935.

Audience: **u,f.**

Cheremisinoff, Nicholas P. TD897.5.E584 2004
(Editor)
Environmental Technologies Handbook. Trade Cloth.
Government Institutes. Blue Ridge Summit, PA. 2005. 328p.
ISBN:0-86587-980-X, ISBN13: 978-0-86587-980-5. Dewey:628.
LCCN:2004-018368.

Audience: **g,f.** *Choice, 2006.*

Corbitt, Robert A. TD145.S72 1998
Standard Handbook of Environmental Engineering. Ed. 2. Cloth
Text. McGraw-Hill Professional Publishing. New York, NY.
1998. 1216p. ISBN:0-07-013160-0, ISBN13:
978-0-07-013160-6. Dewey:628. LCCN:98-031045.

Audience: **u,f.** *Choice, 1990.*

Corbitt, Robert A. TD145.S72 1990
Standard Handbook of Environmental Engineering. Trade Cloth.
McGraw-Hill Professional Publishing. New York, NY. 1989.
1152p. ISBN:0-07-013158-9, ISBN13: 978-0-07-013158-3.
Dewey:628. LCCN:89-012400.

Audience: **u,f.** *Choice, 1990.*

Cowan, James P. NA2800
Handbook of Environmental Acoustics. Wiley. 1993.
ISBN:0-471-28584-6, ISBN13: 978-0-471-28584-7.

Audience: **g.**

Denny, Mark W.   **QH541.5.S35D46 1988**
Biology and the Mechanics of the Wave-Swept Environment.
Trade Cloth. Princeton University Press. Princeton, NJ. 1988.
400p. ISBN:0-691-08486-6, ISBN13: 978-0-691-08486-2.
Dewey:574.5/2638/01532593. LCCN:87-032806.
                              Audience: **u,f.** *Choice, 1989.*

Ehlers, Manfred   **GE45.R44R46 2003**
Remote Sensing for Environmental Monitoring, GIS
Applications, and Geology II. Trade Paper. S P I E-International
Society for Optical Engineering. Bellingham, WA. 2003. 682p.
Proceeding Ser. ISBN:0-8194-4668-8, ISBN13:
978-0-8194-4668-8. Dewey:621.36/78. LCCN:2003-545337.
                              Audience: **u,f.**

Freeman, Harry M.   **TD194.F74 1995**
Industrial Pollution Prevention Handbook. Trade Cloth.
McGraw-Hill Professional Publishing. New York, NY. 1994.
976p. ISBN:0-07-022148-0, ISBN13: 978-0-07-022148-2.
Dewey:363.73/1. LCCN:94-007979.
                              Audience: **u,f.** *Choice, 1996.*

Gray, N. F.   **TD257.G72 1994**
Drinking Water Quality: Problems and Solutions. Wiley. 1994.
ISBN:0-471-94817-9, ISBN13: 978-0-471-94817-9.
                              Audience: **l,u,f.**

Grigg, Neil S.   **HD1691.G75 1996**
Water Resources Management: Principles, Regulations, and
Cases. McGraw-Hill Professional Publishing. 1996.
ISBN:0-07-024782-X, ISBN13: 978-0-07-024782-6.
                              Audience: **u,f.**

Gruden, Dusan (Volume   **QD31**
Editor)
Traffic and Environment. D. Gruden, W. Berg & K. Borgmann
(Contribution by). Mixed Media. Springer. New York, NY. 2004.
XIV, 294p. ISBN:3-540-00050-X, ISBN13: 978-3-540-00050-1.
Dewey:540.
                              Audience: **u,f.**

Heinsohn, Robert Jennings   **TD883.1**
& Cimbala, John M.
Indoor Air Quality Engineering: Environmental Health and
Control of Indoor Pollutants. Paper over Boards. Marcel Dekker
Inc. New York, NY. 2003. 920p. ISBN:0-8247-4061-0, ISBN13:
978-0-8247-4061-0. Dewey:628.53.
                              Audience: **u,f.**

Huffaker, Carl B.   **SB931**
New Technology of Pest Control. Trade Cloth. John Wiley &
Sons, Inc. Hoboken, NJ. 1980. 500p. Environmental Science and
Technology Ser. ISBN:0-471-05336-8, ISBN13:
978-0-471-05336-1. Dewey:632/.7. LCCN:79-004369.
                              Audience: **u,f.**

Hunn, Bruce D. (Editor)   **TJ163.5.B84F86 1996**
Fundamentals of Building Energy Dynamics. Trade Cloth. MIT
Press. Cambridge, MA. 1996. 550p. Solar Heat Technologies
Ser., Vol. 4 ISBN:0-262-08238-1, ISBN13: 978-0-262-08238-9.
Dewey:696. LCCN:95-046158.
                              Audience: **g,u,f.** *Choice, 1997.*

Inhaber, Herbert   **TD195.E49**
Energy Risk Assessment. Bernard L. Cohen (Introduction by).
Cloth Text. Gordon & Breach Publishing Group. New York, NY.

1982. 396p. ISBN:0-677-05980-9, ISBN13: 978-0-677-05980-8.
Dewey:333.79. LCCN:82-003060.
                              Audience: **l,u,f.**

Jarvinen, Alfred W. &   **QH90.57.B5J37 1999**
Ankley, Gerald T.
Linkage of Effects to Tissue Residues: Development of a
Comprehensive Database for Aquatic Organisms Exposed to
Inorganic and Organic Chemicals. Trade Cloth. Society of
Environmental Toxicology and Chemistry. Pensacola, FL. 1998.
15p. ISBN:1-880611-13-9, ISBN13: 978-1-880611-13-5.
Dewey:577.6/27. LCCN:98-022670.
                              Audience: **u,f.**

Kaluarachchi, Jagath J.   **TD427.O7G76 2001**
Groundwater Contamination by Organic Pollutants: Analysis and
Remediation. Trade Cloth. American Society of Civil Engineers.
Reston, VA. 2000. x, 238p. ASCE Manuals and Reports on
Engineering Practice Ser., No. 100 ISBN:0-7844-0527-1,
ISBN13: 978-0-7844-0527-7. Dewey:628.1/68.
LCCN:00-063966.
                              Audience: **u,f.**

Linsley, Ray K., et al.   **TC5**
Water Resources Engineering. Ed. 4. Joseph B. Franzini, David
L. Freyberg & George Tchobanoglous (Authors). Cloth Text.
McGraw-Hill Higher Education. Burr Ridge, IL. 1991. 768p.
Water Resources and Environmental Engineering Ser.
ISBN:0-07-038010-4, ISBN13: 978-0-07-038010-3. Dewey:627.
LCCN:91-040707.
                              Audience: **l,u,f.**

Liu, David H.F.   **TD145.E574 1997**
Environmental Engineers' Handbook. Ed. 2. Lewis. 1997.
ISBN:0-8493-9971-8, ISBN13: 978-0-8493-9971-8.
                              Audience: **l,u,f.**

National Research Council   **VM455.N35 1991**
Staff
Tanker Spills: Prevention by Design. Cloth Text. National
Academies Press. Washington, DC. 1991. 384p.
ISBN:0-309-04377-8, ISBN13: 978-0-309-04377-9.
Dewey:623.8/245. LCCN:91-012489.
                              Audience: **g,u.** *Choice, 1992.*

Odum, Howard T.   **TD196.M4H434 2000**
Heavy Metals in the Environment: Using Wetlands for Their
Removal. Paper over Boards. Lewis Publishers. Boca Raton, FL.
2000. 344p. ISBN:1-56670-401-4, ISBN13: 978-1-56670-401-4.
Dewey:628.5/2. LCCN:99-089022.
                              Audience: **u,f.**

Pfafflin, James R. &   **TD9.E5 2006**
Edward N. Ziegler
Encyclopedia of Environmental Science and Engineering. Ed. 5.
CRC Press. 2006. ISBN:0-8493-9843-6, ISBN13:
978-0-8493-9843-8.
                              Audience: **g,l,u,f.**

Posa, Francesco & Ehlers,   **GE45.R44R46 2004**
Manfred
Remote Sensing for Environmental Monitoring, Gis
Applications, and Geology, IV. Trade Paper. S P I
E-International Society for Optical Engineering. Bellingham,
WA. 2004. 494p. ISBN:0-8194-5521-0, ISBN13:
978-0-8194-5521-5. Dewey:621.36/78. LCCN:2005-278217.
                              Audience: **u,f.**

Saccomanno, Fabio   **TK1007**
Electric Power Systems: Analysis and Control. Trade Cloth.
John Wiley & Sons, Inc. Hoboken, NJ. 2003. 744p. IEEE Press
Series on Power Engineering, Series Editor Ser., :Paul M.
Anderson Ser. ISBN:0-471-23439-7, ISBN13:
978-0-471-23439-5. Dewey:621.3/1.
                                    Audience: **u,f.** *Choice, 2003.*

Saxena, Jitendra (Editor)   **QH545.A1 H38**
Hazard Assessment of Chemicals, Vol. 2. Trade Cloth. Elsevier
Science & Technology Books. Saint Louis, MO. 1983. 332p.
Serial Publication Ser. ISBN:0-12-312402-6, ISBN13:
978-0-12-312402-9. Dewey:363.7/384.
                                              Audience: **l,u.**

Saxena, Jitendra (Editor)   **QH545.A1 H38**
Hazard Assessment of Chemicals, Vol. 6. Library Binding.
Hemisphere Publishing Corporation. Philadelphia, PA. 1988.
400p. Hazard Assessment of Chemicals Ser.
ISBN:0-89116-835-4, ISBN13: 978-0-89116-835-5.
Dewey:363.7/384.
                                              Audience: **l,u.**

Sharma, Hari D. & Reddy,   **TD171.9.S53 2004**
  Krishna R.
Geoenvironmental Engineering: Site Remediation, Waste
Containment, and Emerging Waste Management Technologies.
Trade Cloth. John Wiley & Sons, Inc. Hoboken, NJ. 2004. 992p.
ISBN:0-471-21599-6, ISBN13: 978-0-471-21599-8.
Dewey:628.5. LCCN:2004-007135.
                                              Audience: **u,f.**

Singh, Vijay P.   **QA913**
Kinematic Wave Modeling in Water Resources, Set. Trade
Cloth. John Wiley & Sons, Inc. Hoboken, NJ. 1998. 2272p.
ISBN:0-471-19087-X, ISBN13: 978-0-471-19087-5.
Dewey:532/.051.
                                              Audience: **u,f.**

Tchobanoglous, George,   **TD645.W293 2003**
  et al.
Wastewater Engineering: Treatment and Reuse. Ed. 4. Franklin
L. Burton & H. David Stensel (Authors), Metcalf and Eddy, Inc.
Staff (Contribution by). Paper Text. McGraw-Hill Companies,
The. New York, NY. 2003. xxviii, 1819p. McGraw-Hill Series in
Civil and Environmental Engineering ISBN:0-07-112250-8,
ISBN13: 978-0-07-112250-4. Dewey:628.3.
LCCN:2001-053724.
                                              Audience: **l,u,f.**

Twardowska, I., et al.   **TD794.2.S64 2004**
Solid Waste: Assessment, Monitoring and Remediation. H. E.
Allen, A. F. Kettrup & W. J. Lacy (Authors). Trade Cloth.
Elsevier Science & Technology Books. Saint Louis, MO. 2004.
1222p. Waste Management Ser., Vol. 4 ISBN:0-08-044321-4,
ISBN13: 978-0-08-044321-8. Dewey:363.7285.
LCCN:2006-273066.
                                              Audience: **l,u,f.**

Vaitheeswaran, Vijay V.   **TJ163.2.V335 2003**
Power to the People: How the Coming Energy Revolution Will
Transform an Industry, Change Our Lives, and Maybe Even
Save the Planet. Cloth over Boards. Farrar, Straus & Giroux.
New York, NY. 2003. 368p. ISBN:0-374-23675-5, ISBN13:
978-0-374-23675-5. Dewey:333.79. LCCN:2003-006985.
                                    Audience: **g,l,u,f.** *Choice, 2004.*

Viessman, Warren Jr. &   **TD353.V54 2004**
  Hammer, Mark J.
Water Supply and Pollution Control. Ed. 7. Cloth Text. Prentice
Hall PTR. Upper Saddle River, NJ. 2004. 888p.
ISBN:0-13-140970-0, ISBN13: 978-0-13-140970-5.
Dewey:628.1. LCCN:2004-045395.
                                              Audience: **l,u,f.**

Weber, Walter J. Jr. &   **TD177.W43 1996**
  DiGiano, Francis A.
Process Dynamics in Environmental Systems. Ed. 1. Trade
Cloth. John Wiley & Sons, Inc. Hoboken, NJ. 1996. 968p.
Environmental Science and Technology Ser., Vol. 111:A
Wiley-Interscience Series of Texts and Monographs
ISBN:0-471-01711-6, ISBN13: 978-0-471-01711-0. Dewey:628.
LCCN:94-049669.
                                    Audience: **u,f.** *Choice, 1996.*

Wood, Eric F. & Princeton   **TD223.G76 1984**
  Water Resources Group Staff
Groundwater Contamination from Hazardous Wastes. Cloth
Text. Prentice Hall PTR. Upper Saddle River, NJ. 1983. 192p.
ISBN:0-13-366286-1, ISBN13: 978-0-13-366286-3.
Dewey:628.4/4564. LCCN:83-010948.
                                              Audience: **l,u,f.**

Environmental Movement

                                              HD2769

▢ Worldwatch Institute.
http://www.worldwatch.org/
                                              Audience: **u,f.**

Callicott, J. Baird   **QH81.L563C66 1987**
Companion to a Sand County Almanac: Interpretive and Critical
Essays. Trade Paper. University of Wisconsin Press. Chicago,
IL. 1987. 320p. ISBN:0-299-11234-9, ISBN13:
978-0-299-11234-9. Dewey:508.73. LCCN:87-010396.
                                    Audience: **l,u.** *Choice, 1988.*

Carson, Rachel   **QH545**
Silent Spring. Ed. 40. Dust Jacket. Houghton Mifflin Company
Trade & Reference Division. Boston, MA. 2002. 400p.
ISBN:0-618-25305-X, ISBN13: 978-0-618-25305-0.
Dewey:363.738/4. LCCN:2002-726803.
                                    Audience: **g,l,u,f.**

Collett, Jonathan &   **LC1023.G74 1996**
  Karakashian, Stephen (Editors)
Greening the College Curriculum: A Guide to Environmental
Teaching in the Liberal Arts. Trade Paper. Island Press.
Washington, DC. 1995. 341p. ISBN:1-55963-422-7, ISBN13:
978-1-55963-422-9. Dewey:333.7/0711. LCCN:95-039225.
                                    Audience: **l,u,f.** *Choice, 1996.*

Gorke, Martin   **QH540.5.G6713 2003**
The Death of Our Planet's Species: A Challenge to Ecology and
Ethics. Trade Cloth. Island Press. Washington, DC. 2003. 408p.
ISBN:1-55963-957-1, ISBN13: 978-1-55963-957-6.
Dewey:333.95. LCCN:2003-006059.
                                    Audience: **g,l,u,f.** *Choice, 2004.*

Lacey, Michael J.   **HC110.E5G686 1989**
Government and Environmental Politics: Essays on Historical
Developments since World War II. Trade Paper. Woodrow
Wilson Center Press. Washington, DC. 1981. 336p.

ISBN:0-943875-15-3, ISBN13: 978-0-943875-15-6.
Dewey:363.7/08/09730904. LCCN:89-022761.
Audience: **g,l,u.** *Choice, 1992.*

Leopold, Aldo   **QH31.L618.E77 1999**
The Essential Aldo Leopold: Quotations and Commentaries.
Curt D. Meine & Richard L. Knight (Editors). Trade Cloth.
University of Wisconsin Press. Chicago, IL. 1999. 384p.
ISBN:0-299-16550-7, ISBN13: 978-0-299-16550-5.
Dewey:333.7/2. LCCN:99-006424.
Audience: **g.** *Choice, 2000.*

Mark, Stephen R.   **QE707.M47**
Preserving the Living Past: John C. Merriam's Legacy in the
State and National Parks. California. 2005.
ISBN:0-520-24167-3, ISBN13: 978-0-520-24167-1.
Audience: **g,l,u.**

Marsh, George Perkins   **GF31.M35 2003**
Man and Nature, or, Physical Geography As Modified by
Human Action. David Lowenthal (Editor, Annotations by,
Foreword by), William Cronon (Foreword by). Trade Cloth.
University of Washington Press. Seattle, WA. 2003. 512p.
Weyerhaeuser Environmental Classics Ser. ISBN:0-295-98316-7,
ISBN13: 978-0-295-98316-5. Dewey:304.2.
LCCN:2003-040286.
Audience: **g.** *Choice, 2003.*

McNeill, William H.   **RA649**
Plagues and People. Trade Cloth. Peter Smith Publisher, Inc.
Magnolia, MA. 1992. ISBN:0-8446-6492-8, ISBN13:
978-0-8446-6492-7. Dewey:614.4/9.
Audience: **g,l,u,f.**

Pepper, David   **GE195.P46 1996**
Modern Environmentalism: An Introduction. Ed. 2. Paper over
Boards. Routledge. New York, NY. 1996. 384p.
ISBN:0-415-05744-2, ISBN13: 978-0-415-05744-8.
Dewey:333.7/2. LCCN:95-022324.
Audience: **g,l,u,f.** *Choice, 1996.*

Quammen, David   **QH541.5.I8Q35 1996**
The Song of the Dodo: Island Biogeography in an Age of
Extinctions. Trade Cloth. Simon & Schuster. New York, NY.
1996. 704p. ISBN:0-684-80083-7, ISBN13: 978-0-684-80083-7.
Dewey:574.5/267. LCCN:95-044972.
Audience: **g,l,u,f.** *Choice, 1996.*

World Resources Institute   **HC79.E5**
Staff
World Resources, 1992-93: A Guide to the Global Environment.
Paper Text. Oxford University Press, Inc. New York, NY. 1992.
400p. ISBN:0-19-506231-0, ISBN13: 978-0-19-506231-1.
Dewey:333.7.
Audience: **g,l,u,f.**

Yepsen, Roger B.   **SB974.E53 1984**
The Encyclopedia of Natural Insect and Disease Control. Trade
Cloth. Rodale Press, Inc. Emmaus, PA. 1984. 496p.
ISBN:0-87857-488-3, ISBN13: 978-0-87857-488-9.
Dewey:635/.0494. LCCN:83-024643.
Audience: **g,l.**

Young, Anthony   **HD111 .Y68 1998**
Land Resources: Now and for the Future. Cloth Text.
Cambridge University Press. New York, NY. 1998. 331p.

ISBN:0-521-59003-5, ISBN13: 978-0-521-59003-7.
Dewey:333.73/16. LCCN:97-036654.
Audience: **g,l,u,f.** *Choice, 1999.*

Environmentalists

Cowell, Adrian (Produced   **GF532.A4**
by, Directed By)
The Decade of Destruction Series. Video, VHS Format.
Bullfrog Films, Inc. Oley, PA. 1990. ISBN:1-56029-027-7,
ISBN13: 978-1-56029-027-8. Dewey:333.75/0981/1.
Audience: **g,l,u,f.**

Leopold, Aldo   **QH31.L618.E77 1999**
The Essential Aldo Leopold: Quotations and Commentaries.
Curt D. Meine & Richard L. Knight (Editors). Trade Cloth.
University of Wisconsin Press. Chicago, IL. 1999. 384p.
ISBN:0-299-16550-7, ISBN13: 978-0-299-16550-5.
Dewey:333.7/2. LCCN:99-006424.
Audience: **g.** *Choice, 2000.*

Mark, Stephen R.   **QE707.M47**
Preserving the Living Past: John C. Merriam's Legacy in the
State and National Parks. California. 2005.
ISBN:0-520-24167-3, ISBN13: 978-0-520-24167-1.
Audience: **g,l,u.**

Genetically Modified Foods

Lurquin, Paul F.   **SB123.57.L88 2004**
High Tech Harvest: Understanding Genetically Modified Food
Plants. Trade Paper. Westview Press. Boulder, CO. 2004. 236p.
ISBN:0-8133-4175-2, ISBN13: 978-0-8133-4175-0.
Dewey:631.5/233.
Audience: **l,u,f.** *Choice, 2002.*

Pence, Gregory E.   **TP248.65.F66P46 2002**
Designer Food: Mutant Harvest or Breadbasket of the World?
Trade Cloth. Rowman & Littlefield Publishers, Inc. Lanham,
MD. 2002. 256p. ISBN:0-7425-0839-0, ISBN13:
978-0-7425-0839-2. Dewey:363.19/29. LCCN:2001-041926.
Audience: **g,l,u,f.** *Choice, 2002.*

Plucknett, Donald, et al.   **SB123.3.G46 1987**
Gene Banks and the World's Food. Nigel J. Smith, J. T.
Williams & N. Murthi Anishetty (Authors). Trade Cloth.
Princeton University Press. Princeton, NJ. 1987. 248p.
ISBN:0-691-08438-6, ISBN13: 978-0-691-08438-1.
Dewey:631.5/2. LCCN:86-042841.
Audience: **l,u.** *Choice, 1987.*

Global Warming

Hertsgaard, Mark   **GE149.H47 1998**
Earth Odyssey: Around the World in Search of Our
Environmental Future. Trade Cloth. Broadway Books. New
York, NY. 1998. 384p. ISBN:0-7679-0058-8, ISBN13:
978-0-7679-0058-4. Dewey:363.7. LCCN:98-028202.
Audience: **g.**

Ruddiman, William F.   QC981.R763 2005
Plows, Plagues, and Petroleum: How Humans Took Control of
Climate. Trade Cloth. Princeton University Press. Princeton, NJ.
2005. 272p. ISBN:0-691-12164-8, ISBN13: 978-0-691-12164-2.
Dewey:363.738/74. LCCN:2004-062444.
Audience: **g,l,u,f.** *Choice, 2006.*

Sweet, William   TJ808.S87 2006
Kicking the Carbon Habit: Global Warming and the Case for
Renewable Energy. Trade Cloth. Columbia University Press.
New York, NY. 2006. 272p. ISBN:0-231-13710-9, ISBN13:
978-0-231-13710-2. Dewey:333.79/4. LCCN:2005-035034.
Audience: **g,l.**

Global Warming > Climate Change

Flannery, Tim   QC981.8.C5F438 2006
The Weather Makers: How Man Is Changing the Climate and
What It Means for Life on Earth. Cloth over Boards.
Grove/Atlantic, Inc. New York, NY. 2006. 384p.
ISBN:0-87113-935-9, ISBN13: 978-0-87113-935-1.
Dewey:363.738/74. LCCN:2005-052350.
Audience: **g.**

Hall, Colin M.   G155.A1H347 1994
Tourism and Politics: Policy, Power and Place. Trade Cloth.
John Wiley & Sons, Inc. Hoboken, NJ. 1995. 248p.
ISBN:0-471-94919-1, ISBN13: 978-0-471-94919-0.
Dewey:338.4/791. LCCN:94-018156.
Audience: **l,u,f.** *Choice, 1995.*

Haslett, Simon K.   QE741.Q28 2002
Quaternary Environmental Micropalaeontology. Cloth Text.
Oxford University Press, Inc. New York, NY. 2002. 288p.
ISBN:0-340-76197-0, ISBN13: 978-0-340-76197-7.
Dewey:560.779. LCCN:2003-268637.
Audience: **u.** *Choice, 2003.*

Houghton, John T. (Editor),   QC981.8.C5.C5125
    et al.
Climate Change 1994: Radiative Forcing of Climate Change and
an Evaluation of the IPCC 1992 IS92 Emission Scenarios. L. G.
Filho, James P. Bruce, Hoesung Lee, Bruce A. Callander, E. F.
Haites, N. B. Harris & K. Maskell (Editors). Trade Cloth.
Cambridge University Press. New York, NY. 1995. 347p.
ISBN:0-521-55055-6, ISBN13: 978-0-521-55055-0.
Dewey:363.73/87. LCCN:95-001166.
Audience: **u,f.** *Choice, 1996.*

Kellogg, William W. &   QC879.8 .K44
    Schware, Robert
Climate Change and Society: Consequences of Increasing
Atmospheric Carbon Dioxide. Walter O. Roberts (Foreword by).
Paper Text. Westview Press. Boulder, CO. 1981. 170p. Special
Studies ISBN:0-86531-180-3, ISBN13: 978-0-86531-180-0.
Dewey:363.7/392. LCCN:80-054157.
Audience: **l,u.**

Kidder, Stanley Q. &   QC879.5.K53 1995
    Vonder Haar, Thomas H.
Satellite Meteorology: An Introduction. Cloth Text. Elsevier
Science & Technology Books. Saint Louis, MO. 1995. 466p.
ISBN:0-12-406430-2, ISBN13: 978-0-12-406430-0.
Dewey:551.6/354. LCCN:94-042859.
Audience: **u,f.** *Choice, 1996.*

Kolbert, Elizabeth   QC981.8.G56K655 2006
Field Notes from a Catastrophe: Man, Nature, and Climate
Change. Cloth over Boards. Bloomsbury Publishing. New York,
NY. 2006. 192p. ISBN:1-59691-125-5, ISBN13:
978-1-59691-125-3. Dewey:363.738/74. LCCN:2005-030972.
Audience: **g.**

Lacey, Michael J.   HC110.E5G686 1989
Government and Environmental Politics: Essays on Historical
Developments since World War II. Trade Paper. Woodrow
Wilson Center Press. Washington, DC. 1981. 336p.
ISBN:0-943875-15-3, ISBN13: 978-0-943875-15-6.
Dewey:363.7/08/09730904. LCCN:89-022761.
Audience: **g,l,u.** *Choice, 1992.*

Maunder, W. J.   QC981.8.C5M38 1992
[e] Dictionary of Global Climate Change. E-Book. NetLibrary,
Inc. Boulder, CO. 1992. ISBN:0-585-29573-5, ISBN13:
978-0-585-29573-2. Dewey:551.6.
Audience: **g.**

Mintzer, Irving M.   QC981.8.C5 C68 1992
Confronting Climate Change: Risks, Implications and
Responses. Trade Cloth. Cambridge University Press. New York,
NY. 1992. 396p. ISBN:0-521-42091-1, ISBN13:
978-0-521-42091-4. Dewey:551.6. LCCN:92-250185.
Audience: **g,l,u,f.** *Choice, 1992.*

Seinfeld, John H. & Pandis,   QC879.6.S45 2006
    Spyros N.
Atmospheric Chemistry and Physics: From Air Pollution to
Climate Change. Ed. 2. Trade Cloth. John Wiley & Sons, Inc.
Hoboken, NJ. 2006. 1203p. ISBN:0-471-72017-8, ISBN13:
978-0-471-72017-1. Dewey:551.5/11.
Audience: **l,u,f.** *Choice, 1998.*

Shiklomanov, I. A. &   GB661.2
    Rodda, John C. (Editors)
World Water Resources at the Beginning of the Twenty-First
Century. Trade Paper. Cambridge University Press. New York,
NY. 2004. 449p. International Hydrology Ser.
ISBN:0-521-61722-7, ISBN13: 978-0-521-61722-2.
Dewey:553.7/09/05. LCCN:2002-031201.
Audience: **u,f.** *Choice, 2004.*

Young, Anthony   HD111 .Y68 1998
Land Resources: Now and for the Future. Cloth Text.
Cambridge University Press. New York, NY. 1998. 331p.
ISBN:0-521-59003-5, ISBN13: 978-0-521-59003-7.
Dewey:333.73/16. LCCN:97-036654.
Audience: **g,l,u,f.** *Choice, 1999.*

Heavy Metals: Environmental Aspects

Bradl, Heike   TD196.M4
Heavy Metals in the Environment: Origin, Interaction and
Remediation. Elsevier. 2005. ISBN:0-12-088381-3, ISBN13:
978-0-12-088381-3.
Audience: **g,l,u,f.**

Heavy Metals: Environmental Aspects > Cadmium

Scoullos, Michael J., et al. TD196.M38M463 2001
Mercury - Cadmium - Lead: Handbook for Sustainable Heavy
Metals Policy and Regulation. Gerrit H. Vonkeman, Iain
Thornton & Zen Makuch (Authors). Trade Cloth. Springer
London, Ltd. Guildford, 2001. 544p. Environment and Policy
Ser., Vol. 31 ISBN:1-4020-0224-6, ISBN13: 978-1-4020-0224-3.
Dewey:363.17/91. LCCN:2001-050679.

Audience: **u,f.**

Heavy Metals: Environmental Aspects > Lead

Needleman, Herbert L. RC347.5.H86 1991
Human Lead Exposure. CRC Press. 1992. ISBN:0-8493-6034-X,
ISBN13: 978-0-8493-6034-3.

Audience: **g,l,u.**

Odum, Howard T. TD196.M4H434 2000
Heavy Metals in the Environment: Using Wetlands for Their
Removal. Paper over Boards. Lewis Publishers. Boca Raton, FL.
2000. 344p. ISBN:1-56670-401-4, ISBN13: 978-1-56670-401-4.
Dewey:628.5/2. LCCN:99-089022.

Audience: **u,f.**

Scoullos, Michael J., et al. TD196.M38M463 2001
Mercury - Cadmium - Lead: Handbook for Sustainable Heavy
Metals Policy and Regulation. Gerrit H. Vonkeman, Iain
Thornton & Zen Makuch (Authors). Trade Cloth. Springer
London, Ltd. Guildford, 2001. 544p. Environment and Policy
Ser., Vol. 31 ISBN:1-4020-0224-6, ISBN13: 978-1-4020-0224-3.
Dewey:363.17/91. LCCN:2001-050679.

Audience: **u,f.**

Warren, Christian RA1231.L4W37 2000
Brush with Death: A Social History of Lead Poisoning. Trade
Cloth. Johns Hopkins University Press. Baltimore, MD. 2000.
384p. ISBN:0-8018-6289-2, ISBN13: 978-0-8018-6289-2.
Dewey:615.9/25688/0973. LCCN:99-046329.

Audience: **l,u.** *Choice, 2000.*

Warren, Christian RA1231.L4
Brush with Death: A Social History of Lead Poisoning. Trade
Paper. Johns Hopkins University Press. Baltimore, MD. 2001.
384p. ISBN:0-8018-6820-3, ISBN13: 978-0-8018-6820-7.
Dewey:615.9/25688/0973.

Audience: **l,u,f.** *Choice, 2000.*

Wedeen, Richard P. RC918.N37
Poison in the Pot: The Legacy of Lead. Cloth Text. DIANE
Publishing Company. Collingdale, PA. 2000. 274p.
ISBN:0-7881-9172-1, ISBN13: 978-0-7881-9172-5.
Dewey:616.6/12.

Audience: **g,l.**

Heavy Metals: Environmental Aspects > Mercury

Scoullos, Michael J., et al. TD196.M38M463 2001
Mercury - Cadmium - Lead: Handbook for Sustainable Heavy
Metals Policy and Regulation. Gerrit H. Vonkeman, Iain
Thornton & Zen Makuch (Authors). Trade Cloth. Springer
London, Ltd. Guildford, 2001. 544p. Environment and Policy
Ser., Vol. 31 ISBN:1-4020-0224-6, ISBN13: 978-1-4020-0224-3.
Dewey:363.17/91. LCCN:2001-050679.

Audience: **u,f.**

Heavy Metals: Environmental Aspects > Uranium

Oversby, Virginia M. & TD898
Werme, Lars O. (Editors)
Scientific Basis for Nuclear Waste Management XXVII:
Proceedings of 27th International Symposium on Scientific Basis
for Nuclear Waste Management, Vol. 807. Cloth Text. Materials
Research Society. Warrendale, PA. 2004. 966p. Materials
Research Society Conference Proceedings Ser., 807
ISBN:1-55899-752-0, ISBN13: 978-1-55899-752-3.
Dewey:621.4838.

Audience: **u,f.**

Indoor Air Pollution

Heinsohn, Robert Jennings TD883.1
& Cimbala, John M.
Indoor Air Quality Engineering: Environmental Health and
Control of Indoor Pollutants. Paper over Boards. Marcel Dekker
Inc. New York, NY. 2003. 920p. ISBN:0-8247-4061-0, ISBN13:
978-0-8247-4061-0. Dewey:628.53.

Audience: **u,f.**

Leslie, G. B. & Lunau, F. W. RA1226
(Editors)
Indoor Air Pollution: Problems and Priorities. Trade Paper.
Cambridge University Press. New York, NY. 1994. 341p.
ISBN:0-521-47794-8, ISBN13: 978-0-521-47794-9.
Dewey:615.9/02.

Audience: **g,u.** *Choice, 1992.*

Spengler, John D., et al. RA770.I42 2001
Indoor Air Quality Handbook. John F. McCarthy & Jonathan M.
Samet (Authors). Cloth Text. McGraw-Hill Professional
Publishing. New York, NY. 2000. 1488p. Engineering Handbks.
ISBN:0-07-445549-4, ISBN13: 978-0-07-445549-4.
Dewey:613/.5. LCCN:00-048024.

Audience: **l,u,f.**

Turiel, Isaac RA575.5.T87 1985
Indoor Air Quality and Human Health. Trade Cloth. Stanford
University Press. Palo Alto, CA. 1985. xiv, 174p.
ISBN:0-8047-1255-7, ISBN13: 978-0-8047-1255-2.
Dewey:613/.5. LCCN:84-050638.

Audience: **l,u,f.** *Choice, 1985.*

Industrialization: Environmental Aspects

Bradl, Heike   **TD196.M4**
Heavy Metals in the Environment: Origin, Interaction and
Remediation. Elsevier. 2005. ISBN:0-12-088381-3, ISBN13:
978-0-12-088381-3.

Audience: **g,l,u,f.**

Dorfman, Mark, et al.   **TD899.C5.D66 1992**
Environmental Dividends: Cutting More Chemical Wastes.
Catherine Miller & Warren Muir (Authors). Trade Paper.
INFORM, Inc. New York, NY. 1992. 288p.
ISBN:0-918780-50-0, ISBN13: 978-0-918780-50-8. Dewey:660.
LCCN:92-012251.

Audience: **g,l,u.** *Choice, 1993.*

Freeman, Harry M.   **TD194.F74 1995**
Industrial Pollution Prevention Handbook. Trade Cloth.
McGraw-Hill Professional Publishing. New York, NY. 1994.
976p. ISBN:0-07-022148-0, ISBN13: 978-0-07-022148-2.
Dewey:363.73/1. LCCN:94-007979.

Audience: **u,f.** *Choice, 1996.*

Graedel, Thomas &   **TS171.G715 2005**
  Howard-Grenville, Jennifer
Greening the Industrial Facility: Perspectives, Approaches, and
Tools. Trade Cloth. Springer. New York, NY. 2005. XII, 617p.
ISBN:0-387-24306-2, ISBN13: 978-0-387-24306-1. Dewey:628.
LCCN:2005-925872.

Audience: **u,f.**

Jasanoff, Sheila (Editor)   **T174.5.L415 1994**
Learning from Disaster: Risk Management after Bhopal. Trade
Cloth. University of Pennsylvania Press. Philadelphia, PA. 1994.
336p. Law in Social Context Ser. ISBN:0-8122-3250-X,
ISBN13: 978-0-8122-3250-9. Dewey:363.17/91/0954.
LCCN:93-048100.

Audience: **l,u.** *Choice, 1994.*

Kirsch-Volders, Micheline   **RA1229.M87 1984**
  (Editor)
Mutagenicity, Carcinogenicity, and Teratogenicity of Industrial
Pollutants. Trade Cloth. Basic Books. New York, NY. 1984.
350p. ISBN:0-306-41148-2, ISBN13: 978-0-306-41148-9.
Dewey:615.9/02. LCCN:83-011126.

Audience: **u,f.**

Lewis, Ronald L.   **HC107.W5L39 1998**
Transforming the Appalachian Countryside: Railroads,
Deforestation, and Social Change in West Virginia, 1880-1920.
Trade Cloth. University of North Carolina Press. Chapel Hill,
NC. 1998. 368p. ISBN:0-8078-2405-4, ISBN13:
978-0-8078-2405-4. Dewey:338.9754. LCCN:97-036616.

Audience: **g.** *Choice, 1998.*

Ruddiman, William F.   **QC981.R763 2005**
Plows, Plagues, and Petroleum: How Humans Took Control of
Climate. Trade Cloth. Princeton University Press. Princeton, NJ.
2005. 272p. ISBN:0-691-12164-8, ISBN13: 978-0-691-12164-2.
Dewey:363.738/74. LCCN:2004-062444.

Audience: **g,l,u,f.** *Choice, 2006.*

Saxena, Jitendra (Editor)   **QH545.A1 H38**
Hazard Assessment of Chemicals, Vol. 4. Trade Cloth. Elsevier
Science & Technology Books. Saint Louis, MO. 1985.
ISBN:0-12-312404-2, ISBN13: 978-0-12-312404-3.
Dewey:363.7/384.

Audience: **l,u.**

Wise, Marian & Kenworthy,   **TD1050.C57.K47 1993**
  Lauren
Preventing Industrial Toxic Hazards: A Guide for Communities.
Ed. 2. Trade Paper. INFORM, Inc. New York, NY. 1993. 208p.
ISBN:0-918780-60-8, ISBN13: 978-0-918780-60-7.
Dewey:363.72/87525. LCCN:92-041873.

Audience: **g,l.** *Choice, 1994.*

Land Use

Bush, David M., et al.   **TC224.F6B87 2004**
Living with Florida's Atlantic Beaches: Coastal Hazards from
Amelia Island to Key West. Norma J. Longo & William Neal
(Authors). Trade Paper. Duke University Press. Durham, NC.
2004. 368p. Living with the Shore Ser. ISBN:0-8223-3289-2,
ISBN13: 978-0-8223-3289-3. Dewey:333.91/7/09759.
LCCN:2003-021428.

Audience: **g,l,u,f.** *Choice, 2004.*

Foth, Henry D. & Schafer,   **S591**
  John
Soil Geography and Land Use. Cloth Text. John Wiley & Sons,
Inc. Hoboken, NJ. 1980. 484p. ISBN:0-471-01710-8, ISBN13:
978-0-471-01710-3. Dewey:631.4. LCCN:79-027731.

Audience: **u,f.**

Fuller, Margaret C.   **SD421.F84 1991**
Forest Fires: An Introduction to Wildland Fire Behavior,
Management, Firefighting, and Prevention. Trade Paper. John
Wiley & Sons, Inc. Hoboken, NJ. 1991. 238p. Nature Editions
Ser. ISBN:0-471-52189-2, ISBN13: 978-0-471-52189-1.
Dewey:634.9/618. LCCN:90-046331.

Audience: **g.**

Harris, Larry D.   **QH75.H37 1984**
The Fragmented Forest: Island Biogeography Theory and the
Preservation of Biotic Diversity. Kenton R. Miller (Foreword
by). Library Binding. University of Chicago Press. Chicago, IL.
1984. 208p. ISBN:0-226-31763-3, ISBN13: 978-0-226-31763-2.
Dewey:639.9. LCCN:84-000144.

Audience: **l,u,f.**

Laurance, William F. &   **QH541.15.F73T76 1997**
  Bierregaard, Richard O. Jr. (Editors)
Tropical Forest Remnants: Ecology, Management, and
Conservation of Fragmented Communities. Trade Cloth.
University of Chicago Press. Chicago, IL. 1997. 632p.
ISBN:0-226-46898-4, ISBN13: 978-0-226-46898-3.
Dewey:577.34. LCCN:96-038038.

Audience: **l,u,f.** *Choice, 1998.*

Maser, Chris & Silberstein,   **HD205.S55 2000**
  Jane
Land-Use Planning for Sustainable Development. Perfect. Lewis
Publishers. Boca Raton, FL. 2000. 232p. Sustainable
Community Development Ser. ISBN:1-56670-325-5, ISBN13:
978-1-56670-325-3. Dewey:333.73. LCCN:00-033092.

Audience: **g,l.** *Choice, 2001.*

Yeang, Kenneth   **NA6230.Y43 1999**
The Green Skyscraper: The Basis for Designing Sustainable
Intensive Buildings. Trade Paper. Prestel Publishing. New York,
NY. 1999. 304p. ISBN:3-7913-1993-0, ISBN13:
978-3-7913-1993-3. Dewey:720/.47. LCCN:98-034625.
                                                      Audience: **g.**

Young, Anthony   **HD111 .Y68 1998**
Land Resources: Now and for the Future. Cloth Text.
Cambridge University Press. New York, NY. 1998. 331p.
ISBN:0-521-59003-5, ISBN13: 978-0-521-59003-7.
Dewey:333.73/16. LCCN:97-036654.
                          Audience: **g,l,u,f.** *Choice, 1999.*

Legislation

Bingham, Eula, et al.   **RA1229 .P38**
Patty's Industrial Hygiene and Toxicology, Set. Ed. 5. Barbara
Cohrssen & Charles H. Powell (Authors). CD-ROM. John Wiley
& Sons, Inc. Hoboken, NJ. 2005. ISBN:0-471-70057-6,
ISBN13: 978-0-471-70057-9. Dewey:613.6/2.
                                          Audience: **g,l,u,f.**

Brooks, Virginia   **K3585.B76 2002**
Law and Ecology: The Rise of the Ecosystem Regime. Trade
Cloth. Ashgate Publishing, Ltd. Aldershot, 2002. 430p. Ecology
and Law in Modern Society Ser. ISBN:0-7546-2038-7, ISBN13:
978-0-7546-2038-9. Dewey:344.7304/6. LCCN:2002-107427.
                              Audience: **u,f.** *Choice, 2003.*

Lacey, Michael J.   **HC110.E5G686 1989**
Government and Environmental Politics: Essays on Historical
Developments since World War II. Trade Paper. Woodrow
Wilson Center Press. Washington, DC. 1981. 336p.
ISBN:0-943875-15-3, ISBN13: 978-0-943875-15-6.
Dewey:363.7/08/09730904. LCCN:89-022761.
                              Audience: **g,l,u.** *Choice, 1992.*

Rechtschaffen, Clifford &   **KF3775.R385 2002**
Gauna, Eileen P.
Environmental Justice: Law, Policy and Regulation. Trade Paper.
Carolina Academic Press. Durham, NC. 2002. 496p.
ISBN:0-89089-412-4, ISBN13: 978-0-89089-412-5.
Dewey:344.73/046. LCCN:2002-105197.
                              Audience: **u,f.** *Choice, 2003.*

Scoullos, Michael J., et al.   **TD196.M38M463 2001**
Mercury - Cadmium - Lead: Handbook for Sustainable Heavy
Metals Policy and Regulation. Gerrit H. Vonkeman, Iain
Thornton & Zen Makuch (Authors). Trade Cloth. Springer
London, Ltd. Guildford, 2001. 544p. Environment and Policy
Ser., Vol. 31 ISBN:1-4020-0224-6, ISBN13: 978-1-4020-0224-3.
Dewey:363.17/91. LCCN:2001-050679.
                                          Audience: **u,f.**

Noise Pollution

Cowan, James P.   **NA2800**
Handbook of Environmental Acoustics. Wiley. 1993.
ISBN:0-471-28584-6, ISBN13: 978-0-471-28584-7.
                                          Audience: **g.**

Kryter, Karl D.   **RA772.N7.K78 1985**
The Effects of Noise on Man. Ed. 2. Trade Cloth. Elsevier
Science & Technology Books. Saint Louis, MO. 1985. xi, 688

p. :p. ISBN:0-12-427460-9, ISBN13: 978-0-12-427460-0.
Dewey:616.9/896. LCCN:83-003892.
                                          Audience: **g,l,u,f.**

Nuclear Power plants

Duffy, Robert J.   **HD9698.U5D76 1997**
Nuclear Politics in America: A History and Theory of
Government Regulation. Trade Cloth. University Press of
Kansas. Lawrence, KS. 1997. viii, 304p. Studies in Government
and Public Policy ISBN:0-7006-0852-4, ISBN13:
978-0-7006-0852-2. Dewey:333.792/4/0973. LCCN:97-019146.
                              Audience: **g.** *Choice, 1998.*

Glasstone, Samuel   **TK9202**
Nuclear Reactor Engineering. Ed. 4. Chapman & Hall. 1994.
ISBN:0-412-98521-7, ISBN13: 978-0-412-98521-8.
                                          Audience: **u,f.**

Suppes, Galen J. &   **QC173**
Storvick, Truman
Sustainable Nuclear Power. Trade Cloth. Elsevier Science &
Technology Books. Saint Louis, MO. 2006. 416p.
ISBN:0-12-370602-5, ISBN13: 978-0-12-370602-7. Dewey:539.
                                          Audience: **u,f.**

Wolfson, Richard   **TK9148**
Nuclear Choices: A Citizen's Guide to Nuclear Technology.
Trade Cloth. MIT Press. Cambridge, MA. 1991. 428p.
ISBN:0-262-23158-1, ISBN13: 978-0-262-23158-9.
Dewey:333.7924. LCCN:90-013545.
                              Audience: **g,l.** *Choice, 1992, 1991.*

Nuclear Power plants > Radioactive Waste

Gerber, Michele S.   **TD898.12.W2G47 2002**
On the Home Front: The Cold War Legacy of the Hanford
Nuclear Site. Ed. 2. Trade Cloth. University of Nebraska Press.
Lincoln, NE. 2005. 363p. ISBN:0-8032-7101-8, ISBN13:
978-0-8032-7101-2. Dewey:363.72/89/0979751.
LCCN:2001-027956.
                          Audience: **g,l.** *Choice, 2003, 2002, 1993.*

Glasstone, Samuel &   **GE105**
Jordan, Walter H.
Nuclear Power and Its Environmental Effects. Trade Paper.
American Nuclear Society. La Grange Park, IL. 1980. 400p.
ISBN:0-89448-024-3, ISBN13: 978-0-89448-024-9.
Dewey:363.7. LCCN:80-067303.
                                          Audience: **g,l,u,f.**

Gofman, John W.   **RA1231.R2.G56**
Radiation and Human Health: A Comprehensive Investigation of
the Evidence Relating Low-Level Radiation to Cancer and Other
Diseases. Trade Cloth. Sierra Club Books. San Francisco, CA.
1981. 928p. Guides ISBN:0-87156-275-8, ISBN13:
978-0-87156-275-3. Dewey:616.9/897. LCCN:80-026484.
                                          Audience: **g,l.**

Hanchar, John M. (Editor), TD898.S35 2004
et al.
Scientific Basis for Nuclear Waste Management XXVIII: 2004 MRS Spring Meeting Symposium Proceedings, Vol. 824. Simcha Stroes-Gascoyne & Lauren Browning (Editors). Trade Cloth. Materials Research Society. Warrendale, PA. 2004. 619p. Materials Research Society Symposium Proceedings Ser., 824 ISBN:1-55899-774-1, ISBN13: 978-1-55899-774-5. Dewey:621.48/38. LCCN:2005-295007.

Audience: **u,f.**

Hanford Cultural and TK9025.H36 2003
Historic Resources Program Staff (Contribution by)
Hanford Site Historic District: History of the Plutonium Production Facilities, 1943-1990. Trade Cloth. Battelle Press. Columbus, OH. 2003. 624p. ISBN:1-57477-133-7, ISBN13: 978-1-57477-133-6. Dewey:623.4/5119/0979751. LCCN:2002-034473.

Audience: **g,u,f.** *Choice, 2003.*

Oversby, Virginia M. & TD898
Werme, Lars O. (Editors)
Scientific Basis for Nuclear Waste Management XXVII: Proceedings of 27th International Symposium on Scientific Basis for Nuclear Waste Management, Vol. 807. Cloth Text. Materials Research Society. Warrendale, PA. 2004. 966p. Materials Research Society Conference Proceedings Ser., 807 ISBN:1-55899-752-0, ISBN13: 978-1-55899-752-3. Dewey:621.4838.

Audience: **u,f.**

Ozone Depletion

Bower, Frank A. & Ward, QC879.7.S87 1981
Richard B. (Editors)
Stratospheric Ozone and Man: Stratospheric Ozone. Trade Cloth. Franklin Book Company, Inc. Newtown Sq, PA. 1982. 232p. ISBN:0-8493-5753-5, ISBN13: 978-0-8493-5753-4. Dewey:363.7/392. LCCN:80-039562.

Audience: **u,f.**

Lumsden, Peter (Editor) QK757 .P53 1997
Plants and UV-B: Responses to Environmental Change. Trade Cloth. Cambridge University Press. New York, NY. 1997. 375p. Society for Experimental Biology Seminar Ser., Vol. 64 ISBN:0-521-57222-3, ISBN13: 978-0-521-57222-4. Dewey:571.4/56/2. LCCN:96-030065.

Audience: **l,u,f.**

Pollutants

Burger, Joanna TD196.P4B87 1997
Oil Spills. Cloth Text. Rutgers University Press. Piscataway, NJ. 1997. 228p. ISBN:0-8135-2338-9, ISBN13: 978-0-8135-2338-5. Dewey:363.73/82. LCCN:96-008340.

Audience: **u,f.** *Choice, 1997.*

Harrison, R. M. (Editor) TD174
Pollution: Causes, Effects and Control. Ed. 4. Trade Paper. Royal Society of Chemistry, The. Cambridge, 2001. xxiv + 580p. ISBN:0-85404-621-6, ISBN13: 978-0-85404-621-8. Dewey:363.7/3.

Audience: **l,u,f.**

Kaluarachchi, Jagath J. TD427.O7G76 2001
Groundwater Contamination by Organic Pollutants: Analysis and Remediation. Trade Cloth. American Society of Civil Engineers. Reston, VA. 2000. x, 238p. ASCE Manuals and Reports on Engineering Practice Ser., No. 100 ISBN:0-7844-0527-1, ISBN13: 978-0-7844-0527-7. Dewey:628.1/68. LCCN:00-063966.

Audience: **u,f.**

Krimsky, Sheldon RC649
Hormonal Chaos: The Scientific and Social Origins of the Environmental Endocrine Hypothesis. Lynn R. Goldman (Foreword by). Trade Cloth. DIANE Publishing Company. Collingdale, PA. 2004. 284p. ISBN:0-7567-7113-7, ISBN13: 978-0-7567-7113-3. Dewey:616.4/071.

Audience: **g,l.**

Neely, W. Brock RA566.27.N44 1994
Introduction to Chemical Exposure and Risk Assessment. Paper over Boards. Lewis Publishers. Boca Raton, FL. 1994. 208p. ISBN:1-56670-094-9, ISBN13: 978-1-56670-094-8. Dewey:615.9/02. LCCN:94-022452.

Audience: **u,f.** *Choice, 1995.*

Tinsley, Ian J. TD174
Chemical Concepts in Pollutant Behavior. Ed. 2. Trade Cloth. John Wiley & Sons, Inc. Hoboken, NJ. 2004. 402p. ISBN:0-471-09525-7, ISBN13: 978-0-471-09525-5. Dewey:577.27. LCCN:2003-025152.

Audience: **l,u.**

Wilson, Duff TD195.F46W55 2001
Fateful Harvest: The True Story of a Small Town, a Global Industry, and a Toxic Secret. Trade Cloth. HarperCollins Publishers. New York, NY. 2001. 336p. ISBN:0-06-019369-7, ISBN13: 978-0-06-019369-0. Dewey:363.19/2. LCCN:2001-024208.

Audience: **g,l.**

Pollutants > Carcinogens

Higginson, John, et al. RC261.48 .H54 1991
Human Cancer: Epidemiology and Environmental Causes. Calum S. Muir & Nubia Muñoz (Authors). Trade Paper. Cambridge University Press. New York, NY. 2005. 603p. Cambridge Monographs on Cancer Research Ser. ISBN:0-521-02196-0, ISBN13: 978-0-521-02196-8. Dewey:614.5/999. LCCN:91-023259.

Audience: **u,f.**

Kirsch-Volders, Micheline RA1229.M87 1984
(Editor)
Mutagenicity, Carcinogenicity, and Teratogenicity of Industrial Pollutants. Trade Cloth. Basic Books. New York, NY. 1984. 350p. ISBN:0-306-41148-2, ISBN13: 978-0-306-41148-9. Dewey:615.9/02. LCCN:83-011126.

Audience: **u,f.**

Pollutants > Hazardous Wastes

Saxena, Jitendra (Editor) QH545.A1 H38
Hazard Assessment of Chemicals, Vol. 2. Trade Cloth. Elsevier Science & Technology Books. Saint Louis, MO. 1983. 332p. Serial Publication Ser. ISBN:0-12-312402-6, ISBN13: 978-0-12-312402-9. Dewey:363.7/384.

Audience: **l,u.**

Saxena, Jitendra (Editor)   **QH545.A1 H38**
Hazard Assessment of Chemicals, Vol. 6. Library Binding.
Hemisphere Publishing Corporation. Philadelphia, PA. 1988.
400p. Hazard Assessment of Chemicals Ser.
ISBN:0-89116-835-4, ISBN13: 978-0-89116-835-5.
Dewey:363.7/384.

Audience: **l,u.**

Saxena, Jitendra & Fischer,   **QH545.A1 H38**
  Farley (Editors)
Hazard Assessment of Chemicals: Vol. 1, Current Developments.
Trade Cloth. Elsevier Science & Technology Books. Saint
Louis, MO. 1981. Serial Publication Ser. ISBN:0-12-312401-8,
ISBN13: 978-0-12-312401-2. Dewey:363.7/384.

Audience: **l,u.**

Pollution Control Industry

Freeman, Harry M.   **TD194.F74 1995**
Industrial Pollution Prevention Handbook. Trade Cloth.
McGraw-Hill Professional Publishing. New York, NY. 1994.
976p. ISBN:0-07-022148-0, ISBN13: 978-0-07-022148-2.
Dewey:363.73/1. LCCN:94-007979.

Audience: **u,f.** *Choice, 1996.*

Graedel, Thomas &   **TS171.G715 2005**
  Howard-Grenville, Jennifer
Greening the Industrial Facility: Perspectives, Approaches, and
Tools. Trade Cloth. Springer. New York, NY. 2005. XII, 617p.
ISBN:0-387-24306-2, ISBN13: 978-0-387-24306-1. Dewey:628.
LCCN:2005-925872.

Audience: **u,f.**

Heinsohn, Robert Jennings   **TD883.1**
  & Cimbala, John M.
Indoor Air Quality Engineering: Environmental Health and
Control of Indoor Pollutants. Paper over Boards. Marcel Dekker
Inc. New York, NY. 2003. 920p. ISBN:0-8247-4061-0, ISBN13:
978-0-8247-4061-0. Dewey:628.53.

Audience: **u,f.**

Horan, Nigel J. & Lowe,
  Paul
Sewage Processing Guidebook: Production, Energy Recovery,
Recycling and Technology Developments for Biosolids and
Organic Residuals. Trade Cloth. Elsevier Science & Technology
Books. Saint Louis, MO. 2007. 600p. ISBN:0-7506-7955-7,
ISBN13: 978-0-7506-7955-8.

Audience: **u,f.**

Wise, Marian & Kenworthy,   **TD1050.C57.K47 1993**
  Lauren
Preventing Industrial Toxic Hazards: A Guide for Communities.
Ed. 2. Trade Paper. INFORM, Inc. New York, NY. 1993. 208p.
ISBN:0-918780-60-8, ISBN13: 978-0-918780-60-7.
Dewey:363.72/87525. LCCN:92-041873.

Audience: **g,l.** *Choice, 1994.*

Radioactivity

Coggle, J. E.   **QH652.C56 1983**
Biological Effects of Radiation. Trade Cloth. Bow Historical
Books. New Providence, NJ. 1983. xii, 247 p. :p.
ISBN:0-8002-3075-2, ISBN13: 978-0-8002-3075-3.
Dewey:599/.024. LCCN:83-080179.

Audience: **l,u.**

Glasstone, Samuel &   **GE105**
  Jordan, Walter H.
Nuclear Power and Its Environmental Effects. Trade Paper.
American Nuclear Society. La Grange Park, IL. 1980. 400p.
ISBN:0-89448-024-3, ISBN13: 978-0-89448-024-9.
Dewey:363.7. LCCN:80-067303.

Audience: **g,l,u,f.**

Gofman, John W.   **RA1231.R2.G56**
Radiation and Human Health: A Comprehensive Investigation of
the Evidence Relating Low-Level Radiation to Cancer and Other
Diseases. Trade Cloth. Sierra Club Books. San Francisco, CA.
1981. 928p. Guides ISBN:0-87156-275-8, ISBN13:
978-0-87156-275-3. Dewey:616.9/897. LCCN:80-026484.

Audience: **g,l.**

Hoskins, P. W. O. (Editor)   **TD898.2**
Geology and Mineralogy of Radioactive Waste Repositories.
Trade Cloth. Springer. New York, NY. 2005. 450p.
Environmental Science Ser. ISBN:3-540-43919-6, ISBN13:
978-3-540-43919-6. Dewey:621.4/838.

Audience: **u,f.**

Klauenberg, B. Jon &   **QP82.2.R33R33 2000**
  Miklavicic, Damijan
Radio Frequency Radiation Dosimetry and Its Relationship to
the Biological Effects of Elecromagnetic Fields. Trade Cloth.
Springer London, Ltd. Guildford, 2000. 608p. NATO Advanced
Science Institutes Ser., Vol. 82 ISBN:0-7923-6404-X, ISBN13:
978-0-7923-6404-7. Dewey:612/.01448. LCCN:00-034893.

Audience: **u,f.**

Oversby, Virginia M. &   **TD898**
  Werme, Lars O. (Editors)
Scientific Basis for Nuclear Waste Management XXVII:
Proceedings of 27th International Symposium on Scientific Basis
for Nuclear Waste Management, Vol. 807. Cloth Text. Materials
Research Society. Warrendale, PA. 2004. 966p. Materials
Research Society Conference Proceedings Ser., 807
ISBN:1-55899-752-0, ISBN13: 978-1-55899-752-3.
Dewey:621.4838.

Audience: **u,f.**

Ringius, Lasse   **TD898.4.R56 2001**
Radioactive Waste Disposal at Sea: Public Ideas, Transnational
Policy Entrepreneurs, and Environmental Regimes. Trade Cloth.
MIT Press. Cambridge, MA. 2000. 337p. Global Environmental
Accord Ser., :Strategies for Sustainability and Institutional
Innovation ISBN:0-262-18202-5, ISBN13: 978-0-262-18202-7.
Dewey:363.7289. LCCN:00-031879.

Audience: **l,u,f.** *Choice, 2001.*

Resource Recovery

Lund, Herbert F.   **TD794.5.M397 2000**
The McGraw-Hill Recycling Handbook. Ed. 2. Cloth Text.
McGraw-Hill Professional Publishing. New York, NY. 2000.
976p. ISBN:0-07-039156-4, ISBN13: 978-0-07-039156-7.
Dewey:363.72/82. LCCN:00-028382.

Audience: **g,l,u.**

Resource Recovery > Recycling

Andrews, Gerald D. &   **TP1122.E44 1992**
  Subramanian, Pallatheri M. (Editors)
Emerging Technologies in Plastics Recycling. Trade Cloth.

Oxford University Press, Inc. New York, NY. 1992. 322p. ACS Symposium Ser., No. 513 ISBN:0-8412-2499-4, ISBN13: 978-0-8412-2499-5. Dewey:668.4. LCCN:92-027130.

Audience: **l,u,f.** *Choice, 1993.*

Lund, Herbert F.   **TD794.5.M397 2000**
The McGraw-Hill Recycling Handbook. Ed. 2. Cloth Text. McGraw-Hill Professional Publishing. New York, NY. 2000. 976p. ISBN:0-07-039156-4, ISBN13: 978-0-07-039156-7. Dewey:363.72/82. LCCN:00-028382.

Audience: **g,l,u.**

Powelson, David R. &   **TD794.5.P68 1992**
  Powelson, Melinda A.
The Recycler's Manual for Business, Government, and Environmentalists. Cloth Text. John Wiley & Sons, Inc. Hoboken, NJ. 1992. xxxii, 512p. ISBN:0-442-01190-3, ISBN13: 978-0-442-01190-1. Dewey:363.7282. LCCN:92-010099.

Audience: **g,l,u,f.** *Choice, 1993.*

Powelson, David R. &   **TD794.5 .P68**
  Powelson, Melinda A.
The Recycler's Manual for Business, Government, and the Environmental Community. Trade Cloth. John Wiley & Sons, Inc. Hoboken, NJ. 1992. 512p. ISBN:0-471-28499-8, ISBN13: 978-0-471-28499-4. Dewey:363.72/82.

Audience: **g.**

Rathje, William & Murphy,   **TD793.3.R38 2001**
  Cullen
Rubbish!: The Archaeology of Garbage. Trade Cloth. University of Arizona Press. Tucson, AZ. 2001. 263p. ISBN:0-8165-2143-3, ISBN13: 978-0-8165-2143-2. Dewey:363.72/8/097471. LCCN:00-053526.

Audience: **g,l,u,f.**

Stessel, Richard I.   **TD794.5.S75 1996**
Recycling and Resource Recovery Engineering: Principles of Waste Processing. Trade Cloth. Springer. New York, NY. 1996. 263p. Environmental Engineering Ser. ISBN:3-540-61100-2, ISBN13: 978-3-540-61100-4. Dewey:628.4/458. LCCN:96-018936.

Audience: **l,u,f.**

Soil Pollution

Adriano, D. C.   **QH545.T7A37 2001**
Trace Elements in Terrestrial Environments: Biogeochemistry, Bioavailability and Risks of Metals. Ed. 2. Trade Cloth. Springer. New York, NY. 2001. XII, 867p. ISBN:0-387-98678-2, ISBN13: 978-0-387-98678-4. Dewey:577/.14. LCCN:00-061263.

Audience: **l,u,f.**

Maier, Raina M., et al.   **QR100.M345 2000**
Environmental Microbiology. Ian L. Pepper & Charles P. Gerba (Authors). Cloth Text. Elsevier Science & Technology Books. Saint Louis, MO. 2000. 585p. ISBN:0-12-497570-4, ISBN13: 978-0-12-497570-5. Dewey:579/.17. LCCN:00-267828.

Audience: **u,f.**

Pfafflin, James R. &   **TD9.E5 2006**
  Edward N. Ziegler
Encyclopedia of Environmental Science and Engineering. Ed. 5. CRC Press. 2006. ISBN:0-8493-9843-6, ISBN13: 978-0-8493-9843-8.

Audience: **g,l,u,f.**

Rowe, R. Kerry, et al.   **TD795.7.R67 1997**
Clayey Barrier Systems for Waste Disposal Facilities. John R. Booker & Robert M. Quigley (Authors). Trade Paper. Routledge. New York, NY. 1997. 400p. ISBN:0-419-22600-1, ISBN13: 978-0-419-22600-0. Dewey:628.4/4564. LCCN:94-068785.

Audience: **u,f.**

Sharma, Hari D. & Reddy,   **TD171.9.S53 2004**
  Krishna R.
Geoenvironmental Engineering: Site Remediation, Waste Containment, and Emerging Waste Management Technologies. Trade Cloth. John Wiley & Sons, Inc. Hoboken, NJ. 2004. 992p. ISBN:0-471-21599-6, ISBN13: 978-0-471-21599-8. Dewey:628.5. LCCN:2004-007135.

Audience: **u,f.**

Twardowska, I., et al.   **TD794.2.S64 2004**
Solid Waste: Assessment, Monitoring and Remediation. H. E. Allen, A. F. Kettrup & W. J. Lacy (Authors). Trade Cloth. Elsevier Science & Technology Books. Saint Louis, MO. 2004. 1222p. Waste Management Ser., Vol. 4 ISBN:0-08-044321-4, ISBN13: 978-0-08-044321-8. Dewey:363.7285. LCCN:2006-273066.

Audience: **l,u,f.**

Wilson, Duff   **TD195.F46W55 2001**
Fateful Harvest: The True Story of a Small Town, a Global Industry, and a Toxic Secret. Trade Cloth. HarperCollins Publishers. New York, NY. 2001. 336p. ISBN:0-06-019369-7, ISBN13: 978-0-06-019369-0. Dewey:363.19/2. LCCN:2001-024208.

Audience: **g,l.**

Sustainability

                    HD2769
Worldwatch Institute.
http://www.worldwatch.org/

Audience: **u,f.**

Graedel, Thomas &   **TS171.G715 2005**
  Howard-Grenville, Jennifer
Greening the Industrial Facility: Perspectives, Approaches, and Tools. Trade Cloth. Springer. New York, NY. 2005. XII, 617p. ISBN:0-387-24306-2, ISBN13: 978-0-387-24306-1. Dewey:628. LCCN:2005-925872.

Audience: **u,f.**

Klass, Donald L.   **TP339.K54 1998**
Biomass for Renewable Energy, Fuels, and Chemicals. Trade Cloth. Elsevier Science & Technology Books. Saint Louis, MO. 1998. 651p. ISBN:0-12-410950-0, ISBN13: 978-0-12-410950-6. Dewey:662.8/8. LCCN:98-084422.

Audience: **u,f.** *Choice, 1999.*

Maser, Chris & Silberstein,   **HD205.S55 2000**
  Jane
Land-Use Planning for Sustainable Development. Perfect. Lewis Publishers. Boca Raton, FL. 2000. 232p. Sustainable Community Development Ser. ISBN:1-56670-325-5, ISBN13: 978-1-56670-325-3. Dewey:333.73. LCCN:00-033092.

Audience: **g,l.** *Choice, 2001.*

Masters, Gilbert M.   **TK1005.M33 2004**
Renewable and Efficient Electric Power Systems. Trade Cloth. John Wiley & Sons, Inc. Hoboken, NJ. 2004. 680p.

ISBN:0-471-28060-7, ISBN13: 978-0-471-28060-6. Dewey:621.31. LCCN:2003-062035.

Audience: **g,u,f.** *Choice, 2005.*

Norton, Bryan G.   **QH75.N66 2002**
Searching for Sustainability: Interdisciplinary Essays in the Philosophy of Conservation Biology. Trade Cloth. Cambridge University Press. New York, NY. 2002. 564p. Cambridge Studies in Philosophy and Biology ISBN:0-521-80990-8, ISBN13: 978-0-521-80990-0. Dewey:333.95/16. LCCN:2002-017404.

Audience: **u,f.** *Choice, 2003.*

Speth, James Gustave   **GE149.S64 2004**
Red Sky at Morning: America and the Crisis of the Global Environment. Cloth over Boards. Yale University Press. Cumberland, RI. 2004. 320p. ISBN:0-300-10232-1, ISBN13: 978-0-300-10232-1. Dewey:363.7/00973. LCCN:2003-020223.

Audience: **g.** *Choice, 2004.*

Suppes, Galen J. &   **QC173**
   Storvick, Truman
Sustainable Nuclear Power. Trade Cloth. Elsevier Science & Technology Books. Saint Louis, MO. 2006. 416p. ISBN:0-12-370602-5, ISBN13: 978-0-12-370602-7. Dewey:539.

Audience: **u,f.**

World Resources Institute   **HC79.E5**
   Staff
World Resources, 1992-93: A Guide to the Global Environment. Paper Text. Oxford University Press, Inc. New York, NY. 1992. 400p. ISBN:0-19-506231-0, ISBN13: 978-0-19-506231-1. Dewey:333.7.

Audience: **g,l,u,f.**

Toxic Waste

Dorfman, Mark, et al.   **TD899.C5.D66 1992**
Environmental Dividends: Cutting More Chemical Wastes. Catherine Miller & Warren Muir (Authors). Trade Paper. INFORM, Inc. New York, NY. 1992. 288p. ISBN:0-918780-50-0, ISBN13: 978-0-918780-50-8. Dewey:660. LCCN:92-012251.

Audience: **g,l,u.** *Choice, 1993.*

Hoskins, P. W. O. (Editor)   **TD898.2**
Geology and Mineralogy of Radioactive Waste Repositories. Trade Cloth. Springer. New York, NY. 2005. 450p. Environmental Science Ser. ISBN:3-540-43919-6, ISBN13: 978-3-540-43919-6. Dewey:621.4/838.

Audience: **u,f.**

McDermott, Henry J.   **TD890.M38 2004**
Air Monitoring for Toxic Exposures. Ed. 2. Trade Cloth. John Wiley & Sons, Inc. Hoboken, NJ. 2004. 688p. ISBN:0-471-45435-4, ISBN13: 978-0-471-45435-9. Dewey:628.5/3/0287. LCCN:2003-026039.

Audience: **g,u,f.** *Choice, 2005.*

Waste Disposal

Horan, Nigel J. & Lowe,
   Paul
Sewage Processing Guidebook: Production, Energy Recovery, Recycling and Technology Developments for Biosolids and Organic Residuals. Trade Cloth. Elsevier Science & Technology Books. Saint Louis, MO. 2007. 600p. ISBN:0-7506-7955-7, ISBN13: 978-0-7506-7955-8.

Audience: **u,f.**

Powelson, David R. &   **TD794.5 .P68**
   Powelson, Melinda A.
The Recycler's Manual for Business, Government, and the Environmental Community. Trade Cloth. John Wiley & Sons, Inc. Hoboken, NJ. 1992. 512p. ISBN:0-471-28499-8, ISBN13: 978-0-471-28499-4. Dewey:363.72/82.

Audience: **g.**

Rathje, William & Murphy,   **TD793.3.R38 2001**
   Cullen
Rubbish!: The Archaeology of Garbage. Trade Cloth. University of Arizona Press. Tucson, AZ. 2001. 263p. ISBN:0-8165-2143-3, ISBN13: 978-0-8165-2143-2. Dewey:363.72/8/097471. LCCN:00-053526.

Audience: **g,l,u,f.**

Stessel, Richard I.   **TD794.5.S75 1996**
Recycling and Resource Recovery Engineering: Principles of Waste Processing. Trade Cloth. Springer. New York, NY. 1996. 263p. Environmental Engineering Ser. ISBN:3-540-61100-2, ISBN13: 978-3-540-61100-4. Dewey:628.4/458. LCCN:96-018936.

Audience: **l,u,f.**

Twardowska, I., et al.   **TD794.2.S64 2004**
Solid Waste: Assessment, Monitoring and Remediation. H. E. Allen, A. F. Kettrup & W. J. Lacy (Authors). Trade Cloth. Elsevier Science & Technology Books. Saint Louis, MO. 2004. 1222p. Waste Management Ser., Vol. 4 ISBN:0-08-044321-4, ISBN13: 978-0-08-044321-8. Dewey:363.7285. LCCN:2006-273066.

Audience: **l,u,f.**

Water Pollution

Brezonik, Patrick L.   **GB855.B74 1994**
Chemical Kinetics and Process Dynamics in Aquatic Systems. Lewis Publishers. 1994. ISBN:0-87371-431-8, ISBN13: 978-0-87371-431-0.

Audience: **u,f.**

Bubenick, David V.   **TD196.A25.A29 1984**
Acid Rain Information Book. Ed. 2. Trade Cloth. Noyes Data Corporation/Noyes Publications. Park Ridge, NJ. 1984. 397p. ISBN:0-8155-0967-7, ISBN13: 978-0-8155-0967-7. Dewey:363.7/394. LCCN:83-021986.

Audience: **u,f.**

Chanson, Hubert   **TC175.C37 1999**
Hydraulics of Open Channel Flow: An Introduction: Basic Principles, Sediment Motion, Hydraulic Modelling, Design of Hydraulic Structures. Trade Paper. Elsevier Science &

Technology Books. Saint Louis, MO. 1999. 544p.
ISBN:0-340-74067-1, ISBN13: 978-0-340-74067-5.
Dewey:627/.23. LCCN:00-268020.

Audience: **u,f.**

Charbeneau, Randall J.   **TD426**
Groundwater Hydraulics and Pollutant Transport. Trade Cloth.
Simon & Schuster. New York, NY. 2000. ISBN:0-13-016612-X,
ISBN13: 978-0-13-016612-8. Dewey:628.1/68.

Audience: **u,f.** *Choice, 2000.*

Feigin, A., et al.   **TD760.F45 1990**
Irrigation with Treated Sewage Effluent: Management for
Environmental Protection. I. Ravina & J. Shalhevet (Authors),
E. Bresler, G. W. Thomas, L. Dale Van Vleck & B. Yaron
(Editors). Cloth Text. Springer. New York, NY. 1991. 224p.
Advanced Series in Agricultural Sciences, Vol. 17
ISBN:0-387-50804-X, ISBN13: 978-0-387-50804-7.
Dewey:628.3/623. LCCN:90-010199.

Audience: **u,f.** *Choice, 1991.*

Good, Ralph E. (Editor), et   **QH541.5.M3.F74**
al.
Freshwater Wetlands: Ecological Processes and Management
Potential. Dennis F. Whigham & Robert L. Simpson (Editors).
Trade Cloth. Elsevier Science & Technology Books. Saint
Louis, MO. 1978. xvii, 378p. ISBN:0-12-290150-9, ISBN13:
978-0-12-290150-8. Dewey:574.5/2632. LCCN:78-002836.

Audience: **u,f.**

Gray, N. F.   **TD257.G72 1994**
Drinking Water Quality: Problems and Solutions. Wiley. 1994.
ISBN:0-471-94817-9, ISBN13: 978-0-471-94817-9.

Audience: **l,u,f.**

Horan, Nigel J. & Lowe,
Paul
Sewage Processing Guidebook: Production, Energy Recovery,
Recycling and Technology Developments for Biosolids and
Organic Residuals. Trade Cloth. Elsevier Science & Technology
Books. Saint Louis, MO. 2007. 600p. ISBN:0-7506-7955-7,
ISBN13: 978-0-7506-7955-8.

Audience: **u,f.**

Kaluarachchi, Jagath J.   **TD427.O7G76 2001**
Groundwater Contamination by Organic Pollutants: Analysis and
Remediation. Trade Cloth. American Society of Civil Engineers.
Reston, VA. 2000. x, 238p. ASCE Manuals and Reports on
Engineering Practice Ser., No. 100 ISBN:0-7844-0527-1,
ISBN13: 978-0-7844-0527-7. Dewey:628.1/68.
LCCN:00-063966.

Audience: **u,f.**

Maier, Raina M., et al.   **QR100.M345 2000**
Environmental Microbiology. Ian L. Pepper & Charles P. Gerba
(Authors). Cloth Text. Elsevier Science & Technology Books.
Saint Louis, MO. 2000. 585p. ISBN:0-12-497570-4, ISBN13:
978-0-12-497570-5. Dewey:579/.17. LCCN:00-267828.

Audience: **u,f.**

Naidu, R. (Editor), et al.   **TD427.A77M**
Managing Arsenic in the Environment: From Soil to Human
Health. E. Smith, G. Owens, P. Bhattacharya & P. Nadebaum
(Editors). Trade Cloth. Science Publishers. Enfield, NH. 2006.
664p. ISBN:1-57808-425-3, ISBN13: 978-1-57808-425-8.
Dewey:628.5/2. LCCN:2006-042326.

Audience: **u,f.**

National Research Council   **TD427.N87N38 2000**
Staff, et al.
Clean Coastal Waters: Understanding and Reducing the Effects
of Nutrient Pollution. Ocean Studies Board Staff & Water
Science and Technology Board Staff (Authors). Trade Cloth.
National Academies Press. Washington, DC. 2000. xvi, 405p.
ISBN:0-309-06948-3, ISBN13: 978-0-309-06948-9.
Dewey:363.739/4. LCCN:00-009621.

Audience: **g,u,f.** *Choice, 2001.*

Neilson, Alasdair   **QH545.W3N45 1994**
Fate of Organic Chemicals in the Aquatic Environment. Box or
Slipcased. Lewis Publishers. Boca Raton, FL. 1994. 448p.
ISBN:0-87371-597-7, ISBN13: 978-0-87371-597-3.
Dewey:574.5/263. LCCN:94-022460.

Audience: **l,u.** *Choice, 1995.*

Odum, Howard T.   **TD196.M4H434 2000**
Heavy Metals in the Environment: Using Wetlands for Their
Removal. Paper over Boards. Lewis Publishers. Boca Raton, FL.
2000. 344p. ISBN:1-56670-401-4, ISBN13: 978-1-56670-401-4.
Dewey:628.5/2. LCCN:99-089022.

Audience: **u,f.**

Pfafflin, James R. &   **TD9.E5 2006**
Edward N. Ziegler
Encyclopedia of Environmental Science and Engineering. Ed. 5.
CRC Press. 2006. ISBN:0-8493-9843-6, ISBN13:
978-0-8493-9843-8.

Audience: **g,l,u,f.**

Ringius, Lasse   **TD898.4.R56 2001**
Radioactive Waste Disposal at Sea: Public Ideas, Transnational
Policy Entrepreneurs, and Environmental Regimes. Trade Cloth.
MIT Press. Cambridge, MA. 2000. 337p. Global Environmental
Accord Ser., :Strategies for Sustainability and Institutional
Innovation ISBN:0-262-18202-5, ISBN13: 978-0-262-18202-7.
Dewey:363.7289. LCCN:00-031879.

Audience: **l,u,f.** *Choice, 2001.*

Singh, Vijay P.   **QA913**
Kinematic Wave Modeling in Water Resources, Set. Trade
Cloth. John Wiley & Sons, Inc. Hoboken, NJ. 1998. 2272p.
ISBN:0-471-19087-X, ISBN13: 978-0-471-19087-5.
Dewey:532/.051.

Audience: **u,f.**

Smith, Paul G.   **TD9.S37 2005**
Dictionary of Water and Waste Management. Ed. 2. Trade Cloth.
Elsevier Science & Technology Books. Saint Louis, MO. 2005.
480p. ISBN:0-7506-6525-4, ISBN13: 978-0-7506-6525-4.
Dewey:628.4. LCCN:2006-274436.

Audience: **g,l,u,f.**

Tchobanoglous, George,   **TD645.W293 2003**
et al.
Wastewater Engineering: Treatment and Reuse. Ed. 4. Franklin
L. Burton & H. David Stensel (Authors), Metcalf and Eddy, Inc.
Staff (Contribution by). Paper Text. McGraw-Hill Companies,
The. New York, NY. 2003. xxviii, 1819p. McGraw-Hill Series in
Civil and Environmental Engineering ISBN:0-07-112250-8,
ISBN13: 978-0-07-112250-4. Dewey:628.3.
LCCN:2001-053724.

Audience: **l,u,f.**

Tchobanoglous, George,   **TD645.W295 2002**
et al.
Wastewater Engineering: Treatment and Reuse. Ed. 4. Franklin

L. Burton, H. David Stensel & Metcalf and Eddy, Inc. Staff (Authors). Cloth Text. McGraw-Hill Higher Education. Burr Ridge, IL. 2002. 1848p. McGraw-Hill Series in Civil and Environmental Engineering ISBN:0-07-041878-0, ISBN13: 978-0-07-041878-3. Dewey:628.3. LCCN:2001-053724.

Audience: **u,f.**

Wood, Eric F. & Princeton   **TD223.G76 1984**
  Water Resources Group Staff
Groundwater Contamination from Hazardous Wastes. Cloth Text. Prentice Hall PTR. Upper Saddle River, NJ. 1983. 192p. ISBN:0-13-366286-1, ISBN13: 978-0-13-366286-3. Dewey:628.4/4564. LCCN:83-010948.

Audience: **l,u,f.**

Water Pollution > Marine Pollution

Jarvinen, Alfred W. &   **QH90.57.B5J37 1999**
  Ankley, Gerald T.
Linkage of Effects to Tissue Residues: Development of a Comprehensive Database for Aquatic Organisms Exposed to Inorganic and Organic Chemicals. Trade Cloth. Society of Environmental Toxicology and Chemistry. Pensacola, FL. 1998. 15p. ISBN:1-880611-13-9, ISBN13: 978-1-880611-13-5. Dewey:577.6/27. LCCN:98-022670.

Audience: **u,f.**

National Research Council   **VM455.N35 1991**
  Staff
Tanker Spills: Prevention by Design. Cloth Text. National Academies Press. Washington, DC. 1991. 384p. ISBN:0-309-04377-8, ISBN13: 978-0-309-04377-9. Dewey:623.8/245. LCCN:91-012489.

Audience: **g,u.** *Choice, 1992.*

Walker, C. H. &   **QH541.5.S3**
  Livingstone, D. R.
Persistent Pollutants in Marine Ecosystems. Trade Cloth. Elsevier Science & Technology Books. Saint Louis, MO. 1992. 192p. Society of Environment Toxicology and Chemistry Ser. ISBN:0-08-041874-0, ISBN13: 978-0-08-041874-2. Dewey:574.52636. LCCN:92-006423.

Audience: **l,u,f.**

Water Pollution > Water resources

Grigg, Neil S.   **HD1691.G75 1996**
Water Resources Management: Principles, Regulations, and Cases. McGraw-Hill Professional Publishing. 1996. ISBN:0-07-024782-X, ISBN13: 978-0-07-024782-6.

Audience: **u,f.**

Linsley, Ray K., et al.   **TC5**
Water Resources Engineering. Ed. 4. Joseph B. Franzini, David L. Freyberg & George Tchobanoglous (Authors). Cloth Text. McGraw-Hill Higher Education. Burr Ridge, IL. 1991. 768p. Water Resources and Environmental Engineering Ser. ISBN:0-07-038010-4, ISBN13: 978-0-07-038010-3. Dewey:627. LCCN:91-040707.

Audience: **l,u,f.**

Moser, Michael E. &   **QH87.3.W46 1991**
  Finlayson, Max (Editors)
Wetlands. Trade Cloth. Facts On File, Inc.. New York, NY.

1991. 224p. ISBN:0-8160-2556-8, ISBN13: 978-0-8160-2556-5. Dewey:574.5/26325. LCCN:91-023683.

Audience: **g,l.** *Choice, 1992.*

Postel, Sandra   **TD345.P67 1992**
The Last Oasis: Facing Water Scarcity. Trade Cloth. W. W. Norton & Company, Inc. New York, NY. 1992. 128p. Worldwatch Environmental Alert Ser. ISBN:0-393-03428-3, ISBN13: 978-0-393-03428-8. Dewey:333.91. LCCN:92-030356.

Audience: **g,l.** *Choice, 1993.*

Postel, Sandra & Richter,   **QH75.P67 2003**
  Brian D.
Rivers for Life: Managing Water for People and Nature. Trade Cloth. Island Press. Washington, DC. 2003. 220p. ISBN:1-55963-443-X, ISBN13: 978-1-55963-443-4. Dewey:333.91/6216. LCCN:2003-006051.

Audience: **g,l,u,f.** *Choice, 2004.*

Shiklomanov, I. A. &   **GB661.2**
  Rodda, John C. (Editors)
World Water Resources at the Beginning of the Twenty-First Century. Trade Paper. Cambridge University Press. New York, NY. 2004. 449p. International Hydrology Ser. ISBN:0-521-61722-7, ISBN13: 978-0-521-61722-2. Dewey:553.7/09/05. LCCN:2002-031201.

Audience: **u,f.** *Choice, 2004.*

Smith, Paul G.   **TD9.S37 2005**
Dictionary of Water and Waste Management. Ed. 2. Trade Cloth. Elsevier Science & Technology Books. Saint Louis, MO. 2005. 480p. ISBN:0-7506-6525-4, ISBN13: 978-0-7506-6525-4. Dewey:628.4. LCCN:2006-274436.

Audience: **g,l,u,f.**

Vickers, Amy   **TD388.V53 2001**
Handbook of Water Use and Conservation: Homes, Landscapes, Businesses, Industries, Farms. Trade Cloth. WaterPlow Press. Amherst, MA. 2001. 460p. ISBN:1-931579-07-5, ISBN13: 978-1-931579-07-0. Dewey:333.91/16. LCCN:99-025179.

Audience: **l,u,f.** *Choice, 2001.*

Viessman, Warren Jr. &   **TD353.V54 2004**
  Hammer, Mark J.
Water Supply and Pollution Control. Ed. 7. Cloth Text. Prentice Hall PTR. Upper Saddle River, NJ. 2004. 888p. ISBN:0-13-140970-0, ISBN13: 978-0-13-140970-5. Dewey:628.1. LCCN:2004-045395.

Audience: **l,u,f.**

Wildlife Management

Huffaker, Carl B.   **SB931**
New Technology of Pest Control. Trade Cloth. John Wiley & Sons, Inc. Hoboken, NJ. 1980. 500p. Environmental Science and Technology Ser. ISBN:0-471-05336-8, ISBN13: 978-0-471-05336-1. Dewey:632/.7. LCCN:79-004369.

Audience: **u,f.**

Rader, Russell B. (Editor),   **QH77.N56R34 2001**
  et al.
Bioassessment and Management of North American Freshwater Wetlands. Darold P. Batzer & Scott A. Wissinger (Editors). Trade Cloth. John Wiley & Sons, Inc. Hoboken, NJ. 2001. 480p. ISBN:0-471-35234-9, ISBN13: 978-0-471-35234-1. Dewey:333.91/8/097. LCCN:2001-022372.

Audience: **g,f.**

Yepsen, Roger B.   **SB974.E53 1984**
The Encyclopedia of Natural Insect and Disease Control. Trade Cloth. Rodale Press, Inc. Emmaus, PA. 1984. 496p.

ISBN:0-87857-488-3, ISBN13: 978-0-87857-488-9. Dewey:635/.0494. LCCN:83-024643.

Audience: **g,l.**

GENERAL SCIENCE

Literacy in science is a growing concern especially of late, when many feel that science has been usurped or suppressed by political means. It is important that we all are broadly educated to secure understanding, even wisdom, for participation in our self-governing process.

This science collection is based on BCL3 and the Library of Congress classification system, with updates. This listing includes many categories in general science: history, ancient and modern; by countries; societies; biographies, both individual and collective; philosophy; study and teaching; language; methodology; and some data resources. Also included are some history of technology, cybernetics and artificial intelligence. Reference books are included, but not journals, even though in every collection however modestly attempting to cover science, I would recommend a handful of basic science journals and news magazines: Science, Nature, Scientific American, Science News, New Scientist, The Scientist.

— Louise Deis

Q179.97

☐ Science for the Millennium.
http://www.ncsa.uiuc.edu/Cyberia/Expo/
Ed. 3/18/96.

Audience: **g,l,u,f.**

Q179.97

☐ Science.Gov.
http://www.science.gov

Audience: **g,l,u,f.**

☐ SCIRUS.
http://www.scirus.com
Elsevier.

Audience: **g,l,u,f.**

Societies. Collected Works

☐ InterDok.
http://interdok.com/
InterDok Corporation.

Audience: **f.**

Q11

☐ The National Academies.
http://www.nationalacademies.org

Audience: **g,l.**

Q11

☐ Scientific American Archive.
http://www.sciamdigital.com
EBSCO Host.

Audience: **g,l,u,f.**

Caroe, G.   **Q41.R88**
Royal Institution: Informan. Cloth Text. John Murray. London,
1985. xi, 180p. ISBN:0-7195-4245-6, ISBN13:
978-0-7195-4245-9. Dewey:506/.041. LCCN:86-140414.
Audience: **g,f.** *B*

Gibbs, Josiah W.   **Q113 .G44 1993**
The Scientific Papers of J. Willard Gibbs: Thermodynamics, Vol.
1. Trade Paper. Ox Bow Press. Woodbridge, CT. 1993. xxviii,
434p. ISBN:0-918024-77-3, ISBN13: 978-0-918024-77-0.
Dewey:530. LCCN:93-019391.
Audience: **u,f.**

Gibbs, Josiah W.   **Q113.G44 1993**
Scientific Papers of J. Willard Gibbs: Dynamics, Vector
Analysis, Multiple Algebra, Electromagnetic Theory of Light,
Vol. 2. Trade Paper. Ox Bow Press. Woodbridge, CT. 1994. viii,
284p. ISBN:1-881987-06-X, ISBN13: 978-1-881987-06-2.
Dewey:530. LCCN:93-019391.
Audience: **u,f.**

Hahn, Roger   **Q46.A15.H33**
The Anatomy of a Scientific Institution: The Paris Academy of
Sciences, 1666-1803. Trade Cloth. University of California
Press. Berkeley, CA. 1971. xiv, 433p. ISBN:0-520-01818-4,
ISBN13: 978-0-520-01818-1. Dewey:506/.2/44.
LCCN:70-130795.
Audience: **g,f.** *B*

Hall, Marie B.   **Q41.L85H35 1984**
All Scientists Now: The Royal Society in the Nineteenth
Century. Trade Cloth. Cambridge University Press. New York,
NY. 1984. 272p. ISBN:0-521-26746-3, ISBN13:
978-0-521-26746-5. Dewey:506/.041. LCCN:84-007705.
Audience: **g,f.** *B Choice, 1985.*

Hunter, Michael   **Q41.L85**
Royal Society and Its Fellows, 1660-1700: The Morphology of
an Early Scientific Institution. Trade Paper. British Society for
the History of Science Ltd. Fleet, 1982. 276p.
ISBN:0-906450-03-9, ISBN13: 978-0-906450-03-1.
Dewey:506/.041. LCCN:83-209776.
Audience: **g,f.** *B*

McClellan, James E.   **Q10.M38 1985**
Science Reorganized. Trade Cloth. Columbia University Press.
New York, NY. 1985. 413p. ISBN:0-231-05996-5, ISBN13:
978-0-231-05996-1. Dewey:506. LCCN:84-022993.
Audience: **g,f.** *B*

Morrell, Jack & Thackray,   **Q41.B85.M67 1981**
    Arnold W.
Gentlemen of Science: Early Years of the British Association for
the Advancement of Science. Trade Cloth. Oxford University
Press, Inc. New York, NY. 1981. xxiii, 592p.
ISBN:0-19-858163-7, ISBN13: 978-0-19-858163-5.
Dewey:506/.041. LCCN:81-201474.
Audience: **g,f.** *B*

Oehser, Paul H.   **Q11**
Sons of Science: The Story of the Smithsonian Institution and
Its Leaders. Trade Cloth. Greenwood Publishing Group, Inc.
Portsmouth, NH. 1969. 220p. ISBN:0-8371-0185-9, ISBN13:
978-0-8371-0185-9. Dewey:506/.1/73. LCCN:69-010144.
Audience: **g,f.**

Oehser, Paul H. & Ripley, S.   **Q11.S8 O39 1983**
    Dillon
The Smithsonian Institution. Ed. 2. Cloth Text. Westview Press.
Boulder, CO. 1983. 350p. Library of Federal Departments,
Agencies, and Systems Ser. ISBN:0-86531-300-8, ISBN13:
978-0-86531-300-2. Dewey:069/.09753. LCCN:83-007026.
Audience: **g.** *B*

Purver, Margery   **Q41.L86 P86 1967A**
The Royal Society: Concept and Creation. Trade Cloth. MIT
Press. Cambridge, MA. 1967. ISBN:0-262-16018-8, ISBN13:
978-0-262-16018-6. Dewey:506/.2/421.
Audience: **g,f.** *B*

Reingold, Nathan (Editor)   **Q113 .H43**
The Papers of Joseph Henry: The Princeton Years, January
1836-December 1837. Trade Cloth. Smithsonian Institution
Press. Washington, DC. 1979. 585p. ISBN:0-87474-174-2,
ISBN13: 978-0-87474-174-2. Dewey:537/.092/4.
LCCN:72-002005.
Audience: **g,f.**

Reingold, Nathan (Editor)   **Q113 .H43**
The Papers of Joseph Henry: The Princeton Years, January
1838-December 1840. Trade Cloth. Smithsonian Institution
Press. Washington, DC. 1981. 476p. The Joseph Henry Papers
ISBN:0-87474-792-9, ISBN13: 978-0-87474-792-8.
Dewey:537/.092/4. LCCN:72-002005.
Audience: **g,f.**

Reingold, Nathan (Editor)   Q113 .H43
The Papers of Joseph Henry: The Princeton Years, January
1841-December 1843. Trade Cloth. Smithsonian Institution
Press. Washington, DC. 1985. 500p. The Joseph Henry Papers
ISBN:0-87474-793-7, ISBN13: 978-0-87474-793-5.
Dewey:537/.092/4. LCCN:72-002005.
                                                Audience: **g,f.**

Reingold, Nathan (Editor)   Q113 .H43
The Papers of Joseph Henry: The Princeton Years, November
1832-December 1835. Trade Cloth. Smithsonian Institution
Press. Washington, DC. 1976. 564p. ISBN:0-87474-164-5,
ISBN13: 978-0-87474-164-3. Dewey:537/.092/4.
                                                Audience: **g,f.**

Rothenberg, Marc (Editor)   Q113
The Papers of Joseph Henry: January 1858-December 1865, the
Smithsonian Years. Trade Cloth. Watson Publishing
International. Sagamore Beach, MA. 2005. 613p.
ISBN:0-88135-358-2, ISBN13: 978-0-88135-358-7.
Dewey:537/.092/4.
                                                Audience: **g,f.**

Rothenberg, Marc (Editor)   Q113 .H43
The Papers of Joseph Henry: The Princeton Years, January 1844
- December 1846. Trade Cloth. Smithsonian Institution Press.
Washington, DC. 1992. 592p. ISBN:1-56098-112-1, ISBN13:
978-1-56098-112-1. Dewey:537/.092/4. LCCN:72-002005.
                                                Audience: **g,f.**

Rothenberg, Marc   Q113
The Papers of Joseph Henry: The Smithsonian Years, January
1854-December 1857. Library Binding. Watson Publishing
International. Sagamore Beach, MA. 2002. 564p.
ISBN:0-88135-363-9, ISBN13: 978-0-88135-363-1.
Dewey:537/.092/4. LCCN:72-002005.
                                                Audience: **g,f.**

Rothenberg, Marc (Editor)   Q113 .H43
The Papers of Joseph Henry: The Smithsonian Years, January
1850-December 1853. Trade Cloth. Smithsonian Institution
Press. Washington, DC. 1999. 624p. ISBN:1-56098-891-6,
ISBN13: 978-1-56098-891-5. Dewey:537/.092/4.
LCCN:72-002005.
                                                Audience: **g,f.**

Rothenberg, Marc (Editor)   Q113 .H43
The Papers of Joseph Henry: The Smithsonian Years, January
1847 - December 1849. Trade Cloth. Smithsonian Institution
Press. Washington, DC. 1996. 704p. ISBN:1-56098-533-X,
ISBN13: 978-1-56098-533-4. Dewey:537/.092/4.
LCCN:72-002005.
                                                Audience: **g,f.**

Young, Margaret Labash   Q10
  (Editor)
Scientific and Technical Organizations and Agencies Directory.
Ed. 3. Trade Cloth. Thomson Gale. Farmington Hills, MI. 1993.
2618p. ISBN:0-8103-5464-0, ISBN13: 978-0-8103-5464-7.
Dewey:506.
                                                Audience: **l,u,f.**

Dictionaries. Encyclopedias

                                                        Q121
🐝 [Academic Press] Encyclopedia of Physical Science and
Technology. Knight-Ridder Information, Inc.; Mountain View,
CA: San Diego, CA: Academic Press. 1995.
                                                Audience: **l,u,f.**

▢ English-German and French-German Dictionary.
http://dict.leo.org/?lang=en&lp=ende&search=
                                                Audience: **u,f.**

                                                        Q179
▢ Scientific and Technical Acronyms, Symbols and
Abbreviations.
http://www3.interscience.wiley.com/stasa/search.html
Wiley-Interscience.
                                                Audience: **l,u,f.**

American Heritage   Q123.A5178 2005
  Dictionary Editors (Editor)
The American Heritage Science Dictionary. Trade Cloth.
Houghton Mifflin Company Trade & Reference Division.
Boston, MA. 2005. 704p. ISBN:0-618-45504-3, ISBN13:
978-0-618-45504-1. Dewey:503. LCCN:2004-019696.
                                Audience: **g,l.** *Choice, 2005.*

Applebaum, Wilbur   Q125
Encyclopedia of the Scientific Revolution from Copernicus to
Newton. Garland. 2000. ISBN:0-8153-1503-1, ISBN13:
978-0-8153-1503-2.
                                                Audience: **g,l.**

Callaham, Ludmilla   QD5.C33 1996
  Ignatiev, et al.
Callaham's Russian-English Dictionary of Science and
Technology. Ed. 4. Patricia E. Newman & John R. Callaham
(Authors). Trade Cloth. John Wiley & Sons, Inc. Hoboken, NJ.
1996. 848p. ISBN:0-471-61139-5, ISBN13: 978-0-471-61139-4.
Dewey:603. LCCN:94-037599.
                                Audience: **u,f.** *Choice, 1996.*

Cardarelli, Francois   QC94
Encyclopaedia of Scientific Units, Weights, and Measures: Their
SI Equivalences and Origins. Springer. 2003.
ISBN:1-85233-682-X, ISBN13: 978-1-85233-682-0.
                                                Audience: **g,l,u,f.**

Chakalov, G.   Q123
English-Russian Dictionary of Science and Technology. Trade
Cloth. French & European Publications, Inc. New York, NY.
1996. 1134p. ISBN:0-7859-9369-X, ISBN13:
978-0-7859-9369-8. Dewey:503.
                                                Audience: **u,f.**

Clugston, M. J.   Q123
The New Penguin Dictionary of Science. Ed. 2. Trade Paper.
Penguin Group (USA) Inc. New York, NY. 2004. 784p.
ISBN:0-14-101074-6, ISBN13: 978-0-14-101074-8. Dewey:503.
LCCN:2004-273165.
                            Audience: **l,u,f.** *Choice, 2004, 1999.*

Considine, Glenn D.   Q121
Van Nostrand's Scientific Encyclopedia, Set. Ed. 9. Peter Kulik
(Editor). Trade Cloth. John Wiley & Sons, Inc. Hoboken, NJ.

2002. 3936p. ISBN:0-471-33230-5, ISBN13:
978-0-471-33230-5. Dewey:503. LCCN:76-047074.

Audience: **l,u,f.** *Choice, 2002.*

De Vries, Louis & Theo M.   **T9**
Herrmann
German-English Technical and Engineering Dictionary. Ed. 2.
NY: McGraw-Hill. 1965.

Audience: **u,f.**

De Vries, Louis   **Q123**
French-English Science and Technology Dictionary. Ed. 4. rev.
and enlarged by Stanley Hochman. McGraw-Hill. NY:. 1976.
ISBN:0-07-016629-3, ISBN13: 978-0-07-016629-5.

Audience: **u,f.**

Dorian, A. F.   **Q123 .D67 1978**
Dictionary of Science and Technology. Ed. 2. Trade Cloth.
Elsevier. New York, NY. 1981. 1414p. ISBN:0-444-41649-8,
ISBN13: 978-0-444-41649-0. Dewey:503. LCCN:77-016111.

Audience: **u,f.**

Dorian, A. F. (Editor)   **Q123**
Dorian's Dictionary of Science and Technology, Vol. II. Trade
Cloth. Elsevier Science & Technology Books. Saint Louis, MO.
1980. 1096p. ISBN:0-444-41911-X, ISBN13:
978-0-444-41911-8. Dewey:503/.41. LCCN:80-018312.

Audience: **u,f.**

Dorian, A. F.   **Q123**
Dorian's Dictionary of Science and Technology: German -
English. Trade Cloth. French & European Publications, Inc.
New York, NY. 1981. 1120p. ISBN:0-8288-9276-8, ISBN13:
978-0-8288-9276-6. Dewey:503.

Audience: **u,f.**

Dorian, Angelo Francis   **Q123**
Dictionary of Science and Technology: English-French. NY and
Amsterdam: Elsevier. 1979. ISBN:0-444-41829-6, ISBN13:
978-0-444-41829-6.

Audience: **u,f.**

Dorian, Angelo Francis   **Q123**
Dictionary of Science and Technology: German-English. NY and
Amsterdam: Elsevier Scientific. 1981. ISBN:0-444-41997-7,
ISBN13: 978-0-444-41997-2.

Audience: **u,f.**

Erb, Uwe & Keller, Harald   **Q179.E64 2001**
Scientific and Technical Acronyms, Symbols, and Abbreviations.
Trade Cloth. John Wiley & Sons, Inc. Hoboken, NJ. 2001.
2114p. ISBN:0-471-38802-5, ISBN13: 978-0-471-38802-9.
Dewey:501/.48. LCCN:2001-017598.

Audience: **l,u,f.** *Choice, 2001.*

Facts on File, Inc. Staff   **Q123.F334 1999**
The Facts on File Encyclopedia of Science, Set. Trade Cloth.
Facts On File, Inc.. New York, NY. 1999. 840p. Facts on File
Ser. ISBN:0-8160-4008-7, ISBN13: 978-0-8160-4008-7.
Dewey:503. LCCN:98-053201.

Audience: **l,u,f.** *Choice, 1999.*

Geller, Elizabeth &   **Q121.M3 2002**
McGraw-Hill Staff
McGraw-Hill Encyclopedia of Science and Technology, Set. Ed.
9. Trade Cloth. McGraw-Hill Professional Publishing. New

York, NY. 2002. 15600p. ISBN:0-07-913665-6, ISBN13:
978-0-07-913665-7. Dewey:503. LCCN:2001-057910.

Audience: **l,u,f.** *Choice, 2002.*

Hathway, D. C.   **Q123 .H35**
Harrap's French and English Science Dictionary. Trade Cloth.
French & European Publications, Inc. New York, NY. 1983.
320p. ISBN:0-8288-0614-4, ISBN13: 978-0-8288-0614-5.
Dewey:503.

Audience: **u,f.**

Hempstead, Colin A.   **T9.E462 2005**
Encyclopedia of Twentieth-Century Technology. Worthington,
William E. (Editor). Routledge. 2005. ISBN:1-57958-386-5,
ISBN13: 978-1-57958-386-6.

Audience: **l,u,f.**

Kucera, Antonin   **Q123 .K7923 1989**
The Compact Dictionary of Exact Science and Technology:
English - German. Ed. 2. Library Binding. French & European
Publications, Inc. New York, NY. 1989. 1470p.
ISBN:0-8288-4044-X, ISBN13: 978-0-8288-4044-6. Dewey:503.

Audience: **u,f.**

Kucera, Antonin   **Q123 .K7923**
The Compact Dictionary of Exact Science and Technology:
German - English, Vol. 2. Ed. 2. Library Binding. French &
European Publications, Inc. New York, NY. 1994. 825p.
ISBN:0-8288-4045-8, ISBN13: 978-0-8288-4045-3. Dewey:503.

Audience: **u,f.**

Malyavskaya, Greta R. &   **Q123.M23 1999**
Shveyeva, Natalia K.
Russian-English Dictionary of Scientific and Engineering Terms:
A Guide to Usage. Trade Cloth. Begell House Publishers, Inc.
New York, NY. 1999. 6p. ISBN:1-56700-128-9, ISBN13:
978-1-56700-128-0. Dewey:503/.9171. LCCN:99-013566.

Audience: **u,f.** *Choice, 1999.*

McGraw-Hill   **Q1.M13 2005**
McGraw-Hill 2006 Yearbook of Science and Technology. Trade
Cloth. McGraw-Hill Professional Publishing. New York, NY.
2005. 448p. ISBN:0-07-146205-8, ISBN13: 978-0-07-146205-1.
Dewey:505.

Audience: **g,l,u,f.**

McGraw-Hill Staff   **Q121**
McGraw-Hill Concise Encyclopedia of Science and Technology.
Ed. 5. Trade Cloth. McGraw-Hill Professional Publishing. New
York, NY. 2004. 2651p. ISBN:0-07-142957-3, ISBN13:
978-0-07-142957-3. Dewey:503. LCCN:2004-054909.

Audience: **g.**

McGraw-Hill Staff   **Q123.M15 2002**
McGraw-Hill Dictionary of Scientific and Technical Terms. Ed.
6. Trade Cloth. McGraw-Hill Professional Publishing. New
York, NY. 2002. 2380p. ISBN:0-07-042313-X, ISBN13:
978-0-07-042313-8. Dewey:503. LCCN:2002-026436.

Audience: **l,u,f.** *Choice, 2003.*

Meyers, Robert A. (Editor)   **Q123.E497 2002**
Encyclopedia of Physical Science and Technology, Set. Ed. 3.
Trade Cloth, Box or Slipcased. Elsevier Science & Technology
Books. Saint Louis, MO. 2001. 15453p. ISBN:0-12-227410-5,
ISBN13: 978-0-12-227410-7. Dewey:503. LCCN:2001-090661.

Audience: **l,u,f.** *Choice, 2002.*

Neurath, Otto (Editor)   **Q175 .F686 1969**
Foundations of the Unity of Science: Toward an International
Encyclopedia of Unified Science, 1. Library Binding. University
of Chicago Press. Chicago, IL. 1995. Foundations of the Unity
of Science Ser., Vols. 1 & 2 ISBN:0-226-57586-1, ISBN13:
978-0-226-57586-5. Dewey:501. LCCN:56-000553.

Audience: **u,f.**

Neurath, Otto (Editor),   **Q175 .F686 1969**
  et al.
Foundations of the Unity of Science: Toward an International
Encyclopedia of Unified Science. Rudolf Carnap & Charles F.
W. Morris (Editors). Trade Cloth. University of Chicago Press.
Chicago, IL. 1971. 1032p. Foundations of the Unity of Science
Ser., Vols. 1 & 2 ISBN:0-226-57588-8, ISBN13:
978-0-226-57588-9. Dewey:501. LCCN:56-000553.

Audience: **u,f.**

Parker, S.   **Q123.M34 1994**
McGraw-Hill Dictionary of Scientific and Technical Terms. Ed.
5. Trade Cloth. McGraw-Hill Professional Publishing. New
York, NY. 1993. 2200p. ISBN:0-07-042333-4, ISBN13:
978-0-07-042333-6. Dewey:503. LCCN:93-034772.

Audience: **l,u,f.** *Choice, 1994.*

Scientific American Editors   **Q173.S427 1999**
Scientific American Science Desk Reference. Trade Cloth. John
Wiley & Sons, Inc. Hoboken, NJ. 1999. 704p. Scientific
American Ser. ISBN:0-471-35675-1, ISBN13:
978-0-471-35675-2. Dewey:500. LCCN:99-032007.

Audience: **g,l,u.** *Choice, 2000.*

Volti, Rudi   **Q121.V65 1999**
The Facts on File Encyclopedia of Science, Technology and
Society, Set. Trade Cloth. Facts On File, Inc.. New York, NY.
1999. 1328p. Facts on File Ser. ISBN:0-8160-3123-1, ISBN13:
978-0-8160-3123-8. Dewey:503. LCCN:98-039014.

Audience: **l,u,f.** *Choice, 1999.*

History

Bono, James J.   **Q125.2.B66 1995**
The Word of God and the Languages of Man: Interpreting
Nature in Early Modern Science and Medicine. Trade Cloth.
University of Wisconsin Press. Chicago, IL. 1995. 332p. Science
and Literature Ser. ISBN:0-299-14790-8, ISBN13:
978-0-299-14790-7. Dewey:509/.03. LCCN:95-015652.

Audience: **l,u,f.** *Choice, 1996.*

Brown Reference Group   **Q124.97**
Medieval Science, Technology and Medicine: An Encyclopedia.
Steven J. Livesey, Thomas F. Glick, Faith Wallis & Daniel A.
Stout (Editors). Paper over Boards. Routledge. New York, NY.
2005. 624p. The Routledge Encyclopedias of the Middle Ages
Ser., Vol. 11 ISBN:0-415-96930-1, ISBN13: 978-0-415-96930-7.
Dewey:509/.02. LCCN:2005-022223.

Audience: **g,l,u.** *Choice, 2006.*

Clagett, Marshall (Editor)   **Q125**
Critical Problems in the History of Science: Proceedings of the
Institute for the History of Science 1957. Trade Paper.
University of Wisconsin Press. Chicago, IL. 2005. 560p.
ISBN:0-299-01874-1, ISBN13: 978-0-299-01874-0. Dewey:509.
LCCN:59-005304.

Audience: **l,u,f.**

Friedlander, Michael W.   **Q180.55.D57F75 1995**
At the Fringes of Science: Science, Science Contested and
Pseudo-Science. Trade Cloth. Westview Press. Boulder, CO.
1995. 216p. ISBN:0-8133-2200-6, ISBN13: 978-0-8133-2200-1.
Dewey:500. LCCN:94-035048.

Audience: **g,l.** *Choice, 1995.*

Greene, John C.   **Q127.U6.G69 1984**
American Science in the Age of Jefferson. Cloth Text. Blackwell
Publishing Professional. Ames, IA. 1984. 484p.
ISBN:0-8138-0101-X, ISBN13: 978-0-8138-0101-8.
Dewey:509.73. LCCN:83-008513.

Audience: **g,u,f.** *B*

Harding, Sandra (Editor)   **Q175.55 .R3 1993**
The Racial Economy of Science: Toward a Democratic Future.
Trade Paper. Indiana University Press. Bloomington, IN. 1993.
544p. Race, Gender and Science Ser. ISBN:0-253-20810-6,
ISBN13: 978-0-253-20810-1. Dewey:306.4/5. LCCN:92-031286.

Audience: **g.** *Choice, 1994.*

Hassenbruch, Arne (Editor)   **Q125.R335 2000**
Reader's Guide to the History of Science. Trade Cloth. Fitzroy
Dearborn Publishers, Inc. Chicago, IL. 2000. 964p.
ISBN:1-884964-29-X, ISBN13: 978-1-884964-29-9. Dewey:509.
LCCN:2001-270888.

Audience: **g,l,u.** *Choice, 2001.*

Jaffe, Bernard   **Q127.U6 J27 1980**
Men of Science in America: The Story of American Science
Told Through the Lives and Achievements of Twenty
Outstanding Men from Earliest Colonial Times to the Present
Day. I. Bernard Cohen (Editor). Library Binding. Ayer Company
Publishers, Inc. Manchester, NH. 1980. Three Centuries of
Science in America Ser. ISBN:0-405-12551-8, ISBN13:
978-0-405-12551-5. Dewey:509/.2/2. LCCN:79-007969.

Audience: **g,l,u,f.** *B*

Katz, James E.   **Q127.U6.K37**
Presidential Politics and Science Policy. Trade Cloth.
Greenwood Publishing Group, Inc. Portsmouth, NH. 1978. xix,
292 p. ;p. Praeger Special Studies ISBN:0-03-040941-1,
ISBN13: 978-0-03-040941-7. Dewey:509/.73. LCCN:77-014024.

Audience: **g.** *B*

Kohlstedt, Sally G. &   **Q127.U6H54 1986**
  Rossiter, Margaret (Editors)
Historical Writing on American Science: Perspectives and
Prospects. Trade Paper. Johns Hopkins University Press.
Baltimore, MD. 1994. 330p. ISBN:0-8018-3438-4, ISBN13:
978-0-8018-3438-7. Dewey:509/.73. LCCN:86-020890.

Audience: **u,f.** *B*

Kohlstedt, Sally G. &   **Q125**
  Rossiter, Margaret (Editors)
Historical Writing on American Science, Vol. 1. Trade Cloth.
University of Chicago Press. Chicago, IL. 1991. 322p. Osiris
Ser. ISBN:0-934235-02-3, ISBN13: 978-0-934235-02-0.
Dewey:509/.73;.

Audience: **u,f.**

Krebs, Robert E.   **Q124.97.K73 2004**
Groundbreaking Scientific Experiments, Inventions, and
Discoveries of the Middle Ages and the Renaissance. Cloth
Text. Greenwood Publishing Group, Inc. Portsmouth, NH. 2004.
344p. Groundbreaking Scientific Experiments, Inventions, and

Discoveries Through the Ages Ser. ISBN:0-313-32433-6, ISBN13: 978-0-313-32433-8. Dewey:509.4/0902. LCCN:2003-060075.

Audience: **g,l,u.** *Choice, 2004.*

Krebs, Robert E. & Krebs,   **Q124**
  Carolyn A.
Groundbreaking Scientific Experiments, Inventions, and Discoveries of the Ancient World. Cloth Text. Greenwood Publishing Group, Inc. Portsmouth, NH. 2003. 400p. Groundbreaking Scientific Experiments, Inventions, and Discoveries Through the Ages Ser. ISBN:0-313-31342-3, ISBN13: 978-0-313-31342-4. Dewey:509.3. LCCN:2003-045530.

Audience: **g,l,u.**

Laudan, Larry   **Q125.L34**
Progress and Its Problems: Towards a Theory of Scientific Growth. Trade Cloth. University of California Press. Berkeley, CA. 1977. x, 257 p. ;p. ISBN:0-520-03330-2, ISBN13: 978-0-520-03330-6. Dewey:501. LCCN:76-024586.

Audience: **u,f.** *B*

Leroy, Francis (Editor)   **Q141.C252 2003**
A Century of Nobel Prize Recipients: Chemistry, Physics, and Medicine. Paper over Boards. Marcel Dekker Inc. New York, NY. 2003. 300p. ISBN:0-8247-0876-8, ISBN13: 978-0-8247-0876-4. Dewey:509.2/2 B. LCCN:2002-044452.

Audience: **u,f.** *Choice, 2004.*

Lindberg, David C. (Editor)   **Q124.97**
Science in the Middle Ages. Library Binding. University of Chicago Press. Chicago, IL. 1980. xv, 549p. Chicago History of Science and Medicine Ser. ISBN:0-226-48232-4, ISBN13: 978-0-226-48232-3. Dewey:509/.02. LCCN:78-005367.

Audience: **g,l,u.** *B*

Montgomery, Scott L.   **Q124.M66 2000**
Science in Translation: Movements of Knowledge Through Cultures and Time. Trade Cloth. University of Chicago Press. Chicago, IL. 2000. 333p. ISBN:0-226-53480-4, ISBN13: 978-0-226-53480-0. Dewey:500. LCCN:99-053389.

Audience: **g,l,u,f.** *Choice, 2000.*

Price, Derek D.   **Q125**
Science since Babylon. Trade Cloth. Yale University Press. Cumberland, RI. 1975. xvi, 215p. ISBN:0-300-01797-9, ISBN13: 978-0-300-01797-7. Dewey:509. LCCN:74-079976.

Audience: **g,l,u,f.**

Reingold, Nathan (Editor)   **Q127.U6S318 1985**
Science in Nineteenth-Century America: A Documentary History. Trade Paper. University of Chicago Press. Chicago, IL. 1985. 347p. ISBN:0-226-70947-7, ISBN13: 978-0-226-70947-5. Dewey:509.73. LCCN:85-001021.

Audience: **u,f.**

Ronan, Colin A.   **Q125.R7426 1982**
Science: Its History and Development among the World's Cultures. Trade Cloth. Facts On File, Inc.. New York, NY. 1983. 528p. ISBN:0-87196-745-6, ISBN13: 978-0-87196-745-9. Dewey:509. LCCN:82-012176.

Audience: **g.** *B*

Rosenberg, Charles E.   **Q127.U6R618 1997**
No Other Gods: On Science and American Social Thought. Ed. 2. Trade Cloth. Johns Hopkins University Press. Baltimore, MD.

1997. 336p. ISBN:0-8018-5608-6, ISBN13: 978-0-8018-5608-2. Dewey:303.48/3/0973. LCCN:96-051657.

Audience: **u,f.** *B*

Schlagel, Richard H.   **Q174.8.S335 1995**
From Myth to Modern Mind: A Study of the Origins and Growth of Scientific Thought, Vol. I. Ed. 3. Paper Text. Peter Lang Publishing, Inc. New York, NY. 1995. XII, 498p. American University Studies, Vol. 170:Philosophy ISBN:0-8204-2672-5, ISBN13: 978-0-8204-2672-3. Dewey:509. LCCN:94-047030.

Audience: **g,l,u.** *Choice, 1996.*

Schlagel, Richard H.   **Q174.8.S335 1995**
From Myth to Modern Mind: From Copernicus to Quantum Mechanics. Paper Text. Peter Lang Publishing, Inc. New York, NY. 1996. 580p. American University Studies, Vol. 171:Philosophy ISBN:0-8204-2699-7, ISBN13: 978-0-8204-2699-0. Dewey:509. LCCN:94-047030.

Audience: **g,l,u.** *Choice, 1997.*

Selin, Helaine (Editor)   **Q124.8.E53 1997**
Encyclopaedia of the History of Science, Technology, and Medicine in Non-Western Cultures. Trade Cloth. Springer. New York, NY. 1997. 1124p. ISBN:0-7923-4066-3, ISBN13: 978-0-7923-4066-9. Dewey:509. LCCN:96-036625.

Audience: **u,f.** *Choice, 1998.*

Shectman, Jonathan   **Q125**
Groundbreaking Scientific Experiments, Inventions and Discoveries of the 18th Century. Cloth Text. Greenwood Publishing Group, Inc. Portsmouth, NH. 2003. 368p. Groundbreaking Scientific Experiments, Inventions, and Discoveries Through the Ages Ser. ISBN:0-313-32015-2, ISBN13: 978-0-313-32015-6. Dewey:509/.033. LCCN:2002-075306.

Audience: **g.** *Choice, 2004.*

Singer, Charles   **Q125**
Short History of Scientific Ideas to 1900. Trade Cloth. Oxford University Press, Inc. New York, NY. 1962. Oxford Paperbacks Ser. ISBN:0-19-881049-0, ISBN13: 978-0-19-881049-0. Dewey:509.

Audience: **g,l,u.**

Struik, Dirk J.   **Q127.U6S8 1991**
Yankee Science in the Making. Trade Paper. Dover Publications, Inc. Mineola, NY. 1992. 544p. ISBN:0-486-26927-2, ISBN13: 978-0-486-26927-6. Dewey:509.73. LCCN:91-030933.

Audience: **g,l.**

Taton, Rene (Editor)   **Q125 .T23**
Histoire Generale des Sciences. Trade Cloth. French & European Publications, Inc. New York, NY. ISBN:0-318-52025-7, ISBN13: 978-0-318-52025-4. Dewey:509.

Audience: **u,f.**

Wightman, William P.   **Q125 .W66 1974**
The Growth of Scientific Ideas. Trade Cloth. Greenwood Publishing Group, Inc. Portsmouth, NH. 1974. 495p. ISBN:0-8371-7484-8, ISBN13: 978-0-8371-7484-6. Dewey:509. LCCN:74-004732.

Audience: **g,l,u.**

Windelspecht, Michael   **Q125**
Groundbreaking Scientific Experiments, Inventions and Discoveries of the 17th Century. Cloth Text. Greenwood

Publishing Group, Inc. Portsmouth, NH. 2001. 304p. Groundbreaking Scientific Experiments, Inventions and Discoveries Through the Ages Ser. ISBN:0-313-31501-9, ISBN13: 978-0-313-31501-5. Dewey:509/.032. LCCN:2001-023316.

Audience: **g.** *Choice, 2002.*

Windelspecht, Michael   **Q125**
Groundbreaking Scientific Experiments, Inventions and Discoveries of the 19th Century. Cloth Text. Greenwood Publishing Group, Inc. Portsmouth, NH. 2003. 304p. Groundbreaking Scientific Experiments, Inventions, and Discoveries Through the Ages Ser. ISBN:0-313-31969-3, ISBN13: 978-0-313-31969-3. Dewey:509.034. LCCN:2002-075305.

Audience: **g.** *Choice, 2003.*

Modern

Bodanis, David   **QC522**
Electric Universe: How Electricity Switched on the Modern World. Three Rivers Press. 2005. ISBN:0-307-33598-4, ISBN13: 978-0-307-33598-2.

Audience: **g,l.**

Butterfield, Herbert   **Q125**
The Origins of Modern Science. Trade Paper. Simon & Schuster. New York, NY. 1997. 256p. ISBN:0-684-83637-8, ISBN13: 978-0-684-83637-9. Dewey:509.

Audience: **g,l,u,f.**

Bynum, William F. (Editor),   **Q125.D45**
  et al.
Dictionary of the History of Science. E. Janet Browne & Roy Porter (Editors). Trade Cloth. Princeton University Press. Princeton, NJ. 1982. 528p. ISBN:0-691-08287-1, ISBN13: 978-0-691-08287-5. Dewey:509. LCCN:81-047116.

Audience: **g,l,u,f.** *B*

Clagett, Marshall   **Q125 .C49 1988**
Greek Science in Antiquity. Trade Cloth. Ayer Company Publishers, Inc. Manchester, NH. 1977. Essay Index Reprint Ser. ISBN:0-88143-073-0, ISBN13: 978-0-88143-073-8. Dewey:509.38. LCCN:77-142615.

Audience: **g,l.** *B*

Cohen, H. Floris   **Q125.C538 1994**
The Scientific Revolution: A Historiographical Inquiry. Trade Paper. University of Chicago Press. Chicago, IL. 1994. 680p. ISBN:0-226-11280-2, ISBN13: 978-0-226-11280-0. Dewey:509.4/09032. LCCN:93-041784.

Audience: **u,f.** *Choice, 1995.*

Cohen, I. Bernard   **Q125.C54**
Album of Science: From Leonardo to Lavoisier, 1450-1800. Trade Cloth. Thomson Gale. Farmington Hills, MI. 1998. 320p. ISBN:0-684-15377-7, ISBN13: 978-0-684-15377-3. Dewey:509/.03. LCCN:80-015542.

Audience: **g,l.** *B*

Cohen, I. Bernard   **Q125.C542 1985**
Revolution in Science. Trade Cloth. Harvard University Press. Cambridge, MA. 1985. 704p. ISBN:0-674-76777-2, ISBN13: 978-0-674-76777-5. Dewey:509. LCCN:84-012916.

Audience: **g,l.** *B* *Choice, 1986.*

Crombie, A. C.   **Q127.E8C74 1996**
Science, Art and Nature in Medieval and Modern Thought. Trade Cloth. Continuum International Publishing Group, Ltd. London, 2003. 450p. ISBN:1-85285-067-1, ISBN13: 978-1-85285-067-8. Dewey:509/.4. LCCN:95-049964.

Audience: **g,l.**

Crombie, Alistair Cameron   **Q0125**
Medieval and Early Modern Science, Vol. 1. Ed. 2. Trade Paper. Books on Demand. Ann Arbor, MI. 350p. ISBN:0-608-32814-6, ISBN13: 978-0-608-32814-0. Dewey:509. LCCN:63-019150.

Audience: **g.** *B*

Crombie, Alistair Cameron   **Q0125**
Medieval and Early Modern Science, Vol. 2. Ed. 2. Trade Paper. Books on Demand. Ann Arbor, MI. 420p. ISBN:0-608-32815-4, ISBN13: 978-0-608-32815-7. Dewey:509. LCCN:63-019150.

Audience: **g.** *B*

Dampier, William C.   **Q125 .D17**
A History of Science and its Relations with Philosophy and Religion. I. Bernard Cohen (Contribution by). Trade Paper. Cambridge University Press. New York, NY. 1948. 572p. ISBN:0-521-09366-X, ISBN13: 978-0-521-09366-8. Dewey:509.

Audience: **g,l,u,f.**

Dijksterhuis, E. J.   **Q125.D512 1986**
The Mechanization of the World Picture: Pythagoras to Newton. C. Dikshoorn (Translator), Dirk J. Struik (Foreword by). Trade Cloth. Princeton University Press. Princeton, NJ. 1986. 558p. ISBN:0-691-08403-3, ISBN13: 978-0-691-08403-9. Dewey:509. LCCN:85-043374.

Audience: **g,l.** *B*

Gillespie, Charles C.   **QC32.P75 1991**
Edge of Objectivity: An Essay in the History of Scientific Ideas. Trade Cloth. Princeton University Press. Princeton, NJ. 1960. 576p. ISBN:0-691-07952-8, ISBN13: 978-0-691-07952-3. Dewey:530/.076. LCCN:90-047703.

Audience: **l,u,f.**

Goldstein, Thomas   **Q125.2.G64**
Dawn of Modern Science: From the Arabs to Leonardo Da Vinci. Trade Cloth. Houghton Mifflin Company. New York, NY. 1980. xvii, 297p. ISBN:0-395-26298-4, ISBN13: 978-0-395-26298-6. Dewey:509/.024. LCCN:79-023753.

Audience: **g,l.** *B*

Hankins, Thomas L.   **Q125 .H355 1985**
Science and the Enlightenment. Cloth Text. Cambridge University Press. New York, NY. 1985. 224p. Cambridge History of Science Ser. ISBN:0-521-24349-1, ISBN13: 978-0-521-24349-0. Dewey:509. LCCN:84-016988.

Audience: **g,l,u.** *B* *Choice, 1985.*

Holton, Gerald   **Q173.H7342 1995**
Einstein, History and Other Passions. Cloth Text. Springer. New York, NY. 1995. 320p. AIP Masters of Modern Physics Ser. ISBN:1-56396-333-7, ISBN13: 978-1-56396-333-9. Dewey:500. LCCN:94-037483.

Audience: **g,l,u,f.** *Choice, 1995.*

Holton, Gerald   **Q125.H722**
Thematic Origins of Scientific Thought: Kepler to Einstein. Trade Cloth. Harvard University Press. Cambridge, MA. 1973. 300p. ISBN:0-674-87745-4, ISBN13: 978-0-674-87745-0. Dewey:509. LCCN:72-083467.

Audience: **g,l,u,f.** *B*

Kaku, Michio   **QB981**
Parallel Worlds: A Journey Through Creation, Higher
Dimensions, and the Future of the Cosmos. Doubleday. 2005.
ISBN:0-385-50986-3, ISBN13: 978-0-385-50986-2.
Audience: **g.**

Laidler, Keith J.   **Q125.L25 1998**
Light Such a Candle: Chapters in the History of Science and
Technology. Cloth Text. Oxford University Press, Inc. New
York, NY. 1998. 400p. ISBN:0-19-850056-4, ISBN13:
978-0-19-850056-8. Dewey:609. LCCN:97-024690.
Audience: **g,l,u.** *Choice, 1998.*

Menard, Henry W.   **Q125**
Science: Growth and Change. Trade Cloth. Harvard University
Press. Cambridge, MA. 1971. xiv, 215p. ISBN:0-674-79280-7,
ISBN13: 978-0-674-79280-7. Dewey:509. LCCN:77-156138.
Audience: **g,l,u.** *B*

Rossi, Paolo   **Q127.E8R6713 2001**
The Birth of Modern Science. Book, Other. Blackwell
Publishing, Inc. Malden, MA. 2001. 288p. Making of Europe
Ser. ISBN:0-631-20562-4, ISBN13: 978-0-631-20562-3.
Dewey:509.4. LCCN:00-049429.
Audience: **g,l,u,f.** *Choice, 2001.*

Rossi, Paolo   **Q127.E8R6713 2001**
The Birth of Modern Science. Trade Paper. Blackwell
Publishing, Inc. Malden, MA. 2001. 288p. The Making of
Europe Ser. ISBN:0-631-22711-3, ISBN13: 978-0-631-22711-3.
Dewey:509.4. LCCN:00-049429.
Audience: **g,l,u,f.** *Choice, 2001.*

Shea, William R.   **Q125.2.S54 1990**
The Magic of Numbers and Motion: The Scientific Career of
Rene Descartes. Trade Cloth. Watson Publishing International.
Sagamore Beach, MA. 1990. 416p. ISBN:0-88135-098-2,
ISBN13: 978-0-88135-098-2. Dewey:509.2 B.
LCCN:89-010813.
Audience: **g,l,u.** *Choice, 1991.*

Silver, Brian L.   **T14.5**
The Ascent of Science. Trade Paper. Oxford University Press,
Inc. New York, NY. 2000. 552p. ISBN:0-19-513427-3, ISBN13:
978-0-19-513427-8. Dewey:303.48/3.
Audience: **g,l.** *Choice, 1999.*

Williams, L. Pearce   **Q125.6.W54**
Album of Science: The Nineteenth Century. Trade Cloth.
Thomson Gale. Farmington Hills, MI. 1998. 432p.
ISBN:0-684-15047-6, ISBN13: 978-0-684-15047-5.
Dewey:509/.034. LCCN:77-003907.
Audience: **g.** *B*

Special Periods. Special Topics

Abramson, Norman   **Q360 .A2**
Information Theory and Coding. Trade Cloth. McGraw-Hill
Companies, The. New York, NY. 1963. Electronics Ser.
ISBN:0-07-000145-6, ISBN13: 978-0-07-000145-9.
Dewey:519.7.
Audience: **l,u,f.** *B*

Almqvist, Ebbe   **TP242.A38 2002**
History of Industrial Gases. Trade Cloth. Springer. New York,
NY. 2003. 440p. ISBN:0-306-47277-5, ISBN13:
978-0-306-47277-0. Dewey:665.7/09. LCCN:2002-066906.
Audience: **g,l,u,f.** *Choice, 2003.*

Applebaum, Wilbur   **Q125**
Encyclopedia of the Scientific Revolution from Copernicus to
Newton. Garland. 2000. ISBN:0-8153-1503-1, ISBN13:
978-0-8153-1503-2.
Audience: **g,l.**

Asimov, Isaac   **Q125.A765 1994**
Asimov's Chronology of Science and Discovery. Ed. 2. Trade
Cloth. HarperCollins Publishers. New York, NY. 1994. 800p.
ISBN:0-06-270113-4, ISBN13: 978-0-06-270113-8. Dewey:509.
LCCN:94-002504.
Audience: **g,l.** *Choice, 1990.*

Bodanis, David   **QC522**
Electric Universe: How Electricity Switched on the Modern
World. Three Rivers Press. 2005. ISBN:0-307-33598-4, ISBN13:
978-0-307-33598-2.
Audience: **g,l.**

Briggs, Asa   **TJ275.B825 1982**
The Power of Steam: An Illustrated History of the World's
Steam Age. Trade Cloth. University of Chicago Press. Chicago,
IL. 1982. 208p. ISBN:0-226-07495-1, ISBN13:
978-0-226-07495-5. Dewey:621.1/09. LCCN:82-040321.
Audience: **g.**

Debus, Allen George   **Q125.2**
Man and Nature in the Renaissance. Cloth Text. Cambridge
University Press. New York, NY. 1978. 169p. Cambridge
History of Science Ser. ISBN:0-521-21972-8, ISBN13:
978-0-521-21972-3. Dewey:509/.4. LCCN:77-091085.
Audience: **g,l,u.** *B*

Hall, A. Rupert   **Q125**
The Revolution in Science, 1500-1750. Ed. 3. Trade Paper.
Longman Publishing Group. White Plains, NY. 1989. 384p.
ISBN:0-582-49133-9, ISBN13: 978-0-582-49133-5.
Dewey:509/.03. LCCN:82-008978.
Audience: **g,l,u,f.** *B*

Hall, Marie B.   **Q125.2.H35 1994**
Scientific Renaissance, 1450-1630. Trade Paper. Dover
Publications, Inc. Mineola, NY. 1994. 376p.
ISBN:0-486-28115-9, ISBN13: 978-0-486-28115-5.
Dewey:509.4/09024. LCCN:94-026231.
Audience: **g.**

Hanford Cultural and   **TK9025.H36 2003**
   Historic Resources Program Staff (Contribution by)
Hanford Site Historic District: History of the Plutonium
Production Facilities, 1943-1990. Trade Cloth. Battelle Press.
Columbus, OH. 2003. 624p. ISBN:1-57477-133-7, ISBN13:
978-1-57477-133-6. Dewey:623.4/5119/0979751.
LCCN:2002-034473.
Audience: **g,u,f.** *Choice, 2003.*

Holton, Gerald   **Q180.A3H65 2005**
Victory and Vexation in Science: Einstein, Bohr, Heisenberg,
and Others. Trade Cloth. Harvard University Press. Cambridge,
MA. 2005. 244p. ISBN:0-674-01519-3, ISBN13:
978-0-674-01519-7. Dewey:500. LCCN:2004-060572.
Audience: **g,l,u,f.** *Choice, 2005.*

Kaku, Michio   **QB981**
Parallel Worlds: A Journey Through Creation, Higher
Dimensions, and the Future of the Cosmos. Doubleday. 2005.
ISBN:0-385-50986-3, ISBN13: 978-0-385-50986-2.
Audience: **g.**

Nelkin, Dorothy   **Q183.3.A1.N44**
Science Textbook Controversies and the Politics of Equal Time.
Trade Cloth. MIT Press. Cambridge, MA. 1977. xi, 174 p. ;p.
ISBN:0-262-14027-6, ISBN13: 978-0-262-14027-0.
Dewey:507/.1073. LCCN:76-058459.
Audience: **g.** *B*

Ornstein, Martha   **Q125 .O8 1975**
The Role of Scientific Societies in the Seventeenth Century.
Trade Cloth. Ayer Company Publishers, Inc. Manchester, NH.
1980. History, Philosophy, and Sociology of Science Ser.
ISBN:0-405-06609-0, ISBN13: 978-0-405-06609-2.
Dewey:506/.2. LCCN:74-026282.
Audience: **l,u.**

Smith, Pamela H.   **N72.S3S65 2006**
The Body of the Artisan: Art and Experience in the Scientific
Revolution. Trade Paper. University of Chicago Press. Chicago,
IL. 2006. 408p. ISBN:0-226-76423-0, ISBN13:
978-0-226-76423-8. Dewey:509/.4/0903.
Audience: **g,l,u,f.** *Choice, 2004.*

Stuster, Jack   **Q180.55.P75S78 1996**
Bold Endeavors: Lessons from Polar and Space Exploration.
Trade Cloth. Naval Institute Press. Annapolis, MD. 1996. 408p.
ISBN:1-55750-749-X, ISBN13: 978-1-55750-749-5.
Dewey:155.9/6. LCCN:96-008131.
Audience: **g,l,u,f.** *Choice, 1997.*

By Country

Doern, G. Bruce   **Q127.C2**
Science and Politics in Canada. Trade Cloth. McGill-Queen's
University Press. Montreal, PQ. 1972. xiv, 238p.
ISBN:0-7735-0108-8, ISBN13: 978-0-7735-0108-9.
Dewey:354/.71/00855. LCCN:79-180255.
Audience: **u,f.** *B*

Elman, Benjamin A.   **Q127.C5**
A Cultural History of Modern Science in China. Harvard
University Press. 2007.
Audience: **g,l,u,f.**

Farrington, Benjamin   **Q127.G7**
Greek Science: Its Meaning for Us. Trade Cloth. Spokesman
Books. Nottingham, 1981. 320p. ISBN:0-85124-287-1, ISBN13:
978-0-85124-287-3. Dewey:509/.38.
Audience: **l,u,f.** *B*

Gillispie, Charles C.   **Q127.F8.G53**
Science and Polity in France at the End of the Old Regime.
Trade Cloth. Princeton University Press. Princeton, NJ. 1981.
472p. ISBN:0-691-08233-2, ISBN13: 978-0-691-08233-2.
Dewey:509.44. LCCN:80-007521.
Audience: **g,l,u,f.** *B*

Gillispie, Charles Coulston   **Q127.F8G53 2004**
Science and Polity in France: The Revolutionary and
Napoleonic Years. Princeton Univeristy Press. 2004.
ISBN:0-691-11541-9, ISBN13: 978-0-691-11541-2.
Audience: **g,l,u,f.**

Graham, Loren R.   **Q127.S696G73 1987**
Science, Philosophy, and Human Behavior in the Soviet Union.
Cloth Text. Columbia University Press. New York, NY. 1987.
672p. ISBN:0-231-06442-X, ISBN13: 978-0-231-06442-2.
Dewey:509/.47. LCCN:86-026357.
Audience: **g.** *Choice, 1988.*

Graham, Loren R.   **Q127.S696 G729 1993**
Science in Russia and the Soviet Union: A Short History.
George Basalla & Owen Hannaway (Contribution by). Trade
Paper. Cambridge University Press. New York, NY. 1994. 351p.
Cambridge Studies in the History of Science Ser.
ISBN:0-521-28789-8, ISBN13: 978-0-521-28789-0.
Dewey:509.47. LCCN:92-005087.
Audience: **g,u,f.** *Choice, 1993.*

Hunter, Michael   **Q127.G4**
Science and Society in Restoration England. Trade Cloth.
Ashgate Publishing, Ltd. Aldershot, 1992. 260p. Modern
Revivals in History Ser. ISBN:0-7512-0075-1, ISBN13:
978-0-7512-0075-1. Dewey:306/.45/0942.
Audience: **g.** *B*

Institute of National Science   **Q127.C5A74 1983**
  Staff & Chinese Academy of Science Staff
Ancient China's Technology and Science. Trade Cloth. China
Books & Periodicals, Inc. South San Francisco, CA. 1983. 632p.
China Knowledge Ser. ISBN:0-8351-1001-X, ISBN13:
978-0-8351-1001-3. Dewey:509.31. LCCN:83-222110.
Audience: **g.** *B*

Lloyd, G. E. R.   **Q127.G7**
Greek Science after Aristotle. Trade Paper. W. W. Norton &
Company, Inc. New York, NY. 1975. 208p. Ancient Culture and
Society Ser. ISBN:0-393-00780-4, ISBN13: 978-0-393-00780-0.
Dewey:509/.38. LCCN:72-011959.
Audience: **g,l,u,f.** *B*

Lloyd, G. E. R.   **Q127.G7**
Early Greek Science: Thales to Aristotle. Moses I. Finley
(Editor). Trade Paper. W. W. Norton & Company, Inc. New
York, NY. 1974. 174p. Ancient Culture and Society Ser.
ISBN:0-393-00583-6, ISBN13: 978-0-393-00583-7.
Dewey:509/.38.
Audience: **g,l,u,f.** *B*

Macrakis, Kristie   **Q180.G4.M3 1993**
Surviving the Swastika: Scientific Research in Nazi Germany.
Cloth Text. Oxford University Press, Inc. New York, NY. 1993.
320p. ISBN:0-19-507010-0, ISBN13: 978-0-19-507010-1.
Dewey:506/.043/09043. LCCN:93-019919.
Audience: **l,u,f.** *Choice, 1994.*

Needham, Joseph   **Q127.C5.N42 1969**
The Grand Titration; Science and Society in East and West.
Trade Cloth. University of Toronto Press. Toronto, ON. 1969.
350p. ISBN:0-8020-1636-7, ISBN13: 978-0-8020-1636-2.
Dewey:301.2/4. LCCN:76-483302.
Audience: **u,f.** *B*

Needham, Joseph   **Q127.C5.N46 1981**
Science in Traditional China. Trade Cloth. Harvard University
Press. Cambridge, MA. 1981. 144p. ISBN:0-674-79438-9,
ISBN13: 978-0-674-79438-2. Dewey:509.51. LCCN:81-006962.
Audience: **g,l,u,f.** *B*

Formats: Web: ☐   Ebook: 🄴   CD/DVD-ROM: 🚿   BCL3: *B*

Orleans, Leo A. (Editor)   Q180.C6.S33
Science in Contemporary China. Trade Cloth. Stanford
University Press. Palo Alto, CA. 1980. 640p.
ISBN:0-8047-1078-3, ISBN13: 978-0-8047-1078-7.
Dewey:509/.51. LCCN:79-065178.

Audience: **u,f.** *B*

Sardar, Ziauddin   Q180.M62/
Science and Technology in the Middle East: A Guide to Issues,
Organizations and Institutions. Ziauddin Sardar (Editor). Gale
Group. 1993. Longman Guide to World Science and Technology
Ser. ISBN:0-582-90052-2, ISBN13: 978-0-582-90052-3.

Audience: **l,u,f.** *B*

Sarton, George   Q127.G7
Hellenistic Science and Culture in the Last Three Centuries.
Trade Cloth. Peter Smith Publisher, Inc. Magnolia, MA. 1994.
ISBN:0-8446-6736-6, ISBN13: 978-0-8446-6736-2.
Dewey:509.38.

Audience: **g,l,u,f.**

Sigurdson, Jon   Q127.C5
Technology and Science, Peoples Republic of China:
Introduction. Trade Cloth. Pergamon Press. Kidlington, 1980.
vii, 169p. ISBN:0-08-024288-X, ISBN13: 978-0-08-024288-0.
Dewey:509/.51. LCCN:79-040575.

Audience: **l,u,f.** *B*

Simon, Denis F. & Goldman,   Q127.C5S333 1989
   Merle R. (Editors)
Science and Technology in Post-Mao China. Trade Paper.
Harvard University, Asia Center. Cambridge, MA. 1988. 460p.
Harvard Contemporary China Ser., No. 5 ISBN:0-674-79475-3,
ISBN13: 978-0-674-79475-7. Dewey:338.95106.
LCCN:88-028456.

Audience: **u,f.** *Choice, 1989.*

Tang, Tong B.   Q127.C5
Science and Technology in China. Paper Text. Longman
Publishing Group. White Plains, NY. 1991. 269p. Guides to
World Science and Technology Ser. ISBN:0-582-90056-5,
ISBN13: 978-0-582-90056-1. Dewey:509/.51. LCCN:84-132986.

Audience: **g.** *B*

Vucinich, Alexander S.   Q127.R9V8
Science in Russian Culture: A History to 1860. Trade Cloth.
Stanford University Press. Palo Alto, CA. 1963. xv, 463p.
ISBN:0-8047-0157-1, ISBN13: 978-0-8047-0157-0.
Dewey:509.47.

Audience: **g.**

Vucinich, Alexander S.   Q127.R9
Science in Russian Culture, 1861-1917. Trade Cloth. Stanford
University Press. Palo Alto, CA. 1970. xvi, 576p.
ISBN:0-8047-0738-3, ISBN13: 978-0-8047-0738-1.
Dewey:509.47. LCCN:75-107650.

Audience: **g.**

Webster, Charles   Q125.W35 2002
The Great Instauration: Science, Medicine and Reform,
1626-1660. Ed. 2. Paper Text. Peter Lang Publishing, Inc. New
York, NY. 2002. 670p. Studies in the History of Medicine, Vol.
3 ISBN:0-8204-5616-0, ISBN13: 978-0-8204-5616-4.
Dewey:509.42/09/032. LCCN:2002-069528.

Audience: **l,u,f.**

United States

Q179.97
Science.Gov.
http://www.science.gov

Audience: **g,l,u,f.**

Baxter, James Phinney   Q127.U6
Scientists against Time. Trade Cloth. MIT Press. Cambridge,
MA. 1968. ISBN:0-262-02039-4, ISBN13: 978-0-262-02039-8.
Dewey:507.2.

Audience: **l,u,f.** *B*

Daniels, George H.   Q127.U6.D33
Science in American Society; a Social History. Trade Cloth.
Alfred A. Knopf Inc. New York, NY. 1971. xii, 390, x pp.
ISBN:0-394-44386-1, ISBN13: 978-0-394-44386-7.
Dewey:301.2/43/0973. LCCN:79-118708.

Audience: **g,l,u,f.** *B*

Dickson, David   Q127.U6D53 1988
The New Politics of Science. Trade Paper. University of
Chicago Press. Chicago, IL. 1993. 411p. ISBN:0-226-14763-0,
ISBN13: 978-0-226-14763-5. Dewey:306/.45. LCCN:87-034275.

Audience: **g.** *B*

Geiger, Roger L.   Q180.U5G34 1986
To Advance Knowledge: The Growth of American Research
Universities, 1900-1940. Cloth Text. Oxford University Press,
Inc. New York, NY. 1986. 335p. ISBN:0-19-503803-7, ISBN13:
978-0-19-503803-3. Dewey:001.4/0973. LCCN:85-030971.

Audience: **g.** *B Choice, 1987.*

Greene, John C.   Q127.U6.G69 1984
American Science in the Age of Jefferson. Cloth Text. Blackwell
Publishing Professional. Ames, IA. 1984. 484p.
ISBN:0-8138-0101-X, ISBN13: 978-0-8138-0101-8.
Dewey:509.73. LCCN:83-008513.

Audience: **g,u,f.** *B*

Jaffe, Bernard   Q127.U6 J27 1980
Men of Science in America: The Story of American Science
Told Through the Lives and Achievements of Twenty
Outstanding Men from Earliest Colonial Times to the Present
Day. I. Bernard Cohen (Editor). Library Binding. Ayer Company
Publishers, Inc. Manchester, NH. 1980. Three Centuries of
Science in America Ser. ISBN:0-405-12551-8, ISBN13:
978-0-405-12551-5. Dewey:509/.2/2. LCCN:79-007969.

Audience: **g,l,u,f.** *B*

Katz, James E.   Q127.U6.K37
Presidential Politics and Science Policy. Trade Cloth.
Greenwood Publishing Group, Inc. Portsmouth, NH. 1978. xix,
292 p. ;p. Praeger Special Studies ISBN:0-03-040941-1,
ISBN13: 978-0-03-040941-7. Dewey:509/.73. LCCN:77-014024.

Audience: **g.** *B*

Kohlstedt, Sally G. &   Q127.U6H54 1986
   Rossiter, Margaret (Editors)
Historical Writing on American Science: Perspectives and
Prospects. Trade Paper. Johns Hopkins University Press.
Baltimore, MD. 1994. 330p. ISBN:0-8018-3438-4, ISBN13:
978-0-8018-3438-7. Dewey:509/.73. LCCN:86-020890.

Audience: **u,f.** *B*

Kohlstedt, Sally G. &   **Q125**
  Rossiter, Margaret (Editors)
Historical Writing on American Science, Vol. 1. Trade Cloth.
University of Chicago Press. Chicago, IL. 1991. 322p. Osiris
Ser. ISBN:0-934235-02-3, ISBN13: 978-0-934235-02-0.
Dewey:509/.73;.
                                          Audience: **u,f.**

Lambright, W. Henry   **Q127.U6L29 1985**
Presidential Management of Science and Technology: The
Johnson Presidency. Trade Cloth. University of Texas Press.
Austin, TX. 1985. 238p. Administrative History of the Johnson
Presidency Ser. ISBN:0-292-76494-4, ISBN13:
978-0-292-76494-1. Dewey:338.97306. LCCN:84-028420.
                          Audience: **u,f.** ℬ *Choice, 1985.*

Laudan, Larry   **Q125.L34**
Progress and Its Problems: Towards a Theory of Scientific
Growth. Trade Cloth. University of California Press. Berkeley,
CA. 1977. x, 257 p. ;p. ISBN:0-520-03330-2, ISBN13:
978-0-520-03330-6. Dewey:501. LCCN:76-024586.
                                      Audience: **u,f.** ℬ

McGrath, Patrick J.   **2001035149 [Q]**
Scientists, Business and the State, 1890-1960. Trade Cloth.
University of North Carolina Press. Chapel Hill, NC. 2002.
264p. The Luther Hartwell Hodges Series on Business, Society,
and the State ISBN:0-8078-2655-3, ISBN13:
978-0-8078-2655-3. Dewey:338.97306. LCCN:2001-035149.
                          Audience: **g,l,u.** *Choice, 2002.*

Reingold, Nathan (Editor)   **Q127.U6S318 1985**
Science in Nineteenth-Century America: A Documentary
History. Trade Paper. University of Chicago Press. Chicago, IL.
1985. 347p. ISBN:0-226-70947-7, ISBN13: 978-0-226-70947-5.
Dewey:509.73. LCCN:85-001021.
                                          Audience: **u,f.**

Reingold, Nathan &   **Q127.U6**
  Reingold, Ida H. (Editors)
Science in America: A Documentary History, 1900-1939. Trade
Cloth. University of Chicago Press. Chicago, IL. 1982. 497p.
Chicago History of Science and Medicine Ser.
ISBN:0-226-70946-9, ISBN13: 978-0-226-70946-8.
Dewey:509/.73. LCCN:81-002584.
                                      Audience: **u,f.** ℬ

Rosenberg, Charles E.   **Q127.U6R618 1997**
No Other Gods: On Science and American Social Thought. Ed.
2. Trade Cloth. Johns Hopkins University Press. Baltimore, MD.
1997. 336p. ISBN:0-8018-5608-6, ISBN13: 978-0-8018-5608-2.
Dewey:303.48/3/0973. LCCN:96-051657.
                                      Audience: **u,f.** ℬ

Struik, Dirk J.   **Q127.U6S8 1991**
Yankee Science in the Making. Trade Paper. Dover Publications,
Inc. Mineola, NY. 1992. 544p. ISBN:0-486-26927-2, ISBN13:
978-0-486-26927-6. Dewey:509.73. LCCN:91-030933.
                                          Audience: **g,l.**

Trenn, Thaddeus J.   **Q127.U6.T73 1983**
America's Golden Bough: The Science Advisory Intertwist.
Cloth Text. Oelgeschlager, Gunn & Hain, Inc. Weston, MA.
1983. 320p. ISBN:0-89946-160-3, ISBN13: 978-0-89946-160-1.
Dewey:338.4/75/0973. LCCN:82-018873.
                                      Audience: **u,f.** ℬ

U.S. Dept. of Energy, Office   **Q179.97**
  of Scientific and Technical Information
☐ science.gov.
http://www.science.gov
                                      Audience: **g,l,u,f.**

Wiesner, Jerome B.   **Q127.U6 W5**
Where Science and Politics Meet. Trade Cloth. McGraw-Hill
Companies, The. New York, NY. 1965. ISBN:0-07-069063-4,
ISBN13: 978-0-07-069063-9. Dewey:509.73.
                                      Audience: **u,f.** ℬ

Wilson, John T.   **Q127.U6.W534 1983**
Academic Science, Higher Education, and the Federal
Government, 1950-1983: Programs and Policies. Trade Cloth.
University of Chicago Press. Chicago, IL. 1983. 126p.
ISBN:0-226-90051-7, ISBN13: 978-0-226-90051-3.
Dewey:353.0085/5/09. LCCN:83-017964.
                                      Audience: **u,f.** ℬ

Biography

                                                Q141.W7
World Who's Who in Science: From Antiquity to the Present.
Trade Cloth. Marquis Who's Who, LLC. New Providnce, NJ.
1968. xvi, 1855p. ISBN:0-8379-1001-3, ISBN13:
978-0-8379-1001-7. Dewey:509/.22. LCCN:68-056149.
                                      Audience: **u,f.** ℬ

Ambrose, Susan A., et al.   **Q130.J68 1997**
Journeys of Women in Science and Engineering: No Universal
Constants. Kristin L. Dunkle, Barbara B. Lazarus, Indira Nair &
Deborah A. Harkus (Authors). Trade Cloth. Temple University
Press. Philadelphia, PA. 2000. 512p. Labor and Social Change
Ser. ISBN:1-56639-527-5, ISBN13: 978-1-56639-527-4.
Dewey:508.2. LCCN:96-050415.
                                  Audience: **l,u.** *Choice, 1998.*

Asimov, Isaac   **Q141.A74 1982**
Asimov's Biographical Encyclopedia of Science and
Technology: The Lives and Achievements of 1510 Great
Scientists from Ancient Times to the Present, Chronologically
Arranged. Ed. 2. Trade Cloth. Doubleday Canada, Ltd. Toronto,
ON. 1982. 984p. ISBN:0-385-17771-2, ISBN13:
978-0-385-17771-9. Dewey:509/.2/2. LCCN:81-047861.
                                      Audience: **g,l.** ℬ

Bailey, Martha J.   **Q141.B254 1998**
ℯ American Women in Science: 1950 to the Present - A
Biographical Dictionary. E-Book. ABC-CLIO, Inc. Santa
Barbara, CA. 2003. ISBN:1-57607-497-8, ISBN13:
978-1-57607-497-8. Dewey:500/.82/092273.
                                          Audience: **u,f.**

Brian, Denis   **Q141.B817 1995**
The Voice of Genius: Conversations with Nobel Scientists and
Other Luminaries. Basic Books. 1995. ISBN:0-306-45089-5,
ISBN13: 978-0-306-45089-1.
                                          Audience: **g,l.**

Charles Scribners Sons Staff   **Q141.C55 2000**
  (Contribution by)
Concise Dictionary of Scientific Biography. Ed. 2. Trade Cloth.
Thomson Gale. Farmington Hills, MI. 2000. 1097p.
ISBN:0-684-80631-2, ISBN13: 978-0-684-80631-0.
Dewey:509.2/2. LCCN:00-061231.
                              Audience: **g,l,u,f.** *Choice, 2001.*

Creese, Mary R. S. &   **Q141.C693 2004**
  Creese, Thomas M. (Contribution by)
Ladies in the Laboratory II: West European Women in Science,
1800-1900: A Survey of Their Contributions to Research. Trade
Cloth. Scarecrow Press, Inc. Lanham, MD. 2004. 304p.
ISBN:0-8108-4979-8, ISBN13: 978-0-8108-4979-2.
Dewey:500/.82/09409034. LCCN:2003-020846.
                                      Audience: **g.** *Choice, 2004.*

Creese, Mary R.   **Q141.C69 1998**
Ladies in the Laboratory? American and British Women in
Science, 1800-1900: A Survey of Their Contributions to
Research. Thomas M. Creese (Contribution by). Trade Cloth.
Scarecrow Press, Inc. Lanham, MD. 1998. 452p.
ISBN:0-8108-3287-9, ISBN13: 978-0-8108-3287-9.
Dewey:500.8/2. LCCN:97-001125.
                                      Audience: **g.** *Choice, 1998.*

Dunstan, G. R. & Maruice,   **HV4702**
  F. D.
Science and Sensibility. Trade Cloth. State Mutual Book &
Periodical Service, Ltd. Bridgehampton, NY. 1982.
ISBN:0-7855-1116-4, ISBN13: 978-0-7855-1116-8.
Dewey:179/.3.
                                      Audience: **g.**

Elliott, Clark A.   **Q141**
Biographical Dictionary of American Science: The Seventeenth
Through the Nineteenth Centuries. Cloth Text. Greenwood
Publishing Group, Inc. Portsmouth, NH. 1979. 360p.
ISBN:0-313-20419-5, ISBN13: 978-0-313-20419-7.
Dewey:509/.2/2. LCCN:78-004292.
                                      Audience: **g,l,u.** *B*

Gale Research Staff   **Q 141 .A47 2003**
American Men and Women of Science, Set. Ed. 21. Trade
Cloth. Thomson Gale. Farmington Hills, MI. 2002. 9100p.
ISBN:0-7876-6523-1, ISBN13: 978-0-7876-6523-4.
Dewey:509.2273.
                                      Audience: **u,f.** *Choice, 2003.*

Gillispie, Charles C. (Editor)   **Q141.D5 1981**
Dictionary of Scientific Biography, Set. Cloth Text. Thomson
Gale. Farmington Hills, MI. 1981. -18; in 1p.
ISBN:0-684-16962-2, ISBN13: 978-0-684-16962-0.
Dewey:509/.2/2. LCCN:69-018090.
                                      Audience: **l,u,f.** *B*

Hammond, Allen L. (Editor)   **Q141.P374 1985**
A Passion to Know: 20 Profiles in Science. Trade Cloth.
Thomson Gale. Farmington Hills, MI. 1984. 240p.
ISBN:0-684-18209-2, ISBN13: 978-0-684-18209-4.
Dewey:509.2/2 B. LCCN:84-016145.
                                      Audience: **g.** *B*

Holton, Gerald   **Q173.H7342 1995**
Einstein, History and Other Passions. Cloth Text. Springer. New
York, NY. 1995. 320p. AIP Masters of Modern Physics Ser.
ISBN:1-56396-333-7, ISBN13: 978-1-56396-333-9. Dewey:500.
LCCN:94-037483.
                                      Audience: **g,l,u,f.** *Choice, 1995.*

Howsam, Leslie   **Z7401.H66**
Scientists since 1660: A Bibliography of Biographies. Trade
Cloth. Ashgate Publishing, Ltd. Aldershot, 1997. 326p.
ISBN:1-85928-035-8, ISBN13: 978-1-85928-035-5. Dewey:[B].
LCCN:96-041789.
                                      Audience: **l,u,f.** *Choice, 1998.*

Krapp, Kristine (Editor)   **Q141.N726 1999**
Notable Black American Scientists. Trade Cloth. Thomson Gale.
Farmington Hills, MI. 1998. xxvi, 349p. ISBN:0-7876-2789-5,
ISBN13: 978-0-7876-2789-8. Dewey:509.2/273 B.
LCCN:98-036338.
                                      Audience: **l,u,f.** *Choice, 1999.*

Krapp, Kristine (Editor)   **Q141.N73 1995 SUPPL.**
Notable Twentieth-Century Scientists Supplement. Trade Cloth.
Thomson Gale. Farmington Hills, MI. 1998. 617p.
ISBN:0-7876-2766-6, ISBN13: 978-0-7876-2766-9.
Dewey:509.2/2 b. LCCN:98-014016.
                                      Audience: **l,u,f.** *Choice, 1999.*

McGraw-Hill Staff   **Q141.M15 1980**
Modern Scientists and Engineers. Cloth Text. McGraw-Hill
Companies, The. New York, NY. 1980. :p. ISBN:0-07-045266-0,
ISBN13: 978-0-07-045266-4. Dewey:509/.22. LCCN:79-024383.
                                      Audience: **g.** *B*

McMurray, Emily J. &   **Q141.N73 1995**
  Olendorf, Donna (Editors)
Notable Twentieth-Century Scientists. Trade Cloth. Thomson
Gale. Farmington Hills, MI. 1994. 2397p. ISBN:0-8103-9181-3,
ISBN13: 978-0-8103-9181-9. Dewey:509.22. LCCN:94-005263.
                                      Audience: **l,u,f.** *Choice, 1995.*

National Academy of   **Q141**
  Sciences Staff
Biographical Memoirs. Trade Cloth. National Academies Press.
Washington, DC. 400p. ISBN:0-309-06086-9, ISBN13:
978-0-309-06086-8. Dewey:506.
                                      Audience: **g.**

Ogilvie, Marilyn & Harvey,   **Q141.B5285 2000**
  Joy (Editors)
The Biographical Dictionary of Women in Science: Pioneering
Lives from Ancient Times to the Mid-20th Century, Set.
Margaret Rossiter (Introduction by). Paper over Boards.
Routledge. New York, NY. 2000. 1500p. ISBN:0-415-92038-8,
ISBN13: 978-0-415-92038-4. Dewey:509.2/2 B.
LCCN:99-017668.
                                      Audience: **g,l,u,f.** *Choice, 2001.*

Olson, Richard (Editor)   **Q141.B532 1998**
Biographical Encyclopedia of Scientists. Trade Cloth. Marshall
Cavendish Corporation. Tarrytown, NY. 2000. 1,600p.
ISBN:0-7614-7064-6, ISBN13: 978-0-7614-7064-9.
Dewey:509/.2/2. LCCN:97-023877.
                                      Audience: **u,f.** *Choice, 1998.*

Pelletier, Paul A.   **Q141.P398 1994**
Prominent Scientists: An Index to Collective Biographies. Ed. 3.
Trade Cloth. Neal-Schuman Publishers, Inc. New York, NY.
1994. 353p. ISBN:1-55570-114-0, ISBN13: 978-1-55570-114-7.
Dewey:509/.2/2 B. LCCN:93-050176.
                                      Audience: **g.** *Choice, 1994.*

Roe, Anne   **Q141 .R52 1973**
The Making of a Scientist. Trade Cloth. Greenwood Publishing
Group, Inc. Portsmouth, NH. 1974. 244p. ISBN:0-8371-7151-2,
ISBN13: 978-0-8371-7151-7. Dewey:502/.3. LCCN:73-015059.
                                      Audience: **g,l.** *B*

Shea, William R.   **Q125.2.S54 1990**
The Magic of Numbers and Motion: The Scientific Career of
Rene Descartes. Trade Cloth. Watson Publishing International.

Sagamore Beach, MA. 1990. 416p. ISBN:0-88135-098-2, ISBN13: 978-0-88135-098-2. Dewey:509.2 B. LCCN:89-010813.

Audience: **g,l,u.** *Choice, 1991.*

Shearer, Benjamin F. &   **Q141**
  Shearer, Barbara S. (Editors)
Notable Women in the Physical Sciences: A Biographical Dictionary. Cloth Text. Greenwood Publishing Group, Inc. Portsmouth, NH. 1997. 496p. ISBN:0-313-29303-1, ISBN13: 978-0-313-29303-0. Dewey:500.2/092/2 B. LCCN:96-009024.

Audience: **l,u,f.** *Choice, 1997.*

Smith, Roger   **Z7404.S64 1998**
Biographies of Scientists: An Annotated Bibliography. Trade Cloth. Scarecrow Press, Inc. Lanham, MD. 1998. 304p. Magill Bibliographies Ser. ISBN:0-8108-3384-0, ISBN13: 978-0-8108-3384-5. Dewey:016.5092/2. LCCN:98-005954.

Audience: **l,u,f.** *Choice, 1998.*

Thomson Gale Staff   **Q141**
American Men and Women of Science. Ed. 23. Trade Cloth. Thomson Gale. Farmington Hills, MI. 2006. 8,500p. ISBN:1-4144-0086-1, ISBN13: 978-1-4144-0086-0. Dewey:509.22.

Audience: **g,l,u,f.**

Warren, Wini   **Q141.W367 1999**
Black Women Scientists in the United States. Trade Cloth. Indiana University Press. Bloomington, IN. 2000. xx, 366p. ISBN:0-253-33603-1, ISBN13: 978-0-253-33603-3. Dewey:500/.82/0973. LCCN:99-040264.

Audience: **l,u,f.** *Choice, 2000.*

Yount, Lisa   **Q141.Y675 1999**
A to Z of Women in Science and Math. Nicole Brown (Editor). Trade Cloth. Facts On File, Inc.. New York, NY. 1999. 272p. Encyclopedia of Women Ser. ISBN:0-8160-3797-3, ISBN13: 978-0-8160-3797-1. Dewey:509.2/2 B. LCCN:98-046093.

Audience: **g,l.** *Choice, 2000.*

Individual Biography

Batchelor, G. K.   **Q143.T29 B38 1996**
The Life and Legacy of G. I. Taylor. Trade Cloth. Cambridge University Press. New York, NY. 1996. 301p. ISBN:0-521-46121-9, ISBN13: 978-0-521-46121-4. Dewey:620.106092. LCCN:95-047579.

Audience: **g.** *Choice, 1997.*

Biagioli, Mario   **QB36.G2B54 1993**
Galileo, Courtier: The Practice of Science in the Culture of Absolutism. Trade Cloth. University of Chicago Press. Chicago, IL. 1993. 416p. Science and Its Conceptual Foundations Ser. ISBN:0-226-04559-5, ISBN13: 978-0-226-04559-7. Dewey:509.2. LCCN:92-033736.

Audience: **u,f.** *Choice, 1994.*

Brown, Sanborn C.   **Q143.R8**
Benjamin Thompson, Count Rumford. Trade Cloth. MIT Press. Cambridge, MA. 1979. xiii, 361p. ISBN:0-262-02138-2, ISBN13: 978-0-262-02138-8. Dewey:530/.092/4. LCCN:79-009110.

Audience: **g.** *B*

De Terra, Helmut   **Q143.H9 D4 1979**
The Life and Times of Alexander Humboldt. Library Binding. Hippocrene Books, Inc. New York, NY. 1979. 386p. ISBN:0-374-92134-2, ISBN13: 978-0-374-92134-7. Dewey:500.9/2/4. LCCN:78-027653.

Audience: **g.**

Debré, Patrice   **Q143.P2D33 1998**
Louis Pasteur. Elborg Forster (Translator). Trade Cloth. Johns Hopkins University Press. Baltimore, MD. 1998. 600p. ISBN:0-8018-5808-9, ISBN13: 978-0-8018-5808-6. Dewey:[B]. LCCN:97-043686.

Audience: **g,l,u,f.** *Choice, 1999.*

Desmond, Adrian   **Q143.H956D47 1997**
Huxley: From Devil's Disciple to Evolution's High Priest. Cloth Text. Addison-Wesley Longman, Inc. Boston, MA. 1997. 848p. ISBN:0-201-95987-9, ISBN13: 978-0-201-95987-1. Dewey:509.2 B. LCCN:97-022480.

Audience: **g,l,u,f.** *Choice, 1998.*

Dubos, Rene Jules   **Q143.P2 D78 1986**
Louis Pasteur: Free Lance of Science. Ed. 2. Trade Paper. Da Capo Press, Inc. Cambridge, MA. 1986. 462p. Da Capo Series in Science ISBN:0-306-80262-7, ISBN13: 978-0-306-80262-1. Dewey:509.2/4. LCCN:86-000511.

Audience: **g.**

Freedberg, David   **Q127.I8F74 2002**
The Eye of the Lynx: Galileo, His Friends, and the Beginnings of Modern Natural History. Trade Cloth. University of Chicago Press. Chicago, IL. 2002. 528p. ISBN:0-226-26147-6, ISBN13: 978-0-226-26147-8. Dewey:509.45. LCCN:2002-000361.

Audience: **u,f.** *Choice, 2003.*

Geison, Gerald L.   **Q143.P2**
The Private Science of Louis Pasteur. Paper Text. Princeton University Press. Princeton, NJ. 1996. 392p. ISBN:0-691-01552-X, ISBN13: 978-0-691-01552-1. Dewey:509.2 B. LCCN:94-035338.

Audience: **g,l.** *Choice, 1995.*

Gillmor, C. Stewart   **Q143.C65 G55**
Coulomb and the Evolution of Physics and Engineering in Eighteenth Century France. Trade Cloth. Princeton University Press. Princeton, NJ. 1972. 346p. ISBN:0-691-08095-X, ISBN13: 978-0-691-08095-6. Dewey:530/.0924. LCCN:79-155006.

Audience: **g,u.** *B*

Hahn, Roger   **Q143.L36H35313 2005**
Pierre Simon Laplace, 1749-1827: A Determined Scientist. Trade Cloth. Harvard University Press. Cambridge, MA. 2005. 322p. ISBN:0-674-01892-3, ISBN13: 978-0-674-01892-1. Dewey:509.2 B. LCCN:2005-046358.

Audience: **g.** *Choice, 2006.*

Hariot, Thomas   **Q143.H36.T45 2000**
Thomas Harriot: An Elizabethan Man of Science. Robert Fox (Editor). Trade Cloth. Ashgate Publishing, Ltd. Aldershot, 2000. 330p. ISBN:0-7546-0078-5, ISBN13: 978-0-7546-0078-7. Dewey:509.2 B. LCCN:00-102914.

Audience: **g.** *Choice, 2001.*

Hart, Ivor B.   **Q143.L5 H3 1982**
The Mechanical Investigations of Leonardo da Vinci. Ernest A. Moody (Foreword by). Trade Cloth. Greenwood Publishing

Group, Inc. Portsmouth, NH. 1982. 240p. ISBN:0-313-23489-2, ISBN13: 978-0-313-23489-7. Dewey:620.1. LCCN:82-002967.

Audience: **g,l,u,f.**

Kemp, Martin   **Q143.L5A3 1989**
Leonardo da Vinci: Artist - Scientist - Inventor. Trade Cloth. Yale University Press. Cumberland, RI. 1989. 264p. ISBN:0-300-04508-5, ISBN13: 978-0-300-04508-6. Dewey:709.2. LCCN:88-037855.

Audience: **g.** *Choice, 1989.*

Killian, James R. Jr.   **Q127.U6**
Sputnik, Scientists, and Eisenhower: A Memoir of the First Special Assistant to the President for Science and Technology. Trade Cloth. MIT Press. Cambridge, MA. 1977. xxiv, 315p. ISBN:0-262-11066-0, ISBN13: 978-0-262-11066-2. Dewey:353.008/55/0924. LCCN:77-021560.

Audience: **g.** *B*

Macrae, Norman   **QA29.V66M33 1992**
John Von Neumann: The Scientific Genius Who Pioneered the Modern Computer, Game Theory, Nuclear Deterrence and Much More. Trade Cloth. Knopf Publishing Group. New York, NY. 1992. 352p. ISBN:0-679-41308-1, ISBN13: 978-0-679-41308-0. Dewey:510/.92. LCCN:91-050891.

Audience: **g.** *Choice, 1993.*

Macre, Norman   **QA29.V66M334 1999**
John Von Neumann. Cloth Text. American Mathematical Society. Providence, RI. 1999. 406p. ISBN:0-8218-2064-8, ISBN13: 978-0-8218-2064-3. Dewey:510/.92 B. LCCN:99-037303.

Audience: **g.**

Neeley, Kathryn A. &   **Q143.S7 N44 2001**
  Somerville, Mary
Mary Somerville: Science, Illumination, and the Female Mind. Sally Gregory Kohlstedt & David Knight (Contribution by). Trade Cloth. Cambridge University Press. New York, NY. 2001. 280p. Science Biographies Ser. ISBN:0-521-62299-9, ISBN13: 978-0-521-62299-8. Dewey:500.2092 B. LCCN:00-049363.

Audience: **g,l,u,f.** *Choice, 2002.*

Shirley, John W.   **Q143.H36.S46 1983**
Thomas Harriot: A Biography. Trade Cloth. Oxford University Press, Inc. New York, NY. 1983. 192p. ISBN:0-19-822901-1, ISBN13: 978-0-19-822901-8. Dewey:510/.92/4. LCCN:83-003961.

Audience: **g,l,u,f.** *B*

Stegner, Wallace   **Q143.P8**
Beyond the Hundredth Meridian: John Wesley Powell and the Second Opening of the West. Bernard A. De Voto (Introduction by). Trade Cloth. University of Nebraska Press. Lincoln, NE. 1982. xxvi, 458p. ISBN:0-8032-4133-X, ISBN13: 978-0-8032-4133-6. Dewey:551/.092/4. LCCN:81-023090.

Audience: **g,l,u,f.**

White, Michael   **Q143.L5W57 2001**
Leonardo: The First Scientist. Cloth over Boards. St. Martin's Press. Gordonville, VA. 2000. 384p. ISBN:0-312-20333-0, ISBN13: 978-0-312-20333-7. Dewey:509.2 B. LCCN:2001-041958.

Audience: **g,l.**

Wilson, Edward O.   **QH31.W64A3 1994**
Naturalist. Trade Cloth. Island Press. Washington, DC. 1994. 392p. ISBN:1-55963-288-7, ISBN13: 978-1-55963-288-1. Dewey:574/.092. LCCN:94-013111.

Audience: **g.** *Choice, 1995.*

Zammattio, Carlo, et al.   **Q143.L5.Z28 1980**
Leonardo the Scientist. Augusto Marinoni & Anna M. Brizio (Authors). Trade Cloth. McGraw-Hill Companies, The. New York, NY. 1980. 192p. ISBN:0-07-072723-6, ISBN13: 978-0-07-072723-6. Dewey:509/.2/4. LCCN:80-018436.

Audience: **g.** *B*

Directories

HG4057
America's Corporate Families: The Billion Dollar Directory. Dun & Bradstreet, Inc., Parsippany, NJ: annual. 3 v..

Audience: **u,f.**

HD2425
Encyclopedia of Associations. Gale Research Company, Detroit 1961-.

Audience: **u,f.**

Q180.U5
Government Research Directory. Ed. 19. Trade Cloth. Thomson Gale. Farmington Hills, MI. 2005. 1200p. ISBN:0-7876-6906-7, ISBN13: 978-0-7876-6906-5. Dewey:001.4/025/73.

Audience: **g,u,f.**

HC102
Million Dollar Directory: America's Leading Public and Private Companies. Dun's Marketing Services, Parsippany, NJ: 1959-1996. 38 v..

Audience: **u,f.**

HG4961
Moody's Industrial Manual. NY: Moody's Investors Service, 1954- annual.

Audience: **u,f.**

HG4057
Standard and Poor's Register of Corporations, Directors, and Executives, United States and Canada. Standard & Poor's Corp., NY: 1973- annual..

Audience: **u,f.**

T12
Thomas Register of American Manufacturers. Thomas Publishing Company, NY: 1906- annual.

Audience: **u,f.**

AS2
The World of Learning. London: Europa Publications, 1948- annual.

Audience: **u,f.**

Marquis Who's Who, Inc.   **Q141**
Who's Who in Science and Engineering 1998-1999. Ed. 4. Marquis Who's Who. 1997. ISBN:0-8379-5756-7, ISBN13: 978-0-8379-5756-2.

Audience: **u,f.**

Science as a Profession

Ambrose, Susan A., et al.   **Q130.J68 1997**
Journeys of Women in Science and Engineering: No Universal
Constants. Kristin L. Dunkle, Barbara B. Lazarus, Indira Nair &
Deborah A. Harkus (Authors). Trade Cloth. Temple University
Press. Philadelphia, PA. 2000. 512p. Labor and Social Change
Ser. ISBN:1-56639-527-5, ISBN13: 978-1-56639-527-4.
Dewey:508.2. LCCN:96-050415.
Audience: **l,u.** *Choice, 1998.*

Ben-David, Joseph   **Q147.B45 1984**
The Scientist's Role in Society: A Comparative Study with a
New Introduction. Library Binding. University of Chicago Press.
Chicago, IL. 1984. 236p. ISBN:0-226-04227-8, ISBN13:
978-0-226-04227-5. Dewey:303.4/83. LCCN:84-002758.
Audience: **g.**

Ben-David, Joseph   **Q147**
Scientist's Role in Society: A Comparative Study with a New
Introduction. University of Chicago Press. 1984.
ISBN:0-226-04221-9, ISBN13: 978-0-226-04221-3.
Audience: **g.**

Connolly, Terry   **Q147.C57 1983**
Scientists, Engineers and Organizations. Ed. 1. Trade Paper.
Thomson Wadsworth. Belmont, CA. 1983. xii, 388 p. :p.
General Engineering Ser. ISBN:0-534-01409-7, ISBN13:
978-0-534-01409-4. Dewey:650.1/0245. LCCN:82-022703.
Audience: **g.**

Haas, Violet B. & Perrucci,   **Q130.W66 1984**
Carolyn C. (Editors)
Women in Scientific and Engineering Professions. Trade Paper.
University of Michigan Press. Chicago, IL. 1984. 256p. Women
and Culture Ser. ISBN:0-472-08042-3, ISBN13:
978-0-472-08042-7. Dewey:305.4. LCCN:83-023575.
Audience: **g,u,f.**

Humphreys, Sheila M.   **Q130.W65**
Women and Minorities in Science: Strategies for Increasing
Participation. American Association for the Advancement of
Science Staff (Contribution by). Trade Cloth. Westview Press.
Boulder, CO. 1982. xvi, 218 p. :p. ISBN:0-86531-317-2,
ISBN13: 978-0-86531-317-0. Dewey:509. LCCN:81-019843.
Audience: **g,l,u.**

Lederman, Muriel &   **Q130.G43 2000**
Bartsch, Ingrid (Editors)
The Gender and Science Reader. Paper over Boards. Routledge.
New York, NY. 2000. 528p. ISBN:0-415-21357-6, ISBN13:
978-0-415-21357-8. Dewey:500/.82. LCCN:00-044646.
Audience: **l,u,f.** *Choice, 2001.*

Merchant, Carolyn   **Q130.M47 1989**
The Death of Nature: Women, Ecology, and the Scientific
Revolution. Trade Paper. HarperCollins Publishers. New York,
NY. 1990. 384p. ISBN:0-06-250595-5, ISBN13:
978-0-06-250595-8. Dewey:305.4/2. LCCN:89-024516.
Audience: **g.**

National Research Council   **Q130.C54 1983**
Staff
Climbing the Ladder: An Update on the Status of Doctoral
Women Scientists and Engineers. Paper Text. National

Academies Press. Washington, DC. 1983. 112p.
ISBN:0-309-03341-1, ISBN13: 978-0-309-03341-1.
Dewey:331.4/815/0973. LCCN:83-060184.
Audience: **l,u,f.**

Ogilvie, Marilyn B.   **Q141.O34 1986**
Women in Science: Antiquity Through Nineteenth Century - A
Biographical Dictionary with Annotated Bibliography. Trade
Cloth. MIT Press. Cambridge, MA. 1986. 272p.
ISBN:0-262-15031-X, ISBN13: 978-0-262-15031-6.
Dewey:509.2/2 B. LCCN:86-007507.
Audience: **g,l,u,f.** *Choice, 1987.*

Panel to Study Gender   **Q130.L66 2001**
Differences in Career Outcom
From Scarcity to Visibility: Gender Differences in the Careers of
Doctoral Scientists and Engineers. J. Scott Long, Linda C.
Skidmore & Catherine D. Gaddy (Editors). Perfect. National
Academies Press. Washington, DC. 2001. 340p.
ISBN:0-309-05580-6, ISBN13: 978-0-309-05580-2.
Dewey:502.3. LCCN:2001-086800.
Audience: **l,u,f.**

Rossiter, Margaret W.   **Q130**
Women Scientists in America: Struggles and Strategies to 1940.
Trade Cloth. Johns Hopkins University Press. Baltimore, MD.
1989. 464p. ISBN:0-8018-2443-5, ISBN13: 978-0-8018-2443-2.
Dewey:509/.2/2. LCCN:81-020902.
Audience: **l,u,f.**

Rossiter, Margaret W.   **Q130.R683 1995**
Women Scientists in America: Before Affirmative Action,
1940-1972. Johns Hopkins University Press. 1982.
ISBN:0-8018-4893-8, ISBN13: 978-0-8018-4893-3.
Audience: **l,u,f.**

Rothwell, Nancy   **Q147.R68 2002**
Who Wants to Be a Scientist?: Choosing Science As a Career.
Smudge (Illustrator). Cloth Text. Cambridge University Press.
New York, NY. 2002. 176p. ISBN:0-521-81773-0, ISBN13:
978-0-521-81773-8. Dewey:502/.3. LCCN:2002-023868.
Audience: **g,l,u.** *Choice, 2003.*

Sonnert, Gerhard & Holton,   **Q149.U5S56 1995**
Gerald
Gender Differences in Science Careers: The Project Access
Study. Robert K. Merton (Foreword by). Cloth Text. Rutgers
University Press. Piscataway, NJ. 1995. 200p. Arnold and
Caroline Rose Series of the American Sociological Association
ISBN:0-8135-2174-2, ISBN13: 978-0-8135-2174-9.
Dewey:502.3/73. LCCN:94-025219.
Audience: **l,u,f.** *Choice, 1995.*

Wyer, Mary (Editor), et al.   **Q130.W672 2001**
Women, Science and Technology: A Reader in Feminist Science
Studies. Donna Cookmeyer, Mary Barbercheck, Hatice Ozturk
& Marta Wayne (Editors). Paper over Boards. Routledge. New
York, NY. 2000. 400p. ISBN:0-415-92606-8, ISBN13:
978-0-415-92606-5. Dewey:500/.82. LCCN:00-046452.
Audience: **g,l.** *Choice, 2001.*

Xie, Yu & Shauman,   **Q130.Z54 2003**
Kimberlee A.
Women in Science: Career Processes and Outcomes. Trade
Cloth. Harvard University Press. Cambridge, MA. 2003. 336p.
ISBN:0-674-01034-5, ISBN13: 978-0-674-01034-5.
Dewey:305.43/5. LCCN:2003-045274.
Audience: **g,l,u,f.** *Choice, 2004.*

Zuckerman, Harriet   **Q149.U5Z8 1996**
Scientific Elite: Nobel Laureates in the United States. Ed. 2.
Trade Paper. Transaction Publishers. Somerset, NJ. 1995. 335p.
ISBN:1-56000-855-5, ISBN13: 978-1-56000-855-2.
Dewey:509.2/273. LCCN:95-045046.

Audience: **g.** ℬ

Science: Early Works To 1800

Aristotle
Physics. Trade Paper. Oxford University Press, Inc. New York,
NY. 1999. 382p. Oxford World's Classics Ser.
ISBN:0-19-283586-6, ISBN13: 978-0-19-283586-4.
Dewey:530.01.

Audience: **g,l,u,f.**

Aristotle   **QC6**
Aristotle's Physics: A Collection of Essays. Lindsay Judson
(Editor). Paper Text. Oxford University Press, Inc. New York,
NY. 1995. 296p. ISBN:0-19-823602-6, ISBN13:
978-0-19-823602-3. Dewey:530/.01. LCCN:91-019303.

Audience: **u,f.** *Choice, 1992.*

Aristotle   **Q151.A613 1982**
De Generatione et Corruptione. C. J. F. Williams (Translator,
Notes by). Trade Cloth. Oxford University Press, Inc. New
York, NY. 1982. 256p. Clarendon Aristotle Ser.
ISBN:0-19-872062-9, ISBN13: 978-0-19-872062-1. Dewey:500.
LCCN:81-021727.

Audience: **l,u,f.** ℬ

Descartes, Rene   **Q155.D43513 1979**
Le Monde. Michael S. Mahoney (Translator). Library Binding.
OPAL Publishing Corporation. Norwalk, CT. 1979. 224p. Janus
Ser. ISBN:0-913870-35-8, ISBN13: 978-0-913870-35-8.
Dewey:500. LCCN:77-086236.

Audience: **l,u,f.** ℬ

Grant, E.   **Q124.97**
Physical Science in the Middle Ages. Trade Cloth. Cambridge
University Press. New York, NY. 1978. xiii, 128p.
ISBN:0-521-21862-4, ISBN13: 978-0-521-21862-7.
Dewey:500.2/09/021. LCCN:77-008393.

Audience: **g,l,u,f.**

Lang, Helen S.   **Q151.A8.L36 1992**
Aristotle's Physics and Its Medieval Varieties. Cloth Text. State
University of New York Press. Albany, NY. 1992. 322p. SUNY
Series in Ancient Greek Philosophy ISBN:0-7914-1083-8,
ISBN13: 978-0-7914-1083-7. Dewey:500. LCCN:91-035652.

Audience: **g,l,u,f.** *Choice, 1993.*

Murdoch, John E.   **Q222.M87 1984**
Album of Science: Antiquity and the Middle Ages. Trade Cloth.
Thomson Gale. Farmington Hills, MI. 1984. 375p. Album of
Science Ser. ISBN:0-684-15496-X, ISBN13: 978-0-684-15496-1.
Dewey:509/.01. LCCN:84-001400.

Audience: **g.** ℬ

Science: General Works, 1801-

Bryson, Bill   **Q162.B88 2003**
A Short History of Nearly Everything. Trade Cloth. Broadway
Books. New York, NY. 2003. 560p. ISBN:0-7679-0817-1,
ISBN13: 978-0-7679-0817-7. Dewey:500. LCCN:2003-046006.

Audience: **g,l,u,f.** *Choice, 2003.*

Derry, Gregory Neil   **Q158.5.D47 1999**
What Science Is and How It Works. Trade Cloth. Princeton
University Press. Princeton, NJ. 1999. 324p.
ISBN:0-691-05877-6, ISBN13: 978-0-691-05877-1. Dewey:500.
LCCN:99-017186.

Audience: **g,l,u.** *Choice, 2000.*

Duncan, R. &   **Q158.5**
   Weston-Smith, Miranda (Editors)
The Encyclopedia of Ignorance, Vol. 1 & 2. Trade Cloth.
Elsevier Science & Technology Books. Saint Louis, MO. 1978.
ISBN:0-685-04001-1, ISBN13: 978-0-685-04001-0. Dewey:500.

Audience: **g,l,u.**

Gamow, George   **Q162.G23 1988**
One Two Three... Infinity: Facts and Speculations of Science.
Trade Paper. Dover Publications, Inc. Mineola, NY. 1988. 352p.
ISBN:0-486-25664-2, ISBN13: 978-0-486-25664-1. Dewey:500.
LCCN:88-018955.

Audience: **g.**

Goswami, Amit & Goswami,   **Q162.G67 1983**
   Maggie
The Cosmic Dancers: Exploring the Physics of Science Fiction.
Trade Cloth. HarperCollins Publishers. New York, NY. 1983.
288p. ISBN:0-06-015083-1, ISBN13: 978-0-06-015083-9.
Dewey:809.3/876. LCCN:82-048118.

Audience: **g,l,u.** ℬ

Greenwood, Addison &   **Q180.55.D57**
   National Academy of Sciences Staff
Science at the Frontier. Trade Cloth. National Academies Press.
Washington, DC. 1992. 288p. ISBN:0-309-04592-4, ISBN13:
978-0-309-04592-6. Dewey:500. LCCN:93-640608.

Audience: **g,l,u.** *Choice, 1993.*

Valiela, Ivan   **Q180.A1V35 2001**
Doing Science: Design, Analysis, and Communication of
Scientific Research. Trade Cloth. Oxford University Press, Inc.
New York, NY. 2001. 304p. ISBN:0-19-507962-0, ISBN13:
978-0-19-507962-3. Dewey:507.2. LCCN:99-021693.

Audience: **u,f.** *Choice, 2001.*

Weisskopf, Victor F.   **Q162.W4 1979**
Knowledge and Wonder: The Natural World As Man Knows It.
Ed. 2. Trade Cloth. MIT Press. Cambridge, MA. 1979. 304p.
ISBN:0-262-23098-4, ISBN13: 978-0-262-23098-8. Dewey:500.
LCCN:79-019148.

Audience: **l,u,f.** ℬ

Addresses. Essays. Lectures

Blake, R. M.   **Q175.B58 1989**
Theories of Scientific Method: The Renaissance Through the
Nineteenth Century. Paper Text. Taylor & Francis Group.
Philadelphia, PA. 1960. 364p. Classics in the History and
Philosophy of Science Ser., Vol. 2 ISBN:2-88124-351-7,
ISBN13: 978-2-88124-351-6. Dewey:500. LCCN:89-007613.

Audience: **g,l,u.**

Gutting, Gary (Editor)   **Q175.3.P37**
Paradigms and Revolutions: Appraisals and Applications of
Thomas Kuhn's Philosophy of Science. Cloth Text. University
of Notre Dame Press. Notre Dame, IN. 1980. 256p.
ISBN:0-268-01542-2, ISBN13: 978-0-268-01542-8. Dewey:501.
LCCN:80-020745.

Audience: **l,u.** ℬ

Holton, Gerald   **Q175**
Science and Anti-Science. Harvard. 1993. ISBN:0-674-79298-X,
ISBN13: 978-0-674-79298-2.
Audience: **u,f.**

Laudan, Larry   **Q175.L2938 1996**
Beyond Positivism and Relativism: Theory, Method, and
Evidence. Trade Paper. Westview Press. Boulder, CO. 1996.
288p. ISBN:0-8133-2469-6, ISBN13: 978-0-8133-2469-2.
Dewey:501. LCCN:95-040997.
Audience: **l,u.** *Choice, 1996.*

Laudan, Larry   **Q174.8**
Science and Hypothesis: Historical Essays on Scientific
Methodology. Trade Cloth. Springer. New York, NY. 1981.
269p. The University of Western Ontario Series in Philosophy
of Science, No. 19 ISBN:90-277-1315-4, ISBN13:
978-90-277-1315-5. Dewey:501/.8. LCCN:81-015423.
Audience: **g,u,f.** *B*

Levi, Isaac   **Q175 .L445 1973**
Gambling with Truth: An Essay on Induction and the Aims of
Science. Trade Paper. MIT Press. Cambridge, MA. 1974. 266p.
ISBN:0-262-62026-X, ISBN13: 978-0-262-62026-0.
Dewey:501/.8. LCCN:73-003092.
Audience: **u,f.** *B*

Medawar, Peter Brian   **Q175.M433 1984**
The Limits of Science. Trade Cloth. HarperCollins Publishers.
New York, NY. 1984. 124p. ISBN:0-06-039036-0, ISBN13:
978-0-06-039036-5. Dewey:501. LCCN:83-048841.
Audience: **g.** *B*

Reichenbach, Hans   **Q175.3.R43 1981**
Modern Philosophy of Science: Selected Essays. Maria
Reichenbach (Editor), Rudolf Carnap (Foreword by). Library
Binding. Greenwood Publishing Group, Inc. Portsmouth, NH.
1982. ix, 214p. ISBN:0-313-23274-1, ISBN13:
978-0-313-23274-9. Dewey:501. LCCN:81-013344.
Audience: **g,l.** *B*

Salmon, Wesley Charles   **Q175.S2337 1998**
Causality and Explanation. Trade Cloth. Oxford University
Press, Inc. New York, NY. 1998. 448p. ISBN:0-19-510863-9,
ISBN13: 978-0-19-510863-7. Dewey:501. LCCN:96-048651.
Audience: **g,l,u,f.** *Choice, 1998.*

Sarton, George   **Q125 .S323 1971**
Life of Science: Essays in the History of Civilization. Max H.
Fisch (Foreword by). Trade Cloth. Ayer Company Publishers,
Inc. Manchester, NH. 1977. Essay Index Reprint Ser.
ISBN:0-8369-2472-X, ISBN13: 978-0-8369-2472-5. Dewey:509.
LCCN:70-167410.
Audience: **u.** *B*

Whitehead, Alfred North   **Q175**
Essays in Science and Philosophy. Trade Cloth. Greenwood
Publishing Group, Inc. Portsmouth, NH. 1968. 348p.
ISBN:0-8371-0268-5, ISBN13: 978-0-8371-0268-9. Dewey:82.
LCCN:68-021332.
Audience: **g,l,u,f.** *B*

Philosophy. Methodology

Q175
Personal Knowledge: Towards a Post-Critical Philosophy. Trade
Cloth. University of Chicago Press. Chicago, IL. 1974.
ISBN:0-226-67287-5, ISBN13: 978-0-226-67287-8. Dewey:121.
Audience: **g.**

Achinstein, Peter   **Q175**
Concepts of Science: A Philosophical Analysis. Trade Paper.
Johns Hopkins University Press. Baltimore, MD. 1995. 279p.
ISBN:0-8018-1273-9, ISBN13: 978-0-8018-1273-6. Dewey:501.
LCCN:68-015451.
Audience: **g,u,f.** *B*

Appleyard, Bryan   **Q175.A68 1993**
Understanding the Present: Science and the Soul of Modern
Man. Trade Cloth. Doubleday Canada, Ltd. Toronto, ON. 1993.
288p. ISBN:0-385-42071-4, ISBN13: 978-0-385-42071-6.
Dewey:501. LCCN:92-025662.
Audience: **g.**

Aronson, Jerrold L., et al.   **Q175.32.R42A76 1995**
Realism Rescued: How Scientific Progress Is Possible. Rom
Harre & Eileen C. Way (Authors). Trade Cloth. Open Court
Publishing Company. Chicago, IL. 1999. 233p.
ISBN:0-8126-9288-8, ISBN13: 978-0-8126-9288-4.
Dewey:507.2. LCCN:94-047940.
Audience: **g.** *Choice, 1995.*

Blake, R. M.   **Q175.B58 1989**
Theories of Scientific Method: The Renaissance Through the
Nineteenth Century. Paper Text. Taylor & Francis Group.
Philadelphia, PA. 1960. 364p. Classics in the History and
Philosophy of Science Ser., Vol. 2 ISBN:2-88124-351-7,
ISBN13: 978-2-88124-351-6. Dewey:500. LCCN:89-007613.
Audience: **g,l,u.**

Blay, Michel   **QC133 .B53 1999**
Reasoning with the Infinite: From the Closed World to the
Mathematical Universe. M. B. DeBevoise (Translator). Trade
Paper. University of Chicago Press. Chicago, IL. 1999. 226p.
ISBN:0-226-05835-2, ISBN13: 978-0-226-05835-1.
Dewey:530.15.
Audience: **l,u,f.**

Bronowski, Jacob   **Q175**
The Common Sense of Science. Hermann Bondi (Preface by).
Trade Paper. Harvard University Press. Cambridge, MA. 1978.
162p. Harvard Paperbacks Ser. ISBN:0-674-14651-4, ISBN13:
978-0-674-14651-8. Dewey:501. LCCN:53-009924.
Audience: **g,l.** *B*

Bronowski, Jacob   **Q175.B7918**
The Ascent of Man. Miami-Dade Community College Staff
(Editor). Trade Cloth. Little Brown & Company. New York, NY.
1984. ISBN:0-316-56940-2, ISBN13: 978-0-316-56940-8.
Dewey:501.
Audience: **g,l,u,f.** *B*

Bunge, Mario   **Q175 .B823 1975**
Intuition and Science. Library Binding. Greenwood Publishing
Group, Inc. Portsmouth, NH. 1975. 142p. ISBN:0-8371-8066-X,
ISBN13: 978-0-8371-8066-3. Dewey:501. LCCN:75-011792.
Audience: **g.**

Caruana, Louis   **Q175.C38 2000**
Holism and the Understanding of Science: Integrating the
Analytical, Historical and Sociological. Trade Cloth. Ashgate
Publishing, Ltd. Aldershot, 2000. 182p. New Critical Thinking
in Philosophy Ser. ISBN:0-7546-1314-3, ISBN13:
978-0-7546-1314-5. Dewey:501. LCCN:00-133520.
Audience: **g,l.**

Chalmers, Alan F.   **Q175.C446 1999**
What Is This Thing Called Science?: An Assessment of the
Nature and Status of Science and Its Methods. Ed. 3. Library
Binding. Hackett Publishing Company, Inc. Indianapolis, IN.
1999. 200p. ISBN:0-87220-453-7, ISBN13: 978-0-87220-453-9.
Dewey:501. LCCN:99-071498.
Audience: **g,l.** *B* *Choice, 1999.*

Clark, Peter & Hawley,   **Q175**
Katherine (Editors)
Philosophy of Science Today. Trade Cloth. Oxford University
Press, Inc. New York, NY. 2003. 312p. ISBN:0-19-925054-5,
ISBN13: 978-0-19-925054-7. Dewey:501. LCCN:2003-271821.
Audience: **u,f.**

Clarke, Desmond M.   **B1878.S3**
Descartes' Philosophy of Science. Trade Cloth. Manchester
University Press. Manchester, 1982. xii, 249p.
ISBN:0-7190-0868-9, ISBN13: 978-0-7190-0868-9.
Dewey:509/.2/4. LCCN:82-134585.
Audience: **g,l.** *B*

Collins, Harry M. & Pinch,   **Q125.C552 1993**
Trevor
The Golem: What Everyone Should Know about Science. Cloth
Text. Cambridge University Press. New York, NY. 1993. 176p.
ISBN:0-521-35601-6, ISBN13: 978-0-521-35601-5. Dewey:500.
LCCN:92-041631.
Audience: **g.** *Choice, 1994.*

Corsi, Pietro & Weindling,   **Q126.9**
Paul
Information Sources in the History of Science and Medicine.
Cloth Text. Elsevier Science & Technology Books. Saint Louis,
MO. 1983. 531p. ISBN:0-408-10764-2, ISBN13:
978-0-408-10764-8. Dewey:507/.2. LCCN:86-135026.
Audience: **g,f.** *B*

Darian, Steven G.   **Q175.D2685 2003**
Understanding the Language of Science. Trade Cloth. University
of Texas Press. Austin, TX. 2003. 262p. ISBN:0-292-71617-6,
ISBN13: 978-0-292-71617-9. Dewey:501/.4.
LCCN:2002-154613.
Audience: **g,l,u.** *Choice, 2004.*

Del Re, Giuseppe   **Q175.D574 1999**
The Cosmic Dance: Science Discovers the Mysterious Harmony
of the Universe. Thomas F. Torrance (Foreword by). Trade
Cloth. Templeton Foundation Press. Radnor, PA. 2000. 432p.
ISBN:1-890151-25-4, ISBN13: 978-1-890151-25-6. Dewey:501.
LCCN:99-038482.
Audience: **g.** *Choice, 2001.*

Dunstan, G. R. & Maruice,   **HV4702**
F. D.
Science and Sensibility. Trade Cloth. State Mutual Book &
Periodical Service, Ltd. Bridgehampton, NY. 1982.
ISBN:0-7855-1116-4, ISBN13: 978-0-7855-1116-8.
Dewey:179/.3.
Audience: **g.**

Eigen, Manfred & Winkler,   **Q175.E3713 1981**
Ruthild
Laws of the Game: How the Principles of Nature Govern
Chance. Trade Cloth. Random House Children's Books. New
York, NY. 1981. 384p. ISBN:0-394-41806-9, ISBN13:
978-0-394-41806-3. Dewey:574.8/8/015193. LCCN:79-003494.
Audience: **g,l,u,f.** *B*

Faust, David   **Q175.F269 1984**
The Limits of Scientific Reasoning. Paul E. Meehl (Introduction
by). Book, Other. University of Minnesota Press. Minneapolis,
MN. 1984. 226p. ISBN:0-8166-1359-1, ISBN13:
978-0-8166-1359-5. Dewey:501. LCCN:84-005172.
Audience: **g.** *B*

Feigl, Herbert (Editor)   **Q175**
Concepts, Theories and the Mind-Body Problem. Cloth Text.
University of Minnesota Press. Minneapolis, MN. 1972. Studies
in the Philosophy of Science, Vol. 2 ISBN:0-8166-0158-5,
ISBN13: 978-0-8166-0158-5. Dewey:150.82. LCCN:57-012861.
Audience: **g.**

Feyerabend, Paul K.   **Q175.F42 1993**
Against Method: Outline of an Anarchistic Theory of
Knowledge. Ed. 3. Cloth Text. Analytical Psychology Club of
San Francisco, Inc. San Francisco, CA. 1993. 352p.
ISBN:0-86091-481-X, ISBN13: 978-0-86091-481-5. Dewey:501.
LCCN:93-033557.
Audience: **l,u,f.** *B*

Frank, Philipp   **Q175.F782 1974**
Philosophy of Science: The Link Between Science and
Philosophy. Library Binding. Greenwood Publishing Group, Inc.
Portsmouth, NH. 1974. 394p. ISBN:0-8371-6164-9, ISBN13:
978-0-8371-6164-8. Dewey:501. LCCN:73-021286.
Audience: **g.** *B*

Fuller, Steve   **Q175.46.F85 2004**
Kuhn vs. Popper: The Struggle for the Soul of Science. Trade
Cloth. Columbia University Press. New York, NY. 2004. 160p.
ISBN:0-231-13428-2, ISBN13: 978-0-231-13428-6.
Dewey:501/.09/04. LCCN:2004-049393.
Audience: **g,u,f.** *Choice, 2005.*

Giere, Ronald N. &   **Q0175.F72**
Westfall, Richard S. (Editors)
Foundations of Scientific Method: The Nineteenth Century.
Trade Paper. Books on Demand. Ann Arbor, MI. 314p.
ISBN:0-8357-9213-7, ISBN13: 978-0-8357-9213-4.
Dewey:501/.8. LCCN:72-079910.
Audience: **u,f.**

Glass, Hiram B.   **Q175.3 .G56 1981**
Science and Ethical Values. Trade Cloth. Greenwood Publishing
Group, Inc. Portsmouth, NH. 1981. 101p. ISBN:0-313-23141-9,
ISBN13: 978-0-313-23141-4. Dewey:174/.9574.
LCCN:81-013170.
Audience: **l,u,f.**

Gustav, Bergmann   **Q175 .B466 1977**
Philosophy of Science. Trade Cloth. Greenwood Publishing
Group, Inc. Portsmouth, NH. 1982. 181p. ISBN:0-8371-9623-X,
ISBN13: 978-0-8371-9623-7. Dewey:501. LCCN:77-005439.
Audience: **l,u,f.**

Gutting, Gary (Editor)   **Q175**
Continental Philosophy of Science. Trade Cloth. Blackwell
Publishing, Inc. Malden, MA. 2004. 344p. Blackwell Readings
in Continental Philosophy Ser. ISBN:0-631-23609-0, ISBN13:
978-0-631-23609-2. Dewey:501. LCCN:2004-016924.

Audience: **u,f.**

Gutting, Gary (Editor)   **Q175.3.P37**
Paradigms and Revolutions: Appraisals and Applications of
Thomas Kuhn's Philosophy of Science. Cloth Text. University
of Notre Dame Press. Notre Dame, IN. 1980. 256p.
ISBN:0-268-01542-2, ISBN13: 978-0-268-01542-8. Dewey:501.
LCCN:80-020745.

Audience: **l,u.** 𝓑

Hacking, Ian   **Q175 .H2 1983**
Representing and Intervening: Introductory Topics in the
Philosophy of Natural Science. Cloth Text. Cambridge
University Press. New York, NY. 1983. 302p.
ISBN:0-521-23829-3, ISBN13: 978-0-521-23829-8. Dewey:501.
LCCN:83-005132.

Audience: **l.** 𝓑

Hanson, Norwood R.   **Q175**
Patterns of Discovery: An Enquiry into the Conceptual
Foundations of Science. Cloth Text. Cambridge University
Press. New York, NY. 1958. 252p. ISBN:0-521-05197-5,
ISBN13: 978-0-521-05197-2. Dewey:501.

Audience: **l,u.**

Hanson, Norwood R.   **Q175 .H274**
Perception and Discovery: An Introduction to Scientific Inquiry.
Willard C. Humphreys (Editor), Michael Scriven (Preface by).
Paper Text. Freeman, Cooper & Company. San Francisco, CA.
1969. 435p. ISBN:0-87735-510-X, ISBN13: 978-0-87735-510-6.
Dewey:501. LCCN:75-095161.

Audience: **l.**

Harre, Rom   **Q175.H3255 1983**
An Introduction to the Logic of the Sciences. Ed. 2. Cloth Text.
Palgrave Macmillan. New York, NY. 1983. 174p.
ISBN:0-312-42911-8, ISBN13: 978-0-312-42911-9. Dewey:501.
LCCN:82-042709.

Audience: **l.** 𝓑

Harre, Rom   **Q175**
Matter and Method. Library Binding. Ridgeview Publishing
Company. Atascadero, CA. 1977. x, 124p. ISBN:0-917930-28-2,
ISBN13: 978-0-917930-28-7. Dewey:501.09.

Audience: **l,u.**

Harre, Rom   **Q175.H327**
Scientific Thought 1900-1960: A Selective Survey. Trade Cloth.
Oxford University Press, Inc. New York, NY. 1969. viii, 277p.
ISBN:0-19-858125-4, ISBN13: 978-0-19-858125-3.
Dewey:509/.04. LCCN:74-409990.

Audience: **g,l.** 𝓑

Heisenberg, Werner   **Q175 .H393 1970**
The Physicist's Conception of Nature. Arnold J. Pomerans
(Translator). Trade Cloth. Greenwood Publishing Group, Inc.
Portsmouth, NH. 1970. 192p. ISBN:0-8371-3107-3, ISBN13:
978-0-8371-3107-8. Dewey:501. LCCN:72-090526.

Audience: **l,u,f.** 𝓑

Hempel, Carl G.   **Q175**
Aspects of Scientific Explanation. Trade Paper. Simon &
Schuster. New York, NY. 1970. 504p. ISBN:0-02-914340-3,
ISBN13: 978-0-02-914340-7. Dewey:501. LCCN:65-015441.

Audience: **g,u,f.**

Hesse, Mary   **Q175.H4317**
Revolutions and Reconstructions in the Philosophy of Science.
Trade Cloth. Indiana University Press. Bloomington, IN. 1980.
224p. ISBN:0-253-33381-4, ISBN13: 978-0-253-33381-0.
Dewey:501. LCCN:80-007819.

Audience: **l,u.** 𝓑

Holton, Gerald   **Q175**
Science and Anti-Science. Harvard. 1993. ISBN:0-674-79298-X,
ISBN13: 978-0-674-79298-2.

Audience: **u,f.**

Horwich, Paul   **Q175**
Probability and Evidence. Cloth Text. Cambridge University
Press. New York, NY. 1982. 154p. Cambridge Studies in
Philosophy ISBN:0-521-23758-0, ISBN13: 978-0-521-23758-1.
Dewey:501. LCCN:81-018144.

Audience: **g.** 𝓑

Hubner, Kurt   **Q175**
Critique of Scientific Reason. Paul R. Dixon Jr. & Hollis M.
Dixon (Translators). Library Binding. University of Chicago
Press. Chicago, IL. 1997. 296p. ISBN:0-226-35708-2, ISBN13:
978-0-226-35708-9. Dewey:501. LCCN:82-023690.

Audience: **f.** 𝓑

Hutten, Ernest H.   **Q175 .H96 1978**
The Origins of Science: An Inquiry into the Foundations of
Western Thought. Trade Cloth. Greenwood Publishing Group,
Inc. Portsmouth, NH. 1978. 241p. ISBN:0-313-20003-3,
ISBN13: 978-0-313-20003-8. Dewey:501. LCCN:77-013633.

Audience: **l,u,f.** 𝓑

Jeffreys, Harold   **BC21.I6**
Scientific Inference. Ed. 3. Cloth Text. Cambridge University
Press. New York, NY. 1973. 244p. ISBN:0-521-08446-6,
ISBN13: 978-0-521-08446-8. Dewey:501/.8. LCCN:71-179159.

Audience: **l,u.** 𝓑

Jevons, W. Stanley   **Q175 .J4 1874**
Principles of Science. Ed. 2. Library Binding.
Lincoln-Rembrandt Publishing. Charlottesville, VA. 1986.
ISBN:0-935005-47-1, ISBN13: 978-0-935005-47-9. Dewey:501.

Audience: **l,u.**

Joravsky, David   **Q173 .J64**
Soviet Marxism and Natural Science, 1917-1932. Trade Cloth.
Columbia University Press. New York, NY. 1961.
ISBN:0-231-02443-6, ISBN13: 978-0-231-02443-3.
Dewey:530.1. LCCN:60-014070.

Audience: **g.** 𝓑

Jordan, Pascual   **Q125 .J5813 1974**
Science and the Course of History. Ralph Manheim (Translator).
Library Binding. Greenwood Publishing Group, Inc. Portsmouth,
NH. 1974. 139p. ISBN:0-8371-7280-2, ISBN13:
978-0-8371-7280-4. Dewey:509. LCCN:73-017920.

Audience: **g.**

Kaku, Michio   **QB981**
Parallel Worlds: A Journey Through Creation, Higher Dimensions, and the Future of the Cosmos. Doubleday. 2005. ISBN:0-385-50986-3, ISBN13: 978-0-385-50986-2.
Audience: **g.**

Keller, Evelyn F.   **Q175.K28 1985**
Reflections on Gender and Science. Trade Cloth. Yale University Press. Cumberland, RI. 1985. 176p. ISBN:0-300-03291-9, ISBN13: 978-0-300-03291-8. Dewey:501. LCCN:84-017327.
Audience: **l,u,f.** *B*

Kemeny, John G.   **Q175 .K3**
Philosopher Looks at Science. Paper Text. Van Nostrand Reinhold. New York, NY. 1959. ISBN:0-442-04324-4, ISBN13: 978-0-442-04324-7. Dewey:501.
Audience: **g.** *B*

Klee, Robert   **Q175.K548 1997**
Introduction to the Philosophy of Science: Cutting Nature at Its Seams. Paper Text. Oxford University Press, Inc. New York, NY. 1996. 272p. ISBN:0-19-510611-3, ISBN13: 978-0-19-510611-4. Dewey:501. LCCN:96-018851.
Audience: **l,u,f.** *Choice, 1998.*

Krige, John   **Q174.8**
Science, Revolution and Discontinuity. Trade Cloth. Ashgate Publishing, Ltd. Aldershot, 1994. 232p. Modern Revivals in Philosophy Ser. ISBN:0-7512-0294-0, ISBN13: 978-0-7512-0294-6. Dewey:501.
Audience: **g,l,u.**

Kuhn, Thomas S.   **Q175**
The Essential Tension: Selected Studies in Scientific Tradition and Change. Library Binding. University of Chicago Press. Chicago, IL. 1978. xxiii, 366p. ISBN:0-226-45805-9, ISBN13: 978-0-226-45805-2. Dewey:501. LCCN:77-078069.
Audience: **u,f.** *B*

Kuhn, Thomas S.   **Q175.K95 1996**
The Structure of Scientific Revolutions. Ed. 3. Trade Cloth. University of Chicago Press. Chicago, IL. 1996. 226p. ISBN:0-226-45807-5, ISBN13: 978-0-226-45807-6. Dewey:509. LCCN:96-013195.
Audience: **l,u,f.** *B*

Ladyman, James   **Q175.L174 2001**
Understanding the Philosophy of Science. Paper over Boards. Routledge. New York, NY. 2002. 304p. ISBN:0-415-22156-0, ISBN13: 978-0-415-22156-6. Dewey:501. LCCN:2001-048105.
Audience: **l,u.** *Choice, 2002.*

Lakatos, Imre & Musgrave,   **Q175.I514 1965**
 Alan E. (Editors)
Criticism and the Growth of Knowledge: Proceedings of the International Colloquium in the Philosophy of Science, London 1965. T. S. Kuhn (Introduction by). Trade Cloth. Cambridge University Press. New York, NY. 1970. 290p. ISBN:0-521-07826-1, ISBN13: 978-0-521-07826-9. Dewey:501. LCCN:78-105496.
Audience: **u,f.** *B*

Laszlo, Ervin   **Q175.L288 1996**
The Whispering Pond: A Personal Guide to the Emerging Vision of Science. Trade Paper. Element Books, Inc. Boston, MA. 1996. 208p. ISBN:1-85230-899-0, ISBN13: 978-1-85230-899-5. Dewey:501. LCCN:96-032555.
Audience: **g.** *Choice, 1997.*

Laudan, Larry   **Q175.L2938 1996**
Beyond Positivism and Relativism: Theory, Method, and Evidence. Trade Paper. Westview Press. Boulder, CO. 1996. 288p. ISBN:0-8133-2469-6, ISBN13: 978-0-8133-2469-2. Dewey:501. LCCN:95-040997.
Audience: **l,u.** *Choice, 1996.*

Laudan, Larry   **Q125.L34**
Progress and Its Problems: Towards a Theory of Scientific Growth. Trade Cloth. University of California Press. Berkeley, CA. 1977. x, 257 p. ;p. ISBN:0-520-03330-2, ISBN13: 978-0-520-03330-6. Dewey:501. LCCN:76-024586.
Audience: **u,f.** *B*

Medawar, Peter Brian   **Q175.M433 1984**
The Limits of Science. Trade Cloth. HarperCollins Publishers. New York, NY. 1984. 124p. ISBN:0-06-039036-0, ISBN13: 978-0-06-039036-5. Dewey:501. LCCN:83-048841.
Audience: **g.** *B*

Nagel, Ernest   **Q175 .N22**
Structure of Science: Problems in the Logic of Scientific Explanation. Cloth Text. Harcourt College Publishers. Fort Worth, TX. 1961. ISBN:0-15-584665-5, ISBN13: 978-0-15-584665-4. Dewey:501.
Audience: **l,u.** *B*

Needham, Joseph   **T14.5**
Moulds of Understanding: A Pattern of Natural Philosophy. Trade Cloth. Ashgate Publishing, Ltd. Aldershot, 1993. 320p. Modern Revivals in Philosophy Ser. ISBN:0-7512-0209-6, ISBN13: 978-0-7512-0209-0. Dewey:303.4/83.
Audience: **g,l.** *B*

Pearson, Karl   **Q175.P36 2004**
The Grammar of Science. Cloth over Boards. Dover Publications, Inc. Mineola, NY. 2004. 416p. Dover Phoenix Editions Ser. ISBN:0-486-49581-7, ISBN13: 978-0-486-49581-1. Dewey:501. LCCN:2004-047849.
Audience: **g,l,u,f.** *B*

Pickering, Andrew   **Q175.P522 1995**
The Mangle of Practice: Time, Agency, and Science. Trade Cloth. University of Chicago Press. Chicago, IL. 1995. 296p. ISBN:0-226-66802-9, ISBN13: 978-0-226-66802-4. Dewey:501. LCCN:94-044546.
Audience: **g,l,u,f.** *Choice, 1996.*

Poincare, Jules Henri   **Q175**
The Foundations of Science. George B. Halstead (Translator), L. P. Williams & Josiah Royce (Introduction by). Library Binding. University Press of America, Inc. Lanham, MD. 1982. 568p. ISBN:0-8191-2318-8, ISBN13: 978-0-8191-2318-3. Dewey:501. LCCN:81-048682.
Audience: **g,l.**

Popper, Karl R.   **Q175.P8643 1983**
Realism and the Aim of Science. W. W. Bartley III (Editor). Cloth Text. Rowman & Littlefield Publishers, Inc. Lanham, MD. 1983. 464p. Postscript to the Logic of Scientific Discovery Ser. ISBN:0-8476-7015-5, ISBN13: 978-0-8476-7015-4. Dewey:501. LCCN:82-000501.
Audience: **g,l,u,f.** *B*

Reichenbach, Hans   **Q175.3.R43 1981**
Modern Philosophy of Science: Selected Essays. Maria Reichenbach (Editor), Rudolf Carnap (Foreword by). Library

Binding. Greenwood Publishing Group, Inc. Portsmouth, NH. 1982. ix, 214p. ISBN:0-313-23274-1, ISBN13: 978-0-313-23274-9. Dewey:501. LCCN:81-013344.

Audience: **g,l.** ℬ

Rescher, Nicholas   **Q175.R39333**
Peirce's Philosophy of Science: Critical Studies in His Theory of Induction and Scientific Method. Cloth Text. University of Notre Dame Press. Notre Dame, IN. 1978. 160p. ISBN:0-268-01526-0, ISBN13: 978-0-268-01526-8. Dewey:501. LCCN:77-082479.

Audience: **g,l.** ℬ

Russell, Bertrand   **Q175**
Impact of Science on Society. Trade Cloth. A M S Press, Inc. New York, NY. ISBN:0-404-05466-8, ISBN13: 978-0-404-05466-3. Dewey:504. LCCN:68-054290.

Audience: **g,l.** ℬ

Salk, Jonas   **Q175.S2326 1985**
Anatomy of Reality: Merging of Intuition and Reason. Trade Paper. Holt, Rinehart & Winston. Austin, TX. 1984. xxvii, 124p. Convergence Ser. ISBN:0-03-001013-6, ISBN13: 978-0-03-001013-2. Dewey:128. LCCN:84-017920.

Audience: **g,l.** ℬ

Salmon, Wesley Charles   **Q175.S2337 1998**
Causality and Explanation. Trade Paper. Oxford University Press, Inc. New York, NY. 1998. 448p. ISBN:0-19-510864-7, ISBN13: 978-0-19-510864-4. Dewey:501. LCCN:96-048651.

Audience: **g,l,u.** *Choice, 1998.*

Salmon, Wesley Charles   **Q175**
The Foundations of Scientific Inference. Trade Paper. University of Pittsburgh Press. Pittsburgh, PA. 1967. 157p. ISBN:0-8229-5118-5, ISBN13: 978-0-8229-5118-6. Dewey:501. LCCN:67-021649.

Audience: **l,u.** ℬ

Salmon, Wesley Charles   **Q175.S23415 1984**
Scientific Explanation and the Causal Structure of the World. Trade Cloth. Princeton University Press. Princeton, NJ. 1984. 304p. ISBN:0-691-07293-0, ISBN13: 978-0-691-07293-7. Dewey:501. LCCN:84-042562.

Audience: **g,l,u.** ℬ

Scheffler, Israel   **Q175 .S33 1981**
The Anatomy of Inquiry: Philosophical Studies in the Theory of Science. Trade Cloth. Hackett Publishing Company, Inc. Indianapolis, IN. 1981. 350p. ISBN:0-915144-97-2, ISBN13: 978-0-915144-97-6. Dewey:501. LCCN:81-085415.

Audience: **l,u.** ℬ

Simon, Herbert A.   **Q175.S564 1996**
The Sciences of the Artificial. Ed. 3. Trade Cloth. MIT Press. Cambridge, MA. 1996. 215p. ISBN:0-262-19374-4, ISBN13: 978-0-262-19374-0. Dewey:155.9. LCCN:96-012633.

Audience: **l,u,f.** ℬ

Stengers, Isabelle   **Q175.P8822 1984B**
Order Out of Chaos: Man's New Dialogue with Nature. I. (Ilya) Prigogine (Contribution by), Alvin Toffler (Foreword by). Trade Paper. Bantam Books Canada, Inc. Toronto, ON. 1984. "xxxi, 349"p. ISBN:0-553-34082-4, ISBN13: 978-0-553-34082-2. Dewey:501. LCCN:83-021403.

Audience: **g,l.**

Toulmin, Stephen   **Q175**
The Philosophy of Science. Mass Market. HarperCollins Publishers. New York, NY. 1977. ISBN:0-06-130513-8, ISBN13: 978-0-06-130513-9. Dewey:501.

Audience: **g.**

Toulmin, Stephen E.   **Q175 .T64 1981**
Foresight and Understanding: An Enquiry into the Aims of Science. Jacques Barzun (Foreword by). Trade Cloth. Greenwood Publishing Group, Inc. Portsmouth, NH. 1982. 115p. ISBN:0-313-23345-4, ISBN13: 978-0-313-23345-6. Dewey:501. LCCN:81-013446.

Audience: **l,u,f.**

Webster, Charles   **Q125.W35 2002**
The Great Instauration: Science, Medicine and Reform, 1626-1660. Ed. 2. Paper Text. Peter Lang Publishing, Inc. New York, NY. 2002. 670p. Studies in the History of Medicine, Vol. 3 ISBN:0-8204-5616-0, ISBN13: 978-0-8204-5616-4. Dewey:509.42/09/032. LCCN:2002-069528.

Audience: **l,u,f.**

Weizsacker, Carl F. Von   **Q175 .W5117**
History of Nature. Trade Paper. University of Chicago Press. Chicago, IL. 1976. Midway Reprint Ser. ISBN:0-226-89190-9, ISBN13: 978-0-226-89190-3. Dewey:504. LCCN:49-010947.

Audience: **g,l.**

Whewell, William   **Q175 .W55**
The Philosophy of the Inductive Sciences. Ed. 2. Trade Cloth. Johnson Reprint Corporation. New York, NY. ISBN:0-384-67940-4, ISBN13: 978-0-384-67940-5. Dewey:501.

Audience: **f.**

Whitehead, Alfred North   **Q175 .W58**
The Concept of Nature: Tarner Lectures. Trade Cloth. Cambridge University Press. New York, NY. 1920. 212p. ISBN:0-521-06787-1, ISBN13: 978-0-521-06787-4. Dewey:501.

Audience: **l,u,f.**

Whitehead, Alfred North   **Q175**
Essays in Science and Philosophy. Trade Cloth. Greenwood Publishing Group, Inc. Portsmouth, NH. 1968. 348p. ISBN:0-8371-0268-5, ISBN13: 978-0-8371-0268-9. Dewey:82. LCCN:68-021332.

Audience: **g,l,u,f.** ℬ

Whitehead, Alfred North   **Q175**
Nature and Life. Trade Cloth. Greenwood Publishing Group, Inc. Portsmouth, NH. 1970. 46p. ISBN:0-8371-0751-2, ISBN13: 978-0-8371-0751-6. Dewey:501. LCCN:69-014150.

Audience: **g,u,f.** ℬ

Whittaker, Edmund T.   **Q175 .W6513**
From Euclid to Eddington: A Study of Conceptions of the External World. Trade Cloth. A M S Press, Inc. New York, NY. ISBN:0-404-14631-7, ISBN13: 978-0-404-14631-3. Dewey:501. LCCN:75-041295.

Audience: **g,l.**

Wiesner, Jerome B.   **Q127.U6 W5**
Where Science and Politics Meet. Trade Cloth. McGraw-Hill Companies, The. New York, NY. 1965. ISBN:0-07-069063-4, ISBN13: 978-0-07-069063-9. Dewey:509.73.

Audience: **u,f.** ℬ

Winter, Henry J.   **Q127**
Eastern Science: An Outline of Its Scope and Contribution.
Trade Cloth. Greenwood Publishing Group, Inc. Portsmouth,
NH. 1986. 114p. The Wisdom of the East Ser.
ISBN:0-313-23155-9, ISBN13: 978-0-313-23155-1.
Dewey:509.5. LCCN:85-024804.

                   Audience: **l,u,f.**

Yost, Jeffrey R.   **Z7405**
A Bibliographic Guide to Resources in Scientific Computing,
1945-1975. Cloth Text. Greenwood Publishing Group, Inc.
Portsmouth, NH. 2002. 272p. Bibliographies and Indexes in
Library and Information Science, No. 15 ISBN:0-313-31681-3,
ISBN13: 978-0-313-31681-4. Dewey:016.502/85.
LCCN:2002-069622.

         Audience: **l,u,f.** *Choice, 2003.*

Ziman, John M.   **Q175**
Reliable Knowledge. Cloth Text. Cambridge University Press.
New York, NY. 1979. 224p. ISBN:0-521-22087-4, ISBN13:
978-0-521-22087-3. Dewey:501. LCCN:78-003792.

         Audience: **l,u.** *B*

General

            Z1035
Choice: Current Reviews for College Libraries. Chicago:
American Library Association, March 1964- 11 issues/yr.

                   Audience: **u,f.**

Eventline. The Netherlands: Excerpta Medica Medical
Communications, 1989-.

                   Audience: **u,f.**

ISI Proceedings. Science & Technology edition. Philadelphia:
Thomson/ISI, 2001- (Part of ISI Web of Knowledge).

                   Audience: **u,f.**

            Z7403
Science Books & Films. Washington, DC: American Association
for the Advancement of Science. 5/yr.

                   Audience: **u,f.**

            Z1035.1
Walford's Guide to Reference Material, Vol. 1. Ed. 7. Trade
Cloth. K. G. Saur Verlag GmbH & Company. Munchen 70,
1996. xii, 967p. ISBN:3-598-11346-3, ISBN13:
978-3-598-11346-8. Dewey:011/.02.

                   Audience: **u,f.**

            Q11
World Meetings: United States and Canada. NY: Macmillan
Information, v. 1- , Sept. 1963-.

                   Audience: **u,f.**

Balay, Robert (Editor)   **Z1035.1.S43 1986**
Guide to Reference Books: Covering Materials from 1985-1990,
Supplement to the Tenth Edition. Cloth Text. American Library
Association. Chicago, IL. 1992. 624p. ISBN:0-8389-0588-9,
ISBN13: 978-0-8389-0588-3. Dewey:011.02. LCCN:92-006463.

                   Audience: **u,f.**

Balay, Robert (Editor), et al.   **Z1035.1.G89 1996**
Guide to Reference Books. Ed. 11. Vee F. Carrington & Murray
S. Martin (Editors). Trade Cloth. American Library Association.

Chicago, IL. 1996. 2,040p. ISBN:0-8389-0669-9, ISBN13:
978-0-8389-0669-9. Dewey:011/.02. LCCN:95-026322.

         Audience: **u,f.** *Choice, 1996.*

Burr, John R. & Burr,   **B801**
  Charlotte A.
World Philosophy: A Contemporary Bibliography, No. 3. Cloth
Text. Greenwood Publishing Group, Inc. Portsmouth, NH. 1993.
400p. Bibliographies and Indexes in Philosophy Ser., No. 3
ISBN:0-313-24032-9, ISBN13: 978-0-313-24032-4.
Dewey:016.109047. LCCN:93-018031.

         Audience: **u.** *Choice, 1994.*

Bynagle, Hans E.   **Z7125**
Philosophy: A Guide to Reference Literature. Ed. 2. James
Rettig (Editor). Book, Other. Libraries Unlimited, Inc. Westport,
CT. 1996. 233p. Reference Sources in the Humanities Ser.
ISBN:1-56308-376-0, ISBN13: 978-1-56308-376-1.
Dewey:016.1. LCCN:96-031379.

         Audience: **u,f.** *Choice, 1997, 1986.*

Grogan, Denis Joseph   **Q223.G76 1970**
Science and Technology; an Introduction to the Literature. Trade
Cloth. Shoe String Press, Inc. North Haven, CT. 1970. 231p.
ISBN:0-208-00888-8, ISBN13: 978-0-208-00888-6. Dewey:507.
LCCN:75-013921.

                   Audience: **l,u,f.**

Hurt, C. D.   **Z7401.H85 1998**
Information Sources in Science and Technology. Ed. 3. Trade
Paper. Libraries Unlimited, Inc. Westport, CT. 1998. 346p.
Library and Information Science Text Ser. ISBN:1-56308-531-3,
ISBN13: 978-1-56308-531-4. Dewey:016.5. LCCN:98-019547.

         Audience: **u,f.** *Choice, 1999.*

Kathryl Wolff, Susan M.   **Q181**
  O'Connell, and Valerie J. Montenegro, comp. and ed.
AAAS Science Book List, 1978-1986. Washington, DC:
American Association for the Advancement of Science. 1986.
ISBN:0-87168-315-6, ISBN13: 978-0-87168-315-1.

                   Audience: **u,f.**

Roth, John K. (Editor)   **B104.W67 2000**
World Philosophers and Their Works, 3 vols. Christian J. Moose
(Editor-In-Chief), Rowena Wildin (Editorial Coordinator).
Library Binding. Salem Press, Inc. Hackensack, NJ. 2000.
2066p. ISBN:0-89356-878-3, ISBN13: 978-0-89356-878-8.
Dewey:109. LCCN:99-055143.

         Audience: **g,l.** *Choice, 2001.*

Von Baeyer, Hans Christian   **Q223.V66 2004**
Information: The New Language of Science. Trade Cloth.
Harvard University Press. Cambridge, MA. 2004. 272p.
ISBN:0-674-01387-5, ISBN13: 978-0-674-01387-2.
Dewey:501.4. LCCN:2003-068570.

         Audience: **g,l.** *Choice, 2004.*

General > Addresses, Essays, Lectures

Raymo, Chet   **QB224**
Walking Zero: Discovering Cosmic Space and Time along the
Prime Meridian. Walker & Co. 2006. ISBN:0-8027-1494-3,
ISBN13: 978-0-8027-1494-7.

                   Audience: **g,l.**

Terminology

Darian, Steven G.   **Q175.D2685 2003**
Understanding the Language of Science. Trade Cloth. University
of Texas Press. Austin, TX. 2003. 262p. ISBN:0-292-71617-6,
ISBN13: 978-0-292-71617-9. Dewey:501/.4.
LCCN:2002-154613.

Audience: **g,l,u.** *Choice, 2004.*

Nybakken, Oscar E.   **Q179 .N9**
Greek and Latin in Scientific Terminology. Trade Paper.
Blackwell Publishing Professional. Ames, IA. 1985. 322p.
ISBN:0-8138-0721-2, ISBN13: 978-0-8138-0721-8.
Dewey:501.4. LCCN:59-005992.

Audience: **l,u.** *B*

Research. Study and Teaching. Tables

☐ Applied Science & Technology Full Text.
http://www.hwwilson.com/
H.W. Wilson.

Audience: **l,u,f.**

Z7403

☐ General Science Full Text.
http://www.hwwilson.com/
H.W. Wilson.

Audience: **l,u,f.**

Q199

☐ Knovel Critical Tables.
http://www.knovel.com/knovel2/Toc.jsp?BookID=761&
VerticalID=0
Knovel Corporation (Knovel Library).

Audience: **u,f.**

QD8

☐ NIST Chemistry Webbook.
http://webbook.nist.gov/chemistry/

Audience: **l,u,f.**

Q224

☐ NIST Physical Reference Data.
http://physics.nist.gov/PhysRefData/contents.html

Audience: **g,l,u,f.**

Q224

☐ NSDL The National Science Digital Library.
http://nsdl.org/
National Science Foundation.

Audience: **l,u,f.**

Q224

☐ Office of Scientific and Technical Information.
http://www.osti.gov
Ed. 2006.

Audience: **g,l,u,f.**

General Works. History

Hobart, Michael E. &   **T14.5**
  Schiffman, Zachary S.
Information Ages: Literacy, Numeracy and the Computer
Revolution. Trade Paper. Johns Hopkins University Press.
Baltimore, MD. 2000. 320p. ISBN:0-8018-6412-7, ISBN13:
978-0-8018-6412-4. Dewey:303.4/83.

Audience: **u,f.**

Hunter, Louis C.   **HD1694.A5H76 1991**
ⓔ A History of Industrial Power in the United States,
1780-1930. E-Book. NetLibrary, Inc. Boulder, CO. 1991.
ISBN:0-585-35402-2, ISBN13: 978-0-585-35402-6.
Dewey:338.4/0973.

Audience: **u,f.** *Choice, 1986.*

Lienhard, John H.   **E169.1.L53945 2003**
Inventing Modern: Growing up with X-Rays, Skyscrapers, and
Tailfins. Trade Cloth. Oxford University Press, Inc. New York,
NY. 2003. 304p. ISBN:0-19-516032-0, ISBN13:
978-0-19-516032-1. Dewey:303.48/3/097309045.
LCCN:2002-156634.

Audience: **g.** *Choice, 2004.*

Thiher, Allen   **PN3352.S34T55 2005**
Fiction Refracts Science: Modernist Writers from Proust to
Borges. Saddle Stitched, Cloth over Boards, Dust Jacket.
University of Missouri Press. Columbia, MO. 2005. 297p.
ISBN:0-8262-1580-7, ISBN13: 978-0-8262-1580-2.
Dewey:809.9336. LCCN:2004-029232.

Audience: **g,f.** *Choice, 2005.*

General Works. History > Special Topics. Methodology

Yost, Jeffrey R.   **Z7405**
A Bibliographic Guide to Resources in Scientific Computing,
1945-1975. Cloth Text. Greenwood Publishing Group, Inc.
Portsmouth, NH. 2002. 272p. Bibliographies and Indexes in
Library and Information Science, No. 15 ISBN:0-313-31681-3,
ISBN13: 978-0-313-31681-4. Dewey:016.502/85.
LCCN:2002-069622.

Audience: **l,u,f.** *Choice, 2003.*

Study and Teaching. Tables

☐ Materials Properties Locator Database.
http://libweb.lib.buffalo.edu/sel/searchSelMaterials.html

Audience: **u,f.**

Ackermann, Robert J.   **Q175.A269 1985**
Data, Instruments and Theory: A Dialectical Approach to
Understanding Science. Trade Cloth. Princeton University Press.
Princeton, NJ. 1985. 224p. ISBN:0-691-07296-5, ISBN13:
978-0-691-07296-8. Dewey:501. LCCN:84-015938.

Audience: **g,l.** *B*

Collette, Alfred T.   **Q183.3.A1.C637 1984**
Science Instruction in the Middle and Secondary Schools. Trade
Cloth. Times Mirror Magazines, Incorporated, Book Division.
New York, NY. 1984. xvi, 565, 42,p. ISBN:0-8016-1095-8,

ISBN13: 978-0-8016-1095-0. Dewey:507.1/273.
LCCN:83-012126.

Audience: **l,u.** 𝐵

H. Bennett, (Editor)   **TP151**
The Chemical Formulary. Brooklyn, NY: Chemical Publ. Co., v.
1, 1933-v. 15, 1970; 3 v.; irregular.

Audience: **l,u,f.**

Hall, Carl W.   **Q40**
Laws and Models: Science, Engineering, and Technology. Boca
Raton, FL: CRC Press. 2000. ISBN:0-8493-2018-6, ISBN13:
978-0-8493-2018-7.

Audience: **u,f.**

Hiscox, Gardner Dexter   **T49**
Henley's Twentieth Century Book of Formulas, Processes, and
Trade Secrets. Sloane, T. O'Connor & Eisenson, Harry E.
(Editors). Publishers Agency. 1981. ISBN:0-87781-028-1,
ISBN13: 978-0-87781-028-5.

Audience: **g,l,u,f.**

Horvath, Ari L.   **TA151**
Conversion Tables of Units in Science & Engineering. NY:
Macmillan. 1986. ISBN:0-444-01150-1, ISBN13:
978-0-444-01150-3.

Audience: **l,u,f.**

Nelkin, Dorothy   **Q183.3.A1.N44**
Science Textbook Controversies and the Politics of Equal Time.
Trade Cloth. MIT Press. Cambridge, MA. 1977. xi, 174 p. ;p.
ISBN:0-262-14027-6, ISBN13: 978-0-262-14027-0.
Dewey:507/.1073. LCCN:76-058459.

Audience: **g.** 𝐵

Shamos, Morris H.   **Q183.3.A1S45 1995**
The Myth of Scientific Literacy. Mary B. Rowe (Foreword by).
Cloth Text. Rutgers University Press. Piscataway, NJ. 1995.
300p. ISBN:0-8135-2196-3, ISBN13: 978-0-8135-2196-1.
Dewey:507.1/073. LCCN:94-041057.

Audience: **l,u.** *Choice, 1995.*

Shortland, Michael   **Q223 .S48 1991**
Communicating Science Handbook. Trade Paper. Longman
Publishing Group. White Plains, NY. 1991. 200p.
ISBN:0-582-05709-4, ISBN13: 978-0-582-05709-8.
Dewey:501.4. LCCN:90-046395.

Audience: **g,l,u,f.**

Skolnick, Joan, et al.   **Q183.3.A1**
How To Encourage Girls in Math and Science: Strategies for
Parents and Educators. Carol Langbort & Lucille Day (Authors).
Trade Cloth. Prentice-Hall. Upper Saddle, NJ. 1982. 192p.
ISBN:0-13-405670-1, ISBN13: 978-0-13-405670-8.
Dewey:507/.1073.

Audience: **g.** 𝐵

Von Baeyer, Hans Christian   **Q223.V66 2004**
Information: The New Language of Science. Trade Cloth.
Harvard University Press. Cambridge, MA. 2004. 272p.
ISBN:0-674-01387-5, ISBN13: 978-0-674-01387-2.
Dewey:501.4. LCCN:2003-068570.

Audience: **g,l.** *Choice, 2004.*

Winter, Mark   **QD467**
⬚ WebElements.

http://www.webelements.com/
Ed. 2006.

Audience: **g,l,u.**

System Theory

Iberall, A. S.   **Q295**
Toward a General Science of Viable Systems. Cloth Text.
McGraw-Hill Companies, The. New York, NY. 1971. xvi, 414p.
ISBN:0-07-031672-4, ISBN13: 978-0-07-031672-0. Dewey:003.
LCCN:77-128790.

Audience: **u,f.** 𝐵

Vemuri, V. Rao   **Q295.V45**
Modeling of Complex Systems. Trade Cloth. Elsevier Science &
Technology Books. Saint Louis, MO. 1978. xvi, 448 p. :p.
Operations Research and Industrial Engineering Ser.
ISBN:0-12-716550-9, ISBN13: 978-0-12-716550-9. Dewey:003.
LCCN:77-077246.

Audience: **u,f.** 𝐵

Weinberg, Gerald M.   **Q295.W44 2001**
An Introduction to General Systems Thinking: Silver
Anniversary Edition. Trade Paper. Dorset House Publishing.
New York, NY. 2001. xxi, 279p. ISBN:0-932633-49-8, ISBN13:
978-0-932633-49-1. Dewey:003. LCCN:00-052289.

Audience: **u,f.**

Cybernetics

Alpaydin, Ethem   **Q325.5**
Introduction to Machine Learning. Cloth Text. MIT Press.
Cambridge, MA. 2004. 400p. Adaptive Computation and
Machine Learning Ser. ISBN:0-262-01211-1, ISBN13:
978-0-262-01211-9. Dewey:006.3/1. LCCN:2004-109627.

Audience: **u,f.**

Arbib, Michael A.   **Q310**
The Metaphorical Brain: An Introduction to Cybernetics as
Artificial Intelligence and Brain Theory. Trade Cloth. John
Wiley & Sons, Inc. Hoboken, NJ. 1972. 243p.
ISBN:0-471-03249-2, ISBN13: 978-0-471-03249-6.
Dewey:001.53. LCCN:72-002490.

Audience: **g.** 𝐵

Arbib, Michael A.   **Q310.A7193 1989**
The Metaphorical Brain 2: Neural Networks and Beyond. Ed. 2.
Trade Cloth. John Wiley & Sons, Inc. Hoboken, NJ. 1989. 458p.
ISBN:0-471-09853-1, ISBN13: 978-0-471-09853-9.
Dewey:006.3. LCCN:88-027877.

Audience: **g,l,u.** *Choice, 1990.*

Cristianini, Nello &   **Q325.5 .C75 2000**
  Shawe-Taylor, John
An Introduction to Support Vector Machines and Other
Kernel-Based Learning Methods. Trade Cloth. Cambridge
University Press. New York, NY. 2000. 204p.
ISBN:0-521-78019-5, ISBN13: 978-0-521-78019-3.
Dewey:006.3/1. LCCN:99-054716.

Audience: **l,u,f.**

Duda, Richard O., et al.   **Q327.D83 2000**
Pattern Classification, Part 1. Ed. 2. Peter E. Hart & David G.
Stork (Authors). Trade Cloth. John Wiley & Sons, Inc.
Hoboken, NJ. 2000. 680p. ISBN:0-471-05669-3, ISBN13:
978-0-471-05669-0. Dewey:006.4. LCCN:99-029981.

Audience: **u,f.**

Friedman, J. H., et al.   **Q325.75.F75 2001**
The Elements of Statistical Learning: Data Mining, Inference, and Prediction. Trevor Hastie & Robert Tibshirani (Authors). Trade Cloth. Springer. New York, NY. 2003. 552p. Series in Statistics ISBN:0-387-95284-5, ISBN13: 978-0-387-95284-0. Dewey:006.3/1. LCCN:2001-031433.

Audience: **u,f.**

Hassenstein, B.   **QP363.3**
Information and Control in the Living Organism: An Elementary Introduction. Ed. 99. Trade Paper. John Wiley & Sons, Inc. Hoboken, NJ. 1971. 159p. ISBN:0-470-35887-4, ISBN13: 978-0-470-35887-0. Dewey:591.1/88.

Audience: **g,l.** *B*

Mitchell, Thomas M.   **Q325.5.M58 1997**
Machine Learning. Cloth Text. McGraw-Hill Higher Education. Burr Ridge, IL. 1997. 432p. ISBN:0-07-042807-7, ISBN13: 978-0-07-042807-2. Dewey:006.3/1. LCCN:97-007692.

Audience: **u.**

Rheingold, Howard   **Q183.9**
Virtual Reality: The Revolutionary Technology of Computer-Generated Artificial Worlds - and How It Promises to Transform Society. Trade Paper. Simon & Schuster. New York, NY. 1992. 416p. ISBN:0-671-77897-8, ISBN13: 978-0-671-77897-2. Dewey:006.

Audience: **g.**

Weiss, Sholom M. &   **Q325.5.W45 1990**
 Kulikowski, Casimir A. (Editors)
Computer Systems That Learn: Classification and Prediction Methods from Statistics, Neural Nets, Machine Learning and Expert Systems. Trade Cloth. Elsevier Science & Technology Books. Saint Louis, MO. 1990. 223p. Machine Learning Ser. ISBN:1-55860-065-5, ISBN13: 978-1-55860-065-2. Dewey:006.3. LCCN:90-048187.

Audience: **g,l,u.**

Wiener, Norbert   **Q175 .W6516 1961**
Cybernetics or Control and Communication in the Animal and the Machine. Ed. 2. Trade Cloth. MIT Press. Cambridge, MA. 1961. 212p. ISBN:0-262-23007-0, ISBN13: 978-0-262-23007-0. Dewey:003.5.

Audience: **g,l.** *B*

Wiener, Norbert   **Q310.W5 1988**
Human Use of Human Beings: Cybernetics and Society. Trade Paper. Da Capo Press, Inc. Cambridge, MA. 1988. 200p. Quality Paperbacks Ser. ISBN:0-306-80320-8, ISBN13: 978-0-306-80320-8. Dewey:303.4/83. LCCN:87-037102.

Audience: **g,l.** *B*

Information Theory

Abramson, Norman   **Q360 .A2**
Information Theory and Coding. Trade Cloth. McGraw-Hill Companies, The. New York, NY. 1963. Electronics Ser. ISBN:0-07-000145-6, ISBN13: 978-0-07-000145-9. Dewey:519.7.

Audience: **l,u,f.** *B*

Brillouin, Leon   **Q175.B786 2004**
Science and Information Theory. Ed. 2. Cloth over Boards. Dover Publications, Inc. Mineola, NY. 2004. 368p. Dover

Phoenix Editions Ser. ISBN:0-486-43918-6, ISBN13: 978-0-486-43918-1. Dewey:003/.54. LCCN:2004-051975.

Audience: **g,l,u.** *B*

Campbell, Jeremy   **Q360.C33 1982**
Grammatical Man: Information, Entropy, Language and Life. Trade Cloth. Simon & Schuster. New York, NY. 1982. 320p. ISBN:0-671-44061-6, ISBN13: 978-0-671-44061-9. Dewey:001.53/9. LCCN:82-003272.

Audience: **g.** *B*

Kippenhahn, Rudolf   **Z103.K5613 1999**
Code Breaking: A History and Exploration. Trade Cloth. Overlook Press, The. New York, NY. 1999. 326p. ISBN:0-87951-919-3, ISBN13: 978-0-87951-919-3. Dewey:652.8/09. LCCN:98-048791.

Audience: **g.** *Choice, 1999.*

McEliece, Robert J.   **QA268**
Theory of Information and Coding. G. C. Rota, B. Doran, P. Flajolet, M. Ismail, T. Y. Lam, E. Lutwak & E. Wutwak (Contribution by). Cloth Text. Cambridge University Press. New York, NY. 2004. 410p. Encyclopedia of Mathematics and its Applications Ser., Vol. 86 ISBN:0-521-83185-7, ISBN13: 978-0-521-83185-7. Dewey:003/.54. LCCN:2005-280163.

Audience: **l,u.**

Stoll, Clifford   **HM851**
Silicon Snake Oil: Second Thoughts on the Information Highway. Trade Paper. Knopf Publishing Group. New York, NY. 1996. 256p. ISBN:0-385-41994-5, ISBN13: 978-0-385-41994-9. Dewey:303.48/33. LCCN:95-002537.

Audience: **g.** *Choice, 1995.*

Von Baeyer, Hans Christian   **Q223.V66 2004**
Information: The New Language of Science. Trade Cloth. Harvard University Press. Cambridge, MA. 2004. 272p. ISBN:0-674-01387-5, ISBN13: 978-0-674-01387-2. Dewey:501.4. LCCN:2003-068570.

Audience: **g,l.** *Choice, 2004.*

Scientific method

Ackoff, Russell L.   **T57.6 .A24 1984**
Scientific Method: Optimizing Applied Research Decisions. Cloth Text. Krieger Publishing Company. Melbourne, FL. 1984. 476p. ISBN:0-89874-661-2, ISBN13: 978-0-89874-661-7. Dewey:001.4/2. LCCN:83-012060.

Audience: **l,u.** *B*

Beveridge, William I.   **Q180.A1B48**
Art of Scientific Investigation. Trade Cloth. W. W. Norton & Company, Inc. New York, NY. 1957. ISBN:0-393-06287-2, ISBN13: 978-0-393-06287-8. Dewey:507.2.

Audience: **u,f.**

Conant, James B.   **Q175 .C64**
Science and Common Sense. Trade Cloth. Yale University Press. Cumberland, RI. 1951. Terry Lectures ISBN:0-300-00380-3, ISBN13: 978-0-300-00380-2. Dewey:507.2.

Audience: **g,l,u.**

Cox, David R. Q175 .C8
Planning of Experiments. Cloth Text. John Wiley & Sons, Inc. Hoboken, NJ. 1958. 308p. Probability and Statistics Ser. ISBN:0-471-18183-8, ISBN13: 978-0-471-18183-5. Dewey:001.434. LCCN:58-013457.

Audience: **f.**

Drew, Clifford J. Q180.55.M4.D73 1980
Introduction to Designing and Conducting Research. Ed. 2. Trade Cloth. Mosby. London, 1980. xi, 356 p. :p. ISBN:0-8016-1460-0, ISBN13: 978-0-8016-1460-6. Dewey:001.4/2. LCCN:79-025403.

Audience: **u,f.** *B*

Harre, Rom Q175
Great Scientific Experiments: Twenty Experiments That Changed Our View of the World. Trade Cloth. Oxford University Press, Inc. New York, NY. 1983. 224p. ISBN:0-19-520436-0, ISBN13: 978-0-19-520436-0. Dewey:507/.2.

Audience: **g,l.** *B*

John, J. A. & Quenouille, M. H. Q182.3 .J64 1977
Experiments: Design and Analysis. Ed. 2. Trade Cloth. Lubrecht & Cramer, Ltd. Port Jervis, NY. 1977. 296p. ISBN:0-85264-222-9, ISBN13: 978-0-85264-222-1. Dewey:001.4/24. LCCN:78-314211.

Audience: **f.** *B*

Laudan, Larry Q174.8
Science and Hypothesis: Historical Essays on Scientific Methodology. Trade Cloth. Springer. New York, NY. 1981. 269p. The University of Western Ontario Series in Philosophy of Science, No. 19 ISBN:90-277-1315-4, ISBN13: 978-90-277-1315-5. Dewey:501/.8. LCCN:81-015423.

Audience: **g,u,f.** *B*

Leedy, Paul D. & Ormrod, Jeanne Ellis Q180.55.M4L43 2005
Practical Research: Planning and Design. Ed. 8. Trade Paper. Prentice Hall PTR. Upper Saddle River, NJ. 2004. 352p. ISBN:0-13-110895-6, ISBN13: 978-0-13-110895-0. Dewey:001.4/2. LCCN:2003-066035.

Audience: **l,u,f.**

Levi, Isaac Q175 .L445 1973
Gambling with Truth: An Essay on Induction and the Aims of Science. Trade Paper. MIT Press. Cambridge, MA. 1974. 266p. ISBN:0-262-62026-X, ISBN13: 978-0-262-62026-0. Dewey:501/.8. LCCN:73-003092.

Audience: **u,f.** *B*

Morris, Richard B. Q175.M869 1983
Dismantling the Universe: The Nature of Scientific Discovery. Trade Cloth. Simon & Schuster. New York, NY. 1983. 224p. ISBN:0-671-45239-8, ISBN13: 978-0-671-45239-1. Dewey:501. LCCN:83-011324.

Audience: **g,l.** *B*

Popper, Karl R. Q175
The Logic of Scientific Discovery: 14th Printing. Ed. 2. Paper over Boards. Routledge. New York, NY. 2002. 544p. Classics Ser. ISBN:0-415-27843-0, ISBN13: 978-0-415-27843-0. Dewey:501.

Audience: **g,u,f.**

Salmon, Wesley Charles Q175.S2337 1998
Causality and Explanation. Trade Cloth. Oxford University Press, Inc. New York, NY. 1998. 448p. ISBN:0-19-510863-9, ISBN13: 978-0-19-510863-7. Dewey:501. LCCN:96-048651.

Audience: **g,l,u,f.** *Choice, 1998.*

Sindermann, C. J. Q175
Winning the Games Scientists Play. Trade Cloth. Springer. New York, NY. 1982. 304p. ISBN:0-306-41075-3, ISBN13: 978-0-306-41075-8. Dewey:502/.3. LCCN:82-012225.

Audience: **u,f.** *B*

Stock, M. Q180.55.M4S86 1985
A Practical Guide to Graduate Research. Cloth Text. McGraw-Hill Companies, The. New York, NY. 1985. 176p. ISBN:0-07-061583-7, ISBN13: 978-0-07-061583-0. Dewey:001.4. LCCN:84-007927.

Audience: **u,f.** *B*

Valiela, Ivan Q180.A1V35 2001
Doing Science: Design, Analysis, and Communication of Scientific Research. Trade Cloth. Oxford University Press, Inc. New York, NY. 2001. 304p. ISBN:0-19-507962-0, ISBN13: 978-0-19-507962-3. Dewey:507.2. LCCN:99-021693.

Audience: **u,f.** *Choice, 2001.*

Weimer, Walter B. (Editor) Q180.55.M4.W44
Notes on the Methodology of Scientific Research. Trade Cloth. John Wiley & Sons, Inc. Hoboken, NJ. 1979. 257p. ISBN:0-470-26650-3, ISBN13: 978-0-470-26650-2. Dewey:507/.2. LCCN:78-031093.

Audience: **u,f.** *B*

Zuckerman, Solly Q180.A1Z85 1971
Beyond the Ivory Tower: The Frontiers of Public and Private Science. Trade Cloth. Taplinger Publishing Company, Inc. Marlboro, NJ. 1971. ISBN:0-8008-0733-2, ISBN13: 978-0-8008-0733-7. Dewey:500. LCCN:72-137412.

Audience: **u.** *B*

Science and culture

Q175.4 .S6
Social Implications of the Scientific and Technological Revolution: UNESCO. Trade Paper. Bernan Associates. Lanham, MD. 1981. 408p. ISBN:92-3-101664-4, ISBN13: 978-92-3-101664-6. Dewey:303.4/83. LCCN:81-169437.

Audience: **g,l.** *B*

Bodanis, David QC522
Electric Universe: How Electricity Switched on the Modern World. Three Rivers Press. 2005. ISBN:0-307-33598-4, ISBN13: 978-0-307-33598-2.

Audience: **g,l.**

Botkin, Daniel B. QH31.T485B68 2001
No Man's Garden: Thoreau and a New Vision for Civilization and Nature. Trade Cloth. Island Press. Washington, DC. 2000. 288p. ISBN:1-55963-465-0, ISBN13: 978-1-55963-465-6. Dewey:304.2. LCCN:00-010445.

Audience: **g,l,u,f.** *Choice, 2001.*

Brannigan, Augustine Q180.55.S62
The Social Basis of Scientific Discoveries. Trade Cloth. Cambridge University Press. New York, NY. 1981. 224p.

ISBN:0-521-23695-9, ISBN13: 978-0-521-23695-9.
Dewey:306/.45. LCCN:81-006129.

Audience: **g.** *B*

Capra, Fritjof   Q175.C246 1982
The Turning Point: Science, Society and the Rising Culture.
Trade Cloth. Simon & Schuster. New York, NY. 1982. 464 p. :p.
ISBN:0-671-24423-X, ISBN13: 978-0-671-24423-1. Dewey:501.
LCCN:81-016584.

Audience: **g.** *B*

Cole, Jonathan R. & Cole,   Q149.U/
  Stephen
Social Stratification in Science. Library Binding. University of
Chicago Press. Chicago, IL. 1973. xiv, 283p.
ISBN:0-226-11338-8, ISBN13: 978-0-226-11338-8.
Dewey:305.55. LCCN:73-078166.

Audience: **g.** *B*

Cole, Leonard A.   Q175.52.U5.C653 1983
Politics and the Restraint of Science. Book, Other. Rowman &
Littlefield Publishers, Inc. Lanham, MD. 1983. 200p.
ISBN:0-86598-125-6, ISBN13: 978-0-86598-125-6. Dewey:500.
LCCN:83-002992.

Audience: **l,u.** *B*

Durbin, Paul T. (Editor)   Q175.5.G84 1984
A Guide to the Culture of Science, Technology, and Medicine.
Trade Cloth. Simon & Schuster. New York, NY. 1984. 784p.
ISBN:0-02-907890-3, ISBN13: 978-0-02-907890-7.
Dewey:303.4/83. LCCN:84-008140.

Audience: **g.** *B*

Easlea   Q175.52.E85 E2
Witch Hunting, Magic and the New Philosophy: An Introduction
to Debates of the Scientific Revolution, 1450-1750. Trade Paper.
Brill Academic Publishers, Inc. Boston, MA. 1981. 283p.
Harvester Studies in Philosophy, No. 14 ISBN:0-391-01808-6,
ISBN13: 978-0-391-01808-2. Dewey:303.4/83/094.
LCCN:81-119864.

Audience: **l,u.** *B*

Elman, Benjamin A.   Q127.C5
A Cultural History of Modern Science in China. Harvard
University Press. 2007.

Audience: **g,l,u,f.**

Gould, Stephen Jay   Q175.55
The Hedgehog, the Fox, and the Magister's Pox: Mending the
Gap Between Science and the Humanities. Trade Paper. Crown
Publishing Group. New York, NY. 2004. 288p.
ISBN:1-4000-5153-3, ISBN13: 978-1-4000-5153-3.
Dewey:303.483.

Audience: **g,l** *Choice, 2003.*

Graham, Loren R.   Q175.5
Between Science and Values. Trade Cloth. Columbia University
Press. New York, NY. 1981. 449p. ISBN:0-231-05192-1,
ISBN13: 978-0-231-05192-7. Dewey:303.4/83.
LCCN:81-004436.

Audience: **g.** *B*

Haas, Ernst B., et al.   Q175.5
Scientists and World Order: The Uses of Technical Knowledge
in International Organizations. Mary P. Williams & Don Babai
(Authors). Trade Cloth. University of California Press. Berkeley,

CA. 1978. xi, 368p. Studies in International Political Economy,
Vol. 1 ISBN:0-520-03341-8, ISBN13: 978-0-520-03341-2.
Dewey:301.24/3. LCCN:76-047981.

Audience: **u.** *B*

Jevons, Frederick Raphael   Q125
Science Observed: Science As a Social and Intellectual Activity.
Trade Cloth. Allen & Unwin, Ltd. London, 1973. 186p.
ISBN:0-04-502001-9, ISBN13: 978-0-04-502001-0.
Dewey:301.24/3. LCCN:73-173011.

Audience: **g.** *B*

Lienhard, John H.   E169.1.L53945 2003
Inventing Modern: Growing up with X-Rays, Skyscrapers, and
Tailfins. Trade Cloth. Oxford University Press, Inc. New York,
NY. 2003. 304p. ISBN:0-19-516032-0, ISBN13:
978-0-19-516032-1. Dewey:303.48/3/097309045.
LCCN:2002-156634.

Audience: **g.** *Choice, 2004.*

Lowrance, William W.   Q175.5.L68 1985
Modern Science and Human Values. Trade Cloth. Oxford
University Press, Inc. New York, NY. 1985. 256p.
ISBN:0-19-503605-0, ISBN13: 978-0-19-503605-3.
Dewey:303.4/83. LCCN:84-029609.

Audience: **g.** *B* *Choice, 1985.*

McMullin, Ernan (Editor)   Q175.5.S589 1992
The Social Dimensions of Science. Cloth Text. University of
Notre Dame Press. Notre Dame, IN. 1992. 328p. Studies in
Science and the Humanities from the Reilly Center, Vol. III
ISBN:0-268-01741-7, ISBN13: 978-0-268-01741-5.
Dewey:306.4/5. LCCN:91-050577.

Audience: **g.** *Choice, 1993.*

Nelkin, Dorothy   Q180.55.C5/
Science As Intellectual Property. Trade Cloth. Macmillan
Publishing Company, Inc. Old Tappan, NJ. 1984. 140p.
ISBN:0-02-949080-4, ISBN13: 978-0-02-949080-8.
Dewey:507/.2. LCCN:83-003805.

Audience: **g,l.** *B*

Postlewait, Thomas &   Q11.N5 VOL. 360
  Paradis, James G. (Editors)
Victorian Science and Victorian Values: Literary Perspectives.
Trade Cloth. New York Academy of Sciences. New York, NY.
1981. 362p. ISBN:0-89766-109-5, ISBN13: 978-0-89766-109-6.
Dewey:820/.9/008. LCCN:80-029513.

Audience: **u.** *B*

Richta, Radovan   CB478 .R4713
Civilization at the Crossroads: Social and Human Implications
of the Scientific and Technological Revolution. Trade Cloth. M.
E. Sharpe Inc. Armonk, NY. 1969. 372p. ISBN:0-87332-028-X,
ISBN13: 978-0-87332-028-3. Dewey:301.2/4. LCCN:68-014154.

Audience: **g.**

Rosenberg, Charles E.   Q127.U6R618 1997
No Other Gods: On Science and American Social Thought. Ed.
2. Trade Cloth. Johns Hopkins University Press. Baltimore, MD.
1997. 336p. ISBN:0-8018-5608-6, ISBN13: 978-0-8018-5608-2.
Dewey:303.48/3/0973. LCCN:96-051657.

Audience: **u,f.** *B*

Sarton, George   Q125 .S323 1971
Life of Science: Essays in the History of Civilization. Max H.
Fisch (Foreword by). Trade Cloth. Ayer Company Publishers,

Inc. Manchester, NH. 1977. Essay Index Reprint Ser.
ISBN:0-8369-2472-X, ISBN13: 978-0-8369-2472-5. Dewey:509.
LCCN:70-167410.

Audience: **u.** ℬ

Schroeer, Dietrich   **Q125**
Physics and Its 5th Dimension: Society. Cloth Text.
Addison-Wesley Longman, Inc. Boston, MA. 1972. xvi, 378p.
ISBN:0-201-06767-6, ISBN13: 978-0-201-06767-5.
Dewey:301.24/3. LCCN:75-184158.

Audience: **g,l,u.**

Spiegel-Rosing, Ina & Price,   **Q175.5.S373**
  Derek De Solla (Editors)
Science, Technology and Society: A Cross-Disciplinary
Perspective. Trade Cloth. SAGE Publications, Inc. Thousand
Oaks, CA. 1977. 607p. ISBN:0-8039-9858-9, ISBN13:
978-0-8039-9858-2. Dewey:500. LCCN:76-055928.

Audience: **g,l,u.** ℬ

Ziman, John M.   **Q175.5**
The Force of Knowledge. Trade Cloth. Cambridge University
Press. New York, NY. 1976. 383p. ISBN:0-521-20649-9,
ISBN13: 978-0-521-20649-5. Dewey:306/.45/09.
LCCN:75-023529.

Audience: **g.** ℬ

Ziman, John M.   **Q175.5**
Puzzles, Problems and Enigmas: Occasional Pieces on the
Human Aspects of Science. Trade Cloth. Cambridge University
Press. New York, NY. 1981. 378p. ISBN:0-521-23659-2,
ISBN13: 978-0-521-23659-1. Dewey:306/.45. LCCN:80-042112.

Audience: **g.** ℬ

Science and culture > Science and art

Pickover, Clifford A.   **QA614.86 .F6845 1996**
Fractal Horizons: The Future Uses of Fractals. Trade Cloth.
Palgrave Macmillan. New York, NY. 1996. 256p.
ISBN:0-312-12599-2, ISBN13: 978-0-312-12599-8.
Dewey:514/.74. LCCN:95-026043.

Audience: **g.** *Choice, 1997.*

Smith, Pamela H.   **N72.S3S65 2006**
The Body of the Artisan: Art and Experience in the Scientific
Revolution. Trade Paper. University of Chicago Press. Chicago,
IL. 2006. 408p. ISBN:0-226-76423-0, ISBN13:
978-0-226-76423-8. Dewey:509/.4/0903.

Audience: **g,l,u,f.** *Choice, 2004.*

Thiher, Allen   **PN3352.S34T55 2005**
Fiction Refracts Science: Modernist Writers from Proust to
Borges. Saddle Stitched, Cloth over Boards, Dust Jacket.
University of Missouri Press. Columbia, MO. 2005. 297p.
ISBN:0-8262-1580-7, ISBN13: 978-0-8262-1580-2.
Dewey:809.9336. LCCN:2004-029232.

Audience: **g,f.** *Choice, 2005.*

Science and Politics. Science and Technology Policy

Q175.4 .S6
Social Implications of the Scientific and Technological
Revolution: UNESCO. Trade Paper. Bernan Associates. Lanham,
MD. 1981. 408p. ISBN:92-3-101664-4, ISBN13:
978-92-3-101664-6. Dewey:303.4/83. LCCN:81-169437.

Audience: **g,l.** ℬ

Brannigan, Augustine   **Q180.55.S62**
The Social Basis of Scientific Discoveries. Trade Cloth.
Cambridge University Press. New York, NY. 1981. 224p.
ISBN:0-521-23695-9, ISBN13: 978-0-521-23695-9.
Dewey:306/.45. LCCN:81-006129.

Audience: **g.** ℬ

Cole, Jonathan R. & Cole,   **Q149.U/**
  Stephen
Social Stratification in Science. Library Binding. University of
Chicago Press. Chicago, IL. 1973. xiv, 283p.
ISBN:0-226-11338-8, ISBN13: 978-0-226-11338-8.
Dewey:305.55. LCCN:73-078166.

Audience: **g.** ℬ

Cole, Leonard A.   **Q175.52.U5.C653 1983**
Politics and the Restraint of Science. Book, Other. Rowman &
Littlefield Publishers, Inc. Lanham, MD. 1983. 200p.
ISBN:0-86598-125-6, ISBN13: 978-0-86598-125-6. Dewey:500.
LCCN:83-002992.

Audience: **l,u.** ℬ

Dickson, David   **Q127.U6D53 1988**
The New Politics of Science. Trade Paper. University of
Chicago Press. Chicago, IL. 1993. 411p. ISBN:0-226-14763-0,
ISBN13: 978-0-226-14763-5. Dewey:306/.45. LCCN:87-034275.

Audience: **g.** ℬ

Durbin, Paul T. (Editor)   **Q175.5.G84 1984**
A Guide to the Culture of Science, Technology, and Medicine.
Trade Cloth. Simon & Schuster. New York, NY. 1984. 784p.
ISBN:0-02-907890-3, ISBN13: 978-0-02-907890-7.
Dewey:303.4/83. LCCN:84-008140.

Audience: **g.** ℬ

Easlea   **Q175.52.E85 E2**
Witch Hunting, Magic and the New Philosophy: An Introduction
to Debates of the Scientific Revolution, 1450-1750. Trade Paper.
Brill Academic Publishers, Inc. Boston, MA. 1981. 283p.
Harvester Studies in Philosophy, No. 14 ISBN:0-391-01808-6,
ISBN13: 978-0-391-01808-2. Dewey:303.4/83/094.
LCCN:81-119864.

Audience: **l,u.** ℬ

Ehrlich, Paul R. & Ehrlich,   **GE195.E37 1996**
  Anne H.
Betrayal of Science and Reason: How Anti-Environmental
Rhetoric Threatens Our Future. Trade Cloth. Island Press.
Washington, DC. 1996. 348p. ISBN:1-55963-483-9, ISBN13:
978-1-55963-483-0. Dewey:333.7. LCCN:96-034249.

Audience: **g.** *Choice, 1997.*

Graham, Loren R.   **Q175.5**
Between Science and Values. Trade Cloth. Columbia University
Press. New York, NY. 1981. 449p. ISBN:0-231-05192-1,

ISBN13: 978-0-231-05192-7. Dewey:303.4/83.
LCCN:81-004436.

Audience: **g.** *B*

Haas, Ernst B., et al.   **Q175.5**
Scientists and World Order: The Uses of Technical Knowledge
in International Organizations. Mary P. Williams & Don Babai
(Authors). Trade Cloth. University of California Press. Berkeley,
CA. 1978. xi, 368p. Studies in International Political Economy,
Vol. 1 ISBN:0-520-03341-8, ISBN13: 978-0-520-03341-2.
Dewey:301.24/3. LCCN:76-047981.

Audience: **u.** *B*

Jevons, Frederick Raphael   **Q125**
Science Observed: Science As a Social and Intellectual Activity.
Trade Cloth. Allen & Unwin, Ltd. London, 1973. 186p.
ISBN:0-04-502001-9, ISBN13: 978-0-04-502001-0.
Dewey:301.24/3. LCCN:73-173011.

Audience: **g.** *B*

Katz, James E.   **Q127.U6.K37**
Presidential Politics and Science Policy. Trade Cloth.
Greenwood Publishing Group, Inc. Portsmouth, NH. 1978. xix,
292 p. ;p. Praeger Special Studies ISBN:0-03-040941-1,
ISBN13: 978-0-03-040941-7. Dewey:509/.73. LCCN:77-014024.

Audience: **g.** *B*

Lambright, W. Henry   **Q127.U6L29 1985**
Presidential Management of Science and Technology: The
Johnson Presidency. Trade Cloth. University of Texas Press.
Austin, TX. 1985. 238p. Administrative History of the Johnson
Presidency Ser. ISBN:0-292-76494-4, ISBN13:
978-0-292-76494-1. Dewey:338.97306. LCCN:84-028420.

Audience: **u,f.** *B Choice, 1985.*

Lowrance, William W.   **Q175.5.L68 1985**
Modern Science and Human Values. Trade Cloth. Oxford
University Press, Inc. New York, NY. 1985. 256p.
ISBN:0-19-503605-0, ISBN13: 978-0-19-503605-3.
Dewey:303.4/83. LCCN:84-029609.

Audience: **g.** *B Choice, 1985.*

Macrakis, Kristie   **Q180.G4.M3 1993**
Surviving the Swastika: Scientific Research in Nazi Germany.
Cloth Text. Oxford University Press, Inc. New York, NY. 1993.
320p. ISBN:0-19-507010-0, ISBN13: 978-0-19-507010-1.
Dewey:506/.043/09043. LCCN:93-019919.

Audience: **l,u,f.** *Choice, 1994.*

Martino, Joseph P.   **Q180.U5M326 1992**
Science Funding: Politics and Porkbarrel. Trade Cloth.
Transaction Publishers. Somerset, NJ. 1992. 336p.
ISBN:1-56000-033-3, ISBN13: 978-1-56000-033-4.
Dewey:507/.2/073. LCCN:91-029638.

Audience: **l,u,f.** *Choice, 1993.*

McGrath, Patrick J.   **2001035149 [Q]**
Scientists, Business and the State, 1890-1960. Trade Cloth.
University of North Carolina Press. Chapel Hill, NC. 2002.
264p. The Luther Hartwell Hodges Series on Business, Society,
and the State ISBN:0-8078-2655-3, ISBN13:
978-0-8078-2655-3. Dewey:338.97306. LCCN:2001-035149.

Audience: **g,l,u.** *Choice, 2002.*

Nelkin, Dorothy   **Q180.55.C5/**
Science As Intellectual Property. Trade Cloth. Macmillan
Publishing Company, Inc. Old Tappan, NJ. 1984. 140p.

ISBN:0-02-949080-4, ISBN13: 978-0-02-949080-8.
Dewey:507/.2. LCCN:83-003805.

Audience: **g,l.** *B*

Nelkin, Dorothy   **Q183.3.A1.N44**
Science Textbook Controversies and the Politics of Equal Time.
Trade Cloth. MIT Press. Cambridge, MA. 1977. xi, 174 p. ;p.
ISBN:0-262-14027-6, ISBN13: 978-0-262-14027-0.
Dewey:507/.1073. LCCN:76-058459.

Audience: **g.** *B*

Postlewait, Thomas &   **Q11.N5 VOL. 360**
  Paradis, James G. (Editors)
Victorian Science and Victorian Values: Literary Perspectives.
Trade Cloth. New York Academy of Sciences. New York, NY.
1981. 362p. ISBN:0-89766-109-5, ISBN13: 978-0-89766-109-6.
Dewey:820/.9/008. LCCN:80-029513.

Audience: **u.** *B*

Richta, Radovan   **CB478 .R4713**
Civilization at the Crossroads: Social and Human Implications
of the Scientific and Technological Revolution. Trade Cloth. M.
E. Sharpe Inc. Armonk, NY. 1969. 372p. ISBN:0-87332-028-X,
ISBN13: 978-0-87332-028-3. Dewey:301.2/4. LCCN:68-014154.

Audience: **g.**

Spiegel-Rosing, Ina & Price,   **Q175.5.S373**
  Derek De Solla (Editors)
Science, Technology and Society: A Cross-Disciplinary
Perspective. Trade Cloth. SAGE Publications, Inc. Thousand
Oaks, CA. 1977. 607p. ISBN:0-8039-9858-9, ISBN13:
978-0-8039-9858-2. Dewey:500. LCCN:76-055928.

Audience: **g,l,u.** *B*

Trenn, Thaddeus J.   **Q127.U6.T73 1983**
America's Golden Bough: The Science Advisory Intertwist.
Cloth Text. Oelgeschlager, Gunn & Hain, Inc. Weston, MA.
1983. 320p. ISBN:0-89946-160-3, ISBN13: 978-0-89946-160-1.
Dewey:338.4/75/0973. LCCN:82-018873.

Audience: **u,f.** *B*

Walker, J. Samuel   **TK1345.H37 W35 2004**
Three Mile Island: A Nuclear Crisis in Historical Perspective.
Trade Cloth. University of California Press. Berkeley, CA. 2004.
315p. ISBN:0-520-23940-7, ISBN13: 978-0-520-23940-1.
Dewey:363.17/99/0974818. LCCN:2003-010137.

Audience: **g,l,u,f.** *Choice, 2004.*

Wiesner, Jerome B.   **Q127.U6 W5**
Where Science and Politics Meet. Trade Cloth. McGraw-Hill
Companies, The. New York, NY. 1965. ISBN:0-07-069063-4,
ISBN13: 978-0-07-069063-9. Dewey:509.73.

Audience: **u,f.** *B*

Wilson, John T.   **Q127.U6.W534 1983**
Academic Science, Higher Education, and the Federal
Government, 1950-1983: Programs and Policies. Trade Cloth.
University of Chicago Press. Chicago, IL. 1983. 126p.
ISBN:0-226-90051-7, ISBN13: 978-0-226-90051-3.
Dewey:353.0085/5/09. LCCN:83-017964.

Audience: **u,f.** *B*

Ziman, John M.   **Q175.5**
The Force of Knowledge. Trade Cloth. Cambridge University
Press. New York, NY. 1976. 383p. ISBN:0-521-20649-9,
ISBN13: 978-0-521-20649-5. Dewey:306/.45/09.
LCCN:75-023529.

Audience: **g.** *B*

Ziman, John M.   **Q175.5**
Puzzles, Problems and Enigmas: Occasional Pieces on the
Human Aspects of Science. Trade Cloth. Cambridge University
Press. New York, NY. 1981. 378p. ISBN:0-521-23659-2,
ISBN13: 978-0-521-23659-1. Dewey:306/.45. LCCN:80-042112.
                                    Audience: **g.** *B*

Science and ethics

Lowrance, William W.   **Q175.5.L68 1985**
Modern Science and Human Values. Trade Cloth. Oxford
University Press, Inc. New York, NY. 1985. 256p.
ISBN:0-19-503605-0, ISBN13: 978-0-19-503605-3.
Dewey:303.4/83. LCCN:84-029609.
                        Audience: **g.** *B Choice, 1985.*

Science and humor

Berenbaum, May R.   **QL463**
Buzzwords: A Scientist Muses on Sex, Bugs, and Rock 'n' Roll.
National Academies Press. 2000. Joseph Henry Press
ISBN:0-309-07081-3, ISBN13: 978-0-309-07081-2.
                                    Audience: **g,l.**

Scientific notation

Cardarelli, Francois   **QC94**
Encyclopaedia of Scientific Units, Weights, and Measures: Their
SI Equivalences and Origins. Springer. 2003.
ISBN:1-85233-682-X, ISBN13: 978-1-85233-682-0.
                                    Audience: **g,l,u,f.**

War and Science

Hanford Cultural and   **TK9025.H36 2003**
  Historic Resources Program Staff (Contribution by)
Hanford Site Historic District: History of the Plutonium
Production Facilities, 1943-1990. Trade Cloth. Battelle Press.
Columbus, OH. 2003. 624p. ISBN:1-57477-133-7, ISBN13:
978-1-57477-133-6. Dewey:623.4/5119/0979751.
LCCN:2002-034473.
                        Audience: **g,u,f.** *Choice, 2003.*

GEOLOGY

This section contains resources related to the study of general geology, as well as specific subjects in the earth sciences. It includes resources related to the study of the Earth, its history, surface and subsurface features, rock types, resources, processes, past life, as well as references to the geology of World regions.

Since the third edition of Books for College Libraries was published, the role of plate tectonics in Earth processes has become more clearly understood and incorporated into books for every reading level. As a result, the very few of the titles from BCL3 have been retained. However, this should not be used as a reason to weed titles that are no longer included, as many of the titles in BCL3 are classic texts related to the history of geology.

The resources on this list include textbooks commonly used in undergraduate earth science courses, reference works, including encyclopedias and dictionaries, web sites and general titles on hot topics, such as earthquakes, volcanoes and natural hazards.

Where possible, the most recent edition of a title is recommended, although some classic titles that are only available as reprints and a few out of print titles are also included on the list.

— Andrea Twiss-Brooks and Linda Zellmer

General Geology/Physical Geography

American Geological   QE26.3
  Institute
☐ Earth Science World Image Bank.
http://www.earthscienceworld.org/images/index.html
American Geological Institute.
                                           Audience: **g,l,u,f.**

National Aeronautics and   TL793.5
  Space Administration
☐ NASA Image Exchange (NIX).
http://nix.nasa.gov/
National Aeronautics and Space Administration.
                                           Audience: **g,l,u,f.**

National Oceanic and   QC981
  Atmospheric Administration
☐ NOAA Photo Library.
http://www.photolib.noaa.gov/
National Oceanic and Atmospheric Administration.
                                           Audience: **g,l,u,f.**

U.S. Geological Survey   QE522
☐ USGS Earth Science Photographic Library Archive.
http://libraryphoto.cr.usgs.gov/
U.S. Geological Survey.
                                           Audience: **g,l,u,f.**

General Geology/Physical Geography > Reference Works

                                                           QE645
☐ Geologic Names Lexicon: GEOLEX.
http://ngmdb.usgs.gov/Geolex/geolex_home.html
                                           Audience: **l,u,f.**

                                                           G70.2
☐ National Geologic Maps Database: Geologic Map Image
Library.
http://purl.access.gpo.gov/GPO/LPS68723
                                           Audience: **l,u,f.**

Bates, Robert & Jackson,   QE5.B38 1997
  Julia A.
Glossary of Geology. Ed. 4. Trade Cloth. American Geological
Institute. Alexandria, VA. 2000. 800p. ISBN:0-922152-34-9,
ISBN13: 978-0-922152-34-6. Dewey:550/.3. LCCN:87-003579.
                                           Audience: **l,u,f.** ℬ

Dasch, E. Julius (Editor)   QE5.E5137 1996
Macmillan Encyclopedia of Earth Sciences, Set. Trade Cloth.
Thomson Gale. Farmington Hills, MI. 1996. 1272p.
ISBN:0-02-883000-8, ISBN13: 978-0-02-883000-1.
Dewey:550/.3. LCCN:96-011302.
                                    Audience: **l,u,f.** *Choice, 1997.*

Finkl, Charles W. (Editor)   QE5 .E5
ⓔ The Encyclopedia of Applied Geology. E-Book. Springer.
New York, NY. 2006. ISBN:0-387-30842-3, ISBN13:
978-0-387-30842-5. Dewey:624.1/51/0321.
                                           Audience: **u,f.**

Finkl, Charles W. (Editor)   QE5 .E515
ⓔ The Encyclopedia of Field and General Geology. E-Book.
Springer. New York, NY. 2006. ISBN:0-387-30844-X, ISBN13:
978-0-387-30844-9. Dewey:550/.3/21.
                                           Audience: **u,f.**

Goudie, Andrew S.   GB10.D53 2000
The Dictionary of Physical Geography. Ed. 3. David S. Thomas
(Editor). Trade Paper. Blackwell Publishing, Inc. Malden, MA.
2000. 624p. ISBN:0-631-20473-3, ISBN13: 978-0-631-20473-2.
Dewey:910/.02/03. LCCN:99-049818.
                                    Audience: **g,l,u,f.** *Choice, 2001.*

Goudie, Andrew (Editor)   GB400.3.E53 2003
Encyclopedia of Geomorphology. Mario Panizza (Foreword by).
Paper over Boards. Routledge. New York, NY. 2003. 1200p.
ISBN:0-415-27298-X, ISBN13: 978-0-415-27298-8.
Dewey:551.41/03. LCCN:2005-440494.
                                    Audience: **l,u,f.** *Choice, 2004.*

Kusky, Timothy M.   QE5.K85 2004
Encyclopedia of Earth Science. Trade Cloth. Facts On File, Inc..
New York, NY. 2005. 528p. Science Encyclopedia Ser.
ISBN:0-8160-4973-4, ISBN13: 978-0-8160-4973-8.
Dewey:550/.3. LCCN:2004-004389.
                                    Audience: **g,l,u,f.** *Choice, 2005.*

McGraw-Hill   QE5
McGraw-Hill Concise Encyclopedia of Earth Science. Ed. 5.
Trade Paper. McGraw-Hill Professional Publishing. New York,
NY. 2005. 400p. ISBN:0-07-143954-4, ISBN13:
978-0-07-143954-1. Dewey:550/.3. LCCN:2004-061052.
                                           Audience: **l,u.**

National Audubon Society   QE718
  Staff & Thompson, Ida
Field Guide to Fossils: North America. Carol Nehring
(Illustrator), Townsend P. Dickinson (Photographer). Trade
Cloth. Alfred A. Knopf Inc. New York, NY. 1982. 848p.
Audubon Society Field Guide Ser. ISBN:0-394-52412-8,
ISBN13: 978-0-394-52412-2. Dewey:560/.973.
LCCN:81-084772.
                                           Audience: **g,l,u,f.**

Nierenberg, William A.   QE5.E514 1991
  (Editor)
Encyclopedia of Earth System Science, 4. Cloth Text. Elsevier
Science & Technology Books. Saint Louis, MO. 1991. 3264p.
ISBN:0-12-226725-7, ISBN13: 978-0-12-226725-3.
Dewey:550/.3. LCCN:90-029045.
                                    Audience: **l,u.** *Choice, 1992.*

General Geology/Physical Geography > History, Biography, Directories

☐ Guide to Geoscience Careers and Employers.
http://guide.agiweb.org/employer/index.html
American Geological Institute.
                                           Audience: **g,l,u,f.**

                                                    TK5105.875.I57
☐ Guide to Geoscience Departments.
http://guide.agiweb.org/ggd/
                                           Audience: **g,l,u,f.**

Adams, Frank D. QE11 .A19 1954
Birth and Development of the Geological Sciences. Trade Paper.
Dover Publications, Inc. Mineola, NY. 1990. 510p.
ISBN:0-486-26372-X, ISBN13: 978-0-486-26372-4.
Dewey:550.9. LCCN:55-001083.

Audience: **u,f.**

Dean, Dennis R. QE26.D43 1992
James Hutton and the History of Geology. Book, Other. Cornell
University Press. Ithaca, NY. 1992. 312p. ISBN:0-8014-2666-9,
ISBN13: 978-0-8014-2666-7. Dewey:550/.9. LCCN:91-055545.

Audience: **u,f.** *Choice, 1992.*

Drake, Ellen T. & Jordan, QE13.U6G466 1985
William M. (Editors)
Geologists and Ideas: A History of North American Geology.
Trade Cloth. Geological Society of America, Inc. Boulder, CO.
1986. 520p. DNAG Centennial Special Volumes Ser., Vol. 1
ISBN:0-8137-5301-5, ISBN13: 978-0-8137-5301-0.
Dewey:550/.973. LCCN:85-017631.

Audience: **l,u,f.**

Faul, Henry & Faul, Carol QE11
It Began with a Stone: A History of Geology from the Stone
Age to the Age of Plate Tectonics. Trade Paper. John Wiley &
Sons, Inc. Hoboken, NJ. 1983. 264p. ISBN:0-471-89605-5,
ISBN13: 978-0-471-89605-0. Dewey:551/.09. LCCN:83-003683.

Audience: **l,u,f.** *B*

Geikie, Archibald Sir QE11
The Founders of Geology. Ed. 2. Dover: New York. 1962.

Audience: **u,f.**

Greene, Mott T. QE11 .G73
Geology in the Nineteenth Century: Changing Views of a
Changing World. Book, Other. Cornell University Press. Ithaca,
NY. 1985. 328p. History of Science Ser. ISBN:0-8014-9295-5,
ISBN13: 978-0-8014-9295-2. Dewey:551/.09/034.
LCCN:82-007456.

Audience: **g,l,u,f.** *B*

Laudan, Rachel QE11
From Mineralogy to Geology: The Foundations of a Science,
1650-1830. Trade Paper. University of Chicago Press. Chicago,
IL. 1994. 285p. Science and Its Conceptual Foundations Ser.
ISBN:0-226-46947-6, ISBN13: 978-0-226-46947-8.
Dewey:550/.9.

Audience: **u,f.** *Choice, 1988.*

Mather, Kirtley F. QE3
Source Book in Geology, 1900-1950. Harvard University Press,
Cambridge. 1967. Source books in the history of the sciences

Audience: **u,f.**

Mather, Kirtley F. & Mason, QE0003.M38
Shirley L.
A Source Book in Geology, 1400-1900. Trade Paper. Books on
Demand. Ann Arbor, MI. 726p. Source Books in the History of
the Sciences ISBN:0-7837-3850-1, ISBN13: 978-0-7837-3850-5.
Dewey:550.82. LCCN:67-012100.

Audience: **u,f.**

Merrill, George P. QE13.U6 M6
First One Hundred Years of American Geology. Library
Binding. Lubrecht & Cramer, Ltd. Port Jervis, NY. 1969. 773p.
ISBN:0-02-849180-7, ISBN13: 978-0-02-849180-6. Dewey:550.

Audience: **l,u,f.** *B*

Oldroyd, David R. QE11.O43 1996
Thinking about the Earth: A History of Ideas in Geology. Trade
Cloth. Harvard University Press. Cambridge, MA. 1996. 440p.
ISBN:0-674-88382-9, ISBN13: 978-0-674-88382-6. Dewey:551.
LCCN:95-048234.

Audience: **u,f.** *Choice, 1997.*

Oreskes, Naomi QE511.4
Plate Tectonics: An Insider's History of the Modern Theory of
the Earth. Trade Paper. Westview Press. Boulder, CO. 2003.
448p. ISBN:0-8133-4132-9, ISBN13: 978-0-8133-4132-3.
Dewey:551.1/36.

Audience: **l,u,f.** *Choice, 2003.*

Porter, Roy QE13.G7P67
The Making of Geology: Earth Science in Britain, 1660-1815.
Trade Paper. Books on Demand. Ann Arbor, MI. 300p.
ISBN:0-608-13048-6, ISBN13: 978-0-608-13048-4.
Dewey:550/.941. LCCN:76-056220.

Audience: **u,f.** *B*

Rudwick, Martin J. QE881
Georges Cuvier, Fossil Bones, and Geological Catastrophes:
New Translations and Interpretations of the Primary Texts. Trade
Paper. University of Chicago Press. Chicago, IL. 1998. 318p.
ISBN:0-226-73107-3, ISBN13: 978-0-226-73107-0. Dewey:569.

Audience: **u,f.** *Choice, 1998.*

Thompson, Susan J. QE11.T47 1988
A Chronology of Geological Thinking from Antiquity to 1899.
Trade Paper. Scarecrow Press, Inc. Lanham, MD. 1988. 328p.
ISBN:0-8108-2121-4, ISBN13: 978-0-8108-2121-7.
Dewey:550/.9. LCCN:88-001493.

Audience: **g,l,u,f.** *Choice, 1989.*

Wilhelms, Don E. QB592
To a Rocky Moon: A Geologist's History of Lunar Exploration.
Trade Paper. University of Arizona Press. Tucson, AZ. 1994.
477p. ISBN:0-8165-1443-7, ISBN13: 978-0-8165-1443-4.
Dewey:559.9/1. LCCN:92-033228.

Audience: **g,l,u,f.** *Choice, 1993.*

General Geology/Physical Geography > General Works

☐ This Dynamic Earth.
http://pubs.usgs.gov/gip/dynamic/dynamic.html
U.S. Geological Survey.

Audience: **g,l.**

☐ USGS Geology in the Parks.
http://www2.nature.nps.gov/geology/usgsnps/project/home.html

Audience: **g,l.**

Duff, P. M. (Editor) QE28.2
Holmes' Principles of Physical Geology. Ed. 4. Trade Paper.
Nelson Thornes Ltd. Cheltenham, 1993. 807p.
ISBN:0-7487-4381-2, ISBN13: 978-0-7487-4381-0. Dewey:551.

Audience: **l,u.**

Hamblin, W. Kenneth & QE28.2
Christiansen, Eric H.
Earth's Dynamic Systems. Ed. 10. Trade Paper. Prentice Hall

PTR. Upper Saddle River, NJ. 2003. 816p.
ISBN:0-13-142066-6, ISBN13: 978-0-13-142066-3. Dewey:550.
LCCN:2003-054839.

Audience: **l,u.**

Harris, David V. & Kiver,   QE77.H368 1985
Eugene P.
The Geologic Story Of National Parks and Monuments. Ed. 4.
Paper Text. John Wiley & Sons, Inc. Hoboken, NJ. 1985. 480p.
ISBN:0-471-87224-5, ISBN13: 978-0-471-87224-5.
Dewey:557.3. LCCN:85-005286.

Audience: **l,u.**

Kiver, Eugene P. & Harris,   QE77.K59 1999
David V.
Geology of U. S. Parklands. Ed. 5. Trade Cloth. John Wiley &
Sons, Inc. Hoboken, NJ. 1999. 912p. ISBN:0-471-33218-6,
ISBN13: 978-0-471-33218-3. Dewey:557.3. LCCN:98-031447.

Audience: **l,u.**

Lamb, Simon & Sington,   QE26.2.L33 1998
David
Earth Story: The Forces That Have Shaped Our Planet. Trade
Paper. Princeton University Press. Princeton, NJ. 2003. 240p.
ISBN:0-691-11662-8, ISBN13: 978-0-691-11662-4.

Audience: **g,l.**

Lambert, David & Diagram   QE28 .L22 1998
Group
The Field Guide to Geology. Trade Paper. Facts On File, Inc..
New York, NY. 2003. 256p. ISBN:0-8160-3823-6, ISBN13:
978-0-8160-3823-7. Dewey:550. LCCN:98-168173.

Audience: **g,l.**

Luhr, James F. (Editor)   QE501.E27 2003
Earth. Trade Cloth. Dorling Kindersley Publishing, Inc. New
York, NY. 2003. 520p. Smithsonian Handbooks Ser.
ISBN:0-7894-9643-7, ISBN13: 978-0-7894-9643-0. Dewey:550.
LCCN:2003-051573.

Audience: **g,l.**   *Choice, 2004.*

Mathez, Edmond A. &   QB631.M32 2004
Webster, James D.
The Earth Machine: The Science of a Dynamic Planet. Trade
Paper. Columbia University Press. New York, NY. 2004. xiv,
335p. ISBN:0-231-12579-8, ISBN13: 978-0-231-12579-6.
Dewey:550. LCCN:2003-055213.

Audience: **g,l,u.**   *Choice, 2004.*

Meissner, Rolf   QB631
[e] The Little Book of Planet Earth. E-Book. Springer. New
York, NY. 2004. Little Book Ser. ISBN:0-387-21800-9, ISBN13:
978-0-387-21800-7. Dewey:550.

Audience: **g,l,u.**

Plummer, Charles C., et al.   QE28.2.P58 2007
Physical Geology. Ed. 11. Diane H. Carlson & David McGeary
(Authors). Trade Cloth. McGraw-Hill Companies, The. New
York, NY. 2005. xxi, 617p. ISBN:0-07-282692-4, ISBN13:
978-0-07-282692-0. Dewey:550. LCCN:2005-024100.

Audience: **l.**

Press, Frank, et al.   QE28.2
Understanding Earth. Ed. 2. Peter L. Kresan, Reed Mencke &
Raymond Siever (Authors). Trade Paper. W. H. Freeman &
Company. New York, NY. 2003. 320p. ISBN:0-7167-5776-1,
ISBN13: 978-0-7167-5776-4. Dewey:551.

Audience: **g,l,u,f.**

Woodhead, James A.   QE5.G465 1999
(Editor)
Geology, 2 vols. Library Binding. Salem Press, Inc. Hackensack,
NJ. 1999. 752p. Geology Ser. ISBN:0-89356-522-9, ISBN13:
978-0-89356-522-0. Dewey:550/.3. LCCN:98-053009.

Audience: **g,l,u.**   *Choice, 1999.*

General Geology/Physical Geography > Geology Study and Teaching

QE3

☐ DLESE: Digital Library for Earth System Education.
http://www.dlese.org/

Audience: **l,u,f.**

Z6034.N7

☐ Geologic Guidebooks of North America Database.
http://guide.georef.org/dbtw-wpd/guideens.htm
American Geological Institute.

Audience: **l,u,f.**

TK5105.875.I57

☐ Guide to Geoscience Departments.
http://guide.agiweb.org/ggd/

Audience: **g,l,u,f.**

Compton, Robert R.   QE45.C63 1985
Geology in the Field. Ed. 1. Trade Cloth. John Wiley & Sons,
Inc. Hoboken, NJ. 1985. 416p. ISBN:0-471-82902-1, ISBN13:
978-0-471-82902-7. Dewey:551/.0723. LCCN:85-002325.

Audience: **l,u,f.** *B̶ Choice, 1986.*

Davis, John C.   QE48.8
Statistics and Data Analysis in Geology. Ed. 3. Trade Cloth.
John Wiley & Sons, Inc. Hoboken, NJ. 2002. 638p.
ISBN:0-471-17275-8, ISBN13: 978-0-471-17275-8.
Dewey:550/.72. LCCN:2004-270387.

Audience: **l,u,f.** *B̶*

Swan, A. R. H. &   QE33.2.S82S93 1995
Sandilands, M. H.
Introduction to Geological Data Analysis. Blackwell Science.
1995. ISBN:0-632-03224-3, ISBN13: 978-0-632-03224-2.

Audience: **u,f.**

Geology: Special Topics > Computer Applications

Davis, John C.   QE48.8
Statistics and Data Analysis in Geology. Ed. 3. Trade Cloth.
John Wiley & Sons, Inc. Hoboken, NJ. 2002. 638p.
ISBN:0-471-17275-8, ISBN13: 978-0-471-17275-8.
Dewey:550/.72. LCCN:2004-270387.

Audience: **l,u,f.** *B̶*

Geology: Special Topics > Statistics

Davis, John C.   QE48.8
Statistics and Data Analysis in Geology. Ed. 3. Trade Cloth.
John Wiley & Sons, Inc. Hoboken, NJ. 2002. 638p.
ISBN:0-471-17275-8, ISBN13: 978-0-471-17275-8.
Dewey:550/.72. LCCN:2004-270387.

Audience: **l,u,f.** *B̶*

Hohn, Michael Edward   **TN871**
Geostatistics and Petroleum Geology. Ed. 2. Trade Cloth.
Springer. New York, NY. 1998. 248p. ISBN:0-412-75780-X,
ISBN13: 978-0-412-75780-8. Dewey:553.28015195.
Audience: **u,f.**

Swan, A. R. H. &   **QE33.2.S82S93 1995**
  Sandilands, M. H.
Introduction to Geological Data Analysis. Blackwell Science.
1995. ISBN:0-632-03224-3, ISBN13: 978-0-632-03224-2.
Audience: **u,f.**

Geology: Special Topics > Mathematical Geology

Turcotte, Donald L.   **QE33.2.M3 T87 1997**
Fractals and Chaos in Geology and Geophysics. Ed. 2. Trade
Paper. Cambridge University Press. New York, NY. 1997. 412p.
ISBN:0-521-56733-5, ISBN13: 978-0-521-56733-6.
Dewey:550.1/51. LCCN:96-031558.
Audience: **u,f.** *Choice, 1993.*

Waltham, David   **QE33.2.M3W35 2000**
Mathematics: A Simple Tool for Geologists. Ed. 2. Trade Paper.
Blackwell Publishing, Inc. Malden, MA. 2000. 208p.
ISBN:0-632-05345-3, ISBN13: 978-0-632-05345-2.
Dewey:510.2/4553. LCCN:99-053787.
Audience: **l,u,f.**

Geology: Special Topics > Urban Geology

McCall, G. J. & De Mulder,   **HT166**
  E. F.
Urban Geoscience. Paper over Boards. Taylor & Francis Group.
Abingdon, 1996. 280p. AGID Special Publication Ser., No. 20
ISBN:90-5410-643-3, ISBN13: 978-90-5410-643-2.
Dewey:307.1216.
Audience: **l,u,f.**

Geology: Special Topics > Field Geology

Barnes, John W. & Lisle,   **QE36.B33 1995**
  Richard J.
Basic Geological Mapping. Ed. 4. Trade Paper. John Wiley &
Sons, Inc. Hoboken, NJ. 2004. 196p. Geological Field Guide
Ser. ISBN:0-470-84986-X, ISBN13: 978-0-470-84986-6.
Dewey:551.8. LCCN:2003-062753.
Audience: **l,u,f.**

Compton, Robert R.   **QE45.C63 1985**
Geology in the Field. Ed. 1. Trade Cloth. John Wiley & Sons,
Inc. Hoboken, NJ. 1985. 416p. ISBN:0-471-82902-1, ISBN13:
978-0-471-82902-7. Dewey:551/.0723. LCCN:85-002325.
Audience: **l,u,f.** *B Choice, 1986.*

Dutro, J. T. Jr. (Editor),   **QE52.A36 1989**
  et al.
AGI Data Sheets: For Geology In The Field, Laboratory and
Office. Ed. 3. R. V. Dietrich & R. M. Foose (Editors). Trade
Paper. American Geological Institute. Alexandria, VA. 2000.
294p. ISBN:0-922152-01-2, ISBN13: 978-0-922152-01-8.
Dewey:550. LCCN:89-032854.
Audience: **u,f.**

Fry, Norman   **QE475 A2 T4 1992**
The Field Description of Metamorphic Rocks. Ed. 1. Trade
Paper. John Wiley & Sons, Inc. Hoboken, NJ. 1991. 128p.
Geological Society of London Handbook Ser., Vol. 14
ISBN:0-471-93221-3, ISBN13: 978-0-471-93221-5.
Dewey:552.4.
Audience: **l,u,f.**

Maley, Terry S.   **QE45.M35 2005**
Field Geology Illustrated. Ed. 1. Trade Paper. Mineral Land
Publications. Boise, ID. 2005. 704p. ISBN:0-940949-05-9,
ISBN13: 978-0-940949-05-8. Dewey:550.72.
LCCN:2005-924583.
Audience: **l,u,f.**

McClay, Kenneth R.   **QE501.3.M42 1987**
The Mapping of Geological Structures. Trade Paper. John Wiley
& Sons, Inc. Hoboken, NJ. 1988. 161p. Geological Society of
London Handbook Ser. ISBN:0-470-20355-2, ISBN13:
978-0-470-20355-2. Dewey:551/.022/2. LCCN:86-009919.
Audience: **l,u,f.**

O'Reilly, Gerald (Editor)   **QE45.P53 1992**
Planning for Field Safety. Paper Text. American Geological
Institute. Alexandria, VA. 1992. 197p. ISBN:0-913312-93-2,
ISBN13: 978-0-913312-93-3. Dewey:550/.723.
LCCN:89-083681.
Audience: **l,u,f.**

Thorpe, Richard S. &   **QE461 .T45Y 1993**
  Brown, Geoffrey C.
The Field Description of Igneous Rocks. Ed. 1. Trade Paper.
John Wiley & Sons, Inc. Hoboken, NJ. 1991. 160p. Geological
Society of London Handbook Ser., Vol. 11 ISBN:0-471-93275-2,
ISBN13: 978-0-471-93275-8. Dewey:552.1. LCCN:84-025182.
Audience: **l,u,f.**

Tucker, Maurice E.   **QE471**
Sedimentary Rocks in the Field. Ed. 3. Trade Paper. John Wiley
& Sons, Inc. Hoboken, NJ. 2003. 244p. The Geological Field
Guide Ser. ISBN:0-470-85123-6, ISBN13: 978-0-470-85123-4.
Dewey:552/.5. LCCN:2003-045080.
Audience: **l,u,f.**

Geology: Special Topics > Remote Sensing (Satellite Applications)

Drury, S. A.   **QE33.2.R4D78 2001**
Image Interpretation in Geology. Ed. 3. Trade Paper. Blackwell
Publishing, Inc. Malden, MA. 2002. 304p. ISBN:0-632-05408-5,
ISBN13: 978-0-632-05408-4. Dewey:550/.22/2.
LCCN:00-057197.
Audience: **u,f.**

Gupta, Ravi P.   **QE33.2.R4G86 2002**
Remote Sensing Geology. Ed. 2. Trade Cloth. Springer. New
York, NY. 2003. 424 schw.-w. u. 29 farb. Abb., 53 schw.-w.
Tab., 193 schw.-w. u. 29 farb. Fotos, 231 schw.-w. Zeichn. XX,
655p. ISBN:3-540-43185-3, ISBN13: 978-3-540-43185-5.
Dewey:550/.28. LCCN:2002-021145.
Audience: **u,f.**

National Aeronautics &   **QC981.8.C5**
  Space Administration
☐ Earth Observatory.

http://bibpurl.oclc.org/web/7914
National Aeronautics and Space Administration.

Audience: **g,l,u,f.**

Prost, Gary L.   **TN870.5**
Remote Sensing for Geologists: A Guide to Image Interpretation
A. CRC Press. 2002. ISBN:90-5702-629-5, ISBN13:
978-90-5702-629-4.

Audience: **u,f.**

U.S. Geological Survey   **QE26.3**
  EROS Data Center
☐ EROS Image Gallery Collections.
http://edcw2ks15.cr.usgs.gov:8090/ImageGallery/SilverStream/
Pages/pgcollectiondisplay.html
U.S. Geological Survey EROS Data Center.

Audience: **g,l,u,f.**

Geology: Special Topics > Engineering Geology

Bell, F. G.   **TA705.B329 2004**
Engineering Geology and Construction. Paper over Boards.
Routledge. New York, NY. 2004. 816p. ISBN:0-415-25939-8,
ISBN13: 978-0-415-25939-2. Dewey:624.1/51.
LCCN:2003-015438.

Audience: **l,u,f.**

Bell, F. G., et al.   **TA706**
Sinkholes and Subsidence: Karst and Cavernous Rocks in
Engineering and Construction. Anthony C. Waltham & Martin
G. Culshaw (Authors). Trade Cloth. Springer. New York, NY.
2004. XXXI, 382p. Springer Praxis Books. Geophysical
Sciences Ser. ISBN:3-540-20725-2, ISBN13:
978-3-540-20725-2. Dewey:624.1/51. LCCN:2004-112901.

Audience: **l,u,f.** *Choice, 2005.*

Bell, Frederic G.   **TA0710.B424**
Engineering Properties of Soils and Rocks. Ed. 3. Trade Paper.
Books on Demand. Ann Arbor, MI. 1992. 353p.
ISBN:0-608-04413-X, ISBN13: 978-0-608-04413-2.
Dewey:624.1/513. LCCN:91-039429.

Audience: **u,f.**

Bowles, Joseph E.   **TA775.B63 1996**
Foundation Analysis and Design. Ed. 5. Mixed Media, Trade
Cloth, Diskette. McGraw-Hill Higher Education. Burr Ridge, IL.
1995. 1024p. ISBN:0-07-912247-7, ISBN13:
978-0-07-912247-6. Dewey:624.15. LCCN:95-037880.

Audience: **u,f.** *B*

Chen, Fu Hua   **TA710.C5185**
Soil Engineering: Testing, Design, and Remediation. CRC Press.
2000. ISBN:0-8493-2294-4, ISBN13: 978-0-8493-2294-5.

Audience: **u,f.**

Coduto, Donald P.   **TA705.C62 1998**
Geotechnical Engineering: Principles and Practices. Mixed
Media. Prentice Hall PTR. Upper Saddle River, NJ. 1998. 800p.
ISBN:0-13-576380-0, ISBN13: 978-0-13-576380-3.
Dewey:624.1/51. LCCN:98-022191.

Audience: **u,f.**

Cornforth, Derek   **TA710.C65 2004**
Landslides in Practice: Investigation, Analysis, and
Remedial/Preventative Options in Soils. Trade Cloth. John Wiley
& Sons, Inc. Hoboken, NJ. 2005. 624p. ISBN:0-471-67816-3,
ISBN13: 978-0-471-67816-8. Dewey:624.1/51363.
LCCN:2004-007921.

Audience: **l,u,f.**

Das, Braja M.   **TA775.D37 2004**
Principles of Foundation Engineering. Ed. 5. Cloth Text. Nelson
Thomson Learning. Scarborough, ON. 2003. 768p.
ISBN:0-534-40752-8, ISBN13: 978-0-534-40752-0.
Dewey:624.1/5. LCCN:2002-038362.

Audience: **u,f.** *B*

Day, Robert   **TA654.6.D39 2002**
Geotechnical Earthquake Engineering Handbook. Trade Cloth.
McGraw-Hill Professional Publishing. New York, NY. 2001.
700p. McGraw-Hill Handbooks Ser. ISBN:0-07-137782-4,
ISBN13: 978-0-07-137782-9. Dewey:624.1/762.
LCCN:2002-278152.

Audience: **u,f.**

Fang, Hsai-Yang   **TA775.F675 1991**
Foundation Engineering Handbook. Cloth Text. Chapman &
Hall. New York, NY. 1990. xvii, 923 p. :p.
ISBN:0-442-22487-7, ISBN13: 978-0-442-22487-5.
Dewey:624.1/5. LCCN:89-070490.

Audience: **u,f.**

Goodman, Richard E.   **TA706.G644 1993**
Engineering Geology: Rock in Engineering Construction. Ed. 1.
Trade Cloth. John Wiley & Sons, Inc. Hoboken, NJ. 1993. 432p.
ISBN:0-471-54424-8, ISBN13: 978-0-471-54424-1.
Dewey:624.151. LCCN:92-026854.

Audience: **u,f.** *Choice, 1993.*

Holtz, Robert D. & Kovacs,   **TA705**
  William D.
Introduction to Geotechnical Engineering. Ed. 2. Cloth Text.
Prentice Hall PTR. Upper Saddle River, NJ. 2006. 775p.
ISBN:0-13-031721-7, ISBN13: 978-0-13-031721-6.
Dewey:624.1/51.

Audience: **u,f.**

Hunt, Roy E.   **TA705**
Geotechnical Engineering Investigation Handbook. Ed. 2. CRC
Press. 2005. ISBN:0-8493-2182-4, ISBN13: 978-0-8493-2182-5.

Audience: **u,f.**

Johnson, Robert B. &   **TA705.J65 1988**
  DeGraff, Jerome V.
Principles of Engineering Geology. Ed. 99. Trade Cloth. John
Wiley & Sons, Inc. Hoboken, NJ. 1988. 512p.
ISBN:0-471-03436-3, ISBN13: 978-0-471-03436-0.
Dewey:624.1/51. LCCN:88-005510.

Audience: **u,f.**

Kiersch, George A.   **TA705.H47 1991**
Heritage of Engineering Geology - The First 100 Years. Trade
Cloth. Geological Society of America, Inc. Boulder, CO. 1991.
619p. DNAG Centennial Special Volumes Ser., Vol. 3
ISBN:0-8137-5303-1, ISBN13: 978-0-8137-5303-4.
Dewey:624.1/51/09. LCCN:90-025229.

Audience: **g,l,u,f.**

Lambrechts, James R.　　　　**TA703.B54 1998**
　(Editor), et al.
Big Digs Around the World: Proceedings of Sessions of
Geo-Congress 98, Sponsored by the Geo-Institute of the
American Society of Civil Engineers, October 18-21, 1998,
Boston, Massachusetts. Richard Hwang & Alfredo Urzua
(Editors). Trade Cloth. American Society of Civil Engineers.
Reston, VA. 1998. 432p. Geotechnical Special Publication Ser.
ISBN:0-7844-0398-8, ISBN13: 978-0-7844-0398-3.
Dewey:624.1/5132. LCCN:98-040669.

Audience: **u,f.**

Marr, W. Allen (Editor)　　　　**TA705.H58 2002**
A History of Progress: Selected U. S. Papers in Geotechnical
Engineering. American Society of Civil Engineers, Geo-Institute
Staff (Contribution by). Trade Cloth. American Society of Civil
Engineers. Reston, VA. 2002. 2356p. Geotechnical Special
Publication Ser., No. 118 ISBN:0-7844-0656-1, ISBN13:
978-0-7844-0656-4. Dewey:624.1/51. LCCN:2002-038604.

Audience: **u,f.**

McCalpin, James P. &　　　　**QE521.3**
　Nelson, Alan R. (Editors)
Paleoseismology. Trade Paper. Elsevier Science & Technology
Books. Saint Louis, MO. 1998. 588p. International Geophysics
Ser. ISBN:0-12-481826-9, ISBN13: 978-0-12-481826-2.
Dewey:551.2/2. LCCN:96-002096.

Audience: **u,f.**

Mitchell, James K. & Soga,　　　　**TA710.M577 2005**
　Kenichi
Fundamentals of Soil Behavior. Ed. 3. Trade Cloth. John Wiley
& Sons, Inc. Hoboken, NJ. 2005. 592p. ISBN:0-471-46302-7,
ISBN13: 978-0-471-46302-3. Dewey:624.1/5136.
LCCN:2004-025690.

Audience: **u,f.** *B*

Murthy, V. N.　　　　**TA705.M85 2002**
Geotechnical Engineering: Principles and Practices of Soil
Mechanics and Foundation Engineering, Vol. 10. Paper over
Boards. Marcel Dekker Inc. New York, NY. 2002. 1048p. Civil
and Environmental Engineering Ser., Vol. 10
ISBN:0-8247-0873-3, ISBN13: 978-0-8247-0873-3.
Dewey:624.1/51. LCCN:2002-073993.

Audience: **u,f.**

Nelson, John D. & Miller,　　　　**TA711.5.N5**
　Debora J.
Expansive Soils: Problems and Practice in Foundation and
Pavement Engineering. Ed. 1. Trade Paper. John Wiley & Sons,
Inc. Hoboken, NJ. 1997. 288p. Professional Ser.
ISBN:0-471-18114-5, ISBN13: 978-0-471-18114-9.
Dewey:624.15136. LCCN:91-042720.

Audience: **u,f.** *Choice, 1993.*

Powrie, William　　　　**TA710**
Soil Mechanics: Concepts and Applications. Ed. 2. Paper over
Boards. Routledge. New York, NY. 2004. 704p.
ISBN:0-415-31155-1, ISBN13: 978-0-415-31155-7.
Dewey:624.1/5136. LCCN:2004-002128.

Audience: **u,f.**

Rahn, Perry H.　　　　**TA705.R28 1996**
Engineering Geology: An Environmental Approach. Ed. 2. Trade
Paper. Prentice Hall PTR. Upper Saddle River, NJ. 1996. 657p.
ISBN:0-13-177403-4, ISBN13: 978-0-13-177403-2.
Dewey:624.1/51. LCCN:96-007193.

Audience: **u,f.**

Rowe, R. K.　　　　**TA705.G427 2001**
Geotechnical and Geoenvironmental Engineering Handbook.
Trade Cloth. Springer. New York, NY. 2001. 1160p.
ISBN:0-7923-8613-2, ISBN13: 978-0-7923-8613-1.
Dewey:624.1/51. LCCN:99-037319.

Audience: **u,f.**

Schroeder, W. L., et al.　　　　**TA710.S286 2004**
Soils in Construction. Ed. 5. Stephen Dickenson & D. C.
Warrington (Authors). Cloth Text. Prentice Hall PTR. Upper
Saddle River, NJ. 2003. 368p. ISBN:0-13-048917-4, ISBN13:
978-0-13-048917-3. Dewey:624.1/5136. LCCN:2003-051758.

Audience: **u,f.** *B*

Sharma, Hari D. & Reddy,　　　　**TD171.9.S53 2004**
　Krishna R.
Geoenvironmental Engineering: Site Remediation, Waste
Containment, and Emerging Waste Management Technologies.
Trade Cloth. John Wiley & Sons, Inc. Hoboken, NJ. 2004. 992p.
ISBN:0-471-21599-6, ISBN13: 978-0-471-21599-8.
Dewey:628.5. LCCN:2004-007135.

Audience: **u,f.**

Terzaghi, Karl, et al.　　　　**TA710.T39 1996**
Soil Mechanics in Engineering Practice. Ed. 3. Ralph B. Peck &
Gholamreza Mesri (Authors). Trade Cloth. John Wiley & Sons,
Inc. Hoboken, NJ. 1996. 592p. ISBN:0-471-08658-4, ISBN13:
978-0-471-08658-1. Dewey:624.1/5136. LCCN:95-006166.

Audience: **u,f.** *B Choice, 1996.*

Turner, A. Keith & Schuster,　　　　**QE599.2.L36 1996**
　Robert L. (Editors)
Landslides: Investigation and Mitigation. Trade Paper. National
Academies Press. Washington, DC. 1996. 673p. Special Report,
Transportation Research Board, National Research Council Ser.,
Vol. 247 ISBN:0-309-06208-X, ISBN13: 978-0-309-06208-4.
Dewey:551.3/07. LCCN:95-040780.

Audience: **u,f.**

Underwood, James R. &　　　　**TA705.R4 VOL.13**
　Guth, Peter L.
Military Geology in War and Peace. Trade Cloth. Geological
Society of America, Inc. Boulder, CO. 1998. 245p. Reviews in
Engineering Geology Ser., Vol. 13 ISBN:0-8137-4113-0,
ISBN13: 978-0-8137-4113-0. Dewey:623/.01/55.
LCCN:98-007163.

Audience: **u,f.**

Waltham, Tony　　　　**TA705.W34 2001**
Foundations of Engineering Geology. Ed. 2. Paper over Boards.
Routledge. New York, NY. 2002. 104p. ISBN:0-415-25449-3,
ISBN13: 978-0-415-25449-6. Dewey:624.1/51.
LCCN:2001-049532.

Audience: **u,f.**

Wickert, Jonathan　　　　**TA710**
Principles of Geotechnical Engineering.Txt. Ed. 6. Cloth Text.
Thomson Wadsworth. Belmont, CA. 2005. 672p.
ISBN:0-534-55144-0, ISBN13: 978-0-534-55144-5.
Dewey:624.1/5136.

Audience: **u,f.**

Yong, Raymond N.　　　　**TD878.Y65 2001**
Geoenvironmental engineering: contaminated soils, pollutant
fate, and mitigation. CRC Press. 2001. ISBN:0-8493-8289-0,
ISBN13: 978-0-8493-8289-5.

Audience: **u,f.**

Geology: Special Topics > Natural Hazards

Bell, F. G. **GB5014.B45 1999**
Geological Hazards: Their Assessment, Avoidance and Mitigation. Paper over Boards. Routledge. New York, NY. 1999. 656p. ISBN:0-419-16970-9, ISBN13: 978-0-419-16970-3. Dewey:363.34/9. LCCN:98-039190.

Audience: **g,l,u,f.**

Bryant, Edward **GB5014.B79 2004**
Natural Hazards. Ed. 2. Trade Paper. Cambridge University Press. New York, NY. 2004. 328p. ISBN:0-521-53743-6, ISBN13: 978-0-521-53743-8. Dewey:363.34. LCCN:2004-018299.

Audience: **l,u,f.** *Choice, 2005.*

Cutter, Susan L. (Editor) **GB5010.A43 2001**
American Hazardscapes: The Regionalization of Hazards and Disasters. Trade Cloth. National Academies Press. Washington, DC. 2001. 250p. Natural Hazards and Disasters Ser. ISBN:0-309-07443-6, ISBN13: 978-0-309-07443-8. Dewey:363.34/0973. LCCN:2001-003606.

Audience: **u,f.**

Kusky, Timothy M. **QE501**
Geological Hazards: A Sourcebook. Cloth Text. Greenwood Publishing Group, Inc. Portsmouth, NH. 2003. 312p. Oryx Sourcebooks on Hazards and Disasters Ser. ISBN:1-57356-469-9, ISBN13: 978-1-57356-469-4. Dewey:363.34. LCCN:2002-192773.

Audience: **g,l,u,f.**

Mileti, Dennis **HV551.3.M55 1999**
Disasters by Design: A Reassessment of Natural Hazards in the United States. Trade Cloth. National Academies Press. Washington, DC. 1999. 376p. Natural Hazards and Disasters Ser. ISBN:0-309-06360-4, ISBN13: 978-0-309-06360-9. Dewey:363.34/0973. LCCN:99-029511.

Audience: **u,f.**

Tierney, Kathleen J., et al. **HV551.3.T54 2001**
Facing the Unexpected: Disaster Preparedness and Response in the United States. Michael K. Lindell & Ronald W. Perry (Authors). Trade Cloth. National Academies Press. Washington, DC. 2001. 318p. Natural Hazards and Disasters Ser. ISBN:0-309-06999-8, ISBN13: 978-0-309-06999-1. Dewey:363.34/8/0973. LCCN:2001-003004.

Audience: **u,f.**

Geologic Maps and Mapping

G70.2
National Geologic Maps Database: Geologic Map Image Library.
http://purl.access.gpo.gov/GPO/LPS68723

Audience: **l,u,f.**

Barnes, John W. & Lisle, Richard J. **QE36.B33 1995**
Basic Geological Mapping. Ed. 4. Trade Paper. John Wiley & Sons, Inc. Hoboken, NJ. 2004. 196p. Geological Field Guide Ser. ISBN:0-470-84986-X, ISBN13: 978-0-470-84986-6. Dewey:551.8. LCCN:2003-062753.

Audience: **l,u,f.**

Bobrowsky, P. T. **QE36**
Geoenvironmental Mapping: Method, Theory and Practice. Paper over Boards. Taylor & Francis Group. Abingdon, 2001. 750p. ISBN:90-5410-487-2, ISBN13: 978-90-5410-487-2. Dewey:550.0223. LCCN:2001-052525.

Audience: **g,l,u,f.**

Environmental Geology

Andrews, J. E., et al. **QE516.4.I57 2004**
An Introduction to Environmental Chemistry. Ed. 2. Peter Brimblecombe, Tim D. Jickells, Peter S. Liss & Brian J. Reid (Authors). Trade Paper. Blackwell Publishing, Inc. Malden, MA. 2003. 320p. ISBN:0-632-05905-2, ISBN13: 978-0-632-05905-8. Dewey:551.9. LCCN:2003-002757.

Audience: **l,u.** *Choice, 2004.*

Chamley, Herve (Editor) **QE38.C48 2003**
Geosciences, Environment and Man. Trade Cloth. Elsevier Science & Technology Books. Saint Louis, MO. 2003. 550p. Developments in Earth & Environmental Sciences Ser., Vol. 1 ISBN:0-444-51422-8, ISBN13: 978-0-444-51422-6. Dewey:551. LCCN:2003-056111.

Audience: **l,u,f.** *Choice, 2004.*

Eby, G. Nelson **QE516.4.E39 2004**
Principles of Environmental Geochemistry. Cloth Text. Brooks/Cole. Pacific Grove, CA. 2003. 528p. ISBN:0-12-229061-5, ISBN13: 978-0-12-229061-9. Dewey:551.9. LCCN:2002-033358.

Audience: **l,u,f.**

Keller, Edward A. **QE38.K45 1996**
Environmental Geology. Ed. 7. Trade Cloth. Prentice Hall PTR. Upper Saddle River, NJ. 1995. 560p. ISBN:0-02-363281-X, ISBN13: 978-0-02-363281-5. Dewey:551. LCCN:95-041079.

Audience: **l.**

Montgomery, Carla W. **QE38.M66 2006**
Environmental Geology. Ed. 7. Trade Cloth. McGraw-Hill Companies, The. New York, NY. 2005. xix, 540p. ISBN:0-07-252816-8, ISBN13: 978-0-07-252816-9. Dewey:550. LCCN:2004-020080.

Audience: **l.**

Surficial Geology (GB) > Geomorphology

Allen, P. A. **QB631.A386 1997**
Earth Surface Processes. Trade Paper. Blackwell Publishing Ltd. Oxford, 1997. 416p. ISBN:0-632-03507-2, ISBN13: 978-0-632-03507-6. Dewey:551.3. LCCN:96-039095.

Audience: **u,f.**

Allison, Robert J. (Editor) **GB401.5.A67 2002**
Applied Geomorphology: Theory and Practice. Trade Cloth. John Wiley & Sons, Inc. Hoboken, NJ. 2002. 492p. International Association of Geomorphologists Ser. ISBN:0-471-89555-5, ISBN13: 978-0-471-89555-8. Dewey:551.41. LCCN:2001-046745.

Audience: **u,f.**

Bird, Eric C. **GB451.2.B55 2000**
Coastal Geomorphology: An Introduction. Trade Paper. John Wiley & Sons, Inc. Hoboken, NJ. 2000. 340p.

ISBN:0-471-89977-1, ISBN13: 978-0-471-89977-8.
Dewey:551.45/7. LCCN:00-032095.

Audience: **l,u,f.** *Choice, 2001.*

Bloom, Arthur L.   **GB 401.5 .B55 2004**
Geomorphology: A Systematic Analysis of Late Cenozoic
Landforms. Ed. 3. Cloth Text. Waveland Press, Inc. Prospect
Heights, IL. 2004. 494p. ISBN:1-57766-354-3, ISBN13:
978-1-57766-354-6. Dewey:551.41.

Audience: **g,l,u,f.** *B*

Burbank, Douglas W. &   **GB401.5.B86 2001**
 Anderson, Robert S.
Tectonic Geomorphology. Trade Paper. Blackwell Publishing,
Inc. Malden, MA. 2000. 288p. ISBN:0-632-04386-5, ISBN13:
978-0-632-04386-6. Dewey:551.41. LCCN:00-063021.

Audience: **u,f.**

Cooke Ronald U. et al   **GB61**
Desert Geomorphology. Goudie Andrew S., Warren Andrew
(Authors). Taylor & Francis. 1993. ISBN:1-85728-017-2,
ISBN13: 978-1-85728-017-3.

Audience: **g,l.**

Gerrard, John   **S591.G44 2000**
Fundamentals of Soils. Paper over Boards. Routledge. New
York, NY. 2000. 264p. Fundamentals of Physical Geography
Ser. ISBN:0-415-17004-4, ISBN13: 978-0-415-17004-8.
Dewey:631.4. LCCN:99-054629.

Audience: **u,f.** *Choice, 2001.*

Mares, Michael A.   **GB611.E65 1999**
Encyclopedia of Deserts. Trade Cloth. University of Oklahoma
Press. Norman, OK. 1999. 672p. ISBN:0-8061-3146-2, ISBN13:
978-0-8061-3146-7. Dewey:910/.02154/03. LCCN:98-044437.

Audience: **g,l,u,f.** *Choice, 1999.*

Masselink, Gerd & Hughes,   **GB450**
 Michael
An Introduction to Coastal Processes and Geomorphology. Trade
Paper. Oxford University Press, Inc. New York, NY. 2003. 368p.
A Hodder Arnold Publication ISBN:0-340-76411-2, ISBN13:
978-0-340-76411-4. Dewey:551.4/57. LCCN:2004-271233.

Audience: **u,f.** *Choice, 2004.*

Ritter, Dale F., et al.   **GB402.R57 2002**
Process Geomorphology. Ed. 4. R. Craig Kochel & Jerry R.
Miller (Authors). Paper Text. McGraw-Hill Higher Education.
Burr Ridge, IL. 2001. 576p. ISBN:0-697-34411-8, ISBN13:
978-0-697-34411-3. Dewey:551.41. LCCN:2001-031509.

Audience: **u,f.**

Thomas, David S. G.   **GB611.A75 1997**
 (Editor)
Arid Zone Geomorphology: Process, Form and Change in
Drylands. Ed. 2. Trade Paper. John Wiley & Sons, Inc.
Hoboken, NJ. 1998. 732p. ISBN:0-471-97610-5, ISBN13:
978-0-471-97610-3. Dewey:551.4/09154. LCCN:96-028792.

Audience: **u,f.**

Thornbury, William D.   **QE601**
Principles of Geomorphology. Paper Text. Textbook Publishers.
Temecula, CA. 2003. 618p. ISBN:0-7581-0453-7, ISBN13:
978-0-7581-0453-3. Dewey:551.4.

Audience: **g,l,u,f.** *B*

Woodroffe, C. D.   **GB451.2.W65 2002**
Coasts: Form, Process and Evolution. Trade Paper. Cambridge
University Press. New York, NY. 2002. 638p.
ISBN:0-521-01183-3, ISBN13: 978-0-521-01183-9.
Dewey:551.45/7. LCCN:2002-017418.

Audience: **u,f.** *Choice, 2003.*

Surficial Geology (GB) > Caves

Ford, Derek C. & Williams,   **GB600 .F66**
 Paul
Karst Hydrogeology and Geomorphology. Trade Cloth. John
Wiley & Sons, Inc. Hoboken, NJ. 2007. 568p.
ISBN:0-470-84996-7, ISBN13: 978-0-470-84996-5.
Dewey:551.44/7. LCCN:2006-029323.

Audience: **g,l,u,f.**

Gillieson, David   **GB601.G5 1996**
Caves: Processes, Development, Management. Trade Paper.
Blackwell Publishing, Inc. Malden, MA. 1996. 336p. The
Natural Environment Ser. ISBN:0-631-19175-5, ISBN13:
978-0-631-19175-9. Dewey:551.4/47. LCCN:96-012123.

Audience: **u,f.** *Choice, 1997.*

Gunn, John (Editor)   **GB601.E535 2003**
Encyclopedia of Caves and Karst Science. Library Binding.
Fitzroy Dearborn Publishers, Inc. Chicago, IL. 2003. 896p.
ISBN:1-57958-399-7, ISBN13: 978-1-57958-399-6.
Dewey:551.44/7/03. LCCN:2003-006469.

Audience: **g,l,u,f.** *Choice, 2004.*

Jennings, J. N.   **GB600.J46 1985**
Karst Geomorphology. Trade Paper. Blackwell Publishing, Inc.
Malden, MA. 1985. 320p. ISBN:0-631-14032-8, ISBN13:
978-0-631-14032-0. Dewey:551.4/47. LCCN:84-021589.

Audience: **u,f.** *B Choice, 1986.*

Moore, George W. &   **GB601.M58 1997**
 Sullivan, Nicholas
Speleology: Caves and the Cave Environment. Ed. 3. John C.
Schoenherr (Illustrator). Trade Cloth. Cave Books. Trenton, NJ.
1997. xiv, 176p. ISBN:0-939748-46-0, ISBN13:
978-0-939748-46-4. Dewey:551.44/7. LCCN:77-018176.

Audience: **g,l,u,f.** *Choice, 1997.*

Veni, George, et al.   **GB600.2.L58 2001**
Living with Karst: A Fragile Foundation. Harvey DuChene &
Nicholas C. Crawford (Authors). Trade Paper. American
Geological Institute. Alexandria, VA. 2001. 64p. AGI
Environmental Awareness Ser., Vol. 4 ISBN:0-922152-58-6,
ISBN13: 978-0-922152-58-2. Dewey:551.44/7.
LCCN:2003-271959.

Audience: **g,l,u,f.**

Surficial Geology (GB) > Glaciers and Glacial Geology

Benn, Douglas I. & Evans,   **GB2403.8**
 David J. A.
Glaciers and Glaciation. Paper Text. Oxford University Press,
Inc. New York, NY. 1997. 760p. An Arnold Publication Ser.
ISBN:0-340-58431-9, ISBN13: 978-0-340-58431-6.
Dewey:551.31/2.

Audience: **u,f.** *Choice, 1998.*

Bennett, Matthew R. &   **GB581.B45 1996**
  Glasser, Neil F.
Glacial Geology: Ice Sheets and Landforms. Ed. 1. Trade Paper.
John Wiley & Sons, Inc. Hoboken, NJ. 1996. 376p.
ISBN:0-471-96345-3, ISBN13: 978-0-471-96345-5.
Dewey:551.3/1. LCCN:95-046353.
                                             Audience: **u,f.**

Ehlers, J. & Gibbard, P. L.   **QC884**
Quaternary Glaciations - Extent and Chronology: South
America, Asia, Africa, Australia, Antarctica. Trade Cloth,
CD-ROM. Elsevier Science & Technology Books. Saint Louis,
MO. 2004. 390p. Developments in Quaternary Sciences Ser.,
Vol. 2, Pt. III ISBN:0-444-51593-3, ISBN13:
978-0-444-51593-3. Dewey:551.79. LCCN:2006-276073.
                                             Audience: **u,f.**

Ehlers, J. & Gibbard, P. L.   **QC884**
Quaternary Glaciations - Extent and Chronology: Europe. Trade
Cloth, CD-ROM. Elsevier Science & Technology Books. Saint
Louis, MO. 2004. 488p. Developments in Quaternary Sciences
Ser., Vol. 2 ISBN:0-444-51462-7, ISBN13: 978-0-444-51462-2.
Dewey:551.79. LCCN:2006-276073.
                            Audience: **u,f.** *Choice, 2005.*

Ehlers, J. & Gibbard, P. L.   **QC884**
Quaternary Glaciations - Extent and Chronology: North
America. Trade Cloth, CD-ROM. Elsevier Science &
Technology Books. Saint Louis, MO. 2004. 450p. Developments
in Quaternary Sciences Ser., Vol. 2, Pt. II ISBN:0-444-51592-5,
ISBN13: 978-0-444-51592-6. Dewey:551.79.
LCCN:2006-276073.
                                             Audience: **u,f.**

Flint, Richard F.   **QE696.F553**
Glacial and Quaternary Geology. Cloth Text. John Wiley &
Sons, Inc. Hoboken, NJ. 1977. 892p. ISBN:0-471-26435-0,
ISBN13: 978-0-471-26435-4. Dewey:551.7/9. LCCN:74-141198.
                                    Audience: **u,f.** *B*

Gibbard, Philip L.   **QE696.E2813 1996**
Quaternary and Glacial Geology. Ed. 1. Jurgen Ehlers
(Translator). Trade Cloth. John Wiley & Sons, Inc. Hoboken,
NJ. 1996. 590p. ISBN:0-471-95576-0, ISBN13:
978-0-471-95576-4. Dewey:551.7/9. LCCN:95-052107.
                            Audience: **u,f.** *Choice, 1997.*

Hambrey, Michael J.   **GB2403.2**
Glacial Environments. Trade Paper. University of British
Columbia Press. Vancouver, BC. 1994. 304p.
ISBN:0-7748-0510-2, ISBN13: 978-0-7748-0510-0.
Dewey:551.3/12.
                            Audience: **l,u,f.** *Choice, 1995.*

Hambrey, Michael J. &   **QE471.15.T5**
  Harland, W. B.
Earth's Pre-Pleistocene Glacial Record. Cloth Text. Cambridge
University Press. New York, NY. 1981. 1024p. Cambridge Earth
Science Ser. ISBN:0-521-22860-3, ISBN13: 978-0-521-22860-2.
Dewey:552/.5. LCCN:80-041613.
                                             Audience: **u,f.**

Hambrey, Michael & Alean,   **GB2403.2.H36 2004**
  Jürg
Glaciers. Ed. 2. Cloth Text. Cambridge University Press. New
York, NY. 2004. 394p. ISBN:0-521-82808-2, ISBN13:
978-0-521-82808-6. Dewey:551.31/2. LCCN:2004-043585.
                            Audience: **l,u,f.** *Choice, 2005.*

Menzies, John   **GB2403.2.M632 2001**
Modern and Past Glacial Environments. Ed. 2. Paper Text.
Elsevier Science & Technology Books. Saint Louis, MO. 2002.
576p. ISBN:0-7506-4226-2, ISBN13: 978-0-7506-4226-2.
Dewey:551.31. LCCN:2001-052844.
                                             Audience: **u,f.**

Meteorology and Climatology

Alverson, Keith D. (Editor),   **QC884.P257 2002**
  et al.
Paleoclimate, Global Change and the Future. Raymond S.
Bradley & Thomas F. Pedersen (Editors). Trade Cloth. Springer.
New York, NY. 2003. XIV, 221p. Global Change, :The IGBP
Ser. ISBN:3-540-42402-4, ISBN13: 978-3-540-42402-4.
Dewey:551.6/09/01. LCCN:2002-191204.
                            Audience: **u,f.** *Choice, 2003.*

Andrews, David G.   **QC863 .A596 2000**
An Introduction to Atmospheric Physics. Cloth Text. Cambridge
University Press. New York, NY. 2000. 240p.
ISBN:0-521-62051-1, ISBN13: 978-0-521-62051-2.
Dewey:551.51. LCCN:99-020191.
                            Audience: **u,f.** *Choice, 2001.*

Brock, Fred V. &   **QC876.B758 2001**
  Richardson, Scott J.
Meteorological Measurement Systems. Trade Cloth. Oxford
University Press, Inc. New York, NY. 2001. 304p.
ISBN:0-19-513451-6, ISBN13: 978-0-19-513451-3.
Dewey:551.5/028/7. LCCN:00-028551.
                                             Audience: **u,f.**

Bryant, Edward   **QC981.8.C5 B76 1997**
Climate Process and Change. Cloth Text. Cambridge University
Press. New York, NY. 1997. 225p. ISBN:0-521-48189-9,
ISBN13: 978-0-521-48189-2. Dewey:551.6. LCCN:97-003764.
                            Audience: **l,u,f.** *Choice, 1998.*

Crowley & North   **Q49**
Paleoclimatology. Trade Paper. Oxford University Press, Inc.
New York, NY. 1996. 356p. Series on Geology and Geophysics,
No. 18 ISBN:0-19-510533-8, ISBN13: 978-0-19-510533-9.
Dewey:551.6/09. LCCN:89-026604.
                                             Audience: **u.**

Drake, Frances   **QC981.8.G56D73 2000**
Global Warming: The Science of Climate Change. Cloth Text.
Oxford University Press, Inc. New York, NY. 2000. 288p. An
Arnold Publication Ser. ISBN:0-340-65301-9, ISBN13:
978-0-340-65301-2. Dewey:363.738/74. LCCN:00-711952.
                            Audience: **l,u,f.** *Choice, 2001.*

Fagan, Brian M.   **QC989.A1F34 2000**
Little Ice Age: How Climate Made History 1300-1850. Trade
Cloth. Basic Books. New York, NY. 2000. 272p.
ISBN:0-465-02271-5, ISBN13: 978-0-465-02271-7.
Dewey:551.694. LCCN:00-048627.
                            Audience: **g,l,u,f.** *Choice, 2001.*

Glickman, Todd S.   **QC854.G55 2000**
Glossary of Meteorology. Ed. 2. American Meteorological
Society Staff (Contribution by). Cloth Text. American
Meteorological Society. Boston, MA. 2000. xii, 855p.
ISBN:1-878220-34-9, ISBN13: 978-1-878220-34-9.
Dewey:551.5/03. LCCN:2001-271658.
                                         Audience: **g,l,u,f.**

Grazulis, Thomas P.   QC955.G74 2001
The Tornado: Nature's Ultimate Windstorm. Trade Cloth.
University of Oklahoma Press. Norman, OK. 2001. 352p.
ISBN:0-8061-3258-2, ISBN13: 978-0-8061-3258-7.
Dewey:551.55/3. LCCN:00-032609.

Audience: **g,l,u,f.** *Choice, 2001.*

Grove, Jean M.   QC981.8.I23G76 2004
Little Ice Ages: Ancient and Modern. Ed. 2. Paper over Boards.
Routledge. New York, NY. 2004. 328p. Routledge Studies in
Physical Geography and Environment, Vol. 5
ISBN:0-415-33423-3, ISBN13: 978-0-415-33423-5.
Dewey:551.6/09. LCCN:2003-016884.

Audience: **l,u,f.**

Hardy, John T.   QC981.8.C5
Climate Change: Causes, Effects, and Solutions. Trade Cloth.
John Wiley & Sons, Inc. Hoboken, NJ. 2003. 260p.
ISBN:0-470-85018-3, ISBN13: 978-0-470-85018-3.
Dewey:551.6. LCCN:2003-045073.

Audience: **l,u,f.**

Hartmann, Dennis L.   QC981.H32 1994
Global Physical Climatology. Cloth Text. Elsevier Science &
Technology Books. Saint Louis, MO. 1994. 411p. International
Geophysics Ser., Vol. 56 ISBN:0-12-328530-5, ISBN13:
978-0-12-328530-0. Dewey:551.6. LCCN:93-039578.

Audience: **u,f.** *Choice, 1994.*

Houghton, John T.   QC981.8.G56H68 2004
Global Warming: The Complete Briefing. Ed. 3. Cloth Text.
Cambridge University Press. New York, NY. 2004. 382p.
ISBN:0-521-81762-5, ISBN13: 978-0-521-81762-2.
Dewey:363.738/74. LCCN:2003-068735.

Audience: **g,l,u,f.** *Choice, 2005, 1998.*

Jacobson, Michael, et al.   QH344 .E37 2000
Earth System Science: From Biogeochemical Cycles to Global
Changes. Ed. 2. Robert J. Charlson, Gordon H. Orians &
Henning Rodhe (Authors). Paper Text. Elsevier Science &
Technology Books. Saint Louis, MO. 2000. 527p. International
Geophysics Ser., Vol. 73 ISBN:0-12-379370-X, ISBN13:
978-0-12-379370-6. Dewey:550.

Audience: **u.**

Linden, Eugene   QC981.8.C5L567 2006
The Winds of Change: Climate, Weather, and the Destruction of
Civilizations. Trade Cloth. Simon & Schuster. New York, NY.
2006. 320p. ISBN:0-684-86352-9, ISBN13: 978-0-684-86352-8.
Dewey:551.609/01. LCCN:2005-054434.

Audience: **l,u,f.** *Choice, 2006.*

McElroy, Michael B.   QC861.3.M34 2002
The Atmospheric Environment: Effects of Human Activity.
Trade Cloth. Princeton University Press. Princeton, NJ. 2002.
360p. ISBN:0-691-00691-1, ISBN13: 978-0-691-00691-8.
Dewey:551.51. LCCN:2001-032106.

Audience: **l,u,f.** *Choice, 2004.*

National Oceanic &   QC875
  Atmospheric Administration (NOAA)
☐ NOAA Home Page - Weather Theme Page.
http://www.noaa.gov/wx.html
National Oceanic & Atmospheric Administration (NOAA).

Audience: **g,l,u,f.**

National Oceanic and   QC945
  Atmospheric Administration
☐ Hurricanes.
http://hurricanes.noaa.gov/
National Oceanic and Atmospheric Administration.

Audience: **g,l,u,f.**

National Oceanic and   QC955.2
  Atmospheric Administration
☐ Tornadoes.
http://www.noaa.gov/tornadoes.html
National Oceanic and Atmospheric Administration.

Audience: **g,l,u,f.**

NOAA National Climatic   QC982
  Data Center
☐ National Climatic Data Center Home Page.
http://www.ncdc.noaa.gov/oa/ncdc.html
National Climatic Data Center.

Audience: **g,l,u,f.**

O'Hare, Greg, et al.   QC981.8.C5
Weather, Climate and Climate Change: Human Perspectives.
John Sweeney & Rob Wilby (Authors). Trade Paper. Prentice
Hall PTR. Upper Saddle River, NJ. 2005. 444p.
ISBN:0-13-028319-3, ISBN13: 978-0-13-028319-1.
Dewey:551.6. LCCN:2004-048650.

Audience: **l,u,f.**

Oliver, John E. (Editor)   QC854.E526 2005
The Encyclopedia of World Climatology. Trade Cloth. Springer.
New York, NY. 2005. XX, 854p. Encyclopedia of Earth
Sciences Ser. ISBN:1-4020-3264-1, ISBN13:
978-1-4020-3264-6. Dewey:551.603. LCCN:2005-296425.

Audience: **g,l,u,f.** *Choice, 2006.*

Oliver, John E. Jr. &   QC981.O393 2002
  Hidore, John J.
Climatology: An Atmospheric Science. Ed. 2. Trade Cloth.
Pearson Education. Boston, MA. 2001. 410p.
ISBN:0-13-092205-6, ISBN13: 978-0-13-092205-2.
Dewey:551.5. LCCN:2001-033228.

Audience: **l,u,f.**

Peixoto, J. P.   QC981.P434 1991
Physics of Climate. Trade Paper. Springer. New York, NY. 1992.
560p. ISBN:0-88318-712-4, ISBN13: 978-0-88318-712-8.
Dewey:551.5. LCCN:91-011565.

Audience: **u,f.** *Choice, 1993.*

Potter, Thomas D. &   GB661.2
  Colman, Bradley R. (Editors)
Handbook of Weather, Climate and Water: Dynamics, Climate,
Physical Meteorology, Weather Systems and Measurements.
Trade Cloth. John Wiley & Sons, Inc. Hoboken, NJ. 2003.
1000p. ISBN:0-471-21490-6, ISBN13: 978-0-471-21490-8.
LCCN:2003-003584.

Audience: **l,u,f.**

Robinson, Andrew   GB5014.R63 2002
Earthshock: Hurricanes, Volcanoes, Earthquakes, Tornadoes, and
Other Forces of Nature. Ed. 2. Trade Paper. Thames & Hudson.
New York, NY. 2002. 304p. ISBN:0-500-28304-4, ISBN13:
978-0-500-28304-2. Dewey:363.34. LCCN:2001-093919.

Audience: **g,l,u,f.**

Savage, Candace C.   QC971.S28 1994
Aurora: The Mysterious Northern Lights. Trade Cloth. Sierra
Club Books. San Francisco, CA. 1994. 144p. Guides
ISBN:0-87156-419-X, ISBN13: 978-0-87156-419-1.
Dewey:538.7/68. LCCN:94-001458.
                                    Audience: **g,l,u,f.** *Choice, 1995.*

Seinfeld, John H. & Pandis,   QC879.6.S45 2006
  Spyros N.
Atmospheric Chemistry and Physics: From Air Pollution to
Climate Change. Ed. 2. Trade Cloth. John Wiley & Sons, Inc.
Hoboken, NJ. 2006. 1203p. ISBN:0-471-72017-8, ISBN13:
978-0-471-72017-1. Dewey:551.5/11.
                                    Audience: **l,u,f.** *Choice, 1998.*

Thompson, Russell D. &   QC981.A57 1997
  Perry, Allen H.
Applied Climatology: Principles and Practice. Paper over
Boards. Routledge. New York, NY. 1997. 388p.
ISBN:0-415-14100-1, ISBN13: 978-0-415-14100-0.
Dewey:551.6. LCCN:96-043022.
                                    Audience: **l,u,f.** *Choice, 1998.*

Weart, Spencer R.   QC981.8.G56
The Discovery of Global Warming. Trade Paper. Harvard
University Press. Cambridge, MA. 2004. 240p. New Histories of
Science, Technology, and Medicine Ser. ISBN:0-674-01637-8,
ISBN13: 978-0-674-01637-8. Dewey:551.6.
                                    Audience: **g,l**

Hydrology and Hydrogeology > Surficial Hydrogeology (Rivers, Lakes, Streams, etc.)

Bridge, J. S.   GB1203.2.B75 2002
Rivers and Floodplains: Forms, Processes and Sedmentary
Record. Trade Paper. Blackwell Publishing, Inc. Malden, MA.
2002. 504p. ISBN:0-632-06489-7, ISBN13: 978-0-632-06489-2.
Dewey:551.48/3. LCCN:2002-066648.
                                    Audience: **l,f.** *Choice, 2003.*

Cohen, Andrew S.   QE39.5.P3C63 2003
Paleolimnology: The History and Evolution of Lake Systems.
Trade Cloth. Oxford University Press, Inc. New York, NY. 2003.
528p. ISBN:0-19-513353-6, ISBN13: 978-0-19-513353-0.
Dewey:551.48. LCCN:2002-002722.
                                    Audience: **u,f.** *Choice, 2004.*

Kalff, Jacob   QH96.K24 2002
Limnology. Paper Text. Prentice Hall PTR. Upper Saddle River,
NJ. 2001. 592p. ISBN:0-13-033775-7, ISBN13:
978-0-13-033775-7. Dewey:577.6. LCCN:2001-032745.
                                    Audience: **l,u,f.**

Knighton, David   GB561.K65 1998
Fluvial Forms and Processes: A New Perspective. Ed. 2. Paper
Text. Oxford University Press, Inc. New York, NY. 1998. 400p.
An Arnold Publication Ser. ISBN:0-340-66313-8, ISBN13:
978-0-340-66313-4. Dewey:551.48/3. LCCN:98-171285.
                                    Audience: **l,u,f.**

Leopold, Luna B., et al.   GB55.L4 1995
Fluvial Processes in Geomorphology. M. Gordon Wolman &
John P. Miller (Authors). Trade Paper. Dover Publications, Inc.

Mineola, NY. 1995. 535p. ISBN:0-486-68588-8, ISBN13:
978-0-486-68588-5. Dewey:551.3/5. LCCN:95-020080.
                                    Audience: **l,u,f.** *B*

Lerman, A. (Editor)   GB1603.2.L34
Lakes: Chemistry, Geology, Physics. Trade Cloth. Springer. New
York, NY. 1978. x, 363p. ISBN:0-387-90322-4, ISBN13:
978-0-387-90322-4. Dewey:551.4/82. LCCN:78-017842.
                                    Audience: **u,f.** *B*

Lerman, Abraham (Editor),   GB1603.8
  et al.
Physics and Chemistry of Lakes. Ed. 2. Joel R. Gat & D.
Imboden (Editors). Cloth Text. Springer. New York, NY. 1995.
350p. ISBN:0-387-57891-9, ISBN13: 978-0-387-57891-0.
Dewey:551.48/2.
                                    Audience: **u,f.**

Miall, Andrew D.   QE471.2.M53 1996
The Geology of Fluvial Deposits: Sedimentary Facies, Basin
Analysis and Petroleum Geology. Trade Cloth. Springer. New
York, NY. 1996. XVI, 582p. ISBN:3-540-59186-9, ISBN13:
978-3-540-59186-3. Dewey:551.3/5. LCCN:96-031798.
                                    Audience: **u,f.** *Choice, 1996.*

Morisawa, Marie E.   GB1203.8
Rivers. Trade Paper. John Wiley & Sons, Inc. Hoboken, NJ.
1986. 224p. ISBN:0-470-20548-2, ISBN13: 978-0-470-20548-8.
Dewey:551.48/3.
                                    Audience: **u,f.** *B*

Richards, Keith   GB1205
Rivers: Form and Process in Alluvial Channels. Trade Cloth.
Routledge. New York, NY. 1982. 272p. ISBN:0-416-74900-3,
ISBN13: 978-0-416-74900-7. Dewey:551.48/3.
LCCN:82-008133.
                                    Audience: **u,f.** *B*

Richards, Keith   GB1205.R5 2004
Rivers: Forms and Process in Alluvial Channels. Perfect.
Blackburn Press, The. Caldwell, NJ. 2004. 361p.
ISBN:1-930665-97-0, ISBN13: 978-1-930665-97-2.
Dewey:551.48/3. LCCN:2004-101478.
                                    Audience: **u,f.**

Robert, Andre   GB1201
River Processes: An Introduction to Fluvial Dynamics. Trade
Cloth. Oxford University Press, Inc. New York, NY. 2003. 240p.
An Arnold Publication ISBN:0-340-76338-8, ISBN13:
978-0-340-76338-4. Dewey:551.48/3. LCCN:2004-271234.
                                    Audience: **u,f.**

Schumm, Stanley A.   GB561.S35 2003
The Fluvial System. Perfect. Blackburn Press, The. Caldwell,
NJ. 2003. 358p. ISBN:1-930665-79-2, ISBN13:
978-1-930665-79-8. Dewey:551.48/3. LCCN:2003-105827.
                                    Audience: **u,f.**

Wetzel, Robert G.   QH96.W47 2001
Limnology: Lake and River Ecosystems. Ed. 3. Cloth Text.
Elsevier Science & Technology Books. Saint Louis, MO. 2001.
1006p. ISBN:0-12-744760-1, ISBN13: 978-0-12-744760-5.
Dewey:577.6. LCCN:00-110178.
                                    Audience: **u,f.**

Hydrology and Hydrogeology > Groundwater/aquifer

Domenico, et al.   GB1003.2S39 2002
Fundamentals of Ground Water. Franklin W. Schwartz & Hubao
Zhang (Authors). Trade Cloth. John Wiley & Sons, Inc.
Hoboken, NJ. 2002. 592p. ISBN:0-471-13785-5, ISBN13:
978-0-471-13785-6. Dewey:551.49. LCCN:2002-028811.
Audience: **u,f.**

Freeze, Alan R. & Cherry,   GB1003.2.F73
  John A.
Groundwater. Ed. 1. Trade Cloth. Prentice Hall PTR. Upper
Saddle River, NJ. 1979. 604p. ISBN:0-13-365312-9, ISBN13:
978-0-13-365312-0. Dewey:551.4/98. LCCN:78-025796.
Audience: **u,f.** *B*

Higgins, C. G. & Coates, D.   GB1001.2G765 1990
  R. (Editors)
Groundwater Geomorphology: The Role of Subsurface Water in
Earth-Surface Processes and Landforms. Trade Paper. Geological
Society of America, Inc. Boulder, CO. 1991. 380p. Special
Papers, No. 252 ISBN:0-8137-2252-7, ISBN13:
978-0-8137-2252-8. Dewey:551.3/5. LCCN:90-013852.
Audience: **u,f.**

Ingebritsen, Steven E. &   GB1003.2
  Sanford, Ward E.
Groundwater in Geologic Processes. Trade Cloth. Cambridge
University Press. New York, NY. 1998. 365p.
ISBN:0-521-49608-X, ISBN13: 978-0-521-49608-7.
Dewey:551.49. LCCN:97-018014.
Audience: **u,f.**

Todd, David Keith & Mays,   GB1003.2.T6 2005
  Larry W.
Groundwater Hydrology. Ed. 3. Trade Cloth. John Wiley &
Sons, Inc. Hoboken, NJ. 2004. 656p. ISBN:0-471-05937-4,
ISBN13: 978-0-471-05937-0. Dewey:45/21.
LCCN:2004-557944.
Audience: **l,u,f.**

U.S. Geological Survey   G1201.C34
☐ Ground Water Atlas of the United States.
http://purl.access.gpo.gov/GPO/LPS9905
U.S. Geological Survey. ISBN:0-607-89828-3, ISBN13:
978-0-607-89828-6.
Audience: **g,l,u,f.**

Marine Geology/Oceanography

                                        QE39
☐ Marine Realms Information Bank.
http://mrib.usgs.gov/
Audience: **g,l,u,f.**

                                        GC37
☐ National Oceanographic Data Center (NODC).
http://www.nodc.gov/
Audience: **u,f.**

                                        GC21.5
☐ WINDandSEA: The Oceanoic and Atmospheric Siences
Internet Locator.
http://www.lib.noaa.gov/docs/windandsea.html
Audience: **g,l.**

Cone, Joseph   GB1198 .C66 1991
Fire under the Sea: The Discovery of the Most Extraordinary
Environment on Earth - Volcanic Hot Springs on the Ocean
Floor. Trade Paper. HarperCollins Publishers. New York, NY.
1992. 304p. ISBN:0-688-11905-0, ISBN13: 978-0-688-11905-8.
Dewey:551.2/3. LCCN:92-008802.
Audience: **l,u.**

Earle, Sylvia   G2800.E2 2001
Atlas of the Ocean: The Deep Frontier. Trade Cloth. National
Geographic Society. Washington, DC. 2001. 192p.
ISBN:0-7922-6426-6, ISBN13: 978-0-7922-6426-2.
Dewey:551.4/6/00223. LCCN:2001-034566.
Audience: **l,u,f.**

Ellis, Richard   GC9.E38 2000
Encyclopedia of the Sea. Trade Cloth. Alfred A. Knopf Inc.
New York, NY. 2000. 400p. ISBN:0-375-40374-4, ISBN13:
978-0-375-40374-3. Dewey:551.46/003. LCCN:99-042401.
Audience: **g,l,u.** *Choice, 2001.*

Erickson, Jon   QE39.E68 2003
Marine Geology: Exploring the New Frontiers of the Ocean. Ed.
2. Timothy Kusky (Foreword by). Trade Cloth. Facts On File,
Inc.. New York, NY. 2002. 336p. The Facts on File Science
Library ISBN:0-8160-4874-6, ISBN13: 978-0-8160-4874-8.
Dewey:551.46/08. LCCN:2002-001295.
Audience: **g,l.**

Garrison, Tom S.   GC11.2.G37 2005
Oceanography: An Invitation to Marine Science. Ed. 5. Cloth
Text. Brooks/Cole. Pacific Grove, CA. 2004. 544p.
ISBN:0-534-40887-7, ISBN13: 978-0-534-40887-9.
Dewey:551.46. LCCN:2003-115986.
Audience: **l,u.**

Kunzig, Robert   GC21.K949 2000
Mapping the Deep: The Extraordinary Story of Ocean Science.
Trade Paper. W. W. Norton & Company, Inc. New York, NY.
2000. 352p. ISBN:0-393-32063-4, ISBN13: 978-0-393-32063-3.
Dewey:551.46. LCCN:00-046078.
Audience: **l,u.**

Lawrence, David M.   GC87.L38 2002
Upheaval from the Abyss: Ocean Floor Mapping and the Earth
Science Revolution. Trade Cloth. Rutgers University Press.
Piscataway, NJ. 2002. 284p. ISBN:0-8135-3028-8, ISBN13:
978-0-8135-3028-4. Dewey:551.46/084/0223.
LCCN:2001-031789.
Audience: **g,l,u,f.** *Choice, 2002.*

Martin, Seelye   GC10.4.R4M375 2004
An Introduction to Ocean Remote Sensing. Cloth Text.
Cambridge University Press. New York, NY. 2004. 454p.
ISBN:0-521-80280-6, ISBN13: 978-0-521-80280-2.
Dewey:551.46/028. LCCN:2003-061380.
Audience: **u,f.** *Choice, 2005.*

McCutcheon, Scott &   GC24.M43 2003
  McCutcheon, Bobbi
The Facts on File Marine Science Handbook. Trade Paper. Facts

On File, Inc.. New York, NY. 2003. 272p. The Facts on File Science Handbooks ISBN:0-8160-4883-5, ISBN13: 978-0-8160-4883-0. Dewey:551.46. LCCN:2003-000275.

Audience: **g,l.** *Choice, 2003.*

Monahan, Dave (Editor) G2800.W4413 2001
World Atlas of the Oceans. Trade Cloth. Firefly Books, Ltd. Tonawanda, NY. 2001. 80 deep-sea charts, 80 relief maps, 40 thematic maps, 7 special charts of the North Sea and the Baltic Sea published for the first time, full color throughout, index, maps, sidebars 264p. ISBN:1-55209-585-1, ISBN13: 978-1-55209-585-0. Dewey:551.46/0022/3. LCCN:00-030005.

Audience: **g,l,u.** *Choice, 2002.*

Nybakken, James Willard GC9.I58 2002
(Editor), et al.
Interdisciplinary Encyclopedia of Marine Sciences. William W. Broenkow & T. L. Vallier (Editors). Trade Cloth. Scholastic Library Publishing. Danbury, CT. 2002. 1425p. ISBN:0-7172-5946-3, ISBN13: 978-0-7172-5946-5. Dewey:551.46/003. LCCN:2002-192707.

Audience: **g,l,u.** *Choice, 2003.*

Prager, Ellen & Earle, GC21.5
Sylvia
The Oceans. Trade Paper. McGraw-Hill Companies, The. New York, NY. 2001. 316p. ISBN:0-07-138177-5, ISBN13: 978-0-07-138177-2. Dewey:551.4/6.

Audience: **l,u,f.**

Rozwadowski, Helen M. GC65.R695 2005
Fathoming the Ocean: The Discovery and Exploration of the Deep Sea. Sylvia A. Earle (Foreword by). Trade Cloth. Harvard University Press. Cambridge, MA. 2005. 304p. ISBN:0-674-01691-2, ISBN13: 978-0-674-01691-0. Dewey:551.46. LCCN:2004-057083.

Audience: **l,u,f.** *Choice, 2005.*

Schwartz, M. (Editor) GB450.4
Encyclopedia of Coastal Science. Trade Cloth. Springer. New York, NY. 2005. XXXV, 1211p. Encyclopedia of Earth Sciences Ser. ISBN:1-4020-1903-3, ISBN13: 978-1-4020-1903-6. Dewey:551.45/7. LCCN:2005-281028.

Audience: **l,u,f.** *Choice, 2006.*

Seibold, Eugen & Berger, QE39
W. H.
The Sea Floor: An Introduction to Marine Geology. Ed. 3. Trade Cloth. Springer. New York, NY. 1996. XIII, 356p. ISBN:3-540-60191-0, ISBN13: 978-3-540-60191-3. Dewey:551.4/6/08.

Audience: **g,l,u.** *Choice, 1996.*

Steele, John H. (Editor), GC9.E57 2001
et al.
Encyclopedia of Ocean Sciences, Set. Steve A. Thorpe & Karl K. Turekian (Editors). Trade Cloth. Elsevier Science & Technology Books. Saint Louis, MO. 2001. 3399p. ISBN:0-12-227430-X, ISBN13: 978-0-12-227430-5. Dewey:551.46/003. LCCN:2001-092473.

Audience: **l,u,f.** *Choice, 2002.*

Summerhayes, C. P. & GC11.2 B .S96
Thorpe, S. A.
Oceanography: An Illustrated Text. Trade Paper. John Wiley & Sons, Inc. Hoboken, NJ. 1999. 352p. ISBN:0-470-34537-3, ISBN13: 978-0-470-34537-5. Dewey:551.46.

Audience: **l,u.**

Sverdrup, Keith A., et al. GC11.2.D89
An Introduction to the World's Oceans. Ed. 8. Alyn C. Duxbury & Alison B. Duxbury (Authors). Trade Cloth. McGraw-Hill Higher Education. Burr Ridge, IL. 2004. ISBN:0-07-294555-9, ISBN13: 978-0-07-294555-3. Dewey:551.46.

Audience: **l,u.**

Tomczak, Matthias & GC11.2.T66
Godfrey, J. Stuart
Regional Oceanography: An Introduction. Ed. 2. Trade Paper. Daya Publishing House. Delhi, 2003. ISBN:81-7035-307-6, ISBN13: 978-81-7035-307-2. Dewey:551.46.

Audience: **u,f.** *Choice, 1994.*

Marine Geology/Oceanography > Chemical Oceanography

Broecker, Wallace S. GC116
Tracers in the Sea. Cloth Text. Eldigio Press. Palisades, NY. 1982. 700p. ISBN:0-9617511-0-X, ISBN13: 978-0-9617511-0-4. Dewey:551.46.

Audience: **u,f.** *B*

Chester, Roy GC101.2
Marine Geochemistry. Ed. 2. Trade Paper. Blackwell Publishing, Inc. Malden, MA. 2003. 520p. ISBN:1-4051-0172-5, ISBN13: 978-1-4051-0172-1. Dewey:551.46/01.

Audience: **u,f.** *Choice, 1991.*

Follows, Mick & Oguz, GC117.C37
Temel (Editors)
The Ocean Carbon Cycle and Climate: Proceedings of the NATO asi on Ocean Carbon Cylce and Climate, Ankara, Turkey, from 5 to 16 August 2002. Trade Paper. Springer. New York, NY. 2004. XII, 395p. NATO Science Ser., Vol. 40:Earth and Environmental Sciences 29 ISBN:1-4020-2086-4, ISBN13: 978-1-4020-2086-5. Dewey:551.46/6.

Audience: **u,f.**

Gianguzza, Antonio (Editor), GC111.2.C435 2002
et al.
Chemistry of Marine Water and Sediments. Ezio Pelizzetti & Silvio Sammartano (Editors). Trade Cloth. Springer. New York, NY. 2002. XVIII, 508p. Environmental Science Ser. ISBN:3-540-42055-X, ISBN13: 978-3-540-42055-2. Dewey:551.46/01. LCCN:2002-021060.

Audience: **u,f.**

Open University Staff GC111.2
Seawater: Its Composition, Properties and Behaviour. Ed. 2. Paper Text. Elsevier Science & Technology Books. Saint Louis, MO. 1995. 166p. ISBN:0-7506-3715-3, ISBN13: 978-0-7506-3715-2. Dewey:551.46/01.

Audience: **u,f.**

Sarmiento, Jorge Louis & GC116S27 2006
Gruber, Nicolas
Ocean Biogeochemical Dynamics. Trade Cloth. Princeton University Press. Princeton, NJ. 2006. 464p. ISBN:0-691-01707-7, ISBN13: 978-0-691-01707-5. Dewey:551.46/6. LCCN:2005-050465.

Audience: **u,f.**

Marine Geology/Oceanography > Physical Oceanography

Emery, William J.   GC57.E46 2001
Data Analysis Methods in Physical Oceanography. Ed. 2. R. E. Thomson (Editor). Trade Paper, Perfect. Elsevier Science & Technology Books. Saint Louis, MO. 2001. 654p. ISBN:0-444-50757-4, ISBN13: 978-0-444-50757-0. Dewey:551.46. LCCN:2001-268500.

Audience: **u,f.**

Jochum, Markus &   GC11.2
  Murtugudde, Raghu (Editors)
Physical Oceanography: Developments Since 1950. Trade Cloth. Springer. New York, NY. 2006. xii, 250p. ISBN:0-387-30261-1, ISBN13: 978-0-387-30261-4. Dewey:551.46. LCCN:2005-935458.

Audience: **u,f.**

Knauss, John A.   GC150.5.K6
Introduction to Physical Oceanography. Ed. 2. Paper Text. Waveland Press, Inc. Prospect Heights, IL. 2005. 309p. ISBN:1-57766-429-9, ISBN13: 978-1-57766-429-1. Dewey:551.46.

Audience: **l,u.** 𝓑

Pickard, George L. &   GC150.5.P52 1990
  Emery, W. J.
Descriptive Physical Oceanography: An Introduction. Ed. 5. Trade Paper. Elsevier Science & Technology Books. Saint Louis, MO. 1990. 336p. ISBN:0-7506-2759-X, ISBN13: 978-0-7506-2759-7. Dewey:551.46/01.

Audience: **l,u.**

Pond, S. & Pickard,   GC228.5
  George L.
Introductory Dynamical Oceanography. Ed. 2. Paper Text. Elsevier Science & Technology Books. Saint Louis, MO. 1983. 349p. ISBN:0-7506-2496-5, ISBN13: 978-0-7506-2496-1. Dewey:551.4/7.

Audience: **u,f.**

Thomas, D. N. &   GB2403.2.S43 2003
  Dieckmann, G. S. (Editors)
Sea Ice: An Introduction to its Physics, Chemistry, Biology and Geology. Trade Cloth. Blackwell Publishing, Inc. Malden, MA. 2003. 416p. ISBN:0-632-05808-0, ISBN13: 978-0-632-05808-2. Dewey:551.34/3. LCCN:2002-038346.

Audience: **u,f.**

Marine Geology/Oceanography > Waves, Tides, and Currents

Janssen, Peter   GC190.2.J36 2004
The Interaction of Ocean Waves and Wind. Trade Cloth. Cambridge University Press. New York, NY. 2004. 308p. ISBN:0-521-46540-0, ISBN13: 978-0-521-46540-3. Dewey:551.46/3. LCCN:2004-045181.

Audience: **u,f.**

Komen, G. J., et al.   GC211.2.D96 1994
Dynamics and Modelling of Ocean Waves. L. Cavaleri, M. Donelan, Klaus Hasselmann, S. Hasselmann & P. A. Janssen

(Authors). Trade Paper. Cambridge University Press. New York, NY. 1996. 554p. ISBN:0-521-57781-0, ISBN13: 978-0-521-57781-6. Dewey:551.4/702.

Audience: **u,f.**

Open University Staff   GC228.5.O25 2001
Ocean Circulation. Ed. 2. Paper Text. Elsevier Science & Technology Books. Saint Louis, MO. 2001. 286p. ISBN:0-7506-5278-0, ISBN13: 978-0-7506-5278-0. Dewey:551.47/01. LCCN:2001-280099.

Audience: **l,u.**

Open University Staff   GC211.2.W39 1999
Waves, Tides and Shallow-Water Processes. Ed. 2. Trade Paper. Elsevier Science & Technology Books. Saint Louis, MO. 2000. 228p. ISBN:0-7506-4281-5, ISBN13: 978-0-7506-4281-1. Dewey:551.47. LCCN:00-268315.

Audience: **l,u.**

Philander, S. George   GC296.8.E4P485 2006
Our Affair with el Nino: How We Transformed an Enchanting Peruvian Current into a Global Climate Hazard. Trade Paper. Princeton University Press. Princeton, NJ. 2006. 296p. ISBN:0-691-12622-4, ISBN13: 978-0-691-12622-7. Dewey:551.6.

Audience: **g,l,u,f.** *Choice, 2004.*

Marine Geology/Oceanography > Environmental Oceanography and Marine Resources

Gerdes, Louise I. (Editor)   GC1018.E53 2004
Endangered Oceans. Trade Paper. Thomson Gale. Farmington Hills, MI. 2004. 220p. ISBN:0-7377-2275-4, ISBN13: 978-0-7377-2275-8. Dewey:333.95/616. LCCN:2003-054015.

Audience: **g,l,u,f.**

Helvarg, David   GC1020.H45 2006
Blue Frontier: Dispatches from America's Ocean Wilderness. Ed. 2. Trade Paper. Sierra Club Books. San Francisco, CA. 2006. 336p. ISBN:1-57805-157-6, ISBN13: 978-1-57805-157-1. Dewey:333.91/64160973. LCCN:2005-056339.

Audience: **g,l,u,f.**

Jacques, Peter & Smith,   GC64.J33 2003
  Zachary A.
Ocean Politics and Policy: A Reference Handbook. Mildred Vasan (Editor). Library Binding. ABC-CLIO, Inc. Santa Barbara, CA. 2003. 267p. Contemporary World Issues Ser. ISBN:1-57607-622-9, ISBN13: 978-1-57607-622-4. Dewey:333.91/64. LCCN:2002-156284.

Audience: **g,l,u.** *Choice, 2003.*

Vallega, Adalberto   GC1018.V35 2000
Sustainable Ocean Governance: A Geographical Perspective. Paper over Boards. Routledge. New York, NY. 2000. 304p. Ocean Management and Policy Ser. ISBN:0-415-18916-0, ISBN13: 978-0-415-18916-3. Dewey:333.91/6416. LCCN:00-029103.

Audience: **g,l,u.**

Wilder, Robert J.   GC11.2.W55 1998
Listening to the Sea: The Politics of Improving Environmental Protection. Trade Paper. University of Pittsburgh Press.

Pittsburgh, PA. 1998. 316p. Pitt Series in Policy and Institutional Studies ISBN:0-8229-5663-2, ISBN13: 978-0-8229-5663-1. Dewey:333.91/6415. LCCN:98-008947.

Audience: **u,f.** *Choice, 1999.*

Marine Geology/Oceanography > Biological Oceanography

Jumars, Peter A.   **QH541.5.S3.J85 1993**
Concepts in Biological Oceanography: An Interdisciplinary Primer. Trade Cloth. Oxford University Press, Inc. New York, NY. 1993. 360p. ISBN:0-19-506732-0, ISBN13: 978-0-19-506732-3. Dewey:574.5/2636. LCCN:92-039069.

Audience: **u,f.** *Choice, 1993.*

Knox, George A.   **QH95.58 .K58 1994**
The Biology of the Southern Ocean. Trade Cloth. Cambridge University Press. New York, NY. 1994. 458p. Studies in Polar Research ISBN:0-521-32211-1, ISBN13: 978-0-521-32211-9. Dewey:574.924. LCCN:93-028273.

Audience: **u,f.** *Choice, 1995.*

Lalli, Carol M. & Parsons,   **QH91.16**
  Timothy
Biological Oceanography: An Introduction. Ed. 2. Trade Paper. Elsevier Science & Technology Books. Saint Louis, MO. 1997. 320p. ISBN:0-7506-3384-0, ISBN13: 978-0-7506-3384-0. Dewey:574.92. LCCN:96-042139.

Audience: **u,f.** *Choice, 1994.*

Miller, Charles B.   **QH541.5.S3M55 2003**
Biological Oceanography. Trade Paper. Blackwell Publishing, Inc. Malden, MA. 2003. 416p. ISBN:0-632-05536-7, ISBN13: 978-0-632-05536-4. Dewey:577.7. LCCN:2003-004622.

Audience: **u,f.** *Choice, 2004.*

Mills, Eric L.   **QH91.25.M55 1989**
Biological Oceanography: An Early History, Eighteen Seventy to Nineteen Sixty. Book, Other. Cornell University Press. Ithaca, NY. 1989. 368p. A Comstock Bk. ISBN:0-8014-2340-6, ISBN13: 978-0-8014-2340-6. Dewey:574.92/09. LCCN:89-033048.

Audience: **u,f.** *Choice, 1990.*

Regional Geology > North America

                                        Z6034.N7
☐ Geologic Guidebooks of North America Database. http://guide.georef.org/dbtw-wpd/guideens.htm American Geological Institute.

Audience: **l,u,f.**

☐ The North American Tapestry of Time and Terrain. http://purl.access.gpo.gov/GPO/LPS37342 U.S. Geological Survey.

Audience: **l,u,f.**

Bally, A. W. & Palmer, A. R.   **QE71.G48 1986 VOL. A**
  (Editors)
Geology of North America: An Overview. Trade Cloth. Geological Society of America, Inc. Boulder, CO. 1989. 629p.

DNAG, Geology of North America Ser., Vol. A ISBN:0-8137-5207-8, ISBN13: 978-0-8137-5207-5. Dewey:557 s. LCCN:89-007536.

Audience: **l,u,f.**

Beus, Stanley S. (Editor)   **QE77**
Rocky Mountain Section Field Guide. Trade Cloth. Geological Society of America, Inc. Boulder, CO. 1987. 489p. DNAG Centennial Field Guides Ser., No. 2 ISBN:0-8137-5402-X, ISBN13: 978-0-8137-5402-4. Dewey:557.3.

Audience: **l,u,f.**

Biggs, D. L. (Editor)   **QE77; QE78.7**
North-Central Section Field Guide. Trade Cloth. Geological Society of America, Inc. Boulder, CO. 1988. 490p. DNAG Centennial Field Guides Ser., No.3 ISBN:0-8137-5403-8, ISBN13: 978-0-8137-5403-1. Dewey:557.3.

Audience: **l,u,f.**

Drake, Ellen T. & Jordan,   **QE13.U6G466 1985**
  William M. (Editors)
Geologists and Ideas: A History of North American Geology. Trade Cloth. Geological Society of America, Inc. Boulder, CO. 1986. 520p. DNAG Centennial Special Volumes Ser., Vol. 1 ISBN:0-8137-5301-5, ISBN13: 978-0-8137-5301-0. Dewey:550/.973. LCCN:85-017631.

Audience: **l,u,f.**

Ehlers, J. & Gibbard, P. L.   **QC884**
Quaternary Glaciations - Extent and Chronology: North America. Trade Cloth, CD-ROM. Elsevier Science & Technology Books. Saint Louis, MO. 2004. 450p. Developments in Quaternary Sciences Ser., Vol. 2, Pt. II ISBN:0-444-51592-5, ISBN13: 978-0-444-51592-6. Dewey:551.79. LCCN:2006-276073.

Audience: **u,f.**

Frazier, W. J. &   **QE651.F75 1987**
  Schwimmer, D. R.
Regional Stratigraphy of North America. Trade Cloth. Basic Books. New York, NY. 1987. 744p. ISBN:0-306-42324-3, ISBN13: 978-0-306-42324-6. Dewey:557. LCCN:87-007019.

Audience: **u,f.** *Choice, 1988.*

Graf, W. L. (Editor)   **GB427 .G46 1987**
Geomorphic Systems of North America. Trade Cloth. Geological Society of America, Inc. Boulder, CO. 1987. 661p. DNAG Centennial Special Volume Ser., Vol. 2 ISBN:0-8137-5302-3, ISBN13: 978-0-8137-5302-7. Dewey:551.4/097. LCCN:87-008411.

Audience: **u,f.**

Hayward, O. T. (Editor)   **QE77**
South-Central Section Field Guide. Trade Cloth. Geological Society of America, Inc. Boulder, CO. 1988. 475p. DNAG Centennial Field Guides Ser., No. 4 ISBN:0-8137-5404-6, ISBN13: 978-0-8137-5404-8. Dewey:557.3.

Audience: **l,u,f.**

Hazen, Robert M. (Editor)   **QE71.N67**
North American Geology: Early Writings. Trade Cloth. John Wiley & Sons, Inc. Hoboken, NJ. 1983. 356p. Benchmark Papers in Geology, Vol. 51 ISBN:0-87933-345-6, ISBN13: 978-0-87933-345-4. Dewey:557. LCCN:79-000708.

Audience: **l,u,f.** *B*

Hill, M. L. (Editor)   **QE77**
Cordilleran Section Field Guide. Trade Cloth. Geological
Society of America, Inc. Boulder, CO. 1987. 532p. DNAG
Centennial Field Guides Ser., No. 1 ISBN:0-8137-5401-1,
ISBN13: 978-0-8137-5401-7. Dewey:557.3.
                                          Audience: **l,u,f.**

King, Phillip B.   **QE71**
The Evolution of North America. Trade Cloth. Princeton
University Press. Princeton, NJ. 1977. 216p.
ISBN:0-691-08195-6, ISBN13: 978-0-691-08195-3. Dewey:557.
LCCN:77-071987.
                                      Audience: **l,u,f.** *B*

McPhee, John   **QE77**
Annals of the Former World, Set. Trade Paper. Farrar, Straus &
Giroux. New York, NY. 2000. 696p. ISBN:0-374-51873-4,
ISBN13: 978-0-374-51873-8. Dewey:557.3. LCCN:97-039660.
                          Audience: **g,l,u,f.** *Choice, 1999.*

Moran-Zenteno, Dante   **QE201.M6713 1994**
The Geology of the Mexican Republic. James L. Wilson & Luis
Sanchez-Barreda (Translators). Trade Cloth. American
Association of Petroleum Geologists. Tulsa, OK. 1994. 160p.
Studies in Geology, No. 39 ISBN:0-89181-047-1, ISBN13:
978-0-89181-047-6. Dewey:557.2. LCCN:95-100129.
                                            Audience: **u,f.**

Neathery, T. L. (Editor)   **QE77 .C46**
Southeastern Section Field Guide. Trade Cloth. Geological
Society of America, Inc. Boulder, CO. 1986. 477p. DNAG
Centennial Field Guides Ser., No. 6 ISBN:0-8137-5406-2,
ISBN13: 978-0-8137-5406-2. Dewey:557.3. LCCN:86-011986.
                                          Audience: **l,u,f.**

Redfern, Ron   **QE99**
The Making of a Continent. Trade Paper. Random House, Inc.
New York, NY. 1986. 256p. ISBN:0-8129-1617-4, ISBN13:
978-0-8129-1617-1. Dewey:557. LCCN:86-004374.
                                            Audience: **g,l.**

Reed, John Calvin et. al
Geologic Map of North America, Decade of North American
Geology Project. Continental-Scale Map. Boulder, Colo.:
Geological Society of America. 2005.
                                          Audience: **l,u,f.**

Roy, D. C. (Editor)   **QE77; QE78.7**
Northeastern Section Field Guide. Trade Cloth. Geological
Society of America, Inc. Boulder, CO. 1987. 517p. DNAG
Centennial Field Guides Ser., No. 5 ISBN:0-8137-5405-4,
ISBN13: 978-0-8137-5405-5. Dewey:557.3.
                                          Audience: **l,u,f.**

Regional Geology > South America

Jenks, William Furness   **QE0230**
Handbook of South American Geology: An Explanation of the
Geologic Map of South America. . . Trade Paper. Books on
Demand. Ann Arbor, MI. 453p. Memoir 65 Ser.
ISBN:0-598-64623-X, ISBN13: 978-0-598-64623-1. Dewey:558.
LCCN:56-058161.
                                      Audience: **u,f.** *B*

Lamb, Simon   **QE230.L36 2004**
Devil in the Mountain: A Search for the Origin of the Andes.
Trade Cloth. Princeton University Press. Princeton, NJ. 2004.

336p. ISBN:0-691-11596-6, ISBN13: 978-0-691-11596-2.
Dewey:558. LCCN:2003-064124.
                                            Audience: **l,u,f.**

Regional Geology > Europe

Blundell, D. J. (Editor),   **QE633.A1C66 1992**
et al.
A Continent Revealed: The European Geotraverse, Structure and
Dynamic Evolution. R. Freeman & Stephan Mueller (Editors).
Trade Paper. Cambridge University Press. New York, NY. 1992.
287p. ISBN:0-521-42948-X, ISBN13: 978-0-521-42948-1.
Dewey:551.8/094. LCCN:93-112407.
                          Audience: **u,f.** *Choice, 1994, 1993.*

Ehlers, J. & Gibbard, P. L.   **QC884**
Quaternary Glaciations - Extent and Chronology: Europe. Trade
Cloth, CD-ROM. Elsevier Science & Technology Books. Saint
Louis, MO. 2004. 488p. Developments in Quaternary Sciences
Ser., Vol. 2 ISBN:0-444-51462-7, ISBN13: 978-0-444-51462-2.
Dewey:551.79. LCCN:2006-276073.
                              Audience: **u,f.** *Choice, 2005.*

Moores, Eldridge M. &   **QE260**
Fairbridge, Rhodes W. (Editors)
Encyclopedia of European and Asian Regional Geology. Cloth
Text. Springer U S A, Inc. Las Vegas, NV. 1998. 896p.
Encyclopedia of Earth Sciences Ser. ISBN:0-412-74040-0,
ISBN13: 978-0-412-74040-4. Dewey:554. LCCN:96-086585.
                                            Audience: **l,u,f.**

Ziegler, P. A.   **QE260 .Z53 1982**
Geological Atlas of Western and Central Europe. Trade Cloth.
Elsevier. New York, NY. 1982. 130p. ISBN:0-444-42084-3,
ISBN13: 978-0-444-42084-8. Dewey:554. LCCN:82-193535.
                                            Audience: **l,u,f.**

Regional Geology > Asia

Hall, R. & Blundell, D. J.   **QE634 .A785 T43 1996**
(Editors)
Tectonic Evolution of Southeast Asia. Trade Cloth. Geological
Society Publishing House. Bath, 1996. xiv, 566p. Geological
Society Special Publication Ser., Series 106
ISBN:1-897799-52-7, ISBN13: 978-1-897799-52-9.
Dewey:551.8/0959. LCCN:2002-427068.
                                            Audience: **u,f.**

Kimura, Toshio, et al.   **QE304 .K54 1991**
Geology of Japan. Ed. 2. Itaru Hayami & Shizuo Yoshida
(Authors). Trade Cloth. University of Tokyo Press. 1991. 320p.
ISBN:0-86008-474-4, ISBN13: 978-0-86008-474-7.
Dewey:555.2. LCCN:91-204158.
                                            Audience: **u,f.**

Moores, Eldridge M. &   **QE260**
Fairbridge, Rhodes W. (Editors)
Encyclopedia of European and Asian Regional Geology. Cloth
Text. Springer U S A, Inc. Las Vegas, NV. 1998. 896p.
Encyclopedia of Earth Sciences Ser. ISBN:0-412-74040-0,
ISBN13: 978-0-412-74040-4. Dewey:554. LCCN:96-086585.
                                            Audience: **l,u,f.**

Nalivkin, D. V.   **QE276.N2813 1973**
Geology of the U. S. S. R. Nicholas Rast (Translator). Trade
Cloth. University of Toronto Press. Toronto, ON. 1973. xxviii,

855 pp. ISBN:0-8020-1984-6, ISBN13: 978-0-8020-1984-4. Dewey:554.7. LCCN:72-097781.

Audience: **u,f.** *B*

Yin, An & Harrison, Mark   QE634.A1T43 1996
(Editors)
The Tectonic Evolution of Asia. Trade Cloth. Cambridge University Press. New York, NY. 1996. 678p. World and Regional Geology Ser., No. 8 ISBN:0-521-48049-3, ISBN13: 978-0-521-48049-9. Dewey:551.8/095. LCCN:95-020092.

Audience: **u,f.**

Regional Geology > Africa

Cahen, L., et al.   QE320 .C28 1984
The Geochronology and Evolution of Africa. N. J. Snelling, J. Delhal, J. R. Vail, M. Bonhomme & D. Ledent (Authors). Cloth Text. Oxford University Press, Inc. New York, NY. 1984. 526p. ISBN:0-19-857544-0, ISBN13: 978-0-19-857544-3. Dewey:551.7/0096. LCCN:83-012122.

Audience: **u,f.**

Petters, S. W.   QE320 .P48 1991
Regional Geology of Africa. Cloth Text. Springer. New York, NY. 1991. 722p. Lecture Notes in Earth Sciences, Vol. 40 ISBN:0-387-54528-X, ISBN13: 978-0-387-54528-8. Dewey:556. LCCN:91-037239.

Audience: **l,u,f.**

Schlüter, Thomas   QE320 .S35
Geological Atlas of Africa: With Notes on Stratigraphy, Tectonics, Economic Geology, Geohazards and Geosites of Each Country. Trade Cloth. Springer. New York, NY. 2005. XII, 272p. ISBN:3-540-29144-X, ISBN13: 978-3-540-29144-2. Dewey:556.

Audience: **u,f.**

Regional Geology > Australasia

Brown, D. S.   QE340
The Geological Evolution of Australia and New Zealand. Trade Paper. Pergamon Press. Kidlington, 1968. ISBN:0-08-012277-9, ISBN13: 978-0-08-012277-9. Dewey:551.7/00994.

Audience: **u,f.**

Johnson, David   QE340.J64 2004
Geology of Australia. Trade Paper. Cambridge University Press. New York, NY. 2005. 288p. ISBN:0-521-60100-2, ISBN13: 978-0-521-60100-9. Dewey:559.4. LCCN:2004-009885.

Audience: **u,f.**

Regional Geology > Oceans

Naim, A. E., et al.   QE39
The Ocean Basins and Margins: The Tethys Ocean. L. E. Ricou, B. Vrielynck & J. Dercourt (Authors). Trade Cloth. Basic Books. New York, NY. 1996. 517p. ISBN:0-306-45156-5, ISBN13: 978-0-306-45156-0. Dewey:551.4/6. LCCN:72-083046.

Audience: **l,u,f.**

Naim, A. E. & Stehli, F. G.   QE39
The Ocean Basins and Margins: The Pacific Ocean. Trade Cloth. Basic Books. New York, NY. 1985. 748p. ISBN:0-306-37777-2,

ISBN13: 978-0-306-37777-8. Dewey:551.46/08. LCCN:72-083046.

Audience: **l,u,f.** *Choice, 1989, 1986.*

Naim, A. E., et al.   QE39
The Ocean Basins and Margins: The Pacific Ocean. F. G. Stehli & S. Uyeda (Authors). Trade Cloth. Basic Books. New York, NY. 1988. 656p. ISBN:0-306-37778-0, ISBN13: 978-0-306-37778-5. Dewey:551.46/08. LCCN:72-083046.

Audience: **l,u,f.** *Choice, 1989, 1986.*

Nairn, Alan E. & Stehli,   QE39
Francis G. (Editors)
The Ocean Basins and Margins: The Indian Ocean. Trade Cloth. Basic Books. New York, NY. 1982. 794p. ISBN:0-306-37776-4, ISBN13: 978-0-306-37776-1. Dewey:551.46/08. LCCN:72-083046.

Audience: **l,u,f.**

Nairn, Alan E. & Stehli,   QE39.N27
Francis G. (Editors)
Vol. 1, The South Atlantic. Trade Cloth. Springer. New York, NY. 1973. 600p. ISBN:0-306-37771-3, ISBN13: 978-0-306-37771-6. Dewey:551.4/608. LCCN:72-083046.

Audience: **l,u,f.** *B*

Nairn, Alan E. & Stehli,   QE39
Francis G. (Editors)
Vol. 2, The North Atlantic. Trade Cloth. Springer. New York, NY. 1974. 662p. ISBN:0-306-37772-1, ISBN13: 978-0-306-37772-3. Dewey:551.4/608. LCCN:72-083046.

Audience: **l,u,f.**

Nairn, Alan E. & Stehli,   QE39 .N27
Francis G. (Editors)
Vol. 3, The Gulf of Mexico and The Caribbean. Trade Cloth. Springer. New York, NY. 1975. 722p. ISBN:0-306-37773-X, ISBN13: 978-0-306-37773-0. Dewey:551.4/608. LCCN:72-083046.

Audience: **l,u,f.**

Nairn, Alan E. & Stehli,   QE39
Francis G. (Editors)
Vol. 4A, The Eastern Mediterranean. Trade Cloth. Springer. New York, NY. 1977. 520p. ISBN:0-306-37774-8, ISBN13: 978-0-306-37774-7. Dewey:551.46/08. LCCN:72-083046.

Audience: **l,u,f.**

Nairn, Alan E. & Stehli,   QE39
Francis G. (Editors)
Vol. 4B, The Western Mediterranean. Trade Cloth. Springer. New York, NY. 1978. 462p. ISBN:0-306-37779-9, ISBN13: 978-0-306-37779-2. Dewey:551.46/08. LCCN:72-083046.

Audience: **l,u,f.**

Nairn, Alan E. & Stehli,   QE39
Francis G. (Editors)
Vol. 5, The Arctic Ocean. Trade Cloth. Springer. New York, NY. 1981. 686p. ISBN:0-306-37775-6, ISBN13: 978-0-306-37775-4. Dewey:551.46/08. LCCN:72-083046.

Audience: **l,u,f.**

Tomczak, Matthias &   GC11.2.T66
Godfrey, J. Stuart
Regional Oceanography: An Introduction. Ed. 2. Trade Paper. Daya Publishing House. Delhi, 2003. ISBN:81-7035-307-6, ISBN13: 978-81-7035-307-2. Dewey:551.46.

Audience: **u,f.** *Choice, 1994.*

Regional Geology > Polar regions

Anderson, John B. QE350 .A49 1999
Antarctic Marine Geology. Trade Cloth. Cambridge University Press. New York, NY. 1999. 297p. ISBN:0-521-59317-4, ISBN13: 978-0-521-59317-5. Dewey:559.8/9. LCCN:98-037219.
Audience: **u,f.** *Choice, 2000.*

Chester, Jonathan G855.A58 2002
Antarctica: An Encyclopedia from Abbott Ice Shelf to Zooplankton. Mary Trewby (Editor). Trade Cloth. Firefly Books, Ltd. Tonawanda, NY. 2002. 208p. ISBN:1-55297-590-8, ISBN13: 978-1-55297-590-9. Dewey:919.8/9/003. LCCN:2002-514992.
Audience: **g,l,u,f.** *Choice, 2003.*

Fogg, G. E. G860 .F64 1992
A History of Antarctic Science. Margaret Thatcher (Foreword by), L. C. Bliss, A. C. Clarke, D. J. Drewry, M. A. P. Renouf, D. W. H. Walton & P. J. Williams (Contribution by). Trade Paper. Cambridge University Press. New York, NY. 2005. 505p. Studies in Polar Research Ser. ISBN:0-521-67337-2, ISBN13: 978-0-521-67337-2. Dewey:507.20989.
Audience: **l,u,f.** *Choice, 1993.*

Grantz, A. (Editor), et al. QE71.G48 1986 VOL. L
The Arctic Ocean Region. L. Johnson & J. F. Sweeney (Editors). Trade Cloth. Geological Society of America, Inc. Boulder, CO. 1990. 654p. DNAG, Geology of North America Ser., Vol. L ISBN:0-8137-5211-6, ISBN13: 978-0-8137-5211-2. Dewey:557 s. LCCN:90-034734.
Audience: **u,f.**

O'Neill, Dan F951
Last Giant of Beringia: The Mystery of the Bering Land Bridge. Trade Paper. Basic Books. New York, NY. 2005. 240p. ISBN:0-465-05157-X, ISBN13: 978-0-465-05157-1. Dewey:979.8.
Audience: **g,u,f.**

Stonehouse, B. (Editor) G855.E53 2002
Encyclopedia of Antarctica and the Southern Oceans. Trade Cloth. John Wiley & Sons, Inc. Hoboken, NJ. 2002. 404p. ISBN:0-471-98665-8, ISBN13: 978-0-471-98665-2. Dewey:919.8/9/03. LCCN:2002-028879.
Audience: **u,f.**

Woodworth, Lynn (Editor) G587.M388 2001
Antarctica and the Arctic: The Complete Encyclopedia. David McGonigal (Foreword by). CD-ROM, Trade Cloth, Mixed Media. Firefly Books, Ltd. Tonawanda, NY. 2001. 608p. ISBN:1-55297-545-2, ISBN13: 978-1-55297-545-9. Dewey:998. LCCN:2003-273173.
Audience: **g,l,u,f.** *Choice, 2002.*

Regional Geology > Planets and Extraterrestrial Geology

Bevan, Alex & de Laeter, J. R. QB755.B48 2002
Meteorites: A Journey Through Space and Time. Trade Cloth. Smithsonian Institution Press. Washington, DC. 2002. 256p. ISBN:1-58834-021-X, ISBN13: 978-1-58834-021-4. Dewey:523.5/1. LCCN:2001-049551.
Audience: **g,l,u.** *Choice, 2003.*

Boyce, Joseph M. QB641.B68 2002
The Smithsonian Book of Mars. Trade Cloth. Smithsonian Institution Press. Washington, DC. 2002. 288p. Smithsonian Library of the Solar System ISBN:1-58834-074-0, ISBN13: 978-1-58834-074-0. Dewey:523.43. LCCN:2002-018832.
Audience: **l,u.**

Cattermole, Peter QB621
Venus: The Geological Story. Trade Paper. Johns Hopkins University Press. Baltimore, MD. 1994. 256p. ISBN:0-8018-5418-0, ISBN13: 978-0-8018-5418-7. Dewey:559.9/22.
Audience: **u,f.** *Choice, 1994.*

Cole, G. H. A. & Woolfson, M. M. QB601 .C656 2002
Planetary Science: The Science of Planets Around Stars. Institute of Physics Staff (Contribution by). Perfect. Institute of Physics Publishing. Philadelphia, PA. 2002. 528p. ISBN:0-7503-0815-X, ISBN13: 978-0-7503-0815-1. Dewey:523.4/015. LCCN:96-043614.
Audience: **l,u.** *Choice, 2002.*

De Pater, Imke & Lissauer, Jack Jonathan QB601 .D38 2001
Planetary Sciences. Cloth Text. Cambridge University Press. New York, NY. 2001. 544p. ISBN:0-521-48219-4, ISBN13: 978-0-521-48219-6. Dewey:559.9/2. LCCN:00-052938.
Audience: **u,f.**

Frankel, Charles QB603.V65F73 2005
Worlds on Fire: Volcanoes on the Earth, the Moon, Mars, Venus and Io. Cloth Text. Cambridge University Press. New York, NY. 2005. 366p. ISBN:0-521-80393-4, ISBN13: 978-0-521-80393-9. Dewey:551.21/0999/2. LCCN:2004-051274.
Audience: **g,l,u.** *Choice, 2006.*

Hartmann, William K. QB601.H34 2005
Moons and Planets. Ed. 5. Cloth Text. Brooks/Cole. Pacific Grove, CA. 2004. 456p. ISBN:0-534-49393-9, ISBN13: 978-0-534-49393-6. Dewey:523.2. LCCN:2004-091448.
Audience: **g,l,u,f.**

Lopes, Rosaly M. C. & Gregg, Tracy K. P. QB603.V65L67 2004
Volcanic Worlds: Exploring the Solar System's Volcanoes. Trade Cloth. Springer. New York, NY. 2004. XXIV, 236p. Springer Praxis Books. Geophysical Sciences Ser. ISBN:3-540-00431-9, ISBN13: 978-3-540-00431-8. Dewey:551.2109992. LCCN:2004-105865.
Audience: **l,u.** *Choice, 2005.*

Melosh, H. J. QE571
Impact Cratering: A Geologic Process. Paper Text. Oxford University Press, Inc. New York, NY. 1996. 256p. Monographs on Geology and Geophysics, No. 11 ISBN:0-19-510463-3, ISBN13: 978-0-19-510463-9. Dewey:551.4/4.
Audience: **u,f.**

Strom, Robert G. & Sprague, Anne L. QB611
Exploring Mercury: The Iron Planet. Mixed Media. Springer. New York, NY. 2003. XXX, 216p. Springer-Praxis Books in Astronomy and Space Sciences ISBN:1-85233-731-1, ISBN13: 978-1-85233-731-5. Dewey:523.41. LCCN:2003-042781.
Audience: **g,l,u.** *Choice, 2004.*

U.S. Geological Survey   QB603
☐ Astrogeology Research Program.
http://astrogeology.usgs.gov/
U.S. Geological Survey.
         Audience: **g,l,u,f.**

Wilhelms, Don E.   QB592
To a Rocky Moon: A Geologist's History of Lunar Exploration.
Trade Paper. University of Arizona Press. Tucson, AZ. 1994.
477p. ISBN:0-8165-1443-7, ISBN13: 978-0-8165-1443-4.
Dewey:559.9/1. LCCN:92-033228.
         Audience: **g,l,u,f.** *Choice, 1993.*

Wilhelms, Don E.   QB592.W5
☐ The Geologic History of the Moon (USGS Professional
Paper 1348).
http://pubs.er.usgs.gov/pubs/pp/pp1348
With sections by McCauley, John F. & Trask, Newell J.. U. S.
Geological Survey. ISBN:0-607-71416-6, ISBN13:
978-0-607-71416-6.
         Audience: **u,f.**

Mineralogy > Reference. General Works.

Anthony, John W.   QE366.8.H36 1990
Handbook of Mineralogy: Silica, Silicates. Cloth Text. Mineral
Data Publishing. Tucson, AZ. 1995. 904p. ISBN:0-9622097-1-6,
ISBN13: 978-0-9622097-1-0. Dewey:549. LCCN:89-013673.
         Audience: **u,f.** *Choice, 1996.*

Anthony, John W., et al.   QE366.8 .H36 1990
Handbook of Mineralogy: Borates, Carbonates, Sulfates. Richard
A. Bideaux, Ken W. Bladh & Monte C. Nichols (Authors).
Trade Cloth. Mineral Data Publishing. Tucson, AZ. 2004.
ISBN:0-9622097-4-0, ISBN13: 978-0-9622097-4-1. Dewey:549.
LCCN:89-013673.
         Audience: **u,f.**

Berry, L. G.   QE363.2
Mineralogy: Concepts, Descriptions, Determinations. Paper Text.
Textbook Publishers. Temecula, CA. 2003. 612p.
ISBN:0-7581-0695-5, ISBN13: 978-0-7581-0695-7. Dewey:549.
         Audience: **l,u,f.**

Clark, Andrew   QE357.C53 1993
Hey's Mineral Index: Mineral Species, Varieties and Synonyms.
Ed. 2. Chapman & Hall. 1993. ISBN:0-412-39950-4, ISBN13:
978-0-412-39950-3.
         Audience: **l,u,f.**

Embrey, Peter G. & Fuller,   QE357
John P.
A Manual of New Mineral Names, 1892-1978. Trade Cloth.
Oxford University Press, Inc. New York, NY. 1980. 478p.
ISBN:0-19-858501-2, ISBN13: 978-0-19-858501-5.
Dewey:549/.03. LCCN:80-040204.
         Audience: **l,u,f.** *B*

Frye, Keith (Editor)   QE355.E49
The Encyclopedia of Mineralogy. Trade Cloth. Springer London,
Ltd. Guildford, 1982. 816p. Encyclopedia of Earth Sciences
Ser., Vol. 4B ISBN:0-87933-184-4, ISBN13: 978-0-87933-184-9.
Dewey:549/.03/21. LCCN:81-000982.
         Audience: **l,u,f.** *B*

Gaines, Richard V., et al.   QE372.D23 1997
Dana's New Mineralogy: The System of Mineralogy of James
Dwight Dana and Edward Salisbury Dana. Ed. 8. Eugene E.
Foord, Brian Mason, Abraham Rosenzweig & H. Catherine W.
Skinner (Authors), James D. Dana & Edward S. Dana (Editors).
Trade Cloth. John Wiley & Sons, Inc. Hoboken, NJ. 1997.
1872p. ISBN:0-471-19310-0, ISBN13: 978-0-471-19310-4.
Dewey:549. LCCN:96-046965.
         Audience: **l,u,f.**

MacKenzie, W. S. &   QE397.M33 1980
  Guilford, C.
Atlas of Rock-Forming Minerals in Thin Section. Trade Paper.
John Wiley & Sons, Inc. Hoboken, NJ. 1980. 98p.
ISBN:0-470-26921-9, ISBN13: 978-0-470-26921-3.
Dewey:549/.114. LCCN:79-027822.
         Audience: **l,u,f.** *B*

Mitchell, Richard S.   QE357
Mineral Names: What Do They Mean? Trade Cloth. John Wiley
& Sons, Inc. Hoboken, NJ. 1979. xvii, 229p.
ISBN:0-442-24593-9, ISBN13: 978-0-442-24593-1.
Dewey:549/.01/42. LCCN:78-026141.
         Audience: **l,u,f.** *B*

Mohsen Manutchehr-Danai,   QE392
  Regensburg
Dictionary of Gems and Gemology. Ed. 2. Trade Cloth.
Springer. New York, NY. 2005. X, 879p. ISBN:3-540-23970-7,
ISBN13: 978-3-540-23970-3. Dewey:553.803.
LCCN:2004-116870.
         Audience: **g,l,u,f.**

Mottana, Annibale, et al.   QE366.2.M6713
Simon and Schuster's Guide to Rocks and Minerals. Rodolfo
Crespi & Giuseppe Liborio (Authors), Martin Prinz, George
Harlow & Joseph Peters (Editors). Trade Paper. Simon &
Schuster. New York, NY. 1978. 607p. Book Ser.
ISBN:0-671-24417-5, ISBN13: 978-0-671-24417-0.
Dewey:552/.075. LCCN:78-008610.
         Audience: **g,l,u.** *B*

Roberts, Willard L
Encyclopedia of Minerals. Ed. 2. Chapman & Hall. 1989.
ISBN:0-412-07831-7, ISBN13: 978-0-412-07831-6.
         Audience: **g,l,u.**

Zim, Herbert S.   QE365 .Z77
Guide to Rocks and Minerals. Prebound. Turtleback Books.
Madison, WI. 1989. Golden Guides Ser. ISBN:0-606-11806-3,
ISBN13: 978-0-606-11806-4. Dewey:549.
         Audience: **g,l.**

Zoltai, Tibor & Stout, James   QE363.2.Z65 1984
H.
Mineralogy: Concepts and Principles. Trade Cloth. Pearson
Custom Publishing. Boston, MA. 1984. "x, 505"p.
ISBN:0-8087-2606-4, ISBN13: 978-0-8087-2606-7. Dewey:549
19. LCCN:83-020992.
         Audience: **l,u,f.** *B*

Mineralogy > Descriptive and Determinative Mineralogy (Methods of Mineral Analysis)

Barnes, Virgil & Barnes, Mildred (Editors)   QE399 .B34
Tektites. Trade Cloth. John Wiley & Sons, Inc. Hoboken, NJ. 1982. 445p. Benchmark Papers in Geology, Vol. 4 ISBN:0-87933-027-9, ISBN13: 978-0-87933-027-9. Dewey:523.5/1. LCCN:72-095942.

Audience: **u,f.** *B*

Chang, L. L. (Editor), et al.   QE397
Non-Silicates. Ed. 2. R. A. Howie & J Zussman (Editors). Trade Cloth. Geological Society Publishing House. Bath, 1997. 392p. Rock-Forming Minerals Ser., No. 5B ISBN:1-897799-90-X, ISBN13: 978-1-897799-90-1. Dewey:549.

Audience: **u,f.**

Craig, James R. & Vaughan, David J.   QE390.C7 1994
Ore Microscopy and Ore Petrography. Ed. 2. Trade Cloth. John Wiley & Sons, Inc. Hoboken, NJ. 1994. 448p. ISBN:0-471-55175-9, ISBN13: 978-0-471-55175-1. Dewey:549/.12. LCCN:94-002395.

Audience: **u,f.** *B*

Dana, J. D.   QE372
Manual of Mineralogy ... Trade Cloth. Scholarly Publishing Office, University of Michigan Library. Ann Arbor, MI. 2004. ISBN:1-4181-5915-8, ISBN13: 978-1-4181-5915-3. Dewey:549.

Audience: **l,u,f.**

Deer, W. A. (Editor), et al.   Q115
Disilicates and Ring Silicates. Ed. 2. R. A. Howie & J Zussman (Editors). Trade Cloth. Geological Society Publishing House. Bath, 1997. 630p. Rock-Forming Minerals Ser., Vol. 1B ISBN:1-897799-89-6, ISBN13: 978-1-897799-89-5. Dewey:549.6/4.

Audience: **u,f.**

Deer, W. A. (Editor), et al.   QE397.D44
Double-Chain Silicates. Ed. 2. R. A. Howie & J Zussman (Editors). Trade Cloth. Geological Society Publishing House. Bath, 1997. 784p. Rock-Forming Minerals Ser., No. 2B ISBN:1-897799-77-2, ISBN13: 978-1-897799-77-2. Dewey:549.6.

Audience: **u,f.**

Deer, W. A. (Editor), et al.   QE391.Z7
Orthosilicates. Ed. 2. R. A. Howie & J Zussman (Editors). Trade Cloth. Geological Society Publishing House. Bath, 1997. 932p. Rock-Forming Minerals Ser., No. 1A ISBN:1-897799-88-8, ISBN13: 978-1-897799-88-8. Dewey:549.6/2.

Audience: **u,f.**

Deer, W. A. (Editor), et al.   QE389.62 .D48 1997
Single-Chain Silicates. Ed. 2. R. A. Howie & J Zussman (Editors). Trade Cloth. Geological Society Publishing House. Bath, 1997. 680p. Rock-Forming Minerals Ser., No. 2A ISBN:1-897799-85-3, ISBN13: 978-1-897799-85-7. Dewey:549.6.

Audience: **u,f.**

Guilbert, John M. & Park, Charles F. Jr.   QE390.G85 1986
The Geology of Ore Deposits. Cloth over Boards. Worth Publishers, Inc. New York, NY. 1985. 985p. ISBN:0-7167-1456-6, ISBN13: 978-0-7167-1456-9. Dewey:553.4. LCCN:85-010099.

Audience: **u,f.** *B Choice, 1986.*

Peterson, Roger T. & Pough, Frederick H.   QE432.2
A Field Guide to Rocks and Minerals. Ed. 5. Jeffrey A. Scovil (Photographer), Roger Tory Peterson (Contribution by). Trade Paper. Houghton Mifflin Company Trade & Reference Division. Boston, MA. 1998. Covers all the important minerals, as well as others that are rare and intriguing. Includes 385 color photographs. 426p. Peterson Field Guides ISBN:0-395-91096-X, ISBN13: 978-0-395-91096-2. Dewey:552. LCCN:94-049005.

Audience: **g,l.**

Phillips, W. Revell & Griffen, Dana T.   QE369.O6.P44
Optical Mineralogy: The Nonopaque Minerals. Cloth Text. W. H. Freeman & Company. New York, NY. 1981. 677p. ISBN:0-7167-1129-X, ISBN13: 978-0-7167-1129-2. Dewey:549/.125. LCCN:80-012435.

Audience: **u,f.** *B*

Pough, Frederick H.   QE367.2.P68 1976
A Field Guide to Rocks and Minerals. Trade Cloth. Houghton Mifflin Company. New York, NY. 1976. xix, 317 p.,p. ISBN:0-395-08106-8, ISBN13: 978-0-395-08106-8. Dewey:549.1. LCCN:75-022364.

Audience: **g,l.** *B*

Zussman, John (Editor)   QE367.Z8 1977
Physical Methods in Determinative Mineralogy. Ed. 2. Trade Cloth. Elsevier Science & Technology Books. Saint Louis, MO. 1978. xiv, 720 p. :p. ISBN:0-12-782960-1, ISBN13: 978-0-12-782960-9. Dewey:549/.12. LCCN:77-076850.

Audience: **u,f.** *B*

Mineralogy > Crystallography (of Minerals)

Bloss, F. Donald   QD941.B585 1999
Optical Crystallography. Trade Cloth. Mineralogical Society of America. Chantilly, VA. 1999. x, 239p. Monograph Ser. ISBN:0-939950-49-9, ISBN13: 978-0-939950-49-2. Dewey:548/.9. LCCN:00-500595.

Audience: **u,f.**

Hammond, Christopher   QD905.2.H355 2001
The Basics of Crystallography and Diffraction. Ed. 2. Trade Cloth. Oxford University Press, Inc. New York, NY. 2001. 320p. International Union of Crystallography Texts on Crystallography, Vol. 5 ISBN:0-19-850553-1, ISBN13: 978-0-19-850553-2. Dewey:548. LCCN:00-053086.

Audience: **u,f.** *Choice, 2001.*

Sunagawa, Ichiro   QD921
Crystals: Growth, Morphology and Perfection. Trade Cloth. Cambridge University Press. New York, NY. 2005. 308p. ISBN:0-521-84189-5, ISBN13: 978-0-521-84189-4. Dewey:548.5. LCCN:2005-282428.

Audience: **u,f.**

Igneous Rocks (Including Process of Formation)

Best, Myron G.   **QE461.B53 2002**
Igneous and Metamorphic Petrology. Ed. 2. Trade Paper.
Blackwell Publishing, Inc. Malden, MA. 2002. 756p.
ISBN:1-4051-0588-7, ISBN13: 978-1-4051-0588-0.
Dewey:552/.1. LCCN:2002-066697.

Audience: **u,f.** *B*

Bowen, Norman L.   **QE461**
The Evolution of Igneous Rocks. Trade Paper. Dover
Publications, Inc. Mineola, NY. 1928. 334p.
ISBN:0-486-60311-3, ISBN13: 978-0-486-60311-7.
Dewey:552.1.

Audience: **u,f.**

Bowes, D. R.   **QE461 .E56 1989**
The Encyclopedia of Igneous and Metamorphic Petrology. Mass
Market. Chapman & Hall. New York, NY. 1989. 666p.
ISBN:0-442-20623-2, ISBN13: 978-0-442-20623-9.
Dewey:552/.1/0321. LCCN:89-030622.

Audience: **l,u,f.** *Choice, 1990.*

Le Maitre, R. W. (Editor),   **QE461 .I446 2002**
et al.
Igneous Rocks: A Classification and Glossary of Terms:
Recommendations of the International Union of Geological
Sciences Subcommission on the Systematics of Igneous Rocks.
Ed. 2. A. Streckeisen, B. Zanettin, M. J. Le Bas, B. Bonin & P.
Bateman (Editors). Trade Paper. Cambridge University Press.
New York, NY. 2005. 252p. ISBN:0-521-61948-3, ISBN13:
978-0-521-61948-6. Dewey:552/.1. LCCN:2005-278209.

Audience: **u,f.**

MacKenzie, W. S., et al.   **QE461 .M219 1982**
Atlas of Igneous Rocks and Their Textures. C. H. Donaldson &
C. Guilford (Authors). Trade Paper. John Wiley & Sons, Inc.
Hoboken, NJ. 1982. 148p. ISBN:0-470-27339-9, ISBN13:
978-0-470-27339-5. Dewey:552/.1. LCCN:82-002698.

Audience: **l,u,f.**

McBirney, Alexander R.   **QE461 .M46 1993**
Igneous Petrology. Ed. 2. Trade Cloth. Jones & Bartlett
Publishers, Inc. Sudbury, MA. 1992. 520p.
ISBN:0-86720-175-4, ISBN13: 978-0-86720-175-8.
Dewey:552/.1. LCCN:92-018832.

Audience: **u,f.** *Choice, 1986.*

Thorpe, Richard S. &   **QE461 .T45Y 1993**
Brown, Geoffrey C.
The Field Description of Igneous Rocks. Ed. 1. Trade Paper.
John Wiley & Sons, Inc. Hoboken, NJ. 1991. 160p. Geological
Society of London Handbook Ser., Vol. 11 ISBN:0-471-93275-2,
ISBN13: 978-0-471-93275-8. Dewey:552.1. LCCN:84-025182.

Audience: **l,u,f.**

Winter, John D.   **QE461.W735 2001**
An Introduction to Igneous and Metamorphic Petrology. Cloth
Text. Prentice Hall PTR. Upper Saddle River, NJ. 2001. 699p.
ISBN:0-13-240342-0, ISBN13: 978-0-13-240342-9.
Dewey:552/.1. LCCN:00-049196.

Audience: **u,f.**

Yoder, H. S. Jr.   **QE461**
The Evolution of the Igneous Rocks: Fiftieth Anniversary
Perspectives. Cloth Text. Princeton University Press. Princeton,
NJ. 1979. 600p. ISBN:0-691-08223-5, ISBN13:
978-0-691-08223-3. Dewey:552/.1. LCCN:79-084023.

Audience: **u,f.**

Young, Davis A.   **QE461.Y66 2003**
Mind over Magma: The Story of Igneous Petrology. Trade
Cloth. Princeton University Press. Princeton, NJ. 2003. 704p.
ISBN:0-691-10279-1, ISBN13: 978-0-691-10279-5.
Dewey:552/.1. LCCN:2002-030790.

Audience: **l,u,f.** *Choice, 2004.*

Igneous Rocks (Including Process of Formation) > Volcanoes/Volcanism

de Boer, Jelle Zeilinga &   **QE522.Z435 2002**
Sanders, Donald Theodore
Volcanoes in Human History: The Far-Reaching Effects of
Major Eruptions. Cloth Text. Princeton University Press.
Princeton, NJ. 2001. 320p. ISBN:0-691-05081-3, ISBN13:
978-0-691-05081-2. Dewey:363.34/95. LCCN:2001-095818.

Audience: **g,l,u,f.** *Choice, 2002.*

Decker, Robert & Decker,   **QE522**
Barbara
Volcanoes. Ed. 4. Trade Paper. W. H. Freeman & Company.
New York, NY. 2005. 32p. ISBN:0-7167-8929-9, ISBN13:
978-0-7167-8929-1. Dewey:551.21. LCCN:2005-929602.

Audience: **g,l,u,f.**

Francis, Peter &   **QE522.F73 2003**
Oppenheimer, Clive
Volcanoes. Ed. 2. Paper Text. Oxford University Press, Inc. New
York, NY. 2003. 534p. ISBN:0-19-925469-9, ISBN13:
978-0-19-925469-9. Dewey:551.21. LCCN:2004-268873.

Audience: **u,f.**

Lopes, Rosaly M. C. &   **QB603.V65L67 2004**
Gregg, Tracy K. P.
Volcanic Worlds: Exploring the Solar System's Volcanoes. Trade
Cloth. Springer. New York, NY. 2004. XXIV, 236p. Springer
Praxis Books. Geophysical Sciences Ser. ISBN:3-540-00431-9,
ISBN13: 978-3-540-00431-8. Dewey:551.2109992.
LCCN:2004-105865.

Audience: **l,u.** *Choice, 2005.*

Ritchie, David & Gates,   **QE521.R58 2001**
Alexander E.
Encyclopedia of Earthquakes and Volcanoes. Ed. 2. Trade Cloth.
Facts On File, Inc.. New York, NY. 2001. 320p. The Facts on
File Science Library ISBN:0-8160-4372-8, ISBN13:
978-0-8160-4372-9. Dewey:551.2/03. LCCN:00-049492.

Audience: **g,l,u,f.** *Choice, 2002, 1994.*

Schmincke, Hans-Ulrich   **QE522**
Volcanism. Trade Cloth. Springer. New York, NY. 2005. X,
324p. ISBN:3-540-43650-2, ISBN13: 978-3-540-43650-8.
Dewey:551.21. LCCN:2003-056723.

Audience: **u,f.** *Choice, 2004.*

Sigurdsson, Haraldur   **QE522.S548 1999**
Melting the Earth: The History of Ideas on Volcanic Eruptions.
Trade Cloth. Oxford University Press, Inc. New York, NY. 1999.

272p. ISBN:0-19-510665-2, ISBN13: 978-0-19-510665-7. Dewey:551.21. LCCN:98-020299.

Audience: **g,l,u,f.** *Choice, 1999.*

Sigurdsson, Haraldur, et al.   **QE522.E53 2000**
Encyclopedia of Volcanoes. Bruce Houghton, Steve McNutt, Hazel Rymer & John Stix (Authors), Robert D. Ballard (Foreword by). Trade Cloth. Elsevier Science & Technology Books. Saint Louis, MO. 1999. 1417p. ISBN:0-12-643140-X, ISBN13: 978-0-12-643140-7. Dewey:551.21/03. LCCN:99-062781.

Audience: **l,u,f.** *Choice, 2000.*

Sedimentary Rocks, Sedimentation, Sedimentology, Sedimentary Processes

Adams, A. E., et al.   **QE471.A28 1984**
Atlas of Sedimentary Rocks under the Microscope. W. S. MacKenzie & C. Guilford (Authors). Trade Paper. John Wiley & Sons, Inc. Hoboken, NJ. 1984. 104p. ISBN:0-470-27476-X, ISBN13: 978-0-470-27476-7. Dewey:552/.5. LCCN:83-012379.

Audience: **u,f.** *B*

Allen, John R.   **QE471.A5597 1985**
Principles of Physical Sedimentology. Cloth Text. Routledge. New York, NY. 1985. 400p. ISBN:0-04-551095-4, ISBN13: 978-0-04-551095-5. Dewey:551.3. LCCN:85-006006.

Audience: **u,f.**

Allen, P. A. & Allen, John R.   **QE571.A45 2005**
Basin Analysis: Principles and Applications. Ed. 2. Trade Paper. Blackwell Publishing, Inc. Malden, MA. 2005. 560p. ISBN:0-632-05207-4, ISBN13: 978-0-632-05207-3. Dewey:552/.5. LCCN:2004-005965.

Audience: **u,f.** *Choice, 2005.*

Boggs, Sam Jr.   **QE571.B66 2006**
Principles of Sedimentology and Stratigraphy. Ed. 4. Trade Paper. Prentice Hall PTR. Upper Saddle River, NJ. 2005. 688p. ISBN:0-13-154728-3, ISBN13: 978-0-13-154728-5. Dewey:552/.5. LCCN:2005-047667.

Audience: **l,u,f.**

Busby, C.   **QE571.T355 1995**
Tectonics of Sedimentary Basis. Trade Cloth. Blackwell Publishing, Inc. Malden, MA. 1995. 400p. ISBN:0-86542-245-1, ISBN13: 978-0-86542-245-2. Dewey:551.4/4. LCCN:94-039440.

Audience: **u,f.**

Einsele, Gerhard   **QE571.E36 2000**
Sedimentary Basins: Evolution, Facies and Sediment Budget. Ed. 2. Trade Cloth. Springer. New York, NY. 2000. XII, 792p. ISBN:3-540-66193-X, ISBN13: 978-3-540-66193-1. Dewey:551.44. LCCN:00-037339.

Audience: **u,f.**

Gierlowski-Kordesch, E. &   **QE39.5.P3 G54 1994**
Kelts, Kerry
Global Geological Record of Lake Basins, Vol. 1. Trade Cloth. Cambridge University Press. New York, NY. 1994. 461p. World and Regional Geology Ser., No. 4 ISBN:0-521-41452-0, ISBN13: 978-0-521-41452-4. Dewey:551.482. LCCN:93-028336.

Audience: **u,f.**

Kiessling, Wolfgang; Flügel,   **QE565**
Erik; Golonka, Jan
Phanerozoic reef patterns. Society for Sedimentary Geology. 2002. SEPM special publication no. 72 ISBN:1-56576-081-6, ISBN13: 978-1-56576-081-3.

Audience: **u,f.**

Leeder, M. R.   **QE471.L375 1999**
Sedimentology and Sedimentary Basins: From Turbulence to Tectonics. Trade Paper. Blackwell Publishing, Inc. Malden, MA. 1999. 608p. ISBN:0-632-04976-6, ISBN13: 978-0-632-04976-9. Dewey:552/.5. LCCN:98-053090.

Audience: **l,u,f.**

Miall, Andrew D.   **QE615.M3 2000**
Principles of Sedimentary Basin Analysis. Ed. 3. Trade Cloth. Springer. New York, NY. 1999. XII, 616p. ISBN:3-540-65790-8, ISBN13: 978-3-540-65790-3. Dewey:552/.5. LCCN:99-036198.

Audience: **l,u,f.** *B Choice, 1990.*

Middleton, Gerard V.   **QE471.2.E53 2003**
(Editor)
Encyclopedia of Sediments and Sedimentary Rocks. Michael A. Church, Mario Coniglio, L. A. Hardie & F. J. Longstaffe (Associate Editors). Trade Cloth. Springer. New York, NY. 2005. 928p. Encyclopedia of Earth Sciences Ser. ISBN:1-4020-0872-4, ISBN13: 978-1-4020-0872-6. Dewey:552/.5/03. LCCN:2002-033956.

Audience: **l,u,f.** *Choice, 2004.*

Pettijohn, F. J., et al.   **QE471.2.P47 1987**
Sand and Sandstone. Ed. 2. P. E. Potter & Raymond Siever (Authors). Trade Paper. Springer. New York, NY. 1987. XIX, 553p. Springer Study Edition Ser. ISBN:0-387-96350-2, ISBN13: 978-0-387-96350-1. Dewey:552/.5. LCCN:86-017925.

Audience: **u,f.** *B*

Potter, P. E., et al.   **QE471.2**
Mud and Mudstone: Introduction and Overview. Barry Maynard & Pedro Depetris (Authors). Trade Cloth. Springer. New York, NY. 2005. XI, 297p. ISBN:3-540-22157-3, ISBN13: 978-3-540-22157-9. Dewey:551.3/04. LCCN:2004-106315.

Audience: **u,f.** *Choice, 2005.*

Reading, Harold G. (Editor)   **QE471.S378 1996**
Sedimentary Environments: Processes, Facies and Stratigraphy. Ed. 3. Trade Paper. Blackwell Publishing, Inc. Malden, MA. 1996. 704p. ISBN:0-632-03627-3, ISBN13: 978-0-632-03627-1. Dewey:539.7/4. LCCN:95-048457.

Audience: **u,f.** *B*

Reineck, H. E. & Singh,   **QE471.R425 1980**
I. B.
Depositional Sedimentary Environments with Reference to Terrigenous Classics. Ed. 2. Cloth Text. Springer. New York, NY. 1992. 570p. ISBN:0-387-10189-6, ISBN13: 978-0-387-10189-7. Dewey:551.3/03. LCCN:80-020429.

Audience: **u,f.** *B*

Renaut, R. W. & Last,   **QE39.5.P3S43 1994**
W. M. (Editors)
Sedimentology and Geochemistry of Modern and Ancient Saline Lakes. Cloth Text. SEPM (Society for Sedimentary Geology). Tulsa, OK. 1994. 348p. Special Publications, No. 50 ISBN:1-56576-014-X, ISBN13: 978-1-56576-014-1. Dewey:551.46/09. LCCN:95-107859.

Audience: **u,f.**

Tucker, M. E.   QE471.T827 2001
Sedimentary Petrology. Ed. 3. Trade Paper. Blackwell
Publishing, Inc. Malden, MA. 2001. 272p. ISBN:0-632-05735-1,
ISBN13: 978-0-632-05735-1. Dewey:552/.5.
LCCN:2001-025550.

Audience: **l,u,f.**

Weaver, C. E.   QE471.3.W43 1989
Clays, Muds, and Shales. Trade Cloth. Elsevier. New York, NY.
1989. 820p. Developments in Sedimentology Ser., Vol. 44
ISBN:0-444-87381-3, ISBN13: 978-0-444-87381-1.
Dewey:552/.5. LCCN:89-023611.

Audience: **u,f.**

Sedimentary Rocks, Sedimentation, Sedimentology, Sedimentary Processes > Weathering

Bland, Will & Rolls, David   QE570.B5685 1998
Weathering: An Introduction to the Scientific Principles. Trade
Cloth. Oxford University Press, Inc. New York, NY. 1998. 288p.
An Arnold Publication Ser. ISBN:0-340-67745-7, ISBN13:
978-0-340-67745-2. Dewey:551.3/02. LCCN:98-034261.

Audience: **l,u,f.** *Choice, 1999.*

Robinson, D. A. & Williams,   QE570.R63 1994
R. B. G. (Editors)
Rock Weathering and Landform Evolution. Trade Cloth. John
Wiley & Sons, Inc. Hoboken, NJ. 1995. 544p. British
Geomorphological Research Group Symposia Ser., Vol. 10
ISBN:0-471-95119-6, ISBN13: 978-0-471-95119-3.
Dewey:551.3/02. LCCN:94-004636.

Audience: **u,f.**

Sedimentary Rocks, Sedimentation, Sedimentology, Sedimentary Processes > Erosion

Pye, Kenneth (Editor)   QE571 .S415 1994
Sediment Transport and Depositional Processes. Trade Paper.
Blackwell Publishing, Inc. Malden, MA. 1994. 330p.
ISBN:0-632-03112-3, ISBN13: 978-0-632-03112-2.
Dewey:551.303. LCCN:93-017446.

Audience: **u,f.**

Sedimentary Rocks, Sedimentation, Sedimentology, Sedimentary Processes > Deposition

Pye, Kenneth (Editor)   QE571 .S415 1994
Sediment Transport and Depositional Processes. Trade Paper.
Blackwell Publishing, Inc. Malden, MA. 1994. 330p.
ISBN:0-632-03112-3, ISBN13: 978-0-632-03112-2.
Dewey:551.303. LCCN:93-017446.

Audience: **u,f.**

Sedimentary Rocks, Sedimentation, Sedimentology, Sedimentary Processes > Sedimentary Structures

Allen, J. R.   QE472 .A44
Sedimentary Structures, Vol. 2. Trade Cloth. Elsevier. New York,
NY. 1982. 594p. Developments in Sedimentology Ser., Vol. 30B
ISBN:0-444-41945-4, ISBN13: 978-0-444-41945-3.
Dewey:551.3/05. LCCN:81-012561.

Audience: **u,f.**

Allen, J. R.   QE471
Sedimentary Structures, 1 Vol. Trade Cloth. Elsevier. New York,
NY. 1982. 594p. Developments in Sedimentology Ser., Vol. 30B
ISBN:0-444-41935-7, ISBN13: 978-0-444-41935-4.
Dewey:551.3/05.

Audience: **u,f.**

Pettijohn, F. J. & Potter,   QE471.P44
P. E.
Atlas and Glossary of Primary Sedimentary Structures. Trade
Cloth. Springer. New York, NY. 1964. ISBN:0-387-03194-4,
ISBN13: 978-0-387-03194-1. Dewey:552.5084.

Audience: **l,u,f.** *B*

Reineck, H. E. & Singh,   QE471.R425 1980
I. B.
Depositional Sedimentary Environments with Reference to
Terrigenous Classics. Ed. 2. Cloth Text. Springer. New York,
NY. 1992. 570p. ISBN:0-387-10189-6, ISBN13:
978-0-387-10189-7. Dewey:551.3/03. LCCN:80-020429.

Audience: **u,f.** *B*

Sedimentary Rocks, Sedimentation, Sedimentology, Sedimentary Processes > Carbonate Rocks

Bathurst, R. G.   QD466.5
Carbonate Sediments and Their Diagenesis. Ed. 2. Trade Paper.
Elsevier Science & Technology Books. Saint Louis, MO. 1983.
660p. Developments in Sedimentology Ser., Vol. 12
ISBN:0-444-41353-7, ISBN13: 978-0-444-41353-6.
Dewey:547.1/388. LCCN:76-023181.

Audience: **u,f.**

Flngel, Erik   QE719.F58 2004
Microfacies of Carbonate Rocks. Mixed Media. Springer. New
York, NY. 2004. 318 schw.-w. u. 22 farb. Abb., 7 schw.-w. Tab.,
137 schw.-w. u. 22 farb. Fotos, 181 schw.-w. Zeichn., 151 plates
(7 in color), CD (mit reference list) auf U3 XX, 976p.
ISBN:3-540-22016-X, ISBN13: 978-3-540-22016-9.
Dewey:560/.47. LCCN:2004-104816.

Audience: **u,f.** *Choice, 2005.*

Scholle, Peter A. &   QE471.15.C3S34 2003
Ulmer-Scholle, Dana S.
A Color Guide to the Petrography of Carbonate Rocks: Grains,
Textures, Porosity, Diagenesis. Trade Cloth. American
Association of Petroleum Geologists. Tulsa, OK. 2003. 474p.
Aapg Memoir Ser., Vol. 77 ISBN:0-89181-358-6, ISBN13:
978-0-89181-358-3. Dewey:552/.58. LCCN:2004-299868.

Audience: **u,f.**

Metamorphic Rocks and Processes (Metamorphism)

Bucher, Kurt & Frey, Martin   QE475.A2B84 2002
Petrogenesis of Metamorphic Rocks. Ed. 7. Trade Cloth.
Springer. New York, NY. 2002. XVI, 341p.
ISBN:3-540-43130-6, ISBN13: 978-3-540-43130-5.
Dewey:552/.4. LCCN:2002-070560.
Audience: **u,f.**

Fry, Norman   QE475 A2 T4 1992
The Field Description of Metamorphic Rocks. Ed. 1. Trade
Paper. John Wiley & Sons, Inc. Hoboken, NJ. 1991. 128p.
Geological Society of London Handbook Ser., Vol. 14
ISBN:0-471-93221-3, ISBN13: 978-0-471-93221-5.
Dewey:552.4.
Audience: **l,u,f.**

Kornprobst, Jacques   QE475.A2K668 2002
Metamorphic Rocks and Their Geodynamic Significance: A
Petrological Handbook. Trade Cloth. Springer. New York, NY.
2002. 224p. Petrology and Structural Geology Ser., Vol. 11
ISBN:1-4020-0893-7, ISBN13: 978-1-4020-0893-1.
Dewey:552/.4. LCCN:2002-033952.
Audience: **u,f.**

Miyashiro, A.   QE475.A2
Metamorphism and Metamorphic Belts. Ed. 99. Trade Paper.
John Wiley & Sons, Inc. Hoboken, NJ. 1978. 492p.
ISBN:0-470-99390-1, ISBN13: 978-0-470-99390-3.
Dewey:552/.4. LCCN:72-013983.
Audience: **u,f.**

Yardley, Bruce W.   QE475.A2
Atlas of Metamorphic Rocks and Their Textures. Ed. 1. Trade
Paper. Prentice Hall PTR. Upper Saddle River, NJ. 1996. 115p.
ISBN:0-582-30166-1, ISBN13: 978-0-582-30166-5.
Dewey:552/.4. LCCN:90-033566.
Audience: **l,u,f.**

Yardley, Bruce W.   QE475.A2
An Introduction to Metamorphic Petrology. Trade Paper.
Prentice Hall PTR. Upper Saddle River, NJ. 1996. 264p.
ISBN:0-582-30096-7, ISBN13: 978-0-582-30096-5.
Dewey:552/.4. LCCN:88-018734.
Audience: **u,f.**

Geochemistry

Anderson, Greg M. & Crerar, David A.   QE515.A6 1993
Thermodynamics in Geochemistry: The Equilibrium Model.
Trade Cloth. Oxford University Press, Inc. New York, NY. 1993.
608p. ISBN:0-19-506464-X, ISBN13: 978-0-19-506464-3.
Dewey:551.9. LCCN:91-018041.
Audience: **u,f.**

Appelo, C. A. & Postma, D.   GB855 .A62 1999
Geochemistry, Groundwater and Pollution. Ed. 4. Paper over
Boards. Taylor & Francis Group. Abingdon, 1993. 522p.
ISBN:90-5410-105-9, ISBN13: 978-90-5410-105-5.
Dewey:551.49. LCCN:99-227635.
Audience: **u,f.**

Dickin, Alan P.   QE501.4.N9D53 2004
Radiogenic Isotope Geology. Ed. 2. Cloth Text. Cambridge
University Press. New York, NY. 2005. 508p.
ISBN:0-521-82316-1, ISBN13: 978-0-521-82316-6.
Dewey:551.701. LCCN:2003-069588.
Audience: **u,f.** *Choice, 1996.*

Engel, M. & Macko, S.   QE516.5.O7 1993
Organic Geochemistry: Principles and Applications. Trade Cloth.
Basic Books. New York, NY. 1993. 884p. Topics in Geobiology
Ser., Vol. 11 ISBN:0-306-44378-3, ISBN13: 978-0-306-44378-7.
Dewey:551.9. LCCN:93-028298.
Audience: **u,f.** *Choice, 1994.*

Hoefs, Jochen   QE515.H54 2003
Stable Isotope Geochemistry. Ed. 5. Trade Cloth. Springer. New
York, NY. 2004. XII, 244p. ISBN:3-540-40227-6, ISBN13:
978-3-540-40227-5. Dewey:551.9. LCCN:2003-061089.
Audience: **u,f.**

Krauskopf, Konrad B. & Bird, Dennis K.   QE515.K7 1995
Introduction to Geochemistry. Ed. 3. Trade Cloth. McGraw-Hill
Higher Education. Burr Ridge, IL. 1994. 640p. International
Earth and Planetary Sciences Ser. ISBN:0-07-035820-6,
ISBN13: 978-0-07-035820-1. Dewey:551.9. LCCN:94-010069.
Audience: **u,f.** *B*

Li, Yuan-Hui   QE515.L385 2000
A Compendium of Geochemistry: From Solar Nebula to the
Human Brain. Trade Cloth. Princeton University Press.
Princeton, NJ. 2000. 490p. ISBN:0-691-00938-4, ISBN13:
978-0-691-00938-4. Dewey:551.9. LCCN:99-089467.
Audience: **l,u,f.** *Choice, 2001.*

Marshall, Clare P. & Fairbridge, Rhodes W. (Editors)   QE515.E48 1999
Encyclopedia of Geochemistry. Trade Cloth. Springer London,
Ltd. Guildford, 1999. 768p. Encyclopedia of Earth Sciences Ser.
ISBN:0-412-75500-9, ISBN13: 978-0-412-75500-2.
Dewey:551.9/03. LCCN:98-034743.
Audience: **l,u,f.**

McSween, Harry Y. Jr., et al.   QE515.R53 2003
Geochemistry: Pathways and Processes. Ed. 2. Steven McAfee
Richardson, Maria E. Uhle & Steven McAfee Richardson
(Authors). Trade Cloth. Chinese University of Hong Kong, The.
Hong Kong SAR, 2003. 432p. ISBN:0-231-12440-6, ISBN13:
978-0-231-12440-9. Dewey:551.9. LCCN:2003-051638.
Audience: **u,f.**

Nordstrown, Kirk & Munoz, James L.   QE515.5.T46N67 1994
Geochemical Thermodynamics. Ed. 2. Trade Cloth. Blackwell
Publishing, Inc. Malden, MA. 1994. 504p. ISBN:0-86542-274-5,
ISBN13: 978-0-86542-274-2. Dewey:551.9. LCCN:93-023633.
Audience: **u,f.** *Choice, 1995.*

Schlesinger, William H.   QH343.7.S35 1991
Biogeochemistry: An Analysis of Global Change. Trade Cloth.
Elsevier Science & Technology Books. Saint Louis, MO. 1991.
423p. ISBN:0-12-625156-8, ISBN13: 978-0-12-625156-2.
Dewey:577.1/4. LCCN:90-014401.
Audience: **u,f.**

Geochemistry > Environmental Geochemistry

Berner, Elizabeth K. &   **GB848.B47 1986**
  Berner, Robert A.
The Global Water Cycle: Geochemistry and Environment. Ed. 1.
Trade Cloth. Prentice Hall PTR. Upper Saddle River, NJ. 1998.
397p. ISBN:0-13-357195-5, ISBN13: 978-0-13-357195-0.
Dewey:551.48. LCCN:86-022603.
> Audience: **u,f.** *Choice, 1987.*

Drever, James I.   **GB855.D73 1997**
The Geochemistry of Natural Waters: Surface and Groundwater
Environments. Ed. 3. Cloth Text. Prentice Hall PTR. Upper
Saddle River, NJ. 1997. 436p. ISBN:0-13-272790-0, ISBN13:
978-0-13-272790-7. Dewey:551.48. LCCN:96-051617.
> Audience: **u,f.**

Eby, G. Nelson   **QE516.4.E39 2004**
Principles of Environmental Geochemistry. Cloth Text.
Brooks/Cole. Pacific Grove, CA. 2003. 528p.
ISBN:0-12-229061-5, ISBN13: 978-0-12-229061-9.
Dewey:551.9. LCCN:2002-033358.
> Audience: **l,u,f.**

Structural Geology > General Works

⊡ Structural Geology on the Web.
http://www.science.smith.edu/departments/Geology/
Structure_Resources/
> Audience: **l,u,f.**

Bayly, M. Brian   **QE601.B36 1992**
Mechanics in Structural Geology. Cloth Text. Springer. New
York, NY. 1991. 253p. ISBN:0-387-97615-9, ISBN13:
978-0-387-97615-0. Dewey:551.801531. LCCN:91-017251.
> Audience: **u,f.** *Choice, 1992.*

Bennison, George M. &   **QE601**
  Moseley, Keith
An Introduction to Geological Structures and Maps. Ed. 7.
Trade Paper. Oxford University Press, Inc. New York, NY. 2003.
176p. An Arnold Publication ISBN:0-340-80956-6, ISBN13:
978-0-340-80956-3. Dewey:551.8/022/3.
> Audience: **l,u,f.**

Davis, G. H.   **QE601 .D3**
Structural Geology of Rocks and Regions. Ed. 3. Trade Cloth.
John Wiley & Sons, Inc. Hoboken, NJ. 2004. 635p.
ISBN:0-471-15231-5, ISBN13: 978-0-471-15231-6.
Dewey:551.8.
> Audience: **l,u.**

Hancock, Paul L. (Editor)   **QE0501.C6148**
Continental Deformation. Trade Paper. Books on Demand. Ann
Arbor, MI. 1994. 433p. ISBN:0-608-07924-3, ISBN13:
978-0-608-07924-0. Dewey:551.8. LCCN:93-007258.
> Audience: **u,f.** *Choice, 1994.*

Lisle, Richard J.   **QE601.2**
Geological Structures and Maps: A Practical Guide. Ed. 3. Paper
Text. Elsevier Science & Technology Books. Saint Louis, MO.
2003. 120p. ISBN:0-7506-5780-4, ISBN13: 978-0-7506-5780-8.
Dewey:551.8/0223.
> Audience: **l,u.**

Mitra, Shankar   **QE0606.S768**
Structural Geology of Fold and Thrust Belts. Trade Paper.
Books on Demand. Ann Arbor, MI. 264p. The Johns Hopkins
Studies in Earth and Space Sciences ISBN:0-608-08791-2,
ISBN13: 978-0-608-08791-7. Dewey:551.87. LCCN:91-044214.
> Audience: **u,f.** *Choice, 1993.*

Poag, C. Wylie   **QE613.5.C48P6 1999**
Chesapeake Invader: Discovering America's Giant Meteorite
Crater. Trade Cloth. Princeton University Press. Princeton, NJ.
1999. 168p. ISBN:0-691-00919-8, ISBN13: 978-0-691-00919-3.
Dewey:551.3/97/0916347. LCCN:99-024115.
> Audience: **l,u.** *Choice, 2000.*

Price, Neville J. &   **QE601.P694 1990**
  Cosgrove, John W.
Analysis of Geological Structures. Trade Paper. Cambridge
University Press. New York, NY. 1990. 516p.
ISBN:0-521-31958-7, ISBN13: 978-0-521-31958-4.
Dewey:551.8. LCCN:88-034089.
> Audience: **u,f.** *Choice, 1991.*

Ramsay, John G. & Huber,   **QE601**
  Martin
The Techniques of Modern Structural Geology: Folds and
Fractures. Paper Text. Elsevier Science & Technology Books.
Saint Louis, MO. 1987. 391p. Modern Structural Geology Ser.,
Vol. 2 ISBN:0-12-576922-9, ISBN13: 978-0-12-576922-8.
Dewey:551.8.
> Audience: **l,u.**

Ramsay, John G. & Huber,   **QE601**
  Martin
The Techniques of Modern Structural Geology: Strain Analyses.
Paper Text. Elsevier Science & Technology Books. Saint Louis,
MO. 1984. 307p. ISBN:0-12-576921-0, ISBN13:
978-0-12-576921-1. Dewey:551.8. LCCN:82-074569.
> Audience: **l,u.**

Ramsay, John G. & Lisle,   **QE601**
  Richard J.
The Techniques of Modern Structural Geology: Applications of
Continuum Mechanics in Structural Geology. Trade Cloth.
Elsevier Science & Technology Books. Saint Louis, MO. 2000.
1061p. Modern Structural Geology Ser., Vol. 3
ISBN:0-12-576923-7, ISBN13: 978-0-12-576923-5.
Dewey:551.8/01531.
> Audience: **u,f.**

Rowland, Steve, et al.   **QE501.R73 2006**
Structural Analysis and Synthesis: A Laboratory Course in
Structural Geology. Ed. 3. Ernest Duebendorfer, Ilsa
Schiefelbein & Stephen M. Rowland (Authors). Spiral.
Blackwell Publishing, Inc. Malden, MA. 2006. 304p.
ISBN:1-4051-1652-8, ISBN13: 978-1-4051-1652-7.
Dewey:551.8/078. LCCN:2005-021041.
> Audience: **l,u.**

Twiss, Robert J. & Moores, Eldridge M.   QE601 .T894 1992
Structural Geology. Cloth over Boards. Worth Publishers, Inc. New York, NY. 1992. 532p. ISBN:0-7167-2252-6, ISBN13: 978-0-7167-2252-6. Dewey:551.8. LCCN:92-004058.
Audience: **l,u.**

Structural Geology > Earth Structure

Karato, Shun'ichirao   QE509.K3713 2003
The Dynamic Structure of the Deep Earth: An Interdisciplinary Approach. Trade Cloth. Princeton University Press. Princeton, NJ. 2003. 264p. ISBN:0-691-09511-6, ISBN13: 978-0-691-09511-0. Dewey:551.1/1. LCCN:2002-029298.
Audience: **u,f.** *Choice, 2003.*

Van der Pluijm, Ben A. & Marshak, Stephen   QE601.V363 2003
Earth Structure: An Introduction to Structural Geology and Tectonics. Ed. 2. Trade Cloth. W. W. Norton & Company, Inc. New York, NY. 2003. xvi, 656p. ISBN:0-393-92467-X, ISBN13: 978-0-393-92467-1. Dewey:551.8. LCCN:2003-063957.
Audience: **l,u.**

Structural Geology > Plate Tectonics

Condie, Kent C.   QE511.4
Plate Tectonics and How the Earth Works. CD-ROM. Tasa Graphic Arts, Inc. Taos, NM. 2005. ISBN:1-58256-042-0, ISBN13: 978-1-58256-042-7. Dewey:551.136.
Audience: **u,f.**

Davies, Geoffrey F.   QE509.4 .D38 1999
Dynamic Earth: Plates, Plumes and Mantle Convection. Trade Paper. Cambridge University Press. New York, NY. 1999. 470p. ISBN:0-521-59933-4, ISBN13: 978-0-521-59933-7. Dewey:551.1/16. LCCN:98-051722.
Audience: **u,f.** *Choice, 2000.*

Gubbins, David   QE534.2 .G83 1990
Seismology and Plate Tectonics. Trade Paper. Cambridge University Press. New York, NY. 1990. 340p. ISBN:0-521-37995-4, ISBN13: 978-0-521-37995-3. Dewey:551.2/2. LCCN:89-025291.
Audience: **u,f.**

Peltier, W. Richard (Editor)   QE509
Mantle Convection: Plate Tectonics and Global Dynamics. Trade Cloth. Gordon & Breach Publishing Group. New York, NY. 1988. 882p. ISBN:0-677-22102-9, ISBN13: 978-0-677-22102-1. Dewey:551.1/16.
Audience: **u,f.**

Rogers, John J. W. & Santosh, M.   QE511.R59 2004
Continents and Supercontinents. Trade Cloth. Oxford University Press, Inc. New York, NY. 2004. 298p. ISBN:0-19-516589-6, ISBN13: 978-0-19-516589-0. Dewey:551.1/36. LCCN:2003-022676.
Audience: **u,f.** *Choice, 2005.*

Structural Geology > Earthquakes

USGS Earthquake Hazards Program.   QE534.2
http://earthquake.usgs.gov/
Audience: **g,l,u,f.**

Bolt, Bruce   QE534.3.B65 2003
Earthquakes. Ed. 5. Trade Paper. Worth Publishers, Inc. New York, NY. 2003. 320p. ISBN:0-7167-5618-8, ISBN13: 978-0-7167-5618-7. Dewey:551.22. LCCN:2003-061112.
Audience: **g,l,u.**

Hough, Susan Elizabeth   QE534.3.H68 2004
Earthshaking Science: What We Know (and Don't Know) about Earthquakes. Trade Paper. Princeton University Press. Princeton, NJ. 2004. 256p. ISBN:0-691-11819-1, ISBN13: 978-0-691-11819-2. Dewey:551.22.
Audience: **g,l,u,f.** *Choice, 2003, 2002.*

Ritchie, David & Gates, Alexander E.   QE521.R58 2001
Encyclopedia of Earthquakes and Volcanoes. Ed. 2. Trade Cloth. Facts On File, Inc.. New York, NY. 2001. 320p. The Facts on File Science Library ISBN:0-8160-4372-8, ISBN13: 978-0-8160-4372-9. Dewey:551.2/03. LCCN:00-049492.
Audience: **g,l,u,f.** *Choice, 2002, 1994.*

Yeats, Robert S., et al.   QE534.2.Y43 1997
Geology of Earthquakes. Clarence R. Allen & Kerry E. Sieh (Authors). Cloth Text. Oxford University Press, Inc. New York, NY. 1997. 576p. ISBN:0-19-507827-6, ISBN13: 978-0-19-507827-5. Dewey:551.2/2. LCCN:95-004903.
Audience: **u,f.**

Zeilinga de Boer, Jelle & Sanders, Donald Theodore   QE521.Z45 2005
Earthquakes in Human History: The Far-Reaching Effects of Seismic Disruptions. Trade Cloth. Princeton University Press. Princeton, NJ. 2004. 264p. ISBN:0-691-05070-8, ISBN13: 978-0-691-05070-6. Dewey:363.34/95/09. LCCN:2004-040122.
Audience: **l,u,f.** *Choice, 2005.*

Structural Geology > Seismology

Aki, Keiiti & Richards, Paul G.   QE539.2.M37A45 2002
Quantitative Seismology: Theory and Methods. Ed. 2. Trade Cloth. University Science Books. Sausalito, CA. 2002. 550p. ISBN:0-935702-96-2, ISBN13: 978-0-935702-96-5. Dewey:551.22. LCCN:2002-071360.
Audience: **u,f.**

Lee, William H. K. (Editor), et al.   QE537.3 .I68 2002
International Handbook of Earthquake and Engineering Seismology. Hiroo Kanamori, Paul C. Jennings & Carl Kisslinger (Editors). Trade Cloth. Elsevier Science & Technology Books. Saint Louis, MO. 2002. 976p. ISBN:0-12-440653-X, ISBN13: 978-0-12-440653-7. Dewey:551.22.
Audience: **u,f.**

Stein, Seth & Wysession, Michael   QE534.3.S74 2002
Introduction to Seismology, Earthquakes and Earth Structure.

Formats: Web: ☐ Ebook: *e* CD/DVD-ROM: ✿ BCL3: *B*

Trade Paper. Blackwell Publishing, Inc. Malden, MA. 2002. 512p. ISBN:0-86542-078-5, ISBN13: 978-0-86542-078-6. Dewey:551.22. LCCN:2001-052639.

Audience: **u,f.** *Choice, 2003.*

Geophysics > General

Ahrens, T. J. (Editor)   QC808.8.G56 1995
Global Earth Physics: A Handbook of Physical Constants. Trade Cloth. American Geophysical Union. Washington, DC. 1995. 380p. AGU Reference Shelf Ser., Vol. 1 ISBN:0-87590-851-9, ISBN13: 978-0-87590-851-9. Dewey:550. LCCN:94-044745.

Audience: **l,u,f.** *Choice, 1996.*

Fowler, C. M. R.   QC806.F625 2004
The Solid Earth: An Introduction to Global Geophysics. Ed. 2. Trade Paper. Cambridge University Press. New York, NY. 2004. 704p. ISBN:0-521-89307-0, ISBN13: 978-0-521-89307-7. Dewey:550. LCCN:2003-065424.

Audience: **l,u.**

Gubbins, David   QC809.M37G83 2004
Time Series Analysis and Inverse Theory for Geophysicists. Trade Paper. Cambridge University Press. New York, NY. 2004. 272p. ISBN:0-521-52569-1, ISBN13: 978-0-521-52569-5. Dewey:550/.1/51. LCCN:2003-055730.

Audience: **u,f.**

James, David E   QE501.E58 1989
Encyclopedia of Geophysics. Chapman & Hall. 1989. ISBN:0-442-24366-9, ISBN13: 978-0-442-24366-1.

Audience: **l,u,f.**

Matzner, Richard A., ed.   QB14.D53 2001
Dictionary of Geophysics, Astrophysics, and Astronomy. CRC Press. 2001. ISBN:0-8493-2891-8, ISBN13: 978-0-8493-2891-6.

Audience: **l,u,f.**

Menke, William   QC802.A1M46 1989
Geophysical Data Analysis. Ed. 2. Trade Cloth. Elsevier Science & Technology Books. Saint Louis, MO. 1989. 289p. International Geophysics Ser. ISBN:0-12-490921-3, ISBN13: 978-0-12-490921-2. Dewey:551. LCCN:89-031224.

Audience: **l,u,f.**

Geophysics > Geodesy and Gravity

Smith, James R.   QB281.S55 1996
Introduction to Geodesy: The History and Concepts of Modern Geodesy. Ed. 1. Trade Paper. John Wiley & Sons, Inc. Hoboken, NJ. 1997. 240p. Wiley Series in Surveying and Boundary Control Ser., Vol. 1 ISBN:0-471-16660-X, ISBN13: 978-0-471-16660-3. Dewey:526/.1. LCCN:96-033301.

Audience: **l,u.** *Choice, 1998.*

Torge, Wolfgang   QB281.T5813 2001
Geodesy. Ed. 3. Trade Cloth. Walter De Gruyter Inc. Ossining, NY. 2001. xv, 416p. ISBN:3-11-017072-8, ISBN13: 978-3-11-017072-6. Dewey:526/.1. LCCN:2001-028639.

Audience: **u,f.**

Geophysics > Geodynamics

Davies, Geoffrey F.   QE509.4 .D38 1999
Dynamic Earth: Plates, Plumes and Mantle Convection. Trade Paper. Cambridge University Press. New York, NY. 1999. 470p.

ISBN:0-521-59933-4, ISBN13: 978-0-521-59933-7. Dewey:551.1/16. LCCN:98-051722.

Audience: **u,f.** *Choice, 2000.*

Karato, Shun'ichirao   QE509.K3713 2003
The Dynamic Structure of the Deep Earth: An Interdisciplinary Approach. Trade Cloth. Princeton University Press. Princeton, NJ. 2003. 264p. ISBN:0-691-09511-6, ISBN13: 978-0-691-09511-0. Dewey:551.1/1. LCCN:2002-029298.

Audience: **u,f.** *Choice, 2003.*

Oreskes, Naomi   QE511.4
Plate Tectonics: An Insider's History of the Modern Theory of the Earth. Trade Paper. Westview Press. Boulder, CO. 2003. 448p. ISBN:0-8133-4132-9, ISBN13: 978-0-8133-4132-3. Dewey:551.1/36.

Audience: **l,u,f.** *Choice, 2003.*

Rogers, John J. W. &   QE511.R59 2004
  Santosh, M.
Continents and Supercontinents. Trade Cloth. Oxford University Press, Inc. New York, NY. 2004. 298p. ISBN:0-19-516589-6, ISBN13: 978-0-19-516589-0. Dewey:551.1/36. LCCN:2003-022676.

Audience: **u,f.** *Choice, 2005.*

Sullivan, Walter   QE511.5 .S93 1991
Continents in Motion. Ed. 2. Trade Paper. Springer. New York, NY. 1991. 425p. ISBN:0-88318-704-3, ISBN13: 978-0-88318-704-3. Dewey:551.1/36. LCCN:90-022116.

Audience: **g,l.** 🅱 *Choice, 1992.*

Turcotte, Donald L. &   QE501 .T83 2002
  Schubert, Gerald
Geodynamics. Ed. 2. Trade Paper. Cambridge University Press. New York, NY. 2002. 472p. ISBN:0-521-66624-4, ISBN13: 978-0-521-66624-4. Dewey:551. LCCN:2001-025802.

Audience: **u,f.**

Geophysics > Geomagnetism and Paleomagnetism

QC815.2

▢ USGS National Geomagnetism Program. http://geomag.usgs.gov/

Audience: **l,u,f.**

Campbell, Wallace H.   QC815.2.C364 2003
Introduction to Geomagnetic Fields. Ed. 2. Trade Paper. Cambridge University Press. New York, NY. 2003. 350p. ISBN:0-521-52953-0, ISBN13: 978-0-521-52953-2. Dewey:538/.72. LCCN:2002-031468.

Audience: **u,f.**

McElhinny, Michael W. &   QE501.4.P35M35 2000
  McFadden, Phillip L.
Paleomagnetism: Continents and Oceans. Ed. 2. Renata Dmowska, James R. Holton & H. Thomas Rossby (Contribution by). Trade Cloth. Elsevier Science & Technology Books. Saint Louis, MO. 1999. 386p. International Geophysics Ser., Vol. 73 ISBN:0-12-483355-1, ISBN13: 978-0-12-483355-5. Dewey:538/.727. LCCN:99-065104.

Audience: **u,f.** *Choice, 2000.*

Merrill, Richard T., et al.   QC816.M47 1996
The Magnetic Field of the Earth: Paleomagnetism, the Core, and
the Deep Mantle. Ed. 2. Michael W. McElhinny & Phillip L.
McFadden (Authors). Trade Cloth. Elsevier Science &
Technology Books. Saint Louis, MO. 1996. 531p. International
Geophysics Ser., Vol. 62 ISBN:0-12-491245-1, ISBN13:
978-0-12-491245-8. Dewey:538/.72. LCCN:96-028566.
     Audience: **l,u.** *Choice, 1997.*

Geophysics > Heat Flow

Beardsmore, G. R. & Cull,   QE509.8 .B43 2001
  J. P.
Crustal Heat Flow: A Guide to Measurement and Modelling.
Trade Cloth. Cambridge University Press. New York, NY. 2001.
334p. ISBN:0-521-79289-4, ISBN13: 978-0-521-79289-9.
Dewey:551.14. LCCN:00-048634.
     Audience: **u,f.**

Geophysics > Isotopes and Geochronology

Dalrymple, G. Brent   QE508.D28
Age of the Earth. Trade Paper. Stanford University Press. Palo
Alto, CA. 1994. 492p. ISBN:0-8047-2331-1, ISBN13:
978-0-8047-2331-2. Dewey:551.1.
     Audience: **u,f.**

Dickin, Alan P.   QE501.4.N9D53 2004
Radiogenic Isotope Geology. Ed. 2. Trade Paper, Perfect.
Cambridge University Press. New York, NY. 2005. 510p.
ISBN:0-521-53017-2, ISBN13: 978-0-521-53017-0.
Dewey:551.701. LCCN:2003-069588.
     Audience: **u,f.** *Choice, 1996.*

Faure, Gunter & Mensing,   QE501.4.N9F38 2005
  Teresa M.
Isotopes: Principles and Applications. Ed. 3. Trade Cloth. John
Wiley & Sons, Inc. Hoboken, NJ. 2004. 928p.
ISBN:0-471-38437-2, ISBN13: 978-0-471-38437-3.
Dewey:551.9. LCCN:2003-022089.
     Audience: **u,f.**

Gradstein, Felix M. (Editor),   QE508.G3956 2004
  et al.
A Geologic Time Scale 2004. Ed. 3. James G. Ogg & Alan G.
Smith (Editors). Trade Paper, Poster. Cambridge University
Press. New York, NY. 2005. 610p. ISBN:0-521-78673-8,
ISBN13: 978-0-521-78673-7. Dewey:551.701.
LCCN:2004-043586.
     Audience: **u,f.** *Choice, 2005.*

Geophysics > Seismology

Aki, Keiiti & Richards,   QE539.2.M37A45 2002
  Paul G.
Quantitative Seismology: Theory and Methods. Ed. 2. Trade
Cloth. University Science Books. Sausalito, CA. 2002. 550p.
ISBN:0-935702-96-2, ISBN13: 978-0-935702-96-5.
Dewey:551.22. LCCN:2002-071360.
     Audience: **u,f.**

Bacon, Mike, et al.   QE539.B24 2003
3-D Seismic Interpretation. A. Ronald Masters, Rob Simmonds,
Tom Redshaw & R. Simm (Authors). Trade Cloth. Cambridge

University Press. New York, NY. 2003. 222p.
ISBN:0-521-79203-7, ISBN13: 978-0-521-79203-5.
Dewey:622/.1592. LCCN:2003-041201.
     Audience: **u,f.**

Gubbins, David   QE534.2 .G83 1990
Seismology and Plate Tectonics. Trade Paper. Cambridge
University Press. New York, NY. 1990. 340p.
ISBN:0-521-37995-4, ISBN13: 978-0-521-37995-3.
Dewey:551.2/2. LCCN:89-025291.
     Audience: **u,f.**

Stein, Seth & Wysession,   QE534.3.S74 2002
  Michael
Introduction to Seismology, Earthquakes and Earth Structure.
Trade Paper. Blackwell Publishing, Inc. Malden, MA. 2002.
512p. ISBN:0-86542-078-5, ISBN13: 978-0-86542-078-6.
Dewey:551.22. LCCN:2001-052639.
     Audience: **u,f.** *Choice, 2003.*

Geophysics > Space Physics (Solar Terrestrial Physics)

Carlowicz, Michael J. &   QB505
  Lopez, Ramon E.
Storms from the Sun: The Emerging Science of Space Weather.
Trade Paper. National Academies Press. Washington, DC. 2003.
256p. ISBN:0-309-08940-9, ISBN13: 978-0-309-08940-1.
Dewey:629.4/16.
     Audience: **g,l,u.** *Choice, 2003, 2002.*

Gombosi, Tamas I.   QC861.2 .G64 1998
Physics of the Space Environment. Alexander J. Dessler, John T.
Houghton & Michael J. Rycroft (Contribution by). Trade Paper.
Cambridge University Press. New York, NY. 2004. 357p.
Cambridge Atmospheric and Space Science Ser.
ISBN:0-521-60768-X, ISBN13: 978-0-521-60768-1.
Dewey:551.51/4.
     Audience: **u,f.** *Choice, 1999.*

Parks, George   QC809.P5P37 2003
Physics of Space Plasmas: An Introduction. Ed. 2. Trade Paper.
Westview Press. Boulder, CO. 2003. 616p. ISBN:0-8133-4129-9,
ISBN13: 978-0-8133-4129-3. Dewey:523.01.
LCCN:2003-065660.
     Audience: **u,f.**

Phillips, Tony   QB505
⬜ SpaceWeather.com -- News and Information about the
Sun-Earth Environment.
http://www.spaceweather.com
     Audience: **g,l,u,f.**

Savage, Candace   QC971 .S27 2001
Aurora: The Mysterious Northern Lights. Trade Paper. Firefly
Books, Ltd. Tonawanda, NY. 2001. 144p. ISBN:1-55209-583-5,
ISBN13: 978-1-55209-583-6. Dewey:538.
     Audience: **g,l,u.**

Geophysics > Applied and Exploration Geophysics

Kearey, P., et al.   TN269.K37 2001
An Introduction to Geophysical Exploration. Ed. 3. M. Brooks & Ian Hill (Authors). Trade Paper. Blackwell Publishing Ltd. Oxford, 2002. 288p. ISBN:0-632-04929-4, ISBN13: 978-0-632-04929-5. Dewey:622/.15. LCCN:2001-052638.
         Audience: **l,u.**

Sharma, Prem V.   TA705 .S515 1997
Environmental and Engineering Geophysics. Trade Paper. Cambridge University Press. New York, NY. 1997. 499p. ISBN:0-521-57632-6, ISBN13: 978-0-521-57632-1. Dewey:624.1/51. LCCN:96-037797.
         Audience: **u,f.** *Choice, 1998.*

Sheriff, Robert E.   TN269.S524 2002
Encyclopedic Dictionary of Applied Geophysics. Ed. 4. Trade Cloth. Society of Exploration Geophysicists. Tulsa, OK. 2002. 429p. Geophysical References Ser., Vol. 13 ISBN:1-56080-118-2, ISBN13: 978-1-56080-118-4. Dewey:622/.1592. LCCN:2002-075884.
         Audience: **l,u,f.**

Telford, W. M., et al.   TN269
Applied Geophysics. Ed. 2. L. P. Geldart & R. E. Sheriff (Authors). Trade Paper. Cambridge University Press. New York, NY. 1990. 790p. ISBN:0-521-33938-3, ISBN13: 978-0-521-33938-4. Dewey:622/.15. LCCN:88-038761.
         Audience: **l,u.** *B*

Historical Geology > History of the earth

Fortey, Richard   QE28.3 .F66 2004
Earth: An Intimate History. Trade Paper. Knopf Publishing Group. New York, NY. 2005. 448p. ISBN:0-375-70620-8, ISBN13: 978-0-375-70620-2. Dewey:551.7. LCCN:2006-272680.
         Audience: **l,u.** *Choice, 2005.*

Knoll, Andrew H.   QH325.K54 2004
Life on a Young Planet: The First Three Billion Years of Evolution on Earth. Trade Paper. Princeton University Press. Princeton, NJ. 2004. 304p. Princeton Science Library ISBN:0-691-12029-3, ISBN13: 978-0-691-12029-4. Dewey:576.8/3.
         Audience: **l,u,f.** *Choice, 2003.*

Lamb, Simon & Sington, David   QE26.2.L33 1998
Earth Story: The Forces That Have Shaped Our Planet. Trade Paper. Princeton University Press. Princeton, NJ. 2003. 240p. ISBN:0-691-11662-8, ISBN13: 978-0-691-11662-4.
         Audience: **g,l.**

MacDougall, J. D.   QE28.3
A Short History of Planet Earth: Mountains, Mammals, Fire, and Ice. Trade Paper. John Wiley & Sons, Inc. Hoboken, NJ. 1998. 272p. Popular Science Ser. ISBN:0-471-19703-3, ISBN13: 978-0-471-19703-4. Dewey:551.7. LCCN:95-046399.
         Audience: **g,l.** *Choice, 1997.*

Prothero, Donald R. & Dott, Robert H.   QE283.P75 2004
Evolution of the Earth. Ed. 7. Paper Text. McGraw-Hill Higher Education. Burr Ridge, IL. 2003. 576p. ISBN:0-07-252808-7, ISBN13: 978-0-07-252808-4. Dewey:551.7. LCCN:2003-051153.
         Audience: **l,u.**

Redfern, Ron   QE28.3.R45 2001
Origins: The Evolution of Continents, Oceans, and Life. Trade Cloth. University of Oklahoma Press. Norman, OK. 2001. 360p. ISBN:0-8061-3359-7, ISBN13: 978-0-8061-3359-1. Dewey:551.7. LCCN:2001-027134.
         Audience: **g,l.** *Choice, 2002.*

Rogers, John James William   QE28.3.R64 1993
A History of the Earth. Trade Paper. Cambridge University Press. New York, NY. 1993. 326p. ISBN:0-521-39782-0, ISBN13: 978-0-521-39782-7. Dewey:551.7. LCCN:93-001661.
         Audience: **u,f.**

Historical Geology > Paleoclimatology

         QC884
☐ NOAA Paleoclimatology.
http://www.ncdc.noaa.gov/paleo/
         Audience: **g,l,u,f.**

Bradley, Raymond S.   QC884.B614 1999
Paleoclimatology: Reconstructing Climates of the Quaternary, Vol. 68. Ed. 2. Cloth Text. Elsevier Science & Technology Books. Saint Louis, MO. 1999. 613p. International Geophysics Ser. ISBN:0-12-124010-X, ISBN13: 978-0-12-124010-3. Dewey:551.6/09/01. LCCN:98-083154.
         Audience: **u,f.** *Choice, 1999.*

Crowley & North   Q49
Paleoclimatology. Trade Paper. Oxford University Press, Inc. New York, NY. 1996. 356p. Series on Geology and Geophysics, No. 18 ISBN:0-19-510533-8, ISBN13: 978-0-19-510533-9. Dewey:551.6/09. LCCN:89-026604.
         Audience: **u.**

Huber, Brian T. (Editor), et al.   QC884 .W37 2000
Warm Climates in Earth History. Kenneth G. MacLeod & Scott L. Wing (Editors). Trade Cloth. Cambridge University Press. New York, NY. 1999. 480p. ISBN:0-521-64142-X, ISBN13: 978-0-521-64142-5. Dewey:551.6/09/01. LCCN:98-051724.
         Audience: **u,f.** *Choice, 2000.*

Historical Geology > Paleogeography

         QE501.4.P3
☐ PALEOMAP Project.
http://www.scotese.com/
         Audience: **l,u,f.**

Osborne, Roger (Editor), et al.   QE28.3.H57 1996
The Historical Atlas of the Earth: A Visual Exploration of the Earth's Physical Past. Donald H. Tarling & Stephen Jay Gould (Editors). Cloth over Boards. Henry Holt & Company. New York, NY. 1996. 192p. ISBN:0-8050-4552-X, ISBN13: 978-0-8050-4552-9. Dewey:551.7. LCCN:95-079328.
         Audience: **l.** *Choice, 1996.*

Stratigraphy > General Works

Boggs, Sam Jr.   **QE571.B66 2006**
Principles of Sedimentology and Stratigraphy. Ed. 4. Trade
Paper. Prentice Hall PTR. Upper Saddle River, NJ. 2005. 688p.
ISBN:0-13-154728-3, ISBN13: 978-0-13-154728-5.
Dewey:552/.5. LCCN:2005-047667.

Audience: **l,u,f.**

Donovan, Stephen K. &   **QE711.2.A33 1998**
Paul, Christopher R.
The Adequacy of the Fossil Record. Trade Cloth. John Wiley &
Sons, Inc. Hoboken, NJ. 1998. 322p. ISBN:0-471-96988-5,
ISBN13: 978-0-471-96988-4. Dewey:560/.17. LCCN:98-010110.

Audience: **u,f.**

Doyle, Peter, et al.   **QE651.D64 2001**
The Key to Earth History: An Introduction to Stratigraphy. Ed.
2. Matthew R. Bennett & Alistair N. Baxter (Authors). Trade
Paper. John Wiley & Sons, Inc. Hoboken, NJ. 2001. 304p.
ISBN:0-471-49215-9, ISBN13: 978-0-471-49215-3.
Dewey:551.7. LCCN:00-068516.

Audience: **l,u,f.** *Choice, 1995.*

Einsele, G. (Editor), et al.   **QE651.C9 1991**
Cycles and Events in Stratigraphy. W. Ricken & A. Seilacher
(Editors). Trade Cloth. Bow Historical Books. New Providence,
NJ. 1991. 955p. ISBN:3-540-52784-2, ISBN13:
978-3-540-52784-8. Dewey:551.7. LCCN:91-011656.

Audience: **l,u,f.**

Myers, Keith   **QE651.S458 1996**
Sequence Stratigraphy. Ed. 4. Dominic Emery (Editor). Trade
Paper. Blackwell Publishing, Inc. Malden, MA. 1996. 304p.
ISBN:0-632-03706-7, ISBN13: 978-0-632-03706-3.
Dewey:551.7. LCCN:95-021377.

Audience: **l,u.**

Nichols, Gary J.   **QE571.N53 1999**
Sedimentology and Stratigraphy. Trade Paper. Blackwell
Publishing, Inc. Malden, MA. 1999. 368p. ISBN:0-632-03578-1,
ISBN13: 978-0-632-03578-6. Dewey:551.3/03.
LCCN:98-007562.

Audience: **l,u.**

Salvador, Amos (Editor)   **QE645.I57 1994**
International Stratigraphic Guide: A Guide to Stratigraphic
Classification, Terminology, and Procedure. Ed. 2. Trade Cloth.
Geological Society of America, Inc. Boulder, CO. 1994. IUGS
Publication Ser., No. 001 ISBN:0-8137-7401-2, ISBN13:
978-0-8137-7401-5. Dewey:551.7/0012. LCCN:94-013276.

Audience: **u,f.**

Stratigraphy > Geologic Time

Brush, Stephen G.   **QB601 .B89 1996 VOL**
A History of Modern Planetary Physics: Transmuted Past: The
Age of the Earth and the Evolution of the Elements from Lyell
to Patterson. Cloth Text. Cambridge University Press. New
York, NY. 1996. 144p. ISBN:0-521-55213-3, ISBN13:
978-0-521-55213-4. Dewey:523.1. LCCN:95-032974.

Audience: **f.** *Choice, 1996.*

Dalrymple, G. Brent   **QB631.D34 2004**
Ancient Earth, Ancient Skies: The Age of Earth and Its Cosmic
Surroundings. Trade Cloth. Stanford University Press. Palo Alto,
CA. 2004. 248p. ISBN:0-8047-4932-9, ISBN13:
978-0-8047-4932-9. Dewey:525. LCCN:2003-024023.

Audience: **g,l,u,f.** *Choice, 2004.*

Gould, Stephen Jay   **QE508.G68**
Time's Arrow, Time's Cycle: Myth and Metaphor in the
Discovery of Geological Time. Trade Paper. Harvard University
Press. Cambridge, MA. 1987. 240p. The Jerusalem-Harvard
Lectures ISBN:0-674-89199-6, ISBN13: 978-0-674-89199-9.
Dewey:551.7/01.09.

Audience: **g,l,u,f.** *B Choice, 1988.*

Gradstein, Felix M. (Editor),   **QE508.G3956 2004**
et al.
A Geologic Time Scale 2004. Ed. 3. James G. Ogg & Alan G.
Smith (Editors). Trade Paper, Poster. Cambridge University
Press. New York, NY. 2005. 610p. ISBN:0-521-78673-8,
ISBN13: 978-0-521-78673-7. Dewey:551.701.
LCCN:2004-043586.

Audience: **u,f.** *Choice, 2005.*

Powell, James Lawrence   **QE508.P68 2001**
The Mysteries of Terra Firma: The Age and Evolution of the
Earth. Trade Cloth. Simon & Schuster. New York, NY. 2001.
272p. ISBN:0-684-87282-X, ISBN13: 978-0-684-87282-7.
Dewey:551.7/01. LCCN:2001-051123.

Audience: **l,u,f.**

Stratigraphy > Stratigraphic Units and Sequences

North American   **QE645**
Commission on Stratigraphic Nomenclature and American
Association of Petroleum Geologists
☐ North American Stratigraphic Code.
http://www.agiweb.org/nacsn/code2.html

Audience: **u,f.**

Salvador, Amos (Editor)   **QE645.I57 1994**
International Stratigraphic Guide: A Guide to Stratigraphic
Classification, Terminology, and Procedure. Ed. 2. Trade Cloth.
Geological Society of America, Inc. Boulder, CO. 1994. IUGS
Publication Ser., No. 001 ISBN:0-8137-7401-2, ISBN13:
978-0-8137-7401-5. Dewey:551.7/0012. LCCN:94-013276.

Audience: **u,f.**

Paleontology > Reference, General Works

Bottjer, David J., et al.   **QE766.E93 2001**
Exceptional Fossil Preservation: A Unique View on the
Evolution of Marine Life. Walter Etter, James W. Hagadorn &
Carol M. Tang (Authors). Trade Paper. Columbia University
Press. New York, NY. 2002. 424p. The Critical Moments and
Perspectives in Earth History and Paleobiology Ser.
ISBN:0-231-10255-0, ISBN13: 978-0-231-10255-1.
Dewey:560/.457. LCCN:2001-042434.

Audience: **l,u,f.**

Donovan, Stephen K.   **QE721.2.F6P76 1991**
The Processes of Fossilization. Trade Cloth. Columbia
University Press. New York, NY. 1991. 303p.

ISBN:0-231-07674-6, ISBN13: 978-0-231-07674-6. Dewey:560.
LCCN:91-016327.

Audience: **l,u,f.** *Choice, 1992.*

Eldredge, Niles & Alcosser, QE711.2.E47 1997
Murray
Fossils: The Evolution and Extinction of Species. Trade Paper.
Princeton University Press. Princeton, NJ. 1996. 240p.
ISBN:0-691-02695-5, ISBN13: 978-0-691-02695-4. Dewey:560.
LCCN:96-026969.

Audience: **g,l,u.**

Fortey, Richard A. QE711.3.F67 2002
Fossils: The Key to the Past. Ed. 3. Book, Other. Smithsonian
Institution Press. Washington, DC. 2002. 352p.
ISBN:1-58834-023-6, ISBN13: 978-1-58834-023-8. Dewey:560.
LCCN:2001-049439.

Audience: **l,u.** *Choice, 1992.*

Goldring, Roland QE711.2.G65 1991
Fossils in the Field: Information Potential and Analysis. Trade
Paper. Addison-Wesley Longman, Ltd. Harlow, 1991. 256p.
ISBN:0-582-06261-6, ISBN13: 978-0-582-06261-0. Dewey:560.
LCCN:90-033994.

Audience: **l,u.** *Choice, 1992.*

Knoll, Andrew H. QH325.K54 2004
Life on a Young Planet: The First Three Billion Years of
Evolution on Earth. Trade Paper. Princeton University Press.
Princeton, NJ. 2004. 304p. Princeton Science Library
ISBN:0-691-12029-3, ISBN13: 978-0-691-12029-4.
Dewey:576.8/3.

Audience: **l,u,f.** *Choice, 2003.*

Martin, Robert A. QL607.5.M36 2003
Missing Links: Evolutionary Concepts and Transistions Through
Time. Trade Paper. Jones & Bartlett Publishers, Inc. Sudbury,
MA. 2003. 304p. The Jones and Bartlett Series in Biology
ISBN:0-7637-2196-4, ISBN13: 978-0-7637-2196-1. Dewey:566.
LCCN:2002-041049.

Audience: **l,u.**

Martin, Ronald E. QE721.2.F6 M37 1999
Taphonomy: A Process Approach. D. E. G. Briggs, P. Dodson,
B. J. MacFadden, J. J. Sepkoski & R. A. Spicer (Contribution
by). Trade Paper. Cambridge University Press. New York, NY.
1999. 524p. Paleobiology Ser. ISBN:0-521-59833-8, ISBN13:
978-0-521-59833-0. Dewey:560. LCCN:98-032341.
Audience: **u,f.**

National Audubon Society QE718
Staff & Thompson, Ida
Field Guide to Fossils: North America. Carol Nehring
(Illustrator), Townsend P. Dickinson (Photographer). Trade
Cloth. Alfred A. Knopf Inc. New York, NY. 1982. 848p.
Audubon Society Field Guide Ser. ISBN:0-394-52412-8,
ISBN13: 978-0-394-52412-2. Dewey:560/.973.
LCCN:81-084772.

Audience: **g,l,u,f.**

Singer, Ronald (Editor) QE703.E523 1999
Encyclopedia of Paleontology, Set. Trade Cloth. Fitzroy
Dearborn Publishers, Inc. Chicago, IL. 2000. 1467p.
ISBN:1-884964-96-6, ISBN13: 978-1-884964-96-1.
Dewey:560/.3. LCCN:00-271769.

Audience: **g,l,u,f.** *Choice, 2000.*

University of California QE704.3
Museum of Paleontology, The Paleontological Society,
Society of Vertebrate Paleontology, and United States
Geological Survey
☐ The Paleontology Portal.
http://www.paleoportal.org

Audience: **g,l,u,f.**

Paleontology > Invertebrate Paleontology

Boardman, R., et al. QE770
Fossil Invertebrates. A. Cheetham & A. Rowell (Authors). Trade
Cloth. Blackwell Publishing, Inc. Malden, MA. 1987. 728p.
ISBN:0-86542-302-4, ISBN13: 978-0-86542-302-2. Dewey:562.
LCCN:84-028403.

Audience: **l,u,f.**

Clarkson, Euan N. K. QE770.C56 1998
Invertebrate Palaeontology and Evolution. Ed. 4. Trade Paper.
Blackwell Publishing, Inc. Malden, MA. 1998. 468p.
ISBN:0-632-05238-4, ISBN13: 978-0-632-05238-7. Dewey:562.
LCCN:2001-265988.

Audience: **l,u.**

Doyle, Peter QE770.D69 1996
Understanding Fossils: An Introduction to Invertebrate
Palaeontology. Ed. 1. Florence M. Lowry (Contribution by).
Trade Paper. John Wiley & Sons, Inc. Hoboken, NJ. 1996. 426p.
ISBN:0-471-96351-8, ISBN13: 978-0-471-96351-6. Dewey:562.
LCCN:95-049411.

Audience: **l,u.** *Choice, 1997.*

Levin, Harold L. QE770.L485 1999
Ancient Invertebrates and Their Living Relatives. Trade Paper.
Prentice Hall PTR. Upper Saddle River, NJ. 1998. 358p.
ISBN:0-13-748955-2, ISBN13: 978-0-13-748955-8.
LCCN:98-002690.

Audience: **l,u.** *Choice, 1999.*

Schopf, J. William QH325
Cradle of Life: The Discovery of Earth's Earliest Fossils. Trade
Paper. Princeton University Press. Princeton, NJ. 2001. 384p.
ISBN:0-691-08864-0, ISBN13: 978-0-691-08864-8.
Dewey:576.8/3.

Audience: **g,l,u,f.** *Choice, 2000.*

Paleontology > Vertebrate Paleontology

Benton, M. J. QE841.B44 2005
Vertebrate Palaeontology. Ed. 3. Trade Paper. Blackwell
Publishing, Inc. Malden, MA. 2004. 472p. ISBN:0-632-05637-1,
ISBN13: 978-0-632-05637-8. Dewey:566. LCCN:2003-028152.
Audience: **g,l,u,f.**

Carroll, Robert L. QE841.C254 1988
Vertebrate Paleontology and Evolution. Trade Cloth. W. H.
Freeman & Company. New York, NY. 1987. 698p. Geology Ser.
ISBN:0-7167-1822-7, ISBN13: 978-0-7167-1822-2. Dewey:566.
LCCN:86-031808.

Audience: **l,u.** *Choice, 1988.*

Carroll, Robert Lynn QE841 .C2538 1997
Patterns and Processes of Vertebrate Evolution. D. E. G. Briggs,
P. Dodson, B. J. MacFadden, J. J. Sepkoski & R. A. Spicer

(Contribution by). Trade Paper. Cambridge University Press. New York, NY. 1997. 464p. Cambridge Paleobiology Ser., No. 2 ISBN:0-521-47809-X, ISBN13: 978-0-521-47809-0. Dewey:596.138. LCCN:96-044161.
Audience: **g,l,u,f.** *Choice, 1997.*

Lyman, R. Lee　　　　　　　　　　　**CC79.5.A5 L96 1994**
Vertebrate Taphonomy. Graeme Barker, Peter Bogucki, Elizabeth Slater & Don Brothwell (Contribution by). Trade Paper. Cambridge University Press. New York, NY. 1994. 550p. Cambridge Manuals in Archaeology Ser. ISBN:0-521-45840-4, ISBN13: 978-0-521-45840-5. Dewey:930.1. LCCN:93-028675.
Audience: **g,u.** *Choice, 1995.*

Minkoff, Eli C., et al.　　　　　　　　**QE841.C68 2001**
Evolution of the Vertebrates: A History of the Backboned Animals Through Time. Ed. 5. Edwin H. Colbert & Michael Morales (Authors). Trade Cloth. John Wiley & Sons, Inc. Hoboken, NJ. 2001. 576p. ISBN:0-471-38461-5, ISBN13: 978-0-471-38461-8. Dewey:566. LCCN:2001-024230.
Audience: **g,l,u.**

Thomason, Jeffrey J.　　　　　　　　　**QE841 .F86 1997**
　(Editor)
Functional Morphology in Vertebrate Paleontology. Trade Paper. Cambridge University Press. New York, NY. 1997. 293p. ISBN:0-521-62921-7, ISBN13: 978-0-521-62921-8. Dewey:566.
Audience: **u,f.**

Paleontology > Vertebrate Paleontology > Dinosaurs

Currie, Philip J. & Padian,　　　　**QE862.D5E53 1997**
　Kevin (Editors)
Encyclopedia of Dinosaurs. Trade Cloth. Elsevier Science & Technology Books. Saint Louis, MO. 1997. 869p. ISBN:0-12-226810-5, ISBN13: 978-0-12-226810-6. Dewey:567.9/03. LCCN:97-023430.
Audience: **g,l,u,f.** *Choice, 1998.*

Fastovsky, David E. &　　　　　　**QE861.6.E95F37 2005**
　Weishampel, David B.
The Evolution and Extinction of the Dinosaurs. Ed. 2. John Sibbick (Illustrator). Cloth Text. Cambridge University Press. New York, NY. 2005. 500p. ISBN:0-521-81172-4, ISBN13: 978-0-521-81172-9. Dewey:567.9. LCCN:2004-049261.
Audience: **g,l,u.** *Choice, 1996.*

Gillette, David D. &　　　　　　　**QE862.D5 D496 1989**
　Lockley, Martin (Editors)
Dinosaur Tracks and Traces. Trade Paper. Cambridge University Press. New York, NY. 1991. 472p. ISBN:0-521-40788-5, ISBN13: 978-0-521-40788-5. Dewey:567.9/1. LCCN:88-034049.
Audience: **u,f.** *Choice, 1990.*

Parsons, Keith M.　　　　　　　　　**QE861.4.P38 2003**
The Great Dinosaur Controversy: A Guide to the Debates. Library Binding. ABC-CLIO, Inc. Santa Barbara, CA. 2003. 350p. Controversies in Science Ser. ISBN:1-57607-922-8, ISBN13: 978-1-57607-922-5. Dewey:567.9. LCCN:2003-017991.
Audience: **g,l,u.** *Choice, 2004.*

Thulborn, Tony　　　　　　　　　　　　　**QE862.D5**
Dinosaur Tracks. Chapman & Hall. 1990. ISBN:0-412-32890-9, ISBN13: 978-0-412-32890-9.
Audience: **l,u.**

Weishampel, David B., et al.　　　　**QE861.4 .D55 2004**
The Dinosauria. Ed. 2. Peter Dodson & Halszka Osmolska (Authors). Trade Cloth. University of California Press. Berkeley, CA. 2004. 880p. ISBN:0-520-24209-2, ISBN13: 978-0-520-24209-8. Dewey:567.9. LCCN:2004-049804.
Audience: **u,f.** *Choice, 2005, 1991.*

Paleontology > Vertebrate Paleontology > Mammals

Agustí, Jordi & Antón,　　　　　　　**QE881.A35 2005**
　Mauricio
Mammoths, Sabertooths, and Hominids: 65 Million Years of Mammalian Evolution in Europe. Trade Paper. Columbia University Press. New York, NY. 2005. 328p. ISBN:0-231-11641-1, ISBN13: 978-0-231-11641-1. Dewey:569.094.
Audience: **l,u,f.**

Kemp, Tom　　　　　　　　　　　　　　　**QL708.5**
The Origin and Evolution of Mammals. Trade Paper. Oxford University Press, Inc. New York, NY. 2005. 341p. Oxford Biology Ser. ISBN:0-19-850761-5, ISBN13: 978-0-19-850761-1. Dewey:599.1'38. LCCN:2005-295996.
Audience: **u,f.** *Choice, 2005.*

Kielan-Jaworowska, Zofia,　　　　　**QE881.K53 2004**
　et al.
Mammals from the Age of Dinosaurs: Origins, Evolution and Structure. Richard Cifelli & Zhe-Xi Luo (Authors). Trade Cloth. Edinburgh University Press. Edinburgh, 2004. 700p. ISBN:0-231-11918-6, ISBN13: 978-0-231-11918-4. Dewey:569. LCCN:2004-052897.
Audience: **u,f.** *Choice, 2005.*

Kurtén, Bjö & Anderson,　　　　　　　　**QE881**
　Elaine
Pleistocene Mammals of North America. Trade Cloth. Columbia University Press. New York, NY. 1980. 442p. ISBN:0-231-03733-3, ISBN13: 978-0-231-03733-4. Dewey:569/.097. LCCN:79-026679.
Audience: **u,f.** *B*

Paleontology > Micropaleontology

Armstrong, Howard &　　　　　　　　　**QE719**
　Brasier, Martin
Microfossils. Ed. 2. Trade Paper. Blackwell Publishing, Inc. Malden, MA. 2005. 304p. ISBN:0-632-05279-1, ISBN13: 978-0-632-05279-0. Dewey:560. LCCN:2004-003936.
Audience: **u,f.** *Choice, 2005.*

Haslett, Simon K.　　　　　　　　　　**QE741.Q28 2002**
Quaternary Environmental Micropalaeontology. Trade Paper. Oxford University Press, Inc. New York, NY. 2002. 288p. A Hodder Arnold Publication ISBN:0-340-76198-9, ISBN13: 978-0-340-76198-4. Dewey:560.779. LCCN:2003-268637.
Audience: **u.** *Choice, 2003.*

Schopf, J. William   **QH325**
Cradle of Life: The Discovery of Earth's Earliest Fossils. Trade
Paper. Princeton University Press. Princeton, NJ. 2001. 384p.
ISBN:0-691-08864-0, ISBN13: 978-0-691-08864-8.
Dewey:576.8/3.

Audience: **g,l,u,f.** *Choice, 2000.*

Paleontology > Paleobotany

Andrews, Henry N.   **QE904.A1**
The Fossil Hunters: In Search of Ancient Plants. Book, Other.
Cornell University Press. Ithaca, NY. 1980. 420p.
ISBN:0-8014-1248-X, ISBN13: 978-0-8014-1248-6.
Dewey:561/.09. LCCN:79-024101.

Audience: **g,l,u,f.** *B*

Kenrick, Paul & Crane,   **QK980.K44 1997**
  Peter R.
The Origin and Early Diversification of Land Plants: A Cladistic
Study. Trade Paper. Smithsonian Institution Press. Washington,
DC. 1997. 456p. Series in Comparative Evolutionary Biology
ISBN:1-56098-729-4, ISBN13: 978-1-56098-729-1.
Dewey:581.3/8. LCCN:97-024710.

Audience: **u,f.** *Choice, 1998.*

Kenrick, Paul & Davis, Paul   **QE905.K46 2004**
Fossil Plants. Natural History Museum (London, England) Staff
(Contribution by). Trade Cloth. Smithsonian Institution Press.
Washington, DC. 2004. 232p. ISBN:1-58834-181-X, ISBN13:
978-1-58834-181-5. Dewey:561. LCCN:2003-045658.

Audience: **l,u.**

Niklas, Karl J.   **QK980.N55 1997**
The Evolutionary Biology of Plants. Trade Paper. University of
Chicago Press. Chicago, IL. 1997. 470p. ISBN:0-226-58083-0,
ISBN13: 978-0-226-58083-8. Dewey:581.3/8. LCCN:96-031060.

Audience: **u,f.** *Choice, 1998.*

Tidwell, William D.   **QE935.T5 1998**
Common Fossil Plants of Western North America. Ed. 2. Trade
Paper. Smithsonian Institution Press. Washington, DC. 1998.
252p. ISBN:1-56098-758-8, ISBN13: 978-1-56098-758-1.
Dewey:561.1978. LCCN:97-011386.

Audience: **g,l,u,f.**

Traverse, A.   **QE993 .T67 1988**
Paleopalynology. Paper Text. Routledge. New York, NY. 1985.
500p. ISBN:0-04-561002-9, ISBN13: 978-0-04-561002-0.
Dewey:561/.13. LCCN:88-006317.

Audience: **u,f.** *Choice, 1988.*

Willis, Kathy & McElwain,   **QK980.W56 2002**
  Jenny
The Evolution of Plants. Paper Text. Oxford University Press,
Inc. New York, NY. 2002. 378p. ISBN:0-19-850065-3, ISBN13:
978-0-19-850065-0. Dewey:581.3/8. LCCN:2002-280029.

Audience: **l,u,f.** *Choice, 2003.*

Paleontology > Paleoecology

Allmon, Warren & Bottjer,   **QE721.2.E87E96 2001**
  David J. (Editors)
Evolutionary Paleoecology: The Ecological Context of
Macroevolutionary Change. Trade Paper. Columbia University

Press. New York, NY. 2001. 320p. ISBN:0-231-10995-4,
ISBN13: 978-0-231-10995-6. Dewey:560/.45. LCCN:00-064522.

Audience: **u,f.** *Choice, 2001.*

Behrensmeyer, Anna K.,   **QE720**
  et al.
Terrestrial Ecosystems Through Time: Evolutionary
Paleoecology of Terrestrial Plants and Animals. John D.
Damuth, William A. DiMichele, Richard Potts, Hans-Dieter Sues
& Scott L. Wing (Authors). Trade Paper. University of Chicago
Press. Chicago, IL. 1992. 588p. ISBN:0-226-04155-7, ISBN13:
978-0-226-04155-1. Dewey:560/.45. LCCN:91-044166.

Audience: **u,f.** *Choice, 1993.*

Brenchley, ; Harper,   **QE720.B74 1998**
Introduction to Palaeoecology. Chapman & Hall. 1998.
ISBN:0-412-43450-4, ISBN13: 978-0-412-43450-1.

Audience: **l,u.**

Cohen, Andrew S.   **QE39.5.P3C63 2003**
Paleolimnology: The History and Evolution of Lake Systems.
Trade Cloth. Oxford University Press, Inc. New York, NY. 2003.
528p. ISBN:0-19-513353-6, ISBN13: 978-0-19-513353-0.
Dewey:551.48. LCCN:2002-002722.

Audience: **u,f.** *Choice, 2004.*

Newton, Cathryn &   **QE720.N49 1989**
  Laporte, Leo F.
Ancient Environments. Ed. 3. Trade Paper. Prentice Hall PTR.
Upper Saddle River, NJ. 1997. 208p. ISBN:0-13-036476-2,
ISBN13: 978-0-13-036476-0. Dewey:560/.45. LCCN:88-007880.

Audience: **l,u,f.**

Pielou, E. C.   **QE721.2.P24P54 1991**
After the Ice Age: The Return of Life to Glaciated North
America. Trade Paper. University of Chicago Press. Chicago, IL.
1992. 376p. ISBN:0-226-66812-6, ISBN13: 978-0-226-66812-3.
Dewey:560/.1/78. LCCN:90-011024.

Audience: **g,l,u.** *Choice, 1991.*

Ridinger, Robert B. &   **QE720.E27 2001**
  Zhuravlev, Andrey (Editors)
The Ecology of the Cambrian Radiation. Trade Paper. Columbia
University Press. New York, NY. 2000. 576p. Perspectives in
Paleobiology and Earth History Ser. ISBN:0-231-10613-0,
ISBN13: 978-0-231-10613-9. Dewey:560/.1723.
LCCN:00-063901.

Audience: **u,f.**

Paleontology > Extinction Theories

Alvarez, Walter   **QE506.A48 1997**
T. Rex and the Crater of Doom. Trade Cloth. Princeton
University Press. Princeton, NJ. 1997. 198p.
ISBN:0-691-01630-5, ISBN13: 978-0-691-01630-6.
Dewey:576.8/4. LCCN:96-049208.

Audience: **l,u,f.** *Choice, 1997.*

Courtillot, Vincent   **QE506 .C7513 1999**
Evolutionary Catastrophes: The Science of Mass Extinction. Joe
McClinton (Translator), Claude Allegre (Foreword by). Trade
Paper. Cambridge University Press. New York, NY. 2002. 188p.
ISBN:0-521-89118-3, ISBN13: 978-0-521-89118-9.
Dewey:576.84.

Audience: **g,l,u,f.** *Choice, 2000.*

Donovan, Stephen K.   QC721.2.E97
  (Editor)
Mass Extinctions: Processes and Evidence. Paper Text. Columbia University Press. New York, NY. 1991. 266p. ISBN:0-231-07091-8, ISBN13: 978-0-231-07091-1. Dewey:575/.7.

        Audience: **u,f.** *Choice, 1990.*

Hallam, Tony   QB981
Catastrophes and Lesser Calamities: The Causes of Mass Extinctions. Trade Paper. Oxford University Press, Inc. New York, NY. 2005. 240p. ISBN:0-19-280668-8, ISBN13: 978-0-19-280668-0. Dewey:576.8/4. LCCN:2004-301672.

        Audience: **g,l,u,f.** *Choice, 2005.*

Walker, Gabrielle   PR9387.9.E36
Snowball Earth: The Story of a Maverick Scientist and His Theory of the Global Catastrophe That Spawned Life as We Know It. Trade Paper. Crown Publishing Group. New York, NY. 2004. 288p. ISBN:1-4000-5125-8, ISBN13: 978-1-4000-5125-0. Dewey:823.

        Audience: **g,l,u,f.**

Ward, Peter D.   QE721.2.E97W38 2000
Rivers in Time: The Search for Clues to Earth's Mass Extinctions. Trade Paper. Columbia University Press. New York, NY. 2002. 320p. ISBN:0-231-11863-5, ISBN13: 978-0-231-11863-7. Dewey:576.8/4.

        Audience: **g,l,u,f.** *Choice, 2001.*

Paleontology > Trace fossils

Bromley, Richard
Trace Fossils: Biology, Taphonomy and Applications. Ed. 2. Chapman & Hall. 1996. ISBN:0-412-61480-4, ISBN13: 978-0-412-61480-4.

        Audience: **u,f.**

Gillette, David D. &   QE862.D5 D496 1989
  Lockley, Martin (Editors)
Dinosaur Tracks and Traces. Trade Paper. Cambridge University Press. New York, NY. 1991. 472p. ISBN:0-521-40788-5, ISBN13: 978-0-521-40788-5. Dewey:567.9/1. LCCN:88-034049.
        Audience: **u,f.** *Choice, 1990.*

Thulborn, Tony   QE862.D5
Dinosaur Tracks. Chapman & Hall. 1990. ISBN:0-412-32890-9, ISBN13: 978-0-412-32890-9.

        Audience: **l,u.**

Economic Geology and Mineral Resources

Kogel, Jessica Elzea   TN799.5.A43 2006
Industrial Minerals & Rocks: Commodities, Markets, and Uses. Ed. 7. Society for Mining, Metallurgy, and Exploration (U.S.) Staff (Contribution by). Trade Cloth. Society for Mining, Metallurgy & Exploration, Inc. Littleton, CO. 2006. xvi, 1548p. ISBN:0-87335-233-5, ISBN13: 978-0-87335-233-8. Dewey:553. LCCN:2006-042200.

        Audience: **g,l,u,f.**

U. S. Bureau of Mines Staff   TN9.D564 1997
  & American Geological Institute Staff
Dictionary of Mining, Mineral and Related Terms. Ed. 2. Trade

Cloth. American Geological Institute. Alexandria, VA. 2000. 800p. ISBN:0-922152-36-5, ISBN13: 978-0-922152-36-0. Dewey:622/.03. LCCN:97-021272.

        Audience: **g,l,u,f.**

United States Geological   TN23
  Survey
⬜ Minerals Yearbook.
http://purl.access.gpo.gov/GPO/LPS5003
U.S. Government Printing Office.
        Audience: **g,l,u,f.**

Economic Geology and Mineral Resources > Ore (Metallic Mineral) Deposits

Barnes, Hubert Lloyd   QE390.5.G43 1997
  (Editor)
Geochemistry of Hydrothermal Ore Deposits. Ed. 3. Trade Cloth. John Wiley & Sons, Inc. Hoboken, NJ. 1997. 992p. ISBN:0-471-57144-X, ISBN13: 978-0-471-57144-5. Dewey:553. LCCN:96-034529.

        Audience: **u,f.** *Choice, 1997.*

Guilbert, John M. & Park,   QE390.G85 1986
  Charles F. Jr.
The Geology of Ore Deposits. Cloth over Boards. Worth Publishers, Inc. New York, NY. 1985. 985p. ISBN:0-7167-1456-6, ISBN13: 978-0-7167-1456-9. Dewey:553.4. LCCN:85-010099.
        Audience: **u,f.** *B Choice, 1986.*

Robb, L. J.   QE390.R32 2004
Introduction to Ore-Forming Processes. Trade Paper. Blackwell Publishing, Inc. Malden, MA. 2004. 384p. ISBN:0-632-06378-5, ISBN13: 978-0-632-06378-9. Dewey:553/.1. LCCN:2003-014049.

        Audience: **u,f.** *Choice, 2004.*

Economic Geology and Mineral Resources > Non-Metallic Resource Deposits > Coal, Peat, Natural Carbons, Oil Shales

Freese, Barbara   HD9540
Coal: A Human History. Trade Cloth. Basic Books. New York, NY. 2002. 320p. ISBN:0-7382-0400-5, ISBN13: 978-0-7382-0400-0. Dewey:553.2/4. LCCN:2002-114066.
        Audience: **g,l,u,f.** *Choice, 2003.*

Salvador, Amos   TJ163.2
Energy: A Historical Perspective and 21st Century Forecast. American Association of Petroleum Geologists. 2005. AAPG studies in geology 54 ISBN:0-89181-061-7, ISBN13: 978-0-89181-061-2.

        Audience: **u,f.**

Thomas, Larry   TN799.9
Coal Geology. Trade Cloth. John Wiley & Sons, Inc. Hoboken, NJ. 2002. 396p. ISBN:0-471-48531-4, ISBN13: 978-0-471-48531-5. Dewey:553.2/4. LCCN:2002-027204.
        Audience: **u,f.**

U.S. Geological Survey   **TN805**
☐ National Coal Assessment.
http://energy.cr.usgs.gov/coal/nca/index.htm
U.S. Geological Survey.

Audience: **g,l,u,f.**

Economic Geology and Mineral Resources > Non-Metallic Resource Deposits > Petroleum Geology

Ahmed, Tarek   **TN871**
Reservoir Engineering Handbook. Ed. 3. Cloth Text. Elsevier Science & Technology Books. Saint Louis, MO. 2006. 1376p. ISBN:0-7506-7972-7, ISBN13: 978-0-7506-7972-5. Dewey:622.3382. LCCN:2006-279890.

Audience: **u,f.**

Dake, L. P.   **TN871**
Fundamentals of Reservoir Engineering. Ed. 19. Trade Paper, Perfect. Elsevier Science & Technology Books. Saint Louis, MO. 2001. 462p. Development in Petroleum Science Ser., Vol. 8 ISBN:0-444-41830-X, ISBN13: 978-0-444-41830-2. Dewey:622/.3382. LCCN:77-018701.

Audience: **u,f.**

Dake, L. P.   **TN871.D35 2001**
The Practice of Reservoir Engineering. Trade Cloth. Elsevier Science & Technology Books. Saint Louis, MO. 2001. 572p. Development in Petroleum Science Ser., Vol. 36 ISBN:0-444-50670-5, ISBN13: 978-0-444-50670-2. Dewey:622/.3382. LCCN:2001-023426.

Audience: **u,f.**

Deffeyes, Kenneth S.   **TN870.D37 2003**
Hubbert's Peak: The Impending World Oil Shortage. Trade Paper. Princeton University Press. Princeton, NJ. 2003. 224p. ISBN:0-691-11625-3, ISBN13: 978-0-691-11625-9. Dewey:333.8/23211.

Audience: **g,l,u,f.** *Choice, 2002.*

Gluyas, Jon & Swarbrick,   **TN870.5.G58 2003**
  Richard
Petroleum Geoscience. Trade Paper. Blackwell Publishing, Inc. Malden, MA. 2003. 376p. ISBN:0-632-03767-9, ISBN13: 978-0-632-03767-4. Dewey:553.2/8. LCCN:2002-015310.

Audience: **u,f.** *Choice, 2004.*

Hunt, John M.   **TN870.5.H86 1996**
Petroleum Geochemistry and Geology. Ed. 2. Cloth over Boards. Worth Publishers, Inc. New York, NY. 1995. 743p. ISBN:0-7167-2441-3, ISBN13: 978-0-7167-2441-4. Dewey:553.2/8. LCCN:79-001281.

Audience: **u,f.**

Hyne, Norman J.   **TN865.H96 1990**
Dictionary of Petroleum Exploration, Drilling and Production. Trade Cloth. PennWell Corporation. Tulsa, OK. 1991. 625p. ISBN:0-87814-352-1, ISBN13: 978-0-87814-352-8. Dewey:622/.3382/03. LCCN:90-028584.

Audience: **g,l,u,f.**

Hyne, Norman J.   **TN870.5.H9624 2001**
Nontechnical Guide to Petroleum Geology, Exploration, Drilling, and Production. Ed. 2. Trade Cloth. PennWell

Corporation. Tulsa, OK. 2001. 598p. ISBN:0-87814-823-X, ISBN13: 978-0-87814-823-3. Dewey:665.5. LCCN:2002-279429.

Audience: **g,l,u,f.**

Lyons, William C. & Plisga,   **TN870.S6233 2005**
  Gary J.
Standard Handbook of Petroleum and Natural Gas Engineering. Ed. 2. Trade Cloth. Elsevier Science & Technology Books. Saint Louis, MO. 2004. 1568p. ISBN:0-7506-7785-6, ISBN13: 978-0-7506-7785-1. Dewey:665.5. LCCN:2004-056285.

Audience: **u,f.**

Selley, Richard C.   **TN870.5.S425 1998**
Elements of Petroleum Geology. Ed. 2. Cloth Text. Elsevier Science & Technology Books. Saint Louis, MO. 1997. 470p. ISBN:0-12-636370-6, ISBN13: 978-0-12-636370-8. Dewey:553.2/82. LCCN:97-074392.

Audience: **u,f.**

USGS World Energy   **G3201.H8**
  Assessment Team
☐ U.S. Geological Survey World Petroleum Assessment 2000: Description and Results.
http://purl.access.gpo.gov/GPO/LPS28935
U.S. Geological Survey.

Audience: **g,l,u,f.**

Economic Geology and Mineral Resources > Non-Metallic Resource Deposits > Evaporites

Laszlo, Pierre & Mader,   **TN900**
  Mary Beth
Salt: Grain of Life. Trade Cloth. DIANE Publishing Company. Collingdale, PA. 2005. 193p. ISBN:0-7567-8836-6, ISBN13: 978-0-7567-8836-0. Dewey:553.6/3.

Audience: **g,l,u,f.** *Choice, 2002.*

Schreiber, B. Charlotte   **QE471.15.E8E925 1988**
  (Editor)
Evaporites and Hydrocarbons. Cloth Text. Columbia University Press. New York, NY. 1988. 496p. ISBN:0-231-06530-2, ISBN13: 978-0-231-06530-6. Dewey:552/.5. LCCN:88-013998.

Audience: **u,f.** *Choice, 1989.*

Warren, J. K.   **QE471.15.E8**
Evaporites: Sedimentology, Resources and Hydrocarbon. Trade Cloth. Springer. New York, NY. 2006. xvi, 1036p. ISBN:3-540-26011-0, ISBN13: 978-3-540-26011-0. Dewey:552.5. LCCN:2005-932089.

Audience: **u,f.** *Choice, 2006.*

Economic Geology and Mineral Resources > Non-Metallic Resource Deposits > Building Stone

U.S. Geological Survey   **TA426**
☐ Dimension Stone: Statistics and Information.
http://purl.access.gpo.gov/GPO/LPS56599
U.S. Geological Survey.

Audience: **g,l,u,f.**

Winkler, E. M.   TA426 .W55 1994
Stone in Architecture: Properties, Durability. Ed. 3. Trade Cloth.
Springer. New York, NY. 2002. XVI, 313p.
ISBN:3-540-57626-6, ISBN13: 978-3-540-57626-6.
Dewey:624.1/832. LCCN:94-020332.
         Audience: **u,f.**

Economic Geology and Mineral Resources > Non-Metallic Resource Deposits > Aggregates

Langer, William H.   TN939
Natural Aggregates of the Conterminous United States. U.S.
Geological Survey. 1988. USGS Bulletin 1594
         Audience: **g,l,u,f.**

Langer, William H.   TN939
☐ Natural Aggregates of the Conterminous United States
(USGS Bulletin 1594).
http://purl.access.gpo.gov/GPO/LPS50662
U.S. Government Printing Office; U.S. Geological Survey.
         Audience: **g,l,u,f.**

Langer, William H. &   TN939
   Glanzman, V. M.
Natural Aggregate: Building America's Future. U.S. Government
Printing Office; U.S. Geological Survey. 1993. U.S. Geological
Survey Circular 1110
         Audience: **g,l,u,f.**

Langer, William H. &   TN939
   Glanzman, V. M.
☐ Natural Aggregate: Building America's Future (USGS
Circular 1110).
http://pubs.er.usgs.gov/usgspubs/cir/cir1110
U.S. Government Printing Office; U.S. Geological Survey.
         Audience: **g,l,u,f.**

U.S. Geological Survey   TN939
☐ Natural Aggregates.
http://minerals.usgs.gov/minerals/pubs/commodity/aggregates/
U.S. Geological Survey.
         Audience: **g,l,u,f.**

Economic Geology and Mineral Resources > Gemology

Kievlenko Evgenii   QE392.K475 2003
   IAkovlevich
Geology of Gems. Art Soregaroli. Ocean Pictures. 2003.
ISBN:5-900395-25-1, ISBN13: 978-5-900395-25-8.
         Audience: **u,f.**

Mohsen Manutchehr-Danai,   QE392
   Regensburg
Dictionary of Gems and Gemology. Ed. 2. Trade Cloth.
Springer. New York, NY. 2005. X, 879p. ISBN:3-540-23970-7,
ISBN13: 978-3-540-23970-3. Dewey:553.803.
LCCN:2004-116870.
         Audience: **g,l,u,f.**

O'Donoghue, Michael   QE392
   (Editor)
Gems. Ed. 6. Trade Cloth. Elsevier Science & Technology
Books. Saint Louis, MO. 2006. 936p. ISBN:0-7506-5856-8,
ISBN13: 978-0-7506-5856-0. Dewey:553.8.
         Audience: **g,l,u,f.**

Economic Geology and Mineral Resources > Energy

Berinstein, Paula   TJ808
Alternative Energy: Facts, Statistics and Issues. Paper Text.
Greenwood Publishing Group, Inc. Portsmouth, NH. 2001. 232p.
Alternative Energy Ser. ISBN:1-57356-248-3, ISBN13:
978-1-57356-248-5. Dewey:333.79/4. LCCN:2001-021653.
         Audience: **g,l,u,f.** *Choice, 2002.*

Deffeyes, Kenneth S.   HD9560.4
Beyond Oil: The View from Hubbert's Peak. Trade Paper.
Farrar, Straus & Giroux. New York, NY. 2006. 224p.
ISBN:0-8090-2957-X, ISBN13: 978-0-8090-2957-0.
Dewey:333.8/23211.
         Audience: **g,l,u,f.** *Choice, 2005.*

Energy Information   TJ163
   Administration, National Energy Information Center, U.S.
   Dept. of Energy
☐ EIA - Energy Data and Analysis Publications, Reports,
Articles, and brochures.
http://purl.access.gpo.gov/GPO/LPS50025
Energy Information Administration, National Energy Information
Center, U.S. Dept. of Energy.
         Audience: **g,l,u,f.**

Energy Information   HD9502
   Administration, U.S. Department of Energy
☐ Energy Information Administration: EIA : eia.doe.gov:
Official Energy Statistics from the U. S. Government.
http://www.eia.doe.gov/
         Audience: **l,u,f.**

Goldemberg, Josbe, et al.   TJ163.2.W657 2000
World Energy Assessment: Energy and the Challenge of
Sustainability: Overview. United Nations Development
Programme Staff, United Nations Staff & World Energy Council
Staff (Authors). Trade Paper. United Nations Publications. New
York, NY. 2005. 516p. ISBN:92-1-126126-0, ISBN13:
978-92-1-126126-4. Dewey:333.79. LCCN:00-012327.
         Audience: **l,u,f.**

Salvador, Amos   TJ163.2
Energy: A Historical Perspective and 21st Century Forecast.
American Association of Petroleum Geologists. 2005. AAPG
studies in geology 54 ISBN:0-89181-061-7, ISBN13:
978-0-89181-061-2.
         Audience: **u,f.**

Tester, Jefferson W., et al.   TJ808.S85 2005
Sustainable Energy: Choosing among Options. Elisabeth M.
Drake, Michael J. Driscoll, Michael W. Golay & William A.
Peters (Authors). Trade Cloth. MIT Press. Cambridge, MA.
2005. 872p. ISBN:0-262-20153-4, ISBN13: 978-0-262-20153-7.
Dewey:333.79/4. LCCN:2005-041652.
         Audience: **l,u,f.**

Zumerchik, John   **TJ163.28.M33 2001**
Macmillan Encyclopedia of Energy. Ed. 3. Trade Cloth.
Macmillan Publishing Company, Inc. Old Tappan, NJ. 2000.

ISBN:0-02-865020-4, ISBN13: 978-0-02-865020-3.
Dewey:621.042/03. LCCN:00-062498.

Audience: **g,l,u,f.**

MATHEMATICS

This selection was designed to serve two main functions of a college library mathematics collection: to provide standard textbooks and teaching resources to support the undergraduate liberal arts curriculum, but also to go beyond it in delivering resources that satisfy the independent learner and intrigue the general reader. The General, Reference, and Recreational Mathematics sections provide broad math information and stimulation, from dictionaries to entertaining puzzles at various levels to accessible explorations of recent mathematics research. Textbooks are organized into subject categories roughly corresponding to common curriculum divisions; these reflect recent trends, such as lesser emphasis placed on plane geometry and greater on discrete mathematics, mathematical biology, number theory for computer cryptographic applications, financial mathematics, and fractals and chaotic systems. Most material is aimed at the undergraduate student or general reader with little math background, but some standard graduate-level resources are included for faculty use in preparing lectures and problem sets or for upper-level undergraduate special projects.

— Kristine Fowler

General

QA8.4
☐ Math Archives: Lessons, Tutorials and Lecture Notes.
http://archives.math.utk.edu/tutorials.html

Audience: **l,u,f.**

Aigner, Martin & Ziegler,   **QA36.A36 2004**
  Günter M.
Proofs from the Book. Ed. 3. K. H. Hofmann (Illustrator). Trade
Cloth. Springer. New York, NY. 2003. VIII, 240p.
ISBN:3-540-40460-0, ISBN13: 978-3-540-40460-6. Dewey:510.
LCCN:2003-060832.

Audience: **u,f.**

Alexanderson, Gerald   **QA43 .W553 2003**
  (Editor), et al.
The William Lowell Putnam Mathematical Competition:
Problems and Solutions 1965-1984. Leonard Klosinski & Loren
Larson (Editors). Paper Text. Cambridge University Press. New
York, NY. 2004. 160p. ISBN:0-88385-463-5, ISBN13:
978-0-88385-463-1. Dewey:510.76.

Audience: **u,f.**

Ascher, Marcia   **GN476.15**
Ethnomathematics: A Multicultural View of Mathematical Ideas.
Brooks/Cole Pub. Co.. 1991. ISBN:0-534-14880-8, ISBN13:
978-0-534-14880-5.

Audience: **g.**

Ascher, Marcia   **GN476.15**
Mathematics Elsewhere: An Exploration of Ideas Across
Cultures. Trade Paper. Princeton University Press. Princeton, NJ.
2004. 224p. ISBN:0-691-12022-6, ISBN13: 978-0-691-12022-5.
Dewey:510.

Audience: **g.** *Choice, 2003.*

Benson, Donald C.   **QA21.B46 2003**
A Smoother Pebble: Mathematical Explorations. Trade Cloth.
Oxford University Press, Inc. New York, NY. 2003. 278p.
ISBN:0-19-514436-8, ISBN13: 978-0-19-514436-9. Dewey:510.
LCCN:2002-042515.

Audience: **g.** *Choice, 2004.*

Berlekamp, Elwyn R., et al.   **QA95.B446 2001**
Winning Ways for Your Mathematical Plays, Vol. 2. Ed. 2. John
H. Conway & Richard K. Guy (Authors). Paper Text. A K
Peters, Ltd. Wellesley, MA. 2003. 473p. ISBN:1-56881-142-X,
ISBN13: 978-1-56881-142-0. Dewey:793.7/4. LCCN:00-048541.

Audience: **u,f.**

Berlekamp, Elwyn R., et al.   **QA95 .B446 2001**
Winning Ways for Your Mathematical Plays, Vol. 4. Ed. 2. John
H. Conway & Richard K. Guy (Authors). Paper Text. A K
Peters, Ltd. Wellesley, MA. 2004. 155p. ISBN:1-56881-144-6,
ISBN13: 978-1-56881-144-4. Dewey:793.7/4. LCCN:00-048541.

Audience: **u,f.**

Berlekamp, Elwyn R., et al.   **QA95.B446 2001**
Winning Ways for Your Mathematical Plays, Vol. 1. Ed. 2. John
H. Conway & Richard K. Guy (Authors). Paper Text. A K
Peters, Ltd. Wellesley, MA. 2002. 276p. ISBN:1-56881-130-6,
ISBN13: 978-1-56881-130-7. Dewey:793.7/4. LCCN:00-048541.

Audience: **u,f.**

Berlekamp, Elwyn R., et al.   **QA95**
Winning Ways for Your Mathematical Plays, Vol. 3. Ed. 2. John
H. Conway & Richard K. Guy (Authors). Paper Text. A K
Peters, Ltd. Wellesley, MA. 2003. 800p. ISBN:1-56881-143-8,
ISBN13: 978-1-56881-143-7. Dewey:793.7/4.

Audience: **u,f.**

Borwein, Jonathan, et al.   **QA12.B67 2003**
Experimentation in Mathematics: Computational Paths to
Discovery. David Bailey & Roland Girgensohn (Authors). Cloth
Text. A K Peters, Ltd. Wellesley, MA. 2004. 360p.
ISBN:1-56881-136-5, ISBN13: 978-1-56881-136-9.
Dewey:510/.72. LCCN:2003-062324.

Audience: **u,f.** *Choice, 2004.*

Burger, Edward B. &   **QA39.2.B846**
  Starbird, Michael
The Heart of Mathematics: A Guide to Effective Thinking. Trade
Cloth. Springer. New York, NY. 1999. 680p. TIMS Ser.
ISBN:0-387-98811-4, ISBN13: 978-0-387-98811-5. Dewey:510.

Audience: **g.**

Campbell, D. M., Higgins,   **QA7**
  C. (Editors)
Mathematics: People, Problems, Results. Wadsworth. 1984.
ISBN:0-534-02879-9, ISBN13: 978-0-534-02879-4.

Audience: **g.**

Casti, John L.   **QA26**
Five Golden Rules: Great Theories of 20th-Century
Mathematics-and Why They Matter. Trade Paper. John Wiley &
Sons, Inc. Hoboken, NJ. 1997. 256p. ISBN:0-471-19337-2,
ISBN13: 978-0-471-19337-1. Dewey:510.9/04.
LCCN:94-044470.

Audience: **g.**

Chang, Gengzhe &   **QA601.C53 1997**
  Sederberg, Thomas
Over and over Again. Trade Paper. Mathematical Association of
America. Washington, DC. 1998. 323p. New Mathematical
Library ISBN:0-88385-641-7, ISBN13: 978-0-88385-641-3.
Dewey:511.4. LCCN:97-074344.

Audience: **g,l,u.** *Choice, 1998.*

Cipra, Barry   **QA303.C578 2000**
Misteaks... and How to Find Them Before the Teacher Does: A
Calculus Supplement. Ed. 3. Paper Text. A K Peters, Ltd.
Wellesley, MA. 2000. 69p. ISBN:1-56881-122-5, ISBN13:
978-1-56881-122-2. Dewey:515. LCCN:00-024778.

Audience: **l,u.**

Cipra, Barry   **QA3**
What's Happening in the Mathematical Sciences. Trade Paper.
American Mathematical Society. Providence, RI. 2002. 95p.
What's Happening in the Mathematical Sciences Ser., Vol. 5
ISBN:0-8218-2904-1, ISBN13: 978-0-8218-2904-2. Dewey:510.

Audience: **g,l,u,f.**

Cole, K. C.   **QA36 .C65 1999**
The Universe and the Teacup: The Mathematics of Truth and
Beauty. Trade Paper. Harcourt Trade Publishers. New York, NY.
1999. 224p. ISBN:0-15-600656-1, ISBN13: 978-0-15-600656-9.
Dewey:510.

Audience: **g.**

Conquest, Wendy (Produced by), et al.   GV791

The Math Life. Bob Drake & Daniel N. Rockmore (Produced by). Video, VHS Format. Films Media Group. Princeton, NJ. 2002. ISBN:0-7365-5978-7, ISBN13: 978-0-7365-5978-2. Dewey:797.1/23.

Audience: **g.**

Courant, Richard, et al.   QA37.2.C69 1996

What Is Mathematics?: An Elementary Approach to Ideas and Methods. Ed. 2. Herbert Robbins & Ian Stewart (Authors). Paper Text. Oxford University Press, Inc. New York, NY. 1996. 592p. ISBN:0-19-510519-2, ISBN13: 978-0-19-510519-3. Dewey:510. LCCN:95-053803.

Audience: **g,l,u,f.** *B*

Daepp, Ulrich & Gorkin, Pamela   QA13.D34 2003

Reading, Writing, and Proving: A Closer Look at Mathematics. Trade Cloth. Springer. New York, NY. 2003. 408p. Undergraduate Texts in Mathematics Ser. ISBN:0-387-00834-9, ISBN13: 978-0-387-00834-9. Dewey:510. LCCN:2003-045420.

Audience: **l,u.** *Choice, 2004.*

De Pillis, John   QA99

777 Mathematical Conversation Starters. Paper Text. Mathematical Association of America. Washington, DC. 2004. 360p. MAA-Spectrum Ser. ISBN:0-88385-540-2, ISBN13: 978-0-88385-540-9. Dewey:510.2. LCCN:2002-107969.

Audience: **g.** *Choice, 2003.*

Devlin, Keith J.   QA93

Millennium Problems: The Seven Greatest Unsolved Mathematical Puzzles of Our Time. Paper Text. Basic Books. New York, NY. 2003. 256p. ISBN:0-465-01730-4, ISBN13: 978-0-465-01730-0. Dewey:510. LCCN:2003-535468.

Audience: **g.** *Choice, 2003.*

Dyke, Philip Peter George   QA20

Managing Mathematical Projects - With Success!. Trade Paper. Springer. New York, NY. 2003. XIX, 266p. Springer Undergraduate Mathematics Ser. ISBN:1-85233-736-2, ISBN13: 978-1-85233-736-0. Dewey:510/.71/1. LCCN:2003-060692.

Audience: **l,u,f.**

Fowler, Kristine K.   Z6651

Using the Mathematics Literature, Vol. 66. Paper over Boards. Marcel Dekker Inc. New York, NY. 2004. 475p. Library and Information Science Ser., Vol. 64 ISBN:0-8247-5035-7, ISBN13: 978-0-8247-5035-0. Dewey:510. LCCN:2005-302046.

Audience: **u,f.**

Gaither, Carl C. & Cavazos-Gaither, Alma E.   QA99.M363 1998

Mathematically Speaking: A Dictionary of Quotations. Perfect. Institute of Physics Publishing. Philadelphia, PA. 1998. 484p. Speaking Ser. ISBN:0-7503-0503-7, ISBN13: 978-0-7503-0503-7. Dewey:510. LCCN:98-006351.

Audience: **g.** *Choice, 1999.*

Gleason, A. M. (Editor), et al.   QA43

The William Lowell Putnam Mathematical Competition: Problems and Solutions, 1938-1964. R. E. Greenwood & L. M. Kelly (Editors). Trade Cloth. Mathematical Association of America. Washington, DC. 1980. 652p. ISBN:0-88385-428-7, ISBN13: 978-0-88385-428-0. Dewey:510.76. LCCN:80-080493.

Audience: **u,f.**

Gowers, Timothy   QA93.G69 2002

Mathematics: A Very Short Introduction. Other. Oxford University Press, Inc. New York, NY. 2002. 156p. Very Short Introductions Ser. ISBN:0-19-285361-9, ISBN13: 978-0-19-285361-5. Dewey:510. LCCN:2002-072741.

Audience: **g.**

Hardy, G. H.   QA7 .H3 1992

A Mathematician's Apology. C. P. Snow (Foreword by). Trade Paper. Cambridge University Press. New York, NY. 1992. 153p. A Canto Book Ser. ISBN:0-521-42706-1, ISBN13: 978-0-521-42706-7. Dewey:510. LCCN:91-036386.

Audience: **g.** *B*

Hayes, David & Shubin, Tatiana (Editors)   QA7.M34443 2004

Mathematical Adventures for Students and Amateurs. Trade Paper. Mathematical Association of America. Washington, DC. 2004. 304p. MAA-Spectrum Ser. ISBN:0-88385-548-8, ISBN13: 978-0-88385-548-5. Dewey:510. LCCN:2004-104647.

Audience: **g,l,u.**

Hazewinkel, Michiel   QA5

Encyclopaedia of Mathematics. Ed. 2. Trade Cloth. Springer London, Ltd. Guildford, 2000. 620p. ISBN:0-7923-6114-8, ISBN13: 978-0-7923-6114-5. Dewey:510/.3.

Audience: **l,u,f.**

Henrion, Claudia   QA27.5.H46 1997

Women in Mathematics: The Addition of Difference. Trade Cloth. Indiana University Press. Bloomington, IN. 1997. 328p. ISBN:0-253-33279-6, ISBN13: 978-0-253-33279-0. Dewey:305.43/51. LCCN:97-002546.

Audience: **l,u,f.** *Choice, 1998.*

Higham, Nicholas J.   QA42.H54 1998

Handbook of Writing for the Mathematical Sciences. Ed. 2. Trade Cloth. Society for Industrial & Applied Mathematics. Philadelphia, PA. 1998. xvi + 302p. Miscellaneous Titles in Applied Mathematics Ser., No. OT63 ISBN:0-89871-420-6, ISBN13: 978-0-89871-420-3. Dewey:808/.06651. LCCN:98-007284.

Audience: **u.**

Hilton, Peter J., et al.   QA93.H533 2000

Mathematical Vistas: From a Room with Many Windows. Derek A. Holton & Jean J. Pedersen (Authors), Sheldon J. Axler, F. W. Gehring & K. A. Ribet (Editors). Trade Cloth. Springer. New York, NY. 2002. XIV, 335p. Undergraduate Texts in Mathematics ISBN:0-387-95064-8, ISBN13: 978-0-387-95064-8. Dewey:510. LCCN:00-056268.

Audience: **l,u.**

James, Glenn & James, Robert C.   QA5

The Mathematics Dictionary. Ed. 4. Cloth Text. John Wiley & Sons, Inc. Hoboken, NJ. 1976. 517p. ISBN:0-442-24091-0, ISBN13: 978-0-442-24091-2. Dewey:510/.3/21. LCCN:76-000233.

Audience: **g.** *B*

Kedlaya, Kiran S., et al.   QA43 .W542 2002

The William Lowell Putnam Mathematical Competition, 1985-2000: Problems, Solutions and Commentary. Bjorn Poonen & Ravi Vakil (Authors). Cloth Text. Mathematical Association of America. Washington, DC. 2003. 352p. Spectrum Ser.

ISBN:0-88385-807-X, ISBN13: 978-0-88385-807-3.
Dewey:510.76. LCCN:2002-107972.
Audience: **u,f.** *Choice, 2003.*

King, Jerry P.   **QA36.K47 2006**
The Art of Mathematics. Trade Paper. Dover Publications, Inc.
Mineola, NY. 2006. 320p. ISBN:0-486-45020-1, ISBN13:
978-0-486-45020-9. Dewey:510. LCCN:2005-056062.
Audience: **g.** *Choice, 1992.*

Krantz, Steven   **QA63.K73 1997**
Techniques of Problem Solving. Trade Paper. American
Mathematical Society. Providence, RI. 1996. 465p.
ISBN:0-8218-0619-X, ISBN13: 978-0-8218-0619-7.
Dewey:510/.76. LCCN:96-023878.
Audience: **l,u.** *Choice, 1997.*

Krantz, Steven George   **QA42.K73 1997**
A Primer of Mathematical Writing: Being a Disquisition on
Having Your Ideas Recorded, Typeset, Published, Read and
Appreciated. Trade Paper. American Mathematical Society.
Providence, RI. 1996. 223p. ISBN:0-8218-0635-1, ISBN13:
978-0-8218-0635-7. Dewey:808/.0665. LCCN:96-045732.
Audience: **u.** *Choice, 1997.*

Kuczma, Marcin   **QA43**
International Mathematical Olympiads, 1986-1999. Trade Paper.
Mathematical Association of America. Washington, DC. 2003.
202p. Problem Bks. ISBN:0-88385-811-8, ISBN13:
978-0-88385-811-0. Dewey:510/.76. LCCN:2003-103065.
Audience: **l,u,f.** *Choice, 2004.*

Körner, T. W.   **QA93 .K65 1996**
The Pleasures of Counting. Trade Cloth. Cambridge University
Press. New York, NY. 1996. 544p. ISBN:0-521-56087-X,
ISBN13: 978-0-521-56087-0. Dewey:510. LCCN:97-108334.
Audience: **g.** *Choice, 1997.*

Lambert, Stephen E. &   **QA10.5.L36 2006**
  Decotis, Ruth
Great Jobs for Math Majors. Ed. 2. Trade Paper, Perfect.
McGraw-Hill Companies, The. New York, NY. 2005. 208p.
ISBN:0-07-144859-4, ISBN13: 978-0-07-144859-8.
Dewey:510/.23. LCCN:2005-047956.
Audience: **l,u.**

Lang, Serge A.   **QA7.L286 1999**
Math Talks for Undergraduates. Trade Cloth. Springer. New
York, NY. 1999. X, 121p. ISBN:0-387-98749-5, ISBN13:
978-0-387-98749-1. Dewey:510. LCCN:98-055410.
Audience: **l,u.** *Choice, 2000.*

Liebeck, M. W.   **QA8.4**
Concise Introduction to Pure Mathematics. Chapman &
Hall/CRC. 2000. ISBN:1-58488-193-3, ISBN13:
978-1-58488-193-3.
Audience: **l,u.**

Nelsen, Roger B.   **QA90.N385 1993**
Proofs Without Words: Exercises in Visual Thinking. Paper Text.
Mathematical Association of America. Washington, DC. 1997.
160p. Classroom Resource Materials Ser. ISBN:0-88385-700-6,
ISBN13: 978-0-88385-700-7. Dewey:510. LCCN:93-086338.
Audience: **l,u,f.** *Choice, 1994.*

Nelsen, Roger B. (Editor)   **QA90.N383 2000**
Proofs Without Words II: More Exercises in Visual Thinking.
Paper Text. Mathematical Association of America. Washington,

DC. 2000. 142p. Classroom Resource Materials Ser.
ISBN:0-88385-721-9, ISBN13: 978-0-88385-721-2. Dewey:510.
LCCN:00-108051.
Audience: **l,u,f.**

Newman, James R. (Editor)   **QA37.2**
The World of Mathematics, Set. Trade Paper. Dover
Publications, Inc. Mineola, NY. 2003. ISBN:0-486-43268-8,
ISBN13: 978-0-486-43268-7. Dewey:510.
Audience: **g.**

Nolan, Deborah (Editor)   **QA27.5.W68 1997**
Women in Mathematics: Scaling the Heights. Trade Paper.
Mathematical Association of America. Washington, DC. 1998.
131p. Notes Ser. ISBN:0-88385-156-3, ISBN13:
978-0-88385-156-2. Dewey:510/.82/0973. LCCN:97-074342.
Audience: **l,u,f.** *Choice, 1998.*

Odifreddi, Piergiorgio   **QA26.O3513 2004**
The Mathematical Century: The 30 Greatest Problems of the
Last 100 Years. Arturo Sangalli (Translator). Trade Cloth.
Princeton University Press. Princeton, NJ. 2004. 224p.
ISBN:0-691-09294-X, ISBN13: 978-0-691-09294-2.
Dewey:510/.9/04. LCCN:2003-056324.
Audience: **l,u,f.** *Choice, 2004.*

Olive, Jenny   **QA39.2.O434 2003**
Maths: A Self-Help Workbook for Science and Engineering
Students. Ed. 2. Trade Paper. Cambridge University Press. New
York, NY. 2003. 648p. ISBN:0-521-01707-6, ISBN13:
978-0-521-01707-7. Dewey:510.
Audience: **l.**

Olson, Steve   **QA20.3.O47 2004**
Count Down: Six Kids Vie for Glory at the World's Toughest
Math Competition. Trade Cloth. Houghton Mifflin Company
Trade & Reference Division. Boston, MA. 2004. 256p.
ISBN:0-618-25141-3, ISBN13: 978-0-618-25141-4.
Dewey:510/.79. LCCN:2003-056897.
Audience: **g.**

Parker, Marla (Editor)   **QA27.5.S53 1995**
She Does Math!: Real-Life Problems from Women on the Job.
Paper Text. Mathematical Association of America. Washington,
DC. 1995. 272p. Classroom Resource Materials Ser.
ISBN:0-88385-702-2, ISBN13: 978-0-88385-702-1.
Dewey:510/.23. LCCN:95-076294.
Audience: **g,l,u,f.** *Choice, 1996.*

Peterson, Ivars   **QA93**
The Mathematical Tourist: New and Updated Snapshots of
Modern Mathematics. Trade Paper. Henry Holt & Company.
New York, NY. 1998. 288p. ISBN:0-8050-7159-8, ISBN13:
978-0-8050-7159-7. Dewey:510.
Audience: **g.**

Peterson, Ivars   **QA99.P47 2002**
Mathematical Treks: From Surreal Numbers to Magic Circles.
Trade Paper. Mathematical Association of America. Washington,
DC. 2002. 182p. Spectrum Ser. ISBN:0-88385-537-2, ISBN13:
978-0-88385-537-9. Dewey:510. LCCN:2001-098094.
Audience: **g.** *Choice, 2002.*

Polya, G.   QA63.P6 2004
How to Solve It: A New Aspect of Mathematical Method. Ed. 2.
Trade Paper. Princeton University Press. Princeton, NJ. 2004.
288p. Princeton Science Library ISBN:0-691-11966-X, ISBN13:
978-0-691-11966-3. Dewey:510. LCCN:2004-100613.

Audience: **l,u.**

Rothstein, Edward   ML3800.R62 2006
Emblems of Mind: The Inner Life of Music and Mathematics.
Trade Paper. University of Chicago Press. Chicago, IL. 2006.
284p. ISBN:0-226-72954-0, ISBN13: 978-0-226-72954-1.
Dewey:780/.051. LCCN:2005-032822.

Audience: **g.** *Choice, 1995.*

Schattschneider, Doris &   NC263.E83S3 2004
  Escher, M. C.
M. C. Escher: Visions of Symmetry. Ed. 2. Trade Cloth. Harry
N. Abrams, Inc. New York, NY. 2004. 384p.
ISBN:0-8109-4308-5, ISBN13: 978-0-8109-4308-7.
Dewey:760/.092. LCCN:2003-025109.

Audience: **g.** *Choice, 2004.*

Schoenfeld, Alan H.   QA63.S35 1985
Mathematical Problem Solving. Trade Cloth. Elsevier Science &
Technology Books. Saint Louis, MO. 1985.
ISBN:0-12-628870-4, ISBN13: 978-0-12-628870-4.
Dewey:511.3. LCCN:85-001360.

Audience: **l,u,f.**

Sterrett, Andrew (Editor)   QA10.5.A15 2002
101 Careers in Mathematics. Ed. 2. Perfect. Mathematical
Association of America. Washington, DC. 2002. 360p.
Classroom Resource Materials Ser. ISBN:0-88385-728-6,
ISBN13: 978-0-88385-728-1. Dewey:510/.23.
LCCN:2002-114178.

Audience: **g,l,u,f.** *Choice, 1997.*

Stewart, Ian   QA93.S736 1997
The Magical Maze: Seeing the World Through Mathematical
Eyes. Trade Cloth. John Wiley & Sons, Inc. Hoboken, NJ. 1998.
268p. ISBN:0-471-19297-X, ISBN13: 978-0-471-19297-8.
Dewey:510. LCCN:98-013185.

Audience: **g.** *Choice, 1998.*

Tannenbaum, Peter &   QA36.T35 2006
  Arnold, Robert
Excursions in Modern Mathematics. Ed. 6. Cloth Text. Pearson
Education. Boston, MA. 2006. 640p. ISBN:0-13-187363-6,
ISBN13: 978-0-13-187363-6. Dewey:510. LCCN:2006-044809.

Audience: **g.**

Tanton, James   QA43.T36 2001
Solve This: Math Activities for Students and Clubs. Paper Text.
Mathematical Association of America. Washington, DC. 2001.
232p. Classroom Resource Materials Ser. ISBN:0-88385-717-0,
ISBN13: 978-0-88385-717-5. Dewey:510/.76.
LCCN:2002-278862.

Audience: **g,l,u,f.** *Choice, 2002.*

Ueno, Kenji, et al.   QA445.U3613 2003
A Mathematical Gift I: The Interplay Between Topology,
Functions, Geometry, and Algebra. Kaoji Shiga & S. Morita
(Authors). Trade Paper. American Mathematical Society.
Providence, RI. 2003. 136p. Mathematical World Ser., Vol. 19
ISBN:0-8218-3282-4, ISBN13: 978-0-8218-3282-0. Dewey:516.
LCCN:2003-062778.

Audience: **l,u,f.**

Vaderlind, Paul, et al.   QA63
The Inquisitive Problem Solver. Richard Guy & Loren Larson
(Authors). Trade Paper. Mathematical Association of America.
Washington, DC. 2002. 344p. MAA Problem Books
ISBN:0-88385-806-1, ISBN13: 978-0-88385-806-6.
Dewey:510/.76. LCCN:2001-097391.

Audience: **l,u,f.** *Choice, 2003.*

Weisstein   QA8.4
☐ Eric Weisstein's World of Mathematics.
http://mathworld.wolfram.com/

Audience: **l,u,f.**

Weisstein, Eric W.   QA5.W45 2002
CRC Concise Encyclopedia of Mathematics. Ed. 2. CRC Press.
2003. ISBN:1-58488-347-2, ISBN13: 978-1-58488-347-0.

Audience: **l,u,f.**

Reference

                                                 QA8.4
☐ Math Archives: Lessons, Tutorials and Lecture Notes.
http://archives.math.utk.edu/tutorials.html

Audience: **l,u,f.**

                                                 QA1
☐ MathSciNet/Mathematical Reviews (MR).
http://www.ams.org/mathscinet/

Audience: **u,f.**

Abell, Martha L. &   QA76.95
  Braselton, James P.
Maple by Example. Ed. 3. Cloth Text. Elsevier Science &
Technology Books. Saint Louis, MO. 2005. 568p.
ISBN:0-12-088526-3, ISBN13: 978-0-12-088526-8.
Dewey:510/.28553. LCCN:2005-277776.

Audience: **l,u,f.**

Abramowitz, Milton &   QA55
  Stegun, Irene A. (Editors)
Handbook of Mathematical Functions with Formulas, Graphs
and Mathematical Tables. Trade Paper. Dover Publications, Inc.
Mineola, NY. 1965. 1046p. ISBN:0-486-61272-4, ISBN13:
978-0-486-61272-0. Dewey:515/.0212.

Audience: **u,f.**

Beyer, William H.   QA47 .H324 1978
CRC Handbook of Mathematical Sciences. Ed. 5. Trade Cloth.
C R C Press LLC. Boca Raton, FL. 1978. 992p.
ISBN:0-8493-0655-8, ISBN13: 978-0-8493-0655-6.
Dewey:510/.21/2. LCCN:78-010602.

Audience: **u,f.**

Beyer, William H. (Editor)   QA276.25.C72 1990
CRC Standard Probability and Statistics Tables and Formulae.
CRC Press. 1990. ISBN:0-8493-0680-9, ISBN13:
978-0-8493-0680-8.

Audience: **l,u,f.**

De Pillis, John   QA99
777 Mathematical Conversation Starters. Paper Text.
Mathematical Association of America. Washington, DC. 2004.
360p. MAA-Spectrum Ser. ISBN:0-88385-540-2, ISBN13:
978-0-88385-540-9. Dewey:510.2. LCCN:2002-107969.

Audience: **g.** *Choice, 2003.*

Fowler, Kristine K.   **Z6651**
Using the Mathematics Literature, Vol. 66. Paper over Boards. Marcel Dekker Inc. New York, NY. 2004. 475p. Library and Information Science Ser., Vol. 64 ISBN:0-8247-5035-7, ISBN13: 978-0-8247-5035-0. Dewey:510. LCCN:2005-302046.

         Audience: **u,f.**

Gaither, Carl C. &   **QA99.M363 1998**
  Cavazos-Gaither, Alma E.
Mathematically Speaking: A Dictionary of Quotations. Perfect. Institute of Physics Publishing. Philadelphia, PA. 1998. 484p. Speaking Ser. ISBN:0-7503-0503-7, ISBN13: 978-0-7503-0503-7. Dewey:510. LCCN:98-006351.

         Audience: **g.** *Choice, 1999.*

Gradshteyn, I. S.   **QA55.G6613 2000**
Table of Integrals, Series, and Products. Ed. 6. Alan Jeffrey & Daniel Zwillinger (Editors). Cloth Text. Elsevier Science & Technology Books. Saint Louis, MO. 2000. 1163p. ISBN:0-12-294757-6, ISBN13: 978-0-12-294757-5. Dewey:515/.0212. LCCN:00-104373.

         Audience: **u,f.**

Gratzer, George A.   **Z253.4.L38G745 2000**
Math into LaTeX. Ed. 3. Trade Cloth. Birkhauser Boston. Cambridge, MA. 2000. xxxviii, 584p. ISBN:3-7643-4131-9, ISBN13: 978-3-7643-4131-2. Dewey:686.2/2544536. LCCN:00-036088.

         Audience: **u.**

Hanselman, Duane &   **QA297.H293 2001**
  Littlefield, Bruce R.
Mastering MATLAB 6. Paper Text. Prentice Hall PTR. Upper Saddle River, NJ. 2000. 832p. ISBN:0-13-019468-9, ISBN13: 978-0-13-019468-8. Dewey:519.4/0285/53042. LCCN:00-051643.

         Audience: **l,u.**

Hazewinkel, Michiel   **QA5**
Encyclopaedia of Mathematics. Ed. 2. Trade Cloth. Springer London, Ltd. Guildford, 2000. 620p. ISBN:0-7923-6114-8, ISBN13: 978-0-7923-6114-5. Dewey:510/.3.

         Audience: **l,u,f.**

Higham, Nicholas J.   **QA42.H54 1998**
Handbook of Writing for the Mathematical Sciences. Ed. 2. Trade Cloth. Society for Industrial & Applied Mathematics. Philadelphia, PA. 1998. xvi + 302p. Miscellaneous Titles in Applied Mathematics Ser., No. OT63 ISBN:0-89871-420-6, ISBN13: 978-0-89871-420-3. Dewey:808/.06651. LCCN:98-007284.

         Audience: **u.**

Iyanaga, Shokichi &   **QA5**
  Kawada, Yukiyosi (Editors)
Encyclopedic Dictionary of Mathematics. Cloth Text. MIT Press. Cambridge, MA. 1977. xv, 1750p. ISBN:0-262-09016-3, ISBN13: 978-0-262-09016-2. Dewey:510/.3. LCCN:77-001129.

         Audience: **u,f.** *B*

James, Glenn & James,   **QA5**
  Robert C.
The Mathematics Dictionary. Ed. 4. Cloth Text. John Wiley & Sons, Inc. Hoboken, NJ. 1976. 517p. ISBN:0-442-24091-0, ISBN13: 978-0-442-24091-2. Dewey:510/.3/21. LCCN:76-000233.

         Audience: **g.** *B*

Knuth, Donald E.   **Z253.4.T47K58 1986**
The Texbook, Vol. A. Trade Paper. Addison Wesley Professional. Boston, MA. 1984. 496p. Computers and Typesetting Ser. ISBN:0-201-13448-9, ISBN13: 978-0-201-13448-3. Dewey:686.2/2544. LCCN:83-000830.

         Audience: **u.**

Kopka, Helmut & Daly,   **Z253.4.L38K66 2004**
  Patrick W.
Guide to LaTeX. Ed. 4. Mixed Media, CD-ROM, Book, Other, Trade Paper. Addison Wesley Professional. Boston, MA. 2003. 624p. ISBN:0-321-17385-6, ISBN13: 978-0-321-17385-0. Dewey:686.2/2544536. LCCN:2003-060364.

         Audience: **u.**

Krantz, Steven G.   **Z253.4.T47**
Handbook of Typography for the Mathematical Sciences. Chapman & Hall/CRC. 2001. ISBN:1-58488-149-6, ISBN13: 978-1-58488-149-0.

         Audience: **u.**

Krantz, Steven George   **QA42.K73 1997**
A Primer of Mathematical Writing: Being a Disquisition on Having Your Ideas Recorded, Typeset, Published, Read and Appreciated. Trade Paper. American Mathematical Society. Providence, RI. 1996. 223p. ISBN:0-8218-0635-1, ISBN13: 978-0-8218-0635-7. Dewey:808/.0665. LCCN:96-045732.

         Audience: **u.** *Choice, 1997.*

Lamport, Leslie   **Z253.4.L38L35 1994**
LaTeX: A Document Preparation System. Ed. 2. Trade Paper. Addison Wesley Professional. Boston, MA. 1994. 288p. ISBN:0-201-52983-1, ISBN13: 978-0-201-52983-8. Dewey:682.2/2544536. LCCN:93-039691.

         Audience: **u.**

Pearson, Carl E. (Editor)   **QA36**
Handbook of Applied Mathematics: Selected Results and Methods. Ed. 2. Cloth Text. John Wiley & Sons, Inc. Hoboken, NJ. 1983. 1304p. ISBN:0-442-23866-5, ISBN13: 978-0-442-23866-7. Dewey:510. LCCN:82-020223.

         Audience: **u,f.** *B*

Rade, Lennart &   **QA41**
  Westergren, Bertil
Mathematics Handbook for Science and Engineering. Ed. 5. Trade Cloth. Springer. New York, NY. 2004. 562p. ISBN:3-540-21141-1, ISBN13: 978-3-540-21141-9. Dewey:510. LCCN:96-124564.

         Audience: **l,u,f.** *Choice, 1996.*

Swanson, Ellen & O'Sean,   **T11.S77 1999**
  Arlene A.
Mathematics into Type. Ed. 2. Trade Paper. American Mathematical Society. Providence, RI. 1999. 102p. ISBN:0-8218-1961-5, ISBN13: 978-0-8218-1961-6. Dewey:808/.06651. LCCN:99-025448.

         Audience: **u.**

Weisstein   **QA8.4**
☐ Eric Weisstein's World of Mathematics.
http://mathworld.wolfram.com/

         Audience: **l,u,f.**

Weisstein, Eric W.   **QA5.W45 2002**
CRC Concise Encyclopedia of Mathematics. Ed. 2. CRC Press. 2003. ISBN:1-58488-347-2, ISBN13: 978-1-58488-347-0.

         Audience: **l,u,f.**

Wolfram, Stephen   QA76.95.W65 2003
The Mathematica Book. Ed. 5. Trade Cloth. Penguin Group
(USA) Inc. New York, NY. 2004. 1464p. ISBN:1-57955-022-3,
ISBN13: 978-1-57955-022-6. Dewey:510/.285/5369.
LCCN:2003-053794.
                                              Audience: **l,u.**

Zwillinger, Daniel   QA371
Handbook of Differential Equations. Ed. 3. Trade Cloth. Elsevier
Science & Technology Books. Saint Louis, MO. 1997. 801p.
ISBN:0-12-784395-7, ISBN13: 978-0-12-784395-7.
Dewey:515.3/5. LCCN:97-038072.
                             Audience: **u,f.** *Choice, 1989.*

Zwillinger, Daniel (Editor)   QA47
CRC Standard Mathematical Tables and Formulas. Ed. 31. CRC
Press. 2003. ISBN:1-58488-291-3, ISBN13: 978-1-58488-291-6.
                                            Audience: **l,u,f.**

Mathematics Education

Bishop, Alan J. & Clements,   QA11.2
M. A. (Ken)
Second International Handbook of Mathematics Education. Ed.
2. Christine Keitel, Jeremy Kilpatrick & Frederick K. S. Leung
(Editors). Trade Cloth. Springer. New York, NY. 2003. 1000p.
Kluwer International Handbooks of Education, Vol. 10
ISBN:1-4020-1008-7, ISBN13: 978-1-4020-1008-8.
Dewey:510/.71. LCCN:2002-044708.
                                              Audience: **u,f.**

Campbell, Stephen R. &   QA241
Zazkis, Rina (Editors)
Learning and Teaching Number Theory: Research in Cognition
and Instruction. Trade Cloth. Greenwood Publishing Group, Inc.
Portsmouth, NH. 2001. 256p. Mathematics, Learning, and
Cognition Ser., Vol. 2 ISBN:1-56750-652-6, ISBN13:
978-1-56750-652-5. Dewey:510 s 512/.7071.
LCCN:2001-031649.
                             Audience: **u,f.** *Choice, 2002.*

Carpenter, Thomas P., et al.   QA135.5.C4947 1999
Children's Mathematics: Cognitively Guided Instruction.
Elizabeth Fennema, Susan B. Empson, Megan Loef Franke &
Linda Levi (Authors). CD-ROM. Heinemann. Portsmouth, NH.
1999. 128p. ISBN:0-325-00137-5, ISBN13: 978-0-325-00137-1.
Dewey:372.7/044. LCCN:98-49595.
                                                Audience: **u.**

Chapin, Suzanne H. &   QA135.5.C455 2000
Johnson, Art
Math Matters: Understanding the Math You Teach, Grades K-6.
Trade Paper. Math Solutions Publications. Sausalito, CA. 2000.
238p. ISBN:0-941355-26-8, ISBN13: 978-0-941355-26-1.
Dewey:372.7. LCCN:00-032423.
                                              Audience: **l,u.**

Crannell, Annalisa (Author,   QA43.W75 2004
Author, Author)
Writing Projects for Mathematics Courses: Crushed Clowns,
Cars, and Coffee to Go. Perfect. Mathematical Association of
America. Washington, DC. 2003. 128p. Classroom Resource
Materials Ser. ISBN:0-88385-735-9, ISBN13:
978-0-88385-735-9. Dewey:510/.76. LCCN:2003-113542.
                                                Audience: **f.**

Dalton, LeRoy C. & Snyder,   QA7 .T63 1983
Henry D.
Topics for Mathematics Clubs. Ed. 2. Trade Paper. National
Council of Teachers of Mathematics. Reston, VA. 1983. 106p.
ISBN:0-87353-208-2, ISBN13: 978-0-87353-208-2. Dewey:510.
LCCN:83-008296.
                                             Audience: **l,u,f.**

Day, Roger   QA461.N3143 2001
Navigating Through Geometry in Grades 9-12. Johnny W. Lott
& Peggy House (Editors). Trade Paper. National Council of
Teachers of Mathematics. Reston, VA. 2002. 152p. Navigating
Through Geometry Ser. ISBN:0-87353-514-6, ISBN13:
978-0-87353-514-4. Dewey:516/.0071/273. LCCN:2001-055854.
                                              Audience: **l,u.**

Driscoll, Mark J.   QA159.D74 1999
Fostering Algebraic Thinking: A Guide for Teachers, Grades
6-10. Trade Paper. Heinemann. Portsmouth, NH. 1999. 176p.
ISBN:0-325-00154-5, ISBN13: 978-0-325-00154-8.
Dewey:512/.071/2. LCCN:98-51138.
                                                Audience: **u.**

Easterday, Kenneth et al   QA16
Activities for Junior High and Middle School Mathematics, Vol.
1. Henry, Loren & Simpson, F. Morgan: Kenneth Easterday
(Editor) ; Loren Henry (Editor) ; F. Morgan Simpson (Editor).
National Council of Teachers of Mathematics. 1981.
ISBN:0-87353-188-4, ISBN13: 978-0-87353-188-7.
                                                Audience: **u.**

Easterday, Kenneth (Editor),   QA16 .A27 1981
et al.
Activities for Junior High and Middle School Mathematics, Vol.
2. Loren Henry & F. Morgan Simpson (Editors). Trade Paper.
National Council of Teachers of Mathematics. Reston, VA.
1999. 391p. ISBN:0-87353-465-4, ISBN13: 978-0-87353-465-9.
Dewey:510/.7/12. LCCN:81-014024.
                                                Audience: **u.**

Ernest, Paul A.   QA11.E74 1990
The Philosophy of Mathematics Education. Trade Paper. Taylor
& Francis Group. Philadelphia, PA. 1991. 346p.
ISBN:1-85000-667-9, ISBN13: 978-1-85000-667-1.
Dewey:510/.71. LCCN:90-003618.
                              Audience: **u.** *Choice, 1991.*

Friel, Susan N. & House,   QA461.N32 2002
Peggy A. (Editors)
Navigating Through Geometry in Grades 6-8. Trade Paper.
National Council of Teachers of Mathematics. Reston, VA.
2002. 128p. Principles and Standards for School Mathematics
Navigations Ser. ISBN:0-87353-513-8, ISBN13:
978-0-87353-513-7. Dewey:516/.0071/2. LCCN:2002-283284.
                                                Audience: **u.**

Gavosto, Estela A. (Editor),   QA11.A1 C68 1999
et al.
Contemporary Issues in Mathematics Education. Steven George
Krantz & William McCallum (Editors), Silvio Levy
(Contribution by). Trade Paper. Cambridge University Press.
New York, NY. 1999. 190p. Mathematical Sciences Research
Institute Publications, No. 36 ISBN:0-521-65471-8, ISBN13:
978-0-521-65471-5. Dewey:510/.71. LCCN:99-034737.
                                              Audience: **u,f.**

Hoyles, Celia   QA11.R484 1999
Rethinking the Mathematics Curriculum. Paper over Boards.
Taylor & Francis Group. Philadelphia, PA. 1998. 270p.
ISBN:0-7507-0939-1, ISBN13: 978-0-7507-0939-2.
Dewey:510/.71. LCCN:99-171094.
                              Audience: **u,f.**

Johnson, David   QA11
Every Minute Counts: Making Your Math Class Work. Paper
Text. Dale Seymour Publications. White Plains, NY. 1997. 66p.
ISBN:0-86651-081-8, ISBN13: 978-0-86651-081-3.
Dewey:510.712.
                              Audience: **u.**

Johnson, David   QA11.J5823 1994
Motivation Counts. Paper Text. Dale Seymour Publications.
White Plains, NY. 1997. 98p. ISBN:0-86651-740-5, ISBN13:
978-0-86651-740-9. Dewey:510.7. LCCN:94-179123.
                              Audience: **u.**

Katz, Victor & Michalowica,   QA21
Karen Dee (Editors)
Historical Modules for the Teaching and Learning of
Mathematics. CD-ROM. Mathematical Association of America.
Washington, DC. 2005. Classroom Resource Material Ser.
ISBN:0-88385-741-3, ISBN13: 978-0-88385-741-0.
Dewey:372.7.
                              Audience: **u,f.**

Kilpatrick, J Swafford.   QA135.5
Findell, B. (eds.)
Adding It Up: Helping Children Learn Mathematics.
http://books.nap.edu/books/0309069955/html/index.html
                              Audience: **u.**

Kilpatrick, Jeremy (Editor),   QA13.R462 2003
et al.
A Research Companion to "Principles and Standards for School
Mathematics". W. Gary Martin & Deborah Schifter (Editors).
Trade Paper. National Council of Teachers of Mathematics.
Reston, VA. 2003. 413p. ISBN:0-87353-537-5, ISBN13:
978-0-87353-537-3. Dewey:510/.71/073. LCCN:2003-273035.
                              Audience: **u,f.**

Kilpatrick, Jeremy (Editor),   QA135.5.A32 2001
et al.
Adding It Up: Helping Children Learn Mathematics. Jane
Swafford & Bradford Findell (Editors). Trade Cloth. National
Academies Press. Washington, DC. 2001. 480p.
ISBN:0-309-06995-5, ISBN13: 978-0-309-06995-3.
Dewey:372.7. LCCN:2001-001734.
                              Audience: **l,u.**

Lajoie, Susanne P. (Editor)   QA276.18.R44 1998
Reflections on Statistics: Agendas for Learning, Teaching, and
Assessment in K-12. Cloth over Boards. Lawrence Erlbaum
Associates, Inc. Mahwah, NJ. 1998. 360p. The Studies in
Mathematical Thinking and Learning ISBN:0-8058-1971-1,
ISBN13: 978-0-8058-1971-7. Dewey:519.5/071.
LCCN:97-007357.
                              Audience: **u.**

Lampert, Magdalene   QA135.6.L36 2001
Teaching Problems and the Problems of Teaching. Cloth over
Boards. Yale University Press. Cumberland, RI. 2001. 512p.
ISBN:0-300-08973-2, ISBN13: 978-0-300-08973-8.
Dewey:372.7/044/0973. LCCN:2001-002322.
                              Audience: **u.** *Choice, 2002.*

Lampert, Magdalene & Ball,   QA135.5.L25 1998
Deborah
Teaching, Multimedia and Mathematics: Investigations of Real
Practice. Trade Paper. Teachers College Press, Teachers College,
Columbia University. New York, NY. 1998. 380p. The
Practitioner Inquiry Ser. ISBN:0-8077-3757-7, ISBN13:
978-0-8077-3757-6. Dewey:372.7. LCCN:98-017105.
                              Audience: **u.** *Choice, 1999.*

Meier, John & Rishel,   QA11.M4817 1998
Thomas
Writing in the Teaching and Learning of Mathematics. Trade
Paper. Mathematical Association of America. Washington, DC.
1998. 114p. Notes Ser. ISBN:0-88385-158-X, ISBN13:
978-0-88385-158-6. Dewey:507.1. LCCN:98-086032.
                              Audience: **u,f.**

National Council of   QA13.P735 2000
Teachers of Mathematics Staff
Principles and Standards for School Mathematics. Trade Cloth.
National Council of Teachers of Mathematics. Reston, VA.
2000. xv, 402p. ISBN:0-87353-480-8, ISBN13:
978-0-87353-480-2. Dewey:510/.71. LCCN:00-032109.
                              Audience: **l,u,f.**

National Research Council   QA13.E94 1989
Staff
Everybody Counts: A Report to the Nation on the Future of
Mathematics Education. Paper Text. National Academies Press.
Washington, DC. 1989. 128p. ISBN:0-309-03977-0, ISBN13:
978-0-309-03977-2. Dewey:510/.7/1073. LCCN:88-037684.
                              Audience: **g.**

National Research Council   QA13.N37 1993
Staff
Measuring What Counts: A Conceptual Guide for Mathematics
Assessment. Paper Text. National Academies Press. Washington,
DC. 1993. 236p. ISBN:0-309-04981-4, ISBN13:
978-0-309-04981-8. Dewey:510/.71/2. LCCN:93-085917.
                              Audience: **u.**

National Research Council   QA159.N38 1998
Staff
The Nature and Role of Algebra in the K - 14 Curriculum:
Proceedings of a National Symposium. Paper Text. National
Academies Press. Washington, DC. 1998. 206p.
ISBN:0-309-06147-4, ISBN13: 978-0-309-06147-6.
Dewey:512/.071/073. LCCN:99-179839.
                              Audience: **u,f.**

National Research Council   QA13.O53 1990
Staff
On the Shoulders of Giants: New Approaches to Numeracy.
Lynn A. Steen (Editor). Trade Cloth. National Academies Press.
Washington, DC. 1990. 144p. ISBN:0-309-04234-8, ISBN13:
978-0-309-04234-5. Dewey:513/.071073. LCCN:90-041566.
                              Audience: **u.** *Choice, 1991.*

NCTM Commission on   QA11.N29 1991
Teaching Standards for School M
Professional Standards for Teaching Mathematics. Trade Paper.
National Council of Teachers of Mathematics. Reston, VA.
1991. 196p. ISBN:0-87353-307-0, ISBN13: 978-0-87353-307-2.
Dewey:510/.71. LCCN:90-026154.
                              Audience: **u,f.**

Nolan, Deborah (Editor)   QA27.5.W68 1997
Women in Mathematics: Scaling the Heights. Trade Paper.
Mathematical Association of America. Washington, DC. 1998.
131p. Notes Ser. ISBN:0-88385-156-3, ISBN13:
978-0-88385-156-2. Dewey:510/.82/0973. LCCN:97-074342.
Audience: **l,u,f.** *Choice, 1998.*

Polya, George   QA43 .P62
Mathematical Discovery: On Understanding, Learning, and
Teaching Problem Solving. Paper Text. Textbook Publishers.
Temecula, CA. 2003. ISBN:0-7581-0509-6, ISBN13:
978-0-7581-0509-7. Dewey:510/.76.
Audience: **u,f.** *B*

Powell, Arthur B. &   GN476.15.E85 1997
  Frankenstein, Marilyn (Editors)
Ethnomathematics: Challenging Eurocentrism in Mathematics
Education. Cloth Text. State University of New York Press.
Albany, NY. 1997. 440p. SUNY Series, Reform in Mathematics
Education ISBN:0-7914-3351-X, ISBN13: 978-0-7914-3351-5.
Dewey:510/.7. LCCN:96-024925.
Audience: **u,f.**

Rubenstein, Rheta Norma   QA13.R83 2003
  Pollock, et al.
Teaching and Learning Middle Grades Mathematics. Charlene E.
Beckmann & Denisse Rubilee Thompson (Authors). Trade
Cloth. Key College Publishing. Emeryville, CA. 2003. xxvi,
326p. ISBN:1-930190-94-8, ISBN13: 978-1-930190-94-8.
Dewey:510/.71/2. LCCN:2003-062039.
Audience: **u.**

Schoenfeld, Alan H.   QA63.S35 1985
Mathematical Problem Solving. Trade Cloth. Elsevier Science &
Technology Books. Saint Louis, MO. 1985.
ISBN:0-12-628870-4, ISBN13: 978-0-12-628870-4.
Dewey:511.3. LCCN:85-001360.
Audience: **l,u,f.**

Secada, Walter G. (Editor),   QA13 .N49 1995
  et al.
New Directions for Equity in Mathematics Education. Elizabeth
Fennema & Lisa Byrd (Editors). Trade Cloth. Cambridge
University Press. New York, NY. 1995. 376p.
ISBN:0-521-47152-4, ISBN13: 978-0-521-47152-7.
Dewey:510/.71. LCCN:94-019250.
Audience: **u.**

Seeger, Falk (Editor), et al.   QA11 .C785 1998
The Culture of the Mathematics Classroom: Analyses and
Changes. Jvrg Voigt & Ute Waschescio (Editors). Trade Cloth.
Cambridge University Press. New York, NY. 1998. 412p.
ISBN:0-521-57107-3, ISBN13: 978-0-521-57107-4.
Dewey:510.7/019. LCCN:97-005755.
Audience: **u.**

Skemp, Richard R.   QA11.2
Psychology of Learning Mathematics. Ed. 2. Trade Paper.
Penguin Books, Ltd. London, 1994. 304p. ISBN:0-14-013619-3,
ISBN13: 978-0-14-013619-7. Dewey:510.1/9.
Audience: **u.**

Steen, Lynn Arthur (Editor)   QA13.M1518 2001
Mathematics and Democracy: The Case for Quantitative
Literacy. National Council on Education and the Disciplines
Staff (Contribution by). Trade Cloth. Woodrow Wilson National
Fellowship Foundation. Princeton, NJ. 2001. xx, 121p.
ISBN:0-9709547-0-0, ISBN13: 978-0-9709547-0-1.
Dewey:372.7/2. LCCN:2001-275688.
Audience: **g.**

Steffe, Leslie P.   QA11.A1
Theories of Mathematics Learning. Nesher, Pearla; Cobb, Paul
(Editors). Lawrence Erlbaum. 1996. ISBN:0-8058-1661-5,
ISBN13: 978-0-8058-1661-7.
Audience: **u.**

Tobias, Sheila   Q181
They're Not Dumb, They're Different: Stalking the Second Tier.
Trade Paper. Research Corporation. Tucson, AZ. 1990. 94p.
ISBN:0-9633504-0-4, ISBN13: 978-0-9633504-0-4.
Dewey:507.1.
Audience: **u,f.**

Van de Walle, John   QA135.6.V36 2007
Elementary and Middle School Mathematics: Teaching
Developmentally. Ed. 6. Trade Paper. Allyn & Bacon, Inc.
Boston, MA. 2006. 576p. ISBN:0-205-48392-5, ISBN13:
978-0-205-48392-1. Dewey:510.71/2. LCCN:2005-057485.
Audience: **u.**

Waismann, Friedrich   QA9.W33213 2003
Introduction to Mathematical Thinking: The Formation of
Concepts in Modern Mathematics. Trade Paper. Dover
Publications, Inc. Mineola, NY. 2003. 272p. Mathematics Ser.
ISBN:0-486-42804-4, ISBN13: 978-0-486-42804-8.
Dewey:510/.1. LCCN:2002-041200.
Audience: **l,u,f.**

Mathematics History

Albers, Donald J. &   QA28.M37 1984
  Alexanderson, G. L. (Editors)
Mathematical People: Profiles and Interviews. Trade Cloth.
Birkhauser Boston. Cambridge, MA. 1986. 260p.
ISBN:0-8176-3191-7, ISBN13: 978-0-8176-3191-8.
Dewey:510/.92/2 B. LCCN:84-021602.
Audience: **g.**

Albers, Donald J. (Editor),   QA28.M67 1994
  et al.
More Mathematical People: Contemporary Conversations. Ed. 2.
Gerald L. Alexanderson & Constance Reid (Editors). Trade
Paper. Elsevier Science & Technology Books. Saint Louis, MO.
1994. 375p. ISBN:0-12-048251-7, ISBN13: 978-0-12-048251-1.
Dewey:510/.92/2. LCCN:94-021956.
Audience: **g.**

American Council of   QA28.B534 1991
  Learned Societies Staff (Editor)
Biographical Dictionary of Mathematicians, Set. Trade Cloth.
Thomson Gale. Farmington Hills, MI. 1991. 2000p.
ISBN:0-684-19282-9, ISBN13: 978-0-684-19282-6.
Dewey:510/.92/2 B. LCCN:90-052920.
Audience: **g.**

Anderson, Marlow, et al.   QA21
Sherlock Holmes in Babylon and Other Tales of Mathematical
History. Victor Katz & Robin Wilson (Authors). Cloth Text.
Mathematical Association of America. Washington, DC. 2004.
398p. Spectrum Ser. ISBN:0-88385-546-1, ISBN13:
978-0-88385-546-1. Dewey:510.9. LCCN:2003-113541.
Audience: **g.** *Choice, 2004.*

Apostol, Tom M.   **QA484**
Early History of Mathematics. Video, Other. Springer. New York, NY. 2003. 16p. ISBN:3-540-92648-8, ISBN13: 978-3-540-92648-1. Dewey:516.15.

Audience: **l,u,f.**

Ascher, Marcia   **GN476.15**
Ethnomathematics: A Multicultural View of Mathematical Ideas. Brooks/Cole Pub. Co.. 1991. ISBN:0-534-14880-8, ISBN13: 978-0-534-14880-5.

Audience: **g.**

Ascher, Marcia   **GN476.15**
Mathematics Elsewhere: An Exploration of Ideas Across Cultures. Trade Paper. Princeton University Press. Princeton, NJ. 2004. 224p. ISBN:0-691-12022-6, ISBN13: 978-0-691-12022-5. Dewey:510.

Audience: **g.** *Choice, 2003.*

Bashmakova, Isabella &   **QA151.B37 2000**
  Smirnova, Galina
The Beginnings and Evolution of Algebra. Paper Text. Mathematical Association of America. Washington, DC. 2000. 196p. Dolciani Mathematical Expositions Ser., No. 23 ISBN:0-88385-329-9, ISBN13: 978-0-88385-329-0. Dewey:512/.009. LCCN:99-068950.

Audience: **l,u,f.**

Benson, Donald C.   **QA21.B46 2003**
A Smoother Pebble: Mathematical Explorations. Trade Cloth. Oxford University Press, Inc. New York, NY. 2003. 278p. ISBN:0-19-514436-8, ISBN13: 978-0-19-514436-9. Dewey:510. LCCN:2002-042515.

Audience: **g.** *Choice, 2004.*

Berlinghoff, William &   **QA21**
  Gouvea, Fernando
Math Through the Ages: A Gentle History for Teachers and Others. Ed. 2. Cloth Text. Mathematical Association of America. Washington, DC. 2004. 288p. Classroom Resource Material Ser. ISBN:0-88385-736-7, ISBN13: 978-0-88385-736-6. Dewey:510.9. LCCN:2003-114603.

Audience: **g,l,u,f.** *Choice, 2004.*

Boyer, Carl B.   **QA21.B767 1991**
A History of Mathematics. Ed. 2. Trade Paper. John Wiley & Sons, Inc. Hoboken, NJ. 1991. 736p. ISBN:0-471-54397-7, ISBN13: 978-0-471-54397-8. Dewey:510.9. LCCN:89-005325.

Audience: **u.** *B Choice, 1989.*

Burger, Edward B. &   **QA39.2.B846**
  Starbird, Michael
The Heart of Mathematics: A Guide to Effective Thinking. Trade Cloth. Springer. New York, NY. 1999. 680p. TIMS Ser. ISBN:0-387-98811-4, ISBN13: 978-0-387-98811-5. Dewey:510.

Audience: **g.**

Clawson, Calvin C.   **QA93.C62 2001**
Mathematical Sorcery: Revealing the Secrets of Numbers. Trade Paper. Perseus Books Group. New York, NY. 2001. 312p. ISBN:0-7382-0496-X, ISBN13: 978-0-7382-0496-3. Dewey:510. LCCN:2001-097886.

Audience: **g.** *Choice, 2000.*

Devlin, Keith J.   **QA93**
Millennium Problems: The Seven Greatest Unsolved Mathematical Puzzles of Our Time. Paper Text. Basic Books.

New York, NY. 2003. 256p. ISBN:0-465-01730-4, ISBN13: 978-0-465-01730-0. Dewey:510. LCCN:2003-535468.

Audience: **g.** *Choice, 2003.*

Dick, Auguste   **QA29.N6D513**
Emmy Noether, 1882-1935. Trade Cloth. Birkhauser Boston. Cambridge, MA. 1981. 192p. ISBN:0-8176-3019-8, ISBN13: 978-0-8176-3019-5. Dewey:512/.0092/4 B.

Audience: **l,u,f.**

Dijksterhuis, E. J.   **QA31.D4813 1987**
Archimedes. Wilbur R. Knorr (Foreword by). Trade Cloth. Princeton University Press. Princeton, NJ. 1987. 434p. ISBN:0-691-08421-1, ISBN13: 978-0-691-08421-3. Dewey:510/.92/4. LCCN:86-043144.

Audience: **g.**

Dunham, William   **QA29.E8D86 1999**
Euler: The Master of Us All, Vol. 22. Paper Text. Mathematical Association of America. Washington, DC. 1999. 180p. Dolciani Mathematical Expositions Ser., Vol. 22 ISBN:0-88385-328-0, ISBN13: 978-0-88385-328-3. Dewey:510/.92 B. LCCN:98-088271.

Audience: **g.** *Choice, 1999.*

Dunnington, Waldo   **QA29.G3**
Gauss: Titan of Science. Cloth Text. Mathematical Association of America. Washington, DC. 2004. 600p. Spectrum Ser. ISBN:0-88385-538-0, ISBN13: 978-0-88385-538-6. Dewey:510.9/2.

Audience: **g.**

Edwards, C. H. Jr.   **QA303.E224**
The Historical Development of the Calculus. Ed. 3. Trade Paper. Springer. New York, NY. 1994. XII, 368p. ISBN:0-387-94313-7, ISBN13: 978-0-387-94313-8. Dewey:515/.09.

Audience: **l,u,f.** *B*

Euclid   **QA31**
The Thirteen Books of Euclid's Elements, Vol. 1. Thomas L. Heath (Editor). Trade Paper. Dover Publications, Inc. Mineola, NY. 1956. 443p. Dover Phoenix Editions Ser. ISBN:0-486-60088-2, ISBN13: 978-0-486-60088-8. Dewey:513.

Audience: **g.** *B*

Euclid   **QA31**
The Thirteen Books of Euclid's Elements, Vol. 3. Thomas L. Heath (Editor). Trade Paper. Dover Publications, Inc. Mineola, NY. 1956. 546p. Dover Phoenix Editions Ser. ISBN:0-486-60090-4, ISBN13: 978-0-486-60090-1. Dewey:513.

Audience: **g.**

Euclid   **QA31**
The Thirteen Books of Euclid's Elements, Vol. 2. Thomas L. Heath (Editor). Trade Paper. Dover Publications, Inc. Mineola, NY. 1956. 436p. Dover Phoenix Editions Ser. ISBN:0-486-60089-0, ISBN13: 978-0-486-60089-5. Dewey:513.

Audience: **g.** *B*

Eves, Howard W.   **QA21**
An Introduction to the History of Mathematics. Ed. 6. Cloth Text. Brooks/Cole. Pacific Grove, CA. 1990. 800p. Saunders Ser. ISBN:0-03-029558-0, ISBN13: 978-0-03-029558-4. Dewey:510/.9. LCCN:89-043140.

Audience: **l,u.**

Fauvel, John and Gray,   QA21
  Jeremy (Editors)
History of Mathematics: A Reader. Macmillan Education in
association with the Open University. 1987.
ISBN:0-333-42791-2, ISBN13: 978-0-333-42791-0.
                        Audience: **l,u,f.**

Gazale, Midhat J.   QA141.G39 1999
Number: From Ahmes to Cantor. Trade Cloth. Princeton
University Press. Princeton, NJ. 2000. 314p.
ISBN:0-691-00515-X, ISBN13: 978-0-691-00515-7. Dewey:513.
LCCN:99-036677.
            Audience: **l,u.** *Choice, 2000.*

Grattan-Guinness, Ivor   QA21.C645 2003
  (Editor)
Companion Encyclopedia of the History and Philosophy of the
Mathematical Sciences, Vol. 2. Trade Paper. Johns Hopkins
University Press. Baltimore, MD. 2003. 976p.
ISBN:0-8018-7397-5, ISBN13: 978-0-8018-7397-3.
Dewey:510.9. LCCN:2002-043285.
            Audience: **u,f.** *Choice, 1994.*

Grattan-Guinness, Ivor   QA21
Rainbow of Mathematics: A History of the Mathematical
Sciences. Trade Paper. W. W. Norton & Company, Inc. New
York, NY. 2000. 832p. ISBN:0-393-32030-8, ISBN13:
978-0-393-32030-5. Dewey:510.9.
                        Audience: **l,u.**

Gray, Jeremy   QA21.G7 1989
Ideas of Space: Euclidean, Non-Euclidean, and Relativistic. Ed.
2. Trade Cloth. Oxford University Press, Inc. New York, NY.
1989. 254p. ISBN:0-19-853935-5, ISBN13: 978-0-19-853935-3.
Dewey:516. LCCN:89-003012.
                        Audience: **u,f.**

Guicciardini, Niccoló   QA803 .G85 1999
Reading the Principia: The Debate on Newton's Mathematical
Methods for Natural Philosophy from 1687 to 1736. Trade
Paper. Cambridge University Press. New York, NY. 2003. 291p.
ISBN:0-521-54403-3, ISBN13: 978-0-521-54403-0. Dewey:531.
                        Audience: **l,u,f.**

Halmos, P. R.   QA28.H345 1987
I Have a Photographic Memory. Cloth Text. American
Mathematical Society. Providence, RI. 1988. 342p.
ISBN:0-8218-0115-5, ISBN13: 978-0-8218-0115-4.
Dewey:510./92/2. LCCN:87-033450.
                        Audience: **g.**

Hartshorne, Robin   QA451.H37 2000
Geometry: Euclid and Beyond. Trade Cloth. Springer. New
York, NY. 2000. XII, 532p. Undergraduate Texts in Mathematics
ISBN:0-387-98650-2, ISBN13: 978-0-387-98650-0. Dewey:516.
LCCN:99-044789.
            Audience: **l,u.** *Choice, 2001.*

Heath, Thomas L.   QA22
History of Greek Mathematics, Vol. 1. Trade Paper. Dover
Publications, Inc. Mineola, NY. 1981. 461p. Dover Phoenix
Editions Ser. ISBN:0-486-24073-8, ISBN13: 978-0-486-24073-2.
Dewey:510./938. LCCN:80-070126.
                        Audience: **l,u.**

Heath, Thomas L.   QA22
A History of Greek Mathematics, Vol. 2. Trade Paper. Dover
Publications, Inc. Mineola, NY. 1981. 597p. Dover Phoenix
Editions Ser. ISBN:0-486-24074-6, ISBN13: 978-0-486-24074-9.
Dewey:510./938. LCCN:80-070126.
                        Audience: **l,u.**

Heilbron, J. L.   QA455 .H45X 2000
Geometry Civilized: History, Culture, and Technique. Trade
Paper. Oxford University Press, Inc. New York, NY. 2000. 318p.
ISBN:0-19-850690-2, ISBN13: 978-0-19-850690-4. Dewey:516.
                        Audience: **l,u.**

Henrion, Claudia   QA27.5.H46 1997
Women in Mathematics: The Addition of Difference. Trade
Cloth. Indiana University Press. Bloomington, IN. 1997. 328p.
ISBN:0-253-33279-6, ISBN13: 978-0-253-33279-0.
Dewey:305.43/51. LCCN:97-002546.
            Audience: **l,u,f.** *Choice, 1998.*

Heyde, C. C. & Seneta, E.   QA276.156.S73 2001
  (Editors)
Statisticians of the Centuries. Trade Cloth. Springer. New York,
NY. 2001. XII, 500p. ISBN:0-387-95329-9, ISBN13:
978-0-387-95329-8. Dewey:519.5/092/2 B. LCCN:2001-031422.
            Audience: **g.** *Choice, 2002.*

Hilbert, David   QA681 .H6
The Foundations of Geometry. Ed. 2. Leo Unger (Translator).
Trade Cloth. Open Court Publishing Company. Chicago, IL.
1980. 226p. ISBN:0-87548-163-9, ISBN13: 978-0-87548-163-0.
Dewey:513. LCCN:73-110344.
                        Audience: **u,f.**

Hoffman, Paul   QA29.R3
The Man Who Loved Only Numbers: The Story of Paul Erdos
and the Search for Mathematical Truth. Trade Paper. Hyperion
Press. New York, NY. 1999. 352p. ISBN:0-7868-8406-1,
ISBN13: 978-0-7868-8406-3. Dewey:510/.92 B.
LCCN:98-014027.
                        Audience: **g.**

James, Ioan   QA28.J36 2002
Remarkable Mathematicians: From Euler to Von Neumann.
Trade Paper. Cambridge University Press. New York, NY. 2003.
448p. ISBN:0-521-52094-0, ISBN13: 978-0-521-52094-2.
Dewey:510/.92/2 B. LCCN:2002-022266.
            Audience: **g.** *Choice, 2003.*

Joseph, George G.   QA22 .J67 2000
The Crest of the Peacock: The Non-European Roots of
Mathmatics. Ed. 2. Trade Paper. Princeton University Press.
Princeton, NJ. 2000. 416p. ISBN:0-691-00659-8, ISBN13:
978-0-691-00659-8. Dewey:510/.9. LCCN:00-102425.
                     Audience: **g,l,u,f.**

Kanigel, Robert   QA29.R3 K36 1992
The Man Who Knew Infinity. Trade Paper. Simon & Schuster.
New York, NY. 1992. 464p. ISBN:0-671-75061-5, ISBN13:
978-0-671-75061-9. Dewey:510/.92.
LCCN:91-037763.
                        Audience: **g.**

Katz, Victor J.   QA21 .K33 1993
History of Mathematics. Trade Paper. Addison-Wesley
Educational Publishers, Inc. Boston, MA. 1997. 800p.
ISBN:0-673-38039-4, ISBN13: 978-0-673-38039-5.
Dewey:510/.9. LCCN:92-020989.
                        Audience: **u.**

Katz, Victor & Michalowica,   QA21
  Karen Dee (Editors)
Historical Modules for the Teaching and Learning of
Mathematics. CD-ROM. Mathematical Association of America.
Washington, DC. 2005. Classroom Resource Material Ser.
ISBN:0-88385-741-3, ISBN13: 978-0-88385-741-0.
Dewey:372.7.
         Audience: **u,f.**

Kline, Morris   QA21
Mathematical Thought from Ancient to Modern Times, Vol. 3.
Trade Paper. Oxford University Press, Inc. New York, NY. 1990.
436p. ISBN:0-19-506137-3, ISBN13: 978-0-19-506137-6.
Dewey:510/.9.
         Audience: **u.** ℬ

Kline, Morris   QA21
Mathematical Thought from Ancient to Modern Times, Vol. 2.
Trade Paper. Oxford University Press, Inc. New York, NY. 1990.
462p. ISBN:0-19-506136-5, ISBN13: 978-0-19-506136-9.
Dewey:510/.9.
         Audience: **u.** ℬ

Kline, Morris   QA21.K516 1990
Mathematical Thought from Ancient to Modern Times, Vol. 1.
Trade Paper. Oxford University Press, Inc. New York, NY. 1990.
428p. ISBN:0-19-506135-7, ISBN13: 978-0-19-506135-2.
Dewey:510/.9. LCCN:89-025520.
         Audience: **u.** ℬ

Kline, Morris   QA21
Mathematics in Western Culture. Paper Text. Textbook
Publishers. Temecula, CA. 2003. 484p. ISBN:0-7581-7049-1,
ISBN13: 978-0-7581-7049-1. Dewey:510/.9.
         Audience: **l,u.**

Laugwitz, Detlef   QA29.R425L3813 1998
Bernhard Riemann, 1826-1866: Turning Points in the
Conception of Mathematics. Abe Shenitzer (Translator). Trade
Cloth. Birkhauser Boston. Cambridge, MA. 1998.
ISBN:3-7643-4040-1, ISBN13: 978-3-7643-4040-7. Dewey:[B].
LCCN:98-017834.
         Audience: **u.**

Livio, Mario   QA466
The Golden Ratio: The Story of Phi, the World's Most
Astonishing Number. Trade Paper. Broadway Books. New York,
NY. 2003. 304p. ISBN:0-7679-0816-3, ISBN13:
978-0-7679-0816-0. Dewey:516.2/04.
         Audience: **g.** *Choice, 2003.*

Morrow, Charlene & Perl,   QA28
  Teri (Editors)
Notable Women in Mathematics: A Biographical Dictionary.
Cloth Text. Greenwood Publishing Group, Inc. Portsmouth, NH.
1998. 320p. ISBN:0-313-29131-4, ISBN13: 978-0-313-29131-9.
Dewey:510/.92/2 B. LCCN:97-018598.
         Audience: **g.** *Choice, 1998.*

Newton, Isaac   QA803.N413 1999
The Principia: Mathematical Principles of Natural Philosophy. I.
Bernard Cohen & Anne Whitman (Translators), I. Bernard
Cohen (Supplement by). Trade Cloth. University of California
Press. Berkeley, CA. 1999. 994p. ISBN:0-520-08816-6, ISBN13:
978-0-520-08816-0. Dewey:531. LCCN:99-010278.
         Audience: **l,u,f.**

O'Connor, J. J., and   QA21
  Robertson, E. F. (Editors)
☐ MacTutor History of Mathematics Archive.
http://www-history.mcs.st-andrews.ac.uk/history
         Audience: **g.**

Odifreddi, Piergiorgio   QA26.O3513 2004
The Mathematical Century: The 30 Greatest Problems of the
Last 100 Years. Arturo Sangalli (Translator). Trade Cloth.
Princeton University Press. Princeton, NJ. 2004. 224p.
ISBN:0-691-09294-X, ISBN13: 978-0-691-09294-2.
Dewey:510/.9/04. LCCN:2003-056324.
         Audience: **l,u,f.** *Choice, 2004.*

Osen, Lynn M.   QA28
Women in Mathematics. Trade Paper. MIT Press. Cambridge,
MA. 1975. 185p. ISBN:0-262-65009-6, ISBN13:
978-0-262-65009-0. Dewey:510/.92/2. LCCN:73-019506.
         Audience: **g.** ℬ

Pesic, Peter   QA212.P47 2004
Abel's Proof: An Essay on the Sources and Meaning of
Mathematical Unsolvability. Trade Paper. MIT Press.
Cambridge, MA. 2004. 221p. ISBN:0-262-66182-9, ISBN13:
978-0-262-66182-9. Dewey:512.9/4.
         Audience: **u.** *Choice, 2004.*

Peterson, Ivars   QA93
The Mathematical Tourist: New and Updated Snapshots of
Modern Mathematics. Trade Paper. Henry Holt & Company.
New York, NY. 1998. 288p. ISBN:0-8050-7159-8, ISBN13:
978-0-8050-7159-7. Dewey:510.
         Audience: **g.**

Phillips, G. M.   QA99.P48 2000
Two Millennia of Mathematics: From Archimedes to Gauss.
Trade Cloth. Springer. New York, NY. 2000. XII, 223p. CMS
Books in Mathematics, Vol. 6 ISBN:0-387-95022-2, ISBN13:
978-0-387-95022-8. Dewey:510. LCCN:00-023807.
         Audience: **l,u.** *Choice, 2001.*

Porter, Theodore M.   QA276.P64P67 2004
Karl Pearson: The Scientific Life in a Statistical Age. Trade
Cloth. Princeton University Press. Princeton, NJ. 2004. 352p.
ISBN:0-691-11445-5, ISBN13: 978-0-691-11445-3.
Dewey:519.5092. LCCN:2003-054820.
         Audience: **l,u,f.** *Choice, 2004.*

Reid, Constance   QA29.H5R4 1996
Hilbert. Paper Text. Springer. New York, NY. 1996. 230p.
ISBN:0-387-94674-8, ISBN13: 978-0-387-94674-0.
Dewey:510/.0924. LCCN:96-033753.
         Audience: **l,u,f.** ℬ

Salsburg, David   Q175
The Lady Tasting Tea: How Statistics Revolutionized Science in
the Twentieth Century. Trade Paper. Henry Holt & Company.
New York, NY. 2002. 352p. ISBN:0-8050-7134-2, ISBN13:
978-0-8050-7134-4. Dewey:001.4/22/0904.
         Audience: **g.**

Selin, Helaine   QA21.M3612 2000
Mathematics Across Cultures: The History of Nonwestern
Mathematics. Trade Cloth. Springer London, Ltd. Guildford,
2000. 512p. Science Across Cultures Ser., Vol. 2
ISBN:0-7923-6481-3, ISBN13: 978-0-7923-6481-8.
Dewey:510/.9. LCCN:00-056016.
         Audience: **l,u.** *Choice, 2001.*

Singh, Simon   QA244.S55 1997
Fermat's Enigma: The Quest to Solve the World's Greatest
Mathematical Problem. Trade Cloth. Walker & Company. New
York, NY. 1997. 288p. ISBN:0-8027-1331-9, ISBN13:
978-0-8027-1331-5. Dewey:512.74. LCCN:97-020748.
                                          Audience: **g.** *Choice, 1998.*

Stahl, Saul   QA162.S73 1997
Introductory Modern Algebra: A Historical Approach. Ed. 1.
Trade Cloth. John Wiley & Sons, Inc. Hoboken, NJ. 1996. 336p.
ISBN:0-471-16288-4, ISBN13: 978-0-471-16288-9.
Dewey:512/.2. LCCN:96-019469.
                                          Audience: **l,u,f.** *Choice, 1997.*

Stein, Sherman K.   QA22
Archimedes: What Did He Do Beside Cry Eureka? Paper Text.
Mathematical Association of America. Washington, DC. 1999.
166p. Classroom Resource Materials Ser. ISBN:0-88385-718-9,
ISBN13: 978-0-88385-718-2. Dewey:510. LCCN:99-062795.
                                          Audience: **g.** *Choice, 2000.*

Stigler, Stephen M.   QA276.15 .S75
The History of Statistics: The Measurement of Uncertainty
Before 1900. Trade Paper. Harvard University Press. Cambridge,
MA. 1990. 432p. Belknap Ser. ISBN:0-674-40341-X, ISBN13:
978-0-674-40341-3. Dewey:519.5/09.
                                                     Audience: **l,u.**

Stigler, Stephen M.   QA276.15.S755 1999
Statistics on the Table: The History of Statistical Concepts and
Methods. Trade Cloth. Harvard University Press. Cambridge,
MA. 1999. 510p. ISBN:0-674-83601-4, ISBN13:
978-0-674-83601-3. Dewey:519.5/09. LCCN:99-013719.
                                          Audience: **l,u.** *Choice, 2000.*

Stopple, Jeffrey   QA241.S815 2003
A Primer of Analytic Number Theory: From Pythagoras to
Riemann. Cloth Text. Cambridge University Press. New York,
NY. 2003. 398p. ISBN:0-521-81309-3, ISBN13:
978-0-521-81309-9. Dewey:512/.7. LCCN:2002-041263.
                                                     Audience: **u.**

Struik, Dirk J.   QA21.S87 1987
Concise History of Mathematics. Ed. 4. Trade Paper. Dover
Publications, Inc. Mineola, NY. 1987. 288p.
ISBN:0-486-60255-9, ISBN13: 978-0-486-60255-4.
Dewey:510/.09. LCCN:86-008855.
                                                     Audience: **u.**

Swetz, Frank J. (Editor),   QA21.L38 1995
   et al.
Learn from the Masters. John Fauvel, Victor J. Katz, Otto
Bekken & Bengt Johannson (Editors). Paper Text. Mathematical
Association of America. Washington, DC. 1997. 313p.
Classroom Resource Materials Ser. ISBN:0-88385-703-0,
ISBN13: 978-0-88385-703-8. Dewey:510. LCCN:95-078461.
                                                     Audience: **l,u,f.**

Waismann, Friedrich   QA9.W33213 2003
Introduction to Mathematical Thinking: The Formation of
Concepts in Modern Mathematics. Trade Paper. Dover
Publications, Inc. Mineola, NY. 2003. 272p. Mathematics Ser.
ISBN:0-486-42804-4, ISBN13: 978-0-486-42804-8.
Dewey:510/.1. LCCN:2002-041200.
                                                     Audience: **l,u,f.**

Weil, Andre   QA241.W3418 1984
Number Theory: An Approach Through History. from
Hammurapi to Legendre. Ed. 2. Trade Cloth. Springer. New
York, NY. 1987. 400p. ISBN:0-8176-3141-0, ISBN13:
978-0-8176-3141-3. Dewey:512/.7/09. LCCN:83-011857.
                                          Audience: **u,f.** *B*

Westfall, Richard S.   N56.W52
The Life of Isaac Newton. Trade Paper. Cambridge University
Press. New York, NY. 1994. 350p. A Canto Book Ser.
ISBN:0-521-47737-9, ISBN13: 978-0-521-47737-6.
Dewey:530.092. LCCN:92-003377.
                                          Audience: **g,l,u,f.** *Choice, 1993.*

Wilson, Robin   QA612.19.W54 2002
Four Colors Suffice: How the Map Problem Was Solved. Trade
Cloth. Princeton University Press. Princeton, NJ. 2003. 280p.
ISBN:0-691-11533-8, ISBN13: 978-0-691-11533-7.
Dewey:511.5. LCCN:2002-114311.
                                          Audience: **g.** *Choice, 2003.*

Yandell, Benjamin   QA26.Y36 2001
The Honors Class: Hilbert's Problems and Their Solvers. Cloth
Text. A K Peters, Ltd. Wellesley, MA. 2001. 486p.
ISBN:1-56881-141-1, ISBN13: 978-1-56881-141-3.
Dewey:510/.9/04. LCCN:2001-036795.
                                          Audience: **l,u,f.** *Choice, 2002.*

Recreational Mathematics

Ball, W. W. Rouse   QA95
Mathematical Recreations and Essays. Trade Paper. Kessinger
Publishing, LLC. Whitefish, MT. 2004. ISBN:1-4179-2126-9,
ISBN13: 978-1-4179-2126-3. Dewey:793.7/4.
                                                     Audience: **g.**

Berlekamp, Elwyn R., et al.   QA95.B446 2001
Winning Ways for Your Mathematical Plays, Vol. 2. Ed. 2. John
H. Conway & Richard K. Guy (Authors). Paper Text. A K
Peters, Ltd. Wellesley, MA. 2003. 473p. ISBN:1-56881-142-X,
ISBN13: 978-1-56881-142-0. Dewey:793.7/4. LCCN:00-048541.
                                                     Audience: **u,f.**

Berlekamp, Elwyn R., et al.   QA95 .B446 2001
Winning Ways for Your Mathematical Plays, Vol. 4. Ed. 2. John
H. Conway & Richard K. Guy (Authors). Paper Text. A K
Peters, Ltd. Wellesley, MA. 2004. 155p. ISBN:1-56881-144-6,
ISBN13: 978-1-56881-144-4. Dewey:793.7/4. LCCN:00-048541.
                                                     Audience: **u,f.**

Berlekamp, Elwyn R., et al.   QA95.B446 2001
Winning Ways for Your Mathematical Plays, Vol. 1. Ed. 2. John
H. Conway & Richard K. Guy (Authors). Paper Text. A K
Peters, Ltd. Wellesley, MA. 2002. 276p. ISBN:1-56881-130-6,
ISBN13: 978-1-56881-130-7. Dewey:793.7/4. LCCN:00-048541.
                                                     Audience: **u,f.**

Berlekamp, Elwyn R., et al.   QA95
Winning Ways for Your Mathematical Plays, Vol. 3. Ed. 2. John
H. Conway & Richard K. Guy (Authors). Paper Text. A K
Peters, Ltd. Wellesley, MA. 2003. 800p. ISBN:1-56881-143-8,
ISBN13: 978-1-56881-143-7. Dewey:793.7/4.
                                                     Audience: **u,f.**

Carroll, Lewis   QA95.D6
Mathematical Recreations of Lewis Carroll. Dover. 1958.
                                                     Audience: **g.**

Dudeney, Henry E.   QA95.D83
Five Hundred Thirty-Six Puzzles and Curious Problems. Trade Paper. Thomson Gale. Farmington Hills, MI. 1970. 448p. ISBN:0-684-71755-7, ISBN13: 978-0-684-71755-5. Dewey:510.076. LCCN:67-015488.

              Audience: **g.**

Eiss, Harry E.   QA95
Dictionary of Mathematical Games, Puzzles, and Amusements. Cloth Text. Greenwood Publishing Group, Inc. Portsmouth, NH. 1988. 292p. ISBN:0-313-24714-5, ISBN13: 978-0-313-24714-9. Dewey:793.7/4/0321. LCCN:87-000280.

              Audience: **g.** *Choice, 1988.*

Frederickson, Greg N.   QA95 .F68 1997
Dissections: Plane and Fancy. Trade Paper. Cambridge University Press. New York, NY. 2003. 322p. ISBN:0-521-52582-9, ISBN13: 978-0-521-52582-4. Dewey:793.7/4.

              Audience: **g.**

Gardner, Martin   QA95
Martin Gardner's Mathematical Games: The Entire Collection of his Scientific American Columns. CD-ROM. Mathematical Association of America. Washington, DC. 2005. MAA-Spectrum Ser. ISBN:0-88385-545-3, ISBN13: 978-0-88385-545-4. Dewey:793.74.

              Audience: **g.**

Golomb, Solomon W.   QA166.75
Polyominoes: Puzzles, Patterns, Problems, and Packings. Ed. 2. Trade Paper. Princeton University Press. Princeton, NJ. 1996. 198p. Princeton Science Library ISBN:0-691-02444-8, ISBN13: 978-0-691-02444-8. Dewey:511/.6. LCCN:93-041756.

              Audience: **g.**

Hordern, Edward   GV1493.H62 1986
Sliding Piece Puzzles. Trade Cloth. Oxford University Press, Inc. New York, NY. 1987. 256p. Recreations in Mathematics Ser., No. 4 ISBN:0-19-853204-0, ISBN13: 978-0-19-853204-0. Dewey:793.7/4. LCCN:86-018204.

              Audience: **g.** *Choice, 1987.*

Joyner, David   QA174.2.J69 2002
Adventures in Group Theory: Rubik's Cube, Merlin's Machine and Other Mathematical Toys. Trade Paper. Johns Hopkins University Press. Baltimore, MD. 2002. 280p. ISBN:0-8018-6947-1, ISBN13: 978-0-8018-6947-1. Dewey:512/.2. LCCN:2001-050252.

              Audience: **g.** *Choice, 2003.*

Klarner, David A. (Editor)   QA95 .M3676
The Mathematical Gardner. Trade Cloth. John Wiley & Sons, Inc. Hoboken, NJ. 1982. 382p. ISBN:0-442-25336-2, ISBN13: 978-0-442-25336-3. Dewey:793.7/4.

              Audience: **g.**

Konhauser, Joseph D., et al.   QA43.K643 1996
Which Way Did the Bicycle Go?: And Other Intriguing Mathematical Mysteries. Dan Velleman & Stan Wagon (Authors). Paper Text. Mathematical Association of America. Washington, DC. 1997. 253p. Dolciani Mathematical Expositions Ser., Vol. 18 ISBN:0-88385-325-6, ISBN13: 978-0-88385-325-2. Dewey:793.7/4. LCCN:95-081495.

              Audience: **l,u.** *Choice, 1997.*

Kraitchik, Maurice   QA95 .K72 1953
Mathematical Recreations. Ed. 2. Trade Paper. Dover Publications, Inc. Mineola, NY. 1953. 330p. ISBN:0-486-20163-5, ISBN13: 978-0-486-20163-4. Dewey:793.74. LCCN:53-009354.

              Audience: **g.**

Lang, Robert J.   TT870.L2614 2003
Origami Design Secrets: Mathematical Methods for an Ancient Art. Paper Text. A K Peters, Ltd. Wellesley, MA. 2003. 585p. ISBN:1-56881-194-2, ISBN13: 978-1-56881-194-9. Dewey:736/.982. LCCN:2003-043317.

              Audience: **g.** *Choice, 2004.*

Loyd, Sam   GV1493
Best Mathematical Puzzles of Sam Loyd. Martin Gardner (Editor). Trade Paper. Dover Publications, Inc. Mineola, NY. 1959. 167p. ISBN:0-486-20498-7, ISBN13: 978-0-486-20498-7. Dewey:793.73.

              Audience: **g.**

Nahin, Paul J.   QA273
Duelling Idiots and Other Probability Puzzlers. Trade Paper. Princeton University Press. Princeton, NJ. 2002. 280p. ISBN:0-691-10286-4, ISBN13: 978-0-691-10286-3. Dewey:519.2.

              Audience: **g,l,u.** *Choice, 2001.*

Peterson, Ivars   QA99.P47 2002
Mathematical Treks: From Surreal Numbers to Magic Circles. Trade Paper. Mathematical Association of America. Washington, DC. 2002. 182p. Spectrum Ser. ISBN:0-88385-537-2, ISBN13: 978-0-88385-537-9. Dewey:510. LCCN:2001-098094.

              Audience: **g.** *Choice, 2002.*

Pook, Les   QA95
Flexagons Inside Out. Trade Cloth. Cambridge University Press. New York, NY. 2003. 182p. ISBN:0-521-81970-9, ISBN13: 978-0-521-81970-1. Dewey:516/.156. LCCN:2003-273864.

              Audience: **g.**

Shasha, Dennis   QA95
The Puzzling Adventures of Dr. Ecco. Trade Paper. Dover Publications, Inc. Mineola, NY. 1998. 192p. ISBN:0-486-29615-6, ISBN13: 978-0-486-29615-9. Dewey:793.7/4. LCCN:97-043592.

              Audience: **g.**

Stewart, Ian   QA95.S723 2004
Another Fine Math You've Got Me Into. Martin Gardner (Foreword by). Trade Paper. Dover Publications, Inc. Mineola, NY. 2004. 288p. ISBN:0-486-43181-9, ISBN13: 978-0-486-43181-9. Dewey:793.74. LCCN:2003-067494.

              Audience: **g.**

Tanton, James   QA43.T36 2001
Solve This: Math Activities for Students and Clubs. Paper Text. Mathematical Association of America. Washington, DC. 2001. 232p. Classroom Resource Materials Ser. ISBN:0-88385-717-0, ISBN13: 978-0-88385-717-5. Dewey:510/.76. LCCN:2002-278862.

              Audience: **g,l,u,f.** *Choice, 2002.*

Vaderlind, Paul, et al.   QA63
The Inquisitive Problem Solver. Richard Guy & Loren Larson (Authors). Trade Paper. Mathematical Association of America. Washington, DC. 2002. 344p. MAA Problem Books

---

ISBN:0-88385-806-1, ISBN13: 978-0-88385-806-6.
Dewey:510/.76. LCCN:2001-097391.
Audience: **l,u,f.** *Choice, 2003.*

Watkins, John J.   **QA95.W35 2004**
Across the Board: The Mathematics of Chessboard Problems.
Trade Cloth. Princeton University Press. Princeton, NJ. 2004.
264p. ISBN:0-691-11503-6, ISBN13: 978-0-691-11503-0.
Dewey:793.74. LCCN:2003-062308.
Audience: **g.** *Choice, 2005.*

Winkler, Peter   **QA95.W646 2004**
Mathematical Puzzles: A Connoisseur's Collection. Paper Text.
A K Peters, Ltd. Wellesley, MA. 2004. 163p.
ISBN:1-56881-201-9, ISBN13: 978-1-56881-201-4.
Dewey:793.74. LCCN:2003-064797.
Audience: **l,u,f.** *Choice, 2004.*

Logic, Foundations, and Philosophy

Ayoub, Raymond   **QA7.M87 2004**
Musings of the Masters: An Anthology of Mathematical
Reflections. Cloth Text. Mathematical Association of America.
Washington, DC. 2004. 288p. Spectrum Ser.
ISBN:0-88385-549-6, ISBN13: 978-0-88385-549-2. Dewey:510.
LCCN:2004-104239.
Audience: **l,u,f.** *Choice, 2005.*

Barwise, J. (Editor)   **QA9**
Handbook of Mathematical Logic. Ed. 8. Trade Paper. Elsevier
Science & Technology Books. Saint Louis, MO. 1982. 1166p.
Studies in Logic and the Foundations of Mathematics, No. 90
ISBN:0-444-86388-5, ISBN13: 978-0-444-86388-1.
Dewey:511/.3.
Audience: **u,f.**

Chang, C. C. & Keisler, H.   **QA9.7.C45 1990**
  Jerome
Model Theory. Ed. 3. Trade Cloth. Elsevier Science &
Technology Books. Saint Louis, MO. 1990. 650p. Studies in
Logic and the Foundations of Mathematics, No. 73
ISBN:0-444-88054-2, ISBN13: 978-0-444-88054-3.
Dewey:511/.8. LCCN:89-071124.
Audience: **u.** *B*

Cole, K. C.   **QA36 .C65 1999**
The Universe and the Teacup: The Mathematics of Truth and
Beauty. Trade Paper. Harcourt Trade Publishers. New York, NY.
1999. 224p. ISBN:0-15-600656-1, ISBN13: 978-0-15-600656-9.
Dewey:510.
Audience: **g.**

Edwards, Harold M.   **QA9.56.E39 2004**
Essays in Constructive Mathematics. Trade Cloth. Springer. New
York, NY. 2004. XIX, 211p. ISBN:0-387-21978-1, ISBN13:
978-0-387-21978-3. Dewey:511.3. LCCN:2004-049156.
Audience: **u,f.**

George, Alexander &   **QA8.4.G46 2002**
  Velleman, Daniel J.
Philosophies of Mathematics. Trade Cloth. Blackwell
Publishing, Inc. Malden, MA. 2001. 240p. ISBN:0-631-19543-2,
ISBN13: 978-0-631-19543-6. Dewey:510/.1.
LCCN:2001-037590.
Audience: **l,u.** *Choice, 2003, 2002.*

Hacking, Ian   **BC141 .H33 2001**
An Introduction to Probability and Inductive Logic. Trade Cloth.
Cambridge University Press. New York, NY. 2001. 320p.
ISBN:0-521-77287-7, ISBN13: 978-0-521-77287-7. Dewey:160.
LCCN:00-045503.
Audience: **u,f.**

Hofstadter, Douglas R.   **QA9.8.H63 1980**
  (Author, Preface by)
Gödel, Escher, Bach: An Eternal Golden Braid. Ed. 20. Paper
Text. Basic Books. New York, NY. 1999. 832p.
ISBN:0-465-02656-7, ISBN13: 978-0-465-02656-2.
Dewey:511.3. LCCN:80-011354.
Audience: **g.**

Kleene, S. C.   **QA9**
Introduction to Metamathematics. Ed. 13. Trade Cloth. Elsevier
Science & Technology Books. Saint Louis, MO. 1980. 560p.
Bibliotheca Mathematica Ser., Vol. 1 ISBN:0-7204-2103-9,
ISBN13: 978-0-7204-2103-3. Dewey:510.1.
Audience: **u.**

Laczkovich, Miklos   **QA9.54.L33 2001**
Conjecture and Proof. Paper Text. Mathematical Association of
America. Washington, DC. 2002. 128p. Classroom Resource
Materials Ser. ISBN:0-88385-722-7, ISBN13:
978-0-88385-722-9. Dewey:511.3. LCCN:2001-095773.
Audience: **u,f.** *Choice, 2002.*

Lakatos, Imre (Editor),   **QA9.54 1976**
  et al.
Proofs and Refutations: The Logic of Mathematical Discovery.
John Worrall & Elie Zahar (Editors). Trade Paper. Cambridge
University Press. New York, NY. 1976. 186p.
ISBN:0-521-29038-4, ISBN13: 978-0-521-29038-8.
Dewey:511.3. LCCN:75-032478.
Audience: **u.**

Lucas, J. R.   **QA8.4.L833 2000**
Conceptual Roots of Mathematics. Paper over Boards.
Routledge. New York, NY. 1999. 472p. International Library of
Philosophy, Psychology, and Scientific Method
ISBN:0-415-20738-X, ISBN13: 978-0-415-20738-6.
Dewey:510/.1. LCCN:99-020193.
Audience: **l,u.** *Choice, 2000.*

Marker, David   **QA9.7.M367 2002**
Model Theory: An Introduction. Trade Cloth. Springer. New
York, NY. 2002. VIII, 342p. Graduate Texts in Mathematics,
Vol. 216 ISBN:0-387-98760-6, ISBN13: 978-0-387-98760-6.
Dewey:511.3. LCCN:2002-024184.
Audience: **u.** *Choice, 2003.*

Nagel, Ernest & Newman,   **QA9.65.N34 2002**
  James R.
Godel's Proof. Douglas R. Hofstadter (Foreword by). Trade
Cloth. New York University Press. New York, NY. 2001. 125p.
ISBN:0-8147-5816-9, ISBN13: 978-0-8147-5816-8.
Dewey:511.3. LCCN:2001-044481.
Audience: **l,u.**

Pedrycz, Witold & Gomide,   **QA248.5.P38 1998**
  Fernando
An Introduction to Fuzzy Sets: Analysis and Design. Trade
Cloth. MIT Press. Cambridge, MA. 1998. 465p. Complex
Adaptive Systems Ser. ISBN:0-262-16171-0, ISBN13:
978-0-262-16171-8. Dewey:006.3/01/51132. LCCN:97-034598.
Audience: **u.** *Choice, 1998.*

Pesic, Peter   QA212.P47 2004
Abel's Proof: An Essay on the Sources and Meaning of
Mathematical Unsolvability. Trade Paper. MIT Press.
Cambridge, MA. 2004. 221p. ISBN:0-262-66182-9, ISBN13:
978-0-262-66182-9. Dewey:512.9/4.
                     Audience: **u.** *Choice, 2004.*

Putnam, Hilary (Editor),   QA8.4 .P48 1983
  et al.
Philosophy of Mathematics: Selected Readings. Ed. 2. Hilary
Benacerraf & Paul Benacerraf (Editors). Trade Paper. Cambridge
University Press. New York, NY. 1984. 608p.
ISBN:0-521-29648-X, ISBN13: 978-0-521-29648-9.
Dewey:510.1. LCCN:85-025257.
                     Audience: **l,u.**

Solow, Daniel   QA9.54.S65 2005
How to Read and Do Proofs: An Introduction to Mathematical
Thought Processes. Ed. 4. Trade Paper. John Wiley & Sons, Inc.
Hoboken, NJ. 2004. 288p. ISBN:0-471-68058-3, ISBN13:
978-0-471-68058-1. Dewey:511.3/6. LCCN:2004-058651.
                     Audience: **l,u.**

Suppes, Patrick & Hill,   QA9.S88 2002
  Shirley A.
The First Course in Mathematical Logic. Trade Paper. Dover
Publications, Inc. Mineola, NY. 2002. 288p.
ISBN:0-486-42259-3, ISBN13: 978-0-486-42259-6.
Dewey:511.3. LCCN:2002-017411.
                     Audience: **l,u.**

Wolf, Robert S.   QA9.W748 1998
Proof, Logic, and Conjecture: The Mathematician's Toolbox.
Cloth over Boards. Worth Publishers, Inc. New York, NY. 1997.
4p. ISBN:0-7167-3050-2, ISBN13: 978-0-7167-3050-7.
Dewey:511.3. LCCN:97-031940.
                     Audience: **l,u.**

Logic, Foundations, and Philosophy > Set theory

Halmos, P. R.   QA248 .H26 1974
Naive Set Theory. Trade Cloth. Springer. New York, NY. 1998.
VII, 104p. Undergraduate Texts in Mathematics
ISBN:0-387-90092-6, ISBN13: 978-0-387-90092-6.
Dewey:511/.3. LCCN:74-010687.
                     Audience: **u.**

Kamke, E.   QA248.K33 2006
Theory of Sets. Frederick Bagemihl (Translator). Cloth over
Boards. Dover Publications, Inc. Mineola, NY. 2006. 160p.
Dover Phoenix Editions Ser. ISBN:0-486-45083-X, ISBN13:
978-0-486-45083-4. Dewey:511.3/22. LCCN:2005-056926.
                     Audience: **u.**

Lawvere, F. William &   QA248.L28 2002
  Rosebrugh, Robert
Sets for Mathematics. Trade Paper. Cambridge University Press.
New York, NY. 2003. 276p. ISBN:0-521-01060-8, ISBN13:
978-0-521-01060-3. Dewey:511.3/22. LCCN:2002-071478.
                     Audience: **l,u.** *Choice, 2003.*

Levy, Azriel   QA248.L398 2002
Basic Set Theory. Trade Paper. Dover Publications, Inc.
Mineola, NY. 2002. 416p. ISBN:0-486-42079-5, ISBN13:
978-0-486-42079-0. Dewey:511.3/22. LCCN:2002-022292.
                     Audience: **l,u.**

Vereshchagin, Nikolai   QA248.V4613 2002
  Konstantinovich & Shen, A.
Basic Set Theory. Trade Paper. American Mathematical Society.
Providence, RI. 2002. viii, 116p. Student Mathematical Library,
Vol. 17 ISBN:0-8218-2731-6, ISBN13: 978-0-8218-2731-4.
Dewey:511.3/22. LCCN:2002-066533.
                     Audience: **l,u.**

Logic, Foundations, and Philosophy > Theory of Computing

Davis, Martin   QA9.615
Computability and Unsolvability. Trade Paper. Dover
Publications, Inc. Mineola, NY. 1985. 288p. Mathematics Ser.
ISBN:0-486-61471-9, ISBN13: 978-0-486-61471-7.
Dewey:511.3. LCCN:82-007287.
                     Audience: **u.**

Davis, Martin D., et al.   QA267.D38 1994
Computability, Complexity, and Languages: Fundamentals of
Theoretical Computer Science. Ed. 2. Elaine J. Weyuker & Ron
Sigal (Authors). Cloth Text. Elsevier Science & Technology
Books. Saint Louis, MO. 1994. 609p. Computer Science and
Scientific Computing Ser. ISBN:0-12-206382-1, ISBN13:
978-0-12-206382-4. Dewey:511.3. LCCN:93-026807.
                     Audience: **u.** *Choice, 1994.*

Garey, Michael R. &   QA297
  Johnson, David S.
Computers and Intractability: A Guide to the Theory of
NP-Completeness. Trade Paper. Worth Publishers, Inc. New
York, NY. 1979. 340p. Series of Books in the Mathematical
Sciences ISBN:0-7167-1045-5, ISBN13: 978-0-7167-1045-5.
Dewey:519.4/0285. LCCN:78-012361.
                     Audience: **u,f.** *B*

Parkes, Alan   QA267.3.P37 2001
Introduction to Languages, Machines and Logic: Computable
Machines, Abstract Machines and Formal Logic. Ed. 2. Trade
Paper. Springer. New York, NY. 2002. XI, 351p.
ISBN:1-85233-464-9, ISBN13: 978-1-85233-464-2.
Dewey:511.3. LCCN:2001-054282.
                     Audience: **u.** *Choice, 2002.*

Rogers, Hartley Jr.   QA9.615.R64 1987
Theory of Recursive Functions and Effective Computability.
Trade Paper. MIT Press. Cambridge, MA. 1987. 504p.
ISBN:0-262-68052-1, ISBN13: 978-0-262-68052-3.
Dewey:511.3. LCCN:86-033764.
                     Audience: **u.** *B*

Algebra and Number Theory

                     QA244
The Proof. Video, VHS Format. W G B H Boston Video.
South Burlington, VT. 1997. NOVA Ser. ISBN:1-57807-072-4,
ISBN13: 978-1-57807-072-5. Dewey:512.74.
                     Audience: **g.**

Bashmakova, Isabella &   QA151.B37 2000
  Smirnova, Galina
The Beginnings and Evolution of Algebra. Paper Text.
Mathematical Association of America. Washington, DC. 2000.
196p. Dolciani Mathematical Expositions Ser., No. 23
ISBN:0-88385-329-9, ISBN13: 978-0-88385-329-0.
Dewey:512/.009. LCCN:99-068950.

Audience: **l,u,f.**

Pesic, Peter   QA212.P47 2004
Abel's Proof: An Essay on the Sources and Meaning of
Mathematical Unsolvability. Trade Paper. MIT Press.
Cambridge, MA. 2004. 221p. ISBN:0-262-66182-9, ISBN13:
978-0-262-66182-9. Dewey:512.9/4.

Audience: **u.** *Choice, 2004.*

Stillwell, John C.   QA155.S75 1994
Elements of Algebra: Geometry, Numbers, Equations. Ed. 3.
Trade Cloth. Springer. New York, NY. 1994. 200p.
Undergraduate Texts in Mathematics ISBN:0-387-94290-4,
ISBN13: 978-0-387-94290-2. Dewey:512/.02. LCCN:94-010085.

Audience: **l,u.** *Choice, 1995.*

Algebra and Number Theory > College Algebra

Kaufmann, Jerome E. &   QA154.3.K36 2004
  Schwitters, Karen L.
Algebra for College Students. Ed. 7. Cloth Text, CD-ROM.
Brooks/Cole. Pacific Grove, CA. 2003. 912p.
ISBN:0-534-40032-9, ISBN13: 978-0-534-40032-3.
Dewey:512.9. LCCN:2003-106901.

Audience: **l.**

Larson, Ron, et al.   QA154.3 .L35 2006
College Algebra: Concepts and Models. Ed. 5. Robert P.
Hostetler & Anne V. Hodgkins (Authors). Cloth Text. Houghton
Mifflin College Division. Boston, MA. 2005. 465p.
ISBN:0-618-49281-X, ISBN13: 978-0-618-49281-7.
Dewey:512.9.

Audience: **l.**

Sullivan, Michael   QA154.2
Algebra for Review. Ed. 5. Other. Prentice Hall (School
Division). Needham Heights, MA. 1996. College Algebra
ISBN:0-13-590621-0, ISBN13: 978-0-13-590621-7. Dewey:512.
Audience: **l.**

Algebra and Number Theory > Linear Algebra

Axler, Sheldon J.   QA184.A96 1997
Linear Algebra Done Right. Ed. 2. Trade Cloth. Springer. New
York, NY. 1997. XV, 251p. Undergraduate Texts in Mathematics
ISBN:0-387-98259-0, ISBN13: 978-0-387-98259-5.
Dewey:512/.5. LCCN:97-016664.

Audience: **l,u.** *Choice, 1996.*

Blyth, T. S. & Robertson,   QA184.2.B58 2002
  E. F.
Basic Linear Algebra. Ed. 2. Trade Paper. Springer. New York,
NY. 2002. XI, 232p. Springer Undergraduate Mathematics Ser.
ISBN:1-85233-662-5, ISBN13: 978-1-85233-662-2.
Dewey:512/.5. LCCN:2002-070836.

Audience: **l,u.**

Carlson, David (Editor),   QA184.R48 1997
  et al.
Resources for Teaching Linear Algebra. David C. Lay, Charles
R. Johnson, A. Duane Porter, Ann Watkins & William Watkins
(Editors). Trade Cloth. Mathematical Association of America.
Washington, DC. 1997. 306p. Notes Ser., No. 42
ISBN:0-88385-150-4, ISBN13: 978-0-88385-150-0.
Dewey:512/.5/071. LCCN:97-070503.

Audience: **f.** *Choice, 1998.*

Demmel, James W.   QA184.D455 1997
Applied Numerical Linear Algebra. Trade Cloth. Society for
Industrial & Applied Mathematics. Philadelphia, PA. 1997. xii +
419p. Miscellaneous Bks., OT56 ISBN:0-89871-389-7, ISBN13:
978-0-89871-389-3. Dewey:512/.5. LCCN:97-017290.

Audience: **u,f.** *Choice, 1998.*

Gantmakher, F. R. (Feliks   QA263
  Ruvimovich)
Theory of Matrices, 2 v. Chelsea Publishing Company. 1959.

Audience: **u,f.**

Gilbert, Jimmie & Gilbert,   QA184.G525 2004
  Linda
Linear Algebra and Matrix Theory. Ed. 2. Cloth Text.
Brooks/Cole. Pacific Grove, CA. 2004. 552p.
ISBN:0-534-40581-9, ISBN13: 978-0-534-40581-6.
Dewey:512/.5. LCCN:2003-117069.

Audience: **l,u.**

Golub, Gene H. & Van   QA188.G65 1996
  Loan, Charles F.
Matrix Computations. Ed. 3. Trade Cloth. Johns Hopkins
University Press. Baltimore, MD. 1996. 728p. Johns Hopkins
Studies in the Mathematical Sciences ISBN:0-8018-5413-X,
ISBN13: 978-0-8018-5413-2. Dewey:512.9/434.
LCCN:96-014291.

Audience: **u,f.**

Halmos, P. R.   QA186 .H34 1974
Finite-Dimension Vector Spaces. Ed. 2. Trade Cloth. Springer.
New York, NY. 1993. 200p. Undergraduate Texts in
Mathematics ISBN:0-387-90093-4, ISBN13: 978-0-387-90093-3.
Dewey:512/.523. LCCN:74-010688.

Audience: **u.**

Hoffman, Kenneth & Kunze,   QA184
  Ray
Linear Algebra. Ed. 3. Trade Cloth. Prentice Hall PTR. Upper
Saddle River, NJ. 1999. 608p. ISBN:0-13-181496-6, ISBN13:
978-0-13-181496-7. Dewey:512/.5.

Audience: **l,u.**

Lay, David C.   QA184.2.L39 2006
Linear Algebra and Its Applications. Ed. 3. Trade Cloth,
CD-ROM. Addison Wesley. Boston, MA. 2005. 576p.
ISBN:0-321-28713-4, ISBN13: 978-0-321-28713-7.
Dewey:512/.5. LCCN:2005-042186.

Audience: **l,u.**

Lipschutz, Seymour and   QA188
  Lipson, Marc
Schaum's Outline of Theory and Problems of Linear Algebra.
Ed. 3. McGraw-Hill. 2001. Schaum's Outline Series
ISBN:0-07-136012-2, ISBN13: 978-0-07-136200-9.

Audience: **l.**

Strang, Gilbert   **QA184**
Linear Algebra and Its Applications. Ed. 4. Cloth Text.
Brooks/Cole. Pacific Grove, CA. 1998. 496p.
ISBN:0-03-010567-6, ISBN13: 978-0-03-010567-8.
Dewey:512/.5. LCCN:2005-923623.

Audience: **u.**

Wilkinson, J. Harvie   **QA218.W5 1988**
The Algebraic Eigenvalue Problem. Trade Paper. Oxford
University Press, Inc. New York, NY. 1988. 680p. Monographs
on Numerical Analysis ISBN:0-19-853418-3, ISBN13:
978-0-19-853418-1. Dewey:512.9/4. LCCN:87-028274.

Audience: **u,f.**

Algebra and Number Theory > Abstract Algebra

Anderson, Marlow & Feil,   **QA162.A53 1995**
Todd
A First Course in Abstract Algebra: Rings, Groups, and Fields.
Ed. 1. Mass Market. Brooks/Cole. Pacific Grove, CA. 1994.
480p. ISBN:0-534-19110-X, ISBN13: 978-0-534-19110-8.
Dewey:512/.02. LCCN:94-010521.

Audience: **u.**

Ayres, Frank   **QA162**
Schaum's Outline of Theory and Problems of Modern Abstract
Algebra. McGraw-Hill. 1965. Schaum's Outline Series
ISBN:0-07-002655-6, ISBN13: 978-0-07-002655-1.

Audience: **u.**

Berrick, A. J. & Keating,   **QA169 .B473 2000**
M. E.
Categories and Modules with K-Theory in View. B. Bollobas,
W. Fulton, A. Katok, F. Kirwan, P. Sarnak & B. Simon
(Contribution by). Trade Cloth. Cambridge University Press.
New York, NY. 2000. 380p. Cambridge Studies in Advanced
Mathematics, Vol. 67 ISBN:0-521-63276-5, ISBN13:
978-0-521-63276-8. Dewey:511.3. LCCN:99-025756.

Audience: **u,f.**

Birkhoff, Garrett D. & Mac   **QA162.B57 1997**
Lane, Saunders
A Survey of Modern Algebra. Ed. 5. Cloth Text. A K Peters,
Ltd. Wellesley, MA. 1996. 500p. ISBN:1-56881-068-7, ISBN13:
978-1-56881-068-3. Dewey:512/.02. LCCN:97-000372.

Audience: **u.**

Conway, John & Smith,   **QA196.C66 2002**
Derek
On Quaternions and Octonions. Cloth Text. A K Peters, Ltd.
Wellesley, MA. 2003. 159p. ISBN:1-56881-134-9, ISBN13:
978-1-56881-134-5. Dewey:512/.5. LCCN:2002-035555.

Audience: **u,f.** *Choice, 2003.*

Dummit, David S. & Foote,   **QA162.D85 2004**
Richard M.
Abstract Algebra. Ed. 3. Trade Cloth. John Wiley & Sons, Inc.
Hoboken, NJ. 2003. 944p. ISBN:0-471-43334-9, ISBN13:
978-0-471-43334-7. Dewey:512/.02. LCCN:2003-057652.

Audience: **u.**

Hadlock, Charles   **QA247 .H24 2000**
Field Theory and Its Classical Problems. Paper Text.
Mathematical Association of America. Washington, DC. 2000.

340p. Carus Mathematical Monographs, No. 19
ISBN:0-88385-032-X, ISBN13: 978-0-88385-032-9.
Dewey:512.3. LCCN:78-071937.

Audience: **u,f.**

Herstein, I. N. (Text by)   **QA251.5**
Noncommutative Rings. Trade Paper. Mathematical Association
of America. Washington, DC. 2005. 228p. Carus Monograph
Ser. ISBN:0-88385-039-7, ISBN13: 978-0-88385-039-8.
Dewey:512.4/6.

Audience: **u,f.**

Herstein, Israel N.   **QA162**
Topics in Algebra. Ed. 2. Trade Cloth. John Wiley & Sons, Inc.
Hoboken, NJ. 1975. 400p. ISBN:0-471-01090-1, ISBN13:
978-0-471-01090-6. Dewey:512/.02. LCCN:74-082577.

Audience: **u,f.**

Humphreys, James E.   **QA251 .H83**
Introduction to Lie Algebras and Representation Theory. Trade
Cloth. Springer. New York, NY. 1994. XII, 173p. Graduate Texts
in Mathematics ISBN:0-387-90053-5, ISBN13:
978-0-387-90053-7. Dewey:512/.55. LCCN:72-085951.

Audience: **u,f.**

Jacobson, Nathan   **QA154.2.J32 1985**
Basic Algebra I. Ed. 2. Cloth Text. W. H. Freeman & Company.
New York, NY. 1985. 499p. ISBN:0-7167-1480-9, ISBN13:
978-0-7167-1480-4. Dewey:512.9. LCCN:84-025836.

Audience: **u,f.** *B*

Jacobson, Nathan   **QA154.2 .J32 1985**
Basic Algebra II. Ed. 2. Cloth Text. W. H. Freeman &
Company. New York, NY. 1989. 686p. ISBN:0-7167-1933-9,
ISBN13: 978-0-7167-1933-5. Dewey:512.9. LCCN:84-025836.

Audience: **u,f.**

Lane, Saunders Mac &   **QA162**
Birkhoff, Garrett D.
Algebra. Ed. 3. Trade Cloth. American Mathematical Society.
Providence, RI. 1999. 626p. Chelsea Publishing Ser.
ISBN:0-8218-1646-2, ISBN13: 978-0-8218-1646-2.
Dewey:512.02.

Audience: **u,f.**

Lawvere, F. William &   **QA169.L355 1997**
Schanuel, Stephen Hoel
Conceptual Mathematics: A First Introduction to Categories.
Trade Paper. Cambridge University Press. New York, NY. 1997.
374p. ISBN:0-521-47817-0, ISBN13: 978-0-521-47817-5.
Dewey:511.3.

Audience: **u,f.** *Choice, 1998.*

Lidl, Rudolf & Pilz, Günter   **QA162.L53 1998**
Applied Abstract Algebra. Ed. 2. F. W. Gehring & P. R. Halmos
(Editors). Trade Cloth. Springer. New York, NY. 1997. XVI,
508p. Undergraduate Texts in Mathematics
ISBN:0-387-98290-6, ISBN13: 978-0-387-98290-8.
Dewey:512/.02. LCCN:97-022883.

Audience: **u.**

Little, John, et al.   **QA564.C688 1997**
Ideals, Varieties, and Algorithms: An Introduction to
Computational Algebraic Geometry and Commutative Algebra.
Ed. 2. David Cox & Donal O'Shea (Authors). Trade Cloth.

Springer. New York, NY. 1996. XIII, 556p. Undergraduate Texts in Mathematics ISBN:0-387-94680-2, ISBN13: 978-0-387-94680-1. Dewey:516.3/5. LCCN:96-008023.

Audience: **u,f.**

McCoy, Neal H.   **QA247.M2**
Rings and Ideals. Trade Cloth. Mathematical Association of America. Washington, DC. 1948. 216p. Carus Monographs, No. 8 ISBN:0-88385-008-7, ISBN13: 978-0-88385-008-4. Dewey:512.81.

Audience: **u.**

Reid, Miles   **QA251.3 .R45 1995**
Undergraduate Commutative Algebra. C. M. Series & J. W. Bruce (Contribution by). Trade Cloth. Cambridge University Press. New York, NY. 1995. 167p. London Mathematical Society Student Texts Ser., No. 29 ISBN:0-521-45255-4, ISBN13: 978-0-521-45255-7. Dewey:512/.24. LCCN:94-027644.

Audience: **u.**

Rotman, Joseph J.   **QA3.P8 VOL. 85**
Introduction to Homological Algebra, No. 85. Trade Cloth. Elsevier Science & Technology Books. Saint Louis, MO. 1979. 400p. Pure and Applied Mathematics Ser., 85 ISBN:0-12-599250-5, ISBN13: 978-0-12-599250-3. Dewey:512/.55. LCCN:78-020001.

Audience: **u,f.** *B*

Samuel, Pierre & Zariski, Oscar   **QA251**
Commutative Algebra, Vol. 2. Trade Cloth. Springer. New York, NY. 1997. 432p. Graduate Texts in Mathematics, Vol. 29 ISBN:0-387-90171-X, ISBN13: 978-0-387-90171-8. Dewey:512.24. LCCN:75-017751.

Audience: **u,f.**

Serre, Jean Pierre   **QA564.S4313 2000**
Local Algebra. C. W. Chin (Translator). Cloth Text. Springer. New York, NY. 2000. 108p. Monographs in Mathematics ISBN:3-540-66641-9, ISBN13: 978-3-540-66641-7. Dewey:516.3/5. LCCN:00-032970.

Audience: **u,f.**

Smith, Jonathan D. H. & Romanowska, Anna B.   **QA155.S62 1999**
Post-Modern Algebra. Trade Cloth. John Wiley & Sons, Inc. Hoboken, NJ. 1999. 384p. Pure and Applied Mathematics Ser., Vol. 26:A Wiley-Interscience Series of Texts, Monographs and Tracts ISBN:0-471-12738-8, ISBN13: 978-0-471-12738-3. Dewey:512. LCCN:98-023909.

Audience: **u,f.** *Choice, 1999.*

Stahl, Saul   **QA162.S73 1997**
Introductory Modern Algebra: A Historical Approach. Ed. 1. Trade Cloth. John Wiley & Sons, Inc. Hoboken, NJ. 1996. 336p. ISBN:0-471-16288-4, ISBN13: 978-0-471-16288-9. Dewey:512/.2. LCCN:96-019469.

Audience: **l,u,f.** *Choice, 1997.*

Stewart, Ian   **QA214.S74 1989**
Galois Theory. Ed. 2. Cloth Text. Chapman & Hall. New York, NY. 1990. 288p. ISBN:0-412-34540-4, ISBN13: 978-0-412-34540-1. Dewey:512/.3. LCCN:89-015884.

Audience: **u,f.**

Ueno, Kenji, et al.   **QA445.U3613 2003**
A Mathematical Gift I: The Interplay Between Topology, Functions, Geometry, and Algebra. Kaoji Shiga & S. Morita (Authors). Trade Paper. American Mathematical Society. Providence, RI. 2003. 136p. Mathematical World Ser., Vol. 19 ISBN:0-8218-3282-4, ISBN13: 978-0-8218-3282-0. Dewey:516. LCCN:2003-062778.

Audience: **l,u,f.**

Waerden, Bartel L. van der
Algebra, Vol. I. F. Blum & J. R. Schulenberg (Translators). Trade Paper. Springer. New York, NY. 2003. XIV, 265p. ISBN:0-387-40624-7, ISBN13: 978-0-387-40624-4. Dewey:512/.02.

Audience: **u,f.**

Waerden, Bartel L. van der
Algebra, Vol. II. J. R. Schulenberger (Translator). Trade Paper. Springer. New York, NY. 2003. XII, 284p. ISBN:0-387-40625-5, ISBN13: 978-0-387-40625-1. Dewey:512/.02.

Audience: **u,f.**

Zariski, Oscar & Samuel, Pierre   **QA251.3.Z37 1975**
Commutative Algebra, Volume 1. Springer-Verlag. 1975. ISBN:0-387-90089-6, ISBN13: 978-0-387-90089-6.

Audience: **u,f.**

Algebra and Number Theory > Abstract Algebra > Group Theory

Armstrong, M. A.   **QA372.I68 1990**
Groups and Symmetry. Ed. 2. Trade Cloth. Springer. New York, NY. 1997. 186p. Undergraduate Texts in Mathematics ISBN:0-387-96675-7, ISBN13: 978-0-387-96675-5. Dewey:515/.35. LCCN:89-021765.

Audience: **u.** *Choice, 1989.*

Hall, Marshall   **QA174.2.H35 1999**
The Theory of Groups. Trade Cloth. American Mathematical Society. Providence, RI. 1999. 434p. ISBN:0-8218-1967-4, ISBN13: 978-0-8218-1967-8. Dewey:512/.2. LCCN:99-015536.

Audience: **u.**

Joyner, David   **QA174.2.J69 2002**
Adventures in Group Theory: Rubik's Cube, Merlin's Machine and Other Mathematical Toys. Trade Paper. Johns Hopkins University Press. Baltimore, MD. 2002. 280p. ISBN:0-8018-6947-1, ISBN13: 978-0-8018-6947-1. Dewey:512/.2. LCCN:2001-050252.

Audience: **g.** *Choice, 2003.*

Kurzweil, Hans & Stellmacher, Bernd   **QA177.K87 2004**
The Theory of Finite Groups: An Introduction. Trade Cloth. Springer. New York, NY. 2003. XII, 387p. ISBN:0-387-40510-0, ISBN13: 978-0-387-40510-0. Dewey:512/.2. LCCN:2003-054313.

Audience: **u.**

Lima, Elon Lages   **QA612.L4713 2003**
Fundamental Groups and Covering Spaces. Cloth Text. A K Peters, Ltd. Wellesley, MA. 2003. 210p. ISBN:1-56881-131-4, ISBN13: 978-1-56881-131-4. Dewey:514/.2. LCCN:2003-048719.

Audience: **u,f.** *Choice, 2004.*

Magnus, Wilhelm, et al.   QA174.2.M36 2004
Combinatorial Group Theory: Presentations of Groups in Terms
of Generators and Relations. Ed. 2. Abraham Karrass & Donald
Solitar (Authors). Trade Paper. Dover Publications, Inc.
Mineola, NY. 2004. 464p. ISBN:0-486-43830-9, ISBN13:
978-0-486-43830-6. Dewey:512/.2. LCCN:2004-056124.

Audience: **u,f.**

Parker, Ellen M.   QA174.62.C65P37 1996
Laboratory Experiences in Group Theory. Paper Text.
Mathematical Association of America. Washington, DC. 1996.
112p. Classroom Resource Materials Ser. ISBN:0-88385-705-7,
ISBN13: 978-0-88385-705-2. Dewey:512/.2/07855369.
LCCN:96-077787.

Audience: **f.** *Choice, 1997.*

Rossman, Wulf   QA387.R68 2002
Lie Groups: An Introduction Through Linear Groups. Cloth
Text. Oxford University Press, Inc. New York, NY. 2002. 276p.
Oxford Graduate Texts in Mathematics, Vol. 5
ISBN:0-19-859683-9, ISBN13: 978-0-19-859683-7.
Dewey:512/.55. LCCN:2001-050008.

Audience: **u,f.**

Rotman, Joseph J.   QA174.2.R67 1995
An Introduction to the Theory of Groups. Ed. 4. Trade Cloth.
Springer. New York, NY. 1999. XV, 540p. Graduate Texts in
Mathematics, Vol. 148 ISBN:0-387-94285-8, ISBN13:
978-0-387-94285-8. Dewey:512/.2. LCCN:94-006507.

Audience: **u.**

Algebra and Number Theory > Number Theory

Apostol, Tom M.   QA241 .A6
Introduction to Analytic Number Theory. Trade Cloth. Springer.
New York, NY. 1998. 338p. Undergraduate Texts in
Mathematics ISBN:0-387-90163-9, ISBN13: 978-0-387-90163-3.
Dewey:512/.73. LCCN:75-037697.

Audience: **u.**

Arndt, Jörg & Haenel,   QA484.A7513 2001
Christoph
Pi - Unleashed. C. Lischka & D. Lischka (Translators). Mixed
Media. Springer. New York, NY. 2001. XII, 276p.
ISBN:3-540-66572-2, ISBN13: 978-3-540-66572-4.
Dewey:516/.15. LCCN:00-066062.

Audience: **l,u.**

Borevich, Z. I. &   QA3 .P8 VOL. 20
Shafarevich, I. R.
Number Theory. Trade Paper. Elsevier Science & Technology
Books. Saint Louis, MO. 1986. 448p. Pure and Applied
Mathematics Ser. ISBN:0-12-117851-X, ISBN13:
978-0-12-117851-2. Dewey:512.81.

Audience: **u,f.** *ℬ*

Borwein, Jonathan M. &   QA241
Borwein, Peter B.
PI and the AGM: A Study in Analytic Number Theory and
Computational Complexity. Trade Paper. John Wiley & Sons,
Inc. Hoboken, NJ. 1998. 432p. Canadian Mathematical Society
Series of Monographs and Advanced Texts
ISBN:0-471-31515-X, ISBN13: 978-0-471-31515-5.
Dewey:512/.7. LCCN:86-015811.

Audience: **u,f.**

Bressoud, D. M.   QA161.F3B73 1989
Factorization and Primality Testing. Cloth Text. Springer. New
York, NY. 1997. 237p. Undergraduate Texts in Mathematics
ISBN:0-387-97040-1, ISBN13: 978-0-387-97040-0.
Dewey:512/.74. LCCN:89-019690.

Audience: **u.** *Choice, 1990.*

Bressoud, David M. &   QA241.B788 2000
Wagon, Stan
A Course in Computational Number Theory. Mixed Media. Key
Curriculum Press. Emeryville, CA. 2000. XII, 367p.
ISBN:1-930190-10-7, ISBN13: 978-1-930190-10-8.
Dewey:512/.7. LCCN:99-016037.

Audience: **u.** *Choice, 2000.*

Burger, Edward B.   QA242.B96 2000
Exploring the Number Jungle: A Journey into Diophantine
Analysis. Trade Paper. American Mathematical Society.
Providence, RI. 2000. vi, 151p. STML Ser., Vol. 8
ISBN:0-8218-2640-9, ISBN13: 978-0-8218-2640-9.
Dewey:512/.74. LCCN:00-033180.

Audience: **g,l,u.**

Burger, Edward B. &   QA247.5.B87 2004
Tubbs, Robert
Making Transcendence Transparent: An Intuitive Approach to
Classical Transcendental Number Theory. Trade Cloth. Springer.
New York, NY. 2004. IX, 263p. ISBN:0-387-21444-5, ISBN13:
978-0-387-21444-3. Dewey:512.7/3. LCCN:2004-048101.

Audience: **u.**

Burn, R. P.   QA241 .B827 1997
A Pathway into Number Theory. Ed. 2. Trade Paper. Cambridge
University Press. New York, NY. 1996. 278p.
ISBN:0-521-57540-0, ISBN13: 978-0-521-57540-9.
Dewey:512.7. LCCN:96-022448.

Audience: **l,u,f.**

Conway, John H. & Guy,   QA241.C6897 1996
Richard K.
The Book of Numbers. Cloth Text. Springer. New York, NY.
1998. 318p. ISBN:0-387-97993-X, ISBN13: 978-0-387-97993-9.
Dewey:512.7. LCCN:95-032588.

Audience: **u,f.** *Choice, 1997.*

Derbyshire, John   QA246.D47 2003
Prime Obsession: Bernhard Riemann and the Greatest Unsolved
Problem in Mathematics. Trade Cloth. National Academies
Press. Washington, DC. 2003. 304p. ISBN:0-309-08549-7,
ISBN13: 978-0-309-08549-6. Dewey:512.7/3.
LCCN:2002-156310.

Audience: **g.** *Choice, 2003.*

Esmonde, Jody & Murty,   QA247.E76 2004
Maruti Ram
Problems in Algebraic Number Theory. Ed. 2. Trade Cloth.
Springer. New York, NY. 2004. XVI, 352p. Graduate Texts in
Mathematics Ser., Vol. 190 ISBN:0-387-22182-4, ISBN13:
978-0-387-22182-3. Dewey:512.7/4. LCCN:2004-052213.

Audience: **u,f.**

Eymard, Pierre & Lafon,   QA484.E96 2004
J. P.
The Number [pi]. Trade Paper. American Mathematical Society.
Providence, RI. 2004. 322p. ISBN:0-8218-3246-8, ISBN13:
978-0-8218-3246-2. Dewey:516.22. LCCN:2003-063768.

Audience: **l,u.**

Flannery, Sarah & Flannery,   **QA29.F6A3 2003**
David
In Code: A Mathematical Journey. Trade Paper. Algonquin
Books of Chapel Hill. Chapel Hill, NC. 2002. 352p.
ISBN:1-56512-377-8, ISBN13: 978-1-56512-377-9.
Dewey:005.8/2/092. LCCN:2002-033225.

Audience: **g.**

Garrett, Paul   **QA275.G26 2003**
The Mathematics of Coding Theory. Cloth Text. Prentice Hall
PTR. Upper Saddle River, NJ. 2003. 408p.
ISBN:0-13-101967-8, ISBN13: 978-0-13-101967-6.
Dewey:511.4/3. LCCN:2003-065646.

Audience: **u.**

Gazale, Midhat J.   **QA141.G39 1999**
Number: From Ahmes to Cantor. Trade Cloth. Princeton
University Press. Princeton, NJ. 2000. 314p.
ISBN:0-691-00515-X, ISBN13: 978-0-691-00515-7. Dewey:513.
LCCN:99-036677.

Audience: **l,u.** *Choice, 2000.*

Gouvea, Fernando Q.   **QA241.G64 1997**
P-Adic Numbers: An Introduction. Ed. 2. Trade Paper. Springer.
New York, NY. 1997. VI, 302p. Universitext Ser.
ISBN:3-540-62911-4, ISBN13: 978-3-540-62911-5.
Dewey:512.7/4. LCCN:2003-270626.

Audience: **u.**

Hardy, Godfrey H. &   **QA241**
Wright, E. M.
Introduction to the Theory of Numbers. Ed. 5. Trade Cloth.
Oxford University Press, Inc. New York, NY. 1980. xvi, 426p.
ISBN:0-19-853170-2, ISBN13: 978-0-19-853170-8.
Dewey:512/.7.

Audience: **u,f.**

Hellegouarch, Yves   **QA244.H2913 2002**
Invitation to the Mathematics of Fermat-Wiles. Trade Cloth.
Elsevier Science & Technology Books. Saint Louis, MO. 2001.
400p. ISBN:0-12-339251-9, ISBN13: 978-0-12-339251-0.
Dewey:512/.74. LCCN:2001-089851.

Audience: **u,f.** *Choice, 2002.*

Honsberger, Ross   **QA164**
Mathematical Gems from Elementary Combinatorics, Number
Theory, and Geometry. Mathematical Association of America.
1973. ISBN:0-88385-300-0, ISBN13: 978-0-88385-300-9.

Audience: **l,u,f.**

Ireland, Kenneth & Rosen,   **QA241.I667 1990**
Michael
A Classical Introduction to Modern Number Theory. Ed. 2. J. H.
Ewing, F. W. Gehring & P. R. Halmos (Editors). Trade Cloth.
Springer. New York, NY. 1998. XIV, 389p. Graduate Texts in
Mathematics, Vol. 84 ISBN:0-387-97329-X, ISBN13:
978-0-387-97329-6. Dewey:512.7. LCCN:90-009848.

Audience: **u,f.** *B*

Kaplan, Robert   **QA141.K36 2000**
The Nothing That Is: A Natural History of Zero. Ellen Kaplan
(Illustrator). Trade Cloth. Oxford University Press, Inc. New
York, NY. 1999. 240p. ISBN:0-19-512842-7, ISBN13:
978-0-19-512842-0. Dewey:511.2'11. LCCN:99-029000.

Audience: **g.** *Choice, 2001.*

Koblitz, Neal   **QA564**
Introduction to Elliptic Curves and Modular Forms. Ed. 2. Trade
Cloth. Springer. New York, NY. 1993. 268p. Graduate Texts in
Mathematics, Vol. 97 ISBN:0-387-97966-2, ISBN13:
978-0-387-97966-3. Dewey:516.3/5. LCCN:92-041778.

Audience: **u,f.** *B Choice, 1985.*

Landman, Bruce M. &   **QA166.L34 2003**
Robertson, Aaron
Ramsey Theory on the Integers. Trade Paper. American
Mathematical Society. Providence, RI. 2003. 327p. Student
Mathematical Library, Vol. 24 ISBN:0-8218-3199-2, ISBN13:
978-0-8218-3199-1. Dewey:511/.66. LCCN:2003-062937.

Audience: **l,u.**

LeVeque, William J.   **QA241 .S82**
(Editor)
Studies in Number Theory. Trade Cloth. Mathematical
Association of America. Washington, DC. 1969. 212p. Studies
in Mathematics, No. 6 ISBN:0-88385-106-7, ISBN13:
978-0-88385-106-7. Dewey:512/.81. LCCN:75-076868.

Audience: **l,u.**

Lewand, Robert Edward   **QA268.L48 2000**
Cryptological Mathematics. Paper Text. Mathematical
Association of America. Washington, DC. 2000. 214p.
Classroom Resource Materials Ser. ISBN:0-88385-719-7,
ISBN13: 978-0-88385-719-9. Dewey:003/.54. LCCN:00-105256.

Audience: **u,f.** *Choice, 2001.*

Livio, Mario   **QA466**
The Golden Ratio: The Story of Phi, the World's Most
Astonishing Number. Trade Paper. Broadway Books. New York,
NY. 2003. 304p. ISBN:0-7679-0816-3, ISBN13:
978-0-7679-0816-0. Dewey:516.2/04.

Audience: **g.** *Choice, 2003.*

Mazur, Barry   **QA255.M39 2002**
Imagining Numbers: (Particularly the Square Root of Minus
Fifteen). Trade Paper. Picador. New York, NY. 2004. 288p.
ISBN:0-312-42187-7, ISBN13: 978-0-312-42187-8. Dewey:512.
LCCN:2002-075402.

Audience: **g.**

Mollin, Richard A.   **QA247**
Algebraic Number Theory. Chapman & Hall/CRC. 1999. Series
on Discrete Mathematics and Its Applications
ISBN:0-8493-3989-8, ISBN13: 978-0-8493-3989-9.

Audience: **u,f.**

Nahin, Paul J.   **QA255.N34 1998**
An Imaginary Tale: The Story of (The Square Root of Minus
One). Cloth Text. Princeton University Press. Princeton, NJ.
1998. 274p. ISBN:0-691-02795-1, ISBN13: 978-0-691-02795-1.
Dewey:515/.9. LCCN:97-052082.

Audience: **g.** *Choice, 1999.*

Niven, Ivan (Text by)   **QA247.5 .N57**
Irrational Numbers. Paper Text. Mathematical Association of
America. Washington, DC. 2005. 228p. Carus Monograph Ser.
ISBN:0-88385-038-9, ISBN13: 978-0-88385-038-1.
Dewey:512.81.

Audience: **l,u.**

Niven, Ivan, et al.   **QA241.N56 1991**
An Introduction to the Theory of Numbers. Ed. 5. Hugh L.
Montgomery & Herbert S. Zuckerman (Authors). Trade Cloth.

John Wiley & Sons, Inc. Hoboken, NJ. 1991. 544p.
ISBN:0-471-62546-9, ISBN13: 978-0-471-62546-9.
Dewey:512/.7. LCCN:90-013013.
Audience: **l,u.**

Olds, C., et al.   QA241.5.O38 2000
The Geometry of Numbers. Anneli Lax & Giuliana Davidoff
(Authors). Paper Text. Mathematical Association of America.
Washington, DC. 2001. 192p. New Mathematical Library
ISBN:0-88385-643-3, ISBN13: 978-0-88385-643-7.
Dewey:512.7/5. LCCN:00-110657.
Audience: **l,u.**

Parent, D. P.   QA241.P2913 1984
Exercises in Number Theory. Martina Cole (Translator). Trade
Cloth. Springer. New York, NY. 1984. 539p. Problem Books in
Mathematics ISBN:0-387-96063-5, ISBN13: 978-0-387-96063-0.
Dewey:512/.7. LCCN:84-016056.
Audience: **u,f.**

Pless, Vera   QA268.P55 1998
Introduction to the Theory of Error-Correcting Codes. Ed. 3.
Trade Cloth. John Wiley & Sons, Inc. Hoboken, NJ. 1998. 224p.
Wiley-Interscience Series in Discrete Mathematics Ser., Vol. 48
ISBN:0-471-19047-0, ISBN13: 978-0-471-19047-9.
Dewey:005.7/2. LCCN:97-049834.
Audience: **u.**

Rademacher, Hans   QA241 .R22 1977
Lectures on Elementary Number Theory. Library Binding.
Krieger Publishing Company. Melbourne, FL. 1977. 156p.
ISBN:0-88275-499-8, ISBN13: 978-0-88275-499-4.
Dewey:512/.7. LCCN:76-030495.
Audience: **l,u.** *B*

Serre, Jean Pierre   QA243.S4713 1973
A Course in Arithmetic. Ed. 5. Trade Cloth. Springer. New
York, NY. 1996. 115p. Graduate Texts in Mathematics, Vol. 7
ISBN:0-387-90040-3, ISBN13: 978-0-387-90040-7.
Dewey:512/.73. LCCN:70-190089.
Audience: **u,f.** *B*

Silverman, Joseph   QA241.S497 2006
A Friendly Introduction to Number Theory. Ed. 3. Cloth Text.
Prentice Hall PTR. Upper Saddle River, NJ. 2005. 448p.
ISBN:0-13-186137-9, ISBN13: 978-0-13-186137-4.
Dewey:512.7. LCCN:2005-042950.
Audience: **l,u.**

Singh, Simon   QA244.S55 1997
Fermat's Enigma: The Quest to Solve the World's Greatest
Mathematical Problem. Trade Cloth. Walker & Company. New
York, NY. 1997. 288p. ISBN:0-8027-1331-9, ISBN13:
978-0-8027-1331-5. Dewey:512.74. LCCN:97-020748.
Audience: **g.** *Choice, 1998.*

Stillwell, John   QA39.2.S755 1998
Numbers and Geometry. F. W. Gehring & P. R. Halmos
(Editors). Trade Cloth. Springer. New York, NY. 1997. 364p.
Undergraduate Texts in Mathematics ISBN:0-387-98289-2,
ISBN13: 978-0-387-98289-2. Dewey:510. LCCN:97-022858.
Audience: **u.** *Choice, 1998.*

Stopple, Jeffrey   QA241.S815 2003
A Primer of Analytic Number Theory: From Pythagoras to
Riemann. Cloth Text. Cambridge University Press. New York,
NY. 2003. 398p. ISBN:0-521-81309-3, ISBN13:
978-0-521-81309-9. Dewey:512/.7. LCCN:2002-041263.
Audience: **u.**

Tenenbaum, Gerald &   QA246.T3613 2000
  Mendaes France, Michel
The Prime Numbers and Their Distribution. Trade Paper.
American Mathematical Society. Providence, RI. 2000. xix,
115p. Student Mathematical Library, Vol. 6
ISBN:0-8218-1647-0, ISBN13: 978-0-8218-1647-9.
Dewey:512/.72. LCCN:00-020740.
Audience: **l,u.** *Choice, 2000.*

Weil, Andre   QA241.W3418 1984
Number Theory: An Approach Through History. from
Hammurapi to Legendre. Ed. 2. Trade Cloth. Springer. New
York, NY. 1987. 400p. ISBN:0-8176-3141-0, ISBN13:
978-0-8176-3141-3. Dewey:512/.7/09. LCCN:83-011857.
Audience: **u,f.** *B*

Weil, Andre   QA241 .W342
Number Theory for Beginners. Trade Paper. Springer. New
York, NY. 1985. ISBN:0-387-90381-X, ISBN13:
978-0-387-90381-1. Dewey:512/.7. LCCN:79-010764.
Audience: **u.**

Discrete Mathematics

Anderson, Ian   QA39.2.A533 2000
A First Course in Discrete Mathematics. Trade Paper. Springer.
New York, NY. 2000. VIII, 200p. Undergraduate Mathematics
Ser. ISBN:1-85233-236-0, ISBN13: 978-1-85233-236-5.
Dewey:510. LCCN:00-063762.
Audience: **l,u.**

Balakrishnan, V. K.   QA39.2.B357 1996
Introductory Discrete Mathematics. Trade Paper. Dover
Publications, Inc. Mineola, NY. 1996. 248p.
ISBN:0-486-69115-2, ISBN13: 978-0-486-69115-2. Dewey:511.
LCCN:95-052384.
Audience: **l,u.**

Elaydi, Saber   QA614.8
Discrete Chaos. Chapman & Hall/CRC. 2000.
ISBN:1-58488-002-3, ISBN13: 978-1-58488-002-8.
Audience: **u.**

Goldstein, Larry Joel, et al.   QA39.2.G643 2003
Finite Mathematics and Its Applications. Ed. 8. David I.
Schneider & Martha J. Siegel (Authors). Cloth Text. Prentice
Hall PTR. Upper Saddle River, NJ. 2003. 768p.
ISBN:0-13-046620-4, ISBN13: 978-0-13-046620-4. Dewey:510.
LCCN:2002-029303.
Audience: **l,u.**

Holmgren, Richard A.   QA614.8.H65 1996
A First Course in Discrete Dynamical Systems. Ed. 2. Trade
Paper. Springer. New York, NY. 2000. XV, 223p. Universitext
Ser. ISBN:0-387-94780-9, ISBN13: 978-0-387-94780-8.
Dewey:514/.74. LCCN:96-014777.
Audience: **u.** *Choice, 1994.*

Kemeny, John G., et al.   QA39.2
Introduction to Finite Mathematics. Ed. 3. J. Laurie Snell &
Gerald L. Thompson (Authors). Cloth Text. Prentice Hall PTR.
Upper Saddle River, NJ. 1974. 512p. ISBN:0-13-483834-3,
ISBN13: 978-0-13-483834-2. Dewey:510. LCCN:73-016326.

Audience: **l.**

Lipschutz, Seymour &   QA162.L56 1997
Lipson, Marc Lars
Schaum's Outline of Theory and Problems of Discrete
Mathematics. Ed. 2. Paper Text. McGraw-Hill Companies, The.
New York, NY. 1997. 528p. Schaum's Outline Ser.
ISBN:0-07-038045-7, ISBN13: 978-0-07-038045-5.
Dewey:512/.02. LCCN:97-019341.

Audience: **l,u.**

Lovász, Laszlo, et al.   QA39.3.L68 2003
Discrete Mathematics: Elementary and Beyond. Jozsef Pelikán
& Katalin L. Vesztergombi (Authors). Trade Cloth. Springer.
New York, NY. 2003. IX, 290p. Undergraduate Texts in
Mathematics Ser. ISBN:0-387-95584-4, ISBN13:
978-0-387-95584-1. Dewey:510. LCCN:2002-030585.

Audience: **l,u.** *Choice, 2003.*

Maurer, Stephen B. &   QA39.3.M435 2004
Ralston, Anthony
Discrete Algorithmic Mathematics. Ed. 3. Cloth Text. A K
Peters, Ltd. Wellesley, MA. 2004. 600p. ISBN:1-56881-166-7,
ISBN13: 978-1-56881-166-6. Dewey:510. LCCN:2004-044529.

Audience: **u,f.**

Wilf, Herbert S.   QA353.G44W55 2005
Generating Functionology. Ed. 3. Cloth Text. A K Peters, Ltd.
Wellesley, MA. 2006. 185p. ISBN:1-56881-279-5, ISBN13:
978-1-56881-279-3. Dewey:515/.55. LCCN:2005-054995.

Audience: **u,f.** *Choice, 1994.*

Discrete Mathematics > Combinatorics

Ahuja, Ravindra K., et al.   T57.85 .A37 1993
Network Flows: Theory, Algorithms, and Applications. Ed. 1.
Thomas L. Magnanti & James B. Orlin (Authors). Cloth Text.
Prentice Hall PTR. Upper Saddle River, NJ. 1993. 864p.
ISBN:0-13-617549-X, ISBN13: 978-0-13-617549-0.
Dewey:658.4/032. LCCN:92-026702.

Audience: **u.**

Aigner, Martin   QA164.A36 1997
Combinatorial Theory. Trade Paper. Springer. New York, NY.
1997. VIII, 500p. Classics in Mathematics Ser.
ISBN:3-540-61787-6, ISBN13: 978-3-540-61787-7.
Dewey:511/.6. LCCN:96-051833.

Audience: **u,f.**

Balakrishnan, V. K.   QA164
Schaum's Outline of Theory and Problems of Combinatorics.
McGraw-Hill. 1995. ISBN:0-07-003575-X, ISBN13:
978-0-07-003575-1.

Audience: **l,u.**

Benjamin, Arthur & Quinn,   QA164
Jennifer
Proofs That Really Count: The Art of Combinatorial Proof.
Cloth Text. Mathematical Association of America. Washington,

DC. 2003. 208p. Dolciani Mathematical Expositions Ser., 27
ISBN:0-88385-333-7, ISBN13: 978-0-88385-333-7.
Dewey:511/.62. LCCN:2003-108524.

Audience: **u.** *Choice, 2004.*

Björner and RP Stanley   QA164
☐ Combinatorial Miscellany.
http://www-math.mit.edu/~rstan/papers/comb.ps.gz

Audience: **g.**

Bogart, Kenneth P.   QA164.B63 2000
Introductory Combinatorics. Ed. 3. Cloth Text. Brooks/Cole.
Pacific Grove, CA. 2000. 654p. ISBN:0-12-110830-9, ISBN13:
978-0-12-110830-4. Dewey:511/.6. LCCN:99-068562.

Audience: **l,u.** *B*

Bressoud, David M.   QA188 .B73 1999
Proofs and Confirmations: The Story of the Alternating-Sign
Matrix Conjecture. Gerald L. Alexanderson, Dipa Choudhury,
William J. Firey, Dan Kalman, Eleanor Lang, Russell Merris,
Jeffrey L. Nunemacher, Ellen M. Parker, Jean J. Pedersen &
William Watkins (Contribution by). Cloth Text. Cambridge
University Press. New York, NY. 1999. 290p. Spectrum Ser.
ISBN:0-521-66170-6, ISBN13: 978-0-521-66170-6.
Dewey:512.9/434. LCCN:99-020232.

Audience: **u.** *Choice, 2000.*

Brualdi, Richard A.   QA164.B63 2004
Introductory Combinatorics. Ed. 4. Cloth Text. Prentice Hall
PTR. Upper Saddle River, NJ. 2004. 640p.
ISBN:0-13-100119-1, ISBN13: 978-0-13-100119-0.
Dewey:511/.6. LCCN:2004-044455.

Audience: **l,u.**

Cameron, P. J. & Van Lint,   QA166.25 .C36 1991
J. H.
Designs, Graphs, Codes and Their Links. J. W. Bruce
(Contribution by). Cloth Text. Cambridge University Press. New
York, NY. 1991. 250p. London Mathematical Society Student
Texts Ser., No. 22 ISBN:0-521-41325-7, ISBN13:
978-0-521-41325-1. Dewey:511/.6.

Audience: **u.**

Davey, B. A. & Priestley, H.   QA171.5 .D38 2002
A.
Introduction to Lattices and Order. Ed. 2. Trade Paper.
Cambridge University Press. New York, NY. 2002. 310p.
ISBN:0-521-78451-4, ISBN13: 978-0-521-78451-1.
Dewey:511.3/3. LCCN:2001-043910.

Audience: **u,f.**

Godsil, C. D.   QA164
Algebraic Combinatorics. Chapman & Hall. 1993.
ISBN:0-412-04131-6, ISBN13: 978-0-412-04131-0.

Audience: **u.**

Henle, Michael   QA612.H46 1994
A Combinatorial Introduction to Topology. Trade Paper. Dover
Publications, Inc. Mineola, NY. 1994. 310p.
ISBN:0-486-67966-7, ISBN13: 978-0-486-67966-2.
Dewey:514/.2. LCCN:93-050761.

Audience: **u.**

Honsberger, Ross   QA164
Mathematical Gems from Elementary Combinatorics, Number
Theory, and Geometry. Mathematical Association of America.
1973. ISBN:0-88385-300-0, ISBN13: 978-0-88385-300-9.

Audience: **l,u,f.**

Lovász, Laszio   QA164 .L69 1993
Combinatorial Problems and Exercises. Ed. 2. Trade Cloth.
Elsevier Science & Technology Books. Saint Louis, MO. 1993.
636p. ISBN:0-444-81504-X, ISBN13: 978-0-444-81504-0.
Dewey:511.6076.

Audience: **u,f.**

Magnus, Wilhelm, et al.   QA174.2.M36 2004
Combinatorial Group Theory: Presentations of Groups in Terms
of Generators and Relations. Ed. 2. Abraham Karrass & Donald
Solitar (Authors). Trade Paper. Dover Publications, Inc.
Mineola, NY. 2004. 464p. ISBN:0-486-43830-9, ISBN13:
978-0-486-43830-6. Dewey:512/.2. LCCN:2004-056124.

Audience: **u,f.**

Marcus, Daniel M.   QA164.M345 1998
Combinatorics: A Problem Oriented Approach. Paper Text.
Mathematical Association of America. Washington, DC. 1999.
152p. Classroom Resource Materials Ser. ISBN:0-88385-710-3,
ISBN13: 978-0-88385-710-6. Dewey:511/.6. LCCN:98-085594.

Audience: **u,f.** *Choice, 1999.*

Nemhauser, George L. &   T57.74
  Wolsey, Laurence A.
Integer and Combinatorial Optimization. Trade Paper. John
Wiley & Sons, Inc. Hoboken, NJ. 1999. 784p.
Wiley-Interscience Series in Discrete Mathematics, Vol. 55
ISBN:0-471-35943-2, ISBN13: 978-0-471-35943-2.
Dewey:519.7/7.

Audience: **u,f.**

Niven, Ivan   QA164.N58 1965
The Mathematics of Choice. Paper Text. Mathematical
Association of America. Washington, DC. 1965. 202p. New
Mathematical Library, No. 15 ISBN:0-88385-615-8, ISBN13:
978-0-88385-615-4. Dewey:511.6. LCCN:65-017470.

Audience: **l,u.**

Pach, János & Agarwal,   QA167.P33 1995
  Pankaj K.
Combinatorial Geometry. Ed. 1. Trade Cloth. John Wiley &
Sons, Inc. Hoboken, NJ. 1995. 376p. Wiley-Interscience Series
in Discrete Mathematics Ser., Vol. 37 ISBN:0-471-58890-3,
ISBN13: 978-0-471-58890-0. Dewey:516/.13. LCCN:94-048203.

Audience: **u.** *Choice, 1996.*

Roberts, Fred & Tesman,   QA164.R6 2005
  Barry
Applied Combinatorics. Ed. 2. Cloth Text. Prentice Hall PTR.
Upper Saddle River, NJ. 2004. 848p. ISBN:0-13-079603-4,
ISBN13: 978-0-13-079603-5. Dewey:511/.6.
LCCN:2005-273841.

Audience: **u.**

Rota, Gian-Carlo (Editor)   QA164 .S84
Studies in Combinatorics. Cloth Text. Mathematical Association
of America. Washington, DC. 1978. 273p. Studies in
Mathematics, No. 17 ISBN:0-88385-117-2, ISBN13:
978-0-88385-117-3. Dewey:511/.6. LCCN:78-060730.

Audience: **u.**

Ryser, Herbert J.   QA165 .R95
Combinatorial Mathematics. Trade Cloth. Mathematical
Association of America. Washington, DC. 1963. 154p. Carus
Mathematical Monographs, No. 14 ISBN:0-88385-014-1,
ISBN13: 978-0-88385-014-5. Dewey:512.5. LCCN:65-012288.

Audience: **u.**

Sachov, V. N.   QA164 .S2313 1997
Probabilistic Methods in Combinatorial Analysis. V. A. Vatutin
(Translator). Trade Cloth. Cambridge University Press. New
York, NY. 1997. 256p. Encyclopedia of Mathematics and Its
Applications Ser., No. 56 ISBN:0-521-45512-X, ISBN13:
978-0-521-45512-1. Dewey:519.2. LCCN:94-030891.

Audience: **u,f.**

Stanley, Richard P.   QA164.8 .S73 1997
Enumerative Combinatorics, Vol. 2. B. Bollobas (Contribution
by), Sergey Fomin (Appendix by), W. Fulton, A. Katok, F.
Kirwan, P. Sarnak & B. Simon (Contribution by). Trade Paper.
Cambridge University Press. New York, NY. 2001. 598p.
Cambridge Studies in Advanced Mathematics, Vol. 62
ISBN:0-521-78987-7, ISBN13: 978-0-521-78987-5.
Dewey:511/.62.

Audience: **u,f.** *Choice, 1999.*

Stanley, Richard P.   QA164.8 .S73 1997
Enumerative Combinatorics, Vol. 1. Gian-Carlo Rota (Foreword
by), B. Bollobas, W. Fulton, A. Katok, F. Kirwan, P. Sarnak &
B. Simon (Contribution by). Trade Paper. Cambridge University
Press. New York, NY. 2000. 338p. Cambridge Studies in
Advanced Mathematics, No. 49 ISBN:0-521-66351-2, ISBN13:
978-0-521-66351-9. Dewey:511/.62. LCCN:96-044267.

Audience: **u,f.** *Choice, 1999.*

Stanton, D. W. & White,   QA164.S79 1986
  D. E.
Constructive Combinatorics. Trade Paper. Springer. New York,
NY. 1986. 204p. Undergraduate Texts in Mathematics
ISBN:0-387-96347-2, ISBN13: 978-0-387-96347-1.
Dewey:511/.6. LCCN:86-006585.

Audience: **u.** *Choice, 1986.*

Thompson, Thomas   QA177
From Error Correcting Codes through Sphere Packings to
Semigroups. William Watkins (Contribution by). Trade Paper.
Mathematical Association of America. Washington, DC. 2004.
244p. Carus Mathematical Monographs ISBN:0-88385-037-0,
ISBN13: 978-0-88385-037-4. Dewey:512.2/3.

Audience: **u.**

Tucker, Alan   QA164.T83 2002
Applied Combinatorics. Ed. 4. Trade Cloth. John Wiley & Sons,
Inc. Hoboken, NJ. 2001. 464p. ISBN:0-471-43809-X, ISBN13:
978-0-471-43809-0. Dewey:511/.6. LCCN:2001-035224.

Audience: **u.** *B*

van Lint, Jacobus H. &   QA164 .L56 2001
  Wilson, Richard M.
A Course in Combinatorics. Ed. 2. Cloth Text. Cambridge
University Press. New York, NY. 2001. 616p.
ISBN:0-521-80340-3, ISBN13: 978-0-521-80340-3.
Dewey:511/.6. LCCN:2002-276170.

Audience: **u.** *Choice, 1994.*

Discrete Mathematics > Graph Theory

Balakrishnan, V. K.   QA166
Schaum's Outline of Theory and Problems of Graph Theory.
McGraw-Hill. 1997. ISBN:0-07-005489-4, ISBN13:
978-0-07-005489-9.

Audience: **u.**

Biggs, Norman L.   QA166 .B53 1993
Algebraic Graph Theory. Ed. 2. Trade Paper. Cambridge
University Press. New York, NY. 1994. 213p. Cambridge
Mathematical Library ISBN:0-521-45897-8, ISBN13:
978-0-521-45897-9. Dewey:511/.5. LCCN:73-086042.

Audience: **u.**

Bondy, Adrian J. & Murty,   QA166
U. S. R.
Graph Theory with Applications. Trade Cloth. John Wiley &
Sons, Inc. Hoboken, NJ. 2005. 296p. ISBN:0-471-36324-3,
ISBN13: 978-0-471-36324-8. Dewey:511.5.

Audience: **u.**

Chartrand, Gary and   QA166
Lesniak, Linda
Graphs and Digraphs. Ed. 4. Chapman & Hall/CRC. 2005.
ISBN:1-58488-390-1, ISBN13: 978-1-58488-390-6.

Audience: **u,f.**

Chartrand, Gary & Zhang,   QA166.C455 2005
Ping
Introduction to Graph Theory (reprint). Cloth Text. McGraw-Hill
Higher Education. Burr Ridge, IL. 2004. 484p. The Walter
Rudin Student Series in Advanced Mathematics
ISBN:0-07-320416-1, ISBN13: 978-0-07-320416-1.
Dewey:511/.5. LCCN:2004-104286.

Audience: **u.**

Gross, Jonathan L. &   QA166.G76 1987
Tucker, Thomas W.
Topological Graph Theory. Ed. 99. Trade Cloth. John Wiley &
Sons, Inc. Hoboken, NJ. 1987. 351p. Interscience Series in
Discrete Mathematics ISBN:0-471-04926-3, ISBN13:
978-0-471-04926-5. Dewey:511/.5. LCCN:87-006221.

Audience: **u,f.**

Harris, John M., et al.   QA165.H37 2000
Combinatorics and Graph Theory. Jeffry L. Hirst & Michael J.
Mossinghoff (Authors). Trade Cloth. Springer. New York, NY.
2000. 304p. Undergraduate Texts in Mathematics
ISBN:0-387-98736-3, ISBN13: 978-0-387-98736-1.
Dewey:511/.6. LCCN:99-049806.

Audience: **u.** *Choice, 2001.*

Hartsfield, Nora & Ringel,   QA166
Gerhard (Editors)
Pearls in Graph Theory: A Comprehensive Introduction. Ed. 2.
Trade Cloth. Elsevier Science & Technology Books. Saint
Louis, MO. 1994. 249p. ISBN:0-12-328553-4, ISBN13:
978-0-12-328553-9. Dewey:511/.5.

Audience: **u,f.** *Choice, 1991.*

Kocay, William, and Donald   QA166.245
L. Kreher
Graphs, Algorithms and Optimization. Chapman & Hall/CRC.
2005. ISBN:1-58488-396-0, ISBN13: 978-1-58488-396-8.

Audience: **u.**

Watkins, John J.   QA95.W35 2004
Across the Board: The Mathematics of Chessboard Problems.
Trade Cloth. Princeton University Press. Princeton, NJ. 2004.
264p. ISBN:0-691-11503-6, ISBN13: 978-0-691-11503-0.
Dewey:793.74. LCCN:2003-062308.

Audience: **g.** *Choice, 2005.*

West, Douglas B.   QA166.W43 2001
Introduction to Graph Theory. Ed. 2. Cloth Text. Prentice Hall
PTR. Upper Saddle River, NJ. 2000. 470p.
ISBN:0-13-014400-2, ISBN13: 978-0-13-014400-3.
Dewey:511/.5. LCCN:00-039993.

Audience: **u.**

Wilson, Robin   QA612.19.W54 2002
Four Colors Suffice: How the Map Problem Was Solved. Trade
Cloth. Princeton University Press. Princeton, NJ. 2003. 280p.
ISBN:0-691-11533-8, ISBN13: 978-0-691-11533-7.
Dewey:511.5. LCCN:2002-114311.

Audience: **g.** *Choice, 2003.*

Wilson, Robin J.   QA166
Introduction to Graph Theory. Ed. 4. Trade Paper.
Addison-Wesley Longman, Inc. Boston, MA. 1996. 184p.
ISBN:0-582-24993-7, ISBN13: 978-0-582-24993-6.
Dewey:511/.5.

Audience: **u.**

Statistics and Probability

Ash, Robert B. &   QA273.A775 2000
Doleans-Dade, Catherine A.
Probability and Measure Theory. Ed. 2. Cloth Text. Elsevier
Science & Technology Books. Saint Louis, MO. 1999. 516p.
ISBN:0-12-065202-1, ISBN13: 978-0-12-065202-0.
Dewey:519.2. LCCN:99-065669.

Audience: **u.**

Bennett, Deborah J.   QA273.15.B46 1998
Randomness. Trade Cloth. Harvard University Press. Cambridge,
MA. 1998. 256p. ISBN:0-674-10745-4, ISBN13:
978-0-674-10745-8. Dewey:519.2. LCCN:97-035054.

Audience: **g.** *Choice, 1998.*

Beyer, William H. (Editor)   QA276.25.C72 1990
CRC Standard Probability and Statistics Tables and Formulae.
CRC Press. 1990. ISBN:0-8493-0680-9, ISBN13:
978-0-8493-0680-8.

Audience: **l,u,f.**

Bolstad, William M.   QA279.5.B65 2004
Introduction to Bayesian Statistics. Trade Cloth. John Wiley &
Sons, Inc. Hoboken, NJ. 2004. 376p. ISBN:0-471-27020-2,
ISBN13: 978-0-471-27020-1. Dewey:519.5/42.
LCCN:2003-057660.

Audience: **u,f.** *Choice, 2004.*

Cleveland, William S.   QA90.C54 1994
The Elements of Graphing Data. Library Binding. Hobart Press.
Summit, NJ. 1994. 323p. ISBN:0-9634884-1-4, ISBN13:
978-0-9634884-1-1. Dewey:001.4/226. LCCN:94-075052.

Audience: **l,u.** *Choice, 1995, 1985.*

Devore, Jay L.   QA273.D46 2004
Probability and Statistics for Engineering and the Sciences. Ed.
6. Cloth Text. Brooks/Cole. Pacific Grove, CA. 2003. 816p.
ISBN:0-534-39933-9, ISBN13: 978-0-534-39933-7.
Dewey:519.2. LCCN:2003-101979.

Audience: **l,u.**

Durrett, Richard   QA273.D865 2005
Probability: Theory and Examples. Ed. 3. Cloth Text.
Brooks/Cole. Pacific Grove, CA. 2004. 528p. Duxbury
Advanced Ser. ISBN:0-534-42441-4, ISBN13:
978-0-534-42441-1. Dewey:519.2. LCCN:2004-541125.
Audience: **u.**

Evans, Merran, et al.   QA273.6.E92 2000
Statistical Distributions. Ed. 3. Nicholas Hastings & J. Brian
Peacock (Authors). Trade Paper. John Wiley & Sons, Inc.
Hoboken, NJ. 2000. 248p. Wiley Series in Probability and
Statistics, Vol. 359 ISBN:0-471-37124-6, ISBN13:
978-0-471-37124-3. Dewey:519.2/4. LCCN:99-088655.
Audience: **u,f.**

Freedman, David, et al.   QA276.F683 1998
Statistics. Ed. 3. Robert Pisani & Roger Purves (Authors). Trade
Cloth. W. W. Norton & Company, Inc. New York, NY. 1997.
720p. ISBN:0-393-97083-3, ISBN13: 978-0-393-97083-8.
Dewey:519.5. LCCN:97-021345.
Audience: **l.**

Gigerenzer, Gerd   QA273.15.G54 2002
Calculated Risks: How to Know When Numbers Deceive You.
Trade Cloth. Simon & Schuster. New York, NY. 2002. 320p.
ISBN:0-7432-0556-1, ISBN13: 978-0-7432-0556-6.
Dewey:519.2. LCCN:2002-017010.
Audience: **g.** *Choice, 2002.*

Gross, David, et al.   T57.9.G76 1998
Fundamentals of Queueing Theory. Ed. 3. Carl M. Harris &
Donald Gross (Authors). Trade Cloth. John Wiley & Sons, Inc.
Hoboken, NJ. 1998. 464p. Wiley Series in Probability and
Statistics, Vol. 327 ISBN:0-471-17083-6, ISBN13:
978-0-471-17083-9. Dewey:519.8/2. LCCN:97-013171.
Audience: **u,f.**

Haigh, John   QA273.15.H35 2003
Taking Chances: Winning with Probability. Ed. 2. Trade Paper.
Oxford University Press, Inc. New York, NY. 2003. 400p.
ISBN:0-19-852663-6, ISBN13: 978-0-19-852663-6.
Dewey:519.2. LCCN:2003-269210.
Audience: **g.**

Heyde, C. C. & Seneta, E.   QA276.156.S73 2001
(Editors)
Statisticians of the Centuries. Trade Cloth. Springer. New York,
NY. 2001. XII, 500p. ISBN:0-387-95329-9, ISBN13:
978-0-387-95329-8. Dewey:519.5/092/2 B. LCCN:2001-031422.
Audience: **g.** *Choice, 2002.*

Kotz, Samuel (Editor)   QA276.14
Encyclopedia of Statistical Sciences: Including Supplements and
Updates, Set. Trade Cloth. John Wiley & Sons, Inc. Hoboken,
NJ. 2003. 8811p. ISBN:0-471-46519-4, ISBN13:
978-0-471-46519-5. Dewey:519.5/03/21.
Audience: **l,u,f.**

Lindsey, J. K.   QA278.L5538 1995
Modelling Frequency and Count Data. Trade Cloth. Oxford
University Press, Inc. New York, NY. 1995. 300p. Oxford
Statistical Science Ser., No. 15 ISBN:0-19-852331-9, ISBN13:
978-0-19-852331-4. Dewey:519.5/36. LCCN:94-046457.
Audience: **u.** *Choice, 1996.*

Moore, David S. & Notz,   QA276.12 .M66 2006
William I.
Statistics: Concepts and Controversies. Ed. 6. Trade Paper. W.

H. Freeman & Company. New York, NY. 2005. 480p.
ISBN:0-7167-8636-2, ISBN13: 978-0-7167-8636-8.
Dewey:519.5. LCCN:2005-931294.
Audience: **l.**

Romano, Joseph P. and   QA273.R58 1986
Siegel, Andrew F.
Counterexamples in Probability and Statistics. Wadsworth &
Brooks/Cole Advanced Books & Software. 1986.
Statistics/Probability Ser. ISBN:0-534-05568-0, ISBN13:
978-0-534-05568-4.
Audience: **u,f.**

Salsburg, David   Q175
The Lady Tasting Tea: How Statistics Revolutionized Science in
the Twentieth Century. Trade Paper. Henry Holt & Company.
New York, NY. 2002. 352p. ISBN:0-8050-7134-2, ISBN13:
978-0-8050-7134-4. Dewey:001.4/22/0904.
Audience: **g.**

Stigler, Stephen M.   QA276.15 .S75
The History of Statistics: The Measurement of Uncertainty
Before 1900. Trade Paper. Harvard University Press. Cambridge,
MA. 1990. 432p. Belknap Ser. ISBN:0-674-40341-X, ISBN13:
978-0-674-40341-3. Dewey:519.5/09.
Audience: **l,u.**

Stigler, Stephen M.   QA276.15.S755 1999
Statistics on the Table: The History of Statistical Concepts and
Methods. Trade Cloth. Harvard University Press. Cambridge,
MA. 1999. 510p. ISBN:0-674-83601-4, ISBN13:
978-0-674-83601-3. Dewey:519.5/09. LCCN:99-013719.
Audience: **l,u.** *Choice, 2000.*

Tufte, Edward R.   QA276.3.T83 2001
The Visual Display of Quantitative Information. Ed. 2. Cloth
Text. Graphics Press. Cheshire, CT. 2001. 197p.
ISBN:0-9613921-4-2, ISBN13: 978-0-9613921-4-7.
Dewey:001.4/226. LCCN:2001-271866.
Audience: **g,l,u,f.**

Von Mises, Richard   QA273
Probability, Statistics and Truth. Ed. 2. Hilda Geiringer
(Translator). Trade Paper. Dover Publications, Inc. Mineola, NY.
1981. 244p. ISBN:0-486-24214-5, ISBN13: 978-0-486-24214-9.
Dewey:519.2. LCCN:81-067040.
Audience: **g.**

Walpole, Ronald E., et al.   TA340.P738 2006
Probability and Statistics for Engineers and Scientists. Ed. 8.
Raymond Myers, Sharon L. Myers & Keying Ye (Authors).
Cloth Text. Prentice Hall PTR. Upper Saddle River, NJ. 2006.
848p. ISBN:0-13-187711-9, ISBN13: 978-0-13-187711-5.
Dewey:519.02/462. LCCN:2005-058605.
Audience: **l,u.**

Statistics and Probability > Experimental Methodology/Design

Box, George E. P., et al.   QA279
Statistics for Experimenters: An Introduction to Design, Data
Analysis, and Model Building. William G. Hunter & J. Stuart
Hunter (Authors). Trade Cloth. John Wiley & Sons, Inc.

Hoboken, NJ. 1978. 672p. Wiley Series in Probability and Statistics, Vol. 154 ISBN:0-471-09315-7, ISBN13: 978-0-471-09315-2. Dewey:519.5. LCCN:77-015087.

Audience: **u.**

Lehmann, E. L. & Romano,　　　　**QA277.L425 2005**
Joseph P.
Testing Statistical Hypotheses. Ed. 3. Trade Cloth. Springer. New York, NY. 2006. XIV, 786p. Springer Texts in Statistics Ser. ISBN:0-387-98864-5, ISBN13: 978-0-387-98864-1. Dewey:519.5/6. LCCN:2004-051464.

Audience: **u.**

Mendenhall, William, et al.　　　　**QA276.6.S385 2006**
Elementary Survey Sampling. Ed. 6. R. Lyman Ott & Richard L. Scheaffer (Authors). Cloth Text. Brooks/Cole. Pacific Grove, CA. 2005. 480p. Duxbury Advanced Ser. ISBN:0-534-41805-8, ISBN13: 978-0-534-41805-2. Dewey:519.5/2. LCCN:2004-112934.

Audience: **u.**

Oehlert, Gary W.　　　　**QA279.O34 2000**
A First Course in Design and Analysis of Experiments. Cloth over Boards. Worth Publishers, Inc. New York, NY. 2000. 600p. ISBN:0-7167-3510-5, ISBN13: 978-0-7167-3510-6. Dewey:519.5. LCCN:99-059934.

Audience: **u.**

Statistics and Probability > Statistical Inference and Techniques

Abell, Martha L., et al.　　　　**QA276.4.A24 1999**
Statistics with Mathematica. James P. Braselton & John A. Rafter (Authors). Trade Cloth. Elsevier Science & Technology Books. Saint Louis, MO. 1998. 632p. ISBN:0-12-041554-2, ISBN13: 978-0-12-041554-0. Dewey:519.5/0285/53. LCCN:98-027879.

Audience: **l,u.**　*Choice, 1999.*

Albert, Jim　　　　**QA276.18.A44 2003**
Teaching Statistics Using Baseball. Perfect. Mathematical Association of America. Washington, DC. 2003. 304p. Classroom Resource Materials Ser. ISBN:0-88385-727-8, ISBN13: 978-0-88385-727-4. Dewey:519.5. LCCN:2003-103273.

Audience: **f.**　*Choice, 2004.*

Efron, Bradley; Tibshirani,　　　　**QA276.8**
Robert
Introduction to the Bootstrap. Chapman & Hall. 1993. ISBN:0-412-04231-2, ISBN13: 978-0-412-04231-7.

Audience: **u,f.**

Ewens, Warren J. & Grant,　　　　**QH324.2.E97 2004**
Gregory
Statistical Methods in Bioinformatics: An Introduction. Ed. 2. Trade Cloth. Springer. New York, NY. 2005. XX, 588p. Statistics for Biology and Health Ser. ISBN:0-387-40082-6, ISBN13: 978-0-387-40082-2. Dewey:572.8/0285. LCCN:2004-056491.

Audience: **u,f.**

Fisher, R. A.　　　　**QA276.F497 1990**
Statistical Methods, Experimental Design, and Scientific Inference: A Re-issue of Statistical Methods for Research Workers, the Design of Experiments, and Statistical Methods and Scientific Inference. J. H. Bennett (Editor), F. Yates (Foreword by). Trade Paper. Oxford University Press, Inc. New York, NY. 1990. 832p. ISBN:0-19-852229-0, ISBN13: 978-0-19-852229-4. Dewey:519.5. LCCN:90-006726.

Audience: **u,f.**

Hoaglin, David C. (Editor),　　　　**QA276.U5 2000**
et al.
Understanding Robust and Exploratory Data Analysis. Frederick Mosteller & John W. Tukey (Editors). Trade Paper. John Wiley & Sons, Inc. Hoboken, NJ. 2000. 472p. Wiley Classics Library, Vol. 76 ISBN:0-471-38491-7, ISBN13: 978-0-471-38491-5. Dewey:001.4/22. LCCN:00-028322.

Audience: **u.**

Hoel, Paul G.　　　　**QA276.H573**
Introduction to Statistical Theory. Ed. 1. Cloth Text. Houghton Mifflin Company. New York, NY. 1972. 237p. ISBN:0-395-04637-8, ISBN13: 978-0-395-04637-1. Dewey:519.5. LCCN:70-136172.

Audience: **l,u.**

Hollander, Myles & Wolfe,　　　　**QA278.8.H65 1999**
Douglas A.
Nonparametric Statistical Methods. Ed. 2. Trade Cloth. John Wiley & Sons, Inc. Hoboken, NJ. 1999. 816p. Wiley Series in Probability and Statistics, Vol. 336 ISBN:0-471-19045-4, ISBN13: 978-0-471-19045-5. Dewey:519.5/3. LCCN:98-003314.

Audience: **u.** *B*

Kendall, Maurice　　　　**QA279.5**
Kendall's Advanced Theory of Statistics, Set. Trade Cloth. Hodder Education. London, 2005. A Hodder Arnold Publication ISBN:0-340-81493-4, ISBN13: 978-0-340-81493-2. Dewey:519.5/42.

Audience: **u,f.**

Lindgren　　　　**QA276**
Statistical Theory. Ed. 3. Cloth Text. Prentice Hall PTR. Upper Saddle River, NJ. 1976. xv, 614p. ISBN:0-02-370830-1, ISBN13: 978-0-02-370830-5. Dewey:519.5. LCCN:74-033099.

Audience: **u,f.**

Lomax, Richard G.　　　　**QA276.12.L66 2000**
Statistical Concepts: A Second Course for Education and the Behavioral Sciences. Ed. 2. Trade Paper. Lawrence Erlbaum Associates, Inc. Mahwah, NJ. 2000. 336p. ISBN:0-8058-3783-3, ISBN13: 978-0-8058-3783-4. Dewey:519.5. LCCN:00-059299.

Audience: **u.** *Choice, 1998.*

Moore, Thomas (Editor)　　　　**QA276.18 .T45 2000**
Teaching Statistics: Resources for Undergraduate Instructors. Paper Text. Mathematical Association of America. Washington, DC. 2000. 260p. Notes Ser., Vol. 52 ISBN:0-88385-162-8, ISBN13: 978-0-88385-162-3. Dewey:QA276.18 .T45 2000. LCCN:00-103315.

Audience: **f.** *Choice, 2002.*

Muirhead, Robb J.　　　　**QA278**
Aspects of Multivariate Statistical Theory. Trade Paper. John Wiley & Sons, Inc. Hoboken, NJ. 2005. 712p. Wiley Series in Probability and Statistics Ser. ISBN:0-471-76985-1, ISBN13: 978-0-471-76985-9. Dewey:519.5/35. LCCN:2006-273238.

Audience: **u.**

Rencher, Alvin C.   QA278.R45 2001
Methods of Multivariate Analysis: Basic Applications. Ed. 2.
Trade Cloth. John Wiley & Sons, Inc. Hoboken, NJ. 2002. 738p.
Wiley Series in Probability and Statistics, Vol. 409
ISBN:0-471-41889-7, ISBN13: 978-0-471-41889-4.
Dewey:519.5/35. LCCN:2001-046735.
Audience: **u.** *Choice, 1995.*

Snedecor, George W. &   QA276.12.S59 1989
  Cochran, William G.
Statistical Methods. Ed. 8. ISU Statistics Dept. Staff (Revised
by), D. F. Cox (Contribution by). Trade Cloth. Blackwell
Publishing Professional. Ames, IA. 1989. 524p.
ISBN:0-8138-1561-4, ISBN13: 978-0-8138-1561-9.
Dewey:519.5. LCCN:89-015405.
Audience: **u,f.**

Sobol, Ilya M.   QA298
Primer for the Monte Carlo Method. CRC Press. 1994.
ISBN:0-8493-8673-X, ISBN13: 978-0-8493-8673-2.
Audience: **u.**

Tanur, Judith M., et al.   HA29.S7847
  (Editors)
Statistics: A Guide to Business and Economics. Holden-Day.
1976. Series in Probability and Statistics ISBN:0-8162-8614-0,
ISBN13: 978-0-8162-8614-0.
Audience: **l,u.**

Tanur, Judith M., et al.   HA29.S78474
  (Editors)
Statistics: A Guide to Political and Social Issues. Holden-Day.
1977. ISBN:0-8162-8574-8, ISBN13: 978-0-8162-8574-7.
Audience: **l,u.**

Tanur, Judith M., et al.   QA276.16.S84 2006
Statistics: A Guide to the Unknown. Ed. 4. George Casella,
George W. Cobb, Roger Hoerl, Deborah Nolan & Roxy Peck
(Authors). Paper Text. Brooks/Cole. Pacific Grove, CA. 2005.
464p. ISBN:0-534-37282-1, ISBN13: 978-0-534-37282-8.
Dewey:591.5. LCCN:2004-116710.
Audience: **l.**

Wheater, C. Philip & Cook,   QA276.12.W52 2000
  Penny A.
Statistics for Environmental Investigations. Paper over Boards.
Routledge. New York, NY. 2000. 272p. Introduction to
Environment Ser. ISBN:0-415-19887-9, ISBN13:
978-0-415-19887-5. Dewey:519.5. LCCN:99-040009.
Audience: **l,u.** *Choice, 2001.*

Statistics and Probability > Statistical Inference and Techniques > Regression and Analysis of Variance

Allen, Michael Patrick   QA278.2.A434
Understanding Regression Analysis. Trade Paper. Springer. New
York, NY. 2004. 232p. ISBN:0-306-48433-1, ISBN13:
978-0-306-48433-9. Dewey:519.5/36.
Audience: **l,u.** *Choice, 1998.*

Chatterjee, Samprit, et al.   QA278.2.C5 2000
Regression Analysis by Example. Ed. 3. Ali S. Hadi & Bertram
Price (Authors). Trade Cloth. John Wiley & Sons, Inc. Hoboken,

NJ. 1999. 384p. Wiley Series in Probability and Statistics, Vol.
320 ISBN:0-471-31946-5, ISBN13: 978-0-471-31946-7.
Dewey:519.5/36. LCCN:99-053575.
Audience: **u.**

Cook, R. Dennis &   QA278.2.C663 1994
  Weisberg, Sanford
An Introduction to Regression Graphics. Ed. 1. Trade Cloth.
John Wiley & Sons, Inc. Hoboken, NJ. 1994. 280p. Wiley
Series in Probability and Statistics, Vol. 242
ISBN:0-471-00839-7, ISBN13: 978-0-471-00839-2.
Dewey:519.5/36/078. LCCN:94-019291.
Audience: **u.**

Muller, Keith E. &   QA278.2.M82 2002
  Fetterman, Bethel A.
Regression and Anova: An Integrated Approach Using SAS
Software. Trade Cloth. SAS Publishing. Cary, NC. 2004. 578p.
ISBN:1-58025-890-5, ISBN13: 978-1-58025-890-6.
Dewey:519.536. LCCN:2002-514452.
Audience: **u.**

Weisberg, Sanford   QA278.2.W44 2005
Applied Linear Regression. Ed. 3. Trade Cloth. John Wiley &
Sons, Inc. Hoboken, NJ. 2005. 336p. Wiley Series in Probability
and Statistics ISBN:0-471-66379-4, ISBN13:
978-0-471-66379-9. Dewey:519.5/36. LCCN:2004-050920.
Audience: **u.**

Statistics and Probability > Probability and Stochastic Processes

Beichelt, Frank E.   QA274
Stochastic Processes and Their Applications. Taylor & Francis.
2002. ISBN:0-415-27232-7, ISBN13: 978-0-415-27232-2.
Audience: **u.**

Chung, Kai Lai & AitSahlia,   QA273.C5775 2003
  Farid
Elementary Probability Theory: With Stochastic Processes and
an Introduction to Mathematical Finance. Ed. 4. Trade Cloth.
Springer. New York, NY. 2003. XIII, 402p. Undergraduate Texts
in Mathematics Ser. ISBN:0-387-95578-X, ISBN13:
978-0-387-95578-0. Dewey:519.2. LCCN:2002-030573.
Audience: **u.**

Doob, Joseph L.   QA273
Stochastic Processes. Trade Paper. John Wiley & Sons, Inc.
Hoboken, NJ. 1990. 664p. Wiley Classics Library, Vol. 24
ISBN:0-471-52369-0, ISBN13: 978-0-471-52369-7.
Dewey:519.2.
Audience: **u.**

Dudley, Richard M.   QA273.67 .D84 1999
Uniform Central Limit Theorems. B. Bollobas, W. Fulton, A.
Katok, F. Kirwan, P. Sarnak & B. Simon (Contribution by).
Trade Cloth. Cambridge University Press. New York, NY. 1999.
450p. Cambridge Studies in Advanced Mathematics, No. 63
ISBN:0-521-46102-2, ISBN13: 978-0-521-46102-3.
Dewey:519.2. LCCN:98-035562.
Audience: **u,f.**

Durrett, Rick   QA274.D87 1999
Essentials of Stochastic Processes. G. Casella, S. Fienberg & I.
Olkin (Editors). Trade Cloth. Springer. New York, NY. 2001.

VIII, 281p. Texts in Statistics ISBN:0-387-98836-X, ISBN13: 978-0-387-98836-8. Dewey:519.2. LCCN:99-014733.

Audience: **u.** *Choice, 2000.*

Feller, William   QA273
An Introduction to Probability Theory and Its Applications, Vol. 2. Ed. 2. Trade Paper. John Wiley & Sons, Inc. Hoboken, NJ. 1991. 704p. Wiley Series in Probability and Statistics, Vol. 81 ISBN:0-471-25709-5, ISBN13: 978-0-471-25709-7. Dewey:519.2. LCCN:57-010805.

Audience: **u,f.** *B*

Feller, William   QA273 .F37 1968
An Introduction to Probability Theory and Its Applications, Vol. 1. Ed. 3. Trade Cloth. John Wiley & Sons, Inc. Hoboken, NJ. 1968. 528p. Wiley Series in Probability and Statistics, Vol. 82 ISBN:0-471-25708-7, ISBN13: 978-0-471-25708-0. Dewey:519.2. LCCN:68-011708.

Audience: **u,f.** *B*

Gut, Allan   QA273.G8685 1995
An Intermediate Course in Probability. Trade Paper. Springer. New York, NY. 1995. XIII, 278p. ISBN:0-387-94507-5, ISBN13: 978-0-387-94507-1. Dewey:519.2. LCCN:95-011995.

Audience: **u.**

Hacking, Ian   BC141 .H33 2001
An Introduction to Probability and Inductive Logic. Trade Cloth. Cambridge University Press. New York, NY. 2001. 320p. ISBN:0-521-77287-7, ISBN13: 978-0-521-77287-7. Dewey:160. LCCN:00-045503.

Audience: **u,f.**

Hoel, Paul G.   QA273.H684
Introduction to Probability Theory. Ed. 1. Cloth Text. Houghton Mifflin Company. New York, NY. 1972. 258p. ISBN:0-395-04636-X, ISBN13: 978-0-395-04636-4. Dewey:519.2. LCCN:74-136173.

Audience: **l,u.**

Hoel, Paul G., et al.   QA274 .H6
Introduction to Stochastic Processes. Sidney C. Port & Charles J. Stone (Authors). Paper Text. Waveland Press, Inc. Prospect Heights, IL. 1987. 203p. ISBN:0-88133-267-4, ISBN13: 978-0-88133-267-4. Dewey:519.2.

Audience: **l,u.**

Meester, Ronald   QA274.M6 2003
A Natural Introduction to Probability Theory. Trade Cloth. Birkhauser Boston. Cambridge, MA. 2003. ISBN:0-8176-2188-1, ISBN13: 978-0-8176-2188-9. Dewey:519.2/3. LCCN:2003-062969.

Audience: **u.**

Mills, T. M.   QA273.25 .M55 2001
Problems in Probability. Trade Cloth. World Scientific Publishing Company, Inc. Hackensack, NJ. 2001. 181p. Series on Concrete and Applicable Mathematics, Vol. 2 ISBN:981-02-4598-X, ISBN13: 978-981-02-4598-6. Dewey:519.2/076. LCCN:2002-265582.

Audience: **u,f.**

Mitrani, Isi   QA273 .M595 1998
Probabilistic Modelling. Ed. 2. Cloth Text. Cambridge University Press. New York, NY. 1997. 233p. ISBN:0-521-58511-2, ISBN13: 978-0-521-58511-8. Dewey:003/.85. LCCN:97-026099.

Audience: **u.** *Choice, 1999.*

Nahin, Paul J.   QA273
Duelling Idiots and Other Probability Puzzlers. Trade Paper. Princeton University Press. Princeton, NJ. 2002. 280p. ISBN:0-691-10286-4, ISBN13: 978-0-691-10286-3. Dewey:519.2.

Audience: **g,l,u.** *Choice, 2001.*

Packel, Edward W.   QA271.P3
The Mathematics of Games and Gambling. Paper Text. Mathematical Association of America. Washington, DC. 1996. 151p. New Mathematical Library, No. 28 ISBN:0-88385-628-X, ISBN13: 978-0-88385-628-4. Dewey:519. LCCN:80-085037.

Audience: **l,u.**

Protter, Philip   QA274.22.P76 2004
Stochastic Integration and Differential Equations. Ed. 2. Trade Cloth. Springer. New York, NY. 2005. XIII, 419p. Applications of Mathematics Ser., Vol. 21 ISBN:3-540-00313-4, ISBN13: 978-3-540-00313-7. Dewey:519.2. LCCN:2003-059169.

Audience: **u,f.**

Roman, Steven A.   QA273
Counting and Probability. Ed. 3. Paper Text. Innovative Textbooks. Irvine, CA. 1999. 102p. ISBN:1-878015-18-4, ISBN13: 978-1-878015-18-1. Dewey:519.2.

Audience: **l.**

Rothschild, V. & Logothetis,   QA273.6.R67 1986
Nicholas
Probability Distributions. Paper Text. John Wiley & Sons, Inc. Hoboken, NJ. 1986. 51p. ISBN:0-471-83814-4, ISBN13: 978-0-471-83814-2. Dewey:519.2. LCCN:85-020308.

Audience: **u,f.**

Sachov, V. N.   QA164 .S2313 1997
Probabilistic Methods in Combinatorial Analysis. V. A. Vatutin (Translator). Trade Cloth. Cambridge University Press. New York, NY. 1997. 256p. Encyclopedia of Mathematics and Its Applications Ser., No. 56 ISBN:0-521-45512-X, ISBN13: 978-0-521-45512-1. Dewey:519.2. LCCN:94-030891.

Audience: **u,f.**

Sobel, Matthew J. &   T57.6 H49
Heyman, Daniel P.
Stochastic Models in Operations Research: Stochastic Optimization. Trade Paper. Dover Publications, Inc. Mineola, NY. 2003. 576p. 0 ISBN:0-486-43260-2, ISBN13: 978-0-486-43260-1. Dewey:003.

Audience: **u,f.**

Sobel, Matthew J. &   T57.6H49 2004
Heyman, Daniel P.
Stochastic Models in Operations Research: Stochastic Processes and Operating Characteristics. Trade Paper. Dover Publications, Inc. Mineola, NY. 2003. 560p. 0 ISBN:0-486-43259-9, ISBN13: 978-0-486-43259-5. Dewey:003. LCCN:2003-068673.

Audience: **u,f.**

Weaver, Warren   QA273
Lady Luck: The Theory of Probability. Peg Hosford (Illustrator). Trade Paper. Dover Publications, Inc. Mineola, NY. 1982. 384p. Popular Science Ser. ISBN:0-486-24342-7, ISBN13: 978-0-486-24342-9. Dewey:519.2. LCCN:82-007396.

Audience: **g.**

Calculus

QA303 .S398

Selected Papers on Calculus. Trade Cloth. Mathematical
Association of America. Washington, DC. 1969. 397p.
ISBN:0-88385-201-2, ISBN13: 978-0-88385-201-9.
Dewey:517/.08.

Audience: **l,u,f.**

Adams, Colin C., et al.   **QA303.3.A332 2001**
How to Ace the Rest of Calculus: The Streetwise Guide -
Including Multi-Variable Calculus. Joel Hass & Abigail
Thompson (Authors). Trade Paper. W. H. Freeman & Company.
New York, NY. 2001. 304p. ISBN:0-7167-4174-1, ISBN13:
978-0-7167-4174-9. Dewey:515. LCCN:00-066292.

Audience: **l,u.**

Adams, Colin, et al.   **QA303.3 .A33 1998**
How to Ace Calculus: The Streetwise Guide. Joel Hass &
Abigail Thompson (Authors). Trade Paper. W. H. Freeman &
Company. New York, NY. 1998. 256p. ISBN:0-7167-3160-6,
ISBN13: 978-0-7167-3160-3. Dewey:515/.071.
LCCN:97-051944.

Audience: **l,u.**

Ayres, Frank & Mendelson,   **QA303.A96 1999**
  Elliott
Schaum's Outline of Calculus. Ed. 4. Paper Text. McGraw-Hill
Companies, The. New York, NY. 1999. 578p. Schaum's Outline
Ser. ISBN:0-07-041973-6, ISBN13: 978-0-07-041973-5.
Dewey:515. LCCN:99-038252.

Audience: **l,u.**

Berlinski, David   **QA303.B488 1995**
A Tour of the Calculus. Trade Cloth. Knopf Publishing Group.
New York, NY. 1996. 352p. ISBN:0-679-42645-0, ISBN13:
978-0-679-42645-5. Dewey:515. LCCN:95-004042.

Audience: **l,f.** *Choice, 1996.*

Comenetz, Michael   **QA303.2.C66 2002**
Calculus: The Elements. Trade Cloth. World Scientific
Publishing Company, Inc. Hackensack, NJ. 2002. 540p.
ISBN:981-02-4903-9, ISBN13: 978-981-02-4903-8. Dewey:515.
LCCN:2002-069008.

Audience: **l,f.** *Choice, 2003.*

Edwards, C. H. Jr.   **QA303.E224**
The Historical Development of the Calculus. Ed. 3. Trade Paper.
Springer. New York, NY. 1994. XII, 368p. ISBN:0-387-94313-7,
ISBN13: 978-0-387-94313-8. Dewey:515/.09.

Audience: **l,u,f.** ℬ

Gootman, Elliot C.   **QA303.G65 1997**
Calculus. Trade Paper. Barron's Educational Series, Inc.
Hauppauge, NY. 1997. 342p. Barron's College Review Ser.
ISBN:0-8120-9819-6, ISBN13: 978-0-8120-9819-8. Dewey:515.
LCCN:97-013991.

Audience: **l.**

Neuhauser, Claudia   **QH323.5.N46 2003**
Calculus for Biology and Medicine. Ed. 2. Cloth Text. Prentice
Hall PTR. Upper Saddle River, NJ. 2003. 822p.
ISBN:0-13-045516-4, ISBN13: 978-0-13-045516-1. Dewey:515.
LCCN:2003-048212.

Audience: **l,u.**

Sawyer, W. W.   **QA303 .S2 1961**
What Is Calculus About? Paper Text. Mathematical Association
of America. Washington, DC. 1961. 118p. New Mathematical
Library, No. 2 ISBN:0-88385-602-6, ISBN13:
978-0-88385-602-4. Dewey:515. LCCN:61-006227.

Audience: **l.**

Stewart, James   **QA303.S8825 2003**
Calculus: Early Transcendentals. Ed. 5. Cloth Text, CD-ROM.
Brooks/Cole. Pacific Grove, CA. 2002. 1320p.
ISBN:0-534-39321-7, ISBN13: 978-0-534-39321-2. Dewey:515.
LCCN:2002-112185.

Audience: **l.**

Thomas   **DF78.B398**
Calculus and Analytic Geometry. Ed. 9. Trade Cloth.
Addison-Wesley Longman, Inc. Boston, MA. 1998.
ISBN:0-201-47057-8, ISBN13: 978-0-201-47057-4.
Dewey:949.5.

Audience: **l.**

Calculus > Precalculus

Apostol, Tom M. (Editor)   **QA7 .S44**
Selected Papers on Precalculus. Cloth Text. Mathematical
Association of America. Washington, DC. 1977. 469p. Raymond
W. Brink Selected Mathematical Papers, Vol. 1
ISBN:0-88385-202-0, ISBN13: 978-0-88385-202-6. Dewey:515.
LCCN:77-079279.

Audience: **l,f.**

Demana, Franklin D., et al.   **QA154.2 .D444 1994**
Precalculus Mathematics: A Graphing Approach. Ed. 3. Bert K.
Waits, Stanley R. Clemens, Alan Osborne & Gregory D. Foley
(Authors). Cloth Text. Prentice Hall (School Division). Needham
Heights, MA. 1994. ISBN:0-201-52905-X, ISBN13:
978-0-201-52905-0. Dewey:512/.13/028541. LCCN:92-044754.

Audience: **l.**

Maor, Eli   **QA531.M394 1998**
Trigonometric Delights. Trade Paper. Princeton University Press.
Princeton, NJ. 2002. 250p. ISBN:0-691-09541-8, ISBN13:
978-0-691-09541-7. Dewey:516.24/2.

Audience: **l,f.** *Choice, 1998.*

McKeague, Charles P. &   **QA531.M47 2004**
  Turner, Mark
Trigonometry. Ed. 5. Cloth Text. Brooks/Cole. Pacific Grove,
CA. 2003. 576p. ISBN:0-534-40392-1, ISBN13:
978-0-534-40392-8. Dewey:516.2/4. LCCN:2003-111537.

Audience: **l.**

Ruud, Warren L.   **QA39.2**
Prelude to Calculus. Ed. 3. Cloth Text. Brooks/Cole. Pacific
Grove, CA. 1999. Mathematics Ser. ISBN:0-534-94848-0,
ISBN13: 978-0-534-94848-1. Dewey:510.

Audience: **l.**

Sullivan, Michael   **QA154.3.S85 2005**
Precalculus. Ed. 7. Trade Cloth. Prentice Hall PTR. Upper
Saddle River, NJ. 2005. xx, 1001p. ISBN:0-13-191399-9,
ISBN13: 978-0-13-191399-8. Dewey:512. LCCN:2003-066398.

Audience: **l.**

Calculus > Advanced Calculus

Apostol, Tom M.   **QA300 .A572 1967**
Calculus: One-Variable Calculus with an Introduction to Linear Algebra. Ed. 2. Trade Cloth. John Wiley & Sons, Inc. Hoboken, NJ. 1967. 688p. Calculus Ser., Vol. 1 ISBN:0-471-00005-1, ISBN13: 978-0-471-00005-1. Dewey:515. LCCN:73-020899.

Audience: **l,u.**

Apostol, Tom M.   **QA300 .A572 1967**
Calculus: Multi-Variable Calculus and Linear Algebra with Applications. Ed. 2. Trade Cloth. John Wiley & Sons, Inc. Hoboken, NJ. 1969. 704p. Calculus Ser., Vol. 2 ISBN:0-471-00007-8, ISBN13: 978-0-471-00007-5. Dewey:515. LCCN:67-014605.

Audience: **l,u.**

Courant, Richard   **QA303**
Differential and Integral Calculus. Trade Paper. John Wiley & Sons, Inc. Hoboken, NJ. 2003. Wiley Classics Library ISBN:0-471-48173-4, ISBN13: 978-0-471-48173-7. Dewey:515.

Audience: **l,u.**

Folland, Gerald B.   **QA303.2.F67 2002**
Advanced Calculus. Cloth Text. Prentice Hall PTR. Upper Saddle River, NJ. 2001. 480p. ISBN:0-13-065265-2, ISBN13: 978-0-13-065265-2. Dewey:515. LCCN:2001-055359.

Audience: **u.**

Gradshteyn, I. S.   **QA55.G6613 2000**
Table of Integrals, Series, and Products. Ed. 6. Alan Jeffrey & Daniel Zwillinger (Editors). Cloth Text. Elsevier Science & Technology Books. Saint Louis, MO. 2000. 1163p. ISBN:0-12-294757-6, ISBN13: 978-0-12-294757-5. Dewey:515/.0212. LCCN:00-104373.

Audience: **u,f.**

Spivak, Michael   **QA612**
Calculus on Manifolds: A Modern Approach to Classical Theorems of Advanced Calculus. Trade Paper. Westview Press. Boulder, CO. 2000. 160p. ISBN:0-8053-9021-9, ISBN13: 978-0-8053-9021-6. Dewey:514.3.

Audience: **u,f.**

Calculus > Vector and Tensor Calculus

Barr, Thomas H.   **QA433.B35 2000**
Vector Calculus. Ed. 2. Trade Cloth. Prentice Hall PTR. Upper Saddle River, NJ. 2000. 429p. ISBN:0-13-088005-1, ISBN13: 978-0-13-088005-5. Dewey:515/.63. LCCN:00-056491.

Audience: **u.**

Hay, George E.   **QA261.H39**
Vector and Tensor Analysis. Paper Text. Dover Publications, Inc. Mineola, NY. 1953. 193p. ISBN:0-486-60109-9, ISBN13: 978-0-486-60109-0. Dewey:512.89.

Audience: **u.**

Schey, H. M.   **QA433.S28 2004**
Div, Grad, Curl, and All That: An Informal Text on Vector Calculus. Ed. 4. Trade Paper. W. W. Norton & Company, Inc. New York, NY. 2004. 200p. ISBN:0-393-92516-1, ISBN13: 978-0-393-92516-6. Dewey:515/.63. LCCN:2004-053199.

Audience: **l,u.**

Simmonds, J. G.   **QA433.S535**
A Brief on Tensor Analysis. Ed. 2. Trade Cloth. Springer. New York, NY. 1997. XIV, 112p. Undergraduate Texts in Mathematics ISBN:0-387-94088-X, ISBN13: 978-0-387-94088-5. Dewey:515/.63.

Audience: **u.**

Trotter, Hale F. &   **QA184.W54 2003**
  Williamson, Richard E.
Multivariable Mathematics. Ed. 4. Cloth Text. Prentice Hall PTR. Upper Saddle River, NJ. 2003. 864p. ISBN:0-13-067276-9, ISBN13: 978-0-13-067276-6. Dewey:512/.15. LCCN:2003-049839.

Audience: **u.**

Differential and Integral Equations

Boyce, William E. &   **QA564**
  DiPrima, Richard C.
Elementary Differential Equations: With Solutions Manual. Ed. 8. Trade Cloth. John Wiley & Sons, Inc. Hoboken, NJ. 2004. 918p. ISBN:0-471-69766-4, ISBN13: 978-0-471-69766-4.

Audience: **u.**

Bronson, Richard & Costa,   **QA372**
  Gabriel
Differential Equations. Ed. 3. Paper Text. McGraw-Hill Companies, The. New York, NY. 2006. 384p. ISBN:0-07-145687-2, ISBN13: 978-0-07-145687-6. Dewey:515.3/5.

Audience: **u.**

Davis, Harold T.   **QA303**
Introduction to Nonlinear Differential and Integral Equations. Trade Paper. Dover Publications, Inc. Mineola, NY. 1962. 566p. ISBN:0-486-60971-5, ISBN13: 978-0-486-60971-3. Dewey:517.

Audience: **u.**

Goldberg, Samuel   **QA431.G59 1986**
Introduction to Difference Equations: With Illustrative Examples from Economics, Psychology and Sociology. Trade Paper. Dover Publications, Inc. Mineola, NY. 1986. 260p. ISBN:0-486-65084-7, ISBN13: 978-0-486-65084-5. Dewey:515/.625. LCCN:85-031131.

Audience: **u,f.**

Iserles, Arieh (Editor)   **QA371 .I813 1996**
A First Course in the Numerical Analysis of Differential Equations. M. J. Ablowitz, S. H. Davis, E. J. Hinch, J. Ockendon, P. J. Olver & A. Iserles (Contribution by). Cloth Text. Cambridge University Press. New York, NY. 1996. 396p. Texts in Applied Mathematics , No. 15 ISBN:0-521-55376-8, ISBN13: 978-0-521-55376-6. Dewey:515/.35. LCCN:96-139924.

Audience: **u.**

POLKING, et al.   **QA371.P565 2006**
Differential Equations. Ed. 2. David Arnold, Al Boggess & John Polking (Authors). Cloth Text. Prentice Hall PTR. Upper Saddle River, NJ. 2005. 656p. ISBN:0-13-143738-0, ISBN13: 978-0-13-143738-8. Dewey:515/.35. LCCN:2005-048914.

Audience: **u.**

Protter, Philip QA274.22.P76 2004
Stochastic Integration and Differential Equations. Ed. 2. Trade
Cloth. Springer. New York, NY. 2005. XIII, 419p. Applications
of Mathematics Ser., Vol. 21 ISBN:3-540-00313-4, ISBN13:
978-3-540-00313-7. Dewey:519.2. LCCN:2003-059169.
Audience: **u,f.**

Rassias, J. M. QA377
Counter-Examples in Differential Equations and Related Topics.
Cloth Text. World Scientific Publishing Company, Inc.
Hackensack, NJ. 1991. 192p. ISBN:981-02-0460-4, ISBN13:
978-981-02-0460-0. Dewey:515.353.
Audience: **u,f.**

Zwillinger, Daniel QA371
Handbook of Differential Equations. Ed. 3. Trade Cloth. Elsevier
Science & Technology Books. Saint Louis, MO. 1997. 801p.
ISBN:0-12-784395-7, ISBN13: 978-0-12-784395-7.
Dewey:515.3/5. LCCN:97-038072.
Audience: **u,f.** *Choice, 1989.*

Differential and Integral Equations > Ordinary Differential Equations

Arnold, V. I. QA372
Geometrical Methods in the Theory of Ordinary Differential
Equations. Ed. 2. Mark Levi (Editor), J. Szücs (Translator).
Trade Cloth. Springer. New York, NY. 1996. 351p. Grundlehren
Ser., Vol. 250 ISBN:0-387-96649-8, ISBN13:
978-0-387-96649-6. Dewey:515.3/52.
Audience: **u,f.** *B*

Birkhoff, Garrett D. & Rota, Gian-Carlo QA372.B58 1989
Ordinary Differential Equations. Ed. 4. Trade Cloth. John Wiley
& Sons, Inc. Hoboken, NJ. 1989. 416p. ISBN:0-471-86003-4,
ISBN13: 978-0-471-86003-7. Dewey:515.3/52.
LCCN:88-014231.
Audience: **u.** *B*

Coddington, Earl A. & Levinson, Norman QA372.C6 1984
Theory of Ordinary Differential Equations. Library Binding.
Krieger Publishing Company. Melbourne, FL. 1984. 444p.
ISBN:0-89874-755-4, ISBN13: 978-0-89874-755-3.
Dewey:515.3/52. LCCN:84-004438.
Audience: **u,f.**

Hurewicz, Witold QA371
Lectures on Ordinary Differential Equations. Cloth over Boards.
Dover Publications, Inc. Mineola, NY. 2002. 144p. Dover
Phoenix Editions Ser. ISBN:0-486-49510-8, ISBN13:
978-0-486-49510-1. Dewey:515/.35.
Audience: **u.** *B*

O'Malley, Robert E. Jr. QA372 .O57 1997
Thinking about Ordinary Differential Equations. D. G. Crighton,
M. J. Ablowitz, S. H. Davis, E. J. Hinch, A. Iserles, J.
Ockendon & P. J. Olver (Contribution by). Trade Cloth.
Cambridge University Press. New York, NY. 1997. 259p. Texts
in Applied Mathematics , No. 18 ISBN:0-521-55314-8, ISBN13:
978-0-521-55314-8. Dewey:515.3/5. LCCN:96-014825.
Audience: **u,f.** *Choice, 1997.*

Sanchez, David A. QA372.S175 2002
Ordinary Differential Equations: A Brief Eclectic Tour. Paper
Text. Mathematical Association of America. Washington, DC.
2002. 144p. Classroom Resource Material Ser.
ISBN:0-88385-723-5, ISBN13: 978-0-88385-723-6.
Dewey:515/.35. LCCN:2002-101380.
Audience: **u,f.** *Choice, 2002.*

Shampine, Lawrence F. QA372.S417 1994
Numerical Solution of Ordinary Differential Equations.
Chapman & Hall. 1994. ISBN:0-412-05151-6, ISBN13:
978-0-412-05151-7.
Audience: **u.**

Differential and Integral Equations > Partial Differential Equations

Arnold, Vladimir I. QA377.A815 2004
Lectures on Partial Differential Equations. R. Cooke
(Translator). Trade Paper. Springer. New York, NY. 2004. X,
157p. Universitext Ser. ISBN:3-540-40448-1, ISBN13:
978-3-540-40448-4. Dewey:515/.353. LCCN:2003-060468.
Audience: **u,f.** *Choice, 2005.*

Bleecker, David & Csordas, George (Editors) QA374
Basic Partial Differential Equations. Trade Cloth. International
Press of Boston, Inc. Somerville, MA. 1997. 756p.
Undergraduate Texts Ser. ISBN:1-57146-036-5, ISBN13:
978-1-57146-036-3. Dewey:515.353.
Audience: **u.**

Brown, James Ward & Churchill, Ruel V. QA404.B76 2001
Fourier Series and Boundary Value Problems. Ed. 6. Cloth Text.
McGraw-Hill Higher Education. Burr Ridge, IL. 2000. 360p.
ISBN:0-07-232570-4, ISBN13: 978-0-07-232570-6.
Dewey:515/.2433. LCCN:00-028168.
Audience: **u.**

Constanda, Christian QA377.C7629 2002
Solution Techniques for Elementary Partial Differential
Equations. Chapman & Hall/CRC. 2002. ISBN:1-58488-257-3,
ISBN13: 978-1-58488-257-2.
Audience: **u.**

DuChateau, Paul QA374.D8 1986
Schaum's Outline of Theory and Problems of Partial Differential
Equations. McGraw-Hill. 1986. Schaum's Outline Series
ISBN:0-07-017897-6, ISBN13: 978-0-07-017897-7.
Audience: **u.**

Evans, Lawrence C. QA377.E95 1998
Partial Differential Equations. Trade Cloth. American
Mathematical Society. Providence, RI. 1998. 662p. Graduate
Studies in Mathematics ISBN:0-8218-0772-2, ISBN13:
978-0-8218-0772-9. Dewey:515/.353. LCCN:97-041033.
Audience: **u,f.**

Gockenbach, Mark S. QA377.G63 2002
Partial Differential Equations: Analytical and Numerical
Methods. Trade Cloth, CD-ROM. Society for Industrial &
Applied Mathematics. Philadelphia, PA. 2002. xxii + 614p.
ISBN:0-89871-518-0, ISBN13: 978-0-89871-518-7.
Dewey:515/.353. LCCN:2002-029411.
Audience: **u,f.**

Quarteroni, Alfio & Valli, A.   QA377.Q37 1994
Numerical Approximation of Partial Differential Equations.
Cloth Text. Springer. New York, NY. 1997. 543p. Computational
Mathematics Ser., Vol. 23 ISBN:0-387-57111-6, ISBN13:
978-0-387-57111-9. Dewey:515/.353. LCCN:94-021763.

Audience: **u,f.**

Weinberger, Hans F.   QA374.W43 1995
A First Course in Partial Differential Equations with Complex
Variables and Transform Methods. Trade Paper. Dover
Publications, Inc. Mineola, NY. 1995. 480p.
ISBN:0-486-68640-X, ISBN13: 978-0-486-68640-0.
Dewey:515/.353. LCCN:95-007393.

Audience: **u.**

Differential and Integral Equations > Integral Equations

Atkinson, Kendall E.   QA431 .A837 1997
The Numerical Solution of Integral Equations of the Second
Kind. P. G. Ciarlet, A. Iserles, R. V. Kohn, M. H. Wright, M. J.
Ablowitz, S. H. Davis, E. J. Hinch, J. Ockendon & P. J. Olver
(Contribution by). Trade Cloth. Cambridge University Press.
New York, NY. 1997. 570p. Monographs on Applied and
Computational Mathematics, No. 4 ISBN:0-521-58391-8,
ISBN13: 978-0-521-58391-6. Dewey:515.4/5. LCCN:96-045961.

Audience: **u.**

Davis, Harold T.   QA303
Introduction to Nonlinear Differential and Integral Equations.
Trade Paper. Dover Publications, Inc. Mineola, NY. 1962. 566p.
ISBN:0-486-60971-5, ISBN13: 978-0-486-60971-3. Dewey:517.

Audience: **u.**

Groetsch, Charles W.   QA371
Inverse Problems in the Mathematical Sciences. Trade Cloth.
Informatica International, Inc. Hauppauge, NY. 1993. vi, 152p.
ISBN:3-528-06545-1, ISBN13: 978-3-528-06545-4.
Dewey:530.15535.

Audience: **u,f.**

Kress, Rainer   QA1.A647 VOL.82 1999
Linear Integral Equations. Ed. 2. J. E. Marsden & L. Sirov
(Editors). Trade Cloth. Springer. New York, NY. 1999. XIV,
388p. Applied Mathematical Sciences Ser., Vol. 82
ISBN:0-387-98700-2, ISBN13: 978-0-387-98700-2. Dewey:510
s 515/.45. LCCN:98-051753.

Audience: **u.**

Tricomi, F. G.   QA431.T73 1985
Integral Equations. Trade Paper. Dover Publications, Inc.
Mineola, NY. 1985. 238p. Mathematics Ser.
ISBN:0-486-64828-1, ISBN13: 978-0-486-64828-6.
Dewey:515.4/5. LCCN:84-025917.

Audience: **u.**

Wing, G. Milton   QA431 .W644 1991
A Primer on Integral Equations of the First Kind. Trade Paper.
Society for Industrial & Applied Mathematics. Philadelphia, PA.
1991. xiv, 135p. Miscellaneous Bks., No. 27
ISBN:0-89871-263-7, ISBN13: 978-0-89871-263-6.
Dewey:515/.45. LCCN:91-038059.

Audience: **u,f.**

Differential and Integral Equations > Dynamical Systems and Chaos

Devaney, Robert L.   QA614.8 .D49 1992
First Course in Chaotic Dynamical Systems. Trade Cloth.
Westview Press. Boulder, CO. 1992. 320p. Studies in
Nonlinearity ISBN:0-201-55406-2, ISBN13: 978-0-201-55406-9.
Dewey:515/.352. LCCN:91-038310.

Audience: **u.**

Diacu, Florin & Holmes,   QB362.M3D53 1996
Philip
Celestial Encounters: The Origins of Chaos and Stability. Trade
Cloth. Princeton University Press. Princeton, NJ. 1996. 280p.
Princeton Science Library ISBN:0-691-02743-9, ISBN13:
978-0-691-02743-2. Dewey:521. LCCN:96-000108.

Audience: **u.** *Choice, 1997.*

Drazin, P. G.   QA427 .D7 1992
Nonlinear Systems. D. G. Crighton, M. J. Ablowitz, S. H.
Davis, E. J. Hinch, A. Iserles, J. Ockendon & P. J. Olver
(Contribution by). Trade Paper. Cambridge University Press.
New York, NY. 1992. 331p. Texts in Applied Mathematics , No.
10 ISBN:0-521-40668-4, ISBN13: 978-0-521-40668-0.
Dewey:515/.355. LCCN:91-027971.

Audience: **u,f.**

Glass, Leon & Kaplan,   QA845.K36 1995
Daniel
Understanding Nonlinear Dynamics. Trade Paper. Springer. New
York, NY. 1997. XIX, 420p. Textbooks in Mathematical
Sciences ISBN:0-387-94440-0, ISBN13: 978-0-387-94440-1.
Dewey:515/.352. LCCN:94-043113.

Audience: **u.** *Choice, 1995.*

Gleick, James   Q172.5.C45G54 1988
Chaos: The Making of a New Science. Trade Paper. Penguin
Group (USA) Inc. New York, NY. 1988. 368p.
ISBN:0-14-009250-1, ISBN13: 978-0-14-009250-9. Dewey:003.
LCCN:88-017448.

Audience: **g.**

Hirsch, Morris W., et al.   QA372.H67 2003
Differential Equations, Dynamical Systems, and an Introduction
to Chaos. Ed. 2. Stephen Smale & Robert Devaney (Authors).
Trade Cloth. Elsevier Science & Technology Books. Saint
Louis, MO. 2003. 425p. ISBN:0-12-349703-5, ISBN13:
978-0-12-349703-1. Dewey:515/.35. LCCN:2003-058255.

Audience: **u.**

Holmgren, Richard A.   QA614.8.H65 1996
A First Course in Discrete Dynamical Systems. Ed. 2. Trade
Paper. Springer. New York, NY. 2000. XV, 223p. Universitext
Ser. ISBN:0-387-94780-9, ISBN13: 978-0-387-94780-8.
Dewey:514/.74. LCCN:96-014777.

Audience: **u.** *Choice, 1994.*

Peitgen, Heinz-Otto, et al.   Q172.5.C45P45 2004
Chaos and Fractals: New Frontiers of Science. Ed. 2. Hartmut
Jürgens & Dietmar Saupe (Authors). Trade Cloth. Springer. New
York, NY. 2004. XIII, 864p. ISBN:0-387-20229-3, ISBN13:
978-0-387-20229-7. Dewey:003/.857. LCCN:2003-063341.

Audience: **u.** *Choice, 1993.*

Yorke, James A.   **QA614.8.A44 1996**
Chaos: An Introduction to Dynamical Systems. Kathleen
Alligood & Tim Sauer (Editors). Trade Paper. Springer. New
York, NY. 2000. XVIII, 603p. ISBN:0-387-94677-2, ISBN13:
978-0-387-94677-1. Dewey:515.3/52.

Audience: **u.** *Choice, 1997.*

Analysis

Abbott, Stephen   **QA300.A18 2001**
Understanding Analysis. Sheldon J. Axler, F. W. Gehring & K.
A. Ribet (Editors). Trade Cloth. Springer. New York, NY. 2002.
XII, 257p. Undergraduate Texts in Mathematics
ISBN:0-387-95060-5, ISBN13: 978-0-387-95060-0. Dewey:515.
LCCN:00-058308.

Audience: **l,u.**

Browder, Andrew   **QA300.B727 1996**
Mathematical Analysis: An Introduction. Sheldon J. Axler, F. W.
Gehring & P. R. Halmos (Editors). Cloth Text. Springer. New
York, NY. 1995. 333p. Undergraduate Texts in Mathematics
ISBN:0-387-94614-4, ISBN13: 978-0-387-94614-6. Dewey:515.
LCCN:95-044877.

Audience: **u.** *Choice, 1996.*

Gelbaum, Bernard R. &   **QA36.G45 1990**
  Olmsted, J. M.
Theorems and Counterexamples in Mathematics. P. R. Halmos
(Editor). Trade Cloth. Springer. New York, NY. 1993. XXXIV,
305p. Problem Books in Mathematics ISBN:0-387-97342-7,
ISBN13: 978-0-387-97342-5. Dewey:510. LCCN:90-009899.

Audience: **l,u,f.** *Choice, 1991.*

Hardy, G. H.   **QA303 .H24 1992**
A Course of Pure Mathematics. Ed. 10. Trade Paper. Cambridge
University Press. New York, NY. 1993. 522p. Cambridge
Mathematical Library ISBN:0-521-09227-2, ISBN13:
978-0-521-09227-2. Dewey:515. LCCN:94-107425.

Audience: **l,u.** *B*

Hardy, Godfrey H., et al.   **QA303**
Inequalities. Ed. 2. J. E. Littlewood & G. Pólya (Authors).
Trade Paper. Cambridge University Press. New York, NY. 1988.
336p. Cambridge Mathematical Library ISBN:0-521-35880-9,
ISBN13: 978-0-521-35880-4. Dewey:515.

Audience: **u.**

Kaczor, W. J. & Nowak,   **QA300.K32513 2000**
  M. T.
Problems in Mathematical Analysis: Continuity and
Differentiation. Ed. 2. Trade Paper. American Mathematical
Society. Providence, RI. 2001. 416p. Student Mathematical
Library, Vol. 12 ISBN:0-8218-2051-6, ISBN13:
978-0-8218-2051-3. Dewey:515/.076. LCCN:99-087039.

Audience: **l,u,f.**

Kaczor, W. J. & Nowak,   **QA300.K32513 2000**
  M. T.
Problems in Mathematical Analysis I: Real Numbers, Sequences
and Series. Trade Paper. American Mathematical Society.
Providence, RI. 2000. xiv, 380p. STML Ser., Vol. 4
ISBN:0-8218-2050-8, ISBN13: 978-0-8218-2050-6.
Dewey:515/.076. LCCN:99-087039.

Audience: **l,u,f.**

Lieb, Elliott H. & Loss,   **QA300.L54 2001**
  Michael
Analysis. Ed. 2. Trade Cloth. American Mathematical Society.
Providence, RI. 2001. xxii, 346p. Graduate Studies in
Mathematics, Vol. 14 ISBN:0-8218-2783-9, ISBN13:
978-0-8218-2783-3. Dewey:515. LCCN:2001-018215.

Audience: **u,f.** *Choice, 1997.*

Niven, Ivan   **QA306.N58 2006**
Maxima and Minima Without Calculus. Edward J. Barbeau,
Donna L. Beers, Robert B. Burckel, Guiliana Davidoff, Susan C.
Geller, Lester H. Lance, Daniel J. Velleman, William Watkins &
William S. Zwicker (Contribution by). Cloth Text. Cambridge
University Press. New York, NY. 1982. 320p. Dolciani
Mathematical Expositions Ser., Vol. 6 ISBN:0-88385-306-X,
ISBN13: 978-0-88385-306-1. Dewey:511.66. LCCN:80-081045.

Audience: **l,u.**

Polya, George, et al.   **QA301.P64413 1998**
Problems and Theorems in Analysis: Integral Calculus. Theory
of Functions. Gabor Szego & Gabor Szegö (Authors), Dorothee
Aeppli & C. E. Billigheimer (Translators). Trade Paper.
Springer. New York, NY. 1997. XXI, 389p. Classics in
Mathematics Ser., Vol. I ISBN:3-540-63640-4, ISBN13:
978-3-540-63640-3. Dewey:515/.076. LCCN:97-047108.

Audience: **u,f.**

Robert, Alain   **QA299.82.R5813 2003**
Nonstandard Analysis. Trade Paper. Dover Publications, Inc.
Mineola, NY. 2003. 176p. ISBN:0-486-43279-3, ISBN13:
978-0-486-43279-3. Dewey:515. LCCN:2003-055217.

Audience: **u,f.**

Rudin, Walter   **QA303**
Principles of Mathematical Analysis. Ed. 3. Cloth Text.
McGraw-Hill Higher Education. Burr Ridge, IL. 1976. 352p.
International Series in Pure and Applied Mathematics
ISBN:0-07-054235-X, ISBN13: 978-0-07-054235-8. Dewey:515.
LCCN:75-017903.

Audience: **u.** *B*

Rudin, Walter   **QA300.R82 1987**
Real and Complex Analysis. Ed. 3. Cloth Text. McGraw-Hill
Higher Education. Burr Ridge, IL. 1986. 430p. International
Series in Pure and Applied Mathematics ISBN:0-07-054234-1,
ISBN13: 978-0-07-054234-1. Dewey:515. LCCN:86-000007.

Audience: **u.** *B*

Simmons, George F.   **QA611 .S49 1983**
Introduction to Topology and Modern Analysis. Library Binding.
Krieger Publishing Company. Melbourne, FL. 1983. 384p.
ISBN:0-89874-551-9, ISBN13: 978-0-89874-551-1. Dewey:514.
LCCN:82-014845.

Audience: **u.**

Smith, K. T.   **QA300**
Primer of Modern Analysis. Ed. 2. Trade Cloth. Springer. New
York, NY. 1997. 468p. Undergraduate Texts in Mathematics
ISBN:0-387-90797-1, ISBN13: 978-0-387-90797-0. Dewey:515.

Audience: **u.**

Stroock, Daniel W.   **QA312.S78 1999**
A Concise Introduction to the Theory of Integration. Ed. 3.
Trade Cloth. Birkhauser Boston. Cambridge, MA. 1998. 253p.
ISBN:0-8176-4073-8, ISBN13: 978-0-8176-4073-6.
Dewey:515/.42. LCCN:98-042436.

Audience: **u,f.**

Whittaker, E. T. & Watson, G. N.   IN PROCESS
A Course of Modern Analysis. Ed. 4. Trade Paper. Cambridge University Press. New York, NY. 1996. 616p. Cambridge Mathematical Library ISBN:0-521-58807-3, ISBN13: 978-0-521-58807-2. Dewey:515.243.

Audience: **u,f.**

Analysis > Real Analysis

Boas, Ralph P. Jr.   QA331.5.B57 1996
A Primer of Real Functions. Ed. 4. Harold P. Boas (Revised by), William Watkins (Contribution by). Cloth Text. Mathematical Association of America. Washington, DC. 1997. 319p. Carus Mathematical Monographs, No. 13/R ISBN:0-88385-029-X, ISBN13: 978-0-88385-029-9. Dewey:515/.8. LCCN:96-077785.

Audience: **l,u.**

Brabenec, Robert   QA301.B73 2004
Resources for the Study of Real Analysis. Cloth Text. Mathematical Association of America. Washington, DC. 2004. 244p. Classroom Resource Materials Ser. ISBN:0-88385-737-5, ISBN13: 978-0-88385-737-3. Dewey:515. LCCN:2004-102964.

Audience: **u,f.** *Choice, 2005.*

Bressoud, David   QA300.B685 1994
A Radical Approach to Real Analysis. Paper Text. Mathematical Association of America. Washington, DC. 1996. 336p. Classroom Resource Materials Ser. ISBN:0-88385-701-4, ISBN13: 978-0-88385-701-4. Dewey:515. LCCN:93-080613.

Audience: **u,f.** *Choice, 1994.*

Folland, Gerald B.   QA300.F67 1999
Real Analysis: Modern Techniques and Their Applications. Ed. 2. Trade Cloth. John Wiley & Sons, Inc. Hoboken, NJ. 1999. 408p. Pure and Applied Mathematics, Vol. 40:A Wiley-Interscience Series of Texts, Monographs and Tracts ISBN:0-471-31716-0, ISBN13: 978-0-471-31716-6. Dewey:515. LCCN:98-037260.

Audience: **u.**

Hardy, G. H.   QA295
Divergent Series. Ed. 2. Trade Paper. American Mathematical Society. Providence, RI. 2000. Chelsea Publishing Ser. ISBN:0-8218-2649-2, ISBN13: 978-0-8218-2649-2. Dewey:515/.243.

Audience: **u.**

Makarov, B. M., et al.   QA331.5 .I9313 1992
Selected Problems in Real Analysis. M. G. Goluzina, A. A. Lodkin & A. N. Podkorytov (Authors). Paper Text. American Mathematical Society. Providence, RI. 1992. 370p. Translations of Mathematical Monographs, 0065-9282, Vol. 107 ISBN:0-8218-4559-4, ISBN13: 978-0-8218-4559-2. Dewey:515/.8. LCCN:92-015594.

Audience: **u,f.**

Natanson, I. P.   QA331.5 .N314
Theory of Functions of a Real Variable, Vol.1. Leo F. Boron & Edwin Hewitt (Editors). Trade Cloth. Frederick Ungar A Book. Dulles, VA. 1961. 278p. ISBN:0-8044-4702-0, ISBN13: 978-0-8044-4702-7. Dewey:517.52. LCCN:61-014620.

Audience: **u,f.**

Pugh, C. C.   QA300.P994 2001
Real Mathematical Analysis. F. W. Gehring & P. R. Halmos (Editors). Trade Cloth. Springer. New York, NY. 2003. XI, 437p.

Undergraduate Texts in Mathematics ISBN:0-387-95297-7, ISBN13: 978-0-387-95297-0. Dewey:515. LCCN:2001-032814.

Audience: **u.** *Choice, 2002.*

Wheeden, Richard & Zygmund, Antoni   QA312 .W43
Measure and Integral: An Introduction to Real Analysis. Paper over Boards. Marcel Dekker Inc. New York, NY. 1977. 288p. Pure and Applied Mathematics Ser., Vol. 43 ISBN:0-8247-6499-4, ISBN13: 978-0-8247-6499-9. Dewey:515/.42. LCCN:77-014167.

Audience: **u.**

Analysis > Complex Analysis

Ahlfors, Lars V.   QA331.A45 1979
Complex Analysis. Ed. 3. Cloth Text. McGraw-Hill Higher Education. Burr Ridge, IL. 1979. 345p. International Series in Pure and Applied Mathematics, Vol. 7 ISBN:0-07-000657-1, ISBN13: 978-0-07-000657-7. Dewey:515/.93. LCCN:78-017078.

Audience: **u,f.** *B*

Bak, Joseph & Newman, D. J.   QA331.7.B35 1997
Complex Analysis. Ed. 2. Trade Cloth. Springer. New York, NY. 1999. X, 294p. Undergraduate Texts in Mathematics ISBN:0-387-94756-6, ISBN13: 978-0-387-94756-3. Dewey:515/.9. LCCN:96-012475.

Audience: **u.**

Beardon, Alan   QA333
A Primer on Riemann Surfaces. Trade Paper. Cambridge University Press. New York, NY. 1984. 198p. London Mathematical Society Lecture Note Ser., No. 78 ISBN:0-521-27104-5, ISBN13: 978-0-521-27104-2. Dewey:514/.3. LCCN:82-004439.

Audience: **u,f.**

Brown, James Ward & Churchill, Ruel V.   QA331.7.B76 2002
Complex Variables and Applications. Ed. 7. Cloth Text. McGraw-Hill Higher Education. Burr Ridge, IL. 2003. 480p. International Series in Pure and Applied Mathematics ISBN:0-07-287252-7, ISBN13: 978-0-07-287252-1. Dewey:515/.9. LCCN:2002-043104.

Audience: **l,u.**

Conway, J. B.   QA331.7.C68 1978
Functions of One Complex Variable I. Ed. 2. Trade Cloth. Springer. New York, NY. 1995. 317p. Graduate Texts in Mathematics, Vol. 11 ISBN:0-387-90328-3, ISBN13: 978-0-387-90328-6. Dewey:515.9/3. LCCN:78-018836.

Audience: **u.**

Conway, John B.   QA331.7.C682 1995
Functions of One Complex Variable II. Trade Cloth. Springer. New York, NY. 1996. 394p. Graduate Texts in Mathematics, Vol. 158 ISBN:0-387-94460-5, ISBN13: 978-0-387-94460-9. Dewey:515/.93. LCCN:95-002331.

Audience: **u.**

D'Angelo, John P.   QA331.7.D34 2002
Inequalities from Complex Analysis. Cloth Text. Mathematical Association of America. Washington, DC. 2002. 280p. Carus Monographs, Vol. 28 ISBN:0-88385-033-8, ISBN13: 978-0-88385-033-6. Dewey:515/.9. LCCN:2002-101375.

Audience: **u.** *Choice, 2003.*

Howie, John Mackintosh   QA300.H694 2003
Complex Analysis. Trade Paper. Springer. New York, NY. 2006.
XI, 260p. Springer Undergraduate Mathematics Ser.
ISBN:1-85233-733-8, ISBN13: 978-1-85233-733-9. Dewey:515.
LCCN:2003-042772.

Audience: **u.** *Choice, 2003.*

Kirwan, Frances   QA565 .K57 1992
Complex Algebraic Curves. Cloth Text. Cambridge University
Press. New York, NY. 1992. 272p. London Mathematical
Society Student Texts Ser., No. 23 ISBN:0-521-41251-X,
ISBN13: 978-0-521-41251-3. Dewey:516.352.
LCCN:92-192303.

Audience: **u.** *Choice, 1993.*

Krantz, S. G.   QA331.7.K744 1999
Handbook of Complex Variables. Trade Cloth. Springer. New
York, NY. 1999. XXIV, 290p. ISBN:0-8176-4011-8, ISBN13:
978-0-8176-4011-8. Dewey:515/.9. LCCN:99-020156.

Audience: **u,f.** *Choice, 2000.*

Krantz, Steven   QA300
Complex Analysis: The Geometric Viewpoint. Ed. 2. Trade
Cloth. Mathematical Association of America. Washington, DC.
2004. 234p. Carus Mathematical Monographs, No. 23
ISBN:0-88385-035-4, ISBN13: 978-0-88385-035-0.
Dewey:515/.9. LCCN:2003-114309.

Audience: **u,f.**

Needham, Tristan   QA331.7
Visual Complex Analysis. Paper Text. Oxford University Press,
Inc. New York, NY. 1999. 616p. ISBN:0-19-853446-9, ISBN13:
978-0-19-853446-4. Dewey:515.9.

Audience: **u,f.** *Choice, 1998.*

Palka, B. P.   QA331.7.P35 1991
An Introduction to Complex Function Theory. J. H. 117 et al
Ewing, F. W. Gehring & P. R. Halmos (Editors). Trade Cloth.
Springer. New York, NY. 1995. XVII, 559p. Undergraduate
Texts in Mathematics ISBN:0-387-97427-X, ISBN13:
978-0-387-97427-9. Dewey:515/.9. LCCN:90-047375.

Audience: **u.** *Choice, 1991.*

Siegel, Carl L.   QA331 .S4713
Topics in Complex Function Theory. Trade Cloth. John Wiley &
Sons, Inc. Hoboken, NJ. 9999. Pure and Applied Mathematics
Ser. ISBN:0-318-56448-3, ISBN13: 978-0-318-56448-7.
Dewey:515/.9. LCCN:69-019931.

Audience: **u,f.**

Weinberger, Hans F.   QA374.W43 1995
A First Course in Partial Differential Equations with Complex
Variables and Transform Methods. Trade Paper. Dover
Publications, Inc. Mineola, NY. 1995. 480p.
ISBN:0-486-68640-X, ISBN13: 978-0-486-68640-0.
Dewey:515/.353. LCCN:95-007393.

Audience: **u.**

Analysis > Numerical Analysis

Acton, Forman S.   QA297
Numerical Methods That Work. Paper Text. Mathematical
Association of America. Washington, DC. 1997. 569p. Spectrum
Ser. ISBN:0-88385-450-3, ISBN13: 978-0-88385-450-1.
Dewey:519.4. LCCN:90-062538.

Audience: **l,u.**

Allen, Myron B. III &   QA297.A53 1998
Isaacson, Eli L.
Numerical Analysis for Applied Science. Ed. 1. Trade Cloth.
John Wiley & Sons, Inc. Hoboken, NJ. 1997. 492p. Pure and
Applied Mathematics, Vol. 35:A Wiley-Interscience Series of
Texts, Monographs and Tracts ISBN:0-471-55266-6, ISBN13:
978-0-471-55266-6. Dewey:519.4. LCCN:97-016688.

Audience: **u.** *Choice, 1998.*

Atkinson, Kendall E.   QA431 .A837 1997
The Numerical Solution of Integral Equations of the Second
Kind. P. G. Ciarlet, A. Iserles, R. V. Kohn, M. H. Wright, M. J.
Ablowitz, S. H. Davis, E. J. Hinch, J. Ockendon & P. J. Olver
(Contribution by). Trade Cloth. Cambridge University Press.
New York, NY. 1997. 570p. Monographs on Applied and
Computational Mathematics, No. 4 ISBN:0-521-58391-8,
ISBN13: 978-0-521-58391-6. Dewey:515.4/5. LCCN:96-045961.

Audience: **u.**

Atkinson, Kendall E. &   QA320.A85 2005
Han, Weimin
Theoretical Numerical Analysis: A Functional Analysis
Framework. Ed. 2. Trade Cloth. Springer. New York, NY. 2005.
XVIII, 576p. Texts in Applied Mathematics Ser., Vol. 39
ISBN:0-387-25887-6, ISBN13: 978-0-387-25887-4. Dewey:515.
LCCN:2005-925512.

Audience: **u,f.**

Braess, Dietrich   TA347.F5 B7313 2001
Finite Elements: Theory, Fast Solvers, and Applications in Solid
Mechanics. Ed. 2. Larry L. Schumaker (Translator). Trade
Paper. Cambridge University Press. New York, NY. 2001. 370p.
ISBN:0-521-01195-7, ISBN13: 978-0-521-01195-2.
Dewey:620/.001/51535. LCCN:00-069656.

Audience: **u,f.** *Choice, 1998.*

Burden, Richard L. &   QA297.B84 2005
Faires, J. Douglas
Numerical Analysis. Ed. 8. Cloth Text. Brooks/Cole. Pacific
Grove, CA. 2004. 864p. ISBN:0-534-39200-8, ISBN13:
978-0-534-39200-0. Dewey:518. LCCN:2004-113929.

Audience: **u.**

Chen, Goong & Zhou,   TA347.B69 C44 1992
Jingmin
Boundary Element Methods. Trade Cloth. Elsevier Science &
Technology Books. Saint Louis, MO. 1992. 646p.
Computational Mathematics and Its Applications Ser.
ISBN:0-12-170940-X, ISBN13: 978-0-12-170940-2.
Dewey:620.001515353.

Audience: **u.**

Cheney, E. W.   QA221.C47
Introduction to Approximation Theory. Ed. 2. Trade Cloth.
American Mathematical Society. Providence, RI. 1999. 259p.
ISBN:0-8218-1374-9, ISBN13: 978-0-8218-1374-4.
Dewey:511/.4.

Audience: **u.**

Davis, Philip J.   QA320
Interpolation and Approximation. Paper Text. Dover
Publications, Inc. Mineola, NY. 1975. 393p.
ISBN:0-486-62495-1, ISBN13: 978-0-486-62495-2.
Dewey:515/.7. LCCN:75-002568.

Audience: **u.**

Davis, Philip J. &   **QA299.3**
Rabinowitz, Philip
Methods of Numerical Integration. Ed. 2. Trade Cloth. Elsevier
Science & Technology Books. Saint Louis, MO. 1984. xiv,
612p. Computer Science and Mathematics Monograph
ISBN:0-12-206360-0, ISBN13: 978-0-12-206360-2.
Dewey:515/.624. LCCN:83-013522.

Audience: **u.**

Evans, Gwynne A.   **QA299.3.E93 1993**
Practical Numerical Integration. Ed. 1. Trade Cloth. John Wiley
& Sons, Inc. Hoboken, NJ. 1993. 340p. ISBN:0-471-93898-X,
ISBN13: 978-0-471-93898-9. Dewey:515.624.
LCCN:92-041108.

Audience: **u.**

Gautschi, Walter   **QA297.G35 1997**
Numerical Analysis: An Introduction. Trade Cloth. Birkhauser
Boston. Cambridge, MA. 1997. 500p. ISBN:3-7643-3895-4,
ISBN13: 978-3-7643-3895-4. Dewey:519.4. LCCN:97-000186.

Audience: **u.**

Gockenbach, Mark S.   **QA377.G63 2002**
Partial Differential Equations: Analytical and Numerical
Methods. Trade Cloth, CD-ROM. Society for Industrial &
Applied Mathematics. Philadelphia, PA. 2002. xxii + 614p.
ISBN:0-89871-518-0, ISBN13: 978-0-89871-518-7.
Dewey:515/.353. LCCN:2002-029411.

Audience: **u,f.**

Iserles, Arieh (Editor)   **QA371 .I813 1996**
A First Course in the Numerical Analysis of Differential
Equations. M. J. Ablowitz, S. H. Davis, E. J. Hinch, J.
Ockendon, P. J. Olver & A. Iserles (Contribution by). Cloth
Text. Cambridge University Press. New York, NY. 1996. 396p.
Texts in Applied Mathematics , No. 15 ISBN:0-521-55376-8,
ISBN13: 978-0-521-55376-6. Dewey:515/.35. LCCN:96-139924.

Audience: **u.**

Kincaid, David & Cheney,   **QA297.K563 2001**
E. W.
Numerical Analysis: Mathematics of Scientific Computing. Ed.
3. Cloth Text. Brooks/Cole. Pacific Grove, CA. 2001. 816p.
ISBN:0-534-38905-8, ISBN13: 978-0-534-38905-5.
Dewey:519.4. LCCN:2001-043470.

Audience: **u.**

Nocedal, Jorge & Wright,   **QA402.5.N62 1999**
Stephen J.
Numerical Optimization. Trade Cloth. Springer. New York, NY.
2000. XXI, 636p. Series in Operations Research
ISBN:0-387-98793-2, ISBN13: 978-0-387-98793-4.
Dewey:519.3. LCCN:99-013263.

Audience: **u.**

Press, William H., et al.   **HQ76.2.U5**
Numerical Recipes. Saul A. Teukolsky, William T. Vetterling &
Brian P. Flannery (Authors). Quantity Pack, Trade Cloth, Trade
Paper. Cambridge University Press. New York, NY. 1996.
1356p. ISBN:0-521-57438-2, ISBN13: 978-0-521-57438-9.
Dewey:305.389664.

Audience: **u.**

Quarteroni, Alfio, et al.   **QA297.Q83 2000**
Numerical Mathematics. Riccardo Sacco & Fausto Saleri
(Authors). Trade Cloth. Springer. New York, NY. 2000. XX,

680p. Texts in Applied Mathematics, Vol. 37
ISBN:0-387-98959-5, ISBN13: 978-0-387-98959-4.
Dewey:519.4. LCCN:99-059414.

Audience: **u,f.**

Quarteroni, Alfio & Valli, A.   **QA377.Q37 1994**
Numerical Approximation of Partial Differential Equations.
Cloth Text. Springer. New York, NY. 1997. 543p. Computational
Mathematics Ser., Vol. 23 ISBN:0-387-57111-6, ISBN13:
978-0-387-57111-9. Dewey:515/.353. LCCN:94-021763.

Audience: **u,f.**

Schatzman, Michelle   **QA297**
Numerical Analysis: A Mathematical Introduction. Paper Text.
Oxford University Press, Inc. New York, NY. 2002. 516p.
ISBN:0-19-850852-2, ISBN13: 978-0-19-850852-6.
Dewey:519.4. LCCN:2002-041475.

Audience: **u.** *Choice, 2003.*

Scheid, Francis J.   **QA297**
Schaum's Outline of Theory and Problems of Numerical
Analysis. Ed. 2. McGraw-Hill. 1989. Schaum's Outline Series in
Mathematics ISBN:0-07-055221-5, ISBN13: 978-0-07-055221-0.

Audience: **u.**

Shampine, Lawrence F.   **QA372.S417 1994**
Numerical Solution of Ordinary Differential Equations.
Chapman & Hall. 1994. ISBN:0-412-05151-6, ISBN13:
978-0-412-05151-7.

Audience: **u.**

Wilkinson, J. Harvie   **QA218.W5 1988**
The Algebraic Eigenvalue Problem. Trade Paper. Oxford
University Press, Inc. New York, NY. 1988. 680p. Monographs
on Numerical Analysis ISBN:0-19-853418-3, ISBN13:
978-0-19-853418-1. Dewey:512.9/4. LCCN:87-028274.

Audience: **u,f.**

Analysis > Calculus of Variations, Optimization and Control

Barnett, S. & Cameron,   **QA402.3.B347 1985**
R. G.
Introduction to Mathematical Control Theory. Ed. 2. Paper Text.
Oxford University Press, Inc. New York, NY. 1990. 416p.
Oxford Applied Mathematics and Computing Science Ser.
ISBN:0-19-859639-1, ISBN13: 978-0-19-859639-4.
Dewey:629.8/312. LCCN:85-021589.

Audience: **u.**

Bertsekas, Dimitri P.   **T57.8B47 1999**
Nonlinear Programming. Ed. 2. Cloth Text. Athena Scientific.
Belmont, MA. 1999. 780p. ISBN:1-886529-00-0, ISBN13:
978-1-886529-00-7. Dewey:519.7/6. LCCN:99-073208.

Audience: **u.**

Chvatal, Vasek   **T57.74**
Linear Programming. Trade Paper. Worth Publishers, Inc. New
York, NY. 1983. 478p. Series of Books in the Mathematical
Sciences ISBN:0-7167-1587-2, ISBN13: 978-0-7167-1587-0.
Dewey:519.7/2. LCCN:82-021132.

Audience: **u.** *B*

Dantzig, George B. &   **QA265**
Thapa, Mukund N.
Linear Programming: Theory and Extensions. Trade Cloth.

Formats: Web: ☐   Ebook: 🄴   CD/DVD-ROM: 🔊   BCL3: *B*

Springer. New York, NY. 2003. XXV, 448p. Springer Series in Operations Research ISBN:0-387-98613-8, ISBN13: 978-0-387-98613-5. Dewey:519.7/2. LCCN:96-036411.

Audience: **u,f.**

Dantzig, George B. & Thapa, Mukund N. T57.74.D365 1997
Linear Programming: Introduction. Mixed Media. Springer. New York, NY. 1997. XXXVIII, 435p. Series in Operations Research ISBN:0-387-94833-3, ISBN13: 978-0-387-94833-1. Dewey:519.7/2. LCCN:96-036411.

Audience: **u.**

Gel'fand, I. M. & Fomin, S. V. QA315.G41713 2000
Calculus of Variations. Richard A. Silverman (Translator). Trade Paper. Dover Publications, Inc. Mineola, NY. 2000. 240p. ISBN:0-486-41448-5, ISBN13: 978-0-486-41448-5. Dewey:515/.64. LCCN:00-057099.

Audience: **u,f.** *B*

Hillier, Frederick S. & Lieberman, Gerald J. T57.6 .H54
Introduction to Operations Research. Ed. 8. Mixed Media, Trade Cloth, CD-ROM. McGraw-Hill Higher Education. Burr Ridge, IL. 2005. ISBN:0-07-321114-1, ISBN13: 978-0-07-321114-5. Dewey:658.4034.

Audience: **u.** *B*

Nemhauser, George L. & Wolsey, Laurence A. T57.74
Integer and Combinatorial Optimization. Trade Paper. John Wiley & Sons, Inc. Hoboken, NJ. 1999. 784p. Wiley-Interscience Series in Discrete Mathematics, Vol. 55 ISBN:0-471-35943-2, ISBN13: 978-0-471-35943-2. Dewey:519.7/7.

Audience: **u,f.**

Nocedal, Jorge & Wright, Stephen J. QA402.5.N62 1999
Numerical Optimization. Trade Cloth. Springer. New York, NY. 2000. XXI, 636p. Series in Operations Research ISBN:0-387-98793-2, ISBN13: 978-0-387-98793-4. Dewey:519.3. LCCN:99-013263.

Audience: **u.**

Scales, L.E. QA402.5.S33 1985
Introduction to Non-Linear Optimization. Cloth Text. Springer. New York, NY. 1987. xi, 243 p. :p. ISBN:0-387-91252-5, ISBN13: 978-0-387-91252-3. Dewey:519. LCCN:84-010553.

Audience: **u,f.** *B*

Sobel, Matthew J. & Heyman, Daniel P. T57.6 H49
Stochastic Models in Operations Research: Stochastic Optimization. Trade Paper. Dover Publications, Inc. Mineola, NY. 2003. 576p. 0 ISBN:0-486-43260-2, ISBN13: 978-0-486-43260-1. Dewey:003.

Audience: **u,f.**

Sobel, Matthew J. & Heyman, Daniel P. T57.6H49 2004
Stochastic Models in Operations Research: Stochastic Processes and Operating Characteristics. Trade Paper. Dover Publications, Inc. Mineola, NY. 2003. 560p. 0 ISBN:0-486-43259-9, ISBN13: 978-0-486-43259-5. Dewey:003. LCCN:2003-068673.

Audience: **u,f.**

Van Brunt, Bruce QA315.V35 2003
The Calculus of Variations. Trade Cloth. Springer. New York, NY. 2003. XII, 302p. ISBN:0-387-40247-0, ISBN13: 978-0-387-40247-5. Dewey:515/.64. LCCN:2003-050661.

Audience: **u.** *Choice, 2004.*

Analysis > Functional and Harmonic Analysis

Abramowitz, Milton & Stegun, Irene A. (Editors) QA55
Handbook of Mathematical Functions with Formulas, Graphs and Mathematical Tables. Trade Paper. Dover Publications, Inc. Mineola, NY. 1965. 1046p. ISBN:0-486-61272-4, ISBN13: 978-0-486-61272-0. Dewey:515/.0212.

Audience: **u,f.**

Andrews, George E., et al. QA351.A74 1999
Special Functions. Richard Askey & Ranjan Roy (Authors), B. Doran, P. Flajolet, M. Ismail, T. Y. Lam, E. Lutwak, G. C. Rota & E. Wutwak (Contribution by). Trade Paper, Perfect. Cambridge University Press. New York, NY. 2001. 680p. Encyclopedia of Mathematics and Its Applications Ser., No. 71 ISBN:0-521-78988-5, ISBN13: 978-0-521-78988-2. Dewey:515/.5.

Audience: **u,f.**

Aubin, Jean Pierre QA320.A913 2000
Applied Functional Analysis. Ed. 2. Trade Cloth. John Wiley & Sons, Inc. Hoboken, NJ. 2000. 520p. Pure and Applied Mathematics, Vol. 47:A Wiley-Interscience Series of Texts, Monographs and Tracts ISBN:0-471-17976-0, ISBN13: 978-0-471-17976-4. Dewey:515/.7. LCCN:99-015355.

Audience: **u,f.**

Conway, J. B. QA320.C658 1990
A Course in Functional Analysis. Ed. 2. P. R. Halmos, F. W. Gehring & C. C. Moore (Editors). Trade Cloth. Springer. New York, NY. 1994. 399p. Graduate Texts in Mathematics, Vol. 96 ISBN:0-387-97245-5, ISBN13: 978-0-387-97245-9. Dewey:515.7. LCCN:90-009585.

Audience: **u,f.**

Daubechies, Ingrid QA403.3 .D38 1992
Ten Lectures on Wavelets. Trade Cloth. Society for Industrial & Applied Mathematics. Philadelphia, PA. 1992. xx + 357p. CBMS-NSF Regional Conference Series in Applied Mathematics, No. 61 ISBN:0-89871-274-2, ISBN13: 978-0-89871-274-2. Dewey:515/.2433. LCCN:92-013201.

Audience: **u,f.**

Gillman, L. & Jerison, M. QA323 .G5 1976
Rings of Continuous Functions. J. H. Ewing, F. W. Gehring & P. R. Halmos (Editors). Trade Cloth. Springer. New York, NY. 1993. XIII, 300p. Graduate Texts in Mathematics, Vol. 43 ISBN:0-387-90198-1, ISBN13: 978-0-387-90198-5. Dewey:512/.4. LCCN:76-020442.

Audience: **u,f.**

Grafakos, Loukas QA403.5.G73 2003
Classical and Modern Fourier Analysis. Cloth Text. Prentice Hall PTR. Upper Saddle River, NJ. 2003. 870p. ISBN:0-13-035399-X, ISBN13: 978-0-13-035399-3. Dewey:515/.2433. LCCN:2003-051280.

Audience: **u.**

Hernández, Eugenio and   **QA403.3**
  Guido L. Weiss
First Course on Wavelets. CRC Press. 1996. Studies in
Advanced Mathematics ISBN:0-8493-8274-2, ISBN13:
978-0-8493-8274-1.
                                                 Audience: **u.**

Jaffard, Stephane, et al.   **QA403.3.J34 2001**
Wavelets: Tools for Science and Technology. Ed. 2. Yves Meyer
& Robert D. Ryan (Authors). Trade Cloth. Society for Industrial
& Applied Mathematics. Philadelphia, PA. 2001. xiv + 256p.
ISBN:0-89871-448-6, ISBN13: 978-0-89871-448-7.
Dewey:515/.2433. LCCN:00-051607.
                              Audience: **u.** *Choice, 2002.*

Krantz, Steven G.   **QA403.K63 1999**
A Panorama of Harmonic Analysis. Trade Cloth. Mathematical
Association of America. Washington, DC. 1999. 374p. Carus
Mathematical Monographs, No. 27 ISBN:0-88385-031-1,
ISBN13: 978-0-88385-031-2. Dewey:515/.2433.
LCCN:99-062756.
                                                 Audience: **u.**

Palka, B. P.   **QA331.7.P35 1991**
An Introduction to Complex Function Theory. J. H. 117 et al
Ewing, F. W. Gehring & P. R. Halmos (Editors). Trade Cloth.
Springer. New York, NY. 1995. XVII, 559p. Undergraduate
Texts in Mathematics ISBN:0-387-97427-X, ISBN13:
978-0-387-97427-9. Dewey:515/.9. LCCN:90-047375.
                              Audience: **u.** *Choice, 1991.*

Rudin, Walter   **QA320.R83 1991**
Functional Analysis. Ed. 2. Cloth Text. McGraw-Hill Higher
Education. Burr Ridge, IL. 1991. 448p. International Series in
Pure and Applied Mathematics ISBN:0-07-054236-8, ISBN13:
978-0-07-054236-5. Dewey:515/.7. LCCN:90-005677.
                                     Audience: **u.** *B*

Saxe, Karen   **QA320.S28 2002**
Beginning Functional Analysis. Trade Cloth. Springer. New
York, NY. 2001. XII, 197p. Undergraduate Texts in Mathematics
ISBN:0-387-95224-1, ISBN13: 978-0-387-95224-6.
Dewey:515/.7. LCCN:00-067916.
                                                 Audience: **u.**

Siegel, Carl L.   **QA331 .S4713**
Topics in Complex Function Theory. Trade Cloth. John Wiley &
Sons, Inc. Hoboken, NJ. 9999. Pure and Applied Mathematics
Ser. ISBN:0-318-56448-3, ISBN13: 978-0-318-56448-7.
Dewey:515/.9. LCCN:69-019931.
                                                 Audience: **u,f.**

Stein, Elias M. & Shakarchi,   **QA403.5**
  Rami
Fourier Analysis: An Introduction. Trade Cloth. Princeton
University Press. Princeton, NJ. 2003. 320p.
ISBN:0-691-11384-X, ISBN13: 978-0-691-11384-5.
Dewey:515/.2433. LCCN:2003-103688.
                                                 Audience: **u.**

Ueno, Kenji, et al.   **QA445.U3613 2003**
A Mathematical Gift I: The Interplay Between Topology,
Functions, Geometry, and Algebra. Kaoji Shiga & S. Morita
(Authors). Trade Paper. American Mathematical Society.
Providence, RI. 2003. 136p. Mathematical World Ser., Vol. 19
ISBN:0-8218-3282-4, ISBN13: 978-0-8218-3282-0. Dewey:516.
LCCN:2003-062778.
                                                 Audience: **l,u,f.**

Zygmund, A.   **QA404.Z9 2002**
Trigonometric Series. Ed. 3. Robert Fefferman (Foreword by).
Trade Paper. Cambridge University Press. New York, NY. 2003.
390p. Cambridge Mathematical Library ISBN:0-521-89053-5,
ISBN13: 978-0-521-89053-3. Dewey:515/.2433.
LCCN:2002-067363.
                                     Audience: **u.** *B*

Geometry and Topology

Abbott, Edwin A.   **BL624**
Flatland: A Romance of Many Dimensions. Thomas Banchoff
(Introduction by). Trade Paper, Perfect. Princeton University
Press. Princeton, NJ. 2005. 136p. Princeton Science Library
ISBN:0-691-12366-7, ISBN13: 978-0-691-12366-0.
Dewey:530.1/1.
                                                 Audience: **g,l.**

Apostol, Tom (Editor), et al.   **QA447.A73 1995**
🍄 Arabesques and Geometry. J. P. Bourguignon, Michele
Emmer, H. -C Hege & K. Polthier (Editors), A. F. Costa & B.
Gomez (Contribution by). Video, Other. Springer. New York,
NY. 2000. VideoMath Ser. ISBN:3-540-92639-9, ISBN13:
978-3-540-92639-9. Dewey:516.
                                                 Audience: **g.**

Armstrong, M. A.   **QA372.I68 1990**
Groups and Symmetry. Ed. 2. Trade Cloth. Springer. New York,
NY. 1997. 186p. Undergraduate Texts in Mathematics
ISBN:0-387-96675-7, ISBN13: 978-0-387-96675-5.
Dewey:515/.35. LCCN:89-021765.
                              Audience: **u.** *Choice, 1989.*

Arnold, V. I.   **QA372**
Geometrical Methods in the Theory of Ordinary Differential
Equations. Ed. 2. Mark Levi (Editor), J. Szücs (Translator).
Trade Cloth. Springer. New York, NY. 1996. 351p. Grundlehren
Ser., Vol. 250 ISBN:0-387-96649-8, ISBN13:
978-0-387-96649-6. Dewey:515.3/52.
                                     Audience: **u,f.** *B*

Banchoff, Thomas F.   **QA691.B26 1990**
Beyond the Third Dimension: Geometry, Computer Graphics
and Higher Dimensions. Trade Cloth. Henry Holt & Company.
New York, NY. 1990. 210p. ISBN:0-7167-5025-2, ISBN13:
978-0-7167-5025-3. Dewey:516.3/6/0285/6693.
LCCN:90-008522.
                              Audience: **u.** *Choice, 1991.*

Bennett, M. K.   **QA477.B46 1995**
Affine and Projective Geometry. Ed. 1. Trade Cloth. John Wiley
& Sons, Inc. Hoboken, NJ. 1995. 248p. ISBN:0-471-11315-8,
ISBN13: 978-0-471-11315-7. Dewey:516/.4. LCCN:94-044365.
                              Audience: **u,f.** *Choice, 1996.*

Brannan, David A., et al.   **QA445 .B688 1999**
Geometry. Matthew F. Esplen & Jeremy J. Gray (Authors).
Trade Paper. Cambridge University Press. New York, NY. 1999.
510p. ISBN:0-521-59787-0, ISBN13: 978-0-521-59787-6.
Dewey:516. LCCN:97-018015.
                                                 Audience: **l,u.**

Coxeter, Harold S. M. QA445 .C67 1989
Introduction to Geometry. Ed. 2. Trade Paper. John Wiley &
Sons, Inc. Hoboken, NJ. 1989. 496p. Wiley Classics Library,
Vol. 19 ISBN:0-471-50458-0, ISBN13: 978-0-471-50458-0.
Dewey:516.
Audience: **l,u.**

Coxeter, Harold S. M. QA471.C67 1987
Projective Geometry. Ed. 2. Trade Cloth. Springer. New York,
NY. 1998. 162p. ISBN:0-387-96532-7, ISBN13:
978-0-387-96532-1. Dewey:516.5. LCCN:87-009750.
Audience: **u.**

Coxeter, Harold S. M. & QA473 .C6 1967
 Greitzer, S. L.
Geometry Revisited. Paper Text. Mathematical Association of
America. Washington, DC. 1996. 207p. New Mathematical
Library, No. 19 ISBN:0-88385-619-0, ISBN13:
978-0-88385-619-2. Dewey:516. LCCN:67-020607.
Audience: **l,u.**

Euclid QA31
The Thirteen Books of Euclid's Elements, Vol. 1. Thomas L.
Heath (Editor). Trade Paper. Dover Publications, Inc. Mineola,
NY. 1956. 443p. Dover Phoenix Editions Ser.
ISBN:0-486-60088-2, ISBN13: 978-0-486-60088-8. Dewey:513.
Audience: **g.** *B*

Euclid QA31
The Thirteen Books of Euclid's Elements, Vol. 3. Thomas L.
Heath (Editor). Trade Paper. Dover Publications, Inc. Mineola,
NY. 1956. 546p. Dover Phoenix Editions Ser.
ISBN:0-486-60090-4, ISBN13: 978-0-486-60090-1. Dewey:513.
Audience: **g.**

Euclid QA31
The Thirteen Books of Euclid's Elements, Vol. 2. Thomas L.
Heath (Editor). Trade Paper. Dover Publications, Inc. Mineola,
NY. 1956. 436p. Dover Phoenix Editions Ser.
ISBN:0-486-60089-0, ISBN13: 978-0-486-60089-5. Dewey:513.
Audience: **g.** *B*

Eves, Howard W. QA445 .E92 1972
Survey of Geometry. Cloth Text. McGraw-Hill Higher
Education. Burr Ridge, IL. 1972. ISBN:0-205-03226-5, ISBN13:
978-0-205-03226-6. Dewey:516.
Audience: **l,u.**

Gray, Jeremy QA21.G7 1989
Ideas of Space: Euclidean, Non-Euclidean, and Relativistic. Ed.
2. Trade Cloth. Oxford University Press, Inc. New York, NY.
1989. 254p. ISBN:0-19-853935-5, ISBN13: 978-0-19-853935-3.
Dewey:516. LCCN:89-003012.
Audience: **u,f.**

Hartshorne, Robin QA451.H37 2000
Geometry: Euclid and Beyond. Trade Cloth. Springer. New
York, NY. 2000. XII, 532p. Undergraduate Texts in Mathematics
ISBN:0-387-98650-2, ISBN13: 978-0-387-98650-0. Dewey:516.
LCCN:99-044789.
Audience: **l,u.** *Choice, 2001.*

Heilbron, J. L. QA455 .H45X 2000
Geometry Civilized: History, Culture, and Technique. Trade
Paper. Oxford University Press, Inc. New York, NY. 2000. 318p.
ISBN:0-19-850690-2, ISBN13: 978-0-19-850690-4. Dewey:516.
Audience: **l,u.**

Hilbert, David & QA685.H515 1999
 Cohn-Vossen, S.
Geometry and the Imagination. Ed. 2. Trade Cloth. American
Mathematical Society. Providence, RI. 1999. 357p.
ISBN:0-8218-1998-4, ISBN13: 978-0-8218-1998-2.
Dewey:516.9. LCCN:99-015535.
Audience: **g.** *B*

Hilbert, David QA681 .H6
The Foundations of Geometry. Ed. 2. Leo Unger (Translator).
Trade Cloth. Open Court Publishing Company. Chicago, IL.
1980. 226p. ISBN:0-87548-163-9, ISBN13: 978-0-87548-163-0.
Dewey:513. LCCN:73-110344.
Audience: **u,f.**

Hildebrandt, Stefan & BH301.N3
 Tromba, Anthony J.
Mathematics and Optimal Form. Cloth Text. W. H. Freeman &
Company. New York, NY. 1984. 215p. Scientific American
Library ISBN:0-7167-5009-0, ISBN13: 978-0-7167-5009-3.
Dewey:117. LCCN:84-023461.
Audience: **u.**

Honsberger, Ross QA164
Mathematical Gems from Elementary Combinatorics, Number
Theory, and Geometry. Mathematical Association of America.
1973. ISBN:0-88385-300-0, ISBN13: 978-0-88385-300-9.
Audience: **l,u,f.**

Klein, Felix QA461.K4513 2004
Elementary Mathematics from an Advanced Standpoint:
Geometry. Trade Paper. Dover Publications, Inc. Mineola, NY.
2004. 224p. ISBN:0-486-43481-8, ISBN13: 978-0-486-43481-0.
Dewey:372.7. LCCN:2004-045586.
Audience: **u,f.** *B*

Krantz, Steven QA300
Complex Analysis: The Geometric Viewpoint. Ed. 2. Trade
Cloth. Mathematical Association of America. Washington, DC.
2004. 234p. Carus Mathematical Monographs, No. 23
ISBN:0-88385-035-4, ISBN13: 978-0-88385-035-0.
Dewey:515/.9. LCCN:2003-114309.
Audience: **u,f.**

Ryan, Patrick J. QA445 .R93 1986
Euclidean and Non-Euclidean Geometry: An Analytic Approach.
Trade Paper. Cambridge University Press. New York, NY. 1986.
240p. ISBN:0-521-27635-7, ISBN13: 978-0-521-27635-1.
Dewey:516. LCCN:85-017146.
Audience: **u.** *Choice, 1987.*

Singer, I. M. & Thorpe, QA611 .S498 1976
 J. A.
Lecture Notes on Elementary Topology and Geometry. Trade
Cloth. Springer. New York, NY. 1996. VIII, 244p.
Undergraduate Texts in Mathematics ISBN:0-387-90202-3,
ISBN13: 978-0-387-90202-9. Dewey:514. LCCN:76-026137.
Audience: **u.** *B*

Stehney, Ann K., et al., eds. QA446
Selected Papers on Geometry. Mathematical Association of
America. 1979. ISBN:0-88385-204-7, ISBN13:
978-0-88385-204-0.
Audience: **l,u,f.**

Stewart, Ian PR6015.I3
Flatterland: Like Flatland, Only More So. Trade Paper. Perseus
Books Group. New York, NY. 2002. 320p. Art of Mentoring Ser.

ISBN:0-7382-0675-X, ISBN13: 978-0-7382-0675-2.
Dewey:823.9/14.

Audience: **g,l,u.**

Stillwell, John   QA39.2.S755 1998
Numbers and Geometry. F. W. Gehring & P. R. Halmos
(Editors). Trade Cloth. Springer. New York, NY. 1997. 364p.
Undergraduate Texts in Mathematics ISBN:0-387-98289-2,
ISBN13: 978-0-387-98289-2. Dewey:510. LCCN:97-022858.

Audience: **u.** *Choice, 1998.*

Thurston, William P.   QA685.T49 1997
Three-Dimensional Geometry and Topology. Silvio Levy
(Editor). Trade Cloth. Princeton University Press. Princeton, NJ.
1997. 320p. Princeton Mathematical Ser. ISBN:0-691-08304-5,
ISBN13: 978-0-691-08304-9. Dewey:516/.07. LCCN:96-045578.

Audience: **u.** *Choice, 1998.*

Ueno, Kenji, et al.   QA445.U3613 2003
A Mathematical Gift I: The Interplay Between Topology,
Functions, Geometry, and Algebra. Kaoji Shiga & S. Morita
(Authors). Trade Paper. American Mathematical Society.
Providence, RI. 2003. 136p. Mathematical World Ser., Vol. 19
ISBN:0-8218-3282-4, ISBN13: 978-0-8218-3282-0. Dewey:516.
LCCN:2003-062778.

Audience: **l,u,f.**

Walser, Hans   Q172.5.S95.W3 2000
Symmetry. Peter Hilton (Translator). Paper Text. Mathematical
Association of America. Washington, DC. 2001. 108p. Spectrum
Ser. ISBN:0-88385-532-1, ISBN13: 978-0-88385-532-4.
Dewey:516.1. LCCN:00-107972.

Audience: **l,u.** *Choice, 2001.*

Weinreich, Gabriel   QC20.7.V4W45 1998
Geometrical Vectors. Trade Paper. University of Chicago Press.
Chicago, IL. 1998. 126p. Chicago Lectures in Physics Ser.
ISBN:0-226-89048-1, ISBN13: 978-0-226-89048-7.
Dewey:630.15/6182. LCCN:97-051855.

Audience: **l,u.** *Choice, 1998.*

Wells, David   QA441.W45 1991
The Penguin Dictionary of Curious and Interesting Geometry.
John Sharp (Illustrator). Trade Paper. Penguin Group (USA) Inc.
New York, NY. 1992. 304p. ISBN:0-14-011813-6, ISBN13:
978-0-14-011813-1. Dewey:516. LCCN:92-131759.

Audience: **g.**

Weyl, Hermann   N76
Symmetry. Trade Paper. Princeton University Press. Princeton,
NJ. 1983. 176p. Princeton Science Library ISBN:0-691-02374-3,
ISBN13: 978-0-691-02374-8. Dewey:701.17.

Audience: **u.**

Geometry and Topology > Differential Geometry

DoCarmo, Manfredo P.   QA641.C33
Differential Geometry of Curves and Surfaces. Ed. 1. Cloth
Text. Prentice Hall PTR. Upper Saddle River, NJ. 1976. 503p.
ISBN:0-13-212589-7, ISBN13: 978-0-13-212589-5.
Dewey:516/.36. LCCN:75-022094.

Audience: **u.** *B*

DoCarmo, Manfredo   QA649.C2913 1992
Riemannian Geometry. Ed. 4. Francis Flaherty (Translator).
Trade Cloth. Birkhauser Boston. Cambridge, MA. 1992. XVI,
300p. Mathematics Ser., :Theory and Applications Ser.
ISBN:0-8176-3490-8, ISBN13: 978-0-8176-3490-2.
Dewey:516.3/73. LCCN:91-037377.

Audience: **u,f.** *Choice, 1992.*

Frankel, Theodore   QC20
The Geometry of Physics: An Introduction. Ed. 2. Cloth Text.
Cambridge University Press. New York, NY. 2003. 720p.
ISBN:0-521-83330-2, ISBN13: 978-0-521-83330-1.
Dewey:530.15/636. LCCN:2003-044030.

Audience: **u,f.**

Henderson, David W.   QA641
Differential Geometry: A Geometric Introduction. Prentice Hall.
1998. ISBN:0-13-569963-0, ISBN13: 978-0-13-569963-8.

Audience: **u.**

Jost, Jurgen   QA649
Riemannian Geometry and Geometric Analysis. Ed. 4. Trade
Paper, Perfect. Springer. New York, NY. 2005. XIII, 566p.
Universitext Ser. ISBN:3-540-25907-4, ISBN13:
978-3-540-25907-7. Dewey:516.3/73. LCCN:2005-925885.

Audience: **u,f.**

Lipschutz, Martin   QA641
Schaum's Outline of Differential Geometry. Cloth Text.
McGraw-Hill Companies, The. New York, NY. 1969. 288p.
Schaum's ISBN:0-07-037985-8, ISBN13: 978-0-07-037985-5.
Dewey:516.36.

Audience: **u.**

Morgan, Frank   QA685.M76 1998
Riemannian Geometry: A Beginner's Guide. Ed. 2. Cloth Text.
A K Peters, Ltd. Wellesley, MA. 1997. 150p.
ISBN:1-56881-073-3, ISBN13: 978-1-56881-073-7.
Dewey:516.3/73. LCCN:97-035094.

Audience: **u.** *Choice, 1993.*

O'Neill, Barrett   QA641
Elementary Differential Geometry. Ed. 2. Academic Press. 1996.
ISBN:0-12-526745-2, ISBN13: 978-0-12-526745-8.

Audience: **u.**

Porteous, I. R.   QA641 .P65 2001
Geometric Differentiation: For the Intelligence of Curves and
Surfaces. Ed. 2. Trade Paper. Cambridge University Press. New
York, NY. 2001. 350p. ISBN:0-521-00264-8, ISBN13:
978-0-521-00264-6. Dewey:516.3/6. LCCN:2002-276171.

Audience: **u.**

Spivak, Michael   QA641
A Comprehensive Introduction to Differential Geometry, Vol. 2.
Ed. 3. Cloth Text. Publish or Perish, Inc. Houston, TX. 1999.
xiv, 361p. ISBN:0-914098-71-3, ISBN13: 978-0-914098-71-3.
Dewey:516.3/6.

Audience: **u,f.** *B*

Spivak, Michael   QA641 .S59 1999
A Comprehensive Introduction to Differential Geometry, Vol. 5.
Ed. 3. Cloth Text. Publish or Perish, Inc. Houston, TX. 1999. x,
467p. ISBN:0-914098-74-8, ISBN13: 978-0-914098-74-4.
Dewey:516.3/6. LCCN:2002-283516.

Audience: **u,f.** *B*

Spivak, Michael **QA641**
A Comprehensive Introduction to Differential Geometry, Vol. 1.
Ed. 3. Cloth Text. Publish or Perish, Inc. Houston, TX. 1999.
xviii, 491p. ISBN:0-914098-70-5, ISBN13: 978-0-914098-70-6.
Dewey:516.3/6.

Audience: **u,f.** *B*

Spivak, Michael **QA641**
A Comprehensive Introduction to Differential Geometry, Vol. 4.
Ed. 3. Cloth Text. Publish or Perish, Inc. Houston, TX. 1999. x,
390p. ISBN:0-914098-73-X, ISBN13: 978-0-914098-73-7.
Dewey:516.3/6.

Audience: **u,f.** *B*

Spivak, Michael **QA641**
A Comprehensive Introduction to Differential Geometry, Vol. 3.
Ed. 3. Cloth Text. Publish or Perish, Inc. Houston, TX. 1999.
xii, 314p. ISBN:0-914098-72-1, ISBN13: 978-0-914098-72-0.
Dewey:516.3/6.

Audience: **u,f.** *B*

Thorpe, J. A. **QA641 .T36**
Elementary Topics in Differential Geometry. Trade Cloth.
Springer. New York, NY. 1994. XIII, 253p. Undergraduate Texts
in Mathematics ISBN:0-387-90357-7, ISBN13:
978-0-387-90357-6. Dewey:516/.36. LCCN:78-023308.

Audience: **u.**

Geometry and Topology > Algebraic Geometry

Griffiths, Phillip & Harris, **QA564**
 Joseph
Principles of Algebraic Geometry. Ed. 1. Trade Paper. John
Wiley & Sons, Inc. Hoboken, NJ. 1994. 832p. Wiley Classics
Library, Vol. 52 ISBN:0-471-05059-8, ISBN13:
978-0-471-05059-9. Dewey:516.3/5.

Audience: **u,f.** *B*

Harris, Joe **QA564.H24 1992B**
Algebraic Geometry: A First Course. Trade Cloth. Springer.
New York, NY. 1995. XIX, 328p. Graduate Texts in
Mathematics, Vol. 133 ISBN:0-387-97716-3, ISBN13:
978-0-387-97716-4. Dewey:516.3/5. LCCN:96-105844.
Audience: **u,f.** *Choice, 1993.*

Hartshorne, Robin **QA564**
Algebraic Geometry. Trade Cloth. Springer. New York, NY.
1997. 512p. Graduate Texts in Mathematics, Vol. 52
ISBN:0-387-90244-9, ISBN13: 978-0-387-90244-9.
Dewey:516/.35.

Audience: **u,f.**

Hulek, Klaus **QA565.H85 2003**
Elementary Algebraic Geometry. Trade Paper. American
Mathematical Society. Providence, RI. 2003. 213p. Student
Mathematical Library, Vol. 20 ISBN:0-8218-2952-1, ISBN13:
978-0-8218-2952-3. Dewey:516.3/5. LCCN:2002-038457.
Audience: **u.**

Kirwan, Frances **QA565 .K57 1992**
Complex Algebraic Curves. Cloth Text. Cambridge University
Press. New York, NY. 1992. 272p. London Mathematical
Society Student Texts Ser., No. 23 ISBN:0-521-41251-X,

ISBN13: 978-0-521-41251-3. Dewey:516.352.
LCCN:92-192303.

Audience: **u.** *Choice, 1993.*

Koblitz, Neal **QA564**
Introduction to Elliptic Curves and Modular Forms. Ed. 2. Trade
Cloth. Springer. New York, NY. 1993. 268p. Graduate Texts in
Mathematics, Vol. 97 ISBN:0-387-97966-2, ISBN13:
978-0-387-97966-3. Dewey:516.3/5. LCCN:92-041778.
Audience: **u,f.** *B Choice, 1985.*

Little, John, et al. **QA564.C688 1997**
Ideals, Varieties, and Algorithms: An Introduction to
Computational Algebraic Geometry and Commutative Algebra.
Ed. 2. David Cox & Donal O'Shea (Authors). Trade Cloth.
Springer. New York, NY. 1996. XIII, 556p. Undergraduate Texts
in Mathematics ISBN:0-387-94680-2, ISBN13:
978-0-387-94680-1. Dewey:516.3/5. LCCN:96-008023.

Audience: **u,f.**

McLeod, Robin J. Y. & **QA565 .M39 1998**
 Baart, M. Louisa
Geometry and Interpolation of Curves and Surfaces. Trade
Cloth. Cambridge University Press. New York, NY. 1998. 428p.
ISBN:0-521-32153-0, ISBN13: 978-0-521-32153-2.
Dewey:516.3/52. LCCN:97-043729.

Audience: **u.**

Reid, Miles **QA564 .R45 1988**
Undergraduate Algebraic Geometry. C. M. Series & J. W. Bruce
(Contribution by). Trade Paper. Cambridge University Press.
New York, NY. 1988. 144p. London Mathematical Society
Student Texts Ser., No. 12 ISBN:0-521-35662-8, ISBN13:
978-0-521-35662-6. Dewey:516.3/5. LCCN:88-023793.
Audience: **u.** *Choice, 1989.*

Silverman, J. H. & Tate, **QA567.2.E44**
 John
Rational Points on Elliptic Curves. Trade Cloth. Springer. New
York, NY. 1994. 281p. Undergraduate Texts in Mathematics
ISBN:0-387-97825-9, ISBN13: 978-0-387-97825-3.
Dewey:516.3/52.

Audience: **u.**

Smith, Karen E., et al. **QA564.I62 2000**
An Invitation to Algebraic Geometry. Lauri Kahanpaeae & W.
N. Traves (Authors). Trade Cloth. Springer. New York, NY.
2004. XVI, 161p. Universitext Ser. ISBN:0-387-98980-3,
ISBN13: 978-0-387-98980-8. Dewey:516.3/5. LCCN:00-026595.
Audience: **u.** *Choice, 2001.*

Geometry and Topology > Discrete and Computational Geometry

Barvinok, Alexander **QA639.5.B37 2002**
A Course in Convexity. Trade Cloth. American Mathematical
Society. Providence, RI. 2002. 366p. Graduate Studies in
Mathematics, Vol. 54 ISBN:0-8218-2968-8, ISBN13:
978-0-8218-2968-4. Dewey:516/.08. LCCN:2002-028208.
Audience: **u,f.**

Coxeter, Harold S. M. **QA691 .C68 1973**
Regular Polytopes. Trade Paper. Dover Publications, Inc.
Mineola, NY. 1973. 321p. ISBN:0-486-61480-8, ISBN13:
978-0-486-61480-9. Dewey:513.8. LCCN:73-084364.
Audience: **l,u.**

Cromwell, Peter R. QA491.C76 1997
Polyhedra. Trade Paper. Cambridge University Press. New York, NY. 1999. 466p. ISBN:0-521-66405-5, ISBN13: 978-0-521-66405-9. Dewey:516.1/5. LCCN:96-009420.
Audience: **l,u.** *Choice, 1998.*

Edgar, Gerald A. QA614.86.E34 1990
Measure, Topology and Fractal Geometry. J. H. Ewing, F. W. Gehring & P. R. Halmos (Editors). Trade Cloth. Springer. New York, NY. 1995. 230p. Undergraduate Texts in Mathematics ISBN:0-387-97272-2, ISBN13: 978-0-387-97272-5. Dewey:514/.74. LCCN:90-033060.
Audience: **u.** *Choice, 1991.*

Grunbaum, Branko & QA164
Shephard, Geoffrey C.
Tilings and Patterns. Ed. 1. Paper Text. W. H. Freeman & Company. New York, NY. 1991. 700p. ISBN:0-7167-1194-X, ISBN13: 978-0-7167-1194-0. Dewey:511/.6. LCCN:86-002007.
Audience: **l,u.** *Choice, 1987.*

Hubbard, John L. QA297.8
(Featuring)
⊕ The Beauty and Complexity of the Mandelbrot Set: University Edition. Video, VHS Format. Science Television Company. New York, NY. 1989. ISBN:1-878310-02-X, ISBN13: 978-1-878310-02-6. Dewey:511.4.
Audience: **g.**

Kazarinoff, Nicholas D. QA481 .K35
Geometric Inequalities. Paper Text. Mathematical Association of America. Washington, DC. 1961. 132p. New Mathematical Library, No. 4 ISBN:0-88385-604-2, ISBN13: 978-0-88385-604-8. Dewey:513.1. LCCN:61-006229.
Audience: **u.** *B*

Lay, Steven R. QA640.L38 1991
Convex Sets and Their Applications. Trade Cloth. Krieger Publishing Company. Melbourne, FL. 1992. 262p. ISBN:0-89464-537-4, ISBN13: 978-0-89464-537-2. Dewey:511.3/2. LCCN:90-049488.
Audience: **u,f.**

Mandelbrot, Benoit B. QA445
The Fractal Geometry of Nature. Cloth over Boards. W. H. Freeman & Company. New York, NY. 1982. 480p. ISBN:0-7167-1186-9, ISBN13: 978-0-7167-1186-5. Dewey:516/.15. LCCN:81-015085.
Audience: **g.** *B*

Mandelbrot, Benoit B. QA447.M3613
Fractals: Form, Chance, and Dimension. Cloth Text. W. H. Freeman & Company. New York, NY. 1977. 365p. Mathematics Ser. ISBN:0-7167-0473-0, ISBN13: 978-0-7167-0473-7. Dewey:516/.15. LCCN:76-057947.
Audience: **g.** *B*

Minsky, Marvin L. & Q327.M55 1988
Papert, Seymour A.
Perceptrons: An Introduction to Computational Geometry. Trade Paper. MIT Press. Cambridge, MA. 1987. 275p. ISBN:0-262-63111-3, ISBN13: 978-0-262-63111-2. Dewey:006.3. LCCN:87-030990.
Audience: **u.**

Miyazaki, Koji N7430.5.M59 1986
An Adventure in Multidimensional Space: The Art and Geometry of Polygons, Polyhedra and Polytopes. Ed. 1. Trade Cloth. John Wiley & Sons, Inc. Hoboken, NJ. 1986. 112p. ISBN:0-471-81648-5, ISBN13: 978-0-471-81648-5. Dewey:701. LCCN:85-022595.
Audience: **l,u.**

Pach, János & Agarwal, QA167.P33 1995
Pankaj K.
Combinatorial Geometry. Ed. 1. Trade Cloth. John Wiley & Sons, Inc. Hoboken, NJ. 1995. 376p. Wiley-Interscience Series in Discrete Mathematics Ser., Vol. 37 ISBN:0-471-58890-3, ISBN13: 978-0-471-58890-0. Dewey:516/.13. LCCN:94-048203.
Audience: **u.** *Choice, 1996.*

Pickover, Clifford A. QA614.86 .F6845 1996
Fractal Horizons: The Future Uses of Fractals. Trade Cloth. Palgrave Macmillan. New York, NY. 1996. 256p. ISBN:0-312-12599-2, ISBN13: 978-0-312-12599-8. Dewey:514/.74. LCCN:95-026043.
Audience: **g.** *Choice, 1997.*

Radin, Charles A. QA166.8.R33 1999
Miles of Tiles. Trade Paper. American Mathematical Society. Providence, RI. 1999. xii, 120p. Student Mathematical Library, Vol. 1 ISBN:0-8218-1933-X, ISBN13: 978-0-8218-1933-3. Dewey:516. LCCN:99-020662.
Audience: **l,u.**

Schroeder, Manfred R. QC174.17.S9 S38
Fractals, Chaos and Power Laws: Minutes from an Infinite Paradise. Trade Paper. W. H. Freeman & Company. New York, NY. 1992. 429p. ISBN:0-7167-2357-3, ISBN13: 978-0-7167-2357-8. Dewey:530.1. LCCN:90-036763.
Audience: **l,u.**

Geometry and Topology > Topology

Adams, Colin Conrad QA612.2.A33 2004
The Knot Book: An Elementary Introduction to the Mathematical Theory of Knots. Trade Paper. American Mathematical Society. Providence, RI. 2004. 307p. ISBN:0-8218-3678-1, ISBN13: 978-0-8218-3678-1. Dewey:514/.2242. LCCN:2004-054429.
Audience: **l,u.**

Armstrong, M. A. QA611 .A68 1983
Basic Topology. Trade Cloth. Springer. New York, NY. 1997. 251p. Undergraduate Texts in Mathematics ISBN:0-387-90839-0, ISBN13: 978-0-387-90839-7. Dewey:514. LCCN:83-000655.
Audience: **u.**

Edgar, Gerald A. QA614.86.E34 1990
Measure, Topology and Fractal Geometry. J. H. Ewing, F. W. Gehring & P. R. Halmos (Editors). Trade Cloth. Springer. New York, NY. 1995. 230p. Undergraduate Texts in Mathematics ISBN:0-387-97272-2, ISBN13: 978-0-387-97272-5. Dewey:514/.74. LCCN:90-033060.
Audience: **u.** *Choice, 1991.*

Flapan, Erica QD455.3.T65 F53 2000
When Topology Meets Chemistry: A Topological Look at Molecular Chirality. John Barrow, Fan Chung, Ingrid Daubechies, Persi W. Diaconis, Ronald Graham & Don Zagier

Formats: Web: ☐ Ebook: ℮ CD/DVD-ROM: ⊕ BCL3: *B*

(Contribution by). Cloth Text. Cambridge University Press. New York, NY. 2000. 256p. Outlooks Ser. ISBN:0-521-66254-0, ISBN13: 978-0-521-66254-3. Dewey:541/.01/514. LCCN:00-027517.

Audience: **u,f.** *Choice, 2001.*

Gamelin, Theodore W. & QA611.G35 1999
  Greene, Robert E.
Introduction to Topology. Ed. 2. Trade Paper. Dover Publications, Inc. Mineola, NY. 1999. 24p. ISBN:0-486-40680-6, ISBN13: 978-0-486-40680-0. Dewey:514. LCCN:99-014612.

Audience: **u.**

Gilmore, Robert & Lefranc, QA614.813.G55 2002
  Marc
The Topology of Chaos: Alice in Stretch and Squeezeland. Trade Cloth. John Wiley & Sons, Inc. Hoboken, NJ. 2002. 518p. ISBN:0-471-40816-6, ISBN13: 978-0-471-40816-1. Dewey:514/.74. LCCN:2002-072153.

Audience: **u.** *Choice, 2003.*

Gross, Jonathan L. & QA166.G76 1987
  Tucker, Thomas W.
Topological Graph Theory. Ed. 99. Trade Cloth. John Wiley & Sons, Inc. Hoboken, NJ. 1987. 351p. Interscience Series in Discrete Mathematics ISBN:0-471-04926-3, ISBN13: 978-0-471-04926-5. Dewey:511/.5. LCCN:87-006221.

Audience: **u,f.**

Hatcher, Allen QA612 .H42 2002
Algebraic Topology. Trade Cloth. Cambridge University Press. New York, NY. 2001. 556p. ISBN:0-521-79160-X, ISBN13: 978-0-521-79160-1. Dewey:514/.2. LCCN:00-065166.

Audience: **u,f.** *Choice, 2002.*

Henle, Michael QA612.H46 1994
A Combinatorial Introduction to Topology. Trade Paper. Dover Publications, Inc. Mineola, NY. 1994. 310p. ISBN:0-486-67966-7, ISBN13: 978-0-486-67966-2. Dewey:514/.2. LCCN:93-050761.

Audience: **u.**

Huggett, Stephen & Jordan, QA611.H797 2001
  David
A Topological Aperitif. Trade Paper. Springer. New York, NY. 2001. IX, 166p. Undergraduate Mathematics Ser. ISBN:1-85233-377-4, ISBN13: 978-1-85233-377-5. Dewey:514. LCCN:00-069236.

Audience: **u.**

James, I. M. QA611.J33 1984
General Topology and Homotopy Theory. Cloth Text. Springer. New York, NY. 1984. 248p. ISBN:0-387-90970-2, ISBN13: 978-0-387-90970-7. Dewey:514. LCCN:84-005435.

Audience: **u,f.** *B*

Lickorish, W. B. QA612.2.L53 1997
An Introduction to Knot Theory. Trade Cloth. Springer. New York, NY. 1997. X, 220p. Graduate Texts in Mathematics Ser., Vol. 175 ISBN:0-387-98254-X, ISBN13: 978-0-387-98254-0. Dewey:514/.224. LCCN:97-016660.

Audience: **u.** *Choice, 1998.*

Lima, Elon Lages QA612.L4713 2003
Fundamental Groups and Covering Spaces. Cloth Text. A K Peters, Ltd. Wellesley, MA. 2003. 210p. ISBN:1-56881-131-4,

ISBN13: 978-1-56881-131-4. Dewey:514/.2. LCCN:2003-048719.

Audience: **u,f.** *Choice, 2004.*

Livingston, Charles QA612.2.L58 1993
Knot Theory. Cloth Text. Mathematical Association of America. Washington, DC. 1996. 258p. Carus Monographs ISBN:0-88385-027-3, ISBN13: 978-0-88385-027-5. Dewey:514.2/24. LCCN:93-087341.

Audience: **l,u.** *Choice, 1994.*

Matsumoto, Y. QA331.M442713 2002
An Introduction to Morse Theory. Trade Paper. American Mathematical Society. Providence, RI. 2002. 232p. Iwanami Series in Modern Mathematics, Vol. 208 ISBN:0-8218-1022-7, ISBN13: 978-0-8218-1022-4. Dewey:514. LCCN:2001-045751.

Audience: **u,f.**

Messer, Robert & Straffin, QA611.17
  Philip
Topology Now!. William Watkins, , Andrew Sterrett Jr., Frank A. Farris, Stephen B. Maurer, Julian Fleron, William A. Marion, Sheldon P. Gordon, Edward P. Merkes, Yvette C. Hester & Daniel E. Otero (Contribution by). Cloth Text. Mathematical Association of America. Washington, DC. 2006. 250p. ISBN:0-88385-744-8, ISBN13: 978-0-88385-744-1. Dewey:514. LCCN:2005-937270.

Audience: **u,f.**

Milnor, John QA613.6.M55 1997
Topology from the Differentiable Viewpoint. Trade Paper. Princeton University Press. Princeton, NJ. 1997. 76p. Princeton Landmarks in Mathematics and Physics Ser. ISBN:0-691-04833-9, ISBN13: 978-0-691-04833-8. Dewey:514/.72. LCCN:97-030986.

Audience: **u,f.**

Munkres, James R. QA611.M82 2000
Topology. Ed. 2. Cloth Text. Prentice Hall PTR. Upper Saddle River, NJ. 1999. 537p. ISBN:0-13-181629-2, ISBN13: 978-0-13-181629-9. Dewey:514. LCCN:99-052942.

Audience: **u.**

Prasolov, V. V. QA611.13.P73 1995
Intuitive Topology. A. B. Sossinsky (Translator). Trade Paper. American Mathematical Society. Providence, RI. 1994. 93p. Mathematical World Ser., 4 ISBN:0-8218-0356-5, ISBN13: 978-0-8218-0356-1. Dewey:514. LCCN:94-023133.

Audience: **l,u.**

Simmons, George F. QA611 .S49 1983
Introduction to Topology and Modern Analysis. Library Binding. Krieger Publishing Company. Melbourne, FL. 1983. 384p. ISBN:0-89874-551-9, ISBN13: 978-0-89874-551-1. Dewey:514. LCCN:82-014845.

Audience: **u.**

Spivak, Michael QA612
Calculus on Manifolds: A Modern Approach to Classical Theorems of Advanced Calculus. Trade Paper. Westview Press. Boulder, CO. 2000. 160p. ISBN:0-8053-9021-9, ISBN13: 978-0-8053-9021-6. Dewey:514.3.

Audience: **u,f.**

Willard, Stephen   QA611.W55 2004
General Topology. Trade Paper. Dover Publications, Inc.
Mineola, NY. 2004. 384p. ISBN:0-486-43479-6, ISBN13:
978-0-486-43479-7. Dewey:514. LCCN:2003-068793.

Audience: **u.**

Applied Mathematics

Bender, Carl M. & Orszag,   QA371.B43 1999
  Steven A.
Advanced Mathematical Methods for Scientists and Engineers:
Asymptotic Methods and Perturbation Theory. Trade Cloth.
Springer. New York, NY. 1999. XIV, 593p.
ISBN:0-387-98931-5, ISBN13: 978-0-387-98931-0.
Dewey:515/.35. LCCN:99-044783.

Audience: **u.**

Eriksson, K., et al.   QA273
Applied Mathematics: Body and Soul: Derivatives and
Geometry in IR3. D. Estep & C. Johnson (Authors). Trade
Cloth. Springer. New York, NY. 2003. XLIV, 426p.
ISBN:3-540-00890-X, ISBN13: 978-3-540-00890-3. Dewey:519.
LCCN:2003-066672.

Audience: **u.**

Friedman, A. & Littman, W.   QA37.2.F735 1994
Industrial Mathematics: A Course in Solving Real-World
Problems. Trade Paper. Society for Industrial & Applied
Mathematics. Philadelphia, PA. 1994. xiii, 136p. Miscellaneous
Titles Ser., No. 42 ISBN:0-89871-324-2, ISBN13:
978-0-89871-324-4. Dewey:515. LCCN:94-020770.

Audience: **u,f.**

Gershenfeld, Neil   QA401 .G47 1999
The Nature of Mathematical Modeling. Cloth Text. Cambridge
University Press. New York, NY. 1998. 356p.
ISBN:0-521-57095-6, ISBN13: 978-0-521-57095-4.
Dewey:511/.8. LCCN:98-022029.

Audience: **u.**   *Choice, 1999.*

Kalman, Dan   QA401.K24 1997
Elementary Mathematical Models: Order Aplenty and a Glimpse
of Chaos. Paper Text. Mathematical Association of America.
Washington, DC. 1998. 361p. Classroom Resource Materials
Ser. ISBN:0-88385-707-3, ISBN13: 978-0-88385-707-6.
Dewey:511/.8. LCCN:97-074331.

Audience: **u,f.**   *Choice, 1998.*

Klamkin, Murray S.   QA401.M3937 1987
  (Editor)
Mathematical Modelling: Classroom Notes in Applied
Mathematics. Trade Cloth. Society for Industrial & Applied
Mathematics. Philadelphia, PA. 1987. xiv + 338p. Miscellaneous
Bks., No. 15 ISBN:0-89871-204-1, ISBN13: 978-0-89871-204-9.
Dewey:001.4/34. LCCN:86-060090.

Audience: **u,f.**

Mooney, Douglas D. &   QA401
  Swift, Randall
A Course in Mathematical Modeling. Paper Text. Mathematical
Association of America. Washington, DC. 1999. 452p.
Classroom Resource Materials Ser. ISBN:0-88385-712-X,
ISBN13: 978-0-88385-712-0. Dewey:511/.8. LCCN:98-085688.

Audience: **u,f.**   *Choice, 2000.*

Pearson, Carl E. (Editor)   QA36
Handbook of Applied Mathematics: Selected Results and
Methods. Ed. 2. Cloth Text. John Wiley & Sons, Inc. Hoboken,
NJ. 1983. 1304p. ISBN:0-442-23866-5, ISBN13:
978-0-442-23866-7. Dewey:510. LCCN:82-020223.

Audience: **u,f.** *B*

Rade, Lennart &   QA41
  Westergren, Bertil
Mathematics Handbook for Science and Engineering. Ed. 5.
Trade Cloth. Springer. New York, NY. 2004. 562p.
ISBN:3-540-21141-1, ISBN13: 978-3-540-21141-9. Dewey:510.
LCCN:96-124564.

Audience: **l,u,f.**   *Choice, 1996.*

Strang, Gilbert   QA37.2.S87 1986
Introduction to Applied Mathematics. Trade Cloth.
Wellesley-Cambridge Press. Wellesley, MA. 1986. 750p.
ISBN:0-9614088-0-4, ISBN13: 978-0-9614088-0-0. Dewey:510.
LCCN:84-052450.

Audience: **u.** *B*

Sullivan, Michael &   HF5691
  Mizrahi, Abe
Mathematics: An Applied Approach. Ed. 8. Trade Cloth. John
Wiley & Sons, Inc. Hoboken, NJ. 2004. 1256p.
ISBN:0-471-32784-0, ISBN13: 978-0-471-32784-4.
Dewey:650/.01/513. LCCN:2004-042255.

Audience: **l,u.**

Applied Mathematics > Applications in the Physical Sciences or Engineering

Braess, Dietrich   TA347.F5 B7313 2001
Finite Elements: Theory, Fast Solvers, and Applications in Solid
Mechanics. Ed. 2. Larry L. Schumaker (Translator). Trade
Paper. Cambridge University Press. New York, NY. 2001. 370p.
ISBN:0-521-01195-7, ISBN13: 978-0-521-01195-2.
Dewey:620/.001/51535. LCCN:00-069656.

Audience: **u,f.**   *Choice, 1998.*

Courant, Richard   QA401
Methods of Mathematical Physics. Trade Cloth. John Wiley &
Sons, Inc. Hoboken, NJ. 2004. 576p. ISBN:0-471-67476-1,
ISBN13: 978-0-471-67476-4. Dewey:530.1/5.

Audience: **u.**

Courant, Richard &   QC20
  Hilbert, D.
Methods of Mathematical Physics, Vol. 2. Trade Paper. John
Wiley & Sons, Inc. Hoboken, NJ. 1996. 1390p. Classics Library
ISBN:0-471-55760-9, ISBN13: 978-0-471-55760-9.
Dewey:530.1/5.

Audience: **u.** *B*

Devore, Jay L.   QA273.D46 2004
Probability and Statistics for Engineering and the Sciences. Ed.
6. Cloth Text. Brooks/Cole. Pacific Grove, CA. 2003. 816p.
ISBN:0-534-39933-9, ISBN13: 978-0-534-39933-7.
Dewey:519.2. LCCN:2003-101979.

Audience: **l,u.**

Feeman, Timothy G.   GA13.F44 2002
Portraits of the Earth: A Mathematician Looks at Maps. Trade
Paper. American Mathematical Society. Providence, RI. 2002.

xiii, 123p. Mathematical World Ser., Vol. 18
ISBN:0-8218-3255-7, ISBN13: 978-0-8218-3255-4. Dewey:526.
LCCN:2002-027950.

Audience: **l,u.**

Flapan, Erica   **QD455.3.T65 F53 2000**
When Topology Meets Chemistry: A Topological Look at
Molecular Chirality. John Barrow, Fan Chung, Ingrid
Daubechies, Persi W. Diaconis, Ronald Graham & Don Zagier
(Contribution by). Cloth Text. Cambridge University Press. New
York, NY. 2000. 256p. Outlooks Ser. ISBN:0-521-66254-0,
ISBN13: 978-0-521-66254-3. Dewey:541/.01/514.
LCCN:00-027517.

Audience: **u,f.** *Choice, 2001.*

Frankel, Theodore   **QC20**
The Geometry of Physics: An Introduction. Ed. 2. Cloth Text.
Cambridge University Press. New York, NY. 2003. 720p.
ISBN:0-521-83330-2, ISBN13: 978-0-521-83330-1.
Dewey:530.15/636. LCCN:2003-044030.

Audience: **u,f.**

Glass, Leon & Kaplan,   **QA845.K36 1995**
  Daniel
Understanding Nonlinear Dynamics. Trade Paper. Springer. New
York, NY. 1997. XIX, 420p. Textbooks in Mathematical
Sciences ISBN:0-387-94440-0, ISBN13: 978-0-387-94440-1.
Dewey:515/.352. LCCN:94-043113.

Audience: **u.** *Choice, 1995.*

Graver, Jack   **TA407.G68 2001**
Counting on Frameworks: Mathematics to Aid the Design of
Rigid Structures. Paper Text. Mathematical Association of
America. Washington, DC. 2001. 192p. Dolciani Mathematical
Expositions Ser., Vol. 25 ISBN:0-88385-331-0, ISBN13:
978-0-88385-331-3. Dewey:624.1/7. LCCN:2001-089227.

Audience: **l,u.** *Choice, 2002.*

Greenberg, Michael D.   **QA303**
Foundations of Applied Mathematics. Cloth Text. Prentice Hall
PTR. Upper Saddle River, NJ. 1978. xix, 636p.
ISBN:0-13-329623-7, ISBN13: 978-0-13-329623-5. Dewey:515.
LCCN:77-011125.

Audience: **u.**

Jaffard, Stephane, et al.   **QA403.3.J34 2001**
Wavelets: Tools for Science and Technology. Ed. 2. Yves Meyer
& Robert D. Ryan (Authors). Trade Cloth. Society for Industrial
& Applied Mathematics. Philadelphia, PA. 2001. xiv + 256p.
ISBN:0-89871-448-6, ISBN13: 978-0-89871-448-7.
Dewey:515/.2433. LCCN:00-051607.

Audience: **u.** *Choice, 2002.*

Knobel, Roger   **QA927.K693 2000**
An Introduction to the Mathematical Theory of Waves. Trade
Paper. American Mathematical Society. Providence, RI. 1999.
xiv, 196p. Student Mathematical Library ISBN:0-8218-2039-7,
ISBN13: 978-0-8218-2039-1. Dewey:531/.1133.
LCCN:99-039055.

Audience: **l,u.** *Choice, 2000.*

Kreyszig, Erwin   **QA401**
Advanced Engineering Mathematics. Ed. 9. Trade Paper. John
Wiley & Sons, Inc. Hoboken, NJ. 2006. 260p.
ISBN:0-471-72644-3, ISBN13: 978-0-471-72644-9.
Dewey:510/.2462. LCCN:2004-065932.

Audience: **u.** *B*

Lin, C. C. & Segel, Lee A.   **QA37.2 .L55 1988**
Mathematics Applied to Deterministic Problems in the Natural
Sciences. Trade Paper. Society for Industrial & Applied
Mathematics. Philadelphia, PA. 1988. xxi, 609p. Classics in
Applied Mathematics, No. 1 ISBN:0-89871-229-7, ISBN13:
978-0-89871-229-2. Dewey:510. LCCN:88-062304.

Audience: **u,f.**

O'Neil, Peter V.   **QA331.3**
Advanced Engineering Mathematics. Ed. 6. Cloth Text.
Thomson Learning. Independence, KY. 2006. 1216p.
ISBN:0-534-55208-0, ISBN13: 978-0-534-55208-4.
Dewey:515/.1.

Audience: **u.**

Starck, Jean-Luc   **Q183.9 .S83 1998**
Image Processing and Data Analysis: The Multiscale Approach.
Trade Cloth. Cambridge University Press. New York, NY. 1998.
297p. ISBN:0-521-59084-1, ISBN13: 978-0-521-59084-6.
Dewey:621.36/7/0245. LCCN:97-017393.

Audience: **u.**

Walpole, Ronald E., et al.   **TA340.P738 2006**
Probability and Statistics for Engineers and Scientists. Ed. 8.
Raymond Myers, Sharon L. Myers & Keying Ye (Authors).
Cloth Text. Prentice Hall PTR. Upper Saddle River, NJ. 2006.
848p. ISBN:0-13-187711-9, ISBN13: 978-0-13-187711-5.
Dewey:519.02/462. LCCN:2005-058605.

Audience: **l,u.**

Wolfram, Stephen   **QA267.5.C45W67 2002**
A New Kind of Science. Trade Cloth. Wolfram Media, Inc.
Champaign, IL. 2003. 1197p. ISBN:1-57955-008-8, ISBN13:
978-1-57955-008-0. Dewey:500. LCCN:2001-046603.

Audience: **u,f.** *Choice, 2003.*

Applied Mathematics > Applications in the Biological Sciences

Allen, Linda J. S.   **QA274.A63 2003**
An Introduction to Stochastic Processes with Biology
Applications. Cloth Text. Prentice Hall PTR. Upper Saddle
River, NJ. 2003. 385p. ISBN:0-13-035218-7, ISBN13:
978-0-13-035218-7. Dewey:519.2/3. LCCN:2003-051267.

Audience: **u.**

Anderson, Roy M. & May,   **RA643.A56 1991**
  Robert M.
Infectious Diseases of Humans: Dynamics and Control. Trade
Cloth. Oxford University Press, Inc. New York, NY. 1991. 768p.
ISBN:0-19-854599-1, ISBN13: 978-0-19-854599-6.
Dewey:614.4. LCCN:90-014312.

Audience: **u,f.**

Clark, Colin W. & Mangel,   **QL751.65.M3C58 2000**
  Marc
Dynamic State Variable Models in Ecology: Methods and
Applications. Trade Cloth. Oxford University Press, Inc. New
York, NY. 2000. 302p. Oxford Series in Ecology and Evolution
ISBN:0-19-512266-6, ISBN13: 978-0-19-512266-4.
Dewey:577/.01/5118. LCCN:99-012265.

Audience: **u.** *Choice, 2001.*

Clote, Peter & Backofen,   **QH438.4.M3C565 2000**
  Rolf
Computational Molecular Biology: An Introduction. Trade Cloth.

John Wiley & Sons, Inc. Hoboken, NJ. 2000. 300p. Wiley Series in Mathematical and Computational Biology Ser., Vol. 1 ISBN:0-471-87251-2, ISBN13: 978-0-471-87251-1. Dewey:572.8/01/5118. LCCN:00-038169.

Audience: **u,f.**

Ewens, Warren J. & Grant,   QH324.2.E97 2004
  Gregory
Statistical Methods in Bioinformatics: An Introduction. Ed. 2. Trade Cloth. Springer. New York, NY. 2005. XX, 588p. Statistics for Biology and Health Ser. ISBN:0-387-40082-6, ISBN13: 978-0-387-40082-2. Dewey:572.8/0285. LCCN:2004-056491.

Audience: **u,f.**

Gibson, Greg & Muse,   QH447.G534 2004
  Spencer V.
A Primer of Genome Science. Ed. 2. Trade Cloth. Sinauer Associates, Inc. Sunderland, MA. 2004. 350p. ISBN:0-87893-232-1, ISBN13: 978-0-87893-232-0. Dewey:572.8/6. LCCN:2004-024285.

Audience: **u,f.** *Choice, 2002.*

Hadlock, Charles   TD177
Mathematical Modeling in the Environment. Paper Text. Mathematical Association of America. Washington, DC. 1999. 316p. Classroom Resource Materials Ser. ISBN:0-88385-709-X, ISBN13: 978-0-88385-709-0. Dewey:363.7/015118. LCCN:98-086932.

Audience: **u,f.** *Choice, 1999.*

Haefner, James W.   QH323.5.H34 2005
Modeling Biological Systems: Principles and Applications. Ed. 2. Mixed Media. Springer. New York, NY. 2005. XVI, 480p. ISBN:0-387-25011-5, ISBN13: 978-0-387-25011-3. Dewey:570.1/1. LCCN:2005-042543.

Audience: **u.**

Hastings, Alan   QH352 .H38
Population Biology: Concepts and Models. Ed. 2. Trade Cloth. Springer. New York, NY. 2005. 320p. ISBN:0-387-98852-1, ISBN13: 978-0-387-98852-8. Dewey:574.5/248/0151.

Audience: **u.**

Keener, James, et al.   QP33.6.M36K44 1998
Mathematical Physiology. James Sneyd, L. Sirovich, S. Wiggins, L. P. Kadanoff & J. E. Marsden (Authors). Trade Cloth. Springer. New York, NY. 2001. XIX, 766p. Interdisciplinary Applied Mathematics Ser., Vol. 8 ISBN:0-387-98381-3, ISBN13: 978-0-387-98381-3. Dewey:571/.01/51. LCCN:98-014499.

Audience: **u,f.**

Keyfitz, Nathan   HB850.3 .K49 1984
Demography Through Problems. Trade Cloth. Springer. New York, NY. 1990. VIII, 141p. Problem Books in Mathematics ISBN:0-387-90836-6, ISBN13: 978-0-387-90836-6. Dewey:304.6/076. LCCN:83-006775.

Audience: **u,f.**

Lesk, Arthur M.   QH441.2
Introduction to Bioinformatics. Ed. 2. Paper Text. Oxford University Press, Inc. New York, NY. 2005. 390p. ISBN:0-19-927787-7, ISBN13: 978-0-19-927787-2. Dewey:570/.285. LCCN:2005-279076.

Audience: **u,f.**

Mandelbrot, Benoit B.   QA445
The Fractal Geometry of Nature. Cloth over Boards. W. H. Freeman & Company. New York, NY. 1982. 480p. ISBN:0-7167-1186-9, ISBN13: 978-0-7167-1186-5. Dewey:516/.15. LCCN:81-015085.

Audience: **g.** *B*

Murray, James D.   QH323.5.M88 2001
Mathematical Biology: An Introduction. Ed. 3. Trade Cloth. Springer. New York, NY. 2004. XXIII, 551p. Interdisciplinary Applied Mathematics Ser. ISBN:0-387-95223-3, ISBN13: 978-0-387-95223-9. Dewey:570/.1/5118. LCCN:2001-020448.

Audience: **u,f.**

Neuhauser, Claudia   QH323.5.N46 2003
Calculus for Biology and Medicine. Ed. 2. Cloth Text. Prentice Hall PTR. Upper Saddle River, NJ. 2003. 822p. ISBN:0-13-045516-4, ISBN13: 978-0-13-045516-1. Dewey:515. LCCN:2003-048212.

Audience: **l,u.**

Okubo, A.   QH541.15.M3 O38
Diffusion and Ecological Problems: Mathematical Models. K. Krickeberg & S. A. Levin (Editors). Trade Cloth. Springer. New York, NY. 1980. Biomathematics Ser., Vol. 10 ISBN:0-387-09620-5, ISBN13: 978-0-387-09620-9. Dewey:574.5. LCCN:79-019975.

Audience: **u.**

Roughgarden, Jonathan   QH455.R68
Theory of Population Genetics and Evolutionary Ecology: An Introduction. Trade Cloth. Macmillan Publishing Company, Inc. Old Tappan, NJ. 1979. x, 634 p. :p. ISBN:0-02-403180-1, ISBN13: 978-0-02-403180-8. Dewey:575.1/5. LCCN:78-007245.

Audience: **u.** *B*

Segel, Lee A.   QH506 .S44 1984
Modeling Dynamic Phenomena in Molecular and Cellular Biology. Cloth Text. Cambridge University Press. New York, NY. 1984. 304p. ISBN:0-521-25465-5, ISBN13: 978-0-521-25465-6. Dewey:574.8/8/0724. LCCN:83-015172.

Audience: **u.** *B*

Stewart, Ian   QH323.5.S747 2001
What Shape Is a Snowflake?: Magical Numbers in Nature. Cloth over Boards. Henry Holt & Company. New York, NY. 2001. 200p. ISBN:0-7167-4794-4, ISBN13: 978-0-7167-4794-9. Dewey:510. LCCN:2002-280019.

Audience: **g.**

Waterman, Michael   QH438.4.M33 W38 1995
Introduction to Computational Biology: Maps, Sequences and Genomes. Chapman and Hall/CRC. 1995. ISBN:0-412-99391-0, ISBN13: 978-0-412-99391-6.

Audience: **u.**

Wheater, C. Philip & Cook,   QA276.12.W52 2000
  Penny A.
Statistics for Environmental Investigations. Paper over Boards. Routledge. New York, NY. 2000. 272p. Introduction to Environment Ser. ISBN:0-415-19887-9, ISBN13: 978-0-415-19887-5. Dewey:519.5. LCCN:99-040009.

Audience: **l,u.** *Choice, 2001.*

Yeargers, E. K., et al.   QH323.5.Y435 1996
An Introduction to the Mathematics of Biology: With Computer Algebra Models. R. W. Shonkwiler & J. V. Herod (Authors).

Trade Cloth. Springer. New York, NY. 1996. 432p.
ISBN:0-8176-3809-1, ISBN13: 978-0-8176-3809-2.
Dewey:574/.01/51. LCCN:96-001385.
Audience: **u.** *Choice, 1997.*

Yodzis, Peter   **QH541.Y63 1989**
Introduction to Theoretical Ecology. Trade Paper.
Addison-Wesley Educational Publishers, Inc. Boston, MA. 1989.
384p. ISBN:0-06-047369-X, ISBN13: 978-0-06-047369-3.
Dewey:574.5/01. LCCN:88-031050.
Audience: **u.**

Applied Mathematics > Applications in Business and the Social Sciences

Balinski, M. L. & Young,   **JF1075.U6B3 2001**
Peyton H.
Fair Representation: Meeting the Ideal of One Man, One Vote.
Ed. 2. Trade Cloth. Brookings Institution Press. Washington,
DC. 2001. 192p. ISBN:0-8157-0090-3, ISBN13:
978-0-8157-0090-6. Dewey:328.73/07347/09. LCCN:00-067500.
Audience: **g.**

Barnett, Raymond A., et al.   **QA37.3.B37 2005**
College Mathematics for Business, Economics, Life Sciences
and Social Sciences. Ed. 10. Michael R. Ziegler & Karl E.
Byleen (Authors). Trade Cloth. Prentice Hall PTR. Upper
Saddle River, NJ. 2004. 1314p. ISBN:0-13-143209-5, ISBN13:
978-0-13-143209-3. Dewey:510. LCCN:2004-044667.
Audience: **l.**

Baxter, Martin W. &   **HG6024.A3 B39 1996**
Rennie, Andrew J. O.
Financial Calculus: An Introduction to Derivative Pricing. Trade
Cloth. Cambridge University Press. New York, NY. 1996. 243p.
ISBN:0-521-55289-3, ISBN13: 978-0-521-55289-9.
Dewey:332.63222. LCCN:96-009219.
Audience: **u.**

Capinski, Marek &   **HF5691**
Zastawniak, Tomasz
Mathematics for Finance: An Introduction to Financial
Engineering. Trade Paper. Springer. New York, NY. 2004. X,
310p. Springer Undergraduate Mathematics Ser.
ISBN:1-85233-330-8, ISBN13: 978-1-85233-330-0.
Dewey:332.6/01/51. LCCN:2003-045431.
Audience: **u.**

Chung, Kai Lai & AitSahlia,   **QA273.C5775 2003**
Farid
Elementary Probability Theory: With Stochastic Processes and
an Introduction to Mathematical Finance. Ed. 4. Trade Cloth.
Springer. New York, NY. 2003. XIII, 402p. Undergraduate Texts
in Mathematics Ser. ISBN:0-387-95578-X, ISBN13:
978-0-387-95578-0. Dewey:519.2. LCCN:2002-030573.
Audience: **u.**

Clark, Colin W.   **QH705**
Mathematical Bioeconomics: The Optimal Management of
Renewable Resources. Ed. 2. Trade Paper, Perfect. John Wiley
& Sons, Inc. Hoboken, NJ. 2005. 386p. Pure and Applied
Mathematics Ser., :A Wiley-Interscience Series of Texts,
Monographs and Tracts Ser. ISBN:0-471-75152-9, ISBN13:
978-0-471-75152-6. Dewey:333.95/01/1.
Audience: **u.**

Goldberg, Samuel   **QA431.G59 1986**
Introduction to Difference Equations: With Illustrative Examples
from Economics, Psychology and Sociology. Trade Paper. Dover
Publications, Inc. Mineola, NY. 1986. 260p.
ISBN:0-486-65084-7, ISBN13: 978-0-486-65084-5.
Dewey:515/.625. LCCN:85-031131.
Audience: **u,f.**

Gross, Maurice   **P123**
Mathematical Models in Linguistics. Trade Cloth. Prentice Hall
PTR. Upper Saddle River, NJ. 1972. 176p. Foundations of
Modern Linguistics Ser. ISBN:0-13-561696-4, ISBN13:
978-0-13-561696-3. Dewey:410/.1/84. LCCN:75-181401.
Audience: **u.**

Haeussler, Ernest F., et al.   **QA300.H328 2005**
Introductory Mathematical Analysis for Business, Economics
and the Life and Social Sciences. Ed. 11. Richard S. Paul & R.
J. Wood (Authors). Cloth Text. Prentice Hall PTR. Upper Saddle
River, NJ. 2004. 1056p. ISBN:0-13-113948-7, ISBN13:
978-0-13-113948-0. Dewey:515/.1. LCCN:2004-044607.
Audience: **g,l,u.**

Hoffmann, Laurence D.,   **QA303.2.H64 2007**
et al.
Calculus for Business, Economics, and the Social and Life
Sciences. Ed. 9. Gerald L. Bradley & Kenneth H. Rosen
(Authors). Trade Cloth. McGraw-Hill Companies, The. New
York, NY. 2005. xxx, 758p. ISBN:0-07-305191-8, ISBN13:
978-0-07-305191-8. Dewey:515. LCCN:2005-025832.
Audience: **l,u.**

Hull, John C.   **HG6024.A3H85 2002**
Options, Futures, and Other Derivatives. Ed. 5. Cloth Text.
Prentice Hall PTR. Upper Saddle River, NJ. 2002. 744p.
Prentice Hall Finance Ser. ISBN:0-13-009056-5, ISBN13:
978-0-13-009056-0. Dewey:332.64/5. LCCN:2002-025234.
Audience: **u.**

Lindsey, J. K.   **QA278.L5538 1995**
Modelling Frequency and Count Data. Trade Cloth. Oxford
University Press, Inc. New York, NY. 1995. 300p. Oxford
Statistical Science Ser., No. 15 ISBN:0-19-852331-9, ISBN13:
978-0-19-852331-4. Dewey:519.5/36. LCCN:94-046457.
Audience: **u.** *Choice, 1996.*

Lomax, Richard G.   **QA276.12.L66 2000**
Statistical Concepts: A Second Course for Education and the
Behavioral Sciences. Ed. 2. Trade Paper. Lawrence Erlbaum
Associates, Inc. Mahwah, NJ. 2000. 336p. ISBN:0-8058-3783-3,
ISBN13: 978-0-8058-3783-4. Dewey:519.5. LCCN:00-059299.
Audience: **u.** *Choice, 1998.*

Olinick, Michael   **H61.25**
Introduction to Mathematical Models in the Social and Life
Sciences. Ed. 1. Cloth Text. Addison-Wesley Longman, Inc.
Boston, MA. 1978. xiii, 466p. ISBN:0-201-05448-5, ISBN13:
978-0-201-05448-4. Dewey:574/.0724. LCCN:77-077758.
Audience: **l,u.**

Prichett, Gordon D. &   **HF5691 .B69 1994**
Saber, John C.
Mathematics with Applications in Management and Economics.
Ed. 7. Cloth Text. McGraw-Hill Higher Education. Burr Ridge,
IL. 1993. 1088p. ISBN:0-256-09237-0, ISBN13:
978-0-256-09237-0. Dewey:510. LCCN:92-036042.
Audience: **l,u.**

Raiffa, Howard   **BF637.N4**
The Art and Science of Negotiation. Trade Cloth. Harvard
University Press. Cambridge, MA. 1982. 384p.
ISBN:0-674-04812-1, ISBN13: 978-0-674-04812-6.
Dewey:302.3. LCCN:82-006170.

Audience: **l,u.**

Saari, D.   **JF1001.S227 2001**
Chaotic Elections!: A Mathematician Looks at Voting. Trade
Paper. American Mathematical Society. Providence, RI. 2001.
xiii, 159p. ISBN:0-8218-2847-9, ISBN13: 978-0-8218-2847-2.
Dewey:324.9. LCCN:2001-022386.

Audience: **l,u,f.**

Tanur, Judith M., et al.   **HA29.S7847**
  (Editors)
Statistics: A Guide to Business and Economics. Holden-Day.
1976. Series in Probability and Statistics ISBN:0-8162-8614-0,
ISBN13: 978-0-8162-8614-0.

Audience: **l,u.**

Tanur, Judith M., et al.   **HA29.S78474**
  (Editors)
Statistics: A Guide to Political and Social Issues. Holden-Day.
1977. ISBN:0-8162-8574-8, ISBN13: 978-0-8162-8574-7.

Audience: **l,u.**

Wagner, Harvey M.   **T57.6**
Principles of Operations Research with Applications to
Managerial Decisions. Ed. 2. Cloth Text. Prentice Hall PTR.
Upper Saddle River, NJ. 1975. 1088p. ISBN:0-13-709592-9,
ISBN13: 978-0-13-709592-6. Dewey:658.4/034.
LCCN:74-029418.

Audience: **u.** *B*

Applied Mathematics > Applications in Business and the Social Sciences > Actuarial Science

Bowers, Newton L. Jr., et al.   **HG8781**
Actuarial Mathematics. Ed. 2. Hans U. Gerber, James C.
Hickman, Donald Jones & Cecil J. Nesbitt (Authors). Cloth
Text. Society of Actuaries. Schaumburg, IL. 1997. 650p.
ISBN:0-938959-10-7, ISBN13: 978-0-938959-10-6.
Dewey:368/.01. LCCN:86-061747.

Audience: **u.**

Broverman, Samuel A.   **HG8781.S626**
Actex Study Manual. SOA Exam P, CAS Exam 1. Actex
Publications. 2005. ISBN:1-56698-500-5, ISBN13:
978-1-56698-500-0.

Audience: **u.**

Casualty Actuarial Society   **HG9956.F68 2001**
  Staff (Contribution by)
Foundations of Casualty Actuarial Science. Ed. 4. Cloth Text.
Casualty Actuarial Society. Arlington, VA. 2001. xiii, 817p.
ISBN:0-9624762-2-6, ISBN13: 978-0-9624762-2-8.
Dewey:368.5/01. LCCN:2001-088378.

Audience: **u.**

Kammen, Daniel M;   **GE105.K35 1999**
  Hassenzahl, David M
Should We Risk It?: Exploring Environmental, Health, and
Technological Problem Solving. Princeton University Press.
1999. ISBN:0-691-00426-9, ISBN13: 978-0-691-00426-6.

Audience: **u.**

Kellison, Stephen G.   **HB539.K28 1991**
Theory of Interest. Ed. 2. Cloth Text. McGraw-Hill Higher
Education. Burr Ridge, IL. 1991. 448p. ISBN:0-256-09150-1,
ISBN13: 978-0-256-09150-2. Dewey:332.8. LCCN:91-016494.

Audience: **u.**

London, Richard L. and   **HG8781.S626**
  Nicholas Mocciolo
Actex Study Manual. SOA Exam FM, CAS Exam 2. Actex
Publications. 2005. ISBN:1-56698-501-3, ISBN13:
978-1-56698-501-7.

Audience: **u.**

Applied Mathematics > Applications in Business and the Social Sciences > Game Theory

Aumann, R. J. & Hart,   **HB144.H36 1992**
  S. R. (Editors)
Handbook of Game Theory with Economic Applications, Vol. 1.
Ed. 3. Trade Cloth. Elsevier Science & Technology Books. Saint
Louis, MO. 1992. 760p. Handbooks in Economics , Vol. 11
ISBN:0-444-88098-4, ISBN13: 978-0-444-88098-7.
Dewey:519.3. LCCN:91-038429.

Audience: **u,f.**

Aumann, R. J. & Hart,   **HB144 .H36 1992**
  S. R. (Editors)
Handbook of Game Theory with Economic Applications. Ed. 2.
Trade Cloth. Elsevier Science & Technology Books. Saint
Louis, MO. 1994. 818p. Handbooks in Economics , Vol. 11
ISBN:0-444-89427-6, ISBN13: 978-0-444-89427-4.
Dewey:519.3. LCCN:91-038429.

Audience: **u,f.**

Aumann, Robert J. & Hart,   **QA269**
  Sergiu (Editors)
Handbook of Game Theory with Economic Applications, Vol. 3.
Trade Cloth. Elsevier Science & Technology Books. Saint
Louis, MO. 2002. 890p. Handbooks in Economics
ISBN:0-444-89428-4, ISBN13: 978-0-444-89428-1.
Dewey:519.3.

Audience: **u,f.**

Luce, R. Duncan & Raiffa,   **QA269.L8 1989**
  Howard
Games and Decisions: Introduction and Critical Survey. Trade
Paper. Dover Publications, Inc. Mineola, NY. 1989. 509p.
ISBN:0-486-65943-7, ISBN13: 978-0-486-65943-5.
Dewey:519.3. LCCN:88-033460.

Audience: **u.**

Osborne, Martin J. &   **HB144.O733 1994**
  Rubinstein, Ariel
A Course in Game Theory. Trade Paper. MIT Press. Cambridge,
MA. 1994. 368p. ISBN:0-262-65040-1, ISBN13:
978-0-262-65040-3. Dewey:658.4/0353. LCCN:94-008308.

Audience: **u,f.**

Stahl, Saul QA269.S695 1999
A Gentle Introduction to Game Theory. Trade Paper. American
Mathematical Society. Providence, RI. 1998. 176p.
Mathematical World Ser., Vol. 13 ISBN:0-8218-1339-0,
ISBN13: 978-0-8218-1339-3. Dewey:519.3. LCCN:98-037248.
Audience: **l,u.** *Choice, 1999.*

von Neumann, John & QA269.V65 2004
 Morgenstern, Oskar
Theory of Games and Economic Behavior. Ed. 60. Harold
William Kuhn (Introduction by), Ariel Rubinstein (Afterword
by). Trade Cloth. Princeton University Press. Princeton, NJ.
2004. 704p. Princeton Classic Editions Ser.
ISBN:0-691-11993-7, ISBN13: 978-0-691-11993-9.
Dewey:519.3. LCCN:2004-100346.
Audience: **u,f.**

Williams, J. D. QA270.W5 1986
The Compleat Strategyst: Being a Primer on the Theory of
Games of Strategy. Trade Paper. Dover Publications, Inc.
Mineola, NY. 1986. 268p. ISBN:0-486-25101-2, ISBN13:
978-0-486-25101-1. Dewey:519.3. LCCN:86-001067.
Audience: **u.**

MEDICINE

The titles selected for this section were selected to support primarily the following curricula:

- Premed
- Nursing
- Allied Health
- Respiratory Therapy
- Speech Therapy
- Dental Hygiene
- Medical Biology

Effort was made to include medical texts, nursing texts, and, where possible and appropriate, titles for the informed lay person. In this selection, there is an emphasis on books which provide a clinical or practitioner perspective. Recommendations for databases and multimedia resources have been included.

— Ralph Arcari

Z695.1N8

□ CINAHL®.
http://www.cinahl.com/
EBSCO Industries, Inc..

Audience: **g,l,u,f.**

R118.4.U6

□ MD Consult.
http://www.mdconsult.com/offers/standard.html
Elsevier, Inc..

Audience: **l,u,f.**

RC41

□ MedlinePlus: A Service of the National Library of Medicine
and the National Institutes of Health.
http://medlineplus.com/
U.S. National Library of Medicine.

Audience: **g,l,u,f.**

RC46

□ UpToDate.
http://www.uptodate.com/
UpToDate.

Audience: **l,u,f.**

R735.E4

□ www.eMedicine.com.
http://www.emedicine.com/
WebMD.

Audience: **g,l,u,f.**

Medicine: General

R118.2

□ Stat!Ref Electronic Resources for Healthcare Professionals.
http://www.statref.com/
Teton Data Systems.

Audience: **l,u,f.**

Kongstvedt, Peter   **RA413.E87 2003**
Essentials of Managed Health Care. Ed. 4. Paper Text. Jones &
Bartlett Publishers, Inc. Sudbury, MA. 2003. xvii, 883p.
ISBN:0-7637-2496-3, ISBN13: 978-0-7637-2496-2.
Dewey:362.1/04258. LCCN:2003-047430.

Audience: **l,u,f.**

Kongstvedt, Peter R.   **RA413.5.U5K655 2003**
Managed Care: What It Is and How It Works. Ed. 2. Trade
Paper. Jones & Bartlett Publishers, Inc. Sudbury, MA. 2003.
329p. ISBN:0-7637-2498-X, ISBN13: 978-0-7637-2498-6.
Dewey:362.1/04258/0973. LCCN:2003-054646.

Audience: **l,u.**

Nuland, Sherwin B.   **QP34.5**
The Wisdom of the Body. Trade Cloth. DIANE Publishing
Company. Collingdale, PA. 2001. 395p. ISBN:0-7881-9609-X,
ISBN13: 978-0-7881-9609-6. Dewey:612.
Audience: **g,l,u,f.** *Choice, 1998.*

Medicine: General > Dictionaries. Terminology

R362.11 AME
AHA Guide to the Health Care Field. Trade Paper. Health
Forum. Chicago, IL. 2000. AHA Guide to the Health Care Field

Ser. ISBN:0-87258-757-6, ISBN13: 978-0-87258-757-1.
Dewey:362.110.

Audience: **g,l,u,f.**

American Medical   **R840**
  Association Staff
Graduate Medical Education Directory 2004-2005. Trade Paper.
American Medical Association. Chicago, IL. 2004. 1300p.
ISBN:1-57947-486-1, ISBN13: 978-1-57947-486-7.
Dewey:610.7117.

Audience: **u,f.**

Dorland, Newman W.   **R121 .D73 2003**
Dorland's Illustrated Medical Dictionary. Ed. 30. Trade Cloth.
Elsevier - Health Sciences Division. Philadelphia, PA. 2003.
2144p. ISBN:0-7216-0281-9, ISBN13: 978-0-7216-0281-3.
Dewey:610.3.

Audience: **g,l,u,f.** *ℬ*

Jablonski, Stanley   **R123**
Dictionary of Medical Acronyms and Abbreviations. Ed. 5.
Mixed Media. Elsevier - Health Sciences Division. Philadelphia,
PA. 2004. ISBN:1-56053-652-7, ISBN13: 978-1-56053-652-9.
Dewey:610/.1/48.

Audience: **g,l,u,f.**

Magalini, Sabina I. &   **RC69.M33 1997**
  Magalini, Sergio C.
Dictionary of Medical Syndromes. Ed. 4. Trade Cloth.
Lippincott Williams & Wilkins. Philadelphia, PA. 1996. 976p.
ISBN:0-397-58418-0, ISBN13: 978-0-397-58418-5.
Dewey:616/.003. LCCN:96-041119.

Audience: **g,l,u,f.**

Stedman's Staff   **R121.S8 2006**
Medical Dictionary. Ed. 28. Trade Cloth. Lippincott Williams &
Wilkins. Philadelphia, PA. 2005. 2100p. ISBN:0-7817-3390-1,
ISBN13: 978-0-7817-3390-8. Dewey:610/.3.
LCCN:2005-021544.

Audience: **g,l,u,f.**

Venes, Donald   **R121**
Taber's Cyclopedic Medical Dictionary. Ed. 20. Book, Other. F.
A. Davis Company. Philadelphia, PA. 2005. 2800p.
ISBN:0-8036-1308-3, ISBN13: 978-0-8036-1308-9.
Dewey:610/.3.

Audience: **g,l,u,f.**

Medicine: General > History. Biography

Bliss, Michael   **R134.B55 1999**
William Osler: A Life in Medicine. Trade Cloth. Oxford
University Press, Inc. New York, NY. 1999. 596p.
ISBN:0-19-512346-8, ISBN13: 978-0-19-512346-3.
Dewey:610/.92 B. LCCN:99-032066.

Audience: **g,u,f.** *Choice, 2000.*

Bordley, James III &   **R151**
  Harvey, A. McGehee
Two Centuries of American Medicine, 1776-1976. Cloth Text.
Elsevier - Health Sciences Division. Philadelphia, PA. 1976.
750p. ISBN:0-7216-1873-1, ISBN13: 978-0-7216-1873-9.
Dewey:610/.973. LCCN:75-019841.

Audience: **g,l,u,f.** *ℬ*

Fenn, Elizabeth Anne   **RC183.49.F46 2001**
Pox Americana: The Great Smallpox Epidemic of 1775-1782.
Cloth over Boards. Farrar, Straus & Giroux. New York, NY.
2001. 320p. ISBN:0-8090-7820-1, ISBN13: 978-0-8090-7820-2.
Dewey:614.5/21/097309033. LCCN:2001-016886.
                                    Audience: **g,l,u,f.** *Choice, 2002.*

Hippocrates   **PA3612**
Ancient Medicine, Airs, Waters, Places, Epidemics 1 and 3, the
Oath, Precepts, Nutriment, Vol. 1. W. H. Jones (Translator).
Trade Cloth. Harvard University Press. Cambridge, MA. 1923.
432p. Ancient Medicine, Airs, Waters, Places, Epidemics 1 and
2. Oat Ser., No. 147 ISBN:0-674-99162-1, ISBN13:
978-0-674-99162-0. Dewey:610.9.
                                                   Audience: **u,f.**

Hippocrates   **PA3612**
Hippocrates: Diseases 3, Internal Affections, Regimen in Acute
Diseases. Paul Potter (Translator). Trade Cloth. Harvard
University Press. Cambridge, MA. 1988. 392p. Loeb Classical
Library, No. 473 ISBN:0-674-99522-8, ISBN13:
978-0-674-99522-2. Dewey:610.
                                                   Audience: **u,f.**

Hippocrates   **R126.H6E62513 1994**
Hippocrates: Epidemics 2, 4-6. Wesley Smith (Editor). Trade
Cloth. Harvard University Press. Cambridge, MA. 1994. 432p.
Loeb Classical Library, No. 477 ISBN:0-674-99526-0, ISBN13:
978-0-674-99526-0. Dewey:616. LCCN:93-019601.
                                                   Audience: **u,f.**

Hippocrates   **PA3612**
On Wounds in the Head, in the Surgery, on Fractures, on Joints,
Mochlikon, Vol. 3. E. T. Withington (Translator). Trade Cloth.
Harvard University Press. Cambridge, MA. 1928. 488p. Loeb
Classical Library, No.149 ISBN:0-674-99165-6, ISBN13:
978-0-674-99165-1. Dewey:610.9.
                                                   Audience: **u,f.**

Jones, W. H. (Translator)   **PA3612**
Heracleitus - On the Universe: Nature of Man, Regimen in
Health, Humours, Amorphisms, Regimen 1-3, Dreams., Vol. 4.
Trade Cloth. Harvard University Press. Cambridge, MA. 1931.
592p. Nature of Man, Regimen in Health, Humours,
Amorphisms and Regim Ser., No. 150 ISBN:0-674-99166-4,
ISBN13: 978-0-674-99166-8. Dewey:610.9.
                                                   Audience: **u,f.**

Jones, W. H. (Translator)   **PA3612**
Prognostic, Regimen in Acute Diseases, the Sacred Disease, the
Art, Breaths, Law, Decorum, Physician (Ch. 1), Dentition, Vol.
2. Trade Cloth. Harvard University Press. Cambridge, MA.
1923. 416p. Medical Works, No. 148 ISBN:0-674-99164-8,
ISBN13: 978-0-674-99164-4. Dewey:610.9.
                                                   Audience: **u,f.**

Kolata, Gina   **RA644.I6**
Flu: The Story of the Great Influenza Pandemic of 1918 and the
Search for the Virus That Caused It. Trade Cloth. DIANE
Publishing Company. Collingdale, PA. 2002. 330p.
ISBN:0-7567-5625-1, ISBN13: 978-0-7567-5625-3.
Dewey:614.5/18/0904.
                                    Audience: **g,l,u,f.** *Choice, 2000.*

Lindemann, Mary   **RA418.3.E85 L55 1999**
Medicine and Society in Early Modern Europe. William Beik, T.
C. W. Blanning & Brendan Simms (Contribution by). Cloth
Text. Cambridge University Press. New York, NY. 1999. 263p.

New Approaches to European History Ser., No. 16
ISBN:0-521-41254-4, ISBN13: 978-0-521-41254-4.
Dewey:306.4/61/094. LCCN:99-017819.
                                    Audience: **u,f.** *Choice, 2000.*

Lyons, Albert S. &   **R131**
 Petrucelli, Joseph A.
Medicine: An Illustrated History. Trade Cloth. Harry N. Abrams,
Inc. New York, NY. 1997. 616p. ISBN:0-8109-8080-0, ISBN13:
978-0-8109-8080-8. Dewey:610.9. LCCN:87-011569.
                                    Audience: **g,l,u,f.** *B*

McMullen, Emerson   **QP101.4.H375 2005**
 Thomas (Editor, Translator)
William Harvey's de Motu Cordis: A New Translation and Latin
Edition. Library Binding. Academica Press, LLC. Bethesda,
MD. 2005. 264p. ISBN:1-933146-02-8, ISBN13:
978-1-933146-02-7. Dewey:612.1/3. LCCN:2005-001299.
                                                   Audience: **u,f.**

Morgagni, Giambattista   **RB24**
The Seats and Causes of Diseases. Alexander, Benjamin
(Translator). Classics of Medicine Library. 1983.
                                                   Audience: **u,f.**

Nuland, Sherwin B.   **R134.N85 1988**
Doctors: The Biography of Medicine. Trade Cloth. Alfred A.
Knopf Inc. New York, NY. 1988. 512p. ISBN:0-394-55130-3,
ISBN13: 978-0-394-55130-2. Dewey:610.92/2 B.
LCCN:87-040489.
                                    Audience: **g,l,u,f.** *Choice, 1988.*

Osler, William, Sir   **RC46**
The Principles and Practice of Medicine. Ed. 21. Harvey, A.
McGehee (Editor). Appleton-Century-Crofts. 1984.
ISBN:0-8385-7928-0, ISBN13: 978-0-8385-7928-2.
                                                   Audience: **u,f.**

Porter, Roy   **R131.P59 1998**
The Greatest Benefit to Mankind: A Medical History of
Humanity from Antiquity to the Present. Trade Cloth. W. W.
Norton & Company, Inc. New York, NY. 1998. 800p.
ISBN:0-393-04634-6, ISBN13: 978-0-393-04634-2.
Dewey:610.9. LCCN:98-010219.
                                                   Audience: **g,l,u,f.**

Potter, Paul (Translator)   **PA3612.H65 1923**
Hippocrates: Affections, Diseases 1, Diseases 2. Trade Cloth.
Harvard University Press. Cambridge, MA. 1988. 352p. Loeb
Classical Library, No. 472 ISBN:0-674-99520-1, ISBN13:
978-0-674-99520-8. Dewey:610. LCCN:23-012030.
                                                   Audience: **u,f.**

Starr, Paul   **RA395.A3S77 1982**
Social Transformation of American Medicine: The Rise of a
Sovereign Profession and the Making of a Vast Industry. Trade
Paper. Basic Books. New York, NY. 1984. 528p.
ISBN:0-465-07935-0, ISBN13: 978-0-465-07935-3.
Dewey:305/.961/0973. LCCN:81-068412.
                                    Audience: **g,l,u,f.** *B*

Vesalius, Andreas et al   **QM25**
The Illustrations from the Works of Andreas Vesalius of
Brussels: With Annotations and Translations, a Discussion of the
Plates and Their Background, Authorship and Influence, and a
Biographical Sketch of Vesalius. Saunders, J. B. de C. M. (John

Bertrand de Cusance Morant); O'Malley, Charles Donald. Classics of Medicine Library. 1993.

Audience: **g,u,f.**

Medicine: General > Medical Ethics

AMA Staff (Editor)   **PN2267.C5**
Code of Medical Ethics, Current Opinions with Annotations 2004-2005. Trade Paper. American Medical Association. Chicago, IL. 2004. 228p. ISBN:1-57947-561-2, ISBN13: 978-1-57947-561-1. Dewey:792/.0223/0973.

Audience: **u,f.**

Beauchamp, Thomas L. &   **R724.B36 2001**
Childress, James F.
Principles of Biomedical Ethics. Ed. 5. Trade Paper. Oxford University Press, Inc. New York, NY. 2001. 468p. ISBN:0-19-514332-9, ISBN13: 978-0-19-514332-4. Dewey:174/.2. LCCN:00-062394.

Audience: **g,u,f.**

Bishop, Anne & Scudder,   **RT85.B57 2001**
Jack
Nursing Ethics: Holistic Caring Practice. Ed. 2. Trade Paper. Jones & Bartlett Publishers, Inc. Sudbury, MA. 2000. 136p. Nursing Theory Ser. ISBN:0-7637-1426-7, ISBN13: 978-0-7637-1426-0. Dewey:174/.2. LCCN:00-037113.

Audience: **u,f.**

Burkhardt, Margaret A. &   **RT85.B766 2002**
Nathaniel, Alvita K.
Ethics and Issues in Contemporary Nursing. Ed. 2. Paper Text. Thomson Delmar Learning. Albany, NY. 2001. 456p. ISBN:0-7668-3629-0, ISBN13: 978-0-7668-3629-7. Dewey:174/.2. LCCN:2001-032503.

Audience: **l,u.**

Mappes, Thomas A. &   **R724.B49 2005**
DeGrazia, David
Biomedical Ethics. Ed. 6. Paper Text. McGraw-Hill Higher Education. Burr Ridge, IL. 2005. 752p. ISBN:0-07-297644-6, ISBN13: 978-0-07-297644-1. Dewey:174.2. LCCN:2005-017337.

Audience: **g,l,u.**

Sugarman, Jeremy &   **R724.M43 2001**
Sulmasy, Daniel P. (Editors)
Methods in Medical Ethics. Trade Paper. Georgetown University Press. Washington, DC. 2001. xiv, 314p. ISBN:0-87840-873-8, ISBN13: 978-0-87840-873-3. Dewey:174/.2. LCCN:2001-023268.

Audience: **u,f.** *Choice, 2002.*

Veatch, Robert M.   **R725.5.C76 2000**
Cross Cultural Perspectives in Medical Ethics: Readings. Ed. 2. Trade Paper. Jones & Bartlett Publishers, Inc. Sudbury, MA. 2000. 400p. ISBN:0-7637-1332-5, ISBN13: 978-0-7637-1332-4. Dewey:174/.2. LCCN:99-089318.

Audience: **g,u,f.**

Public Aspects of Medicine > Medical Economics

Culyer, A. J. & Newhouse,   **RA410.H255 2000**
J. P. (Editors)
Handbook of Health Economics. Trade Cloth. Elsevier Science

& Technology Books. Saint Louis, MO. 2000. 1996p. Handbooks in Economics ISBN:0-444-82290-9, ISBN13: 978-0-444-82290-1. Dewey:338.4/33621. LCCN:2001-275530.

Audience: **u,f.**

Davis, John Bryan   **RA410.5.D38 2000**
The Social Economics of Health Care. Paper over Boards. Routledge. New York, NY. 2001. 304p. Advances in Social Economics Ser. ISBN:0-415-20765-7, ISBN13: 978-0-415-20765-2. Dewey:338.4/73621. LCCN:00-051778.

Audience: **u,f.**

Folland, Sherman, et al.   **RA410.F65 2003**
The Economics of Health and Health Care. Ed. 4. Allen C. Goodman & Miron Stano (Authors). Trade Cloth. Pearson Education. Boston, MA. 2003. 648p. Prentice-Hall Series in Economics ISBN:0-13-100067-5, ISBN13: 978-0-13-100067-4. Dewey:338.4/33621. LCCN:2003-045980.

Audience: **u.**

Phelps, Charles E.   **RA410.P48 2003**
Health Economics. Ed. 3. Cloth Text. Addison-Wesley Longman, Inc. Boston, MA. 2002. 688p. Addison-Wesley Series in Economics ISBN:0-321-06898-X, ISBN13: 978-0-321-06898-9. Dewey:338.4/33621. LCCN:2002-021518.

Audience: **l,u.**

Scott, Claudia D.   **RA395.O28S36 2001**
Public and Private Roles in Health Care Systems: Experiences from Seven Countries. Cloth Text. McGraw-Hill Education. Maidenhead, 2001. 184p. State of Health Ser. ISBN:0-335-20460-0, ISBN13: 978-0-335-20460-1. Dewey:362.1. LCCN:00-050153.

Audience: **u,f.**

Public Aspects of Medicine > Medicine and Society. Medical Sociology

Armstrong, David   **R133.A75 2002**
A New History of Identity: A Sociology of Medical Knowledge. Cloth over Boards. Palgrave Macmillan. New York, NY. 2002. 225p. ISBN:0-333-96892-1, ISBN13: 978-0-333-96892-5. Dewey:306.4/61. LCCN:2001-058213.

Audience: **u,f.**

Bloom, Samuel William   **RA418.3.U6B56 2002**
The Word as Scalpel: A History of Medical Sociology. Trade Cloth. Oxford University Press, Inc. New York, NY. 2002. 356p. ISBN:0-19-507232-4, ISBN13: 978-0-19-507232-7. Dewey:306.4/61/0973. LCCN:2001-037042.

Audience: **l,u,f.** *Choice, 2003.*

Scambler, Graham & Higgs,   **RA418.M66 1998**
Paul
Modernity, Medicine and Health: Medical Sociology Towards 2000. Library Binding. Routledge. New York, NY. 1998. 264p. ISBN:0-415-14938-X, ISBN13: 978-0-415-14938-9. Dewey:306.4/61. LCCN:97-034889.

Audience: **u,f.**

Turner, Bryan S.   **HM110.T87 1992**
Regulating Bodies: Essays in Medical Sociology. Paper over Boards. Routledge. New York, NY. 1992. 288p. ISBN:0-415-06963-7, ISBN13: 978-0-415-06963-2. Dewey:306.461. LCCN:92-004229.

Audience: **u,f.**

Public Aspects of Medicine > Public Health

Agarwal, Dharam P. &   **RA1242.A35A425 2001**
  Seitz, Helmut K. (Editors)
Alcohol in Health and Disease. Paper over Boards. Marcel
Dekker Inc. New York, NY. 2001. 648p. ISBN:0-8247-0533-5,
ISBN13: 978-0-8247-0533-6. Dewey:616.86/1.
LCCN:2001-028634.

Audience: **l,u,f.**

Babor, Thomas   **HV5020**
Alcohol and Public Policy: No Ordinary Commodity. Trade
Paper. Oxford University Press, Inc. New York, NY. 2003. 301p.
ISBN:0-19-263261-2, ISBN13: 978-0-19-263261-6.
Dewey:362.2928. LCCN:2004-298606.

Audience: **u,f.**

Begleiter, Henri & Kissin,   **RC565**
  Benjamin (Editors)
The Biology of Alcoholism: Pathogenesis of Alcoholism:
Biological Factors. Trade Cloth. Basic Books. New York, NY.
1983. 666p. ISBN:0-306-41053-2, ISBN13: 978-0-306-41053-6.
Dewey:616.86/1071. LCCN:82-022284.

Audience: **u,f.**

Frances, Richard J.   **RC564.C55 2005**
  (Editor), et al.
Clinical Textbook of Addictive Disorders. Ed. 3. Sheldon Irvin
Miller & Avram H. Mack (Editors). Cloth over Boards. Guilford
Publications, Inc. New York, NY. 2005. 684p.
ISBN:1-59385-174-X, ISBN13: 978-1-59385-174-3.
Dewey:616.86. LCCN:2004-026092.

Audience: **l,u,f.**

Galanter, Marc & Kleber,   **RC564.A526 2004**
  Herbert D.
The American Psychiatric Publishing Textbook of Substance
Abuse Treatment. Ed. 3. Trade Cloth. American Psychiatric
Publishing, Inc. Arlington, VA. 2004. 168p.
ISBN:1-58562-099-8, ISBN13: 978-1-58562-099-9.
Dewey:616.86/06. LCCN:2003-058354.

Audience: **l,u.**

Kissin, Benjamin &   **HV5035**
  Begleiter, Henri (Editors)
The Biology of Alcoholism: Pathogenesis of Alcoholism:
Psychosocial Factors. Trade Cloth. Basic Books. New York, NY.
1983. 734p. ISBN:0-306-41052-4, ISBN13: 978-0-306-41052-9.
Dewey:362.2/92. LCCN:82-019029.

Audience: **u,f.**

Lowinson, Joyce H., et al.   **RC564.S826 2004**
Substance Abuse: A Comprehensive Textbook. Ed. 4. John G.
Langrod & Robert B. Millman (Authors). Trade Cloth.
Lippincott Williams & Wilkins. Philadelphia, PA. 2004. 1200p.
ISBN:0-7817-3474-6, ISBN13: 978-0-7817-3474-5.
Dewey:362.29. LCCN:2004-019274.

Audience: **l,u,f.**

McCrady, Barbara S. &   **RC564.M327 1999**
  Epstein, Elizabeth E. (Editors)
Addictions: A Comprehensive Guidebook. Trade Cloth. Oxford
University Press, Inc. New York, NY. 1999. 663p.
ISBN:0-19-511489-2, ISBN13: 978-0-19-511489-8.
Dewey:616.86. LCCN:98-051552.

Audience: **l,u,f.**

Miller, William R. &   **RC564.M545 2006**
  Carroll, Kathleen M. (Editors)
Rethinking Substance Abuse: What the Science Shows, and
What We Should Do about It. Cloth over Boards. Guilford
Publications, Inc. New York, NY. 2006. 320p.
ISBN:1-57230-231-3, ISBN13: 978-1-57230-231-0.
Dewey:362.29. LCCN:2005-020524.

Audience: **g,l,u,f.**

Ott, Peggy J., et al.   **RC564.S66 1999**
Sourcebook on Substance Abuse: Etiology, Epidemiology,
Assessment, and Treatment. Ed. 1. Ralph E. Tarter & Robert T.
Ammerman (Authors). Cloth Text. Allyn & Bacon, Inc. Boston,
MA. 1999. 472p. ISBN:0-205-19802-3, ISBN13:
978-0-205-19802-3. Dewey:616.86. LCCN:98-035240.

Audience: **g,l,u,f.**

Rassool, Hussein   **RC564.68**
Dual Diagnosis: Substance Misuse and Psychiatric Disorders.
Trade Paper. Blackwell Publishing, Inc. Malden, MA. 2001.
224p. ISBN:0-632-05621-5, ISBN13: 978-0-632-05621-7.
Dewey:616.86/075. LCCN:2001-035734.

Audience: **u,f.**

Sloboda, Zili & Bukoski,   **HV5801.H282 2002**
  William J. (Editors)
Handbook of Drug Abuse Prevention: Theory, Science, and
Practice. Trade Cloth. Springer. New York, NY. 2003. 698p.
Handbooks of Sociology and Social Research
ISBN:0-306-47342-9, ISBN13: 978-0-306-47342-5.
Dewey:362.29/17. LCCN:2002-072682.

Audience: **u,f.**

Straussner, Shulamith Lala   **RC564.E785 2001**
  Ashenberg (Editor)
Ethnocultural Factors in Substance Abuse Treatment. Cloth over
Boards. Guilford Publications, Inc. New York, NY. 2001. 447p.
ISBN:1-57230-630-0, ISBN13: 978-1-57230-630-1.
Dewey:616.86/06. LCCN:00-067723.

Audience: **u,f.** *Choice, 2001.*

Tabakoff, Boris (Editor)   **RC565**
Medical and Social Aspects of Alcohol Abuse. Trade Cloth.
Basic Books. New York, NY. 1983. 420p. ISBN:0-306-41221-7,
ISBN13: 978-0-306-41221-9. Dewey:616.86/1.
LCCN:83-004786.

Audience: **g,l,u,f.** *B*

Wekerle, Christine   **HV4998.W45 2001**
Violence and Addiction Equation: Theoretical and Clinical
Issues in Substance Abuse and Relationship Violence. Paper
over Boards. Brunner-Routledge. Philadelphia, PA. 2002. 352p.
ISBN:0-87630-959-7, ISBN13: 978-0-87630-959-9.
Dewey:362.82/92. LCCN:2001-037778.

Audience: **u,f.**

Public Aspects of Medicine > Nutrition

Alpers, David H., et al.   **RM217.2.A47 2002**
Manual of Nutritional Therapeutics. Ed. 4. William F. Stenson &
Dennis M. Bier (Authors). Perfect. Lippincott Williams &
Wilkins. Philadelphia, PA. 2002. 656p. ISBN:0-7817-3122-4,
ISBN13: 978-0-7817-3122-5. Dewey:615.8/54.
LCCN:2001-029923.

Audience: **l,u,f.**

Pennington, Jean A.   **TX551.P385 2004**
Food Values of Portions Commonly Used. Ed. 18. Trade Paper.
Lippincott Williams & Wilkins. Philadelphia, PA. 2004. 496p.
ISBN:0-7817-4429-6, ISBN13: 978-0-7817-4429-4.
Dewey:641.1. LCCN:2003-066133.
Audience: **g,l,u,f.** *B*

Stipanuk, Martha H.   **QP141.B57 2006**
Biochemical, Physiological and Molecular Aspects of Human
Nutrition. Ed. 2. Cloth Text. Elsevier - Health Sciences
Division. Philadelphia, PA. 2006. 1232p. ISBN:1-4160-0209-X,
ISBN13: 978-1-4160-0209-3. Dewey:612.39.
Audience: **l,u,f.**

Temple, Norman J., et al.   **RA645.N87**
Nutritional Health: Strategies for Disease Prevention. Ed. 2. Ted
Wilson & David R. Jacobs Jr. (Authors), Norman J. Temple, Ted
Wilson & David R. Jacobs Jr. (Editors). Trade Cloth. Humana
Press. Totowa, NJ. 2005. 380p. Nutrition and Health Ser.
ISBN:1-59259-980-X, ISBN13: 978-1-59259-980-6.
Dewey:614.5/939. LCCN:2005-013116.
Audience: **l,u,f.**

Public Aspects of Medicine > Mental Health

Committee on Integrating   **HQ767.9.F76 2000**
  the Science of Early Childhood Development, et al.
From Neurons to Neighborhoods: The Science of Early
Childhood Development. Board on Children, Youth and Families
Staff & Institute of Medicine Staff (Authors), Jack P. Shonkoff
& Deborah A. Phillips (Editors). Trade Cloth. National
Academies Press. Washington, DC. 2000. 612p.
ISBN:0-309-06988-2, ISBN13: 978-0-309-06988-5.
Dewey:305.231. LCCN:00-010760.
Audience: **g,l,u,f.**

Erikson, Erik H.   **HQ767.9**
Childhood and Society. Trade Paper. W. W. Norton & Company,
Inc. New York, NY. 1993. 446p. ISBN:0-393-31068-X, ISBN13:
978-0-393-31068-9. Dewey:305.2/3. LCCN:93-011229.
Audience: **g,l,u,f.** *B*

Erikson, Erik H.   **BF697**
Identity Youth and Crisis. Trade Paper. W. W. Norton &
Company, Inc. New York, NY. 1994. 336p.
ISBN:0-393-31144-9, ISBN13: 978-0-393-31144-0. Dewey:155.
Audience: **g,l,u,f.**

Harris, Judith Rich   **HQ767.9**
The Nurture Assumption: Why Children Turn Out the Way They
Do. Steven Pinker (Foreword by). Trade Paper. Simon &
Schuster. New York, NY. 1999. 480p. ISBN:0-684-85707-3,
ISBN13: 978-0-684-85707-7. Dewey:305.2/31.
Audience: **g,l,u,f.** *Choice, 1999.*

Helton, Lonnie R. & Smith,   **RJ499.H524 2004**
  Mieko Kotake
Mental Health Practice for Children and Youth: A Strengths and
Well-Being Model. Cloth Text. Haworth Press, Incorporated,
The. Binghamton, NY. 2004. 258p. ISBN:0-7890-1574-9,
ISBN13: 978-0-7890-1574-7. Dewey:362.2/083.
LCCN:2003-021017.
Audience: **l,u,f.**

Piaget, Jean   **BF719**
Origin of Intelligence in the Child, Vol. 3. Library Binding.
Routledge. New York, NY. 1998. 440p. ISBN:0-415-16892-9,
ISBN13: 978-0-415-16892-2. Dewey:155.422.
Audience: **l,u,f.**

Steiner, Hans (Editor)   **RJ499**
Handbook of Mental Health Interventions in Children and
Adolescents: An Integrated Developmental Approach. Trade
Cloth. John Wiley & Sons, Inc. Hoboken, NJ. 2004. 1120p.
ISBN:0-7879-6154-X, ISBN13: 978-0-7879-6154-1.
Dewey:618.92/8914. LCCN:2004-040719.
Audience: **u,f.**

Public Aspects of Medicine > Hospitals. Nursing Homes

                                                   G1201.E5 D3
Dartmouth Atlas of Health Care in the United States. Ed. 2.
Trade Cloth. Health Forum. Chicago, IL. 1997.
ISBN:1-55648-186-1, ISBN13: 978-1-55648-186-4.
Dewey:362.1/0973/022.
Audience: **u,f.**

Gamble, Vanessa N.   **RA981.A45G363 1995**
Making a Place for Ourselves: The Black Hospital Movement,
1920-1945. Trade Cloth. Oxford University Press, Inc. New
York, NY. 1995. 284p. ISBN:0-19-507889-6, ISBN13:
978-0-19-507889-3. Dewey:362.1/1/08996073.
LCCN:93-000617.
Audience: **g,l,u,f.** *Choice, 1995.*

Hubbard, Michael W., et al.   **KF1183.H83 2003**
HIPAA Policies and Procedures Desk Reference. Karen E.
Glover & Carolyn P. Hartley (Authors). Trade Cloth. American
Medical Association. Chicago, IL. 2003. 496p.
ISBN:1-57947-362-8, ISBN13: 978-1-57947-362-4.
Dewey:344.73/022. LCCN:2003-040325.
Audience: **l,u,f.**

Knickman, James R.   **RA395.A3J656 2005**
  (Editor)
Jonas and Kovner's Health Care Delivery in the United States.
Ed. 8. Perfect, Paper over Boards. Springer Publishing
Company, Inc. New York, NY. 2005. 753p.
ISBN:0-8261-2087-3, ISBN13: 978-0-8261-2087-8.
Dewey:362.1/0973. LCCN:2005-006979.
Audience: **l,u,f.**

Rosenberg, Charles E.   **RA981.A2R59 1995**
The Care of Strangers: The Rise of America's Hospital System.
Trade Paper. Johns Hopkins University Press. Baltimore, MD.
1995. 456p. ISBN:0-8018-5082-7, ISBN13: 978-0-8018-5082-0.
Dewey:362.1/1/0973. LCCN:94-036036.
Audience: **g,l,u,f.** *Choice, 1988.*

Shelton, Patrick J.   **RA399.A1S47 2000**
Measuring and Improving Patient Satisfaction. Trade Cloth.
Jones & Bartlett Publishers, Inc. Sudbury, MA. 2000. 510p.
ISBN:0-8342-1074-6, ISBN13: 978-0-8342-1074-5.
Dewey:362.1/068/5. LCCN:00-020622.
Audience: **l,u,f.**

Stevens, Rosemary   **RA981.A2S74 1999**
In Sickness and in Wealth: American Hospitals in the Twentieth
Century. Trade Paper. Johns Hopkins University Press.
Baltimore, MD. 1999. 472p. ISBN:0-8018-6049-0, ISBN13:
978-0-8018-6049-2. Dewey:362.1/1/0973. LCCN:98-038184.

Audience: **g,l,u,f.** *Choice, 1989.*

Sultz, Harry A. & Young,   **RA395.A3S897 2006**
  Kristina M.
Health Care, USA: Understanding Its Organization and Delivery.
Ed. 5. Trade Paper. Jones & Bartlett Publishers, Inc. Sudbury,
MA. 2005. 557p. ISBN:0-7637-3625-2, ISBN13:
978-0-7637-3625-5. Dewey:362.1/0973. LCCN:2005-007394.

Audience: **g,l,u,f.**

Vogel, Morris J.   **RA0982.B7V63**
The Invention of the Modern Hospital, Boston, 1870-1930.
Trade Paper. Books on Demand. Ann Arbor, MI. 181p.
ISBN:0-608-09545-1, ISBN13: 978-0-608-09545-5.
Dewey:362.1/1/0974461. LCCN:79-026052.

Audience: **g,l,u,f.**

Wolper, Lawrence F.   **RA971.H384 2003**
Health Care Administration: Planning, Implementing, and
Managing Organized Delivery Systems. Ed. 4. Trade Cloth.
Jones & Bartlett Publishers, Inc. Sudbury, MA. 2004. 750p.
ISBN:0-7637-3144-7, ISBN13: 978-0-7637-3144-1.
Dewey:362.1/068. LCCN:2003-051683.

Audience: **u,f.**

Public Aspects of Medicine > Toxicology

Carson, Rachel   **QH545**
Silent Spring. Ed. 40. Dust Jacket. Houghton Mifflin Company
Trade & Reference Division. Boston, MA. 2002. 400p.
ISBN:0-618-25305-X, ISBN13: 978-0-618-25305-0.
Dewey:363.738/4. LCCN:2002-726803.

Audience: **g,l,u,f.** *B*

Casarett, Louis J., et al.   **RA1211.C298 2003**
Casarett and Doull's Essentials of Toxicology. Curtis D.
Klaassen & John B. Watkins (Authors). Paper Text.
McGraw-Hill Professional Publishing. New York, NY. 2003.
512p. ISBN:0-07-138914-8, ISBN13: 978-0-07-138914-3.
Dewey:615.9. LCCN:2002-043077.

Audience: **l,f.**

Ford, Marsha, et al.   **RA1211.C587 2001**
Clinical Toxicology. Kathleen Delaney, Louis Ling, S.
Rutherford Rose & Timothy Erickson (Authors). Trade Paper.
Elsevier - Health Sciences Division. Philadelphia, PA. 2000.
1138p. ISBN:0-7216-5485-1, ISBN13: 978-0-7216-5485-0.
Dewey:515.9. LCCN:00-029712.

Audience: **u,f.**

Goldfrank, Lewis R., et al.   **RA1224.5.G65 2006**
Toxicologic Emergencies. Ed. 8. Neal E. Flomenbaum, Mary
Ann Howland, Robert S. Hoffman & Richard S. Weisman
(Authors). Trade Cloth. McGraw-Hill Professional Publishing.
New York, NY. 2006. 2064p. ISBN:0-07-143763-0, ISBN13:
978-0-07-143763-9. Dewey:615.9. LCCN:2006-044926.

Audience: **u,f.**

Pathology

Burton, Gwendolyn R. &   **QR41.2.B88 2003**
  Englekirk, Paul
Microbiology for the Health Sciences. Ed. 7. Trade Paper.
Lippincott Williams & Wilkins. Philadelphia, PA. 2003. 579p.
ISBN:0-7817-4000-2, ISBN13: 978-0-7817-4000-5.
Dewey:616/.01. LCCN:2002-043425.

Audience: **l,u.**

Crowley, Leonard V.   **RB112.C76 2004**
An Introduction to Human Disease: Pathology and
Pathophysiology Correlations. Ed. 6. Trade Cloth. Jones &
Bartlett Publishers, Inc. Sudbury, MA. 2004. xxvii, 797p.
ISBN:0-7637-0727-9, ISBN13: 978-0-7637-0727-9.
Dewey:616.07. LCCN:2004-000435.

Audience: **l,u.**

Damjanov, Ivan   **RB25.D26 2006**
Pathology for the Health Professions. Ed. 3. Paper Text. Elsevier
- Health Sciences Division. Philadelphia, PA. 2005. 560p.
ISBN:1-4160-0031-3, ISBN13: 978-1-4160-0031-0.
Dewey:616.07. LCCN:2005-048838.

Audience: **l,u.**

Huether, Sue E. &   **RB113.H77 2004**
  McCance, Kathryn L.
Understanding Pathophysiology. Ed. 3. Paper Text. Elsevier -
Health Sciences Division. Philadelphia, PA. 2003. 1264p.
ISBN:0-323-02368-1, ISBN13: 978-0-323-02368-9.
Dewey:616.07. LCCN:2003-065146.

Audience: **l,u.**

Kumar, Vinay, et al.   **RB111.R62 2004**
Robbins and Cotran Pathological Basis of Disease: With Student
Consult Access. Ed. 7. Abul K. Abbas & Nelson Fausto
(Authors). Cloth Text. Elsevier - Health Sciences Division.
Philadelphia, PA. 2004. 1552p. ISBN:0-7216-0187-1, ISBN13:
978-0-7216-0187-8. Dewey:616.07. LCCN:2004-046835.

Audience: **l,u.**

Tamparo, Carol D. & Lewis,   **RC46.T27 2005**
  Marcia A.
Diseases of the Human Body. Ed. 4. Trade Paper, Perfect. F. A.
Davis Company. Philadelphia, PA. 2005. 512p.
ISBN:0-8036-1245-1, ISBN13: 978-0-8036-1245-7. Dewey:616.
LCCN:2005-002186.

Audience: **l,u,f.**

Virchow, Rudolf Ludwig   **RB25**
  Karl
Cellular Pathology as Based upon Physiological and
Pathological Histology. Dover Publications. 1971.
ISBN:0-486-22698-0, ISBN13: 978-0-486-22698-9.

Audience: **u,f.**

Internal Medicine. Practice of Medicine

                                          RC55
ACP Medicine. Ringbound. WebMD Professional Publishing.
New York, NY. 2004. ISBN:0-9748327-1-5, ISBN13:
978-0-9748327-1-5. Dewey:616.

Audience: **u,f.**

Brooks, Geo. F., et al.   QR46.B76 2004
Jawetz, Melnick, and Adelberg's Medical Microbiology. Ed. 23.
Janet S. Butel & Stephen A. Morse (Authors). Paper Text.
McGraw-Hill Professional Publishing. New York, NY. 2004.
704p. ISBN:0-07-141207-7, ISBN13: 978-0-07-141207-0.
Dewey:616.9/401.

Audience: **l,u.**

Dawson, Beth & Trapp,   QH323.5
  Robert G.
Basic and Clinical Biostatistics. Ed. 4. Mixed Media, Trade
Paper, CD-ROM. McGraw-Hill Professional Publishing. New
York, NY. 2004. 416p. ISBN:0-07-141017-1, ISBN13:
978-0-07-141017-5. Dewey:610.1/5195. LCCN:2005-283683.

Audience: **l,u.**

Glantz, Stanton A.   R853.S7
Primer of Biostatistics. Ed. 6. Mixed Media, Trade Paper, Book,
Other, CD-ROM. McGraw-Hill Companies, The. New York, NY.
2005. 500p. ISBN:0-07-144781-4, ISBN13: 978-0-07-144781-2.
Dewey:610/.72/7.

Audience: **l,u.**

Goldman   RC46.C423 2004
Cecil Textbook of Medicine. Ed. 22. Cloth Text. W. B. Saunders
Company. Philadelphia, PA. 2003. ISBN:0-8089-2292-0,
ISBN13: 978-0-8089-2292-6. Dewey:616. LCCN:2003-042825.

Audience: **u,f.**

Kasper, Dennis L., et al.   RC46
Principles of Internal Medicine: Digital Edition. Ed. 16. Eugene
Braunwald, Anthony Fauci, Stephen Hauser, Dan Longo & J.
Larry Jameson (Authors). Trade Cloth, Digital, Other.
McGraw-Hill Companies, The. New York, NY. 2004. 2680p.
ISBN:0-07-144554-4, ISBN13: 978-0-07-144554-2. Dewey:616.

Audience: **u,f.**

Koneman, Elmer W., et al.   QR67.C64 2006
Koneman's Color Atlas and Textbook of Diagnostic
Microbiology. Ed. 6. Paul C. Schreckenberger, William M.
Janda, Stephen D. Allen, Washington C. Winn, Gary W. Procop
& Gail L. Woods (Authors). Trade Cloth. Lippincott Williams &
Wilkins. Philadelphia, PA. 2005. 1736p. ISBN:0-7817-3014-7,
ISBN13: 978-0-7817-3014-3. Dewey:616.9/041.
LCCN:2005-008049.

Audience: **l,u.**

Merck Staff, et al.   RC55.M4 2006
The Merck Manual of Diagnosis and Therapy. Ed. 18. Mark H.
Beer, Thomas V. Jones & Robert S. Porter (Authors). Trade
Cloth. John Wiley & Sons, Inc. Hoboken, NJ. 2006. 3000p.
ISBN:0-911910-18-2, ISBN13: 978-0-911910-18-6. Dewey:616.
Audience: **g,l,u,f.** *Choice, 2006.*

Pfaller, Michael A., et al.   QR46.M4683 2005
Medical Microbiology: With Student Consult Access. Ed. 5. Ken
S. Rosenthal & Patrick R. Murray (Authors). Paper Text.
Elsevier - Health Sciences Division. Philadelphia, PA. 2005.
976p. ISBN:0-323-03303-2, ISBN13: 978-0-323-03303-9.
Dewey:616.9/041. LCCN:2005-047941.

Audience: **l,u,f.**

Riegelman, Richard K.   R118.6.R54 2005
Studying a Study and Testing a Test: How to Read the Medical
Evidence. Ed. 5. Trade Paper. Lippincott Williams & Wilkins.
Philadelphia, PA. 2004. 328p. ISBN:0-7817-4576-4, ISBN13:
978-0-7817-4576-5. Dewey:610/.72. LCCN:2004-020605.

Audience: **l,u.**

Tierney, Lawrence M. Jr.   RC71
  (Editor)
Current Medical Diagnosis and Treatment. Ed. 45. Paper Text.
McGraw-Hill Medical Publishing Division. New York, NY.
2005. 1884p. ISBN:0-07-145410-1, ISBN13:
978-0-07-145410-0. Dewey:616.075.

Audience: **g,l,u,f.**

Internal Medicine. Practice of Medicine > Diseases

Koff, Raymond S. (Editor)   RC848
Chronic Viral Hepatitis: Diagnosis and Therapeutics. Wu,
George Y. (Editor). Humana Press. 2002. ISBN:0-89603-880-7,
ISBN13: 978-0-89603-880-6.

Audience: **u,f.**

Internal Medicine. Practice of Medicine > Diseases > AIDS

Buckley, R. Michael &   RC606.6.H586 2002
  Gluckman, Stephen John
HIV Infection in Primary Care. Trade Cloth. Elsevier - Health
Sciences Division. Philadelphia, PA. 2002. 315p.
ISBN:0-7216-8601-X, ISBN13: 978-0-7216-8601-1.
Dewey:616.97/92. LCCN:2002-017603.

Audience: **l,u,f.**

Dolin, Raphael, et al.   RC606.6.A37 2002
AIDS Therapy. Ed. 2. Henry Masur & Michael S. Saag
(Authors). Trade Cloth. Elsevier - Health Sciences Division.
Philadelphia, PA. 2002. 1024p. ISBN:0-443-06594-2, ISBN13:
978-0-443-06594-1. Dewey:616.97/9206. LCCN:2001-055272.

Audience: **u,f.**

Morse, Stephen A., et al.   RC200
Atlas of Sexually Transmitted Diseases and AIDS. Ed. 3. King
K. Holmes, Ronald C. Ballard & Adele A. Moreland (Authors).
Trade Cloth. Elsevier - Health Sciences Division. Philadelphia,
PA. 2002. 416p. ISBN:0-7234-3227-9, ISBN13:
978-0-7234-3227-2. Dewey:616.9/51.

Audience: **l,u,f.**

Pizzo, Philip A. & Wilfert,   RJ387.A25P43 1998
  Catherine M. (Editors)
Pediatric AIDS: The Challenge of HIV Infection in Infants,
Children and Adolescents. Ed. 3. Trade Cloth. Lippincott
Williams & Wilkins. Philadelphia, PA. 1998. 1000p.
ISBN:0-683-30399-6, ISBN13: 978-0-683-30399-5.
Dewey:618.92/9792. LCCN:98-006398.

Audience: **u,f.**

Ropka, Mary & Williams,   RC607.A26 H5764 1998
  Ann
HIV Nursing and Symptom Management. Trade Paper. Jones &
Bartlett Publishers, Inc. Sudbury, MA. 1998. 832p. Nursing Ser.
ISBN:0-7637-0544-6, ISBN13: 978-0-7637-0544-2.
Dewey:616.97/92. LCCN:98-013527.

Audience: **l,u,f.**

Sande, Merle A. &   RC607.A26M43 1999
  Volberding, Paul A.
The Medical Management of AIDS. Ed. 6. Trade Paper. Elsevier

- Health Sciences Division. Philadelphia, PA. 1999. 638p. ISBN:0-7216-8102-6, ISBN13: 978-0-7216-8102-3. Dewey:616.97/92. LCCN:98-043930.

Audience: **l,u,f.**

Internal Medicine. Practice of Medicine > Diseases > Sexually Transmitted Diseases

Brandt, Allan M.   **RC201.47.B73 1987**
No Magic Bullet: A Social History of Venereal Disease in the United States Since 1880. Paper Text. Oxford University Press, Inc. New York, NY. 1987. 290p. ISBN:0-19-504237-9, ISBN13: 978-0-19-504237-5. Dewey:362.1/9695/100973. LCCN:87-139908.

Audience: **g,l,u,f.** B

Faro, Sebastian   **RA644.V4S3779 2003**
Sexually Transmitted Diseasees in Obstetrics and Gynecology. Trade Paper. Lippincott Williams & Wilkins. Philadelphia, PA. 2003. 260p. ISBN:0-397-51303-8, ISBN13: 978-0-397-51303-1. Dewey:616.95/1/0082. LCCN:2003-044602.

Audience: **u,f.**

Holmes, King K.   **RC200.S49 1999**
  (Editor), et al.
Sexually Transmitted Diseases. Ed. 3. P. Frederick Sparling, Per-Anders Mardh, Stanley M. Lemon, Walter E. Stamm, Peter Piot & Judith Wasserheit (Editors). Cloth Text. McGraw-Hill Professional Publishing. New York, NY. 1998. 1344p. ISBN:0-07-029688-X, ISBN13: 978-0-07-029688-6. Dewey:616.95/1. LCCN:98-031523.

Audience: **l,u,f.**

Morse, Stephen A., et al.   **RC200**
Atlas of Sexually Transmitted Diseases and AIDS. Ed. 3. King K. Holmes, Ronald C. Ballard & Adele A. Moreland (Authors). Trade Cloth. Elsevier - Health Sciences Division. Philadelphia, PA. 2002. 416p. ISBN:0-7234-3227-9, ISBN13: 978-0-7234-3227-2. Dewey:616.9/51.

Audience: **l,u,f.**

Internal Medicine. Practice of Medicine > Neurology and Psychiatry. Neuropsychiatry

Klawans, Harold L.   **RC351.K57 1989**
Toscanini's Fumble and Other Tales of Clinical Neurology. Trade Paper. Bantam Books. New York, NY. 1989. 240p. ISBN:0-553-34662-8, ISBN13: 978-0-553-34662-6. Dewey:616.8. LCCN:88-008109.

Audience: **l,u,f.**

Menkes, John H.   **RJ486.C455 2005**
Child Neurology. Ed. 7. Trade Cloth. Lippincott Williams & Wilkins. Philadelphia, PA. 2005. 1100p. ISBN:0-7817-5104-7, ISBN13: 978-0-7817-5104-9. Dewey:618.92/8. LCCN:2005-021542.

Audience: **u,f.**

Rowland, Lewis P.   **RC346.M4 2005**
Merritt's Neurology: Integrating the Physical Exam and Echocardiography. Ed. 11. Trade Cloth. Lippincott Williams & Wilkins. Philadelphia, PA. 2005. 1200p. ISBN:0-7817-5311-2, ISBN13: 978-0-7817-5311-1. Dewey:616.8. LCCN:2005-003408.

Audience: **l,u,f.**

Sacks, Oliver   **RC351.S195**
The Man Who Mistook His Wife for a Hat: And Other Clinical Tales. Trade Paper. Simon & Schuster. New York, NY. 1998. 256p. ISBN:0-684-85394-9, ISBN13: 978-0-684-85394-9. Dewey:616.8. LCCN:98-004723.

Audience: **g,l,u,f.**

Siegel, George J.   **QP356.3**
  (Editor), et al.
Basic Neurochemistry: Molecular, Cellular and Medical Aspects. Ed. 7. R. Wayne Albers, Donald L. Price & Scott T. Brady (Editors), American Society for Neurochemistry Staff (Editor-In-Chief). Trade Cloth. Elsevier Science & Technology Books. Saint Louis, MO. 2005. 1016p. ISBN:0-12-088397-X, ISBN13: 978-0-12-088397-4. Dewey:612.8/042.

Audience: **l,u.**

Temkin, Owsei   **RC372**
The Falling Sickness: A History of Epilepsy from the Greeks to the Beginnings of Modern Neurology. Ed. 2. Trade Paper. Johns Hopkins University Press. Baltimore, MD. 1994. 488p. ISBN:0-8018-4849-0, ISBN13: 978-0-8018-4849-0. Dewey:616.85/3/009.

Audience: **g,l,u,f.** B

Waxman, Stephen G.   **QM451.W39 2003**
Clinical Neuroanatomy. Ed. 25. Paper Text. McGraw-Hill Professional Publishing. New York, NY. 2002. 400p. LANGE Basic Science Ser. ISBN:0-07-139238-6, ISBN13: 978-0-07-139238-9. Dewey:611.8.

Audience: **l,u,f.**

Internal Medicine. Practice of Medicine > Psychiatry. Mental retardation

PsycINFO: Your Source for Psychological Abstracts. http://www.apa.org/psycinfo/ American Psychological Association.

Audience: **g,l,u,f.**

American Psychiatric   **RC455.2.C4D536 2000**
  Association Staff
DSM-IV-TR Diagnostic and Statistical Manual of Mental Disorders: Text Revision. Ed. 4. Trade Paper. American Psychiatric Publishing, Inc. Arlington, VA. 2000. 216p. ISBN:0-89042-025-4, ISBN13: 978-0-89042-025-6. Dewey:616.89/075. LCCN:00-024852.

Audience: **u,f.**

Babor, Thomas F. & Del   **RC565.T72 2002**
  Boca, Frances K. (Editors)
Treatment Matching in Alcoholism. Griffith Edwards (Contribution by). Trade Cloth. Cambridge University Press. New York, NY. 2002. 292p. International Research Monographs in the Addictions ISBN:0-521-65112-3, ISBN13: 978-0-521-65112-7. Dewey:616.861/06. LCCN:2002-067652.

Audience: **u,f.**

Beirne-Smith, Mary R.,   **RC570.B45 2006**
  et al.
Mental Retardation: An Introduction to Intellectual Disability.
Ed. 7. James R. Patton & Shannon H. Kim (Authors). Trade
Paper. Prentice Hall PTR. Upper Saddle River, NJ. 2005. 576p.
ISBN:0-13-118189-0, ISBN13: 978-0-13-118189-2.
Dewey:362.3. LCCN:2005-003472.

                            Audience: **g,l,u.**

Beirne-Smith, Mary, et al.   **RC570.M386 2002**
Mental Retardation. Ed. 6. Richard Ittenbach & James R. Patton
(Authors). Trade Paper. Prentice Hall PTR. Upper Saddle River,
NJ. 2001. 570p. ISBN:0-13-032990-8, ISBN13:
978-0-13-032990-5. Dewey:362.3. LCCN:00-051951.

                            Audience: **l,u,f.**

✓**Burack, Jacob A., et al.**   **RJ506.M4 H36 1998**
Handbook of Mental Retardation and Development. Robert M.
Hodapp & Edward F. Zigler (Authors). Trade Paper. Cambridge
University Press. New York, NY. 1998. 782p.
ISBN:0-521-44668-6, ISBN13: 978-0-521-44668-6.
Dewey:618.9/2/8588. LCCN:96-050378.

                            Audience: **u,f.**

✓**Goodwin, Frederick K. &**   **RC516.G66 1990**
  Jamison, Kay R.
Manic-Depressive Illness. Trade Cloth. Oxford University Press,
Inc. New York, NY. 1990. 962p. ISBN:0-19-503934-3, ISBN13:
978-0-19-503934-4. Dewey:616.89/5. LCCN:89-016396.

                            Audience: **u,f.**

Hales, Robert E. (Editor),   **RC454.A419 1999**
  et al.
The American Psychiatric Press Textbook of Psychiatry. Ed. 3.
Stuart C. Yudofsky & John A. Talbott (Editors). Cloth Text.
American Psychiatric Publishing, Inc. Arlington, VA. 1999.
xxvii, 1762p. ISBN:0-88048-819-0, ISBN13:
978-0-88048-819-8. Dewey:616.89. LCCN:98-043411.

                            Audience: **u,f.**

Janicak, Philip G., et al.   **RC483**
Principles and Practice of Psychopharmacotherapy. Ed. 3. John
M. Davis, Sheldon H. Preskorn & Frank J. Ayd Jr. (Authors).
Trade Cloth. Lippincott Williams & Wilkins. Philadelphia, PA.
2001. 720p. ISBN:0-7817-2794-4, ISBN13: 978-0-7817-2794-5.
Dewey:616.89/18. LCCN:2001-018654.

                            Audience: **u,f.**

Kupfer, David J. & Bloom,   **RM315.P762 1995**
  Floyd E. (Editors)
Psychopharmacology: The Fourth Generation of Progress. Ed. 4.
Trade Cloth. Lippincott Williams & Wilkins. Philadelphia, PA.
1994. 2048p. ISBN:0-7817-0166-X, ISBN13:
978-0-7817-0166-2. Dewey:615/.78. LCCN:94-007409.

                            Audience: **u,f.**

Luckasson, Ruth A.   **RC570.C515 2002**
Mental Retardation: Definition, Classification, and Systems of
Supports. Ed. 10. Trade Cloth. American Association on Mental
Retardation. Washington, DC. 2002. 238p. ISBN:0-940898-81-0,
ISBN13: 978-0-940898-81-3. Dewey:616.85/88/0012.
LCCN:2002-066469.

                            Audience: **g,l,u,f.**

McCrady, Barbara S. &   **RC564.M327 1999**
✓**Epstein, Elizabeth E. (Editors)**
Addictions: A Comprehensive Guidebook. Trade Cloth. Oxford
University Press, Inc. New York, NY. 1999. 663p.

ISBN:0-19-511489-2, ISBN13: 978-0-19-511489-8.
Dewey:616.86. LCCN:98-051552.

                            Audience: **l,u,f.**

Sadock, Benjamin J.   **RC454.C637 2004**
  (Author, Author)
Kaplan and Sadock's Comprehensive Textbook of Psychiatry.
Ed. 8. Trade Cloth. Lippincott Williams & Wilkins.
Philadelphia, PA. 2004. 4480p. ISBN:0-7817-3434-7, ISBN13:
978-0-7817-3434-9. Dewey:616.89. LCCN:2004-018805.

                            Audience: **u,f.**

Wehmeyer, Michael L. &   **HV3004.M369 2000**
  Patton, James R.
Mental Retardation in the 21st Century. Trade Cloth. PRO-ED,
Inc. Austin, TX. 1999. xxiii, 457p. ISBN:0-89079-819-2,
ISBN13: 978-0-89079-819-5. Dewey:362.3/0973.
LCCN:99-013073.

                            Audience: **g,l,u,f.**

Internal Medicine. Practice of Medicine > Immunological Diseases. Allergy

Glauser, Michel P. & Pizzo,   **RC606**
  Philip A.
Management of Infections in Immunocompromised Patients.
Trade Cloth. Elsevier - Health Sciences Division. Philadelphia,
PA. 2000. 496p. ISBN:0-7020-2506-2, ISBN13:
978-0-7020-2506-8. Dewey:616.9/79.

                            Audience: **u,f.**

Grammer, Leslie C.   **RC584.A34 2002**
Allergic Diseases: Diagnosis and Management. Ed. 6. Trade
Cloth. Lippincott Williams & Wilkins. Philadelphia, PA. 2002.
848p. ISBN:0-7817-2386-8, ISBN13: 978-0-7817-2386-2.
Dewey:616.97. LCCN:2001-050524.

                            Audience: **u,f.**

Lahita, Robert G., et al.   **RC600**
Textbook of the Autoimmune Diseases. Nicholas Chiorazzi &
Westley H. Reeves (Authors). Trade Cloth. Lippincott Williams
& Wilkins. Philadelphia, PA. 2000. 912p. ISBN:0-7817-1505-9,
ISBN13: 978-0-7817-1505-8. Dewey:616.978.
LCCN:99-054064.

                            Audience: **l,u.**

Lieberman, Phil L. & Blaiss,   **RC585.A87 2005**
  Michael S.
Atlas of Allergic Diseases. Ed. 2. Trade Cloth. Current
Medicine. Philadelphia, PA. 2005. ISBN:1-57340-234-6,
ISBN13: 978-1-57340-234-7. Dewey:616.97.
LCCN:2005-045587.

                            Audience: **u,f.**

Lieberman, Phil &   **RC583**
  Anderson, John A.
Allergic Diseases: Diagnosis and Treatment. Ed. 3. Trade Cloth.
Humana Press. Totowa, NJ. 2005. 450p. Current Clinical
Practice Ser. ISBN:1-58829-603-2, ISBN13: 978-1-58829-603-0.
Dewey:616.97. LCCN:2006-018113.

                            Audience: **u,f.**

Nairn, Roderick & Helbert, Matthew   QR181 .N357 2002
Immunology for Medical Students. Trade Paper. Elsevier - Health Sciences Division. Philadelphia, PA. 2002. 344p. ISBN:0-7234-3190-6, ISBN13: 978-0-7234-3190-9. Dewey:616.07/9. LCCN:2002-511550.

Audience: **u.**

Patrick, Christian C.   RJ387.D42C56 2001
Clinical Management of Infections in Immunocompromised Infants and Children. Cloth Text. Lippincott Williams & Wilkins. Philadelphia, PA. 2000. 672p. ISBN:0-7817-1718-3, ISBN13: 978-0-7817-1718-2. Dewey:618.92. LCCN:00-060888.

Audience: **u,f.**

Rosen, Fred S. & Strom, Terry B.   RM275
Therapeutic Immunology. Ed. 2. K. Frank Austen & S. J. Burakoff (Editors). Trade Cloth. Blackwell Publishing, Inc. Malden, MA. 2001. 672p. ISBN:0-632-04359-8, ISBN13: 978-0-632-04359-0. Dewey:615/.37. LCCN:00-044408.

Audience: **u,f.**

Internal Medicine. Practice of Medicine > Blood Diseases, Endocrinology

Felig, Philip & Frohman, Lawrence A.   RC648
Endocrinology and Metabolism. Ed. 4. Cloth Text. McGraw-Hill Professional Publishing. New York, NY. 2001. 1562p. ISBN:0-07-022001-8, ISBN13: 978-0-07-022001-0. Dewey:616.4. LCCN:00-035134.

Audience: **l,u,f.**

Gardner, David G. & Shoback, Dolores M.   RC648
Greenspan's Basic and Clinical Endocrinology. Ed. 8. Paper Text. McGraw-Hill Medical Publishing Division. New York, NY. 2006. 960p. ISBN:0-07-144011-9, ISBN13: 978-0-07-144011-0. Dewey:616.4.

Audience: **l,u,f.**

Livolsi, Virginia A. & Asa, Sylvia   RC648
Endocrine Pathology. Trade Cloth. Elsevier - Health Sciences Division. Philadelphia, PA. 2002. 384p. ISBN:0-443-06595-0, ISBN13: 978-0-443-06595-8. Dewey:616.4. LCCN:00-065823.

Audience: **u,f.**

Porte, Daniel, et al.   RC660.D542 2003
Ellenberg and Rifkin's Diabetes Mellitus: Theory and Practice. Ed. 6. Robert S. Sherwin, Alain Baron, Max Ellenberg & Harold Rifkin (Authors). Trade Cloth. McGraw-Hill Professional Publishing. New York, NY. 2002. 1047p. ISBN:0-8385-2178-9, ISBN13: 978-0-8385-2178-6. Dewey:616.4/62. LCCN:2002-016657.

Audience: **u,f.**

Williams, Robert Hardin, et al.   RC648.T48 2002
Williams Textbook of Endocrinology. Ed. 10. P. Reed Larsen, Henry M. Kronenberg, Shlomo Melmed & Kenneth S. Polonsky (Authors). Trade Cloth. Elsevier - Health Sciences Division. Philadelphia, PA. 2002. 1968p. ISBN:0-7216-9184-6, ISBN13: 978-0-7216-9184-8. Dewey:616.4. LCCN:2002-019193.

Audience: **u.**

Internal Medicine. Practice of Medicine > Respiratory Diseases

Andrews, Moya L.   RF510.A53 2006
Manual of Voice Treatment: Pediatrics Through Geriatrics. Ed. 3. Spiral. Thomson Delmar Learning. Albany, NY. 2006. 760p. Clinical Competence Ser. ISBN:1-4180-0957-1, ISBN13: 978-1-4180-0957-1. Dewey:616.85/5. LCCN:2005-037320.

Audience: **u,f.**

Baken, Ronald J. & Orlikoff, Robert F.   RC423.B28 2000
Clinical Measurement of Speech and Voice. Ed. 2. Paper Text. Thomson Delmar Learning. Albany, NY. 1999. 624p. ISBN:1-56593-869-0, ISBN13: 978-1-56593-869-4. Dewey:616.85/5075. LCCN:99-024709.

Audience: **l,u,f.**

Crapo, James D. (Editor), et al.   RC756.T48 2004
Textbook of Pulmonary Diseases. Ed. 7. Jeffrey Glassroth, Joel Karlinsky & Talmadge E. King (Editors). Trade Cloth. Lippincott Williams & Wilkins. Philadelphia, PA. 2003. 1455p. ISBN:0-7817-3727-3, ISBN13: 978-0-7817-3727-2. Dewey:616.2/4. LCCN:2003-047508.

Audience: **u,f.**

Hyatt, Robert E., et al.   RC734.P84H93 2003
Interpretation of Pulmonary Function Tests: A Practical Guide. Ed. 2. Paul D. Scanlon & Masao Nakamura (Authors). Trade Paper. Lippincott Williams & Wilkins. Philadelphia, PA. 2003. 200p. ISBN:0-7817-3682-X, ISBN13: 978-0-7817-3682-4. Dewey:616.2/4075. LCCN:2002-043394.

Audience: **l,u,f.**

Kacmarek, Robert M.   RC735.I5
Essentials of Respiratory Care. Ed. 4. Cloth Text. Mosby, Inc. Saint Louis, MO. 9999. ISBN:0-8151-4962-X, ISBN13: 978-0-8151-4962-0. Dewey:616.2/0046.

Audience: **u,f.**

Internal Medicine. Practice of Medicine > Geriatrics

Brocklehurst, J. C. & Fillit, Howard M.   RC952
Geriatric Medicine and Gerontology. Ed. 6. Raymond Tallis (Editor). Trade Cloth. Elsevier - Health Sciences Division. Philadelphia, PA. 2002. 1576p. ISBN:0-443-07087-3, ISBN13: 978-0-443-07087-7. Dewey:618.9/7.

Audience: **u,f.**

Cassel, Christine K. (Editor), et al.   RC952.G393 2002
Geriatric Medicine: An Evidence-Based Approach. Ed. 4. Harvey Jay Cohen, Eric B. Larson, Rosanne M. Leipzig & Diane E. Meier (Editors). Trade Cloth. Springer. New York, NY. 2003. XXV, 1318p. ISBN:0-387-95514-3, ISBN13: 978-0-387-95514-8. Dewey:618.97. LCCN:2002-070548.

Audience: **u,f.**

Eliopoulos, Charlotte K.   RC954.E44 2005
Gerontological Nursing. Ed. 6. Trade Paper. Lippincott Williams & Wilkins. Philadelphia, PA. 2004. 624p. ISBN:0-7817-4428-8,

ISBN13: 978-0-7817-4428-7. Dewey:618.97/0231.
LCCN:2003-026731.

Audience: **l,u,f.**

Hazzard, William R., et al.   **RC952**
Principles of Geriatric Medicine and Gerontology. Ed. 5. John P.
Blass, Jeffrey B. Halter, Joseph G. Ouslander & Mary Tinetti
(Authors). Trade Cloth. McGraw-Hill Professional Publishing.
New York, NY. 2003. 1536p. ISBN:0-07-140216-0, ISBN13:
978-0-07-140216-3. Dewey:618.97. LCCN:2003-054011.

Audience: **u,f.**

Miller, Carol A.   **RC954.M55 2003**
Nursing Care of Older Adults: Theory and Practice. Ed. 4. Trade
Cloth. Lippincott Williams & Wilkins. Philadelphia, PA. 2003.
688p. ISBN:0-7817-3808-3, ISBN13: 978-0-7817-3808-8.
Dewey:618.97/0231. LCCN:30-588160.

Audience: **l,u,f.**

Mittelman, Mary S., et al.   **RC523.M575 2003**
Counseling the Alzheimer's Caregiver: A Resource for
Healthcare Professionals. Cynthia Epstein & Alicia Pierzchala
(Authors). Trade Paper. American Medical Association. Chicago,
IL. 2002. 256p. ISBN:1-57947-262-1, ISBN13:
978-1-57947-262-7. Dewey:362.1/96831. LCCN:2002-008433.

Audience: **l,u,f.**

Tideiksaar, Rein   **RC952.5.T53 1997**
Falling in Old Age: Prevention and Management. Ed. 2. Trade
Cloth. Springer Publishing Company, Inc. New York, NY. 1997.
408p. Springer Series on Adulthood and Aging
ISBN:0-8261-5291-0, ISBN13: 978-0-8261-5291-6.
Dewey:613/.0438. LCCN:96-003017.

Audience: **l,u,f.**

Internal Medicine. Practice of Medicine > Sports Medicine. Physiology of Sports

American College of Sports   **RM725.A48 2005**
Medicine
ACSM's Guidelines for Exercise Testing and Prescription. Ed.
7. Spiral. Lippincott Williams & Wilkins. Philadelphia, PA.
2005. 366p. ISBN:0-7817-4506-3, ISBN13: 978-0-7817-4506-2.
Dewey:615.8/2. LCCN:2004-057756.

Audience: **l,u,f.**

Anderson, Marcia   **RD97.A527 2002**
Fundamentals of Sports Injury Management. Ed. 2. Trade Cloth.
Lippincott Williams & Wilkins. Philadelphia, PA. 2002. 480p.
ISBN:0-7817-3272-7, ISBN13: 978-0-7817-3272-7.
Dewey:617.1/027. LCCN:2002-072941.

Audience: **l,u.**

Brown, Stanley   **QP301**
Exercise Physiology. Trade Paper. Lippincott Williams &
Wilkins. Philadelphia, PA. 2005. 672p. ISBN:0-7817-3592-0,
ISBN13: 978-0-7817-3592-6. Dewey:612/.04.
LCCN:2005-022533.

Audience: **l,u,f.**

Garrett, William E. Jr.,   **RD97.P77 2000**
et al.
Principles and Practice of Orthopaedic Sports Medicine. Kevin
P. Speer & Donald T. Kirkendall (Authors). Trade Cloth.

Lippincott Williams & Wilkins. Philadelphia, PA. 2000. 796p.
ISBN:0-7817-2578-X, ISBN13: 978-0-7817-2578-1.
Dewey:617.1/027. LCCN:00-027377.

Audience: **u,f.**

McArdle   **QP301.M375 2006**
Exercise Physiology: Energy, Nutrition, and Human
Performance. Ed. 6. Trade Cloth. Lippincott Williams &
Wilkins. Philadelphia, PA. 2006. 1184p. ISBN:0-7817-4990-5,
ISBN13: 978-0-7817-4990-9. Dewey:612/.044.
LCCN:2005-029306.

Audience: **l,u,f.**

Prentice, William E.   **RD97**
Arnheim's Principles of Athletic Training: A Competency-Based
Approach. Ed. 12. Trade Cloth. McGraw-Hill Higher Education.
Burr Ridge, IL. 2005. 1002p. ISBN:0-07-313890-8, ISBN13:
978-0-07-313890-9. Dewey:617.1027.

Audience: **l,u.**

Wilk, Kevin E.   **RD97.P49 2004**
Physical Rehabilitation of the Injured Athlete. Ed. 3. James
Andrews & Gary Harrelson (Editors). Trade Cloth. Elsevier -
Health Sciences Division. Philadelphia, PA. 2004. 704p.
ISBN:0-7216-0014-X, ISBN13: 978-0-7216-0014-7.
Dewey:617.1/027. LCCN:2003-053884.

Audience: **u,f.**

Internal Medicine. Practice of Medicine > Gastrointestinal Diseases

Fenoglio-Preiser, Cecilia M.,   **RC802.9**
et al.
Gastrointestinal Pathology: An Atlas and Text. Ed. 2. Patrick E.
Lantz, Margaret Listrom, Amy Noffsinger & Franco Rilke
(Authors). CD-ROM. Lippincott Williams & Wilkins.
Philadelphia, PA. 1998. 1312p. ISBN:0-7817-1929-1, ISBN13:
978-0-7817-1929-2. Dewey:616.3/307.

Audience: **u,f.**

Friedman, Lawrence S.   **RC801.G384 2006**
(Editor), et al.
Sleisenger and Fordtran's Gastrointensinal and Liver Disease:
Pathophysiology, Diagnosis, Management. Ed. 8. Lawrence J.
Brandt & Mark Feldman (Editors). Trade Cloth. Elsevier -
Health Sciences Division. Philadelphia, PA. 2006. 3112p.
ISBN:1-4160-0245-6, ISBN13: 978-1-4160-0245-1.
Dewey:616.3/3. LCCN:2005-049767.

Audience: **u,f.**

Kelly, Deirdre A. (Editor)   **RJ456.L5**
Diseases of the Liver and Biliary System in Children. Ed. 2.
Trade Cloth. Blackwell Publishing, Inc. Malden, MA. 2003.
512p. ISBN:1-4051-0660-3, ISBN13: 978-1-4051-0660-3.
Dewey:618.92/362. LCCN:2003-016894.

Audience: **u,f.**

Internal Medicine. Practice of Medicine > Musculoskeletal Diseases

Harris, Edward D. Jr., et al.   **RC927.T49 2005**
Rheumatology, Set. Ed. 7. Ralph C. Budd, Gary S. Firestein,
Mark C. Genovese, Shaun Ruddy, John S. Sergent & Clement

B. Sledge (Authors). Trade Cloth. Elsevier - Health Sciences Division. Philadelphia, PA. 2004. 2064p. ISBN:0-7216-0141-3, ISBN13: 978-0-7216-0141-0. Dewey:616.7/23. LCCN:2004-052586.

Audience: **l,u,f.**

Internal Medicine. Practice of Medicine > Oncology

DeVita, Vincent T., et al.   **RC254**
Cancer: Principles and Practice of Oncology. Ed. 7. Samuel Hellman & Steven A. Rosenberg (Authors). Trade Cloth. Lippincott Williams & Wilkins. Philadelphia, PA. 2004. 3120p. ISBN:0-7817-4450-4, ISBN13: 978-0-7817-4450-8. Dewey:616.994. LCCN:2004-019888.

Audience: **l,u,f.**

Gossfeld, Lynn M., et al.   **RC280.G5S65 2000**
Women and Cancer: A Gynecologic Oncology Nursing Perspective. Ed. 2. Beth Colvin Huff & Giselle Moore-Higgs (Authors), Giselle J. Moore (Editor), Society of Gynecologic Nurse Oncologists Staff (Contribution by). Trade Cloth. Jones & Bartlett Publishers, Inc. Sudbury, MA. 2000. 608p. Series in Oncology ISBN:0-7637-1166-7, ISBN13: 978-0-7637-1166-5. Dewey:616.99/465. LCCN:99-040657.

Audience: **u,f.**

Haskell, Charles M.   **RC270.8.C38 2001**
Cancer Treatment. Ed. 5. Trade Cloth. Elsevier - Health Sciences Division. Philadelphia, PA. 2000. 1712p. ISBN:0-7216-7833-5, ISBN13: 978-0-7216-7833-7. Dewey:616.9/9/4/06. LCCN:99-089086.

Audience: **u,f.**

Mendelsohn, Berk, et al.   **RC268.5.M632 2001**
The Molecular Basis of Cancer. Ed. 2. John Mendelsohn, Peter M. Howley, Mark A. Israel & Lance A. Liotta (Authors). Trade Cloth. Elsevier - Health Sciences Division. Philadelphia, PA. 2001. 720p. ISBN:0-7216-7291-4, ISBN13: 978-0-7216-7291-5. Dewey:616.99/4071. LCCN:2001-020592.

Audience: **l,u,f.**

Miaskowski, Christine &   **RC266 .O544 1999**
Buchsel, Patricia
Oncology Nursing: Assessment and Clinical Care. Trade Cloth. Elsevier - Health Sciences Division. Philadelphia, PA. 1999. 1700p. ISBN:0-8151-6990-6, ISBN13: 978-0-8151-6990-1. Dewey:610.7/3698. LCCN:2002-275930.

Audience: **u,f.**

Otto, Shirley E.   **RC266**
Oncology Nursing. Ed. 4. Cloth Text. Elsevier - Health Sciences Division. Philadelphia, PA. 2001. 1074p. ISBN:0-323-01217-5, ISBN13: 978-0-323-01217-1. Dewey:610.73/698. LCCN:00-049545.

Audience: **u,f.**

Pizzo, Philip A.   **RC281.C4P65 2005**
Principles and Practice of Pediatric Oncology. Ed. 5. Trade Cloth. Lippincott Williams & Wilkins. Philadelphia, PA. 2005. 1780p. ISBN:0-7817-5492-5, ISBN13: 978-0-7817-5492-7. Dewey:618.92/994. LCCN:2005-031028.

Audience: **u,f.**

Vogelstein, Bert & Kinzler,   **RC268.4**
Kenneth W.
The Genetic Basis of Human Cancer. Ed. 2. Trade Cloth. McGraw-Hill Professional Publishing. New York, NY. 2002. 821p. ISBN:0-07-137050-1, ISBN13: 978-0-07-137050-9. Dewey:616.99/4042. LCCN:2001-044560.

Audience: **u,f.**

Internal Medicine. Practice of Medicine > Cardiology

Arnold, M. Katz   **QP111.4.K38 2006**
Physiology of the Heart. Ed. 4. Trade Cloth. Lippincott Williams & Wilkins. Philadelphia, PA. 2005. 640p. ISBN:0-7817-5501-8, ISBN13: 978-0-7817-5501-6. Dewey:612.1/7. LCCN:2005-017130.

Audience: **l,u.**

Kaplan, Norman M. &   **RC685.H8K35 2006**
Flynn, Joseph T.
Clinical Hypertension. Ed. 9. Trade Cloth. Lippincott Williams & Wilkins. Philadelphia, PA. 2005. 528p. ISBN:0-7817-6198-0, ISBN13: 978-0-7817-6198-7. Dewey:616.1/32. LCCN:2005-017049.

Audience: **u,f.**

Wilansky, Susan &   **RC682.H3835 2001**
Willerson, James T.
Heart Disease in Women. Trade Cloth. Elsevier - Health Sciences Division. Philadelphia, PA. 2002. 672p. ISBN:0-443-07900-5, ISBN13: 978-0-443-07900-9. Dewey:616.1/2/0082. LCCN:2001-017366.

Audience: **u,f.**

Zipes, Douglas P., et al.   **RC681.H36 2005**
Braunwald's Heart Disease: A Textbook of Cardiovascular Medicine. Ed. 7. Robert O. Bonow, Eugene Braunwald & Peter Libby (Authors). Trade Cloth. Elsevier - Health Sciences Division. Philadelphia, PA. 2004. 2400p. ISBN:0-7216-0509-5, ISBN13: 978-0-7216-0509-8. Dewey:616.1/2. LCCN:2004-050808.

Audience: **u,f.**

Internal Medicine. Practice of Medicine > Medical Diagnosis

Bickley, Lynn S. & Szilagyi,   **RC76.B38 2007**
Peter G.
Bates' Guide to Physical Examination and History Taking. Ed. 9. Trade Cloth. Lippincott Williams & Wilkins. Philadelphia, PA. 2005. 992p. ISBN:0-7817-6718-0, ISBN13: 978-0-7817-6718-7. Dewey:616.07/54. LCCN:2005-023366.

Audience: **u,f.**

DeGowin, Richard L., et al.   **RC76.D45 2004**
DeGowin's Diagnostic Examination. Ed. 8. Richard F. LeBlond & Donald D. Brown (Authors). Paper Text. McGraw-Hill Professional Publishing. New York, NY. 2004. 1040p. ISBN:0-07-140923-8, ISBN13: 978-0-07-140923-0. Dewey:616.07/54. LCCN:2003-061420.

Audience: **u,f.**

Seidel, Henry M., et al.   RC76.M63 2006
Mosby's Guide to Physical Examination. Ed. 6. Jane W. Ball,
Joyce E. Dains & G. William Benedict (Authors). Cloth Text.
Elsevier - Health Sciences Division. Philadelphia, PA. 2006.
1040p. ISBN:0-323-02888-8, ISBN13: 978-0-323-02888-2.
Dewey:616.07/54.

Audience: **u,f.**

Seller, Robert H.   RC71.5.S45 2000
Differential Diagnosis of Common Complaints. Ed. 4. Ray
Kersey (Editor). Trade Paper. Elsevier - Health Sciences
Division. Philadelphia, PA. 1999. 442p. ISBN:0-7216-8017-8,
ISBN13: 978-0-7216-8017-0. Dewey:616.07/5.
LCCN:99-027918.

Audience: **u,f.**

Swartz, Mark H.   RC76.S95 2006
Textbook of Physical Diagnosis: History and Examination with
Student Consult Access. Ed. 5. Cloth Text. Elsevier - Health
Sciences Division. Philadelphia, PA. 2005. 928p.
ISBN:1-4160-0307-X, ISBN13: 978-1-4160-0307-6.
LCCN:2005-042850.

Audience: **u,f.**

Internal Medicine. Practice of Medicine > Hematology

Brenner, Benjamin, et al.   RC647.C55W665 2001
Women's Issues in Thrombosis and Hemostasis. Victor J.
Marder & Jacqueline Conard (Authors). Trade Cloth. Taylor &
Francis Group. Abingdon, 2002. 350p. ISBN:1-84184-003-3,
ISBN13: 978-1-84184-003-1. Dewey:616.1/57/0082.
LCCN:2002-416672.

Audience: **l,u,f.**

Lichtman, Marshall Al ,   RC633.H43 2006
et al.
Williams Hematology. Ed. 7. Ernest Beutler, Kenneth
Kaushansky, Thomas J. Kipps, Josef Prchal & Uri Seligsohn
(Authors). Trade Cloth. McGraw-Hill Companies, The. New
York, NY. 2005. 1856p. ISBN:0-07-143591-3, ISBN13:
978-0-07-143591-8. Dewey:616.1/5. LCCN:2004-055200.

Audience: **l,u,f.**

Nathan, David G., et al.   RJ411.N37 2003
Hematology of Infancy and Childhood. Ed. 6. Frank A. Oski,
David Ginsburg, A. Thomas Look & Stuart H. Orkin (Authors).
Trade Cloth. Elsevier - Health Sciences Division. Philadelphia,
PA. 2003. 2060p. ISBN:0-7216-9317-2, ISBN13:
978-0-7216-9317-0. Dewey:618.92/15. LCCN:2002-026919.

Audience: **l,u,f.**

Stamatoyannopoulos,   RC636
George, et al.
Molecular Basis of Blood Diseases. Ed. 3. Philip W. Majerus,
Roger M. Perlmutter & Harold Varmus (Authors). Trade Cloth.
Elsevier - Health Sciences Division. Philadelphia, PA. 2000.
1064p. ISBN:0-7216-7671-5, ISBN13: 978-0-7216-7671-5.
Dewey:616.1/507. LCCN:00-029714.

Audience: **l,u,f.**

Internal Medicine. Practice of Medicine > Substance Abuse and Alcoholism

Agarwal, Dharam P. &   RA1242.A35A425 2001
  Seitz, Helmut K. (Editors)
Alcohol in Health and Disease. Paper over Boards. Marcel
Dekker Inc. New York, NY. 2001. 648p. ISBN:0-8247-0533-5,
ISBN13: 978-0-8247-0533-6. Dewey:616.86/1.
LCCN:2001-028634.

Audience: **l,u,f.**

Babor, Thomas   HV5020
Alcohol and Public Policy: No Ordinary Commodity. Trade
Paper. Oxford University Press, Inc. New York, NY. 2003. 301p.
ISBN:0-19-263261-2, ISBN13: 978-0-19-263261-6.
Dewey:362.2928. LCCN:2004-298606.

Audience: **u,f.**

Begleiter, Henri & Kissin,   RC565
  Benjamin (Editors)
The Biology of Alcoholism: Pathogenesis of Alcoholism:
Biological Factors. Trade Cloth. Basic Books. New York, NY.
1983. 666p. ISBN:0-306-41053-2, ISBN13: 978-0-306-41053-6.
Dewey:616.86/1071. LCCN:82-022284.

Audience: **u,f.**

Benjamin Kissin (Editor)   HV5292
Social Aspects of Alcoholism. Henri Begleiter (Editor). Plenum
Press. 1976. The Biology of Alcoholism, Vol. 4

Audience: **u,f.**

Benjamin Kissin (Editor)   RC565
Treatment and Rehabilitation of the Chronic Alcoholic. Henri
Begleiter (Editor). Plenum Press. 1977. The Biology of
Alcoholism, Vol. 5

Audience: **u,f.**

Frances, Richard J.   RC564.C55 2005
  (Editor), et al.
Clinical Textbook of Addictive Disorders. Ed. 3. Sheldon Irvin
Miller & Avram H. Mack (Editors). Cloth over Boards. Guilford
Publications, Inc. New York, NY. 2005. 684p.
ISBN:1-59385-174-X, ISBN13: 978-1-59385-174-3.
Dewey:616.86. LCCN:2004-026092.

Audience: **l,u,f.**

Galanter, Marc & Kleber,   RC564.A526 2004
  Herbert D.
The American Psychiatric Publishing Textbook of Substance
Abuse Treatment. Ed. 3. Trade Cloth. American Psychiatric
Publishing, Inc. Arlington, VA. 2004. 168p.
ISBN:1-58562-099-8, ISBN13: 978-1-58562-099-9.
Dewey:616.86/06. LCCN:2003-058354.

Audience: **l,u.**

Kissin, Benjamin (Editor)   RC565
Biochemistry. Begleiter, Henri (Editor). Plenum Press. 1971.
The Biology of Alcoholism, Vol. 1 ISBN:0-306-37111-1,
ISBN13: 978-0-306-37111-0.

Audience: **u,f.**

Kissin, Benjamin (Editor)   RC565
Clinical Pathology. Begleiter, Henri (Editor). Plenum Press.
1974. The Biology of Alcoholism, Vol. 3 ISBN:0-306-37113-8,
ISBN13: 978-0-306-37113-4.

Audience: **u,f.**

Kissin, Benjamin (Editor)   **RC565**
Physiology and Behavior. Begleiter, Henri (Editor). Plenum
Press. 1972. The Biology of Alcoholism, Vol. 2
ISBN:0-306-37112-X, ISBN13: 978-0-306-37112-7.

Audience: **u,f.**

Kissin, Benjamin &   **HV5035**
  Begleiter, Henri (Editors)
The Biology of Alcoholism: Pathogenesis of Alcoholism:
Psychosocial Factors. Trade Cloth. Basic Books. New York, NY.
1983. 734p. ISBN:0-306-41052-4, ISBN13: 978-0-306-41052-9.
Dewey:362.2/92. LCCN:82-019029.

Audience: **u,f.**

Lowinson, Joyce H., et al.   **RC564.S826 2004**
Substance Abuse: A Comprehensive Textbook. Ed. 4. John G.
Langrod & Robert B. Millman (Authors). Trade Cloth.
Lippincott Williams & Wilkins. Philadelphia, PA. 2004. 1200p.
ISBN:0-7817-3474-6, ISBN13: 978-0-7817-3474-5.
Dewey:362.29. LCCN:2004-019274.

Audience: **l,u,f.**

McCrady, Barbara S. &   **RC564.M327 1999**
  Epstein, Elizabeth E. (Editors)
Addictions: A Comprehensive Guidebook. Trade Cloth. Oxford
University Press, Inc. New York, NY. 1999. 663p.
ISBN:0-19-511489-2, ISBN13: 978-0-19-511489-8.
Dewey:616.86. LCCN:98-051552.

Audience: **l,u,f.**

Miller, William R. &   **RC564.M545 2006**
  Carroll, Kathleen M. (Editors)
Rethinking Substance Abuse: What the Science Shows, and
What We Should Do about It. Cloth over Boards. Guilford
Publications, Inc. New York, NY. 2006. 320p.
ISBN:1-57230-231-3, ISBN13: 978-1-57230-231-0.
Dewey:362.29. LCCN:2005-020524.

Audience: **g,l,u,f.**

Ott, Peggy J., et al.   **RC564.S66 1999**
Sourcebook on Substance Abuse: Etiology, Epidemiology,
Assessment, and Treatment. Ed. 1. Ralph E. Tarter & Robert T.
Ammerman (Authors). Cloth Text. Allyn & Bacon, Inc. Boston,
MA. 1999. 472p. ISBN:0-205-19802-3, ISBN13:
978-0-205-19802-3. Dewey:616.86. LCCN:98-035240.

Audience: **g,l,u,f.**

Rassool, Hussein   **RC564.68**
Dual Diagnosis: Substance Misuse and Psychiatric Disorders.
Trade Paper. Blackwell Publishing, Inc. Malden, MA. 2001.
224p. ISBN:0-632-05621-5, ISBN13: 978-0-632-05621-7.
Dewey:616.86/075. LCCN:2001-035734.

Audience: **u,f.**

Sloboda, Zili & Bukoski,   **HV5801.H282 2002**
  William J. (Editors)
Handbook of Drug Abuse Prevention: Theory, Science, and
Practice. Trade Cloth. Springer. New York, NY. 2003. 698p.
Handbooks of Sociology and Social Research
ISBN:0-306-47342-9, ISBN13: 978-0-306-47342-5.
Dewey:362.29/17. LCCN:2002-072682.

Audience: **u,f.**

Straussner, Shulamith Lala   **RC564.E785 2001**
  Ashenberg (Editor)
Ethnocultural Factors in Substance Abuse Treatment. Cloth over
Boards. Guilford Publications, Inc. New York, NY. 2001. 447p.

ISBN:1-57230-630-0, ISBN13: 978-1-57230-630-1.
Dewey:616.86/06. LCCN:00-067723.

Audience: **u,f.** *Choice, 2001.*

Tabakoff, Boris (Editor)   **RC565**
Medical and Social Aspects of Alcohol Abuse. Trade Cloth.
Basic Books. New York, NY. 1983. 420p. ISBN:0-306-41221-7,
ISBN13: 978-0-306-41221-9. Dewey:616.86/1.
LCCN:83-004786.

Audience: **g,l,u,f.** *B*

Wekerle, Christine   **HV4998.W45 2001**
Violence and Addiction Equation: Theoretical and Clinical
Issues in Substance Abuse and Relationship Violence. Paper
over Boards. Brunner-Routledge. Philadelphia, PA. 2002. 352p.
ISBN:0-87630-959-7, ISBN13: 978-0-87630-959-9.
Dewey:362.82/92. LCCN:2001-037778.

Audience: **u,f.**

Surgery. Orthopedia

Brunicardi, F. Charles, et al.   **RD37.P74 2006**
Schwartz's Manual of Surgery. Ed. 8. Anderson, Timothy R.
Billiar, David L. Dunn, John G. Hunter & Raphael E. Pollock
(Authors). Trade Paper. McGraw-Hill Professional Publishing.
New York, NY. 2006. 1008p. ISBN:0-07-144688-5, ISBN13:
978-0-07-144688-4. Dewey:617. LCCN:2005-052273.

Audience: **u,f.**

Phipps, Wilma J., et al.   **RT41.M49 2003**
Medical-Surgical Nursing: Health and Illness Perspectives. Ed.
7. Frances Donovan. Monahan, Judith K. Sands, Jane F. Marek
& Marianne Neighbors (Authors). Cloth Text. Elsevier - Health
Sciences Division. Philadelphia, PA. 2002. 2176p.
ISBN:0-323-01804-1, ISBN13: 978-0-323-01804-3.
Dewey:610.73. LCCN:2002-029353.

Audience: **l,u,f.**

Smeltzer, Suzanne C.   **RT41**
  O'Connell, et al.
Brunner And Suddarth's Textbook of Medical-Surgical Nursing.
Ed. 10. Brenda G. Bare & Mary Jo Boyer (Authors). Book,
Other. Lippincott Williams & Wilkins. Philadelphia, PA. 2005.
ISBN:0-7817-6576-5, ISBN13: 978-0-7817-6576-3.
Dewey:610.73.

Audience: **u.**

Thal, Erwin R., et al.   **RD93.3**
Operative Trauma Management. Ed. 2. John A. Weigelt & C.
James Carrico (Authors), Rebekah Dodson (Illustrator). Paper
Text. McGraw-Hill Professional Publishing. New York, NY.
2001. 556p. ISBN:0-8385-7388-6, ISBN13: 978-0-8385-7388-4.
Dewey:617.1. LCCN:2001-030147.

Audience: **u,f.**

Thompson, June M., et al.   **RT41**
Mosby's Clinical Nursing. Ed. 5. Jane E. Hirsch, Gertrude K.
McFarland & Susan Martin Tucker (Authors). Trade Cloth.
Elsevier - Health Sciences Division. Philadelphia, PA. 2001.
1696p. ISBN:0-323-01195-0, ISBN13: 978-0-323-01195-2.
Dewey:610.73. LCCN:2002-511702.

Audience: **l,u,f.**

Townsend, Courtney M. Jr.   RD31.T4732 2004
Pocket Companion to Sabiston Textbook of Surgery. Ed. 17.
Trade Paper. Elsevier - Health Sciences Division. Philadelphia,
PA. 2004. 1184p. ISBN:0-7216-0482-X, ISBN13:
978-0-7216-0482-4. Dewey:617. LCCN:2004-046836.
Audience: **u,f.**

Audiology

Martin, Frederick N. &   RF290.M34 2006
Clark, John Greer
Introduction to Audiology. Ed. 9. Trade Paper. Allyn & Bacon,
Inc. Boston, MA. 2005. 504p. ISBN:0-205-45330-9, ISBN13:
978-0-205-45330-6. Dewey:617.8. LCCN:2004-060247.
Audience: **g,l,u.** *B*

Newby, Hayes A. & Popelka,   RF290.N47 1992
Gerald R.
Audiology. Ed. 6. Cloth Text. Allyn & Bacon, Inc. Boston, MA.
1992. 512p. ISBN:0-13-051921-9, ISBN13: 978-0-13-051921-4.
Dewey:617.8/9. LCCN:91-032038.
Audience: **u,f.** *B*

Northern, Jerry   RF291.5.C45N67 2001
Hearing in Children. Ed. 5. Trade Cloth. Lippincott Williams &
Wilkins. Philadelphia, PA. 2001. 450p. ISBN:0-683-30764-9,
ISBN13: 978-0-683-30764-1. Dewey:618.92/0978.
LCCN:2001-038193.
Audience: **u,f.**

Gynecology. Obstetrics

Aguirre-Molina, Marilyn &   WA309
Molina, Carlos W. (Editors)
Latina Health in the United States: A Public Health Reader.
Trade Paper. John Wiley & Sons, Inc. Hoboken, NJ. 2003. 688p.
ISBN:0-7879-6579-0, ISBN13: 978-0-7879-6579-2.
Dewey:613/.08968/073. LCCN:2003-006260.
Audience: **g,l,u,f.**

Ammer, Christine   RA778.A494 2006
The New A to Z of Women's Health. Ed. 5. Joann E. Manson &
Elizabeth F. Brigham (Foreword by). Trade Paper, Perfect. Facts
On File, Inc.. New York, NY. 2005. 434p. Facts on File Library
of Health and Living ISBN:0-8160-5791-5, ISBN13:
978-0-8160-5791-7. Dewey:613/.04244/03. LCCN:2004-019065.
Audience: **g,l,u.**

Boston Women's Health   RA778.N49 2005
Book Collective Staff & Boston Women's Health Book
Collective
Our Bodies, Ourselves: A New Edition for a New Era. Ed. 35.
Trade Paper. Simon & Schuster. New York, NY. 2005. 848p.
ISBN:0-7432-5611-5, ISBN13: 978-0-7432-5611-7.
Dewey:613/.04244. LCCN:2004-065374.
Audience: **g,l,u.**

Carlson, Karen J., et al.   RA778.C2164 2004
The New Harvard Guide to Women's Health. Stephanie A.
Eisenstat & Terra Diane Ziporyn (Authors). Trade Cloth.
Harvard University Press. Cambridge, MA. 2004. 704p. Harvard
University Press Reference Library ISBN:0-674-01282-8,
ISBN13: 978-0-674-01282-0. Dewey:616/.0082.
LCCN:2003-063680.
Audience: **g,l,u.**

Colditz, Graham A.   RG121.H435 2001
(Editor), et al.
Healthy Women, Healthy Lives: A Guide to Preventing Disease,
from the Landmark Nurses' Health Study. Joann E. Manson &
Frank Speizer (Editors), Susan E. Hankinson (As told by). Trade
Paper. Simon & Schuster. New York, NY. 2002. 576p.
ISBN:0-7432-1774-8, ISBN13: 978-0-7432-1774-3.
Dewey:613/.04244. LCCN:2001-034154.
Audience: **g,l,u.**

Gilbert, Dorie J. & Wright,   RA643
Ednita M. (Editors)
African American Women and HIV/AIDS: Critical Responses.
Mindy Thompson Fullilove (Foreword by). Trade Cloth.
Greenwood Publishing Group, Inc. Portsmouth, NH. 2003. 288p.
ISBN:0-275-97127-9, ISBN13: 978-0-275-97127-4.
Dewey:362.1/969792. LCCN:2001-058040.
Audience: **g,l,u,f.** *Choice, 2004.*

Gossfeld, Lynn M., et al.   RC280.G5S65 2000
Women and Cancer: A Gynecologic Oncology Nursing
Perspective. Ed. 2. Beth Colvin Huff & Giselle Moore-Higgs
(Authors), Giselle J. Moore (Editor), Society of Gynecologic
Nurse Oncologists Staff (Contribution by). Trade Cloth. Jones &
Bartlett Publishers, Inc. Sudbury, MA. 2000. 608p. Series in
Oncology ISBN:0-7637-1166-7, ISBN13: 978-0-7637-1166-5.
Dewey:616.99/465. LCCN:99-040657.
Audience: **u,f.**

Leavitt, Judith W.   RA778.W744 1998
Women and Health in America: Historical Readings. Ed. 2.
Trade Cloth. University of Wisconsin Press. Chicago, IL. 1999.
560p. ISBN:0-299-15960-4, ISBN13: 978-0-299-15960-3.
Dewey:362.1/082/0973. LCCN:98-014446.
Audience: **g,l,u,f.**

Lemcke, Dawn P., et al.   RC48.6
Current Care of Women: Diagnosis and Treatment. Julie
Pattison, Lorna A. Marshall & Deborah S. Cowley (Authors).
Trade Paper. McGraw-Hill Professional Publishing. New York,
NY. 2003. 632p. ISBN:0-07-138770-6, ISBN13:
978-0-07-138770-5. Dewey:616.0082. LCCN:2004-272544.
Audience: **l,u,f.**

Minkin, Mary Jane &   RG121.M667 2003
Wright, Carol V.
The Yale Guide to Women's Reproductive Health: From
Menarche to Menopause. Cloth over Boards. Yale University
Press. Cumberland, RI. 2003. 464p. ISBN:0-300-09820-0,
ISBN13: 978-0-300-09820-4. Dewey:618.1.
LCCN:2002-035738.
Audience: **g,l,u,f.** *Choice, 2003.*

Minkin, Mary & Wright,   RG186.M573 2004
Carol
A Woman's Guide to Menopause and Perimenopause. Trade
Paper. Yale University Press. Cumberland, RI. 2004. 432p. Yale
University Press Health and Wellness Ser. ISBN:0-300-10435-9,
ISBN13: 978-0-300-10435-6. Dewey:618.1/75.
LCCN:2004-014636.
Audience: **g,l,u.**

Minkin, Mary & Wright,   RA788
Carol
A Woman's Guide to Sexual Health. Trade Paper. Yale
University Press. Cumberland, RI. 2004. 464p. Yale University

---

Press Health and Wellness Ser. ISBN:0-300-10594-0, ISBN13: 978-0-300-10594-0. Dewey:613.9/54.

Audience: **g,l,u.**

Morgen, Sandra   **RG103.M67 2002**
Into Our Own Hands: The Women's Health Movement in the United States, 1969-1990. Trade Cloth. Rutgers University Press. Piscataway, NJ. 2004. 320p. ISBN:0-8135-3071-7, ISBN13: 978-0-8135-3071-0. Dewey:362.1/98/0973. LCCN:2001-048614.

Audience: **g,l,u,f.** *Choice, 2002.*

Oaks, Laury   **RG627.6.T6O25 2001**
Smoking and Pregnancy: The Politics of Fetal Protection. Trade Paper. Rutgers University Press. Piscataway, NJ. 2004. 256p. ISBN:0-8135-2888-7, ISBN13: 978-0-8135-2888-5. Dewey:618.2/4. LCCN:00-039036.

Audience: **g,l,u,f.** *Choice, 2001.*

Quilligan, Edward J. &   **RG125.C87 2000**
Zuspan, Frederick P.
Current Therapy in Obstetrics and Gynecology. Ed. 5. William Schmitt (Editor). Trade Cloth. Elsevier - Health Sciences Division. Philadelphia, PA. 1999. 538p. ISBN:0-7216-7579-4, ISBN13: 978-0-7216-7579-4. Dewey:618/.046. LCCN:99-016181.

Audience: **u,f.**

Ratcliff, Kathryn S.   **RA564.85.R38 2002**
Women and Health: Power, Technology, Inequality and Conflict in a Gendered World. Trade Paper. Allyn & Bacon, Inc. Boston, MA. 2001. 416p. ISBN:0-205-30597-0, ISBN13: 978-0-205-30597-1. Dewey:362.1/082. LCCN:2001-018866.
Audience: **g,l,u,f.** *Choice, 2002.*

Reindl, Sheila M.   **RC552.B84**
Sensing the Self: Women's Recovery from Bulimia. Trade Paper. Harvard University Press. Cambridge, MA. 2002. 350p. ISBN:0-674-01011-6, ISBN13: 978-0-674-01011-6. Dewey:616.85/263.

Audience: **g,l,u,f.** *Choice, 2001.*

Sherwin, Susan & Parish,   **R725.5.W66 2001**
Barbara
Women, Medicine, Ethics and the Law. Trade Cloth. Ashgate Publishing, Ltd. Aldershot, 2002. 462p. The International Library of Medicine, Ethics and Law ISBN:0-7546-2046-8, ISBN13: 978-0-7546-2046-4. Dewey:174/.2/082. LCCN:00-053126.

Audience: **u,f.**

Sloan, Ethel &   **RG121.S637 2002**
Sloane-White, Patricia
Biology of Women. Ed. 4. Cloth Text. Thomson Delmar Learning. Albany, NY. 2001. 672p. ISBN:0-7668-1142-5, ISBN13: 978-0-7668-1142-3. Dewey:613/.04244. LCCN:00-065690.

Audience: **l,u,f.**

Worcester, Nancy &   **RA564.85**
Whately, Marianne
Women's Health: Readings on Social, Economic, and Political Issues. Ed. 4. Trade Paper. Kendall/Hunt Publishing Company. Dubuque, IA. 2004. 580p. ISBN:0-7575-0809-X, ISBN13: 978-0-7575-0809-7. Dewey:362.1/082.

Audience: **g,l,u,f.**

Youngkin, Ellis Quinn &   **RA564.85.W6668 2004**
Davis, Marcia Szmania
Women's Health: A Primary Care Clinical Guide. Ed. 3. Trade Paper. Prentice Hall PTR. Upper Saddle River, NJ. 2003. 960p. ISBN:0-13-110026-2, ISBN13: 978-0-13-110026-8. Dewey:613/.04244. LCCN:2003-008428.

Audience: **l,u,f.**

Gynecology. Obstetrics > Obstetrics

Creasy, Robert K., et al.   **RG526.M34 2004**
Maternal-Fetal Medicine. Ed. 5. Jay D. Iams & Robert Resnik (Authors). Trade Cloth. Elsevier - Health Sciences Division. Philadelphia, PA. 2003. 1376p. ISBN:0-7216-0004-2, ISBN13: 978-0-7216-0004-8. Dewey:618.2. LCCN:2003-041522.

Audience: **u,f.**

Cunningham, Gary, et al.   **RG524.W7 2005**
Williams Obstetrics. Ed. 22. Kenneth J. Leveno, Larry C. Gilstrap, John C. Hauth, Katharine D. Wenstrom & Steven L. Bloom (Authors). Trade Cloth. McGraw-Hill Companies, The. New York, NY. 2005. 1600p. ISBN:0-07-141315-4, ISBN13: 978-0-07-141315-2. Dewey:618.2. LCCN:2004-061105.

Audience: **u,f.**

Lowdermilk, Deitra   **RG951**
Leonard & Perry, Shannon E.
Maternity Nursing. Ed. 7. Cloth Text. Elsevier - Health Sciences Division. Philadelphia, PA. 2006. 1024p. ISBN:0-323-03366-0, ISBN13: 978-0-323-03366-4. Dewey:618.2/0231. LCCN:2005-058449.

Audience: **l,u,f.**

Newman, Roger B. & Luke,   **RG567.N49 2000**
Barbara
Multifetal Pregnancy: A Handbook for Care of the Pregnant Patient. Trade Paper. Lippincott Williams & Wilkins. Philadelphia, PA. 2000. 288p. ISBN:0-7817-2217-9, ISBN13: 978-0-7817-2217-9. Dewey:618.2/5. LCCN:00-030145.

Audience: **u,f.**

Speroff, Leon   **RG101**
Clinical Gynecologic Endocrinology and Infertility. Ed. 7. Cloth Text. Lippincott Williams & Wilkins. Philadelphia, PA. 2005. ISBN:0-7817-6398-3, ISBN13: 978-0-7817-6398-1. Dewey:618.1.

Audience: **u,f.**

Pediatrics

Behrman, Richard E.   **RJ45.N4 2004**
Nelson's Textbook of Pediatrics. Ed. 17. Cloth Text. W. B. Saunders Company. Philadelphia, PA. 2003. xlviii, 2618p. ISBN:0-8089-2269-6, ISBN13: 978-0-8089-2269-8. Dewey:618.92. LCCN:2002-030990.

Audience: **u,f.**

Betz, Cecily Lynn &   **RJ245.M675 2004**
Sowden, Linda A.
Mosby's Pediatric Nursing Reference. Ed. 5. Paper Text. Elsevier - Health Sciences Division. Philadelphia, PA. 2003. 832p. ISBN:0-323-01979-X, ISBN13: 978-0-323-01979-8. Dewey:610.73/62. LCCN:2003-054094.

Audience: **l,u,f.**

Fanaroff, Avroy A., et al.   RJ254.N456 2006
Neonatal-Perinatal Medicine: Diseases of the Fetus and Infant.
Ed. 8. Richard J. Martin & Michele C. Walsh (Authors). Trade
Cloth. Elsevier - Health Sciences Division. Philadelphia, PA.
2005. 2036p. ISBN:0-323-02966-3, ISBN13:
978-0-323-02966-7. Dewey:618.92/01. LCCN:2005-047980.

Audience: **u,f.**

Friedman, Marilyn M., et al.   RT120.F34F75 2003
Family Nursing: Research, Theory, and Practice. Ed. 5. Vicky R.
Bowden & Elaine Jones (Authors). Trade Paper. Prentice Hall
PTR. Upper Saddle River, NJ. 2002. 714p.
ISBN:0-13-060824-6, ISBN13: 978-0-13-060824-6.
Dewey:610.73. LCCN:2002-025198.

Audience: **u,f.**

Hay, William W., et al.   RJ50
Current Pediatric Diagnosis and Treatment. Ed. 17. Judith M.
Sondheimer, Robin R. Deterding & Myron J. Levin (Authors).
Paper Text. McGraw-Hill Professional Publishing. New York,
NY. 2004. 1420p. ISBN:0-07-142960-3, ISBN13:
978-0-07-142960-3. Dewey:618.9/2.

Audience: **l,u,f.**

Hockenberry, Marilyn J.   RJ245.H59 2004
Wong's Clinical Manual of Pediatric Nursing. Ed. 6. Paper Text.
Elsevier - Health Sciences Division. Philadelphia, PA. 2003.
784p. ISBN:0-323-01958-7, ISBN13: 978-0-323-01958-3.
Dewey:610.73/62. LCCN:2003-052715.

Audience: **l,u,f.**

Jackson Allen, Patricia &   RJ380
   Vessey, Judith A.
Primary Care of the Child with a Chronic Condition. Ed. 4.
Cloth Text. Elsevier - Health Sciences Division. Philadelphia,
PA. 2003. 832p. ISBN:0-323-02364-9, ISBN13:
978-0-323-02364-1. Dewey:610.7/362.

Audience: **l,u,f.**

Pizzo, Philip A.   RC281.C4P65 2005
Principles and Practice of Pediatric Oncology. Ed. 5. Trade
Cloth. Lippincott Williams & Wilkins. Philadelphia, PA. 2005.
1780p. ISBN:0-7817-5492-5, ISBN13: 978-0-7817-5492-7.
Dewey:618.92/994. LCCN:2005-031028.

Audience: **u,f.**

Rudolph, Colin David   RJ45.R87 2003
   (Editor)
Rudolph's Pediatrics. Ed. 21. Paper Text. McGraw-Hill
Companies, The. New York, NY. 2003. xxxiv, 2688p.
ISBN:0-07-112457-8, ISBN13: 978-0-07-112457-7.
Dewey:618.92. LCCN:00-068714.

Audience: **l,u,f.**

Wright, Lorraine M. &   RT120.F34W75 2005
   Leahey, Maureen
Nurses and Families: A Guide to Family Assessment and
Intervention. Ed. 4. Trade Paper, Perfect. F. A. Davis Company.
Philadelphia, PA. 2005. 345p. ISBN:0-8036-1211-7, ISBN13:
978-0-8036-1211-2. Dewey:610.73. LCCN:2005-007107.

Audience: **l,u,f.**

Dentistry

Beemsterboer, Phyllis L.,   RK361
   et al.
Periodontology for the Dental Hygienist. Ed. 2. Dorothy A.

Perry & Edward J. Taggart (Authors), Saunders, W. B.
Publishing Staff (Contribution by). Trade Paper. Elsevier -
Health Sciences Division. Philadelphia, PA. 2000. 429p.
ISBN:0-7216-8559-5, ISBN13: 978-0-7216-8559-5.
Dewey:617.6/32. LCCN:00-057416.

Audience: **l,u.**

Bird, Doni L. & Robinson,   RK60.5
   Debbie S.
Student Workbook to Accompany Torres and Ehrlich Modern
Dental Assisting. Ed. 8. Paper Text. Elsevier - Health Sciences
Division. Philadelphia, PA. 2005. 560p. ISBN:0-7216-3908-9,
ISBN13: 978-0-7216-3908-6.

Audience: **l,u.**

Burt, Brian A. & Eklund,   RK52
   Steven
Dentistry, Dental Practice, and the Community. Ed. 6. Trade
Paper. Elsevier - Health Sciences Division. Philadelphia, PA.
2005. 440p. ISBN:0-7216-0515-X, ISBN13: 978-0-7216-0515-9.
Dewey:617.6.

Audience: **u,f.**

Davison, Judith A.   KF2910.D3D38 2000
Legal and Ethical Considerations for Dental Hygienists and
Assistants. Trade Paper. Elsevier - Health Sciences Division.
Philadelphia, PA. 1999. 378p. ISBN:1-55664-422-1, ISBN13:
978-1-55664-422-1. Dewey:344.73/0413. LCCN:00-699155.

Audience: **l,u,f.**

Frommer, Herbert H. &   RK309.F76 2005
   Stabulas-Savage, Jeanine J.
Radiology for the Dental Professional. Ed. 8. Paper Text.
Elsevier - Health Sciences Division. Philadelphia, PA. 2005.
576p. ISBN:0-323-03071-8, ISBN13: 978-0-323-03071-7.
Dewey:617.607572.

Audience: **l,u,f.**

Ibsen, Olga A.   RK470
Oral Pathology for the Dental Hygienist. Cloth Text. Elsevier -
Health Sciences Division. Philadelphia, PA. 2003.
ISBN:0-8089-2272-6, ISBN13: 978-0-8089-2272-8.
Dewey:617.5/22.

Audience: **l,u.**

Melfi, Rudy C., et al.   RK280.P4 2000
Oral Embryology and Microscopic Anatomy: A Textbook for
Students in Dental Hygiene. Ed. 10. Keith E. Alley & Dorothy
Permar (Authors). Trade Paper. Lippincott Williams & Wilkins.
Philadelphia, PA. 2000. 332p. ISBN:0-683-30644-8, ISBN13:
978-0-683-30644-6. Dewey:611/.018931. LCCN:00-021829.

Audience: **l,u.**

Ring, Malvin E.   RK29.R54 1985
Dentistry: An Illustrated History. Trade Cloth. Harry N. Abrams,
Inc. New York, NY. 1985. 320p. ISBN:0-8109-1100-0, ISBN13:
978-0-8109-1100-0. Dewey:617.6/009. LCCN:85-003883.

Audience: **g,l,u,f.**   ℬ *Choice, 1986.*

Scheid, Rickne C. &   QM311.W64 2002
   Woelfel, Julian B.
Dental Anatomy: Its Relevance to Dentistry. Ed. 6. Trade Paper.
Lippincott Williams & Wilkins. Philadelphia, PA. 2001. 464p.
ISBN:0-7817-2797-9, ISBN13: 978-0-7817-2797-6.
Dewey:611/.314. LCCN:2001-038187.

Audience: **l,u,f.**

Therapeudics. Pharmacology

Brown, Meta & Mulholland, Joyce L.   RS57.B76 2003
Drug Calculations: Process and Problems for Clinical Practice. Ed. 7. Paper Text. Elsevier - Health Sciences Division. Philadelphia, PA. 2003. 448p. ISBN:0-323-02562-5, ISBN13: 978-0-323-02562-1. Dewey:615/.14. LCCN:2003-059906.

Audience: **u,f.**

Conte, John E. Jr.   RM267.C63 2002
Manual of Antibiotics and Infectious Diseases: Treatment and Prevention. Ed. 5. Trade Paper. Lippincott Williams & Wilkins. Philadelphia, PA. 2001. 784p. ISBN:0-7817-2316-7, ISBN13: 978-0-7817-2316-9. Dewey:615/.329. LCCN:2001-038998.

Audience: **u,f.**

Fong, I. W. & Drlica, Karl (Editors)   QR177.R446 2003
Reemergence of Established Pathogens in the 21st Century. Trade Cloth. Springer. New York, NY. 2003. 312p. Emerging Infectious Diseases of the 21st Century Ser. ISBN:0-306-47500-6, ISBN13: 978-0-306-47500-9. Dewey:616.9. LCCN:2002-040669.

Audience: **u,f.**

Matzke, Gary R., et al.   RM263.P56
Pharmacotherapy: A Pathophysiologic Approach. Ed. 6. L. Michael Posey, Robert L. Talbert, Barbara G. Wells, Gary C. Yee & Joseph T. DiPiro (Authors). Trade Cloth, Mixed Media. McGraw-Hill Companies, The. New York, NY. 2005. 2400p. ISBN:0-07-141613-7, ISBN13: 978-0-07-141613-9. Dewey:615.58.

Audience: **u,f.**

McKenry, Leda M., et al.   RM300
Mosby's Pharmacology in Nursing. Ed. 22. Ed Tessier & Mary Ann Hogan (Authors). Cloth Text. Elsevier - Health Sciences Division. Philadelphia, PA. 2005. 1360p. ISBN:0-323-03008-4, ISBN13: 978-0-323-03008-3. Dewey:615/.1.

Audience: **l,u,f.**

Parker, Keith L., et al.   RM300.G644 2005
Goodman and Gilman's the Pharmacological Basis of Therapeutics. Ed. 11. Laurence Brunton & John Lazo (Authors). Cloth Text. McGraw-Hill Companies, The. New York, NY. 2005. 1984p. ISBN:0-07-142280-3, ISBN13: 978-0-07-142280-2. Dewey:615/.7. LCCN:2004-063122.

Audience: **l,u,f.**

Plotkin, Mark J. & Shnayerson, Michael   QR177.S43 2002
The Killers Within: The Deadly Rise of Drug-Resistant Bacteria. Trade Cloth. Little Brown & Company. New York, NY. 2002. 336p. ISBN:0-316-71331-7, ISBN13: 978-0-316-71331-3. Dewey:616/.01. LCCN:2002-024177.

Audience: **g,l,u.** *Choice, 2003.*

Pharmacy. Materia Medica

Margolis, Simeon   RM301.12.J636 2005
Johns Hopkins Consumer Guide to Drugs 2005. Trade Cloth. Medletter Associates, Inc. Redding, CT. 2005. 840p. ISBN:1-933087-18-8, ISBN13: 978-1-933087-18-4. Dewey:615/.1. LCCN:2005-277209.

Audience: **g,l,u.**

Medical Economics Staff   RM301.15.P39 2000
The PDR Family Guide to Prescription Drugs: America's Leading Drug Guide for over 60 Years. Ed. 8. Trade Paper. Crown Publishing Group. New York, NY. 2001. 944p. Physicians' Desk Reference Family Guide to Prescription Drugs Ser. ISBN:0-609-80766-8, ISBN13: 978-0-609-80766-8. Dewey:615/.1. LCCN:2002-280129.

Audience: **g,l,u.**

Medical Economics Staff, et al.   PL782.E5F44
PDR for Nutritional Supplements. Sheldon Saul Hendler, David Rorvik & PDR Staff (Authors). Trade Cloth. Thomson Healthcare. Montvale, NJ. 2001. 1200p. ISBN:1-56363-364-7, ISBN13: 978-1-56363-364-5. Dewey:895.6/2/008.

Audience: **g,l,u,f.**

PDR Staff   QV 740 AA1 U11 2006
Usp Di: Advice for the Patient, Drug Information in Lay Language, Vol. 2. Ed. 2. Thomson (Author, Photographer). Trade Cloth. Thomson Healthcare. Montvale, NJ. 2006. 256p. ISBN:1-56363-540-2, ISBN13: 978-1-56363-540-3. Dewey:615.1.

Audience: **g,l,u.**

PDR Staff   QV 740 AA1 U11 2006
Usp Di: Drug Information for the Healthcare Professional. Thomson (Author, Photographer). Trade Cloth. Thomson Healthcare. Montvale, NJ. 2006. ISBN:1-56363-539-9, ISBN13: 978-1-56363-539-7. Dewey:615.1.

Audience: **u,f.**

PDR Staff   QV 740 AA1 U11 2006
Usp Di: Approved Drug Products and Legal Requirements, Vol. 3. Thomson (Author, Photographer). Trade Cloth. Thomson Healthcare. Montvale, NJ. 2006. ISBN:1-56363-541-0, ISBN13: 978-1-56363-541-0. Dewey:615.1.

Audience: **u,f.**

Reader's Digest Editors   QK99.A1M325 1986
Magic and Medicine of Plants. Trade Cloth. Reader's Digest Association, Incorporated, The. Pleasantville, NY. 1986. 464p. ISBN:0-89577-221-3, ISBN13: 978-0-89577-221-3. Dewey:615/.321. LCCN:85-030101.

Audience: **g,l,u.**

Sweetman, Sean   RS141.3
Martindale: The Complete Drug Reference. Ed. 34. Pharmaceutical Press. 2004. ISBN:0-85369-550-4, ISBN13: 978-0-85369-550-9.

Audience: **g,l,u,f.**

Thomson PDR Staff   RM666.H33
PDR® for Herbal Medicines. Ed. 3. Book, Other. Thomson Healthcare. Montvale, NJ. 2004. 1250p. ISBN:1-56363-512-7, ISBN13: 978-1-56363-512-0. Dewey:615.321.

Audience: **g,l,u,f.**

Nursing

     RJ245
☐ Mosby's Nursing Consult: The Latest Knowledge for the Greatest Care.
http://www.nursingconsult.com/offers/standard.html
Elsevier, Inc..

Audience: **u,f.**

Andrist, Linda C., et al. **RT31**
A History of Nursing Ideas. Patrice K. Nicholas & Karen A. Wolf (Authors). Trade Paper. Jones & Bartlett Publishers, Inc. Sudbury, MA. 2005. 504p. ISBN:0-7637-2289-8, ISBN13: 978-0-7637-2289-0. Dewey:610.73/09. LCCN:2005-011493.
Audience: **l,u,f.**

Baer, Ellen D. **RT4.E53 2001**
Enduring Issues in American Nursing. Trade Cloth. Springer Publishing Company, Inc. New York, NY. 2000. x, 377p. ISBN:0-8261-1373-7, ISBN13: 978-0-8261-1373-3. Dewey:610.73/0973. LCCN:00-063528.
Audience: **l,u,f.** *Choice, 2001.*

Betz, Cecily Lynn & Sowden, Linda A. **RJ245.M675 2004**
Mosby's Pediatric Nursing Reference. Ed. 5. Paper Text. Elsevier - Health Sciences Division. Philadelphia, PA. 2003. 832p. ISBN:0-323-01979-X, ISBN13: 978-0-323-01979-8. Dewey:610.73/62. LCCN:2003-054094.
Audience: **l,u,f.**

Boykin, Anne & O'Bryan-Schoenhofer, Savina **RT84.5.B69 2001**
Nursing As Caring: A Model for Transforming Practice. Trade Paper. Jones & Bartlett Publishers, Inc. Sudbury, MA. 2000. 71p. Nursing Theory Ser. ISBN:0-7637-1643-X, ISBN13: 978-0-7637-1643-1. Dewey:610.73. LCCN:00-048369.
Audience: **u,f.**

Cowen, Perle Slavik, et al. **RT41**
Current Issues in Nursing. Ed. 7. Sue Moorhead, Joanne McCloskey Dochterman & Helen Kennedy Grace (Authors). Paper Text. Elsevier - Health Sciences Division. Philadelphia, PA. 2006. 896p. ISBN:0-323-03652-X, ISBN13: 978-0-323-03652-8. Dewey:610.73.
Audience: **l,u,f.**

Curtin, Leah L. **RT4.C87 1996**
Nursing into the 21st Century. Trade Paper. Lippincott Williams & Wilkins. Philadelphia, PA. 1995. 352p. New Nursing Photobooks Ser. ISBN:0-87434-834-X, ISBN13: 978-0-87434-834-7. Dewey:610.73. LCCN:95-000595.
Audience: **l,u.**

Dossey, Barbara Montgomery **RT37.N5D67 2000**
Florence Nightingale: Mystic, Visionary, Reformer. Trade Cloth. Lippincott Williams & Wilkins. Philadelphia, PA. 1999. 448p. ISBN:0-87434-984-2, ISBN13: 978-0-87434-984-9. Dewey:610.73/092 B. LCCN:99-023725.
Audience: **g,l,u,f.** *Choice, 2000.*

Edelman, Carole Lium & Mandle, Carol Lynn **RT90.3.H435 2006**
Health Promotion Throughout the Life Span. Ed. 6. Paper Text. Elsevier - Health Sciences Division. Philadelphia, PA. 2005. 720p. ISBN:0-323-03128-5, ISBN13: 978-0-323-03128-8. Dewey:613/.07/1. LCCN:2006-297243.
Audience: **l,u,f.**

Fahey, Victora A. **RC674.V37 2003**
Vascular Nursing. Ed. 4. Cloth Text. Elsevier - Health Sciences Division. Philadelphia, PA. 2003. 528p. ISBN:0-7216-9567-1, ISBN13: 978-0-7216-9567-9. Dewey:616.1/3.
Audience: **u,f.**

Gulanick, Meg & Myers, Judith L. (Editors) **RT49.N87 2003**
Nursing Care Plans: Nursing Diagnosis and Intervention. Ed. 5. Trade Paper. Elsevier - Health Sciences Division. Philadelphia, PA. 2002. 1136p. ISBN:0-323-01627-8, ISBN13: 978-0-323-01627-8. Dewey:610.73. LCCN:2002-070278.
Audience: **l,u,f.**

Henderson, Virginia A. **RT84.5.H46 1991**
The Nature of Nursing: Reflections after 25 Years. Ed. 2. Margaret Cushman (Foreword by). Paper Text. National League for Nursing Press (N L N Press). New York, NY. 1991. 128p. ISBN:0-88737-494-8, ISBN13: 978-0-88737-494-4. Dewey:610.73. LCCN:93-113247.
Audience: **g,l,u,f.**

Higgins, Loretta P. (Editor), et al. **RT34**
Dictionary of American Nursing Biography. Alice H. Friedman & Joellen Watson Hawkins (Editors), Martin Kaufman (Contribution by). Cloth Text. Greenwood Publishing Group, Inc. Portsmouth, NH. 1988. 472p. ISBN:0-313-24520-7, ISBN13: 978-0-313-24520-6. Dewey:610.73/092/2 B. LCCN:87-025454.
Audience: **g,l,u,f.** *Choice, 1988.*

Hobbs, Colleen A. **RT37.N5H62 1997**
Florence Nightingale. Trade Cloth. Thomson Gale. Farmington Hills, MI. 1997. xiv, 110p. Twayne's English Authors Ser., Vol. 538 ISBN:0-8057-7802-0, ISBN13: 978-0-8057-7802-1. Dewey:610.73/092 B. LCCN:97-018783.
Audience: **g,l,u,f.**

Hockenberry, Marilyn J. **RJ245.H59 2004**
Wong's Clinical Manual of Pediatric Nursing. Ed. 6. Paper Text. Elsevier - Health Sciences Division. Philadelphia, PA. 2003. 784p. ISBN:0-323-01958-7, ISBN13: 978-0-323-01958-3. Dewey:610.73/62. LCCN:2003-052715.
Audience: **l,u,f.**

Joel, Lucille A. & Kelly, Lucie Young **RT82.J635 2003**
Kelly's Dimensions of Professional Nursing. Ed. 9. Paper Text. McGraw-Hill Professional Publishing. New York, NY. 2003. 759p. ISBN:0-07-140639-5, ISBN13: 978-0-07-140639-0. Dewey:610.73. LCCN:2002-043249.
Audience: **l,u,f.**

Kalisch, Philip Arthur, et al. **RT4.K34 2004**
American Nursing: A History. Ed. 4. Beatrice J. Kalisch & Philip Arthur Kalisch (Authors). Trade Cloth. Lippincott Williams & Wilkins. Philadelphia, PA. 2003. 512p. ISBN:0-7817-3969-1, ISBN13: 978-0-7817-3969-6. Dewey:362.1/73/0973. LCCN:2003-054517.
Audience: **g,l,u,f.**

Kee, Joyce LeFever **RT48.5.K44 2005**
Laboratory and Diagnostic Tests with Nursing Implications. Ed. 7. Trade Paper. Prentice Hall PTR. Upper Saddle River, NJ. 2004. 832p. ISBN:0-13-118267-6, ISBN13: 978-0-13-118267-7. Dewey:616.07/56. LCCN:2004-020140.
Audience: **l,u,f.**

Melnyk, Bernadette (Author, Author)   RT42.M44 2005
Evidence-Based Practice in Nursing and Healthcare: A Guide to Best Practice. Trade Paper. Lippincott Williams & Wilkins. Philadelphia, PA. 2004. 624p. ISBN:0-7817-4477-6, ISBN13: 978-0-7817-4477-5. Dewey:610.73. LCCN:2004-009913.
Audience: **u,f.**

Miaskowski, Christine & Buchsel, Patricia   RC266 .O544 1999
Oncology Nursing: Assessment and Clinical Care. Trade Cloth. Elsevier - Health Sciences Division. Philadelphia, PA. 1999. 1700p. ISBN:0-8151-6990-6, ISBN13: 978-0-8151-6990-1. Dewey:610.7/3698. LCCN:2002-275930.
Audience: **u,f.**

Nettina, Sandra M.   RT51.B78 2006
Lippincott Manual of Nursing Practice. Ed. 8. Perfect, Paper over Boards. Lippincott Williams & Wilkins. Philadelphia, PA. 2005. 1888p. ISBN:1-58255-342-4, ISBN13: 978-1-58255-342-9. Dewey:610.73. LCCN:2005-003211.
Audience: **l,u,f.**

O'Brien, Mary Elizabeth   RT85.2.O37 2002
Spirituality in Nursing: Standing on Holy Ground. Ed. 2. Trade Paper. Jones & Bartlett Publishers, Inc. Sudbury, MA. 2003. 408p. Other Nursing Titles of Interest Ser. ISBN:0-7637-0052-5, ISBN13: 978-0-7637-0052-2. Dewey:610.73/01. LCCN:2002-021537.
Audience: **u,f.**

O'Connor, Margaret   RT120.I5
Palliative Care Nursing: A Guide to Practice. Sanchia Aranda (Editor). Trade Paper. Ausmed Publications Pty Ltd.. Ascot Vale, VIC. 2003. 389p. ISBN:0-9577988-4-9, ISBN13: 978-0-9577988-4-7. Dewey:610.7/361.
Audience: **l,u,f.**

Otto, Shirley E.   RC266
Oncology Nursing. Ed. 4. Cloth Text. Elsevier - Health Sciences Division. Philadelphia, PA. 2001. 1074p. ISBN:0-323-01217-5, ISBN13: 978-0-323-01217-1. Dewey:610.73/698. LCCN:00-049545.
Audience: **u,f.**

Pender, Nola J., et al.   RT67
Health Promotion in Nursing Practice. Ed. 5. Carolyn L. Murdaugh & Mary Ann Parsons (Authors). Trade Paper. Prentice Hall PTR. Upper Saddle River, NJ. 2005. 384p. ISBN:0-13-119436-4, ISBN13: 978-0-13-119436-6. Dewey:613. LCCN:2005-277018.
Audience: **l,u,f.**

Perry, Anne Griffin & Potter, Patricia Ann   RT51.P365 2002
Clinical Nursing Skills and Techniques. Ed. 6. Paper Text. Elsevier - Health Sciences Division. Philadelphia, PA. 2005. 1648p. ISBN:0-323-02839-X, ISBN13: 978-0-323-02839-4. Dewey:610.73.
Audience: **l,u,f.**

Rn, Lucy Hood   RT41.L53 2005
Leddy and Pepper's Conceptual Bases of Professional Nursing. Ed. 6. Trade Paper. Lippincott Williams & Wilkins. Philadelphia, PA. 2005. 688p. ISBN:0-7817-6100-X, ISBN13: 978-0-7817-6100-0. Dewey:610.73. LCCN:2005-021548.
Audience: **u,f.**

Sparks, Sheila & Cynthia, Taylor   RT48.6.S66 2005
Nursing Diagnosis Reference Manual. Ed. 6. Trade Paper. Lippincott Williams & Wilkins. Philadelphia, PA. 2004. 768p. ISBN:1-58255-292-4, ISBN13: 978-1-58255-292-7. Dewey:610.73. LCCN:2004-017023.
Audience: **l,u,f.**

Springhouse Staff   RT65.P69 2006
Professional Guide to Diseases. Ed. 8. Trade Cloth. Lippincott Williams & Wilkins. Philadelphia, PA. 2005. 1392p. Professional Guide Ser. ISBN:1-58255-370-X, ISBN13: 978-1-58255-370-2. Dewey:616. LCCN:2004-025162.
Audience: **u,f.**

Ulrich, Susan Puderbaugh & Canale, Suzanne Weyland   RT49
Nursing Care Planning Guides: For Adults in Acute, Extended and Home Care Settings. Ed. 6. Trade Paper. Elsevier - Health Sciences Division. Philadelphia, PA. 2004. 912p. ISBN:0-7216-3923-2, ISBN13: 978-0-7216-3923-9. Dewey:610.73.
Audience: **u,f.**

Watson, Jean & NLN Staff   RT84.5
Nursing: Human Science and Human Care. Paper Text. Jones & Bartlett Publishers, Inc. Sudbury, MA. 1999. 111p. ISBN:0-7637-1111-X, ISBN13: 978-0-7637-1111-5. Dewey:610.7301.
Audience: **l,u.**

Wright, Lorraine M. & Leahey, Maureen   RT120.F34W75 2005
Nurses and Families: A Guide to Family Assessment and Intervention. Ed. 4. Trade Paper, Perfect. F. A. Davis Company. Philadelphia, PA. 2005. 345p. ISBN:0-8036-1211-7, ISBN13: 978-0-8036-1211-2. Dewey:610.73. LCCN:2005-007107.
Audience: **l,u,f.**

Nursing > History. Biography

Bullough, Vern L. (Editor), et al.   RT34.A44 1988
American Nursing: A Biographical Dictionary. Lilli Sentz, Olga Church, Sharon Richardson & Bonnie Bullough (Editors). Trade Cloth. Springer Publishing Company, Inc. New York, NY. 2000. 360p. ISBN:0-8261-1296-X, ISBN13: 978-0-8261-1296-5. Dewey:610.73/092/2 B. LCCN:87-029076.
Audience: **g,l,u.** *Choice, 1988.*

Carnegie, M. Elizabeth   RT83.5
The Path We Tread: Blacks in Nursing Worldwide, 1854-1994. Ed. 3. Paper Text. Jones & Bartlett Publishers, Inc. Sudbury, MA. 1999. 328p. ISBN:0-7637-1247-7, ISBN13: 978-0-7637-1247-1. Dewey:610.73/089/96073.
Audience: **g,l,u,f.**

Dossey, Barbara Montgomery   RT37.N5D67 2000
Florence Nightingale: Mystic, Visionary, Reformer. Trade Cloth. Lippincott Williams & Wilkins. Philadelphia, PA. 1999. 448p. ISBN:0-87434-984-2, ISBN13: 978-0-87434-984-9. Dewey:610.73/092 B. LCCN:99-023725.
Audience: **g,l,u,f.** *Choice, 2000.*

Higgins, Loretta P. (Editor),   **RT34**
  et al.
Dictionary of American Nursing Biography. Alice H. Friedman
& Joellen Watson Hawkins (Editors), Martin Kaufman
(Contribution by). Cloth Text. Greenwood Publishing Group,
Inc. Portsmouth, NH. 1988. 472p. ISBN:0-313-24520-7,
ISBN13: 978-0-313-24520-6. Dewey:610.73/092/2 B.
LCCN:87-025454.
> Audience: **g,l,u,f.** *Choice, 1988.*

Hine, Darlene Clark   **RT83.5.H56 1989**
Black Women in White: Racial Conflict and Cooperation in the
Nursing Profession, 1890-1950. Trade Cloth. Indiana University
Press. Bloomington, IN. 1989. 288p. Blacks in the Diaspora Ser.
ISBN:0-253-32773-3, ISBN13: 978-0-253-32773-4.
Dewey:362.1/73/08996073. LCCN:88-046023.
> Audience: **g,l,u,f.** *Choice, 1990.*

Hobbs, Colleen A.   **RT37.N5H62 1997**
Florence Nightingale. Trade Cloth. Thomson Gale. Farmington
Hills, MI. 1997. xiv, 110p. Twayne's English Authors Ser., Vol.
538 ISBN:0-8057-7802-0, ISBN13: 978-0-8057-7802-1.
Dewey:610.73/092 B. LCCN:97-018783.
> Audience: **g,l,u,f.**

Kalisch, Philip Arthur, et al.   **RT4.K34 2004**
American Nursing: A History. Ed. 4. Beatrice J. Kalisch &
Philip Arthur Kalisch (Authors). Trade Cloth. Lippincott
Williams & Wilkins. Philadelphia, PA. 2003. 512p.
ISBN:0-7817-3969-1, ISBN13: 978-0-7817-3969-6.
Dewey:362.1/73/0973. LCCN:2003-054517.
> Audience: **g,l,u,f.**

Keegan, Lynn & Dossey,   **RT34.K44 1998**
  Barbara Montgomery
Profiles of Nurse Healers. Ed. 1. Paper Text. Thomson Delmar
Learning. Albany, NY. 1997. 256p. Nurse as Healer Ser.
ISBN:0-8273-7958-7, ISBN13: 978-0-8273-7958-9.
Dewey:610.73/092/2 B. LCCN:97-007960.
> Audience: **g,l,u,f.**

Schorr, Thelma M. &   **RT4.S375 1999**
  Kennedy, Maureen Shawn
100 Years of American Nursing: Celebrating a Century of
Caring. Trade Cloth. Lippincott Williams & Wilkins.
Philadelphia, PA. 1999. 240p. ISBN:0-7817-1865-1, ISBN13:
978-0-7817-1865-3. Dewey:610.73/0973. LCCN:99-010472.
> Audience: **g,l,u,f.**

Nursing > General Works

Andrist, Linda C., et al.   **RT31**
A History of Nursing Ideas. Patrice K. Nicholas & Karen A.
Wolf (Authors). Trade Paper. Jones & Bartlett Publishers, Inc.
Sudbury, MA. 2005. 504p. ISBN:0-7637-2289-8, ISBN13:
978-0-7637-2289-0. Dewey:610.73/09. LCCN:2005-011493.
> Audience: **l,u,f.**

Friedman, Marilyn M., et al.   **RT120.F34F75 2003**
Family Nursing: Research, Theory, and Practice. Ed. 5. Vicky R.
Bowden & Elaine Jones (Authors). Trade Paper. Prentice Hall
PTR. Upper Saddle River, NJ. 2002. 714p.
ISBN:0-13-060824-6, ISBN13: 978-0-13-060824-6.
Dewey:610.73. LCCN:2002-025198.
> Audience: **u,f.**

Nursing > Study. Teaching

DeYoung, Sandra   **RT71.D553 2003**
Teaching Strategies for Nurse Educators. Trade Paper. Prentice
Hall PTR. Upper Saddle River, NJ. 2002. 280p.
ISBN:0-13-045216-5, ISBN13: 978-0-13-045216-0.
Dewey:610.73/071. LCCN:2002-022005.
> Audience: **u,f.**

Frank-Stromborg, Marilyn   **RT81.5.I57 2004**
  & Olsen, Sharon J. (Editors)
Instruments for Clinical Health-Care Research. Ed. 3. Marilyn
Frank-Stromborg & Sharon J. Olsen (Translators). Trade Paper.
Jones & Bartlett Publishers, Inc. Sudbury, MA. 2003. 713p.
ISBN:0-7637-2252-9, ISBN13: 978-0-7637-2252-4.
Dewey:610.73/072. LCCN:2003-015429.
> Audience: **u,f.**

Keating, Sarah B.   **RT71.K43 2005**
Curriculum Development and Evaluation in Nursing. Trade
Paper. Lippincott Williams & Wilkins. Philadelphia, PA. 2005.
448p. ISBN:0-7817-4770-8, ISBN13: 978-0-7817-4770-7.
Dewey:610.73/071/1. LCCN:2004-025159.
> Audience: **f.**

Morse, Janice M. (Editor)   **RT81.5.C75 1994**
Critical Issues in Qualitative Research Methods. Trade Cloth.
SAGE Publications, Inc. Thousand Oaks, CA. 1993. 401p.
ISBN:0-8039-5042-X, ISBN13: 978-0-8039-5042-9.
Dewey:610.73/072. LCCN:93-034535.
> Audience: **u,f.**

Polit, Denise F.   **RT81.5.P63 2006**
Essentials of Nursing Research: Methods, Appraisal, and
Utilization. Ed. 6. Trade Paper. Lippincott Williams & Wilkins.
Philadelphia, PA. 2005. 336p. ISBN:0-7817-7679-1, ISBN13:
978-0-7817-7679-0. Dewey:610.73/07/2.
> Audience: **u,f.**

Wood, Marilynn J., et al.   **RT81.5.W647 2005**
Basic Steps in Planning Nursing Research. Ed. 6. Janet C. Kerr
& Pamela J. Brink (Authors). Trade Paper. Jones & Bartlett
Publishers, Inc. Sudbury, MA. 2005. 537p.
ISBN:0-7637-3478-0, ISBN13: 978-0-7637-3478-7.
Dewey:610.73/072. LCCN:2005-007398.
> Audience: **l,u,f.**

Nursing > Philosophy. Ethics. Psychological Aspects

Barnum, Barbara Stevens   **RT85.2.B37 2003**
Spirituality in Nursing: From Traditional to New Age. Ed. 2.
Laminated. Springer Publishing Company, Inc. New York, NY.
2003. 216p. ISBN:0-8261-9181-9, ISBN13: 978-0-8261-9181-6.
Dewey:610.73/01. LCCN:2003-042361.
> Audience: **u,f.**

Bishop, Anne & Scudder,   **RT85.B57 2001**
  Jack
Nursing Ethics: Holistic Caring Practice. Ed. 2. Trade Paper.
Jones & Bartlett Publishers, Inc. Sudbury, MA. 2000. 136p.
Nursing Theory Ser. ISBN:0-7637-1426-7, ISBN13:
978-0-7637-1426-0. Dewey:174/.2. LCCN:00-037113.
> Audience: **u,f.**

Burkhardt, Margaret A. &　　　　　**RT85.B766 2002**
Nathaniel, Alvita K.
Ethics and Issues in Contemporary Nursing. Ed. 2. Paper Text. Thomson Delmar Learning. Albany, NY. 2001. 456p. ISBN:0-7668-3629-0, ISBN13: 978-0-7668-3629-7. Dewey:174/.2. LCCN:2001-032503.

Audience: **l,u.**

Chinn, Peggy L. & Watson,　　　　　　　**RT42**
Jean
Art and Aesthetics in Nursing. Trade Paper. Jones & Bartlett Publishers, Inc. Sudbury, MA. 1994. 363p. ISBN:0-88737-609-6, ISBN13: 978-0-88737-609-2. Dewey:610.73.

Audience: **u,f.**

Clifford, Collette & Rutter,　　　　**RT87.S49 C37 2000**
Michael
Caring for Sexuality in Health and Illness. Trade Paper. Harcourt Health Sciences Group. Saint Louis, MO. 2000. 320p. ISBN:0-443-06443-1, ISBN13: 978-0-443-06443-2. Dewey:362.1.

Audience: **u,f.**

McIntyre, Rosemary　　　　　　　　**R726.8**
Nursing Support for Families of Dying Patients. Trade Paper. John Wiley & Sons, Inc. Hoboken, NJ. 2005. 200p. ISBN:1-86156-270-5, ISBN13: 978-1-86156-270-8. Dewey:362.1/75.

Audience: **l,u,f.**

O'Brien, Mary Elizabeth　　　　**RT85.2.O37 2002**
Spirituality in Nursing: Standing on Holy Ground. Ed. 2. Trade Paper. Jones & Bartlett Publishers, Inc. Sudbury, MA. 2003. 408p. Other Nursing Titles of Interest Ser. ISBN:0-7637-0052-5, ISBN13: 978-0-7637-0052-2. Dewey:610.73/01. LCCN:2002-021537.

Audience: **u,f.**

Nursing > Special Topics

Alligood, Martha Raile &　　　　　　**RT84.5**
Marriner Tomey, Ann
Nursing Theory: Utilization and Application. Ed. 3. Paper Text. Elsevier - Health Sciences Division. Philadelphia, PA. 2005. 560p. ISBN:0-323-03133-1, ISBN13: 978-0-323-03133-2. Dewey:610.73.

Audience: **u,f.**

Carter, Bernadette (Editor)　　　**RT87.P35P48 1998**
Perspectives on Pain: Mapping the Territory. Trade Paper. Oxford University Press, Inc. New York, NY. 1998. 336p. An Arnold Publication Ser. ISBN:0-340-69254-5, ISBN13: 978-0-340-69254-7. Dewey:616.0472. LCCN:98-191558.

Audience: **u,f.**

Gossfeld, Lynn M., et al.　　　　**RC280.G5S65 2000**
Women and Cancer: A Gynecologic Oncology Nursing Perspective. Ed. 2. Beth Colvin Huff & Giselle Moore-Higgs (Authors), Giselle J. Moore (Editor), Society of Gynecologic Nurse Oncologists Staff (Contribution by). Trade Cloth. Jones & Bartlett Publishers, Inc. Sudbury, MA. 2000. 608p. Series in Oncology ISBN:0-7637-1166-7, ISBN13: 978-0-7637-1166-5. Dewey:616.99/465. LCCN:99-040657.

Audience: **u,f.**

Institute of Medicine (U.S.)　　**RT87.S24K4473 2005**
Staff (Contribution by)
Keeping Patients Safe: Transforming the Work Environment of Nurses. Trade Cloth. National Academies Press. Washington, DC. 2005. vii, 32p. The Richard and Hinda Rosenthal Lectures, Vol. 2003 ISBN:0-309-09441-0, ISBN13: 978-0-309-09441-2. Dewey:362.17/3 22. LCCN:2005-275669.

Audience: **u,f.**

Leininger, Madeleine M. &　　　**RT86.54.C85 2006**
McFarland, Marilyn
Culture Care Diversity and Universality: A Worldwide Nursing Theory. Ed. 2. Trade Paper. Jones & Bartlett Publishers, Inc. Sudbury, MA. 2005. 413p. ISBN:0-7637-3437-3, ISBN13: 978-0-7637-3437-4. Dewey:610.73/01. LCCN:2005-023891.

Audience: **u,f.**

Leininger, Madeleine &　　　　　　**RT86.54**
McFarland, Marilyn R.
Transcultural Nursing. Ed. 3. Paper Text. McGraw-Hill Professional Publishing. New York, NY. 2002. 621p. ISBN:0-07-135397-6, ISBN13: 978-0-07-135397-7. Dewey:610.73. LCCN:2001-042559.

Audience: **l,u,f.**

Lipson, Juliene G. & Dibble,　　　　**RT86.54**
Suzanne L. (Editors)
Culture and Clinical Care. Ed. 2. Trade Paper. UCSF Nursing Press. San Francisco, CA. 2005. 487p. ISBN:0-943671-22-1, ISBN13: 978-0-943671-22-2. Dewey:362.17.

Audience: **l,u,f.**

Mason, Diana J., et al.　　　　　　**RT86.5.P58**
Policy and Politics in Nursing and Health Care. Ed. 5. Judith K. Leavitt & Mary W. Chaffee (Authors). Paper Text. Elsevier - Health Sciences Division. Philadelphia, PA. 2006. 1104p. ISBN:1-4160-2314-3, ISBN13: 978-1-4160-2314-2. Dewey:362.173.

Audience: **u,f.**

Orem, Dorthea E., et al.　　　　　**RT84.5.O73 2001**
Nursing: Concepts of Practice. Ed. 6. Susan G. Taylor & Kathie McLaughlin Renpenning (Authors). Trade Cloth. Elsevier - Health Sciences Division. Philadelphia, PA. 2001. 542p. ISBN:0-323-00864-X, ISBN13: 978-0-323-00864-8. Dewey:610.73. LCCN:00-049614.

Audience: **l,u.**

Tomey, Ann Marriner &　　　　　**RT84.5.N9 2005**
Alligood, Martha Raile
Nursing Theorists and Their Work. Ed. 6. Paper Text. Elsevier - Health Sciences Division. Philadelphia, PA. 2005. 848p. ISBN:0-323-03010-6, ISBN13: 978-0-323-03010-6. Dewey:610.7301.

Audience: **u,f.**

Nursing > Community Health Nursing

Allender, Judith Ann　　　　　　**RT98.S68 2005**
(Author, Author)
Community Health Nursing: Promoting and Protecting the Public's Health. Ed. 6. Trade Cloth. Lippincott Williams & Wilkins. Philadelphia, PA. 2004. 992p. ISBN:0-7817-4449-0, ISBN13: 978-0-7817-4449-2. Dewey:610.73/43. LCCN:2004-007777.

Audience: **u,f.**

Anderson, Elizabeth T. &   RT98.A533 2004
  McFarlane, Judith M.
Community As Partner: Theory and Practice in Nursing. Ed. 4.
Trade Paper. Lippincott Williams & Wilkins. Philadelphia, PA.
2003. 480p. ISBN:0-7817-4454-7, ISBN13: 978-0-7817-4454-6.
Dewey:610.73/43. LCCN:2003-054599.

                           Audience: **l,u,f.**

Porche, Demetrius James   RT97.P67 2004
Public and Community Health Nursing Practice: A
Population-Based Approach. Cloth Text. SAGE Publications,
Inc. Thousand Oaks, CA. 2003. 528p. ISBN:0-7619-2483-3,
ISBN13: 978-0-7619-2483-8. Dewey:610.73/4.
LCCN:2003-016654.

                           Audience: **u,f.**

Stanhope, Marcia &   RT98
  Lancaster, Jeanette
Community and Public Health Nursing. Ed. 6. Cloth Text.
Elsevier - Health Sciences Division. Philadelphia, PA. 2003.
1232p. ISBN:0-323-02240-5, ISBN13: 978-0-323-02240-8.
Dewey:610.73/43.

                           Audience: **u,f.**

Nursing > Emergency Nursing

Emergency Nurses   RT120
  Association Staff & Newberry, Lorene
Sheehy's Emergency Nursing: Principles and Practice. Ed. 5.
Trade Paper. Elsevier - Health Sciences Division. Philadelphia,
PA. 2002. 856p. ISBN:0-323-01684-7, ISBN13:
978-0-323-01684-1. Dewey:610.73/61. LCCN:2003-270583.
                           Audience: **u,f.**

Fultz, Julia H. & Sturt,   RT120.E4
  Patty Ann
Mosby's Emergency Nursing Reference. Ed. 3. Paper Text.
Elsevier - Health Sciences Division. Philadelphia, PA. 2005.
1024p. ISBN:0-323-03150-1, ISBN13: 978-0-323-03150-9.
Dewey:616.025.

                           Audience: **u,f.**

Proehl, Jean A.   RT120.E4A285 2004
Emergency Nursing Procedures. Ed. 3. Trade Paper. Elsevier -
Health Sciences Division. Philadelphia, PA. 2004. 896p.
ISBN:0-7216-0341-6, ISBN13: 978-0-7216-0341-4.
Dewey:616.025. LCCN:2003-045941.

                           Audience: **u,f.**

Other Systems of Medicine

Blumenthal, Mark   RM666.H33
The Complete German Commission E Monographs: Therapeutic
Guide to Herbal Medicines. Trade Cloth. Integrative Medicine
Communications. Newton, MA. 1999. ISBN:0-9670772-7-3,
ISBN13: 978-0-9670772-7-7. Dewey:615/.321.

                           Audience: **u,f.**

Eliopoulos, Charlotte K.   RT120.I5
Integrating Conventional and Alternative Therapies: Holistic
Care for Chronic Conditions. Trade Paper. Elsevier - Health
Sciences Division. Philadelphia, PA. 1999. 300p.
ISBN:0-8151-2793-6, ISBN13: 978-0-8151-2793-2.
Dewey:610.7/361.

                           Audience: **u,f.**

Faass, Nancy   R733.I57 2001
Integrating Complementary Medicine into Health Systems.
Trade Cloth. Jones & Bartlett Publishers, Inc. Sudbury, MA.
2003. 763p. ISBN:0-8342-1216-1, ISBN13: 978-0-8342-1216-9.
Dewey:362.1. LCCN:00-069523.

                           Audience: **u,f.**

Freeman, Lyn W.   R733
Mosby's Complementary and Alternative Medicine: A
Research-Based Approach. Ed. 2. Cloth Text. Elsevier - Health
Sciences Division. Philadelphia, PA. 2004. 608p.
ISBN:0-323-02626-5, ISBN13: 978-0-323-02626-0.
Dewey:615.5.

                           Audience: **u,f.**

Jonas, Wayne B. & Levin,   R733.E87 1999
  Jeffrey S.
Essentials of Complementary and Alternative Medicine. Paper
Text. Lippincott Williams & Wilkins. Philadelphia, PA. 1999.
604p. ISBN:0-683-30674-X, ISBN13: 978-0-683-30674-3.
Dewey:615.5. LCCN:98-022365.

                           Audience: **l,u,f.**

Lippincott Williams and   R733.N87 2003
  Wilkins Staff (Contribution by)
Nurse's Handbook of Alternative and Complementary Therapies.
Ed. 2. Trade Paper. Lippincott Williams & Wilkins.
Philadelphia, PA. 2002. 480p. ISBN:1-58255-166-9, ISBN13:
978-1-58255-166-1. Dewey:615.5. LCCN:2002-007899.
                           Audience: **l,u,f.**

Micozzi, Mark S (Editor)   R733
Fundamentals of Complementary and Integrative Medicine. Ed.
3. Saunders Elsevier. 2006. ISBN:1-4160-2583-9, ISBN13:
978-1-4160-2583-2.

                           Audience: **l,u.**

Snyder, Mariah &   RT41.I53 2006
  Lindquist, Ruth
Complementary/Alternative Therapies in Nursing. Ed. 5. Trade
Cloth. Springer. New York, NY. 2006. ISBN:0-8261-1447-4,
ISBN13: 978-0-8261-1447-1. Dewey:610.73.
LCCN:2005-027206.

                           Audience: **l,u,f.**

End of Life Care

Beresford, Larry &   R726.8
  Kubler-Ross
The Hospice Handbook: A Complete Guide. Trade Paper. Little
Brown & Company. New York, NY. 1993. 192p.
ISBN:0-316-09138-3, ISBN13: 978-0-316-09138-1.
Dewey:362.1/75. LCCN:92-032814.

                           Audience: **g,l,u,f.**

Byock, Ira   HQ1073
Dying Well: Peace and Possibilities at the End of Life. Trade
Paper. Penguin Group (USA) Inc. New York, NY. 1998. 320p.
ISBN:1-57322-657-2, ISBN13: 978-1-57322-657-8.
Dewey:306.88. LCCN:96-032898.

                           Audience: **g,l,u,f.**

Callanan, Maggie & Kelley,   BF789.O4
  Patricia
Final Gifts: Understanding the Special Awareness, Needs, and
Communications of the Dying. Trade Paper. Bantam Books.

New York, NY. 1997. 256p. ISBN:0-553-37876-7, ISBN13: 978-0-553-37876-4. Dewey:155.937. LCCN:91-043191.

Audience: **g,u,f.**

Frankel, Richard M.   **R723.B495 2003**
  (Editor), et al.
The Biopsychosocial Approach: Past, Present, and Future. Timothy E. Quill & Susan H. McDaniel (Editors). Trade Paper. University of Rochester Press. Rochester, NY. 2003. xii, 298p. ISBN:1-58046-061-5, ISBN13: 978-1-58046-061-3. Dewey:610/.1. LCCN:2003-004093.

Audience: **u,f.**

Kaufman, Sharon R.   **R726.8.K385 2005**
And a Time to Die: How American Hospitals Shape the End of Life. Trade Cloth. Simon & Schuster. New York, NY. 2005. 416p. ISBN:0-7432-6476-2, ISBN13: 978-0-7432-6476-1. Dewey:362.17/5. LCCN:2004-052530.

Audience: **g,l,u,f.** *Choice, 2005.*

Kessler, David   **BF789.D4K47 2000**
The Needs of the Dying: A Guide for Bringing Hope, Comfort, and Love to Life's Final Chapter. Trade Paper. HarperCollins Publishers. New York, NY. 2000. 224p. ISBN:0-06-095821-9, ISBN13: 978-0-06-095821-3. Dewey:155.9/37. LCCN:00-038325.

Audience: **g,l,u.**

Kinzbrunner, Barry M.,   **R726.8**
  et al.
20 Common Problems: End-of-Life Care. Neil J. Weinreb & Joel S. Policzer (Authors). Trade Paper. McGraw-Hill Professional Publishing. New York, NY. 2001. 512p. ISBN:0-07-034883-9, ISBN13: 978-0-07-034883-7. Dewey:362.1/75. LCCN:2001-030452.

Audience: **l,u,f.**

Lynn, Joanne & Schuster,   **R726.8.L96 2000**
  Janice Lynch (Editors)
Improving Care for the End of Life: A Sourcebook for Health Care Managers and Clinicians. Trade Cloth. Oxford University Press, Inc. New York, NY. 2000. 398p. ISBN:0-19-511661-5, ISBN13: 978-0-19-511661-8. Dewey:362.1/75. LCCN:99-045308.

Audience: **l,u,f.**

Nuland, Sherwin B.   **QP87**
How We Die: Reflections on Life's Final Chapter. Trade Paper. Knopf Publishing Group. New York, NY. 1995. 304p. ISBN:0-679-74244-1, ISBN13: 978-0-679-74244-9. Dewey:616.07/8.

Audience: **g,l,u,f.**

Tallmer, Margot, et al.   **R726.8**
The Life-Threatened Elderly. Austin H. Kutscher, Elizabeth R. Prichard & Robert DeBellis (Authors), Mahlon S. Hale & Ivan K. Goldberg (Editors). Trade Cloth. Columbia University Press. New York, NY. 1984. 359p. ISBN:0-231-04966-8, ISBN13: 978-0-231-04966-5. Dewey:362.1/75/0880565. LCCN:83-014263.

Audience: **l,u,f.** *B*

Werth, James L. Jr. (Editor)   **R726.8.P796 2005**
Psychosocial Issues near the End of Life: A Resource for Professional Care Providers. Perfect, Paper over Boards, Dust Jacket. American Psychological Association. Washington, DC.

2005. 258p. ISBN:1-59147-236-9, ISBN13: 978-1-59147-236-0. Dewey:362.17/5. LCCN:2005-002346.

Audience: **l,u,f.**

Communicable Diseases

Committee on the   **RC313**
  Elimination of Tuberculosis in the United States, et al.
Ending Neglect: The Elimination of Tuberculosis in the United States. Division of Health Promotion and Disease Prevention Staff & Institute of Medicine Staff (Authors), Lawrence Geiter (Editor). Cloth Text. National Academies Press. Washington, DC. 2000. 292p. ISBN:0-309-07028-7, ISBN13: 978-0-309-07028-7. Dewey:614.5/42/0973. LCCN:00-056115.

Audience: **g,l,u,f.**

Fenn, Elizabeth Anne   **RC183.49.F46 2001**
Pox Americana: The Great Smallpox Epidemic of 1775-1782. Cloth over Boards. Farrar, Straus & Giroux. New York, NY. 2001. 320p. ISBN:0-8090-7820-1, ISBN13: 978-0-8090-7820-2. Dewey:614.5/21/097309033. LCCN:2001-016886.

Audience: **g,l,u,f.** *Choice, 2002.*

Heymann, David   **RA643 .C65 2004**
Control of Communicable Diseases Manual. Ed. 18. Perfect, Paper over Boards. American Public Health Association Publications. Washington, DC. 2004. 700p. ISBN:0-87553-035-4, ISBN13: 978-0-87553-035-2. Dewey:614.5.

Audience: **l,u,f.**

Katz, Samuel L., et al.   **RJ401.K7 2004**
Krugman's Infectious Diseases of Children. Ed. 11. Anne A. Gershon & Peter J. Hotez (Authors). Trade Cloth. Elsevier - Health Sciences Division. Philadelphia, PA. 2003. 1072p. ISBN:0-323-01756-8, ISBN13: 978-0-323-01756-5. Dewey:618.92/9. LCCN:2003-059984.

Audience: **l,u,f.**

Kelly, John   **RC172.K445 2005**
The Great Mortality: An Intimate History of the Black Death, the Most Devastating Plague of All Time. Trade Cloth. HarperCollins Publishers. New York, NY. 2005. 384p. ISBN:0-06-000692-7, ISBN13: 978-0-06-000692-1. Dewey:614.5/732. LCCN:2004-054213.

Audience: **g,l,u,f.**

Keyes, Daniel C. (Editor),   **RC88.9.T47M43 2005**
  et al.
Medical Response to Terrorism. Jonathan L. Burstein, Richard B. Schwartz & Raymond E. Swienton (Editors). Trade Cloth. Lippincott Williams & Wilkins. Philadelphia, PA. 2004. 581p. ISBN:0-7817-4986-7, ISBN13: 978-0-7817-4986-2. Dewey:362.18. LCCN:2004-020228.

Audience: **g,l,u,f.**

Kolata, Gina   **RA644.I6**
Flu: The Story of the Great Influenza Pandemic of 1918 and the Search for the Virus That Caused It. Trade Cloth. DIANE Publishing Company. Collingdale, PA. 2002. 330p. ISBN:0-7567-5625-1, ISBN13: 978-0-7567-5625-3. Dewey:614.5/18/0904.

Audience: **g,l,u,f.** *Choice, 2000.*

Formats: Web: ☐   Ebook: **e**   CD/DVD-ROM: 🎯   BCL3: *B*

Mandell, Gerald L., et al.   **RC111**
Principles and Practice of Infectious Diseases: Text with
Continually Updated Online Reference. Ed. 6. John E. Bennett
& Raphael Dolin (Authors). Mixed Media, Trade Cloth, Digital,
Other. Elsevier - Health Sciences Division. Philadelphia, PA.
2004. 4000p. ISBN:0-443-06673-6, ISBN13:
978-0-443-06673-3. Dewey:616.9.

Audience: **l,u,f.**

Mayhall, C. Glen   **RA969.H635 2004**
Hospital Epidemiology and Infection Control. Ed. 3. Trade
Cloth. Lippincott Williams & Wilkins. Philadelphia, PA. 2004.
2060p. ISBN:0-7817-4258-7, ISBN13: 978-0-7817-4258-0.
Dewey:614.4/4. LCCN:2003-065937.

Audience: **u,f.**

Oshinsky, David M.   **RC181.U5 O83 2005**
Polio: An American Story. Trade Cloth. Oxford University
Press, Inc. New York, NY. 2005. 352p. ISBN:0-19-515294-8,
ISBN13: 978-0-19-515294-4. Dewey:614.5/49/0973.
LCCN:2004-025249.

Audience: **g,l,u,f.** *Choice, 2005.*

Remington, Jack S., et al.   **RJ275 .I54 2006**
Infectious Diseases of the Fetus and the Newborn Infant. Ed. 6.
Carol Baker, Jerome O. Klein & Christopher B. Wilson
(Authors). Trade Cloth. Elsevier - Health Sciences Division.
Philadelphia, PA. 2005. 1328p. ISBN:0-7216-0537-0, ISBN13:
978-0-7216-0537-1. Dewey:618.92/01. LCCN:2004-051422.

Audience: **u,f.**

Schlossberg, David   **RC311**
Tuberculosis and Nontuberculosis Mycobacterial Infections. Ed.
5. Cloth Text. McGraw-Hill Professional Publishing. New York,
NY. 2005. 400p. ISBN:0-07-143913-7, ISBN13:
978-0-07-143913-8. Dewey:616.99/5. LCCN:2005-052241.

Audience: **u,f.**

Wilson, Daniel J.   **RC180.2.W47 2005**
Living with Polio: The Epidemic and Its Survivors. Trade Cloth.
University of Chicago Press. Chicago, IL. 2005. 312p.
ISBN:0-226-90103-3, ISBN13: 978-0-226-90103-9.
Dewey:616.8/35. LCCN:2004-024170.

Audience: **g,l,u,f.**

Medical Genetics

Jenkins, Jean F.   **RB155.7.J46**
Nursing Care in the Genomic Era: A Care Based Approach.
Trade Paper. Jones & Bartlett Publishers, Inc. Sudbury, MA.
2005. 288p. ISBN:0-7637-3324-5, ISBN13: 978-0-7637-3324-7.
Dewey:616/.042.

Audience: **l,u,f.**

Korf, Bruce R.   **RB155.K666 2006**
Human Genetics: A Problem-Based Approach. Ed. 3. Trade
Paper. Blackwell Publishing, Inc. Malden, MA. 2006. 320p.
ISBN:0-632-04656-2, ISBN13: 978-0-632-04656-0.
Dewey:616/.042. LCCN:2006-014205.

Audience: **l,u.**

Mahowald, Mary B., et al.   **RB155**
Genetics in the Clinic: Clinical, Ethical, and Social Implications
for Primary Care. Timothy Aspinwall, Victor A. McKusick &
Angela Scheuerle (Authors). Trade Paper. Elsevier - Health

Sciences Division. Philadelphia, PA. 2001. 315p.
ISBN:0-323-01203-5, ISBN13: 978-0-323-01203-4.
Dewey:616.042. LCCN:00-135004.

Audience: **u,f.**

Milunsky, Aubrey   **RG628.G46 2004**
Genetic Disorders and the Fetus: Diagnosis, Prevention, and
Treatment. Ed. 5. Trade Cloth. Johns Hopkins University Press.
Baltimore, MD. 2004. 1248p. ISBN:0-8018-7928-0, ISBN13:
978-0-8018-7928-9. Dewey:618.3/2042. LCCN:2003-018312.

Audience: **u,f.**

Scriver, Charles R. (Editor)   **RC627.8.M47 2001**
The Metabolic and Molecular Bases of Inherited Disease. Ed. 8.
Trade Cloth. McGraw-Hill Companies, The. New York, NY.
2001. xlvii, 6338p. ISBN:0-07-136320-3, ISBN13:
978-0-07-136320-4. Dewey:616/.042. LCCN:00-060957.

Audience: **u,f.**

Tudge, Colin   **QH437.T833 2001**
The Impact of the Gene: From Mendel's Peas to Designer
Babies. Trade Cloth. Farrar, Straus & Giroux. New York, NY.
2001. 256p. ISBN:0-374-17523-3, ISBN13: 978-0-374-17523-8.
Dewey:576.5. LCCN:00-067306.

Audience: **g,l,u.** *Choice, 2002.*

Allied Health

                                                  R725.5
Health Care Worker's Primer on Professionalism. Cloth Text.
Prentice Hall PTR. Upper Saddle River, NJ. 1999. 144p.
ISBN:0-13-021416-7, ISBN13: 978-0-13-021416-4.
Dewey:610.69.

Audience: **l,u.**

Badasch, Shirley A. &   **R697.A4.B33 2004**
  Chesebro, Doreen S.
Introduction to Health Occupations: Today's Health Care
Worker. Ed. 6. Trade Cloth. Prentice Hall PTR. Upper Saddle
River, NJ. 2003. 768p. ISBN:0-13-045745-0, ISBN13:
978-0-13-045745-5. Dewey:610.69. LCCN:2002-038100.

Audience: **g,l,u.**

Ramsden, Elsa   **R726.5**
The Person As Patient: Psychosocial Perspectives for the Health
Care Professional. Trade Paper. W. B. Saunders Company.
London, 1999. 288p. ISBN:0-7020-2230-6, ISBN13:
978-0-7020-2230-2. Dewey:610.1/9.

Audience: **l,u.**

Simmers, Louise   **R697.A4S5 2003**
Diversified Health Occupations. Ed. 6. Cloth Text. Thomson
Delmar Learning. Albany, NY. 2003. 960p.
ISBN:1-4018-1456-5, ISBN13: 978-1-4018-1456-4.
Dewey:610.69. LCCN:2002-041716.

Audience: **l,u.**

Stanfield, Peggy S. & Hui,   **R690.S727 2002**
  Y. H.
Introduction to the Health Professions. Ed. 4. Trade Paper. Jones
& Bartlett Publishers, Inc. Sudbury, MA. 2002. 529p. Health
Education Ser. ISBN:0-7637-0049-5, ISBN13:
978-0-7637-0049-2. Dewey:610.69. LCCN:2002-283104.

Audience: **g,l,u.**

Allied Health > Emergency Medical Technician

American Academy of   **RC86.7.A43 2005**
Orthopaedic Surgeons Staff
Emergency Care and Transportation of the Sick and Injured. Ed. 9. Trade Paper, Audio, Other. Jones & Bartlett Publishers, Inc. Sudbury, MA. 2005. 1000p. ISBN:0-7637-4738-6, ISBN13: 978-0-7637-4738-1. Dewey:616.02/5. LCCN:2004-056909.

Audience: **l,u.**

American College of   **RC86.7 .P363**
Emergency Physicians Staff
Paramedic Field Care: A Complaint Based Approach. Peter T. Pons & Debra Cason (Editors). Trade Paper. Mosby, Inc. Saint Louis, MO. 1997. ISBN:0-8151-0088-4, ISBN13: 978-0-8151-0088-1. Dewey:616.02/5.

Audience: **l,u.**

Azzara, Alan J.   **RM300 .A99 2003**
PreHospital Providers' Guide to Medication. Trade Cloth. Elsevier - Health Sciences Division. Philadelphia, PA. 2003. 544p. ISBN:0-323-02440-8, ISBN13: 978-0-323-02440-2. Dewey:615.1.

Audience: **l,u.**

Eichelberger, Martin R.,   **RJ370.P4264 1998**
et al.
Pediatric Emergencies: A Manual for Prehospital Care Providers. Ed. 2. Geraldine S. Pratsch, Jane W. Ball & John R. Clark (Authors), Martin R. Eichelberger & Geraldine S. Pratsch (Editors). Trade Paper. Prentice Hall PTR. Upper Saddle River, NJ. 1997. 272p. ISBN:0-8359-5123-5, ISBN13: 978-0-8359-5123-4. Dewey:618.9/2/0025. LCCN:97-006025.

Audience: **l,u.**

Goldfrank, Lewis R., et al.   **RA1224.5.G65 2006**
Toxicologic Emergencies. Ed. 8. Neal E. Flomenbaum, Mary Ann Howland, Robert S. Hoffman & Richard S. Weisman (Authors). Trade Cloth. McGraw-Hill Professional Publishing. New York, NY. 2006. 2064p. ISBN:0-07-143763-0, ISBN13: 978-0-07-143763-9. Dewey:615.9. LCCN:2006-044926.

Audience: **u,f.**

NAEMT   **RC86.7**
PHTLS Basic and Advanced Prehospital Trauma Life Support. Ed. 6. Paper Text. Elsevier - Health Sciences Division. Philadelphia, PA. 2006. 624p. ISBN:0-323-03331-8, ISBN13: 978-0-323-03331-2. Dewey:616.02/5.

Audience: **l,u.**

Westfal, Richard E. (Editor)   **RC86.8.W474 1997**
Paramedic Protocols. Trade Paper. McGraw-Hill Professional Publishing. New York, NY. 1996. 526p. ISBN:0-07-069318-8, ISBN13: 978-0-07-069318-0. Dewey:616/.025. LCCN:96-023226.

Audience: **l,u.**

Allied Health > Medical Assistant

Bonewit-West, Kathy   **R728.8**
Clinical Procedures for Medical Assistants. Ed. 6. Cloth Text. Elsevier - Health Sciences Division. Philadelphia, PA. 2003. 896p. ISBN:0-7216-0286-X, ISBN13: 978-0-7216-0286-8. Dewey:610.7/37.

Audience: **l,u.**

Molle, Elizabeth A.   **R728.8**
Lippincott Williams and Wilkins' Comprehensive Medical Assisting. Ed. 2. Book, Other. Lippincott Williams & Wilkins. Philadelphia, PA. 2005. ISBN:0-7817-5671-5, ISBN13: 978-0-7817-5671-6. Dewey:610.73/7.

Audience: **l,u.**

Pooler, Marilyn, et al.   **R728.8.T466 2005**
Thomson Delmar Learning's Comprehensive Medical Assisting: Administrative and Clinical Competencies. Ed. 3. Carol Tamparo, Wilburta Lindh & Barbara M. Dahl (Authors). Cloth Text. Thomson Delmar Learning. Albany, NY. 2005. 1360p. ISBN:1-4018-8124-6, ISBN13: 978-1-4018-8124-5. Dewey:610.73/7069. LCCN:2005-050629.

Audience: **l,u.**

Young, Alexandra Patricia   **R728.78**
& Morton, Tammy B.
The Administrative Medical Assistant. Ed. 5. Mixed Media. Elsevier - Health Sciences Division. Philadelphia, PA. 2004. ISBN:1-4160-0238-3, ISBN13: 978-1-4160-0238-3. Dewey:651.961.

Audience: **l,u.**

Allied Health > Physician Assistant

Ballweg, Ruth, et al.   **R697.P45P48 2003**
Physician Assistant: A Guide to Clinical Practice. Ed. 3. Edward M. Sullivan & Sherry Stolberg (Authors). Trade Paper. Elsevier - Health Sciences Division. Philadelphia, PA. 2003. 1072p. ISBN:0-7216-0017-4, ISBN13: 978-0-7216-0017-8. Dewey:610.69/53. LCCN:2003-043468.

Audience: **u,f.**

Moser, Rodney L.   **R847.P75 2001**
Primary Care for Physician Assistants. Ed. 2. Trade Cloth. McGraw-Hill Professional Publishing. New York, NY. 2001. 745p. ISBN:0-07-137014-5, ISBN13: 978-0-07-137014-1. Dewey:616. LCCN:00-049622.

Audience: **u,f.**

Allied Health > Radiology Technician

Adler, Arlene M. & Carlton,   **R898.I565 2003**
Richard R.
Introduction to Radiologic Sciences and Patient Care. Ed. 3. Trade Paper. Elsevier - Health Sciences Division. Philadelphia, PA. 2003. 520p. ISBN:0-7216-9782-8, ISBN13: 978-0-7216-9782-6. Dewey:616.07/572. LCCN:2003-042516.

Audience: **l,u.**

Bushong, Stewart C.   **R895**
Radiologic Science for Technologists: Physics, Biology and Protection. Ed. 8. Cloth Text. Elsevier - Health Sciences Division. Philadelphia, PA. 2004. 656p. ISBN:0-323-02555-2, ISBN13: 978-0-323-02555-3. Dewey:616.07572.

Audience: **l,u,f.**

Woodward, Peggy   **RC78.7.N83M9385 2000**
MRI for Technologists. Ed. 2. Paper Text. McGraw-Hill Professional Publishing. New York, NY. 2000. 408p. ISBN:0-07-135318-6, ISBN13: 978-0-07-135318-2. Dewey:616.07/548. LCCN:00-032110.

Audience: **l,u.**

Formats: Web: ☐   Ebook: 🄮   CD/DVD-ROM: 🗂   BCL3: 𝓑

Allied Health > Occupational Therapy

Anderson, Laura &   **RM735.4.A53 1999**
  Malaski, Christine
Occupational Therapy As a Career: An Introduction to the Field
and a Structured Method for Observation. Trade Paper. F. A.
Davis Company. Philadelphia, PA. 1998. 156p.
ISBN:0-8036-0387-8, ISBN13: 978-0-8036-0387-5.
Dewey:615.8/515/023. LCCN:98-028653.

Audience: **g,l,u.**

Atchison, Ben   **RM735**
Conditions in Occupational Therapy. Ed. 3. Trade Paper.
Lippincott Williams & Wilkins. Philadelphia, PA. 2006. 512p.
ISBN:0-7817-5487-9, ISBN13: 978-0-7817-5487-3.
Dewey:615.8/515. LCCN:2006-014892.

Audience: **l,u,f.**

Bonder, Bette R. & Wagner,   **QP86**
  Marilyn B.
Functional Performance in Older Adults. Ed. 2. Trade Cloth. F.
A. Davis Company. Philadelphia, PA. 2000. 425p.
ISBN:0-8036-0543-9, ISBN13: 978-0-8036-0543-5.
Dewey:612.6/7. LCCN:00-064402.

Audience: **u,f.**

Hansen, Ruth Ann (Editor)   **RM735.C66 2000**
Conditions in Occupational Therapy: Effect on Occupational
Performance. Ed. 2. Trade Cloth. Lippincott Williams &
Wilkins. Philadelphia, PA. 1999. 392p. ISBN:0-683-30417-8,
ISBN13: 978-0-683-30417-6. Dewey:615.8515.
LCCN:99-049311.

Audience: **l,u,f.**

Jacobs, Karen (Editor)   **RM735.E73 1999**
Ergonomics for Therapists. Ed. 2. Trade Cloth. Elsevier - Health
Sciences Division. Philadelphia, PA. 1999. 382p.
ISBN:0-7506-7051-7, ISBN13: 978-0-7506-7051-7.
Dewey:615.8/515. LCCN:98-053102.

Audience: **l,u,f.**

Levy, Barry S.   **RC963.O22 2006**
Occupational and Environmental Health. Ed. 5. Trade Paper.
Lippincott Williams & Wilkins. Philadelphia, PA. 2005. 847p.
ISBN:0-7817-5551-4, ISBN13: 978-0-7817-5551-1.
Dewey:616.9/803. LCCN:2005-022903.

Audience: **l,u,f.**

McCunney, Robert J., et al.   **RC963.H34 2003**
A Practical Approach to Occupational and Environmental
Medicine. Ed. 3. Paul P. Rountree, Jeffrey L. Levinson & Cheryl
S. Barbanel (Authors). Trade Cloth. Lippincott Williams &
Wilkins. Philadelphia, PA. 2003. 912p. ISBN:0-7817-3674-9,
ISBN13: 978-0-7817-3674-9. Dewey:616.9/803.
LCCN:2002-040640.

Audience: **l,u,f.** *Choice, 1995.*

Rogers, Bonnie   **RC966.R64 2003**
Occupational and Environmental Health Nursing: Concepts and
Practice. Ed. 2. Trade Cloth. Elsevier - Health Sciences
Division. Philadelphia, PA. 2003. 640p. ISBN:0-7216-8511-0,
ISBN13: 978-0-7216-8511-3. Dewey:610.73/46.
LCCN:2002-044516.

Audience: **l,u.**

Rosenstock, Linda, et al.   **RC964**
Textbook of Clinical Occupational and Environmental Medicine.
Ed. 2. Carl Andrew Brodkin, Mark R. Cullen & Carrie A.
Redlich (Authors). Trade Cloth. Elsevier - Health Sciences
Division. Philadelphia, PA. 2004. 1328p. ISBN:0-7216-8974-4,
ISBN13: 978-0-7216-8974-6. Dewey:616.9803.

Audience: **l,u,f.**

Solomon, Jean W. &   **RJ53.O25**
  O'Brien, Jane Clifford (Editors)
Pediatric Skills for Occupational Therapy Assistants. Ed. 2.
Paper Text. Elsevier - Health Sciences Division. Philadelphia,
PA. 2005. 624p. ISBN:0-323-03183-8, ISBN13:
978-0-323-03183-7. Dewey:615.8/515/083.

Audience: **l,u.**

Willard, Helen S., et al.   **RM735.O29 2003**
Willard and Spackman's Occupational Therapy. Ed. 10.
Elizabeth Blesedell Crepeau, Ellen S. Cohn & Barbara A. Boyt
Schell (Authors). Trade Cloth. Lippincott Williams & Wilkins.
Philadelphia, PA. 2003. 1088p. ISBN:0-7817-2798-7, ISBN13:
978-0-7817-2798-3. Dewey:615.8/515. LCCN:2002-031288.

Audience: **l,u.**

Allied Health > Physical Therapy

Domholdt, Elizabeth   **RM930.D66 2005**
Rehabilitation Research: Principles and Applications. Ed. 3.
Trade Paper. Elsevier - Health Sciences Division. Philadelphia,
PA. 2004. 592p. ISBN:0-7216-0029-8, ISBN13:
978-0-7216-0029-1. Dewey:617/.03. LCCN:2004-050696.

Audience: **u,f.**

Meadows, James D.   **RD734.O75 1999**
Differential Diagnosis for the Orthopedic Physical Therapist.
Paper Text. McGraw-Hill Professional Publishing. New York,
NY. 1999. 350p. ISBN:0-07-041235-9, ISBN13:
978-0-07-041235-4. Dewey:616.7/075. LCCN:98-049161.

Audience: **u,f.**

Pagliarulo, Michael A.   **RM700.P34 2001**
Introduction to Physical Therapy. Ed. 2. Paper Text. Elsevier -
Health Sciences Division. Philadelphia, PA. 2001. 340p.
ISBN:0-323-01057-1, ISBN13: 978-0-323-01057-3.
Dewey:615.8/2. LCCN:00-068119.

Audience: **l,u.**

Prentice, William E.   **RM700.P78 2005**
Therapeutic Modalities in Rehabilitation. Ed. 3. Cloth Text.
McGraw-Hill Companies, The. New York, NY. 2005. 608p.
ISBN:0-07-144123-9, ISBN13: 978-0-07-144123-0.
Dewey:615.8/2. LCCN:2004-061005.

Audience: **l,u,f.**

Scott, Ron   **RM700.S375 2002**
Foundations of Physical Therapy: A 21st Century-Focused View.
Paper Text. McGraw-Hill Professional Publishing. New York,
NY. 2001. 484p. ISBN:0-07-135590-1, ISBN13:
978-0-07-135590-2. Dewey:615.8/2. LCCN:2001-044041.

Audience: **l,u.**

Allied Health > Respiratory Therapy

Beachey, Will   **QP121.B355 1998**
Respiratory Care Anatomy and Physiology: Foundations for
Clinical Practice. Trade Cloth. Elsevier - Health Sciences
Division. Philadelphia, PA. 1997. 409p. ISBN:0-8151-1198-3,
ISBN13: 978-0-8151-1198-6. Dewey:612.2. LCCN:97-001309.

Audience: **l,u,f.**

Dantzker, David R., et al.   **RC735.I5C65 1995**
Comprehensive Respiratory Care. Neil R. MacIntyre & Eric D.
Bakow (Authors). Trade Cloth. Elsevier - Health Sciences
Division. Philadelphia, PA. 1995. 1344p. ISBN:0-7216-2844-3,
ISBN13: 978-0-7216-2844-8. Dewey:616.2/0046.
LCCN:94-034397.

Audience: **l,u,f.**

Sorenson, Helen & Thorson,   **RC952.S67 1998**
 James A.
Geriatric Respiratory Care. Ed. 1. Paper Text. Thomson Delmar
Learning. Albany, NY. 1998. 224p. Respiratory Care Ser.
ISBN:0-8273-7054-7, ISBN13: 978-0-8273-7054-8.
Dewey:618.97. LCCN:97-009709.

Audience: **l,u,f.**

West, John B.   **QP121.W43**
Respiratory Physiology: The Essentials. Ed. 5. Trade Paper.
Lippincott Williams & Wilkins. Philadelphia, PA. 2004. 208p.
ISBN:0-7817-5152-7, ISBN13: 978-0-7817-5152-0.
Dewey:612.2. LCCN:2004-044149.

Audience: **g,l,u.**

Whitaker, Kent   **RJ434.W47 2001**
Comprehensive Perinatal and Pediatric Respiratory Care. Ed. 3.
Paper Text. Thomson Delmar Learning. Albany, NY. 2001.
832p. ISBN:0-7668-1373-8, ISBN13: 978-0-7668-1373-1.
Dewey:618.92/200428. LCCN:2001-017185.

Audience: **l,u,f.**

Wilkins, Robert L., et al.   **RM161.E37 2003**
Egan's Fundamentals of Respiratory Care. Ed. 8. Craig L.
Scanlan & James K. Stoller (Authors). Trade Cloth. Elsevier -

Health Sciences Division. Philadelphia, PA. 2003. 1408p.
ISBN:0-323-01813-0, ISBN13: 978-0-323-01813-5.
Dewey:615.8/36. LCCN:2003-044930.

Audience: **l,u.**

Medical Anthropology

Baer, Hans A., et al.   **GN296**
Medical Anthropology and the World System. Ed. 2. Merrill
Singer & Ida Susser (Authors). Trade Cloth. Greenwood
Publishing Group, Inc. Portsmouth, NH. 2004. 440p.
ISBN:0-89789-845-1, ISBN13: 978-0-89789-845-4.
Dewey:306.4/61. LCCN:2003-052887.

Audience: **u,f.**

Brown, Peter   **GN296 .U54**
Understanding and Applying Medical Anthropology. Ed. 2.
Paper Text. McGraw-Hill Higher Education. Burr Ridge, IL.
2004. 480p. ISBN:0-7674-2721-1, ISBN13: 978-0-7674-2721-0.
Dewey:306.4/61/01.

Audience: **l,u.**

Janzen, John   **GN296**
The Social Fabric of Health: An Introduction to Medical
Anthropology. Cloth Text. McGraw-Hill Higher Education. Burr
Ridge, IL. 2001. 336p. ISBN:0-07-032831-5, ISBN13:
978-0-07-032831-0. Dewey:306.4/61. LCCN:2001-092036.

Audience: **g,l,u,f.**

Joralemon, Donald   **GN296.J65 2005**
Exploring Medical Anthropology. Ed. 2. Trade Paper. Allyn &
Bacon, Inc. Boston, MA. 2005. 176p. ISBN:0-205-44234-X,
ISBN13: 978-0-205-44234-8. Dewey:306.4/61.
LCCN:2004-060006.

Audience: **g,l,u.**

McElroy, Ann & Townsend,   **GN296.M32 2003**
 Patricia K.
Medical Anthropology in Ecological Perspective. Ed. 4. Trade
Paper. Westview Press. Boulder, CO. 2003. 480p.
ISBN:0-8133-3821-2, ISBN13: 978-0-8133-3821-7.
Dewey:306.4/61. LCCN:2003-006626.

Audience: **g,l,u.**

PHYSICS

Traditionally, physics is a discipline for which undergraduates do little reading beyond their textbooks. In putting together this list of resources, I have attempted to create a collection that will be interesting to the undergraduate population. In particular, I have attempted to do the following:

1) Include classic works by pioneers in physics

2) Include typical textbooks from the physics curricula, to supplement course textbooks

3) Include popular level reading material that is accessible for all students (in and out of physics). This includes a substantial number of popular works, biographies, and histories.

4) Include advanced and hot-topics so that motivated students will have resources beyond their texts. These special topics include, for example, quantum computing, biophysics and environmental physics, phase transitions, and the quantum hall effect.

5) Finally, a small reference collection for quick facts and background information as needed by students

I have not included web sites in the list as yet. In general I am reluctant to, since the content is typically not substantive enough to be worthy of a 'monograph' status.

— Michael Fosmire

General Physics

Bloomfield, Louis A.   QC21.2.B59 2005
How Things Work: The Physics of Everyday Life. Ed. 3. Trade
Paper. John Wiley & Sons, Inc. Hoboken, NJ. 2005. 576p.
ISBN:0-471-46886-X, ISBN13: 978-0-471-46886-8. Dewey:530.
LCCN:2006-271695.

Audience: **l.** *Choice, 1997.*

Chabay, Ruth W. &   QC23.2.C43
  Sherwood, Bruce A.
Matter and Interactions I: Modern Mechanics. Trade Paper. John
Wiley & Sons, Inc. Hoboken, NJ. 2003. 464p.
ISBN:0-471-66328-X, ISBN13: 978-0-471-66328-7. Dewey:530.

Audience: **l.**

Chabay, Ruth W. &   QC23.2 .C43
  Sherwood, Bruce A.
Matter and Interactions II: Electric and Magnetic Interactions
Version 1.2. Trade Paper. John Wiley & Sons, Inc. Hoboken,
NJ. 2003. 528p. ISBN:0-471-66327-1, ISBN13:
978-0-471-66327-0. Dewey:530.

Audience: **l.**

Cutnell, John D. & Johnson,   QC23.2.C87 2007
  Kenneth W.
Physics. Ed. 7. Trade Cloth. John Wiley & Sons, Inc. Hoboken,
NJ. 2006. 1088p. ISBN:0-471-66315-8, ISBN13:
978-0-471-66315-7. Dewey:530. LCCN:2006-004904.

Audience: **l.**

Einstein, Albert   QC7.E52 2005
Einstein's Miraculous Year: Five Papers That Changed the Face
of Physics. John Stachel (Editor), Roger Penrose (Foreword by).
Trade Paper. Princeton University Press. Princeton, NJ. 2005.
248p. ISBN:0-691-12228-8, ISBN13: 978-0-691-12228-1.
Dewey:530.1.

Audience: **l,u.**

Feynman, Richard Phillips   QC21.2
Six Easy Pieces: Essentials of Physics Explained by Its Most
Brilliant Teacher. Paul Davies (Introduction by). Trade Paper.
Perseus Books Group. New York, NY. 1998. 176p.
ISBN:0-7382-0022-0, ISBN13: 978-0-7382-0022-4. Dewey:530.
LCCN:85-755368.

Audience: **l,u.** *Choice, 1995.*

Feynman, Richard Phillips,   QC21.2.F49 2006
  et al.
The Feynman Lectures on Physics, the Definitive Edition
Volume 1. Ed. 2. Robert B. Leighton & Matthew Sands
(Authors). Trade Cloth. Addison-Wesley Longman, Inc. Boston,
MA. 2005. 544p. ISBN:0-8053-9046-4, ISBN13:
978-0-8053-9046-9. Dewey:530. LCCN:2005-280842.

Audience: **l,u.**

Feynman, Richard Phillips,   QC21.2.F49 2006
  et al.
The Feynman Lectures on Physics, the Definitive Edition
Volume 2. Ed. 2. Robert B. Leighton & Matthew Sands
(Authors). Trade Cloth. Addison-Wesley Longman, Inc. Boston,
MA. 2005. 512p. ISBN:0-8053-9047-2, ISBN13:
978-0-8053-9047-6. Dewey:530. LCCN:2005-280842.

Audience: **l,u.**

Feynman, Richard Phillips,   QC21.2.F49 2006
  et al.
The Feynman Lectures on Physics, the Definitive Edition
Volume 3. Ed. 2. Robert B. Leighton & Matthew Sands
(Authors). Trade Cloth. Addison-Wesley Longman, Inc. Boston,
MA. 2005. 384p. ISBN:0-8053-9049-9, ISBN13:
978-0-8053-9049-0. Dewey:530. LCCN:2005-280842.

Audience: **l,u.**

Ford, Kenneth W. & Hewitt,   QC174.12.F68 2004
  Paul
The Quantum World: Quantum Physics for Everyone. Trade
Cloth. Harvard University Press. Cambridge, MA. 2004. 288p.
ISBN:0-674-01342-5, ISBN13: 978-0-674-01342-1.
Dewey:530.12. LCCN:2003-068565.

Audience: **l,u.** *Choice, 2004.*

Gamow, George   QC71 .G25 1993
Mr. Tompkins in Paperback: Comprising 'Mr. Tompkins in
Wonderland' and 'Mr. Tompkins Explores the Atom'. Roger
Penrose (Foreword by). Trade Paper. Cambridge University
Press. New York, NY. 1993. 202p. A Canto Book Ser.
ISBN:0-521-44771-2, ISBN13: 978-0-521-44771-3.
Dewey:530.1. LCCN:93-199164.

Audience: **g,l,u.**

Giambattista, Alan, et al.   QC21.3.G53
College Physics, Vol. 2. Ed. 2. Betty Richardson & Robert C.
Richardson (Authors). Paper Text. McGraw-Hill Higher
Education. Burr Ridge, IL. 2005. ISBN:0-07-325642-0, ISBN13:
978-0-07-325642-9. Dewey:530.

Audience: **l.**

Giancoli, Douglas C.   QC23.G399 2004
Physics: Principles with Applications. Ed. 6. Cloth Text.
Prentice Hall PTR. Upper Saddle River, NJ. 2004. 1040p.
ISBN:0-13-060620-0, ISBN13: 978-0-13-060620-4. Dewey:530.
LCCN:2004-017226.

Audience: **l.**

Gribbin, Mary & Gribbin,   QC16.E5G73 2005
  John
Annus Mirabilis 1905: Albert Einstein, and the Theory of
Relativity. Trade Cloth. Penguin Group (USA) Inc. New York,
NY. 2005. 240p. ISBN:1-59609-144-4, ISBN13:
978-1-59609-144-3. Dewey:530/.092 B. LCCN:2005-040709.

Audience: **l,u.**

Griffith, W. Thomas   QC23.2 .G75
Physics of Everyday Phenomena: A Conceptual Introduction to
Physics. Ed. 4. Trade Cloth. McGraw-Hill Higher Education.
Burr Ridge, IL. 2003. 544p. ISBN:0-07-296959-8, ISBN13:
978-0-07-296959-7. Dewey:530.

Audience: **l.**

Halliday, David, et al.   QC21.2.H35 2004
Fundamentals of Physics: EGrade Plus Stand-Alone Access. Ed.
7. Robert Resnick & Jearl Walker (Authors). Trade Cloth. John
Wiley & Sons, Inc. Hoboken, NJ. 2004. 1136p.
ISBN:0-471-21643-7, ISBN13: 978-0-471-21643-8. Dewey:530.

Audience: **l.**

Hewitt, Paul G. (Illustrator)   QC23.2.H488 2006
Conceptual Physics. Ed. 10. Trade Cloth. Addison-Wesley
Longman, Inc. Boston, MA. 2006. xix, 788p.
ISBN:0-8053-9213-0, ISBN13: 978-0-8053-9213-5. Dewey:530.
LCCN:2005-013760.

Audience: **l.**

March, Robert H.   QC23.2.M37 2003
Physics for Poets. Ed. 5. Paper Text. McGraw-Hill Companies, The. New York, NY. 2002. 288p. ISBN:0-07-119853-9, ISBN13: 978-0-07-119853-0. Dewey:530. LCCN:2002-020019.

Audience: l. *B*

Pais, Abraham   QC7
Inward Bound: Of Matter and Forces in the Physical World. Trade Paper. Oxford University Press, Inc. New York, NY. 1988. 682p. ISBN:0-19-851997-4, ISBN13: 978-0-19-851997-3. Dewey:530. LCCN:85-021587.

Audience: g,l. *B* Choice, 1986.

General Physics > Histories

Dahl, Per F.   QC611.92.D34 1992
Superconductivity. Cloth Text. Springer. New York, NY. 1992. 400p. ISBN:0-88318-848-1, ISBN13: 978-0-88318-848-4. Dewey:537.6/23. LCCN:91-036487.

Audience: l,u. Choice, 1993.

Kragh, Helge   QC7
Quantum Generations: A History of Physics in the Twentieth Century. Trade Paper. Princeton University Press. Princeton, NJ. 2002. 508p. ISBN:0-691-09552-3, ISBN13: 978-0-691-09552-3. Dewey:530/.09/04.

Audience: g. Choice, 2000.

Park, David A.   QC360
The Fire Within the Eye: A Historical Essay on the Nature and Meaning of Light. Trade Paper. Princeton University Press. Princeton, NJ. 1999. 392p. ISBN:0-691-05051-1, ISBN13: 978-0-691-05051-5. Dewey:535.

Audience: g.

Purrington, Robert D.   QC7.P84 1997
Physics in the Nineteenth Century. Paper Text. Rutgers University Press. Piscataway, NJ. 1997. 320p. ISBN:0-8135-2442-3, ISBN13: 978-0-8135-2442-9. Dewey:530/.09/034. LCCN:96-049115.

Audience: l,u. Choice, 1998.

General Physics > Popular Works

Adair, Robert K.   QC26.A23 2002
The Physics of Baseball. Ed. 3. Trade Paper. HarperCollins Publishers. New York, NY. 2002. 192p. ISBN:0-06-008436-7, ISBN13: 978-0-06-008436-3. Dewey:796.357/01/53. LCCN:2001-039886.

Audience: g,l. Choice, 1990.

Capra, Fritjof   QC6.C277 2000
The Tao of Physics: An Exploration of the Parallels Between Modern Physics and Easter Mysticism. Ed. 25. Trade Paper. Shambhala Publications, Inc. Boston, MA. 2000. 366p. ISBN:1-57062-519-0, ISBN13: 978-1-57062-519-0. Dewey:530/.01. LCCN:99-035683.

Audience: g,l.

Chandrasekhar, B. S.   QC173.454 .C49 1998
Why Things Are the Way They Are. Trade Paper. Cambridge University Press. New York, NY. 1997. 264p. ISBN:0-521-45660-6, ISBN13: 978-0-521-45660-9. Dewey:530.4/1. LCCN:96-052937.

Audience: l.

Feynman, Richard Phillips   QC16.E5
No Ordinary Genius: The Illustrated Richard Feynman. Christopher Sykes (Editor). Trade Paper. W. W. Norton & Company, Inc. New York, NY. 1996. 272p. ISBN:0-393-31393-X, ISBN13: 978-0-393-31393-2. Dewey:530/.092 B.

Audience: g,l,u. Choice, 1994.

Fraser, Gordon   QC793.27.F7 1997
The Quark Machines: How Europe Fought the Particle Physics War. Trade Paper. Institute of Physics Publishing. Philadelphia, PA. 1997. 200p. ISBN:0-7503-0447-2, ISBN13: 978-0-7503-0447-4. Dewey:539.7/2. LCCN:97-014853.

Audience: g,l,u. Choice, 1998.

Gamow, George   QC71 .G25 1993
Mr. Tompkins in Paperback: Comprising 'Mr. Tompkins in Wonderland' and 'Mr. Tompkins Explores the Atom'. Roger Penrose (Foreword by). Trade Paper. Cambridge University Press. New York, NY. 1993. 202p. A Canto Book Ser. ISBN:0-521-44771-2, ISBN13: 978-0-521-44771-3. Dewey:530.1. LCCN:93-199164.

Audience: g,l,u.

Gamow, George   QC71 .S775 1999
The New World of Mr. Tompkins. Ed. 3. Russell Stannard (Editor), Michael Edwards (Illustrator). Trade Paper. Cambridge University Press. New York, NY. 2001. 270p. ISBN:0-521-63992-1, ISBN13: 978-0-521-63992-7. Dewey:539. LCCN:98-050379.

Audience: g,l,u.

Gardner, Martin   QC793.3.S9G37 2005
The New Ambidextrous Universe: Symmetry and Asymmetry from Mirror Reflections to Superstrings. Ed. 3. Trade Paper, Perfect. Dover Publications, Inc. Mineola, NY. 2005. 401p. ISBN:0-486-44244-6, ISBN13: 978-0-486-44244-0. Dewey:539.7/2. LCCN:2004-065650.

Audience: g,l.

Gonick, Larry & Huffman, Art   QC24.5.G66 1991
The Cartoon Guide to Physics. Trade Paper. HarperCollins Publishers. New York, NY. 1991. 224p. ISBN:0-06-273100-9, ISBN13: 978-0-06-273100-5. Dewey:530/.0207. LCCN:90-055499.

Audience: g,l.

Gove, H. E.   QC454.A25G68 1999
From Hiroshima to the Iceman: The Development and Applications of Accelerator Mass Spectrometry. Trade Paper. Institute of Physics Publishing. Philadelphia, PA. 1998. 226p. ISBN:0-7503-0558-4, ISBN13: 978-0-7503-0558-7. Dewey:543/.0873. LCCN:98-042786.

Audience: g,l. Choice, 1999.

Gribbin, John   QC173.98G75 1984
In Search of Schrodinger's Cat: Quantum Physics and Reality. Trade Paper. Bantam Books. New York, NY. 1984. 320p. ISBN:0-553-34253-3, ISBN13: 978-0-553-34253-6. Dewey:530.1/2. LCCN:84-002975.

Audience: g,l.

Hawking, Stephen W.   QC174.12.H39 2001
The Universe in a Nutshell. Trade Cloth. Bantam Books. New York, NY. 2001. 224p. ISBN:0-553-80202-X, ISBN13: 978-0-553-80202-3. Dewey:530.12. LCCN:2001-035757.

Audience: g,l,u. Choice, 2003, 2002.

Formats: Web: ☐   Ebook: *e*   CD/DVD-ROM: *✦*   BCL3: *B*

Herbert, Nick   QC174.12.H47 1985
Quantum Reality: Beyond the New Physics. Trade Paper.
Doubleday Publishing. New York, NY. 1987. 288p.
ISBN:0-385-23569-0, ISBN13: 978-0-385-23569-3.
Dewey:530.1/2. LCCN:82-046033.
Audience: **l,u.** *B̶* *Choice, 1985.*

Krauss, Lawrence M.   PN1992.77.S73
The Physics of Star Trek. Trade Paper. HarperCollins Publishers.
New York, NY. 1996. 208p. ISBN:0-06-097710-8, ISBN13:
978-0-06-097710-8. Dewey:791.4/5/72. LCCN:95-033266.
Audience: **g,l.** *Choice, 1996.*

Lederman, Leon & Teresi,   Q175 .L423 1994
  Dick
The God Particle: If the Universe Is the Answer, What Is the
Question? Trade Paper. Dell Publishing. New York, NY. 1994.
448p. ISBN:0-385-31211-3, ISBN13: 978-0-385-31211-0.
Dewey:539.14.
Audience: **g.** *Choice, 1993.*

Leggett, Anthony J.   QC21.2.L44 1987
The Problems of Physics. Trade Paper. Oxford University Press,
Inc. New York, NY. 1988. 204p. ISBN:0-19-289186-3, ISBN13:
978-0-19-289186-0. Dewey:530. LCCN:87-012278.
Audience: **l,u.** *Choice, 1988.*

Penrose, Roger   QC20.P366 2005
The Road to Reality: A Complete Guide to the Laws of the
Universe. Trade Cloth. Alfred A. Knopf Inc. New York, NY.
2005. 1120p. ISBN:0-679-45443-8, ISBN13:
978-0-679-45443-4. Dewey:500.2. LCCN:2004-061543.
Audience: **l,u.** *Choice, 2005.*

Randall, Lisa   QC6.R26 2005
Warped Passages: Unraveling the Mysteries of the Universe's
Hidden Dimensions. Trade Cloth. HarperCollins Publishers.
New York, NY. 2005. 512p. ISBN:0-06-053108-8, ISBN13:
978-0-06-053108-9. Dewey:530/.01. LCCN:2004-056376.
Audience: **l,u.** *Choice, 2006.*

Rees, Martin J.   QB981
Just Six Numbers: The Deep Forces That Shape the Universe.
Trade Paper. Basic Books. New York, NY. 2001. 208p.
ISBN:0-465-03673-2, ISBN13: 978-0-465-03673-8.
Dewey:523.1.
Audience: **g,l.** *Choice, 2000.*

Schlegel, Eric M.   QB472.S35 2002
The Restless Universe: Understanding X-Ray Astronomy in the
Age of Chandra and Newton. Trade Cloth. Oxford University
Press, Inc. New York, NY. 2002. 228p. ISBN:0-19-514847-9,
ISBN13: 978-0-19-514847-3. Dewey:522/.6863.
LCCN:2002-072755.
Audience: **g,l.** *Choice, 2003.*

Springford, Michael (Editor)   QC793.5.E62 E39 1997
Electron: A Centenary Volume. Trade Cloth. Cambridge
University Press. New York, NY. 1997. 342p.
ISBN:0-521-56130-2, ISBN13: 978-0-521-56130-3.
Dewey:539.7/2112. LCCN:96-044744.
Audience: **g.**

Suplee, Curt   QC24.5.S86 2002
Physics in the 20th Century. Trade Paper. Harry N. Abrams, Inc.
New York, NY. 2002. 224p. ISBN:0-8109-9084-9, ISBN13:
978-0-8109-9084-5. Dewey:530.
Audience: **g.** *Choice, 1999.*

Swartz, Clifford E.   QC75.S83 2003
Back-of-the-Envelope Physics. Trade Paper. Johns Hopkins
University Press. Baltimore, MD. 2003. 176p.
ISBN:0-8018-7263-4, ISBN13: 978-0-8018-7263-1. Dewey:530.
LCCN:2002-016143.
Audience: **l.** *Choice, 2004.*

Walker, Jearl   QC0032.W2
The Flying Circus of Physics. Trade Paper. Books on Demand.
Ann Arbor, MI. 1975. 238p. ISBN:0-7837-3492-1, ISBN13:
978-0-7837-3492-7. Dewey:530/.076. LCCN:75-005670.
Audience: **l.**

Weinberg, Steven   QC21.2.W428 1994
Dreams of a Final Theory: The Scientist's Search for the
Ultimate Laws of Nature. Trade Paper. Knopf Publishing Group.
New York, NY. 1994. 352p. ISBN:0-679-74408-8, ISBN13:
978-0-679-74408-5. Dewey:530. LCCN:93-030534.
Audience: **g.**

Zukav, Gary   QC173.98
Dancing Wu Li Masters: An Overview of the New Physics.
Trade Paper. HarperCollins Publishers. New York, NY. 2001.
416p. Perennial Classics Ser. ISBN:0-06-095968-1, ISBN13:
978-0-06-095968-5. Dewey:530.12.
Audience: **g.**

General Physics > Philosophy

Bohm, David   QC174.12.B633 2002
Wholeness and the Implicate Order. Trade Paper. Routledge.
New York, NY. 2002. 304p. Routledge Classics Ser.
ISBN:0-415-28979-3, ISBN13: 978-0-415-28979-5.
Dewey:530.12. LCCN:2002-031676.
Audience: **l,u.** *B̶*

Eddington, Arthur Stanley   QC6.E37
The Philosophy of Physical Science. Paper Text. Textbook
Publishers. Temecula, CA. 2003. ix, 230p. ISBN:0-7581-2054-0,
ISBN13: 978-0-7581-2054-0. Dewey:530.1.
Audience: **l,u.** *B̶*

Einstein, Albert & Infeld,   QC7.E35 1966
  Leopold
The Evolution of Physics: The Growth of Ideas from Early
Concepts to Relativity and Guanta. Trade Paper. Simon &
Schuster. New York, NY. 1967. 0p. ISBN:0-671-20156-5,
ISBN13: 978-0-671-20156-2. Dewey:530.9.
Audience: **l,u.**

Feynman, Richard Phillips   QC71.F44 1994
The Character of Physical Law. James Gleick (Introduction by).
Trade Cloth. Random House, Inc. New York, NY. 1994. 192p.
Modern Library Ser. ISBN:0-679-60127-9, ISBN13:
978-0-679-60127-2. Dewey:530. LCCN:2001-276394.
Audience: **l,u.** *B̶*

Heisenberg, Werner   QC6.2
Philosophical Problems of Quantum Physics. Trade Paper. Ox
Bow Press. Woodbridge, CT. 1979. ISBN:0-918024-15-3,
ISBN13: 978-0-918024-15-2. Dewey:539.7. LCCN:79-089842.
Audience: **u,f.**

Heisenberg, Werner   QC6.H34 1999
Physics and Philosophy: The Revolution in Modern Science. F.
S. C. Northrop (Introduction by). Trade Cloth. Prometheus

Books, Publishers. Amherst, NY. 1999. 228p. Great Minds Ser. ISBN:1-57392-694-9, ISBN13: 978-1-57392-694-2. Dewey:530/.01. LCCN:99-010404.

Audience: **l,u,f.** ℬ

Omnes, Roland   QC6
Quantum Philosophy: Understanding and Interpreting Contemporary Science. Arturo Sangalli (Translator). Trade Paper. Princeton University Press. Princeton, NJ. 2002. 320p. ISBN:0-691-09551-5, ISBN13: 978-0-691-09551-6. Dewey:530/.01.

Audience: **l,u.** *Choice, 1999.*

General Physics > Biographies

Aczel, Amir D.   QC15
Pendulum: Leon Foucault and the Triumph of Science. Trade Paper. Simon & Schuster. New York, NY. 2004. 288p. ISBN:0-7434-6479-6, ISBN13: 978-0-7434-6479-6. Dewey:530/.092 B.

Audience: **g,l.** *Choice, 2004.*

Ajzenberg-Selove, Fay   QC16.A34 A3 1994
A Matter of Choices: Memoirs of a Female Physicist. Ann H. Koblitz (Introduction by). Paper Text. Rutgers University Press. Piscataway, NJ. 1994. 238p. Lives of Women in Science Ser. ISBN:0-8135-2035-5, ISBN13: 978-0-8135-2035-3. Dewey:539.7/092. LCCN:93-028136.

Audience: **l.** *Choice, 1994.*

Bernstein, Jeremy   QC16.O62B43 2004
Oppenheimer: Portrait of an Enigma. Trade Cloth. Ivan R. Dee Publisher. Blue Ridge Summit, PA. 2004. 240p. ISBN:1-56663-569-1, ISBN13: 978-1-56663-569-1. Dewey:530/.092 B. LCCN:2003-066652.

Audience: **g,l.** *Choice, 2004.*

Brennan, Richard P.   QC15
Heisenberg Probably Slept Here: The Lives, Times, and Ideas of the Great Physicists of the 20th Century. Trade Paper. John Wiley & Sons, Inc. Hoboken, NJ. 1998. 274p. Popular Science Ser. ISBN:0-471-29585-X, ISBN13: 978-0-471-29585-3. Dewey:530/.0922. LCCN:96-042935.

Audience: **g,l.** *Choice, 1997.*

Cercignani, Carlo   QC16.B64C47 1998
Ludwig Boltzmann: The Man Who Trusted Atoms. Trade Cloth. Oxford University Press, Inc. New York, NY. 1998. 348p. ISBN:0-19-850154-4, ISBN13: 978-0-19-850154-1. Dewey:530/.092 B. LCCN:98-017743.

Audience: **g.**

Cohen, I. Bernard & Smith,   QC16.N7 C35 2002
  George E. (Editors)
The Cambridge Companion to Newton. Trade Paper. Cambridge University Press. New York, NY. 2002. 514p. Cambridge Companions to Philosophy Ser. ISBN:0-521-65696-6, ISBN13: 978-0-521-65696-2. Dewey:530.092. LCCN:2001-037836.

Audience: **g,l,u,f.** *Choice, 2003.*

Conant, Jennet   QC16.L647
Tuxedo Park: A Wall Street Tycoon and the Secret Palace of Science That Changed the Course of World War II. Trade Paper. Simon & Schuster. New York, NY. 2003. 352p. ISBN:0-684-87288-9, ISBN13: 978-0-684-87288-9. Dewey:530/.092/274731 B. LCCN:2002-021001.

Audience: **g.** *Choice, 2002.*

Dahl, Per F.   QC793.5.E62D34 1997
Flash of the Cathode Rays: A History of J. J. Thomson's Electron. Trade Cloth. Institute of Physics Publishing. Philadelphia, PA. 1997. 472p. ISBN:0-7503-0453-7, ISBN13: 978-0-7503-0453-5. Dewey:539.7/2112/09. LCCN:97-013642.

Audience: **g,l.** *Choice, 1998.*

Dyson, Freeman J.   QC16.E5
Disturbing the Universe. Trade Paper. Basic Books. New York, NY. 1981. 304p. ISBN:0-465-01677-4, ISBN13: 978-0-465-01677-8. Dewey:530/.092/4. LCCN:78-020665.

Audience: **g,l.**

Einstein, Albert   QC16.E5
Out of My Later Years. Trade Paper. Kensington Publishing Corporation. New York, NY. 2000. 288p. ISBN:0-8065-0357-2, ISBN13: 978-0-8065-0357-8. Dewey:530/.092 B.

Audience: **g.** ℬ

Enz, Charles P.   QC16.P37E59 2002
No Time to be Brief: A Scientific Biography of Wolfgang Pauli. Trade Cloth. Oxford University Press, Inc. New York, NY. 2002. 581p. ISBN:0-19-856479-1, ISBN13: 978-0-19-856479-9. Dewey:530/.092 B. LCCN:2002-726902.

Audience: **l,u.** *Choice, 2003.*

Fermi, Laura   QC16.F46 F47 1987
Atoms in the Family: My Life with Enrico Fermi. Trade Cloth. American Institute of Physics. Melville, NY. 1987. 280p. History of Modern Physics and Astronomy Ser. ISBN:0-88318-524-5, ISBN13: 978-0-88318-524-7. Dewey:530/.092/4. LCCN:87-012651.

Audience: **g.** ℬ

Feynman, Richard Phillips   QC16.F49A4 2005
Perfectly Reasonable Deviations from the Beaten Track: The Letters of Richard P. Feynman. Michelle Feynman (Editor), Timothy Ferris (Foreword by). Cloth Text. Basic Books. New York, NY. 2005. 512p. ISBN:0-7382-0636-9, ISBN13: 978-0-7382-0636-3. Dewey:530/.092 B. LCCN:2005-000049.

Audience: **g.** *Choice, 2005.*

Feynman, Richard Phillips   QC16.F49A37 1985
"Surely You're Joking, Mr. Feynman!": Adventures of a Curious Character. Edward Hutchings (Editor), Albert R. Hibbs (Introduction by), Ralph Leighton (As told to). Trade Paper. W. W. Norton & Company, Inc. New York, NY. 1997. 350p. ISBN:0-393-31604-1, ISBN13: 978-0-393-31604-9. Dewey:530/.092/4. LCCN:84-014703.

Audience: **g.**

Feynman, Richard Phillips   QC16 F49.A3 1988
What Do You Care What Other People Think?: Further Adventures of a Curious Character. Ralph Leighton (As told to). Trade Paper. W. W. Norton & Company, Inc. New York, NY. 2001. 256p. ISBN:0-393-32092-8, ISBN13: 978-0-393-32092-3. Dewey:530/.092.

Audience: **g.** *Choice, 1989.*

Folsing, Albrecht   QC16.E5
Albert Einstein: A Biography. Ewald Osers (Translator). Trade Paper. Penguin Group (USA) Inc. New York, NY. 1998. 928p. ISBN:0-14-023719-4, ISBN13: 978-0-14-023719-1. Dewey:530/.092. LCCN:96-026341.

Audience: **g,l.** *Choice, 1997.*

Freeman, Joan   QC16.F713F74 1993
A Passion for Physics: The Story of a Woman Physicist. Trade
Cloth. Institute of Physics Publishing. Philadelphia, PA. 1991.
240p. ISBN:0-7503-0098-1, ISBN13: 978-0-7503-0098-8.
Dewey:530/.092 B. LCCN:99-224371.
                                         Audience: **g.** *Choice, 1991.*

Gamow, George   QC16.G37.A3 1970
My World Line: Fragments of A. Trade Cloth. Penguin Group
(USA) Inc. New York, NY. 1970. xii, 178p.
ISBN:0-670-50376-2, ISBN13: 978-0-670-50376-6.
Dewey:539.7/0924. LCCN:79-094855.
                                                    Audience: **g.**

Gell-Mann, Murray   QC774.G45 A3 1994
The Quark and the Jaguar: Adventures in the Simple and the
Complex. Trade Paper. Henry Holt & Company. New York, NY.
1995. 392p. ISBN:0-8050-7253-5, ISBN13: 978-0-8050-7253-2.
Dewey:530.
                                         Audience: **g.** *Choice, 1994.*

Glashow, Sheldon L. &   Q175 .L423 1994
  Bova, Ben
Interactions: A Journey Through the Mind of a Particle Physicist
and the Matter of This World. Trade Paper. Warner Books, Inc.
New York, NY. 1989. 368p. ISBN:0-446-38946-3, ISBN13:
978-0-446-38946-4. Dewey:539.7.
                                                    Audience: **g.**

Gleick, James   QC16.E5
Genius: The Life and Science of Richard Feynman. Trade Paper.
Knopf Publishing Group. New York, NY. 1993. 560p.
ISBN:0-679-74704-4, ISBN13: 978-0-679-74704-8.
Dewey:530/.092. LCCN:93-007838.
                                         Audience: **g.** *Choice, 1993.*

Goldman, Martin   QC16.M4.G65 1983
The Demon in the Aether: The Story of James Clerk Maxwell.
Trade Cloth. Bow Historical Books. New Providence, NJ. 1983.
224 p., [12]p. ISBN:0-86228-026-5, ISBN13:
978-0-86228-026-0. Dewey:530/.092/4. LCCN:83-200363.
                                             Audience: **g.** *B*

Goodchild, Peter   QC16.O62G66 1985
J. Robert Oppenheimer: Shatterer of Worlds. Trade Paper.
Fromm International Publishing Corporation. New York, NY.
1985. 301p. ISBN:0-88064-021-9, ISBN13: 978-0-88064-021-3.
Dewey:539.7/092/4. LCCN:85-013194.
                                             Audience: **g.** *B*

Heilbron, J. L.   QC16.P6H45 2000
The Dilemmas of an Upright Man: Max Planck and the
Fortunes of German Science. Trade Paper. Harvard University
Press. Cambridge, MA. 2000. 272p. ISBN:0-674-00439-6,
ISBN13: 978-0-674-00439-9. Dewey:530/.092 B.
LCCN:00-040745.
                                                  Audience: **g,l.**

Heilbron, John L. & Seidel,   QC789.2.U62L384 1989
  Robert W.
Lawrence and His Laboratory: A History of the Lawrence
Berkeley Laboratory. Trade Cloth. University of California
Press. Berkeley, CA. 1990. xxvii, 586p. California Studies in the
History of Science Ser. ISBN:0-520-06426-7, ISBN13:
978-0-520-06426-3. Dewey:539.7/0720794/67.
LCCN:89-004820.
                                         Audience: **g.** *Choice, 1990.*

Herken, Gregg   QC16.O62
Brotherhood of the Bomb: The Tangled Lives and Loyalties of
Robert Oppenheimer, Ernest Lawrence, and Edward Teller.
Trade Paper. Henry Holt & Company. New York, NY. 2003.
460p. ISBN:0-8050-6589-X, ISBN13: 978-0-8050-6589-3.
Dewey:539.7/092/273 B.
                                                    Audience: **g.**

Hoddeson, Lillian & Daitch,   QC16.B2763 2005
  Vicki
True Genius: The Life and Science of John Bardeen; the Only
Winner of Two Nobel Prizes in Physics. Trade Paper, Perfect.
National Academies Press. Washington, DC. 2005. 467p.
ISBN:0-309-09511-5, ISBN13: 978-0-309-09511-2.
Dewey:530.092.
                                                    Audience: **g.**

Infeld, Leopold   QC16.I6.A3 1980
Quest: An Autobiography. Ed. 2. Trade Cloth. American
Mathematical Society. Providence, RI. 1997. 361p. Chelsea
Publishing Ser. ISBN:0-8284-0309-0, ISBN13:
978-0-8284-0309-2. Dewey:530/.092/4. LCCN:79-055510.
                                             Audience: **g.** *B*

Johnson, George   QC774
Strange Beauty: Murray Gell-Mann and the Revolution in
Twentieth-Century Physics. UK-Trade Paper. Alfred A. Knopf
Inc. New York, NY. 2000. 464p. ISBN:0-679-75688-4, ISBN13:
978-0-679-75688-0. Dewey:539.7/092. LCCN:99-019952.
                                         Audience: **g.** *Choice, 2000.*

Maxwell, James Clerk   QC517.C35
  (Editor)
Electrical Researches of the Honourable Henry Cavendish.
Paper over Boards. Taylor & Francis Group. Abingdon, 1967.
454p. ISBN:0-7146-1057-7, ISBN13: 978-0-7146-1057-3.
Dewey:537.
                                                  Audience: **l,u.**

McCormmach, Russell K.   QC7.M35
Night Thoughts of a Classical Physicist. Trade Cloth. Harvard
University Press. Cambridge, MA. 1982. 232p.
ISBN:0-674-62460-2, ISBN13: 978-0-674-62460-3.
Dewey:813.54. LCCN:81-006674.
                                           Audience: **l,u.** *B*

Mehra, Jagdish & Milton,   QC15
  Kimball
Climbing the Mountain: The Scientific Biography of Julian
Schwinger. Trade Paper. Oxford University Press, Inc. New
York, NY. 2003. 690p. ISBN:0-19-852745-4, ISBN13:
978-0-19-852745-9. Dewey:530/.092 B.
                                                  Audience: **l,u.**

Oppenheimer, Robert   QC16.062A4
Robert Oppenheimer: Letters and Recollections. Alice K. Smith
& Charles Weiner (Editors). Trade Paper. Harvard University
Press. Cambridge, MA. 1981. 387p. Harvard Paperbacks Ser.
ISBN:0-674-77606-2, ISBN13: 978-0-674-77606-7. Dewey:530.
LCCN:80-010106.
                                                    Audience: **g.**

Pais, Abraham, et al.   QC16.D57 P38 1998
Paul Dirac: The Man and his Work. Maurice Jacob, David I.
Olive & Michael F. Atiyah (Authors). Trade Paper. Cambridge

University Press. New York, NY. 2005. 140p.
ISBN:0-521-01953-2, ISBN13: 978-0-521-01953-8.
Dewey:530.092 B. LCCN:2005-284416.

Audience: **g.**

Pais, Abraham   QC16.E5
Subtle Is the Lord: The Science and the Life of Albert Einstein.
Roger Penrose (Foreword by). Trade Paper, Perfect. Oxford
University Press, Inc. New York, NY. 2005. 576p.
ISBN:0-19-280672-6, ISBN13: 978-0-19-280672-7.
Dewey:530.092 B. LCCN:2005-285161.

Audience: **g,l.** *B*

Rayner-Canham, Marelene   QC16.B79.R39
  F. & Rayner-Canham, Geoffrey W.
Harriet Brooks: Pioneer Nuclear Scientist. Trade Paper.
McGill-Queen's University Press. Montreal, PQ. 1994. 204p.
ISBN:0-7735-1254-3, ISBN13: 978-0-7735-1254-2.
Dewey:539.7092. LCCN:91-090627.

Audience: **g.** *Choice, 1992.*

Schweber, Silvan S.   QC680.S34 1994
QED and the Men Who Made It: Dyson, Feynman, Schwinger,
and Tomonaga. Trade Paper. Princeton University Press.
Princeton, NJ. 1994. 760p. Princeton Series in Physics
ISBN:0-691-03327-7, ISBN13: 978-0-691-03327-3.
Dewey:537.6/7/09. LCCN:93-033550.

Audience: **l,u.**

Segre, Emilio   QC7.S435 1984
From Falling Bodies to Radio Waves: Classical Physicists and
Their Discoveries. Paper Text. W. H. Freeman & Company.
New York, NY. 1984. 298p. ISBN:0-7167-1482-5, ISBN13:
978-0-7167-1482-8. Dewey:530/.09. LCCN:83-016584.

Audience: **g.** *B*

Segre, Emilio   QC7.S4413
From X-Rays to Quarks: Modern Physicists and Their
Discoveries. Trade Cloth. W H Freeman & Company Ltd.
Hampshire, 1980. 337p. ISBN:0-7167-1146-X, ISBN13:
978-0-7167-1146-9. Dewey:530/.09. LCCN:80-000466.

Audience: **g.** *B*

Segrè, Emilio   QC16.S35A3 1993
e A Mind Always in Motion: The Autobiography of Emilio
Segre. E-Book. NetLibrary, Inc. Boulder, CO. 1993.
ISBN:0-585-22847-7, ISBN13: 978-0-585-22847-1.
Dewey:530/.092.

Audience: **g.**

Sime, Ruth L.   QC16.E5
Lise Meitner: A Life in Physics. Trade Paper. University of
California Press. Berkeley, CA. 1997. 540p. California Studies
in the History of Science, Vol. 13 ISBN:0-520-20860-9,
ISBN13: 978-0-520-20860-5. Dewey:530/.092 B.
LCCN:95-035246.

Audience: **g.** *Choice, 1996.*

t' Hooft, Gerard   QC794.6.S75 H66 1997
In Search of the Ultimate Building Blocks. Trade Paper.
Cambridge University Press. New York, NY. 1996. 205p.
ISBN:0-521-57883-3, ISBN13: 978-0-521-57883-7.
Dewey:523/.019/1. LCCN:96-031468.

Audience: **g,l.**

Teller, Edward & Shoolery,   QC16.F46
  Judith
Memoirs: A Twentieth Century Journey in Science and Politics.

Trade Paper. Basic Books. New York, NY. 2002. 672p.
ISBN:0-7382-0778-0, ISBN13: 978-0-7382-0778-0.
Dewey:539.7/092 B.

Audience: **g.** *Choice, 2002.*

Thomson, J. J.   QC16.T45 A3 1975
Recollections and Reflections. Trade Cloth. Ayer Company
Publishers, Inc. Manchester, NH. 1975. History, Philosophy, and
Sociology of Science Ser. ISBN:0-405-06622-8, ISBN13:
978-0-405-06622-1. Dewey:530/.092/4. LCCN:74-026297.

Audience: **g,l.**

Townes, Charles H.   QC16.T65A3 1995
Making Waves. Cloth Text. Springer. New York, NY. 1997.
320p. AIP Masters of Modern Physics Ser. ISBN:1-56396-334-5,
ISBN13: 978-1-56396-334-6. Dewey:507. LCCN:94-028606.

Audience: **g,l.** *Choice, 1995.*

Weinberg, Steven   QC793.2.W44 2003
The Discovery of Subatomic Particles. Ed. 2. Cloth Text.
Cambridge University Press. New York, NY. 2003. 222p.
ISBN:0-521-82351-X, ISBN13: 978-0-521-82351-7.
Dewey:539.7/2. LCCN:2003-283983.

Audience: **g.** *B* *Choice, 2004.*

Weisskopf, Victor   QC15
The Joy of Insight: Passions of a Physicist. Trade Paper. Basic
Books. New York, NY. 1992. 368p. ISBN:0-465-03677-5,
ISBN13: 978-0-465-03677-6. Dewey:530/.092 B.
LCCN:90-049443.

Audience: **g.** *Choice, 1991.*

Westfall, Richard S.   QC16.E5
Never at Rest: A Biography of Isaac Newton. Trade Paper.
Cambridge University Press. New York, NY. 1983. 928p.
ISBN:0-521-27435-4, ISBN13: 978-0-521-27435-7.
Dewey:530/.092. LCCN:79-026294.

Audience: **g.** *B*

Wheeler, John Archibald &   QC16.W48A3 2000
  Ford, Kenneth William
Geons, Black Holes and Quantum Foam: A Life in Physics.
Trade Paper. W. W. Norton & Company, Inc. New York, NY.
2000. 384p. ISBN:0-393-31991-1, ISBN13: 978-0-393-31991-0.
Dewey:530.092. LCCN:97-044566.

Audience: **l,u.** *Choice, 1999.*

White, Michael & Gribbin,   QC16.H33W45 2002
  John
Stephen Hawking: A Life in Science. Ed. 2. Trade Paper.
National Academies Press. Washington, DC. 2002. 360p.
ISBN:0-309-08410-5, ISBN13: 978-0-309-08410-9.
Dewey:530/.092 B. LCCN:2002-011961.

Audience: **g.** *Choice, 2003.*

Reference Works

American Institute of   QC30
  Physics
2006 Graduate Programs in Physics, Astronomy, and Related
Fields. American Institute of Physics. 2006.
ISBN:0-7354-0272-8, ISBN13: 978-0-7354-0272-0.

Audience: **g,l,u,f.**

American Physical Society   QC1
☐ Physics Internet Resources.
http://www.aps.org/resources/
> Audience: **g,l,u,f.**

Daintith, John (Editor)   QC5
A Dictionary of Physics. Ed. 5. Trade Paper, Perfect. Oxford
University Press, Inc. New York, NY. 2005. 592p. Oxford
Paperback Reference Ser. ISBN:0-19-280628-9, ISBN13:
978-0-19-280628-4. Dewey:530.03. LCCN:2005-282728.
> Audience: **g,l,u,f.**

Reference Works > Dictionaries and Encyclopedias

Brown, Laurie M., et al.   QC7.T84 1995
Twentieth Century Physics. Abraham Pais & Brian Pippard
(Authors). Trade Cloth. Institute of Physics Publishing.
Philadelphia, PA. 1995. 2576p. ISBN:0-7503-0310-7, ISBN13:
978-0-7503-0310-1. Dewey:530/.09/04. LCCN:95-041186.
> Audience: **g,l.**

Gaither, Carl C. &   QC5.P47 1997
  Cavazos-Gaither, Alma E.
Physically Speaking: A Dictionary of Quotations on Physics and
Astronomy. Perfect. Institute of Physics Publishing.
Philadelphia, PA. 1997. 504p. Speaking Ser.
ISBN:0-7503-0470-7, ISBN13: 978-0-7503-0470-2. Dewey:530.
LCCN:97-033282.
> Audience: **g,l,u,f.**

Illingworth, Valerie (Editor)   QC5.P46 2000
The Penguin Dictionary of Physics. Ed. 3. Trade Paper. Penguin
Group (USA) Inc. New York, NY. 2001. 512p. Dictionary,
Penguin Ser. ISBN:0-14-051459-7, ISBN13: 978-0-14-051459-9.
Dewey:530/.03. LCCN:2001-267000.
> Audience: **g,l,u,f.**

Lerner, Rita G. & Trigg,   QC5
  George L. (Editors)
Encyclopedia of Physics. Ed. 3. Trade Cloth. John Wiley &
Sons, Inc. Hoboken, NJ. 2005. 3043p. ISBN:3-527-40554-2,
ISBN13: 978-3-527-40554-1. Dewey:530.03.
LCCN:2006-272527.
> Audience: **g,l,u,f.**   *Choice, 2006.*

McGraw-Hill Staff   QC5
Dictionary of Physics. Ed. 3. Sybil P. Parker (Editor). Trade
Paper. McGraw-Hill Professional Publishing. New York, NY.
2003. 483p. ISBN:0-07-141048-1, ISBN13: 978-0-07-141048-9.
Dewey:530/.03. LCCN:2002-033163.
> Audience: **g,l,u,f.**   *Choice, 2003.*

Trigg, George L. (Editor)   QC5
Encyclopedia of Applied Physics. Trade Paper. John Wiley &
Sons, Inc. Hoboken, NJ. 2004. 14576p. ISBN:3-527-40478-3,
ISBN13: 978-3-527-40478-0. Dewey:530.03.
LCCN:2006-280017.
> Audience: **l,u,f.**

Reference Works > Handbooks, Tables, and Formulas

Bass, Michael   QC369.H35 2001
ⓔ Handbook of Optics. Ed. 2. E-Book. McGraw-Hill
Professional Publishing. New York, NY. ISBN:0-07-141479-7,
ISBN13: 978-0-07-141479-1. Dewey:535.
> Audience: **u,f.**

Brookhaven National   QC770
  Laboratory
☐ National Nuclear Data Center.
http://www.nndc.bnl.gov/
> Audience: **u,f.**

Cohen, E. Richard (Editor),   QC61.P49 2000
  et al.
AIP Physics Desk Reference. Ed. 3. David R. Lide & George L.
Trigg (Editors). Trade Cloth. Springer. New York, NY. 2003.
XXXV, 888p. ISBN:0-387-98973-0, ISBN13:
978-0-387-98973-0. Dewey:530. LCCN:99-059693.
> Audience: **g,l,u,f.**   *Choice, 2003.*

Firestone, Richard B.   QD601.2.F57 1996
Table of Isotopes, Vol. 1. Ed. 8. Virginia S. Shirley (Editor),
Coral M. Baglin, S. Y. Chu & Jean Zipkin (Contribution by).
Trade Cloth. John Wiley & Sons, Inc. Hoboken, NJ. 1998.
3000p. ISBN:0-471-07730-5, ISBN13: 978-0-471-07730-5.
Dewey:541.3/884/0212. LCCN:95-046439.
> Audience: **u,f.**

Harris, John W. (Editor),   QC61.H37 2001
  et al.
Handbook of Physics. Horst Stocker, Walter Benenson & Holger
Lutz (Editors). Trade Cloth. Springer. New York, NY. 2006.
XXV, 1181p. ISBN:0-387-95269-1, ISBN13:
978-0-387-95269-7. Dewey:530. LCCN:2001-020442.
> Audience: **l,u,f.**   *Choice, 2002.*

National Institute of   QC61
  Standards and Technology
☐ NIST Physical Reference Data.
http://physics.nist.gov/PhysRefData/contents.html
> Audience: **l,u,f.**

Nuclear Data Evaluation   QC793.5.N82
  Lab
☐ Table of Nuclides.
http://atom.kaeri.re.kr/
> Audience: **u,f.**

Particle Data Group   QC793
☐ Review of Particle Physics.
http://pdg.lbl.gov/
University of California.
> Audience: **u,f.**

Poole, Charles P.   QC61.P65 1998
The Physics Handbook: Fundamentals and Key Equations. Ed.
1. Trade Paper. John Wiley & Sons, Inc. Hoboken, NJ. 1999.
518p. ISBN:0-471-31460-9, ISBN13: 978-0-471-31460-8.
Dewey:530. LCCN:97-045863.
> Audience: **l,u,f.**

Mechanics

Arnold, V. I.   QA805.A6813 1989
Mathematical Methods of Classical Mechanics. Ed. 2. K.
Vogtmann & A. Weinstein (Translators). Trade Cloth. Springer.
New York, NY. 1997. XVI, 509p. Graduate Texts in
Mathematics, Vol. 60 ISBN:0-387-96890-3, ISBN13:
978-0-387-96890-2. Dewey:531/.01515. LCCN:88-039823.
Audience: **u,f.**

Arya, Atam Parkash   QC125.2.A79 1998
Introduction to Classical Mechanics. Ed. 2. Cloth Text. Prentice
Hall PTR. Upper Saddle River, NJ. 1997. 712p.
ISBN:0-13-505223-8, ISBN13: 978-0-13-505223-5. Dewey:531.
LCCN:97-016622.
Audience: **l,u.**

Becker, Robert A.   QA807 .B37
Introduction to Theoretical Mechanics. Paper Text. Textbook
Publishers. Temecula, CA. 2003. 420p. ISBN:0-7581-8493-X,
ISBN13: 978-0-7581-8493-1. Dewey:531.
Audience: **u,f.**

Chandrasekhar, S.   QA808.2
Newton's Principia for the Common Reader. Trade Paper.
Oxford University Press, Inc. New York, NY. 2003. 618p.
ISBN:0-19-852675-X, ISBN13: 978-0-19-852675-9. Dewey:531.
Audience: **g,l,u,f.**

Cohen, I. Bernard   QA803
Introduction to Newton's Principia. Trade Paper. iUniverse, Inc.
Lincoln, NE. 1999. 432p. ISBN:1-58348-601-1, ISBN13:
978-1-58348-601-6. Dewey:531.
Audience: **g,l,u,f.**

Fowles, Grant R. &   QA807.F65 2004
  Cassiday, George L.
Analytical Mechanics. Ed. 7. Cloth Text. Brooks/Cole. Pacific
Grove, CA. 2004. 544p. ISBN:0-534-49492-7, ISBN13:
978-0-534-49492-6. Dewey:531/.01/515. LCCN:2003-115137.
Audience: **l.** *B*

French, Anthony P.   QC125.2
Newtonian Mechanics. Paper Text. W. W. Norton & Company,
Inc. New York, NY. 1971. 743p. M.I.T. Introductory Physics
Ser. ISBN:0-393-09970-9, ISBN13: 978-0-393-09970-6.
Dewey:531.
Audience: **u,f.**

Galilei, Galileo   QC123.G13 1991
Dialogues Concerning Two New Sciences. Henry Crew &
Alfonso De Salvio (Translators). Trade Paper. Prometheus
Books, Publishers. Amherst, NY. 1991. 298p. Great Minds Ser.
ISBN:0-87975-707-8, ISBN13: 978-0-87975-707-6. Dewey:531.
LCCN:91-061910.
Audience: **l,u.**

Galilei, Galileo   QC123 .G1153
On Motion and on Mechanics. I. E. Drabkin (Editor), Stillman
Drake (Translator), M. Clagett (Introduction by). Trade Cloth.
University of Wisconsin Press. Chicago, IL. 1960. 204p.
Medieval Science Publications ISBN:0-299-02030-4, ISBN13:
978-0-299-02030-9. Dewey:531.
Audience: **l,u.**

Goldstein, Herbert, et al.   QA805 .G6 2002
Classical Mechanics. Ed. 3. Charles P. Poole & John L. Safko
(Authors). Cloth Text. Addison-Wesley Longman, Inc. Boston,
MA. 2001. 680p. ISBN:0-201-65702-3, ISBN13:
978-0-201-65702-9. Dewey:531.
Audience: **u,f.** *B*

Gutzwiller, M. C.   QC125.2.G88 1990
Chaos in Classical and Quantum Mechanics. Trade Cloth.
Springer. New York, NY. 1991. XIII, 432p. Interdisciplinary
Applied Mathematics Ser., Vol. 1 ISBN:0-387-97173-4, ISBN13:
978-0-387-97173-5. Dewey:531. LCCN:90-216263.
Audience: **u,f.**

Halliday, David, et al.   QC21.2.H35 2004
Fundamentals of Physics. Ed. 7. Robert Resnick, Jearl Walker &
J. Richard Christman (Authors). Trade Paper. John Wiley &
Sons, Inc. Hoboken, NJ. 2004. 377p. ISBN:0-471-47061-9,
ISBN13: 978-0-471-47061-8. Dewey:530.076.
Audience: **l.**

Hand, Louis N. & Finch,   QA805 .H26 1998
  Janet D.
Analytical Mechanics. Trade Paper. Cambridge University Press.
New York, NY. 1998. 592p. ISBN:0-521-57572-9, ISBN13:
978-0-521-57572-0. Dewey:531/.01/515352. LCCN:97-043334.
Audience: **u,f.**

José, Jorge V. & Saletan,   QA805
  Eugene J.
Classical Dynamics: A Contemporary Approach. Trade Paper.
Cambridge University Press. New York, NY. 1998. 696p.
ISBN:0-521-63636-1, ISBN13: 978-0-521-63636-0.
Dewey:531/.11/01515. LCCN:97-043733.
Audience: **u,f.**

Landau, L. D.   QC21 .L2713
General Physics: Mechanics and Molecular Physics. Trade
Cloth. Elsevier Science & Technology Books. Saint Louis, MO.
1967. ISBN:0-08-009106-7, ISBN13: 978-0-08-009106-8.
Dewey:530.
Audience: **u,f.** *B*

Landau, L. D., et al.   QA931
Theory of Elasticity, Vol. 7. Ed. 3. A. M. Kosevich, E. M.
Lifshitz & L. P. Pitaevskii (Authors). Trade Paper. Elsevier
Science & Technology Books. Saint Louis, MO. 1986. 195p.
ISBN:0-7506-2633-X, ISBN13: 978-0-7506-2633-0.
Dewey:531/.38.
Audience: **u,f.** *B*

Landau, L. D. & Lifshitz,   QA805.L283 2001
  E. M.
Mechanics, Vol. 1. Ed. 3. Paper Text. Elsevier Science &
Technology Books. Saint Louis, MO. 1976. 224p. Course of
Theoretical Physics Ser., Vol. 1 ISBN:0-7506-2896-0, ISBN13:
978-0-7506-2896-9. Dewey:530. LCCN:76-018997.
Audience: **u,f.** *B*

Mahan, Gerald D.   QC176.M24 2000
Many-Particle Physics. Ed. 3. Trade Cloth. Springer. New York,
NY. 2000. 788p. Physics of Solids and Liquids Ser.
ISBN:0-306-46338-5, ISBN13: 978-0-306-46338-9.
Dewey:530.4/1. LCCN:00-039101.
Audience: **u,f.**

McCauley, Joseph L.   QC125.2 .M39 1997
Classical Mechanics: Transformations, Flows, Integrable and Chaotic Dynamics. Trade Cloth. Cambridge University Press. New York, NY. 1997. 487p. ISBN:0-521-48132-5, ISBN13: 978-0-521-48132-8. Dewey:531. LCCN:96-031574.
Audience: **u,f.**

Saletan, Eugene J. &   QA805
  Cromer, Alan H.
Theoretical Mechanics. Ed. 99. Cloth Text. John Wiley & Sons, Inc. Hoboken, NJ. 1971. 376p. ISBN:0-471-74986-9, ISBN13: 978-0-471-74986-8. Dewey:531. LCCN:78-161494.
Audience: **u,f.**

Sommerfeld, Arnold   QC20
Mechanics. Trade Cloth. Elsevier Science & Technology Books. Saint Louis, MO. 1964. Lectures on Theoretical Physics Ser., Vol. 1 ISBN:0-12-654668-1, ISBN13: 978-0-12-654668-2. Dewey:531.
Audience: **u,f.**

Thornton, Stephen T. &   QA845
  Marion, Jerry B.
Classical Dynamics of Particles and Systems. Ed. 5. Cloth Text. Brooks/Cole. Pacific Grove, CA. 2003. 672p. ISBN:0-534-40896-6, ISBN13: 978-0-534-40896-1. Dewey:531/.11. LCCN:2003-105243.
Audience: **u,f.**

Mechanics > Fluid Mechanics

Acheson, D. J.   TA357.A276 1990
Elementary Fluid Dynamics. Paper Text. Oxford University Press, Inc. New York, NY. 1990. 406p. Oxford Applied Mathematics and Computing Science Ser. ISBN:0-19-859679-0, ISBN13: 978-0-19-859679-0. Dewey:532. LCCN:89-022947.
Audience: **u.**

Batchelor, G. K.   QA911
An Introduction to Fluid Dynamics. Trade Paper. Cambridge University Press. New York, NY. 2000. 635p. Cambridge Mathematical Library ISBN:0-521-66396-2, ISBN13: 978-0-521-66396-0. Dewey:532/.05.
Audience: **u,f.** *B*

Chung, T. J.   QA911 .C476 2002
Computational Fluid Dynamics. Trade Cloth. Cambridge University Press. New York, NY. 2002. 1036p. ISBN:0-521-59416-2, ISBN13: 978-0-521-59416-5. Dewey:532/.05/0285. LCCN:00-054671.
Audience: **u,f.** *Choice, 2003, 2002.*

Cohen, Ira M. & Kundu,   QA901
  Pijush K.
Fluid Mechanics. Ed. 3. Cloth Text. Elsevier Science & Technology Books. Saint Louis, MO. 2004. 759p. ISBN:0-12-178253-0, ISBN13: 978-0-12-178253-5. Dewey:620.1/06. LCCN:2004-273176.
Audience: **u,f.**

Davidson, P. A.   QA920 .D38 2001
An Introduction to Magnetohydrodynamics. M. J. Ablowitz, S. H. Davis, E. J. Hinch, A. Iserles, J. Ockendon & P. J. Olver (Contribution by). Trade Paper. Cambridge University Press.

New York, NY. 2001. 452p. Texts in Applied Mathematics ISBN:0-521-79487-0, ISBN13: 978-0-521-79487-9. Dewey:538/.6. LCCN:00-033733.
Audience: **u,f.**

Faber, T. E.   QC151 .F33 1995
Fluid Dynamics for Physicists. Trade Paper. Cambridge University Press. New York, NY. 1995. 466p. ISBN:0-521-42969-2, ISBN13: 978-0-521-42969-6. Dewey:532/.05. LCCN:94-019245.
Audience: **u,f.** *Choice, 1996.*

Frisch, Uriel   QA913 .F74 1995
Turbulence: The Legacy of A. N. Kolmogorov. Trade Paper. Cambridge University Press. New York, NY. 1995. 310p. ISBN:0-521-45713-0, ISBN13: 978-0-521-45713-2. Dewey:532/.0527. LCCN:95-012140.
Audience: **u,f.**

Landau, L. D. & Lifshitz,   QA901 L23ME 1999
  E. M.
Fluid Mechanics, Vol. 6. Ed. 2. Paper Text. Elsevier Science & Technology Books. Saint Louis, MO. 1987. 552p. ISBN:0-7506-2767-0, ISBN13: 978-0-7506-2767-2. Dewey:532.
Audience: **u,f.** *B*

Pope, Stephen Bailey   QA913 .P64 2000
Turbulent Flows. Trade Paper. Cambridge University Press. New York, NY. 2000. 806p. ISBN:0-521-59886-9, ISBN13: 978-0-521-59886-6. Dewey:532/.0527. LCCN:99-044583.
Audience: **u,f.**

Tritton, D. J.   QC151.T74 1988
Physical Fluid Dynamics. Ed. 2. Paper Text. Oxford University Press, Inc. New York, NY. 1988. 536p. ISBN:0-19-854493-6, ISBN13: 978-0-19-854493-7. Dewey:532/.05. LCCN:87-034162.
Audience: **u,f.**

Modern Physics

Beiser, Arthur & Berg,   QC21.3.B45 2002
  Isabel
Concepts of Modern Physics. Ed. 6. Cloth Text. McGraw-Hill Higher Education. Burr Ridge, IL. 2002. 560p. ISBN:0-07-244848-2, ISBN13: 978-0-07-244848-1. Dewey:539. LCCN:2001-044743.
Audience: **l.**

Eisberg, Robert Martin   PN2062.S7513
Fundamentals of Modern Physics. Paper Text. Textbook Publishers. Temecula, CA. 2003. 729p. ISBN:0-7581-0412-X, ISBN13: 978-0-7581-0412-0. Dewey:792/.028.
Audience: **l,u.** *B*

Krane, Kenneth S.   QC21.2.K7 1996
Modern Physics. Ed. 2. Trade Cloth. John Wiley & Sons, Inc. Hoboken, NJ. 1995. 608p. ISBN:0-471-82872-6, ISBN13: 978-0-471-82872-3. Dewey:539. LCCN:95-006382.
Audience: **l,u.**

Tipler, Paul A. & Llewellyn,   QC21.3.T56 2002
  Ralph A.
Modern Physics. Ed. 4. Cloth over Boards. Worth Publishers, Inc. New York, NY. 2002. 700p. ISBN:0-7167-4345-0, ISBN13: 978-0-7167-4345-3. Dewey:530. LCCN:2002-072054.
Audience: **l.**

University of Colorado at   QC21.2
 Boulder
☐ Physics 2000.
http://www.colorado.edu/physics/2000/index.pl

Audience: **g,l.**

Mathematical Physics

Landau, L. D.   Q173.7
Course of Theoretical Physics: The Classical Theory of Fields,
Vol. 2. Ed. 4. M. Hamermesh (Contribution by). Trade Paper.
Elsevier Science & Technology Books. Saint Louis, MO. 1980.
xi, 402p. Course of Theoretical Physics Ser.
ISBN:0-08-025072-6, ISBN13: 978-0-08-025072-4.
Dewey:530.1/4. LCCN:75-004737.

Audience: **u,f.** *B*

Longair, Malcolm S.   QC20.L64 2003
Theoretical Concepts in Physics: An Alternative View of
Theoretical Reasoning in Physics. Ed. 2. Trade Paper.
Cambridge University Press. New York, NY. 2003. 588p.
ISBN:0-521-52878-X, ISBN13: 978-0-521-52878-8.
Dewey:530.1. LCCN:2002-073612.

Audience: **l,u.** *B* *Choice, 2004.*

Morse, Philip McCord   QC20.M6
Methods of Theoretical Physics, Vol. 2. Ed. 1. Trade Cloth.
McGraw-Hill Companies, The. New York, NY. 1999.
ISBN:0-07-043353-4, ISBN13: 978-0-07-043353-3.

Audience: **u,f.**

Thirring, W.   QC20
A Course in Mathematical Physics, Vol II. Cloth Text. Springer.
New York, NY. 1979. 249p. ISBN:0-387-81532-5, ISBN13:
978-0-387-81532-9. Dewey:530.1/5.

Audience: **u,f.**

Mathematical Physics > Group Theory and Symmetry

Cornwell, John F.   QC20.7.G76
Group Theory in Physics: An Introduction. Trade Paper. Elsevier
Science & Technology Books. Saint Louis, MO. 1997. 349p.
Techniques of Physics Ser. ISBN:0-12-189800-8, ISBN13:
978-0-12-189800-7. Dewey:530.1/5/22.

Audience: **u,f.**

Cotton, F. Albert   QD461.C65 1990
Chemical Applications of Group Theory. Ed. 3. Trade Cloth.
John Wiley & Sons, Inc. Hoboken, NJ. 1990. 480p.
ISBN:0-471-51094-7, ISBN13: 978-0-471-51094-9.
Dewey:541/.22/015122. LCCN:89-016434.

Audience: **u,f.** *B* *Choice, 1991.*

Hamermesh, Morton   QA171.H28 1989
Group Theory and Its Application to Physical Problems. Trade
Paper. Dover Publications, Inc. Mineola, NY. 1989. 528p.
ISBN:0-486-66181-4, ISBN13: 978-0-486-66181-0.
Dewey:512/.2. LCCN:89-023257.

Audience: **u,f.**

Singer, Stephanie F.   QA805.S62 2001
Symmetry in Mechanics: A Gentle, Modern Introduction. Trade
Paper. Birkhauser Boston. Cambridge, MA. 2001. XII, 193p.
ISBN:0-8176-4145-9, ISBN13: 978-0-8176-4145-0. Dewey:531.
LCCN:00-049398.

Audience: **u,f.**

Tung, W. K.   QC174.17.G7 T86 1985
Group Theory in Physics: An Introduction to Symmetry
Principles, Group Representations, and Special Functions. Paper
Text. World Scientific Publishing Company, Inc. Hackensack,
NJ. 1985. 336p. ISBN:9971-966-57-3, ISBN13:
978-9971-966-57-7. Dewey:530.1/5222. LCCN:85-003335.

Audience: **u,f.**

Mathematical Physics > Mathematical Methods

Arfken, George B. & Weber,   QA37.3.A74 2005
 Hans J.
Mathematical Methods for Physicists. Ed. 6. Cloth Text.
Elsevier Science & Technology Books. Saint Louis, MO. 2005.
1200p. ISBN:0-12-059876-0, ISBN13: 978-0-12-059876-2.
Dewey:510. LCCN:2005-049844.

Audience: **u,f.**

Arnold, V. I.   QA805.A6813 1989
Mathematical Methods of Classical Mechanics. Ed. 2. K.
Vogtmann & A. Weinstein (Translators). Trade Cloth. Springer.
New York, NY. 1997. XVI, 509p. Graduate Texts in
Mathematics, Vol. 60 ISBN:0-387-96890-3, ISBN13:
978-0-387-96890-2. Dewey:531/.01515. LCCN:88-039823.

Audience: **u,f.**

Boas, Mary L.   QA37.3.B63 2006
Mathematical Methods in the Physical Sciences. Ed. 3. Trade
Cloth. John Wiley & Sons, Inc. Hoboken, NJ. 2005. 864p.
ISBN:0-471-19826-9, ISBN13: 978-0-471-19826-0. Dewey:510.
LCCN:2005-279918.

Audience: **u,f.**

Chow, Tai L.   QC20 .C57 2000
Mathematical Methods for Physicists: A Concise Introduction.
Trade Paper. Cambridge University Press. New York, NY. 2000.
572p. ISBN:0-521-65544-7, ISBN13: 978-0-521-65544-6.
Dewey:530.15. LCCN:99-044592.

Audience: **l,u.**

Lanczos, Cornelius   QA805.L278 1986
The Variational Principles of Mechanics. Trade Paper. Dover
Publications, Inc. Mineola, NY. 1986. 418p.
ISBN:0-486-65067-7, ISBN13: 978-0-486-65067-8.
Dewey:531/.01/51. LCCN:85-029168.

Audience: **u,f.** *B*

Quantum Mechanics/Quantum Theory

Basdevant, Jean-Louis &   QC174.2.B38 2002
 Dalibard, J.
Quantum Mechanics. Trade Cloth, CD-ROM. Springer. New
York, NY. 2002. 534p. Advanced Texts in Physics
ISBN:3-540-42739-2, ISBN13: 978-3-540-42739-1.
Dewey:530.12. LCCN:2002-070768.

Audience: **u,f.**

Bethe, Hans A. & Jackiw, Roman V.   QC174.12.B47 1997
Intermediate Quantum Mechanics. Ed. 3. Trade Paper. Westview Press. Boulder, CO. 1997. 416p. Advanced Book Classics Ser. ISBN:0-201-32831-3, ISBN13: 978-0-201-32831-8. Dewey:530.12. LCCN:97-039327.
Audience: **u,f.**

Bethe, Hans A. & Salpeter, E. E.   QC174.17.P7 B47 1977
Quantum Mechanics of One- and Two-Electron Atoms. Cloth Text. Springer. New York, NY. 1977. 382p. ISBN:0-306-20022-8, ISBN13: 978-0-306-20022-9. Dewey:539.7. LCCN:76-030829.
Audience: **u,f.**

Bjorken, James D.   QC174.45
Relativistic Quantum Mechanics. Paper Text. McGraw-Hill Higher Education. Burr Ridge, IL. 1998. 314p. ISBN:0-07-232002-8, ISBN13: 978-0-07-232002-2. Dewey:530.12.
Audience: **u,f.** B

Bohm, David   QC174.12.B632 1989
Quantum Theory. Trade Paper. Dover Publications, Inc. Mineola, NY. 1998. 655p. ISBN:0-486-65969-0, ISBN13: 978-0-486-65969-5. Dewey:530.1/2. LCCN:89-031187.
Audience: **u,f.** B

Bransden, B. H. & Joachain, C. J.   QC174.12.B74 2000
Quantum Mechanics. Ed. 2. Trade Paper. Prentice Hall PTR. Upper Saddle River, NJ. 2000. 816p. ISBN:0-582-35691-1, ISBN13: 978-0-582-35691-7. Dewey:530.12. LCCN:99-055742.
Audience: **u,f.**

Cohen-Tannoudji, Claude, et al.   QC174.12
Quantum Mechanics, Vol. 2. Ed. 1. Bernard Diu & Frank Laloe (Authors). Trade Paper. John Wiley & Sons, Inc. Hoboken, NJ. 1992. 1524p. ISBN:0-471-56952-6, ISBN13: 978-0-471-56952-7. Dewey:530.1/2.
Audience: **u,f.**

Davydov, A. S.   QC174.12
Quantum Mechanics, Vol. 1. Ed. 2. D. Ter Haar (Translator). Paper Text. Elsevier Science & Technology Books. Saint Louis, MO. 1976. 760p. ISBN:0-08-020437-6, ISBN13: 978-0-08-020437-6. Dewey:530.1/2. LCCN:76-011628.
Audience: **u,f.** B

Dirac, Paul Adrien Maurice   QC174.12
The Principles of Quantum Mechanics. Ed. 4. Paper Text. Oxford University Press, Inc. New York, NY. 1982. 324p. The International Series of Monographs on Physics ISBN:0-19-852011-5, ISBN13: 978-0-19-852011-5. Dewey:530.1/2.
Audience: **u,f.**

Eisberg, Robert M. & Resnick, Robert E.   QC174.12.E34 1985
Quantum Physics of Atoms, Molecules, Solids, Nuclei, and Particles. Ed. 2. Trade Cloth. John Wiley & Sons, Inc. Hoboken, NJ. 1985. 864p. ISBN:0-471-87373-X, ISBN13: 978-0-471-87373-0. Dewey:530.1/2. LCCN:84-010444.
Audience: **u,f.**

Fetter, Alexander L. & Walecka, John Dirk   QC174.17.P7F47 2003
Quantum Theory of Many-Particle Systems. Trade Paper. Dover Publications, Inc. Mineola, NY. 2003. 617p. Physics Ser. ISBN:0-486-42827-3, ISBN13: 978-0-486-42827-7. Dewey:530.14/4. LCCN:2003-043536.
Audience: **u,f.**

Flügge, Siegfried   QC174.12.F5813 1999
Practical Quantum Mechanics. Ed. 2. Trade Paper. Springer. New York, NY. 1998. XVIII, 624p. Classics in Mathematics Ser. ISBN:3-540-65035-0, ISBN13: 978-3-540-65035-5. Dewey:530.12. LCCN:98-045580.
Audience: **u,f.**

French, A. P. & Taylor, E. F.   QC174.12
An Introduction to Quantum Physics. Paper Text. Chapman & Hall. New York, NY. 1991. 696p. MIT Introductory Physics Ser. ISBN:0-412-37580-X, ISBN13: 978-0-412-37580-4. Dewey:530.1/2.
Audience: **u,f.** B

Gasiorowicz, Stephen   QC174.12
Quantum Physics. Ed. 3. Trade Cloth. John Wiley & Sons, Inc. Hoboken, NJ. 2003. 352p. ISBN:0-471-05700-2, ISBN13: 978-0-471-05700-0. Dewey:530.12. LCCN:2003-043271.
Audience: **u,f.**

Gottfried, Kurt & Yan, Tung-Mow   QC174.12.G68 2004
Quantum Mechanics: Fundamentals. Ed. 2. Trade Paper. Springer. New York, NY. 2004. XVII, 620p. ISBN:0-387-22023-2, ISBN13: 978-0-387-22023-9. Dewey:530.12.
Audience: **u,f.**

Greiner, Walter   QC174.12.G745213
Quantum Mechanics: An Introduction. Ed. 4. D. A. Bromley (Foreword by). Trade Paper. Springer. New York, NY. 2000. XXI, 485p. ISBN:3-540-67458-6, ISBN13: 978-3-540-67458-0. Dewey:530.12. LCCN:00-046345.
Audience: **u,f.**

Griffiths, David J.   QC174.12.G75 2005
Introduction to Quantum Mechanics. Ed. 2. Cloth Text. Prentice Hall PTR. Upper Saddle River, NJ. 2004. 480p. ISBN:0-13-111892-7, ISBN13: 978-0-13-111892-8. Dewey:530.12. LCCN:2003-027110.
Audience: **u,f.**

Kleinert, Hagen   QC174.12
Path Integrals in Quantum Mechanics, Statistics and Polymer Physics. Ed. 3. Trade Paper. World Scientific Publishing Company, Inc. Hackensack, NJ. 2004. 1504p. ISBN:981-238-107-4, ISBN13: 978-981-238-107-1. Dewey:530.1/2.
Audience: **u,f.**

Landau, L. D. & Lifshitz, E. M.   QC174.12
Quantum Mechanics Non-Relativistic Theory, Vol. 3. Ed. 3. Paper Text. Elsevier Science & Technology Books. Saint Louis, MO. 1981. 689p. Quantum Mechanics Ser., Vol. 3 ISBN:0-7506-3539-8, ISBN13: 978-0-7506-3539-4. Dewey:530.1/2.
Audience: **u,f.**

Landau, L. D., et al.   QC174.45
Relativistic Quantum Theory, Vol. 4, Pts. 1-2. E. M. Lifshitz &
L. P. Pitaevskii (Authors). Cloth Text. Elsevier. New York, NY.
1974. xv, 375p. ISBN:0-08-016025-5, ISBN13:
978-0-08-016025-2. Dewey:530.1/2. LCCN:78-143989.

      Audience: **u,f.**

Liboff, Richard L.   QC174.12.L52 2003
Introductory Quantum Mechanics. Ed. 4. Trade Cloth.
Addison-Wesley Longman, Inc. Boston, MA. 2002. 900p.
ISBN:0-8053-8714-5, ISBN13: 978-0-8053-8714-8.
Dewey:530.1/2. LCCN:2002-511525.

      Audience: **u,f.**

Merzbacher, Eugen   QC174.12.M47 1998
Quantum Mechanics. Ed. 3. Trade Cloth. John Wiley & Sons,
Inc. Hoboken, NJ. 1998. 672p. ISBN:0-471-88702-1, ISBN13:
978-0-471-88702-7. Dewey:530.12. LCCN:97-020756.

      Audience: **u,f.** *B*

Messiah, Albert   QC174.12.M4813 1999
Quantum Mechanics. Trade Paper. Dover Publications, Inc.
Mineola, NY. 2000. 1152p. ISBN:0-486-40924-4, ISBN13:
978-0-486-40924-5. Dewey:530.12. LCCN:99-055362.

      Audience: **u,f.**

Pauling, Linus & Wilson, E.   QC174.12.P39 1985
   Bright
Introduction to Quantum Mechanics with Applications to
Chemistry. Trade Paper. Dover Publications, Inc. Mineola, NY.
1985. 468p. Physics Ser. ISBN:0-486-64871-0, ISBN13:
978-0-486-64871-2. Dewey:530.1/2. LCCN:84-025919.

      Audience: **u,f.** *B*

Sakurai, J. J. & Taun,   QC174.12 .S25 1994
   San F.
Modern Quantum Mechanics. Ed. 2. Cloth Text.
Addison-Wesley Longman, Inc. Boston, MA. 1993. 500p.
ISBN:0-201-53929-2, ISBN13: 978-0-201-53929-5.
Dewey:530.1/2. LCCN:93-017803.

      Audience: **u,f.**

Schiff, Leonard I.   QC174.12
Quantum Mechanics. Ed. 3. Cloth Text. McGraw-Hill
Companies, The. New York, NY. 1968. xviii, 544p. International
Series in Pure and Applied Physics ISBN:0-07-055287-8,
ISBN13: 978-0-07-055287-6. Dewey:530.12. LCCN:68-025665.

      Audience: **u,f.** *B*

Shankar, R.   QC174.12.S52 1994
Principles of Quantum Mechanics. Ed. 2. Trade Cloth. Springer.
New York, NY. 1994. 694p. ISBN:0-306-44790-8, ISBN13:
978-0-306-44790-7. Dewey:530.1/2. LCCN:94-026837.

      Audience: **u,f.** *Choice, 1995.*

Slater, John C.   QC174.12 .S55
Quantum Theory of Molecules and Solids, Vol. 1, 3 & 4. Other.
McGraw-Hill Companies, The. New York, NY. 9999.
ISBN:0-318-54185-8, ISBN13: 978-0-318-54185-3.
Dewey:530.1/2.

      Audience: **u,f.**

Stöckmann, H. -J.   QC174.17.C45 S84 19
Quantum Chaos: An Introduction. Trade Cloth. Cambridge
University Press. New York, NY. 1999. 380p.
ISBN:0-521-59284-4, ISBN13: 978-0-521-59284-0.
Dewey:530.12. LCCN:98-045454.

      Audience: **u,f.**

Quantum Field Theories

Bogoliubov, M. N. &   QC174.45
   Shirkov, D. V.
Quantum Fields. Trade Cloth. Addison-Wesley Longman, Inc.
Boston, MA. 1983. 653p. ISBN:0-8053-0983-7, ISBN13:
978-0-8053-0983-6. Dewey:530.1/43. LCCN:82-004366.

      Audience: **u,f.** *B*

Chang, S. J.   QC174.45.C445 1990
Introduction to Quantum Field Theory. Paper Text. World
Scientific Publishing Company, Inc. Hackensack, NJ. 1990.
396p. Lecture Notes in Physics Ser., Vol. 29
ISBN:9971-5-0681-5, ISBN13: 978-9971-5-0681-0.
Dewey:530.1/43. LCCN:89-077616.

      Audience: **u,f.**

Das, A.   QC174.52.P37D37 1993
Field Theory: A Path Integral Approach - Lecture Notes in
Physics, Vol. 52. Paper Text. World Scientific Publishing
Company, Inc. Hackensack, NJ. 1993. 416p. Lecture Notes in
Physics Ser. ISBN:981-02-1397-2, ISBN13: 978-981-02-1397-8.
Dewey:530.1/41. LCCN:94-152473.

      Audience: **u,f.**

Kaku, Michio   QC174.45
Quantum Field Theory. Paper Text. Oxford University Press,
Inc. New York, NY. 1994. 804p. ISBN:0-19-509158-2, ISBN13:
978-0-19-509158-8. Dewey:530.1/43.

      Audience: **u,f.**

Patricia Schwarz   QC794.6.S85
⬚ The Official String Theory Web Site.
http://superstringtheory.com/

      Audience: **g,l,u.**

Polyakov, A. M.   QC793.3.F5P66 1987
Gauge Fields and Strings. Paper Text. Gordon & Breach
Publishing Group. New York, NY. 1987. 302p. Contemporary
Concepts in Physics Ser., Vol. 3 ISBN:3-7186-0392-6, ISBN13:
978-3-7186-0392-3. Dewey:530.1/43. LCCN:87-000151.

      Audience: **u,f.**

Ryder, Lewis H.   QC793 .R93 1996
Quantum Field Theory. Ed. 2. Trade Paper. Cambridge
University Press. New York, NY. 1996. 507p.
ISBN:0-521-47814-6, ISBN13: 978-0-521-47814-4.
Dewey:530.1/43. LCCN:95-031119.

      Audience: **u,f.** *Choice, 1986.*

Stone, Michael   QC174.45.S79 2000
The Physics of Quantum Fields. Trade Cloth. Springer. New
York, NY. 1999. XIV, 292p. Graduate Texts in Contemporary
Physics ISBN:0-387-98909-9, ISBN13: 978-0-387-98909-9.
Dewey:530.14/3. LCCN:99-039802.

      Audience: **u,f.**

Zee, A.   QC174.45.Z44 2003
Quantum Field Theory in a Nutshell. Trade Cloth. Princeton
University Press. Princeton, NJ. 2003. 480p.
ISBN:0-691-01019-6, ISBN13: 978-0-691-01019-9.
Dewey:530.14/3. LCCN:2002-031743.

      Audience: **u,f.** *Choice, 2003.*

Zuber, Jean Bernard &   QC174.45.I77 2005
   Itzykson, Claude
Quantum Field Theory. Trade Paper. Dover Publications, Inc.

Mineola, NY. 2006. 752p. Dover Books on Physics
ISBN:0-486-44568-2, ISBN13: 978-0-486-44568-7.
Dewey:530.14/3. LCCN:2005-053026.

Audience: **u,f.**

Computational Physics

Giordano, Nicholas J. &   QC20.7.E4G56 2005
Nakanishi, Hisao
Computational Physics. Ed. 2. Trade Cloth. Prentice Hall PTR.
Upper Saddle River, NJ. 2005. 560p. ISBN:0-13-146990-8,
ISBN13: 978-0-13-146990-7. Dewey:530.15/8.
LCCN:2005-049248.

Audience: **l,u.** *Choice, 1997.*

Koonin, Steven E.   QC20.7.E4 K66
Computational Physics: Fortran Version. Trade Paper. Perseus
Books Group. New York, NY. 1998. 656p. ISBN:0-201-38623-2,
ISBN13: 978-0-201-38623-3. Dewey:530.1/5/02855133.

Audience: **l,u.**

Landau, Rubin H., et al.   QC2082
Computational Physics: Problem Solving with Computers. Ed. 2.
Manuel José Páez Mejía & Cristian C. Bordeianu (Authors).
Trade Cloth. John Wiley & Sons, Inc. Hoboken, NJ. 2004. 550p.
ISBN:0-471-67190-8, ISBN13: 978-0-471-67190-9.
Dewey:530/.0785.

Audience: **l,u.** *Choice, 1998.*

Parr, Robert G. & Weitao,   QC176
Yang
Density-Functional Theory of Atoms and Molecules. Trade
Paper. Oxford University Press, Inc. New York, NY. 1994. 342p.
International Series of Monographs on Chemistry, Vol. 16
ISBN:0-19-509276-7, ISBN13: 978-0-19-509276-9.
Dewey:530.4/1.

Audience: **u,f.**

Thijssen, J. M.   QC20
Computational Physics. Trade Paper. Cambridge University
Press. New York, NY. 1999. 560p. ISBN:0-521-57588-5,
ISBN13: 978-0-521-57588-1. Dewey:530.15. LCCN:99-036458.

Audience: **l,u.**

Computational Physics > Computer Simulations

Allen, M. P. & Tildesley, D.   QD455.3.C64C66 1993
J. (Editors)
Computer Simulation in Chemical Physics. Trade Cloth.
Springer. New York, NY. 1993. 532p. NATO Advanced Science
Institutes Ser., Vol. 397:Mathematical and Physical Science
ISBN:0-7923-2283-5, ISBN13: 978-0-7923-2283-2.
Dewey:539.60113. LCCN:93-017086.

Audience: **u,f.**

Binder, Kurt & Heermann,   QC174.85
Dieter W.
Monte Carlo Simulation in Statistical Physics: An Introduction.
Ed. 4. Trade Cloth. Springer. New York, NY. 2002. XII, 180p.
Series in Solid-State Sciences, Vol. 80 ISBN:3-540-43221-3,
ISBN13: 978-3-540-43221-0. Dewey:530.4/15.
LCCN:2003-537870.

Audience: **u,f.**

Binder, Kurt & Landau,   QC174.85.M64L36 2005
David P.
A Guide to Monte Carlo Simulations in Statistical Physics. Ed.
2. Trade Cloth. Cambridge University Press. New York, NY.
2005. 448p. ISBN:0-521-84238-7, ISBN13: 978-0-521-84238-9.
Dewey:530.13. LCCN:2005-285370.

Audience: **u,f.**

Frenkel, Daan & Smit, B.   QD461
Understanding Molecular Simulation: From Algorithms to
Applications. Ed. 2. Trade Cloth. Elsevier Science &
Technology Books. Saint Louis, MO. 2001. 664p.
Computational Science Ser. ISBN:0-12-267351-4, ISBN13:
978-0-12-267351-1. Dewey:539/.6/0113. LCCN:2001-091477.

Audience: **u,f.**

Haile, J. M.   QD502
Molecular Dynamics Simulation: Elementary Methods. Trade
Paper. John Wiley & Sons, Inc. Hoboken, NJ. 1997. 512p.
Professional Ser. ISBN:0-471-18439-X, ISBN13:
978-0-471-18439-3. Dewey:541.3/94. LCCN:91-031963.

Audience: **u,f.**

Hammersley, J. M. &   QA273
Handscomb, D. C.
Monte Carlo Methods. Trade Cloth. Chapman & Hall. New
York, NY. 1964. Monographs on Statistics and Applied
Probability ISBN:0-412-15870-1, ISBN13: 978-0-412-15870-4.
Dewey:519.

Audience: **u,f.**

Heermann, Dieter W.   G76.5.U5G8
Computer Simulation Methods in Theoretical Physics. Ed. 2.
Trade Paper. Springer. New York, NY. 1995. XII, 145p.
ISBN:3-540-52210-7, ISBN13: 978-3-540-52210-2.
Dewey:910/.7/1173.

Audience: **u,f.**

Hoover, W. G.   QC168.H66 1986
Molecular Dynamics. Cloth Text. Springer. New York, NY.
1986. 138p. Lecture Notes in Physics, Vol. 258
ISBN:0-387-16789-7, ISBN13: 978-0-387-16789-3.
Dewey:533/.2. LCCN:86-020311.

Audience: **u,f.**

Liu, Jun S.   Q180.55.S7L58 2001
Monte Carlo Strategies in Scientific Computing. Trade Cloth.
Springer. New York, NY. 2002. XVI, 343p. Statistics Ser.
ISBN:0-387-95230-6, ISBN13: 978-0-387-95230-7.
Dewey:501/.519282. LCCN:00-069243.

Audience: **u,f.**

Newman, Mark & Barkema,   QC174.85.M64N49 1999
G. T.
Monte Carlo Methods in Statistical Physics. Paper Text. Oxford
University Press, Inc. New York, NY. 1999. 490p.
ISBN:0-19-851797-1, ISBN13: 978-0-19-851797-9.
Dewey:530.13. LCCN:99-213405.

Audience: **u,f.**

Rapaport, D. C. &   QP517.M65
Rapaport, Dennis
The Art of Molecular Dynamics Simulation. Ed. 2. Trade Cloth.
Cambridge University Press. New York, NY. 2004. 564p.
ISBN:0-521-82568-7, ISBN13: 978-0-521-82568-9.
Dewey:539/.6. LCCN:2004-555409.

Audience: **u,f.**

Computational Physics > Quantum Computation

Brown, Julian   QA76.889
The Quest for the Quantum Computer. David Deutsch (Foreword by). Trade Paper. Simon & Schuster. New York, NY. 2001. 400p. ISBN:0-684-87004-5, ISBN13: 978-0-684-87004-5. Dewey:4.1.

Audience: **g,l.**

Milburn, Gerard J.   QA76.889.M55
The Feynman Processor: Quantum Entanglement and the Computing Revolution. Paul Davies (Foreword by). Trade Paper. Basic Books. New York, NY. 1999. 240p. ISBN:0-7382-0173-1, ISBN13: 978-0-7382-0173-3. Dewey:004.1.

Audience: **g,l,u.** *Choice, 1999.*

Williams, Colin &   TK7888.3.W46 1998
  Clearwater, S.
Explorations in Quantum Computing. Mixed Media. Springer. New York, NY. 1997. XX, 307p. ISBN:0-387-94768-X, ISBN13: 978-0-387-94768-6. Dewey:004. LCCN:97-002159.

Audience: **u,f.** *Choice, 1998.*

Particle Physics

Glashow, Sheldon L.   QC776.G59 1991
The Charm of Physics. Cloth Text. Springer. New York, NY. 1991. 312p. ISBN:0-88318-708-6, ISBN13: 978-0-88318-708-1. Dewey:530. LCCN:90-024518.

Audience: **l,u.** *Choice, 1992.*

Gottfried, Kurt &   QC793.2
  Weisskopf, Victor F.
Concepts of Particle Physics, Vol. I. Paper Text. Oxford University Press, Inc. New York, NY. 1986. 204p. ISBN:0-19-504373-1, ISBN13: 978-0-19-504373-0. Dewey:539.7/21.

Audience: **u,f.** *B*

Green, Dan   QC787.C6 G67 2000
The Physics of Particle Detectors. T. Ericson & P. Y. Landshoff (Contribution by). Trade Paper. Cambridge University Press. New York, NY. 2005. 375p. Cambridge Monographs on Particle Physics, Nuclear Physics and Cosmology Ser., Vol. 12 ISBN:0-521-67568-5, ISBN13: 978-0-521-67568-0. Dewey:539.7/7.

Audience: **u,f.**

Greene, Brian   QC794.6
The Elegant Universe: Superstrings, Hidden Dimensions, and the Quest for the Ultimate Theory. Trade Cloth. W. W. Norton & Company, Inc. New York, NY. 2003. 464p. ISBN:0-393-05858-1, ISBN13: 978-0-393-05858-1. Dewey:539.7258.

Audience: **g,l,u.** *Choice, 1999.*

Gribbin, John   QC772
Q Is for Quantum: An Encyclopedia of Particle Physics. Trade Paper. Simon & Schuster. New York, NY. 2000. 560p. ISBN:0-684-86315-4, ISBN13: 978-0-684-86315-3. Dewey:539.7/03.

Audience: **g,l,u.** *Choice, 1999.*

Griffiths, David F.   QC721
Introduction to Elementary Particles. Ed. 1. Trade Cloth. John Wiley & Sons, Inc. Hoboken, NJ. 1987. 399p. ISBN:0-471-60386-4, ISBN13: 978-0-471-60386-3. Dewey:539.7/21.

Audience: **u,f.**

Halzen, Francis & Martin,   QC793.5.Q252
  Alan D.
Quarks and Leptons: An Introductory Course in Modern Particle Physics. Trade Cloth. John Wiley & Sons, Inc. Hoboken, NJ. 1984. 416p. ISBN:0-471-88741-2, ISBN13: 978-0-471-88741-6. Dewey:539.7/211. LCCN:83-014649.

Audience: **u,f.** *B*

Huang, Kerson   QC793.H8 1992
Quarks, Lepton and Gauge Fields. Ed. 2. Paper Text. World Scientific Publishing Company, Inc. Hackensack, NJ. 1992. 348p. ISBN:981-02-0660-7, ISBN13: 978-981-02-0660-4. Dewey:539.7/2167. LCCN:93-158535.

Audience: **u,f.**

Kane, Gordon   QC793
The Particle Garden: Our Universe As Understood by Particle Physicists. Heather Mimnaugh (Editor). Trade Paper. Perseus Books Group. New York, NY. 1996. 240p. Helix Bks. ISBN:0-201-40826-0, ISBN13: 978-0-201-40826-3. Dewey:539.72. LCCN:94-025804.

Audience: **g,l.**

Kane, Gordon   QC174.17.S9K36 2000
Supersymmetry: Unveiling the Ultimate Laws of Nature. Edward Witten (Foreword by). Trade Paper. Perseus Books Group. New York, NY. 2001. 224p. ISBN:0-7382-0489-7, ISBN13: 978-0-7382-0489-5. Dewey:539.7/25. LCCN:2001-094856.

Audience: **g,l.** *Choice, 2000.*

Lawrence Berkeley National   QC173.4.A87
  Laboratory
☐ The Particle Adventure.
http://particleadventure.org/particleadventure/

Audience: **g,l.**

MacKay, William M. &   QC787.P3C65 1991
  Conte, Mario
An Introduction to the Physics of Particle Accelerators. Paper Text. World Scientific Publishing Company, Inc. Hackensack, NJ. 1994. 250p. ISBN:981-02-0813-8, ISBN13: 978-981-02-0813-4. Dewey:539.73. LCCN:95-135912.

Audience: **u,f.** *Choice, 1992.*

Perkins, Donald H.   QC793.2 .P47 2000
Introduction to High Energy Physics. Ed. 4. Cloth Text. Cambridge University Press. New York, NY. 2000. 440p. ISBN:0-521-62196-8, ISBN13: 978-0-521-62196-0. Dewey:539.7/2. LCCN:98-051723.

Audience: **u,f.** *B*

Schwarz, Cindy   QC793.24.S34 1997
A Tour of the Subatomic Zoo: A Guide to Particle Physics. Ed. 2. Trade Paper. Springer. New York, NY. 1996. 136p. ISBN:1-56396-617-4, ISBN13: 978-1-56396-617-0. Dewey:539.7/2. LCCN:96-025726.

Audience: **g,l.**

Formats: Web: ☐   Ebook: *e*   CD/DVD-ROM: *⊛*   BCL3: *B*

Veltman, M. G. QC793.2.V45 2003
Facts and Mysteries in Elementary Particle Physics. Trade Cloth. World Scientific Publishing Company, Inc. Hackensack, NJ. 2003. 348p. ISBN:981-238-148-1, ISBN13: 978-981-238-148-4. Dewey:539.7/2. LCCN:2003-042273.
Audience: **g,l.** *Choice, 2003.*

Veltman, Martinus QC794.6.F4 V45 1994
Diagrammatica: The Path to Feynman Diagrams. Peter Goddard & Julia Yeomans (Contribution by). Trade Paper. Cambridge University Press. New York, NY. 1994. 296p. Cambridge Lecture Notes in Physics Ser., No. 4 ISBN:0-521-45692-4, ISBN13: 978-0-521-45692-0. Dewey:530.1/43. LCCN:95-167612.
Audience: **u,f.**

Weinberg, Steven QC793.2.W44 2003
The Discovery of Subatomic Particles. Ed. 2. Cloth Text. Cambridge University Press. New York, NY. 2003. 222p. ISBN:0-521-82351-X, ISBN13: 978-0-521-82351-7. Dewey:539.7/2. LCCN:2003-283983.
Audience: **g.** ℬ *Choice, 2004.*

Weinberg, Steven QC21.2.W428 1994
Dreams of a Final Theory: The Scientist's Search for the Ultimate Laws of Nature. Trade Paper. Knopf Publishing Group. New York, NY. 1994. 352p. ISBN:0-679-74408-8, ISBN13: 978-0-679-74408-5. Dewey:530. LCCN:93-030534.
Audience: **g.**

Wess, Julius & Bagger, Jonathan QC174.17.S9W47 1992
Supersymmetry and Supergravity. Ed. 2. Trade Paper. Princeton University Press. Princeton, NJ. 1992. 260p. Princeton Series in Physics ISBN:0-691-02530-4, ISBN13: 978-0-691-02530-8. Dewey:530.1/43. LCCN:90-026372.
Audience: **u,f.** ℬ

Nuclear Physics

Abragam, Anatole QC762
Principles of Nuclear Magnetism. Paper Text. Oxford University Press, Inc. New York, NY. 1983. 614p. The International Series of Monographs on Physics, No. 32 ISBN:0-19-852014-X, ISBN13: 978-0-19-852014-6. Dewey:538.
Audience: **u,f.**

Bethe, Hans Albrecht QC173.E358
Elementary Nuclear Theory. Paper Text. Textbook Publishers. Temecula, CA. 2003. 274p. ISBN:0-7581-0414-6, ISBN13: 978-0-7581-0414-4. Dewey:530.1.
Audience: **u,f.** ℬ

Commins, Eugene D. & Bucksbaum, Philip H. QC794.8.W4C65 1983
Weak Interactions of Leptons and Quarks. Trade Paper. Cambridge University Press. New York, NY. 1983. 496p. ISBN:0-521-27370-6, ISBN13: 978-0-521-27370-1. Dewey:539.7/54. LCCN:82-004452.
Audience: **u,f.**

Cottingham, W. Noel & Greenwood, Derek A. QC776 .C63 2001
An Introduction to Nuclear Physics. Ed. 2. Cloth Text. Cambridge University Press. New York, NY. 2001. 288p.

ISBN:0-521-65149-2, ISBN13: 978-0-521-65149-3. Dewey:539.7. LCCN:00-059885.
Audience: **u,f.** *Choice, 2001.*

Garwin, Richard L. & Charpak, Georges QC792.C4713 2001
Megawatts and Megatons: A Turning Point in the Nuclear Age? Trade Cloth. Alfred A. Knopf Inc. New York, NY. 2001. 432p. ISBN:0-375-40394-9, ISBN13: 978-0-375-40394-1. Dewey:333.792/4. LCCN:2001-029863.
Audience: **g.**

Goldberger, Marvin L. & Watson, Kenneth M. QC794.6.C6G64 2004
Collision Theory. Trade Paper. Dover Publications, Inc. Mineola, NY. 2004. 928p. ISBN:0-486-43507-5, ISBN13: 978-0-486-43507-7. Dewey:539.7/57. LCCN:2004-042803.
Audience: **u,f.** ℬ

Heisenberg, Werner QC173 .H3854
Nuclear Physics. Paper Text. Textbook Publishers. Temecula, CA. 2003. 225p. ISBN:0-7581-6375-4, ISBN13: 978-0-7581-6375-2. Dewey:539.7.
Audience: **u,f.** ℬ

Heyde, K. QC776.H49 2004
Basic Ideas and Concepts in Nuclear Physics. Ed. 3. Trade Cloth. Institute of Physics Publishing. Philadelphia, PA. 2004. 600p. Fundamental and Applied Nuclear Physics Ser. ISBN:0-7503-0980-6, ISBN13: 978-0-7503-0980-6. Dewey:539.7. LCCN:2005-270452.
Audience: **u,f.**

Jackson, Daphne F. QC794
Nuclear Reactions. Trade Cloth. Methuen & Company, Ltd. London, 1970. x, 260p. ISBN:0-416-11780-5, ISBN13: 978-0-416-11780-6. Dewey:539.75. LCCN:75-504591.
Audience: **u,f.** ℬ

Segre, Emilio QC0173.S313
Experimental Nuclear Physics, Vol. 1. Trade Paper. Books on Demand. Ann Arbor, MI. 799p. ISBN:0-598-74504-1, ISBN13: 978-0-598-74504-0. Dewey:539.1. LCCN:52-005852.
Audience: **u,f.** ℬ

Smorodinskii, Iakov A. & Landau, L. D. QC173 .L2463 1993
Lectures on Nuclear Theory. Ed. 2. Trade Paper. Dover Publications, Inc. Mineola, NY. 1993. 108p. ISBN:0-486-67513-0, ISBN13: 978-0-486-67513-8. Dewey:539.7. LCCN:92-047392.
Audience: **u,f.**

Walecka, John Dirk QC793.3
Theoretical Nuclear and Subnuclear Physics. Ed. 2. Trade Cloth. World Scientific Publishing Company, Inc. Hackensack, NJ. 2004. 650p. ISBN:981-238-795-1, ISBN13: 978-981-238-795-0. Dewey:539.7. LCCN:94-013930.
Audience: **u,f.**

Williams, W. S. QC776.W55 1990
Nuclear and Particle Physics. Paper Text. Oxford University Press, Inc. New York, NY. 1991. 400p. ISBN:0-19-852046-8, ISBN13: 978-0-19-852046-7. Dewey:539.7/2. LCCN:90-007110.
Audience: **u,f.** *Choice, 1992.*

Wong, Samuel S. M.   QC776.W66 1998
Introductory Nuclear Physics. Ed. 2. Trade Cloth. John Wiley &
Sons, Inc. Hoboken, NJ. 1998. 472p. ISBN:0-471-23973-9,
ISBN13: 978-0-471-23973-4. Dewey:539.7. LCCN:98-003745.
Audience: **u,f.**

Atomic and Molecular Physics

Bohr, Niels Hendrik David   PN2039.A613
Atomic Theory and the Description of Nature. Paper Text.
Textbook Publishers. Temecula, CA. 2003. ISBN:0-7581-3173-9,
ISBN13: 978-0-7581-3173-7. Dewey:792.
Audience: **u,f.** *B*

Born, Max   QC776.B5713 1989
Atomic Physics. Ed. 8. Trade Paper. Dover Publications, Inc.
Mineola, NY. 1989. 495p. ISBN:0-486-65984-4, ISBN13:
978-0-486-65984-8. Dewey:530.1. LCCN:89-012033.
Audience: **u,f.**

Bransden, A.   QC173
The Physics of Atoms and Molecules. Trade Cloth.
Addison-Wesley Longman, Inc. Boston, MA. 1996. 686p.
ISBN:0-582-44401-2, ISBN13: 978-0-582-44401-0. Dewey:539.
LCCN:80-041903.
Audience: **u,f.**

Budker, Dmitry, et al.   QC776
Atomic Physics: An Exploration through Problems and
Solutions. Derek Kimball & David DeMille (Authors). Paper
Text. Oxford University Press, Inc. New York, NY. 2004. 456p.
ISBN:0-19-850950-2, ISBN13: 978-0-19-850950-9.
Dewey:539.7. LCCN:2004-272073.
Audience: **u,f.** *Choice, 2004.*

Fano, Ugo   QC173.F3
Basic Physics of Atoms and Molecules. Paper Text. Textbook
Publishers. Temecula, CA. 2003. 414p. ISBN:0-7581-0438-3,
ISBN13: 978-0-7581-0438-0. Dewey:539.1.
Audience: **u,f.** *B*

Foot, C.   QC776
Atomic Physics. Trade Cloth. Oxford University Press, Inc. New
York, NY. 2005. 346p. Oxford Master Series in Atomic, Optical
and Laser Physics ISBN:0-19-850695-3, ISBN13:
978-0-19-850695-9. Dewey:539.7. LCCN:2005-295406.
Audience: **u,f.** *Choice, 2005.*

Frisch, Otto R.   QC173
The Nature of Matter. Trade Cloth. Thames & Hudson. New
York, NY. 1972. 216p. ISBN:0-500-08006-2, ISBN13:
978-0-500-08006-1. Dewey:530.1. LCCN:72-179319.
Audience: **l,u.**

Gamow, George   QC173.18.B64
The Atom and Its Nucleus. Paper Text. Textbook Publishers.
Temecula, CA. 2003. 153p. ISBN:0-7581-6044-5, ISBN13:
978-0-7581-6044-7. Dewey:530.1.
Audience: **l.** *B*

Ramsey, Norman F.   QC173.4.M65 R36 1985
Molecular Beams. Trade Paper. Oxford University Press, Inc.
New York, NY. 1990. 490p. The International Series of
Monographs on Physics ISBN:0-19-852021-2, ISBN13:
978-0-19-852021-4. Dewey:539. LCCN:2006-271308.
Audience: **u,f.**

Condensed Matter Physics

Ashcroft   QC176
Solid State Physics. Ed. 2. Cloth Text. Harcourt College
Publishers. Fort Worth, TX. 1999. ISBN:0-03-058556-2,
ISBN13: 978-0-03-058556-2. Dewey:530.4/1.
Audience: **u,f.**

Blakemore, J. S.   QC176 .B63 1985
Solid State Physics. Ed. 2. Trade Paper. Cambridge University
Press. New York, NY. 1985. 506p. ISBN:0-521-31391-0,
ISBN13: 978-0-521-31391-9. Dewey:530.4/1. LCCN:85-047879.
Audience: **u,f.** *B*

Chaikin, P. M. & Lubensky,   QC173.3.454.C48 1995
T. C.
Principles of Condensed Matter Physics. Trade Paper.
Cambridge University Press. New York, NY. 2000. 720p.
ISBN:0-521-79450-1, ISBN13: 978-0-521-79450-3.
Dewey:530.4/1. LCCN:93-044244.
Audience: **u,f.**

Hook, J. R. & Hall, H. E.   QC176
Solid State Physics. Ed. 2. Trade Paper. John Wiley & Sons,
Inc. Hoboken, NJ. 1995. 496p. Manchester Physics Ser., Vol. 30
ISBN:0-471-92805-4, ISBN13: 978-0-471-92805-8.
Dewey:530.4/1. LCCN:90-020571.
Audience: **u,f.**

Hudson, John B.   QC173.4.S94H85 1998
Surface Science: An Introduction. Trade Paper. John Wiley &
Sons, Inc. Hoboken, NJ. 1998. 336p. ISBN:0-471-25239-5,
ISBN13: 978-0-471-25239-9. Dewey:530.4/17.
LCCN:97-039020.
Audience: **u,f.** *Choice, 1992.*

Ibach, Harald & Lüth, Hans   QC176
Solid-State Physics: An Introduction to Principles of Materials
Science. Ed. 3. Trade Paper. Springer. New York, NY. 2003.
XII, 501p. Advanced Texts in Physics ISBN:3-540-43870-X,
ISBN13: 978-3-540-43870-0. Dewey:530.4/1.
LCCN:2002-036466.
Audience: **u,f.**

Jones, Richard A.   QC173.458.S62J66
Soft Condensed Matter. Trade Paper. Oxford University Press,
Inc. New York, NY. 2002. 206p. Oxford Master Series in
Condensed Matter Physics, Vol. 6 ISBN:0-19-850589-2,
ISBN13: 978-0-19-850589-1. Dewey:530.4/13.
LCCN:2002-512710.
Audience: **u,f.**

Kittel, Charles   QC176.K5 2005
Introduction to Solid State Physics. Ed. 8. Trade Cloth. John
Wiley & Sons, Inc. Hoboken, NJ. 2004. 704p.
ISBN:0-471-41526-X, ISBN13: 978-0-471-41526-8.
Dewey:530.4/1. LCCN:2004-042250.
Audience: **u,f.** *B*

Madelung, Otfried   QC176.M23213 1978
Introduction to Solid-State Theory. B. C. Taylor (Translator).
Trade Paper. Springer. New York, NY. 1995. XI, 488p. Series in
Solid-State Sciences, Vol. 2 ISBN:3-540-60443-X, ISBN13:
978-3-540-60443-3. Dewey:530.4/1. LCCN:95-042048.
Audience: **u,f.**

Formats: Web: ☐   Ebook: *e*   CD/DVD-ROM: ✎   BCL3: *B*

Marder, Michael P.   QC173.454.M37 2000
Condensed Matter Physics. Trade Cloth. John Wiley & Sons,
Inc. Hoboken, NJ. 2000. 928p. ISBN:0-471-17779-2, ISBN13:
978-0-471-17779-1. Dewey:530.4/1. LCCN:99-036153.

Audience: **u,f.**

Omar, M. Ali   E101.L43
Elementary Solid State Physics: Principles and Applications. Ed.
1. Cloth Text. Addison-Wesley Longman, Inc. Boston, MA.
1993. 688p. ISBN:0-201-60733-6, ISBN13: 978-0-201-60733-8.
Dewey:971.01.

Audience: **u,f.**

Oura, K.   QC173.4.S94S96425
Surface Science: An Introduction. Trade Cloth. Springer. New
York, NY. 1991. XII, 440p. Advanced Texts in Physics
ISBN:3-540-00545-5, ISBN13: 978-3-540-00545-2.
Dewey:530.4/27. LCCN:2003-042812.

Audience: **u,f.**

Peierls, R. E.   QC176.P42 2001
Quantum Theory of Solids. Trade Paper. Oxford University
Press, Inc. New York, NY. 2001. 238p. Oxford Classic Texts in
the Physical Sciences ISBN:0-19-850781-X, ISBN13:
978-0-19-850781-9. Dewey:530.4/1. LCCN:2001-268332.

Audience: **u,f.**

Taylor, Philip L. &   QC173.454 .T39 2002
  Heinonen, Olle G.
A Quantum Approach to Condensed Matter Physics. Trade
Paper. Cambridge University Press. New York, NY. 2002. 424p.
ISBN:0-521-77827-1, ISBN13: 978-0-521-77827-5.
Dewey:530.4/1. LCCN:2001-037339.

Audience: **u,f.** *Choice, 2002.*

Turton, Richard John   QC176.T87 2000
The Physics of Solids. Paper Text. Oxford University Press, Inc.
New York, NY. 2000. 430p. ISBN:0-19-850352-0, ISBN13:
978-0-19-850352-1. Dewey:530.4/1. LCCN:00-026263.

Audience: **l.**

Witten, Thomas A.   QD549.2'C66
Structured Fluids: Polymers, Colloids, Surfactants. Cloth Text.
Oxford University Press, Inc. New York, NY. 2004. 240p.
ISBN:0-19-852688-1, ISBN13: 978-0-19-852688-9.
Dewey:530.4/2. LCCN:2004-299388.

Audience: **u,f.** *Choice, 2004.*

Ziman, J. M.   QC175.2.Z55 2001
Electrons and Phonons: The Theory of Transport Phenomena in
Solids. Trade Paper. Oxford University Press, Inc. New York,
NY. 2001. 568p. Oxford Classic Texts in the Physical Sciences
ISBN:0-19-850779-8, ISBN13: 978-0-19-850779-6.
Dewey:530.4/16. LCCN:2001-268325.

Audience: **u,f.** *B*

Ziman, J. M.   QC176
Principles of the Theory of Solids. Ed. 2. Trade Paper.
Cambridge University Press. New York, NY. 1979. 448p.
ISBN:0-521-29733-8, ISBN13: 978-0-521-29733-2.
Dewey:530.41.

Audience: **u,f.**

Semiconductor Physics

Cohen, M. L. &   QC611.6.O6 C63 1989
  Chelikowsky, J. R.
Electronic Structure and Optical Properties of Semiconductors.
Ed. 2. Paper Text. Springer. New York, NY. 1989. 264p.
Solid-State Sciences Ser., Vol. 75 ISBN:0-387-51391-4,
ISBN13: 978-0-387-51391-1. Dewey:537.6/22.
LCCN:89-208064.

Audience: **u,f.** *Choice, 1989.*

Davies, John H.   QC611.8.L68 D39 1998
The Physics of Low-Dimensional Semiconductors: An
Introduction. Trade Paper. Cambridge University Press. New
York, NY. 1997. 456p. ISBN:0-521-48491-X, ISBN13:
978-0-521-48491-6. Dewey:537.6/221. LCCN:97-000088.

Audience: **u,f.**

Sapoval, Bernard &   QC611
  Hermann, Claudine
Physics of Semiconductors. Trade Paper. Springer. New York,
NY. 2003. IX, 319p. ISBN:0-387-40630-1, ISBN13:
978-0-387-40630-5. Dewey:537.6/22.

Audience: **u,f.**

Seeger, Karlheinz   QC611.S43 2004
Semiconductor Physics: An Introduction. Ed. 9. Trade Cloth.
Springer. New York, NY. 2004. X, 538p. Advanced Texts in
Physics Ser. ISBN:3-540-21957-9, ISBN13: 978-3-540-21957-6.
Dewey:537.6/22. LCCN:2004-105250.

Audience: **u,f.**

Shur, Michael   QC611.S563 1990
Physics of Semiconductor Devices. Ed. 1. Cloth Text. Prentice
Hall PTR. Upper Saddle River, NJ. 1990. 638p. Prentice Hall
Series in Solid State Physical Electronics Ser.
ISBN:0-13-666496-2, ISBN13: 978-0-13-666496-3.
Dewey:537.6/22. LCCN:89-022819.

Audience: **u,f.** *Choice, 1990.*

Sze, Simon M. & Ng,   TK7871.85
  Kwok K,
Physics of Semiconductor Devices. Ed. 3. Trade Cloth. John
Wiley & Sons, Inc. Hoboken, NJ. 2006. 832p.
ISBN:0-471-14323-5, ISBN13: 978-0-471-14323-9.
Dewey:621.3815/2.

Audience: **u,f.** *B*

Gravitation

Chandrasekhar, S.   QA808.2
Newton's Principia for the Common Reader. Trade Paper.
Oxford University Press, Inc. New York, NY. 2003. 618p.
ISBN:0-19-852675-X, ISBN13: 978-0-19-852675-9. Dewey:531.

Audience: **g,l,u,f.**

Cohen, I. Bernard   QA803
Introduction to Newton's Principia. Trade Paper. iUniverse, Inc.
Lincoln, NE. 1999. 432p. ISBN:1-58348-601-1, ISBN13:
978-1-58348-601-6. Dewey:531.

Audience: **g,l,u,f.**

Hawking, Stephen W.   QC6
Black Holes and Baby Universes and Other Essays. Trade Paper.
Bantam Books. New York, NY. 1994. 192p.

ISBN:0-553-37411-7, ISBN13: 978-0-553-37411-7.
Dewey:530.1092. LCCN:93-008269.

Audience: **g,l,u.**

Hawking, Stephen W.   QB981.H377 1998
A Brief History of Time: From the Big Bang to Black Holes.
Ed. 10. Trade Cloth. Bantam Books. New York, NY. 1998.
224p. ISBN:0-553-10953-7, ISBN13: 978-0-553-10953-5.
Dewey:523.1. LCCN:98-021874.

Audience: **g,l,u.** *Choice, 1988.*

Hawking, Stephen W.   QC174.12.H39 2001
The Universe in a Nutshell. Trade Cloth. Bantam Books. New
York, NY. 2001. 224p. ISBN:0-553-80202-X, ISBN13:
978-0-553-80202-3. Dewey:530.12. LCCN:2001-035757.

Audience: **g,l,u.** *Choice, 2003, 2002.*

Misner, Charles W., et al.   QC178 .M57
Gravitation. Kip S. Thorne & John A. Wheeler (Authors). Trade
Paper. Worth Publishers, Inc. New York, NY. 1973. 1215p.
Physics Ser. ISBN:0-7167-0344-0, ISBN13: 978-0-7167-0344-0.
Dewey:531/.14. LCCN:78-156043.

Audience: **u,f.** *B*

Narlikar, Jayant Vishnu   QB331 .N37 1996
The Lighter Side of Gravity. Ed. 2. Trade Paper. Cambridge
University Press. New York, NY. 1996. 229p.
ISBN:0-521-56565-0, ISBN13: 978-0-521-56565-3.
Dewey:521.1. LCCN:96-012581.

Audience: **g,l.** *B*

Newton, Isaac   QA803.N413 1999
The Principia: Mathematical Principles of Natural Philosophy. I.
Bernard Cohen & Anne Whitman (Translators), I. Bernard
Cohen (Supplement by). Trade Cloth. University of California
Press. Berkeley, CA. 1999. 994p. ISBN:0-520-08816-6, ISBN13:
978-0-520-08816-0. Dewey:531. LCCN:99-010278.

Audience: **l,u,f.**

Smolin, Lee   QC178 .S64 2002
Three Roads to Quantum Gravity. Trade Paper. Basic Books.
New York, NY. 2002. 256p. ISBN:0-465-07836-2, ISBN13:
978-0-465-07836-3. Dewey:530.1/43. LCCN:2001-131677.

Audience: **g,l.** *Choice, 2002.*

Wheeler, John A.   QC178
A Journey into Gravity and Spacetime. Trade Paper. Henry Holt
& Company. New York, NY. 1999. 258p. ISBN:0-7167-6034-7,
ISBN13: 978-0-7167-6034-4. Dewey:531.1/4.

Audience: **l,u,f.** *Choice, 1990.*

Gravitation > Relativity

Bohm, David   QC6.4.C3B64 1999
Causality and Chance in Modern Physics. Louis De Broglie
(Foreword by). Book, Other. University of Pennsylvania Press.
Philadelphia, PA. 1971. 184p. ISBN:0-8122-1002-6, ISBN13:
978-0-8122-1002-6. Dewey:530.1/2. LCCN:57-028894.

Audience: **u,f.** *B*

Chandrasekhar, S.   QA808.2
Newton's Principia for the Common Reader. Trade Paper.
Oxford University Press, Inc. New York, NY. 2003. 618p.
ISBN:0-19-852675-X, ISBN13: 978-0-19-852675-9. Dewey:531.

Audience: **g,l,u,f.**

Cohen, I. Bernard   QA803
Introduction to Newton's Principia. Trade Paper. iUniverse, Inc.
Lincoln, NE. 1999. 432p. ISBN:1-58348-601-1, ISBN13:
978-1-58348-601-6. Dewey:531.

Audience: **g,l,u,f.**

D'Inverno, Ray A.   QC173.55.D56 1992
Introducing Einstein's Relativity. Paper Text. Oxford University
Press, Inc. New York, NY. 1992. 394p. ISBN:0-19-859686-3,
ISBN13: 978-0-19-859686-8. Dewey:530.1/1. LCCN:91-024894.

Audience: **u,f.**

Durell, Clement V.   QC173.57.D87 2003
Readable Relativity. Trade Paper. Dover Publications, Inc.
Mineola, NY. 2003. 160p. ISBN:0-486-43257-2, ISBN13:
978-0-486-43257-1. Dewey:530.11. LCCN:2003-055297.

Audience: **l,u.**

Eddington, Arthur S.   QC173.59.M3 E32 1975
The Mathematical Theory of Relativity. Ed. 3. Cloth Text.
American Mathematical Society. Providence, RI. 1975. ix, 270p.
ISBN:0-8284-0278-7, ISBN13: 978-0-8284-0278-1.
Dewey:530.1/1. LCCN:74-001458.

Audience: **u,f.**

Eddington, Arthur S.   QC173.59.S65 E33 19
(Author, Preface by)
Space, Time and Gravitation: An Outline of the General
Relativity Theory. Hermann Bondi (Foreword by). Trade Paper.
Cambridge University Press. New York, NY. 1987. 224p.
Cambridge Science Classics ISBN:0-521-33709-7, ISBN13:
978-0-521-33709-0. Dewey:530.11. LCCN:86-033348.

Audience: **u,f.**

Einstein, Albert   QC173.55.E3613 2001
Relativity: The Special and General Theory. Ed. 2. Trade Paper.
Routledge. New York, NY. 2001. 176p. Classics Ser.
ISBN:0-415-25384-5, ISBN13: 978-0-415-25384-0.
Dewey:530.11. LCCN:2001-048418.

Audience: **u,f.**

Einstein, Albert   QC20
The Meaning of Relativity: Including the Relativistic Theory of
the Non-Symmetric Field. Ed. 5. Brian Greene (Introduction
by). Trade Paper. Princeton University Press. Princeton, NJ.
2004. 192p. Princeton Science Library, Vol. 1921
ISBN:0-691-12027-7, ISBN13: 978-0-691-12027-0.
Dewey:530.11. LCCN:2004-111082.

Audience: **l,u.** *B*

Epstein, Lewis Carroll   QC173.55.E67 1992
Relativity Visualized. Trade Paper. Insight Press. San Francisco,
CA. 1994. 200p. ISBN:0-935218-05-X, ISBN13:
978-0-935218-05-3. Dewey:530.1/1. LCCN:82-084280.

Audience: **l,u.** *B*

Feynman, Richard Phillips   QC173.6
Six Not-So-Easy Pieces: Einstein's Relativity, Symmetry and
Space-Time. Trade Paper. Perseus Books Group. New York, NY.
1998. 192p. Helix Bks. ISBN:0-201-32842-9, ISBN13:
978-0-201-32842-4. Dewey:530.11. LCCN:96-047811.

Audience: **u,f.** *Choice, 1997.*

Fischbach, Ephraim &   QC178 .F53 1999
  Talmadge, Carrick L.
The Search for Non-Newtonian Gravity. Trade Cloth. Springer.
New York, NY. 1998. XVII, 305p. ISBN:0-387-98490-9,
ISBN13: 978-0-387-98490-2. Dewey:531/.14. LCCN:98-013181.
Audience: **u,f.**

French, Anthony P.   QC6 .F68
Special Relativity. Trade Paper. W. W. Norton & Company, Inc.
New York, NY. 1968. M.I.T. Introductory Physics Ser.
ISBN:0-393-09793-5, ISBN13: 978-0-393-09793-1.
Dewey:530.11.
Audience: **u,f.**

Greene, Brian   QB982.G74 2004
The Fabric of the Cosmos: Space, Time, and the Texture of
Reality. Trade Cloth. Knopf Publishing Group. New York, NY.
2004. 592p. ISBN:0-375-41288-3, ISBN13: 978-0-375-41288-2.
Dewey:523.1. LCCN:2003-058918.
Audience: **g,l.** *Choice, 2004.*

Halpern, Paul   QC6.H273 2005
The Great Beyond: Higher Dimensions, Parallel Universes and
the Extraordinary Search for a Theory of Everything. Trade
Paper. John Wiley & Sons, Inc. Hoboken, NJ. 2005. 320p.
ISBN:0-471-74149-3, ISBN13: 978-0-471-74149-7.
Dewey:530/.01.
Audience: **g,l,u.** *Choice, 2005.*

Hawking, Stephen W.   QC6
Black Holes and Baby Universes and Other Essays. Trade Paper.
Bantam Books. New York, NY. 1994. 192p.
ISBN:0-553-37411-7, ISBN13: 978-0-553-37411-7.
Dewey:530.1092. LCCN:93-008269.
Audience: **g,l,u.**

Hawking, Stephen W.   QB981.H377 1998
A Brief History of Time: From the Big Bang to Black Holes.
Ed. 10. Trade Cloth. Bantam Books. New York, NY. 1998.
224p. ISBN:0-553-10953-7, ISBN13: 978-0-553-10953-5.
Dewey:523.1. LCCN:98-021874.
Audience: **g,l,u.** *Choice, 1988.*

Hawking, Stephen W.   QC174.12.H39 2001
The Universe in a Nutshell. Trade Cloth. Bantam Books. New
York, NY. 2001. 224p. ISBN:0-553-80202-X, ISBN13:
978-0-553-80202-3. Dewey:530.12. LCCN:2001-035757.
Audience: **g,l,u.** *Choice, 2003, 2002.*

Kaku, Michio   QC793.3.F5K35 1994
Hyperspace: A Scientific Odyssey Through Parallel Universes,
Time Warps, and the Tenth Dimension. Robert O'Keefe
(Illustrator). Trade Cloth. Oxford University Press, Inc. New
York, NY. 1994. 384p. ISBN:0-19-508514-0, ISBN13:
978-0-19-508514-3. Dewey:530.1/42. LCCN:93-007910.
Audience: **g,l.**

Misner, Charles W., et al.   QC178 .M57
Gravitation. Kip S. Thorne & John A. Wheeler (Authors). Trade
Paper. Worth Publishers, Inc. New York, NY. 1973. 1215p.
Physics Ser. ISBN:0-7167-0344-0, ISBN13: 978-0-7167-0344-0.
Dewey:531/.14. LCCN:78-156043.
Audience: **u,f.** *B*

Narlikar, Jayant Vishnu   QB331 .N37 1996
The Lighter Side of Gravity. Ed. 2. Trade Paper. Cambridge
University Press. New York, NY. 1996. 229p.

ISBN:0-521-56565-0, ISBN13: 978-0-521-56565-3.
Dewey:521.1. LCCN:96-012581.
Audience: **g,l.** *B*

Newton, Isaac   QA803.N413 1999
The Principia: Mathematical Principles of Natural Philosophy. I.
Bernard Cohen & Anne Whitman (Translators), I. Bernard
Cohen (Supplement by). Trade Cloth. University of California
Press. Berkeley, CA. 1999. 994p. ISBN:0-520-08816-6, ISBN13:
978-0-520-08816-0. Dewey:531. LCCN:99-010278.
Audience: **l,u,f.**

Russell, Bertrand   QC173.55 .R85 1999
ABC of Relativity. Ed. 4. Trade Paper. Routledge. New York,
NY. 2001. 176p. ISBN:0-415-15429-4, ISBN13:
978-0-415-15429-1. Dewey:530.1/1. LCCN:2001-278032.
Audience: **l,u.** *B*

Sartori, Leo   QC173.55.S367 1996
Understanding Relativity: A Simplified Approach to Einstein's
Theories. Trade Paper. University of California Press. Berkeley,
CA. 1996. 378p. ISBN:0-520-20029-2, ISBN13:
978-0-520-20029-6. Dewey:530.1/1. LCCN:94-049358.
Audience: **g,l.** *Choice, 1996.*

Smolin, Lee   QC178 .S64 2002
Three Roads to Quantum Gravity. Trade Paper. Basic Books.
New York, NY. 2002. 256p. ISBN:0-465-07836-2, ISBN13:
978-0-465-07836-3. Dewey:530.1/43. LCCN:2001-131677.
Audience: **g,l.** *Choice, 2002.*

Taylor, Edwin F. & Wheeler,   QC173.65T37 1991
  John Archibald
Spacetime Physics. Ed. 2. Trade Paper. Worth Publishers, Inc.
New York, NY. 1992. 32p. ISBN:0-7167-2327-1, ISBN13:
978-0-7167-2327-1. Dewey:530.11. LCCN:92-000722.
Audience: **u,f.** *B*

Thorne, Kip S.   QC6.T526 1993
Black Holes and Time Warps: Einstein's Outrageous Legacy.
Frederick Seitz (Introduction by), Stephen W. Hawking
(Foreword by). Trade Paper. W. W. Norton & Company, Inc.
New York, NY. 1995. 640p. ISBN:0-393-31276-3, ISBN13:
978-0-393-31276-8. Dewey:530.1/1. LCCN:93-002014.
Audience: **l,u.** *Choice, 1994.*

Weinberg, Steven   QB461
Gravitation and Cosmology: Principles and Applications of the
General Theory of Relativity. Trade Cloth. John Wiley & Sons,
Inc. Hoboken, NJ. 1972. 688p. ISBN:0-471-92567-5, ISBN13:
978-0-471-92567-5. Dewey:523.01. LCCN:78-037175.
Audience: **u,f.** *B*

Wheeler, John A.   QC178
A Journey into Gravity and Spacetime. Trade Paper. Henry Holt
& Company. New York, NY. 1999. 258p. ISBN:0-7167-6034-7,
ISBN13: 978-0-7167-6034-4. Dewey:531.1/4.
Audience: **l,u,f.** *Choice, 1990.*

Gravitation > Relativity > Special Relativity

French, Anthony P.   **QC6 .F68**
Special Relativity. Trade Paper. W. W. Norton & Company, Inc.
New York, NY. 1968. M.I.T. Introductory Physics Ser.
ISBN:0-393-09793-5, ISBN13: 978-0-393-09793-1.
Dewey:530.11.

                                    Audience: **u,f.**

Rindler, Wolfgang   **QC173.65.R56 1991**
Introduction to Special Relativity. Ed. 2. Paper Text. Oxford
University Press, Inc. New York, NY. 1991. 180p.
ISBN:0-19-853952-5, ISBN13: 978-0-19-853952-0.
Dewey:530.1/1. LCCN:90-048748.

                          Audience: **l,u,f.** *B*

Gravitation > Relativity > General Relativity

Eddington, Arthur S.   **QC173.59.S65 E33 19**
(Author, Preface by)
Space, Time and Gravitation: An Outline of the General
Relativity Theory. Hermann Bondi (Foreword by). Trade Paper.
Cambridge University Press. New York, NY. 1987. 224p.
Cambridge Science Classics ISBN:0-521-33709-7, ISBN13:
978-0-521-33709-0. Dewey:530.11. LCCN:86-033348.
                                    Audience: **u,f.**

Schutz, Bernard F.   **QC173.6 .S38 1985**
A First Course in General Relativity. Trade Paper. Cambridge
University Press. New York, NY. 1985. 392p.
ISBN:0-521-27703-5, ISBN13: 978-0-521-27703-7.
Dewey:530.1/1. LCCN:83-023205.
                     Audience: **u,f.** *B Choice, 1985.*

Gravitation > Fifth Forces (Intermediate Range Forces)

Fischbach, Ephraim &   **QC178 .F53 1999**
Talmadge, Carrick L.
The Search for Non-Newtonian Gravity. Trade Cloth. Springer.
New York, NY. 1998. XVII, 305p. ISBN:0-387-98490-9,
ISBN13: 978-0-387-98490-2. Dewey:531/.14. LCCN:98-013181.
                                    Audience: **u,f.**

Statistical Mechanics

Abrikosov, A. A., et al.   **QC174.45**
Methods of Quantum Field Theory in Statistical Physics. L. P.
Gorkov & I. E. Dzyaloshinski (Authors), Richard A. Silverman
(Translator). Trade Paper. Dover Publications, Inc. Mineola, NY.
1975. 352p. ISBN:0-486-63228-8, ISBN13: 978-0-486-63228-5.
Dewey:530.1/33. LCCN:75-017174.
                                    Audience: **u,f.**

Balescu, Radu   **QC174.8 .B343 1997**
Statistical Dynamics. Trade Cloth. World Scientific Publishing
Company, Inc. Hackensack, NJ. 1997. 350p.
ISBN:1-86094-045-5, ISBN13: 978-1-86094-045-3.
Dewey:519.2.
                                    Audience: **u,f.**

Binder, Kurt & Heermann,   **QC174.85**
Dieter W.
Monte Carlo Simulation in Statistical Physics: An Introduction.
Ed. 4. Trade Cloth. Springer. New York, NY. 2002. XII, 180p.
Series in Solid-State Sciences, Vol. 80 ISBN:3-540-43221-3,
ISBN13: 978-3-540-43221-0. Dewey:530.4/15.
LCCN:2003-537870.

                                    Audience: **u,f.**

Bowley, Roger & Sanchez,   **QC311.5.B64 1999**
Mariana
Introductory Statistical Mechanics. Ed. 2. Paper Text. Oxford
University Press, Inc. New York, NY. 2000. 368p.
ISBN:0-19-850576-0, ISBN13: 978-0-19-850576-1.
Dewey:530.13. LCCN:99-025577.
                          Audience: **u,f.** *Choice, 1997.*

Chandler, David G.   **QC174.8.C47 1987**
Introduction to Modern Statistical Mechanics. Trade Paper.
Oxford University Press, Inc. New York, NY. 1987. 256p.
ISBN:0-19-504277-8, ISBN13: 978-0-19-504277-1.
Dewey:530.1/3. LCCN:86-017950.

                                    Audience: **u,f.**

Dill, Ken A. & Bromberg,   **QC311.5.D55 2002**
Sarina
Molecular Driving Forces: Statistical Thermodynamics in
Chemistry and Biology. UK-B Format Paperback. Garland
Publishing, Inc. New York, NY. 2002. 704p.
ISBN:0-8153-2051-5, ISBN13: 978-0-8153-2051-7.
Dewey:536/.7. LCCN:2001-053202.

                                    Audience: **u,f.**

Engel, Andreas & Van den   **QA76.87.E45 2001**
Broeck, Christian P. L.
Statistical Mechanics of Learning. Trade Paper. Cambridge
University Press. New York, NY. 2001. 342p.
ISBN:0-521-77479-9, ISBN13: 978-0-521-77479-6.
Dewey:006.3. LCCN:00-058516.
                                    Audience: **u,f.**

Feynman, Richard Phillips   **QC174.8.F48 1998**
Statistical Mechanics: A Set of Lectures. Trade Paper. Perseus
Books Group. New York, NY. 1998. 368p. Advanced Book
Classics Ser. ISBN:0-201-36076-4, ISBN13: 978-0-201-36076-9.
Dewey:530.13. LCCN:98-002741.
                                    Audience: **u,f.**

Gibbs, J. Willard   **QC175**
Elementary Principles of Statistical Mechanics. Trade Paper. Ox
Bow Press. Woodbridge, CT. 1981. 224p. ISBN:0-918024-20-X,
ISBN13: 978-0-918024-20-6. Dewey:536.7. LCCN:80-084972.
                                    Audience: **u,f.**

Heer, C. V.   **QC175**
Statistical Mechanics: Kinetic, Theory and Stochastic Process.
Trade Cloth. Elsevier Science & Technology Books. Saint
Louis, MO. 1972. xvi, 602p. ISBN:0-12-336550-3, ISBN13:
978-0-12-336550-7. Dewey:530.1/3. LCCN:75-137591.
                                    Audience: **u,f.**

Huang, Kerson   **QC174.8.H83 1987**
Statistical Mechanics. Ed. 2. Trade Cloth. John Wiley & Sons,
Inc. Hoboken, NJ. 1987. 512p. ISBN:0-471-81518-7, ISBN13:
978-0-471-81518-1. Dewey:530.1/3. LCCN:86-032466.
                                  Audience: **u,f.** *B*

Landau, L. D., et al.   QC174.8
Statistical Physics, Vol. 9, Pt. 2. Ed. 3. E. M. Lifshitz & L. P. Pitaevskii (Authors). Trade Paper. Elsevier Science & Technology Books. Saint Louis, MO. 1980. 387p. Course of Theoretical Physics Ser., Vol. 2 ISBN:0-7506-2636-4, ISBN13: 978-0-7506-2636-1. Dewey:530.1/3.

Audience: **u,f.** *B*

Ma, Shang-Keng   QC174.8 .M2513 1985
Statistical Mechanics. Cloth Text. World Scientific Publishing Company, Inc. Hackensack, NJ. 1985. 576p. ISBN:9971-966-06-9, ISBN13: 978-9971-966-06-5. Dewey:530.1/3.

Audience: **u,f.** *B*

Mandl, Franz   QC174.8.M27 1988
Statistical Physics. Ed. 2. Trade Paper. John Wiley & Sons, Inc. Hoboken, NJ. 1991. 402p. Manchester Physics Ser., Vol. 14 ISBN:0-471-91533-5, ISBN13: 978-0-471-91533-1. Dewey:530.1/3. LCCN:87-008283.

Audience: **u,f.**

McQuarrie, Donald A.   QC174.8.M3 2000
Statistical Mechanics. Ed. 2. Trade Cloth. University Science Books. Sausalito, CA. 2000. 640p. ISBN:1-891389-15-7, ISBN13: 978-1-891389-15-3. Dewey:530.13. LCCN:00-021962.

Audience: **u,f.**

Newman, Mark & Barkema,   QC174.85.M64N49 1999
  G. T.
Monte Carlo Methods in Statistical Physics. Paper Text. Oxford University Press, Inc. New York, NY. 1999. 490p. ISBN:0-19-851797-1, ISBN13: 978-0-19-851797-9. Dewey:530.13. LCCN:99-213405.

Audience: **u,f.**

Pathria, R. K.   QC174.8.P38 1996
Statistical Mechanics. Ed. 2. Trade Paper. Elsevier Science & Technology Books. Saint Louis, MO. 1996. 576p. ISBN:0-7506-2469-8, ISBN13: 978-0-7506-2469-5. Dewey:530.1/3. LCCN:96-001679.

Audience: **u,f.**

Reichl, Linda E.   QC174.8.R44 1998
A Modern Course in Statistical Physics. Ed. 2. Trade Cloth. John Wiley & Sons, Inc. Hoboken, NJ. 1998. 842p. ISBN:0-471-59520-9, ISBN13: 978-0-471-59520-5. Dewey:530.15/95. LCCN:97-013550.

Audience: **u,f.**

Reif, Frederick   QC175 .R43
Fundamentals of Statistical and Thermal Physics. Cloth Text. McGraw-Hill Higher Education. Burr Ridge, IL. 1965. 651p. ISBN:0-07-051800-9, ISBN13: 978-0-07-051800-1. Dewey:530.13.

Audience: **u,f.**

Stauffer, Dietrich   QC174.85.P45S73 1985
Introduction to Percolation Theory. Ed. 2. Trade Paper. Taylor & Francis Group. Philadelphia, PA. 1985. 130p. ISBN:0-85066-315-6, ISBN13: 978-0-85066-315-0. Dewey:530.1/3. LCCN:85-004793.

Audience: **u,f.**

Tolman, Richard C.   QC174.8
The Principles of Statistical Mechanics. Trade Paper. Dover Publications, Inc. Mineola, NY. 1980. 661p. ISBN:0-486-63896-0, ISBN13: 978-0-486-63896-6. Dewey:530.1/3. LCCN:79-052649.

Audience: **u,f.**

Voit, Johannes   HG176.5.V64 2003
The Statistical Mechanics of Fianancial Markets. Ed. 2. Trade Paper. Springer. New York, NY. 2003. 288p. Texts and Monographs in Physics ISBN:3-540-00978-7, ISBN13: 978-3-540-00978-8. Dewey:332/.041/015195. LCCN:2003-045545.

Audience: **u,f.**

Statistical Mechanics > Phase Transitions

McComb, William David   QC174.17.R46
Renormalization Methods: A Guide for Beginners. Cloth Text. Oxford University Press, Inc. New York, NY. 2004. 348p. ISBN:0-19-850694-5, ISBN13: 978-0-19-850694-2. Dewey:530.14. LCCN:2004-269857.

Audience: **u,f.**

Stanley, H. Eugene   QC175.16.P5 S72 1987
Introduction to Phase Transitions and Critical Phenomena. Paper Text. Oxford University Press, Inc. New York, NY. 1987. 328p. The International Series of Monographs on Physics ISBN:0-19-505316-8, ISBN13: 978-0-19-505316-6. Dewey:530.4. LCCN:87-012357.

Audience: **u,f.** *B*

Yeomans, J. M.   QC175.16.P5Y46 1992
Statistical Mechanics of Phase Transitions. Paper Text. Oxford University Press, Inc. New York, NY. 1992. 164p. ISBN:0-19-851730-0, ISBN13: 978-0-19-851730-6. Dewey:530.1/3.

Audience: **u,f.**

Heat and Thermodynamics

Baierlein, Ralph   QC311 .B293 1999
Thermal Physics. Trade Paper. Cambridge University Press. New York, NY. 1999. 456p. ISBN:0-521-65838-1, ISBN13: 978-0-521-65838-6. Dewey:536/.7. LCCN:98-038617.

Audience: **u,f.** *Choice, 2000.*

Berry, R. Stephen   QC73.B43 1991
Understanding Energy: Energy, Entropy and Thermodynamics for Every Man. Paper Text. World Scientific Publishing Company, Inc. Hackensack, NJ. 1991. 150p. ISBN:981-02-0679-8, ISBN13: 978-981-02-0679-6. Dewey:531/.6. LCCN:91-019564.

Audience: **u,f.**

Callen, Herbert B.   QC311.C25 1985
Thermodynamics and an Introduction to Thermostatistics, Level 4. Ed. 2. Trade Cloth. John Wiley & Sons, Inc. Hoboken, NJ. 1985. 512p. ISBN:0-471-86256-8, ISBN13: 978-0-471-86256-7. Dewey:536/.7. LCCN:85-006387.

Audience: **u,f.**

Fermi, Enrico   **QC311**
Thermodynamics. Trade Paper. Dover Publications, Inc.
Mineola, NY. 1956. 160p. ISBN:0-486-60361-X, ISBN13:
978-0-486-60361-2. Dewey:536.7.

Audience: **u,f.**

Greiner, Walter, et al.   **QC311.G74 1995**
Thermodynamics and Statistical Mechanics. Ludwig Neise &
Horst Stöcker (Authors), D. Rischke (Translator). Trade Paper.
Springer. New York, NY. 2001. 480p. Classical Theoretical
Physics Ser. ISBN:0-387-94299-8, ISBN13: 978-0-387-94299-5.
Dewey:530.1/3. LCCN:94-029072.

Audience: **u,f.**

Kittel, Charles & Kroemer,   **QC311**
  Herbert
Thermal Physics. Ed. 2. Cloth over Boards. Worth Publishers,
Inc. New York, NY. 1980. 496p. ISBN:0-7167-1088-9, ISBN13:
978-0-7167-1088-2. Dewey:536/.7. LCCN:79-016677.

Audience: **u,f.** $\mathcal{B}$

Kondepudi, Dilip K. &   **QC311.K66 1998**
  Prigogine, Ilya
Modern Thermodynamics: From Heat Engines to Dissipative
Structures. Trade Paper. John Wiley & Sons, Inc. Hoboken, NJ.
1998. 508p. ISBN:0-471-97394-7, ISBN13: 978-0-471-97394-2.
Dewey:536/.7. LCCN:97-048745.

Audience: **u,f.** *Choice, 1999.*

Liboff, Richard L.   **QC174.9.L54 2003**
Kinetic Theory: Classical, Quantum, and Relativistic
Descriptions. Ed. 3. Trade Cloth. Springer. New York, NY.
2003. 552p. Graduate Texts in Contemporary Physics Ser.
ISBN:0-387-95551-8, ISBN13: 978-0-387-95551-3.
Dewey:530.13/6. LCCN:2002-026658.

Audience: **u,f.**

Quinn, T. J.   **QC271**
Temperature. Ed. 2. Trade Cloth. Elsevier Science & Technology
Books. Saint Louis, MO. 1991. 495p. Monographs in Physical
Measurement ISBN:0-12-569681-7, ISBN13:
978-0-12-569681-4. Dewey:536/.5/0287.

Audience: **u,f.** $\mathcal{B}$

Schroeder, Daniel V.   **QC311.15.S32**
Introduction to Thermal Physics. Trade Paper. Addison-Wesley
Longman, Inc. Boston, MA. 2000. ISBN:0-201-65680-9,
ISBN13: 978-0-201-65680-0. Dewey:536/.7.

Audience: **u,f.**

Von Baeyer, Hans Christian   **QC318.M35V66 1998**
Maxwell's Demon: Why Warmth Disperses and Time Passes.
Trade Cloth. Fodor's Travel Publications. New York, NY. 1998.
256p. ISBN:0-679-43342-2, ISBN13: 978-0-679-43342-2.
Dewey:536/.71. LCCN:97-041543.

Audience: **g,l.** *Choice, 1998.*

Zemansky, Mark W.   **QC276**
Temperatures Very Low and Very High. Trade Paper. Dover
Publications, Inc. Mineola, NY. 1981. 144p.
ISBN:0-486-24072-X, ISBN13: 978-0-486-24072-5.
Dewey:536/.5. LCCN:80-069673.

Audience: **u,f.** $\mathcal{B}$

Zemansky, Mark W. &   **QC254.2.Z45 1997**
  Dittman, Richard
Heat and Thermodynamics: An Intermediate Textbook. Ed. 7.

Trade Cloth. McGraw-Hill Higher Education. Burr Ridge, IL.
1996. 487p. International Series in Pure and Applied Physics
ISBN:0-07-017059-2, ISBN13: 978-0-07-017059-9. Dewey:536.
LCCN:96-028311.

Audience: **u,f.**

Heat and Thermodynamics > Heat Transfer

Bejan, Adrian & Jones, J. S.   **QC320.B44 1993**
Heat Transfer. Trade Cloth. John Wiley & Sons, Inc. Hoboken,
NJ. 1993. 704p. ISBN:0-471-50290-1, ISBN13:
978-0-471-50290-6. Dewey:621.4022. LCCN:92-025535.

Audience: **u,f.** *Choice, 1993.*

Carslaw, Horatio S. &   **QC321.C28 1986**
  Jaeger, J. C.
Conduction of Heat in Solids. Ed. 2. Trade Paper. Oxford
University Press, Inc. New York, NY. 1986. 520p.
ISBN:0-19-853368-3, ISBN13: 978-0-19-853368-9.
Dewey:526/.23. LCCN:85-026963.

Audience: **u,f.**

Chapman, Alan J.   **QC320.C5**
Heat Transfer. Ed. 5. Trade Cloth. Prentice Hall PTR. Upper
Saddle River, NJ. 2001. ISBN:0-02-321495-3, ISBN13:
978-0-02-321495-0. Dewey:536/.2.

Audience: **u,f.**

Holman, J. P.   **QC320.H64 2002**
Heat Transfer. Ed. 9. Paper Text. McGraw-Hill Companies, The.
New York, NY. 2002. xx, 665p. McGraw-Hill Series in
Mechanical Engineering ISBN:0-07-112230-3, ISBN13:
978-0-07-112230-6. Dewey:536/.2. LCCN:2001-034522.

Audience: **u,f.** $\mathcal{B}$

Incropera, Frank P., et al.   **QC320.I45 2006**
Fundamentals of Heat and Mass Transfer. Ed. 6. David P.
DeWitt, Theodore L. Bergman & Adrienne Lavine (Authors).
Trade Cloth. John Wiley & Sons, Inc. Hoboken, NJ. 2006.
1024p. ISBN:0-471-45728-0, ISBN13: 978-0-471-45728-2.
Dewey:621.402/2. LCCN:2005-058360.

Audience: **u,f.**

Kays, W. M., et al.   **QC327.K37 2005**
Convective Heat and Mass Transfer. Ed. 4. M. E. Crawford &
Bernhard Weigand (Authors). Trade Cloth. McGraw-Hill
Companies, The. New York, NY. 2004. 512p. McGraw-Hill
Series in Mechanical Engineering ISBN:0-07-246876-9,
ISBN13: 978-0-07-246876-2. Dewey:621.4022.
LCCN:2004-040215.

Audience: **u,f.**

Patankar, Suhas V.   **QC320 .P37 1980**
Numerical Heat Transfer and Fluid Flow. Paper over Boards.
Hemisphere Publishing Corporation. Philadelphia, PA. 1980.
214p. ISBN:0-89116-522-3, ISBN13: 978-0-89116-522-4.
Dewey:536.2. LCCN:79-028286.

Audience: **u,f.**

Optics

Als-Nielsen, Jens &   **QC481.A47 2001**
  McMorrow, Des
Elements of Modern X-Ray Physics. Trade Paper. John Wiley &

Sons, Inc. Hoboken, NJ. 2001. 336p. ISBN:0-471-49858-0, ISBN13: 978-0-471-49858-2. Dewey:539.7/222. LCCN:00-063342.

Audience: **u,f**

Bass, Michael   QC369.H35 2001
e Handbook of Optics. Ed. 2. E-Book. McGraw-Hill Professional Publishing. New York, NY. ISBN:0-07-141479-7, ISBN13: 978-0-07-141479-1. Dewey:535.

Audience: **u,f**

Bohren, Craig F. &   QC882 .B63 1998
  Huffman, Donald R.
Absorption and Scattering of Light by Small Particles. Trade Paper. John Wiley & Sons, Inc. Hoboken, NJ. 1998. 544p. ISBN:0-471-29340-7, ISBN13: 978-0-471-29340-8. Dewey:535.

Audience: **u,f**

Born, Max; Wolf, Emil   QC355.2
Principles of Optics: Electromagnetic Theory of Propagation, Interference and Diffraction of Light. Ed. 6. Elsevier Science & Technology Books. 1980. ISBN:0-08-026481-6, ISBN13: 978-0-08-026481-3.

Audience: **u,f** *B*

Fowles, Grant R.   QC395.2.F68 1989
Introduction to Modern Optics. Ed. 2. Trade Paper. Dover Publications, Inc. Mineola, NY. 1989. 336p. ISBN:0-486-65957-7, ISBN13: 978-0-486-65957-2. Dewey:535/.2. LCCN:88-033441.

Audience: **u,f** *B*

Georgi, Howard   QC157.G46 1993
The Physics of Waves. Ed. 1. Cloth Text. Prentice Hall PTR. Upper Saddle River, NJ. 1992. 432p. ISBN:0-13-665621-8, ISBN13: 978-0-13-665621-0. Dewey:530.124. LCCN:92-027348.

Audience: **u,f**

Haken, H.   QC446.2
Light: Laser Light Dynamics. Ed. 2. Trade Cloth. Elsevier Science & Technology Books. Saint Louis, MO. 1986. 336p. ISBN:0-444-86021-5, ISBN13: 978-0-444-86021-7. Dewey:535/.15. LCCN:80-022397.

Audience: **u,f**

Haken, H.   QC446.2
Waves, Photons, Atoms. Ed. 3. Trade Cloth. Elsevier Science & Technology Books. Saint Louis, MO. 1980. 354p. ISBN:0-444-86020-7, ISBN13: 978-0-444-86020-0. Dewey:535/.15. LCCN:80-022397.

Audience: **u,f** *B*

Hecht, Eugene   QC355.3.H43 2002
Optics. Ed. 4. Cloth Text. Addison-Wesley Longman, Inc. Boston, MA. 2001. 680p. ISBN:0-8053-8566-5, ISBN13: 978-0-8053-8566-3. Dewey:535. LCCN:2001-032540.

Audience: **u,f**

Jenkins, Francis A. &   QC355.2 .J46 2001
  White, Harvey E.
Fundamentals of Optics. Ed. 4. Paper Text. McGraw-Hill Higher Education. Burr Ridge, IL. 2001. 768p. ISBN:0-07-256191-2, ISBN13: 978-0-07-256191-3. Dewey:535.

Audience: **u,f** *B*

King, Terry A. & Smith, F.   QC446.2.G73 2000
  Graham
Optics and Photonics: An Introduction. Trade Paper. John Wiley & Sons, Inc. Hoboken, NJ. 2000. 456p. ISBN:0-471-48925-5, ISBN13: 978-0-471-48925-2. Dewey:535. LCCN:99-087078.

Audience: **u,f**

Meyer-Arendt, Jurgen R.   QC355.2.M49 1995
Introduction to Classical and Modern Optics. Ed. 4. Cloth Text. Prentice Hall PTR. Upper Saddle River, NJ. 1994. 480p. ISBN:0-13-124356-X, ISBN13: 978-0-13-124356-9. Dewey:535. LCCN:94-030562.

Audience: **u,f** *B*

Mills, D. L.   QC446.2.M55 1998
Nonlinear Optics: Basic Concepts. Ed. 2. Trade Paper. Springer. New York, NY. 1998. XI, 263p. ISBN:3-540-64182-3, ISBN13: 978-3-540-64182-7. Dewey:535.2. LCCN:98-006385.

Audience: **u,f**

Newton, Isaac   QC353.N53 2003
Opticks: Or Treatise of the Reflections, Inflections, and Colours of Light. Trade Paper. Prometheus Books, Publishers. Amherst, NY. 2004. 350p. Great Minds Ser. ISBN:1-59102-095-6, ISBN13: 978-1-59102-095-0. Dewey:535. LCCN:2003-053868.

Audience: **u,f**

Pedrotti, Frank L., et al.   QC355.3.P43 2007
Introduction to Optics. Ed. 3. Leno M. Pedrotti & Leno S. Pedrotti (Authors). Cloth Text. Prentice Hall PTR. Upper Saddle River, NJ. 2006. 656p. ISBN:0-13-149933-5, ISBN13: 978-0-13-149933-1. Dewey:535. LCCN:2006-041697.

Audience: **u,f**

Shen, Y. R.   QC446.2
The Principles of Nonlinear Optics. Trade Paper. John Wiley & Sons, Inc. Hoboken, NJ. 2002. 576p. ISBN:0-471-43080-3, ISBN13: 978-0-471-43080-3. Dewey:535.2. LCCN:2003-265395.

Audience: **u,f**

Tolansky, S.   QC411 .T58
An Introduction to Interferometry. Paper Text. Textbook Publishers. Temecula, CA. 2003. 223p. ISBN:0-7581-9490-0, ISBN13: 978-0-7581-9490-9. Dewey:535/.4.

Audience: **u,f**

Young, Matt   QC335.2.Y68 2000
Optics and Lasers: Including Fibers and Optical Waveguides. Ed. 5. Trade Cloth. Springer. New York, NY. 2000. XX, 498p. Advanced Texts in Physics ISBN:3-540-65741-X, ISBN13: 978-3-540-65741-5. Dewey:621.36. LCCN:00-059582.

Audience: **u,f**

Optics > Holography

Smith, Howard M.   QC0449.S6
Principles of Holography. Ed. 2. Trade Paper. Books on Demand. Ann Arbor, MI. 293p. ISBN:0-608-16189-6, ISBN13: 978-0-608-16189-1. Dewey:774. LCCN:75-005631.

Audience: **u,f**

Optics > Spectroscopy

Bernath, Peter F.   QC451.B47 2005
Spectra of Atoms and Molecules. Ed. 2. Trade Cloth. Oxford University Press, Inc. New York, NY. 2005. 453p.

ISBN:0-19-517759-2, ISBN13: 978-0-19-517759-6.
Dewey:535.8/4. LCCN:2004-062020.

Audience: **u,f.** *Choice, 2005.*

Condon, E. U. & Shortley,   QC454 .C64
  George H.
The Theory of Atomic Spectra. Trade Paper. Cambridge
University Press. New York, NY. 1935. 460p.
ISBN:0-521-09209-4, ISBN13: 978-0-521-09209-8.
Dewey:535.84.

Audience: **u,f.**

Demtröder, W.   QC454.L3D46 2002
Laser Spectroscopy: Basic Concepts and Instrumentation. Ed. 3.
Trade Cloth. Springer. New York, NY. 2002. XX, 987p.
Advanced Texts in Physics ISBN:3-540-65225-6, ISBN13:
978-3-540-65225-0. Dewey:621.36/6. LCCN:2002-029191.

Audience: **u,f.** *B*

Herzberg, Gerhard   QC454.M6 H4713
Molecular Spectra and Molecular Structure: Infrared and Raman
of Polyatomic Molecules, Vol. 2. Library Binding. Krieger
Publishing Company. Melbourne, FL. 1990. 650p. Molecular
Spectra and Molecular Structure Ser. ISBN:0-89464-269-3,
ISBN13: 978-0-89464-269-2. Dewey:535.8/4. LCCN:88-002933.

Audience: **u,f.**

Herzberg, Gerhard   QC451
Atomic Spectra and Atomic Structure. Ed. 2. J. W. Spinks
(Translator). Trade Cloth. Dover Publications, Inc. Mineola, NY.
1944. 257p. ISBN:0-486-60115-3, ISBN13: 978-0-486-60115-1.
Dewey:539.14.

Audience: **u,f.** *B*

Hollas, J. Michael   QC451
Modern Spectroscopy. Ed. 4. Trade Paper. John Wiley & Sons,
Inc. Hoboken, NJ. 2004. 480p. ISBN:0-470-84416-7, ISBN13:
978-0-470-84416-8. Dewey:535.8/4. LCCN:2004-269787.

Audience: **u,f.** *Choice, 2004, 1987.*

Prasad, Paras N.   TA1520.P73 2004
Nanophotonics. Trade Cloth. John Wiley & Sons, Inc. Hoboken,
NJ. 2004. 432p. ISBN:0-471-64988-0, ISBN13:
978-0-471-64988-5. Dewey:621.36. LCCN:2004-001186.

Audience: **u,f.**

Schawlow, Arthur L. &   QC454.M5
  Townes, C. H.
Microwave Spectroscopy. Trade Paper. Dover Publications, Inc.
Mineola, NY. 1975. 698p. ISBN:0-486-61798-X, ISBN13:
978-0-486-61798-5. Dewey:530.4/3. LCCN:74-083620.

Audience: **u,f.** *B*

Optics > Color

Nassau, Kurt   QC495.N35 2001
The Physics and Chemistry of Color: The Fifteen Causes of
Color. Ed. 2. Trade Cloth. John Wiley & Sons, Inc. Hoboken,
NJ. 2001. 496p. Wiley Series in Pure and Applied Optics Ser.,
Vol. 38 ISBN:0-471-39106-9, ISBN13: 978-0-471-39106-7.
Dewey:535.6. LCCN:2001-024237.

Audience: **l,u.** *Choice, 2002.*

Shevell, S. K. (Editor)   QC+
The Science of Color. Ed. 2. Trade Cloth. Elsevier Science &
Technology Books. Saint Louis, MO. 2003. 350p.

ISBN:0-444-51251-9, ISBN13: 978-0-444-51251-2.
Dewey:535.6. LCCN:2003-106330.

Audience: **l,u.** *Choice, 2004.*

Optics > Quantum Optics

Bachor, Hans A. & Ralph,   QC446.2
  Timothy C.
A Guide to Experiments in Quantum Optics. Ed. 2. Trade Paper.
John Wiley & Sons, Inc. Hoboken, NJ. 2004. 434p. Physics
Textbook Ser. ISBN:3-527-40393-0, ISBN13:
978-3-527-40393-6. Dewey:535. LCCN:2004-273499.

Audience: **u,f.**

Loudon, Rodney   QC446.2.L68 2000
The Quantum Theory of Light. Ed. 3. Paper Text. Oxford
University Press, Inc. New York, NY. 2000. 448p. Oxford
Science Publications ISBN:0-19-850176-5, ISBN13:
978-0-19-850176-3. Dewey:535/.15. LCCN:2001-265846.

Audience: **u,f.**

Scully, Marlan Orvil &   QC446.2 .S4 1997
  Zubairy, Muhammad Suhail
Quantum Optics. Trade Paper. Cambridge University Press. New
York, NY. 1997. 652p. ISBN:0-521-43595-1, ISBN13:
978-0-521-43595-6. Dewey:535. LCCN:94-042949.

Audience: **u,f.**

Experimental Methods > Data Handling

Bevington, Philip R. &   QA278.B48 2002
  Robinson, D. Keith
Data Reduction and Error Analysis for the Physical Sciences.
Ed. 3. Paper Text. McGraw-Hill Higher Education. Burr Ridge,
IL. 2002. 336p. ISBN:0-07-247227-8, ISBN13:
978-0-07-247227-1. Dewey:511/.43. LCCN:2002-070896.

Audience: **g,l,u,f.**

Brandt, Siegmund   QA273.B86213 1998
Data Analysis: Statistical and Computational Methods for
Scientists and Engineers. Ed. 3. Glen Gowan (Translator).
Mixed Media. Springer. New York, NY. 1998. XXXIV, 652p.
ISBN:0-387-98498-4, ISBN13: 978-0-387-98498-8.
Dewey:519.2. LCCN:98-011969.

Audience: **l,u.**

Fruhwirth, R., et al.   QC793.412 .D37 2000
Data Analysis Techniques for High-Energy Physics. Ed. 2. M.
Regler, R. K. Bock, H. Grote & D. Notz (Authors), T. Ericson
& P. Y. Landshoff (Contribution by). Trade Paper. Cambridge
University Press. New York, NY. 2000. 408p. Cambridge
Monographs on Particle Physics, Nuclear Physics and
Cosmology Ser. ISBN:0-521-63548-9, ISBN13:
978-0-521-63548-6. Dewey:530.1/5. LCCN:99-020207.

Audience: **u,f.**

Rabinovich, Semyon   T50
Measurement Errors and Uncertainties: Theory and Practice. Ed.
3. M. E. Alferieff (Translator). Trade Cloth. Springer. New York,
NY. 2005. XII, 308p. ISBN:0-387-25358-0, ISBN13:
978-0-387-25358-9. Dewey:530.8.

Audience: **l,u.**

Taylor, John R.   QC39.T4 1997
An Introduction to Error Analysis: The Study of Uncertainties in Physical Measurements. Ed. 2. Trade Cloth. University Science Books. Sausalito, CA. 1997. 448p. ISBN:0-935702-42-3, ISBN13: 978-0-935702-42-2. Dewey:500. LCCN:96-000953.
Audience: **l,u.** *Choice, 1997.*

Experimental Methods > Laboratory Techniques

Boyes, Walt   QC53.I574 2002
Instrumentation Reference Book. Ed. 3. Trade Cloth. Elsevier Science & Technology Books. Saint Louis, MO. 2002. 1062p. ISBN:0-7506-7123-8, ISBN13: 978-0-7506-7123-1. Dewey:530/.7. LCCN:2002-018480.
Audience: **u,f.**

Dunlap, R. A.   QC33.D86 1988
Experimental Physics: Modern Methods. Trade Cloth. Oxford University Press, Inc. New York, NY. 1988. 386p. ISBN:0-19-504949-7, ISBN13: 978-0-19-504949-7. Dewey:530. LCCN:87-034750.
Audience: **l,u.**

Knoll, Glenn F.   QC787.C6K56 2000
Radiation Detection and Measurement. Ed. 3. Trade Cloth. John Wiley & Sons, Inc. Hoboken, NJ. 2000. 816p. ISBN:0-471-07338-5, ISBN13: 978-0-471-07338-3. Dewey:539.7/7. LCCN:99-034621.
Audience: **u,f.** *B*

Lafferty, James M. (Editor)   QC166.F68 1998
Foundations of Vacuum Science and Technology. Trade Cloth. John Wiley & Sons, Inc. Hoboken, NJ. 1998. 760p. ISBN:0-471-17593-5, ISBN13: 978-0-471-17593-3. Dewey:621.5/5. LCCN:96-029895.
Audience: **u,f.**

Melissinos, Adrian C. &   QC33.M52 2003
 Napolitano, Jim
Experiments in Modern Physics. Ed. 2. Cloth Text. Elsevier Science & Technology Books. Saint Louis, MO. 2003. 640p. ISBN:0-12-489851-3, ISBN13: 978-0-12-489851-6. Dewey:530/.078. LCCN:2002-117796.
Audience: **l,u.**

Pobell, F.   QC192.P63 1991
Matter and Methods at Low Temperatures. Trade Cloth. Springer. New York, NY. 1992. 319p. ISBN:0-387-53751-1, ISBN13: 978-0-387-53751-1. Dewey:536/.56. LCCN:91-031526.
Audience: **u,f.**

Sherman, W. F.   QC0281.S48
Experimental Techniques in High-Pressure Research: W. F. Sherman and A. A. Stadmuller. Trade Paper. Books on Demand. Ann Arbor, MI. 481p. ISBN:0-608-22016-7, ISBN13: 978-0-608-22016-1. Dewey:620.1/04. LCCN:87-008159.
Audience: **u,f.**

White, Guy & Meeson,   QC278.W45 2002
 Philip
Experimental Techniques in Low-Temperature Physics. Ed. 4. Trade Paper. Oxford University Press, Inc. New York, NY. 2002.

292p. Monographs on the Physics and Chemistry of Materials, Vol. 59 ISBN:0-19-851427-1, ISBN13: 978-0-19-851427-5. Dewey:536.5/6. LCCN:2002-283298.
Audience: **u,f.**

Physics Education

Arons, Arnold B.   QC30.A78 1996
Teaching Introductory Physics. Trade Cloth. John Wiley & Sons, Inc. Hoboken, NJ. 1996. 816p. ISBN:0-471-13707-3, ISBN13: 978-0-471-13707-8. Dewey:530/.071/1. LCCN:96-016838.
Audience: **u,f.** *Choice, 1997.*

Christian, Wolfgang &   QC30.C48 2001
 Belloni, Mario
Physlets: Teaching Physics with Interactive Curricular Material. Trade Paper. Prentice Hall PTR. Upper Saddle River, NJ. 2000. 304p. Prentice Hall Series in Educational Innovation ISBN:0-13-029341-5, ISBN13: 978-0-13-029341-1. Dewey:530/.078/5. LCCN:00-055726.
Audience: **f.**

Conner, Donna Berry   QC33
 (Editor)
A Potpourri of Physics Teaching Ideas. Trade Cloth. American Association of Physics Teachers. College Park, MD. 1987. 363p. ISBN:0-917853-27-X, ISBN13: 978-0-917853-27-2. Dewey:530.7.
Audience: **f.**

Epstein, Lewis Carroll   QC32
Thinking Physics: Practical Lessons in Critical Thinking, Gedanken Physics. Trade Paper. Insight Press. San Francisco, CA. 1995. 562p. ISBN:0-935218-06-8, ISBN13: 978-0-935218-06-0. Dewey:530.076.
Audience: **l,u,f.**

Knight, Randall D.   QC30
Five Easy Lessons: Strategies for Successful Physics Teaching. Trade Paper. Addison-Wesley Longman, Inc. Boston, MA. 2002. 330p. ISBN:0-8053-8702-1, ISBN13: 978-0-8053-8702-5. Dewey:530.07.
Audience: **l,f.** *Choice, 2004.*

Kutliroff, David   QC33 .K88
One Hundred One Classroom Demonstrations and Experiments for Teaching Physics. Trade Cloth. Prentice-Hall. Upper Saddle, NJ. 1975. ISBN:0-13-634220-5, ISBN13: 978-0-13-634220-5. Dewey:530/.07/24. LCCN:74-017170.
Audience: **f.**

Mazur, Eric   QC30.M345 1997
Peer Instruction: A User's Manual. Trade Paper. Prentice Hall PTR. Upper Saddle River, NJ. 1996. 253p. Prentice Hall Series in Educational Innovation Ser. ISBN:0-13-565441-6, ISBN13: 978-0-13-565441-5. Dewey:530/.071. LCCN:96-020088.
Audience: **f.**

Meiners, Harry F. (Editor)   QC33 .P45 1985
Physics: Demonstration Experiments. Library Binding. Krieger Publishing Company. Melbourne, FL. 1985. 1518p. ISBN:0-89874-821-6, ISBN13: 978-0-89874-821-5. Dewey:530/.07/8. LCCN:84-023409.
Audience: **f.**

Novak, Gregor, et al.   **QC30.J85 1999**
Just-in-Time Teaching: Blending Active Learning with Web
Technology. Andrew Gavrin, Evelyn Patterson & Wolfgang
Christian (Authors). Trade Paper. Prentice Hall PTR. Upper
Saddle River, NJ. 1999. 188p. ISBN:0-13-085034-9, ISBN13:
978-0-13-085034-8. Dewey:530/.078/54678. LCCN:99-010512.

Audience: **f.**

Redish, Edward F.   **QC30.R348 2003**
Teaching Physics: With the Physics Suite. Trade Paper. John
Wiley & Sons, Inc. Hoboken, NJ. 2003. 232p.
ISBN:0-471-39378-9, ISBN13: 978-0-471-39378-8.
Dewey:530/.071/1. LCCN:2003-278034.

Audience: **f.**

Resnick, Robert E.   **QC30.C639 1993**
Conference on the Introductory Physics Course: On the
Occasion of the Retirement of Robert Resnick. Jack Wilson
(Editor). Trade Cloth. John Wiley & Sons, Inc. Hoboken, NJ.
1996. 348p. ISBN:0-471-15557-8, ISBN13: 978-0-471-15557-7.
Dewey:530/.071/173. LCCN:96-001948.

Audience: **f.**

Biophysics

Berg, Howard C.   **QH323.5 .B45 1993**
Random Walks in Biology. Ed. 2. Trade Paper. Princeton
University Press. Princeton, NJ. 1993. 164p.
ISBN:0-691-00064-6, ISBN13: 978-0-691-00064-0.
Dewey:574/.01/519282. LCCN:93-012708.

Audience: **u,f.**

Boeker, Egbert & Van   **GE105.B65 2001**
Grondelle, Rienk
Environmental Science: Physical Principles and Applications.
Trade Cloth. John Wiley & Sons, Inc. Hoboken, NJ. 2001. 380p.
ISBN:0-471-49576-X, ISBN13: 978-0-471-49576-5. Dewey:628.
LCCN:2001-024907.

Audience: **l,u.**

Denny, Mark W.   **QC161 .D46 1993**
Air and Water: The Biology and Physics of Life's Media. Trade
Paper. Princeton University Press. Princeton, NJ. 1995. 362p.
ISBN:0-691-02518-5, ISBN13: 978-0-691-02518-6.
Dewey:574.191. LCCN:92-020969.

Audience: **l,u.**

Nelson, Philip   **QH505**
Biological Physics: Energy, Information, Life. Cloth over
Boards. Worth Publishers, Inc. New York, NY. 2003. 600p.
ISBN:0-7167-4372-8, ISBN13: 978-0-7167-4372-9.
Dewey:571.4. LCCN:2003-105929.

Audience: **l,u.**

Rubinstein, Michael &   **QC173.4.P65R83 2003**
Colby, Ralph H.
Polymer Physics. Cloth Text. Oxford University Press, Inc. New
York, NY. 2003. 454p. ISBN:0-19-852059-X, ISBN13:
978-0-19-852059-7. Dewey:530.4/13. LCCN:2002-027401.

Audience: **u,f.**

Sertorio, L. (Editor)   **QC311.S512 1990**
Thermodynamics of Complex Systems. Cloth Text. World
Scientific Publishing Company, Inc. Hackensack, NJ. 1990.
220p. ISBN:9971-5-0978-4, ISBN13: 978-9971-5-0978-1.
Dewey:536/.7. LCCN:90-025103.

Audience: **u,f.** *Choice, 1991.*

Vogel, Steven   **QH513**
Cats' Paws and Catapults: Mechanical Worlds of Nature and
People. Trade Paper. W. W. Norton & Company, Inc. New York,
NY. 2000. 384p. ISBN:0-393-31990-3, ISBN13:
978-0-393-31990-3. Dewey:571.4/3. LCCN:97-044807.

Audience: **l,u.**

Vogel, Steven   **QH513.V643 2003**
Comparative Biomechanics: Life's Physical World. Trade Cloth.
Princeton University Press. Princeton, NJ. 2003. 582p.
ISBN:0-691-11297-5, ISBN13: 978-0-691-11297-8.
Dewey:571.4/3. LCCN:2002-042723.

Audience: **l,u.** *Choice, 2004.*

Electricity and Magnetism

Cottingham, W. N. &   **QC760 .C674 1991**
Greenwood, D. A.
Electricity and Magnetism. Cloth Text. Cambridge University
Press. New York, NY. 1991. 215p. ISBN:0-521-36229-6,
ISBN13: 978-0-521-36229-0. Dewey:537. LCCN:90-026471.

Audience: **u,f.**

Duffin, W. J.   **QC522.D83 1990**
Electricity and Magnetism. Ed. 4. Cloth Text. McGraw-Hill
Companies, The. New York, NY. 1990. 442p.
ISBN:0-07-707209-X, ISBN13: 978-0-07-707209-4. Dewey:537.
LCCN:89-037060.

Audience: **l,u.**

Faraday, Michael   **QC503.F21 2004**
Experimental Researches in Electricity. Trade Paper. Dover
Publications, Inc. Mineola, NY. 2004. 352p.
ISBN:0-486-43505-9, ISBN13: 978-0-486-43505-3. Dewey:537.
LCCN:2004-042805.

Audience: **l,u,f.**

Griffiths, David F.   **QC680.G74 1989**
Introduction to Electrodynamics. Ed. 2. Cloth Text. Prentice
Hall PTR. Upper Saddle River, NJ. 1989. 486p.
ISBN:0-13-481367-7, ISBN13: 978-0-13-481367-7.
Dewey:537.6. LCCN:88-036566.

Audience: **u,f.**

Heaviside, Oliver   **QC670 .H43 2003**
Electromagnetic Theory: Including an Account of Heaviside'
Unpublished Notes, Set. Ed. 3. E. Whittaker (Introduction by).
Trade Cloth. American Mathematical Society. Providence, RI.
1971. 504p. AMS/Chelsea Ser., Vol. 237.1.H
ISBN:0-8218-3557-2, ISBN13: 978-0-8218-3557-9.
Dewey:530.141.

Audience: **u,f.**

Jackson, John David   **QC631.J3 1999**
Classical Electrodynamics. Ed. 3. Trade Cloth. John Wiley &
Sons, Inc. Hoboken, NJ. 1998. 832p. ISBN:0-471-30932-X,
ISBN13: 978-0-471-30932-1. Dewey:537.6. LCCN:97-046873.

Audience: **u,f.**

Landau, L. D.   **QC174.26.W28**
The Classical Theory of Fields. Paper Text. Textbook Publishers.
Temecula, CA. 2003. 404p. ISBN:0-7581-6486-6, ISBN13:
978-0-7581-6486-5. Dewey:530.1/4.

Audience: **u,f.**

Formats: Web: ⬜ Ebook: 🄴 CD/DVD-ROM: 🦋 BCL3: 𝓑

Landau, L. D., et al.   QC 661 .L2413 1995
Electrodynamics of Continuous Media, Vol. 8. Ed. 2. E. M.
Lifshitz & L. P. Pitaevskii (Authors). Paper Text. Elsevier
Science & Technology Books. Saint Louis, MO. 1984. 460p.
Course of Theoretical Physics Ser., Vol. 8 ISBN:0-7506-2634-8,
ISBN13: 978-0-7506-2634-7. Dewey:537.

Audience: **u,f.** 𝐵

Marion, Jerry B. & Heald,   QC661.H43 1995
  Mark A.
Classical Electromagnetic Radiation. Ed. 3. Cloth Text.
Brooks/Cole. Pacific Grove, CA. 1994. 584p.
ISBN:0-03-097277-9, ISBN13: 978-0-03-097277-5.
Dewey:539.2. LCCN:94-067490.

Audience: **u,f.**

Maxwell, James Clerk   QC518.M465 1998
A Treatise on Electricity and Magnetism, Vol. 2. Trade Paper.
Oxford University Press, Inc. New York, NY. 1998. 532p.
Oxford Classic Tests in the Physical Sciences
ISBN:0-19-850374-1, ISBN13: 978-0-19-850374-3. Dewey:537.
LCCN:99-169144.

Audience: **u,f.** 𝐵

Maxwell, James Clerk   QC665.E4
A Dynamical Theory of the Electromagnetic Field. Thomas F.
Torrance (Editor). Trade Paper. Wipf & Stock Publishers.
Eugene, OR. 1996. 116p. ISBN:1-57910-015-5, ISBN13:
978-1-57910-015-5. Dewey:537.1.

Audience: **u,f.**

Panofsky, Wolfgang K. H. &   QC518.P337 2005
  Phillips, Melba
Classical Electricity and Magnetism. Ed. 2. Trade Paper. Dover
Publications, Inc. Mineola, NY. 2005. 512p. Dover Books on
Physics ISBN:0-486-43924-0, ISBN13: 978-0-486-43924-2.
Dewey:530.14/1. LCCN:2004-058269.

Audience: **u,f.**

Reitz, John R., et al.   QC670.R4 1979
Foundations of Electromagnetic Theory. Ed. 3. Frederick J.
Milford & Robert W. Christy (Authors). Cloth Text.
Addison-Wesley Longman, Inc. Boston, MA. 1979. x, 534 p. :p.
Physics Ser. ISBN:0-201-06332-8, ISBN13: 978-0-201-06332-5.
Dewey:530.141. LCCN:78-018649.

Audience: **u,f.** 𝐵

Schwinger, Julian Seymour,   QC631.C58 1998
  et al.
Classical Electrodynamics. Lester L. DeRaad Jr., Kimball A.
Milton, Wu-Yang Tsai & Joyce Norton (Authors). Trade Cloth.
Perseus Books Group. New York, NY. 1998. 592p.
ISBN:0-7382-0056-5, ISBN13: 978-0-7382-0056-9.
Dewey:537.6. LCCN:98-086259.

Audience: **u,f.**

Electricity and Magnetism > Superconductivity

Buckel, Werner & Kleiner,   QC611.92
  Reinhold
Superconductivity: Fundamentals and Applications. Ed. 2. Trade
Cloth. John Wiley & Sons, Inc. Hoboken, NJ. 2004. 475p.
Physics Textbook Ser. ISBN:3-527-40349-3, ISBN13:
978-3-527-40349-3. Dewey:537.623. LCCN:2006-280309.

Audience: **u,f.**

Dahl, Per F.   QC611.92.D34 1992
Superconductivity. Cloth Text. Springer. New York, NY. 1992.
400p. ISBN:0-88318-848-1, ISBN13: 978-0-88318-848-4.
Dewey:537.6/23. LCCN:91-036487.

Audience: **l,u.** *Choice, 1993.*

Ketterson, John B. (Editor)   QC611.92.P48 2003
The Physics of Superconductors. K. H. Bennemann (Volume
Editor). Trade Cloth. Springer. New York, NY. 2004. XIV,
1140p. ISBN:3-540-44232-4, ISBN13: 978-3-540-44232-5.
Dewey:532.6/23. LCCN:2002-030322.

Audience: **u,f.**

Kresin, V. Z. & Wolf, S. A.   QC611.92.K74 1990
Fundamentals of Superconductivity. Trade Cloth. Springer. New
York, NY. 1990. 248p. ISBN:0-306-43474-1, ISBN13:
978-0-306-43474-7. Dewey:537.6/23. LCCN:90-042066.

Audience: **u,f.**

Poole, Charles K., et al.   QC611.924.P66 2000
Handbook of Superconductivity. Richard J. Creswick & Horacio
A. Farach (Authors). Trade Cloth. Elsevier Science &
Technology Books. Saint Louis, MO. 1999. 693p.
ISBN:0-12-561460-8, ISBN13: 978-0-12-561460-3.
Dewey:537.6/23. LCCN:99-060091.

Audience: **u,f.**

Schrieffer, J. Robert   QC611.92..S34 1999
Theory of Superconductivity. Ed. 3. Trade Paper. Basic Books.
New York, NY. 1971. 352p. ISBN:0-7382-0120-0, ISBN13:
978-0-7382-0120-7. Dewey:537.6/23. LCCN:99-060035.

Audience: **u,f.**

Tilley, D. R. & Tilley, J.   QC612.S8
Superfluidity and Superconductivity. Ed. 3. Perfect. Institute of
Physics Publishing. Philadelphia, PA. 1990. 240p. Graduate
Student Series in Physics ISBN:0-7503-0033-7, ISBN13:
978-0-7503-0033-9. Dewey:537.623.

Audience: **u,f.**

Tinkham, Michael   QC611.92.T56 2004
Introduction to Superconductivity. Ed. 2. Trade Paper. Dover
Publications, Inc. Mineola, NY. 2004. 480p.
ISBN:0-486-43503-2, ISBN13: 978-0-486-43503-9.
Dewey:537.6/23. LCCN:2004-041434.

Audience: **u,f.** 𝐵

Electricity and Magnetism > Quantum Hall Effect

Chakraborty, Tapash &   QC612.H3C46 1995
  Pietil-Ainen, Pekka
The Fractional Quantum Hall Effect: A Survey of the
Incompressible Quantum Fluid Including the Integer Quantum
Hall Effect. Ed. 2. Trade Cloth. Springer. New York, NY. 1995.
ISBN:0-387-58515-X, ISBN13: 978-0-387-58515-4.
Dewey:537.6/226. LCCN:95-014465.

Audience: **u,f.**

Prange, R. E. & Girvin,   QC612.H3Q36 1990
  S. M. (Editors)
The Quantum Hall Effect. Ed. 2. Trade Paper. Springer. New
York, NY. 1989. XVIII, 473p. Graduate Texts in Contemporary
Physics ISBN:0-387-97177-7, ISBN13: 978-0-387-97177-3.
Dewey:537.6. LCCN:89-021926.

Audience: **u,f.**

Electricity and Magnetism > Magnetism

Craik, Derek J.   QC753.2.C73 1995
Magnetism: Principles and Applications. Ed. 93. Trade Paper.
John Wiley & Sons, Inc. Hoboken, NJ. 1997. 468p.
ISBN:0-471-95417-9, ISBN13: 978-0-471-95417-0. Dewey:538.
LCCN:93-038155.

Audience: **u,f.**

Davidson, P. A.   QA920 .D38 2001
An Introduction to Magnetohydrodynamics. M. J. Ablowitz, S.
H. Davis, E. J. Hinch, A. Iserles, J. Ockendon & P. J. Olver
(Contribution by). Trade Paper. Cambridge University Press.
New York, NY. 2001. 452p. Texts in Applied Mathematics
ISBN:0-521-79487-0, ISBN13: 978-0-521-79487-9.
Dewey:538/.6. LCCN:00-033733.

Audience: **u,f.**

Jiles, David C   QC753.2.J55 1990
Introduction to Magnetism and Magnetic Materials. Chapman &
Hall. 1991. ISBN:0-412-38640-2, ISBN13: 978-0-412-38640-4.
Audience: **u,f.**

Von Molnár, Stephan   TK7874.887W74 2004
Spin Electronics. David D. Awschalom, Robert A. Buhrman,
James M. Daughton & Michael L. Roukes (Editors). Trade
Cloth. Springer. New York, NY. 2003. XXIV, 221p.
ISBN:1-4020-1802-9, ISBN13: 978-1-4020-1802-2.
Dewey:621.3. LCCN:2003-064117.

Audience: **u,f.**

Electricity and Magnetism > Quantum Electrodynamics (QED)

Berestetskii, V. B., et al.   QC680
Quantum Electrodynamics, Vol. 4. Ed. 2. L. D. Landau, E. M.
Lifshitz & L. P. Pitaevskii (Authors). Paper Text. Elsevier
Science & Technology Books. Saint Louis, MO. 1982. 667p.
ISBN:0-7506-3371-9, ISBN13: 978-0-7506-3371-0.
Dewey:537.67.

Audience: **u,f.**

Cohen-Tannoudji, Claude, et al.   QC680
Photons and Atoms: Introduction to Quantum Electrodynamics.
Jacques Dupont-Roc & Gilbert Grynberg (Authors). Trade
Paper. John Wiley & Sons, Inc. Hoboken, NJ. 1997. 486p.
Professional Ser. ISBN:0-471-18433-0, ISBN13:
978-0-471-18433-1. Dewey:537.6/7. LCCN:88-037845.
Audience: **u,f.** *Choice, 1990.*

Feynman, Richard Phillips   QC794.8.P4
QED: The Strange Theory of Light and Matter. Trade Paper.
Princeton University Press. Princeton, NJ. 1988. 170p. Alix G.
Mautner Memorial Lectures ISBN:0-691-02417-0, ISBN13:
978-0-691-02417-2. Dewey:539.7/56. LCCN:85-042685.
Audience: **l,u,f.** *Choice, 1986.*

Schweber, Silvan S.   QC680.S34 1994
QED and the Men Who Made It: Dyson, Feynman, Schwinger,
and Tomonaga. Trade Paper. Princeton University Press.
Princeton, NJ. 1994. 760p. Princeton Series in Physics
ISBN:0-691-03327-7, ISBN13: 978-0-691-03327-3.
Dewey:537.6/7/09. LCCN:93-033550.

Audience: **l,u.**

Electricity and Magnetism > Plasma Physics

Bittencourt, J. A.   QC718.B45 2004
Fundamentals of Plasma Physics. Ed. 3. Trade Cloth. Springer.
New York, NY. 2004. XXIII, 678p. ISBN:0-387-20975-1,
ISBN13: 978-0-387-20975-3. Dewey:530.4/4.
LCCN:2004-041725.

Audience: **u,f.** *Choice, 1987.*

Chen, F. F.   QC718
Introduction to Plasma Physics and Controlled Fusion: Plasma
and Physics. Ed. 2. Trade Cloth. Springer. New York, NY. 1984.
XV, 421p. ISBN:0-306-41332-9, ISBN13: 978-0-306-41332-2.
Dewey:530.4/4. LCCN:83-017666.

Audience: **u,f.**

Frank-Kamenetskii, D. A.   QC718.F713
Plasma: The Fourth State of Matter. Trade Cloth. Springer. New
York, NY. 1972. 160p. ISBN:0-306-30523-2, ISBN13:
978-0-306-30523-8. Dewey:530.4/4. LCCN:71-165695.
Audience: **l,u.** *B*

Gurnett, Donald A. &   QC718.G87 2004
  Bhattacharjee, Amitava
Introduction to Plasma Physics: With Space and Laboratory
Applications. Trade Paper. Cambridge University Press. New
York, NY. 2005. 462p. ISBN:0-521-36730-1, ISBN13:
978-0-521-36730-1. Dewey:530.4/4. LCCN:2003-069745.
Audience: **u,f.** *Choice, 2005.*

Lifshitz, E. M. & Pitaevskii,   QC133.5
  L. P.
Physical Kinetics, Vol. 10. Paper Text. Elsevier Science &
Technology Books. Saint Louis, MO. 1981. 625p. Course of
Theoretical Physics Ser., Vol. 10 ISBN:0-7506-2635-6, ISBN13:
978-0-7506-2635-4. Dewey:531/.113.

Audience: **u,f.**

Nicholson, Dwight R.   QC717.6
Introduction to Plasma Theory. Library Binding. Krieger
Publishing Company. Melbourne, FL. 1992. 304p.
ISBN:0-89464-677-X, ISBN13: 978-0-89464-677-5.
Dewey:530.4/4. LCCN:91-036314.

Audience: **u,f.** *B*

Acoustics

Beyer, Robert T.   QC244.2.B49 1997
Nonlinear Acoustics. Trade Cloth. American Institute of Physics.
Melville, NY. 1997. 452p. ISBN:1-56396-724-3, ISBN13:
978-1-56396-724-5. Dewey:530. LCCN:97-077103.
Audience: **u,f.**

Beyer, Robert T.   QC221.7.B49 1998
Sounds of Our Times: Two Hundred Years of Acoustics. Trade
Cloth. Springer. New York, NY. 1998. XVI, 444p.
ISBN:0-387-98435-6, ISBN13: 978-0-387-98435-3. Dewey:534.
LCCN:98-009607.

Audience: **u,f.**

Dowling, Ann & Williams,   QC225.15
  John E.
Sound and Sources of Sound. Trade Paper. Prentice Hall PTR.

Upper Saddle River, NJ. 1983. 321p. ISBN:0-470-27388-7, ISBN13: 978-0-470-27388-3. Dewey:534/.02462. LCCN:82-015687.

Audience: **u,f.**

Kinsler, Lawrence E., et al.   QC243.F86 2000
Fundamentals of Acoustics. Ed. 4. Austin R. Frey, Alan B. Coppens & James V. Sanders (Authors). Trade Cloth. John Wiley & Sons, Inc. Hoboken, NJ. 1999. 560p. ISBN:0-471-84789-5, ISBN13: 978-0-471-84789-2. Dewey:534. LCCN:99-049667.

Audience: **u,f.**

Morse, Philip M. & Ingard,   QC225.15.M67 1986
K. Uno
Theoretical Acoustics. Trade Paper. Princeton University Press. Princeton, NJ. 1987. 949p. ISBN:0-691-02401-4, ISBN13: 978-0-691-02401-1. Dewey:534. LCCN:86-042860.

Audience: **u,f.**

Rayleigh, Strutt   QC223
Theory of Sound, 1. Ed. 2. Trade Cloth. Dover Publications, Inc. Mineola, NY. 1945. 480p. ISBN:0-486-60292-3, ISBN13: 978-0-486-60292-9. Dewey:534.

Audience: **u,f.**

Rossing, Thomas D. &   TA365.R67 2003
Fletcher, Neville H.
Principles of Vibration and Sound. Ed. 2. Trade Cloth. Springer. New York, NY. 2004. VIII, 330p. ISBN:0-387-40556-9, ISBN13: 978-0-387-40556-8. Dewey:534. LCCN:2003-054413.

Audience: **u,f.**

Rossing, Thomas D., et al.   QC225.15.R67 2002
The Science of Sound. Ed. 3. Richard F. Moore & Paul A. Wheeler (Authors). Trade Cloth. Addison-Wesley Longman, Inc. Boston, MA. 2001. 680p. ISBN:0-8053-8565-7, ISBN13: 978-0-8053-8565-6. Dewey:534. LCCN:2001-053994.

Audience: **u,f.**

Weights and Measures

Fenna, Donald   QC82.F428 2002
A Dictionary of Weights, Measures, and Units. Trade Paper. Oxford University Press, Inc. New York, NY. 2002. 342p. Oxford Paperback Reference Ser. ISBN:0-19-860522-6, ISBN13: 978-0-19-860522-5. Dewey:530.8/1/03. LCCN:2002-072582.

Audience: **g,l,u,f.**

Fenna, Donald   QC82.F43 1999
Elsevier's Encyclopedic Dictionary of Measures: In English (with Definitions). Trade Cloth. Elsevier Science & Technology Books. Saint Louis, MO. 1998. 606p. ISBN:0-444-50046-4, ISBN13: 978-0-444-50046-5. Dewey:530.8/03. LCCN:98-039007.

Audience: **g,l,u,f.**

Jerrard, H G; McNeill, D B
A Dictionary of Scientific Units Including Dimensionless Numbers and Scales. Ed. 6. Chapman & Hall. 1992. ISBN:0-412-46720-8, ISBN13: 978-0-412-46720-2.

Audience: **g,l,u,f.**

Audience: g=general, l=lower division undergraduate, u=upper division undergraduate, f=faculty.

567

PSYCHOLOGY

The RCL section on Psychology comprises a core selection of the most authoritative works from the print and non-print literature, which can be used to build and evaluate library collections that support broad-based undergraduate curricula in psychology. The list can also be used as a point of departure in developing collections that support more advanced study.

The list was compiled by seven bibliographers and includes original and updated resources that appeared in the 1988 BCL3 compilation and are still useful, along with new works that reflect current scholarship or the growth of new areas of interest. The sources are classified according to the American Psychological Association PsycINFO content classification code system , which corresponds more closely to the undergraduate curriculum and includes interdisciplinary subject headings reflecting changes in higher education since 1988.

— Donald Polzella

Educational Psychology

American Education   **LB15 .E48**
   Research Association
Encyclopedia of Educational Research. Ed. 7. Trade Cloth.
Thomson Gale. Farmington Hills, MI. 2001.
ISBN:0-02-864945-1, ISBN13: 978-0-02-864945-0.
Dewey:370/.3.
                  Audience: **g,l,u,f.**

American Educational   **LB1028**
   Research Association
☐ American Educational Research Association.
http://www.aera.net/
                  Audience: **u,f.**

American School Health   **LB3401**
   Association
☐ American School Health Association.
http://www.ashaweb.org
                  Audience: **u,f.**

Berliner, David C. & Calfee,   **LB1051.H2354 1996**
   Robert C. (Editors)
Handbook of Research on Educational Psychology. Trade Cloth.
Thomson Gale. Farmington Hills, MI. 1996. 1200p.
ISBN:0-02-897089-6, ISBN13: 978-0-02-897089-9.
Dewey:370.15. LCCN:95-043348.
           Audience: **f.** *Choice, 1997.*

Bruner, Jerome S.   **LB1051.B74 1971**
The Relevance of Education. Trade Cloth. W. W. Norton &
Company, Inc. New York, NY. 1971. 192p.
ISBN:0-393-04334-7, ISBN13: 978-0-393-04334-1.
Dewey:370.15. LCCN:74-139376.
           Audience: **u,f.** *ℬ*

Center for Psychology in   **LB1027.55**
   Schools
☐ Center for Psychology in Schools.
http://www.apa.org/ed/cpse/
                  Audience: **u,f.**

Child Development Institute,   **LC4019.3**
   University of North Carolina
☐ Child Development Institute, University of North Carolina.
http://www.fpg.unc.edu/
                  Audience: **g,l,u,f.**

Cronbach, Lee J.   **LB1051 .C72 1977**
Educational Psychology. Ed. 3. Cloth Text. Harcourt College
Publishers. Fort Worth, TX. 1977. 875p. ISBN:0-15-520883-7,
ISBN13: 978-0-15-520883-4. Dewey:370.15. LCCN:76-051543.
                  Audience: **u,f.**

Dewey, John   **LB875 .D3943 1997**
Experience and Education. Trade Paper. Simon & Schuster. New
York, NY. 1997. 96p. ISBN:0-684-83828-1, ISBN13:
978-0-684-83828-1. Dewey:370/.1.
           Audience: **u,f.** *ℬ*

Educational Psychology   **LB1051**
   (APA Division 15)
☐ Newsletter for Educational Psychologists.
http://www.apa.org/divisions/div15/
                  Audience: **u,f.**

Fox, Richard   **LB1025.3.F694 2005**
Teaching and Learning: Lessons from Psychology. Trade Cloth.
Blackwell Publishing, Inc. Malden, MA. 2004. 312p.
ISBN:1-4051-1486-X, ISBN13: 978-1-4051-1486-8.
Dewey:371.102. LCCN:2004-009016.
           Audience: **u,f.** *Choice, 2005.*

Gardner, Howard   **BF431.G244 1983**
Frames of Mind: The Theory of Multiple Intelligences. Cloth
Text. Basic Books. New York, NY. 1983. 464p.
ISBN:0-465-02508-0, ISBN13: 978-0-465-02508-4.
Dewey:153.9. LCCN:83-070765.
           Audience: **g,l,u,f.** *ℬ*

Gardner, Howard   **LB1062.G36 1991**
The Unschooled Mind: How Children Think and How Schools
Should Teach. Trade Cloth. Basic Books. New York, NY. 1991.
320p. ISBN:0-465-08895-3, ISBN13: 978-0-465-08895-9.
Dewey:153.083. LCCN:91-070058.
           Audience: **g,l,u,f.** *Choice, 1992.*

Guthrie, Edwin R.   **LB1051 .G85**
The Psychology of Learning. Trade Cloth. Peter Smith
Publisher, Inc. Magnolia, MA. 1952. ISBN:0-8446-1213-8,
ISBN13: 978-0-8446-1213-3. Dewey:154.4.
                  Audience: **f.**

H. W. Wilson Company   **L11**
☐ Education Abstracts.
http://hwwilsonweb.com
H. W. Wilson Co.
                  Audience: **g,l,u,f.**

Kozulin, Alex (Editor), et al.   **LB1051.V943 2003**
Vygotsky's Educational Theory in Cultural Context. Vladimir
Ageyev, Suzanne Miller & Boris Gindis (Editors), John Seely
Brown, Christian Heath & Roy Pea (Contribution by). Trade
Cloth. Cambridge University Press. New York, NY. 2003. 492p.
Learning in Doing Ser. ISBN:0-521-82131-2, ISBN13:
978-0-521-82131-5. Dewey:370.15/23. LCCN:2002-042902.
           Audience: **f.** *Choice, 2004.*

Leonard, David C.   **LB15**
Learning Theories: A to Z. Cloth Text. Greenwood Publishing
Group, Inc. Portsmouth, NH. 2002. 264p. ISBN:1-57356-413-3,
ISBN13: 978-1-57356-413-7. Dewey:370/.3.
LCCN:2001-058792.
           Audience: **l,u.** *Choice, 2003.*

Miller, Gloria E.   **LB1051**
Handbook of Psychology, Educational Psychology, Vol. 7.
William M. Reynolds (Editor), Irving B. Weiner
(Editor-In-Chief). Trade Cloth. John Wiley & Sons, Inc.
Hoboken, NJ. 2003. 688p. ISBN:0-471-38406-2, ISBN13:
978-0-471-38406-9. Dewey:150. LCCN:2002-066380.
                  Audience: **g,l,u.**

Mowrer, O. Hobart   **LB1051 .M737 1973**
Learning Theory and Behavior. Trade Cloth. Krieger Publishing
Company. Melbourne, FL. 1974. 576p. ISBN:0-88275-127-1,
ISBN13: 978-0-88275-127-6. Dewey:153.1/5. LCCN:74-159114.
                  Audience: **f.**

Mowrer, O. Hobart **BF455**
Psychology of Language and Learning. Trade Cloth. Basic
Books. New York, NY. 1980. 312p. Cognition and Language
Ser. ISBN:0-306-40371-4, ISBN13: 978-0-306-40371-2.
Dewey:401/.9. LCCN:79-017959.

Audience: **f.**

National Research Council **LB1060.H672 1999**
　Staff
How People Learn: Brain, Mind, Experience and School. John
D. Bransford, Ann L. Brown & Rodney R. Cocking (Editors).
Trade Cloth. National Academies Press. Washington, DC. 1999.
280p. ISBN:0-309-06557-7, ISBN13: 978-0-309-06557-3.
Dewey:370.15/23. LCCN:98-040290.

Audience: **u,f.**

Novak, Joseph D. **LB1060.N677 1998**
Learning, Creating, and Using Knowledge: Concept Maps As
Facilitative Tools in Schools and Corporations. Cloth over
Boards. Lawrence Erlbaum Associates, Inc. Mahwah, NJ. 1998.
264p. ISBN:0-8058-2625-4, ISBN13: 978-0-8058-2625-8.
Dewey:370.1523. LCCN:97-033965.

Audience: **l,u,f.** *Choice, 1998.*

Nuttall, Ena Vazquez, et al. **BF722.A85 2004**
Assessing and Screening Preschoolers: Psychological and
Educational Dimensions. Ivonne Romero & Joanne Kalesnik
(Authors). Trade Cloth. PRO-ED, Inc. Austin, TX. 2004.
ISBN:1-4164-0001-X, ISBN13: 978-1-4164-0001-1.
Dewey:155.42/3/0287. LCCN:2004-053491.

Audience: **u,f.**

Power, F. Clark, et al. **LC311 .P69**
Lawrence Kohlberg's Approach to Moral Education. Ann
Higgins & Lawrence Kohlberg (Authors). Trade Paper.
Columbia University Press. New York, NY. 1991. 322p.
ISBN:0-231-05977-9, ISBN13: 978-0-231-05977-0.
Dewey:370.11/4/0973. LCCN:88-018970.

Audience: **f.**

Reynolds, Cecil R. & **LC4007.E53 2000**
　Fletcher-Janzen, Elaine
Encyclopedia of Special Education: A Reference for the
Education of the Handicapped and Other Exceptional Children
and Adults. Ed. 2. Trade Cloth. John Wiley & Sons, Inc.
Hoboken, NJ. 1999. 670p. ISBN:0-471-25324-3, ISBN13:
978-0-471-25324-2. Dewey:371.9/03. LCCN:99-015333.

Audience: **g,l,u,f.**

Rieber, Robert W. (Editor) **BF121.V9413 1998**
The Collected Works of L. S. Vygotsky: Child Psychology.
Trade Cloth. Springer. New York, NY. 1998. 380p. Cognition
and Language, :A Series in Psycholinguistics
ISBN:0-306-45707-5, ISBN13: 978-0-306-45707-4. Dewey:150.

Audience: **u,f.**

Rieber, Robert W. (Editor) **BF121.V94 1997**
The Collected Works of L. S. Vygotsky: The History of the
Development of Higher Mental Functions. Marie J. Hall
(Translator), Joseph Glick (Prologue by). Trade Cloth. Basic
Books. New York, NY. 1997. 312p. Cognition and Language
Ser. ISBN:0-306-45609-5, ISBN13: 978-0-306-45609-1.
Dewey:150. LCCN:87-007219.

Audience: **u,f.** *Choice, 1998.*

Rieber, Robert W. & **BF121.V94 1997**
　Wollock, Jeffrey (Editors)
The Collected Works of L. S. Vygotsky: Problems of the Theory
and History of Psychology. Trade Cloth. Basic Books. New
York, NY. 1997. 438p. Cognition and Language Ser.
ISBN:0-306-45488-2, ISBN13: 978-0-306-45488-2. Dewey:150.

Audience: **u,f.** *Choice, 1998.*

Sarason, Seymour Bernard **BF121.S28 2001**
American Psychology and Schools: A Critique. Trade Cloth.
Teachers College Press, Teachers College, Columbia University.
New York, NY. 2001. xii, 199p. ISBN:0-8077-4088-8, ISBN13:
978-0-8077-4088-0. Dewey:370.15. LCCN:00-053270.

Audience: **u,f.** *Choice, 2002.*

Shapiro, Edward S. & **LB1124**
　Kratochwill, Thomas R. (Editors)
Conducting School-Based Assessments of Child and Adolescent
Behavior. Cloth over Boards. Guilford Publications, Inc. New
York, NY. 2000. 318p. Guilford School Practitioner Ser.
ISBN:1-57230-567-3, ISBN13: 978-1-57230-567-0.
Dewey:370/.153. LCCN:00-035421.

Audience: **u,f.**

Smith, M. Cecil & Pourchot, **LC5225.P78A48 1998**
　Thomas (Editors)
Adult Learning and Development: Perspectives from
Educational Psychology. Cloth over Boards. Lawrence Erlbaum
Associates, Inc. Mahwah, NJ. 1998. 288p. The Educational
Psychology Ser. ISBN:0-8058-2523-1, ISBN13:
978-0-8058-2523-7. Dewey:374/.001/9. LCCN:97-030926.

Audience: **u,f.** *Choice, 1998.*

Snow, Richard E., et al. **BF431.S612 2002**
Remaking the Concept of Aptitude: Extending the Legacy of
Richard E. Snow. Joan E. Talbert & Lee J. Cronbach (Authors).
Cloth over Boards. Lawrence Erlbaum Associates, Inc. Mahwah,
NJ. 2001. 312p. The Educational Psychology Ser.
ISBN:0-8058-3532-6, ISBN13: 978-0-8058-3532-8.
Dewey:153.9. LCCN:00-046619.

Audience: **f.**

Sternberg, Robert J. **BF431.S7383 1988**
The Triarchic Mind: A New Theory of Human Intelligence.
Trade Cloth. Penguin Group (USA) Inc. New York, NY. 1988.
384p. ISBN:0-670-80364-2, ISBN13: 978-0-670-80364-4.
Dewey:153.9. LCCN:87-040431.

Audience: **f.** *Choice, 1989.*

Sternberg, Robert J. **BF431.S7385 2003**
Wisdom, Intelligence, and Creativity Synthesized. Trade Cloth.
Cambridge University Press. New York, NY. 2003. 246p.
ISBN:0-521-80238-5, ISBN13: 978-0-521-80238-3.
Dewey:153.9. LCCN:2003-043751.

Audience: **u,f.** *Choice, 2004.*

Sternberg, Robert J. & **BF433.G45G46 2001**
　Grigorenko, Elena (Editors)
The General Factor of Intelligence: How General Is It? Cynthia
A. Berg, J. P. Das & Ian J. Deary (Contribution by). Cloth over
Boards. Lawrence Erlbaum Associates, Inc. Mahwah, NJ. 2002.
512p. ISBN:0-8058-3675-6, ISBN13: 978-0-8058-3675-2.
Dewey:153.9. LCCN:2001-051293.

Audience: **u,f.**

United States Department of Education   **LB5**

☐ Education Resources Information Center.
http://www.eric.ed.gov/

Audience: **g,l,u,f.**

Vygotsky, L. S.   **BF121.V9413 1987**

The Collected Works of L. S. Vygotsky: Fundamentals of Defectology (Abnormal Psychology and Learning Disabilities). Trade Cloth. Basic Books. New York, NY. 1993. 362p. Cognition and Language Ser. ISBN:0-306-42442-8, ISBN13: 978-0-306-42442-7. Dewey:150. LCCN:87-007219.

Audience: **u,f.**

Vygotsky, L. S.   **BF121.V9413 1987**

The Collected Works of L. S. Vygotsky: Problems of General Psychology, Including the Volume "Thinking and Speech". Trade Cloth. Basic Books. New York, NY. 1988. 406p. Cognition and Language Ser. ISBN:0-306-42441-X, ISBN13: 978-0-306-42441-0. Dewey:150. LCCN:87-007219.

Audience: **l,u.**

Vygotsky, L. S.   **BF121**

The Collected Works of L. S. Vygotsky: Scientific Legacy. Robert W. Rieber (Editor), Marie J. Hall (Translator). Trade Cloth. Springer. New York, NY. 1999. 352p. Cognition and Language, :A Series in Psycholinguistics ISBN:0-306-45913-2, ISBN13: 978-0-306-45913-9. Dewey:150. LCCN:87-007219.

Audience: **u,f.**

Weinstein, Rhona S.   **LB1062.6.W45 2002**

Reaching Higher: The Power of Expectations in Schooling. Trade Cloth. Harvard University Press. Cambridge, MA. 2002. 366p. ISBN:0-674-00919-3, ISBN13: 978-0-674-00919-6. Dewey:370.15/4. LCCN:2002-069084.

Audience: **u,f.** *Choice, 2003.*

Zimmerman, Barry J. & Schunk, Dale H. (Editors)   **LB1051.E36214 2003**

Educational Psychology: A Century of Contributions: A Project of Division 15 (educational Psychology) of the American Psychological Society. Lorin W. Anderson, J. William Asher & David C. Berliner (Contribution by). Cloth over Boards. Lawrence Erlbaum Associates, Inc. Mahwah, NJ. 2002. 504p. ISBN:0-8058-3681-0, ISBN13: 978-0-8058-3681-3. Dewey:370.15. LCCN:2002-010674.

Audience: **u,f.** *Choice, 2004.*

Educational Psychology > Educational Administration and Personnel

Kohl, Herbert R.   **LB1025.3.K66 2004**

Stupidity and Tears: Teaching and Learning in Troubled Times. Trade Cloth. New Press, The. New York, NY. 2004. 400p. ISBN:1-56584-851-9, ISBN13: 978-1-56584-851-1. Dewey:371.102. LCCN:2003-044204.

Audience: **g,u.**

Educational Psychology > Curriculum, Programs, and Teaching Methods

Anderson, Lorin W., et al.   **LB17.T29 2001**

A Taxonomy for Learning, Teaching and Assessing: A Revision of Bloom's Taxonomy of Educational Objectives. David R. Krathwohl & Peter W. Airasian (Authors), Benjamin Samuel Bloom (Contribution by). Trade Cloth. Allyn & Bacon, Inc. Boston, MA. 2000. 384p. ISBN:0-321-08405-5, ISBN13: 978-0-321-08405-7. Dewey:370/.1. LCCN:00-063423.

Audience: **u,f.**

Bruner, Jerome S.   **LB1025.3**

Toward a Theory of Instruction. Trade Cloth. Harvard University Press. Cambridge, MA. 1966. 192p. ISBN:0-674-89700-5, ISBN13: 978-0-674-89700-7. Dewey:371.1/02. LCCN:66-013179.

Audience: **f.** *B*

Gage, Nathaniel L.   **LB1025.2.G29**

The Scientific Basis of the Art of Teaching. Trade Paper. Teachers College Press, Teachers College, Columbia University. New York, NY. 1978. 215p. ISBN:0-8077-2537-4, ISBN13: 978-0-8077-2537-5. Dewey:371.1/02. LCCN:78-006250.

Audience: **u,f.** *B*

Gagne, Robert M., et al.   **LB1028.38.G34 2005**

Principles of Instructional Design. Ed. 5. Walter W. Wager, Katharine Golas & John M. Keller (Authors). Cloth Text. Thomson Wadsworth. Belmont, CA. 2004. 408p. ISBN:0-534-58284-2, ISBN13: 978-0-534-58284-5. Dewey:371.3. LCCN:2004-104325.

Audience: **u,f.**

Glaser, Robert (Editor)   **LB1051**

Educational Design and Cognitive Science. John R. Anderson, John D. Bransford & Ann Brown (Contribution by). Cloth over Boards. Lawrence Erlbaum Associates, Inc. Mahwah, NJ. 2000. 416p. Advances in Instructional Psychology Ser., Vol. 5 ISBN:0-8058-2549-5, ISBN13: 978-0-8058-2549-7. Dewey:370.15.

Audience: **u,f.**

Kaplan, Sandra N., et al.   **LC3993.2.P344 2006**

The Parallel Curriculum in the Classroom: Units for Application Across the Content Areas K-12. Jeanne H. Purcell, Jann H. Leppien, Carol Ann Tomlinson, Deborah E. Burns & Cindy A. Strickland (Authors). Trade Paper. Corwin Press. Thousand Oaks, CA. 2005. 392p. ISBN:1-4129-2528-2, ISBN13: 978-1-4129-2528-0. Dewey:371.95/3. LCCN:2005-007504.

Audience: **u,f.**

Pressley, Michael   **LB1573.P72 2006**

Reading Instruction That Works, Third Edition: The Case for Balanced Teaching. Ed. 3. Cloth over Boards. Guilford Publications, Inc. New York, NY. 2005. 469p. Solving Problems in Teaching of Literacy Ser. ISBN:1-59385-229-0, ISBN13: 978-1-59385-229-0. Dewey:372.41. LCCN:2005-022680.

Audience: **g,u,f.**

Rezulli, Joseph S. & Reis, Sally M.   **LC3993.9**

The Schoolwide Enrichment Model: A How-To Guide for Educational Excellence. Ed. 2. Trade Cloth. Creative Learning Press, Inc. Storrs, CT. 1997. 424p. ISBN:0-936386-70-3, ISBN13: 978-0-936386-70-6. Dewey:371.95/0973.

Audience: **u,f.**

Tomlinson, Carol Ann, et al.   LC3993.2.P34 2002
The Parallel Curriculum: A Design to Develop High Potential
and Challenge High-Ability Learners. Sandra N. Kaplan, Joseph
S. Renzulli, Jeanne H. Purcell, Jann Leppien & Deborah Burns
(Authors). Trade Cloth. Corwin Press. Thousand Oaks, CA.
2001. 288p. ISBN:0-7619-4558-X, ISBN13: 978-0-7619-4558-1.
Dewey:371.95/3. LCCN:2001-005340.

Audience: **u,f.** *Choice, 2003.*

Tomlinson, Carol Ann, et al.   LC3993.2.P344 2006
The Parallel Curriculum in the Classroom: Essays for
Application Across the Content Areas K-12. Jann H. Leppien,
Jeanne H. Purcell, Deborah E. Burns, Sandra N. Kaplan &
Cindy A. Strickland (Authors). Trade Cloth. Corwin Press.
Thousand Oaks, CA. 2005. 128p. ISBN:0-7619-2971-1,
ISBN13: 978-0-7619-2971-0. Dewey:371.95/3.
LCCN:2005-007504.

Audience: **u,f.**

Educational Psychology > Academic Learning and Achievement

Ausubel, David P.   LB1051.A7468 2000
The Acquisition and Retention of Knowledge: A Cognitive
View. Trade Cloth. Springer. New York, NY. 2000. 232p.
ISBN:0-7923-6505-4, ISBN13: 978-0-7923-6505-1.
Dewey:153.1/5. LCCN:00-135007.

Audience: **u,f.**

Bloom, Paul   P118
How Children Learn the Meanings of Words. Trade Paper. MIT
Press. Cambridge, MA. 2002. 314p. Learning, Development and
Conceptual Change Ser. ISBN:0-262-52329-9, ISBN13:
978-0-262-52329-5. Dewey:401/.93.

Audience: **g,l,u,f.** *Choice, 2000.*

Chall, Jeanne S.   LB1050.C434 1996
Stages of Reading Development. Ed. 2. Cloth Text. Harcourt
College Publishers. Fort Worth, TX. 1995. 356p.
ISBN:0-15-503081-7, ISBN13: 978-0-15-503081-7.
Dewey:428.4. LCCN:95-079647.

Audience: **u,f.**

Crowder, Robert G.   BF456.R2
The Psychology of Reading: An Introduction. Trade Cloth.
Oxford University Press, Inc. New York, NY. 1982. viii, 269p.
ISBN:0-19-503138-5, ISBN13: 978-0-19-503138-6.
Dewey:428.4/01/9. LCCN:81-022358.

Audience: **u,f.**

Entwhistle, Noel &   LB1060 .E55 1983
Ramsden, Paul
Understanding Student Learning. William G. Perry Jr. (Foreword
by). Trade Cloth. Nichols Publishing Company. East Brunswick,
NJ. 1983. 272p. ISBN:0-89397-171-5, ISBN13:
978-0-89397-171-7. Dewey:370.15/23. LCCN:83-011443.

Audience: **f.**

Goodman, Kenneth S.   LB1575.8.G66 1996
On Reading: A Common-Sense Look at the Nature of Language
and the Science of Reading. Trade Paper. Heinemann.
Portsmouth, NH. 1996. 160p. ISBN:0-435-07200-5, ISBN13:
978-0-435-07200-1. Dewey:372.41. LCCN:96-215414.

Audience: **u,f.**

Lambert, Nadine M. &   LB1060.H674 1998
McCombs, Barbara L. (Editors)
How Students Learn: Reforming Schools Through
Learner-Centered Education. Paper Text. American
Psychological Association. Washington, DC. 1997. 540p.
ISBN:1-55798-464-6, ISBN13: 978-1-55798-464-7.
Dewey:371.1020973. LCCN:97-037185.

Audience: **u,f.**

Medin, Douglas L. (Editor)   BF683
Psychology of Learning and Motivation: Advances in Research
and Theory, Vol. 31. Trade Cloth. Elsevier Science &
Technology Books. Saint Louis, MO. 1994. 366p.
ISBN:0-12-543331-X, ISBN13: 978-0-12-543331-0. Dewey:153.

Audience: **f.**

National Research Council   LB1060
Staff (Editor)
How Students Learn: History, Math, and Science in the
Classroom. Trade Cloth. National Academies Press. Washington,
DC. 2004. 250p. ISBN:0-309-07433-9, ISBN13:
978-0-309-07433-9. Dewey:510/.71. LCCN:2004-026246.

Audience: **u,f.** *Choice, 2005.*

Pollack, Robert & Brenner,   BF181 .B53
Margaret
The Experimental Psychology of Alfred Binet: Selected Papers.
Trade Cloth. Springer Publishing Company, Inc. New York, NY.
1986. ISBN:0-8261-1031-2, ISBN13: 978-0-8261-1031-2.
Dewey:152/.08.

Audience: **f.**

Wolf, Theta H.   BF109.B/
Alfred Binet. Library Binding. University of Chicago Press.
Chicago, IL. 1973. 416p. ISBN:0-226-90498-9, ISBN13:
978-0-226-90498-6. Dewey:150/.92/4. LCCN:72-095957.

Audience: **u,f.**

Educational Psychology > Special and Remedial Education

Council for Exceptional   LC3991
Children
☐ Council for Exceptional Children.
http://www.cec.sped.org/

Audience: **g,l,u,f.**

Council for Exceptional   LC4007
Children
☐ Exceptional Child Education Resources (database).
http://www.ovid.com

Audience: **u,f.**

Porter Sargent Staff (Editor)   LC4007.D5
The Directory for Exceptional Children: A Listing of
Educational and Training Facilities. Ed. 15. Trade Cloth. Porter
Sargent Publishers, Inc. Boston, MA. 2004. 1104p. Handbook
Ser. ISBN:0-87558-150-1, ISBN13: 978-0-87558-150-7.
Dewey:371.92. LCCN:54-004975.

Audience: **g,l,u,f.**

Silver, Archie A. & Hagin,   LC4705.S59 2002
Rosa A.
Disorders of Learning in Childhood. Ed. 2. Trade Cloth. John
Wiley & Sons, Inc. Hoboken, NJ. 2002. 658p.

ISBN:0-471-39259-6, ISBN13: 978-0-471-39259-0.
Dewey:371.92. LCCN:2001-024903.

Audience: **u,f.** *Choice, 1991.*

Swanson, H. Lee (Editor),   **LC4704.H364 2003**
  et al.
Handbook of Learning Disabilities. Karen R. Harris & Steven
Graham (Editors). Cloth over Boards. Guilford Publications, Inc.
New York, NY. 2003. 587p. ISBN:1-57230-851-6, ISBN13:
978-1-57230-851-0. Dewey:371.92/6. LCCN:2002-015272.

Audience: **u,f.** *Choice, 2003.*

Educational Psychology > Gifted and Talented

Bloom, Benjamin S. (Editor)   **BF723.M56D48 1985**
Developing Talent in Young People. Trade Cloth. Ballantine
Books. New York, NY. 1985. 448p. ISBN:0-345-31951-6,
ISBN13: 978-0-345-31951-7. Dewey:155.4/13.
LCCN:84-090809.

Audience: **u,f.** *B*

Burks, Barbara S., et al.   **BF412**
The Promise of Youth: Follow-up Studies of a Thousand Gifted
Children. Dortha W. Jensen & Lewis M. Terman (Authors).
Trade Cloth. Stanford University Press. Palo Alto, CA. 1930.
xiv, 508p. Genetic Studies of Genius, Vol. III
ISBN:0-8047-0011-7, ISBN13: 978-0-8047-0011-5.
Dewey:153.98.

Audience: **u,f.**

Center for Gifted Education,
  College of William and Mary
⊡ Center for Gifted Education, College of William and Mary.
http://cfge.wm.edu

Audience: **u,f.**

Center for Talented Youth,   **LC3991**
  Johns Hopkins University
⊡ Center for Talented Youth, Johns Hopkins University.
http://www.jhu.edu/gifted/

Audience: **g,l,u,f.**

Colangelo, Nicholas &   **LC3993.9.H35 2003**
  Davis, Gary A.
Handbook of Gifted Education. Ed. 3. Cloth Text. Allyn &
Bacon, Inc. Boston, MA. 2002. 640p. ISBN:0-205-34063-6,
ISBN13: 978-0-205-34063-7. Dewey:371.95.
LCCN:2002-071097.

Audience: **u,f.**

Davidson, Jan, et al.   **LC3993.9.D37 2004**
Genius Denied: How to Stop Wasting Our Brightest Young
Minds. Bob Davidson & Laura Vanderkam (Authors). Trade
Cloth. Simon & Schuster. New York, NY. 2004. 256p.
ISBN:0-7432-5460-0, ISBN13: 978-0-7432-5460-1.
Dewey:371.95. LCCN:2003-065905.

Audience: **g,l,u,f.**

Duke University Talent   **LC3991**
  Indentification Program
⊡ Educational Opportunity Guide: A Directory of Programs for
the Gifted.
http://www.duketipeog.com/

Audience: **g.**

Heller, Kurt A. (Editor),   **LC3993 .I596 1993**
  et al.
International Handbook of Research and Development of
Giftedness and Talent. Franz J. Monks & A. Harry Passow
(Editors). Trade Cloth. Elsevier Science & Technology Books.
Saint Louis, MO. 1993. 964p. ISBN:0-08-041398-6, ISBN13:
978-0-08-041398-3. Dewey:371.95. LCCN:93-016813.

Audience: **u,f.**

Holahan, Carole K., et al.   **BF724.85.G54H65 1995**
The Gifted Group in Later Maturity. Robert R. Sears & Lee J.
Cronbach (Authors). Trade Cloth. Stanford University Press.
Palo Alto, CA. 1995. xxiv , 364p. ISBN:0-8047-2407-5,
ISBN13: 978-0-8047-2407-4. Dewey:155.67/087/9.
LCCN:94-004819.

Audience: **u,f.**

Hollingworth, Leta S.   **BF412 .H6 1975**
Children above One Hundred Eighty IQ Stanford-Binet: Origins
and Development. Trade Cloth. Ayer Company Publishers, Inc.
Manchester, NH. 1997. 356p. Classics in Child Development
Ser. ISBN:0-405-06467-5, ISBN13: 978-0-405-06467-8.
Dewey:155.4/5/5. LCCN:74-021417.

Audience: **f.**

Klein, Ann G.   **BF109.H6K57 2002**
A Forgotten Voice: A Biography of Leta Stetter Hollingworth.
Trade Paper. Great Potential Press, Inc. Scottsdale, AZ. 2002.
264p. ISBN:0-910707-53-7, ISBN13: 978-0-910707-53-4.
Dewey:150/.92 B. LCCN:2002-012772.

Audience: **u,f.** *Choice, 2003.*

Maker, C. June & Shiever,   **LC3993.M293 2004**
  Shirley W.
Teaching Models in Education of the Gifted. Ed. 3. Trade Cloth.
PRO-ED, Inc. Austin, TX. 2005. x, 546p. ISBN:0-89079-999-7,
ISBN13: 978-0-89079-999-4. Dewey:371.95.
LCCN:2004-053444.

Audience: **u,f.**

National Association for   **LC3991**
  Gifted Children
⊡ National Association for Gifted Children.
http://www.nagc.org/

Audience: **g,l,u,f.**

National Research Center   **LC3991**
  on the Gifted and Talented (University of Connecticut)
⊡ National Research Center on the Gifted and Talented
(University of Connecticut).
http://www.gifted.uconn.edu/nrcgt.html

Audience: **u,f.**

Nicholas Colangelo, Susan   **LC3991**
  G. Assouline, and Miraca U. M. Gross
⊡ A National Deceived: How Schools Hold Back America's
Brightest Students.
http://nationdeceived.org/
Connie Belin and Jacqueline N. Blank International Center for
Gifted Education and Talent Development, University of Iowa
College of Education

Audience: **g,l,u.**

Office of Educational   **LC3991**
  Research and Improvement, U.S. Department of Education
☐ National Excellence: A Case for Developing America's
Talent.
http://www.ed.gov/pubs/DevTalent/toc.html

                                Audience: **g,l,u,f.**

Renzulli, Joseph S., et al.   **LB1062**
New Directions in Creativity. Carolyn M. Callahan, Linda H.
Smith, Mary J. Renzulli & Barbara G. Ford (Authors). Trade
Cloth. Creative Learning Press, Inc. Storrs, CT. 1986.
Dewey:153.3.

                                     Audience: **f.**

Sternberg, Robert &   **BF412.C66 2005**
  Davidson, Janet (Editors)
Conceptions of Giftedness. Ed. 2. Cloth Text. Cambridge
University Press. New York, NY. 2005. 478p.
ISBN:0-521-83841-X, ISBN13: 978-0-521-83841-2.
Dewey:153.9/8. LCCN:2004-023791.

                                   Audience: **u,f.**

Terman, Lewis M.   **BF723.G5**
Mental and Physical Traits of a Thousand Gifted Children. Ed.
2. Trade Cloth. Stanford University Press. Palo Alto, CA. 1925.
xiii, 648p. Genetic Studies of Genius, Vol. I
ISBN:0-8047-0009-5, ISBN13: 978-0-8047-0009-2.
Dewey:153.98.

                                   Audience: **f.**

Terman, Lewis M. & Oden,   **BF412**
  Melita H.
The Gifted Child Grows Up: Twenty-Five Years' Follow-Up of
a Superior Group. Trade Cloth. Stanford University Press. Palo
Alto, CA. 1947. xiv, 448p. Genetic Studies of Genius, Vol. N
ISBN:0-8047-0012-5, ISBN13: 978-0-8047-0012-2.
Dewey:153.98.

                                   Audience: **f.**

Terman, Lewis M. & Oden,   **HQ773.5**
  Melita H.
The Gifted Group at Mid-Life: Thirty-Five Years' Follow-Up of
the Superior Child. Trade Cloth. Stanford University Press. Palo
Alto, CA. 1959. 200p. Genetic Studies of Genius, Vol. V
ISBN:0-8047-0013-3, ISBN13: 978-0-8047-0013-9.
Dewey:649.155.

                                   Audience: **f.**

Winner, Ellen   **HQ773.5.W55 1996**
Gifted Children: Myths and Realities. Trade Cloth. Basic Books.
New York, NY. 1996. 464p. ISBN:0-465-01760-6, ISBN13:
978-0-465-01760-7. Dewey:155.4/55. LCCN:95-049279.
                      Audience: **g,l,u,f.** *Choice, 1996.*

Educational Psychology > Educational/Vocational Counseling and Student Services

American Association for   **LB1705**
  Career Education
☐ American Association for Career Education.
http://www.acteonline.org/
                                   Audience: **u,f.**

American School Counselor   **LB.51027**
Association
☐ American School Counselor Association.
http://www.schoolcounselor.org/

                                   Audience: **g,l,u,f.**

Brown, Steven D. & Lent,   **HF5381.C265273 2005**
  Robert W. (Editors)
Career Development and Counseling: Putting Theory and
Research to Work. Trade Cloth. John Wiley & Sons, Inc.
Hoboken, NJ. 2004. 682p. ISBN:0-471-28880-2, ISBN13:
978-0-471-28880-0. Dewey:331.702. LCCN:2004-042226.

                                   Audience: **u,f.**

Brown, Steven D. & Lent,   **BF637.C6H315 2000**
  Robert W. (Editors)
Handbook of Counseling Psychology. Ed. 3. Trade Cloth. John
Wiley & Sons, Inc. Hoboken, NJ. 2000. 880p.
ISBN:0-471-25458-4, ISBN13: 978-0-471-25458-4.
Dewey:158/.3. LCCN:99-016054.

                                   Audience: **u,f.**

Division of School   **LB1051**
  Psychology (APA Division 16)
☐ Division of School Psychology (APA Division 16).
http://www.indiana.edu/~div16/index.html
                                   Audience: **u,f.**

Educational Testing Service   **LB3051**
☐ ETS TestLink.
http://www.ets.org/testcoll
                                   Audience: **u,f.**

Jacob, Susan & Hartshorne,   **LB3013.6.J33 2003**
  Timothy S.
Ethics and Law for School Psychologists. Ed. 4. Trade Cloth.
John Wiley & Sons, Inc. Hoboken, NJ. 2003. 408p.
ISBN:0-471-20949-X, ISBN13: 978-0-471-20949-2.
Dewey:174/.93717130683. LCCN:2002-011155.
                                   Audience: **u,f.**

Likoff, Laurie   **HF5381.E52 2005**
Encyclopedia of Careers and Vocational Guidance, Set. Ed. 13.
Trade Cloth. Facts On File, Inc.. New York, NY. 2005. 3776p.
ISBN:0-8160-6055-X, ISBN13: 978-0-8160-6055-9.
Dewey:331.702. LCCN:2004-022855.
                      Audience: **g,l,u.** *Choice, 2006.*

Nastasi, Bonnie K., et al.   **RJ501.A2N28 2003**
School-Based Mental Health Services: Creating Comprehensive
and Culturally Specific Programs. Kristen M. Varjas & Rachel
B. Moore (Authors). Trade Cloth. American Psychological
Association. Washington, DC. 2003. 224p. Applying Psychology
to the Schools Ser. ISBN:1-59147-018-8, ISBN13:
978-1-59147-018-2. Dewey:362.2/083/0973.
LCCN:2003-013782.
                      Audience: **u,f.** *Choice, 2004.*

National Academic Advising   **LB2343**
Association
☐ National Academic Advising Association.
http://www.nacada.ksu.edu/
                                   Audience: **u,f.**

National Association of   **LB1051**
School Psychologists
☐ National Association of School Psychologists.
http://www.nasponline.org/
       Audience: **u,f.**

National O*Net Consortium   **HF5382.5.U5**
☐ O*Net OnLine.
http://online.onetcenter.org/
       Audience: **g,l,u,f.**

Reynolds, Cecil R. &   **LB1051.H2356 1999**
Gutkin, Terry B. (Editors)
The Handbook of School Psychology. Ed. 3. Trade Cloth. John
Wiley & Sons, Inc. Hoboken, NJ. 1998. 1216p.
ISBN:0-471-12205-X, ISBN13: 978-0-471-12205-0.
Dewey:370.15. LCCN:98-017618.
       Audience: **g,l,u.**

Rosenbaum, James E.   **LC1045.R77 2001**
Beyond College for All: Career Paths for the Forgotten Half.
Trade Cloth. Russell Sage Foundation. New York, NY. 2001.
300p. American Sociological Association Rose Series in
Sociology ISBN:0-87154-727-9, ISBN13: 978-0-87154-727-9.
Dewey:331.11/423. LCCN:2001-041783.
       Audience: **g,l,u,f.** *Choice, 2002.*

Super, Donald E.   **HF5381 .S934**
Vocational Development. Cloth Text. Teachers College Press,
Teachers College, Columbia University. New York, NY. 1957.
ISBN:0-8077-2233-2, ISBN13: 978-0-8077-2233-6.
Dewey:371.425. LCCN:57-011370.
       Audience: **f.**

U. S. Department of Labor   **HF5382**
Staff
Occupational Outlook Handbook: 2006-2007 Edition. Trade
Paper. JIST Publishing. Indianapolis, IN. 2006. 704p.
ISBN:1-59357-248-4, ISBN13: 978-1-59357-248-8.
Dewey:331.7/02/0973.
       Audience: **g,l,u,f.**

Industrial and Organizational Psychology
> Occupational Interests and Guidance

Arthur, Michael B. (Editor),   **HF5549.5.C35H36 1989**
et al.
Handbook of Career Theory. Douglas T. Hall & Barbara S.
Lawrence (Editors). Trade Cloth. Cambridge University Press.
New York, NY. 1989. 568p. ISBN:0-521-33015-7, ISBN13:
978-0-521-33015-2. Dewey:650.1/4. LCCN:88-028563.
       Audience: **u,f.** *Choice, 1990.*

Betz, Nancy E., et al.   **HF5382.65.B47 1987**
The Career Psychology of Women. Louise F. Fitzgerald & A. L.
Betz (Authors). Trade Cloth. Elsevier Science & Technology
Books. Saint Louis, MO. 1987. 305p. ISBN:0-12-094405-7,
ISBN13: 978-0-12-094405-7. Dewey:331.7/02/088042.
LCCN:86-022284.
       Audience: **f.**

Brown, Duane (Editor)   **HF5381.C265143 2002**
Career Choice and Development. Ed. 4. Trade Cloth. John
Wiley & Sons, Inc. Hoboken, NJ. 2002. 560p. Jossey Bass
Business and Management Ser. ISBN:0-7879-5741-0, ISBN13:
978-0-7879-5741-4. Dewey:331.7/02. LCCN:2002-005599.
       Audience: **u,f.**

Brown, Steven D. & Lent,   **HF5381.C265273 2005**
Robert W. (Editors)
Career Development and Counseling: Putting Theory and
Research to Work. Trade Cloth. John Wiley & Sons, Inc.
Hoboken, NJ. 2004. 682p. ISBN:0-471-28880-2, ISBN13:
978-0-471-28880-0. Dewey:331.702. LCCN:2004-042226.
       Audience: **u,f.**

Career Planning and Adult   **HF5381.A1**
Development Network
☐ Career Planning and Adult Development Network.
http://www.careernetwork.org
       Audience: **u,f.**

Educational Testing Service   **LB3051**
☐ ETS TestLink.
http://www.ets.org/testcoll
       Audience: **u,f.**

Feldman, Daniel C. (Editor)   **HF5381.W67 2002**
Work Careers: A Developmental Perspective. Trade Cloth. John
Wiley & Sons, Inc. Hoboken, NJ. 2002. 416p. The
Organizational Frontiers Ser. ISBN:0-7879-5916-2, ISBN13:
978-0-7879-5916-6. Dewey:331.7/02. LCCN:2002-008557.
       Audience: **u,f.**

Ginzberg, Eli   **HF5381 .G55**
Occupational Choice: An Approach to a General Theory. Trade
Cloth. Columbia University Press. New York, NY. 1951.
ISBN:0-231-01846-0, ISBN13: 978-0-231-01846-3.
Dewey:371.425. LCCN:51-010961.
       Audience: **f.**

Gottfredson, Gary D. &   **HB2595.G67 1996**
Holland, John L.
Dictionary of Holland Occupational Codes. Ed. 3. Trade Paper.
Psychological Assessment Resources, Inc. Lutz, FL. 1996.
ISBN:0-911907-26-2, ISBN13: 978-0-911907-26-1.
Dewey:331.7/0012. LCCN:96-043949.
       Audience: **g,u,f.**

Holland, John L.   **HF5381.H5668 1997**
Making Vocational Choices: A Theory of Vocational
Personalities and Work Environments. Ed. 3. Trade Cloth.
Psychological Assessment Resources, Inc. Lutz, FL. 1997. 312p.
ISBN:0-911907-27-0, ISBN13: 978-0-911907-27-8.
Dewey:331.7/02. LCCN:97-008435.
       Audience: **u,f.**

Krumboltz, John D. &   **HF5381**
Hamel, Daniel A.
Assessing Career Development. Trade Cloth. Mayfield
Publishing Company. San Francisco, CA. 1982. 296p.
ISBN:0-87484-552-1, ISBN13: 978-0-87484-552-5.
Dewey:331.7/02. LCCN:81-084697.
       Audience: **f.**

Leong, Frederick (Editor)   **HF5549.5.C35C363**
Career Development and Vocational Behavior of Racial and
Ethnic Minorities. Cloth Text. Lawrence Erlbaum Associates,

Inc. Mahwah, NJ. 1995. 312p. Vocational Psychology Ser. ISBN:0-8058-1303-9, ISBN13: 978-0-8058-1303-6. Dewey:331.7/02/089. LCCN:95-021576.

Audience: **u,f.** *Choice, 1996.*

Likoff, Laurie　　　　　　　　**HF5381.E52 2005**
Encyclopedia of Careers and Vocational Guidance, Set. Ed. 13. Trade Cloth. Facts On File, Inc.. New York, NY. 2005. 3776p. ISBN:0-8160-6055-X, ISBN13: 978-0-8160-6055-9. Dewey:331.702. LCCN:2004-022855.

Audience: **g,l,u.** *Choice, 2006.*

Lofquist, Lloyd H. & Dawis,　　　**BF637.C6L65 1991**
Rene V.
Essentials of Person-Environment-Correspondence Counseling. Book, Other. University of Minnesota Press. Minneapolis, MN. 1991. 192p. ISBN:0-8166-1889-5, ISBN13: 978-0-8166-1889-7. Dewey:158/.3. LCCN:90-025916.

Audience: **u,f.**

Lowman, Rodney L.　　　　　　**HF5381.5.L68 1991**
The Clinical Practice of Career Assessment: Abilities, Interests, and Personality. John Holland (Introduction by). Trade Cloth. American Psychological Association. Washington, DC. 1991. 333p. ISBN:1-55798-106-X, ISBN13: 978-1-55798-106-6. Dewey:153.9/4. LCCN:91-004545.

Audience: **u,f.**

National Career　　　　　　　　**HF5381**
Development Association
☐ National Career Development Association. http://www.ncda.org/

Audience: **u,f.**

National O*Net Consortium　　　**HF5382.5.U5**
☐ O*Net OnLine. http://online.onetcenter.org/

Audience: **g,l,u,f.**

Rosenbaum, James E.　　　　　　**LC1045.R77 2001**
Beyond College for All: Career Paths for the Forgotten Half. Trade Cloth. Russell Sage Foundation. New York, NY. 2001. 300p. American Sociological Association Rose Series in Sociology ISBN:0-87154-727-9, ISBN13: 978-0-87154-727-9. Dewey:331.11/423. LCCN:2001-041783.

Audience: **g,l,u,f.** *Choice, 2002.*

Savickas, Mark L. &　　　　　　**HF5381.5.V55 1999**
Spokane, Arnold R. (Editors)
Vocational Interests: Meaning, Measurement and Counseling Use. Trade Cloth. Consulting Psychologists Press, Inc. Mountain View, CA. 1999. 424p. ISBN:0-89106-126-6, ISBN13: 978-0-89106-126-7. Dewey:158.6. LCCN:98-051047.

Audience: **u,f.**

Savickas, Mark L. & Walsh,　　　**HF5381.H1332 1996**
W. Bruce (Editors)
Handbook of Career Counseling Theory and Practice. Trade Cloth. Consulting Psychologists Press, Inc. Mountain View, CA. 1996. 480p. ISBN:0-89106-080-4, ISBN13: 978-0-89106-080-2. Dewey:158.6. LCCN:95-044470.

Audience: **f.**

Super, Charles M., et al.　　　　**HF5549.5.C35L54 1995**
Life Roles, Values, and Careers: International Findings of the Work Importance Study. Branimir Sverko & Donald E. Super

(Authors). Trade Cloth. John Wiley & Sons, Inc. Hoboken, NJ. 1995. 397p. Psychology Ser. ISBN:0-7879-0100-8, ISBN13: 978-0-7879-0100-4. Dewey:306.3/6. LCCN:95-005488.

Audience: **f.**

Super, Donald E.　　　　　　　　**HF5381 .S934**
Vocational Development. Cloth Text. Teachers College Press, Teachers College, Columbia University. New York, NY. 1957. ISBN:0-8077-2233-2, ISBN13: 978-0-8077-2233-6. Dewey:371.425. LCCN:57-011370.

Audience: **f.**

U. S. Department of Labor　　　**HF5382**
Staff
Occupational Outlook Handbook: 2006-2007 Edition. Trade Paper. JIST Publishing. Indianapolis, IN. 2006. 704p. ISBN:1-59357-248-4, ISBN13: 978-1-59357-248-8. Dewey:331.7/02/0973.

Audience: **g,l,u,f.**

U. S. Department of Labor,　　　**HF5382;**
Employment and Training Staff (Contribution by)
The Dictionary of Occupational Titles. Ed. 4. Trade Cloth. JIST Publishing. Indianapolis, IN. 1991. 2870p. ISBN:1-56370-006-9, ISBN13: 978-1-56370-006-4. Dewey:331.7003.

Audience: **g,l,u,f.**

Walsh, W. Bruce &　　　　　　**HF5381.H1335 2005**
Savickas, Mark (Editors)
Handbook of Vocational Psychology: Theory, Research, and Practice. Ed. 3. Steven D. Brown, Timothy R. Elliott & Gary D. Gottfredson (Contribution by). Cloth over Boards. Lawrence Erlbaum Associates, Inc. Mahwah, NJ. 2005. 480p. Contemporary Topics in Vocational Psychology Ser. ISBN:0-8058-4517-8, ISBN13: 978-0-8058-4517-4. Dewey:158.6. LCCN:2004-030573.

Audience: **u,f.**

Industrial and Organizational Psychology > Personnel Attitudes. Job Satisfaction

Blair-Loy, Mary　　　　　　　**HD4904.25.B57 2003**
Competing Devotions: Career and Family among Women Executives. Trade Cloth. Harvard University Press. Cambridge, MA. 2003. 288p. ISBN:0-674-01089-2, ISBN13: 978-0-674-01089-5. Dewey:305.43/658. LCCN:2002-192238.

Audience: **u,f.** *Choice, 2003.*

Brief, Arthur P.　　　　　　　　**HF5549.5.J63.B734**
Attitudes in and Around Organizations, Vol. 9. Trade Cloth. SAGE Publications, Inc. Thousand Oaks, CA. 1998. 280p. Foundations for Organizational Science Ser. ISBN:0-7619-0096-9, ISBN13: 978-0-7619-0096-2. Dewey:158.7. LCCN:98-019719.

Audience: **u,f.** *Choice, 1998.*

Cotton, John L.　　　　　　　　**HD5660.U5.C68 1993**
Employee Involvement: Methods for Improving Performance and Work Attitudes. Trade Cloth. SAGE Publications, Inc. Thousand Oaks, CA. 1993. 320p. ISBN:0-8039-4532-9, ISBN13: 978-0-8039-4532-6. Dewey:658.3/14. LCCN:92-040084.

Audience: **u,f.** *Choice, 1993.*

Drenth, Pieter J. D.   HF5548.8.H2655 1998
Handbook of Work and Organizational Psychology. Ed. 2. Paper over Boards. Taylor & Francis Group. Abingdon, 1998. 1376p. ISBN:0-86377-528-4, ISBN13: 978-0-86377-528-4. Dewey:158.7. LCCN:98-186244.
Audience: **u,f.** *Choice, 1985.*

Freeman, Richard B. &   HF5549.5.J63F74 1999
  Rogers, Joel
What Workers Want. Trade Paper. Cornell University Press. Ithaca, NY. 1999. 224p. ISBN:0-8014-8563-0, ISBN13: 978-0-8014-8563-3. Dewey:331.2/095. LCCN:98-038848.
Audience: **g,l,u,f.** *Choice, 1999.*

Gini, Al   HF5549.5.J63G55 2000
My Job, My Self: Work and Creation of Modern Individual. Paper over Boards. Routledge. New York, NY. 2000. 272p. ISBN:0-415-92635-1, ISBN13: 978-0-415-92635-5. Dewey:331/.01/20973. LCCN:99-048225.
Audience: **u,f.** *Choice, 2000.*

Herzberg, Frederick   HD4908
The Motivation to Work. Ed. 99. Trade Cloth. John Wiley & Sons, Inc. Hoboken, NJ. 1959. 157p. ISBN:0-471-37389-3, ISBN13: 978-0-471-37389-6. Dewey:331.01.
Audience: **f.**

Lawler, Edward E.   HD4909
Pay and Organizational Effectiveness: A Psychological View. Cloth Text. McGraw-Hill Companies, The. New York, NY. 1971. xi, 318p. McGraw-Hill Psychology Ser. ISBN:0-07-036700-0, ISBN13: 978-0-07-036700-5. Dewey:658.32/01/9. LCCN:73-139558.
Audience: **f.**

Lawler, Edward E. III   HF5548.8.L2973 1994
Motivation in Work Organizations. Trade Paper. John Wiley & Sons, Inc. Hoboken, NJ. 1994. 292p. Management Ser. ISBN:1-55542-661-1, ISBN13: 978-1-55542-661-3. Dewey:658.3/14. LCCN:93-050161.
Audience: **u,f.**

Levering, Robert   HF5549.2.U5L385 1988
A Great Place to Work: What Makes Some Employers So Good - And Most So Bad. Trade Cloth. Random House, Inc. New York, NY. 1988. xxii, 312p. ISBN:0-394-55725-5, ISBN13: 978-0-394-55725-0. Dewey:331.2/0973. LCCN:87-043226.
Audience: **g,l,u.** *Choice, 1988.*

Locke, Edwin A. & Latham,   BF503.L63 1990
  Gary P.
A Theory of Goal Setting and Task Performance. Cloth Text. Prentice Hall PTR. Upper Saddle River, NJ. 1989. 544p. ISBN:0-13-913138-8, ISBN13: 978-0-13-913138-7. Dewey:153.8. LCCN:89-016372.
Audience: **u,f.** *Choice, 1990.*

Mayo, Elton   HD6971.M39 2003
The Human Problems of an Industrial Civilization, Vol. 6. Paper over Boards. Routledge. New York, NY. 2003. 204p. The Making of Sociology Ser. ISBN:0-415-27988-7, ISBN13: 978-0-415-27988-8. Dewey:658.3.
Audience: **f.**

Mayo, Elton   HD6955 .M36 1977
The Social Problems of an Industrial Civilization. Leon Stein (Editor). Library Binding. Ayer Company Publishers, Inc. Manchester, NH. 1977. ISBN:0-405-10185-6, ISBN13: 978-0-405-10185-4. Dewey:301.5/5. LCCN:77-070516.
Audience: **f.**

Meyer, John P. & Allen,   HF5549.5.M63M49 1997
  Natalie J.
Commitment in the Workplace: Theory, Research and Application. Trade Cloth. SAGE Publications, Inc. Thousand Oaks, CA. 1997. 160p. Advanced Topics in Organizational Behavior Ser., Vol. 1 ISBN:0-7619-0104-3, ISBN13: 978-0-7619-0104-4. Dewey:658.3/14. LCCN:96-045780.
Audience: **u,f.** *Choice, 1997.*

Military Family Research   UB403
  Institute, Purdue University
Military Family Research Institute, Purdue University. http://www.cfs.purdue.edu/mfri/
Audience: **u,f.**

Organ, Dennis W., et al.   HD58.7.O6682 2006
Organizational Citizenship Behavior: Its Nature, Antecedents, and Consequences. Philip Podsakoff & Scott MacKenzie (Authors). Paper Text. SAGE Publications, Inc. Thousand Oaks, CA. 2005. 360p. Foundations for Organizational Science Ser. ISBN:0-7619-2996-7, ISBN13: 978-0-7619-2996-3. Dewey:158.7. LCCN:2005-008598.
Audience: **u,f.**

Perlow, Leslie A.   HD5106.P42 1997
Finding Time: How Corporations, Individuals, and Families Can Benefit from New Work Practices. Book, Other. Cornell University Press. Ithaca, NY. 1997. 176p. Collection on Technology and Work Ser. ISBN:0-8014-3425-4, ISBN13: 978-0-8014-3425-9. Dewey:331.25/7. LCCN:97-014969.
Audience: **g,l,u,f.** *Choice, 1998.*

Rogelberg, Steven G.   HF5548.8.H2653 2002
  (Editor)
Handbook of Research Methods in Work and Organizational Psychology. Trade Cloth. Blackwell Publishing Ltd. Oxford, 2002. 536p. Blackwell Handbooks of Research Methods in Psychology, Vol. 1 ISBN:0-631-22259-6, ISBN13: 978-0-631-22259-0. Dewey:158.7/07/2. LCCN:2001-043225.
Audience: **u,f.** *Choice, 2003, 2002.*

Spector, Paul E.   HF5549.5.J63.S635
Job Satisfaction: Application, Assessment, Causes, and Consequences, Vol. 3. Trade Cloth. SAGE Publications, Inc. Thousand Oaks, CA. 1997. 104p. Advanced Topics in Organizational Behavior Ser. ISBN:0-7619-8922-6, ISBN13: 978-0-7619-8922-6. Dewey:158.7. LCCN:97-004598.
Audience: **u,f.** *Choice, 1997.*

Trice, Harrison M.   HD6955.T75 1993
Occupational Subcultures in the Workplace. Book, Other. Cornell University Press. Ithaca, NY. 1993. 304p. Cornell Studies in Industrial and Labor Relations, No. 26 ISBN:0-87546-302-9, ISBN13: 978-0-87546-302-5. Dewey:302.3/5. LCCN:92-039034.
Audience: **u,f.** *Choice, 1993.*

Vroom, Victor H.   HF5548.8.V7 1995
Work and Motivation. Trade Paper. John Wiley & Sons, Inc. Hoboken, NJ. 1994. 397p. Management Ser.

ISBN:0-7879-0030-3, ISBN13: 978-0-7879-0030-4.
Dewey:158.7. LCCN:94-028028.

Audience: **u,f.** *B*

Wood, John Cunningham &   HD70.U5G4726 2004
Wood, Michael C.
George Elton Mayo: Critical Evaluations in Business and
Management. Paper over Boards. Routledge. New York, NY.
2004. 504p. Critical Evaluations in Business and Management
Ser. ISBN:0-415-32392-4, ISBN13: 978-0-415-32392-5.
Dewey:306.3/6/092 B. LCCN:2003-064881.

Audience: **u,f.**

Industrial and Organizational Psychology > Working Conditions and Industrial Safety

Aronson, Elliot & Pines,   BF481.P63 1988
Ayala M.
Career Burnout: Causes and Cures. Trade Cloth. Simon &
Schuster. New York, NY. 1988. 240p. ISBN:0-02-925351-9,
ISBN13: 978-0-02-925351-9. Dewey:158.7. LCCN:88-002813.

Audience: **g,l,u.** *Choice, 1988.*

Barling, Julian (Editor),   HF5548.85.H363 2004
et al.
Handbook of Work Stress. E. Kevin Kelloway & Michael
Robert Frone (Editors). Trade Cloth. SAGE Publications, Inc.
Thousand Oaks, CA. 2004. 720p. ISBN:0-7619-2949-5,
ISBN13: 978-0-7619-2949-9. Dewey:158.7/2.
LCCN:2004-008543.

Audience: **u,f.**

Cooper, Cary L. & Dewe,   BF575.S75C646 2004
Philip
Stress: A Brief History. Trade Paper. Blackwell Publishing, Inc.
Malden, MA. 2004. 160p. Blackwell Brief Histories of
Psychology Ser., Vol. 1 ISBN:1-4051-0745-6, ISBN13:
978-1-4051-0745-7. Dewey:155.9/042/09. LCCN:2003-023501.

Audience: **u,f.** *Choice, 2004.*

Families and Work Institute   HD4904.25
☐ Families and Work Institute.
http://www.familiesandwork.org/index.html

Audience: **u,f.**

Hochschild, Arlie Russell   HQ536.H633 1997
The Time Bind: When Work Becomes Home and Home
Becomes Work. Cloth over Boards. Henry Holt & Company.
New York, NY. 1997. 336p. ISBN:0-8050-4470-1, ISBN13:
978-0-8050-4470-6. Dewey:306.3/6. LCCN:97-003411.

Audience: **g,l,u,f.** *Choice, 1997.*

Holman, David (Editor), et   HD6955.N495 2002
al.
The New Workplace: A Guide to the Human Impact of Modern
Working Practices. Chris W. Clegg, Ann Howard, Paul Sparrow
& Toby D. Wall (Editors). Trade Cloth. John Wiley & Sons, Inc.
Hoboken, NJ. 2003. 464p. ISBN:0-471-48543-8, ISBN13:
978-0-471-48543-8. Dewey:331.2. LCCN:2002-028874.

Audience: **u,f.**

International Labour   HD7801
Organisation Library
☐ Labordoc.
http://labordoc.ilo.org/

Audience: **u,f.**

Karasek, Robert A. &   T60.8
Theorell, Torres
Healthy Work: Stress, Productivity, and the Reconstruction of
Working Life. Trade Paper. Basic Books. New York, NY. 1992.
398p. ISBN:0-465-02897-7, ISBN13: 978-0-465-02897-9.
Dewey:658.5/4. LCCN:89-042514.

Audience: **u,f.** *Choice, 1990.*

Kossek, Ellen Ernst &   HD4904.25.W663 2005
Lambert, Susan J. (Editors)
Work and Life Integration: Organizational, Cultural, and
Individual Perspectives. Jeanette N. Cleveland, Cary L. Cooper,
Amy Edmondson, Lotte Bailyn, Susan Eaton, Jeffrey R.
Edwards, Debby D'Amico, Eleanor Drago-Severson & Deborah
Helsing (Contribution by). Cloth over Boards, Saddle Stitched.
Lawrence Erlbaum Associates, Inc. Mahwah, NJ. 2004. 600p.
Series in Applied Psychology ISBN:0-8058-4615-8, ISBN13:
978-0-8058-4615-7. Dewey:306.3/6. LCCN:2004-057709.

Audience: **u,f.**

Maslach, Christina & Leiter,   HF5548.85.M373 1997
Michael P.
The Truth about Burnout: How Organizations Cause Personal
Stress and What to Do about It. Trade Cloth. John Wiley &
Sons, Inc. Hoboken, NJ. 1997. 200p. ISBN:0-7879-0874-6,
ISBN13: 978-0-7879-0874-4. Dewey:158.7/2. LCCN:97-021671.

Audience: **g,l,u,f.**

National Institute for   RC967
**Occupational Safety and Health, Centers for Disease
Control**
☐ NIOSHTIC-2 (bibliographic database).
http://www2.cdc.gov/nioshtic-2/Nioshtic2.htm

Audience: **u,f.**

National Safety Council   HD7262
☐ National Safety Council.
http://www.nsc.org/index.htm

Audience: **g,l,u,f.**

Occupational Safety and   KF3570.Z9
Health Administration, U.S. Department of Labor
☐ Occupational Safety and Health Administration, U.S.
Department of Labor.
http://www.osha.gov/

Audience: **g,l,u,f.**

Perlow, Leslie A.   HD5106.P42 1997
Finding Time: New Work Practice. Trade Paper. Cornell
University Press. Ithaca, NY. 1997. 176p. Collection on
Technology and Work Ser. ISBN:0-8014-8445-6, ISBN13:
978-0-8014-8445-2. Dewey:331.25/7. LCCN:97-014969.

Audience: **g,l,u,f.** *Choice, 1998.*

Population Research Center,   HB850
RAND Corporation
☐ Population Research Center, RAND Corporation.
http://www.rand.org/labor/population/

Audience: **u,f.**

Presser, Harriet B.   HD4904.25.P74 2003
Work in a 24/7 Economy: Challenges for American Families. Trade Cloth. Russell Sage Foundation. New York, NY. 2005. 288p. ISBN:0-87154-670-1, ISBN13: 978-0-87154-670-8. Dewey:331.25. LCCN:2003-047051.
Audience: **u,f.**   *Choice, 2004.*

Quick, James C., et al.   HF5548.85.P762 1997
Preventive Stress Management in Organizations. Ed. 2. Jonathan D. Quick, Debra L. Nelson & Joseph J. Hurrell Jr. (Authors). Cloth Text. American Psychological Association. Washington, DC. 1997. 368p. ISBN:1-55798-432-8, ISBN13: 978-1-55798-432-6. Dewey:658.3/82. LCCN:97-012689.
Audience: **u,f.**

Quick, James C. & Tetrick,   RC967.5.H358 2002
  Lois E. (Editors)
Handbook of Occupational Health Psychology. Trade Cloth. American Psychological Association. Washington, DC. 2002. xvii, 475p. ISBN:1-55798-927-3, ISBN13: 978-1-55798-927-7. Dewey:616.89. LCCN:2002-022843.
Audience: **u,f.**

Schor, Juliet B.   HD4904.6
Overworked American: The Unexpected Decline of Leisure. Trade Paper. Basic Books. New York, NY. 1993. 272p. ISBN:0-465-05434-X, ISBN13: 978-0-465-05434-3. Dewey:306.48. LCCN:91-070057.
Audience: **g,l,u,f.**

Scott, Walter Dill   HF5548.8.S358
Increasing Human Efficiency in Business. Trade Paper. Kessinger Publishing, LLC. Whitefish, MT. 2004. ISBN:1-4191-2628-8, ISBN13: 978-1-4191-2628-4. Dewey:658.409.
Audience: **f.**

Tannen, Deborah   HF5541.T4
Talking from 9 to 5: Women and Men at Work. Trade Paper. HarperCollins Publishers. New York, NY. 1995. 368p. ISBN:0-380-71783-2, ISBN13: 978-0-380-71783-5. Dewey:651.7/3.
Audience: **g,l,u,f.**

Sport Psychology and Leisure

Andersen, Mark B. (Editor)   GV704.S64 2005
Sport Psychology in Practice. Perfect, Trade Paper. Human Kinetics Publishers. Champaign, IL. 2005. 338p. ISBN:0-7360-3711-X, ISBN13: 978-0-7360-3711-2. Dewey:796.01. LCCN:2005-010554.
Audience: **g,l,u.**

Argyle, Michael   GV14.45
Social Psychology of Leisure. Trade Paper. Penguin Books, Ltd. London, 1996. 336p. ISBN:0-14-023887-5, ISBN13: 978-0-14-023887-7. Dewey:306.4/812.
Audience: **l,u.**

Begel, Daniel   RC451.4.A83S65 2000
Sports Psychiatry. Trade Cloth. W. W. Norton & Company, Inc. New York, NY. 1999. 256p. Professional Bks. ISBN:0-393-70295-2, ISBN13: 978-0-393-70295-8. Dewey:616.89/0088/796. LCCN:99-035444.
Audience: **u.**

Berger, Bonnie G., et al.   GV481.2.B47 2002
Foundations of Exercise Psychology. David Pargman & Robert Weinberg (Authors). Trade Cloth. Fitness Information Technology, Inc. Morgantown, WV. 2001. 392p. ISBN:1-885693-34-6, ISBN13: 978-1-885693-34-1. Dewey:796/.01. LCCN:2002-102133.
Audience: **l,u.**

Biller, Henry B.   RA781
Creative Fitness: Applying Health Psychology and Exercise Science to Everyday Life. Trade Cloth. Greenwood Publishing Group, Inc. Portsmouth, NH. 2002. 272p. ISBN:0-86569-325-0, ISBN13: 978-0-86569-325-8. Dewey:613.7. LCCN:2001-053832.
Audience: **l,u.**   *Choice, 2003.*

Black, David R. (Editor)   RC552.E18 B53 1991
Eating Disorder among Athletes: Theory, Issues and Research. Trade Paper. American Alliance for Health, Physical Education, Recreation & Dance. Oxon Hill, MD. 1991. 92p. ISBN:0-88314-497-2, ISBN13: 978-0-88314-497-8. Dewey:616.85/26/0088796. LCCN:91-162937.
Audience: **u.**

Buckworth, Janet &   RA781.B83 2001
  Dishman, Rodney
Exercise Psychology. Trade Cloth. Human Kinetics Publishers. Champaign, IL. 2002. 344p. ISBN:0-7360-0078-X, ISBN13: 978-0-7360-0078-9. Dewey:613.7/1. LCCN:2001-039262.
Audience: **u,f.**

Bull, Stephen J., et al.   GV706.4 .B77 1996
The Mental Game Plan. John G. Albinson & Christopher J. Shambrook (Authors). Trade Paper. Sports Dynamics. Cheltenham, 1996. 216p. ISBN:0-9519543-2-6, ISBN13: 978-0-9519543-2-4. Dewey:796.01.
Audience: **l,u.**

Butler, Richard (Editor)   GV706.4.S6816 1997
Sports Psychology in Performance: Applying Principles to Practice. Trade Paper. Butterworth-Heinemann Ltd. Oxford, 1997. 288p. ISBN:0-7506-2437-X, ISBN13: 978-0-7506-2437-4. Dewey:796/.01/0941. LCCN:96-051509.
Audience: **u,f.**

Carron, Albert V., et al.   RA781.C325 2002
The Psychology of Physical Activity and Exercise. Heather A. Hausenblas & Paul A. Estabrooks (Authors). Trade Cloth. McGraw-Hill Companies, The. New York, NY. 2002. x, 274p. ISBN:0-07-248901-4, ISBN13: 978-0-07-248901-9. Dewey:613.7/01/9. LCCN:2002-019088.
Audience: **l,u.**

Diamant, Louis   GV706.4.M56 1991
Mind-Body Maturity: Psychological Approaches to Sports, Exercise, and Fitness. Paper over Boards. Hemisphere Publishing Corporation. Philadelphia, PA. 1991. 304p. ISBN:0-89116-892-3, ISBN13: 978-0-89116-892-8. Dewey:796/.01. LCCN:90-046147.
Audience: **l,u.**

Diamant, Louis   GV706.4.P695 1991
Psychology of Sports, Exercise and Fitness: Social and Adjustmental Issues. Paper over Boards. Hemisphere Publishing Corporation. Philadelphia, PA. 1991. 256p. ISBN:1-56032-170-9, ISBN13: 978-1-56032-170-5. Dewey:796/.01. LCCN:90-019467.
Audience: **g,u,f.**

Gill, Diane L.   **GV706.4.G55 2000**
Psychological Dynamics of Sport and Exercise. Ed. 2. Trade
Cloth. Human Kinetics Publishers. Champaign, IL. 2000. 368p.
ISBN:0-87322-956-8, ISBN13: 978-0-87322-956-2.
Dewey:796/.01. LCCN:99-057712.

                                    Audience: **l,u,f.**

Goldstein, Jeffrey H.   **GV706.5.S74 1989**
Sports, Games, and Play: Social and Psychological Viewpoints.
Ed. 2. Cloth Text. Lawrence Erlbaum Associates, Inc. Mahwah,
NJ. 1988. 392p. ISBN:0-89859-875-3, ISBN13:
978-0-89859-875-9. Dewey:306/.483. LCCN:87-013731.

                                    Audience: **u,f.**

Hagger, Martin &   **RA781**
  Chatzisarantis, Nikos
Social Psychology of Exercise and Sport. Cloth Text.
McGraw-Hill Education. Maidenhead, 2005. 280p.
ISBN:0-335-21619-6, ISBN13: 978-0-335-21619-2.
Dewey:613.71019.

                                    Audience: **u,f.**

Halden-Brown, Susan   **GV706.4**
Mistakes Worth Making: How to Turn Sports Errors into
Athletic Excellence. Trade Paper. Human Kinetics Publishers.
Champaign, IL. 2003. 34p. ISBN:0-7360-4171-0, ISBN13:
978-0-7360-4171-3. Dewey:796/.01/9. LCCN:2002-151789.

                                    Audience: **u,f.**

Hardy, Lew, et al.   **GV706.4.H373 1996**
Understanding Psychological Preparation for Sport: Theory and
Practice of Elite Performers. J. Graham Jones & Daniel Gould
(Authors). Trade Cloth. John Wiley & Sons, Inc. Hoboken, NJ.
1996. 362p. ISBN:0-471-95023-8, ISBN13: 978-0-471-95023-3.
Dewey:796/.01. LCCN:96-021493.

                        Audience: **l,u.** *Choice, 1997.*

Horn, Thelma   **GV706.4.A38 2002**
Advances in Sport Psychology. Ed. 2. Trade Cloth. Human
Kinetics Publishers. Champaign, IL. 2002. 576p.
ISBN:0-7360-3298-3, ISBN13: 978-0-7360-3298-8.
Dewey:796/.01. LCCN:2002-022912.

                                    Audience: **l,u.**

Kauss, David   **GV706.4.K378 2001**
Mastering Your Inner Game. Trade Paper. Human Kinetics
Publishers. Champaign, IL. 2000. 28p. ISBN:0-7360-0176-X,
ISBN13: 978-0-7360-0176-2. Dewey:790/.01/32.
LCCN:00-031906.

                                    Audience: **l.**

Kremer, John M. & Scully,   **GV706.4.K74 1994**
  Deirdre M.
Psychology in Sport. Trade Cloth. Taylor & Francis Group.
Abingdon, 1994. 208p. Contemporary Psychology Ser.
ISBN:0-7484-0181-4, ISBN13: 978-0-7484-0181-9.
Dewey:796/.01. LCCN:93-046607.

                        Audience: **u,f.** *Choice, 1995.*

Kuehl, Karl, et al.   **GV706.4.K82 2005**
Mental Toughness: A Champion's State of Mind. John Kuehl &
Casey Tefertiller (Authors). Trade Cloth. Ivan R. Dee Publisher.
Blue Ridge Summit, PA. 2005. 304p. ISBN:1-56663-617-5,
ISBN13: 978-1-56663-617-9. Dewey:796/.01.
LCCN:2004-058266.

                      Audience: **g,l,u.** *Choice, 2005.*

Lavalle, David, et al.   **GV706.4.S6813 2003**
Sport Psychology: Contemporary Themes. John Kremer, Aidan
P. Morgan & Mark Williams (Authors). Cloth over Boards.
Palgrave Macmillan. New York, NY. 2004. 272p.
ISBN:1-4039-0467-7, ISBN13: 978-1-4039-0467-6.
Dewey:796/.01. LCCN:2003-058121.

                        Audience: **u,f.** *Choice, 2004.*

Lidor, Ronnie & Henschen,   **GV706.4.P72 2003**
  Keith P. (Editors)
Psychology of Team Sports. Trade Paper. Fitness Information
Technology, Inc. Morgantown, WV. 2001. 278p.
ISBN:1-885693-32-X, ISBN13: 978-1-885693-32-7.
Dewey:796.019. LCCN:2002-116144.

                                  Audience: **l,u,f.**

Lox, Curt, et al.   **GV481.2.L69 2003**
The Psychology of Exercise: Integrating Theory and Practice.
Kathleen Anne Martin & Steven J. Petruzzello (Authors). Trade
Cloth. Holcomb Hathaway, Inc. Scottsdale, AZ. 2003. xiv, 354p.
ISBN:1-890871-47-8, ISBN13: 978-1-890871-47-5.
Dewey:613.7/1019. LCCN:2002-191347.

                      Audience: **l,u.** *Choice, 2003.*

Mannell, Roger C. &   **GV14.4.M35 1997**
  Kleiber, Douglas A.
A Social Psychology of Leisure. Cloth Text. Venture Publishing,
Inc. State College, PA. 1997. 450p. ISBN:0-910251-88-6,
ISBN13: 978-0-910251-88-4. Dewey:790. LCCN:97-060787.

                                  Audience: **l,u.**

May, Jerry R. & Asken,   **GV706.4.S6823 1987**
  Michael J. (Editors)
Sport Psychology: The Psychological Health of the Athlete.
Trade Cloth. P M A Publishing Corporation. Dublin, CA. 1987.
315p. ISBN:0-89335-304-3, ISBN13: 978-0-89335-304-9.
Dewey:796/.01. LCCN:87-787361.

                                  Audience: **l,u.**

Moran, Aidan P.   **GV706.4**
Sport and Exercise Psychology. Paper over Boards. Routledge.
New York, NY. 2004. 368p. ISBN:0-415-16808-2, ISBN13:
978-0-415-16808-3. Dewey:796/.01. LCCN:2003-017078.

                                  Audience: **u,f.**

Mostofsky, David I. &   **RA781.M3925 2002**
  Zaichkowsky, Leonard (Editors)
Medical and Physiological Aspects of Sport Psychology. Trade
Paper. Fitness Information Technology, Inc. Morgantown, WV.
2001. 289p. ISBN:1-885693-29-X, ISBN13: 978-1-885693-29-7.
Dewey:613.7. LCCN:01-132722.

                                  Audience: **u,f.**

Murphy, Shane   **GV706.4.S667 2004**
The Sports Psych Handbook. Trade Paper. Human Kinetics
Publishers. Champaign, IL. 2004. 368p. ISBN:0-7360-4904-5,
ISBN13: 978-0-7360-4904-7. Dewey:796.01.
LCCN:2004-015224.

                                Audience: **g,l,u,f.**

Porter, Kay (As told to)   **GV706.4.P565 2003**
The Mental Athlete. Ed. 2. Trade Paper. Human Kinetics
Publishers. Champaign, IL. 2003. 224p. ISBN:0-7360-4654-2,
ISBN13: 978-0-7360-4654-1. Dewey:796/.01.
LCCN:2003-007591.

                                Audience: **l,u.**

Russell, Gordon W.   GV706.4 .R87 1993
The Social Psychology of Sport. Trade Paper. Springer. New
York, NY. 1998. XIII, 313p. ISBN:0-387-97792-9, ISBN13:
978-0-387-97792-8. Dewey:796/.01. LCCN:92-034893.
                                        Audience: **u,f.**

Silva, John M. & Stevens,   GV706.4.P673 2002
  Diane E.
Psychological Foundations of Sport. Cloth Text.
Benjamin-Cummings Publishing Company. San Francisco, CA.
2001. 560p. ISBN:0-205-33144-0, ISBN13: 978-0-205-33144-4.
Dewey:796/.01. LCCN:00-052200.
                                        Audience: **l,f.**

Singer, Robert N. (Editor),   GV706.4.H37 2001
  et al.
Handbook of Sport Psychology. Ed. 2. Heather Ann Hausenblas
& Christopher Janelle (Editors). Trade Cloth. John Wiley &
Sons, Inc. Hoboken, NJ. 2000. 896p. ISBN:0-471-37995-6,
ISBN13: 978-0-471-37995-9. Dewey:796/.01. LCCN:00-042291.
                      Audience: **l,u,f.** *Choice, 2002.*

Singer, Robert N. (Editor),   GV706.4.H37 1993
  et al.
Handbook of Research on Sport Psychology. Milledge Murphey
& L. Keith Tennant (Editors). Trade Cloth. Macmillan
Publishing Company, Inc. Old Tappan, NJ. 1992. 984p.
ISBN:0-02-897195-7, ISBN13: 978-0-02-897195-7.
Dewey:796/.01. LCCN:92-013400.
                      Audience: **l,u,f.** *Choice, 1993.*

Smith, Edward W.   GV546.4.P78S64 1989
Not Just Pumping Iron: On the Psychology of Lifting Weights.
Paper Text. Charles C Thomas Publisher, Ltd. Springfield, IL.
1989. 176p. ISBN:0-398-05544-0, ISBN13: 978-0-398-05544-8.
Dewey:796.4/1/019. LCCN:88-027569.
                                        Audience: **l,u.**

Stein, Murray & Hollwitz,   GV706.4.P66 1994
  John (Editors)
Psyche and Sports: Baseball, Hockey, Martial Arts, Running,
Swimming, Tennis and Others. Trade Cloth. Chiron
Publications. Wilmette, IL. 1994. 256p. ISBN:0-933029-79-9,
ISBN13: 978-0-933029-79-8. Dewey:796/.01. LCCN:94-028089.
                                        Audience: **l,u.**

Tenenbaum, Gershon   GV706.4 .P62 2001
  (Editor)
The Practice of Sport Psychology. Trade Paper. Fitness
Information Technology, Inc. Morgantown, WV. 2001. 306p.
ISBN:1-885693-30-3, ISBN13: 978-1-885693-30-3.
Dewey:796.01. LCCN:01-126255.
                                        Audience: **l,u.**

Van Raalte, Judy L. &   GV706.4.E96 2002
  Brewer, Britton W. (Editors)
Exploring Sport and Exercise Psychology. Ed. 2. Trade Cloth.
American Psychological Association. Washington, DC. 2002.
xxiii, 561p. ISBN:1-55798-886-2, ISBN13: 978-1-55798-886-7.
Dewey:796/.01. LCCN:2002-020856.
                      Audience: **l,u,f.** *Choice, 1997.*

Weinberg, Robert S. &   GV706.4.W38 2003
  Gould, Daniel
Foundations of Sport and Exercise Psychology. Ed. 3. Trade
Cloth. Human Kinetics Publishers. Champaign, IL. 2005. 608p.

ISBN:0-7360-4419-1, ISBN13: 978-0-7360-4419-6.
Dewey:796.01. LCCN:2002-013861.
                                        Audience: **l,u,f.**

Weiss, Maureen R.   GV706.4.D475 2004
Developmental Sport and Exercise Psychology: A Lifespan
Perspective. Trade Cloth. Fitness Information Technology, Inc.
Morgantown, WV. 2004. 596p. ISBN:1-885693-36-2, ISBN13:
978-1-885693-36-5. Dewey:796/.01. LCCN:2003-108981.
                                        Audience: **g,l,f.**

Whitmarsh, Blair   GV546.5.W48 2001
Mind and Muscle: Psych up, Build Up. Trade Paper. Human
Kinetics Publishers. Champaign, IL. 2001. 296p.
ISBN:0-7360-3753-5, ISBN13: 978-0-7360-3753-2.
Dewey:646.7/5. LCCN:00-054270.
                                        Audience: **g,l.**

Wilson, Gregory S. (Editor)   GV706.4
Applying Sport Psychology: Four Perspectives. Perfect, Trade
Paper. Human Kinetics Publishers. Champaign, IL. 2005. 310p.
ISBN:0-7360-4512-0, ISBN13: 978-0-7360-4512-4.
Dewey:796.01. LCCN:2005-018528.
                                        Audience: **l,u,f.**

Sport Psychology and Leisure > Recreation and Leisure

Csikszentmihalyi, Mihaly   BF515.C74 2000
Beyond Boredom and Anxiety: Experiencing Flow in Work and
Play. Ed. 2. Trade Cloth. John Wiley & Sons, Inc. Hoboken, NJ.
2000. 272p. ISBN:0-7879-5140-4, ISBN13: 978-0-7879-5140-5.
Dewey:152.4/2. LCCN:99-056457.
                                        Audience: **l,u,f.**

Military Psychology

Belenky, Gregory (Editor)   U22
Contemporary Studies in Combat Psychiatry. Trade Cloth.
Greenwood Publishing Group, Inc. Portsmouth, NH. 1987. 291p.
Contributions in Military Studies Ser., No. 62
ISBN:0-313-25513-X, ISBN13: 978-0-313-25513-7.
Dewey:616.85/212. LCCN:86-033660.
                                        Audience: **u,f.**

Binneveld, Hans   UH629 .B56 1997
From Shell Shock to Combat Stress: A Comparative History of
Military Psychiatry. Trade Paper. Amsterdam University Press.
Amsterdam, 2003. 224p. ISBN:90-5356-270-2, ISBN13:
978-90-5356-270-3. Dewey:616.89/0088/355. LCCN:98-170762.
                                        Audience: **l,u,f.**

Britt, Thomas W. (Editor),   U22
  et al.
Military Life: The Psychology of Serving in Peace and Combat
[Four Volumes]. Amy B. Adler & Carl Andrew Castro (Editors).
Cloth Text. Greenwood Publishing Group, Inc. Portsmouth, NH.
2005. 1072p. ISBN:0-275-98300-5, ISBN13:
978-0-275-98300-0. Dewey:355.1/0973. LCCN:2005-017484.
                                        Audience: **l,u,f.**

Evans, Michael & Ryan,   U22.3
  Alan (Editors)
The Human Face of Warfare: Killing, Fear and Chaos in Battle.

Trade Paper. Allen & Unwin Pty., Ltd. Crows Nest, NSW. 2001. 288p. ISBN:1-86508-374-7, ISBN13: 978-1-86508-374-2. Dewey:303.6/6/019.

Audience: **u,f.**

Fitzduff, Mari & Stout,   **U22**
  Chris E. (Editors)
The Psychology of Resolving Global Conflicts: From War to Peace. Trade Cloth. Greenwood Publishing Group, Inc. Portsmouth, NH. 2005. 1088p. Contemporary Psychology Ser. ISBN:0-275-98201-7, ISBN13: 978-0-275-98201-0. Dewey:327.1/72. LCCN:2005-025487.

Audience: **u,f.**

Gabriel, Richard A.   **U22**
The Painful Field: The Psychiatric Dimension of Modern War, 75. Trade Cloth. Greenwood Publishing Group, Inc. Portsmouth, NH. 1988. 207p. Contributions in Military Studies Ser., No. 75 ISBN:0-313-24718-8, ISBN13: 978-0-313-24718-7. Dewey:355/.001/9. LCCN:87-031789.

Audience: **u,f.** *Choice, 1989.*

Gal, Reuven &   **U22.3.H25 1991**
  Mangelsdorff, David (Editors)
Handbook of Military Psychology, Vol. 1. Ed. 1. Trade Cloth. John Wiley & Sons, Inc. Hoboken, NJ. 1992. 812p. Handbook of Military Psychology Ser., Vol. 1 ISBN:0-471-92045-2, ISBN13: 978-0-471-92045-8. Dewey:355/.001/9. LCCN:90-049615.

Audience: **l,u,f.**

Glad, Betty (Editor)   **U0022.3.P77**
Psychological Dimensions of War. Trade Paper. Books on Demand. Ann Arbor, MI. 1990. 384p. Violence, Cooperation, Peace Ser. ISBN:0-608-02772-3, ISBN13: 978-0-608-02772-2. Dewey:355/.001/9. LCCN:90-008755.

Audience: **l,u,f.**

Griffin, Susan   **U22.3 .G75 1992**
Chorus of Stones: The Private Life of War. Trade Cloth. Doubleday Publishing. New York, NY. 1992. 384p. ISBN:0-385-41857-4, ISBN13: 978-0-385-41857-7. Dewey:355/.001/9. LCCN:92-007854.

Audience: **l,u.**

Grossman, Dave   **U22.3.G76 1995**
On Killing: The Psychological Cost of Learning to Kill in War and Society. Other. Little Brown & Company. New York, NY. 1995. 400p. ISBN:0-316-33000-0, ISBN13: 978-0-316-33000-8. Dewey:153.8/5. LCCN:95-013888.

Audience: **g,l,u,f.**

Hillman, James   **U21.2**
A Terrible Love of War. Trade Paper. Penguin Group (USA) Inc. New York, NY. 2005. 272p. ISBN:0-14-303492-8, ISBN13: 978-0-14-303492-6. Dewey:303.6/6.

Audience: **l,u.** *Choice, 2004.*

Hinde, Robert A. & Watson,   **U21.2.W359 1994**
  Helen E. (Editors)
War: A Cruel Necessity. Cloth over Boards. I. B. Tauris & Company, Ltd. London, 1995. 272p. ISBN:1-85043-824-2, ISBN13: 978-1-85043-824-3. Dewey:355.02. LCCN:94-060184.

Audience: **u,f.**

Karsten, Peter (Editor)   **U22.M63 1998**
Motivating Soldiers: Morale or Mutiny. Cloth Text. Garland Publishing, Inc. New York, NY. 1998. 368p. Military and

Society Ser., Vol. 3 ISBN:0-8153-2977-6, ISBN13: 978-0-8153-2977-0. Dewey:355.1/23. LCCN:98-042477.

Audience: **l,u,f.**

Leavitt, Lewis A. & Fox,   **U22.3.P775 1993**
  Nathan A. (Editors)
Psychological Effects of War and Violence on Children. Cloth over Boards. Lawrence Erlbaum Associates, Inc. Mahwah, NJ. 1993. 392p. ISBN:0-8058-1171-0, ISBN13: 978-0-8058-1171-1. Dewey:305.23. LCCN:92-043225.

Audience: **u,f.** *Choice, 1994.*

LeShan, Lawrence   **U22.3.L45 1992**
The Psychology of War: Comprehending Its Mystique and Its Madness. Trade Cloth. Noble Press, Incorporated, The. Chicago, IL. 1992. 163p. ISBN:1-879360-20-9, ISBN13: 978-1-879360-20-4. Dewey:355.0019. LCCN:92-050438.

Audience: **l,u.**

Mansfield, Sue   **U21.2.M34**
The Gestalts of War. Trade Cloth. Doubleday Publishing. New York, NY. 1982. 288p. ISBN:0-385-27219-7, ISBN13: 978-0-385-27219-3. Dewey:355/.0275. LCCN:81-012592.

Audience: **u,f.** *B*

Mosse, George L.   **U22.3.M63 1990**
Fallen Soldiers: Reshaping the Memory of the World Wars. Trade Cloth. Oxford University Press, Inc. New York, NY. 1990. 272p. ISBN:0-19-506247-7, ISBN13: 978-0-19-506247-2. Dewey:303.6/6/09409041. LCCN:89-036202.

Audience: **l,u.** *Choice, 1990.*

Nadelson, Theodore   **U21.5.N33 2005**
Trained to Kill: Soldiers at War. Trade Cloth. Johns Hopkins University Press. Baltimore, MD. 2005. 208p. ISBN:0-8018-8166-8, ISBN13: 978-0-8018-8166-4. Dewey:355.02/01/9. LCCN:2004-021138.

Audience: **l,u,f.** *Choice, 2005.*

Richardson, F. M.   **U22.3**
Fighting Spirit: A Study of Psychological Factors in War. Trade Cloth. Cooper Square Publishers, Inc. New York, NY. 1978. xv, 189p. ISBN:0-85052-236-6, ISBN13: 978-0-85052-236-5. Dewey:355/.02/019. LCCN:78-318970.

Audience: **l,u.**

Rieber, R. W.   **U22.3.P795 1991**
The Psychology of War and Peace: The Image of the Enemy. Trade Cloth. Basic Books. New York, NY. 1990. 302p. ISBN:0-306-43543-8, ISBN13: 978-0-306-43543-0. Dewey:355/.001/9. LCCN:91-010481.

Audience: **l,u,f.**

Rosen, Stephen Peter   **U21.2.R638 2004**
War and Human Nature. Trade Cloth. Princeton University Press. Princeton, NJ. 2004. 216p. ISBN:0-691-11600-8, ISBN13: 978-0-691-11600-6. Dewey:355.02. LCCN:2003-065590.

Audience: **u,f.** *Choice, 2005.*

Shalit, Ben   **U22**
The Psychology of Conflict and Combat. Trade Cloth. Greenwood Publishing Group, Inc. Portsmouth, NH. 1988. 215p. ISBN:0-275-92753-9, ISBN13: 978-0-275-92753-0. Dewey:355/.001/9. LCCN:87-023729.

Audience: **l,u,f.** *Choice, 1988.*

Shephard, Ben   RC550.S535 2001
A War of Nerves: Soldiers and Psychiatrists in the Twentieth Century. Trade Cloth. Harvard University Press. Cambridge, MA. 2001. 512p. ISBN:0-674-00592-9, ISBN13: 978-0-674-00592-1. Dewey:616.8/5212. LCCN:00-066367.
Audience: **l,u,f.**

Stevens, Anthony   U22.3
The Roots of War and Terror. Trade Cloth. Continuum International Publishing Group, Ltd. London, 2003. 192p. ISBN:0-8264-7108-0, ISBN13: 978-0-8264-7108-6. Dewey:355.02019. LCCN:2004-299014.
Audience: **l,u,f.**

Stouffer, Samuel A., et al.   U22.3
The American Soldier: Combat and Its Aftermath, Vol. 2. Arthur A. Lumsdaine & Marion H. Lumsdaine (Authors). Paper Text. M A/A H Publishing. Manhattan, KS. 1949. 675p. ISBN:0-89126-035-8, ISBN13: 978-0-89126-035-6. Dewey:U22.3.
Audience: **u,f.**

Stouffer, Samuel A., et al.   U22.S8
The American Soldier: Adjustment During Army Life, Vol. 1. Edward A. Suchmen, Leland C. DeVinney, Shirley A. Star Jr. & Robin M. Williams (Authors). Paper Text. M A/A H Publishing. Manhattan, KS. 1949. 600p. ISBN:0-89126-034-X, ISBN13: 978-0-89126-034-9. Dewey:U22.3.
Audience: **u,f.** *B*

Watson   U22.3.W37
War on the Mind. Cloth Text. Westview Press. Boulder, CO. 1978. 534p. ISBN:0-465-09065-6, ISBN13: 978-0-465-09065-5. Dewey:355/.001/9. LCCN:77-075237.
Audience: **l,u.** *B*

Webster, Donovan   U21.2.W392 1996
Aftermath: The Landscape of War. Trade Cloth. Knopf Publishing Group. New York, NY. 1996. 288p. ISBN:0-679-43195-0, ISBN13: 978-0-679-43195-4. Dewey:355.02/8. LCCN:96-007649.
Audience: **g,l,u.**

Consumer Psychology

Fromm, Erich   BF698.F746 2005
To Have or to Be? Trade Paper, Perfect. Continuum International Publishing Group, Ltd. London, 2005. 224p. Continuum Impacts Ser. ISBN:0-8264-1738-8, ISBN13: 978-0-8264-1738-1. Dewey:302.
Audience: **g,l,u,f.**

Society for Consumer   HF5415.3
Psychology (APA Division 23)
☐ Society for Consumer Psychology (APA Division 23). http://fisher.osu.edu/marketing/scp/
Audience: **u,f.**

Wachtel, Paul L.   HB74.P8 W3 1983
The Poverty of Affluence: A Psychological Analysis of Life in the Consumer Society. Trade Cloth. Simon & Schuster. New York, NY. 1983. 320p. ISBN:0-02-933540-X, ISBN13: 978-0-02-933540-6. Dewey:339.4/7/0973. LCCN:83-047655.
Audience: **g,l,u,f.**

Consumer Psychology > Consumer Attitudes & Behavior

     HF5415.33.U6
Baby Boom: Americans Born 1946 To 1964. Ed. 4. Trade Cloth. New Strategist Publications, Inc. Ithaca, NY. 2004. 400p. American Generations Ser. ISBN:1-885070-51-9, ISBN13: 978-1-885070-51-7. Dewey:305.2.
Audience: **g,l,u,f.** *Choice, 2005.*

     HF5415.33.U6
Generation X: Americans Born 1965 To 1976. Ed. 4. Trade Cloth. New Strategist Publications, Inc. Ithaca, NY. 2004. 384p. American Generations Ser. ISBN:1-885070-52-7, ISBN13: 978-1-885070-52-4. Dewey:305.235.
Audience: **g,l,u,f.** *Choice, 2005.*

     HQ796
The Millennials: Americans Born 1977 To 1994. Ed. 2. Trade Cloth. New Strategist Publications, Inc. Ithaca, NY. 2004. 402p. American Generations Ser. ISBN:1-885070-53-5, ISBN13: 978-1-885070-53-1. Dewey:305.235.
Audience: **g,l,u,f.** *Choice, 2005.*

     HF5415.3.W67
World Consumer Lifestyles Databook: Key Trends. Ed. 2. Euromonitor International Plc. 2003.
Audience: **u,f.**

Ajzen, Icek   HM251
Attitudes, Personality, and Behavior. Ed. 1. Cloth Text. Brooks/Cole. Pacific Grove, CA. 1988. 175p. ISBN:0-534-10948-9, ISBN13: 978-0-534-10948-6. Dewey:302.
Audience: **u,f.**

Brobeck, Stephen (Editor)   HC79.C63E53 1997
Encyclopedia of the Consumer Movement. Library Binding. ABC-CLIO, Inc. Santa Barbara, CA. 1997. 659p. ISBN:0-87436-987-8, ISBN13: 978-0-87436-987-8. Dewey:381.3/2/03. LCCN:97-041345.
Audience: **g,l,u.** *Choice, 1998.*

Center for Customer Driven   HF5415.32
Quality, Purdue University
☐ Center for Customer Driven Quality, Purdue University. http://www.ccdq.com/
Audience: **u,f.**

Eiser, J. Richard   BF327.E364 1994
Attitudes, Chaos and the Connectionist Mind. Trade Cloth. Blackwell Publishing, Inc. Malden, MA. 1994. 288p. ISBN:0-631-19129-1, ISBN13: 978-0-631-19129-2. Dewey:153. LCCN:93-023963.
Audience: **f.** *Choice, 1994.*

Fishbein, M. & Ajzen, Icek   BF323.C5
Understanding Attitudes and Predicting Social Behavior. Cloth Text. Prentice Hall PTR. Upper Saddle River, NJ. 1980. x, 278p. ISBN:0-13-936443-9, ISBN13: 978-0-13-936443-3. Dewey:301.1. LCCN:79-026063.
Audience: **u,f.**

Gallup, George Jr. (Editor)   HN90.P8G29 1999
The Gallup Poll Cumulative Index: Public Opinion, 1935-1997. Book, Other. Rowman & Littlefield Publishers, Inc. Lanham,

---

MD. 1999. 596p. ISBN:0-8420-2587-1, ISBN13:
978-0-8420-2587-4. Dewey:303.3/8/0973. LCCN:98-045927.

Audience: **g,l,u,f.** *Choice, 2001, 1999.*

Gladwell, Malcolm   **HM1033.G53 2000**
The Tipping Point: How Little Things Can Make a Big
Difference. Trade Cloth. Little Brown & Company. New York,
NY. 2000. 288p. ISBN:0-316-31696-2, ISBN13:
978-0-316-31696-5. Dewey:302. LCCN:99-047576.

Audience: **g,l,u,f.**

Hogg, Margaret (Editor)   **HF5415.32 .C652**
Consumer Behavior II: The Meaning of Consumption. Trade
Cloth. SAGE Publications, Ltd. London, 2006. 1304p.
ISBN:1-4129-0842-6, ISBN13: 978-1-4129-0842-9.
Dewey:658.8342.

Audience: **u,f.**

Hogg, Margaret K. (Editor)   **HF5415.32**
Consumer Behavior: Research and Influences. Trade Cloth.
SAGE Publications, Ltd. London, 2005. 1272p. Sage Library in
Business and Management ISBN:1-4129-0841-8, ISBN13:
978-1-4129-0841-2. Dewey:658.8342. LCCN:2005-900845.

Audience: **u,f.**

Hovland, Carl I.   **P90**
Communication and Persuasion: Psychological Studies of
Opinion Change. Trade Cloth. Yale University Press.
Cumberland, RI. 1953. ISBN:0-300-00573-3, ISBN13:
978-0-300-00573-8. Dewey:808.

Audience: **f.** *B*

Kassarjian, Harold H. &   **HF5415.32.H36 1991**
Robertson, Thomas S.
Handbook of Consumer Behavior. Cloth Text. Prentice Hall
PTR. Upper Saddle River, NJ. 1990. 624p.
ISBN:0-13-372749-1, ISBN13: 978-0-13-372749-4.
Dewey:658.8/342. LCCN:90-040459.

Audience: **u,f.** *Choice, 1991.*

Kasser, Tim   **BF698.35.A36K37 2002**
The High Price of Materialism. Trade Cloth. MIT Press.
Cambridge, MA. 2002. 165p. Bradford Bks.
ISBN:0-262-11268-X, ISBN13: 978-0-262-11268-0.
Dewey:302/.17. LCCN:2002-016506.

Audience: **l,u.** *Choice, 2002.*

Kasser, Tim & Kanner,   **HC110.C6P76 2003**
Allen (Editors)
Psychology and Consumer Culture: The Struggle for a Good
Life in a Materialistic World. Trade Cloth. American
Psychological Association. Washington, DC. 2003. xi, 297p.
ISBN:1-59147-046-3, ISBN13: 978-1-59147-046-5.
Dewey:306.3. LCCN:2003-004965.

Audience: **u,f.**

Lebergott, Stanley   **HC110.C6.L393 1993**
Pursuing Happiness: American Consumers in the Twentieth
Century. Trade Cloth. Princeton University Press. Princeton, NJ.
1993. 202p. ISBN:0-691-04322-1, ISBN13: 978-0-691-04322-7.
Dewey:306.30973. LCCN:92-040491.

Audience: **g,l,u,f.** *Choice, 1994.*

Mintel Group   **HC240.9.C6**
☐ Mintel Reports (database).
http://reports.mintel.com/

Audience: **u,f.**

Mitchell, Susan   **HN90.P8M58 2000**
American Attitudes: Who Thinks What about the Issues That
Shape Our Lives. Ed. 3. Trade Cloth. New Strategist
Publications, Inc. Ithaca, NY. 2000. 500p. American Consumer
Ser. ISBN:1-885070-30-6, ISBN13: 978-1-885070-30-2.
Dewey:303.3/8/0973. LCCN:2002-511417.

Audience: **g,l,u,f.** *Choice, 1999.*

Pooler, Jim   **HF5415**
Why We Shop: Emotional Rewards and Retail Strategies. Trade
Cloth. Greenwood Publishing Group, Inc. Portsmouth, NH.
2003. 216p. ISBN:0-275-98172-X, ISBN13: 978-0-275-98172-3.
Dewey:658.8/342. LCCN:2003-053625.

Audience: **g,l,u.** *Choice, 2004.*

Robert Cialdini Staff   **BF774 .C53**
Influence: Science and Practice. Ed. 4. Trade Cloth. Allyn &
Bacon, Inc. Boston, MA. 2000. ISBN:0-205-32502-5, ISBN13:
978-0-205-32502-3. Dewey:153.8/52.

Audience: **g,l,u.**

Scholarly Resources Staff &   **HN90.P8**
Gallup, George Jr.
The Gallup Poll: Public Opinion 2003. Book, Other. Rowman &
Littlefield Publishers, Inc. Lanham, MD. 2004. 528p.
ISBN:0-8420-5003-5, ISBN13: 978-0-8420-5003-6.
Dewey:303.38.

Audience: **g,l,u,f.**

Shefrin, Hersh   **HG4515.15.S53 2002**
Beyond Greed and Fear: Understanding Behavioral Finance and
the Psychology of Investing. Ed. 2. Trade Cloth. Oxford
University Press, Inc. New York, NY. 1999. 408p. Financial
Management Association Survey and Synthesis Ser.
ISBN:0-19-516121-1, ISBN13: 978-0-19-516121-2.
Dewey:332.6/01/9. LCCN:2002-010047.

Audience: **g,l,u,f.** *Choice, 2003, 2000.*

Vallacher, Robin R. &   **HM251 .D87 1994**
Nowak, Andrzej
Dynamical Systems in Social Psychology. Robin R. Vallacher &
Andrzej Nowak (Editors). Trade Cloth. Elsevier Science &
Technology Books. Saint Louis, MO. 1994. 305p.
ISBN:0-12-709990-5, ISBN13: 978-0-12-709990-3. Dewey:302.
LCCN:93-011325.

Audience: **f.**

van Ginneken, Jaap   **HM1236.G556 2002**
Collective Behavior and Public Opinion: Rapid Shifts in
Opinion and Communication. Cloth over Boards. Lawrence
Erlbaum Associates, Inc. Mahwah, NJ. 2003. 312p. The
European Institute for the Media Ser. ISBN:0-8058-4386-8,
ISBN13: 978-0-8058-4386-6. Dewey:303.3/8.
LCCN:2002-019731.

Audience: **u,f.** *Choice, 2003.*

Wood, Floris W.   **HN90.P8 A53 1990**
An American Profile: Attitude and Behaviors of the American
People, 1972-1989. Trade Cloth. Thomson Gale. Farmington
Hills, MI. 1990. 1200p. ISBN:0-8103-7723-3, ISBN13:
978-0-8103-7723-3. Dewey:303.3/8/097309047.
LCCN:90-220322.

Audience: **g,l,u,f.** *Choice, 1991.*

Consumer Psychology > Marketing and Advertising

Learned, Andrea &   **HC79.C6J64 2004**
  Johnson, Lisa
Don't Think Pink: What Really Makes Women Buy -- and How
to Increase Your Share of This Crucial Market. Trade Cloth.
Amacom. New York, NY. 2004. 224p. ISBN:0-8144-0815-X,
ISBN13: 978-0-8144-0815-5. Dewey:658.8/34/082.
LCCN:2004-005393.
                                 Audience: **g,l,u.**   *Choice, 2004.*

Levine, Robert V.   **BF637.P4L48 2003**
The Power of Persuasion: How We're Bought and Sold. Trade
Cloth. John Wiley & Sons, Inc. Hoboken, NJ. 2003. 288p.
ISBN:0-471-26634-5, ISBN13: 978-0-471-26634-1.
Dewey:153.8/52. LCCN:2002-009952.
                                 Audience: **g,l,u,f.**   *Choice, 2003.*

Levy, Sidney J. & Rook,   **HF5415.1.L48 1999**
  Dennis W. (Editors)
Brands, Consumers, Symbols and Research: Sidney J Levy on
Marketing. Trade Cloth. SAGE Publications, Inc. Thousand
Oaks, CA. 1999. 608p. ISBN:0-7619-1696-2, ISBN13:
978-0-7619-1696-3. Dewey:658.8/243. LCCN:99-006225.
                                 Audience: **u,f.**   *Choice, 2000.*

Schor, Juliet B.   **HF5415.33.U6S355**
Born to Buy: The Commercialized Child and the New
Consumer Culture. Trade Cloth. Simon & Schuster. New York,
NY. 2004. 288p. ISBN:0-684-87055-X, ISBN13:
978-0-684-87055-7. Dewey:305.23/0973. LCCN:2004-045411.
                                 Audience: **g,l,u,f.**   *Choice, 2005.*

Zaltman, Gerald   **HF5415.32.Z35 2003**
How Customers Think: Essential Insights into the Mind of the
Markets. Trade Cloth. Harvard Business School Press. Boston,
MA. 2003. 352p. ISBN:1-57851-826-1, ISBN13:
978-1-57851-826-5. Dewey:658.8/342. LCCN:2002-011666.
                                 Audience: **u,f.**   *Choice, 2003.*

Zollo, Peter   **HF5415.32.Z65 2004**
Getting Wiser to Teens: More Insights into Marketing to
Teenagers. Cloth Text. New Strategist Publications, Inc. Ithaca,
NY. 2003. xvi, 424p. ISBN:1-885070-54-3, ISBN13:
978-1-885070-54-8. Dewey:658.8/34/0835. LCCN:2004-298874.
                                 Audience: **g,l,u.**   *Choice, 2004.*

Engineering and Environmental Psychology

Bechtel, Robert B. &   **BF353.B425 2001**
  Churchman, Arza (Editors)
Handbook of Environmental Psychology. Trade Cloth. John
Wiley & Sons, Inc. Hoboken, NJ. 2002. 736p.
ISBN:0-471-40594-9, ISBN13: 978-0-471-40594-8.
Dewey:155.9. LCCN:2001-026449.
                                 Audience: **u,f.**

Bell, Paul A.   **BF353.E545 2001**
Environmental Psychology. Ed. 5. Cloth Text. Thomson
Wadsworth. Belmont, CA. 2000. 656p. ISBN:0-15-508064-4,
ISBN13: 978-0-15-508064-5. Dewey:155.9. LCCN:00-105961.
                                 Audience: **l,u.**

Cassidy, Tony   **BF353.C38 1997**
Environmental Psychology: Behaviour and Experience in
Context. Paper over Boards. Taylor & Francis Group. Abingdon,
1997. vi, 282p. ISBN:0-86377-480-6, ISBN13:
978-0-86377-480-5. Dewey:155.9. LCCN:97-202071.
                                 Audience: **u.**

Charlton, Samuel G. &   **TA166.H276 2002**
  O'Brien, Thomas G. (Editors)
Handbook of Human Factors Testing and Evaluation. Ed. 2.
Cloth over Boards. Lawrence Erlbaum Associates, Inc. Mahwah,
NJ. 2001. 560p. ISBN:0-8058-3290-4, ISBN13:
978-0-8058-3290-7. Dewey:620.82. LCCN:2001-033265.
                                 Audience: **u,f.**

Dekker, Sidney W. A.   **TL553.6D45 2005**
Ten Questions about Human Error: A New View of Human
Factors and System Safety. Cloth over Boards. Lawrence
Erlbaum Associates, Inc. Mahwah, NJ. 2004. 240p. The Human
Factors in Transportation Ser. ISBN:0-8058-4744-8, ISBN13:
978-0-8058-4744-4. Dewey:363.12. LCCN:2005-297190.
                                 Audience: **l,u,f.**

Fisk, Arthur D.   **TA166.D485 2004**
Designing for Older Adults: Principles and Creative Human
Factors Approaches. Paper over Boards. Taylor & Francis
Group. Philadelphia, PA. 2004. 176p. ISBN:0-415-28611-5,
ISBN13: 978-0-415-28611-4. Dewey:620.8/2.
LCCN:2003-010735.
                                 Audience: **u,f.**

Hancock, Peter A. (Editor)   **TA166**
Human Performance and Ergonomics: Perceptual and Cognitive
Principles. Ed. 2. Cloth Text. Elsevier Science & Technology
Books. Saint Louis, MO. 1999. 397p. Handbook of Perception
and Cognition Ser. ISBN:0-12-322735-6, ISBN13:
978-0-12-322735-5. Dewey:620.8/2. LCCN:99-060088.
                                 Audience: **u,f.**

Hollnagel, Erik (Editor)   **TA167.H35 2003**
Handbook of Cognitive Task Design. Anthony J. Adamski,
James L. Alty & Matthijs Amelink (Contribution by). Cloth over
Boards. Lawrence Erlbaum Associates, Inc. Mahwah, NJ. 2003.
816p. Human Factors and Ergonomics Ser.
ISBN:0-8058-4003-6, ISBN13: 978-0-8058-4003-2.
Dewey:620.8/2. LCCN:2003-042401.
                                 Audience: **u,f.**

Meister, David   **TA166.M395 2003**
Conceptual Foundations of Human Factors Measurement. Cloth
over Boards. Lawrence Erlbaum Associates, Inc. Mahwah, NJ.
2003. 256p. Human Factors and Ergonomics Ser.
ISBN:0-8058-4135-0, ISBN13: 978-0-8058-4135-0.
Dewey:620.8/2. LCCN:2003-052863.
                                 Audience: **u,f.**

Meister, David   **TA166.M396 1999**
The History and Characteristics of Human Factors-Ergonomics.
Cloth over Boards. Lawrence Erlbaum Associates, Inc. Mahwah,
NJ. 1999. 400p. ISBN:0-8058-2768-4, ISBN13:
978-0-8058-2768-2. Dewey:620.8/2/09. LCCN:98-049609.
                                 Audience: **l,u.**

Meister, David &   **TA168.M36 2002**
  Enderwick, Thomas P.
Human Factors in System Design. Cloth over Boards. Lawrence

Erlbaum Associates, Inc. Mahwah, NJ. 2001. 256p.
ISBN:0-8058-3206-8, ISBN13: 978-0-8058-3206-8.
Dewey:620.8/2. LCCN:00-051380.

Audience: **u,f.**

National Research Council   **TA166.E53 1995**
  Staff
Emerging Needs and Opportunities for Human Factors Research.
Raymond Nickerson & Committee on Human Factors (Editors).
Paper Text. National Academies Press. Washington, DC. 1995.
336p. ISBN:0-309-05276-9, ISBN13: 978-0-309-05276-4.
Dewey:620.8. LCCN:95-070762.

Audience: **g,u,f.**

Norman, Donald A.   **BF531.N67 2004**
Emotional Design: Why We Love (or Hate) Everyday Things.
Paper Text. Basic Books. New York, NY. 2005. 272p.
ISBN:0-465-05136-7, ISBN13: 978-0-465-05136-6.
Dewey:155.9/11.

Audience: **g,l,u,f.** *Choice, 2004.*

Proctor, Robert W. &   **TK5105.888.H3635**
  Kim-Phuong, L.Vu (Editors)
Handbook of Human Factors in Web Design. Stanley N.
Roscoe, Greg Vanderheiden, Kim-Phuong L. Vu, Ira H.
Bernstein, Addie Johnson & Celine Mariage (Contribution by).
Cloth over Boards. Lawrence Erlbaum Associates, Inc. Mahwah,
NJ. 2004. 752p. Human Factors/Ergonomics Ser.
ISBN:0-8058-4611-5, ISBN13: 978-0-8058-4611-9.
Dewey:005.7/2. LCCN:2004-018981.

Audience: **u,f.**

Ratner, Julie (Editor)   **TK5105.888.H86 2002**
Human Factors and Web Development. Ed. 2. Johan Aberg,
Brian P. Bailey & Randolph G. Bias (Contribution by). Cloth
over Boards. Lawrence Erlbaum Associates, Inc. Mahwah, NJ.
2002. 352p. ISBN:0-8058-4221-7, ISBN13: 978-0-8058-4221-0.
Dewey:302.23/071/1. LCCN:2002-010673.

Audience: **u,f.**

Reason, James   **BF323.E7 R42 1990**
Human Error. Trade Paper. Cambridge University Press. New
York, NY. 1990. 316p. ISBN:0-521-31419-4, ISBN13:
978-0-521-31419-0. Dewey:153.4/6. LCCN:90-031041.

Audience: **u,f.** *Choice, 1991.*

Salas, Eduardo & Stone,   **TA166**
  Dianna (Editors)
Advances in Human Performance and Cognitive Engineering
Research. Trade Cloth. Elsevier Science & Technology Books.
Saint Louis, MO. 2003. 220p. Advances in Human Performance
and Cognitive Engineering Research Ser. ISBN:0-7623-0986-5,
ISBN13: 978-0-7623-0986-3. Dewey:620.8/2.

Audience: **u,f.**

Salvendy, Gavriel (Editor)   **TA166.H275 2005**
Handbook of Human Factors and Ergonomics. Ed. 3. Trade
Cloth. John Wiley & Sons, Inc. Hoboken, NJ. 2006. 1680p.
ISBN:0-471-44917-2, ISBN13: 978-0-471-44917-1.
Dewey:620.8/2. LCCN:2005-003111.

Audience: **u,f.**

Sternberg, Robert J. &   **T58.5.I565 2005**
  Preiss, David D. (Editors)
Intelligence and Technology: The Impact of Tools on the Nature
and Development of Human Abilities. Carlos Diaz-Canepa,
Patricia M. Greenfield, Jean-Michel Hoc, Edwin Hutchins, Alex

Kirlik & Susanne P. Lajoie (Contribution by). Saddle Stitched,
Cloth over Boards. Lawrence Erlbaum Associates, Inc. Mahwah,
NJ. 2005. 272p. The Educational Psychology Ser.
ISBN:0-8058-4927-0, ISBN13: 978-0-8058-4927-1.
Dewey:153.9. LCCN:2005-004906.

Audience: **u,f.** *Choice, 2005.*

Tsang, Pamela S. &   **RC1085.P75 2002**
  Vidulich, Michael A. (Editors)
Principles and Practices of Aviation Psychology. Robert N.
Buck, Evan A. Byrne & Thomas R. Carretta (Contribution by).
Cloth over Boards. Lawrence Erlbaum Associates, Inc. Mahwah,
NJ. 2002. 624p. Human Factors in Transportation Ser.
ISBN:0-8058-3390-0, ISBN13: 978-0-8058-3390-4.
Dewey:629.132/52/019. LCCN:2002-024377.

Audience: **u,f.**

Tufte, Edward R.   **QA276.3.T83 2001**
The Visual Display of Quantitative Information. Ed. 2. Cloth
Text. Graphics Press. Cheshire, CT. 2001. 197p.
ISBN:0-9613921-4-2, ISBN13: 978-0-9613921-4-7.
Dewey:001.4/226. LCCN:2001-271866.

Audience: **g,l,u,f.**

Wallace, Patricia M.   **BF637.C45 W26 1999**
The Psychology of the Internet. Trade Paper. Cambridge
University Press. New York, NY. 2001. 294p.
ISBN:0-521-79709-8, ISBN13: 978-0-521-79709-2.
Dewey:025.04/01/9. LCCN:99-012696.

Audience: **l,u.**

Walsh, W. Bruce (Editor),   **BF353.P43 2000**
  et al.
Person Environment Psychology: New Directions and
Perspectives. Ed. 2. Kenneth H. Craik & Richard H. Price
(Editors), H. C. Clitheroe, Jack Demick, Carol S. Dweck &
John Finney (Contribution by). Cloth over Boards. Lawrence
Erlbaum Associates, Inc. Mahwah, NJ. 2000. 352p.
ISBN:0-8058-2470-7, ISBN13: 978-0-8058-2470-4.
Dewey:155.9. LCCN:99-030603.

Audience: **u,f.**

Wickens, Christopher D.,   **TA166.W528 2004**
  et al.
Introduction to Human Factors Engineering. Ed. 2. John Lee,
Yili D. Liu & Sallie Gordon-Becker (Authors). Cloth Text.
Prentice Hall PTR. Upper Saddle River, NJ. 2003. 608p.
ISBN:0-13-183736-2, ISBN13: 978-0-13-183736-2.
Dewey:620.8/2. LCCN:2003-020402.

Audience: **l,u.**

Wickens, Christopher D.,   **TL725.3.T7H865 1997**
  et al.
Flight to the Future: Human Factors in Air Traffic Control.
James P. McGee, Anne S. Mavor & Panel on Human Factors in
Air Traffic Control (Authors). Cloth Text. National Academies
Press. Washington, DC. 1997. 384p. ISBN:0-309-05637-3,
ISBN13: 978-0-309-05637-3. Dewey:629.136/6.
LCCN:96-037616.

Audience: **u,f.**

Wogalter, Michael S.   **T10.68.H37 1999**
  (Editor)
Handbook of Warnings. Austin Adams, Adams Austin, Heather
Jane Barnes, A. Jeffrey, Orrock Jeffrey, Brewster Blair & James
P. Bliss (Contribution by). Cloth over Boards. Lawrence

Erlbaum Associates, Inc. Mahwah, NJ. 2006. 864p. Human Factors/Ergonomics Ser. ISBN:0-8058-4724-3, ISBN13: 978-0-8058-4724-6. Dewey:620.8. LCCN:2005-029220.

Audience: **u,f.**

Zsambok, Caroline E. & Klein, Gary A. (Editors)   **BF448.N38 1997**

Naturalistic Decision Making. Trade Cloth. Lawrence Erlbaum Associates, Inc. Mahwah, NJ. 1996. 375p. Expertise Ser., :Research and Applications ISBN:0-8058-1873-1, ISBN13: 978-0-8058-1873-4. Dewey:153.8/3. LCCN:96-027981.

Audience: **u,f.**

Intelligent Systems

Bloom, Charles P. & Loftin, R. Bowen (Editors)   **LB1028.73.F33 1998**

Facilitating the Development and Use of Interactive Learning Environments. Cloth over Boards. Lawrence Erlbaum Associates, Inc. Mahwah, NJ. 1998. 440p. Computers, Cognition, and Work Ser. ISBN:0-8058-1850-2, ISBN13: 978-0-8058-1850-5. Dewey:371.33/4. LCCN:97-044903.

Audience: **u,f.**

Boden, Margaret A. (Editor)   **BD418.8.B63 1996**

The Philosophy of Artificial Life. Paper Text. Oxford University Press, Inc. New York, NY. 1996. 414p. Oxford Readings in Philosophy Ser. ISBN:0-19-875155-9, ISBN13: 978-0-19-875155-7. Dewey:113.8. LCCN:95-043389.

Audience: **u,f.** *Choice, 1996.*

Bullinger, Hans-Jorg & Ziegler, Jurgen   **QA76.9.H85**

Human-Computer Interaction: Ergonomics and User Interfaces. Cloth over Boards. Lawrence Erlbaum Associates, Inc. Mahwah, NJ. 1999. 1384p. ISBN:0-8058-3391-9, ISBN13: 978-0-8058-3391-1. Dewey:004.019.

Audience: **u,f.**

Franklin, Stan   **Q335.F733 1995**

Artificial Minds. Trade Cloth. MIT Press. Cambridge, MA. 1995. 464p. Bradford Bks. ISBN:0-262-06178-3, ISBN13: 978-0-262-06178-0. Dewey:006.3. LCCN:94-038796.

Audience: **u,f.** *Choice, 1996.*

Gorayska, Barbara & Mey, Jacob L. (Editors)   **BF311.C55346 1996**

Cognitive Technology: In Search of a Humane Interface. Trade Cloth. Elsevier Science & Technology Books. Saint Louis, MO. 1995. 434p. Advances in Psychology Ser. ISBN:0-444-82275-5, ISBN13: 978-0-444-82275-8. Dewey:153. LCCN:95-044591.

Audience: **u,f.**

Gordo-Lopez, Angel J. & Parker, Ian (Editors)   **BF38.C93 1999**

Cyberpsychology. Cloth Text. Routledge. New York, NY. 1999. 224p. ISBN:0-415-92496-0, ISBN13: 978-0-415-92496-2. Dewey:150.1. LCCN:99-013198.

Audience: **u,f.**

Jacko, Julie A. & Stephanidis, Constantine (Editors)   **QA76.9.H85**

Human-Computer Interaction, Vol. 1. Cloth over Boards. Lawrence Erlbaum Associates, Inc. Mahwah, NJ. 2003. 1344p. ISBN:0-8058-4930-0, ISBN13: 978-0-8058-4930-1. Dewey:004/.019.

Audience: **u,f.**

Koslow, Stephen H. & Huerta, Michael F. (Editors)   **Q224.E44 2000**

Electronic Collaboration in Science. Floyd E. Bloom, Dan L. Burk & Graham Cameron (Contribution by). Cloth over Boards. Lawrence Erlbaum Associates, Inc. Mahwah, NJ. 2000. 160p. Progress in Neurinformatics Research Ser., Vol. 2 ISBN:0-8058-3106-1, ISBN13: 978-0-8058-3106-1. Dewey:507.2. LCCN:99-053395.

Audience: **u,f.**

Lipson, Carol S. & Day, Michael J. (Editors)   **T11.T2985 2005**

Technical Communication and the World Wide Web. John Barber, John F. Barber, Saul Carliner & Traci Gardner (Contribution by). Cloth over Boards. Lawrence Erlbaum Associates, Inc. Mahwah, NJ. 2005. 376p. ISBN:0-8058-4572-0, ISBN13: 978-0-8058-4572-3. Dewey:808/.0666. LCCN:2005-040902.

Audience: **u,f.** *Choice, 2005.*

Mateas, Michael & Sengers, Phoebe (Editors)   **BF456.N37N37 2002**

Narrative Intelligence. Trade Cloth. John Benjamins Publishing Company. Philadelphia, PA. 2003. viii, 342p. Advances in Consciousness Research Ser., Vol. 46 ISBN:1-58811-274-8, ISBN13: 978-1-58811-274-3. Dewey:153. LCCN:2002-026207.

Audience: **u,f.**

Nehaniv, Chrystopher L. & Dautenhahn, Kerstin (Editors)   **BF357.I47 2002**

Imitation in Animals and Artifacts. Trade Cloth. MIT Press. Cambridge, MA. 2002. 625p. Complex Adaptive Systems Ser. ISBN:0-262-04203-7, ISBN13: 978-0-262-04203-1. Dewey:591.5/14. LCCN:2001-054644.

Audience: **u,f.**

Picard, Rosalind W.   **QA76.9.H85**

Affective Computing. Trade Paper. MIT Press. Cambridge, MA. 2000. 304p. ISBN:0-262-66115-2, ISBN13: 978-0-262-66115-7. Dewey:004/.01/9. LCCN:97-033285.

Audience: **u,f.** *Choice, 1998.*

Ratner, Julie (Editor), et al.   **TK5105.888.H86 1998**

Human Factors and Web Development. Chris Forsythe & Eric Grose (Editors). Trade Cloth. Lawrence Erlbaum Associates, Inc. Mahwah, NJ. 1997. 300p. ISBN:0-8058-2823-0, ISBN13: 978-0-8058-2823-8. Dewey:302.23/071/1. LCCN:97-015656.

Audience: **u,f.**

Roco, Mihail C. & Montemagno, Carlo D.   **Q11.N5 VOL.1013**

The Coevolution of Human Potential and Converging Technologies. Trade Paper. New York Academy of Sciences. New York, NY. 2004. viii, 259p. Annals of the New York Academy of Sciences Ser., Vol. 1013 ISBN:1-57331-501-X, ISBN13: 978-1-57331-501-2. Dewey:500 s 620.8/2. LCCN:2004-007954.

Audience: **u,f.**

Wagman, Morton   **BF311**

Language and Thought in Humans and Computers: Theory and Research in Psychology, Artificial Intelligence and Neural Science. Trade Cloth. Greenwood Publishing Group, Inc. Portsmouth, NH. 1998. 192p. ISBN:0-275-96179-6, ISBN13: 978-0-275-96179-4. Dewey:153. LCCN:97-032997.

Audience: **u,f.**

Intelligent Systems > Artificial Intelligence. Expert Systems

Agre, Philip E.   **Q336 .A37 1997**
Computation and Human Experience. John Seely Brown, Christian Heath & Roy D. Pea (Contribution by). Trade Cloth. Cambridge University Press. New York, NY. 1997. 389p. Learning in Doing, :Social, Cognitive and Computational Perspectives Ser. ISBN:0-521-38432-X, ISBN13: 978-0-521-38432-2. Dewey:006.3/01. LCCN:96-014826.

Audience: **u,f.**

Boden, Margaret A. (Editor)   **Q335.P48 1990**
The Philosophy of Artificial Intelligence. Paper Text. Oxford University Press, Inc. New York, NY. 1990. 460p. Oxford Readings in Philosophy Ser. ISBN:0-19-824854-7, ISBN13: 978-0-19-824854-5. Dewey:006.3/01. LCCN:89-034075.

Audience: **u,f.**

Broadbent, Donald (Editor)   **Q335**
The Simulation of Human Intelligence. Trade Paper. Blackwell Publishing, Inc. Malden, MA. 1993. 232p. ISBN:0-631-18733-2, ISBN13: 978-0-631-18733-2. Dewey:006.3. LCCN:92-017187.

Audience: **u,f.** *Choice, 1993.*

Cooper, Richard P., et al.   **QP395.C66 2002**
Modelling High-Level Cognitive Processes. John Fox, David W. Glasspool & Peter G. Yule (Authors). Cloth over Boards. Lawrence Erlbaum Associates, Inc. Mahwah, NJ. 2002. 424p. ISBN:0-8058-3883-X, ISBN13: 978-0-8058-3883-1. Dewey:612.8/2/0113. LCCN:2002-018862.

Audience: **u,f.**

Feigenbaum, Edward A. &   **Q335.5.C66 1995**
Feldman, Julian (Editors)
Computers and Thought. Trade Paper. MIT Press. Cambridge, MA. 1995. 550p. AAAI Press Ser. ISBN:0-262-56092-5, ISBN13: 978-0-262-56092-4. Dewey:006.3. LCCN:95-215375.

Audience: **u,f.**

Forbus, Kenneth &   **LB1028.73.S53 2001**
Feltovich, Paul (Editors)
Smart Machines in Education. Trade Paper. MIT Press. Cambridge, MA. 2001. 489p. AAAI Press Ser. ISBN:0-262-56141-7, ISBN13: 978-0-262-56141-9. Dewey:371.33/4. LCCN:2001-041247.

Audience: **u,f.** *Choice, 2002.*

Gigerenzer, Gerd, et al.   **BC177**
Simple Heuristics That Make Us Smart. Peter M. Todd & ABC Research Group Staff (Authors). Trade Paper. Oxford University Press, Inc. New York, NY. 2000. 432p. Evolution and Cognition Ser. ISBN:0-19-514381-7, ISBN13: 978-0-19-514381-2. Dewey:128/.33.

Audience: **u,f.**

Haugeland, John   **Q335.5.M492 1997**
Mind Design II: Philosophy, Psychology, Artificial Intelligence. Ed. 2. Trade Paper. MIT Press. Cambridge, MA. 1997. 488p. Bradford Bks. ISBN:0-262-58153-1, ISBN13: 978-0-262-58153-0. Dewey:006.3. LCCN:96-045188.

Audience: **u,f.**

Johnson-Laird, Philip   **BF444 .J64 1993**
Human and Machine Thinking. Cloth over Boards. Lawrence Erlbaum Associates, Inc. Mahwah, NJ. 1992. 200p. MacEachran Lectures ISBN:0-8058-0921-X, ISBN13: 978-0-8058-0921-3. Dewey:153.4/3.

Audience: **u,f.**

Klahr, David & Kotovsky,   **BF444.C66 1989**
K. (Editors)
Complex Information Processing: The Impact of Herbert A. Simon. Trade Cloth. Lawrence Erlbaum Associates, Inc. Mahwah, NJ. 1989. 480p. Carnegie Mellon Symposia on Cognition Ser. ISBN:0-8058-0178-2, ISBN13: 978-0-8058-0178-1. Dewey:153/.092/4. LCCN:88-031004.

Audience: **u,f.**

Lajoie, Susanne (Editor)   **LB1028.5.C5722 2000**
Computers As Cognitive Tools: No More Walls. Ed. 2. Fabio N. Akhras, Roger Azevedo & Tamara Balac (Contribution by). Cloth over Boards. Lawrence Erlbaum Associates, Inc. Mahwah, NJ. 2000. 472p. ISBN:0-8058-2930-X, ISBN13: 978-0-8058-2930-3. Dewey:371.33/4. LCCN:99-088271.

Audience: **u,f.**

Leavitt, David   **QA29.T8L43 2005**
The Man Who Knew Too Much: Alan Turing and the Invention of the Computer. Trade Cloth. W. W. Norton & Company, Inc. New York, NY. 2005. 288p. Great Discoveries Ser. ISBN:0-393-05236-2, ISBN13: 978-0-393-05236-7. Dewey:510/.92 B. LCCN:2005-018034.

Audience: **u,f.**

Schank, Roger C. (Editor)   **P53.28.I57 1997**
Inside Multi-Media Case Based Instruction. Cloth over Boards. Lawrence Erlbaum Associates, Inc. Mahwah, NJ. 1998. 464p. ISBN:0-8058-2537-1, ISBN13: 978-0-8058-2537-4. Dewey:418/.00285. LCCN:97-021714.

Audience: **u,f.**

Steier, David M. & Mitchell,   **BF311.M5534 1996**
Tom (Editors)
Mind Matters: A Tribute to Allen Newell. Cloth Text. Lawrence Erlbaum Associates, Inc. Mahwah, NJ. 1996. 464p. Carnegie Mellon Symposia on Cognition Ser. ISBN:0-8058-1363-2, ISBN13: 978-0-8058-1363-0. Dewey:153. LCCN:95-034683.

Audience: **u,f.**

Trappl, Robert (Editor),   **BF531.E517 2003**
et al.
Emotions in Humans and Artifacts. Paolo Petta & Sabine Payr (Editors). Trade Cloth. MIT Press. Cambridge, MA. 2003. 400p. Bradford Bks. ISBN:0-262-20142-9, ISBN13: 978-0-262-20142-1. Dewey:152.4. LCCN:2002-071829.

Audience: **u,f.** *Choice, 2003.*

Wagman, Morton   **Q335**
Cognitive Science and Concepts of Mind: Toward a General Theory of Human and Artificial Intelligence. Trade Cloth. Greenwood Publishing Group, Inc. Portsmouth, NH. 1991. 208p. ISBN:0-275-94044-6, ISBN13: 978-0-275-94044-7. Dewey:006.3. LCCN:91-010585.

Audience: **u,f.** *Choice, 1992.*

Intelligent Systems > Neural Networks

Abdi, Herve, et al.   QA76.87.A325 1999
Neural Networks, Vol. 124. Dominique Valentin & Betty
Edelman (Authors). Trade Paper. SAGE Publications, Inc.
Thousand Oaks, CA. 1998. 96p. Quantitative Applications in the
Social Sciences Ser. ISBN:0-7619-1440-4, ISBN13:
978-0-7619-1440-2. Dewey:006.3/2. LCCN:98-046918.
Audience: **u,f.**

Churchland, Patricia S. &   QP356.C48 1992
Sejnowski, Terrence J.
The Computational Brain. Trade Cloth. MIT Press. Cambridge,
MA. 1992. 560p. Computational Neuroscience Ser.
ISBN:0-262-03188-4, ISBN13: 978-0-262-03188-2.
Dewey:612.8/2/0113. LCCN:91-028056.
Audience: **u,f.** *Choice, 1992.*

Garson, G. David   QA76.81.G37 1998
Neural Networks: An Introductory Guide for Social Scientists.
Cloth Text. SAGE Publications, Inc. Thousand Oaks, CA. 1998.
208p. Statistics Ser. ISBN:0-7619-5730-8, ISBN13:
978-0-7619-5730-0. Dewey:006.3/2. LCCN:98-061097.
Audience: **u,f.**

Levine, Daniel S.   QP363.3.L48 2000
Introduction to Neural and Cognitive Modeling. Ed. 2. Cloth
over Boards. Lawrence Erlbaum Associates, Inc. Mahwah, NJ.
2000. 512p. ISBN:0-8058-2005-1, ISBN13: 978-0-8058-2005-8.
Dewey:612.8/2/0113. LCCN:99-057795.
Audience: **u,f.**

McLeod, Peter, et al.   QA76.87
Introduction to Connectionist Modelling of Cognitive Proce.
Kim Plunkett & Edmund T. Rolls (Authors). Trade Cloth.
Oxford University Press, Inc. New York, NY. 1998. 404p.
ISBN:0-19-852427-7, ISBN13: 978-0-19-852427-4.
Dewey:006.3/2. LCCN:97-041671.
Audience: **u,f.**

Spitzer, Manfred   QP363.3.S55 1999
The Mind Within the Net: Models of Learning, Thinking and
Acting. Trade Cloth. MIT Press. Cambridge, MA. 1999. 359p. A
Bradford Book Ser. ISBN:0-262-19406-6, ISBN13:
978-0-262-19406-8. Dewey:612.8/2. LCCN:98-010911.
Audience: **u,f.** *Choice, 1999.*

Forensic Psychology and Legal Issues

Ackerman, Marc J.   RA1148.A28 1999
Essentials of Forensic Psychological Assessment. Trade Paper.
John Wiley & Sons, Inc. Hoboken, NJ. 1999. 304p. Essentials
of Psychological Assessment, Vol. 8 ISBN:0-471-33186-4,
ISBN13: 978-0-471-33186-5. Dewey:614/.1. LCCN:99-018558.
Audience: **u.**

Adler, Joanna (Editor)   K2100
Forensic Psychology: Concepts, Debates and Practice. Trade
Cloth. Willan Publishing. Devon, 2004. 333p.
ISBN:1-84392-010-7, ISBN13: 978-1-84392-010-6.
Dewey:347/.066/019. LCCN:2004-299162.
Audience: **u,f.**

Alison, Laurence John   HV6080
(Editor)
The Forensic Psychologist's Casebook: Psychological Profiling
and Criminal Investigation. Trade Cloth. Willan Publishing.
Devon, 2005. 410p. ISBN:1-84392-113-8, ISBN13:
978-1-84392-113-4. Dewey:364.3. LCCN:2005-531290.
Audience: **u,f.**

Arrigo, Bruce A. & Shipley,   RA1148
Stacey L.
Introduction to Forensic Psychology: Issues and Controversies in
Crime and Justice. Ed. 2. Cloth Text. Elsevier Science &
Technology Books. Saint Louis, MO. 2004. 600p.
ISBN:0-12-064351-0, ISBN13: 978-0-12-064351-6.
Dewey:614/.1. LCCN:2004-276462.
Audience: **u,f.**

Bartol, Anne M. & Bartol,   RA1148.B37 2004
Curt
Introduction to Forensic Psychology: Research and Application.
Cloth Text. SAGE Publications, Inc. Thousand Oaks, CA. 2004.
520p. ISBN:0-7619-2606-2, ISBN13: 978-0-7619-2606-1.
Dewey:614/.15. LCCN:2003-021875.
Audience: **u,f.**

Bartol, Anne M. & Bartol,   HV6080.C87 2006
Curt R. (Editors)
Current Perspectives in Forensic Psychology and Criminal
Justice. Paper Text. SAGE Publications, Inc. Thousand Oaks,
CA. 2005. 296p. ISBN:1-4129-2590-8, ISBN13:
978-1-4129-2590-7. Dewey:614/.15. LCCN:2005-019685.
Audience: **u,f.**

Bartol, Curt R. & Bartol,   KF8922
Anne M.
Psychology and Law: Theory, Research, and Application. Ed. 3.
Cloth Text. Thomson Wadsworth. Belmont, CA. 2003. 608p.
ISBN:0-534-52818-X, ISBN13: 978-0-534-52818-8.
Dewey:345/.001/9. LCCN:2003-107739.
Audience: **l,u.**

Bartol, Curt R. & Bartol,   KF8922.B37 1994
Anne M.
Psychology and Law: Research and Application. Ed. 2. Mass
Market. Brooks/Cole. Pacific Grove, CA. 1993. 480p.
ISBN:0-534-16320-3, ISBN13: 978-0-534-16320-4.
Dewey:345/.001/9. LCCN:93-039459.
Audience: **l,u.**

Blau, Theodore H.   KF8965 B57 2002
The Psychologist as Expert Witness. Ed. 2. Trade Paper. John
Wiley & Sons, Inc. Hoboken, NJ. 2001. 608p.
ISBN:0-471-11366-2, ISBN13: 978-0-471-11366-9.
Dewey:347.73067.
Audience: **l,u,f.**

Brewer, Neil & Wilson,   HV7936.P75P78 1995
Carlene (Editors)
Psychology and Policing. Cloth over Boards. Lawrence Erlbaum
Associates, Inc. Mahwah, NJ. 1995. 504p. ISBN:0-8058-1418-3,
ISBN13: 978-0-8058-1418-7. Dewey:363.2/01/9.
LCCN:95-001425.
Audience: **u,f.**

Carson, David & Bull, Ray   K346.H36 2003
(Editors)
Handbook of Psychology in Legal Contexts. Ed. 2. Trade Cloth.

John Wiley & Sons, Inc. Hoboken, NJ. 2003. 688p. ISBN:0-471-49874-2, ISBN13: 978-0-471-49874-2. Dewey:347/.066/019. LCCN:2002-033069.

Audience: **u,f.**

Cooke, David J., et al.   **HV6089.C66**
Psychology in Prisons. Pamela J. Baldwin & Jacqueline Howison (Authors). Trade Paper. Routledge. New York, NY. 1993. ISBN:0-04-159414-2, ISBN13: 978-0-04-159414-0. Dewey:364.3. LCCN:92-047425.

Audience: **l,u.**

Cutler, Brian L. & Penrod,   **KF9672 .C87 1995**
Steven D.
Mistaken Identification: The Eyewitness, Psychology and the Law. Trade Paper. Cambridge University Press. New York, NY. 1995. 300p. ISBN:0-521-44572-8, ISBN13: 978-0-521-44572-6. Dewey:363.2/58. LCCN:94-045187.

Audience: **u,f.** *Choice, 1996.*

Frost, Lynda E. & Bonnie,   **KF3828.E94 2001**
Richard J. (Editors)
The Evolution of Mental Health Law. Trade Cloth. American Psychological Association. Washington, DC. 2001. xiv, 336p. Law and Public Policy Ser., :Psychology and the Social Sciences ISBN:1-55798-746-7, ISBN13: 978-1-55798-746-4. Dewey:344.73/044. LCCN:2001-018897.

Audience: **u,f.**

Heckel, Robert V. &   **RJ506**
Shumaker, David M.
Children Who Murder: A Psychological Perspective. Eugene Arthur Moore (Foreword by). Trade Cloth. Greenwood Publishing Group, Inc. Portsmouth, NH. 2001. 200p. ISBN:0-275-96618-6, ISBN13: 978-0-275-96618-8. Dewey:618.92/85844. LCCN:00-042776.

Audience: **l,u.** *Choice, 2001.*

Heilbrun, Kirk   **RA1148.H45 2001**
Principles of Forensic Mental Health Assessment. Trade Cloth. Springer. New York, NY. 2001. 360p. Perspectives in Law and Psychology Ser., Vol. 12 ISBN:0-306-46538-8, ISBN13: 978-0-306-46538-3. Dewey:614/.1. LCCN:00-067432.

Audience: **u,f.**

Heilbrun, Kirk, et al.   **RA1148.H452 2002**
Forensic Mental Health Assessment: A Casebook. Geffory Marczyk & David DeMatteo (Authors). Trade Cloth. Oxford University Press, Inc. New York, NY. 2002. 548p. ISBN:0-19-514568-2, ISBN13: 978-0-19-514568-7. Dewey:614/.1. LCCN:2001-047644.

Audience: **u,f.**

Horowitz, Irwin A.   **K487.P75H67 1998**
The Psychology of Law: Integrations and Applications. Ed. 2. Trade Cloth. Allyn & Bacon, Inc. Boston, MA. 1997. 560p. ISBN:0-321-00600-3, ISBN13: 978-0-321-00600-4. Dewey:340/.01/9. LCCN:97-037879.

Audience: **l,u.**

Howitt, Dennis   **HV6080.H69 2002**
Forensic and Criminal Psychology. Ed. 2. Trade Paper. Prentice Hall PTR. Upper Saddle River, NJ. 2002. 448p. ISBN:0-13-016985-4, ISBN13: 978-0-13-016985-3. Dewey:364.3. LCCN:2005-053908.

Audience: **l,u.**

Kagehiro, D. & Laufer,   **K487.P75H36 1991**
William S. (Editors)
Handbook of Psychology and Law. Cloth Text. Springer. New York, NY. 1991. 628p. ISBN:0-387-97568-3, ISBN13: 978-0-387-97568-9. Dewey:340/.01/9. LCCN:91-011801.

Audience: **u,f.**

Kapardis, Andreas   **K487.P75K36 2003**
Psychology and Law: A Critical Introduction. Ed. 2. Cloth Text. Cambridge University Press. New York, NY. 2002. 440p. ISBN:0-521-82530-X, ISBN13: 978-0-521-82530-6. Dewey:340/.19. LCCN:2002-035087.

Audience: **u,f.**

Levine, Martin L. (Editor)   **K487.P75L378 1995**
Law and Psychology. Trade Cloth. New York University Press. New York, NY. 1995. 416p. International Library of Essays in Law and Legal Theory, No. 16 ISBN:0-8147-5064-8, ISBN13: 978-0-8147-5064-3. Dewey:340/.01/9. LCCN:95-007995.

Audience: **u,f.**

Levine, Murray & Wallach,   **KF8965.L48 2002**
Leah
Psychological Problems, Social Issues and Law. Cloth Text. Allyn & Bacon, Inc. Boston, MA. 2001. 592p. ISBN:0-321-05672-8, ISBN13: 978-0-321-05672-6. Dewey:614.1/0973. LCCN:2001-026671.

Audience: **l,u.**

Loftus, Elizabeth F.   **KF9672.L65 1991**
Witness for the Defense: The Accused, the Eyewitness and the Expert Who Puts Memory on Trial. Trade Cloth. St. Martin's Press. Gordonville, VA. 1991. 288p. ISBN:0-312-05537-4, ISBN13: 978-0-312-05537-0. Dewey:345.73/066. LCCN:90-048523.

Audience: **l,u,f.**

Memon, Amina, et al.   **HV8073.M38 2003**
Psychology and Law: Truthfulness, Accuracy and Credibility. Ed. 2. Aldert Vrij & Ray Bull (Authors). Trade Cloth. John Wiley & Sons, Inc. Hoboken, NJ. 2003. 236p. Wiley Series in Psychology of Crime, Policing, and Law ISBN:0-470-85060-4, ISBN13: 978-0-470-85060-2. Dewey:363.25. LCCN:2003-002099.

Audience: **l,u,f.**

O'Donohue, William T. &   **RA1148.H362 2003**
Levensky, Eric R. (Editors)
Handbook of Forensic Psychology: Resource for Mental Health and Legal Professionals. Cloth Text. Elsevier Science & Technology Books. Saint Louis, MO. 2003. 1064p. ISBN:0-12-524196-8, ISBN13: 978-0-12-524196-0. Dewey:614/.15. LCCN:2003-057757.

Audience: **u,f.** *Choice, 2004.*

Ogloff, James R. (Editor)   **K487.P75 L38 1992**
Law and Psychology: The Broadening of the Discipline. Trade Cloth, Box or Slipcased. Carolina Academic Press. Durham, NC. 1992. 464p. ISBN:0-89089-475-2, ISBN13: 978-0-89089-475-0. Dewey:340/.01/9. LCCN:92-071726.

Audience: **u.**

Perlin, Michael L.   **KF480.A7P47 1999**
Mental Disability Law: Cases and Materials. Trade Cloth, Box or Slipcased. Carolina Academic Press. Durham, NC. 1999. 1080p. ISBN:0-89089-882-0, ISBN13: 978-0-89089-882-6. Dewey:344.73/044. LCCN:98-089959.

Audience: **u.**

Raskin, David (Editor)   **KF9660.P87 1989**
Psychological Methods in Criminal Investigation and Evidence. Trade Cloth. Springer Publishing Company, Inc. New York, NY. 1989. 416p. ISBN:0-8261-6450-1, ISBN13: 978-0-8261-6450-6. Dewey:345.73/06. LCCN:89-004301.

Audience: **u.**

Ribner, Neil G. (Editor)   **RA1148.C35 2002**
California School of Professional Psychology Handbook of Juvenile Forensic Psychology. Trade Cloth. John Wiley & Sons, Inc. Hoboken, NJ. 2002. 704p. ISBN:0-7879-5948-0, ISBN13: 978-0-7879-5948-7. Dewey:614/.1. LCCN:2002-003290.

Audience: **u,f.**

Rogers, Richard & Shuman, Daniel W.   **KF8965.R64 2005**
Fundamentals of Forensic Practice: Mental Health and Criminal Law. Trade Cloth. Springer. New York, NY. 2005. viii, 445p. ISBN:0-387-25227-4, ISBN13: 978-0-387-25227-8. Dewey:347.7367. LCCN:2005-923617.

Audience: **u,f.**

Saks, Elyn R. & Behnke, Stephen H.   **RA1152.M84S25 1997**
Jekyll on Trial: Multiple Personality Disorder and Criminal Law. Trade Cloth. New York University Press. New York, NY. 1997. 272p. ISBN:0-8147-8042-3, ISBN13: 978-0-8147-8042-8. Dewey:614/.1. LCCN:96-035676.

Audience: **u,f.**

Simon, Robert I. & Gold, Liza H.   **RA1151.A47 2004**
The American Psychiatric Publishing Textbook of Forensic Psychiatry. Trade Cloth. American Psychiatric Publishing, Inc. Arlington, VA. 2004. 248p. ISBN:1-58562-087-4, ISBN13: 978-1-58562-087-6. Dewey:614/.15. LCCN:2003-069699.

Audience: **u,f.**

Van (Editor)   **HV6080**
Psychology and Law: Inside and Outside the Courtroom. Cloth Text. Addison-Wesley Educational Publishers, Inc. Boston, MA. 1998. ISBN:0-321-01134-1, ISBN13: 978-0-321-01134-3. Dewey:364.3.

Audience: **u.**

Van Dorsten, Brent (Editor)   **RA1148.F558 2002**
Forensic Psychology: From Classroom to Courtroom. Trade Cloth. Springer. New York, NY. 2002. 332p. ISBN:0-306-47270-8, ISBN13: 978-0-306-47270-1. Dewey:614/.1. LCCN:2002-028657.

Audience: **u.** *Choice, 2003.*

Walker, Lenore E. & Shapiro, David L.   **RA1148.W34 2004**
Introduction to Forensic Psychology: Clinical and Social Psychological Perspectives. Trade Cloth. Springer. New York, NY. 2003. 444p. ISBN:0-306-47908-7, ISBN13: 978-0-306-47908-3. Dewey:614/.15. LCCN:2003-060286.

Audience: **l,u.**

Weiner, Irving B. & Hess, Allen K. (Editors)   **RA1148.H36 2006**
The Handbook of Forensic Psychology. Ed. 3. Trade Cloth. John Wiley & Sons, Inc. Hoboken, NJ. 2005. 912p. ISBN:0-471-69232-8, ISBN13: 978-0-471-69232-4. Dewey:614/.15. LCCN:2005-020236.

Audience: **u,f.**

Wrightsman, Lawrence S.   **RA1148.W75 2001**
Forensic Psychology. Trade Cloth, Box or Slipcased. Thomson Wadsworth. Belmont, CA. 2000. 420p. ISBN:0-534-52679-9, ISBN13: 978-0-534-52679-5. Dewey:614/.15. LCCN:00-039886.

Audience: **l,u.**

Wrightsman, Lawrence S., et al.   **KF8700.W75 2002**
Psychology and the Legal System. Ed. 5. William H. Fortune, Edith Greene & Michael T. Nietzel (Authors). Cloth Text. Thomson Wadsworth. Belmont, CA. 2001. 608p. ISBN:0-534-36544-2, ISBN13: 978-0-534-36544-8. Dewey:347.73/001/9. LCCN:2001-026526.

Audience: **u.**

General Psychology

                                        BF141
☐ American Psychological Association (APA). http://www.apa.org/

Audience: **g,l,u,f.**

☐ Association for Psychological Science (APS). http://www.psychologicalscience.org/

Audience: **g,l,u,f.**

Aiken, Lewis R.   **BF697.A55 1999**
Human Differences. Cloth over Boards. Lawrence Erlbaum Associates, Inc. Mahwah, NJ. 1999. 352p. ISBN:0-8058-3091-X, ISBN13: 978-0-8058-3091-0. Dewey:155.2/2. LCCN:99-011092.

Audience: **l,u.** *Choice, 1999.*

Aspinwall, Lisa G. & Staudinger, Ursula M. (Editors)   **BF121.P763 2002**
A Psychology of Human Strengths: Fundamental Questions and Future Directions for a Positive Psychology. Trade Cloth. American Psychological Association. Washington, DC. 2002. 369p. ISBN:1-55798-931-1, ISBN13: 978-1-55798-931-4. Dewey:150.19/8. LCCN:2002-008033.

Audience: **u,f.** *Choice, 2003.*

Colman, Andrew   **BF31.C65 2006**
A Dictionary of Psychology. Ed. 2. Trade Cloth. Oxford University Press, Inc. New York, NY. 2006. 880p. ISBN:0-19-280632-7, ISBN13: 978-0-19-280632-1. Dewey:150.3. LCCN:2005-031810.

Audience: **g,l,u,f.** *Choice, 2006.*

Dunn, Dana, et al.   **BF77.M385 2004**
Measuring Up: Educational Assessment Challenges and Practices for Psychology. Chandra Mehrotra & Jane S. Halonen (Authors). Trade Cloth. American Psychological Association. Washington, DC. 2004. 312p. ISBN:1-59147-108-7, ISBN13: 978-1-59147-108-0. Dewey:150/.71. LCCN:2004-004235.

Audience: **l,u,f.** *Choice, 2005.*

Garfield, Jay L.   **BF38.G295 1988**
🄴 Belief in Psychology: A Study in the Ontology of Mind. E-Book. NetLibrary, Inc. Boulder, CO. 1988. ISBN:0-585-33609-1, ISBN13: 978-0-585-33609-1. Dewey:153/.01.

Audience: **u,f.** *Choice, 1988.*

Garner, Wendell R.   **BF38**
Uncertainty and Structure As Psychological Concepts. Paper
Text. Textbook Publishers. Temecula, CA. 2003. ix, 369p.
ISBN:0-7581-0504-5, ISBN13: 978-0-7581-0504-2.
Dewey:150.18.

                                        Audience: **u,f.**

Gholson, Barry (Editor),   **Q175 .P8965 1989**
   et al.
Psychology of Science: Contributions to Metascience. William
R. Shadish Jr., Robert A. Neimeyer & Arthur C. Houts (Editors).
Cloth Text. Cambridge University Press. New York, NY. 1989.
480p. ISBN:0-521-35410-2, ISBN13: 978-0-521-35410-3.
Dewey:501. LCCN:88-018901.
                              Audience: **u,f.** *Choice, 1990.*

Harré, Rom   **BF204**
Physical Being: A Theory for a Corporeal Psychology. Trade
Paper. Blackwell Publishing, Inc. Malden, MA. 1994. 272p.
ISBN:0-631-19505-X, ISBN13: 978-0-631-19505-4.
Dewey:150.19/8. LCCN:90-020581.

                                        Audience: **u,f.**

James, William   **BF38**
The Principles of Psychology. Library Binding. Reprint Services
Company. Temecula, CA. 1992. Notable American Authors Ser.
ISBN:0-7812-3472-7, ISBN13: 978-0-7812-3472-6.
Dewey:150/.1.
                                        Audience: **g,l,u,f.**

Kazdin, Alan E.   **BF31.E52 2000**
Encyclopedia of Psychology. Trade Cloth. American
Psychological Association. Washington, DC. 2000. 29p.
ISBN:1-55798-650-9, ISBN13: 978-1-55798-650-4.
Dewey:150.3. LCCN:99-055239.
                              Audience: **g,l,u,f.** *Choice, 2000.*

Massironi, Manfredo   **BF241.M345 2002**
The Psychology of Graphic Images: Seeing, Drawing,
Communicating. Cloth over Boards. Lawrence Erlbaum
Associates, Inc. Mahwah, NJ. 2001. 328p. ISBN:0-8058-2932-6,
ISBN13: 978-0-8058-2932-7. Dewey:302.2/22.
LCCN:2001-016019.
                              Audience: **u,f.** *Choice, 2002.*

McManus, Chris   **QP385.5.M38 2002**
Right Hand, Left Hand: The Origins of Asymmetry in Brains,
Bodies, Atoms and Cultures. Trade Cloth. Harvard University
Press. Cambridge, MA. 2002. 432p. ISBN:0-674-00953-3,
ISBN13: 978-0-674-00953-0. Dewey:152.3/35.
LCCN:2002-017275.
                              Audience: **l,u,f.** *Choice, 2003.*

Miller, George A., et al.   **BF311.M52 1986**
Plans and the Structure of Behavior. Eugene Galanter & Karl H.
Pribram (Authors), Donald E. Broadbent (Introduction by).
Cloth Text. Adams, Bannister, Cox Publishers. New York, NY.
1986. 226p. ISBN:0-937431-00-1, ISBN13: 978-0-937431-00-9.
Dewey:153.8/3. LCCN:86-025934.
                                        Audience: **u,f.**

O'Donohue, William T. &   **BF76.4.H36 2003**
   Ferguson, Kyle E. (Editors)
Handbook of Professional Ethics for Psychologists: Issues,
Questions, and Controversies. Cloth Text. SAGE Publications,
Inc. Thousand Oaks, CA. 2003. 488p. ISBN:0-7619-1188-X,

ISBN13: 978-0-7619-1188-3. Dewey:174/.915.
LCCN:2002-013230.
                              Audience: **u,f.** *Choice, 2003.*

Reber, Arthur S. & Reber,   **BF31.R43 2001**
   Emily S.
The Penguin Dictionary of Psychology. Ed. 3. Trade Paper.
Penguin Group (USA) Inc. New York, NY. 2002. 864p.
Dictionary, Penguin Ser. ISBN:0-14-051451-1, ISBN13:
978-0-14-051451-3. Dewey:150/.3/21. LCCN:2002-276265.
                              Audience: **g,l,u,f.** *Choice, 2002.*

Scheibe, Karl E.   **BF121.S328 2000**
The Drama of Everyday Life. Trade Cloth. Harvard University
Press. Cambridge, MA. 2000. 304p. ISBN:0-674-00231-8,
ISBN13: 978-0-674-00231-9. Dewey:150. LCCN:99-043533.
                              Audience: **l,u.** *Choice, 2000.*

Schinka, John A. & Velicer,   **BF121.H1955 2004**
   Wayne F.
Handbook of Psychology, Set. Irving B. Weiner
(Editor-In-Chief). Trade Paper. John Wiley & Sons, Inc.
Hoboken, NJ. 2004. 7995p. ISBN:0-471-66675-0, ISBN13:
978-0-471-66675-2. Dewey:150.
                              Audience: **u,f.** *Choice, 2003.*

Sexton, Virginia S. &   **BF121.I5645 1992**
   Hogan, John D. (Editors)
International Psychology: Views from Around the World. Trade
Cloth. University of Nebraska Press. Lincoln, NE. 1992. 524p.
ISBN:0-8032-4184-4, ISBN13: 978-0-8032-4184-8. Dewey:150.
LCCN:91-032299.
                              Audience: **l,u,f.** *Choice, 1993.*

Sternberg, Robert J.   **BF38.U55 2004**
Unity in Psychology: Possibility or Pipedream? Trade Cloth.
American Psychological Association. Washington, DC. 2004.
200p. ISBN:1-59147-156-7, ISBN13: 978-1-59147-156-1.
Dewey:150/.1. LCCN:2004-003908.
                              Audience: **u,f.** *Choice, 2005.*

Uttal, William R.   **BF38.5.U88 2003**
Psychomythics: Sources of Artifacts and Misconceptualizations
in Scientific Psychology. Cloth over Boards. Lawrence Erlbaum
Associates, Inc. Mahwah, NJ. 2003. 216p. ISBN:0-8058-4584-4,
ISBN13: 978-0-8058-4584-6. Dewey:150/.1.
LCCN:2003-040828.
                              Audience: **u,f.** *Choice, 2003.*

Wedding, Danny & Stevens,   **BF121.H2115 2004**
   Michael J. (Editors)
Handbook of International Psychology. Paper over Boards.
Brunner-Routledge. Philadelphia, PA. 2004. 560p.
ISBN:0-415-94612-3, ISBN13: 978-0-415-94612-4.
Dewey:150/.9. LCCN:2004-000334.
                              Audience: **u,f.** *Choice, 2005.*

Werner, Heinz   **BF123**
Comparative Psychology of Mental Development. Paper Text.
Eliot Werner Publications, Inc. Clinton Corners, NY. 2004.
604p. Foundations of Psychology ISBN:0-9719587-1-8,
ISBN13: 978-0-9719587-1-5. Dewey:150. LCCN:2002-104253.
                                        Audience: **l,u.**

General Psychology > History and Systems

History of Psychology.
http://elvers.stjoe.udayton.edu/history/history.htm

Audience: **g,l,u,f.**

Appignanesi, Lisa &   **BF109.F74A86 2001**
   Forrester, John
Freud's Women. Ed. 2. Trade Paper. Other Press, LLC. New
York, NY. 2001. 600p. ISBN:1-892746-94-8, ISBN13:
978-1-892746-94-8. Dewey:150.19/52/082. LCCN:2001-053095.

Audience: **u,f.**

Ash, Mitchell G.   **N/A**
Gestalt Psychology in German Culture, 1890-1967: Holism and
the Quest for Objectivity. William R. Woodward (Contribution
by). Trade Cloth. Cambridge University Press. New York, NY.
1996. 527p. Cambridge Studies in the History of Psychology
ISBN:0-521-47540-6, ISBN13: 978-0-521-47540-2.
Dewey:150.1/982/0943. LCCN:94-036273.

Audience: **u,f.**

Bair, Deirdre   **BF109.J8B35 2003**
Jung: A Biography. Trade Cloth. Little Brown & Company. New
York, NY. 2003. 896p. ISBN:0-316-07665-1, ISBN13:
978-0-316-07665-4. Dewey:150.19/9/54/092.
LCCN:2003-047472.

Audience: **u,f.** *Choice, 2004.*

Benjamin, Ludy Jr.   **BF95.B44 2005**
A History of Psychology in Letters. Ed. 2. Trade Paper.
Blackwell Publishing, Inc. Malden, MA. 2005. 264p.
ISBN:1-4051-2612-4, ISBN13: 978-1-4051-2612-0.
Dewey:150/.9. LCCN:2005-015448.

Audience: **u,f.**

Benjamin, Ludy T. & Baker,   **BF75 .B46 2004**
   David
From Seance to Science: A History of the Profession and
Practice of Psychology in America. Paper Text. Thomson
Wadsworth. Belmont, CA. 2003. 288p. ISBN:0-15-504264-5,
ISBN13: 978-0-15-504264-3. Dewey:150.973.
LCCN:2003-104451.

Audience: **l,u.**

Bjork, Daniel W.   **BF109.S55B46 1997**
B. F. Skinner: A Life. Ed. 2. Trade Paper. American
Psychological Association. Washington, DC. 1997. 298p.
ISBN:1-55798-416-6, ISBN13: 978-1-55798-416-6.
Dewey:150.19/434/092 B. LCCN:96-040385.

Audience: **l,u,f.** *Choice, 1994.*

Bolles, Robert C.   **BF95.B57 1993**
The Story of Psychology: A Thematic History. Ed. 1. Mass
Market. Brooks/Cole. Pacific Grove, CA. 1993. xii, 445p.
ISBN:0-534-19668-3, ISBN13: 978-0-534-19668-4.
Dewey:150.9. LCCN:92-034713.

Audience: **l,u.** *Choice, 1994.*

Boring, Edwin G.   **BF95 .B6**
History of Experimental Psychology. Ed. 2. Cloth Text. Prentice
Hall PTR. Upper Saddle River, NJ. 1950. ISBN:0-13-390039-8,
ISBN13: 978-0-13-390039-2. Dewey:150.72.

Audience: **u,f.**

Breger, Louis   **BF109.F74**
Freud: Darkness in the Midst of Vision. Trade Paper. John
Wiley & Sons, Inc. Hoboken, NJ. 2001. 480p.
ISBN:0-471-07858-1, ISBN13: 978-0-471-07858-6.
Dewey:150.19/52/092 B.

Audience: **u,f.** *Choice, 2001.*

Brett, George Sidney   **BF121**
A History of Psychology: Mediaeval and Early Modern Period,
Vol. 2. Paper over Boards. Routledge. New York, NY. 2004.
400p. Muirhead Library of Philosophy Ser.
ISBN:0-415-29609-9, ISBN13: 978-0-415-29609-0. Dewey:150.

Audience: **u,f.**

Brett, George Sidney   **BF121**
A History of Psychology: Ancient and Patristic, Vol. 1. Paper
over Boards. Routledge. New York, NY. 2004. 408p. Muirhead
Library of Philosophy Ser. ISBN:0-415-29608-0, ISBN13:
978-0-415-29608-3. Dewey:150.

Audience: **u,f.**

Brett, George Sidney   **BF81 .B7**
A History of Psychology: Modern Psychology, Vol. 3. Paper
over Boards. Routledge. New York, NY. 2004. 328p. Muirhead
Library of Philosophy Ser. ISBN:0-415-29610-2, ISBN13:
978-0-415-29610-6. Dewey:150.9.

Audience: **u,f.**

Bringmann, Wolfgang G.   **BF81.P47 1997**
   (Editor), et al.
A Pictorial History of Psychology. Helmut E. Luck & Rudolf
Miller (Editors), Wolfgang G. Bringmann, Helmut E. Luck &
Rudolf Miller (Introduction by, Preface by). Trade Cloth.
Quintessence Publishing Company, Inc. Hanover Park, IL. 1997.
656p. ISBN:0-86715-292-3, ISBN13: 978-0-86715-292-0.
Dewey:150/.9/022. LCCN:96-024728.

Audience: **u,f.** *Choice, 1997.*

Bryher, H. D. & H. D.   **BF109.F74A845 2002**
Analyzing Freud: Letters of H. D., Bryher and Their Circle.
Susan Stanford Friedman (Editor). Trade Cloth. New Directions
Publishing Corporation. New York, NY. 2002. 640p.
ISBN:0-8112-1499-0, ISBN13: 978-0-8112-1499-5.
Dewey:150.19/52/092. LCCN:2002-003980.

Audience: **u,f.** *Choice, 2003.*

Buckley, Kerry W.   **BF109.W39B83 1989**
Mechanical Man: John B. Watson and the Beginnings of
Behaviorism. Cloth over Boards. Guilford Publications, Inc.
New York, NY. 1989. 233p. ISBN:0-89862-744-3, ISBN13:
978-0-89862-744-2. Dewey:150.19/432/0924 B.
LCCN:88-024081.

Audience: **u,f.** *Choice, 1990.*

Candland, Douglas K   **BF95.C36 1993**
Feral Children and Clever Animals: Reflections on Human
Nature. Oxford University Press, Inc. 1993.
ISBN:0-19-507468-8, ISBN13: 978-0-19-507468-0.

Audience: **l,u,f.**

Demorest, Amy   **BF109.A1D45 2004**
Psychology's Grand Theorists: How Personal Experiences
Shaped Professional Ideas. Cloth over Boards. Lawrence
Erlbaum Associates, Inc. Mahwah, NJ. 2004. 216p.
ISBN:0-8058-5107-0, ISBN13: 978-0-8058-5107-6.
Dewey:150.19. LCCN:2004-007577.

Audience: **u,f.** *Choice, 2005.*

Dyer, Donald   **Z8458.75 .D94**
Cross-Currents of Jungian Thought: An Annotated Bibliography.
Trade Paper. Shambhala Publications, Inc. Boston, MA. 2001.
504p. ISBN:1-57062-956-0, ISBN13: 978-1-57062-956-3.
Dewey:016.15019/54.

Audience: **u,f.**

Fancher, Raymond E.   **BF95.F3 1996**
Pioneers of Psychology. Ed. 3. Trade Paper. W. W. Norton &
Company, Inc. New York, NY. 1996. 528p.
ISBN:0-393-96994-0, ISBN13: 978-0-393-96994-8.
Dewey:150/.92/2. LCCN:96-006403.

Audience: **l,u.**

Fletcher, Garth   **BF38.F584 1995**
The Scientific Credibility of Folk Psychology. Trade Paper.
Lawrence Erlbaum Associates, Inc. Mahwah, NJ. 1995. 120p.
ISBN:0-8058-1571-6, ISBN13: 978-0-8058-1571-9.
Dewey:150/.1. LCCN:95-024235.

Audience: **u,f.** *Choice, 1996.*

Freedheim, Donald K.   **BF81**
    (Editor)
Handbook of Psychology, History of Psychology, Vol. 1. Irving
B. Weiner (Editor-In-Chief). Trade Cloth. John Wiley & Sons,
Inc. Hoboken, NJ. 2003. 608p. ISBN:0-471-38320-1, ISBN13:
978-0-471-38320-8. Dewey:150.9. LCCN:2002-066380.

Audience: **u,f.**

Freud, Sigmund & Jung,   **BF109.F4A4 1994**
    C. G.
The Freud-Jung Letters: The Correspondence Between Sigmund
Freud and C. G. Jung. William McGuire (Editor), Ralph
Manheim & R. F. C. Hull (Translators), Alan McGlashan
(Abridged by). Trade Paper. Princeton University Press.
Princeton, NJ. 1994. 328p. Bollingen Series (General) Ser.
ISBN:0-691-03643-8, ISBN13: 978-0-691-03643-4.
Dewey:150.19/52 B. LCCN:93-046096.

Audience: **g,l,u,f.** *B*

Geuter, Ulfried   **BF108.G3 G4813 1992**
The Professionalization of Psychology in Nazi Germany.
Richard Holmes (Translator). Trade Cloth. Cambridge
University Press. New York, NY. 1992. 359p. Cambridge
Studies in the History of Psychology ISBN:0-521-33297-4,
ISBN13: 978-0-521-33297-2. Dewey:150/.943/09043.
LCCN:91-026576.

Audience: **u,f.** *Choice, 1993.*

Green, Christopher D.   **BF81**
Classics in the History of Psychology.
http://psychclassics.yorku.ca/

Audience: **g,l,u,f.**

Green, Christopher D. &   **BF91**
    Groff, Philip R.
Early Psychological Thought: Ancient Accounts of Mind and
Soul. Trade Cloth. Greenwood Publishing Group, Inc.
Portsmouth, NH. 2003. 208p. ISBN:0-313-31845-X, ISBN13:
978-0-313-31845-0. Dewey:150/.9. LCCN:2002-029760.

Audience: **l,u,f.** *Choice, 2004.*

Green, Christopher D., et al.   **BF103.T73 2001**
The Transformation of Psychology: Influences of 19th Century
Philosophy, Technology and Nature Science. Marlene Gay Shore
& Thomas F. Teorey (Authors). Trade Cloth. American

Psychological Association. Washington, DC. 2001. 245p.
ISBN:1-55798-776-9, ISBN13: 978-1-55798-776-1.
Dewey:150/.9/034. LCCN:00-068985.

Audience: **u,f.** *Choice, 2001.*

Guthrie, Robert V.   **BF105.G87 2004**
Even the Rat Was White: A Historical View of Psychology. Ed.
2. Trade Paper. Allyn & Bacon, Inc. Boston, MA. 2003. 304p.
ISBN:0-205-39264-4, ISBN13: 978-0-205-39264-3.
Dewey:150/.89/96073. LCCN:2003-041826.

Audience: **g,l,u,f.** *B*

Heidbreder, Edna   **BF95.H4 1933**
Seven Psychologies. Paper Text. Prentice Hall PTR. Upper
Saddle River, NJ. 1963. viii, 450p. ISBN:0-13-807354-6,
ISBN13: 978-0-13-807354-1. Dewey:150. LCCN:33-013339.

Audience: **u,f.** *B*

Herman, Ellen   **BF108.U5H47 1995**
The Romance of American Psychology: Political Culture in the
Age of Experts. Trade Cloth. University of California Press.
Berkeley, CA. 1995. 512p. ISBN:0-520-08598-1, ISBN13:
978-0-520-08598-5. Dewey:150/.973/09045. LCCN:94-026930.

Audience: **u,f.** *Choice, 1995.*

Herrnstein, Richard J. &   **BF81 .H4**
    Boring, Edwin G. (Editors)
A Source Book in the History of Psychology. Trade Cloth.
Harvard University Press. Cambridge, MA. 1965. 658p. Source
Books in the History of the Sciences ISBN:0-674-82410-5,
ISBN13: 978-0-674-82410-2. Dewey:150.

Audience: **u,f.**

Hothersall, David   **BF95.H67 2004**
History of Psychology. Ed. 4. Paper Text. McGraw-Hill Higher
Education. Burr Ridge, IL. 2003. 624p. ISBN:0-07-284965-7,
ISBN13: 978-0-07-284965-3. Dewey:150/.9.
LCCN:2003-046392.

Audience: **g,l,u.**

Jaynes, Julian   **BD418.3**
The Origin of Consciousness in the Breakdown of the Bicameral
Mind. Trade Paper. Houghton Mifflin Company Trade &
Reference Division. Boston, MA. 2000. 512p.
ISBN:0-618-05707-2, ISBN13: 978-0-618-05707-8.
Dewey:128/.2.

Audience: **u,f.** *B*

Johnson, Michael G. &   **BF109.J28R44 1990**
    Henley, Tracy B. (Editors)
Reflections on the Principles of Psychology: William James after
a Century. Cloth over Boards. Lawrence Erlbaum Associates,
Inc. Mahwah, NJ. 1990. 344p. ISBN:0-8058-0205-3, ISBN13:
978-0-8058-0205-4. Dewey:150/.92. LCCN:90-035867.

Audience: **u,f.** *Choice, 1991.*

Joynson, R. B.   **BF109.B88J68 1989**
The Burt Affair. Trade Cloth. Routledge. New York, NY. 1989.
400p. General Psychology Ser. ISBN:0-415-01039-X, ISBN13:
978-0-415-01039-9. Dewey:150/.92/4. LCCN:88-027096.

Audience: **u,f.** *Choice, 1990.*

Keen, Ernest   **BF105**
A History of Ideas in American Psychology. Trade Cloth.
Greenwood Publishing Group, Inc. Portsmouth, NH. 2001. 288p.
ISBN:0-275-97205-4, ISBN13: 978-0-275-97205-9.
Dewey:150/.973. LCCN:2001-021160.

Audience: **l,u.** *Choice, 2002.*

Kimble, Gregory A.   **BF109.A1**
Portraits of Pioneers in Psychology, Vol. 4. Trade Cloth.
American Psychological Association. Washington, DC. 2000.
360p. Portraits of Pioneers in Psychology Ser., Vol. 4
ISBN:1-55798-712-2, ISBN13: 978-1-55798-712-9.
Dewey:150/.92/2 B. LCCN:91-007226.
Audience: **l,u,f.** *Choice, 2003, 1998, 1992.*

King, D. Brett &   **BF109.W47K56 2004**
  Wertheimer, Michael
Max Wertheimer and Gestalt Theory. Trade Cloth. Transaction
Publishers. Somerset, NJ. 2004. 438p. ISBN:0-7658-0258-9,
ISBN13: 978-0-7658-0258-3. Dewey:150.19/82/092 B.
LCCN:2004-058038.
Audience: **u,f.** *Choice, 2005.*

Klein, Ann G.   **BF109.H6K57 2002**
A Forgotten Voice: A Biography of Leta Stetter Hollingworth.
Trade Paper. Great Potential Press, Inc. Scottsdale, AZ. 2002.
264p. ISBN:0-910707-53-7, ISBN13: 978-0-910707-53-4.
Dewey:150/.92 B. LCCN:2002-012772.
Audience: **u,f.** *Choice, 2003.*

Koch, Sigmund & Leary,   **BF149 .C36 1992**
  David E. (Editors)
A Century of Psychology As Science. Cloth Text. American
Psychological Association. Washington, DC. 1992. 1008p.
ISBN:1-55798-171-X, ISBN13: 978-1-55798-171-4.
Dewey:150/.9. LCCN:92-020981.
Audience: **u,f.** B *Choice, 1985.*

Kozulin, Alex   **BF109.V95K69**
Vygotsky's Psychology: A Biography of Ideas. Trade Paper.
Harvard University Press. Cambridge, MA. 1999. 296p.
ISBN:0-674-94366-X, ISBN13: 978-0-674-94366-7.
Dewey:150.92. LCCN:90-039118.
Audience: **u,f.** *Choice, 1991.*

Lamiell, James T.   **BF105.L36 2003**
Beyond Individual and Group Differences: Human Individuality,
Scientific Psychology, and William Stern's Critical Personalism.
Cloth Text. SAGE Publications, Inc. Thousand Oaks, CA. 2003.
360p. ISBN:0-7619-2172-9, ISBN13: 978-0-7619-2172-1.
Dewey:155.2. LCCN:2003-008606.
Audience: **u,f.** *Choice, 2004.*

Leahey, Thomas H.   **BF105.L43 2001**
A History of Modern Psychology. Ed. 3. Cloth Text. Prentice
Hall PTR. Upper Saddle River, NJ. 2000. 422p.
ISBN:0-13-017573-0, ISBN13: 978-0-13-017573-1.
Dewey:150/.9. LCCN:00-029807.
Audience: **l,u.**

Lindzey, Gardner (Editor)   **BF105**
A History of Psychology in Autobiography, Vol. VII. Cloth Text.
W. H. Freeman & Company. New York, NY. 1980. 472p. A
Series of Books in Psychology ISBN:0-7167-1119-2, ISBN13:
978-0-7167-1119-3. Dewey:150.9. LCCN:30-020129.
Audience: **u,f.**

Lindzey, Gardner (Editor)   **BF105**
A History of Psychology in Autobiography, Vol. VIII. Trade
Cloth. Stanford University Press. Palo Alto, CA. 1989. 504p.
ISBN:0-8047-1492-4, ISBN13: 978-0-8047-1492-1.
Dewey:150.9. LCCN:30-020129.
Audience: **u,f.**

Lindzey, Gardner   **BF105**
A History of Psychology in Autobiography, Vol. 6. Cloth Text.
Prentice-Hall. Upper Saddle, NJ. 1974. 480p.
ISBN:0-13-392274-X, ISBN13: 978-0-13-392274-5.
Dewey:150.9.
Audience: **u,f.**

MacNamara, John   **BF105.M33 1999**
Through the Rearview Mirror: Historical Reflections on
Psychology. Trade Cloth. MIT Press. Cambridge, MA. 1999.
301p. Bradford Bks. ISBN:0-262-13352-0, ISBN13:
978-0-262-13352-4. Dewey:150/.9. LCCN:98-050264.
Audience: **u,f.** *Choice, 2000.*

Messerly, John G.   **BF109.P5M47 1996**
Piaget's Conception of Evolution: Beyond Darwin and Lamarck.
Richard J. Blackwell (Foreword by). Trade Paper. Rowman &
Littlefield Publishers, Inc. Lanham, MD. 1996. 184p.
ISBN:0-8476-8243-9, ISBN13: 978-0-8476-8243-0.
Dewey:155.4/13/092. LCCN:96-013049.
Audience: **u,f.** *Choice, 1997.*

Minton, Henry L.   **BF109.T39M56**
Lewis M. Terman: Pioneer in Educational Testing. Trade Paper.
New York University Press. New York, NY. 1990. 254p. The
American Social Experience Ser., No. 12 ISBN:0-8147-5452-X,
ISBN13: 978-0-8147-5452-8. Dewey:153.9/3/0924 B.
LCCN:88-012274.
Audience: **l,u,f.** *Choice, 1989.*

Mook, Douglas   **BF198**
Classic Experiments in Psychology. Cloth Text. Greenwood
Publishing Group, Inc. Portsmouth, NH. 2004. 384p.
ISBN:0-313-31821-2, ISBN13: 978-0-313-31821-4.
Dewey:150/.72/4. LCCN:2004-023845.
Audience: **g,l,u.** *Choice, 2005.*

Nicholson, Ian A. M.   **BF109.A54N53 2003**
Inventing Personality: Gordon Allport and the Science of
Selfhood. Trade Cloth. American Psychological Association.
Washington, DC. 2002. x, 301p. ISBN:1-55798-929-X, ISBN13:
978-1-55798-929-1. Dewey:155.2/092. LCCN:2002-033217.
Audience: **u,f.** *Choice, 2003.*

Noll, Richard   **BF109.J8N65 1997**
The Jung Cult: Origins of a Charismatic Movement. Trade
Paper. Simon & Schuster. New York, NY. 1997. 416p.
ISBN:0-684-83423-5, ISBN13: 978-0-684-83423-8.
Dewey:150.1/954. LCCN:97-009823.
Audience: **u,f.**

Parkes, Graham   **BF109.N54P37 1995**
Composing the Soul: Reaches of Nietzsche's Psychology. Trade
Cloth. University of Chicago Press. Chicago, IL. 1994. 496p.
ISBN:0-226-64686-6, ISBN13: 978-0-226-64686-2. Dewey:193.
LCCN:94-012479.
Audience: **u,f.** *Choice, 1995.*

Pattie, Frank A.   **RZ430.P38 1994**
Mesmer and Animal Magnetism: A Chapter in the History of
Medicine. Ellen Walker (Designed by), Ernest R. Hilgard
(Foreword by), Louis J. West (Introduction by). Trade Cloth.
Edmonston Publishing, Inc. Hamilton, NY. 1994. 316p.
ISBN:0-9622393-5-6, ISBN13: 978-0-9622393-5-9.
Dewey:615.8/512/092 B. LCCN:93-041168.
Audience: **g,l,u,f.** *Choice, 1994.*

Petocz, Agnes   **BF109.F74 P48 1999**
Freud, Psychoanalysis and Symbolism. Trade Cloth. Cambridge University Press. New York, NY. 1999. 296p. ISBN:0-521-59152-X, ISBN13: 978-0-521-59152-2. Dewey:150.1952. LCCN:98-039047.

Audience: **u,f.** *Choice, 2000.*

Pickren, Wade E. &   **BF105.E87 2002**
  Dewsbury, Donald A. (Editors)
Evolving Perspectives on the History of Psychology. Paper Text. American Psychological Association. Washington, DC. 2002. 608p. ISBN:1-55798-882-X, ISBN13: 978-1-55798-882-9. Dewey:150/.9. LCCN:2001-045909.

Audience: **u,f.** *Choice, 2002.*

Popplestone, John A. &   **E702**
  McPherson, Marion White
An Illustrated History of American Psychology. Ed. 2. Trade Cloth. University of Akron Press, The. Akron, OH. 1999. 222p. ISBN:1-884836-39-9, ISBN13: 978-1-884836-39-8. Dewey:150/0.973.

Audience: **g,l,u.**

Robinson, Daniel N.   **BF81.R65 1995**
An Intellectual History of Psychology. Ed. 3. Trade Paper. University of Wisconsin Press. Chicago, IL. 1995. 392p. ISBN:0-299-14844-0, ISBN13: 978-0-299-14844-7. Dewey:150/.9. LCCN:95-005697.

Audience: **u,f.**

Robinson, Daniel N.   **BF103**
Toward a Science of Human Nature: Aspirations of Nineteenth Century Psychology. Trade Cloth. Columbia University Press. New York, NY. 1982. 258p. ISBN:0-231-05174-3, ISBN13: 978-0-231-05174-3. Dewey:150/.1. LCCN:81-038458.

Audience: **u,f.** *B*

Robinson, Daniel N.   **K5077.R63 1996**
Wild Beasts and Idle Humors: The Insanity Defense from Antiquity to the Present. Trade Cloth. Harvard University Press. Cambridge, MA. 1996. 320p. ISBN:0-674-95289-8, ISBN13: 978-0-674-95289-8. Dewey:346/.0138. LCCN:96-005644.

Audience: **g,l,u,f.** *Choice, 1997.*

Roudinesco, Elizabeth   **BF109.L28R6613 1997**
Jacques Lacan: His Life and Work. Barbara Bray (Translator). Cloth Text. Columbia University Press. New York, NY. 1997. 464p. European Perspectives, :Social Thought and Culturall Criticism Ser. ISBN:0-231-10146-5, ISBN13: 978-0-231-10146-2. Dewey:[B]. LCCN:96-030125.

Audience: **u,f.** *Choice, 1997.*

Rychlak, Joseph F.   **BF121.R93 2003**
The Human Image and Postmodern America. Trade Cloth. American Psychological Association. Washington, DC. 2003. 175p. ISBN:1-55798-986-9, ISBN13: 978-1-55798-986-4. Dewey:150. LCCN:2002-015069.

Audience: **u,f.** *Choice, 2003.*

Scarborough, Elizabeth Ann   **BF109.A1**
  & Furumoto, Laurel
Untold Lives: The First Generation of American Women Psychologists. Trade Paper. Columbia University Press. New York, NY. 1989. 236p. ISBN:0-231-05155-7, ISBN13: 978-0-231-05155-2. Dewey:150/.88042. LCCN:86-020715.

Audience: **g,l,u,f.** *Choice, 1987.*

Schur, Max   **BF 109 F74 S38**
Freud: Living and Dying. Trade Paper. International Universities Press, Inc. Madison, CT. 1972. 587p. ISBN:0-8236-8052-5, ISBN13: 978-0-8236-8052-8. Dewey:150/.19/52. LCCN:71-143379.

Audience: **g,u,f.**

Sheehy, Noel   **BF109.A1S49 2003**
Fifty Key Thinkers in Psychology. Paper over Boards. Routledge. New York, NY. 2003. 288p. Fifty Key Thinkers Ser. ISBN:0-415-16774-4, ISBN13: 978-0-415-16774-1. Dewey:150/.92/2. LCCN:2003-007402.

Audience: **g,l,u.**

Sheehy, Noel (Editor), et al.   **BF109.A1**
Biographical Dictionary of Psychology. Antony J. Chapman & Wendy A. Conroy (Editors). Trade Paper. Routledge. New York, NY. 2002. 704p. World Reference Ser. ISBN:0-415-28561-5, ISBN13: 978-0-415-28561-2. Dewey:150.9/22.

Audience: **g,l,u,f.** *Choice, 1997.*

Shimizu, Hidetada &   **BF108.J3 J36 2001**
  Levine, Robert A. (Editors)
Japanese Frames of Mind: Cultural Perspectives on Human Development. Trade Cloth. Cambridge University Press. New York, NY. 2002. 300p. ISBN:0-521-78159-0, ISBN13: 978-0-521-78159-6. Dewey:155.8952. LCCN:2001-025172.

Audience: **u,f.** *Choice, 2002.*

Simonton, Dean Keith   **BF109.A1S56 2002**
Great Psychologists and Their Times: Scientific Insights into Psychology's History. Trade Cloth. American Psychological Association. Washington, DC. 2002. xii, 550p. ISBN:1-55798-896-X, ISBN13: 978-1-55798-896-6. Dewey:150/.92/2. LCCN:2001-055302.

Audience: **u,f.** *Choice, 2002.*

Sternberg, Robert J.   **BF105.A46 2003**
  (Editor)
The Anatomy of Impact: What Makes the Great Works of Psychology Great. Trade Cloth. American Psychological Association. Washington, DC. 2003. 272p. ISBN:1-55798-980-X, ISBN13: 978-1-55798-980-2. Dewey:150/.9. LCCN:2002-151478.

Audience: **u,f.** *Choice, 2003.*

Wade, Nicholas   **BF241.W3195 2005**
Perception and Illusion: Historical Perspectives. E-Book. Springer. New York, NY. 2005. xiv, 250p. Library of the History of Psychological Theories ISBN:0-387-22723-7, ISBN13: 978-0-387-22723-8. Dewey:152.1/4. LCCN:2004-056968.

Audience: **u,f.**

Wittels, Fritz   **BF109.W58A3 1995**
Freud and the Child Woman: The Memoirs of Fritz Wittels. Edward Timms (Editor). Cloth over Boards. Yale University Press. Cumberland, RI. 1996. 200p. ISBN:0-300-06485-3, ISBN13: 978-0-300-06485-8. Dewey:150.19/5/092 B. LCCN:95-021047.

Audience: **u,f.** *Choice, 1996.*

Zusne, Leonard   **BF109.A1 Z85 1984**
Biographical Dictionary of Psychology. Cloth Text. Greenwood Publishing Group, Inc. Portsmouth, NH. 1984. 563p. ISBN:0-313-24027-2, ISBN13: 978-0-313-24027-0. Dewey:150/.92/2. LCCN:83-018326.

Audience: **g,l,u,f.** *B*

Psychometrics, Statistics, and Methodology

Anastasi, Anne & Urbina, Susana   BF176.A5 1997
Psychological Testing. Ed. 7. Cloth Text. Prentice Hall PTR.
Upper Saddle River, NJ. 1996. 721p. ISBN:0-02-303085-2,
ISBN13: 978-0-02-303085-7. Dewey:150.2/87.
LCCN:96-041155.

Audience: **u,f.**

Bootzin, Richard R. & McKnight, Patrick E.   RC467.8.S8 2006
Strengthening Research Methodology: Psychological
Measurement and Evaluation. Trade Cloth. American
Psychological Association. Washington, DC. 2006. xix, 299p.
ISBN:1-59147-324-1, ISBN13: 978-1-59147-324-4.
Dewey:616.89/0072. LCCN:2005-020255.

Audience: **l,u.**

Cliff, Norman & Keats, John A.   BF39.C525 2003
Ordinal Measurement in the Behavioral Sciences. Cloth over
Boards. Lawrence Erlbaum Associates, Inc. Mahwah, NJ. 2002.
240p. The Applied Psychology Ser. ISBN:0-8058-2093-0,
ISBN13: 978-0-8058-2093-5. Dewey:150/.28/7.
LCCN:2002-727168.

Audience: **u,f.**

Coombs, Clyde Hamilton   BF39.C62
Mathematical Psychology; an Elementary Introduction. Trade
Cloth. Prentice-Hall. Upper Saddle, NJ. 1970. xi, 419p.
ISBN:0-13-562157-7, ISBN13: 978-0-13-562157-8.
Dewey:150/.1/51. LCCN:73-101580.

Audience: **u,f.**

Coombs, Clyde Hamilton   BF0039.C64
A Theory of Psychological Scaling. Trade Paper. Books on
Demand. Ann Arbor, MI. 107p. Engineering Research Institute
Bulletin Ser., No. 34 ISBN:0-598-91301-7, ISBN13:
978-0-598-91301-2. Dewey:150.15195. LCCN:52-062777.

Audience: **u,f.**

Eid, Michael & Diener, Ed   BF39.H2644 2005
Handbook of Multimethod Measurement in Psychology. Trade
Cloth. American Psychological Association. Washington, DC.
2005. 736p. ISBN:1-59147-318-7, ISBN13: 978-1-59147-318-3.
Dewey:150/.28/7. LCCN:2005-015922.

Audience: **u,f.**

Glass, Gene V. & Hopkins, Kenneth D.   LB2846.G55 1995
Statistical Methods in Education and Psychology. Ed. 3. Cloth
Text. Allyn & Bacon, Inc. Boston, MA. 1995. 608p.
ISBN:0-205-14212-5, ISBN13: 978-0-205-14212-5. Dewey:519.
LCCN:95-013309.

Audience: **l,u.**

Graham, John R. & Naglieri, Jack A. (Editors)   BF121.H1955 2004
Handbook of Psychology, Assessment Psychology, Vol. 10.
Irving B. Weiner (Editor-In-Chief). Trade Paper. John Wiley &
Sons, Inc. Hoboken, NJ. 2004. 630p. ISBN:0-471-66673-4,
ISBN13: 978-0-471-66673-8. Dewey:155.93.

Audience: **u,f.**

Guilford, J. P.   BF39
Psychometric Methods. Paper Text. Textbook Publishers.
Temecula, CA. 2003. 597p. ISBN:0-7581-8574-X, ISBN13:
978-0-7581-8574-7. Dewey:152.8.

Audience: **u,f.**

Lewis, Don   BF39
Quantitative Methods in Psychology. Paper Text. Textbook
Publishers. Temecula, CA. 2003. 558p. ISBN:0-7581-8568-5,
ISBN13: 978-0-7581-8568-6. Dewey:150.7253.

Audience: **u,f.**

Michell, Joel   BF39 .M545 1999
Measurement in Psychology: A Critical History of a
Methodological Concept. Lorraine Daston, Dorothy Ross,
Quentin Skinner & James Tully (Contribution by). Trade Cloth.
Cambridge University Press. New York, NY. 1999. 266p. Ideas
in Context Ser., No. 53 ISBN:0-521-62120-8, ISBN13:
978-0-521-62120-5. Dewey:150/.28/7. LCCN:98-039566.

Audience: **u,f.**

Nunnally, Jum C. & Bernstein, Ira H.   BF39.N8 1994
Psychometric Theory. Ed. 3. Cloth Text. McGraw-Hill Higher
Education. Burr Ridge, IL. 1994. 736p. Series in Social
Psychology ISBN:0-07-047849-X, ISBN13: 978-0-07-047849-7.
Dewey:150/.28/7. LCCN:93-022756.

Audience: **u,f.**

Schiffman, Susan, et al.   BF39.S33
Introduction to Multidimensional Scaling: Theory, Methods, and
Applications. M. Lance Reynolds & Forrest W. Young
(Authors). Trade Cloth. Elsevier Science & Technology Books.
Saint Louis, MO. 1981. 440p. ISBN:0-12-624350-6, ISBN13:
978-0-12-624350-5. Dewey:001.4/226. LCCN:81-010842.

Audience: **u,f.**

Thorndike, Edward Lee   HA33
An Introduction to the Theory of Mental and Social
Measurements. Robert H. Wozniak (Editor). Trade Cloth.
Continuum International Publishing Group, Ltd. London, 228p.
Classics in Psychology Ser. ISBN:1-85506-689-0, ISBN13:
978-1-85506-689-2. Dewey:150.287.

Audience: **u,f.**

Torgerson, Warren S.   BF39 .T6
Theory and Methods of Scaling. Paper Text. Textbook
Publishers. Temecula, CA. 2003. 460p. ISBN:0-7581-0471-5,
ISBN13: 978-0-7581-0471-7. Dewey:152.83.

Audience: **u,f.**

Zenderland, Leila   BF431 .Z46 1998
Measuring Minds: Henry Herbert Goddard and the Origins of
American Intelligence Testing. Mitchell G. Ash & William R.
Woodward (Contribution by). Cloth Text. Cambridge University
Press. New York, NY. 1998. 478p. Cambridge Studies in the
History of Psychology ISBN:0-521-44373-3, ISBN13:
978-0-521-44373-9. Dewey:153.9/3/097309041.
LCCN:97-006101.

Audience: **u,f.** *Choice, 1998.*

Psychometrics, Statistics, and Methodology > Tests and Testing

✓ **Aiken, Lewis R. &**   **BF176.A48 2006**
  Groth-Marnat, Gary
Psychological Testing and Assessment. Ed. 12. Trade Cloth.
Allyn & Bacon, Inc. Boston, MA. 2005. 552p.
ISBN:0-205-45742-8, ISBN13: 978-0-205-45742-7.
Dewey:150/.28/7. LCCN:2005-045343.

                              Audience: **l,u.**

1985 **American Psychological**   **LB3051.A693**
  Association Staff
Standards for Educational and Psychological Tests Prepared by a
Joint Committee of the American Psychological Association,
American Educational Research Association and National
Council on Measurement in Education. Trade Paper. Books on
Demand. Ann Arbor, MI. 78p. ISBN:0-7837-0495-X, ISBN13:
978-0-7837-0495-1. Dewey:371.26. LCCN:74-075734.

                         Audience: **g,l,u,f.**

✓ **Boudett, Kathryn Parker**   **LB2822.75**
  (Editor), et al.
Data Wise: A Step-by-Step Guide to Using Assessment Results
to Improve Teaching and Learning. Elizabeth A. City & Richard
J. Murnane (Editors), Tom Buffett, Jonna Sullivan Casey, Sarah
E. Fiarman, Shannon T. Hodge, Melissa Kagle, Jane E. King,
Daniel M. Koretz, Gerardo Martinez, Ethan Mintz, Liane
Moody, Jennifer Price, Mary Russo, Nancy S. Sharkey, Jennifer
L. Steele, Mark B. Teoh & John B. Willett (Contribution by).
Paper Text. Harvard Education Publishing Group (H E P G).
Cambridge, MA. 2005. 212p. ISBN:1-891792-67-9, ISBN13:
978-1-891792-67-0. Dewey:378.125. LCCN:2005-931449.

             Audience: **l,u.** *Choice, 2006.*

Bryon, Mike   **HF5549.5.E5**
Psychometric Tests, Vol. 1. CD-ROM. Kogan Page, Ltd.
London, 2002. Testing Ser. ISBN:0-7494-3757-X, ISBN13:
978-0-7494-3757-2. Dewey:153.94.

                       Audience: **g,l,u,f.**

✓ **Buros, Institute**   **BF176**
Tests in Print VII. Linda L. Murphy & Barbara S. Plake
(Editors). Trade Cloth. Buros Institute of Mental Measurements.
Lincoln, NE. 2006. 1200p. ISBN:0-910674-59-0, ISBN13:
978-0-910674-59-1. Dewey:150.287.

                       Audience: **g,l,u,f.**

✓ **Condon, Margaret E., et al.**   **BF176.T47 2002**
Exercises in Psychological Testing. Lisa Hollis-Sawyer &
George C. Thornton (Authors). Trade Paper. Allyn & Bacon,
Inc. Boston, MA. 2001. 302p. ISBN:0-205-33787-2, ISBN13:
978-0-205-33787-3. Dewey:150/.28/7. LCCN:2002-282687.

                            Audience: **l,u.**

✓ **Downing, Steven &**   **LB3051.H31987 2006**
  Haladyna, Thomas M. (Editors)
Handbook of Test Development. Jamal Abedi, Rebecca
Baranowski, Douglas D. Becker, Chad W. Buckendahl, Dan
Campion & Gregory J. Cizek (Contribution by). Trade Paper.
Lawrence Erlbaum Associates, Inc. Mahwah, NJ. 2006. 792p.
ISBN:0-8058-5265-4, ISBN13: 978-0-8058-5265-3.
Dewey:371.26/1. LCCN:2005-030881.

                            Audience: **u,f.**

✓ **Eid, Michael & Diener, Ed**   **BF39.H2644 2005**
Handbook of Multimethod Measurement in Psychology. Trade
Cloth. American Psychological Association. Washington, DC.
2005. 736p. ISBN:1-59147-318-7, ISBN13: 978-1-59147-318-3.
Dewey:150/.28/7. LCCN:2005-015922.

                            Audience: **u,f.**

✓ **Embretson, Susan E. &**   **BF39.N44 1998**
  Hershberger, Scott L. (Editors)
The New Rules of Measurement: What Every Psychologist and
Educator Should Know. Cloth over Boards. Lawrence Erlbaum
Associates, Inc. Mahwah, NJ. 1999. 272p. ISBN:0-8058-2860-5,
ISBN13: 978-0-8058-2860-3. Dewey:150/.28/7.
LCCN:98-024513.

                            Audience: **u,f.**

✓ **Embretson, Susan E. &**   **BF39.E495 2000**
  Reise, Steven P.
~~Psychometric Methods~~: Item Response Theory for Psychologists.
Cloth over Boards. Lawrence Erlbaum Associates, Inc. Mahwah,
NJ. 2000. 376p. Multivariate Applications Ser.
ISBN:0-8058-2818-4, ISBN13: 978-0-8058-2818-4.
Dewey:150/.28/7. LCCN:99-048454.

                            Audience: **u,f.**

✓ **Gopaul-McNicol,**   **RC473.P79G673 2002**
  Sharon-Ann & Armour-Thomas, Eleanor
ⓔ Assessment and Culture: Psychological Tests with Minority
Populations. E-Book. NetLibrary, Inc. Boulder, CO. 2002.
ISBN:0-585-46910-5, ISBN13: 978-0-585-46910-2.
Dewey:616.89/0089.

                            Audience: **u,f.**

✓ **Greene, Lord, et al.**   *tests*   **BF39.G725 2005**
Learning to Use Statistical ~~Skills~~ in Psychology. Ed. 3. Judith
Greene & Manuela D'Oliveira (Authors). Paper Text.
McGraw-Hill Education. Maidenhead, 2005. 232p.
ISBN:0-335-21680-3, ISBN13: 978-0-335-21680-2.
Dewey:150.727.

                            Audience: **l,u.**

✓ **Gregory, Robert J.**   **BF176.G74 2004**
Psychological Testing: History, Principles, and Applications. Ed.
4. Trade Paper. Allyn & Bacon, Inc. Boston, MA. 2003. 720p.
ISBN:0-205-35472-6, ISBN13: 978-0-205-35472-6.
Dewey:150.28/7. LCCN:2003-051829.

                            Audience: **l,u.**

✓ **Hambleton, Ronald K.**   **LB3060.65.A33 2005**
  (Editor), et al.
Adapting Educational and Psychological Tests for Cross-Cultural
Assessment. Peter F. Merenda & Charles D. Spielberger
(Editors), Ronald K. Hambleton, Peter F. Merenda, Charles D.
Spielberger, Michal Beller, Catherine Brown, James N. Butcher,
Linda L. Cook & Fritz Drasgow (Contribution by). Cloth over
Boards. Lawrence Erlbaum Associates, Inc. Mahwah, NJ. 2004.
392p. The Applied Psychology Ser. ISBN:0-8058-3025-1,
ISBN13: 978-0-8058-3025-5. Dewey:371.26/1.
LCCN:2003-060545.

                            Audience: **u,f.**

✓ **Heiman, Gary W.**   **BF76.5.H435 2001**
Understanding Research Methods and Statistics: An Integrated
Introduction for Psychology. Ed. 2. Cloth Text. Houghton
Mifflin College Division. Boston, MA. 2000. 779p.
ISBN:0-618-04304-7, ISBN13: 978-0-618-04304-0.
Dewey:150/.7/2. LCCN:00-133834.

                            Audience: **l,u.**

Hogan, Thomas P.   **LB3051.H682 2007**
Educational Assessment. Trade Paper. John Wiley & Sons, Inc. Hoboken, NJ. 2005. 448p. ISBN:0-471-47248-4, ISBN13: 978-0-471-47248-3. Dewey:371.26. LCCN:2005-015355.

Audience: **u,f.**

Howell, Scott L. & Hricko,   **LB3060.55.O65 2006**
   Mary
Online Assessment and Measurement: Case Studies from Higher Education, K-12 and Corporate. Saddle Stitched, Cloth over Boards. Idea Group Publishing. Hershey, PA. 2005. 280p. ISBN:1-59140-720-6, ISBN13: 978-1-59140-720-1. Dewey:371.26/0285. LCCN:2005-013552.

Audience: **u,f.**

Irvine, Sidney H. &   **LB3060.65.I84 2002**
   Kyllonen, Patrick C. (Editors)
Item Generation for Test Development. Russell G. Almond, David Bartram, Isaac I. Bejar & Randy Elliot Bennett (Contribution by). Cloth over Boards. Lawrence Erlbaum Associates, Inc. Mahwah, NJ. 2002. 440p. ISBN:0-8058-3441-9, ISBN13: 978-0-8058-3441-3. Dewey:371.26/1. LCCN:2002-283146.

Audience: **u,f.**

Janda, Louis   **BF176.J35 1998**
Psychological Testing: Theory and Applications. Ed. 1. Trade Paper. Allyn & Bacon, Inc. Boston, MA. 1997. 455p. ISBN:0-205-19434-6, ISBN13: 978-0-205-19434-6. Dewey:150/.28/7. LCCN:97-033720.

Audience: **l,u.**

Keyser, Daniel J. &   **BF176**
   Sweetland, Richard C. (Editors)
Test Critiques, Vol. X. Trade Cloth. Thomson Gale. Farmington Hills, MI. 1994. 700p. ISBN:0-89079-596-7, ISBN13: 978-0-89079-596-5. Dewey:150.28.

Audience: **u,f.** *Choice, 1986.*

Kline, Theresa J. B.   **BF176.K583 2005**
Psychological Testing: A Practical Approach to Design and Evaluation. Cloth Text. SAGE Publications, Inc. Thousand Oaks, CA. 2005. 368p. ISBN:1-4129-0544-3, ISBN13: 978-1-4129-0544-2. Dewey:150/.28/7. LCCN:2004-022907.

Audience: **u,f.**

Kolen, Michael J. &   **LB3060.77.K65 2004**
   Brennan, Robert L.
Test Equating, Scaling, and Linking: Methods and Practices. Ed. 2. Trade Cloth. Springer. New York, NY. 2004. XXVI, 548p. Statistics in Social Sciences and Public Policy Ser. ISBN:0-387-40086-9, ISBN13: 978-0-387-40086-0. Dewey:371.27/1. LCCN:2004-045617.

Audience: **u,f.**

Maydeu-Olivares, Albert &   **BF39**
   McArdle, John J. (Editors)
Contemporary Psychometrics: A Festschrift for Roderick P. Mcdonald. Harvey Goldstein, David Grayson & Lisa L. Harlow (Contribution by). Cloth over Boards. Lawrence Erlbaum Associates, Inc. Mahwah, NJ. 2005. 600p. Multivariate Applications Book Ser. ISBN:0-8058-4608-5, ISBN13: 978-0-8058-4608-9. Dewey:150/.1/5195. LCCN:2005-003324.

Audience: **u,f.**

McIntire, Sandra A. &   **PS3334.W39**
   Miller, Leslie A.
Foundations of Psychological Testing. Trade Paper.

McGraw-Hill Higher Education. Burr Ridge, IL. 1999. ISBN:0-07-233596-3, ISBN13: 978-0-07-233596-5. Dewey:150/.28/7.

Audience: **u,f.**

Messick, Samuel   **BF176.U64 2002**
The Role of Constructs in Psychological and Educational Measurement. Henry I. Braun, Douglas Northrop Jackson & David E. Wiley (Editors). Cloth over Boards. Lawrence Erlbaum Associates, Inc. Mahwah, NJ. 2001. 336p. ISBN:0-8058-3798-1, ISBN13: 978-0-8058-3798-8. Dewey:150/.28/7. LCCN:2001-042311.

Audience: **u,f.**

Murphy, Kevin R. &   **BF176.M87 2005**
   Davidshofer, Charles O.
Psychological Testing: Principles and Applications. Ed. 6. Cloth Text. Prentice Hall PTR. Upper Saddle River, NJ. 2004. 624p. ISBN:0-13-189172-3, ISBN13: 978-0-13-189172-2. Dewey:150/.28/7. LCCN:2004-013297.

Audience: **l,u.**

Murphy, Linda L. (Editor),   **Z5814.E9; LB3051**
   et al.
Tests in Print, No. IV. Jane Close Conoley & James C. Impara (Editors). Cloth Text. Buros Institute of Mental Measurements. Lincoln, NE. 1994. 1473p. ISBN:0-910674-53-1, ISBN13: 978-0-910674-53-9. Dewey:016.3712/6; 371.26.

Audience: **g,l,u,f.**

Newmark, Charles S.   **BF176.M35 2005**
Major Psychological Assessment Instruments. Ed. 2. Trade Cloth. PRO-ED, Inc. Austin, TX. 2005. ISBN:1-4164-0007-9, ISBN13: 978-1-4164-0007-3. Dewey:150/.28/7. LCCN:2004-053410.

Audience: **l,u.**

Osterlind, Steven J.   **BF39.O82 2005**
Modern Measurement: Theory, Principles, and Applications of Mental Appraisal. Cloth Text. Prentice Hall PTR. Upper Saddle River, NJ. 2005. 512p. ISBN:0-13-025590-4, ISBN13: 978-0-13-025590-7. Dewey:150/.28/7. LCCN:2005-004717.

Audience: **u,f.**

Robert Gregory Staff   **BF176 .G74**
Psychological Testing: History Principals and Applications. Ed. 3. Trade Cloth. Allyn & Bacon, Inc. Boston, MA. 1999. ISBN:0-205-31487-2, ISBN13: 978-0-205-31487-4. Dewey:150.28/7.

Audience: **l,u.**

Rust, John & Golombok,   **BF39.R85 1999**
   Susan
Modern Psychometrics: The Science of Psychological Assessment. Ed. 2. UK-B Format Paperback. Routledge. New York, NY. 1999. 256p. International Library of Philosophy, Psychology, and Scientific Method ISBN:0-415-20341-4, ISBN13: 978-0-415-20341-8. Dewey:150/.28/7. LCCN:98-047962.

Audience: **u,f.**

Spies, Robert A. (Editor),   **Z5814.P8**
   et al.
Mental Measurements Yearbook, Vol. 16. Ed. 16. Barbara S. Plake & Linda L. Murphy (Editors). Trade Cloth. Buros Institute of Mental Measurements. Lincoln, NE. 2005. 1100p.

ISBN:0-910674-58-2, ISBN13: 978-0-910674-58-4. Dewey:16.3714.

Audience: **g,l,u,f.**

Stafford, Mary E. &   **LB3051.K87 2006**
  Robinson-Kurpius, Sharon E.
Testing and Measurement: A User-Friendly Guide. Paper Text. SAGE Publications, Inc. Thousand Oaks, CA. 2005. 200p. ISBN:1-4129-1002-1, ISBN13: 978-1-4129-1002-6. Dewey:371.26/071/1. LCCN:2005-008152.

Audience: **l,u.**

Thompson, Bruce   **BF176.T45 2002**
Score Reliability: Contemporary Thinking on Reliability Issues. Paper Text. SAGE Publications, Inc. Thousand Oaks, CA. 2002. 296p. ISBN:0-7619-2626-7, ISBN13: 978-0-7619-2626-9. Dewey:150/.28/7. LCCN:2002-006881.

Audience: **u,f.**

Thorndike, Robert M.   **LB1131.M433 2004**
Measurement and Evaluation in Psychology and Education. Ed. 7. Trade Cloth. Prentice Hall PTR. Upper Saddle River, NJ. 2004. 528p. ISBN:0-13-019998-2, ISBN13: 978-0-13-019998-0. Dewey:371.2/6. LCCN:2004-007704.

Audience: **u.**

Tokunaga, Howard &
  Keppel, Geoffrey
Basic Introduction to Statistics for the Behavioral Sciences. Cloth Text. W. H. Freeman & Company. New York, NY. 2005. ISBN:0-7167-3320-X, ISBN13: 978-0-7167-3320-1.

Audience: **l,u.**

Urbina, Susana   **BF176.U73 2004**
e Essentials of Psychological Testing. E-Book. John Wiley & Sons, Inc. Hoboken, NJ. 2004. 304p. Essentials of Behavioral Science Ser. ISBN:0-471-67901-1, ISBN13: 978-0-471-67901-1. Dewey:150/.28/7.

Audience: **l,u.**

Walz, Garry Richard &   **LB3051.A79 2005**
  Bleuer, Jeanne
Assessment: Issues and Challenges for the Millennium. ERIC Counseling and Student Services Clearinghouse Staff (Contribution by). Trade Paper. PRO-ED, Inc. Austin, TX. 2005. ISBN:1-4164-0013-3, ISBN13: 978-1-4164-0013-4. Dewey:371.26. LCCN:2004-057282.

Audience: **g,l,u,f.**

Psychometrics, Statistics, and Methodology > Developmental Scales and Schedules

Andrews, Jac J. W. (Volume   **LB3051.H31985 2001**
  Editor), et al.
Handbook of Psychoeducational Assessment: A Practical Handbook. Henry L. Janzen & Donald H. Saklofske (Volume Editors), Gary D. Phye (Contribution by). Trade Cloth. Elsevier Science & Technology Books. Saint Louis, MO. 2002. 512p. Educational Psychology Ser. ISBN:0-12-058570-7, ISBN13: 978-0-12-058570-0. Dewey:370.15. LCCN:2001-086089.

Audience: **u,f.** *Choice, 2002.*

Bracken, Bruce A. (Editor)   **LB3051**
The Psychoeducational Assessment of Preschool Children. Ed. 3. Cloth over Boards. Lawrence Erlbaum Associates, Inc. Mahwah, NJ. 2004. 496p. ISBN:0-8058-5327-8, ISBN13: 978-0-8058-5327-8. Dewey:372.12/6.

Audience: **u,f.**

DelCarmen-Wiggins,   **RJ503.5.H375 2004**
  Rebecca & Carter, Alice (Editors)
Handbook of Infant, Toddler, and Preschool Mental Health Assessment. Trade Cloth. Oxford University Press, Inc. New York, NY. 2004. 552p. ISBN:0-19-514438-4, ISBN13: 978-0-19-514438-3. Dewey:618.92/89075. LCCN:2003-024325.

Audience: **u,f.**

Flanagan, Dawn P. &   **BF431.C66 2005**
  Harrison, Patti L. (Editors)
Contemporary Intellectual Assessment: Theories, Tests and Issues. Ed. 2. Cloth over Boards. Guilford Publications, Inc. New York, NY. 2005. 667p. ISBN:1-59385-125-1, ISBN13: 978-1-59385-125-5. Dewey:153.9/3. LCCN:2004-016931.

Audience: **u,f.**

Lidz, Carol S.   **BF722.3.L53 2002**
Early Childhood Assessment. Trade Cloth. John Wiley & Sons, Inc. Hoboken, NJ. 2002. 313p. ISBN:0-471-41984-2, ISBN13: 978-0-471-41984-6. Dewey:155.42/3/0287. LCCN:2002-028827.

Audience: **u,f.**

Merrell, Kenneth W.   **BF722.M45 2002**
Behavioral, Social, and Emotional Assessment of Children and Adolescents. Ed. 2. Cloth over Boards. Lawrence Erlbaum Associates, Inc. Mahwah, NJ. 2002. 472p. ISBN:0-8058-3907-0, ISBN13: 978-0-8058-3907-4. Dewey:155.4/028/7. LCCN:2002-074235.

Audience: **u,f.**

Reynolds, Cecil R. &   **BF722.H33 2003**
  Kamphaus, Randy W. (Editors)
Handbook of Psychological and Educational Assessment of Children: Personality, Behavior and Context. Ed. 2. Cloth over Boards. Guilford Publications, Inc. New York, NY. 2003. 539p. ISBN:1-57230-884-2, ISBN13: 978-1-57230-884-8. Dewey:155.4/028/7. LCCN:2003-005957.

Audience: **u,f.**

Reynolds, Cecil R. &   **BF722.H33 2003**
  Kamphaus, Randy W. (Editors)
Handbook of Psychological and Educational Assessment of Children: Intelligence, Aptitude, and Achievement. Ed. 2. Cheryl N. Hendry (Translator). Cloth over Boards. Guilford Publications, Inc. New York, NY. 2003. 718p. ISBN:1-57230-883-4, ISBN13: 978-1-57230-883-1. Dewey:155.4/028/7. LCCN:2003-006119.

Audience: **u,f.**

Sattler, Jerome M.   **BF432.C48S28 2001**
Assessment of Children: Cognitive Applications. Ed. 4. Trade Cloth. Jerome M. Sattler Publisher, Inc. La Mesa, CA. 2001. xxvii, 931p. ISBN:0-9618209-7-7, ISBN13: 978-0-9618209-7-8. Dewey:155.4/1393. LCCN:00-192723.

Audience: **u,f.**

Sattler, Jerome M.   BF722.3.S38 2002
Assessment of Children: Behavioral and Clinical Applications. Ed. 4. Trade Cloth. Jerome M. Sattler Publisher, Inc. La Mesa, CA. 2002. xviii, 620p. ISBN:0-9618209-8-5, ISBN13: 978-0-9618209-8-5. Dewey:155.4. LCCN:2001-117982.
Audience: **u,f.**

Wodrich, David L.   BF722.W63 1997
Children's Psychological Testing: A Guide for Nonpsychologists. Ed. 3. Paper Text. Paul H. Brookes Publishing Company. Baltimore, MD. 1997. 416p. ISBN:1-55766-277-0, ISBN13: 978-1-55766-277-4. Dewey:155.4/028/7. LCCN:96-038720.
Audience: **g,l,u,f.**

Psychometrics, Statistics, and Methodology > Personality Scales and Inventories

Aiken, Lewis R.   BF698.4.A36 1999
Personality Assessment: Methods and Practices. Ed. 3. Trade Cloth. Hogrefe & Huber Publishers. Cambridge, MA. 1999. x, 524p. ISBN:0-88937-209-8, ISBN13: 978-0-88937-209-2. Dewey:155.2/8. LCCN:99-071723.
Audience: **u,f.**

Aiken, Lewis R.   BF176.A483 1997
Questionnaires and Inventories: Surveying Opinions and Assessing Personality. Ed. 1. Mixed Media. John Wiley & Sons, Inc. Hoboken, NJ. 1997. 319p. ISBN:0-471-16871-8, ISBN13: 978-0-471-16871-3. Dewey:150/.28/7. LCCN:96-053659.
Audience: **u,f.**

Aiken, Lewis R.   BF39.A43 1996
Rating Scales and Checklists: Evaluating Behavior, Personality, and Attitudes. Diskette, Trade Cloth. John Wiley & Sons, Inc. Hoboken, NJ. 1996. 320p. ISBN:0-471-12787-6, ISBN13: 978-0-471-12787-1. Dewey:004.1/2. LCCN:95-039106.
Audience: **u,f.**

Beutler, Larry E. &   BF698.4.I58 2003
Groth-Marnat, Gary
Integrative Assessment of Adult Personality. Ed. 2. Cloth over Boards. Guilford Publications, Inc. New York, NY. 2003. 508p. ISBN:1-57230-670-X, ISBN13: 978-1-57230-670-7. Dewey:155.2/8. LCCN:2003-001946.
Audience: **u,f.**

Craig, Robert J.   BF698.5.C73 1999
Interpreting Personality Tests: A Clinical Manual for the MMPI-2, MCMI-III, CPI-R, And 16PF. Trade Cloth. John Wiley & Sons, Inc. Hoboken, NJ. 1999. 272p. ISBN:0-471-34818-X, ISBN13: 978-0-471-34818-4. Dewey:155.2/83. LCCN:98-054152.
Audience: **l,u,f.**

Dana, Richard (Editor)   RC473.P79H36 2000
Handbook of Cross-Cultural and Multicultural Personality Assessment. Jim Allen, Anne Andronikof-Sanglade & Alejandro Avila Espada (Contribution by). Cloth over Boards. Lawrence Erlbaum Associates, Inc. Mahwah, NJ. 2000. 736p. Personality and Clinical Psychology Ser. ISBN:0-8058-2789-7, ISBN13: 978-0-8058-2789-7. Dewey:616.89/075/089. LCCN:99-030954.
Audience: **u,f.**

Goldberg, Lewis R.   BF698.4
☐ International Personality Item Pool.
http://ipip.ori.org/
Oregon Research Institute.
Audience: **l,u,f.**

**Hersen, Michel
(Editor-In-Chief), et al.**   BF176.C654 2003
Comprehensive Handbook of Psychological Assessment, Personality Assessment, Vol. 2. Mark J. Hilsenroth & Daniel L. Segal (Editor-In-Chiefs). Trade Cloth. John Wiley & Sons, Inc. Hoboken, NJ. 2003. 688p. ISBN:0-471-41612-6, ISBN13: 978-0-471-41612-8. Dewey:150.287. LCCN:2002-193381.
Audience: **g,l,u,f.**

Lanyon, Richard I. &   BF698.4.L34 1997
Goodstein, Leonard D.
Personality Assessment. Ed. 3. Trade Cloth. John Wiley & Sons, Inc. Hoboken, NJ. 1996. 448p. Wiley Series on Personality Processes, Vol. 179 ISBN:0-471-55562-2, ISBN13: 978-0-471-55562-9. Dewey:155.2/8. LCCN:96-018061.
Audience: **l,u,f.**

Paul, Annie Murphy   BF698.5.P38 2004
The Cult of Personality: How Personality Tests Are Leading Us to Miseducate Our Children, Mismanage Our Companies, and Misunderstand Ourselves. Trade Cloth. Simon & Schuster. New York, NY. 2004. 320p. ISBN:0-7432-4356-0, ISBN13: 978-0-7432-4356-8. Dewey:155.2/8. LCCN:2004-047186.
Audience: **g,l,u,f.** *Choice, 2005.*

Raad, Boele De & Perugini,   BF698.4.B52 2002
Marco (Editors)
Big Five Assessment. Trade Cloth. Hogrefe & Huber Publishers. Cambridge, MA. 2002. 504p. ISBN:0-88937-242-X, ISBN13: 978-0-88937-242-9. Dewey:155.2/8. LCCN:2002-102111.
Audience: **u,f.**

Revelle, William, Director   BF698.4
☐ The Personality Project.
http://www.personality-project.org/
Northwestern University, Department of Psychology.
Audience: **g,l,u,f.**

Robinson, John P. (Editor),   BF698.4.M38 1990
et al.
Measures of Personality and Social Psychological Attitudes, Vol. 1. Phillip R. Shaver & Lawrence S. Wrightsman (Editors). Paper Text. Elsevier Science & Technology Books. Saint Louis, MO. 1990. 753p. Measures of Personality and Social Psychological Attitudes Ser. ISBN:0-12-590244-1, ISBN13: 978-0-12-590244-1. Dewey:155.2/8. LCCN:90-000091.
Audience: **u,f.**

Wiggins, Jerry S.   BF698.4.W525 2003
Paradigms of Personality Assessment. Cloth over Boards. Guilford Publications, Inc. New York, NY. 2003. 386p. ISBN:1-57230-913-X, ISBN13: 978-1-57230-913-5. Dewey:155.2/8. LCCN:2003-005958.
Audience: **l,u,f.** *Choice, 2004.*

Wiggins, Jerry S.   BF698.4.W53 1988
Personality and Prediction: Principals of Personality Assessment. Library Binding. Krieger Publishing Company. Melbourne, FL. 1988. 704p. ISBN:0-89464-239-1, ISBN13: 978-0-89464-239-5. Dewey:155.2/8. LCCN:87-017348.
Audience: **l,u,f.**

Psychometrics, Statistics, and Methodology > Educational Measurement

American Educational   **LB3051.A693 1999**
Research Association; American Psychological Association; National Council on Measurement in Education; Joint Committee on Standards for Educational and Psychological Testing (U.S.)
Standards for Educational and Psychological Testing. American Educational Research Association. 1999. ISBN:0-935302-25-5, ISBN13: 978-0-935302-25-7.

Audience: **l,u,f.**

Gullickson, Arlen R.   **LB3051.J575 2003**
The Student Evaluation Standards: How to Improve Evaluations of Students. Trade Cloth. Corwin Press. Thousand Oaks, CA. 2002. 264p. 1-Off Ser. ISBN:0-7619-4662-4, ISBN13: 978-0-7619-4662-5. Dewey:371.26/4. LCCN:2002-014621.

Audience: **l,u,f.** *Choice, 2003.*

Linn, Robert L. (Editor)   **LB3051.E266**
Educational Measurement. Ed. 3. Trade Cloth. Macmillan Publishing Company, Inc. Old Tappan, NJ. 1988. 784p. Ace-Macmillan Series on Higher Education ISBN:0-318-41133-4, ISBN13: 978-0-318-41133-0. Dewey:371.2/6.

Audience: **u,f.**

Linn, Robert L. & Miller,   **LB3051.L545 2005**
M. David
Measurement and Assessment in Teaching. Ed. 9. Cloth Text. Prentice Hall PTR. Upper Saddle River, NJ. 2004. 576p. ISBN:0-13-113772-7, ISBN13: 978-0-13-113772-1. Dewey:371.26. LCCN:2004-044543.

Audience: **u.**

Mehrens, William A. &   **LB3051**
Lehmann, Irvin J.
Measurement and Evaluation in Education and Psychology. Ed. 3. Cloth Text. Thomson Wadsworth. Belmont, CA. 1991. 608p. ISBN:0-03-030407-5, ISBN13: 978-0-03-030407-1. Dewey:371.2/64. LCCN:91-150715.

Audience: **u.**

National Council on   **LB3051**
Measurement in Education
National Council on Measurement in Education. http://www.ncme.org/
National Council on Measurement in Education.

Audience: **l,u,f.**

Thorndike, Robert M.   **LB1131.M433 2004**
Measurement and Evaluation in Psychology and Education. Ed. 7. Trade Cloth. Prentice Hall PTR. Upper Saddle River, NJ. 2004. 528p. ISBN:0-13-019998-2, ISBN13: 978-0-13-019998-0. Dewey:371.2/6. LCCN:2004-007704.

Audience: **u.**

Psychometrics, Statistics, and Methodology > Consumer Opinion and Attitude Testing

Ajzen, Icek   **HM251**
Attitudes, Personality, and Behavior. Ed. 1. Cloth Text. Brooks/Cole. Pacific Grove, CA. 1988. 175p. ISBN:0-534-10948-9, ISBN13: 978-0-534-10948-6. Dewey:302.

Audience: **u,f.**

Association for Consumer   **HF5415.32**
Research
Association for Consumer Research. http://www.acrwebsite.org/

Audience: **u,f.**

Center for Customer Driven   **HF5415.32**
Quality, Purdue University
Center for Customer Driven Quality, Purdue University. http://www.ccdq.com/

Audience: **u,f.**

Earl, P. E. & Kemp, S.   **HF5415.32**
(Editors)
The Elgar Companion to Consumer Research and Economic Psychology. Trade Paper. Edward Elgar Publishing, Inc. Northampton, MA. 2002. 672p. ISBN:1-84376-060-6, ISBN13: 978-1-84376-060-3. Dewey:658.8/34. LCCN:98-038240.

Audience: **u,f.**

Fishbein, M. & Ajzen, Icek   **BF323.C5**
Understanding Attitudes and Predicting Social Behavior. Cloth Text. Prentice Hall PTR. Upper Saddle River, NJ. 1980. x, 278p. ISBN:0-13-936443-9, ISBN13: 978-0-13-936443-3. Dewey:301.1. LCCN:79-026063.

Audience: **u,f.**

Hogg, Margaret K. (Editor)   **HF5415.32**
Consumer Behavior: Research and Influences. Trade Cloth. SAGE Publications, Ltd. London, 2005. 1272p. Sage Library in Business and Management ISBN:1-4129-0841-8, ISBN13: 978-1-4129-0841-2. Dewey:658.8342. LCCN:2005-900845.

Audience: **u,f.**

Osgood, Charles E., et al.   **B840**
The Measurement of Meaning. George J. Suci & Percy H. Tannenbaum (Authors). Trade Paper. University of Illinois Press. Champaign, IL. 1967. 360p. ISBN:0-252-74539-6, ISBN13: 978-0-252-74539-3. Dewey:153.1. LCCN:56-005684.

Audience: **u,f.**

Human Experimental Psychology

Block, R. A. (Editor)   **BF468.C55 1990**
Cognitive Models of Psychological Time. Cloth Text. Lawrence Erlbaum Associates, Inc. Mahwah, NJ. 1990. 304p. ISBN:0-8058-0359-9, ISBN13: 978-0-8058-0359-4. Dewey:153.7/53. LCCN:89-037741.

Audience: **u,f.**

Bruner, Jerome S.   **BF455.B74**
Acts of Meaning: Four Lectures on Mind and Culture. Trade Paper. Harvard University Press. Cambridge, MA. 1990. 208p.

Jerusalem Lectures ISBN:0-674-00361-6, ISBN13:
978-0-674-00361-3. Dewey:150.
Audience: **g,l,u,f.** *Choice, 1991.*

Caterette, Edward C.   **BF201.P47 1998**
(Editor), et al.
Perception and Cognition at Century's End: History, Philosophy,
Theory. Ed. 2. Morton P. Friedman & Julian Hochberg (Editors).
Trade Cloth. Elsevier Science & Technology Books. Saint
Louis, MO. 1998. 487p. Handbook of Perception and Cognition
Ser. ISBN:0-12-301160-4, ISBN13: 978-0-12-301160-2.
Dewey:153. LCCN:98-084439.
Audience: **u,f.**

Dalgleish, Tim & Power,   **BF531.H314 1999**
Mick (Editors)
Handbook of Cognition and Emotion. Trade Cloth. John Wiley
& Sons, Inc. Hoboken, NJ. 1999. 866p. ISBN:0-471-97836-1,
ISBN13: 978-0-471-97836-7. Dewey:153. LCCN:98-027102.
Audience: **u,f.**

Druckman, Daniel & Bjork,   **BF481**
Robert A.
In the Mind's Eye: Enhancing Human Performance. Trade
Paper. National Academies Press. Washington, DC. 1992. 304p.
ISBN:0-309-04747-1, ISBN13: 978-0-309-04747-0. Dewey:158.
Audience: **g,l,u,f.**

Gescheider, George A.   **QP431.G473 1997**
Psychophysics: The Fundamentals. Ed. 3. Cloth over Boards.
Lawrence Erlbaum Associates, Inc. Mahwah, NJ. 1997. 440p.
ISBN:0-8058-2281-X, ISBN13: 978-0-8058-2281-6.
Dewey:152.1. LCCN:96-041791.
Audience: **u,f.**

Goldstone, Robert L.   **BF311**
(Editor), et al.
Perceptual Learning: Advances in Research and Theory, Vol. 36.
Philippe G. Schyns & Douglas L. Medin (Editors). Trade Cloth.
Elsevier Science & Technology Books. Saint Louis, MO. 1997.
393p. The Psychology of Learning and Motivation Ser., Vol. 36
ISBN:0-12-543336-0, ISBN13: 978-0-12-543336-5. Dewey:153.
Audience: **u,f.**

Harnad, Stevan R. (Editor)   **BF445 .C38 1987**
Categorical Perception: The Groundwork of Cognition. Trade
Cloth. Cambridge University Press. New York, NY. 1987. 616p.
ISBN:0-521-26758-7, ISBN13: 978-0-521-26758-8. Dewey:153.
LCCN:86-034286.
Audience: **u,f.**

Hochberg, Julian E.   **BF241.H55 2006**
(Editor), et al.
In the Mind's Eye: Julian Hochberg on the Perception of
Pictures, Films, and the World. Mary A. Peterson, Barbara
Gillam & H. A. Sedgwick (Editors). Trade Cloth. Oxford
University Press, Inc. New York, NY. 2006. 704p.
ISBN:0-19-517691-X, ISBN13: 978-0-19-517691-9.
Dewey:152.14. LCCN:2005-019299.
Audience: **u,f.**

Holding, Dennis H. (Author,   **BF0295.H9**
Editor)
Human Skills. Ed. 2. Trade Paper. Books on Demand. Ann
Arbor, MI. 348p. Wiley Series on Studies in Human
Performance ISBN:0-598-03238-X, ISBN13:
978-0-598-03238-6. Dewey:152.3/5. LCCN:88-017410.
Audience: **l,u,f.**

Julesz, Bela, et al.   **QP475.J84 2006**
Foundations of Cyclopean Perception. Thomas V. Papathomas &
Flip Phillips (Authors). Trade Cloth. MIT Press. Cambridge,
MA. 2006. 428p. ISBN:0-262-10113-0, ISBN13:
978-0-262-10113-4. Dewey:152.1/4.
Audience: **u,f.**

Kessen, William (Editor),   **BF311.M445 1991**
et al.
Memories, Thoughts and Emotions: Essays in Honor of George
Mandler. Andrew Ortony & Fergus I. Craik (Editors). Cloth
Text. Lawrence Erlbaum Associates, Inc. Mahwah, NJ. 1991.
376p. ISBN:0-8058-0869-8, ISBN13: 978-0-8058-0869-8.
Dewey:153. LCCN:91-008792.
Audience: **u,f.**

Kintsch, Walter   **BF318**
Memory and Cognition. Trade Cloth. Krieger Publishing
Company. Melbourne, FL. 1982. 496p. ISBN:0-89874-403-2,
ISBN13: 978-0-89874-403-3. Dewey:153.1. LCCN:81-018648.
Audience: **l,u,f.**

Levine, Gustav &   **BF181.L48 1994**
Parkinson, Stanley
Experimental Methods in Psychology. Cloth Text. Lawrence
Erlbaum Associates, Inc. Mahwah, NJ. 1994. 496p.
ISBN:0-8058-1438-8, ISBN13: 978-0-8058-1438-5.
Dewey:150/.724. LCCN:93-035652.
Audience: **u,f.** *Choice, 1994.*

National Research Council   **BF481.L43 1994**
Staff
Learning, Remembering, Believing: Enhancing Human
Performance. Daniel Druckman & Robert A. Bjork (Editors).
Trade Cloth. National Academies Press. Washington, DC. 1994.
416p. ISBN:0-309-04993-8, ISBN13: 978-0-309-04993-1.
Dewey:153.1. LCCN:94-021350.
Audience: **g,l,u,f.** *Choice, 1995.*

Reed, Graham   **BF491.R43 1988**
The Psychology of Anomalous Experience. Ed. 2. Trade Paper.
Prometheus Books, Publishers. Amherst, NY. 1988. 213p.
Psychology Ser. ISBN:0-87975-435-4, ISBN13:
978-0-87975-435-8. Dewey:152. LCCN:88-061531.
Audience: **g,l,u.**

Schneider, David J.   **BF323.S63S36 2003**
The Psychology of Stereotyping. Cloth over Boards. Guilford
Publications, Inc. New York, NY. 2003. 704p. Distinguished
Contributions in Psychology Ser. ISBN:1-57230-929-6, ISBN13:
978-1-57230-929-6. Dewey:303.3/85. LCCN:2003-008819.
Audience: **l,u,f.** *Choice, 2004.*

Stevens, S. S.   **BF181**
Handbook of Experimental Psychology. Paper Text. Textbook
Publishers. Temecula, CA. 2003. xi, 1436p.
ISBN:0-7581-0347-6, ISBN13: 978-0-7581-0347-5. Dewey:150.
Audience: **u,f.**

Human Experimental Psychology >
Sensory Perception

Allport, Floyd Henry   **BF311**
Theories of Perception and the Concept of Structure: A Review
and Critical Analysis with an Introduction to a Dynamic. Paper

Text. Textbook Publishers. Temecula, CA. 2003. 709p.
ISBN:0-7581-0489-8, ISBN13: 978-0-7581-0489-2.
Dewey:153.7/33.

Audience: **u,f.**

Bolles, Robert C. (Editor)   **BF261.H43 1991**
Hedonics of Taste. Trade Cloth. Lawrence Erlbaum Associates,
Inc. Mahwah, NJ. 1991. 224p. ISBN:0-8058-0366-1, ISBN13:
978-0-8058-0366-2. Dewey:152.1/67. LCCN:90-022079.

Audience: **u,f.**

Carterette, Edward C.   **QP456.T372 1997**
(Editor), et al.
Tasting and Smelling. Ed. 2. Morton P. Friedman, Gary K.
Beauchamp & Linda Bartoshuk (Editors). Trade Cloth. Elsevier
Science & Technology Books. Saint Louis, MO. 1997. 231p.
Handbook of Perception and Cognition Ser.
ISBN:0-12-161958-3, ISBN13: 978-0-12-161958-9.
Dewey:612.8/7. LCCN:97-022352.

Audience: **u,f.** *Choice, 1998.*

Commons, Michael L., et al.   **BF319**
Signal Detection: Mechanisms, Models, and Applications. J. A.
Nevin & M. C. Davison (Authors). Cloth Text. Lawrence
Erlbaum Associates, Inc. Mahwah, NJ. 1991. 304p.
ISBN:0-8058-0823-X, ISBN13: 978-0-8058-0823-0.
Dewey:152.82.

Audience: **u,f.**

Ellis, Willis D.   **BF203**
A Source Book of Gestalt Psychology. Ed. 2. Library Binding.
Routledge. New York, NY. 1999. 420p. International Library of
Psychology ISBN:0-415-20957-9, ISBN13: 978-0-415-20957-1.
Dewey:150.1924.

Audience: **u,f.**

Gibson, James J.   **BF311**
The Senses Considered As Perceptual Systems. Trade Cloth.
Greenwood Publishing Group, Inc. Portsmouth, NH. 1983. 335p.
ISBN:0-313-23961-4, ISBN13: 978-0-313-23961-8. Dewey:153.
LCCN:83-001716.

Audience: **u,f.**

Green, David M. & Swets,   **BF237**
John A.
Signal Detection Theory and Psychophysics. Trade Cloth.
Peninsula Publishing. Los Altos, CA. 1989. 521p.
ISBN:0-932146-23-6, ISBN13: 978-0-932146-23-6.
Dewey:152.1. LCCN:88-062297.

Audience: **u,f.**

Hartmann, William M.   **BF251.H35 1997**
Signals, Sound, and Sensation. Trade Cloth. Springer. New
York, NY. 1997. 670p. Modern Acoustics and Signal Processing
Ser. ISBN:1-56396-283-7, ISBN13: 978-1-56396-283-7.
Dewey:621.3/822. LCCN:96-043808.

Audience: **u,f.** *Choice, 1997.*

Heller, Morton & Schiff,   **BF275.P79 1992**
William (Editors)
The Psychology of Touch. Trade Paper. Lawrence Erlbaum
Associates, Inc. Mahwah, NJ. 1991. 408p. ISBN:0-8058-0751-9,
ISBN13: 978-0-8058-0751-6. Dewey:152.1/82.
LCCN:91-014484.

Audience: **u,f.** *Choice, 1992.*

Kohler, Wolfgang   **BF203.K6 1992**
Gestalt Psychology. Ed. 2. Trade Paper. W. W. Norton &
Company, Inc. New York, NY. 1992. 378p.
ISBN:0-87140-218-1, ISBN13: 978-0-87140-218-9.
Dewey:150.19/82. LCCN:72-114375.

Audience: **u,f.**

Kruger, Lawrence (Editor)   **BF275.P35 1996**
Pain and Touch. Ed. 2. Edward C. Carterette & Morton P.
Friedman (Contribution by). Trade Cloth. Elsevier Science &
Technology Books. Saint Louis, MO. 1996. 394p. Handbook of
Perception and Cognition Ser. ISBN:0-12-426910-9, ISBN13:
978-0-12-426910-1. Dewey:152.1/82. LCCN:96-022523.

Audience: **u,f.** *Choice, 1997.*

Uttal, William R.   **BF241.U854 1988**
On Seeing Forms. Trade Cloth. Lawrence Erlbaum Associates,
Inc. Mahwah, NJ. 1988. 352p. ISBN:0-89859-994-6, ISBN13:
978-0-89859-994-7. Dewey:152.1/423. LCCN:88-000421.

Audience: **u,f.** *Choice, 1989.*

Human Experimental Psychology >
Visual Perception

Byrne, Alexander   **QC495.R32 1997**
The Science of Color. David R. Hilbert (Editor). Trade Paper.
MIT Press. Cambridge, MA. 1997. 465p. Readings on Color
Ser., Vol. 2 ISBN:0-262-52231-4, ISBN13: 978-0-262-52231-1.
Dewey:152.14/5. LCCN:96-044539.

Audience: **g,l,u,f.** *Choice, 1998.*

Findlay, John M. &   **BF241**
Gilchrist, Iain D.
Active Vision: The Psychology of Looking and Seeing. Trade
Paper. Oxford University Press, Inc. New York, NY. 2003. 234p.
Oxford Psychology Ser., No. 37 ISBN:0-19-852479-X, ISBN13:
978-0-19-852479-3. Dewey:152.14. LCCN:2003-273823.

Audience: **u,f.** *Choice, 2004.*

Goodale, Melvyn & Milner,   **BF241**
David
Sight Unseen: An Exploration of Conscious and Unconscious
Vision. Trade Cloth. Oxford University Press, Inc. New York,
NY. 2004. 146p. ISBN:0-19-851052-7, ISBN13:
978-0-19-851052-9. Dewey:152.14. LCCN:2004-298027.

Audience: **u,f.** *Choice, 2004.*

Gregory, Richard   **BF241.G735 1997**
Mirrors in Mind. Cloth Text. W. H. Freeman & Company. New
York, NY. 1997. 304p. ISBN:0-7167-4511-9, ISBN13:
978-0-7167-4511-2. Dewey:152.1/4. LCCN:96-020953.

Audience: **l,u.** *Choice, 1997.*

Hecht, Heiko (Editor), et al.   **BF243.L66 2003**
Looking into Pictures: An Interdisciplinary Approach to Pictorial
Space. Robert Schwartz & Margaret Atherton (Editors). Trade
Cloth. MIT Press. Cambridge, MA. 2003. 435p. Bradford Bks.
ISBN:0-262-08310-8, ISBN13: 978-0-262-08310-2.
Dewey:152.14. LCCN:2002-070319.

Audience: **u,f.**

Hershenson, Maurice   **BF469.H45 1998**
Visual Space Perception: A Primer. Trade Paper. MIT Press.
Cambridge, MA. 1998. 248p. Bradford Bks.

ISBN:0-262-58167-1, ISBN13: 978-0-262-58167-7. Dewey:152.14/2. LCCN:98-004970.

Audience: **l,u**. *Choice, 1999.*

Hoffman, David & Hoffman, Donald D.   **BF241.H56 1998**

Visual Intelligence: How We Create What We See. Trade Cloth. W. W. Norton & Company, Inc. New York, NY. 1998. 288p. ISBN:0-393-04669-9, ISBN13: 978-0-393-04669-4. Dewey:152.14. LCCN:98-006181.

Audience: **g,l,u**. *Choice, 1999.*

Jacob, Pierre & Jeannerod, Marc   **BF241**

Ways of Seeing: The Scope and Limits of Visual Cognition. Trade Paper. Oxford University Press, Inc. New York, NY. 2003. 312p. Oxford Cognitive Science Ser. ISBN:0-19-850921-9, ISBN13: 978-0-19-850921-9. Dewey:152.14. LCCN:2004-299281.

Audience: **u,f**. *Choice, 2004.*

Lamb, Trevor & Bourriau, Janine (Editors)   **QC495 .C75 1995**

Colour: Art and Science. Trade Cloth. Cambridge University Press. New York, NY. 1995. 237p. The Darwin College Lectures ISBN:0-521-49645-4, ISBN13: 978-0-521-49645-2. Dewey:535.6. LCCN:95-157646.

Audience: **l,u,f**. *Choice, 1995.*

Massironi, Manfredo   **BF241.M345 2002**

The Psychology of Graphic Images: Seeing, Drawing, Communicating. Cloth over Boards. Lawrence Erlbaum Associates, Inc. Mahwah, NJ. 2001. 328p. ISBN:0-8058-2932-6, ISBN13: 978-0-8058-2932-7. Dewey:302.2/22. LCCN:2001-016019.

Audience: **u,f**. *Choice, 2002.*

Noë, Alva & Thompson, Evan T. (Editors)   **B828.45.V565 2002**

Vision and Mind: Selected Readings in the Philosophy of Perception. Trade Cloth. MIT Press. Cambridge, MA. 2002. 605p. Bradford Bks. ISBN:0-262-14078-0, ISBN13: 978-0-262-14078-2. Dewey:121/.34. LCCN:2002-023533.

Audience: **l,u**.

Parks, Theodore E. (Editor)   **BF241.L64 2000**

Looking at Looking: An Introduction to the Intelligence of Vision. Paper Text. SAGE Publications, Inc. Thousand Oaks, CA. 2000. 144p. ISBN:0-7619-2204-0, ISBN13: 978-0-7619-2204-9. Dewey:152.14. LCCN:00-009062.

Audience: **u,f**.

Rock, Irvin   **BF311.I46 1997**

Indirect Perception. Trade Cloth. MIT Press. Cambridge, MA. 1997. 350p. Cognitive Psychology Ser. ISBN:0-262-18177-0, ISBN13: 978-0-262-18177-8. Dewey:153.7. LCCN:96-026924.

Audience: **u,f**.

Schaal, Benoist (Editor), et al.   **QP456.O445 2002**

Olfaction, Taste, and Cognition. Catherine Rouby, Andri Holley, Danièle Dubois & Rémi Gervais (Editors). Trade Cloth. Cambridge University Press. New York, NY. 2002. 484p. ISBN:0-521-79058-1, ISBN13: 978-0-521-79058-1. Dewey:612.8/6. LCCN:2001-043456.

Audience: **u,f**.

West, Thomas G.   **BF426.W47 1997**

In the Mind's Eye: Visual Thinkers, Gifted People with Dyslexia and Other Learning Difficulties, Computer Images and the Ironies of Creativity. Ed. 2. Trade Cloth. Prometheus Books, Publishers. Amherst, NY. 1997. 397p. ISBN:1-57392-155-6, ISBN13: 978-1-57392-155-8. Dewey:153.9. LCCN:97-019570.

Audience: **g,l,u**. *Choice, 1998.*

Yantis, Steven (Editor)   **QP491.V577 2001**

Visual Perception: Essential Readings. Paper over Boards. Taylor & Francis Group. Philadelphia, PA. 2000. 432p. Key Readings in Cognition Ser. ISBN:0-86377-597-7, ISBN13: 978-0-86377-597-0. Dewey:152.14. LCCN:00-042311.

Audience: **l,u**.

Human Experimental Psychology > Auditory and Speech Perception

Bregman, Albert S.   **BF251**

Auditory Scene Analysis: The Perceptual Organization of Sound. Trade Paper. MIT Press. Cambridge, MA. 1994. 792p. Bradford Bks. ISBN:0-262-52195-4, ISBN13: 978-0-262-52195-6. Dewey:152.1/5.

Audience: **u,f**. *Choice, 1990.*

Deutsch, Diana (Editor)   **ML3830.P9 1999**

The Psychology of Music. Ed. 2. Paper Text. Elsevier Science & Technology Books. Saint Louis, MO. 1998. 807p. Academic Press Ser. ISBN:0-12-213565-2, ISBN13: 978-0-12-213565-1. Dewey:781/.11. LCCN:98-085210.

Audience: **u,f**. *B Choice, 1999.*

Helmholtz, Hermann   **ML3800**

On the Sensations of Tone. Ed. 2. Henry Margenau (Introduction by). Trade Paper. Dover Publications, Inc. Mineola, NY. 1954. 576p. ISBN:0-486-60753-4, ISBN13: 978-0-486-60753-5. Dewey:781.1.

Audience: **u,f**.

Moore, Brian C. (Editor)   **BF251.M65 1995**

Hearing. Ed. 2. Cloth Text. Elsevier Science & Technology Books. Saint Louis, MO. 1995. 468p. Handbook of Perception and Cognition Ser. ISBN:0-12-505626-5, ISBN13: 978-0-12-505626-7. Dewey:152.1/5. LCCN:95-001082.

Audience: **u,f**.

Plack, Christopher J.   **BF251.P57 2005**

The Sense of Hearing. Paper over Boards, Perfect. Lawrence Erlbaum Associates, Inc. Mahwah, NJ. 2005. 267p. ISBN:0-8058-4883-5, ISBN13: 978-0-8058-4883-0. Dewey:152.1/5. LCCN:2005-006662.

Audience: **l,u,f**.

Plomp, Reinier   **QP465.P564 2002**

The Intelligent Ear: On the Nature of Sound and Perception. Cloth over Boards. Lawrence Erlbaum Associates, Inc. Mahwah, NJ. 2001. 184p. ISBN:0-8058-3867-8, ISBN13: 978-0-8058-3867-1. Dewey:612.8/5. LCCN:2001-023646.

Audience: **l,u,f**. *Choice, 2002.*

Human Experimental Psychology > Motor Processes

Rosenbaum, David A.   **BF295.R67 1991**
Human Motor Control. Cloth Text. Elsevier Science &
Technology Books. Saint Louis, MO. 1990. 300p.
ISBN:0-12-597300-4, ISBN13: 978-0-12-597300-7.
Dewey:152.3. LCCN:90-001063.

Audience: **u,f.**

Human Experimental Psychology > Cognitive Processes

Barsalou, Lawrence W.   **BF201.B37 1992**
Cognitive Psychology: An Overview for Cognitive Scientists.
Cloth Text. Lawrence Erlbaum Associates, Inc. Mahwah, NJ.
1992. 424p. Tutorial Essays in Cognitive Science Ser.
ISBN:0-8058-0691-1, ISBN13: 978-0-8058-0691-5. Dewey:153.
LCCN:91-037192.

Audience: **u,f.** *Choice, 1992.*

Bartlett, Frederic Charles   **BF455**
Thinking: An Experimental and Social Study. Trade Cloth.
Greenwood Publishing Group, Inc. Portsmouth, NH. 1982. 203p.
ISBN:0-313-23412-4, ISBN13: 978-0-313-23412-5.
Dewey:153.42. LCCN:82-000983.

Audience: **g,l,u,f.**

Bruer, John T.   **BF318.B79 1999**
The Myth of the First Three Years: A New Understanding of
Early Brain Development and Lifelong Learning. Trade Cloth.
Simon & Schuster. New York, NY. 1999. 256p.
ISBN:0-684-85184-9, ISBN13: 978-0-684-85184-6.
Dewey:155.4/13. LCCN:99-034934.

Audience: **g,l,u.** *Choice, 2000.*

Devlin, Ann Sloan   **BF469**
Mind and Maze: Spatial Cognition and Environmental Behavior.
Trade Cloth. Greenwood Publishing Group, Inc. Portsmouth,
NH. 2001. 296p. ISBN:0-275-96784-0, ISBN13:
978-0-275-96784-0. Dewey:153.7/52. LCCN:00-052859.

Audience: **l,u.** *Choice, 2002.*

Donald, Merlin   **BF311.D57 2001**
A Mind So Rare: The Evolution of Human Consciousness.
Trade Cloth. W. W. Norton & Company, Inc. New York, NY.
2001. 416p. ISBN:0-393-04950-7, ISBN13: 978-0-393-04950-3.
Dewey:153. LCCN:00-053721.

Audience: **g,l,u.** *Choice, 2001.*

Fauconnier, Gilles, et al.   **BF443.F38 2003**
Way We Think: Conceptual Blending and the Mind's Hidden
Complexities. A. Turner & Mark Turner (Authors). Trade Paper.
Basic Books. New York, NY. 2003. 464p. ISBN:0-465-08786-8,
ISBN13: 978-0-465-08786-0. Dewey:153.4.

Audience: **u,f.** *Choice, 2002.*

Fish, Jefferson M. (Editor)   **BF431.R27 2002**
Race and Intelligence: Separating Science from Myth. Cloth
over Boards. Lawrence Erlbaum Associates, Inc. Mahwah, NJ.
2001. 448p. ISBN:0-8058-3757-4, ISBN13: 978-0-8058-3757-5.
Dewey:305.9/082. LCCN:00-033164.

Audience: **l,u,f.** *Choice, 2002.*

Fullilove, Mindy Thompson   **BF353**
The House of Joshua: Meditations on Family and Place. Trade
Cloth. University of Nebraska Press. Lincoln, NE. 1999. 168p.
Texts and Contexts Ser. ISBN:0-8032-6906-4, ISBN13:
978-0-8032-6906-4. Dewey:155.9/092 B.

Audience: **l,u,f.** *Choice, 1999.*

Gardner, Howard   **BF432.3**
Intelligence Reframed: Multiple Intelligences for the 21st
Century. Trade Paper. Basic Books. New York, NY. 2000. 304p.
ISBN:0-465-02611-7, ISBN13: 978-0-465-02611-1.
Dewey:153.9. LCCN:99-042468.

Audience: **g,l,u,f.** *Choice, 2000.*

Gould, Stephen Jay   **BF431.G68 1996**
The Mismeasure of Man. Ed. 2. Trade Cloth. W. W. Norton &
Company, Inc. New York, NY. 1996. 100p.
ISBN:0-393-03972-2, ISBN13: 978-0-393-03972-6.
Dewey:153.9. LCCN:95-044442.

Audience: **g,l,u,f.** *B Choice, 1996.*

Halpern, Diane F.   **BF311**
Thought and Knowledge: An Introduction to Critical Thinking.
Ed. 4. Trade Cloth. Lawrence Erlbaum Associates, Inc. Mahwah,
NJ. 2003. 304p. ISBN:0-8058-4549-6, ISBN13:
978-0-8058-4549-5. Dewey:153.

Audience: **u,f.**

Healy, Alice F.   **BF201.E945 2004**
Experimental Cognitive Psychology and Its Applications. Trade
Cloth. American Psychological Association. Washington, DC.
2004. 328p. Decade of Behavior Ser. ISBN:1-59147-183-4,
ISBN13: 978-1-59147-183-7. Dewey:153. LCCN:2004-008268.

Audience: **u,f.** *Choice, 2005.*

Herrnstein, Richard J.   **BF431.H398 1996**
The Bell Curve: Intelligence and Class Structure in American
Life. Charles Murray (Based on a work by). Trade Paper. Simon
& Schuster. New York, NY. 1996. 912p. A Meditation Bk.
ISBN:0-684-82429-9, ISBN13: 978-0-684-82429-1.
Dewey:305.5/0973. LCCN:95-042934.

Audience: **g,l.** *Choice, 1995.*

Kahneman, Daniel (Editor), et al.   **BF441 .J8 1982**
Judgment under Uncertainty: Heuristics and Biases. Paul Slovic
& Amos Tversky (Editors). Trade Paper. Cambridge University
Press. New York, NY. 1982. 544p. ISBN:0-521-28414-7,
ISBN13: 978-0-521-28414-1. Dewey:153.4/6. LCCN:81-010042.

Audience: **u,f.**

Kimura, Doreen   **BF311.K485 1999**
Sex and Cognition. Trade Cloth. MIT Press. Cambridge, MA.
1999. 272p. A Bradford Book Ser. ISBN:0-262-11236-1,
ISBN13: 978-0-262-11236-9. Dewey:153.3/3. LCCN:98-026802.

Audience: **l,u,f.** *Choice, 2000.*

Levitin, Daniel J. (Editor)   **BF201.L48 2002**
Foundations of Cognitive Psychology: Core Readings. Trade
Cloth. MIT Press. Cambridge, MA. 2002. 832p. Bradford Bks.
ISBN:0-262-12247-2, ISBN13: 978-0-262-12247-4. Dewey:153.
LCCN:2002-022662.

Audience: **u.** *Choice, 2003.*

Myers, David G.   **BF315.5.M94 2003**
Intuition: Its Powers and Perils. Cloth over Boards. Yale
University Press. Cumberland, RI. 2002. 336p.

Formats: Web: ▢ Ebook: **e** CD/DVD-ROM: ✿ BCL3: **B**

ISBN:0-300-09531-7, ISBN13: 978-0-300-09531-9.
Dewey:153.4/4. LCCN:2002-000881.

Audience: **l,u.** *Choice, 2003.*

Nadel, Lynn (Editor)   **BF311.E53 2003**
Encyclopedia of Cognitive Science. Library Binding. Nature
Publishing Group. New York, NY. 2002. 4343p.
ISBN:0-333-79261-0, ISBN13: 978-0-333-79261-2.
Dewey:153.03. LCCN:2003-011554.

Audience: **g,l,u,f.** *Choice, 2003.*

Parker, Sue Taylor &   **QL785**
McKinney, Michael L.
Origins of Intelligence: The Evolution of Cognitive
Development in Monkeys, Apes, and Humans. Trade Paper.
Johns Hopkins University Press. Baltimore, MD. 2000. 424p.
ISBN:0-8018-6671-5, ISBN13: 978-0-8018-6671-5.
Dewey:156.3.

Audience: **l,u.**

Plous, Scott   **BF448**
The Psychology of Judgment and Decision Making. Paper Text.
McGraw-Hill Higher Education. Burr Ridge, IL. 1993. 352p.
McGraw-Hill Series in Social Psychology ISBN:0-07-050477-6,
ISBN13: 978-0-07-050477-6. Dewey:153.83. LCCN:92-038542.

Audience: **l,u.** *Choice, 1994.*

Reason, James   **BF323.E7 R42 1990**
Human Error. Trade Paper. Cambridge University Press. New
York, NY. 1990. 316p. ISBN:0-521-31419-4, ISBN13:
978-0-521-31419-0. Dewey:153.4/6. LCCN:90-031041.

Audience: **u,f.** *Choice, 1991.*

Solso, Robert L.   **N71**
Cognition and the Visual Arts. Trade Paper. MIT Press.
Cambridge, MA. 1996. 312p. Cognitive Psychology Ser., :A
Bradford Book ISBN:0-262-69186-8, ISBN13:
978-0-262-69186-4. Dewey:701/.15.

Audience: **l,u.** *Choice, 1995.*

Sternberg, Robert J.   **BF311 .S6778 1997**
Thinking Styles. Cloth Text. Cambridge University Press. New
York, NY. 1997. 192p. ISBN:0-521-55316-4, ISBN13:
978-0-521-55316-2. Dewey:153.4. LCCN:97-001586.

Audience: **u,f.** *Choice, 1998.*

Sternberg, Robert J.   **BF431.W535 2002**
(Editor)
Why Smart People Can Be So Stupid. Cloth over Boards. Yale
University Press. Cumberland, RI. 2002. 272p.
ISBN:0-300-09033-1, ISBN13: 978-0-300-09033-8.
Dewey:153.9. LCCN:2001-005846.

Audience: **g,l,u.** *Choice, 2003, 2002.*

Sternberg, Robert J. &   **BF311**
Davidson, Janet (Editors)
The Nature of Insight. Trade Paper. MIT Press. Cambridge, MA.
1996. 640p. Bradford Bks. ISBN:0-262-69187-6, ISBN13:
978-0-262-69187-1. Dewey:153.4.

Audience: **u,f.** *Choice, 1995.*

Ward, Lawrence   **BF311.W2695 2001**
Dynamical Cognitive Science. Trade Cloth. MIT Press.
Cambridge, MA. 2001. 371p. Bradford Bks.
ISBN:0-262-23217-0, ISBN13: 978-0-262-23217-3. Dewey:153.
LCCN:2001-044336.

Audience: **u,f.**

Wegner, Daniel M.   **BF441**
White Bears and Other Unwanted Thoughts: Suppression,
Obsession and the Psychology of Mental Control. Trade Paper.
Guilford Publications, Inc. New York, NY. 1994. 207p.
ISBN:0-89862-223-9, ISBN13: 978-0-89862-223-2.
Dewey:153.42.

Audience: **l,u.**

Wilson, Robert A. & Keil,   **BF311**
Frank (Editors)
The MIT Encyclopedia of the Cognitive Sciences (MITECS).
Trade Cloth. MIT Press. Cambridge, MA. 1999. 1096p. A
Bradford Book Ser. ISBN:0-262-23200-6, ISBN13:
978-0-262-23200-5. Dewey:153/.03. LCCN:99-011115.

Audience: **u,f.** *Choice, 1999.*

Zenderland, Leila   **BF431 .Z46 1998**
Measuring Minds: Henry Herbert Goddard and the Origins of
American Intelligence Testing. Mitchell G. Ash & William R.
Woodward (Contribution by). Cloth Text. Cambridge University
Press. New York, NY. 1998. 478p. Cambridge Studies in the
History of Psychology ISBN:0-521-44373-3, ISBN13:
978-0-521-44373-9. Dewey:153.9/3/097309041.
LCCN:97-006101.

Audience: **u,f.** *Choice, 1998.*

Human Experimental Psychology > Learning and Memory

Baddeley, Alan D.   **BF371**
Working Memory. Trade Paper. Oxford University Press, Inc.
New York, NY. 1987. 304p. Oxford Psychology Ser., No. 11
ISBN:0-19-852133-2, ISBN13: 978-0-19-852133-4.
Dewey:153.1/2.

Audience: **l,u,f.**

Baddeley, Alan D. (Editor),   **BF371.E65 2002**
et al.
Episodic Memory: New Directions in Research. Martin Conway
& John P. Aggleton (Editors). Trade Paper. Oxford University
Press, Inc. New York, NY. 2002. 304p. ISBN:0-19-850880-8,
ISBN13: 978-0-19-850880-9. Dewey:153.13.
LCCN:2002-510597.

Audience: **u,f.** *Choice, 2002.*

Bowers, Jeffrey S. &   **RC394.M46R485 2002**
Marsolek, Chad J. (Editors)
Rethinking Implicit Memory. Cloth Text. Oxford University
Press, Inc. New York, NY. 2003. 300p. ISBN:0-19-263233-7,
ISBN13: 978-0-19-263233-3. Dewey:616.8/4.
LCCN:2002-075722.

Audience: **u,f.**

Campbell, Sue   **BF378.A87C36 2003**
Relational Remembering: Rethinking the Memory Wars. Book,
Other. Rowman & Littlefield Publishers, Inc. Lanham, MD.
2003. 238p. Feminist Constructions Ser. ISBN:0-7425-3280-1,
ISBN13: 978-0-7425-3280-9. Dewey:153.13.
LCCN:2003-008534.

Audience: **l,u.** *Choice, 2004.*

Carterette, Edward C.   **BF371**
(Editor), et al.
Memory. Ed. 2. Morton P. Friedman, Elizabeth L. Bjork &
Robert A. Bjork (Editors). Trade Paper. Elsevier Science &

Technology Books. Saint Louis, MO. 1998. 586p. Handbook of Perception and Cognition Ser. ISBN:0-12-102571-3, ISBN13: 978-0-12-102571-7. Dewey:153.1/2.

Audience: **u,f.**

Cohen, Gillian   **BF371**
Memory in the Real World. Ed. 2. Paper over Boards. Taylor & Francis Group. Philadelphia, PA. 1996. 368p. ISBN:0-86377-728-7, ISBN13: 978-0-86377-728-8. Dewey:153.1/2.

Audience: **l,u.** *Choice, 1990.*

Collins, Alan F. (Editor),   **BF371.T44 1993**
et al.
Theories of Memory. Susan E. Gathercole, Martin A. Conway & Peter E. Morris (Editors). Paper over Boards. Lawrence Erlbaum Associates, Inc. Mahwah, NJ. 1993. 440p. ISBN:0-86377-290-0, ISBN13: 978-0-86377-290-0. Dewey:153.12. LCCN:94-121217.

Audience: **u,f.** *Choice, 1994.*

Draaisma, Douwe   **BF378.A87D7313 2004**
Why Life Speeds up As You Get Older: How Memory Shapes our Past. Arnold Pomerans & Erica Pomerans (Translators). Cloth Text. Cambridge University Press. New York, NY. 2004. 288p. ISBN:0-521-83424-4, ISBN13: 978-0-521-83424-7. Dewey:153.1/3. LCCN:2004-049441.

Audience: **l,u.** *Choice, 2005.*

Flora, Stephen Ray   **BF319.5.R4F58 2004**
The Power of Reinforcement. Cloth Text. State University of New York Press. Albany, NY. 2004. 269p. SUNY Series, Alternatives in Psychology ISBN:0-7914-5915-2, ISBN13: 978-0-7914-5915-7. Dewey:153.8/5. LCCN:2002-045264.

Audience: **l,u.** *Choice, 2004.*

Gorfein, David S. &   **BF318**
Hoffman, Robert R. (Editors)
Memory and Learning: The Ebbinghaus Centennial Conference. Trade Cloth. Lawrence Erlbaum Associates, Inc. Mahwah, NJ. 1987. 458p. ISBN:0-89859-653-X, ISBN13: 978-0-89859-653-3. Dewey:153.1. LCCN:86-024195.

Audience: **u,f.**

Gross, David   **BF378.S65G76 2000**
Lost Time: On Remembering and Forgetting in Late Modern Culture. Cloth Text. University of Massachusetts Press. Amherst, MA. 2000. 216p. Critical Perspectives on Modern Culture Ser. ISBN:1-55849-254-2, ISBN13: 978-1-55849-254-7. Dewey:128/.3. LCCN:00-036383.

Audience: **g,l,u.** *Choice, 2001.*

Healy, Alice F. & Bourne,   **P53.7.F67 1998**
Lyle E. Jr. (Editors)
Foreign Language Learning: Psycholinguistic Studies on Training and Retention. Cloth over Boards. Lawrence Erlbaum Associates, Inc. Mahwah, NJ. 1998. 440p. ISBN:0-8058-2754-4, ISBN13: 978-0-8058-2754-5. Dewey:401/.93. LCCN:98-008507.

Audience: **u,f.**

Izawa, Chizuko (Editor)   **BF371.O5 1999**
On Human Memory: Evolution, Progress, and Reflections on the 30th Anniversary of the Atkinson-Shiffrin Model. Cloth over Boards. Lawrence Erlbaum Associates, Inc. Mahwah, NJ. 1999. 304p. ISBN:0-8058-2952-0, ISBN13: 978-0-8058-2952-5. Dewey:153.1/2. LCCN:99-021291.

Audience: **u,f.**

Luria, Aleksandr R.   **BF376.L813 1987**
The Mind of a Mnemomist: A Little Book about a Vast Memory. Jerome S. Bruner (Foreword by). Trade Paper. Harvard University Press. Cambridge, MA. 1987. 192p. ISBN:0-674-57622-5, ISBN13: 978-0-674-57622-3. Dewey:616.85/8. LCCN:86-031847.

Audience: **g,l,u,f.**

Lynn, Steven Jay &   **RC455.2.F35T78 1998**
McConkey, Kevin M. (Editors)
Truth in Memory. Cloth over Boards. Guilford Publications, Inc. New York, NY. 1998. 508p. ISBN:1-57230-345-X, ISBN13: 978-1-57230-345-4. Dewey:616.85/822390651. LCCN:98-006870.

Audience: **l,u.** *Choice, 1998.*

McGaugh, James L.   **BF378.A87M34 2003**
Memory and Emotion: The Making of Lasting Memories. Trade Cloth. Columbia University Press. New York, NY. 2003. 192p. Maps of the Mind Ser. ISBN:0-231-12022-2, ISBN13: 978-0-231-12022-7. Dewey:153.1/2. LCCN:2003-051480.

Audience: **u,f.** *Choice, 2004.*

Reisberg, Daniel & Hertel,   **BF378.A87M46 2003**
Paula (Editors)
Memory and Emotion. Trade Cloth. Oxford University Press, Inc. New York, NY. 2003. 428p. Series in Affective Science ISBN:0-19-515856-3, ISBN13: 978-0-19-515856-4. Dewey:152.4. LCCN:2003-006595.

Audience: **u,f.**

Rubin, David C. (Editor)   **BF378.A87 R45 1996**
Remembering Our Past: Studies in Autobiographical Memory. Trade Cloth. Cambridge University Press. New York, NY. 1996. 458p. ISBN:0-521-46145-6, ISBN13: 978-0-521-46145-0. Dewey:153.1/2. LCCN:94-046448.

Audience: **l,u,f.**

Schacter, Daniel L.   **BF371**
Searching for Memory: The Brain, the Mind, and the Past. Trade Paper. Basic Books. New York, NY. 1997. 416p. ISBN:0-465-07552-5, ISBN13: 978-0-465-07552-2. Dewey:153.1/2. LCCN:96-019521.

Audience: **l,u.** *Choice, 1996.*

Schacter, Daniel L.   **BF371**
The Seven Sins of Memory: How the Mind Forgets and Remembers. Trade Paper. Houghton Mifflin Company Trade & Reference Division. Boston, MA. 2002. 288p. ISBN:0-618-21919-6, ISBN13: 978-0-618-21919-3. Dewey:153.1/2.

Audience: **l,u.** *Choice, 2001.*

Thompson, Charles P.   **BF723.M4E94 1998**
(Editor), et al.
Eyewitness Memory. Douglas Herrmann, Darryl Bruce, J. Don Read & Mike Toglia (Editors). Cloth over Boards. Lawrence Erlbaum Associates, Inc. Mahwah, NJ. 1997. 192p. ISBN:0-8058-2794-3, ISBN13: 978-0-8058-2794-1. Dewey:153.1/2. LCCN:97-008625.

Audience: **l,u,f.**

Thompson, Richard F. &   **BF371.T484 2005**
Madigan, Stephen A.
Memory: The Key to Consciousness. Trade Cloth. National Academies Press. Washington, DC. 2005. vii, 280p.

ISBN:0-309-54949-3, ISBN13: 978-0-309-54949-3.
Dewey:153.12. LCCN:2005-007404.

Audience: **g,l,u,f.** *Choice, 2006.*

Tulving, Endel & Craik,   **BF371**
  Fergus I. M. (Editors)
The Oxford Handbook of Memory. Trade Paper. Oxford
University Press, Inc. New York, NY. 2005. 720p.
ISBN:0-19-518200-6, ISBN13: 978-0-19-518200-2.
Dewey:153.1/2. LCCN:99-027533.

Audience: **u,f.** *Choice, 2000.*

Human Experimental Psychology > Attention

Itti, Laurent (Editor), et al.   **QP405.N48 2005**
Neurobiology of Attention. Geraint Rees & John K. Tsotsos
(Editors). Trade Cloth. Elsevier Science & Technology Books.
Saint Louis, MO. 2005. 744p. ISBN:0-12-375731-2, ISBN13:
978-0-12-375731-9. Dewey:612.8233733. LCCN:2005-297397.

Audience: **u,f.**

Johnson, Addie & Proctor,   **BF321.J56 2004**
  Robert W.
Attention: Theory and Practice. Cloth Text. SAGE Publications,
Inc. Thousand Oaks, CA. 2003. 488p. ISBN:0-7619-2760-3,
ISBN13: 978-0-7619-2760-0. Dewey:153.7/33.
LCCN:2003-016015.

Audience: **u,f.**

Langer, Ellen J.   **BF321.L23 1989**
Mindfulness. Cloth Text. Addison-Wesley Longman, Inc.
Boston, MA. 1989. ISBN:0-201-09502-5, ISBN13:
978-0-201-09502-9. Dewey:153. LCCN:88-033293.

Audience: **l,u.**

Mack, Arien & Rock, Irvin   **BF241.M26 1998**
Inattentional Blindness. Trade Cloth. MIT Press. Cambridge,
MA. 1998. 296p. MIT Press/Bradford Books Series in Cognitive
Psychology ISBN:0-262-13339-3, ISBN13: 978-0-262-13339-5.
Dewey:153.7/33. LCCN:97-028254.

Audience: **u,f.** *Choice, 1998.*

Pashler, Harold E.   **BF321**
The Psychology of Attention. Trade Paper. MIT Press.
Cambridge, MA. 1999. 510p. Bradford Bks.
ISBN:0-262-66156-X, ISBN13: 978-0-262-66156-0.
Dewey:153.7/33.

Audience: **u,f.**

Posner, Michael I. (Editor)   **QP405.C7125 2004**
Cognitive Neuroscience of Attention. Cloth over Boards.
Guilford Publications, Inc. New York, NY. 2004. 466p.
ISBN:1-59385-048-4, ISBN13: 978-1-59385-048-7.
Dewey:153.7/33. LCCN:2004-006240.

Audience: **u,f.**

Human Experimental Psychology > Motivation and Emotion

Argyle, Michael   **BF575.H27A74 2001**
The Psychology of Happiness. Ed. 2. Paper over Boards. Taylor
& Francis Group. Philadelphia, PA. 2002. 288p.

ISBN:0-415-22664-3, ISBN13: 978-0-415-22664-6.
Dewey:152.4/2. LCCN:2001-018072.

Audience: **l,u,f.**

Barrett, Lisa Feldman   **BF311.E4855 2005**
  (Editor), et al.
Emotion and Consciousness. Paula M. Niedenthal & Piotr
Winkielman (Editors). Cloth over Boards. Guilford Publications,
Inc. New York, NY. 2005. 420p. ISBN:1-59385-188-X, ISBN13:
978-1-59385-188-0. Dewey:152.4. LCCN:2005-001276.

Audience: **u,f.** *Choice, 2006.*

Berkowitz, Leonard   **BF531 .B45 2000**
Causes and Consequences of Feelings. Antony Manstead &
Keith Oatley (Contribution by). Trade Cloth. Cambridge
University Press. New York, NY. 2000. 266p. Studies in
Emotion and Social Interaction ISBN:0-521-63325-7, ISBN13:
978-0-521-63325-3. Dewey:152.4. LCCN:99-040249.

Audience: **u,f.** *Choice, 2001.*

Darwin, Charles   **QP401.D3 1998**
The Expression of the Emotions in Man and Animals. Ed. 3.
Paul Ekman (Introduction by, Afterword by, Commentaries by).
Trade Cloth. Oxford University Press, Inc. New York, NY. 1998.
512p. Series in Affective Science ISBN:0-19-511271-7, ISBN13:
978-0-19-511271-9. Dewey:591.5. LCCN:97-036434.

Audience: **g,l,u,f.**

Davidson, Richard J.   **BF511.H35 2002**
  (Editor), et al.
Handbook of Affective Sciences. Klaus R. Scherer & H. Hill
Goldsmith (Editors). Trade Cloth. Oxford University Press, Inc.
New York, NY. 2002. 1,218p. Series in Affective Science
ISBN:0-19-512601-7, ISBN13: 978-0-19-512601-3.
Dewey:152.4. LCCN:2001-045163.

Audience: **u,f.**

Ekman, Paul & Davidson,   **BF531.N38 1994**
  Richard J.
The Nature of Emotion: Fundamental Questions. Paper Text.
Oxford University Press, Inc. New York, NY. 1994. 510p. Series
in Affective Science ISBN:0-19-508944-8, ISBN13:
978-0-19-508944-8. Dewey:152.4. LCCN:94-018638.

Audience: **l,u,f.**

Frijda, Nico H. (Editor),   **BF531.E513 2000**
  et al.
Emotions and Beliefs: How Feelings Influence Thoughts. A. S.
R. Manstead & Sacha Bem (Editors). Trade Cloth. Cambridge
University Press. New York, NY. 2000. vi, 249p. Studies in
Emotion and Social Interaction ISBN:2-7351-0879-1, ISBN13:
978-2-7351-0879-4. Dewey:152.4. LCCN:99-059880.

Audience: **l,u.**

Fromm, Erich   **BF575.L8F76 2000**
The Art of Loving. Trade Cloth. Continuum International
Publishing Group, Ltd. London, 2000. 144p.
ISBN:0-8264-1260-2, ISBN13: 978-0-8264-1260-7.
Dewey:152.4/1. LCCN:00-021030.

Audience: **g,l,u,f.**

Hewstone, Miles   **BF531.E4826 2004**
Emotion and Motivation. Marilynn B. Brewer (Editor). Trade
Paper. Blackwell Publishing, Inc. Malden, MA. 2004. 352p.
Perspectives on Social Psychology Ser. ISBN:1-4051-1068-6,
ISBN13: 978-1-4051-1068-6. Dewey:152.4.
LCCN:2003-011036.

Audience: **l,u.**

Hope, Debra A. (Editor)   **152.46**
Nebraska Symposium on Motivation 1995: Perspectives on Anxiety, Panic, and Fear. Cloth Text. University of Nebraska Press. Lincoln, NE. 1996. 351p. ISBN:0-8032-2382-X, ISBN13: 978-0-8032-2382-0. Dewey:152.46. LCCN:53-011655.
Audience: **u,f.**

Izard, Carroll E.   **BF531.I96**
Psychology of Emotions. Trade Paper. Springer. New York, NY. 2004. 476p. ISBN:0-306-48445-5, ISBN13: 978-0-306-48445-2. Dewey:152.4.
Audience: **l,u.**

Juslin, Patrik N. & Sloboda, John A. (Editors)   **ML3830.M965 2001**
Music and Emotion: Theory and Research. Trade Paper. Oxford University Press, Inc. New York, NY. 2001. 498p. Series in Affective Science ISBN:0-19-263188-8, ISBN13: 978-0-19-263188-6. Dewey:781/.11. LCCN:2001-036068.
Audience: **u,f.** *Choice, 2002.*

Lane, Richard D. & Nadel, Lynn (Editors)   **BF531.C55 2000**
Cognitive Neuroscience of Emotion. Trade Cloth. Oxford University Press, Inc. New York, NY. 1999. 442p. Series in Affective Science ISBN:0-19-511888-X, ISBN13: 978-0-19-511888-9. Dewey:152.4. LCCN:99-017111.
Audience: **u,f.**

Lazarus, Richard S.   **BF531.L37 1991**
Emotion and Adaptation. Trade Cloth. Oxford University Press, Inc. New York, NY. 1991. 570p. ISBN:0-19-506994-3, ISBN13: 978-0-19-506994-5. Dewey:152.4. LCCN:91-009611.
Audience: **l,u,f.** *Choice, 1992.*

Manstead, Antony S. R. (Editor), et al.   **BF531.F445 2003**
Feelings and Emotions: The Amsterdam Symposium. Nico H. Frijda & Agneta H. Fischer (Editors), Keith Oatley & Antony Manstead (Contribution by). Trade Paper. Cambridge University Press. New York, NY. 2004. 498p. Studies in Emotion and Social Interaction Ser. ISBN:0-521-52101-7, ISBN13: 978-0-521-52101-7. Dewey:152.4. LCCN:2003-043960.
Audience: **u,f.**

Parkinson, Brian   **BF311.P31367 1995**
Ideas and Realities of Emotion. UK-B Format Paperback. Routledge. New York, NY. 1995. 352p. International Library of Philosophy, Psychology, and Scientific Method ISBN:0-415-02859-0, ISBN13: 978-0-415-02859-2. Dewey:152.4. LCCN:95-001096.
Audience: **l,u.** *Choice, 1996.*

Rachlin, Howard   **BF632.R3 2000**
The Science of Self-Control. Trade Cloth. Harvard University Press. Cambridge, MA. 2000. 240p. ISBN:0-674-00093-5, ISBN13: 978-0-674-00093-3. Dewey:153.8. LCCN:99-045204.
Audience: **u,f.** *Choice, 2001.*

Steen, R. Grant   **BF341**
DNA and Destiny: Nature and Nurture in Human Behavior. Trade Paper. Perseus Books Group. New York, NY. 2001. 304p. ISBN:0-7382-0619-9, ISBN13: 978-0-7382-0619-6. Dewey:155.7.
Audience: **l,u,f.** *Choice, 1996.*

Human Experimental Psychology > Consciousness States

Baars, Bernard J. (Editor), et al.   **QP411.E85 2003**
Essential Sources in the Scientific Study of Consciousness. James B. Newman & William P. Banks (Editors). Trade Cloth. MIT Press. Cambridge, MA. 2003. 1206p. Bradford Bks. ISBN:0-262-02496-9, ISBN13: 978-0-262-02496-9. Dewey:153. LCCN:2002-029376.
Audience: **u,f.**

Baruess, Imants   **BF1045.A48B37 2003**
Alterations of Consciousness: An Empirical Analysis for Social Scientists. American Psychological Association Staff (Contribution by). Trade Cloth. American Psychological Association. Washington, DC. 2003. 291p. ISBN:1-55798-993-1, ISBN13: 978-1-55798-993-2. Dewey:154.4. LCCN:2002-038313.
Audience: **l,u,f.** *Choice, 2003.*

Classen, Constance   **BF233.C56 1999**
The Color of Angels: Cosmology, Gender and the Aesthetic Imagination. Paper over Boards. Routledge. New York, NY. 1998. 256p. ISBN:0-415-18073-2, ISBN13: 978-0-415-18073-3. Dewey:152.1/09. LCCN:98-021837.
Audience: **g,l.** *Choice, 1999.*

Dennett, Daniel Clement   **BD450**
Consciousness Explained. Trade Paper. Little Brown & Company. New York, NY. 1992. 528p. ISBN:0-316-18066-1, ISBN13: 978-0-316-18066-5. Dewey:126.
Audience: **g,l,u,f.**

Donald, Merlin   **BF311.D57 2001**
A Mind So Rare: The Evolution of Human Consciousness. Trade Cloth. W. W. Norton & Company, Inc. New York, NY. 2001. 416p. ISBN:0-393-04950-7, ISBN13: 978-0-393-04950-3. Dewey:153. LCCN:00-053721.
Audience: **g,l,u.** *Choice, 2001.*

Ellman, Steven J. & Antrobus, John S. (Editors)   **QP425.M56 1991**
The Mind in Sleep: Psychology and Psychophysiology. Ed. 2. Trade Cloth. John Wiley & Sons, Inc. Hoboken, NJ. 1991. 588p. Wiley Series on Personality Processes, Vol. 166 ISBN:0-471-52556-1, ISBN13: 978-0-471-52556-1. Dewey:154.6. LCCN:90-039136.
Audience: **l,u.**

Eysenck, Hans Jürgen   **BF412 .E97 1995**
Genius: The Natural History of Creativity. Michael Gelder, Jeffrey Gray, Richard Gregory, Robert Hinde & Christopher Lonquet-Higgins (Contribution by). Trade Paper. Cambridge University Press. New York, NY. 1995. 354p. Problems in the Behavioral Sciences Ser., No. 12 ISBN:0-521-48508-8, ISBN13: 978-0-521-48508-1. Dewey:153.9/8. LCCN:94-032136.
Audience: **g,l,u,f.**

Gauld, Alan   **BF1125**
A History of Hypnotism. Trade Paper. Cambridge University Press. New York, NY. 1995. 758p. ISBN:0-521-48329-8, ISBN13: 978-0-521-48329-2. Dewey:154.709.
Audience: **g,l,u,f.** *Choice, 1993.*

Hameroff, Stuart R.   BF311.T66 1998
(Editor), et al.
Toward a Science of Consciousness: The First Tucson
Discussions and Debates. Alfred W. Kaszniak & Alwyn C. Scott
(Editors). Trade Cloth. MIT Press. Cambridge, MA. 1996. 804p.
Complex Adaptive Systems Ser. ISBN:0-262-08249-7, ISBN13:
978-0-262-08249-5. Dewey:153. LCCN:98-154523.

Audience: **u,f.**

Hartmann, Ernest   BF1091
Dreams and Nightmares: The Origin and Meaning of Dreams.
Trade Paper. Basic Books. New York, NY. 2000. 336p.
ISBN:0-7382-0359-9, ISBN13: 978-0-7382-0359-1.
Dewey:154.6/3.

Audience: **g,l.**

Hull, Clark L.   BF1141
Hypnosis and Suggestibility: An Experimental Approach. Trade
Cloth. Crown House Publishing. Carmarthen, 2003. 436p.
ISBN:1-899836-93-4, ISBN13: 978-1-899836-93-2.
Dewey:154.7. LCCN:2002-110666.

Audience: **l,u,f.**

Hurley, S. L.   B808.9.H87 1998
Consciousness in Action. Trade Cloth. Harvard University Press.
Cambridge, MA. 1998. 520p. ISBN:0-674-16420-2, ISBN13:
978-0-674-16420-8. Dewey:126. LCCN:98-012790.

Audience: **g,u,f.** *Choice, 1999.*

Jouvet, Michel   QP426.J68313 1999
The Paradox of Sleep: The Story of Dreaming. Laurence Garey
(Translator). Trade Cloth. MIT Press. Cambridge, MA. 1999.
227p. Bradford Bks. ISBN:0-262-10080-0, ISBN13:
978-0-262-10080-9. Dewey:612.8/21. LCCN:98-050198.

Audience: **l,u,f.** *Choice, 2000.*

Kellerman, Henry (Editor)   BF1099.N53N54 1986
The Nightmare: Psychological and Biological Foundations.
Trade Cloth. Columbia University Press. New York, NY. 1987.
376p. ISBN:0-231-05892-6, ISBN13: 978-0-231-05892-6.
Dewey:154.6/32. LCCN:86-013675.

Audience: **l,u,f.**

Lehar, Steven   BF311.L44 2003
The World in Your Head: A Gestalt View of the Mechanism
of Conscious Experience. E-Book. Lawrence Erlbaum
Associates, Inc. Mahwah, NJ. ISBN:1-4106-0654-6, ISBN13:
978-1-4106-0654-9. Dewey:153.7.

Audience: **u,f.**

Metzinger, Thomas   QP411.N48 2000
Neural Correlates of Consciousness: Empirical and Conceptual
Questions. Trade Cloth. MIT Press. Cambridge, MA. 2000.
360p. Bradford Bks. ISBN:0-262-13370-9, ISBN13:
978-0-262-13370-8. Dewey:612.8/2. LCCN:99-087947.

Audience: **u,f.**

Moorcroft, William H. &   RC547.M667 2003
Belcher, Paula
Understanding Sleep and Dreaming. Trade Cloth. Springer. New
York, NY. 2003. 360p. ISBN:0-306-47425-5, ISBN13:
978-0-306-47425-5. Dewey:612.8/21. LCCN:2002-034181.

Audience: **g,l,u.**

Neher, Andrew   BF1031.N43 1990
The Psychology of Transcendence. Trade Paper. Dover
Publications, Inc. Mineola, NY. 1990. 384p.

ISBN:0-486-26167-0, ISBN13: 978-0-486-26167-6.
Dewey:133.8/01/9. LCCN:89-027954.

Audience: **g,l,u.**

Sternberg, Robert J.   BF431.S7385 2003
Wisdom, Intelligence, and Creativity Synthesized. Trade Cloth.
Cambridge University Press. New York, NY. 2003. 246p.
ISBN:0-521-80238-5, ISBN13: 978-0-521-80238-3.
Dewey:153.9. LCCN:2003-043751.

Audience: **u,f.** *Choice, 2004.*

Waterfield, Robin   RC495.W345 2002
Hidden Depths: The Story of Hypnosis. Trade Cloth. Macmillan
Publishers Ltd. London, 2002. 495p. ISBN:0-333-77949-5,
ISBN13: 978-0-333-77949-1. Dewey:154.7/09.
LCCN:2002-421811.

Audience: **g,l,u.**

Human Experimental Psychology > Parapsychology

Alcock, James E.   BF1045.S33A42 1990
Science and Supernature: A Critical Appraisal of
Parapsychology. Trade Cloth. Prometheus Books, Publishers.
Amherst, NY. 1990. 186p. ISBN:0-87975-548-2, ISBN13:
978-0-87975-548-5. Dewey:133.8. LCCN:89-070033.

Audience: **g,l,u.** *Choice, 1990.*

Blackmore, Susan J.   BF1031.B57 1996
In Search of the Light: The Adventures of a Parapsychologist.
Ed. 2. Trade Paper. Prometheus Books, Publishers. Amherst,
NY. 1996. 286p. ISBN:1-57392-061-4, ISBN13:
978-1-57392-061-2. Dewey:133.8/092 B. LCCN:96-016260.

Audience: **g,l,u.** *Choice, 1996.*

Cardena, Etzel, et al.   BF1031.V37 2000
Varieties of Anomalous Experience: Examining the Scientific
Evidence. Steven Jay Lynn & Stanley Krippner (Authors). Cloth
Text. American Psychological Association. Washington, DC.
2000. 488p. ISBN:1-55798-625-8, ISBN13: 978-1-55798-625-2.
Dewey:133. LCCN:99-045473.

Audience: **g,l,u.** *Choice, 2000.*

Hansel, C. E. M.   BF1031.H256 1989
The Search for Psychic Power: ESP and Parapsychology
Revisited. Ed. 3. Trade Cloth. Prometheus Books, Publishers.
Amherst, NY. 1989. 312p. ISBN:0-87975-516-4, ISBN13:
978-0-87975-516-4. Dewey:133.8/072. LCCN:89-003665.

Audience: **g,l,u,f.** *Choice, 1990.*

Hines, Terence   BF1042.H55 2002
Pseudoscience and the Paranormal. Ed. 2. Trade Paper.
Prometheus Books, Publishers. Amherst, NY. 2002. 425p.
ISBN:1-57392-979-4, ISBN13: 978-1-57392-979-0. Dewey:133.
LCCN:2002-068086.

Audience: **g,l,u.**

James, William   BF1031.J225 1986
Essays in Psychical Research. Robert A. McDermott
(Introduction by). Trade Cloth. Harvard University Press.
Cambridge, MA. 2002. 728p. Works of William James, Vol. 16
ISBN:0-674-26708-7, ISBN13: 978-0-674-26708-4.
Dewey:133.8. LCCN:85-007595.

Audience: **g,l,u,f.**

Zusne, Leonard & Jones, Warren H. (Editors)　　BF1040.Z87 1989
Anomalistic Psychology: A Study of Magical Thinking. Ed. 2. Cloth Text. Lawrence Erlbaum Associates, Inc. Mahwah, NJ. 1989. 328p. ISBN:0-8058-0507-9, ISBN13: 978-0-8058-0507-9. Dewey:133.8/01/9. LCCN:89-001050.
Audience: **g,l,u.** *Choice, 1990.*

Animal Experimental and Comparative Psychology

Abramson, Charles I.　　QL364.2.A28 1994
A Primer of Invertebrate Learning: The Behavioral Perspective. Trade Paper. American Psychological Association. Washington, DC. 1994. 273p. ISBN:1-55798-228-7, ISBN13: 978-1-55798-228-5. Dewey:592/.051. LCCN:94-004300.
Audience: **l,u,f.**

Amsel, Abram　　BF575.F7 A553 1992
Frustration Theory: An Analysis of Dispositional Learning and Memory. Michael Gelder, Jeffrey Gray, Richard Gregory, Robert Hinde & Christopher Lonquet-Higgins (Contribution by). Trade Cloth. Cambridge University Press. New York, NY. 1992. 294p. Problems in the Behavioral Sciences Ser., No. 11 ISBN:0-521-24784-5, ISBN13: 978-0-521-24784-9. Dewey:153.153. LCCN:91-042414.
Audience: **u,f.**

Barash, David P. & Lipton, Judith Eve　　QL761
The Myth of Monogamy: Fidelity and Infidelity in Animals and People. Trade Paper. Henry Holt & Company. New York, NY. 2002. 240p. ISBN:0-8050-7136-9, ISBN13: 978-0-8050-7136-8. Dewey:591.562.
Audience: **g,l,u.** *Choice, 2001.*

Bekoff, Marc & Byers, John A. (Editors)　　QL763.5 .A54 1998
Animal Play: Evolutionary, Comparative and Ecological Perspectives. Trade Cloth. Cambridge University Press. New York, NY. 1998. 290p. ISBN:0-521-58383-7, ISBN13: 978-0-521-58383-1. Dewey:591.56/3. LCCN:97-022056.
Audience: **u,f.** *Choice, 1998.*

Boinski, Sue & Garber, Paul Alan (Editors)　　QL775.O6 2000
On the Move: How and Why Animals Travel in Groups. Trade Cloth. University of Chicago Press. Chicago, IL. 2000. 822p. ISBN:0-226-06339-9, ISBN13: 978-0-226-06339-3. Dewey:591.56. LCCN:99-013382.
Audience: **g,l,u.** *Choice, 2000.*

Candland, Douglas K.　　BF81
Feral Children and Clever Animals: Reflections on Human Nature. Trade Paper. Oxford University Press, Inc. New York, NY. 1995. 432p. ISBN:0-19-510284-3, ISBN13: 978-0-19-510284-0. Dewey:150.9.
Audience: **g,l,u,f.** *Choice, 1994.*

Carroll, Marilyn E. & Overmier, J. Bruce (Editors)　　BF671.A56 2001
Animal Research and Human Health: Advancing Human Welfare Through Behavioral Science. Trade Cloth. American Psychological Association. Washington, DC. 2001. xviii, 385p. Decade of Behavior Ser. ISBN:1-55798-788-2, ISBN13: 978-1-55798-788-4. Dewey:616.89/027. LCCN:2001-018885.
Audience: **u,f.** *Choice, 2002.*

De Waal, Frans　　BJ1335.W33 1996
Good Natured: The Origins of Right and Wrong in Humans and Other Animals. Trade Cloth. Harvard University Press. Cambridge, MA. 1996. 368p. ISBN:0-674-35660-8, ISBN13: 978-0-674-35660-3. Dewey:599.1/78. LCCN:95-046032.
Audience: **l,u,f.**

De Waal, Frans B. M. & Tyack, Peter L. (Editors)　　QL775
Animal Social Complexity: Intelligence, Culture, and Individualized Societies. Trade Paper. Harvard University Press. Cambridge, MA. 2005. 640p. ISBN:0-674-01823-0, ISBN13: 978-0-674-01823-5. Dewey:599.156.
Audience: **u,f.** *Choice, 2003.*

Dewsbury, Donald A. (Editor)　　QL26
Leaders in the Study of Animal Behavior. Trade Cloth. Bucknell University Press. Cranbury, NJ. 1985. 512p. ISBN:0-8387-5052-4, ISBN13: 978-0-8387-5052-0. Dewey:591.51/092/2. LCCN:83-046153.
Audience: **g,l,u.** *Choice, 1985.*

Dewsbury, Donald A.　　QL737.P9D49 2006
Monkey Farm: A History of the Yerkes Laboratories of Primate Biology, Orange Park, Florida, 1930-1965. Trade Cloth. Bucknell University Press. Cranbury, NJ. 2005. 352p. ISBN:0-8387-5593-3, ISBN13: 978-0-8387-5593-8. Dewey:599.8/072/075916. LCCN:2005-014999.
Audience: **u,f.**

Haug, Marc & Whalen, Richard E. (Editors)　　BF671.A55 1999
Animal Models of Human Emotion and Cognition. Cloth Text. American Psychological Association. Washington, DC. 1999. 341p. ISBN:1-55798-583-9, ISBN13: 978-1-55798-583-5. Dewey:156. LCCN:99-030612.
Audience: **u,f.**

Hauser, Marc　　QL785.H359 2000
Wild Minds: What Animals Really Think. Cloth over Boards. Henry Holt & Company. New York, NY. 2000. 320p. ISBN:0-8050-5669-6, ISBN13: 978-0-8050-5669-3. Dewey:591.5/13. LCCN:99-036204.
Audience: **g,l.** *Choice, 2000.*

Hepper, Peter G. (Editor)　　QL761.5 .K49 1991
Kin Recognition. Trade Cloth. Cambridge University Press. New York, NY. 1991. 469p. ISBN:0-521-37267-4, ISBN13: 978-0-521-37267-1. Dewey:591.56. LCCN:90-021776.
Audience: **u,f.** *Choice, 1992.*

Houck, Lynne D. & Drickamer, Lee C. (Editors)　　QL751.6.F66 1996
Foundations of Animal Behavior: Classic Papers with Commentaries. Trade Cloth. University of Chicago Press. Chicago, IL. 1996. 858p. ISBN:0-226-35456-3, ISBN13: 978-0-226-35456-9. Dewey:591.51. LCCN:96-033734.
Audience: **l,u.**

Hughes, Howard C.　　QP355.2
Sensory Exotica: A World Beyond Human Experience. Library Binding. Sagebrush Education Resources. Caledonia, MN. 2001. ISBN:0-613-35436-2, ISBN13: 978-0-613-35436-3. Dewey:573.8.
Audience: **g,l.**

Hull, Clark Leonard   **BF199**
A Behavior System: An Introduction to Behavior Theory
Concerning the Individual Organism. Paper Text. Textbook
Publishers. Temecula, CA. 2003. 372p. ISBN:0-7581-0048-5,
ISBN13: 978-0-7581-0048-1. Dewey:150.

Audience: **u,f.**

Kohler, Wolfgang   **QL737.P96**
The Mentality of Apes. Library Binding. Routledge. New York,
NY. 1999. 386p. International Library of Psychology
ISBN:0-415-20979-X, ISBN13: 978-0-415-20979-3.
Dewey:599/.884.

Audience: **l,u,f.**

Ladygina-Kohts, N. N.   **QL785.L28 2000**
Infant Chimpanzee and Human Child: A Classic 1935
Comparative Study of Ape Emotions and Intelligence. Frans B.
M. De Waal (Editor), Boris Vekker (Translator). Trade Cloth.
Oxford University Press, Inc. New York, NY. 2002. 468p. Series
in Affective Science ISBN:0-19-513565-2, ISBN13:
978-0-19-513565-7. Dewey:599.885/139. LCCN:00-028546.

Audience: **l,u,f.** *Choice, 2003.*

Lehner, Philip N.   **QL751.7**
Handbook of Ethological Methods. Ed. 2. Trade Paper.
Cambridge University Press. New York, NY. 1998. 692p.
ISBN:0-521-63750-3, ISBN13: 978-0-521-63750-3.
Dewey:591.5/1/028.

Audience: **u,f.** *Choice, 1997.*

Maestripieri, Dario (Editor)   **BF671**
Primate Psychology. Trade Paper, Perfect. Harvard University
Press. Cambridge, MA. 2005. 640p. ISBN:0-674-01847-8,
ISBN13: 978-0-674-01847-1. Dewey:156.

Audience: **l,u,f.** *Choice, 2004.*

Masson, Jeffrey Moussaieff   **QL751**
When Elephants Weep: The Emotional Lives of Animals.
Library Binding. Sagebrush Education Resources. Caledonia,
MN. 1996. ISBN:0-613-65682-2, ISBN13: 978-0-613-65682-5.
Dewey:591.51.

Audience: **g,l.**

McGrew, William C.   **QL737.P96M442 2004**
The Cultured Chimpanzee: Reflections on Cultural Primatology.
Cloth Text. Cambridge University Press. New York, NY. 2004.
244p. ISBN:0-521-82841-4, ISBN13: 978-0-521-82841-3.
Dewey:156. LCCN:2004-045828.

Audience: **u,f.** *Choice, 2005.*

Mitchell, Robert W.   **QL785.A74 1997**
(Editor), et al.
Anthropomorphism, Anecdotes, and Animals. Nicholas S.
Thompson & H. Lyn Miles (Editors). Trade Cloth. State
University of New York Press. Albany, NY. 1996. 518p.
ISBN:0-7914-3125-8, ISBN13: 978-0-7914-3125-2.
Dewey:591.51. LCCN:97-026611.

Audience: **l,u.**

Novak, Melinda A. & Petto,   **SF407.P7T49 1991**
Andrew J. (Editors)
Through the Looking Glass: Issues of Psychological Well-Being
in Captive Nonhuman Primates. Cloth Text. American
Psychological Association. Washington, DC. 1991. 285p.
ISBN:1-55798-087-X, ISBN13: 978-1-55798-087-8.
Dewey:636/.98. LCCN:90-027583.

Audience: **u,f.**

Parker, Sue Taylor (Editor),   **BF697.5.S43 S43 1994**
et al.
Self-Awareness in Animals and Humans: Developmental
Perspectives. Robert W. Mitchell & Maria L. Boccia (Editors).
Trade Cloth. Cambridge University Press. New York, NY. 1994.
464p. ISBN:0-521-44108-0, ISBN13: 978-0-521-44108-7.
Dewey:156.37. LCCN:93-024656.

Audience: **u,f.**

Pfungst, Oskar   **QL751**
Clever Hans (The Horse of Mr. Von Osten). Robert H. Wozniak
(Editor). Trade Cloth. Continuum International Publishing
Group, Ltd. London, 286p. Classics in Psychology Ser.
ISBN:1-85506-697-1, ISBN13: 978-1-85506-697-7.
Dewey:591.5.

Audience: **g,l,u,f.**

Rumbaugh, Duane M. &   **QL737.P96R855 2003**
Washburn, David A.
Intelligence of Apes and Other Rational Beings. Cloth over
Boards. Yale University Press. Cumberland, RI. 2003. 352p.
Current Perspectives in Psychology Ser. ISBN:0-300-09983-5,
ISBN13: 978-0-300-09983-6. Dewey:156. LCCN:2002-156629.

Audience: **l,u,f.** *Choice, 2004.*

Savage-Rumbaugh, E. Sue,   **QL737.P96S254 1998**
et al.
Apes, Language, and the Human Mind. Stuart G. Shanker &
Talbot J. Taylor (Authors). Trade Cloth. Oxford University
Press, Inc. New York, NY. 1998. 254p. ISBN:0-19-510986-4,
ISBN13: 978-0-19-510986-3. Dewey:599.885159/4.
LCCN:98-014600.

Audience: **l,u.**

Skinner, B. F.   **BF21**
Cumulative Record: Definitive Edition. Trade Cloth. Copley
Publishing Group. Acton, MA. 1999. 700p. B. F. Skinner
Reprint Ser. ISBN:1-58390-005-5, ISBN13: 978-1-58390-005-5.
Dewey:150.81.

Audience: **u,f.**

Sorabji, Richard   **HV4708**
Animal Minds and Human Morals: The Origins of the Western
Debate. Trade Paper. Cornell University Press. Ithaca, NY. 1995.
224p. Studies in Classical Philology - Townsend Lectures
ISBN:0-8014-8298-4, ISBN13: 978-0-8014-8298-4.
Dewey:179/.3.

Audience: **l,u.** *Choice, 1994.*

Thorndike, Edward Lee   **QL785.T5 2000**
Animal Intelligence: Experimental Studies. Ed. 2. Darryl Bruce
(Introduction by). Trade Paper. Transaction Publishers. Somerset,
NJ. 2000. 297p. ISBN:0-7658-0482-4, ISBN13:
978-0-7658-0482-2. Dewey:591.5/13. LCCN:99-011926.

Audience: **u,f.** *Choice, 2000.*

Tinbergen, Niko   **QL781.T58 1969**
The Study of Instinct. Trade Cloth. Oxford University Press,
Inc. New York, NY. 1969. xx, 228p. ISBN:0-19-857343-X,
ISBN13: 978-0-19-857343-2. Dewey:591.51. LCCN:74-452984.

Audience: **l,u,f.**

Vauclair, Jacques   **QL785.V335 1996**
Animal Cognition: An Introduction to Modern Comparative
Psychology. Trade Cloth. Harvard University Press. Cambridge,
MA. 1996. 222p. ISBN:0-674-03703-0, ISBN13:
978-0-674-03703-8. Dewey:591.51. LCCN:95-046951.

Audience: **l,u.** *Choice, 1997.*

Washburn, Margaret F.　　　　　**QL785**
The Animal Mind. Robert H. Wozniak (Editor). Trade Cloth. Continuum International Publishing Group, Ltd. London, 402p. Classics in Psychology Ser. ISBN:1-85506-695-5, ISBN13: 978-1-85506-695-3. Dewey:156.3.

Audience: **l,u,f.**

Watson, John B.　　　　　　　　**BF671**
Behavior: An Introduction to Comparative Psychology. Trade Cloth. Library Reprints, Inc.. Temecula, CA. 1914. 439p. ISBN:0-7222-2069-3, ISBN13: 978-0-7222-2069-6. Dewey:156.

Audience: **u,f.**

Whishaw, Ian Q. & Kolb, Bryan　　　**QL737.R666W52 2004**
The Behavior of the Laboratory Rat: A Handbook with Tests. Trade Cloth. Oxford University Press, Inc. New York, NY. 2004. 520p. ISBN:0-19-516285-4, ISBN13: 978-0-19-516285-1. Dewey:616/.02733. LCCN:2004-041514.

Audience: **l,u.**

Wrangham, Richard W. (Editor), et al.　　　**QL737.P96**
Chimpanzee Cultures. William C. McGrew, Paul G. Heltne & Frans B. M. De Waal (Editors), Jane Goodall (Foreword by). Trade Paper. Harvard University Press. Cambridge, MA. 1996. 448p. ISBN:0-674-11663-1, ISBN13: 978-0-674-11663-4. Dewey:599.88.

Audience: **l,u,f.**

Wynne, Clive D. L.　　　　　**QL785.W9525 2004**
Do Animals Think? Trade Cloth. Princeton University Press. Princeton, NJ. 2004. 288p. ISBN:0-691-11311-4, ISBN13: 978-0-691-11311-1. Dewey:591.5/13. LCCN:2003-060019.

Audience: **l,u.** *Choice, 2004.*

Yerkes, Robert M.　　　　　**QL737.P9 Y49**
Mental Life of Monkeys and Apes. Trade Cloth. Scholars' Facsimiles & Reprints. Carefree, AZ. 1979. 180p. History of Psychology Ser. ISBN:0-8201-1341-7, ISBN13: 978-0-8201-1341-8. Dewey:156/.32. LCCN:79022241.

Audience: **u,f.**

Yerkes, Robert M. & Stevenson, Fanny　　　**QL737.R6 Y5**
The Dancing Mouse A Study in Animal Behavior. Trade Paper. Kessinger Publishing, LLC. Whitefish, MT. 2004. ISBN:1-4191-5853-8, ISBN13: 978-1-4191-5853-7. Dewey:599.323.

Audience: **u,f.**

Animal Experimental and Comparative Psychology > Learning and Motivation

Spence, Kenneth Wartenbee　　　**BF319**
Behavior Theory and Conditioning. Paper Text. Textbook Publishers. Temecula, CA. 2003. 262p. ISBN:0-7581-0050-7, ISBN13: 978-0-7581-0050-4. Dewey:153.

Audience: **u,f.**

Physiological Psychology and Neuroscience

Cacioppo, John T. (Editor), et al.　　　**QP360.5.S636 2006**
Social Neuroscience: People Thinking about Thinking People. Penny S. Visser & Cynthia L. Pickett (Editors). Trade Cloth. MIT Press. Cambridge, MA. 2005. 328p. Social Neuroscience Ser. ISBN:0-262-03335-6, ISBN13: 978-0-262-03335-0. Dewey:153. LCCN:2005-041691.

Audience: **u,f.** *Choice, 2006.*

Churchland, Paul M.　　　　　**QP356**
The Engine of Reason, the Seat of the Soul: A Philosophical Journey into the Brain. Trade Paper. MIT Press. Cambridge, MA. 1996. 344p. Bradford Bks. ISBN:0-262-53142-9, ISBN13: 978-0-262-53142-9. Dewey:612.8/2/01.

Audience: **g,l,u,f.** *Choice, 1995.*

Cytowic, Richard E.　　　　　**QP435.C97 2002**
Synesthesia: A Union of the Senses. Ed. 2. Trade Cloth. MIT Press. Cambridge, MA. 2002. 424p. Bradford Bks. ISBN:0-262-03296-1, ISBN13: 978-0-262-03296-4. Dewey:612.8. LCCN:2001-056242.

Audience: **l,u,f.**

DeArmond, Stephen J., et al.　　　**QM455.D4 1989**
Structure of the Human Brain: A Photographic Atlas. Ed. 3. Madeline M. Fusco & Maynard M. Dewey (Authors). Spiral. Oxford University Press, Inc. New York, NY. 1989. 208p. ISBN:0-19-504357-X, ISBN13: 978-0-19-504357-0. Dewey:611/.81/0222. LCCN:88-019551.

Audience: **g,l,u,f.**

DeCoursey, Patricia J.　　　　**QP84.6.C453 2004**
Chronobiology: Biological Timekeeping. Jay C. Dunlap & Jennifer J. Loros (Editors). Trade Cloth. Sinauer Associates, Inc. Sunderland, MA. 2003. 382p. ISBN:0-87893-149-X, ISBN13: 978-0-87893-149-1. Dewey:571.7/7. LCCN:2003-004552.

Audience: **u,f.** *Choice, 2004.*

Eibl-Eibesfeldt, Irenaus　　　　**BF701.E4313 1989**
Human Ethology. Trade Cloth. Aldine Transaction. Somerset, NJ. 1989. 848p. Evolutionary Foundations of Human Behavior Ser. ISBN:0-202-02030-4, ISBN13: 978-0-202-02030-3. Dewey:304.5. LCCN:88-038152.

Audience: **g,l,u,f.** *Choice, 1989.*

Finger, Stanley　　　　　　**QP353.F548 2005**
Minds behind the Brain: A History of the Pioneers and Their Discoveries. Trade Paper. Oxford University Press, Inc. New York, NY. 2004. 378p. ISBN:0-19-518182-4, ISBN13: 978-0-19-518182-1. Dewey:612.8/2/09.

Audience: **g,l,u.**

Finger, Stanley　　　　　　**QP353**
Origins of Neuroscience: A History of Explorations into Brain Function. Trade Paper. Oxford University Press, Inc. New York, NY. 2001. 480p. ISBN:0-19-514694-8, ISBN13: 978-0-19-514694-3. Dewey:612.8/09.

Audience: **l,u.** *Choice, 1994.*

Freeman, Walter J.　　　　　**QP409.F73 2001**
How Brains Make up Their Minds. Trade Cloth. Columbia University Press. New York, NY. 2001. 146p. Maps of the Mind

Ser. ISBN:0-231-12008-7, ISBN13: 978-0-231-12008-1. Dewey:612.8/2. LCCN:00-063864.

Audience: **g,l,u.** *Choice, 2001.*

Gallagher, Michela &   **QP360**
  Nelson, Randy J. (Editors)
Handbook of Psychology: Biological Psychology. Irving B. Weiner (Editor-In-Chief). Trade Cloth. John Wiley & Sons, Inc. Hoboken, NJ. 2003. 752p. ISBN:0-471-38403-8, ISBN13: 978-0-471-38403-8. Dewey:152. LCCN:2002-066380.

Audience: **u,f.**

Gazzaniga, Michael S.   **QP360.5.N4986 2004**
  (Editor)
The Cognitive Neurosciences. Ed. 3. Trade Cloth. MIT Press. Cambridge, MA. 2004. 1440p. Bradford Bks. ISBN:0-262-07254-8, ISBN13: 978-0-262-07254-0. Dewey:153. LCCN:2004-052587.

Audience: **u,f.** *Choice, 2005, 1995.*

Gazzaniga, Michael S.   **QP360.5.G393 2005**
The Ethical Brain. Trade Cloth. Dana Press, The. Washington, DC. 2005. 232p. ISBN:1-932594-01-9, ISBN13: 978-1-932594-01-0. Dewey:174.2/928233. LCCN:2004-026860.

Audience: **g,l,u,f.** *Choice, 2005.*

Gazzaniga, Michael S.   **BF701.G33 1992**
Nature's Mind: The Biological Roots of Thinking, Emotions, Sexuality, Language, and Intelligence. Trade Paper. Basic Books. New York, NY. 1994. 240p. ISBN:0-465-04863-3, ISBN13: 978-0-465-04863-2. Dewey:155.7. LCCN:91-059010.

Audience: **g,l,u,f.**

Hebb, D. O.   **BF181.H4 2002**
The Organization of Behavior: A Neuropsychological Theory. Cloth over Boards. Lawrence Erlbaum Associates, Inc. Mahwah, NJ. 2002. 368p. ISBN:0-8058-4300-0, ISBN13: 978-0-8058-4300-2. Dewey:150.19/8. LCCN:2002-018867.

Audience: **u,f.**

Hubel, David H. & Wiesel,   **QP475.H815 2005**
  Torsten N.
Brain and Visual Perception: The Story of a 25-Year Collaboration. Trade Cloth. Oxford University Press, Inc. New York, NY. 2004. 738p. ISBN:0-19-517618-9, ISBN13: 978-0-19-517618-6. Dewey:152.14. LCCN:2004-049553.

Audience: **u.**

Johnson, Steven   **RC341.J648 2004**
Mind Wide Open: Your Brain and the Neuroscience of Everyday Life. Trade Cloth. Simon & Schuster. New York, NY. 2004. 288p. ISBN:0-7432-4165-7, ISBN13: 978-0-7432-4165-6. Dewey:612.8/2. LCCN:2003-063308.

Audience: **g,l.** *Choice, 2004.*

Kandel, Eric R.   **RC435.2.K36 2005**
Psychiatry, Psychoanalysis, and the New Biology of Mind. Trade Cloth. American Psychiatric Publishing, Inc. Arlington, VA. 2005. 398p. ISBN:1-58562-199-4, ISBN13: 978-1-58562-199-6. Dewey:616.89. LCCN:2004-029916.

Audience: **u,f.**

Lashley, Karl S.   **BF181**
The Neuropsychology of Lashley: Selected Papers,. Paper Text. Textbook Publishers. Temecula, CA. 2003. 564p. ISBN:0-7581-8533-2, ISBN13: 978-0-7581-8533-4. Dewey:131.

Audience: **u,f.**

Marshall, Louise H. &   **QP353.M367 1998**
  Magoun, Horace W. (Editors)
Discoveries in the Human Brain: Neuroscience Prehistory, Brain Structure, and Function. Book, Other. Humana Press. Totowa, NJ. 1997. 336p. ISBN:0-89603-435-6, ISBN13: 978-0-89603-435-8. Dewey:612.8/09. LCCN:97-042118.

Audience: **l,u.** *Choice, 1998.*

Morris, Desmond   **QD415**
The Human Zoo. UK-B Format Paperback. Knopf Publishing Group. New York, NY. 1994. 166p. ISBN:0-09-948211-8, ISBN13: 978-0-09-948211-6. Dewey:572.

Audience: **g,l,u,f.**

Nestler, Eric J.   **RC341.N393 2003**
Neurobiology of Mental Illness. Ed. 2. Dennis S. Charney & Eric J. Nestler (Editors). Trade Cloth. Oxford University Press, Inc. New York, NY. 2004. 1,250p. ISBN:0-19-514962-9, ISBN13: 978-0-19-514962-3. Dewey:616.89/07. LCCN:2003-048618.

Audience: **u,f.**

Parasuraman, Raja   **QP405.A876 1998**
The Attentive Brain. Trade Cloth. MIT Press. Cambridge, MA. 1998. 577p. Bradford Bks. ISBN:0-262-16172-9, ISBN13: 978-0-262-16172-5. Dewey:612.8/2. LCCN:97-022985.

Audience: **u,f.**

Posner, Michael J. &   **QP376**
  Raichle, Marcus E.
Images of Mind. Trade Paper. W. H. Freeman & Company. New York, NY. 1997. 256p. ISBN:0-7167-6019-3, ISBN13: 978-0-7167-6019-1. Dewey:612.8/2. LCCN:97-049413.

Audience: **u,f.**

Ramachandran, V. S.   **BF311**
A Brief Tour of Human Consciousness: From Impostor Poodles to Purple Numbers. Trade Cloth. Penguin Group (USA) Inc. New York, NY. 2004. 208p. ISBN:0-13-148686-1, ISBN13: 978-0-13-148686-7. Dewey:612.82. LCCN:2004-304062.

Audience: **g,u,f.** *Choice, 2005.*

Ramachandran, V. S. &   **RC351.R24 1998**
  Blakeslee, Sandra
Phantoms in the Brain: Probing the Mysteries of the Human Mind. Trade Cloth. HarperCollins Publishers. New York, NY. 1998. 320p. ISBN:0-688-15247-3, ISBN13: 978-0-688-15247-5. Dewey:612.8/2. LCCN:98-003953.

Audience: **l,u,f.** *Choice, 1999.*

Rees, Dai & Rose, Steven   **RC341.N53 2004**
  (Editors)
The New Brain Sciences: Perils and Prospects. Cloth Text. Cambridge University Press. New York, NY. 2004. 316p. ISBN:0-521-83009-5, ISBN13: 978-0-521-83009-6. Dewey:612.8/01. LCCN:2004-045660.

Audience: **l,u.** *Choice, 2005.*

Schulkin, Jay   **QP356.45 .S38 1999**
The Neuroendocrine Regulation of Behavior. Trade Cloth. Cambridge University Press. New York, NY. 1998. 334p. ISBN:0-521-45385-2, ISBN13: 978-0-521-45385-1. Dewey:612.8. LCCN:97-041739.

Audience: **u,f.** *Choice, 1999.*

Siegel, Jerome H.   **QP425.S585 2002**
The Neural Control of Sleep and Waking. Trade Paper. Springer. New York, NY. 2002. XVI, 211p. ISBN:0-387-95492-9,

ISBN13: 978-0-387-95492-9. Dewey:612.8/21.
LCCN:2002-067019.

Audience: **u,f.** *Choice, 2003.*

Stebbins, William C. QP461
The Acoustic Sense of Animals. Trade Cloth. Harvard
University Press. Cambridge, MA. 1983. 192p.
ISBN:0-674-00326-8, ISBN13: 978-0-674-00326-2.
Dewey:591.1/825. LCCN:82-021350.

Audience: **u,f.**

Swanson, Larry W. QL937.S93 2003
Brain Maps: Structure of the Rat Brain. Ed. 3. Spiral. Elsevier
Science & Technology Books. Saint Louis, MO. 2003. 215p.
ISBN:0-12-610582-0, ISBN13: 978-0-12-610582-7.
Dewey:573.8/6331935. LCCN:2003-111106.

Audience: **l,u,f.**

Tancredi, Laurence R. BJ45.5.T36 2005
Hardwired Behavior: What Neuroscience Reveals about
Morality. Trade Cloth. Cambridge University Press. New York,
NY. 2005. 240p. ISBN:0-521-86001-6, ISBN13:
978-0-521-86001-7. Dewey:153. LCCN:2005-051318.

Audience: **l,u.** *Choice, 2006.*

Uttal, William R. QP360.5.U87 2005
Neural Theories of Mind: Why the Mind-Brain Problem May
Never Be Solved. Cloth over Boards, Saddle Stitched. Lawrence
Erlbaum Associates, Inc. Mahwah, NJ. 2005. 288p.
ISBN:0-8058-5484-3, ISBN13: 978-0-8058-5484-8. Dewey:153.
LCCN:2004-061915.

Audience: **u,f.** *Choice, 2006.*

Zeman, Adam QP411.Z46 20002
Consciousness: A User's Guide. Cloth over Boards. Yale
University Press. Cumberland, RI. 2003. 416p.
ISBN:0-300-09280-6, ISBN13: 978-0-300-09280-6. Dewey:153.
LCCN:2002-007032.

Audience: **l,u.** *Choice, 2003.*

Psychology and the Humanities

Arnheim, Rudolf N70
Art and Visual Perception: A Psychology of the Creative Eye.
Paper Text. Textbook Publishers. Temecula, CA. 2003. x, 408p.
ISBN:0-7581-2744-8, ISBN13: 978-0-7581-2744-0.
Dewey:701/.15.

Audience: **u,f.**

Arnheim, Rudolf N71
New Essays on the Psychology of Art. Trade Paper. University
of California Press. Berkeley, CA. 1986. 348p.
ISBN:0-520-05554-3, ISBN13: 978-0-520-05554-4.
Dewey:701/.1/5. LCCN:85-001062.

Audience: **l,u,f.**

Berlyne, D. E. (Editor) N0071.B42
Studies in the New Experimental Aesthetics. Trade Paper. Books
on Demand. Ann Arbor, MI. 348p. ISBN:0-8357-9148-3,
ISBN13: 978-0-8357-9148-9. Dewey:701/.1/7.
LCCN:74-013600.

Audience: **u,f.**

Langfeld, Herbert Sidney BH201
The Aesthetic Attitude. Trade Paper. Kessinger Publishing, LLC.
Whitefish, MT. 2004. ISBN:1-4179-6364-6, ISBN13:
978-1-4179-6364-5. Dewey:111.85.

Audience: **u,f.**

Paglia, Camille PN751.P34 1990
Sexual Personae: Art and Decadence from Nefertiti to Emily
Dickinson. Cloth over Boards. Yale University Press.
Cumberland, RI. 1990. 712p. ISBN:0-300-04396-1, ISBN13:
978-0-300-04396-9. Dewey:704.9/428. LCCN:89-031659.

Audience: **g,u,f.** *Choice, 1990.*

Psychology and the Humanities > Literature and Fine Arts

Aiello, Rit & Sloboda, ML3830
John A. (Editors)
Musical Perceptions. Trade Paper. Oxford University Press, Inc.
New York, NY. 1994. 304p. ISBN:0-19-506476-3, ISBN13:
978-0-19-506476-6. Dewey:781/.11. LCCN:93-028888.

Audience: **l,u.** *Choice, 1994.*

Benzon, William ML3830.B35 2001
Beethoven's Anvil: Music in Mind and Culture. Trade Paper.
Basic Books. New York, NY. 2002. 352p. ISBN:0-465-01544-1,
ISBN13: 978-0-465-01544-3. Dewey:781/.11.

Audience: **g,l,u.** *Choice, 2002.*

Cook, Nicholas ML3845
Music, Imagination, and Culture. Trade Paper. Oxford
University Press, Inc. New York, NY. 1992. 272p.
ISBN:0-19-816303-7, ISBN13: 978-0-19-816303-9.
Dewey:781.17. LCCN:89-003352.

Audience: **u,f.**

Cupchik, Gerald C. & BH301.P78 E56 1992
László, Janos (Editors)
Emerging Visions of the Aesthetic Process: In Psychology,
Semiology, and Philosophy. Trade Cloth. Cambridge University
Press. New York, NY. 1992. 343p. ISBN:0-521-40051-1,
ISBN13: 978-0-521-40051-0. Dewey:111.85. LCCN:91-034584.

Audience: **u,f.**

Deutsch, Diana (Editor) ML3830.P9 1999
The Psychology of Music. Ed. 2. Paper Text. Elsevier Science
& Technology Books. Saint Louis, MO. 1998. 807p. Academic
Press Ser. ISBN:0-12-213565-2, ISBN13: 978-0-12-213565-1.
Dewey:781/.11. LCCN:98-085210.

Audience: **u,f.** *B Choice, 1999.*

Gardner, Howard & NX0180.C45A7
Perkins, D. N. (Editors)
Art, Mind, and Education: Research from Project Zero. Trade
Paper. Books on Demand. Ann Arbor, MI. 183p.
ISBN:0-7837-5736-0, ISBN13: 978-0-7837-5736-0.
Dewey:700/.7. LCCN:88-029583.

Audience: **l,u,f.**

Hargreaves, David & North, ML3830.S57 1997
Adrian C. (Editors)
The Social Psychology of Music. Trade Paper. Oxford
University Press, Inc. New York, NY. 1997. 324p.
ISBN:0-19-852383-1, ISBN13: 978-0-19-852383-3.
Dewey:781.1/1. LCCN:96-045586.

Audience: **u,f.** *Choice, 1998.*

Juslin, Patrik N. & Sloboda, John A. (Editors)   ML3830.M965 2001
Music and Emotion: Theory and Research. Trade Paper. Oxford University Press, Inc. New York, NY. 2001. 498p. Series in Affective Science ISBN:0-19-263188-8, ISBN13: 978-0-19-263188-6. Dewey:781/.11. LCCN:2001-036068.
Audience: **u,f.** *Choice, 2002.*

Kemp, Anthony E.   ML3838.K46 1996
The Musical Temperament: Psychology and Personality of Musicians. Trade Paper. Oxford University Press, Inc. New York, NY. 1996. 296p. ISBN:0-19-852362-9, ISBN13: 978-0-19-852362-8. Dewey:781/.11. LCCN:95-039981.
Audience: **u,f.** *Choice, 1997.*

Kris, Ernst   N70 .K84
Psychoanalytic Explorations in Art. Trade Cloth. International Universities Press, Inc. Madison, CT. 377p. ISBN:0-8236-4440-5, ISBN13: 978-0-8236-4440-7. Dewey:701.1.
Audience: **u,f.**

Martindale, Colin (Editor), et al.   BH39.E95 2006
Evolutionary and Neurocognitive Approaches to Aesthetics, Creativity, and the Arts. Paul Locher, Vladimir M. Petrov & Arnold Berleant (Editors). Trade Cloth. Baywood Publishing Company, Inc. Amityville, NY. 2006. 238p. Foundations and Frontiers in Aesthetics Ser. ISBN:0-89503-306-2, ISBN13: 978-0-89503-306-2. Dewey:153.3/5.
Audience: **u,f.**

Sloboda, John (Editor)   ML3838.G38 2000
Generative Processes in Music: The Psychology of Performance, Improvisation, and Composition. Trade Paper. Oxford University Press, Inc. New York, NY. 2001. 316p. ISBN:0-19-850846-8, ISBN13: 978-0-19-850846-5. Dewey:781.4/3111. LCCN:2001-271717.
Audience: **u,f.** *Choice, 2001.*

Sloboda, John A.   ML3830.S52 2005
Exploring the Musical Mind: Cognition, Emotion, Ability, Function. Trade Cloth. Oxford University Press, Inc. New York, NY. 2005. 472p. ISBN:0-19-853012-9, ISBN13: 978-0-19-853012-1. Dewey:781/.11. LCCN:2005-560241.
Audience: **u,f.**

Solso, Robert L.   N71
Cognition and the Visual Arts. Trade Paper. MIT Press. Cambridge, MA. 1996. 312p. Cognitive Psychology Ser., :A Bradford Book ISBN:0-262-69186-8, ISBN13: 978-0-262-69186-4. Dewey:701/.15.
Audience: **l,u.** *Choice, 1995.*

Solso, Robert L.   BF311.S652 2003
The Psychology of Art and the Evolution of the Conscious Brain. Trade Cloth. MIT Press. Cambridge, MA. 2003. 294p. Cognitive Psychology Ser., :A Bradford Book ISBN:0-262-19484-8, ISBN13: 978-0-262-19484-6. Dewey:701/.15. LCCN:2003-042131.
Audience: **l,u,f.** *Choice, 2004.*

Storr, Anthony   ML3830
Music and the Mind. Trade Paper. Ballantine Books. New York, NY. 1993. 224p. ISBN:0-345-38318-4, ISBN13: 978-0-345-38318-1. Dewey:781.1/1.
Audience: **g,l.** *Choice, 1993.*

Zaidel, Dahlia W.   QP430.Z35 2005
Neuropsychology of Art: Neurological, Cognitive and Evolutionary Perspectives. Paper over Boards. Taylor & Francis Group. Abingdon, 2005. 288p. ISBN:1-84169-363-4, ISBN13: 978-1-84169-363-7. Dewey:612.8/2. LCCN:2005-011761.
Audience: **u,f.**

Psychology and the Humanities > Philosophy

Flanagan, Owen   BD450.F535 2003
The Problem of the Soul: Two Visions of Mind and How to Reconcile Them. Trade Paper. Basic Books. New York, NY. 2003. 384p. ISBN:0-465-02461-0, ISBN13: 978-0-465-02461-2. Dewey:128.
Audience: **u,f.**

Frankl, Viktor E.   D805.G3
Man's Search for Meaning. Gordon W. Allport (Preface by). Trade Cloth. Beacon Press. Boston, MA. 2000. 256p. ISBN:0-8070-1426-5, ISBN13: 978-0-8070-1426-4. Dewey:150.1957.
Audience: **g,l,u,f.**

Groddeck, Georg Walther   BF175.5.S48
Book of the It. Trade Cloth. Creation Books. New York, NY. 2005. 256p. ISBN:1-84068-127-6, ISBN13: 978-1-84068-127-7. Dewey:150.195.
Audience: **g,l,u,f.**

Lakoff, George   P37
Women, Fire, and Dangerous Things. Trade Paper. University of Chicago Press. Chicago, IL. 1990. 632p. ISBN:0-226-46804-6, ISBN13: 978-0-226-46804-4. Dewey:401.9. LCCN:86-019136.
Audience: **u,f.**

Popper, Karl R. & Eccles, John C.   BF161
The Self and Its Brain. Cloth Text. Springer. New York, NY. 1985. 597p. ISBN:0-387-08307-3, ISBN13: 978-0-387-08307-0. Dewey:128/.2.
Audience: **l,u,f.**

Robinson, Daniel N.   BF38
Philosophy of Psychology. Trade Paper. Columbia University Press. New York, NY. 1989. 188p. ISBN:0-231-05923-X, ISBN13: 978-0-231-05923-7. Dewey:150/.1. LCCN:84-023878.
Audience: **u,f.** *Choice, 1985.*

Searle, John R.   BD418.3.S4 2004
Mind: A Brief Introduction. Trade Cloth. Oxford University Press, Inc. New York, NY. 2004. 336p. Fundamentals of Philosophy Ser. ISBN:0-19-515733-8, ISBN13: 978-0-19-515733-8. Dewey:128/.2. LCCN:2004-049546.
Audience: **g,l,u,f.** *Choice, 2005.*

Wegner, Daniel M.   BF611.W38 2002
The Illusion of Conscious Will. Trade Cloth. MIT Press. Cambridge, MA. 2002. 408p. Bradford Bks. ISBN:0-262-23222-7, ISBN13: 978-0-262-23222-7. Dewey:153.8. LCCN:2001-054608.
Audience: **u,f.** *Choice, 2003, 2002.*

Wilson, Edward O.   GN365.9.W54 2004
On Human Nature. Ed. 25. Trade Paper. Harvard University Press. Cambridge, MA. 2004. 284p. ISBN:0-674-01638-6,

ISBN13: 978-0-674-01638-5. Dewey:304.5.
LCCN:2004-052605.

Audience: **g,l,u,f.**

Communication Systems

Aitchison, Jean   **P140**
The Seeds of Speech: Language Origin and Evolution. Trade
Paper. Cambridge University Press. New York, NY. 2000. 294p.
A Canto Book Ser. ISBN:0-521-78571-5, ISBN13:
978-0-521-78571-6. Dewey:417.7.

Audience: **g,l,u.** *Choice, 1997.*

Anderson, Rob (Editor),   **P95.455.D54 2003**
et al.
Dialogue: Theorizing Difference in Communication Studies.
Leslie A. Baxter & Kenneth N. Cissna (Editors). Cloth Text.
SAGE Publications, Inc. Thousand Oaks, CA. 2003. 344p.
ISBN:0-7619-2670-4, ISBN13: 978-0-7619-2670-2.
Dewey:302.3/46. LCCN:2003-011937.

Audience: **u,f.** *Choice, 2004.*

Berger, Arthur A.   **P99.B437 1999**
Signs in Contemporary Culture: An Introduction to Semiotics.
Ed. 2. Paper Text. Sheffield Publishing Company. Salem, WI.
1998. 255p. ISBN:1-879215-37-3, ISBN13: 978-1-879215-37-5.
Dewey:302.2. LCCN:98-234718.

Audience: **l,u.**

Biocca, Frank & Levy,   **QA76.9.H85C655 1994**
Mark R. (Editors)
Communication in the Age of Virtual Reality. Cloth Text.
Lawrence Erlbaum Associates, Inc. Mahwah, NJ. 1995. 408p.
Communication Ser. ISBN:0-8058-1549-X, ISBN13:
978-0-8058-1549-8. Dewey:302.23. LCCN:94-020994.

Audience: **g,l,u,f.** *Choice, 1995.*

Chomsky, Noam   **P106 .C524 2000**
New Horizons in the Study of Language and Mind. Neil Smith
(Foreword by). Cloth Text. Cambridge University Press. New
York, NY. 2000. 248p. ISBN:0-521-65147-6, ISBN13:
978-0-521-65147-9. Dewey:401. LCCN:99-036753.

Audience: **l,u,f.** *Choice, 2001.*

Clark, Eve V.   **P118.C547 2002**
First Language Acquisition. Trade Paper. Cambridge University
Press. New York, NY. 2002. 534p. ISBN:0-521-62997-7,
ISBN13: 978-0-521-62997-3. Dewey:401/.93.
LCCN:2002-071574.

Audience: **u,f.** *Choice, 2003.*

Copley, Paul   **P121.R692 2001**
Routledge Companion to Linguistics and Semiotics. Paper over
Boards. Routledge. New York, NY. 2001. 352p. Routledge
Companions Ser. ISBN:0-415-24313-0, ISBN13:
978-0-415-24313-1. Dewey:410. LCCN:2001-019312.

Audience: **g,u,f.** *Choice, 2002.*

Crystal, David   **P29.C65 2003**
A Dictionary of Linguistics and Phonetics. Ed. 5. Trade Paper.
Blackwell Publishing, Inc. Malden, MA. 2003. 536p. The
Language Library ISBN:0-631-22664-8, ISBN13:
978-0-631-22664-2. Dewey:410/.3. LCCN:2002-007797.

Audience: **l,u,f.** *Choice, 2003, 1997.*

Dates, Jannette L. &   **P94.5.A372**
Barlow, William (Editors)
Split Image: African Americans in the Mass Media. Ed. 2. Trade
Cloth. Howard University Press. Washington, DC. 1993. 574p.
ISBN:0-88258-178-3, ISBN13: 978-0-88258-178-1.
Dewey:302.23/089/96073. LCCN:92-047367.

Audience: **g,l,u,f.**

Davies, Alan & Elder,   **P129.H33 2004**
Catherine (Editors)
The Handbook of Applied Linguistics. Trade Cloth. Blackwell
Publishing, Inc. Malden, MA. 2004. 888p. Blackwell Handbooks
in Linguistics, Vol. 17 ISBN:0-631-22899-3, ISBN13:
978-0-631-22899-8. Dewey:418. LCCN:2003-021505.

Audience: **u,f.** *Choice, 2004.*

Dindia, Kathryn & Canary,   **P96.S48S49 2006**
Daniel J. (Editors)
Sex Differences and Similarities in Communication. Ed. 2. Janet
K. Alberts, Jess Alberts, Mike Allen, Peter A. Andersen,
Elizabeth Aries, J. Pete Blair & Renee Reiter Boburka
(Contribution by). Cloth over Boards. Lawrence Erlbaum
Associates, Inc. Mahwah, NJ. 2006. 464p. LEA's
Communication Ser. ISBN:0-8058-5141-0, ISBN13:
978-0-8058-5141-0. Dewey:155.3/3. LCCN:2005-030783.

Audience: **u,f.**

Douglas, Susan J.   **P94.5.W65**
Where the Girls Are: Growing up Female with the Mass Media.
Trade Paper. Crown Publishing Group. New York, NY. 1995.
368p. ISBN:0-8129-2530-0, ISBN13: 978-0-8129-2530-2.
Dewey:302.2/3/082.

Audience: **u,f.** *Choice, 1995.*

Frawley, William J. (Editor)   **P29.I58 2003**
International Encyclopedia of Linguistics, Set. Ed. 2. Trade
Cloth. Oxford University Press, Inc. New York, NY. 2003.
2,200p. ISBN:0-19-513977-1, ISBN13: 978-0-19-513977-8.
Dewey:410/.3. LCCN:2003-000430.

Audience: **l,u,f.** *Choice, 2003.*

Fussell, Susan R. & Kreuz,   **BF637.C45S63 1998**
Roger J. (Editors)
Social and Cognitive Approaches to Interpersonal
Communication. Cloth over Boards. Lawrence Erlbaum
Associates, Inc. Mahwah, NJ. 1998. 312p. ISBN:0-8058-2269-0,
ISBN13: 978-0-8058-2269-4. Dewey:302.2. LCCN:97-021638.

Audience: **u,f.** *Choice, 1999.*

Gilyard, Keith   **P40.45.U5G55 1991**
Voices of the Self: A Study of Language Competence. Paper
Text. Wayne State University Press. Detroit, MI. 1991. 178p.
African American Life Ser. ISBN:0-8143-2225-5, ISBN13:
978-0-8143-2225-3. Dewey:306.4/4. LCCN:90-024737.

Audience: **g,l,u,f.** *Choice, 1992.*

Greenspan, Stanley I. &   **BF458**
Shanker, Stuart
The First Idea: How Symbols, Language, and Intelligence
Evolved in Early Primates and Humans. Trade Cloth. Basic
Books. New York, NY. 2004. 512p. ISBN:0-7382-0680-6,
ISBN13: 978-0-7382-0680-6. Dewey:153.7.
LCCN:2004-010658.

Audience: **u,f.** *Choice, 2005.*

Habermas, Jürgen   **B831.5.H33 1998**
On the Pragmatics of Communication. Trade Cloth. MIT Press.
Cambridge, MA. 1998. 416p. Studies in Contemporary German

Social Thought ISBN:0-262-08265-9, ISBN13:
978-0-262-08265-5. Dewey:306.4/4. LCCN:98-018171.
Audience: **g,u,f.** *Choice, 1999.*

Harris, Randy A. P69
The Linguistics Wars. Trade Paper. Oxford University Press, Inc.
New York, NY. 1995. 368p. ISBN:0-19-509834-X, ISBN13:
978-0-19-509834-1. Dewey:410/.904.
Audience: **g,l,u.** *Choice, 1994.*

Hauser, Marc D. QL776
The Evolution of Communication. Trade Paper. MIT Press.
Cambridge, MA. 1997. 770p. Bradford Bks.
ISBN:0-262-58155-8, ISBN13: 978-0-262-58155-4.
Dewey:591.5/9.
Audience: **u,f.** *Choice, 1997.*

Hewes, Dean E. (Editor) HM132
The Cognitive Bases of Interpersonal Communication. Cloth
over Boards. Lawrence Erlbaum Associates, Inc. Mahwah, NJ.
1995. 264p. Communication Ser. ISBN:0-8058-0469-2, ISBN13:
978-0-8058-0469-0. Dewey:302/.12.
Audience: **u,f.** *Choice, 1995.*

Hoggart, Richard HM1206
Mass Media in a Mass Society: Myth and Reality. Trade Cloth.
Continuum International Publishing Group, Ltd. London, 2004.
192p. ISBN:0-8264-7285-0, ISBN13: 978-0-8264-7285-4.
Dewey:306/.0941. LCCN:2004-299464.
Audience: **g,l,u,f.** *Choice, 2004.*

Homer, Bruce D. & BF721.D428 2005
Tamis-LeMonda, Catherine S. (Editors)
The Development of Social Cognition and Communication.
Robyn Fivush & Catherine A. Haden (Contribution by). Cloth
over Boards. Lawrence Erlbaum Associates, Inc. Mahwah, NJ.
2005. 400p. ISBN:0-8058-4322-1, ISBN13: 978-0-8058-4322-4.
Dewey:155.4/13. LCCN:2005-040252.
Audience: **u,f.** *Choice, 2006.*

Jacyna, L. S. RC425.J33 2000
Lost Words: Narratives of Language and the Brain, 1825-1926.
Trade Cloth. Princeton University Press. Princeton, NJ. 2000.
254p. ISBN:0-691-00413-7, ISBN13: 978-0-691-00413-6.
Dewey:616.85/52/009. LCCN:99-089724.
Audience: **u,f.** *Choice, 2001.*

Janda, Richard D. P120.S48H36 2003
The Handbook of Historical Linguistics. Brian D. Joseph
(Editor). Trade Cloth. Blackwell Publishing, Inc. Malden, MA.
2003. 904p. Handbooks in Linguistics, Vol. 13
ISBN:0-631-19571-8, ISBN13: 978-0-631-19571-9.
Dewey:417/.7. LCCN:2002-074363.
Audience: **l,u,f.** *Choice, 2003.*

Jones, Steve (Editor) QA76.575.E5368 2003
Encyclopedia of New Media: An Essential Reference Guide to
Communication and Technology. Trade Cloth. SAGE
Publications, Inc. Thousand Oaks, CA. 2002. 544p.
ISBN:0-7619-2382-9, ISBN13: 978-0-7619-2382-4.
Dewey:302.23/4/03. LCCN:2002-013229.
Audience: **l,u,f.** *Choice, 2003.*

Kent, Raymond D. (Editor) RC423.M56 2003
The MIT Encyclopedia of Communication Disorders. Trade
Cloth. MIT Press. Cambridge, MA. 2003. 648p. Bradford Bks.

ISBN:0-262-11278-7, ISBN13: 978-0-262-11278-9.
Dewey:616.85/5/003. LCCN:2003-059941.
Audience: **u,f.** *Choice, 2004.*

Kitch, Carolyn 2001027415 [P]
The Girl on the Magazine Cover: The Origins of Visual
Stereotypes in American Mass Media. Trade Paper. University
of North Carolina Press. Chapel Hill, NC. 2001. 272p.
ISBN:0-8078-4978-2, ISBN13: 978-0-8078-4978-1.
Dewey:302.23/082/0973. LCCN:2001-027415.
Audience: **l,u,f.** *Choice, 2002.*

Oostendorp, Herre Van T58.5.C74 2005
(Editor), et al.
Creation, Use, and Deployment of Digital Information. Leen
Breure & Andrew Dillon (Editors). Cloth over Boards.
Lawrence Erlbaum Associates, Inc. Mahwah, NJ. 2005. 344p.
ISBN:0-8058-4781-2, ISBN13: 978-0-8058-4781-9.
Dewey:025.04. LCCN:2005-045524.
Audience: **g,l,u.** *Choice, 2005.*

Peters, John Durham P90
Speaking into the Air: A History of the Idea of Communication.
Trade Paper. University of Chicago Press. Chicago, IL. 2001.
304p. ISBN:0-226-66277-2, ISBN13: 978-0-226-66277-0.
Dewey:302.2/01.
Audience: **u,f.** *Choice, 2000.*

Pinker, Steven P106
The Language Instinct: How the Mind Creates Language. Trade
Paper. HarperCollins Publishers. New York, NY. 2000. 544p.
Perennial Classics Ser. ISBN:0-06-095833-2, ISBN13:
978-0-06-095833-6. Dewey:400.
Audience: **g,l,u.**

Pinker, Steven P302
Words and Rules: The Ingredients of Language. Trade Cloth.
DIANE Publishing Company. Collingdale, PA. 2002. 348p.
ISBN:0-7567-5611-1, ISBN13: 978-0-7567-5611-6.
Dewey:401.4/1.
Audience: **g,l,u,f.** *Choice, 2000.*

Rawlins, William K. HM132.5.R38 1991
Friendship Matters: Communication, Dialectics, and the Life
Course. Trade Cloth. Aldine Transaction. Somerset, NJ. 1992.
307p. Communication and Social Order Ser.
ISBN:0-202-30403-5, ISBN13: 978-0-202-30403-8.
Dewey:302.3/4. LCCN:91-030676.
Audience: **u,f.** *Choice, 1992.*

Rieber, Robert W. (Editor) BF121.V94 1997
The Collected Works of L. S. Vygotsky: The History of the
Development of Higher Mental Functions. Marie J. Hall
(Translator), Joseph Glick (Prologue by). Trade Cloth. Basic
Books. New York, NY. 1997. 312p. Cognition and Language
Ser. ISBN:0-306-45609-5, ISBN13: 978-0-306-45609-1.
Dewey:150. LCCN:87-007219.
Audience: **u,f.** *Choice, 1998.*

Ruscher, Janet B. BF575.P9R87 2001
Prejudiced Communication: A Social Psychological Perspective.
Cloth over Boards. Guilford Publications, Inc. New York, NY.
2001. 240p. ISBN:1-57230-638-6, ISBN13: 978-1-57230-638-7.
Dewey:303.3/85. LCCN:00-054356.
Audience: **u,f.** *Choice, 2001.*

Sealey, Alison & Carter, Bob   **P129**
Applied Linguistics as Social Science. Trade Cloth. Continuum International Publishing Group, Ltd. London, 2004. 224p. Advances in Applied Linguistics Ser. ISBN:0-8264-5519-0, ISBN13: 978-0-8264-5519-2. Dewey:418. LCCN:2004-301173.
Audience: **l,u**. *Choice, 2005.*

Shane, Ed   **P92.U5S48 2001**
Disconnected America: The Consequences of Mass Media in a Narcissistic World. Donald A. Fishman (Foreword by). Trade Cloth. M. E. Sharpe Inc. Armonk, NY. 2000. xv, 205p. Media, Communication, and Culture in America Ser. ISBN:0-7656-0526-0, ISBN13: 978-0-7656-0526-9. Dewey:302.23/0973. LCCN:00-059503.
Audience: **g,l,u**. *Choice, 2001.*

Skinner, B. F.   **BF455**
Verbal Behavior. Cloth Text. Copley Publishing Group. Acton, MA. 2002. 515p. ISBN:1-58390-021-7, ISBN13: 978-1-58390-021-5. Dewey:158.83.
Audience: **u,f.**

Todorov, Tzvetan   **P99.T613 1982**
Theories of the Symbol. Catherine Porter (Translator). Trade Cloth. Cornell University Press. Ithaca, NY. 1984. 302p. ISBN:0-8014-1192-0, ISBN13: 978-0-8014-1192-2. Dewey:001.51. LCCN:81-017420.
Audience: **u,f.**

Trask, R. L. (Editor)   **P143**
Dictionary of Historical and Comparative Linguistics. Trade Cloth. Fitzroy Dearborn Publishers, Inc. Chicago, IL. 2001. 500p. ISBN:1-57958-218-4, ISBN13: 978-1-57958-218-0. Dewey:417.703.
Audience: **l,u,f.** *Choice, 2001.*

Trask, R. L.   **P29.T687 1998**
Key Concepts in Language and Linguistics. Paper over Boards. Routledge. New York, NY. 1998. 400p. Key Concepts Ser. ISBN:0-415-15741-2, ISBN13: 978-0-415-15741-4. Dewey:410/.3. LCCN:98-024025.
Audience: **l,u,f.** *Choice, 1999.*

Trevor, Harley   **P37**
Psychology of Language: From Data to Theory. Ed. 2. Paper over Boards. Taylor & Francis Group. Abingdon, 2001. 544p. ISBN:0-86377-866-6, ISBN13: 978-0-86377-866-7. Dewey:401.9.
Audience: **u,f.**

Turnbull, William   **BF637.C45T86 2003**
Language in Action: Psychological Models of Conversation. Paper over Boards. Routledge. New York, NY. 2003. 248p. International Series in Social Psychology ISBN:0-415-19867-4, ISBN13: 978-0-415-19867-7. Dewey:153.6. LCCN:2002-012280.
Audience: **u,f.** *Choice, 2004.*

Vallacher, Robin R. & Nowak, Andrzej   **HM251 .D87 1994**
Dynamical Systems in Social Psychology. Robin R. Vallacher & Andrzej Nowak (Editors). Trade Cloth. Elsevier Science & Technology Books. Saint Louis, MO. 1994. 305p. ISBN:0-12-709990-5, ISBN13: 978-0-12-709990-3. Dewey:302. LCCN:93-011325.
Audience: **f.**

van Ginneken, Jaap   **HM1236.G556 2002**
Collective Behavior and Public Opinion: Rapid Shifts in Opinion and Communication. Cloth over Boards. Lawrence Erlbaum Associates, Inc. Mahwah, NJ. 2003. 312p. The European Institute for the Media Ser. ISBN:0-8058-4386-8, ISBN13: 978-0-8058-4386-6. Dewey:303.3/8. LCCN:2002-019731.
Audience: **u,f.** *Choice, 2003.*

Vangelisti, Anita L. (Editor)   **HQ519.H36 2003**
Handbook of Family Communication. Cloth over Boards. Lawrence Erlbaum Associates, Inc. Mahwah, NJ. 2003. 792p. LEA's Communication Ser. ISBN:0-8058-4130-X, ISBN13: 978-0-8058-4130-5. Dewey:306.87. LCCN:2003-015733.
Audience: **u,f.** *Choice, 2004.*

Vygotsky, L. S.   **BF121.V9413 1987**
The Collected Works of L. S. Vygotsky: Problems of General Psychology, Including the Volume "Thinking and Speech". Trade Cloth. Basic Books. New York, NY. 1988. 406p. Cognition and Language Ser. ISBN:0-306-42441-X, ISBN13: 978-0-306-42441-0. Dewey:150. LCCN:87-007219.
Audience: **l,u.**

Williams, Angela & Nussbaum, Jon F.   **HM726.W56 2001**
Intergenerational Communication Across the Lifespan. Cloth over Boards. Lawrence Erlbaum Associates, Inc. Mahwah, NJ. 2001. 352p. LEA's Communication Ser. ISBN:0-8058-2248-8, ISBN13: 978-0-8058-2248-9. Dewey:306.87. LCCN:99-056785.
Audience: **l,u,f.** *Choice, 2001.*

Communication Systems > Linguistics and Language & Speech

Aitchison, Jean   **P140**
The Seeds of Speech: Language Origin and Evolution. Trade Paper. Cambridge University Press. New York, NY. 2000. 294p. A Canto Book Ser. ISBN:0-521-78571-5, ISBN13: 978-0-521-78571-6. Dewey:417.7.
Audience: **g,l,u.** *Choice, 1997.*

Bruner, Jerome S.   **P37**
Child's Talk: Learning to Use Language. Trade Paper. W. W. Norton & Company, Inc. New York, NY. 1985. 144p. ISBN:0-393-95345-9, ISBN13: 978-0-393-95345-9. Dewey:401/.9. LCCN:83-042676.
Audience: **l,u,f.**

Cameron, Deborah   **P106**
Feminism and Linguistic Theory. Ed. 2. Trade Paper. Palgrave Macmillan. New York, NY. 1992. 257p. ISBN:0-312-08376-9, ISBN13: 978-0-312-08376-2. Dewey:400. LCCN:92-008906.
Audience: **l,u,f.**

Chomsky, Noam   **P107**
Language and Mind. Ed. 3. Trade Cloth. Cambridge University Press. New York, NY. 2006. 208p. ISBN:0-521-85819-4, ISBN13: 978-0-521-85819-9. Dewey:401/.9.
Audience: **u,f.**

Chomsky, Noam   **P107.C535 2004**
Rules and Representations. Norbert Hornstein (Foreword by). Trade Paper. Columbia University Press. New York, NY. 2005. 368p. Columbia Classics in Philosophy Ser.

ISBN:0-231-13271-9, ISBN13: 978-0-231-13271-8. Dewey:401. LCCN:2004-061788.

Audience: **u,f.**

Chomsky, Noam P106 .C524 2000
New Horizons in the Study of Language and Mind. Neil Smith (Foreword by). Cloth Text. Cambridge University Press. New York, NY. 2000. 248p. ISBN:0-521-65147-6, ISBN13: 978-0-521-65147-9. Dewey:401. LCCN:99-036753.

Audience: **l,u,f.** *Choice, 2001.*

Clark, Eve V. P118.C547 2002
First Language Acquisition. Trade Paper. Cambridge University Press. New York, NY. 2002. 534p. ISBN:0-521-62997-7, ISBN13: 978-0-521-62997-3. Dewey:401/.93. LCCN:2002-071574.

Audience: **u,f.** *Choice, 2003.*

Copley, Paul P121.R692 2001
Routledge Companion to Linguistics and Semiotics. Paper over Boards. Routledge. New York, NY. 2001. 352p. Routledge Companions Ser. ISBN:0-415-24313-0, ISBN13: 978-0-415-24313-1. Dewey:410. LCCN:2001-019312.

Audience: **g,u,f.** *Choice, 2002.*

Crystal, David P29.C65 2003
A Dictionary of Linguistics and Phonetics. Ed. 5. Trade Paper. Blackwell Publishing, Inc. Malden, MA. 2003. 536p. The Language Library ISBN:0-631-22664-8, ISBN13: 978-0-631-22664-2. Dewey:410/.3. LCCN:2002-007797.

Audience: **l,u,f.** *Choice, 2003, 1997.*

Davies, Alan & Elder, Catherine (Editors) P129.H33 2004
The Handbook of Applied Linguistics. Trade Cloth. Blackwell Publishing, Inc. Malden, MA. 2004. 888p. Blackwell Handbooks in Linguistics, Vol. 17 ISBN:0-631-22899-3, ISBN13: 978-0-631-22899-8. Dewey:418. LCCN:2003-021505.

Audience: **u,f.** *Choice, 2004.*

Farb, Peter P40
Word Play: What Happens When People Talk. Trade Paper. Random House, Inc. New York, NY. 1993. 384p. ISBN:0-679-73408-2, ISBN13: 978-0-679-73408-6. Dewey:301.2/1. LCCN:92-056361.

Audience: **g,l,u,f.**

Frawley, William J. (Editor) P29.I58 2003
International Encyclopedia of Linguistics, Set. Ed. 2. Trade Cloth. Oxford University Press, Inc. New York, NY. 2003. 2,200p. ISBN:0-19-513977-1, ISBN13: 978-0-19-513977-8. Dewey:410/.3. LCCN:2003-000430.

Audience: **l,u,f.** *Choice, 2003.*

Goffman, Erving P95
Forms of Talk. Book, Other. University of Pennsylvania Press. Philadelphia, PA. 1981. 344p. University of Pennsylvania Publications in Conduct and Communication ISBN:0-8122-1112-X, ISBN13: 978-0-8122-1112-2. Dewey:001.54/2. LCCN:80-052806.

Audience: **l,u,f.**

Greenspan, Stanley I. & Shanker, Stuart BF458
The First Idea: How Symbols, Language, and Intelligence Evolved in Early Primates and Humans. Trade Cloth. Basic

Books. New York, NY. 2004. 512p. ISBN:0-7382-0680-6, ISBN13: 978-0-7382-0680-6. Dewey:153.7. LCCN:2004-010658.

Audience: **u,f.** *Choice, 2005.*

Gumperz, John J. (Editor, Contribution by) P40 .L289 1982
Language and Social Identity. Ed. 2. Paul Drew, Marjorie Harness Goodwin & Deborah Schiffrin (Contribution by). Trade Paper. Cambridge University Press. New York, NY. 1983. 288p. Studies in Interactional Sociolinguistics, No. 2 ISBN:0-521-28897-5, ISBN13: 978-0-521-28897-2. Dewey:401/.9. LCCN:82-004331.

Audience: **u,f.**

Harris, Randy A. P69
The Linguistics Wars. Trade Paper. Oxford University Press, Inc. New York, NY. 1995. 368p. ISBN:0-19-509834-X, ISBN13: 978-0-19-509834-1. Dewey:410/.904.

Audience: **g,l,u.** *Choice, 1994.*

Hauser, Marc D. QL776
The Evolution of Communication. Trade Paper. MIT Press. Cambridge, MA. 1997. 770p. Bradford Bks. ISBN:0-262-58155-8, ISBN13: 978-0-262-58155-4. Dewey:591.5/9.

Audience: **u,f.** *Choice, 1997.*

Jacyna, L. S. RC425.J33 2000
Lost Words: Narratives of Language and the Brain, 1825-1926. Trade Cloth. Princeton University Press. Princeton, NJ. 2000. 254p. ISBN:0-691-00413-7, ISBN13: 978-0-691-00413-6. Dewey:616.85/52/009. LCCN:99-089724.

Audience: **u,f.** *Choice, 2001.*

Janda, Richard D. P120.S48H36 2003
The Handbook of Historical Linguistics. Brian D. Joseph (Editor). Trade Cloth. Blackwell Publishing, Inc. Malden, MA. 2003. 904p. Handbooks in Linguistics, Vol. 13 ISBN:0-631-19571-8, ISBN13: 978-0-631-19571-9. Dewey:417/.7. LCCN:2002-074363.

Audience: **l,u,f.** *Choice, 2003.*

Pinker, Steven P106
The Language Instinct: How the Mind Creates Language. Trade Paper. HarperCollins Publishers. New York, NY. 2000. 544p. Perennial Classics Ser. ISBN:0-06-095833-2, ISBN13: 978-0-06-095833-6. Dewey:400.

Audience: **g,l,u.**

Pinker, Steven P302
Words and Rules: The Ingredients of Language. Trade Cloth. DIANE Publishing Company. Collingdale, PA. 2002. 348p. ISBN:0-7567-5611-1, ISBN13: 978-0-7567-5611-6. Dewey:401.4/1.

Audience: **g,l,u,f.** *Choice, 2000.*

Rieber, Robert W. (Editor) BF121.V94 1997
The Collected Works of L. S. Vygotsky: The History of the Development of Higher Mental Functions. Marie J. Hall (Translator), Joseph Glick (Prologue by). Trade Cloth. Basic Books. New York, NY. 1997. 312p. Cognition and Language Ser. ISBN:0-306-45609-5, ISBN13: 978-0-306-45609-1. Dewey:150. LCCN:87-007219.

Audience: **u,f.** *Choice, 1998.*

Sapir, Edward   **P105**
Language an Introduction to the Study of Speech. Trade Paper. Kessinger Publishing, LLC. Whitefish, MT. 2005. ISBN:0-7661-9576-7, ISBN13: 978-0-7661-9576-9. Dewey:404.
Audience: **g,l,u,f.**

Sapir, Edward   **P27.S33**
Selected Writings of Edward Sapir in Language, Culture, and Personality. David G. Mandelbaum (Editor). Trade Paper. University of California Press. Berkeley, CA. 1949. 653p. ISBN:0-520-05594-2, ISBN13: 978-0-520-05594-0. Dewey:408.9.
Audience: **u,f.**

Sealey, Alison & Carter, Bob   **P129**
Applied Linguistics as Social Science. Trade Cloth. Continuum International Publishing Group, Ltd. London, 2004. 224p. Advances in Applied Linguistics Ser. ISBN:0-8264-5519-0, ISBN13: 978-0-8264-5519-2. Dewey:418. LCCN:2004-301173.
Audience: **l,u.** *Choice, 2005.*

Sinclair, A. (Editor), et al.   **P118.C48**
The Child's Conception of Language. R. J. Jarvella & Willem J. Levelt (Editors). Cloth Text. Springer. New York, NY. 1980. viii, 268p. Language and Communication Ser., Vol. 2 ISBN:0-387-09153-X, ISBN13: 978-0-387-09153-2. Dewey:401/.9. LCCN:80-512674.
Audience: **l,u,f.**

Skinner, B. F.   **BF455**
Verbal Behavior. Cloth Text. Copley Publishing Group. Acton, MA. 2002. 515p. ISBN:1-58390-021-7, ISBN13: 978-1-58390-021-5. Dewey:158.83.
Audience: **u,f.**

Thorne, Barrie (Editor)   **P120.S48.L36 1983**
Language, Gender and Society. Trade Paper. Thomson Heinle. Boston, MA. 1983. "x, 342"p. ISBN:0-88377-268-X, ISBN13: 978-0-88377-268-3. Dewey:401/.9. LCCN:82-022537.
Audience: **g,l,u.**

Trask, R. L. (Editor)   **P143**
Dictionary of Historical and Comparative Linguistics. Trade Cloth. Fitzroy Dearborn Publishers, Inc. Chicago, IL. 2001. 500p. ISBN:1-57958-218-4, ISBN13: 978-1-57958-218-0. Dewey:417.703.
Audience: **l,u,f.** *Choice, 2001.*

Trask, R. L.   **P29.T687 1998**
Key Concepts in Language and Linguistics. Paper over Boards. Routledge. New York, NY. 1998. 400p. Key Concepts Ser. ISBN:0-415-15741-2, ISBN13: 978-0-415-15741-4. Dewey:410/.3. LCCN:98-024025.
Audience: **l,u,f.** *Choice, 1999.*

Trevor, Harley   **P37**
Psychology of Language: From Data to Theory. Ed. 2. Paper over Boards. Taylor & Francis Group. Abingdon, 2001. 544p. ISBN:0-86377-866-6, ISBN13: 978-0-86377-866-7. Dewey:401.9.
Audience: **u,f.**

Turnbull, William   **BF637.C45T86 2003**
Language in Action: Psychological Models of Conversation. Paper over Boards. Routledge. New York, NY. 2003. 248p. International Series in Social Psychology ISBN:0-415-19867-4,

ISBN13: 978-0-415-19867-7. Dewey:153.6. LCCN:2002-012280.
Audience: **u,f.** *Choice, 2004.*

Vygotsky, L. S.   **BF121.V9413 1987**
The Collected Works of L. S. Vygotsky: Problems of General Psychology, Including the Volume "Thinking and Speech". Trade Cloth. Basic Books. New York, NY. 1988. 406p. Cognition and Language Ser. ISBN:0-306-42441-X, ISBN13: 978-0-306-42441-0. Dewey:150. LCCN:87-007219.
Audience: **l,u.**

Whorf, Benjamin Lee   **P27.W53**
Language, Thought, and Reality: Selected Writings. Paper Text. Textbook Publishers. Temecula, CA. 2003. xi, 278p. ISBN:0-7581-3222-0, ISBN13: 978-0-7581-3222-2. Dewey:404.
Audience: **g,l,u,f.** *B*

Communication Systems > Mass Media Communications

Biocca, Frank & Levy, Mark R. (Editors)   **QA76.9.H85C655 1994**
Communication in the Age of Virtual Reality. Cloth Text. Lawrence Erlbaum Associates, Inc. Mahwah, NJ. 1995. 408p. Communication Ser. ISBN:0-8058-1549-X, ISBN13: 978-0-8058-1549-8. Dewey:302.23. LCCN:94-020994.
Audience: **g,l,u,f.** *Choice, 1995.*

Chomsky, Noam   **P106 .C524 2000**
New Horizons in the Study of Language and Mind. Neil Smith (Foreword by). Cloth Text. Cambridge University Press. New York, NY. 2000. 248p. ISBN:0-521-65147-6, ISBN13: 978-0-521-65147-9. Dewey:401. LCCN:99-036753.
Audience: **l,u,f.** *Choice, 2001.*

Dates, Jannette L. & Barlow, William (Editors)   **P94.5.A372**
Split Image: African Americans in the Mass Media. Ed. 2. Trade Cloth. Howard University Press. Washington, DC. 1993. 574p. ISBN:0-88258-178-3, ISBN13: 978-0-88258-178-1. Dewey:302.23/089/96073. LCCN:92-047367.
Audience: **g,l,u,f.**

Douglas, Susan J.   **P94.5.W65**
Where the Girls Are: Growing up Female with the Mass Media. Trade Paper. Crown Publishing Group. New York, NY. 1995. 368p. ISBN:0-8129-2530-0, ISBN13: 978-0-8129-2530-2. Dewey:302.2/3/082.
Audience: **u,f.** *Choice, 1995.*

Hoggart, Richard   **HM1206**
Mass Media in a Mass Society: Myth and Reality. Trade Cloth. Continuum International Publishing Group, Ltd. London, 2004. 192p. ISBN:0-8264-7285-0, ISBN13: 978-0-8264-7285-4. Dewey:306/.0941. LCCN:2004-299464.
Audience: **g,l,u,f.** *Choice, 2004.*

Hovland, Carl Iver   **P90**
Communication and Persuasion: Psychological Studies of Opinion Change,. Paper Text. Textbook Publishers. Temecula, CA. 2003. xii, 315p. ISBN:0-7581-0148-1, ISBN13: 978-0-7581-0148-8. Dewey:808.
Audience: **u,f.**

Jones, Steve (Editor)   QA76.575.E5368 2003
Encyclopedia of New Media: An Essential Reference Guide to Communication and Technology. Trade Cloth. SAGE Publications, Inc. Thousand Oaks, CA. 2002. 544p. ISBN:0-7619-2382-9, ISBN13: 978-0-7619-2382-4. Dewey:302.23/4/03. LCCN:2002-013229.

            Audience: **l,u,f.** *Choice, 2003.*

Kitch, Carolyn   2001027415 [P]
The Girl on the Magazine Cover: The Origins of Visual Stereotypes in American Mass Media. Trade Paper. University of North Carolina Press. Chapel Hill, NC. 2001. 272p. ISBN:0-8078-4978-2, ISBN13: 978-0-8078-4978-1. Dewey:302.23/082/0973. LCCN:2001-027415.

            Audience: **l,u,f.** *Choice, 2002.*

McLuhan, Marshall &   P90.M258 1996
   Fiore, Quentin
The Medium Is the Message. Jerome Agel (Contribution by). Trade Paper. Wired Books, Inc. San Francisco, CA. 1996. 160p. ISBN:1-888869-02-X, ISBN13: 978-1-888869-02-6. Dewey:302.23. LCCN:98-164370.

            Audience: **g,l,u,f.**

McLuhan, Marshall   P90.M26 2003
Understanding Media: The Extensions of Man (Critical Edition). Terrence Gordon (Editor). Trade Cloth. Gingko Press, Inc. Corte Madera, CA. 2005. 640p. ISBN:1-58423-073-8, ISBN13: 978-1-58423-073-1. Dewey:302.23. LCCN:2003-012174.

            Audience: **u,f.** *B*

Oostendorp, Herre Van   T58.5.C74 2005
   (Editor), et al.
Creation, Use, and Deployment of Digital Information. Leen Breure & Andrew Dillon (Editors). Cloth over Boards. Lawrence Erlbaum Associates, Inc. Mahwah, NJ. 2005. 344p. ISBN:0-8058-4781-2, ISBN13: 978-0-8058-4781-9. Dewey:025.04. LCCN:2005-045524.

            Audience: **g,l,u.** *Choice, 2005.*

Shane, Ed   P92.U5S48 2001
Disconnected America: The Consequences of Mass Media in a Narcissistic World. Donald A. Fishman (Foreword by). Trade Cloth. M. E. Sharpe Inc. Armonk, NY. 2000. xv, 205p. Media, Communication, and Culture in America Ser. ISBN:0-7656-0526-0, ISBN13: 978-0-7656-0526-9. Dewey:302.23/0973. LCCN:00-059503.

            Audience: **g,l,u.** *Choice, 2001.*

van Ginneken, Jaap   HM1236.G556 2002
Collective Behavior and Public Opinion: Rapid Shifts in Opinion and Communication. Cloth over Boards. Lawrence Erlbaum Associates, Inc. Mahwah, NJ. 2003. 312p. The European Institute for the Media Ser. ISBN:0-8058-4386-8, ISBN13: 978-0-8058-4386-6. Dewey:303.3/8. LCCN:2002-019731.

            Audience: **u,f.** *Choice, 2003.*

Developmental Psychology

Adams, Gerald R. &   BF724.B487 2003
   Berzonsky, Michael D. (Editors)
Blackwell Handbook of Adolescence. Trade Cloth. Blackwell Publishing, Inc. Malden, MA. 2003. 680p. Blackwell Handbooks

of Developmental Psychology Ser., Vol. 4 ISBN:0-631-21919-6, ISBN13: 978-0-631-21919-4. Dewey:155.5. LCCN:2002-151837.

            Audience: **l,u.** *Choice, 2003.*

Adams, Gerald R. &   RJ503.H266 2005
   Gullotta, Thomas P. (Editors)
Handbook of Adolescent Behavioral Problems: Evidence-Based Approaches to Prevention and Treatment. Trade Cloth. Springer. New York, NY. 2006. XXIV, 666p. ISBN:0-387-23845-X, ISBN13: 978-0-387-23845-6. Dewey:616.89/00835. LCCN:2004-062642.

            Audience: **u,f.** *Choice, 2006.*

Bank, Stephen & Kahn,   BF723.S43
   Michael
Sibling Bond. Trade Paper. Basic Books. New York, NY. 2003. 400p. ISBN:0-465-07843-5, ISBN13: 978-0-465-07843-1. Dewey:155.9/24.

            Audience: **g,l,u,f.**

Bloom, Benjamin S.   BF723.M56D48 1985
Developing Talent in Young People. Trade Paper. Ballantine Books. New York, NY. 1985. 572p. ISBN:0-345-31509-X, ISBN13: 978-0-345-31509-0. Dewey:155.4/13. LCCN:84-090809.

            Audience: **g,l,u,f.**

Bronfenbrenner, Urie   BF721
The Ecology of Human Development: Experiments by Nature and Design. Trade Paper. Harvard University Press. Cambridge, MA. 1979. 348p. ISBN:0-674-22457-4, ISBN13: 978-0-674-22457-5. Dewey:155.4. LCCN:78-027232.

            Audience: **l,u,f.**

Cassidy, Jude & Shaver,   BF575.A86H36 1999
   Phillip R. (Editors)
Handbook of Attachment: Theory, Research, and Clinical Applications. Paper over Boards. Guilford Publications, Inc. New York, NY. 1999. 925p. ISBN:1-57230-087-6, ISBN13: 978-1-57230-087-3. Dewey:155.9/2. LCCN:98-053527.

            Audience: **u,f.** *Choice, 1999.*

Clark, Kenneth B.   BF723.R3C5 1988
Prejudice and Your Child. Stuart W. Cook (Foreword by). Trade Paper. Wesleyan University Press. Middletown, CT. 1988. 327p. ISBN:0-8195-6155-X, ISBN13: 978-0-8195-6155-8. Dewey:155.4/18. LCCN:85-017862.

            Audience: **g,l,u.**

Coopersmith, Stanley   BF723.S3.C6
The Antecedents of Self-Esteem. Trade Cloth. W. H. Freeman & Company. New York, NY. 1967. "ix, 283"p. A Series of Books in Behavioral Science Ser. ISBN:0-7167-0912-0, ISBN13: 978-0-7167-0912-1. Dewey:155.41/8. LCCN:67-021126.

            Audience: **g,l,u,f.**

Cruikshank, Margaret   BF724.55.A35C78 2002
Learning to Be Old: Gender, Culture, and Aging. Book, Other. Rowman & Littlefield Publishers, Inc. Lanham, MD. 2002. 256p. ISBN:0-8476-9848-3, ISBN13: 978-0-8476-9848-6. Dewey:305.26. LCCN:2002-005352.

            Audience: **l,u,f.** *Choice, 2003.*

Damon, William   BF721.H242 1998
Handbook of Child Psychology, Set. Ed. 5. Trade Paper. John Wiley & Sons, Inc. Hoboken, NJ. 2000. 680p.

ISBN:0-471-37789-9, ISBN13: 978-0-471-37789-4.
Dewey:155.4.

Audience: **l,u,f.**

Davidman, Lynn   **BF575.G7**
Motherloss. Trade Paper. University of California Press.
Berkeley, CA. 2002. 308p. ISBN:0-520-23200-3, ISBN13:
978-0-520-23200-6. Dewey:155.937. LCCN:99-053072.

Audience: **l,u,f.** *Choice, 2000.*

Demick, Jack & Andreoletti,   **BF724.5.H36 2002**
  Carrie (Editors)
Handbook of Adult Development. Trade Cloth. Springer. New
York, NY. 2003. 614p. The Plenum Series in Adult
Development and Aging ISBN:0-306-46758-5, ISBN13:
978-0-306-46758-5. Dewey:155.6. LCCN:2002-025686.

Audience: **u,f.** *Choice, 2004.*

Dunn, Judy   **BF723.S6D86 1988**
The Beginnings of Social Understanding. Trade Cloth. Harvard
University Press. Cambridge, MA. 1988. 240p. The Developing
Child Ser. ISBN:0-674-06453-4, ISBN13: 978-0-674-06453-9.
Dewey:155.4/23. LCCN:88-000766.

Audience: **u,f.** *Choice, 1989.*

Dunn, Judy   **HQ784.F7D86 2004**
Children's Friendships: The Beginnings of Intimacy. Trade
Paper. Blackwell Publishing, Inc. Malden, MA. 2004. 224p.
Understanding Children's Worlds Ser. ISBN:1-4051-1448-7,
ISBN13: 978-1-4051-1448-6. Dewey:302.3/4/083.
LCCN:2004-009018.

Audience: **g,l,u,f.** *Choice, 2005.*

Elkind, David   **BF723.S75**
Hurried Child: Growing up Too Fast Too Soon. Ed. 25. Trade
Paper. Da Capo Press, Inc. Cambridge, MA. 2006. 288p.
ISBN:0-7382-1082-X, ISBN13: 978-0-7382-1082-7.
Dewey:305.23.

Audience: **g,l,u,f.**

Elkind, David   **HQ536.E44 1994**
Ties That Stress: The New Family Imbalance. Trade Cloth.
Harvard University Press. Cambridge, MA. 1998. 272p.
ISBN:0-674-89149-X, ISBN13: 978-0-674-89149-4.
Dewey:306.85/0973. LCCN:94-011126.

Audience: **g,l,u,f.**

Ellis, Bruce J. & Bjorklund,   **BF711.O75 2004**
  David F. (Editors)
Origins of the Social Mind: Evolutionary Psychology and Child
Development. Cloth over Boards. Guilford Publications, Inc.
New York, NY. 2004. 540p. ISBN:1-59385-103-0, ISBN13:
978-1-59385-103-3. Dewey:155.7. LCCN:2004-022693.

Audience: **u,f.** *Choice, 2005.*

Engel, Susan L.   **BF723.C5E49 2005**
Real Kids: Creating Meaning in Everyday Life. Trade Cloth.
Harvard University Press. Cambridge, MA. 2005. 240p.
ISBN:0-674-01883-4, ISBN13: 978-0-674-01883-9.
Dewey:155.4/13. LCCN:2005-046005.

Audience: **g,l,u,f.** *Choice, 2006.*

Flavell, John H., et al.   **BF723.C5F62 2002**
Cognitive Development. Ed. 4. Patricia H. Miller & Scott A.
Miller (Authors). Trade Paper. Prentice Hall PTR. Upper Saddle
River, NJ. 2001. 423p. ISBN:0-13-791575-6, ISBN13:
978-0-13-791575-0. Dewey:155.4/13. LCCN:00-051593.

Audience: **g,l,u.**

Fogel, Alan   **RJ131.B475 2001**
Blackwell Handbook of Infant Development. Gavin Bremner (Editor).
Trade Cloth. Blackwell Publishing, Inc. Malden, MA. 2002.
792p. Handbooks of Developmental Psychology
ISBN:0-631-21234-5, ISBN13: 978-0-631-21234-8.
Dewey:305.231. LCCN:2001-025582.

Audience: **g,l,u.** *Choice, 2002.*

Garton, Alison   **BF723.P8G37 2004**
Exploring Cognitive Development: The Child As Problem
Solver. Trade Paper. Blackwell Publishing, Inc. Malden, MA.
2004. 160p. ISBN:0-631-23458-6, ISBN13: 978-0-631-23458-6.
Dewey:155.4/1343. LCCN:2003-017215.

Audience: **g,u,f.** *Choice, 2004.*

Gauvain, Mary   **BF723.C5G38 2001**
The Social Context of Cognitive Development. Cloth over
Boards. Guilford Publications, Inc. New York, NY. 2000. 249p.
Series on Social and Emotional Development
ISBN:1-57230-516-9, ISBN13: 978-1-57230-516-8.
Dewey:155.4/13. LCCN:00-062259.

Audience: **l,u,f.** *Choice, 2001.*

Gesell, Arnold L.   **RJ131 .G467**
The Embryology of Behavior. T. B. Brazelton (Foreword by),
McKeith Press Staff (Contribution by). Trade Cloth. MacKeith
Press. London, 1988. 274p. Classics in Developmental Medicine
Ser., No. 3 ISBN:0-521-41328-1, ISBN13: 978-0-521-41328-2.
Dewey:155.4.

Audience: **l,u,f.**

Getzels, Jacob W.   **BF723.G5**
Creativity and Intelligence: Explorations with Gifted Students,.
Paper Text. Textbook Publishers. Temecula, CA. 2003. 293p.
ISBN:0-7581-0503-7, ISBN13: 978-0-7581-0503-5.
Dewey:136.765.

Audience: **l,u.**

Gielen, Uwe P. &   **BF721**
  Roopnarine, Jaipaul L. (Editors)
Childhood and Adolescence: Cross-Cultural Perspectives and
Applications. Trade Cloth. Greenwood Publishing Group, Inc.
Portsmouth, NH. 2004. 504p. Advances in Applied
Developmental Psychology Ser., No. 23 ISBN:1-56750-660-7,
ISBN13: 978-1-56750-660-0. Dewey:155.4.
LCCN:2004-042785.

Audience: **u,f.** *Choice, 2005.*

Goldstein, Sam & Brooks,   **BF723.R46H36 2004**
  Robert B. (Editors)
Handbook of Resilience in Children. Trade Cloth. Springer. New
York, NY. 2005. XX, 416p. ISBN:0-306-48571-0, ISBN13:
978-0-306-48571-8. Dewey:155.4/1824. LCCN:2004-042176.

Audience: **u,f.** *Choice, 2005.*

Goswami, Usha (Editor)   **BF723.C5B5 2002**
Blackwell Handbook of Childhood Cognitive Development.
Trade Cloth. Blackwell Publishing, Inc. Malden, MA. 2002.
776p. Handbooks of Developmental Psychology
ISBN:0-631-21840-8, ISBN13: 978-0-631-21840-1.
Dewey:155.4/13. LCCN:2002-023054.

Audience: **u,f.** *Choice, 2003.*

Graber, Julia A. (Editor),   **BF724.T64 1996**
  et al.
Transitions Through Adolescence: Interpersonal Domains and
Context. Jeanne Brooks-Gunn & Anne C. Petersen (Editors).

Cloth over Boards. Lawrence Erlbaum Associates, Inc. Mahwah, NJ. 1996. 416p. ISBN:0-8058-1594-5, ISBN13: 978-0-8058-1594-8. Dewey:305.23/55. LCCN:95-041221.

Audience: **u,f.** *Choice, 1996.*

Grossmann, Klaus E.   BF575.A86A78 2005
 (Editor), et al.
Attachment from Infancy to Adulthood: The Major Longitudinal Studies. Karin Grossmann & Everett Waters (Editors). Cloth over Boards. Guilford Publications, Inc. New York, NY. 2005. 332p. ISBN:1-59385-145-6, ISBN13: 978-1-59385-145-3. Dewey:155.2. LCCN:2004-023994.

Audience: **u,f.** *Choice, 2006.*

Gruber, Howard E. &   BF723.C5P494213 1995
 Voneche, J. Jacques (Editors)
The Essential Piaget: An Interpretive Reference and Guide. Ed. 100. Trade Paper. Rowman & Littlefield Publishers, Inc. Lanham, MD. 1995. 952p. ISBN:1-56821-520-7, ISBN13: 978-1-56821-520-4. Dewey:155.4/13. LCCN:95-034259.

Audience: **l,u.**

Haslett, Beth & Samter,   BF723.C57H37 1997
 Wendy
Children Communicating: The First Five Years (& a Little Bit Beyond...). Trade Cloth. Lawrence Erlbaum Associates, Inc. Mahwah, NJ. 1997. 320p. LEA's Communication Ser. ISBN:0-8058-0066-2, ISBN13: 978-0-8058-0066-1. Dewey:155.42/236. LCCN:96-037758.

Audience: **l,u,f.** *Choice, 1998.*

Hauser, Stuart T. &   HQ798
 Kasendorf, E.
Black and White Identity Formation. Ed. 2. Trade Paper. Krieger Publishing Company. Melbourne, FL. 1983. 252p. ISBN:0-89874-055-X, ISBN13: 978-0-89874-055-4. Dewey:155.5/32. LCCN:82-016221.

Audience: **l,u,f.**

Herron, R. E. &   BF717
 Sutton-Smith, Brian
Child's Play. Cloth Text. Krieger Publishing Company. Melbourne, FL. 1982. 400p. ISBN:0-89874-406-7, ISBN13: 978-0-89874-406-4. Dewey:155.4/18. LCCN:81-018560.

Audience: **l,u,f.**

Humphrey, James Harry   BF723.S75H842 2004
Childhood Stress in Contemporary Society. Mixed Media. Haworth Press, Incorporated, The. Binghamton, NY. 2004. 173p. ISBN:0-7890-2265-6, ISBN13: 978-0-7890-2265-3. Dewey:155.4/18. LCCN:2003-025570.

Audience: **g,l,u,f.**

Johoda, Gustav & Lewis,   BF723.S6A25 1988
 Ioan M. (Editors)
Acquiring Culture: Cross-Cultural Studies in Child Development. Library Binding. Croom Helm, Ltd. London, 1988. 288p. ISBN:0-7099-4335-0, ISBN13: 978-0-7099-4335-8. Dewey:155.4. LCCN:87-020060.

Audience: **u,f.** *Choice, 1989.*

Kagan, Jerome   BF721.K158 1994
The Nature of the Child. Ed. 10. Trade Paper. Basic Books. New York, NY. 1994. 352p. ISBN:0-465-04852-8, ISBN13: 978-0-465-04852-6. Dewey:155.4. LCCN:94-172119.

Audience: **l,u,f.**

Kagan, Jerome & Gall,   HQ772.G27 1998
 Susan (Editors)
The Gale Encyclopedia of Childhood and Adolescence. Trade Cloth. Thomson Gale. Farmington Hills, MI. 1997. 752p. ISBN:0-8103-9884-2, ISBN13: 978-0-8103-9884-9. Dewey:305.231/03. LCCN:97-029270.

Audience: **g,l,u.**

Kastenbaum, Robert J.   BF724.5.E53 1993
Encyclopedia of Adult Development. Cloth Text. Greenwood Publishing Group, Inc. Portsmouth, NH. 1993. 592p. ISBN:0-89774-669-4, ISBN13: 978-0-89774-669-4. Dewey:155.6. LCCN:92-046666.

Audience: **g,l,u,f.** *Choice, 1994.*

Kegan, Robert   BF723.M54
The Evolving Self: Problem and Process in Human Development. Trade Paper. Harvard University Press. Cambridge, MA. 1983. 336p. ISBN:0-674-27231-5, ISBN13: 978-0-674-27231-6. Dewey:155.2/5.

Audience: **u,f.**

Ladd, Gary W.   BF723.I646L33 2005
Children's Peer Relations and Social Competence: A Century of Progress. Saddle Stitched, Cloth over Boards, Dust Jacket. Yale University Press. Cumberland, RI. 2005. 448p. Current Perspectives in Psychology Ser. ISBN:0-300-10643-2, ISBN13: 978-0-300-10643-5. Dewey:155.4/18. LCCN:2005-002379.

Audience: **u,f.** *Choice, 2006.*

Lefkowitz, M. M.   BF723.A35
Growing up to Be Violent: A Longitudinal Study of the Development of Aggression. Trade Cloth. Pergamon Press. Kidlington, 1977. ix, 236p. ISBN:0-08-019515-6, ISBN13: 978-0-08-019515-5. Dewey:155.4/18. LCCN:75-044349.

Audience: **l,u,f.**

Lerner, Richard M.   BF713.L47 2002
Concepts and Theories of Human Development. Ed. 3. Cloth over Boards. Lawrence Erlbaum Associates, Inc. Mahwah, NJ. 2001. 632p. ISBN:0-8058-2798-6, ISBN13: 978-0-8058-2798-9. Dewey:155. LCCN:2001-040282.

Audience: **u,f.**

Lichtenberg, Joseph D.   BF719
Psychoanalysis and Infant Research. Trade Paper. Analytic Press. Hillsdale, NJ. 1991. 280p. Psychoanalytic Inquiry Bk., Vol. 2 ISBN:0-88163-145-0, ISBN13: 978-0-88163-145-6. Dewey:155.4/22.

Audience: **g,l,f.**

Light, Leah L. & Burke,   BF724.85.M45L36 1988
 Deborah M. (Editors)
Language, Memory, and Aging. Trade Cloth. Cambridge University Press. New York, NY. 1988. 296p. ISBN:0-521-32942-6, ISBN13: 978-0-521-32942-2. Dewey:155.67/1. LCCN:88-001068.

Audience: **g,l,u,f.** *Choice, 1989.*

Mahler, Margaret S., et al.   BF723
Psychological Birth of the Human Infant: Symbiosis and Individuation. Anni Bergman & Fred Pine (Authors). Trade Paper. Basic Books. New York, NY. 2000. 336p. ISBN:0-465-09554-2, ISBN13: 978-0-465-09554-4. Dewey:155.4/22.

Audience: **l,u,f.**

Maier, Henry W.   **BF721.M196 1988**
Three Theories of Child Development. Ed. 3. Trade Paper.
University Press of America, Inc. Lanham, MD. 1988. 292p.
ISBN:0-8191-6765-7, ISBN13: 978-0-8191-6765-1.
Dewey:155.4/01. LCCN:87-031702.

Audience: **l,u,f.**

Mauthner, Melanie L.   **BF723.S43M385 2002**
Sistering: Power and Change in Female Relationships. Cloth
over Boards. Palgrave Macmillan. New York, NY. 2003. 240p.
ISBN:0-333-80080-X, ISBN13: 978-0-333-80080-5.
Dewey:306.875. LCCN:2002-072320.

Audience: **l,u,f.** *Choice, 2003.*

Miller, Alice   **RC569.5.C55M55313**
The Drama of the Gifted Child: The Search for the True Self.
Ed. 3. Ruth Ward (Translator), Alice Miller (Foreword by).
Paper Text. Basic Books. New York, NY. 1996. 144p. Art of
Mentoring Ser. ISBN:0-465-01690-1, ISBN13:
978-0-465-01690-7. Dewey:616.85/82239. LCCN:97-047532.

Audience: **g,l,u,f.**

Moeller, Thomas G.   **BF724.3.A34M64 2001**
Youth Aggression and Violence: A Psychological Approach.
Cloth over Boards. Lawrence Erlbaum Associates, Inc. Mahwah,
NJ. 2001. 424p. ISBN:0-8058-3713-2, ISBN13:
978-0-8058-3713-1. Dewey:155.4/18232. LCCN:00-068145.

Audience: **g,l,u,f.** *Choice, 2002.*

Mortimer, Jeylan T. &   **BF713**
Shanahan, Michael J. (Editors)
Handbook of the Life Course. Trade Paper. Springer. New York,
NY. 2006. XX, 732p. ISBN:0-387-32457-7, ISBN13:
978-0-387-32457-9. Dewey:305.2.

Audience: **u,f.** *Choice, 2004.*

Piaget, Jean   **BF723.N8**
The Child's Conception of Number. Paper Text. Textbook
Publishers. Temecula, CA. 2003. ix, 248p. ISBN:0-7581-4577-2,
ISBN13: 978-0-7581-4577-2. Dewey:136.745101.

Audience: **l,u,f.**

Piaget, Jean   **BF723.C5**
The Child's Conception of Physical Causality. Library Binding.
Routledge. New York, NY. 1999. 320p. International Library of
Psychology ISBN:0-415-20998-6, ISBN13: 978-0-415-20998-4.
Dewey:155.4/13.

Audience: **l,u,f.**

Piaget, Jean   **BF723.S63**
Child's Conception of Space, Vol. 1. Library Binding.
Routledge. New York, NY. 1998. 504p. ISBN:0-415-16889-9,
ISBN13: 978-0-415-16889-2. Dewey:155.412142.

Audience: **l,u,f.**

Piaget, Jean   **BF721**
The Child's Conception of the World: A 20th-Century Classic of
Child Psychology. Trade Paper. National Book Network.
Lanham, MD. 1975. 397p. Quality Paperback Ser., No. 213
ISBN:0-8226-0213-X, ISBN13: 978-0-8226-0213-2.
Dewey:155.4.

Audience: **l,u,f.**

Piaget, Jean   **BF723.E6**
Play, Dreams and Imitation in Childhood. Library Binding.
Routledge. New York, NY. 1999. 308p. International Library of

Psychology Ser. ISBN:0-415-21005-4, ISBN13:
978-0-415-21005-8. Dewey:155.412.

Audience: **l,u,f.**

Piaget, Jean   **BF721 .P473**
Origins of Intelligence in Children. Margaret Cook (Translator).
Cloth Text. International Universities Press, Inc. Madison, CT.
1966. 419p. ISBN:0-8236-3900-2, ISBN13: 978-0-8236-3900-7.
Dewey:136.72.

Audience: **l,u,f.**

Piaget, Jean   **BF723.C5**
Genetic Epistemology. Eleanor Duckworth (Translator). Trade
Paper. W. W. Norton & Company, Inc. New York, NY. 1971.
ISBN:0-393-00596-8, ISBN13: 978-0-393-00596-7.
Dewey:155.41/3.

Audience: **u,f.**

Piaget, Jean & Inhelder,   **BF721**
Barbel
The Growth of Logical Thinking from Childhood to
Adolescence. Library Binding. Routledge. New York, NY. 1999.
384p. International Library of Psychology ISBN:0-415-21002-X,
ISBN13: 978-0-415-21002-7. Dewey:155.

Audience: **l,u,f.**

Piaget, Jean & Inhelder,   **BF721.P481**
Barbel
Psychology of the Child. Helen Weaver (Translator). Trade
Paper. Basic Books. New York, NY. 1972. 192p.
ISBN:0-465-09500-3, ISBN13: 978-0-465-09500-1.
Dewey:155.4. LCCN:73-078449.

Audience: **g,l,u,f.**

Pinker, Steven   **BF341.P47 2002**
The Blank Slate: The Modern Denial of Human Nature. Trade
Cloth. Penguin Group (USA) Inc. New York, NY. 2002. 528p.
ISBN:0-670-03151-8, ISBN13: 978-0-670-03151-1.
Dewey:155.2. LCCN:2002-022719.

Audience: **l,u,f.** *Choice, 2003.*

Poon, Leonard W. (Editor),   **BF724.5**
et al.
Everyday Cognition in Adulthood and Late Life. David C.
Rubin, Barbara C. Wilson & Barbara A. Wilson (Editors). Trade
Paper. Cambridge University Press. New York, NY. 1992. 720p.
ISBN:0-521-42860-2, ISBN13: 978-0-521-42860-6.
Dewey:155.6. LCCN:88-029974.

Audience: **l,u,f.** *Choice, 1990.*

Rotenberg, K. J. (Editor)   **BF723.T78C55 1991**
Children's Interpersonal Trust: Sensitivity to Lying, Deception
and Promise Violations. Cloth Text. Springer. New York, NY.
1991. 172p. ISBN:0-387-97511-X, ISBN13: 978-0-387-97511-5.
Dewey:155.4/18. LCCN:90-025448.

Audience: **u,f.** *Choice, 1992.*

Salthouse, T. A. (Editor)   **BF724.55.C63S24 1991**
Theoretical Perspectives on Cognitive Aging. Cloth over Boards.
Lawrence Erlbaum Associates, Inc. Mahwah, NJ. 1991. 448p.
ISBN:0-8058-0424-2, ISBN13: 978-0-8058-0424-9.
Dewey:155.67. LCCN:91-012732.

Audience: **u,f.** *Choice, 1992.*

Sanders, Robert &   **BF723.S43S159 2004**
Campling, Jo
Sibling Relationships: Theory and Issues for Practice. Cloth over

Formats: Web: ☐ Ebook: 🄴 CD/DVD-ROM: 🐝 BCL3: 𝓑

Boards. Palgrave Macmillan. New York, NY. 2004. 240p. ISBN:0-333-96410-1, ISBN13: 978-0-333-96410-1. Dewey:306.875. LCCN:2003-062092.

Audience: **u.** *Choice, 2004.*

Sayers, Janet   **BF724.S325 1998**
Boy Crazy: Remembering Adolescence, Memories and Dreams. Paper over Boards. Routledge. New York, NY. 1998. 200p. ISBN:0-415-19084-3, ISBN13: 978-0-415-19084-8. Dewey:155.5. LCCN:98-010662.

Audience: **l,u,f.** *Choice, 1999.*

Schneider, Wolfgang &   **BF723.M4S35 1997**
   Pressley, Michael
Memory Development Between 2 and 20. Ed. 2. Cloth over Boards. Lawrence Erlbaum Associates, Inc. Mahwah, NJ. 1997. 424p. ISBN:0-8058-2437-5, ISBN13: 978-0-8058-2437-7. Dewey:155.4/1312. LCCN:96-036766.

Audience: **u.**

Singer, Dorothy G. &   **BF723.C5S6 1996**
   Revenson, Tracey A.
A Piaget Primer: How a Child Thinks. Trade Paper. Penguin Group (USA) Inc. New York, NY. 1996. 160p. ISBN:0-452-27565-2, ISBN13: 978-0-452-27565-2. Dewey:155.4/13. LCCN:96-001932.

Audience: **g,l,u,f.** *Choice, 1998.*

Sroufe, L. Alan, et al.   **HQ767.9.D477 2005**
The Development of the Person: The Minnesota Study of Risk and Adaptation from Birth to Adulthood. Elizabeth Carlson, W. Andrew Collins & Byron Egeland (Authors). Cloth over Boards. Guilford Publications, Inc. New York, NY. 2005. 384p. ISBN:1-59385-158-8, ISBN13: 978-1-59385-158-3. Dewey:305.231. LCCN:2004-026206.

Audience: **u,f.** *Choice, 2005.*

Stern, Daniel N.   **BF719**
Interpersonal World of the Infant: A View from Psychoanalysis and Developmental Psychology. Trade Paper. Basic Books. New York, NY. 2000. 352p. ISBN:0-465-09589-5, ISBN13: 978-0-465-09589-6. Dewey:155.422.

Audience: **l,u,f.**

Sugar, Max (Editor)   **BF724**
Female Adolescent Development. Ed. 2. Albert J. Solnit (Foreword by). UK-B Format Paperback. Brunner-Routledge. Philadelphia, PA. 1993. 272p. ISBN:0-87630-715-2, ISBN13: 978-0-87630-715-1. Dewey:305.23/55. LCCN:92-041570.

Audience: **l,u,f.**

Thomas, R. Murray   **BF723**
Moral Development Theories - Secular and Religious: A Comparative Study. Trade Cloth. Greenwood Publishing Group, Inc. Portsmouth, NH. 1997. 328p. Contributions to the Study of Education Ser. ISBN:0-313-30236-7, ISBN13: 978-0-313-30236-7. Dewey:155.2/5. LCCN:96-033070.

Audience: **l,u.** *Choice, 1997.*

Toman, Walter   **BF723.B5**
Family Constellation: Its Effects on Personality and Social Behavior. Ed. 4. Trade Cloth. Springer Publishing Company, Inc. New York, NY. 1992. 320p. ISBN:0-8261-0496-7, ISBN13: 978-0-8261-0496-0. Dewey:155.9/24. LCCN:92-002396.

Audience: **l,u,f.**

Underwood, Marion K.   **BF723.A35U53 2003**
Social Aggression among Girls. Cloth over Boards. Guilford Publications, Inc. New York, NY. 2003. 300p. Guilford Series on Social and Emotional Development Ser. ISBN:1-57230-866-4, ISBN13: 978-1-57230-866-4. Dewey:302.5/4/08342. LCCN:2002-152968.

Audience: **u,f.** *Choice, 2004.*

Ungar, Michael (Editor)   **BF723.R46H357 2005**
Handbook for Working with Children and Youth: Pathways to Resilience Across Cultures and Contexts. Trade Cloth. SAGE Publications, Inc. Thousand Oaks, CA. 2005. 552p. ISBN:1-4129-0405-6, ISBN13: 978-1-4129-0405-6. Dewey:362.7. LCCN:2004-028633.

Audience: **u,f.** *Choice, 2005.*

Wallach, Michael A. &   **BF723.C5**
   Kogan, Nathan
Modes of Thinking in Young Children: A Study of the Creativity-Intelligence Distinction. Trade Cloth. Greenwood Publishing Group, Inc. Portsmouth, NH. 1984. 357p. ISBN:0-313-23249-0, ISBN13: 978-0-313-23249-7. Dewey:155.4/13. LCCN:84-015865.

Audience: **l,u,f.**

Waskow, Arthur I. &   **BF723.S43W37 1993**
   Waskow, Howard
Becoming Brothers. Reinforced. Simon & Schuster. New York, NY. 1993. 218p. ISBN:0-02-933997-9, ISBN13: 978-0-02-933997-8. Dewey:306.875/2/0922. LCCN:93-016701.

Audience: **g,l,u,f.** *Choice, 1993.*

Willats, John   **BF723.D7**
Making Sense of Children's Drawings. Paper over Boards, Perfect. Lawrence Erlbaum Associates, Inc. Mahwah, NJ. 2005. 261p. ISBN:0-8058-4537-2, ISBN13: 978-0-8058-4537-2. Dewey:155.4. LCCN:2004-056419.

Audience: **u,f.** *Choice, 2006.*

Worden, J. William   **BF723.G75W67 1996**
Children and Grief: When a Parent Dies. Cloth over Boards. Guilford Publications, Inc. New York, NY. 1996. 225p. ISBN:1-57230-148-1, ISBN13: 978-1-57230-148-1. Dewey:155.9/37/083. LCCN:96-029010.

Audience: **g,l,u,f.** *Choice, 1997.*

Wrightsman, Lawrence S.   **BF724.85.P47W74 1994**
Adult Personality Development: Applications. Trade Paper. SAGE Publications, Inc. Thousand Oaks, CA. 1994. 248p. ISBN:0-8039-4402-0, ISBN13: 978-0-8039-4402-2. Dewey:155.6. LCCN:93-043076.

Audience: **l,u.**

Wrightsman, Lawrence S.   **BF724.85.P47W74 1994**
Adult Personality Development: Theories and Concepts. Trade Cloth. SAGE Publications, Inc. Thousand Oaks, CA. 1994. 227p. ISBN:0-8039-4399-7, ISBN13: 978-0-8039-4399-5. Dewey:155.6. LCCN:93-043076.

Audience: **l,u.**

Developmental Psychology > Cognitive and Perceptual Development

Flavell, John H., et al.   **BF723.C5F62 2002**
Cognitive Development. Ed. 4. Patricia H. Miller & Scott A. Miller (Authors). Trade Paper. Prentice Hall PTR. Upper Saddle

River, NJ. 2001. 423p. ISBN:0-13-791575-6, ISBN13: 978-0-13-791575-0. Dewey:155.4/13. LCCN:00-051593.

Audience: **g,l,u.**

Garton, Alison **BF723.P8G37 2004**
Exploring Cognitive Development: The Child As Problem Solver. Trade Paper. Blackwell Publishing, Inc. Malden, MA. 2004. 160p. ISBN:0-631-23458-6, ISBN13: 978-0-631-23458-6. Dewey:155.4/1343. LCCN:2003-017215.

Audience: **g,u,f.** *Choice, 2004.*

Gauvain, Mary **BF723.C5G38 2001**
The Social Context of Cognitive Development. Cloth over Boards. Guilford Publications, Inc. New York, NY. 2000. 249p. Series on Social and Emotional Development ISBN:1-57230-516-9, ISBN13: 978-1-57230-516-8. Dewey:155.4/13. LCCN:00-062259.

Audience: **l,u,f.** *Choice, 2001.*

Getzels, Jacob W. **BF723.G5**
Creativity and Intelligence: Explorations with Gifted Students,. Paper Text. Textbook Publishers. Temecula, CA. 2003. 293p. ISBN:0-7581-0503-7, ISBN13: 978-0-7581-0503-5. Dewey:136.765.

Audience: **l,u.**

Goswami, Usha (Editor) **BF723.C5B5 2002**
Blackwell Handbook of Childhood Cognitive Development. Trade Cloth. Blackwell Publishing, Inc. Malden, MA. 2002. 776p. Handbooks of Developmental Psychology ISBN:0-631-21840-8, ISBN13: 978-0-631-21840-1. Dewey:155.4/13. LCCN:2002-023054.

Audience: **u,f.** *Choice, 2003.*

Gruber, Howard E. & **BF723.C5P494213 1995**
Voneche, J. Jacques (Editors)
The Essential Piaget: An Interpretive Reference and Guide. Ed. 100. Trade Paper. Rowman & Littlefield Publishers, Inc. Lanham, MD. 1995. 952p. ISBN:1-56821-520-7, ISBN13: 978-1-56821-520-4. Dewey:155.4/13. LCCN:95-034259.

Audience: **l,u.**

Light, Leah L. & Burke, **BF724.85.M45L36 1988**
Deborah M. (Editors)
Language, Memory, and Aging. Trade Cloth. Cambridge University Press. New York, NY. 1988. 296p. ISBN:0-521-32942-6, ISBN13: 978-0-521-32942-2. Dewey:155.67/1. LCCN:88-001068.

Audience: **g,l,u,f.** *Choice, 1989.*

Moore, Chris (Author, **BF721 .M7235**
Editor)
The Development of Commonsense Psychology. Cloth over Boards. Lawrence Erlbaum Associates, Inc. Mahwah, NJ. 2006. 248p. The Developing Mind Ser. ISBN:0-8058-4174-1, ISBN13: 978-0-8058-4174-9. Dewey:155.4/18. LCCN:2006-296265.

Audience: **l,u,f.** *Choice, 2006.*

Piaget, Jean **BF723.N8**
The Child's Conception of Number. Paper Text. Textbook Publishers. Temecula, CA. 2003. ix, 248p. ISBN:0-7581-4577-2, ISBN13: 978-0-7581-4577-2. Dewey:136.745101.

Audience: **l,u,f.**

Piaget, Jean **BF723.C5**
The Child's Conception of Physical Causality. Library Binding. Routledge. New York, NY. 1999. 320p. International Library of

Psychology ISBN:0-415-20998-6, ISBN13: 978-0-415-20998-4. Dewey:155.4/13.

Audience: **l,u,f.**

Piaget, Jean **BF723.S63**
Child's Conception of Space, Vol. 1. Library Binding. Routledge. New York, NY. 1998. 504p. ISBN:0-415-16889-9, ISBN13: 978-0-415-16889-2. Dewey:155.412142.

Audience: **l,u,f.**

Piaget, Jean **BF721**
The Child's Conception of the World: A 20th-Century Classic of Child Psychology. Trade Paper. National Book Network. Lanham, MD. 1975. 397p. Quality Paperback Ser., No. 213 ISBN:0-8226-0213-X, ISBN13: 978-0-8226-0213-2. Dewey:155.4.

Audience: **l,u,f.**

Piaget, Jean **BF721 .P473**
Origins of Intelligence in Children. Margaret Cook (Translator). Cloth Text. International Universities Press, Inc. Madison, CT. 1966. 419p. ISBN:0-8236-3900-2, ISBN13: 978-0-8236-3900-7. Dewey:136.72.

Audience: **l,u,f.**

Piaget, Jean **BF723.C5**
Genetic Epistemology. Eleanor Duckworth (Translator). Trade Paper. W. W. Norton & Company, Inc. New York, NY. 1971. ISBN:0-393-00596-8, ISBN13: 978-0-393-00596-7. Dewey:155.41/3.

Audience: **u,f.**

Piaget, Jean & Inhelder, **BF721**
Barbel
The Growth of Logical Thinking from Childhood to Adolescence. Library Binding. Routledge. New York, NY. 1999. 384p. International Library of Psychology ISBN:0-415-21002-X, ISBN13: 978-0-415-21002-7. Dewey:155.

Audience: **l,u,f.**

Poon, Leonard W. (Editor), **BF724.5**
et al.
Everyday Cognition in Adulthood and Late Life. David C. Rubin, Barbara C. Wilson & Barbara A. Wilson (Editors). Trade Paper. Cambridge University Press. New York, NY. 1992. 720p. ISBN:0-521-42860-2, ISBN13: 978-0-521-42860-6. Dewey:155.6. LCCN:88-029974.

Audience: **l,u,f.** *Choice, 1990.*

Schneider, Wolfgang & **BF723.M4S35 1997**
Pressley, Michael
Memory Development Between 2 and 20. Ed. 2. Cloth over Boards. Lawrence Erlbaum Associates, Inc. Mahwah, NJ. 1997. 424p. ISBN:0-8058-2437-5, ISBN13: 978-0-8058-2437-7. Dewey:155.4/1312. LCCN:96-036766.

Audience: **u.**

Wallach, Michael A. & **BF723.C5**
Kogan, Nathan
Modes of Thinking in Young Children: A Study of the Creativity-Intelligence Distinction. Trade Cloth. Greenwood Publishing Group, Inc. Portsmouth, NH. 1984. 357p. ISBN:0-313-23249-0, ISBN13: 978-0-313-23249-7. Dewey:155.4/13. LCCN:84-015865.

Audience: **l,u,f.**

Developmental Psychology > Psychosocial and Personality Development

Bank, Stephen & Kahn, Michael   BF723.S43
Sibling Bond. Trade Paper. Basic Books. New York, NY. 2003. 400p. ISBN:0-465-07843-5, ISBN13: 978-0-465-07843-1. Dewey:155.9/24.
Audience: **g,l,u,f.**

Cassidy, Jude & Shaver, Phillip R. (Editors)   BF575.A86H36 1999
Handbook of Attachment: Theory, Research, and Clinical Applications. Paper over Boards. Guilford Publications, Inc. New York, NY. 1999. 925p. ISBN:1-57230-087-6, ISBN13: 978-1-57230-087-3. Dewey:155.9/2. LCCN:98-053527.
Audience: **u,f.** *Choice, 1999.*

Clark, Kenneth B.   BF723.R3C5 1988
Prejudice and Your Child. Stuart W. Cook (Foreword by). Trade Paper. Wesleyan University Press. Middletown, CT. 1988. 327p. ISBN:0-8195-6155-X, ISBN13: 978-0-8195-6155-8. Dewey:155.4/18. LCCN:85-017862.
Audience: **g,l,u.**

Coopersmith, Stanley   BF723.S3.C6
The Antecedents of Self-Esteem. Trade Cloth. W. H. Freeman & Company. New York, NY. 1967. "ix, 283"p. A Series of Books in Behavioral Science Ser. ISBN:0-7167-0912-0, ISBN13: 978-0-7167-0912-1. Dewey:155.41/8. LCCN:67-021126.
Audience: **g,l,u,f.**

Dunn, Judy   BF723.S6D86 1988
The Beginnings of Social Understanding. Trade Cloth. Harvard University Press. Cambridge, MA. 1988. 240p. The Developing Child Ser. ISBN:0-674-06453-4, ISBN13: 978-0-674-06453-9. Dewey:155.4/23. LCCN:88-000766.
Audience: **u,f.** *Choice, 1989.*

Dunn, Judy   HQ784.F7D86 2004
Children's Friendships: The Beginnings of Intimacy. Trade Paper. Blackwell Publishing, Inc. Malden, MA. 2004. 224p. Understanding Children's Worlds Ser. ISBN:1-4051-1448-7, ISBN13: 978-1-4051-1448-6. Dewey:302.3/4/083. LCCN:2004-009018.
Audience: **g,l,u,f.** *Choice, 2005.*

Grossmann, Klaus E. (Editor), et al.   BF575.A86A78 2005
Attachment from Infancy to Adulthood: The Major Longitudinal Studies. Karin Grossmann & Everett Waters (Editors). Cloth over Boards. Guilford Publications, Inc. New York, NY. 2005. 332p. ISBN:1-59385-145-6, ISBN13: 978-1-59385-145-3. Dewey:155.2. LCCN:2004-023994.
Audience: **u,f.** *Choice, 2006.*

Johoda, Gustav & Lewis, Ioan M. (Editors)   BF723.S6A25 1988
Acquiring Culture: Cross-Cultural Studies in Child Development. Library Binding. Croom Helm, Ltd. London, 1988. 288p. ISBN:0-7099-4335-0, ISBN13: 978-0-7099-4335-8. Dewey:155.4. LCCN:87-020060.
Audience: **u,f.** *Choice, 1989.*

Ladd, Gary W.   BF723.I646L33 2005
Children's Peer Relations and Social Competence: A Century of Progress. Saddle Stitched, Cloth over Boards, Dust Jacket. Yale University Press. Cumberland, RI. 2005. 448p. Current Perspectives in Psychology Ser. ISBN:0-300-10643-2, ISBN13: 978-0-300-10643-5. Dewey:155.4/18. LCCN:2005-002379.
Audience: **u,f.** *Choice, 2006.*

Mauthner, Melanie L.   BF723.S43M385 2002
Sistering: Power and Change in Female Relationships. Cloth over Boards. Palgrave Macmillan. New York, NY. 2003. 240p. ISBN:0-333-80080-X, ISBN13: 978-0-333-80080-5. Dewey:306.875. LCCN:2002-072320.
Audience: **l,u,f.** *Choice, 2003.*

Moeller, Thomas G.   BF724.3.A34M64 2001
Youth Aggression and Violence: A Psychological Approach. Cloth over Boards. Lawrence Erlbaum Associates, Inc. Mahwah, NJ. 2001. 424p. ISBN:0-8058-3713-2, ISBN13: 978-0-8058-3713-1. Dewey:155.4/18232. LCCN:00-068145.
Audience: **g,l,u,f.** *Choice, 2002.*

Rotenberg, K. J. (Editor)   BF723.T78C55 1991
Children's Interpersonal Trust: Sensitivity to Lying, Deception and Promise Violations. Cloth Text. Springer. New York, NY. 1991. 172p. ISBN:0-387-97511-X, ISBN13: 978-0-387-97511-5. Dewey:155.4/18. LCCN:90-025448.
Audience: **u,f.** *Choice, 1992.*

Sanders, Robert & Campling, Jo   BF723.S43S159 2004
Sibling Relationships: Theory and Issues for Practice. Cloth over Boards. Palgrave Macmillan. New York, NY. 2004. 240p. ISBN:0-333-96410-1, ISBN13: 978-0-333-96410-1. Dewey:306.875. LCCN:2003-062092.
Audience: **u.** *Choice, 2004.*

Sayers, Janet   BF724.S325 1998
Boy Crazy: Remembering Adolescence, Memories and Dreams. Paper over Boards. Routledge. New York, NY. 1998. 200p. ISBN:0-415-19084-3, ISBN13: 978-0-415-19084-8. Dewey:155.5. LCCN:98-010662.
Audience: **l,u,f.** *Choice, 1999.*

Stern, Daniel N.   BF719
Interpersonal World of the Infant: A View from Psychoanalysis and Developmental Psychology. Trade Paper. Basic Books. New York, NY. 2000. 352p. ISBN:0-465-09589-5, ISBN13: 978-0-465-09589-6. Dewey:155.422.
Audience: **l,u,f.**

Toman, Walter   BF723.B5
Family Constellation: Its Effects on Personality and Social Behavior. Ed. 4. Trade Cloth. Springer Publishing Company, Inc. New York, NY. 1992. 320p. ISBN:0-8261-0496-7, ISBN13: 978-0-8261-0496-0. Dewey:155.9/24. LCCN:92-002396.
Audience: **l,u,f.**

Waskow, Arthur I. & Waskow, Howard   BF723.S43W37 1993
Becoming Brothers. Reinforced. Simon & Schuster. New York, NY. 1993. 218p. ISBN:0-02-933997-9, ISBN13: 978-0-02-933997-8. Dewey:306.875/2/0922. LCCN:93-016701.
Audience: **g,l,u,f.** *Choice, 1993.*

Wrightsman, Lawrence S.   BF724.85.P47W74 1994
Adult Personality Development: Applications. Trade Paper.
SAGE Publications, Inc. Thousand Oaks, CA. 1994. 248p.
ISBN:0-8039-4402-0, ISBN13: 978-0-8039-4402-2.
Dewey:155.6. LCCN:93-043076.
         Audience: **l,u.**

Wrightsman, Lawrence S.   BF724.85.P47W74 1994
Adult Personality Development: Theories and Concepts. Trade
Cloth. SAGE Publications, Inc. Thousand Oaks, CA. 1994.
227p. ISBN:0-8039-4399-7, ISBN13: 978-0-8039-4399-5.
Dewey:155.6. LCCN:93-043076.
         Audience: **l,u.**

Developmental Psychology > Gerontology

Cruikshank, Margaret   BF724.55.A35C78 2002
Learning to Be Old: Gender, Culture, and Aging. Book, Other.
Rowman & Littlefield Publishers, Inc. Lanham, MD. 2002.
256p. ISBN:0-8476-9848-3, ISBN13: 978-0-8476-9848-6.
Dewey:305.26. LCCN:2002-005352.
         Audience: **l,u,f.** *Choice, 2003.*

Light, Leah L. & Burke,   BF724.85.M45L36 1988
Deborah M. (Editors)
Language, Memory, and Aging. Trade Cloth. Cambridge
University Press. New York, NY. 1988. 296p.
ISBN:0-521-32942-6, ISBN13: 978-0-521-32942-2.
Dewey:155.67/1. LCCN:88-001068.
         Audience: **g,l,u,f.** *Choice, 1989.*

Mortimer, Jeylan T. &   BF713
Shanahan, Michael J. (Editors)
Handbook of the Life Course. Trade Paper. Springer. New York,
NY. 2006. XX, 732p. ISBN:0-387-32457-7, ISBN13:
978-0-387-32457-9. Dewey:305.2.
         Audience: **u,f.** *Choice, 2004.*

Salthouse, T. A. (Editor)   BF724.55.C63S24 1991
Theoretical Perspectives on Cognitive Aging. Cloth over Boards.
Lawrence Erlbaum Associates, Inc. Mahwah, NJ. 1991. 448p.
ISBN:0-8058-0424-2, ISBN13: 978-0-8058-0424-9.
Dewey:155.67. LCCN:91-012732.
         Audience: **u,f.** *Choice, 1992.*

Social Processes and Social Issues

Chin, Jean Lau (Editor)   BF575
The Psychology of Prejudice and Discrimination. Cloth Text.
Greenwood Publishing Group, Inc. Portsmouth, NH. 2004.
1,000p. Race and Ethnicity in Psychology Ser.
ISBN:0-275-98234-3, ISBN13: 978-0-275-98234-8.
Dewey:303.3/85/0973. LCCN:2004-042289.
         Audience: **l,u.** *Choice, 2005.*

Herrnstein, Richard J.   BF431.H398 1996
The Bell Curve: Intelligence and Class Structure in American
Life. Charles Murray (Based on a work by). Trade Paper. Simon
& Schuster. New York, NY. 1996. 912p. A Meditation Bk.
ISBN:0-684-82429-9, ISBN13: 978-0-684-82429-1.
Dewey:305.5/0973. LCCN:95-042934.
         Audience: **g,l.** *Choice, 1995.*

Pyszczynski, Thomas A.,   HV6432.P97 2003
et al.
In the Wake of 9/11: The Psychology of Terror. Jeff Greenberg
& Sheldon Solomon (Authors). Trade Cloth. American
Psychological Association. Washington, DC. 2002. 227p.
ISBN:1-55798-954-0, ISBN13: 978-1-55798-954-3.
Dewey:155.9/35. LCCN:2002-067561.
         Audience: **u,f.** *Choice, 2003.*

Taylor, Donald M.   HM753
The Quest for Identity: From Minority Groups to Generation
Xers. Trade Cloth. Greenwood Publishing Group, Inc.
Portsmouth, NH. 2002. 144p. ISBN:0-275-97309-3, ISBN13:
978-0-275-97309-4. Dewey:302.4. LCCN:2002-022440.
         Audience: **l,u,f.** *Choice, 2004.*

Social Processes and Social Issues > Religion

Andresen, Jensine (Editor)   BL48 .R424 2001
Religion in Mind: Cognitive Perspectives on Religious Belief,
Ritual, and Experience. Trade Cloth. Cambridge University
Press. New York, NY. 2001. 306p. ISBN:0-521-80152-4,
ISBN13: 978-0-521-80152-2. Dewey:153. LCCN:00-045522.
         Audience: **l,u,f.**

Argyle, Michael   BF51.A73 2000
Psychology and Religion: Introduction. Paper over Boards.
Routledge. New York, NY. 2000. 304p. ISBN:0-415-18906-3,
ISBN13: 978-0-415-18906-4. Dewey:200/.1/9.
LCCN:99-016956.
         Audience: **l,u.** *Choice, 2000.*

Ashbrook, James B.   BL53.B654 1993
Brain, Culture and the Human Spirit: Essays from an Emergent
Evolutionary Perspective. Trade Cloth. University Press of
America, Inc. Lanham, MD. 1992. 222p. ISBN:0-8191-8853-0,
ISBN13: 978-0-8191-8853-3. Dewey:128.2. LCCN:92-024726.
         Audience: **g,l,u,f.**

Atran, Scott   BL53.A88 2002
In Gods We Trust: The Evolutionary Landscape of Religion.
Trade Cloth. Oxford University Press, Inc. New York, NY. 2002.
400p. Evolution and Cognition Ser. ISBN:0-19-514930-0,
ISBN13: 978-0-19-514930-2. Dewey:200/.1/9.
LCCN:2002-074884.
         Audience: **l,u,f.**

Austin, James H.   BQ9288.A96 1998
Zen and the Brain: Toward an Understanding of Meditation and
Consciousness. Trade Cloth. MIT Press. Cambridge, MA. 1998.
896p. ISBN:0-262-01164-6, ISBN13: 978-0-262-01164-8.
Dewey:294.3/422. LCCN:97-024693.
         Audience: **l,u,f.** *Choice, 1999.*

Barnett-Friel, Patricia   BL53.B33 2000
Aspects of Personal Faith: Personality and Religion in Western
and Eastern Traditions. Trade Cloth. University Press of
America, Inc. Lanham, MD. 2000. 88p. ISBN:1-57309-414-5,
ISBN13: 978-1-57309-414-6. Dewey:200/.1/9.
LCCN:00-035085.
         Audience: **l,u.**

Batson, C. Daniel, et al.   BL53.B35 1993
Religion and the Individual: A Social-Psychological Perspective.
Ed. 2. Patricia Schoenrade & W. Larry Ventis (Authors). Cloth

Formats: Web: ☐   Ebook: 🅔   CD/DVD-ROM: 🌦   BCL3: 𝓑

Text. Oxford University Press, Inc. New York, NY. 1993. 440p. ISBN:0-19-506208-6, ISBN13: 978-0-19-506208-3. Dewey:200.19. LCCN:92-028606.

Audience: **l,u.**

Batson, C. Daniel, et al.   **BL53**
Religion and the Individual: A Social-Psychological Perspective. Ed. 2. Patricia Schoenrade & W. Larry Ventis (Authors). Trade Paper. Oxford University Press, Inc. New York, NY. 1993. 436p. ISBN:0-19-506209-4, ISBN13: 978-0-19-506209-0. Dewey:200.19. LCCN:92-028606.

Audience: **l,u,f.**

Beit-Hallahmi, Benjamin   **Z7204**
Psychoanalytic Studies of Religion: A Critical Assessment and Annotated Bibliography. Cloth Text. Greenwood Publishing Group, Inc. Portsmouth, NH. 1996. 208p. Bibliographies and Indexes in Religious Studies, Vol. 39 ISBN:0-313-27362-6, ISBN13: 978-0-313-27362-9. Dewey:016.2/001/9. LCCN:96-018524.

Audience: **u,f.** *Choice, 1997.*

Boyer, Pascal   **BL48.B6439 1994**
The Naturalness of Religious Ideas: A Cognitive Theory of Religion. Trade Cloth. University of California Press. Berkeley, CA. 1994. 340p. ISBN:0-520-07559-5, ISBN13: 978-0-520-07559-7. Dewey:200.19. LCCN:92-037506.

Audience: **u,f.**

Boyer, Pascal   **BL48.B6438 2001**
Religion Explained: The Evolutionary Origins of Religious Thought. Paper Text. Basic Books. New York, NY. 2002. 384p. ISBN:0-465-00696-5, ISBN13: 978-0-465-00696-0. Dewey:200. LCCN:00-054661.

Audience: **g,l,u,f.**

Browning, Don S.   **BF51**
Religious Thought and the Modern Psychologies. Ed. 2. Trade Paper. Augsburg Fortress, Publishers. Minneapolis, MN. 2004. 304p. ISBN:0-8006-3659-7, ISBN13: 978-0-8006-3659-3. Dewey:150.19. LCCN:2004-302507.

Audience: **g,l,u.**

Coles, Robert   **BL65.C8**
The Secular Mind. Trade Paper. Princeton University Press. Princeton, NJ. 2001. 200p. ISBN:0-691-08862-4, ISBN13: 978-0-691-08862-4. Dewey:291.1/7.

Audience: **g,l,u,f.** *Choice, 1999.*

Coles, Robert   **BL2760.C65 1999**
The Secular Mind. Trade Cloth. Princeton University Press. Princeton, NJ. 1999. 198p. ISBN:0-691-05805-9, ISBN13: 978-0-691-05805-4. Dewey:291.1/7. LCCN:98-039388.

Audience: **g,l,u,f.** *Choice, 1999.*

Collins, John J.   **BL2525.C63 1991**
The Cult Experience: An Overview of Cults, Their Traditions and Why People Join Them. Cloth Text. Charles C Thomas Publisher, Ltd. Springfield, IL. 1991. 142p. ISBN:0-398-05721-4, ISBN13: 978-0-398-05721-3. Dewey:291. LCCN:90-049591.

Audience: **g,l,u.**

Corbett, Lionel   **BL53.C657 1996**
The Religious Function of the Psyche. Paper over Boards. Routledge. New York, NY. 1996. 272p. ISBN:0-415-14400-0, ISBN13: 978-0-415-14400-1. Dewey:200.1/9. LCCN:95-025778.

Audience: **u.**

Corrigan, John (Author, Editor)   **BL65.E46R45 2004**
Religion and Emotion: Approaches and Interpretations. Trade Cloth. Oxford University Press, Inc. New York, NY. 2004. 368p. ISBN:0-19-516624-8, ISBN13: 978-0-19-516624-8. Dewey:200/1/9. LCCN:2003-056467.

Audience: **u,f.**

Corrigan, John, et al.   **Z7785**
Emotion and Religion: A Critical Assessment and Annotated Bibliography. Eric Crump & John M. Kloos Jr. (Authors). Cloth Text. Greenwood Publishing Group, Inc. Portsmouth, NH. 2000. 256p. ISBN:0-313-30600-1, ISBN13: 978-0-313-30600-6. Dewey:016.2/001/9. LCCN:00-035372.

Audience: **u,f.** *Choice, 2001.*

Coward, Harold   **BF51.C69 2002**
Yoga and Psychology: Language, Memory, and Mysticism. Cloth Text. State University of New York Press. Albany, NY. 2002. x, 115p. SUNY Series in Religious Studies ISBN:0-7914-5499-1, ISBN13: 978-0-7914-5499-2. Dewey:181/.45. LCCN:2002-017732.

Audience: **l,u,f.** *Choice, 2003.*

De Silva, Padmasiri   **BQ4570.P76D47 2005**
An Introduction to Buddhist Psychology. Ed. 4. John Hick (Foreword by). Trade Paper, Perfect. Palgrave Macmillan. New York, NY. 2005. 216p. Library of Philosophy and Religion ISBN:1-4039-9245-2, ISBN13: 978-1-4039-9245-1. Dewey:150/.1. LCCN:2005-042910.

Audience: **g,l,u,f.**

Dupreez, Peter   **JA74.5.D8 1980**
The Politics of Identity. Cloth Text. Palgrave Macmillan. New York, NY. 1980. 178p. ISBN:0-312-62697-5, ISBN13: 978-0-312-62697-6. Dewey:320/.01/9. LCCN:80-019996.

Audience: **l,u.** *B*

Ellens, J. Harold & Rollins, Wayne G. (Editors)   **BS645**
Psychology and the Bible: A New Way to Read the Scriptures. Trade Cloth. Greenwood Publishing Group, Inc. Portsmouth, NH. 2004. 1,315p. Psychology, Religion, and Spirituality Ser. ISBN:0-275-98347-1, ISBN13: 978-0-275-98347-5. Dewey:220.6/01/9. LCCN:2004-050863.

Audience: **g,l,u,f.** *Choice, 2005.*

Faber, M. D.   **BL51**
The Magic of Prayer: An Introduction to the Psychology of Faith. Trade Cloth. Greenwood Publishing Group, Inc. Portsmouth, NH. 2001. 168p. ISBN:0-275-97385-9, ISBN13: 978-0-275-97385-8. Dewey:291.4/2. LCCN:2001-032913.

Audience: **g,l,u.**

Faber, M. D.   **BL51.F295 2004**
The Psychological Roots of Religious Belief: Searching for Angels and the Parent-God. Trade Cloth. Prometheus Books, Publishers. Amherst, NY. 2004. 290p. ISBN:1-59102-267-3, ISBN13: 978-1-59102-267-1. Dewey:200/.1/9. LCCN:2004-014877.

Audience: **g,l,u.** *Choice, 2005.*

Fenn, Richard K. & Capps, Donald (Editors)   **BL290.O5 1995**
On Losing the Soul: Essays in the Social Psychology of Religion. Cloth Text. State University of New York Press.

Audience: g=general, l=lower division undergraduate, u=upper division undergraduate, f=faculty.

633

Albany, NY. 1995. 249p. ISBN:0-7914-2493-6, ISBN13: 978-0-7914-2493-3. Dewey:306.6. LCCN:94-031494.

Audience: **l,u,f.**

Fontana, David   BL53.F57 2003
Psychology, Religion and Spirituality. Trade Cloth. British Psychological Society. Leicester, 2003. 272p. ISBN:1-4051-0805-3, ISBN13: 978-1-4051-0805-8. Dewey:200/.1/9. LCCN:2002-010324.

Audience: **l,u,f.** *Choice, 2003.*

Forman, Robert K. (Editor)   BL625.I56 1998
The Innate Capacity: Mysticism, Psychology, and Philosophy. Trade Cloth. Oxford University Press, Inc. New York, NY. 1997. 264p. ISBN:0-19-511697-6, ISBN13: 978-0-19-511697-7. Dewey:291.4/22. LCCN:97-001585.

Audience: **u,f.** *Choice, 1998.*

Freud, Sigmund   BL53.F67 1989
The Future of an Illusion. James Strachey (Editor). Trade Paper. W. W. Norton & Company, Inc. New York, NY. 1989. xxiii, 80p. ISBN:0-393-00831-2, ISBN13: 978-0-393-00831-9. Dewey:302.

Audience: **g,l,u,f.** *B*

Friedman, Maurice   BF51.F73 1992
Religion and Psychology: A Dialogical Approach. Trade Paper. Paragon House Publishers. Saint Paul, MN. 1992. 240p. ISBN:1-55778-346-2, ISBN13: 978-1-55778-346-2. Dewey:291.1/75. LCCN:91-030769.

Audience: **u.** *Choice, 1993.*

Gorsuch, Richard L.   BF51
Integrating Psychology and Spirituality? Trade Cloth. Greenwood Publishing Group, Inc. Portsmouth, NH. 2002. 208p. ISBN:0-275-97372-7, ISBN13: 978-0-275-97372-8. Dewey:291.1/75. LCCN:2002-021573.

Audience: **l,u.**

Hamer, Dean H.   BL53.H285 2004
The God Gene: How Faith Is Hardwired into Our Genes. Trade Cloth. Doubleday Publishing. New York, NY. 2004. 256p. ISBN:0-385-50058-0, ISBN13: 978-0-385-50058-6. Dewey:200/.1/9. LCCN:2004-047808.

Audience: **g,l,u.** *Choice, 2005.*

Hamer, Dean H.   BL53
The God Gene: How Faith Is Hardwired into Our Genes. Trade Paper. Knopf Publishing Group. New York, NY. 2005. 256p. ISBN:0-385-72031-9, ISBN13: 978-0-385-72031-1. Dewey:200/.1/9.

Audience: **g,l,u,f.** *Choice, 2005.*

Helminiak, Daniel A.   BL624.H384 1996
The Human Core of Spirituality: Mind as Psyche and Spirit. Cloth Text. State University of New York Press. Albany, NY. 1996. 307p. ISBN:0-7914-2949-0, ISBN13: 978-0-7914-2949-5. Dewey:291.4/4. LCCN:95-031717.

Audience: **l,u,f.**

Helminiak, Daniel A.   BL624.H386 1998
Religion and the Human Sciences: An Approach via Spirituality. Cloth Text. State University of New York Press. Albany, NY. 1998. 320p. ISBN:0-7914-3805-8, ISBN13: 978-0-7914-3805-3. Dewey:291.4. LCCN:97-036986.

Audience: **l,u,f.**

Hood, Ralph W. Jr., et al.   BL238.H66 2005
The Psychology of Religious Fundamentalism. Peter C. Hill & W. Paul Williamson (Authors). Paper over Boards. Guilford Publications, Inc. New York, NY. 2005. 247p. ISBN:1-59385-150-2, ISBN13: 978-1-59385-150-7. Dewey:200/.1/9. LCCN:2004-030394.

Audience: **g,l,u.** *Choice, 2006.*

Jacobs, Janet Liebman & Capps, Donald (Editors)   BF175.R437 1997
Religion, Society, and Psychoanalysis: Readings in Contemporary Theory. Trade Paper. Westview Press. Boulder, CO. 1997. 288p. ISBN:0-8133-2648-6, ISBN13: 978-0-8133-2648-1. Dewey:210. LCCN:97-000573.

Audience: **u.**

James, William   BL53.J36 1994
The Varieties of Religious Experience: A Study in Human Nature. Ed. 19. Trade Cloth. Random House, Inc. New York, NY. 1994. 608p. Modern Library Ser. ISBN:0-679-60075-2, ISBN13: 978-0-679-60075-6. Dewey:291.4/2. LCCN:93-040461.

Audience: **g,l,u,f.**

Johnson, Eric L. & Jones, Stanton L. (Editors)   BR110.P77 2000
Psychology and Christianity: Four Views. Gary Collins (Contribution by). Trade Paper. InterVarsity Press. Downers Grove, IL. 2000. 271p. ISBN:0-8308-2263-1, ISBN13: 978-0-8308-2263-8. Dewey:261.5/15. LCCN:00-040951.

Audience: **g,l,u.**

Jones, James W.   BF175.4.R44J655 1996
Religion and Psychology in Transition: Psychoanalysis, Feminism and Theology. Cloth over Boards. Yale University Press. Cumberland, RI. 1996. 176p. ISBN:0-300-06769-0, ISBN13: 978-0-300-06769-9. Dewey:291.1/75. LCCN:96-015777.

Audience: **u,f.** *Choice, 1997.*

Jung, C. G.   BL53 .J8 1992
Psychology and Religion. Trade Paper. Yale University Press. Cumberland, RI. 1960. 138p. Terry Lectures ISBN:0-300-00137-1, ISBN13: 978-0-300-00137-2. Dewey:200/.1/9. LCCN:91-038405.

Audience: **l,u,f.** *B*

Kirkpatrick, Lee A.   BL53.K56 2004
Attachment, Evolution, and the Psychology of Religion. Cloth over Boards. Guilford Publications, Inc. New York, NY. 2004. 400p. ISBN:1-59385-088-3, ISBN13: 978-1-59385-088-3. Dewey:200/.1/9. LCCN:2004-013003.

Audience: **u,f.** *Choice, 2005.*

Koenig, Harold George (Editor)   BL65.M45H26 1998
Handbook of Religion and Mental Health. Cloth Text. Elsevier Science & Technology Books. Saint Louis, MO. 1998. 408p. ISBN:0-12-417645-3, ISBN13: 978-0-12-417645-4. Dewey:291.1/78322. LCCN:98-084981.

Audience: **l,u,f.**

Lawson, E. Thomas & McCauley, Robert N.   BL41
Rethinking Religion: Connecting Cognition and Culture. Trade Paper. Cambridge University Press. New York, NY. 1993. 204p. ISBN:0-521-43806-3, ISBN13: 978-0-521-43806-3. Dewey:200.

Audience: **u,f.** *Choice, 1990.*

Link, Stuart B   BF51.L56 1999
Psychological Perspectives on Traditional Jewish Practices.
Trade Cloth. Rowman & Littlefield Publishers, Inc. Lanham,
MD. 1999. 244p. ISBN:0-7657-6036-3, ISBN13:
978-0-7657-6036-4. Dewey:296.4/01/9. LCCN:99-013643.
Audience: **g,l,u.**

Maslow, Abraham H.   BL53.M38
Religions, Values and Peak Experiences. Trade Cloth. Peter
Smith Publisher, Inc. Magnolia, MA. 1983. 123p.
ISBN:0-8446-6070-1, ISBN13: 978-0-8446-6070-7.
Dewey:201.6.
Audience: **g,l,u,f.**

McCauley, Robert N. &   BL600 .M36 2002
   Lawson, E. Thomas
Bringing Ritual to Mind: Psychological Foundations of Cultural
Forms. Cloth Text. Cambridge University Press. New York, NY.
2002. 250p. ISBN:0-521-81559-2, ISBN13: 978-0-521-81559-8.
Dewey:291.38019. LCCN:2002-073463.
Audience: **l,u,f.**

Miller, Melvin E. &   BL624.P79 2000
   Young-Eisendrath, Polly (Editors)
The Psychology of Mature Spirituality: Integrity, Wisdom,
Transcendence. Paper over Boards. Routledge. New York, NY.
2000. 224p. ISBN:0-415-17959-9, ISBN13: 978-0-415-17959-1.
Dewey:291.4. LCCN:00-025538.
Audience: **l,u.**

Miller, William R. &   BF51.J83 2004
   Delaney, Harold D.
Judeo-Christian Perspectives on Psychology: Human Nature,
Motivation, and Change. Trade Cloth. American Psychological
Association. Washington, DC. 2004. 336p. ISBN:1-59147-161-3,
ISBN13: 978-1-59147-161-5. Dewey:261.5/15.
LCCN:2004-009504.
Audience: **l,u,f.** *Choice, 2005.*

Newberg, Andrew, et al.   BF773.N48 2001
Why God Won't Go Away: Brain Science and the Biology of
Belief. Eugene D'Aquili & Vince Rause (Authors). Trade Cloth.
Ballantine Books. New York, NY. 2001. 240p.
ISBN:0-345-44033-1, ISBN13: 978-0-345-44033-4.
Dewey:200/.1/9. LCCN:2001-269244.
Audience: **g,l,u,f.** *Choice, 2001.*

Noble, Kate   BL624.N63 2001
Riding the Windhorse: Spiritual Intelligence and the Growth of
the Self. Paper Text. Hampton Press, Inc. Cresskill, NJ. 2001.
vii, 149p. ISBN:1-57273-374-8, ISBN13: 978-1-57273-374-9.
Dewey:291.4/2. LCCN:2001-024128.
Audience: **g,l.**

Palmer, Michael F.   BF175.4.R44P35 1997
Freud and Jung on Religion. Paper over Boards. Routledge.
New York, NY. 1997. 256p. ISBN:0-415-14746-8, ISBN13:
978-0-415-14746-0. Dewey:200/.1/9. LCCN:96-051720.
Audience: **l,u,f.**

Paloutzian, Raymond F. &   BL53.H288 2005
   Park, Crystal L. (Editors)
Handbook of the Psychology of Religion and Spirituality. Cloth
over Boards. Guilford Publications, Inc. New York, NY. 2005.
590p. ISBN:1-57230-922-9, ISBN13: 978-1-57230-922-7.
Dewey:200/.1/9. LCCN:2005-015576.
Audience: **g,l,u,f.** *Choice, 2006.*

Pargament, Kenneth I.   BL53
The Psychology of Religion and Coping: Theory, Research,
Practice. Trade Paper. Guilford Publications, Inc. New York, NY.
2001. 548p. ISBN:1-57230-664-5, ISBN13: 978-1-57230-664-6.
Dewey:200/.1/9.
Audience: **u,f.** *Choice, 1997.*

Persinger, Michael A.   QP360
Neuropsychological Bases of God Beliefs. Trade Cloth.
Greenwood Publishing Group, Inc. Portsmouth, NH. 1987. 175p.
ISBN:0-275-92648-6, ISBN13: 978-0-275-92648-9.
Dewey:200/.1/9. LCCN:87-014689.
Audience: **l,u,f.**

Plante, Thomas G. &   BL65.M4F35 2001
   Sherman, Allen C. (Editors)
Faith and Health: Psychological Perspectives. Cloth over
Boards. Guilford Publications, Inc. New York, NY. 2001. 416p.
ISBN:1-57230-682-3, ISBN13: 978-1-57230-682-0.
Dewey:291.1/78321. LCCN:2001-042932.
Audience: **u,f.** *Choice, 2002.*

Pyysiainen, Ilkka &   BL53.C787 2002
   Anttonen, Veikko (Editors)
Current Approaches in the Cognitive Science of Religion. Trade
Cloth. Continuum International Publishing Group, Ltd. London,
2002. 288p. ISBN:0-8264-5709-6, ISBN13: 978-0-8264-5709-7.
Dewey:200/.1/9. LCCN:2001-047579.
Audience: **l,u.**

Rabin, Albert I.   BF51.R33 1998
Psychological Issues in Biblical Lore: Explorations in the Old
Testament. Trade Cloth. Springer Publishing Company, Inc. New
York, NY. 1998. 222p. Series on Social Work
ISBN:0-8261-1212-9, ISBN13: 978-0-8261-1212-5.
Dewey:221.6/01/9. LCCN:98-017874.
Audience: **l.**

Rank, Otto   BF38.R314 1998
Psychology and the Soul: A Study of Origin, Conceptual
Evolution and Nature of the Soul. Gregory C. Richter & E.
James Lieberman (Translators). Trade Cloth. Johns Hopkins
University Press. Baltimore, MD. 1998. 176p.
ISBN:0-8018-5739-2, ISBN13: 978-0-8018-5739-3.
Dewey:128/.1. LCCN:97-030223.
Audience: **l,u,f.**

Richards, P. Scott & Bergin,   RC489.R46H36 2000
   Allen E. (Editors)
Handbook of Psychotherapy and Religious Diversity. Cloth Text.
American Psychological Association. Washington, DC. 1999.
518p. ISBN:1-55798-624-X, ISBN13: 978-1-55798-624-5.
Dewey:616.89/14. LCCN:99-046210.
Audience: **u,f.**

Rue, Loyal D.   BL53.R82 2005
Religion Is Not about God: How Spiritual Traditions Nurture
Our Biological Nature and What to Expect When They Fail.
Trade Cloth. Rutgers University Press. Piscataway, NJ. 2005.
400p. ISBN:0-8135-3511-5, ISBN13: 978-0-8135-3511-1.
Dewey:200/.1/9. LCCN:2004-007531.
Audience: **g,l,u,f.** *Choice, 2005.*

Schneiderman, Leo   **BL50**
The Psychology of Myth, Folklore and Religion. Trade Cloth.
Rowman & Littlefield Publishers, Inc. Lanham, MD. 1981.
232p. ISBN:0-88229-659-0, ISBN13: 978-0-88229-659-3.
Dewey:291/.01/9. LCCN:81-009471.

Audience: **l,u.**

Segal, Robert A. (Editor,   **BL304.P88 1996**
  Introduction by)
Psychology and Myth. Cloth Text. Garland Publishing, Inc. New
York, NY. 1995. 416p. Theories of Myth Ser., Vol. 1
ISBN:0-8153-2255-0, ISBN13: 978-0-8153-2255-9.
Dewey:291.1/3/019. LCCN:95-038826.

Audience: **l,u.**

Shermer, Michael   **BL240.2.S545 2000**
How We Believe: The Search for God in an Age of Science.
Trade Cloth. W. H. Freeman & Company. New York, NY. 1999.
288p. ISBN:0-7167-3561-X, ISBN13: 978-0-7167-3561-8.
Dewey:215. LCCN:99-040406.

Audience: **g,l,u.**   *Choice, 2000.*

1985
Spilka, Bernard, et al.   **BL53.P625 2003**
The Psychology of Religion: An Empirical Approach. Ed. 3.
Richard Gorsuch, Ralph W. Hood Jr. & Bruce Hunsberger
(Authors). Cloth over Boards. Guilford Publications, Inc. New
York, NY. 2003. 671p. ISBN:1-57230-901-6, ISBN13:
978-1-57230-901-2. Dewey:200/.1/9. LCCN:2003-011806.

Audience: **l,u,f.**

Stein, Samuel (Editor)   **JFE 00-7502**
Beyond Belief: Psychotherapy and Religion. Trade Paper.
Karnac Books. London, 1999. 232p. ISBN:1-85575-186-0,
ISBN13: 978-1-85575-186-6. Dewey:616.8914.

Audience: **l,u.**

Taves, Ann   **BL53.T38 1999**
Fits, Trances, and Visions: Experiencing Religion and
Explaining Experience from Wesley to James. Trade Cloth.
Princeton University Press. Princeton, NJ. 1999. 448p.
ISBN:0-691-02876-1, ISBN13: 978-0-691-02876-7.
Dewey:291.4/2. LCCN:99-029754.

Audience: **l,u,f.**   *Choice, 2000.*

Taylor, Charles   **BL53.J363T39 2002**
Varieties of Religion Today: William James Revisited. Trade
Cloth. Harvard University Press. Cambridge, MA. 2002. 142p.
Institute for Human Sciences Vienna Lectures Ser.
ISBN:0-674-00760-3, ISBN13: 978-0-674-00760-4.
Dewey:291.4/2. LCCN:2001-039872.

Audience: **l,u,f.**   *Choice, 2003.*

Taylor, Eugene   **BL2525**
Shadow Culture: Psychology and Spirituality in America. Trade
Cloth. Addison-Wesley Longman, Inc. Boston, MA. 1999.
ISBN:0-201-60880-4, ISBN13: 978-0-201-60880-9.
Dewey:200/.973.

Audience: **g,l,u.**   *Choice, 1999.*

Ulanov, Barry & Ulanov,   **BL53 .U45**
  Ann Belford
Religion and the Unconscious. Trade Cloth. Westminster John
Knox Press. Louisville, KY. 1975. 288p. ISBN:0-664-20799-5,
ISBN13: 978-0-664-20799-1. Dewey:200/.19. LCCN:75-016302.

Audience: **g,l,u,f.** *B*

Vergote, A.   **BL53**
Religion, Belief and Unbelief: A Psychological Study. Trade
Paper. Leuven University Press. Leuven, 1996. 344p.
ISBN:90-6186-751-7, ISBN13: 978-90-6186-751-7.
Dewey:200/.1/9.

Audience: **u,f.**

Washburn, Michael   **BF204.7.W372 2003**
Embodied Spirituality in a Sacred World. Cloth Text. State
University of New York Press. Albany, NY. 2003. 256p. SUNY
Series in Transpersonal and Humanistic Psychology
ISBN:0-7914-5847-4, ISBN13: 978-0-7914-5847-1.
Dewey:150.19/8. LCCN:2003-052606.

Audience: **l,u,f.**   *Choice, 2004.*

Wilber, Ken   **BF311.W5765 2000**
Integral Psychology: Consciousness, Spirit, Psychology,
Therapy. Trade Paper. Shambhala Publications, Inc. Boston,
MA. 2000. xiii, 303p. ISBN:1-57062-554-9, ISBN13:
978-1-57062-554-1. Dewey:150. LCCN:99-053186.

Audience: **g,l,u.**

Wulff, David H.   **BL53.W77 1997**
Psychology of Religion: Classic and Contemporary. Ed. 2. Trade
Cloth. John Wiley & Sons, Inc. Hoboken, NJ. 1996. 784p.
ISBN:0-471-03706-0, ISBN13: 978-0-471-03706-4.
Dewey:200/.1/9. LCCN:96-043970.

Audience: **l,u.**

Social Processes and Social Issues >
Culture and Ethnology

Atkinson, Donald R. &   **BF637.C6C6372 1995**
  Hackett, Gail
Counseling Diverse Populations. Cloth Text. Brown &
Benchmark. Madison, WI. 1994. 400p. ISBN:0-697-21129-0,
ISBN13: 978-0-697-21129-3. Dewey:158/.3/08.
LCCN:94-070182.

Audience: **l,u,f.**

Bernal, Guillermo (Editor),   **GN502.H3635 2003**
  et al.
Handbook of Racial and Ethnic Minority Psychology, Vol. 4.
Joseph E. Trimble, Ann Kathleen Burlew & Frederick T. L.
Leong (Editors). Trade Cloth. SAGE Publications, Inc.
Thousand Oaks, CA. 2002. 720p. Racial and Ethnic Minority
Psychology Ser., Vol. 4 ISBN:0-7619-1965-1, ISBN13:
978-0-7619-1965-0. Dewey:155.8/2. LCCN:2002-006456.

Audience: **l,u,f.**   *Choice, 2003.*

Brammer, Robert   **BF637.C6B677 2002**
Diversity in Counseling. Cloth Text. Thomson Wadsworth.
Belmont, CA. 2003. 400p. ISBN:0-87581-449-2, ISBN13:
978-0-87581-449-0. Dewey:158/.3. LCCN:2002-113037.

Audience: **l,u.**

Davis-Russell, Elizabeth   **BF637.C6C27 2002**
  (Editor)
The California School of Professional Psychology: Handbook of
Multicultural Education, Research, Intervention, and Training.
Trade Cloth. John Wiley & Sons, Inc. Hoboken, NJ. 2002. 368p.
ISBN:0-7879-5763-1, ISBN13: 978-0-7879-5763-6.
Dewey:150/.7. LCCN:2002-016069.

Audience: **u,f.**

Koslow, Diane R. & Salett,   **BF637.C6**
   Elizabeth P. (Editors)
Crossing Cultures in Mental Health. Trade Paper. N M C I
Publications. Washington, DC. 1989. 154p.
ISBN:0-933934-15-7, ISBN13: 978-0-933934-15-3.
Dewey:158.3.

Audience: **u,f.**

Lee, Wanda M. L.   **BF637.C6L415 1999**
Introduction to Multicultural Counseling. Paper over Boards.
Hemisphere Publishing Corporation. Philadelphia, PA. 1999.
274p. ISBN:1-56032-567-4, ISBN13: 978-1-56032-567-3.
Dewey:158/.3. LCCN:99-017941.

Audience: **l,u.**

Lee, Yueh-Ting (Editor),   **BF698.9.C8P54 1998**
   et al. *Personality and person perception across cultures*
Through the Looking-Glass: Personality in Culture. Clark
McCauley & Juris Draguns (Editors). Cloth over Boards.
Lawrence Erlbaum Associates, Inc. Mahwah, NJ. 1998. 320p.
ISBN:0-8058-2813-3, ISBN13: 978-0-8058-2813-9.
Dewey:155.8. LCCN:98-016383.

Audience: **u,f.** *Choice, 1999.*

Nisbett, Richard E.   **BF311.N565 2003**
The Geography of Thought: How Asians and Westerners Think
Differently... and Why. Trade Cloth. Simon & Schuster. New
York, NY. 2003. 288p. ISBN:0-7432-1646-6, ISBN13:
978-0-7432-1646-3. Dewey:153.4. LCCN:2002-032178.

Audience: **g,l,u.**

Nisbett, Richard E. &   **HN79.A13V56 1996**
   Cohen, Dov
Culture of Honor: The Psychology of Violence in the South.
Trade Paper. Westview Press. Boulder, CO. 1996. 144p. New
Directions in Social Psychology Ser. ISBN:0-8133-1993-5,
ISBN13: 978-0-8133-1993-3. Dewey:303.6/0975.
LCCN:96-166629.

Audience: **g,l,u.**

Palmer, Stephen &   **BF637.C6C665 1999**
   Laungani, Pittu D. (Editors)
Counselling in a Multicultural Society. Cloth Text. SAGE
Publications, Ltd. London, 1999. 224p. Clinical and Counseling
Ser. ISBN:0-7619-5064-8, ISBN13: 978-0-7619-5064-6.
Dewey:158/.3. LCCN:98-075103.

Audience: **u,f.**

Palmer, Stephen (Author,   **BF637.C6M8365 2002**
   Editor)
Multicultural Counselling: A Reader. Cloth Text. SAGE
Publications, Inc. Thousand Oaks, CA. 2002. 280p.
ISBN:0-7619-6375-8, ISBN13: 978-0-7619-6375-2.
Dewey:158/.3. LCCN:2002-511616.

Audience: **u,f.**

Parker, Woodrow M.   **BF637.C6P27 1998**
   (Editor)
Consciousness-Raising: A Primer for Multicultural Counseling.
Ed. 2. Cloth Text. Charles C Thomas Publisher, Ltd. Springfield,
IL. 1998. 326p. ISBN:0-398-06828-3, ISBN13:
978-0-398-06828-8. Dewey:158/.3. LCCN:97-031597.

Audience: **u,f.**

Pedersen, Paul   **BF637.C6P336 2000**
A Handbook for Developing Multicultural Awareness. Ed. 3.
Paper Text. American Counseling Association. Alexandria, VA.
2000. 230p. ISBN:1-55620-177-X, ISBN13: 978-1-55620-177-6.
Dewey:158/.3. LCCN:99-055851.

Audience: **u,f.**

Pedersen, Paul B. (Editor)   **BF637**
Handbook of Cross-Cultural Counseling and Therapy. Cloth
Text. Greenwood Publishing Group, Inc. Portsmouth, NH. 1985.
376p. ISBN:0-313-23914-2, ISBN13: 978-0-313-23914-4.
Dewey:158/.3. LCCN:84-012832.

Audience: **u,f.** *B*

Pedersen, Paul, et al.   **BF637.C6C63 2002**
Counseling Across Cultures. Ed. 5. Juris Draguns, Walter J.
Lonner & Joseph E. Trimble (Authors). Cloth Text. SAGE
Publications, Inc. Thousand Oaks, CA. 2002. 472p.
ISBN:0-7619-2085-4, ISBN13: 978-0-7619-2085-4.
Dewey:616.89/14. LCCN:2001-005392.

Audience: **u,f.**

Perez, Ruperto M. (Editor),   **BF637.C6H3125 2000**
   et al.
Handbook of Counseling and Psychotherapy with Lesbian, Gay
and Bisexual Clients. Kurt A. DeBord & Kathleen J. Bieschke
(Editors). Cloth Text. American Psychological Association.
Washington, DC. 1999. xvi, 484p. ISBN:1-55798-610-X,
ISBN13: 978-1-55798-610-8. Dewey:158/.3/0866.
LCCN:99-032399.

Audience: **u,f.**

Pope-Davis, Donald, et al.   **BF637.C6H3173 2003**
Handbook of Multicultural Competencies in Counseling and
Psychology. Martin Heesacker, Hardin L. K. Coleman, William
Ming Liu & Rebecca L. Toporek (Authors). Trade Cloth. SAGE
Publications, Inc. Thousand Oaks, CA. 2003. 672p.
ISBN:0-7619-2306-3, ISBN13: 978-0-7619-2306-0.
Dewey:158/.3. LCCN:2003-005186.

Audience: **u,f.** *Choice, 2004.*

Roysircar, Gargi (Editor),   **BF637.C6M836 2003**
   et al.
Multicultural Competencies: A Guidebook of Practices. Daya
Singh Sandhu & Victor E. Bibbins (Editors). Trade Cloth.
American Counseling Association. Alexandria, VA. 2003. xxxii,
285p. ISBN:1-55620-198-2, ISBN13: 978-1-55620-198-1.
Dewey:158/.3. LCCN:2002-151998.

Audience: **u,f.**

Schaller, Mark & Crandall,   **GN514.P78 2003**
   Christian S. (Editors)
The Psychological Foundations of Culture. Cloth over Boards.
Lawrence Erlbaum Associates, Inc. Mahwah, NJ. 2003. 392p.
ISBN:0-8058-3839-2, ISBN13: 978-0-8058-3839-8. Dewey:306.
LCCN:2003-040839.

Audience: **u,f.**

Shweder, Richard A.   **GN502.S59 2003**
Why Do Men Barbecue?: Recipes for Cultural Psychology.
Trade Cloth. Harvard University Press. Cambridge, MA. 2003.
430p. ISBN:0-674-01057-4, ISBN13: 978-0-674-01057-4.
Dewey:155.82. LCCN:2002-038818.

Audience: **g,l,u.**

√ **Smith, Timothy B.**   **BF637.C6P7 2004**
Practicing Multiculturalism: Affirming Diversity in Counseling
and Psychology. Trade Paper. Allyn & Bacon, Inc. Boston, MA.
2003. 360p. ISBN:0-205-33640-X, ISBN13: 978-0-205-33640-1.
Dewey:158/.3. LCCN:2003-040433.

Audience: **u,f.**

√ **Sue, David & Sue, Derald**   **BF637.C6S85 2002**
   Wing
Counseling the Culturally Diverse: Theory and Practice. Ed. 4.
Trade Cloth. John Wiley & Sons, Inc. Hoboken, NJ. 2002. 528p.
ISBN:0-471-41980-X, ISBN13: 978-0-471-41980-8.
Dewey:158/.3. LCCN:2002-071444.

Audience: **u,f.**

√ **Tomasello, Michael**   **BF611**
The Cultural Origins of Human Cognition. Trade Paper. Harvard
University Press. Cambridge, MA. 2001. 256p.
ISBN:0-674-00582-1, ISBN13: 978-0-674-00582-2. Dewey:153.
LCCN:99-035902.

Audience: **g,l,u,f.**

√ **Velasquez, Roberto (Editor),**   **RC451.5.M48H36 2004**
   et al.
The Handbook of Chicana/o Psychology and Mental Health.
Leticia M. Arellano & Brian McNeill (Editors), Christina
Ayala-Alcantar, Louise Baca & Manuel Barrera Jr. (Contribution
by). Cloth over Boards. Lawrence Erlbaum Associates, Inc.
Mahwah, NJ. 2004. 544p. ISBN:0-8058-4158-X, ISBN13:
978-0-8058-4158-9. Dewey:362.2/089/68073.
LCCN:2003-045646.

Audience: **u,f.** *Choice, 2004.*

Ward, Colleen A. (Editor)   **RA790.5.A44 1989**
Altered States of Consciousness and Mental Health: A
Cross-Cultural Perspective. Trade Cloth. SAGE Publications,
Inc. Thousand Oaks, CA. 1989. 320p. Cross-Cultural Research
and Methodology Ser., Vol. 12 ISBN:0-8039-3277-4, ISBN13:
978-0-8039-3277-7. Dewey:616.89. LCCN:89-005872.

Audience: **u,f.**

Social Processes and Social Issues > Marriage and Family

√ **Arendell, Terry (Editor)**   **HQ755.8.C655 1997**
Contemporary Parenting: Challenges and Issues, Vol. 9. Trade
Cloth. SAGE Publications, Inc. Thousand Oaks, CA. 1997.
360p. Understanding Families Ser., Vol. 9 ISBN:0-8039-7268-7,
ISBN13: 978-0-8039-7268-1. Dewey:649/.1. LCCN:97-004678.

Audience: **u.**

√ **Bianchi, Suzanne M.**   **HD4904.25.W77 2003**
   (Editor), et al.
Work, Family, Health, and Well-Being. Lynne Casper, Lynne M.
Casper & Rosalind B. King (Editors), Suzanne M. Bianchi,
Susan M. McHale, Harry J. Holzer, Amy Kolak, Laura Lein,
Robert Kaestner, Lars Smith-Hansen, Cameron Mustard, Mary
Noonan, Harriet B. Presser, David Prottas, Susan Jekielek,
Jeanine Andreasse, Sara Raley, Zakia Redd, Rena L. Repetti,
Christopher Ruhm, Stephanie Simmons, Lotte Bailyn, Pamela J.
Smock, Ross M. Stolzenberg, Cynthia A. Thompson, Linda J.
Waite, Jane Waldfogel, Dave Wertheimer, Maureen
Perry-Jenkins, Linda Waite, Martha Zaslow, Susan Lambert,
Richard Wertheimer, Cam Mustard, Jeanette N. Cleveland, Ann

C. Crouter, Eliza K. Pavalko, Ellen Ernst Kossek, Susan J.
Lambert, Kristin A. Moore, Barbara Schneider, Sanders
Korenman, Benjamin C. Amick, Jeanine Andreassi, Tage S.
Kristensen, Ann Bookman, Linda M. Burton, Janet Currie,
Charles N. Darrah, Allard E. Dembe, Alison Earle, Joyce K.
Fletcher, Megan Gallagher, Jennifer Glass, Fang Gong, Julia
Henly, Jody Heymann, Nicole Jansen & Arleen A. Leibowitz
(Contribution by) Saddle Stitched, Cloth over Boards. Lawrence
Erlbaum Associates, Inc. Mahwah, NJ. 2005. 600p.
ISBN:0-8058-5254-9, ISBN13: 978-0-8058-5254-7.
Dewey:306.3/61/0973. LCCN:2004-056394.

Audience: **u,f.** *Choice, 2005.*

√ **Blieszner, Rosemary H. &**   **HQ1061**
   Bedford, Victoria H. (Editors)
Handbook of Aging and the Family. Cloth Text. Greenwood
Publishing Group, Inc. Portsmouth, NH. 1995. 536p.
ISBN:0-313-28395-8, ISBN13: 978-0-313-28395-6.
Dewey:305.26. LCCN:94-017988.

Audience: **u,f.** *Choice, 1995.*

√ **Boss, P. (Editor), et al.**   **HQ728.S638 1993**
Sourcebook of Family Theories and Methods: A Contextual
Approach. W. Doherty, Ralph LaRossa, W. R. Schumm & S. K.
Steinmetz (Editors). Trade Cloth. Basic Books. New York, NY.
1993. 772p. ISBN:0-306-44264-7, ISBN13: 978-0-306-44264-3.
Dewey:306.85. LCCN:92-049046.

Audience: **u,f.**

√ **Coontz, Stephanie**   **HQ503.C66 2005**
Marriage, a History: From Obedience to Intimacy, or How Love
Conquered Marriage. Trade Cloth. Penguin Group (USA) Inc.
New York, NY. 2005. 448p. ISBN:0-670-03407-X, ISBN13:
978-0-670-03407-9. Dewey:306.81/09. LCCN:2005-041497.

Audience: **g,l.**

√ **Demo, David H. (Editor),**   **HQ518.H1538 2000**
   et al.
Handbook of Family Diversity. Katherine R. Allen & Mark A.
Fine (Editors). Cloth Text. Oxford University Press, Inc. New
York, NY. 1999. 480p. ISBN:0-19-512038-8, ISBN13:
978-0-19-512038-7. Dewey:306.85. LCCN:99-015341.

Audience: **u,f.**

√ **Fincham, Frank D. &**   **RC488.5.P786 1990**
   Bradbury, Thomas N. (Editors)
The Psychology of Marriage: Basic Issues and Applications.
Cloth over Boards. Guilford Publications, Inc. New York, NY.
1990. 432p. ISBN:0-89862-433-9, ISBN13: 978-0-89862-433-5.
Dewey:616.89/156. LCCN:90-003038.

Audience: **u.** *Choice, 1990.*

Hawes, Joseph M. & Shores,   **HQ536.H365 2001**
Elizabeth F. (Editors)
The Family in America: An Encyclopedia, Set. Library Binding.
ABC-CLIO, Inc. Santa Barbara, CA. 2002. 1075p. The
American Family Ser. ISBN:1-57607-232-0, ISBN13:
978-1-57607-232-5. Dewey:306.85/0973/03.
LCCN:2002-000394.

Audience: **g,l,u,f.** *Choice, 2003, 2002.*

√ **Macmillan Library**   **HQ9.E52 2003**
   Reference Staff
International Encyclopedia of Marriage and Family, Set. Ed. 2.
Trade Cloth. Thomson Gale. Farmington Hills, MI. 1905. 2000p.
ISBN:0-02-865672-5, ISBN13: 978-0-02-865672-4.
Dewey:306.8/03. LCCN:2002-014107.

Audience: **u.** *Choice, 2003.*

McHale, James P. &   **HQ10.R46 2001**
  Grolnick, Wendy S. (Editors)
Retrospect and Prospect in the Psychological Study of Families.
Cloth over Boards. Lawrence Erlbaum Associates, Inc. Mahwah,
NJ. 2001. 392p. ISBN:0-8058-3797-3, ISBN13:
978-0-8058-3797-1. Dewey:306.85/07/2. LCCN:2001-042310.
                       Audience: **u,f.**

Muncie, John (Editor), et al.   **HQ518**
Understanding the Family. Ed. 2. Margaret Wetherell, Allan
Douglas Cochrane, Rudi Dallos & Mary Langan (Editors). Paper
Text. SAGE Publications, Ltd. London, 1999. 336p.
ISBN:0-7619-5307-8, ISBN13: 978-0-7619-5307-4.
Dewey:306.8/5. LCCN:96-069546.
                       Audience: **l,u.**

Nichols, William C. (Editor),   **RC489.F33.H36 2000**
  et al.
Handbook of Family Development and Intervention. Mary Anne
Pace-Nichols, Dorothy S. Becvar & Augustus Napier (Editors).
Trade Cloth. John Wiley & Sons, Inc. Hoboken, NJ. 2000. 504p.
Wiley Series in Couples and Family Dynamics and Treatment
Ser., Vol. 14 ISBN:0-471-29967-7, ISBN13: 978-0-471-29967-7.
Dewey:616.89/156. LCCN:99-037989.
                       Audience: **u,f.**

Noller, Patricia & Feeney,   **HQ728.U54 2002**
  Judith A. (Editors)
Understanding Marriage: Developments in the Study of Couple
Interaction. Mary Anne Fitzpatrick, Harry Reis & Anita
Vangelista (Contribution by). Trade Cloth. Cambridge University
Press. New York, NY. 2002. 584p. Advances in Personal
Relationships Ser. ISBN:0-521-80370-5, ISBN13:
978-0-521-80370-0. Dewey:306.81. LCCN:2001-052759.
                       Audience: **u,f.**

O'Connell, Mark   **HQ756.O25 2005**
The Good Father: On Men, Masculinity, and Life in the Family.
Trade Cloth. Simon & Schuster. New York, NY. 2005. 304p.
ISBN:0-7432-5801-0, ISBN13: 978-0-7432-5801-2.
Dewey:306.874/2. LCCN:2004-052109.
                       Audience: **g,l.**

Pinsof, William M. &   **HQ728.F3225 2005**
  Lebow, Jay
Family Psychology: The Art of the Science. Trade Cloth. Oxford
University Press, Inc. New York, NY. 2005. 608p. Oxford Series
in Clinical Psychology ISBN:0-19-513557-1, ISBN13:
978-0-19-513557-2. Dewey:306.85/019. LCCN:2004-017539.
                       Audience: **l,u,f.**

Scarf, Maggie   **RC488.5.S28 1995**
Intimate Worlds: Life Inside the Family. Trade Cloth. Random
House, Inc. New York, NY. 1995. 466p. ISBN:0-394-56543-6,
ISBN13: 978-0-394-56543-9. Dewey:616.89/156.
LCCN:95-000827.
               Audience: **g,l.** *Choice, 1996.*

Thornton, Arland (Editor)   **HQ767.9.W455 2001**
The Well-Being of Children and Families: Research and Data
Needs. Trade Cloth. University of Michigan Press. Chicago, IL.
2001. 480p. ISBN:0-472-09758-X, ISBN13: 978-0-472-09758-6.
Dewey:305.23/0973. LCCN:00-011173.
                       Audience: **u,f.**

Vangelisti, Anita L. (Editor)   **HQ519.H36 2003**
Handbook of Family Communication. Cloth over Boards.
Lawrence Erlbaum Associates, Inc. Mahwah, NJ. 2003. 792p.

LEA's Communication Ser. ISBN:0-8058-4130-X, ISBN13:
978-0-8058-4130-5. Dewey:306.87. LCCN:2003-015733.
               Audience: **u,f.** *Choice, 2004.*

Walsh, Froma (Editor)   **HQ728.N83 2002**
Normal Family Processes: Growing Diversity and Complexity.
Ed. 3. Cloth over Boards. Guilford Publications, Inc. New York,
NY. 2002. 678p. ISBN:1-57230-816-8, ISBN13:
978-1-57230-816-9. Dewey:306.85. LCCN:2002-015629.
                       Audience: **l,u.**

White, James M.   **HQ503.W69 1991**
Dynamics of Family Development: A Theoretical Perspective.
Cloth over Boards. Guilford Publications, Inc. New York, NY.
1991. 254p. Perspectives on Marriage and the Family Ser.
ISBN:0-89862-080-5, ISBN13: 978-0-89862-080-1.
Dewey:306.85. LCCN:91-009053.
               Audience: **l,u.** *Choice, 1991.*

Social Processes and Social Issues > Divorce and Remarriage

Beer, William R.   **HQ759.92.B44 1991**
American Stepfamilies. Trade Cloth. Transaction Publishers.
Somerset, NJ. 1991. 226p. ISBN:0-88738-436-6, ISBN13:
978-0-88738-436-3. Dewey:306.874. LCCN:91-008924.
                       Audience: **g,l,u,f.**

Booth, Alan & Dunn, Judith   **HQ759.92.S76 1994**
  (Editors)
Stepfamilies: Who Benefits? Who Does Not? Cloth over Boards.
Lawrence Erlbaum Associates, Inc. Mahwah, NJ. 1994. 256p.
ISBN:0-8058-1544-9, ISBN13: 978-0-8058-1544-3.
Dewey:306.874. LCCN:94-013294.
               Audience: **u,f.** *Choice, 1995.*

Cath, Stanley H. (Editor),   **HQ759.92.S736 2001**
  et al.
Stepparenting: Creating and Recreating Families in America
Today. Moisy Shopper & Lora H. Tessman (Editors). Cloth over
Boards. Analytic Press. Hillsdale, NJ. 2001. 360p.
ISBN:0-88163-176-0, ISBN13: 978-0-88163-176-0.
Dewey:306.874. LCCN:2001-041317.
               Audience: **l,u.** *Choice, 2002.*

Clarke-Stewart, Alison &   **HQ814.C55 2006**
  Brentano, Cornelia
Divorce: Causes and Consequences. Cloth over Boards. Yale
University Press. Cumberland, RI. 2006. 368p. Current
Perspectives in Psychology Ser. ISBN:0-300-11044-8, ISBN13:
978-0-300-11044-9. Dewey:306.89. LCCN:2005-018881.
                       Audience: **l,u,f.**

Deater-Deckard, Kirby D.   **HQ755.83D43 2004**
Parenting Stress. Cloth over Boards. Yale University Press.
Cumberland, RI. 2004. 220p. Current Perspectives in
Psychology Ser. ISBN:0-300-10393-X, ISBN13:
978-0-300-10393-9. Dewey:155.9/042/085. LCCN:2004-049707.
                       Audience: **l,u.**

Emery, Robert E.   **RJ507.D59E44 1999**
Marriage, Divorce, and Children's Adjustment, Vol. 14. Ed. 2.
Trade Paper. SAGE Publications, Inc. Thousand Oaks, CA.

1999. 176p. Developmental Clinical Psychology and Psychiatry Ser. ISBN:0-7619-0252-X, ISBN13: 978-0-7619-0252-2. Dewey:155.4. LCCN:98-040280.

Audience: **u,f.**

Furstenberg, Frank F. Jr. &   HQ777.5.F87 1991
  Cherlin, Andrew J.
Divided Families: What Happens to Children When Parents Part. Trade Cloth. Harvard University Press. Cambridge, MA. 1991. 152p. The Family and Public Policy Ser., No. 1 ISBN:0-674-65576-1, ISBN13: 978-0-674-65576-8. Dewey:306.8/9/0973. LCCN:90-048171.

Audience: **l,u,f.**   *Choice, 1991.*

Ganong, Lawrence H. &   HQ759.92.S7294 2004
  Coleman, Marilyn
Stepfamily Relationships: Development, Dynamics, and Interventions. Trade Cloth. Springer. New York, NY. 2003. 284p. ISBN:0-306-47997-4, ISBN13: 978-0-306-47997-7. Dewey:306.874/7. LCCN:2003-060446.

Audience: **u,f.**   *Choice, 2004.*

Guttman, Joseph   HQ814.G94 1993
Divorce in Psychosocial Perspective: Theory and Research. Cloth Text. Lawrence Erlbaum Associates, Inc. Mahwah, NJ. 1993. 288p. ISBN:0-8058-0347-5, ISBN13: 978-0-8058-0347-1. Dewey:306.89. LCCN:92-033412.

Audience: **u,f.**   *Choice, 1994.*

Hetherington, E. Mavis &   HQ814.H47 2002
  Kelly, John
For Better or for Worse: Divorce Reconsidered. Trade Cloth. W. W. Norton & Company, Inc. New York, NY. 2002. 320p. ISBN:0-393-04862-4, ISBN13: 978-0-393-04862-9. Dewey:306.89. LCCN:2001-044319.

Audience: **g,l,u.**

Kaslow, Florence W. &   HQ814.K37 1987
  Schwartz, Lita L.
The Dynamics of Divorce: A Life Cycle Perspective. Paper over Boards. Brunner-Routledge. Philadelphia, PA. 1987. 346p. Frontiers in Couples and Family Therapy Ser., No. 1 ISBN:0-87630-455-2, ISBN13: 978-0-87630-455-6. Dewey:306.8/9. LCCN:87-000693.

Audience: **g,l,u.**

Marquardt, Elizabeth   HQ777.5.M3746 2005
Between Two Worlds: The Inner Lives of Children of Divorce. Trade Cloth. Crown Publishing Group. New York, NY. 2005. 255p. ISBN:0-307-23710-9, ISBN13: 978-0-307-23710-1. Dewey:306.89. LCCN:2005-008032.

Audience: **l.**

Pam, Alvin & Pearson,   HQ814.P35 1998
  Judith
Splitting Up: Enmeshment and Estrangement in the Process of Divorce. Cloth over Boards. Guilford Publications, Inc. New York, NY. 1998. 448p. ISBN:1-57230-367-0, ISBN13: 978-1-57230-367-6. Dewey:306.89. LCCN:98-022648.

Audience: **u.**   *Choice, 1999.*

Riley, Glenda   HQ834.R55 1997
Divorce: An American Tradition. Trade Cloth. University of Nebraska Press. Lincoln, NE. 1997. 262p. ISBN:0-8032-8969-3, ISBN13: 978-0-8032-8969-7. Dewey:306.89/0973. LCCN:97-012258.

Audience: **l.**   *Choice, 1991.*

Schwartz, Lita Linzer &   HQ814.S38 1997
  Kaslow, Florence W.
Painful Partings: Divorce and Its Aftermath. Trade Cloth. John Wiley & Sons, Inc. Hoboken, NJ. 1997. 320p. Wiley Series in Couples and Family Dynamics and Treatment Ser., Vol. 4 ISBN:0-471-11009-4, ISBN13: 978-0-471-11009-5. Dewey:306.89. LCCN:96-019118.

Audience: **l,u.**   *Choice, 1997.*

Stewart, Abigail J., et al.   RC473.C37H46 1997
Separating Together: How Divorce Transforms Families. Anne P. Copeland, Nia Lane Chester, Janet E. Malley & Nicole B. Barenbaum (Authors). Cloth over Boards. Guilford Publications, Inc. New York, NY. 1997. 293p. ISBN:1-57230-235-6, ISBN13: 978-1-57230-235-8. Dewey:616.89/14. LCCN:97-008707.

Audience: **l,u.**   *Choice, 1998.*

Thompson, Ross A. &   HQ834.P68 1999
  Amato, Paul R. (Editors)
The Postdivorce Family: Children, Parenting, and Society. Trade Cloth. SAGE Publications, Inc. Thousand Oaks, CA. 1999. 272p. ISBN:0-7619-1489-7, ISBN13: 978-0-7619-1489-1. Dewey:306.89. LCCN:99-006018.

Audience: **u,f.**

Wallerstein, Judith S., et al.   HQ834.W356 2000
The Unexpected Legacy of Divorce: The 25 Year Landmark Study. Julia Lewis & Sandra Blakeslee (Authors). Trade Cloth. Hyperion Press. New York, NY. 2000. 352p. ISBN:0-7868-6394-3, ISBN13: 978-0-7868-6394-5. Dewey:306.8/9/0973. LCCN:00-035071.

Audience: **l,u.**   *Choice, 2001.*

Social Processes and Social Issues > Childrearing and Child Care

Adams, Gerald R. &   BF724.B487 2003
  Berzonsky, Michael D. (Editors)
Blackwell Handbook of Adolescence. Trade Cloth. Blackwell Publishing, Inc. Malden, MA. 2003. 680p. Blackwell Handbooks of Developmental Psychology Ser., Vol. 4 ISBN:0-631-21919-6, ISBN13: 978-0-631-21919-4. Dewey:155.5. LCCN:2002-151837.

Audience: **l,u.**   *Choice, 2003.*

Barber, Nigel &   HQ755
  Donnelly, K.
Why Parents Matter: Parental Investment and Child Outcomes. Trade Cloth. Greenwood Publishing Group, Inc. Portsmouth, NH. 2000. 232p. ISBN:0-89789-725-0, ISBN13: 978-0-89789-725-9. Dewey:649/.1. LCCN:99-055886.

Audience: **g,l.**

Bergum, Vangie   HQ759
A Child on Her Mind: The Experience of Becoming a Mother. Trade Cloth. Greenwood Publishing Group, Inc. Portsmouth, NH. 1997. 208p. ISBN:0-89789-446-4, ISBN13: 978-0-89789-446-3. Dewey:306.874/3. LCCN:96-009032.

Audience: **g,l.**

Bornstein, Marc H. (Editor)   HQ755.8.H357 2002
Handbook of Parenting: Social Conditions and Applied Parenting. Ed. 2. Sandra T. Azar, Ruth K. Chao & Moncrieff Cochran (Contribution by). Cloth over Boards. Lawrence

Erlbaum Associates, Inc. Mahwah, NJ. 2002. 576p.
ISBN:0-8058-3781-7, ISBN13: 978-0-8058-3781-0.
Dewey:649/.1. LCCN:2001-058458.

Audience: **u,f.**

Bornstein, Marc H. (Editor)   HQ755.8.H357 2002
Handbook of Parenting: Biology and Ecology of Parenting. Ed.
2. Kim A. Bard, Kay Bathurst & David F. Bjorklund
(Contribution by). Cloth over Boards. Lawrence Erlbaum
Associates, Inc. Mahwah, NJ. 2002. 552p. ISBN:0-8058-3779-5,
ISBN13: 978-0-8058-3779-7. Dewey:649/.1.
LCCN:2001-058458.

Audience: **u,f.**

Bornstein, Marc H. (Editor)   HQ755.8.H357 2002
Handbook of Parenting: Being and Becoming a Parent. Ed. 2.
Kathryn E. Barnard, Jay Belsky & David F. Bjorklund
(Contribution by). Cloth over Boards. Lawrence Erlbaum
Associates, Inc. Mahwah, NJ. 2002. 792p. ISBN:0-8058-3780-9,
ISBN13: 978-0-8058-3780-3. Dewey:649/.1.
LCCN:2001-058458.

Audience: **u,f.**

Bornstein, Marc H. (Editor)   HQ755.8.H357 2002
Handbook of Parenting: Practical Issues in Parenting. Ed. 2.
Diana Baumrind, Ellen W. Clayton & Keith Crnic (Contribution
by). Cloth over Boards. Lawrence Erlbaum Associates, Inc.
Mahwah, NJ. 2002. 696p. ISBN:0-8058-3782-5, ISBN13:
978-0-8058-3782-7. Dewey:649/.1. LCCN:2001-058458.

Audience: **u,f.**

Bornstein, Marc H. (Editor)   HQ755.8.H357 2002
Handbook of Parenting: Children and Parenting. Ed. 2. David
M. Brodzinsky, W. Andrew Collins & Barbara A. DiVitto
(Contribution by). Cloth over Boards. Lawrence Erlbaum
Associates, Inc. Mahwah, NJ. 2002. 600p. ISBN:0-8058-3778-7,
ISBN13: 978-0-8058-3778-0. Dewey:649/.1.
LCCN:2001-058458.

Audience: **u,f.**

Brazelton, T. Berry &   BF721
Greenspan, Stanley I.
The Irreducible Needs of Children: What Every Child Must
Have to Grow, Learn and Flourish. Trade Paper. Perseus Books
Group. New York, NY. 2001. 248p. ISBN:0-7382-0516-8,
ISBN13: 978-0-7382-0516-8. Dewey:155.4.

Audience: **g,l,u.**

Brodzinsky, David M. &   HV875
Palacios, Jesus (Editors)
Psychological Issues in Adoption: Research and Practice. Trade
Cloth. Greenwood Publishing Group, Inc. Portsmouth, NH.
2005. 336p. Advances in Applied Developmental Psychology
Ser., No. 24 ISBN:0-275-97970-9, ISBN13: 978-0-275-97970-6.
Dewey:362.734/01/9. LCCN:2005-004053.

Audience: **l,u,f.** *Choice, 2006.*

Deater-Deckard, Kirby D.   HQ755.83D43 2004
Parenting Stress. Cloth over Boards. Yale University Press.
Cumberland, RI. 2004. 220p. Current Perspectives in
Psychology Ser. ISBN:0-300-10393-X, ISBN13:
978-0-300-10393-9. Dewey:155.9/042/085. LCCN:2004-049707.

Audience: **l,u.**

Dixon, Wallace E.   BF721.D59 2002
Twenty Studies That Revolutionized Child Psychology. Trade
Paper. Prentice Hall PTR. Upper Saddle River, NJ. 2002. 296p.
ISBN:0-13-041572-3, ISBN13: 978-0-13-041572-1.
Dewey:155.4. LCCN:2002-074982.

Audience: **g,l.**

Elkind, David   BF723
Hurried Child: Growing up Too Fast Too Soon. Ed. 3. Trade
Paper. Basic Books. New York, NY. 2001. 272p.
ISBN:0-7382-0441-2, ISBN13: 978-0-7382-0441-3.
Dewey:305.23. LCCN:2002-279985.

Audience: **g,l,u.**

Halfon, Neal (Editor), et al.   HQ769.C4493 2002
Child Rearing in America: Challenges Facing Parents with
Young Children. Kathryn Taaffe McLearn & Mark A. Schuster
(Editors). Trade Cloth. Cambridge University Press. New York,
NY. 2002. 448p. ISBN:0-521-81320-4, ISBN13:
978-0-521-81320-4. Dewey:649/.1/0973. LCCN:2001-043679.

Audience: **l,u.**

Hoghughi, Masud S. &   HQ755.8
Long, Nicholas (Editors)
The Handbook of Parenting: Theory, Research and Practice.
Trade Cloth. SAGE Publications, Inc. Thousand Oaks, CA.
2004. 416p. ISBN:0-7619-7104-1, ISBN13: 978-0-7619-7104-7.
Dewey:306.8/74. LCCN:2003-105476.

Audience: **u,f.**

Kindlon, Daniel J., et al.   HQ775.K56 1999
Raising Cain: Protecting the Emotional Life of Boys. Michael
Thompson & Teresa Barker (Authors). Trade Cloth. Ballantine
Books. New York, NY. 1999. 304p. ISBN:0-345-42457-3,
ISBN13: 978-0-345-42457-0. Dewey:649.1/32.
LCCN:98-054182.

Audience: **g,l,u.** *Choice, 1999.*

Kuczynski, Leon (Editor)   HQ755.85.K8 2002
Handbook of Dynamics in Parent-Child Relations. Trade Cloth.
SAGE Publications, Inc. Thousand Oaks, CA. 2002. 492p.
ISBN:0-7619-2364-0, ISBN13: 978-0-7619-2364-0.
Dewey:306.874. LCCN:2002-011092.

Audience: **u,f.**

Lamb, Michael E. (Editor)   HQ734.N68 1998
Parenting and Child Development in Nontraditional Families.
Cloth over Boards. Lawrence Erlbaum Associates, Inc. Mahwah,
NJ. 1998. 368p. ISBN:0-8058-2747-1, ISBN13:
978-0-8058-2747-7. Dewey:306.85. LCCN:98-018422.

Audience: **u,f.**

Lamb, Sharon   HQ777.L35 2002
The Secret Lives of Girls: What Good Girls Really Do--Sex
Play, Aggression, and Their Guilt. Trade Cloth. Simon &
Schuster. New York, NY. 2002. 272p. ISBN:0-7432-0107-8,
ISBN13: 978-0-7432-0107-0. Dewey:305.23.
LCCN:2001-054755.

Audience: **g,l.**

Lerner, Richard M.   BF721.H242 2006
Handbook of Child Psychology, Set. Ed. 6. William Damon
(Editor). Trade Cloth. John Wiley & Sons, Inc. Hoboken, NJ.
2006. 1250p. ISBN:0-471-27287-6, ISBN13:
978-0-471-27287-8. Dewey:155.4. LCCN:2005-043951.

Audience: **l,u,f.**

Lerner, Richard M. &   **BF724.L367 2004**
  Steinberg, Laurence (Editors)
Handbook of Adolescent Psychology. Ed. 2. Trade Cloth. John
Wiley & Sons, Inc. Hoboken, NJ. 2004. 864p.
ISBN:0-471-20948-1, ISBN13: 978-0-471-20948-5.
Dewey:155.5. LCCN:2003-049664.

Audience: **u,f.**

Lieberman, Alicia F.   **HQ774.5.L54 1993**
Emotional Life of the Toddler. Children's Board Books. Simon
& Schuster. New York, NY. 1993. 256p. ISBN:0-02-919021-5,
ISBN13: 978-0-02-919021-0. Dewey:649/.122.
LCCN:93-008018.

Audience: **g,l.**

Newberger, Eli H.   **HQ775**
The Men They Will Become: The Nature and Nurture of the
Male Character. Trade Paper. Basic Books. New York, NY.
2000. 384p. A Merloyd Lawrence Book Ser.
ISBN:0-7382-0363-7, ISBN13: 978-0-7382-0363-8.
Dewey:155.432.

Audience: **g,l,u.**

Phares, Vicky   **BF723**
Poppa Psychology: The Role of Fathers in Children's Mental
Well Being. Trade Cloth. Greenwood Publishing Group, Inc.
Portsmouth, NH. 1999. 168p. ISBN:0-275-96367-5, ISBN13:
978-0-275-96367-5. Dewey:155.9/24. LCCN:98-033614.

Audience: **l,u.** *Choice, 1999.*

Pipher, Mary   **HQ798.P57 1994**
Reviving Ophelia: Saving the Selves of Adolescent Girls. Trade
Cloth. Penguin Group (USA) Inc. New York, NY. 1994. 320p.
ISBN:0-399-13944-3, ISBN13: 978-0-399-13944-4.
Dewey:305.23/5. LCCN:93-038964.

Audience: **g,l,u,f.**

Pollack, William   **HQ775.P65 1998**
Real Boys: Rescuing Our Sons from the Myths of Boyhood.
Trade Cloth. Random House, Inc. New York, NY. 1998. 288p.
ISBN:0-375-50131-2, ISBN13: 978-0-375-50131-9.
Dewey:305.23. LCCN:98-015282.

Audience: **g,l.**

Roberts, Michael C. (Editor)   **RJ47.5.H38 2003**
Handbook of Pediatric Psychology. Ed. 3. Cloth over Boards.
Guilford Publications, Inc. New York, NY. 2003. 772p.
ISBN:1-57230-906-7, ISBN13: 978-1-57230-906-7.
Dewey:618.92/0001/9. LCCN:2003-010143.

Audience: **u,f.**

Worell, Judy (Editor)   **HQ1206.H23855 2005**
Handbook of Girls' and Women's Psychological Health. Trade
Cloth. Oxford University Press, Inc. New York, NY. 2005. 527p.
Oxford Series in Clinical Psychology ISBN:0-19-516203-X,
ISBN13: 978-0-19-516203-5. Dewey:155.3/33.
LCCN:2004-027119.

Audience: **l,u,f.** *Choice, 2006.*

Social Processes and Social Issues >
Political Processes and Political Issues

Alford, C. Fred   **HM133.A45 1994**
Group Psychology and Political Theory. Cloth over Boards. Yale
University Press. Cumberland, RI. 1994. 240p.

ISBN:0-300-05958-2, ISBN13: 978-0-300-05958-8.
Dewey:302.3/4. LCCN:94-006774.

Audience: **u,f.** *Choice, 1995.*

Almond, Gabriel Abraham   **JA74.A4 1989**
  & Verba, Sidney (Editors)
The Civic Culture: Political Attitudes and Democracy in Five
Nations. Trade Paper. SAGE Publications, Inc. Thousand Oaks,
CA. 1989. 392p. ISBN:0-8039-3558-7, ISBN13:
978-0-8039-3558-7. Dewey:306/.2. LCCN:79-089764.

Audience: **l,u,f.** *B*

Ascher, William &   **JA74.5.A77 2004**
  Hirschfelder-Ascher, Barbara
Revitalizing Political Psychology: The Legacy of Harold D.
Lasswell. Cloth over Boards. Lawrence Erlbaum Associates, Inc.
Mahwah, NJ. 2004. 216p. ISBN:0-8058-5206-9, ISBN13:
978-0-8058-5206-6. Dewey:320/.01/9. LCCN:2004-046928.

Audience: **u,f.**

Bangura, Abdul Karim, et   **JA75.7.P646 1996**
al.
Political Behavior. Dawit Isayas, Gerald Smith & Michael O.
Thomas (Authors). Trade Cloth. University Press of America,
Inc. Lanham, MD. 1996. 176p. ISBN:0-7618-0222-3, ISBN13:
978-0-7618-0222-8. Dewey:306.2. LCCN:95-039480.

Audience: **u.**

Barner-Barry, Carol &   **JA74.5 .B37**
  Rosenwein, Robert
Psychological Perspectives on Politics. Paper Text. Waveland
Press, Inc. Prospect Heights, IL. 1991. 342p.
ISBN:0-88133-619-X, ISBN13: 978-0-88133-619-1.
Dewey:320/.01/9.

Audience: **l,u.**

Cottam, Martha L., et al.   **JA74.5.C665 2004**
Introduction to Political Psychology. Beth Dietz-Uhler, Elena M.
Mastors & Thomas Preston (Authors). Trade Paper. Lawrence
Erlbaum Associates, Inc. Mahwah, NJ. 2004. 360p.
ISBN:0-8058-3770-1, ISBN13: 978-0-8058-3770-4.
Dewey:320/.01/9. LCCN:2003-025976.

Audience: **l,u,f.**

Davies, James C.   **JA74.5 .D38 1978**
Human Nature in Politics: The Dynamics of Political Behavior.
Trade Cloth. Greenwood Publishing Group, Inc. Portsmouth,
NH. 1978. 403p. ISBN:0-8371-9870-4, ISBN13:
978-0-8371-9870-5. Dewey:320/.01/9. LCCN:77-013870.

Audience: **l,u.**

Dean, Kathryn   **JA74.5.P644 1997**
Politics and the Ends of Identity. Trade Cloth. Ashgate
Publishing, Ltd. Aldershot, 1997. 312p. Avebury Series in
Philosophy ISBN:1-85972-372-1, ISBN13: 978-1-85972-372-2.
Dewey:126. LCCN:97-073873.

Audience: **u.**

Edelman, Murray   **JA74.5.E43 1985**
The Symbolic Uses of Politics: With a New Afterward. Ed. 2.
Trade Paper. University of Illinois Press. Champaign, IL. 1985.
232p. ISBN:0-252-01202-X, ISBN13: 978-0-252-01202-0.
Dewey:320/.01/9. LCCN:84-016195.

Audience: **l,u,f.**

Edelman, Murray J.   **JA74.5.E39 1988**
Constructing the Political Spectacle. Trade Paper. University of
Chicago Press. Chicago, IL. 1988. 142p. ISBN:0-226-18399-8,

ISBN13: 978-0-226-18399-2. Dewey:320/.01/9.
LCCN:87-016239.

Audience: **u,f.** *Choice, 1988.*

Elster, Jon   **JA74.5 .E47 1993**
Political Psychology. Cloth Text. Cambridge University Press.
New York, NY. 1993. 214p. ISBN:0-521-41110-6, ISBN13:
978-0-521-41110-3. Dewey:320.019. LCCN:92-017779.

Audience: **u.**

Feldman, Ofer & Valenty,   **BF698**
  Linda O. (Editors)
Profiling Political Leaders: Cross-Cultural Studies of Personality
and Behavior. Trade Cloth. Greenwood Publishing Group, Inc.
Portsmouth, NH. 2001. 320p. ISBN:0-275-97036-1, ISBN13:
978-0-275-97036-9. Dewey:303.3/4/019. LCCN:00-052866.

Audience: **u,f.** *Choice, 2002.*

Goff, Patricia M. & Dunn,   **JA74.5.I35 2004**
  Kevin C. (Editors)
Identity and Global Politics: Theoretical and Empirical
Elaborations. Patricia M. Goff & Kevin C. Dunn (Translators).
Cloth over Boards. Palgrave Macmillan. New York, NY. 2004.
284p. Culture and Religion in International Relations Ser.
ISBN:1-4039-6379-7, ISBN13: 978-1-4039-6379-6.
Dewey:306.2. LCCN:2003-058036.

Audience: **u,f.** *Choice, 2004.*

Hall, Cheryl Ann   **JA74.5.H34 2005**
Trouble with Passion: Political Theory Beyond the Reign of
Reason. Paper over Boards. Routledge. New York, NY. 2005.
176p. ISBN:0-415-93405-2, ISBN13: 978-0-415-93405-3.
Dewey:320/.01/9. LCCN:2004-027358.

Audience: **l,u.**

Hoover, Kenneth R., et al.   **JA74.5.H66 1997**
The Power of Identity: Politics in a New Key. James E. Marcia
& Kristen D. Parris (Authors). Paper Text. CQ Press.
Washington, DC. 1997. 176p. Chatham House Studies in
Political Thinking ISBN:1-56643-051-8, ISBN13:
978-1-56643-051-7. Dewey:320/.01/9. LCCN:96-051258.

Audience: **g,u.** *Choice, 1998.*

Hughes, Alan   **JA74.5**
Psychology and the Political Experience. Cloth Text. Cambridge
University Press. New York, NY. 1975. 234p.
ISBN:0-521-20594-8, ISBN13: 978-0-521-20594-8.
Dewey:320/.01/9. LCCN:74-012961.

Audience: **u.**

Iyengar, Shanto & McGuire,   **JA74.5.E96 1993**
  William J. (Editors)
Explorations in Political Psychology. Cloth Text. Duke
University Press. Durham, NC. 1993. 495p. Duke Studies in
Political Psychology ISBN:0-8223-1301-4, ISBN13:
978-0-8223-1301-4. Dewey:320.019. LCCN:92-027503.

Audience: **u,f.** *Choice, 1993.*

Jost, John T. & Sidanius,   **JA74.5**
  James (Editors) *key*
Political Psychology: Essential Readings. Paper over Boards.
Routledge. New York, NY. 2004. 512p. Key Readings in Social
Psychology Ser. ISBN:1-84169-069-4, ISBN13:
978-1-84169-069-8. Dewey:320/.01/9. LCCN:2003-010695.

Audience: **l,u.**

Kuklinski, James H. (Editor,   **JA74.5 .C59 2001**
  Contribution by)
Citizens and Politics: Perspectives from Political Psychology.
Dennis Chong (Contribution by). Trade Cloth. Cambridge
University Press. New York, NY. 2001. 534p. Studies in
Political Psychology and Public Opinion ISBN:0-521-59376-X,
ISBN13: 978-0-521-59376-2. Dewey:320/.01/9.
LCCN:00-059876.

Audience: **u,f.** *Choice, 2003, 2002.*

Kuklinski, Jim (Editor)   **JA74.5 .T43 2002**
Thinking about Political Psychology. Cloth Text. Cambridge
University Press. New York, NY. 2002. 366p. Studies in
Political Psychology and Public Opinion ISBN:0-521-59377-8,
ISBN13: 978-0-521-59377-9. Dewey:320/.01/9.
LCCN:2001-035589.

Audience: **l,u.** *Choice, 2003.*

Lane, Robert E.   **JA74 .L25**
Political Life. Paper Text. Simon & Schuster. New York, NY.
1965. ISBN:0-02-917870-3, ISBN13: 978-0-02-917870-6.
Dewey:329. LCCN:58-006485.

Audience: **g,l.**

Lerner, A. W.   **JA74.5.L47 1990**
The Manipulators: Personality and Politics in Multiple
Perspectives. Cloth Text. Lawrence Erlbaum Associates, Inc.
Mahwah, NJ. 1989. 168p. ISBN:0-8058-0335-1, ISBN13:
978-0-8058-0335-8. Dewey:320/.01/9. LCCN:89-026045.

Audience: **u,f.** *Choice, 1990.*

Lodge, Milton & McGraw,   **JA74.5.P623 1995**
  Kathleen M. (Editors)
Political Judgment: Structure and Process. Trade Cloth.
University of Michigan Press. Chicago, IL. 1995. 320p.
ISBN:0-472-10541-8, ISBN13: 978-0-472-10541-0.
Dewey:324/.01/9. LCCN:94-034167.

Audience: **u,f.** *Choice, 1995.*

Lorion, Raymond P.   **BF76.3.P78 1996**
  (Editor), et al.
Psychology and Public Policy: Balancing Public Service and
Professional Need. Ira Iscoe, Patrick H. DeLeon & Gary R.
VandenBos (Editors). Paper Text. American Psychological
Association. Washington, DC. 1996. 417p.
ISBN:1-55798-347-X, ISBN13: 978-1-55798-347-3. Dewey:150.
LCCN:95-026810.

Audience: **u,f.**

Ludwig, Arnold M.   **JC330.3.L83 2001**
King of the Mountain: The Nature of Political Leadership. Trade
Cloth. University Press of Kentucky. Lexington, KY. 2002.
432p. ISBN:0-8131-2233-3, ISBN13: 978-0-8131-2233-5.
Dewey:303.3/4. LCCN:2001-007227.

Audience: **g,l,u.** *Choice, 2003, 2002.*

Mackenzie, W. J.   **JA74.5 .M32 1978**
Political Identity. Cloth Text. Palgrave Macmillan. New York,
NY. 1978. ISBN:0-312-62308-9, ISBN13: 978-0-312-62308-1.
Dewey:320/.01/9. LCCN:77-026851.

Audience: **l,u.**

Marcus, George E., et al.   **JA74.5 .E94 1995**
With Malice Toward Some: How People Make Civil Liberties
Judgments. John L. Sullivan, Elizabeth Theiss-Morse & Sandra
L. Wood (Authors). Trade Cloth. Cambridge University Press.

New York, NY. 1995. 304p. Studies in Political Psychology and Public Opinion ISBN:0-521-43396-7, ISBN13: 978-0-521-43396-9. Dewey:323/.019. LCCN:95-006151.

Audience: **u,f.** *Choice, 1996.*

Marcuse, Herbert   **BF175**
Five Lectures. Trade Paper. Beacon Press. Boston, MA. 1970. ISBN:0-8070-1549-0, ISBN13: 978-0-8070-1549-0. Dewey:320.5. LCCN:73-103936.

Audience: **g,l,u,f.**

McDermott, Rose   **JA74.5.M4 2004**
Political Psychology in International Relations. Trade Cloth. University of Michigan Press. Chicago, IL. 2004. 320p. Analytical Perspectives on Politics Ser. ISBN:0-472-09701-6, ISBN13: 978-0-472-09701-2. Dewey:327.1/01/9. LCCN:2003-026180.

Audience: **l,u.**

Milburn, Michael A. &   **JA74.5**
  Conrad, Sheree D.
The Politics of Denial. Trade Paper. MIT Press. Cambridge, MA. 1998. 304p. ISBN:0-262-63184-9, ISBN13: 978-0-262-63184-6. Dewey:320/.019.

Audience: **l,u,f.**

Monroe, Kristen Renwick   **JA74.5.P634 2002**
  (Editor)
Political Psychology. Cloth over Boards. Lawrence Erlbaum Associates, Inc. Mahwah, NJ. 2001. 464p. ISBN:0-8058-3886-4, ISBN13: 978-0-8058-3886-2. Dewey:320/.01/9. LCCN:2001-033185.

Audience: **u,f.** *Choice, 2002.*

Norton, Anne   **JA74.5.N67 1988**
Reflections on Political Identity. Trade Cloth. Johns Hopkins University Press. Baltimore, MD. 1988. 224p. Constitutional Thought Ser. ISBN:0-8018-3694-8, ISBN13: 978-0-8018-3694-7. Dewey:320/.01/9. LCCN:88-045400.

Audience: **l,u.** *Choice, 1989.*

Offerman-Zuckerberg, J.   **JA74.5.P643 1991**
Politics and Psychology: Contemporary Psychodynamic Perspectives. Trade Cloth. Basic Books. New York, NY. 1991. 336p. ISBN:0-306-43864-X, ISBN13: 978-0-306-43864-6. Dewey:320/.01/9. LCCN:91-028033.

Audience: **l,u.**

Ottati, Victor C. (Editor),   **JA74.5.S635 2002**
  et al.
The Social Psychology of Politics. R. Scott Tindale, John Edwards, Fred B. Bryant, Linda Heath, Daniel C. O'Connell, Yolanda Suarez-Balcazar & Emil J. Posavac (Editors). Trade Cloth. Springer. New York, NY. 2002. 254p. Social Psychological Applications to Social Issues Ser., Vol. 5 ISBN:0-306-46723-2, ISBN13: 978-0-306-46723-3. Dewey:320/.01/9. LCCN:2002-020828.

Audience: **l,u.**

Payne, James L., et al.   **JA74.5**
The Motivation of Politicians. Oliver H. Woshinsky, Eric P. Veblen, William H. Coogan & Gene E. Bigler (Authors). Book, Other. Rowman & Littlefield Publishers, Inc. Lanham, MD. 1984. 216p. ISBN:0-88229-824-0, ISBN13: 978-0-88229-824-5. Dewey:320/.01/9. LCCN:83-026853.

Audience: **l,u.**

Post, Jerrold M. (Editor)   **JC330.3**
The Psychological Assessment of Political Leaders: With Profiles of Saddam Hussein and Bill Clinton. Trade Paper. University of Michigan Press. Chicago, IL. 2005. 480p. ISBN:0-472-06838-5, ISBN13: 978-0-472-06838-8. Dewey:320/.01/9.

Audience: **l,u,f.**

Post, Jerrold M.   **JC330.3.P68 2004**
Leaders and Their Followers in a Dangerous World: The Psychology of Political Behavior. Alexander George (Foreword by). Trade Cloth. Cornell University Press. Ithaca, NY. 2004. 320p. Psychoanalysis and Social Theory Ser. ISBN:0-8014-4169-2, ISBN13: 978-0-8014-4169-1. Dewey:320/.01/9. LCCN:2003-021237.

Audience: **l,u,f.** *Choice, 2005.*

Renshon, Stanley A.   **JA74.5**
Psychological Needs and Political Behavior: A Theory of Personality and Political Efficacy. Children's Board Books. Simon & Schuster. New York, NY. 1974. 288p. ISBN:0-02-926320-4, ISBN13: 978-0-02-926320-4. Dewey:320/.01/9. LCCN:73-011735.

Audience: **l,u.** *B*

Renshon, Stanley A. &   **JA74.5.P367 2000**
  Duckitt, John (Editors)
Political Psychology: Cultural and Cross-Cultural Foundations. Trade Cloth. New York University Press. New York, NY. 2000. 400p. ISBN:0-8147-7536-5, ISBN13: 978-0-8147-7536-3. Dewey:320/.01/9. LCCN:99-026248.

Audience: **u,f.**

Roazen, Paul   **JA74.5**
Cultural Foundations of Political Psychology. Trade Cloth. Transaction Publishers. Somerset, NJ. 2003. 295p. ISBN:0-7658-0182-5, ISBN13: 978-0-7658-0182-1. Dewey:320/.01/9. LCCN:2003-050773.

Audience: **l,u,f.**

Roazen, Paul   **JA74.5**
Political Theory and the Psychology of the Unconscious: Freud, J. S. Mill, Nietzsche, Dostoevsky, Fromm, Bettelheim, and Erikson. Trade Paper. Open Gate Press. London, 2002. 160p. ISBN:1-871871-48-4, ISBN13: 978-1-871871-48-7. Dewey:320/.01/9.

Audience: **l,u,f.** *Choice, 2003.*

Robin, Corey   **JA74.5R48 2004**
Fear: The History of a Political Idea. Trade Cloth. Oxford University Press, Inc. New York, NY. 2004. 326p. ISBN:0-19-515702-8, ISBN13: 978-0-19-515702-4. Dewey:320/.01/9. LCCN:2004-006813.

Audience: **g,l,u.** *Choice, 2005.*

Robins, Robert S. & Post,   **JA74.5.R55 1997**
  Jerrold M.
Political Paranoia: The Psychopolitics of Hatred. Cloth over Boards. Yale University Press. Cumberland, RI. 1997. 408p. ISBN:0-300-07027-6, ISBN13: 978-0-300-07027-9. Dewey:302/.17. LCCN:96-040336.

Audience: **u,f.**

Robinson, John P. (Editor),   **JA74.5.M43 1999**
  et al.
Measures of Political Attitudes. Phillip R. Shaver & Lawrence S. Wrightsman (Editors). Cloth Text. Elsevier Science &

Technology Books. Saint Louis, MO. 1998. 801p. The Measures of Social Psychological Attitudes Ser., Vol. 2 ISBN:0-12-590242-5, ISBN13: 978-0-12-590242-7. Dewey:320/.01/9. LCCN:98-084427.

Audience: **l,u,f.**

Rosenberg, Shawn, et al.   JA74.5.R67 1988
Political Reasoning and Cognition: A Piagetian View. Dana Ward & Stephen Chilton (Authors). Cloth Text. Duke University Press. Durham, NC. 1988. 192p. ISBN:0-8223-0856-8, ISBN13: 978-0-8223-0856-0. Dewey:320/.01/9. LCCN:88-016225.

Audience: **u,f.** *Choice, 1989.*

Samuels, Andrew   BF175.4.S65S25 1993
The Political Psyche. UK-B Format Paperback. Routledge. New York, NY. 1993. 400p. ISBN:0-415-08102-5, ISBN13: 978-0-415-08102-3. Dewey:150.195. LCCN:92-039941.

Audience: **l,u.**

Sears, David O. (Editor),   JA74.5.H355 2003
  et al.
Oxford Handbook of Political Psychology. Leonie Huddy & Robert L. Jervis (Editors). Paper Text. Oxford University Press, Inc. New York, NY. 2003. 832p. ISBN:0-19-516220-X, ISBN13: 978-0-19-516220-2. Dewey:320/.01/9. LCCN:2002-012893.

Audience: **g,l,u,f.**

Segall, Marshall H.   HM251
Human Behavior and Public Policy - Political Psychology. Cloth Text. Elsevier Science & Technology Books. Saint Louis, MO. 1977. xiv, 321p. ISBN:0-08-017087-0, ISBN13: 978-0-08-017087-9. Dewey:302. LCCN:75-035631.

Audience: **u,f.**

Simon, Laurence R.   RC480
Psychology, Psychotherapy, Psychoanalysis, and the Politics of Human Relationships. Trade Cloth. Greenwood Publishing Group, Inc. Portsmouth, NH. 2003. 248p. ISBN:0-275-97471-5, ISBN13: 978-0-275-97471-8. Dewey:616.89/14. LCCN:2002-190858.

Audience: **u,f.**

Sniderman, Paul M., et al.   HN90.P8 R43 1991
Reasoning and Choice: Explorations in Political Psychology. Richard A. Brody & Phillip E. Tetlock (Authors), Dennis Chong & James H. Kuklinski (Contribution by). Trade Cloth. Cambridge University Press. New York, NY. 1991. 320p. Cambridge Studies in Political Psychology and Public Opinion Ser. ISBN:0-521-40255-7, ISBN13: 978-0-521-40255-2. Dewey:303.3/8. LCCN:90-021145.

Audience: **u,f.**

Stone, William F. &   JA74.5.S8 1988
  Shaffner, P. E.
The Psychology of Politics. Ed. 2. Cloth Text. Springer. New York, NY. 1988. 331p. ISBN:0-387-96674-9, ISBN13: 978-0-387-96674-8. Dewey:320/.01/9. LCCN:87-032313.

Audience: **l,u.**

Sullivan, John L., et al.   JA74.5
Political Tolerance and American Democracy. James Piereson & George E. Marcus (Authors). Trade Paper. University of Chicago Press. Chicago, IL. 1993. 288p. ISBN:0-226-77992-0, ISBN13: 978-0-226-77992-8. Dewey:306/.2/0973. LCCN:81-016406.

Audience: **u,f.**

Tetlock, Philip E.   JA74.5.T38 2005
Expert Political Judgment: How Good Is It? How Can We Know? Trade Cloth. Princeton University Press. Princeton, NJ. 2005. 280p. ISBN:0-691-12302-0, ISBN13: 978-0-691-12302-8. Dewey:320/.01/9. LCCN:2004-061694.

Audience: **g,l,u.** *Choice, 2006.*

Valenty, Linda O. &   BF698
  Feldman, Ofer (Editors)
Political Leadership for the New Century: Personality and Behavior among American Leaders. Trade Cloth. Greenwood Publishing Group, Inc. Portsmouth, NH. 2002. 288p. ISBN:0-275-97037-X, ISBN13: 978-0-275-97037-6. Dewey:352.23/6/0973. LCCN:2001-036411.

Audience: **l,u.** *Choice, 2003.*

Social Psychology

Baumeister, Roy F.   BF57.B35 2005
The Cultural Animal. Trade Cloth. Oxford University Press, Inc. New York, NY. 2005. 464p. ISBN:0-19-516703-1, ISBN13: 978-0-19-516703-0. Dewey:302. LCCN:2004-002990.

Audience: **g,l,u,f.**

Blass, Thomas   HM1031.M55B57 2004
The Man Who Shocked the World: The Life and Legacy of Stanley Milgram. Trade Cloth. Basic Books. New York, NY. 2004. 392p. Art of Mentoring Ser. ISBN:0-7382-0399-8, ISBN13: 978-0-7382-0399-7. Dewey:302/.092 B. LCCN:2003-023841.

Audience: **g,l.** *Choice, 2004.*

DeLamater, John D.   HM1033.H36 2003
  (Editor)
Handbook of Social Psychology. Trade Cloth. Springer. New York, NY. 2003. 592p. Handbooks of Sociology and Social Research ISBN:0-306-47695-9, ISBN13: 978-0-306-47695-2. Dewey:302. LCCN:2002-042770.

Audience: **u,f.** *Choice, 2004.*

Festinger, Leon   BF1809.F4
When Prophecy Fails. Paper Text. Textbook Publishers. Temecula, CA. 2003. vii, 256p. ISBN:0-7581-1978-X, ISBN13: 978-0-7581-1978-0. Dewey:133.3.

Audience: **l,u,f.**

Fromm, Erich   HM271.F74 1994
Escape from Freedom. Trade Paper. Henry Holt & Company. New York, NY. 1994. 320p. ISBN:0-8050-3149-9, ISBN13: 978-0-8050-3149-2. Dewey:323.44. LCCN:94-005689.

Audience: **g,l,u,f.**

Fromm, Erich   HM271.F75 1990
The Sane Society. Trade Paper. Henry Holt & Company. New York, NY. 1990. 384p. ISBN:0-8050-1402-0, ISBN13: 978-0-8050-1402-0. Dewey:306.3/42. LCCN:55-008006.

Audience: **g,l,u.**

Gilbert, Daniel T. (Editor),   HM251.H224 1998
  et al.
The Handbook of Social Psychology, Set. Ed. 4. Susan T. Fiske & Gardner Lindzey (Editors). Trade Cloth. Oxford University Press, Inc. New York, NY. 1998. 1,984p. ISBN:0-19-521376-9, ISBN13: 978-0-19-521376-8. Dewey:302. LCCN:97-005436.

Audience: **g,l,u.**

Heider, Fritz   BF636 .H383
The Psychology of Interpersonal Relations. Paper Text.
Textbook Publishers. Temecula, CA. 2003. 322p.
ISBN:0-7581-0479-0, ISBN13: 978-0-7581-0479-3.
Dewey:150.13.

Audience: **l,u,f.**

Hewstone, Miles   HM251
The Blackwell Encyclopedia of Social Psychology. Anthony S.
Manstead (Editor, Preface by). Trade Paper. Blackwell
Publishing, Inc. Malden, MA. 1996. 712p. ISBN:0-631-20289-7,
ISBN13: 978-0-631-20289-9. Dewey:302/.03.

Audience: **g,l,u.**   *Choice, 1996.*

Higgins, E. Tory &   HM251.S6743 1996
   Kruglanski, Arie W. (Editors)
Social Psychology: Handbook of Basic Principles. Cloth over
Boards. Guilford Publications, Inc. New York, NY. 1996. 948p.
ISBN:1-57230-100-7, ISBN13: 978-1-57230-100-9. Dewey:302.
LCCN:96-022623.

Audience: **l,u.**   *Choice, 1997.*

Hogg, Michael A. & Cooper,   HM1001
   Joel (Editors)
The SAGE Handbook of Social Psychology. Trade Cloth. SAGE
Publications, Inc. Thousand Oaks, CA. 2003. 526p.
ISBN:0-7619-6636-6, ISBN13: 978-0-7619-6636-4. Dewey:302.
LCCN:2002-114575.

Audience: **u,f.**   *Choice, 2004.*

Holstein, James A. &   HM1033.I56 2002
   Gubrium, Jaber F. (Editors)
Inner Lives and Social Worlds: Readings in Social Psychology.
Paper Text. Oxford University Press, Inc. New York, NY. 2002.
624p. ISBN:0-19-514727-8, ISBN13: 978-0-19-514727-8.
Dewey:302. LCCN:2002-029282.

Audience: **l,u.**

Kelly, Anita E.   BF637.P74K45 2002
The Psychology of Secrets. Trade Cloth. Springer. New York,
NY. 2002. 270p. The Plenum Series in Social/Clinical
Psychology ISBN:0-306-46657-0, ISBN13: 978-0-306-46657-1.
Dewey:155.9/2. LCCN:2001-053920.

Audience: **g,l,u.**   *Choice, 2002.*

Milgram, Stanley, et al.   HM251 .M4639 1992
The Individual in a Social World: Essays and Experiments. Ed.
2. John Sabini & Maury Silver (Authors). Paper Text.
McGraw-Hill Higher Education. Burr Ridge, IL. 1992. 320p.
ISBN:0-07-041936-1, ISBN13: 978-0-07-041936-0. Dewey:302.
LCCN:91-033256.

Audience: **g,l,u,f.**

Perloff, Richard M.   BF637.P4.P39 2003
The Dynamics of Persuasion: Communication and Attitudes in
the 21st Century. Ed. 2. Cloth over Boards. Lawrence Erlbaum
Associates, Inc. Mahwah, NJ. 2002. 416p. Lea's Communication
Ser. ISBN:0-8058-4087-7, ISBN13: 978-0-8058-4087-2.
Dewey:153.852. LCCN:2002-033865.

Audience: **l,u,f.**

Reis, Harry T. & Judd,   HM1019 .H36 2000
   Charles M. (Editors)
Handbook of Research Methods in Social and Personality
Psychology. Trade Cloth. Cambridge University Press. New
York, NY. 2000. 570p. ISBN:0-521-55128-5, ISBN13:
978-0-521-55128-1. Dewey:302/.07/2. LCCN:99-016937.

Audience: **u,f.**

Skinner, B. F.   BF21
Cumulative Record: Definitive Edition. Trade Cloth. Copley
Publishing Group. Acton, MA. 1999. 700p. B. F. Skinner
Reprint Ser. ISBN:1-58390-005-5, ISBN13: 978-1-58390-005-5.
Dewey:150.81.

Audience: **u,f.**

Tesser, Abraham (Editor),   BF697.P765 2000
   et al.
Psychological Perspectives on Self and Identity. Richard B.
Felson & Jerry M. Suls (Editors). Cloth Text. American
Psychological Association. Washington, DC. 2000. x, 252p.
ISBN:1-55798-678-9, ISBN13: 978-1-55798-678-8.
Dewey:155.2. LCCN:00-021139.

Audience: **u,f.**   *Choice, 2001.*

Social Psychology > Group and Interpersonal Processes

Allport, Gordon W.   HM291
The Nature of Prejudice. Ed. 25. Kenneth Clark (Introduction
by), Thomas F. Pettigrew (Preface by). Trade Paper. Da Capo
Press, Inc. Cambridge, MA. 1979. 576p. ISBN:0-201-00179-9,
ISBN13: 978-0-201-00179-2. Dewey:303.3/85.
LCCN:54-005626.

Audience: **g,l,u,f.**

Andersen, Peter A. &   BF637.C45H283 1998
   Guerrero, Laura K. (Editors)
Handbook of Communication and Emotion: Research, Theory,
Applications, and Contexts. Trade Cloth. Elsevier Science &
Technology Books. Saint Louis, MO. 1997. 590p.
ISBN:0-12-057770-4, ISBN13: 978-0-12-057770-5.
Dewey:153.6. LCCN:97-023315.

Audience: **u,f.**   *Choice, 1998.*

Auhagen, Ann Elisabeth &   HM132.Z9213 1996
   Von Salisch, Maria (Editors)
The Diversity of Human Relationships. Ann Robertson
(Translator). Trade Cloth. Cambridge University Press. New
York, NY. 1996. 359p. ISBN:0-521-47463-9, ISBN13:
978-0-521-47463-4. Dewey:158.2. LCCN:96-003885.

Audience: **u,f.**

Binion, Rudolph   HM711.B56 2005
Past Impersonal: Group Process in Human History. Trade Cloth.
Northern Illinois University Press. DeKalb, IL. 2005. 218p.
ISBN:0-87580-345-8, ISBN13: 978-0-87580-345-6.
Dewey:302.3/094. LCCN:2005-007277.

Audience: **u,f.**

Birtchnell, John   HM132
How Humans Relate: A New Interpersonal Theory. Trade Cloth.
Greenwood Publishing Group, Inc. Portsmouth, NH. 1993. 320p.
Human Evolution, Behavior, and Intelligence Ser.
ISBN:0-275-94405-0, ISBN13: 978-0-275-94405-6.
Dewey:158.2. LCCN:93-020296.

Audience: **l,u,f.**   *Choice, 1994.*

Brock, Timothy C. & Green,   BF637.P4P44 2005
   Melanie C. (Editors)
Persuasion: Psychological Insights and Perspectives. Ed. 2.
Paper Text. SAGE Publications, Inc. Thousand Oaks, CA. 2005.
368p. ISBN:0-7619-2809-X, ISBN13: 978-0-7619-2809-6.
Dewey:153.8/52. LCCN:2004-019352.

Audience: **u,f.**

Formats: Web: ▢   Ebook: **e**   CD/DVD-ROM: ✿   BCL3: *B*

Chemers, Martin M. & Ayman, Roya (Editors)   HD57.7.L437 1993
Leadership Theory and Research: Perspectives and Directions. Trade Cloth. Elsevier Science & Technology Books. Saint Louis, MO. 1992. 347p. ISBN:0-12-170609-5, ISBN13: 978-0-12-170609-8. Dewey:303.3/4. LCCN:92-011014.
         Audience: **u,f.** *Choice, 1993.*

Daly, John A. & Wiemann, John M. (Editors)   BF637.C45C638 1993
Strategic Interpersonal Communication. Cloth Text. Lawrence Erlbaum Associates, Inc. Mahwah, NJ. 1994. 320p. Interpersonal Communication Ser. ISBN:0-89859-957-1, ISBN13: 978-0-89859-957-2. Dewey:153.6. LCCN:92-045190.
         Audience: **u,f.**

Deutsch, Morton & Coleman, Peter T. (Editors)   HM1126.H35 2000
The Handbook of Conflict Resolution: Theory and Practice. Ed. 2. Trade Cloth. John Wiley & Sons, Inc. Hoboken, NJ. 2000. 672p. ISBN:0-7879-4822-5, ISBN13: 978-0-7879-4822-1. Dewey:303.6/9. LCCN:2006-022684.
         Audience: **l,u,f.**

Dindia, Kathryn & Duck, Steve (Editors)   HM1116.C65 2000
Communication and Personal Relationships. Trade Paper. John Wiley & Sons, Inc. Hoboken, NJ. 2000. 232p. Wiley Series on Social and Personal Relationships Ser., Vol. 4 ISBN:0-471-49133-0, ISBN13: 978-0-471-49133-0. Dewey:302.3/4. LCCN:00-021833.
         Audience: **u,f.**

Fehr, Beverley   BF575.F66F435 1996
Friendship Processes, Vol. 12. Trade Paper. SAGE Publications, Inc. Thousand Oaks, CA. 1995. 256p. Close Relationships Ser., Vol. 12 ISBN:0-8039-4561-2, ISBN13: 978-0-8039-4561-6. Dewey:158.2/5. LCCN:95-032479.
         Audience: **u,f.** *Choice, 1996.*

Fisher, Erik A. & Sharp, Steven W.   HM1121
The Art of Managing Everyday Conflict: Understanding Emotions and Power Struggles. Trade Cloth. Greenwood Publishing Group, Inc. Portsmouth, NH. 2004. 256p. ISBN:0-275-98184-3, ISBN13: 978-0-275-98184-6. Dewey:303.6/9. LCCN:2003-066140.
         Audience: **l,u.** *Choice, 2004.*

Fitch, Kristine L. & Sanders, Robert E. (Editors)   P40
Handbook of Language and Social Interaction. Mark Aakhus, Robert Arundale & Janet B. Bavelas (Contribution by). Cloth over Boards. Lawrence Erlbaum Associates, Inc. Mahwah, NJ. 2004. 528p. LEA's Communication Ser. ISBN:0-8058-4240-3, ISBN13: 978-0-8058-4240-1. Dewey:306.44. LCCN:2004-016806.
         Audience: **u,f.** *Choice, 2005.*

Fletcher, Garth   BF575.I5.F54 2002
The New Science of Intimate Relationships. Trade Paper. Blackwell Publishing, Inc. Malden, MA. 2002. 336p. ISBN:0-631-22078-X, ISBN13: 978-0-631-22078-7. Dewey:158.2. LCCN:2001-003941.
         Audience: **l,u.** *Choice, 2002.*

Frey, Lawrence R. (Editor)   HM736.N48 2002
New Directions in Group Communication. Cloth Text. SAGE Publications, Inc. Thousand Oaks, CA. 2001. 344p. ISBN:0-7619-1280-0, ISBN13: 978-0-7619-1280-4. Dewey:302.3/4. LCCN:2001-005424.
         Audience: **u,f.**

Gardner, Howard & Laskin, Emma   HM141.G35 1995
Leading Minds: An Anatomy of Leadership. Trade Cloth. Basic Books. New York, NY. 1995. 416p. ISBN:0-465-08279-3, ISBN13: 978-0-465-08279-7. Dewey:158.4. LCCN:95-012088.
         Audience: **g,l,u.** *Choice, 1995.*

Glasser, William   BF121.G559 1998
Choice Theory: A New Psychology of Personal Freedom. Trade Cloth. HarperCollins Publishers. New York, NY. 1998. 352p. ISBN:0-06-019109-0, ISBN13: 978-0-06-019109-2. Dewey:150. LCCN:97-036025.
         Audience: **u.**

Gudykunst, William B.   HM1211.G82 2004
Bridging Differences: Effective Intergroup Communication. Ed. 4. Cloth Text. SAGE Publications, Inc. Thousand Oaks, CA. 2003. 448p. ISBN:0-7619-2936-3, ISBN13: 978-0-7619-2936-9. Dewey:303.48/2. LCCN:2003-010527.
         Audience: **l,u.**

Hare, A. Paul (Editor), et al.   HM133 .S646 1992
Small Group Research: A Handbook. Herbert H. Blumberg, Martin F. Davies & M. Valerie Kent (Editors). Trade Cloth. Greenwood Publishing Group, Inc. Portsmouth, NH. 1994. 592p. ISBN:0-89391-692-7, ISBN13: 978-0-89391-692-3. Dewey:302.3/4. LCCN:91-047016.
         Audience: **u,f.**

Hare, A. Paul, et al.   HM291
Small Groups: An Introduction. Herbert H. Blumberg, Martin F. Davies & M. Valerie Kent (Authors). Cloth Text. Greenwood Publishing Group, Inc. Portsmouth, NH. 1996. 288p. ISBN:0-275-94896-X, ISBN13: 978-0-275-94896-2. Dewey:302.3/4. LCCN:96-015329.
         Audience: **l,u.**

Hartley, Peter   BF637.C45H35 1999
Interpersonal Communication. Ed. 2. Paper over Boards. Routledge. New York, NY. 1999. 264p. ISBN:0-415-20793-2, ISBN13: 978-0-415-20793-5. Dewey:302.2. LCCN:98-047600.
         Audience: **l,u.** *Choice, 1994.*

Haslam, Nick (Editor)   HM1106.R442 2004
Relational Models Theory: A Contemporary Overview. Nicholas Allen, Rebecca Butz & Debra Connelley (Contribution by). Cloth over Boards. Lawrence Erlbaum Associates, Inc. Mahwah, NJ. 2004. 392p. ISBN:0-8058-3915-1, ISBN13: 978-0-8058-3915-9. Dewey:302. LCCN:2004-046925.
         Audience: **u,f.**

Hendrick, Clyde & Hendrick, Susan S. (Editors)   HM1106.C55 2000
Close Relationships: A Sourcebook. Trade Cloth. SAGE Publications, Inc. Thousand Oaks, CA. 2000. 500p. ISBN:0-7619-1605-9, ISBN13: 978-0-7619-1605-5. Dewey:302. LCCN:99-050427.
         Audience: **u.**

√ **Kelley, Harold H., et al.**   HM1106.A85 2002
An Atlas of Interpersonal Situations. John G. Holmes, Norbert
L. Kerr, Harry T. Reis, Caryl E. Rusbult & Paul A. M. Van
Lange (Authors). Trade Cloth. Cambridge University Press. New
York, NY. 2003. 518p. ISBN:0-521-81252-6, ISBN13:
978-0-521-81252-8. Dewey:302. LCCN:2002-067686.
                                    Audience: **u,f.** *Choice, 2003.*

Kelly, Caroline &   HM251.K4465 1996
Breinlinger, Sara
The Social Psychology of Collective Action: Identity, Injustice
and Gender. Library Binding. Taylor & Francis Group.
Philadelphia, PA. 1996. 224p. European Monographs in Social
Psychology Ser. ISBN:0-7484-0510-0, ISBN13:
978-0-7484-0510-7. Dewey:302.3. LCCN:96-223104.
                                    Audience: **u,f.**

√ **Knapp, Mark & Daly, John**   BF637.C45H287 2003
(Editors)
Handbook of Interpersonal Communication. Ed. 3. Trade Cloth.
SAGE Publications, Inc. Thousand Oaks, CA. 2002. 848p.
ISBN:0-7619-2160-5, ISBN13: 978-0-7619-2160-8.
Dewey:302.2. LCCN:2002-007908.
                                    Audience: **u,f.**

Lang, Frieder R. &   HM1106.G76 2003
√ **Fingerman, Karen L.**
Growing Together: Personal Relationships Across the Life Span.
Mary Anne Fitzpatrick, Harry Reis & Anita Vangelista
(Contribution by). Trade Cloth. Cambridge University Press.
New York, NY. 2003. 430p. Advances in Personal Relationships
Ser. ISBN:0-521-81310-7, ISBN13: 978-0-521-81310-5.
Dewey:158.2. LCCN:2002-041683.
                                    Audience: **u,f.** *Choice, 2004.*

√ **Lazare, Aaron**   BF575.A75L39 2004
On Apology. Trade Cloth. Oxford University Press, Inc. New
York, NY. 2004. 320p. ISBN:0-19-517343-0, ISBN13:
978-0-19-517343-7. Dewey:155.9/2. LCCN:2004-043470.
                                    Audience: **g,l,u.** *Choice, 2005.*

√ **Levine, Robert V.**   BF637.P4L48 2003
The Power of Persuasion: How We're Bought and Sold. Trade
Cloth. John Wiley & Sons, Inc. Hoboken, NJ. 2003. 288p.
ISBN:0-471-26634-5, ISBN13: 978-0-471-26634-1.
Dewey:153.8/52. LCCN:2002-009952.
                                    Audience: **g,l,u,f.** *Choice, 2003.*

√ **Mashek, Debra J. & Aron,**   BF575.I5H36 2004
Arthur (Editors)
Handbook of Closeness and Intimacy. Glenn Adams, Joseph K.
Adonu & Christopher R. Agnew (Contribution by). Cloth over
Boards. Lawrence Erlbaum Associates, Inc. Mahwah, NJ. 2004.
464p. ISBN:0-8058-4284-5, ISBN13: 978-0-8058-4284-5.
Dewey:158.2. LCCN:2003-025838.
                                    Audience: **u,f.** *Choice, 2004.*

√ **Messick, David M. &**   BF637.L4P79 2004
Kramer, Roderick Moreland (Editors)
The Psychology of Leadership: New Perspectives and Research.
Scott Allison, Michelle Bligh & Arthur P. Brief (Contribution
by). Cloth over Boards. Lawrence Erlbaum Associates, Inc.
Mahwah, NJ. 2004. 360p. LEA's Organization and Management
Ser. ISBN:0-8058-4094-X, ISBN13: 978-0-8058-4094-0.
Dewey:158/.4. LCCN:2004-047154.
                                    Audience: **u,f.**

√ **Miller, Rowland S.**   BF575.E53M55
Embarrassment: Poise and Peril in Everyday Life. Trade Paper.
Guilford Publications, Inc. New York, NY. 1997. 232p.
Emotions and Social Behavior Ser. ISBN:1-57230-247-X,
ISBN13: 978-1-57230-247-1. Dewey:152.4.
                                    Audience: **l,u.** *Choice, 1997.*

√ **Parks, Craig D. & Sanna,**   HM133.P35 1998
Lawrence J.
Group Performance and Interaction. Trade Paper. Westview
Press. Boulder, CO. 1998. 296p. ISBN:0-8133-3320-2, ISBN13:
978-0-8133-3320-5. Dewey:302.3. LCCN:98-027911.
                                    Audience: **l,u.**

√ **Paulus, Paul B. (Editor),**   BF408.G696 2003
et al.
Group Creativity: Innovation through Collaboration. Bernard
Arjan Nijstad & Bernard A. Nijstad (Editors). Trade Cloth.
Oxford University Press, Inc. New York, NY. 2003. 360p.
ISBN:0-19-514730-8, ISBN13: 978-0-19-514730-8.
Dewey:302.3/4. LCCN:2002-151032.
                                    Audience: **u,f.** *Choice, 2004.*

√ **Planalp, Sally**   BF591 .P57 1999
Communicating Emotion: Social, Moral, and Cultural Processes.
Antony Manstead & Keith Oatley (Contribution by). Trade
Cloth. Cambridge University Press. New York, NY. 1999. 313p.
Studies in Emotion and Social Interaction ISBN:0-521-55315-6,
ISBN13: 978-0-521-55315-5. Dewey:302.2. LCCN:98-049524.
                                    Audience: **l,u.**

√ **Robb, Christina**   HM1106.R63 2006
This Changes Everything: The Relational Revolution in
Psychology. Cloth over Boards. Farrar, Straus & Giroux. New
York, NY. 2006. 480p. ISBN:0-374-27581-5, ISBN13:
978-0-374-27581-5. Dewey:305/.01. LCCN:2005-016270.
                                    Audience: **g,l.** *Choice, 2006.*

√ **Russell, James A. &**   BF592.F33 P78 1997
Fernandez-Dols, Josi-Miguel (Editors)
The Psychology of Facial Expression. George Mandler
(Foreword by), Antony Manstead & Keith Oatley (Contribution
by). Trade Paper. Cambridge University Press. New York, NY.
1997. 415p. Studies in Emotion and Social Interaction
ISBN:0-521-58796-4, ISBN13: 978-0-521-58796-9.
Dewey:153.69. LCCN:96-036250.
                                    Audience: **l,u,f.** *Choice, 1997.*

Salamensky, S. I.   BF637.C45T35 2001
Talk, Talk, Talk: The Cultural Life of Everyday Conversation.
Paper over Boards. Routledge. New York, NY. 2000. 256p.
ISBN:0-415-92170-8, ISBN13: 978-0-415-92170-1.
Dewey:302.3/46. LCCN:00-032301.
                                    Audience: **g,l,u.** *Choice, 2001.*

√ **Shavitt, Sharon**   BF637.P4P44 1994
Persuasion: Psychological Insights and Perspectives. Ed. 1.
Trade Paper. Allyn & Bacon, Inc. Boston, MA. 1994. 464p.
ISBN:0-205-15143-4, ISBN13: 978-0-205-15143-1.
Dewey:153.8/52. LCCN:94-000186.
                                    Audience: **l,u.**

Stephan, Cookie & Stephan,   HM1086 .S74
Walter G.
Improving Intergroup Relations. Trade Cloth. SAGE

Publications, Inc. Thousand Oaks, CA. 2001.
ISBN:0-7619-2022-6, ISBN13: 978-0-7619-2022-9.
Dewey:302/.14.

Audience: **l.**

Surowiecki, James JC328.2
The Wisdom of Crowds. Trade Paper. Knopf Publishing Group.
New York, NY. 2005. 336p. ISBN:0-385-72170-6, ISBN13:
978-0-385-72170-7. Dewey:303.3.

Audience: **g,l,u,f.**

Surowiecki, James JC328.2.S87 2003
The Wisdom of Crowds: Why the Many Are Smarter Than the
Few and How Collective Wisdom Shapes Business, Economies,
Societies and Nations. Trade Cloth. Doubleday Canada, Ltd.
Toronto, ON. 2004. 320p. ISBN:0-385-50386-5, ISBN13:
978-0-385-50386-0. Dewey:303.3/8. LCCN:2003-070095.

Audience: **g,l,u,f.** *Choice, 2004.*

West, Malcolm L. & BF575.A86W47 1994
Sheldon-Keller, Adrienne E.
Patterns of Relating: An Adult Attachment Perspective. Cloth
over Boards. Guilford Publications, Inc. New York, NY. 1994.
210p. ISBN:0-89862-671-4, ISBN13: 978-0-89862-671-1.
Dewey:155.6. LCCN:93-048128.

Audience: **u,f.** *Choice, 1995.*

Williams, Kipling D. HM1131.W55 2001
Ostracism: The Power of Silence. Cloth over Boards. Guilford
Publications, Inc. New York, NY. 2001. 282p. Emotions and
Social Behavior Ser. ISBN:1-57230-689-0, ISBN13:
978-1-57230-689-9. Dewey:302.5/45. LCCN:2001-045132.

Audience: **l,u.** *Choice, 2002.*

Social Psychology > Social Perception and Cognition

Brown, Rupert BF575.P9B74 1995
Prejudice: Its Social Psychology. Trade Paper. Blackwell
Publishing, Inc. Malden, MA. 1995. 336p. ISBN:0-631-18315-9,
ISBN13: 978-0-631-18315-0. Dewey:155.2/32.
LCCN:95-005920.

Audience: **l,u.** *Choice, 1996.*

Dearing, Ronda L. & BF575.S45T36 2002
Tangney, June Price
Shame and Guilt. Cloth over Boards. Guilford Publications, Inc.
New York, NY. 2002. 272p. Emotions and Social Behavior Ser.
ISBN:1-57230-715-3, ISBN13: 978-1-57230-715-5.
Dewey:152.4. LCCN:2001-050143.

Audience: **l,u.** *Choice, 2002.*

Fisher, Adrian T. (Editor), HM756.P79 2002
et al.
Psychological Sense of Community: Research, Applications, and
Implications. Christopher C. Sonn & Brian J. Bishop (Editors).
Trade Cloth. Springer. New York, NY. 2002. 364p. The Plenum
Series in Social/Clinical Psychology ISBN:0-306-47281-3,
ISBN13: 978-0-306-47281-7. Dewey:307. LCCN:2002-066912.

Audience: **u,f.**

Forgas, Joseph P. (Editor) BF511.H34 2001
Handbook of Affect and Social Cognition. Ralph Adolphs, Galen
V. Bodenhausen & Gordon H. Bower (Contribution by). Cloth
over Boards. Lawrence Erlbaum Associates, Inc. Mahwah, NJ.

2000. 472p. ISBN:0-8058-3217-3, ISBN13: 978-0-8058-3217-4.
Dewey:152.4. LCCN:00-034779.

Audience: **u,f.** *Choice, 2001.*

Forgas, Joseph P. (Editor) BF531 .F44 1999
Feeling and Thinking: The Role of Affect in Social Cognition.
Antony Manstead & Keith Oatley (Contribution by). Trade
Cloth. Cambridge University Press. New York, NY. 1999. 438p.
Studies in Emotion and Social Interaction ISBN:0-521-64223-X,
ISBN13: 978-0-521-64223-1. Dewey:152.4. LCCN:99-018219.

Audience: **u,f.** *Choice, 2000.*

Forgas, Joseph P. (Editor), HM1041.S63 2003
et al.
Social Judgments: Implicit and Explicit Processes. Kipling D.
Williams & William Von Hippel (Editors). Trade Cloth.
Cambridge University Press. New York, NY. 2003. 440p.
ISBN:0-521-82248-3, ISBN13: 978-0-521-82248-0.
Dewey:302/.12. LCCN:2002-041239.

Audience: **u,f.**

Gardenfors, Peter BF698.95
How Homo Became Sapiens: On the Evolution of Thinking.
Cloth Text. Oxford University Press, Inc. New York, NY. 2004.
256p. ISBN:0-19-852850-7, ISBN13: 978-0-19-852850-0.
Dewey:155.7. LCCN:2004-298620.

Audience: **l,u.**

Higgins, E. Tory & BF503.H36 1986
Sorrentino, Richard M. (Editors)
Foundations of Social Behavior. Cloth over Boards. Guilford
Publications, Inc. New York, NY. 1990. 621p.
ISBN:0-89862-432-0, ISBN13: 978-0-89862-432-8.
Dewey:153.8. LCCN:85-024916.

Audience: **u,f.**

Hogg, Michael A. HM131.S5843 1999
Social Identity and Social Cognition. Dominic Abrams (Editor).
Trade Paper. Blackwell Publishing, Inc. Malden, MA. 1999.
432p. ISBN:0-631-20643-4, ISBN13: 978-0-631-20643-9.
Dewey:302.4. LCCN:98-029202.

Audience: **u,f.**

Horwitz, A. V. HM291.H67 1990
The Logic of Social Control. Trade Cloth. Basic Books. New
York, NY. 1990. 310p. ISBN:0-306-43475-X, ISBN13:
978-0-306-43475-4. Dewey:303.3/3. LCCN:90-039719.

Audience: **u.**

Kagan, Jerome BF313.K34 2002
Surprise, Uncertainty, and Mental Structures. Trade Cloth.
Harvard University Press. Cambridge, MA. 2002. 272p.
ISBN:0-674-00735-2, ISBN13: 978-0-674-00735-2.
Dewey:153.4. LCCN:2001-051484.

Audience: **g,l,u,f.** *Choice, 2003, 2002.*

Kunda, Ziva BF323.S63K86 1999
Social Cognition: Making Sense of People. Trade Paper. MIT
Press. Cambridge, MA. 1999. 610p. Bradford Bks.
ISBN:0-262-61143-0, ISBN13: 978-0-262-61143-5.
Dewey:302/.12. LCCN:98-056172.

Audience: **l,u,f.**

Lamberts, Koen & BF201
Goldstone, Rob (Editors)
Handbook of Cognition. Trade Cloth. SAGE Publications, Ltd.

Audience: g=general, l=lower division undergraduate, u=upper division undergraduate, f=faculty.

649

London, 2004. 480p. ISBN:0-7619-7277-3, ISBN13: 978-0-7619-7277-8. Dewey:153. LCCN:2005-295835.

Audience: **l,u.** *Choice, 2005.*

Levine, Murray & Perkins,   **RA790.55.L48 2004**
David V.
Principles of Community Psychology: Perspectives and Applications. Ed. 3. Cloth Text. Oxford University Press, Inc. New York, NY. 2004. 560p. ISBN:0-19-514417-1, ISBN13: 978-0-19-514417-8. Dewey:362.2/2. LCCN:2004-049525.

Audience: **u,f.**

Lewis, Thomas, et al.   **BF575.L8L49 2000**
A General Theory of Love. Fari Amini & Richard Lannon (Authors). Trade Cloth. Random House, Inc. New York, NY. 2000. 288p. ISBN:0-375-50389-7, ISBN13: 978-0-375-50389-4. Dewey:152.4/1. LCCN:99-049930.

Audience: **g,l,u.** *Choice, 2000.*

Malle, Bertram F. (Editor),   **BF619.5.I58 2001**
et al.
Intentions and Intentionality: Foundations of Social Cognition. Louis J. Moses & Dare A. Baldwin (Editors). Trade Cloth. MIT Press. Cambridge, MA. 2001. 433p. Bradford Bks. ISBN:0-262-13386-5, ISBN13: 978-0-262-13386-9. Dewey:153.8. LCCN:00-064590.

Audience: **u,f.**

Mills, Judson &   **BF337.C63C64 1999**
Herman-Jones, Eddie (Editors)
Cognitive Dissonance: Progress on a Pivotal Theory in Social Psychology. Trade Cloth. American Psychological Association. Washington, DC. 1999. 411p. Science Conference Ser. ISBN:1-55798-565-0, ISBN13: 978-1-55798-565-1. Dewey:153.4. LCCN:98-049316.

Audience: **u,f.**

Moskowitz, Gordon B.   **BF323.S63M67 2004**
Social Cognition: Understanding Self and Others. Cloth over Boards. Guilford Publications, Inc. New York, NY. 2004. 612p. Texts in Social Psychology Ser. ISBN:1-59385-086-7, ISBN13: 978-1-59385-086-9. Dewey:302/.12. LCCN:2004-017501.

Audience: **l,u.**

Pierce, Gregory R. (Editor),   **HM131.S61869 1997**
et al.
Sourcebook of Social Support and Personality. Brian Lakey, Irwin G. Sarason & Barbara R. Sarason (Editors). Trade Cloth. Basic Books. New York, NY. 1997. 522p. Series in Social/Clinical Psychology ISBN:0-306-45535-8, ISBN13: 978-0-306-45535-3. Dewey:302. LCCN:97-017811.

Audience: **u.**

Pinker, Steven   **BF341.P47 2002**
The Blank Slate: The Modern Denial of Human Nature. Trade Cloth. Penguin Group (USA) Inc. New York, NY. 2002. 528p. ISBN:0-670-03151-8, ISBN13: 978-0-670-03151-1. Dewey:155.2. LCCN:2002-022719.

Audience: **l,u,f.** *Choice, 2003.*

Rappaport, Julian &   **RA790.55.H36 2000**
Seidman, Edward (Editors)
Handbook of Community Psychology. Trade Cloth. Springer. New York, NY. 2000. 982p. ISBN:0-306-46160-9, ISBN13: 978-0-306-46160-6. Dewey:362.2. LCCN:99-049482.

Audience: **u,f.** *Choice, 2000.*

Schneider, David J.   **BF323.S63S36 2003**
The Psychology of Stereotyping. Cloth over Boards. Guilford Publications, Inc. New York, NY. 2003. 704p. Distinguished Contributions in Psychology Ser. ISBN:1-57230-929-6, ISBN13: 978-1-57230-929-6. Dewey:303.3/85. LCCN:2003-008819.

Audience: **l,u,f.** *Choice, 2004.*

Schwartz, Barry   **BF611.S38 2004**
The Paradox of Choice: Why More Is Less. Trade Cloth. HarperCollins Publishers. New York, NY. 2004. 288p. ISBN:0-06-000568-8, ISBN13: 978-0-06-000568-9. Dewey:153.8/3. LCCN:2003-053138.

Audience: **g,l.**

Sober, Elliot & Wilson,   **BJ1474**
David S.
Unto Others: The Evolution and Psychology of Unselfish Behavior. Trade Paper. Harvard University Press. Cambridge, MA. 1999. 416p. ISBN:0-674-93047-9, ISBN13: 978-0-674-93047-6. Dewey:171/.8.

Audience: **l,u,f.**

Sorrentino, Richard M. &   **BF503.H36 1986**
Higgins, E. Tory (Editors)
Foundations of Social Behavior. Cloth over Boards. Guilford Publications, Inc. New York, NY. 1986. 610p. Handbook of Motivation and Cognition Ser., Vol. 1 ISBN:0-89862-667-6, ISBN13: 978-0-89862-667-4. Dewey:153.8. LCCN:85-024916.

Audience: **u,f.**

Sorrentino, Richard M. &   **BF503.H36 1986**
Higgins, E. Tory (Editors)
The Interpersonal Context. Cloth over Boards. Guilford Publications, Inc. New York, NY. 1996. 646p. Handbook of Motivation and Cognition Ser., Vol. 3 ISBN:1-57230-052-3, ISBN13: 978-1-57230-052-1. Dewey:153.8. LCCN:85-024916.

Audience: **u,f.**

Tomasello, Michael   **BF611**
The Cultural Origins of Human Cognition. Trade Paper. Harvard University Press. Cambridge, MA. 2001. 256p. ISBN:0-674-00582-1, ISBN13: 978-0-674-00582-2. Dewey:153. LCCN:99-035902.

Audience: **g,l,u,f.**

van der Velde, Christiaan D.   **BF311.V45 2004**
The Mind: Its Nature and Origin. Trade Cloth. Prometheus Books, Publishers. Amherst, NY. 2004. 200p. ISBN:1-59102-190-1, ISBN13: 978-1-59102-190-2. Dewey:128/.2. LCCN:2004-004498.

Audience: **g,l,u,f.** *Choice, 2005.*

Whitley, Bernard E. & Kite,   **BF575.P9W558 2005**
Mary E.
The Psychology of Prejudice and Discrimination. Paper Text. Thomson Wadsworth. Belmont, CA. 2005. 680p. ISBN:0-534-64271-3, ISBN13: 978-0-534-64271-6. Dewey:303.3. LCCN:2005-925112.

Audience: **l,u.**

Zerubavel, Eviatar   **BF323.S63**
Social Mindscapes: An Invitation to Cognitive Sociology. Trade Paper. Harvard University Press. Cambridge, MA. 1999. 176p. ISBN:0-674-81390-1, ISBN13: 978-0-674-81390-8. Dewey:302/.1.

Audience: **l,u.** *Choice, 1998.*

Personality Psychology > Personality Traits and Processes

Albarracin, Dolores (Editor), et al.   BF327.H36 2005
The Handbook of Attitudes. Blair T. Johnson & Mark P. Zanna (Editors), Icek Ajzen, John N. Bassili & Pablo Brinol (Contribution by). Cloth over Boards. Lawrence Erlbaum Associates, Inc. Mahwah, NJ. 2005. 840p. ISBN:0-8058-4492-9, ISBN13: 978-0-8058-4492-4. Dewey:152.4. LCCN:2005-001804.
Audience: **u,f.** *Choice, 2005.*

Archer, John   BF575.G7A73 1998
The Nature of Grief: The Evolution and Psychology of Reactions to Loss. Paper over Boards. Routledge. New York, NY. 1999. 336p. ISBN:0-415-17857-6, ISBN13: 978-0-415-17857-0. Dewey:155.9/37. LCCN:98-020134.
Audience: **l,u.** *Choice, 2000.*

Arieti, Silvano   BF408
Creativity: The Magic Synthesis. Trade Paper. DIANE Publishing Company. Collingdale, PA. 2000. 448p. ISBN:0-7881-9488-7, ISBN13: 978-0-7881-9488-7. Dewey:153.3/5.
Audience: **u,f.** *B*

Armor, David J.   BF431.A5775 2003
Maximizing Intelligence. Trade Cloth. Transaction Publishers. Somerset, NJ. 2003. 227p. ISBN:0-7658-0185-X, ISBN13: 978-0-7658-0185-2. Dewey:153.9. LCCN:2002-075087.
Audience: **l.** *Choice, 2004.*

Attig, Thomas A.   BF575.G7A79 1996
How We Grieve: Relearning the World. Trade Paper. Oxford University Press, Inc. New York, NY. 1996. 224p. ISBN:0-19-507456-4, ISBN13: 978-0-19-507456-7. Dewey:155.9/37. LCCN:95-031907.
Audience: **l,u.** *Choice, 1997.*

Barber, Nigel   BF637.H4B375 2004
Kindness in a Cruel World: The Evolution of Altruism. Trade Cloth. Prometheus Books, Publishers. Amherst, NY. 2004. 400p. ISBN:1-59102-228-2, ISBN13: 978-1-59102-228-2. Dewey:155.2/32. LCCN:2004-011156.
Audience: **l,u.** *Choice, 2005.*

Baumeister, R. F.   RC455.4.S42S443 1993
Self-Esteem: The Puzzle of Low Self-Regard. Trade Cloth. Basic Books. New York, NY. 1993. 286p. Social - Clinical Psychology Ser. ISBN:0-306-44373-2, ISBN13: 978-0-306-44373-2. Dewey:155.232. LCCN:93-007043.
Audience: **l,u.** *Choice, 1994.*

Bernstein, Judith R.   BF575.G7
When the Bough Breaks: Forever after the Death of a Son or Daughter. Trade Paper. Andrews McMeel Publishing. Kansas City, MO. 1998. 256p. ISBN:0-8362-5282-9, ISBN13: 978-0-8362-5282-8. Dewey:155.9/37/085.
Audience: **l,u.** *Choice, 1998.*

Bornstein, Marc H. (Editor)   BF713.5.W45 2002
Well-Being: Positive Development Across the Life Course. Lisa Bridges, William M. Bukowski & Debra Burock (Contribution by). Cloth over Boards. Lawrence Erlbaum Associates, Inc.

Mahwah, NJ. 2003. 616p. Crosscurrents in Contemporary Psychology Ser. ISBN:0-8058-4035-4, ISBN13: 978-0-8058-4035-3. Dewey:155. LCCN:2002-029756.
Audience: **u,f.** *Choice, 2003.*

Bosma, Harke A. (Author, Editor)   BF0697.I347
Identity and Development: An Interdisciplinary Approach. Tobi L. G. Graafsma, Harold D. Grotevant & David J. de Levita (Editors). Trade Paper. Books on Demand. Ann Arbor, MI. 216p. Sage Focus Editions Ser., Vol. 172 ISBN:0-598-03427-7, ISBN13: 978-0-598-03427-4. Dewey:155.2. LCCN:94-022128.
Audience: **l,u,f.** *Choice, 1995.*

Boss, Pauline   BF575.D35B67 1999
Ambiguous Loss: Learning to Live with Unresolved Grief. Trade Cloth. Harvard University Press. Cambridge, MA. 1999. 176p. ISBN:0-674-01738-2, ISBN13: 978-0-674-01738-2. Dewey:155.9/3. LCCN:98-050585.
Audience: **l,u.** *Choice, 2000.*

Brody, Leslie   RC455.4.E46B76 1999
Gender, Emotion, and the Family. Trade Cloth. Harvard University Press. Cambridge, MA. 1999. 368p. ISBN:0-674-34186-4, ISBN13: 978-0-674-34186-9. Dewey:152.4. LCCN:98-032351.
Audience: **l,u,f.** *Choice, 1999.*

Campbell, Anne   BF575.A3C23
Men, Women, and Aggression. Trade Paper. Basic Books. New York, NY. 1994. 208p. ISBN:0-465-04450-6, ISBN13: 978-0-465-04450-4. Dewey:155.3. LCCN:92-053240.
Audience: **g,l,u.** *Choice, 1993.*

Cassidy, Jude & Shaver, Phillip R. (Editors)   BF575.A86H36 1999
Handbook of Attachment: Theory, Research, and Clinical Applications. Paper over Boards. Guilford Publications, Inc. New York, NY. 1999. 925p. ISBN:1-57230-087-6, ISBN13: 978-1-57230-087-3. Dewey:155.9/2. LCCN:98-053527.
Audience: **u,f.** *Choice, 1999.*

Chamorro-Premuzic, Tomas & Furnham, Adrian   BF698.9.I6C55 2005
Personality and Intellectual Competence. Cloth over Boards. Lawrence Erlbaum Associates, Inc. Mahwah, NJ. 2005. 216p. ISBN:0-8058-5136-4, ISBN13: 978-0-8058-5136-6. Dewey:155.2. LCCN:2004-053322.
Audience: **l,u,f.** *Choice, 2005.*

Chang, Edward C.   BF698.35.O57O68 2001
Optimism and Pessimism: Implications for Theory, Research and Practice. Trade Cloth. American Psychological Association. Washington, DC. 2000. xxi, 395p. ISBN:1-55798-691-6, ISBN13: 978-1-55798-691-7. Dewey:149/.5. LCCN:00-031310.
Audience: **u,f.** *Choice, 2001.*

Chang, Edward C. & Sanna, Lawrence J. (Editors)   BF698.V57 2003
Virtue, Vice, and Personality: The Complexity of Behavior. Trade Cloth. American Psychological Association. Washington, DC. 2003. 224p. ISBN:1-59147-013-7, ISBN13: 978-1-59147-013-7. Dewey:155.2. LCCN:2003-006516.
Audience: **u,f.** *Choice, 2003.*

Collier, Gary   BF341.C57 1994
Social Origins of Mental Ability. Ed. 1. Trade Cloth. John Wiley & Sons, Inc. Hoboken, NJ. 1993. 300p. Wiley Series on

Personality Processes Ser., Vol. 197 ISBN:0-471-30407-7, ISBN13: 978-0-471-30407-4. Dewey:155.92. LCCN:93-003625.
Audience: **l,u,f.** *Choice, 1994.*

Cooper, Cary L. & Dewe, Philip   BF575.S75C646 2004
Stress: A Brief History. Trade Paper. Blackwell Publishing, Inc. Malden, MA. 2004. 160p. Blackwell Brief Histories of Psychology Ser., Vol. 1 ISBN:1-4051-0745-6, ISBN13: 978-1-4051-0745-7. Dewey:155.9/042/09. LCCN:2003-023501.
Audience: **u,f.** *Choice, 2004.*

Crozier, W. Ray   BF575.B3C76 2001
Understanding Shyness: Psychological Perspectives. Cloth over Boards. Palgrave Macmillan. New York, NY. 2001. 270p. ISBN:0-333-77370-5, ISBN13: 978-0-333-77370-3. Dewey:155.2/32. LCCN:00-052439.
Audience: **l,u.** *Choice, 2001.*

Dai, David Yun & Sternberg, Robert J. (Editors)   BF431.M72 2004
Motivation, Emotion, and Cognition: Integrative Perspectives on Intellectual Functioning and Development. Jin Li, Andreas Krapp, Ruth Kanfer, Phillip L. Ackerman, Patricia Alexander & Kurt W. Fischer (Contribution by). Cloth over Boards. Lawrence Erlbaum Associates, Inc. Mahwah, NJ. 2004. 472p. The Educational Psychology Ser. ISBN:0-8058-4556-9, ISBN13: 978-0-8058-4556-3. Dewey:153.9. LCCN:2003-049396.
Audience: **u,f.** *Choice, 2004.*

Davidman, Lynn   BF575.G7
Motherloss. Trade Paper. University of California Press. Berkeley, CA. 2002. 308p. ISBN:0-520-23200-3, ISBN13: 978-0-520-23200-6. Dewey:155.937. LCCN:99-053072.
Audience: **l,u,f.** *Choice, 2000.*

Devlin, Bernie   BF431.I527 1997
Intelligence, Genes and Success: Is It All in the Genes?: Scientists Respond to the Bell Curve. Trade Paper. Springer. New York, NY. 1997. XI, 392p. ISBN:0-387-94986-0, ISBN13: 978-0-387-94986-4. LCCN:97-009792.
Audience: **l,u,f.**

Eagly, Alice & Chaiken, Shelly   BF327.E19 1993
The Psychology of Attitudes. Dawn Youngblood (Editor). Paper Text. Harcourt College Publishers. Fort Worth, TX. 1993. 800p. ISBN:0-15-500097-7, ISBN13: 978-0-15-500097-1. Dewey:153.8. LCCN:92-052667.
Audience: **l,u.** *Choice, 1993.*

Ehrlich, Paul R.   GN281.4.E374 2000
Human Natures: Genes, Cultures and the Human Prospect. Trade Cloth. Island Press. Washington, DC. 2000. 576p. ISBN:1-55963-779-X, ISBN13: 978-1-55963-779-4. Dewey:599.93/8. LCCN:00-010436.
Audience: **g,l.** *Choice, 2001.*

Emmons, Robert A.   BF505.G6E58 1999
The Psychology of Ultimate Concerns: Motivation and Spirituality in Personality. Cloth over Boards. Guilford Publications, Inc. New York, NY. 1999. 230p. ISBN:1-57230-456-1, ISBN13: 978-1-57230-456-7. Dewey:155.2/5. LCCN:99-026409.
Audience: **l,u.** *Choice, 2000.*

Emmons, Robert A. & McCullough, Michael E. (Editors)   BF575.G68P79 2003
The Psychology of Gratitude. Trade Cloth. Oxford University Press, Inc. New York, NY. 2004. 368p. Series in Affective Science ISBN:0-19-515010-4, ISBN13: 978-0-19-515010-0. Dewey:155.2/32. LCCN:2003-005497.
Audience: **u,f.** *Choice, 2004.*

Eysenck, Hans Jürgen   BF412 .E97 1995
Genius: The Natural History of Creativity. Michael Gelder, Jeffrey Gray, Richard Gregory, Robert Hinde & Christopher Lonquet-Higgins (Contribution by). Trade Paper. Cambridge University Press. New York, NY. 1995. 354p. Problems in the Behavioral Sciences Ser., No. 12 ISBN:0-521-48508-8, ISBN13: 978-0-521-48508-1. Dewey:153.9/8. LCCN:94-032136.
Audience: **g,l,u,f.**

Feeney, Judith & Noller, Patricia   BF575.A86F44 1996
Adult Attachment. Trade Paper. SAGE Publications, Inc. Thousand Oaks, CA. 1996. 192p. Series on Close Relationships, Vol. 14 ISBN:0-8039-7224-5, ISBN13: 978-0-8039-7224-7. Dewey:158.2. LCCN:96-004527.
Audience: **u.** *Choice, 1996.*

Fehr, Beverley   BF575.F66F435 1996
Friendship Processes, Vol. 12. Trade Paper. SAGE Publications, Inc. Thousand Oaks, CA. 1995. 256p. Close Relationships Ser., Vol. 12 ISBN:0-8039-4561-2, ISBN13: 978-0-8039-4561-6. Dewey:158.2/5. LCCN:95-032479.
Audience: **u,f.** *Choice, 1996.*

Firestone, Robert & Catlett, Joyce   BF575.I5F57 1999
Fear of Intimacy. Trade Cloth. American Psychological Association. Washington, DC. 1999. 358p. ISBN:1-55798-605-3, ISBN13: 978-1-55798-605-4. Dewey:158.2. LCCN:99-034381.
Audience: **u,f.** *Choice, 2000.*

Fish, Jefferson M. (Editor)   BF431.R27 2002
Race and Intelligence: Separating Science from Myth. Cloth over Boards. Lawrence Erlbaum Associates, Inc. Mahwah, NJ. 2001. 448p. ISBN:0-8058-3757-4, ISBN13: 978-0-8058-3757-5. Dewey:305.9/082. LCCN:00-033164.
Audience: **l,u,f.** *Choice, 2002.*

Fishman, Ethan   BF637.L4T43 2002
Tempered Strength: Studies in the Nature and Scope of Prudential Leadership. Francis Fukuyama (Foreword by). Trade Cloth. Lexington Books. Lanham, MD. 2002. 240p. ISBN:0-7391-0402-0, ISBN13: 978-0-7391-0402-6. Dewey:158/.4. LCCN:2002-004880.
Audience: **u.** *Choice, 2003.*

Flanagan, Owen   BF697
Self Expressions: Mind, Morals, and the Meaning of Life. Trade Paper. Oxford University Press, Inc. New York, NY. 1998. 236p. Philosophy of Mind Ser. ISBN:0-19-512652-1, ISBN13: 978-0-19-512652-5. Dewey:128.2.
Audience: **g,l,u,f.** *Choice, 1996.*

Forgas, Joseph P. (Editor)   BF511.H34 2001
Handbook of Affect and Social Cognition. Ralph Adolphs, Galen V. Bodenhausen & Gordon H. Bower (Contribution by). Cloth over Boards. Lawrence Erlbaum Associates, Inc. Mahwah, NJ. 2000. 472p. ISBN:0-8058-3217-3, ISBN13: 978-0-8058-3217-4. Dewey:152.4. LCCN:00-034779.
Audience: **u,f.** *Choice, 2001.*

Forgas, Joseph P. (Editor)   BF531 .F44 1999
Feeling and Thinking: The Role of Affect in Social Cognition.
Antony Manstead & Keith Oatley (Contribution by). Trade
Cloth. Cambridge University Press. New York, NY. 1999. 438p.
Studies in Emotion and Social Interaction ISBN:0-521-64223-X,
ISBN13: 978-0-521-64223-1. Dewey:152.4. LCCN:99-018219.
                                        Audience: **u,f.** *Choice, 2000.*

Francis, Richard C.   BF698.95.F73 2006
Why Men Won't Ask for Directions: The Seductions of
Sociobiology. Trade Paper. Princeton University Press.
Princeton, NJ. 2005. 352p. ISBN:0-691-12405-1, ISBN13:
978-0-691-12405-6. Dewey:155.7.
                                        Audience: **u,f.** *Choice, 2004.*

Gackenbach, Jayne (Editor)   BF637.C45P79 1998
Psychology and the Internet: Intrapersonal, Interpersonal, and
Transpersonal Implications. Paper Text. Elsevier Science &
Technology Books. Saint Louis, MO. 1998. 369p.
ISBN:0-12-271950-6, ISBN13: 978-0-12-271950-9.
Dewey:303.4833. LCCN:98-085527.
                                        Audience: **u,f.**

Gander, Eric M.   BF701.G26 2003
On Our Minds: How Evolutionary Psychology Is Reshaping the
Nature versus Nurture Debate. Trade Cloth. Johns Hopkins
University Press. Baltimore, MD. 2004. 312p.
ISBN:0-8018-7387-8, ISBN13: 978-0-8018-7387-4.
Dewey:155.7. LCCN:2002-152158.
                                        Audience: **u,f.** *Choice, 2004.*

Gardner, Howard   BF432.3
Intelligence Reframed: Multiple Intelligences for the 21st
Century. Trade Paper. Basic Books. New York, NY. 2000. 304p.
ISBN:0-465-02611-7, ISBN13: 978-0-465-02611-1.
Dewey:153.9. LCCN:99-042468.
                                        Audience: **g,l,u,f.** *Choice, 2000.*

Gaylin, Willard   BF575.H3G39 2004
Hatred: The Psychological Descent into Violence. Trade Paper.
PublicAffairs. New York, NY. 2004. 272p. ISBN:1-58648-260-2,
ISBN13: 978-1-58648-260-2. Dewey:152.4.
                                        Audience: **g,l.** *Choice, 2004.*

Geary, David C.   QP360.5.G43 2004
The Origin of Mind: Evolution of Brain, Cognition, and General
Intelligence. Trade Cloth. American Psychological Association.
Washington, DC. 2004. 432p. ISBN:1-59147-181-8, ISBN13:
978-1-59147-181-3. Dewey:153. LCCN:2004-007707.
                                        Audience: **l,u,f.** *Choice, 2005.*

Glick, Peter & Rudman,   BF575.P9O62 2005
Laurie A.
On the Nature of Prejudice: Fifty Years after Allport. John F.
Dovidio (Editor). Trade Paper. Blackwell Publishing, Inc.
Malden, MA. 2005. 488p. ISBN:1-4051-2751-1, ISBN13:
978-1-4051-2751-6. Dewey:303.3/85. LCCN:2004-029764.
                                        Audience: **l,u,f.** *Choice, 2005.*

Gould, Stephen Jay   BF431.G68 1996
The Mismeasure of Man. Ed. 2. Trade Cloth. W. W. Norton &
Company, Inc. New York, NY. 1996. 100p.
ISBN:0-393-03972-2, ISBN13: 978-0-393-03972-6.
Dewey:153.9. LCCN:95-044442.
                                        Audience: **g,l,u,f.** *Choice, 1996.*

Griffiths, Paul E.   BF511.G75 1997
What Emotions Really Are: The Problem of Psychological
Categories. Trade Cloth. University of Chicago Press. Chicago,
IL. 1997. 293p. Science and Its Conceptual Foundations Ser.
ISBN:0-226-30871-5, ISBN13: 978-0-226-30871-5.
Dewey:128/.37. LCCN:96-048993.
                                        Audience: **l,u.** *Choice, 1998.*

Grotberg, Edith Henderson   BF698
  (Editor)
Resilience for Today: Gaining Strength from Adversity. Trade
Cloth. Greenwood Publishing Group, Inc. Portsmouth, NH.
2003. 296p. Contemporary Psychology Ser.
ISBN:0-275-97984-9, ISBN13: 978-0-275-97984-3.
Dewey:155.2/32. LCCN:2003-051057.
                                        Audience: **l,u.** *Choice, 2004.*

Herrnstein, Richard J.   BF431.H398 1996
The Bell Curve: Intelligence and Class Structure in American
Life. Charles Murray (Based on a work by). Trade Paper. Simon
& Schuster. New York, NY. 1996. 912p. A Meditation Bk.
ISBN:0-684-82429-9, ISBN13: 978-0-684-82429-1.
Dewey:305.5/0973. LCCN:95-042934.
                                        Audience: **g,l.** *Choice, 1995.*

Hesse-Biber, Sharlene   BF697.5.B63H47
Am I Thin Enough Yet?: The Cult of Thinness and the
Commercialization of Identity. Paper Text. Oxford University
Press, Inc. New York, NY. 1997. 200p. ISBN:0-19-511791-3,
ISBN13: 978-0-19-511791-2. Dewey:306.4.
                                        Audience: **g,l,u,f.** *Choice, 1996.*

Hewstone, Miles   BF697.5.S43S429 2003
Self and Social Identity. Marilynn B. Brewer (Editor). Trade
Paper. Blackwell Publishing, Inc. Malden, MA. 2004. 352p.
Perspectives on Social Psychology Ser. ISBN:1-4051-1069-4,
ISBN13: 978-1-4051-1069-3. Dewey:302/.1.
LCCN:2003-004955.
                                        Audience: **l,u,f.** *Choice, 2004.*

Holstein, James A. &   BF697.5.S65H65 2000
  Gubrium, Jaber F.
The Self We Live By: Narrative Identity in a Postmodern World.
Trade Paper. Oxford University Press, Inc. New York, NY. 1999.
282p. ISBN:0-19-511929-0, ISBN13: 978-0-19-511929-9.
Dewey:155.2. LCCN:98-031085.
                                        Audience: **u.** *Choice, 2000.*

Jamison, Kay Redfield   BF575.H27J36 2004
Exuberance: The Passion for Life. Trade Cloth. Knopf
Publishing Group. New York, NY. 2004. 416p.
ISBN:0-375-40144-X, ISBN13: 978-0-375-40144-2.
Dewey:152.4/2. LCCN:2004-046561.
                                        Audience: **g,l.** *Choice, 2005.*

Jankowiak, William (Editor)   BF575.L8R66 1995
Romantic Passion: A Universal Experience? Trade Cloth.
Edinburgh University Press. Edinburgh, 1995. 310p.
ISBN:0-231-09686-0, ISBN13: 978-0-231-09686-7.
Dewey:306.7. LCCN:95-006954.
                                        Audience: **u,f.** *Choice, 1996.*

King, Gillian A. (Editor),   BF698
  et al.
Resilience: Learning from People with Disabilities and the
Turning Points in Their Lives. Elizabeth G. Brown & Linda K.
Smith (Editors). Trade Cloth. Greenwood Publishing Group, Inc.

Portsmouth, NH. 2003. 216p. Praeger Series in Health Psychology ISBN:0-275-97943-1, ISBN13: 978-0-275-97943-0. Dewey:155.9/16. LCCN:2002-044543.

Audience: **u,f.** *Choice, 2004.*

Koestler, Arthur   **BF408**
The Act of Creation. Ed. 2. Trade Cloth. Random House. London, 1976. 4-751 p. :p. ISBN:0-09-128270-5, ISBN13: 978-0-09-128270-7. Dewey:153.35. LCCN:78-310679.

Audience: **g,l,u,f.** *B*

Kovecses, Zoltan   **BF531.K68 1990**
Emotion Concepts. Cloth Text. Springer. New York, NY. 1989. 230p. ISBN:0-387-97115-7, ISBN13: 978-0-387-97115-5. Dewey:152.4. LCCN:89-036504.

Audience: **l.** *Choice, 1990.*

Lampert, Ada   **BF575**
The Evolution of Love. Trade Cloth. Greenwood Publishing Group, Inc. Portsmouth, NH. 1997. 144p. Human Evolution, Behavior, and Intelligence Ser. ISBN:0-275-95907-4, ISBN13: 978-0-275-95907-4. Dewey:155.7. LCCN:97-011073.

Audience: **l.** *Choice, 1998.*

Langford, Wendy   **BF575.L8L266 1999**
Revolutions of the Heart: Gender, Power and the Delusions of Love. Paper over Boards. Routledge. New York, NY. 1999. 192p. ISBN:0-415-16297-1, ISBN13: 978-0-415-16297-5. Dewey:306.7. LCCN:98-050255.

Audience: **l,u.** *Choice, 2000.*

Lazarus, Richard S.   **BF531**
Emotion and Adaptation. Trade Paper. Oxford University Press, Inc. New York, NY. 1994. 576p. ISBN:0-19-509266-X, ISBN13: 978-0-19-509266-0. Dewey:152.4. LCCN:91-009611.

Audience: **l,u,f.** *Choice, 1992.*

Leary, Mark R. &   **BF575.A6L387 1995**
  Kowalski, Robin Mark
Social Anxiety. Cloth over Boards. Guilford Publications, Inc. New York, NY. 1995. 244p. Emotions and Social Behavior Ser. ISBN:1-57230-007-8, ISBN13: 978-1-57230-007-1. Dewey:152.4/6. LCCN:95-032612.

Audience: **l,u.** *Choice, 1996.*

Lefcourt, Herbert M.   **BF575.L3L425 2000**
Humor: The Psychology of Living Buoyantly. Trade Cloth. Springer. New York, NY. 2001. 210p. The Plenum Series in Social/Clinical Psychology ISBN:0-306-46407-1, ISBN13: 978-0-306-46407-2. Dewey:152.4/3. LCCN:00-033112.

Audience: **g,l,u.** *Choice, 2001.*

Levinson, David & Ponzetti,   **BF531.E55 1999**
  James J. Jr.
Encyclopedia of Human Emotions, Vol. 2. Trade Cloth. Simon & Schuster. New York, NY. 1999. ISBN:0-02-864768-8, ISBN13: 978-0-02-864768-5. Dewey:152.4/03. LCCN:99-031198.

Audience: **l,u.** *Choice, 2000.*

Lewis, Thomas, et al.   **BF575.L8 L49 2000**
A General Theory of Love. Fari Amini & Richard Lannon (Authors). Trade Paper. Knopf Publishing Group. New York, NY. 2001. 288p. ISBN:0-375-70922-3, ISBN13: 978-0-375-70922-7. Dewey:152.4/1. LCCN:99-049930.

Audience: **g,l.** *Choice, 2000.*

Lifton, Robert Jay   **BF697.5.S65L53 1999**
The Protean Self: Human Resilience in an Age of Fragmentation. Trade Paper. University of Chicago Press. Chicago, IL. 1999. 272p. ISBN:0-226-48098-4, ISBN13: 978-0-226-48098-5. Dewey:155.2. LCCN:99-035389.

Audience: **u,f.**

Ludwig, Arnold M.   **BF423.L83 1995**
The Price of Greatness: Resolving the Creativity and Madness Controversy. Cloth over Boards. Guilford Publications, Inc. New York, NY. 1995. 310p. ISBN:0-89862-839-3, ISBN13: 978-0-89862-839-5. Dewey:153.3/5. LCCN:94-044905.

Audience: **l,u.** *Choice, 1996.*

Lutz, Tom   **BF575.C88 L87**
Crying: The Natural and Cultural History of Tears. Trade Cloth. DIANE Publishing Company. Collingdale, PA. 2001. 152p. ISBN:0-7567-5214-0, ISBN13: 978-0-7567-5214-9. Dewey:152.4.

Audience: **g,l,u.**

Magai, Carol &   **BF698.9.E45M33 2002**
  Haviland-Jones, Jeannette M.
The Hidden Genius of Emotion: Lifespan Transformations of Personality. Antony Manstead & Keith Oatley (Contribution by). Trade Cloth. Cambridge University Press. New York, NY. 2002. 544p. Studies in Emotion and Social Interaction ISBN:0-521-64094-6, ISBN13: 978-0-521-64094-7. Dewey:152.4. LCCN:2002-019255.

Audience: **u,f.** *Choice, 2003.*

Marar, Ziyad   **BF575.H27**
The Happiness Paradox. Trade Paper. Reaktion Books, Ltd. London, 2004. 186p. Focus on Contemporary Issues Ser. ISBN:1-86189-182-2, ISBN13: 978-1-86189-182-2. Dewey:152.42. LCCN:2004-484218.

Audience: **g,l.** *Choice, 2004.*

Mashek, Debra J. & Aron,   **BF575.I5H36 2004**
  Arthur (Editors)
Handbook of Closeness and Intimacy. Glenn Adams, Joseph K. Adonu & Christopher R. Agnew (Contribution by). Cloth over Boards. Lawrence Erlbaum Associates, Inc. Mahwah, NJ. 2004. 464p. ISBN:0-8058-4284-5, ISBN13: 978-0-8058-4284-5. Dewey:158.2. LCCN:2003-025838.

Audience: **u,f.** *Choice, 2004.*

Matthews, Gerald, et al.   **BF576.M28 2003**
Emotional Intelligence: Science and Myth. Moshe Zeidner & Richard D. Roberts (Authors). Trade Cloth. MIT Press. Cambridge, MA. 2003. 720p. Bradford Bks. ISBN:0-262-13418-7, ISBN13: 978-0-262-13418-7. Dewey:152.4. LCCN:2002-066034.

Audience: **u,f.** *Choice, 2003.*

May, Rollo   **BF408**
The Courage to Create. Trade Cloth. Peter Smith Publisher, Inc. Magnolia, MA. 1995. ISBN:0-8446-6854-0, ISBN13: 978-0-8446-6854-3. Dewey:153.3/5.

Audience: **g,l,u,f.** *B*

May, Rollo   **BF575.A6**
The Meaning of Anxiety. Trade Paper. W. W. Norton & Company, Inc. New York, NY. 1996. 448p. ISBN:0-393-31456-1, ISBN13: 978-0-393-31456-4. Dewey:152.46. LCCN:77-001359.

Audience: **g,l,u,f.** *B*

McAdams, Dan P.   **BF697.M164 1996**
The Stories We Live By: Personal Myths and the Making of the
Self. Trade Paper. Guilford Publications, Inc. New York, NY.
1997. 336p. ISBN:1-57230-188-0, ISBN13: 978-1-57230-188-7.
Dewey:155.2/5. LCCN:96-049264.
                                              Audience: **l,u.**

McAdams, Dan P., et al.   **BF697.I3492 2006**
Identity and Story: Creating Self in Narrative. Ruthellen
Josselson & Amia Lieblich (Authors). Trade Cloth. American
Psychological Association. Washington, DC. 2006. x, 284p. The
Narrative Study of Lives Ser., Vol. 4 ISBN:1-59147-356-X,
ISBN13: 978-1-59147-356-5. Dewey:155.2/5.
LCCN:2005-032036.
                                   Audience: **u,f.** *Choice, 2006.*

McAdams, Dan P. (Editor),   **BF637.L53T87 2001**
  et al.
Turns in the Road: Narrative Studies of Lives in Transition.
Ruthellen Josselson & Amia Lieblich (Editors). Cloth Text.
American Psychological Association. Washington, DC. 2001.
332p. The Narrative Study of Lives Ser. ISBN:1-55798-773-4,
ISBN13: 978-1-55798-773-0. Dewey:155.2/4.
LCCN:2001-022342.
                                   Audience: **u,f.** *Choice, 2002.*

Miller, Arthur G. (Editor)   **HM1116.S63 2004**
The Social Psychology of Good and Evil. Cloth over Boards.
Guilford Publications, Inc. New York, NY. 2004. 498p.
ISBN:1-57230-989-X, ISBN13: 978-1-57230-989-0.
Dewey:303.3/72. LCCN:2003-020008.
                                   Audience: **l,u.** *Choice, 2004.*

Miller, Michael V.   **BF575.L8**
Intimate Terrorism: The Crisis of Love in an Age of Disillusion.
Trade Cloth. W. W. Norton & Company, Inc. New York, NY.
1996. 256p. ISBN:0-393-31532-0, ISBN13: 978-0-393-31532-5.
Dewey:306.7. LCCN:94-041704.
                                             Audience: **g,l,u,f.**

Miller, Rowland S.   **BF575.E53M55**
Embarrassment: Poise and Peril in Everyday Life. Trade Paper.
Guilford Publications, Inc. New York, NY. 1997. 232p.
Emotions and Social Behavior Ser. ISBN:1-57230-247-X,
ISBN13: 978-1-57230-247-1. Dewey:152.4.
                                   Audience: **l,u.** *Choice, 1997.*

Modell, Arnold H.   **BF697.5.S43M63 1993**
The Private Self. Trade Cloth. Harvard University Press.
Cambridge, MA. 1993. 262p. ISBN:0-674-70752-4, ISBN13:
978-0-674-70752-8. Dewey:155.2. LCCN:93-014974.
                                   Audience: **u.** *Choice, 1994.*

Neimeyer, Robert A.   **BF575.D35M43 2001**
  (Editor)
Meaning Reconstruction and the Experience of Loss. Trade
Cloth. American Psychological Association. Washington, DC.
2000. xiii, 359p. ISBN:1-55798-742-4, ISBN13:
978-1-55798-742-6. Dewey:155.9/37. LCCN:00-060602.
                                   Audience: **u,f.** *Choice, 2001.*

Nolen-Hoeksema, Susan &   **BF575.D35N65 1998**
  Larson, Judith
Coping with Loss. Cloth over Boards. Lawrence Erlbaum
Associates, Inc. Mahwah, NJ. 1998. 232p. LEA Series in
Personality and Clinical Psychology Ser. ISBN:0-8058-2139-2,

ISBN13: 978-0-8058-2139-0. Dewey:155.9/37.
LCCN:98-035307.
                                   Audience: **u,f.** *Choice, 1999.*

Nussbaum, Martha C.   **BF531 .N87 2001**
Upheavals of Thought: The Intelligence of Emotions. Trade
Cloth. Cambridge University Press. New York, NY. 2001. 766p.
ISBN:0-521-46202-9, ISBN13: 978-0-521-46202-0.
Dewey:152.4. LCCN:2001-018087.
                                   Audience: **u,f.** *Choice, 2002.*

Oatley, Keith (Author,   **BF511.O37 1991**
  Contribution by)
Best Laid Schemes: The Psychology of the Emotions. Antony S.
R. Manstead (Contribution by). Trade Paper. Cambridge
University Press. New York, NY. 1992. 543p. Studies in
Emotion and Social Interaction ISBN:0-521-42387-2, ISBN13:
978-0-521-42387-8. Dewey:152.4. LCCN:91-017589.
                                   Audience: **u,f.** *Choice, 1993.*

Parducci, Allen   **BF575.H27P37 1995**
Happiness, Pleasure, and Judgment: The Contextual Theory and
Its Applications. Cloth over Boards. Lawrence Erlbaum
Associates, Inc. Mahwah, NJ. 1995. 232p.
ISBN:0-8058-1891-X, ISBN13: 978-0-8058-1891-8. Dewey:150.
LCCN:95-014486.
                                   Audience: **u,f.** *Choice, 1996.*

Parkes, Colin Murray   **BF575.G7P37 1996**
Bereavement: Studies of Grief in Adult Life. Ed. 3. Paper over
Boards. Routledge. New York, NY. 1996. 288p.
ISBN:0-415-11033-5, ISBN13: 978-0-415-11033-4.
Dewey:152.4/34. LCCN:95-047088.
                                   Audience: **l,u.** *Choice, 1988.*

Paul, Annie Murphy   **BF698.5.P38 2004**
The Cult of Personality: How Personality Tests Are Leading Us
to Miseducate Our Children, Mismanage Our Companies, and
Misunderstand Ourselves. Trade Cloth. Simon & Schuster. New
York, NY. 2004. 320p. ISBN:0-7432-4356-0, ISBN13:
978-0-7432-4356-8. Dewey:155.2/8. LCCN:2004-047186.
                                   Audience: **g,l,u,f.** *Choice, 2005.*

Philippot, Pierre &   **BF531.R45 2003**
  Feldman, Robert S. (Editors)
The Regulation of Emotion. Antoine Bechara, Susan Calkins &
Nancy Eisenberg (Contribution by). Cloth over Boards.
Lawrence Erlbaum Associates, Inc. Mahwah, NJ. 2004. 432p.
ISBN:0-8058-4201-2, ISBN13: 978-0-8058-4201-2.
Dewey:152.4. LCCN:2003-064371.
                                   Audience: **u,f.** *Choice, 2005.*

Post, Stephen G., et al.   **BJ1474.A472 2001**
Altruism and Altruistic Love: Science, Philosophy, and Religion
in Dialogue. Lynn G. Underwood, Jeffrey P. Schloss & William
B. Hurlbut (Authors), Stephen Garrard Post (Editor). Trade
Cloth. Oxford University Press, Inc. New York, NY. 2002. 516p.
ISBN:0-19-514358-2, ISBN13: 978-0-19-514358-4.
Dewey:171/.8. LCCN:00-068140.
                                   Audience: **g,l,u,f.** *Choice, 2003.*

Prinz, Jesse J.   **BF531.P75 2004**
Gut Reactions: A Perceptual Theory of Emotion. Trade Cloth.
Oxford University Press, Inc. New York, NY. 2004. 288p.
Philosophy of Mind Ser. ISBN:0-19-515145-3, ISBN13:
978-0-19-515145-9. Dewey:152.4. LCCN:2004-050073.
                                   Audience: **l,u,f.** *Choice, 2005.*

Provine, Robert R.   BF575.L3P76
Laughter: A Scientific Investigation. Trade Cloth. Little Brown & Company. New York, NY. 1999. 288p. ISBN:0-316-71102-0, ISBN13: 978-0-316-71102-9. Dewey:152.4.
                    Audience: **g,l,u.** *Choice, 2001.*

Robbins, Paul R.   RC569.5.A34R62 2000
Anger, Aggression and Violence: An Interdisciplinary Study. Paper Text. McFarland & Company, Incorporated Publishers. Jefferson, NC. 2000. 215p. ISBN:0-7864-0903-7, ISBN13: 978-0-7864-0903-7. Dewey:616.85/82. LCCN:00-41119.
                    Audience: **l,u.** *Choice, 2001.*

Rowe, David C.   BF341
The Limits of Family Influence: Genes, Experience, and Behavior. Trade Paper. Guilford Publications, Inc. New York, NY. 1995. 232p. ISBN:0-89862-148-8, ISBN13: 978-0-89862-148-8. Dewey:155.7. LCCN:93-021876.
                    Audience: **u.** *Choice, 1994.*

Saklofske, Donald H. &   BF698.9.I6I57 1995
Zeidner, Moshe (Editors)
International Handbook of Personality and Intelligence. Trade Cloth. Basic Books. New York, NY. 1995. 800p. Perspectives on Individual Differences Ser. ISBN:0-306-44749-5, ISBN13: 978-0-306-44749-5. Dewey:153.9. LCCN:95-001086.
                    Audience: **l,u.** *Choice, 1996.*

Salovey, Peter (Editor)   BF575.J4P79 1991
The Psychology of Jealousy and Envy. Cloth over Boards. Guilford Publications, Inc. New York, NY. 1991. 293p. ISBN:0-89862-555-6, ISBN13: 978-0-89862-555-4. Dewey:152.4. LCCN:90-023329.
                    Audience: **l,u.** *Choice, 1991.*

Schneider, Benjamin &   BF698.9.O3
Smith, D. Brent (Editors)
Personality and Organizations. Chris Argyris, Murray Barrick & Arthur Brief (Contribution by). Cloth over Boards. Lawrence Erlbaum Associates, Inc. Mahwah, NJ. 2004. 464p. Lea's Organization and Management Ser. ISBN:0-8058-3758-2, ISBN13: 978-0-8058-3758-2. Dewey:158.7.
                    Audience: **u,f.** *Choice, 2004.*

Sidanius, Jim & Pratto,   HM131 .S5832 1999
Felicia
Social Dominance: An Intergroup Theory of Social Hierarchy and Oppression. Trade Paper. Cambridge University Press. New York, NY. 2001. 414p. ISBN:0-521-80540-6, ISBN13: 978-0-521-80540-7. Dewey:305.
                    Audience: **u,f.** *Choice, 2000.*

Simpson, Jeffry A. &   BF575.A86A38 2004
Rholes, W. Steven (Editors)
Adult Attachment: Theory, Research, and Clinical Implications. AnaMarie Guichard (Introduction by). Cloth over Boards. Guilford Publications, Inc. New York, NY. 2004. 482p. ISBN:1-59385-047-6, ISBN13: 978-1-59385-047-0. Dewey:155.9/2. LCCN:2004-007721.
                    Audience: **u,f.** *Choice, 2005.*

Singer, Jerome L.   BF173
Repression and Dissociation: Implications for Personality Theory, Psychopathology and Health. Trade Paper. University of Chicago Press. Chicago, IL. 1995. 536p. The John D. and Catherine T. MacArthur Foundation Series on Mental Health

and De Ser. ISBN:0-226-76106-1, ISBN13: 978-0-226-76106-0. Dewey:150.19/5.
                    Audience: **u,f.** *Choice, 1991.*

Skoyles, John & Sagan,   BF431.S558 2002
Dorion
Up from Dragons: The Evolution of Human Intelligence. Trade Cloth. McGraw-Hill Companies, The. New York, NY. 2002. 448p. ISBN:0-07-137825-1, ISBN13: 978-0-07-137825-3. Dewey:155.7. LCCN:2001-007857.
                    Audience: **g,l.** *Choice, 2003.*

Snyder, C. R. (Editor)   BF335.S69 2001
Coping with Stress: Effective People and Processes. Trade Cloth. Oxford University Press, Inc. New York, NY. 2001. 334p. ISBN:0-19-513044-8, ISBN13: 978-0-19-513044-7. Dewey:155.2/4. LCCN:00-041644.
                    Audience: **l,u.** *Choice, 2002.*

Solomon, Robert C.   BF561.S64
The Passions. Trade Cloth. Doubleday Publishing. New York, NY. 1976. 448p. ISBN:0-385-09740-9, ISBN13: 978-0-385-09740-6. Dewey:152.4. LCCN:74-033691.
                    Audience: **g,l,u.** 𝐵

Steptoe, Andrew (Editor)   BF412.G435 1998
Genius and the Mind: Studies of Creativity and Temperament. Trade Cloth. Oxford University Press, Inc. New York, NY. 1998. 284p. ISBN:0-19-852373-4, ISBN13: 978-0-19-852373-4. Dewey:153.3/5. LCCN:97-051708.
                    Audience: **u,f.** *Choice, 1999.*

Sternberg, Robert J.   BF431
(Editor)
Encyclopedia of Human Intelligence, Vol. 1. Trade Cloth. Macmillan Publishing Company, Inc. Old Tappan, NJ. 1994. xxviii, 623p. ISBN:0-02-897421-2, ISBN13: 978-0-02-897421-7. Dewey:153.9/03. LCCN:93-046975.
                    Audience: **g,l,u,f.** *Choice, 1995.*

Sternberg, Robert J.   BF408 .H285 1999
(Editor)
Handbook of Creativity. Trade Cloth. Cambridge University Press. New York, NY. 1998. 502p. ISBN:0-521-57285-1, ISBN13: 978-0-521-57285-9. Dewey:153.3/5. LCCN:98-035205.
                    Audience: **l,u,f.** *Choice, 1999.*

Sternberg, Robert J.   BF575.H3P74 2004
The Psychology of Hate. Trade Cloth. American Psychological Association. Washington, DC. 2004. 296p. ISBN:1-59147-184-2, ISBN13: 978-1-59147-184-4. Dewey:152.4. LCCN:2004-012194.
                    Audience: **l,u,f.** *Choice, 2005.*

Sternberg, Robert J.   BF431.W535 2002
(Editor)
Why Smart People Can Be So Stupid. Cloth over Boards. Yale University Press. Cumberland, RI. 2002. 272p. ISBN:0-300-09033-1, ISBN13: 978-0-300-09033-8. Dewey:153.9. LCCN:2001-005846.
                    Audience: **g,l,u.** *Choice, 2003, 2002.*

Sternberg, Robert J.   BF431.S7385 2003
Wisdom, Intelligence, and Creativity Synthesized. Trade Cloth. Cambridge University Press. New York, NY. 2003. 246p. ISBN:0-521-80238-5, ISBN13: 978-0-521-80238-3. Dewey:153.9. LCCN:2003-043751.
                    Audience: **u,f.** *Choice, 2004.*

Sternberg, Robert J. & BF575.L8
Barnes, Michael L.
The Psychology of Love. Trade Paper. Yale University Press.
Cumberland, RI. 1989. 383p. ISBN:0-300-04589-1, ISBN13:
978-0-300-04589-5. Dewey:302.

Audience: **l,u.** *Choice, 1988.*

Sternberg, Robert J., et al. BF408.C7548 2004
Creativity: From Potential to Realization. Elena Grigorenko &
Jerome L. Singer (Authors). Trade Cloth. American
Psychological Association. Washington, DC. 2004. 232p.
ISBN:1-59147-120-6, ISBN13: 978-1-59147-120-2.
Dewey:153.3/5. LCCN:2003-022923.

Audience: **u,f.** *Choice, 2005.*

Sternberg, Robert J. BF431.M5584 2002
(Editor), et al.
Models of Intelligence: International Perspectives. Jacques
Lautrey & Todd I. Lubart (Editors). Trade Cloth. American
Psychological Association. Washington, DC. 2002. 424p. Decade
of Behavior Ser. ISBN:1-55798-971-0, ISBN13:
978-1-55798-971-0. Dewey:153.9. LCCN:2002-151674.

Audience: **u,f.** *Choice, 2003.*

Tangney, June Price & BF575.S45
Dearing, Ronda L.
Shame and Guilt. Trade Paper. Guilford Publications, Inc. New
York, NY. 2003. 272p. Emotions and Social Behavior Ser.
ISBN:1-57230-987-3, ISBN13: 978-1-57230-987-6.
Dewey:152.4.

Audience: **l,u.**

Tesser, Abraham (Editor), BF697.P765 2000
et al.
Psychological Perspectives on Self and Identity. Richard B.
Felson & Jerry M. Suls (Editors). Cloth Text. American
Psychological Association. Washington, DC. 2000. x, 252p.
ISBN:1-55798-678-9, ISBN13: 978-1-55798-678-8.
Dewey:155.2. LCCN:00-021139.

Audience: **u,f.** *Choice, 2001.*

Ulanov, Ann & Ulanov, BF575.E65;
Barry
Cinderella and Her Sisters: The Envied and the Envying. Trade
Cloth. Daimon Publishers. Einsiedeln, 1998. 200p.
ISBN:3-85630-563-7, ISBN13: 978-3-85630-563-5.
Dewey:152.4.

Audience: **l,u.**

Watson, David BF698.9.E45W38 2000
Mood and Temperament. Cloth over Boards. Guilford
Publications, Inc. New York, NY. 2000. 340p. Emotions and
Social Behavior Ser. ISBN:1-57230-526-6, ISBN13:
978-1-57230-526-7. Dewey:152.4. LCCN:99-054213.

Audience: **l,u.** *Choice, 2000.*

Wegner, Daniel M. BF611.W38 2002
The Illusion of Conscious Will. Trade Cloth. MIT Press.
Cambridge, MA. 2002. 408p. Bradford Bks.
ISBN:0-262-23222-7, ISBN13: 978-0-262-23222-7.
Dewey:153.8. LCCN:2001-054608.

Audience: **u,f.** *Choice, 2003, 2002.*

West, Malcolm L. & BF575.A86W47 1994
Sheldon-Keller, Adrienne E.
Patterns of Relating: An Adult Attachment Perspective. Cloth
over Boards. Guilford Publications, Inc. New York, NY. 1994.

210p. ISBN:0-89862-671-4, ISBN13: 978-0-89862-671-1.
Dewey:155.6. LCCN:93-048128.

Audience: **u,f.** *Choice, 1995.*

Wilson, Timothy D. BF697.5.S43 2002
Strangers to Ourselves: Discovering the Adaptive Unconscious.
Ed. 25. Trade Cloth. Harvard University Press. Cambridge, MA.
2002. 272p. ISBN:0-674-00936-3, ISBN13: 978-0-674-00936-3.
Dewey:154.2. LCCN:2002-024088.

Audience: **u.** *Choice, 2003.*

Zenderland, Leila BF431 .Z46 1998
Measuring Minds: Henry Herbert Goddard and the Origins of
American Intelligence Testing. Mitchell G. Ash & William R.
Woodward (Contribution by). Cloth Text. Cambridge University
Press. New York, NY. 1998. 478p. Cambridge Studies in the
History of Psychology ISBN:0-521-44373-3, ISBN13:
978-0-521-44373-9. Dewey:153.9/3/097309041.
LCCN:97-006101.

Audience: **u,f.** *Choice, 1998.*

Personality Psychology > Personality Theory

Brody, Leslie RC455.4.E46B76 1999
Gender, Emotion, and the Family. Trade Cloth. Harvard
University Press. Cambridge, MA. 1999. 368p.
ISBN:0-674-34186-4, ISBN13: 978-0-674-34186-9.
Dewey:152.4. LCCN:98-032351.

Audience: **l,u,f.** *Choice, 1999.*

Clore, Gerald L. & Martin, BF531.T52 2001
Leonard L.
Theories of Mood and Cognition: A Users Handbook. Trade
Paper. Lawrence Erlbaum Associates, Inc. Mahwah, NJ. 2001.
224p. ISBN:0-8058-2784-6, ISBN13: 978-0-8058-2784-2.
Dewey:152.4. LCCN:00-042191.

Audience: **u,f.** *Choice, 2001.*

Feeney, Judith & Noller, BF575.A86F44 1996
Patricia
Adult Attachment. Trade Paper. SAGE Publications, Inc.
Thousand Oaks, CA. 1996. 192p. Series on Close Relationships,
Vol. 14 ISBN:0-8039-7224-5, ISBN13: 978-0-8039-7224-7.
Dewey:158.2. LCCN:96-004527.

Audience: **u.** *Choice, 1996.*

Fivush, Robyn & Haden, BF378.A87A883 2002
Catherine A. (Editors)
Autobiographical Memory and the Construction of a Narrative
Self: Developmental and Cultural Perspectives. Cloth over
Boards. Lawrence Erlbaum Associates, Inc. Mahwah, NJ. 2003.
266p. ISBN:0-8058-3756-6, ISBN13: 978-0-8058-3756-8.
Dewey:153.1/3. LCCN:2002-072668.

Audience: **u,f.** *Choice, 2003.*

Francis, Richard C. BF698.95.F73 2006
Why Men Won't Ask for Directions: The Seductions of
Sociobiology. Trade Paper. Princeton University Press.
Princeton, NJ. 2005. 352p. ISBN:0-691-12405-1, ISBN13:
978-0-691-12405-6. Dewey:155.7.

Audience: **u,f.** *Choice, 2004.*

Hogan, Robert (Editor), BF698.H3345 1997
et al.
Handbook of Personality Psychology. John Johnson & Stephen

Briggs (Editors). Paper Text. Elsevier Science & Technology Books. Saint Louis, MO. 1997. 987p. ISBN:0-12-134646-3, ISBN13: 978-0-12-134646-1. Dewey:155.2. LCCN:94-039181.

Audience: **u,f.** *Choice, 1997.*

Joseph, Jay   RC455.4.G4J67 2004
The Gene Illusion: Genetic Research in Psychiatry and Psychology under the Microscope. Trade Cloth. Algora Publishing. New York, NY. 2004. 348p. ISBN:0-87586-344-2, ISBN13: 978-0-87586-344-3. Dewey:616.89/042. LCCN:2004-017619.

Audience: **u,f.** *Choice, 2005.*

L'Abate, Luciano   RC454.L29 2005
Personality in Intimate Relationships: Socialization and Psychopathology. Trade Cloth. Springer. New York, NY. 2005. XVIII, 482p. ISBN:0-387-22605-2, ISBN13: 978-0-387-22605-7. Dewey:158.2/4. LCCN:2004-061909.

Audience: **l,u.** *Choice, 2005.*

Laming, D. R. J.   BF503.L36 2003
Understanding Human Motivation: What Makes People Tick? Trade Paper. Blackwell Publishing, Inc. Malden, MA. 2003. 336p. ISBN:0-631-21983-8, ISBN13: 978-0-631-21983-5. Dewey:153.8. LCCN:2002-154555.

Audience: **g,l.** *Choice, 2004.*

Macmillan, Malcolm   RC387.5
An Odd Kind of Fame: Stories of Phineas Gage. Trade Paper. MIT Press. Cambridge, MA. 2002. 575p. ISBN:0-262-63259-4, ISBN13: 978-0-262-63259-1. Dewey:617.4/81044/092 B.

Audience: **l,u,f.** *Choice, 2001.*

McCrae, Robert R. &   BF698.9.A4M33 2002
  Costa, Paul T. Jr.
Personality in Adulthood: A Five-Factor Theory Perspective. Ed. 2. Cloth over Boards. Guilford Publications, Inc. New York, NY. 2002. 268p. ISBN:1-57230-827-3, ISBN13: 978-1-57230-827-5. Dewey:155.6. LCCN:2002-014633.

Audience: **u,f.**

Mesibov, Gary B., et al.   RJ506.A9M48 1997
Autism: Understanding the Disorder. Lynn W. Adams & Laura G. Klinger (Authors). Trade Paper. Springer. New York, NY. 1998. 140p. Clinical Child Psychology Library ISBN:0-306-45547-1, ISBN13: 978-0-306-45547-6. Dewey:618.92/8982. LCCN:97-035645.

Audience: **l,u,f.** *Choice, 1998.*

Miller, Alice   BF637.F67
Paths of Life: Seven Scenarios. Trade Paper. Knopf Publishing Group. New York, NY. 1999. 208p. ISBN:0-375-70345-4, ISBN13: 978-0-375-70345-4. Dewey:155.9/2.

Audience: **g,l.**

Petrill, Stephen A. (Editor),   BF341.N387 2003
  et al.
Nature, Nurture, and the Transition to Early Adolescence. Robert Plomin, John C. DeFries & John K. Hewitt (Editors). Trade Cloth. Oxford University Press, Inc. New York, NY. 2003. 342p. ISBN:0-19-515747-8, ISBN13: 978-0-19-515747-5. Dewey:155.4/5. LCCN:2002-003903.

Audience: **u,f.** *Choice, 2003.*

Pinker, Steven   BF341.P47 2002
The Blank Slate: The Modern Denial of Human Nature. Trade Cloth. Penguin Group (USA) Inc. New York, NY. 2002. 528p.

ISBN:0-670-03151-8, ISBN13: 978-0-670-03151-1. Dewey:155.2. LCCN:2002-022719.

Audience: **l,u,f.** *Choice, 2003.*

Shapiro, David   RC455.5.T45 S46 2000
Dynamics of Character. Trade Paper. Basic Books. New York, NY. 2002. 192p. ISBN:0-465-09572-0, ISBN13: 978-0-465-09572-8. Dewey:616.89.

Audience: **g,l,u,f.** *Choice, 2000.*

Steen, R. Grant   BF341
DNA and Destiny: Nature and Nurture in Human Behavior. Trade Paper. Perseus Books Group. New York, NY. 2001. 304p. ISBN:0-7382-0619-9, ISBN13: 978-0-7382-0619-6. Dewey:155.7.

Audience: **l,u,f.** *Choice, 1996.*

West, Malcolm L. &   BF575.A86W47 1994
  Sheldon-Keller, Adrienne E.
Patterns of Relating: An Adult Attachment Perspective. Cloth over Boards. Guilford Publications, Inc. New York, NY. 1994. 210p. ISBN:0-89862-671-4, ISBN13: 978-0-89862-671-1. Dewey:155.6. LCCN:93-048128.

Audience: **u,f.** *Choice, 1995.*

Wiggins, Jerry S. (Editor)   BF698.F585 1996
The Five-Factor Model of Personality: Theoretical Perspectives. Cloth over Boards. Guilford Publications, Inc. New York, NY. 1996. 216p. ISBN:1-57230-068-X, ISBN13: 978-1-57230-068-2. Dewey:155.2. LCCN:96-004859.

Audience: **u,f.** *Choice, 1996.*

Wong, Roderick   BF503 .W665 2000
Motivation: A Biobehavioural Approach. Cloth Text. Cambridge University Press. New York, NY. 2000. 292p. ISBN:0-521-56175-2, ISBN13: 978-0-521-56175-4. Dewey:153.8. LCCN:99-054913.

Audience: **u,f.** *Choice, 2001.*

Personality Psychology > Psychoanalytic Theory

Brown, Norman O.   BF175.4.C84B76 1990
Love's Body. Trade Paper. University of California Press. Berkeley, CA. 1990. 285p. ISBN:0-520-07106-9, ISBN13: 978-0-520-07106-3. Dewey:150.19/52. LCCN:90-034738.

Audience: **g,l,u,f.**

Erikson, Erik H.   HQ767.9
Childhood and Society. Trade Paper. W. W. Norton & Company, Inc. New York, NY. 1993. 446p. ISBN:0-393-31068-X, ISBN13: 978-0-393-31068-9. Dewey:305.2/3. LCCN:93-011229.

Audience: **g,l,u,f.** *B*

Freud, Sigmund   BF173
Freud: Standard Edition. Trade Cloth. Random House. London, 1996. 364p. ISBN:0-7012-0516-4, ISBN13: 978-0-7012-0516-4. Dewey:150.19/52.

Audience: **g,l,u,f.**

Freud, Sigmund & Jung,   BF109.F4A4 1994
  C. G.
The Freud-Jung Letters: The Correspondence Between Sigmund Freud and C. G. Jung. William McGuire (Editor), Ralph

Formats: Web: ☐ Ebook: **e** CD/DVD-ROM: 🔥 BCL3: **B**

Manheim & R. F. C. Hull (Translators), Alan McGlashan (Abridged by). Trade Paper. Princeton University Press. Princeton, NJ. 1994. 328p. Bollingen Series (General) Ser. ISBN:0-691-03643-8, ISBN13: 978-0-691-03643-4. Dewey:150.19/52 B. LCCN:93-046096.

Audience: **g,l,u,f.** *B*

Hall, Calvin S.   **BF173.F85 H32**
A Primer of Freudian Psychology. Paper Text. Textbook Publishers. Temecula, CA. 2003. 137p. ISBN:0-7581-0231-3, ISBN13: 978-0-7581-0231-7. Dewey:150.19/52.

Audience: **g,l,u.**

Jung, C. G.   **BF23**
The Collected Works of C. G. Jung, Set. Gerhard Adler, Michael S. Fordham & Herbert Read (Editors). Cloth Text. Princeton University Press. Princeton, NJ. 2000. Collected Works of C. G. Jung Ser. ISBN:0-691-07476-3, ISBN13: 978-0-691-07476-4. Dewey:150.19/54.

Audience: **g,l,u,f.**

Psychological and Physical Disorders > Affective Disorders

Ainsworth, Patricia   **RC537.A39 2000**
Understanding Depression. Trade Cloth. University Press of Mississippi. Jackson, MS. 2000. xii, 174p. Understanding Health and Sickness Ser. ISBN:1-57806-169-5, ISBN13: 978-1-57806-169-3. Dewey:616.85/27. LCCN:99-035416.

Audience: **g,l.** *Choice, 2000.*

Barondes, Samuel H.   **RC537.B3385 1999**
Mood Genes: Hunting for Origins of Mania and Depression. Trade Paper. Oxford University Press, Inc. New York, NY. 1999. 256p. ISBN:0-19-513106-1, ISBN13: 978-0-19-513106-2. Dewey:616.8/95/042. LCCN:99-011427.

Audience: **u,f.** *Choice, 1999.*

Blatt, Sidney J.   **RC537.B525 2004**
Experiences of Depression: Theoretical, Clinical, and Research Perspectives. Trade Cloth. American Psychological Association. Washington, DC. 2004. 400p. ISBN:1-59147-095-1, ISBN13: 978-1-59147-095-3. Dewey:616.85/27. LCCN:2003-016292.

Audience: **u,f.** *Choice, 2004.*

Blazer, Dan G.   **RC537.B527 2005**
The Age of Melancholy: Major Depression and Its Social Origins. Paper over Boards. Routledge. New York, NY. 2005. 264p. ISBN:0-415-95188-7, ISBN13: 978-0-415-95188-3. Dewey:362.2/5. LCCN:2005-006824.

Audience: **l,u,f.** *Choice, 2005.*

Caramagno, Thomas C.   **PR6045.O72.Z566 1992**
The Flight of the Mind: Virginia Woolf's Art and Manic-Depressive Illness. Trade Cloth. University of California Press. Berkeley, CA. 1992. 362p. ISBN:0-520-07280-4, ISBN13: 978-0-520-07280-0. Dewey:823.912. LCCN:91-038836.

Audience: **u,f.** *Choice, 1992.*

Chesler, Phyllis   **RC451.4.W6.C47 1974**
Women and Madness. Trade Cloth. Penguin Books, Ltd. London, 1974. iii-xxi, 338p. ISBN:0-7139-0656-1, ISBN13: 978-0-7139-0656-1. Dewey:616.89/0082. LCCN:74-185752.

Audience: **l,u.** *B* *Choice, 1998.*

Coyne, James C. (Editor)   **RC537.E78 1986**
Essential Papers on Depression. Trade Paper. New York University Press. New York, NY. 1986. 496p. Essential Papers in Psychoanalysis ISBN:0-8147-1399-8, ISBN13: 978-0-8147-1399-0. Dewey:616.85/27. LCCN:85-021498.

Audience: **u,f.** *B*

Formanek, Ruth & Gurian, Anita (Editors)   **RC537.W66 1987**
Women and Depression: A Lifespan Perspective. Trade Cloth. Springer Publishing Company, Inc. New York, NY. 1987. 328p. Focus on Women Ser. ISBN:0-8261-5140-X, ISBN13: 978-0-8261-5140-7. Dewey:616.85/27/088042. LCCN:87-016684.

Audience: **l,u.** *Choice, 1988.*

Gilbert, Paul   **RC537.G53 1992**
Depression: The Evolution of Powerlessness. Ed. 2. Cloth over Boards. Guilford Publications, Inc. New York, NY. 1992. 576p. ISBN:0-89862-884-9, ISBN13: 978-0-89862-884-5. Dewey:616.85/27. LCCN:92-001445.

Audience: **l,u.** *Choice, 1992.*

Gotlib, Ian H. & Hammen, Constance L. (Editors)   **RC537.H3376 2002**
Handbook of Depression. Cloth over Boards. Guilford Publications, Inc. New York, NY. 2002. 624p. ISBN:1-57230-725-0, ISBN13: 978-1-57230-725-4. Dewey:616.85/27. LCCN:2002-003553.

Audience: **u,f.** *Choice, 2003.*

Healy, David   **RM332.H423 2004**
Let Them Eat Prozac: The Unhealthy Relationship Between the Pharmaceutical Industry and Depression. Trade Cloth. New York University Press. New York, NY. 2004. 368p. Disease and Desire Ser. ISBN:0-8147-3669-6, ISBN13: 978-0-8147-3669-2. Dewey:616.85/27061. LCCN:2004-002297.

Audience: **u,f.** *Choice, 2004.*

Hershman, D. Jablow & Lieb, Julian   **BF423.H47 1998**
Manic Depression and Creativity. Trade Paper. Prometheus Books, Publishers. Amherst, NY. 1998. 230p. ISBN:1-57392-241-2, ISBN13: 978-1-57392-241-8. Dewey:153.3/5. LCCN:98-027043.

Audience: **l,u.** *Choice, 1999.*

Hollandsworth, J. G. Jr.   **RC514.H59 1990**
The Physiology of Psychological Disorders: Schizophrenia, Depression, Anxiety, and Substance Abuse. Trade Cloth. Basic Books. New York, NY. 1990. 336p. Behavioral Psychophysiology and Medicine Ser. ISBN:0-306-43353-2, ISBN13: 978-0-306-43353-5. Dewey:616.89/07. LCCN:89-026559.

Audience: **l,u.** *Choice, 1990.*

Jackson, Stanley W.   **RC537**
Melancholia and Depression: From Hippocratic Times to Modern Times. Trade Paper. Yale University Press. Cumberland, RI. 1990. 442p. ISBN:0-300-04614-6, ISBN13: 978-0-300-04614-4. Dewey:616.85/27/009.

Audience: **l,u.** *Choice, 1987.*

Jamison, Kay Redfield   **RC516.J36 1996**
Touched with Fire: Manic-Depressive Illness and the Artistic Temperament. Trade Paper. Simon & Schuster. New York, NY.

1996. 384p. ISBN:0-684-83183-X, ISBN13: 978-0-684-83183-1. Dewey:616.8/95/00887. LCCN:96-021444.

Audience: **g,l,u.** *Choice, 1993.*

✓**Jamison, Kay Redfield**　　　　　**RC516.J363 1995**
An Unquiet Mind: A Memoir of Moods and Madness. Trade Cloth. Random House, Inc. New York, NY. 1995. 240p. ISBN:0-679-44374-6, ISBN13: 978-0-679-44374-2. Dewey:616.8/95/0092. LCCN:95-014273.

Audience: **g,l,u.**

✓**Kendall-Tackett, Kathleen A.**　　　　　**RG852.K448 2005**
Depression in New Mothers: Causes, Consequences, and Treatment Alternatives. Perfect, Paper over Boards. Haworth Press, Incorporated, The. Binghamton, NY. 2005. 255p. ISBN:0-7890-1838-1, ISBN13: 978-0-7890-1838-0. Dewey:618.76. LCCN:2004-022688.

Audience: **l,u.**

✓**Lynch, John & Kilmartin, Christopher T.**　　　　　**RC537.L94 1999**
The Pain Behind the Mask: Overcoming Masculine Depression. Library Binding. Haworth Press, Incorporated, The. Binghamton, NY. 1999. 226p. Haworth Press Advances in Psychology and Mental Health Ser. ISBN:0-7890-0557-3, ISBN13: 978-0-7890-0557-1. Dewey:616.85/27/0081. LCCN:98-045944.

Audience: **u,f.** *Choice, 1999.*

✓**McCullough, James P. Jr.**　　　　　**RC537**
Treatment for Chronic Depression: Cognitive Behavioral Analysis System of Psychotherapy (CBASP). Cloth over Boards. Guilford Publications, Inc. New York, NY. 1999. 326p. ISBN:1-57230-527-4, ISBN13: 978-1-57230-527-4. Dewey:616.85270651.

Audience: **u,f.** *Choice, 2000.*

Morris, W. N.　　　　　**BF521.M67 1989**
Mood. Cloth Text. Springer. New York, NY. 1989. 261p. Social Psychology Ser. ISBN:0-387-96978-0, ISBN13: 978-0-387-96978-7. Dewey:152.4. LCCN:89-021739.

Audience: **l.** *Choice, 1990.*

✓**Nolen-Hoeksema, Susan**　　　　　**RC537.N65 1990**
Sex Differences in Depression. Trade Cloth. Stanford University Press. Palo Alto, CA. 1990. 270p. ISBN:0-8047-1640-4, ISBN13: 978-0-8047-1640-6. Dewey:616.85/27. LCCN:89-027303.

Audience: **l,u.** *Choice, 1991.*

✓**Patterson, Gerald R.**　　　　　**RC537.D4272 1990**
Depression and Aggression in Family Interaction. Cloth Text. Lawrence Erlbaum Associates, Inc. Mahwah, NJ. 1990. 352p. ISBN:0-8058-0137-5, ISBN13: 978-0-8058-0137-8. Dewey:616.85/27. LCCN:89-011829.

Audience: **u,f.** *Choice, 1991.*

✓**Radden, Jennifer (Editor)**　　　　　**BF575.M44**
The Nature of Melancholy: From Aristotle to Kristeva. Trade Paper. Oxford University Press, Inc. New York, NY. 2002. 392p. ISBN:0-19-515165-8, ISBN13: 978-0-19-515165-7. Dewey:152.4.

Audience: **u,f.**

✓**Russell, Denise**　　　　　**RC451.4.W6**
Women, Madness and Medicine. Trade Paper. Blackwell Publishing, Inc. Malden, MA. 1995. 208p.

ISBN:0-7456-1261-X, ISBN13: 978-0-7456-1261-4. Dewey:616.89/0082. LCCN:94-038395.

Audience: **l,u,f.**

✓**Schwartz, Arthur & Schwartz, Ruth M.**　　　　　**RC537.S395 1993**
Depression: Theories and Treatments: Psychological, Biological, and Social Perspectives. Trade Cloth. Columbia University Press. New York, NY. 1993. 533p. ISBN:0-231-06818-2, ISBN13: 978-0-231-06818-5. Dewey:616.85/27. LCCN:92-049525.

Audience: **l,u.** *Choice, 1993.*

Psychological and Physical Disorders > Schizophrenia and Psychotic States

Bentall, Richard P.　　　　　**RC514.R383 1989**
Reconstructing Schizophrenia. UK-B Format Paperback. Routledge. New York, NY. 1992. 336p. ISBN:0-415-07524-6, ISBN13: 978-0-415-07524-4. Dewey:616.89/82. LCCN:89-010209.

Audience: **l,u.** *Choice, 1990.*

✓**Birchwood, Max J. & Jackson, Chris**　　　　　**RC514**
Schizophrenia. Paper over Boards. Taylor & Francis Group. Abingdon, 2001. 192p. ISBN:0-86377-552-7, ISBN13: 978-0-86377-552-9. Dewey:616.8/982.

Audience: **l,u.**

✓**Ciompi, Luc**　　　　　**BF175.C5513 1988**
The Psyche and Schizophrenia: The Bond Between Affect and Logic. Deborah L. Schneider (Translator). Trade Cloth. Harvard University Press. Cambridge, MA. 1988. 320p. ISBN:0-674-71990-5, ISBN13: 978-0-674-71990-3. Dewey:616.89/82. LCCN:88-006768.

Audience: **u.** *Choice, 1989.*

✓**Hollandsworth, J. G. Jr.**　　　　　**RC514.H59 1990**
The Physiology of Psychological Disorders: Schizophrenia, Depression, Anxiety, and Substance Abuse. Trade Cloth. Basic Books. New York, NY. 1990. 336p. Behavioral Psychophysiology and Medicine Ser. ISBN:0-306-43353-2, ISBN13: 978-0-306-43353-5. Dewey:616.89/07. LCCN:89-026559.

Audience: **l,u.** *Choice, 1990.*

✓**Kantor, Martin**　　　　　**RC520**
Understanding Paranoia: A Guide for Professionals, Families, and Sufferers. Trade Cloth. Greenwood Publishing Group, Inc. Portsmouth, NH. 2004. 272p. ISBN:0-275-98152-5, ISBN13: 978-0-275-98152-5. Dewey:616.89/7. LCCN:2004-042205.

Audience: **g,f.** *Choice, 2004.*

✓**Kingdon, David G. & Turkington, Douglas**　　　　　**RC514.K5653 2005**
Cognitive Therapy of Schizophrenia. Cloth over Boards. Guilford Publications, Inc. New York, NY. 2004. 219p. Treatment Manuals for Real World Clinici Ser. ISBN:1-59385-104-9, ISBN13: 978-1-59385-104-0. Dewey:616.89/806. LCCN:2004-012738.

Audience: **u,f.**

Formats: Web: ☐　Ebook: **e**　CD/DVD-ROM: ✦　BCL3: ℬ

Marley, James A.   RC514.M356 2003
Family Involvement in Treating Schizophrenia: Models,
Essential Skills, and Process. Trade Cloth. Haworth Press,
Incorporated, The. Binghamton, NY. 2003. 151p.
ISBN:0-7890-1249-9, ISBN13: 978-0-7890-1249-4.
Dewey:616.89/82. LCCN:2002-154813.
Audience: **u,f.**

McKenna, Peter & Oh,   **RC425**
Tomasina
Schizophrenic Speech: Making Sense of Bathroots and Ponds
that Fall in Doorways. Trade Cloth. Cambridge University Press.
New York, NY. 2005. 220p. ISBN:0-521-81075-2, ISBN13:
978-0-521-81075-3. Dewey:616.8552. LCCN:2005-282389.
Audience: **u,f.**

Nasar, Sylvia   **QA29.N25**
A Beautiful Mind: A Biography of John Forbes Nash, Jr. ,
Winner of the Nobel Prize for Economics 1994. Trade Paper.
Simon & Schuster. New York, NY. 1999. 464p.
ISBN:0-684-85370-1, ISBN13: 978-0-684-85370-3.
Dewey:510.92.
Audience: **g,l,u,f.**

Noll, Richard   RC514.N63 2006
The Encyclopedia of Schizophrenia and Other Psychotic
Disorders. Ed. 3. Susan Naylor (Foreword by). Trade Cloth.
Facts On File, Inc.. New York, NY. 2006. 432p.
ISBN:0-8160-6405-9, ISBN13: 978-0-8160-6405-2.
Dewey:616.89/003. LCCN:2005-056749.
Audience: **l.** *Choice, 2001.*

Shean, Glenn   RC514.S484 2003
Understanding and Treating Schizophrenia: Contemporary
Research, Theory, and Practice. Perfect, Paper over Boards.
Haworth Press, Incorporated, The. Binghamton, NY. 2004. 336p.
Haworth Marriage and the Family Ser. ISBN:0-7890-1887-X,
ISBN13: 978-0-7890-1887-8. Dewey:616.89/82.
LCCN:21-548140.
Audience: **l,u.** *Choice, 2004.*

Siegel, Ronald K.   **RC520**
Whispers: The Voices of Paranoia. Trade Paper. Simon &
Schuster. New York, NY. 1996. 320p. ISBN:0-684-80285-6,
ISBN13: 978-0-684-80285-5. Dewey:616.89/7.
Audience: **l,u.** *Choice, 1994.*

Psychological and Physical Disorders >
Personality Disorders

Carlson, Jon & Sperry, Len   RC488.5.D59 1998
(Editors)
The Disordered Couple. Paper over Boards. Brunner-Routledge.
Philadelphia, PA. 1997. 342p. ISBN:0-87630-815-9, ISBN13:
978-0-87630-815-8. Dewey:616.89/156. LCCN:97-024085.
Audience: **u.** *Choice, 1998.*

Cauchon, Janet Wirth   RC569.5.B67W57 2001
Women and Borderline Personality Disorder: Symptoms and
Stories. Trade Cloth. Rutgers University Press. Piscataway, NJ.
2001. x, 235p. ISBN:0-8135-2890-9, ISBN13:
978-0-8135-2890-8. Dewey:616.85/0082. LCCN:00-039037.
Audience: **u,f.** *Choice, 2002.*

Clarkin, John F. &   RC554.M24 2005
Lenzenweger, Mark F. (Editors)
Major Theories of Personality Disorder. Ed. 2. Cloth over
Boards. Guilford Publications, Inc. New York, NY. 2004. 464p.
ISBN:1-59385-108-1, ISBN13: 978-1-59385-108-8.
Dewey:616.85/81. LCCN:2004-019448.
Audience: **u,f.**

L'Abate, Luciano   RC454.L29 2005
Personality in Intimate Relationships: Socialization and
Psychopathology. Trade Cloth. Springer. New York, NY. 2005.
XVIII, 482p. ISBN:0-387-22605-2, ISBN13:
978-0-387-22605-7. Dewey:158.2/4. LCCN:2004-061909.
Audience: **l,u.** *Choice, 2005.*

Livesley, W. John (Editor)   **RC554**
Handbook of Personality Disorders: Theory, Research, and
Treatment. Cloth over Boards. Guilford Publications, Inc. New
York, NY. 2001. 626p. ISBN:1-57230-629-7, ISBN13:
978-1-57230-629-5. Dewey:616.8/58. LCCN:2001-016208.
Audience: **u,f.**

Magnavita, Jeffrey J.   RC554.H357 2003
(Editor)
Handbook of Personality Disorders: Theory and Practice. Trade
Cloth. John Wiley & Sons, Inc. Hoboken, NJ. 2003. 600p.
ISBN:0-471-20116-2, ISBN13: 978-0-471-20116-8.
Dewey:616.85/8. LCCN:2003-053826.
Audience: **u,f.** *Choice, 2004.*

Maser, Jack D. (Editor),   RC555.H35 1997
et al.
Handbook of Antisocial Behavior. James Breiling & David M.
Stoff (Editors). Trade Cloth. John Wiley & Sons, Inc. Hoboken,
NJ. 1997. 624p. ISBN:0-471-12452-4, ISBN13:
978-0-471-12452-8. Dewey:302.5/4. LCCN:96-053445.
Audience: **u,f.** *Choice, 1998.*

Millon, Theodore (Editor),   RC555.P785 2003
et al.
Psychopathy: Antisocial, Criminal, and Violent Behavior. Erik
Simonsen, Roger Davis & Morten Birket-Smith (Editors). Trade
Paper. Guilford Publications, Inc. New York, NY. 2002. 476p.
ISBN:1-57230-864-8, ISBN13: 978-1-57230-864-0.
Dewey:616.8/582.
Audience: **u,f.**

Petry, Nancy M.   RC569.5.G35P48 2004
Pathological Gambling: Etiology, Comorbidity, and Treatments.
Trade Cloth. American Psychological Association. Washington,
DC. 2004. 384p. ISBN:1-59147-173-7, ISBN13:
978-1-59147-173-8. Dewey:616.85/841. LCCN:2004-014279.
Audience: **u,f.** *Choice, 2005.*

Shapiro, David   RC455.5.T45 S46 2000
Dynamics of Character. Trade Paper. Basic Books. New York,
NY. 2002. 192p. ISBN:0-465-09572-0, ISBN13:
978-0-465-09572-8. Dewey:616.89.
Audience: **g,l,u,f.** *Choice, 2000.*

Simon, Robert I.   **RC569.5.V55**
Bad Men Do What Good Men Dream: A Forensic Psychiatrist
Illuminates the Darker Side of Human Behavior. Trade Paper.
American Psychiatric Publishing, Inc. Arlington, VA. 1999.
248p. ISBN:0-88048-995-2, ISBN13: 978-0-88048-995-9.
Dewey:616.85/82.
Audience: **u,f.** *Choice, 1996.*

Audience: g=general, l=lower division undergraduate, u=upper division undergraduate, f=faculty.   **661**

Psychological and Physical Disorders > Behavior Disorders and Antisocial Behavior

American Psychiatric Association   **RC321**

☐ American Psychiatric Association.
http://www.psych.org/

Audience: **u,f.**

Bandura, Albert   **BF575.A3**

Aggression: A Social Learning Analysis. Cloth Text. Prentice Hall PTR. Upper Saddle River, NJ. 1973. 368p. Social Learning Theory Ser. ISBN:0-13-020743-8, ISBN13: 978-0-13-020743-2. Dewey:302.5/4. LCCN:72-012990.

Audience: **u,f.** *B*

Barkley, Russell A.   **RJ496.A86B37 2006**

Attention-Deficit Hyperactivity Disorder: A Handbook for Diagnosis and Treatment. Ed. 3. Paper over Boards. Guilford Publications, Inc. New York, NY. 2005. 770p. ISBN:1-59385-210-X, ISBN13: 978-1-59385-210-8. Dewey:618.92/8589. LCCN:2005-016986.

Audience: **g,u,f.**

Barkley, Russell A.   **RJ506.B44B36 1997**

Defiant Children: A Clinician's Manual for Assessment and Parent Training. Ed. 2. Trade Paper. Guilford Publications, Inc. New York, NY. 1997. 264p. ISBN:1-57230-123-6, ISBN13: 978-1-57230-123-8. Dewey:618.9289. LCCN:96-047746.

Audience: **u,f.**

Behavior Analysis (APA Division 25)   **BF199**

☐ Behavior Analysis (APA Division 25).
http://www.auburn.edu/~newlamc/apa_div25/

Audience: **u,f.**

Brown, Thomas E.   **RJ506.H9B765 2005**

Attention Deficit Disorder: The Unfocused Mind in Children and Adults. Saddle Stitched, Cloth over Boards, Dust Jacket. Yale University Press. Cumberland, RI. 2005. 384p. Yale University Press Health and Wellness Ser. ISBN:0-300-10641-6, ISBN13: 978-0-300-10641-1. Dewey:616.85/89. LCCN:2005-040895.

Audience: **g,l,u.** *Choice, 2006.*

Cairns, Robert B. & Stoff, David M. (Editors)   **RC569.5.V55A28 1996**

Aggression and Violence: Genetic, Neurobiological, and Biosocial Perspectives. Cloth Text. Lawrence Erlbaum Associates, Inc. Mahwah, NJ. 1996. 416p. ISBN:0-8058-1755-7, ISBN13: 978-0-8058-1755-3. Dewey:616.85/82. LCCN:95-042601.

Audience: **u,f.**

Evans, Glen & Farberow, Norman L.   **HV6545.E87 2003**

The Encyclopedia of Suicide. Ed. 2. Trade Cloth. Facts On File, Inc.. New York, NY. 2003. 368p. Library of Health and Living Ser. ISBN:0-8160-4525-9, ISBN13: 978-0-8160-4525-9. Dewey:362.2/8/03. LCCN:2002-027166.

Audience: **g,l,u.** *Choice, 2003.*

Goldsmith, Sara K. (Editor)   **HV6548.U5R43 2002**

Reducing Suicide: A National Imperative. Institute of Medicine Staff (Contribution by). Trade Cloth. National Academies Press. Washington, DC. 2002. 345p. ISBN:0-309-08321-4, ISBN13: 978-0-309-08321-8. Dewey:362.28/7/0973. LCCN:2002-012032.

Audience: **g,l,u,f.** *Choice, 2003.*

Hill, Jonathan & Maughan, Barbara (Editors)   **RJ499 .C615 2001**

Conduct Disorders in Childhood and Adolescence. Ian M. Goodyer (Contribution by). Trade Paper. Cambridge University Press. New York, NY. 2000. 596p. Cambridge Child and Adolescent Psychiatry Ser. ISBN:0-521-78639-8, ISBN13: 978-0-521-78639-3. Dewey:618.9289. LCCN:99-057084.

Audience: **u,f.**

Lahey, Benjamin B. (Editor), et al.   **RJ506.C65C38 2003**

Causes of Conduct Disorder and Juvenile Delinquency. Terrie E. Moffitt & Avshalom Caspi (Editors). Cloth over Boards. Guilford Publications, Inc. New York, NY. 2003. 370p. ISBN:1-57230-881-8, ISBN13: 978-1-57230-881-7. Dewey:618.92/89. LCCN:2003-000812.

Audience: **u,f.**

Moeller, Thomas G.   **BF724.3.A34M64 2001**

Youth Aggression and Violence: A Psychological Approach. Cloth over Boards. Lawrence Erlbaum Associates, Inc. Mahwah, NJ. 2001. 424p. ISBN:0-8058-3713-2, ISBN13: 978-0-8058-3713-1. Dewey:155.4/18232. LCCN:00-068145.

Audience: **g,l,u,f.** *Choice, 2002.*

Moffitt, Terrie E., et al.   **RJ506.C5 S49 2001**

Sex Differences in Antisocial Behaviour: Conduct Disorder, Delinquency, and Violence in the Dunedin Longitudinal Study. Avshalom Caspi, Michael Rutter & Phil A. Silva (Authors), Alfred Blumstein & David Farrington (Contribution by). Cloth Text. Cambridge University Press. New York, NY. 2001. 296p. Criminology Ser. ISBN:0-521-80445-0, ISBN13: 978-0-521-80445-5. Dewey:616.8900835. LCCN:00-067495.

Audience: **u,f.**

National Center for Post-Traumatic Stress Disorder, U.S. Department of Veterans Affairs   **RC552.P67**

☐ National Center for Post-Traumatic Stress Disorder, U.S. Department of Veterans Affairs.
http://www.ncptsd.va.gov/

Audience: **g,l,u,f.**

Patterson, Gerald R.   **RC537.D4272 1990**

Depression and Aggression in Family Interaction. Cloth Text. Lawrence Erlbaum Associates, Inc. Mahwah, NJ. 1990. 352p. ISBN:0-8058-0137-5, ISBN13: 978-0-8058-0137-8. Dewey:616.85/27. LCCN:89-011829.

Audience: **u,f.** *Choice, 1991.*

Quay, Herbert C. & Hogan, A. E. (Editors)   **RJ506.B44H25 1999**

Handbook of Disruptive Behavior Disorders. Trade Cloth. Springer. New York, NY. 1999. 699p. ISBN:0-306-45974-4, ISBN13: 978-0-306-45974-0. Dewey:618.92/89. LCCN:98-056517.

Audience: **u,f.**

Shneidman, Edwin S.   RC569.S3848 2001
Comprehending Suicide: Landmarks in 20th-Century
Suicidology. Trade Cloth. American Psychological Association.
Washington, DC. 2001. xiv, 215p. ISBN:1-55798-743-2,
ISBN13: 978-1-55798-743-3. Dewey:616.85/8445.
LCCN:00-065066.
                              Audience: **u,f.** *Choice, 2001.*

Shneidman, Edwin S.   RC569.S468 2004
  (Author, Editor)
Autopsy of a Suicidal Mind. Trade Cloth. Oxford University
Press, Inc. New York, NY. 2004. 208p. ISBN:0-19-517273-6,
ISBN13: 978-0-19-517273-7. Dewey:616.85/844509.
LCCN:2003-016303.
                         Audience: **g,l,u,f.** *Choice, 2004.*

Volkmar, Fred R. (Editor),   RJ506.A9
  et al.
Handbook of Autism and Pervasive Developmental Disorders.
Ed. 3. Donald J. Cohen, Ami Klin & Rhea Paul (Editors). Trade
Cloth. John Wiley & Sons, Inc. Hoboken, NJ. 2005. 1200p.
ISBN:0-471-26275-7, ISBN13: 978-0-471-26275-6.
Dewey:618.92/85882.
                                      Audience: **g,l,u,f.**

Wolfe, David A. & Mash,   RJ503.5.B436 2005
  Eric J. (Editors)
Behavioral and Emotional Disorders in Adolescents: Nature,
Assessment, and Treatment. Paper over Boards. Guilford
Publications, Inc. New York, NY. 2005. 719p.
ISBN:1-59385-225-8, ISBN13: 978-1-59385-225-2.
Dewey:618.92/89. LCCN:2005-012856.
                                      Audience: **u,f.**

Zuckerman, Edward L.   RJ503.5
Assessment of Childhood Disorders. Ed. 3. Eric J. Mash & Leif
G. Terdal (Editors). Trade Paper. Guilford Publications, Inc.
New York, NY. 2001. 800p. ISBN:1-57230-587-8, ISBN13:
978-1-57230-587-8. Dewey:618.92/89075.
                                      Audience: **u,f.**

Psychological and Physical Disorders > Substance Abuse and Addiction

Acker, Caroline J. & Tracy,   HV5292.A393 2004
  Sarah W. (Editors)
Altering American Consciouness: Essays on the History of
Alcohol and Drug Use in the United States, 1800-2000. Trade
Cloth. University of Massachusetts Press. Amherst, MA. 2004.
448p. ISBN:1-55849-424-3, ISBN13: 978-1-55849-424-4.
Dewey:362.29/0973/09034. LCCN:2003-013735.
                         Audience: **l,u,f.** *Choice, 2005.*

Blocker, Jack S. Jr.   HV5292
Alcohol, Reform and Society: The Liquor Issue in Social
Context, 83. Trade Cloth. Greenwood Publishing Group, Inc.
Portsmouth, NH. 1979. 289p. Contributions in American History
Ser., No. 83 ISBN:0-313-20889-1, ISBN13: 978-0-313-20889-8.
Dewey:322.4/4/0973. LCCN:78-073800.
                                      Audience: **l,u.** *B*

Blocker, Jack S. Jr., et al.   HV5017.B56 2003
Alcohol and Temperance in Modern History: An Global
Encyclopedia. Ian R. Tyrrell & David M. Fahey (Authors).
Library Binding. ABC-CLIO, Inc. Santa Barbara, CA. 2003.

758p. ISBN:1-57607-833-7, ISBN13: 978-1-57607-833-4.
Dewey:362.292/03. LCCN:2003-008679.
                              Audience: **l,u.** *Choice, 2004.*

Blum, Richard H.   HV5801.B57
Society and Drugs; Social and Cultural Observations. Trade
Cloth. John Wiley & Sons, Inc. Hoboken, NJ. 1969. xvi, 400p.
ISBN:0-87589-033-4, ISBN13: 978-0-87589-033-3.
Dewey:301.47/686/3. LCCN:73-075936.
                                      Audience: **l,u.** *B*

Courtwright, David T.   HV5816.C648 2001
Dark Paradise: A History of Opiate Addiction in America. Ed. 2.
Trade Paper. Harvard University Press. Cambridge, MA. 2001.
352p. ISBN:0-674-00585-6, ISBN13: 978-0-674-00585-3.
Dewey:362.29/3/0973. LCCN:2001-016547.
                                      Audience: **g,l,u,f.**

Crowley, John W.   HV5068.D78 1999
Drunkard's Progress: Narratives of Addiction, Despair, and
Recovery. Trade Paper. Johns Hopkins University Press.
Baltimore, MD. 1999. 216p. ISBN:0-8018-6007-5, ISBN13:
978-0-8018-6007-2. Dewey:362.292. LCCN:98-008732.
                              Audience: **l,u.** *Choice, 1999.*

Deutsch, Charles   HV5132.D43
Broken Bottles, Broken Dreams: Understanding and Helping the
Children of Alcoholics. Trade Cloth. Bow Historical Books.
New Providence, NJ. 1982. xiv, 213p. ISBN:0-8077-2664-8,
ISBN13: 978-0-8077-2664-8. Dewey:362.8/28.
LCCN:81-005729.
                                      Audience: **g,l.** *B*

DiClemente, Carlo C.   RC564.D535 2003
Addiction and Change: How Addictions Develop and Addicted
People Recover. Paper over Boards. Guilford Publications, Inc.
New York, NY. 2003. 318p. Guilford Substance Abuse Ser.
ISBN:1-57230-057-4, ISBN13: 978-1-57230-057-6.
Dewey:616.86/03. LCCN:2002-015477.
                              Audience: **l,u.** *Choice, 2003.*

Duis, Perry R.   HV5201.S6D84 1999
Saloon: Public Drinking in Chicago and Boston, 1880-1920.
Trade Paper. University of Illinois Press. Champaign, IL. 1998.
416p. ISBN:0-252-06781-9, ISBN13: 978-0-252-06781-5.
Dewey:647.9573. LCCN:00-267506.
                                      Audience: **u.**

Furst, Peter T.   HV5822.H25.F87
Hallucinogens and Culture. Botanical Museum of Howard
University Staff (Illustrator). Paper Text. Chandler & Sharp
Publishers, Inc. Novato, CA. 1976. 208p. Cross-Cultural Themes
Ser. ISBN:0-88316-517-1, ISBN13: 978-0-88316-517-1.
Dewey:301.2/2. LCCN:75-025442.
                                      Audience: **l,u,f.** *B*

Gusfield, Joseph R.   HV5292
Symbolic Crusade: Status Politics and the American Temperance
Movement. Trade Cloth. Greenwood Publishing Group, Inc.
Portsmouth, NH. 1980. 198p. ISBN:0-313-22423-4, ISBN13:
978-0-313-22423-2. Dewey:363.4/1/0973. LCCN:80-013342.
                                      Audience: **l,u.** *B*

Himmelstein, Jerome L.   HV5822
The Strange Career of Marihuana: Politics and Ideology of Drug
Control in America, 94. Trade Cloth. Greenwood Publishing
Group, Inc. Portsmouth, NH. 1983. 192p. Contributions in

Political Science Ser., No. 94 ISBN:0-313-23517-1, ISBN13: 978-0-313-23517-7. Dewey:363.4/5. LCCN:82-012181.

Audience: **l,u.** *B*

Krauss, Melvyn B. &   **HV5825**
Lazear, Edward P. (Editors)
Searching for Alternatives: Drug-Control Policy in the United States. Trade Paper. Hoover Institution Press. Stanford, CA. 1993. 454p. Publication Ser., No. 406 ISBN:0-8179-9142-5, ISBN13: 978-0-8179-9142-5. Dewey:363.4/5/0973.

Audience: **u.** *Choice, 1992.*

Lender, Mark Edward &   **HV5292.L4 1987**
Martin, James K.
Drinking in America: A History. Trade Paper. Simon & Schuster. New York, NY. 1987. 256p. ISBN:0-02-918570-X, ISBN13: 978-0-02-918570-4. Dewey:394.1/3/0973. LCCN:86-032885.

Audience: **g,l.**

Leonard, Kenneth E. &   **HV5045.P74 1999**
Blane, Howard Thomas (Editors)
Psychological Theories of Drinking and Alcoholism. Ed. 2. Cloth over Boards. Guilford Publications, Inc. New York, NY. 1999. 467p. Substance Abuse Ser. ISBN:1-57230-410-3, ISBN13: 978-1-57230-410-9. Dewey:616.86/1/0019. LCCN:99-029558.

Audience: **l,u.** *Choice, 2000.*

Lobdell, Jared   **HV5035.L79 2004**
This Strange Illness: Alcoholism and Bill W. Trade Cloth. Aldine Transaction. Somerset, NJ. 2004. 403p. ISBN:0-202-30738-7, ISBN13: 978-0-202-30738-1. Dewey:362.292. LCCN:2003-020359.

Audience: **g,l.** *Choice, 2005.*

Macmillan Library   **HV5804.E53 2001**
Reference Staff
Encyclopedia of Drugs, Alcohol and Addictive Behavior, Set. Ed. 2. Trade Cloth. Thomson Gale. Farmington Hills, MI. 2000. lx, 1863p. ISBN:0-02-865541-9, ISBN13: 978-0-02-865541-3. Dewey:362.29/03. LCCN:00-046068.

Audience: **g,l,u,f.** *Choice, 2001.*

Murdock, Catherine Gilbert   **HV5292**
Domesticating Drink: Women, Men, and Alcohol in America, 1870-1940. Trade Paper. Johns Hopkins University Press. Baltimore, MD. 2002. 264p. Gender Relations in the American Experience Ser. ISBN:0-8018-6870-X, ISBN13: 978-0-8018-6870-2. Dewey:394.1/3/0973.

Audience: **l,u.**

Musto, David F. &   **HV5825.M845 2002**
Korsmeyer, Pamela
The Quest for Drug Control: Politics and Federal Policy in a Period of Increasing Substance Abuse, 1963-1981. Cloth over Boards. Yale University Press. Cumberland, RI. 2002. 338p. ISBN:0-300-09036-6, ISBN13: 978-0-300-09036-9. Dewey:362.29/156/097309045. LCCN:2002-016702.

Audience: **u,f.** *Choice, 2003.*

Platt, Jerome J.   **RC568.C6P53 1997**
Cocaine Addiction: Theory, Research and Treatment. Trade Cloth. Harvard University Press. Cambridge, MA. 1997. 480p. ISBN:0-674-13632-2, ISBN13: 978-0-674-13632-8. Dewey:616.86/47. LCCN:96-037435.

Audience: **l,u,f.** *Choice, 1998.*

Rorabaugh, W. J.   **HV5035**
The Alcoholic Republic: An American Tradition. Trade Paper. Oxford University Press, Inc. New York, NY. 1981. 318p. ISBN:0-19-502990-9, ISBN13: 978-0-19-502990-1. Dewey:362.2/92.

Audience: **l,u.** *B*

Rotskoff, Lori   **2002002093 [HV]**
Love on the Rocks: Men, Women, and Alcohol in Post-World War II America. Trade Cloth. University of North Carolina Press. Chapel Hill, NC. 2002. 336p. Gender and American Culture Ser. ISBN:0-8078-2728-2, ISBN13: 978-0-8078-2728-4. Dewey:394.1/3/09730904. LCCN:2002-002093.

Audience: **u.** *Choice, 2003.*

Saggers, Sherry & Gray,   **HV5198 .S34 1998**
Dennis
Dealing with Alcohol: Indigenous Usage in Australia, New Zealand and Canada. Cloth Text. Cambridge University Press. New York, NY. 1998. 248p. ISBN:0-521-62032-5, ISBN13: 978-0-521-62032-1. Dewey:362.292/089. LCCN:98-007278.

Audience: **u.** *Choice, 1999.*

Seixas, Judith S. & Youcha,   **HV5132.S44 1986**
Geraldine
Children of Alcoholism. Trade Paper. HarperCollins Publishers. New York, NY. 1986. 224p. ISBN:0-06-097020-0, ISBN13: 978-0-06-097020-8. Dewey:362.2/92. LCCN:85-045232.

Audience: **g,l.** *B*

Shaw, Victor N.   **HV4999**
Substance Use and Abuse: Sociological Perspectives. Trade Cloth. Greenwood Publishing Group, Inc. Portsmouth, NH. 2002. 288p. ISBN:0-275-97139-2, ISBN13: 978-0-275-97139-7. Dewey:362.29/1/0973. LCCN:2002-067938.

Audience: **l,u,f.** *Choice, 2003.*

Stephens, Richard C.   **HV5825.S743 1991**
The Street Addict Role: A Theory of Heroin Addiction. Marshall B. Clinard (Introduction by). Cloth Text. State University of New York Press. Albany, NY. 1991. 223p. SUNY Series, the New Inequalities ISBN:0-7914-0619-9, ISBN13: 978-0-7914-0619-9. Dewey:362.29/3/0973. LCCN:90-039205.

Audience: **u.** *Choice, 1992.*

Weissman, James C. &   **HV5825.C74**
DuPont, Robert L. (Editors)
Criminal Justice and Drugs: The Unresolved Connection. Trade Cloth. Associated Faculty Press, Inc. New York, NY. 1982. xii, 204p. Multidisciplinary Studies in Law and Jurisprudence ISBN:0-8046-9291-2, ISBN13: 978-0-8046-9291-5. Dewey:363.4/5. LCCN:81-003701.

Audience: **u.** *B*

Psychological and Physical Disorders > Speech and Language Disorders

Anderson, Noma B. &   **RC423.H847 2006**
Shames, George H.
Human Communication Disorders: An Introduction. Ed. 7. Trade Paper. Allyn & Bacon, Inc. Boston, MA. 2005. 656p. ISBN:0-205-45622-7, ISBN13: 978-0-205-45622-2. Dewey:616.85/5. LCCN:2005-048748.

Audience: **l.**

Bernthal, John E. &   **RC424.7.B47 2004**
Bankson, Nicholas W.
Articulation and Phonological Disorders. Ed. 5. Trade Cloth.
Allyn & Bacon, Inc. Boston, MA. 2003. 448p.
ISBN:0-205-34790-8, ISBN13: 978-0-205-34790-2.
Dewey:616.85/5. LCCN:2003-101684.
                          Audience: **u,f.**

Bloodstein, Oliver   **RC424 .B56 1993**
Stuttering: The Search for a Cause and Cure. Ed. 1. Trade
Paper. Allyn & Bacon, Inc. Boston, MA. 1992. 216p.
ISBN:0-205-13845-4, ISBN13: 978-0-205-13845-6.
Dewey:616.85/54. LCCN:92-011153.
                Audience: **l,u.** *Choice, 1994.*

Jacyna, L. S.   **RC425.J33 2000**
Lost Words: Narratives of Language and the Brain, 1825-1926.
Trade Cloth. Princeton University Press. Princeton, NJ. 2000.
254p. ISBN:0-691-00413-7, ISBN13: 978-0-691-00413-6.
Dewey:616.85/52/009. LCCN:99-089724.
               Audience: **u,f.** *Choice, 2001.*

Kent, Raymond D. (Editor)   **RC423.M56 2003**
The MIT Encyclopedia of Communication Disorders. Trade
Cloth. MIT Press. Cambridge, MA. 2003. 648p. Bradford Bks.
ISBN:0-262-11278-7, ISBN13: 978-0-262-11278-9.
Dewey:616.85/5/003. LCCN:2003-059941.
               Audience: **u,f.** *Choice, 2004.*

Leonard, Laurence B.   **RJ496.L35L46 2000**
Children with Specific Language Impairment. Trade Paper. MIT
Press. Cambridge, MA. 2000. 352p. Language, Speech and
Communication Ser. ISBN:0-262-62136-3, ISBN13:
978-0-262-62136-6. Dewey:618.92/855. LCCN:00-268670.
               Audience: **u.** *Choice, 1998.*

Minifie, Fred D.   **RC423**
Introduction to Communication Science and Disorders. Ed. 2.
Trade Paper. Thomson Learning. Independence, KY. 2000. 708p.
ISBN:1-56593-960-3, ISBN13: 978-1-56593-960-8.
Dewey:616.85/5.
                                Audience: **l.**

Starkweather, C. Woodruff   **RC424.S693 1997**
& Givens-Ackerman, Janet
Stuttering. Paper Text. PRO-ED, Inc. Austin, TX. 1996. 215p.
Studies in Communicative Disorders ISBN:0-89079-699-8,
ISBN13: 978-0-89079-699-3. Dewey:616.85/54.
LCCN:96-020276.
               Audience: **l,u.** *Choice, 1997.*

Vinson, Betsy Partin   **RC423**
Language Disorders Across the Lifespan. Ed. 2. Paper Text.
Thomson Delmar Learning. Albany, NY. 2006. 576p.
ISBN:1-4180-0954-7, ISBN13: 978-1-4180-0954-0.
Dewey:616.85/5. LCCN:2006-018327.
                       Audience: **l,u.**

Worrall, Linda & Hickson,   **RC429.W67 2003**
Louise M.
Communication Disability in Aging: Prevention to Intervention.
Paper Text. Thomson Delmar Learning. Albany, NY. 2003.
420p. ISBN:0-7693-0015-4, ISBN13: 978-0-7693-0015-3.
Dewey:618.97/6855. LCCN:2002-031512.
                       Audience: **u.**

Mental Health Treatment and Prevention > Cognitive Therapy

Beck, Aaron T., et al.   **RC554.B43 2003**
Cognitive Therapy of Personality Disorders. Ed. 2. Denise D.
Davis & Arthur Freeman (Authors). Cloth over Boards. Guilford
Publications, Inc. New York, NY. 2003. 412p.
ISBN:1-57230-856-7, ISBN13: 978-1-57230-856-5.
Dewey:616.85/8. LCCN:2003-017118.
               Audience: **u,f.** *Choice, 1991.*

Ellis, Albert   **RC489.R3E4648 2004**
Rational Emotive Behavior Therapy: It Works for Me--It Can
Work for You. Trade Paper. Prometheus Books, Publishers.
Amherst, NY. 2004. 270p. ISBN:1-59102-184-7, ISBN13:
978-1-59102-184-1. Dewey:616.89/14. LCCN:2004-003664.
                       Audience: **g,l.**

Hersen, Michel (Editor)   **RC489.B4E485 2005**
Encyclopedia of Behavior Modification and Cognitive Behavior
Therapy:Volume I: Adult Clinical Applications Volume II: Child
Clinical Applications Volume III: Educational Applications.
Trade Cloth. SAGE Publications, Inc. Thousand Oaks, CA.
2005. 1856p. ISBN:0-7619-2747-6, ISBN13:
978-0-7619-2747-1. Dewey:616.89/142/003.
LCCN:2004-022910.
               Audience: **u,f.** *Choice, 2005.*

Kingdon, David G. &   **RC514.K5653 2005**
Turkington, Douglas
Cognitive Therapy of Schizophrenia. Cloth over Boards.
Guilford Publications, Inc. New York, NY. 2004. 219p.
Treatment Manuals for Real World Clinici Ser.
ISBN:1-59385-104-9, ISBN13: 978-1-59385-104-0.
Dewey:616.89/806. LCCN:2004-012738.
                       Audience: **u,f.**

Martell, Christopher R.,   **RC451.4.G39M37 2004**
et al.
Cognitive-Behavioral Therapies with Lesbian, Gay and Bisexual
Clients. Steven A. Safren & Stacey E. Prince (Authors). Cloth
over Boards. Guilford Publications, Inc. New York, NY. 2003.
263p. ISBN:1-57230-954-7, ISBN13: 978-1-57230-954-8.
Dewey:616.89/142/08664. LCCN:2003-017548.
               Audience: **u,f.** *Choice, 2004.*

McCullough, James P. Jr.   **RC537**
Treatment for Chronic Depression: Cognitive Behavioral
Analysis System of Psychotherapy (CBASP). Cloth over Boards.
Guilford Publications, Inc. New York, NY. 1999. 326p.
ISBN:1-57230-527-4, ISBN13: 978-1-57230-527-4.
Dewey:616.85270651.
               Audience: **u,f.** *Choice, 2000.*

Nielsen, Stevan Lars &   **RC489.R3N54 2001**
Johnson, W. Brad
Counseling and Psychotherapy with Religious Persons: A
Rational Emotive Behavior Therapy Approach. Cloth over
Boards. Lawrence Erlbaum Associates, Inc. Mahwah, NJ. 2001.
296p. ISBN:0-8058-2878-8, ISBN13: 978-0-8058-2878-8.
Dewey:616.89/14. LCCN:2001-018771.
               Audience: **u,f.** *Choice, 2001.*

Persons, Jacqueline B., et al.   **RC537.P436 2001**
Essential Components of Cognitive-Behavior Therapy for
Depression. Joan Davidson & Michael A. Tompkins (Authors).

Trade Cloth. American Psychological Association. Washington, DC. 2000. x, 256p. ISBN:1-55798-697-5, ISBN13: 978-1-55798-697-9. Dewey:616.85/270651. LCCN:00-038045.

Audience: **u,f.**

Salkovskis, Paul M. (Editor)   **RC489.C63**
Frontiers of Cognitive Therapy. Trade Paper. Guilford Publications, Inc. New York, NY. 1997. 553p. ISBN:1-57230-113-9, ISBN13: 978-1-57230-113-9. Dewey:616.8/9/142.

Audience: **u.**

Schwebel, Andrew I. &   **RC488.5.S384 1994**
   Fine, Mark A.
Understanding and Helping Families: A Cognitive-Behavioral Approach. Cloth Text. Lawrence Erlbaum Associates, Inc. Mahwah, NJ. 1994. 224p. ISBN:0-8058-1225-3, ISBN13: 978-0-8058-1225-1. Dewey:616.89/156. LCCN:93-032023.

Audience: **u,f.** *Choice, 1994.*

Zarb, Janet M.   **RJ505.C63**
Cognitive-Behavioral Assessment and Therapy with Adolescents. Paper over Boards. Brunner-Routledge. Philadelphia, PA. 1992. 272p. ISBN:0-87630-685-7, ISBN13: 978-0-87630-685-7. Dewey:616.89/142/0835. LCCN:92-016165.

Audience: **u.** *Choice, 1993.*

Mental Health Treatment and Prevention > Behavior Therapy and Behavior Modification

Albert Ellis Institute   **RC489.R3**
☐ Albert Ellis Institute.
http://www.rebt.org/

Audience: **g,l,u,f.**

Ammerman, Robert T. &   **RJ505.B4**
   Hersen, Michel (Editors)
Handbook of Child Behavior Therapy in the Psychiatric Setting. Trade Paper. John Wiley & Sons, Inc. Hoboken, NJ. 2001. 528p. Personality Processes Ser., Vol. 205 ISBN:0-471-11393-X, ISBN13: 978-0-471-11393-5. Dewey:618.92/89142.

Audience: **u,f.**

Association for Behavioral   **RC489.B4**
   and Cognitive Therapies
☐ Association for Behavioral and Cognitive Therapies.
http://www.aabt.org/

Audience: **u,f.**

Austin, John & Carr,   **RC473.B43H36 2000**
   James E.
Handbook of Applied Behavior Analysis. Trade Paper. Context Press. Reno, NV. 2000. 488p. ISBN:1-878978-34-9, ISBN13: 978-1-878978-34-9. Dewey:616.89/075. LCCN:00-052362.

Audience: **u,f.**

Bandura, Albert   **RC489.B4.B3**
Principles of Behavior Modification. Trade Cloth. Holt, Rinehart & Winston. Austin, TX. 1969. ix, 677p. ISBN:0-03-081151-1, ISBN13: 978-0-03-081151-7. Dewey:616.89/1. LCCN:74-081173.

Audience: **f.** *B*

Behavior Analyst   **RC473.B43**
   Certification Board
☐ Behavior Analyst Certification Board.
http://www.bacb.com/

Audience: **u,f.**

Bellack, Alan S. (Editor)   **RC489.B4I54 1990**
International Handbook of Behavior Modification and Therapy. Ed. 2. Trade Cloth. Basic Books. New York, NY. 1989. 908p. ISBN:0-306-43348-6, ISBN13: 978-0-306-43348-1. Dewey:616.89/142. LCCN:90-006900.

Audience: **u,f.**

Cambridge Center for   **BF199**
   Behavioral Studies
☐ Cambridge Center for Behavioral Studies.
http://www.behavior.org

Audience: **u,f.**

Cautela, Joseph R. & Ishaq,   **RC489.B4C673 1996**
   Waris (Editors)
Contemporary Issues in Behavior Therapy: Improving the Human Condition. Trade Cloth. Basic Books. New York, NY. 1996. 432p. Applied Clinical Psychology Ser. ISBN:0-306-45168-9, ISBN13: 978-0-306-45168-3. Dewey:616.8/9/142. LCCN:96-018531.

Audience: **u,f.**

Dunlap, Knight   **BF335 .D8**
Habits: Their Making and Unmaking. Trade Paper. Liveright Publishing Corporation. New York, NY. 1949. 336p. ISBN:0-87140-267-X, ISBN13: 978-0-87140-267-7. Dewey:153.1/5. LCCN:77-184102.

Audience: **g,l,u,f.**

Eysenck, Hans J. & Martin,   **RC489.B4T516 1987**
   I.
Theoretical Foundations of Behavior Therapy. Trade Cloth. Basic Books. New York, NY. 1987. 494p. Perspectives on Individual Differences Ser. ISBN:0-306-42634-X, ISBN13: 978-0-306-42634-6. Dewey:616.89/142. LCCN:87-017168.

Audience: **u,f.**

Friedman, Howard S.   **RA790.5.E53 1998**
   (Editor), et al.
Encyclopedia of Mental Health, Set. Nancy E. Adler, Ross D. Parke, Christopher Peterson, Robert Roskoski Jr., Ralf Schwarzer, Roxane Cohen Silver & David Spiegel (Editors). Trade Cloth. Elsevier Science & Technology Books. Saint Louis, MO. 1998. 2398p. ISBN:0-12-226675-7, ISBN13: 978-0-12-226675-1. Dewey:616.89/003. LCCN:98-084208.

Audience: **g,l,u,f.** *Choice, 1998.*

Hersen, Michel   **RC489.B4C578 2002**
Clinical Behavior Therapy: Adults and Children. Trade Cloth. John Wiley & Sons, Inc. Hoboken, NJ. 2002. 513p. ISBN:0-471-39258-8, ISBN13: 978-0-471-39258-3. Dewey:616.89/142. LCCN:2001-058148.

Audience: **u,f.**

Hersen, Michel (Editor)   **RC489.B4E485 2005**
Encyclopedia of Behavior Modification and Cognitive Behavior Therapy:Volume I: Adult Clinical Applications Volume II: Child Clinical Applications Volume III: Educational Applications. Trade Cloth. SAGE Publications, Inc. Thousand Oaks, CA. 2005. 1856p. ISBN:0-7619-2747-6, ISBN13:

978-0-7619-2747-1. Dewey:616.89/142/003.
LCCN:2004-022910.

Audience: **u,f.** *Choice, 2005.*

Hersen, Michel & Bellack,   RC467.C597 1998
  Alan S. (Editors)
Comprehensive Clinical Psychology, Set. Trade Cloth. Elsevier
Science & Technology Books. Saint Louis, MO. 1998. 7000p.
ISBN:0-08-042707-3, ISBN13: 978-0-08-042707-2.
Dewey:616.89. LCCN:97-050185.

Audience: **u,f.** *Choice, 1999.*

Hersen, Michel, et al.   BF637.B4
Progress in Behavior Modification, Vol. 30. Richard M. Eisler &
Peter M. Miller (Authors). Paper Text. Thomson Wadsworth.
Belmont, CA. 1995. 224p. Special Education Ser.
ISBN:0-534-26304-6, ISBN13: 978-0-534-26304-1.
Dewey:153.8/5.

Audience: **u,f.**

Lee, David L. & Axelrod,   BF637.B4A94 2005
  Saul
Behavior Modification: Basic Principles. Ed. 3. Trade Paper.
PRO-ED, Inc. Austin, TX. 2005. x, 149p. Managing Behavior
Ser. ISBN:1-4164-0058-3, ISBN13: 978-1-4164-0058-5.
Dewey:153.8/5. LCCN:2004-062484.

Audience: **u,f.**

Mills, John A.   BF199.M485 1998
Control: A History of Behavioral Psychology. Trade Cloth. New
York University Press. New York, NY. 1998. 246p.
ISBN:0-8147-5611-5, ISBN13: 978-0-8147-5611-9.
Dewey:150.19/43/09. LCCN:98-019699.

Audience: **u,f.** *Choice, 1999.*

O'Donohue, William   RC489.B4L39 1998
Learning and Behavior Therapy. Ed. 1. Trade Paper. Allyn &
Bacon, Inc. Boston, MA. 1997. 568p. ISBN:0-205-18609-2,
ISBN13: 978-0-205-18609-9. Dewey:616.89/142.
LCCN:97-010769.

Audience: **u,f.**

O'Donohue, William T.   RC489.B4H55 2001
  (Editor)
A History of the Behavioral Therapies: Founders' Personal
Theories. Trade Paper. Context Press. Reno, NV. 2001. 357p.
ISBN:1-878978-40-3, ISBN13: 978-1-878978-40-0.
Dewey:616.89/142/09. LCCN:2001-047081.

Audience: **u,f.**

Rehabilitation Research and   RC489.B4
  Training Center, University of South Florida
☐ Rehabilitation Research and Training Center, University of
South Florida.
http://rrtcpbs.fmhi.usf.edu/

Audience: **u,f.**

Van Houten, R. & Axelrod,   RC489.B4B426 1993
  Saul (Editors)
Behavior Analysis and Treatment. Trade Cloth. Basic Books.
New York, NY. 1993. 406p. Applied Clinical Psychology Ser.
ISBN:0-306-44371-6, ISBN13: 978-0-306-44371-8.
Dewey:616.89142. LCCN:93-004431.

Audience: **u,f.**

Wachtel, Paul L.   RC489.B4W32 1997
Psychoanalysis, Behavior Therapy, and the Relational World.
Trade Cloth. American Psychological Association. Washington,

DC. 1997. 485p. APA Psychotherapy Integration Book Ser., Vol.
1 ISBN:1-55798-409-3, ISBN13: 978-1-55798-409-8.
Dewey:616.89/142. LCCN:96-053417.

Audience: **u,f.** *Choice, 1997.*

Watson, T. Steuart &   RJ505.B4H346 1998
  Gresham, Frank M. (Editors)
Handbook of Child Behavior Therapy. Trade Cloth. Basic
Books. New York, NY. 1997. 524p. Issues in Clinical Child
Psychology Ser. ISBN:0-306-45548-X, ISBN13:
978-0-306-45548-3. Dewey:618.92/89142. LCCN:97-040442.

Audience: **u,f.**

Wolpe, Joseph   RC489.C63
The Practice of Behavior Therapy. Ed. 3. Cloth Text. Elsevier
Science & Technology Books. Saint Louis, MO. 1982. 425p.
ISBN:0-08-027165-0, ISBN13: 978-0-08-027165-1.
Dewey:616.89/142.

Audience: **u,f.**

Wolpe, Joseph &   RC480.5
  Lazarus, A.
Behavior Therapy Techniques: Guide to the Treatment of
Neuroses. Trade Cloth. Pergamon Press. Kidlington, 1966.
ISBN:0-08-011793-7, ISBN13: 978-0-08-011793-5.
Dewey:616.89. LCCN:66-018405.

Audience: **u,f.**

Mental Health Treatment and Prevention > Group and Family Therapy

Basham, Kathryn Karusaitis   RC488.5.B365 2004
  & Miehls, Dennis
Transforming the Legacy: Couple Therapy with Survivors of
Childhood Trauma. Trade Cloth. Columbia University Press.
New York, NY. 2004. 368p. ISBN:0-231-12342-6, ISBN13:
978-0-231-12342-6. Dewey:616.89/1562. LCCN:2004-052788.

Audience: **u,f.** *Choice, 2005.*

Boyd-Franklin, Nancy   RC451.5.N4B69 2003
Black Families in Therapy: Understanding the African American
Experience. Ed. 2. Cloth over Boards. Guilford Publications,
Inc. New York, NY. 2003. 368p. ISBN:1-57230-619-X, ISBN13:
978-1-57230-619-6. Dewey:616.89/156/08996073.
LCCN:2003-009245.

Audience: **l,u,f.**

Caffaro, John V. &   RJ507.S53C34 1998
  Conn-Caffaro, Allison
Sibling Abuse Trauma: Assessment and Intervention Strategies
for Children, Families and Adults. Trade Cloth. Haworth Press,
Incorporated, The. Binghamton, NY. 1998. 303p.
ISBN:0-7890-6007-8, ISBN13: 978-0-7890-6007-5.
Dewey:616.85/822. LCCN:98-008166.

Audience: **u.** *Choice, 1999.*

Carlson, Jon & Sperry, Len   RC488.5.D59 1998
  (Editors)
The Disordered Couple. Paper over Boards. Brunner-Routledge.
Philadelphia, PA. 1997. 342p. ISBN:0-87630-815-9, ISBN13:
978-0-87630-815-8. Dewey:616.89/156. LCCN:97-024085.

Audience: **u.** *Choice, 1998.*

Ganong, Lawrence H. &
Coleman, Marilyn HQ759.92.S7294 2004
Stepfamily Relationships: Development, Dynamics, and
Interventions. Trade Cloth. Springer. New York, NY. 2003.
284p. ISBN:0-306-47997-4, ISBN13: 978-0-306-47997-7.
Dewey:306.874/7. LCCN:2003-060446.

Audience: **u,f.** *Choice, 2004.*

Guerin, Philip J. Jr. (Editor) RC488.5 .F35
Family Therapy: Theory and Practice. Cloth Text. Gardner
Press, Inc. Palm Beach Gardens, FL. 1976. 566p.
ISBN:0-89876-020-8, ISBN13: 978-0-89876-020-0.
Dewey:616.8/915. LCCN:76-008409.

Audience: **u.**

Haley, Jay & Hoffman,
Lynn RC488.5.H3213 1994
Techniques of Family Therapy. Trade Cloth. Rowman &
Littlefield Publishers, Inc. Lanham, MD. 1994. 494p.
ISBN:1-56821-329-8, ISBN13: 978-1-56821-329-3.
Dewey:616.89/156. LCCN:94-072313.

Audience: **u,f.**

Johnson, Susan M. RC488.5.J589 2002
Emotionally Focused Couple Therapy with Trauma Survivors:
Strengthening Attachment Bonds. Cloth over Boards. Guilford
Publications, Inc. New York, NY. 2002. 228p. Family Therapy
Ser. ISBN:1-57230-735-8, ISBN13: 978-1-57230-735-3.
Dewey:616.89/156. LCCN:2001-056916.

Audience: **u,f.**

Johnston, Janet R. &
Campbell, Linda E. G. HQ834.J45
Impasses of Divorce: The Dynamics and Resolution of Family
Conflict. Judith S. Wallerstein (Foreword by). Trade Paper.
Simon & Schuster. New York, NY. 1999. 272p.
ISBN:0-684-87101-7, ISBN13: 978-0-684-87101-1.
Dewey:306.89. LCCN:88-011224.

Audience: **u.** *Choice, 1989.*

L'Abate, Luciano RC454.L29 2005
Personality in Intimate Relationships: Socialization and
Psychopathology. Trade Cloth. Springer. New York, NY. 2005.
XVIII, 482p. ISBN:0-387-22605-2, ISBN13:
978-0-387-22605-7. Dewey:158.2/4. LCCN:2004-061909.

Audience: **l,u.** *Choice, 2005.*

McGoldrick, Monica
(Editor), et al. RC451.5.A2E83 2005
Ethnicity and Family Therapy. Ed. 3. Nydia Garcia-Preto & Joe
Giordano (Editors). Saddle Stitched, Cloth over Boards, Dust
Jacket. Guilford Publications, Inc. New York, NY. 2005. 796p.
ISBN:1-59385-020-4, ISBN13: 978-1-59385-020-3.
Dewey:362.2/089/00973. LCCN:2004-029338.

Audience: **u,f.** *B Choice, 1997.*

Micucci, Joseph A. RJ503
The Adolescent in Family Therapy: Breaking the Cycle of
Conflict and Control. Trade Paper. Guilford Publications, Inc.
New York, NY. 2000. 336p. Family Therapy Ser.
ISBN:1-57230-588-6, ISBN13: 978-1-57230-588-5.
Dewey:616.89/156/0835.

Audience: **u.** *Choice, 1999.*

Minuchin, Salvador &
Fishman, H. Charles RC488.5
Family Therapy Techniques. Trade Cloth. Harvard University
Press. Cambridge, MA. 1990. 320p. ISBN:0-674-29410-6,

ISBN13: 978-0-674-29410-3. Dewey:616.89/156.
LCCN:80-025392.

Audience: **u,f.** *B*

Nichols, Michael P. &
Schwartz, Richard C. RC488.5.N53 2007
Family Therapy: Concepts and Methods. Ed. 7. Cloth Text.
Allyn & Bacon, Inc. Boston, MA. 2005. 528p.
ISBN:0-205-47809-3, ISBN13: 978-0-205-47809-5.
Dewey:616.89/156. LCCN:2005-051218.

Audience: **u.** *B*

Paolino, Thomas J. &
McCrady, Barbara S. (Editors) RC488.5.M365
Marriage and Marital Therapy: Psychoanalytic, Behavioral and
Systems Theory Perspectives. Paper over Boards.
Brunner-Routledge. Philadelphia, PA. 1986. 612p.
ISBN:0-87630-171-5, ISBN13: 978-0-87630-171-5.
Dewey:362.8/286. LCCN:78-017398.

Audience: **u.** *B*

Papp, Peggy RC488.5
The Process of Change. Trade Paper. Guilford Publications, Inc.
New York, NY. 1994. 248p. Family Therapy Ser.
ISBN:0-89862-501-7, ISBN13: 978-0-89862-501-1.
Dewey:616.8/9156. LCCN:83-012814.

Audience: **u.** *B*

Revenson, Tracey A., et al. RC488.5.C64343 2005
Couples Coping with Stress: Emerging Perspectives on Dyadic
Coping. Karen Kayser & Guy Bodenmann (Authors). Trade
Cloth. American Psychological Association. Washington, DC.
2005. 256p. APA Science Volumes Ser. ISBN:1-59147-204-0,
ISBN13: 978-1-59147-204-9. Dewey:616.89/1562.
LCCN:2004-020293.

Audience: **u,f.** *Choice, 2005.*

Robin, Arthur L. & Foster,
Sharon L. RJ503.R63 1989
Negotiating Parent-Adolescent Conflict: A Behavioral-Family
Systems Approach. Cloth over Boards. Guilford Publications,
Inc. New York, NY. 1989. 338p. Family Therapy Ser.
ISBN:0-89862-072-4, ISBN13: 978-0-89862-072-6.
Dewey:616.89/022. LCCN:87-031502.

Audience: **u.** *Choice, 1989.*

Sanders, Robert &
Campling, Jo BF723.S43S159 2004
Sibling Relationships: Theory and Issues for Practice. Cloth over
Boards. Palgrave Macmillan. New York, NY. 2004. 240p.
ISBN:0-333-96410-1, ISBN13: 978-0-333-96410-1.
Dewey:306.875. LCCN:2003-062092.

Audience: **u.** *Choice, 2004.*

Schwebel, Andrew I. &
Fine, Mark A. RC488.5.S384 1994
Understanding and Helping Families: A Cognitive-Behavioral
Approach. Cloth Text. Lawrence Erlbaum Associates, Inc.
Mahwah, NJ. 1994. 224p. ISBN:0-8058-1225-3, ISBN13:
978-0-8058-1225-1. Dewey:616.89/156. LCCN:93-032023.

Audience: **u,f.** *Choice, 1994.*

Seligman, Milton & Darling,
Rosalyn Benjamin HV888.5
Ordinary Families, Special Children: A Systems Approach to
Childhood Disability. Ed. 2. Trade Paper. Guilford Publications,

Inc. New York, NY. 1999. 324p. ISBN:1-57230-466-9, ISBN13: 978-1-57230-466-6. Dewey:362.4/043/083.

Audience: **u.** *Choice, 1990.*

Sherman, Robert, et al.   **RC488.S47 1991**
Solving Problems in Couples and Family Therapy: Techniques and Tactics. Paul Oresky & Yvonne B. Rountree (Authors). Paper over Boards. Brunner-Routledge. Philadelphia, PA. 1991. 336p. ISBN:0-87630-647-4, ISBN13: 978-0-87630-647-5. Dewey:616.89/156. LCCN:91-025757.

Audience: **u,f.** *Choice, 1992.*

Solomon, Judith Y.   **RJ507.A77A87 1999**
Attachment Disorganization. Carol George (Editor). Cloth over Boards. Guilford Publications, Inc. New York, NY. 1999. 420p. ISBN:1-57230-480-4, ISBN13: 978-1-57230-480-2. Dewey:618.92/89. LCCN:99-023365.

Audience: **u.** *Choice, 2000.*

Williamson, Donald S.   **RC488.5**
The Intimacy Paradox: Personal Authority in the Family System. Trade Paper. Guilford Publications, Inc. New York, NY. 2002. 305p. Guilford Family Therapy Ser. ISBN:1-57230-815-X, ISBN13: 978-1-57230-815-2. Dewey:616.89/156.

Audience: **u.** *Choice, 1992.*

Yalom, Irvin D. & Leszcz, Molyn   **RC488.Y3 2005**
The Theory and Practice of Group Psychotherapy. Ed. 5. Trade Cloth. Basic Books. New York, NY. 2005. 688p. ISBN:0-465-09284-5, ISBN13: 978-0-465-09284-0. Dewey:616.89/152. LCCN:2005-000056.

Audience: **u,f.**

Mental Health Treatment and Prevention > Self Help Groups

Alcoholics Anonymous World Services, Inc., Staff   **HV5275.W15 1976**
Alcoholics Anonymous. Trade Cloth. Alcoholics Anonymous World Services, Inc. New York, NY. 1939. 400p. ISBN:0-916856-00-3, ISBN13: 978-0-916856-00-7. Dewey:362.2/92. LCCN:76-004029.

Audience: **g,l,u,f.**

Borkman, Thomasina J.   **HV547.B67 1999**
Understanding Self-Help/Mutual-Aid: Experiential Learning in the Commons. Cloth Text. Rutgers University Press. Piscataway, NJ. 1999. 260p. ISBN:0-8135-2629-9, ISBN13: 978-0-8135-2629-4. Dewey:361.4. LCCN:98-050649.

Audience: **u,f.** *Choice, 2000.*

Humphreys, Keith   **RC564.H85 2004**
Circles of Recovery: Self-Help Organizations for Addictions. Griffith Edwards (Contribution by). Trade Cloth. Cambridge University Press. New York, NY. 2003. 238p. International Research Monographs in the Addictions ISBN:0-521-79277-0, ISBN13: 978-0-521-79277-6. Dewey:362.29/18. LCCN:2003-043935.

Audience: **u,f.**

Katz, Alfred H. *in America*   **HV547.K369 1993**
The Self-Help Movement. Trade Cloth. Macmillan Publishing Company, Inc. Old Tappan, NJ. 1992. 250p. Social Movements Past and Present Ser. ISBN:0-8057-3877-0, ISBN13: 978-0-8057-3877-3. Dewey:361.4. LCCN:92-036285.

Audience: **l,f.**

Katz, Alfred H. (Editor)   **RA776.S4536 1991**
Self-Help: Concepts and Applications. C. Everett Koop (Foreword by). Paper Text. Charles Press Publishers. Philadelphia, PA. 1991. 336p. ISBN:0-914783-56-4, ISBN13: 978-0-914783-56-5. Dewey:362.1/0425. LCCN:91-028890.

Audience: **u.** *Choice, 1993.*

McGee, Micki   **BF632.M36 2005**
Self-Help, Inc: Makeover Culture in American Life. Trade Cloth. Oxford University Press, Inc. New York, NY. 2005. 304p. ISBN:0-19-517124-1, ISBN13: 978-0-19-517124-2. Dewey:158/.0973. LCCN:2004-024905.

Audience: **u,f.** *Choice, 2006.*

Norcross, John C., et al.   **RA790.6.A94 2003**
Authoritative Guide to Self-Help Resources in Mental Health, Revised Edition. John W. Santrock, Linda F. Campbell, Thomas P. Smith, Robert Sommer & Edward L. Zuckerman (Authors). Cloth over Boards. Guilford Publications, Inc. New York, NY. 2003. 468p. The Clinician's Toolbox Ser. ISBN:1-57230-896-6, ISBN13: 978-1-57230-896-1. Dewey:362.2/0973. LCCN:2003-002772.

Audience: **g,l,u.**

Powell, Thomas J. (Editor)   **HV547.U53 1994**
Understanding the Self-Help Organization: Frameworks and Findings. Trade Cloth. SAGE Publications, Inc. Thousand Oaks, CA. 1994. 346p. ISBN:0-8039-5487-5, ISBN13: 978-0-8039-5487-8. Dewey:361.4. LCCN:94-003376.

Audience: **u,f.**

Riessman, Frank & Carroll, David   **HV547.R55 1995**
Redefining Self-Help in the Human Services: Policy and Practice. Trade Cloth. John Wiley & Sons, Inc. Hoboken, NJ. 1995. 236p. Health and Social and Behavioral Sciences Ser. ISBN:0-7879-0066-4, ISBN13: 978-0-7879-0066-3. Dewey:362.1/0425. LCCN:94-038982.

Audience: **u,f.**

Steinberg, Dominique Moyse   **HV45.S783 2004**
The Mutual-Aid Approach to Working with Groups: Helping People Help One Another. Ed. 2. Trade Cloth. Haworth Press, Incorporated, The. Binghamton, NY. 2004. 274p. ISBN:0-7890-1461-0, ISBN13: 978-0-7890-1461-0. Dewey:361.4. LCCN:2004-007025.

Audience: **u,f.**

Watson, David L. & Tharp, Roland G.   **BF637.B4W38 2002**
Self-Directed Behavior: Self-Modification for Personal Adjustment. Ed. 8. Paper Text. Thomson Wadsworth. Belmont, CA. 2001. 360p. ISBN:0-534-52736-1, ISBN13: 978-0-534-52736-5. Dewey:158.1. LCCN:2001-035457.

Audience: **u,f.**

White, Barbara J. & Madara, Edward J. (Editors)   **HV547**
Self-Help Group Sourcebook: Your Guide to Community and Online Support Groups. Ed. 7. Alfred H. Katz (Foreword by),

Phyllis Silverman (Introduction by). Otabind. Saint Clare's Health System. Cedar Knolls, NJ. 2002. 448p. ISBN:1-930683-00-6, ISBN13: 978-1-930683-00-6. Dewey:374.22.

Audience: **g.**

Wuthnow, Robert   **BL2525.W885 1994**
Sharing the Journey: Support Groups and America's New Quest for Community. Trade Cloth. Simon & Schuster. New York, NY. 1994. 463p. ISBN:0-02-935625-3, ISBN13: 978-0-02-935625-8. Dewey:302.3/4. LCCN:93-027320.

Audience: **g,l,u,f.** *Choice, 1994.*

Mental Health Treatment and Prevention > Promotion and Maintenance of Health and Wellness

Aspinwall, Lisa G. &   **BF121.P763 2002**
Staudinger, Ursula M. (Editors)
A Psychology of Human Strengths: Fundamental Questions and Future Directions for a Positive Psychology. Trade Cloth. American Psychological Association. Washington, DC. 2002. 369p. ISBN:1-55798-931-1, ISBN13: 978-1-55798-931-4. Dewey:150.19/8. LCCN:2002-008033.

Audience: **u,f.** *Choice, 2003.*

Diener, Ed & Suh,   **B187.H3C85 2003**
Eunkook M. (Editors)
Culture and Subjective Well-Being. Trade Paper. MIT Press. Cambridge, MA. 2003. 365p. Well Being and Quality of Life Ser. ISBN:0-262-54146-7, ISBN13: 978-0-262-54146-6. Dewey:306.

Audience: **u,f.**

Haidt, Jonathan   **BJ1481.H14 2005**
The Happiness Hypothesis: Finding Modern Truth in Ancient Wisdom. Trade Cloth. Basic Books. New York, NY. 2005. 320p. ISBN:0-465-02801-2, ISBN13: 978-0-465-02801-6. Dewey:170. LCCN:2005-021163.

Audience: **l,u.**

Kahneman, Daniel (Editor),   **BF637.C5F68 1999**
et al.
Well-Being: The Foundations of Hedonic Psychology. Edward Diener & Norbert Schwarz (Editors). Trade Cloth. Russell Sage Foundation. New York, NY. 1999. xii, 593p. ISBN:0-87154-424-5, ISBN13: 978-0-87154-424-7. Dewey:152.4/2. LCCN:98-032295.

Audience: **l,u,f.**

Keyes, Corey L. M. &   **BF20.F57 2003**
Haidt, Jonathan (Editors)
Flourishing: Positive Psychology and the Life Well-Lived. Trade Cloth. American Psychological Association. Washington, DC. 2002. xx, 335p. ISBN:1-55798-930-3, ISBN13: 978-1-55798-930-7. Dewey:158. LCCN:2002-033219.

Audience: **u,f.**

Peterson, Christopher &   **BF818.P38 2004**
Seligman, Martin E. P.
Character Strengths and Virtues: A Handbook and Classification. Trade Cloth. Oxford University Press, Inc. New York, NY. 2004. 814p. ISBN:0-19-516701-5, ISBN13: 978-0-19-516701-6. Dewey:155.2/32. LCCN:2003-024320.

Audience: **u,f.** *Choice, 2004.*

Snyder, C. R. & Lopez, S. J.   **BF121.H212 2005**
(Editors)
Handbook of Positive Psychology. Trade Paper. Oxford University Press, Inc. New York, NY. 2005. 848p. ISBN:0-19-518279-0, ISBN13: 978-0-19-518279-8. Dewey:150.19/8. LCCN:2004-057524.

Audience: **u,f.**

Mental Health Treatment and Prevention > Community and Social Services

Advocates for Youth   **HV1437**
Advocates for Youth.
http://www.advocatesforyouth.org/

Audience: **g,l,u.**

Albee, George W. & Joffe,   **RC454**
Justin M. (Editors)
The Issues: An Overview of Primary Prevention. Trade Cloth. University Press of New England. Lebanon, NH. 1977. 440p. Primary Prevention of Psychopathology Ser., Vol. 1 ISBN:0-87451-135-6, ISBN13: 978-0-87451-135-2. Dewey:616.89/05. LCCN:76-053992.

Audience: **u,f.**

Arriaga, Ximena B. &   **HM131.A313 1998**
Oskamp, Stuart (Editors)
Addressing Community Problems: Psychological Research and Interventions. Trade Paper. SAGE Publications, Inc. Thousand Oaks, CA. 1998. 271p. Claremont Symposium on Applied Social Psychology Ser. ISBN:0-7619-1078-6, ISBN13: 978-0-7619-1078-7. Dewey:307/.0973. LCCN:98-019701.

Audience: **u,f.**

Barker, Robert L.   **HV12.B37 2003**
The Social Work Dictionary. Ed. 5. Trade Paper. National Association of Social Workers/N A S W Press. Washington, DC. 2003. 493p. ISBN:0-87101-355-X, ISBN13: 978-0-87101-355-2. Dewey:361.3/03. LCCN:2003-054062.

Audience: **g,l,u,f.** *Choice, 2004.*

Bartkowski, John P. &   **HV530.B37 2003**
Regis, Helen A.
Charitable Choices: Religion, Race, and Poverty in the Post-Welfare Era. Trade Cloth. New York University Press. New York, NY. 2003. 224p. ISBN:0-8147-9901-9, ISBN13: 978-0-8147-9901-7. Dewey:361.7/5/09762. LCCN:2002-010095.

Audience: **u,f.** *Choice, 2003.*

Cambridge Scientific
Abstracts
Social Services Abstracts (bibliographic database).

Audience: **l,u,f.**

Caplan, Gerald   **RA790 .C513**
An Approach to Community Mental Health. Trade Cloth. Harcourt Health Sciences Group. Saint Louis, MO. 1961. 272p. ISBN:0-8089-0093-5, ISBN13: 978-0-8089-0093-1. Dewey:131.329.

Audience: **f.**

Caplan, Gerald   **RJ111 .C33**
Support Systems and Community Mental Health. Cloth Text. Springer. New York, NY. 1974. 267p. ISBN:0-87705-119-4, ISBN13: 978-0-87705-119-0. Dewey:362.2/2. LCCN:73-012398.

Audience: **u,f.**

Center on Urban Poverty   HT108
  and Social Change, Case Western Reserve University
☐ Center on Urban Poverty and Social Change, Case Western
Reserve University.
http://povertycenter.case.edu/
                                                    Audience: **u,f.**

Chapin Hall Center for   HV741.A14
  Children, University of Chicago   1997
☐ Chapin Hall Center for Children, University of Chicago.
http://www.chapinhall.org/
                                                    Audience: **u,f.**

Division of Child, Youth,   HV741
  and Family Services (APA Division 37)
☐ Division of Child, Youth, and Family Services (APA Division
37).
http://www.apa.org/divisions/div37/
                                                    Audience: **u,f.**

Elias, Maurice J., et al.   RA790.5 .D35
Community Psychology: Linking Individuals and Communities.
Ed. 2. Abraham Wandersman & James H. Dalton (Authors).
Cloth Text. Thomson Wadsworth. Belmont, CA. 2006. 640p.
ISBN:0-534-63454-0, ISBN13: 978-0-534-63454-4.
Dewey:362.2.
                                                    Audience: **u,f.**

Felner, Robert D.   RA790 .P7736
Preventive Psychology. Paper Text. Allyn & Bacon, Inc. Boston,
MA. 1983. ISBN:0-205-14326-1, ISBN13: 978-0-205-14326-9.
Dewey:362.2/0425.
                                                    Audience: **u,f.**

Garmezy, Norman   RJ506.S3
Vulnerable and Invulnerable Children: Theory, Research, and
Intervention. Trade Cloth. American Psychological Association.
Washington, DC. 1986. Master Lectures on Developmental
Psychology, Manuscript No. 1337 ISBN:0-912704-32-2,
ISBN13: 978-0-912704-32-6. Dewey:618.928982.
                                                    Audience: **u,f.**

Human Services Policy   HQ536
  Center, University of Washington
☐ Human Services Policy Center, University of Washington.
http://hspc.org/
                                                    Audience: **u,f.**

Joint Commission on Mental   RC455 .J6 1979
  Illness and Health
Action for Mental Health. Gerald N. Grob (Editor). Library
Binding. Ayer Company Publishers, Inc. Manchester, NH. 1980.
Historical Issues in Mental Health Ser. ISBN:0-405-11922-4,
ISBN13: 978-0-405-11922-4. Dewey:362.2. LCCN:78-022569.
                                                    Audience: **u,f.**

Kelly, James G.   HN29.K45 1988
A Guide to Conducting Prevention Research in the Community:
First Steps. Trade Cloth. Haworth Press, Incorporated, The.
Binghamton, NY. 1989. 174p. Prevention in Human Services
Ser., Vol. 6, No. 1 ISBN:0-86656-858-1, ISBN13:
978-0-86656-858-6. Dewey:301/.0723. LCCN:88-024550.
                                                    Audience: **u,f.**

Levin, Bruce Lubotsky   RA790.6.M445 2004
  (Editor), et al.
Mental Health Services: A Public Health Perspective. Ed. 2.

John Petrila & Kevin Hennessy (Editors), Bruce Lubotsky
Levin, John Petrila & Kevin Hennessy (Translators). Trade
Cloth. Oxford University Press, Inc. New York, NY. 2004. 496p.
ISBN:0-19-515395-2, ISBN13: 978-0-19-515395-8.
Dewey:362.2/0973. LCCN:2003-056532.
                                                    Audience: **u,f.**

Levine, Murray & Perkins,   RA790.55.L48 2004
  David V.
Principles of Community Psychology: Perspectives and
Applications. Ed. 3. Cloth Text. Oxford University Press, Inc.
New York, NY. 2004. 560p. ISBN:0-19-514417-1, ISBN13:
978-0-19-514417-8. Dewey:362.2/2. LCCN:2004-049525.
                                                    Audience: **u,f.**

Milbank Memorial Fund   RC0458
Interrelations Between the Social Environment and Psychiatric
Disorders: Papers Presented at the 1952 Annual Conference of
the Milbank Memorial Fund. Trade Paper. Books on Demand.
Ann Arbor, MI. 265p. ISBN:0-598-26347-0, ISBN13:
978-0-598-26347-6. Dewey:616.8. LCCN:53-012536.
                                                    Audience: **f.**

National Association for   RA790.6
  Rural Mental Health
☐ National Association for Rural Mental Health.
http://www.narmh.org
                                                    Audience: **u,f.**

National Center for   HV741
  Children in Poverty, Columbia University
☐ National Center for Children in Poverty, Columbia
University.
http://www.nccp.org/
                                                    Audience: **g,l,u,f.**

National Center for   HV741
  Research and Data, Child Welfare League of America
☐ Center for Research and Data, Child Welfare League of
America.
http://www.cwla.org/programs/researchdata/default.htm
                                                    Audience: **l,u,f.**

National Child Welfare   HV741,A14
  Resource Center, Muskie School of Public Service,
  University of Southern Maine
☐ National Child Welfare Resource Center, Muskie School of
Public Service, University of Southern Maine.
http://muskie.usm.maine.edu/helpkids/
                                                    Audience: **u,f.**

National Institute of Mental   RA790.5
  Health
☐ National Institute of Mental Health.
http://www.nimh.nih.gov/
                                                    Audience: **g,l,u,f.**

National Mental Health   RA790.5
  Association
☐ National Mental Health Association.
http://www.nmha.org/
                                                    Audience: **g,l,u.**

National Research Council   HV1421.L67 1993
  Staff
Losing Generations: Adolescents in High-Risk Settings.
Shepherd Zeldin (Editor). Paper Text. National Academies Press.

Washington, DC. 1993. 288p. ISBN:0-309-04828-1, ISBN13: 978-0-309-04828-6. Dewey:362.7/4/0973. LCCN:93-004358.
Audience: **u,f.** *Choice, 1994.*

Nelson, Geoffrey & Prilleltensky, Isaac — RA790.55.N445 2004
Community Psychology: In Pursuit of Liberation and Well-Being. Cloth over Boards. Palgrave Macmillan. New York, NY. 2005. 450p. ISBN:0-333-92281-6, ISBN13: 978-0-333-92281-1. Dewey:362.2/2. LCCN:2004-051261.
Audience: **u,f.**

Plotnick, Amy (Editor) — HV89
2004 Public Human Services Directory, Vol. 64. Trade Paper. American Public Human Services Association. Washington, DC. 2004. ISBN:0-910106-34-7, ISBN13: 978-0-910106-34-4. Dewey:361.
Audience: **g.**

Rappaport, Julian & Seidman, Edward (Editors) — RA790.55.H36 2000
Handbook of Community Psychology. Trade Cloth. Springer. New York, NY. 2000. 982p. ISBN:0-306-46160-9, ISBN13: 978-0-306-46160-6. Dewey:362.2. LCCN:99-049482.
Audience: **u,f.** *Choice, 2000.*

Schalock, Robert L. — HV11.S36 2000
Outcome-Based Evaluation. Ed. 2. Trade Cloth. Springer. New York, NY. 2000. 292p. ISBN:0-306-46458-6, ISBN13: 978-0-306-46458-4. Dewey:361/.0068. LCCN:00-059659.
Audience: **u,f.**

Search Institute — HQ768.A55
Search Institute.
http://www.search-institute.org
Audience: **g.**

Society for Community Research and Action (APA Division 27) — HV40
Society for Community Research and Action (APA Division 27).
http://www.scra27.org/
Audience: **u,f.**

Society for the Psychological Study of Social Issues (APA Division 9) — HM251.A1
Society for the Psychological Study of Social Issues (APA Division 9).
http://www.spssi.org/
Audience: **u,f.**

U.S. Department of Health and Human Services — HV4999.2
Substance Abuse and Mental Health Services Administration.
http://www.samhsa.gov/
Audience: **g,l,u,f.**

U.S. House of Representatives, Committee on Ways and Means — HJ2052.A2
2004 Green Book.
http://waysandmeans.house.gov/Documents.asp?section=813
Audience: **g,l,u,f.**

United Way — HV97.U553
Outcome Measurement Resource Network.
http://national.unitedway.org/outcomes/
Audience: **u,f.**

Werner, Emmy E. & Smith, Ruth S. — HQ792.U5W4 1989
Vulnerable but Invincible: A Longitudinal Study of Resilient Children and Youth. Ed. 3. Norman Garmezy (Foreword by). Paper Text. Adams, Bannister, Cox Publishers. New York, NY. 1998. 228p. ISBN:0-937431-03-6, ISBN13: 978-0-937431-03-0. Dewey:305.2/3/0996941. LCCN:89-000313.
Audience: **u,f.**

White House Office of Faith-Based and Community Initiatives — HV95
White House Office of Faith-Based and Community Initiatives.
http://www.whitehouse.gov/government/fbci/
Audience: **g,l,u,f.**

World Health Organization — RA790.5
Mental Health.
http://www.who.int/mental_health/en/
Audience: **g,l,u,f.**

Mental Health Treatment and Prevention > Rehabilitation

Frank, Robert G. & Elliott, Timothy R. — R726.7.H366 2000
Handbook of Rehabilitation Psychology. Trade Cloth. American Psychological Association. Washington, DC. 2000. xiv, 727p. ISBN:1-55798-644-4, ISBN13: 978-1-55798-644-3. Dewey:617/.03/019. LCCN:99-087407.
Audience: **u,f.**

Mental Health Treatment and Prevention > Drug and Alcohol Rehabilitation

A. A. Services Staff, A. A. Services — HV5275.W15 2001
Alcoholics Anonymous: The Story of How Many Thousands of Men and Women Have Recovered from Alcoholism. Ed. 4. Trade Cloth. Hazelden Publishing & Educational Services. Center City, MN. 2002. 576p. ISBN:1-893007-16-2, ISBN13: 978-1-893007-16-1. Dewey:362.2/92. LCCN:2001-094693.
Audience: **g,l,u,f.**

A. A. Services Staff, A. A. Services — HV5278
Twelve Steps and Twelve Traditions. Trade Cloth. Hazelden Publishing & Educational Services. Center City, MN. 2002. 194p. ISBN:0-916856-01-1, ISBN13: 978-0-916856-01-4. Dewey:362.292. LCCN:53-005454.
Audience: **g,l,u,f.**

Alcoholics Anonymous World Services, Inc., Staff — HV5278.A78
Alcoholics Anonymous Comes of Age: A Brief History of Alcoholic Anonymous. Trade Cloth. Alcoholics Anonymous World Services, Inc. New York, NY. 1957. 333p. ISBN:0-916856-02-X, ISBN13: 978-0-916856-02-1. Dewey:362.2. LCCN:57-010949.
Audience: **g,l,u,f.**

Brown, Stephanie & Lewis, Virginia M. — HV5132.B748 1998
The Alcoholic Family in Recovery: A Developmental Model.

Cloth over Boards. Guilford Publications, Inc. New York, NY. 1998. 318p. ISBN:1-57230-402-2, ISBN13: 978-1-57230-402-4. Dewey:362.292/3. LCCN:98-036077.

Audience: **u.** *Choice, 1999.*

Crowley, John W.   **HV5068.D78 1999**

Drunkard's Progress: Narratives of Addiction, Despair, and Recovery. Trade Paper. Johns Hopkins University Press. Baltimore, MD. 1999. 216p. ISBN:0-8018-6007-5, ISBN13: 978-0-8018-6007-2. Dewey:362.292. LCCN:98-008732.

Audience: **l,u.** *Choice, 1999.*

Diamond, Jonathan   **RC564.D535 2000**

Narrative Means to Sober Ends: Treating Addiction and Its Aftermath. Cloth over Boards. Guilford Publications, Inc. New York, NY. 2000. 386p. Family Therapy Ser. ISBN:1-57230-566-5, ISBN13: 978-1-57230-566-3. Dewey:616.86/06. LCCN:00-026074.

Audience: **u.** *Choice, 2001.*

DiClemente, Carlo C.   **RC564.D535 2003**

Addiction and Change: How Addictions Develop and Addicted People Recover. Paper over Boards. Guilford Publications, Inc. New York, NY. 2003. 318p. Guilford Substance Abuse Ser. ISBN:1-57230-057-4, ISBN13: 978-1-57230-057-6. Dewey:616.86/03. LCCN:2002-015477.

Audience: **l,u.** *Choice, 2003.*

Ketcham, Katherine, et al.   **HV5035.K53 2000**

Beyond the Influence: Understanding and Defeating Alcoholism. Ed. 2. William F. Asbury, Mel Schulstad & Arthur P. Ciaramicoli (Authors). Trade Paper. Bantam Books. New York, NY. 2000. 368p. ISBN:0-553-38014-1, ISBN13: 978-0-553-38014-9. Dewey:362.292/8. LCCN:99-058107.

Audience: **g,l.**

Kurtz, Ernest   **HV5278 .K85**

Not God: A History of Alcoholics Anonymous. Trade Paper. Hazelden Publishing & Educational Services. Center City, MN. 1998. 456p. ISBN:0-89486-065-8, ISBN13: 978-0-89486-065-2. Dewey:362.2/9286. LCCN:79-088264.

Audience: **g,l,u,f.** *B*

Miller, Peter M. & Nirenberg, Ted D. (Editors)   **HV5035**

Prevention of Alcohol Abuse. Trade Cloth. Basic Books. New York, NY. 1984. 536p. ISBN:0-306-41328-0, ISBN13: 978-0-306-41328-5. Dewey:362.2/9286. LCCN:83-019203.

Audience: **l,u.** *B*

Platt, Jerome J.   **RC568.C6P53 1997**

Cocaine Addiction: Theory, Research and Treatment. Trade Cloth. Harvard University Press. Cambridge, MA. 1997. 480p. ISBN:0-674-13632-2, ISBN13: 978-0-674-13632-8. Dewey:616.86/47. LCCN:96-037435.

Audience: **l,u,f.** *Choice, 1998.*

Rotgers, Frederick (Editor), et al.   **RC564.T734 2003**

Treating Substance Abuse: Theory and Technique. Ed. 2. Jon Morgenstern & Scott T. Walters (Editors). Cloth over Boards. Guilford Publications, Inc. New York, NY. 2003. 374p. Guilford Substance Abuse Ser. ISBN:1-57230-897-4, ISBN13: 978-1-57230-897-8. Dewey:616.86/06. LCCN:2003-012710.

Audience: **u,f.** *Choice, 1996.*

Straussner, Shulamith Lala Ashenberg (Editor)   **RC564.E785 2001**

Ethnocultural Factors in Substance Abuse Treatment. Cloth over Boards. Guilford Publications, Inc. New York, NY. 2001. 447p. ISBN:1-57230-630-0, ISBN13: 978-1-57230-630-1. Dewey:616.86/06. LCCN:00-067723.

Audience: **u,f.** *Choice, 2001.*

Tims, Frank M. (Editor), et al.   **RC564.R4376 2001**

Relapse and Recovery in Addictions. Carl G. Leukefeld & Jerome J. Platt (Editors). Cloth over Boards. Yale University Press. Cumberland, RI. 2001. 432p. ISBN:0-300-08383-1, ISBN13: 978-0-300-08383-5. Dewey:616.86/0651. LCCN:00-043598.

Audience: **u,f.** *Choice, 2001.*

Mental Health Treatment and Prevention > Speech and Language Therapy

Anderson, Noma B. & Shames, George H.   **RC423.H847 2006**

Human Communication Disorders: An Introduction. Ed. 7. Trade Paper. Allyn & Bacon, Inc. Boston, MA. 2005. 656p. ISBN:0-205-45622-7, ISBN13: 978-0-205-45622-2. Dewey:616.85/5. LCCN:2005-048748.

Audience: **l.**

Bernthal, John E. & Bankson, Nicholas W.   **RC424.7.B47 2004**

Articulation and Phonological Disorders. Ed. 5. Trade Cloth. Allyn & Bacon, Inc. Boston, MA. 2003. 448p. ISBN:0-205-34790-8, ISBN13: 978-0-205-34790-2. Dewey:616.85/5. LCCN:2003-101684.

Audience: **u,f.**

Jacyna, L. S.   **RC425.J33 2000**

Lost Words: Narratives of Language and the Brain, 1825-1926. Trade Cloth. Princeton University Press. Princeton, NJ. 2000. 254p. ISBN:0-691-00413-7, ISBN13: 978-0-691-00413-6. Dewey:616.85/52/009. LCCN:99-089724.

Audience: **u,f.** *Choice, 2001.*

Kent, Raymond D. (Editor)   **RC423.M56 2003**

The MIT Encyclopedia of Communication Disorders. Trade Cloth. MIT Press. Cambridge, MA. 2003. 648p. Bradford Bks. ISBN:0-262-11278-7, ISBN13: 978-0-262-11278-9. Dewey:616.85/5/003. LCCN:2003-059941.

Audience: **u,f.** *Choice, 2004.*

Leonard, Laurence B.   **RJ496.L35L46 2000**

Children with Specific Language Impairment. Trade Paper. MIT Press. Cambridge, MA. 2000. 352p. Language, Speech and Communication Ser. ISBN:0-262-62136-3, ISBN13: 978-0-262-62136-6. Dewey:618.92/855. LCCN:00-268670.

Audience: **u.** *Choice, 1998.*

Starkweather, C. Woodruff & Givens-Ackerman, Janet   **RC424.S693 1997**

Stuttering. Paper Text. PRO-ED, Inc. Austin, TX. 1996. 215p. Studies in Communicative Disorders ISBN:0-89079-699-8, ISBN13: 978-0-89079-699-3. Dewey:616.85/54. LCCN:96-020276.

Audience: **l,u.** *Choice, 1997.*

Van Riper, Charles &   **RC423.V35 1996**
   Erickson, Robert L.
Speech Correction: An Introduction to Speech Pathology and
Audiology. Ed. 9. Cloth Text. Allyn & Bacon, Inc. Boston, MA.
1995. 512p. ISBN:0-13-825142-8, ISBN13: 978-0-13-825142-0.
Dewey:616.85/5. LCCN:95-041718.

                                      Audience: **l,u.**

Vinson, Betsy Partin   **RC423**
Language Disorders Across the Lifespan. Ed. 2. Paper Text.
Thomson Delmar Learning. Albany, NY. 2006. 576p.
ISBN:1-4180-0954-7, ISBN13: 978-1-4180-0954-0.
Dewey:616.85/5. LCCN:2006-018327.

                                      Audience: **l,u.**

Professional Psychological and Health Personnel Issues > Professional Ethics, Standards, and Liability

American Counseling   **BF637.C6**
   Association
☐ ACA Code of Ethics.
http://www.counseling.org/Resources/CodeOfEthics/TP/Home/
CT2.aspx

                                      Audience: **g,l,u,f.**

American Psychological   **BF76.4**
   Association
☐ Ethical Principles of Psychologists and Code of Conduct.
http://www.apa.org/ethics/code2002.html

                                      Audience: **g,l,u,f.**

American Psychological   **QL55**
   Association, Committee on Animal Research and Ethics
☐ Guidelines for Ethical Conduct in the Care and Use of
Animals.
http://www.apa.org/science/anguide.html

                                      Audience: **l,u,f.**

Bailey, Jon S. & Burch,   **RC473.B43B355 2005**
   Mary R.
Ethics for Behavior Analysts: A Practical Guide to the Behavior
Analyst Certification Board Guidelines for Responsible Conduct.
Trade Paper. Lawrence Erlbaum Associates, Inc. Mahwah, NJ.
2005. 312p. ISBN:0-8058-5118-6, ISBN13: 978-0-8058-5118-2.
Dewey:174.20973.

                                      Audience: **u,f.**

Beauchamp, Thomas L. &   **R724.B36 2001**
   Childress, James F.
Principles of Biomedical Ethics. Ed. 5. Trade Cloth. Oxford
University Press, Inc. New York, NY. 2001. 472p.
ISBN:0-19-514331-0, ISBN13: 978-0-19-514331-7.
Dewey:174/.2. LCCN:00-062394.

                                      Audience: **u,f.**

Bersoff, Donald N. (Editor)   **BF76.4.E814 2003**
Ethical Conflicts in Psychology. Ed. 3. Trade Cloth. American
Psychological Association. Washington, DC. 2003. 6002p.
ISBN:1-59147-051-X, ISBN13: 978-1-59147-051-9.
Dewey:174/.915. LCCN:2003-048175.

                                      Audience: **u,f.**

Childress, James F. (Editor),   **R853.H8B45 2005**
   et al.
Belmont Revisited: Ethical Principles for Research with Human
Subjects. Eric M. Meslin & Harold T. Shapiro (Editors). Trade
Paper. Georgetown University Press. Washington, DC. 2005.
264p. ISBN:1-58901-062-0, ISBN13: 978-1-58901-062-8.
Dewey:174.2. LCCN:2005-008286.

                                      Audience: **f.**

Fisher, Celia B.   **BF76.4.F57 2003**
Decoding the Ethics Code: A Practical Guide for Psychologists.
Paper Text. SAGE Publications, Inc. Thousand Oaks, CA. 2003.
320p. ISBN:0-7619-2619-4, ISBN13: 978-0-7619-2619-1.
Dewey:174/.915. LCCN:2003-006141.

                                      Audience: **u,f.**

Hanson, Stephanie L., et al.   **R724.H234 2004**
Health Care Ethics for Psychologists: A Casebook. Thomas R.
Kerkhoff & Shane S. Bush (Authors). Trade Cloth. American
Psychological Association. Washington, DC. 2004. 280p.
ISBN:1-59147-152-4, ISBN13: 978-1-59147-152-3.
Dewey:174.2. LCCN:2004-003104.

                                      Audience: **u,f.**

Herlihy, Barbara & Corey,   **BF637.C6A37 2006**
   Gerald
ACA Ethical Standards Casebook. Ed. 6. Trade Cloth. American
Counseling Association. Alexandria, VA. 2006. xv, 264p.
ISBN:1-55620-255-5, ISBN13: 978-1-55620-255-1.
Dewey:174/.91583. LCCN:2005-025160.

                                      Audience: **u,f.**

Nagy, Thomas F.   **BF76.4.N34 2004**
Ethics in Plain English: An Illustrative Casebook for
Psychologists. Ed. 2. Trade Paper. American Psychological
Association. Washington, DC. 2004. 368p. ISBN:1-59147-201-6,
ISBN13: 978-1-59147-201-8. Dewey:174/.915.
LCCN:2004-018052.

                                      Audience: **u,f.**

National Academy Press   **SF406 .G8**
   Staff (Contribution by)
Guide for the Care and Use of Laboratory Animals. Paper Text.
National Academies Press. Washington, DC. 1996. 140p.
ISBN:0-309-05377-3, ISBN13: 978-0-309-05377-8.
Dewey:636.08/85/05.

                                      Audience: **l,u,f.** *Choice, 1997.*

O'Donohue, William T. &   **BF76.4.H36 2003**
   Ferguson, Kyle E. (Editors)
Handbook of Professional Ethics for Psychologists: Issues,
Questions, and Controversies. Cloth Text. SAGE Publications,
Inc. Thousand Oaks, CA. 2003. 488p. ISBN:0-7619-1188-X,
ISBN13: 978-0-7619-1188-3. Dewey:174/.915.
LCCN:2002-013230.

                                      Audience: **u,f.** *Choice, 2003.*

Pack-Brown, Sherlon P. &   **BF637.C6P235 2003**
   Williams, Carmen Braun
Ethics in a Multicultural Context. Cloth Text. SAGE
Publications, Inc. Thousand Oaks, CA. 2003. 280p.
Multicultural Aspects of Counseling Ser., Vol. 19
ISBN:0-7619-2426-4, ISBN13: 978-0-7619-2426-5.
Dewey:174/.9362. LCCN:2002-153687.

                                      Audience: **u,f.**

Pincus, Harold A. (Editor),   RC337.E84 1999
  et al.
Ethics in Psychiatric Research: A Resource Manual on Human Subjects Research. Jeffrey Lieberman & Sandy Ferris (Editors). Trade Cloth. American Psychiatric Publishing, Inc. Arlington, VA. 1999. 576p. ISBN:0-89042-281-8, ISBN13: 978-0-89042-281-6. Dewey:174/.28. LCCN:98-017948.

                             Audience: **f.**

Prilleltensky, Isaac   BF76.4.P75 1994
The Morals and Politics of Psychology: Psychological Discourse and the Status Quo. Cloth Text. State University of New York Press. Albany, NY. 1994. 283p. SUNY Series, Alternatives in Psychology ISBN:0-7914-2037-X, ISBN13: 978-0-7914-2037-9. Dewey:150/.1. LCCN:93-037494.

                 Audience: **u,f.** *Choice, 1995.*

Woody, Robert & Woody,   RC488.5
  Jane (Editors)
Ethics in Marriage and Family Therapy. Perfect. American Association for Marriage & Family Therapy. Alexandria, VA. 2001. ISBN:1-931846-04-9, ISBN13: 978-1-931846-04-2. Dewey:174.915.

                         Audience: **u,f.**

Professional Psychological and Health Personnel Issues > Professional Education and Training

American Board of   BF80.8
  Professional Psychology
☐ American Board of Professional Psychology.
http://www.abpp.org/

                         Audience: **u,f.**

American Psychological   BF77
  Association (Created by)
Graduate Study in Psychology: 2007 Edition. Trade Paper, Perfect. American Psychological Association. Washington, DC. 2005. 832p. Graduate Study in Psychology Ser. ISBN:1-59147-315-2, ISBN13: 978-1-59147-315-2. Dewey:150/.7/1173.

                         Audience: **u.**

American Psychological   BF77
  Association Education Directorate
☐ American Psychological Association Education Directorate.
http://www.apa.org/ed/

                         Audience: **l,u,f.**

American Psychological   BF30.A49
  Association of Graduate Students
☐ American Psychological Association of Graduate Students.
http://www.apa.org/apags/

                         Audience: **u,f.**

Association of Psychology   BF77
  Postdoctoral and Internship Centers
☐ APPIC Online Directory.
http://www.appic.org/directory/search_dol_postdocs.asp

                         Audience: **u,f.**

Benjamin, Ludy T. Jr. &   BF78.A28 1981
  Lowman, Kathleen D. (Editors)
Activities Handbook for the Teaching of Psychology, Vol. 1.

Trade Paper. American Psychological Association. Washington, DC. 1981. 244p. Activities Handbook for the Teaching of Psychology Ser., Vol. 1 ISBN:0-912704-34-9, ISBN13: 978-0-912704-34-0. Dewey:150.7. LCCN:81-001648.

                         Audience: **f.**

Benjamin, Ludy T. Jr.   BF78
  (Editor), et al.
Activities Handbook for the Teaching of Psychology, Vol. 4. Barbara F. Nodine, Randal M. Ernst & Charles Blair-Broeker (Editors). Paper Text. American Psychological Association. Washington, DC. 1999. 408p. Activities Handbook for the Teaching of Psychology Ser., Vol. 4 ISBN:1-55798-537-5, ISBN13: 978-1-55798-537-8. Dewey:150.7.

                         Audience: **f.**

Davis, Stephen F.   BF77.H268 2005
Handbook of the Teaching of Psychology. William Buskist (Editor). Trade Paper, Perfect. Blackwell Publishing, Inc. Malden, MA. 2005. 376p. ISBN:1-4051-3801-7, ISBN13: 978-1-4051-3801-7. Dewey:150/.71/1. LCCN:2005-014828.

                         Audience: **f.**

Dunn, Dana S. & Chew,   BF77.B48 2005
  Stephen L. (Editors)
Best Practices for Teaching Introduction to Psychology. Craig Abrahamson, Drew C. Appleby & Victor Benassi (Contribution by). Trade Paper, Perfect. Lawrence Erlbaum Associates, Inc. Mahwah, NJ. 2005. 304p. ISBN:0-8058-5218-2, ISBN13: 978-0-8058-5218-9. Dewey:150/.71/1. LCCN:2005-041464.

                         Audience: **f.**

Goss Lucas, Sandra &   BF77.G67 2004
  Bernstein, Douglas A.
Teaching Psychology: A Step by Step Guide. Cloth over Boards. Lawrence Erlbaum Associates, Inc. Mahwah, NJ. 2004. 296p. ISBN:0-8058-4224-1, ISBN13: 978-0-8058-4224-1. Dewey:150/.71. LCCN:2004-046911.

                         Audience: **f.**

Kuther, Tara L.   BF77
The Psychology Major's Handbook. Ed. 2. Paper Text. Thomson Wadsworth. Belmont, CA. 2005. 2640p. ISBN:0-534-53387-6, ISBN13: 978-0-534-53387-8. Dewey:150/.71/1.

                         Audience: **l,u.**

Makosky, Vivian P. (Editor),   BF78 .A28 1981
  et al.
Activities Handbook for the Teaching of Psychology, Vol. 3. Chi Chi Sileo, Christine P. Landry, Mary L. Skutley & Linda G. Whittemore (Editors), Charles L. Brewer (Foreword by). Trade Cloth. American Psychological Association. Washington, DC. 1981. 372p. Activities Handbook for the Teaching of Psychology Ser., Vol. 3 ISBN:1-55798-081-0, ISBN13: 978-1-55798-081-6. Dewey:150/.7. LCCN:81-001648.

                         Audience: **f.**

Matthews, Janet R. &   RC467.7.M38 2005
  Walker, C. Eugene
Your Practicum in Psychology: A Guide for Maximizing Knowledge and Competence. Trade Paper. American Psychological Association. Washington, DC. 2005. 320p. ISBN:1-59147-328-4, ISBN13: 978-1-59147-328-2. Dewey:616.89/0071. LCCN:2005-015452.

                         Audience: **l,u.**

McGovern, Thomas V. (Editor)   BF80.7.U6 H36 1993
Handbook for Enhancing Undergraduate Education in Psychology. Paper Text. American Psychological Association. Washington, DC. 1993. 273p. ISBN:1-55798-196-5, ISBN13: 978-1-55798-196-7. Dewey:150/.71/173. LCCN:93-007081.
Audience: **f.**

Neufeldt, Susan A.   RC459.N48 1999
Supervision Strategies for the First Practicum. Ed. 2. Trade Cloth. American Counseling Association. Alexandria, VA. 1999. 243p. ISBN:1-55620-218-0, ISBN13: 978-1-55620-218-6. Dewey:616.89/14/07155. LCCN:98-049915.
Audience: **f.**

Office of Program Consultation and Accreditation   BF77
◻ Accreditation.
http://www.apa.org/ed/accreditation/
Audience: **g,u,f.**

Pedersen, Paul   LC1099.3.P53 2004
110 Experiences for Multicultural Learning. Trade Cloth. American Psychological Association. Washington, DC. 2004. 360p. ISBN:1-59147-082-X, ISBN13: 978-1-59147-082-3. Dewey:370.117. LCCN:2003-020360.
Audience: **f.**

Peterson, Donald R.   BF80.7.U6P48 1997
Educating Professional Psychologists: History and Guiding Conception. Trade Paper. American Psychological Association. Washington, DC. 1997. 281p. ISBN:1-55798-420-4, ISBN13: 978-1-55798-420-3. Dewey:150/.71/173. LCCN:97-014077.
Audience: **f.**

Pope, Kenneth S. & Vasquez, Melba Jean Trinidad   BF75.P66 2005
How to Survive and Thrive As a Therapist: Information, Ideas, and Resources for Psychologists in Practice. Trade Paper. American Psychological Association. Washington, DC. 2005. 496p. ISBN:1-59147-231-8, ISBN13: 978-1-59147-231-5. Dewey:150/.68. LCCN:2004-023318.
Audience: **u,f.**

Prinstein, Mitchell J. & Patterson, Marcus D. (Editors)   BF76.P67 2003
The Portable Mentor: Expert Guide to a Successful Career in Psychology. Trade Cloth. Springer. New York, NY. 2003. 332p. ISBN:0-306-47457-3, ISBN13: 978-0-306-47457-6. Dewey:150/.23. LCCN:2003-051301.
Audience: **l,u.**

Psi Chi   BF11
◻ Psi Chi.
http://www.psichi.org/home.asp
Audience: **l,u.**

Puente, Antonio E. (Editor), et al.   BF80.7.U6.T43 1992
Teaching Psychology in America: A History. Janet R. Matthews & Charles L. Brewer (Editors). Cloth Text. American Psychological Association. Washington, DC. 1992. 578p. ISBN:1-55798-181-7, ISBN13: 978-1-55798-181-3. Dewey:150/.71/173. LCCN:92-032027.
Audience: **g.**   *Choice, 1993.*

Russell-Chapin, Lori Ann & Ivey, Allen E.   RC481.R875 2004
Your Supervised Practicum and Internship: Field Resources for Turning Theory into Action. Paper Text. Thomson Wadsworth. Belmont, CA. 2003. 288p. ISBN:0-534-60615-6, ISBN13: 978-0-534-60615-2. Dewey:616.89/14. LCCN:2003-107200.
Audience: **u.**

Social Psychology Network   BF76
◻ Online Psychology Career Center.
http://www.socialpsychology.org/career.htm
Audience: **g,l,u,f.**

Society for the Teaching of Psychology (APA Division 2)   BF77
◻ Society for the Teaching of Psychology (APA Division 2).
http://teachpsych.lemoyne.edu/
Audience: **f.**

Sternberg, Robert J. (Editor)   BF76.C38 1997
Career Paths in Psychology: Where Your Degree Can Take You. Trade Paper. American Psychological Association. Washington, DC. 1997. 297p. ISBN:1-55798-411-5, ISBN13: 978-1-55798-411-1. Dewey:150.23/73. LCCN:96-039943.
Audience: **l,u.**

Williams-Nickelson, Carol & Prinstein, Mitchell J. (Editors)   BF77.I67 2005
Internships in Psychology: The APAGS Workbook for Writing Successful Applications and Finding the Right Match. Trade Paper. American Psychological Association. Washington, DC. 2004. 152p. ISBN:1-59147-209-1, ISBN13: 978-1-59147-209-4. Dewey:150/.71/55. LCCN:2004-559157.
Audience: **l,u.**

TECHNOLOGY AND ENGINEERING

This section contains works that class in general technology; applied mathematics; industrial, chemical, civil, structural, transportation, environmental, mechanical, aeronautical, electrical and electronic, and nuclear engineering; mining; metallurgy; applied optics; and water resource engineering. Most of these categories have subcategories: Chemical engineering: fuel cells and other energy topics; process, plant, and experimental chemical engineering. General technology: technical writing and industrial safety. Applied mathematics: engineering mathematics and computer applications. Industrial engineering: patents, management, economics, systems, manufacturing. Civil engineering: standards; materials science. Structural engineering: construction—concrete, metal, highways/bridges/roads/buildings; soil mechanics. Environmental engineering: pollution, radioactive waste. Mechanical engineering: power/energy, control, heat/thermodynamics, fluid mechanics, heat transfer, machinery, motor vehicles. Aeronautical engineering: aircraft, rockets, astronautics, space flight. Electrical and electronic engineering: circuit analysis, analog/digital electronics, electric power transmission/distribution, telecommunications, computer networks, antenna theory, microwaves, computer engineering, lasers and optoelectronics. Metallurgy: metallography, corrosion, iron and steel, other ferrous metals, nonferrous metals, alloys, joining, electroplating. Mining: coal, petroleum.

— Antoinette Nelson

General and Reference Works

TA145

☐ Efunda: Engineering Fundamentals.
http://www.efunda.com/home.cfm

Audience: **g,l,u,f.**

Allstetter, William &   **T9.C96 2000**
Schuyler, Tami
The Cutting Edge: An Encyclopedia of Advanced Technologies.
Trade Cloth. Oxford University Press, Inc. New York, NY. 2000.
368p. ISBN:0-19-512899-0, ISBN13: 978-0-19-512899-4.
Dewey:603. LCCN:99-056125.

Audience: **u,f.** *Choice, 2000.*

Berlow, Lawrence H.   **TA15.B42 1998**
Reference Guide to Famous Engineering Landmarks of the
World: Bridges, Tunnels, Dams, Roads and Other Structures.
Cloth Text. Greenwood Publishing Group, Inc. Portsmouth, NH.
1997. 264p. ISBN:0-89774-966-9, ISBN13: 978-0-89774-966-4.
Dewey:620/.009. LCCN:97-036051.

Audience: **g,l,u,f.** *Choice, 1998.*

Erb, Uwe & Keller, Harald   **TA402**
Dictionary of Engineering Materials. Trade Cloth. John Wiley &
Sons, Inc. Hoboken, NJ. 2004. 1328p. ISBN:0-471-44436-7,
ISBN13: 978-0-471-44436-7. Dewey:620.1/1/03.
LCCN:2004-043365.

Audience: **l,u,f.** *Choice, 2004.*

Heisler, Sanford I.   **TA151.H425 1998**
The Wiley Engineer's Desk Reference: A Concise Guide for the
Professional Engineer. Ed. 2. Trade Cloth. John Wiley & Sons,
Inc. Hoboken, NJ. 1998. 712p. ISBN:0-471-16827-0, ISBN13:
978-0-471-16827-0. Dewey:620. LCCN:97-030199.

Audience: **u,f.** *Choice, 1999.*

Hempstead, Colin &   **T9.E462 2005**
Worthington, William E.
Encyclopedia of 20th-Century Technology. Trade Cloth. Fitzroy
Dearborn Publishers, Inc. Chicago, IL. 2005.
ISBN:1-57958-463-2, ISBN13: 978-1-57958-463-4. Dewey:603.
LCCN:2004-004862.

Audience: **l,u,f.**

Karwowski, Waldemar   **TA166.I556 2001**
(Editor)
International Encyclopedia of Ergonomics and Human Factors,
Set. Paper over Boards. Taylor & Francis Group. Abingdon,
2001. 3200p. ISBN:0-7484-0847-9, ISBN13:
978-0-7484-0847-4. Dewey:620.82. LCCN:00-050940.

Audience: **l,u,f.** *Choice, 2002.*

Lord, Charles R.   **T10.7.L67 2000**
Guide to Information Sources in Engineering. Trade Cloth.
Libraries Unlimited, Inc. Westport, CT. 2000. 345p. Reference
Sources in Science and Technology Ser., : ISBN:1-56308-699-9,
ISBN13: 978-1-56308-699-1. Dewey:025.066.
LCCN:00-030929.

Audience: **u,f.** *Choice, 2001.*

McGraw-Hill Staff   **TA402**
McGraw-Hill Dictionary of Materials Science. Paper Text.
McGraw-Hill Professional Publishing. New York, NY. 2003.
397p. ISBN:0-07-142176-9, ISBN13: 978-0-07-142176-8.
Dewey:620.1/1/03. LCCN:2003-051203.

Audience: **u,f.** *Choice, 2003.*

McGraw-Hill Staff   **TA9**
Dictionary of Engineering. Ed. 2. Sybil P. Parker (Editor). Trade
Paper. McGraw-Hill Professional Publishing. New York, NY.
2003. 642p. ISBN:0-07-141050-3, ISBN13: 978-0-07-141050-2.
Dewey:620/.003. LCCN:2002-033178.

Audience: **g,l,u,f.** *Choice, 2003.*

Moschovitis, Christos J. P.,   **TK5105.875.I57H58**
et al.
History of the Internet: A Chronology, 1843 to the Present.
Hilary Poole, Tami Schuyler & Theresa M. Senft (Authors).
Library Binding. ABC-CLIO, Inc. Santa Barbara, CA. 1999.
viii, 312p. ISBN:1-57607-118-9, ISBN13: 978-1-57607-118-2.
Dewey:004.67/8/09. LCCN:99-013275.

Audience: **l,u,f.** *Choice, 1999.*

Nalwa, H.S.   **QC176.8.N35E53 2004**
Dekker Encyclopedia of Nanoscience and Nanotechnology, 10.
Laminated. American Scientific Publishers. Stevenson Ranch,
CA. 2003. 6000p. ISBN:1-58883-001-2, ISBN13:
978-1-58883-001-2. Dewey:620/.5. LCCN:2002-110511.

Audience: **u,f.** *Choice, 2005.*

Oliverson, Ray & McKenna,   **TS9.M43 1997**
Ted
Glossary of Reliability and Maintenance Terms. Trade Cloth.
Elsevier Science & Technology Books. Saint Louis, MO. 1997.
176p. ISBN:0-88415-360-6, ISBN13: 978-0-88415-360-3.
Dewey:658.2/02/03. LCCN:97-017097.

Audience: **l,u,f.** *Choice, 1998.*

Schlein, Alan M.   **TK5105**
Find it Online: The Complete Guide to Online Research. Ed. 3.
Newby, J. J. (Editor); Weber, Peter J. (Editor). Facts on
Demand. 2002. ISBN:1-889150-29-0, ISBN13:
978-1-889150-29-1.

Audience: **g,l,u,f.**

Schwartz, Mel   **TA418.9.S62S39 2002**
Encyclopedia of Materials, Parts, and Finishes. Ed. 2. CRC
Press. 2002. ISBN:1-56676-661-3, ISBN13: 978-1-56676-661-6.

Audience: **l,u,f.**

Schwartz, Mel   **TA418.9.S62E63 2002**
Encyclopedia of Smart Materials. Trade Cloth. John Wiley &
Sons, Inc. Hoboken, NJ. 2002. 1176p. ISBN:0-471-17780-6,
ISBN13: 978-0-471-17780-7. Dewey:620.1/1.
LCCN:2001-056795.

Audience: **l,u,f.** *Choice, 2003.*

Schwarz, James A., et al.   **QC176.8.N35D43 2004**
Dekker Encyclopedia of Nanoscience and Nanotechnology, Vol.
1. Cristian I. Contescu & Karol Putyera (Authors). Paper over
Boards. Marcel Dekker Inc. New York, NY. 2004. 700p. Dekker
Encyclopedias Ser. ISBN:0-8247-5047-0, ISBN13:
978-0-8247-5047-3. Dewey:620/.5. LCCN:2004-051950.

Audience: **u,f.** *Choice, 2005.*

Young, Margaret Levine   **TK5105.875.I57I583**
Internet Millenium Edition. Ed. 3. Paper Text. McGraw-Hill
Osborne. Emeryville, CA. 2003. 956p. Complete Reference Ser.
ISBN:0-07-211942-X, ISBN13: 978-0-07-211942-8.
Dewey:004.67/8. LCCN:00-501674.

Audience: **g,l,u,f.** *Choice, 2000.*

Zierdt-Warshaw, Linda,   **T36.Z54 2000**
et al.
American Women in Technology: An Encyclopedia. Alan

Winkler & Leonard Bernstein (Authors). Library Binding. ABC-CLIO, Inc. Santa Barbara, CA. 2000. 0420p. ISBN:1-57607-072-7, ISBN13: 978-1-57607-072-7. Dewey:604/.82/0973. LCCN:00-021997.

Audience: **g,l,u,f.** *Choice, 2001.*

Technology: General > Technical Writing

Alred, Gerald J., et al.   **T11**
Handbook of Technical Writing. Ed. 8. Charles T. Brusaw & Walter E. Oliu (Authors). Trade Cloth. St. Martin's Press. Gordonville, VA. 2006. 688p. ISBN:0-312-35267-0, ISBN13: 978-0-312-35267-7. Dewey:808/.0666.

Audience: **u,f.**

Barrass, Robert   **T11.B37 2002**
Scientists Must Write: A Guide to Better Writing for Scientists, Engineers and Students. Ed. 2. Trade Paper. Routledge. New York, NY. 2002. 224p. Routledge Study Guides ISBN:0-415-26996-2, ISBN13: 978-0-415-26996-4. Dewey:808/.0666021. LCCN:2002-021341.

Audience: **l,u,f.**

Beer, David F. (Editor)   **T10.5**
Writing and Speaking in the Technology Professions: A Practical Guide. Ed. 2. Trade Paper. John Wiley & Sons, Inc. Hoboken, NJ. 2003. 517p. ISBN:0-471-44473-1, ISBN13: 978-0-471-44473-2. Dewey:808/.0666. LCCN:2003-272849.

Audience: **l,u,f.**

Beer, David F. & McMurrey, David   **T11**
A Guide to Writing as an Engineer. Ed. 2. Trade Paper. John Wiley & Sons, Inc. Hoboken, NJ. 2004. 272p. ISBN:0-471-43074-9, ISBN13: 978-0-471-43074-2. Dewey:808/.0666. LCCN:2004-273792.

Audience: **u,f.**

Bremer, Michael   **T11.B678 1999**
The User Manual Manual: How to Research, Write, Test, Edit and Produce a Software. Trade Paper. UnTechnical Press. Concord, CA. 1999. 314p. Press Books for Writers ISBN:0-9669949-1-4, ISBN13: 978-0-9669949-1-9. Dewey:808/.066004. LCCN:99-090430.

Audience: **u,f.**

Budinski, Kenneth G.   **T11.B83 2001**
Engineers' Guide to Technical Writing. Trade Cloth. A S M International. Materials Park, OH. 2001. 398p. ISBN:0-87170-693-8, ISBN13: 978-0-87170-693-5. Dewey:808/.0666. LCCN:00-046476.

Audience: **u,f.**

Burnett   **T11.B86**
Technical Communication. Ed. 5. Trade Cloth. Thomson Wadsworth. Belmont, CA. 2000. ISBN:0-534-56098-9, ISBN13: 978-0-534-56098-0. Dewey:808.0666.

Audience: **l,u,f.**

Davies, John W.   **T10.5.D38 2000**
Communication Skills: A Guide for Engineering and Applied Science Students. Ed. 2. Trade Paper. Pearson Education. Boston, MA. 2001. 184p. ISBN:0-13-088294-1, ISBN13: 978-0-13-088294-3. Dewey:620/.001/4. LCCN:00-051047.

Audience: **l,u,f.**

Davis, Martha   **T11.D324 2004**
Scientific Papers and Presentations. Ed. 2. Trade Paper. Elsevier Science & Technology Books. Saint Louis, MO. 2004. 384p. ISBN:0-12-088424-0, ISBN13: 978-0-12-088424-7. Dewey:501/.4. LCCN:2004-050500.

Audience: **u,f.**

Day, Robert A. & Gastel, Barbara   **T11**
How to Write and Publish a Scientific Paper. Ed. 6. Trade Cloth. Greenwood Publishing Group, Inc. Portsmouth, NH. 2006. 320p. ISBN:0-313-33027-1, ISBN13: 978-0-313-33027-8. Dewey:808/.0665. LCCN:2005-031621.

Audience: **u,f.** ℬ

Finkelstein, Leo   **T11.F53 2000**
Pocket Book of Technical Writing for Engineers and Scientists. Paper Text. McGraw-Hill Higher Education. Burr Ridge, IL. 1999. 336p. McGraw-Hill's Best - Basic Engineering Series and Tools ISBN:0-07-237080-7, ISBN13: 978-0-07-237080-5. Dewey:808/.0666. LCCN:99-044806.

Audience: **l,u,f.**

Gurak, Laura J. & Lannon, John M.   **T10.5**
A Concise Guide to Technical Communication. Ed. 3. Trade Paper. Longman Publishing. Boston, MA. 2006. 416p. ISBN:0-321-39168-3, ISBN13: 978-0-321-39168-1. Dewey:601/.4. LCCN:2006-022345.

Audience: **l,u,f.**

Hart, Hillary   **TA158.5**
Introduction to Engineering Communication. Trade Paper. Prentice Hall PTR. Upper Saddle River, NJ. 2004. 208p. ISBN:0-13-146102-8, ISBN13: 978-0-13-146102-4. Dewey:620/.001/4. LCCN:2005-295861.

Audience: **l,u,f.**

Harwell, George C.   **PN2287.B5W5**
Technical Communication. Paper Text. Textbook Publishers. Temecula, CA. 2003. 332p. ISBN:0-7581-9267-3, ISBN13: 978-0-7581-9267-7. Dewey:792/.028/0924.

Audience: **l,u,f.**

Holloway, Brian R.   **PE1475.H65 2005**
Technical Writing Basics: A Guide to Style and Form. Ed. 3. Trade Paper. Prentice Hall PTR. Upper Saddle River, NJ. 2004. 240p. ISBN:0-13-114089-2, ISBN13: 978-0-13-114089-9. Dewey:808/.0666. LCCN:2004-005609.

Audience: **l,u,f.**

Kennedy, George E. & Montgomery, Tracy T.   **PE1475.K47 2002**
Professional and Technical Writing: Solving Problems at Work. Trade Paper. Prentice Hall PTR. Upper Saddle River, NJ. 2001. 510p. ISBN:0-13-055072-8, ISBN13: 978-0-13-055072-9. Dewey:808/.0666. LCCN:2001-036654.

Audience: **u,f.**

Lannon, John M.   **T11.L24 2006**
Technical Communication. Ed. 10. Trade Paper. Longman Publishing. Boston, MA. 2005. 832p. ISBN:0-321-27076-2, ISBN13: 978-0-321-27076-4. Dewey:808/.0666. LCCN:2005-272647.

Audience: **l,u,f.**

Malmfors, Birgitta   Q223
Writing and Presenting Scientific Papers. Ed. 2. Nottingham University. 2004. ISBN:1-897676-12-3, ISBN13: 978-1-897676-12-7.
Audience: **l,u,f.**

Markel, Mike   T11
Technical Communication. Ed. 7. Trade Paper. Bedford/Saint Martin's. New York, NY. 2003. 699p. ISBN:0-312-40338-0, ISBN13: 978-0-312-40338-6. Dewey:808.066.
Audience: **l,u,f.**

Miller, Jane E.   T11.M484 2005
The Chicago Guide to Writing about Multivariate Analysis. Trade Paper, Perfect. University of Chicago Press. Chicago, IL. 2005. 424p. Chicago Guides to Writing, Editing, and Publishing Ser. ISBN:0-226-52783-2, ISBN13: 978-0-226-52783-3. Dewey:808/.066519535. LCCN:2004-026821.
Audience: **u,f.** *Choice, 2006.*

Miller, Jane E.   T11.M485 2004
The Chicago Guide to Writing about Numbers. Trade Paper. University of Chicago Press. Chicago, IL. 2004. 312p. Chicago Guides to Writing, Editing, and Publishing Ser. ISBN:0-226-52631-3, ISBN13: 978-0-226-52631-7. Dewey:808/.0665. LCCN:2004-000204.
Audience: **l,u,f.** *Choice, 2005.*

Nagle, Joan G.   TA190.N34 1996
Handbook for Preparing Engineering Documents: From Concept to Completion. Trade Paper. IEEE Computer Society Press. Los Alamitos, CA. 1995. 392p. ISBN:0-7803-1097-7, ISBN13: 978-0-7803-1097-1. Dewey:808/.06662. LCCN:95-014962.
Audience: **u,f.**

Pfeiffer, William S.   PE1475.P465 2004
A Pocket Guide to Technical Writing. Ed. 3. Trade Paper. Prentice Hall PTR. Upper Saddle River, NJ. 2003. 240p. ISBN:0-13-047611-0, ISBN13: 978-0-13-047611-1. Dewey:808/.0666. LCCN:2002-043176.
Audience: **l,u,f.**

Pfeiffer, William S.   PE1475.P47 2006
Technical Communication: A Practical Approach. Ed. 6. Trade Paper. Prentice Hall PTR. Upper Saddle River, NJ. 2005. 720p. ISBN:0-13-119816-5, ISBN13: 978-0-13-119816-6. Dewey:808/.0666. LCCN:2004-053517.
Audience: **l,u,f.**

Raman, M. & Sharma, S.   T10.5.R298 2004
Active Technical Communication: Concepts and Applications. Paper Text. Oxford University Press, Inc. New York, NY. 2005. 608p. ISBN:0-19-566804-9, ISBN13: 978-0-19-566804-9. Dewey:808/.0666. LCCN:2005-297784.
Audience: **u,f.**

Robinson, Patricia A. &   T11.R635 2000
  Etter, Ryn
Writing and Designing Manuals: Operator Manuals, Service and Maintenance Manuals for International Markets. Ed. 3. Paper over Boards. Lewis Publishers. Boca Raton, FL. 2000. 224p. ISBN:1-56670-378-6, ISBN13: 978-1-56670-378-9. Dewey:808/.0666. LCCN:99-086267.
Audience: **u,f.**

Rubens, Philip   T11.S378 2001
Science and Technical Writing: A Manual of Style. Ed. 2. Paper over Boards. Routledge. New York, NY. 2000. 544p. ISBN:0-415-92550-9, ISBN13: 978-0-415-92550-1. Dewey:808.0666. LCCN:00-032837.
Audience: **u,f.**

Sides, Charles H.   T11
How to Write and Present Technical Information. Ed. 3. Trade Paper. Cambridge University Press. New York, NY. 1999. 224p. ISBN:0-521-66693-7, ISBN13: 978-0-521-66693-0. Dewey:808/.0666.
Audience: **u,f.**

Sims, Brenda R.   PE1475.S56 2003
Technical Communication for Readers and Writers. Ed. 2. Paper Text. Houghton Mifflin College Division. Boston, MA. 2002. 685p. ISBN:0-618-22173-5, ISBN13: 978-0-618-22173-8. Dewey:808/.0666. LCCN:2001-133346.
Audience: **l,u,f.**

VanAlstyne, Judith S.   PE1475.V36 2005
Professional and Technical Writing: Communicating in Technology and Science. Ed. 6. Trade Paper. Prentice Hall PTR. Upper Saddle River, NJ. 2004. 752p. ISBN:0-13-191520-7, ISBN13: 978-0-13-191520-6. Dewey:808/.0666. LCCN:2004-015581.
Audience: **l,u,f.**

Technology: General > Industrial Safety

Cadick, John   TK152.C22 1994
Electrical Safety Handbook. Trade Cloth. McGraw-Hill School Education Group. Columbus, OH. 1992. 384p. ISBN:0-07-009514-0, ISBN13: 978-0-07-009514-4. Dewey:621.319/028/9. LCCN:94-013347.
Audience: **l,u,f.** *Choice, 1994.*

Cheremisinoff, Nicholas P. &   T55.3.H3C4859 1996
  Graffia, Madelyn
Safety Management Practices for Hazardous Materials. Paper over Boards. Marcel Dekker Inc. New York, NY. 1995. 368p. ISBN:0-8247-9687-X, ISBN13: 978-0-8247-9687-7. Dewey:363.17/6/0973. LCCN:95-037548.
Audience: **l,f.** *Choice, 1996.*

CoVan, James   T55
Safety Engineering. Ed. 1. Trade Cloth. John Wiley & Sons, Inc. Hoboken, NJ. 1995. 256p. New Dimensions in Engineering Ser., Vol. 9 ISBN:0-471-55612-2, ISBN13: 978-0-471-55612-1. Dewey:620.86. LCCN:93-027077.
Audience: **u,f.** *Choice, 1995.*

Crowl, Daniel A. & Louvar,   TP155.5.C76 1990
  Joseph F.
Chemical Process Safety: Fundamentals with Applications. Trade Cloth. Prentice Hall PTR. Upper Saddle River, NJ. 1989. 528p. Prentice Hall International Series in the Physical and Chemical Engineering Sciences Ser. ISBN:0-13-129701-5, ISBN13: 978-0-13-129701-2. Dewey:660/.2804. LCCN:89-008766.
Audience: **l,u,f.** *Choice, 1990.*

Evans, Leonard   HE5614.2.E958 2004
Traffic Safety. Trade Cloth. Science Serving Society. Bloomfield
Hills, MI. 2004. 445p. ISBN:0-9754871-0-8, ISBN13:
978-0-9754871-0-5. Dewey:363.125. LCCN:2004-095056.

Audience: **u,f.** *Choice, 2005.*

Filskov, Per, et al.   T55.3.H3S83 1996
Substitutes for Hazardous Chemicals in the Workplace. Tea
Johansen & Lena Hoglund (Authors). Paper over Boards. Lewis
Publishers. Boca Raton, FL. 1996. 192p. ISBN:1-56670-021-3,
ISBN13: 978-1-56670-021-4. Dewey:604.7. LCCN:95-049037.

Audience: **u,f.**

Hagan, Philip, et al.   T55.A333 2001
Accident Prevention Manual for Business and Industry:
Administration and Programs. Ed. 12. John F. Montgomery &
James T. O'Reilly (Authors). Trade Cloth. National Safety
Council. Itasca, IL. 2001. x, 836p. Occupational Safety and
Health Ser. ISBN:0-87912-212-9, ISBN13: 978-0-87912-212-6.
Dewey:658.4/08. LCCN:00-046568.

Audience: **u,f.**

Hagan, Philip (Editor), et al.   T55.A333 2001
Accident Prevention Manual for Business and Industry:
Engineering and Technology. Ed. 12. John F. Montgomery &
James T. O'Reilly (Editors), National Safety Council (NSC)
Staff (Contribution by). Trade Cloth. National Safety Council.
Itasca, IL. 2001. x, 877p. Occupational Safety and Health Ser.
ISBN:0-87912-213-7, ISBN13: 978-0-87912-213-3.
Dewey:363.11. LCCN:00-011927.

Audience: **u,f.**

Harris, Robert L. (Editor)   RC967.P37
Patty's Industrial Hygiene, Vol. 4. Ed. 5. Trade Cloth. John
Wiley & Sons, Inc. Hoboken, NJ. 2000. 3552p.
ISBN:0-471-29784-4, ISBN13: 978-0-471-29784-0.
Dewey:613.6/2. LCCN:99-032462.

Audience: **u,f.** *Choice, 2002.*

Koren, Herman   RA566.K59 2004
Illustrated Dictionary and Resource Directory of Environmental
and Occupational Health. Ed. 2. Paper over Boards. Lewis
Publishers. Boca Raton, FL. 2004. 712p. ISBN:1-56670-590-8,
ISBN13: 978-1-56670-590-5. Dewey:616.9/8/003.
LCCN:2003-065998.

Audience: **u,f.** *Choice, 2004.*

Krieger, Gary R.   TD194.A27 2000
Accident Prevention Manual for Business and Industry:
Environmental Management. Ed. 2. Trade Cloth. National Safety
Council. Itasca, IL. 1999. xiv, 539p. Occupational Safety and
Health Ser. ISBN:0-87912-209-9, ISBN13: 978-0-87912-209-6.
Dewey:658.4/08. LCCN:99-030662.

Audience: **u,f.**

Krieger, Gary R. & Balge,   RC967.O26 2000
Marci Z.
Occupational Health and Safety. Ed. 3. Trade Cloth. National
Safety Council. Itasca, IL. 2000. ix, 595p. Occupational Safety
and Health Ser. ISBN:0-87912-203-X, ISBN13:
978-0-87912-203-4. Dewey:616.9/803. LCCN:99-030897.

Audience: **l,u,f.**

Lewis, Richard J.   T55.3.H3L494 2004
Sax's Dangerous Properties of Industrial Materials. Ed. 11.
Trade Cloth. John Wiley & Sons, Inc. Hoboken, NJ. 2005.

4860p. ISBN:0-471-70133-5, ISBN13: 978-0-471-70133-0.
Dewey:604.7. LCCN:2005-273086.

Audience: **u,f.** *Choice, 2005, 2000, 1999, 1997.*

NFPA Staff   TK260
National Electrical Code 2005. Cloth Text. Thomson Delmar
Learning. Albany, NY. 2005. 1250p. ISBN:0-87765-625-8,
ISBN13: 978-0-87765-625-8. Dewey:348.023.

Audience: **l,u,f.**

O'Reilly, James T., et al.   T55.O683 1996
University Hospitals and School Managers Guide to
Environment: A Guide for University, Hospital, and School
Managers. Philip Hagan & Peter de la Cruz (Authors). Cloth
Text. John Wiley & Sons, Inc. Hoboken, NJ. 1996. 368p.
Industrial Health and Safety Ser. ISBN:0-442-02123-2, ISBN13:
978-0-442-02123-8. Dewey:371.6/068/4. LCCN:95-038757.

Audience: **u,f.** *Choice, 1996.*

Pitblado, Robin, et al.   T174.5.R556 1996
Risk Assessment and Management Handbook: For
Environmental, Health, and Safety Professionals. Ed. 1. Scott
Stricoff, Steve Bartell & Rao V. Kolluru (Authors). Trade Cloth.
McGraw-Hill Professional Publishing. New York, NY. 1995.
688p. ISBN:0-07-035987-3, ISBN13: 978-0-07-035987-1.
Dewey:363.1. LCCN:95-021284.

Audience: **g,l,u,f.** *Choice, 1996.*

Sittig, Marshall   RA1215.S58 2002
Handbook of Toxic and Hazardous Chemicals and Carcinogens.
Ed. 4. Richard P. Pohanish (Editor). Trade Cloth. Noyes Data
Corporation/Noyes Publications. Park Ridge, NJ. 2002. 2300p.
ISBN:0-8155-1459-X, ISBN13: 978-0-8155-1459-6.
Dewey:615.9/02. LCCN:2001-056289.

Audience: **u,f.** *Choice, 2003, 2002.*

Urben, Peter   TP149
Bretherick's Handbook of Reactive Chemical Hazards. Ed. 6.
Trade Paper. Elsevier Science & Technology Books. Saint
Louis, MO. 2000. 2100p. ISBN:0-7506-4725-6, ISBN13:
978-0-7506-4725-0. Dewey:660/.2804.

Audience: **u,f.**

Wallace, Ian   TP155.5.W35 1995
Developing Effective Safety Systems. Other. Elsevier Science &
Technology Books. Saint Louis, MO. 1995. 166p.
ISBN:0-88415-205-7, ISBN13: 978-0-88415-205-7.
Dewey:660/.2804. LCCN:94-073482.

Audience: **l,u,f.** *Choice, 1996.*

Woodside, Gayle &   TD145.W67 1997
Kocurek, Dianna
Environmental, Safety, and Health Engineering. Trade Cloth.
John Wiley & Sons, Inc. Hoboken, NJ. 1997. 600p.
ISBN:0-471-10932-0, ISBN13: 978-0-471-10932-7. Dewey:628.
LCCN:96-044717.

Audience: **u,f.** *Choice, 1998.*

Applied Mathematics > Engineering Mathematics

Devore, Jay L.   **QA273.D46 2004**
Probability and Statistics for Engineering and the Sciences. Ed. 6. Cloth Text. Brooks/Cole. Pacific Grove, CA. 2003. 816p. ISBN:0-534-39933-9, ISBN13: 978-0-534-39933-7. Dewey:519.2. LCCN:2003-101979.
                  Audience: **l,u.**

Graver, Jack   **TA407.G68 2001**
Counting on Frameworks: Mathematics to Aid the Design of Rigid Structures. Paper Text. Mathematical Association of America. Washington, DC. 2001. 192p. Dolciani Mathematical Expositions Ser., Vol. 25 ISBN:0-88385-331-0, ISBN13: 978-0-88385-331-3. Dewey:624.1/7. LCCN:2001-089227.
           Audience: **l,u.** *Choice, 2002.*

Kreyszig, Erwin   **QA401**
Advanced Engineering Mathematics. Ed. 9. Trade Paper. John Wiley & Sons, Inc. Hoboken, NJ. 2006. 260p. ISBN:0-471-72644-3, ISBN13: 978-0-471-72644-9. Dewey:510/.2462. LCCN:2004-065932.
                  Audience: **u.** *B*

O'Neil, Peter V.   **QA331.3**
Advanced Engineering Mathematics. Ed. 6. Cloth Text. Thomson Learning. Independence, KY. 2006. 1216p. ISBN:0-534-55208-0, ISBN13: 978-0-534-55208-4. Dewey:515/.1.
                  Audience: **u.**

Walpole, Ronald E., et al.   **TA340.P738 2006**
Probability and Statistics for Engineers and Scientists. Ed. 8. Raymond Myers, Sharon L. Myers & Keying Ye (Authors). Cloth Text. Prentice Hall PTR. Upper Saddle River, NJ. 2006. 848p. ISBN:0-13-187711-9, ISBN13: 978-0-13-187711-5. Dewey:519.02/462. LCCN:2005-058605.
                  Audience: **l,u.**

Applied Mathematics > Computer Applications

Brickman, Louis   **T57.74.B74 1989**
A Mathematical Introduction to Linear Programming and Game Theory. Trade Cloth. Springer. New York, NY. 1989. XI, 130p. Undergraduate Texts in Mathematics ISBN:0-387-96931-4, ISBN13: 978-0-387-96931-2. Dewey:519.7/2. LCCN:89-011257.
           Audience: **l,u,f.** *Choice, 1990.*

Cumberbatch, Ellis & Fitt, Alistair (Editors)   **T57.62 .M38 2001**
Mathematical Modeling: Case Studies from Industry. Trade Cloth. Cambridge University Press. New York, NY. 2001. 316p. ISBN:0-521-65007-0, ISBN13: 978-0-521-65007-6. Dewey:670/.1/5118. LCCN:00-054672.
           Audience: **u,f.** *Choice, 2002.*

Frigon, Normand L. & Mathews, David   **T57.37.F75 1997**
Practical Guide to Experimental Design. Ed. 1. Trade Cloth. John Wiley & Sons, Inc. Hoboken, NJ. 1996. 360p. ISBN:0-471-13919-X, ISBN13: 978-0-471-13919-5. Dewey:658.4/033. LCCN:96-023728.
           Audience: **u,f.** *Choice, 1997.*

Gnedenko, Boris V. & Kovalenko, I. N.   **T57.9.G5813 1989**
Introduction to Queueing Theory. Ed. 2. Trade Cloth. Springer. New York, NY. 1989. 350p. Mathematical Modeling Ser., No. 5 ISBN:0-8176-3423-1, ISBN13: 978-0-8176-3423-0. Dewey:519.8/2. LCCN:89-007306.
           Audience: **l,u,f.** *Choice, 1990.*

Karloff, Howard   **T57.74.K37 1991**
Linear Programming. Ed. 2. Trade Paper. Springer. New York, NY. 1991. 142p. Progress in Theoretical Computer Science Ser. ISBN:0-8176-3561-0, ISBN13: 978-0-8176-3561-9. Dewey:519.7/2. LCCN:91-003387.
           Audience: **l,u,f.** *Choice, 1992.*

Nazareth, J. L.   **T57.74.N38 1987**
Computer Solution of Linear Programs. Cloth Text. Oxford University Press, Inc. New York, NY. 1988. 254p. Monographs on Numerical Analysis ISBN:0-19-504278-6, ISBN13: 978-0-19-504278-8. Dewey:519.7/2. LCCN:86-033108.
           Audience: **u,f.** *Choice, 1988.*

Nering, Evar D. & Tucker, Albert W.   **T57.74.N46 1993**
Linear Programs and Related Problems. Trade Cloth. Elsevier Science & Technology Books. Saint Louis, MO. 1992. 584p. Computer Science and Scientific Computing Ser., Vol. 1 ISBN:0-12-515440-2, ISBN13: 978-0-12-515440-6. Dewey:519.7/2. LCCN:89-017804.
           Audience: **l,u,f.** *Choice, 1993.*

Pannell, David J.   **T57.74.P37 1997**
Introduction to Practical Linear Programming. Ed. 1. Trade Cloth. John Wiley & Sons, Inc. Hoboken, NJ. 1996. 332p. ISBN:0-471-51789-5, ISBN13: 978-0-471-51789-4. Dewey:519.7/2. LCCN:96-006185.
           Audience: **l,u,f.** *Choice, 1997.*

Parlar, Mahmut&   **T57.6.P38 2000**
Interactive Operations Research with Maple: Methods and Models. Trade Cloth. Springer. New York, NY. 2000. XV, 468p. ISBN:0-8176-4165-3, ISBN13: 978-0-8176-4165-8. Dewey:658.4/034/0285. LCCN:00-031232.
           Audience: **u,f.** *Choice, 2001.*

Strayer, J. K.   **T57.74.S82 1989**
Linear Programming and Its Applications. Trade Cloth. Springer. New York, NY. 1989. XI, 284p. Undergraduate Texts in Mathematics ISBN:0-387-96930-6, ISBN13: 978-0-387-96930-5. Dewey:519.7/2. LCCN:89-030834.
           Audience: **l,u,f.** *Choice, 1990.*

Industrial Engineering > Invention and Patents

Smith, Roger (Editor)   **T20.I59 2001**
Inventions and Inventors, Vol. 2. Library Binding. Salem Press, Inc. Hackensack, NJ. 2001. 936p. Magill's Choice Ser. ISBN:1-58765-016-9, ISBN13: 978-1-58765-016-1. Dewey:609. LCCN:2001-049412.
           Audience: **l,u,f.** *Choice, 2002.*

Industrial Engineering > Manufacturing

Bray, Donald E. & Stanley,　　　**TA417.2.B63 1989**
Roderick K.
Nondestructive Evaluation: A Tool in Design, Manufacturing and Service. Cloth Text. McGraw-Hill Companies, The. New York, NY. 1989. 672p. McGraw-Hill Series in Mechanical Engineering ISBN:0-07-007351-1, ISBN13: 978-0-07-007351-7. Dewey:620.1/127. LCCN:88-019015.
Audience: **u,f.** *Choice, 1989.*

Brown, James　　　**TS183.B76 1991**
Modern Manufacturing Processes. Trade Cloth. Industrial Press, Inc. New York, NY. 1991. 256p. ISBN:0-8311-3034-2, ISBN13: 978-0-8311-3034-3. Dewey:670.42. LCCN:90-048046.
Audience: **l,u,f.** *Choice, 1992.*

Dorf, Richard C. & Kusiak,　　　**TS183.H359 1994**
Andrew (Editors)
Handbook of Design, Manufacturing and Automation. Trade Cloth. John Wiley & Sons, Inc. Hoboken, NJ. 1994. 1064p. ISBN:0-471-55218-6, ISBN13: 978-0-471-55218-5. Dewey:670.42/7. LCCN:94-007901.
Audience: **l,u,f.** *Choice, 1995.*

Drexler, K. Eric　　　**T174.7.D74 1992**
Nanosystems: Molecular Machinery, Manufacturing, and Computation. Trade Cloth. John Wiley & Sons, Inc. Hoboken, NJ. 1992. 576p. ISBN:0-471-57547-X, ISBN13: 978-0-471-57547-4. Dewey:620.43. LCCN:92-030870.
Audience: **u,f.** *Choice, 1993.*

Geng, Hwaiyu　　　**TS176.M3615 2004**
Manufacturing Engineering Handbook. Trade Cloth. McGraw-Hill Professional Publishing. New York, NY. 2004. 1088p. McGraw-Hill Handbooks ISBN:0-07-139825-2, ISBN13: 978-0-07-139825-1. Dewey:658.5. LCCN:2004-049949.
Audience: **u,f.** *Choice, 2005.*

Henzold, G.　　　**TS172.H46 1995**
Handbook of Geometrical Tolerancing: Design, Manufacturing and Inspection. Ed. 1. Trade Cloth. John Wiley & Sons, Inc. Hoboken, NJ. 1995. 430p. ISBN:0-471-94816-0, ISBN13: 978-0-471-94816-2. Dewey:620/.0045. LCCN:95-159689.
Audience: **l,u,f.** *Choice, 1996.*

Koshal, D. (Editor)　　　**TS176.M3622 1993**
Manufacturing Engineer's Reference Book, Vol. 13. Ed. 13. Trade Cloth. Elsevier Science & Technology Books. Saint Louis, MO. 1993. 896p. ISBN:0-7506-1154-5, ISBN13: 978-0-7506-1154-1. Dewey:670.42. LCCN:94-121765.
Audience: **u,f.** *Choice, 1994.*

Lim, Kyung S. (Editor)　　　**TS176**
How Products Are Made: An Illustrated Guide to Product Manufacturing. Trade Cloth. Thomson Gale. Farmington Hills, MI. 1995. 520p. ISBN:0-8103-8952-5, ISBN13: 978-0-8103-8952-6. Dewey:670.
Audience: **g,l,u,f.** *Choice, 1996.*

National Academy of　　　**TS155.6.D47 1988**
Engineering Staff
Design and Analysis of Integrated Manufacturing Systems. Cloth Text. National Academies Press. Washington, DC. 1988. 248p. ISBN:0-309-03844-8, ISBN13: 978-0-309-03844-7. Dewey:670.42/7. LCCN:88-001766.
Audience: **u,f.** *Choice, 1988.*

Schlager, Nell Y.　　　**TA5**
How Products Are Made: An Illustrated Guide to Product Manufacturing, Vol. 1. Trade Cloth. Thomson Gale. Farmington Hills, MI. 1993. 524p. ISBN:0-8103-8907-X, ISBN13: 978-0-8103-8907-6. Dewey:620.
Audience: **g,l,u,f.** *Choice, 1994.*

Singh, Nanua　　　**TS155.63.S56 1996**
Systems Approach to Computer-Integrated Design and Manufacturing. Ed. 1. Trade Cloth. John Wiley & Sons, Inc. Hoboken, NJ. 1995. 664p. ISBN:0-471-58517-3, ISBN13: 978-0-471-58517-6. Dewey:670/.285. LCCN:94-040012.
Audience: **l,u,f.** *Choice, 1996.*

Todd, Robert H., et al.　　　**TS183.T63 1994**
Manufacturing Processes Reference Guide. Dell K. Allen & Leo Alting (Authors). Trade Cloth. Industrial Press, Inc. New York, NY. 1994. 512p. ISBN:0-8311-3049-0, ISBN13: 978-0-8311-3049-7. Dewey:671. LCCN:93-031767.
Audience: **u,f.** *Choice, 1994.*

Turbide, David A.　　　**TS155.6.T86 1991**
Computers in Manufacturing. Trade Cloth. Industrial Press, Inc. New York, NY. 1991. 224p. ISBN:0-8311-3033-4, ISBN13: 978-0-8311-3033-6. Dewey:670/.285. LCCN:90-047446.
Audience: **l,u,f.** *Choice, 1991.*

Waldner, J. B.　　　**TS155.6.W3513 1992**
Principles of Computer Integrated Manufacturing. W. J. Duffin (Translator). Trade Paper. John Wiley & Sons, Inc. Hoboken, NJ. 1992. 206p. ISBN:0-471-93450-X, ISBN13: 978-0-471-93450-9. Dewey:670.285. LCCN:92-009522.
Audience: **u,f.** *Choice, 1993.*

Waters, T. F.　　　**TS183.W38 1996**
Fundamentals of Manufacturing for Engineers. UCL PRess. 1996. ISBN:1-85728-338-4, ISBN13: 978-1-85728-338-9.
Audience: **l,u,f.**

Civil Engineering > Standards

　　　TA404.5
ASTM International Standards on Sustainability in Buildings. ASTM. ISBN:0-8031-3341-3, ISBN13: 978-0-8031-3341-9.
Audience: **u,f.**

　　　TA684
Manual of Steel Construction, Load and Resistance Factor Design, 3rd Edition. Trade Cloth. American Institute of Steel Construction. Chicago, IL. 2001. ISBN:1-56424-051-7, ISBN13: 978-1-56424-051-4. Dewey:624.1821.
Audience: **l,u,f.**

　　　TH435 .M44
Square Foot Costs. Ed. 27. Trade Paper, Perfect. R. S. Means Company, Inc. Kingston, MA. 2005. 488p. ISBN:0-87629-794-7, ISBN13: 978-0-87629-794-0. Dewey:621.
Audience: **l,u,f.**

American Institute of　　　**TA666.T47 2004**
Timber Construction Staff
Timber Construction Manual. Ed. 5. Trade Cloth. John Wiley & Sons, Inc. Hoboken, NJ. 2004. 496p. Wiley Survival Guides in Engineering and Science Ser. ISBN:0-471-23687-X, ISBN13: 978-0-471-23687-0. Dewey:694. LCCN:2004-000225.
Audience: **u,f.**

American Society for   **GE45.S25A88 2002**
Testing and Materials Committee D-18 on Soil and Rock &
American Society for Testing and Materials Staff
(Contribution by)
ASTM Standards Related to Environmental Site
Characterization. Ed. 2. Trade Cloth. American Society for
Testing & Materials. West Conshohocken, PA. 2002. 1827p.
ISBN:0-8031-2840-1, ISBN13: 978-0-8031-2840-8.
Dewey:628.5/32. LCCN:2002-018226.

Audience: **u,f.**

American Society of Civil   **TH851.M56 2002**
Engineers Staff
Minimum Design Loads for Buildings and Other Structures.
Trade Cloth. American Society of Civil Engineers. Reston, VA.
2002. 352p. SEI/ASCE Standard, No. 7-02
ISBN:0-7844-0624-3, ISBN13: 978-0-7844-0624-3.
Dewey:624.1/72/021873. LCCN:2002-038610.

Audience: **l,u,f.**

Archdeacon, William   **TD665.A83 2005**
(Editor)
ASCE/EWRI 45-05 (Standard Guidelines for the Design of
Urban Stormwater Systems), ASCE/EWRI 46-05 (Standard
Guidelines for the Installation of Urban Stormwater Systems),
and ASCE/EWRI 47-05 (Standard Guidelines for the Operation
and Maintenance of Urban Stormwater Systems). American
Society of Civil Engineers Staff (Contribution by). Paper Text.
American Society of Civil Engineers. Reston, VA. 2005. 120p.
ISBN:0-7844-0806-8, ISBN13: 978-0-7844-0806-3.
Dewey:628/.212/0218. LCCN:2005-022933.

Audience: **u,f.**

ASTM Subcommittee   **TH153.A86 2004**
E06.81 on Building Economics Staff (Contribution by)
ASTM Standards on Building Economics. Trade Paper.
American Society for Testing & Materials. West Conshohocken,
PA. 2004. 304p. ISBN:0-8031-3148-8, ISBN13:
978-0-8031-3148-4. Dewey:690/.068/1. LCCN:2004-047739.

Audience: **u,f.**

Breyer, Donald E., et al.   **NA4110**
Design of Wood Structures - ASD. Ed. 5. Kelly Cobeen,
Kenneth J. Fridley & David G. Pollock (Authors). Cloth Text.
McGraw-Hill Professional Publishing. New York, NY. 2003.
950p. ISBN:0-07-137932-0, ISBN13: 978-0-07-137932-8.
Dewey:624.1/84. LCCN:2003-279056.

Audience: **l,u,f.**

Chen, W. F.   **TA151.C57 2002**
The Civil Engineering Handbook. Ed. 2. CRC Press. 2003.
ISBN:0-8493-0958-1, ISBN13: 978-0-8493-0958-8.

Audience: **u,f.**

Choi, Ying-Kit   **TH425.C44 2004**
Principles of Applied Civil Engineering Design. Trade Paper.
American Society of Civil Engineers. Reston, VA. 2004. 227p.
ISBN:0-7844-0712-6, ISBN13: 978-0-7844-0712-7. Dewey:624.
LCCN:2003-063835.

Audience: **u,f.**

Colley, Barbara C.   **TA151**
Practical Manual of Land Development. Ed. 4. Trade Cloth.
McGraw-Hill Companies, The. New York, NY. 2005. 416p.
ISBN:0-07-144866-7, ISBN13: 978-0-07-144866-6. Dewey:624.
LCCN:2005-047896.

Audience: **l,u,f.**

Ellingwood, Bruce Jr. &   **TH845.S75 2005**
Kanda, Jun (Editors)
Structural Safety and Its Quality Assurance. Paper Text.
American Society of Civil Engineers. Reston, VA. 2005. 208p.
ISBN:0-7844-0816-5, ISBN13: 978-0-7844-0816-2.
Dewey:624.1/71. LCCN:2005-053573.

Audience: **u,f.**

Grigg, Neil S. & Criswell,   **TA145.C59 2001**
Marvin E.
Civil Engineering Practice in the Twenty-First Century:
Knowledge and Skills for Design and Management. Trade Cloth.
American Society of Civil Engineers. Reston, VA. 2001. 272p.
ISBN:0-7844-0526-3, ISBN13: 978-0-7844-0526-0. Dewey:624.
LCCN:2001-018217.

Audience: **u,f.**

Hicks, Tyler G.   **TA331.H53 2001**
Civil Engineering Formulas: Pocket Guide. Trade Paper.
McGraw-Hill Professional Publishing. New York, NY. 2001.
350p. McGraw-Hill Pocket Reference Ser. ISBN:0-07-135612-6,
ISBN13: 978-0-07-135612-1. Dewey:624/.01/51.
LCCN:2001-034309.

Audience: **l,u,f.**

International Code Council   **HF5351**
International Building Code 2006: Softcover Version. Paper
Text. Thomson Delmar Learning. Albany, NY. 2006.
ISBN:1-58001-251-5, ISBN13: 978-1-58001-251-5. Dewey:650.
Audience: **g,l,u,f.**

International Code Council   **KF3975.I58 2006**
International Fire Code 2006: Softcover Version. Paper Text.
Thomson Delmar Learning. Albany, NY. 2006.
ISBN:1-58001-255-8, ISBN13: 978-1-58001-255-3.
Dewey:344.730537.

Audience: **g,l,u,f.**

International Code Council   **KFN5035**
International Residential Code 2006: Softcover Version. Paper
Text. Thomson Delmar Learning. Albany, NY. 2006.
ISBN:1-58001-253-1, ISBN13: 978-1-58001-253-9.
Dewey:690.837.

Audience: **g,l,u,f.**

Juran, Joseph M. &   **TS156.Q3618 1998**
Godfrey, A. Blanton
Juran's Quality Handbook. Ed. 5. Trade Cloth. McGraw-Hill
Professional Publishing. New York, NY. 1998. 1872p.
ISBN:0-07-034003-X, ISBN13: 978-0-07-034003-9.
Dewey:658.5/62. LCCN:98-043311.

Audience: **u,f.**

Keenan, Andrea & Georges,   **TH880.G74 2002**
Danielle
Green Building: Project Planning and Cost Estimating. Trade
Cloth. R. S. Means Company, Inc. Kingston, MA. 2002. 350p.
Reference Book Publications ISBN:0-87629-659-2, ISBN13:
978-0-87629-659-2. Dewey:690.837. LCCN:2003-266423.

Audience: **l,u,f.**

Lindeburg, Michael R.   **TA159.L53 2006**
Civil Engineering Reference Manual for the PE Exam. Ed. 10.
Trade Cloth. Professional Publications, Inc. Belmont, CA. 2005.
1424p. ISBN:1-59126-043-4, ISBN13: 978-1-59126-043-1.
Dewey:624. LCCN:2005-053516.

Audience: **u,f.**

Masonry Standards Joint   **TA682.24.B85 2005**
  Committee (MSJC), Masonry society
Building Code Requirements and Specification for Masonry
Structures - 2005, ACI 530/ASCE 5-05/TMS 402 and ACI
530.1/ASCE 6-05/TMS 602. ASCE. 2005. ASCE Standard No.
5-05 and 6-05

Audience: **u,f.**

McDonald, Patrick H.   **TA153.M34 2001**
Fundamentals of Infrastructure Engineering: Civil Engineering
Systems, Vol. 7. Ed. 2. Paper over Boards. Marcel Dekker Inc.
New York, NY. 2001. 472p. Civil and Environmental
Engineering Ser., Vol. 7 ISBN:0-8247-0612-9, ISBN13:
978-0-8247-0612-8. Dewey:624. LCCN:2001-042177.

Audience: **u,f.**

Mehta, Kishor   **TH891**
Wind Loads on Structures. American Society of Civil
Engineers. 2002. ISBN:0-9729253-1-7, ISBN13:
978-0-9729253-1-0.

Audience: **u,f.**

Mehta, Kishor C. &   **TH891.M45 2003**
  Delahay, James M.
Guide to the Use of the Wind Load Provisions of ASCE 7-02.
Trade Cloth. American Society of Civil Engineers. Reston, VA.
2004. 144p. ISBN:0-7844-0703-7, ISBN13: 978-0-7844-0703-5.
Dewey:624.1/72/021873. LCCN:2003-063552.

Audience: **u,f.**

Merritt, Frederick S., et al.   **TA151.S8 2003**
Standard Handbook for Civil Engineers. Ed. 5. Jonathan T.
Ricketts & M. Kent Loftin (Authors). Trade Cloth. McGraw-Hill
Professional Publishing. New York, NY. 2003. 1600p. Handbook
Ser. ISBN:0-07-136473-0, ISBN13: 978-0-07-136473-7.
Dewey:624. LCCN:2003-061440.

Audience: **l,u,f.** *Choice, 2004, 1996.*

Narayanan, R. S. & Beeby,   **TA174.N35 2000**
  A. W.
Introduction to Design for Civil Engineers. UK-B Format
Paperback. Routledge. New York, NY. 2000. 208p.
ISBN:0-419-23550-7, ISBN13: 978-0-419-23550-7. Dewey:624.
LCCN:00-044548.

Audience: **u,f.** *Choice, 2001.*

NFPA Staff   **TK260**
National Electrical Code 2005. Cloth Text. Thomson Delmar
Learning. Albany, NY. 2005. 1250p. ISBN:0-87765-625-8,
ISBN13: 978-0-87765-625-8. Dewey:348.023.

Audience: **l,u,f.**

Parmley, Robert O.   **TA151.P33 2003**
Civil Engineer's Illustrated Sourcebook. E-Book.
McGraw-Hill Professional Publishing. New York, NY.
ISBN:0-07-142886-0, ISBN13: 978-0-07-142886-6. Dewey:624.

Audience: **l,u,f.**

Parmley, Robert O.   **TA151.F5 2002**
Field Engineer's Manual. Ed. 3. Spiral. McGraw-Hill
Professional Publishing. New York, NY. 2001. 720p. Portable
Engineering Ser. ISBN:0-07-135624-X, ISBN13:
978-0-07-135624-4. Dewey:624. LCCN:2001-044171.

Audience: **u,f.**

R. S. Means Company Staff   **TH435**
Building Construction Cost Data. Trade Cloth. R. S. Means
Company, Inc. Kingston, MA. 2005. 700p.

ISBN:0-87629-786-6, ISBN13: 978-0-87629-786-5.
Dewey:692.5.

Audience: **l,u,f.**

R. S. Means Company Staff   **TH435.M42 2003**
Means Estimating Handbook. Ed. 2. Trade Cloth. R. S. Means
Company, Inc. Kingston, MA. 2003. xvi, 918p.
ISBN:0-87629-699-1, ISBN13: 978-0-87629-699-8.
Dewey:692/.5. LCCN:2004-555465.

Audience: **l,u,f.**

Ratay, Robert T.   **TA219.F685 2000**
Forensic Structural Engineering Handbook. Trade Cloth.
McGraw-Hill Professional Publishing. New York, NY. 2000.
688p. McGraw-Hill Handbooks Ser. ISBN:0-07-052667-2,
ISBN13: 978-0-07-052667-9. Dewey:624.1/71.
LCCN:00-701354.

Audience: **u,f.**

Reese, Charles D   **TH443.R434 2006**
Handbook of OSHA Construction Safety and Health. Ed. 2.
CRC/Taylor&Francis. 2006. ISBN:0-8493-6546-5, ISBN13:
978-0-8493-6546-1.

Audience: **u,f.**

Simiu, Emil & Miyata,   **TA654.5.S54 2006**
  Toshio
Design of Buildings and Bridges for Wind: A Practical Guide
for ASCE-7 Standard Users and Designers of Special Structures.
Trade Cloth. John Wiley & Sons, Inc. Hoboken, NJ. 2006. 320p.
ISBN:0-471-65743-3, ISBN13: 978-0-471-65743-9.
Dewey:624.1/75. LCCN:2005-021300.

Audience: **l,u,f.**

Structural Engineering   **TK9152.163.S77 2005**
  Institute (Contribution by)
Seismic Design Criteria for Structures, Systems, and
Components in Nuclear Facilities. Trade Paper. American
Society of Civil Engineers. Reston, VA. 2005. 96p.
ISBN:0-7844-0762-2, ISBN13: 978-0-7844-0762-2.
Dewey:621.48/32. LCCN:2005-005011.

Audience: **u,f.**

Taguchi, Genichi, et al.   **TS156.T343 2004**
Taguchi's Quality Engineering Handbook. Subir Chowdhury &
Yuin Wu (Authors). Trade Cloth. John Wiley & Sons, Inc.
Hoboken, NJ. 2004. 1696p. ISBN:0-471-41334-8, ISBN13:
978-0-471-41334-9. Dewey:658.5/62. LCCN:2004-011335.

Audience: **l,u,f.** *Choice, 2006.*

Taylor, Craig E. &   **TA153.I5 2005**
  Vanmarcke, Erik
Infrastructure Risk Management Processes: Natural, Accidental,
and Deliberate Hazards. ASCE Council on Disaster Risk
Management Staff (Contribution by). Paper Text. American
Society of Civil Engineers. Reston, VA. 2005. 304p.
ISBN:0-7844-0815-7, ISBN13: 978-0-7844-0815-5. Dewey:624.
LCCN:2005-044492.

Audience: **u,f.**

Civil Engineering > Materials Science

TA461
Metals and Alloys in the Unified Numbering System. Trade
Paper. Society of Automotive Engineers, Inc. Warrendale, PA.

2004. 500p. ISBN:0-7680-1488-3, ISBN13: 978-0-7680-1488-4. Dewey:669/.01/2.

Audience: **l,u,f.**

TA417
Nondestructive Evaluation and Quality Control. Ed. 9. Trade Cloth. A S M International. Materials Park, OH. 1989. 795p. ASM Handbook Ser., Vol. 17 ISBN:0-87170-023-9, ISBN13: 978-0-87170-023-0. Dewey:620.1.

Audience: **u,f.**

AISE Staff   **TN730.M35 1998**
The Making, Shaping and Treating of Steel: Steelmaking and Refining Volume. Ed. 11. Richard J. Fruehan (Editor). Trade Cloth. Association for Iron & Steel Technology. Warrendale, PA. 1998. 767p. ISBN:0-930767-02-0, ISBN13: 978-0-930767-02-0. Dewey:672. LCCN:98-073477.

Audience: **u,f.**

American Institute of   **TA666.T47 2004**
  Timber Construction Staff
Timber Construction Manual. Ed. 5. Trade Cloth. John Wiley & Sons, Inc. Hoboken, NJ. 2004. 496p. Wiley Survival Guides in Engineering and Science Ser. ISBN:0-471-23687-X, ISBN13: 978-0-471-23687-0. Dewey:694. LCCN:2004-000225.

Audience: **u,f.**

Amstock, Joseph S.   **TA450.A55 1997**
Handbook of Glass in Construction. Trade Cloth. McGraw-Hill Professional Publishing. New York, NY. 1997. 584p. ISBN:0-07-001619-4, ISBN13: 978-0-07-001619-4. Dewey:624.1/838. LCCN:97-001273.

Audience: **u,f.** *Choice, 1998.*

Anderson, T. L.   **TA409 .A493 1991**
Fracture Mechanics: Fundamentals and Application. Library Binding. C R C Press LLC. Boca Raton, FL. 1991. ISBN:0-8493-4422-0, ISBN13: 978-0-8493-4422-0. Dewey:620.1/126. LCCN:91-034305.

Audience: **u,f.**

Ashby, Michael F. & Jones,   **TA403**
  David. R. H.
Engineering Materials 1: An Introduction to Properties, Applications and Design. Ed. 3. Paper Text. Elsevier Science & Technology Books. Saint Louis, MO. 2005. 448p. ISBN:0-7506-6380-4, ISBN13: 978-0-7506-6380-9. Dewey:620.1/1.

Audience: **l,u.**

Askeland, Donald R. &   **TA403**
  Phule, Pradeep P.
Science and Engineering of Materials. Ed. 5. Cloth Text. Nelson Thomson Learning. Scarborough, ON. 2005. 896p. ISBN:0-534-55396-6, ISBN13: 978-0-534-55396-8. Dewey:620.11.

Audience: **l,u.**

Bannantine, Julie A., et al.   **TA460.B23 1990**
Fundamentals of Metal Fatigue Analysis. Ed. 1. Jess J. Comer & James L. Handrock (Authors). Cloth Text. Prentice Hall PTR. Upper Saddle River, NJ. 1989. 273p. ISBN:0-13-340191-X, ISBN13: 978-0-13-340191-2. Dewey:620.1/63. LCCN:88-038653.

Audience: **u,f.** *Choice, 1990.*

Barbero, Ever J.   **TA418.9.C6I599 1998**
Introduction to Composite Materials Design. Paper over Boards. Taylor & Francis Group. Philadelphia, PA. 1998. 354p. ISBN:1-56032-701-4, ISBN13: 978-1-56032-701-1. Dewey:620.1/18. LCCN:98-021968.

Audience: **l,u.**

Bardal, Einar   **TA418.74**
Corrosion and Protection. Trade Cloth. Springer. New York, NY. 2004. 336p. Engineering Materials and Processes Ser. ISBN:1-85233-758-3, ISBN13: 978-1-85233-758-2. Dewey:620.1/1223. LCCN:2003-054415.

Audience: **u,f.** *Choice, 2004.*

Barsom, John M. & Rolfe,   **TA409.B37 1999**
  Stanley T. (Editors)
Fracture and Fatigue Control in Structures: Applications of Fracture Mechanics. Ed. 3. Trade Cloth. American Society for Testing & Materials. West Conshohocken, PA. 1999. 525p. ISBN:0-8031-2082-6, ISBN13: 978-0-8031-2082-2. Dewey:620.1/126. LCCN:99-045439.

Audience: **u,f.**

Bauccio, Michael L. (Editor)   **TA459.A78 1993**
ASM Metals Reference Book. Ed. 3. Trade Cloth. A S M International. Materials Park, OH. 1993. 614p. ISBN:0-87170-478-1, ISBN13: 978-0-87170-478-8. Dewey:620.1/6. LCCN:93-028716.

Audience: **l,u.** *Choice, 1994.*

Beer, Ferdinand Pierre,   **TA405.B39 2004**
  et al.
Mechanics of Materials. Ed. 4. E. Russell Johnston & John T. DeWolf (Authors). Trade Cloth. McGraw-Hill Companies, The. New York, NY. 2004. xix, 787p. ISBN:0-07-298090-7, ISBN13: 978-0-07-298090-5. Dewey:620.1/12. LCCN:2004-058751.

Audience: **u,f.**

Broek, David   **TA409**
Elementary Engineering Fracture Mechanics. Ed. 4. Trade Cloth. Springer. New York, NY. 1982. 524p. ISBN:90-247-2580-1, ISBN13: 978-90-247-2580-9. Dewey:620.1/126. LCCN:82-045135.

Audience: **l,u.** *B*

Brooks, Charles R.   **TA460.B755 1993**
Metallurgical Failure Analysis. Cloth Text. McGraw-Hill Professional Publishing. New York, NY. 1992. 409p. ISBN:0-07-008078-X, ISBN13: 978-0-07-008078-2. Dewey:620.1/66. LCCN:92-024839.

Audience: **u,f.** *Choice, 1993.*

Buch, A.   **TA459.B787 1999**
Pure Metals Properties: A Scientific and Technical Handbook. Trade Cloth. A S M International. Materials Park, OH. 1999. 307p. ISBN:0-87170-637-7, ISBN13: 978-0-87170-637-9. Dewey:546.3. LCCN:2001-316168.

Audience: **u,f.**

Budinski, Ken & Budinski,   **TA403**
  Michael K.
Engineering Materials: Properties and Selection. Ed. 8. Cloth Text. Prentice Hall PTR. Upper Saddle River, NJ. 2004. 880p. ISBN:0-13-183779-6, ISBN13: 978-0-13-183779-9. Dewey:620.1/1.

Audience: **u,f.**

Callister, William D. Jr.   **TA403.C23 2006**
Materials Science and Engineering: An Introduction. Ed. 7.
Trade Cloth. John Wiley & Sons, Inc. Hoboken, NJ. 2006. 832p.
ISBN:0-471-73696-1, ISBN13: 978-0-471-73696-7.
Dewey:620.1/1. LCCN:2005-054228.

Audience: **l,u.**

Cardarelli, Francois   **TA404.8.C37 2000**
Materials Handbook: A Concise Desktop Reference. Trade
Cloth. Springer. New York, NY. 2001. XI, 595p.
ISBN:1-85233-168-2, ISBN13: 978-1-85233-168-9.
Dewey:620.1/1. LCCN:99-020194.

Audience: **l,u,f.**

Cartz, Louis   **TA417.2.C37 1995**
Nondestructive Testing. Trade Cloth. A S M International.
Materials Park, OH. 1995. 229p. ISBN:0-87170-517-6, ISBN13:
978-0-87170-517-4. Dewey:620.1/127. LCCN:94-073646.

Audience: **u,f.** *Choice, 1996.*

Chakrabarty, Jagabanduhu   **TA652.C44 2000**
Applied Plasticity. Trade Cloth. Springer. New York, NY. 2000.
IX, 682p. Mechanical Engineering Ser. ISBN:0-387-98812-2,
ISBN13: 978-0-387-98812-2. Dewey:620.1/1233.
LCCN:99-017361.

Audience: **u,f.**

Chawla, Sohan L. & Gupta,   **TA418.75.C48 1993**
R. K.
Materials Selection for Corrosion Control. Trade Cloth. A S M
International. Materials Park, OH. 1993. 508p.
ISBN:0-87170-474-9, ISBN13: 978-0-87170-474-0.
Dewey:620.1/1223. LCCN:93-038047.

Audience: **u,f.** *Choice, 1994.*

Cheremisinoff, Nicholas P.   **TA418.9.C6H32 1992**
🄴 Handbook of Ceramics and Composites. E-Book. NetLibrary,
Inc. Boulder, CO. 1992. ISBN:0-585-37478-3, ISBN13:
978-0-585-37478-9. Dewey:620.1/18.

Audience: **u,f.**

Cheremisinoff, Nicholas P.   **TA455.P58H36 1997**
Handbook of Engineering Polymeric Materials. Paper over
Boards. Marcel Dekker Inc. New York, NY. 1997. 888p.
ISBN:0-8247-9799-X, ISBN13: 978-0-8247-9799-7.
Dewey:668.9. LCCN:97-020896.

Audience: **u,f.**

Cheremisinoff, Nicholas P. &   **TA410.H233 1995**
Cheremisinoff, Paul N. (Editors)
Handbook of Advanced Materials Testing, Vol. 9. Paper over
Boards. Marcel Dekker Inc. New York, NY. 1994. 1024p.
Engineering Materials Ser., Vol. 9 ISBN:0-8247-9196-7,
ISBN13: 978-0-8247-9196-4. Dewey:620.1/1/0287.
LCCN:94-033625.

Audience: **u,f.**

Dally, James W. & Riley,   **TA407.D32 2005**
William F.
Experimental Stress Analysis. Ed. 4. Cloth Text. College House
Enterprises, LLC. Knoxville, TN. 2005. 686p.
ISBN:0-9762413-0-7, ISBN13: 978-0-9762413-0-0.
Dewey:620.1/123. LCCN:2005-284595.

Audience: **u,f.**

Daniel, Isaac M. & Ishai,   **TA418.9.C6D28 2005**
Ori
Engineering Mechanics of Composite Materials. Ed. 2. Cloth

Text. Oxford University Press, Inc. New York, NY. 2005. 432p.
ISBN:0-19-515097-X, ISBN13: 978-0-19-515097-1.
Dewey:620.1/183. LCCN:2004-065462.

Audience: **u,f.**

Davis, Joseph R. (Editor)   **TA459.M288 1998**
Metals Handbook: Desk Edition. Ed. 2. Book, Other. A S M
International. Materials Park, OH. 1998. 1,521p. Asm
Handbooks Ser. ISBN:0-87170-654-7, ISBN13:
978-0-87170-654-6. Dewey:620.1/6. LCCN:98-045866.

Audience: **l,u,f.**

Den Hartog, J. P.   **TA405**
Advanced Strength of Materials. Paper Text. Textbook
Publishers. Temecula, CA. 2003. 379p. ISBN:0-7581-8430-1,
ISBN13: 978-0-7581-8430-6. Dewey:620.1/12.

Audience: **u,f.**

Dieter, George   **TA405.D53 1986**
Mechanical Metallurgy. Ed. 3. Cloth Text. McGraw-Hill Higher
Education. Burr Ridge, IL. 1986. 800p. Materials Science and
Engineering Ser. ISBN:0-07-016893-8, ISBN13:
978-0-07-016893-0. Dewey:620.1/63. LCCN:85-018229.

Audience: **l,u.**

Felbeck, David K. & Atkins,   **TA405**
Anthony G.
Strength and Fracture of Engineering Solids. Cloth Text.
Prentice Hall PTR. Upper Saddle River, NJ. 1983. 608p.
ISBN:0-13-851709-6, ISBN13: 978-0-13-851709-0.
Dewey:620.1/126. LCCN:83-009488.

Audience: **u,f.**

Forest Products Laboratory   **TA419.W78 1990**
Staff
Wood Engineering Handbook. Ed. 2. Trade Cloth. Prentice Hall
PTR. Upper Saddle River, NJ. 1990. 480p.
ISBN:0-13-963745-1, ISBN13: 978-0-13-963745-2.
Dewey:620.1/2. LCCN:90-042579.

Audience: **u,f.**

Gauthier, Michelle M.   **TA403.4.E64 1995**
ASM Engineered Materials Handbook: Desk Edition. Book,
Other. A S M International. Materials Park, OH. 1995. 1,300p.
Engineered Materials Handbook Ser. ISBN:0-87170-283-5,
ISBN13: 978-0-87170-283-8. Dewey:620.1/1. LCCN:95-035405.
Audience: **l,u,f.** *Choice, 1996.*

Gere, James M.   **TA403**
Mechanics of Materials. Ed. 6. Cloth Text. Nelson Thomson
Learning. Scarborough, ON. 2003. 912p. ISBN:0-534-41793-0,
ISBN13: 978-0-534-41793-2. Dewey:620.1123.
LCCN:2003-113085.

Audience: **u,f.**

Grellmann, Wolfgang &   **TA455.P58D42 2001**
Seidler, Sabine
Deformation and Fracture Behavior of Polymers. Trade Cloth.
Springer. New York, NY. 2001. 625p. Engineering Materials Ser.
ISBN:3-540-41247-6, ISBN13: 978-3-540-41247-2.
Dewey:620.1/920426. LCCN:00-049713.

Audience: **u,f.**

Harvey, Philip (Editor)   **TA472 .E63 1982**
Engineering Properties of Steel. Trade Cloth. A S M
International. Materials Park, OH. 1982. 527p.
ISBN:0-87170-144-8, ISBN13: 978-0-87170-144-2.
Dewey:620.1/7. LCCN:82-008829.

Audience: **u,f.**

Hearn, E. J.   **TA405.H3 1997**
Mechanics of Materials: An Introduction to the Mechanics of
Elastic and Plastic Deformation of Solids and Structural
Materials. Ed. 3. Paper Text. Elsevier Science & Technology
Books. Saint Louis, MO. 1997. 450p. ISBN:0-7506-3265-8,
ISBN13: 978-0-7506-3265-2. Dewey:620.1/123.
LCCN:96-049967.

Audience: **l,u.**

Hearn, E. J.   **TA405.H3 1997**
Mechanics of Materials 2: The Mechanics of Elastic and Plastic
Deformation of Solids and Structural Materials. Ed. 3. Trade
Paper. Elsevier Science & Technology Books. Saint Louis, MO.
1997. 512p. ISBN:0-7506-3266-6, ISBN13: 978-0-7506-3266-9.
Dewey:620.1123. LCCN:96-049967.

Audience: **l,u.**

Hertzberg, Richard W.   **TA417.6.H46 1996**
Deformation and Fracture Mechanics of Engineering Materials.
Ed. 4. Trade Cloth. John Wiley & Sons, Inc. Hoboken, NJ.
1995. 816p. ISBN:0-471-01214-9, ISBN13: 978-0-471-01214-6.
Dewey:620.1/123. LCCN:95-035234.

Audience: **u,f.** *ℬ*

Hibbeler, Russell C.   **TA405.H47 2004**
Mechanics of Materials. Ed. 6. Cloth Text. Prentice Hall PTR.
Upper Saddle River, NJ. 2004. 896p. ISBN:0-13-191345-X,
ISBN13: 978-0-13-191345-5. Dewey:620.1/1.
LCCN:2004-053109.

Audience: **u,f.**

Higdon   **TA405 .M515**
Mechanics of Materials with Tront Eureka. Ed. 4. Cloth Text.
John Wiley & Sons, Inc. Hoboken, NJ. 1988.
ISBN:0-471-61078-X, ISBN13: 978-0-471-61078-6.
Dewey:620.1/12.

Audience: **u,f.**

Holloway, D. G. & Tawney,   **KF8745.S8**
D. A.
The Physical Properties of Glass. Trade Cloth. Taylor & Francis
Group. Philadelphia, PA. 1973. Wykeham Science Ser., No. 24
ISBN:0-8448-1151-3, ISBN13: 978-0-8448-1151-2.
Dewey:923.473.

Audience: **u,f.**

Honeycombe, Robert   **TN690**
Plastic Deformation of Metals. Ed. 2. Trade Paper. Hodder
Education. London, 1984. 496p. ISBN:0-7131-3468-2, ISBN13:
978-0-7131-3468-1. Dewey:620.1/633. LCCN:85-124042.

Audience: **u,f.**

Hull, D. & Clyne, T. W.   **TA418.9.C6 H85 1996**
An Introduction to Composite Materials. Ed. 2. D. R. Clarke, S.
Suresh & I. M. Ward (Contribution by). Cloth Text. Cambridge
University Press. New York, NY. 1996. 342p. Solid State
Science Ser. ISBN:0-521-38190-8, ISBN13: 978-0-521-38190-1.
Dewey:620.1/18. LCCN:96-005701.

Audience: **l,u.** *Choice, 1997.*

Jastrzebski, Zbigniew D.   **TA403.J35 1987**
The Nature and Properties of Engineering Materials. Ed. 3.
Cloth Text. John Wiley & Sons, Inc. Hoboken, NJ. 1987. 633p.
ISBN:0-471-81841-0, ISBN13: 978-0-471-81841-0.
Dewey:620.1/1. LCCN:86-024673.

Audience: **u,f.**

Kaesche, Helmut   **TA462**
Corrosion of Metals. Trade Cloth. Springer. New York, NY.
2003. X, 594p. Engineering Materials and Processes Ser.
ISBN:3-540-00626-5, ISBN13: 978-3-540-00626-8.
Dewey:620.1/623. LCCN:2003-054778.

Audience: **l,u.** *Choice, 2004.*

Kocanda, S.   **TA460 .K5313**
Fatigue Failure of Metals. Trade Cloth. Springer. New York, NY.
1978. 379p. ISBN:90-286-0025-6, ISBN13: 978-90-286-0025-6.
Dewey:620.1/6/3. LCCN:78-378428.

Audience: **u,f.**

Kong, F. K., et al.   **TA439.H275 1983**
Handbook of Structural Concrete. Edward Cohen & R. H. Evans
(Authors). Cloth Text. McGraw-Hill Companies, The. New
York, NY. 1983. 1936p. ISBN:0-07-011573-7, ISBN13:
978-0-07-011573-6. Dewey:624.1/834. LCCN:83-000802.

Audience: **l,u,f.**

Krishnamoorti, Ramanan &   **TA418.9.N35P66 2001**
Vaia, Richard A. (Editors)
Polymer Nanocomposites: Synthesis, Characterization, and
Modeling. Trade Cloth. Oxford University Press, Inc. New York,
NY. 2001. 256p. ACS Symposium Ser., No. 804
ISBN:0-8412-3768-9, ISBN13: 978-0-8412-3768-1.
Dewey:620.1/92. LCCN:2001-046392.

Audience: **u,f.**

Kutz, Myer (Editor)   **TA403.4.H368 2001**
Handbook of Materials Selection. Trade Cloth. John Wiley &
Sons, Inc. Hoboken, NJ. 2002. 1520p. ISBN:0-471-35924-6,
ISBN13: 978-0-471-35924-1. Dewey:620.1/1.
LCCN:2001-046821.

Audience: **l,u,f.**

Lee, Stuart M. (Editor)   **TA418.9.C6**
International Encyclopedia of Composites, Set. Trade Cloth.
John Wiley & Sons, Inc. Hoboken, NJ. 1996. 3293p.
ISBN:0-471-18706-2, ISBN13: 978-0-471-18706-6.
Dewey:620.118.

Audience: **l,u,f.**

Lemaitre, Jean P. (Editor)   **TA404.8.H358 2001**
Handbook of Materials Behavior Models: Nonlinear Models and
Properties. Trade Cloth. Elsevier Science & Technology Books.
Saint Louis, MO. 2001. 1200p. ISBN:0-12-443341-3, ISBN13:
978-0-12-443341-0. Dewey:620.1/1/015118.
LCCN:2001-089698.

Audience: **u,f.**

Malhotra, V. M. & Carino,   **TA440.C72 2004**
Nicholas J.
Handbook on Nondestructive Testing of Concrete. Ed. 2. Trade
Paper. American Society for Testing & Materials. West
Conshohocken, PA. 2003. 392p. ISBN:0-8031-2099-0, ISBN13:
978-0-8031-2099-0. Dewey:620.1/367. LCCN:2004-266422.

Audience: **u,f.**

Mallick, P. K.   **TA418.9.C6.C63193**
Composites Engineering Handbook, Vol. 11. Paper over Boards. Marcel Dekker Inc. New York, NY. 1997. 1248p. Materials Engineering Ser., Vol. 11 ISBN:0-8247-9304-8, ISBN13: 978-0-8247-9304-3. Dewey:620.1/18. LCCN:97-004058.

Audience: **l,u.**

Mamlouk, Michael S. &   **TA403.2.M35 2005**
  Zaniewski, John P.
Materials for Civil and Construction Engineers. Ed. 2. Perfect, Paper over Boards. Prentice Hall PTR. Upper Saddle River, NJ. 2005. 576p. ISBN:0-13-147714-5, ISBN13: 978-0-13-147714-8. Dewey:624.1/8. LCCN:2005-052717.

Audience: **u,f.**

Mark, James E. (Editor)   **TA455.P58P475 1996**
Physical Properties of Polymers Handbook. Cloth Text. Springer. New York, NY. 1996. 744p. Polymers and Complex Materials Ser. ISBN:1-56396-295-0, ISBN13: 978-1-56396-295-0. Dewey:620.1/92. LCCN:95-050256.

Audience: **u,f.** *Choice, 1996.*

Maxwell, Jane & Gretton,   **TA459 .M43**
  Monica (Editors)
ASM Handbook. Ed. 16. Brian Land (Introduction by). Trade Cloth. A S M International, Inc. Fort Lauderdale, FL. 1313p. ISBN:0-614-03408-6, ISBN13: 978-0-614-03408-0. Dewey:620.1/6.

Audience: **l,u,f.**

Mazumdar, Sanjay K.   **TA418.9.C6M34 2002**
Composites Manufacturing: Materials, Product and Process Engineering. Paper over Boards. C R C Press LLC. Boca Raton, FL. 2001. 416p. ISBN:0-8493-0585-3, ISBN13: 978-0-8493-0585-6. Dewey:620.1/18. LCCN:2001-004994.

Audience: **u,f.**

Meyers, Marc A. & Chawla,   **TA460.M466 1984**
  K. K.
Mechanical Metallurgy: Principles and Applications. Cloth Text. Prentice Hall PTR. Upper Saddle River, NJ. 1983. 752p. ISBN:0-13-569863-4, ISBN13: 978-0-13-569863-1. Dewey:620.1/6. LCCN:83-000552.

Audience: **u,f.**

Mix, Paul E.   **TA417.2.M59 2005**
@ Introduction to Nondestructive Testing: A Training Guide. Ed. 2. E-Book. John Wiley & Sons, Inc. Hoboken, NJ. 2005. 560p. ISBN:0-471-71913-7, ISBN13: 978-0-471-71913-7. Dewey:620.1/127.

Audience: **l,u.**

Moore, D. R., et al.   **TA418.9.C6F725 2001**
Fracture Mechanics Testing Methods for Polymers, Adhesives and Composites. A. Pavan & J. G. Williams (Authors). Trade Cloth. Elsevier Science & Technology Books. Saint Louis, MO. 2001. 388p. ESIS Publication Ser., Vol. 28 ISBN:0-08-043689-7, ISBN13: 978-0-08-043689-0. Dewey:620.1/126. LCCN:2001-018979.

Audience: **u,f.**

Murray, G. T. (Editor)   **TA403.4.H37 1997**
Handbook of Materials Selection for Engineering Applications. Paper over Boards. Marcel Dekker Inc. New York, NY. 1997. 632p. Mechanical Engineering Ser., Vol. 113 ISBN:0-8247-9910-0, ISBN13: 978-0-8247-9910-6. Dewey:620.1/1. LCCN:97-020899.

Audience: **l,u,f.**

Nalwa, Hari Singh (Editor)   **TA403.H345 2001**
Handbook of Surfaces and Interfaces of Materials, Set. Trade Cloth. Elsevier Science & Technology Books. Saint Louis, MO. 2001. 2911p. ISBN:0-12-513910-1, ISBN13: 978-0-12-513910-6. Dewey:620.1/1. LCCN:2001-088194.

Audience: **u,f.**

Nalwa, Hari Singh (Editor)   **TA418.9.N35H37 2001**
Nanostructured Materials and Nanotechnology: Concise Edition. Trade Cloth. Elsevier Science & Technology Books. Saint Louis, MO. 2001. 834p. ISBN:0-12-513920-9, ISBN13: 978-0-12-513920-5. Dewey:620/.5. LCCN:2001-089144.

Audience: **u,f.**

Nalwa, Hari Singh (Editor)   **TA418.9.N35H37 2000**
Handbook of Nanostructured Materials and Nanotechnology, Set. George A. Olah (Foreword by). Trade Cloth. Elsevier Science & Technology Books. Saint Louis, MO. 1999. 3461p. ISBN:0-12-513760-5, ISBN13: 978-0-12-513760-7. Dewey:620.5. LCCN:98-043220.

Audience: **u,f.**

Nawy, Edward G.   **TA444 .N38 2005**
Reinforced Concrete, ACI 2005: A Fundamental Approach. Ed. 5. Cloth Text. Pearson Education. Boston, MA. 2004. 840p. ISBN:0-13-149757-X, ISBN13: 978-0-13-149757-3. Dewey:624.1/8341. LCCN:2004-014787.

Audience: **u,f.**

Needleman, A., et al.   **TA481.F87 1993**
Fundamentals of Metal-Matrix Composites. A. Mortensen & Subra Suresh (Authors). Trade Cloth. Elsevier Science & Technology Books. Saint Louis, MO. 1993. 400p. ISBN:0-7506-9321-5, ISBN13: 978-0-7506-9321-9. Dewey:620.16. LCCN:93-004727.

Audience: **u,f.** *Choice, 1994.*

Pollack, H.   **TA403**
Materials Science and Metallurgy. Ed. 4. Trade Paper. Prentice Hall PTR. Upper Saddle River, NJ. 1998. 560p. ISBN:0-8359-4287-2, ISBN13: 978-0-8359-4287-4. Dewey:620.1/1. LCCN:87-007224.

Audience: **u,f.**

Popovics, Sandor (Editor)   **TA439**
Fundamentals of Portland Cement Concrete - A Quantitative Approach: Fresh Concrete, Vol. 1. Trade Cloth. John Wiley & Sons, Inc. Hoboken, NJ. 1982. 477p. ISBN:0-471-86217-7, ISBN13: 978-0-471-86217-8. Dewey:666/.893. LCCN:81-002796.

Audience: **u,f.**

Revie, R. Winston & Uhlig,   **TA462.U4 2000**
  Herbert Henry (Editors)
Uhlig's Corrosion Handbook. Ed. 2. Trade Cloth. John Wiley & Sons, Inc. Hoboken, NJ. 2000. 1344p. Electrochemical Society Ser., Vol. 39 ISBN:0-471-15777-5, ISBN13: 978-0-471-15777-9. Dewey:620.1/1223. LCCN:99-030123.

Audience: **u,f.**

Rosen, Stephen L.   **TA455.P58R63 1993**
Fundamental Principles of Polymeric Materials. Ed. 2. Trade Cloth. John Wiley & Sons, Inc. Hoboken, NJ. 1993. 448p. Society of Plastics Engineers Monographs, Vol. 21 ISBN:0-471-57525-9, ISBN13: 978-0-471-57525-2. Dewey:547.7. LCCN:92-010973.

Audience: **u,f.**

Ross, Robert B.   **TN671**
Metallic Materials Specification Handbook. Ed. 99. Trade Cloth. John Wiley & Sons, Inc. Hoboken, NJ. 1980. 850p. ISBN:0-470-26757-7, ISBN13: 978-0-470-26757-8. Dewey:669.0212. LCCN:79-040761.
            Audience: **u,f.**

Sandor, Bela I.   **TA407**
Fundamentals of Cyclic Stress and Strain. Cloth Text. University of Wisconsin Press. Chicago, IL. 1972. 184p. ISBN:0-299-06100-0, ISBN13: 978-0-299-06100-5. Dewey:620.1/123. LCCN:70-176415.
            Audience: **u,f.**

Sandor, Bela Imre   **TA405.S28**
Strength of Materials. Trade Cloth. Prentice Hall PTR. Upper Saddle River, NJ. 1978. xiv, 432 p. :p. ISBN:0-13-852418-1, ISBN13: 978-0-13-852418-0. Dewey:620.1/12. LCCN:77-015506.
            Audience: **l,u.**

Sanford, R. J.   **TA409.S26 2002**
Principles of Fracture Mechanics. Cloth Text. Prentice Hall PTR. Upper Saddle River, NJ. 2002. 404p. ISBN:0-13-092992-1, ISBN13: 978-0-13-092992-1. Dewey:620.1/126. LCCN:2001-058094.
       Audience: **u,f.** *Choice, 2003.*

Scheirs, John   **TA455.P58S345 2000**
Compositional and Failure Analysis of Polymers: A Practical Approach. Trade Cloth. John Wiley & Sons, Inc. Hoboken, NJ. 2000. 806p. ISBN:0-471-62534-5, ISBN13: 978-0-471-62534-6. Dewey:620.1/920422. LCCN:99-056526.
            Audience: **u,f.**

Schwartz, Mel   **TA418.9.S62E63 2002**
Encyclopedia of Smart Materials. Trade Cloth. John Wiley & Sons, Inc. Hoboken, NJ. 2002. 1176p. ISBN:0-471-17780-6, ISBN13: 978-0-471-17780-7. Dewey:620.1/1. LCCN:2001-056795.
       Audience: **l,u,f.** *Choice, 2003.*

Schwartz, Melvin M.   **TA418.9.C6.S38 1992**
Composite Materials Handbook. Ed. 2. Cloth Text. McGraw-Hill Companies, The. New York, NY. 1992. variousp. ISBN:0-07-055819-1, ISBN13: 978-0-07-055819-9. Dewey:620.1/18. LCCN:91-039341.
       Audience: **l,u,f.** *Choice, 1992.*

Schweitzer, Philip A.   **TA418.74.S379 2004**
Corrosion Resistance Tables: Metals, Nonmetals, Coatings, Mortars, Plastics, Elastomers and Linings, and Fabrics. Ed. 5. Paper over Boards. Marcel Dekker Inc. New York, NY. 2004. 874p. Corrosion Technology Ser. ISBN:0-8247-5676-2, ISBN13: 978-0-8247-5676-5. Dewey:620.1/1223. LCCN:2004-555152.
            Audience: **u,f.**

Schweitzer, Philip A.   **TA459.S44 2003**
Metallic Materials: Physical, Mechanical, and Corrosion Properties, Vol. 19. Paper over Boards. Marcel Dekker Inc. New York, NY. 2003. 712p. Corrosion Technology Ser. ISBN:0-8247-0878-4, ISBN13: 978-0-8247-0878-8. Dewey:620.1/6. LCCN:2002-041426.
            Audience: **u,f.**

Scully, J. C.   **TA462.S39 1990**
The Fundamentals of Corrosion. Ed. 3. Trade Cloth. Elsevier Science & Technology Books. Saint Louis, MO. 1990. 250p.

International Series on Materials Science and Technology ISBN:0-08-037875-7, ISBN13: 978-0-08-037875-6. Dewey:620.1/623. LCCN:89-072143.
            Audience: **l,u.**

Shackelford, James F. &   **TA403.4 .C74 1992**
  Alexander, W.
Materials Science and Engineering Handbook. Trade Cloth. Franklin Book Company, Inc. Newtown Sq, PA. 1992. ISBN:0-8493-4276-7, ISBN13: 978-0-8493-4276-9. Dewey:620.1/1. LCCN:92-102192.
       Audience: **l,u,f.** *Choice, 1995.*

Smith, William F.   **TA481**
Structure and Properties of Engineering Alloys. Ed. 2. Cloth Text. McGraw-Hill Higher Education. Burr Ridge, IL. 1993. 672p. Materials Science and Engineering Ser. ISBN:0-07-059172-5, ISBN13: 978-0-07-059172-1. Dewey:620.16. LCCN:92-006795.
            Audience: **u,f.**

Spencer, Albert & Luy, Jack   **TA419.S73**
Wood and Wood Products. Paper Text. Macmillan Publishing Company, Inc. Old Tappan, NJ. 1986. 256p. Occupational Education Ser. ISBN:0-675-08798-8, ISBN13: 978-0-675-08798-8. Dewey:674. LCCN:74-075406.
            Audience: **l,u.**

Stephens, Ralph I., et al.   **TA460.M4437 2001**
Metal Fatigue in Engineering. Ed. 2. Robert R. Stephens, Henry O. Fuchs & Ali Fatemi (Authors). Trade Cloth. John Wiley & Sons, Inc. Hoboken, NJ. 2000. 496p. ISBN:0-471-51059-9, ISBN13: 978-0-471-51059-8. Dewey:620.1/66. LCCN:00-028972.
            Audience: **u,f.**

Timoshenko, S.   **TA405**
Strength of Materials, Pt. 2: Advanced Theory and Problems, Set. Library Binding. Krieger Publishing Company. Melbourne, FL. 1983. 1,044p. ISBN:0-89874-621-3, ISBN13: 978-0-89874-621-1. Dewey:620.11. LCCN:76-011851.
            Audience: **u,f.**

Timoshenko, Stephen &   **TA405**
  Young, Donovan H.
Elements of Strength of Materials. Ed. 5. Cloth Text. Van Nostrand Reinhold. New York, NY. 1968. ISBN:0-442-08547-8, ISBN13: 978-0-442-08547-6. Dewey:620.1/12.
            Audience: **l,u.**

USDA Forest Products Staff   **TA419**
Wood Handbook: Wood As an Engineering Material. Trade Paper. Forest Products Society. Madison, WI. 1999. 428p. ISBN:1-892529-02-5, ISBN13: 978-1-892529-02-2. Dewey:620.12.
            Audience: **l,u,f.**

Vaccari, John A., et al.   **TA402**
Materials Handbook. Ed. 15. George Stuart Brady & Henry R. Clauser (Authors). Trade Cloth. McGraw-Hill Professional Publishing. New York, NY. 2002. 1244p. Handbook Ser. ISBN:0-07-136076-X, ISBN13: 978-0-07-136076-0. Dewey:620.1/1/03. LCCN:2002-067015.
            Audience: **l,u,f.**

Van Vlack, Lawrence H.   **TA430 .V3**
Physical Ceramics for Engineers. Trade Cloth. Addison-Wesley Longman, Inc. Boston, MA. 1964. ISBN:0-201-08068-0, ISBN13: 978-0-201-08068-1. Dewey:620.14.

Audience: **u,f.**

Wagoner, Robert H. &   **TA460.W318 1997**
  Chenot, Jean-Loup
Fundamentals of Metal Forming. Trade Cloth. John Wiley & Sons, Inc. Hoboken, NJ. 1996. 389p. ISBN:0-471-57004-4, ISBN13: 978-0-471-57004-2. Dewey:620.1/63. LCCN:95-047898.

Wang, Z. L. (Editor), et al.   **TA418.9.N35 H358**
Handbook of Nanophase and Nanostructured Materials: Volume I: Synthesis Volume II: Characterization Volume III: Materials Systems and Applications I Volume IV: Materials Systems and Applications II. Yi Liu & Ze Zhang (Editors). Mixed Media. Springer. New York, NY. 2006. 1200p. ISBN:0-387-33552-8, ISBN13: 978-0-387-33552-0. Dewey:620.1/1299.

Audience: **u,f.**

Wessel, James K.   **TA403.6**
  (Editor-In-Chief)
The Handbook of Advanced Materials: Enabling New Designs. Trade Cloth. John Wiley & Sons, Inc. Hoboken, NJ. 2004. 656p. ISBN:0-471-45475-3, ISBN13: 978-0-471-45475-5. Dewey:620.1/1. LCCN:2004-004219.

Audience: **u,f.**

Williams, David B. (Editor),   **TA418.7.I44 1991**
  et al.
Images of Materials. Alan R. Pelton & Ronald Gronsky (Editors). Cloth Text. Oxford University Press, Inc. New York, NY. 1992. 432p. ISBN:0-19-505856-9, ISBN13: 978-0-19-505856-7. Dewey:620.1/127. LCCN:90-014181.
Audience: **l,u,f.** *Choice, 1992.*

Williams, J. G.   **TA455.P58.W538 1984**
Fracture Mechanics of Polymers. Trade Cloth. Bow Historical Books. New Providence, NJ. 1984. 302 p. :p. ISBN:0-85312-685-2, ISBN13: 978-0-85312-685-0. Dewey:620.1/920426. LCCN:83-026593.

Audience: **l,u.**

Williams, J. G.   **TA455.P58**
Stress Analysis of Polymers. Ed. 2. Trade Cloth. John Wiley & Sons, Inc. Hoboken, NJ. 1980. 360p. Ellis Horwood Series in Engineering Science ISBN:0-470-26964-2, ISBN13: 978-0-470-26964-0. Dewey:620.1/92. LCCN:80-040144.
Audience: **u,f.**

Young, J. Francis, et al.   **TA439.M49 2002**
Concrete. Ed. 2. Sidney Mindess & David Darwin (Authors). Cloth Text. Prentice Hall PTR. Upper Saddle River, NJ. 2002. 644p. ISBN:0-13-064632-6, ISBN13: 978-0-13-064632-3. Dewey:624.1/834. LCCN:2002-070052.
Audience: **l,u.**

Structural Engineering

TA684
Manual of Steel Construction, Load and Resistance Factor Design, 3rd Edition. Trade Cloth. American Institute of Steel

Construction. Chicago, IL. 2001. ISBN:1-56424-051-7, ISBN13: 978-1-56424-051-4. Dewey:624.1821.

Audience: **l,u,f.**

TA682.455.R67 1994
Roller-Compacted Concrete. Trade Cloth. American Society of Civil Engineers. Reston, VA. 1994. 100p. Technical Engineering and Design Guides as Adapted from the U. S. Army Corps of Engineers Ser., No. 5 ISBN:0-87262-999-6, ISBN13: 978-0-87262-999-8. Dewey:624.1/834. LCCN:94-000259.
Audience: **u,f.**

TA645
Structural Engineering, Vol. 2. Trade Cloth. Pearson Custom Publishing. Boston, MA. 1999. 688p. ISBN:0-536-02542-8, ISBN13: 978-0-536-02542-5. Dewey:624.171.
Audience: **u,f.**

Addis, William   **TA633.A33 1990**
Structural Engineering: The Nature of Theory and Design. Trade Cloth. Ellis Horwood Ltd. Hempstead, 1990. xiv, 258 p. :p. ISBN:0-13-850611-6, ISBN13: 978-0-13-850611-7. Dewey:624.1. LCCN:90-039911.
Audience: **u,f.**

AISC Manual Committee   **TA684**
Manual of Steel Construction Allowable Stress Design. Ed. 9. Cloth Text. American Institute of Steel Construction. Chicago, IL. 1991. 1144p. ISBN:1-56424-000-2, ISBN13: 978-1-56424-000-2. Dewey:624.1821.
Audience: **u,f.**

Akin, J. E.   **TA646**
Finite Element Analysis with Error Estimators: An Introduction to the FEM and Adaptive Error Analysis for Engineering Students. Paper Text. Elsevier Science & Technology Books. Saint Louis, MO. 2005. 512p. ISBN:0-7506-6722-2, ISBN13: 978-0-7506-6722-7. Dewey:620.00151825. LCCN:2005-281877.
Audience: **u,f.**

Allen, Edward & Zalewski,   **TA648.Z35 1998**
  Waclaw
Shaping Structures: Statics. Trade Cloth. John Wiley & Sons, Inc. Hoboken, NJ. 1997. 416p. ISBN:0-471-16968-4, ISBN13: 978-0-471-16968-0. Dewey:624.1/71. LCCN:96-037609.
Audience: **l,u,f.** *Choice, 1998.*

Amrhein, James E.   **TA670.A56 1994**
Reinforced Masonry Engineering Handbook Clay and Concrete Masonry. Ed. 5. Trade Cloth. Masonry Institute of America. Torrance, CA. 1994. 469p. ISBN:0-940116-27-8, ISBN13: 978-0-940116-27-6. Dewey:693/.1. LCCN:94-077659.
Audience: **l,u,f.**

Bangash, M. Y. H. &   **TH5667**
  Bangash, T.
Staircases: Structural Analysis and Design. Paper over Boards. Taylor & Francis Group. Abingdon, 1999. 348p. ISBN:90-5410-607-7, ISBN13: 978-90-5410-607-4. Dewey:694.6.
Audience: **u,f.**

Bejan, Adrian   **TA168 .B37 2000**
Shape and Structure, from Engineering to Nature. Cloth Text. Cambridge University Press. New York, NY. 2000. 344p. ISBN:0-521-79049-2, ISBN13: 978-0-521-79049-9. Dewey:620/.0042. LCCN:00-027314.
Audience: **u,f.** *Choice, 2001.*

Bendsoe, Martin P. &   **TA658.8.B463 2002**
  Siegmund, Ole
Topology Optimization: Theory, Methods, and Applications. Ed. 2. Trade Cloth. Springer. New York, NY. 2004. XIV, 370p. Engineering Online Library ISBN:3-540-42992-1, ISBN13: 978-3-540-42992-0. Dewey:624.1/7713. LCCN:2002-030512.
                                     Audience: **u,f.**

Bentur, A., et al.   **TA445.5.B46 1997**
Steel Corrosion in Concrete: Fundamentals and Civil Engineering Practice. S. Diamond & N. Berke (Authors). Paper over Boards. Routledge. New York, NY. 1998. 208p. Modern Concrete Technology Ser. ISBN:0-419-22530-7, ISBN13: 978-0-419-22530-0. Dewey:624.1/8341. LCCN:98-150903.
                                     Audience: **u,f.**

Benvenuto, E.   **TA646.B46 1990**
An Introduction to the History of Structural Mechanics: Vaulted Structures and Elastic Systems. Cloth Text. Springer. New York, NY. 1990. 554p. ISBN:0-387-97187-4, ISBN13: 978-0-387-97187-2. Dewey:624.1/71/09. LCCN:89-026230.
                        Audience: **u,f.** *Choice, 1991.*

Benvenuto, Edoardo   **TA646**
An introduction to the history of structural mechanics: Pt. 1: Statics and resistance of solids. Springer-Verlag. 1991. ISBN:0-387-96227-1, ISBN13: 978-0-387-96227-6.
                                     Audience: **u,f.**

Bhatti, M. Asghar   **TA647.B494 2006**
Advanced Topics in Finite Element Analysis of Structures: With Mathematica and MATLAB Computations. Trade Cloth. John Wiley & Sons, Inc. Hoboken, NJ. 2006. 608p. ISBN:0-471-64807-8, ISBN13: 978-0-471-64807-9. Dewey:624.1/71/0151825. LCCN:2005-005179.
                                     Audience: **u,f.**

Bhatti, M. Asghar   **TA646.B56 2005**
Fundamental Finite Element Analysis and Applications: With Mathematica and Matlab Computations. Trade Cloth. John Wiley & Sons, Inc. Hoboken, NJ. 2005. 720p. ISBN:0-471-64808-6, ISBN13: 978-0-471-64808-6. Dewey:620/.001/51825. LCCN:2004-002270.
                                     Audience: **u,f.**

Britvec, S. J.   **TA660.F53**
Stability and Optimization of Flexible Space Structures. Trade Cloth. Springer. New York, NY. 1995. 352p. ISBN:0-8176-2864-9, ISBN13: 978-0-8176-2864-2. Dewey:624.1/71.
                                     Audience: **u,f.**

Cheng   **TA654**
Matrix Analysis of Structural Dynamics: Applications and Earthquake Engineering. Trade Cloth. Marcel Dekker Inc. New York, NY. 2000. 1014p. ISBN:0-8247-4538-8, ISBN13: 978-0-8247-4538-7. Dewey:624.1/7.
                                     Audience: **u,f.**

Chopra, Anil K.   **TA654.6.C466 1995**
Dynamics of Structures: Theory and Applications to Earthquake Engineering. Ed. 1. Trade Cloth. Prentice Hall PTR. Upper Saddle River, NJ. 1995. 729p. Prentice-Hall International Series in Civil Engineering and Ser. ISBN:0-13-855214-2, ISBN13: 978-0-13-855214-5. Dewey:624.1/762. LCCN:94-046527.
                       Audience: **u,f.** *Choice, 1995.*

Ciarlet, P. G. (Editor), et al.   **TA653.A79 1995**
Asymptotic Methods for Elastic Structures: Proceedings: International Conference on Asymptotic Methods for Elastic Structures (1993: Lisbon, Portugal). Luis Trabucho & Juan M. Viano (Editors). Trade Cloth. Walter De Gruyter Inc. Ossining, NY. 1995. 291p. ISBN:3-11-014731-9, ISBN13: 978-3-11-014731-5. Dewey:624.1/7. LCCN:95-007856.
                                     Audience: **u,f.**

Drew, Horace R. &   **TA645.N46 2002**
  Pellegrino, Sergio
New Approaches to Structural Mechanics, Shells and Biological. Trade Cloth. Springer. New York, NY. 2002. 536p. Solid Mechanics and Its Applications Ser., Vol. 104 ISBN:1-4020-0862-7, ISBN13: 978-1-4020-0862-7. Dewey:624.1. LCCN:2002-030117.
                                     Audience: **u,f.**

Dym, Clive L.   **TA645.D95 1997**
Structural Modeling and Analysis. Cambridge University Press. 1997. ISBN:0-521-49536-9, ISBN13: 978-0-521-49536-3.
                                     Audience: **u,f.**

Dyrbye, Claës & Hansen,   **TA654.5.D97 1997**
  Svend Ole
Wind Loads on Structures. Trade Cloth. John Wiley & Sons, Inc. Hoboken, NJ. 1997. 244p. ISBN:0-471-95651-1, ISBN13: 978-0-471-95651-8. Dewey:624.1/75. LCCN:96-030346.
                       Audience: **u,f.** *Choice, 1998.*

Erdey, Charles K.   **TA654.6.E73 2006**
Earthquake Engineering. Trade Cloth. John Wiley & Sons, Inc. Hoboken, NJ. 2007. 432p. ISBN:0-470-04843-3, ISBN13: 978-0-470-04843-6. Dewey:624.1/762. LCCN:2006-011329.
                                     Audience: **u,f.**

Felton, Lewis P. & Nelson,   **TA642.F45 1997**
  Richard B.
Matrix Structural Analysis. Trade Cloth. John Wiley & Sons, Inc. Hoboken, NJ. 1996. 700p. ISBN:0-471-12324-2, ISBN13: 978-0-471-12324-8. Dewey:624.1/71. LCCN:96-019454.
                                     Audience: **u,f.**

French, Samuel E.   **TA645.F73 1995**
Fundamentals of Structural Analysis. Ed. 1. Trade Cloth, Box or Slipcased. West Publishing Company, College & School Division. Eagan, MN. 1995. 750p. ISBN:0-314-03929-5, ISBN13: 978-0-314-03929-3. Dewey:624.1/71. LCCN:94-002551.
                                     Audience: **u,f.**

Friswell, M. I. &   **TA654.F76 1995**
  Mottershead, J. E.
Finite Element Model Updating in Structural Dynamics. Trade Cloth. Springer. New York, NY. 1995. 300p. Solid Mechanics and Its Applications Ser., Vol. 38 ISBN:0-7923-3431-0, ISBN13: 978-0-7923-3431-6. Dewey:624.1/71. LCCN:95-008173.
                                     Audience: **u,f.**

Fu G Staff   **TA5**
Inspection and Monitoring Techniques for Bridges and Civil Struct. Trade Cloth. Taylor & Francis Group. Philadelphia, PA. 2005. ISBN:0-8493-9544-5, ISBN13: 978-0-8493-9544-4. Dewey:620.
                                     Audience: **l,u,f.**

Gambhir, M. L.   **TA656**
Stability Analysis and Design of Structures. Trade Cloth.
Springer. New York, NY. 2004. XIII, 535p.
ISBN:3-540-20784-8, ISBN13: 978-3-540-20784-9.
Dewey:624.1/71. LCCN:2004-106461.

Audience: **u,f.**

Gatti, Paolo L. & Ferrari,   **TA654.G34 1999**
   Vittorio
Applied Structural and Mechanical Vibrations: Theory Methods
and Measuring Instrumentation. Paper over Boards. Routledge.
New York, NY. 1999. 848p. Civil Engineering Ser.
ISBN:0-419-22710-5, ISBN13: 978-0-419-22710-6.
Dewey:620.3. LCCN:98-053028.

Audience: **u,f.** *Choice, 2000.*

Ghali, A.   **TA439**
Concrete Structures: Stresses and Deformations. Ed. 2. Trade
Cloth. Routledge. New York, NY. 1994. 464p.
ISBN:0-419-17740-X, ISBN13: 978-0-419-17740-1.
Dewey:624.1834.

Audience: **u,f.**

Gioncu, Victor & Mazzolani,   **TA684**
   Federico M.
Global Analysis of Seismic-Resistant Steel Structures. Trade
Cloth. Spon Press. 2006. ISBN:0-415-24263-0, ISBN13:
978-0-415-24263-9. Dewey:624.1762.

Audience: **u,f.**

Grierson, Donald E.   **TA630.P76 1991**
   (Editor), et al.
Progress in Structural Engineering. Alberto Franchi & Paalo
Riva (Editors). Trade Cloth. Springer. New York, NY. 1991.
648p. ISBN:0-7923-1396-8, ISBN13: 978-0-7923-1396-0.
Dewey:624. LCCN:91-025922.

Audience: **u,f.**

Guarracino, F. & Walker, A.   **TA645**
Energy Methods in Structural Mechanics. Trade Cloth. Thomas
Telford Ltd. London, 1999. 270p. ISBN:0-7277-2757-5,
ISBN13: 978-0-7277-2757-2. Dewey:624.1/7.

Audience: **u,f.**

Guran, Ardeshir (Editor), et   **TA654.9.S76 1998**
   al.
Structronic Systems: Active Structures, Devices and Systems.
Horn-Sen Tzou & Gary L. Anderson (Editors). Trade Cloth.
World Scientific Publishing Company, Inc. Hackensack, NJ.
1997. 880p. Series on Stability, Vibration and Control of
Systems, Vol. 4 ISBN:981-02-2652-7, ISBN13:
978-981-02-2652-7. Dewey:624.1. LCCN:98-212843.

Audience: **u,f.**

Hadjian, Asadour
Basic Elements of Earthquake Engineering. Trade Cloth. John
Wiley & Sons Canada, Ltd. Mississauga, ON. 2005. 600p.
ISBN:0-471-49852-1, ISBN13: 978-0-471-49852-0.

Audience: **u,f.**

Hartmann, Friedel & Katz,   **TA645**
   Casimir
Structural Analysis with Finite Elements. Trade Cloth. Springer.
New York, NY. 2004. X, 484p. ISBN:3-540-40416-3, ISBN13:
978-3-540-40416-3. Dewey:624.1/71. LCCN:2003-063958.

Audience: **u,f.**

Heyman, Jacques   **TA645 .H465 1998**
Structural Analysis: A Historical Approach. Trade Cloth.
Cambridge University Press. New York, NY. 1998. 186p.
ISBN:0-521-62249-2, ISBN13: 978-0-521-62249-3.
Dewey:624.1/71/09. LCCN:97-018474.

Audience: **u,f.** *Choice, 1998.*

Hibbeler, R. C. & Tan,   **TA645.H47 2006**
   Kiang Hwee
Structural Analysis. Ed. 6. Trade Paper. Pearson Education, Ltd.
Harlow, 2006. xiv, 644p. ISBN:0-13-197641-9, ISBN13:
978-0-13-197641-2. Dewey:624.171.

Audience: **l,u,f.**

Hohberg, Jorg-Martin   **TC547**
A Joint Element for the Nonlinear Dynamic Analysis of Arch
Dams. Trade Cloth. Springer. New York, NY. 1993. 300p.
ISBN:0-8176-2811-8, ISBN13: 978-0-8176-2811-6.
Dewey:627/.82. LCCN:92-032866.

Audience: **u,f.**

Hori, Muneo   **TA654.6**
Introduction to Computational Earthquake Engineering. Trade
Cloth. Imperial College Press. London, 2006. 380p.
ISBN:1-86094-621-6, ISBN13: 978-1-86094-621-9.
Dewey:624.1/762.

Audience: **u,f.**

Hsu, Teng H.   **TA0633.H77**
Structural Engineering and Applied Mechanics Data Handbook,
Vol. 4. Trade Paper. Books on Demand. Ann Arbor, MI. 1988.
400p. ISBN:0-608-05005-9, ISBN13: 978-0-608-05005-8.
Dewey:624.1. LCCN:88-007227.

Audience: **u,f.**

Hsu, Teng H.   **TA0633.H77**
Structural Engineering and Applied Mechanics Data Handbook:
Frames, Vol. 2. Trade Paper. Books on Demand. Ann Arbor, MI.
1991. 544p. ISBN:0-608-01334-X, ISBN13: 978-0-608-01334-3.
Dewey:624.1. LCCN:88-007227.

Audience: **u,f.**

Hsu, Teng H.   **TA633.H77 1988**
Structural Engineering and Applied Mechanics Data Handbook:
Plates. Trade Cloth. Elsevier Science & Technology Books.
Saint Louis, MO. 1990. 512p. Structural Engineering and
Applied Mechanics Data Handbooks Ser., Vol. 3
ISBN:0-87201-335-9, ISBN13: 978-0-87201-335-3.
Dewey:624.1. LCCN:88-007227.

Audience: **u,f.**

Jennings, Alan   **TA658.2.J46 2004**
Structures: From Theory to Practice. Paper Text. Routledge.
New York, NY. 2004. 648p. ISBN:0-415-26843-5, ISBN13:
978-0-415-26843-1. Dewey:624.1/7. LCCN:2003-027278.

Audience: **u,f.** *Choice, 2005.*

Johnson, David   **TA645**
Advanced Structural Mechanics. Ed. 2. Trade Cloth. Thomas
Telford Ltd. London, 2000. 300p. ISBN:0-7277-2860-1,
ISBN13: 978-0-7277-2860-9. Dewey:624.1/71.

Audience: **u,f.**

Jones, Phil　　　　　　　　　　　　**TA654.5**
Wind Tunnel Modelling and Ventilation Design. Trade Cloth.
Elsevier Science & Technology Books. Saint Louis, MO. 234p.
ISBN:0-7506-5127-X, ISBN13: 978-0-7506-5127-1.
Dewey:624.1/75.
　　　　　　　　　　　　　　　Audience: **u,f.**

Kaveh, A.　　　　　　　　　　**TA642.K38 2004**
Structural Mechanics: Graph and Matrix Methods. Ed. 3. Trade
Cloth. Research Studies Press Ltd. Baldock, 2004. 500p.
Computational Structures Technology Ser., Vol. 1
ISBN:0-86380-304-0, ISBN13: 978-0-86380-304-8.
Dewey:624.1/7. LCCN:2004-009855.
　　　　　　　　　　　Audience: **u,f.** *Choice, 1993.*

Kirsch, Uri　　　　　　　　　　**TA645.K49 2002**
Design-Oriented Analysis of Structures: A Unified Approach.
Trade Cloth. Springer. New York, NY. 2002. 260p. Solid
Mechanics and Its Applications Ser., Vol. 95
ISBN:1-4020-0443-5, ISBN13: 978-1-4020-0443-8.
Dewey:624.1/71. LCCN:2002-066196.
　　　　　　　　　　　　　　　Audience: **u,f.**

Krenk, S.　　　　　　　　　　**TA646.K74 2001**
Mechanics and Analysis of Beams, Columns and Cables: A
Modern Introduction to the Classic Theories. Ed. 2. Trade Cloth.
Springer. New York, NY. 2001. VIII, 245p.
ISBN:3-540-41713-3, ISBN13: 978-3-540-41713-2.
Dewey:624.1/772. LCCN:2001-031132.
　　　　　　　　　　　　　　　Audience: **u,f.**

Kythe, Prem K. & Wei,　　　**TA646.K98 2003**
　Dongming
An Introduction to Linear and Nonlinear Finite Element
Analysis: A Computational Approach. Trade Cloth. Springer.
New York, NY. 2003. XXII, 445p. ISBN:0-8176-4308-7,
ISBN13: 978-0-8176-4308-9. Dewey:620/.0042.
LCCN:2003-057713.
　　　　　　　　　　　　　　　Audience: **u,f.**

Lagnese, John E. &　　　　**TA660.F53L34 1994**
　Schmidt, E. J.
Modeling, Analysis and Control of Dynamic Elastic Multi-Link
Structures. Trade Cloth. Springer. New York, NY. 1994. 388p.
Systems and Control Ser. ISBN:0-8176-3705-2, ISBN13:
978-0-8176-3705-7. Dewey:624.1/7. LCCN:94-003096.
　　　　　　　　　　　　　　　Audience: **u,f.**

Lee, P. K. (Editor)　　　　　　　　**TA630**
Structures in the New Millenium: Proceedings of the 4th
International Kerensky Conference, Hong Kong, 3-5 September
1997. Paper over Boards. Taylor & Francis Group. Abingdon,
1997. 688p. ISBN:90-5410-898-3, ISBN13: 978-90-5410-898-6.
Dewey:624.1. LCCN:99-496425.
　　　　　　　　　　　　　　　Audience: **u,f.**

MacRae, Greg
Structural Earthquake Engineering. Trade Cloth. John Wiley &
Sons Australia, Ltd. Milton, QLD. 2006. 576p.
ISBN:0-470-84845-6, ISBN13: 978-0-470-84845-6.
　　　　　　　　　　　　　　　Audience: **u,f.**

Mak, King K. & Sickling,　　　**TE7.N25 NO.492**
　Dean L.
Roadside Safety Analysis Program (RSAP): Engineer's Manual.
National Cooperative Highway Research Program Staff,
National Research Council (U.S.), Transportation Research

Board Staff & American Association of State Highway and
Transportation Officials Staff (Contribution by). Trade Cloth.
Transportation Research Board. Washington, DC. 2003. 66p.
ISBN:0-309-06812-6, ISBN13: 978-0-309-06812-3.
Dewey:625.8. LCCN:2003-104728.
　　　　　　　　　　　　　　　Audience: **u,f.**

McCormac, Jack C.　　　　　　　**TA645**
Structural Analysis: A Classical and Matrix Approach. Ed. 2.
Trade Cloth. John Wiley & Sons, Inc. Hoboken, NJ. 1997. 624p.
ISBN:0-471-36411-8, ISBN13: 978-0-471-36411-5.
Dewey:624.1/71.
　　　　　　　　　　　　　　　Audience: **u,f.**

Mikhelson, Ilya　　　　　　**TA636.M55 2004**
Structural Engineering Formulas. Cloth Text. McGraw-Hill
Professional Publishing. New York, NY. 2004. 228p.
ISBN:0-07-143911-0, ISBN13: 978-0-07-143911-4.
Dewey:624.1/02/12. LCCN:2004-044803.
　　　　　　　　　　　Audience: **u,f.** *Choice, 2004.*

Milne, R. J.　　　　　　　　**TA636.S77 1997**
Structural Engineering: History and Development. Paper over
Boards. Routledge. New York, NY. 1998. 160p.
ISBN:0-419-20170-X, ISBN13: 978-0-419-20170-0.
Dewey:624.1. LCCN:98-171733.
　　　　　　　　　　　　　　　Audience: **l,u,f.**

Nawy, Edward G.　　　　　**TA683.9.N39 1996**
Prestressed Concrete: A Fundamental Approach. Ed. 2. Cloth
Text. Prentice Hall PTR. Upper Saddle River, NJ. 1995. 800p.
Prentice Hall International Series in Civil Engineering and Ser.
ISBN:0-13-123480-3, ISBN13: 978-0-13-123480-2.
Dewey:624.1/83412. LCCN:95-013788.
　　　　　　　　　　　　　　　Audience: **l,u,f.**

Nawy, Edward G.　　　　　**TA683.9.N39 2003**
Prestressed Concrete: A Fundamental Approach. Ed. 4. Cloth
Text. Prentice Hall PTR. Upper Saddle River, NJ. 2002. 960p.
Prentice-Hall International Series in Civil Engineering and
Engineering Mechanics ISBN:0-13-008391-7, ISBN13:
978-0-13-008391-3. Dewey:624.1/83412. LCCN:2002-006006.
　　　　　　　　　　　　　　　Audience: **l,u,f.**

Nilson, Arthur H. &　　　　**TA683.2.N55 1997**
　Darwin, David
Design of Concrete Structures. Ed. 12. Trade Cloth.
McGraw-Hill Higher Education. Burr Ridge, IL. 1997. 880p.
Construction Engineering and Project Management Ser.
ISBN:0-07-046586-X, ISBN13: 978-0-07-046586-2.
Dewey:624.1/8341. LCCN:96-036814.
　　　　　　　　　　　　　　　Audience: **u,f.**

Oehlers, D. J. & Bradford,　　　**TA664.O34 1995**
　M. A.
Composite Steel and Concrete Structural Members: Fundamental
Behaviour. Trade Cloth. Elsevier Science & Technology Books.
Saint Louis, MO. 1995. 548p. Structural and Multidisciplinary
Optimization Ser. ISBN:0-08-041919-4, ISBN13:
978-0-08-041919-0. Dewey:624.1/8. LCCN:95-031130.
　　　　　　　　　　　Audience: **u,f.** *Choice, 1996.*

Oliveira, Carlos Sousa, et al.　　**QE539.2.S34A77 2006**
Assessing and Managing Earthquake Risk: Geo-Scientific and
Engineering Knowledge for Earthquake Risk Mitigation:
Developments, Tools, Techniques. Antoni Roca & Xavier Goula

(Authors). Trade Cloth. Springer. New York, NY. 2006. xxv, 543p. Geotechnical, Geological, and Earthquake Engineering Ser., Vol. 2 ISBN:1-4020-3608-6, ISBN13: 978-1-4020-3608-8. Dewey:551.22. LCCN:2006-295961.

Audience: **u,f.**

Pilkey, Walter D.   **TA407.2.P55 1994**
Formulas for Stress, Strain, and Structural Matrices. Trade Cloth. John Wiley & Sons, Inc. Hoboken, NJ. 1994. 1488p. ISBN:0-471-52746-7, ISBN13: 978-0-471-52746-6. Dewey:624.1/76/0212. LCCN:94-001008.

Audience: **l,u,f.** *Choice, 1995.*

Pilkey, Walter D.;   **TA407.P48 1994**
Wunderlich, Walter
Mechanics of Structures: Variational and Computational Methods. CRC PRess. 1994. ISBN:0-8493-4435-2, ISBN13: 978-0-8493-4435-0.

Audience: **u,f.**

Rajan, S. D.   **TA645.R325 2000**
Introduction to Structural Analysis and Design. Trade Cloth. John Wiley & Sons, Inc. Hoboken, NJ. 2000. 720p. ISBN:0-471-31997-X, ISBN13: 978-0-471-31997-9. Dewey:624.1/71. LCCN:00-021963.

Audience: **u,f.**

Ross, Carl T.   **TA641.R67 1996**
Finite Element Programs in Structural Engineering and Continuum Mechanics. Trade Paper. Horwood Publishing Ltd. Chichester, 1996. 615p. ISBN:1-898563-28-4, ISBN13: 978-1-898563-28-0. Dewey:624.1/71/028553. LCCN:96-155846.

Audience: **u,f.** *Choice, 1996.*

Ross, Carl T.   **TA642.R67 1996**
Finite Element Techniques in Structural Mechanics. Trade Paper. Horwood Publishing Ltd. Chichester, 1996. 207p. ISBN:1-898563-25-X, ISBN13: 978-1-898563-25-9. Dewey:624.1/71. LCCN:97-155183.

Audience: **u,f.** *Choice, 1997.*

Rossow, Edwin C.   **TA645.R683 1996**
Analysis and Behavior of Structures. Trade Paper. Prentice Hall PTR. Upper Saddle River, NJ. 1995. 735p. ISBN:0-02-403913-6, ISBN13: 978-0-02-403913-2. Dewey:624.1/71. LCCN:95-003647.

Audience: **l,u,f.**

Shaeffer, Ronald E.   **TA645 .S479**
Elementary Structures for Architects and Builders. Ed. 5. Cloth Text. Prentice Hall PTR. Upper Saddle River, NJ. 2006. 544p. ISBN:0-13-118655-8, ISBN13: 978-0-13-118655-2. Dewey:624.171.

Audience: **l,u,f.**

Shanmugam Ne Staff   **TA151**
Analysis and Design of Plated Structures Volume 1 Stability. Trade Cloth. Taylor & Francis Group. Philadelphia, PA. 2005. ISBN:0-8493-9545-3, ISBN13: 978-0-8493-9545-1. Dewey:624.

Audience: **u,f.**

Simiu, Emil & Miyata,   **TA654.5.S54 2006**
Toshio
Design of Buildings and Bridges for Wind: A Practical Guide for ASCE-7 Standard Users and Designers of Special Structures. Trade Cloth. John Wiley & Sons, Inc. Hoboken, NJ. 2006. 320p.

ISBN:0-471-65743-3, ISBN13: 978-0-471-65743-9. Dewey:624.1/75. LCCN:2005-021300.

Audience: **l,u,f.**

Simiu, Emil & Scanlan,   **TA654.5.S55 1996**
Robert H.
Wind Effects on Structures: Fundamentals and Applications to Design. Ed. 3. Trade Cloth. John Wiley & Sons, Inc. Hoboken, NJ. 1996. 704p. ISBN:0-471-12157-6, ISBN13: 978-0-471-12157-2. Dewey:624.1/76. LCCN:96-005238.

Audience: **u,f.** *Choice, 1997.*

Spiegel, Leonard F., et al.   **TA444 .L44**
Reinforced Concrete Design for Engineering Technology. Ed. 6. George F. Limbrunner & Abi Aghayere (Authors). Cloth Text. Prentice Hall PTR. Upper Saddle River, NJ. 2006. 544p. ISBN:0-13-118767-8, ISBN13: 978-0-13-118767-2. Dewey:624.1/8341. LCCN:2005-056572.

Audience: **l,u,f.**

Spiegel, Leonard &   **TA684.S656 1997**
Limbrunner, George F.
Applied Structural Steel Design. Ed. 3. Trade Cloth. Prentice Hall PTR. Upper Saddle River, NJ. 1996. 529p. ISBN:0-13-381583-8, ISBN13: 978-0-13-381583-2. Dewey:624.1/821. LCCN:96-031114.

Audience: **l,u,f.**

Stang, H. & Li, Victor C.   **TA683.2**
Mechanics of Fiber-Reinforced Concrete: Material Design for Structural Applications. Trade Cloth. Research Studies Press Ltd. Baldock, 2003. 300p. Civil and Structural Engineering Ser. ISBN:0-86380-272-9, ISBN13: 978-0-86380-272-0. Dewey:624.1/8341.

Audience: **u,f.**

Stankovic, Sinisa &   **TJ825**
Campbell, Neil
Wind Energy in the Built Environment. Trade Cloth. Earthscan/James & James. London, 2007. 144p. ISBN:1-84407-282-7, ISBN13: 978-1-84407-282-8. Dewey:333.92.

Audience: **u,f.**

Svetlietiskiaei, Valery A.   **TA656.S88 2003**
Statistical Dynamics and Reliability Theory for Mechanical Structures. Trade Cloth. Springer. New York, NY. 2003. XII, 446p. Foundations of Engineering Mechanics Ser. ISBN:3-540-44297-9, ISBN13: 978-3-540-44297-4. Dewey:624.1/71. LCCN:2002-191105.

Audience: **u,f.**

Wang, Chu-Kia & Salmon,   **TA645**
Charles G.
Introductory Structural Analysis. Ed. 1. Trade Paper. Prentice Hall PTR. Upper Saddle River, NJ. 1996. 608p. Prentice-Hall Civil Engineering and Engineering Mechanics Se Ser. ISBN:0-13-501569-3, ISBN13: 978-0-13-501569-8. Dewey:624.1/71. LCCN:82-020429.

Audience: **l,u,f.**

Williams, Alan   **TA683.2**
Civil and Structural Engineering: Design of Reinforced Concrete Structures. Ed. 2. Trade Paper. DP Group, Inc. Chicago, IL. 2004. 400p. ISBN:1-4195-0124-0, ISBN13: 978-1-4195-0124-1. Dewey:624.076.

Audience: **u,f.**

Wolf, John P. & Deeks, Andrew J.　　　　TA775.F6917 2004
Foundation Vibration Analysis: A Strength of Materials Approach. Cloth Text. Elsevier Science & Technology Books. Saint Louis, MO. 2004. 240p. ISBN:0-7506-6164-X, ISBN13: 978-0-7506-6164-5. Dewey:624.1/5. LCCN:2004-040363.
Audience: **u,f.** *Choice, 2004.*

Yang, Bingen　　　　TA648.3
Stress, Strain, and Structural Dynamics: An Interactive Handbook of Formulas, Solutions, and MATLAB Toolboxes. Cloth Text. Elsevier Science & Technology Books. Saint Louis, MO. 2005. 960p. ISBN:0-12-787767-3, ISBN13: 978-0-12-787767-9. Dewey:624.1/7. LCCN:2004-022861.
Audience: **u,f.**

Young-Jin, Kim (Editor)　　　　TF148
Advances in Safety and Structural Integrity. Cloth Text. Trans Tech Publications, Ltd. Aedermannsdorf, 2006. 300p. Solid State Phenomena Ser., Vol. 110 ISBN:3-908451-15-9, ISBN13: 978-3-908451-15-0. Dewey:385. LCCN:2006-277109.
Audience: **u,f.**

Zienkiewicz, O. C. & Taylor, R. L.　　　　TA640.2.Z5 2000
Finite Element Method: The Basis, Vol. 1. Ed. 5. Trade Cloth. Elsevier Science & Technology Books. Saint Louis, MO. 2000. 689p. Finite Element Method Ser., Vol. 1 ISBN:0-7506-5049-4, ISBN13: 978-0-7506-5049-6. Dewey:624.1/7. LCCN:00-710705.
Audience: **u,f.**

Structural Engineering > Construction: Concrete and Metal

　　　　TA484.F37 1995
Fatigue Data Book: Light Structural Alloys. Trade Cloth. A S M International. Materials Park, OH. 1995. 397p. ISBN:0-87170-507-9, ISBN13: 978-0-87170-507-5. Dewey:620.1/66. LCCN:95-039481.
Audience: **l,u,f.** *Choice, 1996.*

Campbell-Allen, Denison & Roper, Harold　　　　TA681.C38 1991
Concrete Structures: Materials, Maintenance and Repair. Trade Cloth. John Wiley & Sons, Inc. Hoboken, NJ. 1991. 369p. Concrete Design and Construction Ser. ISBN:0-470-21727-8, ISBN13: 978-0-470-21727-6. Dewey:624.1/834. LCCN:91-009052.
Audience: **u,f.** *Choice, 1992.*

Heyman, Jacques　　　　TA676.H49 1995
The Stone Skeleton: Structural Engineering of Masonry Architecture. Trade Cloth. Cambridge University Press. New York, NY. 1995. 170p. ISBN:0-521-47270-9, ISBN13: 978-0-521-47270-8. Dewey:693.1. LCCN:94-034084.
Audience: **u,f.** *Choice, 1996.*

Oehlers, D. J. & Bradford, M. A.　　　　TA664.O34 1995
Composite Steel and Concrete Structural Members: Fundamental Behaviour. Trade Cloth. Elsevier Science & Technology Books. Saint Louis, MO. 1995. 548p. Structural and Multidisciplinary Optimization Ser. ISBN:0-08-041919-4, ISBN13: 978-0-08-041919-0. Dewey:624.1/8. LCCN:95-031130.
Audience: **u,f.** *Choice, 1996.*

Russell, Alan & Lee, Kok Loong　　　　TA479.3.R84 2005
Structure-Property Relations in Nonferrous Metals. Trade Cloth. John Wiley & Sons, Inc. Hoboken, NJ. 2005. 520p. ISBN:0-471-64952-X, ISBN13: 978-0-471-64952-6. Dewey:620.1/8. LCCN:2004-054807.
Audience: **u,f.** *Choice, 2005.*

Sharp, Maurice L.　　　　TA690.S44 1993
Behavior and Design of Aluminum Structures. Cloth Text. McGraw-Hill Companies, The. New York, NY. 1992. xi, 309 p. :p. ISBN:0-07-056478-7, ISBN13: 978-0-07-056478-7. Dewey:624.1/826. LCCN:92-022257.
Audience: **u,f.** *Choice, 1993.*

Smith, J. C.　　　　TA684.S584 1996
Structural Steel Design: LRFD Approach. Ed. 2. Trade Cloth. John Wiley & Sons, Inc. Hoboken, NJ. 1996. 560p. ISBN:0-471-10693-3, ISBN13: 978-0-471-10693-7. Dewey:624.1/821. LCCN:95-036503.
Audience: **u,f.** *Choice, 1996.*

Xanthakos, Petros P.　　　　TA772.X36 1991
Ground Anchors and Anchored Structures. Ed. 1. Trade Cloth. John Wiley & Sons, Inc. Hoboken, NJ. 1991. 704p. ISBN:0-471-52520-0, ISBN13: 978-0-471-52520-2. Dewey:624.1/5. LCCN:90-044291.
Audience: **u,f.** *Choice, 1991.*

Structural Engineering > Construction: Highways, Bridges, Roads, and Buildings

Francis, A. J.　　　　TA633.F73 1989
Introducing Structures: Civil and Structural Engineering, Building and Architecture. Ed. 2. Trade Cloth. Prentice Hall PTR. Upper Saddle River, NJ. 1989. 298p. Civil Engineering Ser. ISBN:0-470-21534-8, ISBN13: 978-0-470-21534-0. Dewey:624.1. LCCN:89-015291.
Audience: **u.** *Choice, 1990.*

Gordon, J. E.　　　　TA405.G62 1988
The Science of Structures and Materials. Stephen Wagley (Editor). Cloth over Boards. Henry Holt & Company. New York, NY. 1988. 217p. Scientific American Library ISBN:0-7167-5022-8, ISBN13: 978-0-7167-5022-2. Dewey:620.1/1. LCCN:87-035412.
Audience: **u,f.** *Choice, 1988.*

Jones, Norman　　　　TA654.2 .J66 1997
Structural Impact. Trade Cloth. Cambridge University Press. New York, NY. 1990. 591p. ISBN:0-521-30180-7, ISBN13: 978-0-521-30180-0. Dewey:624.1/71. LCCN:88-031794.
Audience: **u,f.** *Choice, 1990.*

Levy, Matthys & Salvadori, Mario G.　　　　TH441.L48 1992
Why Buildings Fall Down: How Structures Fail. Trade Cloth. W. W. Norton & Company, Inc. New York, NY. 1992. 352p. ISBN:0-393-03356-2, ISBN13: 978-0-393-03356-4. Dewey:690.2/1. LCCN:91-034954.
Audience: **l,u,f.** *Choice, 1992.*

Liu, Henry　　　　TA654.5.L58 1991
Wind Engineering: A Handbook for Structural Engineering. Trade Paper. Prentice Hall PTR. Upper Saddle River, NJ. 1990.

224p. ISBN:0-13-960279-8, ISBN13: 978-0-13-960279-5. Dewey:624.1/75. LCCN:89-048279.

Audience: **l,u.** *Choice, 1991.*

MacLeod, Iain A.   **TA647.M33 1990**
Analytical Modelling of Structural Systems: An Entirely New Approach with Emphasis on Behaviour of Building Structures. Trade Cloth. Ellis Horwood Ltd. Hempstead, 1990. 222p. ISBN:0-13-035254-3, ISBN13: 978-0-13-035254-5. Dewey:624.1/71. LCCN:89-029860.

Audience: **u,f.** *Choice, 1991.*

Melaragno, Michele G.   **TA660.S5M445 1991**
Introduction to Shell Structures: The Art and Science of Vaulting. Cloth Text. Chapman & Hall. New York, NY. 1991. 352p. ISBN:0-442-23725-1, ISBN13: 978-0-442-23725-7. Dewey:624.1/7762. LCCN:90-041113.

Audience: **u,f.** *Choice, 1992.*

Schueller, Wolfgang   **TA658.S15 1996**
The Design of Building Structures. Ed. 1. Trade Cloth. Prentice Hall PTR. Upper Saddle River, NJ. 1995. 868p. International Series in Civil Engineering ISBN:0-13-346560-8, ISBN13: 978-0-13-346560-0. Dewey:690. LCCN:95-013790.

Audience: **u,f.** *Choice, 1996.*

Structural Engineering > Soil Mechanics

Atkinson, John H.   **TA710**
Mechanics of Soil and Foundations. Ed. 2. Cloth Text. Taylor & Francis Group. Philadelphia, PA. 2007. 360p. ISBN:0-415-36255-5, ISBN13: 978-0-415-36255-9. Dewey:624.15136.

Audience: **u,f.**

Barends, F. B. J. (Editor),   **TA710.A1**
  et al.
Geotechnical Engineering for Transportation Infrastructure -Theory and Practice, Planning and Design, Construction and Maintenance: Proceedings of the XIIth ECSMGE Conference, Amsterdam, 7-10 June 1999/Additional Volume. J. Lindenberg, H. J. Luger, L. de Quelery & A. Verruijt (Editors). Paper over Boards. Taylor & Francis Group. Abingdon, 2000. 158p. ISBN:90-5809-134-1, ISBN13: 978-90-5809-134-5. Dewey:624.1/5136.

Audience: **u,f.**

British Tunnelling Society   **TA815**
Closed-face Tunnelling Machines and Ground Stability: A Guideline for Best Practice. Trade Paper. Thomas Telford Ltd. London, 2005. 96p. ISBN:0-7277-3386-9, ISBN13: 978-0-7277-3386-3. Dewey:624.193091732.

Audience: **u,f.**

Budhu, Muniram   **TA710**
Soil Mechanics and Foundations. Ed. 2. Trade Cloth. John Wiley & Sons, Inc. Hoboken, NJ. 2006. 656p. ISBN:0-471-43117-6, ISBN13: 978-0-471-43117-6. Dewey:624.1/5136221.

Audience: **u,f.**

Cornforth, Derek   **TA710.C65 2004**
Landslides in Practice: Investigation, Analysis, and Remedial/Preventative Options in Soils. Trade Cloth. John Wiley & Sons, Inc. Hoboken, NJ. 2005. 624p. ISBN:0-471-67816-3,

ISBN13: 978-0-471-67816-8. Dewey:624.1/51363. LCCN:2004-007921.

Audience: **l,u,f.**

Das   **TA775**
Principles of Foundation and Geotechnical Engineering. Trade Cloth. Thomson Learning EMEA, Ltd. London, 2006. ISBN:0-495-08249-X, ISBN13: 978-0-495-08249-1. Dewey:624.1/5.

Audience: **u,f.**

Davis, R. O. & Selvadurai,   **TA418.14 .D38**
  A. P. S.
Plasticity and Geomechanics. Trade Paper. Cambridge University Press. New York, NY. 2005. 299p. ISBN:0-521-01809-9, ISBN13: 978-0-521-01809-8. Dewey:624.1/51.

Audience: **u,f.** *Choice, 2003.*

Hack, Robert (Editor), et al.   **TA705.4.E85E54 2004**
Engineering Geology and Geotechnics for Infrastructure Development in Europe. Azzam Rafig & Robert Charlier (Editors). Trade Cloth. Springer. New York, NY. 2004. XIX, 803p. Lecture Notes in Earth Sciences Ser., Vol. 104 ISBN:3-540-21075-X, ISBN13: 978-3-540-21075-7. Dewey:624.1/51. LCCN:2004-103475.

Audience: **u,f.**

Han, Jie (Editor), et al.   **TA710.A1G368 2006**
Advances in Earth Structures: Research to Practice: Proceedings of Sessions of GeoShanghai, June 6-8, 2006, Shanghai, China. Jian-Hua Yin, David White & Guoming Lin (Editors). Paper Text. American Society of Civil Engineers. Reston, VA. 2006. 388p. Geotechnical Special Publication Ser., No. 151 ISBN:0-7844-0863-7, ISBN13: 978-0-7844-0863-6. Dewey:624.1/891. LCCN:2006-042773.

Audience: **u,f.**

Highway Innovative   **TA770.E918 2001**
  Technology Evaluation Center Staff (Contribution by)
Evaluation of the Inter-Lok Retaining Wall System. Trade Cloth. American Society of Civil Engineers. Reston, VA. 2002. CERF Report Ser., Vol. 01 ISBN:0-7844-0595-6, ISBN13: 978-0-7844-0595-6. Dewey:624.1/64. LCCN:2001-046447.

Audience: **u,f.**

Highway Innovative   **TA770.E938 2003**
  Technology Evaluation Center Staff (Contribution by)
Evaluation of the Versa-Lok/Miragrid Reinforced Soil Wall System. Trade Cloth. American Society of Civil Engineers. Reston, VA. 2003. Technical Evaluation Report Ser. ISBN:0-7844-0708-8, ISBN13: 978-0-7844-0708-0. Dewey:625.7/3. LCCN:2003-063551.

Audience: **u,f.**

Jefferson, Ian, et al.
Foundations of Geotechnical Engineering. John Greenwood & Matthew Frost (Authors). Trade Cloth. Spon Press. 2006. 88p. ISBN:0-415-27240-8, ISBN13: 978-0-415-27240-7.

Audience: **u,f.**

Katzenbach, Rolf & Turek,   **TA633**
  Jens (Editors)
Interaction Between Structural and Geotechnical Engineers. Trade Paper. Thomas Telford Ltd. London, 2004. 106p. ISBN:0-7277-3126-2, ISBN13: 978-0-7277-3126-5. Dewey:624.1094.

Audience: **u,f.**

Kempfert, Hans-Georg &   QE28.2
  Gebreselassie, Berhane
Excavations and Foundations in Soft Soils. Trade Cloth.
Springer. New York, NY. 2006. xxii, 576p.
ISBN:3-540-32894-7, ISBN13: 978-3-540-32894-0. Dewey:551.
LCCN:2006-921905.
                           Audience: **u,f.**

Luo, Yiqi & Zhou, Xuhui   QC879.8.L86 2006
Soil Respiration and the Environment. Trade Cloth. Elsevier
Science & Technology Books. Saint Louis, MO. 2006. 328p.
ISBN:0-12-088782-7, ISBN13: 978-0-12-088782-8.
Dewey:577/.144. LCCN:2006-024416.
                           Audience: **u,f.**

McCarthy, David F.   TA710 .M3853 2007
Essentials of Soil Mechanics and Foundations: Basic
Geotechnics. Ed. 7. Trade Cloth. Pearson Education. Boston,
MA. 2006. 864p. ISBN:0-13-114560-6, ISBN13:
978-0-13-114560-3. Dewey:624.1/5. LCCN:2006-049454.
                           Audience: **u,f.**

Miller, Gerald A. (Editor),   TA710.A1I5194 2006
  et al.
Unsaturated Soils 2006: Geotechnical Special Publication No.
147. Claudia E. Zapata, Sandra L. Houston & Delwyn G.
Fredlund (Editors). Paper Text. American Society of Civil
Engineers. Reston, VA. 2006. 2581p. Geotechnical Special
Publication Ser., No. 147 ISBN:0-7844-0802-5, ISBN13:
978-0-7844-0802-5. Dewey:624.1/5136. LCCN:2006-045958.
                           Audience: **u,f.**

Ortigao, José A. & Sayao,   TA710.H36 2003
  Alberto (Editors)
Handbook of Slope Stabilisation. Trade Cloth. Springer. New
York, NY. 2004. XX, 498p. ISBN:3-540-41646-3, ISBN13:
978-3-540-41646-3. Dewey:624.1/51363. LCCN:2003-054437.
                  Audience: **u,f.** *Choice, 2004.*

Powrie, William   TA710
Soil Mechanics: Concepts and Applications. Ed. 2. UK-B
Format Paperback. Routledge. New York, NY. 2004. 704p.
ISBN:0-415-31156-X, ISBN13: 978-0-415-31156-4.
Dewey:624.1/5136. LCCN:2004-002128.
                           Audience: **u,f.**

Raghu Dorairaja Staff
Soil Mechanics for Environmental Engineers. Trade Cloth.
Taylor & Francis Group. Philadelphia, PA. 2007.
ISBN:0-8247-5818-8, ISBN13: 978-0-8247-5818-9.
                           Audience: **u,f.**

Schanz, Tom (Editor)   TA710
Unsaturated Soils. Trade Cloth. Springer. New York, NY. 2004.
540p. Springer Proceedings in Physics Ser.
ISBN:3-540-21121-7, ISBN13: 978-3-540-21121-1.
Dewey:624.1/5136. LCCN:2004-109958.
                           Audience: **u,f.**

Schofield, Andrew   TA710.S285 2005
Disturbed Soil Properties and Geotechnical Design. Trade Cloth.
Thomas Telford Ltd. London, 2005. 216p. ISBN:0-7277-2982-9,
ISBN13: 978-0-7277-2982-8. Dewey:624.15136.
LCCN:2006-365850.
                           Audience: **u,f.**

Smith, Ian   TA710
Elements of Soil Mechanics. Ed. 8. Trade Paper. Blackwell
Publishing, Inc. Malden, MA. 2006. 552p. ISBN:1-4051-3370-8,
ISBN13: 978-1-4051-3370-8. Dewey:624.1/5136.
LCCN:2006-045974.
                           Audience: **u,f.**

Wickert, Jonathan   TA710
Principles of Geotechnical Engineering.Txt. Ed. 6. Cloth Text.
Thomson Wadsworth. Belmont, CA. 2005. 672p.
ISBN:0-534-55144-0, ISBN13: 978-0-534-55144-5.
Dewey:624.1/5136.
                           Audience: **u,f.**

Wood, David   TA706
Geotechnical Modelling. Paper over Boards. Routledge. New
York, NY. 2004. 504p. Applied Geotechnics Ser., Vol. 1
ISBN:0-415-34304-6, ISBN13: 978-0-415-34304-6.
Dewey:624.1/5136. LCCN:2003-024081.
                           Audience: **u,f.**

Wright, Stephen G. &   TA710.D868 2005
  Duncan, J. Michael
Soil Strength and Slope Stability. Trade Cloth. John Wiley &
Sons, Inc. Hoboken, NJ. 2005. 312p. ISBN:0-471-69163-1,
ISBN13: 978-0-471-69163-1. Dewey:624.1/51363.
LCCN:2004-019535.
                           Audience: **u,f.**

Wu, Wei & Yu, H. -S.   TA703.5
  (Editors)
Modern Trends in Geomechanics. Trade Cloth. Springer. New
York, NY. 2006. 258 schw.-w. u. 2 farb. Abb., 40 schw.-w. Tab.,
258 schw.-w. u. 2 farb. Zeichn., Coloured pages 255, 310 X,
559p. Springer Proceedings in Physics Ser.
ISBN:3-540-25135-9, ISBN13: 978-3-540-25135-4.
Dewey:624.151. LCCN:2006-921401.
                           Audience: **u,f.**

Yamamuro, Jerry A. &   TA710.A1G344 2005
  Kaliakin, Victor N. (Editors)
Soil Constitutive Models: Evaluation, Selection, and Calibration:
January 24-26, 2005, Austin, Texas. American Society of Civil
Engineers Staff (Contribution by). Paper Text. American Society
of Civil Engineers. Reston, VA. 2005. 512p. Geotechnical
Special Publication Ser., No. 128 ISBN:0-7844-0771-1, ISBN13:
978-0-7844-0771-4. Dewey:624.1/5136/015118.
LCCN:2004-062791.
                           Audience: **u,f.**

Transportation Engineering

Adeli, Hojjat & Karim,   TA1235
  Asim
Wavelets in Intelligent Transportation Systems. Trade Cloth.
John Wiley & Sons, Inc. Hoboken, NJ. 2005. 242p.
ISBN:0-470-86742-6, ISBN13: 978-0-470-86742-6.
Dewey:388.3/12. LCCN:2005-021397.
                           Audience: **u,f.**

Allan, J. (Editor), et al.   TF153
Computers in Railways X: Computer System Design and
Operation in the Railway and Other Transit Systems. Carlos A.
Brebbia, A. F. Rumsey, G. Sciutto, S. Sone & C. J. Goodman

(Editors). Trade Cloth. WIT Press. Ashurst, 2006. 1008p. Transactions on the Built Environment Ser., 88 ISBN:1-84564-177-9, ISBN13: 978-1-84564-177-1. Dewey:385.20285.

Audience: **u,f.**

Chant, Christopher   **HE4211**
Rapid Transit Systems: And the Decline of Steam. John Moore (Editor). Trade Cloth. Universal International Pty, Ltd. Gordon, NSW. 2000. 64p. ISBN:1-84013-359-7, ISBN13: 978-1-84013-359-2. Dewey:388.4/2.

Audience: **g,l,u,f.**

Dahl, Gerhard Melvin   **HE4491.B75D13**
Transit truths, by Gerhard M. Dahl. Trade Cloth. Scholarly Publishing Office, University of Michigan Library. Ann Arbor, MI. 2005. ISBN:1-4181-7077-1, ISBN13: 978-1-4181-7077-6. Dewey:388.

Audience: **l,u,f.**

Edwards, John D.   **HE152.5.T73 1999**
Transportation Planning Handbook. Ed. 2. Cloth Text. Institute of Transportation Engineers. Washington, DC. 1999. 865p. ISBN:0-935403-33-7, ISBN13: 978-0-935403-33-6. Dewey:388/.068. LCCN:99-041567.

Audience: **u,f.**

Fotsch, Paul Mason   **TA1023.F68 2006**
Watching the Traffic Go By: Transportation and Isolation in Urban America. Trade Cloth. University of Texas Press. Austin, TX. 2007. ISBN:0-292-71425-4, ISBN13: 978-0-292-71425-0. Dewey:388.40973. LCCN:2006-008602.

Audience: **l,u,f.**

Fricker, Jon D. & Whitford,   **TA1145**
Robert K.
Fundamentals of Transportation Engineering: A Multimodal Systems Approach. Trade Cloth. Prentice Hall PTR. Upper Saddle River, NJ. 2004. 792p. ISBN:0-13-035124-5, ISBN13: 978-0-13-035124-1. Dewey:629.04. LCCN:2004-040015.

Audience: **u,f.**

Garber   **HE151**
Introduction to Transportation Engineering: A Multimodal Integration. Cloth Text. Thomson Wadsworth. Belmont, CA. 2006. 656p. General Engineering Ser. ISBN:0-534-95289-5, ISBN13: 978-0-534-95289-1. Dewey:388.

Audience: **u,f.**

Garrett, Mark & Wachs,   **HE206.2.G37 1996**
Martin
Transportation Planning on Trial: The Clean Air Act and Travel Forecasting. Trade Cloth. SAGE Publications, Inc. Thousand Oaks, CA. 1996. 232p. Metropolis and Region Ser., Vol. T ISBN:0-8039-7352-7, ISBN13: 978-0-8039-7352-7. Dewey:711.7/0973. LCCN:95-050228.

Audience: **l,u,f.** *Choice, 1996.*

Greene, David L. & Santini,   **TD885.5.G73.T72 1993**
Danilo J.
Transportation and Global Climate Change. Trade Paper. American Council for an Energy Efficient Economy. Washington, DC. 1997. 357p. ISBN:0-918249-17-1, ISBN13: 978-0-918249-17-3. Dewey:363.73/87. LCCN:93-015469.

Audience: **l,u,f.** *Choice, 1994.*

Khisty, C. Jotin & Lall, B.   **TA1145.K48 1998**
Kent
Transportation Engineering: An Introduction. Ed. 2. Trade Cloth. Prentice Hall PTR. Upper Saddle River, NJ. 1997. 720p. ISBN:0-13-157355-1, ISBN13: 978-0-13-157355-0. Dewey:629.04. LCCN:97-017389.

Audience: **l,u,f.** *Choice, 1990.*

Khisty, C. Jotin & Lall, B.   **TA1145.K48 2002**
Kent
Transportation Engineering: An Introduction. Ed. 3. Cloth Text. Prentice Hall PTR. Upper Saddle River, NJ. 2002. 813p. ISBN:0-13-033560-6, ISBN13: 978-0-13-033560-9. Dewey:629.04. LCCN:2002-190384.

Audience: **l,u,f.** *Choice, 1990.*

Korve, Hans W.   **HE4451 .L54**
Light Rail Service: Pedestrian and Vehicular Safety. Paper Text. DIANE Publishing Company. Collingdale, PA. 2001. 141p. ISBN:0-7567-2409-0, ISBN13: 978-0-7567-2409-2. Dewey:363.12/2.

Audience: **u,f.**

Kutz, Myer   **TA1145**
Handbook of Transportation Engineering. Trade Cloth. McGraw-Hill Professional Publishing. New York, NY. 2003. 1000p. ISBN:0-07-139122-3, ISBN13: 978-0-07-139122-1. Dewey:629.04. LCCN:2004-298713.

Audience: **u,f.** *Choice, 2004.*

Marchildon Greg   **RA395.C3**
Health Care Systems in Transit. Trade Paper. University of Toronto Press. Toronto, ON. 2006. 176p. ISBN:0-8020-9400-7, ISBN13: 978-0-8020-9400-1. Dewey:362.1/0971. LCCN:2006-274293.

Audience: **u,f.**

Middleton, William D.   **HE4500.M53 2002**
Metropolitan Railways: Rapid Transit in America. Trade Cloth. Indiana University Press. Bloomington, IN. 2002. 400p. Railroads Past and Present Ser. ISBN:0-253-34179-5, ISBN13: 978-0-253-34179-2. Dewey:388.4/2/0973. LCCN:2002-006588.

Audience: **g,l,u,f.** *Choice, 2003.*

Murthy, A. S. Narasimha &   **TA1145.M88 2001**
Mohle, R. Henry
Transportation Engineering Basics. Ed. 2. Trade Cloth. American Society of Civil Engineers. Reston, VA. 2001. 184p. ISBN:0-7844-0464-X, ISBN13: 978-0-7844-0464-5. Dewey:388. LCCN:00-063965.

Audience: **l,u,f.**

New York (State)   **TF725.N5 A7**
New subways for New York. Trade Cloth. Scholarly Publishing Office, University of Michigan Library. Ann Arbor, MI. 2005. ISBN:1-4181-7072-0, ISBN13: 978-1-4181-7072-1. Dewey:388.42097471.

Audience: **u,f.**

Norbeck, Joseph M. et al.   **TL229**
Hydrogen fuel for surface transportation. Society of Automotive Engineers. 1996. ISBN:1-56091-684-2, ISBN13: 978-1-56091-684-0.

Audience: **u,f.**

Papageorgiou, M. (Editor)   **TA1145.C58 1991**
Concise Encyclopedia of Traffic and Transportation Systems. Ed. 2. Trade Cloth. Elsevier Science & Technology Books. Saint

Louis, MO. 1991. 676p. Advances in Systems Control and Information Engineering Ser., No. 6 ISBN:0-08-036203-6, ISBN13: 978-0-08-036203-8. Dewey:388/.03. LCCN:90-022479.
Audience: **u,f.** *Choice, 1992.*

Riley, Robert Q.   **HD9710.A2R55 1994**
Alternative Cars in the 21st Century: A New Personal Transportation Paradigm. Trade Cloth. Society of Automotive Engineers, Inc. Warrendale, PA. 1994. 400p. ISBN:1-56091-519-6, ISBN13: 978-1-56091-519-5. Dewey:338.4/7629222. LCCN:94-019325.
Audience: **g,l,u,f.** *Choice, 1995.*

Robertson, Douglas (Editor)   **HE333.M28 1994**
Manual of Transportation Engineering Studies. Ed. 5. Cloth Text. Prentice Hall PTR. Upper Saddle River, NJ. 1994. 528p. ISBN:0-13-097569-9, ISBN13: 978-0-13-097569-0. Dewey:629.04. LCCN:93-013519.
Audience: **u,f.** *Choice, 1994.*

Roess, Roger P., et al.   **HE355**
Traffic Engineering. Ed. 3. William R. McShane & Elena S. Prassas (Authors). Cloth Text. Prentice Hall PTR. Upper Saddle River, NJ. 2004. 816p. ISBN:0-13-142471-8, ISBN13: 978-0-13-142471-5. Dewey:388.3/12/0973. LCCN:2004-295239.
Audience: **l,u,f.**

Sperling, Daniel   **TL220.S65 1995**
Future Drive: Electric Vehicles and Sustainable Transportation. A. F. Burke, Patricia M. Davis & Mark A. Delucchi (Other Primary Creators). Trade Cloth. Island Press. Washington, DC. 1994. 191p. ISBN:1-55963-327-1, ISBN13: 978-1-55963-327-7. Dewey:388. LCCN:94-038935.
Audience: **g,l,u,f.** *Choice, 1995.*

Sproule, William J. (Editor), et al.   **TA1207.A987 1998**
Automated People Movers VI: Creative Access for Major Activity Centers: Proceedings of the Sixth International Conference. Edward S. Neumann & Stanford W. Lynch (Editors), American Society of Civil Engineers Staff (Contribution by). Trade Cloth. American Society of Civil Engineers. Reston, VA. 1998. 774p. ISBN:0-7844-0289-2, ISBN13: 978-0-7844-0289-4. Dewey:388.4/1. LCCN:97-031341.
Audience: **u,f.**

Thomson Delmar Learning Staff   **HF5035**
ASE Transit Bus Technician Certification H6: Electrical/Electronic Systems. Trade Paper. Thomson Delmar Learning. Albany, NY. 2006. 112p. ISBN:1-4180-4999-9, ISBN13: 978-1-4180-4999-7. Dewey:338.
Audience: **l,u,f.**

UNC Institute for Transportation Research and Education Staff (Contribution by), et al.   **TA1235.U53 2002**
Guidebook for Selecting Appropriate Technology Systems for Small Urban and Rural Public Transportation Operators. KFH Group Staff, TransCore (Firm) Staff, Transit Cooperative Research Program Staff, National Research Council (U.S.), Transportation Research Board Staff, United States, Federal Transit Administration Staff & Transit Development Corporation Staff (Contribution by). Trade Cloth. National Academies Press. Washington, DC. 2002. vii, 73p. ISBN:0-309-06723-5, ISBN13: 978-0-309-06723-2. Dewey:629. LCCN:2002-101475.
Audience: **u,f.**

United Nations   **HE148.5**
Challenges and Opportunities for further Improving the Transit Systems and Economic Development of Landlocked and Transit Developing Countries. Trade Cloth. United Nations Publications. New York, NY. 2005. 56p. ISBN:92-1-112593-6, ISBN13: 978-92-1-112593-1. Dewey:338.4.
Audience: **u,f.**

Webb, Mary   **HE305**
Jane's Urban Transport Systems 2005-2006. Ed. 24. Trade Cloth. Jane's Information Group. Coulsdon, 2005. 24p. ISBN:0-7106-2709-2, ISBN13: 978-0-7106-2709-4. Dewey:388.4.
Audience: **u,f.**

Whitelegg, John   **TD195**
Transport for a sustainable future: the case for Europe. Bellhaven/Halsted. 1993. ISBN:0-470-22018-X, ISBN13: 978-0-470-22018-4.
Audience: **l,u,f.**

Wright, Paul H., et al.   **TA1145.W75 1998**
Transportation Engineering: Planning and Design. Ed. 4. Norman J. Ashford & Robert J. Stammer (Authors). Trade Cloth. John Wiley & Sons, Inc. Hoboken, NJ. 1997. 688p. ISBN:0-471-17396-7, ISBN13: 978-0-471-17396-0. Dewey:629.04. LCCN:97-015256.
Audience: **u,f.**

Applied Optics

Das, P. K.   **TA1677.D37 1991**
Lasers and Optical Engineering. Trade Cloth. Springer. New York, NY. 1990. 496p. ISBN:0-387-97108-4, ISBN13: 978-0-387-97108-7. Dewey:621.36/6. LCCN:89-026312.
Audience: **l,u,f.** *Choice, 1991.*

Hecht, Jeff   **TA1800.H42 1999**
City of Light: The Story of Fiber Optics. Trade Cloth. Oxford University Press, Inc. New York, NY. 1999. 328p. Sloan Technology Ser. ISBN:0-19-510818-3, ISBN13: 978-0-19-510818-7. Dewey:621.36/92. LCCN:98-006135.
Audience: **g,l,f.** *Choice, 2000.*

Laufer, Gabriel   **TA367.5 .L39 1996**
Introduction to Optics and Lasers in Engineering. Trade Cloth. Cambridge University Press. New York, NY. 1996. 490p. ISBN:0-521-45233-3, ISBN13: 978-0-521-45233-5. Dewey:621.3/6. LCCN:95-044046.
Audience: **u,f.** *Choice, 1997.*

Rogers, Alan J.   **TK5103.59.R64 2001**
Understanding Optical Fiber Communications. Trade Cloth. Artech House, Inc. Norwood, MA. 2001. 232p. Optoelectronics Library ISBN:0-89006-478-4, ISBN13: 978-0-89006-478-8. Dewey:621.382/7. LCCN:00-068930.
Audience: **g,l.** *Choice, 2001.*

Vanderlugt, Anthony   **TA1632.V28 1992**
Optical Signal Processing. Trade Cloth. John Wiley & Sons, Inc. Hoboken, NJ. 1992. 632p. Wiley Series in Pure and Applied Optics Ser., Vol. 10 ISBN:0-471-54682-8, ISBN13: 978-0-471-54682-5. Dewey:621.36/7. LCCN:91-023378.
Audience: **l,u,f.** *Choice, 1993.*

Winch, Robert G.   **TK5101.W48 1993**
Telecommunication Transmission Systems: Microwave, Fiber
Optic, Mobile Cellular Radio, Data, and Digital Multiplexing.
Trade Cloth. McGraw-Hill Companies, The. New York, NY.
1993. 560p. ISBN:0-07-070964-5, ISBN13: 978-0-07-070964-5.
Dewey:621.382. LCCN:92-026723.

Audience: **u,f.** *Choice, 1993.*

Yu, Francis T. S. & Yang,   **TA1750 .Y8 1997**
 Xiangyang
Introduction to Optical Engineering. Cloth Text. Cambridge
University Press. New York, NY. 1997. 423p.
ISBN:0-521-57366-1, ISBN13: 978-0-521-57366-5.
Dewey:621.3/6. LCCN:96-002864.

Audience: **u,f.** *Choice, 1998.*

Water Resource Engineering

Akan, A. Osman &   **TC409.A39 2003**
 Houghtalen, Robert J.
Urban Hydrology, Hydraulics, and Stormwater Quality:
Engineering Applications and Computer Modeling. Trade Cloth.
John Wiley & Sons, Inc. Hoboken, NJ. 2003. 392p.
ISBN:0-471-43158-3, ISBN13: 978-0-471-43158-9.
Dewey:628/.21. LCCN:2003-001377.

Audience: **u,f.**

Billington, David P. &   **TC556.B55 2006**
 Jackson, Donald C.
Big Dams of the New Deal Era: A Confluence of Engineering
and Politics. Trade Cloth. University of Oklahoma Press.
Norman, OK. 2006. 416p. ISBN:0-8061-3795-9, ISBN13:
978-0-8061-3795-7. Dewey:333.9100973/0904.
LCCN:2006-044493.

Audience: **u,f.**

Brandt, Steven A.   **HM51**
Damming the Past: Dams and Cultural Heritage Management.
Trade Cloth. Lexington Books. Lanham, MD. 2007. 500p.
ISBN:0-7391-0885-9, ISBN13: 978-0-7391-0885-7. Dewey:301.

Audience: **l,u,f.**

Brouwer, Roy & Pearce,   **HD1691**
 David
Cost-Benefit Analysis and Water Resources Management. Trade
Cloth. Edward Elgar Publishing, Inc. Northampton, MA. 2005.
432p. ISBN:1-84376-359-1, ISBN13: 978-1-84376-359-8.
Dewey:333.91. LCCN:2005-040693.

Audience: **u,f.**

Chapra, Steven C.   **TD365.C48 1997**
Surface Water Quality Modeling. Cloth Text. McGraw-Hill
Higher Education. Burr Ridge, IL. 1996. 784p. Water Resources
and Environmental Engineering Ser. ISBN:0-07-011364-5,
ISBN13: 978-0-07-011364-0. Dewey:628.1/61/015118.
LCCN:96-015461.

Audience: **u,f.**

Chin, David   **TC405**
Water-Resources Engineering. Ed. 2. Cloth Text. Prentice Hall
PTR. Upper Saddle River, NJ. 2006. 976p.
ISBN:0-13-148192-4, ISBN13: 978-0-13-148192-3. Dewey:627.
LCCN:2006-041989.

Audience: **u,f.**

Delleur, Jacques W. (Editor)   **TD405**
Handbook of Groundwater Engineering. Trade Cloth. Springer.
New York, NY. 1999. XX, 949p. ISBN:3-540-64745-7, ISBN13:
978-3-540-64745-4. Dewey:628.1/14.

Audience: **u,f.**

Doddannavar, Ravi, et al.   **TC5**
Practical Hydraulic Systems: Operation and Troubleshooting for
Engineers and Technicians. Andries Barnard & Jayaraman
Ganesh (Authors), Steve MacKay (Editor). Trade Paper, Perfect.
Elsevier Science & Technology Books. Saint Louis, MO. 2005.
240p. Practical Professional Books from Elsevier
ISBN:0-7506-6276-X, ISBN13: 978-0-7506-6276-5. Dewey:627.
LCCN:2005-296515.

Audience: **u,f.**

Duckstein, Lucien & Plate,   **TC401.N285 1985**
 Erich J. (Editors)
Engineering Reliability and Risk in Water Resources. Trade
Cloth. Springer. New York, NY. 1987. 590p.
ISBN:90-247-3492-4, ISBN13: 978-90-247-3492-4. Dewey:627.
LCCN:87-001722.

Audience: **u,f.**

Ghosh, S. N. & Desai, V. R.   **TC409.G52 2005**
Environmental Hydrology and Hydraulics: Eco-Technological
Practices for Sustainable Development. Trade Cloth. Science
Publishers. Enfield, NH. 2006. 394p. ISBN:1-57808-403-2,
ISBN13: 978-1-57808-403-6. Dewey:627. LCCN:2005-056311.

Audience: **u,f.**

Grover, Velma I.   **TC411.W345 2006**
Water: Global Common and Global Problems. Trade Cloth.
Science Publishers. Enfield, NH. 2006. 532p.
ISBN:1-57808-409-1, ISBN13: 978-1-57808-409-8.
Dewey:363.6/1. LCCN:2005-056109.

Audience: **u,f.**

Herbich, John B. (Editor)   **TC330.H36 1990**
Handbook of Coastal and Ocean Engineering, vol. 1: Wave
Phenomena and Costal Structures. Gulf Publishing. 1990.
ISBN:0-87201-461-4, ISBN13: 978-0-87201-461-9.

Audience: **u,f.**

Herbich, John B. (Editor)   **TC330.H36 1990**
Handbook of Coastal and Ocean Engineering, vol. 2: Offshore
Structures, Marine Foundations, Sediment Processes, and
Modeling. Gulf Publishing. 1991. ISBN:0-87201-462-2,
ISBN13: 978-0-87201-462-6.

Audience: **u,f.**

Herbich, John B. (Editor)   **TC330**
Handbook of Coastal and Ocean Engineering, vol. 3: Harbors,
Navigational Channels, Estuaries, Environmental Effects. Gulf
Publishing. 1992. ISBN:0-87201-452-5, ISBN13:
978-0-87201-452-7.

Audience: **u,f.**

Institution of Mechanical   **TA660.T34**
 Engineers (Great Britain), Pressure Systems Group Staff
 (Contribution by)
Developments in Pressure Equipment: Where to Next? Trade
Cloth. John Wiley & Sons, Inc. Hoboken, NJ. 2005. 144p.
ISBN:1-86058-478-0, ISBN13: 978-1-86058-478-7.
Dewey:681.76041.

Audience: **u,f.**

Joussan, John & Chadwick, Matthew   HD1702

Water Resources and Development. Trade Cloth. Routledge. New York, NY. 2005. 256p. ISBN:0-415-30050-9, ISBN13: 978-0-415-30050-6. Dewey:363.6/1/091724.

Audience: **u,f.**

Kay, B. H.   TC401

Water Resources: Health, Environment and Development. Walter E. Houghton (Editor). Paper over Boards. Routledge. New York, NY. 1999. 272p. ISBN:0-419-22290-1, ISBN13: 978-0-419-22290-3. Dewey:333.9/115. LCCN:99-193422.

Audience: **u,f.**

Maidment, David R.   GB662.5.M35 1993

Handbook of Hydrology. Trade Cloth. McGraw-Hill Professional Publishing. New York, NY. 1993. 1424p. ISBN:0-07-039732-5, ISBN13: 978-0-07-039732-3. Dewey:551.48. LCCN:92-018193.

Audience: **u,f.** *Choice, 1993.*

Mays, Larry W.   TC145.M383 2005

Water Resources Engineering. Ed. 2. Trade Cloth. John Wiley & Sons, Inc. Hoboken, NJ. 2004. 860p. ISBN:0-471-70524-1, ISBN13: 978-0-471-70524-6. Dewey:627. LCCN:2004-058650.

Audience: **u,f.**

Mays, Larry W.   QA901

Water Resources Sustainability. Trade Cloth. McGraw-Hill Professional Publishing. New York, NY. 2006. 480p. ISBN:0-07-146230-9, ISBN13: 978-0-07-146230-3. Dewey:363.6/1. LCCN:2006-025702.

Audience: **u,f.**

McCartney, Bruce L.   TC175.S56345 2005

Ship Channel Design and Operation: (ASCE Manuals and Reports on Engineering Practice No. 107 (revision of MOP 80)). Trade Paper. American Society of Civil Engineers. Reston, VA. 2005. 272p. ASCE Manuals and Reports on Engineering Practice, No. 107 ISBN:0-7844-0770-3, ISBN13: 978-0-7844-0770-7. Dewey:627/.23. LCCN:2005-012333.

Audience: **u,f.**

MONTANES   TC745.L573 2005

Hydraulic Canals Design, Construction, Regulation And Maintenance. Trade Cloth. Taylor & Francis Group. Philadelphia, PA. 2005. 416p. ISBN:0-415-36211-3, ISBN13: 978-0-415-36211-5. Dewey:627/.13. LCCN:2005-013676.

Audience: **u,f.**

National Research Council Staff   TC423.N356 1999

New Directions in Water Resources Planning for the U. S. Army Corps of Engineers. Paper Text. National Academies Press. Washington, DC. 1999. 120p. ISBN:0-309-06097-4, ISBN13: 978-0-309-06097-4. Dewey:333.91/00973. LCCN:99-060701.

Audience: **u,f.**

Novak, Paul   TC163

Hydraulic Modelling. Spon Press. 2006. ISBN:0-419-25020-4, ISBN13: 978-0-419-25020-3.

Audience: **u,f.**

Schwab, Glenn O., et al.   S591

Soil and Water Conservation Engineering. Ed. 4. Delmar D. Fangmeier, William J. Elliot & Richard K. Frevert (Authors).

Trade Cloth. John Wiley & Sons, Inc. Hoboken, NJ. 1992. 528p. ISBN:0-471-57490-2, ISBN13: 978-0-471-57490-3. Dewey:631.4. LCCN:92-010953.

Audience: **u,f.**

Seybert, Thomas A.   TD657.S49 2006

Stormwater Management for Land Development: Methods and Calculations for Quantity Control. Trade Cloth. John Wiley & Sons, Inc. Hoboken, NJ. 2006. 392p. ISBN:0-471-72177-8, ISBN13: 978-0-471-72177-2. Dewey:628.2. LCCN:2006-000885.

Audience: **u,f.**

Singh, Vijay P. (Editor)   GB652.I543 1993

Water Resources Planning and Management. Trade Cloth. Springer. New York, NY. 1995. 368p. Water Science and Technology Library ISBN:0-7923-3653-4, ISBN13: 978-0-7923-3653-2. Dewey:551.48. LCCN:97-117499.

Audience: **u,f.**

Tan & REN   TC540INT

Dam Engineering 2004. Paper over Boards. Taylor & Francis Group. Philadelphia, PA. 2004. 1240p. ISBN:0-415-36240-7, ISBN13: 978-0-415-36240-5. Dewey:627.8.

Audience: **u,f.**

Thompson, Stephen A.   TD223.T527 1999

Water Use, Management, and Planning in the United States. Cloth Text. Elsevier Science & Technology Books. Saint Louis, MO. 1998. 371p. ISBN:0-12-689340-3, ISBN13: 978-0-12-689340-3. Dewey:333.91/00973. LCCN:98-087241.

Audience: **u,f.** *Choice, 1999.*

Torre, Josbe de la, et al.   HD62.4.T67 2000

Environmental Biotechnology: Principles and Applications. Yves L. Doz, Timothy Michael Devinney, William Harley Davidson, Bruce E. Rittmann & Perry L. McCarty (Authors). Cloth Text. McGraw-Hill Higher Education. Burr Ridge, IL. 2000. 768p. McGraw-Hill Series in Water Resources and Environmental Engineering ISBN:0-07-234553-5, ISBN13: 978-0-07-234553-7. Dewey:628.5. LCCN:00-034882.

Audience: **u,f.**

Van der Tuin, J. D.   TC9 .T85 1987

Elsevier's Dictionary of Water and Hydraulic Engineering. Ed. 3. Trade Cloth. Elsevier. New York, NY. 1987. 466p. ISBN:0-444-42768-6, ISBN13: 978-0-444-42768-7. Dewey:627/.03. LCCN:87-005308.

Audience: **u,f.**

Wigmosta, Mark S., et al.   GB661.2.L35 2001

Land Use and Watersheds: Human Influence on Hydrology and Geomorphology in Urban and Forest Areas. Ronald M. Thom, Derek B. Booth, C. Rhett Jackson, David R. Montgomery, Thomas Dunne, Jack Lewis, Laura C. Bowling, Charles H. Luce, Roy C. Sidle & William E. Dietrich (Authors), Mark S. Wigmosta & Stephen J. Burges (Editors), Mark S. Wigmosta (Preface by), Stephen J. Burges (Preface by, Introduction by), Thomas Dunne (Introduction by). Trade Cloth. American Geophysical Union. Washington, DC. 2001. v, 227p. Water Science and Application Ser., Vol. 2 ISBN:0-87590-351-7, ISBN13: 978-0-87590-351-4. Dewey:551.48. LCCN:2001-022667.

Audience: **u,f.**

Environmental Engineering

Brookes, Andrew   TC529.B76 1988
Channelized Rivers: Perspectives for Environmental
Management. Ed. 1. Trade Cloth. John Wiley & Sons, Inc.
Hoboken, NJ. 1991. 342p. ISBN:0-471-91979-9, ISBN13:
978-0-471-91979-7. Dewey:627/.12. LCCN:85-005647.
                    Audience: **u,f.** *Choice, 1989.*

Chapra, Steven C.   TD365.C48 1997
Surface Water Quality Modeling. Cloth Text. McGraw-Hill
Higher Education. Burr Ridge, IL. 1996. 784p. Water Resources
and Environmental Engineering Ser. ISBN:0-07-011364-5,
ISBN13: 978-0-07-011364-0. Dewey:628.1/61/015118.
LCCN:96-015461.
                    Audience: **u,f.**

Cooper, C. David, et al.   TD146.C66 2000
Foundations of Environmental Engineering. John D. Dietz &
Debra R. Reinhart (Authors). Trade Cloth. Waveland Press, Inc.
Prospect Heights, IL. 1999. 369p. ISBN:1-57766-048-X,
ISBN13: 978-1-57766-048-4. Dewey:628. LCCN:00-699769.
                    Audience: **u,f.**

Gupta, Ram S.   GE105.G86 1997
Environmental Engineering and Science: An Introduction. Cloth
Text. Government Institutes. Blue Ridge Summit, PA. 1997.
498p. ISBN:0-86587-548-0, ISBN13: 978-0-86587-548-7.
Dewey:628. LCCN:96-027082.
                    Audience: **l,u,f.** *Choice, 1998.*

Hansen, P. E. & Jorgensen,   TD170.I584 1990
Sven E. (Editors)
Introduction to Environmental Management. Trade Cloth.
Elsevier Science & Technology Books. Saint Louis, MO. 1991.
404p. Developments in Environmental Modelling Ser., Vol. 8
ISBN:0-444-88469-6, ISBN13: 978-0-444-88469-5.
Dewey:363.7. LCCN:91-014791.
                    Audience: **l,u,f.** *Choice, 1992.*

Henry, J. Glynn & Heinke,   GE105.H46 1996
Gary W.
Environmental Science and Engineering. Ed. 2. Ian Burton
(Contribution by). Trade Cloth. Prentice Hall PTR. Upper
Saddle River, NJ. 1996. 778p. ISBN:0-13-120650-8, ISBN13:
978-0-13-120650-2. Dewey:628. LCCN:95-033505.
                    Audience: **l,u.**

Jördening, Hans-Joachim &   TD192.5
Winter, Josef (Editors)
Environmental Biotechnology: Concepts and Applications. Trade
Cloth. John Wiley & Sons, Inc. Hoboken, NJ. 2005. 488p.
ISBN:3-527-30585-8, ISBN13: 978-3-527-30585-8.
Dewey:628.5. LCCN:2005-272400.
                    Audience: **u,f.** *Choice, 2005.*

Landis, Wayne G. & Yu,   QH545.A1L35 1999
Ming-Ho
Introduction to Environmental Toxicology. Ed. 2. Box or
Slipcased. Lewis Publishers. Boca Raton, FL. 1998. 416p.
ISBN:1-56670-265-8, ISBN13: 978-1-56670-265-2.
Dewey:571.9/5. LCCN:97-050324.
                    Audience: **u,f.**

Logan, Bruce E.   TD193.L64 1999
Environmental Transport Processes. Ed. 1. Trade Cloth. John
Wiley & Sons, Inc. Hoboken, NJ. 1998. 672p.
ISBN:0-471-18871-9, ISBN13: 978-0-471-18871-1. Dewey:628.
LCCN:98-008018.
                    Audience: **u,f.**

Manahan, Stanley E.   TD193.M36 1999
Environmental Chemistry. Ed. 7. Paper over Boards. Lewis
Publishers. Boca Raton, FL. 1999. 912p. ISBN:1-56670-492-8,
ISBN13: 978-1-56670-492-2. Dewey:628.5/01/54.
LCCN:99-047521.
                    Audience: **u,f.**

MWH, Inc. Staff   TD430.W375 2004
Water Treatment: Principles and Design. Ed. 2. John Crittenden
(Revised by). Trade Cloth. John Wiley & Sons, Inc. Hoboken,
NJ. 2005. 1968p. ISBN:0-471-11018-3, ISBN13:
978-0-471-11018-7. Dewey:628.1/62. LCCN:2003-024156.
                    Audience: **u,f.**

Newman, Michael C. &   QH545.A1N49 2002
Unger, Michael A.
Fundamentals of Ecotoxicology. Ed. 2. Paper over Boards.
Lewis Publishers. Boca Raton, FL. 2002. 480p.
ISBN:1-56670-598-3, ISBN13: 978-1-56670-598-1.
Dewey:571.9/5. LCCN:2002-034105.
                    Audience: **u,f.**

Powelson, David R. &   TD794.5.P68 1992
Powelson, Melinda A.
The Recycler's Manual for Business, Government, and
Environmentalists. Cloth Text. John Wiley & Sons, Inc.
Hoboken, NJ. 1992. xxxii, 512p. ISBN:0-442-01190-3, ISBN13:
978-0-442-01190-1. Dewey:363.7282. LCCN:92-010099.
                    Audience: **g,l,u,f.** *Choice, 1993.*

Rand, Gary M. & Petrocelli,   QH541.5.W3
Sam R. (Editors)
Fundamentals of Aquatic Toxicology: Methods and Applications.
Trade Paper. Hemisphere Publishing Corporation. Philadelphia,
PA. 1985. 666p. ISBN:0-89116-382-4, ISBN13:
978-0-89116-382-4. Dewey:574.5/263. LCCN:84-004529.
                    Audience: **u,f.**

Raven, Peter H. & Berg,   HD75.6
Linda R.
Environment. Ed. 5. Trade Paper, Mixed Media, Stapled. John
Wiley & Sons, Inc. Hoboken, NJ. 2005. 672p.
ISBN:0-471-70438-5, ISBN13: 978-0-471-70438-6.
Dewey:363.7. LCCN:2006-272535.
                    Audience: **u,f.**

Roberts, L. E., et al.   TD195.E4R64 1990
Power Generation and the Environment. Peter S. Liss & P. A.
Saunders (Authors). Cloth Text. Oxford University Press, Inc.
New York, NY. 1990. 224p. Science, Technology, and Society
Ser., No. 6 ISBN:0-19-858338-9, ISBN13: 978-0-19-858338-7.
Dewey:333.79/3214. LCCN:90-006859.
                    Audience: **l,u,f.** *Choice, 1991.*

Salvato, Joseph A.   TD145
Environmental Engineering and Sanitation, Vol. 1121. Ed. 4.
Trade Cloth. John Wiley & Sons, Inc. Hoboken, NJ. 1992.
1456p. Environmental Science and Technology Ser., Vol. 99:A

Wiley-Interscience Series of Texts and Monographs
ISBN:0-471-52377-1, ISBN13: 978-0-471-52377-2. Dewey:628.
LCCN:91-035168.

Audience: **u,f.**

Seinfeld, John H. & Pandis,   QC879.6.S45 1998
  Spyros N.
Atmospheric Chemistry and Physics: From Air Pollution to
Climate Change. Ed. 1. Trade Paper. John Wiley & Sons, Inc.
Hoboken, NJ. 1997. 1360p. ISBN:0-471-17816-0, ISBN13:
978-0-471-17816-3. Dewey:551.5/11. LCCN:97-007638.

Audience: **u,f.**   *Choice, 1998.*

Snoeyink, Vernon L. &   QD169.W3
  Jenkins, David
Water Chemistry. Trade Cloth. John Wiley & Sons, Inc.
Hoboken, NJ. 1980. 480p. SPE Monographs
ISBN:0-471-05196-9, ISBN13: 978-0-471-05196-1.
Dewey:546/.22. LCCN:79-021331.

Audience: **u,f.**

Sterrett, Frances (Editor)   TD195.E49A44 1995
Alternative Fuels and the Environment. Paper over Boards.
Lewis Publishers. Boca Raton, FL. 1994. 288p.
ISBN:0-87371-978-6, ISBN13: 978-0-87371-978-0.
Dewey:621.042. LCCN:94-025419.

Audience: **l,u,f.**   *Choice, 1995.*

Theodore, Louis & Kunz,   T174.7.T48 2005
  Robert G.
Nanotechnology: Environmental Implications and Solutions.
Trade Cloth. John Wiley & Sons, Inc. Hoboken, NJ. 2005. 400p.
ISBN:0-471-69976-4, ISBN13: 978-0-471-69976-7.
Dewey:620/.5. LCCN:2004-053459.

Audience: **u,f.**   *Choice, 2005.*

Thomas, Randall (Editor)   NA2542.35.E575 1996
Environmental Design: An Introduction for Architects and
Engineers. Trade Paper. Routledge. New York, NY. 1995. 240p.
ISBN:0-419-19930-6, ISBN13: 978-0-419-19930-4.
Dewey:720/.47. LCCN:95-071097.

Audience: **u,f.**   *Choice, 1997.*

Vaccari, David A., et al.   QH308.2.V33 2005
Environmental Biology for Engineers and Scientists. Peter F.
Strom & James E. Alleman (Authors). Trade Cloth. John Wiley
& Sons, Inc. Hoboken, NJ. 2005. 960p. ISBN:0-471-72239-1,
ISBN13: 978-0-471-72239-7. Dewey:570. LCCN:2005-008313.

Audience: **u,f.**   *Choice, 2006.*

Valsaraj, Kalliat T.   TD153.V35 2000
Elements of Environmental Engineering: Thermodynamics and
Kinetics. Ed. 2. Paper over Boards. Lewis Publishers. Boca
Raton, FL. 2000. 712p. ISBN:1-56670-397-2, ISBN13:
978-1-56670-397-0. Dewey:628. LCCN:99-053965.

Audience: **u,f.**   *Choice, 2000.*

Vesilind, P. Aarne & Gunn,   TA157 .V42 1998
  Alastair S.
Engineering, Ethics, and the Environment. Trade Paper.
Cambridge University Press. New York, NY. 1998. 332p.
ISBN:0-521-58918-5, ISBN13: 978-0-521-58918-5.
Dewey:179.1/02462. LCCN:97-000083.

Audience: **u,f.**   *Choice, 1998.*

Weber, Walter J. Jr. &   TD177.W43 1996
  DiGiano, Francis A.
Process Dynamics in Environmental Systems. Ed. 1. Trade

Cloth. John Wiley & Sons, Inc. Hoboken, NJ. 1996. 968p.
Environmental Science and Technology Ser., Vol. 111:A
Wiley-Interscience Series of Texts and Monographs
ISBN:0-471-01711-6, ISBN13: 978-0-471-01711-0. Dewey:628.
LCCN:94-049669.

Audience: **u,f.**   *Choice, 1996.*

Environmental Engineering > Pollution

Carter, F. W. & Turnock,   TD186.E58 1993
  David (Editors)
Environmental Problems in Eastern Europe. Cloth Text.
Routledge. New York, NY. 1993. 312p. The Natural
Environment: Problems and Management Ser.
ISBN:0-415-06229-2, ISBN13: 978-0-415-06229-9.
Dewey:363.730947. LCCN:92-035163.

Audience: **u,f.**   *Choice, 1994.*

Cheremisinoff, Paul N.,   TA9
  Nicholas P. Cheremisinoff, and Su Ling Cheng (Editors)
Civil Engineering Practice: vol. 5: Water
Resources/Environmental. Technomic. 1988.
ISBN:0-87762-540-9, ISBN13: 978-0-87762-540-7.

Audience: **u,f.**

Connell, Des W. & Miller,   QH545.A1
  Gregory J.
Chemistry and Ecotoxicology of Pollution: Environmental
Science and Technology. Trade Cloth. John Wiley & Sons, Inc.
Hoboken, NJ. 1984. 464p. Environmental Science and
Technology Ser., Vol. 65:A Wiley-Interscience Series of Texts
and Monographs ISBN:0-471-86249-5, ISBN13:
978-0-471-86249-9. Dewey:574.5/222. LCCN:83-016794.

Audience: **u,f.**   *Choice, 1985.*

Cooper, C. David & Alley,   TD883.C585 2002
  F. C.
Air Pollution Control: A Design Approach. Ed. 3. Cloth Text.
Waveland Press, Inc. Prospect Heights, IL. 2002. 739p.
ISBN:1-57766-218-0, ISBN13: 978-1-57766-218-1.
Dewey:628.5/3. LCCN:2002-284922.

Audience: **u,f.**

Dorfman, Mark, et al.   TD899.C5.D66 1992
Environmental Dividends: Cutting More Chemical Wastes.
Catherine Miller & Warren Muir (Authors). Trade Paper.
INFORM, Inc. New York, NY. 1992. 288p.
ISBN:0-918780-50-0, ISBN13: 978-0-918780-50-8. Dewey:660.
LCCN:92-012251.

Audience: **g,l,u.**   *Choice, 1993.*

Godish, Thad   TD883.17.G64 2001
Indoor Environment Quality. Paper over Boards. Lewis
Publishers. Boca Raton, FL. 2000. 480p. ISBN:1-56670-402-2,
ISBN13: 978-1-56670-402-1. Dewey:628.5/3. LCCN:00-057400.

Audience: **g,l,u,f.**   *Choice, 2001.*

Hill, Marquita K.   TD174 .H55 1997
Understanding Environmental Pollution: A Primer. Cloth Text.
Cambridge University Press. New York, NY. 1997. 334p.
ISBN:0-521-56210-4, ISBN13: 978-0-521-56210-2.
Dewey:363.73. LCCN:96-052929.

Audience: **g,l.**   *Choice, 1998.*

LaGrega, Michael D., et al.   TD1030.L34 2001
Hazardous Waste Management. Ed. 2. Phillip L. Buckingham,
Jeffrey C. Evans & Environmental Resources Management Staff

(Authors). Cloth Text. McGraw-Hill Higher Education. Burr Ridge, IL. 2000. 1228p. Environmental Engineering and Water Resources ISBN:0-07-039365-6, ISBN13: 978-0-07-039365-3. Dewey:363.72876. LCCN:00-059453.

Audience: **u,f.**

Manahan, Stanley E.   **TS161.M353 1999**
Industrial Ecology. Saddle Stitched. Lewis Publishers. Boca Raton, FL. 1999. 336p. ISBN:1-56670-381-6, ISBN13: 978-1-56670-381-9. Dewey:628.4/2. LCCN:98-049415.

Audience: **l,f.** *Choice, 1999.*

Melosi, Martin V.   **TD788.M45 2004**
Garbage in the Cities: Refuse, Reform, and the Environment. Trade Paper. University of Pittsburgh Press. Pittsburgh, PA. 2004. 320p. History of the Urban Environment Ser. ISBN:0-8229-5857-0, ISBN13: 978-0-8229-5857-4. Dewey:363.72/85/0917320973. LCCN:2004-015714.

Audience: **l,u,f.** *Choice, 2005.*

Mulligan, Catherine N.   **TD192.5.M85 2001**
Environmental Biotreatment: Technologies for Air, Water, Soil, and Waste. Trade Cloth. Government Institutes. Blue Ridge Summit, PA. 2002. 395p. ISBN:0-86587-890-0, ISBN13: 978-0-86587-890-7. Dewey:628.5. LCCN:2001-040712.

Audience: **l,u,f.** *Choice, 2002.*

Nalven, Gail (Editor)   **TD899.C5E545 1996**
Environmental Management and Pollution Prevention. Trade Cloth. American Institute of Chemical Engineers. New York, NY. 1997. 148p. Practical Engineering Perspectives Ser. ISBN:0-8169-0711-0, ISBN13: 978-0-8169-0711-3. Dewey:660. LCCN:96-041208.

Audience: **l,u,f.** *Choice, 1998.*

Page, G. William   **TD1030.P34 1997**
Contaminated Sites and Environmental Cleanup: International Approaches to Prevention, Remediation, and Reuse. Trade Cloth. Elsevier Science & Technology Books. Saint Louis, MO. 1997. 212p. ISBN:0-12-543580-0, ISBN13: 978-0-12-543580-2. Dewey:363.73/84. LCCN:96-029220.

Audience: **u,f.** *Choice, 1997.*

Ripley, Earle A., et al.   **TD195.M5R559 1996**
Environmental Effects of Mining. Ed. 2. Robert E. Redman & A. A. Crowder (Authors). Paper over Boards. Saint Lucie Press. Boca Raton, FL. 1995. 36p. ISBN:1-884015-76-X, ISBN13: 978-1-884015-76-2. Dewey:333.8/54. LCCN:95-210701.

Audience: **g,u,f.** *Choice, 1996.*

Spellman, Frank R.   **TD174.S675 1999**
The Science of Environmental Pollution. Technomic. 1999. ISBN:1-56676-765-2, ISBN13: 978-1-56676-765-1.

Audience: **u,f.**

Stiller, David M.   **TD195.M5S75 2000**
Wounding the West: Montana, Mining and the Environment. Trade Cloth. University of Nebraska Press. Lincoln, NE. 2000. 212p. ISBN:0-8032-4281-6, ISBN13: 978-0-8032-4281-4. Dewey:363.739/42/09786. LCCN:99-048939.

Audience: **g,l,u.** *Choice, 2000.*

Tchobanoglous, George, et al.   **TD645.W295 2002**
Wastewater Engineering: Treatment and Reuse. Ed. 4. Franklin L. Burton, H. David Stensel & Metcalf and Eddy, Inc. Staff

(Authors). Cloth Text. McGraw-Hill Higher Education. Burr Ridge, IL. 2002. 1848p. McGraw-Hill Series in Civil and Environmental Engineering ISBN:0-07-041878-0, ISBN13: 978-0-07-041878-3. Dewey:628.3. LCCN:2001-053724.

Audience: **u,f.**

Environmental Engineering > Radioactive Waste

Eisenbud, Merrill & Gesell, Thomas F.   **TD196.R3E597 1997**
Environmental Radioactivity from Natural, Industrial and Military Sources: From Natural, Industrial and Military Sources. Ed. 4. Trade Cloth. Elsevier Science & Technology Books. Saint Louis, MO. 1997. 656p. ISBN:0-12-235154-1, ISBN13: 978-0-12-235154-9. Dewey:363.1/79. LCCN:96-041834.

Audience: **l,u,f.** *Choice, 1997.*

Ringius, Lasse   **TD898.4.R56 2001**
Radioactive Waste Disposal at Sea: Public Ideas, Transnational Policy Entrepreneurs, and Environmental Regimes. Trade Paper. MIT Press. Cambridge, MA. 2000. 337p. Global Environmental Accord Ser. ISBN:0-262-68118-8, ISBN13: 978-0-262-68118-6. Dewey:363.7289. LCCN:00-031879.

Audience: **u,f.** *Choice, 2001.*

Environmental Engineering > Reference Works

☐ How to Find Out in Environmental Engineering. http://www.hw.ac.uk/libWWW/howto/environ.html

Audience: **u,f.**

Ayres, David C. & Hellier, Desmond (Editors)   **QD5**
Dictionary of Environmentally Important Chemicals. Trade Cloth. Fitzroy Dearborn Publishers, Inc. Chicago, IL. 1999. 600p. ISBN:1-57958-206-0, ISBN13: 978-1-57958-206-7. Dewey:540.3.

Audience: **l,u,f.** *Choice, 2000.*

Burke, Gwendolyn, et al.   **TD145**
Handbook of Environmental Management and Technology. Ed. 2. Ben Ramnarine Singh & Louis Theodore (Authors). Trade Paper. John Wiley & Sons, Inc. Hoboken, NJ. 2004. 824p. ISBN:0-471-72237-5, ISBN13: 978-0-471-72237-3. Dewey:628.

Audience: **g,u,f.**

Corbitt, Robert A.   **TD145.S72 1990**
Standard Handbook of Environmental Engineering. Trade Cloth. McGraw-Hill Professional Publishing. New York, NY. 1989. 1152p. ISBN:0-07-013158-9, ISBN13: 978-0-07-013158-3. Dewey:628. LCCN:89-012400.

Audience: **u,f.** *Choice, 1990.*

Gottlieb, Daniel W.   **TD169.5.G68 2002**
Environmental Technology Resources Handbook. Paper over Boards. Lewis Publishers. Boca Raton, FL. 2002. 240p. ISBN:1-56670-566-5, ISBN13: 978-1-56670-566-0. Dewey:363.7/0025. LCCN:2002-072485.

Audience: **u,f.** *Choice, 2003.*

Greene, Stanley A.   T55.3.H3G743 2002
International Resources Guide to Hazardous Chemicals: Manufacturers, Agencies. Organizations, and Useful Sources of Information. Trade Cloth. William Andrew Publishing. Bighamton, NY. 2002. 950p. ISBN:0-8155-1475-1, ISBN13: 978-0-8155-1475-6. Dewey:363.17. LCCN:2002-016531.
Audience: **u,f.** *Choice, 2003.*

Katz, Michael & Thornton,   GE20
Dorothy
Environmental Management Tools on the Internet: Accessing the World of Environmental Information. UK-B Format Paperback. Saint Lucie Press. Boca Raton, FL. 1996. 184p. ISBN:1-57444-059-4, ISBN13: 978-1-57444-059-1. Dewey:025/.06/3337.
Audience: **u,f.** *Choice, 1997.*

Lee, C. C.   TD145
Environmental Engineering Dictionary. Ed. 3. Cloth Text. Government Institutes. Blue Ridge Summit, PA. 1998. 682p. ISBN:0-86587-620-7, ISBN13: 978-0-86587-620-0. Dewey:628.
Audience: **l,u,f.** *Choice, 1999, 1993.*

Little, Charles E. &   TD9.A84 2001
Ashworth, William
Encyclopedia of Environmental Studies. Ed. 2. Trade Cloth. Facts On File, Inc.. New York, NY. 2001. 608p. The Facts on File Science Library ISBN:0-8160-4255-1, ISBN13: 978-0-8160-4255-5. Dewey:333.7/03. LCCN:00-051379.
Audience: **l,u,f.** *Choice, 2002.*

Liu, David H. and Bela G.   TD145.E574
Liptak, eds.
Environmental Engineers' Handbook. Chapman & Hall/CRCnetBASE. 1999. ISBN:0-8493-2157-3, ISBN13: 978-0-8493-2157-3.
Audience: **u,f.**

Liu, David H.F., ed.   TD145
Environmental Engineers' Handbook. Ed. 2. Lewis Publishers. 1997. ISBN:0-8493-9971-8, ISBN13: 978-0-8493-9971-8.
Audience: **l,u,f.**

Miller, E. Willard & Miller,   TD883.M52 1998
Ruby M.
Indoor Pollution: A Reference Handbook. Library Binding. ABC-CLIO, Inc. Santa Barbara, CA. 1998. 330p. Contemporary World Issues Ser. ISBN:0-87436-895-2, ISBN13: 978-0-87436-895-6. Dewey:363.739/2. LCCN:98-025606.
Audience: **l,u,f.** *Choice, 1999.*

Ryding, Sven-Olof   TD170 .R83 1992
Environmental Management Handbook. Trade Cloth. Lewis Publishers. Boca Raton, FL. 1992. 777p. ISBN:0-87371-753-8, ISBN13: 978-0-87371-753-3. Dewey:363.7.
Audience: **u,f.** *Choice, 1993.*

Smith, P. G. & Scott, J. S.   TD9.S37 2002
Dictionary of Water and Waste Management. Trade Cloth. IWA Publishing. London, 2002. 448p. ISBN:1-84339-015-9, ISBN13: 978-1-84339-015-2. Dewey:628.03.
Audience: **l,u,f.** *Choice, 2003.*

Spellman, Frank R. and   TD145
Nancy E. Whiting
Environmental engineer's mathematics handbook. CRC Press. 2005. ISBN:1-56670-681-5, ISBN13: 978-1-56670-681-0.
Audience: **u,f.**

Staudinger, Jeff   TD171.S734 2002
The Environmental Guidebook: A Selective Reference Guide to Environmental Organizations and Related Entities. Perfect. Environmental Frontlines. Menlo Pk., CA. 2002. 312p. ISBN:0-9720685-0-3, ISBN13: 978-0-9720685-0-5. Dewey:363.7. LCCN:2002-106011.
Audience: **l,u,f.** *Choice, 2003.*

Stevenson, L. Harold &   TD9.W95 2001
Wyman, Bruce
The Facts on File Dictionary of Environmental Science. Ed. 2. Trade Cloth. Facts On File, Inc.. New York, NY. 2001. 464p. The Facts on File Science Library ISBN:0-8160-4233-0, ISBN13: 978-0-8160-4233-3. Dewey:363.7/003. LCCN:00-055554.
Audience: **g,l,u,f.** *Choice, 2001, 1992.*

Wang, Lawrence K.   TD897.5
Handbook of Industrial and Hazardous Waste Treatment: Second Edition, Revised and Expanded. Ed. 2. Paper over Boards. Marcel Dekker Inc. New York, NY. 2004. 1368p. ISBN:0-8247-4114-5, ISBN13: 978-0-8247-4114-3. Dewey:628.4. LCCN:2004-056844.
Audience: **u,f.** *Choice, 2005.*

Webster, L. F. (Editor)   TD9.W43 2000
Dictionary of Environmental & Civil Engineering. Parthenon. 2000. ISBN:1-85070-075-3, ISBN13: 978-1-85070-075-3.
Audience: **l,u,f.**

Mechanical Engineering

Alciatore, David G. &   TJ163.12.H57 2005
Histand, Michael B.
Introduction to Mechatronics and Measurement Systems. Ed. 3. Cloth Text. McGraw-Hill Higher Education. Burr Ridge, IL. 2005. 544p. ISBN:0-07-296305-0, ISBN13: 978-0-07-296305-2. Dewey:621. LCCN:2005-023850.
Audience: **l,u.**

Bhushan, Bharat (Editor)   TJ1075.H245 1995
Handbook of Micro/Nanotribology, Vol. 1. Paper over Boards. C R C Press LLC. Boca Raton, FL. 1995. 640p. Mechanics and Materials Science, Vol. 1 ISBN:0-8493-8401-X, ISBN13: 978-0-8493-8401-1. Dewey:621.8/9. LCCN:94-038829.
Audience: **u,f.**

Bhushan, Bharat & Gupta,   TJ1075.B47 1997
B. K.
Handbook of Tribology: Materials, Coatings, and Surface Treatments. Trade Cloth. Krieger Publishing Company. Melbourne, FL. 1997. 1168p. ISBN:1-57524-050-5, ISBN13: 978-1-57524-050-3. Dewey:621.8/9. LCCN:97-008067.
Audience: **u,f.**

Blau, Peter J.   TJ1075
Friction, Lubrication, and Wear Technology. ASM International, Handbook Committee (Contribution by). Trade Cloth. A S M International. Materials Park, OH. 1992. 942p. ASM Handbook Ser., Vol. 18 ISBN:0-87170-380-7, ISBN13: 978-0-87170-380-4. Dewey:621.8/9.
Audience: **u,f.**

Cameron, A. & Ettles, C. M.   **TJ1075**
Basic Lubrication Theory. Ed. 3. Trade Paper. John Wiley &
Sons, Inc. Hoboken, NJ. 1982. 256p. Ellis Horwood Series in
Engineering Science ISBN:0-470-27554-5, ISBN13:
978-0-470-27554-2. Dewey:621.8/9.

                Audience: **u,f.**

Durst, F.   **TJ935 .D83 1981**
Principles and Practice of Laser-Doppler Anemometry. Ed. 2.
Trade Cloth. Elsevier Science & Technology Books. Saint
Louis, MO. 1981. 437p. ISBN:0-12-225260-8, ISBN13:
978-0-12-225260-0. Dewey:681/.2. LCCN:81-201710.

                Audience: **u,f.**

Fuller, Dudley D.   **TJ1075**
Theory and Practice of Lubrication for Engineers. Ed. 2. Trade
Cloth. John Wiley & Sons, Inc. Hoboken, NJ. 1984. 682p.
ISBN:0-471-04703-1, ISBN13: 978-0-471-04703-2.
Dewey:621.8/9. LCCN:83-027394.

                Audience: **u,f.**

Hamrock, Bernard J.   **TJ1075**
Fundamentals of Fluid Film Lubrication, Vol. 169. Ed. 2. Paper
over Boards. Marcel Dekker Inc. New York, NY. 2004. 728p.
Mechanical Engineering Ser., Vol. 169 ISBN:0-8247-5371-2,
ISBN13: 978-0-8247-5371-9. Dewey:621.8/9.
LCCN:2004-555403.

                Audience: **u,f.**

Hamrock, Bernard J., et al.   **TJ1063.H35 2004**
🄴 Fundamentals of Fluid Film Lubrication. Ed. 2. Steven
Schmid & Bo Jacobson (Authors). E-Book. Marcel Dekker Inc.
New York, NY. 2004. 750p. Mechanical Engineering Ser., Vol.
171 ISBN:0-8247-5120-5, ISBN13: 978-0-8247-5120-3.
Dewey:621.8/9.

                Audience: **u,f.**

Neale, M. J.   **TJ1075.L812 2001**
Lubrication and Reliability Handbook. Trade Cloth. Elsevier
Science & Technology Books. Saint Louis, MO. 2000. 256p.
ISBN:0-7506-5154-7, ISBN13: 978-0-7506-5154-7.
Dewey:621.8/9. LCCN:00-049378.

                Audience: **l,u,f.**

Neale, Michael J.   **TJ1075**
Lubrication: A Tribology Handbook. Trade Cloth. Society of
Automotive Engineers, Inc. Warrendale, PA. 1993. 148p.
ISBN:1-56091-392-4, ISBN13: 978-1-56091-392-4.
Dewey:621.8/9.

                Audience: **l,u,f.**

Pirro, D. M., et al.   **TJ1075.W57 2001**
Lubrication Fundamentals, Vol. 137. Ed. 2. A. A. Wessol & J.
George Wills (Authors). Paper over Boards. Marcel Dekker Inc.
New York, NY. 2001. 544p. Dekker Mechanical Engineering
Ser. ISBN:0-8247-0574-2, ISBN13: 978-0-8247-0574-9.
Dewey:621.8/9. LCCN:2001-042179.

                Audience: **l,u.**

Shigley, Joseph, et al.   **621.815**
Mechanical Engineering Design. Ed. 7. Charles Mischke &
Richard Budynas (Authors). Trade Cloth. McGraw-Hill Higher
Education. Burr Ridge, IL. 2003. 1088p. ISBN:0-07-292193-5,
ISBN13: 978-0-07-292193-9. Dewey:621.8/15.

                Audience: **l,u.**

Mechanical Engineering > Power. Energy

Boyle, Godfrey (Editor)   **TJ808.R46 2003**
Renewable Energy. Ed. 2. Paper Text. Oxford University Press,
Inc. New York, NY. 2004. 464p. ISBN:0-19-926178-4, ISBN13:
978-0-19-926178-9. Dewey:333.79. LCCN:2004-271593.

                Audience: **g,l,u,f.**

C.-J. Winter, R.L. Sizmann,   **TK1056.S627 1990**
  and L.L. Vant-Hull (Editors)
Solar Power Plants: Fundamentals, Technology, Systems,
Economics. Springer-Verlag. 1991. ISBN:0-387-18897-5,
ISBN13: 978-0-387-18897-3.

                Audience: **u,f.**

Chambers, Ann   **TK1061.C49 1999**
Natural Gas and Electric Power in Nontechnical Language.
Trade Cloth. PennWell Corporation. Tulsa, OK. 1999. 258p.
ISBN:0-87814-761-6, ISBN13: 978-0-87814-761-8.
Dewey:621.31. LCCN:99-013897.

         Audience: **g,l,u,f.** *Choice, 2000.*

Cleveland, Cutler J.   **TJ163.28.E53 2004**
  (Editor-In-Chief)
Encyclopedia of Energy, Set. Robert Ayres, Robert Costanza,
Jose Goldemberg, Marija D. Ilic, Eberhard Jochem, Robert
Kaufmann, Amory Lovins, Mohan Munasinghe, Claudia
Sheinbaum Pardo, Per Peterson, Lee Schipper, Margaret Slade,
Vaclav Smil, Ernst Worrell & R. K. Pachauri (Contribution by).
Trade Cloth. Elsevier Science & Technology Books. Saint
Louis, MO. 2004. 5376p. ISBN:0-12-176480-X, ISBN13:
978-0-12-176480-7. Dewey:333.79/03. LCCN:2003-116610.

         Audience: **g,l,u,f.** *Choice, 2004.*

Cleveland, Cutler J. &   **TJ163.28**
  Morris, Christopher (Editors)
Dictionary of Energy. Trade Cloth. Elsevier Science &
Technology Books. Saint Louis, MO. 2005. 512p.
ISBN:0-08-044578-0, ISBN13: 978-0-08-044578-6.
Dewey:333.7903.

         Audience: **u,f.** *Choice, 2006.*

Fairmont Press Staff &   **TK1051**
  Kehlhofer, Rolf H.
Combined-Cycle Gas and Steam Turbine Power Plants. Cloth
Text. Prentice Hall PTR. Upper Saddle River, NJ. 1990. 446p.
ISBN:0-13-151481-4, ISBN13: 978-0-13-151481-2.
Dewey:621.312132.

         Audience: **u,f.** *Choice, 1991.*

Fujii, I.   **TJ810.F85 1990**
From Solar Energy to Mechanical Power. Cloth Text. Gordon &
Breach Publishing Group. New York, NY. 1990. viii, 246p.
ISBN:3-7186-5036-3, ISBN13: 978-3-7186-5036-1.
Dewey:621.47. LCCN:90-084220.

         Audience: **l,u.** *Choice, 1991.*

Gipe, Paul   **TJ820.G565 2003**
Wind Power: Renewable Energy for Home, Farm, and Business.
Ed. 2. Trade Paper. Chelsea Green Publishing. White River
Junction, VT. 2004. 512p. ISBN:1-931498-14-8, ISBN13:
978-1-931498-14-2. Dewey:621.4/5. LCCN:2003-019354.

         Audience: **g,l,u,f.** *Choice, 2004.*

Gipe, Paul   **TJ820.G57 1993**
Wind Power for Home and Business: Renewable Energy for the
1990's and Beyond. Trade Paper. Chelsea Green Publishing.

White River Junction, VT. 1993. 432p. Real Goods Independent Living Books ISBN:0-930031-64-4, ISBN13: 978-0-930031-64-0. Dewey:621.4/5. LCCN:93-009437.

Audience: **g,l,u,f.** *Choice, 1993.*

Heaberlin, S. W. TK9146.H43 2003
A Case for Nuclear-Generated Electricity, or, Why I Think Nuclear Power Is Cool and Why It Is Important That You Think So Too. Trade Cloth. Battelle Press. Columbus, OH. 2003. 326p. ISBN:1-57477-136-1, ISBN13: 978-1-57477-136-7. Dewey:333.792/4. LCCN:2003-052499.

Audience: **l,u,f.** *Choice, 2005.*

Hehn, Anton H. TJ840.H44 1993
Plant Engineering Magazine's Fluid Power Handbook, vol. 1: System Design, Maintenance, and Troubleshooting. Gulf Publishing. 1993. ISBN:0-88415-089-5, ISBN13: 978-0-88415-089-3.

Audience: **u,f.**

Hehn, Anton H. TJ840.H44 1993
Plant Engineering Magazine's Fluid Power Handbook, vol. 2: System Applications and Components. Gulf Publishing. 1993. ISBN:0-88415-072-0, ISBN13: 978-0-88415-072-5.

Audience: **u,f.**

Henderson, Harry TK9146.H45 2000
Nuclear Power: A Reference Handbook. Mildred Vasan (Editor). Library Binding. ABC-CLIO, Inc. Santa Barbara, CA. 2000. 0250p. Contemporary World Issues Ser. ISBN:1-57607-128-6, ISBN13: 978-1-57607-128-1. Dewey:333.792/4/09. LCCN:00-010255.

Audience: **u,f.** *Choice, 2001.*

Hills, Richard Leslie TJ823.H55 1994
Power from Wind: A History of Windmill Technology. Trade Paper. Cambridge University Press. New York, NY. 1996. 334p. ISBN:0-521-56686-X, ISBN13: 978-0-521-56686-5. Dewey:621.4/53/09. LCCN:93-008858.

Audience: **g,l,u,f.** *Choice, 1994.*

Lauber, Volkmar (Editor) TJ808.S89 2005
Switching to Renewable Power: A Framework for the 21st Century. Trade Cloth. Earthscan/James & James. London, 2005. 256p. ISBN:1-84407-241-X, ISBN13: 978-1-84407-241-5. Dewey:333.79/4. LCCN:2005-011832.

Audience: **g,l,u,f.** *Choice, 2006.*

Marston, R.M. TK7881
Power Control Circuits Manual. Ed. 2. Newnes. 1997. ISBN:0-7506-3005-1, ISBN13: 978-0-7506-3005-4.

Audience: **l,u,f.**

Nansen, Ralph TJ810.N33 1995
Sun Power: The Global Solution for the Coming Energy Crisis. Trade Paper. Ocean Press. Seattle, WA. 1996. 252p. ISBN:0-9647021-1-8, ISBN13: 978-0-9647021-1-0. Dewey:333.792/3. LCCN:96-113681.

Audience: **g,l,u,f.** *Choice, 1996.*

Pasqualetti, Martin, et al. TJ820.W5767 2002
Wind Power in View: Energy Landscapes in a Crowded World. Paul Gipe & Robert Righter (Authors). Trade Cloth. Elsevier Science & Technology Books. Saint Louis, MO. 2002. 248p. Sustainable World Series ISBN:0-12-546334-0, ISBN13: 978-0-12-546334-8. Dewey:621.4/5. LCCN:2001-096353.

Audience: **g,l,u,f.** *Choice, 2003.*

Patel, Mukund R. TK1541.P38 2005
Wind and Solar Power Systems: Design, Analysis, and Operation. Ed. 2. Taylor & Francis. 2006. ISBN:0-8493-1570-0, ISBN13: 978-0-8493-1570-1.

Audience: **l,u,f.**

Ramsey, Charles B. & TK9152
Modarres, Mohammad
Commercial Nuclear Power: Assuring Safety for the Future. Trade Cloth. John Wiley & Sons, Inc. Hoboken, NJ. 1998. 508p. ISBN:0-471-29186-2, ISBN13: 978-0-471-29186-2. Dewey:621.4/835. LCCN:97-038062.

Audience: **l,u.** *Choice, 1998.*

Rashid, Muhammad H. TK7881.15.P6733 2001
(Editor)
Power Electronics Handbook. Trade Cloth. Elsevier Science & Technology Books. Saint Louis, MO. 2001. 895p. Series in Engineering ISBN:0-12-581650-2, ISBN13: 978-0-12-581650-2. Dewey:621.31/7. LCCN:2001-088199.

Audience: **u,f.** *Choice, 2002.*

Rifkin, Jeremy TP359.H8R54 2002
The Hydrogen Economy: The Creation of the Worldwide Energy Web and the Redistribution of Power on Earth. Trade Cloth. Penguin Group (USA) Inc. New York, NY. 2002. 304p. ISBN:1-58542-193-6, ISBN13: 978-1-58542-193-0. Dewey:333.8. LCCN:2002-025370.

Audience: **g,l,u,f.** *Choice, 2003.*

Roberts, L. E., et al. TD195.E4R64 1990
Power Generation and the Environment. Peter S. Liss & P. A. Saunders (Authors). Cloth Text. Oxford University Press, Inc. New York, NY. 1990. 224p. Science, Technology, and Society Ser., No. 6 ISBN:0-19-858338-9, ISBN13: 978-0-19-858338-7. Dewey:333.79/3214. LCCN:90-006859.

Audience: **l,u,f.** *Choice, 1991.*

Skvarenina, Tim L. TK7881.15.P673 2001
The Power Electronics Handbook. CRC Press. 2002. ISBN:0-8493-7336-0, ISBN13: 978-0-8493-7336-7.

Audience: **u,f.**

Tarter, Ralph E. TK7881.15.T362 1993
Solid-State Power Conversion Handbook. Trade Cloth. John Wiley & Sons, Inc. Hoboken, NJ. 1993. 736p. ISBN:0-471-57243-8, ISBN13: 978-0-471-57243-5. Dewey:621.3815. LCCN:92-018179.

Audience: **l,u,f.** *Choice, 1993.*

Vaitheeswaran, Vijay V. TJ163.2.V335 2003
Power to the People: How the Coming Energy Revolution Will Transform an Industry, Change Our Lives, and Maybe Even Save the Planet. Cloth over Boards. Farrar, Straus & Giroux. New York, NY. 2003. 368p. ISBN:0-374-23675-5, ISBN13: 978-0-374-23675-5. Dewey:333.79. LCCN:2003-006985.

Audience: **g,l,u,f.** *Choice, 2004.*

Wizelius, Tore TJ825.W59 2006
Developing Wind Power Projects: Theory and Practice. Trade Paper. Earthscan/James & James. London, 2007. 296p. ISBN:1-84407-262-2, ISBN13: 978-1-84407-262-0. Dewey:333.9/2. LCCN:2006-013771.

Audience: **u,f.**

Yeaple, Franklin D. TJ843.Y43 1996
🄴 Fluid Power Design Handbook. Ed. 3. E-Book. NetLibrary,

Audience: g=general, l=lower division undergraduate, u=upper division undergraduate, f=faculty.

709

Inc. Boulder, CO. 1996. ISBN:0-585-24186-4, ISBN13: 978-0-585-24186-9. Dewey:621.2. LCCN:2002-284550.

Audience: **l,u,f.**

Yount, Lisa   **TJ163.2.Y68 2005**
Energy Supply. Trade Cloth. Facts On File, Inc.. New York, NY. 2005. 304p. Library in a Book ISBN:0-8160-5577-7, ISBN13: 978-0-8160-5577-7. Dewey:333.79. LCCN:2004-021607.

Audience: **l,u,f.** *Choice, 2006.*

Mechanical Engineering > Control Engineering

Arkin, Ronald C.   **TJ211.A75 1998**
Behavior-Based Robotics. Trade Cloth. MIT Press. Cambridge, MA. 1998. 491p. Complex Adaptive Systems Ser. ISBN:0-262-01165-4, ISBN13: 978-0-262-01165-5. Dewey:629.8/92. LCCN:97-018389.

Audience: **u,f.** *Choice, 1999.*

Astrom, Karl J. &   **TJ217.A67 1995**
  Wittenmark, Bjorn
Adaptive Control. Ed. 2. Trade Cloth. Prentice Hall PTR. Upper Saddle River, NJ. 1994. 580p. ISBN:0-201-55866-1, ISBN13: 978-0-201-55866-1. Dewey:629.8/36. LCCN:94-012682.

Audience: **u,f.**

Biernson, George A.   **TJ216.B45 1988**
Principles of Feedback Control: Feedback System Design, Vol. 1. Trade Cloth. John Wiley & Sons, Inc. Hoboken, NJ. 1988. 498p. ISBN:0-471-82167-5, ISBN13: 978-0-471-82167-0. Dewey:629.8/312. LCCN:87-030539.

Audience: **u,f.** *Choice, 1989.*

Bollinger, John G. & Duffie,   **TJ213.B5952 1988**
  Neil A.
Computer Control of Machines and Processes. Trade Cloth. Prentice Hall PTR. Upper Saddle River, NJ. 1988. 620p. Addison-Wesley Series in Mechanical Engineering ISBN:0-201-10645-0, ISBN13: 978-0-201-10645-9. Dewey:629.8/95. LCCN:87-014019.

Audience: **u,f.** *Choice, 1990.*

Chen, C. H   **TJ217.5.F9 1996**
Fuzzy Logic and Neural Network Handbook. Cloth Text. McGraw-Hill Companies, The. New York, NY. 1995. Computer Systems Ser. ISBN:0-07-011189-8, ISBN13: 978-0-07-011189-9. Dewey:006.3. LCCN:95-038128.

Audience: **u,f.**

Craig, John J.   **TJ211**
Introduction to Robotics: Mechanics and Control. Ed. 3. Trade Cloth. Prentice Hall PTR. Upper Saddle River, NJ. 2004. 408p. ISBN:0-201-54361-3, ISBN13: 978-0-201-54361-2. Dewey:629.8/92. LCCN:2004-275113.

Audience: **l,u.** *Choice, 1986.*

DiStefano, Joseph J., et al.   **TJ216.5.D57 1995**
Schaum's Outline of Feedback and Control Systems. Ed. 2. Allen J. Stubberud & Ivan J. Williams (Authors). Paper Text. McGraw-Hill Companies, The. New York, NY. 1994. 496p. Schaum's ISBN:0-07-017052-5, ISBN13: 978-0-07-017052-0. Dewey:629.8/3. LCCN:96-224787.

Audience: **u,f.**

Dorf, Richard C. & Bishop,   **TJ216.D67 2004**
  Robert H.
Modern Control Systems. Ed. 10. Cloth Text. Prentice Hall PTR. Upper Saddle River, NJ. 2004. 912p. ISBN:0-13-145733-0, ISBN13: 978-0-13-145733-1. Dewey:629.8/3. LCCN:2004-004466.

Audience: **u,f.**

Driankov, D., et al.   **TJ217.5.D75 1996**
An Introduction to Fuzzy Control. Ed. 2. H. Hellendoorn & M. Reinfrank (Authors). Trade Cloth. Springer. New York, NY. 1996. XV, 316p. ISBN:3-540-60691-2, ISBN13: 978-3-540-60691-8. Dewey:629.8. LCCN:96-001576.

Audience: **l,u.**

Duro, Richard J. (Editor),   **TJ211.B555 2002**
  et al.
Biologically Inspired Robot Behavior Engineering. Jose Santos & Manuel Grana (Editors). Trade Cloth. Physica-Verlag. Heidelberg, 2004. XX, 438p. Studies in Fuzziness and Soft Computing, Vol. 109 ISBN:3-7908-1513-6, ISBN13: 978-3-7908-1513-9. Dewey:629.8/92. LCCN:2002-034601.

Audience: **u,f.**

Ellis, George   **TJ216.E39 2000**
Control System Design Guide: Using Your Computer to Understand and Diagnose Feedback Controllers. Ed. 2. Trade Cloth. Elsevier Science & Technology Books. Saint Louis, MO. 2000. 456p. ISBN:0-12-237465-7, ISBN13: 978-0-12-237465-4. Dewey:629.8/3. LCCN:00-101600.

Audience: **l,u.**

Franklin, Gene F., et al.   **TJ223.M53F73 1998**
Digital Control of Dynamic Systems. Ed. 3. Michael L. Workman & J. David Powell (Authors). Trade Cloth. Prentice Hall PTR. Upper Saddle River, NJ. 1997. 850p. ISBN:0-201-82054-4, ISBN13: 978-0-201-82054-6. Dewey:003.8/5. LCCN:97-035994.

Audience: **u,f.**

Fuller, James L.   **TJ211.F85 1999**
Robotics: Introduction, Programming and Projects. Ed. 2. Cloth Text. Pearson Education. Boston, MA. 1998. 489p. ISBN:0-13-095543-4, ISBN13: 978-0-13-095543-2. Dewey:670.42/72. LCCN:98-004165.

Audience: **u,f.**

Gabasov, R. F., et al.   **TJ216.G33 1995**
Feedback Optimal Control. Faima Kirillova & Svetlana Prischepova (Authors). Paper Text. Springer. New York, NY. 1995. 210p. Lecture Notes in Control and Information Sciences, No. 207 ISBN:3-540-19991-8, ISBN13: 978-3-540-19991-5. Dewey:629.8/3. LCCN:95-038038.

Audience: **l,u.**

Ghosh, Bijoy K., et al.   **TJ211.35.C65 1999**
Control in Robotics and Automation: Sensor Based Integration. Ning Xi & T. J. Tarn (Authors). Trade Cloth. Elsevier Science & Technology Books. Saint Louis, MO. 1999. 428p. Academic Press Series in Engineering ISBN:0-12-281845-8, ISBN13: 978-0-12-281845-5. Dewey:629.8/92. LCCN:98-038975.

Audience: **u,f.**

Horn, Berthold K.   **TJ211.3.H67 1986**
Robot Vision. Trade Cloth. MIT Press. Cambridge, MA. 1986. 480p. MIT Electrical Engineering and Computer Science Ser.

ISBN:0-262-08159-8, ISBN13: 978-0-262-08159-7.
Dewey:629.8/92. LCCN:85-018137.
Audience: **u,f.** *Choice, 1986.*

Hutchinson, Seth, et al.   **TJ211.4.P75 2004**
Principles of Robot Motion: Theory, Algorithms, and
Implementations. George Kantor, Wolfram Burgard, Lydia E.
Kavraki, Sebastian Thrun, Howie Choset & Kevin Lynch
(Authors). Cloth Text. MIT Press. Cambridge, MA. 2005. 550p.
Intelligent Robotics and Autonomous Agents Ser.
ISBN:0-262-03327-5, ISBN13: 978-0-262-03327-5.
Dewey:629.8/92. LCCN:2004-044906.
Audience: **u,f.**

Jacquot, Raymond G.   **TJ223.M53J34 1995**
Modern Digital Control Systems, Vol. 89. Ed. 2. Paper over
Boards. Marcel Dekker Inc. New York, NY. 1994. 432p.
Electrical Engineering and Electronics Ser., Vol. 89
ISBN:0-8247-8914-8, ISBN13: 978-0-8247-8914-5.
Dewey:629.8. LCCN:94-029066.
Audience: **u,f.**

Koren, Yoram   **TJ211.K66 1985**
Robotics for Engineers. Cloth Text. McGraw-Hill Companies,
The. New York, NY. 1985. 352p. ISBN:0-07-035399-9, ISBN13:
978-0-07-035399-2. Dewey:629.8/92. LCCN:84-021316.
Audience: **l,u,f.**

Kuo, Benjamin C.   **TJ223.M53K86 1991**
Digital Control Systems. Ed. 2. Cloth Text. Oxford University
Press, Inc. New York, NY. 1992. 784p. The Oxford Series in
Electrical and Computer Engineering ISBN:0-03-012884-6,
ISBN13: 978-0-03-012884-4. Dewey:629.8/043.
LCCN:91-041422.
Audience: **l,u.**

Kuo, Benjamin C. &   **TJ213.K8354 2003**
  Golnaraghi, Farid
Automatic Control Systems. Ed. 8. Trade Cloth. John Wiley &
Sons, Inc. Hoboken, NJ. 2002. 624p. ISBN:0-471-13476-7,
ISBN13: 978-0-471-13476-3. Dewey:629.8.
LCCN:2002-513209.
Audience: **l,u,f.**

Latombe, Jean-Claude   **TJ211.4.L38 1991**
Robot Motion Planning. Trade Cloth. Springer. New York, NY.
1990. 672p. The International Series in Engineering and
Computer Science Ser. ISBN:0-7923-9129-2, ISBN13:
978-0-7923-9129-6. Dewey:629.8/92. LCCN:90-049962.
Audience: **l,u,f.**

Leigh, J. R.   **TJ223.M53L45 2006**
Applied Digital Control: Theory, Design and Implementation.
Ed. 2. Trade Paper. Dover Publications, Inc. Mineola, NY. 2006.
544p. ISBN:0-486-45051-1, ISBN13: 978-0-486-45051-3.
Dewey:629.8/95. LCCN:2006-041009.
Audience: **l,u,f.**

Lewis, H. W.   **TJ213.L433 1997**
The Foundations of Fuzzy Control. Trade Cloth. Basic Books.
New York, NY. 1997. 318p. IFSR International Series on
Systems Science, Vol. 10 ISBN:0-306-45452-1, ISBN13:
978-0-306-45452-3. Dewey:629.8/9. LCCN:97-014026.
Audience: **l,u,f.** *Choice, 1997.*

Lindsay, James F. & Katz,   **TJ173.L56**
  Silas
Dynamics of Physical Circuits and Systems. Trade Cloth. Weber

Systems, Inc. Beachwood, OH. 1978. 480p.
ISBN:0-916460-21-5, ISBN13: 978-0-916460-21-1.
Dewey:620.1/04. LCCN:78-053838.
Audience: **l,u.**

Lyshevski, Sergey Edward   **TJ213.L94 2000**
Control Systems Theory with Engineering Applications. Mixed
Media. Birkhauser Boston. Cambridge, MA. 2001. XII, 416p.
Control Engineering Ser. ISBN:0-8176-4203-X, ISBN13:
978-0-8176-4203-7. Dewey:629.8. LCCN:00-060868.
Audience: **l,u,f.**

McNeill, F. Martin & Thro,   **TJ213.M355 1994**
  Ellen
Fuzzy Logic: A Practical Approach. Trade Paper. Elsevier
Science & Technology Books. Saint Louis, MO. 1994. 292p.
ISBN:0-12-485965-8, ISBN13: 978-0-12-485965-4.
Dewey:006.3/3. LCCN:94-030787.
Audience: **u,f.**

Menzel, Peter & D'Aluisio,   **TJ211**
  Faith
Robo Sapiens: Evolution of a New Species. Trade Paper. MIT
Press. Cambridge, MA. 2001. 240p. ISBN:0-262-63245-4,
ISBN13: 978-0-262-63245-4. Dewey:629.8/92.
Audience: **u,f.** *Choice, 2001.*

Murphy, Robin R.   **TJ211.M865 2000**
Introduction to AI Robotics. Trade Cloth. MIT Press.
Cambridge, MA. 2000. 486p. Intelligent Robotics and
Autonomous Agents Ser. ISBN:0-262-13383-0, ISBN13:
978-0-262-13383-8. Dewey:629.8/6263. LCCN:00-033251.
Audience: **l,u.**

Nehmzow, Ulrich   **TJ211.415**
Mobile Robotics: A Practical Introduction. Ed. 2. Trade Paper.
Springer. New York, NY. 2003. XVI, 280p.
ISBN:1-85233-726-5, ISBN13: 978-1-85233-726-1.
Dewey:629.8/92. LCCN:2003-045588.
Audience: **l,u.**

Niku, Saeed B.   **TJ211.N547 2001**
Introduction to Robotics: Analysis, Systems, Applications. Cloth
Text. Prentice Hall PTR. Upper Saddle River, NJ. 2001. 349p.
ISBN:0-13-061309-6, ISBN13: 978-0-13-061309-7.
Dewey:629.8/92. LCCN:2002-279536.
Audience: **l,u.** *Choice, 2002.*

Patyra, M. J. & Mlynek, D.   **TJ213.F88 1996**
  J. (Editors)
Fuzzy Logic: Implementation and Applications. Ed. 1. Trade
Cloth. John Wiley & Sons, Inc. Hoboken, NJ. 1996. 346p.
ISBN:0-471-95059-9, ISBN13: 978-0-471-95059-2.
Dewey:629.8. LCCN:95-045241.
Audience: **u,f.** *Choice, 1997.*

Phillips, Charles L.   **TJ216.P54 1996**
Feedback Control Systems. Ed. 3. Trade Cloth. Prentice Hall
PTR. Upper Saddle River, NJ. 1995. 683p.
ISBN:0-13-371691-0, ISBN13: 978-0-13-371691-7.
Dewey:629.8/3. LCCN:95-021166.
Audience: **l,u.** *Choice, 1988.*

Phillips, Charles L. &   **TJ223.M53P47 1995**
  Nagle, H. Troy
Digital Control System Analysis and Design. Ed. 3. Cloth Text.

Prentice Hall PTR. Upper Saddle River, NJ. 1994. 704p.
ISBN:0-13-309832-X, ISBN13: 978-0-13-309832-7.
Dewey:629.8/95. LCCN:94-003482.

Audience: **l,u.**

Rehg, James A.   **TJ211.R422 2003**
Introduction to Robotics in CIM Systems. Ed. 5. Cloth Text.
Pearson Education. Boston, MA. 2002. 510p.
ISBN:0-13-060243-4, ISBN13: 978-0-13-060243-5.
Dewey:670.42/72. LCCN:2001-052086.

Audience: **l,u.**

Schilling, Robert J.   **TJ211.S38 1990**
Fundamentals of Robotics: Analysis and Control. Ed. 1. Cloth
Text. Prentice Hall PTR. Upper Saddle River, NJ. 1990. 464p.
ISBN:0-13-344433-3, ISBN13: 978-0-13-344433-9.
Dewey:629.8/92. LCCN:89-030739.

Audience: **l,u.**

Siegwart, Roland &   **TJ211.415.S54 2004**
  Nourbakhsh, Illah Reza
Introduction to Autonomous Mobile Robots. Trade Cloth. MIT
Press. Cambridge, MA. 2004. 331p. Intelligent Robots and
Autonomous Agents Ser. ISBN:0-262-19502-X, ISBN13:
978-0-262-19502-7. Dewey:629.8/92. LCCN:2003-059349.

Audience: **u.**

Siouris, George M.   **TJ213.S474443 1996**
An Engineering Approach to Optimal Control and Estimation
Theory. Trade Cloth. John Wiley & Sons, Inc. Hoboken, NJ.
1996. 407p. ISBN:0-471-12126-6, ISBN13: 978-0-471-12126-8.
Dewey:629.8. LCCN:95-006633.

Audience: **l,u.** *Choice, 1996.*

Spong, Mark W., et al.   **TJ211.35.S75 2005**
Robot Modeling and Control. Seth Hutchinson & M. Vidyasagar
(Authors). Trade Cloth. John Wiley & Sons, Inc. Hoboken, NJ.
2005. 496p. ISBN:0-471-64990-2, ISBN13: 978-0-471-64990-8.
Dewey:629.8/92. LCCN:2005-054227.

Audience: **l,u.**

Tsui, Chia-Chi   **TJ216**
e Robust Control System Design: Advanced State Space
Techniques. Ed. 2. E-Book. Marcel Dekker Inc. New York, NY.
2004. 500p. Control Engineering Ser., Vol. 16
ISBN:0-8247-5069-1, ISBN13: 978-0-8247-5069-5.
Dewey:629.8/3.

Audience: **u,f.**

Vaccaro, Richard   **TJ223.M53V32 1995**
Digital Control: A State-Space Approach. Ed. 1. Cloth Text.
McGraw-Hill Higher Education. Burr Ridge, IL. 1995. 480p.
McGraw-Hill Series in Electrical and Computer Engineering
ISBN:0-07-066781-0, ISBN13: 978-0-07-066781-5.
Dewey:629.8. LCCN:94-025300.

Audience: **u,f.**

Vidyasagar, M. & Spong,   **TJ211.4.S66 1989**
  Mark W.
Robot Dynamics and Control. Ed. 1. Trade Cloth. John Wiley &
Sons, Inc. Hoboken, NJ. 1989. 352p. ISBN:0-471-61243-X,
ISBN13: 978-0-471-61243-8. Dewey:629.8/92.
LCCN:88-022724.

Audience: **u,f.**

Vincent, Thomas L. &   **TJ216.V56 1997**
  Grantham, Walter J.
Nonlinear and Optimal Control Systems. Ed. 1. Trade Cloth.

John Wiley & Sons, Inc. Hoboken, NJ. 1997. 576p.
ISBN:0-471-04235-8, ISBN13: 978-0-471-04235-8.
Dewey:629.8/312. LCCN:96-037129.

Audience: **u,f.**

White, David A. & Sofge,   **TJ213**
  Donald A.
The Handbook of Intelligent Control. Cloth Text. John Wiley &
Sons, Inc. Hoboken, NJ. 1992. 250p. ISBN:0-442-30857-4,
ISBN13: 978-0-442-30857-5. Dewey:629.8. LCCN:92-073265.

Audience: **u,f.**

Whittle, Peter   **TJ213.W442 1996**
Optimal Control: Basics and Beyond. Ed. 1. Trade Paper. John
Wiley & Sons, Inc. Hoboken, NJ. 1996. 474p. Interscience
Series in Systems and Optimization ISBN:0-471-96099-3,
ISBN13: 978-0-471-96099-7. Dewey:629.8. LCCN:95-022113.

Audience: **u,f.**

Mechanical Engineering > Heat. Thermodynamics

Marquand, C. & Croft, D.   **TJ265.M317 1994**
Thermofluids: An Integrated Approach to Thermodynamics and
Fluid Mechanics Principles. Ed. 1. Trade Paper. John Wiley &
Sons, Inc. Hoboken, NJ. 1994. 418p. ISBN:0-471-94184-0,
ISBN13: 978-0-471-94184-2. Dewey:532.051.
LCCN:93-008776.

Audience: **l,u.** *Choice, 1994.*

Ragone, David V.   **TA418.52.R34 1995**
Thermodynamics of Materials, Vol. 1. Trade Cloth. John Wiley
& Sons, Inc. Hoboken, NJ. 1994. 336p. MIT Series in Materials
Science and Engineering, Vol. 1 ISBN:0-471-30885-4, ISBN13:
978-0-471-30885-0. Dewey:536/.7. LCCN:94-025647.

Audience: **u,f.** *Choice, 1995.*

Ragone, David V.   **TA418.52.R34**
Thermodynamics of Materials, Vol. 2. Trade Cloth. John Wiley
& Sons, Inc. Hoboken, NJ. 1994. 256p. MIT Series in Materials
Science and Engineering, Vol. 2 ISBN:0-471-30886-2, ISBN13:
978-0-471-30886-7. Dewey:536/.7. LCCN:94-025647.

Audience: **u,f.** *Choice, 1995.*

Valsaraj, Kalliat T.   **TD153.V35 2000**
Elements of Environmental Engineering: Thermodynamics and
Kinetics. Ed. 2. Paper over Boards. Lewis Publishers. Boca
Raton, FL. 2000. 712p. ISBN:1-56670-397-2, ISBN13:
978-1-56670-397-0. Dewey:628. LCCN:99-053965.

Audience: **u,f.** *Choice, 2000.*

Winterbone, D. E.   **TJ265**
Advanced Thermodynamics for Engineers. Trade Paper. John
Wiley & Sons, Inc. Hoboken, NJ. 1996. 352p.
ISBN:0-470-23718-X, ISBN13: 978-0-470-23718-2.
Dewey:621.402/1.

Audience: **u,f.** *Choice, 1997.*

Mechanical Engineering > Fluid Mechanics and Heat Transfer

Beattie, Donald A. (Editor)   **TJ809.95.S68**
History and Overview of Solar Heat Technologies. Trade Cloth.
MIT Press. Cambridge, MA. 1997. 250p. Solar Heat

Technologies Ser., Vol. 1:Fundamentals and Applications Ser. ISBN:0-262-02415-2, ISBN13: 978-0-262-02415-0. Dewey:697/.78 s. LCCN:96-034297.

Audience: **l,u,f.** *Choice, 1998.*

Bejan, Adrian & Jones, J. S.   **QC320.B44 1993**
Heat Transfer. Trade Cloth. John Wiley & Sons, Inc. Hoboken, NJ. 1993. 704p. ISBN:0-471-50290-1, ISBN13: 978-0-471-50290-6. Dewey:621.4022. LCCN:92-025535.

Audience: **u,f.** *Choice, 1993.*

Benedict, Robert P.   **TJ935**
Fundamentals of Pipe Flow. Trade Cloth. John Wiley & Sons, Inc. Hoboken, NJ. 1980. 531p. ISBN:0-471-03375-8, ISBN13: 978-0-471-03375-2. Dewey:532/.54. LCCN:79-023924.

Audience: **l,u.**

Casten, Thomas R.   **TJ163.4.U6C38 1998**
Turning off the Heat: Why America Must Double Energy Efficiency to Save Money and Reduce Global Warming. Federico Pena (Foreword by). Trade Cloth. Prometheus Books, Publishers. Amherst, NY. 1998. 273p. ISBN:1-57392-269-2, ISBN13: 978-1-57392-269-2. Dewey:333.7916/0973. LCCN:98-028272.

Audience: **g,l,u,f.** *Choice, 1999.*

Cheremisinoff, Nicholas P.   **TJ0260.H36**
  (Editor)
Handbook of Heat and Mass Transfer, Vol. 1. Trade Paper. Books on Demand. Ann Arbor, MI. 1986. 1470p. ISBN:0-608-04455-5, ISBN13: 978-0-608-04455-2. Dewey:621.4022. LCCN:84-025338.

Audience: **u,f.**

Cheremisinoff, Nicholas P.   **TJ0260.H36**
  (Editor)
Handbook of Heat and Mass Transfer: Advances in Reactor Design and Combustion Science, Vol. 4. Trade Paper. Books on Demand. Ann Arbor, MI. 1990. 1224p. ISBN:0-608-01340-4, ISBN13: 978-0-608-01340-4. Dewey:621.4022. LCCN:84-025338.

Audience: **u,f.**

Cheremisinoff, Nicholas P.   **TJ0260.H36**
Handbook of Heat and Mass Transfer: Catalysis, Kinetics and Reactor Engineering, Vol. 3. Trade Paper. Books on Demand. Ann Arbor, MI. 1990. 1484p. ISBN:0-608-01339-0, ISBN13: 978-0-608-01339-8. Dewey:621.4022. LCCN:84-025338.

Audience: **u,f.**

Cheremisinoff, Nicholas P.   **TJ0260.H36**
  (Editor)
Handbook of Heat and Mass Transfer, Vol. 2. Trade Paper. Books on Demand. Ann Arbor, MI. 1986. 1534p. ISBN:0-608-04456-3, ISBN13: 978-0-608-04456-9. Dewey:621.4022. LCCN:84-025338.

Audience: **u,f.**

Fuhs, Allen E. & Schetz,   **TA357.H286 1996**
  Joseph A. (Editors)
Handbook of Fluid Dynamics and Fluid Machinery, Set. Ed. 99. Trade Cloth. John Wiley & Sons, Inc. Hoboken, NJ. 1996. 2776p. ISBN:0-471-87352-7, ISBN13: 978-0-471-87352-5. Dewey:620.1/06. LCCN:95-005671.

Audience: **u,f.**

Jiji, Latif M.   **QC320.J55 1998**
Heat Transfer Essentials: A Textbook. Trade Cloth. Begell House Publishers, Inc. New York, NY. 1998. 228p. ISBN:1-56700-114-9, ISBN13: 978-1-56700-114-3. Dewey:536/.2. LCCN:98-016085.

Audience: **l.** *Choice, 1999.*

Kadac, Sadik   **TJ263.K25 1998**
Heat Exchangers: Selection, Rating, and Thermal Design. CRC Press. 1998. ISBN:0-8493-1688-X, ISBN13: 978-0-8493-1688-3.

Audience: **l,u,f.**

Karassik, Igor J., et al.   **TJ900.P79 2001**
Pump Handbook. Ed. 3. Paul Cooper, Charles C. Heald & Joseph P. Messina (Authors). Trade Cloth. McGraw-Hill Professional Publishing. New York, NY. 2000. 1765p. Harvard Business Review Book Ser. ISBN:0-07-034032-3, ISBN13: 978-0-07-034032-9. Dewey:621.6/9. LCCN:00-712414.

Audience: **l,u,f.** *Choice, 1986.*

Lakshminarayana, Budugur   **TJ267.L35 1996**
Fluid Dynamics and Heat Transfer of Turbomachinery. Ed. 1. Trade Cloth. John Wiley & Sons, Inc. Hoboken, NJ. 1995. 848p. ISBN:0-471-85546-4, ISBN13: 978-0-471-85546-0. Dewey:621.406. LCCN:94-041844.

Audience: **u,f.** *Choice, 1996.*

Lock, G. S.   **TJ260.L59 1994**
Latent Heat Transfer: An Introduction to Fundamentals. Trade Cloth. Oxford University Press, Inc. New York, NY. 1994. 312p. Engineering Science Ser., Vol. 43 ISBN:0-19-856285-3, ISBN13: 978-0-19-856285-6. Dewey:621.4/022. LCCN:94-011638.

Audience: **u,f.** *Choice, 1995.*

Mikhailov, M. D. & Ozisik,   **QC320**
  M. Necati
Heat Transfer Solver. Paper Text. Prentice Hall PTR. Upper Saddle River, NJ. 1991. 160p. ISBN:0-13-388802-9, ISBN13: 978-0-13-388802-7. Dewey:536.2.

Audience: **l,u.** *Choice, 1992.*

Naterer, Greg F.   **TJ260**
Heat Transfer in Single and Multiphase Systems. CRC Press. 2003. ISBN:0-8493-1032-6, ISBN13: 978-0-8493-1032-4.

Audience: **l,u,f.**

Rohsenow, Warren M., et al.   **QC320.4.H36 1998**
Handbook of Heat Transfer. Ed. 3. James P. Hartnett & Young I. Cho (Authors). Trade Cloth. McGraw-Hill Professional Publishing. New York, NY. 1998. 1344p. McGraw-Hill Handbooks Ser. ISBN:0-07-053555-8, ISBN13: 978-0-07-053555-8. Dewey:621.402/2. LCCN:97-051381.

Audience: **u,f.** *Choice, 1999.*

Thomas, Lindon C.   **QC320.T493 2000**
Heat Transfer. Ed. 2. Trade Cloth. Capstone Publishing Corporation. Tulsa, OK. 2000. 879p. ISBN:1-893317-01-3, ISBN13: 978-1-893317-01-7. Dewey:621.402/2. LCCN:99-067547.

Audience: **l,u,f.**

Webb, Ralph L. & Kim,   **TJ260.W36 2005**
  Nae-Hyun
Principles of Enhanced Heat Transfer. Ed. 2. Paper over Boards. Taylor & Francis Group. Philadelphia, PA. 2005. 824p.

ISBN:1-59169-014-5, ISBN13: 978-1-59169-014-6.
Dewey:621.402/2. LCCN:2004-021960.

Audience: **u,f.** *Choice, 2005, 1994.*

Mechanical Engineering > Machinery

American Society of   **TJ1075**
  Lubrication Engineers Staff
Standard Handbook of Lubrication Engineering. Trade Cloth.
Society of Tribologists & Lubrication Engineers. Park Ridge, IL.
1988. 1016p. ISBN:0-318-12832-2, ISBN13:
978-0-318-12832-0. Dewey:621.8/9.

Audience: **u,f.**

Amiss, John M., et al.   **TJ151**
Machinery's Handbook Guide. Ed. 27. Franklin D. Jones, Henry
H. Ryffel, Christopher J. McCauley & Riccardo Heald
(Authors). Trade Paper. Industrial Press, Inc. New York, NY.
2004. 260p. ISBN:0-8311-2799-6, ISBN13: 978-0-8311-2799-2.
Dewey:621.8/0212.

Audience: **u,f.**

Billingsley, John   **TJ163.12**
Essentials of Mechatronics. Online Resource. John Wiley &
Sons, Inc. Hoboken, NJ. 2006. 370p. ISBN:0-471-79153-9,
ISBN13: 978-0-471-79153-9. Dewey:621.

Audience: **l,u.**

Bishop Robert H Staff   **TJ163.12 .M434**
The Mechatronics Handbook Second Edition. Trade Cloth.
Taylor & Francis Books. New York, NY. 2007.
ISBN:0-8493-9257-8, ISBN13: 978-0-8493-9257-3. Dewey:621.

Audience: **l,u,f.**

Bishop, Robert H.   **TJ163.12.M4315 2005**
Mechatronics: An Introduction. Perfect, Paper over Boards.
Taylor & Francis Group. Philadelphia, PA. 2005. 283p.
ISBN:0-8493-6358-6, ISBN13: 978-0-8493-6358-0.
Dewey:621.3. LCCN:2005-049656.

Audience: **l,u.**

Boldy, Adrian P. & Radha   **TJ840.H93 1997**
  Krishna, Hari C. (Editors)
Hydraulic Design of Hydraulic Machinery. Trade Cloth. Ashgate
Publishing, Ltd. Aldershot, 1997. 594p. Hydraulic Machinery
Ser. ISBN:0-291-39851-0, ISBN13: 978-0-291-39851-2.
Dewey:621.2. LCCN:96-085968.

Audience: **u,f.** *Choice, 1997.*

Conrad, James M.   **TJ211.495**
Stiquito Controlled!: Making a Truly Autonomous Robot. Trade
Paper. John Wiley & Sons, Inc. Hoboken, NJ. 2005. 191p.
Software Engineering Best Practices Ser. ISBN:0-471-48882-8,
ISBN13: 978-0-471-48882-8. Dewey:629.892.

Audience: **u,f.**

Derby, Stephen   **TJ213.D44 2004**
Design of Automatic Machinery. Saddle Stitched. Marcel
Dekker Inc. New York, NY. 2004. 464p. Mechanical
Engineering Ser., Vol. 177 ISBN:0-8247-5369-0, ISBN13:
978-0-8247-5369-6. Dewey:670.42/7. LCCN:2004-055222.

Audience: **l,u.**

Dudley, D. W.   **TJ184.D784 1984**
Handbook of Practical Gear Design. Cloth Text. McGraw-Hill
Companies, The. New York, NY. 1984. 656p.

ISBN:0-07-017951-4, ISBN13: 978-0-07-017951-6.
Dewey:621.8/33. LCCN:84-003860.

Audience: **l,u,f.**

Faulkner, L. L. & Logan,   **TJ170.H365 2001**
  Earl
Handbook of Machinery Dynamics, Vol. 132. Paper over
Boards. Marcel Dekker Inc. New York, NY. 2000. 608p.
Mechanical Engineering Ser. ISBN:0-8247-0386-3, ISBN13:
978-0-8247-0386-8. Dewey:621.8/1. LCCN:00-050929.

Audience: **u,f.**

Faulkner, L. L. & Logan,   **TJ170.H365 2001**
  Earl
[e] Handbook of Machinery Dynamics. E-Book. NetLibrary, Inc.
Boulder, CO. 2001. ISBN:0-585-42704-6, ISBN13:
978-0-585-42704-1. Dewey:621.8/1.

Audience: **u,f.**

Histand, Michael B. &   **TJ163.12.H57 1998**
  Alciatore, David G.
Introduction to Mechatronics and Measurement Systems. Trade
Cloth. McGraw-Hill Higher Education. Burr Ridge, IL. 1998.
432p. ISBN:0-07-029089-X, ISBN13: 978-0-07-029089-1.
Dewey:621. LCCN:98-006438.

Audience: **l,u.**

Jones, Franklin D.   **TJ175**
Ingenious Mechanisms for Designers and Inventors, Vol. 14.
Trade Cloth. Industrial Press, Inc. New York, NY. 1977.
ISBN:0-8311-1084-8, ISBN13: 978-0-8311-1084-0.
Dewey:621.8. LCCN:30-014992.

Audience: **l,u,f.**

Juvinall, Robert C. &   **TJ230.J88 2005**
  Marshek, Kurt M.
Fundamentals of Machine Component Design. Ed. 4. Trade
Cloth. John Wiley & Sons, Inc. Hoboken, NJ. 2005. 848p.
ISBN:0-471-66177-5, ISBN13: 978-0-471-66177-1.
Dewey:621.8/15. LCCN:2005-047031.

Audience: **l,u.**

Krivchenko, G. I.   **TJ840.K76 1994**
Hydraulic Machines: Turbines and Pumps. Ed. 2. Library
Binding. Lewis Publishers. Boca Raton, FL. 1993. 432p.
ISBN:1-56670-001-9, ISBN13: 978-1-56670-001-6.
Dewey:621.2. LCCN:93-008853.

Audience: **l,u.**

Masterson, James W., et al.   **TJ211**
Robotics Technology. Stephen Fardo & Robert L. Towers
(Authors). Trade Paper. Goodheart-Willcox Publisher. Tinley
Park, IL. 1996. 320p. ISBN:1-56637-046-9, ISBN13:
978-1-56637-046-2. Dewey:629.8/92.

Audience: **u,f.**

Miller, Rex & Miller, Mark   **TJ1185**
  Richard
Audel Automated Machines and Toolmaking. Ed. 5. Trade
Paper. John Wiley & Sons, Inc. Hoboken, NJ. 2004. 501p.
Audel Technical Trades Ser. ISBN:0-7645-5528-6, ISBN13:
978-0-7645-5528-2. Dewey:671.3/5. LCCN:2004-296726.

Audience: **u,f.**

Norton, Robert L.   **TJ175.N58 2003**
Design of Machinery: An Introduction to the Synthesis and
Analysis of Mechanisms and Machines. Ed. 3. Cloth Text.

McGraw-Hill Companies, The. New York, NY. 2003. 880p.
McGraw-Hill Series in Mechanical Engineering
ISBN:0-07-247046-1, ISBN13: 978-0-07-247046-8.
Dewey:621.8/15. LCCN:2002-038057.

Audience: **l,u.** *Choice, 1992.*

Oberg, et al.　　　　　　　　　**TJ151.O245 2004**
Machinery's Handbook. Ed. 27. Jones Sr. & Horton (Authors).
Trade Paper. Industrial Press, Inc. New York, NY. 2004. 2693p.
ISBN:0-8311-2700-7, ISBN13: 978-0-8311-2700-8. Dewey:621.

Audience: **l,u,f.**

Onwubolu, Godfrey　　　　　　　　　**TJ163.12**
Mechatronics: Principles and Applications. Paper Text. Elsevier
Science & Technology Books. Saint Louis, MO. 2005. 672p.
ISBN:0-7506-6379-0, ISBN13: 978-0-7506-6379-3. Dewey:621.
LCCN:2005-299897.

Audience: **l,u.**

Phelan, Richard M.　　　　　　　　　**TJ175 .P47**
Dynamics of Machinery. Cloth Text. McGraw-Hill Companies,
The. New York, NY. 1967. ISBN:0-07-049770-2, ISBN13:
978-0-07-049770-2. Dewey:621.811.

Audience: **l,u.**

Riduttori, Bonfiglioli　　　　　　　　　**TJ184 .G3472**
(Editor)
Gear Motor Handbook. D. W. Dudley, J. Sprengers, D. Schroder
& H. Yamashina (Contribution by). Trade Cloth. Springer. New
York, NY. 1996. XXVIII, 606p. ISBN:3-540-58988-0, ISBN13:
978-3-540-58988-4. Dewey:621.8/33.

Audience: **l,u,f.**

Rothbart, Harold A.　　　　　　　　　**TJ230.M43 1985**
Mechanical Design and Systems Handbook. Ed. 2. Trade Cloth.
McGraw-Hill Companies, The. New York, NY. 1985. 1824p.
ISBN:0-07-054020-9, ISBN13: 978-0-07-054020-0.
Dewey:621.8/15. LCCN:84-020128.

Audience: **l,u,f.** *Choice, 1985.*

Rothbart, Harold A. &　　　　　　　　　**TJ230.M433 2006**
Brown, Thomas H.
Mechanical Design Handbook. Ed. 2. Trade Cloth. McGraw-Hill
Professional Publishing. New York, NY. 2006. 900p.
ISBN:0-07-146636-3, ISBN13: 978-0-07-146636-3.
Dewey:621.8/15. LCCN:2006-043833.

Audience: **l,u,f.** *Choice, 1996.*

Sandler, Ben Zion　　　　　　　　　**TJ213.S1157 1999**
Robotics: Designing the Mechanisms for Automated Machinery.
Ed. 2. Cloth Text. Elsevier Science & Technology Books. Saint
Louis, MO. 1999. 433p. ISBN:0-12-618520-4, ISBN13:
978-0-12-618520-1. Dewey:670.42/72. LCCN:98-045839.

Audience: **l,u.**

Sclater, Neil & Chironis,　　　　　　　　　**TJ181.S28 2001**
Nicholas P.
Mechanisms and Mechanical Devices Sourcebook. Ed. 3. Trade
Cloth. McGraw-Hill Professional Publishing. New York, NY.
2001. 500p. Mechanical Engineering Ser. ISBN:0-07-136169-3,
ISBN13: 978-0-07-136169-9. Dewey:621.8.
LCCN:2001-030297.

Audience: **l,u.**

Selig, J. M.　　　　　　　　　**TJ211.S433 2005**
Geometric Fundamentals of Robotics. Ed. 2. Trade Cloth.
Springer. New York, NY. 2004. XVII, 398p. Monographs in
Computer Science ISBN:0-387-20874-7, ISBN13:
978-0-387-20874-9. Dewey:629.8/92. LCCN:2004-059103.

Audience: **l,u.**

Shigley, Joseph, et al.　　　　　　　　　**TJ230**
Standard Handbook of Machine Design. Ed. 3. Charles Mischke
& Thomas H. Brown (Authors). Trade Cloth. McGraw-Hill
Professional Publishing. New York, NY. 2004. 1200p.
ISBN:0-07-144164-6, ISBN13: 978-0-07-144164-3.
Dewey:621.8/15. LCCN:2004-275003.

Audience: **l,u,f.**

Spotts, Merhyle Franklin,　　　　　　　　　**TJ230.S82 2003**
et al.
Design of Machine Elements. Ed. 8. Terry E. Shoup & Lee
Emrey Hornberger (Authors). Cloth Text. Prentice Hall PTR.
Upper Saddle River, NJ. 2003. 944p. ISBN:0-13-048989-1,
ISBN13: 978-0-13-048989-0. Dewey:621.8/15.
LCCN:2003-049879.

Audience: **l,u,f.**

Waldron, Kenneth J. &　　　　　　　　　**TJ170**
Kinzel, Gary L.
Kinematics, Dynamics, and Design of Machinery. Ed. 2. Trade
Cloth. John Wiley & Sons, Inc. Hoboken, NJ. 2003. 680p.
ISBN:0-471-24417-1, ISBN13: 978-0-471-24417-2.
Dewey:621.8/1. LCCN:2003-050053.

Audience: **l,u.**

Wise, Edwin　　　　　　　　　**TJ211.W5628 2004**
Robotics Demystified. Trade Paper. McGraw-Hill Professional
Publishing. New York, NY. 2004. 314p. ISBN:0-07-143678-2,
ISBN13: 978-0-07-143678-6. Dewey:629.8/92.
LCCN:2004-059207.

Audience: **l,u.**

Mechanical Engineering > Motor Vehicles

Abbott, Allan V. & Wilson,　　　　　　　　　**TL154.A23 1995**
David G. (Editors)
Human-Powered Vehicles. Trade Cloth. Human Kinetics
Publishers. Champaign, IL. 1995. 288p. ISBN:0-87322-827-8,
ISBN13: 978-0-87322-827-5. Dewey:629.04. LCCN:95-010636.

Audience: **l,u,f.** *Choice, 1996.*

Bosch, Robert & Robert　　　　　　　　　**TL147**
Bosch GmbH Staff
BOSCH Automotive Handbook. Ed. 6. Trade Cloth. John Wiley
& Sons, Inc. Hoboken, NJ. 2005. 320p. Gasoline-Engine
Management Ser. ISBN:1-86058-474-8, ISBN13:
978-1-86058-474-9.

Audience: **l,u,f.**

Bradsher, Keith　　　　　　　　　**TL230.5.S66B73 2002**
High and Mighty SUV's: The World's Most Dangerous Vehicles
and How They Got That Way. Trade Cloth. PublicAffairs. New
York, NY. 2002. 464p. ISBN:1-58648-123-1, ISBN13:
978-1-58648-123-0. Dewey:629.2/31. LCCN:2002-028722.

Audience: **g,l,u,f.** *Choice, 2003.*

Committee Staff on Fuel　　　　　　　　　**TL151.6 .A927 1992**
Economy of Automobiles and L (Editor)
Automotive Fuel Economy: How Far Can We Go? Paper Text.

National Academies Press. Washington, DC. 1992. 288p. ISBN:0-309-04530-4, ISBN13: 978-0-309-04530-8. Dewey:333.79/68. LCCN:92-015227.

Audience: **l,u,f.**

Dixon, Lloyd, et al.   **TL220.D578 2002**
Driving Emissions to Zero: Are the Benefits of California's Zero Emission Vehicle Program Worth the Costs? Isaac Porche & Jonathan Kulick (Authors). Trade Paper. RAND Corporation, The. Santa Monica, CA. 2002. 140p. ISBN:0-8330-3212-7, ISBN13: 978-0-8330-3212-6. Dewey:363.739/26/09794. LCCN:2002-026552.

Audience: **u,f.**

Dukkipati, Rao V   **TL243.D85 2000**
Vehicle dynamics. CRC Press. 2000. ISBN:0-8493-0976-X, ISBN13: 978-0-8493-0976-2.

Audience: **u,f.**

Ehsani, Mehrdad   **TL221.15.G39 2004**
Modern electric, hybrid electric, and fuel cell vehicles : fundamentals, theory, and design. CRC Press. 2005. ISBN:0-8493-3154-4, ISBN13: 978-0-8493-3154-1.

Audience: **u,f.**

Emadi, Ali   **TL145**
Vehicular Electric Power Systems: Land, Sea, Air, and Space Vehicles, Vol. 22. Paper over Boards. Marcel Dekker Inc. New York, NY. 2003. 520p. Power Engineering Ser., Vol. 22 ISBN:0-8247-4751-8, ISBN13: 978-0-8247-4751-0. Dewey:629.2/5. LCCN:2004-300325.

Audience: **u,f.**

Fujimoto, Takahiro   **TL278.F83 1999**
The Evolution of a Manufacturing System at Toyota. Trade Cloth. Oxford University Press, Inc. New York, NY. 1999. 390p. ISBN:0-19-512320-4, ISBN13: 978-0-19-512320-3. Dewey:629.2/34. LCCN:98-038201.

Audience: **u,f.** *Choice, 2000.*

Fuller, R. & Santos, Jorge   **TL152.3.H76 2002**
   A. (Editors)
Human Factors for Highway Engineers. Trade Cloth. Elsevier Science & Technology Books. Saint Louis, MO. 2002. 342p. ISBN:0-08-043412-6, ISBN13: 978-0-08-043412-4. Dewey:629.283019. LCCN:2001-058569.

Audience: **u,f.**

Goodsell, Don   **TL278**
Dictionary of Automotive Engineering. Trade Cloth. Society of Automotive Engineers, Inc. Warrendale, PA. 1989. 182p. ISBN:0-89883-766-9, ISBN13: 978-0-89883-766-7. Dewey:629.2. LCCN:89-000685.

Audience: **l,u,f.**

Hucho, Wolf   **TL245.A4813 1998**
Aerodynamics of Road Vehicles: From Fluid Mechanics to Vehicle Engineering. Ed. 4. Trade Cloth. Society of Automotive Engineers, Inc. Warrendale, PA. 1998. 956p. ISBN:0-7680-0029-7, ISBN13: 978-0-7680-0029-0. Dewey:629.2/31. LCCN:97-035351.

Audience: **u,f.**

Jurgen, Ronald K.   **TL272.5.A982 1999**
Automotive Electronics Handbook. Ed. 2. Cloth Text. McGraw-Hill Professional Publishing. New York, NY. 1999.

1000p. ISBN:0-07-034453-1, ISBN13: 978-0-07-034453-2. Dewey:629.25/49. LCCN:98-049442.

Audience: **l,u,f.**

Kemper, Steve   **TL410.K46 2003**
Code Name Ginger: The Story Behind Segway and Dean Kamen's Quest to Invent a New World. Trade Cloth. Harvard Business School Press. Boston, MA. 2003. 336p. ISBN:1-57851-673-0, ISBN13: 978-1-57851-673-5. Dewey:629.22/7. LCCN:2002-155932.

Audience: **u,f.**

Larminie, James & Lowry,   **TL220**
   John
Electric Vehicle Technology Explained. Trade Cloth. John Wiley & Sons, Inc. Hoboken, NJ. 2003. 314p. ISBN:0-470-85163-5, ISBN13: 978-0-470-85163-0. Dewey:629.22/93. LCCN:2003-062752.

Audience: **u,f.**

Nader, Ralph   **TL242.N3 1972**
Unsafe at Any Speed; the Designed-in Dangers of the American Automobile. Trade Cloth. Grossman Publishers, Inc. 1972. xciii, 417p. ISBN:0-670-74159-0, ISBN13: 978-0-670-74159-5. Dewey:629.2/3. LCCN:79-179071.

Audience: **g,l,u,f.**

National Research Council   **TL158.N39 2001**
   Staff
Review of the Research Program of the Partnership for a New Generation of Vehicles: Seventh Report. Perfect. National Academies Press. Washington, DC. 2001. 136p. ISBN:0-309-07603-X, ISBN13: 978-0-309-07603-6. Dewey:629.2/07/2073. LCCN:2001-094462.

Audience: **u,f.**

Newton, K., et al.   **TL205.N4 1996**
The Motor Vehicle. Ed. 12. W. Steeds & T. K. Garrett (Authors). Trade Cloth. Society of Automotive Engineers, Inc. Warrendale, PA. 1996. 976p. ISBN:1-56091-898-5, ISBN13: 978-1-56091-898-1. Dewey:629.2. LCCN:96-070164.

Audience: **l,u,f.**

Nieuwenhuis, Paul; Wells,   **TL158.N54 2003**
   P. E.
The automotive industry and the environment : a technical, business and social future. CRC Press. 2003. ISBN:0-8493-2072-0, ISBN13: 978-0-8493-2072-9.

Audience: **u,f.**

Vlacic, Ljubo, et al.   **TL152.8.I573 2001**
Intelligent Vehicle Technologies. Michel Parent & Fumio Harashima (Authors). Trade Paper. Elsevier Science & Technology Books. Saint Louis, MO. 2000. 512p. ISBN:0-7506-5093-1, ISBN13: 978-0-7506-5093-9. Dewey:629.2/3. LCCN:2001-025276.

Audience: **u,f.**

Wong, J. Y.   **TL240.W66 2001**
Theory of Ground Vehicles. Ed. 3. Trade Cloth. John Wiley & Sons, Inc. Hoboken, NJ. 2001. 560p. ISBN:0-471-35461-9, ISBN13: 978-0-471-35461-1. Dewey:629.2/3. LCCN:00-043853.

Audience: **u,f.**

Aeronautical Engineering > Aircraft

Abbott, Ira H. & Von   **TL574.A4**
Doenhoff, Albert E.
Theory of Wing Sections: Including a Summary of Airfoil Data.
Trade Paper. Dover Publications, Inc. Mineola, NY. 1999. 693p.
ISBN:0-486-60586-8, ISBN13: 978-0-486-60586-9.
Dewey:629.1/3432.

Audience: **u,f.**

Abzug, Malcolm J. &   **TL574.S7A2 2002**
Larrabee, E. Eugene
Airplane Stability and Control: A History of the Technologies
That Made Aviation Possible. Ed. 2. Michael J. Rycroft & Wei
Shyy (Contribution by). Trade Cloth. Cambridge University
Press. New York, NY. 2002. 414p. Cambridge Aerospace Ser.,
Vol. 14 ISBN:0-521-80992-4, ISBN13: 978-0-521-80992-4.
Dewey:629.132/36. LCCN:2001-052847.

Audience: **u,f.**

Anderson, John D. Jr.   **TL670.3.A49 2002**
The Airplane, a History of Its Technology. Trade Cloth.
American Institute of Aeronautics & Astronautics. Reston, VA.
2002. viii, 369p. ISBN:1-56347-525-1, ISBN13:
978-1-56347-525-2. Dewey:629.133/34/09. LCCN:2002-153182.

Audience: **l,u,f.** *Choice, 2003.*

Anderson, John D. Jr.   **TL570.A68 2000**
Introduction to Flight. Ed. 4. Cloth Text. McGraw-Hill Higher
Education. Burr Ridge, IL. 1999. 784p. ISBN:0-07-109282-X,
ISBN13: 978-0-07-109282-1. Dewey:629.1. LCCN:99-032638.

Audience: **u,f.**

Baker, A. A., et al.   **TL699.C57C66 2004**
Composite Materials for Aircraft Structures. Ed. 2. S. Dutton &
D. Kelly (Authors). Trade Cloth. American Institute of
Aeronautics & Astronautics. Reston, VA. 2004. 400p.
ISBN:1-56347-540-5, ISBN13: 978-1-56347-540-5.
Dewey:629.134. LCCN:2004-012195.

Audience: **u,f.**

Bilstein, Roger E.   **TL521.B528 2001**
Flight in America: From the Wrights to the Astronauts. Ed. 3.
Trade Paper. Johns Hopkins University Press. Baltimore, MD.
2001. 416p. ISBN:0-8018-6685-5, ISBN13: 978-0-8018-6685-2.
Dewey:629.1/0973. LCCN:00-065494.

Audience: **g,l,u,f.**

Blakelock, John H.   **TL589.4.B55 1991**
Automatic Control of Aircraft and Missiles. Ed. 2. Trade Cloth.
John Wiley & Sons, Inc. Hoboken, NJ. 1991. 672p.
ISBN:0-471-50651-6, ISBN13: 978-0-471-50651-5.
Dewey:629.132/6. LCCN:90-012393.

Audience: **u,f.**

Buck, Robert N.   **TL553.5**
The Pilot's Burden: Flight Safety and the Roots of Pilot Error.
Trade Paper. Blackwell Publishing Professional. Ames, IA.
1999. 252p. ISBN:0-8138-2815-5, ISBN13: 978-0-8138-2815-2.
Dewey:363.12/414. LCCN:99-053504.

Audience: **l,u,f.**

Cook, M. V.   **TL570**
Flight Dynamics Principles. Trade Paper. Elsevier Science &
Technology Books. Saint Louis, MO. 1997. 400p.
ISBN:0-340-63200-3, ISBN13: 978-0-340-63200-0.
Dewey:629.132/3.

Audience: **u,f.**

Corke, Thomas   **TL546.C692 2002**
Design of Aircraft. Cloth Text. Prentice Hall PTR. Upper Saddle
River, NJ. 2002. 391p. ISBN:0-13-089234-3, ISBN13:
978-0-13-089234-8. Dewey:629.134/1. LCCN:2002-027074.

Audience: **l,u,f.**

Cumpsty, Nicholas A.   **TL709**
Jet Propulsion: A Simple Guide to the Aerodynamic and
Thermodynamic Design and Performance of Jet Engines. Ed. 2.
Trade Paper. Cambridge University Press. New York, NY. 2003.
322p. ISBN:0-521-54144-1, ISBN13: 978-0-521-54144-2.
Dewey:629.134/3533. LCCN:2003-047256.

Audience: **u,f.**

Davies, Mark   **TL509.S664 2002**
The Standard Handbook for Aeronautical and Astronautical
Engineers. Trade Cloth. McGraw-Hill Professional Publishing.
New York, NY. 2002. 1360p. McGraw-Hill Standard Handbooks
ISBN:0-07-136229-0, ISBN13: 978-0-07-136229-0.
Dewey:629.1. LCCN:2002-032551.

Audience: **u,f.**

Eshelby, Martin E.   **TL671.4.E84 2000**
Aircraft Performance: Theory and Practice. Trade Cloth.
American Institute of Aeronautics & Astronautics. Reston, VA.
2000. 350p. ISBN:1-56347-398-4, ISBN13: 978-1-56347-398-2.
Dewey:629.132. LCCN:99-089517.

Audience: **u,f.**

Etkin, Bernard & Reid,   **TL570.E75 1996**
Lloyd Duff
Dynamics of Flight: Stability and Control. Ed. 3. Trade Cloth.
John Wiley & Sons, Inc. Hoboken, NJ. 1995. 400p.
ISBN:0-471-03418-5, ISBN13: 978-0-471-03418-6.
Dewey:629.1/32. LCCN:95-020395.

Audience: **u,f.**

Fielding, John P.   **TL671.2**
Introduction to Aircraft Design. Michael J. Rycroft & Wei Shyy
(Contribution by). Trade Paper. Cambridge University Press.
New York, NY. 1999. 277p. Cambridge Aerospace Ser., No. 11
ISBN:0-521-65722-9, ISBN13: 978-0-521-65722-8.
Dewey:629.1/341. LCCN:98-039489.

Audience: **u,f.**

Gillispie, Charles C.   **TL617.M66 G48 1983**
The Montgolfier Brothers and the Invention of Aviation,
1783-1784: With a Word on the Importance of Ballooning for
the Science of Heat and the Art of Building Railroads. Trade
Cloth. Princeton University Press. Princeton, NJ. 1983. 272p.
ISBN:0-691-08321-5, ISBN13: 978-0-691-08321-6.
Dewey:629.13/0092/2. LCCN:82-061363.

Audience: **g,l,u,f.**

Gunston, Bill (Editor)   **TL509.G88 2004**
The Cambridge Aerospace Dictionary. Trade Cloth. Cambridge
University Press. New York, NY. 2004. 750p.
ISBN:0-521-84140-2, ISBN13: 978-0-521-84140-5.
Dewey:629.1/03. LCCN:2004-043530.

Audience: **u,f.** *Choice, 2004.*

Houghton, E. L. &   **TL570.H587 2002**
  Carpenter, P. W.
Aerodynamics for Engineering Students. Ed. 5. Trade Paper.
Elsevier Science & Technology Books. Saint Louis, MO. 2003.
608p. ISBN:0-7506-5111-3, ISBN13: 978-0-7506-5111-0.
Dewey:629.132/3. LCCN:2002-029945.
                                          Audience: **u,f.**

Jones, Robert T.   **TL574.A4J62 1990**
Wing Theory. Cloth Text. Princeton University Press. Princeton,
NJ. 1990. 224p. ISBN:0-691-08536-6, ISBN13:
978-0-691-08536-4. Dewey:629.134/32. LCCN:89-035136.
                                          Audience: **u,f.**

Mattingly, Jack D., et al.   **TL709.5.T87M38 2002**
Aircraft Engine Design. Ed. 2. William H. Heiser & David T.
Pratt (Authors). Trade Cloth. American Institute of Aeronautics
& Astronautics. Reston, VA. 2002. xxvii, 687p. AIAA Education
Ser. ISBN:1-56347-538-3, ISBN13: 978-1-56347-538-2.
Dewey:629.134/353. LCCN:2002-013143.
                                          Audience: **u,f.**

Miyagi, Masako   **TL553.5.M56 2005**
Serious Accidents and Human Factors: Breaking the Chain of
Events Leading to an Accident. Trade Cloth. American Institute
of Aeronautics & Astronautics. Reston, VA. 2005. xxix, 288p.
ISBN:1-56347-745-9, ISBN13: 978-1-56347-745-4.
Dewey:363.12/4. LCCN:2005-002339.
                                          Audience: **u,f.**

National Research Council   **TL725.3.T7F88 1998**
  Staff
The Future of Air Traffic Control: Human Operators and
Automation. Christopher D. Wickens, Anne S. Mavor, Raja
Parasuraman & James P. McGee (Editors). Cloth Text. National
Academies Press. Washington, DC. 1998. 336p.
ISBN:0-309-06412-0, ISBN13: 978-0-309-06412-5.
Dewey:387.7/40426. LCCN:97-045303.
                                          Audience: **u,f.**

Nelson, Robert C.   **TL574.S7N45 1998**
Flight Stability and Automatic Control. Ed. 2. Cloth Text.
McGraw-Hill Higher Education. Burr Ridge, IL. 1997. 456p.
ISBN:0-07-046273-9, ISBN13: 978-0-07-046273-1.
Dewey:629.1/3236. LCCN:97-026109.
                                          Audience: **u,f.**

Phillips, Warren F.   **TL570.P46 2004**
Mechanics of Flight. Trade Cloth. John Wiley & Sons, Inc.
Hoboken, NJ. 2004. 984p. ISBN:0-471-33458-8, ISBN13:
978-0-471-33458-3. Dewey:629.132/3. LCCN:2003-006644.
                                          Audience: **u,f.**

Pierce, G. Alvin & Hodges,   **TL671.6.H565 2002**
  Dewey H.
Introduction to Structural Dynamics and Aeroelasticity. Michael
J. Rycroft & Wei Shyy (Contribution by). Cloth Text.
Cambridge University Press. New York, NY. 2002. 182p.
Cambridge Aerospace Ser., Vol. 15 ISBN:0-521-80698-4,
ISBN13: 978-0-521-80698-5. Dewey:629.134/31.
LCCN:2001-052552.
                              Audience: **u,f.** *Choice, 2003.*

R Spitzer, Cary   **TL695.A8163 2001**
The Avionics Handbook. CRC Press. 2001.
ISBN:0-8493-8348-X, ISBN13: 978-0-8493-8348-9.
                                          Audience: **u,f.**

Singer, Bayla   **TL516.S56 2003**
Like Sex with Gods: An Unorthodox History of Flying. Trade
Cloth. Texas A & M University Press. College Station, TX.
2004. 224p. Centennial of Flight Ser., Vol. 3
ISBN:1-58544-256-9, ISBN13: 978-1-58544-256-0.
Dewey:629.13/009. LCCN:2002-152954.
                          Audience: **g,l,u,f.** *Choice, 2004.*

Stevens, Brian L. & Lewis,   **TL678.S74 2003**
  Frank L.
Aircraft Control and Simulation. Ed. 2. Trade Cloth. John Wiley
& Sons, Inc. Hoboken, NJ. 2003. 680p. ISBN:0-471-37145-9,
ISBN13: 978-0-471-37145-8. Dewey:629.135.
LCCN:2003-043250.
                                          Audience: **u,f.**

Tennekes, Henk   **TL547**
The Simple Science of Flight: From Insects to Jumbo Jets.
Trade Paper. MIT Press. Cambridge, MA. 1997. 137p.
ISBN:0-262-70065-4, ISBN13: 978-0-262-70065-8.
Dewey:629.1/32.
                                          Audience: **u,f.**

Thomas, Andrew   **TL553.52.R45 2003**
Aviation Insecurity: The New Challenges of Air Travel. Trade
Paper. Prometheus Books, Publishers. Amherst, NY. 2003. 260p.
ISBN:1-59102-074-3, ISBN13: 978-1-59102-074-5.
Dewey:363.28/76. LCCN:2003-001479.
                          Audience: **g,l,u,f.** *Choice, 2003.*

Upham, Paul (Editor)   **HE9776**
Towards Sustainable Aviation. Trade Cloth. Earthscan/James &
James. London, 2003. 248p. ISBN:1-85383-817-9, ISBN13:
978-1-85383-817-0. Dewey:629.13. LCCN:2003-000450.
                                          Audience: **u,f.**

Vincenti, Walter G.   **TL515**
What Engineers Know and How They Know It: Analytical
Studies from Aeronautical History. Trade Paper. Johns Hopkins
University Press. Baltimore, MD. 1993. 336p. Studies in the
History of Technology Ser. ISBN:0-8018-4588-2, ISBN13:
978-0-8018-4588-8. Dewey:629.13/09. LCCN:89-049003.
                              Audience: **u,f.** *Choice, 1991.*

Wickens, Christopher D.,   **TL725.3.T7H865 1997**
  et al.
Flight to the Future: Human Factors in Air Traffic Control.
James P. McGee, Anne S. Mavor & Panel on Human Factors in
Air Traffic Control (Authors). Cloth Text. National Academies
Press. Washington, DC. 1997. 384p. ISBN:0-309-05637-3,
ISBN13: 978-0-309-05637-3. Dewey:629.136/6.
LCCN:96-037616.
                                          Audience: **u,f.**

Aeronautical Engineering > Rockets. Astronautics. Space Flight

Ackmann, Martha   **TL789.85.A1A28 2003**
The Mercury 13: The Untold Story of Thirteen American
Women and the Dream of Space Flight. Lynn Sherr (Foreword
by). Trade Cloth. Random House, Inc. New York, NY. 2003.
256p. ISBN:0-375-50744-2, ISBN13: 978-0-375-50744-1.
Dewey:629.45/0082/0973. LCCN:2002-037118.
                          Audience: **g,l,u,f.** *Choice, 2003.*

Booker, P. J.   **TL789.8.U6A523 1969**
Project Apollo: The Way to the Moon. Trade Cloth. Elsevier.
New York, NY. 1970. ISBN:0-444-19705-2, ISBN13:
978-0-444-19705-4. Dewey:629.45/4. LCCN:72-101222.
Audience: **u,f.**

Dethloff, Henry C. &   **TL789.8.U6V683 2003**
  Schorn, Ronald A.
Voyager's Grand Tour: To the Outer Planets and Beyond. Trade
Cloth. Smithsonian Institution Press. Washington, DC. 2003.
272p. Smithsonian History of Aviation and Spaceflight Ser.
ISBN:1-58834-124-0, ISBN13: 978-1-58834-124-2.
Dewey:919.9/204. LCCN:2002-029217.
Audience: **g,l,u,f.**

Dewar, James A.   **TL783.5.D48 2003**
To the End of the Solar System: The Story of the Nuclear
Rocket. Ken Hechler (Foreword by). Trade Cloth. University
Press of Kentucky. Lexington, KY. 2003. 384p.
ISBN:0-8131-2267-8, ISBN13: 978-0-8131-2267-0.
Dewey:629.47/53/0973. LCCN:2003-007973.
Audience: **l,u,f.** *Choice, 2004.*

Dolman, Everett Carl   **TL788.4.D685 2001**
Astropolitik: Classical Geopolitics in the Space Age. Cloth Text.
Taylor & Francis Group. Abingdon, 2002. 224p. Strategy and
History Ser. ISBN:0-7146-5200-8, ISBN13: 978-0-7146-5200-9.
Dewey:327/.0919. LCCN:2001-047183.
Audience: **u,f.** *Choice, 2002.*

Fortescue, Peter W. (Editor),   **TL875.S68 2003**
  et al.
Spacecraft Systems Engineering. Ed. 3. John Stark & Graham
Swinerd (Editors). Trade Cloth. John Wiley & Sons, Inc.
Hoboken, NJ. 2003. 704p. ISBN:0-470-85102-3, ISBN13:
978-0-470-85102-9. Dewey:629.47/4. LCCN:2002-028089.
Audience: **u,f.** *Choice, 1992.*

Gruntman, Mike   **TL781.G78 2004**
Blazing the Trail: The Early History of Spacecraft and Rocketry.
Trade Cloth. American Institute of Aeronautics & Astronautics.
Reston, VA. 2004. 475p. ISBN:1-56347-705-X, ISBN13:
978-1-56347-705-8. Dewey:621.43/56. LCCN:2004-006792.
Audience: **g,l,u,f.** *Choice, 2005.*

Hale, Francis J.   **TL791.H35 1994**
Introduction to Space Flight. Ed. 1. Cloth Text. Prentice Hall
PTR. Upper Saddle River, NJ. 1993. 366p.
ISBN:0-13-481912-8, ISBN13: 978-0-13-481912-9.
Dewey:629.4/1. LCCN:93-022436.
Audience: **l,u,f.** *Choice, 1994.*

Hall, Rex & Shayler, David   **TL789.8.R92S694 2003**
Soyuz: A Universal Spacecraft. Trade Paper. Springer. New
York, NY. 2003. XXXVI, 459p. Springer-Praxis Books in
Astronomy and Space Sciences ISBN:1-85233-657-9, ISBN13:
978-1-85233-657-8. Dewey:629.47/0947. LCCN:2002-191130.
Audience: **u,f.**

Harland, David M.   **TL795.5**
The Story of the Space Shuttle. Trade Paper. Springer. New
York, NY. 2004. XXIV, 444p. Springer Praxis Books / Space
Exploration Ser. ISBN:1-85233-793-1, ISBN13:
978-1-85233-793-3. Dewey:629.44/1/0973. LCCN:2004-041821.
Audience: **g,l,u,f.** *Choice, 2004.*

Harvey, Brian   **TL789.8.R8H37 2001**
Russia in Space: The Failed Frontier? Trade Paper. Springer.
New York, NY. 2001. XIX, 330p. Astronomy and Space
Sciences Bks. ISBN:1-85233-203-4, ISBN13:
978-1-85233-203-7. Dewey:629.4/0947. LCCN:00-049273.
Audience: **u,f.** *Choice, 2001.*

Hill, Philip G. & Peterson,   **TL709.H5 1991**
  Carl R.
Mechanics and Thermodynamics of Propulsion. Ed. 2. Cloth
Text. Prentice Hall PTR. Upper Saddle River, NJ. 1991. 760p.
ISBN:0-201-14659-2, ISBN13: 978-0-201-14659-2.
Dewey:629.132/38. LCCN:91-004691.
Audience: **l,u,f.**

Hofmann-Wellenhof,   **G109.5.H64 2001**
  Bernhard, et al.
Global Positioning System: Theory and Practice. Ed. 5. Herbert
Lichtenegger & James Collins (Authors). Trade Paper. Springer.
New York, NY. 2004. XXII, 382p. ISBN:3-211-83534-2,
ISBN13: 978-3-211-83534-0. Dewey:623.89/3.
LCCN:2001-266601.
Audience: **u,f.**

Hughes, Peter C.   **TL1050.H84 2004**
Spacecraft Attitude Dynamics. Trade Paper. Dover Publications,
Inc. Mineola, NY. 2004. 592p. ISBN:0-486-43925-9, ISBN13:
978-0-486-43925-9. Dewey:629.47/42. LCCN:2004-056225.
Audience: **u,f.**

Jenkins, Dennis R.   **TL795.5.J4624 2001**
Space Shuttle: The History of the National Space Transportation
System. Ed. 3. Trade Cloth. Dennis R. Jenkins Publishing. Cape
Canaveral, FL. 2004. viii, 513p. ISBN:0-9633974-5-1, ISBN13:
978-0-9633974-5-4. Dewey:629.44/1/0973. LCCN:00-091732.
Audience: **g,l,u,f.** *Choice, 2002.*

Jensen, Gordon E. & Netzer,   **TL782**
  David W. (Editors)
Tactical Missile Propulsion. Trade Cloth. American Institute of
Aeronautics & Astronautics. Reston, VA. 1996. 529p. Progress
in Astronautics and Aeronautics Ser., Vol. 170
ISBN:1-56347-118-3, ISBN13: 978-1-56347-118-6.
Dewey:621.43/56. LCCN:95-005943.
Audience: **u,f.**

King-Hele, D. G.   **TL1080 .K55 1992**
A Tapestry of Orbits. Trade Paper. Cambridge University Press.
New York, NY. 2005. 254p. ISBN:0-521-01732-7, ISBN13:
978-0-521-01732-9. Dewey:629.43/4.
Audience: **l,u,f.**

Lambright, W. Henry   **TL789.8.U5S588 2002**
  (Editor)
Space Policy in the Twenty-First Century. Trade Cloth. Johns
Hopkins University Press. Baltimore, MD. 2002. 304p. New
Series in NASA History ISBN:0-8018-7068-2, ISBN13:
978-0-8018-7068-2. Dewey:629.4/0973. LCCN:2001-008648.
Audience: **u,f.** *Choice, 2003.*

Launius, Roger D. &   **TL785.8.L3L385 2002**
  Jenkins, Dennis R. (Editors)
To Reach the High Frontier: A History of U.S. Launch Vehicles.
Trade Cloth. University Press of Kentucky. Lexington, KY.
2002. 480p. ISBN:0-8131-2245-7, ISBN13: 978-0-8131-2245-8.
Dewey:629.47/5. LCCN:2002-011433.
Audience: **g,l,u,f.** *Choice, 2003.*

Logsdon, Tom   **TL1050.L59 1998**
Orbital Mechanics: Theory and Applications. Trade Cloth. John Wiley & Sons, Inc. Hoboken, NJ. 1997. 288p. ISBN:0-471-14636-6, ISBN13: 978-0-471-14636-0. Dewey:629.4/113. LCCN:97-006507.

Audience: **u,f.** *Choice, 1998.*

Meyer, Rudolph X.   **TL795.M48 1999**
Elements of Space Technology. Cloth Text. Elsevier Science & Technology Books. Saint Louis, MO. 1999. 329p. ISBN:0-12-492940-0, ISBN13: 978-0-12-492940-1. Dewey:629.4. LCCN:98-052665.

Audience: **u,f.**

Milne, Antony   **TL1499**
Sky Static: The Space Debris Crisis. Trade Cloth. Greenwood Publishing Group, Inc. Portsmouth, NH. 2002. 200p. ISBN:0-275-97749-8, ISBN13: 978-0-275-97749-8. Dewey:363.728/0919. LCCN:2002-067293.

Audience: **u,f.** *Choice, 2003.*

National Research Council   **GE45.R44N38 2003**
(U.S.), Committee on NASA-NOAA Transition from Research to Operations Staff (Contribution by)
Satellite Observations of the Earth's Environment: Accelerating the Transition of Research to Operations. Trade Paper. National Academies Press. Washington, DC. 2003. xvii, 163p. ISBN:0-309-08749-X, ISBN13: 978-0-309-08749-0. Dewey:551.63/54. LCCN:2003-107186.

Audience: **u,f.** *Choice, 2004.*

Roy, G. D.   **TL783.A38 2001**
Advances in Chemical Propulsion : Science to Technology. CRC Press. 2002. ISBN:0-8493-1171-3, ISBN13: 978-0-8493-1171-0.

Audience: **u,f.**

Ruzic, Neil P.   **TL799.M6**
Where the Winds Sleep : Man's Future on the Moon, a Projected History. Doubleday. 1970.

Audience: **l,u,f.**

Stoewer, Heinz &   **QB500.22**
Feuerbacher, Berndt P. (Editors)
Utilisation of Space: Basics, Fields of Usage, Future Developments. Trade Cloth. Springer. New York, NY. 2005. XX, 410p. ISBN:3-540-25200-2, ISBN13: 978-3-540-25200-9. Dewey:629.4. LCCN:2005-928158.

Audience: **u,f.**

Sutton, George P. & Biblarz,   **TL782.S8 2001**
Oscar
Rocket Propulsion Elements. Ed. 7. Trade Cloth. John Wiley & Sons, Inc. Hoboken, NJ. 2000. 768p. ISBN:0-471-32642-9, ISBN13: 978-0-471-32642-7. Dewey:629.47/5. LCCN:00-027334.

Audience: **u,f.**

Verger, Fernand, et al.   **TL788.V48 2002**
The Cambridge Encyclopedia of Space: Missions, Applications and Exploration. Isabelle Sourbes-Verger, Raymond Ghirardi & Isabelle Sourbès-Verger (Authors), Frances Brown, Stephen Lyle & Paul Reilly (Translators), Xavier Pasco (Contribution by), John M. Logsdon (Foreword by). Trade Cloth. Cambridge University Press. New York, NY. 2003. 428p. ISBN:0-521-77300-8, ISBN13: 978-0-521-77300-3. Dewey:629.4/03. LCCN:2002-067408.

Audience: **l,u,f.**

Williamson, Mark   **TL788 .W54 2001**
The Cambridge Dictionary of Space Technology. Ed. 2. Cloth Text. Cambridge University Press. New York, NY. 2001. 472p. ISBN:0-521-66077-7, ISBN13: 978-0-521-66077-8. Dewey:629.4/03. LCCN:00-059884.

Audience: **l,u,f.** *Choice, 2001.*

Wolfe, Tom   **TL551.5**
The Right Stuff. Trade Cloth. Black Dog & Leventhal Publishers, Inc. New York, NY. 2005. 304p. ISBN:1-57912-458-5, ISBN13: 978-1-57912-458-8. Dewey:629.45.

Audience: **g,l,u,f.**

Electrical and Electronic Engineering > Circuits Analysis

Alexander, Charles &   **TK454.A452 2007**
Sadiku, Matthew
Fundamentals of Electric Circuits. Ed. 3. Trade Cloth. McGraw-Hill Higher Education. Burr Ridge, IL. 2005. xxviii, 901p. ISBN:0-07-325643-9, ISBN13: 978-0-07-325643-6. Dewey:621.319/24. LCCN:2005-052270.

Audience: **l,u,f.**

Attia, John Okyere   **TK7835.A88 2004**
Electronics and Circuit Analysis Using MATLAB. CRC Press. 2004. ISBN:0-8493-1892-0, ISBN13: 978-0-8493-1892-4.

Audience: **u,f.**

Boylestad, Robert L.   **TK7867.B645 2003**
Essentials of Circuit Analysis. Cloth Text. Prentice Hall PTR. Upper Saddle River, NJ. 2003. 880p. ISBN:0-13-061655-9, ISBN13: 978-0-13-061655-5. Dewey:621.3815. LCCN:2003-043364.

Audience: **l,u,f.**

Boylestad, Robert L.   **TK454.B68 2003**
Introductory Circuit Analysis. Ed. 10. Cloth Text. Prentice Hall PTR. Upper Saddle River, NJ. 2002. 1248p. ISBN:0-13-097417-X, ISBN13: 978-0-13-097417-4. Dewey:621.319/2. LCCN:2002-019603.

Audience: **l,u,f.**

Bryant, James S.   **TK454.B766 2005**
Circuit Analysis Essentials: A Signal Processing A. Cloth Text. Thomson Delmar Learning. Albany, NY. 2005. 528p. ISBN:1-4018-5041-3, ISBN13: 978-1-4018-5041-8. Dewey:621.319/2. LCCN:2005-025290.

Audience: **l,u,f.**

Decarlo, Raymond A., et al.   **E591.P84**
Linear Circuit Analysis, Set. Ed. 2. Pen-Min Lin & Allan Kraus (Authors). Cloth Text. Oxford University Press, Inc. New York, NY. 2001. 1,578p. The Oxford Series in Electrical and Computer Engineering ISBN:0-19-515253-0, ISBN13: 978-0-19-515253-1. Dewey:973.7/5.

Audience: **u,f.**

Dorf, Richard C. &   **TK454**
Svoboda, James A.
Introduction to Electric Circuits. Ed. 6. Trade Cloth. John Wiley & Sons, Inc. Hoboken, NJ. 2003. 832p. ISBN:0-471-44795-1, ISBN13: 978-0-471-44795-5. Dewey:621.319/24. LCCN:2003-270579.

Audience: **l,u,f.**

Guru, Bhag & Warrier,   TK454.G87 2005
  Ravi K.
Electric Circuits: Analysis and Design. Cloth Text. Oxford
University Press, Inc. New York, NY. 2005. 816p. The Oxford
Series in Electrical and Computer Engineering Ser.
ISBN:0-19-517723-1, ISBN13: 978-0-19-517723-7.
Dewey:621.319/2. LCCN:2005-051839.

           Audience: **u,f.**

Hayt, William H., et al.   **TK454**
Engineering Circuit Analysis. Ed. 7. Jack Kemmerly & Steven
M. Durbin (Authors). Cloth Text. McGraw-Hill Higher
Education. Burr Ridge, IL. 2006. ISBN:0-07-326318-4, ISBN13:
978-0-07-326318-2. Dewey:621.319/2.

           Audience: **l,u,f.**

Huijsing, J. H. (Editor),   TK7814.654 .W67 2004
  et al.
Analog Circuit Design. Michiel Steyaert & Arthur H. M. van
Roermund (Editors). Trade Cloth. Springer. New York, NY.
2005. X, 406p. ISBN:1-4020-2786-9, ISBN13:
978-1-4020-2786-4. Dewey:621.3815.

           Audience: **l,u,f.**

Irwin, J. David & Nelms, R.   TK454.I78 2004
  Mark
Basic Engineering Circuit Analysis. Ed. 8. Trade Cloth. John
Wiley & Sons, Inc. Hoboken, NJ. 2004. 816p.
ISBN:0-471-48728-7, ISBN13: 978-0-471-48728-9.
Dewey:621.319/2. LCCN:2004-042293.

           Audience: **l,u,f.**

Johnson, David E., et al.   **TK454**
Electric Circuit Analysis. Ed. 3. Johnny R. Johnson, John L.
Hilburn & Peter D. Scott (Authors). Trade Cloth. John Wiley &
Sons, Inc. Hoboken, NJ. 1999. 864p. ISBN:0-471-36571-8,
ISBN13: 978-0-471-36571-6. Dewey:621.3/192.

           Audience: **l,u,f.**

Mersereau, Russell, et al.   TK7867.M39 2006
Circuit Analysis: A Systems Approach. William D. Hunt Jr. &
Joel Jackson (Authors). Cloth Text. Prentice Hall PTR. Upper
Saddle River, NJ. 2005. 464p. ISBN:0-13-093224-8, ISBN13:
978-0-13-093224-2. Dewey:621.319/2. LCCN:2005-048933.

           Audience: **l,u,f.**

Monier, Charles J.   TK454.M645 2000
Electric Circuit Analysis. Cloth Text. Prentice Hall PTR. Upper
Saddle River, NJ. 2000. 923p. ISBN:0-13-014410-X, ISBN13:
978-0-13-014410-2. Dewey:621.319/2. LCCN:00-027423.

           Audience: **l,u,f.**

Nilsson, James W. & Riedel,   TK454.N54 2004
  Susan A.
Electric Circuits. Ed. 7. Cloth Text. Prentice Hall PTR. Upper
Saddle River, NJ. 2004. 992p. ISBN:0-13-146592-9, ISBN13:
978-0-13-146592-3. Dewey:621.3192. LCCN:2004-045370.

           Audience: **l,u,f.**

Robbins, Allan & Miller,   TK454.R56 2003
  Wilhelm
Circuit Analysis: Theory and Practice. Ed. 3. Cloth Text.
Thomson Delmar Learning. Albany, NY. 2003. 1008p.
ISBN:1-4018-1156-6, ISBN13: 978-1-4018-1156-3.
Dewey:621.319/2. LCCN:2003-051418.

           Audience: **l,u,f.**

Robbins, Allan & Miller,   TK454.R5623 2003
  Wilhelm
Circuit Analysis with Devices: Theory and Practice. Ed. 2. Cloth
Text. Thomson Delmar Learning. Albany, NY. 2003. 1280p.
ISBN:1-4018-7984-5, ISBN13: 978-1-4018-7984-6.
Dewey:621.319/2. LCCN:2003-053710.

           Audience: **l,u,f.**

Stanley, William D.   TK454.S7 2003
Transform Circuit Analysis for Engineering and Technology. Ed.
5. Cloth Text. Prentice Hall PTR. Upper Saddle River, NJ. 2002.
487p. ISBN:0-13-060259-0, ISBN13: 978-0-13-060259-6.
Dewey:621.31/042. LCCN:2002-068447.

           Audience: **u,f.**

Steyaert, Michiel (Editor),   TK7874.654.A49 2002
  et al.
Analog Circuit Design. Johan H. Huijsing & Arthur H. M van
Roermund (Editors). Trade Cloth. Springer. New York, NY.
2002. 404p. ISBN:0-7923-7621-8, ISBN13: 978-0-7923-7621-7.
Dewey:621.3815. LCCN:2002-280342.

           Audience: **l,u,f.**

Sudhakar, A.   TK454.2.S889 2006
Circuits and Networks: Analysis and Synthesis. Paper Text.
McGraw-Hill Companies, The. New York, NY. 2006. 852p.
ISBN:0-07-340458-6, ISBN13: 978-0-07-340458-5.
Dewey:621.319/2. LCCN:2006-041928.

           Audience: **l,u,f.**

Thomas, Roland E. & Rosa,   TK454.T466 2004
  Albert J.
The Analysis and Design of Linear Circuits: Laplace Early. Ed.
4. Trade Cloth. John Wiley & Sons, Inc. Hoboken, NJ. 2003.
848p. ISBN:0-471-43299-7, ISBN13: 978-0-471-43299-9.
Dewey:621.319/2. LCCN:2004-268992.

           Audience: **u,f.**

Electrical and Electronic Engineering > Analog and Digital Electronics

Agarwal, Anant & Lang,   **TK7867**
  Jeffrey
Foundations of Analog and Digital Electronic Circuits. Paper
Text. Elsevier Science & Technology Books. Saint Louis, MO.
2005. 1008p. The Morgan Kaufmann Series in Computer
Architecture and Design Ser. ISBN:1-55860-735-8, ISBN13:
978-1-55860-735-4. Dewey:621.3815. LCCN:2005-047954.

           Audience: **u,f.**

Allen, Phillip E. & Holberg,   TK7874.A428 2002
  Douglas R.
CMOS Analog Circuit Design. Ed. 2. Cloth Text. Oxford
University Press, Inc. New York, NY. 2002. 800p. Series in
Electrical and Computer Engineering ISBN:0-19-511644-5,
ISBN13: 978-0-19-511644-1. Dewey:621.39/732.
LCCN:2002-020034.

           Audience: **u,f.**

Aminian, Ali &   TK7870.A527 2003
  Kazimierczuk, Marian
Electronic Devices: A Design Approach. Cloth Text. Prentice
Hall PTR. Upper Saddle River, NJ. 2003. 816p.
ISBN:0-13-013560-7, ISBN13: 978-0-13-013560-5.
Dewey:621.381. LCCN:2002-035536.

           Audience: **l,u,f.**

Beards, P. H. QC685
Analog and Digital Electronics: A First Course. Ed. 2. Trade
Paper. Prentice Hall PTR. Upper Saddle River, NJ. 2002. 672p.
ISBN:0-13-571753-1, ISBN13: 978-0-13-571753-0.
Dewey:537.5.

Audience: **l,u,f.**

Bogart, Theodore F. Jr., TK7867.B57 2004
et al.
Electronic Devices and Circuits. Ed. 6. Jeffrey S. Beasley &
Guillermo Rico (Authors). Cloth Text. Prentice Hall PTR. Upper
Saddle River, NJ. 2003. 896p. ISBN:0-13-111142-6, ISBN13:
978-0-13-111142-4. Dewey:621.3815. LCCN:2003-051282.

Audience: **l,u,f.**

Boylestad, Robert L. & TK7867.B66 2005
Nashelsky, Louis
Electronic Devices and Circuit Theory. Ed. 9. Cloth Text.
Prentice Hall PTR. Upper Saddle River, NJ. 2005. 912p.
ISBN:0-13-118905-0, ISBN13: 978-0-13-118905-8.
Dewey:621.3815. LCCN:2005-007746.

Audience: **l,u,f.** *B*

Comer, David J. & Comer, TK7874.C64623 2003
Donald T.
Fundamentals of Electronic Circuit Design. Trade Cloth. John
Wiley & Sons, Inc. Hoboken, NJ. 2002. 512p.
ISBN:0-471-41016-0, ISBN13: 978-0-471-41016-4.
Dewey:621.3815. LCCN:2002-514134.

Audience: **u,f.**

Cook, Nigel P. TK7868.D5C598 2004
Practical Digital Electronics. Cloth Text. Prentice Hall PTR.
Upper Saddle River, NJ. 2003. 448p. ISBN:0-13-111060-8,
ISBN13: 978-0-13-111060-1. Dewey:621.381.
LCCN:2003-056302.

Audience: **l,u,f.**

Dailey, Denton J. TK7871.9.D33 2001
Electronic Devices and Circuits: Discrete and Integrated. Cloth
Text. Prentice Hall PTR. Upper Saddle River, NJ. 2000. 820p.
ISBN:0-13-081110-6, ISBN13: 978-0-13-081110-3.
Dewey:621.3815/28. LCCN:99-086432.

Audience: **l,u,f.**

Floyd, Thomas L. TK7870.F52 2004
Electronic Devices (Conventional Current Version). Ed. 7. Cloth
Text. Prentice Hall PTR. Upper Saddle River, NJ. 2004. 992p.
ISBN:0-13-114080-9, ISBN13: 978-0-13-114080-6.
Dewey:621.3815. LCCN:2004-046657.

Audience: **l,u,f.**

Fortney, Lloyd R. TK7816 .F67 1987
Principles of Electronics: Analog and Digital. Cloth Text.
Oxford University Press, Inc. New York, NY. 2005. 652p.
ISBN:0-19-517863-7, ISBN13: 978-0-19-517863-0.
Dewey:621.381.

Audience: **l,u,f.**

Gray, Paul R., et al. TK7874.A588 2001
Analysis and Design of Analog Integrated Circuits. Ed. 4. Paul
J. Hurst, Stephen H. Lewis & Robert G. Meyer (Authors). Trade
Cloth. John Wiley & Sons, Inc. Hoboken, NJ. 2001. 896p.
ISBN:0-471-32168-0, ISBN13: 978-0-471-32168-2.
Dewey:621.3815. LCCN:00-043583.

Audience: **u,f.** *B*

Hambley, Allan R. TK7867.H345 2000
Electronics: A Top-down Approach. Ed. 2. Trade Cloth. Prentice
Hall PTR. Upper Saddle River, NJ. 1999. 888p.
ISBN:0-13-691982-0, ISBN13: 978-0-13-691982-7.
Dewey:621.381. LCCN:99-021128.

Audience: **l,u,f.**

Jaeger, Richard C. & TK7874
Blalock, Travis
Microelectronic Circuit Design. Ed. 2. Mixed Media, Trade
Cloth, CD-ROM. McGraw-Hill Higher Education. Burr Ridge,
IL. 2003. ISBN:0-07-250503-6, ISBN13: 978-0-07-250503-0.
Dewey:621.3/815.

Audience: **u,f.**

Jain, R. P. TK7868.D5J34 2006
Modern Digital Electronics. Paper Text. McGraw-Hill
Companies, The. New York, NY. 2006. 636p.
ISBN:0-07-340457-8, ISBN13: 978-0-07-340457-8.
Dewey:621.381. LCCN:2006-041929.

Audience: **u,f.**

Kang, Sung-Mo Steve & TK7871.99.M44K36
Leblebici, Yusuf
CMOS Digital Integrated Circuits Analysis and Design. Ed. 3.
Cloth Text. McGraw-Hill Higher Education. Burr Ridge, IL.
2002. 672p. McGraw-Hill Series in Electrical and Computer
Engineering ISBN:0-07-246053-9, ISBN13: 978-0-07-246053-7.
Dewey:621.39/5. LCCN:2002-026558.

Audience: **u,f.**

Kleitz, William TK7868.D5K55 2004
Digital Electronics: A Practical Approach. Ed. 7. Cloth Text.
Prentice Hall PTR. Upper Saddle River, NJ. 2004. 928p.
ISBN:0-13-114165-1, ISBN13: 978-0-13-114165-0.
Dewey:621.381. LCCN:2004-007371.

Audience: **u,f.**

Neamen, Donald TK7867 .N412
Microelectronic Circuit Analysis and Design. Ed. 3. Trade Cloth.
McGraw-Hill Higher Education. Burr Ridge, IL. 2006.
ISBN:0-07-328596-X, ISBN13: 978-0-07-328596-2.
Dewey:621.3815.

Audience: **u,f.**

Rabaey, Jan M., et al. TK7874.65R33 2003
Digital Integrated Circuits. Ed. 2. Anantha P. Chandrakasan &
Borivoje Nikolic (Authors). Cloth Text. Prentice Hall PTR.
Upper Saddle River, NJ. 2002. 761p. Prentice Hall Electronics
and VLSI Ser. ISBN:0-13-090996-3, ISBN13:
978-0-13-090996-1. Dewey:621.39/5. LCCN:2003-270283.

Audience: **l,u,f.**

Roden, Martin S., et al. TK7867
Electronic Design: From Concept to Reality. Ed. 4. Goldon L.
Carpenter & William R. Wieserman (Authors). Cloth Text.
Discovery Press. Los Angeles, CA. 2002. ISBN:0-9646969-8-3,
ISBN13: 978-0-9646969-8-3. Dewey:621.381/5.

Audience: **l,u,f.**

Spencer, Richard & Ghausi, TK7867.S817 2001
Mohammed
Introduction to Electronic Circuit Design. Mixed Media.
Prentice Hall PTR. Upper Saddle River, NJ. 2002. 1132p.
ISBN:0-201-36183-3, ISBN13: 978-0-201-36183-4.
Dewey:621.3815. LCCN:2001-021251.

Audience: **l,u,f.**

Formats: Web: ☐ Ebook: **e** CD/DVD-ROM: 🎿 BCL3: *B*

Streetman, Ben & Banerjee,   **TK7871.85**
  Sanjay
Solid State Electronic Devices. Ed. 6. Trade Cloth. Prentice Hall
PTR. Upper Saddle River, NJ. 2005. 608p. Prentice Hall Series
in Solid State Physical Electronics ISBN:0-13-149726-X,
ISBN13: 978-0-13-149726-9. Dewey:621.38152.
LCCN:2006-272508.

Audience: **l,u,f.**

Tokheim, Roger L.   **TK7868.D5**
Digital Electronics: Principles and Applications, Student Text
with MultiSIM CD-ROM. Ed. 6. Mixed Media, Trade Cloth,
CD-ROM. Glencoe/McGraw-Hill. Columbus, OH. 2002.
ISBN:0-07-830981-6, ISBN13: 978-0-07-830981-6.
Dewey:621.381.

Audience: **l,u,f.**

Uyemura, John P.   **TK7874.U39 2002**
Introduction to VLSI Circuits and Systems. Trade Cloth. John
Wiley & Sons, Inc. Hoboken, NJ. 2001. 656p.
ISBN:0-471-12704-3, ISBN13: 978-0-471-12704-8.
Dewey:621.39/5. LCCN:2001-026643.

Audience: **u,f.**

Electrical and Electronic Engineering > Electric Power Transmission and Distribution

Agrawal, Jai P.   **TK7881.15.A38 2001**
Power Electronic Systems: Theory and Design. Cloth Text.
Prentice Hall PTR. Upper Saddle River, NJ. 2000. 562p.
ISBN:0-13-442880-3, ISBN13: 978-0-13-442880-2.
Dewey:621.381. LCCN:00-059845.

Audience: **l,u,f.**

Anderson, Paul M.   **TK3226.A55 1995**
Analysis of Faulted Power Systems. Trade Cloth. IEEE
Computer Society Press. Los Alamitos, CA. 2001. 540p. IEEE
Press Series on Power Engineering (Was Power Systems
Engineering), Series Editor Ser., Vol. 11:Paul M. Anderson Ser.
ISBN:0-7803-1145-0, ISBN13: 978-0-7803-1145-9.
Dewey:621.319. LCCN:95-015246.

Audience: **u,f.**

Barnett, Dave   **TK1001.B275 2000**
Electric Power Generation: A Nontechnical Guide. Trade Cloth.
PennWell Corporation. Tulsa, OK. 1999. xviii, 337p.
ISBN:0-87814-753-5, ISBN13: 978-0-87814-753-3.
Dewey:621.31. LCCN:99-056998.

Audience: **g,l.** *Choice, 2000.*

Bartnikas, Ray &   **TK3301.P66 2000**
  Srivastava, K. D.
Power and Communication Cables: Theory and Applications.
Trade Cloth. IEEE Computer Society Press. Los Alamitos, CA.
2003. 880p. ISBN:0-7803-1196-5, ISBN13: 978-0-7803-1196-1.
Dewey:621.319/34. LCCN:99-018442.

Audience: **l.** *Choice, 2000.*

Bates, Regis & Bates,   **TK5101.B3153 2005**
  Marcus
Principles of Voice and Data Communications. Paper Text.

McGraw-Hill Osborne. Emeryville, CA. 2006. 816p.
ISBN:0-07-225732-6, ISBN13: 978-0-07-225732-8.
Dewey:621.382. LCCN:2005-053374.

Audience: **u,f.**

Bollen, Math H. J.   **TK1010.B65 1999**
Understanding Power Quality Problems: Voltage Sags and
Interruptions. Trade Cloth. John Wiley & Sons, Inc. Hoboken,
NJ. 1999. 672p. IEEE Press Series on Power Engineering (Was
Power Systems Engineering), Series Editor Ser., Vol. 5:Paul M.
Anderson Ser. ISBN:0-7803-4713-7, ISBN13:
978-0-7803-4713-7. Dewey:621.319. LCCN:99-023546.

Audience: **u,f.** *Choice, 2000.*

Bose, Bimal K.   **TK2781.B67 2002**
Modern Power Electronics and AC Drives. Trade Paper. Prentice
Hall PTR. Upper Saddle River, NJ. 2001. 736p.
ISBN:0-13-016743-6, ISBN13: 978-0-13-016743-9.
Dewey:621.46. LCCN:2001-032192.

Audience: **l,u,f.**

Casazza, Jack & Delea,   **HD9685**
  Frank
Understanding Electric Power Systems: An Overview of the
Technology and the Marketplace. Trade Paper. John Wiley &
Sons, Inc. Hoboken, NJ. 2003. 232p. IEEE Press Understanding
Science and Technology Series, Series Editor Ser., :Dr.
Mohamed E. El-hawary Ser. ISBN:0-471-44652-1, ISBN13:
978-0-471-44652-1. Dewey:621.319/1. LCCN:2004-297419.

Audience: **u,f.** *Choice, 2004.*

Denny, Fred I. & Dismukes,   **TK1001.D45 2002**
  David E.
Power System Operations and Electricity Markets. CRC Press.
2002. ISBN:0-8493-0813-5, ISBN13: 978-0-8493-0813-0.

Audience: **u,f.**

Glover, Sarma, et al.   **TK1005.G57 2002**
Power System Analysis and Design. Ed. 3. J. Duncan Glover &
Mulukutla S. Sarma (Authors). Cloth Text. Nelson Thomson
Learning. Scarborough, ON. 2001. 672p. Electrical Engineering
Ser. ISBN:0-534-95367-0, ISBN13: 978-0-534-95367-6.
Dewey:621.319. LCCN:2001-052617.

Audience: **l,u,f.**

Green, Martin   **TK2960**
Power to the People: Sunlight to Electriciy Using Solar Cells.
Trade Paper. University of New South Wales Press. Sydney,
NSW. 2000. 128p. ISBN:0-86840-554-X, ISBN13:
978-0-86840-554-4. Dewey:621.3/1244.

Audience: **g,l,u,f.** *Choice, 2000.*

Guru, Bhag S. & Hiziroglu,   **TK2000.G87 2000**
  Huseyin R.
Electric Machinery and Transformers. Ed. 3. Cloth Text. Oxford
University Press, Inc. New York, NY. 2000. 720p. The Oxford
Series in Electrical and Computer Engineering
ISBN:0-19-513890-2, ISBN13: 978-0-19-513890-0.
Dewey:621.31/042. LCCN:00-020034.

Audience: **u,f.**

Helms, Ronald N. &   **TK4175.H45 1991**
  Belcher, M. Clay
Lighting for Energy Efficient Luminous Environments. Ed. 2.
Cloth Text. Prentice Hall PTR. Upper Saddle River, NJ. 1991.

448p. ISBN:0-13-451568-4, ISBN13: 978-0-13-451568-7. Dewey:621.32. LCCN:90-019471.

Audience: **g,l,u,f.** *Choice, 1992.*

Kabisama, Henslay W. TK1005.K32 1993
Electrical Power Engineering. Trade Cloth. McGraw-Hill Companies, The. New York, NY. 1993. 509p. ISBN:0-07-033157-X, ISBN13: 978-0-07-033157-0. Dewey:621.31. LCCN:93-009697.

Audience: **l,u.** *Choice, 1993.*

Kothari, D.P. & Nagrath, I. J. TK1005.K685 2006
Modern Power System Analysis. Paper Text. McGraw-Hill Companies, The. New York, NY. 2006. 708p. ISBN:0-07-340455-1, ISBN13: 978-0-07-340455-4. Dewey:621.319/1. LCCN:2006-041933.

Audience: **u,f.**

Kundur, Prabha TK1005.K86 1994
Power System Stability and Control. Trade Cloth. McGraw-Hill Professional Publishing. New York, NY. 1994. 1176p. Epri Power System Engineering Ser. ISBN:0-07-035958-X, ISBN13: 978-0-07-035958-1. Dewey:621.319. LCCN:93-021456.

Audience: **u,f.**

Masters, Gilbert M. TK1005.M33 2004
Renewable and Efficient Electric Power Systems. Trade Cloth. John Wiley & Sons, Inc. Hoboken, NJ. 2004. 680p. ISBN:0-471-28060-7, ISBN13: 978-0-471-28060-6. Dewey:621.31. LCCN:2003-062035.

Audience: **g,u,f.** *Choice, 2005.*

Pabla, A. S. TK3001
Electric Power Distribution. Cloth Text. McGraw-Hill Companies, The. New York, NY. 2004. 878p. McGraw-Hill Professional Engineering Ser. ISBN:0-07-144783-0, ISBN13: 978-0-07-144783-6. Dewey:621.319. LCCN:2004-061623.

Audience: **u,f.** *Choice, 2005.*

Pansini, Anthony J. TK3001
Guide to Electrical Power Distribution Systems. Prentice-Hall. 1992. ISBN:0-13-059460-1, ISBN13: 978-0-13-059460-0.

Audience: **g,l,u,f.**

Pansini, Anthony J. & Smalling, Kenneth D. TK1001.P35 2005
Guide to Electric Power Generation. Ed. 3. Trade Cloth. Fairmont Press, Inc. Lilburn, GA. 2005. ISBN:0-88173-524-8, ISBN13: 978-0-88173-524-6. Dewey:621.31. LCCN:2005-049470.

Audience: **l,u,f.**

Pete, Geradino A. TK1001.P47 1992
Electric Power Systems Manual. Trade Cloth. McGraw-Hill Companies, The. New York, NY. 1992. xiii, 231p. ISBN:0-07-049530-0, ISBN13: 978-0-07-049530-2. Dewey:621.319/1. LCCN:91-048339.

Audience: **u,f.** *Choice, 1993.*

Rashid, M. H. TK7881.15.R37 2003
Power Electronics: Circuits, Devices and Applications. Ed. 3. Cloth Text. Prentice Hall PTR. Upper Saddle River, NJ. 2003. 912p. ISBN:0-13-101140-5, ISBN13: 978-0-13-101140-3. Dewey:621.317. LCCN:2003-048622.

Audience: **l,u,f.**

Rosengrant, Martha TK5101.R595 2007
Introduction to Telecommunications. Ed. 2. Trade Cloth. Pearson Education. Boston, MA. 2006. 784p. ISBN:0-13-112615-6, ISBN13: 978-0-13-112615-2. Dewey:384. LCCN:2006-046002.

Audience: **l,u,f.**

Saadat, Hadi TK1001
Power Systems Analysis. Ed. 2. Trade Paper. McGraw-Hill Primis Custom Publishing. Hightstown, NJ. 2002. 712p. ISBN:0-07-284869-3, ISBN13: 978-0-07-284869-4. Dewey:621.31.

Audience: **u,f.**

Saccomanno, Fabio TK1007
Electric Power Systems: Analysis and Control. Trade Cloth. John Wiley & Sons, Inc. Hoboken, NJ. 2003. 744p. IEEE Press Series on Power Engineering, Series Editor Ser., :Paul M. Anderson Ser. ISBN:0-471-23439-7, ISBN13: 978-0-471-23439-5. Dewey:621.3/1.

Audience: **u,f.** *Choice, 2003.*

Schiff, Maurice TK5102.5.S355 2006
Introduction to Communication Systems Simulation. Trade Cloth. Artech House, Inc. Norwood, MA. 2006. 238p. Artech House Mobile Communications Library ISBN:1-59693-002-0, ISBN13: 978-1-59693-002-5. Dewey:621.382. LCCN:2005-057173.

Audience: **u,f.**

Short, Tom TK3001.S47 2003
Electric Power Distribution Handbook. CRC Press. 2004. ISBN:0-8493-1791-6, ISBN13: 978-0-8493-1791-0.

Audience: **u,f.**

Skvarenina, Timothy L. & DeWitt, William E. TK1001.S564 2004
Electrical Power and Controls. Ed. 2. Cloth Text. Prentice Hall PTR. Upper Saddle River, NJ. 2004. 752p. ISBN:0-13-113045-5, ISBN13: 978-0-13-113045-6. Dewey:621.4. LCCN:2004-000228.

Audience: **l,u,f.**

Smeloff, Edward & Asmus, Peter HD9685.U5S55 1997
Reinventing Electric Utilities: Competition, Citizen Action and Clean Power. Amory B. Lovins (Foreword by). Trade Paper. Island Press. Washington, DC. 1996. 254p. ISBN:1-55963-455-3, ISBN13: 978-1-55963-455-7. Dewey:333.7/932/0973. LCCN:96-031799.

Audience: **g,l,u,f.** *Choice, 1997.*

Von Meier, Alexandra TK1005.M37 2006
Electric Power Systems: A Conceptual Introduction. Trade Cloth. John Wiley & Sons, Inc. Hoboken, NJ. 2006. 309p. ISBN:0-471-17859-4, ISBN13: 978-0-471-17859-0. Dewey:621.31. LCCN:2005-056773.

Audience: **u,f.**

Willis, H. Lee & Scott, Walter G. (Contribution by) TK1041.W55 2000
Distributed Power Generation: Planning and Evaluation, Vol. 10. Paper over Boards. Marcel Dekker Inc. New York, NY. 2000. 616p. Power Engineering Ser. ISBN:0-8247-0336-7, ISBN13: 978-0-8247-0336-3. Dewey:621.31. LCCN:99-054218.

Audience: **g,l,u,f.** *Choice, 2000.*

Formats: Web: ☐   Ebook: 🄴   CD/DVD-ROM: 💾   BCL3: *B*

Yamayee, Zia A. & Bala,   TK1001.Y36 1994
  Juan L. Jr.
Electromechanical Energy Devices and Power Systems. Trade
Cloth. John Wiley & Sons, Inc. Hoboken, NJ. 1993. 528p.
ISBN:0-471-57217-9, ISBN13: 978-0-471-57217-6.
Dewey:621.319. LCCN:93-005529.

Audience: **u,f.** *Choice, 1994.*

Electrical and Electronic Engineering >
Electric Power Transmission and
Distribution > Transformers, Motors, and
Generators

Caisse, Arthur J. Jr.   TK2182
Electric Motors. Ed. 1. Trade Cloth. Prentice Hall PTR. Upper
Saddle River, NJ. 2001. ISBN:0-13-362971-6, ISBN13:
978-0-13-362971-2. Dewey:321.31/042.

Audience: **l,u,f.**

Fitzgerald, Arthur E., et al.   TK2181.F5 2002
Electric Machinery. Ed. 6. Stephen D. Umans & Charles
Kingsley (Authors). Cloth Text. McGraw-Hill Higher Education.
Burr Ridge, IL. 2002. 704p. McGraw-Hill Series in Electrical
Engineering ISBN:0-07-366009-4, ISBN13: 978-0-07-366009-7.
Dewey:621.31/042. LCCN:2002-070988.

Audience: **l,u,f.** ℬ

Keljik, Jeff   TK2851.K444 2006
Electric Motors and Motor Controls. Ed. 2. Cloth Text.
Thomson Delmar Learning. Albany, NY. 2006. 416p.
ISBN:1-4018-9841-6, ISBN13: 978-1-4018-9841-0.
Dewey:621.46. LCCN:2006-002546.

Audience: **l,u,f.**

Patrick, Dale R.   TK2000
Rotating Electrical Machines and Power Systems. Ed. 2.
Fairmont. 1997. ISBN:0-13-268665-1, ISBN13:
978-0-13-268665-5.

Audience: **l,u,f.**

Toliyat, Hamid A.   TK2511
Handbook of Electric Motors. Ed. 2. Paper over Boards. Marcel
Dekker Inc. New York, NY. 2004. 850p. Environmental and
Energy Engineering Ser. ISBN:0-8247-4105-6, ISBN13:
978-0-8247-4105-1. Dewey:621.46.

Audience: **l,u,f.**

Trzynadlowski, Andrzej M.   TK2785.T75 2001
Control of Induction Motors. Trade Cloth. Elsevier Science &
Technology Books. Saint Louis, MO. 2000. 228p. Academic
Press Series in Engineering ISBN:0-12-701510-8, ISBN13:
978-0-12-701510-1. Dewey:621.46. LCCN:00-104379.

Audience: **u,f.** *Choice, 2001.*

Valentine, Richard   TK7881.2.M68 1998
Motor Control Electronics Handbook. Trade Cloth. McGraw-Hill
Professional Publishing. New York, NY. 1998. 700p.
McGraw-Hill Handbooks Ser. ISBN:0-07-066810-8, ISBN13:
978-0-07-066810-2. Dewey:621.46. LCCN:98-005074.

Audience: **u,f.** *Choice, 1999.*

Electrical and Electronic Engineering >
Telecommunications

Anandalingam, G. &   TK5102.5.T3953 2003
  Raghavan, S. (Editors)
Telecommunications Network Design and Management. Trade
Cloth. Springer. New York, NY. 2002. 352p. Operations
Research/Computer Science Interfaces Ser., Vol. 23
ISBN:1-4020-7318-6, ISBN13: 978-1-4020-7318-2.
Dewey:621.382/1. LCCN:2002-035703.

Audience: **u,f.**

Barry, John R., et al.   TK5103.7.L44 2003
Digital Communication. Ed. 3. Edward A. Lee & David G.
Messerschmitt (Authors). Trade Cloth. Springer. New York, NY.
2003. 856p. ISBN:0-7923-7548-3, ISBN13: 978-0-7923-7548-7.
Dewey:621.382. LCCN:2003-054667.

Audience: **u,f.**

Beasley, Jeffrey S. & Miller,   TK5101.B327 2005
  Gary M.
Modern Electronic Communication. Ed. 8. Cloth Text. Prentice
Hall PTR. Upper Saddle River, NJ. 2004. 960p.
ISBN:0-13-113037-4, ISBN13: 978-0-13-113037-1.
Dewey:621.382. LCCN:2004-040080.

Audience: **l,u,f.**

Carlson, A. Bruce, et al.   TK5102.5.C3 2002
Communication Systems. Ed. 4. P. B. Crilly & Janet Rutledge
(Authors). Cloth Text. McGraw-Hill Higher Education. Burr
Ridge, IL. 2001. 864p. Electrical Engineering Ser.
ISBN:0-07-011127-8, ISBN13: 978-0-07-011127-1.
Dewey:621.382/23. LCCN:2001-030273.

Audience: **u,f.**

Couch, Leon W. II   TK5101.C69 2001
Digital and Analog Communication Systems. Ed. 6. Cloth Text.
Prentice Hall PTR. Upper Saddle River, NJ. 2000. 758p.
ISBN:0-13-081223-4, ISBN13: 978-0-13-081223-0.
Dewey:621.38/0413. LCCN:00-029131.

Audience: **l,u,f.**

Freeman, Roger L.   TK5103.F68 2004
Telecommunication System Engineering. Ed. 4. Trade Cloth.
John Wiley & Sons, Inc. Hoboken, NJ. 2004. 991p. Wiley
Series in Telecommunications and Signal Processing Ser.
ISBN:0-471-45133-9, ISBN13: 978-0-471-45133-4.
Dewey:621.382. LCCN:2003-063763.

Audience: **u,f.** *Choice, 1996.*

Haykin, Simon   TK5101.H37 2000
Communication Systems. Ed. 4. Trade Cloth. John Wiley &
Sons, Inc. Hoboken, NJ. 2000. 840p. ISBN:0-471-17869-1,
ISBN13: 978-0-471-17869-9. Dewey:621.382.
LCCN:99-042977.

Audience: **u,f.**

Haykin, Simon & Moher,   TK5101.A1
  Michael
An Introduction to Digital and Analog Communications. Ed. 2.
Trade Cloth. John Wiley & Sons, Inc. Hoboken, NJ. 2006. 515p.
ISBN:0-471-43222-9, ISBN13: 978-0-471-43222-7.
Dewey:621.382. LCCN:2006-276222.

Audience: **u,f.**

Kurzweil, Jack   TK5103.7.K87 2000
An Introduction to Digital Communications. Ed. 1. Trade Cloth.
John Wiley & Sons, Inc. Hoboken, NJ. 1999. 560p.
ISBN:0-471-15772-4, ISBN13: 978-0-471-15772-4.
Dewey:621.382. LCCN:99-027789.

Audience: **u,f.**

Lathi, Bhagwandas P.   TK5101.L333 1998
Modern Digital and Analog Communication Systems. Ed. 3.
Cloth Text. Oxford University Press, Inc. New York, NY. 1998.
796p. The Oxford Series in Electrical and Computer
Engineering ISBN:0-19-511009-9, ISBN13: 978-0-19-511009-8.
Dewey:621.3/82. LCCN:97-016040.

Audience: **u,f.** *B*

Proakis, John G. & Salehi,   TK5101.P75 2002
  Masoud
Communication Systems Engineering. Ed. 2. Cloth Text.
Prentice Hall PTR. Upper Saddle River, NJ. 2001. 801p.
ISBN:0-13-061793-8, ISBN13: 978-0-13-061793-4.
Dewey:621.382. LCCN:2001-036971.

Audience: **l,u,f.**

Rappaport, Theodore   TK5103.2.R37 2002
Wireless Communications: Principles and Practice. Ed. 2. Trade
Cloth. Prentice Hall PTR. Upper Saddle River, NJ. 2001. 736p.
Prentice Hall Communications Engineering and Emerging
Technologies Ser. ISBN:0-13-042232-0, ISBN13:
978-0-13-042232-3. Dewey:621.382. LCCN:2002-279109.

Audience: **l,u,f.**

Roden, Martin S.   TK5105 .R64 2003
Analog and Digital Communication Systems. Ed. 5. Cloth Text.
Discovery Press. Los Angeles, CA. 2002. 584p.
ISBN:0-9646969-7-5, ISBN13: 978-0-9646969-7-6.
Dewey:621.38.

Audience: **l,u,f.** *B*

Sklar, Bernard   TK5103.7
Digital Communications: Fundamentals and Applications. Ed. 2.
Trade Cloth. Prentice Hall PTR. Upper Saddle River, NJ. 2001.
1104p. ISBN:0-13-084788-7, ISBN13: 978-0-13-084788-1.
Dewey:621.382. LCCN:00-007476.

Audience: **l,u,f.**

Snyder, Gordon F.   TK5101.S59 2003
Introduction to Telecommunications Networks. Paper Text.
Thomson Delmar Learning. Albany, NY. 2002. 352p.
ISBN:1-4018-6486-4, ISBN13: 978-1-4018-6486-6.
Dewey:621.382/1. LCCN:2002-075054.

Audience: **l,u,f.**

Stern, Harold P. &   TK5103.S72 2004
  Mahmoud, Samy
Communication Systems: Analysis and Design. Cloth Text.
Prentice Hall PTR. Upper Saddle River, NJ. 2003. 552p.
ISBN:0-13-040268-0, ISBN13: 978-0-13-040268-4.
Dewey:621.382. LCCN:2003-062300.

Audience: **l,u,f.**

Tranter, William, et al.   TK5102.5.P673 2003
Principles of Communication Systems Simulation with Wireless
Applications. Theodore S. Rappaport, Kurt L. Kosbar & K. Sam
Shanmugan (Authors). Trade Paper. Prentice Hall PTR. Upper
Saddle River, NJ. 2003. 800p. Prentice Hall Communications
Engineering and Emerging Technologies Ser., Vol. 16

ISBN:0-13-494790-8, ISBN13: 978-0-13-494790-7.
Dewey:621.382/01/1. LCCN:2003-063403.

Audience: **l,u,f.**

Young, Paul H.   TK5101.Y68 2004
Electronic Communication Techniques. Ed. 5. Trade Cloth.
Prentice Hall PTR. Upper Saddle River, NJ. 2003. 960p.
ISBN:0-13-048285-4, ISBN13: 978-0-13-048285-3.
Dewey:621.382. LCCN:2003-042543.

Audience: **l,u,f.**

Electrical and Electronic Engineering > Telecommunications > Data Transmission and Distribution

Aboul-Magd, Osama S.   TK5105.5
High Performance Networks. Trade Cloth. John Wiley & Sons,
Inc. Hoboken, NJ. 2007. 500p. ISBN:0-471-65265-2, ISBN13:
978-0-471-65265-6. Dewey:004.6.

Audience: **u,f.**

Anderson, Harry R.   TK5103.4.A53 2003
Fixed Broadband Wireless System Design. Trade Cloth. John
Wiley & Sons, Inc. Hoboken, NJ. 2003. 528p.
ISBN:0-470-84438-8, ISBN13: 978-0-470-84438-0.
Dewey:621.38456. LCCN:2002-033360.

Audience: **u,f.**

Bates, Regis Bud J.   TK5103.4.B38 2002
Broadband Telecommunications Handbook. Ed. 2. Trade Paper.
McGraw-Hill Professional Publishing. New York, NY. 2002.
805p. Professional Telecom Ser. ISBN:0-07-139851-1, ISBN13:
978-0-07-139851-0. Dewey:384. LCCN:2002-021281.

Audience: **u,f.**

Chen, H. -H. & Guizani,   TK5103.2
  Mohsen
Next Generation Wireless Systems and Networks. Trade Cloth.
John Wiley & Sons, Inc. Hoboken, NJ. 2006. 512p.
ISBN:0-470-02434-8, ISBN13: 978-0-470-02434-8.
Dewey:621.3. LCCN:2006-298187.

Audience: **u,f.**

Di Benedetto,   TK5103.2
  Maria-Gabriella & Giancola, Guerino
Understanding Ultra Wide Band Radio Fundamentals. Trade
Paper. Prentice Hall PTR. Upper Saddle River, NJ. 2004. 528p.
Prentice Hall Communications Engineering and Emerging
Technologies Ser. ISBN:0-13-148003-0, ISBN13:
978-0-13-148003-2. Dewey:621.384. LCCN:2005-273502.

Audience: **l,u,f.**

Forouzan, Behrouz A.   TK5105
Data Communications and Networking. Ed. 3. Trade Cloth.
McGraw-Hill Higher Education. Burr Ridge, IL. 2003. 944p.
ISBN:0-07-292354-7, ISBN13: 978-0-07-292354-4.
Dewey:004.6. LCCN:2003-011267.

Audience: **u,f.**

Kota, Sastri L., et al.   TK5103.4885.K68 2003
Broadband Satellite Communications for Internet Access. Kaveh
Pahlavan & Pentti A. Leppanen (Authors). Trade Cloth.

Springer. New York, NY. 2003. 456p. ISBN:1-4020-7659-2, ISBN13: 978-1-4020-7659-6. Dewey:004.67/8. LCCN:2003-063088.

Audience: **u,f.**

Kurose, James F. & Ross,   **TK5105.875.I57K88**
Keith W.
Computer Networking: A Top-down Approach Featuring the Internet. Ed. 3. Cloth Text. Addison-Wesley Longman, Inc. Boston, MA. 2004. 848p. ISBN:0-321-22735-2, ISBN13: 978-0-321-22735-5. Dewey:004.67/8. LCCN:2004-044284.

Audience: **u,f.**

Lang, Jack   **TK7872.M25**
Applications of Ultra Wide Band Wireless. Trade Cloth. John Wiley & Sons, Inc. Hoboken, NJ. 2005. 256p. ISBN:0-470-09243-2, ISBN13: 978-0-470-09243-9. Dewey:621.3/84.

Audience: **u,f.**

Lee, Byeong Gi & Kim,   **TK5103.4.L44 2002**
Woo-June
Integrated Broadband Networks: TCP/IP, ATM, SDH/SONET, and WDM/Optics. Trade Cloth. Artech House, Inc. Norwood, MA. 2002. 605p. Telecommunications Library ISBN:1-58053-163-6, ISBN13: 978-1-58053-163-4. Dewey:621.382. LCCN:2002-023674.

Audience: **u,f.**

Nekoogar, Faranak   **TK5103.4.N45 2005**
Ultra-Wideband Communications: Fundamentals and Applications. Trade Cloth. Prentice Hall PTR. Upper Saddle River, NJ. 2005. 240p. ISBN:0-13-146326-8, ISBN13: 978-0-13-146326-4. Dewey:621.382. LCCN:2005-018370.

Audience: **l,u,f.**

Oppermann, Ian (Author,   **TK5102.9**
Editor)
UWB: Theory and Applications. Matti Hämäläinen & Jari Iinatti (Editors). Trade Cloth. John Wiley & Sons, Inc. Hoboken, NJ. 2004. 248p. ISBN:0-470-86917-8, ISBN13: 978-0-470-86917-8. Dewey:621.3/822.

Audience: **u,f.**

Reed, Jeffrey H.   **TK5103.4**
An Introduction to Ultra Wideband Communication Systems. Trade Cloth. Prentice Hall PTR. Upper Saddle River, NJ. 2005. 504p. Prentice Hall Communications Engineering and Emerging Technologies Ser. ISBN:0-13-148103-7, ISBN13: 978-0-13-148103-9. Dewey:621.38216. LCCN:2004-117283.

Audience: **l,u,f.**

Siwiak, Kazimierz &   **TK6550**
McKeown, Debra
Ultra-Wideband Radio Technology. Trade Cloth. John Wiley & Sons, Inc. Hoboken, NJ. 2004. 264p. ISBN:0-470-85931-8, ISBN13: 978-0-470-85931-5. Dewey:621.384. LCCN:2005-270728.

Audience: **u,f.**

Stallings, William   **TK5105.S73 2003**
Data and Computer Communications. Ed. 7. Cloth Text. Prentice Hall PTR. Upper Saddle River, NJ. 2003. 864p. ISBN:0-13-100681-9, ISBN13: 978-0-13-100681-2. Dewey:004.6. LCCN:2003-051281.

Audience: **u,f.**

Electrical and Electronic Engineering > Computer Networks

Dally, William James &   **TK5105.5.D327 2003**
Towles, Brian Patrick
Principles and Practices of Interconnection Networks. Cloth Text. Elsevier Science & Technology Books. Saint Louis, MO. 2003. 550p. The Morgan Kaufmann Series in Computer Architecture and Design Ser. ISBN:0-12-200751-4, ISBN13: 978-0-12-200751-4. Dewey:004.6/5. LCCN:2003-058915.

Audience: **u,f.**

Forouzan, Behrouz A.   **TK5105**
Data Communications Networking. Ed. 4. Trade Cloth. McGraw-Hill Higher Education. Burr Ridge, IL. 2006. xxxiv, 1134p. McGraw-Hill Forouzan Networking Ser. ISBN:0-07-325032-5, ISBN13: 978-0-07-325032-8. Dewey:004.6. LCCN:2006-000013.

Audience: **u,f.**

Peterson, Larry L. & Davie,   **TK5015.5.P479 2003**
Bruce S.
Computer Networks: A Systems Approach. Ed. 3. Cloth Text. Elsevier Science & Technology Books. Saint Louis, MO. 2003. 813p. The Morgan Kaufmann Series in Networking ISBN:1-55860-832-X, ISBN13: 978-1-55860-832-0. Dewey:004.6/5. LCCN:2003-047589.

Audience: **u,f.**

Pióro, Michal & Medhi,   **TK5101**
Deepankar
Routing, Flow, and Capacity Design in Communication and Computer Networks. Cloth Text. Elsevier Science & Technology Books. Saint Louis, MO. 2004. 800p. The Morgan Kaufmann Series in Networking Ser. ISBN:0-12-557189-5, ISBN13: 978-0-12-557189-0. Dewey:004.6/6. LCCN:2004-301909.

Audience: **u,f.**

Price, Ron   **TK5105.78.P75 2007**
Fundamentals of Wireless Networking. Paper Text. McGraw-Hill School Education Group. Columbus, OH. 2006. 672p. ISBN:0-07-225668-0, ISBN13: 978-0-07-225668-0. Dewey:004.6/8. LCCN:2006-040882.

Audience: **u,f.**

Stallings, William   **TK5105.5.S725 2004**
Computer Networking with Internet Protocols. Cloth Text. Prentice Hall PTR. Upper Saddle River, NJ. 2003. 656p. ISBN:0-13-141098-9, ISBN13: 978-0-13-141098-5. Dewey:004.6/78. LCCN:2004-295130.

Audience: **l,u,f.**

Tanenbaum, Andrew   **TK5105.5.T36 2002**
Computer Networks. Ed. 4. Trade Cloth. Prentice Hall PTR. Upper Saddle River, NJ. 2002. 912p. ISBN:0-13-066102-3, ISBN13: 978-0-13-066102-9. Dewey:004.6. LCCN:2002-029263.

Audience: **u,f.**

Electrical and Electronic Engineering > Antenna Theory

Balanis, Constantine A.   **TK7871.6**
Antenna Theory: Analysis and Design. Ed. 3. Trade Cloth. John Wiley & Sons, Inc. Hoboken, NJ. 2005. 1136p. ISBN:0-471-66782-X, ISBN13: 978-0-471-66782-7. Dewey:621.382/4. LCCN:2005-041794.

Audience: **u,f.** **B**

Boyle, Kevin   **TK7871.6**
Antennas for Multi-band RF Front-end Modules. Trade Paper. IOS Press. Amsterdam, 2004. 339p. ISBN:90-407-2549-7, ISBN13: 978-90-407-2549-4. Dewey:621.3824.

Audience: **u,f.**

Chandran, Satish (Editor)   **TK7871.67.A33C49**
Adaptive Antenna Arrays. Trade Cloth. Springer. New York, NY. 2004. XII, 660p. Signals and Communication Technology Ser. ISBN:3-540-20199-8, ISBN13: 978-3-540-20199-1. Dewey:621.382/4. LCCN:2003-067351.

Audience: **u,f.**

Drabowitch, Serge, et al.   **TK7871.6**
Modern Antennas. Ed. 2. Hugh Griffiths, Albert Papiernik, Bradford Smith & J. Encinas (Authors). Trade Cloth. Springer. New York, NY. 2005. xx, 689p. ISBN:1-4020-3216-1, ISBN13: 978-1-4020-3216-5. Dewey:621.382/4. LCCN:2006-273254.

Audience: **u,f.**

Elliott, Robert S.   **TK7871.6E45 2003**
Antenna Theory and Design. Trade Cloth. John Wiley & Sons, Inc. Hoboken, NJ. 2003. 624p. IEEE Press Series on Electromagnetic Wave Theory, Series Editor Ser., :Donald G. Dudley Ser. ISBN:0-471-44996-2, ISBN13: 978-0-471-44996-6. Dewey:621.382/4. LCCN:2003-277255.

Audience: **u,f.**

Imbriale, W. A.   **TL3026.I46 2003**
Large Antennas of the Deep Space Network. Trade Cloth. John Wiley & Sons, Inc. Hoboken, NJ. 2003. 302p. JPL Deep-Space Communications and Navigation Ser. ISBN:0-471-44537-1, ISBN13: 978-0-471-44537-1. Dewey:621.382/54. LCCN:2002-191014.

Audience: **u,f.**

Josefsson, Lars & Persson, Patrik   **TX7871.6**
Conformal Array Antenna Theory and Design. Trade Cloth. John Wiley & Sons, Inc. Hoboken, NJ. 2006. 488p. IEEE Press Series on Electromagnetic Wave Theory Ser. ISBN:0-471-46584-4, ISBN13: 978-0-471-46584-3. Dewey:621.382/4. LCCN:2006-530414.

Audience: **u,f.**

Kraus, John Daniel & Marhefka, Ronald J.   **TK6565.A6K73 2002**
Antennas for All Applications. Ed. 3. Paper Text. McGraw-Hill Higher Education. Burr Ridge, IL. 2002. xviii, 938p. McGraw-Hill Series in Electrical and Computer Engineering ISBN:0-07-112240-0, ISBN13: 978-0-07-112240-5. Dewey:621.382/4. LCCN:2001-030613.

Audience: **u,f.**

Kraus, John D. & Marhefka, Ronald J.   **TK6565.A6K73 2002**
Antennas. Ed. 3. Cloth Text. McGraw-Hill Higher Education. Burr Ridge, IL. 2001. 960p. Electrical Engineering Ser. ISBN:0-07-232103-2, ISBN13: 978-0-07-232103-6. Dewey:621.382/4. LCCN:2001-030613.

Audience: **u,f.**

Makarov, Sergey N.   **TK6565.A6M283 2002**
Antenna and EM Modeling with MatLab. Trade Cloth. John Wiley & Sons, Inc. Hoboken, NJ. 2002. 288p. ISBN:0-471-21876-6, ISBN13: 978-0-471-21876-0. Dewey:621.382/4/0113. LCCN:2002-027225.

Audience: **u,f.**

Milligan, Thomas A.   **TK7871.6.M54 2005**
Modern Antenna Design. Ed. 2. Trade Cloth. John Wiley & Sons, Inc. Hoboken, NJ. 2005. 632p. ISBN:0-471-45776-0, ISBN13: 978-0-471-45776-3. Dewey:621.382/4. LCCN:2004-059098.

Audience: **u,f.** **B**

Miron, Douglas B.   **TK6565.A6M555 2006**
Small Antenna Design. Paper Text. Elsevier Science & Technology Books. Saint Louis, MO. 2006. 304p. Communications Engineering Ser. ISBN:0-7506-7861-5, ISBN13: 978-0-7506-7861-2. Dewey:621.384/135. LCCN:2005-033797.

Audience: **u,f.**

Rogstad, David H., et al.   **TL3026.R64 2003**
Antenna Arraying Techniques in the Deep Space Network. Alexander Mileant & Timothy T. Pham (Authors). Trade Cloth. John Wiley & Sons, Inc. Hoboken, NJ. 2003. 166p. JPL Deep-Space Communications and Navigation Ser. ISBN:0-471-46799-5, ISBN13: 978-0-471-46799-1. Dewey:629.47/43/0973. LCCN:2003-049656.

Audience: **u,f.**

Sarkar, Tapan, et al.   **TK7871.67.A33S27**
Smart Antennas. Michael Wicks, Robert J. Bonneau & Magdalena Salazar-Palma (Authors). Trade Cloth. John Wiley & Sons, Inc. Hoboken, NJ. 2003. 472p. Wiley Series in Microwave and Optical Engineering ISBN:0-471-21010-2, ISBN13: 978-0-471-21010-8. Dewey:621.382/4. LCCN:2002-032424.

Audience: **u,f.**

Saunders, Simon R.   **TK7871.6.S28 1999**
Antennas and Propagation for Wireless Communication Systems. Trade Cloth. John Wiley & Sons, Inc. Hoboken, NJ. 1999. 426p. ISBN:0-471-98609-7, ISBN13: 978-0-471-98609-6. Dewey:621.382/4. LCCN:99-023322.

Audience: **u,f.**

Schantz, Hans   **TK7871.67.U45S33**
The Art and Science of Ultra-Wideband Antennas. Trade Cloth. Artech House, Inc. Norwood, MA. 2005. 340p. Artech House Antennas and Propagation Library ISBN:1-58053-888-6, ISBN13: 978-1-58053-888-6. Dewey:621.384/135. LCCN:2005-045270.

Audience: **u,f.**

Visser, Hubregt   TK7871.6
Array and Phased Array Antenna Basics. Trade Cloth. John
Wiley & Sons, Inc. Hoboken, NJ. 2005. 376p.
ISBN:0-470-87117-2, ISBN13: 978-0-470-87117-1.
Dewey:621.3824. LCCN:2005-283917.

Audience: **u,f.**

Wong, Kin-Lu   TK7871.67.M5W65 2002
Compact and Broadband Microstrip Antennas. Trade Cloth. John
Wiley & Sons, Inc. Hoboken, NJ. 2002. 344p. Wiley Series in
Microwave and Optical Engineering, Vol. 131
ISBN:0-471-41717-3, ISBN13: 978-0-471-41717-0.
Dewey:621.381/33. LCCN:2001-049241.

Audience: **u,f.**

Wong, Kin-Lu   TK7871.67.M5W6524
Planar Antennas for Wireless Communications. Trade Cloth.
John Wiley & Sons, Inc. Hoboken, NJ. 2003. 320p. Wiley
Series in Microwave and Optical Engineering
ISBN:0-471-26611-6, ISBN13: 978-0-471-26611-2.
Dewey:621.382/4. LCCN:2002-031135.

Audience: **u,f.**

Zhi Ning, Chen & Michael   TK7871.67.U45
  Yan Wah, Chia
Broadband Planar Antennas: Design and Applications. Trade
Cloth. John Wiley & Sons, Inc. Hoboken, NJ. 2006. 258p.
ISBN:0-470-87174-1, ISBN13: 978-0-470-87174-4.
Dewey:621.384/135. LCCN:2005-026868.

Audience: **u,f.**

Electrical and Electronic Engineering >
Microwaves

Chen, Lin-Feng, et al.   TK7876
Microwave Electronics: Measurement and Materials
Characterization. V. K. Varadan, V. V. Varadan, C. P. Neo & C.
K. Ong (Authors). Trade Cloth. John Wiley & Sons, Inc.
Hoboken, NJ. 2004. 552p. ISBN:0-470-84492-2, ISBN13:
978-0-470-84492-2. Dewey:621.3813. LCCN:2004-274185.

Audience: **u,f.**

Collin, Robert E.   TK7876.C645 2001
Foundations for Microwave Engineering. Ed. 2. Trade Cloth.
John Wiley & Sons, Inc. Hoboken, NJ. 2001. 944p. The
IEEE/OUP Series on Electromagnetic Wave Theory (Formerly
IEEE Only), Series Editor Ser., Vol. 11:Donald G. Dudley Ser.
ISBN:0-7803-6031-1, ISBN13: 978-0-7803-6031-0.
Dewey:621.381/3. LCCN:00-053874.

Audience: **u,f.**

Das, Annapurna & Das,   TK7876.D36 2006
  Sisir K.
Microwave Engineering. Paper Text. McGraw-Hill Companies,
The. New York, NY. 2006. 528p. ISBN:0-07-352950-8, ISBN13:
978-0-07-352950-9. Dewey:621.381/3. LCCN:2006-041924.

Audience: **u,f.**

Datta, Asim Kumar &   TP371.8.H36 2001
  Anantheswaran, R. C. (Editors)
The Handbook of Microwave Technology, Vol. 109. Paper over
Boards. Marcel Dekker Inc. New York, NY. 2001. 536p. Food
Science and Technology Ser. ISBN:0-8247-0490-8, ISBN13:
978-0-8247-0490-2. Dewey:664. LCCN:2001-028557.

Audience: **u,f.**

Nusinovich, Gregory S.   TK7876.M62 2004
Modern Microwave and Millimeter-Wave Power Electronics.
Robert J. Barker, Neville C. Luhmann & John H. Booske
(Editors). Trade Cloth. John Wiley & Sons, Inc. Hoboken, NJ.
2005. 872p. ISBN:0-471-68372-8, ISBN13: 978-0-471-68372-8.
Dewey:621.381/3. LCCN:2004-059334.

Audience: **u,f.**

Pozar, David M.   TK7876.P69 2005
Microwave Engineering. Ed. 3. Trade Cloth. John Wiley &
Sons, Inc. Hoboken, NJ. 2004. 720p. ISBN:0-471-44878-8,
ISBN13: 978-0-471-44878-5. Dewey:621.381/3.
LCCN:2003-065001.

Audience: **u,f.**

Santos, Hector J. de los   TK7876.S28 2004
Introduction to Microelectromechanical Microwave Systems. Ed.
2. Trade Cloth. Artech House, Inc. Norwood, MA. 2004. 277p.
Artech House MEMS and Sensors Library ISBN:1-58053-871-1,
ISBN13: 978-1-58053-871-8. Dewey:621.381/3.
LCCN:2004-052959.

Audience: **u,f.**

Vendelin, George D., et al.   TK7876.V47 2005
Microwave Circuit Design Using Linear and Nonlinear
Techniques. Ed. 2. Anthony M. Pavio & Ulrich L. Rohde
(Authors). Trade Cloth. John Wiley & Sons, Inc. Hoboken, NJ.
2005. 1080p. ISBN:0-471-41479-4, ISBN13:
978-0-471-41479-7. Dewey:621.381/32. LCCN:2004-057100.
Audience: **u,f.** *Choice, 1991.*

White, Joseph F.   TK7876.W4897 2004
High Frequency Techniques: An Introduction to RF and
Microwave Engineering. Trade Cloth. John Wiley & Sons, Inc.
Hoboken, NJ. 2004. 528p. ISBN:0-471-45591-1, ISBN13:
978-0-471-45591-2. Dewey:621.384/12. LCCN:2003-010753.
Audience: **u,f.**

Electrical and Electronic Engineering >
Computer Engineering

Comer, Douglas E.   QA76.9.A73C625 2005
Essentials of Computer Architecture. Cloth Text. Prentice Hall
PTR. Upper Saddle River, NJ. 2004. 400p.
ISBN:0-13-149179-2, ISBN13: 978-0-13-149179-3. Dewey:5.8.
LCCN:2004-304438.

Audience: **l,u,f.**

Dueck, Robert K.   TK7872.L64D84 2004
Digital Design with CPLD Applications and VHDL. Ed. 2.
Cloth Text. Thomson Delmar Learning. Albany, NY. 2004.
1024p. ISBN:1-4018-4030-2, ISBN13: 978-1-4018-4030-3.
Dewey:621.39/5. LCCN:2004-045514.

Audience: **l,u,f.**

El-Rewini, Hesham &   QA76.9.A73E47 2004
  Abd-El-Barr, Mostafa
Advanced Computer Architecture and Parallel Processing. Trade
Cloth. John Wiley & Sons, Inc. Hoboken, NJ. 2005. 288p.
Wiley Series on Parallel and Distributed Computing
ISBN:0-471-46740-5, ISBN13: 978-0-471-46740-3.
Dewey:004/.35. LCCN:2004-014922.
Audience: **u,f.** *Choice, 2005.*

Hennessy, John L. &   **QA76.9.A73P377 2003**
  Patterson, David A.
Computer Architecture: A Quantitative Approach. Ed. 3. Cloth
Text. Elsevier Science & Technology Books. Saint Louis, MO.
2002. 1136p. The Morgan Kaufmann Series in Computer
Architecture and Design Ser. ISBN:1-55860-596-7, ISBN13:
978-1-55860-596-1. Dewey:004.2/2. LCCN:2001-099789.

Audience: **l,u.**

Heuring, Vincent P., et al.   **QA76.9.S88H48 2003**
Computer Systems Design and Architecture. Ed. 2. Harry F.
Jordan & Miles J. Murdocca (Authors). Cloth Text. Prentice
Hall PTR. Upper Saddle River, NJ. 2003. 608p.
ISBN:0-13-048440-7, ISBN13: 978-0-13-048440-6.
Dewey:004.2/1. LCCN:2003-064790.

Audience: **l,u,f.**

Juola, Patrick   **QA76**
Principles of Computer Organization and Assembly Language.
Cloth Text. Prentice Hall PTR. Upper Saddle River, NJ. 2006.
439p. ISBN:0-13-148683-7, ISBN13: 978-0-13-148683-6.
Dewey:004.

Audience: **l,u,f.**

Mano, M. Morris   **TK7888.3.M343 2002**
Digital Design. Ed. 3. Mixed Media. Prentice Hall PTR. Upper
Saddle River, NJ. 2001. 516p. ISBN:0-13-062121-8, ISBN13:
978-0-13-062121-4. Dewey:621.395. LCCN:2002-276849.

Audience: **l,u,f.** *B*

Miller, Gene H.   **TK7874.M5247 2003**
Microcomputer Engineering. Ed. 3. Cloth Text. Prentice Hall
PTR. Upper Saddle River, NJ. 2003. 592p.
ISBN:0-13-142804-7, ISBN13: 978-0-13-142804-1.
Dewey:004.16. LCCN:2003-049795.

Audience: **l,u,f.**

Oklobdzija, Vojin   **TK7885.C645 2001**
The Computer Engineering Handbook. CRC Press. 2001.
ISBN:0-8493-0885-2, ISBN13: 978-0-8493-0885-7.

Audience: **u,f.**

Parhami, Behrooz   **QA76.9.A73P375 2005**
Computer Architecture: From Microprocessors to
Supercomputers. Cloth Text. Oxford University Press, Inc. New
York, NY. 2005. 575p. The Oxford Series in Electrical and
Computer Engineering ISBN:0-19-515455-X, ISBN13:
978-0-19-515455-9. Dewey:004.2/2. LCCN:2004-052063.

Audience: **u.**

Rafiquzzaman, M.   **TK7888.4.R34 2005**
Fundamentals of Digital Logic and Microcomputer Design. Ed.
5. Trade Cloth, CD-ROM. John Wiley & Sons, Inc. Hoboken,
NJ. 2005. 840p. ISBN:0-471-72784-9, ISBN13:
978-0-471-72784-2. Dewey:621.39/5. LCCN:2004-065974.

Audience: **u,f.**

Tanenbaum, Andrew S.   **QA76.6.T38 2005**
Structured Computer Organization. Ed. 5. Cloth Text. Prentice
Hall PTR. Upper Saddle River, NJ. 2005. 800p.
ISBN:0-13-148521-0, ISBN13: 978-0-13-148521-1.
Dewey:005.1. LCCN:2005-043004.

Audience: **l,u,f.** *B*

Tocci, Ronald J. &   **QA76.5.T556 2002**
  Ambrosio, Frank J.
Microprocessors and Microcomputers: Hardware and Software.

Ed. 6. Trade Cloth. Prentice Hall PTR. Upper Saddle River, NJ.
2002. 612p. ISBN:0-13-060904-8, ISBN13: 978-0-13-060904-5.
Dewey:004.16. LCCN:2001-051151.

Audience: **u,f.**

Uffenbeck, John E.   **QA76.5.U35 2000**
Microcomputers and Microprocessors: The 8080, 8085, and
Z-80 Programming, Interfacing, and Troubleshooting. Ed. 3.
Cloth Text. Prentice Hall PTR. Upper Saddle River, NJ. 1999.
729p. ISBN:0-13-209198-4, ISBN13: 978-0-13-209198-5.
Dewey:004.165. LCCN:98-050972.

Audience: **l.**

Wakerly, John F.   **TK7874.65.W34 2005**
Digital Design: Principles and Practices. Ed. 4. Cloth Text.
Prentice Hall PTR. Upper Saddle River, NJ. 2005. 928p.
ISBN:0-13-186389-4, ISBN13: 978-0-13-186389-7.
Dewey:621.39/5. LCCN:2005-048710.

Audience: **l,u,f.**

Electrical and Electronic Engineering > Lasers. Optoelectronics

Das, P. K.   **TA1677.D37 1991**
Lasers and Optical Engineering. Trade Cloth. Springer. New
York, NY. 1990. 496p. ISBN:0-387-97108-4, ISBN13:
978-0-387-97108-7. Dewey:621.36/6. LCCN:89-026312.

Audience: **l,u,f.** *Choice, 1991.*

Laufer, Gabriel   **TA367.5 .L39 1996**
Introduction to Optics and Lasers in Engineering. Trade Cloth.
Cambridge University Press. New York, NY. 1996. 490p.
ISBN:0-521-45233-3, ISBN13: 978-0-521-45233-5.
Dewey:621.3/6. LCCN:95-044046.

Audience: **u,f.** *Choice, 1997.*

Metallurgy

     TA140.F9
☐ AIME: The American Institute of Mining, Metallurgical, and
Petroleum Engineers.
http://www.aimeny.org/
AIME.

Audience: **u,f.**

     TN775 (online
☐ Aluminium Industry Abstracts (AIA).
http://www.csa.com/factsheets/aia-set-c.php
CSA.

Audience: **u,f.**

     TA403.4
ASM Desk Editions: Metals Handbook; Engineered Materials
Handbook. Trade Cloth, CD-ROM. A S M International.
Materials Park, OH. 2001.

Audience: **u,f.**

     HD9539.C5
☐ CDA: Copper.org.
http://copper.org/
Copper Development Association.

Audience: **u,f.**

□ e-Library @ Iowa State University: Materials Science Resources on the Web.
http://www.lib.iastate.edu/collections/eresourc/matsci.html
e-Library @ Iowa State University.

Audience: **l,u,f.**

TA403.6 .G85
Guide to Materials Engineering Data and Information. Trade Cloth. A S M International. Materials Park, OH. 1986. 300p. ISBN:0-87170-231-2, ISBN13: 978-0-87170-231-9. Dewey:620.1/107.

Audience: **l,u,f.**

TA401
□ METADEX.
http://www.csa.com/factsheets/metadex-set-c.php
CSA.

Audience: **u,f.**

□ Metallurgy Resources on the Internet.
http://steelynx.net/metallurgy.html
Steelynx.

Audience: **u,f.**

TN1
□ SME: The Society for Mining, Metallurgy and Exploration.
http://www.smenet.org/
SME.

Audience: **u,f.**

TA401
□ TMS OnLine: Home of The Minerals, Metals & Materials Society.
http://tms.org/tmshome.html
The Minerals, Metals & Materials Society.

Audience: **u,f.**

□ Yahoo! Search Directory: Material Science > Metallurgy.
http://dir.yahoo.com/Science/Engineering/Material_Science/
Metallurgy/
Yahoo! Inc..

Audience: **u,f.**

Agricola, Georgius   **TN421**
De Re Metallica. Trade Paper. Dover Publications, Inc. Mineola, NY. 1950. 672p. ISBN:0-486-60006-8, ISBN13: 978-0-486-60006-2. Dewey:622.3/4.

Audience: **l,u,f.** *B*

Avallone, Eugene A. &   **TJ151**
Baumeister, Theodore
Mark's Standard Handbook for Mechanical Engineers on CD-ROM. Ed. 2. Mixed Media, CD-ROM. McGraw-Hill Professional Publishing. New York, NY. 1998. 1792p. ISBN:0-07-134411-X, ISBN13: 978-0-07-134411-1. Dewey:621.
Audience: **u,f.** *Choice, 2000.*

Bauccio, Michael L. (Editor)   **TA459.A78 1993**
ASM Metals Reference Book. Ed. 3. Trade Cloth. A S M International. Materials Park, OH. 1993. 614p. ISBN:0-87170-478-1, ISBN13: 978-0-87170-478-8. Dewey:620.1/6. LCCN:93-028716.
Audience: **l,u.** *Choice, 1994.*

Brown, Colin D.   **TN609.B76 1998**
Dictionary of Metallurgy. Ed. 1. Trade Cloth. John Wiley & Sons, Inc. Hoboken, NJ. 1998. 316p. ISBN:0-471-96155-8, ISBN13: 978-0-471-96155-0. Dewey:669/.03. LCCN:97-027383.
Audience: **u,f.**

Cambridge Scientific   **Z695.1.M55**
Abstracts, Inc.
Thesaurus of Metallurgical Terms : The Vocabulary That Controls Storage and Retrieval of Technical Information in Metallurgy. Ed. 13. Cambridge Scientific Abstracts, Inc.. 2003. ISBN:0-88387-968-9, ISBN13: 978-0-88387-968-9.
Audience: **u,f.**

Carter, Giles F.   **TN0690.C29**
Principles of Physical and Chemical Metallurgy. Trade Paper. Books on Demand. Ann Arbor, MI. 447p. ISBN:0-608-12109-6, ISBN13: 978-0-608-12109-3. Dewey:669.94. LCCN:79-019184.
Audience: **u,f.**

Chandler, Harry   **TN667.C43 1998**
Metallurgy for the Non-Metallurgist. Trade Cloth. A S M International. Materials Park, OH. 1998. 284p. ISBN:0-87170-652-0, ISBN13: 978-0-87170-652-2. Dewey:669. LCCN:98-004664.
Audience: **l,u,f.** *Choice, 1998.*

Chapman, Woodrow W.   **TA403.4.C463514 2004**
Modern Machine Shop Guide to Engineering Materials. Trade Cloth. Hanser-Gardner Publications. Cincinnati, OH. 2004. vi, 380p. ISBN:1-56990-358-1, ISBN13: 978-1-56990-358-2. Dewey:620.1/1. LCCN:2004-000741.
Audience: **u,f.** *Choice, 2004.*

Chapman, Woodrow W.   **TJ1165.M56 2002**
(Editor)
Modern Machine Shop's Machinist's Handbook for the Metalworking Industries. Trade Cloth. Hanser-Gardner Publications. Cincinnati, OH. 2002. xvii, 2347p. ISBN:1-56990-345-X, ISBN13: 978-1-56990-345-2. Dewey:670.42/3. LCCN:2002-005345.
Audience: **l,u,f.** *Choice, 2003.*

Chapman, Woodrow W.   **TJ1330.C37 2004**
Modern Machine Shops Guide to Threads, Threading, and Threaded Fasteners. Trade Cloth. Hanser-Gardner Publications. Cincinnati, OH. 2004. viii, 596p. ISBN:1-56990-359-X, ISBN13: 978-1-56990-359-9. Dewey:621.8/82. LCCN:2004-004400.
Audience: **l,u,f.** *Choice, 2004.*

Courtney, Thomas H.   **TA405**
Mechanical Behavior of Materials. Ed. 2. Cloth Text. Waveland Press, Inc. Prospect Heights, IL. 2005. 733p. ISBN:1-57766-425-6, ISBN13: 978-1-57766-425-3. Dewey:620.1/1292.
Audience: **u,f.** *Choice, 1990.*

Davis, J. R. (Editor)   **TA402.A85 1992**
ASM Materials Engineering Dictionary. Trade Cloth. A S M International. Materials Park, OH. 1992. 555p. ISBN:0-87170-447-1, ISBN13: 978-0-87170-447-4. Dewey:620.1/1/03. LCCN:92-073858.
Audience: **u,f.** *Choice, 1993.*

Gale, William F. &   **TN665**
Totemeier, Terry C. (Editors)
Smithells Metals Reference Book. Ed. 8. Trade Cloth. Elsevier
Science & Technology Books. Saint Louis, MO. 2003. 2080p.
ISBN:0-7506-7509-8, ISBN13: 978-0-7506-7509-3.
Dewey:669.02/12. LCCN:2004-351939.

Audience: **u,f.** *Choice, 2004.*

Gibson, Eleanor B. & Tapia,   **Z6678**
Elizabeth W. (Editors)
Guide to Metallurgical Information. Ed. 2. Trade Paper. Special
Libraries Association. Alexandria, VA. 1965. Bibliography Ser.,
No. 3 ISBN:0-87111-164-0, ISBN13: 978-0-87111-164-7.
Dewey:16.669. LCCN:65-027056.

Audience: **u,f.**

Gottstein, Günter   **TA403.G57513 2004**
Physical Foundations of Materials Science. Trade Cloth.
Springer. New York, NY. 2004. XIV, 502p.
ISBN:3-540-40139-3, ISBN13: 978-3-540-40139-1.
Dewey:620.1/1. LCCN:2004-045239.

Audience: **u,f.** *Choice, 2005.*

Gupta, Chiranjib Kumar   **QD133**
Chemical Metallurgy: Principles and Practice. Trade Cloth. John
Wiley & Sons, Inc. Hoboken, NJ. 2003. 831p. Advances in
Electrochemical Sciences and Engineering Ser.
ISBN:3-527-30376-6, ISBN13: 978-3-527-30376-2.
Dewey:669/.9. LCCN:2004-425637.

Audience: **u,f.**

Habashi, Fathi (Editor)   **TN665.H335 1997**
Handbook of Extractive Metallurgy, Set. Trade Cloth. John
Wiley & Sons, Inc. Hoboken, NJ. 1998. 2435p.
ISBN:3-527-28792-2, ISBN13: 978-3-527-28792-5. Dewey:669.
LCCN:2001-316075.

Audience: **u,f.**

Hausner, H. H. & Mal,   **TN695**
M. K.
Handbook of Powder Metallurgy. Ed. 2. Trade Cloth. Chemical
Publishing Company, Inc. New York, NY. 1982.
ISBN:0-8206-0301-5, ISBN13: 978-0-8206-0301-8.
Dewey:671.37.

Audience: **u,f.**

Hosford, William F.   **TN690.H845 2005**
Physical Metallurgy. Saddle Stitched. Marcel Dekker Inc. New
York, NY. 2005. 520p. Materials Engineering Ser.
ISBN:0-8247-2421-6, ISBN13: 978-0-8247-2421-4.
Dewey:669/.9. LCCN:2004-063430.

Audience: **u,f.** *Choice, 2005.*

Hummel, Rolf E.   **TA401.6.A1H86 2004**
Understanding Materials Science: History, Properties,
Applications. Ed. 2. Trade Cloth. Springer. New York, NY.
2004. XVIII, 452p. ISBN:0-387-20939-5, ISBN13:
978-0-387-20939-5. Dewey:620.1. LCCN:2004-041693.
Audience: **l,u,f.** *Choice, 1998.*

Hyslop, Marjorie R.   **TN675.4 .H95**
A Brief Guide to Sources of Metals Information. Cloth Text.
Information Resources Press. Rocksville, MD. 1973. ix, 180p.
ISBN:0-87815-008-0, ISBN13: 978-0-87815-008-3.
Dewey:669/.007. LCCN:72-087893.

Audience: **u,f.** *B*

Lampman, Steve   **TA409.L58 2005**
Mechanics and Mechanisms of Fracture: An Introduction. Trade
Paper. A S M International, Inc. Fort Lauderdale, FL. 2005.
500p. ISBN:0-87170-802-7, ISBN13: 978-0-87170-802-1.
Dewey:620.1/126. LCCN:2005-042107.

Audience: **u,f.** *Choice, 2006.*

Livingston, James D.   **TK7871.L58 1999**
Electronic Properties of Engineering Materials. Trade Cloth.
John Wiley & Sons, Inc. Hoboken, NJ. 1998. 336p. Mit Series
in Materials Science and Engineering Ser. ISBN:0-471-31627-X,
ISBN13: 978-0-471-31627-5. Dewey:620.1/1297.
LCCN:98-024461.

Audience: **u,f.** *Choice, 1999.*

Martin, John   **TA403 .M35 2002**
Materials for Engineering. Ed. 2. Trade Paper. Maney
Publishing. Leeds, 2002. 248p. ISBN:1-902653-50-5, ISBN13:
978-1-902653-50-1. Dewey:620.1.

Audience: **u,f.** *Choice, 2002.*

McArthur, Hugh &   **TA403.M388 2004**
Spalding, Duncan
Engineering Materials Science: Properties, Uses, Degradation,
Remediation. Trade Paper. Horwood Publishing Ltd. Chichester,
2004. 577p. ISBN:1-898563-11-X, ISBN13: 978-1-898563-11-2.
Dewey:620.1/1. LCCN:2004-303778.

Audience: **u,f.** *Choice, 2005.*

Merriman, A.   **TN609**
Concise Encyclopaedia of Metallurgy. Trade Cloth. Elsevier.
New York, NY. 1965. ISBN:0-444-19857-1, ISBN13:
978-0-444-19857-0. Dewey:669.003.

Audience: **u,f.**

Mitchell, Brian S.   **TA403.M685 2003**
An Introduction to Materials Engineering and Science: For
Chemical and Materials Engineers. Trade Cloth. John Wiley &
Sons, Inc. Hoboken, NJ. 2003. 976p. ISBN:0-471-43623-2,
ISBN13: 978-0-471-43623-2. Dewey:620.11.
LCCN:2003-053451.

Audience: **u,f.** *Choice, 2004.*

Murray, G. T.   **TA403.M84 1993**
Introduction to Engineering Materials: Behavior, Properties, and
Selection, Vol. 2. Paper over Boards. Marcel Dekker Inc. New
York, NY. 1993. 688p. Engineering Materials Ser., Vol. 2
ISBN:0-8247-8965-2, ISBN13: 978-0-8247-8965-7.
Dewey:620.1/1. LCCN:93-012660.

Audience: **u,f.** *Choice, 1994.*

Oberg, et al.   **TJ151.O245 2004**
Machinery's Handbook. Ed. 27. Jones Sr. & Horton (Authors).
Trade Paper. Industrial Press, Inc. New York, NY. 2004. 2693p.
ISBN:0-8311-2700-7, ISBN13: 978-0-8311-2700-8. Dewey:621.

Audience: **l,u,f.**

Oberg, et al.   **TJ151**
Machinery's Handbook. Ed. 26. McCauley, Jones, Horton,
Ryffel, Heald & Hussain (Authors). Trade Cloth, CD-ROM.
Industrial Press, Inc. New York, NY. 2000.
ISBN:0-8311-2666-3, ISBN13: 978-0-8311-2666-7. Dewey:621.

Audience: **l,u,f.**

Patten, M. N. (Editor)   **TA459**
Information Sources in Metallic Materials. Bowker-Saur. 1989.
ISBN:0-408-01491-1, ISBN13: 978-0-408-01491-5.

Audience: **u,f.**

Russell, Alan & Lee, Kok   **TA479.3.R84 2005**
  Loong
Structure-Property Relations in Nonferrous Metals. Trade Cloth.
John Wiley & Sons, Inc. Hoboken, NJ. 2005. 520p.
ISBN:0-471-64952-X, ISBN13: 978-0-471-64952-6.
Dewey:620.1/8. LCCN:2004-054807.

Audience: **u,f.** *Choice, 2005.*

Simons, Eric N.   **TN665**
An Outline of Metallurgy. Muller. 1968. ISBN:0-584-00201-7,
ISBN13: 978-0-584-00201-0.

Audience: **u,f.**

Sinha, Anil Kumar   **TN690.4.S57 2003**
Physical Metallurgy Handbook. Trade Cloth. McGraw-Hill
Professional Publishing. New York, NY. 2002. 1808p.
ISBN:0-07-057986-5, ISBN13: 978-0-07-057986-6.
Dewey:669/.9. LCCN:2002-727138.

Audience: **u,f.**

SME Staff   **TS176**
Tool and Manufacturing Engineers Handbook: Continuous
Improvement. Ed. 4. R. Bakerjian (Editor). Trade Cloth. Society
of Manufacturing Engineers. Dearborn, MI. 1993. 400p.
ISBN:0-87263-420-5, ISBN13: 978-0-87263-420-6. Dewey:670.
LCCN:92-081156.

Audience: **l,u,f.**

SME Staff   **TS176**
Tool and Manufacturing Engineers Handbook: Plastic Part
Manufacturing. Ed. 4. Philip Mitchell (Editor). Trade Cloth.
Society of Manufacturing Engineers. Dearborn, MI. 1996. 650p.
ISBN:0-87263-456-6, ISBN13: 978-0-87263-456-5.
Dewey:621.7. LCCN:82-060312.

Audience: **l,u,f.**

SME Staff   **TS176**
Tool and Manufacturing Engineers Handbook: Material and Part
Handling in Manufacturing. Ed. 4. Philip Mitchell (Editor).
Trade Cloth. Society of Manufacturing Engineers. Dearborn, MI.
1998. 550p. ISBN:0-87263-489-2, ISBN13: 978-0-87263-489-3.
Dewey:670. LCCN:82-060312.

Audience: **l,u,f.**

SME Staff   **TS176**
Tool and Manufacturing Engineers Handbook: Design for
Manufacturability, Vol. 6. Ed. 4. Philip Mitchell (Editor), Ramon
Bakerjian (Introduction by). Trade Cloth. Society of
Manufacturing Engineers. Dearborn, MI. 1992. 675p.
ISBN:0-87263-402-7, ISBN13: 978-0-87263-402-2. Dewey:670.
LCCN:91-060347.

Audience: **l,u,f.**

SME Staff   **TS176**
Tool and Manufacturing Engineers Handbook: Manufacturing
Management. Ed. 4. R. Veilleux & L. Petro (Editors). Trade
Cloth. Society of Manufacturing Engineers. Dearborn, MI. 1988.
600p. ISBN:0-87263-306-3, ISBN13: 978-0-87263-306-3.
Dewey:670. LCCN:82-060312.

Audience: **l,u,f.**

SME Staff   **TS176**
Tool and Manufacturing Engineers Handbook: Materials,
Finishing and Coating. Ed. 4. C. Wick & R. Veilleux (Editors).
Trade Cloth. Society of Manufacturing Engineers. Dearborn, MI.
1985. 864p. ISBN:0-87263-176-1, ISBN13: 978-0-87263-176-2.
Dewey:670. LCCN:82-060312.

Audience: **l,u,f.**

Society of Manufacturing   **TS176**
  Engineers Staff
Tool and Manufacturing Engineers Handbook: Forming. Ed. 4.
C. Wick, J. Benedict & R. Veilleux (Editors). Trade Cloth.
Society of Manufacturing Engineers. Dearborn, MI. 1984. 936p.
ISBN:0-87263-135-4, ISBN13: 978-0-87263-135-9. Dewey:670.
LCCN:82-060312.

Audience: **l,u,f.**

Society of Manufacturing   **TS176 .T63 1983**
  Engineers Staff
Tool and Manufacturing Engineers Handbook: Machining. Ed.
4. C. Wick & T. Drozda (Editors). Trade Cloth. Society of
Manufacturing Engineers. Dearborn, MI. 1983. 1494p.
ISBN:0-87263-085-4, ISBN13: 978-0-87263-085-7. Dewey:670.
LCCN:82-060312.

Audience: **l,u,f.**

Society of Manufacturing   **TS176**
  Engineers Staff
Tool and Manufacturing Engineers Handbook: Quality Control
and Assembly. Ed. 4. C. Wick & R. Veilleux (Editors). Trade
Cloth. Society of Manufacturing Engineers. Dearborn, MI. 1987.
840p. ISBN:0-87263-177-X, ISBN13: 978-0-87263-177-9.
Dewey:670. LCCN:82-060312.

Audience: **l,u,f.**

Tottle, C. R.   **TN665**
An Encyclopaedia of Metallurgy and Materials. Cloth Text.
Ashgate Publishing Company. Williston, VT. 1984. 448p.
ISBN:0-7121-0571-9, ISBN13: 978-0-7121-0571-2.
Dewey:669/.003/21. LCCN:83-008099.

Audience: **u,f.** B

U S Bureau of Mines Staff   **TN23**
Mineral Facts and Problems. U.S. Dept. of the Interior. 1991.

Audience: **l,u,f.**

White, D.   **Z6333.M47**
How to Find Out about Iron and Steel. Cloth Text. Elsevier
Science & Technology Books. Saint Louis, MO. 1970. v, 184p.
ISBN:0-08-015790-4, ISBN13: 978-0-08-015790-0.
Dewey:016.6691.

Audience: **u,f.**

Young, James F. & Shane   **QC21.2**
  (Editors)
Materials and Processes, Set, Pt. A. Ed. 3. Cloth Text. Marcel
Dekker Inc. New York, NY. 1985. 888p. ISBN:0-8247-7197-4,
ISBN13: 978-0-8247-7197-3. Dewey:530.

Audience: **u,f.**

Young & Shane (Editors)   **TA403.8 .M375 1985**
Materials and Processes, Set, Pt. B. Ed. 3. Cloth Text. Marcel
Dekker Inc. New York, NY. 1985. 1688p. ISBN:0-8247-7198-2,
ISBN13: 978-0-8247-7198-0. Dewey:620.1/1. LCCN:85-020432.

Audience: **u,f.**

Metallurgy > Metallography

Vander Voort, George F.   **TN690.V36 1999**
Metallography: Principles and Practice. Trade Cloth. A S M
International. Materials Park, OH. 1984. 752p.
ISBN:0-87170-672-5, ISBN13: 978-0-87170-672-0.
Dewey:669/.95. LCCN:99-024360.

Audience: **u,f.**

Metallurgy > Corrosion

Corrosion Information Server: Internet resources in Corrosion
& Materials.
http://www.cp.umist.ac.uk/cis/links.htm
UMIST Corrosion and Protection Centre.

Audience: **u,f.**

The International Corrosion Council (ICC).
http://icc-net.org/
The International Corrosion Council.

Audience: **u,f.**

National Institute of Corrosion Engineers NACE: Protecting
People, Assets, and the Environment from the Effects of
Corrosion.
http://www.nace.org/nace/index.asp
NACE International.

Audience: **u,f.**

UMIST Corrosion and Protection Centre.
http://www.cp.umist.ac.uk/default.htm
UMIST UMIST Corrosion and Protection Centre.

Audience: **u,f.**

Yahoo! Search Directory: Metallurgy > Corrosion.
http://dir.yahoo.com/Science/Engineering/Material_Science/
Metallurgy/Corrosion/
Yahoo! Inc..

Audience: **u,f.**

Baboian, B. & Dean, S.   **TA462.C664 1990**
(Editors)
Corrosion Testing and Evaluation: Silver Anniversary Volume.
Trade Cloth. American Society for Testing & Materials. West
Conshohocken, PA. 1990. 450p. Corrosion and Degradation Ser.,
No. 1000 ISBN:0-8031-1406-0, ISBN13: 978-0-8031-1406-7.
Dewey:620.1/1223. LCCN:90-045036.

Audience: **u,f.**

Baboian, Robert (Editor)   **TA462.C666 1995**
Corrosion Tests and Standards: Application and Interpretation.
Trade Cloth. American Society for Testing & Materials. West
Conshohocken, PA. 1995. 764p. Manual Ser., Vol. 20
ISBN:0-8031-2058-3, ISBN13: 978-0-8031-2058-7.
Dewey:620.1/1223. LCCN:95-006879.

Audience: **u,f.** *Choice, 1996.*

Bardal, Einar   **TA418.74**
Corrosion and Protection. Trade Cloth. Springer. New York, NY.
2004. 336p. Engineering Materials and Processes Ser.

ISBN:1-85233-758-3, ISBN13: 978-1-85233-758-2.
Dewey:620.1/1223. LCCN:2003-054415.

Audience: **u,f.** *Choice, 2004.*

Brubaker, George R. &   **TA418.74 .C595**
Phipps, P. Beverley (Editors)
Corrosion Chemistry. Trade Cloth. American Chemical Society.
Washington, DC. 1979. ACS Symposium Ser., No. 89
ISBN:0-8412-0471-3, ISBN13: 978-0-8412-0471-3.
Dewey:620.1/6/23. LCCN:78-025554.

Audience: **u,f.**

Chawla, Sohan L. & Gupta,   **TA418.75.C48 1993**
R. K.
Materials Selection for Corrosion Control. Trade Cloth. A S M
International. Materials Park, OH. 1993. 508p.
ISBN:0-87170-474-9, ISBN13: 978-0-87170-474-0.
Dewey:620.1/1223. LCCN:93-038047.

Audience: **u,f.** *Choice, 1994.*

Davis, J. R. (Editor)   **TA462.C668 2000**
Corrosion: Understanding the Basics. Trade Cloth. A S M
International. Materials Park, OH. 2000. 563p.
ISBN:0-87170-641-5, ISBN13: 978-0-87170-641-6.
Dewey:620.1/1223. LCCN:99-057146.

Audience: **u,f.** *Choice, 2000.*

edited by Technische   **TA462**
Universität Dresden, Zentrum für Angewandte
Sprachwissenschaft (Editor)
Dictionary, Corrosion and Corrosion Control: English-German,
German-English. Ed. 2. Verlag Technik. 1991.
ISBN:3-341-00957-4, ISBN13: 978-3-341-00957-4.

Audience: **u,f.**

Fontana, Mars G.   **TA418.74.F6 1986**
Corrosion Engineering. Ed. 3. Cloth Text. McGraw-Hill Higher
Education. Burr Ridge, IL. 1985. 512p. McGraw-Hill Series in
Materials Science and Engineering ISBN:0-07-021463-8,
ISBN13: 978-0-07-021463-7. Dewey:620.1/12/23.
LCCN:85-019713.

Audience: **u,f.**

Jones, Russell H. (Editor)   **TA462.S728 1992**
Stress-Corrosion Cracking: Materials Performance and
Evaluation. Trade Cloth. A S M International. Materials Park,
OH. 1992. 448p. ISBN:0-87170-441-2, ISBN13:
978-0-87170-441-2. Dewey:620.1/1223. LCCN:92-071978.

Audience: **u,f.** *Choice, 1993.*

Kaesche, Helmut   **TA462**
Corrosion of Metals. Trade Cloth. Springer. New York, NY.
2003. X, 594p. Engineering Materials and Processes Ser.
ISBN:3-540-00626-5, ISBN13: 978-3-540-00626-8.
Dewey:620.1/623. LCCN:2003-054778.

Audience: **l,u.** *Choice, 2004.*

Lucas, K. A.   **TA481.L83 1993**
Corrosion of Aluminium-Based Metal Matrix Composites. Trade
Cloth. Bow Historical Books. New Providence, NJ. 1993. xi,
140 p. :p. ISBN:0-86380-148-X, ISBN13: 978-0-86380-148-8.
Dewey:620.1/8623. LCCN:93-026513.

Audience: **u,f.**

Mattsson, Einar   **TA418.74 .M397 2001**
Basic Corrosion Technology for Scientists and Engineers. Ed. 2.
Trade Cloth. Institute of Materials. Leeds, 1999. 224p.
ISBN:1-86125-138-6, ISBN13: 978-1-86125-138-1.
Dewey:620.1/1223. LCCN:2003-447000.
                       Audience: **u,f.**

Roberge, Pierre R.   **TA418.74.R63 2000**
Handbook of Corrosion Engineering. Cloth Text. McGraw-Hill
Professional Publishing. New York, NY. 1999. 1072p. Products
Liability Ser. ISBN:0-07-076516-2, ISBN13:
978-0-07-076516-0. Dewey:620.1/1223. LCCN:99-035898.
               Audience: **u,f.** *Choice, 2000.*

Sauveur, Albert   **TA462.E83 1982**
Metallurgical Reminiscences and Dialogue. Trade Cloth. A S M
International. Materials Park, OH. 1981. 302 p. :p.
ISBN:0-87170-132-4, ISBN13: 978-0-87170-132-9.
Dewey:620.1/623. LCCN:81-017651.
                    Audience: **u,f.** *B*

Schweitzer, Philip A.   **TA418.74**
Concise Encyclopedia of Corrosion Technology. Ed. 2. Paper
over Boards. Marcel Dekker Inc. New York, NY. 2004. 624p.
ISBN:0-8247-4878-6, ISBN13: 978-0-8247-4878-4.
Dewey:620.1/1223. LCCN:2004-300435.
                       Audience: **u,f.**

Schweitzer, Philip A.   **TA418.74.C5928 1989**
Corrosion and Corrosion Protection Handbook, Vol. 1. Ed. 2.
Paper over Boards. Marcel Dekker Inc. New York, NY. 1988.
660p. Corrosion Technology Ser., Vol. 1 ISBN:0-8247-7998-3,
ISBN13: 978-0-8247-7998-6. Dewey:620.1/1223.
LCCN:88-013916.
                       Audience: **u,f.**

Schweitzer, Philip A.   **TA462.C6545 1996**
(Editor)
Corrosion Engineering Handbook, Vol. 11. Paper over Boards.
Marcel Dekker Inc. New York, NY. 1996. 752p. Corrosion
Technology Ser., Vol. 11 ISBN:0-8247-9709-4, ISBN13:
978-0-8247-9709-6. Dewey:620.1/1223. LCCN:96-018884.
                       Audience: **u,f.**

Schweitzer, Philip A.   **TA418.74.S379 2004**
Corrosion Resistance Tables: Metals, Nonmetals, Coatings,
Mortars, Plastics, Elastomers and Linings, and Fabrics. Ed. 5.
Paper over Boards. Marcel Dekker Inc. New York, NY. 2004.
874p. Corrosion Technology Ser. ISBN:0-8247-5674-6, ISBN13:
978-0-8247-5674-1. Dewey:620.1/1223. LCCN:2004-555152.
                       Audience: **u,f.**

Schweitzer, Philip A.   **TA418.74.S379 2004**
Corrosion Resistance Tables: Metals, Nonmetals, Coatings,
Mortars, Plastics, Elastomers and Linings, and Fabrics. Ed. 5.
Paper over Boards. Marcel Dekker Inc. New York, NY. 2004.
874p. Corrosion Technology Ser. ISBN:0-8247-5675-4, ISBN13:
978-0-8247-5675-8. Dewey:620.1/1223. LCCN:2004-555152.
                       Audience: **u,f.**

Schweitzer, Philip A.   **TA418.74.S379 2004**
Corrosion Resistance Tables, Part A. Ed. 5. Paper over Boards.
Marcel Dekker Inc. New York, NY. 2004. 800p. Corrosion
Technology Ser. ISBN:0-8247-5673-8, ISBN13:
978-0-8247-5673-4. Dewey:620.1/223/0212.
LCCN:2004-555152.
                       Audience: **u,f.**

Schweitzer, Philip A.   **TA418.74.S379 2004**
Corrosion Resistance Tables: Metals, Nonmetals, Coatings,
Mortars, Plastics, Elastomers and Linings, and Fabrics. Ed. 5.
Paper over Boards. Marcel Dekker Inc. New York, NY. 2004.
874p. Corrosion Technology Ser. ISBN:0-8247-5676-2, ISBN13:
978-0-8247-5676-5. Dewey:620.1/1223. LCCN:2004-555152.
                       Audience: **u,f.**

Schweitzer, Philip A.   **TA459.S44 2003**
Metallic Materials: Physical, Mechanical, and Corrosion
Properties, Vol. 19. Paper over Boards. Marcel Dekker Inc. New
York, NY. 2003. 712p. Corrosion Technology Ser.
ISBN:0-8247-0878-4, ISBN13: 978-0-8247-0878-8.
Dewey:620.1/6. LCCN:2002-041426.
                       Audience: **u,f.**

Sedriks, A. John   **TA479.S7S4 1996**
Corrosion of Stainless Steels. Ed. 2. Trade Cloth. John Wiley &
Sons, Inc. Hoboken, NJ. 1996. 464p. Corrosion Monograph Ser.,
Vol. 15 ISBN:0-471-00792-7, ISBN13: 978-0-471-00792-0.
Dewey:620.1/7/23. LCCN:95-041698.
               Audience: **u,f.** *Choice, 1997.*

Shreir, L. L., et al.   **TA462.C6513 1994**
Corrosion. Ed. 3. R. Jarman & T. Burstein (Authors). Trade
Cloth. Elsevier Science & Technology Books. Saint Louis, MO.
1994. 3184p. ISBN:0-7506-1077-8, ISBN13:
978-0-7506-1077-3. Dewey:620.1/623. LCCN:93-013859.
               Audience: **u,f.** *Choice, 1995.*

Stanbury, E. E. &   **TA462.S714 2000**
  Buchanan, R. A.
Fundamentals of Electrochemical Corrosion. Trade Cloth. A S M
International. Materials Park, OH. 2000. 487p.
ISBN:0-87170-676-8, ISBN13: 978-0-87170-676-8.
Dewey:620.1/1223. LCCN:99-058428.
                       Audience: **u,f.**

Talbot, David (David E. J.)   **TA462**
  &Talbot, James (James D. R.)
Corrosion Science and Technology. CRC Press. 1998. CRC
series in materials science and technology; Variation: Materials
science and technology (Boca Raton, Fla.) ISBN:0-8493-8224-6,
ISBN13: 978-0-8493-8224-6.
                       Audience: **u,f.**

Trethewey, Kenneth R. &   **TA462**
  Chamberlain, John
Corrosion for Students of Science and Engineering. Trade Paper.
John Wiley & Sons, Inc. Hoboken, NJ. 1988. 382p.
ISBN:0-470-20794-9, ISBN13: 978-0-470-20794-9.
Dewey:620.1/1223. LCCN:86-034417.
                       Audience: **l,u,f.**

Uhlig, Herbert H. & Revie,   **TA462.U39 1985**
  R. Winston
Corrosion and Corrosion Control, No. 3. Ed. 3. Trade Cloth.
John Wiley & Sons, Inc. Hoboken, NJ. 1985. 464p.
ISBN:0-471-07818-2, ISBN13: 978-0-471-07818-0.
Dewey:620.1/623. LCCN:84-013034.
                       Audience: **u,f.**

Metallurgy > Iron and Steel

AISE Staff　　　　　　　　　　　**TN730.M35 1998**
The Making, Shaping and Treating of Steel: Steelmaking and Refining Volume. Ed. 11. Richard J. Fruehan (Editor). Trade Cloth. Association for Iron & Steel Technology. Warrendale, PA. 1998. 767p. ISBN:0-930767-02-0, ISBN13: 978-0-930767-02-0. Dewey:672. LCCN:98-073477.

Audience: **u,f.**

Brooks, Charlie R.　　　　　　　　　　　　**TN731**
Principles of the Surface Treatment of Steels. Technomic Pub. Co.. 1992. ISBN:0-87762-796-7, ISBN13: 978-0-87762-796-8.

Audience: **u,f.**

Davis, Joseph R. (Editor)　　　　**TA479.S7S677 1994**
Stainless Steels. Trade Cloth. A S M International. Materials Park, OH. 1994. 576p. ASM Specialty Handbook Ser. ISBN:0-87170-503-6, ISBN13: 978-0-87170-503-7. Dewey:620.1/7. LCCN:94-023392.

Audience: **u,f.** *Choice, 1995.*

Fruehan, R. J.　　　　　　　　　　**TN730.M35 1998**
The Making, Shaping, and Treating of Steel: Ironmaking Volume. Ed. 11. Trade Cloth, CD-ROM. Association for Iron & Steel Technology. Warrendale, PA. 1999. ISBN:0-930767-03-9, ISBN13: 978-0-930767-03-7. Dewey:672. LCCN:98-073477.

Audience: **l,u,f.**

German, Randall M.　　　　　　　**TN697.I7G47 1998**
Powder Metallurgy of Iron and Steel. Ed. 1. Trade Cloth. John Wiley & Sons, Inc. Hoboken, NJ. 1998. 496p. ISBN:0-471-15739-2, ISBN13: 978-0-471-15739-7. Dewey:672.3/7. LCCN:97-031764.

Audience: **u,f.** *Choice, 1998.*

Gladman, T.　　　　　　　　　　　　**TN693.I7**
The Physical Metallurgy of Microalloyed Steels. Paper Text. Institute of Materials. Leeds, 1997. 376p. ISBN:0-901716-81-2, ISBN13: 978-0-901716-81-1. Dewey:669.142.

Audience: **u,f.** *Choice, 1998.*

Peckner, Donald &　　　　　　　　　　**TA479.S7**
　Bernstein, I. M.
Handbook of Stainless Steels. Cloth Text. McGraw-Hill Companies, The. New York, NY. 1977. 928p. Handbook Ser. ISBN:0-07-049147-X, ISBN13: 978-0-07-049147-2. Dewey:669/.142. LCCN:76-054266.

Audience: **u,f.**

Metallurgy > Other Ferrous Metals

ASM International Staff　　　　　**TA480.N6A28 2000**
Nickel, Cobalt, and Their Alloys. J. R. Davis (Editor). Trade Cloth. A S M International. Materials Park, OH. 2000. 442p. ASM Specialty Handbook Ser. ISBN:0-87170-685-7, ISBN13: 978-0-87170-685-0. Dewey:620.1/88. LCCN:00-059348.

Audience: **u,f.** *Choice, 2001.*

Metallurgy > Nonferrous Metals

Ayres, Robert U., et al.　　　　　**TA480.C7A97 2003**
The Life Cycle of Copper, Its Co-Products and Byproducts. Leslie Ayres & Ingrid Rade (Authors). Trade Cloth. Springer.

New York, NY. 2003. 276p. Eco-Efficiency in Industry and Science Ser. ISBN:1-4020-1552-6, ISBN13: 978-1-4020-1552-6. Dewey:620.1/82. LCCN:2003-058218.

Audience: **u,f.** *Choice, 2004.*

Davis, Joseph R. (Editor)　　　　**TA480.A6A6177 1993**
Aluminum and Aluminum Alloys. Trade Cloth. A S M International. Materials Park, OH. 1993. 784p. ASM Specialty Handbook Ser. ISBN:0-87170-496-X, ISBN13: 978-0-87170-496-2. Dewey:620.1/86. LCCN:93-041647.

Audience: **u,f.** *Choice, 1994.*

Nicholas, Sarah Anne, et al.　　　**TA401.6.A1N53 2000**
Aluminum by Design. Paola Antonelli, Dennis P. Doordan, Robert Friedel, Eric Schatzberg, Penny Sparke & Craig Vogel (Authors). Trade Cloth. Harry N. Abrams, Inc. New York, NY. 2000. 300p. ISBN:0-8109-6721-9, ISBN13: 978-0-8109-6721-2. Dewey:620.1/86. LCCN:00-009918.

Audience: **g,l,u,f.** *Choice, 2001.*

Sharp, Maurice L.　　　　　　　　**TA690.S44 1993**
Behavior and Design of Aluminum Structures. Cloth Text. McGraw-Hill Companies, The. New York, NY. 1992. xi, 309 p. :p. ISBN:0-07-056478-7, ISBN13: 978-0-07-056478-7. Dewey:624.1/826. LCCN:92-022257.

Audience: **u,f.** *Choice, 1993.*

Totten, George &　　　　　　　　**TA480.A6 H36 2003**
　MacKenzie, D. Scott
Handbook of Aluminum: Alloy Production and Materials Manufacturing. Paper over Boards. Marcel Dekker Inc. New York, NY. 2003. 736p. ISBN:0-8247-0896-2, ISBN13: 978-0-8247-0896-2. Dewey:620.186. LCCN:2003-273504.

Audience: **u,f.** *Choice, 2004.*

Totten, George &　　　　　　　　**TA480.A6H36 2003**
　MacKenzie, D. Scott
Handbook of Aluminum: Physical Metallurgy and Processes, Vol. 1. Paper over Boards. Marcel Dekker Inc. New York, NY. 2003. 1403p. ISBN:0-8247-0494-0, ISBN13: 978-0-8247-0494-0. Dewey:620.186. LCCN:2003-273504.

Audience: **u,f.** *Choice, 2004.*

Metallurgy > Alloys

Frick, J. (Editor)　　　　　　　　**TA483.W64 2000**
Woldman's Engineering Alloys. Ed. 9. Trade Cloth. A S M International. Materials Park, OH. 2000. 1,363p. ISBN:0-87170-691-1, ISBN13: 978-0-87170-691-1. Dewey:620.1/6. LCCN:00-046475.

Audience: **u,f.**

Lu, Li & Lai, Man O.　　　　　　　**TN698.L85 1998**
Mechanical Alloying. Trade Cloth. Springer. New York, NY. 1997. 296p. ISBN:0-7923-8066-5, ISBN13: 978-0-7923-8066-5. Dewey:669/.95. LCCN:97-035207.

Audience: **u,f.** *Choice, 1998.*

Metallurgy > Joining

American Welding Society　　　　**TS227 . W388 2001**
Staff
Welding Handbook, (2002), Vol. 1. Ed. 9. Trade Cloth. American Welding Society. Miami, FL. 2002. 932p.

ISBN:0-87171-657-7, ISBN13: 978-0-87171-657-6.
Dewey:671.52. LCCN:2001-089999.

Audience: **l,u,f.**

Humpston, Giles &   **TS610.H85 1993**
  Jacobson, David M.
Principles of Soldering and Brazing. Trade Cloth. A S M
International. Materials Park, OH. 1993. 281p.
ISBN:0-87170-462-5, ISBN13: 978-0-87170-462-7.
Dewey:671.5/6. LCCN:93-070224.

Audience: **l,u,f.** *Choice, 1994.*

Kou, Sindo   **TS227.K649 2002**
Welding Metallurgy. Ed. 2. Trade Cloth. John Wiley & Sons,
Inc. Hoboken, NJ. 2002. 480p. ISBN:0-471-43491-4, ISBN13:
978-0-471-43491-7. Dewey:671.5/2. LCCN:2002-014327.

Audience: **u,f.** *Choice, 2003.*

Lippold, John C. & Kotecki,   **TS227.2.L57 2005**
  Damian J.
Welding Metallurgy and Weldability of Stainless Steels. Trade
Cloth. John Wiley & Sons, Inc. Hoboken, NJ. 2005. 376p.
ISBN:0-471-47379-0, ISBN13: 978-0-471-47379-4.
Dewey:620.1/7. LCCN:2004-058043.

Audience: **u,f.** *Choice, 2005.*

Metallurgy > Electroplating

Durney, Lawrence J.   **TS670.E4614 1984**
Graham's Electroplating Handbook. Ed. 4. Cloth Text. Chapman
& Hall. New York, NY. 1984. ISBN:0-442-22002-2, ISBN13:
978-0-442-22002-0. Dewey:671.7/32. LCCN:84-003548.

Audience: **l,u,f.**

Kanani, N. (Editor)   **TS692.C6**
Electroplating and Electroless Plating of Copper and Its Alloys.
CD-ROM, Trade Cloth. Finishing Publications, Ltd. Stevenage,
2003. 304p. ISBN:0-904477-26-6, ISBN13: 978-0-904477-26-9.
Dewey:671.732.

Audience: **l,u,f.** *Choice, 2004.*

Mining

                    HD9502.U6
☐ EIA Energy Information Administration: Official Energy
Statistics from the U. S. Government.
http://www.eia.doe.gov/
The Energy Information Administration (EIA), U.S. Department
of Energy.

Audience: **u,f.**

☐ NIOSH: The National Institute for Occupational Safety and
Health Mining Safety and Health Research.
http://www.cdc.gov/niosh/mining/
NOISH.

Audience: **u,f.**

American Geological   **TN9**
  Institute Staff (Compiled by)
Dictionary of Mining, Mineral, and Related Terms. Ed. 2. Trade
Cloth. Springer. New York, NY. 2003. x, 646p.
ISBN:3-540-01271-0, ISBN13: 978-3-540-01271-9.
Dewey:622/.03.

Audience: **g,l,u,f.**

Conaway, Charles F.   **TN870. C58 1999**
The Petroleum Industry: A Nontechnical Guide. Trade Cloth.
PennWell Corporation. Tulsa, OK. 1999. 289p. PennWell
Nontechnical Ser. ISBN:0-87814-763-2, ISBN13:
978-0-87814-763-2. Dewey:665.5. LCCN:99-045825.

Audience: **l,u,f.** *Choice, 2000.*

Crickmer, D. F. & Zegeer,   **TN275**
  DAvid A. (Editors)
Elements of Practical Coal Mining. Ed. 2. Trade Cloth. Society
for Mining, Metallurgy & Exploration, Inc. Littleton, CO. 1981.
847p. ISBN:0-89520-270-0, ISBN13: 978-0-89520-270-3.
Dewey:622.334. LCCN:79-057346.

Audience: **l,u,f.** ℬ

Deffeyes, Kenneth S.   **TN870.D37 2003**
Hubbert's Peak: The Impending World Oil Shortage. Trade
Paper. Princeton University Press. Princeton, NJ. 2003. 224p.
ISBN:0-691-11625-3, ISBN13: 978-0-691-11625-9.
Dewey:333.8/23211.

Audience: **g,l,u,f.** *Choice, 2002.*

Dorr, Ann & Paty, Alma   **TN263**
  Hale
Minerals: Foundations of Society. Ed. 3. American Geological
Institute. 2002. ISBN:0-922152-60-8, ISBN13:
978-0-922152-60-5.

Audience: **l,u,f.**

Downey, Marlan W.   **TN870.P498 2001**
  (Editor), et al.
Petroleum Provinces of the Twenty-First Century. Jack C. Threet
& William A. Morgan (Editors). Trade Cloth. American
Association of Petroleum Geologists. Tulsa, OK. 2001. 550p.
AAPG Memoir Ser., No. 74 ISBN:0-89181-355-1, ISBN13:
978-0-89181-355-2. Dewey:553.2/8. LCCN:2002-280923.

Audience: **u,f.**

Freese, Barbara   **HD9540**
Coal: A Human History. Trade Cloth. Basic Books. New York,
NY. 2002. 320p. ISBN:0-7382-0400-5, ISBN13:
978-0-7382-0400-0. Dewey:553.2/4. LCCN:2002-114066.

Audience: **g,l,u,f.** *Choice, 2003.*

Fuerstenau, Maurice C.   **TN500.P66 2003**
  (Editor)
Principles of Mineral Processing. Trade Cloth. Society for
Mining, Metallurgy & Exploration, Inc. Littleton, CO. 2003.
305p. ISBN:0-87335-167-3, ISBN13: 978-0-87335-167-6.
Dewey:622/.7. LCCN:2002-042938.

Audience: **u,f.**

Gambogi, Joseph (Editor)   **TN9**
☐ Minerals Information : U.S.G.S.
http://www.minerals.usgs.gov/minerals/
U.S. Geological Survey.

Audience: **l,u,f.**

Gertsch, Richard E. &   **TN275.T33 1998**
  Bullock, Richard L. (Editors)
Techniques in Underground Mining: Selections from
Underground Mining Methods Handbook. Trade Cloth. Society
for Mining, Metallurgy & Exploration, Inc. Littleton, CO. 1998.
834p. ISBN:0-87335-163-0, ISBN13: 978-0-87335-163-8.
Dewey:622.2. LCCN:98-028643.

Audience: **u,f.**

Gluyas, Jon & Swarbrick,   **TN870.5.G58 2003**
  Richard
Petroleum Geoscience. Trade Paper. Blackwell Publishing, Inc.
Malden, MA. 2003. 376p. ISBN:0-632-03767-9, ISBN13:
978-0-632-03767-4. Dewey:553.2/8. LCCN:2002-015310.
                                        Audience: **u,f.** *Choice, 2004.*

Gregory, Cedric E.   **TN15.G44 2001**
A Concise History of Mining. Ed. 2. Paper over Boards. Taylor
& Francis Group. Abingdon, 2001. 200p. ISBN:90-5809-347-6,
ISBN13: 978-90-5809-347-9. Dewey:622/.09.
LCCN:2001-056068.
                                        Audience: **u,f.** *B*

Hartman, Howard L.   **TN145 .S56 1992**
  (Editor)
SME Mining Engineering Handbook, Set. Ed. 2. Trade Cloth.
Society for Mining, Metallurgy & Exploration, Inc. Littleton,
CO. 1992. 2394p. ISBN:0-87335-100-2, ISBN13:
978-0-87335-100-3. Dewey:622. LCCN:92-061198.
                                        Audience: **u,f.**

Hartman, Howard L. &   **TN275.H35 2002**
  Mutmansky, Jan M.
Introductory Mining Engineering. Ed. 2. Trade Cloth. John
Wiley & Sons, Inc. Hoboken, NJ. 2002. 584p.
ISBN:0-471-34851-1, ISBN13: 978-0-471-34851-1. Dewey:622.
LCCN:2002-071315.
                                        Audience: **u,f.**

Hopler, Robert B. (Editor)   **TN279**
Blasters' Handbook. Ed. 17. Cloth Text. International Society of
Explosives Engineers. Cleveland, OH. 1998. 650p.
ISBN:1-892396-00-9, ISBN13: 978-1-892396-00-6.
Dewey:624.152.
                                        Audience: **l,u,f.**

Hyne, Norman J.   **TN870.5.H9624 2001**
Nontechnical Guide to Petroleum Geology, Exploration,
Drilling, and Production. Ed. 2. Trade Cloth. PennWell
Corporation. Tulsa, OK. 2001. 598p. ISBN:0-87814-823-X,
ISBN13: 978-0-87814-823-3. Dewey:665.5.
LCCN:2002-279429.
                                        Audience: **g,l,u,f.**

Karmis, Michael (Editor)   **RC965.M48M56 2001**
Mine Health and Safety Management. Trade Cloth. Society for
Mining, Metallurgy & Exploration, Inc. Littleton, CO. 2001.
472p. ISBN:0-87335-200-9, ISBN13: 978-0-87335-200-0.
Dewey:618.9/803/088622. LCCN:2001-049135.
                                        Audience: **l,u,f.**

Kennedy, B. A. (Editor)   **TN291 .S78 1990**
Surface Mining, 2e. Ed. 2. Trade Cloth. Society for Mining,
Metallurgy & Exploration, Inc. Littleton, CO. 1990. 1206p.
ISBN:0-87335-102-9, ISBN13: 978-0-87335-102-7.
Dewey:622/.292. LCCN:90-063205.
                                        Audience: **u,f.**

Kesler, Stephen E.   **TN145**
Mineral Resources, Economics, and the Environment. New
York: Macmillan; Toronto: Maxwell Macmillan Canada; New
York: Maxwell Macmillan International. 1994.
ISBN:0-02-362842-1, ISBN13: 978-0-02-362842-9.
                                        Audience: **u,f.**

Langenkamp, Robert D.   **TN865.I43 1994**
The Illustrated Petroleum Reference Dictionary. Ed. 4. Trade
Cloth. PennWell Corporation. Tulsa, OK. 1994. 904p.
ISBN:0-87814-423-4, ISBN13: 978-0-87814-423-5.
Dewey:665.5/03. LCCN:94-034489.
                                        Audience: **l,u,f.**

Leffler, William L. &   **TN870**
  Raymond, Martin S.
Oil and Gas Production in Nontechnical Language. Trade Cloth.
PennWell Corporation. Tulsa, OK. 2005. 221p.
ISBN:1-59370-052-0, ISBN13: 978-1-59370-052-2.
Dewey:622/.338. LCCN:2006-024876.
                                        Audience: **l,u,f.** *Choice, 2006.*

Lyons, William C. & Plisga,   **TN870.S6233 2005**
  Gary J.
Standard Handbook of Petroleum and Natural Gas Engineering.
Ed. 2. Trade Cloth. Elsevier Science & Technology Books. Saint
Louis, MO. 2004. 1568p. ISBN:0-7506-7785-6, ISBN13:
978-0-7506-7785-1. Dewey:665.5. LCCN:2004-056285.
                                        Audience: **u,f.**

Miesner, Thomas O. &   **TN879.5.M53 2006**
  Leffler, William L.
Oil and Gas Pipelines in Nontechnical Language. Trade Cloth.
PennWell Corporation. Tulsa, OK. 2006. 180p.
ISBN:1-59370-058-X, ISBN13: 978-1-59370-058-4.
Dewey:665.5/44. LCCN:2006-003359.
                                        Audience: **l,u,f.**

Schobert, Harold H.   **TP325.S34 1987**
Coal: The Energy Source of the Past and Future. Trade Cloth.
American Chemical Society. Washington, DC. 1987. xi, 280p.
ISBN:0-8412-1171-X, ISBN13: 978-0-8412-1171-1.
Dewey:662.6/2. LCCN:87-011433.
                                        Audience: **l,u,f.**

Selley, Richard C.   **TN870.5.S425 1998**
Elements of Petroleum Geology. Ed. 2. Cloth Text. Elsevier
Science & Technology Books. Saint Louis, MO. 1997. 470p.
ISBN:0-12-636370-6, ISBN13: 978-0-12-636370-8.
Dewey:553.2/82. LCCN:97-074392.
                                        Audience: **u,f.**

Shah, Sonia   **TN870**
Crude: The Story of Oil. Trade Cloth. Seven Stories Press. New
York, NY. 2004. 304p. ISBN:1-58322-625-7, ISBN13:
978-1-58322-625-4. Dewey:665.5. LCCN:2004-012307.
                                        Audience: **l,u,f.**

Thomas, Larry   **TN799.9**
Coal Geology. Trade Cloth. John Wiley & Sons, Inc. Hoboken,
NJ. 2002. 396p. ISBN:0-471-48531-4, ISBN13:
978-0-471-48531-5. Dewey:553.2/4. LCCN:2002-027204.
                                        Audience: **u,f.**

U S Bureau of Mines Staff   **TN23**
Mineral Facts and Problems. U.S. Dept. of the Interior. 1985.
United States. Bureau of Mines. Bulletin ; 675; Variation:
United States; Bureau of Mines; Bulletin ; 675.
                                        Audience: **l,u,f.**

U. S. Bureau of Mines Staff   **TN0023.U425**
Mineral Facts and Problems. Trade Paper. Books on Demand.
Ann Arbor, MI. 1050p. ISBN:0-598-68911-7, ISBN13:
978-0-598-68911-5. Dewey:338.2. LCCN:56-060859.
                                        Audience: **l,u,f.** *B*

U. S. Bureau of Mines Staff   **TN9.D564 1997**
   & American Geological Institute Staff
Dictionary of Mining, Mineral and Related Terms. Ed. 2. Trade
Cloth. American Geological Institute. Alexandria, VA. 2000.
800p. ISBN:0-922152-36-5, ISBN13: 978-0-922152-36-0.
Dewey:622/.03. LCCN:97-021272.
                                        Audience: **g,l,u,f.**

Youngquist, Walter L.   **HD9502.A2Y684 1997**
GeoDestinies: The Inevitable Control of Earth Resources over
Nations and Individuals. Trade Cloth. National Book Co./ERA
Learning. Portland, OR. 1997. 500p. ISBN:0-89420-299-5,
ISBN13: 978-0-89420-299-5. Dewey:304.2/8. LCCN:97-004825.
                                        Audience: **l,u,f.**

Nuclear Engineering

☐ American Nuclear Society.
http://ans.org/
                                        Audience: **g,l,u,f.**

                                        HD9698.5
☐ International Atomic Energy Agency (IAEA).
http://www.iaea.org/
                                        Audience: **g,l,u,f.**

☐ Nuclear Energy Institute.
http://www.nei.org/
                                        Audience: **g,l,u,f.**

                                        TK9006
☐ Nuclear Engineering Virtual Library.
http://www.nuc.berkeley.edu/main/vir_library.html
                                        Audience: **l,u,f.**

☐ Reference Sources: Nuclear Engineering: Subject Guides:
MIT Libraries.
http://libraries.mit.edu/guides/subjects/nuclear/reference.html
                                        Audience: **l,u,f.**

☐ U.S. Nuclear Regulatory Commission.
http://www.nrc.gov/
                                        Audience: **g,l,u,f.**

                                        TJ163.165
World Energy and Nuclear Directory. Ed. 4. Trade Cloth.
Longman Publishing Group. White Plains, NY. 1990. 588p.
ISBN:0-582-07933-0, ISBN13: 978-0-582-07933-5.
Dewey:621.042072.
                                        Audience: **u,f.** *Choice, 1991.*

Angelo, Joseph A.   **TK9145**
Nuclear Technology. Cloth Text. Greenwood Publishing Group,
Inc. Portsmouth, NH. 2004. 656p. Sourcebooks in Modern

Technology ISBN:1-57356-336-6, ISBN13: 978-1-57356-336-9.
Dewey:621.48. LCCN:2004-011238.
                                        Audience: **u,f.** *Choice, 2005.*

Bodansky, David   **TK9145.B54 2003**
Nuclear Energy: Principles, Practices, and Prospects. Ed. 2.
Trade Cloth. Springer. New York, NY. 2004. XXII, 693p.
ISBN:0-387-20778-3, ISBN13: 978-0-387-20778-0.
Dewey:333.792/4. LCCN:2003-070772.
                                        Audience: **u,f.** *Choice, 2005.*

Carlisle, Rodney P.   **TK9202.C23 1996**
Supplying the Nuclear Arsenal: American Production Reactors,
1942-1992. Joan M. Zenzen (As told to). Trade Cloth. Johns
Hopkins University Press. Baltimore, MD. 1990. 296p.
ISBN:0-8018-5207-2, ISBN13: 978-0-8018-5207-7.
Dewey:355.4/3/00973. LCCN:95-044410.
                                        Audience: **u,f.** *Choice, 1997.*

Clason, W. E.   **QC772 .E4 1970**
Elsevier's Dictionary of Nuclear Science and Technology: In
English-American (with Definitions), French, Spanish, Italian,
Dutch and German. Ed. 2. Trade Cloth. Elsevier. New York, NY.
1986. 798p. ISBN:0-444-40810-X, ISBN13: 978-0-444-40810-5.
Dewey:539.7/03. LCCN:72-103357.
                                        Audience: **l,u,f.**

Clasper, James W.
☐ Engineering Library Resources in Nuclear Engineering.
http://www.engrlib.uc.edu/resources/nucl.html
                                        Audience: **l,u,f.**

Dahl, Per F.   **QD169.W3D25 1999**
Heavy Water and the Wartime Race for Nuclear Energy. Saddle
Stitched. Institute of Physics Publishing. Philadelphia, PA. 1999.
399p. ISBN:0-7503-0633-5, ISBN13: 978-0-7503-0633-1.
Dewey:546/.22. LCCN:99-033672.
                                        Audience: **l,u.** *Choice, 2000.*

Domenici, Pete V.   **TK9146.D66 2004**
A Brighter Tomorrow: Fulfilling the Promise of Nuclear Energy.
Trade Cloth. Rowman & Littlefield Publishers, Inc. Lanham,
MD. 2004. 288p. ISBN:0-7425-4188-6, ISBN13:
978-0-7425-4188-7. Dewey:333.792/4. LCCN:2004-010521.
                                        Audience: **l,u.** *Choice, 2005.*

Dresser, Peter D.   **TK9202**
Nuclear Power Plants Worldwide. Trade Cloth. Thomson Gale.
Farmington Hills, MI. 1993. 500p. Environmental Library
ISBN:0-8103-8880-4, ISBN13: 978-0-8103-8880-2.
Dewey:621.483.
                                        Audience: **u,f.** *Choice, 1994.*

Graf, William L.   **TD427.P63G73 1994**
Plutonium and the Rio Grande: Environmental Change and
Contamination in the Nuclear Age. Trade Cloth. Oxford
University Press, Inc. New York, NY. 1994. 346p.
ISBN:0-19-508933-2, ISBN13: 978-0-19-508933-2.
Dewey:628.1/685/097896. LCCN:93-040028.
                                        Audience: **l,u,f.** *Choice, 1995.*

Heaberlin, S. W.   **TK9146.H43 2003**
A Case for Nuclear-Generated Electricity, or, Why I Think
Nuclear Power Is Cool and Why It Is Important That You Think
So Too. Trade Cloth. Battelle Press. Columbus, OH. 2003. 326p.

ISBN:1-57477-136-1, ISBN13: 978-1-57477-136-7.
Dewey:333.792/4. LCCN:2003-052499.

Audience: **l,u,f.** *Choice, 2005.*

Henderson, Harry   **TK9146.H45 2000**
Nuclear Power: A Reference Handbook. Mildred Vasan (Editor).
Library Binding. ABC-CLIO, Inc. Santa Barbara, CA. 2000.
0250p. Contemporary World Issues Ser. ISBN:1-57607-128-6,
ISBN13: 978-1-57607-128-1. Dewey:333.792/4/09.
LCCN:00-010255.

Audience: **u,f.** *Choice, 2001.*

Hope, Marjorie & Young,   **TK9152.16.M33 1998**
  James
Voices of Hope in the Struggle to Save the Planet. Trade Paper.
Apex Press, The. Croton-on-Hudson, NY. 2000. 377p.
ISBN:0-945257-75-9, ISBN13: 978-0-945257-75-2.
Dewey:291.1/78362. LCCN:98-036673.

Audience: **l,u,f.** *Choice, 2000.*

Kruschke, Earl R. &   **HD9698.U52K78 1990**
  Jackson, Byron M.
Nuclear Energy Policy: A Reference Handbook. Library
Binding. ABC-CLIO, Inc. Santa Barbara, CA. 1989. 246p.
Contemporary World Issues Ser. ISBN:0-87436-238-5, ISBN13:
978-0-87436-238-1. Dewey:333.792/4/0973. LCCN:89-018132.

Audience: **l,u,f.** *Choice, 1991.*

Lamarsh, John R. &   **TK9145.L28 2001**
  Baratta, Anthony J.
Introduction to Nuclear Engineering. Ed. 3. Cloth Text. Prentice
Hall PTR. Upper Saddle River, NJ. 2001. 783p. Addison-Wesley
Series in Nuclear Science and Engineering ISBN:0-201-82498-1,
ISBN13: 978-0-201-82498-8. Dewey:621.48.
LCCN:2001-016394.

Audience: **u.**

Lowenthal, Gerhart &   **QC795.7 .L68 2001**
  Airey, Peter
Practical Applications of Radioactivity and Nuclear Radiations.
Trade Cloth. Cambridge University Press. New York, NY. 2001.
366p. ISBN:0-521-55305-9, ISBN13: 978-0-521-55305-6.
Dewey:621.4837. LCCN:2002-265177.

Audience: **u,f.** *Choice, 2002.*

Mounfield, Peter R.   **TK1078.M68 1990**
World Nuclear Power: A Geographical Appraisal. Trade Cloth.
Routledge. New York, NY. 1991. 416p. ISBN:0-415-00463-2,
ISBN13: 978-0-415-00463-3. Dewey:333.792/4.
LCCN:90-045131.

Audience: **u,f.** *Choice, 1991.*

Osif, Bonnie A.; Baratta,   **TK1345.H37**
  Anthony J. & Conkling, Thomas W.
TMI 25 Years Later: The Three Mile Island Nuclear Power
Plant Accident and Its Impact. Pennsylvania State University
Press. 2004. ISBN:0-271-02383-X, ISBN13: 978-0-271-02383-0.

Audience: **l,u.**

Ramsey, Charles B. &   **TK9152**
  Modarres, Mohammad
Commercial Nuclear Power: Assuring Safety for the Future.
Trade Cloth. John Wiley & Sons, Inc. Hoboken, NJ. 1998. 508p.
ISBN:0-471-29186-2, ISBN13: 978-0-471-29186-2.
Dewey:621.4/835. LCCN:97-038062.

Audience: **l,u.** *Choice, 1998.*

Walker, Peter (Editor)   **TK9009.C48 1992**
Chambers Nuclear Energy and Radiation Dictionary. Trade
Cloth. Chambers Harrap Publishers Limited.. Edinburgh, 1992.
352p. ISBN:0-550-13246-5, ISBN13: 978-0-550-13246-8.
Dewey:621.48/03. LCCN:93-111539.

Audience: **u,f.** *Choice, 1993.*

Winkler, Allan M.   **UA23.W485 1993**
Life under a Cloud: American Anxiety about the Atom. Trade
Cloth. Oxford University Press, Inc. New York, NY. 1993. 288p.
ISBN:0-19-507821-7, ISBN13: 978-0-19-507821-3.
Dewey:355/.0335/73. LCCN:92-020013.

Audience: **l,u,f.** *Choice, 1993.*

Chemical Engineering

                                                           Q199
☐ Knovel Critical Tables.
http://www.knovel.com/knovel2/Toc.jsp?BookID=761&
VerticalID=0
Knovel Corporation (Knovel Library).

Audience: **u,f.**

Ali, M. & El, Ali Bassam   **TP151.A57 2005**
Handbook of Industrial Chemistry. Trade Cloth. McGraw-Hill
Professional Publishing. New York, NY. 2004. 628p.
McGraw-Hill Handbooks ISBN:0-07-141037-6, ISBN13:
978-0-07-141037-3. Dewey:661/.8. LCCN:2004-063172.

Audience: **u,f.** *Choice, 2005.*

Baine, Celeste   **TA157.B294 2004**
Is There an Engineer Inside You?: A Comprehensive Guide to
Career Decisions in Engineering. Ed. 2. Trade Cloth.
Professional Publications, Inc. Belmont, CA. 2004. 204p.
ISBN:1-59126-020-5, ISBN13: 978-1-59126-020-2.
Dewey:320.0023. LCCN:2006-272577.

Audience: **l,u,f.**

Bejan, Adrian & Kraus,   **TJ250.B35 2003**
  Allan D. (Editors)
Heat Transfer Handbook. Trade Cloth. John Wiley & Sons, Inc.
Hoboken, NJ. 2003. 1496p. ISBN:0-471-39015-1, ISBN13:
978-0-471-39015-2. Dewey:621.402/2. LCCN:2002-028857.

Audience: **u,f.**

Bohnet, Matthias, et. al.   **TP9**
  (Editors)
Ullmann's Encyclopedia of Industrial Chemistry. Ed. 6.
Wiley-VCH. 2003. ISBN:3-527-30385-5, ISBN13:
978-3-527-30385-4.

Audience: **u,f.**

Branan, Carl R.   **TP151.R85 2005**
Rules of Thumb for Chemical Engineers. Ed. 4. Paper Text.
Elsevier Science & Technology Books. Saint Louis, MO. 2005.
496p. ISBN:0-7506-7856-9, ISBN13: 978-0-7506-7856-8.
Dewey:660. LCCN:2005-048489.

Audience: **l,u,f.**

Cabri, Walter & Fabio,   **RS403.C23 2000**
  Romano Di
From Bench to Market: The Evolution of Chemical Synthesis.
Trade Cloth. Oxford University Press, Inc. New York, NY. 2000.
282p. ISBN:0-19-850384-9, ISBN13: 978-0-19-850384-2.
Dewey:615/.19. LCCN:00-062399.

Audience: **u,f.**

Campbell, W. A.   HD9652.5 .M55 1991
Milestones in 150 Years of the Chemical Industry, No. 96. H. L.
Roberts (Editor). Trade Cloth. Royal Society of Chemistry, The.
Cambridge, 1991. 318p. Special Publications
ISBN:0-85186-456-2, ISBN13: 978-0-85186-456-3.
Dewey:338.4766009. LCCN:92-115112.

Audience: **u,f.**

Committee on Challenges   QD47.B49 2003
for the Chemical Sciences in the 21st Century
Beyond the Molecular Frontier: Challenges for Chemistry and
Chemical Engineering. Trade Paper. National Academies Press.
Washington, DC. 2003. 224p. ISBN:0-309-08477-6, ISBN13:
978-0-309-08477-2. Dewey:540/.72/073. LCCN:2003-100913.

Audience: **u,f.**

Coulson, J. M. &   TP155
Richardson, J. F.
Chemical Engineering, Vol. 3. Ed. 3. Cloth Text. Elsevier. New
York, NY. 1971. xiii, 623p. ISBN:0-08-016438-2, ISBN13:
978-0-08-016438-0. Dewey:660.2. LCCN:63-010117.

Audience: **u,f.**

Coulson, John Metcalfe   TP155
Chemical engineering, Vol. 4, Solutions to the problems in
Chemical engineering, vol. 1. Ed. 2. Richardson, J. F. and
Peacock. Pergamon Press. 1979. ISBN:0-08-042083-4, ISBN13:
978-0-08-042083-7.

Audience: **u,f.**

Coulson, J. & Richardson, J   TP155.C69 1996
Chemical Engineering: Design. Ed. 2. Trade Paper. Elsevier
Science & Technology Books. Saint Louis, MO. 1996. 976p.
Chemical Engineering Ser., Vol. 6 ISBN:0-7506-2558-9,
ISBN13: 978-0-7506-2558-6. Dewey:660.2/812.
LCCN:95-023187.

Audience: **u,f.**

Daubert, T. E. & Foster,   TP200.D39 1989
Diane (Editors)
Physical and Thermodynamic Properties of Pure Chemicals:
Data Compilation. Paper over Boards. Hemisphere Publishing
Corporation. Philadelphia, PA. 1989. 1100p.
ISBN:0-89116-948-2, ISBN13: 978-0-89116-948-2.
Dewey:661/.00212. LCCN:89-031740.

Audience: **u,f.** *Choice, 1990.*

Forsythe, William E.   QD511
☐ Smithsonian Physical Tables.
http://www.knovel.com/knovel2/Toc.jsp?BookID=736
Ed. 9. Knovel Corporation (Knovel Library).

Audience: **u,f.**

Gmehling, J. (Editor)   TP156.E65
Vapor-Liquid Equilibrium Data Collection: Aqueous-Organic
Systems. Ed. 2. Cloth Text. Dechema. 60061 Frankfurt, 1991.
750p. Dechema Chemistry Data Ser., Vol. 1, Pt. 1
ISBN:3-926959-30-4, ISBN13: 978-3-926959-30-0.
Dewey:547.1363.

Audience: **u,f.**

Grandison, A.S. & Lewis,   TP248.65
M.J. (Editors)
Separation Processes in the Food and Biotechnology Industries :
PrInciples and Applicaitons. Woodhead Publishing, Ltd. 1996.
ISBN:1-59124-153-7, ISBN13: 978-1-59124-153-9.

Audience: **u,f.**

Griskey, Richard A.   TP151 .G75 2000
Chemical Engineers' Portable Handbook. Trade Paper.
McGraw-Hill Professional Publishing. New York, NY. 2000.
432p. Portable Handbook Ser. ISBN:0-07-024801-X, ISBN13:
978-0-07-024801-4. Dewey:660.2. LCCN:00-712691.

Audience: **u,f.**

Himmelblau, David M. &   TP151.H5 2004
Riggs, James B.
Basic Principles and Calculations in Chemical Engineering. Ed.
7. Mixed Media, Quantity Pack, CD-ROM, Cloth Text. Prentice
Hall PTR. Upper Saddle River, NJ. 2003. 1072p.
ISBN:0-13-140634-5, ISBN13: 978-0-13-140634-6.
Dewey:660/.2. LCCN:2003-016672.

Audience: **u,f.**

Jankowski, Dorothy A. &   TP149.C4834 1986
Selover, Theodore B. Jr. (Editors)
Chemical Engineering Data Sources. Trade Paper. American
Institute of Chemical Engineers. New York, NY. 1986. 72p.
AIChE Symposium Ser., Vol. 82, No. 247 ISBN:0-8169-0358-1,
ISBN13: 978-0-8169-0358-0. Dewey:025/.0666/02.
LCCN:86-003365.

Audience: **u,f.**

Kirk-Othmer   TP9
Kirk-Othmer Encyclopedia of Chemical Technology. Ed. 5.
Trade Cloth. John Wiley & Sons, Inc. Hoboken, NJ. 2006. 869p.
ISBN:0-471-48502-0, ISBN13: 978-0-471-48502-5.
Dewey:660/.03/21.

Audience: **u,f.**

Perry, Robert H. & Green,   TP151.P45 1997
Donald W.
Perry's Chemical Engineers' Handbook. Ed. 7. Trade Cloth.
McGraw-Hill Professional Publishing. New York, NY. 1997.
2640p. Handbook Ser. ISBN:0-07-049841-5, ISBN13:
978-0-07-049841-9. Dewey:660. LCCN:96-051648.
                    Audience: **u,f.** ℬ *Choice, 1998.*

Riegel, Emil Raymond   TP145.R53 2003
Riegel's Handbook of Industrial Chemistry. Ed. 10. James
Albert Kent (Editor). Trade Cloth. Springer. New York, NY.
2003. 1374p. ISBN:0-306-47411-5, ISBN13:
978-0-306-47411-8. Dewey:660. LCCN:2002-040615.
                            Audience: **u,f.** *Choice, 2004.*

Simrock, K. H., et al.   QD65
Critical Data of Pure Substances, Set, Vol. 2, Pts. 1 & 2. R.
Janowsky & A. Ohnsorge (Authors). Library Binding. Dechema.
60061 Frankfurt, 1986. 1500p. Dechema Chemistry Data Ser.
ISBN:3-921567-77-7, ISBN13: 978-3-921567-77-7.
Dewey:540/.212.

Audience: **u,f.**

Wypych, George   TP247.5
☐ Knovel solvents : a properties database.
http://www.knovel.com/knovel2/Toc.jsp?BookID=635
ChemTech Publishing (Knovel Library).

Audience: **u,f.**

Chemical Engineering > Special Topics

Cassedy, Patrice   LB1775.C37 2002
Engineering. Trade Cloth. Thomson Gale. Farmington Hills, MI.
2003. 112p. Careers for the Twenty-First Century Ser.

ISBN:1-56006-897-3, ISBN13: 978-1-56006-897-6.
Dewey:371.102. LCCN:2002-003298.

Audience: **l,u,f.**

CCPS **TP155.7**
Guidelines for Safe and Reliable Instrumented Protective
Systems. Trade Cloth. American Institute of Chemical
Engineers. New York, NY. 2007. 400p. ISBN:0-471-97940-6,
ISBN13: 978-0-471-97940-1. Dewey:660.2804.

Audience: **u,f.**

Di Ventra, Massimiliano **QC176.8.N35N3556**
 (Editor), et al.
Nanoscale Science and Technology. Stephane Evoy & James R.
Heflin (Editors). Mixed Media. Springer. New York, NY. 2004.
632p. Nanostructure Science and Technology Ser.
ISBN:1-4020-7720-3, ISBN13: 978-1-4020-7720-3.
Dewey:620/.5. LCCN:2003-070222.

Audience: **u,f.**

Jackson, R. G. **TA165**
Novel Sensors and Sensing. Saddle Stitched. Institute of Physics
Publishing. Philadelphia, PA. 2004. 512p. Series in Sensors Ser.
ISBN:0-7503-0989-X, ISBN13: 978-0-7503-0989-9.
Dewey:681.2. LCCN:2005-275405.

Audience: **u,f.**

Prentis, Steve **TP248.2.P74 1984**
Biotechnology. Trade Cloth. George Braziller Inc. New York,
NY. 1984. 192p. ISBN:0-8076-1094-1, ISBN13:
978-0-8076-1094-7. Dewey:660/.62. LCCN:83-026571.

Audience: **u,f.**

Schugerl, K. & Zeng, A. P. **TP248.65.P76**
 (Editors)
Tools and Applications of Biochemical Engineering Science.
Mixed Media. Springer. New York, NY. 2002. XVIII, 274p.
Advances in Biochemical Engineering/Biotechnology Ser., Vol.
74 ISBN:3-540-42250-1, ISBN13: 978-3-540-42250-1.
Dewey:660.6/3.

Audience: **u,f.**

Swern, Daniel (Editor) **TP670**
Bailey's Industrial Oil and Fat Products, Vol. 1. Ed. 4. Trade
Cloth. John Wiley & Sons, Inc. Hoboken, NJ. 1979. 841p.
ISBN:0-471-83957-4, ISBN13: 978-0-471-83957-6. Dewey:665.
LCCN:78-031275.

Audience: **u,f.**

Chemical Engineering > Fuel, Fuel Cells, and Energy Options

Doxon, Lynn Ellen **TP358**
The Alcohol Fuel Handbook. Perfect. Infinity Publishing. West
Conshohocken, PA. 2001. 127p. ISBN:0-7414-0646-2, ISBN13:
978-0-7414-0646-0. Dewey:662.669.

Audience: **l,u,f.**

Farag, Ihab H. & **TJ810 .F86**
 Melsheimer, Stephen S. (Editors)
Fundamentals and Applications of Solar Energy, Pt. II. Trade
Paper. American Institute of Chemical Engineers. New York,
NY. 1981. 96p. AIChE Symposium Ser., Vol. 77, No. 210
ISBN:0-8169-0218-6, ISBN13: 978-0-8169-0218-7.
Dewey:621.47. LCCN:80-016305.

Audience: **l,u,f.**

Guibet, Jean-Claude & **TP343.G8413 1999**
 Faure-Birchem, Emmanuelle
Fuels and Engines: Technology, Energy, Environment. Frank
Carr (Translator), Raymond H. Laevy (Foreword by). Trade
Cloth. Editions Technip. Paris Cedex 15, 1999.
ISBN:2-7108-0751-3, ISBN13: 978-2-7108-0751-3. Dewey:665.
LCCN:00-295175.

Audience: **l,u,f.** *Choice, 2000.*

Hoffmann, Peter **TP359.H8H633 2001**
Tomorrow's Energy: Hydrogen, Fuel Cells, and the Prospects
for a Cleaner Planet. Tom Harkin (Foreword by). Trade Cloth.
MIT Press. Cambridge, MA. 2001. 320p. ISBN:0-262-08295-0,
ISBN13: 978-0-262-08295-2. Dewey:333.79/4.
LCCN:00-054613.

Audience: **l,u,f.** *Choice, 2002.*

Larminie, James & Dicks, **TK2931.L37 2003**
 Andrew
Fuel Cell Systems Explained. Ed. 2. Trade Cloth. John Wiley &
Sons, Inc. Hoboken, NJ. 2003. 428p. ISBN:0-470-84857-X,
ISBN13: 978-0-470-84857-9. Dewey:621.31/2429.
LCCN:2002-192419.

Audience: **u,f.**

Shapouri, Hosein
The Energy Balance of Corn Ethanol : An Update. Duffield,
James A.; Wang, Michael. U.S. Dept. of Agriculture, Office of
the Chief Economist ; Office of Energy Policy and New Uses.
2002.

Audience: **u,f.**

Sperling, Daniel (Editor) **TP360**
Alternative Transportation Fuels: An Environmental and Energy
Solution. Trade Cloth. Greenwood Publishing Group, Inc.
Portsmouth, NH. 1989. 342p. ISBN:0-89930-407-9, ISBN13:
978-0-89930-407-6. Dewey:662/.66. LCCN:89-003759.

Audience: **g,l,u,f.** *Choice, 1990.*

Xianguo, L. **TK2931.L5 2005**
Principles of Fuel Cells. Paper over Boards. Taylor & Francis
Group. Philadelphia, PA. 2005. 592p. ISBN:1-59169-022-6,
ISBN13: 978-1-59169-022-1. Dewey:621.31/2429.
LCCN:2005-021228.

Audience: **u,f.** *Choice, 2006.*

Chemical Engineering > Process Engineering

Azbel, David **TP363.A87 1984**
Fundamentals of Heat Transfer for Process Engineering. Trade
Cloth. Noyes Data Corporation/Noyes Publications. Park Ridge,
NJ. 1984. 382p. ISBN:0-8155-0982-0, ISBN13:
978-0-8155-0982-0. Dewey:660.2/8427. LCCN:84-004213.

Audience: **u,f.**

Couper, Pen **TP157.C414 2004**
Chemical Process Equipment: Selection and Design. Ed. 2.
James R. Fair, James R. Couper, W. Roy Penney & Stanley M.
Walas (Editors). Trade Cloth. Elsevier Science & Technology
Books. Saint Louis, MO. 2004. 776p. ISBN:0-7506-7510-1,
ISBN13: 978-0-7506-7510-9. Dewey:660/.283.
LCCN:2004-026118.

Audience: **u,f.**

Hessel, Volker, et al.   **TP155.7**
Chemical Micro Process Engineering: Fundamentals, Modelling and Reactions. Steffen Hardt & Holger Löwe (Authors). Trade Cloth. John Wiley & Sons, Inc. Hoboken, NJ. 2004. 712p. ISBN:3-527-30741-9, ISBN13: 978-3-527-30741-8. Dewey:660.2/8. LCCN:2004-299394.
       Audience: **u,f.** *Choice, 2004.*

Kessler, David P. &   **TP156.T7K48 1999**
   Greenkorn, Robert A.
Momentum, Heat and Mass Transfer Fundamentals. Paper over Boards. Marcel Dekker Inc. New York, NY. 1999. 1048p. ISBN:0-8247-1972-7, ISBN13: 978-0-8247-1972-2. Dewey:660/.2842. LCCN:99-010432.
       Audience: **u,f.**

Peters, Max Stone   **TP155 .P43 1984**
Elementary Chemical Engineering. Ed. 2. Cloth Text. McGraw-Hill Companies, The. New York, NY. 1984. ISBN:0-07-049586-6, ISBN13: 978-0-07-049586-9. Dewey:660.2. LCCN:83-012058.
       Audience: **u,f.**

Polyanin, Andrei   **TP156.F6**
   Dmitrievich
Hydrodynamics, mass and heat transfer in chemical engineering. Taylor & Francis. 2002. Topics in chemical engineering ISBN:0-415-27237-8, ISBN13: 978-0-415-27237-7.
       Audience: **u,f.**

Smith, Robin   **TP155.7.S57 2003**
Chemical Process: Design and Integration. Ed. 2. Trade Cloth. John Wiley & Sons, Inc. Hoboken, NJ. 2005. 712p. ISBN:0-471-48680-9, ISBN13: 978-0-471-48680-0. Dewey:660/.2812. LCCN:2004-014695.
       Audience: **u,f.**

Ulrich, Gael D.   **TP155.7**
Chemical Engineering Process Design and Economics : A Practical Guide. Ed. 2. Vasudevan, Palligarnai T.. Process Publisher. 2004. ISBN:0-9708768-2-3, ISBN13: 978-0-9708768-2-9.
       Audience: **u,f.**

Chemical Engineering > Experimental Chemical Engineering

Akanazarova, S. L. &   **QA279**
   Kafarov, V. V.
Experiment Optimization in Chemistry and Chemical Engineering. V. M. Matskovsky & A. P. Repyev (Translators). Trade Cloth. Imported Publications, Inc. Chicago, IL. 1982. 312p. ISBN:0-8285-2305-3, ISBN13: 978-0-8285-2305-9. Dewey:519.5.
       Audience: **u,f.**

Churchill, Stuart W.   **TP155.7 .C46**
   (Introduction by)
The Interpretation and Use of Rate Data: The Rate Concept. Paper Text. Hemisphere Publishing Corporation. Philadelphia, PA. 1979. 510p. ISBN:0-89116-234-8, ISBN13: 978-0-89116-234-6. Dewey:660.2/844. LCCN:78-023365.
       Audience: **u,f.**

Lazic, Zivorad R.   **QD43**
Design of Experiments in Chemical Engineering: A Practical Guide. Trade Cloth. John Wiley & Sons, Inc. Hoboken, NJ. 2005. 620p. ISBN:3-527-31142-4, ISBN13: 978-3-527-31142-2. Dewey:660. LCCN:2005-275128.
       Audience: **u,f.**

Chemical Engineering > Safety and Plant Maintenance

American Institute of   **TH9446.5.P45**
   Chemical Engineers Staff
Dow's Fire and Explosion Index Hazard Classification Guide. Ed. 7. Trade Paper. American Institute of Chemical Engineers. New York, NY. 1994. 83p. CEP Technical Manual Ser. ISBN:0-8169-0623-8, ISBN13: 978-0-8169-0623-9. Dewey:628.9222. LCCN:80-029237.
       Audience: **u,f.**

American Institute of   **TS191.G85 2004**
   Chemical Engineers Staff & Center For Chemical Process Safety CCPS Staff
Guidelines for Mechanical Integrity Systems. Trade Cloth. American Institute of Chemical Engineers. New York, NY. 2006. 286p. ISBN:0-8169-0952-0, ISBN13: 978-0-8169-0952-0. Dewey:660/.2830288. LCCN:2006-008220.
       Audience: **u,f.**

American Institute of   **TP155.5.G775 2003**
   Chemical Engineers Staff & Center for Chemical Process Safety Staff
Guidelines for Investigating Chemical Process Incidents. Ed. 2. Trade Cloth. American Institute of Chemical Engineers. New York, NY. 2003. 452p. ISBN:0-8169-0897-4, ISBN13: 978-0-8169-0897-4. Dewey:660/.2804. LCCN:2003-009470.
       Audience: **u,f.**

American Institute of   **TH9445.C47G85 2003**
   Chemical Engineers, Center for Chemical Process Safety Staff (Contribution by)
Guidelines for Fire Protection in Chemical, Petrochemical, and Hydrocarbon Processing Facilities. Trade Cloth. American Institute of Chemical Engineers. New York, NY. 2003. 400p. ISBN:0-8169-0898-2, ISBN13: 978-0-8169-0898-1. Dewey:660/.2804. LCCN:2003-017934.
       Audience: **u,f.**

Center for Chemical Process   **TP150.S24C764 2003**
   Safety Staff & Crowl, Daniel A.
Understanding Explosions. Trade Cloth. American Institute of Chemical Engineers. New York, NY. 2003. 214p. ISBN:0-8169-0779-X, ISBN13: 978-0-8169-0779-3. Dewey:660/.2804. LCCN:2003-004849.
       Audience: **u,f.**

Grossel, Stanley S., et al.   **TS180.8.B8G76 2005**
Guidelines for Safe Handling of Powders and Bulk Solids. Robert G. Zalosh, American Institute of Chemical Engineers Staff & Center for Chemical Process Safety Staff (Authors). Trade Cloth. American Institute of Chemical Engineers. New York, NY. 2004. 796p. ISBN:0-8169-0951-2, ISBN13: 978-0-8169-0951-3. Dewey:604.7. LCCN:2004-027448.
       Audience: **u,f.**

Keith, Lawrence H. &   **TP149**
  Walters, Douglas B.
The Compendium of Safety Data Sheets for Research and
Industrial Chemicals, Set, Vols. 1-6. Trade Cloth. John Wiley &
Sons, Inc. Hoboken, NJ. 1987. 1696p. ISBN:0-89573-289-0,
ISBN13: 978-0-89573-289-7. Dewey:660.2804.
LCCN:84-027107.

                                Audience: **l,u,f.**

King, Lester J. & Opelka,   **TK1345.H37 T46 1982**
  James H. (Editors)
Three Mile Island Clean-Up: Experiences, Waste Disposal and
Environmental Impact. Trade Paper. American Institute of
Chemical Engineers. New York, NY. 1982. AIChE Symposium
Series, Vol. 78 ISBN:0-8169-0224-0, ISBN13:
978-0-8169-0224-8. Dewey:621.48/38. LCCN:82-008817.

                                Audience: **u,f.**

McCabe, Warren L., et al.   **TP155.7.M3 2004**
Unit Operations of Chemical Engineering. Ed. 7. Julian C.
Smith & Peter Harriott (Authors). Cloth Text. McGraw-Hill
Companies, The. New York, NY. 2004. 1152p. McGraw-Hill
Chemical Engineering Ser. ISBN:0-07-284823-5, ISBN13:
978-0-07-284823-6. Dewey:660/.2842. LCCN:2004-055184.

                                Audience: **u,f.**

Zebovitz, Thomas C.   **TP149**
The Compendium of Safety Data Sheets for Research and
Industrial Chemicals: Flavors and Fragrances, Vol. 7. Library
Binding. John Wiley & Sons, Inc. Hoboken, NJ. 1989. 694p.
ISBN:0-89573-764-7, ISBN13: 978-0-89573-764-9.
Dewey:660.2804. LCCN:84-027107.

                                Audience: **l,u,f.**

Author Index

E

H

J

N

O

Q

T

V

X

Y

Z

Title Index

B

E

G

N

O

Q

R

S

W

X

Y